REVISED EDITION

WEBSTER'S CROSSWORD PUZZLE DICTIONARY

REVISED EDITION

WEBSTER'S CROSSWORD PUZZLE DICTIONARY

CREATED IN COOPERATION WITH THE EDITORS OF
MERRIAM-WEBSTER

BARNES & NOBLE

NEW YORK

This 2006 edition published by Barnes & Noble, Inc.
by arrangement with Federal Street Press,
a division of Merriam-Webster, Incorporated

2006 Barnes & Noble Books

ISBN 10   0-7607-8175-3
ISBN 13   978-07607-8175-3

Printed in the United States of America

06 07 08 09 10   5 4 3 2 1

Preface to the Second Edition

This new edition of our Crossword Puzzle Dictionary represents a significant revision of those that have preceded it. Every entry has been reconsidered, the content has been thoroughly updated, and the page design has been enhanced for legibility.

In updating the work, we have added many terms that have recently entered the general English vocabulary: the names of computer languages *(Java, Perl)*, new national currencies *(vatu, nakfa)*, contemporary slang *(slacker, schlep, hoser, chill out, go-to guy, brewski, nebbish)*, and much more. And numerous individuals and institutions that have emerged in recent years—soccer stars *(Hamm, Ronaldo)*, auto companies *(Kia, Daewoo)*, Nobel Prize winners *(Annan, Naipaul)*, actors and actresses *(Depp, Swank)*, and so on—have naturally also been added.

Drawing extensively on actual crossword puzzles, we have made a special effort to add examples of "crosswordese," words that show up unusually often in puzzle grids. Thus, you will find such distinctive words and names as those for Prince Valiant's wife *(Aleta)* and son *(Arn)*, a former newspaper columnist *(Eda)*, a sharp mountain ridge *(arête)*, a hare's tail *(scut)*, an eminent golfer *(Els)*, Peer Gynt's mother *(Ase, Aase)*, a puzzle-cube inventor *(Erno)*, and a Scottish uncle *(eme)*—many of which might have been omitted if frequency of use in everyday English had been our only criterion.

While crossword clues have gotten cleverer in recent years, crossword answer words have gotten simpler, and archaic and obscure terms have gradually been disappearing from puzzle grids. For this new edition, it seemed unnecessary to retain words that were unlikely to show up in even the most challenging modern puzzles, and consequently a number of words that have fallen out of use have been deleted. Their absence has been more than made up for by additional entries and answer words, which now total substantially over 300,000.

We hope our revised edition, with its new orientation, will prove to be the most useful dictionary of its kind for a new century of puzzle solving.

The principal editors of this dictionary's first two editions were James G. Lowe and Michael G. Belanger. Editorial work on the new edition was carried out by Mark A. Stevens and C. Roger Davis with freelance help from Jocelyn White Franklin, Mike Nichols, Francesca M. Forrest, and Doris Maxfield. Eileen M. Haraty and Dr. Thomas W. Adams made valuable vocabulary contributions, and Robert D. Copeland and Ted Atanowski provided essential electronic assistance.

Mark A. Stevens
Editor

Explanatory Notes

This dictionary is organized to make it easy to find answer words with a specific number of letters. Every answer word follows a numeral indicating the number of letters it contains. These words generally run from three to 13 letters. Two-letter words are omitted because such words almost never appear in crossword puzzles, and words longer than 13 letters are omitted because, when a puzzle calls for a longer answer, the answer is usually a phrase or part of a phrase rather than a single word or term. An exception to the 13-letter limit is made for multiword titles of works, which occasionally run as long as 25 letters. The exception allows for those frequent crossword clues that omit one or two words from a title, perhaps enough for a five- or ten-letter answer.

As in any crossword dictionary, a single list of answer words will often include words representing various parts of speech. The entry for **quiet**, for example, includes synonyms for the noun *(silence)*, the adjective *(placid)*, and the verb *(soothe)*, all in a continuous list. Since clues are often intentionally ambiguous as to what part of speech or meaning is intended, listing all the possible synonyms together is probably ideal for the puzzle solver.

Words that share a root with their entry word have usually been omitted from the answer lists, because puzzle creators rarely choose a clue that is related in this way to its answer. Therefore, *singular* does not appear at **single**, *basal* does not appear at **basic**, and *papa* does not appear at **pop**. On the other hand, since clues do occasionally share a standard prefix or suffix (such as *re-* or *-ness*) with an answer word, we have retained many clue/answer-word pairs of this kind.

When one entry word simply adds a suffix to another entry word, as when **keenness** follows **keen**, the answer list for the suffixed entry word will generally omit all the words that merely add the same suffix to a word in the stem word's list. For example, because **keen** includes such answer words as *sharp* and *shrewd,* the list at **keenness** omits *sharpness* and *shrewdness.* When encountering a clue with a common suffix, therefore, the user will occasionally want to look at a neighboring entry to find all the possible synonyms.

When a personal name is entered as an answer term, the first name generally appears in parentheses and is ignored in the letter count. In cases where the first name is the one normally encountered—e.g., for historical figures such as Michelangelo and Raphael or fictional characters such as Tess Durbeyfield and Angel Clare—the last name is generally parenthesized instead. When a title begins with an article *(A, An,* or *The),* the article is parenthesized and omitted from the letter count. In a list of geographic entities such as mountains (lakes, gulfs, etc.), the generic word *Mount (Lake, Gulf,* etc.) is parenthesized and omitted from the letter count. If you find that none of the answers as listed fits the blanks for a given puzzle clue, you should naturally check to see if any of the parenthesized elements might help provide the desired answer.

Many entries are broken into subentries by means of subheadings. Subheadings often consist of a single word, which is usually to be read as either preceding or following the main entry word. Thus, in the entry for **hair,** the subheadings include **animal** (which should be read as "animal hair") and **ornament** (which should be read as "hair ornament"). The subentry **combining form** lists the kinds of word fragments, usually Greek or Latin in origin, that are commonly called *roots.*

The dictionary is best used somewhat imaginatively. If you fail to find a word at its own entry, look up a synonym; only rarely will you fail to find one. If a clue takes a form such as **Australian tree, garden tool,** or **Southeast Asian lake** and the dictionary provides no such entry, check at the entry for the generic term—**tree, tool, lake,** etc.—for a list, perhaps broken down by subheadings.

REVISED EDITION
WEBSTER'S
CROSSWORD
PUZZLE
DICTIONARY

A

A1 4 best, tops **5** prime **7** optimal, perfect **8** superior **9** excellent, first-rate, front-rank, matchless, top-drawer **10** blue-ribbon, first-class

Aaron *brother:* **5** Moses *father:* **5** Amram *sister:* **6** Miriam

aback 7 unaware **8** suddenly, unawares **10** by surprise **12** unexpectedly

abaft 4 back **5** after **6** astern, behind **8** rearward **9** sternward

abalone 7 mollusc, mollusk **9** gastropod

abandon 4 cede, drop, dump, ease, jilt, junk, play, quit **5** cease, chuck, ditch, leave, let go, scrap, yield **6** desert, disown, give up, laxity, maroon, reject, resign, strand, vacate **7** back out, bail out, cast off, discard, drop out, forsake, freedom, liberty, license, pull out, retreat **8** abdicate, give over, hand over, renounce, wildness, withdraw **9** looseness, repudiate, surrender, throw over **10** enthusiasm, exuberance, relinquish, wantonness **11** discontinue, leave behind, naturalness, spontaneity, unrestraint **12** carelessness, heedlessness, intemperance, recklessness, unconstraint **13** impulsiveness

abandoned 4 free, lewd, lorn, wild **5** loose **6** gave up, jilted, vacant, wanton **7** cast off, corrupt, given up, outcast, uncouth **8** cast away, depraved, derelict, deserted, desolate, forsaken, stranded **9** cast aside, debauched, destitute, discarded, dissolute, lecherous, neglected, reprobate, shameless **10** degenerate, dissipated, eliminated, friendless, lascivious, left behind, licentious, profligate, unoccupied **11** uninhibited **12** incorrigible, relinquished, uncontrolled, unrestrained

abase 5 lower, shame **6** debase, defame, demean, demote, grovel, humble, lessen, reduce **7** cheapen, degrade, devalue, put down **8** belittle **9** denigrate, discredit, disparage, downgrade, humiliate **10** depreciate, undervalue

abash 4 faze **5** mix up, shame, upset **6** dismay, puzzle, rattle **7** confuse, mortify, mystify **8** confound **9** discomfit, embarrass **10** discompose, disconcert

abashment 6 unease **7** chagrin **8** disquiet **9** confusion **12** discomfiture, discomposure **13** embarrassment

abate 3 ebb, end **4** ease, fade, fall, omit, slow, void, wane **5** allay, annul, close, let up, quash, taper **6** deduct, lessen, negate, recede, reduce, relent, weaken **7** abolish, decline, deprive, die down, dwindle, ease off, nullify, slacken, subside **8** decrease, diminish, mitigate, moderate **9** alleviate, eradicate **10** invalidate

abatement 6 ebbing, rebate, waning **8** decrease, discount **9** declining, deduction, dwindling, exemption, lessening, reduction, shrinkage **10** diminution, subsidence **11** subtraction

abattoir 8 shambles

abbey 6 friary **7** convent **8** cloister **9** monastery

abbot *female:* **6** abbess

abbreviate 3 cut **4** clip, trim **5** prune **6** cut out, reduce **7** abridge, curtail, cut back, shorten **8** compress, condense, contract, cut short, truncate

abbreviation 5 brief **6** digest, précis, sketch **7** acronym, cutting, outline **8** abstract, clipping, synopsis, trimming **10** abridgment, shortening **11** curtailment **12** condensation

abdicate 4 cede, drop, quit **5** evade, forgo, leave, waive, yield **6** abjure, give up, reject, resign **7** abandon, cast off, discard **8** abnegate, disclaim, hand over, renounce, withdraw **9** repudiate, surrender **10** relinquish

abdomen 3 gut, pot **5** belly, tummy **6** middle, paunch **7** midriff, stomach **8** potbelly **9** bay window **10** midsection **11** breadbasket *depression:* **5** navel

abduct 4 grab, take **5** seize **6** kidnap, remove, snatch **8** carry off, draw away, take away **9** carry away, steal away **10** spirit away **11** make off with

Abduction from the Seraglio composer 6 Mozart (Wolfgang Amadeus)

abecedarian 4 tyro **6** novice **7** amateur, dabbler, learner **8** beginner, initiate, neophyte **9** beginning, smatterer **10** apprentice, dilettante, elementary **11** rudimentary **12** alphabetical

Abel *brother:* **4** Cain, Seth *father:* **4** Adam *mother:* **3** Eve *slayer:* **4** Cain

Abelard *son:* 9 Astrolabe *wife:* 7 Heloise

abele 6 poplar

aberrant 3 odd 7 deviant, strange, unusual 8 abnormal, atypical, peculiar, straying 9 anomalous, deviating, different, eccentric, irregular, unnatural, untypical 11 exceptional, nonstandard

aberration 4 slip 5 quirk 6 change, oddity 7 anomaly, mistake 8 mutation, straying, 9 curiosity, deviation, exception, wandering 10 deflection, difference, distortion, divergence 11 abnormality, peculiarity 12 eccentricity, irregularity

abet 3 aid, egg 4 ally, back, help, prod, spur, urge 5 boost, egg on 6 assist, exhort, foment, incite, second, stir up 7 condone, endorse, forward, promote, support 8 advocate 9 encourage, instigate 11 countenance

abettor 4 aide, ally 6 backup, cohort, helper 7 inciter, partner 8 fomenter 9 accessory, supporter 10 accomplice, instigator 11 confederate, conspirator 12 collaborator

abeyance 4 lull, rest 5 break, lapse, pause 6 recess 7 respite, time-out, waiting 8 breather, interval 10 inactivity, quiescence, suspension 12 intermission, interruption

abeyant 7 dormant 8 deferred, inactive, recessed 9 postponed, quiescent, suspended 11 interrupted

abhor 4 hate 5 scorn 6 detest, loathe, reject, revile, vilify 7 contemn, despise, disdain, dislike 8 execrate 9 abominate, excoriate, repudiate

abhorrence 4 evil, hate 6 hatred, horror 7 disgust 8 aversion, distaste, loathing 9 repulsion, revulsion 10 repugnance 11 abomination, detestation

abhorrent 4 base, foul, vile 5 awful 6 horrid, odious 7 beastly, hateful, heinous 8 damnable, horrible, horrific 9 atrocious, execrable, invidious, loathsome, monstrous, obnoxious, repellent, repugnant, repulsive, revolting 10 abominable, deplorable, despicable, detestable, disgusting 12 contemptible 13 reprehensible

abide 4 bear, last, live, stay, wait 5 await, brook, dwell, exist, stand, tarry 6 accede, accept, comply, endure, keep on, linger, remain, reside, stay on, suffer 7 consent, hang out, inhabit, persist, sojourn, stomach, subsist, swallow, wait for 8 continue, live with, stand for, tolerate 9 put up with, withstand

abiding 4 fast, firm, sure 6 steady 7 durable, eternal, lasting, staying 8 constant, enduring, timeless 9 complying, perpetual, steadfast 10 continuing, persistent, persisting, unchanging 11 everlasting, unfaltering

abigail 4 maid

Abigail *brother:* 5 David *husband:* 5 David, Nabal *mother:* 5 Amasa *son:* 7 Chileah

ability 4 bent, gift 5 craft, flair, knack, might, savvy, skill 6 talent 7 aptness, command, faculty, know-how, mastery, prowess 8 aptitude, capacity, facility 9 adeptness, dexterity, expertise, handiness, ingenuity, potential 10 adroitness, capability, cleverness, competence, efficiency 11 proficiency, skillfulness 13 qualification

abject 3 low 4 base, mean, poor, vile 5 lowly, sorry 6 dismal, humble, shabby, sordid 7 debased, fawning, forlorn, ignoble, pitiful, servile 8 cast down, degraded, dejected, downcast, hopeless, pathetic, pitiable, rejected, resigned, wretched 9 afflicted, destitute, groveling, miserable, worthless 10 deplorable, obsequious, spiritless, submissive 11 deferential, downtrodden, subservient 12 contemptible, dishonorable, ingratiating

abjure 4 cede, deny 5 avoid, spurn 6 desert, disown, recall, recant, reject, refuse, revoke 7 abandon, disavow, decline, forsake, retract 8 disclaim, forswear, renounce, take back, withdraw 9 repudiate, surrender 10 relinquish 11 abstain from

ablaze 5 afire, aglow, fiery 6 aflame, alight, on fire 7 blazing, burning, flaming, excited, flaring, ignited, radiant

able 3 apt, fit 4 keen 5 adept, alert, sharp, smart 6 adroit, clever, expert, facile, suited 7 capable, skilled 8 skillful, talented 9 competent, effective, effectual, efficient, qualified 10 proficient 11 intelligent, resourceful 12 accomplished, enterprising

able-bodied 3 fit 4 hale 5 hardy, lusty, sound, stout 6 brawny, hearty, robust, strong, sturdy 7 capable 8 stalwart, vigorous 9 strapping

ablution 6 laving 7 bathing, washing 8 lavation 9 cleansing, immersion 12 purification

abnegate 4 cede, deny, drop 5 forgo, waive, yield 6 abjure, give up, recant, revoke, vacate 7 disavow, gainsay 8 disallow, disclaim, forswear, renounce, withdraw 9 repudiate, surrender 10 contradict, contravene, relinquish

abnegation 6 denial 9 surrender 10 abstinence, self-denial 12 renouncement, renunciation

Abner *cousin:* 4 Saul *father:* 3 Ner *slayer:* 4 Joab

abnormal 3 odd 5 freak, undue, weird 6 off-key 7 bizarre, deviant, unusual 8 aberrant, atypical, freakish, peculiar 9 anomalous, divergent, eccentric, irregular, unnatural 11 heteroclite 13 heteromorphic, preternatural

abnormality 4 flaw 6 oddity 7 anomaly 8 deviance 9 deviation, exception 10 aberration, difference 12 irregularity

abode 4 home, nest 5 house 7 address, lodging, sojourn 8 domicile, dwelling 9 residence 10 habitation

abolish 3 end 4 undo, kill, void 5 abate, annul, erase, quash 6 cancel, negate, recall, repeal, revoke, vacate 7 destroy, nullify, rescind, retract, reverse, wipe out 8 abrogate, disallow, dissolve, overturn, prohibit 9 eliminate, eradicate, terminate 10 do away with, extinguish, invalidate

abolitionist 4 Mott (Lucretia), Weld (Theodore) 5 Brown (John), Child (Lydia), Lundy (Benjamin), Smith (Gerrit), Stowe (Harriet Beecher) 6 Birney (James), Lowell (James Russell), Parker (Theodore), Tappan (Arthur), Tubman (Harriet) 7 Lincoln (Abraham) 8 Douglass (Frederick), Garrison (William Lloyd), Phillips (Wendell), Whittier (John Greenleaf)

abominable 5 awful, nasty 6 cursed, horrid, odious 7 hateful 8 horrible, shocking, terrible, wretched 9 abhorrent, loathsome, offensive, repellent, repugnant, repulsive, revolting 10 deplorable, despicable, detestable, disgusting 12 contemptible

abominable snowman 4 yeti

abominate 4 damn, hate 5 abhor, curse, scorn 6 detest, loathe, revile 7 despise 8 execrate 9 repudiate

abomination 4 evil, hate 5 scorn 6 hatred, horror, plague 7 disdain, disgust, dislike 8 anathema, aversion, contempt, distaste, loathing 9 repulsion, revulsion 10 abhorrence, repugnance, repugnancy 11 detestation

aboriginal 5 first 6 native 7 ancient, endemic, primary 8 earliest, original, primeval 9 primitive 10 indigenous, primordial 13 autochthonous

aborigine 6 native 7 ancient 8 indigene 10 autochthon

abort 4 drop, halt, stop 5 check, expel, scrap, scrub 6 arrest, cancel 7 abandon, call off 8 cut short 9 interrupt, terminate

abortive 4 vain 5 empty 6 futile, unripe 7 failing, useless 8 immature, unformed 9 fruitless, worthless 10 unavailing, unfruitful 11 ineffective, ineffectual, unavailable, undeveloped 12 unproductive, unsuccessful

abound 4 flow, teem 5 burst, crawl, crowd, flood, swarm, swell 6 be full, throng 7 bristle, jam with 8 overflow, pack with 9 crawl with 11 be plentiful

abounding 4 full, rife 5 laden 6 filled, full of, jammed, packed 7 copious, profuse, replete, stuffed, teeming 8 abundant, swarming, thronged 9 alive with, bristling, plenteous, plentiful 11 overflowing

about 4 as to, back, in re, near, nigh, over 5 again, anent, circa, round 6 almost, around, moving, nearby, nearly 7 apropos, close to, roughly, through 8 backward 9 as regards, engaged in, haphazard, in reverse, in general, regarding 10 as concerns, concerning, encircling, in regard to, more or less, on all sides, oppositely, relating to, respecting 11 any which way, dealing with, on every side, practically, referring to, relative to, surrounding 12 here and there, with regard to 13 approximately, concerned with, in reference to, with respect to

about-face 4 turn 7 reverse 8 reversal 9 turnabout, volte-face

above 3 o'er 4 over, past 5 aloft, supra 6 beyond 8 overhead 9 exceeding *prefix:* 4 over 5 hyper, super, supra

above all 7 chiefly 9 primarily 10 especially 11 principally 12 particularly

aboveboard 4 free, open 5 frank 6 candid, honest, openly 7 frankly, up front 8 candidly, honestly, straight 10 truthfully, forthright, scrupulous

abracadabra 5 charm, magic 6 babble, jargon 9 gibberish 10 double talk, mumbo jumbo 11 incantation 12 gobbledygook 13 mystification

abrade 3 bug, irk, rub 4 burn, fret, gall, rasp, wear 5 annoy, chafe, erode, grate, graze, upset, weary 6 bother, ruffle, scrape 7 corrode, eat away, perturb, provoke, roughen 8 irritate, wear away, wear down 9 aggravate, grind down

Abraham *brother:* 5 Haran, Nahor *concubine:* 5 Hagar *father:* 5 Terah *grandfather:* 5 Nahor *grandson:* 4 Esau *nephew:* 3 Lot *son:* 5 Isaac, Medan, Shuah 6 Midian, Zimran 7 Ishmael *well:* 9 Beer-Sheba *wife:* 5 Sarah 7 Keturah

abrasion 5 chafe, scuff 6 scrape 7 chafing, erosion, grating, rubbing, scratch

8 friction, grinding, scraping, scuffing **10** irritation, scratching

abrasive 5 emery, rough, sharp **6** biting, pumice **7** wearing **8** annoying **9** smoothing, polishing **10** irritating, unpleasant

abreast 6 beside, next to, versed, with-it **7** versant **8** familiar, informed, up-to-date **9** au courant **10** acquainted, conversant **13** knowledgeable

abridge 3 cut **4** pare, trim **5** limit, prune **6** lessen, narrow, reduce **7** curtail, cut back, shorten **8** boil down, compress, condense, cut short, diminish, restrict, truncate **9** summarize **10** abbreviate

abridgment 5 brief **6** digest **7** capsule, cutting, summary **8** abstract, synopsis **9** reduction, short form, **10** diminution, lessening, shortening **11** compression, contraction, curtailment, restriction **12** abbreviation, condensation

abroad 4 afar, away **5** about **6** afield, astray, widely **7** touring **8** overseas **9** elsewhere, traveling

abrogate 3 end **4** undo, void **5** abate, annul, quash **6** cancel, negate, repeal, revoke, vacate **7** abolish, blot out, nullify, rescind, reverse **8** dissolve **9** discharge **10** extinguish, invalidate, obliterate

abrupt 4 curt **5** bluff, blunt, brief, brisk, crisp, gruff, hasty, sharp, sheer, short, steep **6** cut off, snippy, sudden **7** arduous, brusque, hurried, rushing **8** headlong **9** broken off, impetuous **10** unexpected **11** precipitant, precipitate, precipitous **13** unceremonious

abruptly 5 short **6** curtly **7** quickly, steeply **8** suddenly **12** unexpectedly **13** precipitately, precipitously

abruptness 8 curtness **9** steepness **10** brusquerie **12** precipitance

Absalom *commander:* **5** Amasa *father:* **5** David *mother:* **7** Maachah *sister:* **5** Tamar *slayer:* **4** Joab

abscess 4 boil, sore **5** botch, ulcer **6** lesion, pimple, trauma **7** blister, pustule **8** furuncle **9** carbuncle

abscond 4 bolt, flee, quit **5** break, leave **6** decamp, escape, run off **7** run away, take off **8** slip away, sneak off **9** disappear, sneak away, steal away

absence 4 AWOL, lack, need, void, want **6** dearth, defect, vacuum **7** default, drought, failure, vacancy **9** privation **10** deficiency, inadequacy **11** absenteeism, inattention **13** insufficiency

absent 4 away, AWOL, gone, lost **6** no-show **7** bemused, faraway, lacking, missing, omitted, wanting, without **8** distrait, heedless **9** elsewhere, forget-ful, wandering **10** abstracted, distracted, not present **11** inattentive, preoccupied **12** not attentive

absentminded 4 lost **7** bemused, faraway **8** distrait, dreaming, heedless, unseeing **9** forgetful, oblivious, unheeding, unmindful **10** abstracted, distracted, unnoticing **11** inattentive, inconscient, preoccupied, unconscious, unobserving **12** unperceiving

absent without leave 4 AWOL

absolute 4 full, pure, real, true **5** ideal, sheer, total, utter **6** actual, entire, simple **7** eternal, factual, genuine, perfect, supreme, unmixed **8** autarkic, complete, despotic, flawless, infinite, outright, positive, ultimate, simplest, thorough, unflawed **9** arbitrary, autarchic, boundless, downright, embodying, imperious, masterful, sovereign, unalloyed, undiluted, unlimited **10** autocratic, autonomous, consummate, impeccable, monocratic, tyrannical **11** categorical, dictatorial, domineering, fundamental, independent, unequivocal, unmitigated, unqualified **12** indefectible, indisputable, totalitarian, unrestrained, unrestricted **13** authoritarian, incontestable, unconditional

absolutely 5 fully **6** wholly **7** utterly **8** entirely **9** doubtless, perfectly **10** completely, definitely, positively, thoroughly **11** doubtlessly **13** unequivocally

absolution 6 pardon **7** amnesty, freeing, release **9** releasing, remission **10** letting off **11** exculpation, exoneration, forgiveness **12** dispensation

absolutism 9 Caesarism, despotism **12** dictatorship

absolve 4 free **5** clear, let go, remit, spare **6** acquit, excuse, exempt, let off, pardon **7** forgive, release, relieve, set free **8** dispense **9** discharge, exculpate, exonerate, vindicate

absorb 4 bear, blot **5** imbue, learn, sop up, use up **6** assume, embody, endure, engage, imbibe, infuse, ingest, soak up, sponge, suck up, take in, take up **7** acquire, consume, drink in, engross, immerse, involve, receive, sustain **8** permeate **9** preoccupy, transform **10** assimilate **11** incorporate

absorbed 4 deep, into, lost, rapt **6** intent **7** engaged, wrapped **8** caught up, immersed, involved **9** engrossed, wrapped up **10** captivated, fascinated **11** preoccupied

absorbing 9 arresting, consuming **10** engrossing, intriguing **11** captivating, fascinating, interesting **12** monopolizing, preoccupying

abstain 4 curb, deny, diet, fast, keep, pass, stop **5** avoid, forgo, spurn **6** abjure, eschew, give up, pass up, refuse, reject **7** decline, forbear, refrain **8** abnegate, forswear, hold back, keep from, renounce, swear off, teetotal, withhold **9** constrain, do without **11** deny oneself

abstemious 5 sober **6** strict **7** ascetic, austere, chaste, sparing **9** abstinent, continent, temperate **10** restrained **11** self-denying

abstinence 6 denial **7** fasting **8** chastity, sobriety **9** soberness **10** continence, self-denial, temperance **12** renunciation **13** self-restraint

abstract 5 brief, ideal **6** detach, digest, précis **7** epitome, neutral, outline, shorten, summary, utopian **8** academic, breviary, condense, detached, notional, separate, synopsis **9** disengage, summarize **10** abridgment, conceptual, conspectus, disconnect, dissociate, impersonal **11** appropriate, impractical, speculative, theoretical **12** condensation, hypothetical, transcendent **13** disinterested

abstracted 4 lost, rapt **6** absent, intent **7** bemused, faraway **8** absorbed, distrait, heedless **9** engrossed, oblivious, unheeding, unmindful, unminding, withdrawn **11** inattentive, inconscient, preoccupied, unconscious **12** absentminded

abstruse 4 deep **5** heavy **6** knotty, occult **7** complex **8** esoteric, hermetic, involved, profound **9** difficult, intricate, recondite **11** complicated

absurd 5 balmy, comic, crazy, droll, funny, inane, loony, potty, silly, wacky **6** insane **7** asinine, fatuous, foolish, idiotic **8** farcical **9** illogical, laughable, ludicrous **10** irrational, ridiculous **11** harebrained **12** preposterous, unreasonable

absurdity 5 farce, folly **7** inanity **8** insanity, nonsense **9** craziness, dottiness, silliness **11** foolishness, incongruity, witlessness **13** irrationality, ludicrousness, senselessness

abundance 6 bounty, excess, plenty, riches, wealth **9** affluence, profusion **10** lavishness, prosperity **11** prodigality *Scottish:* **5** routh

abundant 4 full, lush, rich, rife **5** ample, thick **6** filled, lavish, plenty **7** copious, crammed, crowded, liberal, profuse, replete **8** adequate, fruitful, generous, prolific **9** abounding, bounteous, boun-

tiful, extensive, luxuriant, plenteous, plentiful **10** sufficient

abuse 3 mar **4** harm, hurt, rail **5** anger, decry, shame, spoil, wrong **6** damage, debase, deride, impair, injure, misuse, revile, vilify **7** calumny, corrupt, cursing, exploit, obloquy, oppress, outrage, pervert, profane, pollute **8** belittle, berating, derision, derogate, discount, disgrace, ill-treat, maltreat, mistreat, reviling, swearing **9** blaspheme, contumely, desecrate, disparage, dispraise, harshness, invective, manhandle, mishandle, persecute, profanity, vehemence **10** defamation, depreciate, impose upon, malignment, revilement, scurrility **11** disapproval **12** billingsgate, condemnation, denunciation, vilification, vituperation

abusive 5 dirty, harsh **6** odious **7** corrupt **8** scurrile **9** injurious, insulting, invective, offending, offensive, truculent **10** calumnious, defamatory, scurrilous **11** blasphemous, castigating, opprobrious **12** calumniating, contumelious, sharp-tongued, vituperative, vituperatory

abut 4 join, link **5** flank, touch, verge **6** adjoin, border, butt on **8** border on, neighbor **9** lie beside **11** butt against, communicate

abutting 4 next **6** beside, joined, next to **7** joining, verging **8** adjacent, next door, touching **9** adjoining, bordering, impinging **10** connecting, contiguous, juxtaposed **11** bordering on, coextensive, coterminous, neighboring **12** conterminous

abysm see ABYSS

abysmal 4 deep, vast **7** endless **8** infinite, profound, unending, wretched **9** boundless, cavernous, plumbless, soundless, unplumbed **10** bottomless, fathomless, unmeasured **11** illimitable, measureless **12** immeasurable, unfathomable

abyss 3 pit **4** gulf, hell, hole, void **5** abysm, chasm, depth, gorge, hades, Sheol **6** Tophet **7** fissure, Gehenna, inferno **8** crevasse, deepness **9** perdition **10** underworld

academia 10 university **12** professoriat

academic 3 don **5** pupil, tutor **6** closet, fellow, master **7** bookish, learned, scholar, student **8** abstract, gownsman, lecturer, pedantic **9** professor, scholarly **10** scholastic **11** book-learned, conjectural, impractical, speculative, theoretical **12** conventional, hypothetical

academic period 4 term **7** quarter **8** semester **9** trimester

academy 6 lyceum 7 college, society 9 institute 10 prep school 12 conservatory

Academy Award winner

picture:

1927-28: 5 Wings *1928-29:* 14 Broadway Melody *1929-30:* 25 All Quiet on the Western Front *1930-31:* 8 Cimarron *1931-32:* 10 Grand Hotel *1932-33:* 9 Cavalcade *1934:* 18 It Happened One Night *1935:* 17 Mutiny on the Bounty *1936:* 16 The Great Ziegfeld *1937:* 15 Life of Emile Zola *1938:* 20 You Can't Take It with You *1939:* 15 Gone with the Wind *1940:* 7 Rebecca *1941:* 19 How Green Was My Valley *1942:* 10 Mrs. Miniver *1943:* 10 Casablanca *1944:* 10 Going My Way *1945:* 11 Lost Weekend (The) *1946:* 19 Best Years of Our Lives (The) *1947:* 19 Gentleman's Agreement *1948:* 6 Hamlet *1949:* 14 All the King's Men *1950:* 11 All About Eve *1951:* 15 American in Paris (An) *1952:* 19 Greatest Show on Earth (The) *1953:* 18 From Here to Eternity *1954:* 15 On the Waterfront *1955:* 5 Marty *1956:* 26 Around the World in Eighty Days *1957:* 20 Bridge on the River Kwai (The) *1958:* 4 Gigi *1959:* 6 Ben-Hur *1960:* 9 Apartment (The) *1961:* 13 West Side Story *1962:* 16 Lawrence of Arabia *1963:* 8 Tom Jones *1964:* 10 My Fair Lady *1965:* 12 Sound of Music (The) *1966:* 16 Man for All Seasons (A) *1967:* 19 In the Heat of the Night *1968:* 6 Oliver *1969:* 14 Midnight Cowboy *1970:* 6 Patton *1971:* 16 French Connection (The) *1972:* 9 Godfather (The) *1973:* 5 Sting (The) *1974:* 9 Godfather (Part Two)(The) *1975:* 25 One Flew over the Cuckoo's Nest *1976:* 5 Rocky *1977:* 9 Annie Hall *1978:* 10 Deer Hunter (The) *1979:* 14 Kramer vs. Kramer *1980:* 14 Ordinary People *1981:* 14 Chariots of Fire *1982:* 6 Gandhi *1983:* 17 Terms of Endearment *1984:* 7 Amadeus *1985:* 11 Out of Africa *1986:* 7 Platoon *1987:* 11 Last Emperor (The) *1988:* 7 Rain Man *1989:* 16 Driving Miss Daisy *1990:* 16 Dances with Wolves *1991:* 17 Silence of the Lambs (The) *1992:* 16 Unforgiven *1993:* 14 Schindler's List *1994:* 11 Forrest Gump *1995:* 10 Braveheart *1996:* 14 English Patient (The) *1997:* 7 Titanic *1998:* 17 Shakespeare in Love *1999:* 14 American Beauty *2000:* 9 Gladiator *2001:* 13 Beautiful Mind (A) *2002:* 7 Chicago *2003:* 14 Lord of the Rings

actor:

1927-28: 8 Jannings (Emil) *1928-29:* 6 Baxter (Warner) *1929-30:* 6 Arliss (George) *1930-31:* 9 Barrymore (Lionel) *1931-32:* 5 Beery (Wallace), March (Fredric) *1932-33:* 8 Laughton (Charles) *1934:* 5 Gable (Clark) *1935:* 8 McLaglen (Victor) *1936:* 4 Muni (Paul) *1937:* 5 Tracy (Spencer) *1938:* 5 Tracy (Spencer) *1939:* 5 Donat (Robert) *1940:* 7 Stewart (James) *1941:* 6 Cooper (Gary) *1942:* 6 Cagney (James) *1943:* 5 Lukas (Paul) *1944:* 6 Crosby (Bing) *1945:* 7 Milland (Ray) *1946:* 5 March (Fredric) *1947:* 6 Colman (Ronald) *1948:* 7 Olivier (Laurence) *1949:* 8 Crawford (Broderick) *1950:* 6 Ferrer (José) *1951:* 6 Bogart (Humphrey) *1952:* 6 Cooper (Gary) *1953:* 6 Holden (William) *1954:* 6 Brando (Marlon) *1955:* 8 Borgnine (Ernest) *1956:* 7 Brynner (Yul) *1957:* 8 Guinness (Alec) *1958:* 5 Niven (David) *1959:* 6 Heston (Charlton) *1960:* 9 Lancaster (Burt) *1961:* 6 Schell (Maximilian) *1962:* 4 Peck (Gregory) *1963:* 7 Poitier (Sidney) *1964:* 8 Harrison (Rex) *1965:* 6 Marvin (Lee) *1966:* 8 Scofield (Paul) *1967:* 7 Steiger (Rod) *1968:* 9 Robertson (Cliff) *1969:* 5 Wayne (John) *1970:* 5 Scott (George C.) *1971:* 7 Hackman (Gene) *1972:* 6 Brando (Marlon) *1973:* 6 Lemmon (Jack) *1974:* 6 Carney (Art) *1975:* 9 Nicholson (Jack) *1976:* 5 Finch (Peter) *1977:* 8 Dreyfuss (Richard) *1978:* 6 Voight (Jon) *1979:* 7 Hoffman (Dustin) *1980:* 6 De Niro (Robert) *1981:* 5 Fonda (Henry) *1982:* 8 Kingsley (Ben) *1983:* 6 Duvall (Robert) *1984:* 7 Abraham (F. Murray) *1985:* 4 Hurt (William) *1986:* 6 Newman (Paul) *1987:* 7 Douglas (Michael) *1988:* 7 Hoffman (Dustin) *1989:* 8 Day-Lewis (Daniel) *1990:* 5 Irons (Jeremy) *1991:* 7 Hopkins (Anthony) *1992:* 6 Pacino (Al) *1993:* 5 Hanks (Tom) *1994:* 5 Hanks (Tom) *1995:* 4 Cage (Nicholas) *1996:* 4 Rush (Geoffrey) *1997:* 9 Nicholson (Jack) *1998:* 7 Benigni (Roberto) *1999:* 6 Spacey (Kevin) *2000:* 5 Crowe (Russell) *2001:* 10 Washington (Denzel) *2002:* 5 Brody (Adrien) *2003:* 4 Penn (Sean)

actress:

1927-28: 6 Gaynor (Janet) *1928-29:* 8 Pickford (Mary) *1929-30:* 7 Shearer (Norma) *1930-31:* 8 Dressler (Marie) *1931-32:* 5 Hayes (Helen) *1932-33:* 7 Hepburn (Katharine) *1934:* 7 Colbert (Claudette) *1935:* 5 Davis (Bette) *1936:* 6 Rainer (Luise) *1937:* 6 Rainer (Luise) *1938:* 5 Davis (Bette) *1939:* 5 Leigh (Vivien) *1940:* 6 Rogers (Ginger) *1941:*

8 Fontaine (Joan) *1942:* 6 Garson (Greer) *1943:* 5 Jones (Jennifer) *1944:* 7 Bergman (Ingrid) *1945:* 8 Crawford (Joan) *1946:* 11 de Havilland (Olivia) *1947:* 5 Young (Loretta) *1948:* 5 Wyman (Jane) *1949:* 11 de Havilland (Olivia) *1950:* 8 Holliday (Judy) *1951:* 5 Leigh (Vivien) *1952:* 5 Booth (Shirley) *1953:* 7 Hepburn (Audrey) *1954:* 5 Kelly (Grace) *1955:* 7 Magnani (Anna) *1956:* 7 Bergman (Ingrid) *1957:* 8 Woodward (Joanne) *1958:* 7 Hayward (Susan) *1959:* 8 Signoret (Simone) *1960:* 6 Taylor (Elizabeth) *1961:* 5 Loren (Sophia) *1962:* 8 Bancroft (Anne) *1963:* 4 Neal (Patricia) *1964:* 7 Andrews (Julie) *1965:* 8 Christie (Julie) *1966:* 6 Taylor (Elizabeth) *1967:* 7 Hepburn (Katharine) *1968:* 7 Hepburn (Katharine) 9 Streisand (Barbra) *1969:* 5 Smith (Maggie) *1970:* 7 Jackson (Glenda) *1971:* 5 Fonda (Jane) *1972:* 8 Minnelli (Liza) *1973:* 7 Jackson (Glenda) *1974:* 7 Burstyn (Ellen) *1975:* 8 Fletcher (Louise) *1976:* 7 Dunaway (Faye) *1977:* 6 Keaton (Diane) *1978:* 5 Fonda (Jane) *1979:* 5 Field (Sally) *1980:* 6 Spacek (Sissy) *1981:* 7 Hepburn (Katharine) *1982:* 6 Streep (Meryl) *1983:* 8 MacLaine (Shirley) *1984:* 5 Field (Sally) *1985:* 4 Page (Geraldine) *1986:* 6 Matlin (Marlee) *1987:* 4 Cher *1988:* 6 Foster (Jodie) *1989:* 5 Tandy (Jessica) *1990:* 5 Bates (Kathy) *1991:* 6 Foster (Jodie) *1992:* 8 Thompson (Emma) *1993:* 6 Hunter (Holly) *1994:* 5 Lange (Jessica) *1995:* 8 Sarandon (Susan) *1996:* 9 McDormand (Frances) *1997:* 4 Hunt (Helen) *1998:* 7 Paltrow (Gwyneth) *1999:* 5 Swank (Hilary) *2000:* 7 Roberts (Julia) *2001:* 5 Berry (Halle) *2002:* 6 Kidman (Nicole) *2003:* 6 Theron (Charlize)

accede 3 let 5 admit, agree, allow, grant, yield 6 accept, assent, comply, concur, give in, permit 7 agree to, approve, concede, consent 9 acquiesce, cooperate, subscribe

accelerando 6 faster 7 speed up 10 speeding up

accelerate 3 gun, rev 4 grow, roll 5 hurry, impel, rev up, speed 6 hasten, open up, step up 7 quicken, speed up 8 expedite, go faster, increase 9 fast track, gain speed 10 move faster, peel rubber

acceleration 7 speedup 8 hurrying, spurring 9 hastening, revving up 10 increasing, quickening, speeding up, stepping up 12 moving faster

accent 4 beat, lilt, tone 5 acute, grave, meter, pulse, throb 6 rhythm, stress, weight 7 cadence 8 emphasis 9 diacritic, pulsation 10 inflection, intonation *Irish:* 6 brogue *Scottish:* 4 burr *Southern:* 5 drawl

accept 3 bow, buy, see 4 bear, gain, okay, take 5 admit, adopt, agree, catch, favor, go for, grasp, yield 6 accede, admire, affirm, assent, endure, follow, take in, take on 7 agree to, approve, believe, receive, respect, swallow, welcome 8 assent to, bear with, hold with, live with, stand for, tolerate, tough out 9 acquiesce, agree with, undertake 10 capitulate, comprehend, concur with, understand 11 acknowledge, countenance, subscribe to

acceptable 4 good, okay 6 decent, worthy 7 average, welcome 8 adequate, all right, bearable, ordinary, passable, pleasing, standard, suitable 9 endurable, tolerable 10 sufficient 11 commonplace, respectable, supportable 12 satisfactory 13 unexceptional, unimpeachable

acceptably 4 well 5 amply, right 7 capably 8 properly, suitably 9 fittingly, tolerably 10 adequately, becomingly, fairly well 11 competently 12 sufficiently 13 appropriately

acceptant 4 open 8 amenable, friendly, swayable 9 favorable, receptive, recipient, welcoming 10 open-minded, responsive 11 persuadable, persuasible, susceptible 13 influenceable

acceptation 4 gist 5 point, sense 6 import 7 meaning, message, purport 9 intention 10 intendment 12 significance, significancy 13 signification, understanding

accepted 5 usual 6 common, normal, proper 7 correct, regular, routine 8 approved, everyday, expected, habitual, ordinary, orthodox, received 9 customary 10 accustomed, recognized, sanctioned 11 established, traditional 12 conventional

access 3 fit, way 4 adit, door, gust, pang, path, road, turn 5 burst, entry, get at, onset, route, sally, spell, throe 6 attack, avenue, entrée 7 contact, flare-up, ingress, passage, seizure 8 approach, entrance, eruption, increase, outburst 9 admission, explosion 10 admittance

accessible 4 near, open 5 handy 6 public, usable 8 possible 9 available, operative, reachable 10 attainable, employable, obtainable 11 practicable 12 approachable, unrestricted

accession 4 rise 5 raise 8 addition, approach, increase, outburst, taking on 9 accretion, adherence, increment, induction 10 admittance, assumption, attainment, succession 11 acquisition 12 augmentation, inauguration

accessory 3 aid 4 aide, trim 5 extra, frill 6 helper 7 abettor, adjunct, fitting, insider, partner 8 addition, adjuvant, appendix 9 accretion, adornment, ancillary, appendage, assistant, associate, auxiliary, increment, secondary, tributary 10 accomplice, coincident, collateral, concurrent, decoration, incidental, subsidiary 11 appurtenant, concomitant, confederate, conspirator, subordinate, subservient 12 appurtenance, contributory 13 accompaniment, coconspirator, supplementary

accident 3 hap, lot 4 fate, luck, odds 5 fluke 6 chance, gamble, hazard, kismet, mishap 7 bad luck, destiny, fortune, lottery 8 calamity, casualty, fortuity, incident 9 adventure, mischance 10 misfortune 12 misadventure

accidental 3 odd 5 fluky 6 casual, chance, random 7 unmeant 8 by chance, careless 9 chromatic, dependent, extempore, impromptu, unplanned, unwitting 10 coincident, contingent, fortuitous, incidental, undesigned, unexpected, unforeseen, unintended, unpurposed 11 conditional, inadvertent 12 coincidental, nonessential, uncalculated 13 unintentional

acclaim 4 hail, clap, laud 5 cheer, éclat, exalt, extol, glory, honor, kudos, roose 6 homage, praise, salute 7 applaud, approve, commend, glorify, magnify, ovation, root for 8 applause, plaudits 10 compliment

acclimate 5 adapt 6 adjust, change, harden, season 7 toughen 9 condition, habituate

accolade 4 bays, fame 5 award, badge, honor, kudos 6 praise 7 laurels, tribute 8 approval 10 decoration 11 distinction

accommodate 3 fit 4 hold, rent, suit 5 adapt, alter, board, defer, favor, house, humor, lodge, put up, yield 6 adjust, attune, bestow, billet, change, encase, harbor, modify, oblige, please, submit, tailor, take in 7 cater to, conform, contain, enclose, furnish, indulge, quarter, receive, shelter 8 accustom, allow for, domicile 9 entertain, harmonize, integrate, reconcile 11 domiciliate, make room for

accommodating 7 amiable, helpful, willing 8 gracious, obliging 9 adaptable 10 hospitable, solicitous, thoughtful 11 considerate, cooperative

accommodations 4 digs, keep, room 5 hotel, motel 7 housing, lodging, shelter 8 lodgment, quarters 9 residence 12 room and board

accompaniment 4 back, mate 6 fellow, backup 7 adjunct, comrade, consort, partner 8 addition 9 accessory, associate, attendant, colleague, companion, corollary 10 assistance, complement, enrichment, equivalent, supplement 11 concomitant, enhancement 12 augmentation

accompany 4 join 5 bring, guide, pilot 6 attend, convoy, escort, go with 7 combine, conduct, consort 8 chaperon, come with 9 associate 10 appear with, go together 11 perform with

accompanying 8 incident 9 accessory, ancillary, attendant, attending, secondary 10 associated, coincident, collateral 11 concomitant

accomplice 4 aide, ally 5 aider 6 flunky, helper, stooge 7 abettor, partner 9 accessory, assistant, associate 11 confederate, conspirator, subordinate 13 coconspirator

accomplish 3 win 4 gain 5 reach, score 6 attain, effect, fulfil, rack up 7 achieve, execute, fulfill, perfect, pull off, realize, succeed 8 bring off, carry out, complete 9 discharge 10 bring about

accomplished 4 able 5 adept 6 expert 7 skilled 8 finished, masterly, skillful, talented 9 perfected, practiced 10 proficient 11 beyond doubt

accomplishment 3 act, art 4 deed, feat 5 craft, doing, skill 6 action, effort, finish, talent 7 ability, exploit 9 adeptness, expertise 10 attainment, capability, completion, expertness 11 achievement, acquirement, acquisition, proficiency

accord 4 deal, fuse, give, jibe, pact 5 agree, award, blend, chime, fit in, grant, match, merge, tally, union 6 affirm, assent, concur, confer, treaty 7 compact, concert, concord, conform, empathy, harmony, rapport 8 affinity, coalesce, coincide, dovetail, sympathy 9 agreement, harmonize, reconcile, vouchsafe 10 attraction, conformity, consonance, correspond, solidarity 11 concordance 13 understanding

accordant 8 agreeing 9 congruous, consonant 10 conforming, harmonious 13 correspondent

accordingly 4 duly, ergo, then, thus

5 hence **9** therefore, thereupon **12** consequently
accost 3 dog **4** call, dare, face, hail
5 annoy, cross, front, hound, worry
6 bother, call to **7** affront, apply to, bespeak, outface, outrage **8** approach, confront **9** challenge **10** buttonhole **11** memorialize
accouchement 7 lying-in **8** childbed, delivery **10** childbirth **11** confinement, giving birth, parturition
account 3 tab, use **4** bill, deem, note, rate, view **5** avail, basis, favor, score, story, track, value, worth **6** assess, client, esteem, reason, reckon, record, regard, report, repute **7** analyze, explain, expound, history, invoice, justify, recital, respect, service, utility, version **8** appraise, consider, customer, estimate **9** advantage, chronicle, narrative, probe into, rationale, reckoning, relevance, statement, valuation
10 admiration, estimation, exposition, importance, reputation, usefulness **11** consequence, distinction, explain away, explanation, performance, rationalize **13** consideration, justification *book:* **6** ledger
accountable 6 liable **8** amenable
10 answerable **11** explainable, responsible
accounting 11 bookkeeping
accoutre 3 arm, rig **4** deck, gear **5** adorn, dress, equip, fix up, ready **6** attire, fit out, outfit, supply **7** appoint, furnish, prepare, provide, turn out **9** provision
accoutrement 3 kit **4** gear **6** outfit, tackle **7** regalia **8** tackling **9** accessory, apparatus, equipment, machinery, trappings **10** provisions **11** furnishings, habiliments **12** appointments **13** paraphernalia
accredit 3 lay **4** okay **5** refer **6** assign, attest, charge, credit, enable **7** approve, ascribe, certify, commend, empower, endorse, license, warrant **8** sanction, validate, vouch for **9** attribute, authorize, recognize, recommend **10** commission, credential
accretion 4 rise **5** raise **6** growth
7 buildup **8** addition, increase **9** accession, appendage, increment **10** attachment **11** enlargement **12** accumulation, augmentation
accrue 4 grow **5** amass **6** gather, pile up **7** build up, collect, compile **8** increase **10** accumulate, amalgamate **11** agglomerate
accumulate 4 heap, grow, mass, pile **5** add to, amass, hoard, lay by, lay in, lay up, stock, store **6** accrue, garner,

gather, pile up, rack up, roll up
7 acquire, backlog, collect, compile, lay down, stack up, store up **8** assemble, increase **9** stockpile
accumulation 4 bank, heap, mass, pile **5** hoard, stock, store, trove **6** growth **7** buildup, reserve **8** increase **9** accretion, amassment **10** collection **11** aggregation, enlargement **13** agglomeration
accumulative 6 heaped **7** growing **8** additive, additory **9** summative **10** collective, increasing **11** aggregative **12** augmentative
accuracy 8 veracity **9** certainty, exactness, precision **10** definition, exactitude **11** correctness, preciseness **12** definiteness
accurate 4 just, nice, true **5** exact, right **6** actual, proper **7** certain, correct, factual, precise **8** definite, reliable, rigorous **9** authentic, error-free, errorless **10** dependable
accursed 4 vile **6** odious **7** hateful **8** damnable **9** abhorrent, execrable, loathsome, offensive, repugnant, revolting **10** abominable, despicable, detestable
accusation 3 rap **6** charge **9** complaint **10** allegation, indictment **12** denunciation *false:* **7** calumny
accuse 3 tax **5** blame, brand **6** allege, charge, delate, finger, impute, indict **7** arraign, ascribe, censure, impeach **8** admonish, denounce, reproach **9** criminate, criticize, inculpate, reprobate **10** denunciate **11** incriminate
accustom 3 use **4** wont **5** adapt, inure **6** adjust, harden, season **7** conform **9** habituate **11** acclimatize, familiarize
accustomed 3 set **5** usual **6** normal **7** chronic, regular, routine **8** accepted, everyday, familiar, habitual, ordinary, standard **9** customary **10** habituated **11** commonplace, established, traditional **12** conventional
ace 3 bit, jot, pip, top **4** atom, hair, iota, mite, star **5** crumb, minim, point, score, speck **6** defeat, master, winner **7** whisker **8** molecule, particle **9** first rate, hole in one **11** hairbreadth, tennis score
ace and face card 7 natural **9** blackjack
acedia 6 apathy **7** boredom
acerbate 3 vex **5** anger, annoy, peeve **6** madden **7** incense, inflame **8** embitter, irritate **9** aggravate **10** exasperate
acerbic 4 acid, sour, tart **5** acrid, harsh, rough, sharp **7** caustic, cutting, satiric **8** stinging **9** acidulous, corrosive, sarcastic **10** astringent
acerbity 7 acidity, sarcasm **8** acrimony,

asperity, sourness, tartness **9** harshness, roughness, surliness **10** bitterness, causticity

Achates' companion 6 Aeneas

ache 3 yen **4** hurt, long, pain, pang, pine, pity, sigh **5** crave, smart, throb, yearn **6** hanker, hunger, stitch, suffer, thirst, twinge **8** yearning **11** commiserate *Scottish:* **6** stound

Acheron 5 Hades, river

achieve 3 get, win **4** gain **5** reach, score **6** attain, effect, finish, obtain, rack up, secure **7** acquire, execute, fulfill, get done, perform, realize, succeed **8** carry out, complete, conclude **9** actualize **10** accomplish

achievement 4 deed, feat **6** finish **7** exploit, success **10** attainment, completion **11** acquisition, tour de force

Achilles *adviser:* **6** Nestor *companion:* **9** Patroclus *father:* **6** Peleus *horse:* **7** Xanthus *lover:* **7** Briseis *mother:* **6** Thetis *slayer:* **5** Paris *victim:* **6** Hector *vulnerable part:* **4** heel

aching 4 hurt, sore **6** in pain **7** hurtful, hurting, painful **8** yearning **9** disturbed **10** afflictive, distressed **13** compassionate

acicular 5 acute, peaky, piked, sharp **6** peaked, pointy, spiked **7** pointed

acid 4 sour, tart **5** acerb **7** acerbic, acetose, caustic **8** stinging **9** corrosive, sarcastic, vitriolic *bleaching:* **6** oxalic *fatty:* **6** capric **7** caproic, stearic **8** caprylic *found in apples:* **5** malic *found in cranberries:* **7** benzoic *found in grapes:* **8** tartaric *found in lemons:* **6** citric *found in rhubarb:* **6** oxalic *found in sour milk:* **6** lactic *indicator:* **6** litmus *kind:* **5** amino, boric, iodic, malic, oleic **6** acetic, bromic, formic, nitric, oxalic, tannic **7** nitrous, silicic **8** carbolic, carbonic, muriatic, sulfuric **9** aqua regia **12** hydrochloric *neutralizer:* **4** base **6** alkali *tanning:* **6** tannic **8** catechin *vinegar:* **6** acetic

acidulous 3 dry **4** sour, tart **5** acerb, harsh, sharp **6** biting **7** acerbic, acetose, cutting, piquant, pungent **9** sarcastic

Acis *lover:* **7** Galatea *slayer:* **10** Polyphemus

acknowledge 3 own **4** avow, deem, tell, view **5** admit, agree, allow, grant, let on, own up **6** accede, accept, fess up, reveal **7** concede, confess, declare, divulge, profess **8** announce, consider, disclose, proclaim **9** recognize

acknowledgment 6 assent, avowal, credit, notice **9** admission **10** confession **11** affirmation, declaration, recognition

acme 3 cap, top **4** apex, peak **6** apogee,

climax, summit, tiptop, vertex, zenith **8** capstone, pinnacle, ultimate **9** high point **10** perfection **11** culmination

acorn sprouter 3 oak

acoustic 5 aural **6** audile **8** auditory **9** unplugged

acquaint 4 clue, tell, warn **6** advise, fill in, inform, notify, orient, reveal, wise up **7** apprise, divulge, present **8** accustom, disclose **9** enlighten, habituate, introduce **11** familiarize

acquaintance 4 mate **5** amigo, crony, grasp **6** friend **7** comrade, contact **9** associate, colleague, companion **10** cognizance, experience **11** familiarity

acquainted 6 versed **7** abreast, in touch **8** familiar, informed, up-to-date **9** au courant **10** conversant

acquiesce 3 bow, yes **5** agree, allow, bow to, yield **6** accede, accept, assent, comply, concur, give in, submit **7** consent, go along **9** reconcile, subscribe

acquiescence 6 assent **7** consent **8** giving in, yielding **9** deference **10** acceptance, compliance, conformity, submission **11** resignation

acquiescent 6 docile **7** passive **8** resigned, yielding **10** submissive **11** unresistant, unresisting **12** nonresistant, nonresisting

acquire 3 add, buy, get, win **4** earn, form, gain, land **5** amass, annex **6** garner, obtain, pick up, secure **7** bring in, collect, develop, procure **10** accumulate

acquirement 8 addition **9** accretion **11** acquisition

acquisition 4 gain **5** prize **7** winning **8** addition, learning, property, purchase **9** accretion

acquisitive 5 eager, itchy **6** grabby, greedy **8** covetous, desirous, grasping **10** avaricious

acquit 3 act **4** bear, free **5** carry, clear, let go **6** behave, deport, let off **7** absolve, comport, conduct, perform, release, set free **8** liberate **9** discharge, exculpate, exonerate, vindicate

acres 4 area, land **5** lands **6** estate **7** demesne, expanse, holding **8** property

acrid 4 acid, sour **5** harsh, nasty, sharp **6** biting, bitter **7** austere, burning, caustic, cutting, pungent **8** stinging **9** trenchant **10** astringent, irritating **11** acrimonious

acrimonious 3 mad **5** angry, cross, irate, sharp, testy **6** biting, bitter, cranky, ireful **7** acerbic, caustic, cutting **9** indignant, irascible, rancorous **11** belligerent, contentious, quarrelsome

acrimony 5 anger, spite **6** animus, malice, rancor **7** ill will **8** acerbity, asperity, mordancy **9** animosity, antipathy, harshness, virulence **10** bitterness **11** malevolence

Acrisius *daughter:* **5** Danaë *slayer:* **7** Perseus

acrobat 7 gymnast **9** aerialist, trapezist **11** funambulist

across 4 over **6** beyond **7** athwart **12** transversely *prefix:* **5** trans

act 3 law, run **4** bear, bill, deed, fake, feat, mime, play, pose, sham, work **5** bluff, feign, front, put-on, serve, stunt **6** affect, appear, behave, shtick **7** exploit, operate, perform, portray, pretend, routine, statute **8** function, pretense, simulate **9** officiate **10** masquerade **11** counterfeit, impersonate

acting 6 pro tem **7** interim, playing **9** ad interim, dramatics, imitating, portrayal, temporary **10** pro tempore **12** entertaining

action 4 case, deed, move, step, stir, suit, work **5** cause, doing **6** battle, bustle, combat **7** lawsuit, process, service **8** activity, behavior, conflict, fighting, function **9** execution, operation, procedure **10** engagement, proceeding **11** performance

action painting 7 tachism

activate 4 stir, wake **5** rally, rouse, set up, waken **6** arouse, awaken, call up, turn on **8** energize, mobilize, motivate, vitalize **9** stimulate

active 4 busy, live, spry **5** agile, alert, alive, brisk, going **6** at work, in play, lively, moving **7** driving, dynamic, flowing, running, working **8** animated, bustling, emitting, erupting, spirited, vigorous **9** effective, energetic, operating, operative, sprightly **11** functioning, industrious **12** enterprising

activity 6 action, bustle, motion **7** process, pursuit, venture **8** exercise, exertion **10** exercising, liveliness **11** undertaking

actor 4 mime, star **5** mimic **6** mummer, player **7** trouper **8** thespian **9** performer **11** participant **12** impersonator *name:* **3** Cox (Wally), Fox (James, Michael J.), Lee (Bruce), Lom (Herbert), Mix (Tom), Ray (Aldo) **4** Alda (Alan, Robert), Bean (Orson), Blue (Ben), Bond (Ward), Caan (James), Cage (Nicholas), Cobb (Lee J.), Coco (James), Culp (Robert), Dean (James), Depp (Johnny), Dern (Bruce), Duff (Howard), Egan (Richard), Falk (Peter), Ford (Glenn, Harrison), Foxx (Redd), Geer (Will), Gere (Richard), Grey (Joel), Hill (Arthur), Hope (Bob), Hurt (John, William), Ives (Burl), Kaye (Danny), Kean (Edmund), Keel (Howard), Ladd (Alan), Lahr (Bert), Lord (Jack), Lowe (Rob), Lunt (Alfred), Marx (Chico, Groucho, Harpo, Zeppo), Muni (Paul), Ngor (Haing S.), Peck (Gregory), Penn (Sean), Pitt (Brad), Raft (George), Roth (Tim), Ryan (Robert), Shaw (Robert), Tati (Jacques), Tone (Franchot), Torn (Rip), Tune (Tommy), Wahl (Ken), Webb (Clifton, Jack), Wynn (Ed, Keenan), York (Michael) **5** Adler (Luther), Allen (Fred, Tim, Woody), Arkin (Adam, Alan), Asner (Ed), Autry (Gene), Ayres (Lew), Bacon (Kevin), Barry (Gene), Bates (Alan), Beery (Wallace), Benny (Jack), Berle (Milton), Boone (Richard), Booth (Edwin), Boyer (Charles), Brand (Neville), Burns (George), Caine (Michael), Candy (John), Chase (Chevy), Clift (Montgomery), Cosby (Bill), Dafoe (Willem), Davis (Clifton, Ossie, Sammy Jr.), Delon (Alain), Donat (Robert), Evans (Maurice), Ewell (Tom), Finch (Peter), Firth (Colin, Peter), Flynn (Errol), Fonda (Henry, Peter), Franz (Dennis), Gabin (Jean), Gable (Clark), Gould (Elliot), Grant (Cary, Hugh), Gwenn (Edmund), Hanks (Tom), Hardy (Oliver), Hauer (Rutger), Hawke (Ethan), Hayes (Gabby), Irons (Jeremy), Jaffe (Sam), Jones (Dean, James Earl, Tommy Lee), Kazan (Elia), Keach (Stacy), Keith (Brian, David), Kelly (Gene), Kiley (Richard), Kline (Kevin), Kotto (Yaphet), Lamas (Fernando, Lorenzo), Lanza (Mario), Lewis (Jerry, Richard), Lloyd (Harold), Lorre (Peter), Lukas (Paul), Lynde (Paul), March (Fredric), Mason (James), McCoy (Tim), Mills (John), Mineo (Sal), Moore (Dudley, Roger, Victor), Neill (Sam), Nimoy (Leonard), Niven (David), Nolte (Nick), Olmos (Edward James), O'Neal (Patrick, Ryan), Payne (John), Perry (Luke, Matthew), Pesci (Joe), Power (Tyrone), Price (Vincent), Pryce (Jonathan), Quaid (Dennis, Randy), Quayle (Anthony), Quinn (Aidan, Anthony), Rains (Claude), Reeve (Christopher), Scott (Campbell, George C., Randolph), Segal (George), Sheen (Charlie, Martin), Smits (Jimmy), Stack (Robert), Stamp (Terence), Sydow (Max von), Tracy (Spencer), Wayne (John), Wilde (Cornel), Wills (Chill), Woods (James), Young (Gig, Robert) **6** Abbott (Bud),

Albert (Eddie), Ameche (Don), Arness (James), Backus (Jim), Balsam (Martin), Barker (Lex), Baxter (Warner), Beatty (Ned, Warren), Begley (Ed), Blades (Ruben), Bogart (Humphrey), Bolger (Ray), Brando (Marlon), Brooks (Albert, Mel), Burton (Richard), Caesar (Sid), Cagney (James), Cantor (Eddie), Cariou (Len), Carney (Art), Carrey (Jim), Carvey (Dana), Chaney (Lon), Cleese (John), Coburn (Charles, James), Colman (Ronald), Conrad (Robert, William), Conway (Tim, Tom), Coogan (Jackie), Cooper (Gary), Cotten (Joseph), Coward (Noël), Crabbe (Buster), Crenna (Richard), Cronyn (Hume), Crosby (Bing), Cruise (Tom), Culkin (Macaulay), Curtis (Tony), Dailey (Dan), Dalton (Timothy), Danson (Ted), Danton (Ray), Darren (James), De Niro (Robert), de Sica (Vittorio), De Vito (Danny), Dillon (Matt), Downey (Robert), Dullea (Keir), Duryea (Dan), Duvall (Robert), Ferrer (José, Mel), Fields (W.C.), Finney (Albert), Garcia (Andy), Garner (James), Gibson (Hoot, Mel), Glover (Danny), Graves (Peter), Greene (Lorne), Grodin (Charles), Harris (Ed, Richard), Harvey (Laurence), Hayden (Sterling), Heflin (Van), Heston (Charlton), Hingle (Pat), Holden (Bill), Hopper (Dennis, William), Howard (Leslie, Ron, Trevor), Hudson (Rock), Hunter (Jeffrey, Tab), Huston (John, Walter), Hutton (Jim, Timothy), Irving (Henry), Jacobi (Derek, Lou), Jagger (Dean), Keaton (Buster, Michael), Keitel (Harvey), Kilmer (Val), Knotts (Don), Landau (Martin), Landon (Michael), Laurel (Stan), Lemmon (Jack), Liotta (Ray), Lugosi (Bela), MacRae (Gordon), Malden (Karl), Martin (Dean, Steve), Marvin (Lee), Massey (Raymond), Mature (Victor), McCrea (Joel), Meeker (Ralph), Menjou (Adolphe), Mifune (Toshiro), Modine (Matthew), Morley (Robert), Mostel (Zero), Murphy (Audie, Eddie), Murray (Bill, Don), Neeson (Liam), Nelson (Ozzie), Newley (Anthony), Newman (Paul), O'Brian (Hugh), O'Brien (Edmund, Pat), Oldman (Gary), O'Toole (Peter), Pacino (Al), Parker (Fess), Poston (Tom), Powell (Dick), Reeves (Keanu, Steve), Reiner (Carl, Rob), Reiser (Paul), Rennie (Michael), Ritter (John, Tex), Rogers (Roy, Wayne, Will), Romero (Cesar), Rooney (Mickey), Rourke (Mickey), Schell (Maximilian), Seagal (Steven), Sharif (Omar), Slezak (Walter), Snipes (Wesley), Spacey (Kevin), Spader (James), Swayze (Patrick), Taylor (Robert, Rod), Thomas (Danny, Richard), Turpin (Ben), Vallee (Rudy), Vaughn (Robert), Voight (Jon), Wagner (Robert), Walker (Robert), Warden (Jack), Wayans (Damon, Keenen Ivory), Weaver (Dennis, Fritz), Welles (Orson), Werner (Oskar), Wilder (Gene), Willis (Bruce) 7 Abraham (F. Murray), Andrews (Dana), Astaire (Fred), Aykroyd (Dan), Baldwin (Alec, Daniel, Stephen, William), Bellamy (Ralph), Bogarde (Dirk), Branagh (Kenneth), Bridges (Beau, Jeff, Lloyd), Bronson (Charles), Brosnan (Pierce), Brynner (Yul), Burbage (Richard), Bushman (Francis X.), Buttons (Red), Calhern (Louis), Calhoun (Rory), Cameron (Rod), Carroll (Leo G.), Chaplin (Charlie), Clooney (George), Connery (Sean), Connors (Chuck), Conried (Hans), Costner (Kevin), Crystal (Billy), Daniels (Jeff), da Silva (Howard), DeLuise (Dom), Dennehy (Brian), Donahue (Troy), Donlevy (Brian), Douglas (Kirk, Melvyn, Michael, Paul), Dreyfuss (Richard), Durante (Jimmy), Edwards (Vince), Feldman (Marty), Fiennes (Ralph), Freeman (Morgan), Garrick (David), Gazzara (Ben), Gielgud (John), Gleason (Jackie), Goodman (John), Gossett (Lou), Grammer (Kelsey), Granger (Farley, Stewart), Guinness (Alec), Hackman (Gene), Henreid (Paul), Hoffman (Dustin), Homolka (Oscar), Hopkins (Anthony), Hoskins (Bob), Janssen (David), Johnson (Ben, Don, Van), Jourdan (Louis), Jurgens (Curt), Karloff (Boris), Kennedy (Arthur, George), Klugman (Jack), Lawford (Peter), Leonard (Robert Sean, Sheldon), Lithgow (John), MacLane (Barton), Maharis (George), Mathers (Jerry), Matthau (Walter), McCarey (Leo), McGavin (Darren), McQueen (Steve), Milland (Ray), Mitchum (Robert), Montand (Yves), Navarro (Ramon), Newhart (Bob), O'Connor (Carroll, Donald), Olivier (Laurence), Palance (Jack), Paulsen (Pat), Peppard (George), Perkins (Anthony), Pickens (Slim), Pidgeon (Walter), Poitier (Sidney), Preston (Robert), Randall (Tony), Redford (Robert), Rickman (Alan), Robards (Jason), Robbins (Tim), Robeson (Paul), Roberts (Pernell, Tony), Sanders (George), Savalas (Telly), Scourby (Alexander), Selleck (Tom),

Sellers (Peter), Shatner (William), Shepard (Sam), Silvers (Phil), Sinatra (Frank), Skelton (Red), Skinner (Otis), Steiger (Rod), Stewart (James, Patrick), Stooges (Three), Tamblyn (Russ), Ustinov (Peter), Van Dyke (Dick, Jerry), Wallach (Eli), Widmark (Richard), Wilding (Michael), Winters (Jonathan), Woolley (Monty) **8** Banderas (Antonio), Barrault (Jean-Louis), Basehart (Richard), Belmondo (Jean-Paul), Berenger (Tom), Blackmer (Sidney), Borgnine (Ernest), Buchanan (Edgar), Buchholz (Horst), Chandler (Jeff), Costello (Lou), Crawford (Broderick, Michael), Cummings (Robert), Day-Lewis (Daniel), DiCaprio (Leonardo), Eastwood (Clint), Forsythe (John), Garfield (John), Goldblum (Jeff), Griffith (Andy), Harrison (Noel, Rex), Hemmings (David), Holbrook (Hal), Holloway (Stanley), Houseman (John), Jannings (Emil), Kingsley (Ben), Langella (Frank), Laughton (Charles), Marshall (E.G., Herbert), McDowall (Roddy), McDowell (Malcolm), McLaglen (Victor), Meredith (Burgess), Rathbone (Basil), Redgrave (Michael), Reynolds (Burt), Ritchard (Cyril), Robinson (Edward G.), Sarrazin (Michael), Scofield (Paul), Seinfeld (Jerry), Stallone (Sylvester), Stroheim (Erich von), Sullivan (Barry), Travolta (John), Turturro (John), Van Damme (Jean-Claude), Von Sydow (Max), Whitmore (James), Williams (Robin) **9** Amsterdam (Morey), Barrymore (John, Lionel), Brandauer (Klaus Maria), Broderick (Matthew), Carnovsky (Morris), Carradine (David, John, Keith, Robert), Courtenay (Tom), Depardieu (Gérard), Fairbanks (Douglas), Fishburne (Larry), Franciosa (Anthony), Hardwicke (Cedric), Harrelson (Woody), Hyde-White (Wilfrid), Lancaster (Burt), MacMurray (Fred), Malkovich (John), Montalban (Ricardo), Nicholson (Jack), Pleasance (Donald), Robertson (Cliff, Dale), Strasberg (Lee), Tarantino (Quentin), Valentino (Rudolph), Zimbalist (Efrem) **10** Fitzgerald (Barry), Hasselhoff (David), Montgomery (Robert), Richardson (Ralph), Sutherland (Donald, Kiefer), Washington (Denzel) **11** Chamberlain (Richard), Greenstreet (Sydney), Mastroianni (Marcello), Trintignant (Jean-Louis) **13** Kristofferson (Kris)

actor's *quest:* 4 part, role *signal:* 3 cue

actress 3 Bow (Clara), Cox (Courtney), Day (Doris), Dee (Ruby, Sandra), Dru (Joanne), Gam (Rita), Loy (Myrna), May (Elaine), Rae (Charlotte) **4** Ball (Lucille), Bara (Theda), Barr (Roseanne), Cass (Peggy), Cher, Coca (Imogene), Cruz (Penelope), Dahl (Arlene), Daly (Tyne), Dern (Laura), Diaz (Cameron), Dors (Diana), Down (Lesley-Ann), Duke (Patty), Duse (Eleonora), Eden (Barbara), Foch (Nina), Garr (Teri), Gish (Dorothy, Lillian), Grey (Jennifer), Gwyn (Nell), Hawn (Goldie), Holm (Celeste), Hunt (Helen, Linda, Marsha), Hurt (Mary Beth), Hyer (Martha), Ivey (Judith), Kahn (Madeline), Kerr (Deborah), Lake (Veronica), Lisi (Virna), Main (Marjorie), Mayo (Virginia), Neal (Patricia), Olin (Lena), Page (Geraldine), Raye (Martha), Rigg (Diana), Ross (Diana, Katharine), Rush (Barbara), Ryan (Meg, Peggy), Shue (Elisabeth), Weld (Tuesday), West (Mae), Wood (Natalie, Peggy), Wray (Fay), York (Susannah) **5** Adams (Maude), Aimee (Anouk), Allen (Joan, Gracie, Karen, Nancy), Alley (Kirstie), Arden (Eve), Astor (Mary), Bates (Kathy), Berry (Halle), Black (Karen), Bloom (Claire), Blyth (Ann), Booth (Shirley), Brice (Fanny), Britt (May), Bruce (Virginia), Buzzi (Ruth), Caron (Leslie), Close (Glenn), Crain (Jeanne), Danes (Claire), Davis (Bette, Geena, Judy), Dench (Judi), Derek (Bo), Dunne (Irene), Eggar (Samantha), Evans (Edith), Falco (Edie), Field (Sally), Fonda (Bridget, Jane), Gabor (Eva, Zsa Zsa), Garbo (Greta), Gless (Sharon), Grant (Lee), Greer (Jane), Grier (Pam), Hagen (Uta), Hasso (Signe), Hayek (Salma), Hayes (Helen), Heche (Anne), Henie (Sonja), Howes (Sally Ann), Jones (Cherry, Jennifer, Shirley), Kazan (Lainie), Kelly (Grace, Patsy), Kurtz (Swoosie), Lahti (Christine), Lange (Hope, Jessica), Leigh (Janet, Jennifer Jason, Vivien), Lenya (Lotte), Lewis (Juliette), Loren (Sophia), Mason (Marsha, Pamela), Meara (Anne), Miles (Sarah, Vera), Moore (Demi, Julianne, Mary Tyler, Terry), North (Sheree), Novak (Kim), O'Hara (Maureen), Olson (Nancy), O'Neal (Tatum), Perez (Rosie), Picon (Molly), Pitts (Zasu), Reese (Della), Ricci (Christina), Roman (Ruth), Ruehl (Mercedes), Ryder (Winona), Saint (Eva Marie), Scott (Lizbeth, Martha), Shire (Talia), Smith (Alexis, Maggie), Stone (Sharon), Storm (Gale), Swank

(Hilary), Tandy (Jessica), Terry (Ellen), Tomei (Marisa), Tyler (Liv), Tyson (Cicely), Watts (Naomi), Welch (Raquel), Wiest (Dianne), Wyatt (Jane), Wyman (Jane), Young (Sean, Loretta) **6** Adjani (Isabelle), Angeli (Pier), Arthur (Beatrice, Jean), Ashley (Elizabeth), Bacall (Lauren), Bardot (Brigitte), Barkin (Ellen), Barrie (Wendy), Baxter (Anne), Bening (Annette), Bergen (Candice, Polly), Bisset (Jacqueline), Blaine (Vivian), Brooks (Louise), Bujold (Genevieve), Butler (Brett), Cannon (Dyan), Carter (Dixie, Lynda, Nell), Cooper (Gladys), Crouse (Lindsay), Curtin (Jane), Curtis (Jamie Lee), Danner (Blythe), Davies (Marion), Delaney (Dana), Del Rio (Dolores), Dennis (Sandy), Diller (Phyllis), Draper (Ruth), Dumont (Margaret), Duncan (Sandy), Durbin (Deanna), Duvall (Shelley), Ekberg (Anita), Ekland (Britt), Fabray (Nanette), Farmer (Frances), Farrow (Mia), Feldon (Barbara), Fisher (Carrie), Foster (Jodie), Garner (Peggy Ann), Garson (Greer), Gaynor (Mitzi), Gordon (Ruth), Grable (Betty), Grimes (Tammy), Hannah (Daryl), Harlow (Jean), Harper (Jessica, Tess, Valerie), Harris (Barbara, Julie, Rosemary), Hedren (Tippi), Hiller (Wendy), Hunter (Holly, Kim), Hussey (Ruth), Huston (Anjelica), Hutton (Betty), Irving (Amy), Keaton (Diane), Keeler (Ruby), Kidman (Nicole), Kinski (Nastassja), Knight (Shirley), Lamarr (Hedy), Lamour (Dorothy), Lasser (Louise), Laurie (Piper), Lillie (Beatrice), Louise (Tina), Lupino (Ida), MacRae (Sheila), Malone (Dorothy), Martin (Mary), Matlin (Marlee), McGraw (Ali), Merkel (Una), Merman (Ethel), Midler (Bette), Miller (Ann), Mirren (Helen), Monroe (Marilyn), Moreau (Jeanne), Moreno (Rita), Oberon (Merle), O'Brien (Margaret), Oliver (Edna May), Palmer (Lili), Paquin (Anna), Parker (Eleanor, MaryLouise, Sarah Jessica, Suzy), Peters (Bernadette), Powers (Stephanie), Prowse (Juliet), Rainer (Luise), Rashad (Phylicia), Remick (Lee), Ritter (Thelma), Rivera (Chita), Rogers (Ginger), Scales (Prunella), Seberg (Jean), Sidney (Sylvia), Somers (Suzanne), Sommer (Elke), Spacek (Sissy), Streep (Meryl), Taylor (Elizabeth), Temple (Shirley), Theron (Charlize), Thomas (Marlo), Tiffin (Pamela), Tomlin (Lily), Turner (Kathleen, Lana), Walker (Nancy), Warren (Lesley Ann), Watson (Emily),

Weaver (Sigourney), Wilson (Marie), Winger (Debra), Wright (Teresa), Wynter (Dana) **7** Allyson (June), Andress (Ursula), Andrews (Julie), Aniston (Jennifer), Bassett (Angela), Bennett (Constance, Joan), Bergman (Ingrid), Binoche (Juliette), Blethyn (Brenda), Buckley (Betty), Bullock (Sandra), Burnett (Carol), Burstyn (Ellen), Campbell (Mrs. Patrick), Colbert (Claudette), Collins (Joan, Pauline), Cornell (Katherine), Cushman (Charlotte), Darnell (Linda), DeCarlo (Yvonne), Deneuve (Catherine), Dukakis (Olympia), Dunaway (Faye), Dunnock (Mildred), Fawcett (Farrah), Fleming (Rhonda), Fricker (Brenda), Gardner (Ava), Garland (Judy), Gingold (Hermione), Goddard (Paulette), Grahame (Gloria), Grayson (Kathryn), Hayward (Susan), Heckart (Eileen), Hepburn (Audrey, Katharine), Hershey (Barbara), Jackson (Anne, Glenda, Kate), Langtry (Lillie), Learned (Michael), Lombard (Carole), MacGraw (Ali), Madonna, Magnani (Anna), Mangano (Silvana), McGuire (Dorothy), McKenna (Siobhan), McQueen (Butterfly), Meadows (Audrey, Jayne), Mimieux (Yvette), Miranda (Carmen), Mulgrew (Kate), Natwick (Mildred), Parsons (Estelle), Perlman (Rhea), Perrine (Valerie), Plummer (Amanda), Podesta (Rosanna), Portman (Natalie), Roberts (Julia), Russell (Jane, Rosalind, Theresa), Scacchi (Greta), Sevigny (Chloë), Shearer (Norma), Shields (Brooke), Siddons (Sarah), Simmons (Jean), Sorvino (Mira), Sothern (Ann), Stevens (Connie, Stella), Stritch (Elaine), Swanson (Gloria), Swinton (Tilda), Thaxter (Phyllis), Thurman (Uma), Tierney (Gene), Ullmann (Liv), Winfrey (Oprah), Winslet (Kate), Winters (Shelley), Withers (Jane), Woodard (Alfre) **8** Anderson (Judith, Loni, Melissa Sue), Arquette (Patricia, Rosanna), Ashcroft (Peggy), Bancroft (Anne), Bankhead (Tallulah), Basinger (Kim), Blondell (Joan), Byington (Spring), Caldwell (Zoe), Channing (Carol, Stockard), Charisse (Cyd), Christie (Julie), Crawford (Joan), DeMornay (Rebecca), Dewhurst (Colleen), Dietrich (Marlene), Dressler (Marie), Fletcher (Louise), Fontaine (Joan), Fontanne (Lynn), Goldberg (Whoopi), Griffith (Melanie), Hayworth (Rita), Holliday (Judy), Lansbury (Angela), Lawrence (Gertrude), Leachman (Cloris),

Leighton (Margaret), Lindfors (Viveca), Lockhart (June), Lovelace (Linda), MacLaine (Shirley), McDaniel (Hattie), Mercouri (Melina), Minnelli (Liza), Nelligan (Kate), Neuwirth (Bebe), O'Donnell (Rosie), Pfeiffer (Michelle), Pickford (Mary), Prentiss (Paula), Redgrave (Lynn, Vanessa), Reynolds (Debbie), Roseanne, Rowlands (Gena), Sarandon (Susan), Shepherd (Cybill), Signoret (Simone), Stanwyck (Barbara), Straight (Beatrice), Sullavan (Margaret), Talmadge (Norma), Thompson (Emma, Sada), Van Doren (Mamie), Williams (Esther), Woodward (Joanne) **9** Alexander (Jane), Barrymore (Drew, Ethel), Bernhardt (Sarah), Blanchett (Cate), Cardinale (Claudia), Christian (Linda), Clayburgh (Jill), Dandridge (Dorothy), DeGeneres (Ellen), Dickinson (Angie), Fairchild (Morgan), Henderson (Florence), Kellerman (Sally), Mansfield (Jayne), McDonnell (Mary), Moorehead (Agnes), O'Sullivan (Maureen), Pleshette (Suzanne), Plowright (Joan), Schneider (Romy), Singleton (Penny), Stapleton (Jean, Maureen), Strasberg (Susan), Streisand (Barbra), Struthers (Sally), Thorndike (Sybil), Vera-Ellen, Zellweger (Renée) **10** Ann-Margret, Lanchester (Elsa), Montgomery (Elizabeth), Richardson (Miranda, Natasha), Rossellini (Isabella), Rutherford (Margaret), Tushingham (Rita) **11** de Havilland (Olivia), McCambridge (Mercedes), Riefenstahl (Leni), Silverstone (Alicia), Steenburgen (Mary) **12** Bonham-Carter (Helena), Lollabrigida (Gina), Mastrantonio (Mary Elizabeth)

actual 4 hard, live, real, true **5** exact **6** extant, living **7** certain, current, factual, genuine **8** absolute, bona fide, concrete, definite, existent, existing, material, physical, positive, tangible **9** authentic, objective **10** legitimate, phenomenal, undeniable **12** indisputable

actuality 4 fact **5** being, truth **7** reality **9** existence, substance **10** embodiment **11** incarnation, materiality

actually 4 very **5** truly **6** indeed, in fact, really **7** de facto, no doubt **9** genuinely, in reality, veritably **10** absolutely

actuate 4 move, spur, stir **5** drive, impel, rouse **6** arouse, excite, propel, set off, turn on **7** provoke, trigger **8** activate, energize, mobilize, motivate, vitalize

act up 5 cut up **7** show off **9** misbehave **11** misfunction

acumen 3 wit **6** acuity, vision, wisdom **7** insight **8** keenness **9** acuteness, sharpness **10** astuteness, perception, shrewdness **11** discernment, penetration, percipience **12** perspicacity

acute 4 dire, keen **5** sharp **6** urgent **7** crucial, exigent, intense, pointed **8** critical, incisive, piercing, shooting, stabbing **9** knifelike, observant, trenchant **10** perceptive **11** penetrating, quickwitted, sharp-witted

ad ___ 3 hoc, lib, rem **7** hominem, interim, nauseam **9** infinitum

adage 3 saw **4** rule **5** axiom, maxim, motto **6** byword, saying, truism **7** proverb **8** aphorism, apothegm

adagio 4 slow **5** tempo

Adah *husband:* **4** Esau **6** Lamech *son:* **5** Jabal, Jubal **7** Eliphaz

Adam *grandson:* **4** Enos **5** Enoch *rib:* **3** Eve *son:* **4** Abel, Cain, Seth *wife:* **3** Eve **6** Lilith

Adam ___ 4 Bede **5** Smith

adamant 3 set **4** firm, hard **5** rigid, stiff, stone, tough **6** flinty **8** immobile, obdurate, resolute **9** immovable, unbending, unswaying **10** determined, inflexible, unbendable, unyielding **11** unbreakable

adapt 3 fit **4** suit **5** alter, shape, yield **6** adjust, change, modify, revise, square, tailor **7** arrange, conform, remodel **9** acclimate, habituate, reconcile **11** acclimatize, accommodate

adaptable 6 mobile, pliant, supple **7** ductile, plastic, pliable **8** flexible, moldable **9** alterable, malleable, versatile **10** adjustable, modifiable **11** conformable

adaptation 6 change **8** revision **9** reworking **10** adjustment, alteration **12** modification

ad astra per ___ 6 aspera

add 3 sum, tot **4** cast, foot, join, tote **5** affix, annex, count, tally, total, unite **6** append, attach, figure, reckon, tack on, take on **7** augment, compute, count up, enlarge, improve, include **8** compound, increase, totalize **9** build onto, calculate **10** supplement

added 3 new **4** else, more **5** extra, fresh, other **7** another, farther, further **8** appended **9** accessory, increased **10** additional **13** supplementary

addendum 5 extra, rider **8** addition **10** supplement

adder 5 snake, viper **10** calculator **12** hognose snake

addict 3 fan, nut **4** bias, buff **5** hound, lover **6** abuser, devote, junkie, zealot **7** booster, devotee, fanatic, groupie, habitué **9** habituate, surrender **10** aficionado, enthusiast

addition 4 plus, rise 5 annex, extra, raise, rider 7 accrual, adjunct 8 addendum, appendix, increase 9 accession, accessory, accretion, extension, increment 10 supplement 11 enlargement 12 appurtenance, augmentation

additional see ADDED

additionally 3 too 4 also, more, then 5 again 6 as well 7 addedly, besides, further 8 likewise, moreover 9 along with 11 furthermore

additive 5 extra 8 extender 9 summative, substance

addle 5 mix up, spoil 6 muddle, puzzle 7 confuse, fluster, nonplus, perplex 8 befuddle, bewilder, confound, distract, throw off 9 dumbfound

add-on 7 adjunct 9 accessory 11 enhancement

address 3 aim, air, set, URL 4 hail, send, tact, talk 5 apply, court, grace, greet, level, place, point, poise, remit, route, skill, speak, treat 6 call to, devote, direct, pursue, relate, salute, speech 7 bearing, consign, deliver, forward, know-how, lecture, speak to, write to 8 appeal to, approach, converse, deal with, deftness, delivery, demeanor, dispatch, identify, location, petition, position, presence, talk with, transmit 9 attention, dexterity, diplomacy, expertise 10 adroitness, competence, directions, efficiency 11 communicate, comportment, designation, proficiency, savoir faire, tactfulness

adduce 3 lay 4 cite 5 claim, offer 6 allege, submit, tender 7 advance, present, proffer, propose, refer to, suggest 8 document 9 exemplify 10 illustrate

add up 3 sum 5 count, tally, total 6 amount, reckon 7 compute 9 make sense

add up to 4 mean 5 spell 6 amount, denote, import, intend 7 compute, connote, express, signify

A Death in the Family author 4 Agee (James)

adept 3 pro 4 deft, whiz 5 crack, savvy 6 adroit, expert, master, wizard 7 skilled 8 masterly, skillful, virtuoso 9 dexterous, masterful 10 proficient 11 crackerjack 12 professional

adequacy 5 might 6 enough 7 ability 8 capacity 10 capability, competence, sufficient 11 sufficiency 13 qualification

adequate 6 common, decent, enough 8 all right, passable, pleasing, standard, suitable 9 competent, sufficing 10 acceptable, sufficient 11 comfortable 12 satisfactory 13 unexceptional, unimpeachable

adequately 4 well 5 amply, right 6 enough 8 all right, passably, properly, suitably 9 fittingly, tolerably 12 sufficiently 13 appropriately

adhere 4 glue 5 cling, paste, stick 6 attach, bind to, cement, cleave, cohere, fasten 7 stick to 8 hold fast

adherence 4 bond 5 cling 7 loyalty 8 adhesion, clinging, cohesion, fidelity, sticking 9 constancy 10 attachment 12 faithfulness

adherent 6 cohort, votary 7 devotee, sectary 8 disciple, follower, henchman, partisan, stalwart 9 satellite, supporter 10 aficionado

adhering 6 clingy, gluing, sticky 7 binding 8 clinging, sticking 9 attaching, cementing

adhesive 4 glue 5 gluey, gooey, gummy, stamp, tacky 6 cement, clingy, gummed, sticky 7 holding, stickum 8 adhering, fastener, mucilage, sticking 9 attaching

adieu 5 congé 6 bye-bye, so long 7 cheerio, good-bye, parting 8 farewell 11 leave-taking

ad interim 6 acting, pro tem 9 temporary 10 pro tempore 11 temporarily

adios 4 by-by, ciao, ta-ta 5 adieu, later 6 bye-bye, so long 7 cheerio, goodbye, toodles 8 farewell, toodle-oo 10 hasta luego

adipose 3 fat 4 oily 5 fatty 6 greasy 7 fat-like

adit 3 way 4 door 5 entry 6 access, entrée, tunnel 7 ingress, passage 8 entrance 9 mine entry 10 passageway 12 mine entrance

adjacent 4 near 5 close 6 beside, nearby, next to 8 abutting, next door, touching 9 adjoining, alongside, bordering 10 contiguous, juxtaposed, near-at-hand 11 close-at-hand, neighboring 12 conterminous

adjoin 3 add 4 abut, link, line, meet 5 annex, touch, verge 6 append, attach, border, butt on, couple 7 connect, impinge 8 neighbor 11 communicate

adjourn 4 move, rise, stay 5 defer, delay 6 hold up, put off, recess, shelve 7 hold off, suspend 8 dissolve, hold over, postpone, prorogue 9 prorogate

adjudge 4 deem, rule 5 award, grant 6 decide, settle, umpire 7 mediate, referee 9 arbitrate 10 adjudicate

adjunct 5 added, affix 6 joined 8 addendum, addition, appanage, appendix, attached 9 accessory, accretion, appendage, assistant, associate, auxiliary 10 attachment 12 appurtenance

adjure 3 beg, bid 4 urge 6 exhort

7 beseech, entreat, command, implore, require 9 importune 10 supplicate

adjust 3 fit, fix, rig 4 suit, tune 5 adapt, order, right 6 accord, attune, modify, orient, settle, square, tailor, tune up 7 arrange, conform, correct, rectify, resolve 8 modulate, regulate 9 habituate, harmonize, reconcile 11 accommodate

adjuvant 4 aide 6 aiding, helper 8 enhancer, modifier 9 accessory, ancillary, assisting, auxiliary 10 collateral, subsidiary 11 appurtenant 12 contributory

ad-lib 9 extempore, improvise, impromptu 10 improvised, off-the-cuff, unprepared 11 extemporize, spontaneous, unrehearsed

Admetus *father:* 6 Pheres *wife:* 8 Alcestis

administer 3 run 4 boss, deal, give, head 5 issue 6 direct, govern, head up, manage 7 conduct, control, deal out, deliver, dole out, execute, give out, mete out, oversee, perform, provide 8 carry out, dispense, share out 9 apportion, supervise 10 distribute, portion out

administration 6 regime 7 control 9 direction 10 governance, presidency *system of:* 11 bureaucracy

administrator 4 boss, exec, head 5 chief 7 manager, officer 8 director, official, overseer 9 executive 10 supervisor

admirable 6 august, worthy 8 laudable 9 deserving, estimable, excellent, meritable 11 commendable, meritorious, outstanding 12 praiseworthy

admiral *American:* 4 Byrd (Richard), Sims (William) 5 Dewey (George), Stark (Harold) 6 Halsey (Bull), Nimitz (Chester) 7 Zumwalt (Elmo) 8 Farragut (David), Rickover (Hyman), Spruance (Raymond) *Confederate:* 6 Semmes (Raphael) *Dutch:* 5 Tromp (Maarten) *English:* 5 Drake (Francis) 6 Nelson (Horatio), Rodney (George), Vernon (Edward) 7 Hawkins (John) 8 Beaufort (Francis), Jellicoe (John), Villiers (George) 11 Mountbatten (Louis) *French:* 10 Villeneuve (Pierre-Charles) *German:* 4 Spee (Graf Maximilian von) 6 Dönitz (Karl), Raeder (Erich) 7 Doenitz (Karl), Tirpitz (Alfred von) *Japanese:* 4 Togo (Hideki) 5 Yonai (Mitsumasa) 8 Yamamoto (Isoroku) *Spanish:* 8 Menéndez (Pedro)

admiration 5 favor 6 esteem, praise, regard 7 account, delight, respect 8 applause, approval, pleasure 9 affection 10 estimation 11 approbation 12 appreciation

admire 5 adore, honor, prize, value

6 esteem, praise, regard, relish, revere 7 adulate, applaud, approve, cherish, commend, respect 8 consider, treasure 9 delight in 10 appreciate

admirer 3 fan 4 beau, buff 7 booster, devotee, fancier 8 believer, follower, partisan 9 supporter 10 enthusiast

admission 3 way 4 door 5 entry 6 access, assent, entrée 7 ingress 8 entrance 10 admittance, concession, confession 11 affirmation

admit 3 own 4 avow, take 5 agree, allow, enter, grant, let in, let on, lodge, own up 6 accept, fess up, harbor, permit, suffer, take in 7 concede, confess, receive, shelter, welcome 9 entertain, introduce, recognize 11 acknowledge

admix 5 blend, merge 6 mingle 7 combine 8 comingle, compound, immingle 9 commingle 11 intermingle

admixture 5 alloy, blend, combo 6 fusion 7 amalgam 8 compound 9 aggregate, composite 12 amalgamation

admonish 4 warn 5 alert, chide 6 lesson, monish, rebuke, talk to 7 caution, counsel, reprove, speak to 8 call down, forewarn, reproach 9 criticize, reprimand

admonition 3 tip 6 caveat, rebuke 7 caution, chiding, reproof, warning 8 reproach 9 criticism, reprimand 11 disapproval, forewarning

ado 4 fuss, stir 5 tizzy, whirl, worry 6 bother, bustle, flurry 7 concern, problem, trouble, turmoil 9 confusion 10 difficulty

adolescence 5 youth 7 puberty 8 minority 9 greenness 10 juvenility, pubescence 12 youthfulness

adolescent 4 teen 5 minor 6 teener 7 teenage 8 immature, preadult, teenager, youthful 9 pubescent

Adonai 3 God 4 YHWH 6 Elohim, Yahweh

Adonijah *brother:* 5 Amnon 7 Absalom, Chileab *father:* 5 David *mother:* 7 Haggith *slayer:* 7 Benaiah

Adonis *lover:* 5 Venus 9 Aphrodite *mother:* 5 Myrrh 6 Myrrha *slayer:* 4 boar

adopt 4 pick, take 5 raise 6 accept, affect, assume, choose, select, take on, take up 7 care for, embrace, endorse, espouse

adoption 6 choice 7 raising, support 8 espousal, taking in 9 embracing, selection 11 embracement

adorable 4 cute, dear 7 darling, lovable, winsome 8 charming, pleasing, precious 9 appealing 10 attractive, delightful

adoration 4 love 5 ardor, honor

6 esteem, praise 7 passion, worship
8 devotion, idolatry 9 adulation, affection, reverence 10 admiration 11 idolization

adore 4 love 5 honor, prize 6 admire,
dote on, esteem, revere 7 cherish, idolize, respect, worship 8 dote upon,
treasure, venerate 9 affection, delight
in, reverence

adorn 4 deck, trim 5 fix up, grace
6 bedeck, enrich, pretty 7 dress up,
enhance, enliven, furbish, garnish,
smarten 8 beautify, decorate, ornament, prettify 9 embellish

adornment 5 decor, frill 6 finery 7 garnish 8 ornament, trimming 9 accessory,
caparison 10 decoration 13 embellishment

ad rem 3 apt 7 apropos, fitting, germane
8 apposite, material, relevant 9 pertinent 10 applicable, relevantly, to the
point 11 applicative, applicatory

adrift 4 asea, lost 5 at sea, loose 6 afloat
7 aimless, mixed up 8 confused, floating, unmoored 10 anchorless, bewildered 11 disoriented, purposeless

adroit 3 apt 4 able, deft 5 adept, canny,
handy, savvy, smart 6 astute, clever,
expert, nimble, shrewd 7 cunning,
skilled 8 skillful, talented 9 dexterous,
ingenious 11 intelligent, quick-witted,
resourceful 13 perspicacious

adroitness 3 art 4 gift 5 craft, flair,
knack, savvy, skill 7 address, cunning,
know-how, prowess 8 deftness 9 adeptness, dexterity, expertise, ingenuity,
readiness 10 cleverness, expertness
12 intelligence

adulation 7 acclaim, baloney, blarney,
fawning, tribute, worship 8 applause,
flattery, soft soap 9 servility, sweet talk
10 overpraise 11 false praise 12 blandishment

adulatory 7 buttery, fawning 8 unctuous
9 kowtowing 10 flattering, obsequious,
oleaginous 11 bootlicking, sycophantic

adult 4 aged, ripe 5 grown 6 mature
7 grown-up, matured, ripened 9 full-
blown 10 fully grown 11 full-fledged

adulterate 3 cut 4 thin 5 alloy, dirty,
taint, water 6 debase, defile, dilute,
doctor, dope up, impair, weaken
7 cheapen, corrupt, defiled, degrade,
devalue, diluted, falsify, pollute, tainted, thinned 8 degraded, denature,
impurify, polluted, spurious 9 water
down 10 tamper with 11 contaminate

adumbrate 3 dim, fog 4 bode, call, hint,
mist, veil 5 augur, cloud 6 darken,
shadow, sketch 7 becloud, bespeak,
betoken, obscure, outline, portend,

predict, presage, suggest 8 block out,
disclose, forebode, forecast, foretell,
indicate, intimate, prophesy 9 obfuscate, prefigure 10 foreshadow, overshadow 11 prefigurate 12 characterize

adumbration 4 hint, sign 5 shade, umbra
6 shadow 7 outline 8 penumbra 10 indication, intimation, suggestion

advance 3 aid 4 cite, help, lend, loan,
move, rise 5 get on, march, money,
raise, serve 6 assist, course, foster,
mature, prefer, supply, uplift 7 deposit,
develop, elevate, forward, furnish, further, headway, ongoing, present, proceed, promote, propose, upgrade
8 approach, get along, heighten,
increase, progress 9 encourage, evolution, provision 10 accelerate, bring
about 11 development, furtherance,
improvement, progression 12 breakthrough

advanced 3 old 5 first 6 far out 7 forward, in front, leading, liberal, radical
8 far ahead, foremost 9 developed
10 precocious 11 broad-minded, progressive

advancement 4 gain, rise 5 boost
6 growth 7 headway 8 progress 9 elevation, promotion 10 betterment, preference 11 improvement, progression

advantage 4 boon, edge, gain, good,
help, lead, odds 5 asset, avail, serve
6 better, profit 7 account, benefit, mastery 8 blessing, interest, leverage
9 allowance, head start, upper hand
10 ascendancy, domination, leadership,
prosperity 11 superiority 12 running
start

advantageous 4 good 6 timely, toward,
useful 7 benefic, gainful, helpful
8 favoring, salutary 9 conducive, desirable, expedient, favorable, fortunate,
promising 10 beneficial, profitable, propitious, worthwhile

advent 5 onset 6 coming 7 arrival
8 approach 9 beginning

adventitious 5 fluky 6 casual, chance
8 by chance 9 unplanned 10 accidental,
contingent, fortuitous, incidental,
unexpected

adventure 3 try 4 feat, risk, trip 5 quest,
wager 6 chance, gamble, hazard
7 exploit 8 escapade 9 undertake
10 enterprise, experience

adventurous 4 bold, rash 5 brash, risky
6 daring 8 intrepid, reckless 9 audacious, dangerous, daredevil, foolhardy,
hazardous, impetuous, imprudent
10 innovative 12 enterprising

adversary 3 con, foe 4 anti 5 enemy,

rival 7 opposer 8 opponent, opposing
10 antagonist, competitor
adverse 3 bad 4 anti 7 counter, harmful,
hostile, hurtful, opposed 8 contrary,
damaging, negative, opposing, opposite
9 injurious 11 deleterious, detrimental,
obstructive, unfavorable 12 antagonistic, antipathetic
adversity 4 dole 5 trial 6 misery, mishap
7 bad luck, bad news, trouble 8 bad
break, distress, hard time, hardship
9 mischance, suffering 10 difficulty, ill
fortune, misfortune
advert 4 cite, note 5 refer 6 allude,
notice, remark 7 bring up, mention,
observe 8 indicate, point out
advertent 5 aware 7 heedful, mindful
9 attentive, intentive, observant,
regardful
advertise 4 drum, hype, plug, puff, push
5 boost, pitch 6 blazon, herald, inform,
notify, report 7 advance, apprise, build
up, declare, promote, publish, sponsor
8 announce, ballyhoo, proclaim
9 broadcast, publicize 10 annunciate,
promulgate
advertisement 4 bill, plug, sign 5 blurb,
flyer, promo 6 notice, poster, want ad
7 affiche 8 circular 9 billboard, broadcast, promotion, publicity 10 commercial 11 declaration, publication
12 announcement, proclamation
advice 3 aid, tip 4 help, news, view, word
5 input 6 notice 7 caution, counsel,
opinion, tidings, warning 8 guidance,
teaching 10 admonition, suggestion
11 information, instruction 12 intelligence
advisable 4 wise 5 sound 6 seemly
7 politic, prudent 8 sensible, suitable,
tactical 9 desirable, expedient, practical
10 worthwhile 11 recommended
12 advantageous
advise 3 tip 4 tell, tout, urge, warn
5 guide 6 clue in, confer, enjoin, fill in,
inform, notify, tip off, wise up 7 apprise,
caution, consult, counsel, suggest
8 acquaint, forewarn, instruct, point
out 9 encourage, prescribe, recommend
Advise and Consent author 5 Drury
(Allen)
advised 7 studied, weighed 8 designed,
intended 10 calculated, considered,
deliberate, thought out 11 intentional
12 premeditated
adviser 5 coach, guide 6 mentor 7 counsel, tipster 9 counselor 10 consultant,
instructor
advisory 7 guiding, helping 9 educative
10 counseling 12 consultative 13 informational

advocacy 3 aid 6 urging 7 backing,
defense, support 9 promotion
advocate 4 back, push, tout, urge
5 favor 6 backer, defend, preach,
uphold 7 promote, propose, support
8 argue for, backstop, champion, exponent, plump for, side with 9 encourage,
expounder, proponent, recommend,
spokesman, supporter 11 countenance
Aeacus *father:* 4 Zeus *mother:* 6 Aegina
son: 6 Peleus 7 Telamon
Aedon *brother:* 7 Amphion *sister-in-law:*
5 Niobe *son (victim):* 6 Itylus
Aeëtes *daughter:* 5 Medea *father:*
6 Helios
aegis 4 care, ward 5 armor, guard
6 charge, shield 7 backing, control,
defense, support 8 auspices, guidance,
security 9 influence, patronage, safeguard 10 protection 11 sponsorship
Aegisthus *father:* 8 Thyestes *lover:*
12 Clytemnestra *mother:* 7 Pelopia *slayer:* 7 Orestes *victim:* 6 Atreus
9 Agamemnon
Aeneas *companion:* 7 Achates *father:*
8 Anchises *mother:* 5 Venus 9 Aphrodite
son: 5 Iulus 8 Ascanius *wife:* 6 Creusa
7 Lavinia
Aeneid *author:* 6 Vergil, Virgil *first words:*
16 arma virumque cano *hero:* 6 Aeneas
Aeolus *daughter:* 7 Alcyone 8 Halcyone
father: 8 Poseidon
aeon 3 age 4 time 6 period 8 blue moon,
duration
aerate 7 lighten, freshen, refresh 9 oxy-
genate, ventilate
aerial 4 high 5 lofty 6 flying, vapory
7 antenna, soaring 8 birdlike, elevated,
ethereal, fanciful, towering, vaporous
9 pneumatic 10 impalpable 11 atmospheric, forward pass
aerie 4 nest 7 citadel, lookout 9 penthouse
aeronaut 4 Fogg (Phileas) 5 pilot 7 aviator 8 Zeppelin (Ferdinand, Graf von)
10 balloonist
Aerope *husband:* 6 Atreus *lover:*
8 Thyestes *son:* 8 Menelaus 9 Agamemnon
aery see AERIAL
Aesculapius *daughter:* 6 Hygeia
7 Panacea *father:* 6 Apollo *slayer:*
4 Zeus 7 Jupiter *teacher:* 6 Chiron *wife:*
6 Epione
Aeson *brother:* 6 Pelias *son:* 5 Jason
aesthete 4 buff 6 expert 7 devotee
9 authority 10 dilettante 11 appreciator,
cognoscente, connoisseur
aesthetic 6 artful 8 artistic, creative,
pleasing 9 beautiful, sensitive 10 attractive, harmonious

afar 5 apart 6 remote 7 distant

affable 4 kind, open, warm 6 at ease, genial, gentle, kindly, polite 7 amiable, cordial 8 friendly, gracious, obliging, pleasant, sociable 9 congenial, courteous

affair 4 case, love 5 amour, worry 6 action, matter 7 concern, liaison, palaver, romance 8 business, function, interest, intrigue, occasion 9 happening, procedure 10 proceeding 12 relationship

affect 3 act 4 fake, move, sham, stir, sway 5 adopt, alter, bluff, fancy, feign, haunt, put on, touch 6 assume, change, strike 7 act upon, disturb, impress, inspire, pretend 8 frequent, simulate 9 cultivate, influence 11 counterfeit

affectation 3 air 4 airs, pose, sham, show 6 facade 8 pretense 9 mannerism 10 pretension 13 artificiality

affected 5 false, moved, put-on 6 phoney 7 altered, assumed, changed, feigned, stilted 8 disposed, inclined, involved, mannered, precious, spurious 9 concerned, conscious, contrived, insincere, pretended, unnatural 10 artificial 11 overrefined, pretentious 13 self-conscious

affecting 3 sad 6 lively, moving 7 pitiful 8 exciting, poignant, touching 9 thrilling 10 disturbing, impressive 11 distressing, influential

affection 4 bias, love 5 trait 6 doting, liking, malady, virtue, warmth 7 ailment, concern, disease, emotion, feature, feeling, illness, leaning, passion, quality 8 devotion, disorder, fondness, interest, penchant, property, sickness, sympathy 9 attention, attribute, character, complaint, condition, sentiment 10 attachment, propensity, tenderness 12 predilection

affectionate 4 dear, fond, warm 6 caring, doting, loving, tender 7 devoted 8 friendly 11 sympathetic

affective 6 moving 7 emotive 8 stirring, touching 9 emotional

affectivity 7 emotion, feeling, passion 9 sentiment

affianced 7 engaged, pledged 8 intended, plighted, promised 9 betrothed, committed 10 contracted

affiche 4 bill, list 6 notice, poster 7 placard 8 handbill

affidavit 4 oath 9 testimony 11 affirmation, declaration

affiliate 4 ally, join 5 annex, unite 6 branch 7 combine, connect, partner 9 associate

affiliated 4 akin 5 bound 6 allied, joined, linked 7 kindred, related 9 connected, dependent 10 associated

affiliation 4 club 5 tie-in, union 6 hookup, league 7 cahoots, company, joining 8 alliance 10 connection, fellowship 11 association, combination, conjunction, partnership

affinity 6 simile 7 analogy, kinship, rapport 8 likeness, relation, sympathy 9 alikeness 10 attraction, similarity, similitude 11 resemblance 13 compatibility

affirm 3 say, yes 4 aver, avow, okay 5 state, swear, vouch 6 assent, assert, attest, depose, ratify, uphold 7 certify, confirm, declare, profess, protest, testify, witness 8 dedicate, validate 9 guarantee

affirmative 3 aye, yea, yes 4 yeah 6 assent 8 approval, positive 9 affirming, approving, asserting, assertion, endorsing, favorable, ratifying 10 confirming, supporting 11 affirmation

affix 3 add, tag 4 bind, glue, join, nail, tack 5 annex, paste, put on, rivet, stick, tag on 6 append, attach, fasten, tack on 7 impress, stick on, subjoin 8 addition 9 appendage 10 attachment

afflict 3 try, vex 4 pain, rack 5 annoy, beset, harry, press, smite, worry, wound, wring 6 bother, burden, harass, harrow, injure, martyr, pester, plague, strike, suffer 7 agonize, anguish, torment, torture, trouble 8 distress

afflicted 6 pained, rueful, woeful 7 doleful, injured, unhappy, worried 8 dolorous, stricken, troubled, wretched 9 disturbed, miserable, sorrowful, tormented 10 distressed

affliction 3 woe 4 care 5 cross, grief, trial 6 ordeal, plague, sorrow 7 anguish, illness, scourge, torment, trouble 8 distress, hardship, sickness 9 adversity, heartache, infirmity 10 misfortune 11 tribulation

afflictive 3 sad 4 dire, sore 6 aching, bitter, woeful 7 galling, hurtful, hurting, painful 8 grievous, mournful 9 sorrowful 10 calamitous, deplorable, lamentable 11 distasteful, distressing, regrettable, troublesome, unfortunate, unpalatable 13 heartbreaking

affluence 5 means, worth 6 bounty, influx, plenty, riches, wealth 8 opulence, property, richness 9 abundance, plenitude, profusion, resources 10 prosperity

affluent 4 full, rich 5 flush 6 loaded 7 copious, flowing, moneyed, opulent, wealthy, well-off 8 abundant, well-to-do

9 bountiful, plentiful, tributary, well-fixed 10 prosperous

afford 4 able, bear, give 5 allow, grant, incur, offer, spare, stand 6 bestow, confer, donate, impart, manage, supply 7 furnish, present, support, sustain

affordable 5 cheap 6 modest 7 low-cost 8 bearable 10 manageable, reasonable 11 inexpensive

affray 3 row 5 clash, fight, melee, scrap 6 fracas, rumpus 7 dispute, quarrel, ruction, scuffle 8 disorder, skirmish

affront 3 vex 4 face, meet, slap, slur 5 abuse, anger, annoy, wrong 6 injury, insult, offend, slight 7 offense, outrage, put down 8 contempt, rudeness 9 aspersion, criticize, encounter, indignity

Afghanistan *capital:* 5 Kabul *city:* 5 Herat 8 Kandahar 12 Mazar-i-Sharif *ethnic group:* 7 Pashtun *language:* 4 Dari 6 Pashto *monetary unit:* 7 Afghani *neighbor:* 4 Iran 5 China 8 Pakistan 10 Tajikistan, Uzbekistan 12 Turkmenistan

aficionado 3 fan 4 buff 5 hound, lover 6 expert 7 admirer, devotee, habitué 10 enthusiast 11 appreciator

afield 4 afar, away, awry 5 amiss, badly, wrong 6 abroad, astray 8 straying 9 elsewhere, off course

afire 3 hot 5 aglow, fiery 6 ablaze, aflame, alight, red-hot 7 blazing, burning, excited, flaming, flaring, ignited 8 inflamed, in flames 9 energized, excitable 10 passionate 11 conflagrant

afloat 4 asea 5 at sea 6 adrift, buoyed 9 supported, sustained

afraid 4 wary 5 chary, jumpy, loath, scary, sorry, timid 6 averse, scared, trepid 7 anxious, fearful, uneager, worried 8 cautious, hesitant, skittish, timorous 9 concerned, regretful, reluctant, unwilling 10 frightened 11 disinclined 12 apprehensive

afresh 3 new 4 anew, over 5 again, newly 6 de novo, encore 8 once more, repeated 9 once again

Africa *country:* 4 Chad, Mali, Togo 5 Benin, Congo, Egypt, Gabon, Ghana, Kenya, Libya, Niger, Sudan, Zaire 6 Angola, Gambia, Guinea, Malawi, Rwanda, Uganda, Zambia 7 Algeria, Burundi, Comoros, Eritrea, Lesotho, Liberia, Morocco, Namibia, Nigeria, Senegal, Somalia, Tunisia 8 Botswana, Cameroon, Djibouti, Ethiopia, Tanzania, Zimbabwe 9 Cape Verde, Mauritius, Swaziland 10 Ivory Coast, Madagascar, Mauritania, Mozambique, Seychelles 11 Burkina Faso, Côte d'Ivoire, Sierra Leone, South Africa

12 Guinea-Bissau *ethnic group:* 3 Ibo 4 Akan, Arab, Boer, Copt, Fula, Issa, Moor, Zulu 5 Bantu, Fulah, Galla, Hausa, Kongo, Mande, Pygmy, Swazi, Wolof 6 Berber, Fulani, Hamite, Herero, Kikuyu, Nubian, Somali, Tuareg, Ubangi, Yoruba 7 Ashanti, Bedouin, Bushman, Malinke, Swahili 8 Egyptian, Mandingo 9 Hottentot *language:* 3 Ibo 5 Bantu, Galla, Hausa 6 Arabic, Berber, Somali, Yoruba 7 Amharic, Bambara, Swahili 8 Malagasy 9 Afrikaans

aft 5 after 6 astern 8 rearmost, rearward 9 sternward

after 3 aft, for 4 back, hind, next, past, rear 5 below, later, since 6 astern, back of, behind, beyond, hinder 7 by and by, ensuing 8 hindmost, in view of 9 following, posterior, sternward 10 subsequent 12 subsequently

after all 3 yet 5 still 6 at last, though 7 finally, however 8 in the end 11 nonetheless 12 nevertheless

aftereffect 5 issue 6 result, upshot 7 fallout, outcome 11 consequence, eventuality

afterlife 6 beyond 8 eternity 9 hereafter

aftermath 4 wake 6 effect, result, upshot 12 consequences, repercussion

afterward 4 next, soon, then 5 later 6 behind 7 by and by, thereon 8 latterly 9 hereafter 10 thereafter 12 subsequently

afterword 8 epilogue

Agag *kingdom:* 6 Amalek *slayer:* 6 Samuel

again 4 also, anew, back, over 6 afresh, de novo, encore 8 once more

again and again 3 oft 4 much 5 often 8 ofttimes 10 frequently, oftentimes, repeatedly

against 6 contra, facing, versus 7 vis-à-vis 8 fronting, opposite, touching *prefix:* 4 anti 6 contra 7 counter

Agamemnon *avenger:* 7 Orestes *brother:* 8 Menelaus *daughter:* 7 Electra 9 Iphigenia *father:* 6 Atreus *slayer:* 9 Aegisthus *son:* 7 Orestes *wife:* 12 Clytemnestra

agape 4 love, open 6 amazed, gaping 7 yawning 8 wide open 9 astounded, love feast 10 astonished, confounded 11 dumbfounded, overwhelmed 13 thunderstruck

agate 3 taw 4 type 6 marble, quartz 7 shooter 8 type size

Agave *father:* 6 Cadmus *husband:* 6 Echion *mother:* 8 Harmonia *sister:* 3 Ino 6 Semele 7 Autonoë *son:* 8 Pentheus

age 3 eon, era 4 aeon, grow, span, time

5 epoch, ripen, stage **6** grow up, mature, mellow, period **7** develop, grow old **8** blue moon, division, interval, lifetime, long time, majority, maturate **9** become old **10** generation

aged 3 old **4** ripe, worn **5** cured, hoary, olden **6** mellow, senior **7** ancient, antique, elderly, matured, ripened **8** grown old, timeworn **9** developed, senescent, venerable **11** patriarchal **12** antediluvian

ageless 7 endless, eternal, lasting **8** dateless, enduring, immortal, timeless **9** immutable **11** everlasting

agency 4 cause, force, means, organ, power **6** action, bureau, medium, office **7** company, channel, vehicle **8** activity, auspices, business, division, function, ministry **9** mechanism, operation **10** department, instrument **12** organization **13** establishment

agenda 6 docket, lineup **7** program **8** calendar, schedule **9** timetable *entry:* **4** item

Agenor *brother:* **5** Belus *daughter:* **6** Europa *father:* **7** Antenor, Neptune **8** Poseidon *mother:* **5** Libya *son:* **6** Cadmus

agent 3 fed, spy **4** tool **5** actor, means, organ, proxy, spook **6** deputy, factor, medium **7** channel, proctor, steward, vehicle **8** assignee, attorney, executor, minister, ministry **9** activator, go-between, middleman, operative **10** instrument, procurator

age-old 5 olden **7** ancient, antique, elderly, forever **8** timeworn **9** venerable **10** immemorial **11** time-honored, traditional

agglomerate 4 heap, mass, pile, rock **6** gather **7** cluster **9** aggregate **10** collection **11** aggregation

agglomeration 4 heap **5** hoard, trove **7** cluster **9** aggregate, amassment, gathering **10** collection, cumulation **11** aggregation

aggrandize 4 hype **5** boost **6** beef up, expand, extend, praise **7** augment, build up, enhance, enlarge, ennoble, glorify, inflate, magnify **8** heighten, increase, multiply **11** distinguish

aggravate 3 vex **4** gall **5** anger, annoy, grate, mount, peeve, pique, rouse, upset **6** burn up, deepen, nettle, worsen **7** bedevil, disturb, enhance, inflame, magnify, perturb, provoke **8** heighten, increase, irritate **9** intensify **10** exacerbate

aggravation 4 pain **5** worry **6** bother **8** increase **9** annoyance, worsening **10** irritation **11** provocation

aggregate 3 all, sum **4** body, bulk, floc **5** add up, gross, total, whole **6** amount **8** entirety, quantity, totality **9** composite **10** cumulative **11** agglomerate **12** conglomerate **13** agglomeration

aggregation 4 body, mass **5** crowd, group, hoard, total, trove **7** cluster, company **8** assembly **9** amassment, gathering **10** assemblage, collection, cumulation **11** agglomerate **12** accumulation

aggression 4 push, raid **5** fight, onset **6** attack **7** assault, offense **8** invasion **9** hostility, incursion, offensive, onslaught, pugnacity **10** assailment **12** belligerence **13** combativeness

aggressive 5 pushy **6** fierce, severe **7** hostile, scrappy, vicious, warlike **8** emphatic, forceful, militant **9** assertive, attacking, combative, energetic, intrusive, offensive **11** belligerent, contentious, domineering, hard-hitting **12** enterprising

aggrieve 4 hurt, pain **5** annoy, harry, upset, worry, wrong **6** harass, injure, plague **7** afflict, oppress, torment, trouble **8** distress **9** constrain, persecute

aghast 4 agog, awed **6** afraid, amazed, scared **7** anxious, fearful, shocked, stunned **8** appalled, dismayed, startled **9** awestruck, horrified, terrified **10** astonished, confounded, frightened **11** dumbfounded, overwhelmed **13** thunderstruck

agile 4 deft, spry **5** alert, brisk, catty, lithe, quick, zippy **6** active, adroit, limber, lively, nimble, supple **7** lissome **9** adaptable, dexterous, sprightly

agitate 4 move, rile, rock, stir, toss **5** argue, churn, peeve, shake, upset **6** arouse, bother, excite, flurry, joggle, ruffle, stir up **7** discuss, dispute, disturb, fluster, perturb, provoke, tempest, trouble, unhinge **8** disquiet, irritate **9** thrash out **10** discompose

agitation 4 flap, fuss, stir, to-do **5** clash **6** bustle, clamor, debate, flurry, lather, tumult **7** dispute, tempest, turmoil **9** commotion, confusion **10** turbulence **11** disturbance

agitator 5 rebel **6** shaker **7** inciter, stirrer **8** fomenter, inflamer **9** disrupter **10** instigator **11** provocateur

Aglaia see GRACES

Aglauros *father:* **7** Cecrops *sister:* **5** Herse **9** Pandrosos

aglow 4 warm **5** afire **6** bright, aflame, alight **7** excited, radiant, shining **8** gleaming, luminous

agnate 4 akin, like **5** alike **6** allied, joined, linked **7** cognate, connate, kindred, kinsman, related, similar **8** relation, relative **9** analogous **10** affiliated **11** consanguine **13** corresponding

agnostic 7 doubter, skeptic **8** doubting **10** questioner, undogmatic **11** uncommitted **12** noncommittal

Agnus ___ 3 Dei

ago 4 back, gone, past, yore **5** since **6** before

agog 4 avid, keen **5** eager **6** roused **7** excited, fervent **8** desirous **9** expectant, impatient **12** enthusiastic

agon 5 clash **6** battle **7** contest **8** conflict, struggle

agonize 4 fret, gall, hurt, pain, rack **5** chafe **6** harrow, squirm, suffer, writhe **7** afflict, torment, torture, trouble **8** distress, stew over, struggle **10** excruciate

agonizing 6 fierce **7** extreme, intense, painful, racking, tearing **9** harrowing, suffering, torturing, torturous **10** tormenting **12** excruciating

agony 4 pain **5** dolor, pangs **6** misery **7** anguish, passion, torment, torture **8** distress, outburst, struggle **9** suffering **10** affliction

agora 11 marketplace **12** meeting place

agrarian 5 rural **6** rustic **8** pastoral **10** campestral **12** agricultural

agree 3 buy, set, yes **4** jibe, okay, suit **5** admit, check, equal, fit in, match, tally **6** accede, accept, accord, assent, concur, settle, square **7** buy into, comport, concede, concert, concord, conform, consent **8** check out, coincide, dovetail, side with **9** acquiesce, harmonize, recognize, subscribe **10** correspond **11** acknowledge

agreeable 4 nice, open **5** ready **7** affable, welcome, willing **8** amenable, in accord, pleasant, pleasing **9** approving, congenial, congruous, consonant, favorable, receptive **10** acceptable, compatible, concurring, consenting, consistent **11** pleasurable, sympathetic

agreed 3 aye, yea, yep, yes **4** okay **6** surely **8** all right, of course **9** certainly **10** definitely, positively

agreement 4 bond, deal, pact **6** accord, assent, treaty **7** bargain, compact, concord, consent, entente, harmony **8** contract, covenant **9** concordat **10** acceptance, consonance **11** arrangement, concordance, concurrence

agree with 3 fit **4** suit **5** befit **6** assist, become **7** support **10** go together

agricultural 7 bucolic **8** agrarian, pastoral

agriculture 7 farming, tillage **8** agronomy, ranching **9** husbandry **11** cultivation, soil culture

Agrippina *brother:* **8** Caligula *husband:* **8** Claudius *son:* **4** Nero

aground 5 stuck **6** ashore, on land **7** beached, on shore **8** disabled, stranded

ague 3 flu **5** fever **7** malaria, shivers **9** influenza, shivering **10** blackwater

Ahab *daughter:* **8** Athaliah *father:* **4** Omri *wife:* **7** Jezebel

Ahasuerus *kingdom:* **6** Persia *wife:* **6** Esther, Vashti

Ahaz *kingdom:* **5** Judah *son:* **8** Hezekiah *wife:* **3** Abi

Ahaziah *father:* **4** Ahab **5** Joram **7** Jehoram *kingdom:* **5** Judah **6** Israel *mother:* **7** Jezebel **8** Athaliah *sister:* **9** Jehosheba **11** Jehosobeath

ahead 4 ante, fore **6** before, onward **7** earlier, forward, in front, leading, onwards **8** foremost, forwards, previous **9** in advance **10** beforehand **11** precedently

Ahinoam *father:* **7** Ahimaaz *husband:* **4** Saul **5** David *son:* **5** Amnon

aid 4 abet, care, hand, help, lift **6** assist, helper, relief, rescue, succor **7** backing, comfort, help out, support, sustain **9** assistant, attendant, subsidize **10** assistance, benefactor, mitigation **11** alleviation

Aida *composer:* **5** Verdi (Giuseppe) *father:* **8** Amonasro *lover:* **7** Radames *rival:* **7** Amneris

aide 6 deputy, helper, second **7** orderly **8** adjutant. **9** assistant, attendant, coadjutor **10** coadjutant, lieutenant

aikido 10 martial art

ail 4 hurt, pain **5** upset, worry **6** bother **7** afflict, disturb, trouble **8** distress

ailing 3 ill, low **4** down, sick, weak **6** in pain, poorly, sickly, unwell **8** below par, diseased **9** enfeebled **10** indisposed **11** debilitated

ailment 6 malady, unrest **7** disease, ferment, illness, turmoil **8** disorder, disquiet, sickness, syndrome **9** affection, complaint, condition, infirmity **10** inquietude, uneasiness **11** disquietude, restiveness **12** restlessness

aim 3 end, try **4** cast, goal, head, mark, mean, plan, want, wish **5** angle, essay, focus, level, point, slant, train **6** aspire, design, desire, direct, intend, object, strive, target, zero in **7** address, attempt, propose, purpose **8** ambition, endeavor **9** objective **11** contemplate

aimless 6 random **7** wayward **8** goalless **9** desultory, haphazard, hit-or-miss, irregular, pointless, unplanned **10** designless **11** purposeless

air 3 sky **4** aura, mien, mood, song, tune, vent **5** style **6** manner, melody, reveal, strain **7** bearing, divulge, express, feeling, quality **8** demeanor **9** broadcast, character, ventilate **10** atmosphere, deportment

aircraft 5 blimp, drone, plane **6** glider **7** airship, balloon, chopper **8** aerodyne, aerostat, airplane, jetliner, zeppelin **9** dirigible **10** helicopter *carrier:* **7** flattop *designer:* **6** Fokker (Anthony), Martin (Glenn) **7** Junkers (Hugo), Tupolev (Andrei) **8** Northrop (Jack), Sikorsky (Igor), Yakovlev (Alexander) **13** Messerschmitt (Willy)

airless 5 close **6** stuffy, sultry **8** stagnant, stifling **11** suffocating

airline 3 JAL, KLM, LOT, TWA **4** BOAC, El Al **5** Delta, Pan Am, USAir, Varig **6** Iberia, Qantas, United, Virgin **7** Eastern, JetBlue, Olympic **8** Aeroflot, Alitalia, American, Swissair **9** Air France, Lufthansa, Northwest, Southwest, U.S. Airways **11** Continental, Pan American

airman 5 flier, flyer, pilot **6** flyboy **7** aviator **8** aeronaut

air movement 4 gust, wind **5** draft **6** breath, breeze **7** updraft **9** downdraft

air navigation system 5 loran, navar, radar

airplane 3 jet **5** avion **6** bomber **7** fighter **8** autogiro, autogyro **9** transport *A-bomb-dropper:* **8** Enola Gay *battle:* **8** dogfight *body:* **8** fuselage *engine:* **3** jet **6** fanjet **7** propjet **8** turbofan, turbojet **9** turboprop *engine casing:* **7** nacelle *engineless:* **6** glider *instrument:* **5** radar, radio **7** compass **9** altimeter, gyroscope **10** tachometer **11** transponder *maneuver:* **4** buzz, dive, loop, roll **8** nosedive **9** chandelle **10** barrel roll *movement:* **3** yaw **4** bank, spin **5** pitch **8** tailspin *part:* **3** fin **4** flap, nose, prop, tail, wing **5** cabin, wheel **6** engine, rudder **7** aileron **8** airscrew, elevator **9** empennage, propeller **10** stabilizer *pilotless:* **5** drone *shelter:* **6** hangar *target:* **6** drogue *vapor:* **8** contrail

air plant 6 orchid **8** epiphyte **9** bromeliad, kalanchoe **11** Spanish moss **12** strangler fig

airport 5 field **7** helipad **8** heliport **9** aerodrome *building:* **8** terminal *flag:* **8** windsock
name:
> Atlanta: **10** Hartsfield Boston: **5** Logan Chicago: **5** O'Hare **6** Midway Dublin: **7** Shannon London: **7** Gatwick **8** Heathrow New York: **3** JFK **7** Kennedy **9** La Guardia Paris: **4** Orly **8** DeGaulle **9** Le Bourget Rome: **7** Da Vinci Washington: **6** Dulles, Reagan

8 National *part:* **5** apron, tower **6** runway **7** taxiway

airs 4 pose, show **5** front **6** vanity **7** hauteur **8** pretense **9** loftiness, mannerism, vainglory **10** pretension **11** affectation, insincerity, ostentation **13** artificiality

airship 3 jet **5** blimp, plane **8** zeppelin **9** dirigible

airtight 4 shut **6** closed, sealed **7** certain **8** hermetic, ironclad **10** impervious **11** impermeable, irrefutable **12** indisputable, invulnerable **13** incontestable

airy 4 open, rare, thin **5** blowy, fresh, gusty, light, lofty, proud, windy **6** aerial, bouncy, breezy, dainty, unreal **7** buoyant, gaseous, soaring, tenuous **8** affected, animated, delicate, ethereal, graceful, illusory, rarefied, spirited, towering, vaporous, volatile **9** expansive, frivolous, pneumatic, resilient, sprightly, vivacious **10** diaphanous, ventilated **11** atmospheric, skyscraping **12** effervescent, high-spirited

A Is for Alibi author 7 Grafton (Sue)

Ajax 4 hero **5** Greek **7** warrior *father:* **6** Oileus **7** Telamon *opponent:* **6** Hector *participant:* **9** Trojan War

akin 4 like, same **5** alike **6** allied **7** kindred, related, similar, uniform **8** parallel **9** analogous, consonant **10** affiliated, comparable, compatible **11** consanguine **13** corresponding

Alabama *capital:* **10** Montgomery *city:* **5** Selma **6** Mobile **10** Birmingham, Huntsville, Tuscaloosa **12** Muscle Shoals *college, university:* **6** Auburn **8** Tuskegee *mountain:* **6** Cheaha *nickname:* **6** Cotton (State) **12** Heart of Dixie *river:* **6** Mobile **7** Alabama **9** Tombigbee *state bird:* **12** yellowhammer *state flower:* **8** camellia *state tree:* **12** longleaf pine

alacrity 8 dispatch **9** briskness, eagerness, quickness, readiness **10** enthusiasm, expedition, liveliness, promptness **11** promptitude, willingness **12** cheerfulness

alamo 6 poplar **10** cottonwood

a la mode 4 chic, tony **6** trendy **7** dashing, stylish **8** up-to-date **9** exclusive **11** fashionable **12** with ice cream

alarm 3 SOS **4** bell, fear, horn **5** alert, dread, panic, scare, siren, spook, upset **6** dismay, excite, fright, signal, terror, tocsin **7** anxiety, disturb, startle, terrify, unnerve, warning **8** distress, frighten **9** terrorize **11** forewarning, trepidation **12** apprehension **13** consternation

alas 3 heu, woe **4** darn, drat **5** alack, oy vey **7** woe is me

Alaska *capital:* **6** Juneau *city:* **4** Nome **5** Sitka **6** Barrow **9** Anchorage, Fairbanks **10** Prudhoe Bay *island group:*

6 Kodiak 8 Aleutian, Pribilof *mountain, range:* 6 Brooks 8 McKinley, Wrangell *nickname:* 12 Last Frontier *park:* 6 Denali, Katmai *river:* 5 Yukon *state bird:* 9 ptarmigan *state flower:* 11 forget-me-not *state tree:* 11 sitka spruce

alb 4 gown 8 vestment

Albania *capital:* 6 Tirana, Tiranë *city:* 5 Korçë, Vlorë 6 Durrës 7 Shkodër *ethnic group:* 4 Gheg, Tosk *monetary unit:* 3 lek *neighbor:* 6 Greece, Serbia 9 Macedonia *part of:* 7 Balkans *peninsula:* 6 Balkan *sea:* 8 Adriatic

albatross 5 check, goony, worry 6 burden, gooney 7 anxiety, seabird 9 hindrance, millstone, restraint 11 encumbrance

Albee *play:* 7 Sandbox (The) 8 Seascape, Zoo Story (The) 9 Tiny Alice 13 American Dream (The) 14 Three Tall Women 16 A Delicate Balance 25 Who's Afraid of Virginia Woolf?

albeit 5 still, while 6 even if, much as, though 7 despite, whereas 8 although 10 even though

Alberta *capital:* 8 Edmonton *city:* 5 Banff 7 Calgary *lake:* 6 Claire, Louise 9 Athabasca *mountain, range:* 7 Rockies 8 Columbia *provincial flower:* 8 wild rose *river:* 4 Milk 5 Peace 9 Athabasca

Albion 7 England

album 4 book 6 jacket, record 7 garland, omnibus 8 notebook, pictures, register 9 anthology, portfolio, scrapbook 10 collection, miscellany, recordings

Alcestis *father:* 6 Pelias *husband:* 7 Admetus *rescuer:* 8 Heracles, Hercules

alchemist 10 Paracelsus

alchemy 5 charm, magic 7 panacea, sorcery 8 wizardry 9 conjuring 10 necromancy

Alcina *sister:* 7 Morgana 10 Logistilla *victim:* 6 Rogero 8 Astolpho, Ruggiero

Alcinous *daughter:* 8 Nausicaa *wife:* 5 Arete

Alcmaeon *father:* 10 Amphiaraus *mother:* 8 Eriphyle *wife:* 10 Callirrhoe

Alcmene *husband:* 10 Amphitryon *son:* 8 Heracles, Hercules

alcohol 4 grog 5 booze, hooch, juice, sauce 6 hootch, liquor, red-eye, rotgut, tipple 7 spirits 8 home brew 9 aqua vitae, firewater, moonshine *name:* 4 amyl 5 butyl, cetyl, ethyl 6 glycol, methyl, sterol 7 butanol, ethanol, mannite, menthol 8 glycerin, glycerol, inositol, mannitol, methanol 9 isopropyl 11 cholesterol *used in perfumes:* 5 nerol 7 borneol 8 geraniol, linalool

alcoholic 4 hard 5 drunk 6 brewed 8 drunkard 9 distilled, fermented, in-ebriant, inebriate, spiritous 10 spirituous 11 dipsomaniac, inebriating 12 intoxicating

alcoholic drink see under BEVERAGE

alcove 4 nook 5 niche 6 gazebo, recess 9 belvedere 11 summerhouse *Japanese:* 8 tokonoma

Alcyone *father:* 5 Atlas 6 Aeolus *husband:* 4 Ceyx *mother:* 7 Pleione *sisters:* 8 Pleiades

ale 4 nog 4 beer, nogg

aleatory 4 iffy 5 dicey, risky, shaky 6 chancy 9 hazardous, uncertain 10 contingent, precarious, vulnerable 11 problematic, speculative 13 unpredictable

alehouse 3 bar, pub 6 bistro, saloon, tavern 7 taproom 8 beer hall 10 beer garden 11 rathskeller

alembic 5 still 6 filter 9 distiller

alert 3 SOS 4 keen, warn 5 alarm, quick, ready, sharp, smart 6 brainy, bright, clever, lively, notify, tip off, tocsin 7 heedful, mindful, on guard, red flag, wakeful 8 animated, forewarn, open-eyed, vigilant, watchful 9 attentive, mercurial, sprightly, wide-awake 10 perceptive 11 intelligent, quick-witted *Scottish:* 4 gleg 8 wakerife

Aleutian island 3 Fox 4 Adak, Atka, Attu, Near 5 Amlia, Kiska 6 Unimak 8 Unalaska 9 Andreanof *town:* 11 Dutch Harbor

alewife 4 fish 7 herring 8 menhaden

Alexander *birthplace:* 5 Pella *conquest:* 4 Tyre 5 Egypt, Issus 6 Greece, Persia 7 Parthia 8 Granicus *father:* 6 Philip *general:* 9 Antipater *horse:* 10 Bucephalus *kingdom:* 9 Macedonia *mother:* 8 Olympias *teacher:* 9 Aristotle *wife:* 6 Roxana

alfalfa 3 hay 5 plant 6 forage, legume 7 lucerne 9 perennial

alfresco 7 open-air, outdoor, outside 8 outdoors 9 out-of-door 10 out-of-doors

alga 6 desmid, diatom 7 seaweed *blue-green:* 6 nostoc *brown:* 4 kelp 5 fucus 8 rockweed *green:* 9 chlorella *red:* 4 nori

algebra term 4 root 6 factor 8 binomial, equation, monomial, variable 9 quadratic 10 polynomial

Algeria *capital:* 7 Algiers *city:* 4 Bône, Oran 6 Annaba 11 Constantine *coast:* 7 Barbary *desert:* 6 Sahara *ethnic group:* 4 Arab 6 Berber *language:* 6 Arabic, Berber *monetary unit:* 5 dinar *mountain range:* 5 Atlas 12 Saharan Atlas *neighbor:* 4 Mali 5 Libya, Niger 7 Morocco, Tunisia 10 Mauritania

Algren novel 17 Walk on the Wild Side (A) 19 Man with the Golden Arm (The)

Ali *son:* 5 Hasan 6 Husayn *wife:* 6 Fatima

alias 3 AKA 6 anonym, handle 7 moniker, pen name 8 nickname 9 false name, pseudonym, stage name 10 also called, nom de plume 11 nom de guerre

alibi 4 plea 5 clear, cover, proof 6 answer, excuse 7 account, cover up, defense, pretext 9 assertion, exonerate 11 explanation

alien 6 exotic 7 foreign, opposed, strange 8 estrange, outsider, stranger, transfer 9 estranged, extrinsic, foreigner, outlander 10 extraneous, outlandish 12 incompatible

alienate 4 part 5 repel 6 assign, convey, divide, offend, oppose 7 break up, turn off 8 disunify, disunite, estrange, separate, sign over, transfer 9 disaffect 10 drive apart, relinquish

alienation 5 break 6 breach 7 discord, divorce, rupture 8 division 10 conveyance, separation 11 breaking off 12 disaffection, estrangement

alight 4 land 5 fiery 6 arrive, bright, on fire, settle 7 blazing, burning, deplane, descend, detrain, flaming, flaring, get down, glowing, ignited, shining 8 dismount 9 touch down 11 conflagrant

align 4 ally, join, line, true 5 agree, array, order, range 6 adjust, follow, line up 8 regulate 9 affiliate, associate 10 straighten

alike 4 akin, same 7 similar 8 parallel 9 analogous, consonant 10 comparable 13 corresponding

alikeness 6 simile 7 analogy 8 affinity, alliance, relation 9 closeness, semblance 10 comparison, connection, similarity, similitude 11 resemblance

aliment 4 eats, fare, feed, food, grub 7 nourish, nurture, sustain 9 nutriment 10 sustenance 11 nourishment

alimentary 9 nutritive 10 nourishing, sustaining 11 nutritional

alimentary canal 7 enteron

alimony 4 keep 5 bread 6 living, upkeep 7 support 9 allowance, provision 10 livelihood, sustenance 11 maintenance, subsistence

alive 4 rife, spry 5 alert, awake, aware, brisk, fresh, quick, ready, vital 6 active, extant, living, moving, viable 7 animate, dynamic, knowing, replete, running, teeming, working, zestful 8 animated, existent, existing, sensible, sentient, swarming, thronged 9 abounding, breathing, cognizant, conscious, energetic, operative, sensitive, wide-awake 11 functioning, overflowing

alkali 4 base, salt 9 substance 11 soluble salt *metal:* 6 cesium, sodium 7 lithium 8 francium, rubidium 9 potassium 10 monovalent *opposite:* 4 acid

alkaline 5 acrid, basic, salty 6 bitter 7 antacid, caustic, soluble 8 chemical

alkaline substance 3 lye 4 lime, soda 5 borax 6 potash 7 ammonia, antacid 8 pearl ash, saltwort 11 caustic soda

alkaloid 4 base *medicinal:* 5 ergot 7 codeine, emetine, eserine, quinine 8 atropine, caffeine, lobeline, morphine 9 ephedrine, quinidine, reserpine 11 scopolamine *narcotic:* 6 heroin 7 cocaine, codeine 8 morphine *poisonous:* 8 atropine, nicotine, solanine 11 scopolamine

all 3 sum 4 each 5 every, gross, total, whole 6 entire, in toto, purely, wholly 7 exactly, totally, utterly 8 complete, entirety, everyone, outright, totality 9 aggregate, everybody 10 altogether, everything

all-around 7 general, overall, skilled 8 complete, sweeping, synoptic 9 adaptable, competent, many-sided, panoramic, universal, versatile 10 consummate, proficient 11 wide-ranging 12 encompassing 13 comprehensive

allay 4 balm, calm, ease, lull 5 abate, quiet, still 6 lessen, reduce, settle, soothe, subdue 7 assuage, compose, lighten, mollify, quieten, relieve 8 decrease, diminish, mitigate, moderate 9 alleviate 11 tranquilize

all but 4 most, much, nigh 5 about 6 almost, nearly 8 as much as, in effect 9 just about, virtually 11 essentially, practically 13 approximately

All Creatures Great and Small author 7 Herriot (James)

allegation 5 claim 6 charge, report 9 assertion, statement 10 contention, profession 11 declaration

allege 3 say 4 avow, cite 5 claim, offer, state 6 adduce, assert, attest, charge, submit 7 advance, contend, declare, present, profess 8 maintain 10 put forward

alleged 6 stated 7 accused, dubious, reputed, suspect 8 asserted, declared, doubtful, so-called, supposed 9 described, pretended, professed, purported, soi-disant 10 ostensible, self-styled 12 questionable

allegiance 4 duty 5 ardor, piety 6 fealty, homage 7 loyalty 8 devotion, fidelity 9 adherence, constancy, obedience 10 dedication, obligation 11 devotedness 12 faithfulness

allegiant 4 firm, true 5 liege, loyal

6 ardent, steady 7 devoted, dutiful, staunch 8 constant, faithful, resolute 9 steadfast 10 dependable

allegorical 5 moral 6 fabled 8 mythical, symbolic 9 legendary, spiritual 10 emblematic, exegetical, fictitious, figurative 12 iconographic, illustrative, metaphorical

allegory 4 myth, tale 5 fable, story 6 emblem, symbol 7 parable 8 apologue 9 symbolism 10 figuration 12 typification

allegro 5 brisk 6 bouncy, lively 8 animated, spirited 9 sprightly

allergy 5 dread 6 hatred 7 disgust, dislike 8 aversion, distaste 9 antipathy, disliking, rejection, repulsion

alleviate 4 cure, ease 5 allay 6 lessen, reduce, remedy 7 assuage, lighten, mollify, relieve 8 decrease, diminish, mitigate

alleviation 4 ease 6 relief 7 decline 8 decrease, easement 9 lessening, reduction 10 diminution, mitigation

alley 4 lane, walk 6 marble, street 7 passage 10 backstreet

all-fired 7 totally, utterly 9 extremely 10 absolutely, completely 11 excessively

alliance 3 tie 4 bond, pact 5 union 6 accord, league, treaty 7 compact, concord 8 affinity, relation 9 coalition 10 connection, federation 11 affiliation, association, combination, confederacy, conjunction, partnership, unification 12 relationship 13 confederation

allied 4 akin 5 bound 6 agnate, joined, linked, united 7 cognate, connate, kindred, related, unified 8 in league 9 connected 10 affiliated, associated, connatural 11 consanguine

alligator 11 crocodilian *relative:* 4 croc 6 caiman, cayman 9 crocodile

alligator pear 7 avocado

all in 4 dead, used, worn 5 spent, tired 6 bushed, done in, used up 7 drained, far-gone, worn-out 8 depleted 9 dead tired, exhausted, washed-out

all in all 5 in all 6 mainly 7 en masse, largely 9 generally 10 altogether, by and large, on the whole

allocate 4 give 5 allot, slice 6 assign, divide 7 dish out, divvy up, dole out, earmark, mete out 8 set apart 9 admeasure, apportion, designate 10 distribute

allocution 4 talk 5 spiel 6 sermon, speech 7 address, lecture, oration, oratory, pep talk 11 exhortation

allot 4 give 5 grant, share 6 accord, assign 7 deal out, divvy up, dole out, mete out 8 allocate, dispense, set aside 9 admeasure, apportion 10 distribute

allotment 3 cut, lot 4 bite, part 5 chunk, piece, quota, share, slice 6 ration 7 measure, portion 9 allowance, provision 13 apportionment

all-out 4 full 5 total 6 entire, utmost 7 maximum 8 absolute, complete, thorough 9 full-blown, full-scale, unlimited 12 totalitarian 13 thoroughgoing

all over 8 wherever 9 all around 10 everyplace, everywhere, far and near, far and wide, high and low, thoroughly, throughout

allow 3 let, lot, own 4 avow, give 5 admit, allot, brook, grant, leave, let on, stand 6 assign, endure, permit, suffer 7 concede, confess, consent, forbear, mete out 8 allocate, tolerate 9 apportion 11 acknowledge

allowance 3 aid, cut, lot, pay, sum 4 bite, edge, help, part 5 grant, leave, piece, quota, share, slice 6 amount, permit, ration 7 consent, handicap, measure, partage, portion, quantum, subsidy, vantage 8 handicap, pittance, quantity, sanction 9 advantage, allotment, head start, reduction 10 adjustment, allocation, assistance, concession, permission, sufferance, toleration 13 accommodation, apportionment, authorization

alloy 5 blend 6 fusion 7 amalgam, mixture 8 compound 9 admixture, composite 10 adulterant 11 interfusion 12 amalgamation, intermixture *brasslike:* 6 latten *copper-sulfur:* 6 niello *copper-tin:* 6 bronze *copper-zinc:* 5 brass 6 tombac *gold-like:* 6 ormolu *gold-silver:* 8 electrum *iron-carbon:* 5 steel *iron-nickel:* 5 invar *mercury:* 7 amalgam *tin-lead:* 5 terne 6 pewter, solder *used in jewelry:* 6 tombac

all-powerful 6 mighty 7 supreme 8 absolute, almighty 10 invincible, omnipotent 11 controlling

all right 3 aye, yea, yep, yes 4 good, okay, safe, well 6 agreed, decent, proper, surely 7 average 8 adequate, of course, passable, passably, pleasing, standard, very well 9 agreeable, certainly, tolerable, tolerably 10 , acceptably, adequately, definitely, positively, sufficient, well enough 12 satisfactory

all round see ALL-AROUND

All the King's Men author 6 Warren (Robert Penn)

All the Way Home author 4 Agee (James)

allude 4 hint 5 imply, point, refer 7 bring up, suggest 8 indicate, intimate

allure 4 draw, pull 5 charm, tempt 6 appeal, entice, lead on, seduce 7 attract, beguile, enchant, glamour, win over 8 charisma, inveigle, persuade

9 captivate, fascinate, magnetism, magnetize **10** attraction **11** enchantment, fascination

alluring 6 lovely **7** winning, winsome **8** charming, inviting, pleasing **9** appealing, beguiling, glamorous, seductive **10** appetizing, attractive, bewitching, enchanting **11** captivating, fascinating

ally 4 join **5** unite **6** friend, helper **7** comrade, partner **8** federate **9** accessory, affiliate, associate, auxiliary, bedfellow, colleague, supporter **10** accomplice **11** confederate **12** collaborator

almighty 4 very **6** hugely, mighty **7** awfully, godlike, supreme **8** absolute **9** extremely **10** invincible, omnipotent **11** all-powerful, exceedingly

almost 4 nigh **5** about **6** all but, nearly **8** as good as, as much as, not quite, well-nigh **9** just about, virtually **11** essentially, practically **13** approximately *Scottish:* **6** feckly

alms 4 gift **6** relief **7** present **8** donation, offering **10** assistance **11** benefaction, beneficence **12** contribution

aloe 9 emollient, succulent

Aloeus *father:* **7** Neptune **8** Poseidon *mother:* **6** Canace *son:* **4** Otus **9** Ephialtes *wife:* **9** Iphimedia

aloft 4 high, over **5** above **6** on high, upward **7** skyward **8** in flight, overhead

aloha 4 by-by, ciao, hail **5** hello, howdy **6** bye-bye, good-by, so long **7** good-bye, welcome **8** farewell, greeting **9** greetings *State:* **6** Hawaii

alone 4 only, sole, solo, stag **5** apart **6** singly, solely, unique, wholly **7** isolate, removed **8** detached, entirely, isolated, peerless, singular, solitary **9** matchless, unequaled, unmatched, unrivaled **10** nothing but, unequalled, unexampled, unexcelled **11** exclusively, unsurpassed **12** incomparable, unparalleled, unrepeatable **13** unaccompanied

aloneness 8 solitude **9** isolation, seclusion **10** uniqueness

along 3 too, yet **4** also, near, with **5** forth, there **6** as well, at hand, on hand, onward **7** besides, forward **8** likewise, moreover **11** furthermore **12** accompanying, additionally

alongside 6 beside, next to **8** touching **9** adjoining, bordering

aloof 3 shy **4** cold, cool **5** apart, proud **6** casual, chilly, frigid, offish, remote **7** distant, haughty, removed, stuck up **8** arrogant, detached, reserved, reticent, solitary **9** incurious, unbending, uncurious, withdrawn **10** disdainful, restrained, unfriendly, unsociable **11** constrained, indifferent, standoffish,

unconcerned **12** uninterested **13** disinterested

alopecia 8 baldness

alp 4 peak **5** mount **8** mountain

alpaca 4 wool **5** cloth **6** mammal *habitat:* **4** Peru **5** Andes **7** Bolivia

alpha 4 dawn **5** first, start **6** outset **7** dawning, genesis, opening **9** beginning **12** commencement

alphabet 4 ABC's **7** letters *Arabic:* **3** ayn, dad, dal, gaf, jim, kaf, kha, lam, mim, nun, qaf, sad, sin, tha, waw, zay **4** alif, dhal, shin **5** ghayn *Greek:* **3** chi, eta, phi, psi, rho, tau **4** beta, iota, zeta **5** alpha, delta, gamma, kappa, omega, sigma, theta **7** lambda **7** epsilon, omicron, upsilon *Hebrew:* **3** mem, nun, sin, taw, tet, vav, waw, yod **4** alef, ayin, beth, heth, kaph, koph, qoph, resh, shin, teth **5** aleph, gimel, lamed, sadhe, tsade, zayin **6** daleth, samekh *Old Irish:* **4** ogam **5** ogham *runic:* **7** futhark

Alpheus *beloved:* **8** Arethusa *father:* **7** Oceanus *form:* **5** river *mother:* **6** Tethys

Alpine *animal:* **4** ibex **7** chamois *dress:* **6** dirndl *house:* **6** chalet *lake:* **4** Como, Iseo **5** Garda **6** Geneva **7** Lucerne **8** Bodensee, Maggiore **9** Constance, Neuchâtel *pass:* **3** col **5** Cenis **7** Brenner, Simplon **9** St. Bernard *peak:* **5** Blanc, Eiger **7** Bernina **8** Jungfrau **10** Matterhorn *plant:* **9** edelweiss *primrose:* **8** auricula *resort:* **5** Davos **7** Bolzano, Zermatt **8** Chamonix, Grenoble **9** Innsbruck **10** Interlaken **11** Saint Moritz *river:* **5** Rhine, Rhône *snowfield:* **4** firn, névé *staff:* **10** alpenstock *state:* **5** Tirol, Tyrol **7** Bavaria *tunnel:* **5** Blanc, Cenis **7** Arlberg, Simplon **10** St. Gotthard *wind:* **4** bora, föhn **5** foehn

already 4 even, once **5** by now, prior **6** before, by then **7** earlier, just now **8** formerly **9** before now **10** by this time, heretofore, previously

also 3 and, too **4** more, plus **5** again, along **6** as well **7** besides, further **8** likewise, moreover **9** along with, including, similarly **10** in addition **11** furthermore **12** additionally

also-ran 3 dud **5** loser **7** failure, washout **8** defeated

altar 6 shrine *boy:* **6** server **7** acolyte *cloth:* **4** pall **7** frontal *constellation:* **3** Ara *hanging:* **6** dorsal, dossal *platform:* **8** predella *screen:* **7** reredos *shelf:* **7** retable *site:* **4** apse, bema *vessel:* **5** cruet, paten **7** chalice **8** ciborium **10** monstrance

alter 3 fix **4** geld, spay, turn, vary **5** adapt **6** adjust, change, doctor, modify,

mutate, neuter, revamp **7** remodel
8 castrate, moderate, modulate
9 refashion
alteration 4 turn **5** shift **6** change
8 mutation, revision **9** variation
10 adaptation, adjustment, changeover,
conversion, remodeling, transition
12 modification
altercate 4 spat, tiff **5** argue, scrap
6 bicker, hassle **7** dispute, quarrel,
wrangle **8** squabble **9** caterwaul
altercation 3 row **4** beef, flap, spat, tiff
5 brawl **6** blowup, combat, fracas, hassle **7** contest, dispute, quarrel, rhubarb,
wrangle **8** argument, squabble **9** bickering **10** falling-out **11** controversy,
embroilment
alternate 3 sub **5** proxy **6** backup, by
turn, change, fill-in, rotate, second
7 another, relieve, stand-in **8** periodic,
rotating **9** change off, fluctuate, recurrent, recurring, replacing, surrogate
10 equivalent, every other, periodical,
substitute **11** every second, pinch hitter, replacement **12** intermittent
alternately 6 in lieu, rather **7** instead
10 preferably
alternative 5 other, proxy **6** backup,
choice, option, second **7** another
8 atypical, druthers, election **9** different, selection, surrogate **10** preference,
substitute **11** contingency, nonstandard,
possibility
Althaea *father:* **8** Thestius *husband:*
6 Oeneus *son (victim):* **8** Meleager
although 4 when **5** still, while **6** albeit,
even if, much as **7** despite, howbeit,
whereas
altitude 6 height **8** eminence **9** elevation,
high level
altitudinous 4 high, tall **7** eminent **8** elevated
altogether 4 nude, well **5** fully, in all,
quite **6** in toto, wholly **7** all told, en
masse, exactly, totally, utterly **8** all in
all, entirely **9** generally, perfectly
10 absolutely, by and large, completely,
on the whole, thoroughly
altruism 7 charity **8** sympathy **10** compassion, generosity **11** benevolence
12 philanthropy, selflessness **13** unselfishness
altruistic 3 big **6** humane **8** generous
9 unselfish **10** benevolent, bighearted,
charitable, open-handed **11** considerate, magnanimous, noble-minded
12 humanitarian **13** philanthropic
alum 4 grad **6** emetic **7** styptic **8** graduate **10** astringent
always 4 ever **7** forever **8** evermore, for
keeps **9** at any rate, endlessly, eternally

10 at all times, constantly, in any event,
invariably **11** continually, forevermore,
in perpetuum, perpetually, unceasingly
12 consistently, continuously
Amahl and the Night Visitors composer
7 Menotti (Gian Carlo)
amalgamate 3 mix **4** ally, fuse, meld,
pool **5** admix, alloy, merge, unify, unite
6 mingle **7** combine **8** coalesce, compound, intermix **9** commingle, integrate **11** consolidate, intermingle
amalgamation 5 alloy, blend, union
6 fusion, merger **7** joining, melding,
merging, mixture, uniting **8** alliance,
compound **9** admixture, coalition,
composite **10** commixture **12** intermixture **13** consolidation
Amalthea *form:* **4** goat *horn:* **10** cornucopia *nursling:* **4** Zeus
amanita 8 death cap, mushroom **9** fly
agaric
amanuensis 6 scribe **7** copyist **9** scrivener, secretary **11** transcriber **12** stenographer
amass 4 bulk, heap, make, pile **5** hoard,
lay up, store, uplay **6** accrue, garner,
gather, pile up, roll up **7** acquire, collect, compile, round up, store up
8 assemble, cumulate **9** aggregate,
stockpile **10** accumulate **12** come
together
amassment 4 pile **5** clump, group,
hoard, stack, stock, store, trove **7** cluster **8** assembly, quantity **9** gathering,
stockpile **10** assemblage, collection,
cumulation **11** aggregation **12** accumulation **13** agglomeration
amateur 4 tyro **6** layman, novice, tinker,
votary **7** admirer, dabbler, devotee,
learner **8** aspirant, beginner, neophyte,
putterer **9** greenhorn, smatterer
10 apprentice, dilettante, enthusiast,
uninitiate **11** abecedarian
amateurish 3 raw **5** green **6** simple **7** artless **8** dabbling, inexpert **9** deficient,
unskilled, untutored **10** dilettante,
unfinished, unpolished, unskillful
12 dilettantist, unproficient **13** inexperienced
amative see AMOROUS
amatory 6 ardent, erotic, loving, tender
7 sensual **8** romantic **9** erogenous,
seductive **10** passionate **11** aphrodisiac
amaze 4 daze **5** floor **6** wonder
7 astound, perplex, startle **8** astonish,
bewilder, blow away, bowl over, confound, surprise **9** dumbfound **10** admiration **11** flabbergast
amazement 3 awe **6** marvel, wonder
8 surprise **9** marveling **10** admiration,

perplexity, wonderment **12** astonishment, bewilderment, confoundment

amazing 7 awesome **8** striking, stunning, wondrous **9** marvelous, startling, wonderful **10** astounding, impressive, miraculous, stupendous, surprising **11** astonishing, bewildering, spectacular **12** breathtaking

Amazon 6 parrot **7** warrior **8** giantess **12** woman warrior

ambassador 5 agent, envoy **6** legate **8** diplomat, emissary **9** messenger *papal:* **6** nuncio

amber 5 ocher, ochre, resin, rosin **6** orange, yellow **7** saffron

ambience 4 mood, tone **6** flavor, medium, milieu **7** climate **10** atmosphere **11** environment **12** surroundings

ambient 5 music **6** milieu **7** general, setting **8** everyday **9** prevalent **10** atmosphere, prevailing **11** atmospheric, environment, mise-en-scène **12** encompassing, surroundings **13** environmental

ambiguity 5 doubt **6** enigma, puzzle **7** evasion **9** equivoque, obscurity, vagueness **11** incertitude, uncertainty **12** doubtfulness, equivocality, equivocation **13** double meaning

ambiguous 5 vague **6** opaque, unsure **7** cryptic, dubious, inexact, obscure, unclear **8** doubtful, puzzling **9** enigmatic, equivocal, tenebrous, uncertain, unsettled **10** indefinite, inexplicit **11** problematic **12** inconclusive, questionable

ambit 4 area, room **5** field, limit, orbit, range, reach, scope, space, sweep **6** border, bounds, extent, limits, radius, sphere **7** breadth, circuit, compass, expanse, purview **8** boundary, confines **9** extension, perimeter, periphery **13** circumference

ambition 3 aim **4** goal, hope, itch, push, wish, zeal **5** ardor, dream, drive, vigor **6** desire, energy, hunger, spirit, target, thirst **7** avidity, craving, purpose **8** appetite, striving, yearning **9** eagerness, intention, objective **10** aspiration, enterprise, enthusiasm, get-up-and-go, initiative, pretension

ambitious 4 avid, bold, keen **5** eager, pushy **6** driven, hungry, intent **7** driving, zealous **8** aspiring, desirous, striving **9** energetic **10** aggressive **11** hardworking **12** enterprising, enthusiastic

ambivalent 5 mixed **6** unsure **7** warring **8** clashing, wavering **9** equivocal, uncertain, undecided, **10** unresolved **11** fluctuating, vacillating **13** contradictory

amble 4 gait, walk **5** dally, drift, mosey **6** dawdle, linger, stroll, wander **7** meander, saunter

ambrosia 6 dainty, regale **7** dessert, perfume **8** delicacy, ointment

ambrosial 5 balmy, spicy, sweet **6** savory **7** scented **8** aromatic, fragrant, heavenly, luscious, perfumed, pleasing, redolent **9** delicious **10** delectable, delightful **11** scrumptious

ambulate 4 hoof, move, pace, step, walk **5** tread, troop **6** foot it, hoof it **7** traipse

ambulatory 6 moving, on foot, roving **7** nomadic, roaming, walking **8** vagabond **9** itinerant **11** peripatetic

ambush 4 jump, lurk, trap **5** snare **6** assail, attack, entrap, lay for, waylay **7** assault, ensnare **8** surprise **9** ambuscade **11** concealment

ameliorate 3 fix **4** help, lift, mend **5** amend, raise **6** better, perk up, remedy, reform **7** elevate, enhance, improve, lighten, relieve, upgrade **8** mitigate **9** alleviate **10** convalesce, recuperate

amenable 4 open, tame **6** docile, liable, pliant, suited **7** plastic, pliable, subdued, subject, willing **8** biddable, in accord, obedient, yielding **9** adaptable, agreeable, complying, malleable, receptive, tractable **10** answerable, consenting, responsive, submissive **11** accountable, acquiescent, cooperative, responsible

amend 3 fix **4** help **5** alter, right **6** better, change, modify, reform, remedy, repair, revise, square **7** correct, improve, rectify **8** put right **9** meliorate **10** ameliorate

amendment 5 rider **6** change, remedy, reform, repair **7** codicil **8** addendum, revision **10** alteration, attachment, correction **11** enhancement, improvement reformation **12** modification **13** rectification

amends 7 redress **8** reprisal **9** indemnity, quittance **10** recompense, reparation **11** restitution **12** compensation

amenities 5 mores **6** polish **7** decorum, manners **8** civility, courtesy **9** etiquette, propriety **12** social graces

amenity 5 charm, frill **6** luxury **7** comfort, quality **8** civility, courtesy, facility **9** advantage, etiquette, geniality, pleasance **10** affability, amiability, betterment, cordiality, enrichment, pleasantry, politeness **11** convenience, enhancement, improvement, sociability **12** agreeability, graciousness, pleasantness

ament 6 catkin

amerce 3 tax **4** dock, fine, levy **5** exact, mulct **6** punish **7** hit with, make pay **8** penalize

amercement 4 fine 5 mulct 7 damages, forfeit, penalty 10 assessment, punishment, reparation

American League *Baltimore:* 7 Orioles *Boston:* 6 Red Sox *Anaheim:* 6 Angels *Chicago:* 8 White Sox *Cleveland:* 7 Indians *Detroit:* 6 Tigers *Kansas City:* 6 Royals *Milwaukee:* 7 Brewers *Minnesota:* 5 Twins *New York:* 7 Yankees *Oakland:* 9 Athletics *Seattle:* 8 Mariners *Tampa Bay:* 9 Devil Rays *Texas:* 7 Rangers *Toronto:* 8 Blue Jays

American Samoa *capital:* 8 Pago Pago *island, island group:* 4 Rose 5 Aunuu, Manua 6 Swains 7 Tutuila *language:* 6 Samoan

America, the Beautiful *music:* 4 Ward (Samuel Augustus) *words:* 5 Bates (Katherine Lee)

Amfortas *father:* 7 Titurel *opera:* 8 Parsifal

amiability 7 amenity 9 geniality, pleasance 10 cordiality 11 sociability 12 complaisance, congeniality, friendliness, pleasantness, sociableness 13 agreeableness, enjoyableness

amiable 4 kind, warm 6 genial, gentle, kindly 7 affable, cordial, likable 8 cheerful, friendly, gracious, likeable, obliging, sociable 9 agreeable, congenial, courteous 10 responsive 11 complaisant, good-humored, good-natured, warmhearted

amicable 7 cordial, pacific 8 empathic, friendly, peaceful, sociable 9 congenial, peaceable 10 harmonious, like-minded, neighborly 11 sympathetic 13 understanding

amid 4 over 5 among, midst 6 during 7 amongst, between 10 throughout

amigo 3 pal 4 chum, mate, pard 6 friend 7 comrade, partner 8 sidekick 9 companion, confidant 12 acquaintance

amino acid 4 dopa 6 leucin, lysine, serine, toluid, valine 7 cystein, cystine, glycine, leucine, proline, toluide 8 cysteine, dopamine, histidin, thyroxin, toluidin, tyrosine

Amis, Kingsley *novel:* 8 Lucky Jim *son:* 6 Martin

amiss 3 bad 4 awry, poor 5 badly, wrong 6 afield, astray, faulty, flawed 7 wrongly 8 erringly, faultily 9 defective, imperfect 10 improperly, mistakenly, out of place 11 erroneously, imperfectly, incorrectly, unfavorably 12 inaccurately 13 inappropriate

amity 5 union 6 accord, comity, unison 7 concert, concord, harmony 8 alliance, goodwill 9 agreement 10 cordiality, friendship, kindliness 11 concurrence 12 friendliness

Ammonite 6 Semite *god:* 6 Molech, Moloch

ammunition 4 shot 5 bombs 6 rounds, shells 7 charges 8 armament, grenades, missiles, ordnance 10 cartridges 11 projectiles

Amneris's rival 4 Aïda

amnesty 6 pardon 7 freeing, release 8 immunity, reprieve 9 discharge 10 absolution 11 forgiveness 12 dispensation

Amnon *father:* 5 David *half sister:* 5 Tamar *mother:* 7 Ahinoam

amoeba 4 blob 8 rhizopod 9 protozoan

Amon *father:* 8 Manasseh *son:* 6 Josiah

Amonasro's daughter 4 Aïda

among 3 mid 4 amid 5 midst 6 amidst, within 7 between *prefix:* 5 inter

amorist 4 rake, wolf 5 lover, Romeo 7 Don Juan, gallant, playboy 8 Casanova, lothario, paramour 9 womanizer 12 heartbreaker

amorous 6 ardent, erotic, in love 7 amative, amatory, lustful 8 enamored, romantic 10 infatuated, passionate 11 aphrodisiac, impassioned

amorousness 4 love, lust 5 amour, ardor 6 desire 7 passion 9 eroticism

amorphous 7 unclear 8 formless, inchoate, nebulous, unformed, unshaped 9 shapeless, undefined 10 indistinct 11 nondescript 12 disorganized 13 characterless

amortize 5 repay 6 pay off, reduce 7 pay down 8 write off

amount 4 bulk, dose 5 add up, equal, price, total 6 dosage, matter, number, upshot 7 purport, quantum 8 quantity 9 aggregate, substance *owed:* 4 debt *small:* 3 bit, jot 4 atom, drop, iota, mite, whit 5 minim, spark, speck, trace 7 modicum, smidgen 8 molecule, particle 9 scintilla

amour 4 love 5 fling, lover 6 affair 7 liaison, passion, romance 8 intimacy, intrigue 9 dalliance 10 love affair 12 entanglement, relationship

amour propre 5 pride 6 egoism, vanity 7 conceit, egotism 8 self-love, vainness 9 vainglory 10 narcissism, self-esteem, self-regard 11 self-conceit, self-respect 12 pridefulness 13 conceitedness

amphetamines 5 speed 6 dexies, hearts, uppers 7 bennies, Dexoxyn 8 greenies, pep pills, Preludin 9 Dexedrine 10 Benzedrine, Methedrine

amphibian *burrowing:* 9 caecilian *legless:* 9 caecilian *tailed:* 3 eft 4 newt 10 salamander *tailless:* 4 frog, toad 8 bullfrog, tree toad 10 batrachian *wormlike:* 9 caecilian *young:* 7 tadpole 8 polliwog

Amphion *brother:* 6 Zethus *conquest:* 6 Thebes *father:* 4 Zeus *mother:* 7 Antiope *sister:* 5 Aedon *wife:* 5 Niobe

amphitheater 4 bowl 5 arena 7 stadium 8 coliseum 10 auditorium, hippodrome

Amphitrite *father:* 6 Nereus *husband:* 7 Neptune 8 Poseidon *mother:* 5 Doris *son:* 6 Triton

Amphitryon's wife 7 Alcmene

amphora 3 jar, jug, urn 4 ewer, vase 5 crock, flask 6 carafe, flagon, vessel

ample 4 wide 5 buxom, great, large, roomy 6 lavish, plenty, portly 7 copious, liberal, profuse 8 abundant, generous, handsome, spacious 9 bounteous, bountiful, capacious, expansive, extensive, plenteous, plentiful 10 commodious, sufficient 11 substantial

amplify 5 boost, raise, swell 6 dilate, expand, extend, jack up 7 augment, develop, distend, enhance, enlarge, inflate, magnify 8 increase 9 elaborate, intensify 10 supplement

amplitude 4 size 5 range, scale, scope, space 6 amount, extent, spread 7 bigness, breadth, expanse, stretch 8 distance, fullness, wideness 9 abundance, expansion, greatness, largeness, magnitude, roominess 12 spaciousness 13 capaciousness

amulet 4 juju, luck 5 charm 6 fetish, grigri, mascot 7 periapt 8 gris-gris, talisman 10 lucky piece, phylactery 11 rabbit's-foot

amuse 4 wile 5 charm, cheer 6 appeal, divert, engage, occupy, please, regale, tickle 7 animate, beguile, delight, enchant, enliven, gladden 8 distract, interest, recreate 9 entertain, fascinate

amusement 3 fun 4 play 7 delight, pastime 8 pleasure 9 diversion, enjoyment 10 recreation 11 distraction 13 entertainment

amusing 3 fun 5 droll, funny 7 comical, risible 8 engaging, humorous, pleasing 9 diverting, enjoyable 9 laughable 12 entertaining

Amycus *father:* 7 Neptune 8 Poseidon *friend:* 8 Heracles, Hercules *mother:* 5 Melia

ana 5 varia 7 sayings 9 anecdotes 10 collection, miscellany 11 memorabilia, miscellanea

anabasis 5 march 7 advance, headway, retreat 8 progress 11 advancement, progression

anagogic 6 arcane, hidden, mystic, occult, secret 7 obscure 8 esoteric,

mystical, telestic 9 spiritual 10 symbolical 11 allegorical

analects 5 album 6 digest 7 garland, omnibus 8 treasury 9 anthology, selection 10 compendium, miscellany 11 compilation, florilegium

analgesic 6 opiate 7 anodyne 10 anesthetic, painkiller

analogous 4 akin, like 5 alike 7 kindred, similar, related, uniform 8 parallel 9 consonant 10 comparable, equivalent, resembling

analogue 5 match 7 cognate 8 parallel 9 correlate 10 similarity 11 correlation, counterpart, equivalence 13 correspondent

analogy 6 simile 8 affinity, likeness, metaphor, parallel, relation 9 agreement, alikeness, semblance 10 comparison, similarity, similitude 11 correlation, equivalence, resemblance

analysis 5 assay, audit, proof, study 6 method, review, report, survey 7 finding, inquiry 8 division 9 breakdown, partition, statement 10 dissection, inspection, resolution, separation 11 examination 13 clarification

analytic 6 cogent, subtle 7 logical, testing 8 studious 9 organized 10 diagnostic, scientific, systematic 11 proposition, questioning 13 investigative, ratiocinative

analyze 4 part, test 5 assay, study 6 divide 7 dissect, examine, inspect, resolve 8 classify, consider, separate 9 anatomize, break down, decompose, interpret 10 decompound, scrutinize 11 deconstruct, distinguish, investigate

analyze grammatically 5 parse

Ananias 4 liar 9 falsifier 12 prevaricator *father:* 9 Nedebaeus *wife (coconspirator):* 8 Sapphira

anarchism 4 riot 6 theory 7 misrule 8 disorder 9 distemper, rebellion 11 lawlessness

anarchist 5 rebel 6 rioter 8 agitator, mutineer, provoker, revolter 9 dissident, insurgent 10 malcontent 11 provocateur 13 revolutionary

anarchy 4 riot 5 chaos 7 misrule, mob rule, turmoil 8 disarray, disorder 9 confusion, distemper, mobocracy, rebellion 10 ochlocracy, revolution 11 lawlessness 13 nongovernment

anathema 3 ban 4 bane 5 curse, enemy, odium, taboo 6 pariah 7 bugbear, censure, malison, outcast, reproof 8 loathing 9 damnation, bête noire 10 black beast, execration 11 abomination, commination, detestation, imprecation, malediction **12** condemnation, denunciation

anathematize 3 ban **4** damn, oust **5** curse, expel **6** banish **7** condemn **8** denounce, execrate **9** objurgate, proscribe **13** excommunicate

anatomical depression 5 fossa, fovea

anatomical tube 3 vas **4** duct **5** canal

anatomist 5 Wolff (Kaspar) **6** Harvey (William) **8** Vesalius (Andreas)

anatomize 5 cut up **7** analyze, dissect **8** separate **9** break down, decompose

anatomy 5 frame, mummy **6** makeup **8** analysis, division, skeleton **9** framework, histology, structure **10** dissection, morphology, physiology **11** examination

Anaxo *brother:* **10** Amphitryon *daughter:* **7** Alcmene *father:* **7** Alcaeus *husband:* **9** Electryon

ancestor 8 forebear, foregoer **9** ascendant, precursor, prototype **10** antecedent, antecessor, forefather, forerunner, progenitor **11** predecessor **12** primogenitor

ancestral 6 family, inborn, inbred, lineal **7** genetic **8** familial **9** inherited **10** bequeathed, hereditary **11** consanguine, patrimonial *sequence:* **8** pedigree **9** bloodline, genealogy

ancestry 4 line, race **5** blood, breed, stock **6** family, origin, source **7** descent, history, kindred, lineage **8** heritage, pedigree **9** parentage **10** derivation, extraction

Anchises' son 6 Aeneas

anchor 4 moor **6** secure **7** grapnel, mooring **8** mainstay *part:* **5** crown, fluke, shank

anchorage 4 port **5** haven, roads **6** harbor, refuge, riding **7** mooring, shelter **9** harborage, roadstead

anchorite 5 loner **6** hermit **7** recluse **8** solitary

anchors ___ **6** aweigh

ancient 3 old **4** aged **5** hoary, olden **6** age-old, primal **7** antique, archaic, elderly **8** Noachian, old-timer, primeval, timeworn **9** venerable **10** primordial **12** antediluvian

ancient capital 4 Susa **5** Aksum, Balkh, Calah, Isker, Kalhu, Ninus, Pella, Petra, Sibir **6** Angkor, Bactra, Nimrud, Sardis **7** Babylon, Knossos, Memphis, Nineveh, Samaria, Shushan **10** Persepolis

ancient city *Asia Minor:* **4** Nice, Teos **5** Tyana **6** Edessa, Nicaea **7** Antioch **13** Halicarnassus *Babylonia:* **4** Sura **5** Agade, Akkad, Eridu, Larsa **7** Ellasar *Bengal:* **4** Gaur **9** Lakhnauti *Canaan:*

5 Gezer *Cyprus:* **7** Salamis *Egypt:* **5** Tanis **6** Thebes **7** Memphis **10** Heliopolis *Etruria:* **4** Veii *Euphrates River:* **7** Babylon *Greece:* **5** Crisa **6** Athens, Sparta **7** Calydon **10** Lacedaemon *Ionia:* **4** Myus, Teos **5** Chios, Samos **6** Priene **7** Ephesus, Lebedos, Miletus, Phocaea **8** Colophon, Erythrae **10** Clazomenae *Italy:* **5** Locri **7** Pompeii **8** Siracusa, Syracuse **11** Herculaneum *Latium:* **5** Gabii **9** Alba Longa *Mayan:* **4** Cobá **5** Tikal, Tulum, Uxmal **8** Palenque **11** Chichén Itzá *Nile River:* **5** Meroë *North Africa:* **5** Utica **8** Carthage *Palestine:* **4** Gaza **5** Ekron, Endor, Sodom **6** Beroea, Bethel, Gilead, Hebron **7** Jericho, Samaria **8** Ashkelon **9** Capernaum, Jerusalem *Peloponnesus:* **5** Tegea **6** Sparta **7** Corinth *Sumeria:* **4** Kish, Uruk **5** Erech, Larsa **6** Lagash *Turkey:* **5** Assos, Assus **9** Byzantium

ancient country *Adriatic coast:* **7** Illyria *Africa:* **10** Mauretania *Arabian Peninsula:* **5** Sheba *Asia:* **4** Aram **5** Media, Minni, Syria **7** Armenia, Ash Sham, Bactria *Asia Minor:* **5** Lydia, Mysia **6** Aeolis, Pontus **7** Cilicia, Phrygia **8** Bithynia *Balkan:* **7** Macedon **9** Macedonia *Black Sea:* **7** Colchis *Dead Sea:* **4** Edom *Euphrates River:* **9** Babylonia *Europe:* **4** Gaul **5** Dacia **6** Gallia *gold-rich:* **5** Ophir *Italy:* **6** Latium **7** Etruria *Nile valley:* **4** Cush *Peloponnesus:* **4** Elis **7** Arcadia *Syria:* **9** Phoenicia

ancient empire 6 Median **7** Hittite, Persian **8** Assyrian, Athenian, Chaldean, Seleucid **9** Ptolemaic **10** Babylonian

ancient kingdom *Anglo-Saxon:* **6** Wessex *Asia:* **4** Ghor, Ghur *Celtic:* **7** Cumbria *China:* **3** Shu *Euphrates valley:* **4** Hira **7** Al-Hirah *Greece:* **8** Pergamon, Pergamum *North Of Assyria:* **3** Van **4** Ararat, Urartu *Palestine:* **5** Judah **6** Israel *Persian Gulf:* **4** Elam *Portugal:* **7** Algarve *Spain:* **4** Leon **6** Aragon **7** Castile, Galicia, Granada, Navarre *Syria:* **4** Moab *Welsh:* **5** Powys *West Sahara:* **4** Gana **5** Ghana

ancient monument 6 sphinx **7** obelisk, pyramid

ancient royal forest 4 Dean **8** Sherwood

ancient town *Africa:* **4** Zama *Armenia:* **4** Dwin, Tvin *Asia Minor:* **4** Soli **5** Derbe, Issus, Soloi *Attica:* **6** Icaria *Black Sea:* **5** Olbia **9** Apollonia *Greece:* **4** Abae, Opus **8** Marathon *Italy:* **4** Elea, Luna **5** Cumae, Velia *Latium:* **5** Ardea, Cures *Macedonia:* **5** Pydna, Stobi **9** Apollonia *Peloponnesus:* **5** Asine *Persia:* **6** Hormuz **8** Harmozia *Sicily:* **5** Hybla *Spain:*

5 Munda *Tatar:* 5 Isker, Sibir *Wendish:*
5 Julin

ancilla 3 aid 4 aide, ally, hand, help
6 helper 9 assistant, attendant, supporter

ancillary 5 extra 8 adjuvant, incident
9 accessory, attendant, attending, auxiliary, satellite, secondary 10 additional,
coincident, collateral, subsidiary, supporting 11 appurtenant, concomitant,
subordinate, subservient 12 accompanying, contributory 13 supplementary

andante 4 slow 5 tempo 7 relaxed, walking 8 moderate

Anderson, Maxwell *play:* 7 High Tor
8 Key Largo 9 Winterset 11 Valley
Forge 14 What Price Glory

Anderson, Sherwood *book:* 9 Poor
White 12 Dark Laughter
13 Winesburg Ohio

Andes native 4 Inca

andiron 7 firedog

Andorra *capital:* 7 Andorra *language:*
7 Catalan *liberator:* 11 Charlemagne
monetary unit: 4 euro *mountain range:*
8 Pyrenees *neighbor:* 5 Spain 6 France
river: 6 Valira

Andrea ___ 5 Doria 8 del Sarto

androgynous 7 epicene 8 bisexual 9 unisexual

android 5 robot 9 automaton

Andromache *husband:* 6 Hector *son:*
8 Astyanax, Molossus

Andromeda *father:* 7 Cepheus *husband:*
7 Perseus *mother:* 10 Cassiopeia *rescuer:*
7 Perseus

___ **and warp** 4 weft, woof

anecdote 4 tale, yarn 5 story 7 account,
episode, recital 8 relation 9 narration,
narrative 12 recollection, reminiscence

anemic 3 wan 4 pale, thin, weak 5 pasty
6 feeble, pallid, sickly, watery 7 insipid
8 ischemic 9 bloodless, colorless
10 spiritless

anemone 9 buttercup 10 windflower

anent 4 as to, in re 5 about, as for
7 apropos 8 touching 9 as regards
10 concerning 13 with respect to

anesthetic 6 opiate 7 anodyne 9 analgesic 10 painkiller, palliative *medical:*
5 ether 6 spinal 8 morphine, procaine
9 halothane, novocaine 10 benzocaine,
chloroform, tetracaine 11 scopolamine
suffix: 5 caine

anesthetize 4 numb, stun 6 benumb,
deaden 8 etherize, knock out 9 narcotize 11 desensitize

anesthetized 4 dead, numb 5 inert
6 asleep, torpid 10 insensible 11 insensitive, unconscious

anew 4 over 5 again 6 afresh, de novo,
lately, of late 8 once more, recently

angel 6 backer, cherub, patron, seraph,
surety 7 sponsor 8 backer-up, guardian
9 celestial, guarantor, supporter
10 benefactor 11 underwriter *biblical:*
5 Uriel 7 Gabriel, Michael, Raphael *fallen:* 7 Lucifer *hierarchy:* 6 powers
7 thrones, virtues 8 cherubim,
seraphim 9 dominions *Mormon:*
6 Moroni *of death:* 6 Azrael

Angel Clare's bride 4 Tess

angelic 4 holy, pure 5 godly 6 divine
7 saintly 8 cherubic, ethereal, heavenly
9 celestial 11 beneficent

Angelica *father:* 9 Galaphron *husband:*
6 Medoro *lover:* 7 Orlando

Angelou work 13 Heart of a Woman
(The) 25 I Know Why the Caged Bird
Sings

anger 3 ire, irk, vex 4 bile, boil, burn,
fume, fury, gall, huff, rage, rant, rave,
rile 5 annoy, pique, storm, upset, wrath
6 blow up, choler, dander, enrage,
madden, nettle, offend, seethe, stir up
7 affront, bristle, dudgeon, flare up,
incense, outrage, provoke, steam up,
umbrage 8 acrimony, boil over, irritate
9 aggravate, annoyance, animosity, displease, infuriate 10 antagonism, antagonize, exasperate 11 displeasure, indignation, infuriation 12 exasperation

angle 3 aim, bow 4 axil, bend, bias, fish,
hand, skew, turn 5 facet, slant 6 aspect,
corner, crotch, dogleg 7 flexure, outlook, turning 9 direction, viewpoint
10 standpoint

angler 6 fisher 8 monkfish 9 fisherman,
goosefish

Anglo-Saxon *assembly:* 4 moot 5 gemot
6 gemote *council:* 9 heptarchy *county:*
5 shire *court:* 4 moot 5 gemot 6 gemote
crown tax: 4 geld *epic:* 7 Beowulf *free
servant:* 5 thane, thegn *god:* 3 Ing *goddess of fate:* 4 Wyrd *historian:* 4 Bede
king: 3 Ine, Ini 4 Edwy 5 Edgar, Edred
6 Alfred, Edmund, Edward, Egbert
8 Ethelred *kingdom:* 4 Kent 5 Essex
6 Mercia, Sussex, Wessex 10 East Anglia
11 Northumbria *king's council:* 5 witan
letter: 3 edh, eth, wen, wyn 4 wynn
5 thorn *nobleman:* 4 earl *poet:* 4 scop
prince: 8 atheling *sheriff:* 5 reeve *slave:*
4 esne *warrior:* 5 thane, thegn

Angola *capital:* 6 Luanda *city:* 6 Huambo
7 Lubango 8 Benguela *exclave:* 7 Cabinda *language:* 10 Portuguese *monetary
unit:* 6 kwanza *neighbor:* 5 Congo
6 Zambia 7 Namibia 11 South Africa
river: 5 Congo

angora 3 cat **4** goat, hair, wool, yarn **6** mohair, rabbit

angry 3 hot, mad **4** sore **5** irate, riled, riley, upset, vexed, wroth **6** fuming, heated, ireful, wrathy **7** enraged, furious, riled up **8** choleric, incensed, inflamed, maddened, wrathful **9** indignant, irritated **10** aggravated, infuriated **11** acrimonious, exasperated

angst 4 fear **5** worry **6** unease **7** anxiety, concern **8** distress **10** insecurity **11** disquietude, fretfulness **12** apprehension

Anguilla *island, island group:* **3** Dog **4** Seal **5** Scrub **7** Leeward *language:* **7** English *location:* **10** West Indies *territory of:* **7** Britain

anguish 3 rue, woe **4** ache, care, dole, hurt, pain, pang **5** agony, dread, grief, throe, worry **6** misery, regret, sorrow, throes **7** anxiety, torment, torture **8** distress, hardship **9** heartache, suffering **10** affliction, heartbreak **12** wretchedness

angular 4 bony, edgy, lank, lean, thin **5** gaunt, lanky, spare, stiff **6** forked, skinny, zigzag **7** pointed, scraggy, scrawny **8** cornered, rawboned, ungainly **9** roughhewn **10** unfinished, ungraceful, unpolished **13** sharp-cornered

ani 6 cuckoo

anima 4 soul **6** psyche, spirit **9** inner self

animadversion 4 slam, slur **7** censure, obloquy **9** aspersion, criticism **10** accusation, imputation, reflection **11** insinuation **12** reprehension

animadvert 6 notice **7** observe **9** criticize

animal 3 beast, brute, feral **6** brutal, carnal, ferine **7** beastly, bestial, brutish, critter, fleshly, sensual, swinish, wilding **8** creature, wildling *antlered:* **3** elk **4** axis, deer **5** moose **7** caribou **8** reindeer *aquatic:* **3** eel **4** fish, frog, seal **5** otter, whale **6** dugong, sea cow, walrus **7** dolphin, manatee, octopus **8** bryozoan, porpoise **9** alligator, crocodile *arboreal:* **4** bird **5** chimp, coati, koala, lemur, sloth **6** gibbon, monkey **7** opossum, tarsier **8** kinkajou, marmoset, squirrel **8** orangutan *burrowing:* **4** mole **5** brock, ratel **6** badger, gopher, marmot, rabbit **7** echidna **9** armadillo, groundhog, woodchuck *castrated:* **5** capon, steer **6** barrow, wether **7** gelding *draft:* **3** ass **4** mule, oxen (plural) **5** horse **6** donkey **8** elephant *exhibit:* **3** zoo *extinct:* **3** moa **4** dodo, urus **6** quagga **7** mammoth **8** dinosaur, eohippus, mastodon **9** trilobite *female:* **3** cow, dam, doe, ewe, hen, pen, roe, sow **4** mare, puss **5** bitch, goose, jenny, nanny, vixen **6** jennet **7** lioness *four-*

footed: **9** quadruped *four-limbed:* **8** tetrapod *free-swimming:* **6** nekton *hibernating:* **4** bear, frog, toad **5** skunk, snake **7** polecat **8** chipmunk **9** groundhog, woodchuck *horned:* **3** ram, yak **4** bull, goat, ibex, kudu **5** addax, bison, eland, rhino **6** cattle, koodoo **7** buffalo, gazelle, giraffe, unicorn **8** antelope *humped:* **3** elk, yak **4** zebu **5** bison, camel, moose *imaginary:* **5** snark *insect-eating:* **4** mole, newt **5** gecko, shrew **7** echidna **8** aardvark, anteater, hedgehog, pangolin, tamandua **10** salamander *male:* **3** cob, ram, tom **4** boar, buck, bull, cock, stag, stud **5** billy, steer **6** gander **7** gobbler, rooster **8** bachelor, stallion *many-celled:* **8** metazoan *many-footed:* **9** centipede, millipede *marsupial:* **5** koala **6** wombat **7** opossum, wallaby **8** kangaroo **9** bandicoot, phalanger *meat-eating:* **9** carnivore *mythical:* **5** Hydra **6** dragon, kraken, sphinx **7** centaur, griffin, mermaid, Pegasus, unicorn **8** basilisk, Cerberus, Minotaur *one-celled:* **9** protozoan *Peruvian:* **5** llama **6** alpaca, vicuña *plant-eating:* **9** herbivore *skin disease:* **5** mange *snouted:* **5** coati, tapir **8** mongoose (see also ANIMAL INSECT-EATING) *spotted:* **4** axis, paca **6** calico, jaguar, ocelot **7** cheetah, leopard, piebald **8** skewbald **9** dalmatian *striped:* **4** kudo **5** tiger, zebra **6** koodoo, quagga **7** warthog **8** elephant *two-footed:* **5** biped *web-footed:* **4** duck, frog, toad **5** goose, otter **6** beaver **8** duckbill, platypus *young:* **3** cub, kid, kit, pup **4** calf, colt, fawn, foal, joey, lamb **5** bunny, chick, kitty, poult, shoat, stirk, whelp **6** cygnet, farrow, heifer, kitten, piglet **7** bullock, gosling, lambkin **8** suckling, yeanling, yearling **9** fledgling

animal behavior *study of:* **8** ethology

animal fat 4 suet **6** tallow

animalism 4 lust **7** abandon **8** vitality **9** carnality **10** sensualism, sensuality **11** lustfulness, physicality, unrestraint

animalize 4 warp **6** debase **7** corrupt, deprave, pervert, vitiate **9** brutalize **10** bestialize, demoralize

animal life 5 fauna

animal sound 3 arf, baa, bay, caw, coo, low, mew, moo **4** bark, bray, buzz, crow, hiss, hoot, howl, meow, purr, roar, yelp **5** bleat, chirp, croak, drone, growl, grunt, miaow, neigh, quack **6** bellow, gibber, gobble, warble **7** screech, twitter

animate 4 fire, live, move, spur, stir,

urge **5** alert, alive, cheer, drive, exalt, impel, liven, nerve, spark, steel, vital **6** active, arouse, excite, inform, kindle, lively, living, moving, viable, vivify **7** actuate, chirk up, dynamic, enliven, hearten, inspire, quicken, refresh **8** activate, embolden, energize, inspirit, motivate, spirited, vitalize **9** breathing, encourage, energized, enhearten, make alive, stimulate **10** invigorate

animated 3 gay **4** keen **5** alert, alive, peppy, quick, vivid, vital **6** lively, living **7** dynamic, excited, vibrant, zestful **8** spirited, vigorous **9** activated, energetic, energized, exuberant, sprightly, vitalized, vivacious **12** high-spirited

animation 3 pep, vim **4** brio, dash, élan, life, zing **5** oomph, verve **6** energy, esprit, gaiety, spirit **8** dynamism, vitality, vivacity **10** liveliness

animato 5 brisk, tempo **6** lively **8** spirited **9** energetic, sprightly

animosity 4 hate **5** venom **6** animus, enmity, hatred, rancor **7** dislike, ill will **8** acrimony **9** antipathy, hostility **10** antagonism, resentment

animus 4 plan, soul **6** design, enmity, intent, pneuma, psyche, rancor, spirit **7** dislike, ill will, meaning, purpose **9** antipathy, élan vital, hostility, intention **10** antagonism, intendment, opposition, vital force **11** disposition, malevolence

Anjou 4 pear *capital:* **6** Angers *native:* **7** Angevin

ankle 6 tarsus

annals 6 record **7** account, history **8** archives, register **9** chronicle

annelid 4 worm **5** leech **9** earthworm

annex 3 add, arm, cop, ell, win **4** gain, hook, join, land, take, wing **5** add on, affix, seize, tag on **6** adjoin, append, attach, fasten, obtain, pick up, secure, tack on, take on **7** acquire, connect, preempt, procure, subjoin **8** accroach, addition, appendix, arrogate, superadd, take over **9** extension **10** attachment, commandeer, subsidiary, supplement **11** appropriate, expropriate, incorporate

Annie Oakley 4 pass **10** free ticket, markswoman

annihilate 4 do in, kill, raze, rout, ruin, undo **5** abate, annul, crush, erase, quash, quell, wrack, wreck **6** murder, negate, quench, rub out, squash, uproot, vanish **7** abolish, blot out, destroy, expunge, nullify, put down, root out, vitiate, wipe out **8** abrogate, demolish, massacre, suppress, vanquish **9** eradicate, extirpate, liquidate, slaugh-

ter **10** extinguish, invalidate, obliterate **11** exterminate

annihilation 7 killing **8** massacre **9** abolition **11** destruction, elimination, liquidation, termination **12** obliteration **13** extermination

anniversary *hundredth:* **9** centenary **10** centennial *tenth:* **9** decennial *thousandth:* **10** millennial

annotate 5 gloss **6** remark **7** comment, explain **8** footnote **9** elucidate, interpret **10** commentate

announce 4 call, tell **5** augur, issue, state, sound **6** attest, blazon, herald, impart, report, reveal, signal **7** bespeak, declare, divulge, forerun, give out, portend, predict, presage, present, publish, release, signify, trumpet **8** disclose, forecast, foreshow, foretell, indicate, proclaim **9** advertise, broadcast, harbinger, make known, publicize **10** give notice, make public, promulgate **11** preindicate

announcement 4 news **6** notice, report **7** message, release **8** briefing, bulletin **9** broadcast, statement **10** communiqué, disclosure **11** declaration, publication **12** proclamation, promulgation **13** advertisement, communication

announcer 5 emcee **6** deejay, herald, veejay **9** anchorman, voice-over **10** disc jockey, disk jockey, newscaster **11** anchorwoman, broadcaster, commentator **12** anchorperson, sportscaster

annoy 3 bug, irk, vex **4** bait, fret, gall, miff **5** chafe, chivy, harry, peeve, tease, upset, worry **6** badger, bother, harass, heckle, hector, needle, nettle, pester, plague, ruffle **7** agitate, bedevil, disturb, hagride, perturb, provoke, tick off **8** distress, irritate **9** beleaguer *Scottish:* **4** fash

annoyance 4 drag, to-do **5** trial, upset, worry **6** bother, nettle, plague, strain **7** problem, trouble **8** distress, headache, irritant, nuisance, vexation **10** affliction, harassment, irritation **11** aggravation, botheration, disturbance, indignation, provocation **12** exasperation

annoying 5 pesky **8** tiresome **9** troubling, vexatious **10** disturbing, irritating **11** aggravating, distressing, troublesome **12** exasperating

annual 5 plant **6** flower, yearly **7** almanac **8** each year, yearbook, yearlong **9** every year

annul 4 undo, void **5** abate, erase, quash **6** cancel, delete, efface, negate, revoke, vacate **7** abolish, blot out, expunge, nullify, redress, rescind, retract, reverse, vitiate, wipe out **8** abrogate,

dissolve 9 cancel out, discharge, frustrate **10** annihilate, counteract, extinguish, invalidate, neutralize, obliterate **11** countermand

annunciate see ANNOUNCE

anodyne 4 balm **5** bland **6** opiate, relief, remedy **7** soother **8** narcotic, nepenthe, painless, sedative **9** analgesic, calmative, innocuous, soporific **10** anesthetic, depressant, pain-killer, palliative **11** inoffensive, unoffending **12** tranquilizer

anoint 3 rub **4** daub, laud, name **5** anele, apply, bless, honor, smear **6** choose, hallow, ordain **7** confirm, massage **8** dedicate, sanctify, set apart, venerate **9** designate **10** consecrate

anomalous 3 odd **6** off-key **7** deviant, strange, unusual **8** aberrant, abnormal, atypical, peculiar **9** deviating, deviatory, divergent, irregular, unnatural, untypical **10** unexpected **11** heteroclite, incongruous, paradoxical **12** inconsistent **13** nonconforming, preternatural

anomaly 5 freak, quirk **6** oddity **9** departure, deviation, exception **10** aberration, divergence **11** abnormality, incongruity, peculiarity **12** idiosyncrasy, irregularity **13** inconsistency

anomie 4 flux **6** unrest **7** anxiety, inertia **10** alienation, insecurity **11** disquietude, instability, uncertainty **12** disaffection, estrangement, indifference, restlessness

anon 4 soon **5** later **7** by and by, shortly **8** directly **9** presently **10** before long **11** after a while

anonym 5 alias **6** handle **7** pen name **8** nickname **9** pseudonym **10** nom de plume **11** assumed name, nom de guerre

anonymous 7 unknown, unnamed **8** nameless, not named, unsigned **9** incognito **10** innominate **11** unspecified **12** undesignated, unidentified, unrecognized

anorak 5 parka

another 3 new **4** else, more **5** added, fresh **7** farther, further, one more **9** different **10** additional **11** alternative, someone else **13** something else

anschluss 5 union **6** league **8** alliance **9** coalition **10** federation **11** confederacy **13** confederation

answer 4 fill, meet, plea **5** atone, plead, rebut, reply, serve, solve **6** come in, refute, rejoin, result, retort, return **7** conform, defense, explain, fulfill, respond, satisfy **8** antiphon, rebuttal, response, solution **9** rejoinder **10** refutation **11** recriminate **13** countercharge

answerable 5 bound **6** liable **7** obliged, subject **8** amenable **9** compelled, dutybound, obligated **11** accountable, constrained, responsible

ant 5 emmet **9** carpenter *relating to:* **6** formic

Antaean 4 huge **5** giant **6** heroic **7** mammoth, titanic **8** colossal, enormous, gigantic **9** cyclopean, Herculean **10** gargantuan

Antaeus *father:* **7** Neptune **8** Poseidon *mother:* **4** Gaea *slayer:* **8** Heracles, Hercules

antagonism 3 con **6** animus, enmity, hatred, rancor **7** discord **8** conflict, friction **9** animosity, antipathy, hostility **10** antithesis, contention, dissension, opposition, resistance **11** contrariety **12** disagreement

antagonist 3 con, foe **4** anti **5** enemy, match **6** muscle **7** opposer **8** chemical, opponent **9** adversary, contender

antagonistic 4 anti **6** averse **7** adverse, hostile, opposed **8** clashing, contrary, inimical, opposing **9** bellicose, combative, rancorous, truculent, vitriolic **10** discordant **11** belligerent, conflicting, contentious **12** antipathetic

Antarctica sea 4 Ross **7** Weddell **8** Amundsen

ante 3 bet, pay, pot **4** cost, risk **5** level, pay up, price, put up, stake, wager **6** stakes **7** produce

anteater see ANIMAL *INSECT-EATING*

antecede 7 forerun, precede, predate **8** foredate, go before

antecedence 8 priority **10** precedence, precession, preference

antecedent 4 fore, line **5** cause, prior **6** former, reason **7** earlier **8** ancestor, anterior, forebear, foregoer, occasion, previous **9** condition, foregoing, precedent, preceding, precursor, prototype **10** forerunner, progenitor **11** determinant, predecessor

antedate 7 forerun, precede **11** anachronize **12** occur earlier

antediluvian 3 old **4** aged, fogy **5** hoary, passé **6** age-old, fogram, fossil, square **7** ancient, antique, archaic **8** mossback, Noachian, obsolete, outdated, outmoded, primeval, timeworn **9** out-of-date, primitive **10** antiquated, fuddy-duddy **12** old-fashioned **13** stick-in-the-mud

antelope 3 gnu **4** kudu, oryx **5** addax, bongo, eland, nyala, serow **6** dik-dik, duiker, impala, koodoo, lechwe **7** blesbok, chamois, gazelle, gemsbok, gerenuk, sassaby **8** bushbuck, reedbuck, steinbok **9** springbok, waterbuck **10** hartebeest *female:* **3** doe *male:* 4 buck *young:* 3 kid (see also GAZELLE)

antenna 4 wire 6 aerial, device, dipole, sensor 8 monopole, receiver

antennae 4 ears 11 sensitivity 13 receptiveness

anterior 4 past 5 prior 6 former 8 previous 9 foregoing, precedent, preceding 10 antecedent

anteroom 5 entry, foyer, lobby 6 alcove 9 vestibule

Anteros *brother:* 4 Eros *father:* 4 Ares, Mars *mother:* 5 Venus 9 Aphrodite *opposite:* 4 Eros

anthem 4 hymn, song 5 chant, paean, psalm 8 canticle

anthology 3 ana 5 album 6 digest, reader 7 garland, omnibus 8 analects, treasury 9 selection 10 assortment, collection, compendium, miscellany 11 compilation, florilegium

anthropoid 3 ape 5 biped 6 monkey 7 bipedal, gorilla, manlike, primate 8 hominoid, humanoid 10 chimpanzee

anthropologist 4 Boas (Franz), Dart (Raymond), Mead (Margaret) 5 Sapir (Edward), Tylor (Edward Burnett) 6 Frazer (James George), Geertz (Clifford), Leakey (Louis), Morgan (Lewis Henry) 7 Bateson (Gregory), Kroeber (Alfred Louis) 8 Benedict (Ruth) 10 Malinowski (Bronisław) 11 Lévi-Strauss (Claude)

anti 3 con 6 averse 7 adverse, against, counter, opposed, opposer 8 contrary, opponent, opposing 9 adversary, opposed to 10 antagonist 12 antagonistic, antipathetic, in opposition

antiaircraft fire 4 flak

antibiotic 7 colicin 8 neomycin, viomycin 9 polymyxin 10 bacitracin, novobiocin, penicillin 11 bacteriocin, tyrothricin 12 streptomycin, tetracycline

antic 3 gag 4 dido, joke, lark, romp 5 caper, comic, prank, trick 6 frisky, frolic, lively 7 comical, foolish, playful 8 escapade, farcical, prankish, spirited 9 high jinks, laughable, ludicrous, sprightly 10 frolicsome, rollicking, shenanigan, tomfoolery 11 mischievous, monkeyshine 12 monkeyshines 13 practical joke

anticipate 3 see 4 wait 5 await, check 6 divine, expect 7 counter, count on, foresee, prepare, presage, prevent, wait for 8 forecast, foreknow, foretell 9 apprehend, forestall, prevision, visualize 10 prepare for

anticipation 7 inkling, outlook, promise 8 awaiting, forecast, prospect 9 aware-ness, foresight, foretaste 10 expectancy 11 expectation, realization 12 apprehension 13 visualization

Anticlea *father:* 9 Autolycus *husband:* 7 Laertes *son:* 7 Ulysses 8 Odysseus

antidote 4 cure, drug 6 remedy 7 negator 8 medicine 9 nullifier 10 corrective, counteract, preventive 11 counterstep, neutralizer 12 counteragent 13 counteractant, counteractive

Antigone *brother:* 9 Polynices 10 Polyneices *father:* 7 Oedipus *mother:* 7 Jocasta *sister:* 6 Ismene *uncle:* 5 Creon

Antigua and Barbuda *capital:* 7 St. Johns *island:* 7 Antigua, Barbuda, Redonda *language:* 7 English *monetary unit:* 6 dollar

Antilochus *father:* 6 Nestor *friend:* 8 Achilles *slayer:* 6 Memnon

Antiope *father:* 6 Asopus *husband:* 5 Lycus 7 Theseus *queen of:* 7 Amazons *son:* 6 Zethus 7 Amphion 10 Hippolytus

antipasto 9 appetizer 11 hors d'oeuvre 12 hors d'oeuvres

antipathetic 5 loath 6 averse, loathe 7 adverse, hostile, opposed 8 aversive, clashing, contrary, inimical, opposing, opposite 9 abhorrent, disliking, loathsome, repellent, repugnant, repulsive 10 discordant, unfriendly 11 conflicting, distasteful, ill-disposed, uncongenial 12 antagonistic 13 contradictory

antipathy 4 hate 6 animus, enmity, hatred, rancor 7 allergy, dislike, ill will 8 aversion, distaste, loathing 9 animosity, hostility 10 abhorrence, antagonism, opposition, repellency

antiphon 5 psalm, reply, verse 6 answer, anthem, return 7 respond 8 response

antipodal 5 polar 7 adverse, counter, opposed, reverse 8 contrary, converse, opposite 9 diametric 11 conflicting, contrasting, diametrical 12 antithetical 13 contradictory

antipode 6 contra 7 counter, reverse 8 contrary, converse, flip side, opposite 9 other side 10 antithesis 11 counterpole

antiquate 7 make old, outdate, outmode 8 obsolete 9 obsolesce 12 superannuate

antiquated 3 old 4 aged 5 dated, fusty, hoary, moldy, passé 6 old hat 7 ancient, antique, archaic 8 obsolete, old-timey, outmoded 9 out-of-date 10 oldfangled, out-of-style 11 discredited, obsolescent 12 antediluvian, old-fashioned 13 inappropriate, superannuated

antique 3 old 4 aged 5 dated, hoary, olden, passé, relic 6 age-old, bygone, rarity 7 ancient, archaic, vintage 8 artifact, heirloom, old-timey, outdated, outmoded, timeworn **9** ancestral, objet d'art, out-of-date, venerable **10** antiquated, oldfangled **12** antediluvian, old-fashioned

antiseptic 6 iodine **7** alcohol, sterile **8** hygienic, peroxide, sanitary **9** boric acid, carvacrol, germicide, merbromin **10** gramicidin, sterilized **12** carbolic acid, disinfectant *pioneer:* **6** Lister (Joseph)

antisocial 7 ascetic, austere, hostile **8** eremitic, solitary **9** alienated, reclusive, withdrawn **10** unfriendly **11** standoffish **12** antagonistic, misanthropic

antithesis 3 con **6** contra **7** counter, reverse **8** antipode, antipole, contrary, contrast, converse, opposite **10** antagonism, opposition **11** counterpole

antithetical 5 polar **7** counter, reverse **8** contrary, converse, opposite **9** antipodal, diametric **10** antipodean **11** diametrical **13** contradictory

antitoxin 4 sera (plural) **5** serum **11** neutralizer

antiwar 6 irenic **8** pacifist **10** nonviolent, pacifistic

Antony, Mark *defeat:* **6** Actium *friend:* **6** Caesar *lover:* **9** Cleopatra *wife:* **7** Octavia

anxiety 4 care, fear **5** doubt, dread, panic, worry **6** unease **7** concern **8** distress, mistrust, suspense **9** self-doubt, suffering **10** uneasiness **11** disquietude, uncertainty **12** apprehension

anxious 4 avid, keen **5** eager **6** afraid, ardent, scared, uneasy **7** alarmed, fearful, worried **8** agitated, desirous, troubled, worrying **9** impatient, perturbed, terrified **10** breathless, disquieted, frightened **12** apprehensive

any 3 all **4** a bit, some **5** at all, every **7** a little, several **8** whatever

anyhow 6 random **7** however **8** at random, randomly **9** hit-or-miss **10** carelessly, regardless **11** any which way, haphazardly **13** helter-skelter

anymore 3 now **5** today **8** nowadays **9** presently, these days

anyone 3 all **9** everybody

anything 5 at all

anytime 4 ever **5** at all **8** whenever

anyway 4 ever, once **5** at all **7** however **12** nevertheless

anywhere 5 at all **7** all over **10** at any point

anywise 5 at all

apace 4 fast **6** versed **7** abreast, flat-out, hastily, quickly, rapidly, swiftly **8** informed, up-to-date, speedily **9** posthaste **12** lickety-split **13** expeditiously

Apache *chief:* **7** Cochise **8** Geronimo *subgroups:* **7** Cibecue **9** Jicarilla, Mescalero **10** Chiricahua

apart 5 alone, aside **6** singly **7** asunder, removed **8** detached, isolated, one by one **9** severally **10** separately **12** individually **13** independently, unaccompanied *prefix:* **3** dis

apart from 3 bar, but **4** save **6** except, saving **7** barring, besides **9** except for, excepting, excluding, other than, outside of **11** exclusive of

apartheid 8 division **9** partition **10** separation, separatism **11** segregation **12** separateness

apartment 4 flat, room **5** rooms, suite **6** rental **7** chamber, housing, lodging **8** building, dwelling **9** residence **13** accommodation

apathetic 4 dull, flat, limp **5** inert **6** stolid, torpid **7** languid, passive, unmoved **8** sluggish **9** impassive, untouched **10** anesthetic, insensible, phlegmatic, spiritless **11** emotionless, indifferent, insensitive **12** unresponsive **13** disinterested

apathy 6 torpor **8** coldness, dullness, lethargy, obduracy, stoicism **9** aloofness, disregard, inertness, lassitude, passivity, stolidity, torpidity, unconcern **10** detachment, dispassion **11** callousness, disinterest, impassivity **12** heedlessness, indifference, listlessness **13** insensibility, insensitivity

ape 4 copy, mime, mock **5** mimic **6** baboon, bonobo, gibbon, monkey, parody, pongid, simian **7** copycat, emulate, gorilla, imitate, siamang, take off **8** simulate, travesty **9** burlesque, orangutan **10** anthropoid, caricature, chimpanzee **11** impersonate

aperçu 5 brief **6** digest, précis, sketch, survey **7** insight, outline **8** syllabus **10** compendium, impression

aperitif 4 whet **5** drink **8** cocktail **9** appetizer

aperture 3 gap **4** hole, vent **6** outlet **7** opening, orifice, pinhole

apery 7 mimicry **9** imitation

apex 3 cap, tip, top **4** acme, cusp, peak, roof **5** crest, crown, limit, point **6** apogee, climax, summit, vertex, zenith **8** capstone, pinnacle, ultimate **9** crescendo, sublimity **11** culmination, ne plus ultra **12** quintessence

aphorism 3 saw **4** rule **5** adage, axiom, maxim, moral **6** dictum, saying, truism **7** precept, proverb **8** apothegm

aphrodisiac 6 erotic **7** amative, amatory, amorous, lustful **8** excitant **10** passionate

Aphrodite *Roman counterpart:* 5 Venus *consort:* 4 Ares 6 Vulcan 10 Hephaestus *father:* 4 Zeus 7 Jupiter *goddess of:* 4 love *mother:* 5 Dione *son:* 4 Eros 6 Aeneas 7 Priapus

apiarist 9 beekeeper

apical 3 top 7 highest, topmost 8 loftiest 9 uppermost

apiculture 10 beekeeping

apiece 3 per 4 a pop, each 6 singly, to each 7 for each 8 one by one 9 per capita, severally 10 separately 12 individually, respectively

apish 5 phony, silly 7 slavish 8 affected 9 emulative, imitative 10 artificial

aplenty 4 full 5 ample 6 galore, indeed 7 copious, greatly 8 abundant, very much 9 extremely

aplomb 4 ease 5 poise 6 polish 8 coolness, easiness 9 assurance, certainty, certitude, composure 10 confidence, equanimity 11 nonchalance, savoir faire 12 self-reliance 13 self-assurance

apocalypse 6 augury, oracle, vision 8 disaster, prophecy 10 Armageddon, prediction, revelation

apocalyptic 4 dire 5 awful 7 baleful, baneful, fateful, fearful, ominous 8 Delphian, dreadful, oracular, terrible 9 appalling, climactic, grandiose, prophetic 10 foreboding, predicting 11 foretelling, prophetical, threatening 12 inauspicious *book:* 10 Revelation 11 Revelations

apocryphal 5 false, wrong 6 untrue 7 dubious 8 doubtful, spurious 9 incorrect, ungenuine 10 ficticious, inaccurate, unverified 11 unauthentic 12 questionable

apogee 4 acme, apex, peak 6 climax, summit, zenith 8 capstone, meridian, pinnacle 9 high point 11 culmination

Apollo 6 Helios 7 Phoebus *beloved:* 6 Cyrene, Daphne 8 Calliope *birthplace:* 5 Delos *father:* 4 Zeus 7 Jupiter *mother:* 4 Leto 6 Latona *oracle:* 6 Delphi *sister:* 5 Diana 7 Artemis *son:* 3 Ion 7 Orpheus *temple:* 6 Delphi

apologetic 5 sorry 6 rueful 8 contrite, penitent 9 regretful, repentant 10 remorseful 11 penitential 12 compunctious

apologia 4 plea 6 excuse, reason 7 defense 8 argument 11 elucidation, explanation 13 clarification, justification

apologize 5 atone 6 lament, regret, repent 7 confess 9 beg pardon 10 make amends

apologue 4 myth, tale 5 fable, story 7 parable 8 allegory

apology 4 plea 6 amends, excuse 7 redress, regrets 8 mea culpa 9 admission, makeshift 10 concession, confession

apostasy 7 perfidy 9 defection, desertion, disavowal, falseness, rejection 11 abandonment, repudiation 12 disaffection, renunciation

apostate 7 heretic, traitor 8 defector, deserter, recreant, renegade, turncoat 9 turnabout

apostatize 4 turn 6 defect, desert 7 abandon, forsake, sell out 8 renounce 9 repudiate

a posteriori 9 inductive

apostle 4 John, Jude, Paul 5 James, Judas, Peter, Silas, Simon 6 Andrew, Philip, Thomas 7 Matthew 8 Barnabas, disciple, follower, Matthias, preacher 9 missioner 10 colporteur, evangelist, missionary 11 Bartholomew 12 propagandist *of Germany:* 8 Boniface *of Ireland:* 7 Patrick *of the English:* 9 Augustine *of the French:* 5 Denis *of the Gauls:* 8 Irenaeus *of the Gentiles:* 4 Paul *of the Goths:* 7 Ulfilas *to the Indians:* 9 John Eliot

apothecary 7 chemist 8 druggist, pharmacy 9 drugstore 10 pharmacist

apothegm see APHORISM

apotheosis 6 height 7 epitome 8 exemplar, last word, ultimate 9 archetype, elevation 10 embodiment, exaltation 11 deification, ennoblement, idolization, lionization 12 enshrinement, quintessence 13 glorification

appall 3 awe 4 faze 5 alarm, shake, shock 6 dismay 7 horrify, outrage, overawe, perturb 8 confound, distress 10 disconcert 11 consternate

appalled 6 aghast 11 dumbfounded

appalling 5 awful 6 horrid 7 fearful 8 daunting, dreadful, horrible, horrific, shocking, terrible 9 atrocious, dismaying, frightful, loathsome 10 disgusting, formidable, horrifying

appanage 5 grant, right 7 adjunct 8 property 9 endowment, privilege 10 birthright, perquisite 11 prerogative

apparatus 4 gear, tool 5 gizmo 6 device, outfit, tackle 7 utensil 8 matériel, tackling 9 equipment, implement, machinery 10 instrument 11 contraption, habiliments 13 accouterments, accoutrements, paraphernalia

apparel 4 clad, duds, garb, gear, robe, suit, togs 5 adorn, array, dress, getup, habit 6 attire, clothe, outfit 7 clothes, costume, garment, raiment, threads 8 clothing, enclothe, glad rags, vestment 9 embellish 11 habiliments

apparent 5 clear, plain 6 patent 7 evident, obvious, seeming, visible 8 distinct, manifest, palpable 9 succedent 10 noticeable, observable 11 discernible, perceivable, unambiguous, unequivocal 12 successional

apparition 5 ghost, shade, umbra 6 shadow, spirit, vision, wraith 7 phantom, specter 8 illusion, phantasm 10 appearance, phenomenon 13 hallucination

appeal 3 ask, beg, bid 4 call, lure, plea, pray, pull, suit, urge 5 apply, brace, charm, crave, plead 6 accuse, allure, charge, excite, invoke, sue for 7 attract, beseech, entreat, glamour, implore, request 8 call upon, charisma, entreaty, interest, intrigue, petition 9 fascinate, importune, magnetism, seduction 10 allurement, attraction, supplicate 11 application, fascination, imploration 12 drawing power, solicitation, supplication

appealing 8 alluring, charming, pleading, pleasant, pleasing 9 agreeable, imploring 10 attracting, attractive, bewitching, enchanting, entreating 11 captivating, fascinating

appear 4 come, look, loom, rise, seem, show 5 arise, issue, occur, sound 6 arrive, emerge, show up 7 be clear, emanate 8 look like, resemble 9 be evident, come forth 10 be manifest 11 materialize

appearance 3 air 4 face, form, look, mien, pose, show 5 debut, dress, front, guise, image 6 advent, aspect, facade, manner 7 arrival, bearing, display, seeming 8 attitude, demeanor, illusion 9 semblance 10 impression, occurrence, simulacrum 11 countenance 13 manifestation

appease 4 calm, ease 5 allay, quiet 6 buy off, pacify, soothe 7 assuage, concede, content, gratify, mollify, placate, relieve, satisfy, sweeten 10 conciliate, propitiate

appellation 4 name 5 brand, label, nomen, style, title 7 moniker 8 cognomen 10 identifier 11 designation 12 denomination

append 3 add 5 add on, affix, annex, tag on 6 adjoin, attach, tack on 7 subjoin 10 supplement

appendage 3 arm, fin, leg, tab, tag 4 barb, flap, horn, limb, seta, tail, wing 5 extra 6 cercus, member 7 adjunct, antenna, elytron, stipule 8 pedipalp, pendicle, tentacle 9 accessory, auxiliary, extremity 10 attachment, collateral, incidental, projection, supplement

appendix 5 notes, rider 7 adjunct, codicil 8 addendum, addition 9 accessory, appendage 10 attachment, supplement 12 appurtenance

apperception 5 grasp 9 awareness 10 cognizance 11 realization, recognition 12 apprehension, assimilation 13 comprehension, introspection, understanding

appertain 4 bear 5 apply, refer 6 bear on, belong, relate 8 bear upon 10 be relevant 11 be connected, be pertinent

appetence 3 yen 5 taste 6 desire, hunger, relish, thirst 7 craving, longing, stomach 8 fondness

appetent 4 agog, avid, keen 5 eager 6 ardent 7 anxious, craving, lusting, thirsty 8 desirous, yearning 9 impatient 10 breathless

appetite 3 yen 4 bent, itch, lust, urge 5 taste 6 desire, hunger, liking, relish 7 craving, leaning, longing, passion, stomach 8 cupidity, fondness, gluttony, penchant, soft spot, voracity, weakness, yearning 9 hankering 10 preference, proclivity, propensity 11 inclination

appetizer 4 whet 5 snack 6 canapé, savory, tidbit 8 aperitif, cocktail, stimulus 9 antipasto 11 hors d'oeuvre

appetizing 5 tasty 6 savory 8 saporous, tempting 9 agreeable, appealing, aperitive, flavorful, palatable, relishing, toothsome 10 delectable, flavorsome 11 tantalizing 13 mouth-watering

applaud 4 clap, hail, laud, root 5 bravo, cheer, extol 6 praise, rise to 7 acclaim, approve, commend 9 recommend 10 compliment

applause 4 hand 5 round 6 bravos, cheers, praise 7 acclaim, hurrahs, ovation, rooting 8 accolade, approval, cheering, clapping, plaudits 11 acclamation 12 commendation

apple 4 crab, Fuji, Gala, pome 6 Empire, pippin, russet 7 Baldwin, costard, Duchess, Winesap 8 Braeburn, Cortland, greening, Jonagold, Jonathan, McIntosh 9 Delicious 10 Rome Beauty 11 Granny Smith, Gravenstein, Northern Spy, Transparent *dessert:* 5 crisp *juice:* 5 cider

applejack 5 cider 6 brandy, liquor 8 calvados 9 hard cider

apple knocker see R

apple-polish 4 fawn 5 toady 6 kowtow 7 cater to, flatter, honey up, truckle 8 butter up 10 curry favor, ingratiate

apple-polisher 5 toady 6 yes-man

8 bootlick, groveler, lickspit **9** flatterer, sycophant **11** lickspittle

applesauce 5 hooey **6** bunkum **7** baloney, rubbish, twaddle **8** malarkey, nonsense **9** poppycock

appliance 6 device **7** utensil **9** implement **10** instrument **11** application *kitchen:* **4** oven **5** mixer, range, stove **6** fridge **7** blender, toaster **9** can opener, microwave **10** dishwasher **12** refrigerator

applicability 3 use **7** account, fitness, utility **9** advantage, relevance **10** usefulness

applicable 3 apt, fit **4** just, meet **5** ad rem **6** seemly, suited, useful **7** apropos, fitting, germane **8** apposite, material, relevant, suitable **9** befitting, pertinent **10** felicitous **11** appropriate

applicant 6 seeker **7** hopeful **8** aspirant, inquirer **9** candidate, job-hunter, job-seeker

application 3 use **4** form, heed, plea, suit **5** study **6** appeal, debate, effort, letter **7** request **8** entreaty, exercise, exertion, industry, petition **9** assiduity, attention, diligence, operation, treatment **10** dedication, employment **11** requisition, utilization **12** solicitation **13** concentration, consideration

appliqué 5 decal

apply 3 dab, use **4** bend, give, turn, urge **5** press, refer **6** accost, affect, appeal, assign, bear on, bestow, devote, direct, employ, engage, handle, relate, resort, take on **7** address, beseech, concern, entreat, execute, implore, involve, pertain, utilize **8** approach, bear upon, exercise, petition, set about **9** appertain, implement, importune, undertake **10** administer, buckle down

appoint 3 arm, fix, rig, set, tap **4** gear, name **5** equip **6** assign, decide, fit out, outfit, supply **7** dress up, furbish, furnish, provide, turn out **8** accouter, accoutre, accredit, delegate, nominate **9** authorize, designate, determine, embellish, provision **10** commission

appointment 3 job **4** date, meet, post, spot **5** berth, place, tryst **6** billet, choice, office **7** meeting **8** election, position **9** equipment, selection, situation **10** assignment, connection, engagement, rendezvous **11** arrangement, assignation, designation

appointments 7 fitting **8** equipage **9** equipment, trappings **12** furnishings **13** accouterments, accoutrements

apportion 3 cut, lot **4** give, mete, part **5** allot, allow, cut up, divvy, quota, serve, share, slice, split **6** assign,

bestow, divide, parcel, ration **7** deal out, dish out, divvy up, dole out, measure, mete out, prorate, split up **8** allocate, dispense, separate, share out **9** admeasure, partition **10** administer, distribute

apportionment 3 cut, lot **4** part **5** piece, quota, share, slice, split **6** ration **7** measure, quantum **9** allotment, allowance **10** allocation, assignment

apposite 3 apt **4** just **5** ad rem **6** proper, suited, timely **7** apropos, fitting, germane, right on **8** material, on target, relevant, suitable **9** pertinent **10** applicable **11** appropriate

appositeness 7 aptness, fitness **9** relevance **10** pertinence, timeliness **11** suitability

appraisal 5 stock **6** rating, survey **7** pricing **8** estimate, judgment **9** valuation **10** assessment, estimation, evaluation

appraise 3 eye, fix, set **4** rate, size **5** assay, audit, gauge, judge, price, set at, value **6** assess, figure, size up, survey **7** adjudge, examine, inspect, measure, valuate **8** estimate, evaluate, look over **9** calculate, figure out

appreciable 5 clear, plain **6** marked **7** evident, obvious **8** apparent, clearcut, concrete, manifest, material, palpable, sensible, tangible **10** detectable, measurable, noticeable, observable **11** discernible, perceptible, substantial **12** considerable

appreciate 4 gain, go up, grow, know, like, love, rise **5** enjoy, grasp, judge, prize, savor, value **6** admire, esteem, fathom, regard, relish **7** apprize, cherish, cognize, enhance, improve, inflate, realize, respect **8** evaluate, increase, treasure **9** apprehend, delight in, recognize **10** comprehend, understand

appreciation 4 gain, rise **6** growth, regard, thanks **7** tribute **8** increase, judgment **9** awareness, gratitude, inflation **10** evaluation, perception **11** recognition, sensitivity, testimonial **12** gratefulness

apprehend 3 dig, get, nab, see **4** bust, fear, grab, know, nail, read, take, twig **5** catch, grasp, pinch, run in, seize, sense **6** absorb, accept, arrest, collar, detain, digest, divine, fathom, pick up, take in, wise up **7** capture, catch on, cognize, compass, foresee, make out, preknow, previse, realize **8** conceive **9** penetrate, recognize, visualize **10** anticipate, appreciate, understand

apprehensible 5 clear, lucid, plain **7** evident, obvious **8** distinct, explicit, knowable, luminous **9** graspable **10** fathomable

apprehension 3 ken **4** care, fear, idea **5** alarm, angst, dread, grasp, pinch, worry **6** arrest, notion, pickup, unease **7** anxiety, capture, concern, seizure, thought **8** disquiet, judgment **9** agitation, awareness, detention, knowledge, misgiving, suspicion **10** conception, foreboding, perception, solicitude, uneasiness **11** disquietude, premonition **13** comprehension, understanding

apprehensive 5 alive, awake, aware, sharp **6** afraid, astute, scared, uneasy **7** anxious, fearful, knowing, uneasy **8** sensible, sentient, troubled **9** cognizant, conscious, observant, sensitive **10** discerning, disquieted, insightful, perceptive

apprentice 4 bind, tyro **5** pupil, serve **6** novice, rookie **7** learner, starter, student, trainee, work for **8** beginner, freshman, neophyte, newcomer **9** novitiate **10** tenderfoot

apprenticed 5 bound **7** obliged, pledged **8** articled **9** obligated **10** indentured

apprise 4 clue, post, tell, warn **6** advise, clue in, fill in, impart, inform, notify, reveal, wise up **7** let know **8** acquaint, announce, describe, disclose **9** make known **11** communicate

apprize 5 value **6** admire, esteem, regard, relish **7** cherish **8** hold dear, treasure **10** appreciate, rate highly

approach 4 near, nigh **5** reach, rival, touch, verge **6** access, advise, amount, avenue, border, gain on **7** address, advance, apply to, attempt, consult, descent, request **8** come up to, draw near, endeavor, overture **9** come close **11** approximate

approachable 7 affable **8** friendly, sociable **9** agreeable, congenial, reachable, receptive **10** accessible, attainable

approaching 6 coming **7** nearing **8** expected, imminent, oncoming, upcoming **11** forthcoming

approbate 4 back, like **5** favor **6** accept, assent, praise **7** applaud, approve, commend, consent, endorse, support **8** sanction **9** recommend **11** countenance

approbation 3 nod **4** okay **5** favor **6** esteem, praise **7** acclaim, consent, support **8** applause, approval, sanction **10** admiration, permission **11** endorsement, recognition **12** commendation

appropriate 3 apt, cop, due, fit **4** grab, just, lift, meet, take, true **5** allot, annex, claim, exact, filch, grasp, pinch, right, seize, steal, swipe, usurp **6** assign,

assume, budget, devote, pilfer, proper, snatch, snitch, timely, useful, worthy **7** apropos, desired, earmark, fitting, germane, merited, preempt, purloin **8** accroach, apposite, arrogate, deserved, eligible, entitled, relevant, rightful, set apart, set aside, suitable **9** befitting, opportune, pertinent, requisite **10** acceptable, admissible, applicable, commandeer, compatible, confiscate, convenient, felicitous, seasonable

appropriately 4 well **5** amply, aptly, right **8** properly, suitably **9** fittingly **10** acceptably, adequately, becomingly

appropriateness 3 use **5** order **7** account, aptness, fitness, service, utility **8** meetness **9** advantage, propriety, relevance, rightness **10** expediency, usefulness **13** applicability

appropriation 5 grant **7** funding, stipend, subsidy **9** allotment, allowance **10** allocation, assignment, earmarking, subvention

approval 4 okay **5** favor, leave **6** assent **7** consent, go-ahead, license, support **8** applause, blessing, sanction, suffrage **10** acceptance, compliment, green light, permission **11** approbation, benediction, concurrence, endorsement **12** commendation, ratification **13** authorization, confirmation

approve 4 okay **5** clear, favor, go for **6** accept, back up, praise, ratify, uphold **7** applaud, certify, commend, condone, confirm, endorse, initial, mandate, stand by, support, sustain **8** accredit, hold with, sanction **9** approbate, authorize, encourage **10** compliment **11** countenance

approximate 4 near **5** close, rough, touch **6** almost **7** similar, verge on **8** approach, come near **10** resembling **11** comparative

approximately 4 most, nigh **5** about, circa **6** all but, almost, nearly **7** close to **8** well-nigh **9** just about, very close **11** practically

approximation 8 likeness, nearness **9** closeness **10** similarity **11** resemblance

appurtenance 7 adjunct **8** addition, appendix, ornament **9** accessory, apparatus, appendage **10** attachment **11** furnishings **13** accompaniment

appurtenant 5 extra **8** adjuvant **9** accessory, ancillary, auxiliary **10** additional, collateral, subsidiary **11** subordinate, subservient **12** accompanying, contributory

a priori 8 provable, reasoned **9** deducible, deductive, derivable, inferable **11** inferential, presumptive

apron 5 stage **6** shield **7** garment
8 pinafore **9** extension

apropos 3 apt **4** as to, in re, meet
5 about, ad rem, anent, aptly, as for
6 proper, timely **7** fitting, germane,
related **8** apposite, material, pointful,
relevant, suitable, suitably, touching
9 as regards, opportune, pertinent,
regarding **10** applicable, as respects,
concerning, relevantly, respecting, seasonably **11** applicative, applicatory,
bearing upon, in respect to, oppor-
tunely, pertinently **13** with respect to

apt 3 fit **4** just **5** alert, given, prone,
quick, ready, savvy, smart **6** bright,
clever, liable, likely, prompt, proper
7 apropos, fitting, germane, tending
8 apposite, disposed, inclined, relevant,
suitable **9** befitting, pertinent, qualified
10 felicitous, responsive **11** appropriate,
intelligent

aptitude 4 bent, gift **5** flair, knack, savvy
6 genius, liking, talent **7** ability, faculty,
fitness **8** capacity, tendency **10** capability, cleverness, proclivity, propensity
11 disposition, inclination, suitability
12 predilection

aptness 4 bent, gift **5** flair, knack, skill
6 genius, talent **7** ability, faculty, fitness
8 tendency **9** propriety, readiness
10 capability, cleverness, expediency,
likelihood **11** inclination, suitability
12 intelligence

aquanaut 5 diver **10** scuba diver

aqua vitae 4 grog **5** booze, drink, hooch
6 liquor, tipple **7** alcohol, spirits

aqueduct 5 canal **6** course **7** channel,
conduit, passage **8** waterway **11** watercourse

aqueous 5 fluid **6** liquid, watery **9** liquefied

Aquila 13 constellation *representation:*
5 eagle *star:* **6** Altair

Aquitaine 7 Guienne *queen:* **7** Eleanor

aquiver 5 shaky **7** quaking, shaking,
trembly **9** shivering, trembling, tremu-
lant, tremulous

Arab *chief:* **4** emir **5** sheik **6** sheikh, sul-
tan *country:* **4** Iraq, Oman **5** Egypt,
Libya, Qatar, Sudan, Syria, Yemen
6 Jordan, Kuwait **7** Algeria, Bahrain,
Lebanon, Morocco, Tunisia **11** Saudi
Arabia

arable 7 fertile **8** fruitful, tillable **10** cultivable, productive

Arachne *father:* **5** Idmon *form:* **6** spider
mother: **6** Cyrene *rival:* **6** Athena **7** Minerva

arachnid 4 mite, tick **6** acarus, spider
8 scorpion **9** arthropod, phalangid,

tarantula **10** harvestman **13** daddy longlegs

arbiter 5 judge **6** expert, umpire **7** referee **8** mediator **9** authority, moderator
11 adjudicator

arbitrary 4 rash **6** chance, random
7 erratic, offhand, wayward, willful
8 fanciful, heedless **9** frivolous, impetuous, whimsical **10** capricious, subjective **10** irrational **12** unreasonable
13 discretionary

arbitrate 5 judge **6** settle, umpire
7 adjudge, mediate, referee **9** intervene
10 adjudicate **12** intermediate

arbitrator 5 judge **6** umpire **7** referee,
settler **8** mediator **9** moderator **11** adjudicator

arbor 4 axle, beam **5** bower, frame, shaft
7 pergola, shelter, spindle

arc 3 bow, lob **4** arch, bend, path
5 curve, round **7** rainbow **9** curvation,
curvature **11** measurement, progression

arcade 6 arches **7** gallery **10** passageway

arcadia 4 Eden, Zion **6** heaven, utopia
7 Elysium, nirvana **8** paradise **9** fairyland, Shangri-la **10** wonderland
12 promised land

arcane 6 hidden, mystic, occult, opaque,
secret **7** obscure, unknown **8** esoteric
9 recondite **10** cabalistic, mysterious,
unknowable **11** inscrutable **12** impenetrable **13** unaccountable

Arcas *father:* **4** Zeus **7** Jupiter *mother:*
8 Callisto

arch 3 bow, coy, sly **4** bend, hump, pert
5 curve, fresh, saucy, vault **6** camber,
cheeky, impish **7** playful, roguish, waggish **8** flippant, malapert **9** curvature
10 coquettish **11** mischievous *inner
curve:* **8** intrados *kind:* **4** ogee **5** ogive,
round, Tudor **6** lancet **7** rampart, trefoil
9 horseshoe, primitive, segmental
10 shouldered **11** equilateral *outer
curve:* **8** extrados *part:* **6** impost **8** keystone, springer, voussoir

archaeological site *Africa:* **8** Zimbabwe
13 Great Zimbabwe *Britain:* **7** Avebury
9 Skara Brae, Sutton Hoo **10** Stonehenge *Cambodia:* **6** Angkor **9** Angkor
Wat *Crete:* **7** Knossos *Egypt:* **4** Giza
5 Luxor **6** Abydos, Karnak, Naqada,
Thebes **7** Memphis **9** El-Bahnasa
11 Oxyrhynchus *Greece:* **6** Delphi
7 Mycenae, Olympia *Guatemala:* **5** Tikal
Honduras: **5** Copán *Indonesia* **9**
Borobudur *Iran:* **10** Persepolis *Iraq:*
4 Isin, Nuzi **6** Nimrud **7** Babylon, Nineveh, Samarra *Israel:* **7** Jericho *Italy:*
7 Pompeii **11** Herculaneum *Lebanon:*
6 Byblos **7** Baalbek *Mexico:* **5** Mitla,
Tulum, Uxmal **8** Palenque **10** Monte

Albán 11 Chichén Itzá *Peru:* 11 Machu
Picchu *Syria:* 7 Palmyra *Tunisia:*
8 Carthage, Kairouan *Turkey:* 4 Troy
6 Knidos 8 Hisarlik, Pergamon
9 Hissarlik *Uzbekistan:* 9 Samarkand
archaeologist 4 Dart (Raymond)
5 Evans (Arthur) 6 Carter (Howard),
Childe (V. Gordon), Kidder (Alfred),
Petrie (Flinders) 7 Thomsen (Christian), Woolley (Leonard), Worsaae
(Jens) 8 Breasted (James Henry),
Goodyear (William) 10 Schliemann
(Heinrich) 11 Champollion (Jean-
François), Winckelmann (Johann)
archaic 3 old 5 dated, olden, passé
6 bygone 7 ancient, antique 8 obsolete,
outdated 9 out-of-date, primitive,
unevolved 10 antiquated 11 undeveloped 12 old-fashioned
archangel 5 Uriel 7 Gabriel, Michael,
Raphael
arched 4 bent 5 bowed, round 6 curved
7 curving, rounded
archer 4 Tell (William) 5 Cupid 6 bowman 9 Robin Hood 11 Sagittarius
archery 9 toxophily
archetypal 5 ideal, model 7 classic, perfect, typical 9 classical, exemplary
10 consummate 12 paradigmatic, prototypical
archetype 4 idea 5 ideal, model 6 mirror
7 epitome, essence, example, pattern
8 exemplar, original, paradigm, standard 9 beau ideal, prototype 10 apotheosis, embodiment, protoplast 12 quintessence
archfiend 5 demon, devil, Satan 6 diablo
7 Lucifer
Archimedes 5 Greek 8 inventor *cry:*
6 eureka *discovery:* 5 screw 8 buoyancy
9 principle 11 water raiser
archipelago *Asian:* 5 Malay *Canada:*
6 Arctic *Japan:* 4 Goto 9 Gotoretto *Norway:* 11 Spitsbergen *Papua New Guinea:*
8 Bismarck 9 Louisiade *Philippines:*
4 Sulu *off Scotland:* 7 Orcades, Orkneys
United States: 9 Alexander
architect 5 maker 7 creator 8 designer,
inventor 9 generator 10 originator
American: 3 Pei (I. M.) 4 Hood (Raymond), Kahn (Louis) 5 Gehry (Frank),
McKim (Charles), Meier (Richard),
Roche (Kevin), Stone (Edward Durell),
Weese (Harry), White (Stanford)
6 Breuer (Marcel), Fuller (Buckminster), Graves (Michael), Morgan
(Julia), Neutra (Richard), Rogers (Isaiah), Soleri (Paolo), Upjohn (Richard),
Walter (Thomas), Warren (William),
Wright (Frank Lloyd) 7 Burnham
(Daniel), Gilbert (Cass), Johnson

(Philip), Latrobe (Benjamin), Olmsted
(Frederick Law), Renwick (James),
Sturgis (John Hubbard), Venturi
(Robert) 8 Bulfinch (Charles), Saarinen
(Eero, Eliel), Sullivan (Louis), Thornton (William), Yamasaki (Minoru)
10 Richardson (Henry Hobson) *Austrian:* 4 Loos (Adolf) 6 Wagner (Otto)
Brazilian: 8 Niemeyer (Oscar) *Canadian:*
6 Safdie (Moshe) *Dutch:* 8 Rietveld
(Gerrit) *English:* 4 Nash (John), Shaw
(Richard), Wood (John), Wren
(Christopher) 5 Jones (Inigo), Scott
(George Gilbert), Wyatt (James) 6 Foster (Norman), Rogers (Richard), Street
(George Edmund), Voysey (Charles)
7 Lutyens (Edwin) 8 Vanbrugh (John)
Finnish: 5 Aalto (Alvar) 8 Saarinen
(Eero, Eliel) *French:* 6 Perret (Auguste)
7 Garnier (Tony), L'Enfant (Pierre-
Charles) 11 Le Corbusier 12 Viollet-le-
Duc (Eugène) *German:* 8 Schinkel
(Karl) 10 Mendelsohn (Erich) *German-
American:* 7 Gropius (Walter) *Israeli:*
6 Safdie (Moshe) *Italian:* 5 Nervi (Pier
Luigi) 6 Romano (Giulio), Soleri
(Paolo) 7 Alberti (Leon Battista), Bernini (Gian Lorenzo), da Vinci (Leonardo), Orcagna, Peruzzi (Baldassare),
Raphael, Vignola (Giacomo da) 8 Bramante (Donato), Leonardo (da Vinci),
Palladio (Andrea), Sangallo (Giuliano
da), Terragni (Giuseppe) 9 Borromini
(Francesco), Sansovino (Jacopo)
12 Michelangelo *Japanese:* 5 Tange
(Kenzo) *Roman:* 9 Vitruvius *Scottish:*
10 Mackintosh (Charles Rennie) *Spanish:* 5 Gaudí (Antonio) *Swedish:*
7 Asplund (Erik Gunnar)
architecture 6 design, makeup 9 formation 11 composition 12 constitution,
construction *ornament:* 4 boss, fret
5 gutta 6 finial, volute 7 cabling, console, crocket, diglyph 8 triglyph,
vignette 9 arabesque, modillion *style:*
5 Doric, Ionic, Tudor 6 Gothic, Norman, Rococo 7 Baroque 8 Colonial,
Georgian 9 Byzantine, Victorian
10 Corinthian, Romanesque
archive 4 file 6 record 7 collect, history,
library, records 8 document, register
9 chronicle 10 collection, repository
archon 10 magistrate
arctic 3 icy 4 cold 5 chill, gelid 6 chilly,
frigid, frosty, wintry 7 glacial, numbing
8 freezing, hibernal 11 hyperborean *animal:* 3 auk, fox 4 bear, hare, seal, vole
5 sable, whale 6 ermine, marten 7 caribou, lemming 8 reindeer 9 polar bear,
ptarmigan *base:* 4 Etah 5 Thule 6 Barrow 11 Point Barrow *bird:* 3 auk

cetacean: 7 narwhal **current:** 8 Labrador **dog:** 5 husky 7 Samoyed 8 malamute **explorer:** 4 Byrd (Richard), Cook (Frederick) 5 Bylot (Robert), Davis (John), Peary (Robert) 6 Baffin (William), Bering (Vitus), Henson (Matthew), Hudson (Henry), Nansen (Fridtjof), Nobile (Umberto) 7 Barents (Willem), Bennett (Floyd), Wilkins (George), Wrangel (Ferdinand) 8 Amundsen (Roald) 9 Ellsworth (Lincoln), Mackenzie (Alexander), MacMillan (Donald) 10 Stefansson (Vilhjalmus) **forest:** 5 taiga **jacket:** 5 parka 6 anorak **people:** 4 Lapp 5 Aleut, Inuit, Yakut 6 Eskimo, Tungus 7 Chukchi, Samoyed **sea:** 4 Kara 6 Laptev 7 Barents, Chukchi 8 Beaufort **transport:** 7 dogsled **treeless plains:** 6 tundra

ardent 3 hot 4 agog, avid, keen, true 5 eager, fiery, loyal 6 fervid, fierce, heated, intent, red-hot, strong, torrid 7 blazing, burning, devoted, earnest, fervent, flaming, glowing, intense, shining, staunch, zealous 8 constant, desirous, faithful, powerful, resolute, sizzling, vehement, white-hot 9 allegiant, impatient, impetuous, impulsive, perfervid, scorching, steadfast 10 breathless, hot-blooded, passionate 11 impassioned 12 enthusiastic

ardor 4 fire, heat, zeal, zest, zing 5 gusto, verve, vigor 6 energy, fealty, fervor, spirit, warmth 7 avidity, loyalty, passion 8 devotion, fidelity 9 eagerness, intensity, vehemence 10 allegiance, enthusiasm, excitement 12 faithfulness

arduous 4 hard 5 harsh, rough, sheer, steep, tight, tough 6 severe, taxing, tiring, trying, uphill 7 labored 8 grueling, rigorous, toilsome 9 difficult, effortful, gruelling, laborious, punishing, strenuous 10 formidable 11 precipitate, precipitous

area 4 belt, turf, zone 5 field, place, range, realm, scene, space, tract 6 domain, locale, region, sector, sphere 7 expanse, stretch 8 district, locality, province, vicinity 9 bailiwick, territory 12 neighborhood **unit:** 4 acre 7 hectare

arena 5 field, scene, stage 6 sphere 7 stadium, theater 8 activity, building, coliseum, province 10 hippodrome 12 amphitheater

Ares **Roman counterpart:** 4 Mars **consort:** 9 Aphrodite **father:** 4 Zeus **mother:** 4 Enyo, Hera **sister:** 4 Eris **son:** 5 Remus 7 Romulus

arête 5 crest, ridge

Arethusa 5 nymph 6 spring 9 wood nymph **pursuer:** 7 Alpheus

argent 6 silver 7 silvern, silvery 9 whiteness

Argentina **capital:** 11 Buenos Aires **city:** 6 Paraná 7 Córdoba, La Plata, Rosario, Santa Fe 11 Mar del Plata **desert:** 9 Patagonia **language:** 7 Spanish **leader:** 5 Perón (Juan) **monetary unit:** 4 peso **mountain, range:** 5 Andes 9 Aconcagua **neighbor:** 5 Chile 6 Brazil 7 Bolivia, Uruguay 8 Paraguay **plain:** 6 Pampas **river:** 5 Plata (Río de la) 6 Paraná 8 Colorado 12 Río de la Plata **volcano:** 5 Maipo 9 Tupungato

Arges 7 Cyclops **brother:** 7 Brontes 8 Steropes **father:** 6 Uranus **mother:** 4 Gaea

Argonaut 4 hero 10 adventurer 13 paper nautilus **leader:** 5 Jason

argosy 4 ship 5 fleet 6 armada, supply 8 flotilla

argot 4 cant 5 idiom, lingo, slang 6 jargon, patois, patter 7 dialect 10 vernacular

arguable 4 moot 7 dubious 8 doubtful 9 debatable, in dispute, uncertain 10 disputable 11 contestable, problematic 12 questionable

argue 5 claim, clash, prove 6 assert, attest, bicker, debate, differ, induce, object, reason 7 agitate, canvass, contend, discuss, dispute, dissent, justify, protest, quarrel, quibble, stickle, testify, witness, wrangle 8 announce, conflict, consider, disagree, indicate, maintain, persuade, polemize, squabble 9 thrash out 10 polemicize 11 expostulate, remonstrate

argument 3 row 4 case, feud, flap, fuss 5 claim, proof, set-to, theme, topic 6 debate, dustup, hassle, motive, reason, rumpus, thesis 7 defense, dispute, polemic, sorites, subject, summary, wrangle 8 abstract, evidence, rebuttal 9 amplitude, assertion, discourse 10 contention, discussion, dissension, squabbling 11 controversy, disputation, embroilment 12 disagreement

argumentation 6 debate 7 dispute, oratory 8 forensic, rhetoric 9 dialectic, reasoning 10 discussion 11 controversy, disputation

argumentative 4 moot 9 in dispute, litigious, polemical 11 contentious, quarrelsome 12 disputatious, questionable 13 controversial

Argus **father:** 4 Zeus **mother:** 5 Niobe **slayer:** 6 Hermes

Argus-eyed 5 alert 9 all-seeing

argyle 4 sock 6 design 7 diamond, pattern 8 Campbell

aria 3 air, lay 4 hymn, lied, solo, song, tune 5 ditty 6 melody 7 descant

Ariadne *father:* 5 Minos *husband:* 7 Theseus *island home:* 5 Naxos *mother:* 8 Pasiphaë

arid 3 dry 4 drab, dull, sere 5 dusty, vapid 6 barren, boring, desert, dreary, jejune 7 bone-dry, insipid, parched, sterile, tedious, thirsty 8 droughty, lifeless, weariful 9 dryasdust, infertile, unwatered, waterless, wearisome 10 lackluster, spiritless, unfruitful 12 moistureless 13 uninteresting

Ariel 6 spirit *master:* 8 Prospero

Aries 3 ram 13 constellation

aright 4 well 5 fitly 6 justly, nicely 8 decently, properly 9 correctly, fittingly, precisely 10 accurately, decorously

Ariosto epic 14 Orlando Furioso

arise 4 go up, lift, soar, wake 5 awake, begin, get up, issue, mount, occur, start 6 appear, ascend, aspire, come up, crop up, emerge, spring, uprear, wake up 7 emanate, proceed 8 commence 9 originate

Aristaeus *father:* 6 Apollo *mother:* 6 Cyrene *son:* 7 Actaeon *wife:* 7 Autonoe

aristocracy 5 elite, state 6 gentry, jet set 7 who's who 8 nobility, noblesse 9 beau monde, blue blood, gentility, haut monde 10 government, patricians, patriciate, upper class, upper crust

aristocrat 9 blue blood, gentleman, patrician *ancient Greek:* 8 eupatrid *Russian:* 5 boyar 6 boyard

aristocratic 5 aloof, elite, noble 6 lordly 7 courtly, elegant, genteel, haughty, refined, stately 8 highborn, well-born, well-bred 9 dignified, exclusive, patrician 10 privileged, upper-class, uppercrust 11 blue-blooded

Aristophanes play 5 Birds (The), Frogs (The), Wasps (The) 6 Clouds (The), Plutus

arithmetic 4 math 8 addition, counting, figuring 9 ciphering, reckoning 10 estimation 11 calculation, computation, mathematics

Arizona *capital:* 7 Phoenix *city:* 4 Mesa, Yuma 5 Tempe 6 Bisbee, Sedona, Tucson 8 Glendale, Prescott 9 Flagstaff 10 Scottsdale *mountain:* 9 Humphreys (Peak) *nickname:* 11 Grand Canyon (State) *park:* 15 Petrified Forest *river:* 4 Gila, Salt 8 Colorado *state bird:* 10 cactus wren *state flower:* 7 saguaro (cactus) *state tree:* 9 palo verde

ark 3 den 4 ship 5 chest, haven 6 adytum, asylum, refuge 7 convent, retreat,

shelter 8 hideaway 9 safe house, sanctuary 10 repository, Torah chest *landfall:* 6 Ararat *wood:* 6 gopher 7 cypress

Arkansas *capital:* 10 Little Rock *city:* 4 Hope 9 Fort Smith, Pine Bluff 10 Hot Springs 11 Bentonville 12 Fayetteville *mountain, range:* 5 Ozark 8 Magazine *nickname:* 17 Land of Opportunity *river:* 3 Red 8 Arkansas *state bird:* 11 mockingbird *state flower:* 12 apple blossom *state tree:* 12 loblolly pine

arm 3 bay, ell, gun, rig 4 cove, gear, gulf, wing 5 annex, bayou, equip, firth, force, inlet, power 6 fit out, harbor, muscle, outfit, slough, weapon 7 appoint, furnish, turn out 8 accouter, strength 9 extension *bone:* 4 ulna 6 radius 7 humerus *combining form:* 6 brachi 7 brachio *muscle:* 6 biceps 7 triceps

armada 4 navy 5 boats, fleet, force, group, ships 7 vessels 8 flotilla, warships

armadillo *relative:* 5 sloth 8 anteater

armament 4 arms 5 armor 6 weapon 7 defense 8 ordnance, security, weaponry 9 munitions, safeguard 10 ammunition, protection

armamentarium 4 fund 5 stock, store 6 supply 9 inventory

armchair 6 remote 8 fauteuil 9 vicarious 11 theoretical

armed forces 4 army, navy 6 troops 8 air force, military 10 servicemen

Armenia *capital:* 7 Yerevan *city:* 6 Gyumri 8 Vanadzor *lake:* 5 Sevan *monetary unit:* 4 dram *mountain, range:* 7 Aragats 8 Caucasus *neighbor:* 4 Iran 6 Turkey 7 Georgia 10 Azerbaijan *river:* 5 Araks

armistice 5 truce 9 agreement, cease-fire 10 suspension

armor 4 mail 5 aegis, cover, guard 6 shield 7 buckler 8 security 9 safeguard 10 protection *arm:* 8 brassard *body:* 7 cuirass *armpit:* 8 pallette *buttocks:* 5 culet *coat:* 7 hauberk 10 brigandine *face:* 5 visor 6 beaver *flexible:* 4 mail *foot:* 8 solleret *hand:* 7 gantlet 8 gauntlet *head:* 6 helmet *horse:* 4 bard 5 barde 8 chamfron *leg:* 6 greave 7 jambeau *mail:* 4 coif 7 hauberk *suit:* 7 panoply *thigh:* 5 tasse 6 tuille *throat:* 6 gorget

armory 4 dump 5 depot, plant, range, store 7 arsenal, factory 8 magazine 10 collection, storehouse

armpit 6 axilla 8 underarm *Scottish:* 5 oxter

arms 7 ensigns, warfare 8 weaponry

army 4 host 5 flock, horde 6 legion 7 militia 9 multitude *combat arm:*

5 armor 8 infantry 9 artillery *commission:* 6 brevet 7 reserve *Fort:* 3 Dix, Lee, Ord 4 Drum, Hood, Knox, Myer, Polk, Sill 5 Bliss, Bragg, Irwin, Lewis, McCoy, Meade, Riley, Story 6 Carson, Eustis, Gillem, Gordon, Greely, McNair, Monroe, Rucker 7 Belvoir, Benning, Detrick, Jackson, Ritchie, Shafter, Stewart 8 Buchanan, Campbell, Hamilton, Holabird, Huachuca, Monmouth 9 McClellan, McPherson 10 Richardson, Sam Houston, Wainwright 11 Leavenworth *mascot:* 4 mule *meal:* 4 chow, mess *mine layer:* 6 sapper *NCO:* 8 corporal, sergeant *officer:* 5 major 7 captain, colonel, general, warrant 10 lieutenant *post:* 4 base, camp, fort *postal abbreviation:* 3 APO *relating to:* 7 martial 8 military *school:* 3 OCS, OTS 7 academy 9 West Point *store:* 10 commissary 12 post exchange *unit:* 5 corps, squad, troop 7 brigade, cavalry, company, platoon 8 division, regiment 9 battalion *vehicle:* 4 jeep, tank 6 Abrams, Humvee 7 Bradley 9 half-track

aroma 4 balm, odor 5 scent, smell, spice 6 flavor 7 bouquet, incense, perfume 9 fragrance, redolence

aromatic 5 balmy, spicy, sweet 6 savory 7 odorous, perfumy, pungent, scented 8 fragrant, perfumed, redolent 9 ambrosial

around 4 near, nigh 5 about, circa 6 nearby 7 through *prefix:* 4 ambi, peri 5 amphi 6 circum

around-the-clock 8 constant, unending 9 ceaseless, continual, incessant, perpetual, unceasing 10 continuous 11 unremitting 13 uninterrupted

arouse 4 fire, stir, wake, whet 5 alert, awake, pique, rally, waken 6 awaken, bestir, excite, fire up, foment, incite, kindle, work up 7 agitate, inflame 9 challenge, stimulate

arraign 3 tax, try 5 blame 6 accuse, charge, indict, summon 9 criminate, inculpate 11 incriminate

arrange 4 plan, sort 5 adapt, array, chart, order, score, unify 6 assort, codify, design, devise, lay out, line up, map out, scheme, set out, settle 7 dispose, marshal, prepare, work out 8 organize, sequence 9 blueprint, harmonize, integrate, methodize 10 bring about, categorize, instrument, symphonize, synthesize 11 choreograph, orchestrate, systematize

arrangement 5 array, order, setup 6 format, layout, lineup, series 8 grouping, ordering, sequence 9 structure 10 adaptation 11 disposition 12 distribution *floral:* 4 posy 7 bouquet, garland

arrant 4 rank 5 gross, total, utter 6 brassy, brazen 7 blatant, extreme, flat-out 8 absolute, complete, impudent, infernal, overbold 9 barefaced, downright, egregious, out-and-out, shameless, unabashed 10 immoderate, unblushing

arras 6 screen 7 drapery 8 curtains, tapestry

array 3 lot 4 clad, garb, pomp, show 5 adorn, batch, bunch, clump, dress, group, order 6 attire, bundle, clothe, draw up, finery, lineup, parade 7 apparel, arrange, cluster, display, dispose, garment, marshal, raiment, variety 8 clothing, decorate, enclothe, organize, spectrum 9 formation 10 assortment 11 systematize

arrears 3 due 4 debt 5 claim, debit 7 deficit 9 liability 10 balance due, obligation 12 indebtedness

arrest 3 nab, tab, tag 4 bust, grab, halt, hold, jail, slow, snag, stay, stem, stop 5 block, catch, check, pinch, run in, seize, stall 6 collar, detain, haul in, lock up, pick up, pull in, retard, take in 7 capture, contain, seizure 8 imprison, obstruct, restrain 9 apprehend, detention, interrupt 11 incarcerate 12 apprehension

arresting 6 marked, signal 7 salient 8 striking 9 affective, appealing, prominent 10 attractive, compelling, enchanting, impressive, noticeable, remarkable 11 conspicuous, eye-catching, outstanding

arrival 6 advent, coming 7 landing, success 8 entrance, incoming 9 emergence 10 appearance

arrive 4 come, land, show 5 get in, get to, reach 6 appear, show up, thrive, turn up 7 prosper, succeed 8 flourish

arriviste 7 parvenu, upstart 8 roturier 12 nouveau riche

arrogance 3 ego 4 airs, gall 5 brass, cheek, pride 6 hubris 7 conceit, disdain, hauteur 8 self-love 9 loftiness 11 haughtiness

arrogant 5 cocky, proud 6 lordly, snooty 7 haughty, pompous 8 cavalier, fastuous, insolent, superior 9 egotistic 10 disdainful, high-handed, peremptory 11 domineering, magisterial, overbearing 12 supercilious 13 high-and-mighty, self-important

arrogate 4 grab, take 5 annex, claim, seize, usurp 6 assume, demand 7 ascribe, preempt 8 accroach, take over 9 sequester 10 commandeer, confiscate 11 appropriate, expropriate

arrow 4 dart 5 shaft *poison:* 4 inée, upas 6 curare

arrowroot 5 plant, tuber 6 starch 7 coontie

Arrowsmith's wife 5 Leora

arroyo 3 gap 4 draw 5 brook, chasm, cleft, clove, creek, gorge, gulch, gully 6 coulee, ravine 7 channel 11 watercourse

arsenal 4 dump 5 depot, stock, store 6 armory, supply 7 factory, weapons 8 magazine, ordnance 9 stockpile 10 depository, repertoire, repository, storehouse

arson 6 firing 8 torching 9 pyromania 12 incendiarism

arsonist 5 firer, torch 7 firebug 10 incendiary

art 5 craft, skill 6 métier 7 finesse, know-how 8 artifice, painting, vocation 9 dexterity, expertise, sculpture 10 handicraft *faddish:* 6 kitsch *style:* 3 pop 4 dada 6 cubist, rococo 7 fauvist, realist, surreal 8 abstract, futurist 9 classical 10 naturalist, surrealist 12 naturalistic, surrealistic 13 expressionist, impressionist

art deco 5 style 6 design *designer:* 4 Erté

Artemis *Roman counterpart:* 5 Diana *birthplace:* 5 Delos *brother:* 6 Apollo *father:* 4 Zeus *mother:* 4 Leto *priestess:* 9 Iphigenia

artery 3 way 4 duct, line, path, road, tube 5 aorta, track 6 avenue, course, street, vessel 7 carotid, channel, conduit, highway, passage, pathway 8 coronary 9 boulevard 12 thoroughfare

artful 3 sly 4 foxy, wily 5 adept, sharp, slick, smart, suave 6 adroit, astute, clever, crafty, shrewd, smooth, tricky 7 cunning 8 guileful, skillful 9 dexterous, ingenious 10 artificial, diplomatic

arthropod 3 bee, fly 4 crab, mite, moth, tick 6 beetle, insect, shrimp, spider 7 lobster 8 arachnid, barnacle, diplopod, myriapod, scorpion 9 butterfly, centipede, cockroach, millipede, trilobite 10 crustacean *body segment:* 6 somite, telson 8 metamere

Arthur see KING ARTHUR

article 3 the 4 bind, item, part 5 essay, paper, piece, point, theme, thing 6 matter, object 7 element, feature, passage, section 10 particular 11 composition, stipulation

articled 5 bound 10 indentured

articulate 3 say 4 join, link, oral, talk 5 clear, hinge, joint, lucid, shape, speak, state, utter, vocal, voice 6 couple, fluent, prolix, relate, spoken, voiced 7 connect, express, jointed 8 coherent, definite, distinct, eloquent, vocalize 9 effective, enunciate, harmonize, integrate, pronounce, verbalize 10 coordinate, expressive 11 concatenate 12 intelligible, smooth-spoken

artifact 5 curio, relic 6 legacy, rarity, trophy 7 remnant, spin-off, vestige 8 creation, heirloom 9 by-product, handcraft, handiwork 10 handicraft 11 contrivance, fabrication

artifice 4 play, ploy, ruse, wile 5 craft, feint, guile, skill, trick 6 deceit, device, gambit 7 cunning, slyness 8 facility, foxiness, trickery, wiliness 9 adeptness, canniness, chicanery, duplicity, ingenuity, stratagem 10 adroitness, artfulness, cleverness, craftiness

artificial 4 fake, faux, mock, sham 5 bogus, dummy, faked, false, phony, put-on 6 ersatz, forced, hollow, unreal 7 assumed, feigned, in vitro, labored, man-made, plastic, pretend 8 affected, mannered, spurious 9 contrived, imitation, insincere, simulated, synthetic, unnatural 10 fabricated, factitious, fictitious, substitute

artillery 4 arms 5 canon, force 6 rocket 7 battery, bazooka, gunnery, weapons 8 cannonry, howitzer, ordnance, weaponry 9 munitions

artisan 6 worker 7 builder, workman 8 producer 9 carpenter, craftsman 12 craftsperson

artist 7 painter 8 sculptor, virtuoso *garb:* 5 smock *knife:* 7 spatula *medium:* 3 oil 5 paint 6 pastel 7 tempera 8 charcoal 10 watercolor *pigment board:* 7 palette *stand:* 5 easel *workshop:* 6 studio 7 atelier (see also PAINTER)

artless 4 free, open, pure, true 5 crude, naive, plain 6 direct, honest, simple 7 genuine, natural, sincere, unaware 8 trusting 9 childlike, guileless, ingenuous, unstudied 10 aboveboard, forthright, unaffected, uncultured, unschooled 12 unartificial, unsuspicious

arty 5 showy 6 pseudo 8 affected, imposing 9 overblown 11 pretentious 12 high-sounding

Aruba *capital:* 10 Oranjestad *language:* 5 Dutch 10 Papiamento *monetary unit:* 6 florin *part of:* 11 Netherlands

as 3 for, who 4 coin, like, that, when 5 being, since, which, while 6 though 7 because 11 considering, for instance

____ **as a pin** 4 neat

as a rule 6 mainly, mostly 7 usually

8 commonly **9** generally **10** frequently, ordinarily

Ascanius 5 Iulus *father:* **6** Aeneas

ascend 4 go up, lift, rise, soar **5** arise, climb, crest, mount, scale **6** aspire, move up, occupy **7** lift off, take off **8** escalade, escalate, surmount

ascendancy 4 rule **5** power, reign **7** command, control, mastery **8** dominion **9** authority, dominance, influence, supremacy **10** domination, prepotency **11** preeminence, sovereignty **13** preponderance

ascendant 6 master, rising **7** regnant **8** ancestor, dominant, forebear, relative, superior **9** paramount, precursor, prevalent, sovereign **10** commanding, forefather, forerunner, prevailing, progenitor **11** controlling, overbearing, predecessor, predominant, predominate **12** preponderant, primogenitor

ascension 4 rise **6** rising **7** going up, scaling **8** climbing, mounting

ascent 4 ramp, rise **5** climb, grade, slope **6** rising **7** advance, incline **8** gradient, progress **9** acclivity, elevation, uplifting

ascertain 5 learn **7** catch on, find out, unearth **8** discover, make sure **9** determine, establish, figure out

ascetic 5 stoic **6** hermit, severe **7** austere, eremite, recluse **9** abstinent, anchoress, anchorite, mortified **10** abstemious, astringent, forbearing, restrained **11** disciplined, self-denying *ancient Hebrew:* **6** Essene *Buddhist:* **5** bonze *early Christian:* **7** stylite *Hindu:* **4** yogi **5** fakir, Yogin

Asclepius see AESCULAPIUS

ascribe 3 lay **4** cite **5** infer, refer **6** assign, charge, credit, impute **8** accredit **9** attribute, reference **10** conjecture

Asenath *husband:* **6** Joseph *son:* **7** Ephraim **8** Manasseh

aseptic 4 cool, flat **5** clean **7** sterile **8** germ-free, hygienic, sanitary **9** unfeeling **10** restrained, sterilized **11** emotionless, unemotional

asexual 6 agamic

as for 4 in re **5** about, anent **7** apropos **9** regarding **10** concerning, respecting **12** with regard to

as good as 4 nigh **6** all but, almost, nearly **8** in effect, well-nigh **9** basically, in essence, just about, virtually **11** essentially, practically

ash 4 soot, tree, wood **7** cinders, residue **8** clinkers

ashamed 6 abased, abject, guilty **7** abashed, humbled **8** contrite, penitent **9** chagrined, mortified, repentant

10 humiliated **11** discomfited, embarrassed

ashen 3 wan **4** gray, pale **5** faded, pasty, waxen **6** doughy, pallid, sallow, sickly **7** ghostly **8** blanched, bleached **9** bloodless, colorless **10** corpselike

Asher *daughter:* **5** Serah *father:* **5** Jacob *mother:* **6** Zilpah *son:* **4** Isui **6** Beriah, Ishuah, Jimnah

ashes 5 ruins **6** pallor **7** remains

ashy 3 wan **4** drab, pale **5** livid, waxen **6** doughy, leaden, pallid **7** ghastly, greyish **8** blanched **9** bloodless, colorless, washed-out **10** cadaverous

Asia *country:* **4** Laos **5** Burma, China, India, Japan, Korea, Nepal **6** Bhutan, Russia, Taiwan **7** Armenia, Georgia, Myanmar, Vietnam **8** Cambodia, Malaysia, Mongolia, Pakistan, Sri Lanka, Thailand **9** Indonesia, Kampuchea, Kazakstan, Singapore **10** Azerbaijan, Bangladesh, Kazakhstan, Kyrgyzstan, North Korea, South Korea, Tajikistan, Uzbekistan **11** Afghanistan, Philippines **12** Turkmenistan *ethnic group:* **3** Han, Lao, Tai **4** Arab, Kurd, Moor, Shan **5** Karen, Khmer, Malay, Tajik, Tamil, Uzbek **6** Burman, Lepcha, Manchu, Mongol, Sindhi **7** Baluchi, Bengali, Persian, Punjabi, Tibetan **8** Armenian, Assyrian, Javanese **9** Dravidian, Indo-Aryan, Sinhalese **10** Circassian, Montagnard, Singhalese *language:* **3** Lao **4** Urdu **5** Hindi, Malay, Tamil, Uzbek **6** Arabic, Bahasa, Korean, Nepali **7** Bengali, Burmese, Khalkha, Kurdish, Persian, Tibetan, Turkish **8** Armenian, Japanese, Javanese, Mandarin **9** Cambodian **10** Vietnamese

Asia Minor 8 Anatolia *country:* **6** Turkey

Asian inland sea 4 Aral

aside 4 away **5** apart **7** tangent **8** away from **9** in reserve, privately **10** digression, discursion **11** parenthesis

aside from 3 bar, but **4** save **6** bating, except **7** barring, besides **9** excepting, excluding, other than, outside of **11** exclusive of

Asimov, Isaac *forte:* **5** sci-fi *work:* **6** I Robot **9** Nightfall **10** Foundation (Trilogy) **14** Gods Themselves (The)

asinine 5 crazy, daffy, silly **6** absurd, simple **7** fatuous, foolish, idiotic, puerile, witless **8** mindless **9** brainless **10** irrational, ridiculous **11** nonsensical

ask 3 beg, bid **4** pray, quiz, seek **5** crave, exact, grill, plead, query **6** appeal, demand, desire, invite **7** beseech, call for, canvass, consult, enquire, entreat, examine, implore, inquire, request, require, solicit **8** petition, question **9** catechize, importune **10** supplicate **11** interrogate *Scottish:* **5** speer, speir

askance 8 sidelong, sideways **9** cynically, obliquely **10** critically, doubtfully, doubtingly, scornfully **11** skeptically **12** suspiciously **13** distrustfully, mistrustfully

asker 6 beggar, prayer, suitor **7** speaker **9** suppliant **10** petitioner, questioner, supplicant **11** supplicator

askew 4 awry **6** turned **8** cockeyed **9** crookedly

aslant 4 awry **5** askew **7** crooked **8** cockeyed, sideways, sidewise **9** obliquely

asleep 4 dead, idle, numb **5** inert **6** dozing, numbed **7** defunct, dormant, napping **8** benumbed, deadened, inactive, in repose, not alert, sluggish **9** senseless, unfeeling **10** insensible, slumbering, unanimated **11** indifferent, unconscious **12** anesthetized

as long as 3 for **5** since **6** seeing **7** because, whereas **10** inasmuch as **11** considering **12** provided that

as much as 6 all but, almost **8** well-nigh **11** essentially, practically

aspect 3 air **4** look, mien, side **5** angle, facet, phase, scene, slant **6** regard, status **7** bearing, seeming **8** exposure, position **9** direction **10** appearance **11** perspective

aspen 4 tree **6** poplar

asperity 5 rigor **8** acerbity, acrimony, grimness, hardness, hardship, mordancy, severity, tartness **9** harshness, roughness, sharpness **10** bitterness, difficulty, unevenness **12** irregularity, irritability

asperse 4 slur **5** libel, smear, sully **6** attack, defame, insult, malign, vilify **7** baptize, slander, tarnish, traduce **8** bad mouth, dishonor, sprinkle **9** denigrate, insinuate **10** calumniate

aspersion 4 muck, slam, slur **5** abuse **7** calumny, obloquy, slander **9** invective, stricture **10** defamation, detraction **11** denigration **12** vilification, vituperation **13** animadversion

asphalt 4 pave **5** bitumen, surface **8** blacktop, pavement

asphyxiate 4 kill **5** choke, drown **6** stifle **7** smother **8** strangle, throttle **9** suffocate

aspirant 6 seeker **7** hopeful, seeking **9** applicant, candidate, contender

aspiration 3 aim **4** goal, urge, wish **5** dream **6** desire, intent, object **7** craving, longing, passion, pursuit **8** ambition, striving, yearning **9** breathing, objective **10** pretension **13** ambitiousness

aspire 3 aim, try **4** long, pant, rise, seek, soar, want, wish **5** arise, mount, yearn **6** ascend, desire, hunger, strive, thirst

aspiring 7 longing, seeking, wanting, wishful **8** striving, vaulting, yearning **9** ambitious

as regards 4 in re **7** apropos **8** touching **10** concerning, respecting

ass 4 dolt, fool, jerk, moke, mule **5** burro, dunce, idiot **6** donkey, nitwit **8** bonehead, imbecile **10** nincompoop *female:* **5** jenny *male:* **4** jack *wild Asian:* **5** kiang **6** onager

assai 4 very

assail 4 bash, beat **5** abuse, beset, blast, pound, storm **6** attack, berate, buffet, charge, fall on, malign, oppugn, pummel, revile, strike, vilify **7** assault, bombard **8** fall upon, lambaste **9** break down

assassin 3 gun **5** bravo **6** gunman, hit man, killer **7** torpedo **8** murderer **9** cutthroat **10** hatchet man, triggerman *of Caesar:* **6** Brutus **7** Cassius *of Garfield:* **7** Guiteau (Charles Julius) *of J. F. Kennedy:* **6** Oswald (Lee Harvey) *of M. L. King:* **3** Ray (James Earl) *of Lincoln:* **5** Booth (John Wilkes) *of Marat:* **6** Corday (Charlotte) *of McKinley:* **8** Czolgosz (Leon) *of R. F. Kennedy:* **6** Sirhan (Sirhan)

assassinate 4 do in, kill, slay **6** finish, murder, rub out **7** bump off, execute, gun down, put away, take out **8** dispatch, knock off **9** eliminate, liquidate

assault 3 mug, war **4** raid **5** beset, fight, onset, set-to, storm **6** assail, attack, charge, fall on, strike, threat **7** aggress, besiege, mugging, offense **8** fall upon, invasion, storming **9** incursion, offensive, onslaught, violation **10** aggression

assay 3 try **4** rate, seek, test **5** judge, offer, prove, trial, value, weigh **6** assess, result, rating, strive, survey **7** analyze, attempt, examine, inspect, measure, valuate, venture **8** analysis, appraise, endeavor, estimate, evaluate, struggle **9** appraisal, undertake, valuation **10** assessment, evaluation, inspection, measurement **11** examination

assemblage 5 crowd, group **6** muster **7** company, turnout **8** audience **9** gathering **10** collection **11** aggregation, composition, convergence **12** congregation

assemble 4 call, form, make, mass, meet, mold **5** amass, build, clump, group, shape, unite **6** gather, muster, summon **7** cluster, collect, convene, convoke, fashion, marshal, produce, round up **8** congress, contrive **9** aggregate, forgather **10** accumulate, congregate **11** fit together, manufacture, put together **12** call together, come together **13** bring together

assembly 4 bevy **5** bunch, covey, crowd, flock, group, party, rally, set-up **6** muster, troupe **7** cluster, meeting **8** conclave **9** congeries, gathering **10** collection **11** association, fabrication, get-together, manufacture **12** congregation, construction *American Indian:* **6** powwow *ancient Greek:* **8** ecclesia *ancient Roman:* **7** comitia *Anglo-Saxon:* **4** moot **5** gemot **6** gemote **8** folkmoot, folkmote *ecclesiastical:* **5** synod **10** consistory *legislative:* **4** diet **6** senate **8** congress **10** parliament *place:* **4** hall, room **5** agora **10** auditorium *Russian:* **4** duma *witches':* **6** sabbat **7** sabbath

assent 3 nod, yes **4** okay **5** agree **6** accede, accord, concur, say yes **7** approve, consent, embrace **8** approval, sanction, thumbs-up **9** accession, acquiesce, admission, agreement, subscribe **10** acceptance, permission **11** affirmation, concurrence **12** acquiescence

assert 3 say **4** aver, avow **5** argue, claim, posit, state, utter, voice **6** adduce, affirm, allege, attest, avouch, defend, depose, insist, submit **7** advance, contend, declare, express, justify, profess, protest, publish, warrant **8** announce, maintain, proclaim **9** broadcast, postulate, predicate **10** promulgate

assertion 6 avowal **8** averment **9** affidavit, statement **10** allegation, avouchment, contention, deposition, disclosure, insistence, profession **11** affirmation, attestation, declaration **12** asseveration **13** pronouncement

assertive 4 firm, sure **5** pushy **6** strong **7** assured, certain, decided, pushing **8** cocksure, emphatic, forceful, positive **9** confident, energetic, insistent **10** aggressive, resounding **11** affirmative, distinctive, self-assured **13** self-confident

assess 3 fix, tax **4** deem, levy, rate **5** assay, exact, judge, put on, set at, value, weigh **6** charge, figure, impose, reckon, survey **7** account, compute, subject, valuate **8** appraise, consider, estimate, evaluate **9** determine

assessment 3 fee, tax **4** duty, levy, toll **6** charge, impost, rating, tariff **8** estimate, judgment **9** appraisal, valuation **10** estimation, evaluation **12** appraisement

asset 4 boon, good **5** merit **6** credit **7** benefit **8** blessing, resource **9** advantage **11** distinction *opposite:* **9** liability

assets 5 items, means, money **6** wealth **7** capital **8** bankroll, property **9** resources, valuables **11** possessions

asseverate 4 aver, avow **5** state **6** affirm, assert, attest, avouch, depose, insist **7** certify, contend, declare, profess **8** maintain, proclaim **9** pronounce

assiduous 4 busy **5** eager **6** active **7** moiling, zealous **8** diligent, sedulous, tireless **9** attentive, laborious **10** persistent, unflagging **11** hard-working, industrious **13** indefatigable

assiduously 4 hard **6** busily **9** earnestly, intensely **10** diligently, thoroughly **11** intensively **12** exhaustively, meticulously, persistently **13** painstakingly, unremittingly

assign 3 fix, lay, set **4** cede, deed, give, name **5** allot, allow, refer **6** charge, convey, credit, define, impute, remise, settle **7** appoint, ascribe, earmark, lay down, mete out, specify, station **8** accredit, allocate, delegate, make over, relegate, sign over, transfer **9** admeasure, apportion, attribute, designate, establish, prescribe **10** pigeonhole

assignation 4 date **5** tryst **7** meeting **9** allotment **10** engagement, rendezvous **11** appointment, get-together

assignee 5 agent, proxy **6** deputy, factor **7** officer **8** attorney, delegate

assignment 3 job **4** beat, duty, post, task, work **5** chore, stint **6** office **8** homework, position, transfer **9** allotment **10** allocation, delegation, obligation **11** designation

assimilate 5 adapt, adopt, grasp, learn, liken, match **6** absorb, adjust, digest, equate, imbibe, soak up, take in, take up **7** blend in, compare, conform **8** parallel **10** comprehend, understand **11** incorporate

assimilation 8 taking in **9** awareness **10** absorption, conversion **11** mindfulness, recognition **12** apperception **13** consciousness, incorporation

assist 3 aid **4** abet, back, help, lift **5** boost, do for, serve, stead **6** relief, succor **7** backing, benefit, comfort, help out, secours, service, support, work for **8** benefact, work with **9** cooperate, open doors

assistance 3 aid **4** hand, help, lift **5** boost **6** relief, succor **7** backing, benefit, comfort, secours, service, subsidy, support **8** abetment **9** upholding **10** subvention, supporting **11** cooperation

assistant 3 aid **4** aide, ally, help **5** aider **6** backer, backup, deputy, flunky, helper, second **7** acolyte, ancilla, orderly **8** adjutant, henchman **9** attendant, auxiliary, coadjutor **10** accomplice, aide-de-camp, coadjutant, lieutenant **12** right-hand man

assistive 6 aiding, useful **7** helpful **10** beneficial **11** serviceable

assize 3 law **4** rule, writ **5** canon, edict **6** decree **7** finding, inquest, precept, statute, verdict **8** standard **9** ordinance, prescript **10** regulation

associate 3 pal **4** ally, chum, join, link, mate, pair, yoke **5** blend, buddy, crony, group, match, merge, unite **6** cohort, comate, couple, fellow, friend, hobnob, relate, worker **7** bracket, combine, compeer, comrade, conjoin, connect, consort, partner **8** confrere, coworker, employee, familiar, federate, identify, intimate **9** affiliate, bedfellow, colleague, companion, copartner, secondary **10** accomplice, amalgamate, compatriot, complement **11** concomitant, confederate, correlative, counterpart, running mate, subordinate **12** acquaintance **13** accompaniment

association 3 tie **4** band, bloc, bond, clan, club, crew, hint **5** group, guild, order, tie-up, union **6** hookup, league **7** circuit, concert, linkage, linking, society **8** alliance, congress, overtone, relation, sodality, teamwork **9** coalition, undertone **10** conference, connection, federation, fellowship, fraternity, mental link, suggestion **11** affiliation, brotherhood, combination, conjunction, connotation, cooperation, implication, partnership **12** conjointment, organization, relationship, togetherness **13** collaboration

assort 5 class, group, order **6** codify, divide **7** arrange **8** classify, stratify **9** associate, designate, harmonize, methodize **10** categorize, distribute, pigeonhole **11** systematize

assorted 4 like **5** mixed **6** fitted, motley, suited, sundry, varied **7** adapted, diverse, matched, similar, various **9** different **11** diversified, conformable **12** conglomerate, multifarious **13** heterogeneous, miscellaneous

assortment 4 olio **5** array, group **6** choice, jumble, medley **7** mélange, mixture, variety **8** mishmash, mixed bag, pastiche **9** diversity, potpourri, selection **10** collection, hodgepodge, miscellany **11** gallimaufry

assuage 4 calm, cool, ease **5** allay, quiet **6** lessen, pacify, quench, reduce, soften, soothe, temper **7** appease, lighten, mollify, placate, relieve, sweeten

8 decrease, mitigate, moderate **9** alleviate **10** conciliate, propitiate

as such 5 per se **8** by itself **9** in essence, virtually **11** essentially **12** by definition **13** fundamentally, intrinsically

assumably 6 likely, surely **7** no doubt **8** probably **9** doubtless **10** most likely, presumably

assume 3 act, don **4** fake, sham, take **5** adopt, bluff, feign, put on, seize, usurp **6** affect, draw on, expect, reckon, slip on, take in, take on, take up **7** believe, imagine, preempt, premise, presume, pretend, receive, suppose, suspect **8** accroach, arrogate, shoulder, simulate, take over **9** undertake **10** commandeer, presuppose, understand **11** appropriate, counterfeit

assumed 4 fake, sham **5** bogus, false, put on, tacit **6** made-up, phoney **7** feigned **8** affected, delusory, putative, spurious, supposed **9** deceptive, pretended, simulated **10** artificial, fictitious

assumption 5 posit **6** belief, thesis **7** conceit, premise, seizure, surmise **8** takeover **9** arrogance, postulate **10** acceptance, arrogation, conjecture, pretension, usurpation **11** expectation, supposition, undertaking **13** appropriation

assurance 4 oath, word **5** nerve, troth **6** aplomb, parole, pledge, safety, surety **7** promise, support, warrant **8** audacity, boldness, safeness, security, sureness, temerity, warranty **9** assertion, brashness, certainty, certitude, cockiness, composure, guarantee, hardiness, self-trust **10** brazenness, confidence, conviction, equanimity, profession **11** affirmation, presumption

assure 4 aver **5** bet on, cinch, swear **6** affirm, attest, ensure, insure, pledge, secure, soothe **7** certify, comfort, confirm, promise, satisfy **8** convince, persuade **9** guarantee **11** make certain

assured 3 set **4** cool **5** fixed **6** secure **7** certain, decided, settled **8** clear-cut, composed, definite, positive, sanguine, **9** assertive, collected, confident, undoubted, unruffled **10** guaranteed, pronounced **11** beyond doubt, made certain, unflappable **13** imperturbable, self-confident, self-satisfied

assuredly 9 certainly, doubtless **10** positively **11** confidently, undoubtedly, without fail

assuredness 6 surety **9** certainty, certitude **10** confidence, conviction

Assyria *capital:* **5** Calah **7** Nineveh *city:* **5** Ashur, Assur *god:* **3** Sin **4** Nabu

5 Ashur, Nusku 6 Tammuz 7 Ninurta
goddess: 6 Ishtar *king:* 3 Pul 6 Sargon
11 Sennacherib, Shalmaneser 12 Ashurbanipal *language:* 7 Aramaic *queen:*
9 Semiramis *river:* 6 Tigris *writing:*
9 cuneiform
asterisk 4 star 6 symbol 9 character
astern 3 aft 4 rear, tail 5 abaft 6 back of,
behind 8 backward, rearmost, rearward
asteroid 5 Ceres
Asterope *father:* 5 Atlas *mother:*
7 Pleione *sisters:* 8 Pleiades
asthma 7 allergy 8 disorder
as to 4 in re 5 about, anent 7 apropos
9 regarding 10 concerning, respecting
11 according to
astonish 4 daze, stun 5 amaze, floor,
shock 7 astound, stagger, startle, stupefy 8 blow away, bowl over, confound,
dumfound, surprise 9 dumbfound, take
aback 11 flabbergast
astonishing 7 amazing 8 stunning, wondrous 9 marvelous, startling, wonderful
10 astounding, miraculous, prodigious,
staggering, stupendous, surprising
11 spectacular 12 breathtaking
astonishment 3 awe 5 shock 6 wonder
8 surprise 9 amazement, confusion
10 perplexity, wonderment 12 bewilderment, stupefaction 13 consternation
astound 4 daze, stun 5 amaze, shock
7 confuse 8 astonish, bewilder, confound, dumfound, surprise 9 dumbfound, overwhelm, take aback 11 flabbergast
Astraea *father:* 4 Zeus 7 Jupiter *mother:*
6 Themis
astral 6 dreamy, starry 7 exalted, highest, stellar 8 elevated, sidereal 9 celestial, top-drawer, unworldly, visionary
10 top-ranking 11 high-ranking 12 otherworldly
astray 4 awry 5 amiss, badly, wrong
6 adrift, afield 7 in error 9 off course
astride 8 bridging, spanning 10 on each
side, straddling
astringent 4 acid, keen 5 acerb, acrid,
harsh, sharp, stern 6 biting, bitter,
severe, strict 7 acerbic, ascetic, austere,
caustic, cutting, puckery, pungent,
styptic 8 incisive, stinging 10 irritating
11 contracting 12 constrictive
astrolabe *successor* 7 sextant
astrologer 5 Dixon (Jeane), Faust
9 stargazer, Zoroaster 11 horoscopist,
Nostradamus
astrological aspect 5 trine 7 sextile
8 quartile 10 opposition 11 conjunction
astronaut 4 Ride (Sally) 5 Glenn (John),
White (Edward), Young (John) 6 Aldrin
(Edwin), Cooper (Gordon), Lovell
(James), Worden (Alfred) 7 Bluford
(Guion), Collins (Michael), Gagarin
(Yuri), Grissom (Gus), Jemison (Mae),
Schirra (Walter), Shepard (Alan),
Yegorov (Boris) 8 Stafford (Thomas)
9 Armstrong (Neil), Carpenter (Scott),
McAuliffe (Christa) 10 Tereshkova
(Valentina)
astronomer *American:* 3 See (Thomas
Jefferson) 5 Sagan (Carl) 6 Hubble
(Edwin), Lowell (Percival) 7 Langley
(Samuel), Newcomb (Simon), Shapley
(Harlow) 8 Bowditch (Nathaniel),
Mitchell (Maria), Tombaugh (Clyde)
9 Pickering (Edward) 11 Schlesinger
(Frank) *Austrian:* 13 Schwarzschild
(Karl) *Danish:* 5 Brahe (Tycho) *Dutch:*
4 Oort (Jan Hendrik) 6 Sitter (Willem
de) 7 Huygens (Christiaan) *English:*
4 Ryle (Martin), Wren (Christopher)
6 Halley (Edmond), Lovell (Bernard)
7 Lockyer (Joseph), Parsons (William)
8 Herschel (Caroline, John, William)
French: 6 Picard (Jean) 7 Laplace
(Pierre-Simon de), Messier (Charles)
German: 4 Wolf (Maximilian) 5 Vogel
(Hermann) 6 Kepler (Johannes),
Müller (Johann), Struve (Otto) *Greek:*
12 Eratosthenes *Italian:* 7 Galileo
(Galilei) 12 Schiaparelli (Giovanni) *Persian:* 11 Omar Khayyám *Polish:*
10 Copernicus (Nicolaus) *Swedish:*
7 Celsius (Anders) *Swiss:* 6 Zwicky
(Fritz)
astute 3 sly 4 deep, foxy, keen, wily
5 cagey, canny, heady, quick, savvy,
sharp 6 artful, clever, crafty, shrewd,
tricky 7 cunning, knowing 8 guileful
9 insidious, sagacious 11 calculating
13 perspicacious
astuteness 3 wit 6 acumen 8 keenness,
wiliness 9 canniness 10 craftiness,
shrewdness 11 discernment, percipience 12 perspicacity
Astyanax *father:* 6 Hector *mother:*
10 Andromache
asunder 4 torn 5 apart, split 7 divided
9 into parts, separated
as usual 8 normally, wontedly 9 routinely 10 habitually, ordinarily 11 customarily 12 consistently
as well 3 and, too, yet 4 also, even, just,
more, plus 7 besides, further 8 likewise,
moreover 9 along with, including, similarly 10 in addition 11 furthermore
12 additionally
as well as 3 and 4 plus 7 besides 9 along
with 11 not counting 12 in addition to,
together with
as yet 5 so far, to now 7 earlier, thus far

8 hitherto, until now **10** to this time
12 to the present
asylum 4 home, port **5** cover, haven
6 covert, harbor, refuge **7** retreat, shelter **8** hospital, security **9** harborage,
safe house, sanctuary **10** protection,
sanatorium **11** institution
asymmetric 6 uneven **7** not even,
unequal **8** lopsided **9** irregular
10 unbalanced **12** overbalanced
Atalanta *husband:* **8** Melanion *suitor:*
10 Hippomenes
at all 4 ever, once **6** anyway **7** anytime
atavism 9 reversion, throwback
10 recurrence
ataxia 5 chaos, snarl **6** huddle, muddle
7 clutter **8** disarray, disorder **9** confusion
atelier 6 studio **8** workroom, workshop
Athamas *daughter:* **5** Helle *father:* **6** Aeolus *son:* **7** Phrixos, Phrixus **8** Learchus
wife: **3** Ino **7** Nephele
Athena *Roman counterpart:* **7** Minerva
attribute: **3** owl **5** Aegis **7** serpent *city:*
6 Athens *father:* **4** Zeus *names:* **4** Nike
6 Pallas **9** Parthenos *shield:* **5** Aegis *statue:* **9** Palladium *temple:* **9** Parthenon
athenaeum 6 museum **7** library
8 archives **10** repository
Athens *citadel:* **9** Acropolis *founder:*
7 Cecrops *last king:* **6** Codrus *marketplace:* **5** agora *rival:* **6** Sparta *senate:*
5 boule *temple:* **9** Parthenon
athirst 4 avid, keen **5** eager **6** ardent
7 anxious **8** desiring, desirous, yearning
9 impatient
athlete 4 jock **5** sport **6** player **7** acrobat,
gymnast, tumbler **9** sportsman **10** competitor **11** sportswoman
athlete's foot 8 ringworm **10** tinea pedis
athletic 6 brawny, robust, sinewy **8**
sporting, vigorous **9** strapping, strenuous *contest:* **4** agon, game **5** match *field:*
4 oval, ring, rink **5** arena, court **7** diamond, stadium **8** gridiron *prize:* **3** cup
5 medal **6** trophy, wreath
athletics 5 games, races **6** events, sports
7 contest **8** exercise **9** exercises **10** gymnastics, recreation **12** calisthenics
athwart 4 over **5** cross **6** across, beyond
9 crossways, crosswise, opposed to
12 transversely
Atlanta's civic center 4 Omni
Atlas *brother:* **10** Prometheus *daughter:*
5 Hyads **6** Hyades **7** Pleiades **10** Atlantides *father:* **7** Iapetus *mother:* **7** Clymene
race: **5** Titan *wife:* **7** Pleione
at last 7 finally
Atli *wife (slayer):* **6** Gudrun
atmosphere 3 air **4** aura, mood, tone
6 medium, milieu **7** ambient, climate,

feeling, quality **8** ambiance, ambience
11 environment, mise-en-scène **12** surroundings *stratum:* **9** exosphere **10** ionosphere, mesosphere **11** chemosphere,
ozonosphere, troposphere **12** stratosphere, thermosphere *sun's:* **12** chromosphere
atmospheric 4 airy **6** aerial **8** ethereal
atoll 6 island *equatorial area:* **5** Baker
Indian Ocean: **4** Male *Kiribati:* **4** Beru
Marshall Islands: **6** Bikini **8** Eniwetok
Tuamotu: **4** Anaa **5** Chain *Tuvalu:*
8 Funafuti
atom 3 bit, jot **4** iota, mite, whit
5 minim, speck, touch, trace **6** tittle
7 modicum, smidgen **8** particle **9** scintilla *charged:* **3** ion **5** anion *group:* **7** radical
atomic particle 3 ion **4** beta, muon, pion
5 alpha, boson, meson **6** baryon,
hadron, lepton, proton **7** fermion,
hyperon, neutron, nucleon **8** electron,
mesotron, neutrino, positron, thermion
hypothetical: **5** quark **6** parton
atomize 4 nuke, ruin **5** smash, wreck
6 divide, rub out **7** break up, destroy,
shatter **9** demolish, destruct, disperse,
dynamite, fragment, nebulize **9** break
down, devastate, pulverize **10** disconnect
at once 3 now **4** away, both **6** pronto
8 directly, first off, right now, together
9 forthwith, instantly, right away
11 immediately, straightway **12** concurrently, straightaway, without delay
atone 3 pay **6** redeem, repair, repent
7 correct, expiate, rectify, redress, satisfy **10** compensate, make amends, recompense
atoner 8 penitent
atop 4 upon
Atossa *father:* **5** Cyrus *husband:* **6** Darius
7 Smerdes **8** Cambyses *son:* **6** Xerxes
at random 5 about **6** anyhow **7** anywise
8 by chance **9** aimlessly, haphazard
10 carelessly **11** any which way, haphazardly **12** accidentally **13** helterskelter
at rest 4 dead **5** still **8** inactive, lifeless,
reposing, sleeping, tranquil, unmoving
9 quiescent **10** motionless, stationary,
untroubled **11** trouble-free
Atreus *brother:* **8** Thyestes *father:*
6 Pelops *mother:* **10** Hippodamia *slayer:*
9 Aegisthus *son:* **8** Menelaus
9 Agamemnon **11** Pleisthenes *victim:*
11 Pleisthenes *wife:* **6** Aerope
atrocious 4 foul, vile **5** awful, cruel
6 brutal, horrid, odious, savage, wicked
7 heinous, noisome, obscene **8** barbaric, horrible, shocking, terrible

9 appalling, desperate, execrable, loathsome, monstrous, offensive, repulsive, revolting, sickening **10** abominable, despicable, detestable, disgusting, horrifying, outrageous, scandalous **12** contemptible

atrocity 4 evil **5** crime **6** horror, infamy **7** cruelty, outrage **8** enormity, savagery **9** barbarity, brutality **11** abomination, heinousness **13** monstrousness

atrophy 7 decline, wasting **9** decadence, waste away **10** devolution **11** declination **12** degeneration **13** deterioration

attach 3 add, fix, tie **4** bind, hook, link, take **5** affix, annex, latch, rivet, stick, unite **6** adhere, append, assign, fasten, secure **7** ascribe, connect **8** make fast **9** associate, attribute

attached 5 fixed **7** sessile

attachment 3 tie **4** bond, link, love **6** fealty **7** loyalty, seizure **8** addition, adhesion, devotion, fastener, fidelity, fondness **9** accessory, adherence, affection, connector, constancy **10** allegiance, connection **12** faithfulness

attack 4 bout, jump, raid, rush **5** beset, blitz, drive, fight, foray, onset, sally, siege, spasm, spell, storm, throe **6** access, ambush, assail, banzai, battle, charge, fall on, harass, have at, invade, irrupt, onrush, sortie, strike, tackle **7** aggress, assault, barrage, besiege, bombard, offense, seizure **8** fall upon, invasion, outbreak, paroxysm **9** beleaguer, incursion, offensive, onslaught, pugnacity **10** aggression, blitzkrieg

attain 3 get, win **4** gain **5** reach, score **6** arrive, come to, effect, make it, obtain, rack up **7** achieve, fulfill, pull off, realize, succeed **8** bring off, complete **10** accomplish

attainment 4 feat **6** finish **7** arrival **10** completion **11** achievement, acquirement, acquisition, fulfillment, realization

attempt 3 bid, try **4** seek, shot, stab **5** assay, crack, essay, offer, trial **6** attack, effort, strive, tackle **7** assault, venture **8** endeavor, striving, struggle **9** undertake **11** undertaking **12** make an effort

attend 3 aid, see **4** be at, go to, hear, heed, help, mark, mind, note **5** apply, catch, nurse, see to, serve, visit, watch **6** assist, convoy, doctor, drop in, escort, go with, listen, notice, show up, turn up, wait on **7** be there, care for, conduct, hearken, oversee, pay heed, work for **8** chaperon, stay with, wait upon **9** accompany, chaperone, companion, look after, supervise **11** concentrate

attendant 4 aide **5** valet **6** escort, helper, lackey **7** orderly, servant **9** ancillary, assistant **10** bridesmaid, coincident **11** chamberlain, concomitant **12** accompanying *ancient Roman:* **6** lictor *in court:* **7** bailiff **8** tipstaff

attendants 5 suite, train **7** cortege, retinue **9** entourage

attendee 4 goer

attention 4 care, heed, mark, note **5** study **6** notice, regard, remark **7** amenity, command, concern, respect, service, thought **8** civility, courtesy, industry, scrutiny **9** assiduity, awareness, deference, diligence, gallantry, spotlight, treatment **10** absorption, cognizance, observance, politeness **11** application, mindfulness, observation, sensibility **12** deliberation **13** concentration, consciousness, consideration

attention getter 4 ahem **5** gavel

attentive 4 kind **5** alert, awake, aware, civil **6** intent, polite **7** devoted, gallant, heedful, mindful **8** gracious, obliging, open-eyed **9** advertent, courteous, observant, regardful **10** interested, respectful, solicitous, thoughtful **11** considerate **13** concentrating

attenuate 3 sap **4** rare, slim, thin **5** abate, blunt, reedy **6** lessen, rarefy, shrink, slight, stalky, subtle, twiggy, weaken **7** cripple, deflate, disable, reduced, slender, squinny, subtile, tenuous, unbrace **8** contract, enfeeble, mitigate, rarefied, tapering, wiredraw **9** constrict, dissipate, undermine **10** become thin, become fine, become less, debilitate

attest 4 aver, show **5** argue, prove, swear, vouch **6** adjure, affirm, assert, verify **7** certify, confirm, declare, display, exhibit, point to, support, sustain, swear to, testify, warrant, witness **8** announce, indicate, manifest **9** establish **10** asseverate **11** bear witness, demonstrate **12** authenticate

attestation 5 proof **7** witness **8** evidence **9** testament, testimony **10** validation **11** declaration, testimonial **12** confirmation

attic 4 loft, room **6** garret **7** storage **8** cockloft

Attica 6 Greece *division:* **4** deme

at times 9 sometimes **10** now and then, on occasion **11** now and again **12** here and there, occasionally

attire 4 clad, duds, garb, gear, togs, wear **5** array, drape, dress, getup, habit, tog up **6** clothe, fit out, outfit **7** apparel, clothes, costume, garment, raiment, threads **8** clothing, garments, glad rags **11** habiliments

attitude 4 pose, view **5** angle, stand **6** manner, stance **7** bearing, mind-set, outlook, posture **8** carriage, demeanor, position, pretense **10** standpoint **11** inclination, perspective, point of view

attitudinize 4 mask, pose, sham **6** affect **7** pass for, pass off, posture, pretend, show off **10** masquerade

attorney 5 agent, proxy **6** deputy, factor, lawyer **7** counsel **8** advocate, assignee **9** barrister, counselor, solicitor **10** counsellor, legal eagle, mouthpiece

attract 4 draw, lure, wile **5** charm, court, tempt **6** allure, appeal, beckon, draw in, entice, invite, seduce **7** beguile, bewitch, enchant, solicit **8** appeal to, interest, intrigue, inveigle **9** captivate, fascinate, influence, magnetize

attraction 4 bait, call, draw, lure, pull **5** charm **6** allure, appeal, liking **8** affinity, cynosure, sympathy **9** affection, chemistry, magnetism, seduction **10** allurement **12** drawing power

attractive 4 cute, fair, sexy **5** bonny, dishy **6** comely, lovely, luring, pretty **7** Circean, likable, winsome **8** alluring, charming, engaging, enticing, fetching, handsome, inviting, magnetic, mesmeric, tempting **9** appealing, beauteous, beautiful, beckoning, glamorous, seductive **10** bewitching, enchanting **11** captivating, fascinating, good-looking, tantalizing **13** prepossessing

attractiveness 5 charm **6** appeal, beauty, glamor **7** glamour

attribute 3 lay **4** mark, sign **5** apply, facet, pin on, point, refer, trait **6** aspect, assign, charge, credit, emblem, impute, symbol, virtue **7** ascribe, connect, earmark, explain, feature, quality **8** accredit, classify, property **9** adjective, character, designate

attrition 3 rue **4** ruth, wear **6** sorrow **7** erosion, penance, remorse, rubbing, wearing **8** abrasion, friction, grinding **9** penitence, penitency, reduction, weakening **10** repentance **12** contriteness

attritional 5 sorry **6** rueful **8** contrite, penitent **9** regretful, repentant **10** apologetic, remorseful **11** penitential

attune 6 accord, adjust **7** balance, conform **9** harmonize, integrate, reconcile **10** coordinate, proportion **11** accommodate

atypical 3 odd **5** queer **7** deviant, strange, unusual **8** aberrant, abnormal, peculiar **9** anomalous, deviative, differ-

ent, divergent, irregular, unnatural **11** exceptional, heteroclite, nonstandard **13** preternatural

auberge 3 inn **5** hotel, lodge **6** hostel, tavern **7** hospice **8** hostelry **9** roadhouse **11** caravansary, public house

Auber opera 10 Fra Diavolo

auburn 4 rust **5** henna **6** russet **8** chestnut **11** burnt sienna **12** reddish-brown

au courant 3 mod **4** up on **5** awake, aware, hep to, hip to, savvy **6** modern, modish, versed **7** abreast, current, in touch, knowing, stylish, versant, witting **8** familiar, informed, sentient, up-to-date **9** cognizant, conscious, plugged in **10** acquainted, conversant **11** fashionable **12** contemporary **13** up-to-the-minute

auction 4 sale, sell

audacious 4 bold, rash **5** brash, brave, cocky, risky, saucy **6** brazen, cheeky, daring **7** valiant **8** arrogant, fearless, impudent, insolent, intrepid, reckless, unafraid, uncurbed **9** daredevil, dauntless, foolhardy, shameless, undaunted, venturous **10** courageous, ungoverned, unhampered **11** adventurous, impertinent, temerarious, uninhibited, untrammeled, venturesome **12** unrestrained **13** adventuresome

audacity 4 gall **5** brass, cheek, moxie, nerve, spunk **6** mettle, spirit **7** courage **8** boldness, chutzpah, rashness, temerity **9** assurance, arrogance, brashness, cockiness, disregard, hardihood, hardiness, impudence, insolence **10** brazenness, effrontery **12** recklessness

audible 5 aural, clear, heard **8** distinct **9** auricular

audibly 5 aloud **7** aurally, clearly, out loud

audience 5 crowd, group, house **6** public **7** hearing, gallery, hearers, meeting **8** admirers, assembly, audition, devotees **9** clientele, following, gathering, interview, listeners **10** assemblage, spectators

audile see AUDITORY

audio 5 sound

audit 4 scan **5** check, probe **6** go over, report, review, survey, verify **7** analyze, balance, checkup, examine, inspect **8** analysis, scrutiny **10** inspection, scrutinize **11** examination **13** investigation

audition 4 test **5** trial **6** tryout **7** hearing, reading

auditor 8 examiner, listener **9** inspector **10** accountant, controller **11** comptroller

auditory 5 aural **8** acoustic

au fait 4 able **5** right **6** decent, proper,

versed **7** abreast, capable, correct, versant **8** becoming, decorous, familiar, informed, revelant **9** befitting, competent, qualified **10** acquainted, conforming, conversant, to the point

au fond 8 at bottom **9** basically, in essence **11** essentially **13** fundamentally

Augean 9 difficult **10** formidable **11** distasteful *stable:* **3** sty **4** sink **5** filth, Sodom **7** cesspit **8** cesspool

auger 3 bit **5** borer, drill, screw **6** gimlet, trepan, wimble **9** corkscrew

Auge's son 8 Telephus

aught 3 all, nil, nix, zip **4** nada, zero **5** zilch **6** cipher **7** nothing **8** anything, goose egg **10** everything

augment 3 wax **4** grow, hike, rise **5** add to, boost, build, exalt, mount, raise **6** beef up, expand, extend **7** build up, develop, enhance, enlarge, magnify **9** intensify, reinforce **8** compound, heighten, increase, multiply **10** aggrandize, supplement **11** make greater

augmentation 4 rise **5** annex, extra, raise **7** adjunct, buildup **8** addition, increase **9** accession, accretion, increment **10** complement, enrichment **11** enhancement, enlargement

augur 4 bode, seer **6** herald, oracle **7** betoken, diviner, portend, predict, presage, promise, prophet, suggest **8** forebode, forecast, foreshow, foretell, indicate, prophesy, soothsay **9** adumbrate, foretoken, harbinger, predictor, prefigure **10** forecaster, foreshadow, foreteller, prophesier, soothsayer, vaticinate **11** Nostradamus **13** prognosticate

augury 4 omen, sign **5** token **6** herald **7** auspice, portent, presage, warning **8** bodement, forecast, prophecy **9** foretoken, harbinger **10** divination, forerunner, prediction, prognostic **11** forewarning

august 5 grand, noble, regal **6** lordly **7** eminent, stately **8** baronial, imposing, majestic, princely, splendid **9** dignified, grandiose **11** magnificent

auk 5 alcid **7** seabird *genus:* **4** Alca
___ **au lait 4** café

au naturel 3 raw **4** nude **5** naked, plain **6** unclad **8** stripped **9** unclothed, undressed **10** stark naked

aura 3 air **4** feel, glow, halo, mood, tone, vibe **5** aroma, vibes **6** nimbus **7** aureole, feeling, quality **8** ambience, mystique, radiance, stimulus **9** emanation, semblance, sensation **10** atmosphere

aural 6 audile **7** audible **8** acoustic, auditory **9** auricular

aureate 6 florid, golden **7** flowery, orotund **8** sonorous **9** bombastic, grandiose, overblown **10** euphuistic, rhetorical **11** declamatory **13** grandiloquent

aureole 4 aura, halo, ring **5** crown, light **6** circle, corona, nimbus **8** radiance

au revoir 4 by-by, ciao, ta-ta **5** adieu, adios **6** bye-bye, so long **7** good-bye **8** farewell **11** arrivederci

auricular see AURAL

Auriga star 7 Capella

aurora 4 dawn, morn **7** dawning, morning, sunrise **8** cockcrow, daybreak

Aurora *Roman counterpart:* **3** Eos *goddess of:* **4** dawn *husband:* **8** Tithonus *son:* **6** Memnon

auslander 5 alien **7** inconnu **8** outsider, stranger **9** foreigner

auspice 4 omen, sign **10** divination

auspices 5 aegis **6** charge **7** backing, support **8** guidance **9** influence, patronage **11** sponsorship, supervision

auspicious 5 lucky **6** bright, timely **7** hopeful **9** favorable, fortunate, opportune, promising, well-timed **10** prosperous **11** encouraging, propitious

Austen, Jane *novel:* **4** Emma **10** Persuasion **13** Mansfield Park **15** Northanger Abbey **17** Pride and Prejudice **19** Sense and Sensibility

Auster see NOTUS

austere 4 bare, cold, dour, firm, grim, hard **5** acrid, bleak, grave, harsh, plain, rigid, sharp, spare, stern **6** bitter, severe, simple, somber, strict **7** ascetic, serious, spartan **8** exacting **9** stringent, unadorned, unfeeling **10** astringent, restrained **11** self-denying

austerity 5 rigor **6** thrift **7** economy **8** acerbity, asperity, coldness, grimness, hardness, rigidity, severity **9** harshness, parsimony, privation, solemnity, spareness, sternness, stiffness **10** self-denial, simplicity, strictness, stringency **11** unadornment **13** self-restraint

Australia *capital:* **8** Canberra *city:* **5** Perth **6** Darwin, Sydney **8** Adelaide, Brisbane **9** Melbourne, Newcastle *desert:* **10** Great Sandy **13** Great Victoria *ethnic group:* **9** Aborigine *island:* **6** Fraser **8** Kangaroo, Melville, Tasmania *lake:* **4** Eyre *monetary unit:* **6** dollar *mountain, range:* **9** Ayers Rock **9** Kosciusko **13** Great Dividing *reef:* **12** Great Barrier *river:* **4** Swan **6** Murray **7** Darling **8** Flinders **11** Cooper Creek **12** Coopers Creek *strait:* **4** Bass **6** Torres

Austria *capital:* **6** Vienna *city:* **4** Graz, Linz **8** Salzburg **9** Innsbruck **10** Klagenfurt *lake:* **10** Neusiedler *monetary unit:* **4** euro *mountain:* **13** Grossglockner *mountain range:* 4 Alps *neighbor:* 5 Italy 7 Croatia, Germany, Hungary 8 Slovakia, Slovenia 11 Switzerland 13 Czech Republic, Liechtenstein *river:* 3 Ems 6 Danube

autarchy see AUTOCRACY

autarkic 4 free 8 separate 9 sovereign 10 autonomous, self-ruling 11 independent, self-reliant 13 self-governing

autarky 7 freedom 8 autonomy 12 independence, self-reliance

authentic 4 real, true 5 legit, pukka, right, solid, sound, valid 6 actual, trusty 7 certain, factual, for real, genuine 8 accurate, bona fide, credible, faithful, reliable 9 undoubted, veritable 10 convincing, dependable, legitimate, sure-enough 11 indubitable, trustworthy 12 questionless

authenticate 5 prove, vouch 6 adduce, attest, verify 7 bear out, certify, confirm, justify, voucher, warrant 8 accredit, validate 11 corroborate 12 substantiate

author 5 maker 6 penman, scribe, writer 7 creator 8 inventor, novelist, prosaist 9 generator 10 originator *American:* 3 Bly (Robert), Fox (Paula), Nin (Anaïs), Poe (Edgar Allan), Tan (Amy) 4 Agee (James), Baum (L. Frank), Buck (Pearl S.), Cook (Robin), Dana (Richard Henry), Fast (Howard), Ford (Richard), Grey (Zane), Jong (Erica), King (Stephen), Mann (Thomas), Puzo (Mario), Rand (Ayn), Rice (Anne), Roth (Philip), Shaw (Irwin), Uris (Leon), West (Nathanael), Wouk (Herman) 5 Aiken (Conrad), Alger (Horatio), Banks (Russell), Barth (John), Benét (Stephen Vincent), Blume (Judy), Boyle (T. Coraghessan), Brown (Rita Mae), Clark (Mary Higgins), Crane (Hart, Stephen), Dunne (Dominick, John Gregory), Elkin (Stanley), Ellis (Bret Easton), Foote (Horton), Harte (Bret), Henry (O.), Jakes (John), James (Henry), Levin (Ira), Lewis (Sinclair), Lurie (Alison), Mason (Bobbie Ann), Oates (Joyce Carol), O'Hara (John), Ozick (Cynthia), Paine (Thomas), Paley (Grace), Potok (Chaim), Price (Reynolds, Richard), Steel (Danielle), Stein (Gertrude), Stone (Irving), Stout (Rex), Stowe (Harriet Beecher), Turow (Scott), Twain (Mark), Tyler (Anne), Vidal (Gore), Welty (Eudora), White (Edmund, E. B., T. H.), Wolfe (Thomas, Tom), Wylie (Elinor) 6 Alcott (Louisa May), Asimov (Isaac), Auster (Paul), Bellow (Saul), Berger (Thomas), Bierce (Ambrose), Bowles (Paul), Cabell

(James Branch), Capote (Truman), Cather (Willa), Chopin (Kate), Clancy (Tom), Conroy (Pat), Cooper (James Fenimore), Dickey (James), Didion (Joan), Ellroy (James), Ferber (Edna), French (Marilyn), Gaddis (William), Gaines (Ernest J.), Gilroy (Frank), Godwin (Gail), Hailey (Arthur), Harris (Frank, Joel Chandler), Hawkes (John), Heller (Joseph), Hersey (John), Hinton (S. E.), Holmes (Oliver Wendell), Hughes (Langston), Irving (John, Washington), Jewett (Sarah Orne), Kidder (Tracy), Koontz (Dean), Krantz (Judith), L'Amour (Louis), L'Engle (Madeleine), Le Guin (Ursula K.), London (Jack), Mailer (Norman), McBain (Ed), Miller (Arthur, Henry, Joaquin, May), Morley (Christopher), Morris (Wright), Mosley (Walter), Norris (Frank), Parker (Dorothy), Piercy (Marge), Porter (Katherine Anne, William Sydney), Proulx (E. Annie), Runyon (Damon), Sarton (May), Singer (Isaac Bashevis), Smiley (Jane), Styron (William), Taylor (Peter), Updike (John), Walker (Alice), Waller (Robert James), Warren (Robert Penn), Wilder (Laura Ingalls, Thornton), Wilson (August, Edmund, Harriet, Lanford), Wister (Owen), Wright (James, Richard) 7 Baldwin (Faith, James), Beattie (Ann), Cheever (John), Clemens (Samuel Langhorne), Collins (Jackie), Connell (Evan), Cozzens (James Gould), DeLillo (Don), Dreiser (Theodore), Ellison (Ralph), Erdrich (Louise), Farrell (James T.), Francis (Dick), Franzen (Jonathan), Gardner (Erle Stanley), Garland (Hamlin), Glasgow (Ellen), Goldman (William), Grafton (Sue), Grisham (John), Hammett (Dashiell), Heyward (DuBose), Howells (William Dean), Hurston (Zora Neale), Jackson (Shirley), Jarrell (Randall), Johnson (Diane, James), Keillor (Garrison), Kennedy (William), Kerouac (Jack), Kincaid (Jamaica), Lardner (Ring), Leonard (Elmore), Malamud (Bernard), Marquis (Don), Masters (Edgar Lee), McCourt (Frank), Mumford (Lewis), Nabokov (Vladimir), O'Connor (Flannery), Pynchon (Thomas), Rexroth (Kenneth), Richter (Conrad), Roberts (Elizabeth Madox, Kenneth, Nora), Saroyan (William), Sheehan (Neil), Sheldon (Sidney), Theroux (Paul), Thoreau (Henry David), Thurber (James), Wallace (Lew), Wharton (Edith) 8 Anderson (Maxwell, Poul, Regina, Sherwood), Benchley (Peter),

Bradbury (Ray), Bradford (Barbara Taylor), Caldwell (Erskine), Chandler (Raymond), Cornwell (Patricia), Crichton (Michael), Doctorow (E. L.), Faulkner (William), Kingston (Maxine Hong), Marquand (John P.), McCarthy (Cormac, Mary), McMillan (Terry), McMurtry (Larry), Melville (Herman), Michener (James), Mitchell (Donald Grant, Margaret, S. Weir), Morrison (Toni), Remarque (Erich Maria), Rinehart (Mary Roberts), Salinger (J. D.), Sandburg (Carl), Sinclair (Upton), Spillane (Mickey), Stockton (Frank R.), Vonnegut (Kurt), Wambaugh (Joseph) **9** Burroughs (Edgar Rice, John, William S.), Dos Passos (John), Hawthorne (Nathaniel), Hemingway (Ernest), Hillerman (Tony), Isherwood (Christopher), McCullers (Carson), Steinbeck (John), Wodehouse (P. G.), Woollcott (Alexander) **10** Cunningham (Michael), Fitzgerald (F. Scott), Kingsolver (Barbara), Tarkington (Booth) **11** Auchincloss (Louis), Matthiessen (Peter) *Argentinian:* **6** Borges (Jorge Luis) *Australian:* **4** West (Morris L.) **5** Stead (Christina), White (Patrick) **6** Davies (Robertson) **7** Clavell (James) **8** Keneally (Thomas) **10** McCullough (Colleen), Richardson (Henry Handel) *Austrian:* **5** Kafka (Franz) **7** Jelinek (Elfriede), Suttner (Bertha) **8** Bernhard (Thomas) **10** Schnitzler (Arthur) *Canadian:* **3** Roy (Camille, Gabrielle) **5** Kirby (William), Moore (Brian), Munro (Alice) **6** Atwood (Margaret), Davies (Robertson) **7** Leacock (Stephen), Raddall (Thomas), Richler (Mordecai), Service (Robert), Shields (Carol) **8** Woodcock (George) **9** de la Roche (Mazo), MacLennan (Hugh) *Chilean:* **6** Donoso (José) **7** Allende (Isabel) *Chinese:* **5** Han Yu *Colombian:* **7** Márquez (Gabriel García) *Czech:* **5** Capek (Karel), Hasek (Jaroslav) **7** Kundera (Milan) *Danish:* **4** Rode (Helge), Wied (Gustav) **6** Jensen (Johannes Vilhelm) **7** Dinesen (Isak), Holberg (Ludwig) *Dutch:* **6** Vondel (Joost van den) *Egyptian:* **7** Mahfouz (Naguib) *English:* **4** Amis (Kingsley, Martin), Dahl (Roald), Ford (Ford Madox, John), Lyly (John), Saki, Snow (C. P.), Ward (Mrs. Humphry), West (Rebecca) **5** Byatt (A. S.), Defoe (Daniel), Doyle (Authur Conan), Eliot (George, Thomas Stearns), Evans (Mary Ann), Frayn (Michael), Hardy (Thomas), James (Henry, P. D.), Lewis (C. S., Monk, Wyndham), Lowry (Malcolm), Milne (A. A.), Munro (H. H.),

Powys (John Cowper, Llewelyn, Theodore Francis), Reade (Charles), Spark (Muriel), Waugh (Alec, Evelyn), Wells (Charles Jeremiah, H. G.), White (T. H.), Wilde (Oscar), Woolf (Leonard, Virginia), Young (Arthur, Edward, Francis Brett) **6** Ambler (Eric), Archer (Jeffrey), Austen (Jane), Belloc (Hilaire), Brontë (Anne, Charlotte, Emily), Bunyan (John), Butler (Samuel), Clarke (Arthur C.), Conrad (Joseph), Fowles (John), Graves (Robert), Greene (Graham, Robert), Hilton (James), Hudson (W. H.), Huxley (Aldous), Malory (Thomas), McEwan (Ian), O'Brian (Patrick), Orwell (George), Potter (Beatrix), Powell (Anthony), Sayers (Dorothy L.), Sterne (Laurence), Stoker (Bram), Storey (David), Walton (Izaak) **7** Ballard (J. G.), Burgess (Anthony), Burnett (Frances Hodgson), Carroll (Lewis), Collins (Wilkie), Dickens (Charles), Dodgson (Charles), Durrell (Lawrence), Fleming (Ian), Follett (Ken), Forster (E. M.), Forsyth (Frederick), Golding (Louis, William), Kipling (Rudyard), Le Carré (John), Lessing (Doris), Lofting (Hugh), Maugham (Robin, W. Somerset), Murdoch (Iris), Naipaul (V. S.), Rendell (Ruth), Rowling (J. K.), Sassoon (Siegfried), Shelley (Mary Wollstonecraft, Percy Bysshe), Sitwell (Edith, Osbert, Sacheverell), Southey (Robert), Stewart (Mary), Surtees (Robert Smith), Tolkien (J. R. R.), Walpole (Horace, Hugh), Wyndham (John) **8** Christie (Agatha), Fielding (Henry), Forester (C. S.), Koestler (Arthur), Lawrence (D. H., T. E.), Macaulay (Rose, Thomas Babington), Meredith (George), Sillitoe (Alan), Smollett (Tobias), Strachey (Lytton), Trollope (Anthony), Zangwill (Israel) **9** De Quincey (Thomas), Du Maurier (Daphne, George), Goldsmith (Oliver), Isherwood (Christopher), Mansfield (Katherine), Masefield (John), Priestley (J. B.), Radcliffe (Ann), Stevenson (Robert Louis), Thackeray (William Makepeace), Wodehouse (P. D.) **10** Chesterton (Gilbert Keith), Galsworthy (John), Richardson (Dorothy, Samuel) **12** Quiller-Couch (Arthur Thomas) *Finnish:* **7** Waltari (Mika) **9** Sillanpää (Frans Eemil) *French:* **4** Gide (André), Hugo (Victor), Kock (Charles-Paul de), Sade (Marquis de), Sand (George), Zola (Emile) **5** Beyle (Marie Henri), Camus (Albert), Dumas

(Alexandre), Genet (Jean), Sagan
(Françoise), Staël (Germaine de), Verne
(Jules), Vigny (Alfred-Victor) 6 Balzac
(Honoré de), Daudet (Alphonse),
France (Anatole), Proust (Marcel),
Sartre (Jean-Paul) 7 Cocteau (Jean),
Colette, Gautier (Léon, Théophile),
Malraux (André), Mauriac (Claude,
François), Maurois (André), Merimée
(Prosper), Rolland (Romain), Romains
(Jules), Simenon (Georges) 8 Beauvoir
(Simone de), Flaubert (Gustave), Mari-
vaux (Pierre), Rabelais (François),
Stendhal, Voltaire 9 Giraudoux (Jean)
10 Maupassant (Guy de), Saint-Simon
(Duke de) 12 Robbe-Grillet (Alain),
Saint-Exupéry (Antoine de) *German:*
4 Böll (Heinrich), Mann (Thomas)
5 Grass (Gunter), Hesse (Hermann),
Kafka (Franz), Storm (Theodor), Tieck
(Ludwig), Zweig (Stefan) 6 Goethe
(Johann Wolfgang von), Toller (Ernst)
7 Fontane (Theodor), Richter (Jean
Paul), Wieland (Christoph Martin)
8 Hoffmann (E.T.A., Heinrich), Remar-
que (Erich Maria), Schlegel (August
Wilhelm von, Friedrich von, Johann
Elias) 9 Hauptmann (Gerhart), Suder-
mann (Hermann) 10 Wassermann
(Jakob) *Greek:* 6 Lucian 11 Kazantzakis
(Nikos) *Hungarian:* 5 Jókai (Mór) *Icelandic:* 7 Laxness (Halldór) *Indian:*
7 Rushdie (Salman) *Irish:* 5 Behan
(Brendan), Doyle (Roddy), Joyce
(James), Moore (Brian), Wilde (Oscar)
6 O'Brien (Edna), Stoker (Bram)
7 Beckett (Samuel), O'Connor (Frank),
Russell (George William) 8 O'Faolain
(Julia, Sean), Stephens (James) 9 O'Fla-
herty (Liam) *Italian:* 3 Eco (Umberto)
5 Verga (Giovanni) 6 Silone (Ignazio)
7 Calvino (Italo), Manzoni (Alessan-
dro), Moravia (Alberto) 9 Boccaccio
(Giovanni), Vittorini (Elio) 10 Pirandello (Luigi), Straparola (Gianfrancesco)
Japanese: 7 Mishima (Yukio) 8 Kawa-
bata (Yasunari), Murakami (Haruki),
Murasaki (Shikibu) 9 Yokomitsu
(Riichi), Yoshikawa (Eiji) *Lebanese:*
6 Gibran (Khalil) 7 Fuentes (Carlos)
Nigerian: 6 Achebe (Chinua) 7 Soyinka
(Wole), Tutuola (Amos) *Norwegian:*
3 Lie (Jonas) 6 Hamsun (Knut),
Undset (Sigrid) 7 Rolvaag (Ole)
8 Bjornson (Bjornstjerne), Kielland
(Alexander) *Peruvian:* 11 Vargas Llosa
(Mario) *Polish:* 7 Reymont (Wladyslaw)
8 Zeromski (Stefan) 11 Sienkiewicz
(Henryk) *Portuguese:* 6 Pessoa (Fernan-
do) 8 Saramago (José) *Roman:* 5 Pliny,
Varro (Marcus Terentius) *Russian:*

5 Gogol (Nikolai), Gorki (Maxim),
Gorky (Maxim) 7 Chekhov (Anton),
Pushkin (Alexander), Tolstoy (Leo)
8 Andreyev (Leonid), Turgenev (Ivan),
Zamyatin (Yevgeny) 9 Ehrenburg (Ilya),
Lermontov (Mikhail), Pasternak
(Boris), Sholokhov (Mikhail) 10 Dosto-
evsky (Fyodor) 11 Dostoyevsky
(Fyodor), Yevtushenko (Yevgeny)
12 Solzhenitsyn (Alexander) *Scottish:*
4 Lang (Andrew) 5 Scott (Alexander,
Walter) 6 Barrie (James M.), Buchan
(John) 8 Urquhart (Thomas) 9 Steven-
son (Robert Louis) *South African:*
6 Fugard (Athol) 8 Gordimer (Nadine)
Spanish: 6 Baroja (Pio) 7 Alarcón
(Pedro Antonio de) 9 Cervantes
(Miguel de) *Swedish:* 7 Johnson
(Eyvind), Rydberg (Viktor) 8 Lagerlöf
(Selma) 10 Lagerkvist (Pär), Strindberg
(August) *Swiss:* 4 Wyss (Johann
Rudolf) 5 Spyri (Johanna) 6 Frisch
(Max) 9 Spitteler (Carl) *Trinidadian:*
7 Naipaul (V. S.) *Welsh:* 4 Owen (Alun,
Daniel, Goronwy, John) 5 Evans
(David, Evan), Wynne (Ellis) *Yiddish:*
4 Asch (Sholem) 6 Singer (Isaac Bashe-
vis) 8 Aleichem (Sholem)

authoritarian 5 harsh, rigid 6 despot,
severe, strict, tyrant 8 absolute, autocrat, despotic, dictator, dogmatic
9 imperious, stringent 10 absolutist,
autocratic, oppressive, totalistic,
tyrannical 11 dictatorial, doctrinaire,
domineering, magisterial 12 totalitarian

authoritative 4 sure, true 5 legal, legit,
sound 6 lawful, proven 7 factual
8 accepted, accurate, approved, attested, dogmatic, official, orthodox, reliable, verified 9 canonical, cathedral,
confirmed, imperious, trustable, validated 10 autocratic, commanding,
definitive, dependable, documented,
dominating, ex cathedra, legitimate,
sanctioned 11 dictatorial, doctrinaire,
domineering, irrefutable, magisterial,
overbearing, trustworthy 12 indisputable

authority 4 rule, sway 5 clout, force,
power, right, say-so 6 agency, charge,
credit, expert, master, weight 7 command, control, grounds, license, mastery, warrant 8 citation, decision,
dominion, prestige 9 influence, testimony 10 domination, governance,
government, management 12 jurisdiction

authorization 4 okay, word 5 leave 6 permit 7 consent, go-ahead, mandate
8 approval, sanction 9 agreement,

allowance, clearance **10** green light, permission, sufferance **11** approbation

authorize 3 let **4** okay, vest **5** allow **6** affirm, enable, invest, permit **7** approve, confirm, empower, endorse, entitle, license, qualify, warrant **8** accredit, sanction, vouch for **9** give leave, recognize **10** commission **11** countenance

auto see AUTOMOBILE

autobahn 7 highway **8** turnpike **10** expressway **12** superhighway

autobiography 4 life, vita **5** diary **6** memoir **7** account, journal **9** life story **11** confessions **13** reminiscences

autochthonous 6 native **7** endemic **8** original **10** aboriginal, indigenous

autocracy 7 czarism, tyranny **8** monarchy **9** despotism, monocracy **12** absolute rule, dictatorship

autocrat 4 czar, duce, emir, lord, raja, shah, tsar, tzar **5** mogul, rajah, ruler **6** caliph, despot, sultan, tyrant **7** magnate, monarch **8** dictator, oligarch, overlord **9** potentate, sovereign **10** absolutist

autocratic 7 haughty **8** absolute, arrogant, despotic **9** arbitrary, imperious, tyrannous **10** monocratic, tyrannical **11** dictatorial, domineering, overbearing

autodidactic 10 self-taught **12** self-educated

autograph 3 ink, pen **4** sign **5** write **7** endorse **8** original **9** signature, subscribe **11** endorsement, John Hancock

Autolycus *daughter:* **8** Anticlea *father:* **6** Hermes **7** Mercury

automated 7 robotic **9** by machine, motorized **10** electrical, electronic, mechanical, mechanized, programmed **12** computerized

automatic 6 reflex **8** habitual **9** impulsive, reflexive **10** mechanical, self-acting, unprompted **11** instinctive, involuntary, perfunctory, spontaneous, unmeditated *prefix:* **4** self

automaton 5 droid, golem, robot **7** android, machine **9** mechanism

automobile 3 bus, car **5** buggy, coupe, racer, sedan **6** jalopy, tourer, wheels **7** flivver, hardtop, machine **8** dragster, motorcar, roadster, runabout **9** hatchback, limousine **11** convertible *American:* **3** Reo **4** Cord, Ford, Jeep, Nash **5** Buick, Dodge, Eagle, Essex, Lexus **6** DeSoto, Hudson, Model A, Model T, Saturn, Willys **7** LaSalle, LeBaron, Lincoln, Maxwell, Mercury, Mustang, Packard, Pontiac, Rambler, Seville **8** Cadillac, Chrysler, Corvette, Eldorado, Franklin, Plymouth **9** Chevrolet, Hupmobile **10** Duesenberg, Oldsmobile, Studebaker **11** Continental, Pierce-Arrow, Thunderbird **12** Kaiser-Frazer *British:* **4** Mini **6** Anglia, Austin, Cooper, DeSoto, Jaguar, Morris **7** Bentley, Daimler, Hillman, Sunbeam, Triumph **8** Vauxhall **10** Range Rover, Rolls-Royce **11** Aston Martin, Land Rover **12** Austin-Healey *French:* **5** Simca **7** Citroën, Peugeot, Renault *German:* **3** BMW **4** Audi, Benz, Opel **7** Daimler, Porsche **8** Mercedes **10** Volkswagen **12** Mercedes-Benz *Italian:* **4** Fiat **6** Lancia **7** Bugatti, Ferrari **8** Maserati **9** Alfa-Romeo **11** Lamborghini *Japanese:* **5** Honda, Isuzu, Mazda **6** Datsun, Nissan, Subaru, Toyota **10** Mitsubishi *Korean:* **3** Kia **6** Daewoo **7** Hyundai *Swedish:* **4** Saab **5** Volvo

automotive pioneer 4 Benz (Carl Friedrich), Ford (Henry), Olds (Ransom), Otto (Nikolaus), Pope (Albert) **5** Evans (Oliver), Rolls (Charles), Roper (Sylvester) **6** Cugnot (Nicholas Joseph), Duryea (Charles E., J. Frank), Lenoir (Etienne), Winton (Alexander) **7** Bugatti (Ettore), Citroën (André-Gustave), Daimler (Gottlieb), Peugeot (Armand), Stanley (Francis, Freelan) **8** Morrison (William) **10** Lanchester (Frederick William)

Autonoë *father:* **6** Cadmus *husband:* **9** Aristaeus *mother:* **8** Harmonia *sister:* **5** Agave *son:* **7** Actaeon

autonomous 4 free **8** autarkic, separate **9** sovereign **10** self-ruling **11** independent, self-reliant **12** self-governed, uncontrolled **13** self-contained, self-governing

autonomy 7 autarky, freedom **8** home rule, self-rule **11** sovereignty **12** independence

autopsy 6 assess **7** examine **8** evaluate, necropsy **10** assessment, dissection, evaluation, postmortem **11** examination

auto racer 4 Foyt (A. J.), Hill (Graham) **5** Clark (Jim), Mears (Rick), Petty (Richard), Unser (Al, Bobby) **6** Carter (Pancho), Fangio (Juan), Vogler (Rich) **7** Brabham (Jack), Stewart (Jackie) **8** Andretti (Mario, Michael), Johncock (Gordon) **9** Earnhardt (Dale) **10** Rutherford (Johnny)

autumn 4 fall **6** season **8** maturity

auxiliary 4 aide **5** spare **6** backup, helper **7** reserve **8** adjutant, adjuvant **9** accessory, ancillary, assistant, coadjutor, secondary **10** accomplice, additional, collateral, subsidiary **11** appurtenant, subservient **12** contributory **13** comple-mentary, supplementary *verb:* **3** are, can, did, had, has, may, was **4** been, does, have, must, were, will **5** could, might, ought, shall, would **6** should

avail 3 aid, use **4** gain, good, help **5** asset, serve **6** profit **7** account, benefit, fitness, satisfy, service **9** advantage, relevance **10** usefulness **13** applicability

available 5 handy, on tap, ready, valid **6** at hand, on hand, usable **7** present, willing **8** prepared **9** qualified **10** accessible, attainable, convenient, obtainable, procurable **11** purchasable

avalanche 4 mass, rush **5** drown, flood, slide **6** deluge **7** overrun, smother **8** inundate, mudslide, overflow, rockfall **9** landslide, overwhelm, rockslide, snowslide **10** inundation **12** accumulation

Avalon 8 paradise

avant-garde 7 radical **8** advanced, contempo **10** innovative, pioneering **11** cutting-edge, leading-edge, progressive **12** experimental **13** up-to-the-minute

avarice 5 greed **7** avidity **8** cupidity, rapacity, voracity **10** greediness **12** covetousness

avaricious 6 grabby, greedy, stingy **7** miserly **8** covetous, esurient, grasping, ravenous **9** mercenary, rapacious **11** acquisitive

avatar 4 type **5** image **7** epitome **8** exemplar **9** archetype **10** apotheosis, embodiment, expression **11** incarnation, reification **13** manifestation

avaunt 4 away **5** hence, leave, scram **6** beat it, depart, get out

ave 4 hail **8** farewell, greeting

avenge 5 repay, right **6** punish **7** get even, pay back, redress, requite **9** fight back, retaliate, vindicate

avenue 3 way **4** path, road **5** drive, means, route, track **6** access, artery, course, street **7** channel, parkway, pathway **8** approach **9** boulevard **10** passageway **12** thoroughfare

aver 4 avow **5** prove, state, swear **6** affirm, allege, assert, attest, avouch, depose, insist, verify **7** declare, profess, protest, testify, warrant **8** maintain **9** guarantee, predicate

average 3 par **4** fair, mean, norm **5** usual **6** common, divide, equate, figure, median, medium, middle, normal **7** balance, even out, typical **8** everyday, midpoint, moderate, ordinary **12** intermediate

averagely 4 so-so **6** enough, fairly, rather **8** passably **9** tolerably **10** moderately

averse 5 balky, loath **6** afraid **7** hostile,

opposed, uneager **8** allergic, hesitant **9** reluctant, resistant, unwilling **10** indisposed **11** disinclined **12** antipathetic

aversion 4 fear, hate **5** dread **6** hatred, horror **7** allergy, disgust, dislike **8** disfavor, distaste, loathing **9** antipathy, disliking, repulsion, revulsion **10** abhorrence, antagonism, repugnance **11** abomination, detestation, displeasure **13** indisposition

aversive 8 ungenial **9** repellent, repugnant **11** uncongenial **12** antipathetic **13** unsympathetic

avert 4 foil, halt, turn, veer, ward **5** avoid, check, deter **6** thwart **7** deflect, fend off, forfend, obviate, prevent, rule out, ward off **8** go around, stave off, turn away **9** forestall, turn aside

avian 6 flying, winged **8** birdlike, ornithic

aviary 4 cage **8** birdcage, dovecote **9** birdhouse, enclosure

aviator 3 ace **4** Post (Wiley) **5** flier, pilot **6** airman, flyboy, Wright (Orville, Wilbur), Yeager (Chuck) **7** birdman, Earhart (Amelia) **8** aeronaut **9** bush pilot, Lindbergh (Charles) **10** Richthofen (Manfred von) **12** Rickenbacker (Eddie)

avid 4 agog, keen **5** eager **6** ardent, greedy, hungry **7** anxious, athirst, craving, fervent, thirsty, zealous **8** appetent, covetous, desirous, grasping **9** impatient **10** breathless, insatiable **12** enthusiastic

avidity 4 zeal **5** greed **6** fervor, thirst **7** avarice, craving **8** cupidity, keenness, rapacity **9** eagerness **10** greediness

Avis *competitor:* **5** Hertz

___ **avis 4** rara

avocation 5 hobby **7** pastime, pursuit **8** sideline **9** amusement, diversion **10** recreation

avoid 4 bilk, duck, miss, shun, snub **5** annul, avert, dodge, elude, evade, shirk, skirt **6** bypass, divert, escape, eschew, pass up **7** abstain, prevent, refrain **8** preclude, sidestep, stay away, withdraw **9** keep clear **11** refrain from **12** keep away from

avoidance 5 dodge **6** escape **7** dodging, elusion, evasion **8** escaping, escapism, eschewal, shirking, shunning **9** runaround **10** abstinence

avouch 3 own **4** aver, avow **5** admit, claim, state, swear **6** affirm, assert, depose, insist **7** certify, confess, confirm, declare, profess, testify **9** predicate, pronounce **11** acknowledge, corroborate

avow 3 own 4 aver 5 admit, allow, grant, let on, own up, state, swear 6 affirm, assert, avouch, depose 7 concede, confess, declare, profess, protest 8 disclose, maintain, proclaim 9 predicate 11 acknowledge

avowal 6 assent 9 admission, assertion, statement 10 profession 11 affirmation, attestation, declaration

avowedly 6 openly 7 frankly 8 candidly 9 allegedly 10 apparently, ostensibly, supposedly

await 4 bide, hope, stay 5 abide 6 expect 7 count on, look for 8 watch for 10 anticipate, hang around

awake 4 stir 5 alert, alive, aware, rouse 6 active, arouse, bestir, excite, revive, roused, stir up 7 animate, aroused, excited, on guard 8 activate, sensible, sentient, vigilant, watchful 9 attentive, cognizant, conscious, observant, stimulate, stirred up

award 4 gift, give, kudo 5 allot, badge, endow, grant, honor, kudos, medal, prize 6 accord, bestow, confer, donate, trophy 7 concede, laurels, tribute 8 accolade, citation, donation 9 vouchsafe 10 blue ribbon, decoration, distribute 11 distinction *motion picture:* 5 Oscar 7 Academy 11 Golden Globe *mystery novel:* 5 Edgar *record:* 6 Grammy *science-fiction:* 4 Hugo *television:* 4 Emmy *theater:* 4 Tony

aware 4 onto 5 alert, alive, awake 7 heedful, knowing, mindful, tuned in, witting 8 informed, sensible, sentient, vigilant 9 attentive, au courant, cognizant, conscious, observant 10 conversant, perceptive 12 apprehensive 13 knowledgeable

awash 4 full 6 afloat, filled, jammed, loaded, packed 7 brimful, covered, crammed, crowded, flooded, run-over, stuffed 8 brimming, chockful 9 chockfull 11 overflowing

away 3 far, fro, now, off, out 4 afar, gone 5 along, apart, aside, forth, hence 6 abroad, absent, afield, far off 7 distant, lacking, missing, not here 9 elsewhere 11 incessantly 12 continuously

away from 6 beyond

awe 5 alarm, amaze, scare 6 wonder 7 inspire, startle 8 astonish 9 amazement, reverence 10 veneration, wonderment 11 flabbergast 12 astonishment

aweless 4 bold 5 brave 7 valiant 8 fearless, intrepid, unafraid 9 dauntless, undaunted 10 courageous

awesome 6 august 7 amazing, sublime 8 imposing, terrific, wondrous 10 for-midable, impressive 11 astonishing 12 breathtaking 13 extraordinary

awful 3 bad 4 very 5 nasty 6 odious 7 hateful 8 dreadful, horrible, horrific, shocking, terrible, terrific 9 appalling, atrocious, extremely, frightful, loath-some, offensive 10 deplorable, disgusting, formidable

awfully 4 much, very 6 hugely, vastly 7 greatly 8 terribly, whopping 9 extremely, immensely 10 dreadfully, enormously 11 exceedingly

awhile 7 briefly 8 for a time 11 temporarily

awkward 5 gawky, inept, messy, nerdy, splay 6 clumsy, gauche, klutzy, wooden 7 artless, gawkish, halting, lumpish, unhandy, unhappy 8 bumbling, bungling, tactless, ungainly 9 graceless, ham-handed, ill-chosen, inelegant, lumbering, maladroit 10 blundering, ungraceful, unskillful 11 heavy-handed, unfortunate 12 embarrassing, incommodious, inconvenient, infelicitous

awl 4 tool 7 piercer

awning 6 canopy 7 marquee 8 sunshade *ancient Roman:* 8 velarium

awry 5 amiss, askew, wrong 6 astray 7 askance, crooked 8 cockeyed 9 cock-a-hoop, crookedly *Scottish:* 5 agley

ax, axe 3 can, hew 4 adze, boot, chop, fire, sack 6 bounce 7 boot out, chopper, cleaver, dismiss, hatchet, kick out 8 tomahawk 9 discharge, terminate *blade:* 3 bit *handle:* 5 helve

axiom 3 law 4 rule 5 adage, maxim, moral, truth 6 dictum, truism 7 precept, theorem 8 aphorism, apothegm 9 postulate, principle 10 principium 11 fundamental

axiomatic 5 given 7 assumed, certain, obvious 8 accepted, absolute, manifest, provable 10 aphoristic, understood 11 fundamental, indubitable, self-evident 12 unquestioned

axis 4 line, pole, stem 5 point, pivot 8 alliance 9 continuum, plant stem 11 partnership 12 straight line, turning point

axle 3 bar, pin, rod 4 beam 5 bogie, shaft 7 spindle, support

aye 3 yea, yep, yes 4 amen, okay, ever, vote 6 agreed, always 8 all right 11 affirmative, continually

Azerbaijan *capital:* 4 Baku *city:* 5 Gäncä 8 Sumqayit *exclave:* 8 Naxçivan 11 Nakhichevan *monetary unit:* 5 manat *neighbor:* 4 Iran 6 Russia 7 Armenia, Georgia *river:* 4 Kura 5 Araks *sea:* 7 Caspian

Azores *capital:* 12 Ponta Delgada *city:*
5 Horta *island:* 4 Pico 5 Corvo, Faial,
Lajes 6 Flores 8 São Jorge, Terceura
9 São Miguel 10 Santa Maria *part of:*
8 Portugal
Aztec *capital:* 12 Tenochtitlán *conqueror:*
6 Cortés, Cortéz *emperor:* 9 Moctezu-
ma, Montezuma *god:* 4 Xipe 6 Tlaloc
9 Xipetotec 12 Quetzalcoatl *hero:*
4 Nata *language:* 7 Nahuatl *temple:*
8 teocalli
azure 3 sky 4 blue 5 color 7 sky blue

B

baa 5 bleat
Babbitt 10 conformist, middlebrow, philistine *author:* 5 Lewis (Sinclair)
babble 3 gab, jaw, yak, yap 4 blab, chat,
go on, gush, rant, rave 5 clack, prate,
run on 6 burble, drivel, gibber, gossip,
jabber, murmur, patter, piffle, rattle,
yammer 7 blabber, blather, chatter,
maunder, palaver, prattle, twaddle
8 nonsense, idle talk 9 gibberish 11 jabberwocky
babe 3 cub, tot 4 doll, girl 5 bairn,
child, chick, cutie, woman 6 infant,
hottie 7 bambino, papoose, neonate,
newborn 8 bantling, nursling
babel 3 ado, din, row 4 to-do 5 hoo-ha
6 bedlam, clamor, hubbub, jangle, outcry, racket, ruckus, tumult, uproar
7 clangor, discord, ferment, turmoil
8 brouhaha, clangour, foofaraw
9 cacophony, commotion, confusion
10 dissonance, hullabaloo, hurly-burly,
turbulence 11 pandemonium 12 vocif-
eration
baboon 3 oaf 4 clod, dolt, goon, lout
6 chacma, galoot, simian 7 palooka
8 lunkhead, mandrill, meathead
9 hamadryas
babushka 6 granny 7 bandana 8 bandanna, kerchief
baby 3 pet, tot 4 tiny 5 bairn, sissy, spoil
6 cocker, coddle, cosset, dote on,
infant, pamper 7 bambino, cater to,
indulge, neonate, newborn, papoose,
toddler 8 bantling, dote upon,
nursling, suckling, weanling 11 mollycoddle *ailment:* 5 colic, croup *bed:*
4 crib 6 cradle 8 bassinet *bedroom:*
7 nursery *breechcloth:* 6 diaper *cap:*
6 biggin, bonnet *carriage:* 4 pram
5 buggy 8 stroller 12 perambulator

doctor: 12 pediatrician *food:* 3 pap
4 milk 6 pablum 7 pabulum *garment:*
7 rompers *Italian:* 7 bambino *napkin:*
3 bib *outfit:* 7 layette *powder:* 4 talc
shoe: 6 bootee *Spanish:* 4 bebé, nene
baby grand 5 piano
babyhood 7 infancy 10 diaper days,
immaturity
babyish 5 petty 7 foolish, puerile,
spoiled 8 childish, immature, juvenile
9 infantile, infantine
Babylonian 6 lavish 9 luxurious *abode of*
the dead: 5 Aralu *capital:* 7 Babylon
chaos: 4 Apsu *city:* 5 Akkad 6 Cunaxa
crown prince: 10 Belshazzar *division:*
5 Akkad, Sumer *earth mother:* 6 Ishtar
first ruler: 6 Nimrod *god:* 3 Bel 6 Marduk, Tammuz *goddess:* 5 Belit 6 Ishtar
hero: 9 Gilgamesh *king:* 6 Sargon
9 Hammurabi 12 Ashurbanipal *river:*
6 Tigris 9 Euphrates *sun god:* 3 Bel
7 Shamash *tower:* 5 Babel 8 ziggurat
waters: 4 Apsu 6 Tiamat *winged dragon:*
6 Tiamat
baccalaureate 6 degree 9 bachelor's
10 graduation
bacchanal 6 maenad see also BACCHA-
NALIA
bacchanalia 4 bash, orgy 5 binge, revel,
spree 6 bender, excess 7 blowout,
carouse, debauch, revelry, wassail
8 carnival, festival, wingding 11 celebration, dissipation, merrymaking
bacchanalian 4 wild 7 drunken, riotous
8 frenzied 9 debauched, orgiastic
12 intoxicating *cry* 4 evoe 5 evohe
Bacchus 8 Dionysus *attendant:* 6 maenad 9 bacchante *father:* 4 Zeus
7 Jupiter *lover:* 5 Venus 9 Aphrodite
mother: 6 Semele *son:* 7 Priapus *staff:*
7 thyrsus

Bach, Johann Sebastian *birthplace:*
8 Eisenach *genre:* 5 fugue, motet, suite
6 sonata 7 cantata, chorale, partita,
prelude, toccata 8 concerto, fantasia,
oratorio, sinfonia *home:* 7 Leipzig
instrument: 5 organ 11 harpsichord
musical style: 7 baroque *religion:*
8 Lutheran

back 3 aft, aid 4 abet, fund, help, hind,
rear 5 abaft, about, dorsa (plural),
spine, stake 6 assist, astern, dorsum,
hinder, recede, uphold 7 endorse,
finance, promote, retract, retreat,
reverse, sponsor, support 8 advocate,
bankroll, champion, rearward, side
with 9 in reverse, posterior, retrocede,
subsidize 10 retrograde *ailment:* 7 lumbago 10 rheumatism *of an arthropod:*
6 tergum *of an insect:* 5 notum *of the
neck:* 4 nape 6 scruff *prefix:* 4 post
5 retro *relating to:* 6 dorsal

back answer 3 lip 6 retort 7 riposte
8 comeback, repartee 9 rejoinder,
wisecrack 10 return, shot
11 parting shot

backbite 4 slam, slur 5 abuse, decry,
knock, libel, smear, sully, taint
6 defame, defile, malign, vilify
7 asperse, put down, run down, slander, traduce 8 bad-mouth, belittle,
besmirch, derogate, diminish 9 denigrate, discredit

backbiter 6 gossip 7 defamer, traitor
9 detractor, slanderer 10 talebearer

backbiting 5 abuse, smear, spite 6 gossip
7 abusing, calumny, obloquy, scandal,
slander 8 libelous, smearing 9 aspersion, cattiness, gossiping, invective,
maligning, traducing, vilifying
10 calumnious, defamation, defamatory, scandalous, slandering, slanderous 11 denigration 12 belittlement,
depreciation, spitefulness, vituperation
13 disparagement

backbone 4 base, grit, guts, will 5 basis,
moxie, nerve, spine, spunk 6 mettle,
pillar, rachis 7 resolve, support 8 mainstay, tenacity 9 character, fortitude,
framework, toughness, vertebrae
10 foundation, moral fiber, resolution
12 spinal column 13 determination,
steadfastness

backbreaking 6 taxing, tiring 7 arduous,
onerous 8 grueling, toilsome 9 fatiguing, gruelling, laborious, punishing,
strenuous, torturous, wearisome
10 burdensome, exhausting

backchat 6 banter, gossip 10 persiflage

backcomb 5 tease

backcountry 4 bush 6 sticks 7 boonies,
outback 8 frontier, interior 9 boondocks 10 hinterland

backcourtman 5 guard

back down 4 balk 5 admit, demur,
welsh, yield 6 beg off, bow out, cry off,
give in, give up, recall, recant, renege
7 concede, disavow, retract, retreat 8
take back, withdraw 9 surrender,
weasel out 10 chicken out

backdrop 6 milieu 7 climate, context,
scenery, setting 8 stage set 10 atmosphere, background 11 environment,
mise-en-scène 12 surroundings

backer 4 ally 5 angel 6 patron, surety
7 sponsor 8 advocate, defender, exponent, follower, investor, promoter
9 auxiliary, guarantor, proponent, supporter 10 bankroller, benefactor, meal
ticket

backfire 4 fail 5 blast 6 fizzle, go awry
7 go amiss, go wrong 8 miscarry, ricochet 9 boomerang, discharge, explosion
10 disappoint, spring back 11 fall
through 13 counteraction

backgammon *board section:* 5 table
piece: 5 stone *wedge:* 5 point

background 4 base, tone 6 milieu 7 history, scenery, setting 8 heritage, training 9 education 10 experience, supporting 13 circumstances, qualification

backhanded 7 devious, oblique 8 indirect, derisive, sneering 9 insulting, sarcastic 10 roundabout 12 disingenuous
13 condescending *compliment:* 6 insult,
slight 7 put-down 9 aspersion

backing 3 aid 4 help 5 aegis, funds 7 harmony, support 8 auspices 9 patronage,
promotion 10 assistance 11 endorsement, sponsorship 13 accompaniment,
encouragement

backland see BACKCOUNTRY

backlash 5 slack 6 recoil 8 kickback,
reaction, response, ricochet 11 retaliation 12 repercussion

backlog 4 pile 5 hoard, stock, store
6 pile up, supply 7 nest egg, reserve
9 inventory, reservoir, stockpile
12 accumulation

back of 5 abaft 6 behind 9 following

back off see BACK DOWN

back out 4 quit 5 leave, welsh, yield
6 beg off, desert, give up, renege 7 forsake 8 withdraw 9 surrender

backpack 4 gear, hike 5 tramp 6 duffel,
ramble 8 knapsack, rucksack 9 haversack

backpedal see BACK DOWN

backset see SETBACK

backside 3 bum 4 butt, rear, rump, seat,
tail, tush 5 fanny, hiney, stern 6 behind,
bottom, breech, far end, heinie 8 but-

tocks, derriere, haunches **9** fundament, posterior **12** hindquarters

backslide 4 fall, sink, slip **5** lapse **6** return, revert **7** go wrong, regress, relapse **9** retrovert **10** degenerate, go downhill, recidivate **11** deteriorate

backstabbing 4 slur **5** smear **6** malice **7** calumny, scandal, slander **8** betrayal **9** treachery **10** defamation, detraction, traitorous **11** treacherous **12** belittlement, depreciation, vilification **13** disparagement

backstairs 6 covert, secret, sneaky, sordid **7** furtive **8** hush-hush **9** secretive **10** scandalous **11** clandestine, underhanded **13** surreptitious

backstop 5 fence **6** screen, uphold **7** bolster, support **8** advocate, champion, side with

back talk 3 lip **4** guff, sass **5** cheek, mouth, sauce **9** freshness, impudence, insolence **12** impertinence

backtrack 7 regress, retrace, retreat, reverse **8** turn tail

backward 4 dull, slow, rear **5** abaft, dense **6** averse, astern, behind, stupid **7** awkward, delayed, moronic **9** ignorant, inverted, rearward, retarded, reversed, stagnant **9** benighted, dimwitted, in reverse **10** half-witted, retrograde, slow-witted, uncultured **11** thickheaded, turned around, undeveloped **12** feebleminded, simpleminded, uncultivated **13** unprogressive

backwoods see BACKCOUNTRY

backwoodsman 4 hick, rube **5** swain, yokel **6** rustic **7** bumpkin, hayseed **9** hillbilly **10** clodhopper, country boy, provincial **11** mountaineer

bacon *side:* **6** flitch, gammon *slice:* **6** rasher

Bacon, Francis *work:* **12** Novum Organum

bacteria 5 cocci **7** bacilli, vibrios **8** spirilla *culture medium:* **4** agar *destroyer:* **10** antibiotic

bacterial disease 6 plague, typhus **7** anthrax, leprosy, tetanus, typhoid **8** botulism, syphilis **9** gonorrhea, infection, pneumonia **10** diphtheria, meningitis **11** shigellosis

bacteriologist *American:* **6** Enders (John Franklin) **7** Noguchi (Hideyo), Theiler (Max) *British:* **7** Fleming (Alexander) *French:* **5** Widal (Fernand) **7** Nicolle (Charles-Jean-Henri), Pasteur (Louis) *German:* **4** Cohn (Ferdinand Julius), Koch (Robert) **5** Klebs (Edwin) **7** Behring (Emil von), Löffler (Friedrich) **10** Wassermann (August von) *Japanese:* **8** Kitasato

(Shibasaburo) *Russian:* **11** Metchnikoff (Elie) *Swiss:* **6** Yersin (Alexandre-Emile-John)

bad 3 ill, low **4** evil, foul, sour **5** amiss, awful, lousy, wrong **6** crummy, putrid, rancid, rotten, sinful, wicked **7** harmful, hateful, hurtful, immoral, naughty, noisome, noxious, spoiled, tainted, vicious **8** damaging, dreadful, inferior, perverse, terrible, wretched **9** abhorrent, defective, execrable, injurious, loathsome, obnoxious, offensive, putrefied, reprobate, repulsive, sickening **10** disgusting, iniquitous **11** deleterious, detrimental, distasteful, intolerable **12** unacceptable **13** objectionable *comparative:* **5** worse *prefix:* **3** dys, mis *superlative:* **5** worst

Badebec *husband:* **9** Gargantua *son:* **10** Pantagruel

Baden 3 spa **6** resort **9** hot spring

badge 3 pin **4** arms, logo, mark, seal, sign **5** award, honor, kudos, medal, token **6** button, emblem, ensign **7** laurels **8** accolade, hallmark, insignia **10** coat of arms, decoration **11** distinction, purple heart

badger 3 bug, nag **4** bait, goad, ride **5** annoy, brock, chivy, harry, hound **6** chivvy, harass, hassle, heckle, hector, needle, pester, plague **7** torment **8** bullyrag **9** importune

Badger State 9 Wisconsin

badinage 4 play **6** banter, joking **7** jesting, joshing, kidding, ribbing, teasing **8** backchat, chitchat, repartee **9** cross talk **10** persiflage

badland 4 wild **5** waste, wilds **6** barren, desert **7** outback **8** wildness **10** wilderness **11** hill country

bad mark 3 gig **7** demerit **9** poor grade

bad-tempered 4 dour, sour **5** cross, sulky, surly, testy **6** crabby, cranky, crusty, grumpy, ornery, sullen, touchy **7** grouchy, peevish **8** choleric, petulant **9** crotchety, dyspeptic, irascible, irritable, splenetic **10** ill-humored, illnatured, unpleasant **11** quarrelsome **12** cantankerous, curmudgeonly, disagreeable, misanthropic

Baedeker 5 guide **6** manual **8** handbook **9** guidebook, vade mecum **10** compendium **11** enchiridion, travel guide

baffle 4 balk, foil **5** addle, block, floor, mix up, stump **6** bemuse, hinder, impede, muddle, puzzle, thwart **7** barrier, confuse, flummox, mystify, nonplus, perplex **8** befuddle, bewilder, confound **9** deflector, dumbfound, frustrate **10** circumvent, disappoint, disconcert

bafflement 9 confusion 10 bemusement, perplexity 12 bewilderment

bag 3 cop, nab, kit, net, sag, win 4 flop, grip, hook, kill, land, nail, poke, sack, tote, trap 5 biddy, bulge, catch, crone, forgo, pouch, purse, seize, shoot, snare, steal, udder 6 beldam, collar, duffel, duffle, give up, secure, valise 7 abandon, acquire, capture, satchel 8 backpack, knapsack, reticule, suitcase 9 apprehend, haversack 12 protuberance

bagatelle 6 trifle, whimsy 9 plaything

baggage 4 gear 5 hussy, stuff, tramp, trull, wench 6 burden, things, wanton 7 carry-on, effects, jezebel, luggage, parcels, trollop 8 obstacle, matériel, slattern, strumpet 9 equipment, hindrance 10 impediment, prostitute 11 impedimenta 13 paraphernalia

baggy 5 loose

Baghdad *founder:* 6 Mansur *river:* 6 Tigris

bagnio 4 crib, stew 7 brothel, lupanar 8 bordello, cathouse 10 bawdy house, whorehouse

bagpipe *part:* 5 drone 7 bourdon, chanter *sound:* 5 skirl

Bahamas *capital:* 6 Nassau *island:* 3 Cat 5 Abaco 6 Andros, Inagua 7 Watling 9 Eleuthera, Mayaguana 11 Grand Bahama, San Salvador 13 New Providence *language:* 7 English *monetary unit:* 6 dollar *neighbor:* 4 Cuba

Bahrain *capital:* 6 Manama *island:* 6 Sitrah 7 Bahrain 10 Al Muharraq *language:* 6 Arabic *monetary unit:* 5 dinar

bail 3 bar, dip 4 bond, flee, lade 5 ladle, scoop 6 handle, pledge, surety 7 release 8 guaranty, security, warranty 9 guarantee 10 collateral 12 recognizance

bailiwick 4 area, turf, zone 5 field, realm 6 domain, sphere 7 demesne, purview, terrain 8 district, dominion, province 9 champaign, specialty, territory 10 discipline 12 jurisdiction

bailout 3 aid 6 relief, rescue 7 subsidy 11 benefaction, deliverance

bairn 3 kid, tot 4 babe, baby, tyke 5 child 6 infant

bait 3 nag, try, vex 4 lure, ride, trap 5 abuse, chase, chivy, decoy, harry, hound, leger, snare, taunt, tease, tempt, worry 6 allure, badger, come-on, entice, entrap, harass, heckle, hector, lead on, molest, pester, seduce 7 beguile, torment, torture 8 bullyrag, inveigle, ridicule 9 persecute, seduction, sweetener 10 attraction, allurement, enticement, temptation *and switch:* 4 lure 5 trick 8 inveigle 10 substitute

bake 4 burn, char, cook, fire, kiln 5 broil, roast, toast 6 scorch 7 scallop, scollop, swelter

baked clay 7 ceramic

baker's dozen 8 thirteen

bakers' yeast 6 leaven 9 leavening

baking 3 hot 5 fiery 6 red-hot, torrid 7 burning 8 broiling, scalding, sizzling, white-hot 9 scorching *chamber:* 4 kiln, oven

baksheesh 3 tip 4 alms 5 bribe, favor 6 grease, reward 7 payment 8 gratuity 9 emolument 12 compensation

Balaam *beast:* 3 ass 6 donkey *father:* 4 Beor

balance 4 rest 5 level, scale, weigh 6 adjust, excess, make up, offset, set off, square, stasis 7 harmony, remains, remnant, residue 8 atone for, equalize, outweigh, residual, residuum, symmetry 9 composure, congruity, equipoise, harmonize, remainder, stability 10 compensate, counteract, difference, equanimity, neutralize, proportion, steadiness 11 consistency, countervail, equilibrium, self-control 12 counterpoise

balanced 4 fair 5 equal 6 offset, stable, steady 7 equable, weighed 9 equitable, impartial 10 evenhanded, harmonized, stabilized

balcony 6 piazza 7 catwalk, gallery 8 platform 9 mezzanine *section:* 4 loge

bald 4 bare, nude 5 blunt, naked, plain, stark 6 barren, severe, shaven, smooth 8 glabrous, hairless, palpable, treeless 9 depilated, unadorned, uncovered 10 deforested, forthright 11 undisguised, unvarnished

baldachin 4 silk 6 canopy, fabric

Balder, Baldur *father:* 4 Odin *mother:* 5 Frigg 6 Frigga *slayer:* 3 Höd 4 Hoth, Loke, Loki 5 Hoder, Hothr *wife:* 5 Nanna

balderdash 3 rot 4 bosh, bull, bunk 5 bilge, crock, hooey 6 blague, bunkum, drivel 7 baloney, eyewash, garbage, hogwash, palaver, rubbish, twaddle 8 buncombe, claptrap, malarkey, nonsense, tommyrot 9 poppycock 10 tomfoolery 11 foolishness 13 horsefeathers

bald-faced 4 bold 6 arrant, brazen 7 blatant, defiant 8 impudent, insolent 9 audacious, shameless, unabashed 11 impertinent

baldness 8 alopecia 12 hairlessness

baldpate 7 widgeon 8 skinhead

Baldwin, James *essay:* 17 Nobody Knows My Name, Notes of a Native Son *novel:* 12 Fire Next Time (The)

13 Giovanni's Room 14 Another Country 21 Go Tell It on the Mountain *play:* 21 Blues for Mister Charlie

balefire 6 beacon 9 watchfire

baleful 4 dire, evil 6 deadly, malign 7 direful, fateful, harmful, hostile, malefic, ominous 8 menacing, sinister 9 ill-boding, ill-omened, malignant 10 maleficent, malevolent, pernicious 11 apocalyptic, threatening 12 unpropitious

balk 3 bar, gag, jib, shy 4 beam, dash, foil, ruin 5 block, check, demur, plank, stall 6 baffle, boggle, desist, flinch, hinder, rafter, refuse, thwart 7 prevent, scruple, stumble 8 hang back, hesitate, obstruct 9 frustrate, hindrance 10 circumvent, disappoint

balky 5 loath 6 averse, ornery, mulish, unruly 7 froward, restive, wayward, willful 8 contrary, hesitant, perverse, stubborn 9 immovable, obstinate, reluctant 10 unreliable 11 intractable, wrongheaded 12 cross-grained, recalcitrant 13 uncooperative, unpredictable

ball 3 orb, wad 4 prom 5 dance, globe, round 6 sphere 8 spheroid *batted high:* 3 fly *batted straight:* 5 liner *of thread or yarn:* 4 clew *ornamental:* 6 pom-pom, pompon *tiny:* 7 globule

ballad 3 lay 4 poem, song *singer:* 8 minstrel 10 troubadour

ballast 4 load 5 poise 6 steady 7 balance, freight 8 balancer 9 stabilize, weigh down 10 dead weight, stabilizer 12 counterpoise 13 counterweight

ballerina 6 dancer 8 coryphée, danseuse 9 toe dancer 11 dancing girl see DANCER

ballet 4 Agon 6 Apollo, Jewels, Sylvia 7 Giselle, Orpheus 8 Bayadère (La), Coppélia, Firebird (The), Raimonda, Raymonda, Swan Lake, Sylphide (La) 9 Fancy Free, Petrushka, Sylphides (Les) 10 Don Quixote, Nutcracker (The), Petrouchka 12 Rite of Spring (The) *costume:* 4 tutu 6 tights 7 leotard *dancer:* 7 danseur 8 coryphée, danseuse 9 ballerina *for two:* 9 pas de deux *handrail:* 5 barre *jump:* 4 jeté 9 entrechat *knee bend:* 4 plié *position:* 6 pointe 8 attitude 9 arabesque *step:* 3 pas 8 glissade *turn:* 6 chaîné 9 pirouette

ball game see at GAME

Ballo in Maschera composer 5 Verdi (Giuseppe)

balloon sail 9 spinnaker

ball-shaped 7 globoid, globose 8 globular, spheroid 9 globulous, spherical

ball up 4 clew, daze 5 addle 6 fuddle, jumble, muddle, puzzle, tangle 7 confuse, fluster 8 befuddle, bewilder, bollix up, confound, distract, throw off 9 disorient

ballyhoo 4 hype, tout 6 blazon, herald, hoopla, hubbub, tumult 7 promote, trumpet 8 brouhaha 9 commotion, publicity 12 extravaganza

balm 4 lull 5 aroma, cream, quiet, salve, scent, spice 6 chrism, relief, remedy, solace 7 anodyne, bouquet, comfort, incense, perfume, soother, unction, unguent 8 easement, ointment 9 emollient, fragrance, redolence 10 palliative 11 consolation, restorative

balmacaan 8 overcoat

balm of Gilead 6 poplar 7 soother 8 restorer 9 balsam fir 11 restorative 12 balsam poplar

balmy 4 calm, daft, mild, nuts, soft 5 crazy, loony, nutty, potty, silly, sweet, wacky 6 gentle, insane, smooth 7 cracked, foolish, lenient, summery 8 aromatic, deranged, fragrant, perfumed, peaceful, pleasant, pleasing, redolent, soothing, tropical 9 agreeable, ambrosial, temperate

baloney 3 rot 4 bosh, bull, bunk 5 bilge, hokum, hooey 6 bunkum, humbug 7 hogwash, rubbish 8 buncombe, claptrap, nonsense 9 poppycock 10 balderdash 11 foolishness

balsam poplar 9 tacamahac 12 balm of Gilead

Balthazar's gift 5 myrrh

Baltic *native:* 4 Lett 7 Latvian 8 Estonian 10 Lithuanian *state:* 6 Latvia 7 Estonia 9 Lithuania

Baltic native 4 Lett, Sorb, Wend 7 Latvian 8 Estonian, Prussian 10 Lithuanian

balustrade 4 rail 5 fence 7 railing 8 banister, handrail

Balzac character 4 Pons (Cousin) 5 Bette (Cousin) 6 Goriot (Père), Vidocq 7 Chabert (Colonel), Eugénie (Grandet), Grandet, Vautrin 8 Rubempré (Lucien de) 9 Birotteau, Rastignac (Eugène de) 13 Henri de Marsay

Bambi author 6 Salten (Felix)

bambino 3 kid, tot 4 babe, baby, tyke 5 bairn, child 6 cherub, Christ, infant, moppet, nipper 7 toddler

bamboozle 3 con 4 bilk, dupe, fool, gull, hoax, scam 5 stump, trick 6 baffle, befool, diddle, puzzle 7 chicane, confuse, deceive, defraud, mislead, perplex, swindle 8 befuddle, confound, flimflam, hoodwink, throw off 9 frustrate 11 hornswoggle

ban 3 bar 5 curse, taboo 6 enjoin, forbid, outlaw 7 censure, exclude 8 anathema, prohibit, suppress 9 damnation, interdict, proscribe 10 injunction 11 forbiddance, malediction, prohibition, suppression **12** denunciation, interdiction, proscription

Ban *ally:* **6** Arthur *son:* **8** Lancelot

banal 4 blah, dull, flat **5** bland, corny, ho-hum, tired, trite, usual, vapid **6** common, jejune, stupid **7** clichéd, humdrum, insipid, prosaic, sapless, trivial **8** ordinary **9** hackneyed, quotidian, wearisome **10** namby-pamby, pedestrian, uninspired, wishy-washy **11** commonplace

banality 5 ennui **6** cliché, old saw, truism **7** bromide, inanity, old song **8** chestnut, monotony, prosaism **9** platitude **10** dreariness, shibboleth, triviality **11** commonplace, old chestnut, tediousness

banausic 4 blah, drab, dull, poky **6** dreary, earthy, stodgy **7** humdrum, mundane, routine, secular, sensual, tedious, worldly **8** everyday, material, plodding, temporal, workaday **9** practical, pragmatic **10** monotonous, pedestrian **11** acquisitive, utilitarian **13** materialistic, uninteresting

band 4 belt, bevy, club, crew, gang, gird, sash, tape **5** bunch, corps, covey, group, horde, party, strap, strip, troop, unite **6** concur, fillet, girdle, league, outfit, ribbon, team up, troupe **7** cluster, combine, company, coterie **8** cincture, engirdle, ensemble, symphony **9** cooperate, orchestra **10** federation *Mexican:* **8** mariachi *neck:* **6** torque *small:* **5** combo

bandage 4 bind **5** cover, dress, gauze, truss **6** swathe **7** plaster, swaddle **8** compress, dressing

bandanna 8 babushka, kerchief **9** headscarf **11** neckerchief

bandeau 3 bra **5** strip **6** fillet, ribbon, stripe **7** tube top **8** swimwear **9** brassiere

banderilla 4 dart

banderole 4 flag, jack **6** banner, burgee, colors, ensign, pennon, scroll **7** pennant **8** bannerol, standard, streamer

bandicoot 3 rat

bandit 6 outlaw, raider, robber, sacker **7** brigand, cateran, forager, ravager **8** marauder, pillager **9** cutthroat, desperado, holdup man, plunderer **10** freebooter, highwayman **11** bushwhacker

bandleader 7 maestro **9** conductor

bandolier 4 belt, sash

bandwagon 3 fad **4** chic, mode, rage **5** craze, style, trend, vogue **7** fashion

bandy 3 bat **4** flip, swap, toss **5** argue, bowed **6** banter **7** discuss, shuffle **8** exchange **9** bowlegged, pass about **11** interchange

bane 3 woe **4** pest, ruin **5** curse, death, venom, virus **6** blight, burden, plague, poison **7** bugaboo, bugbear, scourge, torment, undoing **8** anathema, calamity, downfall, nuisance **9** bête noire, contagion, destroyer, ruination **10** affliction, pestilence **11** destruction

baneful 4 dire, evil **5** fatal **6** deadly **7** fateful, harmful, hurtful, malefic, noxious, ominous **9** ill-boding, ill-omened, injurious, malignant, pestilent, unhealthy **10** disastrous, pernicious **11** apocalyptic, deleterious, pestiferous, threatening **12** pestilential, unpropitious

bang 3 bat, box, hit, pop, rap **4** bash, beat, belt, blow, boom, bump, clap, peal, push, rape, shot, slam, sock, wham, whop **5** blast, burst, crack, crash, noise, pound, punch, smack, smash, sound, vigor, whack **6** fringe, report, strike, thrill, wallop **7** collide, exactly, resound **8** smack-dab, squarely **9** explosion **10** detonation

banger 7 athlete, sausage

Bangkok native 4 Thai

Bangladesh *capital:* **5** Dacca, Dhaka *city:* **6** Khulna **10** Chittagong *former name:* **6** Bengal *language:* **7** Bengali *monetary unit:* **4** taka *neighbor:* **5** Burma, India **7** Myanmar *river:* **5** Padma **6** Ganges, Jamuna **11** Brahmaputra

bangle 4 disk **5** charm **6** anklet, bauble **7** pendant, trinket **8** bracelet, wristlet

bang-up 3 ace **4** fine **5** dandy, primo, super **6** far-out, superb **7** capital **8** champion, fabulous, five-star, splendid, top-notch **9** excellent, first-rate **10** first-class **11** spectacular

banish 3 ban **4** oust **5** debar, eject, evict, exile, expel **6** deport, dispel, put out, run out **7** cast out, dismiss, exclude, shut out, turn out **8** drive out, relegate, send away **9** discharge, ostracize, rusticate, transport **10** expatriate **13** excommunicate

banishment 5 exile **7** banning **8** eviction **9** discharge, expulsion, ostracism **10** dispelling, relegation **11** deportation, dissolution **12** displacement

banister 3 bar **4** rail **7** railing **10** balustrade

bank 3 row **4** edge, heap, hill, mass, pile, rank, save, tier, tilt **5** amass, array, beach, coast, group, hoard, levee, mound, pitch, shore, slope, stack, stash **6** coffer, dealer, invest, margin, rivage, strand **7** deposit, incline, lay away, pyramid **8** lakeside, lay aside, salt away, seafront, set aside, sock away, squirrel, treasury **9** riverside **10** repository, storehouse **11** credit union **12** squirrel away

bank on 5 trust **7** believe
bankroll 4 back, fund **5** endow, funds, stake **6** pay for **7** capital, finance, sponsor, support **9** grubstake, subsidize **10** capitalize, underwrite
bankrupt 4 bare, bust, do in, ruin **5** break, drain, empty, strip, spent, use up, wreck **6** broken, divest, failed, fold up **7** deplete, deprive, exhaust, lacking, sterile **8** depleted, indebted **9** destitute, exhausted, pauperize, penniless **10** impoverish **12** impoverished
bankruptcy 4 lack, ruin **6** penury **7** failure **9** depletion, ruination, sterility, total loss **10** barrenness, exhaustion, insolvency **11** destitution, liquidation
banned 5 taboo **6** barred **7** illegal, illicit, tabooed **8** enjoined, verboten **9** forbidden **10** contraband, disallowed, prohibited, proscribed **11** interdicted
banner 4 flag, jack **6** burgee, ensign, pennon **7** pendant, pennant **8** banderol, gonfalon, standard, streamer **9** banderole *Roman:* **7** labarum **8** vexillum
bannerol see BANDEROLE
banquet 4 feed **5** feast **6** dinner, regale, repast, spread
banquette 4 seat, sofa **5** bench, shelf **8** platform, sidewalk
Banquo 5 ghost *murderer:* **7** Macbeth
banshee 6 keener, wailer
bantam 3 wee **4** arch, fowl, mini, pert, runt, tiny **5** dwarf, saucy, small **6** cheeky, little, petite **8** insolent, malapert **9** combative, undersize **10** diminutive, undersized
banter 3 fun, kid, rag, rib, wit **4** fool, jest, jive, joke, josh, razz **5** chaff, dally, jolly, tease **7** jesting, joshing, kidding, mockery, ragging, razzing, ribbing, teasing **8** backchat, back talk, badinage, chitchat, drollery, exchange, repartee **9** challenge, small talk **10** persiflage, pleasantry **11** give-and-take
bantling 4 babe, baby **5** bairn **6** infant **7** bambino, newborn, papoose
baptize 3 dip, dub **4** call, name, soak **5** douse, title **6** anoint, drench, purify **7** asperse, cleanse, entitle, immerse **8** christen, dedicate, initiate, sprinkle **9** designate **10** consecrate, denominate, regenerate
bar 3 ban, dam, pub, rod, tap **4** curb, dive, halt, save, stop **5** block, court, estop, ingot, limit, stick, strip **6** bistro, except, impede, lounge, saloon, tavern **7** barrier, cantina, delimit, exclude, gin mill, rule out, taproom **8** alehouse, blockade, count out, obstacle, obstruct, restrict, tribunal **9** barricade, eliminate, honky-tonk, nightclub, roadhouse

11 obstruction, rathskeller **12** circumscribe, watering hole *type:* **3** raw **4** cash, fern, open, roll, tiki **6** sports
barb 3 dig **4** dart, hook **5** quill, shaft, thorn
Barbados *capital:* **10** Bridgetown *language:* **7** English *location:* **10** West Indies *monetary unit:* **6** dollar
barbarian 3 Hun **4** Goth, lout, rude, wild **5** beast, crude, brute **6** savage, Vandal **7** lowbrow, uncouth **8** Visigoth **9** foreigner, Ostrogoth, primitive **10** uncultured **11** uncivilized **12** uncultivated
barbaric 4 wild **5** crude, rough **6** brutal, coarse, savage **7** beastly, boorish, brutish, loutish, uncouth **8** churlish **9** atrocious, monstrous, primitive, unrefined **11** uncivilized
barbarism 8 malaprop, rudeness, solecism **9** vulgarism, vulgarity **10** coarseness, corruption **11** impropriety, malapropism **12** backwardness, unseemliness
barbarity 7 cruelty **8** atrocity, savagery **9** brutality, depravity **10** inhumanity, savageness **11** viciousness **12** ruthlessness **13** monstrousness
barbarous 4 base, fell, grim, rude, vile, wild **5** cruel, harsh **6** brutal, fierce, Gothic, savage, unholy, vulgar, wicked **7** brutish, Hunnish, inhuman, lowbrow, uncivil, ungodly, vicious, wolfish **8** backward, fiendish, inhumane, ruthless, sadistic **9** benighted, ferocious, graceless, heartless, merciless, monstrous, primitive, tasteless, truculent **10** abominable, outlandish, outrageous, philistine, unmerciful **11** unchristian, uncivilized **12** uncultivated
Barbary state 5 Tunis **7** Algiers, Morocco, Tripoli
barbecue 5 grill, roast **7** cookout, roaster
barber 3 bob, cut **4** clip, crop, trim **5** shave, shear **6** shaver **7** clipper, cropper **8** coiffeur **9** coiffeuse **10** beautician, haircutter **11** hairdresser, hair stylist
Barber of Seville *author:* **12** Beaumarchais (Pierre-Augustin) *character:* **6** Figaro, Rosina, Rosine **7** Bartolo, Basilio **8** Almaviva, Bartholo *composer:* **7** Rossini (Gioacchino) **9** Paisiello (Giovanni)
bard 4 muse, poet, scop **5** skald **8** jongleur, minstrel **9** balladist **10** Parnassian, troubadour
Bard of Avon 11 Shakespeare (William)
bare 4 bald, mere, nude, void **5** empty, naked, shorn, stark, strip **6** barren, denude, devoid, expose, peeled, reveal, unclad, unveil, vacant **7** denuded, dis-

robe, emptied, exposed, uncover
8 bankrupt, disclose, stripped
9 unclothed, uncovered, undressed
barefaced 4 bald, bold, open 5 blunt,
naked 6 arrant, brassy, brazen 7 blatant, glaring, obvious 8 flagrant, impudent, overbold 9 audacious, beardless,
shameless, unabashed 10 unblushing
11 temerarious, unconcealed
barefoot 6 unshod 8 shoeless 9 discalced
bareheaded 7 hatless
barely 4 just 6 hardly, scarce 7 faintly
8 meagerly, scarcely
bargain 3 buy 4 bond, deal, pact, swap
5 agree, steal, trade, truck, value
6 barter, confer, dicker, haggle, higgle,
palter, pledge 7 chaffer, compact, savings, traffic 8 closeout, contract,
covenant, exchange, giveaway, good
deal, huckster, markdown, transact
9 agreement, good value, negotiate,
reduction 10 compromise, convention,
loss leader, pennyworth 11 arrangement, transaction 13 understanding
barge 4 scow 5 clump, stump 6 lumber
7 galumph, stumble
baritone 4 Prey (Hermann) 5 Gobbi
(Tito) 6 Bailey (Norman), London
(George), Milnes (Sherrill), Terfel
(Bryn), Warren (Leonard) 7 Hampson
(Thomas), MacNeil (Cornell), Merrill
(Robert), Tibbett (Lawrence) 8 Raimondi (Ruggero), Warfield (William)
bark 3 arf, bay, yap, yip 4 snap, woof,
yelp 5 snarl 6 bellow
barkeeper see BARTENDER
barker 6 hawker 8 pitchman
Barlow epic 9 Columbiad
barman see BARTENDER
Barmecidal 5 empty, false 6 unreal 7 fictive 8 apparent, illusive, illusory
9 imaginary 10 chimerical, ostensible
13 insubstantial
barn 6 stable *area of:* 4 loft 7 hayloft
barnacle 5 leech 7 sponger 8 hanger-on,
nuisance, parasite 9 dependent, free
rider 10 crustacean, freeloader
barnstorm 8 campaign
Barnum *elephant:* 5 Jumbo *midget:*
8 Tom Thumb *partner:* 6 Bailey
barnyard 4 foul, rude 5 crass, crude,
dirty, nasty 6 coarse, earthy, filthy, ribald, smutty, vulgar 7 obscene, raunchy,
uncouth 8 indecent 9 tasteless 10 indelicate 12 scatological
baron 4 lord, peer 5 mogul, noble
6 tycoon 7 kingpin, magnate 8 overlord
13 industrialist
baronial 5 ample, grand, noble 6 august,
lordly 7 stately 8 imposing, majestic,

princely 9 grandiose 10 commanding,
impressive 11 magnificent, resplendent
baroque 6 florid, ornate, rococo 7 complex 8 dramatic 9 excessive, grotesque,
irregular 10 flamboyant, ornamented
11 embellished, extravagant 12 ostentatious 13 overdecorated
Baroque *architect:* 4 Wren (Christopher)
7 Bernini (Gian Lorenzo), Guarini
(Guarino), Maderno (Carlo) 9 Borromini (Francesco) *composer:* 4 Bach
(Johann Sebastian) 5 Lully (Jean-Baptiste) 6 Handel (George Frideric),
Rameau (Jean-Philippe), Schütz (Heinrich) 7 Corelli (Arcangelo), Purcell
(Henry), Vivaldi (Antonio) 8 Albinoni
(Tommaso), Couperin (François), Telemann (Georg Philipp) 9 Pachelbel
(Johann), Scarlatti (Alessandro,
Domenico) 10 Monteverdi (Claudio)
painter: 4 Hals (Frans) 5 Steen (Jan)
6 Claude (Lorrain), Rubens (Peter
Paul) 7 El Greco, Holbein (Hans),
Poussin (Nicolas), Van Dyck (Anthony), Vermeer (Jan) 8 Carracci (Agosti-
no, Annibale, Lodovico), Ter Borch
(Gerard) 9 Rembrandt (van Rijn),
Velázquez (Diego) 10 Caravaggio *sculptor:* 5 Puget (Pierre) 7 Bernini (Gian
Lorenzo), Coustou (Guillaume,
Nicholas), Pigalle (Jean-Baptiste)
8 Coysevox (Antoine), Girardon
(François)
barrack 4 jeer, root 5 cheer, scoff, taunt
6 billet, casern, deride, hector 7 caserne
8 quarters
barrage 3 dam 4 fire, hail, mass 5 blitz,
burst, salvo, storm, surge 6 deluge,
shower, stream, volley 7 gunfire, torrent 8 drumfire, shelling 9 broadside,
cannonade, crossfire, fusillade,
onslaught 11 bombardment
barranca 4 bank 5 bluff, gully 6 arroyo
barrel 3 keg, tun, vat 4 butt, cask, drum,
peck, race, rush, tear 5 hurry 6 firkin,
hasten 8 hogshead *maker:* 6 cooper *part:*
4 hoop 5 stave *stopper:* 4 bung *support:*
6 gantry
barrelhouse 4 dive 5 hurry, joint 7 hangout 9 honky-tonk
barren 3 dry 4 arid, bare, poor 5 bleak,
empty, stark, stony, waste 6 desert,
devoid, effete, futile, fallow 7 badland,
lacking, parched, sterile, wanting 8 desolate, heirless, impotent 9 childless,
fruitless, infertile, unbearing, unfertile,
wasteland 10 unfruitful, untillable
11 unrewarding 12 hardscrabble,
unproductive, unprofitable
barricade 5 block, fence 7 barrier
8 blockade 9 roadblock *of trees:* 6 abatis

Barrie character 4 John, Nana 5 Peter, Tommy, Wendy 7 Michael 8 Crichton 9 Tiger Lily 10 Tinker Bell 11 Captain Hook

barrier see BARRICADE

barring 3 but 4 save 6 bating, except, saving 7 besides, without 9 aside from, excluding, excepting, outside of 11 exclusive of

barrio 4 slum, turf, ward 6 ghetto 7 quarter, section 8 district, precinct 12 neighborhood

barrister 6 lawyer 7 counsel 8 advocate, attorney 9 counselor

barroom 3 pub 6 lounge, saloon, tavern 7 gin mill, rum room, taproom 8 alehouse, beer hall, dramshop, drinkery, groggery, grogshop 9 beer joint, roadhouse 12 watering hole

bartender 7 tapster 8 boniface 10 mixologist 12 saloonkeeper

barter 4 swap 5 trade, truck 7 bargain, traffic 8 exchange

Bartered Bride composer 7 Smetana (Bedrich)

Barth novel 7 Chimera 12 Giles Goat-Boy 13 Sot-Weed Factor (The)

Baruch *father:* 6 Neriah, Zabbai *occupation:* 6 scribe

basal 5 basic, vital 6 bottom, lowest 7 minimal, primary, radical 8 simplest 9 beginning, essential, undermost 10 bottommost, elementary, primordial, underlying 11 fundamental, preliminary, rudimentary 12 foundational

base 3 bad, bed, fix, key, low 4 camp, evil, foot, foul, home, mean, poor, post, prop, rest, root, seat, site, ugly, vile 5 build, cheap, dirty, found, hinge, lousy, lowly, nadir, plant, set up, sorry, stand 6 bottom, coarse, common, depend, derive, filthy, ground, humble, menial, origin, paltry, scurvy, shoddy, sleazy, sordid, source, trashy, wicked 7 bedrock, caitiff, essence, footing, ignoble, lowborn, low-down, pitiful, servile, squalid, support 8 beggarly, buttress, cowardly, garrison, inferior, pedestal, plebeian, recreant, unwashed, unworthy, wretched 9 construct, dastardly, degrading, establish, framework, loathsome, low-minded, predicate, principle 10 abominable, despicable, foundation, groundwork, substratum, unennobled 11 disgraceful, humiliating, ignominious 12 contemptible, mean-spirited, substructure, underpinning

baseball *abbreviation:* 3 ERA, LOB, MVP, RBI *reputed founder:* 9 Doubleday (Abner) *glove:* 4 mitt *official:* 3 ump 6 umpire *pitch:* 4 drop, heat 5 curve, smoke 6 change, heater, sinker, slider, slurve 7 spitter 8 change-up, fadeaway, fastball, fork ball, knuckler, palm ball, spitball 9 brushback, screwball 11 knuckleball 12 change of pace, knuckle curve *player:* 6 batter 7 baseman, catcher, fielder, pitcher 9 infielder, shortstop 10 outfielder 11 left fielder 12 right fielder 13 center fielder *term:* 3 bag, bat, box, fan, fly, out, run, tag, tap, tip 4 balk, ball, base, bean, bunt, cage, deck, foul, hook, line, mitt, pill, pole, save, walk 5 alley, apple, bench, bloop, clout, count, drive, error, flare, fungo, glove, homer, liner, mound, pop-up, slide, swing 6 assist, clutch, double, dugout, groove, ground, inning, inside, pop fly, pop-out, powder, putout, rubber, runner, single, strike, triple, windup 7 battery, blooper, bullpen, cleanup, diamond, floater, fly ball, home run, infield, manager, outside, pickoff, rhubarb, sidearm, squeeze, stretch 8 baseline, beanball, delivery, foul ball, grounder, keystone, outfield, pinch-hit, rosin bag, southpaw 9 full count, home plate, hot corner, line drive, sacrifice, strikeout, two-bagger 10 double play, frozen rope, ground ball, scratch hit, strike zone 11 knuckleball, pinch hitter, squeeze play, threebagger

baseballer 3 Ott (Mel) 4 Bell (George), Cobb (Ty), Cone (David), Dean (Dizzy), Fisk (Carlton), Ford (Whitey), Foxx (Jimmy), Kaat (Jim), Mays (Willie), Rice (Jim), Rose (Pete), Ruth (Babe), Ryan (Nolan), Sosa (Sammy) 5 Aaron (Henry), Anson (Cap), Banks (Ernie), Belle (Albert), Bench (Johnny), Berra (Yogi), Boggs (Wade), Bonds (Barry), Brett (George), Brock (Lou), Brown (Kevin), Carew (Rod), Clark (Will), Damon (Johnny), Davis (Mark), Green (Shawn), Grove (Lefty), Gwynn (Tony), Henke (Tom), Jeter (Derek), Kiner (Ralph), Maris (Roger), Mauer (Joe), Paige (Satchel), Perez (Tony), Perry (Gaylord), Smith (Lee), Spahn (Warren), Staub (Rusty), Tiant (Luis), Viola (Frank), Weeks (Rickie), Young (Cy), Yount (Robin) 6 Dawson (Andre), Feller (Bob), Foster (George), Franco (John), Garvey (Steve), Gehrig (Lou), Gibson (Bob, Josh, Kirk), Gooden (Dwight), Herzog (Whitey), Hunter (Catfish), Koufax (Sandy), Lajoie (Nap), Maddux (Greg), Mantle (Mickey), Morgan (Joe), Murphy (Dale), Murray (Eddie), Musial (Stan), Palmer (Jim), Piazza (Mike), Raines (Tim),

Ripken (Cal), Seaver (Tom), Sisler (George), Sutter (Bruce), Sutton (Don), Thomas (Frank), Vaughn (Mo), Wagner (Honus), Walker (Larry) **7** Bagwell (Jeff), Canseco (José), Carlton (Steve), Clemens (Roger), Coleman (Vince), Collins (Eddie), Delgado (Carlos), Fingers (Rollie), Griffey (Ken), Hornsby (Roger), Hubbell (Carl), Jackson (Joe, Reggie), Johnson (Randy, Walter), Justice (David), Leonard (Buck), McGwire (Mark), Mondesi (Raul), Puckett (Kirby), Reardon (Jeff), Schmidt (Mike), Simmons (Al), Speaker (Tris) **8** Anderson (Sparky), Blyleven (Bert), Clemente (Roberto), DiMaggio (Joe), Guerrero (Vladimir), Martinez (Pedro), Mitchell (Kevin), Righetti (Dave), Robinson (Brooks, Frank, Jackie), Williams (Bernie, Ted), Winfield (Dave) **9** Alexander (Grover), Eckersley (Dennis), Gehringer (Charlie), Greenberg (Hank), Henderson (Rickey), Hernandez (Willie), Hershiser (Orel), Killebrew (Harmon), Mathewson (Christy), Mattingly (Don), Rodriguez (Alex), Sheffield (Gary) **10** Campanella (Roy), Conigliaro (Tony), Strawberry (Darryl), Valenzuela (Fernando) **11** Garciaparra (Nomar), Yastrzemski (Carl)

baseball team see AMERICAN LEAGUE; NATIONAL LEAGUE

baseboard 7 molding **8** skirting

baseless 4 idle, thin, vain **5** empty, false, wrong **6** feeble, flimsy **9** frivolous, pointless, senseless, unfounded, untenable **10** fallacious, gratuitous, groundless, inadequate, incredible, ungrounded **11** uncalled-for, unconfirmed, unnecessary, unsupported, unsustained, unwarranted **12** indefensible, contemptible, unpersuasive **13** unjustifiable

basement 6 bottom, cellar, ground **7** bedrock **10** foundation, groundwork, substratum **12** substructure

base on balls 4 walk

bash 3 bat, hit **4** belt, blow, fete, gala, slam, whop **5** blast, crack, crash, party, pound, smack, smash, thump, whack **6** attack, pummel, soiree, strike, wallop **7** blowout, shindig **8** wingding

Bashemath *father:* **7** Ishmael *husband:* **4** Esau *sister:* **8** Nebaioth

bashful 3 coy, shy **5** chary, mousy, timid **6** demure, modest **7** abashed, nervous **8** blushing, reserved, retiring, timorous **9** diffident, reluctant, shrinking, unassured **11** unassertive

basic 3 key **4** main **5** chief **6** bottom **7** capital, central, element, minimum,

primary, radical **8** cardinal, inherent, rudiment **9** beginning, elemental, essential, intrinsic, primitive, principal, unadorned **10** elementary, underlying **11** fundamental **12** foundational

basically 6 au fond, mainly, mostly **7** at heart, chiefly, firstly, overall **8** in effect **9** generally, in essence, primarily

basic point 4 crux, gist, pith **5** heart **6** kernel **7** essence

basilica 6 church **7** minster **9** cathedral

basin 3 dip, pan, sag **4** bowl, sink **6** cirque, hollow **7** sinkage **8** sinkhole, washbowl **9** concavity **10** depression *liturgical:* **5** stoup **7** piscina

basis 3 bed **4** crux, root, seat, seed **5** heart, nexus **6** bottom, ground, reason **7** bedrock, essence, footing, grounds, nucleus, premise, support, warrant **9** authority, postulate, principle **10** assumption, foundation, groundwork, substratum **11** fundamental, presumption **12** substructure, underpinning **13** justification

bask 3 sun **4** loll **5** glory, revel, relax **6** lounge, wallow, welter **7** indulge **8** sunbathe **9** luxuriate

basket 6 bushel, gabion **7** pannier *angler's:* **5** creel

basketball *inventor:* **8** Naismith (James) *official:* **6** umpire **7** referee *player:* **5** cager, guard **6** center **7** forward **8** hoopster, swingman **10** point guard *team:* **4** five **7** quintet *term:* **3** gun, jam, key **4** cage, dunk, pass **5** board, lay-up, press, shoot, tip-in **6** freeze, tap-off, tip-off, travel **7** dribble, keyhole, rebound, throw-in, time-out **8** alley-oop, jump ball, slam dunk **9** backboard, backcourt, field goal, free throw **11** ball control

basketballer 3 Bol (Manute) **4** Bird (Larry), Ming (Yao), Nash (Steve), Redd (Michael), Reed (Willis), West (Jerry, Mark) **5** Allen (Ray), Barry (Rick), Brand (Elton), Cousy (Bob), Davis (Baron), Ewing (Patrick), Mikan (George), O'Neal (Shaquille), Price (Mark) **6** Baylor (Elgin), Blount (Mark), Boozer (Carlos), Bryant (Kobe), Carter (Vince), Cowens (Dave), Duncan (Tim), Erving (Julius), Gervin (George), Jordan (Michael), Malone (Jeff, Karl, Moses), McAdoo (Bob), McHale (Kevin), Miller (Brad, Reggie), Parish (Robert), Pierce (Paul, Ricky), Pippin (Scottie), Rodman (Dennis), Skiles (Scott), Thomas (Kenny), Thorpe (Otis), Walton (Bill), Worthy (James) **7** Barkley (Charles), Billups (Chauncey), Dawkins (Darryl),

Dampier (Erick), Edwards (James), Frazier (Walt), Garnett (Kevin), Hilario (Nene), Houston (Allan), Iverson (Allen), Jackson (Lauren), Jamison (Antawn), Johnson (Magic), McGrady (Tracy), Russell (Bill), Rollins (Tree), Taurasi (Diana), Wallace (Ben), Wilkins (Dominique) **8** Auerbach (Red), Cardinal (Brian), Havlicek (John), Olajuwon (Akeem), Magloire (Jamaal), Nowitzki (Dirk), Randolph (Zach), Robinson (David), Stockton (John), Thompson (Tina), Williams (Buck) **9** Donaldson (James), Ferdinand (Marie), Holdsclaw (Chamique), Robertson (Oscar) **10** Stojakovic (Predrag), Williamson (Corliss) **11** Abdul-Jabbar (Kareem), Chamberlain (Wilt)

Basmath's father 7 Solomon

Basque 6 bodice *cap:* **5** beret *game:* **6** pelota **7** jai alai *mountains:* **8** Pyrenees *province:* **5** Alava **7** Vizcaya **9** Guipúzcoa

bass 3 low **4** deep **6** singer **8** cabrilla *famous:* **5** Hines (Jerome), Pinza (Ezio), Ramey (Samuel), Siepi (Cesare), Tozzi (Giorgio) **6** Hotter (Hans), London (George), Morris (James) **7** Plishka (Paul), Robeson (Paul), Talvela (Martti) **8** Flagello (Ezio), Ghiaurov (Nicolai), Raimondi (Ruggero) **9** Chaliapin (Fyodor), Christoff (Boris)

Bassanio's beloved 6 Portia

bassinet 6 cradle, basket

bastard 5 cross **6** by-blow, hybrid **7** mongrel **9** love child **12** natural child *combining form:* **4** noth **5** notho

bastardize 4 warp **5** taint **6** debase, defile **7** corrupt, debauch, degrade, deprave, pervert, pollute, vitiate **9** brutalize **10** adulterate, bestialize, demoralize, depreciate **11** contaminate

baste 3 sew **4** beat, drub, lash, mill, pelt, rail, tack, whip **5** scold **6** batter, berate, larrup, pummel, revile, stitch, thrash, wallop **7** bawl out, belabor, chew out, clobber, moisten, tell off, trounce, upbraid **8** bless out, chastise **9** dress down **10** tongue-lash

bastille 4 jail **6** prison **9** bridewell

bastinado 3 bat, rod **4** bash, beat, blow, cane, club **5** birch, crack, pound, smack, smash, stick, whack **6** cudgel, paddle, strike, switch, thwack, wallop **8** bludgeon **9** truncheon

bastion 5 tower **7** bulwark, citadel, parapet, rampart, redoubt **8** fastness, fortress **10** breastwork, stronghold **13** fortification

bat 3 bag, bop, hag **4** belt, biff, blow, bust, club, slam, sock, swat, whop,

wink **5** biddy, blink, crone, smack **6** cudgel, thwack **7** meander **8** bludgeon **9** flying fox, truncheon **10** knobkerrie, shillelagh **11** pipistrelle

batch 3 lot, set **5** array, bunch, clump, crowd, group **6** bundle, clutch, parcel **7** cluster **8** quantity, shipment **10** assemblage, assortment, collection **11** aggregation **12** accumulation

bate 3 bar **4** omit **5** check **6** deduct, except, reduce **7** cut back, exclude, suspend **8** diminish, moderate, restrain, subtract

bateau 4 boat, dory **5** craft, skiff **6** dinghy, launch **7** shallop

bath 3 spa, tub **4** soak, wash **5** hydro, wells **6** shower **7** springs **8** ablution **13** watering place

bathe 3 dip, lap, lip, sop, tub, wet **4** bask, lave, soak, soap, swim, wash **5** clean, douse, flood, rinse, flush, souse, steep **6** shower **7** cleanse, immerse, pervade, suffuse **8** irrigate

bathetic 5 mushy, soppy, stale, tired, trite **6** drippy **7** clichéd, cloying, gushing, maudlin, mawkish **9** emotional, hackneyed, schmaltzy **10** lachrymose **11** commonplace, sentimental, stereotyped, tear-jerking **13** anticlimactic, overemotional, stereotypical

bathhouse 5 sauna **6** cabana

bathing suit 6 bikini, trunks **7** bandeau, maillot

bathos 7 letdown **8** banality, comedown **9** triteness **10** anticlimax

bathroom 3 loo **4** john **5** privy **6** toilet **8** lavatory, outhouse

Bathsheba *father:* **5** Eliam *husband:* **5** David, Uriah *son:* **7** Solomon

bathtub gin 5 hooch **6** rotgut **7** bootleg **8** homebrew **9** moonshine **11** mountain dew

Batman creator 4 Kane (Bob)

baton 3 rod **4** club, mace, wand **5** billy, staff, stick **6** cudgel **7** war club **8** bludgeon **9** billy club, truncheon **10** nightstick

___ Bator 4 Ulan

batrachian 4 frog, toad **9** amphibian

battalion 4 army, host, unit **5** force, horde **6** legion, throng, troops **8** squadron **10** contingent, detachment

batter 4 bash, beat, drub, hurt, maul, mush **5** baste, break, dough, paste, pound, wreck **6** bruise, buffet, bung up, hitter, mangle, pommel, pummel, thrash, wallop **7** assault, belabor, bombard, clobber, coating, contuse, cripple, lambast **8** demolish, lambaste

battery 3 lot, set **4** body, guns **5** abuse, array, batch, bunch, clump, group, suite 6 bundle, cannon, series 7 assault, beating, cluster 8 thumping 9 artillery, onslaught 10 energy cell 11 gunnery unit

battery terminal 5 anode 7 cathode

battle 4 fray 5 brush, clash, fight 6 action, assail, attack, combat, sortie 7 assault, contend, contest 8 conflict, skirmish, struggle 9 encounter, onslaught, scrimmage 10 engagement 11 hostilities

battle-ax 5 harpy, scold, shrew 6 virago 8 harridan 9 termagant, Xanthippe

Battle Born State 6 Nevada

battle cry 6 banzai

battlement 4 wall 7 barrier, bastion, bulwark, parapet, rampart 10 protection

batty 3 mad 4 daft, nuts, zany 5 barmy, crazy, kooky, loony, nutty, potty, wacky 6 crazed, cuckoo, insane, maniac, screwy, whacko 7 bananas, bonkers, cracked, idiotic, lunatic 8 deranged 9 bedlamite

bauble 3 toy 5 curio 6 gewgaw, trifle 7 bibelot, novelty, trinket, whatnot 8 gimcrack, ornament 9 objet d'art, plaything 10 knickknack

Baucis's husband 8 Philemon

Bavaria 6 Bayern *capital:* 6 Munich *city:* 8 Augsburg, Bayreuth, Würzburg 9 Nuremberg *king:* 6 Ludwig *patron saint:* 6 Rupert

bawd 4 drab, moll, tart 5 madam, tramp, whore 6 floozy, harlot, hooker 7 trollop 8 strumpet 10 prostitute 11 nightwalker 12 streetwalker

bawdy 4 blue, lewd 5 crude, dirty 6 coarse, erotic, ribald, risqué, smutty, vulgar 7 obscene 8 indecent, prurient 9 lecherous, offensive, salacious 10 lascivious, libidinous, licentious, suggestive

bawdy house 4 crib, stew 6 bagnio 7 brothel, lupanar 8 bordello

bawl 3 cry, sob 4 howl, roar, rout, wail, weep, yell, yowl 5 shout 6 bellow, berate, boohoo, clamor, holler, outcry, scream, shriek, squall 7 blubber, bluster

bawl out 3 wig 4 lash 5 baste, scold 6 berate, rebuke 7 censure, chew out, condemn, tell off, upbraid 8 bless out, castigate, denounce, tear into 9 dress down, reprimand 10 tongue-lash

bay 3 arm 4 cove, gulf, howl, nook, wail 5 award, bight, crown, firth, honor, inlet, niche 6 harbor, laurel, recess 7 garland, laurels 8 accolade 10 decoration *Aegean Sea:* 5 Anzac *Africa:* 6 Walvis *Alaska:* 7 Glacier *Antarctica:* 3 Ice 8 Amundsen *Argentina:* 6 Blanca

Australia: 5 Anson, Shark 6 Botany, Sharks 9 Discovery *Baltic:* 4 Hano, Kiel 6 Danzig, Kieler 9 Pomerania 10 Pomeranian, Pommersche *Beaufort Sea:* 7 Prudhoe 9 Mackenzie *Brazil:* 9 Guanabara *Bristol Channel:* 10 Carmarthen *California:* 5 Morro 8 Monterey, San Diego *Canada:* 5 Fundy *Capetown:* 5 Table *Caribbean Sea:* 5 Limon 8 Chetumal *Central America:* 7 Fonseca *Cuba:* 10 Guantánamo *East River:* 8 Flushing *Egypt:* 6 Abu Qir *Eire:* 4 Clew 7 Brandon *English Channel:* 3 Tor 4 Lyme *Europe:* 6 Biscay *Florida:* 8 Biscayne *Greenland:* 6 Baffin 8 Melville *Gulf of Alaska:* 12 Resurrection *Gulf of California:* 5 Adair *Gulf of Guinea:* 5 Benin 6 Biafra *Gulf of Mexico:* 5 Tampa 6 Mobile 7 Aransas 8 Campeche, Sarasota 9 Matagorda, Pensacola 10 San Antonio, Terrebonne 11 Atchafalaya, Ponce de Leon 12 Apalachicola 13 Corpus Christi *Gulf of St. Lawrence:* 5 Bonne, Gaspé *Hawaii:* 5 Koloa, Lawai *Hong Kong:* 4 Deep *Honshu:* 3 Ise 5 Mutsu, Osaka, Owari, Tokyo 6 Atsuta, Sagami *Indian Ocean:* 6 Bengal *Indonesia:* 8 Humboldt *Irish Sea:* 4 Luce 7 Dundalk *Jamaica:* 4 Long *Japan:* 4 Tosa *Java Sea:* 7 Batavia 8 Djakarta *Lake Erie:* 8 Sandusky *Lake Huron:* 7 Saginaw, Thunder *Lake Michigan:* 5 Green 13 Grand Traverse *Lake Ontario:* 11 Irondequoit *Lake Superior:* 5 Huron 8 Keweenaw 9 Whitefish *Long Island Sound:* 6 Oyster *Maine:* 5 Casco 7 Machias 9 Penobscot *Maryland-Virginia:* 10 Chesapeake 12 Chincoteague *Massachusetts:* 6 Boston 7 Cape Cod 8 Buzzards, Plymouth *New Brunswick:* 13 Passamaquoddy *Newfoundland:* 4 Hare 5 White 7 Fortune *New Jersey:* 5 Great 6 Newark 7 Raritan 8 Barnegat *New York:* 7 Jamaica *North Carolina:* 6 Onslow *Northwest Territories:* 5 Wager 7 Repulse 8 Franklin 9 Frobisher *Oregon:* 4 Coos *Puerto Rico:* 5 Sucia *Quebec:* 6 Ungava *Rhode Island:* 12 Narragansett *Sea of Japan:* 13 Peter the Great *South Carolina:* 4 Bull, Long *South China Sea:* 5 Subic 7 Camranh *Spain:* 5 Cadiz *Strait of Gibraltar:* 7 Tangier *Sydney:* 6 Botany *Tasmania:* 5 Storm *Texas:* 7 Trinity *Tyrrhenian Sea:* 6 Naples 7 Paestum *Wales:* 10 Caernarfon, Caernarvon *Washington:* 5 Dabob 6 Skagit *West Indies:* 5 Coral

bayou 5 creek, marsh 6 slough 9 everglade, tributary *Louisiana:* 5 Macon 9 Barataria, Lafourche 10 Terrebonne *Mississippi:* 9 Chickasaw

Bay State 13 Massachusetts
bay window 3 gut, pot 5 oriel, tummy 6 paunch 8 potbelly 9 beer belly, spare tire 11 corporation, breadbasket
bazaar 4 fair, mall, mart, souk 6 market 7 benefit 8 emporium, exchange 11 marketplace
bazooka's target 4 tank
be 4 live 5 exist
beach 4 bank 5 Cocoa, coast, shore 6 Malibu, Pebble, strand, Venice 7 seaside, shingle, Waikiki 8 cast away, lakeside, littoral, seashore 9 lakeshore 10 Clearwater, Copacabana, oceanfront, run aground
___ **Beach** 3 Amy 4 Long, Palm, Vero 5 Dover, Miami, Omaha 6 Delray, Myrtle, Ormond 7 Daytona, Riviera, Waikiki 8 Imperial, Virginia
beached 6 ashore 7 aground 8 grounded, marooned, stranded 9 abandoned
beachhead 8 foothold
beachwear see BATHING SUIT
beacon 4 buoy, sign 5 flare, guide 6 pharos, signal 7 bonfire, lantern 8 balefire 9 watchfire 10 lighthouse, signal fire 11 inspiration, transmitter 12 guiding light
bead 3 dab, dot, pea 4 blob, drop 6 bubble 7 driblet, globule 8 spherule
beak 3 neb, nib 4 bill, nose 5 snoot, snout, spout 6 pecker, schnoz 7 schnozz 8 mandible 9 proboscis, schnozzle
beaker 3 cup 6 carafe, goblet, vessel 8 decanter
beaklike part 7 rostrum
be-all and end-all 3 sum 4 pith, root, soul 5 total, whole 6 bottom 7 essence 8 entirety, sum total, totality 9 aggregate, substance 10 prime cause 12 quintessence
beam 3 bar, ray 4 balk, boom, burn, glow, grin, spar 5 flare, flash, gleam, joist, plank, shaft, shine, shoot, smile, strut 6 girder, lintel, rafter, signal, streak, stream, timber 7 radiate 8 transmit 9 broadcast
beaming 6 bright, joyful, lucent 7 fulgent, lambent, radiant 8 animated, cheerful, luminous 9 brilliant, effulgent, refulgent 12 incandescent
bean 3 soy, wax 4 bush, conk, dome, head, lima, mung, navy, pate, pole, poll, snap, soya 5 baked, brain, broad, horse, jelly, pinto 6 belfry, coffee, frijol, kidney, legume, noddle, noggin, noodle, string 7 jumping 9 headpiece 10 stringless *of India:* 3 urd
beanery 4 café 5 diner, grill 9 hash

house 10 coffee shop, restaurant 11 greasy spoon 12 luncheonette
beano 5 bingo
Bean Town 6 Boston
bear 3 lug 4 tote 5 abide, allow, beget, bring, brook, bruin, carry, stand, touch 6 accept, behave, convey, deport, endure, permit, suffer 7 comport, condone, conduct, deliver, stomach, support, sustain, swallow, undergo 8 engender, generate, shoulder, tolerate 9 procreate, propagate, reproduce, transport 10 bring forth 11 countenance *Alaskan:* 5 polar 6 Kodiak *Australian:* 5 koala *genus:* 5 Ursus *kind:* 3 sun 5 black, brown, honey, koala, polar, sloth 6 Kodiak 7 grizzly 10 spectacled *relating to:* 6 ursine *young:* 3 cub
bearable 7 livable, tenable 8 adequate, passable 9 allowable, endurable, tolerable 10 acceptable, admissible, good enough, manageable, sufferable 11 supportable, sustainable
bearcat 5 panda
beard 4 dare, defy, face, fuzz 5 brave, front 6 goatee 7 outface, stubble, Vandyke 8 confront, imperial, whiskers 9 challenge *on grain:* 3 awn
bearded 5 bushy, fuzzy, hairy 6 shaggy, tufted 7 bristly, goateed, hirsute, stubbly 8 unshaven 9 whiskered 11 bewhiskered
bear down 4 rout 5 crush, quell 6 burden, defeat, reduce, subdue 7 conquer, overrun, trample 8 overcome, vanquish 9 emphasize, overpower, overwhelm, subjugate
bearer 4 mule 5 envoy 6 coolie, porter, runner 7 carrier, courier 8 conveyor, emissary 9 go-between, messenger 11 internuncio
bear hug 6 clinch
bearing 3 air, set 4 look, mien, pose 5 poise 6 aspect, manner, stance 7 address, conduct, display, posture 8 attitude, behavior, carriage, delivery, demeanor, presence, relation 9 demeanour, direction 10 connection, deportment 11 comportment
bearish 4 curt 5 gruff, rough, terse, surly 6 cranky, ornery 7 anxious, dubious, prickly, uncouth 8 cautious, vinegary 9 crotchety, irascible 10 ill-humored 11 pessimistic 12 cantankerous
bearlike 6 ursine
bear out 4 show 5 prove 6 attest, uphold, verify 7 certify, confirm, justify 8 validate, vouch for 9 vindicate 11 corroborate, demonstrate 12 authenticate, substantiate

bear up 4 cope, fare, prop 5 brace, get by 6 endure, uphold 7 bolster, support, sustain 8 buttress, get along, maintain, underpin

beast 5 brute 6 animal 7 critter, monster, varmint 8 behemoth, creature

beastly 4 foul, mean, vile 5 awful, brute, feral, nasty 6 animal, brutal, odious 7 bestial, brutish, inhuman, ogreish, swinish 8 horrible, terrible 9 barbarous, revolting 10 abominable, detestable

beat 3 box, get, gyp, hit, lam, rap, tan, top 4 balk, belt, best, cane, dash, drub, drum, dump, flap, flog, foil, lash, lick, maul, pelt, rout, ruin, stir, tick, trim, whip, whop 5 baste, cheat, cozen, excel, forge, lay on, meter, outdo, paste, pound, pulse, punch, rhyme, route, scoop, scour, smear, stick, stump, swing, throb, tread, tromp, whack, whisk 6 baffle, batter, better, buffet, cudgel, defeat, diddle, exceed, forage, hammer, larrup, muss up, patrol, pummel, rhythm, rounds, strike, thrash, thresh, thwart, wallop 7 belabor, clobber, circuit, conquer, exhaust, fashion, fatigue, lambast, lay down, prevail, pulsate, ransack, rough up, shellac, surpass, swindle, triumph, trounce 8 bewilder, bludgeon, Bohemian, lambaste, outshine, outsmart, outstrip, overcome, precinct 9 exhausted, frustrate, palpitate, pulsation, transcend, vibration 10 circumvent, pistol-whip 11 oscillation

beating 4 rout 5 lumps 6 defeat, hiding, mayhem 7 assault, setback 9 hammering, pulsation, throbbing 11 palpitation, shellacking

beatitude 3 joy 5 bliss 7 delight, ecstasy, rapture 8 euphoria, gladness, rhapsody 9 happiness, transport 10 exaltation, joyfulness 11 blessedness 12 blissfulness

Beatles 4 John (Lennon), Paul (McCartney) 5 Ringo (Starr) 6 George (Harrison)

beatnik 5 rebel 6 hippie 7 radical 8 Bohemian 9 dissident 11 flower child 13 nonconformist

beat-up 6 shabby 7 rickety, worn-out 8 decrepit, tattered 9 crumbling 10 broken-down, ramshackle, tumble-down 11 dilapidated

beau 4 dandy, flame, lover, swain, wooer 6 steady, suitor 7 admirer, beloved 8 paramour, truelove, young man 9 boyfriend 10 sweetheart

Beau Brummell 3 fop 5 dandy, swell 7 coxcomb, gallant 8 macaroni 11 petit-maître 12 lounge lizard

beau ideal 5 guide, model 6 mirror 7 epitome, example, paragon, pattern 8 exemplar, paradigm, standard 9 archetype 12 quintessence

Beaumarchais hero 6 Figaro

beau monde 5 elite 6 gentry, jet set 7 society 8 smart set 10 glitterati, upper crust

beauteous see BEAUTIFUL

beautiful 4 fair 5 bonny 6 comely, lovely, pretty 7 radiant 8 glorious, gorgeous, handsome, splendid, stunning 9 exquisite 10 attractive 11 good-looking, resplendent, well-favored

beautiful people 6 jet set 8 smart set 9 haut monde 10 glitterati 11 high society

beautify 4 deck, gild, trim 5 adorn, array, fix up, grace, prank, primp 6 bedeck, doll up 7 dress up, festoon, garland, garnish, gussy up, enhance, improve 8 decorate, ornament, prettify, spruce up 9 embellish, glamorize

beauty 5 asset, belle, dream, merit, peach 6 appeal, eyeful, looker, lovely 7 charmer, dazzler, stunner 8 knockout 9 eye-opener, good looks 10 good-looker, loveliness

beaver 6 rodent *project:* 3 dam *home:* 5 lodge *young:* 3 kit, pup

Beaver State 6 Oregon

becalm 3 hush, lull, stop 5 allay, quiet, stall, still 6 arrest, pacify, sedate, settle, soothe, steady, subdue 7 assuage, compose, quieten 11 tranquilize

because 3 for, now 4 that 5 since 7 being as, whereas 8 being how, as long as, seeing as 10 inasmuch as

because of 4 over 5 due to 7 owing to, through 8 thanks to 10 by reason of 11 on account of

Beckett work of 4 Not I, Play, Watt 6 Molloy, Murphy 7 Endgame 9 Happy Days, Unnamable (The) 10 Eleutheria, Malone Dies 14 Krapp's Last Tape 15 Waiting for Godot

beckon 3 bid, nod 4 lure, wave 6 allure, entice, invite, motion, signal, summon 7 attract

becloud 3 dim, fog 4 blur, hide, veil 5 addle, bedim, befog, cloak, muddy 6 impair, darken, muddle, puzzle, shroud 7 confuse, eclipse, obscure, perplex 8 befuddle 9 obfuscate 10 overshadow

become 3 fit, get, wax 4 grow, suit 5 befit 6 go with 7 enhance, flatter 8 turn into

becoming 3 apt 5 right 6 decent, proper, seemly 7 correct, fitting 8 decorous, suitable, tasteful 9 befitting 10 attractive, flattering, well-chosen 11 appropriate, comme il faut

bed 3 cot 4 base, bunk, crib, sack, twin 5 basis, berth, layer 6 bottom, cradle, double, ground, Murphy, pallet 7 bedrock, stratum, trundle 8 rollaway 10 foundation, substratum *of India:* 7 charpoy

bedaub 4 coat 5 cover, smear 6 smudge 7 overlay, plaster

bedazzle 4 daze 5 blind

bedcover 5 duvet, quilt 6 afghan, spread 7 blanket 8 coverlet 9 comforter 11 counterpane

bedeck 4 trim 5 adorn, array, prank 6 attire, bedaub, jazz up 7 appoint, bedizen, dress up, festoon, furbish, garland, garnish, gussy up 8 accouter, accoutre, beautify, decorate, ornament, prettify 9 embellish

bedevil 5 annoy, harry, spoil, tease, worry 6 harass, needle, nettle, pester, plague 7 hagride, provoke, torment, trouble 8 bewilder 10 exasperate

bedevilment 6 bother 7 torment, trouble 8 disorder, vexation 9 annoyance, confusion 10 irritation 11 aggravation 12 bewilderment

bedfellow 4 ally 5 crony 7 comrade 9 associate, colleague 10 compatriot 11 confederate 12 collaborator

bedim 3 fog 4 blur, mask, veil 5 befog, blear, cloud, gloom, shade, 6 darken, muddle, shadow, shroud 7 becloud, confuse, eclipse, obscure 9 obfuscate

bedizen 4 deck, garb, gild 5 adorn, array, endue 6 doll up, dude up, invest, outfit, rig out 7 costume, dandify, dress up, garnish, gussy up, turn out 8 beautify, ornament 9 caparison, embellish

bedlam 3 ado 5 chaos, furor 6 asylum, clamor, furore, hubbub, tumult, uproar, welter 7 turmoil 8 foofaraw, madhouse, upheaval 9 commotion, maelstrom 10 hurly-burly 11 pandemonium

bedlamite 3 mad, nut 4 loon, nuts 5 batty, crazy, loony 6 insane, madman, maniac 7 cracked, lunatic 8 demented, deranged

bedouin 4 Arab 5 nomad

bedraggled 5 faded, seedy 6 shabby, ragtag, untidy 7 muddied, rundown, unkempt 8 decrepit, dripping, slovenly, tattered 10 disheveled, disarrayed, disordered, down-at-heel, ramshackle, threadbare 11 dilapidated

bedridden 6 laid up, shut-in 8 confined 12 hospitalized

bedrock 4 base, core, foot, root 5 axiom, basic, basis, floor, nadir 6 bottom, depths, ground 7 footing, support 10 foundation, groundwork, substra-

tum 11 fundamental 12 substructure, underpinning

bedroom 7 boudoir, chamber

bedspread 8 coverlet 11 counterpane

bed-wetting 8 enuresis

bee *food:* 6 nectar *glue:* 8 propolis *group:* 5 swarm 6 colony *house:* 4 hive 6 apiary *kind:* 5 drone, mason, queen 6 mining, sewing, worker 8 quilting, spelling 9 carpenter *nest:* 4 hive, skep *product:* 3 wax 5 honey *relating to:* 8 apiarian *wax cells:* 9 honeycomb

beechnuts 4 mast

beef 4 crab, fuss, meat 5 bitch, brawn, gripe 6 grouse, muscle 7 grumble 9 bellyache, complaint, grievance *cut:* 3 rib 4 loin, rump, side 5 chuck, flank, plate, round, shank 7 brisket, sirloin 10 tenderloin 11 porterhouse *grade:* 5 prime 6 choice 7 utility 8 standard 10 commercial *order:* 4 rare 6 medium 8 well-done

beefeater 5 guard 6 sentry, warder, yeoman

beefy 5 bulky, burly, hefty, husky, meaty 6 brawny, fleshy, robust, stocky, sturdy 7 massive 8 muscular, thickset 9 strapping 11 substantial

Beehive State 4 Utah

beekeeper 8 apiarist 12 apiculturist

beekeeping 10 apiculture

beeline 3 fly, nip, zip 4 race, whiz 5 hurry, speed 6 bullet, hasten, hustle, rocket 7 hotfoot 8 expedite, highball 10 make tracks 12 shortest path

Beelzebub 5 devil, fiend, Satan 6 diablo 7 Evil One, Lucifer, Old Nick, serpent 8 Apollyon 9 adversary, archfiend

beer 3 ale 4 bock, brew, suds 5 draft, lager, stout, weiss 6 porter 7 brewski, cerveza, pilsner 8 pilsener *vessel:* 3 mug 4 toby 5 stein 6 flagon, seidel 7 tankard 8 schooner 9 blackjack *drinking place:* 3 bar, inn, pub 6 saloon, tavern *ingredient:* 4 hops, malt 5 yeast 6 barley *maker:* 6 brewer *mythical inventor:* 9 Gambrinus *plant:* 7 brewery *Russian:* 5 kvass *Scottish:* 10 barley-bree

beer hall 3 pub 6 saloon, tavern 7 taproom 8 alehouse 11 public house, rathskeller

Beeri *daughter:* 6 Judith *son:* 5 Hosea

beet 5 chard 6 mangel, wurzel 10 Swiss chard *family:* 9 goosefoot

Beethoven, Ludwig van *birthplace:* 4 Bonn *opera:* 7 Fidelio *overture:* 6 Egmont 7 Leonore 10 Coriolanus, Prometheus *sonata:* 7 Tempest 8 Kreutzer 9 Moonlight, Waldstein 10 Pathétique 12 Appassionata *symphony:* 6 Choral, Eroica 8 Pastoral

beetle 3 bug, jut **5** bulge **6** insect, scarab, scurry **7** project **8** overhang, protrude, stand out, stick out *click:* **6** elater **7** firefly *dung:* **6** scarab **9** tumblebug *front wing:* **6** elytra (plural) **7** elytron *fruit-eating:* **8** curculio *insect-eating:* **7** ladybug **8** ladybird *kind:* **4** bean, dung, fire, June, stag **5** click, flour, grain, tiger, water **6** carpet, chafer, ground, May bug, museum **7** blister, cadelle, carabid, firefly, goldbug, goliath, June bug, vedalia **8** ambrosia, Japanese **9** longicorn, potato bug **10** cockchafer, rhinoceros *order:* **10** Coleoptera *snouted:* **6** weevil **7** billbug **8** curculio **9** wood borer *young:* **4** grub **5** larva **6** larvae (plural) **8** wireworm

beet soup 6 borsch **7** borscht

befall 3 hap **5** ensue, occur **6** betide, chance, follow, happen **7** come off, develop, fall out **8** happen to **9** come about, eventuate, transpire

befit 4 meet, suit **6** become, go with **9** agree with, chime with **10** accord with, be right for **11** be proper for

befitting 3 apt **4** just, meet **5** happy, right **6** decent, proper, seemly **7** correct **8** becoming, decorous, suitable **10** conforming, felicitous **11** appropriate, comme il faut

befog 3 dim **4** blur, hide, veil **5** bedim, blear, cloak, cloud, muddy **6** darken, puzzle **7** becloud, confuse, eclipse, envelop, obscure, perplex **8** bewilder, confound **9** obfuscate, overcloud **10** overshadow

befool 4 dupe, gull, hoax, play **5** cozen, trick **6** delude **7** chicane, deceive, mislead **8** hoodwink **9** bamboozle, victimize **11** hornswoggle

before 3 ere **4** ante, once, till, up to **5** ahead, until **6** facing, sooner, up till **7** ahead of, already, earlier, prior to **8** formerly **9** in advance, in front of, preceding **10** previously **11** in advance of *prefix:* **3** pre, pro **4** ante, fore

befoul 3 mar, tar **4** slur, soil **5** dirty, smear, spoil, sully, taint **6** defame, defile, malign, smudge **7** blacken, pollute, profane, spatter, tarnish, traduce **8** besmirch **9** bespatter, denigrate **10** adulterate **11** contaminate

befuddle 4 daze **5** addle, mix up **6** ball up, baffle, bemuse, muddle **7** confuse, fluster, perplex, stupefy **8** bewilder, confound, distract, throw off, **9** disorient

befuddlement 3 fog **4** daze, haze, maze **5** mix-up **6** muddle, stupor **9** confusion **10** perplexity, puzzlement **11** distraction

beg 3 ask, bum, dun, nag, sue **4** pray, urge **5** apply, brace, cadge, crave, evade, hit on, mooch, plead, press, worry **6** adjure, appeal, call on, demand, invoke, pester **7** beseech, besiege, conjure, entreat, implore, request, solicit **8** petition, sidestep **9** importune, panhandle **10** supplicate

beget 4 bear, sire **5** breed, bring, cause, forge, hatch, spawn, yield **6** create, effect, father **7** produce **8** engender, generate, multiply, result in **9** procreate, propagate, reproduce **10** bring about

beggar 4 hobo, defy, ruin **5** tramp **6** bummer, cadger, fellow, pauper, prayer, sponge, suitor **7** moocher, sponger **8** bankrupt, deadbeat, vagabond **9** overwhelm, pauperize, schnorrer, suppliant **10** down-and-out, freeloader, impoverish, panhandler, petitioner, supplicant **11** bindle stiff, supplicator **12** street person

beggared 4 flat, poor **5** broke, needy **6** ruined **7** drained **8** bankrupt, dirt poor, indigent, strapped, wiped out **9** destitute, insolvent, penniless, penurious, tapped out **10** pauperized **11** impecunious, overwhelmed **12** dispossessed, impoverished

beggarly 3 low **4** base, mean, poor **5** cheap, lowly, nasty, petty, sorry **6** cheesy, meager, measly, paltry, scanty, scurvy, shabby, shoddy, trashy **7** ignoble, miserly, pitiful, squalid **8** pitiable, inferior, wretched **9** miserable, niggardly **10** despicable, despisable **11** ignominious **12** contemptible, parsimonious

Beggar's Opera *music:* **7** Pepusch (John) *painting:* **7** Hogarth (William) *text:* **3** Gay (John)

beggarweed 6 dodder **9** knotgrass **11** tick trefoil

beggary 4 need, want **6** penury **7** bumming, cadging, poverty **8** mooching, pleading **9** indigence, neediness, pauperism, privation **10** meagerness, mendicancy **11** destitution, panhandling

begin 4 dawn, open, rise **5** arise, cause, dig in, enter, found, mount, set to, start **6** appear, attack, be born, broach, create, effect, emerge, get off, induce, invent, launch, spring, sprout, tackle, take up, tee off **7** break in, embark on, emanate, jump off, kick off, lead off, prepare, usher in **8** activate, commence, embark on, engender, initiate **9** establish, instigate, institute, introduce, originate **10** embark upon, inaugurate, issue forth **11** break ground

beginner 4 colt, tiro, tyro **6** newbie, new kid, novice, rookie **7** recruit, starter, student, trainee **8** freshman, neophyte, newcomer **9** fledgling, greenhorn, novitiate **10** apprentice, catechumen, tenderfoot **11** abecedarian

beginning 4 dawn, font, rise, root **5** alpha, basal, birth, fount, onset, start **6** day one, origin, outset, primal, source, spring **7** dawning, genesis, infancy, initial, kickoff, nascent, opening **8** creation, exordium, outstart, prologue, rudiment, simplest **9** elemental, emergence, inception, incipient **10** appearance, elementary, incipiency, initiative, initiatory, opening gun, rudimental **11** origination, rudimentary **12** commencement, inauguration, introductory

begird 3 hem **4** belt, bind, ring **5** beset, fence, hem in, round **6** circle, corral, girdle, immure **7** confine, enclose, wreathe **8** encircle, engirdle, surround **9** encompass **12** circumscribe

beg off 5 demur, welsh **6** bow out, cop out, opt out, pass up, refuse, renege **7** back out, bail out, decline, drop out, pull out **8** back down, withdraw

begone 5 leave, scram, split **6** beat it, decamp, depart, get out **7** buzz off, get lost, skiddoo, take off, vamoose **8** clear out, hightail, shove off **9** skedaddle **10** make tracks

begrime 3 tar **4** foul, soil, spot **5** dirty, muddy, smear, spoil, sully, taint **6** defile, mess up, muck up, smirch, smooch, smudge, smutch **7** blacken, corrupt, pollute, tarnish **8** besmirch **11** contaminate

begrudge 4 envy **6** resent

beguile 3 con **4** draw, dupe, fool, hoax, lure, play, snow, wile **5** bluff, charm, fleet, trick **6** beckon, betray, delude, divert, entice, humbug, seduce, take in **7** attract, bewitch, deceive, enchant, engross, exploit, finesse, mislead **8** distract, hoodwink, intrigue, maneuver **9** captivate, fascinate, while away **10** manipulate **11** double-cross

beguiling 4 wily **5** false **6** artful, subtle **8** alluring, deluding, delusive, delusory **9** deceitful, deceiving, deceptive, insidious, seductive **10** bewitching, chimerical, enchanting, fallacious, misleading **11** enthralling

Behan's autobiography 10 Borstal Boy

behave 3 act, run **5** carry, react **6** acquit, be good, deport, direct, manage **7** comport, conduct, disport, perform **8** function

behavior 3 act, air, way **4** mien, tone,

ways **6** action, aspect, custom, habits, manner **7** bearing, conduct **8** demeanor, presence, response **10** deportment **11** comportment

behead 4 head, kill **7** execute **9** decollate **10** decapitate, guillotine

beheaded noblewoman 8 Jane Grey (Lady) **9** Catherine (Howard) **10** Anne Boleyn

behemoth 5 giant, jumbo, whale **7** goliath, mammoth, monster **8** colossus **9** leviathan **11** monstrosity

behemothic 4 huge **5** jumbo **7** mammoth, massive, titanic **8** colossal, gigantic, towering **9** Herculean, monstrous **10** gargantuan **11** elephantine

behest 3 say **4** will, wish, word, writ **5** edict, order **6** charge, demand, urging **7** bidding, command, dictate, mandate, precept, request **9** direction, enjoinder, ordinance, prescript, prompting **10** injunction **11** commandment, exhortation, instruction **12** solicitation

behind 3 can **4** late, next, rump **5** after, fanny **6** back of, bottom, heinie **7** backing **8** backside, buttocks, derriere, trailing **9** following, posterior **10** supporting **12** subsequent to *prefix:* **4** post **5** retro

behindhand 3 lax **4** late, slow **5** slack, tardy **6** in debt, lesser, remiss **7** belated, delayed, laggard, overdue **8** backward, careless, derelict, sluggish **9** in arrears, negligent, unmindful **10** delinquent, neglectful, regardless, unpunctual **11** subordinate, undeveloped **13** unprogressive

behold 3 see **4** espy, note, view **6** descry, notice **7** discern, observe, witness *French:* **5** voilà *Latin:* **4** ecce

beholden 5 bound **7** obliged **8** grateful, indebted **9** duty-bound, obligated

beholder 4 seer **6** gawker, viewer **7** watcher, witness **8** observer, onlooker, passerby **9** bystander, spectator **10** eyewitness **12** rubbernecker

beige 3 tan **4** buff, ecru **7** vanilla

being 3 man **4** body, life, self, soul **5** human, stuff, thing **6** entity, matter, mortal, nature, object, person, spirit **7** essence **8** creature, existent, material **9** actuality, character, existence, personage, something, substance **10** individual **11** personality **12** essentiality **13** individuality

bejeweled 7 studded **8** sequined, spangled **9** encrusted **10** bespangled, gemstudded, ornamented

Bel *Sumerian counterpart:* **5** Enlil *wife:* **5** Belit **6** Beltis

Bel ___ 3 Air **5** Paese

bel ___ 5 canto **6** esprit

Bela *father:* 4 Beor 8 Benjamin *son:* 3 Ard

belabor 4 beat, drub, flog 5 baste, pound, scold 6 batter, berate, buffet, pummel, thrash, wallop 7 lambast, scourge, tell off, upbraid 8 chastise, lambaste, tear into 9 criticize, fulminate, overstate 10 flagellate 11 overexplain

Belarus *capital:* 5 Minsk *city:* 6 Homyel 7 Vitebsk 8 Mahilyow 9 Vitsyebsk *language:* 7 Russian 10 Belarusian 11 Belarussian *monetary unit:* 5 rubel, ruble *neighbor:* 6 Latvia, Poland, Russia 7 Ukraine 9 Lithuania *river:* 3 Bug 5 Neman 7 Dnieper, Pripyat

belated 4 late, slow 5 tardy 6 remiss 7 delayed, laggard, overdue 10 behindhand, behind time, unpunctual

Belau see PALAU

belch 4 burp, emit, gush, spew, vent, void 5 eject, eruct, erupt, expel, issue, spout, spurt, vomit 6 hiccup, irrupt 7 explode, extrude 8 disgorge 10 eructation 11 expectorate

beldam 3 hag 5 crone 8 old woman

beleaguer 3 bug, dog, hem, nag, vex 4 gnaw 5 annoy, beset, harry, hound, siege, storm, tease, worry 6 assail, attack, badger, bother, fall on, harass, invest, pester, plague 7 bedevil, besiege, hagride, put upon, set upon, trouble 8 blockade, fall upon

belfry 7 steeple 8 carillon 9 bell tower, campanile *dweller:* 3 bat

Belgium *capital:* 8 Brussels *city:* 4 Gent 5 Ghent, Liège 7 Antwerp 9 Charleroi *ethnic group:* 7 Fleming, Flemish, Walloon *language:* 5 Dutch 7 Flemish *monetary unit:* 4 euro *neighbor:* 6 France 7 Germany 10 Luxembourg 11 Netherlands *plain:* 8 Flanders *port:* 7 Antwerp 8 Oostende *river:* 4 Yser 5 Meuse 7 Schlede *sea:* 5 North

belie 4 deny, hide, warp 5 color, twist 6 expose, doctor, garble 7 conceal, confute, distort, falsify, gainsay, pervert, trump up 8 confront, denounce, disagree, disguise, disprove, miscolor, misstate, negative 9 disaffirm, gloss over, repudiate 10 contradict, contravene, controvert 11 dissimulate 12 misrepresent

belief 3 ism 4 idea, mind, view 5 axiom, credo, creed, dogma, faith, hunch, tenet, trust 6 assent, avowal, credit, surety, theory, thesis 7 concept, feeling, opinion, precept, surmise, theorem 8 credence, doctrine, firmness, religion, sureness 9 assurance, certainty, certitude, intuition, postulate, principle, sentiment 10 acceptance, assumption, confidence, contention, conviction, hypothesis, impression, persuasion 11 supposition

believable 5 solid, sound, valid 6 cogent, likely, smooth, steady, trusty 7 logical, swaying, tenable, up front 8 credible, possible, probable, rational, reliable 9 authentic, colorable, plausible 10 convincing, creditable, impressive, meaningful, persuasive, presumable, reasonable, satisfying, supposable 11 conceivable, substantial, trustworthy 12 satisfactory

believe 3 buy 4 deem, hold, know 5 lap up, think, trust 6 accept, affirm, assume, credit, expect, reckon 7 fall for, imagine, profess, suppose, suspect, swallow 8 conceive, consider 10 conjecture, presuppose, understand

belittle 3 cut, pan 5 abuse, decry, knock, scorn 6 deride, insult, jeer at, revile 7 cut down, put down, run down, sneer at 8 bad-mouth, derogate, diminish, discount, minimize, write off 9 criticize, discredit, disparage, dispraise, downgrade, underrate 10 depreciate, undervalue 13 underestimate

belittlement 5 abuse, scorn 7 calumny, jeering, scandal, slander 8 derision, ridicule 9 aspersion 10 backbiting, defamation, detraction 11 denigration 12 backstabbing, depreciation 13 disparagement

Belize *capital:* 8 Belmopan *city:* 10 Belize City *ethnic group:* 4 Maya 5 Mayan *language:* 7 English, Spanish *monetary unit:* 6 dollar *mountain:* 8 Victoria *neighbor:* 6 Mexico 9 Guatemala *river:* 5 Hondo *sea:* 9 Caribbean

bell 4 peal 5 chime, knell 6 tocsin

belle 4 siren 6 beauty, eyeful 7 charmer 8 knockout, ornament 11 enchantress, femme fatale

Bellerophon *father:* 7 Glaucus 8 Poseidon *grandfather:* 8 Sisyphus *horse:* 7 Pegasus *victim:* 7 Chimera

belles lettres 10 literature

belletrist 8 novelist 4 poet 6 author, writer 9 dramatist 10 playwright

bellflower 9 campanula

___ **belli** 5 casus

bellicose 6 ornery 7 hawkish, hostile, martial, scrappy, warlike 8 factious, fighting, militant 9 assertive, combative, truculent 10 aggressive, pugnacious, rebellious 11 belligerent, contentious, hot-tempered, quarrelsome 12 disputatious, gladiatorial

belligerence 5 fight 6 attack, enmity, rancor, spleen 7 ill will 9 hostility, mili-

tancy, petulance, pugnacity **10** aggression, antagonism, truculence **11** bellicosity **12** churlishness **13** combativeness
belligerent 6 ardent, fierce **7** fighter, hostile, scrappy, soldier, warlike, warring, warrior **8** battling, churlish, fighting, invading, militant, opponent, petulant **9** aggressor, attacking, bellicose, combatant, combative, disputant, splenetic, truculent **10** aggressive, antagonist, pugnacious **11** contentious, hot-tempered, quarrelsome **12** antagonistic, disputatious
Bellini *opera:* **5** Norma **6** Pirata (Il) **8** Puritani (I) **10** Sonnambula (La) *sleepwalker:* **5** Amina
bell metal 6 bronze
bellow 3 bay, cry, moo **4** bark, bawl, bray, howl, roar, rout, yowl **5** shout **6** clamor, holler **7** bluster
Bellow character 4 Rose (Billy) **5** Chick **6** Herzog (Moses E.) **7** Citrine (Charlie), Sammler (Arthur) **8** Humboldt, Fonstein (Harry) **9** Henderson **10** Ravelstein (Abe), Augie March
bell ringer 6 toller **9** Quasimodo **12** carillonneur **13** campanologist
bell ringing 11 campanology
bell-shaped 11 campanulate
bell sound 4 bong, boom, ding, dong, peal, ring, ting, toll **5** chime, clang, knell **6** tinkle
bell tower 6 belfry **7** clocher **8** carillon **9** campanile
___ **bellum 4** ante, post
bellwether 4 dean, lead **5** doyen, guide, pilot **6** leader **7** pioneer **8** lodestar **9** harbinger **10** forerunner **11** trend setter
belly 3 gut, pot **5** tummy **6** paunch, venter **7** abdomen, midriff, stomach **9** bay window **10** front porch, midsection **11** breadbasket *Scottish:* **4** wame
bellyache 4 beef, carp, crab, fret, fuss, moan, yawp **5** bitch, bleat, colic, gripe, whine **6** grouse, snivel, squawk, yammer **7** grumble **8** complain **11** let off steam **12** collywobbles
bellyacher 4 crab **5** crank **6** griper, grouch, whiner **7** grouser **8** grumbler, sourpuss **10** complainer, crosspatch, malcontent **11** faultfinder
belly button 5 navel
belong 3 fit, set **4** suit, vest **5** agree, apply, befit, chime, fit in, match, tally **6** accord, attach, become, reside **7** pertain **9** correlate, harmonize **10** correspond
belongings 3 kit **4** gear **5** goods, stuff **6** assets, estate, legacy, things **7** baggage, effects **8** chattels, movables, property **9** patrimony **11** attachments,

impedimenta, inheritance, possessions **13** appurtenances
beloved 3 pet **4** baby, beau, dear, idol, love **5** flame, honey, lover, swain, sweet **6** adored, steady **7** darling, dearest, dear one, doted on, sweetie **8** favorite, idolized, ladylove, old flame, precious, truelove **9** boyfriend, cherished, inamorata, treasured **10** girlfriend, heartthrob, sweetheart, sweetie pie
below 5 infra, under **7** beneath **10** underneath *prefix:* **3** sub **5** infra
belt 3 bat, bop **4** area, band, bash, biff, blow, gird, loop, ring, sash, slam, slug, sock, whap, whop, zone **5** smack, smash, strap, strip **6** begird, cestus, circle, engird, girdle, region, wallop **7** baldric, clobber, stretch **8** begirdle, ceinture, cincture, encircle, engirdle **9** bandoleer, bandolier, territory, waistband **10** cummerbund *celestial:* **6** zodiac
beltway 8 ring road
Belus *brother:* **6** Agenor *daughter:* **4** Dido *father:* **7** Neptune **8** Poseidon *mother:* **5** Libya *son:* **6** Danaus **7** Cepheus, Phineus **8** Aegyptus
belvedere 6 alcove, cupola, gazebo, pagoda **7** balcony, terrace **10** widow's walk **11** garden house, summerhouse, observatory
bemedaled 9 decorated **10** beribboned
bemired 4 miry, oozy **5** boggy, dirty, grimy, gummy, gunky, muddy, stuck **6** filthy, soiled, swampy **7** swamped
bemoan 3 rue **4** wail, weep **6** bewail, grieve, lament, oppose, regret **7** deplore **8** complain, object to **10** sorrow over **12** disapprove of
bemuse 4 daze **5** addle **6** absorb, muddle, puzzle **7** confuse, mystify, nonplus, perplex **8** bewilder, distract **10** disconcert
bemused 3 wry **4** lost **6** absent, remote **7** faraway **8** distrait **9** distraite **10** abstracted, distracted **11** preoccupied **12** absentminded **13** lost in thought
bench 5 court **6** settee, settle, thwart **7** counter **8** platform **9** worktable *church:* **3** pew *outdoor:* **6** exedra *upholstered:* **9** banquette
benchmark 4 norm **5** basis, gauge, guide, model, scale **7** measure **8** exemplar, paradigm, standard **9** criterion, guideline, milestone, yardstick **10** touchstone
bend 3 arc, bow, sag **4** arch, bank, cave, curl, flex, hang, hook, lean, mold, sway, tend, tilt, turn, veer, warp **5** angle, crook, curve, round, shape, shift, stoop, twist, yield **6** compel, cor-

ner, buckle, direct, double, fasten,
kowtow, subdue, submit, zigzag
7 deflect, dispose, distort, flexure, turning **8** lean over **9** curvature, deviation,
genuflect **10** compromise, predispose
bendable 5 lithe **6** limber, pliant, supple
7 elastic, plastic, pliable **8** flexible,
moldable **9** malleable, tractable
11 manipulable
bender see BINGE
___ **bene 4** nota
beneath 5 below, under *prefix:* **3** hyp,
sub **4** hypo **5** infra
___ **Benedict 4** eggs
benediction 4 boon, okay **5** favor, grace
6 orison, thanks **7** benefit, benison,
godsend **8** approval, blessing **9** advantage **11** approbation **12** consecration,
thanksgiving
benefaction 4 alms, care, fund, gift, help
5 favor, grant **6** relief **7** charity, comfort, handout, largess, service, subsidy
8 donation, largesse, oblation, offering,
windfall **9** endowment, patronage
10 assistance **12** contribution, ministration
benefactor 5 angel, donor **6** backer,
patron **7** grantor, sponsor **9** supporter,
sustainer **11** contributor, underwriter
beneficence see BENEFACTION
beneficent 4 kind **6** benign, caring, giving **8** generous **10** altruistic, bighearted,
charitable, ungrudging **11** kindhearted,
magnanimous **13** compassionate, philanthropic
beneficial 4 good **5** brave, tonic
6 benign, toward, useful **7** helpful
8 favoring, salutary, valuable **9** favorable, healthful, nurturing, wholesome
10 profitable, propitious, salubrious
12 advantageous, constructive
beneficiary 4 heir **5** donee, payee
7 grantee, heiress, legatee **8** assignee
9 inheritor, recipient
beneficiate 5 treat **6** reduce **7** prepare,
process
benefit 3 aid **4** boon, gain, good, help,
perk, sake **5** avail, extra, favor, serve
6 assist, behalf, better, profit, relief,
succor **7** account, advance, charity, further, godsend, improve, promote,
relieve, welfare **8** blessing, interest
9 advantage, well-being **10** ameliorate,
fund-raiser, prosperity **11** good fortune
12 contribute to
benevolence 4 boon, gift, help **5** amity,
favor, grant **6** comity, relief **7** caritas,
charity **8** altruism, clemency, goodness,
goodwill, humanity, kindness **10** compassion, compliment, kindliness
11 magnanimity

benevolent 4 good, kind, warm **6** caring,
do-good, humane, kindly **7** helpful, liberal **8** generous, tolerant **10** altruistic,
beneficent, bighearted, charitable,
openhanded **11** considerate, magnanimous, warmhearted **12** eleemosynary,
humanitarian **13** compassionate, philanthropic, tenderhearted
Ben Hur author 7 Wallace (Lew)
benighted 6 obtuse, unread **8** backward,
ignorant, untaught **9** untutored, unwitting **10** illiterate, uneducated, uninformed, unlettered, unschooled
11 know-nothing **12** uncultivated
13 unenlightened, unprogressive
benign 4 kind, mild **6** genial, gentle,
humane, kindly, mellow **7** amiable,
clement **8** gracious, harmless, merciful,
pleasant **9** favorable, fortunate, healthful, temperate, wholesome **10** auspicious, benevolent, charitable, forbearing, propitious, remediable
11 good-hearted **12** noncancerous
Benin *capital:* **9** Porto-Novo *city:* **7** Cotonou *coast:* **5** Slave *ethnic group:* **3** Fon
6 Fulani, Yoruba *former name:*
7 Dahomey *language:* **3** Fon **6** French
monetary unit: **5** franc *neighbor:* **4** Togo
5 Niger **7** Nigeria **11** Burkina Faso *river:*
5 Ouémé
benison 5 grace **8** blessing **11** benediction **12** consecration
Benjamin *brother:* **6** Joseph *father:*
5 Jacob *mother:* **6** Rachel
bent 3 set **4** bias, gift **5** arced, bowed,
flair, knack **6** arched, curved, intent,
talent **7** decided, faculty, leaning **8** aptitude, capacity, penchant, resolute,
resolved, tendency **10** determined, proclivity, propensity **11** disposition, inclination **12** predilection
benumb 4 daze, dull, stun **5** blunt, chill
6 deaden, freeze **7** petrify, stupefy
8 etherize, paralyze **10** immobilize
11 desensitize
benumbed 4 cold **6** frozen **9** unfeeling
10 insensible **11** insensitive **12** anesthetized
Beowulf *drink:* **4** mead *monster:* **7** Grendel
bequeath 4 gift, will **5** endow, grant,
leave **6** bestow, commit, confer, devise,
hand on, impart, legate, pass on **7** furnish, present **8** hand down, make over,
transmit
bequest 3 lot **4** gift **5** share, trust
6 devise, estate, legacy **7** portion **8** heritage **10** settlement **11** inheritance
berate 3 jaw **4** rail, rate **5** chide, scold
6 rebuke, revile **7** bawl out, chew out,
condemn, reprove, tell off, upbraid

8 admonish, chastise, reproach **9** castigate, criticize, reprimand **10** tonguelash, vituperate

berceuse 7 lullaby **10** cradlesong

bereave 3 rob **4** lose **5** seize, strip **6** divest, remove **7** deprive **8** take away **10** confiscate, disinherit, dispossess **11** appropriate, requisition

bereaved 8 mourning **9** sorrowful, sorrowing **10** distressed **11** heartbroken **13** grief-stricken

bereavement 3 rue, woe **4** loss **5** dolor, grief **6** misery, pining, regret, sorrow **7** anguish, despair, remorse, sadness **8** grieving, mourning **9** dejection, heartache **10** affliction, depression, desolation **11** deprivation, despondency, lamentation, tribulation

bereft 5 shorn **6** devoid, robbed **7** fleeced, forlorn, wanting **8** beggared, deprived, desolate, divested, stripped **9** destitute **10** despondent **12** disconsolate, dispossessed, impoverished

Bergen's dummy 7 Charlie (McCarthy) **8** Mortimer (Snerd)

Berger novel 12 Little Big Man

Bergman role 4 Ilsa

berm 4 path **5** ledge, mound, shelf **8** shoulder

Bermuda *capital:* **8** Hamilton *territory of:* **7** Britain

Bernice *brother:* **7** Agrippa *father:* **5** Herod *husband:* **6** Polemo *lover:* **5** Titus **9** Vespasian

berry 5 cubeb, fruit, grape **7** currant, madrona, madrone **8** allspice **9** saskatoon

berserk 3 ape **4** amok **5** amuck, crazy **6** crazed, insane **7** bonkers, lunatic **8** demented, deranged, frenzied

berth 3 bed, cot **4** dock, moor, pier, port, post, quay, slip, spot **5** cabin, jetty, levee, place, wharf **6** billet, office **8** position **9** anchorage, situation **10** connection **11** appointment, compartment **13** accommodation

beseech see BEG

beset 3 dog, hem, try, vex **4** gird, ring **5** harry, hem in, storm, worry **6** assail, attack, badger, circle, fall on, harass, infest, pester, plague, strike **7** assault, besiege, overrun, trouble, torture **8** blockade, encircle, fall upon, surround **9** beleaguer, encompass, overswarm

besetment 3 nag **4** bane, pain, pest **5** curse, trial **6** blight, bother, gadfly, pester, plague **7** torment **8** irritant, nuisance, vexation **9** annoyance **10** affliction, botherment, holy terror **11** aggravation, botheration

besetting 6 urgent **7** driving **8** dominant **9** obsessive **10** compelling, persistent **11** omnipresent **12** overwhelming

beside 4 near, nigh **6** next to

besides 3 too **4** also, else, plus, save **5** added, extra **6** and all, as well, beyond, except, to boot **7** barring, farther, further, without **8** as well as, likewise, moreover, more than **9** aside from, along with, exceeding, excluding, other than, otherwise, outside of **10** in addition **11** exclusive of, furthermore, not counting **12** additionally, together with

besiege 3 nag **4** ring, trap **5** beset, hem in, hound **6** assail, attack, circle, girdle, harass, pester, plague **7** assault, confine, environ, trouble **8** blockade, encircle, surround **9** beleaguer, encompass

besmear see SMEAR

besmirch 4 blot, foul, slur, soil **5** dirty, libel, stain, sully, taint **6** defile, damage, impugn, malign **7** asperse, slander, tarnish **8** disgrace, dishonor

besom material 5 twigs

besotted 5 dotty, drunk **7** charmed, muddled, smitten **8** enamored **9** enchanted **10** captivated, fascinated, infatuated, spellbound **11** intoxicated

bespatter see SPATTER

bespeak 3 ask **4** book, hire, show **5** imply **6** accost, attest, desire, evince, reveal **7** address, apply to, betoken, connote, lecture, portend, request, reserve, signify, solicit, suggest, testify, witness **8** announce, approach, foretell, indicate, intimate, petition **9** preengage **10** prearrange

bespoke 8 tailored **10** custom-made

best 3 gem, top **4** beat, pick, tops **5** cream, elite, excel, model, outdo, pride, prime, prize **6** choice, defeat, exceed, finest **7** conquer, leading, optimal, optimum, paragon, premium, supreme, surpass **8** exemplar, foremost, greatest, nonesuch, outshine, outstrip, overcome **9** matchless, nonpareil, number-one, paramount, transcend, unequaled **11** outstanding **12** incomparable *combining form:* **6** aristo

bestial 4 vile, wild **5** brute, cruel, feral **6** animal, brutal, carnal, fierce, malign, savage **7** beastly, brutish, inhuman, swinish, vicious **8** depraved, inhumane **9** ferocious **10** degenerate

bestialize 4 ruin, warp **5** abase **6** debase, defile **7** corrupt, debauch, degrade, deprave, pervert, pollute, subvert, vitiate, violate **9** brutalize **10** bastardize, demoralize

bestir 3 fly, rip 4 dash, flit, goad, race, rush, spur, stir, tear, urge, wake, whet 5 rally, rouse, scoot, waken, whirl 6 arouse, awaken, hasten, hustle, kindle 8 get going, scramble 9 challenge

bestow 4 give 5 apply, award, grant 6 confer, devote, donate, lavish 7 hand out, present 8 bequeath, give away *Scottish:* 7 propine

bestower 5 donor, giver 6 patron 7 donator 8 altruist 9 conferrer, patroness, presenter 10 benefactor 12 benefactress 13 good Samaritan

bestrew 3 dot, sow 6 pepper, shower 7 diffuse, disject, scatter, speckle, stipple 8 disperse, sprinkle 9 broadcast, interlard 10 distribute 11 disseminate

bestride 5 mount, tower 8 dominate, loom over, straddle 9 stand over

bet 3 pot 4 ante, game, play, risk, shot 5 put on, stake, wager 6 gamble, hazard, parlay, pledge 7 lay odds, venture *racing:* 6 exacta 8 perfecta, quinella, quiniela *taker:* 6 bookie

Betelgeuse 4 star *constellation:* 5 Orion

betel palm 5 areca

bête noire 4 hate, ruin 5 trial 6 animus, horror 7 bugbear, scourge, torment, undoing 8 anathema, aversion, downfall 9 ruination 10 black beast

bethink 4 cite, mind 6 call up, recall, remind, retain, review, revive 7 flash on 8 hark back, look back, remember, summon up 9 conjure up, recollect, reminisce 10 call to mind, retrospect

Bethuel *daughter:* 7 Rebekah *father:* 5 Nahor *mother:* 6 Milcah *son:* 5 Laban *uncle:* 7 Abraham

betide 4 fall 5 break, ensue, occur 6 befall, chance, happen 7 come off, develop, fall out 8 commence 9 come about, transpire

betimes 4 anon, soon 5 early 6 pronto, seldom, timely 7 too soon 8 directly, far ahead, fitfully, promptly 9 presently 10 before long, now and then, on occasion, seasonably 11 prematurely 12 occasionally, sporadically

betoken 4 bode, omen, show, warn 5 argue, augur 6 attest, denote, hint at 7 bespeak, point to, portend, presage, promise, signify, suggest, testify, witness 8 announce, forebode, evidence, foreshow, foretell, indicate, intimate, prophesy, prefigure 10 foreshadow 13 prognosticate

betray 4 dupe, jilt, name, sell, show, tell, trap 5 bluff, cheat, knife, rat on, snare, spill, split 6 delude, desert, entrap, evince, finger, inform, reveal, seduce, take in, tattle, tell on, turn in, unmask, unveil 7 abandon, beguile, betoken, deceive, divulge, ensnare, forsake, let down, let slip, mislead, sell out, traduce, uncover 8 blurt out, denounce, disclose, discover, evidence, give away, indicate, manifest 9 deliver up 10 apostatize, break faith, lead astray 11 demonstrate, double-cross 13 inform against

betrayal 4 leak 7 perfidy, treason 8 exposure 9 duplicity, falseness, Judas kiss, treachery 10 disclosure, infidelity, revelation 13 faithlessness

betrayer 3 rat 4 fink, nark 5 Judas 6 snitch 7 stoolie, tattler, traitor 8 apostate, defector, informer, quisling, renegade, squealer, turncoat 10 talebearer, tattletale 11 backstabber, stool pigeon

betroth 3 wed 5 marry 6 pledge 7 espouse 8 affiance

betrothal 6 pledge 8 espousal 10 engagement

betrothed 6 fiancé 7 engaged, fiancée, pledged 8 intended, plighted, promised, wife-to-be 9 affianced, bride-to-be, spoken for 10 contracted 11 husband-to-be

better 3 fix, top, win 4 beat, help, mend, more, well 5 amend, cured, elder, excel, finer, outdo 6 exceed, fitter, repair 7 advance, correct, enhance, further, greater, improve, largest, mending, rectify, success, surpass, triumph, victory 8 greatest, improved, outshine, outstrip, stronger, superior, whip hand, worthier 9 advantage, desirable, excellent, healthier, improving, meliorate, preferred, transcend, upper hand 10 ameliorate, preferable, preferably, recovering, surpassing

bettor 7 gambler, wagerer

between 4 amid 5 among, twixt 6 within 7 betwixt *prefix:* 5 inter, intra

betweentimes 11 at intervals

bevel 4 bias, cant 5 angle, grade, slant, slope 7 chamfer, incline, oblique 8 diagonal

beverage 3 ade, nog, pop, tea 4 cola, maté, milk, soda 5 cider, cocoa, drink, juice, mocha, shake 6 coffee, eggnog, frappe, malted, nectar 7 potable, soda pop 8 lemonade, libation, potation 9 drinkable, milk shake *alcoholic:* 3 ale, gin, rum 4 beer, grog, mead, wine 5 cider, julep, negus, punch, stout, toddy, vodka 6 bishop, brandy, caudle, cooler, liquor, rickey, shandy, sherry, whisky 7 liqueur, martini, sangria, tequila, whiskey 8 cocktail, highball, sillabub, syllabub, vermouth *Arab:* 4 arak 6 arrack *Australasian:* 4 kava *Balkan:* 9 slivovitz *British:* 5 perry, stout

carbonated: 4 cola, soda 6 rickey 7 soda pop 8 root beer 9 ginger ale **central Asian:** 6 kumiss 7 koumiss **Dutch:** 7 schnaps 8 schnapps **from milk:** 5 kefir 6 kumiss 7 koumiss **Greek:** 4 ouzo 7 retsina **Irish:** 6 poteen 10 usquebaugh **medicinal:** 6 elixir **Mexican:** 6 pulque 7 tequila **of the gods:** 6 nectar **Oriental:** 4 arak, sake, saki 6 arrack **Russian:** 5 kefir, kvass, vodka **Scottish:** 6 scotch **South American:** 4 maté 5 yerba 9 yerba maté **Swedish:** 5 glogg **Turkish:** 4 raki **West Indies:** 3 rum

bevy 3 mob 4 band, club, crew, gang, herd, knot, pack 5 bunch, covey, crowd, drove, flock, group, horde, party, swarm 6 clutch, gaggle, troupe 7 cluster, company, coterie 8 assembly 9 menagerie, multitude 10 assemblage, collection

bewail 3 rue 4 keen, moan, weep 5 mourn 6 bemoan, grieve, lament, regret 7 deplore

beware 4 heed, mark, mind, note, shun 5 avoid, watch 6 attend, notice 7 look out 8 take heed, watch out

bewhiskered 5 bushy 7 bearded, goateed, hirsute, stubbly 8 unshaven

bewilder 3 fog 4 daze, stun 5 addle, amaze, befog, mix up, stump 6 baffle, ball up, bemuse, fuddle, muddle, puzzle, rattle 7 confuse, fluster, mystify, nonplus, perplex, stumble 8 befuddle, confound, distract 9 disorient, dumbfound 10 disconcert

bewilderment 3 awe 4 daze 6 wonder 8 surprise 9 amazement, confusion 10 perplexity, puzzlement 11 distraction 12 astonishment, discomfiture, stupefaction 13 consternation

bewitch 3 hex 4 draw, pull, snow, take, wile 5 charm, spell, trick 6 allure, dazzle, seduce, voodoo 7 attract, bedevil, beguile, control, delight, enchant, possess 8 demonize, ensorcel, enthrall, entrance, intrigue, overlook 9 captivate, enrapture, ensorcell, fascinate, hypnotize, magnetize, mesmerize, spellbind

bewitching 4 foxy 5 siren 8 alluring, charming, engaging, enticing, magnetic, mesmeric 9 seductive 10 attractive 12 irresistible

bewitchment 3 hex 4 jinx 5 charm, magic, spell 6 trance 7 evil eye, sorcery 8 black art, wizardry 9 conjuring 10 necromancy 11 conjuration, enchantment, incantation, thaumaturgy

beyond 4 over, past 5 above, after 6 across, beside, yonder 7 besides, further, outside 8 as well as 9 afterlife, hereafter, otherwise 10 afterworld 12 over and above **prefix:** 4 meta, over, para 5 extra, hyper, super, trans, ultra 6 preter

Bhutan capital: 7 Thimphu **ethnic group:** 6 Bhutia 8 Assamese, Nepalese 9 Mongolian, Sharcrops **language:** 8 Dzongkha **monetary unit:** 8 ngultrum **mountain range:** 8 Himalaya 13 Great Himalaya **neighbor:** 5 China, India, Tibet **plain:** 5 Duars

bias 4 bend, bent, skew, sway, tilt, turn 5 angle, bevel, slant 7 beveled, bigotry, dispose, distort, incline, leaning, oblique, slanted 8 diagonal, penchant, slanting, tendency 9 crosswise, inclining, influence, prejudice, proneness, viewpoint 10 diagonally, favoritism, partiality, propensity, predispose, prepossess, proclivity, standpoint, transverse 11 disposition, inclination 12 onesidedness, predilection 13 preconception

biased 6 racist, swayed, unfair, warped 7 bigoted, colored, partial, slanted 8 disposed, inclined, one-sided, partisan, slanting 9 jaundiced, sectarian, unneutral 10 influenced, interested, prejudiced 11 opinionated, predisposed, tendentious

bibelot 5 curio 6 bauble, gewgaw, trifle 7 memento, novelty, trinket, whatnot 8 gimcrack, ornament 9 objet d'art 10 knickknack

Bible abbreviation: 3 Col, Cor, Dan, Eph, Gal, Gen, Hab, Heb, Hos, Jas, Jer, Jon, Lam, Lev, Mal, Mic, Neh, Num, Pet, Rev, Rom, Sam, Tim, Tit 4 Deut, Ezek, Josh, Judg, Obad, Phil, Prov, Zech, Zeph 5 Chron, Thess 6 Eccles, Philem **Apocrypha book:** 5 Tobit 6 Baruch, Esdras, Esther, Judith 7 Susanna 8 Manasseh, Manasses 9 Maccabees **New Testament book:** 4 Acts, John, Jude, Luke, Mark 5 James, Peter, Titus 6 Romans 7 Hebrews, Matthew, Timothy 8 Philemon 9 Ephesians, Galatians 10 Colossians, Revelation 11 Corinthians, Philippians 13 Thessalonians **Old Testament book:** 3 Job 4 Amos, Ezra, Joel, Ruth 5 Hosea, Jonah, Kings, Micah, Nahum 6 Daniel, Esther, Exodus, Haggai, Isaiah, Joshua, Judges, Psalms, Samuel 7 Ezekiel, Genesis, Malachi, Numbers, Obadiah 8 Habakkuk, Jeremiah, Nehemiah, Proverbs 9 Leviticus, Zechariah, Zephaniah 10 Chronicles 11 Deuteronomy 12 Ecclesiastes, Lamentations 13 Song of Solomon **part:** 4 book

5 verse 7 chapter 9 testament *translator:*
4 Knox (Ronald Arbuthnott) 5 Eliot
(John) 6 Jerome, Luther (Martin)
7 Erasmus (Desiderius), Tyndale
(William), Zwingli (Huldrych)
8 Andrewes (Lancelot), Wycliffe (John)
9 Coverdale (Miles) *version:* 5 Douay
6 Coptic, Gothic, Syriac 7 Vulgate
9 Jerusalem, King James, Masoretic
10 New English, Septuagint

Biblical *animal:* 8 behemoth *ascetic
order:* 6 Essene *battle:* 7 Jericho *battle
site:* 10 Armageddon *charioteer:* 4 Jehu
city, town: 4 Cana, Gaza, Tyre, Zoar
5 Endor, Golan, Haifa, Joppa, Sidon,
Sodom 6 Asshur, Bethel, Emmaus, Gil-
gal, Hebron, Mizpah, Shiloh, Smyrna,
Tarsus 7 Antioch, Baalbec, Bethany,
Corinth, Ephesus, Ephraim, Jericho,
Magdala, Nineveh, Samaria 8 Caesarea,
Damascus, Gomorrah, Nazareth,
Philippi, Tiberias 9 Beersheba, Bethle-
hem, Capernaum, Jerusalem *coin:* (see
at HEBREW) *desert:* 5 Sinai *garden:*
4 Eden 8 Paradise *giant:* 7 Goliath *giant
slayer:* 5 David *hill:* 4 Zion 7 Calvary
hunter: 6 Nimrod *judge:* 3 Eli 4 Ehud
6 Gideon, Samson, Samuel 7 Deborah,
Jephtha 8 Jephthah *king:* 3 Asa 4 Ahab,
Amon, Elah, Jehu, Saul 5 David,
Herod, Hiram 6 Josiah 7 Azariah,
Menahem, Solomon 8 Hezekiah, Jer-
oboam, Manasseh, Rehoboam, Zedeki-
ah 9 Zechariah 11 Jehoshaphat *land:*
3 Nod 4 Aram, Elam, Moab, Seba
5 Judah, Judea 6 Canaan, Goshen,
Israel 7 Chaldea, Galilee, Samaria
9 Palestine *land of plenty:* 6 Goshen
measure: (see at HEBREW) *mountain:*
5 Horeb, Sinai 6 Ararat, Carmel,
Gilboa, Gilead, Hermon, Moriah,
Olivet, Pisgah 7 Lebanon *name:* 3 Asa,
Bel, Dan, Eli, Eve, Gad, Ham, Ira, Job,
Lot, Uri 4 Abel, Adam, Ahab, Amon,
Boaz, Cain, Elam, Enos, Esau, Jael,
Jehu, Joel, John, Lael, Leah, Levi,
Mark, Mary, Mica, Moab, Noah, Omar,
Onan, Paul, Reba, Ruth, Sara, Saul,
Seth, Shem 5 Aaron, Abner, Amram,
Asher, Caleb, David, Dinah, Elias,
Enoch, Ethan, Hagar, Heman, Herod,
Hosea, Isaac, Jacob, James, Jared,
Jesse, Jonah, Jubal, Judah, Judas,
Laban, Micah, Moses, Naomi, Peter,
Rufus, Sarah, Sheba, Simon, Tamar,
Tubal, Uriah, Uriel, Zadok 6 Ashhur,
Balaam, Baruch, Canaan, Daniel, Eli-
jah, Elisha, Esther, Gideon, Gilead,
Hannah, Hebron, Isaiah, Israel, Jeshua,
Jethro, Joanna, Joseph, Joshua, Josiah,
Judith, Martha, Miriam, Nathan, Nim-

rod, Pasach, Philip, Pilate, Rachel,
Reuben, Salome, Samson, Samuel,
Simeon, Thomas, Tobias *patriarch:* (see
at HEBREW) *people:* 6 Kenite, Levite
7 Amorite, Edomite, Elamite, Moabite
9 Israelite *plains:* 6 Sharon 7 Jericho
plotter: 5 Haman *poem:* 5 psalm *pool:*
8 Bethesda *priest:* 3 Eli 4 Levi 5 Aaron,
Annas 8 Caiaphas *Promised Land:*
6 Canaan *pronoun:* 3 thy 4 thee, thou
5 thine *prophet:* (see PROPHET) *Psalmist:*
5 David *punishment:* 7 stoning *queen:*
5 Sheba 6 Esther 7 Jezebel *river:* 4 Nile
6 Jordan *sacred object:* 4 urim 7 thum-
min *scribe:* 6 Baruch *sea:* 3 Red 4 Dead
7 Galilee *sea monster:* 9 Leviathan
spice: 5 aloes, myrrh 6 cassia 7 calamus
8 cinnamon 12 frankincense *spy:*
5 Caleb *temptress:* 3 Eve 7 Delilah *thief:*
8 Barabbas *tree:* 5 cedar *valley:* 4 Baca,
Elah 6 Hinnon, Kidron, Shaveh, Siddim
witch's home: 5 Endor

bibliography 4 list 7 catalog, history
8 book list 13 reference list

bibliopole 7 bookman 10 book dealer,
bookseller

bibulous 6 spongy 7 thirsty 8 drinking
9 absorbent 10 absorptive

bicker 3 row 4 spar, spat, tiff 5 argue,
clack, fight, scrap 6 gurgle, hassle
7 brabble, clatter, contend, dispute, fall
out, flicker, quarrel, quibble, wrangle
8 squabble

bickering 3 row 4 spat 5 brawl, run-in
6 blowup, fracas, hassle, ruckus, rumpus, strife 7 discord, dispute, quarrel,
rhubarb, wrangle 8 squabble 11 altercation, embroilment

bicycle 4 bike *brake:* 7 caliper, coaster
for two: 6 tandem *gear shift:*
10 derailleur *rider:* 6 cycler 7 cyclist

bid 3 ask, say, try 4 call, tell, warn, wish
5 essay, greet, offer, order 6 amount,
charge, direct, effort, enjoin, invite,
render, summon, tender 7 attempt,
command, proffer, request, require,
venture 8 endeavor, instruct, proposal
10 invitation, submission 11 proposition

biddable 4 mild 6 docile, pliant 7 amiable, pliable, willing 8 amenable, obedient, obliging 9 tractable 10 governable,
manageable 11 acquiescent, cooperative, good-natured 13 accommodating

bidding 4 call, word 5 offer, order
6 behest, charge, demand, notice, tender 7 auction, command, dictate, mandate, request, summons 9 ordinance,
summoning 10 injunction, invitation
11 commandment, instruction
12 proclamation

biddy 3 bag, bat, hag, hen 4 drab, trot
5 crone, witch 6 beldam 7 chicken
bide 4 live, stay, wait 5 await, dwell,
tarry 6 hang in, linger, remain, reside
7 hang out, sojourn 8 continue, sit
tight, tolerate 10 hang around 11 stick
around
bier 10 catafalque
biff 3 bop, box, hit, jab, zap 4 bash, belt,
blow, clip, ding, nail, slam, slug, sock,
swat, whop 5 blast, catch, clout,
pound, slosh, smack, thump, whack
6 strike, thwack, wallop
bifurcate 3 cut 4 fork 5 halve, split
6 bisect, branch, cleave, divide 8 separate 9 branch out 11 dichotomize,
dichotomous
bifurcation 4 fork 6 branch 8 division
9 dichotomy, partition, radiation
10 separation
big 3 fat 4 full, hard, huge, main, tall,
vast 5 adult, ample, chief, great, grown,
heavy, hefty, husky, large, lofty, major,
proud, roomy 6 bumper, hugely 7 capital, copious, crammed, crowded, eminent, grown-up, hulking, leading, liberal, mammoth, massive, monster,
notable, popular, replete, sizable,
stuffed, swollen, weighty 8 colossal,
enormous, generous, gracious, imposing, inflated, material, oversize, princely, spacious, swelling 9 capacious,
chock-full, distended, extensive, heavy
duty, humongous, important, momentous, overblown, paramount, ponderous, principal, prominent, unselfish
10 commodious, large-scale, preeminent, prodigious, voluminous 11 heavyweight, magnanimous, major league,
overflowing, significant, substantial
12 considerable 13 comprehensive, consequential
big bang theorist 5 Gamow (George)
Big Bertha's birthplace 5 Essen
Big ___, Cal. 3 Sur
Big Dipper *constellation:* 9 Ursa Major
star: 5 Alcor, Dubhe, Merak, Mizar
bigfoot 9 Sasquatch
biggety 4 bold, vain, wise 5 fresh, nervy,
sassy 6 cheeky, snippy, snooty, uppity
7 forward, stuck-up 8 impudent, insolent, puffed up, snobbish 9 conceited
11 smart-alecky 13 self-important
bighearted 6 giving 7 liberal 8 generous
9 forgiving 10 altruistic, benevolent,
charitable, munificent, openhanded
11 magnanimous 13 compassionate
big house 3 can, jug, pen 4 coop, jail
5 clink, joint 6 cooler, lockup, prison
7 slammer 8 bastille, hoosegow, stock-

ade 9 bridewell 11 reformatory 12 penitentiary
bight 3 arm, bay 4 cove, gulf 6 harbor
bigmouthed 4 loud, rude 8 boastful
10 boisterous
bigness 4 size 5 scale, scope 6 extent,
volume 9 amplitude, immensity, magnitude 10 dimensions, importance
bigot 6 racist 8 jingoist 9 extremist,
racialist 10 chauvinist 11 supremacist
bigoted 6 biased, narrow, unfair 9 hidebound, illiberal, sectarian 10 brassbound, intolerant, prejudiced 11 small-
minded 12 narrow-minded
bigotry 4 bias 6 racism 9 apartheid, prejudice 10 xenophobia 11 intolerance
big shot 3 VIP 4 czar 5 celeb, mogul,
nabob 6 bigwig, fat cat, tycoon 7 kingpin, notable, pooh-bah 8 higher-up,
luminary, top brass 9 celebrity, dignitary, personage 13 high-muck-a-muck
big-time 5 major 7 eminent, greatly,
leading 8 renowned 9 high-level,
important, paramount, prominent
10 large-scale 11 influential, major-
league
big top 4 tent 6 circus
bigwig 3 VIP 5 heavy, mogul, nabob
6 honcho, kahuna 7 kingpin, magnate,
notable 8 luminary, somebody 9 dignitary, personage 11 heavy hitter, muckety-muck 13 high-muck-a-muck
bijou 3 gem 5 jewel 8 gemstone
bijouterie 6 jewels 7 jewelry 8 trinkets
10 decoration
bike 5 cycle 7 scooter 10 motorcycle
12 motorscooter
bilge 3 rot 4 bull, bunk, guff 5 hooey,
trash 6 bunkum 7 baloney, garbage,
hogwash, malarky, rubbish, twaddle
8 claptrap, nonsense 9 poppycock, silliness 10 balderdash 11 foolishness
bilk 3 con, gyp 4 balk, beat, dash, duck,
dupe, foil, fool, hoax, hose, kite, milk,
ruin, scam, take 5 avoid, cheat, cozen,
dodge, elude, evade, shake, shaft, skirt,
stiff, trick 6 baffle, chisel, chouse, diddle, double, escape, eschew, fleece, rip
off, sucker, thwart 7 deceive, defraud,
prevent, swindle 8 flimflam, hoodwink,
sidestep, stave off 9 frustrate 10 circumvent
bill 3 dun, fin, neb, nib, tab 4 beak,
bone, buck, chit, list, note, skin
5 check, score, visor 6 charge, damage,
dollar, notice, poster, roster 7 account,
charges, invoice, placard, program,
sawbuck, smacker 8 mandible 9 greenback, reckoning, smackeroo, statement
billet 3 bar, bed, gig, hut, job, rod 4 post,
slab, spar, spot 5 berth, board, house,

ingot, lodge, place, put up, stick, strip **6** bestow, canton, harbor, office **7** quarter **8** domicile, position, quarters, vocation **9** entertain, situation **10** assignment, connection, employment, encampment, livelihood, profession, occupation **11** appointment

billet-doux 8 mash note **10** love letter
billfold 6 wallet
billiards term 3 cue **4** foot, head, jaws, kiss, long, peas, pool, race, rack, spot **5** break, carom, chalk, count, masse **6** bridge, cannon, corner, crotch, inning, miscue, nurses, pocket, stance, string **7** bricole, cue ball, cushion, ferrule, kitchen, pyramid, scratch, shooter, snooker **8** apex ball, balkline, bank shot, cue stick, dead ball, jump shot, rotation, triangle **9** clean bank, eight ball **10** chuck nurse, head string, object ball **12** balance point
billingsgate 5 abuse **6** tirade **7** obloquy **9** contumely, invective **10** revilement, scurrility **12** vilification, vituperation
billion British: 8 milliard **combining form: 4** giga
billionth combining form: 4 nano
bill of fare 4 menu **7** program **11** carte du jour
billow 4 mass, wave **5** bulge, cloud, surge, swell **6** puff up, roller **7** balloon, upsurge
Billy Budd's captain 4 Vere
billy club 4 cane **5** baton **6** cudgel, paddle **8** bludgeon **9** bastinado, truncheon **10** knobkerrie, nightstick
bin 4 crib **5** frame, stall **6** bunker, hamper, trough **9** container **10** receptacle
binary 4 twin, dual **5** duple **6** double, duplex, paired **7** coupled, matched, twofold **9** dualistic
bind 3 tie **4** frap, gird, tape, wrap **5** chain, cinch, strap, tie up, truss **6** cement, commit, fasten, fetter, ligate, pinion **7** bandage, confine, enchain, shackle, trammel **8** enfetter, restrain **9** constrain, constrict, indenture
binder 4 file **5** cover **6** folder, jacket **7** wrapper
binding 8 required **9** mandatory, requisite **10** obligatory
bindlestiff 4 hobo
binge 3 jag **4** orgy, riot, soak, tear, time, toot **5** blast, booze, fling, party, revel, souse, spree, stint **6** bender **7** blowoff, blowout, carouse, debauch, rampage, revelry, shindig, splurge, surfeit, wassail **8** carousal, gluttony **9** bacchanal, brannigan **10** debauchery, indulgence **11** bacchanalia, celebration **12** intemperance

bingo 3 yes **5** beano **7** correct
biographer American: 5 Weems (Parson) **6** Parton (James) **7** Freeman (Douglas) **8** Bradford (Gamaliel), Sandburg (Carl) **10** McCullough (David) **English: 6** Aubrey (John), Morley (John), Walton (Izaak) **8** Strachey (Lytton) **French: 7** Maurois (André) **German: 6** Ludwig (Emil) **Greek: 8** Plutarch **Italian: 6** Vasari (Giorgio) **Roman: 9** Suetonius **Scottish 7** Boswell (James)
biography 3 bio **4** life, obit, vita **5** diary, story **6** memoir **7** history, profile **8** obituary **11** confessions
biological category 5 class, genus, order **6** family, phylum **7** kingdom, species, variety **10** subspecies
bionomics 7 ecology
Bip's creator 7 Marceau (Marcel)
bird African: 6 barbet, bulbul, jabiru, turaco **7** courser, marabou, ostrich, touraco **8** hornbill, oxpecker, parakeet **9** broadbill, francolin **Antarctic: 4** skua **7** penguin **10** sheathbill **aquatic: 3** auk, mew **4** coot, duck, erne, gull, loon, skua, swan, teal, tern **5** booby, cahow, goose, grebe, murre **6** fulmar, gannet, petrel, puffin, scoter, wigeon **7** anhinga, dovekie, mallard, moorhen, pelican, penguin, skimmer, widgeon **8** baldpate, dabchick, murrelet **9** albatross, cormorant, gallinule, guillemot, kittiwake **10** shearwater, sheathbill **arctic: 3** auk **4** knot, skua **5** murre **6** fulmar, jaeger **7** dovekie **9** guillemot, gyrfalcon **Asian: 4** myna, ruff, smew **5** mynah, pewit **6** chukar, drongo, dunlin, hoopoe, peewit **7** courser, lapwing, peacock **8** dotterel, hornbill, parakeet, tragopan, wheatear **9** francolin **Australian: 3** emu **4** lory **5** galah **6** drongo **7** bustard **8** bellbird, cockatoo, lorikeet, lyrebird, parakeet **9** cassowary **blackbird: 3** ani, daw **4** crow, rook **5** merle, ousel, ouzel, raven **6** chough, magpie, thrush **7** grackle, jackdaw, redwing **carrion-eating: 6** condor **7** buzzard, vulture **Central American: 4** guan, ibis **5** booby, macaw **6** barbet, jabiru, toucan **7** bittern, jacamar, quetzal, tinamou **8** curassow, troupial **chimney-nesting: 5** swift **class: 4** Aves **colony: 5** roost **7** rookery **combining form: 5** ornis **6** ornith **7** ornitho **8** ornithes (plural) **crow family: 3** daw, jay **4** rook **5** raven **6** chough, corbie, magpie **7** jackdaw **diving: 3** auk **4** smew **5** grebe, murre **6** petrel **8** murrelet **9** guillemot, merganser **European: 3** mew **4** rook, smew, wren **5** crake, egret, finch, merle, ousel, ouzel, pewit, pipit **6** cuckoo, hoopoe, linnet, martin,

merlin, redleg, thrush **7** bustard, jackdaw, kestrel, lapwing, martlet, ortolan, redwing, sparrow, wagtail **8** blackcap, dabchick, nightjar, nuthatch, redstart, starling, throstle, whimbrel, woodcock **9** chaffinch, crossbill, stonechat **10** chiffchaff, goatsucker, kingfisher **11** lammergeier *extinct:* **3** moa **4** dodo **9** aepyornis, solitaire *fabulous:* **3** roc **7** phoenix *fish-eating:* **4** erne **6** osprey *flightless:* **3** emu, moa **4** dodo, kiwi, rhea **6** kakapo, ratite, takahe **7** apteryx, ostrich, penguin **9** cassowary *game:* **4** duck, rail, teal **5** brant, goose, quail, snipe **6** chukar, grouse, turkey **7** bustard, mallard, pintail, widgeon **8** baldpate, bobwhite, moorfowl, pheasant, shoveler, tragopan, wildfowl, woodcock **9** merganser, partridge, ptarmigan *ground-dwelling:* **5** quail **6** grouse, peahen, turkey **7** chicken, peacock, peafowl **8** bobwhite, moorfowl, pheasant **9** partridge, ptarmigan *Indian:* **6** bulbul **7** peacock **8** adjutant, tragopan *Jamaican:* **7** vervain *large:* **3** emu, moa **5** eagle **6** curlew **7** bustard, ostrich, pelican **8** curassow, shoebill *largest:* **7** ostrich *Madagascar:* **6** drongo **7** anhinga *marsh:* **4** coot, rail **5** crane, snipe, stilt **9** gallinule *Mexican:* **6** jacana *mythical:* **3** roc **7** phoenix *New Zealand:* **3** kea **4** kiwi **6** kakapo **7** apteryx *nocturnal:* **3** owl **5** owlet **7** oilbird **8** guacharo, nightjar **9** nighthawk **10** goatsucker *North American:* **3** ani, tit **4** coot, wren **5** booby, crane, egret, junco, murre, robin, swift, veery, vireo **6** dunlin, fulmar, grouse, phoebe, towhee, turkey, verdin, willet **7** anhinga, blue jay, catbird, flicker, grackle, tanager **8** bobolink, bobwhite, cardinal, killdeer, nuthatch, thrasher, titmouse **9** chickadee, crossbill, nighthawk, partridge, snakebird **10** bufflehead **12** whippoorwill *of Arabian Nights:* **3** roc *of brilliant plumage:* **4** lory **5** macaw **6** oriole, parrot, toucan, trogon **7** jacamar **8** lorikeet, parakeet, pheasant, tragopan *of peace:* **4** dove *of prey:* **3** owl **4** hawk, kite **5** buteo, eagle, harpy **6** condor, falcon, osprey, raptor **7** buzzard, goshawk, harrier, kestrel, vulture **8** caracara **9** accipiter **11** lammergeier *passerine:* (see SONGBIRD below) *razorbilled:* **3** auk *relating to:* **5** avian **6** ornithic *shore:* **3** auk **4** gull, tern **5** snipe, stilt **6** avocet, curlew, dunlin, plover, puffin, willet **7** lapwing, skimmer **8** killdeer, whimbrel, woodcock **9** phalarope, sandpiper, turnstone *small:* **3** tit **4** wren **5** finch, pewee, pipit, vireo **6** canary,

tomtit, verdin **7** sparrow **8** titmouse **9** chickadee *songbird:* **3** jay, tit **4** chat, crow, lark, wren **5** finch, pipit, robin, veery, vireo **6** bulbul, canary, linnet, oriole, shrike, thrush **7** catbird, creeper, kinglet, redwing, skylark, sparrow, swallow, tanager, titlark, wagtail, warbler, waxwing **8** bobolink, brantail, cardinal, nuthatch, Philomel, redstart, starling, thrasher, woodlark **9** chickadee, stonechat **10** chiffchaff, flycatcher **11** nightingale *South American:* **4** guan, loro, rhea **5** egret, macaw **6** jabiru, toucan **7** jacamar, limpkin, oilbird **8** caracara, curassow, guacharo, screamer, troupial **9** trumpeter *talking:* **4** myna **5** mynah **6** parrot *tropical:* **3** ani **6** barbet, drongo, toucan, trogon **7** jacamar, quetzal, sawbill, waxbill **8** troupial *turkey-like:* **8** curassow *unfledged:* **4** eyas **5** chick **8** nestling *wading:* **4** ibis, rail **5** crane, egret, heron, stork **6** godwit, jabiru, jacana **7** bittern, limpkin, tattler **8** flamingo, shoebill **9** spoonbill *web-footed:* **3** auk **4** duck, loon, swan **5** goose, murre **6** avocet, fulmar, gannet, petrel, puffin **7** anhinga, pelican, penguin **8** shoveler **9** albatross, cormorant, guillemot, merganser, razorbill, snakebird **10** shearwater *West Indian:* **3** ani

birdbrain 4 dodo, goof **5** dummy, dunce, idiot, moron, ninny **6** nitwit **7** airhead, dullard, halfwit **8** dumbbell, imbecile, meathead, numskull **9** dumb bunny, ignoramus, numbskull, simpleton **10** nincompoop **11** featherhead

birdcage 6 aviary

birdlife 8 avifauna

bird pepper 9 chiltepin

birds' eggs *study of:* **6** oology

birth 4 dawn, stem **5** arise, issue, onset, start **6** create, outset, spring **7** emanate, genesis, lineage, opening **8** delivery, generate, geniture, nascence, nascency, nativity, pedigree **9** beginning, originate **10** extraction **11** parturition **12** commencement

birth-control leader 6 Sanger (Margaret)

birth flower *April:* **5** daisy *August:* **9** gladiolus *December:* **10** poinsettia *February:* **8** primrose *January:* **9** carnation *July:* **8** sweet pea *June:* **4** rose *March:* **6** violet *May:* **15** lily of the valley *November:* **13** chrysanthemum *October:* **6** dahlia *September:* **5** aster

birthmark 4 mole **5** nevus, point, trait **7** feature **13** discoloration

Birth of a Nation director 8 Griffith (D. W.)

birthright 3 due, lot **6** legacy **7** bequest,

birthroot 8 trillium

portion 8 appanage, heirloom, heritage 9 patrimony 11 entitlement, inheritance

birthstone *April:* 7 diamond 8 sapphire *August:* 7 peridot 8 sardonyx *December:* 6 zircon 9 turquoise *February:* 8 amethyst *January:* 6 garnet *July:* 4 ruby *June:* 5 agate, pearl 11 alexandrite *March:* 6 jasper 10 aquamarine, bloodstone *May:* 7 emerald *November:* 5 topaz *October:* 4 opal 10 tourmaline *September:* 8 sapphire 10 chrysolite

biscuit 4 rusk, snap 6 cookie 7 cracker 8 cracknel, hardtack

bishop *district:* 7 diocese *headdress:* 5 miter, mitre *seat of office:* 3 see *skullcap:* 9 zucchetto *staff:* 7 crosier, crozier *throne:* 8 cathedra

bishopric 3 see 7 diocese

bison *European:* 6 wisent 7 aurochs *family:* 7 Bovidae *North American:* 7 buffalo

bistered 4 dark 5 brown, dusky, swart, tawny 6 brunet, tanned 7 swarthy 8 brunette 11 dark-skinned

bistro 3 bar, pub 4 café 5 joint 6 nitery, tavern 7 barroom, cabaret, hot spot, niterie, taproom 8 snack bar 9 nightclub, night spot 10 coffee shop 11 rathskeller 13 watering place

bit 3 dab, dot, end, jot, tad 4 atom, dash, drop, iota, lump, mite, part, rein, tick, time, whet 5 borer, flake, grain, minim, pinch, scrap, shard, shred, slice, space, speck, spell, trace, while 6 minute, moment, morsel, rather, second 7 portion, segment, smidgen, stretch, trickle 8 fraction, fragment, molecule, mouthful, particle, somewhat

bit by bit 6 evenly 9 by degrees, gradually, piecemeal 12 continuously 13 slow and steady

bitch goddess 7 success

bite 3 cut, eat, lot, nip 4 chaw, chew, edge, etch, food, gnaw, kick, meal, pain, part, rust, snap, tapa, zest 5 champ, chomp, erode, munch, piece, quota, share, slice, snack, stink, taste, tooth 6 crunch, morsel, nibble 7 corrode, eat away, eat into, engrave, portion 8 dissolve, mouthful, piquancy 9 allotment, allowance, masticate, occlusion 10 laceration 11 refreshment

biting 3 raw 4 cold 5 bleak, crisp, harsh, nippy, sharp 6 bitter, severe 7 acerbic, caustic, cutting, mordant, satiric 8 freezing, incisive, piercing, scathing 9 sarcastic, trenchant 11 penetrating

bitter 4 acid, tart 5 acerb, acrid, harsh, sharp 6 severe 7 acerbic, caustic, galling, hostile, painful 8 grievous, ruthless, virulent 9 rancorous, vexa-tious, vitriolic 11 acrimonious, unpalatable 12 antagonistic

bitterness 4 gall 6 rancor 7 ill will 8 acridity, acrimony, asperity, coldness 9 animosity, antipathy 10 resentment

bittersweet 4 vine 8 poignant 10 nightshade

bitumen 3 tar 5 pitch 7 asphalt 8 blacktop

bivalve 4 clam, spat 6 cockle, mussel, oyster 7 geoduck, mollusk, piddock, scallop 9 lampshell 10 brachiopod

bivouac 4 camp, tent 6 billet, encamp, laager, maroon 7 shelter, sojourn 10 encampment

bizarre 3 odd 5 antic, queer, weird 7 curious, oddball, strange, uncanny, unusual 8 abnormal, atypical, freakish, peculiar, quixotic, singular 9 anomalous, eccentric, fantastic, grotesque, unearthly, unnatural 10 outlandish, outrageous 11 extravagant

bizarrerie 5 freak 6 oddity 7 anomaly, caprice, oddness 9 curiosity, weirdness 10 aberration

Bizet opera 6 Carmen

blab 3 gab, gas, jaw, yak 4 chat, leak, talk, tell 5 run on, spill 6 babble, betray, burble, gabble, gossip, inform, jabber, reveal, snitch, squeal, tattle, tell on, yammer 7 blather, chatter, divulge, let slip, palaver, prattle 8 blurt out, disclose, give away, go public

blabber 3 gab, rat 4 chat, fink 5 clack, drool, prate 6 babble, canary, drivel, gabber, gabble, gossip, jabber, magpie, prater, ramble 7 blather, chatter, palaver, prattle, twaddle 8 idle talk, jabberer, prattler 9 chatterer 10 chatterbox, tattletale

blabbermouth 3 rat 4 fink 6 canary, gabber, gossip, magpie, prater, snitch 7 windbag 8 busybody, jabberer, prattler 10 chatterbox, talebearer, tattletale 11 stool pigeon

black 3 jet 4 ebon, inky, noir, onyx 5 ebony, raven, sable 6 pitchy 8 charcoal, funereal 9 pitch-dark *combining form:* 3 mel 4 atro, mela, melo 5 melam, melan 6 melano

blackball 3 bar 4 veto, shun, snub 5 block, spurn 6 ice out, refuse, reject, strike 7 boycott, exclude, keep out, rule out 9 interdict, ostracize 11 vote against

black bass 7 sunfish

black beast see BÊTE NOIRE

Black Beauty author 6 Sewell (Anna)

blackbird see BIRD

black cohosh 7 bugbane

black crappie 7 sunfish 10 calico bass

black death 6 plague 13 bubonic plague
black diamond 4 coal 8 hematite 9 carbonado
blacken 3 dim, fog, ink 4 blot, burn, char, sear, slur, soil, soot 5 cloud, libel, shade, singe, smear, sully, taint 6 bruise, darken, defame, defile, malign, scorch, vilify 7 asperse, cloud up, eclipse, slander, traduce 8 besmirch, dishonor 10 calumniate
black eye 4 blot, onus, slur 5 stain 6 bruise, defeat, shiner, stigma 7 setback
blackfish 5 whale 6 tautog 10 pilot whale
Black Forest 11 Schwarzwald *city:* 10 Baden-Baden *peak:* 8 Feldberg *river:* 5 Rhein, Rhine 6 Danube, Neckar
black gold 3 oil 9 petroleum
blackguard 4 heel, punk 5 abuse, cheat, knave, rogue 6 rascal 7 hoodlum, lowlife, ruffian, villain 8 hooligan, scalawag 9 charlatan, miscreant, reprobate, scoundrel 10 delinquent, mountebank 11 rapscallion
blackhead 3 zit 4 spot 5 sebum 6 pimple 10 larval clam
blackjack 3 oak, sap 4 bash, club, cosh 6 coerce 7 pontoon, tankard 8 bludgeon 9 twenty-one, vingt-et-un 10 sphalerite
black lead 8 graphite
black letter 6 Gothic 10 Old English
blacklist 3 bar 4 oust 5 expel, purge, smear 6 banish, impugn 7 boycott, condemn, exclude, shut out 8 denounce 9 ostracize, proscribe 10 stigmatize
blackmail 5 bleed 6 extort, payoff 7 milking, squeeze 8 chantage, coercion 9 extortion, hush money, shake down
black out 4 edit, wipe 5 annul, erase, faint, swoon 6 cancel, censor, cut off, darken, delete, efface, excise 7 conceal, eclipse, expunge 8 collapse, make dark, sanitize, suppress 9 eradicate, expurgate 10 blue-pencil, obliterate
blackpoll 7 warbler
Black Prince 6 Edward
Black Sea *city:* 5 Yalta 6 Odessa 9 Constanta *peninsula:* 6 Crimea 7 Crimean
Blackshirt 7 fascist
blacksmith 6 forger 7 farrier, striker 10 horseshoer
blacktail 8 mule deer
blackthorn 4 plum, sloe
black widow 6 spider
bladder 3 sac 4 cyst 5 pouch 7 blister, vacuole 7 vesicle
blade 4 beau, buck, dude, edge, leaf 5 knife, sword 6 runner 9 swordsman
blah 4 bosh, dull, flat, tame 5 ho-hum, hooey, tired, vapid 6 boring, bunkum, dreary, humbug, stodgy 7 humdrum

8 banausic, lifeless, mediocre, nonsense, plodding 10 balderdash, lackluster, monotonous, pedestrian 11 indifferent, uninspiring 13 uninteresting
blamable see BLAMEWORTHY
blame 3 rap 4 onus 5 fault, guilt, knock 6 accuse, charge, finger, indict 7 censure, condemn 8 denounce, reproach 9 criticize, liability, reprehend, reprobate 10 accusation, imputation 11 culpability 12 condemnation, denunciation, reprehension *Scottish:* 4 wite, wyte 6 dirdum
blameless 4 good, pure 5 clean, moral 7 perfect, upright 8 innocent, unguilty, virtuous 9 crimeless, exemplary, faultless, guiltless, honorable, lily-white, righteous, unsullied 10 immaculate, impeccable, inculpable 13 unimpeachable
blameworthy 3 lax 5 amiss 6 guilty, liable, sinful 7 at fault 8 criminal, culpable, derelict 9 negligent 10 answerable, censurable, delinquent, indictable, punishable 11 disgraceful, inexcusable, responsible 12 dishonorable 13 reprehensible, objectionable
blanch 4 fade, pale 5 quail, scald, start 6 bleach, shrink, whiten 7 decolor, lighten, parboil 8 etiolate
blanched 3 wan 4 ashy, pale 5 ashen, faded, livid, peaky, waxen, white 6 anemic, doughy, pallid, peaked 7 ghostly 9 bloodless, colorless, washed out 10 cadaverous
Blancheflor's beloved 6 Flores, Floris
bland 4 dull, flat, blah, mild, soft 5 balmy, banal, vapid 6 boring, gentle, pablum 7 insipid, restful, sapless 8 soothing 9 calmative 10 complacent, flavorless, monotonous, namby-pamby, wishy-washy 12 ingratiating 13 nonirritating
blandish 3 con, woo 4 coax, fawn, urge 5 cozen 6 cajole, stroke 7 blarney, flatter, wheedle 8 butter up, inveigle, softsoap 9 importune, sweet-talk 10 curry favor
blandishment 3 oil 5 honey 7 blarney, eyewash, incense, promise 8 flattery, soft soap 9 adulation, seduction, sweet talk 10 allurement, compliment, inducement, sycophancy, temptation
blank 3 gap 4 bare, dull, seal, skip, void 5 chasm, dazed, empty, space 6 stupid, vacant, virgin 7 deadpan, obscure, unfilled, vacuous 8 complete, omission, outright, spotless 9 impassive 10 empty space, interstice, obliterate 11 featureless 12 inexpressive, unexpressive
blanket 4 bury, hide 5 cover, quilt, throw

6 afghan, stroud 7 overlay 8 coverlet, mackinaw, sweeping 10 overspread

blankness 6 vacuum 7 nullity, vacancy, vacuity 9 emptiness 10 desolation

blare 4 roar 5 blast, shout 6 clamor, jangle 7 trumpet

blaring 4 loud 5 sharp 6 brassy, shrill 7 clarion, jarring, roaring 8 blinding, piercing, strident 9 deafening, dissonant 10 stentorian 11 ear-piercing, penetrating, stentorious 12 earsplitting

blarney 3 con, oil 4 coax, bunk 5 charm, honey, hooey 6 bunkum, cajole, humbug 7 baloney, incense, wheedle 8 blandish, buncombe, cajolery, flattery, inveigle, nonsense, soft soap 9 adulation, sweet-talk 11 compliments 12 blandishment, inveiglement

blasé 4 cool 5 bored, jaded, sated 6 breezy 7 knowing, offhand, unmoved, worldly 9 apathetic, incurious, surfeited, unexcited 10 world-weary 11 indifferent, unconcerned, worldlywise 12 disenchanted, uninterested 13 disillusioned, sophisticated

blaspheme 4 cuss 5 abuse, curse, swear 6 revile 7 pollute, profane 8 denounce, execrate 9 castigate, excoriate

blasphemous 6 coarse, sinful 7 godless, impious, obscene, profane, ungodly 10 irreverent 12 sacrilegious 13 disrespectful

blasphemy 3 sin 5 abuse, error 6 heresy 7 cursing, cussing, impiety, mockery 8 swearing 9 profanity, sacrilege, violation 10 execration, heterodoxy, iconoclasm 11 desecration, imprecation, irreverence, malediction, profanation

blast 3 din 4 bang, beat, blow, boom, clap, dash, gale, gust, kill, peal, ruin, slam, toot 5 blare, burst, crack, crash, salvo, shoot, smash, wreck 6 attack, blight, blow up, damage, squall, wallop 7 destroy, lambast, shatter, shrivel, trumpet 8 dynamite, lambaste, outburst 9 explosion, castigate, discharge, overwhelm, shock wave 10 annihilate, detonation

blat 4 bray 5 blurt 6 cry out 7 exclaim 8 blurt out

blatant 4 bald, loud 5 clear, gaudy, naked, noisy, overt, saucy 6 arrant, brassy, brazen, crying, flashy, garish, patent, tawdry, vulgar 7 glaring, jarring, obvious 8 flagrant, immodest, impudent, insolent, manifest, overbold, strident 9 barefaced, clamorous, obtrusive, shameless, unabashed 10 boisterous, outrageous, scurrilous, unblushing, vociferous 11 conspicuous, loud-mouthed, transparent 12 ear-splitting, obstreperous

blather 3 gab, gas, jaw, rot, yak 4 bosh, gush, rave, stir 5 bleat, drool, hokum, prate 6 babble, bunkum, drivel, effuse, gabble, jabber, natter, yammer 7 blabber, chatter, enthuse, palaver, prattle, rubbish, twaddle 8 chitchat, claptrap, idle talk, nonsense 9 commotion 10 balderdash, double-talk, flapdoodle 12 gobbledygook

blaze 4 burn, fire 5 burst, flame, flare, glare, shine 7 flare up 8 eruption, outburst 10 incandesce 13 conflagration *Scottish:* 3 low 4 lowe

blazer 6 marker, reefer 9 sport coat 10 sports coat 12 sports jacket

blazes 4 hell 5 abyss, Hades, Sheol 6 Tophet 7 Gehenna, inferno 9 perdition 11 netherworld

blazing 4 keen 5 afire, fiery 6 aflame, alight, ardent, fervid, on fire, red-hot 7 burning, fervent, flaming, flaring, furious, glowing, ignited, intense, lighted 8 dazzling, feverish, powerful, speeding, white-hot 9 brilliant, perfervid 11 conflagrant, impassioned 12 incandescent 13 scintillating

blazon 4 deck 5 adorn, sound 7 declare, display, publish, trumpet 8 announce, proclaim 9 advertise, broadcast 10 coat of arms, promulgate 11 ostentation

bleach 3 dim 4 fade, pale 5 pale white 6 blanch, blench, purify, whiten 7 decolor, launder, wash out 8 etiolate, peroxide, sanitize 9 whitewash

bleak 3 raw, sad 4 bare, cold, dour, drab, grim, wild 5 chill, drear, empty, harsh, stark 6 barren, chilly, dismal, dreary, gloomy, lonely, severe, somber, wintry 7 austere, exposed, joyless 8 blighted, desolate, funereal, hopeless 9 cheerless, windswept, woebegone 10 depressing, despondent, oppressive, melancholy

blear 3 dim, fog 4 blur, dull, mist, murk, veil 5 bedim, faint, vague 6 hidden, shroud 7 becloud, obscure, shadowy, unclear 10 indistinct

bleary 3 dim 5 all in, faint, filmy, fuzzy, milky, spent, tired, vague 6 pooped, sapped, used-up, wasted 7 blurred, drained, obscure, shadowy, unclear, worn-out 8 depleted 9 enervated, exhausted, washed-out 10 indistinct

bleat 3 baa 4 blat, carp, crab, fuss, yawp 5 gripe, whine 6 bellow, grouse, squawk, yammer 7 blather, grumble, whimper 8 complain 9 bellyache

bleed 3 sap, run 4 milk, ooze, pity, seep 5 drain, exude, leech, mulct 6 extort,

fleece 7 diffuse, extract 9 blackmail
10 hemorrhage

blemish 3 mar 4 blot, flaw, harm, mark,
maim, mole, scar, spot, vice, wart
5 fault, nevus, spoil, stain 6 blotch,
damage, deface, defect, impair, injure,
pimple, stigma 7 blacken, distort,
freckle, pervert, tarnish, vitiate 8 impurity, mutilate, pockmark 9 birthmark
12 imperfection 13 disfigurement

blench 3 shy 4 balk, duck, fade 5 blink,
cower, quail, quake, start, wince
6 flinch, purify, recoil, shrink, whiten
7 launder, shy away, squinch, tremble
8 draw back, etiolate 9 whitewash

blend 3 fit, mix 4 brew, fuse, meld, weld
5 admix, alloy, merge, unify, union,
unite 6 commix, fusion, go with,
hybrid, mingle 7 amalgam, combine,
mélange, mixture 8 beverage, coalesce,
compound, conflate, immingle, infusion, intermix, mishmash 9 admixture,
commingle, composite, harmonize,
integrate 10 amalgamate, commixture,
concoction, synthesize 12 adulteration,
amalgamation, intermixture

blender setting 3 mix 4 whip 5 puree
7 liquefy

blesbok 8 antelope

bless 4 laud 5 exalt, extol, endow, favor,
grace 6 anoint, bestow, hallow, praise,
uphold 7 approve, beatify, glorify, magnify 8 enshrine, eulogize, make holy,
sanctify 10 consecrate

blessed 4 holy 5 happy, lucky 6 joyous,
sacred 7 saintly 8 beatific, hallowed
9 beatified, fortunate, venerated
10 inviolable, sacrosanct, sanctified
11 consecrated

blessedness 5 bliss 8 felicity, sanctity
9 beatitude, godliness, happiness
12 blissfulness

blessing 4 boon, good, okay 5 asset,
favor, grace 6 assent, bounty, thanks
7 benefit, benison, consent, fortune,
godsend, support 8 approval, good
luck, windfall 9 advantage 10 invocation, permission 11 approbation, benediction, endorsement, good fortune,
valediction 12 commendation, consecration, thanksgiving 13 encouragement

"___ **bleu!**" 5 Sacré

blight 3 mar, nip 4 dash, ruin 5 blast,
decay, spoil, wreck 6 canker, wither
7 disease, scourge, shrivel 9 withering
10 pestilence 13 deterioration

blimp 7 airship 8 zeppelin 9 dirigible

blind 4 daze, dull 5 decoy, front, shade,
shill 6 dazzle 7 eyeless, muddled, shutter 8 bedazzle, unseeing 9 sightless
10 visionless

blind alley 6 pocket 7 dead end, impasse
8 cul-de-sac, deadlock 9 stone wall
10 standstill 11 obstruction

blind god 4 Eros, Hodr, Hoth 5 Cupid,
Hoder, Hodur, Hothr

blindworm 8 slowworm

blink 3 bat 4 wink 5 flash, yield 6 give in,
squint 7 flicker, flutter, nictate, twinkle
9 nictitate 11 scintillate

blink at 4 omit 5 clear, let go 6 bypass,
excuse, forget, ignore, slight 7 condone, connive, let pass, neglect 8 discount, overlook, pass over 9 disregard,
exonerate, whitewash

blip 6 censor, screen 9 deviation, expurgate, radar spot 10 bowdlerize

bliss 3 joy 4 Zion 6 Canaan, heaven
7 ecstasy, elysium, nirvana, rapture
8 empyrean, euphoria, paradise 9 beatitude, happiness 10 exaltation 11 blessedness

blissful 5 happy 6 divine, elated, joyful,
joyous 8 beatific, ecstatic, euphoric
9 ambrosial, delighted, entranced, rapturous 10 delightful, entrancing

blissfulness 3 joy 7 ecstasy 8 euphoria
9 beatitude, happiness 10 exaltation
11 contentment

blister 4 bleb, flay, lash 5 blain, bulla,
slash 6 assail, canker, scathe, scorch
7 lambast, scarify, scourge, vesicle
8 lambaste 9 castigate, excoriate

blithe 3 gay 4 boon 5 happy, jolly, merry,
sunny 6 bouncy, casual, cheery, chirpy,
jaunty, jocund, jovial 7 gleeful 8 carefree, careless, cheerful, chirrupy, gladsome, heedless, mirthful 9 lightsome,
sprightly, unworried, vivacious
10 untroubled 11 thoughtless 12 lighthearted

blithesome see BLITHE

blitz 4 raid, rush 7 air raid, bombard,
bombing 8 shelling 9 onslaught 10 mass
attack 11 bombardment

blitzkrieg 6 attack 7 assault, bombing
9 offensive, onslaught 11 bombardment

blizzard 4 gale 6 squall 8 whiteout
9 snowstorm

bloat 5 bulge, swell 6 billow, expand, fatten, puff up 7 balloon, distend, enlarge,
inflate 10 distension

bloated 5 puffy 6 puffed 7 pompous,
swollen 8 arrogant, enlarged, inflated
9 distended, overblown, overlarge
11 pretentious 13 self-important

bloc 4 band, ring 5 cabal, party, union
6 clique, league 7 combine, faction
8 alliance 9 coalition 10 consortium,

contingent, federation **11** association, combination **13** confederation

block 3 bar **4** clog, fill, hunk, plug, slab, stop, wall, wing **5** brick, choke, chunk, close, ingot **6** cut off, hinder, impede **7** barrier, congest, occlude, stopper **8** obstacle, obstruct **9** barricade, hindrance, intercept

blockade 3 bar **4** stop, wall **5** beset, hem in, siege **6** shut in **7** barrier, besiege **8** close off, encircle, obstruct, stoppage **9** barricade, beleaguer, blank wall, hindrance, roadblock **10** impediment **11** obstruction

blockage 3 bar **4** clog, halt **7** barrier **8** obstacle, stoppage **10** impediment **11** obstruction

blockbuster 4 bomb **11** spectacular

blockhead 3 oaf **4** clod, dolt, dope, fool **5** dummy, dunce, idiot, moron, ninny **6** nitwit **7** halfwit, imbecile **8** clodpole, clodpoll, dumbbell, numskull **9** ignoramus, lamebrain, numbskull, simpleton **10** nincompoop **12** featherbrain

blockheaded 4 dull, dumb **5** dense, thick **6** obtuse, stupid **7** doltish **9** brainless, dim-witted **10** slow-witted

block out 4 mark **5** chart, close, draft, frame **6** hinder, screen, sketch **7** obscure, outline, prepare, repress, shut off **8** indicate, obstruct **9** adumbrate, formulate

block up 3 dam **4** clog, fill, plug, stop **5** choke **7** congest

bloke 3 guy, man **4** chap, gent **6** fellow **9** gentleman

blond 4 fair, gold, pale **5** light, sandy, straw, tawny **6** flaxen, golden **7** towhead **8** platinum **9** champagne, towheaded **10** fair-haired **11** sandy-haired **12** honey-colored

blood 4 gore **7** descent, kindred, kinship, lineage **8** ancestry **10** extraction *cancer of:* **8** leukemia *cell:* **3** red **5** white **8** hemocyte, monocyte, platelet **9** corpuscle, leukocyte **10** lymphocyte **11** erythrocyte, granulocyte *clot:* **8** thrombus *coloring matter:* **10** hemoglobin *disease:* **6** anemia **8** leukemia **10** hemophilia *fluid part:* **5** serum **6** plasma *of the gods:* **5** ichor *particle in:* **7** embolus *poisoning:* **6** pyemia **7** toxemia **10** septicemia *pressure:* **8** systolic **9** diastolic *relating to:* **5** hemic *serum:* **6** plasma *study of:* **10** hematology *sugar:* **7** glucose

bloodbath 7 carnage, slaying **8** butchery, massacre **9** slaughter **10** decimation **12** annihilation **13** extermination

bloodless 3 wan **4** ashy, dull, pale, weak **5** ashen, waxen **6** anemic, feeble, pallid,

sallow, torpid **8** listless **9** insensate, unfeeling **10** insensible, nonviolent **11** coldhearted, passionless, unemotional

bloodletting 4 gore **7** carnage, killing **8** butchery, shambles, violence **9** slaughter **10** phlebotomy **11** venesection

bloodline 6 family, strain **7** descent, lineage **8** ancestry, pedigree **10** family tree

bloodroot 7 puccoon

bloodshed 4 gore **7** carnage **9** slaughter

bloodstained 4 gory **6** grisly **7** imbrued, wounded **8** sanguine **10** sanguinary **11** ensanguined, sanguineous

bloodstone 10 chalcedony

bloodsucker 4 tick **5** lamia, leech **6** lizard, sponge **7** sponger, vampire **8** hanger-on, parasite **10** freeloader **12** lounge lizard

bloodthirsty 5 rabid **8** ravening, sanguine **9** cutthroat, homicidal, murdering, murderous, predatory, voracious **10** sanguinary **11** sanguineous

blood vessel 4 vein **5** aorta **6** artery **7** jugular **9** capillary *combining form:* **3** vas **4** angi, vasi, vaso **5** angio

bloody 4 gory, grim, very **5** cruel **6** damage, damned, deadly, grisly **7** blasted, hateful, imbrued, wounded **8** accursed, infernal, sanguine **9** cutthroat, homicidal, murdering, murderous **10** detestable, sanguinary **11** ensanguined, sanguineous **12** death-dealing, slaughtering

bloom 4 blow, glow, open, posy **5** blush **6** floret, flower, thrive, unfold **7** blossom, burgeon, coating, develop, dusting, prosper **8** flourish, rosiness **10** cloudiness, effloresce **13** discoloration

blooper 4 goof, slip, trip **5** boner, break, error, fluff, gaffe, lapse **6** boo-boo, bungle, howler, slipup **7** blunder, faux pas, fly ball, misstep, mistake, offense **8** solecism **9** indecorum, false step **11** impropriety **12** indiscretion

blossom 3 bud, wax **4** blow, glow, grow, open, posy **5** bloom, blush, flush **6** expand, flower, mature, thrive, unfold **7** burgeon, develop, prosper **8** flourish, floweret, progress **10** effloresce, peak period **13** efflorescence

blot 4 blur, mark, onus, slur, smut, soil, spot **5** brand, odium, smear, speck, stain, sully **6** absorb, smudge, stigma **7** bestain, blemish, spatter, tarnish **8** black eye, discolor, disgrace **9** bespatter, moral flaw

blotch 4 mark, spot **5** stain **6** macula,

macule, mottle, smudge 7 blemish,
splotch 12 imperfection

blot out 4 raze, void 5 annul, crush,
erase, quash, quell, scrub 6 cancel,
delete, efface, squash 7 abolish,
destroy, expunge 9 eliminate, eradicate,
extirpate 10 annihilate, extinguish,
obliterate 11 exterminate

blotto see DRUNK

blouse 5 middy, shell, shirt, smock,
tunic 6 guimpe

bloviate 4 rail, rant, rave 5 mouth, orate,
spout 7 bluster, carry on, declaim,
inveigh, soapbox, talk big 8 harangue,
perorate, sound off, splutter 9 hold
forth 10 vociferate

blow 3 bop, fan, hit, jar 4 bang, bash,
belt, biff, bump, cuff, damn, fail, gasp,
gust, huff, pipe, puff, slam, slug, swat,
toot, whop, wind 5 boast, botch, crack,
drive, erupt, leave, pound, punch,
shock, slosh, smack, smash, sound,
spend, waste, whack 6 buffet, depart,
impact, mishap, thwack, wallop
7 assault, breathe, chagrin, consume,
debacle, explode, flutter, fritter, trumpet 8 calamity, disaster, flounder,
knockout, squander 9 bombshell, collision, dissipate, throw away 10 concussion, misfortune, trifle away 11 catastrophe

blow-by-blow 4 full 5 fussy 6 minute
7 careful, precise 8 detailed, itemized,
thorough 10 exhaustive, meticulous,
scrupulous 13 thoroughgoing

blowhard see BO

blow in 4 land 5 pop by 6 appear, arrive,
drop by, show up, turn up 7 hit town
11 materialize

blowout 4 bash, fete, gala, riot, tear
5 binge, blast, break, party, split, spree
6 frolic, shindy 7 shindig, victory
8 carousal, flat tire 9 festivity

blowsy 5 dingy, ruddy 6 florid, frowsy,
sloppy, untidy 7 flushed, healthy,
unkempt 8 blooming, blushing
10 bedraggled

blow up 4 bomb, burn, fume, rage
5 bloat, burst, erupt, flare, go off,
storm, swell 6 expand, seethe 7 bristle,
distend, enlarge, explode, inflate, magnify, rupture, shatter 8 boil over,
demolish, detonate, dynamite, height-
en, mushroom 9 discredit, fulminate,
overstate 10 aggrandize

blowy 4 airy, wild 5 fresh, gusty, windy
6 breezy, stormy 7 squally 8 blustery
9 windswept 11 tempestuous

blubber 3 cry, fat, sob 4 bawl, flab, keen,
lard, pipe, wail, weep 5 flesh 6 snivel
7 carry on 8 whale fat

bludgeon 3 bat 4 club 5 baton, billy,
bully 6 attack, cudgel, hector 7 bluster,
war club 8 browbeat, bulldoze, bullyrag 9 bastinado, billy club, blackjack,
strong-arm, truncheon 10 intimidate,
nightstick *British:* 4 cosh

blue 3 low, sad, sea 4 down, glum, lewd,
navy, racy 5 bawdy, ocean, royal, salty,
spicy 6 cobalt, gloomy, risqué
7 naughty, profane, unhappy 8 dejected, downcast, indecent, off-color
9 depressed, woebegone 10 despondent,
dispirited, melancholy, suggestive
11 downhearted *combining form:* 4 cyan
5 cyano *dark:* 5 perse 6 indigo *grayish:*
5 merle, slate *greenish:* 4 aqua, cyan,
teal 5 beryl 6 cobalt 7 azurite
9 turquoise *reddish:* 5 smalt 6 marine,
purple, violet 7 cyanine, gentian,
lobelia *sky:* 5 azure 8 cerulean

___ **Blue** 3 Ben 9 Little Boy

blue blood 4 lady, lord, peer 5 elite,
noble 6 aristo 7 royalty 8 nobleman
9 gentility, gentleman, patrician 10 aristocrat, noblewoman 11 gentle birth,
gentlewoman

bluebonnet 4 Scot 11 Texas lupine

Blue Boy painter 12 Gainsborough
(Thomas)

bluecoat 3 cop, law 4 fuzz 5 bobby
6 copper 9 constable, patrolman,
policeman

Bluegrass State 8 Kentucky

Blue Grotto site 5 Capri

bluejacket 4 mate, salt, swab 5 limey
6 sailor, seaman 7 swabbie 9 sailorman

blue jeans 5 Levis 6 denims

blue moon 3 age, eon, era 4 aeon
5 epoch 7 dog's age 8 eternity, lifetime
10 generation

bluenose 4 prig 5 prude 7 puritan 9 Mrs.
Grundy, nice Nelly 10 goody-goody

bluenosed 4 prim 5 rigid 6 prissy, proper, square, stuffy 7 prudish 8 overnice,
priggish 9 Victorian 10 scrupulous,
tight-laced 11 puritanical, straitlaced

blue-pencil 3 cut 4 edit, trim 5 emend
6 cut out, delete, excise, remove, revise
7 clean up 8 boil down, cross out
9 strike out, tighten up

bluepoint 6 oyster

blueprint 3 map 4 cast, plan, plot
5 chart, draft, frame, model, trace
6 design, devise, rubric, scheme, set
out, sketch 7 arrange, diagram, outline,
picture, project 8 game plan, strategy
9 delineate 10 conception, rough draft
11 description

blue-ribbon 3 top 5 prime 6 Grade A, tip-
top 7 capital, premier 8 five-star, top-
notch, superior 9 excellent, first-rate,

top-drawer 10 first-class, top-quality, world-class **11** outstanding **12** prize-winning

blues 4 funk **5** dumps, gloom, grief **6** lament **7** sadness, trouble **8** doldrums, glumness **9** dejection, pessimism **10** depression, desolation, low spirits, melancholy, woefulness **11** despondency, melancholia, unhappiness **12** hopelessness, mournfulness

bluff 3 act, con **4** curt, fake, fool, jive, ruse, sham, show **5** blunt, cliff, feign, frank, gruff, rough, trick **6** abrupt, betray, candid, crusty, delude, direct, hearty, humbug **7** beguile, brusque, deceive, fake out, mislead, playact, pretend **8** headland, pretense **9** deception, outspoken, precipice, steep bank **10** escarpment, forthright, no-nonsense, promontory, subterfuge **11** counterfeit, double-cross, plainspoken, shortspoken **13** unceremonious

blunder 4 bull, gaff, goof, mess, muff, slip, trip **5** boner, botch, error, fluff, gaffe, gum up, lapse, lurch **6** bobble, bollix, bumble, bungle, foul up, fumble, goof up, howler, mess up, wander **7** blooper, failure, faux pas, louse up, misstep, mistake, screw up, stumble **8** disaster, flounder **12** indiscretion, misadventure

blunderbuss 3 gun **4** dolt **5** klutz **6** galoot, lummox **7** bungler, firearm **8** bonehead, numskull **9** blockhead, numbskull **10** stumblebum **13** butterfingers

blunt 4 bald, calm, curt **5** allay, bluff, brief, frank, gruff, plain, rough, terse **6** abrupt, benumb, candid, crusty, deaden, direct, lessen, obtuse **7** brusque, rounded, uncivil **8** enfeeble, not sharp, snippety **10** forthright **11** desensitize, insensitive, plainspoken, unvarnished **12** discourteous **13** unceremonious

blur 3 dim, fog **4** blot, dull, mist **5** befog, blear, cloud, muddy, smear, stain, taint **6** smudge, stigma **7** becloud, besmear, confuse, tarnish **8** besmirch, discolor *in printing:* **6** mackle

blurb 4 hype, plug, puff **5** press **6** notice **7** write-up **8** good word **9** promotion **12** commendation

blurry 4 hazy **5** vague **6** cloudy **7** clouded, unclear **9** undefined, unfocused **10** indistinct

blurt 4 blab, blat, bolt **5** spill **6** cry out, let out **7** divulge, exclaim, let slip, spit out **8** disclose, give away **9** ejaculate

blush 4 burn, glow, rose, view **5** bloom, color, flame, flush, rouge **6** mantle, pinken, redden **7** blossom, crimson, redness, turn red **8** mantling, rosiness

bluster 4 bawl, crow, gust, huff, rage, roar, rout **5** blast, bully, prate, storm, strut, vaunt **6** bellow, clamor, hector, lean on **7** bombast, bravado, dragoon, roister, swagger, talk big **8** boasting, browbeat, bulldoze, bullyrag, domineer **9** gasconade **10** grandstand, intimidate **11** braggadocio

blustery 4 wild **5** blowy, gusty, rough **6** drafty, raging, raving, stormy **7** furious, squally, violent **9** truculent, tumultuous, turbulent **10** boisterous **11** tempestuous

boa 5 scarf, snake

boar 3 pig **4** male **5** swine

board 4 fare, feed, food, lath, slab, slat **5** catch, get on, hop on, house, lodge, meals, panel, plank, put up, table **6** billet, embark **7** emplane, entrain, quarter **9** directors **11** directorate *artist's:* **7** palette

boarder 5 guest **6** lodger, renter, roomer, tenant

board game see at GAME

boarding house 6 hostel **7** hospice, lodging, pension **8** pensione

boardwalk 7 gangway **9** esplanade, promenade

boast 3 own **4** blow, brag, crow, have, puff **5** exalt, exult, glory, mouth, prate, preen, strut, vaunt **6** parade **7** bluster, bombast, bravado, contain, enlarge, exhibit, inflate, possess, show off, swagger, talk big **9** gasconade **10** exaggerate, grandstand **11** rodomontade **12** exaggeration

boaster 6 gascon **7** egotist, peacock, show-off **8** big mouth, blowhard, braggart **11** braggadocio, rodomontade

boastful 4 vain **5** cocky **6** braggy **8** arrogant, braggart, puffed-up, vaunting **9** bigheaded, conceited, egotistic **11** egotistical, pretentious, swellheaded **12** vainglorious **13** swelled-headed *Scottish:* **6** vaunty

boat 3 ark, hoy, tug **4** dhow, dory, junk, pram, prau, proa, punt, scow, ship, yawl **5** barge, canoe, coble, ferry, kayak, ketch, scull, shell, skiff, sloop, smack, umiak, yacht **6** bateau, bugeye, caïque, cutter, dinghy, hooker, lateen, lugger, packet, sampan, vessel, wherry **7** caravel, coracle, currach, curragh, gondola, lighter, pinnace, pirogue, pontoon, shallop, steamer, trawler, vedette, vidette **8** schooner, trimaran **9** catamaran, hydrofoil *bottom projection:* **4** keel *captain:* **5** pilot **6** master **7** skipper *dock, basin:* **6** marina *front end of:* **3** bow

4 fore, prow *motor:* 7 cruiser, inboard
8 outboard, runabout *on a ship:* 3 gig
6 launch 7 pinnace *race:* 7 regatta *rear
end of:* 3 aft 5 stern *song:* 6 chanty,
shanty 7 chantey 9 barcarole 10 barcarolle

boatman 4 mate 5 limey 6 Charon, sailor
7 mariner, oarsman, paddler 8 deckhand, water dog 9 gondolier, navigator

boat-shaped 8 scaphoid 9 navicular

Boaz's wife 4 Ruth

bob 3 jig, nod, rap, tap 4 buff, clip, crop,
dock, trim 5 bunch, float 6 bounce,
curtsy, jiggle, jounce, polish, trifle,
wobble 7 cluster, curtsey, nosegay
8 shilling 9 genuflect

bobbery 3 ado, din, row 4 fray, riot
5 babel, noise 6 bedlam, hubbub, racket, ruckus, rumpus 7 ferment, ruction
9 commotion, confusion 10 hullabaloo,
hurly-burly 11 disturbance, pandemonium

bobbin 4 pirn 5 quill, spool, wheel
7 spindle 8 cylinder

bobble 3 bob, dud 4 flub, goof, mess,
muff 5 botch, error, fluff, gum up 6 ball
up, bollix, bumble, bungle, flub up,
fumble, goof up, muff up 7 blooper,
failure, louse up, mistake

bobby 3 law 6 copper, peeler 7 officer
9 constable, patrolman, policeman

bobwhite 5 quail 9 partridge

Boccaccio *beloved:* 9 Fiammetta *tales:*
9 Decameron

bode 4 hint 5 augur 6 signal, warn of
7 betoken, portend, presage, promise,
signify, suggest 8 foreshow, indicate
9 foretoken, prefigure 10 foreshadow

bodega 3 bar, pub 6 saloon 7 barroom,
grocery 8 wineshop 12 general store

bodement 4 omen, sign 5 hunch
6 augury 7 portent, presage 8 prophecy
9 foretoken, harbinger 10 foreboding,
intimation, prediction, prognostic
11 premonition 12 presentiment

bodiless 7 ghostly 8 ethereal, spectral
9 unfleshly 10 discarnate, immaterial,
unphysical 11 disembodied, incorporeal, nonmaterial 12 apparitional
13 insubstantial

bodily 6 carnal 7 en masse, earthly,
fleshly, sensual, somatic, totally 8 corporal, entirely, physical, visceral 9 corporeal 10 altogether, completely
11 unspiritual

bodkin 4 shiv 5 blade, knife, shank
6 dagger, lancet, needle 7 poniard
8 stiletto

___ **bodkins** 4 odds

body 4 bulk, core, form, hull, mass,
soma 5 frame, stiff, stock, torso

6 corpse, corpus 7 anatomy, cadaver,
carcass, chassis, corpora (plural),
remains 8 physique 9 aggregate, substance *combining form:* 4 dema, soma,
some, somi (plural) 5 somat, somia,
somus 6 somata (plural), somato

body cavity 5 cecum, sinus 6 coelom
7 abdomen 8 hemocoel

body check 5 block

bodyguard 7 retinue 9 attendant, protector

body of water 3 bay, sea 4 cove, gulf,
lake, pond, pool 5 bight, brook, creek,
fiord, firth, fjord, inlet, ocean, river
6 harbor, lagoon, puddle, stream
7 channel, estuary 8 reservoir

body passage 4 duct, vein 5 canal
6 artery, meatus, ureter, vagina, venule,
vessel 7 trachea, urethra 8 bronchus
9 arteriole, capillary, esophagus, intestine 10 bronchiole 13 bronchial tube,
fallopian tube

body politic 5 state 6 nation 11 nation-
state

boffo 3 gag, gas, hit 4 wild 5 laugh
6 scream 7 sold-out 8 smash-hit, smashing 10 successful 11 sensational

bog 3 fen 4 mire, quag 5 delay, marsh,
swamp 6 impede, morass, muskeg,
slough, slow up 8 quagmire 9 swampland

Bogart, Humphrey *film:* 6 Sahara 7 Dead
End, Sabrina 8 Big Sleep (The), Key
Largo 10 Casablanca, High Sierra
11 Caine Mutiny (The) 12 African
Queen (The) 13 Maltese Falcon (The)
15 Petrified Forest (The) 16 To Have
and Have Not 24 Treasure of the Sierra
Madre (The) *wife:* 6 Bacall (Lauren)

bog down 4 flag, mire 5 choke, delay,
stall 6 detain, falter, hang up, hinder,
impede, retard, slow up 7 embroil, set
back, slacken 8 encumber, keep back,
obstruct, slow down 9 lose steam
10 decelerate

bogey 5 ghost, haunt, shade, spook
6 scarer, shadow, spirit, wraith 7 phantom, specter 8 phantasm, revenant
10 apparition

bogeyman 5 spook 7 bugbear, chimera,
monster, phantom, specter, spectre
10 apparition

boggle 4 balk, mess, muff, stun 5 amaze,
botch, fudge, gum up, shock, wreck
6 bollix, bungle, cobble, goof up, mess
up, strain 7 astound, louse up, nonplus,
stagger, stumble, stupefy 8 astonish,
bewilder, bowl over, confound 9 dumbfound, mishandle, mismanage, overwhelm, take aback 11 flabbergast

bogus 4 fake, mock, sham 5 false,

phony, snide 6 ersatz, forged, pseudo
7 fictive, pretend 8 invented, specious,
spurious 9 brummagem, concocted,
imitation, pinchbeck, simulated,
trumped up 10 artificial, fabricated,
fraudulent, mendacious 11 counterfeit

Bohème, La *character:* 4 Mimi 7 Rodolfo
composer: 7 Puccini (Giacomo) *setting:*
5 Paris

bohemian 5 artsy, gypsy, hippy 6 hippie
7 beatnik, dropout, oddball, offbeat
8 maverick, vagabond, wanderer
9 eccentric 10 avant-garde, iconoclast,
unorthodox 13 nonconformist

boil 3 jet 4 bolt, brew, burn, cook, dash,
foam, fume, gush, moil, race, rage,
rush, spew, spot, stew, vent 5 anger,
churn, erupt, fling, froth, poach, shoot,
storm, swirl 6 blow up, bubble, charge,
canker, coddle, pimple, seethe, simmer
7 abscess, agitate, bristle, ferment, flare
up, pustule, smolder 8 furuncle 9 carbuncle, discharge 10 effervesce
11 excrescence

boil down 4 pare, trim 6 amount, reduce
7 distill 8 compress, condense, simplify,
truncate 9 summarize, synopsize
10 streamline 11 concentrate, encapsulate

boiler suit 8 coverall

boiling 3 hot 5 fiery 6 baking, red-hot,
sultry, torrid 7 burning, febrile 8 agitated, roasting, scalding, sizzling, tropical 9 scorching 10 blistering

boil over 4 burn, fume, rage 5 erupt
6 blow up, bridle, see red, seethe 7 bristle, flare up

boisterous 4 loud, wild 5 noisy, rowdy
6 lively, stormy, unruly 7 blatant, raucous, riotous 8 strident 9 clamorous,
convivial, turbulent 10 disorderly, dis-
ruptive, rollicking, tumultuous,
uproarious, vociferous 11 loud-
mouthed, tempestuous 12 high-spirited,
obstreperous, rambunctious,
ungovernable, unrestrained

Boito opera 11 Mefistofele

bold 4 free, pert, rude 5 bluff, brave,
fresh, gutsy, nervy, sassy, saucy, sheer,
showy, steep 6 arrant, bright, brazen,
cheeky, daring, heroic 7 doughty, forward, glaring, obvious, valiant 8 cocksure, fearless, impudent, insolent,
intrepid, resolute, unafraid, valorous
9 audacious, dauntless, intrusive,
prominent, shameless, undaunted
10 courageous, pronounced 11 adventurous, impertinent, smart-alecky, venturesome 12 enterprising, presumptuous

boldness 4 gall, grit 5 drive, nerve, valor

6 aplomb, mettle, spirit 8 audacity,
backbone, chutzpah, temerity 9 arrogance, challenge, hardihood, impudence, insolence 10 brazenness, disrespect, effrontery 11 discourtesy
12 impertinence

Bolero composer 5 Ravel (Maurice)

Bolivia *ancient culture:* 4 Inca 10 Tiahua-
naco *capital:* 5 La Paz, Sucre *city:* 6 El
Alto 9 Santa Cruz 10 Cochabamba *conqueror:* 7 Pizarro (Hernando) *Indian
people:* 6 Aymara 7 Quechua *lake:*
5 Poopó 8 Titicaca *language:* 6 Aymara
7 Quechua, Spanish *monetary unit:*
9 boliviano *mountain, range:* 5 Andes
6 Sajama *neighbor:* 4 Peru 5 Chile
6 Brazil 8 Paraguay 9 Argentina *river:*
4 Beni 5 Abuna 6 Mamoré 7 Guaporé
9 Pilcomayo

bollix 4 flub, mess, muff, ruin 5 botch,
gum up, spoil, upset 6 bobble, bumble,
bungle, foul up, fumble, goof up, jumble, mess up, muck up, muddle, muff
up 7 confuse, louse up, screw up
8 dishevel, disorder, scramble, unsettle
9 mishandle, mismanage

bolo 5 knife 7 machete

Bolshevik 3 Red 6 commie 7 comrade
8 Leninist, tovarich, tovarish 9 communist

bolshevism 7 Marxism 8 Leninism
9 communism

bolster 3 aid 4 buoy, gird, help, prop
5 boost, brace, carry, cheer 6 assist,
bear up, buoy up, pillow, upbear,
uphold 7 bulwark, cushion, fortify,
hearten, shore up, support, sustain
8 backstop, buttress, maintain
9 encourage, reinforce 10 strengthen
12 underpinning 13 reinforcement

bolt 3 bar, fly, rod, run 4 cram, dash,
dart, flee, gulp, jump, lock, race, rush,
tear, wolf 5 arrow, blurt, bound, chase,
dowel, flush, rivet, scarf, scoot, shoot,
skirr, slosh, start 6 charge, decamp,
devour, gobble, guzzle, secure, spring
7 abscond, exclaim, hotfoot, make off,
missile, rigidly, scamper, startle, take
off 8 blurt out, hightail 9 skedaddle
10 make tracks, take flight 11 ingurgitate 13 thunderstroke

bomb 3 dud, hit 4 bust, dull, fail, flop,
sink, zero 5 blast, blitz, lemon, loser,
pound, shell 6 blow up 7 debacle,
destroy, failure, home run, success,
washout, wipe out 8 detonate, disaster,
fall flat, long pass, long shot, spray can

bombard 4 pelt 5 blast, blitz, shell, storm
6 attack, assail, cannon, hammer, pepper, shower, strafe, strike 7 assault,
barrage 8 catapult 9 cannonade

bombardment 4 hail 5 burst, salvo 6 attack, shower, volley 7 barrage, battery 8 drumfire 9 broadside, cannonade, fusillade, onslaught

bombardon 4 bass 8 bass tuba

bombast 4 rant 6 hot air 7 bluster, fustian, oration 8 rhapsody, tumidity 9 fancy talk, pomposity, turgidity 10 pretension 11 rodomontade

bombastic 5 wordy 6 prolix 7 aureate, flowery, orotund, pompous, swollen 8 inflated, puffed-up 9 overblown 10 euphuistic, rhetorical 11 declamatory, overwrought 12 magniloquent 13 grandiloquent

bombed 4 high 5 drunk, fried, stiff, tight 6 blotto, stoned, wasted 8 comatose, tanked up 9 plastered 10 inebriated 11 intoxicated

bombinate 3 hum 4 buzz, purr, whir 5 drone, strum, thrum 6 bumble, rumble 7 grumble

bombshell 4 blow, jolt 5 shock 6 marvel 8 surprise 9 curveball, sensation 10 revelation 11 thunderbolt

bona fide 4 real, sure, true 5 valid 6 actual 7 earnest, genuine, sincere 8 sterling 9 authentic, undoubted, veritable 10 legitimate, sure-enough 11 indubitable, in good faith 13 authenticated

bona fides 6 candor 7 probity 8 goodwill 9 good faith, sincerity 10 reputation 11 reliability, sincereness

bonanza 4 mine 5 catch, hoard 7 pay dirt 8 Golconda, gold mine, treasure, treasury, windfall 12 extravaganza 13 treasure trove

bonbon 5 candy, sweet 7 fondant 9 sweetmeat, sugarplum 10 confection

bond 3 tie 4 bail, fuse, knot, link, pact, yoke 5 nexus 6 cement, fetter, pledge, surety 7 bargain, compact, linkage, promise, shackle, warrant 8 adhesive, affinity, cohesion, contract, covenant, guaranty, ligament, ligature, security, vinculum, warranty 9 adherence, agreement, coherence, guarantee 10 attachment, connection, connective, obligation

bondage 4 yoke 6 chains, thrall 7 durance, fetters, helotry, peonage, serfage, serfdom, slavery 9 captivity, detention, servitude, thralldom, vassalage, villenage 10 subjection 11 enslavement, subjugation 12 imprisonment

bondsman 4 peon, serf 5 helot, slave 6 surety 7 chattel

bone *ankle:* 5 talus 6 tarsus *arm:* 4 ulna 6 radius 7 humerus *back:* 5 spine 8 vertebra 9 vertebrae (plural) *breast:* 7 sternum *calf:* 6 fibula *cavity:* 5 fossa *change into:* 6 ossify *cheek:* 5 malar 6 zygoma *chest:* 3 rib *collar:* 8 clavicle *face:* 5 malar, nasal 7 frontal *finger:* 7 phalanx 8 phalange *foot:* 6 tarsus 9 calcaneum, calcaneus 10 astragalus, metatarsus *hand:* 10 metacarpus *head:* 5 skull, vomer 7 cranium 8 parietal, sphenoid 9 occipital *heel:* 9 calcaneum, calcaneus *hip:* 5 ilium, pubis 6 pelvis 7 ischium *jaw:* 7 maxilla 8 mandible *kneecap:* 7 patella *leg:* 5 femur, tibia 6 fibula 7 patella *lower back:* 6 coccyx, sacrum *middle ear:* 5 anvil, incus 6 hammer, stapes 7 malleus, stirrup *pelvis:* 5 ilium *relating to:* 6 osteal *shin:* 5 tibia *shoulder blade:* 7 scapula *small:* 7 ossicle *substance:* 6 ossein *thigh:* 5 femur *toe:* 7 phalanx 8 phalange *U-shaped:* 5 hyoid *wrist:* 6 carpus

bonehead 4 clod 5 dunce, moron 6 cretin, dimwit, nitwit 7 halfwit 8 clodpole, clodpoll, lunkhead, numskull 9 ignoramus, lamebrain, numbskull 12 featherbrain

bonelike 7 osseous, osteoid

boner see BLOOPER

bone up 4 cram 5 study 6 review, revise 8 pore over

bong 4 bell, dong, peal, ring, toll 5 chime, knell, sound 6 hookah, strike 7 resound 9 water pipe 11 reverberate

boniface 7 barkeep 8 publican, taverner 9 barkeeper, innkeeper 12 saloonkeeper

bonkers 3 ape, mad 4 daft, loco, nuts, wild 5 batty, crazy, giddy, loony, potty 6 cuckoo, insane 7 bananas, haywire 8 demented, deranged, unhinged

bon mot 4 jest, quip 5 crack, sally 7 epigram, riposte 8 one-liner, repartee 9 witticism

bonny 4 fair, fine 6 comely, lovely, pretty 7 winsome 8 pleasing 9 beauteous, beautiful, excellent 10 attractive, delightful 11 good-looking

bon ton 4 élan 5 flair, style 6 gentry, jet set 7 fashion, society 8 elegance, smart set 9 haut monde, propriety 11 high society

bonus 4 gift, plus 6 reward 7 benefit, payment, premium 8 dividend 12 compensation 13 fringe benefit

bon vivant 7 epicure, flaneur, gourmet, trifler 8 aesthete, gourmand 10 aficionado, dilettante, gastronome 11 cognoscente, connoisseur 12 boulevardier, gastronomist, man-about-town

bony 4 lank, lean, thin 5 gaunt, lanky, spare 6 barren, skinny, twiggy 7 angular, osseous, scraggy, scrawny, starved

8 rawboned, skeletal, underfed **9** emaciated **10** cadaverous

boo 4 hiss, hoot, jeer, razz **6** bellow, deride, heckle, revile **7** catcall **9** raspberry, shout down

boob 3 oaf **4** dolt, dope, goof, goon, boor **5** chump, dunce, goose, ninny **6** breast, dumb ox **7** blunder, fathead, mistake, tomfool **8** lunkhead **9** simpleton **10** dunderhead, philistine

boo-boo see BLOOPER

booby hatch 6 asylum, bedlam **8** bughouse, loony bin, madhouse, nuthouse **9** funny farm **11** institution

booby trap 4 mine **5** snare **6** hazard **7** pitfall, springe **8** deadfall, land mine

boodle 3 wad **4** bilk, haul, heap, loot, mint, perk, take **5** booty, prize, spoil **6** bundle, packet, payola, spoils **7** fortune, plunder, present **8** kickback **9** incentive **10** bribe money, inducement

book 4 list, text, tome **5** album, bible, codex, enter, folio, novel, tract **6** charge, engage, enroll, folder, line up, manual, octavo, quarto, record, script, volume **7** catalog, edition, reserve **8** hardback, inscribe, register, schedule, softback, treatise **9** hardcover, monograph, paperback, preengage **10** compendium **11** publication *combining form:* **6** biblio *of hours:* **5** Horae *of psalms:* **7** psalter

bookie see BOOKMAKER

bookish 5 nerdy **6** formal **7** erudite, learned **8** academic, cerebral, literary, pedantic, studious, well-read **9** scholarly **10** longhaired **12** intellectual, professorial

bookkeeping term 4 loss **5** asset, audit, check, debit, entry, yield **6** budget, credit, equity, income, ledger, margin, profit, return **7** account, accrual, balance, expense, invoice, revenue, voucher **8** discount, dividend, interest, write off **9** inventory, liability **10** appreciate, depreciate, fiscal year **11** double entry **12** amortization, appreciation, balance sheet, depreciation, variable cost

booklet 8 brochure, opuscule, pamphlet

bookmaker 6 binder, bookie, editor **7** printer **9** bet holder, oddsmaker, publisher

book of account 6 ledger, record **7** journal **8** register

bookplate 5 label **8** ex libris

bookstall 5 kiosk **9** newsstand

boom 3 wax **4** bang, clap, grow, rise, slam, spar, wham **5** blast, boost, burst, crack, crash, sound, smash, swell **6** do

well, expand, growth, rumble, thrive **7** explode, prosper, resound, thunder **8** flourish, kick hard, long beam **9** expansion **10** bull market, detonation, prosperity **11** reverberate

boomerang 6 recoil **7** rebound **8** backfire, backlash, come back, kick back, ricochet **10** bounce back

booming 4 bass, deep **6** robust **7** roaring **8** affluent, resonant, sonorous, thriving **9** deafening **10** prospering, prosperous, successful **11** flourishing

boon 3 aid, gay **4** gift, good, help **5** asset, grant, favor, jolly, merry, token **6** blithe, bounty, jocund, jovial **7** benefit, festive, gleeful, godsend, largess, present **8** blessing, largesse, mirthful, windfall **9** advantage, convivial, privilege **10** indulgence **11** benediction, benefaction

boondocks 5 wilds **6** sticks **7** outback **8** backland, frontier **9** backwater, backwoods, provinces, rural area **10** hinterland **11** backcountry, countryside **12** back of beyond

boondoggle 4 cord, hoax, scam **5** fraud, hokum **6** hustle **7** fast one, hatband, lanyard, swindle **8** flimflam **10** fool around, mess around **11** horse around

boor 3 cad, oaf **4** lout, hick, rube **5** brute, chuff, churl, clown, yahoo, yokel **6** lummox, rustic **7** buffoon, bumpkin, hayseed, peasant **9** ignoramus, vulgarian **10** clodhopper, philistine, provincial

boorish 4 rude **5** crass, crude, rough **6** coarse, common, rugged, vulgar **7** illbred, loutish, lowbred, lumpish, uncivil, uncouth **8** churlish, cloddish, clownish, impolite, insolent, lubberly, swainish **9** graceless, offensive, tasteless, unrefined **10** philistine, provincial, robustious, uncultured, ungracious, unmannerly, unpolished, unsociable **11** bad-mannered, clodhopping, illmannered, uncivilized **12** discourteous, uncultivated **13** disrespectful

boost 3 aid **4** hike, lift, jump, plug, push, rise **5** raise, steal **6** assist, beef up, expand, extend, foster, jack up **7** advance, amplify, augment, elevate, magnify, promote, support **8** heighten, increase, shoplift **9** advertise, encourage, expansion, promotion **10** assistance **11** helping hand **13** encouragement

booster 3 fan **4** hypo, shot **6** backer, patron, rocket, rooter **7** vaccine **8** champion, defender, promoter, upholder **9** amplifier, expositor, injection, proponent, supporter **10** shoplifter **11** inoculation

boot 3 can 4 bang, fire, kick, sack
5 chuck, eject, evict, expel, start
6 bounce, thrill 7 dismiss, kick out,
start up 8 throw out 9 discharge, dismissal, terminate *kind:* 5 wader 6 arctic,
chukka, gaiter, galosh, mukluk 7 jodhpur, shoepac 8 balmoral, cothurni (plural), overshoe, shoepack 9 cothurnus
10 Wellington

Boötes star 8 Arcturus

booth 4 nook 5 berth, bower, kiosk,
stall, stand 6 carrel 9 enclosure 11 compartment

bootleg 3 hot, run 5 hooch 6 pirate
7 illicit, smuggle 9 irregular, moonshine
10 bathtub gin, contraband 11 black
market, mountain dew 12 unauthorized

bootless 4 vain 5 empty 6 futile, hollow
7 useless 8 abortive, impotent, nugatory 9 fruitless, valueless, worthless
10 profitless, unavailing 11 ineffective,
ineffectual 12 unproductive, unprofitable, unsuccessful

bootlick 4 fawn 5 cower, crawl, creep,
toady 6 cringe, grovel, kowtow, stroke
7 cater to, flatter, truckle 8 blandish
9 brownnose, importune, seek favor
10 curry favor 11 apple-polish 12 bow
and scrape

bootlicker 4 toad 5 toady 6 lackey, lapdog, minion, yes-man 7 doormat,
spaniel 8 hanger-on 9 sycophant
11 lickspittle

booty 4 haul, lift, loot, pelf, swag, take
5 prize, spoil, yield 6 spoils 7 pillage,
plunder, rear end, seizure, takings
8 buttocks

booze 4 brew, grog, swig 5 binge, drink,
hooch, juice, quaff, sauce, souse, swill
6 guzzle, imbibe, liquor, rotgut, tank
up, tipple 7 alcohol, carouse, put away,
spirits, swizzle 8 cocktail, liquor up
9 aqua vitae, firewater, knock back,
moonshine

boozehound 3 sot 4 lush, wino 5 drunk,
hoser, souse 7 guzzler 8 drunkard
9 alcoholic, inebriate 11 dipsomaniac

boozer see BOOZEHOUND

bop 3 bat, box, hit, jab, pop, rap 4 bash,
bean, belt, biff, boff, blow, clip, cuff,
jive, slug, sock, swat, whop 5 clock,
pound, smack, thump, whack
8 plant one

borax 4 junk

Bordeaux wine *district:* 5 Médoc
6 Graves *grape:* 6 Malbec, Merlot
8 Cabernet *name:* 5 Arsac, Ludon,
Macau 6 Moulis 7 Labarde, Margaux,
Pomerol 8 Cantenac, St. Julien, Pauillac 9 St. Emilion, St. Estèphe, St. Laurent *red:* 6 claret

bordello see BORTHEL

border 3 hem, lip, rim 4 abut, brim,
edge, join, line, pale, trim 5 bound,
brink, flank, frame, limit, march, skirt,
touch, verge 6 adjoin, bounds, butt on,
define, fringe, limbus, margin, trench
7 contour, outline, selvage 8 approach,
boundary, frontier, neighbor, sideline,
surround 9 marchland, perimeter,
periphery 11 butt against, communicate *inlaid:* 8 purfling *raised:* 7 coaming

bordereau 4 note 6 record 7 account
10 memorandum

bordering 4 nigh 5 close 6 almost, next
to 7 meeting, verging 8 abutting, adjacent, touching 9 adjoining, alongside,
close upon, impinging 10 approximal,
contiguous, juxtaposed 11 coterminous,
neighboring, practically

borderland 5 march 6 fringe, margin
8 frontier 9 marchland

borderline 4 pale 6 almost, nearly
7 dubious, unclear 8 boundary, doubtful, marginal, unstable 9 ambiguous,
debatable, dubitable, equivocal,
perimeter, uncertain, undecided, unsettled 11 demarcation, problematic
12 intermediate 13 indeterminate

border state 8 Delaware, Kentucky,
Maryland, Missouri, Virginia

bore 3 irk 4 drag, drip, mine, peer, pill,
ream, sink, tire, yawn 5 auger, drill,
drone, gouge, prick, punch 6 burrow,
pierce, tunnel 7 bromide, caliber,
fatigue 8 diameter, puncture 9 penetrate, perforate, soporific 10 dullsville

boreal 3 icy 4 cold, cool 5 chill, gelid,
polar 6 arctic, bitter, chilly, frosty,
frigid, tundra 7 glacial, wintery 8 freezing, northern 9 northerly

Boreas *beloved:* 8 Orithyia *brother:*
5 Notus 8 Hesperus, Zephyrus *father:*
8 Astraeus *mother:* 3 Eos *son:* 5 Zetes
6 Calais

boredom 5 blahs, ennui 6 apathy, stupor,
tedium, torpor 7 fatigue 8 doldrums,
dullness, flatness, monotony 9 lassitude, weariness 11 incuriosity, tediousness 12 indifference

Borgia 4 Juan 6 Alonso, Cesare 7 Alfonso, Rodrigo 8 Lucrezia

boring 3 dry 4 arid, drab, dull, flat, zero
5 ho-hum, vapid 6 dreary, stodgy, tiring
7 humdrum, tedious 8 bromidic, drudging, lifeless, tiresome 9 wearisome
10 lackluster, monotonous, pedestrian,
unexciting 13 uninteresting

boring tool 5 drill, auger 6 trepan

Boris Godunov composer 10 Mussorgsky (Modest) 11 Moussorgsky
(Modest)

born 3 née 6 innate, native 8 destined, inherent 9 intrinsic 10 congenital, deep-seated *combining form:* 3 gen 4 gene 6 genous 7 genetic

borne by the wind 6 aeolic, eolian 7 aeolian

Borneo *ethnic group:* 4 Dyak 5 Dayak *mountain:* 8 Kinabalu *nation:* 6 Brunei *river:* 6 Rabang

Borodin opera 10 Prince Igor

borough 4 town 5 burgh 7 village 8 township

bosh see BUNKUM

Bosnia-Herzegovina *capital:* 8 Sarajevo *language:* 7 Serbian 8 Croatian 13 Serbo-Croatian *monetary unit:* 4 mark 5 dinar *neighbor:* 6 Serbia 7 Croatia *part of:* 7 Balkans *sea:* 8 Adriatic

bosom 4 bust, core, soul, teat 5 chest, close, heart 6 breast 7 embrace 8 feelings, intimate 10 affections, conscience

bosomy 5 built, busty, buxom, curvy 6 chesty 7 shapely, stacked 9 Junoesque 11 full-figured

boss 4 head, stud 5 chief 6 direct, honcho, leader, manage, master, survey 7 command, foreman, headman, oversee 8 director, employer, overlook, overseer, superior 9 chieftain, supervise 10 supervisor, taskmaster 11 superintend *African:* 5 bwana

bossy 3 cow 4 calf 7 studded 8 despotic, imperial 9 arbitrary, assertive, imperious, masterful 10 autocratic, high-handed, imperative, oppressive, peremptory, tyrannical 11 controlling, dictatorial, domineering, magisterial, overbearing

botanist *American:* 4 Gray (Asa) 5 Sears (Paul B.) 6 Bailey (Liberty), Bessey (Charles), Carver (George Washington) 7 Bartram (John, William), Burbank (Luther) 9 Fairchild (David) *Austrian:* 6 Mendel (Gregor) *British:* 6 Sloane (Sir Hans) *Danish:* 7 Warming (Johannes) *Dutch:* 7 De Vries (Hugo) *French:* 7 Lamarck (Chevalier de) *German:* 4 Cohn (Ferdinand), Mohl (Hugo von) 5 Sachs (Julius von) *Irish:* 6 Harvey (William) *Scottish:* 5 Brown (Robert) *Swedish:* 8 Linnaeus (Carolus) *Swiss:* 6 Nägeli (Karl) 8 Candolle (Augustin)

botany branch 7 ecology 8 algology, bryology, mycology 9 phycology 10 morphology, palynology, physiology 11 hydroponics, paleobotany, pteridology, systematics 12 bacteriology

botch 4 blow, flop, flub, foul, goof, mess, muck, muff, ruin 5 fluff, gum up, mix-up, snarl, spoil 6 bobble, boggle, bollix, bumble, bungle, fiasco, fumble, goof up, mess up, muddle 7 blunder, confuse, louse up, washout 8 bugger up, disaster, disorder, dishevel, shambles 9 mishandle, mismanage, patchwork 10 discompose, hodgepodge, misconduct, mishmash

botchy 5 messy 6 blowzy, frowsy, frowzy, sloppy, untidy 7 chaotic 8 careless, confused, slapdash, slipshod, slovenly

both *combining form:* 3 bis *prefix:* 4 ambi, amph 5 amphi

bother 3 ado, bug, irk, nag, vex 4 drag, fret, fuss, gall, pest, pain 5 annoy, eat at, harry, trial, upset 6 badger, flurry, harass, needle, pester, plague, ruffle 7 afflict, agitate, anxiety, bedevil, concern, disturb, fluster, perturb, provoke, torment, trouble 8 disquiet, headache, irritant, nuisance, vexation 9 aggravate, annoyance 10 discompose, exasperate, irritation 11 aggravation, intrude upon 12 exasperation 13 inconvenience

botheration 4 damn, pain, pest 5 trial 6 plague 7 torment 8 headache, irritant, nuisance, vexation 9 annoyance 10 difficulty, irritation 11 aggravation, provocation 12 exasperation 13 inconvenience

Botswana *capital:* 8 Gaborone *city:* 11 Francistown *desert:* 8 Kalahari *former name:* 12 Bechuanaland *language:* 6 Tswana 7 English *monetary unit:* 4 pula *neighbor:* 7 Namibia 8 Zimbabwe 11 South Africa *river:* 5 Chobe 6 Molopo 7 Limpopo 8 Okavango

bottle 4 vial 5 cruet, cruse, flask, phial 6 ampule, carafe, fiasco, flacon, magnum, vessel 7 ampoule 8 decanter, jeroboam 9 container

bottle gourd 8 calabash

bottleneck 5 choke 6 hinder, impede, narrow 7 impasse 8 obstacle, obstruct, paralyze, slowdown, throttle 9 hindrance 10 choke point, congestion, traffic jam 11 obstruction

bottom 3 bum 4 base, boat, core, foot, root, pith, rump, seat, ship, sole, soul, tail, tush 5 basal, basic, basis, fanny, found, nadir 6 behind, breech, heinie, lowest, source 7 bedrock, essence, footing, primary, rear end 8 backside, buttocks, derriere, pedestal, pediment 9 establish, fundament, lowermost, posterior, predicate, principle, underbody, undermost, underside 10 foundation, nethermost, underbelly, underlying, underneath 11 fundamental, lowest point 12 undersurface

bottomless 4 deep, vast 7 abysmal, endless **8** baseless, enduring, profound, unending **9** boundless, unlimited **10** gratuitous, groundless, unfillable, ungrounded **11** everlasting, inestimable, never-ending **12** immeasurable, incalculable, unfathomable **13** inexhaustible

bottommost 4 last **5** least **6** lowest **7** deepest

bough 3 arm **4** limb **5** shoot **6** branch **8** offshoot

boulevard 4 road **6** artery, avenue, street **7** terrace **8** main drag **9** esplanade, promenade **10** high street **12** thoroughfare

boulevardier 7 flaneur, trifler **9** bon vivant **10** aficionado, dilettante **11** cognoscente, connoisseur **12** man-about-town

bounce 3 can, hop, pep, vim, zip **4** fire, jump, leap, oust, sack, zest **5** expel, vault, verve, vigor **6** energy, hurdle, spirit, spring **7** bluster, boot out, dismiss, kick out, rebound, saltate, sparkle **8** buoyancy, ricochet, vitality **9** animation, discharge, eliminate, terminate **10** ebullience, elasticity, liveliness

bounce back 5 rally **6** perk up, pick up, recoil, return, revive **7** cheer up, improve, rebound, recover **8** backfire **9** boomerang **10** recuperate, turn around

bounce off 5 carom **7** rebound **8** ricochet

bouncer 4 goon **5** guard **8** houseman, sentinel, watchman **9** muscleman

bouncy 3 gay **4** airy **5** peppy, perky **6** blithe, cheery, jaunty, jocund, lively **7** buoyant, elastic **8** animated, volatile **9** ebullient, energetic, expansive, exuberant, resilient, sprightly **10** unsinkable **12** effervescent, high-spirited **13** irrepressible

bound 3 end, hem, hop, rim **4** bolt, edge, jump, leap, term, skip **5** caper, frisk, hem in, limit, skirt, vault, verge **6** border, bounce, define, demark, driven, finite, fringe, gambol, hurdle, margin, spring, sprint **7** confine, delimit, enclose, hotfoot, limited, mark out, obliged, pledged, rebound, saltate **8** articled, beholden, confined, confines, enslaved, resolved, restrain, surround **9** compelled, demarcate, obligated **10** determined, indentured, limitation **11** apprenticed, responsible **12** circumscribe

boundary 3 hem **4** mete, pale **5** ambit, limit **6** limits, margin **7** compass, outline **8** confines, environs, purlieus **9** perimeter, precincts **10** borderline **13** circumference

bounder 3 cad, cur, dog **4** boor, worm **5** knave, louse, rogue **6** rascal, rotter

boundless 4 vast **5** great **7** endless **8** infinite **9** excessive, limitless, unbounded, unlimited **10** indefinite, unconfined, unmeasured **11** illimitable, measureless **12** immeasurable, unrestricted **13** inexhaustible, unsurpassable

bounteous 5 ample **6** benign, lavish **7** copious, liberal, profuse **8** abundant, generous, handsome, prodigal **9** bountiful, capacious, expansive, extensive, plenteous, plentiful, unsparing **10** beneficent, big-hearted, freehanded, munificent, openhanded, voluminous **11** magnanimous, overflowing

bountiful see BOUNTEOUS

bounty 5 grant, prize, yield **6** deluge, plenty, reward, wealth **7** payment, premium **8** plethora, richness **9** abundance, affluence, plenitude, profusion **10** cornucopia, generosity, inducement, liberality, luxuriance, prosperity **11** benevolence, copiousness **12** compensation

Bounty captain 5 Bligh (William)

bouquet 4 balm, kudo, odor, posy **5** aroma, kudos, scent, spice, spray **6** eulogy, medley **7** acclaim, corsage, essence, garland, incense, nosegay, perfume **8** accolade, encomium **9** fragrance, redolence **10** compliment **11** arrangement, boutonniere **12** commendation

bourgeois 7 burgher **8** ordinary **10** conformist, philistine **11** middle-class **12** conventional

bourgeoisie 11 middle class, third estate

Bourne Identity author 6 Ludlum (Robert)

bout 3 jag, run **4** game, meet, term, tour, turn **5** match, round, shift, siege, spell, spasm, spree, stint, throe, trick **6** attack **7** contest, session **8** outbreak **10** engagement

boutique 4 shop **8** emporium

bovine 3 cow, yak **4** anoa, bull, calf, gaur, neat, zebu **5** bison, steer, stirk **6** heifer, placid, torpid, wisent **7** aurochs, banteng, buffalo, bullock, cowlike **8** longhorn *genus:* **3** Bos *sound:* **3** low, moo

bow 3 arc, bob, dip, nod **4** arch, bend, knot, lout, prow, turn **5** angle, crook, curve, debut, defer, hunch, round, stoop, yield **6** archer, congee, curtsy, give in, kowtow, relent, salaam, salute, submit **7** concede, curtsey, flexure, incline, rainbow, succumb, turning **9** curvation, curvature, genuflect, obeisance, surrender **10** capitulate **11** buckle under **12** knuckle under

Bow, Clara 6 It girl

bowdlerize 4 blip, edit **6** censor, excise, purify, screen **7** abridge, cleanse, distort, launder **8** sanitize **9** expurgate **10** adulterate, blue-pencil

bowed 4 bent **5** arced, bandy **6** arched, curved **11** bandy-legged, curvilinear

bowel 3 gut **6** paunch **9** intestine

bower 5 arbor **6** anchor **7** enclose, pergola, retreat **9** apartment

bowery 7 skid row

bowfin 4 amia **7** mudfish

bowl 5 arena, basin, jorum, mazer, stade, tazza **6** tureen, vessel **7** stadium **8** coliseum **12** amphitheater

bowlegged 5 bandy

bowler 3 hat **5** derby **6** kegler

Bowl game 5 Super *Abilene:* **5** Pecan *Anaheim:* **7** Freedom *Atlanta:* **5** Peach *Dallas:* **6** Cotton *El Paso:* **3** Sun *Fresno:* **10** California *Honolulu:* **5** Aloha *Houston:* **10** Bluebonnet *Jacksonville:* **5** Gator *Memphis:* **7** Liberty *Miami:* **6** Orange **8** Carquest *Mobile:* **6** Senior *New Orleans:* **5** Sugar *Orlando:* **13** Florida Citrus *Pasadena:* **4** Rose *San Diego:* **7** Holiday *Shreveport:* **12** Independence *Tampa:* **10** Hall of Fame *Tempe:* **6** Fiesta *Tucson:* **6** Copper

bowling 7 kegling *British:* **8** skittles *Italian:* **5** bocce, bocci **6** boccie *term:* **3** pin **4** hook, lane, spot **5** curve, frame, spare, split **6** gutter, strike, string, turkey **7** duckpin **9** candlepin

bowl over 3 awe, wow **4** daze, fell, stun **5** floor, shock, throw **6** boggle, dismay **7** astound, flatten, impress, stupefy **8** blow away, surprise **9** bring down, dumbfound, knock down, overwhelm **10** disconcert

bow out 4 exit, fold, quit **5** leave, welsh **6** beg off, give up, retire **8** withdraw **9** surrender

box 3 bin **4** case, cell, chop, cuff, duke, loge, slap, sock, spar **5** booth, chest, clout, crate, fight, punch, smack, stall, trunk **6** buffet, carton, casket, coffer, coffin, encase, hopper, packet **7** confine, enclose, package **9** container, enclosure, rectangle **10** pigeonhole, receptacle **11** compartment

boxer 7 fighter, palooka **8** pugilist **9** flyweight **11** heavyweight, lightweight **12** bantamweight, middleweight, welterweight **13** featherweight *champ:* **3** Ali (Muhammad) **4** Bowe (Riddick) **5** Bruno (Frank), Jones (Roy), Lewis (Lennox), Louis (Joe), Moore (Archie), Tyson (Mike) **6** Hagler (Marvin), Hearns (Thomas), Holmes (Larry), McCall (Oliver), Moorer (Michael), Seldon (Bruce), Spinks (Leon, Michael), Tunney (Gene), Walker (Mickey) **7** Charles (Ezzard), Corbett (James), Dempsey (Jack), Douglas (Buster), Foreman (George), Frazier (Joe), Johnson (Jack), LaMotta (Jake), Leonard (Sugar Ray), Sharkey (Jack), Walcott (Joe) **8** Marciano (Rocky), Robinson (Sugar Ray), Sullivan (John L.) **9** Armstrong (Henry), Holyfield (Evander), Patterson (Floyd), Schmeling (Max)

boxing 8 pugilism **10** fisticuffs **13** prizefighting *term:* **3** jab, TKO **4** blow, bout, duck, foul, hook, ring, rope, spar **5** break, count, feint, glove, match, parry, punch, round, swing **6** bucket, canvas, corner **7** low blow, referee **8** heavy bag, knockout, uppercut **9** knockdown **11** punching bag

boy 3 lad, son, tad **5** gamin, puppy, sonny **6** laddie, nipper, shaver **9** shaveling, stripling, youngster *combining form:* **3** ped **4** paed, paid, pedo **5** paedo, paido *errand:* **5** gofer **8** lobbygow *French:* **6** garçon *Latin:* **4** puer *mischievous:* **6** urchin *Spanish:* **4** niño

boyfriend 4 beau **5** swain **6** fiancé, old man, suitor **7** main man **9** inamorato

Boy Scout *founder:* 11 Baden-Powell (Robert) *gathering:* **8** jamboree *motto:* **10** be prepared *rank:* **4** Life (Scout), Star (Scout) **5** Eagle (Scout) **10** Tenderfoot *unit:* **5** troop **6** patrol

Boys Town *founder:* 8 Flanagan (Edward) *state:* **8** Nebraska

bozo 3 oaf **4** boob, clod, dodo, dolt, dope, fool, goof, jerk, mutt, simp, yo-yo **5** chump, dummy, dunce, idiot, moron, ninny, noddy, stupe **6** dimwit, donkey, dum-dum, nitwit, noodle **7** airhead, dullard, pinhead **8** bonehead, clodpoll, dumbbell, dumbhead, imbecile, lunkhead, meathead, numskull **9** birdbrain, blockhead, ignoramus, lamebrain, numbskull, simpleton, thickhead **10** dunderhead, hammerhead, nincompoop **11** chowderhead, chucklehead, knucklehead

B.P.O.E. member 3 Elk

Brabantio's daughter 9 Desdemona

brabble 3 row **4** beef, feud, flap, riot, spat, tiff **5** argue, scrap, set to **6** bicker, blowup, fracas, grouse **7** dispute, fall out, palaver, quarrel, rhubarb, scuffle, wrangle **8** argument, squabble **9** altercate, bickering, brannigan, caterwaul, wrangling **10** falling-out **11** altercation, disputation, embroilment

brace 3 arm, bar, duo, tie **4** dyad, gird,

pair, prop, stay **5** clamp, ready, shore, steel, strut, truss **6** accost, bear up, column, couple, demand, splint, steady, uphold **7** bolster, bracket, enliven, fortify, freshen, prepare, refresh, shore up, support, sustain, tighten, twosome **8** buttress **9** reinforce **10** cantilever, exhilarate, invigorate, strengthen **12** underpinning **13** underpropping

bracelet 6 bangle **7** manacle **8** wristlet

bracing 4 keen **5** brisk, crisp, fresh, nippy, sharp, tonic **6** biting, chilly **7** rousing **8** stirring **9** animating **10** energizing, quickening **11** restorative, stimulating, stimulative **12** exhilarating, invigorating

bracken 4 fern **5** brake, brush, scrub **11** undergrowth

bracket 3 arm **4** join, link, omit **5** brace **6** couple, relate, remove **7** combine, compare, conjoin, connect, embrace, enclose, include, support **8** buttress, encircle, leave out, put aside, set aside **9** associate, encompass **11** parenthesis **12** strengthener

brackish 4 sour **5** acrid, briny, salty **6** saline, salted **9** repulsive, sickening **10** nauseating

bract 4 leaf **5** glume **6** paleat, spathe **8** phyllary

brad 4 nail

Bradamant *brother:* **7** Rinaldo *husband:* **6** Rogero **8** Ruggiero

Bradbury's forte 5 sci-fi **7** fantasy

brae 4 bank, hill **5** slope **8** hillside

brag 3 gas **4** blow, crow, puff **5** boast, mouth, prate, vaunt **7** show off, swagger, talk big **9** cockiness, gasconade **10** grandstand **11** rodomontade

braggadocio 6 hot air **7** boaster, bombast, bravado, conceit, puffery, swagger, windbag **8** blowhard, boasting, braggart, bragging **9** arrogance, cockiness, pomposity **10** cockalorum, pretension, swaggering **11** fanfaronade

braggart 6 blower **7** boaster, egotist, vaunter, windbag **8** big mouth, blowhard **9** big talker, know-it-all, swaggerer, vulgarian **11** braggadocio

Brahmin 8 highbrow **9** blueblood, patrician **10** aristocrat

braid 4 plat **5** plait, queue **7** galloon, pigtail **8** soutache **9** interlace **10** intertwine, interweave

brain 3 wit **4** bean, conk, mind **7** concuss **9** intellect **10** gray matter **12** intelligence *bone:* **5** skull **7** cranium *clot:* **10** thrombosis *gland:* **6** pineal **9** pituitary *layer:* **6** cortex *lobe:* **6** limbic, vermis **7** frontal **8** parietal, temporal **9** occipital *membrane:* **3** pia **4** dura **6** meninx **8** pia

mater **9** arachnoid, dura mater *part:* **4** lobe **7** medulla **8** cerebrum, thalamus **9** sensorium, ventricle **10** cerebellum, hemisphere **12** diencephalon *relating to:* **8** cerebral **10** encephalic *ridge:* **4** gyri (plural) **5** gyrus *vertebrate:* **10** encephalon *wave record:* **3** EEG

brainchild 4 idea, opus, work **6** animus, scheme, theory **7** coinage **9** handiwork, invention **10** hypothesis, innovation **11** achievement, chef-d'oeuvre, contrivance

brainiac 4 whiz **6** genius **7** prodigy

brainless 3 dim **5** dense, silly, thick **6** simple, stupid **7** asinine, foolish, idiotic, moronic, vacuous, witless **9** dimwitted, nitwitted **10** acephalous **12** feebleminded

brainpower 3 wit **5** sense **6** smarts **8** aptitude, capacity, sagacity **9** intellect, mentality, mother wit **10** perception **11** discernment, penetration **12** intelligence **13** comprehension

brainsick 3 mad **4** daft **5** batty, crazy, manic, potty **6** crazed, insane, mental **7** cracked, haywire, lunatic **8** aberrant, demented, deranged, maniacal, unhinged **9** bedlamite, delirious, disturbed **10** disordered, incoherent, irrational, unbalanced

brainstorm 3 rap, jaw **4** idea **6** confer, huddle **7** dream up, think up **8** cogitate, discuss, mull over **9** mental fit **10** groupthink, kick around, toss around **11** inspiration, put together

brainteaser 5 poser, rebus **6** puzzle, riddle **7** stumper **9** conundrum **10** cryptogram

brainwashing 10 propaganda **11** mind control, reeducation

brainy 4 keen **5** quick, savvy, sharp, smart **6** adroit, astute, bright, clever **9** eggheaded, brilliant, sagacious **10** discerning, precocious **11** intelligent, quick-witted, ready-witted **13** knowledgeable, perspicacious

brake 4 curb, slow, stop **5** block **6** damper, hinder, impede, retard, slough **7** barrier, bracken, slacken **8** blockade, obstacle, obstruct, slow down **9** deterrent, hindrance **10** constraint, decelerate **11** bracken fern

bramble 4 burr **5** brier, furze, gorse, hedge, shrub, thorn **6** nettle **7** thistle

branch 3 arm **4** fork, limb, rami (plural), wing **5** bough, ramus **6** ramify **7** diverge, outpost **8** division **9** tributary **10** subsidiary

branched 6 ramate, ramose

brand 4 blot, blur, logo, make, mark, onus, sear, slur, sort, spot, type

5 badge, class, odium, stain, stamp, sword, taint, torch **6** accuse, charge, impute, stigma, stripe **7** species, variety **8** black eye, disgrace, insignia, logotype **9** trademark **10** stigmatize

brandish 4 wave **5** flash, shake, sport, swing, wield **6** flaunt, parade **7** display, exhibit, show off **8** flourish

brand-new 4 mint **5** fresh **6** latest, unused, virgin **8** up-to-date **9** untouched **11** cutting-edge **13** inexperienced

brandy 4 marc, ouzo, raki **5** Pisco **6** cognac, grappa, kirsch, Metaxa **7** liqueur **8** Armagnac, calvados, digestif, eau-de-vie **9** applejack, framboise, slivovitz

brannigan 3 row **4** bust, flap, spat, tiff **5** binge, fight, set-to, spree **6** bender, blowup, hassle, ruckus **7** brabble, discord, dispute, quarrel, wassail, wrangle **8** squabble **10** falling-out **11** altercation

brash 4 bold, flip, pert **5** cocky, gutsy, hasty, nervy, saucy **6** brassy, brazen, cheeky, madcap, uppish, uppity **7** brittle, forward **8** arrogant, cocksure, flippant, impudent, insolent, reckless, tactless **9** audacious, bumptious, ebullient, energetic, exuberant, hot-headed, impetuous, impolitic, maladroit, unabashed, untactful **10** ill-advised, incautious **11** overweening, thoughtless **12** high-spirited, presumptuous, undiplomatic, unrestrained **13** disrespectful, inconsiderate, irrepressible, self-assertive

brashness 4 gall, grit, guts **5** brass, cheek, crust, nerve, pluck **6** aplomb, daring, mettle, spirit **8** audacity, chutzpah, temerity **9** assurance **10** confidence, effrontery **11** presumption

brass 4 gall **5** cheek, nerve **8** audacity, chutzpah **9** brashness, impudence, insolence **10** confidence, effrontery **11** presumption **12** impertinence

brassbound 3 set **5** brash, rigid **6** brazen, narrow **7** adamant, bigoted, forward **8** obdurate **9** illiberal, presuming, obstinate, unbending **10** implacable, inflexible, intolerant, relentless, unswayable, unyielding **11** opinionated, small-minded, unrelenting **12** narrow-minded, presumptuous, single-minded **13** dyed-in-the-wool, self-asserting, self-assertive

brasserie 10 restaurant

brass hat 3 VIP **4** boss **5** elder **6** better, senior **7** big shot **8** big whell, higher-up, superior

brassica 4 kale, rape **5** colza **6** turnip **7** cabbage, mustard **8** broccoli, collards, kohlrabi, rutabaga **11** cauliflower

brass tacks 5 facts **7** details **11** nitty-gritty, particulars

brass worker 7 brazier

brassy see BRAZEN

brat 3 imp **4** punk **6** urchin **10** holy terror

bravado 5 bluff **6** hot air **7** bluster, bombast **8** audacity, boasting, boldness, bragging, defiance, vaunting **9** gasconade **10** blustering, pretension, swaggering **11** braggadocio, grandiosity **12** boastfulness

brave 4 bold, dare, defy, face, game, meet, risk **5** beard, gutsy, hardy, manly, nervy, noble, stout **6** daring, heroic, manful, plucky, spunky, take on **7** defiant, doughty, gallant, valiant, venture **8** confront, face down, fearless, intrepid, reckless, resolute, spirited, splendid, stalwart, unafraid, valorous **9** audacious, challenge, dauntless, excellent, steadfast, undaunted, withstand **10** courageous **11** boldhearted, indomitable, lionhearted, undauntable, unflinching, venturesome **12** stouthearted **13** adventuresome

Brave New World author 6 Huxley (Aldous)

bravery 4 grit, guts **5** nerve, pluck, valor **6** daring, mettle, spirit **7** courage, heroism **8** audacity, boldness, temerity **9** derring-do, fortitude, gallantry **11** intrepidity **12** fearlessness, intrepidness *false:* **7** bravado

bravo 3 olé **4** rave **5** cheer **6** gunman, hit man, killer **7** ovation, plaudit, villain **8** applause, assassin **9** desperado

bravura 4 bold **5** showy **6** daring, florid, ornate **8** dazzling, skillful, virtuoso **9** brilliant

brawl 3 row **4** feud, flap, fray, fuss, maul, riot, spar, spat, tiff **5** clash, broil, fight, melee, scrap, set-to **6** affray, battle, bicker, dustup, fracas, rumble, tussle **7** bobbery, brabble, contend, quarrel, rhubarb, ruction, scuffle, wrangle **8** dogfight, eruption, skirmish, slugfest, squabble, upheaval **9** fistfight, imbroglio, scrimmage **10** donnybrook, fisticuffs, free-for-all **11** altercation, disturbance **13** confrontation

brawn 4 beef, meat, thew **5** clout, flesh, might, power, sinew **6** muscle **8** strength **9** puissance **10** headcheese

brawny 5 beefy, burly, husky, lusty, tough **6** robust, sinewy, stocky, strong, sturdy **8** athletic, muscular, powerful, thickset, vigorous **9** strapping, well-built **10** able-bodied

bray 4 mill **5** crush, grind, pound **6** bellow, pestle, powder **7** atomize,

brazen 4 bold, loud **5** brash, gaudy, noisy, showy **6** arrant, brassy, cheeky **7** blatant, defiant, forward, glaring, jarring **8** flagrant, impudent, insolent **9** audacious, barefaced, obtrusive, shameless, unabashed **10** outrageous, procacious, unblushing **11** conspicuous, impertinent **12** contumelious, presumptuous **13** disrespectful

Brazil *capital:* **8** Brasília *city:* **5** Belém **6** Recife **8** Salvador, São Paulo **12** Rio de Janeiro **13** Belo Horizonte *discoverer:* **6** Cabral (Pedro) *island:* **6** Marajó **7** Caviana *language:* **10** Portuguese *monetary unit:* **4** real *neighbor:* **4** Peru **6** Guyana **7** Bolivia, Uruguay **8** Colombia, Paraguay, Suriname **9** Argentina, Venezuela **12** French Guiana *river:* **6** Amazon **8** Parnaíba **10** Alto Paraná **12** São Francisco

breach 3 gap **4** gash, hole, open, rent, rift, slit **5** break, chasm, cleft, crack, split **6** hiatus, lacuna, schism **7** break in, discord, disrupt, fissure, infract, interim, opening, rupture, violate **8** aperture, disunity, division, fracture, infringe, interval, trespass **9** disregard, severance, violation **10** alienation, contravene, infraction, separation, transgress **11** delinquency, dereliction **12** disaffection, disobedience, estrangement, infringement, interruption **13** contravention, discontinuity, noncompliance, nonobservance, transgression

bread 3 bun **4** food, pita, rusk **5** bagel, money, toast **6** living, muffin, sippet **7** biscuit, crouton, edibles, stollen **8** victuals, zwieback **9** provender **10** livelihood, provisions, sustenance **11** comestibles, maintenance, subsistence *communion:* **4** host **5** wafer **9** Eucharist *from heaven:* **5** manna *ingredient:* **4** meal **5** flour, yeast **6** leaven *Jewish:* **5** matzo **6** hallah, matzoh **7** challah *maker:* **5** baker *Scottish:* **7** bannock *spread:* **3** jam **4** oleo **5** jelly **6** butter **9** margarine *unleavened:* **5** matzo **6** matzoh

bread and butter 4 keep, work **6** basics, living **7** support **8** mainstay, victuals **10** employment, livelihood, occupation, sustenance **9** nutriment **11** maintenance, necessities, subsistence **12** alimentation

breadbasket 3 gut **5** belly, tummy **6** paunch **7** abdomen, stomach **8** potbelly **9** bay window, beer belly

breadth 4 area, size, span **5** range, reach, scope, space, sweep, width **6** extent, spread **7** compass, expanse, stretch **8** distance, fullness, latitude, vastness, wideness **9** amplitude, expansion, magnitude **10** liberality

break 3 gap **4** bust, dash, halt, leak, luck, rest, rift, ruin, tame **5** burst, clear, crack, inure, sever, solve, spell **6** breach, chance, decode, divide, escape, exceed, hiatus, impair, lacuna, refute, relief, reveal **7** destroy, divulge, fall out, interim, lighten, opening, respite, rupture, shatter, surpass, suspend, time-out, violate **8** accustom, bankrupt, breather, decipher, disclose, division, downtime, fracture, good luck, interval, moderate **9** interlude, interrupt **10** annihilate, controvert, impoverish **11** discontinue, disjunction, dislocation, opportunity, suspensions **12** intermission, interruption **13** discontinuity

breakable 4 weak **5** frail **6** flimsy **7** brittle, fragile, friable **8** delicate **9** frangible

breakaway 4 prop **7** escapee **8** offshoot, renegade, seceding

break down 4 fail, fold, sort, wilt **5** class, decay, index **6** cave in, digest, give in **7** analyze, clarify, crumble, crumple, elucidate, give out, give way, go crazy, succumb **8** classify, collapse, dissolve **9** anatomize, decompose, fall apart **12** disintegrate

breakdown 5 crash, decay, smash, study, wreck **6** mishap **7** crack-up, debacle, failure, smashup **8** analysis, collapse, taxonomy **9** cataclysm, partition **10** disruption, dissection, resolution **11** dysfunction, examination, prostration

breaker 4 wave **6** billow, comber, roller

Breakfast at Tiffany's *author* **6** Capote (Truman)

breakfront 7 cabinet **8** bookcase

break in 4 tame **5** train **6** breach, burgle, gentle, invade **7** intrude **8** initiate **9** condition, habituate, interfere, interpose, interrupt

breakneck 4 fast **5** fleet, hasty, quick, rapid, swift **6** racing, speedy, unsafe **8** meteoric **10** harefooted **11** precipitous

break off 3 end **4** drop, halt, kill, stop **5** abort, cease, scrub, sever **6** cancel, detach **7** curtail, scratch, suspend **8** cut short **9** terminate **11** discontinue

break out 4 bolt, flee **5** arise, erupt, flare **6** emerge, escape **7** explode **8** mushroom, separate

break through 5 burst **6** breach, emerge, pierce **7** rupture, surface **8** overcome **9** penetrate

breakthrough 4 find, gain, hike, leap, rise **5** boost **7** advance, radical, upgrade **8** advanced, increase, landmark **9** invention, milestone **10** avant-garde, innovation 11 cutting-edge, development, exceptional, progressive, quantum leap

break up 3 end 4 halt, part 6 divide, sunder 7 destroy, disband, disjoin, disrupt, rupture, scatter, shatter 8 disperse, dissever, dissolve, disunite, separate 9 decompose, dismantle, pulverize, terminate 12 disintegrate

breakup 4 rift 5 split 7 divorce, parting 8 analysis 9 dispersal 10 dissection, separation 11 dissolution

breakwater 5 jetty

breast 5 bosom, chest, heart *animal:* 7 brisket *combining form:* 3 maz 4 mast, mazo 5 masto, stern, steth 6 mastia (plural), sterno, stetho

breastbone 7 sternum

breast-feed 5 nurse 6 suckle 7 nourish

breastwork 7 barrier, bastion, bulwark, defense, parapet, rampart 9 barricade, earthwork 10 embankment 13 fortification, reinforcement

breath 4 gasp, gust, hint, puff 5 let-up, pause, trace, whiff 6 breeze 7 respite 10 exhalation, inhalation, suggestion

breathe 4 emit, sigh 5 exude, utter, voice 6 endure, exhale, expire, inhale, murmur 7 confide, express, give off, inspire, persist, radiate, respire, subsist, survive, whisper

breather 4 lull, rest, stay, vent 5 break, let-up, pause, spell 6 hiatus, recess 7 caesura, respite 8 downtime 9 remission 12 interruption

breathing *labored:* 7 dyspnea *normal:* 6 eupnea *rapid:* 8 polypnea

breathing apparatus 10 respirator *underwater:* 5 scuba

breathing orifice 4 nose 5 mouth 8 blowhole, spiracle

breathless 4 agog, avid, keen 5 eager 6 ardent 7 anxious, gasping, intense 8 gripping 9 expectant, impatient 11 short-winded 13 on tenterhooks

breathtaking 6 moving 7 awesome 8 dramatic, exciting, imposing, stunning, wondrous 9 panoramic, thrilling 10 impressive, staggering 11 astonishing, magnificent, spectacular 12 awe-inspiring, overwhelming 13 heart-stirring

Brecht play 4 Baal 13 Life of Galileo (The), Mother Courage 15 Seven Deadly Sins (The), Threepenny Opera (The) 20 Caucasian Chalk Circle (The)

breech 3 bum 4 duff, rear, rump, seat, tail 5 fanny 6 behind, bottom, heinie 7 keester, keister, rear end 8 backside, buttocks, derriere, haunches 9 fundament, posterior 12 hindquarters

breechclout 9 loincloth

breed 3 ilk 4 bear, grow, kind, make, mate, race, rear, sire, sort, type 5 beget, brand, cause, class, cross, genus, hatch, likes, raise, stock, yield 6 couple, create, father, induce, nature, strain, stripe 7 bring up, develop, educate, lineage, nurture, produce, species, variety 8 copulate, engender, generate, mate with, multiply 9 cultivate, procreate, propagate, reproduce 10 discipline, extraction, give rise to, impregnate, inseminate

breeding 4 line 5 grace, taste 6 polish 7 culture, decorum, lineage, manners 8 ancestry, civility, courtesy, pedigree 9 genealogy, gentility, propriety 10 refinement, upbringing 11 cultivation

breeding ground 6 hotbed, origin 8 hothouse 10 forcing bed, mating spot 12 forcing house

breeze 3 zip 4 flit, sail, snap, waft 5 cinch, draft, waltz 6 zephyr 8 duck soup, kid stuff 10 child's play

breezy 4 airy, cool 5 fresh, gusty, windy 6 blithe, casual, drafty 7 offhand, relaxed 8 carefree, careless, detached, informal 9 easygoing 10 insouciant, nonchalant 11 unconcerned 12 devil-may-care, lighthearted

Breton 4 Celt

___ breve 4 alla

breviary 5 brief 6 digest, précis 7 epitome, essence, outline, rundown, summary 8 abstract, boildown, synopsis 9 reduction 10 abridgment, conspectus, prayer book 11 abridgement 12 condensation, divine office

brevity 7 economy 8 laconism 9 briefness, concision, crispness, pithiness, shortness, terseness 10 transience

brew 3 ale, tea 4 beer, loom, mull, plan, plot 5 drink 6 cook up, foment, gather, impend, infuse, scheme, stir up 7 concoct, ferment 8 contrive

briar 4 burr, pipe 5 furze, gorse, shrub, thorn 6 nettle 7 bramble, thistle

Briareus 7 Aegaeon *father:* 6 Uranus *mother:* 4 Gaea

bribe 3 buy, fix, sop 6 buy off, payoff, payola, square, suborn 7 corrupt 9 incentive 10 enticement, inducement, tamper with

bric-a-brac 6 curios 8 trinkets 9 ornaments 10 knicknacks, objets d'art 11 gingerbread 13 embellishment

brick 5 block *layer:* 5 mason *laying:* 7 masonry *material:* 4 clay, marl *oven:* 4 kiln *row:* 6 course *sun-dried:* 5 adobe *trough for carrying:* 3 hod

bridal 7 nuptial, spousal 8 conjugal 9 connubial 11 matrimonial

bridal wreath 6 spirea

bridewell 3 can, jug, pen 4 coop, jail 5 clink, joint 6 lockup, prison 7 slammer 8 bastille 12 penitentiary

bridge 4 join, link, span 5 unite 7 connect 8 overpass, traverse *great:* 8 Brooklyn 10 Golden Gate *kind:* 4 arch, draw, rope 5 swing, truss 7 bascule, covered, natural, pontoon, trestle, viaduct 10 cantilever, suspension *term:* 3 bid 4 book, east, pass, ruff, slam, suit, void, west 5 bonus, dummy, north, raise, south, trick, trump 6 double, renege, rubber 7 auction, finesse, notrump, overbid 8 contract, jump call, redouble 9 grand slam, overtrick, singleton 10 little slam, undertrick, vulnerable

bridgelike game 5 whist 6 hearts

bridle 3 bit 4 curb, fume, rein, rule 5 check, flare, quell 6 govern, halter, hold in, manage, master, rein in, ruffle, seethe, subdue 7 bristle, control, flare up, inhibit, repress 8 hold back, moderate, restrain, suppress, withhold 9 constrain, deterrent, hackamore, restraint

brief 4 curt 5 pithy, short, terse 6 abrupt, digest, inform 7 brusque, concise, epitome, laconic, outline, passing, summary 8 abstract, breviary, fleeting, succinct, synopsis 9 momentary, transient 10 abridgment, conspectus 11 abridgement, compendious 12 condensation 13 short and sweet

brig 3 can, jug, pen 4 coop, jail 5 clink 6 cooler, lockup, prison 7 slammer 8 stockade 9 guardroom 10 guardhouse

brigade 4 army, unit 5 force, group 6 troops 10 contingent, detachment

brigand 6 bandit, bummer, looter, pirate, raider 7 cateran, corsair, forager, rustler 8 marauder, pillager 9 buccaneer, plunderer 10 freebooter, highwayman

brigandage 7 pillage, sacking 10 despoiling, ransacking 11 depredation

bright 4 fair, keen 5 aglow, alert, clear, light, lucid, quick, shiny, smart, sunny, vivid 6 brainy, cheery, clever, lively, lucent 7 beaming, blazing, flaming, fulgent, glowing, lambent, lighted, radiant 8 cheerful, dazzling, gleaming, luminous, lustrous, sunshiny 9 brilliant, effulgent, favorable, refulgent, sparkling 10 auspicious, glittering, precocious, propitious, shimmering 11 illuminated, intelligent, quick-witted 12 incandescent 13 scintillating

brighten 4 buoy 5 cheer, clear, shine

6 look up, perk up, polish, revive, solace 7 burnish, cheer up, clear up, enhance, enliven, furbish, gladden, hearten, improve 8 illumine 10 illuminate

brightness 5 éclat, shine 6 luster, lustre 8 radiance, splendor 10 brilliance, effulgence, luminosity *measure of:* 3 lux 5 lumen 6 candle 7 candela 10 footcandle

brilliance see BRIGHTNESS

brilliant 6 ablaze, brainy, genius, lucent, superb 7 beaming, fulgent, lambent, radiant, shining, stellar 8 dazzling, luminous, masterly, striking 9 effulgent, ingenious, refulgent, sparkling 10 glittering 11 exceptional 12 incandescent

brilliantine 6 pomade 9 hair cream

brim 3 hem, lip, rim 4 edge, fill, well 5 brink, skirt, verge, visor 6 border, fill up, fringe, margin 7 run over 8 overflow, well over 9 perimeter, periphery 13 circumference

brimful see BRIMMING

brimming 4 full 5 awash, flush 6 filled, jammed, loaded, packed 7 crammed, crowded, replete, stuffed, teeming, welling 8 bursting, overfull, suffused, swarming, swelling 9 chock-full, jampacked 11 chockablock, running over

brimstone 6 sulfur

brine 3 sea 4 deep, main 5 ocean 8 seawater 9 salt water

bring 3 lug 4 lead, pack, tote 5 carry, fetch, gross, yield 6 convey 7 attract, produce 9 transport

bring about 3 win 5 beget, cause 6 create, draw on, effect, secure 7 procure, produce, trigger 8 engender, generate, result in 10 accomplish, effectuate, give rise to

bring around 4 hook, sway, turn 7 convert, win over 8 convince, persuade, talk into 9 argue into, prevail on, sweet-talk 11 prevail upon

bring back 5 renew 6 recall, recoup, return, revive 7 recover, reprise, restore, salvage 8 retrieve, revivify 9 reinstate 10 repatriate 11 reestablish

bring down 3 bag, hew 4 drop, fell, raze 5 floor, level, shoot 6 defeat, depose, ground, humble, lay low, reduce 7 depress, flatten 8 demolish, overturn 9 humiliate, overthrow, prostrate, undermine

bring forth 4 bear 5 beget, yield 6 create, elicit, invent 7 deliver, produce 8 generate 9 propagate, reproduce 10 give rise to

bring forward 6 adduce, submit, tender,

unveil **7** advance, present, produce, proffer **9** introduce

bring in 3 pay, net, win **4** draw, earn, gain, sell **5** fetch, gross, yield **6** garner, return, secure **7** acquire, be worth, realize **9** introduce

bring off 6 effect, finish, rescue **7** achieve, execute, realize, succeed **8** carry out **9** discharge, implement **10** accomplish, consummate, effectuate **12** carry through

bring out 4 cull **5** educe, utter, voice **6** elicit, reveal **7** declare, enhance, explain, extract **8** disclose, showcase **9** elucidate, highlight, introduce

bring together 3 mix, wed **4** herd, join, link, yoke **5** amass, batch, blend, group, marry, merge, rally, unify, unite **6** corral, muster **7** collect, compact, compile, convene, round up **8** assemble **9** aggregate, integrate, reconcile, stockpile **10** synthesize **11** consolidate

bring up 4 moot, rear **5** breed, raise, refer, teach, train, vomit **6** advert, allude, broach, foster, school **7** advance, educate, mention, nurture, propose, suggest, touch on **8** point out, instruct **9** cultivate, introduce **10** put forward **11** regurgitate

brink 3 hem **4** bank, brim, edge **5** point, skirt, verge **6** border, fringe, margin **9** extremity, perimeter, periphery, threshold

briny 5 salty **6** saline

brio 3 pep, vim, zip **4** dash, élan, fire, life, zest, zing **5** ardor, flair, gusto, oomph, style, verve, vigor **6** bounce, esprit, fervor, spirit **7** panache, passion, sparkle **8** dynamism, vivacity **9** animation

brioche 4 roll

Briseis' lover 8 Achilles

brisk 4 busy, fast, keen, spry, yare **5** agile, fresh, nippy, quick, sharp, zippy **6** lively, nimble, snappy, speedy **7** bracing **8** animated, bustling, vigorous **9** energetic, sprightly **10** refreshing **11** stimulating **12** invigorating

bristle 4 boil, burn, fume, seta **5** anger, quill, setae (plural), spine **6** arista, chaeta, seethe **7** chaetae (plural) *Scottish:* **5** birse

British *air force:* **3** RAF *cathedral city:* **3** Ely **4** York **5** Ripon, Truro, Wells **6** Durham, Exeter **7** Chester, Lincoln **8** Coventry, Hereford, St. David's **9** Lichfield, Salisbury, Wakefield, Worcester **10** Canterbury, Gloucester *Channel Island:* **4** Sark **6** Jersey **8** Alderney, Guernsey *coin, current:* **5** pence (plural), penny, pound *coin, old:* **3** bob **5** crown, groat, noble **6** bawbee, florin, George, guinea, tanner, teston **8** farthing, shilling **9** halfcrown, halfpenny, sovereign **10** threepence *colony, former:* **4** Aden, Cape **5** Adana, Kenya, Malta, Natal **6** Ceylon, Cyprus, Gambia **7** Jamaica, Sarawak **9** Gold Coast, Singapore, Transvaal **10** Basutoland, New Zealand **11** Orange River, Sierra Leone **12** Bechuanaland *county:* **4** Avon, Kent, York **5** Derby, Devon, Essex, Gwent **6** Dorset, Durham, Oxford, Surrey, Sussex **7** Bedford, Cumbria, Norfolk, Rutland, Suffolk, Warwick **8** Cheshire, Cornwall, Hereford, Hertford, Somerset, Stafford **9** Berkshire, Cleveland, Hampshire, Lancaster, Leicester, Wiltshire, Worcester **10** Cumberland, Gloucester, Humberside, Lancashire, Merseyside, Shropshire **11** Westmorland **12** Lincolnshire *court, local:* **8** hustings *court, medieval:* **4** eyre *forest:* **5** Arden, weald **8** Sherwood *king, legendary:* **3** Lud **4** Beli, Bran **6** Arthur **7** Artegal, Belinus, Elidure **8** Brannius *language, ancient:* **6** Celtic, Cymric **9** Brythonic *legislature:* **10** Parliament *news agency:* **7** Reuters *nobleman:* **4** duke, earl, peer **5** baron **6** prince **8** marquess, viscount *order:* **6** Garter *people, early:* **5** Celts, Iceni, Jutes, Picts **6** Angles, Saxons *political party:* **4** Tory, Whig **6** Labour **12** Conservative *pope:* **8** Adrian IV *prince:* **5** Harry **6** Andrew, Edward **7** Charles, William *princess:* **4** Anne **5** Diana **8** Margaret *prison:* **5** Tower (of London) **7** Newgate **8** Dartmoor *queen, ancient:* **8** Boadicea, Boudicca *resort:* **4** Bath **7** Margate **8** Brighton **9** Blackpool *royal house:* **4** York **5** Tudor **6** Stuart **7** Hanover, Windsor **9** Lancaster **11** Plantagenet *royal residence:* **7** Windsor **8** Balmoral **10** Buckingham *school:* **4** Eton **5** Rugby **6** Harrow **10** Winchester *school, military:* **9** Sandhurst *spa:* **4** Bath **5** Epsom **6** Buxton **7** Malvern, Matlock **8** Brighton **9** Harrogate **10** Cheltenham

British Columbia *capital:* **8** Victoria *city:* **6** Surrey **7** Burnaby **8** Richmond **9** Vancouver *mountain:* **11** Fairweather *provincial flower:* **7** dogwood (Pacific)

British Honduras 6 Belize

brittle 4 curt **5** crisp, frail, stiff **6** infirm **7** crumbly, fragile, friable **9** breakable, frangible, inelastic, irritable, sensitive **10** perishable, transitory

broach 3 tap **4** moot **6** open up **7** bring up, mention, propose, suggest **8** initiate **9** introduce **10** put forward

broad 4 wide **7** general, liberal **8** extended, generous, spacious, sweeping, tolerant 9 expansive, extensive *combining form:* 4 eury, lati, plat 5 platy

broadcast 3 air, sow 4 beam, show 5 radio, strew 6 blazon, report, spread 7 bestrew, declare, publish, scatter 8 announce, proclaim, televise, transmit 9 advertise, publicize 10 bruit about, promulgate 11 communicate, declaration, disseminate, publication 12 announcement, proclamation, promulgation, transmission

broaden 4 open 5 swell, widen 6 dilate, expand, extend, fatten, spread 7 amplify, augment, distend, enlarge, thicken 8 increase 10 supplement

broadloom 6 carpet

broad-minded 4 open 7 liberal 8 catholic, eclectic, flexible, tolerant, unbiased 9 accepting, indulgent, unbigoted 10 forbearing, undogmatic 11 progressive 12 unjudgmental, unprejudiced

broadsheet 7 tabloid 9 newspaper

broadside 4 hail 5 burst, salvo, sheet, storm 6 shower, volley 7 barrage, torrent 8 at random 9 cannonade, fusillade, laterally, obliquely 11 bombardment

broadtail 4 hawk 5 sheep 7 karakul 8 lambskin

Brobdingnagian 4 huge 5 giant, jumbo 7 hulking, immense, mammoth, massive, titanic 8 colossal, gigantic, towering 9 cyclopean, humongous, monstrous 10 gargantuan, prodigious 11 elephantine

brochette 4 spit 6 skewer

brochure 5 flier, flyer 7 booklet 8 pamphlet

brogue 4 lilt, shoe 6 accent, oxford 7 dialect

broil 3 row 4 bake, burn, char, cook, fray, riot, sear 5 brawl, clash, fight, grill, melee, roast, run-in, toast 6 affray, fracas, scorch, tumult 7 bobbery, rhubarb, ruction, swelter, wrangle 8 disorder, squabble 10 donnybrook, free-for-all 11 disturbance

broiling 3 hot 5 fiery 6 baking, red-hot, torrid 7 blazing, burning 8 ovenlike, scalding, sizzling, white-hot 9 scorching 10 blistering, oppressive, sweltering

broke 4 poor 5 needy, spent 6 busted, ruined 7 drained 8 bankrupt, beggared, dirt poor, indigent, strapped, wiped out 9 destitute, insolvent, out of cash, penniless, penurious, played out 10 cleaned out 11 impecunious

broke-in 4 tame 5 tamed 6 docile

broken 4 shot 5 tamed 6 beaten, busted, cut off, faulty 7 crushed, haywire,

humbled, subdued 8 bankrupt, defeated, violated, weakened 9 depressed, disrupted, fractured, heartsick, shattered, sorrowful 11 discouraged, demoralized, interrupted 12 disconnected, disheartened 13 discontinuous

broken-down 7 rickety 8 battered, decaying, decrepit 9 crumbling, neglected 10 threadbare, ramshackle 11 debilitated, dilapidated 12 deteriorated

brokenhearted 7 crushed, unhappy 8 dejected, dolorous, hopeless, wretched 9 depressed, heartsick, sorrowful 10 despairing, despondent 12 inconsolable 13 grief-stricken

broker 5 agent 6 factor 8 diplomat, mediator 9 financier, go-between, middleman 10 interagent, interceder, matchmaker, negotiator 11 intercessor 12 intermediary 13 intermediator

brolly 8 umbrella

bromide 4 bore, drip, lump, pill, yawn 5 drone, grind 6 cliché, old saw, truism 7 proverb 8 banality, chestnut, prosaism, sedative 9 platitude, soporific 10 shibboleth, triviality 11 commonplace, rubber stamp

bromidic 3 dry 4 arid, dull 5 banal, bland, dusty, stale, trite 6 boring 7 humdrum, insipid, tedious 8 shopworn, tiresome 9 dryasdust, motheaten, wearisome 10 monotonous, pedestrian, unoriginal 11 commonplace 13 unimaginative, uninteresting

bronco 5 horse 6 cayuse 7 mustang *Australian:* 6 brumby

Brontë *character:* 9 Catherine, Rochester 10 Heathcliff *novel:* 7 Shirley 8 Jane Eyre, Villette 16 Wuthering Heights *sisters:* 4 Anne 5 Emily 9 Charlotte

Bronx cheer 3 boo 4 hoot, jeer, razz 5 taunt 7 catcall 9 raspberry

brooch 3 pin 4 clip 5 clasp 8 fastener

brood 3 set, sit 4 fret, mope, muse, stew, sulk 5 cover, flock, gloom, hatch, worry 6 litter, ponder, repine 7 despond, progeny 8 children, meditate, ruminate 9 offspring

brook 4 bear, burn, gill, race, rill 5 abide, creek, stand 6 arroyo, endure, rillet, runnel, stream, suffer 7 rivulet, stomach, swallow 8 stand for, tolerate *Scottish:* 6 burnie

Brookner *novel* 10 Hotel du Lac

broom 5 besom, brush, shrub, sweep, whisk 7 heather

broth 5 stock 8 bouillon, consommé

brothel 4 crib, stew 6 bagnio 7 lupanar 8 bordello, cathouse 9 call house 10 bawdy house, whorehouse

brother 3 kin 4 monk 5 friar 7 comrade, sibling *French:* 5 frère *Italian:* 3 fra 5 frate 8 fratello *Latin:* 6 frater *relating to:* 9 fraternal *Spanish:* 7 hermano

brotherhood 4 club, gang 5 amity, guild, order, union 6 league 7 kinship, society 8 alliance, sodality 10 fellowship, fraternity, friendship 11 association, camaraderie, comradeship, confederacy 12 togetherness 13 consanguinity, secret society

brotherly 9 fraternal

Brothers Karamazov 4 Ivan 5 Mitya 6 Alexei, Alexey, Dmitri, Dmitry 7 Alyosha 10 Smerdyakov

brouhaha 3 din 4 coil, flap, fuss, riot, to-do 5 babel, broil, hoo-ha, whirl 6 bedlam, clamor, fracas, furore, hubbub, hurrah, jangle, pother, racket, ruckus, rumpus, shindy, tumult, uproar 7 ferment 8 foofaraw 9 agitation, commotion 10 excitement, hullabaloo, hurly-burly 11 pandemonium

brow 3 top 4 mien 5 front, crest, crown 8 forehead 9 gangplank 10 expression 11 countenance

browbeat 3 cow 5 beset, bully, harry, press 6 badger, carp at, coerce, harass, hector, lean on 7 bluster, dragoon 8 bludgeon, bulldoze, bullyrag, domineer, overbear, pressure 9 tyrannize 10 intimidate

brown 4 sear 5 dusky, toast 6 scorch, tanned 7 swarthy *dark:* 5 sepia, umber 9 chocolate *grayish:* 3 dun 6 bister, bistre *light:* 3 tan 4 ecru, fawn 5 beige, hazel, khaki, tawny *moderate:* 4 teak 6 sienna *reddish:* 3 bay 4 roan 5 henna 6 auburn, russet, sorrel, titian 8 chestnut *yellowish:* 6 bronze 12 butterscotch

Brown Bomber 5 Louis (Joe)

brown coal 7 lignite

brownie 3 elf, fay 5 fairy, pixie 6 sprite

Browning poem 8 Prospice, Sordello 11 Aurora Leigh, Pippa Passes 12 Rabbi Ben Ezra 13 Fra Lippo Lippi, My Last Duchess 14 How Do I Love Thee?

brown recluse 6 spider

brownshirt 4 Nazi 12 storm trooper

browse 4 crop, feed, scan, shop, skim 5 graze, munch 6 forage, nibble, peruse 7 dip into, pasture 8 glance at, look over 10 glance over 11 flip through, leaf through, look through, skim through 12 thumb through

bruin 4 bear

bruise 5 pound, wound 6 batter, damage, injure, injury 7 contuse 8 abrasion, discolor 9 contusion 13 discoloration

bruit about 6 blazon, gossip, report, spread 7 declare, publish 8 announce, proclaim 9 advertise, broadcast, circu-

late 10 annunciate, pass around, promulgate 11 blaze abroad

brume 3 fog 4 film, haze, mist, murk 5 vapor 6 miasma 8 haziness 11 obscuration

brummagem 4 fake, sham 5 bogus, false, gaudy, phony, showy 6 ersatz, pseudo, tinsel, tawdry 7 chintzy 8 spurious 9 imitation, pinchbeck, tasteless 10 fabricated, fictitious 11 counterfeit, make-believe

Brunei *capital:* 17 Bandar Seri Begawan *island:* 6 Borneo *language:* 5 Malay *monetary unit:* 6 dollar *neighbor:* 8 Malaysia *sea:* 10 South China

brunet 3 jet 4 dark, onyx 5 dusky, ebony, raven, sable, sooty, swart 6 swarth 7 swarthy 8 bistered, obsidian 10 dark-haired 11 brown-haired

Brunhild 5 queen 7 heroine 8 Valkyrie *husband:* 6 Gunnar 7 Gunther *lover:* 9 Siegfried

brunt 4 jolt 5 shock 6 burden, impact

brush 4 clip, kiss, skim 5 broom, clash, graze, run-in, scrap, scrub, shave, sweep, whisk 6 glance, scrape, tussle 7 contact, thicket 8 skirmish 9 encounter, shrubbery, sideswipe 11 undergrowth

brusque 4 curt, tart 5 bluff, blunt, brief, gruff, rough, short, surly, terse 6 abrupt, crusty, snippy 7 uncivil 8 impolite, snippety, succinct 10 peremptory, ungracious 11 ill-mannered 12 discourteous

brutal 4 hard 5 cruel, feral, harsh 6 rugged, savage, severe 7 beastly, bestial, callous, inhuman, swinish, ruthless 8 barbaric, pitiless, ruthless, sadistic 9 barbarous, ferocious, merciless 10 relentless 11 cold-blooded, remorseless 12 bloodthirsty

brutalize 5 abuse 6 debase, harden 7 corrupt, debauch, deprave, pervert, roughen, subvert, vitiate 8 maltreat, mistreat 9 manhandle 10 bestialize

brute 4 ogre 5 beast, cruel, feral 6 animal, savage 7 beastly, bestial, inhuman, piggish, swinish, varmint 8 creature 10 troglodyte 11 instinctive

brutish 3 low 4 base, vile 5 crude, feral, gross, rough, stony 6 animal, carnal, coarse, scurvy, strong 7 beastly, bestial, boorish, inhuman, obscene, piggish, swinish, uncivil, uncouth 8 barbaric, degraded, depraved, inhumane, physical, sadistic 9 primitive, truculent, unrefined 11 animalistic, uncivilized

bryophyte 4 moss 8 hornwort 9 liverwort

Brythonic see CYMRIC

bubble 3 sac 4 blob, boil, dome, fizz, foam, moil 5 churn, froth, slosh, spume, swash 6 burble, gurgle, seethe, simmer 7 ferment, globule, vesicle 10 effervesce

bubbly 5 alive, fizzy, foamy, jolly, perky 6 cheery, frothy, lively 7 buoyant, excited 8 animated, effusive 9 champagne, ebullient, exuberant, sparkling 10 carbonated

buccaneer 5 rover 6 cowboy, pirate, sea dog 7 corsair, sea wolf 8 picaroon, sea rover 9 sea robber 10 freebooter

buck 3 fop, guy, lad, lug 4 balk, bear, bill, chap, dude, jerk, load, move, note, oner, pack, stag, tote, trip 5 cadet, carry, dandy, ferry, fight, money, pitch, repel, stark, throw 6 combat, dollar, fellow, oppose, resist, unseat 7 coxcomb, trestle 8 antelope, bank note, sawhorse, traverse 9 greenback, withstand, workhorse 10 completely 11 Beau Brummel

bucket 3 fly, run 4 pail, rush, whiz 5 hurry, speed 6 barrel, basket, hasten, hustle, vessel 9 clamshell 10 receptacle

Buckeye State 4 Ohio

buckle 4 bend, clip, fold, hasp, kink, warp 5 catch, clamp, clasp, heave, yield 6 cave in, fasten 7 contort, crumple, harness 8 collapse 9 fastening 10 coffee cake

buckle under 3 bow 4 cave, fold, give 5 defer, yield 6 cave in, submit 7 concede, succumb 8 collapse 9 surrender 10 capitulate 11 admit defeat

Buck novel 9 Good Earth (The)

buckram 4 taut 5 stiff 6 wooden 8 starched 9 cardboard, unbending 10 inflexible 11 interlining

bucks 5 kale 5 bread, dough, money, moola 6 dinero, do-re-mi, moolah 7 lettuce 10 greenbacks

buck up 4 buoy, lift 5 cheer, rally 6 solace 7 comfort, console, gladden, improve, refresh, smarten 8 brighten 9 encourage 10 strengthen

___ **buco** 4 osso

bucolic 5 rural 6 rustic 7 georgic, halcyon, idyllic 8 agrarian, arcadian, pastoral 10 campestral, provincial 11 countrified, picturesque

bud 4 germ, seed 5 gemma, spark 6 sprout 7 burgeon 9 pullulate 10 primordium *combining form:* 5 blast 6 blasto

Buddha 7 Gautama 10 Siddhartha *dialogues:* 5 sutra *disciple:* 6 Ananda *enemy:* 4 Mara *Japanese:* 5 Amida, Amita *mother:* 4 Maya *son:* 6 Rahula *teachings:* 6 dharma *wife:* 9 Yasodhara

Buddhism 3 Son, Zen 4 Chan 5 Kegon 6 Huayan, Tendai 7 Tiantai 8 Hinayana, Mahayana, Nichiren, Pure Land 9 Theravada, Vajrayana

Buddhist *chant:* 6 mantra *dialogues:* 5 sutra *enlightenment:* 6 satori *evil spirit:* 4 Mara *fate:* 5 karma *language:* 4 Pali *monk:* 4 lama 5 arhat, bonze *sacred city:* 5 Lhasa *saint:* 5 arhat *scripture:* 5 sutra 6 sutras 9 Pali canon *sect:* 3 Zen *shrine:* 4 tope 5 stupa 7 chorten *spell:* 6 mantra *spiritual leader:* 4 guru 9 Dalai Lama *state of happiness:* 7 nirvana *temple:* 6 pagoda *title:* 7 mahatma *tree of enlightenment:* 5 bodhi, pipal

buddy 3 mac, pal 4 chum, mate 5 crony 6 comate, fellow, friend 7 compeer, comrade, partner 8 coworker, playmate, sidekick 9 associate, companion 10 accomplice 11 confederate

buddy-buddy 5 close, pally, thick, tight 6 chummy 8 intimate 10 palsy-walsy 11 inseparable

budge 4 move 5 shift, yield 7 give way

budgerigar 6 parrot 8 parakeet

budget 5 funds, means 6 amount, ration, supply 8 allocate, estimate 9 allowance, apportion, resources

Buenos ___ 5 Aires

buff 3 fan, nut, rub, tan 4 fawn, sand, wipe 5 beige, brush, fiend, freak, glaze, gloss, lover, shine 6 addict, expert, polish, votary 7 admirer, burnish, devotee, fanatic, fancier, furbish, groupie, habitué 8 follower 9 yellowish 10 aficionado, altogether, enthusiast 11 connoisseur, yellow-brown

buffalo 4 bilk, faze 5 bison, bovid, stump 6 baffle, muddle, rattle 7 carabao, confuse, defraud, flummox, fluster, nonplus, perplex, swindle 8 befuddle, bewilder, confound, hoodwink 9 bamboozle, dumbfound

buffalo grass 5 grama

buffer 6 screen, shield 7 buckler, bulwark, cushion 8 absorber, mediator, polisher 9 safeguard 10 protection 12 intermediary

buffet 3 box, hit, rap 4 beat, blip, blow, bump, chop, cuff, drub, jolt, move, poke, slap, sock 5 clout, drive, force, pound, punch, smack, spank 6 batter, hammer, pummel, thrash, wallop 7 belabor, clobber, counter, lambast 8 lambaste, salad bar 9 sideboard

buffoon 3 wag 4 dolt, fool, goof, lout, zany 5 antic, clown, comic, droll, dunce, joker, yokel 6 jester 7 bumpkin, dullard 8 bonehead 9 blockhead, harlequin 10 clodhopper 11 merry-andrew

bug 3 fad, fan, irk, nag, nut, spy, tap, vex 4 buff, flaw, fret, gall, germ, rage 5 annoy, bulge, craze, fiend, freak, mania, peeve 6 badger, bother, defect, insect, malady, needle, nettle, pester, plague, zealot 7 disease, fanatic, microbe, provoke, wiretap **8** irritate, listen in, protrude, sickness **9** eavesdrop, infection, obsession **10** enthusiast **12** imperfection **13** microorganism

bugaboo see BUGBEAR

bugbear 4 bane, bogy, fear, ogre **5** bogey, bogie, poser **6** goblin, teaser **7** bugaboo, problem, specter, spectre **8** anathema, bogeyman, phantasm **9** bête noire, boogerman, boogeyman, hobgoblin **10** black beast **11** abomination

buggy 4 cart, tram **6** go-cart, jalopy **8** carriage

bugle *call:* **4** mess, taps **5** drill **6** sennet, tattoo **7** fanfare, retreat, tantara **8** assembly, reveille *relative:* **6** cornet **7** trumpet **10** flugelhorn

build 3 wax **4** body, form, make, mode, mold, rise **5** boost, erect, forge, frame, habit, mount, put up, raise, set up, shape, swell **6** expand, figure **7** amplify, augment, compose, enlarge, fashion, magnify, produce, upsurge **8** assemble, compound, engineer, escalate, heighten, increase, multiply, physique **9** construct, establish, fabricate, institute, intensify, originate **10** accelerate, inaugurate, strengthen **11** fit together, manufacture **12** conformation, constitution

builder 5 mason **9** carpenter **10** bricklayer, contractor

builder's knot 10 clove hitch

building 3 hut **5** house **7** edifice **8** dwelling **9** structure *addition:* **3** ell **4** wing **5** annex *compartment:* **3** bay **4** room **6** office *connector:* **9** breezeway *farm:* **4** barn, crib, shed, silo *for apartments:* **8** tenement *for arms:* **7** arsenal *for gambling:* **6** casino *for grain:* **4** silo **7** granary **8** elevator *for horses:* **6** stable *for manufacture:* **4** shop **5** plant **7** factory *for music:* **10** auditorium *for sports:* **3** gym **4** bowl **5** arena **7** stadium **8** coliseum **9** gymnasium **10** hippodrome *material:* **4** iron, wood **5** adobe, brick, glass, steel, stone **6** cement **8** concrete *projection:* **3** bay, ell **4** wing **5** annex **6** dormer **7** cornice *round:* **7** rotunda

building kit 5 Legos **10** Erector set **11** Lincoln Logs

build up 4 hype, plug, puff **5** boost, brace, erect **6** accrue, expand, extend, praise **7** collect, develop, enhance, fortify, improve, promote **8** buttress, heighten, increase **9** advertise, construct, establish, intensify, publicize **10** accumulate, aggrandize, strengthen

buildup 4 hype, puff, to-do **6** growth, hoopla **8** increase, ballyhoo **9** accretion, expansion, promotion, publicity **10** escalation **11** development, enhance-

ment, enlargement **12** accumulation, augmentation **13** strengthening

built-in 6 inborn, inbred, innate **8** included, inherent **9** essential, ingrained, intrinsic **10** congenital, deep-seated, indwelling **11** established, fundamental **12** constitutive, incorporated

bulb 4 leek, lily, sego **5** onion, tulip **6** allium, garlic, squill **8** daffodil, hyacinth **9** amaryllis, narcissus *segment:* **5** clove

bulb-like bud 4 corm **5** tuber **7** rhizome

Bulgaria *capital:* **5** Sofia *city:* **4** Ruse **5** Stara, Varna **6** Burgas, Pleven, Zagora **7** Plovdiv *monetary unit:* **3** lev *mountain, range:* **6** Balkan, Musala **7** Rhodope *neighbor:* **6** Greece, Serbia, Turkey **7** Romania **9** Macedonia *part of:* **7** Balkans *river:* **6** Danube **7** Maritsa *sea:* **5** Black

bulge 3 bag, jut, sac, sag **4** blob, bump, edge, lump, poke **5** bloat, pouch, swell **6** beetle, billow, bubble, bug out, dilate, excess, expand **7** balloon, distend, inflate, project, puff out **8** overhang, protrude, stand out, stick out, swelling **9** allowance, head start **10** distension, projection, promontory, protrusion **11** excrescence, protuberate **12** protuberance

bulk 4 body, core, loom, mass **5** fiber, swell, total **6** amount, corpus, expand, volume **7** bigness, quantum **8** majority, quantity, stand out **9** aggregate, magnitude, substance

bulky 3 fat **5** beefy, hefty, husky, large, obese, stout **7** massive **8** cumbrous, unwieldy **9** corpulent, ponderous **10** cumbersome, overweight **11** substantial

bull 4 bunk, male, slip, toro, trip **5** boner, edict, error, fluff, force, hooey, lapse **6** bovine, bungle, decree **7** baloney, blooper, blunder, hogwash, mistake **8** nonsense **9** detective *combining form:* **4** taur **5** tauri, tauro

bulldoze 3 cow **4** move, push, raze **5** abash, bully, clear, cream, elbow, force, level, press, scare, shove **6** coerce, hector, hustle, jostle, lean on, menace, propel, thrust **7** bluster, clobber, dragoon, flatten, oppress, trounce **8** bludgeon, browbeat, bullyrag, demolish, domineer, restrain, shoulder **9** terrorize, tyrannize **10** intimidate, obliterate

bullet 6 dumdum, tracer **9** cartridge **10** projectile *size:* **7** caliber, calibre

bulletin 4 news **5** flash, scoop **6** notice, report **7** account, catalog, gazette, message, missive, release **8** briefing, calen-

dar, dispatch, magazine, register 9 catalogue, statement 10 communiqué, periodical 12 announcement
bull fiddle 10 contrabass, double bass
bullfighter 6 torero 7 matador, picador 8 toreador 11 cuadrillero 12 banderillero *famous:* 6 Arruza 7 Ordóñez 8 Belmonte, Joselito, Manolete 9 Dominguin 10 El Cordobés
bullfighting *arena:* 5 plaza *cheer:* 3 olé *hero:* 6 torero 7 matador *lancer:* 7 picador *red cloth:* 6 muleta *Spanish:* 7 corrida *team:* 9 cuadrilla
bullheaded 6 mulish 7 adamant, willful 8 contrary, obdurate, perverse, stubborn 9 insistent, obstinate, pigheaded 10 headstrong, refractory, self-willed, unyielding 11 intractable, stiff-necked 12 intransigent, pertinacious, strong-willed
bullish 4 rosy 6 brawny, rising, upbeat 7 booming 9 advancing, expanding, favorable 10 optimistic
bully 3 cow 4 goon, pimp, punk, thug 5 abuse, heavy, meany, tease, tough 6 harass, hector, meanie, menace, pander, pick on, rascal 7 bluster, buffalo, dragoon, harrier, oppress, ruffian, torment, torture 8 bludgeon, browbeat, bulldoze, bullyrag, harasser, threaten 9 bulldozer, persecute, victimize, tormenter, tyrannize 10 browbeater, corned beef, intimidate, persecutor 11 intimidator
bullyrag see BULLDOZE
bulrush 4 reed 5 sedge 7 cattail, papyrus
bulwark 4 wall 6 screen, shield 7 barrier, bastion, parapet, rampart, seawall 8 buttress, fortress, palisade 9 earthwork, safeguard 10 breakwater, breastwork, embankment, stronghold 13 fortification
bum 3 beg, vag 4 bust, hobo, idle, laze, lazy, loaf, loll, slug 5 binge, cadge, drunk, hit up, idler, mooch, tramp 6 bottom, dawdle, loafer, loiter, lounge, slouch, unfair 7 depress, drifter, feel low, goof off, rear end, vagrant, wheedle 8 buttocks, derelict, fainéant, slugabed, sluggard, vagabond 9 do-nothing, goldbrick, importune, lazybones, panhandle, transient
bumbershoot 8 umbrella
bumble 3 mar 4 blow, flub, muff 5 botch, fluff, gum up, lurch 6 bobble, bollix, bungle, falter, fumble, mess up, muck up, rumble, slip up, teeter, totter 7 blunder, screw up, stagger, stumble 8 flounder
bumbling 5 inept, gawky 6 clumsy, gauche, klutzy 7 awkward, halting,

unhandy 8 ungainly 9 all thumbs, graceless, ham-handed, maladroit, unskilled 11 heavy-handed, incapable, incompetent 13 butterfingers, uncoordinated
bummer 3 dud 4 drag, flop, hobo 5 tramp 6 beggar, cadger, downer, sponge, too bad 7 failure, forager, moocher, sponger 8 deadbeat, vagabond 9 tough luck 10 freebooter, panhandler, rotten luck, wet blanket
bump 3 bop, hit, jar, ram, rap, wen 4 bang, bash, bust, jolt, knot, lump, oust, slam 5 break, carom, clash, crack, crash, gnarl, knock, prang, shift, shock, shove, wound 6 demote, growth, impact, injury, jostle, jounce, nodule, remove, strike, wallop 7 collide, degrade, demerit, pothole, run into 8 demotion, dislodge, displace, swelling 9 carbuncle, collision, contusion, convexity 10 concussion, projection, protrusion 12 protuberance
bumpkin 3 oaf 4 boor, hick, lout, rube 5 clown, swain, yokel 6 rustic 7 hayseed, peasant 9 chawbacon, hillbilly, simpleton 10 clodhopper, country boy, countryman, provincial
bump off 3 ice 4 do in, kill, slay 5 erase, snuff 6 murder, rub out 7 butcher, execute, take out 8 knock off 9 eliminate, liquidate 11 assassinate
Bumppo, Natty *alias:* 7 Hawkeye 10 Deerslayer, Pathfinder *creator:* 6 Cooper (James Fenimore)
bumptious 5 cocky, pushy 8 arrogant, impudent 9 audacious, obnoxious, obtrusive, officious 13 self-assertive
bumpy 5 jerky, nubby, ridgy, rough 6 bouncy, jouncy, knobby, knotty, patchy, pimply, uneven 7 jolting, nodular 9 difficult, irregular
bun 4 load, roll 6 pastry
bunch 3 lot, set, wen 4 band, bevy, bump, clot, crew, knot, lump, mass, push 5 batch, clump, covey, crowd, flock, group, party, spray, stack, swell 6 bundle, circle, clutch, gather, huddle, parcel, throng 7 bouquet, collect, cluster 8 assembly, protrude, swelling 9 gathering 10 assemblage, assortment, collection, congregate 11 aggregation 12 accumulation
bunco steerer 3 gyp 6 con man 7 cheater, diddler, grifter, sharper 8 swindler 9 defrauder, trickster 12 double-dealer 13 confidence man
bundle 3 lot, pot, set, wad 4 bale, body, heap, mint, pack, pile, wrap 5 array, batch, bunch, clump, group, sheaf,

truss **6** fardel, packet, parcel **7** cluster, fortune **10** assortment

bungalow 5 cabin, lodge **6** chalet **7** cottage

bungle 4 flub, goof, mess, muff, slip, trip **5** boner, botch, error, fluff, gum up, lapse, mix up, spoil **6** bollix, bumble, fiasco, foozle, foul up, fumble, goof up, mess up, muck up, muddle **7** blooper, blunder, failure, louse up, misstep, mistake, stumble **9** mishandle, mismanage

bungler 3 oaf **4** clod, dolt, goof **5** klutz **7** screw-up, tomfool **8** bonehead, goofball, shlemiel **9** blunderer, schlemiel **10** stumblebum **11** blunderbuss, incompetent **13** butterfingers

bunglesome 6 clumsy, klutzy **7** awkward **8** bumbling **9** all thumbs **13** uncoordinated

bung up 4 beat, hurt **5** abuse, pound **6** batter, bruise, injure **7** contuse, disable **9** disfigure, manhandle

bunion 4 lump **8** swelling **10** protrusion, tumescence **11** enlargement

bunk 3 bed, cot, kip, rot **4** bosh, bull, guff, jazz **5** bilge, board, crash, hokum, hooey, house, lodge, put up **6** humbug, pallet, piffle **7** eyewash, baloney, hogwash, rubbish, twaddle **8** claptrap, domicile, flimflam, malarkey, nonsense, tommyrot **9** poppycock **10** balderdash

bunker 3 bin **6** dugout **7** bastion, chamber **10** embankment, stronghold **11** compartment

bunkum 3 rot **4** bosh, bull, guff, jazz **5** bilge, hokum, hooey **6** humbug, piffle **7** baloney, hogwash, rubbish, twaddle **8** claptrap, flimflam, malarkey, nonsense, tommyrot **9** poppycock **10** balderdash

bunting 5 flags **9** streamers

Bunyanesque 4 huge **5** giant, jumbo **7** mammoth, massive, titanic **8** behemoth, colossal, gigantic, towering **9** Herculean **10** gargantuan, prodigious

Bunyan's ox 4 Babe

buoy 4 lift, prop **5** boost, cheer, float, raise **6** assist, beacon, bear up, buck up, signal, solace, uphold, uplift **7** bolster, comfort, gladden, hearten, support, sustain **9** encourage

buoyancy 6 bounce, levity **7** jollity **8** airiness **10** ebullience, exuberance, exuberancy, liveliness, resilience **12** floatability **13** effervescence

buoyant 3 gay **4** airy **5** sunny **6** afloat, bouncy **7** elastic **8** cheerful, floating, volatile **9** expansive, floatable, resilient

10 unsinkable, weightless **12** effervescent, lighthearted

burble 3 gas, yak **4** blab, chat, gush, talk, wash **5** clack, plash, run on, slosh, swash **6** babble, bubble, gabble, gurgle, murmur, rattle, splash, yammer **7** chatter, prattle, sparkle

burden 3 tax, try **4** care, clog, core, duty, gist, haul, lade, load, onus, pile, pith, task, text **5** brunt, cargo, press, theme, weigh **6** amount, charge, chorus, cumber, hamper, lading, lumber, saddle, strain, stress, thrust, upshot, weight **7** afflict, anxiety, freight, oppress, payload, refrain, purport **8** encumber, handicap, obligate, overload **9** millstone, substance, weigh down **10** deadweight **11** encumbrance

burdensome 5 tough **6** taxing, trying **7** arduous, exigent, irksome, onerous, weighty **8** crushing, exacting, grievous **9** demanding, difficult, fatiguing, ponderous **10** exhausting, oppressive **11** troublesome **12** backbreaking, unmanageable

bureau 4 unit **5** chest **6** agency **7** dresser, section **8** ministry **10** department, chiffonier **11** writing desk

bureaucrat 8 mandarin, minister, official **11** functionary **12** civil servant, officeholder

burg 4 city, town **7** borough **8** fortress **10** metropolis, walled town **12** municipality

burgee 4 flag **6** banner, ensign, pennon **7** pendant, pennant **8** standard, streamer

burgeon 4 blow, boom, open **5** bloom, build, mount, run up **6** emerge, expand, flower, sprout, thrive, unfold **7** augment, blossom, develop, enlarge, fill out, prosper, run riot **8** flourish, heighten, increase, multiply, mushroom, snowball **9** germinate **10** burst forth, effloresce

burghal 5 civic, urban **8** citified **9** municipal **12** metropolitan

burgher 7 citizen, denizen **8** townsman

burglar 4 yegg **5** thief *loot:* **4** swag

burglarize see BURGLE

burglary 5 heist, theft **7** larceny

burgle 3 rob **4** lift, loot **5** heist, steal, strip **6** rip off, thieve **7** despoil, plunder, ransack **9** break into, knock over **10** housebreak

burgomaster 5 mayor **10** magistrate

Burgundy wine *grape:* **5** Gamay **9** Pinot Noir **10** Chardonnay *red:* **8** Mercurey **10** Beaujolais *white:* **5** Rully **6** Chagny **7** Chablis **10** Montrachet **13** Pouilly-Fuissé

burial 4 tomb **5** grave **7** funeral **9** inter-ment, obsequies, sepulcher, sepulchre, sepulture **10** entombment, inhumation *box:* **6** casket, coffin *ceremony:* **7** funeral, obsequy **9** obsequies *mound:* **6** barrow **7** tumulus *tomb:* **9** mausoleum, sepulcher, sepulchre

burial ground 8 boot hill, cemetery **8** boneyard, God's acre **9** graveyard **10** churchyard, necropolis **12** memorial park, potter's field *early Christian:* **8** catacomb

Burkina Faso *capital:* **11** Ouagadougou *ethnic group:* **3** Gur **5** Mossi **7** Voltaic *former name:* **10** Upper Volta *language:* **4** Moré **5** Dyula **6** French *monetary unit:* **5** franc *neighbor:* **4** Mali, Togo **5** Benin, Ghana, Niger **10** Ivory Coast *river:* **5** Volta (Black, Red) **6** Nazion **7** Mouhoun, Nakanbe **8** Red Volta **10** Black Volta

burlap 5 gunny **6** fabric **7** bagging, sacking *fiber:* **4** hemp, jute

burlesque 3 ape **4** mock, sham **5** farce, spoof **6** parody, satire, send-up **7** lampoon, mockery, mocking, takeoff **8** pastiche, skin show, travesty **10** caricature, distortion, girlie show, lampoonery

burly 4 hale **5** beefy, hefty, husky, tough **6** brawny, robust, strong, stocky **8** athletic, heavyset, muscular, powerful, stalwart, thickset, vigorous **9** strapping

Burma see MYANMAR

burn 4 bake, char, cook, fire, fume, rage, sear **5** anger, blaze, broil, creek, flame, flare, gleam, roast, scald, singe, smart, smoke, sting, toast **6** ignite, kindle, scorch, seethe **7** bristle, combust, consume, cremate, flare up, inflame, radiate, smolder, swelter **8** smoulder **9** carbonize, cauterize **10** incinerate

burnable 8 volatile **9** flammable, ignitable **10** incendiary **11** combustible, inflammable

burned-out 4 beat, shot **5** spent, weary **6** sapped **7** drained, worn-out **8** consumed, fatigued **9** destroyed, exhausted, played-out **10** broken-down **11** debilitated **12** extinguished

burner 3 hob

burning 3 hot **5** afire, aglow, fiery **6** ablaze, aflame, alight, ardent, fervid, heated, hectic, red-hot, torrid, urgent **7** blazing, fervent, fevered, glowing, ignited, kindled, searing **8** broiling, feverish, pressing, sizzling, white-hot **9** scorching **10** imperative, passionate **11** conflagrant, impassioned **12** incandescent *combining form:* **4** igni *malicious:* **5** arson

burnish 3 rub, wax **4** buff **5** glaze, gloss,

scour, sheen, shine **6** luster, patina, polish, smooth **7** furbish, varnish **8** brighten

burnished 5 shiny **6** glossy, satiny, sheeny **7** lambent, radiant, shining **8** gleaming, lustrous, polished **9** brilliant **10** glistening **11** resplendent

burnsides 8 whiskers **9** sideburns **10** sideboards **11** dundrearies, muttonchops **12** side-whiskers

burp 5 belch, eruct, expel

burro 3 ass **6** donkey **7** jackass

Burroughs hero 6 Tarzan

burrow 3 den, dig **4** hole, lair, mine, nook, snug **5** delve, gouge, lodge **6** cavity, cuddle, nestle, nuzzle, tunnel **7** snuggle **10** excavation

burst 3 pop, run **4** bang, boom, clap, gush, gust, rive, rush, slam, wham **5** blast, crack, crash, erupt, flare, go off, lunge, sally, salvo, smash, spasm, split, storm, surge **6** access, blow up, emerge, launch, plunge, shiver, spring, shower, volley **7** assault, barrage, explode, flareup, fly open, rupture, shatter, torrent **8** detonate, drumfire, eruption, fragment, outbreak, splinter, splitter **9** broadside, cannonade, explosion, fusillade, onslaught **11** bombardment

Burundi *capital:* **9** Bujumbura *ethnic group:* **4** Hutu **5** Tutsi *former name:* **6** Urundi *lake:* **10** Tanganyika *language:* **5** Rundi **6** French **7** Kirundi *monetary unit:* **5** franc *neighbor:* **5** Congo **6** Rwanda **8** Tanzania

bury 4 hide, sink, stow **5** cache, cover, embed, inter, plant, stash **6** absorb, entomb, inhume, mantle, shroud **7** blanket, conceal, cover up, implant, lay away, overlay, put away, secrete **8** ensconce, submerge

bus 5 clear **7** missile, trolley, vehicle **9** hand truck **10** spacecraft

bush 4 rose **5** lilac, shrub, wahoo **6** azalea, cassis, privet **7** currant, thicket, weigela **8** backland, barberry, hazelnut **9** backwater, backwoods, forsythia, manzanita **10** gooseberry, hinterland, wilderness **11** pussy willow **12** rhododendron

bushel 3 ton **4** heap, load, pile **6** basket, hamper **7** pannier

bush-league 5 minor **6** junior, two-bit **8** inferior, mediocre, small-fry **9** smalltime **10** inadequate, second-rate **11** lightweight **13** insignificant

bushranger 6 outlaw **8** woodsman **12** frontiersman

bushwhack 4 trap **6** ambush, assail, attack, entrap, waylay **7** assault **8** surprise **9** blindside

bushwhacker 6 bandit, outlaw, raider, sniper 8 guerilla, woodsman 9 guerrilla 10 highwayman

bushy 5 bosky, fuzzy, hairy, leafy 6 fluffy, woolly 7 hirsute, unkempt 9 bristling, luxuriant, overgrown 10 disordered 11 flourishing

business 3 job 4 firm, line, work 5 trade 6 affair, custom, matter, métier, office, outfit, racket 7 calling, company, concern, pursuit, traffic 8 commerce, function, industry 9 patronage 10 employment, enterprise, livelihood, occupation 11 corporation 13 establishment *expense:* 8 overhead *syndicate:* 6 cartel

businesslike 6 formal 7 orderly, serious 8 diligent, thorough 9 competent, efficient, practical, pragmatic 10 impersonal, methodical, no-nonsense, purposeful, systematic 11 disciplined, hardworking 12 professional

businessman 6 broker, dealer, trader, tycoon 7 magnate 8 investor, merchant 9 bourgeois, financier, tradesman, executive 10 capitalist, trafficker 12 entrepreneur, merchandiser 13 industrialist

busker 8 minstrel, musician 11 entertainer

buss 4 kiss, peck 5 smack 6 smooch 8 osculate

bust 3 bag, cop, dud, hit, jag, nab, net 4 bomb, bump, fail, flop, fold, raid, ruin, slug, sock, tear, tour 5 binge, bosom, break, broke, burst, catch, chest, crash, lemon, loser, punch, smash, spell, spree, stint, torso, trash 6 arrest, bender, breast, collar, demote, pick up 7 break up, carouse, degrade, demerit, destroy, exhaust, failure, rupture, wear out 8 bankrupt, demolish, fracture 9 apprehend, break down, destitute, downgrade, penniless 10 impoverish, police raid

bustle 3 ado, fly, run 4 flit, fuss, rush, stir, tear, teem, to-do 5 hurry, whirl, whisk 6 action, be busy, bestir, clamor, flurry, furore, hassle, hasten, hubbub, hustle, motion, pother, scurry, tumult, uproar 7 ferment, turmoil 8 activity, to-and-fro 9 commotion, whirlpool, whirlwind 10 hurly-burly, excitement, liveliness

bustling 4 busy, rife 5 brisk, fussy, peppy 6 active, hectic, lively 7 dynamic, festive, hopping, humming, jumping 8 animated, swarming, vigorous 9 energetic 10 tumultuous 11 hardworking, industrious

busty 5 ample, buxom, curvy 6 bosomy, chesty, zaftig 7 shapely, stacked 10 curvaceous, voluptuous 11 full-bosomed, well-rounded

busy 5 brisk, fussy 6 active, at work, lively, on duty, tied up 7 crowded, engaged, hopping, humming, swamped, teeming, working 8 bustling, diligent, employed, hustling, meddling, occupied, overdone, sedulous 9 assiduous, congested, elaborate, energetic, intrusive, obtrusive, officious 10 meddlesome, overworked 11 impertinent, industrious, interfering, unavailable

busybody 5 prier, pryer, snoop, yenta 6 butt-in, gossip, old hen 7 meddler 8 informer, kibitzer, quidnunc 9 pragmatic 10 chatterbox, newsmonger, pragmatist, talebearer, tattletale 11 nosey parker, rumormonger 12 gossipmonger, rubbernecker, troublemaker

but 3 bar, yet 4 just, only, save 5 alone 6 except, merely, saving, unless 7 barring, besides, however 8 entirely 9 aside from, excepting, excluding, outside of 13 on the contrary

butcher 4 ruin, slay 5 botch, carve, clean, spoil, wreck 6 bollix, killer, mess up, slayer 7 cut meat, destroy, meat man 8 mutilate 9 slaughter 11 slaughterer

butcher-bird 6 shrike

butcherly 5 cruel 6 bloody, clumsy, savage 7 awkward 8 sadistic 9 ferocious, merciless 10 unskillful

butchery 7 carnage 8 abattoir, genocide, massacre 9 bloodbath, bloodshed, holocaust, slaughter 10 mass murder 12 annihilation 13 extermination

buteo 4 hawk 7 buzzard

butler 5 valet 7 steward 10 manservant

Butler, Samuel *novel:* 7 Erewhon 13 Way of All Flesh (The) *poem:* 8 Hudibras

butt 3 end, keg, tip, ram, tun, vat 4 base, cask, drum, dupe, join, push, rump, stub, tail 5 chump, fanny, patsy, stump, touch, verge 6 adjoin, barrel, border, bottom, firkin, pigeon, sucker, target, thrust, victim 7 collide, fall guy, rear end, run itno 8 derriere, hogshead, neighbor 9 cigarette, fundament, lie beside, pilgarlic, posterior, remainder 11 communicate, sitting duck 12 hindquarters 13 laughingstock

butter *artificial:* 4 oleo 9 margarine 13 oleomargarine *Indian:* 4 ghee *piece:* 3 pat *semifluid:* 4 ghee *tree:* 4 shea

butterball 5 blimp, whale 8 dumpling, elephant 10 bufflehead

butterfish 6 gunnel

butterfly 4 blue 5 diana, satyr, zebra

6 copper, morpho 7 admiral, buckeye, monarch, satyrid, skipper, sulphur, vanessa, viceroy 8 crescent, grayling, milkweed, victoria 9 aphrodite, metalmark, nymphalid, wood nymph 10 fritillary, hairstreak 11 swallowtail *bush:* 8 buddleia *fish:* 6 blenny, chiton 7 gurnard *larva:* 11 caterpillar *lily:* 8 mariposa *order:* 11 Lepidoptera *plant:* 8 oncidium *pupa:* 9 chrysalis *scientist:* 13 lepidopterist

butter up 4 coax 5 charm 6 cajole, kowtow, praise, stroke 7 adulate, beguile, blarney, flatter, massage, wheedle 8 blandish, bootlick, soft-soap 9 brownnose, sweet-talk 10 overpraise

butt in 6 kibitz, meddle 7 intrude, obtrude 8 busybody, overstep 9 interfere, interlope, interpose, interrupt

buttinsky 7 meddler 8 busybody, kibitzer, quidnunc 9 loudmouth 10 trespasser 12 troublemaker

buttocks 4 rear, rump, seat, tail 5 fanny, nates 6 behind, bottom, breech, heinie 7 hind end, hunkers, keister, rear end, tail end 8 backside, derriere, haunches 9 fundament, posterior

buttonball 8 sycamore 9 plane tree

button-down 6 square, stuffy 8 decorous, orthodox, straight 10 restrained 11 straitlaced, traditional 12 conservative, conventional

buttonwood 8 sycamore 9 plane tree

buttress 4 pier, prop, stay 5 brace, carry, shore, strut, truss 6 back up, bear up, hold up, column, uphold 7 bolster, bulwark, fortify, shore up, support, sustain 9 reinforce, stanchion 10 strengthen 12 underpinning 13 fortification, reinforcement

buxom 5 ample, busty, curvy 6 bosomy, chesty, zaftig 7 shapely, stacked 10 curvaceous, voluptuous 11 full-bosomed, full-figured, well-rounded

buy 5 bribe 6 obtain, ransom, redeem 7 acquire, bargain, believe 8 purchase

buy back 6 ransom, recoup, redeem, regain 8 retrieve 10 repurchase

buyer 6 client, patron, vendee 7 shopper 8 consumer, customer 9 purchaser

buy off 3 fix, sop 5 bribe 6 settle 7 corrupt, silence 9 influence 10 manipulate, tamper with

buzz 3 fad, hum 4 call, fizz, high, hiss, news, purr, ring, talk, whir, whiz 5 craze, drone, hurry, rumor, strum, thrum, whirr, whish 6 bumble, fizzle, gossip, murmur, natter, report, rumble, sizzle, summon, wheeze, whoosh 7 chatter, scandal, whisper 8 sibilate

9 bombinate 11 reverberate, scuttlebutt

buzzard 5 buteo 7 vulture 13 turkey vulture

by 3 per, via 4 away, near, nigh, past 5 along, aside 6 at hand, beside, next to 7 through 9 alongside 10 incidental 11 according to 12 not later than

by and by 4 anon, soon 5 after, later 7 shortly 8 directly, latterly 9 afterward, presently 10 before long 12 subsequently

by and large 7 all told, broadly, en masse, overall, usually 8 all in all, normally 9 generally, typically 10 altogether, on the whole, ordinarily 11 principally

by dint of see BY MEANS OF

bye-bye 4 ciao, ta-ta 5 adieu, adios 6 so long 7 cheerio 8 au revoir, farewell, sayonara, toodle-oo

bygone 3 old 4 dead, late, lost, once, past 5 dated, of old, olden 6 former, fossil, of yore, remote, whilom 7 antique, archaic, belated, defunct, extinct, old-time, onetime, quondam, vintage 8 departed, sometime, obsolete, outdated, outmoded, vanished 9 erstwhile, out-of-date 10 antiquated, oldfangled 12 antediluvian, old-fashioned

by means of 3 per, via 4 with 5 using 7 through 9 employing, utilizing

byname 6 handle 7 epithet, moniker 8 cognomen 9 sobriquet 10 diminutive, hypocorism 11 appellation

bypass 4 omit 5 avoid, burke, shunt, skirt 6 detour, ignore 7 highway 8 outflank, ring road, sidestep 10 circumvent, pass around 11 deviate from

by-product 5 yield 6 effect, result 7 outcome, residue, spin-off 8 offshoot 9 outgrowth 10 derivative, descendant 11 aftereffect, consequence 12 repercussion

Byron work 4 Cain, Lara 5 Beppo 6 Giaour (The), Werner 7 Corsair (The), Don Juan, Manfred 12 Childe Harold

bystander 6 gawker, viewer 7 watcher, witness 8 beholder, observer, onlooker, passerby 9 spectator 10 eyewitness 12 rubbernecker

by stealth 5 slyly 7 sub rosa 8 covertly, in secret, secretly 9 furtively, privately 10 under cover 11 insidiously 13 clandestinely

by virtue of see BY MEANS OF

by way of see BY MEANS OF

byword 3 saw 5 adage, axiom, maxim, motto, nomen 6 dictum, phrase, saying, slogan, truism 7 epigram, epithet, precept, proverb, refrain **8** aphorism, cognomen, nickname **9** platitude, prescript, sobriquet **10** hypocorism, shibboleth **11** catchphrase, commonplace, rallying cry

Byzantine 6 daedal, knotty **7** complex, devious **8** involved **9** elaborate, intri- cate **10** convoluted **11** complicated **12** labyrinthine **13** sophisticated, surreptitious *emperor:* **3** Leo **4** Zeno **5** Basil **6** Bardas, Justin, Phocas **7** Michael, Romanus **9** Heraclius, Justinian **10** Nicephorus, Theodosius *empress:* **3** Zoe **5** Irene **8** Theodora

C

cab 4 hack, taxi **6** jitney **7** hackney **8** carriage

cabal 3 mob **4** clan, club, plot, ring **5** coven, group, junta, mafia **6** cartel, circle, clique **7** coterie, faction, ingroup **8** intrigue **9** camarilla **10** conspiracy **11** machination

cabaletta 4 aria, song

cabalistic 6 arcane, mystic, occult **8** esoteric **9** recondite **10** mysterious **11** inscrutable **12** impenetrable

caballero 6 knight **7** paladin **8** cavalier, horseman **9** chevalier

cabana 3 hut **5** shack **7** shelter

cabaret 4 café **6** bistro, nitery **7** hot spot **9** nightclub, nightspot **10** supper club **12** watering hole

cabbage 3 nab, nip **4** cash, hook, lift, palm **5** bread, dough, filch, kraut, money, moola, pinch, steal, swipe **6** dinero, do-re-mi, moolah, pilfer **7** purloin, scratch **10** greenbacks, sauerkraut *disease of:* **6** mildew, mosaic **7** root rot, yellows **8** blackleg, club root *family:* **4** cole, kale, rape **5** colza, savoy **6** turnip **7** collard, mustard **8** broccoli, colewort, kohlrabi, rutabaga **11** cauliflower

cabbagehead see DUNCE

cabdriver 4 hack **5** cabby **6** cabbie

cabin 3 hut **4** camp, shed **5** berth, hovel, lodge, shack **6** cabana, chalet, lean-to, shanty **7** bivouac, cottage **9** stateroom

cabin cruiser 5 yacht **9** motorboat, powerboat

cabinet 4 case **6** bureau **7** armoire, chamber, commode, console, council, dresser **8** advisers, advisors, cupboard, ministry **9** presidium **10** chiffonier, collection, counselors

cabinetmaker *American:* **5** Eames (Charles), Phyfe (Duncan) **6** Belter (John Henry) **7** Goddard (John, Stephen, Thomas) **8** McIntire (Samuel), Townsend (Christopher, Edmund, James, Job, John) *English:* **4** Adam (James, Robert), Hope (Thomas), Kent (William) **8** Sheraton (Thomas) **11** Chippendale (Thomas), Hepplewhite (George) *French:* **6** Boulle (André-Charles) **8** Caffieri (Jacques, Jean-Jacques, Philippe), Cressent (Charles) *German:* **10** Weisweiler (Adam)

cable 4 rope, wire **5** braid, chain **6** stitch **8** transmit **9** telegraph

cabriolet 5 coupe **8** carriage

cache 4 bury, hide **5** cover, plant, stash, store **6** memory, wealth **7** conceal, lay away, nest egg, put away, reserve, secrete **8** ensconce, treasure **9** stockpile **10** accumulate **11** hiding place

cachet 4 rank, seal **5** motto, state **6** slogan, status **7** dignity, stature **8** approval, position, prestige, standing **11** consequence

cachinnate 4 crow, howl, roar **5** laugh, whoop **6** guffaw, shriek

cackle 3 gab, jaw **4** blab, chat, crow **5** clack, cluck **6** babble, burble, gabble, gaggle, gobble **7** blabber, blatter, chatter, prattle

cacoëthes 4 zeal **5** mania **6** desire **9** obsession

cacomistle 5 civet **7** raccoon **8** civet cat, ringtail

cacophonic 5 harsh **8** tuneless **9** dissonant, unmusical **10** discordant **11** unmelodious **12** unharmonious

cacophony 9 harshness **10** dissonance

cactus 5 nopal **6** cereus, cholla, mescal,

peyote 7 opuntia, saguaro
11 prickly pear
cad 3 cur, dog 4 boor, heel, lout, rake
5 creep, knave, louse, rogue 6 rascal,
rotter 7 bounder 9 conductor,
scoundrel
cadaver 4 body, mort 5 stiff 6 corpse
7 carcass, remains 8 deceased
cadaverous 5 ashen, gaunt, livid 6 pallid, wasted 7 deathly, ghastly, ghostly,
shadowy 8 skeletal, spectral 9 deathlike, emaciated, ghostlike 10 corpselike
caddy 3 bin, box 4 aide 5 toter 6 casket
8 canister, tea chest
cadence 4 beat, flow, lilt 5 meter, pulse
6 rhythm 9 pulsation 10 conclusion,
inflection, intonation
cadet 4 pimp 5 plebe 7 student, trainee
cadge 3 beg, bum 5 mooch 6 hustle,
sponge 8 freeload, scrounge 9 panhandle
Cadmus *daughter:* 3 Ino 5 Agave
6 Semele 7 Autonoë *father:* 6 Agenor
sister: 6 Europa *victim:* 6 dragon *wife:*
8 Harmonia
cadre 4 cell, core 5 frame, staff 6 cohort
7 in-group 9 framework
caducity 3 age 6 dotage, old age 8 senility 10 senescence 11 senectitude
Caesar *assassin:* 6 Brutus (Marcus
Junius) 7 Cassius (Gaius) *battle:* 4 Zela
9 Pharsalus *conquest:* 4 Gaul 7 Britain
eulogist: 6 Antony (Marc) 7 Anthony
(Mark) 8 Antonius (Marcus) *message:*
12 Veni vidi vici *river:* 7 Rubicon *utterance:* 9 Et tu Brute *wife:* 7 Pompeia
8 Cornelia 9 Calpurnia
Caesarism 7 tyranny 9 authority, autocracy, despotism 10 absolutism 12 dictatorship
caesura 5 break, pause 12 interruption
café 5 diner 6 bistro, nitery 7 barroom,
beanery, cabaret, hot spot 8 cookshop
9 lunchroom, nightclub, nightspot
10 coffee shop, restaurant, supper club
12 luncheonette, watering hole
13 watering place
café ___ 4 noir 6 au lait, filtre 7 society
caftan 4 gown, robe 6 muumuu 12 dressing gown
cage 3 hem, pen 4 cell, coop, jail 5 score
6 corral, immure, lock up, shut in
7 close in, enclose, impound 8 imprison
9 enclosure 11 incarcerate
cagey 3 sly 4 foxy, wary, wily 5 canny,
sharp 6 astute, clever, crafty, shrewd
cahier 6 record, report, review
cahoots 6 hookup, league 8 alliance
9 collusion 10 complicity 11 partnership
caiman 9 crocodile 11 crocodilian
Cain *brother:* 4 Abel, Seth *father:* 4 Adam

land: 3 Nod *mother:* 3 Eve *nephew:*
4 Enos *son:* 5 Enoch *victim:* 4 Abel
Caine Mutiny author 4 Wouk (Herman)
Cain novel 8 Serenade 13 Mildred Pierce
23 Postman Always Rings Twice (The)
cajole 3 con 4 coax, dupe 6 entice,
seduce 7 beguile, blarney, deceive,
wheedle 8 blandish, inveigle, maneuver,
persuade, soft-soap 9 sweet-talk
cake 3 dry, set 4 coat, loaf, rime 5 cover,
crust 6 harden, pastry 7 congeal,
encrust, incrust 8 solidify *almond:*
8 macaroon *flat:* 5 cooky 6 cookie *oatmeal:* 4 farl 5 scone 7 bannock *ring-
shaped:* 5 donut 6 jumble 8 doughnut
rum-soaked: 4 baba *Scottish:* 4 farl
5 scone *shell-shaped:* 9 madeleine *topping:* 5 icing 8 frosting, streusel *without
flour:* 5 torte *without shortening:*
6 sponge
Cakes and Ale author 7 Maugham (W.
Somerset)
cakewalk 4 romp, rout, snap 5 cinch,
dance, strut 6 breeze, prance
8 pushover, walkover
calaboose 3 can 4 brig, coop, jail, tank
5 clink, pokey 6 cooler, lockup, prison
7 slammer 8 hoosegow 9 jailhouse
calamitous 4 dire 5 fatal 6 woeful
7 ruinous 8 grievous 10 disastrous, lamentable 11 cataclysmic, devastating,
unfortunate 12 catastrophic 13 heartbreaking
calamity 4 ruin 5 wreck 7 tragedy 8 disaster, downfall 9 cataclysm 11 catastrophe, tribulation
Calamity ___ 4 Jane
calculate 4 rely 5 assay, count, gauge,
judge, solve, tally, tot up, value
6 assess, cipher, figure, intend, reckon
7 compute, measure, work out
8 appraise, estimate, evaluate, forecast
9 ascertain, determine, figure out
calculated 6 likely 7 planned 8 intended
9 worked out 10 deliberate 12 aforethought, premeditated
calculating 3 sly 4 wary, wily 5 canny,
chary, sharp 6 artful, crafty, shrewd
7 careful, cunning, devious, politic
8 cautious, discreet, guileful, scheming
9 designing 11 circumspect
calculating device 6 abacus *Peruvian:*
5 quipu
calculation 8 analysis, counting, estimate, figuring, prudence 9 ciphering,
reckoning 10 arithmetic, estimation,
prediction 11 computation
Caledonia 8 Scotland
calendar 3 log 4 card, sked 6 agenda,
docket 7 almanac, program 8 schedule
9 timetable *abbreviation:* 3 Apr, Aug,

Dec, Feb, Fri, Jan, Mar, Mon, Nov, Oct, Sat, Sep, Sun, Tue, Wed 4 Sept 5 Thurs *ecclesiastical:* 4 ordo

calenture 4 fire, zeal 5 ardor, fever 6 fervor 7 passion 10 enthusiasm

calf *hide:* 3 kip *leather:* 3 elk *meat:* 4 veal *stray:* 5 dogie *unbranded:* 8 maverick

Caliban 5 slave *master:* 8 Prospero *witch-mother:* 7 Sycorax

caliber 4 bore 5 class, gauge, grade, merit, value, worth 6 virtue 7 ability, quality, stature 8 diameter

calibrate 3 set 6 adjust, polish 7 measure 8 fine-tune, regulate 9 ascertain 11 standardize

California *capital:* 10 Sacramento *city:* 4 Napa 6 Fresno, Sonoma 7 Anaheim, Oakland, San Jose 8 San Diego, Santa Ana 9 Long Beach, Santa Cruz 10 Los Angeles 12 San Francisco *college, university:* 3 USC 4 UCLA 5 Mills 6 Pomona 8 Berkeley, Stanford, Whittier 9 Loma Linda 10 Golden Gate, Occidental, Pepperdine, Santa Clara *desert:* 6 Mohave *fault zone:* 10 San Andreas *lake:* 5 Owens, Tahoe 9 Salton Sea *lowest spot:* 11 Death Valley *motto:* 6 Eureka *mountain, range:* 5 Coast 6 Lassen (Peak), Shasta 7 Whitney 12 Sierra Nevada *nickname:* 6 Golden (State) *park:* 7 Sequoia 8 Yosemite 11 Kings Canyon 14 Channel Islands *river:* 10 Sacramento, San Joaquin *state bird:* 5 quail *state flower:* 11 golden poppy *state tree:* 7 redwood, sequoia *wine region:* 4 Napa 6 Sonoma

caliginous 3 dim 4 dark, dusk 5 dusky, foggy, misty, murky 6 gloomy 7 obscure, sunless 8 nebulous 9 lightless, tenebrous

Caligula's mother 9 Agrippina

caliph's name 3 Ali 7 Abu Bakr

Calista's seducer 8 Lothario

calisthenics 7 workout 9 exercises

call 3 bid, cry 4 buzz, hail, lure, name, page, ring, yell 5 phone, pop in, shout, visit 6 bellow, come by, drop by, drop in, holler, salute, stop by, stop in, summon 7 convene, convoke, summons 8 estimate 9 designate, telephone

calla 4 lily

call down 5 chide, scold 6 rebuke 7 censure, reprove 8 admonish, reproach 9 reprimand

called 5 named 6 chosen, picked, yclept 7 ycleped 8 selected

caller 5 guest 6 suitor 7 visitor

call for 3 ask, beg 4 seek 5 crave, plead 6 demand, entail, pick up 7 beseech, entreat, implore, involve, require 11 necessitate

call forth 5 awake, educe, evoke, rouse 6 arouse, elicit 7 conjure, provoke 9 conjure up

calligrapher 6 penman, scribe 7 copyist 9 engrosser, scrivener

calligraphy 4 hand 6 script 7 writing 8 longhand 10 penmanship 11 handwriting

call in 5 phone 6 summon 7 convene, reclaim 8 retrieve, withdraw 9 repossess, telephone

calling 3 job 4 duty, work 5 craft, trade 6 career, métier 7 mission, pursuit, yelling 8 business, lifework, shouting, vocation 10 employment, obligation, occupation, profession

call in sick 7 book off

Calliope 4 Muse *father:* 4 Zeus 7 Jupiter *mother:* 9 Mnemosyne *son:* 7 Orpheus

Callisto *lover:* 4 Zeus 7 Jupiter *son:* 5 Arcas

Call It Sleep author 4 Roth (Henry)

call off 4 halt 5 abort, scrub 6 cancel, divert 8 distract

Call of the Wild *author:* 6 London (Jack) *dog:* 4 Buck

call on 5 visit 6 oblige 7 require

callosity 8 hardness 9 thickness

callous 5 stony 8 hardened, obdurate, uncaring 9 heartless, indurated, unfeeling 10 hard-bitten, hard-boiled 11 cold-hearted, hardhearted, insensitive, unemotional 12 case-hardened, stony-hearted 13 unsympathetic

callow 3 raw 5 fresh, green, naive, young 7 puerile 8 immature, juvenile, youthful 9 unfledged 10 unseasoned 13 inexperienced, unexperienced

call's partner 4 beck

call up 5 draft, evoke 6 summon 8 mobilize, retrieve 9 conscript

calm 4 cool, ease, hush, lull 5 allay, peace, quiet, relax, salve, still 6 hushed, pacify, placid, poised, repose, sedate, serene, settle, smooth, soothe, stable, steady, stilly 7 appease, assuage, compose, halcyon, mollify, pacific, placate, restful, resting 8 composed, inactive, peaceful, reposing, serenity, tranquil 9 collected, composure, easygoing, impassive, possessed, quiescent, unruffled 10 phlegmatic, untroubled 11 tranquility, tranquilize, unflappable 12 even-tempered, self-composed, tranquillity 13 imperturbable, self-possessed

calmative 8 quietive, relaxing, sedative 9 soporific 12 tranquilizer

calmness 4 lull 5 quiet 6 phlegm 8 coolness, serenity 9 composure, placidity, sangfroid **10** equanimity **11** tranquility **12** tranquillity

calumet 4 pipe **9** peace pipe

calumniate 5 libel, smear **6** defame, malign, vilify **7** asperse, slander, tarnish, traduce **8** besmirch **9** denigrate **10** scandalize

calumnious 8 libelous **9** maligning, traducing, vilifying **10** backbiting, defamatory, detracting, scandalous, slanderous

calumny 7 scandal, slander **9** aspersion **10** backbiting, defamation, detraction **11** denigration **12** backstabbing, belittlement, depreciation **13** disparagement

calvados 6 brandy **9** applejack

calvary 5 agony, cross, trial **6** misery, ordeal **7** anguish **8** distress **9** suffering **10** affliction, visitation **11** tribulation

Calypso *beloved:* **7** Ulysses **8** Odysseus *island:* **6** Ogygia

calyx part 3 cup **5** sepal

camaraderie 5 cheer **7** jollity **10** affability, fellowship **12** conviviality

camarilla 3 mob **4** camp, clan, ring **5** cabal, mafia **6** circle, clique **7** coterie, ingroup

Cambodia 9 Kampuchea *capital:* **9** Phnom Penh *city:* **10** Battambang **11** Kompong Cham *ethnic group:* **8** Mon-Khmer *lake:* **8** Tonle Sap *language:* **5** Khmer *leader:* **6** Pol Pot *monetary unit:* **4** riel *neighbor:* **4** Laos **7** Vietnam **8** Thailand *river:* **6** Mekong *ruin:* **9** Angkor Wat

camel *one-humped:* **9** dromedary *two-humped:* **8** Bactrian

camel-hair fabric 3 aba

camelopard 7 giraffe

Camelot 6 palace *lord:* **6** Arthur

Camembert 6 cheese

cameo 6 brooch, relief, walk-on **8** portrait

cameraman 6 photog **7** lensman **12** photographer

Cameroon *capital:* **7** Yaoundé *ethnic group:* **4** Fang **5** Duala, Pygmy **6** Fulani **8** Bamileke *largest city:* **6** Douala *monetary unit:* **5** franc *neighbor:* **4** Chad **5** Congo, Gabon **7** Nigeria *river:* **5** Nyong **6** Sanaga

Camille's creator 5 Dumas (Alexandre)

Camino ___ 4 Real

camouflage 4 mask **5** cloak **7** conceal, deceive **8** disguise **9** dissemble **11** dissimulate

camp 3 hut **4** bloc, shed **5** cabin, lodge, shack **6** clique, shanty **7** bivouac, coterie, cottage, faction **10** settlement

campaign 4 push **5** blitz, drive, fight, lobby, stump **6** attack **7** agitate, canvass, crusade **8** movement, politick **9** barnstorm, offensive **10** engagement, expedition **11** electioneer, whistle-stop

campaigner 8 activist **9** candidate

campanile 6 belfry **8** carillon **9** bell tower

campesino 6 farmer **7** peasant

campestral 5 rural **6** rustic, sylvan **7** bucolic, country, idyllic **8** agrarian, pastoral **10** provincial **11** countrified

campus see COLLEGE

Camus work 4 Fall (The) **5** Rebel (The) **6** Plague (The) **8** Caligula, Stranger (The)

can 3 may, tin **4** boot, fire, sack **5** let go, put up **7** dismiss **9** container, discharge **10** receptacle

Canaan 4 Zion **12** Promised Land *father:* **3** Ham *grandfather:* **4** Noah

Canaanite god 3 Mot **4** Baal **6** Molech, Moloch

Canada *bay:* **5** Fundy, James **6** Baffin, Hudson, Ungava **8** Georgian **9** Frobisher *capital:* **6** Ottawa *city:* **6** London, Oshawa, Quebec, Regina, Surrey **7** Burnaby, Calgary, Halifax, Moncton, Toronto, Windsor **8** Edmonton, Hamilton, Montreal, Moose Jaw, Victoria, Winnipeg **9** Longueuil, North York, Saskatoon, Vancouver **10** Lethbridge, Thunder Bay **11** Fredericton, Scarborough **13** Charlottetown, Mississisauga *district:* **6** riding *explorer:* **6** Hudson (Henry) **7** Cartier (Jacques) **9** Champlain (Samuel de) *Indian people:* **4** Cree, Inuk **5** Blood, Haida, Huron, Inuit, Métis, Niska, Slave **6** Abnaki, Beaver, Eskimo, Micmac, Mohawk, Nootka, Ojibwa, Ojibwe, Ottawa, Piegan, Seneca, Stoney **7** Kutenai, Naskapi, Ojibwa, Siksika, Wyandot **8** Algonkin, Chippewa, Iroquois, Kootenai, Kootenay, Kwakiutl, Salishan, Tsattine **9** Algonkian, Algonquin, Blackfeet, Blackfoot, Chipewyan, Tsimshian **10** Algonquian, Athapascan, Gros Ventre, Montagnais **11** Assiniboine *island, island group:* **5** Banks, Devon **6** Baffin **7** Belcher **8** Melville, Victoria **9** Anticosti, Ellesmere, Vancouver **10** Cape Breton **11** Southampton **12** Newfoundland, Prince Edward *lake:* **6** Louise **7** Nipigon **8** Reindeer, Winnipeg **9** Athabasca, Champlain, Great Bear **10** Great Slave *language:* **6** French **7** English *monetary unit:* **6** dollar *mountain, range:* **5** Coast, Logan, Rocky **10** Laurentian *national park:* **5** Banff, Fundy **6** Jasper **7** Glacier, Nahanni **8** Kootenay **9** Gros Morne **10** Grasslands, Point Pelee **11** Georgian Bay, Wood Buffalo *peninsula:* **5** Bruce,

Gaspé 6 Ungava 8 Labrador *prime minister:* 4 King (W. L. Mackenzie) 5 Clark (Joe) 6 Abbott (John), Borden (Robert Laird), Bowell (Mackenzie), Martin (Paul), Tupper (Charles), Turner (John) 7 Bennett (Richard Bedford), Laurier (Wilfrid), Meighen (Arthur), Pearson (Lester), Trudeau (Pierre Elliott) 8 Campbell (Kim), Chrétien (Jean), Mulroney (Brian), Thompson (John) 9 MacDonald (John), Mackenzie (Alexander), St. Laurent (Louis) 11 Diefenbaker (John) *province:* 6 Quebec 7 Alberta, Nunavut, Ontario 8 Manitoba 10 Nova Scotia 12 New Brunswick, Newfoundland (and Labrador), Saskatchewan 15 British Columbia 18 Prince Edward Island *provincial park:* 3 Gas 7 Rondeau 9 Garibaldi *river:* 3 Red 5 Liard, Slave, Yukon 6 Albany, Fraser, Nelson, Ottawa, Severn 8 Columbia, Saguenay 9 Athabasca, Churchill, Mackenzie 10 St. Lawrence *sea:* 8 Beaufort, Labrador *symbol:* 9 maple leaf *territory:* 5 Yukon 9 Northwest

Canadian insurgent 4 Riel (Louis)

canaille 3 mob 6 masses, rabble 8 riffraff, unwashed 9 hoi polloi 11 proletarian, proletariat

canal 4 duct 6 course 7 channel, conduit 8 aqueduct 11 watercourse *Africa:* 4 Suez 8 Ismailia *Belgium:* 6 Albert *Canada:* 7 Welland *Central America:* 6 Panama *China:* 7 Da Yunhe *Florida:* 10 Saint Lucie *Germany:* 4 Kiel *Greece:* 7 Corinth *Michigan:* 3 Soo *New York:* 4 Erie 6 Oswego 9 Champlain *Ontario:* 6 Rideau *Venice:* 5 Grand

canapé 6 morsel 9 appetizer 11 hors d'oeuvre *spread:* 4 paté

canard 3 fib, lie 4 tale, yarn 5 fraud, rumor, spoof 6 deceit 7 falsity, untruth 8 chestnut 9 falsehood

canary 3 rat 4 fink, wine 5 finch 6 snitch 7 rat fink, stoolie 8 informer, squealer 11 stool pigeon

Canary Islands 5 Ferro, Lobos, Palma 6 Gomera, Hierro 7 Inferno 8 Graciosa, Tenerife 9 Alegranza, Lanzarote

cancel 3 end 4 drop, undo, x out 5 abort, annul, erase, scrub 6 delete, efface, negate, offset, repeal, revoke 7 blot out, call off, destroy, expunge, nullify, rescind, wipe out 8 black out, deletion 9 terminate 10 invalidate, neutralize, obliterate

cancer 5 tumor 9 carcinoma 10 malignancy *treatment:* 5 chemo, X-rays 9 radiation 12 chemotherapy

cancer-causing 12 carcinogenic *substance:* 10 carcinogen

candescent 7 glowing 8 dazzling 9 refulgent

Candia 5 Crete

candid 4 fair, just, open 5 blunt, frank, plain 6 honest 7 sincere 8 unbiased 9 equitable, guileless, impartial, objective 10 aboveboard, forthright, scrupulous, unreserved 11 openhearted, unconcealed, undisguised 12 unprejudiced 13 dispassionate

candidate 6 seeker 7 hopeful, nominee, stumper 8 aspirant 9 applicant, contender 10 campaigner, contestant

Candide *author:* 8 Voltaire *lover:* 9 Cunegonde *tutor:* 8 Pangloss *valet:* 7 Cacambo

candle 5 taper 6 bougie *holder:* 6 sconce 7 menorah, pricket 9 girandole 10 candelabra 11 candelabrum *material:* 3 wax 4 wick 6 tallow 7 beeswax, stearin 8 paraffin *religious:* 6 votive 7 paschal

candlefish 8 eulachon *relative:* 5 smelt

candlelit service 5 vigil

candlepins 7 bowling

candor 7 honesty 8 fairness, openness 9 frankness, sincerity, whiteness 11 artlessness 13 guilelessness

candy 7 sweeten 9 sugarcoat 10 confection *kind:* 4 rock 5 fudge, lolly, sweet, taffy 6 bonbon, comfit, dragée, jujube, nougat, toffee 7 brittle, caramel, fondant, gumdrop, penuche, praline 8 licorice, lollipop, lollypop, marzipan, sourball 9 chocolate, jelly bean, nonpareil, sweetmeat 10 confection 12 butterscotch *medicated:* 7 lozenge 9 cough drop

cane 3 rod 4 beat, drub, flog, lash, reed, stem, swat 5 flail, grass, spank, staff, stave, stick, weave, whale 6 batter, buffet, cudgel, larrup, paddle, rattan, thrash, wallop 7 lambast, sorghum 8 lambaste 12 walking stick

Canea's land 5 Crete

canine 3 dog 4 tyke 5 hound, pooch

caning material 5 istle

Canis Major star 6 Sirius

Canis Minor star 7 Procyon

canker 5 rust, sore 5 stain 6 debase, infect 7 corrupt, debauch, deprave, pervert, vitiate 8 necrosis 10 demoralize

cankered 8 infested, infected

canker sore 5 ulcer 6 lesion 10 ulceration

cannabis 3 pot 4 hemp 5 bhang, ganja, grass 7 hashish 9 marijuana

canned 5 drunk, fired 6 potted 11 prerecorded

Cannery Row author 9 Steinbeck (John)

canniness 7 caution, cunning, slyness **8** prudence, wiliness **9** cageyness, foresight **10** artfulness, cleverness, craftiness, discretion, precaution, providence, shrewdness **11** forethought

cannon 6 pom-pom **8** howitzer, ordnance **9** artillery *part:* **5** chase **6** breech **8** cascabel, trunnion

cannonade 4 bomb **5** blitz, burst, salvo, shell **6** shower, volley **7** barrage, bombard **8** drumfire, shelling **9** broadside, fusillade **11** bombardment

cannonball 4 dive **5** speed **7** missile

cannoneer 6 gunner

cannon fodder 6 troops **8** infantry, soldiers

canny 3 sly **4** wary, wise **5** acute, cagey, chary, quick, sharp, smart **6** adroit, clever, frugal, saving, shrewd **7** cunning, knowing, prudent, thrifty **9** ingenious, provident **10** economical **11** quick-witted, sharp-witted **12** nimble-witted

canoe 6 dugout **7** pirogue *ancient:* **7** coracle *Eskimo:* **5** kayak, umiak

canon 3 law **4** list, rule **5** dogma, edict, round, tenet **6** decree **7** precept, statute **8** doctrine, standard **9** clergyman, criterion, ordinance **10** regulation

canonical 5 sound **6** lawful **7** classic **8** accepted, approved, official, orthodox, received **10** authorized, recognized, sanctioned **13** authoritative

canonical hour 4 none, sext **5** lauds, prime, terce **6** matins, tierce **7** vespers **8** compline

canonicals 9 vestments

canoodle 3 hug, pet **5** spoon **6** caress, cuddle, fondle

can opener 9 church key

canopy 5 cover, shade **6** awning **7** marquee, shelter **8** covering, sunshade **9** baldachin **10** baldachino *canvas:* **4** tilt

cant 3 tip **4** heel, lean, list, tilt **5** angle, argot, bevel, idiom, lingo, piety, slang, slant, slope **6** humbug, jargon, patois, patter, speech **7** dialect, diction, incline, lexicon, palaver, recline **8** language, singsong **9** hypocrisy **10** dictionary, pharisaism, sanctimony, vernacular **11** inclination, insincerity **12** pecksniffery

cantaloupe 5 melon **9** muskmelon

cantankerous 4 dour, sour **5** cross, huffy, testy, waspy **6** crabby, cranky, crusty, grumpy, morose, ornery **7** bearish, crabbed, grouchy, peevish, prickly, waspish **8** cankered, liverish, petulant, snappish, stubborn, vinegary **9** crotchety, difficult, dyspeptic, irascible, irrita-

ble, obstinate **10** ill-natured, irritating, vinegarish **12** cross-grained

canter 3 bum **4** gait, hobo, lope **5** tramp **6** beggar **7** drifter, vagrant **8** derelict, vagabond **11** bindle stiff

Canterbury *Archbishop:* **3** Oda **6** Anselm, Becket (Thomas á), Parker (Matthew) **7** Cranmer (Thomas), Dunstan **9** Augustine

Canterbury Tales *author:* **7** Chaucer (Geoffrey) *character:* **8** Griselda, pardoner, summoner **10** wife of Bath *inn:* **6** Tabard

canticle 3 ode **4** hymn, song **6** Te Deum **10** Benedicite, Benedictus, Magnificat **12** Nunc Dimittis

canticles 11 Song of Songs **13** Song of Solomon

cantilever 4 beam **6** bridge **7** bracket, support

cantillate 4 sing **5** chant **6** intone, recite

cantina 3 bar, pub **6** saloon, tavern **7** barroom

canton 5 state **6** billet **7** quarter, section **8** district, division

cantor 5 hazan **6** singer **9** precentor

canvas 4 duck, sail, tarp, tent **7** tenting **8** painting **9** sailcloth, tarpaulin

canvasback 4 duck

canvass 3 con, vet **5** argue, study **6** debate, survey **7** discuss, dispute, examine, inspect, solicit **8** campaign **9** check over **10** scrutinize **11** electioneer **12** authenticate

canyon 4 Glen, Zion **5** Bryce, chasm, gorge, Grand, gulch, Hells **6** Copper, coulee, ravine, valley

cap 3 tam, top **4** best **5** beret, cover, crest, crown, limit, trump **6** beanie, exceed, top off **7** calotte **9** culminate *clergyman's:* **7** biretta **9** zucchetto *hoodlike:* **4** coif *hunter's:* **7** montero *jester's:* **7** coxcomb **9** cockscomb *Jewish:* **8** yarmulke *knitted:* **5** toque, tuque **9** balaclava *military:* **4** kepi *mushroom:* **6** pileus *part:* **4** bill, brim, flap, peak **5** visor **7** earflap *Roman:* **6** pileus *Scottish:* **3** tam **8** balmoral **9** glengarry **11** tam-o'-shanter *Turkish:* **6** calpac **7** calpack

capability 5 craft, means, skill **7** ability, potency **8** adequacy, aptitude, capacity, efficacy, facility **9** potential **10** competence, efficiency **12** potentiality **13** effectiveness, qualification

capable 3 apt **4** able **5** adept **6** adroit, au fait **9** competent, efficient, qualified **10** proficient **11** susceptible

capacious 4 wide **5** ample, roomy **7** sizable **8** abundant, spacious **9** extensive **10** commodious **11** substantial

capacitance *unit of:* **5** farad

capacity 4 bent, gift, rank, role, room 5 knack, range, reach, scope, skill, space 6 output, status, talent 7 ability, caliber, faculty 8 adequacy, aptitude, facility, position, standing 10 capability, competence 11 proficiency 13 qualification *unit of:* 4 gill, peck, pint 5 liter, litre, minim, quart 6 bushel, gallon 10 fluid ounce, milliliter

Capaneus *slayer:* 4 Zeus *wife:* 6 Evadne

caparison 5 adorn 6 finery 7 apparel, panoply, raiment 9 adornment, trappings

cape 4 cope, ness 5 cloak, point 6 capote, mantle, tabard, tippet 7 manteau, pelisse 8 foreland, headland, mantelet, mantilla, pelerine 9 peninsula 10 promontory *clergyman's:* 8 mozzetta

Cape *Africa:* 4 Juby, Yubi 5 Blanc 6 Blanco 7 Agulhas *Alaska:* 3 Icy 4 Nome 11 Krusenstern *Algeria:* 3 Fer *Antarctica:* 3 Ann 4 Dart 5 Adare *Arctic:* 8 Nordkaap *Asia:* 5 Aniva *Australia:* 5 Byron, Otway, Sandy, Smoky 6 Arnhem 9 Van Diemen *Baffin Island:* 4 Dyer *Black Sea:* 5 Yasun *Borneo:* 4 Datu 6 Datoek *Brazil:* 4 Frio, Raso *California:* 9 Mendocino *Colombia:* 5 Aguja *Costa Rica:* 5 Velas *Crete:* 5 Plaka *Croatia:* 5 Ploca 6 Planka *Cuba:* 4 Cruz 5 Maisi *Denmark:* 4 Skaw 6 Skagen *Desolación Island:* 5 Pilar 6 Pillar *Djibouti:* 3 Bir *Egypt:* 5 Banas *England:* 8 Bolerium, Lands End *Florida:* 5 Sable 7 Kennedy 9 Canaveral *Greece:* 4 Busa 5 Gallo, Malea, Papas, Vouxa 6 Araxos, Maleas 7 Akritas *Guinea:* 5 Verga *Gulf of California:* 5 Lobos *Gulf of Guinea:* 5 Lopez *Gulf of Mexico:* 4 Rojo *Hawaii:* 5 Ka Lae 10 South Point 11 Diamond Head *Hispaniola:* 5 Beata *Honshu:* 3 Iro, Oma 5 Inubo, Kyoga, Nyudo *Indonesia:* 4 Vals 5 False *Japan:* 4 Esan, Nomo, Sata, Soya 5 Erimo, Kamui *Libya:* 3 Tin 4 Milh *Long Island Sound:* 10 Throgs Neck *Malay Peninsula:* 5 Bulat *Malaysia:* 4 Piai 5 Sirik *Massachusetts:* 3 Ann, Cod *Mediterranean:* 5 Ajdir *Mexico:* 4 Buey *Morocco:* 3 Sim 4 Guir, Rhir *Namibia:* 4 Fria *Newfoundland:* 5 Bauld *New Jersey:* 3 May *New Zealand:* 5 Brett *North Carolina:* 4 Fear 7 Lookout 8 Hatteras *Northwest Territories:* 8 Bathurst *Nova Scotia:* 5 Canso 6 Breton *Oman:* 3 Nus 4 Hadd *Ontario:* 4 Hurd, Rich *Pakistan:* 5 Monze, Muari *Portugal:* 4 Roca *Puerto Rico:* 4 Rojo *Quebec:* 5 Gaspé *Red Sea:* 5 Kasar *Sicily:* 4 Boeo, Faro 7 Lilibeo, Passero, Pelorus *Solomon Islands:* 5 Zelee *Somalia:* 4 Asir 5 Assir, Hafun *South Africa:* 8 Good Hope *South America:* 4 Horn *Spain:* 3 Nao 4 Gata 5 Creus, Penas *Syria:* 5 Basit *Taiwan:* 5 O-Iuan 7 Garam Bi *Tierra del Fuego:* 5 Penas *Tunisia:* 5 Blanc *Turkey:* 3 Boz 4 Baba, Ince, Kara, Krio 6 Lectum 8 Bozburun 9 Inceburun, Karaburun *Vancouver Island:* 5 Scott *Virginia:* 5 Henry *Washington:* 5 Alava

Căpek, Karel *coinage:* 5 robot *play:* 3 R.U.R.

caper 4 dido, lark, leap, romp 5 antic, frisk, prank, revel, shine, theft, trick 6 cavort, frolic, gambol, prance 7 roguery, rollick 8 escapade, mischief 10 shenanigan, tomfoolery 11 monkeyshine

Cape Town's famous son 5 Smuts (Jan)

Cape Verde *capital:* 5 Praia *city:* 7 Mindelo *island:* 3 Sal 4 Fogo, Maio 5 Brava 8 Boa Vista, São Tiago 10 São Vicente, São Nicolau, Santa Luzia, Santo Antão *language:* 7 Crioulo 10 Portuguese *monetary unit:* 6 escudo

capillary 4 tube 6 tubule 8 hairlike 11 blood vessel

capital 4 main 5 basic, chief, funds, major, prime 6 assets, lethal, wealth 8 cardinal 9 essential, excellent, financing, first-rate, principal, resources 10 first-class, investment, preeminent, underlying 11 fundamental, outstanding, predominant, wherewithal *Afghanistan:* 5 Kabul *Albania:* 6 Tirana, Tiranë *Alberta:* 8 Edmonton *Algeria:* 7 Algiers *Angola:* 6 Luanda *Antigua and Barbuda:* 7 St. John's 10 Saint John's *Argentina:* 11 Buenos Aires *Armenia:* 7 Yerevan *Assam:* 6 Dispur *Australia:* 8 Canberra *Austria:* 4 Wien 6 Vienna *Azerbaijan:* 4 Baku *Bahamas:* 6 Nassau *Bahrain:* 6 Manama *Bangladesh:* 5 Dhaka *Barbados:* 10 Bridgetown *Belarus:* 5 Minsk *Belgium:* 8 Brussels *Belize:* 8 Belmopan *Benin:* 9 Porto-Novo *Bhutan:* 7 Thimphu *Bolivia:* 5 La Paz *Bosnia and Herzegovina:* 8 Sarajevo *Botswana:* 8 Gaborone *Brazil:* 8 Brasília *Bulgaria:* 5 Sofia *Burkina Faso:* 11 Ouagadougou *Burma:* 6 Yangon 7 Rangoon *Burundi:* 9 Bujumbura *Cambodia:* 9 Phnom Penh *Cameroon:* 7 Yaoundé *Canada:* 6 Ottawa *Cape Verde:* 5 Praia *Central African Republic:* 6 Bangui *Chad:* 8 N'Djamena *Chile:* 8 Santiago *China:* 6 Peking 7 Beijing *Colombia:* 6 Bogotá *Comoros:* 6 Moroni *Congo (Zaire):* 8 Kinshasa *Costa Rica:* 7 San José *Côte d'Ivoire:* 7 Abidjan 12 Yamoussoukro *Croatia:* 6 Zagreb *Cuba:* 6 Havana *Cyprus:* 7 Nicosia *Czech Republic:* 6 Prague *Denmark:* 10 Copenhagen

Dominica: 6 Roseau *Dominican Republic:* 12 Santo Domingo *East Timor:* 4 Dili *Ecuador:* 5 Quito *Egypt:* 5 Cairo *El Salvador:* 11 San Salvador *Equatorial Guinea:* 6 Malabo *Eritrea:* 6 Asmara *Estonia:* 7 Tallinn *Ethiopia:* 10 Addis Ababa *Faeroe Islands:* 8 Tórshavn *Falkland Islands:* 7 Stanley *Fiji:* 4 Suva *Finland:* 8 Helsinki *France:* 5 Paris *French Guiana:* 7 Cayenne *Gabon:* 10 Libreville *Galápagos Islands:* 12 San Cristóbal *Gambia:* 6 Banjul *Georgia, Republic of:* 6 Tiflis 7 Tbilisi *Germany:* 6 Berlin *Ghana:* 5 Accra *Greece:* 6 Athens *Greenland:* 8 Godthaab *Grenada:* 9 St. George's 12 Saint George's *Guam:* 5 Agana *Guinea:* 7 Conakry *Guyana:* 10 Georgetown *Haiti:* 12 Port-au-Prince *Honduras:* 11 Tegucigalpa *Hungary:* 8 Budapest *Iceland:* 9 Reykjavík *India:* 8 New Delhi *Indonesia:* 7 Jakarta 8 Djakarta *Iran:* 6 Tehran 7 Teheran *Iraq:* 7 Baghdad *Ireland:* 6 Dublin *Israel:* 7 Tel-Aviv 9 Jerusalem *Italy:* 4 Rome *Jamaica:* 8 Kingston *Japan:* 5 Tokyo *Jordan:* 5 Amman *Kazakhstan:* 7 Astana 7 Alma-Ata *Kenya:* 7 Nairobi *Kiribati:* 6 Tarawa 11 South Tarawa *Korea, North:* 9 Pyongyang *Korea, South:* 5 Seoul *Kuwait:* 10 Kuwait City *Kyrgyzstan:* 7 Bishkek *Laos:* 9 Vientiane *Latvia:* 4 Riga *Lebanon:* 6 Beirut *Lesotho:* 6 Maseru *Libya:* 7 Tripoli *Liechtenstein:* 5 Vaduz *Lithuania:* 7 Vilnius *Macedonia:* 6 Skopje *Madagascar:* 12 Antananarivo *Malawi:* 8 Lilongwe *Malaysia:* 11 Kuala Lumpur *Maldives:* 4 Male *Mali:* 6 Bamako *Malta:* 8 Valletta *Manitoba:* 8 Winnipeg *Marshall Islands:* 6 Majuro *Mauritania:* 10 Nouakchott *Mauritius:* 9 Port Louis *Micronesia:* 7 Palikir *Moldova:* 8 Kishinev 9 Chişinaău *Mongolia:* 9 Ulan Bator *Montserrat:* 8 Plymouth *Morocco:* 5 Rabat *Mozambique:* 6 Maputo *Myanmar:* 6 Yangon 7 Rangoon *Namibia:* 8 Windhoek *Nauru:* 5 Yaren *Nepal:* 8 Katmandu 9 Kathmandu *Netherlands:* 9 Amsterdam *Newfoundland:* 10 Saint Johns *New Zealand:* 10 Wellington *Nicaragua:* 7 Managua *Niger:* 6 Niamey *Nigeria:* 5 Abuja *Northern Ireland:* 7 Belfast *Northern Territory:* 6 Darwin *North-West Frontier Province:* 8 Peshawar *Northwest Territories:* 11 Yellowknife *Norway:* 4 Oslo *Nova Scotia:* 7 Halifax *Oman:* 6 Muscat *Pakistan:* 9 Islamabad *Palau:* 5 Koror 10 Babelthuap *Papua New Guinea:* 11 Port Moresby *Paraguay:* 8 Asunción *Peru:* 4 Lima *Philippines:* 6 Manila *Poland:* 6 Warsaw *Portugal:* 6 Lisbon

Prince Edward Island: 13 Charlottetown *Puerto Rico:* 7 San Juan *Qatar:* 4 Doha *Queensland:* 8 Brisbane *Réunion:* 7 St. Denis 10 Saint Denis *Romania:* 9 Bucharest *Russia:* 6 Moscow *Rwanda:* 6 Kigali *Saint Helena:* 9 Jamestown *Saint Kitts and Nevis:* 10 Basseterre *Saint Lucia:* 8 Castries *Samoa:* 4 Apia *Saskatchewan:* 6 Regina *Saudi Arabia:* 6 Riyadh *Scotland:* 9 Edinburgh *Senegal:* 5 Dakar *Serbia and Montenegro:* 8 Belgrade *Seychelles:* 8 Victoria *Shetland:* 7 Lerwick *Sicily:* 7 Palermo *Sierra Leone:* 8 Freetown *Sikkim:* 7 Gangtok *Sind:* 7 Karachi *Slovakia:* 10 Bratislava *Slovenia:* 9 Ljubljana *Solomon Islands:* 7 Honiara *Somalia:* 9 Mogadishu *South Africa:* 8 Cape Town, Pretoria 12 Bloemfontein *South Australia:* 8 Adelaide *South-West Africa:* 8 Windhoek *Spain:* 6 Madrid *Sri Lanka:* 7 Colombo *Sudan:* 8 Khartoum *Suriname:* 10 Paramaribo *Swaziland:* 7 Mbabane *Sweden:* 9 Stockholm *Switzerland:* 4 Bern 5 Berne *Syria:* 8 Damascus *Tahiti:* 7 Papeete *Taiwan:* 6 Taipei *Tajikistan:* 8 Dushanbe *Tanzania:* 6 Dodoma 11 Dar es Salaam *Tasmania:* 6 Hobart *Thailand:* 7 Bangkok *Tibet:* 5 Lhasa *Tirol:* 9 Innsbruck *Togo:* 4 Lomé *Tonga:* 9 Nuku'alofa *Trinidad and Tobago:* 11 Port-of-Spain *Tunisia:* 5 Tunis *Turkey:* 6 Ankara *Turkmenistan:* 8 Ashgabat 9 Ashkhabad *Tuvalu:* 8 Funafuti *Uganda:* 7 Kampala *Ukraine:* 4 Kiev *United Arab Emirates:* 8 Abu Dhabi *United Kingdom:* 6 London *Uruguay:* 10 Montevideo *Uttar Pradesh:* 7 Lucknow *Uzbekistan:* 8 Tashkent *Vanuatu:* 4 Vila *Venezuela:* 7 Caracas *Victoria:* 9 Melbourne *Vietnam:* 5 Hanoi *Wales:* 7 Cardiff *Western Australia:* 5 Perth *Yemen:* 4 Sana 5 Sanaa *Yugoslavia:* 8 Belgrade *Yukon:* 10 Whitehorse *Zambia:* 6 Lusaka *Zimbabwe:* 6 Harare

capitalist 6 backer, tycoon 7 magnate 8 investor 9 bourgeois, financier, plutocrat 12 entrepreneur
capitalistic 9 bourgeois
capitalize 4 back, fund 5 stake 6 profit 7 convert, finance, promote, sponsor, support 8 bankroll 9 grubstake, subsidize
capital sin see DEADLY SIN
capitation 3 tax 7 payment, poll tax
Capitol Hill sound 3 aye, nay
capitulate 3 bow 4 cave 5 defer, yield 6 cave in, give in, give up, relent, submit 7 concede, succumb 9 acquiesce, surrender 12 knuckle under
capitulation 9 surrender 10 submission

capo 3 bar **4** boss, head **5** chief **9** godfather

capote 4 cope **5** cloak **6** mantle, tabard **7** manteau, pelisse **8** overcoat

capper 4 lure **5** blind, decoy, shill **6** climax, finale **8** clincher

capriccio 4 whim **5** caper, fancy, prank **6** notion, vagary, whimsy **7** impulse

caprice 3 bee **4** mood, vein, whim **5** fancy, freak, humor **6** foible, maggot, megrim, notion, vagary, whimsy **7** conceit **8** crotchet

capricious 4 iffy **5** flaky, moody **6** chancy, fickle **7** erratic, flighty, wayward **8** fanciful, unstable, variable, volatile **9** arbitrary, impulsive, mercurial, uncertain, whimsical **10** changeable, inconstant **12** effervescent, incalculable **13** temperamental, unpredictable

caprid 4 goat

capriole 4 leap **5** caper

capsize 4 keel, roll, sink **5** upset **7** founder, tip over **8** collapse, overturn, turn over

capstone 4 acme, apex, peak **6** apogee, climax, coping, summit, zenith **8** pinnacle **9** high point **11** culmination

capsule 6 canned, pocket, potted **7** compact, outline **9** condensed

capsulize 6 reduce **7** enclose **8** compress, condense **9** summarize, synopsize

captain 6 master **7** skipper *fictional:* **4** Ahab, Nemo **5** Queeg *historical:* **5** Bligh (William) *pirate:* **4** Kidd (William)

Captains Courageous author 7 Kipling (Rudyard)

caption 5 title **6** legend, rubric **7** cutline, heading **8** subtitle **9** underline

captious 5 testy **7** carping, peevish **8** caviling, contrary, critical, exacting, petulant, snappish **9** demanding, irritable **10** censorious, nit-picking **12** faultfinding, overcritical **13** hypercritical

captivate 4 draw, grip, hold, take **5** charm **6** allure, dazzle, please, ravish, seduce **7** attract, beguile, bewitch, delight, enchant, gratify **8** enthrall **9** enrapture, fascinate, hypnotize, infatuate, magnetize, mesmerize, spellbind

captivating 8 charming, enticing, fetching, magnetic, riveting **9** appealing, glamorous, seductive **10** bewitching, engrossing, intriguing **11** enthralling, fascinating

captive 5 bound, caged, taken **6** jailed **7** hostage **8** confined, detainee, internee, prisoner **10** enthralled, hypnotized, imprisoned

captivity 7 bondage, custody, slavery

9 detention **10** internment **11** confinement **12** imprisonment

capture 3 bag, get, nab, net, win **4** nail, take, trap **5** catch, lasso, prize, seize, snare **6** arrest, collar, entrap, occupy, secure **7** conquer, ensnare **8** preserve

Capuan 4 lush **5** plush **6** deluxe **7** opulent **8** luscious, palatial **9** luxuriant, luxurious, sumptuous **11** upholstered

car 4 auto, heap **5** buggy, coach, crate, sedan, wreck **6** jalopy, junker, wheels **7** clunker, flivver **8** roadster **10** automobile (see also AUTOMOBILE)

carafe 4 ewer **5** cruet **6** bottle, flacon, flagon **8** decanter

caravan 6 convoy, safari

caravansary 3 inn **4** khan **5** hotel, lodge, serai **6** hostel, tavern **10** campground

carbohydrate 5 sugar **6** starch **7** amylose, glucose, lactose, maltose, sucrose **8** fructose, glycogen **9** cellulose, galactose

carbolic acid 6 phenol

carbon 4 coal, coke, soot **8** charcoal, graphite, plumbago **9** lampblack

carbonate 6 aerate

carbon copy 4 dupe, twin **5** clone, ditto, mimeo, repro, Xerox **7** replica **8** knockoff **9** duplicate, facsimile **10** dead ringer **11** replication **12** reproduction

carbonize 4 burn, char, sear **5** singe, toast **6** scorch

carbuncle 4 boil, sore **5** ulcer **6** garnet, pimple **7** abscess, pustule **8** cabochon

carcass 4 body, hulk, mort **5** frame, shell, stiff **6** corpse **7** cadaver, remains **8** skeleton

carcinoid 5 tumor **8** neoplasm

carcinoma 5 tumor **6** cancer **8** neoplasm

card 3 wag, wit **4** menu, sked **5** joker **6** agenda, docket **7** program **8** calendar, comedian, humorist, schedule **9** timetable *fortune-telling:* **5** tarot *performer's:* **3** cue *spot:* **3** pip

cardboard 5 stiff **6** unreal, wooden **7** bristol, buckram, stilted **8** lifeless **10** unlifelike **11** stereotyped, unrealistic

card-carrying 4 true **7** genuine **8** bona fide **9** authentic, certified **11** fullfledged

card game see at GAME

cardiac stimulant 7 ouabain **9** digitalis

cardinal 3 key **4** main **5** basic, chief, prime, vital **6** ruling **7** central, leading, pivotal, primary **9** essential, important, principal **10** overriding, overruling **11** fundamental **12** constitutive *point:* **4** east, west **5** north, south *suffix:* **4** teen *virtue:* **7** justice **8** prudence **9** fortitude **10** temperance

care 3 rue, woe **4** fear, heed, mind, tend,

ward **5** alarm, grief, nurse, pains, serve, trust, watch, worry **6** attend, charge, dismay, effort, mother, regard, regret, sorrow, strain, stress, unease, wait on **7** anguish, anxiety, concern, conduct, custody, keeping, trouble **8** disquiet, exertion, handling, interest, suspense **9** attention, curiosity, misgiving, oversight, vigilance **10** affliction, foreboding, management, solicitude, uneasiness **11** disquietude, heedfulness, maintenance, safekeeping, supervision **12** apprehension, guardianship, watchfulness **13** consciousness, consideration, consternation

careen 4 race, sway, tilt **5** lurch, pitch, speed, swing, weave **6** repair, wobble **7** stagger

career 3 job **4** race, rush, tear, work **5** chase, speed **6** charge, course **7** calling, passage **8** lifework, vocation **9** encounter **10** livelihood, profession

care for 4 like, love, mind, tend **5** nurse, treat **6** attend, foster **7** cherish, nurture **8** preserve **9** cultivate, look after

carefree 4 wild **6** blithe, breezy, jaunty **8** reckless **10** insouciant, untroubled **12** happy-go-lucky, lighthearted **13** irresponsible

careful 4 safe, wary **5** chary, exact, fussy **7** dutiful, guarded, precise, prudent, studied **8** accurate, cautious, critical, discreet, gingerly, thorough **9** attentive, provident **10** deliberate, meticulous, particular, scrupulous **11** calculating, circumspect, considerate, foresighted, painstaking, punctilious **13** conscientious

carefully 6 warily **8** gingerly **10** cautiously, discreetly **12** meticulously, scrupulously **13** painstakingly, punctiliously

careless 3 lax **5** hasty, messy, slack **6** casual, remiss, sloppy, untidy **7** cursory, offhand, unkempt **8** feckless, heedless, reckless, slapdash, slipshod, slovenly **9** forgetful, negligent, oblivious, unheeding, unmindful, unstudied **10** disheveled, inaccurate, incautious, neglectful, unthinking, untroubled **11** inadvertent, inattentive, indifferent, perfunctory, spontaneous, thoughtless, unconcerned **12** uninterested, unreflective **13** irresponsible

caress 3 pat, pet, toy **4** kiss, love **5** dally, touch **6** coddle, cosset, cuddle, dandle, fondle, nuzzle, pamper, stroke **7** cherish, indulge **8** canoodle **10** endearment

caressive 7 calming **8** soothing

caretaker 6 warden **7** curator, janitor **9** custodian

careworn 3 wan **5** drawn, faded, jaded **7** haggard, pinched, wearied **8** fatigued, troubled **9** exhausted **10** distressed

cargo 4 haul, load **6** burden, lading **7** freight, payload **8** shipload, shipment **11** consignment

caribe 7 piranha

caribou 4 deer **8** reindeer

caricature 4 mock, sham **5** farce, phony **6** parody **7** cartoon, lampoon, mockery, takeoff **8** travesty **9** burlesque **10** distortion, pasquinade **12** exaggeration

Carlsbad feature 4 cave **6** cavern

Carmen *author:* **7** Mérimée (Prosper) *composer:* **5** Bizet (Georges) *lover:* **7** Don José **9** Escamillo

carnage 4 gore **8** butchery, hecatomb, massacre **9** bloodbath, bloodshed, slaughter

carnal 4 lewd **6** animal, bodily, coarse, earthy, sexual, vulgar, wanton **7** earthly, fleshly, lustful, mundane, obscene, sensual, worldly **8** corporal, material, physical, sensuous, temporal **9** corporeal **10** lascivious

carnation 4 pink **5** color **6** flower

carnival 4 fair, fete **6** fiesta *attraction:* **4** ride **6** midway **8** sideshow **10** concession *character:* **5** shill **6** barker, hawker **7** grifter, spieler *New Orleans:* **9** Mardi Gras *performer:* **4** geek

carnivore 9 meat-eater **10** flesh-eater

carol 4 song **6** ballad *Christmas:* **4** noel

carom 6 bounce, glance **7** rebound **8** ricochet

Caron role 4 Gigi, Lili **5** Fanny

carotid's relative 5 aorta

carousal 3 bat, jag **4** bash, tear **5** binge, booze, drunk, fling, revel, spree **6** bender, frolic **7** blowout, debauch, shindig **8** wingding **9** brannigan *Scottish:* **6** splore

carouse 5 revel **6** cavort, frolic **7** roister *Scottish:* **4** birl

carp 3 nag **4** fuss **5** bream, cavil, scold **6** peck at, pester **7** henpeck **8** complain, cyprinid, sea bream **9** complaint, criticize, find fault

carpe ___ 4 diem

carpenter 3 ant, bee **6** joiner, wright **7** builder, workman **10** woodworker

carpentry 7 joinery **10** timberwork

carper 6 critic, nagger **7** caviler, knocker **9** nitpicker **10** complainer, criticizer **11** faultfinder

carpet 3 mat, rug **4** Agra **5** Herat, Heriz, Koula, Ladik, Sarok, tapis **6** Herati, Kerman, Keshan, Kirman, Sarouk, Tabriz, Wilton **8** moquette **9** Axminster, broadloom

carpet beetle 10 buffalo bug

carping 7 blaming, fussing, nagging, railing **8** captious, caviling, critical, scolding **9** pestering **10** censorious, upbraiding **11** criticizing, reproachful **12** faultfinding, overcritical

carrageen 7 seaweed **9** Irish moss

carrefour 5 plaza **6** square **10** crossroads

carriage 3 rig **4** pose **5** coach **6** stance **7** posture, transit **8** attitude **9** transport **10** conveyance, deportment *American:* **5** buggy **8** rockaway **9** buckboard *attendant:* **6** flunky **7** footman *baby:* **4** pram **5** buggy **8** stroller **12** perambulator *driver:* **4** hack **5** cabby **8** coachman *folding top:* **6** calash *four-wheeled:* **4** trap **5** buggy, coupe **6** calash, fiacre, landau, surrey **7** hackney, phaeton **8** barouche, brougham, carryall, rockaway, stanhope, victoria **9** buckboard *Indian:* **6** gharry *man-drawn:* **8** rickshaw **10** jinricksha, jinrikisha *Russian:* **6** troika **7** droshky *stately:* **7** caroche *three-horse:* **6** troika *two-wheeled:* **3** gig **4** shay, trap **5** buggy, sulky **6** chaise, hansom **7** calèche, dogcart, tilbury **9** cabriolet *with attendants:* **8** equipage

carriage trade 5 elite **6** gentry **7** quality **9** blue blood, gentility **10** upper class, upper crust **11** aristocracy

carrick bend 4 knot

carrier 4 mule **5** envoy **6** bearer, porter, runner, vector **7** airline, courier, shipper, vehicle **8** conveyor, emissary **9** go-between, messenger **11** internuncio, transporter

Carroll character 5 Alice, Bruno, Snark **6** Boojum, Sylvie **8** Dormouse, Red Queen **9** Mad Hatter, March Hare **10** Mock Turtle **11** White Rabbit **12** Humpty Dumpty

carrot 5 prize **6** reward **9** incentive **10** inducement

carry 3 get, lug **4** bear, haul, have, hump, keep, move, pack, send, take, tote, wear **5** bring, ferry, fetch, range, stock **6** affect, bear up, convey, uphold **7** comport, conduct, portage, possess, support, sustain **8** buttress, transfer, transmit **9** influence, transport

carrying case 7 holdall, satchel **8** carryall

carry off 4 kill **6** abduct, kidnap, remove, spirit away **7** achieve, destroy, execute, perform, realize **8** complete, conclude, dispatch, shanghai **10** accomplish

carry on 3 run **4** go on, keep, rant, rave, wage **6** direct, endure, manage, ordain **7** conduct, operate, persist, prattle, proceed **8** continue, sound off **9** persevere

carry out 6 effect, govern, render **7** achieve, execute, fulfill, oversee, perform, realize **8** bring off, complete, finalize, transact **9** discharge, prosecute **10** accomplish, administer, effectuate **12** administrate

carry over 6 deduct **7** persist **8** postpone, transfer

carry through 4 last **5** abide **6** effect, endure, execute, perdure, perform, persist, survive **8** bring off, complete, continue **10** accomplish, effectuate

Carson work 11 Sea Around Us (The) **12** Silent Spring

cart 3 gig **4** dray, haul **5** buggy, carry **6** barrow, convey, schlep **7** schlepp, trundle, tumbrel, tumbril **8** carriage **9** transport **11** wheelbarrow *Indian:* **5** tonga *racing:* **5** sulky

___ **carte 3** à la

___ **Carte 5** D'Oyly

carte blanche 3 say **5** power, right, say-so **7** freedom, license **8** free hand, free rein **9** authority **10** blank check **11** prerogative

carte du jour 4 menu

cartel 4 bloc, pool **5** trust **7** combine **9** syndicate **10** consortium **12** conglomerate

Carthaginian *goddess of the moon:* **5** Tanit **6** Tanith *queen:* **4** Dido **6** Elissa

cartilage 7 gristle

cartographer *English:* **5** Smith (William) *Flemish:* **6** Kremer (Gerhard) **8** Mercator (Gerardus), Ortelius *German:* **13** Waldseemüller (Martin) *Greek:* **7** Ptolemy

cartography 9 mapmaking

carton 3 box **4** pack

cartoonist 3 Lee (Stan) **4** Capp (Al), Kane (Bob), Nast (Thomas), Szep (Paul) **5** Adams (Scott), Booth (George), Chast (Roz), Crumb (R.), Davis (Jim), Gould (Chester), Hanna (Bill), Jones (Chuck), Kelly (Walt), Steig (William), Young (Chic) **6** Addams (Charles), Caniff (Milton), Disney (Walt), Larson (Gary), Martin (Don), Schulz (Charles), Walker (Mort) **7** Barbera (Joe), Feiffer (Jules), Ketcham (Hank), Mauldin (Bill), Thurber (James), Trudeau (Garry) **8** Goldberg (Rube), Groening (Matt), Herblock, Hokinson (Helen), MacNelly (Jeff), Oliphant (Pat) **9** Fleischer (Max) **10** Hirschfeld (Al)

cartouche 5 frame **6** shield **9** cartridge

cartridge 4 case, tube **5** shell **8** cassette, cylinder **9** cartouche, container

cartwheel 4 coin **6** dollar, tumble **10** handspring

carve 3 cut, hew 4 chip, etch, form, hack 5 shape, slice 6 chisel, cleave, incise, sculpt 7 dissect, engrave, whittle 9 sculpture

Casablanca *actor:* 5 Lorre (Peter), Rains (Claude) 6 Bogart (Humphrey) 7 Bergman (Ingrid) 11 Greenstreet (Sydney) *character:* 4 Ilsa (Lund), Rick (Blaine) 6 Laszlo (Victor) *director:* 6 Curtiz (Michael)

Casanova 4 rake, roué, wolf 5 Romeo 6 lecher, masher, tomcat 7 amorist, Don Juan, gallant, playboy, seducer 8 lothario, paramour 9 adulterer, ladies' man, libertine, womanizer 10 lady-killer, voluptuary 11 philanderer

cascade 4 fall, gush, lace, pour, spew 5 chute, falls, flood, spill 6 deluge, plunge, rapids, shower, tumble 7 Niagara, torrent 8 cataract 9 avalanche, waterfall 10 outpouring

Cascade Mountains peak 6 Lassen, Shasta 7 Rainier

case 3 box, con, vet 4 etui, hull, husk, skin, suit 5 cause, event, shell 6 action, sample, sheath 7 episode, examine, example, inspect, lawsuit 8 argument, covering, incident, instance, sampling, specimen 9 check over, condition, situation 10 occurrence, proceeding, scrutinize 11 eventuality 12 circumstance *grammatical:* 6 dative 8 ablative, genitive, vocative 9 objective 10 accusative, nominative, possessive

casebearer 5 larva 11 caterpillar

case-hardened 5 tough 7 callous 8 obdurate 9 indurated, insensate, toughened, unfeeling 11 insensitive 12 thick-skinned

casement 4 sash 6 window

Casey at the Bat poet 6 Thayer (Ernest Lawrence)

cash 4 coin, jack 5 bread, dough, money, scrip 6 dinero, redeem, wampum 7 cabbage, lettuce, scratch 8 currency 10 greenbacks, ready money 11 legal tender

cashier 4 boot, fire, oust, sack 5 clerk, eject, expel, scrap 6 banker, bounce, bursar, reject, teller 7 boot out, discard, dismiss, kick out 8 jettison, throw out 9 discharge, eliminate, terminate, throw away 10 bookkeeper 11 bean counter, comptroller

cash in 3 die 4 conk, drop 5 croak 6 expire, pop off, redeem, retire 7 kick off, succumb 8 check out, drop dead, pass away, settle up 9 liquidate

casing 4 hull, husk, pipe, rind, skin, tire 5 frame, shell, space 7 wrapper 8 membrane

casino *attendant:* 6 dealer 8 croupier *game:* 4 faro 5 craps, monte, poker 6 tierce 8 baccarat, roulette 9 blackjack

cask 3 keg, tun 4 butt, drum, pipe 6 barrel, firkin 8 hogshead

casket 3 box 5 chest 6 coffer, coffin 8 jewel box

Caspian Sea *city:* 4 Baku *feeder:* 4 Ural

Cassandra 4 seer 7 prophet, seeress 8 doomster 9 doomsayer, pessimist, worrywart 10 prophetess *brother:* 7 Helenus *father:* 5 Priam *lover:* 9 Agamemnon *mother:* 6 Hecuba *slayer:* 12 Clytemnestra

casserole 4 dish 5 crock 6 tureen

Cassiopeia 13 constellation *daughter:* 9 Andromeda *husband:* 7 Cepheus

Cassio's mistress 6 Bianca

cassock 4 robe 7 soutane 8 vestment

cast 3 add, hue, sum, tot 4 drop, face, fire, form, hurl, kind, look, mold, shed, sort, tint, tone, toss, turn, type 5 color, fling, heave, leave, pitch, range, shade, shape, strew, throw, tinge, total, touch 6 actors, design, devise, direct, figure, nature, reject, slough, troupe, visage 7 arrange, company, quality, replica, scatter 8 abdicate, disperse, jettison, sprinkle 9 character, prognosis, throw away 10 appearance, conjecture, distribute, expression, prediction, strabismus, suggestion 11 countenance *a spell on:* 3 hex 5 charm 7 beguile, bewitch 8 enthrall 9 captivate, enrapture, fascinate, hypnotize, infatuate, mesmerize, spellbind *overboard:* 7 deep-six 8 jettison

cast about 4 hunt, seek 5 grope 6 search 7 seek out 8 contrive 9 search for, search out

castaway 5 leper, tramp 6 beggar, maroon, pariah 7 Ishmael, outcast, vagrant 8 deadbeat, derelict 10 Ishmaelite

cast down see DOW

caste 5 class 6 degree, estate, status 7 station 8 division, prestige

cast head 4 bust

castigate 4 beat, flay, rail, whip 5 baste, chide, scold, slash 6 berate, pummel, punish, rebuke, scorch, thrash 7 belabor, blister, chasten, chew out, lambast, reprove, scarify, scourge, upbraid 8 chastise, lambaste, penalize 9 criticize, dress down, excoriate, reprimand 10 discipline, tongue-lash

castigation 3 rod 6 rebuke 7 reproof 8 punition, scolding 10 correction, discipline, punishment 12 chastisement

castle 5 manor, villa 7 alcazar, château, citadel, mansion 8 fortress 10 stronghold *adjunct:* 4 moat *gate:* 10 portcullis *ledge:* 7 rampart *structure:* 6 turret *tower:* 4 keep 6 donjon *wall:* 6 bailey 10 battlement

cast off 5 fling, flung, let go, loose, untie 6 jilted, untied 7 unhitch 8 cut loose, forsaken, rejected, unfasten, unmoored 9 discarded, unhitched 10 left behind, unfastened

Castor *brother:* 6 Pollux 10 Polydeuces *constellation:* 6 Gemini *father:* 4 Zeus 9 Tyndareus *mother:* 4 Leda *sister:* 5 Helen *slayer:* 4 Idas

castor oil 8 laxative 9 cathartic, lubricant, purgative

cast out 4 oust 5 eject, evict, exile, expel 6 banish, deport 7 discard 9 eliminate, ostracize

castrate 3 fix 4 geld, spay 5 alter, unman, unsex 6 neuter 7 unnerve 8 enervate, mutilate 9 sterilize 10 emasculate 11 desexualize

castrato singer 9 Farinelli

casual 5 light, minor 6 breezy, chance, random, remote 7 natural, offhand, relaxed, trivial, unfussy 8 detached, informal, laid-back 9 easygoing, impromptu, irregular, uncurious, unplanned, unserious 10 accidental, contingent, fortuitous, improvised, incidental, insouciant, nonchalant, occasional 11 indifferent, low-pressure, spontaneous, unconcerned, unimportant 12 uninterested 13 disinterested, insignificant

casualty 4 prey 5 death 6 mishap, victim 8 accident, calamity, disaster, fatality 9 mischance 10 misfortune 11 catastrophe 12 misadventure

casuistry 7 sophism 9 deception, sophistry 12 equivocation, speciousness 13 deceptiveness

casus ___ 5 belli

cat 4 lion, lynx, puma, puss 5 felid, kitty, liger, ounce, pussy, tiger, tigon 6 cougar, feline, jaguar, mouser, ocelot 7 caracal, cheetah, leopard, panther 12 mountain lion *Alice's:* 5 Dinah *catlike animal:* 5 civet, genet 7 linsang *combining form:* 5 ailur 6 ailuro *disease:* 9 distemper *domestic:* 3 Mau, Rex 4 Manx 5 tabby 6 Angora, Birman, calico, exotic, Ocicat, Somali 7 bobtail, Burmese, Persian, Ragdoll, Siamese 8 longhair, Wirehair 9 Himalayan, Maine coon, shorthair, Tonkinese 10 Abyssinian *extinct:* 10 saber-tooth *fastest:* 7 cheetah *female:* 5 queen 7 lioness, tigress 9 grimalkin *genus:* 5 Felis *grinning:* 8 Cheshire *male:* 3 gib, tom *relating to:* 6 feline *ring-tailed:* 6 serval *sound:*

3 mew 4 hiss, meow, purr, roar 9 caterwaul *spotted:* 4 pard 6 jaguar, margay, ocelot, serval 7 cheetah, leopard, panther *striped:* 5 tiger *tailless:* 4 Manx *young:* 6 kitten

cataclysm 5 flood 6 deluge 7 Niagara, torrent, tragedy 8 calamity, cataract, disaster, flooding 10 inundation 11 catastrophe, devastation

cataclysmic 5 fatal 7 ruinous 10 calamitous, disastrous 11 devastating 12 catastrophic

catacomb 5 crypt, vault 8 cemetery 10 necropolis, undercroft

catafalque 4 bier

catalog 4 list, roll 5 enter, index, tally 6 enroll, roster 7 itemize, program 8 classify, inscribe, register, roll call, schedule, syllabus 9 enumerate, inventory 10 prospectus *of books:* 11 bibliotheca *of saints:* 9 hagiology

catalyst 4 goad, spur 7 impetus, impulse 8 stimulus 9 incentive, stimulant 10 incitation, incitement, motivation

catamaran 4 boat, raft

catamount 4 lynx, puma 6 bobcat, cougar 7 panther, wildcat

cataract 5 falls, flood, rapid 6 deluge, rapids 7 cascade, Niagara, torrent 8 downpour 9 waterfall 10 inundation

catastrophe 3 woe 6 deluge, fiasco 7 debacle, tragedy 8 calamity, disaster, meltdown 9 cataclysm, emergency 11 devastation

catastrophic 5 fatal 6 deadly, tragic 7 ruinous 10 calamitous, disastrous 11 cataclysmic

Catawba 4 wine 5 river 6 Indian

catcall 4 hiss, hoot, jeer, razz 9 criticism, raspberry 10 Bronx cheer

catch 3 bag, get, nab, net, see, wed 4 dupe, find, fool, grab, grip, gull, haul, hoax, hook, nail, snag, sock, spot, take, trap 5 block, clasp, clout, grasp, hit on, marry, reach, round, seize, smite, snare, stick, stump, trick, watch, whack 6 accept, anchor, arrest, clutch, collar, cut off, descry, detect, engage, entrap, fasten, flurry, follow, put out, rattle, secure, snatch, strike, take in, tangle, turn up 7 capture, confuse, deceive, disturb, ensnare, grapple, hit upon, perplex, receive 8 confound, contract, entangle, flimflam, fragment, hoodwink, kick over, meet with, overhaul, overtake 9 apprehend, bamboozle, embarrass, encounter, intercept 10 comprehend, understand 12 come down with

Catch-22 author 6 Heller (Joseph)

catchall term 3 etc.

Catcher in the Rye *author:* **8** Salinger (J. D.) *character:* **9** Caulfield (Holden)

catcher's glove 4 mitt

catching 6 taking **10** contagious, infectious **12** communicable

catch on 3 see **4** hear **5** learn **7** find out **8** discover **9** ascertain, determine, figure out

catchphrase see CATCHWORD

catch up 4 hold **6** gain on **7** close in, ensnare **8** entangle, enthrall **9** fascinate, mesmerize, spellbind

catchword 5 maxim, motto **6** slogan **10** shibboleth

catchy 6 fitful, spotty, tricky **7** erratic **8** sporadic **9** appealing, desultory, irregular, memorable, spasmodic

catechist 7 teacher

catechize 3 ask **4** quiz **5** grill, query, train **7** examine, inquire **8** instruct, question **9** inculcate **11** interrogate

catechumen 6 novice **7** convert, student, trainee **8** initiate, neophyte

categorical 7 certain, decided, express **8** absolute, clear-cut, definite, emphatic, explicit, positive **9** downright **10** definitive, forthright **11** unambiguous, unequivocal, unqualified

categorize 3 peg **4** sort **5** class, group **7** put down **8** classify, identify **10** pigeonhole

category 4 rank, tier **5** class, genre, grade, group **6** league **7** section **8** division, grouping **10** pigeonhole

catenation 4 link **5** chain **6** series, string **7** linkage **10** connection, succession

catercorner 9 obliquely, slantways, slantwise **10** cornerwise, diagonally

caterpillar 5 larva **7** cutworm, webworm **8** armyworm, silkworm **10** casebearer

cater to 5 humor **6** pamper, supply **7** furnish, gratify, indulge

caterwaul 4 howl, meow, yowl **5** miaow **6** squall

catfish see FISH

catharsis 5 purge, tonic **7** purging **8** curative **9** cleansing, purgation, purgative **10** lustration **11** expurgation, restorative **12** purification

cathartic 5 purge, tonic **8** curative **9** castor oil, purgative **11** restorative, therapeutic

Cathay 5 China

cathedral 5 duomo **6** church **8** basilica *feature:* **4** apse, nave **5** altar **6** chapel **7** chancel **10** clerestory **8** buttress, transept

Cather novel 8 Lost Lady (A) **9** My Antonia, One of Ours, O Pioneers **13** Song of the Lark **15** Professor's House (The) **16** Shadows on the Rock **23** Youth and the Bright Medusa

catholic 5 broad **6** global **7** general, liberal **8** eclectic, tolerant **9** expansive, inclusive, undivided, universal, worldwide **10** ecumenical **12** cosmopolitan **13** comprehensive

catholicity 7 breadth **9** tolerance **10** liberality **11** magnanimity **12** universality

catholicon 6 elixir **7** cure-all, nostrum, panacea

catkin 5 ament

catlike 6 feline **7** furtive **8** stealthy

catnap 3 nap **4** doze **6** siesta, snooze **10** forty winks

Cato *title:* **6** aedile, censor, consul **7** praetor, tribune **8** quaestor

Cat on a ___ Tin Roof 3 Hot

cat's-paw 4 dupe, knot, pawn, tool **5** patsy **6** puppet, stooge

cattail 4 reed, rush

cattle 4 cows, kine, neat, oxen **7** bovines **9** livestock *breed:* **5** Angus, Devon, Kerry **6** Durham, Jersey, Sussex **7** Brahman, Hariana, Red Poll **8** Ayrshire, Galloway, Guernsey, Hereford, Highland, Holstein, Limousin, Longhorn **9** Charolais, Red Polled, Shorthorn, Simmental **10** Brown Swiss **11** Dutch Belted *catching rope:* **5** lasso **6** lariat *cry:* **3** low, moo **4** poll *dehorn:* **4** poll *disease:* **4** loco **5** bloat **6** nagana **7** anthrax, locoism, measles, murrain **8** blackleg, lumpy jaw, mastitis, staggers **10** rinderpest, Texas fever **11** brucellosis *extinct breed:* **9** Teeswater *family:* **7** Bovidae *feed:* **6** fodder *genus:* **3** Bos *goddess:* **6** Bubona *grazing land:* **5** range **7** pasture *group:* **4** herd **5** drove *herdsman:* **6** cowboy, drover, gaucho **7** vaquero **8** wrangler **10** cowpuncher *identification:* **5** brand *pen:* **6** corral *round up:* **7** wrangle *stable:* **4** barn, byre **6** rustle *wild flight:* **8** stampede

catty 4 mean **5** nasty **6** barbed, bitchy, feline **7** furtive, vicious **8** spiteful, stealthy **9** malicious **10** backbiting, malevolent

Caucasian *capital:* **4** Baku **6** Tiflis **7** Tbilisi, Yerevan *republic:* **7** Armenia, Georgia **10** Azerbaijan

Caucasus *peak:* **6** Elbrus *people:* **5** Osset

caucus 4 bloc, sect **5** cabal, lobby **6** parley, powwow **7** faction

caudal appendage 4 tail

caudillo 6 despot, tyrant **8** dictator **9** strongman

cauldron 3 pot **6** boiler, kettle **8** crucible

cause 4 case, make, root **5** evoke, hatch **6** compel, effect, elicit, induce, motive, origin, reason, source, spring **7** produce, provoke **8** engender, generate, movement **9** necessity, principle **10** antecedent, bring about, inducement, originator **11** determinant, precipitate **13** consideration

cause ___ **7** célèbre

causerie 4 chat **5** essay **6** column **7** article, feature **8** colloquy, dialogue **12** conversation

caustic 4 acid, keen, tart **5** acerb, acrid, sharp **6** biting, bitter, ironic **7** acerbic, cutting, mordant, pungent **8** scathing, stinging **9** corrosive, sarcastic, trenchant **10** astringent *solution:* **3** lye

cauterize 4 burn, numb, sear **6** deaden **11** anesthetize

caution 4 warn **6** caveat **7** warning **8** forewarn, monition, prudence **9** canniness, chariness, foresight, vigilance **10** admonition, discretion, providence **11** carefulness, forethought, forewarning **12** admonishment, discreetness

cautionary 7 warning **8** monitory **10** admonitory

cautious 4 wary **5** alert, cagey, canny, chary, leery **6** shrewd **7** careful, guarded, politic, prudent **8** discreet, gingerly, vigilant, watchful **9** judicious, provident **11** circumspect, considerate, foresighted

cavalcade 6 parade, series **7** cortege **8** sequence **10** procession, succession

cavalier 5 lofty, proud **6** casual, knight, lordly **7** gallant, haughty, offhand **8** arrogant, debonair, horseman, scornful, superior **9** caballero, gentleman **10** disdainful, dismissive, insouciant, nonchalant **12** aristocratic, supercilious

cavalryman 6 lancer **7** dragoon, trooper *Algerian:* **5** spahi *horse:* **5** waler *Prussian:* **5** uhlan *Russian:* **7** cossack *Turkish:* **5** spahi *weapon:* **5** lance, saber **7** carbine

cave 3 bow, den **4** bend, drop, give, grot, lair **5** antre, break, defer, yield **6** fold up, grotto, hollow, submit **7** crumple, knuckle, succumb **8** collapse **9** break down **10** capitulate, subterrane **11** buckle under **12** knuckle under, subterranean *dweller:* **3** bat **4** bear, lion **6** hermit **9** Cro-Magnon **10** troglodite **11** Neanderthal *explorer:* **9** spelunker *formation:* **10** stalactite, stalagmite *France:* **7** Lascaux **10** Rouffignac *Iceland:* **7** Singing *Indiana:* **9** Wyandotte *Iraq:* **8** Shanidar *Kentucky:* **7** Mammoth *New Zealand:* **7** Waitomo *rock:* **8** dolomite **9** limestone *Scotland:* **7** Fingal's *South Africa:* **5** Cango *Spain:* **8** Altamira *study of:* **10** speleology

caveat 6 notice **7** caution, warning **8** monition **10** admonition **11** explanation, forewarning

caveat ___ **6** emptor

caveman 5 brute **6** savage **9** barbarian, Cro-Magnon **10** troglodyte

cavern 6 grotto **12** subterranean *Capri:* **10** Blue Grotto *Montana:* **13** Lewis and Clark *New Mexico:* **8** Carlsbad *Tennessee:* **10** Cumberland *Virginia:* **5** Luray

cavernous 4 vast **6** gaping, hollow **7** yawning

caviar 3 roe **4** eggs **6** relish *source:* **6** beluga **8** sturgeon

cavil 4 carp **7** nitpick, quibble **9** criticize, find fault

caviler 6 carper, critic **7** knocker **8** quibbler **10** criticizer **11** faultfinder

caviling 5 fussy **7** carping, finicky, nagging **8** captious, contrary, critical, exacting, niggling **10** censorious, nitpicking **12** faultfinding **13** hairsplitting

cavity 3 pit **4** bore, hole, void **5** decay **6** caries, hollow **7** vacuity **10** interstice *body:* **5** antra (plural), sinus **6** antrum **8** follicle, hemocoel

cavort 4 leap, romp **5** caper, cut up, frisk, sport **6** frolic, gambol, prance **7** carry on, rollick **10** roughhouse **11** horse around

cavy 4 paca **6** rodent **9** guinea pig

caw 4 crow, yawp **6** squall, squawk

cay 3 key **4** isle, reef **5** islet **6** island

cayenne 6 pepper *genus:* **8** Capsicum

cayman see CAIMAN

Cayman Islands *capital:* **10** George Town *discoverer:* **8** Columbus (Christopher) *territory of:* **7** Britain

Cayuga chief 5 Logan (James)

cease 3 die, end **4** halt, quit, stop **5** close **6** desist, ending, finish **8** conclude, give over, knock off, leave off **9** terminate **10** conclusion **11** discontinue, termination

cease-fire 5 truce **9** armistice **10** suspension

ceaseless 7 endless, eternal, nonstop **8** constant, immortal, unending **9** continual, incessant, perennial, perpetual, sustained, unabating **10** continuing, continuous **11** everlasting, neverending, unremitting **12** interminable **13** uninterrupted

Cecrops' daughter 5 Herse **8** Aglauros, Aglaurus **9** Pandrosos, Pandrosus

cede 4 deed **5** grant, leave, yield **6** assign, convey, give up **7** abandon, concede **8** alienate, hand over, make over, part with, renounce, sign over, transfer **9** surrender, vouchsafe **10** relinquish

ceinture 4 belt, sash **6** girdle **9** waistband

Celaeno *father:* **5** Atlas *mother:* **7** Pleione *sisters:* **8** Pleiades

celebrate 4 fete, hold, hymn, keep, laud **5** bless, cry up, exalt, extol, honor, party, revel **6** praise **7** carouse, glorify, maffick, observe, perform, rejoice **8** eulogize **9** solemnize **11** commemorate

celebrated 5 famed, great, noted **6** famous **7** eminent, notable, partied **8** caroused, rejoiced, renowned **9** prominent, well-known **11** illustrious **13** distinguished

celebration 4 bash, fete, gala **5** party **6** fiesta **7** blowout, jubilee, revelry **8** ceremony, festival, jamboree, wingding **10** observance

___ **célèbre 5** cause

celebrity 3 VIP **4** fame, hero, lion, name, star **5** éclat, glory **6** renown, repute **7** notable **8** eminence, luminary, prestige, somebody **9** notoriety, personage, superstar **10** notability, prominence, reputation

celerity 4 pace **5** speed **8** alacrity, dispatch, rapidity, velocity **9** briskness, fleetness, quickness, swiftness **10** speediness

celestial 6 divine **7** blessed, elysian, sublime **8** beatific, empyreal, empyrean, ethereal, heavenly, Olympian, supernal **9** unearthly **12** otherworldly

celestial body 3 sun **4** moon, star **5** comet **6** meteor, nebula, planet **8** asteroid **9** satellite

Celestial Empire 5 China

celibate 5 unwed **6** chaste, single, virgin **8** virginal, virtuous **9** abstinent, continent

cell 4 room **5** cubby, zooid **6** alcove **7** chamber, cubicle **9** corpuscle, cubbyhole **11** compartment *blood:* **8** hemocyte *disease:* **6** cancer *division:* **7** meiosis, mitosis *fertilized egg:* **6** zygote *material:* **3** DNA, RNA **7** protein **9** chromatin, cytoplasm **10** protoplasm *nerve:* **6** neuron *part:* **4** gene **7** nucleus, vacuole **8** ribosome **9** centriole **10** chromosome *reproductive:* **3** egg **4** germ, ovum **5** sperm **6** gamete **8** gonidium

cellar 5 store **7** shelter **8** basement

cellist *American:* **4** Rose (Leonard) **6** Lesser (Laurence), Parnas (Leslie) **7** Nelsova (Zara), Parisot (Aldo), Starker (Janos) **8** Fournier (Pierre), Schuster (Joseph) **10** Greenhouse (Bernard) *English:* **5** du Pré (Jacqueline) *Russian:* **11** Piatigorsky (Gregor) **12** Rostropovich (Mstislav) *Spanish:* **6** Casals (Pablo)

cellophane 4 wrap **7** wrapper **8** wrapping **9** packaging

celluloid 4 film **7** plastic

Celt 4 Gael, Scot **6** Breton **8** Irishman, Welshman **10** Cornishman, Highlander

Celtic *deity:* **4** Bran **5** Epona, Lugus, Macha **6** Brigit **8** Rhiannon **9** Cernunnos *festival:* **7** Beltane, Samhain

cement 4 bind, glue, join **5** grout, unify, unite **6** mortar **8** concrete *ingredient:* **4** lime **6** silica **7** alumina **8** magnesia, pozzolan **9** iron oxide, pozzolana

cemetery 8 boneyard, boot hill **8** God's acre **9** graveyard **10** churchyard, necropolis **12** burial ground, memorial park, potter's field *underground:* **8** catacomb

cenotaph 4 tomb **6** marker **8** memorial, monument

censer 8 thurible *carrier:* **8** thurifer

censor 3 ban, cut **4** blip, edit **5** bleep, purge **6** cut out, delete, excise, purify, screen **7** clean up **8** black out, restrict, suppress, withhold **9** expurgate, redpencil **10** blue-pencil, bowdlerize

censorious 6 severe **7** carping **8** captious, critical **10** accusatory, condemning **11** reproachful **12** condemnatory, denunciatory, disapproving, faultfinding, overcritical, reprehending **13** hypercritical

censurable 5 wrong **6** guilty, sinful **7** heinous **8** blamable, blameful, culpable, improper, wrongful **9** incorrect **10** deplorable, despicable, detestable **11** blameworthy, disgraceful, impeachable **12** unacceptable **13** discreditable, objectionable, reprehensible

censure 5 blame, scold **6** rebuke, strafe **7** condemn, reprove, upbraid **8** chastise, denounce, disallow, reproach **9** castigate, criticize, reprehend, reprimand, reprobate **10** disapprove

centaur 6 Chiron, Nessus

Centaurus star 4 Beta **5** Alpha

Centennial State 8 Colorado

center 3 hub **4** axis, core, crux, mean, pith, root, seat **5** focus, heart, midst, pivot **6** inside, medial, median, middle, source **7** central, essence **8** interior, midpoint, omphalos **10** focal point **11** equidistant **12** intermediary, intermediate

centerboard 4 keel

centerfold 7 foldout **8** gatefold

central 3 hub, key, mid **4** main, mean **5** basic, chief, focal **6** medial, median, middle **7** leading, pivotal, primary, salient **8** cardinal, dominant, exchange, foremost, moderate **9** essential, paramount, principal **10** overriding **11** fundamental, outstanding, predominant **12** intermediate

Central African Republic *capital:* **6** Bangui *former name:* **11** Ubangi-Shari *language:* **5** Sango, Zande **6** French *monetary unit:* **5** franc *neighbor:* **4** Chad **5** Congo, Sudan **8** Cameroon

Central America *country:* **6** Panama **8** Honduras **9** Costa Rica, Guatemala, Nicaragua **10** El Salvador *language:* **7** Nahuatl, Spanish

centralize 5 focus, unify **11** concentrate, consolidate

centripetal 8 afferent, focusing, unifying **10** converging **11** integrative **12** centralizing **13** concentrating, consolidating

centurion 7 officer **9** commander

century plant 5 agave

cephalopod 5 squid **7** mollusc, mollusk, octopus **10** cuttlefish

Cepheus *daughter:* **9** Andromeda *kingdom:* **8** Ethiopia *wife:* **10** Cassiopeia

cerate 4 balm **5** cream, salve **6** chrism **7** unction, unguent **8** dressing, liniment, ointment **9** demulcent, emollient

Cerberus 5 guard **8** guardian, sentinel, watchdog *father:* **6** Typhon *form:* **3** dog *mother:* **7** Echidna

cereal 4 meal, mush, samp **5** gruel **6** farina **7** oatmeal **8** cornmeal, porridge *grass:* **3** rye **4** corn, oats, ragi, rice **5** emmer, maize, spelt, wheat **6** barley, millet **7** sorghum **9** buckwheat *North African:* **8** couscous *Russian:* **5** kasha

cerebral 6 mental **7** bookish **8** highbrow **9** scholarly **10** highbrowed **12** intellectual

cerebrate 5 think **6** reason **7** reflect **8** cogitate **9** speculate **10** deliberate

cerebration 7 thought **9** brainwork **10** cogitation, reflection **11** speculation **12** deliberation

ceremonial 6 august, formal, ritual, solemn **7** courtly, stately, studied **8** mannered, stylized **10** liturgical **11** ritualistic **12** conventional

ceremonious 6 formal, proper, seemly, solemn **7** courtly, stately **8** decorous, imposing, majestic **9** dignified, grandiose **10** impressive **11** punctilious **12** conventional

ceremony 4 form, pomp, rite **6** ritual **7** decorum, liturgy, service **8** protocol **9** formality **10** observance *Jewish:* **8** habdalah, havdalah **10** bar mitzvah, bat mitzvah *university:* **8** encaenia

Ceres *Greek counterpart:* **7** Demeter *daughter:* **10** Persephone, Proserpina, Proserpine *father:* **6** Cronus, Saturn *mother:* **3** Ops **4** Rhea

certain 3 set **4** firm, some, sure, true **5** fated, fixed **6** divers, stated, sundry **7** assured, settled, several, various **8** cocksure, credible, definite, destined, positive, provable, reliable, sanguine, specific, surefire, unerring **9** authentic, certified, confident, convinced, necessary, plausible, warranted **10** conclusive, dependable, guaranteed, inarguable, inevitable, infallible, stipulated, undeniable, verifiable **11** confirmable, indubitable, ineluctable, inescapable, trustworthy, unavoidable **12** demonstrable, indisputable, well-grounded **13** incontestable, predetermined, uncontestable

certainty 5 faith **6** surety **8** firmness, sureness **9** assurance, certitude, sure thing **10** confidence, conviction **11** assuredness, staunchness **12** absoluteness, definiteness, positiveness

certificate 7 diploma, license, voucher **8** contract, document **9** affidavit **10** credential

certifier 6 notary **7** auditor **9** registrar

certify 4 aver, avow, okay **5** state, swear, vouch **6** assert, assure, attest, verify **7** approve, confirm, endorse, license, testify, warrant, witness **8** accredit, guaranty, notarize **9** authorize, guarantee, recognize **10** commission **12** authenticate

Cervantes' hero 10 Don Quixote

cessation 3 end **4** halt, rest, stop **5** break, cease, close, letup, pause **6** ending, finish, freeze, hiatus, period, recess **7** respite **10** conclusion, suspension **11** termination **12** interruption

cesspool 3 den, pit, sty **4** sink **5** sewer, Sodom **6** cloaca, gutter, pigsty **8** Gomorrah **12** Augean stable

cetacean 5 whale **7** dolphin **8** porpoise

Cetus star 4 Mira

Ceylon 8 Sri Lanka

cgs unit 3 erg **4** dyne, gram, phot **5** gauss, poise, stilb **6** second, stokes **7** lambert, maxwell, oersted **10** centimeter

Chablis 4 wine **8** Burgundy **9** white wine

Chad *capital:* **8** N'Djamena *city:* **4** Sarh **6** Abéché **7** Moundou *lake:* **4** Chad *language:* **6** Arabic, French *monetary unit:* **5** franc *neighbor:* **5** Libya, Niger, Sudan **7** Nigeria **8** Cameroon *river:* **5** Chari **6** Logone

chafe 3 irk, rub, vex **4** fret, gall, peel, rage, skin, wear **5** annoy, erode **6** abrade, bother, scrape **7** provoke **8** irritate, vexation

chaff 3 kid, rag, rib **4** jest, joke, josh, razz **5** dregs, husks, tease **6** banter, debris, refuse **7** remains **8** detritus **9** sweepings

chaffer 6 barter, dicker, haggle, higgle, palter **7** bargain, chatter **8** exchange, huckster

chagrin 3 ire, irk, vex **5** abash, annoy, peeve, pique, upset **6** dismay **7** perturb **8** disquiet, distress, unsettle, vexation **9** annoyance, discomfit, displease, embarrass, humiliate, petulance **10** disappoint, discompose, disconcert, irritation **11** frustration, humiliation **12** discomfiture

chagrined 4 hurt **5** upset, vexed **6** shamed **7** ashamed **8** dismayed **9** disturbed, mortified, perturbed, unsettled **10** distressed, humiliated **11** discomposed, embarrassed **12** disappointed, disconcerted

chain 3 row **4** bind, bond, gyve **5** group, train, trust **6** cartel, catena, fetter, hobble, series, string, tether **7** combine, manacle, shackle **8** handcuff, sequence **9** syndicate **10** succession **11** concatenate, progression **12** conglomerate **13** concatenation *adjunct:* **8** sprocket *collar:* **6** torque *gang:* **6** coffle *ornamental:* **10** chatelaine *sound:* **5** clank

chain ___ 3 saw **4** gang, mail **5** store **6** letter **8** reaction

Chained Lady 9 Andromeda

chair 4 seat **5** stool **6** rocker, settee, settle **7** preside *back:* **5** splat *bishop's:* **8** cathedra *designer:* **5** Eames *portable:* **5** sedan *reclining:* **12** chaise longue, chaise lounge *royal:* **6** throne *type:* **4** club, easy **6** morris **7** rocking **8** captain's, electric **9** director's, reclining **10** Adirondack, ladder-back

chaise 4 sofa **5** chair, coach, divan **8** carriage

chalcedony 4 onyx, sard **5** agate, chert **6** jasper, quartz **9** carnelian, cornelian **10** bloodstone **11** chrysoprase

chalet 3 hut **4** camp **5** lodge **7** cottage

chalice 3 cup **5** grail **6** goblet

chalk out 5 draft **6** sketch **7** outline **8** block out, rough out **11** skeletonize **12** characterize

chalk up 3 get, win **4** gain **6** attain, credit, impute, obtain, secure **7** achieve, acquire, ascribe, procure, realize **9** attribute

challenge 3 try **4** dare, defy, face, stir, wake **5** brave, claim, demur, doubt, exact, rouse, waken **6** arouse, awaken, demand, impugn, invite, kindle **7** calling, dispute, protest, require, solicit, venture **8** confront, defiance, demurral, demurrer, question, struggle **9** objec-

tion, postulate, stimulate **10** difficulty, insistence **12** remonstrance

challenger 5 rival **8** aspirant, opponent **9** adversary, contender **10** antagonist, competitor, contestant

chamber 4 cell, hall, room **5** haven, house **7** cubicle **9** apartment, enclosure **11** compartment *underground:* **8** hypogeum

chambered seashell 8 nautilus

chamberlain 6 priest **7** officer, servant **9** attendant, treasurer

chameleon 6 lizard

chameleonic 6 fickle **7** protean **9** mercurial **10** changeable, inconstant

chamfer 5 bevel **6** groove

chamois 6 shammy **7** leather **8** antelope, ruminant *habitat:* **4** Alps *Old Testament:* **6** aoudad

chamois-like animal 4 goat, ibex

champ 3 gum **4** bite, chew, mash **5** gnash, munch **7** trample **8** macerate, ruminate **9** masticate

champagne 4 wine **6** bubbly *center:* **5** Reims **6** Rheims

Champagne *capital:* **6** Troyes

champaign 5 field, plain **7** expanse, terrain **11** battlefield

champignon 6 fungus **8** mushroom

champion 4 back, hero **5** first, prime **6** uphold, victor, winner **7** capital, contend, leading, paladin, premier, support, titlist **8** advocate, defender, exponent, fight for, foremost, medalist, unbeaten **9** excellent, nonpareil, number one, principal, proponent, protector, supporter **11** illustrious, outstanding, titleholder, white knight

championship 5 crown, title **6** laurel, trophy **7** contest, defense, laurels, pennant **8** advocacy **10** blue ribbon

chance 4 hap, hit, lot, odd **4** fate, luck, meet, odds, risk, shot **5** break, fluke, light, wager **6** befall, casual, gamble, happen, hazard **7** fortune, offhand, stumble, venture **8** accident, fortuity, occasion, prospect **9** advantage, transpire **10** accidental, fortuitous, incidental, likelihood **11** contingency, opportunity, possibility, probability *even:* **6** toss-up

chancellor 5 judge **8** minister **9** secretary *German:* **4** Kohl (Helmut) **6** Brandt (Willy), Erhard (Ludwig), Hitler (Adolf) **7** Schmidt (Helmut) **8** Adenauer (Konrad), Bismarck (Otto von) **9** Schroeder (Gerhard)

chancy 4 iffy **5** dicey, fluky, hairy, risky **6** touchy, tricky **8** perilous, ticklish **9** dangerous, haphazard, hazardous, uncertain **10** capricious, precarious

11 speculative, treacherous 12 incalculable 13 unpredictable

Chandler, Raymond *character:* 7 Marlowe (Philip) *novel:* 8 Big Sleep (The) 11 Long Good-Bye (The) 13 Murder My Sweet 16 Farewell My Lovely *screenplay:* 10 Blue Dahlia (The) 15 Double Indemnity

change 3 fix 4 swap, turn, vary 5 alter, coins, money, morph, shift, trade 6 adjust, evolve, modify, mutate, reform, remake, revamp, revert, revise, switch 7 commute, convert, novelty, replace, reverse 8 exchange, mutation, revision, transfer 9 alternate, deviation, diversify, fluctuate, refashion, transform, transmute, transpose, variation 10 alteration, conversion, divergence, innovation, substitute 11 interchange, permutation, transfigure, vicissitude 12 metamorphose, modification, transmogrify 13 metamorphosis, transmutation *sudden:* 8 peripety 10 peripeteia

changeable 5 fluid 6 fickle, labile, pliant, shifty 7 flighty, mutable, plastic, protean, unfixed, varying 8 restless, shifting, slippery, ticklish, unstable, unsteady, variable, volatile 9 adaptable, alterable, impulsive, mercurial, uncertain, unsettled, whimsical 10 capricious, inconstant 11 chameleonic, fluctuating, vacillating 13 kaleidoscopic, temperamental, unpredictable

change decor 4 redo 10 redecorate

changeless 5 fixed 6 steady 7 abiding, regular, uniform 8 constant, enduring, resolute 9 immutable, perpetual, steadfast, unvarying 10 invariable

change off 6 rotate 9 alternate

change of heart 8 reversal

change of life 9 menopause 11 climacteric

change of pace 5 pitch, shift 9 slow pitch

changeover 5 shift 10 alteration, conversion, transition

channel 3 way 4 band, duct, pass, path, pipe 5 agent, canal, carry 6 agency, convey, course, funnel, groove, gutter, medium, siphon, strait, trough, tunnel 7 conduct, conduit, passage, vehicle 8 aqueduct, pipeline, transmit 10 instrument 11 watercourse *Africa-Madagascar:* 10 Mozambique *Atlantic-Nantucket Sound:* 8 Muskeget *Atlantic-North Sea:* 7 English *Ellesmere-Greenland:* 7 Robeson *Ganges:* 5 Hugli 7 Hooghly *Hawaii:* 5 Kaiwi, Kauai *Japan:* 5 Bungo *Northwest Territories:* 9 M'Clintock *Pakistan:* 4 Nara *Scotland:* 5 Minch *Tierra del*

Fuego: 6 Beagle *Tigris-Euphrates:* 11 Shatt al Arab *Virginia:* 12 Hampton Roads *West Indies:* 9 Old Bahama

channel bass 4 drum 7 red drum, redfish

Channel Islands *capital:* 8 St. Helier 11 St. Peter Port *dependency of:* 7 Britain *island:* 4 Sark 6 Jersey 8 Alderney, Guernsey

chanson 4 song

"Chanson ___ " 6 Triste

chanson de ___ 5 geste

chant 4 sing, tune 5 drone 6 intone 8 vocalize 10 cantillate *Gregorian:* 9 plainsong 12 cantus firmus *Jewish:* 6 Hallel

chanteuse 6 singer 7 artiste 10 cantatrice

chanticleer 4 cock 7 rooster

chaos 6 bedlam, muddle 7 anarchy, clutter, entropy, turmoil 8 disarray, disorder 9 confusion 11 lawlessness

Chaos *daughter:* 3 Nox, Nyx 4 Gaea *son:* 6 Erebus

chaotic 7 jumbled, lawless 8 anarchic, confused, formless 9 amorphous, haphazard, scrambled 10 disordered, disorderly, topsy-turvy, tumultuous 11 harum-scarum, unorganized 12 disorganized 13 helter-skelter, unpredictable

chap 3 guy 4 gent 5 bloke 6 fellow

chaparral 5 scrub 7 thicket

chaparral cock 10 roadrunner

chapeau 3 hat 6 topper

chapel 6 bethel, church, shrine 7 chantry 9 sanctuary

chaperone 5 guide 6 attend, duenna, escort, matron 7 oversee 9 accompany, companion, supervise 11 superintend

chapfallen SEE CRESTFALLEN

chaplain 5 padre 6 pastor 8 minister, sky pilot

chaplet 5 crown 6 anadem, laurel, rosary, wreath 7 coronal, coronet, garland

chapter 4 unit 5 phase, stage 6 branch, period 7 episode, section 8 division 9 affiliate

char 4 burn 9 carbonize

character 3 ilk 4 bent, case, cast, kind, mark, mind, name, rank, role, sign, sort, type 5 state, trait 6 cipher, device, letter, makeup, nature, oddity, repute, spirit, status, stripe, symbol, temper, virtue 7 feature, oddball, persona, quality, station, variety 8 capacity, eminence, identity, position, standing 9 attribute, eccentric, rectitude, situation 10 reputation, uniqueness 11 description, disposition, personality, temperament 13 individuality *chief:*

4 hero **11** protagonist *defect:* **8** hamartia
character assassination 5 libel **7** calumny, scandal, slander **10** backbiting, defamation **12** backstabbing
characteristic 4 mark, sign **5** badge, point, token, trait **6** aspect, innate, normal, proper **7** feature, natural, quality, special, typical **8** especial, peculiar, property, specific, tendency **9** attribute, birthmark, component, mannerism, trademark **10** diagnostic, emblematic, individual, particular **11** distinction, distinctive, peculiarity, singularity **12** idiosyncrasy **13** idiosyncratic
characterize 4 mark **5** draft **6** define, sketch, typify **7** outline, portray **8** describe, identify **10** constitute, pigeonhole **11** distinguish, individuate, personalize **12** discriminate **13** differentiate, individualize
characterless 4 flat **5** mousy **7** humdrum, insipid, vacuous **8** mediocre **9** colorless **10** namby-pamby, wishy-washy **11** nondescript
charade 4 sham **5** farce, put-on **6** parody **8** disguise, pretense, travesty **9** deception **11** make-believe
chare see CHORE
charge 3 ask, bid, fee, lay, tab, tax **4** bill, care, cost, duty, fill, heap, kick, load, onus, race, rate, rush, task, tell, toll, warn **5** choke, debit, order, place, price, refer, trust **6** accuse, assign, attack, burden, credit, direct, enjoin, exhort, impugn, impute, indict, saddle, thrill **7** arraign, ascribe, bidding, command, conduct, entrust, expense, impeach, mandate, request, solicit **8** accredit, handling, instruct, price tag, reproach, stampede **9** attribute, committal, electrify, inculpate **10** accusation, allegation, commitment, injunction, management, obligation **11** incriminate, instruction, requirement, supervision
chargeable 6 liable **7** subject **11** accountable, responsible
chargeless 4 free **6** gratis **8** costless **10** gratuitous **13** complimentary
charger 5 horse, mount, steed **6** salver **7** courser, platter **8** trencher, warhorse
chariness 7 caution **8** prudence **9** integrity **10** discretion
chariot 8 carriage *four-horse:* **8** quadriga
charioteer 6 Auriga, driver
charisma 5 charm **6** allure, appeal, duende **7** glamour **9** magnetism **10** attraction **11** fascination
charitable 6 benign, giving, humane, kindly **7** clement, lenient, liberal **8** generous, merciful, obliging, tolerant

9 forgiving, indulgent **10** altruistic, beneficent, benevolent, forbearing, thoughtful **11** considerate, kindhearted, sympathetic **12** eleemosynary, humanitarian **13** philanthropic
charity 4 alms, love **5** grace, mercy **6** lenity, relief **7** caritas **8** altruism, clemency, donation, goodwill, leniency, offering **10** generosity, humaneness, kindliness **11** benefaction, beneficence, benevolence **12** contribution
charivari 5 babel, melee **6** jangle, jumble, medley, racket, ruckus, uproar **7** farrago **8** serenade, shivaree **9** cacophony, confusion **10** hodgepodge **11** celebration
charlatan 4 sham **5** bluff, faker, fraud, quack **6** con man **8** imposter, impostor, swindler **10** mountebank **11** quacksalver **13** confidence man
Charlemagne *brother:* **8** Carloman *father:* **5** Pepin *knight:* **6** Oliver, Roland **7** Olivier, paladin **8** douzeper *nephew:* **6** Roland **7** Orlando *sword:* **7** Joyeuse *traitor:* **4** Gano **7** Ganelon
Charles's Wain 9 Big Dipper, Ursa Major
charleston 5 dance
Charley's Aunt author 6 Thomas (Brandon)
Charlie and the Chocolate Factory author 4 Dahl (Roald)
Charlie Brown creator 6 Schulz (Charles)
Charlie McCarthy 5 dummy **6** stooge *friend:* **5** Snerd (Mortimer) *voice:* **6** Bergen (Edgar)
charm 3 hex **4** juju, lure, mojo, rune, take, wile **5** grace, quark, spell **6** allure, amulet, appeal, enamor, fetish, mascot, seduce, voodoo **7** attract, beguile, bewitch, enchant, glamour **8** enthrall, entrance, talisman, witchery **9** captivate, enrapture, ensorcell, fascinate, hypnotize, magnetism, mesmerize **10** allurement, attraction, phylactery, witchcraft **11** fascination, incantation **13** agreeableness
charmed 5 lucky **7** blessed **8** enamored **9** bewitched, enchanted, entranced, fortunate **10** captivated, fascinated, infatuated
charmer 4 roué **5** magus **6** wizard **7** seducer, warlock **8** conjurer, lothario, magician, sorcerer **9** enchanter **11** spellbinder
charming 7 winsome **8** adorable, alluring, inviting, magnetic **9** appealing, glamorous, seductive **10** attractive, delightful, enchanting, entrancing **11** captivating
Charon 7 boatman **8** ferryman *father:* **6** Erebus *mother:* **3** Nox *river:* **4** Styx

Charpentier opera 6 Louise
charpoy 3 bed, cot
chart 3 map 4 plan, plat, plot 5 graph, table 6 design, lay out, map out, sketch 7 arrange, diagram, outline, project 9 blueprint 10 tabulation
charter 3 let 4 deed, hire, rent 5 grant, lease 10 conveyance 12 constitution
Chartreuse 7 liqueur
chary 4 wary 5 cagey, canny 6 frugal, stingy 7 careful, guarded, miserly, prudent, sparing, thrifty 8 cautious, discreet, gingerly, hesitant 9 provident, reluctant 10 economical, restrained, suspicious, unwasteful 11 calculating, circumspect, constrained, disinclined
Charybdis 9 whirlpool *rock associated with:* 6 Scylla
chase 3 run 4 bolt, dash, game, hunt, prey, race, rush, tear 5 chivy, drive, eject, evict, hound, shoot, speed, trail 6 career, charge, course, follow, hasten, pursue, quarry 7 boot out, hunting, kick out, pursuit 8 run after, throw out
chase away 4 rout, shoo
chaser 4 wolf 6 masher 7 Don Juan 8 Casanova 9 ladies' man, womanizer 10 lady-killer 11 philanderer
chasm 3 gap 4 gulf, rift 5 abyss, cleft, clove, flume, gorge, gulch, split 6 ravine 8 crevasse
chasmal 6 gaping 7 echoing, yawning 9 cavernous
chassepot 5 rifle
chaste 4 pure 5 clean, moral 6 decent, modest, proper, seemly, vestal, virgin 7 austere, prudish 8 celibate, decorous, innocent, maidenly, platonic, spotless, virginal, virtuous 9 abstinent, continent, stainless, undefiled, unsullied 10 immaculate 11 unblemished
chasten 5 abase, scold 6 humble, punish, rebuke, refine, subdue 7 correct, upbraid 8 chastise 9 castigate, humiliate, reprimand 10 discipline
chastise 4 beat, flog, whip 5 scold 6 punish, rebuke, thrash 7 belabor, censure, chasten, correct, reprove, scourge, upbraid 9 castigate 10 discipline
chastisement 3 rod 7 reproof 8 punition 10 correction, discipline, punishment 11 castigation
chastity 6 purity, virtue 7 modesty 8 celibacy 9 innocence, integrity, virginity 10 abstention, continence, maidenhood
chasuble 8 vestment
chat 3 gab, jaw, rap, yak, yap 4 blab, gush, talk 5 prate, visit 6 babble, confab, gossip, jabber, natter, parley, pat-

ter, yak-yak 7 chatter, palaver, prattle, twaddle 8 causerie, colloquy, converse, dialogue, schmooze 9 tête-à-tête, yakety-yak 11 confabulate 12 conversation, tittle-tattle 13 confabulation
château 5 manor, villa 6 castle, estate 7 mansion 8 fortress 12 country house
chateaubriand 5 steak 10 tenderloin
Chateaubriand novel 4 René 5 Atala
chatelain 6 warden 8 governor 9 castellan
chatelaine 4 hook, wife 5 clasp 8 mistress
chattel 4 serf 5 slave 7 bondman 8 bondsman, property
chatter 3 gab, jaw, yak 4 blab, bull 5 prate 6 babble, gabble, gibber, gossip, jabber, natter, patter, yak-yak, yammer 7 blabber, blather, palaver, prattle, vibrate 9 small talk, yakety-yak 12 tittle-tattle
chatterbox 6 gabber, gossip, magpie, prater 7 blabber 8 jabberer, prattler 12 blabbermouth
chatty 5 gabby 7 voluble 9 garrulous, talkative 10 loquacious
Chaucer pilgrim 4 Cook, Monk 5 Clerk, Friar, Reeve 6 Miller, Parson, Squire 8 Franklin, Manciple, Merchant, Summoner 10 Nun's Priest, Wife of Bath
chauffeur 5 drive 6 driver 9 transport
chauvinism 6 sexism 8 jingoism 10 partiality, patriotism 11 nationalism
cheap 4 mean, poor 5 junky, tight 6 cheesy, common, cruddy, flashy, measly, paltry, shabby, shoddy, sleazy, stingy, tawdry, trashy 7 chintzy, cutrate, low-cost, reduced, thrifty 8 inferior, trifling, uncostly 9 brummagem, low-priced 10 economical 11 inexpensive 12 contemptible, meretricious
cheapen 5 decry, lower 6 debase, reduce 7 devalue 8 mark down 9 devaluate, downgrade 10 depreciate, undervalue
cheapjack 5 junky 6 hawker, cheesy, cruddy, shoddy, sleazy, tawdry, trashy 7 haggler, higgler, packman, peddler 8 huckster, inferior, rubbishy 9 worthless 13 opportunistic
cheapskate 5 miser 7 niggard, scrooge 8 tightwad 9 skinflint 11 cheeseparer
cheat 3 con, gyp 4 bilk, burn, dupe, fool, gull, hoax, milk, ream, scam 5 bunco, cozen, crook, fraud, fudge, gouge, hocus, put-on, screw, shaft, short, slick 6 chisel, chouse, con man, deceit, delude, diddle, extort, fleece, humbug, rip-off, sucker, take in 7 beguile, chicane, deceive, defraud, diddler, mislead, sharper, shyster, swindle, two-time 8 flimflam, hoodwink,

swindler, trickery **9** bamboozle, chicanery, deception, defrauder, imposture, overreach, trickster **11** double-cross **12** double-dealer **13** confidence man *on a check:* **4** kite

check 3 tab, try **4** bill, curb, halt, jibe, stay, stop, test, tick **5** block, brake, draft, prove, score, stall **6** accord, arrest, baffle, bridle, damage, desist, hold in, square, thwart, verify **7** compare, conform, control, examine, inhibit, repress, setback **8** dovetail, hold back, hold down, preclude, restrain, reversal, suppress **9** constrain, criterion, interrupt, restraint **10** correspond, inspection **11** examination **13** investigation

checkered 5 plaid **6** motley **7** mutable, spotted **9** patchwork, patterned **10** variegated **11** diversified

checklist 7 catalog **9** catalogue, inventory **11** enumeration

checkmate 4 beat **6** corner, defeat **7** outplay **8** vanquish **9** finish off

check out 3 die, eye **5** leave **6** assess **7** examine, inspect **8** appraise, evaluate, look over

check over 3 con, vet **4** scan **5** audit, study **6** review, survey **7** analyze, canvass, examine, inspect **10** scrutinize

checkup 4 exam **8** physical **10** inspection **11** examination

cheek 4 gall **5** brass, nerve **8** audacity, chutzpah, temerity **9** brashness, impudence, insolence **10** confidence, effrontery **11** presumption **12** impertinence

cheekbone 5 malar

cheeky 4 bold, flip, pert, wise **5** brash, cocky, fresh, nervy, sassy, saucy, smart **6** brazen **7** forward **8** flippant, impudent, insolent **11** impertinent, smart-alecky **12** presumptuous

cheep 4 peep **5** chirp, tweet **7** chirrup, chitter, twitter

cheer 3 rah **4** buoy, hail, root **5** bravo, huzza, nerve **6** buck up, gaiety, hoorah, hooray, hurrah, hurray, huzzah, solace, spirit **7** animate, applaud, comfort, console, enliven, gladden, hearten **8** embolden, inspirit **9** animation, encourage **10** strengthen *corrida:* **3** olé

cheerful 3 gay **4** glad, rosy **5** jolly, merry, perky, sunny **6** blithe, bouncy, bright, chirpy, hearty, jaunty, jocund, lively **7** beamish, buoyant, radiant **8** animated, carefree, chirrupy **9** vivacious **12** lighthearted

cheerio 3 bye **4** ta-ta **5** adieu **6** bye-bye, good-by, so long **7** good-bye, toodles **8** farewell, toodle-oo

cheerless 4 dour, drab, grim **5** bleak

6 dismal, dreary, gloomy, somber, sombre **7** forlorn, joyless **8** desolate, dolorous, funereal, mournful **9** dejecting **10** depressing, melancholy, oppressive, tenebrific **11** dispiriting

cheers 5 salud, skoal **6** cincin, l'chaim, prosit **7** l'chayim, sláinte **8** applause, approval, chinchin **9** bottoms up **10** jubilation **11** acclamation, approbation

cheery 5 happy, jolly, merry, sunny **6** blithe, bouncy, chirpy, lively, upbeat **7** buoyant, chipper, festive, gleeful **8** animated, carefree, gladsome **9** convivial, sparkling **12** lighthearted

cheese 3 pot **4** blue, jack **5** brick, cream **6** farmer **7** cottage, process, ricotta **9** smearcase *American:* **8** Longhorn **11** Liederkranz **12** Monterey Jack *Belgian:* **9** Limburger *curdling agent:* **6** rennet, rennin *Danish:* **7** Havarti *dish:* **6** fondue **7** rarebit, soufflé *Dutch:* **4** Edam **5** Gouda **6** Leyden *English:* **7** cheddar, Stilton **8** Cheshire **10** Lancashire *French:* **4** Brie **7** fromage, Livarot **9** Camembert, Reblochon, Roquefort **10** Neufchâtel **11** Pont l'Évêque, Port du Salut *German:* **6** Tilsit **7** Munster **8** Muenster, Tilsiter *Greek:* **4** feta *green:* **7** sapsago *Italian:* **6** Asiago, Romano **7** fontina, ricotta **8** Bel Paese, Parmesan, pecorino **9** provolone **10** Gorgonzola, mozzarella *lover:* **9** turophile *main ingredient:* **6** casein *Norwegian:* **9** Jarlsberg *protein:* **6** casein *Scottish:* **6** Dunlop, Orkney **7** kebbock, kebbuck *Swiss:* **6** Saanen **7** Gruyère, sapsago **8** Vacherin **10** Emmentaler **11** Emmenthaler *uncured:* **7** cottage *Welsh:* **10** Caerphilly

cheesecloth 5 gauze

cheeselike 6 caseic **7** caseous

cheeseparer 5 miser **7** niggard, scrooge **8** tightwad **9** skinflint **10** cheapskate, pinchpenny

cheeseparing 4 mean **5** chary, cheap, mingy, tight **6** frugal, shabby, stingy **7** chintzy, miserly, thrifty **8** grudging, skimping **9** niggardly, penurious **11** closefisted, tightfisted **12** parsimonious **13** penny-pinching

cheesy 4 poor **5** cheap **6** common, shabby, shoddy, sleazy, tawdry, trashy **7** caseous **8** rubbishy

Cheever, John *novel:* **8** Falconer **14** Wapshot Scandal (The) **16** Wapshot Chronicle (The) *story:* **7** Swimmer (The)

chef 4 cook

chef d'oeuvre 7 classic **9** showpiece **10** magnum opus, masterwork **11** masterpiece, tour de force

Chekhov, Anton *play:* 6 Ivanov 7 Seagull (The) 10 Uncle Vanya 12 Three Sisters 13 Cherry Orchard (The) *story:* 9 Black Monk (The)

chelonian 6 turtle 8 tortoise

chemical *agent:* 8 catalyst *combining power:* 7 valence *compound:* 4 acid, base, diol, enol, imid, oxim, salt, tepa, urea 5 amide, amine, diene, ester, imide, imine, indol, orcin, oxime, purin, pyran, salol, tolan, triol 6 alkali, benzin, benzol, diamin, emodin, guanin, halide, hydrid, indole, inulin, ionone, isatin, isolog, isomer, ketone, lactam, maltol, metepa, natron, nitril, pterin, purine, pyrone, pyrrol, quinol, retene, silane, skatol, tannin, tetryl, thiram, thymol, tolane, triene, trimer, uracil, ureide, yttria, zeatin 7 barilla, benzene, benzole, cumarin, diamide, diamine, diazine, diazole, diester, flavone, guanine, heptose, hydride, indamin, indican, indoxyl, isatine, levulin, metamer, monomer, naphtol, nitrile, orcinol, oxazine, phytane, picolin, polyene, polymer, pyrrole, quinoid, quinone, salicin, skatole, steroid, taurine, terpene, thiazin, thiazol, thymine, tolidin, triazin, urethan, uridine, vitamer, xylidin 8 cephalin, cyanamid, disulfid, elaterin, fluorene, furfural, guaiacol, hematein, hexamine, indamine, isologue, kephalin, lichenin, limonene, melamine, naloxone, naphthol, palmitin, phenazin, phosphid, phthalin, picoline, piperine, pristane, quinolin, resorcin, salicine, santonin, siloxane, sodamide, sorbitol, spermine, squalene, stilbene, strontia, tautomer, thiazine, thiazole, thiophen, thiotepa, thiourea, tolidine, triazine, triazole, triptane, tyramine, urethane, vanillin, warfarin, xanthene, xanthine, xanthone, xylidine, ytterbia, zaratite, zirconia (see at ELEMENT) *quantity:* 4 mole *radical:* 4 acyl, amyl, cyan 5 allyl, butyl, ethyl, tolyl 6 acetyl, formyl, methyl, oxalic, phenyl, propyl, toluyl 7 benzoyl *reaction:* 5 redox *salt:* 5 niter, nitre, urate, ziram 6 haloid, humate, malate, oleate, phytin 7 ferrate, formate, gallate, maleate, pectate, persalt, picrate, tannate, toluate, zincate 8 fumarate, pyruvate, racemate, selenate, silicate, stearate, tartrate, thionate, titanate, valerate, vanadate, xanthate *suffix:* 3 ane, ase, ate, ein, ene, ide, ile, ine, ite, ium, oic, oin, one, ose, ous, yne 4 eine, idin, itol, oate, olic, onic 5 idine, onium, oside, ylene *warfare agent:* 7 tear gas 8 vesicant 10 mustard gas

chemin de fer 5 train 7 railway 8 railroad

chemise 4 slip

chemist 7 analyst 8 druggist 10 apothecary, pharmacist *American:* 4 Urey (Harold) 6 Remsen (Ira), Sumner (James) 7 Onsager (Lars), Pauling (Linus), Seaborg (Glenn) 8 Hoffmann (Roald), Langmuir (Irving), Mulliken (Robert), Richards (Theodore), Woodward (Robert) *Austrian:* 4 Kuhn (Richard) 5 Pregl (Fritz) *British:* 4 Abel (Frederick), Davy (Humphry), Todd (Alexander) 5 Boyle (Robert), Soddy (Frederick) 6 Dalton (John), Ramsay (William) 7 Faraday (Michael) 8 Smithson (James) 9 Priestley (Joseph), Wollaston (William) 10 Williamson (Alexander) *Dutch:* 8 van't Hoff (Jacobus) *French:* 5 Curie (Irene, Marie, Pierre) 7 Moissan (Henri), Pasteur (Louis) 8 Sabatier (Paul) 9 Gay-Lussac (Joseph), Lavoisier (Antoine), Berthelot (Marcellin) *German:* 5 Haber (Fritz) 6 Bunsen (Robert), Liebig (Justus von), Nernst (Walther), Wittig (Georg), Wohler (Friedrich) 7 Fischer (Emil, Ernst, Hans), Hofmann (August), Ostwald (Friedrich), Wallach (Otto), Wieland (Heinrich), Windaus (Adolf), Ziegler (Karl) 9 Zsigmondy (Richard) 10 Erlenmeyer (Richard), Staudinger (Hermann) 11 Willstatter (Richard) *Italian:* 5 Natta (Giulio) 8 Avogadro (Amedeo) *Russian:* 8 Semyonov (Nikolay), Zelinsky (Nikolay) 10 Mendeleyev (Dmitry) *Swedish:* 8 Svedberg (The, Theodor) 9 Berzelius (J. J.) *Swiss:* 6 Karrer (Paul), Werner (Alfred) (see also under NOBEL PRIZE WINNER)

chemist's vessel 4 vial 5 flask, phial 6 ampule, beaker, mortar, retort 7 ampoule 8 crucible, test tube

chemoreceptor 8 taste bud

cheongsam 5 dress

Cheops 5 Khufu

cherish 4 keep, save 5 adore, guard, honor, nurse, prize, value 6 admire, cosset, defend, dote on, esteem, foster, harbor, relish, revere, shield 7 apprize, care for, nourish, nurture, shelter, worship 8 conserve, hold dear, preserve, treasure, venerate 9 cultivate, delight in, entertain, reverence, safeguard 10 appreciate

Cherokee *chief:* 4 Ross (John) *historian:* 7 Sequoia, Sequoya 8 Sequoyah

cherry *dark:* 4 bing *family:* 4 rose 8 Rosaceae *genus:* 6 Prunus *hybrid:* 4 Duke *sour:* 7 morello *sweet:* 4 bing 7 mazzard, oxheart *wild:* 7 mazzard 10 maraschino

cherry bomb 11 firecracker
Cherry Orchard author 7 Chekhov (Anton)
cherrystone 4 clam 6 quahog
Chersonese 9 peninsula
cherub 4 babe, baby 5 angel, child, cupid, putto 6 infant 7 bambino 8 amoretto, innocent
cherubic 4 cute, rosy 6 chubby 7 angelic 8 adorable, innocent
chess *champion:* 3 Tal (Mikhail) 4 Euwe (Max) 6 Karpov (Anatoly), Lasker (Emanuel) 7 Fischer (Bobby), Kramnik (Vladimir), Smyslov (Vassily), Spassky (Boris) 8 Alekhine (Alexander), Kasparov (Garry), Steinitz (Wilhelm) 9 Botvinnik (Mikhail), Petrosian (Tigran) 10 Capablanca (José) *draw game:* 9 stalemate *goal:* 4 mate 9 checkmate *move:* 6 castle, gambit *opening:* 6 gambit *piece:* 4 king, pawn, rook 5 queen 6 bishop, knight *risk:* 6 gambit *term:* 5 check 7 capture, endgame
chest 3 box 4 kist 5 bosom, torso, trunk 6 breast, bureau, coffer, thorax 7 cabinet 8 cupboard, treasury 9 exchequer
chesterfield 4 sofa 5 divan 8 overcoat 9 davenport
chestnut 4 tree 5 color, horse 6 cliché, marron 10 chinquapin *extract:* 6 tannin *water:* 4 ling
cheval glass 6 mirror
chevalier 5 noble 7 knight 8 horseman 9 caballero, gentleman
chevet 4 apse
chevron 6 stripe
chew 3 eat, gum 4 bite, gnaw 5 champ, chomp, munch 6 crunch, devour, nibble 7 consume 8 ruminate 9 masticate
chewing gum 6 chicle
chew out 3 jaw 5 scold 6 rebuke, revile 7 bawl out, reprove, tell off, upbraid 8 lambaste, reproach 9 castigate, criticize, reprimand 10 tongue-lash, vituperate
Chiang ___ 7 Kai-shek
chic 4 mode, rage, tony 5 smart, style, swank, swish, vogue 6 modish, trendy, with-it 7 dashing, elegant, fashion, stylish 10 dernier cri 11 fashionable
chicane 4 dupe, fool, gull, hoax, ploy, ruse, wile 5 cavil, cheat, feint, fraud, trick 6 gambit 8 artifice, flimflam, hoodwink, trickery 9 bamboozle, deception, duplicity, stratagem, victimize 10 dishonesty, hanky-panky 13 double-dealing
chicanery 4 plot, ruse 5 fraud, trick 6 gambit 8 intrigue, trickery 9 deception, duplicity 10 subterfuge 11 machination, skulduggery

chichi 4 arty 5 gaudy, showy, swank 6 dressy, frilly, la-di-da 7 splashy 8 affected, précieux, precious 10 flamboyant, preciosity 11 affectation, fashionable, overrefined, pretentious 12 ostentatious 13 ornamentation
chick 3 kid, tot 4 girl 5 child 6 moppet, nipper, pullet 7 toddler 8 juvenile, young one 9 youngster
chickadee 8 titmouse *family:* 7 Paridae
chicken 4 fowl, funk 5 sissy, timid 6 coward, craven 7 dastard, gutless 8 cowardly, poltroon 11 lily-livered, yellowbelly 13 pusillanimous *breed:* 4 Java 6 Cochin 7 Cornish, Leghorn 9 Dominique, Orpington, Wyandotte 11 Jersey Giant, Rock Cornish *castrated:* 5 capon *cooking:* 5 fryer 7 broiler, roaster *disease:* 8 pullorum 11 coccidiosis *female:* 3 hen 6 pullet *genus:* 6 Gallus *male:* 4 cock 7 rooster 8 cockerel *pen:* 4 coop *small:* 6 bantam *sound:* 6 cackle
chicken feed 7 peanuts 8 pittance 11 chump change
chicken pox 9 varicella
chickpea 4 gram 8 garbanzo
chickweed 4 pink 7 potherb
chicle 3 gum 10 chewing gum
chicory 6 endive 7 witloof 9 radicchio
chide 3 kid 5 scold 6 berate, rebuke 7 chew out, lecture, reprove, upbraid 8 admonish, call down, reproach 9 castigate, reprimand
chiding 6 rebuke 7 reproof 8 reproach 9 reprimand 10 admonition 12 admonishment
chief 3 key 4 arch, boss, duce, head, lion, main, star 5 first, major, prime 6 führer, honcho, leader, master, primal, ruling, sachem 7 fuehrer, headman, highest, leading, premier, primary 8 cardinal, champion, dictator, dominant, eminence, foremost 9 numberone, principal, prominent 10 preeminent 11 outstanding, predominant *commander:* 4 CINC *prefix:* 4 arch *Spanish:* 4 jefe
Chief Justice 3 Jay (John) 4 Taft (William Howard) 5 Chase (Salmon), Stone (Harlan Fiske), Taney (Roger), Waite (Morrison), White (Edward) 6 Burger (Warren), Fuller (Melville) Hughes (Charles Evans), Vinson (Fred), Warren (Earl) 8 Marshall (John), Rutledge (John) 9 Ellsworth (Oliver), Rehnquist (William)
chiefly 6 mainly, mostly, notably 7 largely, overall 9 generally, primarily 10 especially 11 principally 12 preeminently 13 predominantly

chiffchaff 4 bird 7 warbler
chiffonier 5 chest 6 bureau 7 armoire, dresser
chigger 4 mite 6 chigoe, red bug
chignon 3 bun 4 knot
chilblain 4 sore 8 swelling 12 inflammation
child 3 kid 4 brat 5 minor, youth 6 cherub, infant, moppet, nipper, shaver, urchin 7 bambino, toddler 8 juvenile, small fry 9 youngling, youngster *combining form:* 3 ped 4 paed, pedo 5 paedo *gifted:* 7 prodigy *homeless:* 4 waif *parentless:* 6 orphan *Scottish:* 5 bairn *spoiled:* 4 brat *young:* 3 tot 4 baby, tike, tyke 6 infant, kiddie 8 bantling, weanling
childish 5 naive 7 puerile 8 arrested, immature 9 infantile
childless 6 barren 7 sterile
childlike 5 naive 6 docile, filial 7 natural, puerile 8 innocent, trustful, trusting 9 ingenuous
children 4 kids, seed 5 brood, heirs, issue 6 scions 7 progeny 9 offspring, posterity 11 descendants
child's play 4 snap 5 cinch, setup 6 breeze, picnic 8 cakewalk, duck soup, kid stuff, pushover 11 piece of cake
Chile *capital:* 8 Santiago *city:* 6 Temuco 10 Concepción, Talcahuano, Valparaíso, Viña del Mar 11 Antofagasta *conqueror:* 7 Almagro (Diego de) 8 Valdivia (Pedro de) *desert:* 7 Atacama *island:* 6 Easter 13 Juan Fernández *lake:* 10 Llanquihue *language:* 7 Spanish *leader:* 7 Allende (Salvador) 8 Pinochet (Augusto) *monetary unit:* 4 peso *mountain range:* 5 Andes *neighbor:* 4 Peru 7 Bolivia 9 Argentina *passage:* 5 Drake *river:* 6 Bío-Bío *strait:* 8 Magellan
Chileab *father:* 5 David *mother:* 7 Abigail
chili con ___ 5 carne
Chilion *father:* 9 Elimelech *mother:* 5 Naomi
chill 3 icy, raw 4 ague, cold, cool, hang 5 gelid, nippy 6 arctic, formal, freeze, frigid, frosty, wintry 7 distant, glacial, hostile 8 dispirit, freezing 10 demoralize, discourage, dishearten 11 emotionless, refrigerate
chiller 7 shocker 8 thriller
chilly 3 raw 4 cold 5 algid, brisk, crisp, nippy 6 frigid 7 bracing, coldish, hostile 10 unfriendly
chilopod 9 centipede
chime 3 din 4 bell, bong, dong, peal, ring, toll, tune 5 agree, clang, knell, sound 6 accord, strike 7 concord, harmony 8 carillon 9 agreement, harmonize 10 consonance, correspond

chime in 3 say 4 tell 5 state, utter 6 inject 7 break in, declare 9 interrupt
chimera 5 dream, fancy 7 fantasy, figment, monster, specter, spectre 8 illusion, phantasy 9 nightmare, pipe dream
Chimera *father:* 6 Typhon *mother:* 7 Echidna *slayer:* 11 Bellerophon
chimerical 6 absurd, unreal 7 fictive, utopian 8 delusive, delusory, fabulous, fanciful, illusory, mythical, spurious 9 ambitious, beguiling, deceptive, fantastic, fictional, imaginary, visionary 10 far-fetched, fictitious, improbable, outlandish 11 extravagant, unrealistic 12 preposterous, supposititious
chiming 8 harmonic 9 consonant 10 harmonious
chimney 3 lum 4 flue, tube, vent 5 stack 10 smokestack *corner:* 8 fireside 9 inglenook *output:* 4 soot 5 fumes, smoke
chimpanzee 3 ape 7 primate 10 anthropoid *kin:* 6 bonobo, gibbon 7 gorilla 9 orangutan
chin 3 gab, jaw, rap, yak 4 blab, chat, talk 8 converse
china 6 dishes 7 ceramic 8 crockery 9 porcelain, tableware 11 earthenware *maker:* 3 Bow 5 Hizen, Imari, Spode 6 Doccia, Sèvres 7 Bristol, Chelsea, Dresden, Limoges, Meissen 8 Caughley, Haviland, Wedgwood
China *bay:* 8 Hangzhou *capital:* 7 Beijing *city:* 4 Sian, Xi'an 5 Wuhan 6 Canton, Harbin, Mukden 7 Nanjing, Nanking, Tianjin 8 Shanghai, Shenyang, Tientsin 9 Chongqing, Guangzhou *desert:* 4 Gobi 10 Taklimakan *dynasty:* 3 Han, Sui 4 Ch'in, Chou, Ming, Sung, Tang, Yüan 5 Ch'ing, Shang 6 Manchu *ethnic group:* 3 Han *gulf:* 5 Bo Hai *heritage site:* 9 Great Wall *island:* 6 Hainan 8 Hong Kong *lake:* 5 Tai Hu 8 Hongze Hu, Poyang Hu 10 Dongting Hu *language:* 3 Han 8 Mandarin *leader:* 9 Mao Zedong, Sun Yat-sen 10 Kublai Khan, Mao Tse-tung 12 Deng Xiaoping 13 Chiang Kai-shek, Teng Hsiao-p'ing *monetary unit:* 4 yuan *monetary unit, former:* 4 tael *mountain, range:* 6 Kunlun 8 Himalaya 9 Altai Shan, Altay Shan, Himalayan 10 Gongga Shan *old name:* 6 Cathay *peninsula:* 7 Leizhou 8 Liaodong, Shandong *province:* 5 Anhui, Gansu, Hevei, Henan, Hubei, Hunan, Jilin 6 Fujian, Shanxi, Yunnan 7 Guizhou, Jiangsu, Jiangxi, Qinghai, Shaanxi, Sichuan 8 Liaoning, Shandong, Szechuan, Szechwan, Zhejiang 9 Guangdong 12 Heilongjiang *region:* 5 Tibet 6 Xizang 10 Nei Monggol

12 Ningxia Huizu 13 Inner Mongolia, Xinjiang Uygur *river:* 4 Amur 5 Chang, Huang, Tarim 6 Mekong, Yellow, Zangbo 7 Salween, Yangtze

china clay 6 kaolin

chinchilla 3 fur 6 rodent

chine 5 crest, ridge, spine 7 hogback 8 backbone

Chinese *aromatic root:* 7 ginseng *bamboo:* 7 whangee *boat:* 4 junk 6 sampan *bow:* 6 kowtow *cabbage:* 7 bok choy, pak choi *card game:* 6 fan-tan *cauterizing agent:* 4 moxa *prefix:* 4 Sino *conveyance:* 7 pedicab 8 rickshaw 10 jinricksha, jinrikisha *date:* 6 jujube *dialect:* 4 Amoy 8 Mandarin 9 Cantonese, Pekingese *dictator:* 9 Mao Zedong 10 Mao Tsetung 12 Deng Xiaoping 13 Teng Hsiaop'ing *dog:* 4 chow, Peke 8 chow chow 9 Pekingese *dynasty:* 3 Ch'i, Han, Qin, Sui, Wei, Yin 4 Ch'en, Ch'in, Chou, Hsia, Ming, Qing, Song, Sung, T'ang, Tsin, Yuan 5 Ch'ing, Liang, Shang 6 Manchu, Mongol, Shu Han *fabric:* 6 pongee, tussah 8 shantung *feminine principle:* 3 yin *feudal state:* 3 Wei *food:* 6 dim sum, lo mein, mantou, subgum, wonton 8 chop suey, chow mein 9 fried rice 10 egg foo yong, egg foo yung, Peking duck 11 egg foo young *fruit:* 6 lichee, litchi, lychee, loquat 7 kumquat 8 mandarin *gambling game:* 6 fan-tan *gong:* 6 tam-tam *gruel:* 6 congee *herb:* 5 ramie 7 ginseng *idol:* 4 joss *laborer:* 6 coolie *legendary emperor:* 7 Huangdi, Huang-ti *mandarin's residence:* 5 yamen *masculine principle:* 4 yang *money, silver:* 5 sycee *musical instrument:* 4 pipa *nurse:* 4 amah *official:* 8 mandarin *official seal:* 4 chop *oil:* 4 tung *ox:* 4 zebu *porcelain:* 4 Ming 7 celadon, Nankeen 8 mandarin *pottery:* 4 Kuan, Ming 5 Chien *puzzle:* 7 tangram *race:* 3 Mongoloid *religion:* 6 Taoism 8 Buddhism 12 Confucianism *sauce:* 3 soy *secret society:* 4 tong *sheep:* 5 urial *silkworm:* 6 tussah *tea:* 5 bohea, hyson 6 congou, oolong 8 souchong *temple:* 6 pagoda *tree:* 4 tung 6 ginkgo, loquat 7 kumquat *vine:* 5 kudzu

chink 4 rift, slit 5 caulk, cleft, crack, split 6 cranny 7 crevice, fissure, opening 8 aperture

chinquapin 3 nut 8 chestnut

chintzy 4 loud 5 cheap, gaudy, showy, tacky 6 flashy, garish, stingy, tawdry, vulgar 9 tasteless 12 meretricious

chip 4 flaw, nick 5 flake, notch, shard, slice, split, wafer, wedge 6 chisel, defect, paring, sliver 7 counter

chip in 6 ante up, kick in 7 pitch in 10 contribute 11 come through

chipper 4 spry 5 alert, brisk, perky, zesty 6 bright, lively, nimble 8 animated, spirited 9 sprightly, vivacious

chirk 4 buoy 5 cheer 7 animate, enliven, hearten 8 energize, inspirit 9 encourage 10 strengthen

chirography 6 script 8 longhand 10 penmanship 11 calligraphy, handwriting

chiromancy 9 palmistry

Chiron 7 centaur *father:* 6 Cronus *mother:* 7 Philyra *pupil:* 5 Jason 8 Achilles, Heracles, Hercules 9 Asclepius 11 Aesculapius

chiropody 8 podiatry

chiropractic founder 6 Palmer (Daniel)

chirp 4 chip, peep, sing 5 cheep, trill, tweet 6 warble 7 chirrup, twitter

chirpy 3 gay 5 sunny 6 blithe, cheery, sparky 7 buoyant, sparkly 8 cheerful, sunbeamy 9 lightsome

chirrup 4 chip, peep, sing 5 cheep, tweet 6 warble 7 chipper, twitter

chisel 3 gyp, hew 4 beat, bilk, scam 5 carve, cheat, cozen, cut in, gouge, trick 6 butt in, diddle, fleece, horn in, sculpt 7 defraud, engrave, intrude, swindle

chit 3 IOU, kid 4 memo, note, slip 5 child 6 moppet 7 invoice, voucher 8 notation 9 youngster 10 memorandum

chitchat 3 gab 5 chaff 6 babble, banter, gossip 7 chatter, palaver, prattle 8 badinage 9 small talk 12 tittle-tattle

chitter 4 chip, peep, sing 5 cheep, chirp, tweet 6 warble 7 chatter, chirrup, twitter

chivalric see CHIVALROUS

chivalrous 5 lofty, manly, noble 7 courtly, gallant, valiant 8 generous, gracious, knightly 9 honorable 10 benevolent, courageous 11 considerate, gentlemanly, magnanimous

chivy, chivvy 4 bait, ride 5 annoy, tease 6 badger, heckle, hector 7 torment 8 bullyrag

Chloe 11 shepherdess *beloved:* 7 Daphnis

chlordane 11 insecticide

Chloris *father:* 7 Amphion *husband:* 6 Neleus 8 Zephyrus *mother:* 5 Niobe *son:* 6 Nestor

chloroform 7 anodyne, solvent 10 anesthetic 11 anaesthetic

chockablock 4 full 6 jammed, loaded, packed 7 brimful, crammed, crowded, stuffed 9 jam-packed

chocolate 5 brown, cacao, cocoa

Chocolate Soldier composer 6 Straus (Oscar)

chocolate tree 5 cacao

choice 3 top **4** best, pick, rare, vote **5** cream, elite, prime, prize **6** chosen, dainty, option, rating, select **7** elegant, verdict **8** decision, delicate, druthers, election, judgment, selected, superior, volition **9** exquisite, selection **9** selection **10** preference **11** alternative **13** determination *even:* **6** toss-up

choir 6 chorus **7** chorale *area:* **4** loft **7** chancel, gallery *leader:* **6** cantor **8** choragus **9** precentor *member:* **9** chorister *section:* **4** alto, bass **5** tenor **7** soprano *vestment:* **4** gown, robe **5** cotta **8** surplice

choke 3 gag **4** clog, plug, stop **5** block, close **6** stifle **7** congest, occlude, silence, smother **8** obstruct, strangle, throttle **9** constrict, suffocate **10** asphyxiate

choking 8 quashing, stifling **10** repression, smothering, squelching, strangling **11** suppression

choleric 5 angry, fiery, irate **6** fierce, heated **7** enraged **8** incensed, wrathful **9** irascible, splenetic **10** infuriated **11** hot-tempered **13** quick-tempered

cholla 6 cactus **7** opuntia

Chomolungma 7 Everest (Mt.)

chomp 4 bite, chew **5** munch **6** crunch **9** masticate

choose 3 opt **4** cull, mark, pick, take, want **5** adopt, elect, favor **6** decide, desire, opt for, prefer, select **7** embrace, pick out **8** decide on, handpick **9** single out

choosy 5 fussy, picky **7** finical, finicky **9** finicking, selective **10** fastidious, particular, pernickety **11** persnickety

chop 3 cut, hew **4** dice, fell, hack, hash, seal, veer **5** cut up, grade, mince **7** quality

chop-chop 4 fast **5** quick **6** presto, pronto **7** quickly, rapidly **8** promptly, speedily **9** posthaste **12** lickety-split

chophouse 10 restaurant

Chopin, Frédéric *birthplace:* **6** Poland *instrument:* **5** piano *lover:* **4** Sand (George) *work:* **7** mazurka **8** nocturne **9** polonaise

choppy 4 wavy **5** jerky, rough **6** ripply, stormy, uneven **7** erratic **8** variable **9** turbulent, unsettled

choral section 5 altos **6** basses, tenors **8** sopranos

chord 5 triad **6** tetrad **7** harmony *sequence:* **7** cadence **11** progression

chore 3 job **4** duty, task **5** stint, trial **6** devoir, effort **7** routine **10** assignment, obligation **11** tribulation

choreograph 6 devise, direct, map out **7** arrange, compose **11** orchestrate

choreographer *American:* **4** Feld (Elliot), Holm (Hanya), Lang (Pearl) **5** Ailey (Alvin), Fosse (Bob), Limón (José), Shawn (Ted), Tharp (Twyla) **6** Duncan (Isadora), Dunham (Katherine), Fokine (Michel), Graham (Martha), Morris (Mark), Taylor (Paul), Tetley (Glen) **7** de Mille (Agnes), Jamison (Judith), Joffrey (Robert), Martins (Peter), Massine (Leonide), Robbins (Jerome), St. Denis (Ruth), Tamiris (Helen), Weidman (Charles) **8** Champion (Gower, Marge), Humphrey (Doris), Nikolais (Alwin), Villella (Edward) **10** Balanchine (George), Cunningham (Merce) *Australian:* **8** Helpmann (Robert) *Cuban:* **6** Alonso (Alicia) *Danish:* **5** Bruhn (Erik) **7** Martins (Peter) **12** Bournonville (August) *English:* **5** Dolin (Anton), Tudor (Antony) **6** Ashton (Frederick), Weaver (John) **7** Markova (Alicia), Rambert (Marie) **8** de Valois (Ninette), Helpmann (Robert) **9** MacMillan (Kenneth) *French:* **5** Lifar (Serge) **6** Béjart (Maurice), Perrot (Jules), Petipa (Marius) **7** Camargo (Marie), Massine (Léonide), Noverre (Jean-Georges) *German:* **5** Jooss (Kurt) *Hungarian:* **5** Laban (Rudolf) *Mexican:* **5** Limón (José) *Russian:* **5** Lifar (Serge) **6** Fokine (Michel), Petipa (Marius) **8** Nijinska (Bronislava), Nijinsky (Vaslav)

chorography 3 map **7** mapping **8** features **9** mapmaking

chortle 5 laugh **6** giggle, guffaw, hee-haw, titter **7** chuckle, snicker

chorus 5 choir **7** refrain

chorus girl 7 chorine

chosen 4 pick **5** elect, elite, named **6** called, marked, pegged, picked, select **7** blessed **8** selected **9** appointed, delegated, exclusive

Chou ___ 5 En-lai

chouse 3 gyp **4** bilk, clip, dupe, herd **5** cheat, cozen, drive, trick **6** diddle, fleece **7** defraud, swindle **8** flimflam

chow 4 eats, feed, food, grub, meal

chowchow 6 medley, relish **7** mélange

chowderhead 4 boob, clod, dodo, dolt, dope, fool **5** chump, dunce, idiot, noddy **6** dimwit, nitwit, noodle **7** halfwit, schnook **8** dumbbell, numskull **9** lamebrain, numbskull

chowhound 7 glutton **8** gourmand

chrism 3 oil **4** balm **5** cream, salve **6** cerate **7** unction, unguent **8** ointment

christen 3 dub **4** call, name, term **5** title

7 asperse, baptize, immerse 8 dedicate, sprinkle 9 designate

christening 7 baptism

Christian *denomination:* 6 Mormon, Quaker 7 Baptist, Friends 8 Anglican, Catholic, Lutheran, Moravian, Nazarene, Reformed 9 Calvinist, Episcopal, Mennonite, Methodist, Unitarian 10 Anabaptist 11 Pentecostal 12 Episcopalian, Presbyterian, Universalist *Eastern rite:* 5 Uniat 6 Uniate *Egyptian:* 4 Copt *love feast:* 5 agape *martyr, first:* 7 Stephen *symbol:* 3 IHS 4 fish, rood 5 cross 6 Chi-Rhos 7 ichthus

Christiania 4 Oslo

Christian Science founder 4 Eddy (Mary Baker)

Christie, Agatha *character:* 6 Marple (Jane), Poirot (Hercule) *novel:* 14 Death on the Nile 24 Murder on the Orient Express *play:* 9 Mousetrap (The) 24 Witness for the Prosecution

Christina's World painter 5 Wyeth (Andrew)

Christmas 4 Noel, yule 8 Nativity, yuletide *symbol:* 7 Yule log

Christmas Carol, A *author:* 7 Dickens (Charles) *character:* 7 Scrooge (Ebenezer), Tiny Tim 8 Cratchit (Bob)

Christogram 6 Chi-Rho

Christopher Robin creator 5 Milne (A. A.)

chromatic 8 colorful 10 accidental

chromatin thread 7 spireme

chromosome component 3 DNA 4 gene 8 telomere 10 centromere, chromomere

chronic 5 usual 6 wonted 7 routine 8 constant, enduring, habitual 9 ceaseless, confirmed, continual, customary, incessant, perennial, perpetual, recurrent, recurring 10 accustomed, continuing, habituated, inveterate, persisting 11 unrelenting

chronicle 4 list 6 annals, record, relate, report 7 account, history, narrate, recital, recount 8 describe 9 narration, narrative

chronicler 8 narrator, recorder, reporter 9 historian

chronograph 5 clock, watch 9 timepiece

chronology 5 annal 6 annals, record 7 history 8 calendar, register, schedule 9 timetable

chronometer 5 clock, watch 9 timepiece

chrysalis 4 pupa 8 covering

Chryses *captor:* 9 Agamemnon *father:* 7 Chryses

Chrysippus *father:* 6 Pelops *slayer:* 6 Atreus 8 Thyestes

chthonic 6 Hadean, nether 7 hellish, satanic 8 accursed, infernal, plutonic 9 plutonian, Tartarean 10 sulphurous

chubby 5 hefty, husky, plump, podgy, pudgy, round, tubby 6 chunky, fleshy, portly, rotund, stocky, zaftig 8 plumpish, roly-poly

chuck 3 pat, tap 4 beef. cast, hurl, junk, oust, shed, toss 5 ditch, fling, heave, nudge, pitch, scrap, throw 6 give up, reject 7 abandon, boot out, discard, dismiss, kick out 8 jettison, throw out 9 throw away

chucker 7 bouncer

chuckle 5 laugh 6 giggle, guffaw, heehaw, titter 7 chortle, snicker

chucklehead see CHOWDERHEAD

chuff 3 oaf 4 boor, lout, rube 5 churl, clown, yahoo, yokel 7 bumpkin, hayseed 10 clodhopper

chum 3 pal 4 mate 5 buddy, crony 6 friend, salmon 7 comrade 8 sidekick 9 companion

chummy 4 cozy 5 close, pally, palsy, thick 8 familiar, intimate 10 buddy-buddy, palsy-walsy

chump 3 oaf, sap 4 boob, dolt, dope, dupe, fool, goof, goon, gull, mark 5 booby, dummy, dunce, patsy 6 pigeon, sucker, turkey 7 fall guy, fathead 8 dolthead, lunkhead

chunk 3 sum, wad 4 clod, hunk, lump, slab 5 clump 6 nugget

chunky 5 beefy, dumpy, hefty, husky, plump, pudgy, squat, stout 6 chubby, fleshy, portly, rotund, stocky, stubby, stumpy 8 heavyset, thickset

church 4 cult, fane, kirk, sect 5 creed, faith 6 temple 7 minster 8 basilica, religion 9 cathedral, communion 10 tabernacle 12 denomination *adjunct:* 6 belfry 7 steeple 9 bell tower *basin:* 4 font 5 stoup *bench:* 3 pew *bishop's:* 9 cathedral *calendar:* 4 ordo *caretaker:* 6 sexton *chapel:* 7 oratory *council:* 5 synod *court:* 4 rota 10 consistory *creed:* 6 Nicene 8 Apostles' *district:* 6 parish 7 diocese *father:* 5 Basil 6 Jerome, Justin, Origen 7 Ambrose, Clement 8 Ignatius 9 Augustine 10 Chrysostom, Tertullian, theologian *fund-raiser:* 6 bazaar *governing body:* 5 curia 7 classis 10 consistory, presbytery *head:* 4 pope 7 pontiff *law:* 5 canon *member:* 11 communicant *of a monastery:* 7 minster *officer:* 5 elder, vicar 6 beadle, deacon, sexton, verger, warden 9 presbyter, sacristan *part:* 4 apse, bema, loft, nave 5 aisle, altar, choir 6 vestry 7 chancel, gallery, narthex, steeple 8 sacristy, transept 9 baptistry, sanctuary 10 baptistery, clerestory *porch:* 6 parvis 7 galilee *reader:* 6 lector *recess:* 4 apse *revenue:* 5 tithe *room:* 6 vestry 8 sacristy *Scottish:*

4 kirk *seats for clergy:* 7 sedilia *service:*
4 mass 6 matins 7 vespers 8 evensong
9 communion *small:* 6 chapel *tribunal:*
4 rota *vault:* 5 crypt

Churchill, Winston *daughter:* 4 Mary
5 Diana, Sarah *father:* 8 Randolph *mother:* 6 Jennie *Order:* 6 Garter *phrase:*
11 Iron Curtain *son:* 8 Randolph *trademark:* 5 cigar *wife:* 10 Clementine

church key 9 can opener

churchman 6 bishop, cleric, divine, parson, pastor, priest 8 minister, preacher,
reverend 9 clergyman 12 ecclesiastic

churl 3 oaf 4 boor, clod, lout, rube
5 chuff, clown, yahoo, yokel 6 mucker
7 bumpkin, hayseed 10 clodhopper

churlish 4 base, curt, dour, rude 5 blunt,
crude, gruff, surly 6 coarse, crusty, oafish, vulgar 7 boorish, brusque, loutish,
lowbred, uncivil 8 cloddish, clownish
10 unmannerly 11 clodhopping, uncivilized 12 discourteous

churn 4 boil, foam, roil, stir 5 froth,
swirl 6 bubble, seethe, simmer, stir up
7 agitate, ferment, smolder

chute 4 fall, ramp 5 falls, rapid, slide,
spout 6 rapids 7 cascade, channel,
descent 8 cataract 9 spinnaker, waterfall

chutzpah 4 gall 5 brass, cheek, moxie,
nerve, spunk 8 audacity, temerity
10 effrontery

CIA *predecessor:* 3 OSS

ciao 4 by-by, ta-ta 5 adieu, adios, aloha,
hello, howdy 6 bye-bye, good-by, so
long 7 good-bye, welcome 8 farewell
9 greetings

cicatrix 4 scar 13 scarification

Cicero *forte:* 7 oratory *target:* 8 Catiline
10 Mark Antony

cicerone 4 guru 5 coach, guide, tutor
6 docent, escort, mentor 7 adviser
9 counselor, tour guide

Cid, El (Le) 4 epic, hero, play, poem
5 opera *composer:* 8 Massenet (Jules)
meaning: 4 lord *name:* 4 Díaz (Rodrigo,
Ruy) 5 Bivar *playwright:* 9 Corneille
(Pierre) *sword:* 6 Colada, Tizona *wife:*
6 Jimena, Ximena

cigar 5 stogy 6 corona, Havana, stogie
7 cheroot 8 panatela, perfecto *case:*
7 humidor *color:* 5 claro 6 maduro
8 colorado

cigarette 3 fag 4 butt 5 smoke 6 gasper
10 coffin nail

cilium 4 hair, lash 7 eyelash

Cimmerian 4 dark 5 dusky, murky
6 gloomy 7 hellish, shadowy, stygian
8 infernal, plutonic 9 plutonian

cinch 4 snap 5 girth, setup 6 assure,
breeze, ensure, fasten, insure, picnic,

secure, shoo-in 8 duck soup, kid stuff,
pushover 9 certainty 10 child's play

cinchona bark extract 7 quinine

cincture 4 band, belt, sash 6 girdle
9 waistband

cinders 3 ash 4 coal, lava, slag 5 ashes,
dross 6 embers 8 clinkers

cinema 4 film, show 5 flick, movie
6 movies 7 picture, theater, theatre
12 silver screen 13 motion picture

cinereous 4 ashy, gray, grey 5 ashen
7 ashlike

cinnabar 3 ore 7 mineral, pigment 9 vermilion *color:* 3 red

cinnamon bark 6 cassia

cinnamon stone 6 garnet 8 essonite

cipher 4 code, zero 5 aught, count, digit
6 figure, naught, nobody, number,
reckon, symbol 7 compute, integer,
numeral 8 estimate, monogram 9 calculate, nonentity 11 whole number

ciphering 8 figuring 9 computing, reckoning 10 arithmetic 11 calculation,
computation

circa 4 near, nigh 5 about 6 around
7 roughly 13 approximately

circadian 5 daily 6 cyclic 7 diurnal, regular 9 quotidian

Circe 5 siren 9 sorceress *brother:*
6 Aeëtes *father:* 3 Sol 6 Helios *home:*
5 Aeaea *lover:* 7 Ulysses 8 Odysseus
niece: 5 Medea *son:* 5 Comus
9 Telegonus

Circean 6 luring 8 alluring, enticing,
fetching, tempting 10 bewitching

circinate 6 coiled 7 rounded

circle 4 belt, gyre, hoop, loop, ring
5 crowd, cycle, group, orbit, wheel,
whorl 6 clique, corona, girdle, gyrate,
rotary, rotate 7 compass, coterie, cro-
nies, friends, revolve, rondure 8 surround 9 encompass 10 associates, com-
panions, revolution *bisector:* 8 diameter
colored: 6 areola *combining form:* 3 gyr
4 cycl, gyro 5 cyclo *graph:* 8 pie chart
luminous: 4 aura, halo 6 corona, nimbus 7 aureole *part:* 3 arc 6 sector
8 quadrant *small:* 4 disk 7 annulet

circlet 4 band, ring 6 bangle, diadem
8 bracelet, headband *for head or helmet:*
7 coronal

circuit 3 lap, way 4 loop, tour, trip, turn
5 ambit, cycle, orbit, round, route,
track 6 course, hookup, league 7 compass, journey, pathway, travels 8 district, rotation 9 perimeter, periphery,
round trip 10 revolution, roundabout
11 association, circulation 13 circumference

circuitous 7 devious, oblique, winding
8 circular, indirect, tortuous 10 collat-

eral, convoluted, meandering, round-about

circuit rider 5 judge **8** minister, preacher **9** clergyman

circular 4 bill **5** flier, flyer, round **7** annular, cycloid, discoid, handout, leaflet **8** handbill **9** throwaway *file:* **11** wastebasket *motion:* **4** eddy, gyre, spin **5** whirl **8** gyration, rotation **10** revolution *plate:* **4** disc, dish, disk

circularize 4 poll **6** survey **7** canvass **9** advertise, publicize

circulate 4 flow **6** rotate, spread **7** diffuse, radiate, revolve **8** disperse **9** propagate **10** distribute **11** disseminate

circulation 4 flow **6** spread **8** currency **9** diffusion **11** propagation **12** transmission **13** dissemination

circumciser 5 mohel

circumcision, Jewish 4 bris **9** Brit Milah

circumference 3 rim **5** ambit **6** border, bounds, limits, margin **7** circuit, compass **8** boundary, confines **9** perimeter, periphery

circumflex 9 diacritic

circumjacent 11 surrounding

circumlocution 8 pleonasm, verbiage **9** euphemism, loquacity, prolixity, verbosity, wordiness **10** redundancy **11** periphrasis, verboseness

circumnavigate 5 skirt **6** bypass, detour **8** sidestep

circumnavigator 4 Cook (James) **5** Drake (Francis) **8** Magellan (Ferdinand), van Noort (Olivier) **9** Cavendish (Thomas)

circumscribe 5 cramp, limit **6** fetter, hamper **7** confine, delimit, enclose, mark off, outline, trammel **8** restrict, surround **9** constrict

circumscribed 5 bound, fixed **6** finite, narrow, strait **7** bounded, cramped, limited, precise **8** confined, definite, hampered **10** restrained, restricted **11** determinate

circumscription 5 cramp, limit, stint **6** border, margin **8** boundary **9** perimeter, restraint, stricture **10** constraint, definition, limitation **11** confinement, restriction **12** ball and chain, delimitation **13** constrainment

circumspect 4 safe, wary **5** chary **7** careful, guarded, prudent **8** cautious, discreet, gingerly **11** calculating

circumstance 4 fact, item **5** event, thing **6** detail, factor **7** adjunct, element, episode, feature **8** accident, incident, occasion **9** component, condition, happening **10** occurrence, particular **11** concomitant, constituent, eventuality

circumstantial 4 full **5** close, exact **6** strict **7** precise, replete **8** accurate, complete, detailed, thorough **9** elaborate, pertinent **10** blow-by-blow, ceremonial, exhaustive, incidental, particular

circumvent 5 avoid, elude, evade, hem in, skirt **6** bypass, detour **8** outflank, sidestep

circumvolution 4 gyre, turn **5** wheel, whirl **8** gyration, rotation **10** revolution

circus 4 ring **5** arena **6** big top **9** spectacle **12** amphitheater *animal:* **4** bear, flea, lion, seal **5** horse, tiger **8** elephant *attraction:* **5** freak **8** sideshow *owner:* **6** Bailey (James), Barnum (P. T.) **8** Ringling (Bros.) *performer:* **5** clown, tamer **7** acrobat, athlete, juggler, tumbler **9** aerialist, fire eater *worker:* **10** roustabout

citadel 4 fort **7** redoubt **8** fastness, fortress **10** stronghold *of Carthage:* **5** Bursa, Byrsa *Russian:* **7** Kremlin

citation 5 quote **6** eulogy **7** excerpt, mention, summons, tribute **8** accolade, encomium **9** panegyric, quotation, reference **12** commendation

cite 4 name, tell **5** offer, quote **6** adduce, recall, summon **7** arraign, mention, present, refer to, specify **8** point out, remember **9** recollect

citizen 7 burgess, burgher, subject **8** civilian, national, resident, townsman **10** inhabitant

Citizen Kane director 6 Welles (Orson)

citron 4 tree **5** melon

citrus *family:* **3** rue **8** Rutaceae *fruit:* **4** lime, ugli **5** lemon **6** citron, orange, pomelo **7** kumquat, tangelo **8** bergamot, mandarin, shaddock **9** tangerine **10** grapefruit

city 4 burg **5** urban **7** burghal **9** municipal **10** metropolis *combining form:* **5** polis *Eternal:* **4** Rome *French:* **5** ville *heavenly:* **4** Sion, Zion *Latin:* **4** urbs *Motor:* **7** Detroit *of Bells:* **10** Strasbourg *of Bridges:* **6** Bruges *of Brotherly Love:* **12** Philadelphia *of David:* **9** Jerusalem *official:* **5** mayor **7** manager **8** alderman **10** councilman *of God:* **6** heaven **8** paradise *of Gold:* **8** Eldorado *of Kings:* **4** Lima *of Lights:* **5** Paris *of Lilies:* **8** Florence *of Masts:* **6** London *of Rams:* **6** Canton *of Refuge:* **6** Medina *of Saints:* **8** Montreal *of Seven Hills:* **4** Rome *of the dead:* **10** necropolis *of Victory:* **5** Cairo *planner:* **8** urbanist *section:* **4** slum, ward **5** block, plaza **6** barrio, ghetto, square, uptown **8** business, downtown, red-light **11** residential *slicker:* **4** dude *windy:* **7** Chicago

city-state, Greek 5 Argos, polis 6 Athens, Delphi, poleis (plural), Sparta, Thebes 7 Corinth

city, town, village (see also CAPITAL) *Afghanistan:* 5 Balkh, Farah, Herat, Kushk 6 Konduz 8 Kandahar, Qandahar 9 Jalalabad *Alabama:* 3 Opp 4 Arab, Boaz, Elba 5 Selma 6 Athens, Dothan, Mobile 7 Decatur, Florala 8 Prichard 10 Birmingham, Huntsville, Scottsboro, Tuscaloosa 12 Muscle Shoals *Alaska:* 4 Nome 5 Kenai, Sitka 6 Barrow, Bethel, Kodiak, Valdez 9 Anchorage, Fairbanks, Ketchikan 11 Point Barrow *Albania:* 4 Fier 5 Berat, Korçë, Kukës, Vlorë *Alberta:* 4 Olds 5 Hanna, Leduc, Taber 7 Calgary 8 Edmonton 10 Lethbridge 11 Medicine Hat *Algeria:* 4 Bône, Oran 5 Batna, Blida, Médéa, Saïda, Sétif 6 Annaba, Bechar 11 Constantine *Angola:* 6 Huambo 7 Lubango 8 Benguela *Argentina:* 4 Azul, Goya 5 Junin, Lanus, Lujan, Merlo, Salta, Tigre 6 Parana 7 Córdoba, La Plata, La Rioja, Mendoza, Rosario, San Juan, Santa Fe 9 Catamarca 11 Bahía Blanca, Mar del Plata *Arizona:* 3 Ajo 4 Eloy, Mesa, Yuma 5 Globe, Tempe 6 Tucson 7 Sun City, Winslow 8 Glendale, Prescott 9 Flagstaff, Tombstone 10 Casa Grande, Scottsdale *Arkansas:* 4 Mena 5 Beebe, Cabot, Earle, Ozark, Wynne 9 Fort Smith, Pine Bluff, Texarkana 10 Hot Springs *Armenia:* 6 Gyumri 8 Vanadzor *Australia:* 3 Ayr 5 Dalby, Dubbo, Perth, Unley 6 Darwin, Sydney 8 Adelaide, Brisbane, Randwick 9 Bankstown, Blacktown, Gold Coast, Melbourne, Newcastle 10 Kalgoorlie, Parramatta, Sutherland, Wollongong 12 Alice Springs *Austria:* 4 Enns, Graz, Linz, Wels 5 Steyr, Traun 8 Salzburg 9 Innsbruck 10 Klagenfurt *Azerbaijan:* 5 Gäncä 8 Sumqayit 9 Kirovabad *Bahamas:* 8 Freeport *Bangladesh:* 5 Bogra, Pabna 6 Khulna, Sylhet 7 Barisal, Comilla, Jessore, Rangpur, Saidpur 10 Chittagong *Belarus:* 5 Brest, Gomel, Mozyr, Pinsk 6 Grodno, Homyel', Hrodna 7 Mogilev, Vitebsk 8 Babruysk, Mahilyow 9 Vitsyebsk *Belgium:* 3 Ath, Hal, Huy, Mol 4 Amay, Dour, Geel, Genk, Gent, Hoei, Luik, Mons, Vise 5 Aalst, Arlon, Diest, Evere, Ghent, Halle, Ieper, Jumet, Leuze, Liège, Namur, Ronse, Theux, Wavre, Ypres 6 Bruges, Brugge 7 Antwerp, Hasselt, Louvain 8 Oostende 9 Charleroi *Benin:* 5 Kandi 6 Abomey 7 Parakou *Bolivia:* 5 Oruro, Uyuni 6 Potosí 9 Santa Cruz 10 Cochabamba

Bosnia and Herzegovina: 5 Bihac, Brcko, Jajce, Tuzla 6 Mostar, Zenica 9 Banja Luka *Botswana:* 4 Maun 5 Kanye 11 Francistown *Brazil:* 4 Codo, Pará 5 Bahia, Bauru, Belém, Ceara, Natal 6 Campos, Canoas, Caxias, Ilheus, Maceio, Manaus, Olinda, Recife, Santos 7 Aracaju, Caruaru, Goiania, Jundiai, Marilia, Niteroi, Pelotas, São Luis, Uberaba, Vitória 8 Campinas, Colatina, Curitiba, Londrina, Salvador, Santarém, São Paulo, Sorocaba, Teresina 9 Caratinga, Fortaleza, Guarulhos, Rio Grande 10 Guarapuava, Joao Pessoa, Juiz de Fora, Nova Iguaçu, Pernambuco, Petropolis, Piracicaba, Pôrto Velho, Santa Maria, Santo André, São Gonçalo, Uberlândia 11 Campo Grande, Caxias do Sul, Ponta Grossa, Pôrto Alegre 12 Montes Claros, Rio de Janeiro, Teófilo Otoni, Volta Redonda 13 Belo Horizonte, Campina Grande, Duque de Caxias, Florianopolis, Mogi das Cruzes, Riberião Prêto *British Columbia:* 5 Comox 6 Surrey 7 Burnaby 8 Richmond 9 Vancouver *Bulgaria:* 3 Lom 4 Ruse 5 Varna, Vidin 6 Burgas 7 Plovdiv 11 Stara Zagora *California:* 4 Brea, Galt, Lodi, Ojai 5 Arvin, Azusa, Ceres, Chico, Chino, Dixon, Hemet, Indio, Norco, Ripon, Ukiah, Wasco, Yreka 6 Downey, Encino, Fresno, Oxnard, Pomona, Sonoma 7 Anaheim, Burbank, Compton, Fremont, Hayward, Modesto, Oakland, San Jose, Seaside, Soledad, Van Nuys 8 Berkeley, Glendale, Palo Alto, Pasadena, San Diego, Santa Ana, Stockton, Torrance, Yuba City 9 El Segundo, Hollywood, Long Beach, Menlo Park, Riverside, Sausalito 10 Chula Vista, Culver City, Los Angeles, San Leandro, Santa Clara 11 Bakersfield, Laguna Beach, Pebble Beach, Redwood City, San Clemente, Santa Monica 12 Beverly Hills, Mission Viejo, Redondo Beach, San Francisco, Santa Barbara 13 San Bernardino, San Luis Obispo *Cambodia:* 8 Siem Reap 10 Battambang 11 Kompong Cham *Cameroon:* 4 Buea, Edea 5 Kribi, Lomie 6 Douala 7 Bamenda, Foumban 9 Bafoussam *Canada:* 4 York 5 Banff 6 London, Oshawa, Ottawa, Regina, St. John 7 Brandon, Burnaby, Calgary, Halifax, Iqaluit, Red Deer, St. John's, Sudbury, Toronto, Windsor 8 Hamilton, Montreal, Moose Jaw, North Bay, Victoria, Winnipeg 9 Dartmouth, Kitchener, Longueuil, North York, Saint John, Saskatoon, Vancouver 10 Lethbridge, Saint John's, Sherbrooke, Thunder

Bay, Whitehorse **11** Fredericton, Medicine Hat, Mississauga, Scarborough, Yellowknife **12** Peterborough, Prince Albert, Prince George **13** Charlottetown, Trois-Rivières *Central African Republic:* **5** Bouar **7** Bambari *Chad:* **4** Sarh **6** Abéché *Chile:* **4** Lebu, Lota, Tomé **5** Ancud, Angol, Arica, Maipu, Penco, Rengo, Talca **6** Temuco **7** Copiapó, Iquique **8** Rancagua **10** Concepción, Talcahuano, Valparaíso **11** Antofagasta *China:* **4** Amoy, Jian, Luan, Xi'an, Yaan **5** Hefei, Jilin, Jinan, Lhasa, Qinan, Ssuan, Wuhan, Yibin, Yumen **6** Andong, Anqing, Anshan, Anshun, Anyang, Beihai, Canton, Dalian, Datong, Foshan, Fushun, Fuzhou, Guilin, Haikou, Handan, Harbin, Hohhot, Hoihao, Jilong, Luzhou, Mukden, Ningbo, Pengbu, Suzhou, Ürümqi, Xiamen, Xining, Xuzhou, Yanggu, Yichun, Yining, Zhangi, Zhaoan **7** Baoding, Changan, Chengdu, Dandong, Guiyang, Huainan, Jiamusi, Jiaxing, Kaifeng, Kunming, Lanzhou, Luoshan, Luoyang, Nanking, Nanjiang, Nanning, Shantou, Tianjin, Taiyuan, Wanxian, Weifang, Yizhang, Zhuzhou **8** Changchi, Changsha, Dangshan, Hangzhou, Hanzhong, Hengyang, Huangshi, Jiangmen, Jiujiang, Kueiyang, Liaoyang, Nanchang, Shanghai, Shangrao, Shaoyang, Shenyang, Tianshui, Yinchuan, Zhenjing **9** Changchun, Chenjiang, Chongqing, Chungking, Guangzhou, Huangshih, Zhengzhou, Zhenjiang **10** Jingdezhen, Laojunmiao **11** Qinhuangdao, Zhangjiakou *Colombia:* **4** Buga, Cali **5** Bello, Mocoa, Neiva, Ocaña, Pasto, Tuluá, Tunja **6** Cúcuta, Ibagué **7** Ciénaga, Palmira, Pereira, Popayán **8** Medellín, Montería **9** Cartagena, Manizales **10** Santa Marta **11** Bucaramanga **12** Barranquilla *Colorado:* **6** Arvada, Aurora, Golden, Salida **7** Alamosa, Boulder, Durango, Greeley, La Junta **8** Brighton, Gunnison, Lakewood, Longmont, Loveland, Montrose, Thornton **9** Englewood, Estes Park, Leadville, Littleton, Rocky Ford, Telluride **10** Broomfield, Castle Rock, Fort Lupton, Fort Morgan, Monte Vista, Northglenn, Wheat Ridge **11** Fort Collins **13** Grand Junction *Congo (Zaire):* **4** Boma **6** Bukavu **7** Kolwezi **8** Bandundu **9** Kisangani **10** Lubumbashi **12** Stanleyville *Congo-Brazzaville:* **11** Pointe-Noire *Connecticut:* **5** Byram **6** Darien, Easton, Granby, Groton,

Haddam **7** Ansonia, Bethany, Danbury, Enfield, Meriden, Milford, Newtown, Niantic, Norwalk, Norwich, Old Lyme, Pomfret, Windham **8** Branford, Cromwell, East Lyme, Guilford, New Haven, Simsbury, Stamford, Suffield, Westport **9** Greenwich, New Canaan, Newington, New London, Rocky Hill, Southbury, Waterbury, Waterford **10** Bridgeport, Brookfield, East Haddam, Farmington, Kensington, Litchfield, New Britain, New Milford, North Haven, Plainville, Ridgefield, Stonington, Torrington **11** Beacon Falls, Glastonbury, Middlefield, Old Saybrook, Southington, Wallingford, Willimantic **12** Wethersfield *Costa Rica:* **8** Alajuela **10** Puntarenas **11** Puerto Limón *Croatia:* **4** Pula **5** Sisak, Split, Zadar **6** Osijek, Rijeka, Zagreb **9** Dubrovnik *Cuba:* **5** Banes, Bauta **6** Bayamo **7** Holguín **8** Camagüey, Marianao, Matanzas, Santiago **10** Cienfuegos, Guantánamo **11** Pinar del Río *Cyprus:* **7** Kyrenia, Larnaca, Nicosia **8** Limassol **9** Famagusta *Czech Republic:* **4** Brno, Zlín **5** Plzen **7** Liberec, Olomouc, Ostrava **10** Bratislava *Delaware:* **5** Lewes **7** Seaford **10** Harrington, Wilmington, Winterthur *Denmark:* **5** Århus, Skive, Vejle **6** Alborg, Odense, Viborg **13** Frederiksberg *Dominican Republic:* **4** Azua, Bani, Moca **5** Bonao, Nagua **8** Barahona, Santiago *Ecuador:* **4** Loja **5** Canar, Daule, Manta, Pinas **7** Machala **8** Riobamba **9** Guayaquil *Egypt:* **4** Giza, Idfu, Isna, Qena **5** Aswan, Asyut, Benha, Disuq, Girga, Luxor, Minuf, Tahta, Tanta **6** Helwan **7** El Arish, Zagazig **8** Damanhur, Damietta, El Faiyum, Ismailia, Port Said **10** Alexandria *Eire:* **4** Athy, Birr, Cobh, Cork, Naas, Tuam **5** Ennis, Sligo **6** Carlow, Galway, Tralee **7** Dundalk, Kildare, Wexford, Wicklow **8** Drogheda, Kilkenny, Limerick, Monaghan **9** Castlebar, Killarney, Tipperary, Waterford **10** Balbriggan *El Salvador:* **7** La Unión **8** Santa Ana **9** Sonsonate *England:* **4** Bath, Eton, Hove, Ryde, York **5** Brent, Brigg, Colne, Corby, Cowes, Derby, Dover, Egham, Eling, Esher, Eston, Goole, Leeds, Leigh, Lewes, Luton, Poole, Ryton, Wigan **6** Bexley, Bolton, Dudley, Durham, Exeter, Merton, Oldham, Oxford, Torbay, Warley, Welwyn **7** Bristol, Bromley, Croydon, Hackney, Ipswich, Malvern, Norwich, Salford, Seaford, Walsall **8** Abingdon, Basildon, Bradford, Brighton, Coventry, Hastings, Hatfield, Havering, Hertford,

Kingston, Lewisham, Plymouth, Wallsend **9** Aylesbury, Blackpool, Cambridge, Islington, Leicester, Liverpool, Newcastle, Sheffield, Stratford **10** Birkenhead, Birmingham, Canterbury, Colchester, Manchester, Nottingham, Portsmouth, Sunderland **11** Bournemouth, Northampton, Southampton **12** Peterborough, Stoke-on-Trent, West Bromwich **13** Southend-on-Sea, Wolverhampton *Estonia:* **5** Narva, Pärnu, Tartu *Ethiopia:* **5** Aksum, Harer **6** Nazret **8** Dire Dawa *Finland:* **4** Kemi, Oulu, Pori **5** Espoo, Hango, Kotka, Lahti, Rauma, Turku, Vaasa **6** Vantaa **7** Tampere *Florida:* **5** Largo, Miami, Ocala, Ocoee, Oneco, Tampa **6** DeLand, Naples **7** Hialeah, Key West, Orlando, Sebring **8** Gulfport, Key Largo, Lakeland, Opa-Locka, Sarasota **9** Boca Raton, Bradenton, Fort Myers, Hollywood, Kissimmee, Palm Beach, Pensacola, Vero Beach **10** Clearwater, Cocoa Beach, Fort Pierce, Miami Beach, Punta Gorda, Titusville **11** Coral Gables, Gainesville, Key Biscayne, St. Augustine, Winter Haven **12** Apalachicola, Daytona Beach, Ft. Lauderdale, Jacksonville, Pompano Beach, St. Petersburg **13** Chattahoochee *France:* **3** Dax, Pau **4** Agde, Agen, Albi, Ales, Auch, Caen, Gien, Laon, Lyon, Metz, Nice, Orly, Rezé, Sens, Sète, Vire **5** Arles, Arras, Auray, Auton, Avion, Berck, Blois, Bondy, Brest, Creil, Digne, Dijon, Douai, Dreux, Flers, Gagny, Laval, Le Puy, Lille, Lunel, Lyons, Mâcon, Meaux, Melun, Muret, Nîmes, Niort, Noyon, Reims, Revin, Rodez, Rouen, Royan, Tours, Tulle, Vichy, Vitre **6** Amiens, Angers, Calais, Cannes, Dieppe, Evreux, Le Mans, Nantes, Nevers, Rennes, Rheims, Thiers, Toulon, Troyes **7** Ajaccio, Antibes, Avignon, Béthune, Bourges, Le Havre, Limoges, Lorient, Lourdes, Orléans, Roubaix **8** Beauvais, Besançon, Biarritz, Bordeaux, Chartres, Gentilly, Grenoble, Nanterre, Poitiers, Toulouse **9** Cherbourg, Dunkerque, Le Creusot, Marseille, Montreuil, Perpignan **10** Draguignan, Marseilles, Strasbourg, Versailles **11** Carcassonne, Montpellier **12** Saint-Etienne **13** Aix-en-Provence *Gabon:* **4** Oyem **5** Bitam **10** Port-Gentil **11** Franceville *Gambia:* **9** Serekunda *Georgia:* **4** Adel, Alma, Arco **5** Jesup, Macon, McRae **6** Albany, Athens **7** Augusta, Calhoun **8** Americus, Columbus, Marietta, Savannah, Val-

dosta **9** Brunswick *Georgia, Republic of:* **6** Batumi **7** Kutaisi, Rustavi, Sukhumi *Germany:* **3** Aue, Hof, Ulm **4** Bonn, Gera, Goch, Hamm, Jena, Kehl, Kiel, Köln, Marl, Suhl **5** Aalen, Ahlen, Borna, Bruhl, Calbe, Celle, Düren, Emden, Essen, Forst, Fulda, Furth, Gotha, Greiz, Hagen, Halle, Hanau, Herne, Hurth, Kleve, Lemgo, Lobau, Mainz, Neuss, Peine, Pirna, Riesa, Stade, Thale, Trier, Wesel, Zeitz **6** Aachen, Bremen, Coburg, Dachau, Dessau, Erfurt, Kassel, Lübeck, Munich, Rheydt **7** Cologne, Cottbus, Dresden, Hamburg, Hanover, Koblenz, Krefeld, Leipzig, München, Munster, Potsdam, Rostock, Zwickau **8** Augsburg, Bayreuth, Chemnitz, Cuxhaven, Dortmund, Duisburg, Freiburg, Hannover, Mannheim, Nürnberg, Würzburg **9** Bielefeld, Brunswick, Darmstadt, Frankfurt, Göttingen, Karlsruhe, Magdeburg, Nuremberg, Offenbach, Oldenburg, Osnabrück, Remscheid, Stuttgart, Wiesbaden, Wuppertal **10** Baden-Baden, Düsseldorf, Heidelberg, Oberhausen, Regensburg, Salzgitter **11** Brandenburg, Bremerhaven, Saarbrücken **12** Braunschweig **13** Gelsenkirchen *Ghana:* **4** Axim, Keta, Tema **5** Lawra, Yendi **6** Kumasi *Greece:* **3** Kos **4** Arta **5** Argos, Lamia, Nemea, Volos **6** Sparta, Thebes **7** Corinth, Khalkis, Larissa, Piraeus, Tríkala **8** Salonika **12** Thessaloniki *Guatemala:* **5** Cobán **13** Quezaltenango *Guinea:* **4** Labé **6** Kankan, Kindia *Haiti:* **8** Gonaïves **10** Cap Haitien *Hawaii:* **4** Aiea, Hilo, Laie **5** Kapaa, Lihue, Maili **6** Kailua **7** Kaneohe, Waikiki, Wailuku *Honduras:* **5** Danlí **7** La Ceiba **12** San Pedro Sula *Hong Kong:* **7** Kowloon *Hungary:* **3** Ozd **4** Eger, Györ, Pécs **5** Abony, Bekes **6** Szeged **7** Miskolc **8** Debrecen *Idaho:* **4** Buhl **5** Nampa **6** Dubois, Moscow **7** Gooding, Payette, Rexburg **8** Caldwell **9** Blackfoot, Pocatello, Sandpoint, Sun Valley, Twin Falls **11** Coeur d'Alene, Grangeville **12** Mountain Home, Saint Anthony *Illinois:* **6** DeKalb, Galena, Hardin, Joliet, Macomb, Moline, Paxton, Peoria, Skokie, Urbana **7** Chicago, Decatur, Glencoe, Oak Lawn, Oak Park, Tuscola, Watseka, Wheaton **8** Carthage, Evanston, Kankakee, La Grange, Monmouth, Rockford, Vandalia, Waukegan **9** Belvidere, Effingham, Galesburg, Park Ridge, Yorkville **10** Belleville, Carbondale, Carrollton, Des Plaines,

Metropolis, Northbrook, Rock Island **11** Carlinville, Jerseyville, Lindenhurst, Murphysboro, Taylorville **12** Highland Park, Mount Carroll *India:* **3** Mau **4** Agra, Ahwa, Bhuj, Durg, Gaya, Kota, Mhow, Pune, Puri, Rewa, Tonk, Ziro **5** Adoni, Aimer, Akola, Alwar, Arcot, Arrah, Banda, Barsi, Bidar, Bihar, Churu, Damoh, Delhi, Dewas, Eluru, Gonda, Jalna, Jammu, Karur, Miraj, Morvi, Nasik, Patan, Patna, Poona, Sagar, Satna, Sikar, Simla, Surat, Thana **6** Baroda, Bhopal, Bombay, Cochin, Guntur, Howrah, Indore, Jaipur, Jhansi, Kanpur, Madras, Meerut, Mysore, Nagpur, Raipur, Rajkot, Ranchi, Ujjain **7** Aligarh, Asansol, Belgaum, Bikaner, Burdwan, Cuttack, Gauhati, Gwalior, Jodhpur, Kurnool, Lucknow, Madurai, Mathura, Nellore, Patiala, Vellore **8** Amritsar, Bhatpara, Calcutta, Dehra Dun, Kolhapur, Ludhiana, Sholapur, Srinagar, Varanasi **9** Ahmadabad, Allahabad, Bangalore, Hyderabad **10** Ahmadnagar, Chandigarh, Trivandrum **11** Pondicherry *Indiana:* **4** Gary **5** Berne, Paoli, Vevay **6** Delphi, Kokomo, Marlon, Muncie, Tipton **7** Bedford, Corydon, Elkhart, La Porte, Winamac **8** Bluffton, Kentland **9** Boonville, Fort Wayne, New Albany, Rushville, South Bend, Vincennes **10** Crown Point, Evansville, Logansport, Scottsburg, Terre Haute, Valparaiso **11** Bloomington, Greencastle, Noblesville, Shelbyville **12** Connersville, Lawrenceburg, Martinsville *Indonesia:* **4** Pati **5** Ambon, Bogor, Garut, Kudus, Medan, Tegal, Turen **6** Batang, Kediri, Madiun, Malang, Manado, Padang **7** Bandung, Kendari **8** Semarang, Surabaja, Surabaya, Tjirebon **9** Palembang, Pontianak, Surakarta **10** Pekalongan **11** Tasikmalaja **12** Bandjarmasin *Iowa:* **5** Onawa, Pella **6** Eldora, Harlan, Keokuk, Le Mars, Red Oak **7** Allison, Anamosa, Carroll, Clinton, Corydon, Denison, Dubuque, Marengo, Osceola, Waverly **8** Clarinda, Ida Grove, Waterloo **9** Davenport, Fort Dodge, Indianola, Mason City, Muscatine, Oskaloosa, Sioux City, Storm Lake, West Union, Winterset **10** Emmetsburg, Rock Rapids, Spirit Lake **11** Cedar Rapids, Fort Madison **13** Council Bluffs *Iran:* **3** Qom, Qum **4** Amul, Arak, Khoi, Sari, Yazd, Yezd **5** Ahvaz, Ahwaz, Babol, Rasht **6** Abadan, Meshed, Shiraz, Tabriz **7** Esfahan, Hamadan, Isfahan, Mashhad **9** Bakhtaran *Iraq:* **3** Ana, Kut

4 Kufa **5** Al Kut, Amara, Basra, Erbil, Hilla, Mosul, Najaf, Rutba **6** Amarah, Hillah, Kirkuk, Ramadi, Rutbah **7** Falluja, Samarra **8** Fallujah, Nasiriya **9** Nasiriyah *Ireland:* (see *Eire*, above) *Israel:* **5** Afula, Haifa, Holon, Jaffa **7** Rehovot **8** Ashqelon, Nazareth, Ramat Gan **9** Beersheba *Italy:* **4** Acri, Alba, Asti, Bari, Enna, Este, Fano, Gela, Iesi, Lodi, Lugo, Pisa **5** Adria, Agira, Anzio, Aosta, Arola, Cantù, Capua, Carpi, Crema, Cuneo, Eboli, Fermo, Fondi, Forli, Gaeta, Genoa, Imola, Ivrea, Lecce, Lecco, Lucca, Massa, Melfi, Menfi, Milan, Monza, Padua, Parma, Prato, Siena, Turin **6** Ancona, Assisi, Foggia, Mantua, Milano, Modena, Naples, Napoli, Rimini, Torino, Venice, Verona **7** Bergamo, Bologna, Bolzano, Brescia, Catania, Firenze, Leghorn, Messina, Palermo, Perugia, Pescara, Potenza, Ravenna, Salerno, San Remo, Taranto, Trieste, Venezia **8** Brindisi, Cagliari, Florence, La Spezia, Piacenza, Siracusa, Syracuse *Ivory Coast:* **6** Bouaké *Jamaica:* **6** May Pen **10** Montego Bay *Japan:* **3** Ina, Ise, Ito, Ota, Tsu, Ube, Uji, Yao **4** Ageo, Anan, Gifu, Hagi, Himi, Hofu, Iida, Joyo, Kaga, Kobe, Kofu, Kure, Miki, Mito, Naha, Nara, Noda, Oita, Otsu, Saga, Saku, Soka, Tosu, Ueda, Yono **5** Akita, Atami, Beppu, Chiba, Imari, Itami, Iwaki, Iwata, Izumi, Izumo, Kiryu, Kochi, Kyoto, Minoo, Odate, Ogaki, Okawa, Okaya, Omiya, Omuta, Osaka, Otaru, Oyama, Sabae, Saiki, Sakai, Sanjo, Suita, Tenri, Urawa **6** Akashi, Aomori, Himeji, Kadoma, Kurume, Matsue, Mitaka, Nagano, Nagoya, Numazu, Sasebo, Sendai, Suzuka, Toyama, Yonago **7** Fukuoka, Hitachi, Ibaraki, Imabari, Muroran, Niigata, Niihama, Nobeoka, Obihiro, Odawara, Okayama, Okazaki, Sapporo **8** Ashikaga, Fujisawa, Fukuyama, Hirakata, Hirosaki, Ichihara, Ichikawa, Kakogawa, Kamakura, Kanazawa, Kawasaki, Miyazaki, Nagasaki, Onomichi, Shizuoka, Takasaki, Toyonaka, Wakayama, Yamagata, Yokohama, Yokosuka **9** Fukushima, Funabashi, Hiroshima, Kawaguchi, Yamaguchi, Yokkaichi *Jordan:* **5** Aqaba, Irbid *Kansas:* **4** Gove, Iola **5** Colby, Hoxie, Lakin, Leoti, Paola, Pratt **6** Atwood, Beloit, Girard, Holton, Salina **7** Abilene, Emporia, Garnett, Kinsley, Wichita **8** Cimarron, Goodland, La Crosse, Sublette **9** Coldwater, Fort Scott, Great Bend, Oskaloosa **10** Hutchinson

11 Leavenworth 12 Council Grove, Overland Park 13 Medicine Lodge *Kazakhstan:* 5 Semey 6 Almaty, Aqtöbe, Guryev, Uralsk 7 Alma-Ata, Zhambyl 8 Balkhash, Chimkent, Dzhambul, Kyzl Orda, Pavlodar, Shymkent 9 Karaganda 10 Aktyubinsk *Kentucky:* 4 Inez 5 Cadiz, Hyden, McKee 6 Elkton, Harlan 7 Ashland, Campton, Greenup, Hindman, Paducah, Stanton 8 Fort Knox, Mayfield 9 Bardstown, Covington, Cynthiana, Lexington, Maysville, Owensboro, Pikeville, Pineville, Southgate, Vanceburg 10 Booneville, Hawesville, Louisville, Whitesburg 11 Hardinsburg, Harrodsburg, Hodgenville, Leitchfield, Morganfield 12 Bowling Green *Kenya:* 4 Embu 5 Nyeri 6 Kisumu, Nakuru 7 Mombasa *Kyrgyzstan:* 3 Osh 5 Naryn *Laos:* 5 Pakse 11 Savannakhet *Latvia:* 7 Jelgava, Liepaja 9 Ventspils 10 Daugavpils *Lebanon:* 4 Tyre 5 Sidon, Zahlé 7 Juniyah, Tripoli *Libya:* 4 Homs 5 Derna, Zawia 6 Tobruk 8 Benghazi, Misratah *Lithuania:* 6 Kaunas 8 Klaipeda *Louisiana:* 4 Jena 5 Amite, Arabi, Houma, Mamou, Norco, Rayne 6 Colfax, Edgard, Gretna, Minden, Ruston 7 Arcadia, Bastrop, Marrero, Oberlin 8 Bogalusa, De Ridder, Metairie, New Roads, Oak Grove, Westwego 9 Abbeville, Chalmette, Hahnville, Leesville, New Iberia, Opelousas, Port Allen, Thibodaux, Winnfield, Winnsboro 10 New Orleans, Plaquemine, Shreveport 11 Lake Charles 12 Natchitoches *Macedonia:* 6 Bitola, Prilep, Tetovo *Maine:* 4 Saco 5 Orono 6 Auburn, Bangor, Gorham 7 Berwick, Kittery, Machias, Rumford 8 Lewiston, Portland, Rockland 9 Bar Harbor, Biddeford, Brunswick, Ellsworth, Kennebunk, Skowhegan, Wiscasset 11 Millinocket, Presque Isle 13 Kennebunkport *Malawi:* 5 Mzuzu, Zomba 8 Blantyre *Malaysia:* 4 Ipoh 5 Gemas, Klang 6 Kelang, Penang, Pinang 11 Johore Bahru *Mali:* 5 Kayes, Mopti, Ségou 7 Sikasso *Malta:* 10 Birkirkara *Maryland:* 5 Bowie 6 Denton, Elkton, Towson 8 Bethesda, Landover, Snow Hill 9 Baltimore, Rockville 10 Beltsville, Hagerstown 11 Chestertown, College Park, Leonardtown 12 Havre de Grace, Silver Spring *Massachusetts:* 4 Ayer 5 Acton, Lenox, Salem 6 Agawam, Boston, Dedham, Lowell, Malden, Monson, Natick, Saugus, Woburn 7 Amherst, Danvers, Duxbury, Holyoke, Hyannis, Medford, Methuen, Needham, Swansea, Taunton, Walpole, Waltham, Wareham 8 Brockton, Chicopee, Falmouth, Plymouth, Rockport, Scituate, Yarmouth 9 Attleboro, Braintree, Brookline, Cambridge, Edgartown, Fall River, Fitchburg, Haverhill, Lexington, Nantucket, Southwick, Wilbraham, Worcester 10 Barnstable, Framingham, Gloucester, Greenfield, Leominster, New Bedford, North Adams, Pittsfield, Somerville, Swampscott 11 Northampton, Springfield 12 Mattapoisett, Provincetown, Williamstown *Mauritania:* 4 Atar 5 Kaedi 6 Dakhla *Mexico:* 4 León 5 Ameca, Choix, Tepic 6 Cancún, Celaya, Colima, Jalapa, Juárez, Mérida, Oaxaca, Puebla, Toluca, Tuxtla 7 Durango, Guasave, Morelia, Obregón, Reynosa, Tampico, Tijuana, Tlalpán, Torreón, Uruapan, Zapopan 8 Chetumal, Coyoacán, Culiacán, Ensenada, Mazatlan, Mexicali, Saltillo, Tuxtepec 9 Chihuahua, Fresnillo, Ixtacalco, Monterrey, Querétaro, Salamanca, Tapachula, Zacatecas 10 Cuernavaca, Hermosillo, Ixtapalapa, Xochimilco 11 Guadalajara, Nuevo Laredo 13 San Luis Potosí *Michigan:* 4 Alma, Holt 5 Flint, Ionia, L'Anse, Niles 6 Otsego, Paw Paw, Warren 7 Allegan, Corunna, Detroit, Gladwin, Livonia, Midland, Saginaw 8 Ann Arbor, Bessemer, Dearborn, Escanaba, Grayling, Hastings, Houghton, Muskegon, Newberry, Petoskey, Sandusky 9 Cheboygan, Coldwater, Hillsdale, Kalamazoo, Menominee, Port Huron, Roscommon, Ypsilanti 10 Charlevoix, Grand Haven, West Branch, White Cloud 11 Battle Creek, Grand Rapids, Harrisville, Saint Ignace 12 Highland Park, Iron Mountain *Minnesota:* 3 Ely 4 Mora 5 Anoka, Edina, Osseo 6 Aitkin, Benson, Duluth, Waseca, Windom, Winona 7 Glencoe, Hibbing, Mankato, Red Wing, St. Cloud, Wabasha 8 Brainerd, Elk River, Moorhead, Shakopee 9 Caledonia, Crookston, Faribault, Pipestone, Rochester, Saint Paul, Silver Bay 10 Park Rapids, Saint Cloud, Saint James, Saint Peter, Stillwater, Two Harbors 11 Bloomington, Fergus Falls, Long Prairie, Minneapolis, Worthington 12 Breckenridge, Granite Falls, Redwood Falls *Mississippi:* 4 Iuka 5 Amory 6 Biloxi, Leland, McComb, Purvis, Sardis, Sumner, Tupelo, Winona 7 Belzoni, Brandon, Okolona, Quitman, Wiggins 8 Gulfport, Hernando, Meridian, Paulding, Rosedale, Walthall

9 Greenwood, Indianola, New Albany, Pittsboro, Vicksburg 10 Batesville, Booneville, Brookhaven, Clarksdale, Ellisville, Greenville, Hazlehurst, Pascagoula, Port Gibson, Starkville, Waynesboro 11 Coffeeville, Hattiesburg, Poplarville 12 Holly Springs *Missouri:* 3 Ava 4 Linn 5 Eldon, Hayti, Ladue, Rolla 6 Galena, Neosho, Potosi 7 Hermann, Ironton, Kennett, Linneus, Osceola, Palmyra, Sedalia, St. Louis 8 Gallatin, Hannibal 9 Boonville, Hartville, Hillsboro, Maryville, Pineville, Tuscumbia, Warrenton 10 Kansas City, Kirksville, Marble Hill, Marshfield, Perryville, Saint Louis, Springfield, Steelville, Unionville, West Plains 11 Poplar Bluff, Saint Joseph, Warrensburg 12 Independence, Saint Charles *Moldova:* 5 Balti 7 Tighina 8 Tiraspol *Mongolia:* 5 Kobdo 6 Darhan 10 Choybalsan *Montana:* 5 Butte, Havre, Libby 6 Hardin, Polson 7 Bozeman 8 Billings, Missoula, Red Lodge 10 Great Falls *Montenegro:* 8 Titograd 9 Podgorica *Morocco:* 3 Fès 4 Safi, Salé, Taza 5 Nador, Oujda 6 Agadir, Meknès 7 Kenitra, Tangier 8 Marrakech, Marrakesh 10 Casablanca *Mozambique:* 5 Beira 7 Chimoio, Nampula 9 Quelimane, Quilimane *Myanmar:* 3 Pyu 4 Paan 5 Akyab, Bhamo, Chauk, Katha, Magwe, Minbu, Mogok, Tavoy 7 Bassein 8 Mandalay, Moulmein *Namibia:* 5 Outjo 6 Tsumeb 8 Oshakati 12 Keetmanshoop *Nebraska:* 3 Ord 5 Cozad, Omaha, Ponca, Tryon, Wahoo 6 Elwood, Gering, McCook, Minden, Wilber 7 Burwell, Fremont, Kearney, Kimball, Osceola, Tekamah 8 Beatrice, Fairbury, Hastings, Ogallala, Red Cloud, Schuyler, Tecumseh, Thedford 9 Fullerton, Papillion 10 Springview, Stockville 11 Grand Island, Hayes Center, North Platte, Plattsmouth *Netherlands:* 3 Ede, Epe, Oss 4 Echt, Tiel, Uden 5 Aalst, Assen, Breda, Delft, Emmen, Hague, Soest, Vaals, Venlo, Vught, Weert, Wesp, Zeist 6 Arnhem 7 Haarlem, Tilburg, Utrecht 8 Enschede, Nijmegen, The Hague 9 Apeldoorn, Eindhoven, Groningen, Rotterdam, Zandvoort 10 Maastricht *Nevada:* 3 Ely 4 Elko, Reno 6 Fallon, Minden, Pioche 7 Tonopah 8 Las Vegas, Lovelock 9 Goldfield, Yerington 10 Winnemucca *New Brunswick:* 5 Minto 6 St. John 7 Moncton 9 Dalhousie, Saint John 10 Edmundston, Richibucto 12 Hopewell Cape, Perth Andover, Saint Andrews *Newfoundland:*

5 Burin 6 Wabana 10 Mount Pearl 11 Corner Brook *New Hampshire:* 5 Derry, Dover, Keene 6 Berlin, Exeter, Gorham, Nashua 7 Hanover, Laconia, Lebanon, Ossipee 8 Hinsdale, Seabrook 9 Littleton, Merrimack 10 Manchester, Portsmouth, Woodsville *New Jersey:* 4 Atco, Lodi 6 Camden, Newark, Nutley, Rahway, Rumson 7 Bayonne, Cape May, Clifton, Hoboken, Paramus, Passaic, Raritan, Teaneck 8 Freehold, Metuchen, Paterson, Vauxhall, Woodbury 9 Belvidere, Bridgeton, Elizabeth, Glassboro, Lakehurst, Maplewood, Menlo Park, Montclair, Princeton, Riverside, Toms River 10 Asbury Park, Bloomfield, Cherry Hill, East Orange, Flemington, Hackensack, Jersey City, Morristown, Mount Holly, Perth Amboy, Piscataway, Plainfield, Somerville, West Orange 11 Mays Landing, South Orange 12 Atlantic City, New Brunswick 13 Palisades Park *New Mexico:* 4 Taos 5 Belen, Hobbs, Raton 6 Clovis, Deming, Grants 7 Roswell, Socorro 8 Estancia, Los Lunas, Portales 9 Carrizozo, Las Cruces, Los Alamos, Lovington, Tucumcari 10 Alamogordo, Bernalillo, Fort Sumner 11 Albuquerque *New York:* 4 Elma, Ovid, Troy 5 Depew, Ilion, Islip, Le Roy, Nyack, Olean, Owego, Utica 6 Attica, Cohoes, Delmar, Elmira, Hudson, Ithaca, Oneida 7 Batavia, Buffalo, Corning, Geneseo, Katonah, Mineola, Penn Yan, Suffern, Yonkers 8 Bay Shore, Cortland, Herkimer, Hyde Park, Kingston, Lockport, Mayville, Ossining, Syracuse, Valhalla 9 Greenport, Hempstead, Patchogue, Riverhead, Rochester, Scarsdale, Schoharie 10 Binghamton, Glens Falls, Haverstraw, Huntington, Lackawanna, Lake George, Lake Placid, Mamaroneck, Massapequa, Mount Kisco, Plattsburg, Rensselaer, Watervliet 11 Canajoharie, Canandaigua, Cooperstown, Farmingdale, Hudson Falls, Plattsburgh, Port Chester, Saint George, Schenectady, Southampton, Watkins Glen, White Plains 12 Lake Pleasant, Poughkeepsie 13 Mechanicville, Port Jefferson *New Zealand:* 4 Hutt, Tawa 5 Levin, Taupo, Waihi 7 Dunedin, Manukau 8 Auckland 12 Christchurch *Nicaragua:* 4 León 5 Boaco, Rivas 6 Masaya 7 Granada *Nigeria:* 3 Aba, Ado, Ede, Ife, Ila, Iwo, Jos, Owo, Oyo 4 Kano, Ondo 5 Akure, Enugu, Gusau, Lagos, Okene, Zaria 6 Ibadan, Ilesha, Ilorin, Kaduna, Mushin, Sokoto 7 Onitsha, Oshogbo

8 Abeokuta **9** Maiduguri, Ogbomosho
12 Port Harcourt *North Carolina:*
4 Dunn **5** Ayden, Elkin, Erwin, Oteen,
Sylva **6** Dobson, Durham, Lenoir, Man-
teo, Marlon, Shelby, Winton **7** Bay-
boro, Brevard, Edenton, Kinston, New
Bern, Newland, Roxboro, Sanford, Tar-
boro **8** Asheboro, Beaufort, Gastonia,
Hatteras, Snow Hill **9** Albemarle,
Asheville, Charlotte, Currituck, High
Point, Kitty Hawk, Louisburg, Lum-
berton, Morganton **10** Chapel Hill,
Greensboro, Mocksville, Smithfield,
Wilkesboro **11** Statesville, Yanceyville
12 Murfreesboro, Winston-Salem *North
Dakota:* **4** Mott **5** Cando, Fargo, Minot,
Rolla **6** Amidon, Ashley, Bowman, For-
mon, Lakota, Linton, Medora, Mohall
8 Wahpeton, Washburn **9** Dickinson,
Williston **10** Devils Lake, Grand Forks
Northern Ireland: **5** Derry, Larne, Newry,
Omagh **6** Antrim, Armagh **9** Bally-
mena, Coleraine, Craigavon, Dungan-
non **10** Ballymoney **11** Ballycastle,
Downpatrick, Enniskillen, Londonder-
ry **13** Carrickfergus *North Korea:*
5 Haeju, Nampo **6** Wonsan **7** Hamhung,
Kaesong, Sinuiju **8** Ch'ongjin, Kim-
chaek **9** P'yongyang *Northwest Territories:* **6** Dawson **10** Whitehorse **11** Yellowknife *Norway:* **4** Bodo **5** Hamar,
Skien, Vardo **6** Bergen, Tromso
8 Kirkenes **9** Stavanger, Trondheim
10 Hammerfest **12** Kristiansand *Nova
Scotia:* **5** Digby **6** Pictou **7** Arichat, Bad-
deck **8** Port Hood **9** Dartmouth,
Kentville, Lunenburg, Shelburne,
Westville **10** Antigonish **11** Guysbor-
ough *Ohio:* **4** Kent **5** Akron, Berea,
Bryan, Carey, Eaton, Heath, Logan,
Niles, Parma, Piqua, Solon, Xenia
6 Canton, Celina, Dayton, Elyria,
Euclid, Kenton, Lorain, Marion, Medi-
na, Sidney, Tiffin, Toledo **7** Ashland,
Batavia, Bucyrus, Chardon, Findlay,
Ironton, Oakwood, Pomeroy, Ravenna,
Wauseon, Wooster **8** Conneaut, Mariet-
ta, Sandusky **9** Ashtabula, Cleveland,
Coshocton, Mansfield **10** Cincinnati,
Gallipolis, Wapakoneta, Zanesville
11 Chillicothe, Circleville, Millersburg,
Mount Gilead, Painesville, Port Clinton
12 Steubenville **13** Bellefontaine, Cuyahoga Falls *Oklahoma:* **3** Ada **4** Alva,
Enid **5** Altus, Atoka, Sayre, Tulsa
6 Durant, El Reno, Guymon, Idabel,
Lawton, Okemah, Poteau, Wewoka
7 Antlers, Ardmore, Cordell, Eufaula,
Newkirk, Purcell, Sapulpa, Watonga
8 Anadarko, Okmulgee, Pawhuska, Sal-
lisaw, Stilwell **9** Chickasha, Claremore,

Frederick, McAlester, Wilburton
10 Stillwater, Tishomingo **11** Pauls Valley **12** Bartlesville *Oman:* **3** Sur
6 Matrah **7** Salalah *Ontario:* **4** Ajax,
Wawa, York **6** Barrie, Guelph, Kenora,
London, Oshawa, Sarnia, Simcoe
7 Cobourg, Markham, Napanee, Sudbury, Windsor **8** Brampton, Cochrane,
Goderich, Hamilton, North Bay, Pem-
broke, Prescott **9** Brantford, Etobicoke, Kitchener, L'Original, Newmarket, North York, Owen Sound,
Walkerton **10** Belleville, Brockville,
Burlington, Haileybury, Parry Sound,
Thunder Bay **11** Bracebridge, Fort
Frances, Mississauga, Scarborough
12 Peterborough, St. Catharines *Oregon:* **5** Canby, Nyssa **6** Eugene
8 Coquille, La Grande, Portland, Rose-
burg **9** Clackamas, Corvallis, Gold
Beach, Pendleton, The Dalles, Tilla-
mook **10** Grants Pass **12** Klamath Falls
Pakistan: **5** Bannu, Bhera, Kasur, Kohat
6 Gujrat, Lahore, Mardan, Multan,
Quetta, Sukkur **7** Karachi, Sialkot
8 Lyallpur, Peshawar, Sargodha
9 Hyderabad **10** Bahawalpur, Faisalabad, Gujranwala, Rawalpindi
Paraguay: **3** Itá **4** Yuty **5** Luque, Pilar
7 Caacupé, Caazapa **9** Paraguarí **10** San
Lorenzo *Papua New Guinea:* **3** Lae
10 Mount Hagen, Popondetta *Pennsylvania:* **4** Erie, York **5** Avoca, Darby,
Muncy, Paoli **6** Easton **7** Altoona, Bedford, Clarion, Hanover, Hershey,
Latrobe, Reading, Ridgway, Sunbury
8 Carlisle, Edinboro, Hazleton, Mont-
rose, Scranton, Somerset **9** Allentown,
Ebensburg, Honesdale, Jim Thorpe,
Lancaster, Lewisburg, Lock Haven,
Meadville, New Castle, Wellsboro
10 Bloomsburg, Brookville, Carbon-
dale, Clearfield, Gettysburg, Greens-
burg, Huntingdon, Kittanning, Mc-
Keesport, Middleburg, Pittsburgh,
Pottsville, Waynesburg **11** Stroudsburg,
Valley Forge, West Chester, Wilkes-
Barre **12** Philadelphia, State College,
Williamsport *Peru:* **3** Ica, Ilo **5** Ancon,
Cuzco, Jauja, Junin, Lamas, Pisco,
Piura, Tacna **6** Callao **8** Arequipa, Chi-
clayo, Chimbote, Trujillo *Philippines:*
3 Iba **4** Bago, Bais, Boac, Bogo, Cebu,
Daet, Jolo, Lipa, Mati **5** Basco, Bulan,
Cadiz, Danao, Davao, Digos, Gapan,
Gubat, Iriga, Laoag, Ormoc, Pasay,
Silay, Tagum, Vigan **6** Butuan, Iloilo,
Quezon **7** Angeles, Bacolod, Basilan
8 Batangas, Calbayog, Caloocan **9** Zam-
boanga **10** Quezon City *Poland:* **4** Lodz,
Nysa, Pila, Zary **5** Bytom, Bytow,

Chelm, Kutno, Lomza, Luban, Lubin, Plock, Radom, Torun, Tychy **6** Elblag, Gdansk, Gdynia, Kalisz, Kielce, Krakow, Lublin, Poznan, Rybnik, Zabrze **7** Chorzow, Dabrowa, Gliwice, Rzeszow, Wroclaw **8** Gornicza, Katowice, Szczecin **9** Bialystok, Bydgoszcz, Sosnowiec, Walbrzych **11** Czestochowa *Portugal:* **4** Faro **5** Braga, Evora, Porto **6** Almada, Oporto, Queluz **7** Amadora **8** Barreiro, Santarém *Prince Edward Island:* **10** Summerside *Puerto Rico:* **5** Ponce **6** Caguas **7** Arecibo, Bayamón **8** Carolina, Guaynabo, Mayagüez *Quebec:* **4** Alma **5** Amqui, Anjou, Gaspé, Laval, Lévis, Magog, Percé, Rouyn **6** Granby, Ham Sud, Matane, Ste.-Foy, Val d'Or **7** Bedford, Lachute **8** Beauport, Cap Santé, Joliette, Lac Brome, Maniwaki, Montreal, Rimouski, Roberval, Sept-Iles, Waterloo **9** Bécancour, Cookshire, Iberville, Inverness, La Malbaie, La Prairie, Longueuil, Montmagny, Sainte-Foy, Saint Jean, Tadoussac, Vaudreuil **10** Baie-Comeau, Chicoutimi **11** Beauharnois, Louiseville, Mont-Laurier **12** Charlesbourg **13** Trois-Rivières *Rhode Island:* **7** Newport, Rumford, Warwick **8** Apponaug, Coventry, Cranston, Tiverton, Westerly **9** Hopkinton, Pawtucket **10** Woonsocket **12** Narragansett, West Kingston *Romania:* **3** Dej **4** Aiud, Arad, Cluj, Deva, Husi, Iasi **5** Anina, Bacau, Buzau, Carei, Lugoj, Sibiu, Turda **6** Braila, Brasov, Galati, Oradea **7** Craiova **8** Ploiesti **9** Constanta, Timisoara **10** Cluj-Napoca *Russia:* **3** Kem, Ufa **4** Inta, Luga, Okha, Omsk, Orel, Orsk, Perm, Tula, Tura, Zima **5** Aldan, Artem, Chita, Ishim, Kansk, Kazan, Lysva, Onega, Penza, Pskov, Rzhev, Salsk, Serov, Sochi, Sokol, Tomsk, Tulun, Volsk, Yurga **6** Bratsk, Grozny, Kaluga, Kovrov, Kurgan, Rostov, Ryazan, Samara, Syzran, Tambov, Tyumen, Vyborg, Yelets **7** Irkutsk, Ivanovo, Izhevsk, Kalinin, Kolomna, Lipetsk, Magadan, Norilsk, Rybinsk, Saransk, Saratov, Shakhty, Vologda, Yakutsk, Zhdanov **8** Belgorod, Kemerovo, Kostroma, Murmansk, Nakhodka, Novgorod, Orenburg, Smolensk, Taganrog, Vladimir, Volzhski, Voronezh **9** Archangel, Astrakhan, Berezniki, Krasnodar, Serpukhov, Stavropol, Ulyanovsk, Volgograd, Yaroslavl **10** Cheboksary, Dzerzhinsk **11** Arkhangel'sk, Chelyabinsk, Cheremkhovo, Cherepovets, Kaliningrad, Krasnoyarsk, Novosibirsk,

St. Petersburg, Vladivostok **13** Yekaterinburg *Saskatchewan:* **8** Moose Jaw **9** Saskatoon **10** Assiniboia **12** Prince Albert *Saudi Arabia:* **4** Jauf, Taif **5** Jedda, Jidda, Mecca, Tabuk **6** Jeddah, Jiddah, Medina **8** Buraydah *Scotland:* **3** Ayr **4** Alva, Caol, Dyce, Oban **5** Alloa, Annan, Beith, Cowie, Cupar, Dalry, Ellon, Kelso, Kelty, Largs, Leven, Nairn, Patna, Troon **6** Dundee **7** Glasgow, Paisley **8** Aberdeen, Greenock, Hamilton **9** Inverness, Lockerbie **10** Kilmarnock **11** Dunfermline, John o'Groats *Senegal:* **5** Thiès **6** Kaolak **7** Kaolack **10** Saint-Louis *Serbia:* **3** Bor, Nis, Pec **4** Ruma **5** Becej, Cacak, Pirot, Sabac, Senta, Vrbas, Vrsac **7** Novi Sad **8** Subotica **10** Kragujevac *Slovakia:* **5** Nitra **6** Kosice, Presov, Zilina *Slovenia:* **4** Bled **5** Celje, Koper, Kranj **7** Maribor *Somalia:* **3** Eil **5** Afgoi, Alula, Brava, Burao, Marka, Obbia **7** Berbera, Kismayu **8** Hargeysa, Kismaayo *South Africa:* **5** Brits, Ceres, De Aar, Nigel, Paarl **6** Benoni, Durban, Soweto **7** Springs **8** Boksburg, Mafeking **9** Germiston, Kimberley, Ladysmith, Uitenhage **10** East London **11** Krugersdorp, Vereeniging **12** Johannesburg **13** Port Elizabeth *South Carolina:* **5** Aiken, Cayce, Saxon **6** Sumter **7** Gaffney, Laurens, Manning, Pickens **8** Beaufort, Newberry, Rock Hill, Walhalla **9** Abbeville, Allendale, Greenwood, Kingstree, McCormick, Winnsboro **10** Charleston, Darlington, Greenville, Hilton Head, Orangeburg, Walterboro **11** Bishopville, Myrtle Beach, Spartanburg **12** Moncks Corner *South Dakota:* **7** Sturgis, Yankton **8** Deadwood, Elk Point **9** Brookings, Rapid City **10** Sioux Falls *South Korea:* **3** Iri **4** Yosu **5** Cheju, Masan, Mokpo, Pusan, Suwon, Taegu, Ulson, Wonju **6** Chinju, Chonju, Inchon, Kunsan, Taejon **7** Kwangju *Spain:* **4** Adra, Baza, Elda, Jaca, Jaén, León, Loja, Lugo, Olot, Reus, Vich, Vigo **5** Albox, Alcoy, Alora, Baena, Cádiz, Ceuta, Cieza, Ecija, Eibar, Elche, Gijón, Ibiza, Jodar, Lorca, Mahon, Oliva, Osuna, Palma, Ronda, Soria, Ubeda **6** Bilbao, Burgos, Cuenca, Huelva, Lérida, Málaga, Mérida, Murcia, Oviedo, Toledo **7** Almadén, Almería, Cáceres, Córdoba, Durango, Granada, Segovia, Sevilla, Seville, Tarrasa, Vitoria **8** Albacete, Alicante, La Coruña, Pamplona, Sabadell, Valencia, Zaragoza **9** Algeciras, Barcelona, Salamanca, Santander, Saragossa, Tarrago-

na 10 Hospitalet, Valladolid 12 San
Sebastián *Sri Lanka:* 5 Galle, Kandy
6 Jaffna 8 Dehiwala, Moratuwa 10 Batticaloa *Sudan:* 4 Juba 5 Kodok, Kosti
7 El Obeid, Kassala 8 Omdurman *Sweden:* 4 Lund, Täby, Umea 5 Falun,
Gävle, Lulea, Malmö, Växjö, Visby
6 Orebro 7 Uppsala 8 Göteborg, Halm-
stad 9 Jönköping, Linköping 12 Kris-
tianstad *Switzerland:* 3 Zug 4 Biel, Chur,
Sion, Thun 5 Aarau, Arbon, Baden,
Basel, Koniz 6 Geneva, Lugano, St.
Gall, Zürich 7 Lucerne, Zermatt 8 Lausanne, Montreux, St. Moritz 9 Neuchâtel, Saint Moritz 11 Saint Moritz *Syria:*
4 Hama, Homs 5 Idlib 6 Aleppo, Tartus
7 Latakia *Taiwan:* 5 Chia-i 6 T'ai-nan
7 Chi-lung, Hsin-chu 8 Feng-shan, Pan-
ch'iao, San-ch'ung, T'ai-chung 9 Kao-
hsiung *Tanzania:* 5 Lindi, Mbeya, Tanga
6 Arusha, Dodoma, Kigoma, Mwanza
8 Morogoro, Zanzibar 11 Dar es
Salaam *Tennessee:* 5 Alcoa, Erwin,
Rives 6 Loudon, Ripley, Selmer
7 Memphis, Waverly 8 Gallatin, Oak
Ridge, Rutledge, Tazewell, Wartburg
9 Dandridge, Dyersburg, Jacksboro,
Jonesboro, Knoxville, Lewisburg,
Maryville 10 Cookeville, Crossville,
Somerville, Waynesboro 11 Blountville,
Chattanooga, Clarksville, Greeneville,
McMinnville, Rogersville, Sevierville,
Shelbyville 12 Elizabethton, Lawrence-
burg, Madisonville, Murfreesboro
Texas: 4 Azle, Waco 5 Alvin, Anson,
Baird, Bowie, Bryan, Clute, Cuero,
Emory, Ennis, Freer, Hondo, Marfa,
Mexia, Olney, Pampa, Pecos, Pharr,
Plano, Sealy, Vidor, Wylie 6 Belton,
Boerne, Bonham, Burnet, Conroe, Dal-
las, Del Rio, Denton, El Paso, Gilmer,
Goliad, Jayton, Lamesa, Laredo, Lin-
den, Lufkin, Odessa, Seguin, Sinton,
Uvalde 7 Abilene, Anahuac, Bandera,
Bastrop, Brenham, Denison, Dimmitt,
Houston, Kaufman, Kountze, Lub-
bock, Midland, Wharton 8 Amarillo,
Angleton, Beaumont, Beeville, Cle-
burne, Eastland, Giddings, Gonzales,
Granbury, Groveton, Hemphill, La
Grange, Lampasas, Longview, McKin-
ney, Monahans, Montague, Pearsall,
Rockwall, Stinnett 9 Arlington,
Ballinger, Bellville, Big Spring, Brown-
wood, Corsicana, Crosbyton, Eagle
Pass, Fort Worth, Galveston, Groes-
beck, Henrietta, Hillsboro, Kerrville,
Levelland, Palo Pinto, Plainview, San
Angelo, San Marcos, Woodville
10 Brownfield, Coldspring, Gatesville,
Jourdanton, Kingsville, Port Arthur,

Port Lavaca, San Antonio, Sweetwater,
Waxahachie 11 Brownsville, Floresville,
Littlefield, Nacogdoches, Weatherford
12 Breckenridge, Daingerfield, Fort
Stockton, New Braunfels, Ray-
mondville, Stephenville, Wichita Falls
13 Corpus Christi, Hallettsville *Thailand:* 3 Nan, Tak 5 Phrae, Roi Et, Surin
8 Songkhla 9 Chiang Mai 10 Non-
thaburi *Tunisia:* 4 Béja, Sfax 5 Gabès,
Gafsa, Susah 6 Ariana 7 Bizerte,
Safaqis *Turkey:* 5 Adana, Bursa, Izmir,
Konya, Sivas 6 Edirne, Erzurm, Sam-
sun 7 Antakya, Antalya, Antioch, Kay-
seri, Malatya 8 Istanbul 9 Eskisehir,
Gallipoli, Gaziantep 10 Diyarbakir
Turkmenistan: 8 Nebit Dag 9 Chardzhou, Dashhowuz *Uganda:* 5 Jinja,
Mbale 7 Entebbe *Ukraine:* 4 Lviv, Lvov,
Sumy 5 Lutsk, Rovno, Yalta 6 Odessa
7 Donetsk, Kharkiv, Kharkov, Kherson,
Luhansk, Poltava 8 Mariupol, Vinnitsa,
Zhitomir 9 Chernigov, Chernobyl,
Krivoy Rog, Krivyy Rih, Nikolayev
10 Kirovograd, Sebastopol, Sevastopol,
Simferopol, Zaporozhye *United Arab
Emirates:* 5 Ajman, Dubai 6 Dubayy
8 Fujairah, Fujayrah *Uruguay:* 4 Melo
5 Minas, Pando, Rocha, Salto 6 Rivera
8 Paysandú 10 Las Piedras *Utah:* 3 Loa
4 Lehi, Orem 5 Manti, Ogden, Provo,
Sandy 6 Dugway, Tooele 7 Parowan
8 Duchesne 9 Coalville 11 Saint George
Uzbekistan: 5 Nukus 6 Kokand
7 Bukhara, Fergana 8 Andizhan,
Chirchik, Namangan 9 Samarkand,
Samarqand *Venezuela:* 4 Coro 5 Anaco,
Cagua 6 Cumaná, Mérida, Petare
7 Cabimas, Guayana, Maracay 8 Valen-
cia 9 Maracaibo 12 Barquisimeto, San
Cristóbal *Vermont:* 5 Barre 7 Rutland
8 St. Albans 10 Bennington, Burlington,
Middlebury 11 Brattleboro, Saint
Albans, St. Johnsbury *Vietnam:* 3 Hue
4 Vinh 5 Da Lat, Hoi An, My Tho 6 Can
Tho, Da Nang, Saigon 7 Bien Hoa,
Nam Dinh, Qui Nhon 8 Haiphong, Nha
Trang, Thanh Hoa 9 Long Xuyen *Vir-
ginia:* 4 Tabb 5 Luray 6 Grundy 7 Acco-
mac, Boydton, Fairfax, Hampton, New
Kent, Norfolk 8 Abingdon, Culpeper,
Leesburg, Manassas, Montross, Not-
toway, Poquoson, Powhatan, Rustburg,
Tazewell 9 Arlington, Clintwood,
Courtland, Dinwiddie, Eastville, Farm-
ville, Fincastle, Goochland, Lunen-
burg, Lynchburg 10 Alexandria, Appo-
mattox, Berryville, Front Royal,
Hillsville, Jonesville, King George,
Lovingston, Pearisburg, Portsmouth,
Rocky Mount, Wytheville 11 Heaths-

ville, King William, Newport News **12** Chesterfield, Prince George, Spotsylvania, Williamsburg **Wales:** **4** Rhyl **5** Neath, Risca, Tenby, Tywyn **7** Cardiff, Cwmbran, Denbigh, Harlech, Newport, Swansea **8** Aberdare, Bridgend **10** Caernarfon, Caernarvon, Llangollen **11** Aberystwyth **Washington:** **4** Omak **5** Brier, Camas, Kelso, Lacey, Pasco, Selah **6** Asotin, Colfax, Tacoma, Yakima **7** Ephrata, Everett, Prosser, Redmond, Seattle, Spokane **8** Bellevue, Chehalis, Colville, Okanogan **9** Montesano, Ritzville, Snohomish, Wenatchee **10** Bellingham, Coupeville, Ellensburg, Goldendale, Walla Walla, Waterville **11** Port Angeles, Port Orchard **12** Friday Harbor, Port Townsend **West Virginia:** **5** Nitro, Welch **6** Elkins, Hamlin, Hinton, Keyser, Ripley **7** Beckley, Weirton **8** Kingwood, Philippi, Wheeling **9** Pineville, Wellsburg **10** Buckhannon, Clarksburg, Huntington, Moorefield, Morgantown, Petersburg, Williamson **11** Harrisville, Martinsburg, Moundsville, Parkersburg **12** Harpers Ferry, Summersville **13** New Cumberland, Point Pleasant **Wisconsin:** **4** Kiel **5** Ripon, Tomah **6** Antigo, Barron, Oconto, Racine, Wausau **7** Baraboo, Chilton, Elkhorn, Hayward, Kenosha, Mauston, Merrill, Oshkosh, Shawano, Viraqua, Waupaca, Wautoma **8** Appleton, Green Bay, Kewaunee, La Crosse, Montello, Phillips, Washburn, Waukesha, West Bend **9** Eau Claire, Ellsworth, Fond du Lac, Green Lake, Ladysmith, Manitowoc, Marinette, Menomonie, Milwaukee, Sheboygan, Shell Lake, Wauwatosa, West Allis, Whitehall **10** Balsam Lake, Darlington, Dodgeville, Eagle River, Grantsburg, Janesville **11** Neillsville, Sturgeon Bay **12** Stevens Point, Whitefish Bay **Wyoming:** **6** Casper, Lander **7** Laramie, Rawlins **8** Gillette, Kemmerer, Sheridan **10** Green River **11** Rock Springs **Yemen:** **4** Aden **5** Taizz **7** Hodeida, Mukalla **8** Hudaydah **Zambia:** **5** Kabwe, Kitwe, Mansa, Mbala, Mongu, Ndola **6** Kasama **7** Chipata **Zimbabwe:** **5** Gweru **6** Hwange, Kadoma, Kwekwe, Mutare, Umtali **7** Mashava **8** Bulawayo, Masvingo

civet **3** cat **Madagascar:** **5** fossa **relative:** **5** genet

civic **5** urban **6** public, social **8** communal, national, societal **9** municipal

civil **6** polite, public, seemly, urbane **7** affable, cordial, courtly, genteel, refined **8** decorous, gracious, mannerly, national, obliging, well-bred **9** courte-

ous, political **10** diplomatic **12** well-mannered **13** accommodating

civility **6** comity **7** amenity, decency, decorum, manners **8** courtesy **9** etiquette, gentility, propriety **10** politeness **11** correctness

civilization **7** culture

civilized **6** decent, proper, urbane **7** genteel, refined **8** decorous, mannerly, tasteful **9** courteous **10** cultivated **13** sophisticated

civil rights **leader:** **4** King (Martin Luther) **organization:** **4** ACLU, CORE **5** NAACP

Civil War **admiral:** **8** Buchanan (Franklin), Farragut (David) **battle:** **6** Shiloh **7** Bull Run **8** Antietam, Manassas **9** Mobile Bay, Nashville, Vicksburg **10** Cold Harbor, Gettysburg **11** Chattanooga, Chickamauga **general:** **3** Lee (Robert E.) **4** Hood (John Bell), Pope (John) **5** Bragg (Braxton), Buell (Don Carlos), Ewell (Richard Stoddart), Grant (Ulysses S.), Meade (George), Sykes (George) **6** Hooker (Joseph) **7** Forrest (Nathan Bedford), Jackson (Thomas "Stonewall"), Sherman (Thomas West, William Tecumseh) **8** Burnside (Ambrose), Johnston (Albert Sidney, Joseph Eggleston), Sheridan (Philip) **9** McClellan (George Brinton), Rosecrans (William), Schofield (John) **10** Beauregard (Pierre) **ship:** **7** Monitor **9** Merrimack

civil wrong **4** tort

clabber **5** curds

clack **3** gab, jaw, yak **4** blab, chat **5** prate **6** babble, cackle, gabble, gossip, jabber, rattle **7** blabber, chatter, clatter, palaver, prattle **9** yakety-yak

clad **4** face, side, skin **5** dress, faced **6** clothe, decked, garbed, outfit **7** attired, clothed, covered, dressed, overlay, sheathe **8** costumed, overlaid, sheathed **9** outfitted

claim **4** call, dibs, hold, plea, take **5** argue, exact, right, share, stake, title **6** adduce, allege, assert, defend, demand, insist **7** advance, call for, contend, declare, justify, profess, purport, require, solicit, warrant **8** interest, maintain **9** assertion, challenge, postulate, privilege **10** allegation, birthright **11** affirmation, declaration, prerogative, requisition **12** protestation

clairvoyance **3** ESP **7** insight **9** intuition, telepathy **10** sixth sense **11** penetration, second sight **12** precognition

clairvoyant **4** seer **5** sibyl **7** diviner **8** telepath **10** soothsayer

clam **4** buck **5** razor **6** dollar, quahog

7 bivalve, coquina, geoduck, mollusc, mollusk, smacker, steamer 11 cherrystone *genus:* 3 Mya

clamant 4 dire 6 crying, urgent 7 blatant, burning, exigent 8 pressing 9 insistent 10 compelling, imperative

clamber 5 climb, crawl, scale, swarm 8 scrabble, scramble, struggle

clammy 4 cool, dank, damp 5 close, moist, slimy 6 sticky

clamor 3 cry, din 4 bawl, roar, to-do 5 babel, hoo-ha, noise 6 bellow, demand, hubbub, jangle, outcry, racket, ruckus, tumult, uproar 7 agitate, dispute, ferment, protest, turmoil 8 brouhaha, shouting 9 agitation, commotion 10 hullabaloo, hurly-burly 11 pandemonium

clamorous 5 noisy, vocal 6 crying, shrill, urgent 7 blatant, exigent, raucous, voluble 8 strident, vehement 9 insistent 10 boisterous, imperative, tumultuous, vociferous 11 importunate 12 obstreperous

clamp 4 grip, hold, vise 5 clasp, grasp 6 clench, clinch, clutch, fasten, secure 7 grapple

clamshell 6 bucket 7 grapple

clan 3 mob 4 camp, folk, ring, sept 5 cabal, house, stock, tribe 6 circle, clique, family 7 coterie, kindred, lineage 9 camarilla *emblem:* 5 totem

Clancy novel 12 Patriot Games 13 Sum of All Fears (The) 17 Hunt for Red October (The) 21 Clear and Present Danger

clandestine 6 covert, secret, sneaky 7 furtive, illicit 8 hush-hush, stealthy 10 undercover, under wraps 11 underhanded 12 hugger-mugger, illegitimate 13 surreptitious, under-the-table

clang 3 cry, din 4 ding, peal, slam 6 jangle 8 ding-dong

clangor 3 din 5 noise 6 clamor, jangle, racket, rattle, tumult, uproar 7 clatter, ringing 9 stridency 13 reverberation

clangorous 5 noisy 7 booming, rackety, ringing 8 clattery, sonorous 9 deafening 12 earsplitting

clap 3 pat 4 bang, blow, boom, slam, slap 5 blast, burst, crack, crash, whack 6 strike 7 applaud 8 applause

claptrap 4 bull, bunk 5 cheap, hokum, showy, trash 6 bunkum, drivel, humbug, vulgar 7 baloney, eyewash, hogwash, twaddle 8 malarkey, nonsense 9 poppycock 10 balderdash, flapdoodle

Clara Bow 6 It girl

Clare Boothe ___ 4 Luce

claret 3 red 4 wine 8 Bordeaux

clarify 5 clean, clear 6 define, filter, purify 7 analyze, cleanse, clear up, explain, resolve 8 simplify 9 elucidate 10 illuminate 13 straighten out

clarion 5 clear 7 ringing, rousing, trumpet 8 gleaming, stirring 9 brilliant

clarity 6 purity 8 accuracy, lucidity 9 clearness, limpidity, precision 10 exactitude, simplicity 12 transparency

Clarke novel 10 Earthlight 19 Fountains of Paradise (The)

clash 4 bump, jolt 5 brawl, crash, melee, set-to, smash 6 battle, fracas, impact, jangle 7 collide 8 conflict, mismatch, skirmish 9 collision, encounter 10 engagement 11 embroilment

clasp 3 hug, pin 4 clip, grip, hold 5 clamp, grasp, press 6 brooch, buckle, clench, clinch, clutch, enfold 7 embrace, grapple, squeeze 10 chatelaine

class 3 ilk 4 hold, kind, mark, part, rank, rate, sort, tier, type 5 allot, brand, caste, gauge, genre, genus, grade, grain, group, judge, order, score, stamp, style 6 assess, assign, assort, branch, course, league, nature, reckon, regard, stripe 7 bracket, caliber, quality, section, species, variety 8 appraise, category, consider, division, evaluate, grouping, separate 10 categorize, pigeonhole 11 description 12 denomination *middle:* 11 bourgeoisie *school:* 6 junior, senior 8 freshman 9 sophomore *working:* 11 proletariat

classic 5 ideal, model, prime 7 capital, typical, vintage 8 champion, enduring, standard, superior, top-notch 9 authentic, canonical, classical, excellent, exemplary, memorable, tradition 10 magnum opus, masterwork 11 chef d'oeuvre, masterpiece, tour de force, traditional 12 paradigmatic, prototypical 13 authoritative

classical 4 pure 5 Attic, Greek, ideal, Latin, Roman 7 ancient, fitting, Grecian, perfect, typical, vintage 8 Hellenic, standard, sterling 9 canonical, exemplary 10 consummate 11 traditional 13 authoritative

classical musician 4 Böhm (Karl), Hess (Myra), Lind (Jenny), Muti (Riccardo), Pons (Lily), Shaw (Robert) 5 Arrau (Claudio), Biggs (E. Power), Borge (Victor), Boult (Adrian), Davis (Colin), du Pré (Jacqueline), Gould (Glenn), Masur (Kurt), Mehta (Zubin), Melba (Nellie), Ozawa (Seiji), Patti (Adelina), Pinza (Ezio), Price (Leontyne), Ramey (Samuel), Sills (Beverly), Stern (Isaac), Szell (George) 6 Abbado (Claudio),

Battle (Kathleen), Boulez (Pierre), Callas (Maria), Caruso (Enrico), Casals (Pablo), Galway (James), Levine (James), Maazel (Lorin), Midori, Norman (Jessye), Peters (Roberta), Previn (André), Rampal (Jean-Pierre), Rattle (Simon), Reiner (Fritz), Serkin (Peter, Rudolf), Terfel (Bryn), Tucker (Richard), Upshaw (Dawn), Walter (Bruno) **7** Bartoli (Cecilia), Beecham (Thomas), Bocelli (Andrea), Brendel (Alfred), Cliburn (Van), Corelli (Franco), Domingo (Plácido), Farrell (Eileen), Fiedler (Arthur), Fleming (Renée), Glennie (Evelyn), Haitink (Bernard), Heifetz (Jascha), Karajan (Herbert von), Menuhin (Yehudi), Nilsson (Birgit), Ormandy (Eugene), Perlman (Itzhak), Pollini (Maurizio), Sargent (Malcolm), Segovia (Andrés), Tebaldi (Renata) **8** Anderson (Marian), Argerich (Martha), Bergonzi (Carlo), Carreras (José), Flagstad (Kirsten), Horowitz (Vladimir), Kreisler (Fritz), Marriner (Neville), Oistrakh (David), Schnabel (Artur), Te Kanawa (Kiri), Zukerman (Pinchas) **9** Barenboim (Daniel), Bernstein (Leonard), Chaliapin (Feodor), Klemperer (Otto), Landowska (Wanda), Pavarotti (Luciano), Stokowski (Leopold), Toscanini (Arturo) **10** Rubinstein (Arthur), Sutherland (Joan), Tetrazzini (Luisa) **11** Furtwängler (Wilhelm), Kostelanetz (André), Schwarzkopf (Elisabeth) **12** Rostropovich (Mstislav)

classification 4 sort, type **5** genre, genus, grade, order **6** family, phylum, rating **7** sorting, species **8** category, division, grouping, ordering, taxonomy, typology **11** arrangement, cataloguing

classified 6 secret, sorted **7** divided, ordered **9** top secret **11** categorized **12** confidential

classify 4 rank, rate, sort **5** grade, group **6** assort **7** arrange **9** break down **10** categorize, pigeonhole

classy 4 chic, tony **5** swank **6** modish **7** dashing, elegant, refined, stylish **8** gracious, tasteful, well-bred **9** courteous **11** fashionable

clatter 4 to-do **6** clamor, hubbub, pother, rattle, tumult, uproar **7** turmoil **9** commotion **10** hurly-burly *Scottish:* **7** brattle

clattery 5 noisy **7** rackety **10** clangorous

Claudia's husband 6 Pilate

Claudio's beloved 4 Hero

Claudius *nephew:* **6** Hamlet *predecessor:* **8** Caligula *slayer:* **6** Hamlet **9** Agrippina

successor: **4** Nero *wife:* **8** Gertrude **9** Agrippina

Clavell novel 6 Gai-Jin, Shogun, Tai-Pan **7** King Rat

claw 3 dig **4** nail, rake, tear **5** chela, talon, uncus **6** scrape **7** scratch

clay 3 cob **4** loam, lute, marl **5** argil, brick, earth, gault, loess, ocher, ochre **6** kaolin **10** terra-cotta *baked:* **4** tile **5** adobe, brick *box:* **6** saggar, sagger *building:* **5** adobe *ceramic:* **10** terra-cotta *constituent:* **6** silica **8** feldspar, silicate **9** kaolinite *in glass:* **4** tear *made of:* **7** fictile *porcelain:* **6** kaolin *red:* **8** laterite *rock:* **5** shale *tobacco pipe:* **6** dudeen *watery mixture:* **4** slip *white:* **6** kaolin

clay pigeon 6 target

clean 4 dust, fair, pure, swab, tidy, wash, wipe **5** bathe, fresh, groom, purge, scour, scrub, sweep **6** bright, chaste, decent, neaten, purify, spruce, vacuum, washed **7** clarify, launder, sinless **8** hygienic, innocent, sanitary, sanitize, spotless, unsoiled **9** blameless, faultless, sparkling, stainless, undefiled, unsullied, untainted, wholesome **10** antiseptic, immaculate **11** unblemished **12** spick-and-span

clean-cut 4 trim **7** defined, precise **8** definite, explicit, specific **9** wholesome **10** definitive **11** categorical, unambiguous, well-groomed

cleaner see CLEANSER

cleanhanded 8 innocent **9** blameless

clean-limbed 4 trim **7** shapely **8** handsome **10** statuesque

cleanse 4 wash **5** purge, rinse **6** purify, refine **7** clarify, launder **8** lustrate, sanitize **9** disinfect, expurgate, sterilize

cleanser 3 lye **4** soap **9** detergent **10** antiseptic **12** disinfectant

cleansing 7 purging **8** ablution **9** catharsis, purgation **10** lustration **11** expurgation **12** purification

clear 3 get, net, pay, rid, win **4** earn, fade, fair, fine, free, gain, leap, lose, make, pure, well **5** close, empty, exact, fully, glean, lucid, overt, pay up, plain, quite, repay, solve, stark, sunny **6** acquit, gather, hurdle, limpid, obtain, pay off, pick up, secure, settle, simple, square, vacant, vacate, vanish **7** absolve, acquire, approve, audible, clarify, clarion, cleanse, clean up, defined, evident, explain, improve, legible, obvious, precise, rule out, satisfy, utterly **8** apparent, definite, distinct, entirely, explicit, knowable, luminous, manifest, palpable, pleasant, scot-free, shake off, surmount **9** authorize, cloudless, discharge, eliminate, elucidate, evaporate, exculpate, exonerate, extricate, liquidate, meliorate, negotiate, perfectly, unblurred, unclouded, vindicate **10** ameliorate, completely, illuminate, illustrate, openhanded, seethrough **11** conspicuous, disentangle, open-and-shut, perceptible, translucent, transparent, unambiguous, unequivocal **12** recognizable, unmistakable **13** uncomplicated

clearance 3 gap **4** sale **7** go-ahead, removal **8** approval **10** green light, permission **13** authorization

clear away 6 remove **7** take out

clear-cut 5 crisp, exact, plain **7** decided, precise **8** definite, distinct, explicit, manifest **10** definitive, pronounced, undisputed **11** categorical, indubitable, unambiguous, unequivocal **12** unquestioned

clear-eyed 6 astute **9** judicious, observant **10** discerning, perceptive

clearheaded 4 calm, cool **10** perceptive

clearing 3 gap **5** field, glade **7** opening **10** settlement

clear out 5 scoot, scram, split **6** beat it, begone, bug off, decamp, depart **7** buzz off, skiddoo, take off, vamoose **8** shove off **9** drive away, skedaddle **10** hightail it

clear-sightedness 6 acuity, acumen **8** keenness, sagacity **10** astuteness, shrewdness **11** discernment, penetration, percipience **12** perspicacity

clear up 5 solve **6** cipher, unfold **7** clarify, dope out, explain, resolve, unravel **8** decipher **9** elucidate, figure out **10** illuminate

clearwing 4 moth

cleat 4 bitt **5** chock **6** batten **7** bollard, dolphin

cleavage 4 rift **5** chasm, cleft, split **6** schism **7** fissure **8** crevasse **9** splitting

cleave 3 cut, hew **4** chop, join, link, rend, rive **5** carve, cling, sever, slice, split, stick, unite **6** adhere, divide, sunder **7** combine **8** dissever, separate

cleft 3 gap **4** rift **5** chasm, chink, clove, crack, gorge, gulch, split **6** clough, ravine, schism **7** crevice, fissure **8** cleavage

clemency 5 grace, mercy **6** lenity **7** caritas, charity **8** kindness, lenience, leniency, mildness **9** tolerance **10** compassion, gentleness, indulgence, sufferance, toleration **11** forbearance

clement 4 fair, kind, mild **5** balmy **6** benign, humane, kindly **7** lenient **8** merciful, tolerant **9** indulgent **10** benevolent, charitable, forbearing **13** compassionate

clench 4 grip, grit, hold **5** clamp, clasp, grasp **6** clutch **7** grapple

Cleopatra *attendant:* **4** Iras **8** Charmian *brother:* **7** Ptolemy *husband:* **7** Ptolemy *killer:* **3** asp *lover:* **6** Antony (Marc), Caesar (Julius) **7** Anthony (Mark) *river:* **4** Nile

Cleopatra's Needle 7 obelisk

clepsydra 9 timepiece **10** water clock

clerestory 7 gallery

clergy 7 canonry **8** ministry **9** churchmen, diaconate, pastorate, rabbinate **10** priesthood **11** cardinalate **13** ecclesiastics

clergyman 5 clerk, padre, vicar **6** bishop, cleric, curate, divine, father, parson, pastor, priest, rector **7** dominie, prelate **8** chaplain, clerical, minister, preacher, reverend, shepherd, sky pilot **9** churchman, pulpiteer **10** evangelist, missionary, sermonizer **12** ecclesiastic *American:* **4** Hale (Edward Everett), King (Martin Luther, Thomas Starr) **5** Eliot (John), Moody (Dwight), Stone (Barton Warren), Weems (Parson) **6** Dwight (Timothy), Finney (Charles), Graham (Billy), Holmes (John Haynes), Hooker (Thomas), Mather (Cotton, Increase, Richard), Merton (Thomas), Parker (Samuel, Theodore), Sunday (Billy), Taylor (Edward, Graham, Nathaniel William) **7** Beecher (Henry Ward, Lyman), Edwards (Jonathan), Harvard (John), Russell (Charles Taze) **10** Muhlenberg (Frederick Augustus, Henry Melchior, John Peter Gabriel) *English:* **4** Ward (Nathaniel, Seth, William George) **5** Donne (John), Paley (William), Smith (Henry "Silver-Tongued," John "The Sebaptist," Sidney) **6** Cotton (John), Fuller (Andrew, Thomas), Taylor (Jeremy, Rowland), Wesley (Charles, John) **7** Cranmer (Thomas), Parsons (Robert) **8** Kingsley (Charles) **10** Whitefield (George) *home:* **5** manse **6** priory **7** rectory **8** vicarage **9** monastery, parsonage *traveling:* **12** circuit rider

cleric see CLERGYMAN

clerisy 8 literati **10** illuminati **13** intellectuals

clerk 7 cashier **8** salesman **9** secretary **10** accountant, bookkeeper **11** salesperson **12** stenographer

clever 3 apt, sly **4** able, deft, good, keen **5** adept, alert, canny, funny, handy, quick, savvy, sharp, smart, witty **6** adroit, astute, brainy, bright, crafty, expert, shrewd, tricky **7** amusing, capable, cunning, knowing, skilled **8** fanciful, humorous, pleasing, skillful, talented **9** competent, dexterous, ingenious **10** proficient **11** intelligent, quickwitted, resourceful **12** entertaining

cliché 3 saw **6** truism **7** bromide **8** banality, buzzword, chestnut **9** platitude **10** shibboleth, stereotype **11** commonplace

clichéd 5 banal, bland, musty, stale, tired, trite, vapid **6** old-hat **7** humdrum, insipid, worn-out **8** bromidic, shopworn, timeworn **9** hackneyed **10** pedestrian, unoriginal **11** stereotyped **13** platitudinous, unimaginative

click 3 fit **4** snap, tick, work **5** agree, match **6** go over, pan out **7** come off, succeed

client 6 patron **7** patient, protégé **8** customer **9** dependent

clientele 4 fans **5** trade, train **6** custom, market, public **7** patrons, traffic **8** audience, patients, regulars, shoppers **9** customers **10** purchasers, supporters **12** constituency

cliff 4 crag **5** bluff, scarp **8** headland, palisade **9** precipice **10** escarpment

climacteric 4 apex, crux, cusp **5** acute **6** crisis **7** crucial **8** critical **9** menopause **11** culmination **12** change of life, turning point

climactic 4 peak **7** crucial, pivotal **8** critical, decisive, dramatic **9** momentous **10** definitive **11** culminating, determining

climate 6 medium, milieu **7** ambient **8** ambience **10** atmosphere **11** environment **12** surroundings

climax 3 cap **4** acme, apex, peak **5** crown **6** apogee, summit, top off **8** capstone, meridian, pinnacle **9** culminate **11** culmination

climb 4 go up, rise, soar **5** mount, scale, slope **6** ascend **7** clamber **8** escalate, increase

climbing 8 scandent

climbing iron 7 crampon

clinch 3 hug **4** grip, hold, seal **5** clamp, clasp, grasp, sew up **6** clutch, decide, ensure, lock up **7** confirm, embrace, grapple, squeeze **8** nail down

clincher 4 tire **5** proof **6** kicker **7** quietus **9** deathblow **10** smoking gun **11** affirmation, attestation, coup de grâce **12** confirmation **13** corroboration

cling 4 bond **5** stick **6** adhere, cleave, clutch, hold on, linger **8** adhesion **9** adherence

clingstone 5 peach

clink 3 can, jug, pen **4** brig, cell, coop, jail, stir **5** pokey, pound **6** cooler, jingle, lockup, prison, tingle, tinkle **7** slammer **8** hoosegow **9** calaboose

clinker 3 dud **4** bomb, bust, flop, goof, slag **5** botch, brick, error, lemon, loser **6** bummer, bungle, fiasco, howler, turkey **7** bloomer, blunder, failure, faux pas, mistake

clinkers 3 ash **4** slag **5** ashes **7** cinders

clinquant 5 gaudy **6** flashy, garish, tawdry, tinsel **8** specious **10** glittering **11** superficial

Clio see MUSE

clip 3 bob, cut, mow, pin **4** crop, hasp, pare, snip, sock, trim **5** block, clasp, prune, punch, shave, shear, slash **6** broach, brooch, fleece, reduce **7** curtail, cut back, cut down, shorten **8** magazine, truncate **10** abbreviate, overcharge

clique 3 set **4** camp, clan, club, gang, ring **5** cabal, crowd, mafia **6** circle **7** coterie, faction, in-group **9** camarilla

cloak 4 cape, mask, robe, veil, wrap **5** cover, guise **6** facade, joseph, mantle, screen, shroud, veneer **7** blanket, conceal, curtain, dress up, manteau, obscure **8** disguise **9** dissemble, semblance **10** camouflage **11** dissimulate *ancient Greek:* **7** chlamys *ancient Roman:* **7** pallium *Arab:* **3** aba *fur:* **7** pelisse *hooded:* **6** capote **7** burnous **8** burnoose *liturgical:* **4** cope *Moroccan:* **8** djellaba *over armor:* **6** tabard **7** surcoat *Spanish:* **5** manta

clobber 4 belt, drub, flay, lick, slam, slug, whip, whup **5** blast, brain, clout, pound, smash **6** hammer, thrash, wallop **7** shellac, trounce **8** demolish, lambaste

clochard 3 bum, vag **4** hobo **5** tramp **6** beggar, canter **7** drifter, floater, moocher, vagrant **8** deadbeat, derelict, vagabond **9** transient **10** freeloader, panhandler **11** bindle stiff

cloche 3 hat **5** cover, toque, tuque

clock 4 time **9** timepiece **11** chronometer *water:* **9** clepsydra

clocklike 5 exact **6** minute, prompt, strict, timely **7** precise, regular **8** accurate, punctual, reliable, thorough **9** assiduous **10** dependable, meticulous, scrupulous **11** painstaking **13** conscientious

clockmaker 10 horologist

clockwise 6 deasil **7** dextral **11** righthanded

Clockwork Orange author 7 Burgess (Anthony)

clod 3 gob, wad **4** boob, dolt, dope, hunk, lump, soil **5** chump, chunk, clump, dummy, dunce, earth **6** dimwit **8** dumbbell **9** blockhead, lamebrain

cloddish 7 boorish, ill-bred, loutish,

uncouth 8 churlish, clownish 9 unrefined 10 uncultured, unpolished 11 uncivilized

clodhopper 4 boor, boot, hick, lout 5 chuff, churl, clown, yokel 6 rustic 7 bumpkin, hayseed, redneck 9 chawbacon

clog 3 gum, jam, tax 4 fill, glut, load, plug, stop 5 block, choke, close, stuff 6 hamper, hinder 7 congest 8 encumber, obstruct, overload 10 impediment 11 encumbrance

cloister 5 abbey, court 6 arcade, garden 7 convent, retreat, seclude, shelter 9 courtyard, monastery, sequester

Cloister and the Hearth author 5 Reade (Charles)

cloistered 7 recluse 8 confined, hermetic, secluded 9 seclusive, withdrawn 11 sequestered

cloistered one 3 nun 4 monk

clone 4 copy 5 ditto 6 double, carbon 7 replica 9 duplicate, facsimile, replicate, reproduce 10 carbon copy, simulacrum 12 reproduction

Clorinda *beloved:* 7 Tancred *father:* 6 Senapo *guardian:* 6 Arsete *slayer:* 7 Tancred

close 3 end 4 near, nigh, shut, slam 5 block, cease, choke, humid, muggy, tight 6 ending, finale, finish, narrow, nearby, sticky, stuffy, sultry, windup, wrap up 7 airless, compact, crowded, stopper 8 abutting, adjacent, complete, conclude, finalize, intimate, obstruct, stifling 9 adjoining, cessation, condensed, terminate 10 conclusion, consummate, convenient, near-at-hand 11 constricted, neighboring, termination 12 confidential

closed-minded 4 deaf 6 narrow 8 obdurate 9 hidebound, obstinate, pigheaded, unbending 10 bullheaded, hardheaded 11 intractable

closefisted 5 cheap, mingy 6 frugal, stingy 7 miserly, thrifty 9 niggardly, penurious 13 penny-pinching

close in 3 hem 4 cage 5 fence, hedge 6 corral, immure 7 advance, confine, enclose, envelop, impound 8 approach, converge, encircle, enshroud, imprison, surround

close-knit 8 intimate

closely 4 hard 7 sharply 8 intently, minutely 9 carefully 11 searchingly 12 meticulously, scrupulously, thoughtfully 13 punctiliously

close match 6 toss-up

closemouthed 3 mum 4 mute 6 silent 7 laconic 8 reserved, reticent, taciturn 12 tight-mouthed

closeness 8 intimacy

close off 4 clog, plug 5 block 6 stop up 7 isolate, occlude 8 insulate 9 segregate, sequester

closet 6 covert, inside, office 7 cabinet, chamber, furtive, private 8 wardrobe 11 speculative, theoretical

closing 3 end 4 last, stop 5 final 6 ending, finish, latest, period, windup, wrap-up 7 curtain 8 eventual, terminal, ultimate 9 cessation 10 concluding 11 termination

closure 3 cap, end, lid 6 ending, finish 8 fastener 9 cessation

clot 3 gel, set 4 curd, glob, jell, lump 5 clump 6 curdle, gelate 7 congeal 8 coagulum, thrombus 9 coagulate 10 gelatinize *combining form:* 6 thromb 7 thrombo

cloth see FABRIC

clothe 3 tog 4 deck, do up, garb, robe 5 array, cloak, couch, drape, dress, endow, equip 6 attire, bedeck, outfit, swathe 7 apparel, costume, dress up 8 accouter

clothes 3 rig 4 duds, garb, rags, togs 5 array, dress, getup, habit 6 attire, outfit, things 7 apparel, costume, raiment, rigging, threads, toggery, vesture 8 garments, glad rags 9 vestments 11 habiliments *basket:* 6 hamper *civilian:* 5 mufti

clothes-moth genus 5 Tinea

clothespress 7 armoire 8 wardrobe

cloud 3 dim, fog, tar 4 blur, haze, mist, murk 5 addle, befog, brume, gloom, muddy, plume, smear, sully, taint 6 muddle, nebula, puzzle, shadow, smudge 7 besmear, confuse, obscure, perplex, tarnish 8 befuddle, besmirch, discolor, distract, overcast 9 obfuscate *type:* 6 cirrus, nimbus 7 cumulus, stratus 11 altocumulus, altostratus 12 cirrocumulus, cirrostratus, cumulonimbus, nimbostratus 13 stratocumulus

cloudburst 6 deluge, shower 7 monsoon, torrent 8 downpour, drencher, rainfall 10 outpouring

clouded 5 dusky, murky, shady 6 dreary, gloomy, somber, sombre 7 dubious, ominous, sunless, unclear 8 doubtful, overcast 9 ambiguous, equivocal, uncertain, unsettled 11 problematic

cloudless 4 fair, fine 5 clear, sunny 7 clarion 8 pleasant, rainless, sunshiny

cloud-like mass 6 nebula

cloudy 4 dull, hazy 5 dusky, foggy, heavy, misty, murky, vague 6 gloomy, opaque, somber, sombre 7 louring, obscure, tainted, unclear 8 confused, darkened, lowering, nebulous, overcast, vaporous 10 indistinct

clout 3 box, hit, rag 4 blow, cuff, poke, pull, slam, slap, slug, sock, swat, sway 5 paste, power, punch, smack, smite, whack 6 strike 9 influence

clove 4 bulb 5 spice 7 chopped, severed

clove hitch 4 knot

clover 5 lotus 6 alsike, ladino, lucern 7 alfalfa, berseem, lucerne, melilot, trefoil 8 four-leaf, shamrock 9 lespedeza *family:* 3 pea *genus:* 9 Trifolium

clown 3 wag 4 mime, zany 5 cutup, joker, Punch 6 jester, mummer 7 buffoon 8 comedian, jokester 9 harlequin, prankster 11 merry-andrew *French:* 7 Pierrot *operatic:* 5 buffo *Spanish:* 8 gracioso

clownish 4 rude 6 clumsy, gauche, oafish 7 awkward, boorish, ill-bred, loutish, lumpish, uncouth 8 churlish, cloddish 9 unrefined

cloy 4 fill, glut, jade, pall, sate 5 gorge 6 sicken 7 satiate, surfeit 8 overfill

cloying 4 icky 5 gushy, mushy, sappy, soppy 6 sticky, sugary 7 fulsome, gushing, maudlin, mawkish 9 excessive, schmaltzy, sickening 10 disgusting, lovey-dovey, nauseating, saccharine 11 distasteful, sentimental

club 3 bat, sap 4 beat, cosh, iron, mace 5 baton, billy, guild, lodge, order, union 6 cudgel, league 7 society 8 bludgeon, sodality, sorority 9 blackjack, truncheon 10 fellowship, fraternity, knobkerrie, nightstick 11 association, brotherhood *Australian:* 5 waddy *Irish:* 10 shillelagh

clubfoot 7 talipes

cluck 4 dodo, dolt, dope, fool 5 dunce 6 dimwit, nitwit 7 pinhead

clue 3 cue 4 hint, idea, lead, sign, tell, warn 6 advise, inform, notify, notion, tip-off 7 inkling 8 evidence, telltale 10 indication, intimation, suggestion

clump 3 gob, wad 4 clod, hunk, lump, mass, mess, plod 5 batch, bunch, chunk, group, stomp, tramp 6 bumble, bundle, lumber, parcel 7 cluster, galumph, stumble

clump of grass 4 tuft 6 tuffet 7 tussock

clumsy 5 bulky, gawky, inept, splay 6 clunky, gauche, klutzy, wooden 7 awkward, hulking, lumpish, uncouth, unhandy 8 bumbling, bungling, tactless, ungainly, unsubtle, unwieldy 9 all thumbs, graceless, ham-handed, inelegant, lumbering, maladroit 11 heavy-handed, inefficient

clumsy one 3 oaf 4 clod, goon, lout, slob 5 klutz 6 baboon, galoot, lummox 7 bumpkin, bungler, palooka 13 butterfingers

clunk 4 thud 5 clout, thump, whack 6 thwack, wallop

clunker 4 bomb, heap 5 crate, wreck 6 jalopy, junker 7 stinker 10 rattletrap

cluster 3 lot, set 4 band, bevy, crew, knot, pack 5 array, batch, bunch, clump, covey, group 6 bundle, clutch, gather 7 collect, package 8 assemble, assembly 9 aggregate, associate, gathering 10 accumulate

cluster bean 4 guar

clutch 4 grab, grip, hold, keep 5 catch, clamp, clasp, grasp, pinch, seize 6 bundle, clench, clinch, snatch 7 cluster, grapple

clutter 4 hash, mash, mess, muss, ruck 5 chaos, snarl, strew 6 jumble, litter, muddle 7 mélange, rummage 8 disarray, disorder, mishmash, shambles 9 confusion 10 hodgepodge

Clydesdale 5 horse 10 draft horse

Clymene *father:* 7 Oceanus *husband:* 7 Iapetus *mother:* 6 Tethys *son:* 5 Atlas 10 Epimetheus, Prometheus

Clytemnestra *brother:* 6 Castor, Pollux 10 Polydeuces *daughter:* 7 Electra 9 Iphigenia *father:* 9 Tyndareus *husband:* 9 Agamemnon *lover:* 9 Aegisthus *mother:* 4 Leda *slayer:* 7 Orestes *son:* 7 Orestes *victim:* 9 Agamemnon, Cassandra

Clytie *beloved:* 6 Apollo *form:* 9 sunflower 10 heliotrope

coach 3 bus, car 5 drill, stage, train, tutor 6 chaise, mentor 7 prepare, trainer 8 carriage, instruct 10 instructor

coadjutor 3 aid 4 aide 6 bishop, deputy 9 assistant 10 aide-de-camp, lieutenant

coagulate 3 gel, set 4 clot, jell 5 curdle 7 congeal, jellify, thicken 8 coalesce, condense, solidify 10 gelatinize, inspissate 11 concentrate, consolidate

coal *distillate:* 3 tar *dust:* 4 smut, soot 5 slack *element:* 6 carbon *fused leavings:* 4 slag 7 clinker *glowing:* 5 ember, gleed *hard:* 10 anthracite *lump:* 3 cob *miner:* 7 collier *region:* 4 Saar *residue:* 4 coke *soft:* 6 cannel 10 bituminous

coalesce 3 mix 4 fuse, join, link 5 blend, merge, unite 6 mingle 7 combine, conjoin 10 amalgamate

coalition 4 bloc, ring 5 party, union 6 fusion, league, merger 7 combine, melding, merging 8 alliance 9 anschluss 10 federation 11 affiliation, association, combination, confederacy, integration, unification 13 confederation, consolidation

coarse 3 raw 4 rude 5 bawdy, crass, crude, dirty, gross, rough, tacky 6 common, filthy, grainy, ribald, smutty, vul-

gar **7** boorish, obscene, raffish,
raunchy, uncouth **8** granular, indecent
9 inelegant, roughneck, unrefined
10 uncultured **11** particulate **12** uncultivated

coast 4 bank **5** beach, drift, shore, slide
6 strand **7** seaside **8** littoral, seashore *of
Antarctica:* **4** Knox

coastal 7 seaside **8** littoral, riverine

coaster 4 sled, tray **6** trader

coat 5 crust, glaze, gloss, layer, parka,
plate, tunic **6** blazer, duster, finish,
jacket, patina, raglan, reefer, ulster,
veneer **7** cutaway **8** covering, mackinaw, tegument **9** newmarket, redingote
10 integument, mackintosh **11** wind-
breaker *animal:* **3** fur **4** hide, pelt, wool
6 pelage *fur-lined:* **7** pelisse *kind:* **3** pea,
top **5** frock **6** trench *Levantine:* **6** caftan
of arms: **5** crest **6** blazon, emblem,
shield, tabard **8** blazonry **10** escutcheon
of egg white: **5** glair **6** glaire *of mail:*
7 hauberk *soldier's:* **5** frock, tunic
6 capote *waterproof:* **7** slicker **10** mackintosh

coating 4 film, leaf, scum, skin **5** glaze,
gloss, layer **6** finish, patina, veneer
7 dusting, lacquer, overlay, surface,
varnish **8** covering

coax 4 lure, urge **5** cable, press, tempt
6 cajole, entice, induce **7** blarney,
wheedle **8** blandish, butter up, inveigle,
persuade, soft-soap **9** importune,
sweet-talk

cob 3 ear **4** swan **5** adobe, horse

cobble 4 make, mend **5** patch, stone
6 repair **11** paving stone

cobbler 3 pie **5** drink **8** cocktail **9** shoemaker

cobbler's form 4 last

cobelligerent 4 ally

cobweb 3 net **4** mesh, trap **8** gossamer
9 confusion, spiderweb **12** entanglement

coccyx 8 tailbone

cochineal 3 dye **6** insect

cock 3 tap **4** boss, head, heap, hill, lord,
mass, pile, rick, tilt **5** chief, mound,
stack, strut, valve **6** faucet, honcho,
leader, master, spigot **7** headman,
hydrant, rooster, swagger **11** chanticleer

cock-a-hoop 4 awry **5** askew **7** askance,
crooked **8** boastful, exultant, exulting,
jubilant **9** triumphal **10** triumphant

Cockaigne 6 utopia **7** arcadia **9** Shangri-
la **10** wonderland

cockalorum 7 bluster, bombast, bravado
8 blowhard, boasting, braggart,
leapfrog **11** braggadocio

cockamamy 5 batty, crazy, daffy, flaky,
kooky, loony, nutty, wacky **6** absurd

9 ludicrous **10** incredible, ridiculous
11 harebrained

cock-and-bull story 5 crock **6** canard
7 whopper **9** fairy tale

cockcrow 4 dawn, morn **5** sunup
7 morning, sunrise **8** daybreak, daylight

cocker 4 baby **5** humor, spoil **6** coddle,
cosset, pamper **7** indulge, spaniel
11 mollycoddle

cockeyed 4 awry **5** askew **8** lopsided
11 harebrained

cockle 5 shell **6** dimple, furrow, groove,
pucker, ripple **7** bivalve, mollusc, mollusk, wrinkle

cockleshell 4 boat

cockscomb see COXCOMB

cocksure 5 brash **6** cheeky **9** bumptious
13 overconfident

cocktail 5 Bronx, drink **6** gibson, gimlet,
mai tai, mimosa, mojito, Rob Roy,
zombie **7** gin fizz, martini, sidecar,
stinger **8** aperitif, daiquiri, pink lady,
salty dog, sombrero **9** Cuba libre, manhattan, margarita, mint julep, rusty nail
10 Bloody Mary, Tom Collins, wall-
banger **11** grasshopper, screwdriver,
whiskey sour **12** black russian, cosmopolitan, old-fashioned *fruit:* **9** mace-
doine *gasoline:* **7** Molotov

Cocktail Party author 5 Eliot (T. S.)

cocky 4 bold, sure **5** brash, pushy, sassy,
saucy **6** brassy, cheeky, jaunty **8** arrogant, impudent, insolent **9** conceited
10 swaggering **11** self-assured **12** enterprising **13** overconfident, self-confident

coconspirator 7 abettor **9** accessory
10 accomplice **11** confederate

coconut *husk fiber:* **4** coir *meat:* **5** copra

coda 5 envoi, envoy **6** ending, finale
7 summary **8** epilogue, follow-up
9 afterword **10** conclusion

coddle 4 baby **5** humor, spoil **6** cosset,
pamper **7** cater to, indulge

code 6 cipher, symbol **7** encrypt **8** encipher *kind:* **3** zip **4** area **5** Morse, legal,
penal *message in:* **10** cryptogram
11 cryptograph

code word see COMMUNICATIONS CODE
WORD

codger 6 duffer, fellow

codicil 5 rider **8** addendum, addition,
appendix **10** postscript, supplement

codswallop see NONSENSE

coefficient 6 factor **7** measure **8** constant

coelenterate 5 coral **7** anemone, hydroid
9 cnidarian, jellyfish **10** sea anemone

coerce 3 cow **5** bully, force, impel, press
6 compel, menace, oblige **8** browbeat,
bulldoze, dominate, threaten **9** blackjack, constrain, strong-arm, terrorize
10 intimidate

coercion 5 force **6** duress, menace, threat **8** pressure **10** compulsion, constraint
Coeur d'___ 5 Alene
coeval see CONTEMPORARY
coexistent see CONTEMPORARY
coffee *alkaloid:* **8** caffeine *bean:* **3** nib *cake:* **6** kuchen *cup:* **9** demitasse *French:* **4** café *grinder:* **4** mill *kind:* **4** drip, java **5** decaf, latte, mocha **7** arabica, instant **8** espresso **9** Americano, macchiato **10** café au lait, cappuccino *maker:* **10** percolator *pot:* **3** urn
coffee shop 4 café **5** diner **8** snack bar **9** cafeteria, hash house, lunchroom **11** greasy spoon **12** luncheonette
coffer 5 chest **6** casket **8** treasury **9** exchequer, strongbox
coffin 3 box **4** kist **6** casket *carrier:* **6** hearse **10** pallbearer *nail:* **9** cigarette *stand:* **4** bier **10** catafalque
cogency 5 force, point, power, punch **7** potency **8** strength, validity **9** relevance **10** conviction, pertinence **13** effectiveness
cogent 5 solid, sound, valid **6** potent **7** telling, weighty **8** forceful, powerful, relevant **9** pertinent **10** compelling, convincing, meaningful, persuasive **11** influential, well-founded **12** well-grounded **13** consequential
cogitate 4 muse **5** think **6** ponder, reason **7** reflect **8** conceive, consider, meditate, mull over, ruminate **9** cerebrate, speculate **10** deliberate
cogitation 7 thought **10** meditation, reflection, rumination **11** cerebration, speculation **12** deliberation **13** consideration
cogitative 7 pensive **10** meditative, reflective, ruminative, thoughtful **11** speculative **13** contemplative
Cogito ___ sum 4 ergo
cognac 6 brandy
cognate 4 akin, like **5** alike **6** allied, common **7** kindred, related, similar **8** parallel **10** affiliated, associated
cognition 9 awareness, knowledge, sentience **10** perception
cognizance 4 heed, note **6** notice **9** attention, awareness, knowledge **12** jurisdiction
cognizant 5 aware **7** knowing, mindful **8** informed, sensible **9** conscious **13** knowledgeable
cognize 4 know **5** grasp **6** fathom **7** realize **8** perceive **9** apprehend **10** appreciate, comprehend, understand
cognomen 4 name **5** alias, title **7** epithet, moniker, surname **8** nickname **11** appellation, appellative, designation **12** denomination

cognoscente 5 judge **6** critic, expert **7** epicure **8** aesthete **9** authority **10** specialist **11** connoisseur
cognoscible 8 knowable **10** fathomable **13** apprehensible
cohere 4 fuse, join **5** agree, blend, cling, merge, stick, unite **6** accord **7** combine, comport, conform, connect **8** coalesce, dovetail **10** correspond **11** consolidate
coherence 4 bond **5** union, unity **8** adhesion, cohesion **9** agreement, congruity, integrity **10** conformity, connection, consonance, solidarity **11** consistency, integration
coherent 5 sound **7** logical, ordered, unified **8** rational **10** consistent, integrated, meaningful **11** coordinated
cohesion see COHERENCE
coho 6 salmon **12** silver salmon
cohort 3 pal **4** ally, band, chum, crew, mate **5** buddy, crony, group **6** fellow, friend **7** comrade, partner **8** adherent, confrere, disciple, follower, henchman, sidekick **9** assistant, associate, colleague, companion, supporter **10** accomplice **11** demographic **12** collaborator
coif 3 cap, cut **4** hood, perm **6** hairdo **7** haircut **8** skullcap
coiffeur 6 barber **10** haircutter **11** hairdresser, hairstylist
coiffure 6 hairdo *aid:* **3** net, rat **5** snood
coil 4 curl, loop, ring, turn, wind **5** helix, twine, twist **6** rotate, spiral **7** entwine, revolve, wreathe **8** curlicue **9** corkscrew
coiled 6 spiral, volute **7** helical, voluted, whorled **9** circinate
coin 4 mint **6** invent, make up, strike *Afghanistan:* **3** pul **7** afghani *Albania:* **3** lek **9** quindarka *Algeria:* **5** dinar **7** centime *ancient Greek:* **4** obol *ancient Muslim:* **5** dinar *ancient Roman:* **8** denarius *Argentina:* **4** peso **7** centavo *Austria:* **4** euro **8** groschen **9** schilling *Bahrain:* **4** fils **5** dinar *Belgium:* **4** euro **5** franc **7** centime *Benin:* **5** franc **7** centime *Bhutan:* **7** chetrum **8** ngultrum *Bolivia:* **7** centavo **9** boliviano *Botswana:* **4** pula **5** thebe *Brazil:* **4** real **7** centavo **8** cruzeiro *Bulgaria:* **3** lev **8** stotinka *Burundi:* **5** franc **7** centime *Cameroon:* **5** franc **7** centime *Canada:* **6** loonie, toonie, twonie *Cape Verde Islands:* **6** escudo **7** centavo *Chile:* **4** peso **7** centavo *China:* **3** fen **4** jiao, yuan *Columbia:* **4** peso **7** centavo *Costa Rica:* **5** colón **7** centimo *Cuba:* **4** peso **7** centavo *Czech Republic:* **5** haler **6** koruna *defective:* **4** fido *Denmark:* **3** ore **5** krone *Dominican Republic:* **4** peso **7** centavo *Ecuador:*

5 sucre 7 centavo *edge:* 7 milling *Egypt:* 7 piastre *European gold:* 5 ducat *Finland:* 4 euro 5 penni 6 markka *former:* 3 ecu, mil, pie, sol, sou 4 anna, besa, doit, duit, kran, para, pice, reis (plural) 5 fanam, litas, mohur, paisa, rupia, shahi, soldo, toman 6 centas, denier, heller, macuta, pagoda, tangka 7 santims, sapeque 8 maravedi, skilling 9 rigsdaler 10 Indian head, reichsmark 13 reichspfennig *France:* 4 euro 5 franc 7 centime *Gambia:* 5 butut 6 dalasi *Germany:* 4 euro, mark 7 pfennig *Ghana:* 4 cedi 6 pesewa *Great Britain:* 3 bob 5 crown, penny 6 guinea 7 ha'penny 8 farthing, shilling, sixpence 9 halfpenny, sovereign 10 threepence *Greece:* 4 euro 6 lepton 7 drachma *Guatemala:* 7 centavo, quetzal *Guinea-Bissau:* 4 peso *Haiti:* 6 gourde 7 centime *Honduras:* 7 centavo, lempira *Hungary:* 5 pengo 6 filler, forint *Iceland:* 5 aurar (plural), eyrir, krona *India:* 5 paisa, rupee *Indonesia:* 3 sen 6 rupiah *Iran:* 4 rial 5 dinar *Iraq:* 4 fils 5 dinar *Ireland:* 4 euro 5 penny 8 farthing *Israel:* 5 agora 6 shekel *Italy:* 4 euro, lira 5 scudo *Japan:* 3 rin, sen, yen *Jordan:* 4 fils 5 dinar *Kenya:* 8 shilling *Korea, North and South:* 3 won 4 chon *Kuwait:* 4 fils 5 dinar *large:* 9 cartwheel *Lebanon:* 5 livre 7 piastre *Lesotho:* 4 loti 7 licente, lisente *Libya:* 5 dinar 6 dirham *Luxembourg:* 4 euro 5 franc *Madagascar:* 5 franc *Malawi:* 6 kwacha 7 tambala *Mauritania:* 5 khoum 7 ouguiya *Mauritius:* 5 rupee *Mexico:* 4 peso 7 centavo *Monaco:* 4 euro 5 franc *Morocco:* 6 dirham *Mozambique:* 7 metical *Nepal:* 5 paisa, rupee *Netherlands:* 4 euro 6 florin, gulden 7 guilder *Nicaragua:* 7 centavo, córdoba *Nigeria:* 4 kobo 5 naira *Norway:* 3 ore 5 krone *Oman:* 4 rial 5 baiza *Pakistan:* 5 paisa, rupee *Panama:* 6 balboa 9 centesimo *Papua New Guinea:* 4 kina, toea *Paraguay:* 7 centimo, guarani *Peru:* 3 sol 7 centimo *Philippines:* 4 piso 7 sentimo *Poland:* 5 grosz, zloty *Portugal:* 4 euro 6 escudo 7 centavo *Qatar:* 5 riyal 6 dirham *Roman:* 6 aureus, bezant 7 solidus *Romania:* 3 ban, leu *Russia:* 5 kopek, ruble 6 kopeck *San Marino:* 4 lira *Saudi Arabia:* 4 rial 6 halala *Seychelles:* 5 rupee *side of a:* 7 obverse *Slovakia:* 5 haler 6 koruna *South Africa:* 4 rand 10 Krugerrand *Spain:* 4 euro 6 peseta 7 centimo *Sri Lanka:* 5 rupee *stamping metal:* 8 planchet *Suriname:* 6 florin, gulden 7 guilder *Swaziland:* 9 lilangeni *Sweden:* 3 ore 5 krona 8 skilling *Switzer-*

-land: 5 franc 6 rappen *Syria:* 7 piastre *Tanzania:* 8 shilling *Thailand:* 4 baht 5 tical 6 satang *Tonga:* 6 pa'anga, seniti *Tunisia:* 5 dinar *Turkey:* 4 lira 5 kurus *Uganda:* 8 shilling *United Arab Emirates:* 6 dirham *United States:* 4 dime 5 penny 6 dollar, nickel 7 quarter 10 half-dollar *Uruguay:* 4 peso 9 centesimo *Vatican City:* 4 lira *Venezuela:* 7 bolivar *Samoa:* 4 sene, tala *Zambia:* 5 ngwee 6 kwacha

coinage 7 new word 8 creation, currency 9 invention, neologism 10 brainchild 11 contrivance

coincide 4 jibe 5 agree, equal, match, tally 6 accord, concur, square 7 comport, conform 8 dovetail 9 harmonize 10 correspond

coincident 7 similar 9 consonant 10 concurrent 11 concomitant, synchronous 12 accompanying, contemporary, simultaneous

coincidentally 8 by chance, together 12 accidentally, concurrently, fortuitously

coin-shaped 8 nummular

col 4 pass 5 ridge 6 saddle

___ **colada** 4 piña

colander's cousin 5 sieve 6 sifter 8 strainer

cold ___ 3 war 4 call, cash, cuts, feet, fish, sore, wave 5 cream, frame, front, patch, steel, sweat, water 6 turkey 7 comfort, storage 8 shoulder

cold 3 icy, raw 4 cool, dead, iced 5 aloof, chill, crisp, frore, gelid, nippy, polar 6 arctic, biting, chilly, frigid, frosty, frozen, wintry 7 bracing, glacial, shivery 8 chilling, comatose, freezing, lifeless 11 emotionless, passionless, unconscious, unemotional 12 unresponsive *combining form:* 4 cryo, kryo *common:* 6 coryza *symptom:* 5 cough, fever 6 sneeze 7 catarrh

cold-blooded 5 cruel 6 brutal 7 callous 8 hardened, obdurate, pitiless, ruthless 9 heartless, impassive, unfeeling 10 hard-boiled, impersonal 11 emotionless, hard-hearted 12 matter-of-fact, stonyhearted 13 dispassionate, unimpassioned

cold feet 4 fear 5 alarm, doubt, dread, panic, worry 6 dismay, fright, terror 7 anxiety, jitters 8 timidity 9 cowardice 11 trepidation 12 apprehension

coldhearted see COLD-BLOODED

cold-shoulder 3 cut 4 snub 6 ignore, slight 9 ostracize

cold storage 8 abeyance, dormancy 10 quiescence, suspension 12 intermission, interruption

cole 4 kale, rape 7 cabbage 8 brassica, broccoli, kohlrabi 11 cauliflower

Coleridge poem 9 Dejection, Kubla Khan 10 Christabel

Colette character 4 Gigi 5 Cheri 8 Claudine

colewort 4 kale 7 cabbage

colic 5 gripe 9 bellyache 11 stomachache 12 collywobbles

coliseum 4 bowl 5 arena, stade 6 circus 7 stadium

collaborate 6 team up 7 collude 8 conspire 9 cooperate

collaborator 4 ally 6 helper 7 abettor, partner, traitor 8 coworker, henchman, quisling 9 accessory, assistant, associate, auxiliary, colleague 10 accomplice 11 confederate, conspirator

collapse 4 cave, drop, fail, ruin 5 break, crash, smash, wreck 6 buckle, cave in, fold up 7 breakup, crack-up, crumple, debacle, deflate, downfall, failure, founder, give out, give way, pass out, shatter, smashup, succumb 8 condense 9 breakdown, cataclysm, fall apart, ruination 10 disruption 11 catastrophe, destruction, prostration 12 disintegrate

collar 3 bag, nab 4 grab, hook, nail, take 5 catch, seize 6 arrest, secure 7 capture 9 apprehend *armor:* 6 gorget *boy's:* 4 Eton *chain:* 4 torc 6 torque *jeweled:* 8 carcanet *lace-edged:* 6 rebato *metal:* 4 torc 6 torque *pleated:* 4 ruff

collarbone 8 clavicle

collate 5 group, order 7 arrange, collect, compare, compile 8 assemble, contrast, organize 9 integrate

collateral 4 bond 6 allied, lineal, pledge, surety 7 cognate, kindred, oblique, related, subject 8 indirect, parallel, security 9 accessory, ancillary, attendant, auxiliary, dependent, secondary, tributary 10 coincident, coordinate, reciprocal, subsidiary 11 concomitant, subordinate, subservient 12 accompanying, confirmatory, contributory 13 complementary, corresponding, corroborative

colleague 4 aide 6 cohort, fellow, helper 7 partner 8 confrere, coworker, teammate 9 assistant, associate, companion 10 compatriot 11 confederate 12 collaborator

collect 4 draw 5 group, infer, raise 6 deduce, derive, gather, muster, prayer 7 build up, compile, compose, convene, dispose, marshal, round up 8 assemble, conclude, converge 10 accumulate, congregate, rendezvous

collected 4 calm, cool 5 quiet, still 6 poised, serene 7 assured 8 complete, composed, sanguine, tranquil 9 assembled, confident, unruffled 11 unflappable 13 imperturbable, self-possessed

collection 3 ana, kit, lot 4 band, bevy, crew, olio, ruck 5 bunch, crowd, hoard, trove 6 medley, muster 7 cluster, variety 8 assembly, caboodle 9 aggregate, anthology, congeries, gathering, stockpile 10 assemblage, assortment, cumulation, miscellany 11 aggregation 12 accumulation, congregation 13 agglomeration *miscellaneous:* 4 hash, olio 6 jumble, medley 7 mélange, mixture 8 mishmash, pastiche 9 potpourri 10 hodgepodge, salmagundi 11 olla podrida *of anecdotes:* 3 ana *of animals:* 3 zoo 9 menagerie *of artistic works:* 6 museum 7 gallery *of clothes:* 8 wardrobe *of dried plants:* 9 herbarium *of literary pieces:* 8 analects 9 anthology *of reports:* 4 file 7 dossier *of trinkets:* 10 bijouterie

collective 5 joint 7 commune, kibbutz, kolkhoz 11 cooperative

collector *of bird's eggs:* 8 oologist *of books:* 11 bibliophile *of coins:* 11 numismatist *of fares:* 9 conductor *of phonograph records:* 10 discophile *of stamps:* 11 philatelist

colleen 4 girl, lass 6 maiden *country:* 4 Eire, Erin 7 Ireland

college *building:* 3 gym, lab 4 dorm, hall *campus area:* 4 quad 10 quadrangle *class meeting:* 3 lab 7 lecture, seminar 8 tutorial, workshop *degree:* 3 BLS, DST, LLB, LLD, MBA, MEd, MFA, MLS, PhD 5 LittD *graduate:* 6 alumna, alumni (plural) 7 alumnae (plural), alumnus *official:* 4 dean 5 prexy 6 bursar, regent 7 proctor, provost 9 registrar *oldest in U.S.:* 7 Harvard *oldest women's in U.S.:* 12 Mount Holyoke *relating to:* 8 academic 10 collegiate *social group:* 4 frat 8 sorority 10 fraternity *song:* 9 alma mater *student class:* 4 soph 5 frosh 6 junior, senior 8 freshman 9 sophomore *teacher:* 3 don 4 prof 8 academic 9 professor *term:* 7 quarter, session 8 semester 9 trimester *VIP:* 4 BMOC *woman:* 4 coed

college team *Air Force:* 7 Falcons *Alabama:* 11 Crimson Tide *Arizona:* 8 Wildcats *Arizona State:* 9 Sun Devils *Arkansas:* 10 Razorbacks *Arkansas State:* 7 Indians *Army:* 6 Cadets *Auburn:* 6 Tigers *Baylor:* 5 Bears *Boston College:* 6 Eagles *Boston University:* 8 Terriers *Brigham Young:* 7 Cougars *Brown:* 5 Bears *California:* 11 Golden Bears *Central Michigan:* 9 Chippewas *Cincinnati:* 8 Bearcats *Citadel:* 8 Bulldogs *Clemson:*

6 Tigers *Colgate:* 10 Red Raiders *Colorado:* 9 Buffaloes *Colorado State:* 4 Rams *Columbia:* 5 Lions *Connecticut:* 7 Huskies *Cornell:* 6 Big Red *Dartmouth:* 8 Big Green *Davidson:* 8 Wildcats *Delaware State:* 7 Hornets *Drake:* 8 Bulldogs *Duke:* 10 Blue Devils *Eastern Kentucky:* 8 Colonels *Eastern Michigan:* 6 Eagles *Florida:* 6 Gators *Florida State:* 9 Seminoles *Fresno State:* 8 Bulldogs *Furman:* 8 Palidans *Georgia:* 8 Bulldogs *Georgia Tech:* 13 Yellow Jackets *Harvard:* 7 Crimson *Hawaii:* 15 Rainbow Warriors *Holy Cross:* 9 Crusaders *Houston:* 7 Cougars *Howard:* 6 Bisons *Idaho:* 7 Vandals *Idaho State:* 7 Bengals *Illinois:* 14 Fighting Illini *Illinois State:* 8 Redbirds *Indiana:* 8 Hoosiers *Indiana State:* 9 Sycamores *Iowa:* 8 Hawkeyes *Iowa State:* 8 Cyclones *Kansas:* 8 Jayhawks *Kansas State:* 8 Wildcats *Kent State:* 13 Golden Flashes *Kentucky:* 8 Wildcats *Lehigh:* 9 Engineers *Louisiana State:* 6 Tigers *Louisiana Tech:* 8 Bulldogs *Maine:* 10 Black Bears *Maryland:* 5 Terps 9 Terrapins *Massachusetts:* 9 Minutemen *Miami (Florida):* 10 Hurricanes *Miami (Ohio):* 8 Redskins *Michigan:* 10 Wolverines *Michigan State:* 8 Spartans *Minnesota:* 7 Gophers *Mississippi:* 6 Rebels *Mississippi State:* 8 Bulldogs *Missouri:* 6 Tigers *Montana:* 9 Grizzlies *Montana State:* 7 Bobcats *Navy:* 10 Midshipmen *Nebraska:* 11 Cornhuskers *Nevada:* 6 Rebels 8 Wolfpack *New Hampshire:* 8 Wildcats *New Mexico:* 5 Lobos *New Mexico State:* 6 Aggies *North Carolina:* 8 Tar Heels *North Carolina State:* 8 Wolfpack *Northeastern:* 7 Huskies *Northwestern:* 8 Wildcats *Notre Dame:* 13 Fighting Irish *Ohio State:* 8 Buckeyes *Ohio University:* 7 Bobcats *Oklahoma:* 7 Sooners *Oklahoma State:* 7 Cowboys *Oregon:* 5 Ducks *Oregon State:* 7 Beavers *Pennsylvania:* 7 Quakers *Pennsylvania State:* 12 Nittany Lions *Pittsburgh:* 8 Panthers *Princeton:* 6 Tigers *Purdue:* 12 Boilermakers *Rhode Island:* 4 Rams *Rice:* 4 Owls *Rutgers:* 14 Scarlet Knights *San Diego State:* 6 Aztecs *San Jose State:* 8 Spartans *South Carolina:* 9 Gamecocks *South Carolina State:* 8 Bulldogs *Southern California:* 7 Trojans *Southern Illinois:* 7 Salukis *Southern Methodist:* 8 Mustangs *Stanford:* 9 Cardinals *Syracuse:* 9 Orangemen *Temple:* 4 Owls *Tennessee:* 10 Volunteers *Tennessee State:* 6 Tigers *Tennessee Tech:* 12 Golden Eagles *Texas:* 9 Longhorns *Texas A&M:* 6 Aggies *Texas Christian:* 11 Horned Frogs *Texas Southern:* 6 Tigers *Texas*

Tech: 10 Red Raiders *Toledo:* 7 Rockets *Tulane:* 9 Green Wave *UCLA:* 6 Bruins *UNLV:* 12 Runnin' Rebels *Utah:* 4 Utes *Utah State:* 6 Aggies *Vanderbilt:* 10 Commodores *Villanova:* 8 Wildcats *Virginia:* 9 Cavaliers *VMI:* 7 Keydets *VPI:* 8 Gobblers *Wake Forest:* 12 Demon Deacons *Washington:* 7 Huskies *Washington State:* 7 Cougars *West Virginia:* 12 Mountaineers *William & Mary:* 5 Tribe *Wisconsin:* 7 Badgers *Wyoming:* 7 Cowboys *Yale:* 4 Elis 8 Bulldogs

collide 3 hit, ram 4 bump 5 clash, crash, smash 6 impact, strike 7 impinge 8 conflict

collision 4 bump, jolt 5 clash, crash, shock, smash, wreck 6 impact 7 crackup, smashup 10 concussion

collocate 7 arrange 8 position 9 juxtapose

collogue 6 confer, huddle, parley, powwow 7 consult

colloid 3 gel, sol 4 agar 7 mixture 8 hydrogel, hydrosol

colloquial 6 casual, vulgar 7 demotic 8 familiar, informal 9 idiomatic 10 vernacular

colloquium 5 forum 7 palaver, seminar 9 symposium 10 conference, roundtable

colloquy 4 chat, talk 5 forum 6 debate, parley 7 palaver, seminar 8 dialogue 9 symposium 10 conference, discussion, roundtable 12 conversation 13 confabulation

collude 4 plot 6 devise, scheme 7 connive 8 conspire, contrive, intrigue 9 machinate

collusion 4 plot 8 intrigue, skin game 10 conspiracy

collywobbles 5 colic, gripe 9 bellyache 11 stomachache

Colombia *capital:* 6 Bogotá *city:* 4 Cali 6 Ibagué 8 Medellín 9 Cartagena 12 Barranquilla *language:* 7 Spanish *liberator:* 7 Bolivar (Simón) *monetary unit:* 4 peso *mountain, range:* 5 Andes, Chita 6 Puracé, Tolima 9 Cristóbal *neighbor:* 4 Peru 6 Brazil, Panama 7 Ecuador 9 Venezuela *river:* 6 Chauca 7 Orinoco 9 Magdalena *sea:* 9 Caribbean

Colonel Blimp 4 fogy, Tory 6 fossil 7 old fogy 8 mossback 10 fuddy-duddy 11 reactionary

colonnade 4 stoa 9 peristyle

colony 7 outpost 9 satellite 10 settlement

color 3 dun, dye, hue, red, tan 4 aqua, blue, cast, glow, gold, gray, grey, jade, lime, navy, pink, puce, rose, teal, tint, tone 5 amber, azure, beige, belie, black, blush, brown, coral, ebony, flush, green, hazel, henna, ivory, khaki, lilac, mauve, ocher, ochre, olive, paint, peach, rouge, shade, stain, taupe, tinge, umber **6** auburn, bronze, canary, copper, indigo, maroon, orange, purple, redden, salmon, sienna, silver, violet, yellow **7** crimson, emerald, magenta, pigment, saffron, scarlet **8** chestnut, dyestuff, lavender, tincture **9** embellish, embroider, turquoise, vermilion **10** aquamarine, exaggerate **12** pigmentation **band:** **5** facia, vitta **6** fascia **combining form:** **5** chrom **6** chromo **7** chromat **8** chromato **primary:** **3** red **4** blue **6** yellow **relating to:** **9** chromatic **secondary:** **5** green **6** orange, purple **soft:** **6** pastel

Colorado **capital:** **6** Denver **city:** **4** Vail **5** Aspen **6** Aurora, Pueblo **7** Boulder **8** Lakewood **11** Fort Collins **college, university:** **5** Regis **9** Fort Lewis **mountain, range:** **5** Longs (Peak), Pikes (Peak), Rocky **6** Elbert **7** Rockies **nickname:** **10** Centennial (State) **park:** **9** Mesa Verde **river:** **8** Arkansas, Colorado **9** Rio Grande **state bird:** **11** lark bunting **state flower:** **9** columbine **state tree:** **10** blue spruce

colorant **3** dye **5** stain **7** pigment **8** dyestuff, tincture

colored **6** biased, warped **8** one-sided, partisan **9** jaundiced **10** prejudiced **11** tendentious

colorful **3** gay **5** gaudy, showy, vivid **6** bright, flashy, florid, garish, motley **7** splashy

coloring **4** cast, tint **5** front, tinge **6** facade, nuance **7** pigment **8** overtone **10** camouflage, complexion **12** embroidering **13** embellishment

colorless **3** wan **4** ashy, drab, dull, flat, pale **5** ashen, pasty, prosy, waxen, white **6** albino, doughy, pallid **7** insipid, neutral, prosaic **8** abstract, blanched, bleached **10** achromatic, lackluster

Color Purple author **6** Walker (Alice)

colossal **4** huge, vast **7** immense, mammoth, massive, titanic **9** cyclopean, monstrous **10** gargantuan, stupendous **11** astonishing, elephantine

colossus **5** giant, titan **6** statue **7** goliath, mammoth, monster **8** behemoth **9** leviathan

Colossus of ___ **6** Rhodes

colporteur **10** evangelist, missionary **12** propagandist

colt **4** foal, tyro **6** novice, rookie **8** beginner, freshman, neophyte, newcomer **9** fledgling **10** tenderfoot

coltish **6** frisky, impish **7** playful **10** frolicsome

Columbine **beloved:** **9** Harlequin **father:** **9** Pantaloon

Columbus, Christopher **birthplace:** **5** Genoa **patron:** **8** Isabella **9** Ferdinand **ship:** **4** Niña **5** Pinta **10** Santa Maria **son:** **5** Diego **starting point:** **5** Palos

column **3** row **4** pier **5** shaft, stela **6** pillar **7** obelisk **8** pilaster **angle:** **5** arris **base:** **4** ordo **5** socle **6** plinth **9** stylobate **bulge:** **7** entasis **female figure:** **8** caryatid **male figure:** **5** atlas **7** telamon **8** atlantes (plural) **style:** **5** Doric, Ionic **10** Corinthian **top:** **7** capital **8** chapiter

coma **6** stupor, torpor **8** blackout, hebetude, lethargy **9** lassitude

comate **3** pal **4** chum **5** buddy, crony **7** comrade, partner **9** associate, colleague, companion

comatose **5** dopey **6** stupid, torpid **7** out cold **8** sluggish **9** lethargic **10** insensible **11** unconscious

comb **4** rake, sift, sort **5** crest, curry, probe, scour, sweep, tease **6** search, winnow **7** ransack **8** untangle **10** straighten **11** investigate

combat **3** war **4** buck, duel, fray **5** fight, repel **6** action, battle, oppose, resist, strife **7** contend, contest, dispute **8** skirmish, struggle **9** withstand **11** controversy

combatant **7** battler, fighter, soldier, warrior **9** militant, opponent **9** adversary, aggressor, assailant, contender, disputant, mercenary **10** antagonist, challenger, competitor, contestant **11** belligerent

combative **6** feisty **7** scrappy, warlike **8** militant **9** agonistic, bellicose, truculent **10** aggressive, pugnacious **11** belligerent, contentious, quarrelsome **12** disputatious, militaristic

combativeness **9** pugnacity **10** aggression, truculence **11** bellicosity **12** belligerence

combe **4** dale, dell, glen, vale **6** dingle, valley

combination **3** mix **4** bloc, pool, ring **5** blend, union **6** fusion, hookup, merger **7** melding, merging **8** alliance **9** aggregate, coalition, composite, synthesis **10** connection **11** affiliation, association, conjunction, partnership, unification **13** consolidation

combine **3** add, mix, wed **4** band, bloc, fuse, join, link, pool, ring **5** blend, chain, group, marry, merge, trust, unify, union, unite **6** cartel, league, mingle **7** bracket, conjoin, connect, faction **8** coadjute, coalesce **9** associate, coalition, commingle, cooperate, integrate, syndicate **10** amalgamate **11** con-

solidate, incorporate 12 conglomerate
Japanese: 8 keiretsu, zaibatsu *Korean:*
7 chaebol, jaebeol
combined action 7 synergy 9 synergism
combo 4 band, trio 5 group 6 septet,
sextet 7 quartet, quintet 8 ensemble
combust 4 burn 6 ignite, kindle 10 incinerate
combustible 4 edgy, fuel 8 burnable,
volatile 9 excitable, flammable, ignitable 11 inflammable *material:* 3 gas, oil
4 coal, peat, wood 6 tinder
combustion 4 riot 7 burning 8 eruption,
ignition, kindling 9 explosion, oxida-
tion 13 thermogenesis
come 4 flow, hail, stem 5 arise, issue,
occur 6 arrive, derive, show up, spring,
turn up 7 advance, emanate, proceed
8 approach 9 originate *a cropper:* 4 fail,
fall *across:* 4 find, meet 8 discover
9 encounter *apart:* 12 disintegrate *at:*
6 attack *away:* 5 leave 6 depart *before:*
7 precede *clean:* 7 confess *forth:* 5 issue
6 appear, emerge *forward:* 7 advance
9 volunteer *into:* 5 enter 7 acquire *near:*
5 verge 8 approach *round:* 5 rally 7 get
well, recover *to pass:* 5 occur 6 happen
up: 5 arise *upon:* 4 find, meet 8 discover
9 encounter
comeback 5 rally 6 answer, retort,
return 7 rebound, revival, riposte
8 rebuttal, recovery, repartee, response
11 improvement 12 counterclaim, recu-
peration
come by 4 call 5 pop in, visit 6 drop in,
look in 7 acquire, collect, inherit
comedian 3 wag, wit 4 card 5 clown,
comic, droll, joker 6 jester 7 farceur
8 funnyman, humorist, jokester, quipster 11 entertainer
comedo 9 blackhead
comedown 4 dive, fall, ruin 5 crash
7 decline, descent, failure, setback
8 collapse 9 ruination
come down with 3 get 5 catch 7 develop
8 contract
comedy 5 farce, humor 6 levity
8 drollery, hilarity 9 drollness, wittiness
come in 5 enter, reply 6 answer
7 respond
comely 4 fair 5 bonny, sonsy 6 lovely,
pretty, proper, sonsie 7 winsome
8 becoming, decorous, handsome,
pleasing 9 beauteous, beautiful, befitting 10 attractive 11 good-looking
come off 4 fare, seem 5 click, occur
6 appear, go over, happen, pan out
7 develop, succeed 8 prove out 9 transpire
come-on 4 bait, lure, trap 5 decoy, snare
9 seduction 10 allurement, enticement,

inducement, invitation, temptation
12 blandishment, inveiglement, solicitation
come out 4 leak 5 break, debut, end up
6 emerge 9 transpire
come out with 3 say 4 tell 5 state, utter
6 report 7 declare, deliver, publish,
release 8 announce, proclaim
comestible 6 edible 7 eatable 8 esculent
comestibles 4 feed, food 6 viands 7 edibles 8 victuals 9 provender 10 provisions
come through 6 chip in, endure 7 pitch
in, prevail, survive 8 transmit 10 contribute
come together 4 mass, meet 5 merge,
swarm 6 gather, huddle 7 cluster, collect, combine, convene 8 assemble,
converge 10 congregate
come upon 4 find 7 run into, uncover,
unearth 8 bump into, discover, trip
over 9 encounter, run across
comeuppance 3 due 5 lumps 7 deserts
comfort 3 aid 4 help 5 cheer 6 assist,
buck up, luxury, relief, solace, soothe,
succor 7 amenity, cheer up, console,
relieve, support 8 reassure, sympathy
10 assistance, sympathize 11 commiserate, consolation, contentment
comfortable 4 cozy, easy, homy, snug,
soft 5 ample, cushy, homey, roomy
7 content, easeful, restful, well-off
8 adequate, homelike, pleasant, pleasing, spacious, well-to-do 9 agreeable,
satisfied, well-fixed 10 commodious,
prosperous, sufficient, well-heeled
11 substantial 12 satisfactory
comforter 4 down, pouf, puff 5 duvet,
quilt 9 eiderdown
comfy 4 cozy, homy 5 cushy, homey
comic 3 wag, wit 5 antic, droll, funny,
joker 6 jester 7 risible 8 comedian, farcical, funnyman, humorist, jokester,
quipster 9 laughable, ludicrous
10 ridiculous
comical 4 zany 5 droll, funny, goofy,
silly 6 absurd 7 amusing, foolish, risible, waggish 8 farcical 9 laughable,
ludicrous 10 ridiculous
comic strip 4 Pogo, Shoe 5 Hazel, Henry,
Nancy 6 Archie, Popeye 7 Blondie, Dil-
bert, Far Side (The), Peanuts 8 Alley
Oop, Andy Capp, Garfield, Krazy Kat,
Li'l Abner, Superman 9 Betty Boop,
Dick Tracy, Flash Gordon, Marmaduke, Mary Worth, Spider-Man, Yellow Kid (The) 10 Doonesbury, Joe
Palooka, Little Nemo 11 Bloom County, Brenda Starr, Mutt and Jeff, Rex
Morgan M.D., Steve Canyon 12 Beetle

Bailey 13 Captain Marvel, Gasoline Alley, Prince Valiant

coming 3 due 4 next 5 fated, onset 6 advent, future 7 arrival, ensuing, nearing 8 approach, expected, foreseen, imminent 9 following, impending 11 approaching *forth:* 7 issuant

comity 5 amity 7 concord, harmony 8 goodwill 10 friendship 11 benevolence, camaraderie 12 friendliness

comma 4 lull 5 pause 8 interval

command 3 bid 4 rule, sway 5 order 6 adjure, behest, charge, compel, direct, enjoin 7 bidding, conduct, control, dictate, mandate, mastery, precept 9 authority, direction, directive, expertise, ordinance 10 domination, injunction 11 instruction 12 jurisdiction *to go:* 4 mush 6 avaunt, begone 7 giddyap, giddyup *to stop:* 4 whoa 5 avast

commandeer 4 take 5 annex, seize, usurp 6 assume, hijack 7 preempt 8 accroach, arrogate 9 conscript, sequester 10 confiscate 11 appropriate, expropriate, requisition

commander 4 boss, head 6 honcho, leader, master 7 captain, general, headman, officer

commandment 3 law 4 fiat, rule 5 edict, order 6 decree 7 mitzvah, precept, statute

commedia dell' ___ 4 arte

comme il faut 6 decent, polite, proper, seemly 7 correct 8 becoming, decorous, suitable

commemorate 4 keep 7 observe 8 eulogize, monument 9 celebrate, solemnize 11 memorialize 13 monumentalize

commemorative 8 memorial 10 dedicatory 11 celebratory

commence 5 begin, start 6 launch, set out 7 kick off 8 embark on, initiate 10 embark upon, inaugurate

commencement 4 dawn 5 birth, onset, start 6 outset 7 dawning, genesis, opening 9 beginning, inception 10 graduation 12 inauguration

commend 4 hail, laud 5 extol 6 commit, kudize, praise, salute, tender 7 acclaim, applaud, approve, consign, entrust 8 hand over, relegate, turn over 10 compliment

commendable 6 worthy 8 laudable 9 admirable, deserving, estimable, meritable, venerable 10 creditable 11 meritorious 12 praiseworthy

commensurable see COMMENSURATE

commensurate 4 even 5 equal 10 comparable 11 coextensive 12 proportional 13 corresponding, proportionate

comment 4 note 5 opine 6 remark 7 mention, observe 8 critique, point out 9 criticism, interject 10 animadvert 11 observation 12 obiter dictum

commentary 5 gloss 6 review 8 analysis, critique, exegesis 9 editorial, narration, voice-over 10 annotation, exposition 11 explanation, observation 12 appreciation, obiter dictum

commerce 5 trade 7 contact, traffic 8 business, congress, dealings, exchange, industry 9 communion 11 interchange 13 communication

commercial 6 advert 8 economic 10 mercantile 13 advertisement

commie 3 Red 5 pinko 6 bolshy 7 bolshie 9 Bolshevik

commination 5 curse 8 anathema 10 accusation, execration 11 imprecation, malediction 12 denunciation

commingle 3 mix 4 meld 5 blend, merge, unify 8 compound, intermix 9 integrate 10 amalgamate

comminute 4 bray 5 crush, grind 9 granulate, pulverize

commiserate 4 pity 7 condole, feel for 9 empathize 10 sympathize 13 compassionate

commiseration 4 pity, ruth 7 empathy 8 sympathy 10 compassion, condolence

commission 3 bid, fee 4 name 5 board, order 6 agency, assign, charge, enable, engage, enjoin, enlist 7 appoint, command, council, empower, license, warrant 8 accredit, delegate, deputize 9 authorize, designate 10 delegation, deputation, percentage 11 certificate

commit 4 bind 5 allot, grant, refer 6 assign, convey, invest, ordain, pledge, record, reveal 7 achieve, consign, deposit, entrust, execute, perform, promise, pull off, trustee 8 allocate, carry out, hand over, obligate, relegate, turn over 10 accomplish, perpetrate

commitment 3 vow 4 bond, deal, duty 6 charge, devoir, pledge 7 promise 8 contract 9 agreement, assurance, guarantee 10 obligation 11 undertaking

committal see COMMITMENT

commixture 5 blend 6 fusion 7 amalgam, melange 8 compound, mingling 9 composite

commodious 4 wide 5 ample, roomy 8 spacious 9 capacious, expansive, luxurious 11 comfortable

commodities 5 goods, items, wares 8 articles, products 9 vendibles 11 merchandise

common 4 park 5 banal, daily, joint, plaza, trite, usual 6 mutual, normal, shared 7 general, generic, prosaic, regular, routine, typical 8 adequate, communal, conjoint, conjunct, déclassé, everyday, familiar, frequent, habitual, ordinary, standard, workaday 9 customary, prevalent, tolerable, universal 10 collective, pedestrian, prevailing, unexciting, widespread 12 conventional, run-of-the-mill, satisfactory 13 unexceptional, uninteresting

commonalty 3 mob 5 plebs 6 masses, people, plebes, public, rabble 7 commune 8 populace 9 hoi polloi, multitude, plebeians 11 proletariat, rank and file, third estate

commoners see COMMONALTY

commonplace 5 stale, tired, trite, usual 6 cliché, normal, truism 7 bromide, clichéd, humdrum, mundane, obvious, prosaic, regular, routine, typical 8 banality, bromidic, chestnut, everyday, habitual, mediocre, ordinary, wellworn, workaday 9 hackneyed, platitude, prevalent 10 pedestrian, shibboleth, stereotype, uneventful 11 stereotyped 12 conventional, run-of-the-mill, unremarkable 13 stereotypical, unexceptional, uninteresting

common sense 6 wisdom 8 judgment, prudence 10 shrewdness

Common Sense author 5 Paine (Thomas)

commotion 3 ado, din, row 4 flap, fuss, moil, riot, stew, stir, to-do 5 storm, whirl 6 bustle, clamor, dither, flurry, fracas, furore, hoopla, hubbub, hurrah, lather, outcry, pother, racket, ruckus, rumpus, shindy, tumult, uproar, upturn 7 ferment, tempest, turmoil 8 brouhaha, foofaraw 9 agitation, confusion 10 convulsion, hullabaloo, hurly-burly, turbulence 11 pandemonium

commove 5 rouse 6 excite 7 agitate, inspire, provoke 9 electrify, galvanize, stimulate

communal 5 civil, joint 6 common, mutual, public, shared 10 collective 11 socialistic

commune 10 collective *Israeli:* 7 kibbutz *Russian:* 3 mir 7 kolkhoz

communicable 8 catching 10 contagious, infectious 13 transmissible, transmittable

communicate 4 tell 6 convey, impart, inform, pass on, relate, reveal, signal 7 connect, contact, divulge 8 disclose, transmit 9 make known

communication 4 talk 7 contact, message, missive, talking 8 converse, exchange 9 directive 10 discussing, discussion 11 interchange, intercourse 12 conversation *means:* 3 Web 4 drum,

mail, note 5 e-mail, media, phone, radio 6 letter, medium, pigeon, speech 8 Internet 9 telegraph, telephone 10 television *system:* 8 language

communications code word 4 Alfa, Echo, Golf, Kilo, Lima, Mike, Papa, Xray, Zulu 5 Alpha, Bravo, Delta, Hotel, India, Oscar, Romeo, Tango 6 Quebec, Sierra, Victor, Yankee 7 Charlie, Foxtrot, Juliett, Uniform, Whiskey 8 November

communicative 5 vocal 6 fluent, prolix 7 verbose, voluble 8 eloquent 9 expansive, garrulous, talkative 10 articulate, expressive, loquacious

communion 7 rapport, sharing 9 Eucharist, sacrament 10 connection, fellowship *cloth:* 8 corporal *cup:* 7 chalice *plate:* 5 paten

communism 7 Marxism 8 Leninism 10 bolshevism 12 collectivism

Communist 3 red 5 lefty, pinko 6 bolshy, Maoist 7 bolshie, comrade, Marxist 8 Leninist 9 Bolshevik, Stalinist 10 Bolshevist, Trotskyist

Communist leader *Chinese:* 3 Mao 4 Deng 5 Jiang 8 Hu Jintao 9 Mao Zedong 10 Jiang Zemin, Mao Tse-tung 12 Deng Xiaoping 13 Teng Hsiao-p'ing *Russian:* 5 Lenin (Vladimir Ilyich) 6 Stalin (Joseph) 7 Kosygin (Aleksey), Trotsky (Leon) 8 Andropov (Yuri), Brezhnev (Leonid) 9 Chernenko (Konstantin), Gorbachev (Mikhail) 10 Khrushchev (Nikita)

community 4 town 7 enclave, society 12 neighborhood *ecological:* 10 biocenosis 11 biocoenosis

commute 5 alter 6 change, make up, modify, soften, travel 7 convert, curtail, shorten, shuttle 8 decrease, exchange, mitigate, transfer 9 transform, translate, transmute, transpose 10 compensate, substitute 11 interchange

Como está ___ ? 5 usted

Comoros *capital:* 6 Moroni *island:* 6 Mohéli 7 Anjouan 12 Grande Comore *language:* 6 Arabic, French 8 Comorian *monetary unit:* 5 franc *volcano:* 8 Karthala

compact 4 bond 5 close, dense, unify 7 bargain, bunched, crowded, pressed 8 compress, condense, contract, covenant 9 agreement, concordat 10 convention 11 concentrate, consolidate, transaction

compadre 3 pal 4 chum, mate 5 amigo, buddy, crony 6 friend 7 comrade, partner 8 confrere, sidekick, intimate 9 associate, colleague, companion

companion 3 pal 4 chum, mate 5 buddy,

crony 6 cohort, escort **7** comrade, consort, partner **8** sidekick **9** associate, attendant, colleague

companionable 6 genial, social **7** affable, amiable **8** outgoing, sociable **9** agreeable, congenial, convivial **10** gregarious **11** good-natured

companionship 7 company, society **8** intimacy **10** fellowship **11** camaraderie

company 4 band, club, crew, firm, gang, team **5** corps, group, party, troop **6** circle, clique, guests, outfit, troupe **7** concern, coterie, retinue, society, visitor **8** assembly, business, ensemble, visitors **9** gathering **10** assemblage, enterprise, fellowship **11** association, camaraderie, corporation **12** congregation **13** companionship, establishment

comparable 4 akin, like **5** alike **6** agnate **7** similar, uniform **8** parallel **9** analogous **10** equivalent, homologous **12** commensurate **13** corresponding

comparative 4 near **8** relative **11** approximate

compare 5 liken, match **6** equate, relate **7** collate **8** contrast, parallel **9** correlate **10** assimilate

comparison 6 simile **7** analogy **8** affinity, contrast, likeness **9** collation, semblance **10** similarity, similitude **11** correlation, resemblance

compartment 3 bay **4** cell, nook, part, slot **5** berth, booth, niche, stall **6** alcove, carrel, locker **7** chamber, cubicle, section **8** division **9** cubbyhole **10** pigeonhole **11** subdivision

compass 3 hem **4** ring **5** ambit, field, grasp, orbit, range, reach, scope, sweep **6** bounds, circle, domain, extent, girdle, limits, radius, sphere **7** circuit, environ, purview **8** boundary, confines, environs **9** enclosure, extension, perimeter, periphery **13** circumference *kind:* **4** gyro **5** solar **8** magnetic *stand:* **8** binnacle

compassion 4 pity, ruth **5** mercy **7** charity, empathy **8** clemency, humanity, kindness, sympathy **9** condolence, humaneness **11** benevolence **13** commiseration, fellow feeling

compassionate 4 pity, warm **6** humane, tender **7** clement **8** merciful **10** benevolent, charitable, solicitous **11** commiserate, kindhearted, softhearted, sympathetic, warmhearted

compassionless 5 stony **7** callous **8** obdurate **9** heartless, unfeeling **11** coldblooded, hard-hearted, ironhearted **12** stonyhearted

compass point 3 ENE, ESE, NNE, NNW, SSE, SSW, WNW, WSW **4** east, west **5** north, rhumb, south **7** bearing *Scottish:* **4** airt

compatible 6 proper **8** suitable **9** agreeable, congenial, congruous, consonant **10** consistent, harmonious, like-minded **11** appropriate, sympathetic

compatriot 8 confrere **9** associate, colleague, companion

compeer see COMPANION

compel 4 hale, urge **5** drive, force **6** coerce, impose, oblige **7** enforce **9** constrain

compelling 4 dire **5** acute **6** cogent, crying, urgent **7** clamant, exigent, telling, weighty **8** forceful, pressing **10** convincing, persuasive **11** importunate, significant **12** well-grounded **13** authoritative

compendious 5 brief, pithy, short **7** compact, concise, summary **8** succinct **9** condensed **11** abbreviated

compendium 4 list **5** brief, guide **6** aperçu, digest, manual, précis, sketch, survey **7** epitome, summary **8** abstract, Baedeker, handbook, overview, syllabus, synopsis **9** anthology, guidebook, vade mecum **10** abridgment, collection, conspectus **11** abridgement, compilation, enchiridion

compensate 3 pay **5** atone, repay **6** make up, offset, pay off, redeem, set off **7** balance, guerdon, requite, satisfy **8** outweigh **9** indemnify, reimburse **10** counteract, neutralize, recompense, remunerate **11** countervail

compensation 6 amends, reward, salary **7** damages, payment, redress **8** earnings, reprisal, requital, solatium **9** atonement, indemnity, quittance, repayment **10** recompense, reparation **11** restitution **12** remuneration

compete 3 vie **4** spar **5** fight **6** battle, strive **7** contend **8** contest, struggle

competence 5 skill **7** ability, know-how **8** adequacy, aptitude, capacity, facility **9** expertise **10** capability **11** proficiency, sufficiency **13** qualification

competent 3 fit **4** able **5** adept **6** au fait, decent, proper **7** capable, skilled **8** adequate **9** efficient, qualified **10** proficient, sufficient **12** satisfactory

competition 4 bout, game, meet, race **5** clash, fight, match, rival **6** strife **7** contest, matchup, rivalry **8** concours, conflict, striving, struggle, tug-of-war **10** antagonism, contention, tournament

competitor 5 enemy, rival **8** opponent **9** adversary **10** antagonist, contestant, opposition

compile 4 edit **5** amass **6** gather, select

7 build up, collate, collect 8 assemble 9 construct 10 accumulate 11 anthologize

complacency 5 pride 7 conceit 8 smugness 10 narcissism

complacent 4 smug 6 serene 7 assured 9 conceited, confident 11 self-assured, unconcerned 13 self-confident, self-contented, self-possessed, self-satisfied

complain 3 nag 4 beef, crab, fret, fuss, wail 5 gripe, grump, whine 6 grouch, grouse, lament, yammer 7 grizzle, grumble, protest 9 bellyache

complainer 4 crab 5 crank 6 griper, grouch 7 grouser 8 grumbler, sourpuss 10 malcontent 11 faultfinder

complaint 5 gripe 6 grouse, lament, malady 7 ailment, disease, protest 8 disorder, sickness, syndrome 9 condition, criticism, grievance, infirmity, objection 10 affliction, allegation 12 protestation

complaisant 4 easy, mild 7 amiable, lenient 8 generous, obliging 9 agreeable, compliant, easygoing, indulgent 11 deferential, good-humored, good-natured 12 good-tempered 13 accommodating

complement 4 crew, rest 9 correlate, remainder 10 supplement 11 counterpart

complete 3 end 4 done, full, halt 5 close, ended, total, utter, whole 6 entire, finish, intact, wind up, wrap up 7 achieve, fulfill, perfect, perform, plenary 8 absolute, conclude, finalize, finished, integral, round out, thorough 9 concluded, out-and-out, terminate 10 accomplish, consummate, exhaustive, unabridged 11 categorical, unmitigated 13 thoroughgoing

completed 4 done, over 5 ended 7 through 8 done with, executed, finished 9 concluded, fulfilled 10 terminated 11 consummated 12 accomplished

completion 3 end 6 finish, windup, wrap-up 8 fruition 10 conclusion

complex 6 daedal, knotty, system, varied 7 chelate, gordian, network 8 abstruse, compound, involved, syndrome, tortuous 9 aggregate, Byzantine, composite, elaborate, intricate 10 convoluted 11 complicated 12 conglomerate, labyrinthine 13 heterogeneous, sophisticated

complexion 3 hue 4 cast, tint, tone 5 color, humor, tinge 6 aspect, makeup, nature, temper 8 tincture 9 character 10 appearance, coloration 11 disposi-

tion, temperament 12 pigmentation 13 individuality

compliance 7 consent 8 docility 9 agreement, deference, obedience 10 acceptance, conformity, submission 11 amenability, flexibility, resignation 12 acquiescence, tractability

complicate 5 mix up, ravel, snarl 6 jumble, muddle, tangle 7 confuse, involve 8 confound, disorder, entangle 9 aggravate, convolute 10 disarrange, exacerbate

complicated 6 daedal, knotty 7 complex, gordian, tangled 8 abstruse, involved, tortuous 9 Byzantine, elaborate, intricate, recondite 10 convoluted 12 labyrinthine 13 heterogeneous, sophisticated

complicity 8 abetment 9 collusion 10 connivance 11 involvement

compliment 4 hail, kudo, laud 5 extol, honor, kudos 6 praise, salute 7 acclaim, applaud, bouquet, commend, regards, tribute 8 accolade, encomium 9 laudation, recommend 11 recognition 12 appreciation, commendation, congratulate

complimentary 4 free 6 gratis 8 costless 9 favorable, laudatory 10 chargeless, gratuitous 12 appreciative

comply 4 obey 5 yield 6 accede, submit 7 conform 9 acquiesce

component 4 part 5 piece 6 factor 7 element, segment 10 ingredient 11 constituent

comport 4 bear, jibe 5 agree, carry, fit in, match, tally 6 accord, acquit, behave, demean, square 7 conduct 8 coincide, dovetail 9 harmonize 10 correspond

comportment 3 air 4 mien 7 address, bearing, conduct 8 attitude, behavior, carriage, demeanor, presence

compose 4 calm, cool, form, lull, make 5 forge, quiet, relax, still, write 6 becalm, create, devise, draw up, indite, invent, make up, settle, solace, soothe 7 collect, console, contain, control 8 comprise 9 construct, fabricate, formulate, originate 10 constitute *type:* 3 set

composed 4 calm, cool 5 staid 6 poised, sedate, serene 9 collected, unruffled 11 unflappable 13 imperturbable, self-possessed

composer 6 scorer 8 melodist 9 balladist, songsmith, tunesmith 10 songwriter *American:* 3 Kay (Hershy, Ulysses) 4 Bock (Jerry), Cage (John), Hill (Edward Burlingame), Ives (Charles), Kern (Jerome), King

(Carole), Lane (Burton), Monk (Thelonious), Work (Henry Clay) **5** Adams (John), Arlen (Harold), Beach (Amy), Blake (Eubie), Bland (James A.), Bloch (Ernest), Cohan (George M.), Friml (Rudolf), Glass (Philip), Gould (Morton), Grofé (Ferde), Handy (W. C.), Loewe (Frederick), Mason (Daniel Gregory, Lowell), Moore (Douglas), Reich (Steve), Sousa (John Philip), Still (William Grant), Styne (Jule), Zappa (Frank) **6** Barber (Samuel), Berlin (Irving), Carter (Elliott), Cowell (Henry), Emmett (Daniel), Foster (Stephen), Hanson (Howard), Harris (Roy), Herman (Jerry), Joplin (Scott), Kander (John), McHugh (Jimmy), McKuen (Rod), Menken (Alan), Morton ("Jelly Roll"), Oliver ("King"), Parker (Charlie "Bird," Horatio), Piston (Walter), Porter (Cole), Previn (André), Seeger (Pete), Taylor (Deems), Varèse (Edgard), Warren (Harry) **7** Babbitt (Milton), Brubeck (Dave), Copland (Aaron), Gilbert (Henry F.), Gilmore (Patrick), Goldman (Edwin Franko), Herbert (Victor), Loesser (Frank), Mancini (Henry), Menotti (Gian Carlo), Rodgers (Richard), Romberg (Sigmund), Schuman (William), Thomson (Virgil), Tiomkin (Dimitri), Willson (Meredith), Youmans (Vincent) **8** Anderson (Leroy), Billings (William), Burleigh (Henry Thacker), Damrosch (Leopold, Walter), Gershwin (George), Hamlisch (Marvin), Herrmann (Bernard), Korngold (Erich Wolfgang), Kreisler (Fritz), Marsalis (Wynton), Schuller (Gunther), Sessions (Roger), Sondheim (Stephen), Williams (John) **9** Bacharach (Burt), Bernstein (Elmer, Leonard), Donaldson (Walter), Ellington (Duke), Hovhaness (Alan), MacDowell (Edward) **10** Blitzstein (Marc), Carmichael (Hoagy), Gottschalk (Louis Moreau) *Argentinian:* **9** Ginastera (Alberto) *Australian:* **8** Grainger (Percy) *Austrian:* **4** Berg (Alban), Wolf (Hugo) **5** Haydn (Franz Joseph) **6** Czerny (Karl), Mahler (Gustav), Mozart (Leopold, Wolfgang Amadeus), Straus (Oscar), Webern (Anton) **7** Strauss (Eduard, Johann, Josef) **8** Bruckner (Anton), Schubert (Franz) **10** Schoenberg (Arnold) *Belgian:* **5** Ysaÿe (Eugène) **6** Franck (César) *Brazilian:* **5** Jobim (Antonio Carlos) **10** Villa-Lobos (Heitor) *Czech:* **3** Suk (Josef) **6** Dvořák (Antonín) **7** Janáček (Leoš), Martinu (Bohuslav), Smetana (Bedřich) *Danish:* **7** Nielsen (Carl) *Dutch:* **9** Sweel-

inck (Jan Pieterszoon) *English:* **4** Arne (Thomas Augustine), Byrd (William) **5** Elgar (Edward), Holst (Gustav) **6** Delius (Frederick), Morley (Thomas), Tallis (Thomas), Walton (William), Wesley (Charles, Samuel) **7** Britten (Benjamin), Dowland (John), Gibbons (Orlando), Purcell (Henry), Weelkes (Thomas) **8** Sullivan (Arthur) **9** Dunstable (John) **11** Lloyd Webber (Andrew) *Finnish:* **8** Palmgren (Selim), Sibelius (Jean) *Flemish:* **5** Dufay (Guillaume), Lasso (Orlando di) **6** Lassus (Orlande de) **8** Willaert (Adriaan) *French:* **4** Indy (Vincent d'), Lalo (Edouard) **5** Auber (Esprit), Bizet (Georges), Dukas (Paul), Fauré (Gabriel), Ibert (Jacques), Jarre (Maurice), Lully (Jean-Baptiste), Ravel (Maurice), Satie (Erik), Widor (Charles-Marie) **6** Boulez (Pierre), Campra (André), Franck (César), Gounod (Charles), Rameau (Jean-Philippe), Thomas (Ambroise) **7** Berlioz (Hector), Debussy (Claude), Delibes (Léo), Machaut (Guillaume de), Milhaud (Darius), Poulenc (Francis) **8** Chabrier (Emmanuel), Couperin (François, Louis), Honegger (Arthur), Massenet (Jules), Messiaen (Olivier) **9** Meyerbeer (Giacomo), Offenbach (Jacques) **10** Saint-Saëns (Camille) *German:* **4** Bach (C. P. E., Johann Christian, Johann Sebastian, Wilhelm Friedemann), Orff (Carl) **5** Bruch (Max), Gluck (Christoph Willibald von), Reger (Max), Spohr (Louis, Ludwig), Weber (Carl Maria von), Weill (Kurt) **6** Brahms (Johannes), Handel (George Frideric), Schütz (Heinrich), Vogler (Abt), Wagner (Richard) **7** Hassler (Hans Leo), Strauss (Richard) **8** Korngold (Erich Wolfgang), Schumann (Robert), Telemann (Georg Philipp) **9** Beethoven (Ludwig van), Buxtehude (Dietrich), Hindemith (Paul), Meyerbeer (Giacomo), Pachelbel (Johann) **10** Praetorius (Michael) **11** Humperdinck (Engelbert), Mendelssohn (Felix), Stockhausen (Karlheinz) *Hungarian:* **5** Léhar (Franz), Liszt (Franz) **6** Bartók (Béla), Kodály (Zoltán), Ligeti (György) **8** Dohnányi (Erno) *Italian:* **4** Peri (Jacopo), Rota (Nino) **5** Berio (Luciano), Boito (Arrigo), Verdi (Giuseppe) **6** Busoni (Ferruccio) **7** Bellini (Vincenzo), Caccini (Giulio), Corelli (Arcangelo), Martini (Padre), Puccini (Giacomo), Rossini (Gioacchino), Salieri (Antonio), Tartini (Giuseppe), Vivaldi (Antonio) **8** Albinoni (Tomaso), Clementi (Muzio),

Gabrieli (Andrea, Giovanni), Mascagni (Pietro), Paganini (Niccolò), Respighi (Ottorino) 9 Cherubini (Luigi), Donizetti (Gaetano), Pergolesi (Giovanni Battista), Scarlatti (Alessandro, Domenico), Tommasini (Vincenzo) 10 Boccherini (Luigi), Monteverdi (Claudio), Palestrina (G. P. da), Ponchielli (Amilcare), Zingarelli (Niccolò) 11 Frescobaldi (Girolamo), Leoncavallo (Ruggero) 12 Dallapiccola (Luigi) *Mexican:* 6 Chávez (Carlos) *Norwegian:* 5 Grieg (Edvard) *Polish:* 6 Chopin (Frédéric) 7 Gorecki (Henryk) 10 Paderewski (Ignacy Jan), Penderecki (Krzysztof), Wieniawski (Henryk) 11 Lutoslawski (Witold), Szymanowski (Karol) *Romanian:* 7 Xenakis (Iannis) *Russian:* 6 Glinka (Mikhail) 7 Borodin (Aleksandr) 8 Glazunov (Aleksandr), Scriabin (Aleksandr) 9 Balakirev (Mily), Prokofiev (Sergey), Schnittke (Alfred) 10 Kabalevsky (Dmitri), Mussorgsky (Modest), Rubinstein (Anton), Stravinsky (Igor), Tcherepnin (Nikolay) 11 Tchaikovsky (Pyotr Ilich) 12 Khachaturian (Aram), Rachmaninoff (Sergey), Shostakovich (Dmitry) *Spanish:* 5 Falla (Manuel de) 7 Albéniz (Isaac), Rodrigo (Joaquin) 8 Granados (Enrique), Victoria (Tomas Luis de)

composite 3 mix 5 blend 6 fusion, hybrid 7 amalgam, complex, mixture 8 compound 11 combination 12 amalgamation

composition 4 opus 5 essay, paper, theme 6 design, layout, makeup 7 article 11 formation 12 architecture, constitution, construction *choral:* 4 mass 5 motet 8 oratorio *for eight:* 5 octet *for five:* 7 quintet *for four:* 7 quartet *for nine:* 5 nonet *for one:* 4 aria, solo *for seven:* 6 septet *for six:* 6 sextet *for three:* 4 trio *for two:* 4 duet *instrumental:* 3 jig 4 reel 5 étude, fugue, gigue, march, rondo, suite 6 sonata 7 caprice, partita, prelude, scherzo 8 concerto, fantasia, overture, rhapsody, saraband, sinfonia, symphony, tone poem 9 allemande, capriccio, sarabande 10 intermezzo *vocal:* 4 aria, lied, mass, song 5 carol, chant, motet, opera, round 6 arioso, ballad, chanty 7 cantata, chanson, chantey, chorale, lullaby, requiem 8 berceuse, madrigal, oratorio 9 plainsong, spiritual

compos mentis 4 sane 5 lucid, sound 6 normal

composure 4 calm 5 poise 7 balance, dignity 8 calmness, coolness, evenness, serenity, sobriety 9 sangfroid 10 equanimity 11 equilibrium

compound 3 mix 4 join, link 5 admix, alloy, blend, union, unite 6 expand, extend, fusion, make up, mingle 7 amalgam, augment, complex, compost, enlarge, magnify, mixture 8 coalesce, comingle, heighten, increase, intermix, multiply 9 admixture, aggravate, associate, commingle, composite, intensify, synthesis 10 commixture, exacerbate 11 intermingle 12 amalgamation *chemical:* (see at CHEMICAL) *medicinal:* 8 magnesia *protein:* 7 peptone *sulfur:* 5 thiol 7 sulfide, sulfone 8 sulfonyl, sulfuryl, sulphide

comprehend 4 know 5 catch, grasp 6 absorb, accept, embody, fathom, take in 7 cognize, compass, contain, discern, embrace, include, involve, subsume 8 comprise, perceive 9 encompass 10 appreciate, understand

comprehensible 8 knowable 9 graspable 10 fathomable 12 intelligible

comprehension 3 ken 5 grasp 9 awareness, knowledge 10 cognizance, conception, perception 11 discernment 12 apperception 13 understanding

comprehensive 4 full, wide 5 broad 6 global 7 general, overall 8 catholic, complete, sweeping 9 all-around, extensive, inclusive, universal 10 exhaustive 12 all-inclusive, encyclopedic

comprehensiveness 5 range, reach, scope 7 breadth 8 fullness 9 amplitude

compress 3 jam 4 cram, push 5 crush, press 6 reduce, shrink, squash, squish, shrink 7 bandage, compact, squeeze 8 condense, contract 11 concentrate

comprise 4 form 6 make up 7 compose, contain, embrace, include, subsume 10 comprehend, constitute

compromise 4 mean, pact, risk 6 settle 7 bargain, compact 8 contract, endanger, trade off 9 agreement, middle way 10 concession, golden mean, jeopardize, settlement 12 middle ground

compulsion 4 itch, need, urge 5 drive, force 8 coercion 9 necessity 10 constraint

compulsive 7 driving 9 besetting, obsessive 12 irresistible, overwhelming

compulsory 7 binding 8 coercive, enforced, required 9 mandatory, requisite 10 imperative, obligatory

compunction 4 pang 5 demur, qualm 6 regret, unease 7 remorse, scruple 8 distress 9 hesitancy, misgiving 10 conscience, hesitation

compunctious 5 sorry 8 contrite, penitent 9 regretful, repentant 10 apologetic, remorseful 11 penitential

computation 8 figuring 9 ciphering, reckoning 10 arithmetic, estimation 11 calculation

compute 5 tally, total 6 cipher, figure, reckon 8 estimate 9 calculate, determine

computer 6 abacus, laptop 7 desktop 9 mainframe 10 calculator *component:* 3 CPU 4 chip 5 mouse, tower 7 monitor 8 keyboard 9 hard drive *information:* 4 data *instruction:* 5 macro *inventor:* 7 Babbage (Charles) *language:* 3 Ada, APL 4 Java, Lisp, Perl 5 ALGOL, BASIC, COBOL 6 Pascal 7 FORTRAN *type:* 6 analog 7 digital

comrade 3 pal 4 ally, chum, mate 5 buddy, crony 6 cohort, comate, fellow 7 consort 8 sidekick, tovarich, tovarish 9 associate, colleague, companion

con 3 gyp, vet 4 anti, bilk, coax, dupe, fool, hoax, rook, scam 5 cheat, fraud, learn, study, trick 6 cajole, fleece, gammon, inmate, survey 7 against, blarney, canvass, chicane, convict, deceive, defraud, examine, inspect, swindle, wheedle 8 blandish, flimflam, hoodwink, inveigle, jailbird, memorize, negative, opponent, persuade, prisoner, soft-soap 9 bamboozle, check over, sweet-talk 10 antithesis, manipulate, scrutinize 11 hornswoggle 12 tuberculosis

concatenate 4 join, link 5 unite 7 connect

concavity 3 dip, sag 4 bowl, dent, sink 5 basin 6 crater, hollow, trough 7 sinkage 8 sinkhole 10 depression

conceal 4 bury, hide, mask, veil 5 cache, cloak, cover, stash 6 screen 7 obscure, secrete 8 ensconce, enshroud, palliate 10 camouflage

concealed 5 privy 6 buried, covert, hidden, secret 8 obscured, shrouded, ulterior 11 clandestine

concede 3 own 4 avow, fold 5 admit, allow, award, grant, yield 6 accept, accord 7 confess 9 surrender, vouchsafe 10 capitulate, relinquish 11 acknowledge

conceit 4 idea, whim 5 fancy, pride 6 egoism, megrim, notion, vagary, vanity 7 caprice, egotism, thought 8 crotchet, metaphor, self-love, smugness, snobbery 9 self-pride, vainglory 10 narcissism, self-esteem 11 complacence, complacency, self-opinion, swelled head

conceited 4 vain 6 snobby, snooty 7 pompous, stuck-up 8 immodest,

puffed up, snobbish 12 narcissistic, vainglorious

conceitedness 6 vanity 8 self-love 9 vainglory 10 narcissism

conceivable 8 possible 9 plausible, thinkable 10 imaginable, supposable

conceive 4 form 5 beget, fancy, grasp, think 6 accept, assume, devise, expect, follow, gather, ideate, ponder 7 believe, dream up, feature, imagine, realize, suppose, suspect, think up 8 cogitate, envisage, envision, meditate, ruminate 9 apprehend, formulate, originate, speculate, visualize 10 comprehend, excogitate, understand

concentrate 4 mass 5 focus 6 gather, shrink 7 collect, compact 8 assemble, compress, condense, contract, converge 10 accumulate 11 consolidate

concentrated 5 thick 6 intent, strong 7 focused, intense 8 vehement 9 intensive, undiluted, undivided 12 undistracted

concentration 5 field, major, study 9 attention 10 absorption 11 application

concept 4 idea 5 image 6 notion, theory 7 conceit, thought 10 impression, perception

conception 4 idea 5 birth, image, start 6 notion, origin, outset, theory 7 conceit, genesis, thought 9 beginning 10 impression, perception

conceptual 5 ideal 8 abstract, notional 9 imaginary, visionary 10 ideational 11 theoretical 12 hypothetical, intellectual

concern 4 care, firm, heed 5 doubt, worry 6 affair, bear on, bother, engage, gadget, matter, occupy, outfit, regard, unease 7 anxiety, company, disturb, involve, perturb, trouble 8 business, deal with, disquiet, interest, mistrust 9 attention, curiosity, misgiving, suspicion 10 enterprise, skepticism, solicitude, uneasiness 11 carefulness, contrivance, uncertainty 12 apprehension 13 consciousness, consideration, establishment

concerned 7 anxious, worried 8 affected, involved 10 implicated, interested

concerning 4 as to, in re 5 about, anent, as for 7 apropos 9 as regards, regarding 10 relating to, relative to, respecting

concert 5 agree, union 6 accord, concur, settle, soiree 7 arrange, concord, harmony, recital 8 coincide, musicale 9 agreement, cooperate, harmonize, negotiate 11 performance

concerted 5 joint 6 mutual, united 7 unified 8 combined 11 coordinated 13 collaborative

concert hall 5 arena, odeum 7 theater, theatre 10 auditorium

concession 5 favor, grant 8 giveback 9 admission, allowance, privilege 10 compromise 12 acquiescence

conch 5 shell 7 mollusc, mollusk

concierge 6 porter, warden 7 doorman, janitor 9 custodian 10 doorkeeper

conciliate 4 calm, ease 6 disarm, pacify, soothe 7 appease, assuage, mollify, placate, sweeten, win over 9 reconcile 10 propitiate

concise 5 brief, pithy, short, terse 7 compact, laconic, summary 8 abridged, succinct 9 condensed 10 compressed, contracted 11 compendious 13 short and sweet

conclave 5 synod 6 caucus, powwow 7 meeting, session 8 assembly 9 gathering 10 conference, consistory, convention 11 convocation

conclude 3 end 4 halt, stop 5 close, infer, judge 6 decide, deduce, derive, effect, figure, finish, gather, reason, settle, wind up, wrap up 7 collect, resolve 8 complete 9 determine, terminate

concluding 4 last 5 final 6 latest, latter 7 closing 8 eventual, terminal, ultimate

conclusion 3 end 4 stop 5 cease, close 6 ending, epilog, finale, finish, period, result, windup 7 closing, closure, outcome, verdict 8 decision, epilogue, judgment, sequitur 9 cessation, deduction, inference, summation 10 completion, denouement, resolution, settlement 11 culmination, termination 13 determination

conclusive 4 last 5 final 6 cogent 8 deciding, decisive, ultimate 9 clinching 10 compelling, convincing, definitive, undeniable 11 determinant, determinate, irrefutable 12 irrefragable, unanswerable 13 determinative

concoct 3 mix 4 brew, cook 5 frame, hatch 6 cook up, create, devise, invent 7 dream up 8 conceive, contrive 9 fabricate, formulate, originate

concoction 4 brew, plan 5 blend 7 mixture, project 8 compound, creation 9 invention 11 combination, contrivance, fabrication, preparation

concomitant 7 adjunct 8 adjuvant 9 accessory, ancillary, associate, attendant, attending, companion, satellite 10 coincident, collateral 12 accompanying 13 accompaniment, supplementary

concord 4 pact 5 amity, peace, unity 6 accord, comity, treaty 7 concert, entente, harmony, rapport 8 goodwill 9 agreement 10 consonance

concordant 8 agreeing 9 congruous,

consonant 10 compatible, consistent, harmonious 11 appropriate

concourse 5 foyer 6 throng 7 joining, meeting 8 junction 9 gathering 10 confluence, crossroads

concrete 5 solid 6 actual 8 specific, tangible 10 particular 11 substantial *component:* 4 sand 5 water 6 gravel

concubine 7 hetaera, hetaira 8 mistress 9 courtesan, odalisque

concupiscence 4 lust 5 ardor 6 desire 7 lechery, passion 9 prurience, pruriency 11 lustfulness 13 lickerishness

concupiscent 3 hot 7 aroused, goatish, lustful 8 prurient 9 lecherous, lickerish, salacious 10 lascivious, libidinous, lubricious, passionate

concur 4 jibe 5 agree, unite 6 accord, assent 7 approve, combine, concord, consent, go along 8 coincide 9 cooperate, harmonize

concurrent 6 coeval 8 parallel 10 coexistent, coexisting, convergent, synchronic 11 synchronous 12 contemporary, simultaneous

concurrently 6 at once 8 together 12 coincidently

concuss 3 jar 4 rock, stun 5 shake, shock 7 agitate

concussion 3 jar 4 bump, jolt 5 clout, crash, shock 6 impact 7 jarring, jolting, shaking 8 pounding 9 agitation, collision

condemn 3 rap 4 damn, doom 5 blame, decry, knock, seize 7 censure, convict, deplore 8 denounce, sentence 9 criticize, deprecate, proscribe, reprehend, reprobate 10 denunciate

condensation 3 dew 5 brief 6 digest, précis 7 epitome, outline, summary 8 abstract, synopsis 9 reduction 10 abridgment, conspectus 11 abridgement

condense 5 sum up 6 digest, reduce, shrink 7 abridge, compact, shorten 8 boil down, compress, contract 9 constrict, epitomize, summarize, synopsize 10 abbreviate 11 concentrate, consolidate, precipitate

condensed 7 concise, summary 10 boiled down 11 compendious

condescend 5 deign, stoop 6 unbend

condescending 6 lofty 6 lordly, snobby, snooty, uppish, uppity 7 haughty, pompous 8 affected, arrogant, cavalier, snobbish, superior 10 disdainful 11 patronizing, pretentious 12 supercilious

condign 3 apt, due, fit 4 fair, just 5 right 6 proper 7 fitting, merited 8 deserved, rightful, suitable **9** equitable, justified **11** appropriate

condiment 5 curry, sauce, spice **6** catsup, relish, tamari **7** chutney, ketchup, mustard **8** dressing, soy sauce **9** seasoning **10** mayonnaise

___ **con Dios! 4** Vaya

condition 5 shape, state, terms **6** fettle, malady, status **7** ailment, disease, fitness, proviso **8** syndrome **9** complaint, essential, exception, necessity, provision, requisite, situation **10** limitation, sine qua non **11** requirement, reservation, stipulation **12** prerequisite **13** qualification

conditional 7 reliant **8** relative **9** dependent, provisory, qualified, tentative, uncertain **10** contingent, restricted **11** provisional

condolence 3 rue **4** pity, ruth **6** solace **7** comfort **8** sympathy **10** compassion **13** commiseration

condonable 7 tenable **9** excusable, tolerable **10** acceptable, defensible, pardonable **11** justifiable

condone 5 remit **6** excuse, pardon **7** forgive **8** overlook

conduce 4 lead, tend **7** redound **10** contribute

conducive 7 helpful, leading, tending **9** favorable **10** beneficial, salubrious **11** efficacious, serviceable, stimulating **12** advantageous, contributory, instrumental **13** accommodating

conduct 3 act, run **4** bear, head, lead, show **5** guide, pilot, steer, usher **6** attend, behave, charge, convey, demean, deport, direct, escort, handle, manage **7** arrange, bearing, comport, control, manners, operate, oversee **8** behavior, demeanor, handling, shepherd, transmit **9** accompany, oversight, supervise **10** administer, deportment, management **11** comportment, supervision

conductor 5 guide **6** escort, leader **7** maestro **8** motorman **10** bandleader *American:* **4** Shaw (Robert) **5** Stock (Frederick), Szell (George) **6** Levine (James), Maazel (Lorin), Previn (André), Reiner (Fritz), Thomas (Theodore, Michael Tilson), Walter (Bruno) **7** Fennell (Frederick), Fiedler (Arthur), Monteux (Pierre), Ormandy (Eugene), Schwarz (Gerard), Slatkin (Leonard) **8** Damrosch (Leopold, Walter), Williams (John) **9** Bernstein (Leonard), Leinsdorf (Erich), Rodzinski (Artur), Steinberg (William), Stokowski (Leopold) **11** Kostelanetz (André), Mitropoulos (Dimitri) *Argen-*

tinian: **7** Kleiber (Carlos) **9** Barenboim (Daniel) *Australian:* **7** Bonynge (Richard) *Austrian:* **4** Böhm (Karl) **6** Mahler (Gustav) **7** Karajan (Herbert von) **11** Weingartner (Felix) *Belgian:* **5** Ysaÿe (Eugene) *British:* **5** Solti (Georg) *Canadian:* **6** Dutoit (Charles) **9** MacMillan (Ernest) *Czech:* **7** Kubelik (Jan, Rafael) *Dutch:* **7** Haitink (Bernard) **10** Mengelberg (Willem) *English:* **4** Wood (Henry) **5** Boult (Adrian), Davis (Colin) **6** Rattle (Simon) **7** Beecham (Thomas), Leppard (Raymond), Malcolm (George), Pinnock (Trevor), Sargent (Malcolm) **8** Goossens (Eugene), Marriner (Neville) **9** Mackerras (Charles) **10** Barbirolli (John) *Finnish:* **7** Salonen (Esa-Pekka) *French:* **5** Munch (Charles) **6** Boulez (Pierre), Prêtre (Georges) **7** Monteux (Pierre) *German:* **4** Muck (Carl, Karl) **5** Masur (Kurt) **6** Jochum (Eugen) **7** Kleiber (Erich) **9** Klemperer (Otto), Scherchen (Hermann) **10** Sawallisch (Wolfgang) **11** Furtwängler (Wilhelm), Mendelssohn (Felix) *Greek:* **11** Mitropoulos (Dimitri) *Hungarian:* **5** Seidl (Anton) **6** Doráti (Antal), Reiner (Fritz) **7** Nikisch (Arthur), Ormandy (Eugene), Richter (Hans) *Indian:* **5** Mehta (Zubin) *Italian:* **4** Muti (Riccardo) **6** Abbado (Claudio) **7** Chailly (Riccardo), Giulini (Carlo Maria) **8** Cantelli (Guido), Sinopoli (Giuseppe) **9** Toscanini (Arturo) *Japanese:* **5** Ozawa (Seiji) *Polish:* **9** Rodzinski (Artur) *Russian:* **7** Gergiev (Valery) **10** Temirkanov (Yuri) **12** Koussevitzky (Serge) *Spanish:* **6** Iturbi (José) *Swiss:* **8** Ansermet (Ernest) *stick:* **5** baton

conduit 4 duct, main, pipe **5** canal **6** course **7** channel **8** aqueduct, penstock, pipeline **11** watercourse

coney 4 pika **5** hyrax, lapin **6** rabbit **10** butterfish

confab 4 chat, talk **6** confer, huddle, parley, powwow **7** consult **8** collogue, colloquy, dialogue **10** conference, discussion **12** conversation, deliberation

confabulate see CONFAB

confabulation see CONFAB

confection see CANDY

confederacy 5 cabal, union **6** league **7** compact **8** alliance **9** coalition, syndicate **10** conspiracy, federation

confederate 3 reb **4** ally **5** rebel, unite **6** fellow **7** abettor, partner **9** accessory, associate, colleague, Johnny Reb **10** accomplice **11** conspirator **12** collaborator **13** coconspirator *admiral:* **6** Semmes *capital:* **8** Richmond *color:*

4 gray *general:* **3** Lee (Robert E.) **4** Hill (Ambrose), Hood (John Bell) **5** Bragg (Braxton), Ewell (Richard Stoddart), Price (Sterling), Smith (Edmund Kirby) **6** Morgan (John Hunt), Stuart (J. E. B.) **7** Forrest (Nathan Bedford), Hampton (Wade), Jackson (Thomas Jonathan "Stonewall"), Pickett (George) **8** Johnston (Albert Sidney, Joseph Eggleston) **9** Pemberton (John Clifford) **10** Beauregard (Pierre G. T.), Longstreet (James) *president:* **5** Davis (Jefferson) *soldier:* **9** butternut *spy:* **4** Boyd (Belle) *vice-president:* **8** Stephens (Alexander)

confederation see CONFEDERACY

confer 4 give, meet, talk **5** allot, award, grant, speak **6** accord, advise, bestow, confab, donate, huddle, parley, pow-wow **7** consult, discuss, present **8** collogue, converse **10** deliberate **11** confabulate

conference 4 talk **5** forum, synod **6** caucus, league, parley, powwow **7** meeting, palaver, seminar **8** assembly, colloquy, congress **9** symposium **10** colloquium, discussion, round-robin, roundtable **11** association, convocation **12** consultation, deliberation **13** confabulation

confess 3 own **4** avow, sing **5** admit, allow, grant, let on, own up **6** reveal **7** concede, divulge, profess **8** disclose **9** come clean **11** acknowledge

confession 5 creed **6** avowal **7** peccavi **9** admission, statement **10** disclosure

confidant 8 familiar, intimate

confide 4 tell **5** trust **6** bestow, commit, reveal **7** commend, consign, entrust, whisper **8** hand over, relegate, turn over

confidence 5 faith, poise, stock, trust **6** aplomb, surety **8** credence, reliance, sureness **9** assurance, certainty, certitude **10** conviction, equanimity *game:* **4** scam **5** bunco, bunko, grift, sting **7** swindle **8** flimflam

confidence man 3 gyp **5** shark **7** diddler, grifter, scammer, sharper, sharpie **8** swindler **9** charlatan, defrauder, trickster **11** bunco artist

confident 4 bold, sure **5** brash, brave, cocky **6** secure **7** assured, certain **8** cocksure, fearless, intrepid, positive, sanguine, unafraid **9** dauntless, undaunted **10** courageous, undoubtful **11** self-assured, self-reliant **13** self-assertive, self-possessed

confidential 5 close, privy **6** hushed, inside, secret **7** private **8** familiar, hush-hush, intimate **9** auricular **10** classified

configuration 4 cast, form **5** shape **6** figure, layout, makeup **7** contour, gestalt, outline, pattern **9** structure **12** conformation

confine 3 box, mew, pen **4** cage, coop, crib, jail, term **5** bound, cramp, hem in, limit **6** immure, intern, lock up, shut in, shut up **7** delimit, enclose, impound, put away **8** encircle, imprison, localize, restrict **9** constrain **11** incarcerate **12** circumscribe

confinement 7 custody, lying-in **8** childbed **9** captivity, detention, restraint **10** constraint **12** accouchement, imprisonment **13** incarceration

confines 6 bounds, limits **7** borders, compass **8** boundary, environs, purlieus **9** precincts **10** boundaries

confirm 3 fix, set **5** check, prove, vouch **6** attest, ratify, uphold, verify **7** approve, bear out, certify, concede, endorse, justify, support **8** buttress, check out, validate **9** ascertain, reinforce **10** strengthen **11** corroborate **12** authenticate, substantiate

confirmation 5 proof **7** support, witness **8** approval, evidence **9** testimony **10** validation **11** attestation, endorsement, testimonial **12** ratification, verification **13** certification, corroboration

confirmed 3 set **5** fixed, sworn **6** proven **7** chronic, settled **8** deep-dyed, definite, habitual, hardened, ratified **10** accustomed, deep-rooted, deep-seated, entrenched, habituated, inveterate, persistent **13** bred-in-the-bone, dyed-in-the-wool

confiscate 4 grab, take **5** annex, seize, usurp **7** escheat, impound, preempt **8** arrogate **9** sequester **10** commandeer **11** appropriate, expropriate

confiture 3 jam **8** conserve, preserve **9** marmalade, preserves

conflagrant 5 afire, fiery **6** ablaze, aflame, alight **7** blazing, burning, flaming

conflagration 3 war **4** fire **5** blaze **7** inferno **8** conflict **9** holocaust

conflate 3 mix **4** fuse, join, meld, weld **5** blend, merge, mix up **6** mingle, muddle **7** combine, confuse, mistake **8** coalesce, confound **9** commingle

conflict 3 row, war **4** bout, duel, rift, vary **5** brawl, clash, fight, set-to **6** battle, combat, differ, fracas, strife **7** contend, contest, discord, dispute, rivalry, warfare **8** argument, disagree, mismatch, struggle, tug-of-war, variance **9** encounter, rencontre **10** contention, engagement **11** competition

conflicting 6 at odds **7** opposed, warring **8** clashing, contrary, opposing **9** dissonant **10** contending, discordant, discrepant **11** incongruent, incongruous, inconsonant **12** antagonistic, antipathetic, incompatible, inconsistent, inharmonious **13** contradictory

confluence 6 merger **7** joining, meeting, merging **8** junction **9** concourse, gathering **11** convergence

conform 3 fit **4** jibe, obey, suit **5** adapt, agree, fit in, match, yield **6** accord, adjust, attune, comply, follow, square, submit, tailor **8** dovetail **9** acquiesce, harmonize, reconcile **10** coordinate, correspond, proportion **11** accommodate

conformable 6 fitted, suited **7** adapted, matched **8** amenable, obedient, suitable **9** agreeable, compliant, congenial, consonant **10** submissive

conformation 4 cast, form **5** shape **6** figure **7** anatomy **9** structure **10** adaptation **11** arrangement **13** configuration

conforming 3 apt **6** decent, proper, seemly **7** correct, uniform **8** becoming, decorous, suitable **9** befitting, civilized **10** compatible, consistent **11** comme il faut

conformity 6 accord **7** decorum, harmony **9** agreement, coherence, congruity, obedience, orthodoxy **10** accordance, allegiance, compliance, consonance, observance, submission **11** consistency **12** acquiescence

confound 4 damn, faze **5** befog, mix up, stump **6** baffle, puzzle, rattle, refute **7** confuse, mistake, mystify, nonplus, perplex, stupefy **8** befuddle, bewilder, disprove **9** discomfit, dumbfound, embarrass, frustrate **10** controvert, disconcert **11** misidentify

confounded 5 utter **6** blamed, cursed, cussed, damned **7** blasted, blessed, doggone, shocked **8** absolute, accursed, dismayed, infernal, outright **9** consarned, dad-blamed, execrable, out-and-out **11** dumbfounded, overwhelmed, unmitigated **13** thunderstruck

confrere see COLLEAGUE

confront 4 defy, face, meet **5** beard, brave, cross **6** accost, breast, oppose, take on **9** challenge, encounter

Confucian way of life 3 tao

confuse 3 fog **4** blur, daze, faze **5** abash, addle, befog, cloud, dizzy, mix up, muddy, stump, upset **6** baffle, ball up, bemuse, flurry, foul up, fuddle, garble, jumble, mess up, muddle, puzzle, rattle **7** agitate, becloud, derange, disrupt, distort, flummox, fluster, mislead, mistake, mystify, nonplus, perplex, perturb, snarl up **8** bedazzle, befuddle,

bewilder, confound, disorder, disquiet, distract, throw off, unsettle **9** discomfit, disorient, embarrass **10** complicate, disarrange, discompose, disconcert **11** disorganize, misidentify **12** misrepresent

confused 4 lost **5** dazed, messy, muddy, muzzy, vague **6** addled **7** at a loss, chaotic, mixed up, muddled, puzzled **9** flustered, perplexed, unsettled **10** bewildered, nonplussed, topsy-turvy **11** disoriented **12** disconcerted

confusion 3 ado, din **4** flap, mess, stew **5** babel, chaos, havoc, mix-up, snafu, snarl **6** bedlam, dither, foul-up, hubbub, huddle, jumble, lather, muddle, tumult, unease **7** anarchy, clutter, turmoil **8** disarray, disorder, shambles **9** abashment, agitation, commotion, imbroglio **10** hullabaloo, perplexity, puzzlement, turbulence, uneasiness **11** derangement, disturbance, pandemonium **12** bewilderment **13** embarrassment

confute 4 deny **5** evert, rebut **6** defeat, negate **8** confound, disprove, puncture **10** controvert, disconfirm

congé 3 bow **5** adieu **6** good-by **7** goodbye, molding, parting, sendoff **8** farewell **9** dismissal **11** leave-taking

congeal 3 dry, gel, set **4** clot, jell **5** jelly **6** curdle, harden **7** stiffen, thicken **8** solidify **9** coagulate **10** gelatinize

congener 6 agnate **7** cognate, sibling **8** relation, relative

congenial 4 nice **6** social **7** affable, amiable, cordial, kindred, welcome **8** amicable, friendly, gracious, pleasant, pleasing, sociable, suitable **9** agreeable, congruous, consonant, favorable **10** compatible, consistent, gratifying, harmonious **11** cooperative, pleasurable, sympathetic **13** companionable

congenital 6 inborn, inbred, innate, native **7** natural **8** inherent **9** essential, ingrained, intrinsic **10** deep-seated, indigenous, indwelling

conger 3 eel

congeries 5 group **7** company **8** assembly **9** gathering **10** assemblage, collection **11** aggregation **12** congregation

congest 3 jam **4** clog, fill, plug, stop **5** block, choke, close, crowd **6** plug up **7** occlude **8** obstruct

conglobate 4 ball **6** sphere **8** ensphere **9** spherical

conglomerate 4 mass, pool **5** chain, group, mixed, trust **6** cartel, motley **7** chaebol, combine **8** keiretsu, zaibatsu **9** aggregate, syndicate **11** aggregation **12** multifarious **13** heterogeneous

conglomeration 5 hoard, trove 8 mishmash 9 aggregate 10 collection, cumulation, hodgepodge, miscellany 11 agglomerate, aggregation 12 accumulation

Congo, Democratic Republic of the *capital:* 8 Kinshasa *city:* 7 Kolwezi 9 Mbuji-Mayi 10 Lubumbashi *explorer:* 7 Stanley (Henry Morton) *former name:* 5 Zaire 12 Belgian Congo *lake:* 4 Kivu 5 Mweru 6 Albert, Edward 10 Tanganyika *language:* 6 French 7 English *monetary unit:* 5 franc *neighbor:* 5 Congo, Sudan 6 Angola, Rwanda, Uganda, Zambia 7 Burundi 8 Tanzania *river:* 5 Congo

Congo, Republic of *capital:* 11 Brazzaville *city:* 11 Pointe-Noire *former name:* 11 Middle Congo *language:* 6 French *monetary unit:* 5 franc *neighbor:* 5 Congo, Gabon 6 Angola 7 Cabinda 8 Cameroon *river:* 5 Congo

congratulate 4 laud 6 salute 10 compliment, felicitate

congregate 4 meet 5 swarm 6 gather, muster 7 collect, convene 8 assemble, converge 9 forgather 10 foregather, rendezvous

congregation 4 mass 5 crowd, flock, group 7 meeting 8 assembly, audience 9 gathering 10 assemblage, collection 11 churchgoers 12 parishioners

congress 4 diet 5 synod 6 league 7 meeting, society 8 assembly, conclave 10 convention, parliament 11 association, Capitol Hill, legislature

congressman 5 solon 7 senator 8 delegate, lawmaker 10 legislator 14 representative

congruity 9 agreement, coherence 10 conformity 11 consistency

congruous 3 apt, fit 7 fitting 9 agreeable, befitting, congenial, consonant 10 compatible, concordant, consistent, harmonious 11 appropriate, sympathetic

conifer 3 fir, yew 4 pine 5 cedar, larch 6 spruce 7 cypress, hemlock, juniper 8 softwood 9 evergreen 10 arborvitae

conjectural 7 reputed 8 putative, supposed 11 speculative, theoretical 12 hypothetical, suppositious 13 suppositional

conjecture 5 guess, infer 6 assume, theory 7 presume, suppose, surmise, suspect 8 theorize 9 inference, speculate 11 hypothesize, proposition, speculation, supposition

conjoin 3 wed 4 band, link, yoke 5 unite 6 couple 7 combine, connect 8 federate 9 affiliate, associate, cooperate 11 consolidate

conjoint 6 common, mutual, public, shared, united 7 unified 8 combined, communal 9 concerted 10 collective 11 coefficient, cooperative, intermutual

conjointly 8 mutually, together

conjugal 6 wedded 7 marital, married, nuptial, spousal 8 hymeneal 9 connubial 11 matrimonial

conjugality 7 wedlock 8 marriage 9 matrimony

conjugate 4 fuse, join, link, pair, yoke 5 yoked 6 couple, joined, linked 7 bracket, combine, conjoin, connect, coupled 9 associate, connected

conjunct 5 joint 6 common, joined, mutual, shared, united

conjunction 3 and, but, for, nor, yet 4 lest, once, than, then, when 5 after, since, union, until, where, which, while 6 before, either, though, unless 7 because, however, neither, whereas, whether 8 alliance, although, moreover, whenever 9 therefore 10 connection 11 affiliation, association, combination, concurrence

conjuration 4 oath 5 charm, spell, trick 7 sorcery 10 adjuration, hocus-pocus, invocation 11 abracadabra, incantation

conjure 3 beg 4 urge 6 appeal, invoke, summon 7 beseech, entreat, imagine, implore 8 contrive 9 importune 10 supplicate

conjurer 4 mage, seer 5 magus 6 Magian, wizard 7 warlock 8 magician, sorcerer 9 enchanter, trickster 11 illusionist, necromancer

conjuring 5 magic 7 sorcery 8 wizardry 10 hocus-pocus, necromancy 11 abracadabra, legerdemain, thaumaturgy

conk 3 die, hit, rap 4 belt, swat 5 croak, faint, knock, thump, whack 8 knock out

con man see CONFIDENCE MAN

connate 4 akin 6 allied, inborn, native 7 kindred, related 8 inherent 9 congenial, elemental, essential, ingrained, inherited, intrinsic 10 affiliated, congenital, indigenous, indwelling 11 consanguine

connect 3 tie, wed 4 ally, bind, join, link, yoke 5 marry, unite 6 attach, bridge, couple, fasten, relate 7 combine, conjoin 8 transfer 9 affiliate, associate, interlock

Connecticut *capital:* 8 Hartford *city:* 4 Avon 6 Darien 8 New Haven, Stamford 9 Greenwich, New London, Waterbury 10 Bridgeport *college, university:* 4 Yale 7 Trinity 8 Wesleyan 9 Fairfield 10 Quinnipiac *nickname:* 6 Nutmeg (State) 12 Constitution

(State) *river:* **6** Thames **10** Housatonic **11** Connecticut *state bird:* **5** robin (American) *state flower:* **14** mountain laurel *state tree:* **8** white oak

connection 3 tie **4** bond, link **5** joint, nexus, tie-in, union **6** hookup **7** joining, kinship, network **8** affinity, alliance, coupling, junction, juncture **9** coherence, communion, fastening **10** attachment, catenation, continuity **11** affiliation, association, combination, conjunction, partnership **12** relationship

connective 3 and, nor, not **4** then **6** either **7** neither **8** syndetic **11** conjunction, conjunctive

conniption 3 fit **4** bout **5** furor, spasm, spate, spell, throe **6** attack, frenzy **7** seizure, tantrum **8** outburst, paroxysm **10** convulsion

connivance 8 intrigue **9** collusion **10** complicity, conspiracy

connive 4 plot, wink **5** blink **6** devise, scheme, wink at **7** blink at, collude **8** conspire, contrive, intrigue **9** machinate

connoisseur 4 buff **6** expert **7** epicure, gourmet **8** aesthete, gourmand, highbrow **9** authority, bon vivant **10** dilettante, gastronome **11** cognoscente

connotation 4 hint **7** meaning **8** overtone **9** undertone **10** intimation, suggestion **11** association, implication **13** signification

connote 4 hint, mean **5** imply, spell **6** hint at, intend **7** betoken, express, signify, suggest **8** indicate, intimate **9** insinuate

connubial 6 wedded **7** marital, married, nuptial, spousal **8** conjugal, hymeneal **11** matrimonial

connubiality 7 wedlock **8** marriage **9** matrimony **11** conjugality

conquer 4 beat, best, lick, tame, whip **5** crush **6** defeat, master, subdue **8** overcome, surmount, vanquish **9** checkmate, overpower, overthrow, overwhelm, subjugate

conquest 3 win **4** rout **7** triumph, victory **9** overthrow, seduction **11** subjugation

Conrad, Joseph *character:* **3** Jim **4** Axel, Lena **5** Flora, Kurtz **6** Marlow, Verloc **7** Almayer **8** MacWhirr, Nostromo *work:* **5** Youth **6** Chance **7** Lord Jim, Typhoon, Victory **8** Nostromo **11** Secret Agent (The) **13** Almayer's Folly **15** Heart of Darkness

Conroy novel 10 Beach Music **11** Water Is Wide (The) **12** Great Santini (The) **13** Prince of Tides (The) **17** Lords of Discipline (The)

consanguineous 4 akin **6** agnate **7** cognate, connate, kindred, related

conscience 5 demur, honor, qualm **6** ethics, virtue **7** decency, remorse, scruple **8** morality, scruples **9** integrity **10** contrition **11** compunction

conscienceless 6 amoral **7** immoral **9** unethical **12** unprincipled, unscrupulous

conscientious 4 fair, just, true **5** exact **6** honest **7** careful, dutiful, upright **8** diligent, reliable, studious **9** honorable **10** high-minded, meticulous, principled, scrupulous **11** hard-working, painstaking, punctilious

conscious 5 alive, awake, aware **7** knowing, mindful, witting **8** sensible, sentient **9** attentive, cognizant **10** deliberate, perceptive

consciousness 4 heed, mind **6** regard **7** concern **9** alertness, awareness, knowledge **10** cognizance, perception **11** realization, recognition

conscribe 5 draft, limit **6** call up, enlist, enroll, muster **7** recruit

conscript 5 draft, elect **6** called, choose, chosen, enlist, enroll, induct, select **7** drafted, dragoon, impress, recruit, soldier **8** selected

consecrate 5 bless **6** anoint, devote, hallow, ordain, pledge **8** dedicate, sanctify

consecrated 4 holy **6** sacred **7** blessed **8** hallowed **10** sanctified *oil:* **6** chrism

consecution see SEQUENCE

consecutive 4 next **5** later **6** serial **7** ensuing, ordered, sequent **9** following, succedent **10** sequential, subsequent, succeeding, successive **11** progressive **12** successional

consent 3 yes **4** okay **5** agree, allow, leave, yield **6** accede, accord, assent, comply, concur, permit **7** approve, go-ahead **8** approval, sanction **9** acquiesce, agreement, allowance, subscribe **10** compliance, permission **12** acquiescence **13** authorization, understanding

consequence 4 fame, note, rank **5** issue, state **6** cachet, effect, import, moment, renown, repute, result, sequel, status, upshot, weight **7** account, conceit, dignity, fallout, outcome, stature **8** eminence, interest, position, prestige, reaction, standing **9** aftermath, inference, magnitude **10** importance, reputation **11** aftereffect, weightiness **12** repercussion, significance **13** momentousness

consequent 5 later, sound **7** ensuing, logical **8** rational **9** deduction, following, resulting

consequential 3 big **5** major **7** serious, weighty **8** egoistic, indirect, material

9 conceited, egotistic, important, momentous **10** collateral, incidental, meaningful, subsidiary **11** significant, substantial **12** considerable **13** self-important

consequently 4 ergo, thus **5** hence **9** as a result, therefore, thereupon **10** inevitably **11** accordingly

conservation 4 care **7** control **9** attention, husbandry **10** management, protection **11** safekeeping **12** guardianship, preservation

conservative 4 tory **6** proper **7** diehard, old-line **8** cautious, discreet, old-guard, orthodox, rightist, standpat **9** right-wing, temperate **10** restrained **11** circumspect, reactionary, right-winger, standpatter, traditional

conservatory 6 school **7** academy, nursery **8** hothouse **10** greenhouse **11** music school

conserve 3 can, jam **4** keep, save **5** hoard, lay up, put up, skimp, store **6** keep up **7** husband, protect, support, sustain **8** maintain, set aside, withhold **9** confiture, economize, safeguard, sweetmeat

consider 3 see **4** deem, feel, mind, muse, note, rate, view **5** fancy, judge, sense, study, think, weigh **6** credit, look at, notice, ponder, reason, reckon, regard **7** account, believe, examine, imagine, inspect, reflect, respect, suppose **8** appraise, cogitate, conceive, conclude, envisage, meditate, mull over, ruminate **9** speculate, think over **10** deliberate, excogitate, scrutinize, think about **11** contemplate

considerable 3 big **5** ample, hefty, large, major **7** notable, sizable, weighty **8** material, sensible, sizeable **9** extensive, important, momentous, plentiful - **10** large-scale, meaningful **11** respectable, significant, substantial **13** consequential

considerably 3 far **4** well **5** quite **6** rather **7** notably **8** somewhat **10** noticeably **11** appreciably **13** significantly, substantially

considerate 4 kind **6** kindly, polite, tender **7** amiable, careful, patient, tactful **8** discreet, generous, obliging **9** attentive **10** chivalrous, forbearing, solicitous, thoughtful **11** circumspect, complaisant, sympathetic, warmhearted **13** compassionate

consideration 3 fee **4** heed, tact **5** cause, favor, issue, study **6** esteem, factor, motive, reason, regard **7** account, concern, payment, respect, thought **8** kindness **9** attention, awareness **10** admira-tion, cogitation, discussion, estimation, inducement, recompense, reflection, solicitude **11** application, forbearance, mindfulness **12** deliberation **13** attentiveness, concentration

considered 7 advised, studied, weighed **8** studious **10** deliberate, thought-out **11** intentional **12** aforethought, premeditated

consign 4 give, send, ship **5** agree, allot, award, remit, yield **6** commit, convey, devote, submit **7** address, commend, confide, deliver, entrust, forward **8** dispatch, hand over, relegate, transmit, turn over **9** surrender

consist 3 lie **4** rest **5** abide, agree, dwell, exist, fit in **6** accord, inhere, reside **7** comport, conform, consort, subsist **8** dovetail **10** correspond

consistency 7 aptness, concord, density, fitness, harmony, texture **8** evenness, firmness, likeness **9** agreement, coherence, congruity, thickness, viscosity **10** conformity, consonance, similarity **11** suitability

consistent 4 even, true **6** steady **7** regular, uniform **8** constant **9** accordant, agreeable, congenial, congruous, consonant, unfailing, unvarying **10** compatible, conforming, dependable, invariable, unchanging **11** homogeneous, sympathetic, undeviating

consistently 8 wontedly **9** regularly, routinely **10** habitually, invariably **11** customarily

console 4 calm, case **5** cheer **6** buck up, solace **7** cabinet, comfort, hearten

consolidate 3 mix, set **4** fuse, join, meld, pool **5** blend, merge, unify, unite **6** firm up, secure **7** compact, fortify **8** compress, condense, federate, solidify **9** integrate **10** amalgamate, strengthen **11** concentrate

consolidation 5 union **6** merger **7** melding, merging **9** coalition **11** combination, integration, unification **12** amalgamation

consonance 6 accord **7** concord, harmony **9** agreement, congruity, resonance **10** congruence

consonant 4 akin, like **6** agnate **7** musical, similar **8** blending, harmonic, resonant **9** congruous **10** compatible, harmonious **11** conformable **13** corresponding *kind:* **4** stop, surd **5** nasal, velar **6** atonic, voiced **7** lateral, palatal, spirant **8** alveolar, bilabial, unvoiced **9** fricative, voiceless

consort 3 set **4** mate, wife **5** agree, group, tally, unite **6** accord, attend, fellow, spouse, square, troupe **7** company,

comport, conform, husband, partner
8 assembly, chaperon, dovetail
9 accompany, associate, companion,
harmonize **10** correspond
consortium 4 bloc, club, ring **5** guild,
trust, union **6** cartel, league **7** combine,
society **8** alliance, congress **9** coalition,
syndicate **10** federation **11** association
12 conglomerate
conspectus 5 brief **6** digest, précis,
sketch, survey **7** epitome, outline, summary **8** abstract, overview, synopsis
9 reduction **10** abridgment **11** abridgement **12** condensation
conspicuous 5 clear, overt, showy
6 marked, patent, signal **7** blatant, evident, glaring, notable, obvious, pointed, salient **8** apparent, distinct, flagrant,
manifest, striking **9** arresting, egregious, notorious, obtrusive, prominent
10 celebrated, noticeable, pronounced,
remarkable **11** eye-catching, illustrious,
outstanding **12** ostentatious
conspiracy 4 plan, plot **5** cabal **6** scheme
8 intrigue **11** machination
conspirator 7 abettor, plotter, schemer
9 accessory, intriguer **10** accomplice
11 confederate
conspire 4 plot **5** cabal **6** scheme **7** collude, connive **8** intrigue **9** machinate
constable 6 deputy, lawman, warden
7 marshal, sheriff
constancy 5 faith **6** fealty **7** loyalty,
resolve **8** adhesion, devotion, fidelity,
firmness **9** adherence, diligence,
endurance, fortitude **10** allegiance,
attachment, dedication, resolution,
steadiness **11** staunchness **12** faithfulness, perseverance **13** dependability,
steadfastness
constant 4 even, fast, firm, true **5** fixed,
loyal **6** dogged, stable, steady, trusty
7 abiding, chronic, endless, equable,
lasting, nonstop, staunch, uniform
8 enduring, faithful, habitual, resolute,
unending **9** ceaseless, confirmed, continual, immovable, immutable, incessant, obstinate, perpetual, steadfast,
sustained, unceasing, unfailing, unmovable, unvarying **10** changeless, consistent, continuous, dependable, inflexible, invariable, inveterate, persistent,
persisting, unchanging, unwavering
11 everlasting, inalterable, unalterable,
unrelenting, unremitting **12** interminable, unchangeable
Constantine *birthplace:* **4** Nish *mother:*
6 Helena *son:* **7** Crispus *victim:* **6** Fausta
7 Crispus *wife:* **6** Fausta
constantly 4 ever **5** often **6** always **7** forever **9** eternally **10** frequently, invari-

ably, repeatedly **11** incessantly, perpetually **12** continuously
constellation 5 group **7** pattern
10 assemblage, collection **11** arrangement *Altar:* **3** Ara *Archer:* **11** Sagittarius
Arrow: **7** Sagitta *Balance:* **5** Libra **9** Ursa
Major *Bear, Little:* **9** Ursa Minor *Big Dipper:* **9** Ursa Major *Bird of Paradise:*
4 Apus *Bull:* **6** Taurus *Centaur:* **9** Centaurus *Chained Lady:* **9** Andromeda
Chameleon: **10** Chamaeleon *Champion:*
7 Perseus *Charioteer:* **6** Auriga *Clock:*
10 Horologium *Colt:* **8** Equuleus *Crab:*
6 Cancer *Crane:* **4** Grus *Cross:* **4** Crux
Crow: **6** Corvus *Crown:* **6** Corona *Cup:*
6 Crater *Dolphin:* **9** Delphinus *Dove:*
7 Columba *Dragon:* **5** Draco *Eagle:*
6 Aquila *Fishes:* **6** Pisces *Fly:* **5** Musca
Flying Fish: **6** Volans *Furnace:* **6** Fornax
Graving Tool: **6** Caelum *Great Bear:*
9 Ursa Major *Greater Dog:* **10** Canis
Major *Hare:* **5** Lepus *Herdsman:*
6 Boötes *Horned Goat:* **11** Capricornus
Hunter: **5** Orion *Indian:* **5** Indus *Keel:*
6 Carina *Lady in the Chair:* **10** Cassiopeia
Larger Bear: **9** Ursa Major *Larger Dog:*
10 Canis Major *Lesser Dog:* **10** Canis
Minor *Lion:* **3** Leo *Little Bear:* **9** Ursa
Minor *Little Dipper:* **9** Ursa Minor *Little
Fox:* **9** Vulpecula *Lizard:* **7** Lacerta *Lyre:*
4 Lyra *Mariner's Compass:* **5** Pyxis
Monarch: **7** Cepheus *Net:* **9** Reticulum
Painter's Easel: **6** Pictor *Pair of Com-
passes:* **8** Circinus *Peacock:* **4** Pavo
Pump: **6** Antlia *Ram:* **5** Aries *Rescuer:*
7 Perseus *River Po:* **8** Eridanus *Sails:*
4 Vela *Scorpion:* **8** Scorpius *Serpent:*
7 Serpens *Serpent Holder:* **9** Ophiuchus
Sextant: **7** Sextans *Shield:* **6** Scutum
Smaller Bear: **9** Ursa Minor *Square:*
5 Norma *Stern:* **6** Puppis *Swan:*
6 Cygnus *Table:* **5** Mensa *Toucan:*
6 Tucana *Triangle:* **10** Triangulum *Twins:*
6 Gemini *Unicorn:* **9** Monoceros *Virgin:*
5 Virgo *Water Carrier:* **8** Aquarius *Water
Monster:* **5** Hydra *Water Snake:* **6** Hydrus
Whale: **5** Cetus *Winged Horse:* **7** Pegasus
Wolf: **5** Lupus
consternate 5 alarm, daunt, shake,
shock **6** appall, dismay **7** horrify,
unnerve **8** distress
consternation 4 fear **5** alarm, dread,
panic, shock **6** dismay, fright, horror,
terror **11** trepidation **12** bewilderment
constituent 4 part **5** piece, voter **6** factor,
member **7** element, portion **8** division,
fraction **9** component, elemental, principal **10** ingredient
constitute 4 form, make **5** enact, found,
set up, start **6** create, embody, make up
7 appoint, compose **8** complete, com-

prise, organize **9** establish, institute, represent

constitution 3 law **4** code **5** build, canon **6** design, makeup, nature **7** charter **8** physique **9** formation, structure **11** composition **12** architecture, construction

constitutional 4 walk **6** inborn, inbred, innate, lawful **7** built-in, organic **8** inherent **9** essential, ingrained, intrinsic **10** congenital, deep-seated

Constitution State 11 Connecticut

Constitution, U.S.S. 12 Old Ironsides

constitutive 5 vital **8** cardinal **9** essential **11** fundamental **12** constructive

constrain 3 bar **4** curb, deny, jail **5** chain, check, crush, force, impel, limit, press **6** bridle, coerce, compel, enjoin, oblige, secure, squash, squish **7** confine, deprive, inhibit, refrain, squeeze **8** compress, hold back, hold down, imprison, restrain, restrict **11** incarcerate

constraint 4 bond **5** check, force **6** duress **8** coercion, pressure **9** captivity, detention, restraint **10** compulsion, diffidence, inhibition, limitation, repression **11** confinement, restriction, suppression **13** embarrassment

constrict 4 curb **5** cramp, limit, pinch, strap **6** hamper, narrow, shrink **7** confine, inhibit, squeeze, tighten **8** compress, condense, contract, restrain, strangle, stultify **9** constrain **12** circumscribe

constrictor 3 boa **5** snake **6** muscle **8** anaconda **9** sphincter, strangler

construct 4 form, make **5** build, erect, forge, frame, put up, raise, set up, shape **6** create, devise **7** build up, compile, fashion, produce **8** assemble, engineer **9** establish, fabricate **11** manufacture, put together

construction 6 design, makeup **7** edifice, shaping **8** assembly, building **9** formation **10** fashioning **11** arrangement, engineering, fabrication, manufacture **12** architecture, constitution

constructive 6 useful **7** helpful, implied, virtual **8** implicit, positive, valuable **9** practical **10** beneficial

construe 5 educe, gloss, parse **6** induct **7** analyze, explain, expound **9** explicate, interpret **10** paraphrase, understand

consuetude 5 habit, usage **6** custom, manner **8** practice **10** convention

consult 3 ask **6** advise, confer, huddle, parley **7** examine, refer to **8** collogue, consider **11** confabulate

consume 3 eat, use **4** down, gulp, ruin **5** drain, drink, eat up, gorge, spend,

use up, waste **6** absorb, devour, expend, finish, ingest, obsess, take up **7** deplete, destroy, engross, exhaust, put away, put down, swallow **8** squander **9** dissipate, finish off, polish off **10** annihilate, extinguish, monopolize, run through

consumer 4 user **5** buyer **6** client **7** shopper, end user **8** customer **9** purchaser

consumer advocate 5 Nader (Ralph)

consuming 6 ardent **7** fervent, intense **8** gripping, riveting **9** absorbing **10** engrossing **11** enthralling **12** monopolizing

consummate 3 end **4** ripe **5** close, crown, ideal, utter **6** finish, superb, wind up, wrap up **7** achieve, perfect, supreme **8** absolute, complete, conclude, finished, flawless, peerless, ultimate **9** faultless, matchless, perfected, virtuosic **10** accomplish, impeccable, inimitable **11** superlative **12** accomplished **13** thoroughgoing

consumption 3 use **5** decay, waste **6** intake **7** wasting **8** phthisis **9** depletion, ingestion **10** absorption **11** dissipation **12** tuberculosis

contact 4 meet **5** reach, touch **8** tangency, touching **9** closeness, communion, proximity **10** connection, contiguity **11** association, contingence **13** communication

contagion 3 pox **4** bane, meme **5** taint, venom, virus **6** miasma, plague, poison **7** disease, infection, scourge **8** epidemic **9** pollution **10** corruption, pestilence **13** contamination

contagious 6 catchy **8** catching, epidemic **10** infectious **12** communicable, pestilential **13** transmissible, transmittable

contain 4 hold, keep **5** check, house **6** embody, take in **7** collect, control, embrace, enclose, include, receive, repress, subsume **8** comprise, restrain **9** encompass **10** comprehend **11** accommodate

container 3 bag, bin, box, can, cup, jar, keg, mug, pod, pot, tin, tub, urn, vat **4** cage, case, cask, drum, etui, ewer, pail, sack, silo, tank, vase, vial, well **5** chest, crate, cruet, flask, glass, gourd, phial, pouch **6** basket, bottle, carafe, carton, casket, coffin, cooler, goblet, hamper, hatbox, holder, inkpot, shaker **7** bandbox, capsule, chalice, inkwell, package, pitcher, thermos **8** canister, catchall, decanter, envelope, hogshead, jerrican, puncheon **10** receptacle *liturgical:* **3** pyx **7** chalice **8** ciborium

contaminate 4 foul, soil **5** dirty, spoil,

stain, sully, taint 6 befoul, debase, defile, infect, injure, poison 7 corrupt, deprave, pervert, pollute, profane, tarnish, vitiate 9 desecrate 10 adulterate

conte 4 tale 5 story 9 narrative

contemn 4 snub 5 abhor, scorn, spurn 6 deride 7 deplore, despise, disdain 8 ridicule 10 look down on

contemplate 4 mull, muse, view 5 study, think, weigh 6 behold, debate, gaze at, intend, look at, ponder, regard 7 examine, inspect, propose, reflect 8 consider, gaze upon, look upon, meditate, mull over, ruminate, think out 9 think over 10 deliberate, excogitate, scrutinize

contemplation 5 study 6 musing 7 thought 8 thinking 9 intention, pondering 10 cogitation, meditation, reflection, rumination 11 cerebration, expectation, speculation 12 deliberation 13 consideration

contemplative 6 musing 7 pensive 10 cogitative, meditative, reflecting, reflective, ruminative, thoughtful 11 speculative 13 introspective

contemporary 3 new 6 coeval, extant, modern, recent 7 current, present, topical 8 existent, existing, up-to-date 9 au courant 10 coexistent, coexisting, coincident, concurrent, present-day, synchronic 11 synchronous 12 simultaneous

contempt 5 scorn, shame 7 despite, disdain, mockery 8 aversion, defiance, disfavor, disgrace, dishonor, distaste, ignominy 9 antipathy, discredit, disesteem, disrepute 10 disrespect, opprobrium, repugnance 12 disobedience, stubbornness

contemptible 3 low 4 base, mean, poor, vile 5 cheap, sorry 6 abject, odious, paltry, scummy, scurvy, shabby, sordid 7 hateful, ignoble, pitiful, squalid 8 inferior, pitiable, shameful, unworthy, wretched 9 abhorrent, loathsome 10 despicable, detestable, disgusting 11 ignominious 12 dishonorable

contemptuous 7 haughty 8 arrogant, derisive, scornful 10 disdainful 12 supercilious 13 condescending, disrespectful

contend 3 vie, war 4 aver, avow, cope, face, urge 5 argue, brawl, claim, fight 6 affirm, allege, assert, battle, charge, combat, debate, defend, insist, oppose, report, strive 7 compete, contest 8 confront, maintain, struggle 9 encounter, withstand

contender 5 match, rival 6 player 8 opponent 9 adversary, candidate,

combatant 10 antagonist, challenger, competitor, contestant

____ **contendere** 4 nolo

content 4 cozy, gist 5 happy 6 at ease, serene 7 appease, gratify, meaning, placate, satisfy 9 gratified, satisfied, substance 11 comfortable 12 significance

contention 3 war 4 beef, feud 6 combat, rumpus, strife, thesis 7 discord, dispute, dissent, quarrel, rivalry, wrangle 8 argument, conflict, disunity, squabble 10 difference, dissension, dissidence 11 altercation, competition, controversy *Scottish:* 5 sturt

contentious 5 fiery 7 carping, froward, peppery, scrappy, warlike 8 captious, caviling, contrary, militant, perverse 9 bellicose, combative, hotheaded, litigious, polemical, truculent 10 pugnacious 11 belligerent, quarrelsome 12 disputatious, faultfinding 13 argumentative, controversial

conterminous 10 coincident 11 coextensive

contest 3 vie 4 bout, duel, feud, fray, game, meet, race, tilt 5 clash, fight, match, repel, rival, trial 6 battle, combat, debate, oppose, resist, strife, strive 7 compete, dispute, rivalry, warfare 8 argument, conflict, endeavor, skirmish, struggle, tug-of-war 9 challenge, encounter, rencontre 10 engagement, tournament 11 competition

contiguity 9 adjacency, immediacy, proximity 11 propinquity

contiguous 4 next 8 abutting, adjacent, touching 9 adjoining, bordering 10 juxtaposed

continence 6 purity, virtue 8 chastity, sobriety 9 austerity 10 abnegation, abstinence, asceticism, chasteness, moderation, temperance 11 forbearance 12 renunciation 13 self-restraint

continent 4 Asia, mass 5 sober 6 Africa, chaste, Europe 8 celibate, mainland 9 abstinent, Australia, temperate 10 abstemious, Antarctica, restrained 11 abstentious 12 North America, South America *lost:* 8 Atlantis

contingence 5 touch 7 contact 8 tangency, touching

contingency 4 pass 5 event 6 chance, crisis 8 exigency, juncture, occasion 9 emergency 10 likelihood 11 opportunity, possibility, probability, uncertainty

contingent 3 odd 4 band 5 group, party, troop 6 casual, chance, likely 7 reliant 8 possible, probable, relative 9 dependent, empirical, entourage, uncertain 10 accidental, delegation, deputation,

detachment, fortuitous, incidental, unforeseen **11** conditional **13** unanticipated, unforeseeable, unpredictable
continual 6 steady **7** abiding, endless, nonstop, regular, running **8** constant, enduring, timeless, unbroken, unending **9** ceaseless, incessant, perpetual, perennial, recurrent, recurring, unceasing, unfailing, unvarying **10** persistent, persisting, relentless, unchanging, unflagging **11** everlasting, unremitting **12** interminable **13** uninterrupted
continually 4 ever **6** always **7** forever **8** together **9** endlessly **10** constantly **11** incessantly, night and day **12** interminably, persistently, relentlessly, successively **13** consecutively
continuance 3 run **4** stay **5** delay **6** sequel **8** duration, survival **9** longevity **10** permanence **11** adjournment, persistence **12** postponement, prolongation
continuation 3 run **4** coda **6** sequel **8** appendix, duration, epilogue **9** endurance, extension **10** resumption **11** persistence, protraction **12** prolongation
continue 4 go on, last, stay **5** abide, renew, run on **6** endure, hang in, keep at, keep on, keep up, pick up, push on, remain, reopen, resume, retain, take up **7** carry on, persist, press on, proceed, prolong, restart, survive **8** maintain, postpone **9** carry over, persevere **10** recommence
continuing 5 fixed **6** steady **7** abiding, chronic, durable, eternal, lasting, ongoing **8** constant, enduring, lifelong, stubborn **9** long-lived, obstinate, perennial, prolonged, steadfast, tenacious, unabating **10** inveterate, persistent, persisting **11** long-lasting
continuity 4 flow **6** script **8** duration, scenario, sequence **9** endurance **11** persistence, progression
continuous see CONTINUAL
continuously see CONTINUALLY
contort 4 knot, warp **5** twist, wring **6** deform, wrench, writhe **7** distort, grimace, torture **9** convolute, corkscrew, disfigure
contortionist 7 acrobat
contour 4 form, line **5** curve, lines, shape **6** figure **7** outline, pattern, profile **9** lineament, lineation **10** silhouette **11** delineation
contra 6 facing, toward **7** against, counter, reverse, vis-à-vis **8** converse, fronting, opposite **10** conversely
contraband 3 hot **5** taboo **6** banned **7** bootleg, illegal, illicit, smuggle **8** unlawful **9** forbidden **10** prohibited,

proscribed **11** black market, bootlegging, trafficking
contract 4 bond, hire, pact, sink **5** catch, incur, lease **6** engage, induce, lessen, reduce, shrink, treaty, weaken **7** abridge, acquire, afflict, bargain, decline, dwindle, shorten, shrivel **8** compress, condense, covenant, decrease, diminish **9** agreement, constrict, succumb to **11** concentrate, transaction **12** come down with *part:* **6** clause **7** article, proviso
contraction 3 he'd, he's, I'll, it's, I've, tic **4** ain't, can't, don't, flex, he'll, isn't, let's, she'd, she's, won't, you'd **5** aren't, cramp, didn't, hadn't, hasn't, she'll, spasm, they'd, wasn't, you'll, you're, you've **6** haven't, mustn't, needn't, they'll, they've, weren't **7** couldn't, elision, mightn't, wouldn't **8** shouldn't **9** reduction, shrinkage **10** abridgment **12** abbreviation *heart's:* **7** systole *poetic:* **3** e'en, e'er, o'er, 'tis **4** ne'er, 'twas **5** 'twere, 'twill
contradict 4 deny **5** belie, cross, rebut **6** impugn, negate, refute, take on **7** confute, dispute, gainsay **8** negative, traverse **9** challenge, disaffirm
contradiction 6 denial **7** paradox **8** antinomy, negation, rebuttal, variance **9** disparity **10** gainsaying, opposition, refutation **11** discrepancy, incongruity **12** disagreement, protestation **13** inconsistency
contradictory 7 counter, reverse **8** contrary, converse, negating, opposite **9** antipodal **10** antipodean, antithesis, nullifying **12** antithetical
contraption 3 rig **5** gizmo **6** device, doodad, gadget **7** machine **9** apparatus, doohickey **11** contrivance
contrariety 10 antagonism, antithesis, opposition, perversity, unlikeness
contrariwise 9 vice versa **10** conversely, oppositely
contrary 5 balky **6** averse, ornery, unruly **7** adverse, counter, froward, reverse, wayward **8** converse, opposite, perverse, stubborn **9** antipodal, diametric, dissident, obstinate, vice versa **10** conversely, discordant, headstrong, oppositely, rebellious, refractory **11** conflicting, intractable, wrongheaded **12** antagonistic, antipathetic, antithetical, contumacious, cross-grained, recalcitrant *prefix:* **7** counter
contrast 6 differ **7** collate, compare, diverge **8** conflict, disagree **9** disparity, diversity **10** comparison, difference, divergence **11** distinction, distinguish **13** dissimilarity

contravene 4 defy, deny **5** break, cross, fight **6** abjure, breach, disown, impugn, negate, offend, oppose, reject **7** disobey, gainsay, violate **8** disclaim, infringe, renege on **9** disaffirm, go against, repudiate **10** contradict, transgress

contravention 6 breach **7** offense **8** trespass **9** violation **10** infraction **12** infringement **13** nonobservance, transgression

contretemps 3 row **4** slip, tiff **5** clash, run-in **6** dustup, mishap, slip-up **7** dispute, quarrel **8** argument **9** mischance **10** falling-out, misfortune

contribute 3 add **4** give, help, tend **5** grant **6** chip in, donate, kick in, submit, supply **7** conduce, pitch in, redound **9** subscribe **11** come through

contribution 4 alms, gift **5** input, share **7** charity, payment, present **8** donation, offering **11** benefaction, beneficence

contributory 8 adjuvant **9** accessory, ancillary, auxiliary **10** collateral, subsidiary, supporting **11** appurtenant, subservient

contrite 5 sorry **8** penitent **9** regretful, repentant **10** apologetic, remorseful **11** penitential

contriteness see CONTRITION

contrition 3 rue **4** ruth **6** regret **7** penance, remorse **9** penitence **10** repentance **11** compunction **12** self-reproach

contrivance 4 ruse **6** device, gadget **7** gimmick **8** artifice **9** apparatus, expedient, invention, stratagem **10** brainchild **11** contraption

contrive 3 rig **4** fake, make, move, plan, plot **5** frame, hatch **6** cook up, devise, invent, make up, manage, scheme, vamp up, wangle **7** arrange, concoct, connive, develop, dream up, fashion, project, work out **8** cogitate, conspire, engineer, intrigue **9** construct, elaborate, fabricate, formulate, machinate

contrived 5 hokey **6** forced **7** labored **8** strained **9** concocted, insincere **10** artificial, fabricated, factitious

control 3 run **4** curb, rein, rule, sway **5** guide, power, steer **6** bridle, direct, govern, handle, manage, master, rein in, subdue **7** command, conduct, mastery, oversee, repress, reserve **8** dominate, dominion, regulate, restrain **9** authority, direction, restraint, supervise, supremacy **10** discipline, domination, management **11** supervision **12** jurisdiction

controlled 8 discreet, reserved **9** temperate **10** restrained

controversial 5 risky **6** touchy **7** awkward, charged, eristic **8** delicate, disputed, ticklish **9** explosive, litigious, polemical **11** contentious, problematic **12** disputatious **13** argumentative

controversy 3 row **5** clash **6** debate, rumpus, strife **7** dispute, quarrel, wrangle **8** argument, squabble **10** contention, falling-out **11** altercation, disputation, embroilment

controvert 4 deny **5** rebut **6** debate, oppose, oppugn, refute **7** confute, counter, dispute, gainsay **8** disprove, question **9** challenge, repudiate

contumacious 7 froward **8** contrary, insolent, mutinous, obdurate, perverse **9** obstinate **10** rebellious, refractory **11** disobedient, intractable **12** recalcitrant **13** insubordinate

contumacy 8 contempt, defiance **9** insolence **10** perversity **12** stubbornness **13** recalcitrance

contumelious 7 abusive **8** derisive, insolent, scornful **9** insulting, truculent **10** disdainful, scurrilous **11** opprobrious **12** vituperative

contumely 5 abuse **6** insult **7** affront, mockery, obloquy **8** contempt, ridicule, sneering **9** aspersion, invective **10** scurrility **12** vituperation

contuse 6 batter, bruise, injure **7** blacken

conundrum 5 poser **6** enigma, puzzle, riddle **7** baffler, mystery, problem, puzzler, stumper **10** puzzlement **13** Chinese puzzle

convalesce 4 heal, mend **7** improve, recover **10** recuperate

convene 4 call, meet **6** call in, gather, muster, summon **7** convoke, summons **8** assemble **9** forgather **10** congregate **12** come together

convenience 4 ease **7** amenity, benefit, comfort, leisure **8** facility **9** handiness **10** assistance **13** accessibility

convenient 3 fit **4** near **5** close, handy, ready **6** at hand, nearby, proper, useful **7** close by, helpful **8** suitable **9** available, immediate, opportune **10** accessible **11** appropriate, comfortable **12** advantageous

convent 5 abbey **6** priory **7** nunnery **8** cloister **9** monastery, sanctuary

convention 3 law **4** bond, code, pact, rule **5** canon, usage **6** accord, custom, treaty **7** compact, meeting, precept **8** assembly, congress, contract, covenant, practice, protocol **9** agreement, concordat, formality, gathering, propriety, tradition **11** convocation **13** understanding

conventional 5 trite, usual **6** formal, normal, proper, seemly, solemn, square **7** correct, regular, routine, typical **8** everyday, habitual, moderate, ordinary, orthodox, standard, straight **9** bourgeois, customary **10** button-down, conforming, prevailing, restrained, unoriginal **11** commonplace, traditional **12** conservative

conventionalize 5 adapt **7** conform, stylize

converge 4 join, meet **5** focus, merge, unite **11** concentrate **12** come together

conversant 8 familiar **9** au courant **10** acquainted **11** experienced

conversation 4 chat, talk **6** confab, debate, parley **7** palaver, talking **8** causerie, colloquy, dialogue, duologue, exchange, repartee **9** discourse, tête-à-tête **10** discussion **13** confabulation

conversation piece 5 curio **6** oddity **9** curiosity

converse 3 gab **4** chat, chin, talk **5** speak, visit **6** confer, contra, parley **7** chatter, counter, reverse **8** antipode, contrary, opposite **9** antipodal, diametric **10** antithesis **12** antithetical **13** contradictory

conversely 9 vice versa **10** oppositely **12** contrariwise

conversion 5 shift **6** change, switch **7** novelty, rebirth, turning **8** mutation, reversal **9** about-face **10** alteration, changeover **11** permutation **12** modification, regeneration **13** metamorphosis, transmutation

convert 4 sway **5** alter **6** change, modify, redeem, reform, switch **7** commute, remodel **8** persuade, renovate **9** proselyte, transform, translate, transmute, transpose **11** transfigure **12** metamorphose, transmogrify *Christian:* **10** catechumen

convex 5 bowed, toric **6** arched, curved **7** bulging, curving, gibbous, rounded

convey 3 lug **4** bear, cart, cede, deed, pack, send, tell, tote **5** bring, carry, ferry **6** assign, impart, pass on **7** channel, conduct, consign, deliver, express, project **8** make over, sign over, transfer, transmit **9** transport **11** communicate

conveyance 3 car **4** auto, cart, deed, sled **5** coach, sedan, stage, title, wagon **7** charter, trailer, transit, vehicle **8** carriage, carrying **9** transport **10** automobile **12** transporting *public:* **3** bus, cab **4** taxi, tram **5** plane, train **6** subway **7** trolley **8** airplane, monorail, railroad, rickshaw **9** streetcar **10** jinricksha, jinrikisha

convict 5 felon, lifer **6** inmate, send up **7** condemn, put away **8** criminal, jailbird, prisoner, sentence, yardbird **10** find guilty

conviction 4 view **5** creed, faith **6** belief, surety **7** opinion **8** doctrine, sentence, sureness **9** assurance, certainty, certitude, sentiment **10** confidence, persuasion **12** condemnation

convince 6 assure, induce, prompt **7** satisfy, win over **8** persuade, talk into **9** influence, prevail on **11** bring around, prevail upon

convincing 5 solid, sound, valid **6** cogent **8** credible, faithful **9** plausible **10** believable, conclusive, persuasive, satisfying **11** trustworthy

convivial 3 gay **5** jolly, merry **6** hearty, jocund, jovial, lively, social **7** festive **8** mirthful, sociable **9** fun-loving, vivacious **10** gregarious **13** companionable

convocation 5 synod **7** council, meeting **8** assembly, conclave **9** gathering **10** assemblage **12** congregation

convoke 4 call **6** gather, invite, muster, summon **7** collect, convene **8** assemble **12** call together

convoluted 6 coiled **7** complex, tangled, winding **8** involved, tortuous **9** intricate **10** circuitous **11** anfractuous, complicated **12** labyrinthine

convoy 6 attend, escort **7** conduct **9** accompany

convulse 4 rock **5** shake **7** agitate, concuss **8** tetanize

convulsion 3 fit **5** spasm **6** attack, tumult, uproar **7** quaking, rocking, seizure, shaking **8** disaster, paroxysm, upheaval **9** commotion, trembling

cook 3 fix, fry **4** bake, boil, chef, heat, melt, stew **5** broil, grill, poach, roast, sauté, steam **6** braise, doctor, simmer **7** falsify, parboil, prepare, swelter

cooked 4 done, sham **5** bogus, faked, phony **6** made-up **7** altered **8** doctored, spurious **10** fictitious

cookery 7 cuisine *expert:* **3** Yan (Martin) **4** Chen (Joyce), Kerr (Graham), Puck (Wolfgang), Root (Waverley) **5** Beard (James), Child (Julia), David (Elizabeth), Hines (Duncan), Smith (Jeff) **6** Bocuse (Paul), Carême (Marie-Antoine), Farmer (Fannie), Fisher (M. F. K.), Franey (Pierre), Waters (Alice) **7** Crocker (Betty), Stewart (Martha) **8** Bourdain (Anthony), Rombauer (Irma) **9** Claiborne (Craig), Escoffier (Auguste), Prudhomme (Paul)

cookie 4 snap **7** biscuit, brownie **10** gingersnap

cooking *appliance:* **4** oven **5** mixer,

range, stove **7** blender, toaster
9 microwave **10** rotisserie *implement:*
3 cup, pan, pot, wok **4** olla **5** ladle,
sieve, spoon, whisk **6** grater, masher,
sifter, tureen **7** griddle, skillet, spatula,
steamer **8** colander, teaspoon **9** eggbeater, frying pan **10** rolling pin, table-
spoon **12** measuring cup *room:* **6** galley
7 kitchen

Cook Islands *capital:* **6** Avarua *dependency of:* **10** New Zealand *island:* **9** Raro-
tonga

cool 3 hep, hip, icy **4** calm, cold **5** abate,
aloof, chill, gelid, nippy **6** arctic, chilly,
frigid, frosty **7** assured, compose, control, decline, distant, dwindle, repress,
subside **8** composed, decrease,
detached, diminish, reserved, suppress
9 collected, confident, impassive,
unruffled **10** nonchalant, phlegmatic,
unsociable **11** indifferent, standoffish,
unflappable **13** dispassionate, imperturbable, self-possessed

cooler 3 fan, jug, pen **4** brig, coop, jail
5 clink, pokey **6** fridge, icebox, lockup,
prison **7** freezer, slammer **9** calaboose
11 refrigerant **12** refrigerator

cooling device 3 fan **6** fridge, icebox
7 freezer **12** refrigerator

coolness 5 chill, poise **6** aplomb,
phlegm **7** reserve **9** composure, frigidi-
ty, sangfroid **10** dispassion, equanimity
11 nonchalance, self-control

coop 3 hem, jug, mew, pen **4** brig, cage,
jail **5** cramp, fence, pokey **6** cooler, corral, lockup, prison, shut in **7** close in,
confine, enclose, slammer **9** calaboose,
enclosure

cooperate 5 agree, unite **6** concur,
league **7** combine, conjoin, pitch in
8 coincide, conspire **11** collaborate,
participate **12** work together

cooperation 8 alliance, teamwork
13 confederation

cooperative 5 joint **6** common, mutual,
shared **8** coactive, conjoint, obliging
9 collegial, concerted **10** collective, syn-
ergetic **11** coordinated **13** accommodating, collaborative, uncompetitive

Cooper hero 7 Hawkeye **10** Deerslayer,
Pathfinder **11** Natty Bumppo

coordinate 4 mate, mesh **5** align, equal,
match, order **6** adjust, relate **7** coequal,
conform **8** organize, parallel **9** companion, correlate, harmonize, integrate,
reconcile **10** proportion, reciprocal
11 accommodate, correlative, counterpart

coot 4 bird, fogy **6** dotard, duffer, fellow,
oddity, scoter, weirdo **7** oddball **9** character, eccentric

cootie 5 louse **9** body louse

cop 3 nab **4** lift, take **5** adopt, catch,
filch, pinch, steal, swipe **6** pilfer **7** capture, officer **8** bluecoat **9** patrolman,
policeman

copacetic 3 A-OK **4** fine, jake, okay
5 dandy, great, nifty **8** all right **9** excellent **12** satisfactory

cope 4 cape, hack **5** cloak, cover, get by,
match, vault **6** canopy, endure, make
do, manage, mantle **7** carry on, survive
8 vestment

copestone 5 crown

copious 4 lush, rich **5** ample **6** lavish,
plenty **7** liberal, profuse, replete
8 abundant, generous **9** abounding,
bounteous, bountiful, exuberant, luxuriant, plenteous, plentiful

Copland work 5 Rodeo **11** Billy the Kid
17 Appalachian Spring

cop-out 5 dodge **6** excuse **7** evasion, pretext, retreat

copper 4 cent, coin **5** metal, penny,
token **9** butterfly, policeman *item:*
4 cent **5** penny **6** kettle *sulfate:* **7** vitriol
9 bluestone **11** blue vitriol

copperhead 5 snake, viper **8** pit viper

coppice 4 bosk, wood **5** copse, grove,
woods **6** bosque, forest, growth **7** thicket **9** brushwood, underwood

copse see COPPICE

Copt 8 Egyptian

copula 4 bond, link **5** joint, union **7** coupler

copy 3 ape **4** echo, fake, mock, sham
5 clone, ditto, forge, mimic, model
6 carbon, parrot, repeat **7** emulate, forgery, imitate, replica, takeoff **8** knockoff, likeness, simulate **9** duplicate, facsimile, imitation, replicate, reproduce
10 impression, simulacrum, simulation,
transcribe, transcript **11** counterfeit,
counterpart, reduplicate, replication
12 reproduction

copyist 5 clerk **6** scribe **8** imitator
9 engrosser **10** plagiarist **12** transcriber

copyread 4 edit

coquet 3 toy **4** fool, vamp **5** dally, flirt,
tease **6** trifle

coquette 4 vamp **5** flirt, tease

coquettish 3 coy **6** fickle **9** frivolous, kittenish **11** flirtatious

coral 3 red **4** pink, rosy **5** polyp **9** limestone

coral reef 3 cay, key **5** atoll *off Australia:*
5 Wreck *world's largest:* **12** Great Barrier

cord 3 tie **4** band, lace, pile, rope, whip,
yarn **5** cable, nerve, stack **6** strand,
string, tendon *twisted:* **7** torsade

cordage 4 rope 5 ropes 7 rigging *fiber:* 4 bast, hemp, jute, pita 5 sisal

Corday's victim 5 Marat (Jean-Paul)

Cordelia *father:* 4 Lear *sister:* 5 Regan 7 Goneril

cordial 4 warm 6 genial, hearty, jovial, tender 7 affable, liqueur, sincere 8 cheerful, friendly, gracious, sociable 9 congenial, convivial, heartfelt 10 hospitable 11 sympathetic, warmhearted 12 wholehearted

cordiality 6 warmth 7 amenity 9 geniality 10 amiability 12 agreeability, friendliness

cordon 4 lace, line, ring 5 braid 6 circle, ribbon 7 barrier 8 espalier *bleu:* 4 chef, cook 6 ribbon 10 blue ribbon, decoration, master chef

core 3 hub, nub 4 base, crux, gist, meat, pith, root 5 basis, focus, heart, midst 6 center, depths, kernel, middle, upshot 7 essence, nucleus 8 interior, midpoint 9 substance 10 foundation

corium 5 cutis 6 dermis

cork 4 bark, plug, seal, stop 5 float 6 bobber 7 stopper, stopple

corker 4 lulu 5 beaut, dandy, dilly, doozy 6 doozie, killer 8 jim-dandy, knockout 9 humdinger 11 crackerjack 12 lollapalooza

corkscrew 4 coil, wind 5 helix, twist 6 spiral

cormorant 4 bird, shag 7 glutton

corn 5 grain, maize 6 hominy 9 granulate *bread:* 4 pone 7 bannock *Indian:* 5 maize 6 mealie *kind:* 3 pop 5 flint, flour, sweet 6 Indian *pest:* 5 borer *piece:* 3 cob, ear 5 spike 6 kernel, nubbin

Corncracker State 8 Kentucky

corner 3 box, fix, jam, nab 4 hole, nook, trap, tree 5 angle, catch, coign, niche, seize 6 collar, cranny, dogleg, pickle, plight, recess, scrape 7 capture, dilemma, impasse, trouble 8 bottle up, monopoly 10 bring to bay 11 predicament 12 intersection *of eye:* 7 canthus

cornerstone 4 base 5 basis 7 support 8 rudiment 10 foundation, groundwork

cornet 4 cone, horn 7 officer, trumpet 10 instrument

Cornhusker State 8 Nebraska

cornice 3 cap 4 band, eave 5 crown 7 molding

cornmeal 4 masa, samp 5 grits 6 hominy 7 hoecake *mush:* 7 polenta

cornucopia 4 cone, horn 6 bounty, plenty, wealth 9 abundance, profusion 12 horn of plenty

Cornwallis, Charles *adversary:* 6 Greene (Nathanael) *surrender site:* 8 Yorktown

corny 5 banal, sappy, stale, trite 6 old hat 7 clichéd, mawkish 8 shopworn 9 hackneyed, schmaltzy 11 sentimental, stereotyped

corollary 6 effect, result, sequel, upshot 8 parallel, sequence 9 resulting 10 associated, end product, equivalent 11 aftereffect, consequence

corona 4 aura, glow, halo 5 cigar, crown, glory 6 circle, nimbus 7 aureola, aureole

coroner 8 examiner

coronet 5 crown, tiara 6 anadem, circle, diadem, wreath 7 chaplet, circlet, garland 8 headband

Coronis *form:* 4 crow *son:* 9 Asclepius 11 Aesculapius

corporal 3 NCO 6 bodily, carnal 7 fleshly, somatic 8 physical

corporate 7 unified 8 combined 9 aggregate

corporeal 6 bodily, carnal, mortal 7 fleshly, somatic 8 material, physical, tangible 9 objective 10 phenomenal 11 substantial

corps 4 band, body 5 group, party, troop 6 outfit, troupe 7 company

corpse 4 body 5 bones, stiff 7 cadaver, carcass, carrion, remains *combining form:* 4 necr 5 necro

corpselike 4 dead 5 gaunt 7 deathly, ghastly, macabre 8 lifeless, skeletal 10 cadaverous

corpulence 7 fatness, obesity 9 adiposity, rotundity 10 fleshiness

corpulent 3 fat 5 bulky, gross, heavy, obese, plump, stout 6 fleshy, portly, rotund 7 porcine, weighty 9 overblown 10 overweight

corpus 4 body, bulk, core, mass 6 oeuvre 9 principal, substance 10 collection 11 compilation

corpuscle 4 cell 8 hemocyte, monocyte 9 blood cell, leukocyte 10 lymphocyte 11 erythrocyte, granulocyte

corral 3 mew, pen 5 fence 6 gather, shut in 7 close in, collect, confine, enclose, round up 8 surround 9 enclosure

correct 3 fit, fix 4 edit, just, mend, true 5 amend, emend, exact, right 6 adjust, decent, proper, punish, reform, remedy, repair, revise, seemly 7 chasten, fitting, improve, perfect, precise, rectify, redress 8 accurate, becoming, chastise, decorous, flawless, set right 9 castigate, faultless 10 conforming, discipline, impeccable, legitimate, meticulous, scrupulous 11 appropriate, comme il faut, punctilious 12 conventional *combining form:* 4 orth 5 ortho

correction 3 rod 6 rebuke 7 reproof

8 revision **9** amendment **10** adjustment, discipline, emendation, punishment **11** castigation

corrective 4 cure **6** remedy **8** antidote, punitive, remedial **10** beneficial **11** counterstep, restorative **12** counteragent **13** counteractive

correctness 7 decorum **8** accuracy, fidelity **9** precision, propriety **10** exactitude

correlate 5 match **6** analog **7** pendant **8** analogue, coincide, dovetail, parallel **9** harmonize **10** complement, correspond **11** counterpart

correlative 3 and, nor **4** both, then **6** either **7** neither, related **10** complement, reciprocal **11** counterpart **13** complementary, corresponding

correspond 4 jibe **5** agree, equal, match, write **6** accord, concur **7** comport, conform **8** dovetail **9** harmonize **11** communicate

correspondence 4 mail **7** analogy, letters **8** symmetry **9** agreement, congruity **10** conformity, similarity **11** consistency, correlation *mathematical:* **7** mapping **8** function

correspondent 5 match **6** analog, pen pal, writer **7** fitting **8** analogue, parallel, reporter, suitable **9** correlate **10** conforming, journalist **11** commentator, contributor, counterpart

corresponding 4 akin, like **5** alike **6** agnate **7** related, similar **8** matching, parallel **9** analogous, consonant **10** comparable **11** correlative

correspondingly 4 also **7** equally **8** likewise **9** similarly **11** analogously

corrida 9 bullfight *shout:* **3** olé

corridor 4 hall, lane, path **5** aisle, route, strip **6** artery, avenue **7** hallway, passage **10** passageway

corroborate 5 prove **6** uphold, verify **7** approve, bear out, certify, confirm, endorse, justify, support **8** document, validate **9** vindicate **12** authenticate, substantiate

corroborative 9 ancillary, auxiliary **10** collateral, supporting, supportive **12** confirmatory

corrode 4 rust **7** eat away, eat into, oxidize **8** wear away **9** undermine

corrosive 5 acerb **6** biting **7** acerbic, caustic, cutting **9** sarcastic

corrosiveness 7 sarcasm **8** acerbity

corrugation 4 fold, ruck **5** plica, ridge **6** crease, furrow, groove **7** crinkle, wrinkle

corrupt 3 rot **5** bribe, decay, spoil, stain, taint, venal **6** befoul, debase, defile, molder, rotten, smirch **7** crooked,

debauch, degrade, deprave, pervert, putrefy, tarnish, vitiate **8** bribable, degraded, depraved, infected, perverse **9** decompose, dishonest, miscreant, reprobate, unethical **10** bastardize, degenerate **12** unprincipled, unscrupulous **13** untrustworthy

corruptible 5 venal **7** buyable **8** bribable

corruption 4 vice **5** decay, fraud, graft **7** bribery, jobbery **9** barbarism, depravity, turpitude **10** immorality, wickedness **11** impropriety

corsair 5 rover **6** pirate **8** picaroon, sea rover **9** buccaneer, pickaroon, privateer **10** freebooter

corset 5 stays **6** bodice, girdle **7** support

cortege 5 train **6** parade **7** retinue **9** entourage **10** attendants, procession

cortex 4 bark, husk, peel, rind **6** casing **8** peridium

Cortland 5 apple

corundum 4 ruby **5** emery, topaz **7** emerald **8** abrasive, amethyst, sapphire

coruscate 5 flash, gleam, glint, shine **7** glisten, glitter, sparkle, twinkle **11** scintillate

corvid 3 jay **4** crow **5** raven **6** magpie **9** passerine

Corvino's wife 5 Celia

corybantic 3 mad **4** wild **5** rabid **6** crazed **7** frantic, furious **8** ecstatic, frenetic, frenzied **9** delirious

coryphée 6 dancer **8** danseuse **9** ballerina

Cosí Fan Tutte composer 6 Mozart (Wolfgang Amadeus)

cosmetic 4 kohl **5** blush, rouge **6** ceruse, makeup, powder **7** blusher, bronzer, mascara **8** lip gloss, lipstick **9** eye shadow **10** decorative, nail polish, ornamental **11** beautifying, superficial

cosmetologist 10 beautician

cosmic 4 huge, vast **7** immense **8** infinite **9** planetary, spiritual, unbounded, universal **12** astronomical, metaphysical

cosmopolitan 6 global, urbane **7** worldly **8** catholic, cultured, polished **9** civilized, universal, worldwide **10** cultivated, ecumenical **11** worldly-wise **13** sophisticated

cosmos 6 flower **8** creation, universe

Cossack *army:* **3** Don **4** Ural **5** Kuban *land:* **7** Ukraine *leader:* **5** Razin (Stenka) **6** ataman, hetman, Mazepa (Ivan) **7** Bulavin (Kondraty) **8** Pugachov (Yemelyan) *novel:* **10** Taras Bulba

cosset 3 pet **4** baby, lamb, love **5** humor, spoil **6** caress, cocker, coddle, cuddle, dandle, dote on, fondle, pamper **7** cater to, indulge **11** mollycoddle

cost 3 tab **4** rate, toll **5** price **6** charge,

damage, outlay, tariff **7** expense, payment **8** price tag **9** sacrifice **11** expenditure **12** disbursement *business:* **8** overhead

Costa Rica *bay:* **8** Coronado *capital:* **7** San José *city:* **8** Alajuela **10** Puntarenas **11** Puerto Limón *discoverer:* **8** Columbus (Christopher) *language:* **7** Spanish *leader:* **5** Arias (Oscar) *monetary unit:* **5** colón *neighbor:* **6** Panama **9** Nicaragua *peninsula:* **3** Osa **6** Nicoya *river:* **7** San Juan *volcano:* **5** Barba, Irazú **9** Turrialba

costermonger 6 hawker **7** peddler **9** barrow boy

costive 4 mean, slow **5** bound, close, tight **6** frugal, stingy **7** miserly **9** penurious **10** hardfisted, pinchpenny **11** closefisted **12** cheeseparing, parsimonious

costless 4 free **6** gratis **10** gratuitous **13** complimentary

costly 4 dear, rich **5** fancy **6** lavish, pricey **7** opulent, premium **8** precious, splendid, valuable **9** expensive, luxurious, priceless **10** exorbitant, highpriced, invaluable **11** extravagant

costume 3 rig **4** duds, garb, mode **5** dress, getup, guise, habit, style **6** attire, outfit **7** apparel, clothes, fashion, threads, turnout, uniform **8** disguise, ensemble, garments **9** trappings

cot 3 bed, hut **4** camp **5** cabin, lodge, shack **6** shanty *wheeled:* **6** gurney

coterie 4 band, camp, clan, club, ring **5** cabal **6** circle, clique **7** in-group **9** camarilla

cotillion 4 ball, prom **5** dance

cottage 3 hut **4** camp **5** cabin, lodge, shack **6** shanty **8** bungalow *Russian:* **5** dacha *Swiss:* **6** chalet

cotton *cleaner:* **3** gin **6** linter *cloth:* **4** duck, jean, mull **5** baize, chino, denim, drill, khaki, scrim, terry, wigan **6** calico, canvas, chintz, dimity, muslin, oxford, sateen, velour **7** batiste, etamine, fustian, gingham, jaconet, nankeen, organdy, percale **8** corduroy, dungaree, moleskin, nainsook, tarlatan **9** grenadine, percaline, stockinet, swansdown **10** balbriggan **11** stockinette *cloth, Indian:* **5** surah **6** madras **7** dhurrie, khaddar *comb:* **4** card *fuzz remover:* **6** linter *measure:* **4** hank, pick, yard **5** count, skein *pad:* **7** pledget *pod:* **4** boll *refuse:* **5** flock *seed separator:* **3** gin *sheet:* **4** batt *thread:* **5** lisle

Cotton State 7 Alabama

cottonwood 5 alamo **6** poplar

cottony 4 soft **6** fluffy

___ Coty 4 René

couch 3 den, put **4** lair, sofa, word **5** divan, lodge **6** burrow, chaise, daybed, lounge, phrase **7** express, lie down, recline **9** davenport, formulate **12** chesterfield

couch potato 7 slacker

cougar 3 cat **4** puma **7** panther **9** catamount **12** mountain lion

cough 4 hack, hawk

cough drop 6 troche **7** lozenge

cough up 3 pay **5** spend **6** lay out, pay out **7** deliver, dole out, fork out **8** fork over, hand over, shell out

couloir 5 chasm, gorge, gulch, gully **6** ravine

council 4 diet **5** board, junta **6** powwow, senate **7** cabinet, meeting **8** assembly, conclave, congress, ministry **10** conference, federation **12** consultation *ancient Greek:* **5** boule *church:* **5** synod **10** consistory *medieval English:* **4** moot **5** gemot **6** gemote **8** hustings *Muslim:* **5** divan *Russian:* **4** duma **6** soviet *secret:* **5** cabal, junto **9** camarilla *Spanish:* **7** cabildo

counsel 4 urge, warn **6** advice, advise, charge, direct, enjoin, lawyer **7** consult, suggest **8** advocate, attorney **9** prescribe, recommend **10** advisement **12** deliberation *British:* **9** barrister, solicitor

count 3 add, sum, tot **4** bank, earl, mean, rely, tote **5** issue, score, tally, total, tot up, weigh **6** census, charge, depend, expect, figure, matter, number, reckon, result, tote up **7** compute, signify **8** estimate, militate, numerate, quantify **9** calculate, enumerate **10** allegation

countenance 3 mug **4** back, cast, face, look, mien, phiz **5** favor, go for **6** accept, visage **7** approve, commend, condone, endorse, support **8** advocate, features, hold with, sanction, tolerate **9** approbate, composure, encourage **10** expression **11** physiognomy

counter 3 pit, vie **4** anti **5** asset, check, match, polar, shelf **6** offset, oppose **7** adverse, against, hostile, obverse, opposed, reverse **8** antipode, contrary, converse, opposing, opposite **9** antipodal, diametric **10** antipodean, antithesis, contravene **12** antagonistic, antipathetic, antithetical **13** contradictory

counteract 3 fix **4** foil **5** annul **6** cancel, negate, oppose, resist, thwart **7** balance, correct, nullify, prevent, rectify, redress **8** negative **9** cancel out, frustrate **10** balance out, neutralize

counteragent 4 cure **6** remedy **8** antidote **9** antitoxin, antivenin **10** corrective

counterbalance 6 cancel, make up, offset, redeem, set off **7** ballast, correct, even out, rectify, redress **8** equalize, outweigh **10** compensate

counterblow 7 revenge **8** reprisal, requital, revanche **9** vengeance **11** retaliation, retribution

counterclockwise 4 levo **12** levorotatory

counterfeit 4 copy, fake, hoax, sham **5** bluff, bogus, dummy, false, feign, forge, fraud, mimic, phony **6** affect, assume, deceit, ersatz, forged, pseudo **7** feigned, imitate, pretend **8** delusive, delusory, knock off, simulate, spurious **9** brummagem, deception, deceptive, fabricate, imitation, imposture, insincere, pinchbeck, pretended, simulated **10** fraudulent, misleading, simulacrum *prefix:* **5** pseud **6** pseudo

counterpane 4 pouf, puff **5** duvet **6** spread **8** bedcover, coverlet **9** bedspread, comforter, eiderdown

counterpart 4 like, twin **5** equal, match **6** analog, double **7** vis-à-vis **8** analogue, parallel **9** correlate, duplicate **10** complement, coordinate, equivalent **11** correlative **13** correspondent

counterpoise 6 make up, offset, redeem, set off **7** balance, ballast **8** outweigh **9** stabilize **10** compensate

countersign 8 password **9** watchword

countervail 4 foil **6** cancel, offset, oppose, redeem, set off, thwart **7** balance, correct, nullify, rectify **8** outweigh **9** frustrate **10** compensate, neutralize

countless 6 legion, myriad, untold **7** umpteen **11** innumerable

Count of Monte Cristo 6 Dantès (Edmond) *author:* **5** Dumas (Alexandre)

count out 5 expel **6** except **7** exclude **9** disregard, eliminate

countrified 5 rural **6** rustic **7** bucolic **8** homespun, pastoral **10** campestral

country 4 home, land, soil **5** rural **6** nation, region, rustic, sticks **7** boonies, bucolic, outland **8** homeland, pastoral **9** backwoods, boondocks **10** campestral, fatherland, motherland, provincial *dance:* **3** jig **4** reel **10** strathspey *home:* **5** manor, ranch, villa **8** hacienda *music:* **9** bluegrass *road:* **4** lane, path **5** byway

coup 4 blow, feat **5** upset **6** putsch, stroke **8** takeover

couple 3 duo **4** bond, dyad, fuse, join, link, mate, pair, span, team, yoke **5** brace, hitch, marry, merge, unite **6** hook up, link up **7** bracket, combine, conjoin, connect, doublet, harness, twosome

coupler 4 link, ring **5** hitch, joint

6 hookup **7** shackle **8** ligature *railroad:* **7** drawbar

couplet 3 duo **4** dyad, pair **5** twins **7** distich, doublet, twosome

coupling 4 link, seam **5** joint, union **7** joining, pairing **8** junction, juncture **9** connector **10** connection

courage 4 dash, grit, guts **5** heart, moxie, nerve, pluck, spunk, valor **6** daring, mettle, spirit **7** bravery, heroism **8** audacity, backbone, boldness, firmness, temerity, tenacity, valiance, valiancy **9** assurance, fortitude, gallantry **10** resolution **11** doughtiness, intrepidity **12** fearlessness **13** dauntlessness

courageous 4 bold **5** brave, gutsy, nervy, stout **6** daring, heroic, manful, plucky, spunky, strong **7** doughty, gallant, valiant **8** fearless, intrepid, resolute, stalwart, unafraid, valorous **9** audacious, dauntless, tenacious, undaunted **11** venturesome **12** stouthearted

courier 5 envoy **6** legate, runner **8** emissary **9** go-between, messenger **11** internuncio

course 3 row, run, way **4** dart, dash, duct, flow, line, path, plan, race, road, rush, tack, tear **5** canal, chain, chase, class, hurry, orbit, order, range, route, scoot, scope, speed, surge, track, trend **6** career, design, hasten, hustle, manner, policy, polity, scheme, sequel, series, string, system **7** advance, channel, circuit, conduit, passage, pattern, program, regimen, routine, seminar **8** aqueduct, duration, progress, sequence, syllabus **9** procedure, racetrack **10** curriculum, succession **11** progression *dinner:* **4** soup **5** salad **6** entrée **7** dessert **9** appetizer, blue plate

courser 4 bird **5** horse **7** charger **8** huntsman, warhorse

court 3 bar, woo **4** date, quad, yard **5** charm, motel, spark, suite, tempt **6** allure, homage, invite, palace, pursue **7** address, flatter, justice, retinue, romance, solicit **8** assembly, cloister, tribunal **9** captivate, curtilage, enclosure, entourage **10** magistrate, parliament, quadrangle **11** legislature *action:* **4** suit **5** trial **6** appeal, assize **7** hearing, inquest, lawsuit **10** proceeding *calendar:* **6** docket *call to:* **7** summons **9** subpoena **11** arraignment *circuit:* **4** eyre *crier's call:* **4** oyez *decision:* **6** assize **7** finding, verdict **8** judgment *ecclesiastical:* **4** rota **5** Curia **10** consistory *Indian:* **6** durbar *kind:* **4** moot **5** civil **6** county, family **7** circuit, customs, federal, supreme **8** chancery, criminal, district, juvenile, kangaroo, superior 9 appellate, municipal 11 territorial *medieval English:* 4 eyre, moot 5 gemot 6 gemote 8 hustings *of equity:* 8 chancery *officer:* 5 clerk, crier, judge 7 bailiff, justice, marshal, sheriff 10 prosecutor *order:* 4 writ 5 edict 6 decree 7 summons 8 mandamus, subpoena *panel:* 4 jury *relating to:* 8 judicial 9 juridical *session:* 6 assize 7 sitting 8 sederunt

courteous 5 civil 6 polite 7 courtly, gallant, genteel 8 mannerly, well-bred 9 attentive 10 chivalrous, thoughtful 11 considerate 12 well-mannered

courtesy 7 amenity, decorum, manners, service 8 chivalry, civility 9 attention, etiquette, gallantry 10 cordiality, indulgence 11 courtliness 12 graciousness 13 attentiveness, consideration

court game see under GAME

courtly 5 noble 6 august, formal, urbane 7 elegant, gallant, refined, stately 8 gracious 9 dignified 10 chivalrous, flattering 11 ceremonious

courtship 4 suit 6 dating, wooing 7 romance 10 flirtation *former custom of:* 8 bundling

courtyard 4 quad 5 garth, patio 9 curtilage 10 quadrangle

cousin 3 kin 7 kinsman 8 relative

Cousteau, Jacques *ship:* 7 Calypso *vehicle:* 11 bathysphere

couturier 8 clothier, costumer, designer 10 dressmaker

cove 3 arm, bay 4 nook 5 bight, firth, inlet, niche 6 harbor, recess 9 concavity

covenant 3 vow 4 bond, pact 5 agree, swear 6 pledge, treaty 7 compact, promise 8 contract 9 agreement 10 convention

Covent Garden offering 5 opera

cover 3 cap, lid 4 bury, hide, hood, mask, wrap 5 alibi, cloak, front, guise, stash, track 6 enfold, enwrap, facade, hiding, insure, refuge, screen, secure, shield, shroud, travel 7 blanket, conceal, embrace, enclose, envelop, obscure, overlay, protect, secrete, shelter, write up 8 disguise, ensconce, enshroud, traverse 9 encompass, safeguard, sanctuary, superpose 10 overspread 11 concealment, superimpose *rooflike:* 6 awning, canopy *the eyes:* 9 blindfold *the face:* 4 mask, veil *the mouth:* 6 muzzle *with asphalt:* 4 pave *with cloth:* 5 drape *with dirt:* 7 begrime, blacken 8 besmirch *with straw:* 6 thatch

coverall 8 jumpsuit 10 boilersuit

covered wagon 9 Conestoga

covering *anatomical:* 5 theca, velum 6 tegmen 7 velamen 8 tegument 10 integument *close-fitting:* 6 sheath

9 sheathing *cloth:* 5 sheet *flap:* 9 operculum *for a book:* 4 case 6 jacket *for a cigar:* 7 wrapper *for a coffin:* 4 pall *for a corpse:* 6 shroud 8 cerement *for a package:* 7 wrapper *for concealment:* 10 camouflage *for food:* 4 cosy, cozy *for soil:* 5 mulch *metal:* 4 mail 5 armor *of a diatom:* 6 lorica *of a plant ovary:* 8 pericarp *of a seed:* 4 aril, case 5 testa *of fruits:* 4 peel, rind *of gloom:* 4 pall *of grain:* 4 hull, husk 5 chaff *shell-like:* 8 carapace *thin:* 4 film 6 patina, veneer *waterproof:* 4 tarp 9 tarpaulin

coverlet 4 pouf, puff 5 duvet 6 spread 8 bedcover 9 bedspread, comforter 11 counterpane

covert 4 lair 5 haven, privy 6 hidden, masked, refuge, secret, veiled 7 feather, furtive, retreat, shelter, sub-rosa, thicket 8 hush-hush, shrouded, stealthy 9 concealed, disguised, sanctuary, sheltered 10 undercover 11 camouflaged, clandestine, hiding place, underhanded 12 hugger-mugger 13 surreptitious, under-the-table

covertly 7 sub-rosa 9 by stealth 12 hugger-mugger

covet 4 want 5 crave 6 desire

covetous 4 avid, keen 5 itchy 6 grabby, greedy 7 envious 8 desirous, esurient, grasping, ravenous 9 rapacious, voracious 10 avaricious, gluttonous 11 acquisitive

covey 4 band, bevy, crew, nest 5 brood, bunch, flock, group, party, troop 6 gaggle, troupe 7 cluster, company

cow (see also CATTLE) 4 faze, kine (plural), neat 5 abash, bossy, bully, daunt 6 appall, bovine, dismay, hector, rattle 7 bluster, dragoon 8 bludgeon, browbeat, bulldoze, bullyrag 9 discomfit, embarrass, strong-arm 10 disconcert, intimidate *cud:* 5 rumen *French:* 5 vache *hornless:* 5 muley 7 pollard *mammary gland:* 5 udder *pen:* 6 corral *shed:* 4 barn, byre *Spanish:* 4 vaca *young:* 4 calf 5 stirk 6 heifer

coward 6 craven 7 caitiff, chicken, dastard, milksop, nebbish 8 poltroon, recreant 9 jellyfish 10 scaredy-cat 11 yellowbelly

___ **Coward** 4 Noël

cowardly 5 timid, wimpy 6 afraid, craven, yellow 7 caitiff, chicken, fearful, gutless 8 poltroon, recreant, timorous 9 dastardly 11 lily-livered, milk-livered, poltroonish 12 apprehensive, fainthearted, poor-spirited, white-livered 13 pusillanimous

cowboy 5 rogue, waddy 6 drover, herder, waddie 7 puncher, rancher 8 buckaroo, herdsman, maverick, wrangler **9** cattleman, ranch hand **10** cowpuncher **12** broncobuster *contest:* **5** rodeo *gear:* **5** cuffs, quirt, spurs **6** duster **7** bedroll, slicker, Stetson *legendary:* **9** Pecos Bill *leggings:* **5** chaps *movie:* **3** Mix (Tom) **4** Hart (William S.) **5** Autry (Gene), Wayne (John) **6** Gibson (Hoot), McCrea (Joel), Murphy (Audie), Ritter (Tex), Rogers (Roy, Will) **8** Cisco Kid, Eastwood (Clint) *rope:* **5** lasso, reata, riata **6** lariat *Spanish-American:* **6** charro, gaucho **7** vaquero

cower 5 quail, wince **6** blench, cringe, flinch, recoil, shrink

cowfish 6 dugong, sea cow **7** grampus, manatee **8** sirenian

cowl 4 cape, hood **5** cloak **6** mantle **7** capuche

cowpox 8 vaccinia

cowpuncher see COWBOY

coxcomb 3 fop **4** beau, buck, dude, fool **5** blood, dandy, swell **7** peacock **8** macaroni **9** exquisite **11** Beau Brummel **12** clotheshorse, fashion plate, lounge lizard

coy 3 shy **4** arch, cute, pert **5** saucy, timid **6** demure, modest **7** bashful, evasive, playful **8** blushing, decorous, skittish **9** diffident, kittenish **10** capricious, coquettish **11** flirtatious, mischievous **12** noncommittal

Coyote State 11 South Dakota

coypu 6 rodent *fur:* **6** nutria

cozen 3 gyp **4** bilk, scam **5** cheat, trick **6** diddle, fleece, take in **7** beguile, deceive, defraud, swindle, wheedle **8** flimflam **9** bamboozle **11** double-cross

cozy 4 safe, snug, soft **5** comfy, cushy, pally, tight **6** chummy, secure **8** familiar, intimate **11** comfortable

crab 3 nag **4** beef, fuss, yawp **5** gripe, sidle **6** grinch, griper, grouch, kvetch, squawk, yammer **7** decapod, grouser, growler **8** arthopod, complain, grumbler, sourpuss **9** bellyache, shellfish **10** bellyacher, complainer, crosspatch, crustacean, curmudgeon **11** faultfinder *claw:* **5** chela **6** nipper *constellation:* **6** Cancer *genus:* **3** Uca **6** Birgus **7** Limulus, Pagurus *kind:* **3** pea **4** blue, king, pine, rock **5** ghost, purse **6** hermit, spider **7** fiddler **9** Dungeness, horseshoe *king, horseshoe:* **7** limulus

crabbed 4 dour, glum, grim, sour **5** gruff, surly **6** crusty, gloomy, morose, sullen **9** illegible, irascible, saturnine, splenetic

crablike 8 cancroid

crabwise 8 sidelong, sideward, sideways **9** laterally

crack 3 gag, gap, rap, try **4** bang, bash, belt, blow, boom, clap, flaw, jest, joke, open, peal, quip, rift, roll, shot, slam, slap, snap, stab, wham, whop **5** adept, break, burst, chink, cleft, crash, craze, knock, smack, smash, solve, split, whack, whirl, wreck **6** breach, cranny, decode, expert, master, moment, thwack **7** break up, crevice, decrypt, destroy, fissure, instant, shatter, skilled **8** crevasse, decipher, disorder, interval, masterly, skillful, superior **9** break into, excellent, interrupt, masterful, witticism **10** percussion, proficient

crackbrain 3 nut **4** kook **5** crank, wacko **6** cuckoo **7** dingbat, lunatic **9** ding-a-ling, fruitcake, screwball

crackdown 5 purge **8** quashing **10** repression **11** suppression

cracked 3 mad **4** daft, nuts **5** balmy, batty, crazy, daffy, loony, nutty **6** broken, crazed, cuckoo, insane, screwy **7** bonkers, lunatic, smashed **8** demented, deranged

cracker 5 wafer **6** hacker, rustic **7** biscuit, saltine, snapper **8** Georgian **9** Floridian

crackerjack 3 ace **4** lulu **5** dandy, nifty, sharp **6** corker, killer **8** jim-dandy, knockout **9** humdinger **12** lollapalooza

crackle 4 snap **7** glitter, sparkle, twinkle **9** crepitate **10** effervesce **13** effervescence

crackpot 3 nut **4** case, kook, loon **5** crank, loony, wacko **6** cuckoo, madman **7** dingbat, lunatic, oddball **9** ding-a-ling, eccentric, fruitcake, harebrain, screwball

crack-up, crack up 5 crash, smash, wreck **6** fiasco **7** debacle **8** accident, collapse, disaster **9** breakdown **11** catastrophe

cradlesong 7 lullaby **8** berceuse

craft 3 art, job **5** guile, knack, skill, trade, wiles **6** career, deceit, métier **7** ability, calling, cunning, know-how, slyness **8** artifice, caginess, foxiness, vocation, wiliness **9** adeptness, canniness, dexterity, duplicity, expertise, ingenuity, technique **10** adroitness, artfulness, competence, occupation, profession, shrewdness **11** proficiency

craftiness 5 guile **7** cunning **8** artifice, subtlety

craftsman 5 smith **6** carter, carver, potter, weaver, wright **7** artisan, builder, cobbler, jeweler **9** carpenter **10** blacksmith

crafty 3 sly **4** foxy, keen, wily **5** acute, cagey, canny, sharp, slick **6** adroit, artful, astute, clever, shrewd, tricky **7** cunning, devious, fawning, vulpine **8** guileful, scheming, skillful, slippery **9** deceitful, designing, ingenious, insidious **11** calculating, duplicitous *Scottish:* **7** sleekit

crag 3 tor **4** hill **5** cliff

craggy 5 harsh, rocky, rough **6** jagged, rugged, uneven

cram 3 jam, ram **4** bolt, fill, gulp, heap, load, pack, wolf **5** crowd, crush, drive, force, press, shove, study, stuff, wedge **6** gobble, review, squash, thrust **7** jam-pack, overeat, squeeze

crammed 4 full **5** awash, flush **7** brimful **8** brimming **9** chock-full

cramp 4 kink, pain, pang **5** crick, limit, spasm **6** hamper, stitch **7** confine, inhibit, shackle **8** confined, restrain, restrict **9** restraint, stricture **10** constraint, limitation **11** confinement, restriction

cramped 5 close, tight **6** narrow **9** confining, two-by-four

crane 4 bird, boom, rail **5** heron **7** derrick, stretch **arm: 3** jib **genus: 4** Grus **ship's: 5** davit

Crane hero 12 Henry Fleming

cranium 5 skull **9** braincase

crank 3 nut **4** crab, kook **5** fancy **6** griper, grouch, notion, rotate, turn up, vagary **7** caprice, conceit, fanatic, grouser, oddball **8** crackpot, crotchet, grumbler, sourpuss **9** eccentric, screwball **10** bellyacher, crosspatch

cranky 5 cross, testy **6** crabby, crusty, cussed, grumpy, ornery, tetchy, touchy **7** bearish, crabbed, peevish, prickly **8** contrary, petulant, tortuous, vinegary **9** crotchety, irascible, irritable, obstinate **10** bad-humored, ill-humored **12** cantankerous, disagreeable **13** unpredictable

cranny 3 gap **4** nook, slit **5** chink, crack, niche **6** corner **7** crevice

crash 3 din, jar, ram **4** bang, boom, bump, bust, clap, fail, fold, jolt, peal, slam, wham **5** blast, break, burst, crack, shock, smash, wreck **6** impact, pileup **7** collide, crack-up, debacle, decline, failure, smashup **8** accident, collapse **9** breakdown, collision **10** concussion

crass 4 rude **5** crude, gross **6** coarse, vulgar **7** boorish, loutish, uncouth **8** churlish **9** unrefined **13** materialistic

crate 3 box **4** heap **5** wreck **6** jalopy, junker **7** clunker

crater 3 pit **4** dent, hole, pock **5** crash **6** cavity, dimple, hollow, trough **7** caldera **8** collapse **10** depression **Hawaiian: 7** Kilauea

cravat 3 tie **4** band **5** ascot, scarf **7** necktie

crave 3 ask, beg **4** need, want, wish **5** covet **6** demand, desire **7** call for, entreat, implore, long for, require **8** yearn for

craven 4 funk **6** abject, coward **7** caitiff,

chicken, dastard, fearful, gutless, ignoble **8** cowardly, cringing, poltroon, recreant **9** dastardly **11** lily-livered, poltroonish, yellowbelly **13** pusillanimous, yellowbellied

craving 4 itch, lust, urge **6** desire, hunger, thirst **7** longing, passion **8** appetite, yearning **9** hankering

crawl 4 flow, inch, teem **5** creep, swarm **6** abound, grovel **7** slither, wriggle **9** pullulate

crawling 6 repent

craze 3 fad **4** chic, rage **5** crack, fever, furor, mania, trend, vogue **6** dement, enrage, frenzy, furore, madden **7** derange, fashion, unhinge **9** unbalance **10** dernier cri, enthusiasm

craziness 5 folly, mania **6** lunacy **8** hysteria, insanity **9** absurdity

crazy 3 fey, mad **4** daft, gaga, loco, nuts, wild **5** balmy, barmy, batty, daffy, dotty, goofy, kooky, loony, loopy, nutty, rabid, silly, wacko, wacky **6** absurd, cuckoo, fruity, insane, mental, psycho, screwy, teched, whacky **7** berserk, bonkers, cracked, foolish, frantic, lunatic, smitten, tetched, touched, unsound **8** cockeyed, crackpot, demented, deranged, frenetic, frenzied, maniacal, unhinged **9** bedlamite, delirious, eccentric, fanatical, foolhardy, ludicrous, possessed, screwball, senseless **10** crackbrain, moonstruck, ridiculous, unbalanced **11** harebrained, nonsensical **12** preposterous **British: 5** potty **6** scatty **Scottish: 3** wud

creak 4 rasp **5** grate, grind **6** scrape, squeak, squeal **7** grating, screech **9** squeaking

creaky 4 aged **5** rusty **7** rickety, rundown, squeaky, unsound, worn-out **8** decrepit **9** tottering **10** broken-down, ramshackle

cream 3 top **4** balm, beat, best, drub, pick, whip, whup **5** blast, elite, prime, salve **6** cerate, choice, defeat, finest, thrash **7** clobber, destroy, trounce, unguent **8** lambaste, liniment, ointment

crease 4 fold, ruck **5** graze, plica, ridge **6** furrow, groove, rumple **7** crinkle, wrinkle

create 3 dub **4** form, make, sire **5** beget, build, cause, forge, found, hatch, set up, spawn, start **6** author, design, devise, father, invent **7** compose, concoct, develop, fashion, produce **8** conceive, engender, generate, occasion **9** construct, establish, fabricate, formulate, institute, originate **10** constitute

creation 5 birth, world **6** cosmos, nature

7 genesis **8** universe **9** inception, macrocosm **10** conception **11** macrocosmos

creative 7 fertile **8** artistic, inspired, original **9** deceptive, demiurgic, ingenious, inventive **10** innovative, innovatory **11** imaginative **12** innovational

creator 3 god **6** author **8** inventor **9** architect, generator, patriarch **10** originator, progenitor

creature 3 man **5** beast, being, brute, human **6** animal, mortal, person **7** critter, varmint *fabled:* **3** elf, imp, orc, roc **4** ogre, puck, yeti **5** dwarf, fairy, ghost, giant, gnome, harpy, nymph, pixie, troll **6** dragon, goblin, gorgon, kraken, merman, sphinx, sprite **7** bigfoot, brownie, bugbear, centaur, chimera, gremlin, griffin, mermaid, monster, unicorn, vampire, wendigo **8** minotaur, werewolf **9** hobgoblin, manticore, sasquatch **10** cockatrice, hippogriff, leprechaun (see also MON

credence 5 faith, trust **6** belief, credit **8** reliance **9** sideboard **10** acceptance, confidence

credentials 6 papers **9** documents **10** references **12** certificates, testimonials **13** documentation

credenza 6 buffet **8** bookcase **9** sideboard

credible 5 solid, sound, valid **6** trusty **8** reliable **9** authentic, colorable, plausible **10** believable, convincing, persuasive, reasonable **11** trustworthy **12** satisfactory

credit 4 deem, feel **5** asset, faith, honor, refer, sense, think, trust **6** accept, assign, belief, charge, impute, notice, weight **7** ascribe, believe **8** consider, credence, prestige, reliance **9** attribute, authority, influence **10** confidence, reputation **11** recognition

creditable 6 worthy **8** laudable, reliable **9** colorable, deserving, estimable, plausible, reputable **10** believable **11** commendable, meritorious, respectable **12** praiseworthy

credo 5 canon, creed, dogma, tenet **6** belief, tenets **7** beliefs, precept **8** doctrine, ideology **9** catechism, principle

credulous 5 naive **6** unwary **8** gullible, trustful, trusting **9** believing **12** unsuspecting, unsuspicious **13** unquestioning

creed 4 sect **5** canon, dogma, faith, tenet **6** belief, church, tenets **7** beliefs, precept **8** doctrine, ideology, religion **9** catechism, communion, principle **12** denomination

creek 4 burn, rill **5** brook **6** arroyo, rillet, runlet, runnel, stream **7** freshet, rivulet **8** brooklet **9** streamlet

creep 4 drag, edge, inch, lurk, slip **5** crawl, glide, shirk, skulk, slide, slink, snake, sneak, steal **6** spread, tiptoe **7** gumshoe, slither, wriggle **9** pussyfoot

creeping 6 repent **7** gradual **9** prostrate

creepy 5 eerie, weird **6** spooky **7** anxious, macabre, ominous, strange, uncanny **8** ghoulish, menacing, sinister **9** unnerving **10** disturbing, unpleasant, unsettling **11** hair-raising

crème de la crème 4 best **5** elect, elite **6** finest **8** very best

Cremona family 5 Amati **8** Guarneri

Creon *daughter:* 6 Creusa, Glauce, Glauke *sister:* **7** Jocasta *son:* **6** Haemon *victim:* **8** Antigone

crescendo 4 acme, apex, peak, rise **5** crest, surge, swell **6** apogee, climax, growth, height, zenith **8** increase, pinnacle **9** high point **11** culmination

crescent-shaped 5 bowed **6** lunate, sickle **7** falcate *body or surface:* **8** meniscus

crest 3 cap, top **4** acme, apex, comb, noon, peak, roof, tuft **5** arête, chine, crown, plume, ridge **6** apogee, climax, summit, vertex **7** hogback **8** pinnacle, surmount **9** high point **10** coat of arms, prominence **11** culmination *of a wave:* **8** whitecap

crestfallen 3 low **4** blue, down **6** droopy **8** dejected, downcast, drooping **9** depressed **10** dispirited **11** discouraged, downhearted **12** disappointed, disconsolate, disheartened

Crete *ancient city:* 7 Cnossus, Knossos **8** Phaistos *ancient name:* **6** Candia *capital:* **5** Canea *goddess:* **8** Dictynna **11** Britomartis *guard:* **5** Talos *king:* **5** Minos **9** Idomeneus *maze:* **9** labyrinth *monster:* **8** Minotaur *mountain:* **3** Ida *princess:* **7** Ariadne

cretin 3 oaf **4** boob, clod, dolt, dope, fool, lout **5** dumbo, dummy, dunce, idiot, moron **6** dimwit, nitwit **7** half-wit **8** imbecile, lunkhead, numskull **9** lamebrain, numbskull, simpleton

Creusa *father:* 5 Priam *husband:* **6** Aeneas *mother:* **6** Hecuba *son:* **3** Ion **8** Ascanius

crevice 3 gap **4** seam, slit **5** chink, cleft, crack **6** cranny **7** fissure **8** cleavage **10** interstice

crew 4 band, bevy, gang, team **5** bunch, covey, group, party **6** rowers, rowing **7** company, sailors

crib 3 bed, bin, box, hut, key **4** pony, trot **5** cheat, crate, hovel, shack, stall, steal, theft **6** cradle, crèche, manger, pilfer **7** barrier, brothel **8** bassinet, bedstead, bordello **9** enclosure **10** plagiarism, plagiarize

Crichton novel 11 Terminal Man (The)
12 Jurassic Park 15 Andromeda Strain
(The)

cricket *period of play:* 7 innings *team:*
6 eleven *term:* 3 leg, off, rot 4 bowl
5 pitch 6 bowler, wicket, yorker 7 bats-
man, striker 9 fieldsman *turn at bat:*
4 over

crime 3 sin 4 evil, tort, vice 5 caper
6 breach, delict, felony 7 misdeed,
offense 8 atrocity, iniquity 9 diablerie,
violation 10 corruption, illegality,
infraction, wrongdoing 11 misdemeanor 13 transgression *instructor:*
5 Fagin

Crimea *city:* 5 Kerch, Yalta
10 Sebastopol, Sevastopol, Simferopol
river: 4 Alma *sea:* 4 Azov *strait:* 5 Kerch

criminal 4 hood, thug 5 crook, felon,
shady 6 outlaw 7 convict, corrupt,
crooked, hoodlum, illegal, illicit, lawless, mobster 8 culpable, fugitive, gangster, jailbird, offender, scofflaw, unlawful, wrongful 9 desperado, felonious,
miscreant, nefarious, racketeer, wrongdoer 10 delinquent, lawbreaker, malefactor, trespasser 12 illegitimate, transgressor *habitual:* 8 repeater 10 recidivist

criminate see INCRIMINATE

crimp 4 bend, curb, wave 5 frizz
6 crease, hamper, hold in 7 crinkle,
inhibit, wrinkle 8 hold back, obstacle,
restrain 9 constrain, restraint 10 impediment 11 obstruction

crimson 3 red 4 rose 5 blush, color, flush
6 redden

cringe 4 duck 5 cower, hunch, quail,
wince 6 blench, flinch, recoil, shrink

crinkle 4 ruck 5 crimp, plica, ridge
6 crease, furrow, pucker, ruck up, rumple, rustle 7 crackle, crumple, scrunch,
wrinkle 11 corrugation

crinkly 5 crepy 6 crepey, frizzy 7 frizzed
8 wrinkled

cripple 4 lame, maim 6 mangle 7 disable
8 mutilate, paralyze 9 hamstring,
undermine 10 debilitate 12 incapacitate

crippled 4 halt, lame 6 maimed
7 gnarled, mangled 8 battered,
deformed, disabled, weakened 9 enfeebled, misshapen, mutilated, paralyzed
11 debilitated, handicapped

crisis 4 crux, pass 5 pinch 6 climax,
crunch, height, strait 7 impasse, straits
8 disaster, exigency, juncture, zero
hour 9 emergency, extremity 10 crossroads 11 catastrophe, contingency
12 turning point

crisp 4 cold, cool, curl, deft, keen, neat,
wavy 5 brisk, clean, crimp, curly, fresh,
nippy, pithy, sharp, short 6 biting,

chilly, lively, ripple, spruce 7 bracing,
brittle, crunchy, cutting, wrinkle
8 clean-cut, clear-cut, incisive 9 trenchant 11 stimulating 12 invigorating

crisscross 3 net 4 grid, mesh 5 weave
7 network, overlap 8 reticule 9 confusion, decussate, intersect, reticular
10 reticulate

criterion 4 norm 5 canon, gauge, ideal,
model, tenet 7 measure, precept
8 exemplar, paradigm, standard
9 benchmark, yardstick 10 touchstone

critic 5 judge 6 carper, pundit 7 arbiter,
caviler 8 caviller, censurer, quibbler,
reviewer 9 belittler, nitpicker 10 dispar-
ager, mudslinger 11 commentator, connoisseur, faultfinder

critical 4 dire 5 acute, fussy 7 carping,
crucial, finicky, pivotal, weighty 8 captious, caviling, decisive 9 desperate,
important, momentous 10 belittling,
censorious, conclusive, precarious
11 disparaging, significant 12 faultfinding 13 consequential, determinative,
hairsplitting *study:* 6 examen 8 exegesis

criticism 4 flak, slap 5 blame, cavil,
swipe 6 rebuke, review 7 censure, comment, opinion, reproof 8 analysis, judgment, reproach 9 appraisal, objection
10 assessment, commentary, evaluation,
nitpicking 11 examination, observation
12 faultfinding

criticize 3 pan, rap 4 bash, carp 5 blame,
blast, cavil, chide, fault, judge, knock,
roast, scold 6 assess, rebuke, review,
scathe 7 censure, condemn, nitpick,
reprove 8 appraise, badmouth, chastise,
denounce, evaluate, lambaste 9 castigate, disparage, dress down, excoriate,
find fault, reprehend, reprimand,
reprobate

critique see CRITICISM

critter 5 beast 6 animal 7 varmint

Crius *father:* 6 Uranus *mother:* 4 Gaea
son: 8 Astraeus

croak 3 die 6 cackle, expire, squawk
7 grumble

croaky 5 gruff, husky, raspy 6 hoarse
8 gravelly

Croatia *capital:* 6 Zagreb *city:* 5 Split
6 Osijek, Rijeka 9 Dubrovnik *monetary
unit:* 4 kuna *neighbor:* 7 Hungary
8 Slovenia *part of:* 7 Balkans *region:*
8 Dalmatia, Slavonia

crock 3 jar, lie, pot 4 tale 6 tureen 7 cripple, disable, fiction 9 break down
11 fabrication

crocked 3 lit 4 high 5 drunk, lit up,
oiled, tipsy 6 bashed, blotto, bombed,
juiced, potted, soaked, soused, stewed,
stoned, tanked, wasted, zonked

7 drunken, pickled, pie-eyed, sloshed, smashed **9** plastered **10** inebriated, liquored up **11** intoxicated
crocodile 7 reptile *bird:* **6** plover *Indian:* **6** gavial **7** gharial *relative:* **9** alligator *South American:* **6** caiman, cayman *Southeast Asian:* **6** mugger
Croesus' kingdom 5 Lydia
croft 4 farm **5** field
crofter 4 hind **6** farmer
Cromwell, Oliver 13 lord protector *battle:* **6** Naseby **11** Marston Moor *regiment:* **9** Ironsides *son:* **7** Richard
crone 3 hag **4** trot **5** biddy, witch **6** beldam **7** beldame
Cronus 5 Titan **6** Saturn *daughter:* **4** Hera **6** Hestia **7** Demeter *father:* **6** Uranus *mother:* **4** Gaea *sister:* **4** Rhea **6** Cybele, Tethys *son:* **4** Zeus **5** Hades **7** Jupiter, Neptune **8** Poseidon *wife:* **4** Rhea **6** Cybele
crony 3 pal **4** chum **5** buddy **6** cohort **7** comrade **8** sidekick **9** associate, companion **10** accomplice **11** confederate
crook 3 bow **4** bend, flex, hook, wind **5** angle, curve, staff, thief **6** bandit, robber **7** burglar, crosier, hoodlum, pothook **8** criminal
crooked 4 awry **5** askew, lying, shady, venal **6** curved, errant, jagged, shifty, skewed, zigzag **7** bending, corrupt, devious, illegal, illicit, slanted **8** cockeyed, criminal, ruthless, tortuous, twisting **9** deceitful, dishonest, nefarious, underhand, unethical **10** fraudulent, mendacious, untruthful **11** duplicitous, underhanded **12** unscrupulous **13** double-dealing
croon 4 sing **6** murmur, warble
crooner 4 Cole (Nat "King"), Como (Perry) **5** Laine (Frankie), Tormé (Mel) **6** Crosby (Bing), Martin (Dean), singer, Vallee (Rudy) **7** Astaire (Fred), Bennett (Tony), Sinatra (Frank) **8** Eckstine (Billy), vocalist, Williams (Andy)
crop 3 bob, cut, hew, lop, mow **4** chop, clip, pare, snip, trim **5** prune, shave, shear, stock, yield **6** gullet, handle, output **7** harvest, produce **8** fruitage, truncate **10** collection
croquet 5 roque
crosier 5 crook, staff
cross 3 mad **4** mule, rood, span **5** angry, surly, testy, trial **6** betray, bridge, crabby, cranky, grumpy, hybrid, negate, oppose, ordeal, tetchy, touchy **7** athwart, calvary, carping, gainsay, grouchy, mongrel, peevish **8** captious, choleric, confront, traverse **9** decussate, half blood, half-breed, hybridize, intersect, irascible, irritable, querulous,

splenetic **10** affliction, contradict, contravene, interbreed, transverse **11** tribulation **12** cantankerous **13** quick-tempered *a river:* **4** ford *bearer:* **8** crucifer *decoration:* **4** Iron **8** Victoria *Egyptian:* **4** ankh *kind:* **3** tau **5** Greek, Latin, papal **6** Celtic, fleury, formée, moline, pommée, potent **7** avellan, botonée, Calvary, Maltese **8** crucifix, fourchée, Lorraine, quadrate **11** patriarchal **12** Saint Andrew's **13** Saint Anthony's *section:* **5** slice *stroke of a letter:* **5** serif
crossbow 8 arbalest, arbalist
crossbreed 4 mule **6** hybrid **7** bastard, mongrel **9** half blood, half-breed, hybridize **10** interbreed
cross-eye 6 squint **10** strabismus
crossing 8 junction, overpass, traverse **9** traversal, underpass **10** transverse **11** decussation, interchange, transversal **12** intersection
cross out 5 erase **6** cancel, delete, efface, excise **7** expunge
crosspatch 4 crab **5** crank, grump **6** griper, grouch **7** grouser **8** grumbler, sorehead, sourpuss **10** complainer, curmudgeon
crossroads 4 crux, pass **5** pinch **6** crisis, strait **8** exigency, juncture, zero hour **9** carrefour, emergency **11** contingency **12** intersection, turning point *goddess:* **6** Hecate, Hekate, Trivia
cross-shaped 8 cruciate **9** cruciform
crossways 6 aslant **7** athwart, oblique **8** diagonal **9** obliquely **10** diagonally, transverse **11** kitty-corner **12** transversely
crotchet 3 bee **4** whim **5** fancy, freak, quirk, trick **6** foible, megrim, notion, vagary **7** caprice, conceit **11** quarter note **12** eccentricity
crotchety 5 testy **6** crabby, cranky, crusty, ornery, tetchy, touchy **7** bearish, peevish, prickly **8** contrary, snappish, vinegary **9** difficult, eccentric, irascible **10** vinegarish **11** ill-tempered **12** cantankerous, cross-grained
crouch 4 bend, duck **5** cower, hunch, squat, stoop **6** cringe, huddle, shrink **10** hunker down
croup 3 bum **4** butt, hack, rear, rump, seat, tail **5** cough, edema, whoop **6** behind **7** keister, rear end, tail end **8** backside, buttocks, derriere, haunches **9** posterior
crow 4 blow, brag, puff **5** boast, exult, gloat, prate, vaunt **6** cackle **7** bluster **9** gasconade, humble pie *colony:* **7** rookery *cry:* **3** caw *family:* **6** corvid **8** Corvidae *genus:* **6** Corvus *relating to:*

7 corvine *relative:* 3 daw, jay 4 rook
5 raven 6 chough, magpie 7 jackdaw
crowbar 3 pry 5 jimmy, lever
crowd 3 jam, mob 4 army, bear, cram,
fill, herd, host, mass, pack, pile, push,
rout, ruck 5 bunch, crush, drove,
flock, flood, group, horde, hurry, press,
serry, shove, surge, swarm, troop 6 circle, clique, gaggle, huddle, jostle,
legion, rabble, squash, squish, stream,
throng 7 cluster, collect, company,
coterie, squeeze 8 assembly 9 gathering, multitude 10 assemblage, collection 11 aggregation 12 congregation
crowded 4 full 5 awash, close, dense,
thick, tight 6 loaded 7 brimful, compact, teeming 8 brimming, populous,
swarming 9 chock-full, congested, jam-
packed
crow-like 7 corvoid
crown 3 cap, top 4 acme, apex, peak,
roof 5 cover, crest, tiara 6 climax, diadem, laurel, summit, top off, vertex,
wreath, zenith 7 chaplet, coronal, coronet, garland, overlay, perfect 8 pinnacle,
round off, surmount 9 culminate, finish
off 10 consummate 11 culmination
crucial 4 dire 5 acute, vital 6 urgent
7 central, pivotal 8 critical, deciding,
decisive 9 desperate, essential, important, momentous, necessary 10 imperative 11 climacteric, significant
crucible 4 test 5 trial 6 ordeal 8 acid test
10 melting pot
crucifix 4 rood 5 cross
crucifixion site 7 Calvary 8 Golgotha
crucify 4 rack 6 impale, martyr 7 mortify,
pillory, torment, torture 10 excruciate
crud 3 goo 4 glop, gook, gunk, junk,
muck 5 dreck, filth, slime, trash
6 debris, sludge 7 deposit, garbage, rubbish 12 incrustation
crude 3 raw 4 poor 5 crass, dirty, gross,
rough 6 coarse, earthy, gauche, impure,
ribald, risqué, vulgar 7 boorish, ill-
bred, loutish, lowbred, obscene, obvious, raunchy, uncivil, uncouth 8 backward, cloddish, homespun, ignorant,
indecent, inferior 9 elemental, graceless, inelegant, makeshift, primitive,
rough-hewn, unrefined 10 amateurish,
unfinished, unpolished
cruel 4 fell, grim, mean 5 harsh 6 brutal,
fierce, savage 7 bestial, brutish, callous,
heinous, vicious 8 inhumane, ruthless,
sadistic 9 atrocious, barbarous, ferocious, heartless, merciless, monstrous,
truculent 12 bloodthirsty
cruise 4 roam, rove, sail, surf, tour 5 drift,
jaunt 6 junket, voyage 9 excursion
cruiser 4 boat 5 yacht 7 warship 8 squad
car 9 patrol car, powerboat

crumb 3 bit 4 iota 5 ounce, scrap, shred
6 morsel, sliver 7 smidgen 8 fragment,
particle
crumble 5 decay 8 collapse 9 break
down, decompose 11 deteriorate 12 disintegrate
crumbly 7 friable
crummy 4 poor 5 dingy, lousy, seedy,
tacky 6 cruddy, flimsy, shoddy, sleazy
8 inferior
crumple 3 wad 4 cave 5 crimp 6 buckle,
cave in, ruck up 7 crinkle, scrunch,
wrinkle 8 collapse
crunch 4 chew 5 champ, chomp, grind,
munch, sit-up 6 crisis 7 compute,
process, squeeze 8 shortage, showdown
crusade 5 cause, drive 6 appeal 7 holy
war 8 campaign, movement 9 offensive
10 expedition 11 undertaking
Crusader *English:* 7 Richard (Lionheart)
French: 5 Louis (IX) 6 Philip, Robert
7 Baldwin, Charles, Godfrey, Raymond, Raymund 8 Boniface, Montfort,
Philippe, Theobald *German:* 6 Conrad
9 Frederick, Friedrich 10 Barbarossa
Norman: 7 Tancred 8 Bohemund *Preacher:* 5 Peter (the Hermit), Urban (II)
7 Adhémar, Bernard 8 Innocent (III),
Pelagius
crusading 11 evangelical 12 evangelistic
crush 3 jam, mob 4 cram, mash, pulp,
push, ruin 5 crowd, drove, grind,
horde, pound, press, quash, quell,
smash, wreck 6 bruise, burden, defeat,
reduce, squash, squish, subdue, throng
7 conquer, destroy, mortify, oppress,
passion, put down, repress, scrunch,
squeeze, squelch, trample 8 bear down,
beat down, demolish, overcome, suppress, vanquish 9 humiliate, multitude,
overpower, overwhelm, pulverize,
puppy love, subjugate 10 annihilate,
extinguish, obliterate 11 infatuation
crust 4 cake, coat, rime, scab 7 coating,
deposit 8 covering
crustacean 4 crab, flea 5 louse, prawn
6 isopod, shrimp, slater, sow bug
7 copepod, daphnia, decapod, lobster,
pill bug 8 amphipod, barnacle, crawfish, crayfish, ostracod, sand flea
9 arthropod, beach flea, shellfish, water
flea, wood louse 10 stomatopod, whale
louse 11 branchiopod *aggregate of:*
5 krill *appendage:* 7 pleopod *body segment:* 6 somite, telson 8 metamere *claw:*
5 chela 6 pincer *covering substance:*
6 chitin *larva:* 8 nauplius
crusty 4 curt 5 bluff, blunt, gross, gruff,
short, surly 6 cranky 7 brusque,
crabbed, prickly 8 choleric 9 irascible,
irritable, saturnine, splenetic
crux 3 nub 4 core, gist, meat, pith

5 focus, heart **6** kernel, thrust **7** essence, purport **9** substance
cry (see also EXCLAMATION) **3** sob **4** bawl, blub, call, howl, keen, mewl, moan, pule, wail, weep, yawp, yell, yowl **5** bleat, motto, mourn, shout, whine, whoop **6** boohoo, furore, holler, lament, scream, snivel, squall, squawk, squeak, squeal **7** blubber, screech, ululate, whimper **10** vociferate *bacchanals':* **4** evoe *calf:* **5** bleat *cat:* **3** mew **4** meow **5** miaow *cattle:* **3** low, moo *chick:* **4** peep **5** cheep *court:* **4** oyez *crane:* **5** clang *crow:* **3** caw *dog:* **3** arf **4** bark, woof *donkey:* **4** bray **6** hee-haw *duck:* **5** quack *frog:* **5** croak *goat:* **5** bleat *goose:* **4** honk **5** clang *hen:* **6** cackle *horse:* **5** neigh **6** nicker, whinny **7** whicker *lion:* **4** roar *owl:* **4** hoot *pig:* **4** oink **5** grunt *raven:* **5** croak *sheep:* **5** bleat *songbird:* **5** chirp, tweet *turkey:* **6** gobble
cry down 5 decry **6** defame, deride, malign, revile, vilify **7** condemn **8** belittle, denounce, derogate, diminish **9** denigrate, deprecate, discredit, disparage **10** calumniate, depreciate **11** detract from, disparage
crying 4 dire **5** acute, vital **6** urgent **7** blatant, burning, clamant, exigent, heinous **8** flagrant, pressing, shocking **9** atrocious, clamorous, desperate, monstrous, notorious **10** compelling, imperative, outrageous, scandalous **11** importunate
crypt 5 vault **7** chamber **8** catacomb **9** mausoleum **10** undercroft
cryptic 5 vague **6** arcane, occult, opaque, secret **7** Delphic, obscure, unclear **8** abstruse, Delphian, esoteric, puzzling **9** ambiguous, enigmatic, recondite, tenebrous **10** mysterious, mystifying **12** unfathomable
crystal 4 lens **5** clear, lucid **6** limpid, lucent, quartz **8** clear-cut, luminous, pellucid **9** glassware, unblurred **11** translucent, transparent **12** transpicuous *gazer:* **4** seer **7** psychic **11** clairvoyant
Cry, the Beloved Country author 5 Paton (Alan)
cry up 4 laud, puff **5** boost, extol **6** praise **7** acclaim
cub 3 pup **4** baby, tyro **6** novice, rookie **8** neophyte **9** offspring, youngster **10** apprentice
Cuba capital: **6** Havana *city:* **7** Holguín **8** Camagüey, Santiago **10** Guantánamo, Santa Clara *discoverer:* **8** Columbus (Christopher) *language:* **7** Spanish *leader:* **6** Castro (Fidel) **7** Batista (Fulgencio) *monetary unit:* **4** peso **6** dollar *sea:* **9** Caribbean
cubbyhole 5 niche **6** alcove, recess **7** cubicle

cube 4 dice **5** mince
Cub Scout rank: **4** Bear, Lion, Wolf **6** Bobcat **7** Webelos *unit:* **3** den **4** pack
Cuchulain father: **3** Lug **4** Lugh **5** Lugus *foe:* **4** Medb **5** Maeve *kingdom:* **6** Ulster *lord:* **9** Conchobar *mother:* **8** Dechtire *son:* **8** Conlaoch *victim:* **8** Conlaoch *wife:* **4** Emer
cuckoo 3 mad, nut **4** daft, kook, nuts **5** batty, crank, crazy, daffy, loony, loopy, nutty, potty, silly, wacko, wacky **6** crazed, fruity, insane, screwy, whacky **7** bonkers, cracked, idiotic, lunatic, nutcase **8** crackpot, demented **9** ding-a-ling, harebrain, screwball **12** crackbrained *bird:* **3** ani
cucumber 4 pepo **7** gherkin
cuddle 3 hug, pet **4** neck, snug **5** spoon **6** burrow, caress, clinch, cosset, dandle, fondle, nestle, nuzzle **7** embrace, snuggle, squeeze **8** canoodle
cuddlesome 7 lovable, snuggly **8** huggable **11** embraceable
cudgel 3 bat, sap **4** club, cosh, mace **5** baton, billy **7** war club **8** bludgeon **9** bastinado, billy club, blackjack, truncheon **10** knobkerrie, nightstick, shillelagh
cue 3 key, nod, rod, tip **4** clue, hint, lead, prod, sign **6** insert, notion, prompt, signal, tip-off **7** inkling, warning **8** high sign, reminder, telltale **10** indication, intimation, suggestion
cuff 3 box, hit **4** belt, blip, clip, poke, slap, sock **5** clout, fight, punch, smack, whack **6** bangle, buffet, wallop **7** clobber, scuffle **8** bracelet, wristlet
cul-de-sac 5 pouch **6** pocket **7** dead end, impasse **10** blind alley **12** diverticulum
cull 4 pick, sift, thin **5** elect, glean **6** choose, garner, gather, select, winnow **7** extract, thin out
culminate 4 peak **5** crest **6** climax
culmination 3 top **4** acme, apex, peak **6** apogee, capper, climax, height, payoff, summit, zenith **8** capstone, pinnacle **11** ne plus ultra **12** consummation
culpability 4 onus **5** blame, fault, guilt
culpable 6 guilty, liable, sinful **7** at fault **8** blamable, blameful **10** censurable, delinquent **11** blameworthy, impeachable, responsible **13** reprehensible
cult 3 fad **4** sect **5** creed, faith **6** church **8** religion **10** persuasion **12** denomination
cultivable 6 arable **8** tillable
cultivate 4 farm, grow, tend, till **5** breed, nurse, raise **6** enrich, foster, refine **7** cherish, develop, further, improve, nourish, nurture, produce, promote **9** encourage, propagate
cultivated 6 urbane **7** genteel, refined **8** cultured, polished, well-bred

cultivation 6 polish 7 culture 8 breeding
10 refinement 11 development
culture 4 grow 5 taste 6 foster 7 nurture
9 cultivate, erudition, gentility
10 refinement 11 cultivation 12 civilization 13 enlightenment
cultured 6 urbane 7 erudite, genteel,
learned, refined 8 educated, highbrow,
literate, polished, well-bred 9 civilized
10 cultivated 11 enlightened
culture medium 4 agar
cum ___ salis 5 grano
cumber 4 clog, lade, load 6 burden, hinder, hobble, impede, saddle 7 clutter
8 handicap 9 hindrance
cumbersome 5 bulky, heavy, hefty
6 clumsy 7 awkward 8 unwieldy 9 lumbering, ponderous 10 slow-moving
cumbrous see CUMBERSOME
cumshaw 3 fee, tip 5 bribe 6 payoff
7 present 8 gratuity, largesse
9 lagniappe, pourboire 10 perquisite
cumulate 4 heap 5 amass, hoard, lay up,
store 6 garner, gather, pile up 7 collect,
combine, store up 9 stockpile
cumulation 4 heap, mass, pile 5 cache,
hoard, trove 9 stockpile 10 collection
11 aggregation 13 agglomeration
cumulative 8 additive, compound 9 summative 10 compounded, increasing
cunning 3 sly 4 cute, foxy, keen, wary,
wily 5 acute, cagey, canny, craft, guile,
savvy, sharp, skill, slick, smart 6 adroit,
artful, astute, clever, crafty, deceit,
shifty, tricky 7 finesse, know-how, slyness 8 artifice, deftness, facility, foxiness, guileful, slippery, subtlety, wiliness 9 adeptness, cageyness, canniness,
dexterity, dexterous, duplicity, ingenious, ingenuity, insidious, sharpness,
slickness 10 adroitness, artfulness, cleverness, craftiness, shiftiness, shrewdness, trickiness
cup 3 mug 4 toby 5 grail, jorum, stein
6 beaker, goblet, seidel 7 chalice,
tankard 8 schooner *handle:* 3 ear, lug
liturgical: 5 calix 7 chalice *small:* 6 noggin 8 cannikin, pannikin 9 demitasse
sports: 5 Davis, Ryder, World 6 Curtis,
Nextel 7 Stanley 8 America's, Wightman
cupbearer of the gods 4 Hebe
8 Ganymede
cupboard 5 ambry, cuddy 6 buffet, closet, larder, pantry 7 armoire, cabinet
8 credence, credenza 9 sideboard
Cupid 4 Amor, Eros 5 putto 6 cherub
8 amoretto *beloved:* 6 Psyche *brother:*
7 Anteros *father:* 6 Hermes 7 Mercury
mother: 5 Venus 9 Aphrodite *title:* 3 Dan
cupidity 4 lust 5 greed 6 desire 7 avarice,
avidity, craving, lechery, passion
8 rapacity, voracity 9 eagerness, esuri-

ence 10 greediness 11 infatuation
12 covetousness 13 rapaciousness
cupola 4 dome 5 vault 6 turret 7 furnace, lookout
cur 3 dog 4 mutt 7 mongrel
curate 6 cleric, priest 9 churchman, clergyman
curative 4 pill 5 tonic 6 elixir, relief,
remedy 7 healing, nostrum, panacea,
therapy 8 antidote, remedial, salutary,
sanative, solution 9 healthful, medicinal, remedying, treatment, wholesome
10 beneficial, corrective 11 restorative,
therapeutic 12 health-giving
curator 6 keeper, warden 9 caretaker,
custodian 11 conservator
curb 3 bit 4 deny 5 check, frame, leash,
tie up 6 border, bridle, edging, fetter,
hamper, hobble, hold in, subdue
7 abstain, contain, control, inhibit,
refrain, repress 8 hold back, hold down,
restrain, suppress, withhold 9 constrain,
entrammel, restraint *British:* 4 kerb
curdle 4 clot, sour, turn 5 spoil 7 clabber, congeal, thicken 9 coagulate
cure 3 age, spa 4 heal, mend 5 treat
6 elixir, kipper, physic, pickle, relief,
remedy 7 rectify, relieve, restore, therapy 8 antidote, medicant, medicine, preserve, recovery, solution 10 ameliorate,
corrective 12 counteragent 13 counteractive
cure-all 6 elixir 7 nostrum, panacea
10 catholicon
curio 6 oddity, whimsy 7 novelty
curiosity 5 freak 6 marvel, oddity, rarity,
whimsy, wonder 7 anomaly, concern,
novelty 8 interest, nonesuch
curious 3 odd 4 nosy 5 nosey, novel,
queer, weird 6 exotic, prying, quaint,
snoopy 7 bizarre, oddball, strange,
unusual 8 meddling, peculiar, puzzling,
singular 9 inquiring, intrusive
11 inquisitive, questioning
curl 4 coil, kink, wind 5 frizz, twine, twist
6 spiral 7 contort, crinkle, entwine, frizzle, ringlet, wreathe 9 corkscrew
curling *match:* 8 bonspiel *period of play:*
3 end *team:* 4 four *term:* 3 tee 4 hack,
rink 5 house, stone
curly 4 wavy 5 kinky 6 frizzy
currency 4 cash, coin 5 dough, lucre,
money, scrip 7 coinage 8 banknote
10 acceptance, prevalence 11 legal tender *unit:* (see INDIVIDUAL COUNTRY)
current 4 eddy, flow, flux, rush, tide
5 drift, flood, spate, tenor, trend
6 extant, modern, strain, stream
7 instant, ongoing, popular, present, regnant, topical 8 accepted, existent, existing, tendency, up-to-date 9 prevalent
10 present-day, prevailing, widespread

11 fashionable 12 contemporary *air:*
4 gale, gust, wind 5 blast, draft 6 breeze,
squall, zephyr 7 cyclone, indraft,
updraft 9 downdraft 10 slipstream
ocean: 7 riptide 8 undertow 9 maelstrom, whirlpool *unit:* 3 amp 6 ampere
Currier's partner 4 Ives (James)
curry 4 beat, comb, seek, whip 5 groom
6 thrash
curse 4 bane, cuss, damn, evil, jinx, oath
5 swear 6 blight, plague, whammy
7 afflict, damning, malison, scourge,
torment 8 anathema, cussword, execrate 9 bête noire, blaspheme, blasphemy, expletive, imprecate, profanity,
swearword 10 affliction, execration,
misfortune, pestilence 11 commination,
imprecation, malediction, profanation
12 anathematize, denunciation
cursed 6 damned 7 blasted, dratted
8 damnable, infernal 9 execrable
10 confounded 13 blankety-blank
cursive 6 fluent, smooth 7 flowing, running
cursory 5 hasty, quick, rapid 6 casual
7 hurried, shallow, sketchy 8 careless
10 uncritical 11 perfunctory, superficial
curt 4 rude 5 bluff, blunt, brief, gruff,
short, terse 6 abrupt, crusty 7 brusque,
concise 8 succinct 10 peremptory
curtail 3 cut 4 clip, dock, trim 5 prune,
slash 6 lessen, reduce 7 abridge, cut
back, shorten 8 diminish, pare down,
retrench, truncate 10 abbreviate
curtain 4 drop, veil 5 drape 6 screen
7 barrier *doorway:* 8 portiere *holder:*
3 rod *Indian:* 6 purdah *rod concealer:*
7 valance *sash:* 7 tieback *stage:* 4 drop
5 scrim 8 backdrop
curtains 3 end 4 ruin 5 death 6 demise,
finish 7 decease 8 disaster
curtilage 4 quad, yard 5 court 8 cloister
9 courtyard, enclosure 10 quadrangle
curvaceous 5 buxom 7 rounded, shapely
9 Junoesque 10 statuesque, voluptuous
13 well-developed
curvature *of the spine:* 8 kyphosis, lordosis 9 scoliosis
curve 3 arc, bow 4 arch, bend, turn,
veer, wind 5 crook, round, twist 6 convex, spiral, swerve 7 concave, flexure,
rondure *of an arch:* 8 extrados, intrados
pitcher's: 4 hook *plane:* 7 cycloid,
limaçon 8 parabola, sinusoid, trochoid
9 hyperbola *S-shaped:* 3 ess 4 ogee 7 sigmoid
curved 4 bent 5 arced, bowed, round
6 arched 7 arcuate, bending, embowed,
falcate, rounded, sigmoid, sinuous,
twisted *implement:* 6 sickle *molding:*
4 ogee *sword:* 5 kukri, saber, sabre
7 cutlass 8 scimitar

curvilinear see CURVED
curvy see CURVACEOUS; CURVED
Cush *father:* 3 Ham *son:* 6 Nimrod
cushion 3 mat, pad 5 squab 6 absorb,
buffer, pillow, soften 7 bolster, hassock,
pillion 8 palliate, woolsack
cushy 4 cozy, easy, soft 11 comfortable,
undemanding
cusp 3 tip 4 apex, edge, peak 5 point,
verge 12 turning point
cuspid 6 canine 8 eyetooth
cuspidate 5 sharp 6 peaked, pointy
7 pointed
cuss 3 guy, man 4 chap, damn, dude,
oath 5 curse, swear 6 fellow 9 expletive
cussed 4 dour 5 crude, gruff 6 crusty,
cursed, grumpy, ornery 7 boorish,
brusque, grouchy 8 churlish 9 obstinate
10 unyielding 11 contentious 12 antagonistic, cantankerous
cussword 4 oath 5 curse 9 expletive,
swearword
custard 4 flan 7 pudding
custodian 5 super 6 keeper, porter, warden 7 curator, steward 8 guardian,
overseer, watchdog, watchman 9 caretaker, concierge, protector 10 supervisor 11 conservator
custody 4 care, ward 5 guard, trust
6 charge 7 keeping 9 captivity, detention 10 caretaking, management, protection 11 confinement, safekeeping,
supervision 12 guardianship
custom 3 use 4 norm 5 habit, mores
(plural), trade, usage 6 groove, manner,
praxis, ritual 7 folkway, precept, routine, traffic 8 business, habitude, practice 9 patronage 10 consuetude, convention
customary 5 usual 6 common, normal,
wonted 7 general, regular, routine
8 accepted, everyday, familiar, frequent, habitual, ordinary, orthodox,
standard 10 accustomed 11 established,
traditional 12 conventional
custom-built 7 bespoke 10 tailor-made
11 made-to-order
customer 5 buyer 6 client, patron
7 shopper 8 consumer 9 purchaser *frequent:* 7 habitué
customized see CUSTOM-BUILT
custom-made see CUSTOM-BUILT
cut 3 bob, hew, lop, mow, saw 4 bite,
chop, clip, crop, dice, dock, fell, gash,
hack, nick, pare, reap, sawn, slit, snip,
snub, trim 5 carve, filet, lathe, lower,
mince, notch, piece, prune, quota,
sawed, sever, share, shave, shear, slash,
slice, split, wound 6 cleave, delete,
dilute, divide, excise, fillet, incise,
reduce, scythe, sickle, sunder
7 abridge, curtail, dissect, operate, por-

tion, scissor, section, segment, shorten 8 amputate, decrease, dissever, division, mark down, separate, truncate 9 allotment, allowance, reduction 10 abbreviate 12 cold-shoulder *of beef:* 3 rib 4 loin, rump 5 chine, chuck, flank, roast, shank, steak, T-bone 6 saddle 7 brisket, sirloin 9 aitchbone 11 porterhouse

cut across 6 bisect 8 transect 9 transcend

cut-and-dried 5 stock 7 routine 9 formulaic 10 unoriginal 11 predictable 13 unimaginative

cutaneous 6 dermal

cutaway 4 coat, dive 5 tails

cut back 3 zag 4 clip, curb, dock, pare, trim 5 lower, prune, shave, slash 6 lessen, reduce 7 abridge, curtail, shorten 8 decrease, retrench, truncate 10 abbreviate

cut down 3 axe 4 chop, clip, fell, pare 5 lower, shave, slash 6 digest, reduce 7 abridge, shorten 10 abbreviate

cute 6 dainty, pretty 7 cunning 8 affected 10 attractive 11 impertinent, smartalecky

cut in 7 include, intrude, obtrude 9 introduce

cutlass 5 saber, sabre, sword 7 machete 8 scimitar

cut off 3 axe, bar, end, lop 4 halt, kill, stop 5 abort, block, sever 6 disown 7 curtail, destroy, isolate, suspend 8 amputate, obstruct, renounce, separate, truncate 9 intercept, interrupt, terminate 10 disinherit 11 discontinue

cut out 3 end 4 halt 5 leave, scram, usurp 6 beat it, delete, depart, escape, excise, remove, resect 7 defraud, deprive, take off 8 displace, supplant 9 eliminate, extirpate 10 disconnect

cutpurse 5 thief 10 pickpocket

cut short 3 bob 4 clip, crop, dock, halt, poll 5 abort, check, scrub, shear 7 abridge, curtail 8 break off 9 interrupt, terminate 10 abbreviate

cuttable 7 sectile 8 scissile

cutthroat 5 bravo 6 gunman, hit man, killer 7 torpedo 8 assassin, murderer 10 hatchet man, triggerman

cutting 8 incisive, piercing 9 sarcastic, trenchant 11 penetrating *edge:* 5 blade *remark:* 3 dig 4 barb 5 taunt *tool:* 3 axe, hob, saw 4 adze 5 knife, lathe, mower, plane, razor 6 reaper, scythe, shears, sickle 7 hatchet 8 scissors, tomahawk

cuttlefish 7 mollusc, mollusk 10 cephalopod *ink:* 5 sepia *relative:* 5 squid 7 octopus

cut up 4 dice, hash, romp 5 caper, clown, mince, slash 6 cavort 7 carry on, show off 9 misbehave 10 roughhouse

cutup 3 wag 4 zany 5 clown, joker 6 madcap 7 buffoon, farceur 8 jokester

cyan 4 blue

Cybele 4 Rhea *beloved:* 5 Attis *brother:* 6 Cronus *father:* 6 Uranus *husband:* 6 Cronus *mother:* 4 Gaea *son:* 4 Zeus 7 Jupiter, Neptune 8 Poseidon

cyber 5 wired 10 electronic

cybernetics founder 6 Wiener (Norbert)

cycle 3 age, lap, set 4 bike, loop, ring 5 chain, orbit, recur, round, wheel 6 circle, course, period, series 7 circuit 8 rotation, sequence 9 vibration 10 revolution, succession, two-wheeler, velocipede 11 oscillation

cyclic 7 regular 8 periodic, repeated, rhythmic 9 iterative, recurring, repeating 10 isochronal 12 intermittent

cyclone 7 tornado, twister

cyclopean 4 huge 7 immense, mammoth, massive, titanic 8 colossal, enormous, gigantic 9 monstrous 10 gargantuan, tremendous 11 elephantine

Cyclops 5 Arges 7 Brontes 8 Steropes 10 Polyphemus

Cycnus *father:* 4 Ares, Mars *slayer:* 8 Heracles, Hercules

cygnet 4 swan *dam (mother):* 3 pen *sire (father):* 3 cob

Cygnus *form:* 4 swan *friend:* 7 Phaeton *star:* 5 Deneb

cylinder 4 drum, pipe, tube 5 spool 6 barrel, bobbin, platen, roller

cylindrical 6 terete 7 tubular 8 tubelike

Cymbeline *daughter:* 6 Imogen *son:* 9 Arviragus, Guiderius *son-in-law:* 9 Posthumus

Cymric 5 Welsh 6 Celtic 9 Brythonic *bard:* 8 Taliesin *Elysium:* 6 Annwfn *god:* 5 Lludd *of Elysium:* 5 Arawn *of the dead:* 5 Pwyll *of the seas:* 3 Ler 4 Llyr 5 Dylan *of the sky:* 7 Gwydion *of the sun:* 4 Lleu, Llew *of the underworld:* 4 Gwyn *goddess:* 3 Don 9 Arianrhod *magician:* 6 Merlin

Cymru 5 Wales

cynical 8 derisive, sardonic, scornful 12 misanthropic

Cynthia 4 Luna, moon 5 Diana 7 Artemis

cyprian 4 bawd, jade, slut, tart 5 hussy, tramp 6 floozy, harlot, hooker, wanton 7 jezebel, trollop 8 slattern, strumpet 10 prostitute

Cyprus *capital:* 7 Nicosia 8 Lefkosia *city:* 7 Larnaca 8 Limassol *language:* 5 Greek 7 Turkish *monetary unit:* 4 lira 5 pound *mountain:* 7 Olympus *port:* 9 Famagusta *sea:* 13 Mediterranean

Cyrano de Bergerac 4 poet 7 duelist 8 duellist *author:* 7 Rostand (Edmond) *beloved:* 6 Roxane *feature:* 4 nose *rival:* 9 Christian

Cyrus *conquest:* 5 Lydia, Media 7 Babylon *daughter:* 6 Atossa *empire:* 7 Persian *father:* 8 Cambyses *son:* 8 Cambyses

cyst 3 sac, wen 4 sore 5 pouch, spore 6 growth 7 abscess, blister, capsule, vesicle 8 swelling

Cytherea 4 isle 5 Venus 6 island 9 Aphrodite

czar 5 chief, mogul 6 despot, honcho, tycoon, tyrant 7 emperor, kingpin, magnate 8 autocrat *Russian:* 4 Ivan 5 Basil, Boris, Peter 6 Alexis, Dmitry, Feodor, Fyodor, Vasily 7 Dimitri, Michael, Romanov 8 Nicholas, Romanoff, Theodore 9 Alexander 12 Boris Godunov

czar's wife 7 czarina

Czech Republic *capital:* 6 Prague *city:* 4 Brno 7 Ostrava *monetary unit:* 6 koruna *neighbor:* 6 Poland 7 Austria, Germany 8 Slovakia *region:* 7 Bohemia, Moravia *river:* 4 Labe, Oder 5 March 6 Morava

D

dab 3 bit, pat 4 blob, blow, daub, peck, poke, spot 5 smear, touch 6 bedaub 7 besmear, plaster, splotch 8 flatfish

dabble 3 dip, dot, toy 4 fool, stud 5 fleck 6 dampen, fiddle, monkey, pepper, putter, splash, tinker 7 freckle, spatter, stipple 8 sprinkle 9 bespeckle, muck about 10 muck around

dabbler 4 duck, tyro 7 amateur 8 putterer, tinkerer 9 smatterer 10 dilettante

dabchick 5 grebe

dacha 5 villa 7 cottage 12 country house

dad 3 pop 4 papa 5 padre, pater 6 father, old man, parent

Dadaist 3 Arp (Jean), Ray (Man) 4 Ball (Hugo) 5 Ernst (Max), Grosz (George), Tzara (Tristan) 7 Duchamp (Marcel), Picabia (Francis) 10 Schwitters (Kurt)

daedal 6 knotty 7 complex 8 artistic, involved, skillful 9 elaborate, intricate 11 complicated 12 labyrinthine 13 sophisticated

Daedalus 7 builder 9 architect, artificer *construction:* 9 Labyrinth *father:* 6 Metion *son:* 6 Icarus *victim:* 5 Talos 6 Perdix

daffy see DAFT

daft 3 mad 4 loco, nuts 5 balmy, crazy, dopey, flaky, loony, nutty, potty, silly, wacko, wacky 6 absurd, crazed, cuckoo, insane, screwy 7 cracked, foolish, idiotic, lunatic, witless 8 demented 10 unbalanced 11 harebrained

Dag *father:* 7 Delling *horse:* 9 Skinfaksi *mother:* 4 Nott

Dagda *chief god of the:* 5 Gaels, Irish *daughter:* 6 Brigit *instrument:* 4 harp *son:* 6 Aengus *wife:* 5 Boann

dagger 4 dirk 5 skean, skene 6 bodkin, stylet 7 dudgeon, poniard 8 stiletto *handle:* 4 hilt *Malay:* 4 kris

___ **Dahl** 5 Roald 6 Arlene

daikon 6 radish

daily 7 diurnal 8 everyday 9 circadian, quotidian

dainty 5 goody, tasty, treat 6 choice, morsel, select, tidbit 7 elegant, fragile 8 delicacy, delicate, ethereal, graceful, kickshaw 9 exquisite, recherché 10 delightful

dairy 8 creamery

dais 5 stage 6 podium 7 rostrum 8 platform

daisy 5 oxeye 6 Shasta *British:* 10 moonflower *Scottish:* 5 gowan

Daisy Miller author 5 James (Henry)

Dakota dialect 5 Teton

Daksha's father 6 Brahma

dale 4 dell, glen, vale 6 dingle, valley

dally 3 lag, pet, toy 4 drag, idle, play 5 delay, flirt, tarry 6 coquet, dawdle, diddle, linger, loiter, trifle 8 lollygag 9 hang about, waste time 10 fool around

dam 4 weir 5 block, check 7 barrier 8 hold back, restrain *major:* 4 Oahe

6 Hoover 7 San Luis 8 Fort Peck, Garrison, Oroville 10 Bonneville, Glen Canyon 11 Grand Coulee

damage 3 mar 4 blot, harm, hurt, loss, maim, ruin 5 abuse, burst, cloud, spoil, stain, wound 6 blight, deface, impair, injure, injury, mangle, ravage, scathe 7 blemish, destroy, marring, tarnish, vitiate 8 maltreat, mischief, mistreat, mutilate, sabotage 9 devastate, vandalism 10 impairment 11 devastation

damaged 4 hurt, rent 6 broken, busted, dinged, flawed, marred 7 injured, spoiled, totaled 8 battered, impaired, ruptured 9 blemished, fractured, imperfect, shattered 10 fragmented

damaging 6 nocent 7 harmful, hurtful, nocuous 9 injurious 11 deleterious, detrimental, prejudicial

dame 4 lady 5 woman 6 gammer, matron 7 dowager 9 matriarch

Damien's island 7 Molokai

Damkina's son 6 Marduk

damn 4 cuss, darn, doom, drat 5 curse, swear 7 condemn, doggone 8 execrate, sentence 9 imprecate 10 vituperate 12 anathematize

damnable 6 blamed, cursed, cussed 7 blasted, dratted 8 accursed, infernal 9 abhorrent, execrable 10 abominable, detestable

damned 5 utter 6 blamed, cursed, cussed, darned, dashed, doomed 7 awfully, blasted, doggone, dratted, goldarn 8 accursed, infernal 9 condemned 10 confounded 13 anathematized

Damocles' ___ 5 sword

Damon's friend 7 Pythias

damp 3 wet 4 dank, dewy 5 check, choke, humid, moist, musty 6 clammy 7 bedewed 8 humidify, humidity

dampen 4 cool, curb 5 chill 6 deaden 7 depress, moisten 8 diminish

damsel 3 gal 4 girl, lass, maid, miss 5 filly, wench 6 lassie, maiden

Dan *father:* 5 Jacob *mother:* 6 Bilhah *son:* 6 Hushim

Danaë *father:* 8 Acrisius *lover:* 4 Zeus *son:* 7 Perseus

Danaus *brother:* 8 Aegyptus *daughters:* 7 Danaïds 8 Danaïdes *father:* 5 Belus *founder of:* 5 Argos *grandfather:* 7 Neptune 8 Poseidon

dance 3 hop, jig, tap 4 ball, flit, foot, heel, hoof, juba, leap, lope, reel, step, trip 5 bamba, brawl, galop, gigue, hover, lindy, mambo, mixer, polka, rumba, stomp, swing, tread 6 ballet, bolero, boogie, Boston, cancan, chassé, foot it, formal, frolic, German, hoof it,

rhumba, shimmy 7 beguine, coranto, courant, flicker, flitter, flutter, hoedown, one-step, shuffle 8 cakewalk, flamenco, galliard, glissade, rigadoon, rigaudon 9 allemande, cotillion, jitterbug, pas de deux *art of:* 12 choreography *Austrian:* 7 ländler *ballroom:* 5 rumba, tango 6 cha-cha, rhumba 7 fox-trot, mazurka, two-step 8 merengue 9 cotillion 10 Charleston *Bohemian:* 5 polka *Brazilian:* 5 samba 6 maxixe 7 lambada 8 capoeira 9 bossa nova *combining form:* 5 chore 6 choreo, chorio *country:* 4 reel 8 hornpipe *couple:* 5 polka 9 cotillion, malaguena 11 square dance *court:* 6 canary, pavane 8 saraband 9 allemande, sarabande *Cuban:* 5 conga, mambo, rumba 6 rhumba 8 habanera *designer:* 13 choreographer *English:* 6 morris *formal:* 4 ball, prom 9 cotillion *French:* 6 cancan 7 bourrée, gavotte 9 allemande 10 carmagnole *garment:* 4 tutu 7 leotard *Haitian:* 4 juba 8 merengue *Hungarian:* 7 czardas *Indian:* 6 nautch 7 bhangra *instrument:* 8 castanet *Israeli:* 4 hora *Italian:* 3 jig 4 reel, trot 5 galop, gigue, polka, rumba 6 rhumba 7 bourrée 8 fandango, hornpipe, rigadoon, rigaudon 9 farandole, shakedown 10 Charleston, saltarello, tarantella *movement:* 4 plié, step 8 capriole, glissade 9 pirouette *Muse of:* 11 Terpsichore *1920's:* 10 Charleston *Polish:* 5 polka 7 mazurka 9 polonaise *Polynesian:* 4 hula *Scottish:* 3 bob 4 reel 5 fling 10 strathspey 11 schottische 13 Highland fling *shoes:* 5 pumps 8 slippers *slipper:* 7 toeshoe *slow:* 6 adagio, minuet, pavane 8 habanera *South American:* 7 carioca *Spanish:* 4 jota 6 bolero 7 zapateo 8 cachucha, chaconne, fandango, flamenco, saraband 9 malaguena, sarabande 10 seguidilla *springy:* 3 jig *square:* 7 hoedown, lancers 9 cotillion, quadrille *stately:* 5 pavan 6 pavane 8 saraband 9 polonaise, sarabande *step:* 3 pas *woman's:* 6 cancan

dancer 6 hoofer 7 chorine, clogger, danseur, stepper 8 coryphée, danseuse 9 ballerina, chorus boy 10 cakewalker, chorus girl *American:* 4 Feld (Elliot), Holm (Hanya), Lang (Pearl), Tune (Tommy) 5 Ailey (Alvin), Fosse (Bob), Kelly (Gene), Shawn (Ted), Tharp (Twyla) 6 Castle (Irene, Vernon), Duncan (Isadora), Dunham (Katherine), Graham (Martha), Morris (Mark), Taylor (Paul), Verdon (Gwen) 7 Astaire (Fred), Bujones (Fernando), de Mille

(Agnes), Farrell (Suzanne), Gregory (Cynthia), Jamison (Judith), Joffrey (Robert), Martins (Peter), Massine (Leonide), McBride (Patricia), Robbins (Jerome), St. Denis (Ruth), Tamiris (Helen) **8** Champion (Gower, Marge), d'Amboise (Jacques), Humphrey (Doris), Kirkland (Gelsey), Mitchell (Arthur), Nikolais (Alwin), Villella (Edward) **9** Tallchief (Maria) **10** Cunningham (Merce) *Cuban:* **6** Alonso (Alicia) *Danish:* **5** Bruhn (Erik) **7** Martins (Peter) **8** Tomasson (Helgi) *English:* **5** Dolin (Anton), Somes (Michael), Tudor (Antony) **7** Fonteyn (Margot), Markova (Alicia), Rambert (Marie) **8** de Valois (Ninette), Helpmann (Robert) *French:* **5** Lifar (Serge) **6** Béjart (Maurice), Perrot (Jules), Petipa (Marius) **7** Camargo (Marie), Massine (Leonide) *German:* **5** Jooss (Kurt) *Italian:* **5** Grisi (Carlotta) *Mexican:* **5** Limón (José) *Russian:* **5** Lifar (Serge) **6** Fokine (Michel), Petipa (Marius) **7** Massine (Leonide), Nureyev (Rudolf), Pavlova (Anna), Ulanova (Galina) **8** Danilova (Aleksandra), Makarova (Natalia), Nijinska (Bronislava), Nijinsky (Vaslav), Vaganova (Agrippina) **9** Karsavina (Tamara), Semyonova (Marina) **11** Baryshnikov (Mikhail), Plisetskaya (Maya) *Scottish:* **7** Shearer (Moira)

dancing 6 ballet **12** choreography *mania:* **9** tarantism

dandle 3 pet **4** play **6** caress, cosset, cradle, cuddle, pamper

dandruff 5 scall, scurf

dandy 3 fop **4** beau, buck, dude, fine, toff **5** nifty, swell **6** peachy **7** coxcomb, foppish **8** terrific **9** excellent, first-rate, hunky-dory **11** Beau Brummel, crackerjack **12** lounge lizard

dang 4 damn, darn **6** cursed, cussed, damned, darned **7** blasted, dratted, goldarn **8** infernal **10** confounded

danger 4 risk **5** peril **6** crisis, hazard, menace, plight, threat **7** pitfall, trouble **8** distress, jeopardy **9** emergency *signal:* **4** bell **5** alarm, siren **6** tocsin

dangerous 5 risky **6** unsafe **7** parlous **8** insecure, menacing, perilous, unstable **9** hazardous **10** precarious **11** threatening

dangle 4 hang **5** droop, swing **6** depend **7** suspend

Daniel ___ pioneer: **5** Boone *statesman:* **7** Webster

Danish hero: **5** Ogier *king:* **9** Christian, Frederick *queen:* **9** Margrethe

dank 3 wet **4** damp **5** humid, moist **6** clammy **8** dripping

Dante beloved: **8** Beatrice *birthplace:* **8** Florence *daughter:* **7** Antonia *deathplace:* **7** Ravenna *party:* **6** Guelph **7** Bianchi *patron:* **5** Scala *teacher:* **6** Latini *wife:* **5** Gemma *work:* **7** Inferno **8** Commedia, Paradiso **9** Vita Nuova **10** Purgatorio **12** Divine Comedy (The)

Dantean division 5 canto

Danton's colleague 5 Marat (Jean-Paul) **11** Robespierre (Maximilien)

Danzig 6 Gdańsk

Daphne father: **5** Ladon **6** Peneus *form:* **6** laurel **10** laurel tree *pursuer:* **6** Apollo **9** Leucippus

Daphnis' lover 5 Chloe

dapper 4 neat, trim **5** doggy, natty, sassy, smart, swank **6** classy, jaunty, rakish, snazzy, spiffy, spruce, sprucy **7** bandbox, dashing, doggish, foppish, stylish **11** well-groomed

dapple 4 spot **5** fleck, patch **6** mottle **7** speckle, stipple

dappled 4 pied **6** motley **7** flecked, mottled, patched, piebald, spotted **8** brindled **10** variegated **11** varicolored

Dardanelles 10 Hellespont

Dardanus descendants: **7** Trojans *father:* **4** Zeus **7** Jupiter *mother:* **7** Electra

dare 3 try **4** defy, risk **5** beard, brave **6** hazard **7** attempt, venture **8** confront, defiance **9** challenge

daredevil see DARING

darer 4 hero **6** risker

daring 4 bold, guts, rash **5** brash, brave, gutsy, moxie, nerve, nervy, pluck, valor **6** heroic, plucky **7** bravery, courage, heroism **8** audacity, boldness, fearless, reckless **9** audacious, derring-do, fortitude, venturous **10** courageous **11** adventurous, venturesome **13** adventuresome

Darius battle: **8** Marathon *father:* **9** Hystaspes *country:* **6** Persia **7** Parthia *son:* **6** Xerxes *wife:* **6** Atossa

Darjeeling 3 tea

dark 3 dim **4** dusk, inky, murk **5** black, blind, cloud, dingy, dusky, ebony, murky, night, sable, shady, sooty, swart, umber, unlit, vague **6** brunet, cloudy, dismal, gloomy, opaque, somber, sombre, wicked **7** obscure, ominous, rayless, satanic, shadowy, stygian, subfusc, sunless, swarthy, unclear **8** bistered, brunette, infernal, sinister **9** enigmatic, lightless, secretive, tenebrous, unlighted **10** caliginous, indistinct, mysterious, mystifying, pitchblack **11** crepuscular **13** unilluminated *poetic:* **4** ebon

darken 3 dim **5** bedim, cloud, gloom, lower, shade, sully, umber **6** shadow **7** becloud, blacken, eclipse, obscure, tarnish **8** melanize, overcast **9** obfuscate, overcloud **10** overshadow *Scottish:* **5** gloam

dark-haired *female:* **8** brunette *male:* **6** brunet

darkness 4 dusk, evil, murk **5** black, gloom, night, shade **6** shadow **8** blackout **9** nightfall, obscurity

darling 3 hon, pet **4** dear, duck, love **5** angel, deary, ducky, flame, honey, loved, sugar, sweet **7** beloved, dearest, sweetie **8** adorable, charming, favorite, precious **10** sweetheart, sweetie pie

darn 4 knit, mend **5** patch **6** blamed, cursed, cussed, damned, shucks **7** blasted, doggone, dratted **8** infernal **9** embroider **10** confounded

darn it *French:* **3** zut

Darrow client 4 Debs (Eugene), Loeb (Richard) **6** Scopes (John) **7** Haywood (William), Leopold (Nathan)

dart 3 fly, run, zip **4** barb, bolt, buzz, dash, flit, leap, rush, sail, scud, skim, tear **5** arrow, bound, hurry, lance, pitch, scamp, scoot, shaft, shoot, skirr, spear, speed, spurt **6** glance, hasten, scurry, spring, sprint **7** javelin, missile, scamper *barbed:* **10** banderilla

D'Artagnan's friends 5 Athos **6** Aramis **7** Porthos **10** musketeers

Dartmouth location 5 Devon **7** Hanover **12** New Hampshire

darts term 3 leg **4** bust **5** split **6** double, flight, hockey, treble **8** bull's-eye

Darwin, Charles *colleague:* **7** Wallace (Alfred Russel) *ship:* **6** Beagle *theory:* **9** evolution, selection

dash 3 fly, nip, run **4** bolt, brio, cast, damn, dart, élan, foil, hurl, race, ruin, rush, slam, tear, zing **5** break, chase, flair, fling, pinch, smash, style, trace **6** esprit, hyphen, pizazz, scurry, splash, sprint, thrust, thwart **7** bravura, depress, destroy, pizzazz, shatter, smidgen, spatter **8** confound **9** animation, frustrate

dashboard reading 4 fuel **5** speed **7** mileage **8** pressure **11** temperature

dashing 4 bold **5** smart **6** dapper, jaunty, lively, modish **7** gallant, stylish **8** animated, spirited **11** adventurous, fashionable

Das Kapital author 4 Marx (Karl)

dassie 4 pika **5** coney, hyrax

dastard 6 coward, craven **7** chicken, quitter **8** poltroon, recreant **9** scoundrel

dastardly 3 low **4** base, mean **6** craven, yellow **8** cowardly, shameful, skulking **11** treacherous, underhanded **13** pusillanimous

data 4 info **5** facts, input **7** figures **9** documents **11** information

date 3 age, era, woo **5** court, epoch, tryst **6** cutoff, escort **7** take out **8** deadline **9** accompany **10** engagement, rendezvous **11** anniversary, appointment, assignation

dated 3 old **5** passé **6** démodé, old hat **7** archaic, outworn **8** obsolete, outmoded **10** antiquated **12** old-fashioned **13** unfashionable

datum 4 fact

daub 4 blob, blot, spot **5** fleck, paint, smear **6** dapple, smudge, splash **7** besmear, dribble, plaster, speckle, splotch

daughter *Blythe Danner's:* **7** Paltrow (Gwyneth) *Bruce Dern's:* **5** Laura *Bush's:* **5** Jenna **7** Barbara *Carter's:* **3** Amy *Cash's:* **7** Rosanne *Cher's:* **8** Chastity *Clinton's:* **7** Chelsea *Cole's:* **7** Natalie *Coppola's:* **5** Sofia *Danny Thomas's:* **5** Marlo *Debbie Reynolds's:* **6** Carrie (Fisher) *Eddie Fisher's:* **6** Carrie *Elizabeth II's:* **4** Anne *Elvis's:* **9** Lisa Marie *Fonda's:* **4** Jane *Ford's (Gerald):* **5** Susan *Freud's:* **4** Anna *Garland's:* **12** Liza Minnelli *Goldie Hawn's:* **10** Kate Hudson *Ingrid Bergman's:* **8** Isabella (Rossellini) *Janet Leigh's:* **8** Jamie Lee (Curtis) *Joel Grey's:* **8** Jennifer *Johnson's (Lyndon):* **4** Lucy **5** Linda *Jon Voight's:* **8** Angelina (Jolie) *Kennedy's (John F.):* **8** Caroline *Klaus Kinski's:* **9** Nastassja *Maureen O'Sullivan's:* **3** Mia (Farrow) *Naomi Judd's:* **7** Wynonna *Nat King Cole's:* **7** Natalie *Nixon's:* **5** Julie **6** Tricia *Pat Boone's:* **5** Debby *Ravi Shankar's:* **10** Norah Jones *Reagan's:* **5** Patti **7** Maureen *Richard Burton's:* **4** Kate *Ryan O'Neal's:* **5** Tatum *Sinatra's:* **5** Nancy *Tony Curtis's:* **8** Jamie Lee (Curtis)

Daughter of the Moon 7 Nokomis

daunt 3 cow **5** alarm, deter **6** dismay, subdue **7** terrify **8** frighten **10** disconcert, discourage, dishearten, intimidate

daunting 7 awesome **8** imposing **9** dismaying, unnerving **10** forbidding, formidable **11** dispiriting **12** discouraging, intimidating, overwhelming

dauntless 4 bold, game **5** brave **6** daring **7** gallant, valiant **8** fearless, unafraid **9** unfearful, unfearing **10** courageous **11** lionhearted **12** stouthearted

dauntlessness 4 guts **5** heart, nerve, pluck, spunk, valor **6** daring, mettle, spirit **7** bravery, cojones, courage **8** boldness **10** resolution **12** fearlessness

davenport 4 desk, sofa 5 couch, divan 6 daybed 12 chesterfield

David *commander:* 4 Joab 5 Amasa *companion:* 8 Jonathan *daughter:* 5 Tamar *father:* 5 Jesse *rebuker:* 6 Nathan *son:* 5 Amnon 7 Absalom, Solomon 8 Adoijah *wife:* 6 Michal 7 Abigail, Ahinoam 9 Bathsheba

___ **David** 4 Camp 5 Magen, Mogen 6 Star of

David Copperfield *author:* 7 Dickens (Charles) *character:* 4 Dora, Heep 5 Uriah 6 Barkis 8 Micawber, Peggotty 9 Murdstone 10 Steerforth

Da Vinci Code author 5 Brown (Dan)

davit 5 crane

dawdle 3 lag 4 idle, laze, loaf, loll 5 dally, delay, tarry 6 diddle, linger, loiter, lounge 8 lollygag 10 dillydally

dawn 4 morn 5 sunup 6 aurora 7 morning, sunrise 8 cockcrow, daybreak, daylight 9 beginning 10 first light *goddess:* 3 Eos 6 Aurora

day *abbreviation:* 3 Fri, Mon, Sat, Sun, Thu, Tue, Wed 4 Thur, Tues 5 Thurs *before:* 3 eve *church calendar:* 5 feria *French:* 4 jour *German:* 3 Tag *holy:* 5 feast *hour:* 4 noon *Latin:* 4 dies *Spanish:* 3 día

daybreak 4 dawn, morn 5 sunup 6 aurora 7 dawning, morning, sunrise 8 cockcrow, daylight

daydream 4 muse 5 fancy 6 vision 7 fantasy, reverie 8 phantasy 9 fantasize 10 woolgather 13 woolgathering

daystar 3 Sol, sun 5 Venus 7 phoebus

daze 3 fog 4 haze, stun 5 amaze, blind 6 dazzle, stupor, trance 7 astound, confuse, stupefy 8 astonish, bedazzle, befuddle, confound 9 dumbfound

dazed 5 woozy 6 groggy, punchy 7 dazzled, stunned 8 confused 9 stupefied 10 punch-drunk

___ **d'Azur** 4 Côte

dazzle 5 amaze, blind, éclat, glitz, shine 7 impress 8 astonish, bewilder, confound, outshine 9 overpower

dazzling 6 flashy, garish 7 radiant 8 splendid, stunning 9 brilliant 11 confounding, resplendent 12 overpowering

deacon 6 clergy, cleric, layman 8 reverend 9 churchman

dead 4 cold, gone, late 5 passé, slain, stiff 6 buried, fallen 7 defunct, done for, expired, extinct 8 deceased, departed, lifeless 9 senseless 10 corpselike 11 unconscious 12 extinguished

deadbeat 3 bum 5 idler 6 debtor, loafer, slouch 7 lounger, shirker, slacker 10 delinquent, malingerer

dead duck 5 goner 8 casualty, fatality

deaden 4 dull, kill, mute, numb, stun 5 blunt, quiet 6 benumb, dampen, lessen, muffle, obtund, reduce, stifle 7 smother, stupefy 8 suppress 11 anesthetize, desensitize

dead end 4 halt, stop 6 pocket, unruly 7 impasse 8 cul-de-sac, standoff 9 stalemate, terminate 10 blind alley, bottleneck, standstill

deadened 4 numb 6 asleep, dulled, killed, numbed 7 blunted 8 benumbed, impaired 12 anesthetized

deadeye 5 block 8 marksman 12 sharpshooter

deadfall 4 trap 7 springe 9 booby trap, mousetrap

deadliness 8 fatality 9 lethality, mortality

deadlock 3 tie 4 draw 7 impasse 8 standoff, stoppage 9 checkmate, stalemate 10 standstill

deadly 5 fatal, toxic 6 lethal, mortal 7 capital, killing 8 lethally, unerring 10 implacable 11 destructive 12 pestilential

deadpan 5 blank, empty 6 vacant 9 impassive 10 poker-faced 11 inscrutable 12 inexpressive, unexpressive

Dead Souls author 5 Gogol (Nikolay)

dead to rights 9 red-handed

deadweight 4 load 6 weight

deal 4 dole, sale, sell 5 allot, serve, shake, share, trade, treat 6 barter, dicker, parcel 7 bargain, deliver, dish out, dole out, mete out, package, portion, traffic, wrestle 8 contract, disburse, dispense, share out 9 agreement, apportion, negotiate 10 administer, compromise, distribute, measure out 11 arrangement, transaction 13 understanding *great:* 4 gobs, heap, lots, tons 5 heaps, horde, loads, scads 6 oodles, plenty, stacks *out:* 8 disburse, dispense 9 apportion 10 administer, distribute *with:* 5 serve, treat 6 handle, regard 7 concern, involve

dealer 5 agent 6 broker, seller, trader, vendor 8 chandler, merchant, operator 9 tradesman 10 negotiator, trafficker 11 businessman, distributer, distributor 12 merchandiser *British:* 5 coper 6 draper, jobber, mercer 7 chapman

dealings 5 trade, truck 7 affairs, matters, traffic 8 business, commerce, concerns 11 intercourse 12 interactions, transactions, undertakings

dean 4 head 5 chief, doyen, elder 6 leader

dear 3 pet 4 fond, lamb, love 5 honey, loved, sweet 6 costly, doting, loving,

prized, scarce 7 beloved, darling, devoted, lovable, machree, querida, tootsie **8** favorite, precious, valuable **9** cherished, expensive, heartfelt, treasured **10** fair-haired, honeybunch, sweetheart **12** affectionate *French:* **4** cher **5** chère **6** cherie

dearth 4 lack, want **6** famine **7** absence, default, paucity **8** scarcity, shortage, sparsity **9** privation, scantness **10** deficiency, meagerness, scantiness

death 3 end **4** exit **6** demise, ending, expiry **7** decease, passing, quietus **8** casualty, curtains, fatality, necrosis, thanatos **9** bloodshed, departure **10** expiration, extinction, grim reaper **11** dissolution, termination **12** annihilation *after:* **10** posthumous *combining form:* **6** thanat **7** thanato *music:* **5** dirge, elegy **8** threnody *notice:* **4** obit **8** obituary **9** necrology *of tissue:* **8** gangrene *personification:* **10** grim reaper *put to:* **3** gas, hit, ice, zap **4** do in, hang, kill, slay **5** drown, lynch, snuff, waste **6** murder, poison, rub out **7** bump off, butcher, execute, smother, wipe out **8** blow away, dispatch, immolate, knock off, strangle, throttle **9** slaughter, suffocate **10** asphyxiate **11** assassinate, electrocute *rate:* **9** mortality *rites:* **7** funeral **8** exequies **9** interment, obsequies

deathless 7 abiding, eternal, lasting, undying **8** enduring, immortal **11** everlasting **12** imperishable

deathlike see DEATHLY

deathly 5 fatal **6** lethal, mortal **7** macabre, stygian **12** pestilential

debacle 4 rout **6** defeat, fiasco **7** breakup, failure **8** collapse, disaster **9** breakdown, cataclysm **10** disruption

debar 3 ban **4** stop **6** forbid, outlaw **7** exclude, prevent, rule out **8** preclude, prohibit **9** interdict

debark 4 land **6** alight, get off **11** decorticate

debase 3 mar **4** harm **5** lower, stain **6** damage, defile, demean, dilute, impair, reduce, weaken **7** cheapen, corrupt, degrade, devalue, pervert, pollute, vitiate **8** dishonor **9** undermine **10** adulterate, depreciate **11** contaminate

debatable 4 iffy, moot **7** dubious **8** arguable, doubtful **9** contested, uncertain, undecided **10** disputable, unresolved **11** problematic **12** questionable

debate 4 moot **5** argue, bandy, plead **7** contend, contest, discuss, dispute, quarrel, wrangle **8** argument, consider, forensic, question **9** dialectic, thrash

out **10** controvert, toss around **11** application, controversy, disputation **12** deliberation **13** argumentation *art of:* **9** forensics *expert:* **7** eristic *place for:* **5** forum

debauch 4 orgy, warp **6** seduce **7** corrupt, deprave, pervert, vitiate **9** bacchanal, brutalize **10** lead astray, saturnalia **11** bacchanalia

debauched 6 wanton **8** degraded, depraved, vitiated **9** corrupted, dissolute, libertine, perverted **10** degenerate, licentious

debilitate 3 sap **6** impair, weaken **7** cripple, disable **8** enfeeble **9** attenuate, undermine **10** devitalize

debilitated 4 weak **6** feeble, infirm, sapped **7** run-down, worn-out **8** weakened **9** enfeebled

debility 7 disease, malaise **8** weakness **9** infirmity **10** feebleness, infirmness, sickliness **11** decrepitude

Debir *kingdom:* **5** Eglon *slayer:* **6** Joshua

debit 4 bill, levy **6** charge **7** deficit **8** drawback **9** liability **11** encumbrance, shortcoming

debonair 5 suave **6** smooth, urbane **7** dashing, elegant **10** nonchalant **12** lighthearted

Deborah's husband 9 Lappidoth

debris 4 junk, slag **5** trash, waste **6** litter, refuse, rubble, spilth **7** garbage, rubbish **8** detritus, riffraff, wreckage *rock:* **5** scree, talus **8** colluvia **9** colluvium

debt 3 due, sin **6** arrear, red ink **7** arrears, default, deficit **8** mortgage, trespass **9** arrearage, liability **10** obligation **11** delinquency *acknowledgment:* **3** IOU **4** bill **5** check

debtless 7 solvent

debunk 6 expose, reveal, show up, unmask **7** lay bare, lay open, uncloak, uncover, undress **8** unshroud **9** demystify, discredit

Debussy's La ___ 3 Mer

debut 3 bow **5** entry **6** entree **7** come out, opening, present **8** entrance, premiere **9** beginning, coming out, introduce **12** introduction, presentation

decadence 5 decay **7** decline **10** degeneracy, regression **11** degradation **12** degeneration **13** deterioration

decadent 6 effete **7** debased **8** decaying, degraded, depraved **9** debauched, declining, dissolute **10** degenerate **13** self-indulgent

Decalogue verb 5 shalt

Decameron, The *author:* **9** Boccaccio (Giovanni) *heroine:* **8** Griselda

decamp 4 blow, bolt, exit, flee **5** leave, scram, split **6** beat it, begone, cut out, escape, get out, retire 7 abscond, make off, pull out, run away, skiddoo, take off, vamoose 8 clear out, withdraw 9 skedaddle

decant 4 pour 7 draw off, pour out 8 transfer

decanter 5 cruet, flask 6 bottle, carafe, flagon, vessel

decapitate 4 head 6 behead 9 decollate 10 guillotine

decapod 7 mollusc, mollusk 10 crustacean

decathlon champ 6 Jenner (Bruce), Morris (Glenn), O'Brien (Dan), Schenk (Christian), Sebrle (Roman), Toomey (Bill), Zmelik (Robert) 7 Doherty (Ken), Johnson (Rafer), Mathias (Bob) 8 Campbell (Milton), Thompson (Daley)

decay 3 rot 4 ruin, wane 5 spoil, waste 6 molder, wither 7 atrophy, crumble, decline, putrefy, rotting 8 putresce, spoilage 9 decompose 11 deteriorate 12 dilapidation, putrefaction 13 deterioration

decayed 6 putrid, rotted, rotten, ruined 7 carious, spoiled 8 decadent, moldered, overripe 9 putrefied 10 decomposed, degenerate

decease 3 die, end 4 fail, pass 5 death, dying, sleep 6 demise, depart, expire, finish, pass on, perish 7 passing, quietus, release, succumb 8 pass away 9 departure 10 expiration

deceased 4 body, dead, late 6 corpse 7 cadaver, carcass, expired, remains 8 departed, lifeless 9 inanimate

deceit 3 gyp 4 hoax, ruse, sham 5 fraud, guile, trick 6 humbug 7 swindle 8 artifice, flimflam, trickery 9 chicanery, deception, duplicity, imposture 10 dishonesty 13 double-dealing

deceitful 3 sly 4 wily 5 false, lying 6 crafty, sneaky, tricky 7 cunning, knavish, roguish 8 guileful, two-faced 9 deceptive, dishonest, underhand 10 mendacious 11 underhanded 13 double-dealing

deceive 3 con 4 bilk, dupe, fool, gull, hoax 5 bluff, cozen, lie to, trick 6 delude, humbug, palter, take in 7 beguile, mislead, sandbag, two-time 8 flimflam, hoodwink 9 bamboozle, four-flush 11 double-cross

deceiving 5 false 6 tricky 8 deluding, delusive, delusory, guileful, two-faced 9 beguiling, deceptive 10 fallacious, misleading 11 duplicitous, underhanded

decelerate 4 slow 5 delay 6 retard, slow up 7 slacken 8 slow down

decency 7 decorum, dignity, fitness, modesty 8 civility 9 etiquette, propriety 10 conformity, seemliness

decennium 6 decade

decent 4 fair, good 5 right 6 honest, modest, proper, seemly 7 correct, fitting, upright 8 adequate, all right 9 competent, honorable, tolerable 10 acceptable, conforming, sufficient 11 comme il faut, presentable, respectable 12 satisfactory

deception 3 gyp 4 gaff, hoax, hype, ruse, sham, wile 5 cheat, fraud, guile, put-on, trick 6 deceit, dupery, humbug, mirage 7 chicane, cunning, fallacy, fantasm, knavery, sophism 8 flimflam, illusion, intrigue, phantasm, trickery, trumpery, wiliness 9 casuistry, chicanery, duplicity, imposture, sophistry, treachery 10 artfulness, dishonesty, hanky-panky, subterfuge 11 indirection 12 speciousness, spuriousness 13 double-dealing

deceptive 5 false, phony 6 tricky 8 deluding, delusory, illusory, specious 9 beguiling, deceitful, deceiving 10 fallacious, misleading

decide 3 opt 4 rule, will 5 judge 6 settle 7 adjudge, resolve 8 conclude 9 determine 10 adjudicate

decided 3 set 4 firm 5 fixed 6 intent 7 assured, certain, obvious, settled 8 definite, resolute, resolved 10 determined, pronounced 11 established, unequivocal

decimate 4 raze, ruin 5 wreck 7 abolish, destroy, wipe out 8 demolish, massacre 9 slaughter 10 annihilate, obliterate 11 exterminate

decipher 4 read 5 break, crack, solve 6 decode, reveal 7 decrypt, resolve, unravel 8 unriddle 9 figure out, interpret, puzzle out, translate 12 cryptanalyze

decision 4 fiat 6 choice, ruling 7 finding, resolve, verdict 8 firmness, judgment, sentence 9 selection 10 conclusion, resolution, settlement 13 determination
rabbinical: 9 responsum

decisive 3 set 7 crucial, settled 8 critical, resolute 10 conclusive, convincing, determined, imperative, peremptory 11 determining 12 unmistakable

deck 4 trim 5 adorn, array, dress, equip, floor, level, porch, prank 6 attire, blazon, clothe 7 apparel, appoint, furnish, garland, garnish, terrace 8 accouter, accoutre, beautify, decorate, emblazon, ornament, platform 9 embellish *chief:* 4 bos'n 9 boatswain *high:* 4 poop *lowest:* 5 orlop *out:* 5 array, fix up, slick, spiff,

tog up **6** clothe, doll up **7** dress up, gussy up **8** spruce up *part:* **7** scupper
deckhand 3 gob **4** jack, swab **6** sailor, seaman **7** jack-tar, rouster, swabbie **10** bluejacket
declaim 4 rant **5** mouth, orate, speak **6** recite **7** deliver, lecture **8** bloviate, harangue, perorate **9** hold forth
declamatory 5 tumid, windy, wordy **6** florid, turgid **7** aureate, flowery, fustian, orotund, pompous, ranting, verbose **8** sonorous **9** bombastic, highflown, overblown **10** euphuistic, oratorical, rhetorical **12** magniloquent **13** grandiloquent
declaration 5 edict **6** avowal, notice, report **7** promise **8** document, pleading **9** affidavit, manifesto, statement, testimony **10** confession, deposition, disclosure, expression, profession **11** affirmation, attestation **12** announcement, notification, proclamation **13** advertisement, pronouncement
declare 3 say, vow **4** aver, avow, tell, vent **5** claim, sound, state, swear, utter, voice **6** affirm, allege, assert, avouch, blazon, depone, depose, herald, insist, ordain, report, reveal **7** certify, confirm, deliver, divulge, express, profess, signify, testify **8** announce, disclose, indicate, maintain, manifest, proclaim, propound **9** advertise, broadcast, enunciate, predicate, pronounce **10** annunciate, asseverate, promulgate **11** come out with, disseminate *a saint:* **8** canonize *in cards:* **3** bid **4** meld *invalid:* **5** annul
declass 4 bump, bust **5** abase, lower **6** demote, reduce **7** degrade, set back **9** downgrade
déclassé 4 mean, poor **6** common, vulgar **7** ignoble, lowered **8** inferior, lowgrade, mediocre, middling **10** secondrate **11** second-class
declension 5 class, slope **7** decline, descent **8** downfall **9** downgrade **10** inflection **12** dégringolade **13** deterioration
declination 3 ebb **5** slant, slide **6** ebbing **7** refusal, incline **8** downturn **9** downgrade **10** deflection **12** dégringolade, turning aside **13** deterioration
decline 3 dip, ebb, jib, rot, sag, set **4** balk, dive, drop, fade, fail, fall, flag, loss, sink, slip, wane **5** abate, avoid, demur, droop, lapse, lower, say no, slide, slope, slump, spurn **6** ebbing, go down, recede, refuse, reject, renege, waning, weaken, worsen **7** abstain, atrophy, descend, descent, devolve, dismiss, drop-off, dwindle, failure, falloff, forbear, refrain, relapse, sell-off, sink-

age, subside **8** comedown, decrease, downfall, downturn, languish, lowering, turn down **9** backslide, decadence, downgrade, downslide, downswing, downtrend, reprobate, repudiate, weakening **10** degeneracy, degenerate, depression, devolution, disapprove, falling off **11** backsliding, deteriorate **12** degeneration, dégringolade **13** deterioration
declivitous 5 steep **6** sloped **7** pitched, sloping **8** inclined **9** inclining **10** descending
declivity 3 dip **4** drop, fall **5** slope **7** decline, descent **8** downturn, gradient **9** downgrade **11** inclination
decode see DECIPHER
decollate 4 head, kill **6** behead **10** decapitate, guillotine
decolor 6 blanch, bleach, blench, whiten **7** wash out **11** achromatize
decompose 3 rot **5** decay, spoil, taint **6** fester, molder **7** analyze, break up, crumble, putrefy, resolve **8** dissolve, separate **9** anatomize, break down **12** disintegrate
decor 7 setting **8** backdrop, stage set **11** furnishings **13** ornamentation
decorate 4 do up, pink, trim **5** adorn, dress, frill **6** bedeck **7** bedizen, dress up, enhance, festoon, furnish, garnish **8** appliqué, beautify, emblazon, ornament **9** embellish *a border:* **6** purfle
decorated 6 ornate **7** adorned, honored, wrought **9** bemedaled, decked out, garnished **10** beribboned, ornamented **11** embellished
decoration 4 bays **5** award, badge, honor, kudos, medal **6** doodad, plaque **7** garnish, laurels **8** accolade, filigree, fretting, fretwork, frippery, furbelow, ornament, trimming, vignette **11** distinction *cutout:* **8** appliqué *furniture:* **4** buhl **6** boulle
decorous 3 fit **4** meet, prim **5** right **6** au fait, comely, decent, proper, seemly **7** correct, elegant, fitting **8** becoming, mannerly, suitable, tasteful **9** befitting, civilized, de rigueur, dignified **10** conforming **11** appropriate, respectable, well-behaved
decorously 5 fitly **7** rightly **8** decently, properly, suitably **9** correctly, fittingly **11** befittingly, respectably
decorousness 7 decency **8** civility **9** propriety, rightness **10** seemliness **11** correctness, orderliness **12** correctitude
decorticate 4 bare, bark, flay, hull, husk, pare, peel, skin **5** scale, scalp, shell, shuck, strip **6** denude **7** lay bare, pull off
decorum 5 order **7** decency, dignity, fit-

ness, modesty, protocol 9 etiquette, propriety 10 properness, seemliness 11 correctness, orderliness 12 correctitude

decoy 4 bait, fake, lure 5 plant, shill, tempt 6 allure, capper, delude, entice, lead on, pigeon, seduce 7 deceive, mislead 8 inveigle 10 red herring

decrease 3 cut, ebb 4 bate, drop, ease, fall, loss, wane 5 allay, lower 6 lessen, reduce, shrink 7 abridge, curtail, cut back, cutback, cut down, decline, die down, drop off, dwindle, fall off, lighten, shorten, slacken, subside 8 diminish, downturn, moderate, rollback, taper off 9 abatement, alleviate, reduction 10 abbreviate, depreciate, diminution, falling off

decree 4 fiat, rule 5 canon, edict, enact, judge, order, ukase 6 behest, charge, dictum, impose, ordain, ruling 7 adjudge, appoint, bidding, command, declare, dictate, lay down, mandate, precept, statute 8 judgment, proclaim, sentence 9 directive, judgement, ordinance, prescribe, prescript, pronounce 10 adjudicate, injunction, regulation 11 declaration 12 adjudication, announcement, proclamation, promulgation 13 pronouncement *Muslim:* 5 fatwa

decrepit 4 aged, weak, worn 5 frail, seedy, tacky 6 creaky, feeble, infirm, senile, shabby, wasted, weakly 7 fragile, run-down, worn-out 8 battered, impaired, weakened 10 bedraggled, broken-down, down-at-heel, ramshackle 11 dilapidated

decrepitude 4 ruin 5 decay 7 frailty, wasting 8 collapse, debility, weakness 9 disrepair, infirmity 10 exhaustion, feebleness, infirmness 12 dilapidation, enfeeblement 13 deterioration

decretal 4 fiat, writ 5 edict, order, ukase 6 assize, dictum, letter, ruling 7 dictate 8 decision, judgment 11 declaration 13 pronouncement

decry 3 boo 4 bash, slam, slur 5 abuse 6 berate, malign, vilify 7 asperse, censure, condemn, degrade, devalue, put down 8 bad-mouth, belittle, denounce, derogate, reproach 9 criticize, deprecate, discredit, disparage, dispraise, reprehend, reprobate 10 depreciate, disapprove 11 rail against

decrypt see DECIPHER

decumbent 4 flat 5 prone 6 supine 9 lying down, prostrate, reclining 10 horizontal

decussate 5 cross 8 crosscut 9 intersect 10 crisscross, intercross

dedicate 3 vow 5 bless 6 commit, devote, hallow, pledge 7 address 8 inscribe, restrict, set apart 10 consecrate

deduce 5 infer, judge, trace 6 derive, evolve, gather, reason, reckon 7 discern, make out, surmise 8 conclude 9 figure out

deduct 4 bate 5 abate, infer, judge 6 gather, remove 7 make out, take off, take out 8 conclude, knock off, perceive, subtract, take away

deduction 3 cut 8 discount, illation, judgment, sequitur, write-off 9 abatement, inference, reasoning 10 conclusion 11 subtraction

deductive 7 a priori 8 dogmatic, illative, provable, reasoned 9 derivable, inferable 10 consequent 11 inferential 13 ratiocinative

deed 3 act 4 cede, fact, feat, pact 5 doing, title 6 action, assign, convey, escrow, remise 7 charter, exploit 8 alienate, contract, covenant, make over, sign over, transfer 9 adventure 10 conveyance, enterprise 11 achievement, performance, tour de force *brutal:* 8 atrocity *evil:* 3 sin 11 malefaction *good:* 7 mitzvah

deem 4 feel, hold 5 judge, think 7 account, adjudge, believe 8 consider

de-emphasize 8 downplay, minimize, play down 9 gloss over, soft-pedal, underplay 13 underestimate

deep 3 low 4 bass, rapt, sunk 5 abyss, grave, ocean 6 occult, orphic, secret 7 abyssal, obscure 8 abstruse, esoteric, hermetic, profound 9 engrossed, recondite 10 bottomless, fathomless, mysterious *combining form:* 5 bathy

deepen 6 darken, worsen 7 enhance, enlarge, magnify, thicken 8 heighten 9 aggravate, intensify 10 strengthen

deepness 5 abyss 9 intensity 10 profundity

deep-seated 6 inborn, inbred, innate 7 settled 8 inherent, lifelong, profound, stubborn 9 confirmed, ingrained, intrinsic 10 congenital, entrenched, indwelling, inveterate 11 established 12 long-standing 13 bred-in-the-bone, dyed-in-the-wool, thoroughgoing

deep-six 4 dump, toss 5 chuck, scrap 6 unload 7 discard 8 jettison 9 eliminate

deep water 7 trouble 8 distress 10 difficulty

deer 3 elk, roe 4 buck, musk, stag 5 moose 6 wapiti 7 caribou, venison *Asian:* 4 axis 6 sambar 7 muntjac *British:* 4 hart *female:* 3 doe 4 hind *Japanese:* 4 sika *male:* 4 buck, hart, stag 7 roebuck *meat:* 5 jerky 7 venison *path:*

3 run 5 trail *red:* 7 brocket *relating to:*
7 cervine *track:* 4 slot 5 spoor *young:*
3 kid 4 fawn
Deerslayer (The) *author:* 6 Cooper
(James Fenimore) *character:* 5 Harry
(Hurry) 6 Hutter (Thomas), Judith
(Hutter) 11 Natty Bumppo 12 Chingachgook
deface 3 mar 4 harm, ruin 6 damage,
deform, impair, injure 9 disfigure, vandalize
de facto 6 actual, really 8 actually, existing
defalcation 7 default, failing, failure
10 embezzling, inadequacy, negligence
12 embezzlement
defamation 5 libel, smear 7 calumny,
obloquy, slander 10 backbiting 11 traducement 12 backstabbing 13 disparagement
defamatory 8 libelous 9 maligning, traducing, vilifying 10 backbiting, calumnious, slanderous 11 denigrating
defame 5 abase, libel, smear 6 malign,
vilify 7 asperse, blacken, blemish, slander, traduce 8 dishonor 9 denigrate,
discredit 10 calumniate
default 4 fail 5 welsh 7 absence, exclude,
failure, forfeit, neglect 9 selection
defeasance 4 deed 6 defeat 9 overthrow
11 termination
defeat 3 tan 4 beat, best, down, drub,
edge, foil, lick, loss, rout, sink, undo,
whip, whup 5 crush, outdo, skunk,
swamp, upset, waste, whomp 6 outgun,
reduce, subdue, wallop 7 beating, conquer, destroy, failure, licking, mow
down, nose out, nullify, outplay, overrun, setback, shellac, trounce, wipe out
8 knock out, outfight, outflank, overcome, vanquish, waterloo 9 frustrate,
overpower, overthrow, overtrump, subjugate, thrashing, trouncing 10 obliterate 11 shellacking
defeatist 8 doomster 9 doomsayer,
Gloomy Gus, pessimist, worrywart
defect 3 bug 4 flaw, lack, vice, want
5 botch, error, fault 6 damage, dearth,
desert, foible, injury 7 blemish, default,
failing 8 drawback, weakness 9 birthmark, deformity 10 apostatize, deficiency 11 shortcoming 12 imperfection,
tergiversate *timber:* 4 knot *visual:*
6 myopia, squint 9 amblyopia, hyper-
opia 10 presbyopia, strabismus
defection 8 apostasy 9 desertion, forsaking, recreancy 10 disloyalty 11 abandonment
defective 5 amiss 6 broken, faulty,
flawed 7 damaged, lacking, unsound,
wanting 8 impaired 9 corrupted, defi-

cient, imperfect 10 inaccurate, inadequate, incomplete 12 insufficient
defector 5 Judas 7 traitor 8 apostate,
quisling, recreant, renegade, turncoat
9 turnabout 13 double-crosser
defend 4 back, hold, save 5 argue, cover,
guard 6 screen, secure, shield, uphold
7 contend, justify, protect, support
8 advocate, champion, maintain, plead
for, preserve 9 safeguard
defendable see DEFENSIBLE
defendant 7 accused, libelee 8 libellee
defender 7 paladin, tribune 8 advocate,
champion, guardian 9 protector
11 white knight
defense 4 fort, ward 5 aegis, alibi,
armor, guard 6 excuse, sconce, shield
7 bulwark, rampart, shelter 8 apologia,
armament, fastness, fortress, muni-
ment, security 9 safeguard 10 protection, stronghold 11 exculpation, explanation 13 justification *organization:*
4 NATO 5 NORAD, SEATO
10 Warsaw Pact
defenseless 4 open 7 exposed, unarmed
8 helpless, wide open 9 unguarded
10 vulnerable 11 unprotected
defensible 5 valid 7 tenable 8 passable
9 excusable, plausible 10 condonable,
reasonable 11 justifiable
defer 3 bow 4 stay, wait 5 delay, remit,
stall, table, yield 6 accede, hold up, put
off, shelve, submit 7 hold off, lay over,
put over, suspend 8 hold over, postpone, prorogue 9 acquiesce 13 procrastinate
deference 5 honor 6 esteem, homage,
regard 7 respect 8 courtesy 9 obeisance
11 recognition
deferential 8 obliging 9 disarming,
regardful 10 respectful 11 complaisant
defiance 4 dare 5 moxie 7 bravado
8 audacity, contempt 9 challenge, contumacy, impudence, insolence 10 brazenness, effrontery 12 contrariness,
stubbornness
defiant 4 bold 5 brash, gutsy, sassy,
saucy 6 brazen, cheeky, daring 8 arrogant, impudent, insolent 9 audacious,
obstinate, resistant 10 refractory
12 recalcitrant
deficiency 4 flaw, lack, want 5 fault,
minus 6 dearth 7 absence, blemish,
demerit, failing, failure, paucity
8 scarcity, shortage, weakness 9 privation 10 inadequacy, scantiness 11 defalcation, shortcoming 12 imperfection
mental: 6 idiocy 7 amentia
deficient 3 shy 5 minus, scant, short
6 faulty, flawed, meager, meagre,
measly, scanty, scarce 7 failing, lacking,

unsound, wanting 8 exiguous, impaired 9 defective, imperfect 10 inadequate, incomplete

deficit 4 lack, loss 6 red ink 8 shortage 10 impairment, inadequacy 12 disadvantage 13 insufficiency

defile 3 tar 4 foul, pass, rape, soil 5 dirty, gorge, march, shame, smear, spoil, stain, sully, taint 6 befoul, debase, ravish 7 besmear, corrupt, pollute, profane, tarnish, violate 8 deflower, dishonor 9 desecrate 11 contaminate

defiled 5 raped 6 impure 7 stained, unclean 8 profaned, polluted, ravished, violated 9 corrupted 10 deflowered, desecrated 12 contaminated

define 3 fix, hem, rim, set 4 edge 5 limit 6 assign, border, detail 7 clarify, delimit, lay down, mark off, mark out, outline, specify 9 delineate, demarcate, determine, establish 11 distinguish 12 characterize

definite 3 set 4 sure 5 clear, final, fixed, sharp, solid 7 certain, decided, express, precise, settled 8 clear-cut, distinct, explicit, specific 10 conclusive, pronounced 11 unambiguous, unequivocal 12 unmistakable

definiteness 8 accuracy, sureness 9 certainty, certitude, exactness, precision 10 exactitude

definitive 5 final 7 express 8 clear-cut, complete, explicit, settling, specific, ultimate 10 concluding, conclusive, exhaustive 11 categorical, determining, unambiguous 13 authoritative

deflate 4 dash 6 humble, reduce, shrink 7 devalue, put down 8 contract, ridicule 9 humiliate, shoot down

deflect 5 avert, parry 6 divert 7 deviate, diverge, hold off 9 turn aside

deflection 3 yaw 4 bend, tack, turn, veer 5 carom, curve, shift 6 double, swerve 7 bending, rebound, turning, veering 8 swerving 9 departure, deviation, diversion 10 divergence

deflower 4 rape 5 spoil 6 defile, ravish 7 despoil, violate 9 desecrate

Defoe, Daniel *character:* 6 Crusoe (Robinson), Friday, Roxana 12 Moll Flanders

deform 4 warp 5 spoil 6 deface 7 contort, distort 8 misshape 9 disfigure

deformed 4 awry, bent 5 askew, bowed 6 warped 7 buckled, crooked 8 crippled 9 contorted, misshapen, unshapely

deformity 4 flaw 6 defect 7 blemish 11 abnormality 12 imperfection, irregularity, malformation 13 disfigurement

___ **de France** 3 Île

defraud 3 con, gyp 4 bilk, dupe, rook,

scam 5 cheat, cozen, mulct, trick 6 fleece, rip off 7 swindle 8 flimflam 9 bamboozle

deft 3 apt 4 able 5 adept, agile, handy 6 adroit, clever 7 skilled 8 dextrous, skillful 9 dexterous

deftness 5 knack, skill 7 address, prowess 8 facility 9 adeptness, dexterity 10 capability

defunct 4 cold, dead, late 5 kaput 7 extinct 8 deceased, departed, lifeless, vanished

defy 4 dare, face, gibe, jeer, mock 5 beard, brave, flout, stump 6 resist 7 affront, outdare, outface 8 confront 9 challenge, disregard, withstand

dégagé 6 breezy, casual 7 relaxed, unfussy 8 informal 9 easygoing 10 nonchalant, unreserved 13 unconstrained

degeneracy see DEGENERATION

degenerate 4 sink 6 rotten, sunken, worsen 7 corrupt, debased, decayed, decline, descend, immoral, pervert, vicious, vitiate 8 decadent, degraded, depraved 9 backslide, dissolute 11 deteriorate

degeneration 7 atrophy, decline 8 downfall, lowering 9 decadence, depravity, downgrade 10 debasement, perversion, regression 11 degradation 12 dégringolade 13 deterioration

degradation 4 fall 7 decline, descent 8 demotion 9 abasement, decadence, depravity, downgrade, reduction 10 corruption, debasement, degeneracy, perversion 11 downgrading 12 degeneration

degrade 4 bump, bust 5 abase, break, decry, lower 6 debase, demean, demote, impair, lessen, reduce 7 corrupt, declass, pervert, put down 8 belittle, cast down, derogate, diminish 9 decompose, discredit, disparage, downgrade, humiliate

degree 3 peg 4 heat, rank, rate, rung, step, term, tier 5 grade, honor, notch, order, pitch, point, ratio, scale, shade, stage, stair 6 amount, extent, status 7 measure, station 8 standing 9 dimension, intensity, magnitude 10 proportion *academic:* 3 BFA, BSc, DDS, LLB, LLD, LLM, MBA, MFA, MSc, PhD 5 MPhil 7 master's 9 bachelor's, doctorate *highest:* 8 cum laude 13 magna cum laude, summa cum laude *of combining power:* 7 valence *of height:* 5 grade *of importance:* 7 caliber, calibre *of outward slope:* 5 splay *seeker:* 9 candidate *slight:* 4 hair *utmost:* 4 acme

dégringolade see DEGENERATION

___ **de guerre** 3 nom

dehydrate 3 dry **4** sear **5** parch **9** desiccate, exsiccate

Deianira *brother:* **8** Meleager *father:* **6** Oeneus *husband:* **8** Heracles, Hercules *mother:* **7** Althaea *victim:* **8** Heracles, Hercules

deific 5 godly **6** divine **7** godlike

deification 8 idolatry **10** apotheosis, glorifying **13** glorification

deify 5 exalt **7** glorify, idolize, worship **8** sanctify, venerate **11** apotheosize

deign 5 stoop **7** descend **9** vouchsafe **10** condescend

Deiphobus *brother:* **5** Paris **6** Hector *father:* **5** Priam *mother:* **6** Hecuba *wife:* **5** Helen

Deirdre *beloved:* **5** Noisi *father:* **5** Felim

deity 3 god **4** Lord **7** goddess, godhead, godhood **8** Almighty, divinity **12** supreme being (see also at GREEK; HINDU; NORSE; ROMAN)

deject 5 chill, cloud, daunt **6** dampen, dismay **7** depress **8** dispirit **9** disparage **10** demoralize, discourage, dishearten

dejected 3 low, sad **4** blue, down, glum, sunk **6** gloomy, morose, somber, sombre **7** doleful, hangdog, humbled, unhappy **8** downcast, wretched **9** cheerless, depressed, woebegone **10** despondent, spiritless **11** crestfallen, downhearted **12** disconsolate, disheartened

dejection 5 dumps, gloom **7** despair, sadness **10** melancholy **11** despondency, unhappiness **12** mournfulness

Delaware *capital:* **5** Dover *city:* **10** Wilmington *nickname:* **5** First (State) **7** Diamond (State) *state bird:* **14** blue hen chicken *state flower:* **12** peach blossom *state tree:* **13** American holly

delay 3 lag **4** drag, hold, slow, stay, wait **5** dally, defer, stall, tarry, trail **6** dawdle, detain, hang up, hinder, holdup, impede, linger, loiter, put off, retard, slow up **7** bog down, hold off, respite, set back, slacken, suspend **8** hesitate, hold over, postpone, prorogue, reprieve, slow down **10** dillydally, moratorium, suspension **13** procrastinate

delaying 8 dawdling, dilatory **10** postponing, putting off

delectable 5 tasty, yummy **6** choice, savory **8** charming, heavenly, luscious, pleasing **9** ambrosial, delicious, enjoyable, exquisite, toothsome **10** delightful, enchanting **11** scrumptious **13** mouthwatering

delectation 3 fun, joy **4** zest **5** gusto **6** relish **7** delight **8** gladness, pleasure **9** enjoyment

delegate 4 name, send **5** agent, envoy,

proxy **6** assign, depute, deputy, legate **7** appoint, consign, entrust **8** deputize, emissary, transfer **9** authorize, catchpole, designate, spokesman **10** commission, mouthpiece, procurator

delete 4 drop, omit, x out **5** erase, purge **6** cancel, censor, cut out, efface, excise, remove **7** blot out, destroy, expunge, take out, wipe out **8** black out, cross out **9** eliminate, eradicate, strike out **10** blue-pencil, obliterate

deleterious 3 bad **6** nocent **7** baneful, harmful, hurtful, nocuous, noxious, ruinous **8** damaging **9** injurious **10** pernicious **11** destructive, detrimental, mischievous, prejudicial

deletion 7 erasure, voiding **9** canceling **10** deficiency **11** elimination **12** cancellation

deliberate 4 chaw, cool, muse, pore, slow **5** chary, meant, study, think, weigh **6** chew on, ponder, reason **7** careful, heedful, planned, reflect, studied, willful, willing, witting **8** cautious, cogitate, consider, intended, measured, meditate, mull over, ruminate, talk over **9** cerebrate, conscious, unhurried **10** calculated, considered, purposeful, thought-out **11** circumspect, intentional **12** premeditated

deliberately 9 knowingly, on purpose, purposely, willfully, wittingly **11** consciously **12** purposefully **13** intentionally

deliberation 5 study **6** debate **7** thought **10** conference, discussion, reflection **13** consideration

Delibes, Léo *ballet:* **6** Sylvia **8** Coppélia, La Source *opera:* **5** Lakmé

delicacy 5 goody, treat **6** dainty, luxury, morsel, nicety, tidbit **7** frailty **8** kickshaw, fineness **9** fragility, precision **10** daintiness, difficulty, indulgence, stickiness **11** awkwardness **12** ticklishness

delicate 4 fine, lacy, weak **5** frail **6** choice, dainty, flimsy, petite, queasy, sickly, slight, subtle, tender, touchy, tricky **7** elegant, fragile, refined, tactful, tenuous **8** ethereal, feathery, finespun, gossamer, graceful, pleasing, ticklish **9** exquisite, sensitive, squeamish **10** precarious

delicatessen 11 charcuterie

delicious 5 tasty, yummy **6** choice, divine, savory **8** heavenly, luscious **9** ambrosial, exquisite, toothsome **10** delectable, delightful **11** scrumptious **13** mouthwatering

delight 3 joy **4** glee **5** amuse, bliss, charm, enjoy, exult, glory, mirth, revel

6 divert, please, regale, relish 7 ecstasy, enchant, gladden, gratify, jollity, rapture, rejoice 8 enravish, entrance, fruition, hilarity, pleasure 9 delectate, enjoyment, enrapture, entertain 11 delectation *in:* 4 love 5 adore, enjoy, savor 6 admire, relish 7 cherish 10 appreciate

delighted 4 glad 5 happy 6 joyful 8 ecstatic, euphoric

delightful 5 yummy 6 dreamy, lovely 8 charming, heavenly, luscious, pleasant, pleasing 9 congenial, enjoyable 10 delectable, enchanting, satisfying 11 captivating, fascinating, pleasurable, scrumptious 12 entertaining

Delilah's victim 6 Samson

DeLillo novel 5 Libra, Mao II 10 Underworld, White Noise

delimit 3 bar 5 bound, hem in 6 demark, define 7 confine, enclose 8 restrict 9 demarcate, determine 12 circumscribe

delineate 3 map 4 etch, limn 5 chart, image, trace 6 define, depict, detail, render 7 outline, picture, portray 8 describe, spell out 9 elucidate, interpret, represent 10 illustrate

delineation 5 draft, story 6 report 7 account, contour, drawing, outline, picture, profile 9 depiction, rendering 11 presentment

delinquency 4 debt 5 crime, fault, lapse 7 default, failure, misdeed, neglect, offense 8 omission 9 oversight 10 misconduct, nonpayment, wrongdoing 11 dereliction, misbehavior

delinquent 3 lax 5 slack 6 debtor 7 overdue 8 careless, offender 9 defaulter, in arrears, negligent 10 behindhand, neglectful

deliquesce 3 rot, run 4 flux, fuse, melt, thaw 5 decay 6 render, soften 7 liquefy, putrefy 8 dissolve, fluidize 9 decompose, disappear, waste away 12 disintegrate

delirious 3 mad 4 wild 5 crazy 6 crazed, insane, raving 7 frantic, lunatic 8 confused, demented, deranged, ecstatic, frenetic, frenzied, rambling 9 rapturous 10 bewildered, corybantic, distracted, irrational 11 lightheaded, overexcited, overwrought

delirium 5 furor, mania 6 fervor, frenzy 7 ecstasy, jimjams, rapture, seizure 8 dementia, hysteria 13 hallucination

delirium ___ 7 tremens

deliver 4 bear, deal, feed, find, give, hand, save, send, ship, sing, take 5 bring, serve, speak, state, throw, utter 6 convey, redeem, rescue, strike, sup-

ply 7 consign, present, produce, provide, set free, release 8 hand over, liberate, turn over 9 pronounce, surrender 10 bring forth, emancipate 11 come out with, come through

deliverance 6 rescue 7 freeing, opinion, release, verdict 8 decision 9 acquittal, discharge, salvation 10 absolution, liberation

Deliverance author 6 Dickey (James)

delivery 4 drop 5 birth, labor 6 rescue 7 address, bearing 8 birthing, shipment 9 elocution, rendition, salvation 10 childbirth, conveyance, liberation 11 consignment, parturition, transferral 12 childbearing, transmission

dell 4 dale, glen, vale 6 dingle, hollow, valley

Delphic 4 dark 5 vatic 6 arcane, hidden, mantic, mystic, occult, veiled 7 cryptic, obscure 8 auguring, divining, esoteric, mystical, oracular 9 ambiguous, enigmatic, equivocal, prophetic, recondite, sibylline, vaticinal 10 mystifying, portentous 11 prophesying, prophetical

delta 5 plain 6 letter, symbol 7 deposit 8 triangle 9 increment

delude 3 con 4 dupe, fool, gull, hoax 5 bluff, cozen, trick 6 betray, humbug, juggle, take in 7 beguile, deceive, mislead 8 flimflam, hoodwink 11 doublecross

deluge 4 drown, flood, swamp 6 drench, engulf 7 Niagara, torrent 8 cataract, downpour, drencher, flooding, inundate, overflow 9 cataclysm, overwhelm 10 cloudburst, outpouring, inundation

delusion 4 hoax, sham 5 dream, fancy, snare 6 mirage 7 chimera, fallacy, fantasy, figment, phantom, specter 8 daydream, phantasm 9 deception 10 apparition 11 ignis fatuus 13 hallucination

delusive 5 false 8 fanciful, illusory, specious 9 beguiling, deceiving, deceptive, imaginary 10 chimerical, fallacious, misleading

delusory see DELUSIVE

deluxe 4 lush, posh 5 grand, plush, ritzy, swank 6 choice, costly, swanky 7 elegant, opulent 8 luscious, splendid 9 expensive, exquisite, luxuriant, luxurious, sumptuous 10 first class

delve 3 dig, dip 4 mine 5 probe 6 dredge, fathom, hollow, quarry, search, shovel 7 inquire 8 excavate *into:* 4 sift 5 probe 7 explore 8 prospect 11 investigate

delving 6 asking 7 inquest, inquiry, probing 8 research 9 inquiring, searching

demagnetize 7 degauss

demagogue 6 leader 7 inciter 8 agitator, fomenter 9 firebrand 10 instigator 11 provocateur 12 rabble-rouser

demand 3 ask, use 4 call, need, urge, want 5 claim, crave, exact, force, order 6 compel, direct, expect, insist 7 call for, request, require 11 requirement, requisition

demanding 4 hard 5 pushy, tough 6 taxing, trying 7 exigent, onerous, weighty 8 exacting, forceful, rigorous 9 assertive, difficult, insistent, strenuous, stringent 10 aggressive, burdensome, oppressive 11 challenging

demarcate 5 bound, limit 6 define, set off 7 delimit, mark off, outline 8 separate, set apart 9 delineate, determine 11 distinguish 12 circumscribe 13 differentiate

demarcation 9 outlining 10 border line, separation 11 distinction 12 delimitation

démarche 4 plan, ploy, ruse 5 feint 6 action, device, gambit, scheme, tactic 7 protest 8 artifice, maneuver, petition 9 stratagem 10 initiative 11 contrivance, machination

demean 4 bear 5 abase, carry, decry, lower 6 acquit, behave, debase, deport, humble 7 comport, conduct, degrade, detract 8 bad-mouth, belittle 9 disparage, humiliate

demeanor 3 air 4 look, mien 6 aspect, manner 7 address, bearing, conduct 8 behavior, carriage, presence 10 deportment 11 comportment

demented 3 mad 5 crazy, loony, nutty, wacko 6 crazed, insane, psycho 7 lunatic, unsound 8 deranged, frenzied, maniacal 9 delirious 10 hysterical, unbalanced 12 psychopathic

___ de mer 3 mal

demerit 4 mark 5 fault, stain 6 defect 7 blemish, penalty 9 downgrade 10 deficiency, punishment 11 shortcoming 12 imperfection

demesne 5 field, realm 6 domain, estate, region, sphere 7 terrain 8 dominion, province 9 bailiwick, champaign, territory *house:* 5 manor

Demeter see CERES

demigod 4 diva, idol 8 superman 9 superstar

demise 3 die, end 4 drop, pass 5 death, dying, sleep 6 cash in, depart, ending, expire 7 decease, passing, quietus, release, silence, succumb 8 pass away 9 cessation, departure 10 expiration, extinction

demit 4 quit 6 bow out, give up, resign

8 abdicate, renounce, step down, withdraw

demiurgic 8 creative, original 9 formative, ingenious, inventive 10 innovative 11 originative 12 innovational

demobilize 7 break up, disband, dismiss, scatter 8 disperse, separate 9 discharge, disengage, muster out

democratic 7 popular 8 populist 10 self-ruling 11 egalitarian 13 self-governing

Democrats' symbol 6 donkey

démodé 5 dated, passé 7 antique, archaic 8 old-timey, outdated 9 out-of-date 12 old-fashioned

demoiselle 6 damsel, lassie, maiden 10 damselfish

demolish 4 raze, ruin 5 crush, level, smash, total, wrack, wreck 7 destroy, flatten, wipe out 8 decimate, tear down 9 finish off 10 annihilate, obliterate

demolition 6 razing 8 leveling, wrecking 10 bulldozing 11 destruction 12 annihilation

demolition bomb 11 blockbuster

demon 3 imp 5 devil, fiend, genie, ghoul, jinni, Satan 7 hellion, incubus 9 archfiend *Arabic:* 5 afrit 6 afreet *female:* 5 lamia 7 succuba, succubi (plural) 8 succubae (plural), succubus

demonic 6 wicked 7 satanic 8 devilish, diabolic, fiendish, infernal 9 possessed 10 diabolical

demonize 6 malign, revile, vilify 7 bedevil, censure, slander 8 denounce 9 diabolize

demonstrate 3 try 4 mark, show, test 5 prove, rally 7 confirm, display, exhibit, explain, make out, protest 8 evidence, manifest, proclaim, validate 9 determine, establish 10 illustrate 12 authenticate

demonstration 4 expo, show, test 5 march, proof, rally, trial 6 picket 7 display, protest 9 spectacle 10 exhibition, exposition, validation 12 presentation 13 corroboration, manifestation

demonstrative 4 open 8 effusive, outgoing, specific 9 emotional, expansive, exuberant, outspoken 10 outpouring, unreserved, validating 12 affectionate, unrestrained 13 unconstrained

demoralize 5 chill, daunt, shake, unman, upset 6 dampen, debase, deject, rattle, weaken 7 corrupt, debauch, deprave, unnerve, vitiate 8 dispirit, psych out 9 undermine 10 discourage, dishearten

Demosthenes 6 orator *oration:* 9 Philippic

demote 4 bump, bust 5 lower 6 reduce 7 declass, degrade 9 downgrade

demulcent 4 balm 5 jelly, salve

7 unguent 8 liniment, ointment, soothing 9 softening

demur 5 qualm 6 object, oppose, resist 7 dispute, protest 8 question 9 challenge, hesitancy, objection 10 hesitation, indecision, reluctance 11 compunction, remonstrate

demure 3 coy, shy 5 timid 6 modest 7 bashful 8 reserved, reticent, retiring 9 diffident 11 unassertive 12 self-effacing

demurral 7 protest 9 challenge, objection 12 remonstrance 13 remonstration

demurrer see DEMURRAL

den 4 base, cave, home, lair, nest, room 5 study 6 burrow, cavern, hollow 7 dayroom, hideout, sanctum 8 hideaway, playroom *rabbit:* 6 warren

denial 3 nay 6 heresy 7 refusal 8 disproof, negation, rebuttal 9 disavowal, rejection 10 abnegation, gainsaying, refutation 11 repudiation 12 renunciation

denigrate 5 decry, libel, smear, stain, sully 6 darken, defame, defile, impugn, malign, vilify 7 asperse, devalue, put down, slander, tarnish, traduce 8 belittle, dishonor, tear down 9 discredit, disparage 10 calumniate, scandalize

denims 5 jeans 8 overalls 9 blue jeans, dungarees

denizen 5 liver 6 native 7 dweller, habitué, haunter, resider 8 habitant, occupant, resident 9 indweller, inhabiter 10 frequenter, inhabitant

Denmark *capital:* 10 Copenhagen *city:* 5 Århus 6 Ålborg, Odense 11 Helsingborg 13 Frederiksberg *island:* 3 Fyn 7 Falster, Zealand 8 Bornholm 9 Sjaelland *monetary unit:* 5 krone *neighbor:* 6 Sweden 7 Germany *part of:* 11 Scandinavia *peninsula:* 7 Jutland *possession:* 9 Greenland 12 Faroe Islands 13 Faeroe Islands *sea:* 5 North 6 Baltic *strait:* 5 Lille, Store 9 Langeland

denominate 3 dub 4 call, name, term 5 label, style, title 7 baptize, entitle 8 christen 9 designate

denomination 4 cult, name, sect 5 creed, faith, style, title 6 church 8 category, cognomen, religion 9 communion 10 persuasion *religious:* 5 Amish 6 Mormon 7 Baptist 8 Lutheran, Moravian, Reformed 9 Adventist, Episcopal, Mennonite, Methodist, Unitarian 11 Pentecostal 12 Presbyterian, Universalist 13 Roman Catholic

denotation 4 name, sign 5 sense 6 import 7 meaning 10 indication, signifying 11 designation 13 signification, specification

denote 4 mark, mean, name, show 5 spell 6 import 7 add up to, betoken, express 8 announce, indicate 9 designate, represent

denouement 6 effect, result, upshot 7 outcome 10 conclusion 11 consequence, culmination

denounce 3 rap 4 skin 5 blame, blast, decry, knock 6 rebuke, scathe 7 censure, condemn, upbraid 8 derogate, reproach 9 castigate, criticize, dress down, excoriate, reprehend, reprobate 10 denunciate, vituperate 11 incriminate 12 anathematize

de novo 4 anew, over 5 again, newly 6 afresh 8 once more 9 over again 11 from scratch

dense 4 dull, dumb 5 close, heavy, solid, thick, tight 6 obtuse, opaque, stupid 7 compact, crammed, crowded, doltish, serried 9 fatheaded, jam-packed 10 numskulled 11 blockheaded, numbskulled, thickheaded 12 impenetrable

dent 4 bash, ding, flaw, nick 5 tooth 6 dimple, hollow 10 depression, impression

denticulate 6 ridged 7 dentate, notched, serrate, serried, toothed 8 saw-edged, sawtooth, serrated 10 saw-toothed

dentin 6 enamel

denude 4 bare 5 strip 6 divest 7 disrobe, uncover, undress 8 unclothe

denunciate see DENOUNCE

deny 5 cross, rebut 6 disown, forbid, negate, refuse, refute, reject, renege 7 disavow, gainsay 8 abnegate, disallow, disclaim, forswear, renounce, traverse, withhold 9 disaffirm 10 contradict, contravene

depart 3 die 4 exit, flee, pass, quit 5 leave, scram, split 6 begone, decamp, demise, desert, escape, expire, go away, move on, pass on, perish, skidoo 7 decease, deviate, go forth, move out, pull out, skiddoo, take off, vamoose 8 pass away, shove off, slip away, withdraw 9 skedaddle, take leave

departing 6 egress, exodus 7 good-bye 8 farewell 9 desertion 11 leave-taking, valedictory

department 5 arena 6 branch, domain, sphere 7 section 8 category, division, province 9 bailiwick, territory 11 subdivision

departure 4 exit 5 adieu, break, congé, going 6 egress, exodus, flight 7 leaving 8 farewell 9 deviation, diversion 10 aberration, decampment, deflection, divergence, embarkment, setting-out, withdrawal 11 embarkation, leave-taking *of a ship:* 6 sortie *point:* 7 outport

dependable 4 sure, true 5 loyal, solid, tried 6 secure, steady, trusty 7 certain, staunch 8 accurate, constant, faithful, reliable, surefire 9 authentic, steadfast, unfailing 11 responsible, trustworthy 12 tried and true 13 authoritative *Scottish:* 6 sicker

dependence 4 need 5 faith, habit, stock, trust 8 reliance 9 addiction 11 contingency, habituation

dependent 5 child 6 minion, vassal 7 reliant, relying 9 secondary 10 contingent, equivalent 11 conditional, subordinate

depend on 5 bet on, trust 6 bank on, hang on, look to, rely on, turn on 7 build on, count on, hinge on, stand on, swear by

depict 4 draw, limn, show 5 image, paint 6 relate, render, sketch 7 express, picture, portray 8 describe 9 delineate, represent 10 illustrate

depiction 5 image 6 sketch 7 drawing, picture 9 portrayal, rendering 11 delineation, portraiture, presentment 12 illustration, presentation

deplete 3 sap 4 milk 5 bleed, drain, eat up, empty, leech, use up 6 expend, lessen, reduce 7 consume, draw off, exhaust 8 decrease, diminish, draw down 9 undermine 10 run through

depleted 6 sapped, used up 7 drained, reduced 8 consumed, expended 9 exhausted, washed-out

deplorable 5 awful 6 rotten, woeful 8 dreadful, god-awful, grievous, terrible, wretched 9 execrable, miserable, sickening 10 calamitous, disastrous, lamentable 11 distressing, intolerable 12 contemptible, disreputable, heartrending 13 heartbreaking, reprehensible

deplore 3 rue 5 abhor, mourn 6 bemoan, bewail, grieve, lament, regret 7 condemn 8 denounce, object to 9 deprecate 10 disapprove

deploy 3 use 5 array 6 muster, unfold 7 arrange, display, dispose, marshal, utilize 8 position

___ de plume 3 nom

depone 5 state, swear 6 affirm, assert, attest 7 certify, confirm, declare, testify, warrant 11 corroborate 12 authenticate

deport 3 act 4 bear 5 carry, exile, expel 6 acquit, banish, behave, demean 7 conduct 8 displace, relegate 10 expatriate

deportee 5 exile 8 expellee

deportment 3 air, set 4 mien, port 6 aspect, manner 7 address, bearing, conduct, manners 8 behavior, carriage, demeanor, presence

depose 4 aver, avow, oust 5 state, swear 6 affirm, assert, avouch, remove, topple, unmake 7 declare, profess, testify, uncrown 8 dethrone, displace, throw out, unthrone 9 overthrow

deposit 3 lay 4 bank, drop, dump, fund, lees, pawn, save, stow 5 cache, chest, dregs, place, put by, stash, store 6 settle 7 consign, grounds, lay away 8 put aside, security, sediment, sock away 9 settlings 11 precipitate 13 precipitation *alluvial:* 5 delta *black:* 4 soot *calcium carbonate:* 10 stalactite, stalagmite *containing gold:* 6 placer *eggs:* 5 spawn *geologic:* 7 horizon *glacial:* 4 till 5 drift, esker 7 moraine *loam:* 5 loess *mineral:* 4 lode 10 concretion *muddy:* 6 sludge *sand:* 4 bank 5 beach *sedimentary:* 4 silt *skeletal:* 5 coral *stolen goods:* 5 fence *stream:* 8 alluvium, sediment *tooth:* 6 tartar

deposition 6 avowal 7 ousting, placing 9 affidavit, dismissal, testimony 10 testifying 11 attestation, declaration

depository 4 bank, dump, safe 5 attic, cache, depot, store, vault 7 archive, arsenal 8 magazine 9 warehouse 10 storehouse *for bones:* 7 ossuary

depot 4 dump 5 cache, store 6 armory, garage 7 arsenal, station 8 magazine, terminal, terminus 9 warehouse 10 depository, repository, storehouse 12 station house

deprave 4 warp 6 debase 7 corrupt, debauch, pervert, vitiate 9 brutalize 10 bastardize, bestialize, demoralize

depraved 3 bad, low 4 base, evil, ugly, vile 6 putrid, rotten, wanton, warped, wicked 7 bestial, corrupt, debased, immoral, twisted, vicious 8 degraded, perverse, vitiated 9 corrupted, debauched, miscreant, nefarious, perverted, reprobate 10 degenerate

depravity 4 vice 8 baseness 9 abasement, decadence 10 corruption, debasement, debauchery, degeneracy, immorality, perversion 12 degeneration

deprecate 7 frown on, put down 8 belittle, derogate, disfavor, object to, play down, pooh-pooh 9 disparage 10 disapprove 12 disapprove of

depreciate 4 drop, fall 5 abate, decry, erode, lower 6 lessen, reduce, slight 7 cheapen, devalue, put down 8 belittle, decrease, derogate, diminish, discount, mark down, write off 9 devaluate, disparage, downgrade, underrate 10 devalorize, undervalue 11 detract from

depreciation 8 discount **11** denigration **12** belittlement **13** disparagement
depreciative 9 slighting **10** derogatory, detracting, pejorative **11** disparaging, underrating **12** undervaluing
depredate 4 sack **5** waste **6** ravage **7** despoil, pillage, plunder **8** desolate, lay waste, prey upon, spoliate **9** desecrate, devastate, vandalize
depredation 4 sack **5** havoc **7** pillage, plunder, sacking **8** ravaging **9** marauding, ruination **10** spoliation **11** desecration, destruction, devastation **12** despoliation
depredator 6 looter, raider, vandal **7** forager, spoiler **8** marauder **9** plunderer **10** freebooter
depress 4 damp, dash, dent **5** chill, daunt, lower **6** dampen, deject, dismay, sadden **7** afflict, trouble **8** dispirit, enfeeble **9** disparage, weigh down **10** discourage, dishearten
depressed 3 low, sad **4** blue, down, glum, sunk **6** broody, gloomy, glumpy, lonely, somber **8** cast down, dejected, downcast **9** bummed out, flattened, woebegone **10** dispirited, lugubrious, melancholy, spiritless **11** crestfallen, downhearted, melancholic **12** disconsolate **13** disadvantaged
depressing 3 sad **5** bleak **6** dismal, dreary, gloomy, somber, sombre **7** joyless **8** funereal, mournful **9** saddening **10** melancholy, oppressive **11** melancholic **13** disheartening
depression 3 dip, low, pit, sag **4** bust, drop, funk, hole, sink, vale **5** basin, blues, dolor, dumps, ennui, gloom, scoop, slump **6** cavity, crater, hollow, pocket, valley **7** cyclone, decline, sadness, sinkage **8** downturn, sinkhole **9** concavity, dejection **10** desolation, melancholy **11** melancholia, unhappiness *anatomical:* **5** fossa, fovea **6** foveae (plural) *geographic:* **7** Qattara *in ridge:* **3** col *in snow:* **8** sitzmark *small:* **4** dent **6** dimple
depressive 4 blue, dour, glum **6** woeful **7** doleful **8** downbeat, downcast, mournful **9** miserable, woebegone **10** despondent, melancholy **11** lowspirited
deprivation 4 lack, loss **6** denial **7** forfeit, removal **10** forfeiture **11** bereavement, divestiture **13** dispossession
deprive 3 rob **5** strip **6** divest **8** disseise, disseize **10** disinherit, dispossess *of brilliancy:* **4** dull **6** deaden *of courage:* **7** unnerve *of sensation:* **6** benumb
depth 4 base, drop, gulf **5** abyss, chasm, gorge **7** lowness **10** profundity *measure:* **6** fathom *of water:* **5** draft **7** draught
depthless 7 cursory, shallow, sketchy **10** uncritical **11** superficial
Dept. of ___ **5** Labor, State **6** Energy **7** Defense, Justice **8** Commerce, Interior, Treasury **9** Education **11** Agriculture
deputize 4 name **6** assign **7** appoint, empower, warrant **8** delegate **9** authorize, designate **10** commission
deputy 4 aide **5** agent, proxy **6** backup, factor **8** delegate **9** assistant, catchpole, surrogate
derange 4 muss **5** craze, upset **6** madden, mess up **7** confuse, perturb, unhinge **8** confound, disarray, disorder, distract, unsettle **9** interrupt, unbalance **10** discompose **11** disorganize
deranged 3 mad **4** loco **5** crazy, wacko **6** crazed, insane, maniac **7** berserk, cracked, haywire, lunatic, unsound **8** demented, maniacal **9** disturbed **10** disordered, flipped out, unbalanced
derangement 4 mess **5** chaos, mania **6** lunacy, muddle **7** madness **8** dementia, disorder, insanity **9** confusion, unbalance **10** hodgepodge **11** distraction, disturbance, psychopathy
derby 3 hat **4** race **7** contest **9** horse race
derelict 4 bum **4** hobo, lorn **5** tramp **6** remiss, shabby **7** drifter, outcast, rundown, uncouth, vagrant **8** careless, deserted, vagabond **9** abandoned, negligent **10** neglectful **11** dilapidated **12** disregardful, undependable **13** irresponsible
dereliction 5 fault **7** default, failure, neglect **9** deviation, disregard, oversight **11** abandonment, delinquency, shortcoming
deride 3 rag, rap **4** gibe, jeer, jibe, lout, mock, quiz, razz, twit **5** fleer, rally, scoff, scout, sneer, taunt **6** dump on, insult **7** catcall **8** ridicule
de rigueur 5 right **6** au fait, decent, proper **7** correct **8** becoming, decorous, required **9** essential, mandatory, requisite **10** compulsory, obligatory, prescribed **11** comme il faut
derision 5 abuse, scorn **7** disdain, mockery, ribbing **8** contempt, raillery, ridicule, scoffing **9** contumely, invective
derisive 7 abusive, jeering, mocking **8** sardonic, scoffing, scornful, taunting **9** insulting, sarcastic **10** disdainful **12** contemptuous
derivable 7 a priori **9** deducible, deductive, traceable **10** obtainable **11** extractable **12** attributable, determinable
derivation 4 root **6** origin, source

7 descent 9 etymology 10 provenance, wellspring 11 origination, provenience
derivative 5 banal 7 spin-off 8 acquired, offshoot 9 by-product, imitative, outgrowth, secondary 10 descendant, unoriginal
derive 3 get 4 draw, flow, rise, stem, take 5 adapt, arise, educe, infer, issue, trace 6 deduce, deduct, evolve, gather, obtain 7 descend, emanate, extract, proceed, work out 8 arrive at, conclude 9 formulate, originate
dernier cri 3 fad 4 chic, rage 5 craze, vogue 8 last word
derogate 5 decry 6 berate, dump on, insult 7 put down 8 bad-mouth, belittle, diminish, minimize, write off 9 disparage, dispraise 10 depreciate 11 detract from
derogatory 5 snide 8 decrying, scornful, spiteful 9 degrading, demeaning, maligning, slighting 10 belittling, detracting, disdainful, pejorative 11 disparaging 12 contumelious, depreciative
derrick 5 hoist
derriere 3 bum 4 beam, butt, rear, rump, seat, tail 5 fanny 6 behind, bottom 7 rear end 8 backside, buttocks 9 posterior
derring-do 4 guts 5 nerve, pluck, spunk, valor 6 daring, mettle 7 bravado, bravery, bravura, courage 8 boldness 9 gallantry 12 fearlessness 13 dauntlessness
dervish 4 monk, Sufi 9 mendicant *in Arabian Nights:* 4 Agib *practice:* 7 dancing 8 whirling *wandering:* 5 fakir 8 calender
descant 4 sing 6 melody, remark, treble 7 comment, discuss, melisma, melodia, oration, soprano 9 discourse, expatiate 12 counterpoint
Descartes's axiom 13 cogito ergo sum
descend 4 dive, drop, fall, pass, sink 5 slide, stoop, swoop 6 alight, derive, go down, plunge, worsen 7 decline 8 come down, dismount 9 originate 10 degenerate, retrograde *by rope:* 6 rappel
descendant 4 heir 5 scion 7 progeny, spin-off 8 offshoot, relative 9 byproduct, offspring, outgrowth 10 derivative
descendants 4 seed 5 brood, heirs, issue, spawn 6 litter 7 progeny 8 children 9 offspring, posterity 11 progeniture
descent 3 dip 4 drop, fall 5 birth, blood, slide, slope 6 origin, plunge, tumble 7 decline, drop-off, incline, lineage, sinkage 8 ancestry, comedown, gradient, pedigree 9 declivity, downgrade 10 derivation, devolution, extraction *airplane:* 8 approach *parachute:* 4 jump 7 bailout
describe 4 limn 6 denote, depict, recite,

relate, render, report 7 explain, express, mark out, narrate, outline, picture, portray, recount 9 delineate, represent 10 illustrate 12 characterize
description 3 ilk 4 kind, sort, type 6 nature, report 7 account, picture, species 9 character, depiction, narrative, portrayal 10 recounting
descry 3 see 4 espy, spot 6 behold, detect, spy out, turn up 7 discern, find out, hit upon 8 discover, meet with, perceive 9 encounter, recognize
Desdemona *father:* 9 Brabantio *husband:* 7 Othello *slanderer:* 4 Iago *slayer:* 7 Othello
desecrate 4 sack 5 stain, sully, waste 6 befoul, debase, defile, ravage 7 corrupt, degrade, despoil, pillage, pollute, profane, violate 8 spoliate 9 depredate, devastate
desecration 5 abuse 7 impiety 9 blasphemy, sacrilege 10 debasement, defilement, spoliation 11 profanation 12 despoliation
desensitize 4 dull, numb 5 blunt 6 benumb, dampen, deaden, freeze, sedate 11 anesthetize
desert 4 flee, quit 5 leave, waste 6 barren, betray, decamp, defect, escape, maroon, strand 7 abandon, abscond, badland, forsake 8 renounce 9 repudiate, wasteland 10 apostatize, wilderness 12 tergiversate *African:* 5 Namib 6 Libyan, Sahara 7 Arabian 8 Kalahari *Arizona:* 7 Painted *Asian:* 4 Gobi, Thar 6 Syrian 7 Kara-Kum 8 Kyzyl Kum, Qizilkum 10 Great Sandy *basin bottom:* 5 playa *beast:* 5 camel 9 dromedary *California:* 5 Mohave, Mojave *Chilean:* 7 Atacama *clay:* 5 adobe *dweller:* 4 Arab 5 nomad 6 Berber, Libyan, Malian, Nubian 7 bedouin 8 Algerian, Egyptian, Maghrebi, Maghribi, Sudanese 11 Mauritanian *Egyptian:* 7 Arabian *fertile area:* 5 oases (plural), oasis *garb:* 3 aba *hallucination:* 6 mirage *Israeli:* 5 Negev *region:* 3 erg *Saudi Arabia:* 7 Al-Nafud, An Nafud *Sudan:* 6 Nubian *travel group:* 7 caravan *wind:* 7 sirocco
deserted 4 bare, lorn 6 barren, vacant 8 derelict, desolate, forsaken, solitary 9 abandoned, neglected 11 uninhabited
deserter 3 rat 4 AWOL 6 bolter 7 runaway 8 apostate, defector, fugitive, renegade, runagate, turncoat
desertion 7 perfidy 8 apostasy 9 defection, forsaking 11 abandonment, dereliction
deserts 3 due 6 reward 8 requital 9 reckoning 10 recompense 11 comeuppance

deserve 3 win **4** earn, gain, rate **5** merit **6** demand **7** justify, warrant
deserved 3 apt, due **4** just **5** right **7** fitting, merited **8** rightful, suitable **9** befitting **11** appropriate **13** rhadamanthine
deserving 3 due **6** worthy **8** laudable **9** admirable, estimable **10** creditable **11** commendable, meritorious, thankworthy **12** praiseworthy
desiccate 3 dry **5** dry up, parch, wizen **6** wither **7** shrivel **9** dehydrate **10** devitalize
desiderate 4 want, wish **5** covet, crave **6** desire **7** long for, wish for **8** yearn for
design 3 aim **4** cast, draw, form, mean, mind, plan, plot, will **5** chart, draft, frame, model, motif **6** create, device, devise, figure, intend, intent, invent, lay out, makeup, map out, motive, scheme, set out, sketch, tailor **7** arrange, diagram, drawing, execute, fashion, meaning, outline, pattern, prepare, project, propose, tracing **8** contrive, creation, game plan, intrigue, strategy, thinking **9** blueprint, construct, delineate, direction, formation, intention, invention **10** decoration, figuration **11** arrangement, composition **12** architecture, construction **book:** **8** vignette **carpet:** **3** gul **9** medallion **incised:** **8** intaglio **Indonesian:** **5** batik **inlaid:** **6** mosaic **intricate:** **9** arabesque **of squares:** **5** check **openwork:** **8** filigree **perforated:** **7** stencil **raised:** **8** repoussé **skin:** **6** tattoo **textile:** **8** polka dot **velvety:** **8** flocking
designate 3 dub, tap **4** call, name, pick, term **5** allot, elect, label, style, title **6** assign, choose, denote, depute, select **7** appoint, declare, earmark, reserve, signify, specify **8** allocate, christen, delegate, identify, set aside, stand for **9** apportion, stipulate **10** decide upon **11** appropriate **12** characterize
designation 4 name, sign **5** class, nomen, style, title **6** naming **8** cognomen, monicker **11** appellation
designed 7 devised, planned **8** intended, resolved **9** contrived, patterned **10** considered, deliberate, determined, thought-out **12** premeditated
designedly 9 expressly, knowingly, on purpose, purposely, willfully, wittingly **11** consciously, purposively **12** deliberately **13** intentionally
desirable 8 enviable, fetching **9** advisable, agreeable, preferred **10** attractive, beneficial **12** advantageous
desire 3 aim, yen **4** envy, eros, itch, lust, want, wish **5** covet, crave, fancy, go for, greed **6** pining, thirst **7** avarice, craving, long for, longing, passion **8** appetite, cupidity, petition, yearn for, yearning **9** eroticism, hankering, prurience, pruriency **10** aphrodisia, attraction, preference **11** inclination, lustfulness **13** concupiscence, lickerishness
desired 6 wanted **8** hoped-for **9** preferred, requested
desirous 6 greedy **7** athirst, craving, envious, longing, wishful, wishing **8** covetous, grasping **10** solicitous
desist 6 halt, quit, stop **5** cease, yield **7** forbear, hold off, refrain **8** knock off, leave off, surcease **11** discontinue
desistance 3 end **4** halt, stop **5** cease, close **6** ending, finish, period **8** stoppage, stopping **9** cessation **10** conclusion **11** termination
desk 5 booth, stand, table **7** counter, lectern, rolltop **8** lapboard **9** secretary **10** escritoire **adjunct:** **8** inkstand, standish **item:** **3** pad **7** blotter, inkwell **library:** **6** carrel
desolate 4 bare, lorn, sack **5** alone, bleak, drear, stark, waste **6** barren, devoid, dismal, dreary, gloomy, ravage **7** despoil, forlorn, joyless, pillage, plunder **8** dejected, derelict, deserted, desolate, downcast, forsaken, lay waste, lifeless, lonesome, solitary, spoliate **9** abandoned, cheerless, depredate, desecrate, destitute, devastate, sorrowful **10** despondent **11** dilapidated **12** inconsolable **13** disheartening
desolation 3 woe **4** ruin **5** gloom, grief, waste **6** misery, sorrow **7** anguish, despair, sadness **8** bareness **9** bleakness, dejection, wasteland **10** loneliness **11** abandonment, devastation **12** wretchedness
despair 6 give up **8** lose hope
despairing 7 anxious, doleful, forlorn **8** dejected, desolate, hopeless, wretched **9** depressed **10** despondent **11** downhearted **12** disconsolate **13** brokenhearted
desperado 6 bandit, gunman, outlaw **7** bandito, brigand, convict, ruffian **8** criminal **9** cutthroat **10** gunslinger, highwayman, lawbreaker
desperate 4 bold, dire, rash **5** acute, risky **6** daring, futile **7** crucial, forlorn, frantic, useless, violent **8** critical, headlong, hopeless, reckless, shocking **9** foolhardy, impetuous **10** despondent, frustrated, outrageous, scandalous **11** climacteric, precipitate **12** overpowering **13** irretrievable
desperation 5 agony **7** anguish, despair **8** distress **11** distraction **12** hopelessness, wretchedness

despicable 3 low 4 base, foul, grim, mean, ugly, vile 5 awful, cheap, gross, sorry 6 abject, scurvy, shabby, sordid 7 beastly, hateful, ignoble, pitiful 8 pitiable, shameful, wretched 9 degrading, loathsome 10 deplorable, detestable 11 disgraceful, ignominious 12 contemptible, disreputable 13 reprehensible

despise 4 hate, shun, snub 5 abhor, avoid, scorn, spurn 6 detest, loathe, reject 7 contemn 8 execrate 9 abominate

despised one 6 pariah 7 outcast

despisement 4 hate 5 scorn 6 hatred, malice 7 disdain, ill will 8 aversion, contempt, loathing 9 antipathy, contumely 10 abhorrence 11 detestation

despite 8 although 11 in the face of 12 regardless of

despiteful 4 evil, mean 5 catty 6 bitchy, horrid, malign, odious, wicked 7 baleful, baneful, hostile, vicious 8 vengeful 9 malicious, rancorous, repellent 10 despicable, malevolent

despoil 4 sack 5 blast, strip, waste, wreck 6 denude, devour, maraud, ravage 7 pillage, plunder 8 desolate, spoliate 9 depredate, desecrate, devastate, strip away, vandalize 10 wreak havoc

despoiler 6 looter, sacker, vandal 7 ravager, wrecker 8 marauder, pillager 9 plunderer, spoliator 10 depredator, freebooter

despond 4 fret, mope, wilt 5 brood, droop, worry 6 give up, sorrow 8 languish 9 dejection 12 hopelessness

despondency 5 blues, dumps, gloom 6 misery, sorrow 7 anguish, despair, sadness 8 glumness 9 dejection 10 depression, melancholy 11 desperation, unhappiness 12 hopelessness

despondent 3 low, sad 4 blue, down, glum 7 doleful, forlorn 8 cast down, dejected, downcast, grieving, hopeless, mourning 9 depressed, desperate, heartsick, heartsore, sorrowful, woebegone 10 dispairing, dispirited, melancholy 11 discouraged, downhearted 12 disconsolate, disheartened

despot 4 czar, duce, tsar, tzar 5 ruler 6 tyrant 7 autarch, emperor 8 autocrat, dictator 9 oppressor, strong man

despotic 8 absolute 9 arbitrary, autarchic, imperious, tyrannous 10 autocratic, monocratic, tyrannical 11 dictatorial 12 totalitarian

despotism 7 czarism, tsarism, tyranny, tzarism 8 autarchy 9 autocracy 10 absolutism, domination 12 dictatorship

desquamate 4 pare, peel 5 scale 7 peel off 8 flake off, scale off 9 exfoliate

dessert 3 ice, pie 4 cake, flan, fool, tart 5 Betty, bombe, crepe, crisp, fruit, grunt, halva, Jell-O, melba, s'more, sweet, torte 6 afters, blintz, Danish, éclair, fondue, frappe, gâteau, halvah, hermit, junket, kuchen, mousse, pastry, sorbet, sundae, trifle 7 brownie, cobbler, compote, custard, gelatin, parfait, pudding, sabayon, sherbet, soufflé, spumoni, strudel 8 ambrosia, Bismarck, crostata, flummery, ice cream, macaroon, meringue, napoleon, pandowdy, streusel, tiramisu, turnover 9 charlotte, cream puff, fruitcake, petit four, shortcake 10 blancmange, brown Betty, cheesecake, frangipane, icebox cake, zabaglione 11 baked Alaska, banana split, crème brûlée, gingerbread 12 hasty pudding, zuppa inglese *French:* 5 bombe 6 éclair, frappe, gâteau, mousse 7 parfait, sabayon 9 petit four 10 blancmange, frangipane *frozen:* 5 bombe 7 parfait, sherbet *German:* 6 kuchen 7 strudel *Italian:* 7 Fannoli, spumoni 8 tiramisu 10 zabaglione 12 zuppa inglese *Turkish:* 5 halva 6 halvah

destination 3 aim, end, use 6 object, target 7 purpose 8 terminus 9 objective 10 appointing

destine 4 fate 6 assign, direct, intend 8 dedicate, set aside 9 designate, determine, preordain 10 foreordain 12 predetermine

destiny 3 lot 4 doom, fate 5 karma 6 design, future, kismet, Moirai 7 fortune, portion 8 prospect 9 hereafter 12 circumstance

destitute 4 bare, poor, void 5 broke, empty, needy 6 bereft, devoid, ruined 7 drained, lacking 8 bankrupt, depleted, dirt poor, divested, indigent, strapped, stripped 9 deficient, exhausted, penurious 10 bankrupted, stonebroke 11 impecunious 12 impoverished

destitution 6 penury 7 poverty 9 indigence, privation

destroy 3 axe, zap 4 doom, down, kill, nuke, raze, ruin, sack, slay, undo 5 crush, erase, quash, quell, smash, total, trash, waste, wrack, wreck 6 finish, lay low, mangle, ravage, rubble, rub out 7 abolish, atomize, despoil, expunge, nullify, pillage, shatter, wipe out 8 decimate, demolish, dispatch, dynamite, lay waste, pull down, snuff out, stamp out, tear down 9 devastate, dismantle, eradicate, extirpate, liquidate, pulverize 10 annihilate, extinguish 11 exterminate

destroyer 4 bane, ruin 6 tin can, vandal 7 undoing, warship 8 downfall

destruction 4 loss, ruin 5 havoc 7 killing, sacking, undoing 8 downfall 9 ruination 10 extinction 11 devastation, liquidation 12 annihilation

destructive 7 baneful, harmful, ruinous 8 damaging 9 corrosive, injurious 10 shattering 11 deleterious, detrimental

desuetude 6 disuse 7 closure, neglect 9 cessation 11 abandonment

desultory 6 casual, chance, fitful, random, spotty 7 aimless, erratic, offhand, vagrant 8 shifting, slipshod, sporadic, wavering 9 haphazard, hit-or-miss, unplanned 10 capricious, digressive, disjointed 11 purposeless 12 unmethodical, unsystematic

detach 4 free, part, undo, wean 5 sever 6 cut off, remove, sunder 7 disjoin, divorce, release 8 separate, uncouple, withdraw 9 disengage 10 disconnect 12 disaffiliate

detached 5 alone, aloof, apart 6 remote 7 distant, neutral, removed, severed 8 abstract, isolated, separate, unbiased 9 incurious, withdrawn 10 impersonal 11 indifferent, unconcerned, unconnected 12 uninterested 13 disinterested, dispassionate, unaccompanied

detachment 5 squad 7 divorce, rupture 8 disunion, division 9 partition 10 neutrality, separation 11 dissolution

detail 4 item, list, part 5 point 6 assign, nicety, relate, report 7 appoint, article, element, itemize, listing, minutia, specify 8 allocate, spell out 9 enumerate, stipulate 10 assignment, particular 12 circumstance 13 particularize

detailed 4 full 6 minute 8 itemized, complete, thorough 10 blow-by-blow, exhaustive, meticulous, particular 13 thoroughgoing

detain 3 nab 4 bust, curb, hold, keep, mire, snag 5 check, delay, run in 6 arrest, collar, hang up, hinder, hold up, impede, pick up, retard, slow up 7 bog down, reserve, set back 8 hold back, keep back, restrain, slow down, withhold 9 apprehend 10 buttonhole *in conversation:* 10 buttonhole

detect 4 espy, find, spot 5 catch, dig up, hit on, scent 6 descry, notice, turn up 7 discern, hit upon, uncover, unearth 8 discover, meet with 9 ascertain, encounter, ferret out, track down

detectable 6 patent 7 evident, visible 8 sensible, tangible 10 noticeable, observable 11 discernible, perceptible

detection 9 discovery 10 unearthing *system:* 5 radar, sofar

detective 4 dick, G-man 6 shamus, sleuth 7 gumshoe 8 hawkshaw, informer, sherlock 9 inspector 10 private eye 12 investigator *fictional:* 4 Chan (Charlie), Gray (Cordelia), Moto (Mr.) 5 Banks (Alan), Bosch (Harry), Brown (Father), Dupin (Auguste), Lecoq, Lupin (Arsène), McGee (Travis), Morse (Inspector), Queen (Ellery), Rebus (John), Saint, Spade (Sam), Trent (Philip), Vance (Philo), Wolfe (Nero) 6 Alleyn (Roderick), Archer (Lew), Carter (Nick), Hammer (Mike), Holmes (Sherlock), Marple (Miss Jane), McCone (Sharon), Poirot (Hercule), Wimsey (Peter) 7 Campion (Albert), Charles (Nick, Nora), Maigret (Jules), Marlowe (Philip) 8 Drummond (Bulldog), Millhone (Kinsey) 9 Dalgleish (Adam) 10 Robicheaux (Dave), Warshawski (V. I.) 11 Father Brown

detective-story writer 3 Poe (Edgar Allan), Tey (Josephine) 4 Carr (John Dickson), Knox (Ronald) 5 Blake (Nicholas), Block (Lawrence), Cross (Amanda), Doyle (Arthur Conan), Green (Anna Katherine), Innes (Michael), James (P. D.), Marsh (Ngaio), Queen (Ellery), Stout (Rex) 6 Bramah (Ernest), Buchan (John), Hansen (Joseph), McBain (Ed), Mosley (Walter), Parker (Robert), Peters (Ellis), Sayers (Dorothy L.) 7 Bentley (E. C.), Biggers (Earl Derr), Collins (Wilkie), Francis (Dick), Freeman (Austin), Gardner (Erle Stanley), Grafton (Sue), Hammett (Dashiell), Hornung (E. W.), Rendell (Ruth), Simenon (Georges), Van Dine (S. S.), Wallace (Edgar) 8 Chandler (Raymond), Christie (Agatha), Gaboriau (Emile), Marquand (John), Paretsky (Sara), Rinehart (Mary Roberts), Spillane (Mickey) 9 Allingham (Margery), Hillerman (Tony), Lockridge (Frances, Richard), Macdonald (Ross) 10 Chesterton (Gilbert Keith)

detention 6 arrest 7 holding 10 internment 11 confinement 12 imprisonment

deter 5 avert, block 6 divert, hinder, impede, thwart 7 forfend, inhibit, obviate, prevent, rule out, shut out, ward off 8 dissuade, preclude, restrain, stave off 9 forestall, turn aside 10 discourage

deterge 4 wash 7 cleanse, wash off

detergent 4 soap 8 cleanser

deteriorate 3 rot 4 fade, fail, flag, sink, wear 5 decay, lapse, slide, spoil 6 weaken, worsen 7 decline, regress 8 languish 9 decompose, fall apart 10 debilitate, degenerate, depreciate, go downhill, retrograde, retrogress 12 disintegrate

deterioration 4 ruin 5 decay 6 ebbing, waning 7 atrophy, decline, erosion, failing, rotting 8 decaying, spoiling 9 crumbling, decadence, downgrade 10 debasement, degeneracy 12 degeneration, dégringolade

determinant 4 gene 5 agent, basis, cause, trait 6 factor, ground, reason 7 epitope, radical 9 attribute, influence

determinate 5 fixed 6 cymose 7 limited, precise, settled 8 constant, definite 10 definitive, restricted 11 established 13 circumscribed

determination 5 drive, spunk 6 fixing, mettle 7 finding, opinion, purpose, resolve, verdict 8 decision, firmness, judgment, tenacity 9 assurance, hardihood, impulsion, intention, resolving, willpower 10 conclusion, dedication, definition, doggedness, resolution, settlement 11 decidedness, intrepidity 12 perseverance, resoluteness, stubbornness 13 purposiveness

determine 3 fix, set 4 rule 5 bound, limit, prove 6 decide, figure, ordain, settle 7 control, delimit, find out, mark out, measure, preform, unearth 8 conclude, discover, regulate 9 ascertain, demarcate, establish, preordain, resolve on 10 delimitate, foreordain, predestine, predispose

determined 3 set 4 bent 5 fixed 6 driven, intent 7 decided, earnest, serious, settled 8 decisive, hellbent, resolute, resolved, stubborn 9 tenacious 10 persistent, purposeful, unwavering 11 established, persevering, unfaltering 12 foreordained, unhesitating

detest 4 hate 5 abhor, spurn 6 loathe 7 despise, dislike 8 execrate 9 abominate, repudiate

detestable 4 foul, vile 6 damned, horrid, odious 7 hateful, heinous 9 abhorrent, execrable, loathsome 10 abominable, despicable 12 contemptible

detestation 4 hate 6 hatred 8 anathema, aversion, loathing 9 repulsion, revulsion 10 abhorrence, execration, repugnance

dethrone 4 oust 6 depose 7 uncrown 8 displace

detonate 5 blast, burst, go off, spark 6 blow up, set off 7 explode 8 touch off

detonator 3 cap 4 fuse 9 explosive 11 blasting cap

detour 5 avoid, skirt 6 bypass 9 diversion

detract 6 divert, lessen, reduce

8 decrease, diminish, minimize 10 depreciate

detraction 9 aspersion, maligning, traducing 10 backbiting, belittling, derogation, slandering 11 denigration, deprecation, traducement 12 backstabbing, belittlement 13 disparagement

detractive 9 maligning, slighting, traducing, vilifying 10 defamatory, derogatory, pejorative 11 denigrating, disparaging 12 depreciative, depreciatory

detriment 4 harm, loss 6 damage, injury 7 marring 8 drawback 10 impairment 12 disadvantage

detrimental 3 bad, ill 7 adverse, harmful, hurtful, nocuous 8 damaging, negative 9 injurious 11 deleterious, unfavorable

detritus 4 tufa, tuff 5 scree, talus 6 debris, rubble 7 remains 11 odds and ends

Detroit *county:* 5 Wayne *founder:* 8 Cadillac (Sieur de) *lake:* 4 Erie 10 Saint Clair *sobriquet:* 6 Motown 9 Motor City

de trop 5 extra, spare 7 too much, surplus 9 excessive, redundant 10 gratuitous 11 superfluous 13 supernumerary

Deucalion *father:* 10 Prometheus *kingdom:* 6 Phthia *mother:* 7 Clymene *son:* 6 Hellen *wife:* 6 Pyrrha

Deutschland über ___ 5 alles

Devaki's son 7 Krishna

___ De Valera 5 Eamon

devaluate 5 abase, decry, lower 6 reduce, weaken 7 cheapen, degrade 8 mark down, write off 9 undermine, underrate, write down 10 depreciate

devaluation 7 decline 10 debasement, declension 11 declination

devalue see DEPRECIATE

devastate 4 raze, ruin, sack 5 waste 6 ravage 7 despoil, pillage, plunder 8 demolish, desolate, lay waste, overcome, spoliate 9 depredate, desecrate, overpower, overwhelm

devastation 4 loss, ruin 5 chaos, havoc, waste 6 ravage 7 pillage, plunder 8 disorder 9 confusion, ruination 10 demolition, desolation, spoliation 11 depredation

develop 3 age 4 form, grow 5 occur, reach, ripen 6 attain, dilate, evolve, expand, grow up, happen, mature, mellow, open up, thrive, unfold, unfurl 7 achieve, acquire, advance, burgeon, enlarge, expound, promote 8 flourish 9 actualize, elaborate, establish, transpire 11 come to light, materialize

development 5 phase 6 growth, result, spread 7 advance, buildup, outcome 8 ontogeny, progress, ripening 9 evolution, expansion, flowering, phylogeny,

unfolding 10 maturation 11 elaboration, progression *of life:* 10 biogenesis
Devi 7 goddess *consort:* 5 Shiva *father:* 7 Himavat *name:* 3 Uma 4 Kali 5 Durga, Gauri 6 Chandi 7 Parvati
deviant 4 bent 5 kinky, queer 6 off-key 7 twisted, wayward 8 aberrant, abnormal, atypical, perverse 9 anomalous, different, divergent, irregular, unnatural 11 heteroclite
deviate 3 err, yaw 4 turn, vary, veer 5 sheer, stray 6 depart, swerve, wander 7 digress, diverge 8 aberrant 9 eccentric, turn aside
deviation 3 yaw 4 bend, tack, turn 5 error, shift 6 change 7 anomaly, turning, veering 8 variance 9 departure, diversion 10 aberration, alteration, deflection, divergence
device 4 ploy, tool 5 feint, gizmo, means, motif, motto, shift, thing, trick 6 dingus, doodad, emblem, figure, gadget, gambit, hickey, jigger, medium, motive, symbol, widget 7 gimmick, machine, utensil, whatnot, whatsit 8 artifice, creation, insignia 9 apparatus, appliance, doohickey, expedient, implement, invention, makeshift, mechanism, thingummy 10 instrument 11 contraption, contrivance, inclination, thingamabob, thingamajig, thingumajig *automatic:* 5 servo *binding:* 5 clamp *fastening:* 6 zipper *grasping:* 4 tong *heating:* 8 radiator *hoisting:* 5 crane, lewis 8 windlass *holding:* 4 vise 5 clamp
devil 5 beast, cloot, demon, fiend, rogue, Satan, scamp 6 Belial, diablo, dybbuk, rascal, spirit 7 Clootie, dickens, Lucifer, Old Nick, serpent, tempter, villain 8 Apollyon, Mephisto, scalawag, succubus 9 archfiend, Beelzebub, cacodemon, scoundrel, skeezicks 10 blackguard, Old Scratch 11 rapscallion
devilfish 3 ray 5 manta 7 octopus 8 manta ray 10 cephalopod
devilish 3 bad 4 evil 6 cursed, wicked 7 demonic, hellish, roguish, satanic 8 accursed, damnable, diabolic, fiendish, infernal, sinister 9 nefarious 10 diabolical, iniquitous, villainous 11 mischievous
devil-may-care 3 gay 4 rash, wild 6 rakish, sporty 7 raffish 8 carefree, rakehell, reckless 9 easygoing
devilry 7 knavery, roguery, sorcery, waggery 8 mischief 9 diablerie 10 wickedness, witchcraft 11 roguishness, waggishness 12 sportiveness
devious 3 sly 4 foxy, wily 6 artful, crafty, errant, erring, roving, shifty, sneaky,

tricky 7 bending, crooked, cunning, curving, erratic, winding 8 aberrant, guileful, indirect, scheming, sneaking, twisting 9 deceptive, underhand, wandering 10 roundabout 11 out-of-the-way, underhanded
devise 4 form, plan, plot, will 5 chart, forge, frame, shape 6 cook up, create, design, invent, legacy, legate, scheme 7 arrange, bequest, concoct, connive, dope out, dream up, hatch up, project 8 bequeath, property 9 determine, formulate 11 inheritance
devitalize 3 sap 5 drain 6 deaden, weaken 7 exhaust 8 enfeeble 9 desiccate 10 eviscerate
devoid of 7 lacking, wanting 8 free from
devoir 3 job 4 duty, task, work 5 chore, stint 6 charge 9 committal 10 assignment, commitment, obligation
devolution 5 decay 7 decline, passing 8 receding, transfer 9 conferral, decadence, recession, surrender 10 conveyance, declension, degeneracy, regression, relegation, transferal 11 degradation 12 degeneration, dégringolade, retrograding, transference 13 retrogression
devolve 4 give, pass 6 pass on 8 hand down, hand over, relegate, transfer 10 degenerate
devote 5 apply 6 commit, direct, donate, hallow 7 reserve 8 dedicate, give over, sanctify 9 confirm in, habituate 10 consecrate
devoted 4 dear, fond, true 5 loyal 6 ardent, caring, doting, fervid, loving 7 dutiful, fervent, zealous 8 constant, faithful 9 dedicated 10 thoughtful 12 affectionate *religiously:* 6 oblate
devotee 3 fan, nut 4 buff 5 hound, lover 6 addict, votary, zealot 7 admirer, amateur, fanatic, fancier, habitué 8 follower 9 supporter 10 aficionado, enthusiast
devotion 4 love, zeal 5 ardor, piety 6 fealty, fervor, prayer 7 loyalty, passion 8 fidelity, fondness 9 adherence, adoration, reverence 10 allegiance, attachment, dedication, enthusiasm 12 faithfulness
devour 3 eat 5 eat up, enjoy 6 absorb, feed on 7 consume, destroy, feast on, pillage 8 prey upon, wolf down 9 delight in, feast upon, polish off, swallow up 10 annihilate
devouring 4 avid 6 greedy 8 esurient, ravenous 9 voracious 10 gluttonous
devout 4 holy 5 godly, loyal, pious 6 ardent 7 earnest, fervent, serious, sincere, zealous 8 faithful, reverent 9 pietistic, prayerful, religious

devoutness 4 zeal **5** ardor, piety **9** reverence **10** commitment

dew 5 sweat, tears **8** moisture **11** precipitate **12** perspiration **13** precipitation

dewy 3 wet **4** damp, pure **5** fresh, moist, naive **7** artless, natural **8** innocent, wide-eyed **9** credulous, guileless, ingenuous, unworldly

dexter 5 right

dexterity 4 ease **5** craft, grace, skill **7** ability, aptness, know-how, prowess, sleight **8** deftness, facility **9** adeptness, expertise, readiness **10** adroitness, nimbleness, smoothness **12** skillfulness

dexterous 3 apt **4** able, deft **5** adept, agile, handy **6** adroit, artful, facile, nimble, smooth **7** skilled **8** masterly, skillful **10** proficient

___ **Dhabi 3** Abu

diablerie 7 devilry, roguery, sorcery, waggery **8** deviltry, iniquity, mischief, satanism **9** devilment **10** black magic, wickedness, witchcraft, wrongdoing **11** roguishness, waggishness **12** sportiveness

diabolical 4 evil **5** awful **6** impish, wicked **7** beastly, demonic, heinous, hellish, puckish, roguish, satanic **8** demoniac, devilish, dreadful, fiendish, god-awful, hellborn, infernal, rascally, sinister **9** execrable, malicious, monstrous, nefarious **10** degenerate, demoniacal, horrendous, iniquitous, scandalous, villainous **11** mischievous

diabolism see DIABLERIE

diacritic 5 acute, breve, grave, haček, tilde **6** macron, umlaut **7** cedilla **8** dieresis **9** diaeresis **10** circumflex *Arabic:* **5** hamza **6** hamzah

diadem 5 crown **6** wreath **7** chaplet, coronal, coronet **8** headband

diagnose 4 spot **5** place **8** identify, pinpoint **9** determine, interpret, recognize **11** distinguish

diagnostic 8 analytic **10** analytical, expository, indicating, indicative **11** explanatory, exploratory **12** interpretive

diagonal 4 bias **5** bevel **6** biased **7** beveled, oblique, slanted **8** inclined, slanting **9** inclining, slantways, slantwise

diagonally 9 slantways, slantwise **10** cornerwise **11** catercorner, kitty-corner

diagram 3 map **5** chart, graph **6** design, layout, sketch **7** drawing, isotype **9** represent

dial 4 call, face, knob, tune, turn **5** phone **6** rotate **7** control **10** manipulate

dialect 4 cant, jive **5** argot, idiom, koine, lingo, slang **6** creole, jargon, patois, patter, pidgin, speech, tongue **8** language, localism **10** vernacular **11** regionalism, terminology **13** provincialism *Georgia:* **6** Gullah *London:* **7** cockney

dialectic 5 logic **6** debate **8** dialogue, forensic **9** reasoning **10** discussion **11** disputation **13** argumentation, investigation

dialogue 4 chat, talk **6** confer, parley, script **8** colloquy, converse **12** conversation **13** confabulation

diameter 4 bore **5** chord, width **7** breadth, caliber **8** bisector, wideness **9** broadness

diametric 7 counter, opposed **8** contrary, converse, opposite **12** antithetical **13** contradictory

diamond 3 gem **5** field, stone *element:* **6** carbon *famous:* **4** Hope, Pitt **5** Sancy **6** Orloff, Regent **8** Braganza, Cullinan, Kohinoor **9** Excelsior **10** Great Mogul *inferior:* **4** bort *oval:* **9** briolette *pattern:* **6** argyle *playing card:* **7** lozenge *state:* **8** Delaware *surface:* **5** facet

Diana see ARTEMIS

diapason 4 peal, stop **5** range, scale, scope **7** compass, measure **8** spectrum **10** tuning fork

diaper 5 nappy **7** pattern **8** ornament

diaphanous 5 filmy, gauzy, sheer, vague **6** flimsy **8** ethereal, gossamer **11** transparent **13** insubstantial

diaphragm 4 stop **6** septum **8** membrane **9** partition

diarist 4 Gide (André) **5** Frank (Anne), Pepys (Samuel), Scott (Walter), Swift (Jonathan), Woolf (Virginia) **6** Burney (Fanny), Evelyn (John) **7** Boswell (James) **8** Robinson (Henry Crabb) **10** chronicler, journalist

diary 3 log **6** record **7** daybook, diurnal, journal, logbook **8** notebook, register **9** chronicle

diastase 6 enzyme **8** catalyst, reactant

diatribe 6 tirade **7** polemic **8** harangue, jeremiad **9** criticism, philippic **11** castigation **12** denunciation

dibs 4 gelt **5** claim, dough, money, title **6** rights **11** reservation

dice 4 cast, cube **5** bones, cubes, ivory, mince **11** devil's-bones *game:* **5** craps *losing throw:* **7** missout *singular:* **3** die *throw:* **7** boxcars **9** snake eyes

dicer 5 loser **6** risker **7** gambler

dicey 4 iffy **5** risky **6** chancy, tricky **8** ticklish **9** uncertain, whimsical **10** precarious, speculative **11** problematic **13** unpredictable

dichotomize 5 halve **7** dissect **8** hemisect **9** bifurcate

dichotomous 5 split **6** forked **7** pronged **9** bifurcate **10** bifurcated

dichotomy 7 forking **8** division **9** bisection, branching, splitting **11** bifurcation **13** contradiction

Dickens, Charles *birthplace:* **10** Portsmouth *captain:* **6** Cuttle *character:* **3** Ada (Clare), Pip, Tim **4** Dick (Mr.), Dora, Gamp (Sairey), Heep (Uriah), Nell **5** Drood (Edwin), Emily, Fagin, Lucie (Manette), Sikes (Bill) **6** Barkis, Bumble (Mr.), Carton (Sydney), Cuttle (Capt.), Darnay (Charles), Dombey (Fanny, Florence, Paul), Dorrit (Amy), Oliver (Twist) **7** Barnaby (Rudge), Dedlock (Lady), Defarge, Gargery (Joe), Manette (Dr.), Scrooge (Ebenezer), Tiny Tim **8** Cratchit (Bob), Havisham (Miss), Jarndyce (John), Magwitch (Abel), Micawber (Mr.), Nickleby (Nicholas), Peggotty (Clara, Daniel, Ham), Pickwick (Mr.) **9** Bill Sikes, Gradgrind (Mr.), Murdstone (Mr.), Pecksniff (Mr.), Uriah Heep **10** Chuzzlewit (Anthony, Jonas, Martin), Steerforth **11** Copperfield (David) *hero:* **6** Carton (Sydney) *nationality:* **7** English *pen name:* **3** Boz *villain:* **5** Fagin *work:* **9** Hard Times **10** Bleak House **11** Oliver Twist **12** Barnaby Rudge, Dombey and Son, Little Dorrit **14** Christmas Carol (A), Pickwick Papers (The) **15** Our Mutual Friend, Tale of Two Cities (A) **16** David Copperfield, Martin Chuzzlewit, Nicholas Nickleby **17** Great Expectations

dicker 4 deal, swap **5** argue, trade **6** barter, haggle, higgle, palter **7** bargain, chaffer **8** contract, huckster **9** negotiate

dickey 10 shirtfront

Dickey novel 11 Deliverance

dictate 3 set **4** lead, rule, word **5** edict, order, tenet **6** behest, decree, direct, enjoin, govern, impose, ordain, recite **7** bidding, command, control, lay down, mandate, read off, summons **9** determine, direction, directive, prescribe, principle, pronounce, verbalize **10** injunction **12** prescription

dictative 5 bossy **8** despotic, dogmatic **9** imperious **10** peremptory **11** doctrinaire, magisterial **13** authoritarian

dictator 4 czar, duce **6** caesar, despot, tyrant **8** autocrat, martinet **9** oppressor, strongman *German:* **6** Hitler (Adolf) *Italian:* **9** Mussolini (Benito) *military:* **8** caudillo *Spanish:* **6** Franco (Francisco)

dictatorial 5 bossy **8** despotic, dogmatic **9** arbitrary, imperious, masterful

10 autocratic, iron-handed, peremptory, tyrannical **11** doctrinaire, domineering, overbearing **12** totalitarian **13** authoritarian

dictatorship 7 tyranny **9** autocracy, Caesarism, despotism, supremacy **10** absolutism

diction 6 phrase, speech **7** wordage, wording **8** delivery, language, parlance, phrasing, rhetoric, verbiage **9** elocution, verbalism **11** enunciation, phraseology

dictionary 7 lexicon **8** glossary, wordbook **10** repository **13** reference book *compiler:* **7** Johnson (Samuel), Webster (Noah) **13** lexicographer *geographical:* **9** gazetteer *of synonyms:* **8** thesauri (plural) **9** thesaurus

dictum 4 fiat **5** adage, axiom, edict, maxim, moral **6** ruling **7** mandate, opinion, precept, proverb **11** declaration **13** pronouncement

didactic 5 moral **6** teachy **7** donnish, preachy **8** advisory, edifying, pedantic, sermonic, teaching **9** hortative, pedagogic, teacherly **10** moralizing **11** informative, instructive

diddle 3 con, gyp, toy **4** beat, bilk, dupe, hoax, fool, idle, laze, loaf, loll, rook, scam **5** cheat, cozen, delay, drone, trick **6** chisel, chouse, dabble, dawdle, delude, fiddle, fleece, loiter, lounge, rope in, take in **7** deceive, defraud, goof off, mislead, swindle **8** flimflam, fool with, hoodwink, lollygag **9** bamboozle, overreach, victimize, waste time **10** dilly-dally, fool around, hang around

diddler 3 gyp **4** sham **5** cheat, faker, fraud, rogue **6** con man **7** grifter, shammer, sharper **8** swindler **9** con artist, defrauder, trickster **11** flimflammer **12** double-dealer **13** confidence man

dido 4 jest, lark **5** antic, caper, curio, frill, prank **6** bauble, frolic, gewgaw, trifle, whimsy **7** bibelot, novelty, trinket **8** furbelow, gimcrack, kickshaw, mischief **9** bagatelle, plaything **10** knickknack, tomfoolery

Dido 6 Elissa *brother:* **9** Pygmalion *city founded by:* **8** Carthage *father:* **5** Belus **6** Mutton *husband:* **7** Acerbas **8** Sichaeus *lover:* **6** Aeneas

Dido and Aeneas composer 7 Purcell (Henry)

die 4 drop, fall, mold, pass, stop, wane **5** cease, croak **6** cash in, demise, expire, go west, matrix, pass on, peg out, perish, pop off **7** decease, go south, kick off, snuff it, succumb **8** cash it in, check out, drop dead, pass away **9** disappear 10 buy the farm 12 join the choir 13 kick the bucket *from hunger:* 6 starve *loaded:* 6 fulham ___ die 4 sine

diehard 7 devoted, fanatic 8 true-blue 9 dogmatist 10 determined 11 bitterender, doctrinaire, reactionary, standpatter 12 conservative, intransigent 13 stick-in-the-mud

___ **diem** 3 per 5 carpe

Dies ___ 4 Irae

diet 4 eats, fare, fast, feed, menu 6 ration, reduce, regime 7 regimen 8 assembly, victuals 10 parliament 11 legislature, nourishment

Diet of ___ 5 Worms 6 Speyer, Spires 8 Augsburg

Dieu ___ **(British motto)** 10 et mon droit ___-**dieu** 4 prie

differ 4 vary 5 demur 7 deviate 8 disagree

difference 7 discord, dispute, dissent 8 conflict, contrast, variance 9 departure, deviation, disparity, otherness, variation 10 dissension, divergence, unlikeness 11 controversy, discrepancy, distinction 12 disagreement 13 dissimilarity

different 5 other 6 divers, single, sundry, unlike 7 another, deviant, distant, diverse, several, special, unalike, unequal, unusual, various 8 discrete, distinct, peculiar, separate 9 disparate, divergent 10 dissimilar, individual, particular 11 contrasting, distinctive

differentiate 4 vary 5 adapt 6 change, modify 8 contrast, separate 9 diversify, transform 11 distinguish, individuate 12 characterize, discriminate

difficult 4 hard 5 tough 6 thorny, uphill 7 arduous, awkward, labored, obscure, operose 8 exacting, perverse, puzzling, stubborn 9 demanding, effortful, herculean, laborious, strenuous 10 refractory 11 problematic

difficulty 3 ado, fix, jam 4 beef 4 pass, snag 5 hitch, nodus, pinch, rigor, worry 6 bother, hang-up, hassle, pickle, plight, scrape, strait 7 dilemma, pitfall, problem, trouble 8 distress, hardness, hardship, hot water, obstacle, quandary, quagmire, question, squabble 9 adversity, bickering, challenge, deep water, objection 10 falling-out, impediment 11 aggravation, altercation, arduousness, controversy, obstruction, predicament, vicissitude 12 complication, disagreement 13 embarrassment, inconvenience

diffidence 7 modesty, reserve, shyness 8 distrust, meekness, timidity 9 quietness, restraint, timidness 10 hesitation 11 bashfulness

diffident 3 shy 4 meek 5 timid 7 bashful 8 hesitant, reserved, retiring, timorous 9 reluctant, unassured 11 unassertive 12 self-effacing

diffuse 5 strew, wordy 6 prolix, spread 7 scatter, verbose 8 disperse, rambling 9 broadcast, dispersed, propagate, scattered, spreading, spread out 10 distribute, long-winded, widespread 11 disseminate, distributed

diffusion 6 spread 7 osmosis 9 broadcast, dispersal, prolixity, spreading 10 dispersion, scattering 11 circulation, propagation 12 broadcasting, promulgation

dig 3 jab 4 barb, grub, hole, like, mine, poke, prod, root, site, stab 5 delve, ditch, enjoy, gouge, nudge, probe, scoop, spade, taunt 6 burrow, plunge, quarry, relish, rootle, shovel, thrust, trench, tunnel 7 explore, root out, unearth 8 excavate, prospect 10 excavation 11 investigate *up:* 6 exhume 7 unearth

digest 5 sum up 6 absorb, codify, précis 7 consume, stomach, summate, swallow 8 abstract, boil down, classify, compress, condense, syllabus, synopsis 9 summarize, summation, synopsize 10 abridgment 12 condensation

digger 4 plow 5 miner 6 shovel 7 soldier

digit 3 toe 5 thumb 6 cipher, figure, finger, number, pinkie 7 integer, numeral 9 character 11 whole number

dignified 4 prim 6 august, formal, proper, seemly 7 courtly, elegant, stately 8 cultured, decorous, ennobled, polished 9 distingué, patrician

dignify 5 adorn, exalt, grace, honor 7 ennoble, elevate, glorify, sublime 11 distinguish

dignitary 3 VIP 4 lion 5 chief, nabob 6 leader, worthy 7 notable 8 eminence, luminary 9 personage 10 notability 11 muckety-muck 13 high-muck-a-muck

dignity 4 rank 5 honor, merit, poise, pride, worth 6 cachet, status, virtue 7 address, decorum, gravity, hauteur, majesty, stature 8 grandeur, nobility, position, prestige, standing 9 propriety 10 augustness, seemliness 11 consequence, self-respect

digress 5 stray 6 depart, ramble, swerve, wander 7 deviate, diverge 8 divagate

digression 5 aside 7 episode, tangent 8 drifting, excursus, rambling, straying 9 deviation, wandering 10 deflection, divagation, divergence 11 parenthesis

dig up 4 find **6** expose, reveal **7** nose out, root out, uncover, unearth **8** discover **9** ferret out, run across, search out, track down

dik-dik 8 antelope

dike 3 dam **4** bank **5** ditch, drain, levee **7** barrier **8** causeway **10** embankment **11** watercourse

dilapidate 4 ruin **5** decay, wreck **7** break up, crumble, decline, neglect **9** break down, decompose, disregard **10** deliquesce **12** disintegrate

dilapidated 5 dingy, seedy **6** beat-up, ragtag, ruined, shabby **7** decayed, rundown **8** battered, crumbled, decrepit **9** crumbling **10** broken-down, down-at-heel, ramshackle **12** deteriorated

dilapidation 4 ruin **5** decay **7** atrophy **8** collapse, decaying **9** crumbling, decadence, disrepair **11** decrepitude **13** decomposition, deterioration

dilate 5 swell, widen **6** expand, extend **7** distend, enlarge, expound **9** discourse, expatiate

dilatory 4 idle, slow **5** slack, tardy **7** laggard **8** dallying, delaying, sluggish **9** leisurely, lingering, unhurried **11** time-wasting

dilemma 3 box, fix, jam **4** bind, hole, spot **6** choice, corner, pickle, plight, scrape **7** catch-22, problem **8** argument, quandary **10** difficulty **11** predicament

dilettante 4 tyro **7** amateur, dabbler **8** aesthete, putterer **9** smatterer

dilettantish see AMATEURISH

diligence 4 zeal **8** industry **9** assiduity **10** commitment **11** application, persistence **12** perseverance, sedulousness **13** assiduousness

diligent 8 sedulous **9** assiduous **10** persistent, persisting, unflagging **11** hardworking, industrious, painstaking, persevering

dilly 4 lulu **5** dandy, doozy, peach **6** corker, doozie, pippin, ripper, rouser **8** jimdandy, knockout **9** humdinger **10** ripsnorter **11** crackerjack

dillydally see DELAY

dilute 3 cut **4** thin, weak **5** water **6** watery, weaken **8** diminish, weakened **9** attenuate, water down **11** watered-down

dim 4 dull, dumb, hazy, pale, slow **5** befog, blear, blind, cloud, dense, dusky, faint, muddy, murky, muted, thick, vague **6** bleary, gloomy, stupid **7** becloud, low beam, obscure, shadowy, subdued, unclear **9** tenebrous **10** ill-defined, indistinct, lackluster, lusterless **11** unpromising

dime novel 4 pulp **7** chiller, shocker

dreadful, thriller 12 bloodcurdler **13** penny dreadful

dimension 4 size **5** reach, scale, scope, width **6** aspect, extent, spread **7** compass, expanse, measure, quality **9** amplitude, magnitude

diminish 3 ebb **4** bate, wane **5** abate, peter, quell, taper **6** lessen, reduce, subdue, temper, weaken **7** curtail, dwindle, subside **8** belittle, decrease, minimize, moderate, restrain, taper off **9** attenuate, disparage, dispraise **10** depreciate **11** detract from

diminishing 6 waning **8** receding **9** declining, dwindling, lessening, subsiding, weakening **10** curtailing, decreasing **11** attenuating **12** depreciating

diminutive 3 wee **4** tiny **5** bitsy, dwarf, pygmy, small, teeny, weeny **6** bantam, little, midget, minute, peewee, petite, teensy **9** miniature, pint-sized, undersize **10** teeny-weeny **11** lilliputian **12** teensy-weensy

___ **dimittis 4** Nunc

dimple 3 pit **4** dent, dint, fret, nick **5** notch **6** ripple **8** pockmark **10** depression **11** indentation

dimwit 3 oaf **4** clod, dodo, dolt, dope, fool, simp, yo-yo **5** booby, chump, cluck, dummy, dunce, idiot, moron, stupe **6** dum-dum **7** airhead, dullard, fathead, pinhead **8** bonehead, dumbbell, imbecile, lunkhead, meathead, numskull **9** birdbrain, blockhead, dumb bunny, dumb cluck, ignoramus, lamebrain, numbskull, simpleton **10** dunderhead, nincompoop **11** featherhead, knucklehead **12** featherbrain

dim-witted 4 dull, dumb, slow **6** stupid **7** doltish, foolish, idiotic, moronic **8** backward, imbecile, retarded **9** brainless, half-baked, imbecilic **11** birdbrained, lamebrained **12** feebleminded, simpleminded

din 3 row **4** roar **5** babel, clash, noise **6** bedlam, clamor, deafen, hubbub, racket, rattle, tumult, uproar **7** clangor, clatter, resound **8** brouhaha **9** commotion, stridency **10** hullabaloo, hurlyburly **11** pandemonium **13** clamorousness

Dinah *brother:* **4** Levi **6** Simeon *father:* **5** Jacob *mother:* **4** Leah

dine 3 eat, sup **4** feed **5** feast **6** eat out **7** banquet, nourish

diner 4 café **5** eater **6** eatery **7** canteen **8** snack bar **9** hash house **10** coffee shop, restaurant **11** greasy spoon **12** lunch counter, luncheonette, sandwich shop

ding 3 mar **4** dent, nick **5** clang **7** blemish
ding-a-ling 3 nut **4** kook, yo-yo **5** flake, loony, wacko **6** cuckoo, nitwit, weirdo **7** lunatic **8** crackpot **9** fruitcake, harebrain, lamebrain, screwball **10** crackbrain **12** scatterbrain
dinghy 5 skiff **7** rowboat, shallop **8** lifeboat, life raft, sailboat
dingle 4 dale, dell, glen, vale **6** ravine, valley
dingus 5 gizmo **6** doodad, gadget, jigger, widget **7** whatsit **9** doohickey, thingummy **11** thingamabob, thingamajig, thingumajig
dingy 4 foul, mean **5** dirty, seedy, tacky **6** filthy, grubby, grungy, scuzzy, shabby, soiled, sordid **7** run-down, squalid, sullied, unclean **8** begrimed
dinky 3 toy **4** tiny **5** small, teeny **9** undersize **10** locomotive
"Dinner ___" 7 at Eight
dinner 4 meal **5** feast **6** regale, repast, spread, supper **7** banquet **8** luncheon **9** collation **10** table d'hôte *course:* **4** meat, soup **5** salad **6** entrée **7** dessert **9** appetizer *jacket:* **3** tux **6** tuxedo
dinosaur 6 fossil **7** has-been **8** theropod **11** anachronism
dinosauric 4 huge **5** passé **6** bygone **7** extinct, mammoth **8** colossal, enormous, obsolete, outmoded **9** cyclopean, leviathan, out-of-date **10** antiquated, behemothic, fossilized, gargantuan, mastodonic, oldfangled **11** elephantine **12** antediluvian, old-fashioned, out-of-fashion **13** anachronistic
dint 4 nick **5** force, might, power **6** dimple, virtue **7** drive in, impress **10** impression **11** indentation
diocese 3 see **9** bishopric *Eastern Orthodox:* **7** eparchy *subdivision:* **6** parish
diode 9 rectifier **10** vacuum tube **12** electron tube *component:* **5** anode **7** cathode **9** electrode
Diomedes *city founded by:* **4** Arpi *father:* **4** Ares, Mars **6** Tydeus *foe:* **6** Aeneas, Hector *slayer:* **8** Hercules *victim:* **6** Rhesus
Dione 5 Titan *cult partner:* **4** Zeus *daughter:* **5** Venus **9** Aphrodite *father:* **7** Oceanus *lover:* **4** Zeus *mother:* **6** Tethys
Dionysus see BACCHUS
Dionyza's husband 5 Cleon
Dioscuri 5 twins **6** Castor, Gemini, Pollux *father:* **4** Zeus **9** Tyndareus *mother:* **4** Leda *sister:* **5** Helen
dip 3 sag **4** bail, draw, drop, duck, dunk, fall, lade, sink, skid, slip, slue, swim **5** basin, ladle, lower, pitch, sauce, scoop, slope, slump, spoon, stoop **6** go down, hollow, plunge **7** decline, descend, descent, falloff, immerse, sinkage **8** decrease, downturn, sinkhole, submerge, submerse **9** concavity, declivity, downswing, downtrend, immersion **10** depression
diphthong 7 digraph **8** ligature
diploma 6 degree **7** charter **8** document **9** sheepskin **10** credential
diplomacy 4 tact **7** address, finesse **8** delicacy **10** artfulness, discretion, statecraft **11** negotiation, savoir faire, tactfulness
diplomatic 4 deft **5** bland, suave **6** artful, astute, polite, smooth, urbane **7** courtly, politic, tactful **8** delicate, discreet **9** courteous **12** conciliating, conciliatory, paleographic **13** accommodating
diplomat's office 7 embassy, mission
diplopod 9 millipede
dipper 3 cup **4** bird **5** ladle, ouzel, scoop, stars **6** bucket **10** pickpocket, water ouzel
dippy 4 daft, zany **5** crazy, daffy, flaky, goofy, kooky, loony, nutty, silly, wacky **6** stupid **7** doltish, foolish, witless **9** half-baked **11** harebrained **12** preposterous
dipsomania 10 alcoholism
dire 4 grim **5** acute, awful **6** dismal, horrid, tragic, urgent, woeful **7** baleful, baneful, crucial, extreme, fateful, ominous, ruinous **8** alarming, critical, dreadful, grievous, horrible, horrific, menacing, shocking, sinister, terrible **9** appalling, desperate, frightful, illboding **10** calamitous, deplorable, depressing, foreboding, malevolent, oppressing, oppressive, pernicious **11** apocalyptic, distressing, threatening
direct 4 head, lead, show **5** apply, frank, guide, label, level, order, pilot, plain, point, route, steer, train **6** assign, charge, define, devote, divert, enjoin, escort, extend, govern, lineal, linear, manage, ordain, settle **7** address, carry on, command, conduct, control, genuine, nonstop, operate, oversee, preside, project, request **8** dispatch, instruct, regulate, shepherd, straight, unbroken, verbatim **9** determine, firsthand, immediate, prescribe **10** administer, contiguous, continuous, inevitable **11** categorical, undeviating, unequivocal, word for word *a helmsman:* **4** conn *proceedings:* **7** preside
direction 3 way **4** east, line, path, side, west **5** angle, north, point, south, trend **6** course, design **7** bearing, channel, command, purpose **8** guidance, tendency **9** clockwise, oversight, viewpoint **10** management, standpoint, trajectory

11 instruction, supervision *blowing:*
7 leeward 8 windward *horizontal:*
7 azimuth *main line of:* 4 axis (see also
COMPASS POINT)
directive 4 fiat, memo, word, writ
5 edict, order, ukase 6 charge, decree,
dictum, notice, ruling 7 bidding, command, dictate, mandate 8 deciding,
managing 9 presiding 10 assignment,
injunction, memorandum 11 instruction, supervising, supervisory 12 policymaking 13 communication, pronouncement
directly 3 due 4 anon, soon 5 right, spang
6 at once, pronto 7 bluntly, by and by,
shortly 8 first off, in person, promptly,
squarely, straight, verbatim 9 forthwith,
instanter, instantly, presently, right
away 10 face-to-face 11 immediately,
straight off, straightway, word for word
12 contiguously, straightaway
director 4 boss, head 5 chief 6 leader,
top dog 7 manager 8 overseer 9 conductor, organizer 10 head honcho,
supervisor
directory 4 list 5 guide, index 6 folder
7 catalog 8 register 9 catalogue 11 compilation
dirge 6 lament 7 requiem 8 threnody
11 lamentation *Gaelic:* 8 coronach
dirigible 5 blimp 7 airship 8 zeppelin
9 steerable
dirk 4 stab 5 sword 6 dagger 7 poniard
dirt 3 mud 4 clay, dust, land, loam, mire,
muck, porn, smut, soil, spot 5 earth,
filth, fraud, grime, stain 6 gossip,
ground 7 chicane, squalor 9 chicanery,
excrement, indecency 10 corruption,
hanky-panky 11 pornography
dirt-poor 4 bust 5 broke 8 beggared,
indigent 9 destitute, flat broke, penniless, penurious 10 stone-broke
12 impoverished
dirty 3 low, tar 4 base, foul, lewd, smut,
soil 5 bawdy, foggy, grimy, messy,
mucky, muddy, murky, nasty, smear,
sooty, stain, sully, taint 6 basely, befoul,
coarse, debase, defile, filthy, grubby,
impure, smudge, smutty, soiled, sordid,
vulgar 7 corrupt, defiled, hateful,
immoral, obscene, raunchy, smutchy,
spotted, squalid, squally, sullied, tainted, tarnish, unclean, unkempt
8 begrimed, besmirch, blustery, indecent, off-color, polluted, unchaste,
unwashed 9 ill-gotten, uncleanly
10 abominable, blustering, scandalous,
scurrilous 11 disgraceful, distasteful,
distressing, tempestuous, unlaundered
12 contaminated, contemptible, disagreeable, dishonorable, scatological

Dis see PLUTO
disability 7 ailment 8 drawback, handicap 9 detriment, hindrance, infirmity,
unfitness 10 affliction, impairment,
impediment, incapacity 11 restriction,
shortcoming 12 disadvantage
disable 3 sap 4 maim 5 spoil 6 hobble,
weaken 7 cripple 8 enfeeble, handicap,
paralyze, sabotage 9 hamstring, undermine 10 debilitate, immobilize 12 incapacitate *a racehorse:* 6 nobble
disabled 7 hobbled 8 crippled 9 arthritic,
paralyzed, rheumatic 11 handicapped
13 incapacitated
disabuse 4 free 5 emend, purge 7 correct, deliver, rectify, redress, release,
relieve 8 liberate, unburden 9 enlighten, undeceive 10 illuminate 11 disencumber, disillusion
disaccharide 7 lactose, maltose, sucrose
disaccord 3 jar, war 4 vary 5 brawl,
clash 6 combat, debate, differ 7 contest,
contend, dispute, dissent, quarrel
8 conflict, disagree 12 disharmonize
disadvantage 3 bar 4 harm, loss 6 burden, damage, hamper 7 barrier, setback
8 drawback, handicap, obstacle 9 detriment, hindrance, liability, prejudice
10 impairment, impediment, imposition, limitation 11 deprivation, obstruction
disadvantaged 7 lacking 8 deprived
11 handicapped
disaffect 4 wean 5 alien, repel 8 alienate,
disquiet, disunite, estrange 10 antagonize
disaffirm 4 deny 5 annul, belie, cross
6 abjure, impugn, negate, refute, reject
7 confute, explode, gainsay, reverse
8 disclaim, disprove, negative, traverse
9 repudiate 10 contradict, contravene
disagree 4 vary 5 argue, clash 6 bicker,
differ, divide, haggle 7 contend, contest, dispute, dissent 8 conflict
disagreeable 4 ugly 7 peevish 8 annoying, petulant 9 offensive 10 unpleasant
11 disobliging, distressing, ill-tempered
disagreement 5 clash 6 debate 7 discord,
dispute, quarrel, wrangle 8 argument,
conflict, squabble, variance 9 disparity
10 contention, difference, dissension,
divergence, unlikeness 11 altercation,
controversy, discrepancy, incongruity
disallow 4 deny, veto 5 debar 6 enjoin,
forbid, refuse, reject 7 disavow, dismiss,
exclude, rule out, shut out 8 disclaim,
prohibit 9 interdict, proscribe, repudiate
disallowance 4 veto 5 taboo 6 denial
7 refusal 9 disavowal, dismissal, exclu-

sion, rejection **11** prohibition, repudiation **12** interdiction, proscription

____**-disant 3** soi

disappear 3 die **5** clear, leave **6** depart, die out, vanish **8** evanesce, fade away, melt away, pass away, slip away **9** evaporate, sneak away, steal away **13** dematerialize

disappoint 4 dash, foil, ruin **6** baffle, defeat, thwart **7** let down **9** frustrate **10** discourage, dishearten

disappointment 4 blow **6** bummer, defeat, downer **7** failure, letdown **8** comedown **9** bringdown **11** frustration

disapproval 4 veto **6** rebuke **7** censure, dislike, obloquy, reproof **8** reproach **9** criticism, objection, rejection *expression of:* **3** boo **4** hiss, hoot, jeer **7** catcall **9** raspberry **10** Bronx cheer

disapprove 4 veto **6** oppose, reject **7** decline, dislike, dismiss, frown on **8** disfavor, turn down **9** dispraise

disarm 5 charm **6** allure **7** win over **8** sideline **9** captivate **10** neutralize

disarming 5 silky **6** silken **7** amiable, likable, winning, winsome **8** likeable, pleasing **9** endearing **10** convincing, persuasive, saccharine **11** deferential, insinuating **12** ingratiating

disarrange 4 mess **5** mix up, upset **6** jumble, mess up, mislay, muddle, muss up **7** confuse, disturb **8** disorder, displace, misplace, unsettle **10** discompose **11** disorganize

disarray 5 chaos **6** bedlam, jumble, mess up, muddle **7** clutter, undress **8** disorder, shambles, unsettle **9** confusion **10** discompose, dishabille

disassemble 6 detach **7** scatter **8** dismount, disperse, separate, take down, tear down **9** break down, come apart, dismantle, dismember, take apart

disassociate 5 sever, unfix **6** detach, sunder **7** back off **8** abstract, alienate, back down, disunite, liberate, separate, uncouple, withdraw **9** disengage **10** disconnect

disaster 3 woe **6** fiasco **7** debacle, failure, tragedy **8** calamity **9** cataclysm, ruination **11** catastrophe, devastation

disastrous 4 dire **5** fatal **6** tragic **7** fateful, ruinous **8** terrible **10** calamitous, horrendous **11** cataclysmic, destructive, devastating **12** catastrophic

disavow 4 deny **6** abjure, disown, impugn, negate, recant, reject **7** forsake, gainsay, retract **8** abnegate, disclaim, forswear, negative, renounce **9** repudiate

disband 3 end **4** part **5** sever **6** divide, sunder **7** break up, dissect, divorce, scatter **8** disperse, dissolve, separate

disbelieve 5 doubt, scorn, scout **6** eschew, reject **7** scoff at, suspect **8** discount, distrust, mistrust, question **9** discredit, repudiate

disbeliever 5 cynic **7** doubter, sceptic, scoffer, skeptic **9** dissenter **10** questioner **11** freethinker

disbelieving 4 wary **5** leery **6** show-me **7** cynical, dubious **8** doubting **9** quizzical, skeptical **11** incredulous, mistrustful, questioning, unconvinced

disburden 4 shed **6** unlade, unload, unship, unstow **7** off-load, relieve **8** disgorge **9** discharge

disburse 3 pay **5** allot, issue **6** lay out, pay out, supply **7** deliver, dole out, furnish, provide **8** dispense, disperse **9** apportion, partition **10** distribute, measure out

disbursement 4 cost **5** funds **6** outlay **7** expense, payment **9** allotment **11** expenditure **12** distribution

discard 4 cast, drop, dump, junk, shed, toss, waif **5** chuck, ditch, eject, let go, scrap **6** reject **7** cast off, castoff, deepsix, wash out **8** get rid of, jettison, shuck off, throw out **9** throw away, toss aside

discarnate 8 bodiless, ethereal, spectral **9** asomatous, unfleshly **10** immaterial, unembodied, unphysical, wraithlike **11** disembodied, incorporeal, nonphysical **12** otherworldly **13** insubstantial

discern 3 see **4** know, note **5** grasp, sense **6** behold, detect, divine, notice **7** observe **8** identify, perceive **9** apprehend, ascertain, recognize **10** comprehend, understand **11** distinguish **12** discriminate **13** differentiate

discernible 7 visible **8** apparent, palpable **10** detectable, noticeable, observable **11** appreciable, perceivable **12** recognizable

discerning 4 keen **5** acute, aware **6** astute **7** knowing **9** clear-eyed, insighted, observant, sagacious **10** insightful, perceptive **12** clear-sighted **13** knowledgeable, perspicacious

discernment 6 acumen **7** insight **8** keenness, sagacity **9** intuition **10** astuteness, perception, shrewdness **11** penetration, percipience, recognition **12** perspicacity **13** comprehension, sagaciousness

discharge 3 can, pay **4** drop, emit, fire, free, gush, oust, quit, sack, spew, vent, void **5** annul, clear, demob, eject, empty, expel, exude, let go, loose, pay up, quash, salvo, shoot, utter **6** bounce, excuse, expend, let fly, let off, loosen, outlet, remove, settle, unbind, unload, vacate **7** absolve, boot out, barrage, cashier, deliver, dismiss, exclude, excrete, execute, fulfill, give off, kick out, manumit, off-load, release, relieve, removal, satisfy, unchain 8 abrogate, aquittal, dispense, displace, dissolve, ejection, emission, get rid of, liberate, separate, throw off 9 acquittal, dismissal, eliminate, explosion, expulsion, muster out, pour forth, send forth, terminate, unshackle 10 deactivate, demobilize, emancipate, inactivate, liberation, separation 11 exoneration, fulfillment *electrical:* 5 spark 6 leader 8 streamer 9 lightning

disciple 3 fan 6 minion 7 apostle, devotee, learner 8 adherent, follower, henchman, partisan, retainer 9 supporter 10 enthusiast

disciplinarian 8 enforcer, martinet 10 taskmaster 11 slave driver

disciplinary 8 punitive 9 punishing 10 corrective

discipline 4 curb, rule, will 5 check, drill, field, guide, order, teach, train 6 bridle, direct, method, punish, school, subdue 7 chasten, conduct, control, correct, educate 8 approach, chastise, instruct, penalize, restrain, training 9 castigate, obedience, subjugate, willpower 10 correction, punishment 11 castigation, self-control, self-mastery 12 chastisement 13 self-restraint

disclaim 4 deny 6 abjure, reject 7 disavow, gainsay, retract 8 disallow, forswear, renounce, traverse 9 repudiate 10 contradict

disclose 3 own 4 avow, tell 5 spill 6 expose, impart, relate, report, reveal, unmask, unveil 7 display, divulge, uncover 8 discover, give away, unclothe 9 make known

disclosure 6 exposé 8 exposure 10 revelation 11 declaration

discolor 3 tar 4 blot, dull, fade, smut, soil 5 smear, stain, sully, taint, tinge 6 defile, smudge 7 besmear, bestain, tarnish 8 besmirch

discoloration 4 spot 5 stain, taint 6 blotch, bruise, smudge 7 blemish 9 birthmark

discomfit 3 irk, vex 4 faze 5 abash, annoy, upset 6 baffle, bother, defeat, rattle, thwart 7 fluster, nonplus, perturb, unnerve 8 confound 9 embarrass 10 discompose, disconcert

discomfiture 5 upset 6 unease 8 disquiet 9 abashment, agitation, confusion 10 uneasiness 11 frustration 12 discomposure, perturbation 13 embarrassment, inconvenience

discomfort 3 irk, vex 4 ache, pain 5 annoy 6 bother, unease 7 malaise 8 vexation 9 annoyance 10 uneasiness 13 embarrassment

discomforting see UNCOMFORTABLE

discommend 5 decry 7 censure, frown on, put down 8 admonish, disfavor, object to 9 criticize, deprecate, disesteem, disparage, reprehend 10 disapprove

discommode 3 irk, vex 5 annoy, upset 6 bother, burden, flurry, put out 7 disturb, fluster, perturb, trouble 8 encumber 9 aggravate, disoblige 13 inconvenience

discompose 3 irk, vex 5 annoy, harry, upset, worry 6 bother, dismay, flurry, harass, pester, plague, ruffle, untune 7 agitate, disturb, fluster, perturb, unhinge 8 disarray, disorder, unsettle 9 embarrass 10 disarrange 11 disorganize

discomposure 5 upset, worry 6 bother, unease 8 vexation 9 abashment, agitation, annoyance, confusion 10 discomfort, irritation, perplexity, uneasiness 11 disquietude 12 discomfiture, perturbation 13 consternation, embarrassment

disconcert 4 faze 5 abash, upset, worry 6 bemuse, bother, puzzle, rattle, ruffle 7 confuse, disturb, nonplus, perplex, perturb, trouble 8 bewilder, confound, disquiet 9 discomfit, embarrass, frustrate

disconfirm 4 deny 5 rebut 6 refute, negate 7 gainsay 8 abnegate, confound, disclaim, disprove 10 contradict, controvert

disconnect 3 cut, gap 5 break, sever, unfix 6 cut off, detach 7 disjoin 8 separate, uncouple 9 disengage 10 dissociate

disconnected 7 muddled 8 detached, separate 10 disjointed, incoherent, unattached 11 fragmentary, unorganized 13 discontinuous

disconsolate 3 low, sad 4 blue, down 5 bleak, drear 6 abject, dreary, gloomy, woeful 7 doleful, forlorn, joyless, unhappy 8 dejected, downcast, wretched 9 cheerless, depressed, miserable, sorrowful, woebegone 10 dispirited, melancholy 11 comfortless, crestfallen, downhearted

discontent 4 envy 9 dysphoria 10 depression, inquietude, uneasiness 11 displeasure 12 disaffection, restlessness

discontented 5 upset 6 uneasy 7 annoyed, fretful, unhappy 8 restless 9 disturbed, irritated, perturbed 10 displeased 11 complaining, disgruntled, ungratified, unsatisfied 12 dissatisfied

discontinuation 3 end 4 stop 5 cease, close, pause 6 ending, finish 7 closing 8 abeyance 9 cessation 10 conclusion, desistance, moratorium, suspension 12 postponement

discontinue 3 end 4 halt, quit, stay, stop

5 cease, close, sever 6 desist, give up, wind up, wrap up 8 break off, close out, conclude, knock off, leave off, shut down, surcease 9 terminate

discontinuity 3 gap 4 hole, rent, rift 5 break, cleft, crack, split 6 breach, lacuna 7 fissure, opening, rupture

discontinuous 6 fitful 7 muddled 8 discrete, separate 9 spasmodic 10 incoherent, incohesive 11 unconnected 12 disconnected, intermittent 13 nonsequential

discord 5 clash 6 enmity, rancor, strife 7 rupture 8 conflict, contrast, disunity, division, friction, mismatch, variance 9 animosity, antipathy, hostility 10 antagonism, contention, difference, dissension, dissidence, dissonance, opposition 12 inconsonance, polarization 13 inconsistency *goddess:* 3 Ate 4 Eris

discordant 5 harsh 6 at odds 7 jarring 8 clashing, contrary, jangling, strident 9 dissonant 10 cacophonic, unpleasant 11 cacophonous, conflicting, disagreeing, inconsonant, quarrelsome, unmelodious 12 unharmonious

discotheque 6 bistro, nitery 7 hot spot 9 dance club, nightclub, night spot

discount 5 doubt, lower 6 deduct, ignore, reduce, slight 7 neglect, take off 8 belittle, derogate, decrease, diminish, knock off, mark down, markdown, minimize, overlook, roll back, rollback, subtract, take away 9 abatement, deduction, disregard, reduction, substract, underrate 13 underestimate

discountenance 4 faze 5 abash 6 rattle 7 frown on 8 confound, disfavor 9 deprecate, discomfit, embarrass 10 disapprove, disconcert, discourage

discourage 4 damp 5 daunt, check, chill, deter 6 dampen, deject, divert, hinder, impede 7 depress, inhibit, trouble 8 disfavor, dissuade, suppress 10 demoralize, dishearten

discouraging 5 bleak 7 unhappy 8 daunting 9 deterring, troubling 10 depressing 11 unfavorable, unpromising 12 unpropitious 13 disappointing, disheartening

discourse 4 talk 5 argue, essay, orate, speak, spiel, voice 6 sermon, speech, thesis 7 amplify, descant, enlarge, explain, expound, lecture 8 converse, harangue, perorate, rhetoric, speaking, treatise 9 expatiate, hold forth, monograph, sermonize, utterance 10 expression 11 interchange 12 conversation 13 verbalization *art of:* 8 rhetoric *religious:* 6 homily, sermon

discourteous 4 rude 6 unkind 7 boorish, brusque, ill-bred, uncivil, uncouth 8 impolite 10 ungracious, unmannerly 11 ill-mannered, impertinent 13 disrespectful

discover 4 espy, find, spot 5 learn 6 betray, detect, expose, reveal, unmask 7 divulge, find out, observe, unearth 8 come upon, perceive, proclaim, unshroud 9 ascertain, determine, encounter, make known 10 come across

discovery 4 find 5 trove 6 espial, strike 7 finding 8 locating, sighting 9 detection 10 revelation, unearthing

discredit 4 slur, ruin 5 doubt, shame 6 defame, malign, show up 7 asperse, degrade, put down, run down, slander, traduce 8 disgrace, ignominy 9 disparage, disrepute 10 disbelieve, opprobrium

discreditable 5 shady 6 shabby, shoddy 8 shameful, unworthy 9 degrading 10 inglorious 11 blameworthy, disgraceful, ignominious 12 contemptible, dishonorable, disreputable

discreet 4 wary 5 chary, muted, plain 6 modest, simple 7 careful, guarded, prudent, tactful 8 cautious, moderate 9 unadorned 10 controlled, reasonable, restrained 11 circumspect, considerate, unelaborate, unobtrusive 12 unnoticeable 13 unpretentious

discrepancy 3 gap 8 alterity, conflict, variance 9 disparity, otherness, variation 10 difference, divergence, divergency, unlikeness 12 disagreement 13 inconsistency

discrepant 6 unlike 7 diverse, varying 8 contrary 9 different, differing, disparate, divergent 11 conflicting, disagreeing 12 incompatible, inconsistent 13 contradictory

discrete 8 detached, distinct, separate 9 countable, different 12 disconnected 13 discontinuous, noncontinuous

discretion 4 care, tact 7 caution, reserve 8 delicacy, judgment, prudence, wariness 9 canniness, chariness, restraint 13 judiciousness

discriminate 5 judge 6 assess 7 compare, discern, make out 8 contrast, disfavor, evaluate, perceive, separate 9 segregate, tell apart 11 distinguish 13 differentiate

discriminating 6 choosy, select 7 finical, finicky 8 eclectic 9 judicious, selective 10 discerning 11 prejudicial

discrimination 5 taste 6 acumen 7 bigotry, insight 8 inequity, judgment 9 prejudice 10 astuteness, favoritism, partiality, perception 11 discernment, intolerance, penetration

discriminatory 6 biased 7 partial, unequal 8 partisan 9 jaundiced 10 prejudiced 11 inequitable, predisposed

discursive 5 windy, wordy 6 chatty, prolix 7 diffuse, logical, verbose 8 rambling, tortuous 9 desultory 10 analytical, circuitous, digressive, long-winded, meandering 11 wide-ranging

discuss 4 moot 5 argue, weigh 6 debate, parley 7 canvass, expound 8 consider, converse, hash over, talk over 9 elucidate, expatiate, interpret, talk about, thrash out, ventilate 10 deliberate, toss around *business:* 8 talk shop *lightly:* 5 bandy *thoroughly:* 7 exhaust

discussion 3 rap 4 chat, talk 6 confab, debate, parley, powwow 7 canvass, palaver 8 argument, colloquy 10 conference, rap session 11 bull session, ventilation 12 conversation, deliberation 13 confabulation

discus thrower 6 Alekna (Virgilijus), Marten (Maritza), Oerter (Al) 10 discobolus 11 Rashchupkin (Viktor)

disdain 5 abhor, scorn, scout, spurn 6 deride, refuse, reject, slight 7 contemn, despise, despite, hauteur, put down 8 aversion, belittle, contempt, disprize, misprize 9 antipathy 10 repugnance, undervalue

disdainful 5 aloof, proud 6 averse, lordly, snooty, uppity 7 haughty 8 arrogant, cavalier, derisive, insolent, scorning, spurning, superior, toplofty 11 overbearing 12 antipathetic, contemptuous, supercilious 13 high and mighty

disease 3 bug, ill 5 upset, virus 6 blight, malady 7 ailment, anthrax, illness, malaise, mycosis, purpura 8 debility, disorder, epidemic, myxedema, pandemic, sickness, syndrome, zoonoses (plural), zoonosis 9 affection, black lung, complaint, condition, contagion, ill health, infection, infirmity, sclerosis 10 affliction, alteration, blackwater, bronchitis, feebleness, impairment, infirmness, sickliness 11 decrepitude, derangement 13 unhealthiness *animal:* 5 mange, surra 6 rabies 7 bighead 8 enzootic, zoonosis 9 distemper, tularemia 10 rinderpest *blood:* 8 leukemia, leukoses (plural), leukosis *cabbage:* 8 clubroot *cattle:* 6 cowpox 7 foot rot, locoism, murrain 8 blackleg, vaccinia 9 vibriosis 10 rinderpest 11 brucellosis *cereal grass:* 4 bunt, smut 5 ergot *children's:* 5 mumps 7 measles, rubella 10 chicken pox 13 whooping cough *citrus tree:* 8 tristeza *classifica-*

tion: 8 nosology *combining form:* 4 path 5 patho *communicable:* 4 mono 5 mumps, polio 6 dengue, herpes, plague, rabies 7 cholera, leprosy, malaria, measles, rubella, tetanus, typhoid 8 impetigo 9 hepatitis, influenza 10 giardiasis 12 tuberculosis *deficiency:* 6 scurvy 7 rickets 8 beriberi, pellagra *disseminator:* 6 vector 7 carrier *eye:* 8 glaucoma, trachoma 9 retinitis *hair follicle:* 7 sycoses (plural), sycosis *heart:* 11 cardiopathy *horse:* 6 nagana, spavin 7 locosim, sarcoid 8 glanders 9 strangles *identification of:* 9 diagnosis *industrial:* 10 byssinosis *infectious:* 4 mono, yaws 6 dengue, typhus 7 leprosy, malaria, tetanus, typhoid 9 tularemia, vibriosis 10 rinderpest 13 whooping cough *liver:* 9 cirrhosis, hepatitis *livestock:* 7 locoism 9 vibriosis 10 rinderpest *lung:* 8 phthisic, phthisis 9 pneumonia 10 byssinosis 12 tuberculosis *lymph glands:* 8 scrofula *metabolic:* 4 gout *nervous system:* 4 kuru 6 rabies 10 diphtheria *of beets:* 8 heartrot *of mammals:* 6 rabies 7 malaria 9 distemper 10 babesiosis, rinderpest *parasitic:* 3 rot 4 smut 5 mange 7 malaria 8 hookworm, kala-azar 9 heartworm *plant:* 4 rust, scab, smut, wilt 5 blast, edema, scald, scurf, stunt 6 blight, blotch, canker, mosaic, streak 7 blister, crinkle, foot rot, frogeye, red leaf, root rot 8 clubroot, curly top, fusarium, gummosis, leaf curl, leaf roll, leaf rust, leaf spot, ring spot, root knot, stem rust 9 chlorosis, crown gall, white rust 10 blackheart, leaf scorch *poultry:* 8 leukosis *respiratory:* 6 asthma, coryza 10 byssinosis *sheep:* 3 gid 7 scrapie 9 vibriosis 10 bluetongue *skin:* 4 acne, yaws 5 favus, hives, lupus, mange, pinta, tinea 6 eczema, tetter 7 leprosy, prurigo, sarcoid, scabies 8 impetigo, miliaria, pyoderma, ringworm, vitiligo 9 pemphigus, psoriasis 10 erysipelas 11 scleroderma *syphilitic:* 5 tabes *throat:* 5 croup *thyroid:* 6 struma *tropical:* 4 yaws 5 pinta, sprue, surra 6 dengue 8 kala-azar *venereal:* 8 syphilis 9 chancroid, gonorrhea *viral:* 3 flu 4 AIDS, noma 5 Ebola, mumps, polio 6 dengue, grippe, herpes, rabies, zoster 7 measles, rubella, rubeola, variola 8 morbilli, shingles, smallpox 9 hepatitis, influenza, varicella 13 poliomyelitis

diseased 3 ill 6 ailing, infirm, sickly, unwell 7 fevered, unsound 8 feverish, infected

disembark 4 land 6 alight 7 deplane, detrain 8 go ashore

disembarrass 3 rid 4 free 7 release, relieve 8 liberate, unburden, untangle 9 extricate 11 disencumber, disentangle
disembodied 7 ghostly 8 ethereal, spectral 9 asomatous, unfleshly 10 immaterial, unphysical, wraithlike 11 incorporeal, nonmaterial, nonphysical 13 insubstantial
disembogue 4 flow, gush, pour, spew 5 empty 7 pour out 9 discharge
disembowel 3 gut 10 eviscerate, exenterate
disenchanted 5 blasé, jaded 6 soured 7 cynical 9 jaundiced 10 undeceived 11 worldly-wise 12 disappointed, dissatisfied 13 disenthralled, disillusioned
disencumber 4 free 7 lighten, release, relieve, sort out 8 free from, liberate, unburden 9 alleviate, disburden, extricate
disengage 4 free, part 5 loose, unfix 6 detach, opt out, unbind 7 back out, drop out, release, unloose 8 cut loose, liberate, separate, uncouple, unfasten, unloosen, withdraw 10 disconnect
disentangle 5 untie 6 detach 7 resolve, sort out, unravel, unsnarl, untwine 8 separate 9 extricate 10 unscramble 11 disencumber 13 straighten out
disenthrall 4 free 7 manumit, release 8 liberate 10 emancipate
disfavor 7 dislike 8 aversion, distrust, mistrust 9 deprecate, disesteem, disregard, disrepute 10 disrespect 11 disapproval 12 disadvantage, unpopularity
disfigure 3 mar 4 maim, scar 6 deface, defile, deform, impair, injure, mangle 7 blemish, distort 8 mutilate
disfranchise 3 bar 7 exclude 8 take away 9 deprive of 10 disentitle
disgorge 4 barf, spew 5 belch, eject, eruct, erupt, expel, vomit 6 give up, irrupt, spit up 7 release, throw up, upchuck 9 discharge
disgrace 5 odium, shame 6 stigma 7 attaint, mortify, obloquy 8 black eye, contempt, dishonor, ignominy, reproach 9 discredit, disrepute, humiliate 10 opprobrium, stigmatize 11 degradation, humiliation
disgraceful 7 ignoble 8 shameful 9 degrading 10 deplorable, inglorious, unbecoming 11 humiliating, ignominious, reproachful 12 dishonorable, disreputable
disgruntled 5 vexed 6 cranky, put out 7 annoyed, beefing, griping 8 grousing 9 irritated 10 discontent, displeased, ill-humored, malcontent 11 ungratified 12 discontented, malcontented
disguise 4 hide, mask, sham, veil 5 belie, cloak, feign, put on 6 facade

7 conceal, falsify, obscure 8 artifice, pretense 9 deception 10 camouflage, false front, pretension 12 misrepresent
disguised 6 masked, veiled 7 cloaked, feigned 9 incognito 10 undercover 11 camouflaged
disguisement 4 mask, veil 5 cloak, front 6 facade 8 pretense 9 deception 10 false front, pretention
disgust 6 nausea, offend, revolt, sicken 8 aversion, gross out, loathing, nauseate 9 antipathy, repulsion, revulsion 10 abhorrence, repugnance 13 squeamishness
disgusted 5 fed up 8 offended, repelled, repulsed, revolted, sickened 9 nauseated, squeamish 10 grossed out
disgusting 4 foul, icky, vile 5 gross, nasty, yucky 7 noisome 9 loathsome, offensive, repellent, repugnant, repulsive, revolting, sickening 10 nauseating
dish 4 bowl, buzz, food, talk, tray 5 plate 6 course, gossip, tureen 7 chatter, hearsay, platter, scandal, slander 9 casserole, container 11 scuttlebutt *baked:* 7 soufflé *baking:* 7 cocotte, scallop 9 casserole 12 scallop shell *cheese:* 6 fondue 7 ramekin, rarebit 8 raclette, ramequin *Chinese:* 6 dim sum, lo mein, subgum, wonton 8 chop suey, chow mein 10 egg foo yong, egg foo yung 11 egg foo young *deep:* 9 casserole *Hungarian:* 7 goulash *Italian:* 5 penne, pesto, pizza 6 scampi 7 cannoli, lasagna, polenta, ravioli 8 calamari, linguine, linguini, osso buco, rigatoni 9 foccacia, manicotti 10 cannelloni, scaloppine, tortellini 11 saltimbocca *Japanese:* 7 sashimi, tempura 8 sukiyaki *Mexican:* 4 taco 5 chili 6 fajita, flauta, nachos, tamale 7 burrito, chalupa 8 frijoles 9 enchilada, guacamole 10 carne asada 11 chimichanga 12 refried beans 13 chili con carne *Middle Eastern:* 5 halva, kebab, kibbe, kibbi 6 halvah, hummus, kibbeh 7 baklava, falafel 8 couscous, moussaka 10 shish kebab 11 baba ghanouj 12 baba ghanoush *principal:* 6 entrée *rice:* 7 risotto *rice and meat:* 5 pilaf *Scottish:* 5 brose 6 haggis *shallow:* 6 saucer *Thai:* 7 pad thai
disharmonize 3 jar, war 5 clash 6 jangle 7 discord 8 conflict, mismatch 9 disaccord
disharmony 6 strife 7 discord 8 conflict, disunion, disunity, friction, variance 9 cacophony 10 contention, difference, dissension, dissonance
dishearten 3 cow 5 chill, crush, daunt, shake 6 dampen, deject, dismay, sadden 7 depress, unnerve 8 dispirit, distress 10 demoralize, discourage, intimidate

disheartening 8 daunting 9 dismaying, saddening 10 depressing 11 dispiriting 12 demoralizing, discouraging, intimidating

dishes 4 ware *clay:* 7 pottery *porcelain:* 5 china

dishevel 5 touse 6 muss up, rumple, tousle 8 disarray, disorder 10 disarrange, discompose

disheveled 5 messy 7 ruffled, rumpled, tousled, unkempt 8 ill-kempt, mussed up, uncombed 10 disarrayed, disordered 11 discomposed

dishonest 5 false, lying, rogue, snide 6 tricky, unfair 7 corrupt, crooked, knavish 8 cheating, cozening, two-faced 9 deceitful, deceiving, deceptive, swindling 10 defrauding, fraudulent, mendacious, untruthful 13 double-dealing, untrustworthy

dishonesty 5 fraud, guile 6 deceit 7 falsity, knavery, roguery 8 flimflam, pretense, trickery 9 chicanery, deception, duplicity, falsehood, hypocrisy 10 corruption 11 crookedness 13 double-dealing

dishonor see DISGRACE

dishonorable see DISGRACEFUL

dish out 5 ladle, serve 6 pile on, supply 7 deliver, present, serve up 8 allocate, disburse, dispense 10 distribute

disillusioned see DISENCHANTED

disinclination 7 dislike 8 aversion, distaste 9 antipathy, objection 10 reluctance 13 indisposition, unwillingness

disinclined 5 loath 6 averse 7 balking, opposed 8 boggling, hesitant 9 reluctant, resistant, unwilling 10 hesitating, indisposed 12 antipathetic 13 unsympathetic

disinfect 6 purify 8 sanitize 9 autoclave, sterilize 13 decontaminate

disingenuous 3 sly 4 foxy, wily 5 false 6 artful, crafty, tricky 7 cunning, devious, feigned 8 delusive, guileful, indirect, specious 9 deceitful, deceiving, deceptive, dishonest, insidious, insincere, sophistic 10 misleading 11 calculating, casuistical, sophistical

disinherit 6 cut off 7 bereave, exclude 9 deprive of, repudiate 10 dispossess

disintegrate 3 rot 4 turn 5 break, burst, decay, spoil, taint 6 molder 7 crumble, scatter, shatter 8 splinter 9 break down, decompose, fall apart 10 deliquesce

disinter 5 dig up 6 exhume, unbury 7 unearth 8 exhumate 9 resurrect

disinterest 6 apathy 7 neglect 8 coolness, lethargy 9 aloofness, disregard, unconcern 10 detachment, dispassion, neutrality 11 impassivity, inattention,

insouciance, nonchalance, objectivity 12 indifference

disinterested 4 fair, just 5 aloof 6 candid 7 neutral 8 detached, unbiased 9 impartial, impassive, incurious, objective 10 even-handed, impersonal, neglectful, nonchalant 11 inattentive, indifferent, unconcerned

disjoin 4 part 5 sever, unfix 6 detach, divide, sunder, unlink 7 break up, divorce 8 disunite, separate, uncouple, unfasten 9 disengage, take apart 10 dissociate 12 disaffiliate, disassociate

disjointed 7 jumbled, muddled 8 confused, inchoate, rambling 9 displaced 10 disordered, incoherent, incohesive 11 unconnected, unorganized 13 discontinuous

disk 4 puck 5 wafer 6 record *metal:* 4 slug *ornamental:* 6 bangle, sequin

dislike 4 hate, shun 5 abhor, scorn, spurn 6 animus, detest, loathe, oppose, reject, resent 7 deplore, despise, frown on 8 aversion, disfavor, distaste, execrate 9 animosity, antipathy 10 alienation, disapprove, repugnance 11 detestation, disapproval 13 indisposition

dislimn 3 dim 5 bedim 6 darken 7 becloud, obscure 9 obfuscate

dislocate 5 break 7 disrupt, unhinge 9 disengage 10 disconnect 13 disarticulate

dislodge 4 oust 5 eject, evict, expel 6 remove, uproot 8 displace, drive out, force out

disloyal 5 false 6 untrue 8 apostate, recreant 9 alienated, faithless 10 perfidious, traitorous, unfaithful 11 disaffected, treacherous

disloyalty 7 falsity, perfidy, treason 8 apostasy 9 falseness, recreancy, treachery 10 alienation, infidelity 12 disaffection 13 faithlessness

dismal 5 bleak 6 dreary, gloomy, horrid, somber, sombre 7 joyless 8 desolate, dreadful, funereal, lowering 9 atrocious, cheerless, depressed, tenebrous 10 depressing, depressive 11 dispiriting 12 discouraging 13 disheartening

dismantle 4 raze, undo 5 strip, unrig, wreck 6 denude, divest 7 break up, destroy 8 demolish, pull down, take down 9 break down, knock down, take apart 11 disassemble

dismay 4 faze, fear 5 abash, alarm, daunt, dread, panic, scare, shake, upset 6 appall, fright, horror, rattle 7 agitate, fluster, horrify, perturb, unnerve 8 affright, bewilder, confound, dispirit, distress, frighten 9 discomfit, dumbfound, embarrass 10 discompose, disconcert, discourage, dishearten 11 trepidation **12** perturbation **13** consternation

dismayed 5 upset **6** afraid, aghast, scared, shaken **7** fearful, shocked **9** disturbed

dismember 4 maim **7** disjoin **8** mutilate **9** dismantle, take apart

dismiss 3 axe, can **4** drop, fire, oust, sack, shed **5** chuck, eject, evict, let go, scorn, spurn **6** bounce, depose, deride, lay off, reject, remove, retire, shelve, unseat **7** boot out, cashier, contemn, decline, disband, kick out, kiss off, turn off **8** displace, furlough, poohpooh, ridicule, throw out, turn away, turn down **9** discharge, repudiate, terminate **11** send packing

dismissal 5 congé **6** firing, layoff, ouster **7** removal **8** brush-off, bum's rush **9** discharge, expulsion **10** cashiering

dismount 6 alight, debark, get off **7** deplane, detrain **9** disembark **10** alight from **11** descend from

Disney, Walt 10 cartoonist *character:* **4** Gyro, Huey, Lady **5** Ariel, Bambi, Daisy, Dewey, Dumbo, Goofy, Louie, Mulan, Pluto, Simba, Tramp **6** Beauty, Donald, Mickey, Minnie, Mowgli **7** Aladdin, Scrooge **9** Gladstone, Pinocchio **10** Beagle Boys, Clarabelle, Pocahontas *classic:* **5** Bambi, Dumbo **8** Fantasia **9** Pinocchio **10** Jungle Book (The) **15** Lady and the Tramp

disobedient 6 unruly **7** naughty, wayward, willful **8** contrary **10** headstrong, ill-behaved, rebellious, refractory, uncompliant **11** misbehaving **12** contumacious, noncompliant, obstreperous, recalcitrant **13** insubordinate

disoblige 5 annoy **6** bother, offend, put out **7** affront, disturb, trouble **9** displease, incommode **10** discommode **13** inconvenience

disorder 3 ill **4** mess, riot **5** chaos, mix up, snarl, upset **6** ataxia, hubbub, jumble, malady, mess up, muddle, muss up, ruckus, rumple, tumble, tumult, unrest, uproar **7** ailment, anarchy, clutter, confuse, disease, embroil, illness, misdeed, shuffle, turmoil **8** disarray, sickness, syndrome, unsettle, upheaval **9** affection, agitation, commotion, complaint, confusion, infirmity **10** affliction, turbulence, untidiness *mental:* **5** mania **8** delirium, insanity, neurosis, paranoia **9** psychosis **11** psychopathy **13** schizophrenia

disordered 6 roiled **7** jumbled, muddled **8** confused, inchoate, shuffled **9** displaced **10** disjointed, dislocated, incoherent, incohesive **11** disarranged,

unconnected, unorganized **13** discontinuous

disorderly 5 rowdy **6** unruly, untidy **7** jumbled, raucous, unkempt **8** confused **9** cluttered, offensive, turbulent **10** boisterous, topsy-turvy, tumultuous **12** disorganized, rambunctious, unsystematic

disorganize 5 upset **6** jumble, mess up **7** break up, confuse, derange, disband, disrupt **8** disorder, disperse, unsettle **10** disarrange

disoriented 4 lost **7** mixed up **8** confused **9** displaced, perplexed, unsettled **10** bewildered

disown 4 deny, dump **6** desert, reject **7** cast off, disavow **8** disclaim, renounce **9** repudiate

disparage 5 decry **6** defame, slight **7** condemn, degrade, devalue, dismiss, put down, run down **8** bad-mouth, belittle, derogate, discount, downplay, minimize, pooh-pooh **9** denigrate, deprecate, discredit, dispraise, downgrade, underrate **10** demoralize, depreciate, undervalue **11** detract from

disparagement 5 scorn **7** calumny, censure, despite, scandal, slander **8** contempt, despisal, reproach **9** aspersion, discredit, stricture **10** backbiting, defamation, derogation, detraction, diminution **11** degradation **12** backstabbing, depreciation **13** animadversion

disparate 6 at odds, divers, unlike, varied **7** diverse, unalike, unequal, various, varying **8** discrete, distinct, separate **9** different, divergent, unsimilar **10** dissimilar **11** distinctive, incongruous, inconsonant **12** incompatible, inconsistent

disparity 3 gap **8** contrast **9** imbalance **10** difference, divergence, divergency, inequality **11** discrepancy **13** disproportion, dissimilarity

dispassionate 4 calm, fair, just **7** neutral **8** composed, detached, unbiased **9** equitable, impartial, objective, unruffled **10** impersonal **11** unemotional **12** unprejudiced **13** disinterested

dispatch 4 kill, send, ship, slay **5** haste, hurry, scrag, speed **6** defeat, murder **7** bump off, execute, forward, killing, message, put away **8** alacrity, get rid of, shipment, transmit **9** dispose of, eliminate, swiftness **10** expedition, put to death, speediness **11** assassinate, promptitude

dispel 6 banish **7** cast out, scatter **8** disperse **9** clear away, dissipate, drive away

dispensable 5 minor **7** trivial **8** needless,

unneeded **10** disposable, expendable, unrequired **11** superfluous, unessential, unimportant, unnecessary **12** nonessential

dispensary 6 clinic

dispensation 4 plan **5** favor, share **7** license, portion, service **8** bestowal, courtesy, kindness, ordering **9** allotment, exception, exemption, privilege, remission **10** indulgence, management **12** disbursement, distribution **13** apportionment, authorization

dispense 5 allot, apply, wield **6** assign, divide, excuse, exempt, ration, supply **7** absolve, deal out, deliver, dish out, dole out, furnish, give out, mete out, portion, provide, release **8** allocate, carry out, disburse, share out, transfer **9** apportion, discharge, partition **10** administer, distribute, measure out, portion out

disperse 3 sow **5** spray, strew **6** dispel, divide, spread, vanish **7** break up, diffuse, disband, radiate, scatter **9** broadcast, dissipate, partition, propagate **10** distribute

dispersion 6 spread **7** breakup, colloid **9** diffusion, spreading **10** scattering **11** dissipation **12** distribution **13** dissemination

dispirit 3 cow **5** chill, daunt **6** deject, dismay, sadden **7** depress, oppress **8** distress **10** demoralize, discourage, dishearten

dispirited 3 low, sad **4** blue, down, glum **5** cowed **6** morose **7** daunted **8** cast down, dejected, dismayed, downcast, saddened **9** bummed out, depressed, oppressed, woebegone **10** distressed, melancholy **11** crestfallen, demoralized, discouraged, downhearted **12** disconsolate, disheartened

dispiriting 4 blue **6** dismal, dreary, gloomy **8** daunting, dolorous, funereal **9** cheerless, dismaying, saddening **10** depressing, oppressive **12** demoralizing, disconsolate, discouraging **13** disheartening

displace 4 oust, sack **5** exile, expel, usurp **6** banish, deport, depose, remove **7** succeed **8** dethrone, supplant **9** supersede, transport **10** expatriate, substitute

display 4 pomp, show **5** array, model **6** evince, expose, flaunt, lay out, parade, reveal, spread, unfold, unfurl, unveil **7** exhibit, panoply, present, showing, show off, trot out, uncover **8** brandish, evidence, manifest, showcase **9** showiness, spectacle **10** exhibiting, exhibition **11** demonstrate, ostentation **13** demonstration, manifestation

displeasing 6 vexing **7** irksome **8** annoying **10** bothersome, unpleasant **12** disagreeable **13** objectionable

displeasure 8 aversion, disfavor, vexation **9** annoyance **10** discomfort, discontent, irritation, uneasiness **11** indignation, unhappiness **13** indisposition

disport 4 show **5** amuse **6** acquit, behave, divert, expose, flaunt, frolic, parade **7** conduct, display, exhibit, show off, trot out **9** entertain

disposal 5 order **7** removal **8** bestowal, chucking, jettison, ordering, transfer **9** clearance **10** allocation, assignment, demolition, discarding, regulation, relegation **11** arrangement, consignment, destruction, disposition **12** distribution, transference

dispose 4 bend, bias, rank **5** array, order, range **6** settle **7** arrange, incline, marshal, prepare **8** organize, regulate **9** make ready **11** systematize *of:* **4** dump, junk, sell **5** chuck, scrap **6** finish, handle, unload **7** deep-six, destroy, discard **8** deal with, throw out, transfer **9** eighty-six, eliminate **10** distribute

disposed 3 apt **4** fain, game **5** prone, ready **6** biased, minded **7** partial, willing **8** arranged, inclined **9** persuaded

disposition 4 bent, cast, mood, tone, type, vein **5** being, order, stamp **6** makeup, nature, temper **7** control, leaning, mind-set **8** ordering, penchant, riddance, sequence, tendency, transfer **9** character, direction **10** management, proclivity, propensity, settlement **11** arrangement, inclination, personality, temperament **12** constitution, predilection **13** individuality *favorable:* **8** optimism *unfavorable:* **9** pessimism

dispossess 3 rob **4** oust **5** eject, strip **6** divest **7** bereave, deprive

dispossession 4 loss **6** ouster **7** seizure **9** privation **10** divestment **11** deprivation, divestiture **13** expropriation

dispraise 3 pan **5** decry **6** censor, deride, dump on **7** put down, run down **8** badmouth, belittle, derogate **9** criticize, deprecate, discredit, disparage **10** depreciate, disapprove **11** detract from **12** depreciation

disproportion 8 imparity, mismatch **9** disparity **10** inequality, unevenness **12** lopsidedness

disproportionate 6 uneven **7** unequal **8** lopsided **10** unbalanced

disprove 5 belie, rebut **6** refute, negate **7** confute, explode **8** confound, overturn, puncture, traverse **9** discredit, overthrow **10** invalidate

disputable 4 iffy, moot **7** dubious

8 arguable, doubtful **9** debatable, uncertain, unsettled **10** unresolved **11** problematic **12** questionable **13** controversial

disputation 6 debate **8** argument, forensic, polemics **9** dialectic **11** controversy **13** argumentation

dispute 4 buck, duel, moot, tiff **5** argue, fight, rebut, repel **6** bicker, combat, debate, hassle, impugn, negate, oppose, refute, resist, rumpus, strife **7** confute, contend, contest, discuss, gainsay, quarrel, quibble, wrangle **8** argument, conflict, question, squabble **9** bickering, challenge, thrash out, withstand **10** contention, controvert, falling-out **11** altercation, controversy, embroilment

disputed 7 debated **8** arguable **9** contested, uncertain **12** questionable **13** controversial

disqualified 5 unfit **8** unfitted **10** ineligible, unequipped

disqualify 3 bar **5** debar **6** except **7** exclude, rule out, suspend **9** eliminate *as judge:* **6** recuse

disquiet 5 alarm, angst, upset, worry **6** bother, flurry, unease, unrest **7** agitate, anxiety, concern, disturb, ferment, fluster, perturb, trouble, turmoil **10** discompose, uneasiness **11** disturbance, restiveness **12** restlessness **13** Sturm und Drang

disquietude 4 care **5** worry **6** unease, unrest **7** anxiety, concern, ferment, turmoil **9** agitation, misgiving **10** foreboding, uneasiness **11** nervousness, restiveness **12** apprehension, restlessness **13** Sturm und Drang

Disraeli, Benjamin *novel:* **5** Sybil **7** Lothair, Tancred **8** Endymion **9** Coningsby *opponent:* **4** Peel (Robert) **9** Gladstone (William) *queen:* **8** Victoria

disregard 6 forget, ignore, slight **7** neglect, tune out **8** overlook **9** unconcern **12** heedlessness, indifference

disregardful 3 lax **5** slack **6** remiss **8** careless, derelict, heedless **9** forgetful, unheeding, negligent, unmindful **10** neglectful, regardless, unthinking **11** indifferent, unconcerned **12** absentminded

disremember 6 forget

disreputable 4 base **5** dingy, seamy, seedy, shady **6** scurvy, shabby, shoddy, sordid **7** run-down **8** decrepit, infamous, shameful **10** inglorious **11** dilapidated, disgraceful, ignominious **12** contemptible, unprincipled **13** discreditable, unrespectable

disrepute 5 odium, shame **7** obloquy

8 disfavor, disgrace, dishonor, ignominy **9** disesteem **10** opprobrium

disrespect 6 insult **7** disdain **8** boldness, contempt, rudeness **9** disregard, flippancy, impudence, insolence **10** incivility **11** discourtesy, presumption **12** impertinence, impoliteness

disrespectful 4 flip, rude **5** sassy, saucy **7** ill-bred, uncivil **8** flippant, impolite, impudent, insolent **10** ungracious **11** ill-mannered, impertinent **12** contemptuous, discourteous

disrobe 4 bare, peel **5** strip **6** denude, divest **7** undress **8** unclothe

disrupt 5 upset **6** mess up **7** break up, rupture **8** disorder, unsettle

dissatisfaction 6 dismay **9** annoyance, complaint **10** discontent, irritation, uneasiness **11** displeasure, frustration

dissatisfied 5 irked, vexed **7** annoyed **8** bothered **10** begrudging, discontent, displeased, malcontent **11** complaining, disaffected, unfulfilled **12** disappointed, discontented, malcontented

dissect 5 probe, study **7** analyze, examine, inspect **9** anatomize, break down, take apart **10** scrutinize

dissection 7 autopsy **8** analysis, necropsy *of animals:* **7** zootomy

dissemble 4 hide, mask **5** cloak, feign **7** conceal, cover up, dress up, falsify **8** disguise, simulate **9** whitewash **10** camouflage **11** counterfeit

dissembler 4 fake **5** faker, fraud, phony **8** deceiver, imposter, impostor, pharisee **9** hypocrite, pretender

disseminate 3 sow **5** strew **6** blazon, spread **7** bestrew, diffuse, publish, scatter, send out **8** announce, disperse, proclaim **9** advertise, broadcast, circulate, propagate, publicize **10** promulgate

dissension 5 fight **6** strife **7** discord, dispute, faction, quarrel, wrangle **8** argument, clashing, conflict, disunity, friction, variance **9** bickering **10** contention, difference, quarreling **11** altercation, controversy **12** disagreement

dissent 5 demur **6** differ, heresy, object **8** conflict, variance **9** misbelief **10** contention, difference, heterodoxy, opposition, resistance **11** unorthodoxy **12** nonagreement **13** nonconformism, nonconformity

dissenter 7 heretic **8** apostate, defector, deserter, partisan, recreant **10** schismatic, separatist **11** misbeliever, schismatist **13** nonconformist

dissertation 6 thesis **8** tractate, treatise **9** discourse, monograph **10** commentary, exposition **11** disputation **12** disquisition **13** argumentation

disservice 4 harm **6** damage, injury, insult **8** disfavor, meanness, mischief **9** detriment **10** misfortune

dissever 3 cut, hew **4** hack, part **5** carve, slice, split **6** cleave, detach, divide, sunder **7** disjoin, divorce **8** disjoint, disunite, separate, uncouple **10** disconnect

dissidence 6 heresy, schism, strife **7** discord, dispute, dissent, faction **8** conflict, friction, variance **10** contention, disharmony, dissension, heterodoxy, opposition **11** discordance, unorthodoxy **12** disagreement **13** nonconformism, nonconformity

dissident 7 heretic **8** partisan, recusant **9** differing, dissenter, heretical, heterodox, protestor **10** schismatic, separatist, unorthodox **11** contentious, disagreeing, misbeliever, nonbeliever, quarrelsome, schismatist **12** disputatious, unharmonious **13** nonconformist

dissimilar 6 unlike **7** diverse, unalike, unequal, various **8** distinct **9** different, disparate, divergent **13** heterogeneous

dissimilarity 8 contrast, variance **9** disparity, diversity, variation **10** difference, divergence, divergency, unlikeness **11** incongruity **13** heterogeneity, inconsistency

dissimulate see DISSEMBLE

dissimulation 5 fraud, guile, lying **6** deceit **7** cunning **8** artifice, flimflam, pretense **9** deception, duplicity, hypocrisy, mendacity, sophistry **10** craftiness, pharisaism **11** beguilement, smoke screen

dissipate 4 blow **5** use up, waste **6** burn up, spread, vanish **7** break up, scatter **8** disperse, evanesce, melt away, misspend, squander **9** evaporate, throw away **11** fritter away

dissipated 6 rakish, wanton, wasted **8** depraved **9** debauched, reprobate **10** degenerate, licentious, profligate **11** intemperate

dissociate 4 part **5** unfix **6** cut off, detach **7** disband, disjoin **8** alienate, disunite, estrange, separate, uncouple **9** disengage **10** disconnect

dissolute 3 lax **4** fast, wild **5** loose, slack **6** rakish, wanton **7** raffish, wayward **8** decadent, depraved **9** abandoned, debauched, indulgent, reprobate **10** degenerate, dissipated, licentious, profligate **12** unprincipled, unrestrained

dissolution 5 death, decay, split **6** demise **7** breakup, divorce, rupture, split-up **8** division **9** dispersal, partition **10** detachment, disbanding, profligacy **11** evaporation **12** liquefaction

dissolvable 7 soluble **8** meltable

dissolve 3 end **4** flux, melt, thaw, undo, void **5** annul, quash **6** recess, vacate, vanish **7** adjourn, break up, destroy, diffuse, disband, liquefy, resolve, shatter, unravel **8** abrogate, demolish, disperse, evanesce, fade away, get rid of, melt away, prorogue, separate **9** decompose, dissipate, evaporate, prorogate, terminate, waste away **10** deliquesce, do away with **12** disintegrate

dissonance 6 strife **7** discord **8** clashing, conflict **9** cacophony, harshness **10** contention, difference, disharmony **11** incongruity **12** disagreement **13** inconsistency

dissonant 5 harsh **7** grating, jarring, raucous **8** strident **9** unmusical **10** cacophonic, discordant, inharmonic **11** cacophonous, conflicting, incongruous **12** incompatible, inharmonious

dissuade 5 deter **7** turn off **10** discourage, disincline

distaff 6 female **8** maternal

distance 4 area **5** ambit, lapse, orbit, range, reach, scope, space, sweep **6** course, degree, extent, length, radius, remove, spread **7** breadth, compass, expanse, horizon, mileage, reserve, spacing, stretch **8** coldness, interval **9** amplitude, disparity, expansion, extension **10** divergence, divergency, remoteness, separation **11** distinction, perspective **13** dissimilarity *angular:* **8** latitude **9** longitude *between levels:* **4** drop *between rails:* **4** gage *between supports:* **4** span *from bottom to top:* **6** height *geometric:* **8** altitude *greatest perpendicular:* **6** camber *measuring instrument:* **8** odometer **9** pedometer, telemeter **11** range finder *minute:* **4** hair *perpendicular:* **5** depth *shortest:* **7** beeline **12** straight line *the wind blows:* **5** fetch

distant 3 far, shy **4** afar, cold, cool **5** aloof, apart **6** absent, far-off, remote **7** faraway, haughty, obscure, removed, spacial, spatial **8** far-flung, isolated, outlying, reserved, secluded, solitary **9** separated, unsimilar, withdrawn **10** unsociable **11** out-of-the-way, sequestered, standoffish *combining form:* **3** tel **4** tele, telo

distaste 7 disgust, dislike **8** aversion, loathing **9** antipathy, hostility, revulsion **10** abhorrence, repugnance **13** indisposition

distasteful 8 unsavory **9** loathsome, obnoxious, offensive, repellent, repugnant, repulsive **10** abominable, unpleasant **11** displeasing, unpalatable **12** disagreeable, unappetizing 13 objectionable

distemper 6 malady 7 ailment, disease 8 disorder 9 contagion, strangles 10 affliction 11 derangement 13 panleucopenia

distend 5 bloat, bulge, swell, widen 6 dilate, expand, extend, puff up 7 amplify, augment, enlarge, inflate, stretch 8 increase, lengthen 10 stretch out

distill 6 refine 7 extract 8 boil down 11 concentrate, precipitate

distinct 4 sole 5 clear, lucid, plain 6 marked, patent, single, unique 7 audible, defined, diverse, evident, express, notable, obvious, special, unusual 8 apparent, clear-cut, definite, discrete, especial, explicit, manifest, palpable, peculiar, separate, specific 9 different, divergent 10 individual, noticeable, particular 11 categorical, unambiguous, unequivocal 12 unmistakable

distinction 4 bays, rank 5 award, badge, grade, honor, kudos 6 nicety, renown 7 laurels 8 accolade, eminence, prestige 10 difference, divergence, divergency, prominence, unlikeness 11 differentia, peculiarity, preeminence, recognition 12 significance 13 dissimilarity

distinctive 6 proper, single, unique 7 special 8 peculiar, separate, singular 10 individual 13 idiosyncratic

distingué 6 classy, urbane 7 courtly, elegant, eminent, genteel, refined 8 cultured, decorous, highbrow, mannerly, polished, well-bred 9 dignified, high-class 10 cultivated 13 sophisticated

distinguish 4 mark, note, spot, view 5 honor, place 6 descry, notice, set off 7 dignify, make out, mark off, observe, pick out 8 classify, identify, perceive, separate 9 recognize, single out 10 categorize 12 characterize, discriminate 13 differentiate, individualize

distinguished 5 famed, noted 6 famous 7 eminent, notable, stately 8 esteemed, imposing, renowned 9 dignified, prominent 10 celebrated 11 illustrious

distort 4 bend, warp, wind 5 alter, color, twist 6 deform, garble 7 contort, falsify, pervert, torture 8 misstate 11 misconstrue 12 misinterpret, misrepresent

distortion 8 twisting 9 deformity

distract 5 addle, mix up 6 ball up, bemuse, divert, puzzle 7 confuse, fluster, mislead, perplex 8 befuddle, bewilder, confound, throw off 9 sidetrack, unbalance

distracted 8 confused, deranged, maddened, troubled 9 oblivious 10 non-plussed 11 disoriented, inattentive, preoccupied 12 absentminded

distraction 5 upset 9 agitation, amusement, confusion, diversion 10 perplexity 12 interruption 13 entertainment

distrait 5 upset 7 anxious, bemused, faraway, worried 8 confused, deranged, harassed, maddened, troubled 9 tormented, withdrawn 10 abstracted, distracted, distraught 11 inattentive, preoccupied 12 absentminded, apprehensive

distraught 5 upset 6 addled, crazed 7 anxious, frantic, muddled, rattled, shook up, unglued, worried 8 agitated, confused, demented, deranged, frenzied, harassed, troubled, worked up 9 flustered, perturbed, tormented, wigged-out 10 distressed, bewildered, freaked out, nonplussed 11 overwrought

distress 3 ail, irk, mar, try, vex, woe 4 ache, care, hurt, pain, pang, rack 5 agony, annoy, cross, dolor, grief, rigor, throe, trial, upset, worry 6 bother, grieve, harass, misery, pester, plague, sorrow, strain, strait, twinge 7 afflict, anguish, anxiety, exhaust, torment, torture, trouble 8 aggrieve, calamity, exigency, hardship 9 adversity, constrain, hard times, suffering 10 affliction, difficulty, heartbreak, misfortune, visitation 11 tribulation, vicissitude **call:** 6 Mayday **signal:** 3 SOS 5 alarm

distressing 4 dire 6 woeful 8 alarming, grievous, shocking 9 offensive 10 deplorable, lamentable 11 dispiriting, regrettable, unfortunate 13 heartbreaking

distribute 4 deal, mete 5 allot, place, strew 6 assign, assort, divide, donate, parcel, ration, spread 7 deal out, deliver, diffuse, dish out, divvy up, dole out, dribble, give out, hand out, mete out, prorate, radiate, scatter, slice up 8 allocate, classify, disburse, dispense, position, separate 9 apportion, circulate, partition, propagate, spread out 10 administer, measure out 11 disseminate **in a tournament:** 4 seed

distribution 7 density 8 delivery, dividend, grouping, ordering, sequence 9 allotment, allotting, diffusion, dispersal, marketing, placement, spreading 10 dispersion, scattering 11 arrangement, probability, propagation 12 apportioning, dispensation 13 apportionment, dissemination

distributor 5 agent 6 broker, jobber 7 carrier 10 wholesaler 12 intermediate

district 4 area, ward 5 tract 6 barrio, locale, parcel, region, sector 7 borough, quarter, section 8 division, locality, precinct, vicinage, vicinity 11 subdivision 12 neighborhood *ecclesiastical:* 5 synod 6 parish 7 diocese *Greek:* 4 deme *Indian:* 6 tahsil *judicial:* 7 circuit *London:* 4 Soho 7 Chelsea, Mayfair 9 Docklands, Greenwich, Southwark 10 Kensington, Piccadilly 11 Canary Wharf, Notting Hill 13 Knightsbridge *New York:* 4 Soho 7 Chelsea, Tribeca *theater:* 6 rialto

District of Columbia *college, university:* 6 Howard 8 American, Catholic 9 Gallaudet 10 Georgetown *motto:* 13 E Pluribus Unum *official bird:* 10 wood thrush *official flower:* 18 American Beauty rose

distrust 5 doubt 7 suspect 8 question, wariness 9 disbelief, discredit, misgiving, suspicion 10 disbelieve

distrustful 4 wary 5 chary, leery 7 cynical, dubious, jealous 8 doubtful, doubting 10 suspicious 12 questionable

distrusting 4 wary 5 chary, leery 7 cynical, dubious, jealous 8 doubtful, doubting 10 suspicious

disturb 4 faze 5 alarm, daunt, rouse, upset, worry 6 bother, harass, meddle, mess up, pester, stir up 7 agitate, break up, disrupt, fluster, perplex, trouble, unnerve 8 bewilder, distress, unsettle 9 incommode, interrupt 10 discompose, disconcert, tamper with 13 inconvenience, interfere with

disturbance 4 flap, fuss, stir, to-do 5 stink 6 clamor, hubbub, rumpus, tumult, unrest, uproar 7 bobbery, turmoil 8 disorder 9 agitation, commotion, confusion 10 alteration, disruption, turbulence 11 derangement, distraction 12 interruption *atmospheric:* 5 storm 7 cyclone, tornado 9 hurricane *mental:* 6 frenzy 8 delirium, neurosis 9 psychosis *oceanic:* 7 tsunami

disturbed 5 upset 6 insane, shaken 7 anxious, puzzled, rattled, worried 8 bothered, demented, deranged, troubled 9 concerned, psychotic, unsettled 10 distracted, distressed 12 disconcerted

disunion 7 divorce, rupture, split-up 8 division, severing, variance 9 partition 10 detachment, difference, separation 13 disconnection

disunite 4 part 6 divide, sunder 7 break up, disjoin, divorce, split up 8 dissever, separate, uncouple 9 disengage, fall apart 10 disconnect 12 disaffiliate

disunity 6 strife, schism 7 discord 8 conflict, division, variance 10 alienation, contention, disharmony, dissension 12 disaffection, disagreement, estrangement

disused 5 passé 8 obsolete, outdated, outmoded 9 abandoned, discarded 10 antiquated, superseded

ditch 3 dig, pit 4 drop, dump, foss, junk, moat 5 chuck, fosse, leave, scrap, swale 6 reject, trench, trough 7 abandon, cashier, discard, dismiss, forsake, foxhole 8 jettison, throw out 9 crash-land, dispose of, throw away 10 excavation

dither 4 fuss, stew 5 quake, shake, tizzy, waver 6 falter, flurry, quaver, shiver 7 flutter, tremble, twitter, whiffle 8 hesitate 9 agitation, commotion, confusion, vacillate 10 excitement, turbulence 12 shilly-shally

dithyramb 4 hymn, poem 5 chant

dithyrambic 6 ardent, fervid 9 perfervid, rhapsodic 10 boisterous, passionate 11 impassioned

ditto 4 copy, same 5 clone, me too, Xerox 6 carbon, repeat 7 replica, reprint, similar 9 duplicate, facsimile, photocopy 10 carbon copy, mimeograph 11 replication 12 reproduction 13 reduplication

ditty 3 air, lay 4 song, tune 5 carol, chant 6 ballad

diurnal 5 daily 7 daytime 8 daylight 9 circadian, ephemeral, quotidian

diva 7 goddess 10 prima donna 11 leading lady

divagate 4 turn, veer 5 drift, stray 6 depart, ramble, wander 7 deviate, digress, diverge

divan 4 sofa 5 couch 6 settee 7 chamber, council 9 davenport 12 chesterfield

dive 3 bar, pub 4 dash, dump, hole, jump, leap 5 joint, lunge, pitch, sound, swoop 6 header, lounge, plunge, saloon, tavern 7 barroom, decline, descend, descent, hangout, plummet, taproom 8 submerge 9 honky-tonk, roadhouse 10 cannonball *type:* 4 pike, swan, tuck 6 gainer 7 cutaway 9 belly flop, jackknife

diver 4 loon

diverge 4 part, vary 5 stray 6 depart, differ, swerve 7 deflect, deviate, digress 8 disagree, separate 9 bifurcate, branch off, draw apart

divergence 7 parting 9 departure, deviation, differing 10 aberration, deflection, difference, digression, separation 11 disagreeing, discrepancy, distinction 12 disagreement

divergent 6 unlike 8 aberrant, abnormal,

atypical **9** anomalous, different, differing, disparate, irregular **10** dissimilar
divers 6 sundry **7** several, various **8** assorted **9** different, disparate **13** miscellaneous
diverse 5 mixed **6** motley, sundry, unlike, varied **7** several, unalike, unequal, various, varying **8** assorted, discrete, distinct, manifold, separate **9** different, differing, disparate, multiform, multiplex, unsimilar **10** contrasted, dissimilar **11** contrasting, contrastive **12** multifarious **13** contradictory, miscellaneous *meanings:* **8** polysemy
diversion 5 sport **7** pastime, turning **8** pleasure, sideshow **9** amusement, deviation, enjoyment **10** aberration, deflection, recreation, red herring **11** distraction **13** entertainment
diversity 7 variety **10** assortment, difference, unlikeness **11** variegation **12** multiformity **13** dissimilarity, heterogeneity
divert 4 turn, veer **5** amuse **6** regale, swerve **7** beguile, deflect, delight, deviate, digress **8** distract, redirect **9** entertain, turn aside
divest 3 rid, rob **4** free **5** spoil, strip **6** denude **7** bereave, deprive, despoil, disrobe, undress **8** take away **9** dismantle **10** disinherit, dispossess
divide 3 cut **4** fork, part **5** allot, cut up, sever, share **6** assign, cleave, parcel, ration, sunder **7** break up, dissect, divorce, dole out, isolate, prorate, quarter, share in, split up **8** allocate, classify, dispense, disunite, separate **9** apportion, branch out, partition, watershed **10** distribute, measure out **11** dichotomize, distinguish *into four parts:* **7** quarter *into three parts:* **7** trisect *into two parts:* **5** halve **6** bisect **9** bifurcate
divided 4 rent **5** riven, split **6** cloven **7** asunder, partite **8** ruptured
dividend 5 bonus, share **6** return, reward **7** benefit, guerdon, portion, premium **9** allotment **12** dispensation
divider 6 border, screen **9** partition
divination 6 augury **7** insight **8** prophecy **11** foretelling, soothsaying *by communication with the dead:* **10** necromancy *by figures:* **8** geomancy *by lots:* **9** sortilege *by numbers:* **10** numerology *by rods:* **7** dowsing **11** rhabdomancy *by stars:* **9** astrology
divine 4 holy **5** clerk, godly, infer **6** cleric, deduce, deific, intuit, parson, priest, sacred, superb **7** foresee, godlike **8** clerical, foreknow, heavenly, luscious, minister, preacher, prophesy, reverend

9 apprehend, churchman, clergyman, marvelous, religious, visualize **10** anticipate, conjecture, sanctified, superhuman, theologian **11** scrumptious **12** ecclesiastic
diviner 4 seer **5** augur, sibyl **6** oracle **7** palmist, prophet **8** haruspex **10** forecaster, prophetess, soothsayer
divinity 3 god **5** deity, fudge **7** goddess, godhead, godhood **8** theology
division 3 cut **4** part, unit **5** class, piece, slice, split **6** branch, moiety, parcel, schism, sector **7** breakup, discord, dissent, divorce, parting, portion, rupture, section, segment, split-up **8** category, conflict, district, disunion, disunity, variance **9** partition **10** detachment, difference, disharmony, dissidence, separation **11** dissolution **12** disagreement **13** apportionment *Bible:* **5** verse *book:* **7** chapter *British territorial:* **5** shire *building:* **4** wing *cell:* **7** meiosis, mitosis *city:* **4** ward **7** borough **8** precinct *contest:* **4** heat **6** inning, period *corolla:* **5** petal *country:* **5** state **6** canton **8** province **10** department, prefecture *family:* **4** side **6** branch *geologic time:* **3** eon, era **5** epoch **6** period *hospital:* **4** ward, wing *into two:* **9** bisection **11** bifurcation, bipartition *meal:* **6** course *music:* **3** bar **4** beat **7** measure **8** movement *opera, play:* **3** act **5** scena, scene *poem:* **5** canto, verse **6** stanza *population:* **7** segment, stratum *race:* **3** lap **4** heat *social:* **5** caste, class, tribe *state:* **6** county, parish *term:* **8** quotient *time:* **3** day, eon **4** week, year **5** month **6** decade, minute, moment, second **7** century, weekend **9** fortnight *tribal:* **4** clan *word:* **8** syllable *zodiac:* **4** sign
divisive 8 factious **11** disunifying
divorce 4 part **5** sever, split **6** divide, sunder **7** break up, breakup, disjoin, rupture **8** disjoint, dissever, disunion, disunite, separate **9** partition, severance **10** detachment, separation **11** dissolution
divot 3 sod **4** turf **5** clump
divulge 4 blab, leak, tell **5** spill **6** betray, expose, gossip, reveal, tattle **7** let slip, uncover **8** disclose, give away
Dixie composer 6 Emmett (Daniel D.)
dizziness 7 vertigo **9** giddiness
dizzy 5 addle, dazed, giddy, mix up, silly, tipsy **6** addled **7** confuse, dazzled, flighty, foolish, fuddled, muddled, puzzled, reeling **8** confused, swimming, whirling **9** befuddled, confusing **10** bewildered, confounded, distracted, exorbitant, immoderate, inordinate

11 extravagant, light-headed, vertiginous

Djibouti *capital:* 8 Djibouti *language:* 6 Arabic, French *monetary unit:* 5 franc *neighbor:* 7 Eritrea, Somalia 8 Ethiopia *sea:* 3 Red

DNA *component:* 7 adenine, guanine, thymine 8 cytosine 10 nucleotide 11 deoxyribose *segment:* 7 cistron

doable 8 feasible, possible, workable 9 realistic 10 achievable, attainable 11 performable

do away with 3 end, nix, zap 4 kill, slay 5 annul, erase, whack 6 cancel, finish, murder, remove, repeal, revoke, rub out 7 abolish, bump off, deep-six, destroy, discard, expunge, rescind, squelch, wipe out 8 abrogate, blow away, demolish, dispatch, dissolve, massacre, stamp out 9 dispose of, eliminate, eradicate, extirpate, finish off, liquidate, slaughter 10 extinguish, obliterate 11 discontinue, exterminate

docent 5 guide 6 leader 7 teacher 8 lecturer 10 instructor

docile 4 tame 6 pliant 7 ductile, pliable 8 amenable, biddable, obedient, yielding 9 adaptable, compliant, teachable, tractable 10 submissive 11 acquiescent

dock 3 bob, cut 4 crop, fine, pier, quay, rump, slip 5 berth, jetty, levee, tie up, wharf 6 anchor, hangar, lessen, marina, reduce 7 abridge, landing, shorten 8 cut short, platform, truncate *worker:* 6 lumper 9 stevedore 12 longshoreman

docket 4 card 6 agenda, lineup, record 7 program 8 abstract, calendar, caseload, register, schedule 9 timetable

doctor 3 fix, vet 4 mend 5 adapt, alter, medic, treat 6 medico, repair 7 croaker, dentist, falsify, scholar, surgeon 8 sawbones 9 clinician, internist, physician 10 adulterate, specialist 11 medicine man, recondition, reconstruct *animal:* 3 vet 12 veterinarian *children's:* 12 pediatrician *famous:* 4 Koop (C. Everett) 5 Galen, Spock (Benjamin) 6 Atkins (Robert), Chopra (Deepak), Ornish (Dean) 9 Kevorkian (Jack) 10 Schweitzer (Albert) 11 Hippocrates, Livingstone (David) *foot:* 10 podiatrist 11 chiropodist *heart:* 12 cardiologist *teeth:* 7 dentist *women's:* 12 gynecologist

Doctor of the Church 5 Basil 6 Jerome 7 Ambrose, Gregory 9 Augustine 10 Athanasius

Doctorow *novel* 7 Ragtime 9 City of God (The) 10 Waterworks, World's Fair 12 Book of Daniel (The) 13 Billy Bathgate 18 Welcome to Hard Times

doctrinaire 5 rigid 8 dogmatic 9 obstinate 10 unyielding 11 domineering, magisterial 13 authoritarian

doctrine 3 ism 5 axiom, basic, canon, credo, creed, dogma, faith, tenet 7 precept 8 teaching 9 principle 11 fundamental

document 4 deed 5 paper 6 record 8 evidence, monument 9 testimony 10 instrument 11 certificate *travel:* 8 passport

dodder 4 limp 5 shake 6 falter, hobble, totter 7 shamble, shuffle, stagger, tremble 12 morning glory

doddering 5 shaky 6 doting, feeble, senile 7 fragile 8 unsteady, weakened 9 faltering

dodge 4 duck, jink, ruse, slip 5 avoid, elude, evade, fence, parry, shirk, skirt, slide, trick 6 escape, scheme, weasel 7 evasion 8 sidestep 9 avoidance, deception, expedient

Dodger 5 Davis (Tommy) 6 Garvey (Steve), Karros (Eric), Koufax (Sandy), Piazza (Michael), Snider (Duke), Sutton (Don) 8 Newcombe (Don), Robinson (Jackie) 9 Hershiser (Orel) 10 Campanella (Roy) *field:* 7 Ebbetts *manager:* 6 Alston (Walter) 7 Lasorda (Tommy)

dodger 6 outlaw, screen 7 escapee 8 circular, deceiver, deserter, fugitive, handbill, runagate 9 throwaway

dodgy 4 iffy 5 fishy, vague 6 tricky 7 cryptic, obscure 8 doubtful, unproven 9 ambiguous, enigmatic, uncertain 10 indefinite, suspicious, unreliable 11 problematic 12 questionable 13 controversial

dodo 3 oaf 4 bird, boob, clod, dolt, dope, goof, yo-yo 5 chump, dummy, dunce, idiot, moron, ninny, noddy, stupe 6 dimwit, dum-dum, nitwit 7 airhead, dullard, pinhead 8 bonehead, dumbbell, imbecile, lunkhead, meathead, numskull 9 birdbrain, blockhead, ignoramus, lamebrain, numbskull, simpleton 10 dunderhead, nincompoop 11 chowderhead, chucklehead

doe 4 deer 6 female, rabbit 8 kangaroo

doff 4 shed 6 remove 7 take off

dog 3 cur, pug, pup, tag 4 chow, fice, mutt, peke, puli, tail, tyke 5 Akita, boxer, feist, frank, hound, husky, lemon, pooch, puppy, spitz, trail 6 Afghan, beagle, bowwow, briard, canine, collie, detent, poodle, pursue, rascal, saluki, setter, shadow, vizsla, wiener, wretch 7 andiron, Maltese, mastiff, mongrel, pointer, Samoyed, spaniel, terrier, whippet 8 Airedale, Brittany, inferior, keeshond, papillon,

Pekinese, pinscher, spurious, wirehair
9 Chihuahua, dachshund, dalmation,
Great Dane, greyhound, Pekingese,
retriever, schnauzer **10** bloodhound,
Pomeranian, rottweiler, Weimaraner
11 bullmastiff, frankfurter, wienerwurst
12 Newfoundland, Saint Bernard
13 cocker spaniel *Alaskan:* **8** malamute,
malemute *Australian:* **5** dingo *barkless:*
7 basenji *bird:* **6** setter **7** pointer, spaniel
9 retriever *Bush's:* **6** Millie *Buster
Brown's:* **4** Tige *Charlie Brown's:*
6 Snoopy *command:* **3** sit **4** heel, stay
Dorothy's: **4** Toto *Eskimo:* **5** husky *family:* **7** Canidae *FDR's:* **4** Fala *fictional:*
4 Buck **5** Astro, Pluto **6** Big Red
8 McBarker **9** Marmaduke, Old Yeller,
Scooby-Doo, White Fang *"Garfield":*
4 Odie *genus:* **5** Canis *Hungarian:* **6** vizsla *hunting:* **5** hound **6** beagle, borzoi,
saluki, setter, Talbot, vizsla **7** harrier,
pointer, redbone **8** elkhound, foxhound
9 wolfhound **10** bloodhound **11** basset
hound *Indian:* **5** dhole *L.B.J.'s:* **3** Her
long-bodied: **9** dachshund *movie:* **4** Asta,
Toto **5** Benji, Tramp **6** Lassie
9 Beethoven, Old Yeller, Rin Tin Tin
name: **4** Fido, Spot **5** Rover **6** Bowser
Nixon's: **8** Checkers *Odysseus's:* **5** Argos
of Hades: **8** Cerberus *Orphan Annie's:*
5 Sandy *powerful:* **11** bullmastiff *Roy
Rogers's:* **6** Bullet *Russian:* **6** borzoi
7 Samoyed *shaggy-coated:* **8** komondor,
sheepdog *deerhound short-legged:*
5 corgi *small:* **3** pom, pug, pup **4** peke
8 Pekinese **9** Chihuahua, Pekingese
10 Pomeranian *space traveler:* **5** Laika
Steinbeck's: **7** Charley *television:* **4** King
5 Eddie, Tramp **6** Lassie, Murray
8 Wishbone **9** Rin Tin Tin *terrier:*
7 Scottie *three-headed:* **8** Cerberus
Tibetan: **9** Lhasa apso *tiny:* **9** Chihuahua
tooth: **4** fang *tracking:* **10** bloodhound
two-headed: **6** Orthos *Wallace's:*
6 Gromit *Welsh:* **5** corgi *Wendy's:*
4 Nana *wild:* **5** dingo *young:* **3** pup
5 puppy, whelp
dog days 6 August **9** canicular
dogfight 3 row **4** fray **5** brawl, broil,
melee, set-to **6** fracas, ruckus **7** ruction
10 donnybrook, free-for-all
dogfish 6 bowfin, burbot **8** mud puppy
dogged 7 adamant **8** obdurate, resolute,
stubborn **9** insistent, steadfast, obstinate, tenacious, unbending **10** bullheaded, hardheaded, persistent,
persisting, unshakable, unyielding
11 persevering, unremitting **12** pertinacious
doggone 4 damn, dang, darn, rank
5 utter **6** cursed, damned, darned

7 blasted, blessed, dratted **8** absolute,
accursed, infernal, outright **9** out-and-
out **10** confounded **11** unmitigated
13 blankety-blank
dogma 4 code, rule **5** canon, credo,
creed, tenet **6** belief, gospel **7** precept
8 doctrine, ideology **9** orthodoxy, postulate, teachings **10** conviction, persuasion
dogmatic 8 oracular, orthodox
9 assertive, canonical, doctrinal **11** dictatorial, doctrinaire, magisterial
13 authoritarian, authoritative
Dog of Flanders author 5 Ouida
dog-paddle 4 swim
dog's age 3 eon **4** aeon **8** blue moon,
eternity
Dog Star 6 Sirius
dogwood 6 cornel, Cornus **8** red osier
do in 4 kill, ruin, slay **5** cheat, wreck
6 defeat, finish, murder, rub out **7** blot
out, bump off, destroy, execute,
exhaust, frazzle, take out, wear out,
wipe out **8** dispatch, knock off, knock
out **9** eliminate, liquidate, prostrate,
run ragged, shipwreck **11** assassinate
doing 3 act **6** action **8** activity *good:*
10 beneficent *evil:* **10** maleficent
doit 3 bit, jot **4** coin, damn, dram, drop,
hoot, iota, mite, whit **6** trifle **8** particle
doldrums 5 blahs, blues, dumps, ennui,
gloom, slump **6** apathy, tedium, torpor
7 boredom **9** dejection **10** depression,
inactivity, quiescence, stagnation
12 listlessness
doleful 3 sad **4** down **7** forlorn, ruthful
8 cast down, dejected, dolorous, downcast, grieving, mournful, mourning
9 afflicted, cheerless, depressed, miserable, plaintive, sorrowful, sorrowing,
woebegone **10** dispirited, lamentable,
lugubrious, melancholy **11** crestfallen,
downhearted **12** disconsolate
dole out 4 deal **5** allot **6** divide, parcel,
ration **7** divvy up **8** disburse, dispense,
disperse **9** apportion, partition
10 administer, distribute
doll 3 Ken **6** Barbie, figure, Kewpie,
puppet **10** Betsy Wetsy, Raggedy Ann
11 Raggedy Andy *grotesque:* **8** golliwog
dollar 3 one **4** bill, buck, clam, oner,
peso **5** taler **6** single **7** ringgit, smacker
8 simoleon **9** cartwheel, greenback
dollop 4 blob, glob, lump **7** portion
Doll's House, A author: 5 Ibsen (Henrik)
heroine: **4** Nora
dolly 4 cart **7** stirrer **8** platform **10** locomotive
dolomite 6 marble **9** limestone
dolor 5 agony, grief **6** misery, sorrow

7 anguish, passion 8 distress 9 suffering
10 affliction
dolorous 6 rueful, woeful 7 ruthful
8 grievous, mournful, wretched
9 afflicted, anguished, miserable, plaintive, sorrowful 10 lamentable, lugubrious, melancholy 13 heartbreaking
dolphin 5 whale 7 bollard 8 porpoise
dolt 3 ass, oaf 4 boob, clod, dodo, dork,
fool, goof, goon, lout, yo-yo 5 booby,
chump, dunce, idiot 6 nitwit 7 dullard,
fathead, halfwit, jughead, saphead,
schnook 8 bonehead, dumbbell,
dummkopf, imbecile, lunkhead, meathead, numskull 9 blockhead, lamebrain, numbskull, simpleton
doltish 4 dull, dumb 5 dense, thick
6 oafish, obtuse, stupid 7 idiotic,
moronic 8 ignorant, mindless 9 dimwitted, fatheaded, imbecile
domain 4 land, rule, turf 5 field, realm
6 estate, sphere 7 kingdom, terrain
8 dominion, province 9 bailiwick, territory
dome 4 head, hill, roof 5 mound 6 cupola 7 ceiling 8 mountain
domestic 4 help, home, tame 6 family,
native 7 servant 8 houseboy, internal,
national 9 charwoman, household
10 indigenous 11 chambermaid
domesticate 4 tame 5 adapt, adopt, train
10 housebreak
domicile 3 pad 4 home 5 abode, house,
lodge, put up 6 bestow, billet, harbor
7 quarter 8 dwelling, quarters 9 residence, residency 10 habitation
domiciliate 4 bunk, tame 5 house, lodge,
put up 6 billet, harbor, reside 7 quarter
dominance 4 rule, sway 5 power 7 command, control 7 mastery 9 supremacy
10 ascendancy, prepotency 11 preeminence, sovereignty
dominant 4 main 5 chief, first, major
6 ruling 7 leading, supreme 8 foremost,
powerful, reigning 9 ascendant, governing, number-one, paramount, prevalent, principal 10 commanding, preeminent, prevailing, successful, surpassing
11 controlling, outweighing, overbearing 12 preponderant
dominate 4 rule 5 reign 6 direct, govern,
obsess 7 control, prevail, repress
8 bestride, hold sway, look down, loom
over, overlook 9 subjugate, tower over,
tyrannize 10 tower above
domination 4 rule, sway 5 might, power
7 command, control, mastery 9 authority, supremacy 10 ascendancy, prepotency, suzerainty 11 preeminence, sovereignty 13 preponderancy
dominator 4 boss, head 5 chief, ruler

6 honcho, leader, master, top dog
7 headman 8 director, hierarch, kingfish 9 chieftain, commander
domineer 5 bully 6 hector 7 swagger
8 browbeat, bulldoze 9 tyrannize
10 intimidate
domineering 5 bossy 6 lordly 8 arrogant,
despotic 9 imperious, masterful
10 autocratic, high-handed, oppressive,
tyrannical 11 dictatorial, magisterial,
overbearing
Dominica *capital:* 6 Roseau *discoverer:*
8 Columbus (Christopher) *language:*
7 English *location:* 10 West Indies *monetary unit:* 6 dollar *sea:* 9 Caribbean
Dominican Republic *capital:* 12 Santo
Domingo *island:* 10 Hispaniola *language:* 7 Spanish *location:* 10 West
Indies *monetary unit:* 4 peso *mountain:*
6 Duarte *neighbor:* 5 Haiti *sea:*
9 Caribbean
dominion 3 raj 4 rule, sway, turf 5 realm,
power 6 domain, empery, empire, regnum, sphere 7 demesne, kingdom, terrain 8 province 9 ascendant, ownership,
supremacy, territory 10 ascendancy,
possession 11 preeminence, sovereignty
domino 4 mask 5 amice, cloak, visor
6 vizard 8 disguise *spot:* 3 pip
don 3 sir 4 lord 5 get on, put on, tutor
6 assume, fellow, take on 9 professor,
undertake
Donalbain *brother:* 7 Malcolm *father:*
6 Duncan
donate 4 give 5 grant 6 chip in, supply
7 dish out, hand out, present, provide
8 give away, shell out, transfer 10 contribute
donation 3 aid 4 alms, gift 5 grant
7 bequest, handout 8 offering 9 endowment 11 benefaction, beneficence
12 contribution, philanthropy
Don Carlos *author:* 8 Schiller (Friedrich
von) *composer:* 5 Verdi (Giuseppe)
father: 6 Philip
done 4 over 5 all in, ended, ready, spent
6 bushed, decent, doomed, gone by,
proper, used up 7 correct, drained,
dressed, far-gone, settled, through,
worn-out 8 becoming, complete,
depleted, finished, washed-up 9 befitting, completed, concluded, exhausted
10 terminated 12 accomplished *poetic:*
3 o'er
donee 7 grantee 8 receiver 9 recipient
11 beneficiary
done for 4 gone, sunk 5 kaput 6 beaten,
doomed, ruined 7 wrecked 8 finished,
stricken
done in 5 spent 6 effete, used up 7 far

gone, worn out **8** depleted **9** exhausted, washed out

Don Giovanni composer 6 Mozart (Wolfgang Amadeus)

Donizetti, Gaetano *hero:* **7** Roberto (Devereux) *opera:* **5** Lucia (di Lammermoor) **10** Anna Bolena, La Favorita **11** Don Pasquale **12** Maria Stuarda

Don Juan 4 rake, roué, wolf **5** Romeo **6** chaser, masher **7** amorist, gallant, playboy, seducer **8** Casanova, lothario, paramour **9** ladies' man, libertine, womanizer **10** lady-killer, profligate **11** philanderer *drama:* **10** Stone Guest (The) *home:* **7** Seville *mother:* **4** Inez *poet:* **5** Byron (Lord) **7** Pushkin (Alexander)

donkey 3 ass **4** mule **5** burro **7** jackass *female:* **5** jenny

donkeywork 4 moil, toil **5** grind, labor **7** travail **8** drudgery

donnybrook 3 row **4** fray **5** brawl, broil, fight, melee, set-to **6** fracas, ruckus, rumpus, tumult, uproar **7** dispute, quarrel, rhubarb, ruction **10** free-for-all **11** altercation

donor 5 giver **6** patron **7** granter, grantor **8** bestower **9** conferrer, presenter **10** benefactor **11** contributor

do-nothing 3 bum **4** slug **5** idler **6** loafer, slouch **7** goof-off, slacker **8** deadbeat, fainéant, layabout, slugabed, sluggard **9** lazybones, vegetable **11** couch potato

Don Pasquale composer 9 Donizetti (Gaetano)

Don Quixote *author:* **9** Cervantes (Miguel de) *beloved:* **8** Dulcinea *companion (squire):* **11** Sancho Panza *giant:* **8** windmill *home:* **8** La Mancha *horse:* **9** Rocinante, Rosinante, Rozinante

doodad 5 gizmo, thing **6** bauble, dingus, entity, gadget, gewgaw, jigger, widget **7** trinket, whatsit **8** gimcrack **9** doohickey, thingummy **10** attachment, decoration, knickknack **11** thingamabob, thingamajig, thingumajig

doodle 6 dabble, dawdle, fiddle, potter, putter, sketch, tinker, trifle **7** cartoon, drawing **8** scribble **10** mess around

doodlebug 7 ant lion, missile **8** buzz bomb

doohickey see DOODAD

doom 4 damn, fate, ruin **5** death **6** decree, demise, kismet **7** condemn, destiny, tragedy **8** calamity, disaster, judgment, sentence **11** catastrophe **12** annihilation, last judgment

doomful 4 dire **7** baleful, baneful, direful, fateful, malefic, ominous, unlucky

8 dreadful, ill-fated, sinister **10** foreboding, portentous **11** apocalyptic

doomsayer 7 killjoy **9** Cassandra, defeatist, Gloomy Gus, pessimist

___ Doone 5 Lorna

door 3 way **4** adit, exit **5** entry **6** access, egress, entrée, portal **7** gateway, ingress, opening **8** entrance, entryway **9** admission **10** admittance **11** entranceway *rear:* **7** postern

doorkeeper 6 porter

doorway 5 entry **6** portal **8** entrance, entryway **11** entranceway

doozy 3 ace, pip **5** dandy **7** paragon **8** standout **10** phenomenon **11** crackerjack

dope 3 oaf **4** clod, dodo, dolt, drug, goof, news, yo-yo **5** chump, drugs, dummy, dunce, facts, idiot, moron, ninny, noddy, stupe **6** dimwit, dumdum, heroin, nitwit, opiate, sedate, skinny **7** airhead, cocaine, details, dullard, lowdown, pinhead **8** bonehead, dumbbell, imbecile, lunkhead, meathead, narcotic, numskull **9** birdbrain, blockhead, ignoramus, lamebrain, marijuana, narcotize, numbskull, simpleton **10** dunderhead, nincompoop **11** anesthetize, chowderhead, chucklehead, information, preparation

doped 4 high **5** dazed **6** stoned, zonked **7** drugged, tuned-in **8** hopped-up, tripping, turned on, wiped out **9** spacedout, strung out, stupefied **10** narcotized

dopey 4 dumb **5** silly **6** dulled, stupid, torpid **7** fatuous, fuddled, muddled **8** comatose, sluggish **9** lethargic, senseless, stupefied

Doris *brother:* **6** Nereus *daughters:* **7** Nereids *father:* **7** Oceanus *husband:* **6** Nereus

dormancy 5 sleep **6** repose **7** latency, slumber **8** abeyance, diapause, doldrums, downtime **9** torpidity **10** inactivity, quiescence, suspension **11** cold storage **12** intermission, interruption

dormant 5 inert **6** asleep, drowsy, fallow, latent, torpid **7** abeyant **8** comatose, inactive, sluggish **9** lethargic, potential, quiescent, suspended **10** slow-moving, slumbering

dormer 3 bay **4** nook **5** niche **6** window

dorsal 6 aboral **7** abaxial

___ d'Orsay 4 Quai

dorsum 4 back

Dorus *brother:* **6** Aeolus *father:* **6** Hellen

dory 4 bark, boat **5** craft, skiff **6** barque, bateau **7** shallop **8** lifeboat

dose 3 fix, hit **4** dram, shot, slug **7** measure, portion **8** medicate, quantity

Dos Passos trilogy 3 U.S.A.
dossier 4 file **6** folder **9** portfolio
dot 4 mark, mote, stud **5** dower, dowry,
point, speck **6** bestud, period
7 freckle, speckle, stipple **8** flyspeck,
sprinkle **9** bespeckle **12** decimal point
dotage 8 senility **11** decrepitude, senectitude
dote on 5 adore, enjoy, fancy, prize
7 cherish, idolize **8** treasure **9** delight in
doting 4 dear, fond **6** loving **7** adoring,
devoted **12** affectionate
dotted 6 spotty **8** punctate, stippled
dotty 4 gaga **5** crazy, loony, wacky
6 absurd, insane **7** foolish, smitten
8 enamored **9** eccentric **10** captivated,
enraptured, infatuated **12** preposterous
double 4 copy, dual, fold, mate, tack,
twin **5** clone, duple, image, match,
twice **6** bifold, binary, duplex, paired,
ringer **7** dualize, enlarge, magnify,
replica, twofold **8** alter ego, geminate,
increase **9** companion, dualistic, duplicate,
look-alike, replicate **10** dead
ringer, reciprocal, simulacrum, understudy
13 spitting image
double-barreled 4 dual **5** duple **6** bifold,
binary, duplex, paired **7** twofold **9** dualistic
double bass 10 bull fiddle
double-cross 3 con **4** dupe **5** cheat, trick
6 betray, delude, humbug, juggle, take
in **7** beguile, deceive, sell out, two-time
8 flimflam, hoodwink **9** four-flush
double dagger 6 diesis
double-dealer 3 gyp **5** cheat, knave **6** con
man **7** cozener, diddler, sharper
8 deceiver, swindler **9** defrauder
11 flimflammer **13** confidence man
double-dealing 5 fraud **6** deceit **7** chicane
8 flimflam, trickery **9** chicanery,
deceitful, deception, duplicity, two-
timing **10** hanky-panky **11** duplicitous
double-dome 7 egghead **8** Einstein, highbrow
10 pointy-head **12** intellectual
double-faced 9 deceitful, deceptive,
equivocal, insincere **10** reversible
12 hypocritical **13** untrustworthy
doublet 3 duo **4** dyad, pair, span **5** brace
6 couple, jacket **7** twosome
double-talk 4 bosh, bunk **5** hokum,
hooey **6** babble, bunkum, drivel, jabber
7 blather, hogwash, twaddle **8** flimflam,
nonsense **9** gibberish, poppycock
10 balderdash **12** gobbledygook
double vision 8 diplopia
doubt 5 qualm **7** concern, dispute, dubiety,
suspect **8** distrust, mistrust, question
9 challenge, disbelief, misgiving,
suspicion **10** skepticism **11** dubiousness,
incertitude, incredulity, uncertainty

doubtable 4 hazy, iffy, moot **7** dubious,
suspect **8** arguable **9** ambiguous, debatable,
equivocal, uncertain, undecided
10 disputable, borderline, indefinite
11 problematic **12** questionable
doubter 5 cynic **6** Thomas **7** skeptic
8 agnostic **10** Pyrrhonist, questioner,
unbeliever **11** freethinker
doubtful 4 hazy, iffy, moot **5** fishy, shady,
shaky **6** chancy, unsure **7** clouded,
dubious, obscure, suspect, unclear
8 arguable, unlikely **9** ambiguous,
debatable, dubitable, equivocal, uncertain,
undecided, unsettled **10** borderline,
disputable, improbable **11** problematic,
speculative **12** questionable
doubtfulness 7 concern, dubiety **8** mistrust
9 ambiguity, misgiving, suspicion
10 indecision, skepticism, uneasiness
11 dubiousness, incertitude, uncertainty
13 indeterminacy
doubting Thomas see DOUBTER
doubtless 6 likely, surely **7** certain,
clearly **8** of course, probably
10 absolutely, definitely, positively, presumably
11 indubitably **12** indisputably
13 presumptively, unequivocally
douceur 3 tip **4** gift **5** bribe **7** present
8 gratuity
dough 4 cash **5** bread, money **6** dinero,
moolah **7** cabbage, lettuce, scratch
8 currency **11** legal tender **inflator:**
5 yeast
doughboy 7 dogface **11** infantryman
doughty 4 bold **5** brave, gutsy, manly,
stout **6** daring, heroic, plucky, spunky,
strong **7** gallant, valiant **8** fearless,
intrepid, resolved, stalwart, unafraid,
valorous **9** dauntless, undaunted
10 courageous **12** stouthearted
doughy 3 wan **4** pale **5** pasty, waxen
6 pallid **8** blanched **9** colorless
do up 3 can, fix **4** mend, wash, wrap
5 clean, patch **6** clothe, doctor, fasten,
repair, revamp **7** exhaust, festoon,
launder, package, prepare, rebuild,
wear out **8** decorate, gift wrap, ornament,
overhaul **9** embellish **11** recondition,
reconstruct
dour 4 glum, grim **5** bleak, harsh, rigid,
stern, surly **6** gloomy, morose, severe,
strict, sullen **7** austere, crabbed, peevish
9 obstinate, saturnine, stringent
10 forbidding, unyielding
douse 3 sop **4** duck, dunk, soak **5** bathe,
drown, plash, slosh, souse **6** drench,
put out, quench, splash, strike
7 immerse, slacken **8** inundate, saturate,
snuff out, submerge, submerse
10 extinguish

dove 6 culver, pigeon 8 pacifist *call:*
3 coo *genus:* 7 Columba
dovecote 6 aviary 9 birdhouse
dovetail 3 fit 4 jibe, mesh 5 agree,
match, tally 6 accord, splice, square
7 comport, conform 8 check out 9 harmonize, interlock, intermesh 10 correspond
dovish 4 mild 6 gentle 7 antiwar, pacific
8 pacifist 9 peaceable 10 nonviolent,
pacifistic 11 peace-loving 12 conciliatory
dowager 4 dame 5 widow 6 matron
9 matriarch 10 grande dame 11 grandmother
dowdy 4 drab 5 dated, frump, passé,
seedy, tacky 6 blowsy, bygone, démodé,
frowsy, frowzy, frumpy, old hat, shabby 7 rundown, unkempt 8 frumpish,
outdated, outmoded, slattern, slovenly
9 out-of-date, unstylish 10 antiquated,
bedraggled, slatternly 11 draggle-tail
12 old-fashioned 13 draggletailed
dowel 3 bar, peg, pin, rod 5 stick
dower 4 gift 5 endow, endue 6 legacy, talent 8 bequeath
dowitcher 5 snipe 9 sandpiper
do without 5 forgo, waive 6 abjure,
eschew, give up, pass up 8 renounce
down 3 eat, fur, ill, low, off, sad 4 blue,
fell, fuzz, lint, pile, sick 5 below, ended,
floor, floss, fluff, level, lower, under
6 defeat, fallen, finish, lay low, nether
7 conquer, consume, destroy, flatten,
swallow, unhappy 8 bowl over, complete, defeated, dejected, dispatch,
feathers, finished, inferior, overcome,
sluggish, surmount 9 completed, concluded, depressed, earthward, miserable 10 dispirited, groundward
down-and-out 5 broke, needy 6 hard-up,
ruined 8 beggared, derelict, homeless
9 destitute, penniless, penurious
12 impoverished
down-and-outer 3 bum 6 beggar, pauper,
wretch 7 have-not 9 mendicant 10 supplicant
down-at-heels 4 mean 5 dingy, ratty,
seedy, tacky 6 ragged, ragtag, shabby,
shoddy 7 ignoble, run-down, worn-out
8 decrepit, tattered 10 bedraggled,
threadbare 11 dilapidated 12 deteriorated, disreputable
downbeat 3 low, sad 4 blue, glum
6 droopy, gloomy, morose 7 decline,
doleful 8 dejected 9 depressed 10 dispirited, melancholy 11 discouraged, pessimistic 12 disconsolate, disheartened,
heavyhearted
downcast 3 low, sad 4 blue, glum, sunk
5 moody, mopey 6 droopy, gloomy,

morose 7 doleful, forlorn, unhappy
8 dejected, dismayed, listless, soul-sick,
troubled 9 depressed, heartsick, heartsore, miserable, oppressed, woebegone
10 chapfallen, despondent, dispirited,
distressed, melancholy, spiritless
11 crestfallen, discouraged, low-spirited
12 disconsolate, disheartened
downfall 4 bane, ruin 6 demise 7 decline,
undoing 8 collapse, Waterloo 9 ruination 10 devolution 11 declination,
destruction 12 degeneration, dégringolade 13 deterioration
downgrade 4 bump, bust 5 abase, lower
6 demote 7 decline, demerit, descent,
devalue 8 belittle, diminish, discount,
minimize, relegate 9 denigrate, deprecate, devaluate, discredit, disparage,
humiliate 10 depreciate, undervalue
12 degeneration, dégringolade 13 deterioration
downhearted see DOWNCAST
down-in-the-mouth see DOWNCAST
down payment 5 token 6 pledge
7 advance, deposit, earnest
downplay 8 belittle, discount, minimize,
pooh-pooh 11 de-emphasize
downpour 6 deluge 7 monsoon
8 drencher 9 drenching, rainstorm
10 cloudburst, inundation 11 gully
washer
downright 5 blunt, gross, total, truly,
utter 7 blatant, flat-out 8 absolute,
complete, explicit, positive, thorough
9 out-and-out 10 absolutely, sureenough 11 indubitable, unequivocal,
unmitigated, unqualified 13 thoroughgoing
downslide 3 dip, sag 4 drop, slip 5 slump
7 decline, drop-off, falloff 8 decrease
9 declivity, reduction
downstairs 6 cellar 8 basement
down-to-earth 8 rational 9 practical,
pragmatic, realistic 10 hard-boiled,
hardheaded, no-nonsense, reasonable
11 common-sense, plain-spoken
12 matter-of-fact 13 unpretentious,
unsentimental
downtrend see DOWNSLIDE
downtrodden 6 abject, abused
9 oppressed 10 maltreated, mistreated,
persecuted, tyrannized
downturn see DOWNSLIDE
downward 8 dropping 9 declining
10 descending
downy 4 soft 5 fuzzy 6 fleecy, fluffy
7 velvety 8 feathery *filler:* 5 eider
dowry 4 gift 6 talent *French:* 3 dot
doxy 4 moll, tart 5 wench 6 floozy, harlot 7 trollop 8 mistress 10 prostitute
doyen 4 dean, head 5 chief, maven

6 expert, leader, master, wizard **7** maestro **8** virtuoso **9** authority, patriarch **10** past master

Doyle's detective 6 Holmes (Sherlock)

D'Oyly Carte offering 8 operetta

doze 3 nap **5** sleep **6** catnap, drowse, nod off, snooze **7** drop off, slumber **8** drift off **10** forty winks

dozy see DROWSY

DP 5 exile **6** émigré **7** evacuee, outcast, refugee **8** deportee, emigrant, fugitive **10** expatriate

drab 4 dull, flat **5** bleak, brown, dingy, faded, mousy, muddy, olive, vapid **6** dismal, dreary, mousey **7** subfusc **8** lifeless **9** cheerless, colorless **10** lackluster **11** dispiriting

draconian 5 cruel, harsh, rigid **6** severe, strict **7** callous **8** ironclad, rigorous, ruthless **9** merciless, stringent **10** inflexible, ironfisted, ironhanded

Dracula author 6 Stoker (Bram)

draft 3 tap **4** dose, haul, plan, plot, pull, pump, swig **5** check, claim, drink, frame, press, swill **6** breeze, call up, demand, design, devise, enlist, enroll, induct, potion, scheme, select, siphon, sketch **7** compose, concoct, current, outline, portion, prepare, project, recruit **8** block out, contrive, rough out, skeleton, traction **9** adumbrate, allowance, blueprint, conscribe, conscript, fabricate, formulate, muster out **11** delineation, skeletonize *avoider:* **6** dodger *of a law:* **4** bill

drag 3 lug, tow, tug **4** bore, haul, puff, pull, swig **5** dally, delay, draft, tarry, trail **6** burden, dawdle, harrow, loiter, schlep, search, sledge **7** schlepp **8** friction, straggle **9** lag behind **13** procrastinate

dragging 4 beat, long **5** all in, spent, weary **6** pooped **7** drained, lengthy, tedious **8** drawn-out, extended, fatigued, overlong, sluggish, wiped out **9** exhausted, lethargic, long-drawn, pooped out, prolonged, washed-out, wearisome **10** protracted, slow-moving **12** interminable, long-drawn-out

draggle 3 lag **4** rove **5** stray, trail **8** straggle, trail off **10** fall behind

draggle-tail 4 bawd, drab, slut **5** wench, whore **6** harlot **8** slattern **10** prostitute **11** nightwalker **12** streetwalker

draggletailed 6 blowsy, frowsy, frowzy, sordid, untidy **8** slattern, sluttish **10** slatternly

dragnet 4 trap **5** snare, trawl **7** network

drag off 4 cart, haul

dragon 5 beast **8** basilisk **10** cockatrice *biblical:* **5** Rahab *Canaanite:* **3** Yam

4 Yamm **5** Lotan *Chinese:* **4** lung *French:* **8** Tarasque *genus:* **5** Draco *Greek:* **5** Ladon **9** Eurythion *slayer:* **4** Baal, Enki, Zeus **5** Indra **6** Cadmus, George (St.), Marduk, Sigurd **7** Beowulf, Jupiter, Michael (St.), Ninurta, Perseus **8** Margaret (St.) *Sumerian:* **3** Kur *Wagnerian:* **6** Fafnir

dragoon 3 cow **5** bully **6** badger, coerce, harass, hector **8** bludgeon, browbeat, bulldoze, bullyrag, threaten **9** persecute, strong-arm, terrorize **10** cavalryman, intimidate

drain 3 dry, tap **4** pump, sink, sump, swig, tire, vent, wear **5** bleed, draft, drink, empty, leech, sewer, swill, use up, weary **6** burden, gutter, siphon, trench **7** conduit, culvert, deplete, dwindle, draw off, exhaust, fatigue, outflow **8** bankrupt, draw down, wear down **9** discharge **10** impoverish **11** watercourse

drain away 3 ebb **4** drop, sink, wane **5** abate **6** lessen, reduce, remove **7** draw off, dwindle, retreat, subside **8** decrease, diminish, draw back, taper off, withdraw

drained 4 beat **5** all-in, spent, weary **6** bleary, pooped, used up **7** far-gone, worn-out **8** depleted, dragging, weakened, wiped out **9** exhausted, pooped out, washed-out

drainpipe 4 duct **5** sewer, spout **7** conduit **9** downspout

dram 3 bit, dab, nip, tot **4** atom, dash, drop, iota, jolt, mite, shot, slug, spot, swig, whit **5** crumb, grain, ounce, pinch, scrap, shred, snort, speck **6** morsel, sliver **7** modicum, smidgen, snifter, snippet, soupçon **8** particle

drama 4 play **7** pageant, theater, theatre, tragedy *award:* **4** Tony *former English:* **6** masque *Japanese:* **3** Noh *main part:* **8** epitasis *musical:* **5** opera **8** operetta *suspenseful:* **11** cliff-hanger

dramatic 5 vivid **8** striking, thespian **10** histrionic, theatrical *conflict:* **4** agon

dramatis personae 4 cast **5** parts, roles **6** actors, troupe **7** company **10** characters

dramatist 10 playwright *American:* **4** Hart (Moss), Inge (William), Rabe (David), Rice (Elmer), Uhry (Alfred) **5** Albee (Edward), Barry (Philip), Foote (Horton), Guare (John), Hecht (Ben), Mamet (David), Odets (Clifford), Parks (Suzan-Lori), Payne (John Howard), Simon (Neil) **6** Ferber (Edna), Gurney (A. R.), Henley (Beth), Miller (Arthur), Norman (Marsha), O'Neill (Eugene), Thomas (Augustus), Wilder (Thornton), Wilson (August, Lanford, Robert) 7 Hellman (Lillian), Kaufman (George S.), Kushner (Tony), Shanley (John Patrick), Shepard (Sam) 8 Anderson (Maxwell, Robert), Caldwell (Erskine), Connolly (Marc), Sherwood (Robert), Williams (Tennessee) 9 Chayefsky (Paddy), Fierstein (Harvey), Hansberry (Lorraine) 11 Hammerstein (Oscar), Wasserstein (Wendy) *Austrian:* 10 Schnitzler (Arthur) *Belgian:* 11 Maeterlinck (Maurice) *Czech:* 5 Havel (Vaclav) *English:* 3 Fry (Christopher), Gay (John) 4 Hare (David), Rowe (Nicholas), Tate (Nahum) 5 Frayn (Michael), Milne (A. A.), Orton (Joe), Peele (George), Wilde (Oscar) 6 Barrie (James), Coward (Nöel), Dryden (John), Jonson (Ben), Pinero (Arthur Wing), Pinter (Harold), Steele (Richard), Storey (David) 7 Delaney (Shelagh), Marlowe (Christopher), Marston (John), Osborne (John), Shaffer (Anthony, Peter), Webster (John) 8 Congreve (William), Rattigan (Terrence), Shadwell (Thomas), Stoppard (Tom), Tourneur (Cyril), Vanbrugh (John), Zangwill (Israel) 9 Ayckbourn (Alan), Churchill (Caryl), Goldsmith (Oliver), Middleton (Thomas), Wycherley (William) 11 Shakespeare (William) *French:* 5 Camus (Albert), Genet (Jean) 6 Musset (Alfred de), Racine (Jean), Sardou (Victorien), Sartre (Jean-Paul), Scribe (Eugène) 7 Anouilh (Jean), Ionesco (Eugène), Labiche (Eugène), Molière, Rostand (Edmond) 8 Marivaux (Pierre) 9 Corneille (Pierre), Crébillon, Giraudoux (Jean) 12 Beaumarchais (P. A. Caron de) *German:* 5 Weiss (Peter) 6 Brecht (Bertolt), Goethe (Johann Wolfgang von), Kleist (Heinrich von) 8 Schiller (Friedrich von) 9 Hauptmann (Gerhart), Zuckmayer (Carl) *Greek:* 8 Menander 9 Aeschylus, Euripides, Sophocles 12 Aristophanes *Hindu:* 8 Kalidasa *Irish:* 4 Shaw (George Bernard) 5 Behan (Brendan), Friel (Brian), Synge (John Millington), Yeats (William Butler) 6 O'Casey (Sean) 7 Beckett (Samuel), Gregory (Lady Augusta) 8 Sheridan (Richard Brinsley) *Italian:* 5 Gozzi (Carlo), Verga (Giovanni) 7 Alfieri (Vittorio), Ariosto (Ludovico), Giacosa (Giuseppe), Goldoni (Carlo) 8 Trissino (Gian Giorgio) 9 D'Annunzio (Gabriele) 10 Metastasio (Pietro), Pirandello (Luigi) *Japanese:* 5 Zeami *Nigerian:* 7 Soyinka (Wole) *Norwegian:* 5 Ibsen (Henrik) 8 Bjornson

(Bjornstjerne) *Roman:* 6 Seneca 7 Plautus, Terence *Romanian:* 7 Ionesco (Eugene) *Russian:* 7 Chekhov (Anton) 8 Zamyatin (Yevgeny) *South African:* 6 Fugard (Athol) *Spanish:* 4 Vega (Lope de) 5 Lorca (Federico García) 7 Alberti (Rafael), Arrabal (Fernando) 8 Quintero (Serafín, Joaquín) 9 Benavente (Jacinto) 11 García Lorca (Federico), Valle-Inclán (R. M. del) *Swedish:* 5 Sachs (Nelly) 10 Strindberg (August) *Swiss:* 6 Frisch (Max)

drape 4 fold, hang, roll 5 adorn, array, cloak, cover 6 clothe, enwrap, swathe, wrap up 7 curtain, swaddle 8 enswathe, envelope, swathe in

drapery 7 curtain, hanging 8 curtains, hangings

drastic 4 dire 5 harsh 6 severe 7 extreme, radical 9 desperate 10 exorbitant

draw 3 gut, tie, tow, tug 4 etch, haul, limn, lure, puff, pull, pump 5 draft, drain, infer, judge, trace 6 allure, appeal, deduce, depict, derive, elicit, entice, extend, gather, indite, inhale, pencil, siphon, sketch 7 attract, deplete, exhaust, extract, outline, portray, prolong, spin out, win over 8 conclude, contract, convince, dead heat, deadlock, lengthen, protract, standoff 9 delineate, formulate, represent, stalemate 10 allurement, attraction, disembowel, eviscerate, exenterate *forth:* 5 educe 6 elicit 7 extract *from:* 4 milk, pump 5 bleed *together:* 3 tie 4 join, lace

draw back 4 duck 5 cower, quail, wince 6 blench, flinch, recoil, shrink 7 back off, retreat, take off 9 turn aside

drawback 4 flaw, snag 5 fault, hitch 6 defect, refund 7 failing, trouble 8 weakness 9 detriment, hindrance 10 deficiency, difficulty, impediment 11 shortcoming 12 disadvantage 13 inconvenience

draw down 4 milk 5 drain, spend, use up 6 expend, reduce 7 deplete, exhaust 8 decrease, diminish 9 reduction, siphon off

drawer 9 draftsman *for money:* 4 till

drawers 5 pants 6 undies 8 trousers 10 underpants

draw in 6 enmesh, entice, induce, prompt 7 involve, retract, win over 8 convince, persuade, pull back 9 prevail on 11 bring around, prevail upon

drawing 6 doodle, sketch 7 cartoon, outline

drawing power 4 lure, pull 6 appeal 9 magnetism 10 attraction

drawn 4 taut, worn 6 peaked 7 fraught, haggard, pinched 8 careworn, fatigued, pictured, strained, stressed **9** attracted **10** delineated

drawn-out 4 long **7** lengthy, tedious **8** extended, overlong **9** prolonged **10** protracted

draw off 3 tap **4** pump **5** bleed, draft, drain **6** siphon

draw out 6 extend **7** prolong, stretch **8** elongate, lengthen, protract

draw up 4 balk, halt, lift, make, stop **5** array, draft, frame, order, raise, write **6** deploy, map out **7** compose, concoct, dispose, marshal, prepare, set down **8** organize, write out **9** formulate

dray 4 cart, drag **5** wagon **6** barrow, sledge **7** travois **9** stoneboat

dread 4 fear **5** alarm, panic **6** dismay, fright, horror, phobia, terror **7** anxiety **10** foreboding **11** trepidation **12** apprehension **13** consternation

dreadful 5 awful **6** tragic **7** awesome, extreme, fearful, ghastly, hideous, ominous **8** alarming, horrible, horrific, shocking, terrible **9** appalling, frightful, revolting **11** distressing, frightening

dreadfully 7 awfully **8** horribly **9** decidedly, extremely, fearfully, hideously, seriously **10** strikingly, tragically **11** appallingly, exceedingly, frightfully

dreadnought 10 battleship

dream 4 ache, long, wish **5** crave, fancy, ideal **6** bubble, desire, hanker, vision **7** chimera, fantasy, imagine, rainbow, reverie, specter, spectre **8** ambition, delusion, illusion, phantasm, phantasy **9** fantasize, nightmare **10** aspiration *divination by:* **11** oneiromancy *god:* **8** Morpheus

dreamer 7 utopian **8** idealist **9** visionary **10** Don Quixote, lotus-eater **13** castle-builder

dreamlike 5 ideal, vague **6** unreal **7** shadowy, surreal **8** fanciful, illusory, nebulous **9** imaginary, visionary **12** otherworldly

Dream of Gerontius composer 5 Elgar (Edward)

dream up 5 frame, hatch **6** cook up, create, devise, invent **7** concoct, imagine **8** conceive, contrive, envisage, envision **9** formulate, visualize

dreamy 7 pensive **9** unworldly, visionary **10** idealistic **11** impractical **12** otherworldly **13** introspective

dreary 4 blah, drab, dull **5** bleak **6** boring, dismal, gloomy, somber, sombre **7** forlorn, humdrum, joyless, tedious **8** banausic, tiresome, wretched **9** cheerless **10** depressing, depressive, monotonous, oppressive, pedestrian **11** dispiriting **12** discouraging

dreck 3 mud **4** junk, muck, slop **5** offal, swill, trash, waste **6** litter, refuse, sewage **7** garbage, rubbish **9** sweepings

dredge 3 dig **5** barge, scoop **6** deepen, dig out, gather **8** excavate, scoop out **9** hollow out, scrape out

dregs 4 lees, scum **5** trash **6** grouts **7** deposit, grounds, remains, residue **8** sediment **9** settlings **11** precipitate

drei 5 three

dreidel 3 top

Dreiser, Theodore *character:* **5** Clyde (Griffiths) **6** Carrie (Meeber), Eugene (Witla), Sondra (Finchley) **7** Roberta (Alden) **9** Hurstwood (George) **10** Cowperwood (Frank) *novel:* **5** Stoic (The), Titan (The) **6** Genius (The) **9** Financier (The) **12** Sister Carrie **14** Jennie Gerhardt **15** American Tragedy (An)

drench 3 sop **4** dunk, soak **5** douse, souse, steep, swill **6** deluge, seethe **7** immerse **8** inundate, saturate, submerge, waterlog

dress 3 gut **4** bind, clad, deck, doll, duds, garb, gown, sack, togs **5** adorn, align, array, frock, getup, guise, habit, smock, weeds **6** attire, bedeck, caftan, clothe, dirndl, enrobe, outfit, sacque **7** apparel, bandage, bedizen, chemise, clothes, costume, garment, garnish, raiment, threads, turnout, uniform **8** beautify, clothing, covering, decorate, ensemble, ornament, wardrobe **9** embellish, make ready **11** habiliments *a wound:* **7** bandage *designer:* **4** Dior (Christian), Erté, Head (Edith) **5** Blass (Bill), Bohan (Marc), Karan (Donna), Klein (Calvin), Pucci (Emilio), Quant (Mary), Worth (Charles Frederick) **6** Armani (Giorgio), Cardin (Pierre), Jacobs (Marc), Lauren (Ralph), Miyake (Issey), Poiret (Paul) **7** Balmain (Pierre), Cassini (Oleg), Halston, Lacroix (Christian), Mizrahi (Isaac), Versace (Gianni) **8** Galliano (John), Givenchy (Hubert) **9** Courrèges (André), de la Renta (Oscar), Gernreich (Rudi), Lagerfeld (Karl), Valentino **10** Balenciaga (Cristóbal) **12** Saint-Laurent (Yves), Schiaparelli (Elsa) *finically:* **5** primp *hair:* **4** coif **6** barber *line:* **3** hem *mode of:* **5** habit *oriental:* **9** cheongsam *part:* **5** skirt **6** bodice *South Seas:* **6** sarong *with the beak:* **5** preen *with vulgarity:* **7** bedizen

dress down 5 chide, scold **6** berate, rail at, rebuke, revile **7** bawl out, reprove, tell off, upbraid **8** admonish, chastise, reproach **9** castigate, reprimand **10** tongue-lash

dresser 5 chest **6** bureau **7** commode, highboy **10** chiffonier *gaudy:* **9** butterfly

dressing 5 sauce **6** catsup **7** bandage, catchup, ketchup **8** stuffing *salad:* **5** ranch **6** French **7** Italian, Russian **10** blue cheese **11** vinaigrette **12** green goddess

dressing room 6 vestry **8** vestiary

dressmaker 7 modiste **9** couturier **10** couturiere, seamstress

dress up 6 attire, clothe, rig out, tog out **7** apparel, deck out **8** beautify, disguise, prettify, trick out **9** embellish **10** camouflage

dressy 4 chic **5** showy, smart **6** classy, formal, frilly, ornate **7** duded up, elegant, stylish **9** rigged out

Dreyfus's defender 4 Zola (Emile)

dribble 4 drip, leak, weep **5** drool **6** bounce, drivel, slaver **7** distill, drizzle, slobber, trickle **8** salivate, sprinkle

driblet 4 drop **6** gobbet **7** globule, smidgen **8** particle, pittance

dried grape 6 raisin

dried meat 5 jerky

dried plum 5 prune

drift 3 bat, gad **4** flow, flux, gist, roam, sail, skim, tide, waft, wash **5** amble, coast, creep, float, mosey, range, slide, stray, trend **6** bummel, linger, ramble, stream, stroll, wander **7** current, maunder, meander, meaning, saunter **8** movement, penchant, sideslip, tendency **9** deviation **10** propensity **11** disposition, inclination, progression **12** predilection

drifter 3 bum, vag **4** hobo **5** gypsy, nomad, tramp **7** floater, migrant, vagrant **8** derelict, vagabond **9** transient **11** beachcomber **12** rolling stone

drill 3 bit, dig **4** bore **5** auger, borer, punch, train **6** pierce, trepan, wimble **7** routine, wildcat, workout **8** exercise, practice, practise, rehearse **9** penetrate, rehearsal **10** discipline *command:* **6** at ease **8** left face **9** about face, attention, right face

drink 3 ade, lap, nip, sea, sip, tea **4** belt, brew, deep, down, grog, gulp, soak, swig, tope, toss **5** booze, draft, drain, ocean, quaff, slurp, swill, toast **6** absorb, brandy, cognac, guzzle, imbibe, jigger, liquid, liquor, pledge, potion, tank up, tipple **7** consume, potable, schnaps, spirits, swallow, swizzle, toss off **8** aperitif, beverage, libation, liquor up, schnapps **9** aqua vitae *after-dinner:* **6** frappé **7** cordial, liqueur *drugged:* **6** Mickey **10** Mickey Finn *honey:* **4** mead *hot:* **5** negus, toddy *liquor:* **5** booze, hooch **6** red-eye **9** fire-

water, moonshine *mixed:* **3** nog **5** julep **6** Gibson, gimlet, mai tai, mimosa, mojito, rickey, Rob Roy, zombie **7** gin fizz, martini, sidecar, stinger **8** daiquiri, pink lady **9** alexander, Cuba libre, manhattan, margarita, mint julep, rusty nail **10** Bloody Mary, piña colada, Tom Collins **11** gin and tonic, grasshopper, screwdriver, whiskey sour **12** black Russian, old-fashioned *mixer:* **7** swirler *noisily:* **5** slurp *of liquor:* **4** dram, shot, slug **5** snort **8** highball *of the gods:* **6** nectar *soft:* **3** pop **4** cola, soda **5** tonic **7** soda pop **8** root beer **9** ginger ale **12** sarsaparilla *stimulating:* **6** bracer (see also BEVERAGE)

drinkable 6 liquor **7** potable **8** beverage, libation, potation

drinking 8 potation *fountain:* **7** bubbler *horn:* **6** rhyton *spree:* **3** jag **4** tear, toot **5** binge, spree **6** bender **7** carouse **8** carousal

drip 4 leak, plop, weep **7** dribble, droplet, trickle **8** sprinkle

dripping 3 wet **5** runny, soppy **6** soaked, soused **7** drizzly, soaking, sopping **8** drenched **9** saturated **11** wringing-wet

drippy 5 mushy, rainy, sappy, sobby, soppy, soupy, teary, weepy **6** slushy, syrupy **7** drizzly, maudlin, mawkish, soaking, sopping, tearful **9** schmaltzy **11** sentimental

drive 3 pep, ram **4** goad, herd, push, spur, taxi, trip, urge **5** chase, force, guide, impel, jaunt, lunge, motor, moxie, oomph, pilot, pound, spunk, steer, surge, vigor **6** compel, convey, exhort, hammer, outing, plunge, propel, strike, thrust **7** actuate, impetus, operate, produce **8** ambition, mobilize, momentum, navigate, shepherd, vitality **9** chauffeur, excursion, urge along **10** enterprise, get-up-and-go, initiative, motivation *away:* **4** shoo **5** exile **6** aroint *back:* **5** repel **6** defend **7** repulse *off:* **6** dispel *out:* **8** exorcise

drivel 3 rot **4** bosh, bunk **5** drool, hokum, hooey, prate **6** babble, bunkum, gabble, jabber, slaver **7** baloney, blabber, blather, dribble, hogwash, prattle, rubbish, slobber, twaddle **8** claptrap, flimflam, nonsense, salivate **9** gibberish, poppycock **10** balderdash, double-talk, flapdoodle **12** blatherskite, gobbledygook

driver 4 jehu **5** cabby **6** cabbie, cabman, hackie, mallet **7** hackman **8** coachman, motorist, muleteer, operator **9** chauffeur, dowitcher **10** taskmaster **11** tamping iron *of an elephant:* **6** mahout *Roman:* **10** charioteer *truck:* **8** teamster

driving 7 dynamic, powered **8** forceful, vigorous **9** energetic, inspiring **10** compelling

drizzle 4 mist, rain **7** dribble, spatter **8** droplets, sprinkle **10** sprinkling **13** precipitation

Dr. Jekyll and Mr. ___ 4 Hyde

droll 3 odd **5** comic, funny, nutty, witty **7** comical, risible **8** farcical, humorous **9** eccentric, laughable, ludicrous, whimsical

drollery 5 humor **6** comedy, joking, whimsy **7** jesting

dromedary 5 camel

drone 3 bee, hum **4** buzz, idle, laze, loaf, loll **5** idler **6** drudge, loiter, lounge, murmur **7** bagpipe **8** aircraft, parasite **9** bombinate **10** pedal point

drool 4 gush, rave **5** froth **6** dote on, drivel, saliva, slaver **7** blather, dribble, enthuse, slobber **8** salivate **10** rhapsodize

droop 3 sag **4** fall, flag, hang, loll, sink, swag, wilt **5** slump **6** dangle, slouch, weaken **7** decline, let down, subside **8** languish

droopy 4 blue, down, weak **5** baggy **6** gloomy **7** doleful, languid, sagging, slouchy, wilting **8** cast down, dejected, downcast **9** depressed **10** dispirited **11** downhearted

drop 3 dip, nip, sag, tot **4** down, drib, dump, fall, fell, jolt, lose, slip, slug, tear **5** cease, depth, lapse, lower, pitch, plump, scrub, slide, snort, speck, spend **6** cancel, cave in, demise, depart, expire, fumble, give up, go down, ground, plunge, reduce, smitch, topple, unload, vanish **7** abandon, decease, decline, deposit, descend, descent, distill, dribble, driblet, fall off, forfeit, give out, globule, pendant, plummet, trickle **8** bowl over, break off, collapse, comedown, downturn, keel over, nosedive **9** declivity, discharge, downslide, downswing, downtrend, prostrate, reduction, terminate **10** depository

drop by 4 call **5** pop in, visit **6** stop in **8** come over

droplet 4 drib, tear **7** globule

drop off 3 nap, sag **4** doze, fall, slip **5** slide, slump **6** catnap, drowse, lessen, snooze **7** decline, deliver, deposit, slacken **8** diminish, fall away, hand over **10** fall asleep

dropsical 5 puffy, tumid **6** turgid **7** swollen **8** inflated **9** edematous, tumescent

dropsy 5 edema **8** anasarca

dross 4 junk, scum, slag **5** dregs, offal, waste **6** debris, scoria **7** remains,

residue, schlock **8** detritus, impurity, leavings

drossy 4 base **6** impure, scummy **7** trivial **8** inferior, unworthy **9** worthless

drought 4 lack, need, want **6** dearth **7** aridity, dryness **8** scarcity, shortage **10** deficiency

droughty 3 dry **4** arid, sere **7** bone-dry, dried up, parched, thirsty **10** desiccated

drove 3 mob **4** army, herd, host, mass, pack **5** crowd, flock, horde, troop **6** myriad, pushed, school, throng **7** phalanx **9** multitude

drover 6 cowboy **8** shepherd

drown 4 sink, soak **5** douse, flood, souse, swamp **6** deluge, drench, engulf **7** immerse, repress, smother **8** inundate, submerge **9** overpower, overwhelm, suffocate **10** asphyxiate, extinguish

drowse 3 nod **4** doze **5** sleep **6** catnap, snooze **7** doze off, drop off, shut-eye, slumber **10** forty winks

drowsy 4 dozy **5** dopey **6** droopy, sleepy, torpid **7** languid **8** indolent, sluggish **9** lethargic, somnolent, soporific **10** slumberous **13** lackadaisical

Dr. Seuss 6 Geisel (Theodor Seuss) *book:* **11** Cat in the Hat (The) **15** Green Eggs and Ham, Yertle the Turtle **19** Horton Hatches the Egg **26** How the Grinch Stole Christmas

drub 3 tan, wax, zap **4** bash, beat, club, deck, drum, flay, flog, lash, lick, mash, maul, pelt, trim, whip **5** baste, cream, crush, paste, pound, score, slash, smash, smear, spank, stamp, thump, wreck **6** batter, berate, bruise, buffet, deface, hammer, master, pummel, punish, revile, scorch, thrash, thresh, wallop **7** belabor, blister, censure, clobber, cripple, lambast, scourge, shatter, shellac, trounce **8** bulldoze, lambaste, lash into, outclass, outshine **9** castigate, excoriate, overwhelm

drubbing 4 loss, rout **6** defeat **7** setback **10** defeasance **11** shellacking

drudge 4 grub, hack, moil, peon, plod, slog **5** grind, slave **6** menial, slavey **7** grubber, plodder **8** dogsbody

drudgery 4 moil, toil **5** chore, grind **7** travail **9** grunt work **10** donkeywork **11** backbreaker

drudging 6 boring, tiring **7** irksome, tedious **8** dragging, tiresome **9** fatiguing, laborious, wearisome **10** monotonous

drug 4 dope, lull **5** sulfa **6** downer, ipecac, opiate, physic, poison, potion, remedy, statin **7** fen-phen, generic, stupefy **8** biologic, medicine, narcotic, nepenthe, relaxant, sedative 9 ibuprofen, medicinal, methadone 10 antibiotic, medicament, medication 11 thalidomide *addict:* 6 junkie *agent:* 4 narc *calming:* 8 sedative *experience:* 4 trip *illicit:* 3 ice, kif, LSD, pot 4 acid, coke, dope, hash, meth, scag, snow, weed 5 crack, grass, opium, smack, speed 6 heroin, peyote 7 cocaine, crystal, hashish 8 cannabis, goofball 9 mescaline 10 methadrine, psilocybin *seller:* 10 pharmacist *sleep-inducing:* 8 hypnotic 9 soporific 11 barbiturate

drugged 4 high 5 dazed, doped, dopey 6 flying, loaded, stoned, zonked 8 benumbed, hopped-up, turned on 9 spaced-out, stupefied 10 narcotized

druggist 7 chemist 10 apothecary, pharmacist

drugstore 8 pharmacy 10 apothecary

druid 4 Celt 6 priest 7 prophet *sacred object:* 3 oak 9 mistletoe

drum 3 keg, vat 4 beat, cask 5 conga, tabor 6 barrel, tom-tom, tympan 7 tambour, timpani (plural), tympani (plural) 8 cylinder *Indian:* 5 tabla 8 mridanga *Irish:* 7 bodhran *large:* 4 bass 7 timbale *small:* 5 bongo, tabor 7 timbrel *string:* 5 snare

drumbeat 4 flam, roll, tuck 6 ruffle, tattoo 7 booming, pit-a-pat, rat-a-tat 8 rataplan

drumfire 5 salvo 6 volley 7 barrage, booming 9 broadside, cannonade, fusillade 11 bombardment

drumhead 4 skin 7 summary

drummer 4 Rich (Buddy) 5 Krupa (Gene), Roach (Max), Starr (Ringo), Watts (Charlie) 6 Blakey (Art), hawker, Puente (Tito), vendor 7 peddler 8 pitchman, salesman

drum up 6 invent 7 canvass, solicit 9 originate *interest:* 8 ballyhoo

drunk 3 lit, sot 4 lush, soak, wino 5 lit up, souse, tight, tipsy 6 blotto, boozer, juiced, soused, stewed, stinko, tiddly, wasted, zonked 7 crocked, guzzler, pie-eyed, sloshed, squiffy, tippler 8 squiffed 9 inebriate, plastered 10 boozehound, inebriated 11 intoxicated

drunkard 3 sot 4 lush, soak, wino 5 rummy, souse, stiff, toper 6 bibber, boozer, soaker 7 guzzler, swiller, tippler, tosspot 9 alcoholic, inebriate, juicehead 10 boozehound 11 dipsomaniac

Drusilla *brother:* 8 Caligula *father:* 5 Herod 10 Germanicus *husband:* 5 Felix *mother:* 9 Agrippina *sister:* 8 Berenice 9 Agrippina

dry 3 set 4 arid, brut, dull, sere, sour, tart 5 baked, dusty, parch, stale, wizen 6 barren, desert, harden, stolid, thirst, wither 7 congeal, deadpan, parched, shrivel, sterile, thirsty 8 rainless, solidify, tearless, teetotal, withered 9 anhydrous, dehydrate, desiccate, evaporate, unwatered 10 dehydrated, desiccated 11 unemotional 12 matter-of-fact 13 uninteresting *combining form:* 3 xer 4 xero *goods:* 6 linens, napery 8 clothing, textiles *out:* 5 sober 8 soberize *period:* 7 drought *wine:* 3 sec 4 brut

dryasdust 4 arid, dull 5 banal, inane, vapid 6 boring, stodgy 7 insipid, prosaic, tedious 9 wearisome 10 uninspired 13 uninteresting

dry measure 4 peck, pint 5 quart 6 bushel

Dryope *form:* 5 lotus *husband:* 9 Andraemon *sister:* 4 Iole

dry up 4 wilt 5 wizen 6 wither 7 deplete, exhaust, mummify, shrivel 9 desiccate, disappear, evaporate

dual 3 two 4 twin 5 duple 6 bifold, binary, double, duplex, paired 7 coupled, matched, twofold 8 matching 9 duplicate

dualistic 5 duple 6 bifold, binary, double, duplex, paired 7 twofold 9 Manichean 10 Manichaean

dualize 4 copy, dupe 5 clone 6 double 9 duplicate, replicate, reproduce

dub 4 call, name, term, trim 5 style, title 6 duffer 7 baptize, bungler, entitle, fumbler 8 christen, nickname, rerecord 9 blunderer, designate 10 denominate

dubiety 5 doubt 7 concern 8 mistrust 9 confusion, suspicion 10 skepticism 11 incertitude, incredulity, uncertainty 12 doubtfulness

dubious 4 iffy 5 fishy 6 unsure 7 suspect, unclear 8 doubtful, hesitant, unlikely 9 equivocal, skeptical, uncertain, undecided 10 improbable, unreliable 11 mistrustful, problematic, questioning, unconvinced, unpromising 12 questionable, undependable, undetermined

dubitable 5 fishy 7 suspect 8 doubtful, marginal 9 ambiguous, uncertain, unsettled 10 borderline 11 problematic 13 indeterminate

duce 5 ruler 6 despot, leader, tyrant 8 dictator 9 Mussolini (Benito), oppressor, strongman

duck 3 bob, bow, dip, shy 4 bend, dive, dunk, shun 5 avoid, dodge, douse, elude, evade, fence, parry, shirk, stoop 6 escape, plunge 7 back out, immerse 8 sidestep, submerge, submerse 10 canvasback *Asian:* 5 Pekin 8 mandarin *dabbling:* 7 gadwall, mallard *diving:* 4 smew

7 pochard **9** merganser **10** bufflehead *Eurasian:* **4** smew *European:* **8** shelduck *genus:* **4** Anas *group:* **4** team **5** brace, flock, skein **6** flight *hunter's screen:* **5** blind *male:* **5** drake *red-wattled:* **7** Muscovy *river:* **4** teal **6** wigeon **7** pintail, widgeon *scaup:* **8** bluebill *sea:* **5** eider, scaup **6** scoter

duckbill 8 platypus **9** hadrosaur, monotreme

duck soup 4 easy, snap **5** cinch **6** breeze, picnic, simple **8** kid stuff, painless, pushover **10** child's play **11** piece of cake

ducky 4 cute **5** swell **6** lovely, peachy **7** darling **9** hunky-dory **10** peachy-keen

duct 4 pipe, tube **5** canal **6** course, runway **7** channel, conduit **11** watercourse *anatomical:* **3** vas **4** vasa (plural)

ductile 6 pliant, supple **7** plastic, pliable **8** flexible, moldable **9** adaptable, compliant, malleable, tractable *metal:* **4** wire

ductless gland see ENDOCRINE GLAND

dud 3 dog **4** bomb, bust, flop **5** lemon, loser **6** bummer, misfit, turkey **7** debacle, failure, washout **8** abortion **9** valueless **11** ineffective

dude 3 fop, guy **4** beau, buck, rake **5** blood, dandy **6** fellow **7** coxcomb **8** macaroni **9** exquisite **12** Beau Brummell, lounge lizard

dudgeon 3 ire **4** fury, huff, miff, rage **5** anger, pique, wrath **7** chagrin, offense, outrage, umbrage **8** vexation **10** resentment **11** indignation **12** exasperation

duds 3 rig **4** garb, gear, rags, togs **5** dress, getup, weeds **6** attire, things **7** apparel, clothes, raiment, threads, toggery **8** clothing, garments **9** trappings, vestments **11** habiliments

due 4 debt, just, owed **5** lumps, owing, right **6** direct, earned, lawful, proper, unpaid **7** arrears, condign, deserts, exactly, merited, payable, payment, regular **8** adequate, deserved, directly, expected, rightful, suitable **9** deserving, equitable, liability, requisite, scheduled **10** ascribable, obligatory, receivable, satisfying, sufficient **11** appropriate, outstanding **12** compensation, satisfaction

duel 4 tilt **5** fight, joust **6** combat **7** contest, dispute **8** conflict

duenna 8 chaperon **9** chaperone, companion, governess

duet *dancer's:* **9** pas de deux

due to 4 over **7** owing to, through **9** because of **11** considering

duff 3 can **4** buns, butt, rear, rump, tail, tush **5** fanny, slack **6** bottom **7** keister, pudding, rear end **8** backside, buttocks, coal dust, derriere, fine coal

duffer 4 boob, clod, dolt, dope, yo-yo **5** chump, dunce, klutz **6** dimwit, dumdum, lubber, nitwit **7** dullard, fumbler, peddler, pinhead **8** bonehead, dumbbell, lunkhead, numskull **9** blockhead, ignoramus, numbskull, simpleton **10** nincompoop, stumblebum **11** incompetent

dugout 5 canoe **6** trench **7** piragua, pirogue, shelter

duiker 8 antelope

dukedom 5 duchy **6** domain

dulcet 5 sweet **7** melodic, tuneful **8** charming, cheerful, engaging, euphonic, pleasant, pleasing, soothing **9** agreeable, melodious **10** euphonious **11** mellifluous

dulcimer 6 zither **8** psaltery *Hungarian:* **8** cimbalom *Persian:* **6** santir **7** santour

dull 3 dim, dun, mat **4** arid, blah, blur, drab, flat, numb **5** blunt, dense, dusty, faded, ho-hum, inert, matte, muddy, muted **6** benumb, blurry, boring, deaden, dreary, gloomy, leaden, obtuse, stodgy, stupid **7** blunted, humdrum, insipid, muffled, prosaic, stupefy, subdued, tarnish, tedious **8** banausic, bromidic, deadened, discolor, lifeless, listless, monotone, plodding, sluggish **9** bloodless, colorless, dim-witted, dryasdust, insensate, ponderous, wearisome **10** dispirited, indistinct, insensible, lackluster, lusterless, monotonous, pedestrian **11** commonplace, desensitize, insensitive, thickheaded, thickwitted, unsharpened **12** simpleminded **13** uninteresting

dullard 3 oaf **4** bird, boob, clod, dolt, dope, yo-yo **5** chump, dummy, dunce, idiot, moron, ninny, noddy, stupe **6** dimwit, dum-dum, nitwit **7** airhead, pinhead **8** bonehead, dumbbell, imbecile, lunkhead, meathead, numskull **9** birdbrain, blockhead, ignoramus, lamebrain, numbskull, simpleton **10** dunderhead **11** chowderhead, chucklehead

dullness 5 ennui **6** apathy, stupor, tedium, torpor **7** boredom, languor **8** hebetude, lethargy, monotony **9** bluntness, denseness, lassitude, stupidity, torpidity **12** indifference, listlessness, sluggishness

duly 8 properly, suitably **9** correctly, regularly **12** sufficiently **13** appropriately

duma 7 council **8** assembly, congress **11** legislature

Dumas character 5 Athos **6** Aramis,

Dantès (Edmond) 7 Camille, Porthos
9 D'Artagnan
dumb 3 mum 4 dull, mute 5 dense,
quiet, thick 6 deaden, obtuse, silent,
stupid 7 doltish, foolish, idiotic,
moronic 8 duncical, ignorant, taciturn,
wordless 9 dim-witted, fatheaded,
voiceless 10 speechless, tongue-tied
11 blockheaded, thick-witted, tight-
lipped 12 closemouthed, inarticulate,
simple-minded, tight-mouthed, unresponsive
dumbbell see DULLARD
dumbfound 5 amaze 6 boggle, puzzle
7 astound, nonplus, perplex, stagger
8 astonish, bewilder, bowl over, confound, distract, surprise 9 take aback
11 flabbergast
dumbfounded 5 agape 6 amazed 7 puzzled, shocked 8 startled 9 astounded,
perplexed, staggered, surprised
10 astonished, bewildered, bowled over,
confounded, distracted, nonplussed,
taken aback 13 thunderstruck
dummkopf 3 oaf 4 boob, clod, dodo, dolt,
dope, fool, goof, jerk, mutt, simp, yo-yo
5 chump, dummy, dunce, idiot, moron,
ninny, noddy, stupe 6 dimwit, donkey,
dum-dum, nitwit, noodle 7 airhead,
dullard, pinhead, schnook 8 bonehead,
clodpoll, dumbbell, dumbhead, imbecile, lunkhead, meathead, numskull
9 birdbrain, blockhead, ignoramus,
lamebrain, numbskull, simpleton, thickhead 10 dunderhead, hammerhead, nincompoop 11 chowderhead, chucklehead, knucklehead
dummy 4 boob, clod, dodo, dolt, mock,
sham, yo-yo 5 chump, dunce, false,
idiot, model, moron, ninny, noddy,
stupe 6 dimwit, dum-dum, effigy,
ersatz, layout, mock-up, nitwit, puppet, stooge 7 airhead, dullard, manikin,
pinhead, stand-in 8 bonehead, dumbbell, imbecile, lunkhead, mannekin,
meathead, numskull 9 birdbrain,
blockhead, ignoramus, imitation, lamebrain, numbskull, simpleton, simulated
10 artificial, dunderhead, fictitious,
nincompoop, substitute 11 chowderhead, chucklehead
dump 4 drop, junk 5 chuck, depot,
ditch, scrap 6 armory, pigpen, pigsty,
plunge 7 abandon, arsenal, deep-six,
discard 8 jettison, magazine, throw out
9 stockpile, throw away 10 depository
dumpling 5 dough 8 quenelle 10 butterball
dumps 4 funk 5 blues, dolor, gloom,
mopes, slump 7 sadness 8 doldrums
9 dejection 10 depression, gloominess,

melancholy 11 despondency, unhappiness 12 mournfulness
dumpy 5 dingy, seedy, squat, stout
6 chubby, chunky, shabby, slummy,
stocky, stubby, stumpy 7 run-down
8 heavyset, thickset 9 shapeless 10 broken-down 11 dilapidated, thick-bodied
dun 3 dim, fly 4 dull, drab, gray 5 annoy,
brown, dusky, horse, murky, press
6 demand, gloomy, mayfly, needle,
pester, plague, somber, sombre
9 ephemerid, importune
Duncan's slayer 7 Macbeth
dunce 3 oaf 4 boob, clod, dodo, dolt,
dope, goof, mutt, simp, yo-yo 5 booby,
chump, dummy, idiot, moron, ninny,
noddy, stupe 6 dimwit, donkey, duffer,
dum-dum, nitwit, noodle, stupid 7 airhead, dullard, fathead, pinhead 8 bonehead, clodpoll, dumbbell, imbecile,
lunkhead, meathead, numskull 9 birdbrain, blockhead, ignoramus, lamebrain, numbskull, simpleton 10 dunderhead, hammerhead, nincompoop
11 chowderhead, chucklehead, knucklehead
Dunciad author 4 Pope (Alexander)
dundrearies 9 burnsides, sideburns
11 muttonchops 12 side-whiskers
dune 8 sandbank *area:* 3 erg
dung 4 muck 6 manure, ordure 9 excrement *beetle:* 6 scarab 9 tumblebug
dungeon 4 jail 5 vault 6 prison 9 black
hole, oubliette
dunghill 6 midden
dunk 3 dip, sop 4 soak 5 douse, drown,
souse 6 drench 7 immerse 8 saturate,
submerge, submerse
dunlin 9 sandpiper
duo 4 duet, dyad, pair 5 brace 6 couple
7 doublet, twosome
dupe 3 con, kid, sap 4 butt, fool, gull,
hoax, mark 5 cheat, chump, cozen,
patsy, spoof, trick 6 befool, delude,
double, outwit, pigeon, sucker 7 chicane, deceive, defraud, mislead 8 flimflam, hoodwink 9 bamboozle, victimize
11 double-cross, hornswoggle
dupery 3 con 4 scam, sham 5 cheat,
fraud 6 deceit, humbug, hustle 7 chicane 8 cheating, flimflam, trickery
9 chicanery, deception, duplicity,
imposture, swindling 10 dishonesty,
hanky-panky 11 hoodwinking
13 double-dealing, sharp practice
duple 4 dual, twin 6 bifold, binary, double, duplex, paired 7 coupled, doubled,
twofold 9 dualistic
duplex see DUPLE
duplicate 4 copy, fake, mate, redo,
same, twin 5 clone, ditto, equal, match,

mimeo, repro **6** carbon, double **7** dualize, imitate, replica **8** knockoff **9** companion, facsimile, identical, imitation, look-alike, replicate, reproduce **10** carbon copy, dead ringer, equivalent, reciprocal **11** counterfeit, counterpart, replication **12** reproduction

duplicitous 5 phony **6** shifty, sneaky **7** devious **8** delusive, guileful, scheming, sneaking, two-faced **9** deceitful, deceiving, deceptive, dishonest, underhand **10** fraudulent **11** underhanded **12** disingenuous **13** double-dealing

duplicity 5 fraud, guile **6** deceit **7** cunning, perfidy **8** scheming, trickery **9** chicanery, deception, treachery **10** dishonesty, doubleness **11** skulduggery **12** dissemblance, skullduggery **13** dissimulation, double-dealing

durability 4 wear **8** firmness **9** endurance, longevity, stability **10** permanence

durable 5 stout **6** stable, strong, sturdy **7** lasting **8** enduring **9** permanent, tenacious **10** dependable **11** long-lasting

durance 7 bondage **9** captivity, detention, restraint **11** confinement **12** enthrallment, imprisonment **13** incarceration

duration 3 run **4** term, time **6** extent, period **7** interim **8** interval **11** persistence

duress 5 force **6** menace, threat **8** bullying, coercion, menacing, pressure **9** restraint **10** compulsion, constraint **11** restriction **12** intimidation

during 4 amid **10** throughout

durra 7 sorghum **12** grain sorghum

durum 5 wheat

dusk 4 dark **7** evening **8** darkness, eventide, gloaming, twilight **9** nightfall **12** semidarkness

dusky 3 dim **4** dark **5** murky, swart **6** brunet, gloomy, opaque, twilit **7** obscure, shadowy, swarthy **8** funereal, nubilous, overcast, twilight **9** tenebrous **10** caliginous **11** dark-skinned

dust 4 grit, sand, sift, soot **5** ashes, grime **6** powder **8** sprinkle **10** besprinkle, sprinkling

dustbowl victim 4 Okie

dustup 3 row **4** spat **5** fight, melee, run-in, set-to **6** battle, fracas, hassle, tussle **7** dispute, quarrel, rhubarb, scuffle **8** argument, skirmish **9** bickering, brannigan **10** falling-out **11** altercation

dusty 3 dry **4** arid, dull **5** stale **7** parched, powdery, tedious, unswept

Dutch 7 trouble **8** hot water **African: 9** Afrikaans **ceramics: 5** delft **cheese: 4** Edam **5** Gouda **dog breed: 7** griffon

8 keeshond **painter: 3** Dou (Gerrit, Gerard) **4** Cuyp (Aelbert Jacobsz), Gogh (Vincent van), Hals (Frans) **5** Bosch (Hieronymus), Hooch (Pieter de), Steen (Jan) **7** de Hooch (Pieter), Hobbema (Meindert), van Gogh (Vincent), Vermeer (Jan) **8** Mondrian (Piet), Ruysdael (Jacob van, Salomon van), Terborch (Gerard) **9** de Kooning (Willem), Honthorst (Gerrit van), Rembrandt (van Rijn) **philosopher: 7** Spinoza (Benedict de) **scholar: 7** Erasmus (Desiderius)

Dutch South African 4 Boer

dutiful 7 devoted **8** faithful **9** compliant **10** respectful **13** conscientious

duty 3 job, tax, use **4** levy, onus, role, task, work **5** chare, chore, stint **6** burden, charge, devoir, impost, office, tariff **7** respect, service **8** function **10** allegiance, assessment, assignment, commitment, obligation

dwarf 4 runt **5** gnome, pygmy, stunt, troll **6** midget, peewee **7** manikin **8** Tom Thumb **9** miniature **10** diminutive, homunculus **11** hop-o'-my-thumb, lilliputian **in Snow White: 3** Doc **5** Dopey, Happy **6** Grumpy, Sleepy, Sneezy **7** Bashful **Scottish: 7** blastie

dwarfish 5 pygmy, small **6** midget **7** minikin, stunted **8** inferior, pint-size **9** miniature, pint-sized **10** diminutive, undersized **11** lilliputian

dweeb 4 dork, drip, geek, nerd, wimp, wuss **5** loser **7** nebbish

dwell 3 lie **4** bide, live, stay **5** abide, exist **6** locate, remain, repose, reside, settle **7** hang out

dweller 7 citizen, denizen, settler **8** habitant, occupant, resident **10** inhabitant

dwelling 3 pad **4** casa, digs, home, nest **5** abode, haunt, house **7** address, habitat, lodging **8** domicile, quarters **9** residence **10** brownstone, habitation **American Indian: 4** tipi **5** hogan, tepee **6** pueblo, teepee, wigwam **clergyman's: 5** manse **7** rectory **8** vicarage **9** parsonage **crude: 3** hut **4** camp **5** cabin, hovel, shack **6** cabana, shanty **7** barrack **8** barracks **Eskimo: 5** igloo **grand: 5** manor, manse, villa **6** palace **7** château, mansion **Hindu: 6** ashram **Navajo: 5** hogan **Russian: 5** dacha **small: 3** cot, hut **5** hovel **7** cottage **8** bungalow

dwindle 3 ebb **4** fade, fall, wane **5** abate, taper **6** lessen, recede, reduce, shrink, weaken, wither **7** decline, die away, die down, shrivel, slacken, subside **8** decrease, diminish, taper off **9** attenuate, drain away

dyad 3 duo, two **4** pair, yoke **5** brace, twins **6** couple **7** doublet, twosome

dye 4 tint 5 color, stain, tinge 7 pigment 8 colorant, pyronine, tincture *blue:* 4 woad 6 indigo 7 cyanine *for hair:* 5 henna *plant:* 4 woad 5 sumac 6 madder *red:* 5 eosin, henna 6 kermes, ruddle 7 cudbear, fuchsin, magenta 8 alizarin, fuchsine, amaranth, safranin 9 cochineal, rhodamine, safranine 10 erythrosin *violet:* 6 archil *yellow:* 7 flavine 8 orpiment *yellowish red:* 7 annatto

dyed-in-the-wool 5 loyal, sworn 7 devoted, die-hard, old-line, settled, staunch 8 faithful, hard-core, orthodox, standpat, true-blue 9 confirmed, hard-shell, steadfast 10 deep-rooted, deep-seated, entrenched, inveterate, unwavering 11 established 13 bred-in-the-bone, thoroughgoing

dyewood 6 fustic 10 brazilwood

dying 6 demise 7 done for, quietus 8 moribund 9 departure 10 extinction, in extremis 12 annihilation

dynamic 7 driving, intense 8 forceful, forcible, powerful, vigorous 9 energetic, strenuous 10 compelling, energizing

dynamite 4 raze 5 blast 6 blow up 7 destroy, explode, shatter 8 demolish 9 explosive 10 annihilate *inventor:* 5 Nobel (Alfred)

dynamo 8 go-getter, live wire 9 generator 10 ball of fire 11 self-starter

dysentery 4 flux 6 scours 8 diarrhea

dyslogistic 7 adverse 10 derogatory, pejorative 11 deleterious, disparaging, prejudicial, unfavorable

dyspepsia 5 gloom 6 dismay 7 chagrin, pyrosis 8 glumness 9 dejection, heartburn 10 gloominess 11 frustration, indigestion

dyspeptic 5 cross, surly 6 crabby, morose, ornery 9 irritable 10 ill-humored, ill-natured 11 disgruntled, ill-tempered

dysphoria 4 funk 5 blues, dumps, gloom, mopes 6 sorrow 7 sadness 9 dejection 10 depression, gloominess, melancholy 11 unhappiness 12 mournfulness, wretchedness 13 cheerlessness

E

each 3 all, per 4 a pop 5 every 6 apiece 8 everyone 9 per capita, everybody

eager 3 hot 4 agog, avid, keen, wild 5 antsy, hyper, itchy, pushy, ready, vital 6 ardent, fervid, gung ho, heated, hungry, intent, pining, raring 7 anxious, athirst, burning, craving, earnest, fervent, longing, restive, thirsty, wishful 8 appetent, aspiring, covetous, desirous, restless, striving, vehement, yearning 9 ambitious, energetic, hankering, impatient, voracious 10 breathless, solicitous 11 impassioned 12 enthusiastic

eagerness 4 push, urge, zeal, zest, zing 5 ardor, gusto 6 desire, fervor, hunger, spirit, thirst 7 avidity, craving, itching, longing, passion 8 alacrity, ambition, appetite, fervency, vitality, yearning 9 intensity, quickness, vehemence 10 enthusiasm, impatience, resolution

eagle 4 hawk 9 accipiter *nest:* 4 aery 5 aerie, eyrie *North American:* 4 bald 6 golden *sea:* 4 erne 6 osprey

eagle-eyed 8 vigilant, watchful 9 attentive, observant 10 perceptive 12 sharp-sighted

ear 6 notice 7 auricle 9 attention *bone:* 5 anvil, incus 6 hammer, stapes 7 malleus, stirrup *canal:* 5 scala *combining form:* 3 aur, oto 4 auri, otic *doctor:* 9 otologist *inner:* 9 labyrinth *middle:* 8 tympanum *outer:* 5 pinna *part:* 4 drum, lobe 5 canal 6 tragus 7 cochlea *relating to:* 5 aural 9 auricular *science:* 7 otology

eardrum 8 tympanum

___ **Earhart** 6 Amelia

earl 4 lord, peer 5 count, noble 8 nobleman, seigneur 9 patrician 10 aristocrat

earlier 3 ere, yet 4 once 5 as yet, so far 6 before, sooner 7 already, thus far 8 formerly, hitherto, previous 9 erstwhile, preceding 10 beforehand, heretofore, previously

earlier than 3 pre 6 before

earliest 5 first, prime 6 maiden, primal 7 initial, pioneer, primary 8 original,

primeval, pristine **10** aboriginal, primordial
earlike projection 3 lug
early 3 old **5** first, prior **6** primal, timely **7** ancient, betimes **8** original, previous, primeval, pristine, untimely **9** preceding, premature, primitive **10** antecedent, antiquated, precocious, primordial **11** prematurely *prefix:* **5** paleo
earn 3 bag, get, net, win **4** gain, make, rate, reap **5** amass, clear, gross, merit, score **6** attain, come by, obtain, pick up, rack up, secure, wangle **7** acquire, bring in, collect, deserve, harvest, procure, produce, realize, receive **8** pull down **9** bring home, knock down
earnest 3 vow **4** bond, busy, firm, keen, pawn, true, warm **5** grave, sober, token **6** active, ardent, intent, pledge, solemn, somber, surety **7** deposit, genuine, intense, serious, sincere, up front, warrant, zealous **8** contract, covenant, diligent, interest, security, sedulous, studious **9** assiduous, heartfelt **10** determined, no-nonsense, passionate, sobersided, thoughtful, unaffected **11** industrious **12** enthusiastic, wholehearted
earnestly 5 madly **7** for real, like mad
earnestness 6 fervor **7** gravity, honesty, passion, resolve **8** sobriety **9** sincerity **10** absorption, doggedness **11** engrossment, persistence **12** perseverance **13** concentration, determination
earnings 3 net, pay **4** gain **5** lucre, wages **6** income, profit, return, salary **7** profits **8** proceeds, take-home **9** emolument **10** bottom line
ear shell see ABALONE
earshot 5 range, sound **7** hearing
earsplitting 4 loud **6** shrill **7** blaring, grating, raucous, roaring **8** piercing, strident **9** deafening, dissonant **10** screeching, stentorian **11** fullmouthed
earth 3 orb, sod **4** dirt, land, soil, turf **5** globe, world **6** ground, planet, sphere **7** dry land, terrain **8** creation **10** terra firma *combining form:* **3** geo **4** geog **6** tellur **7** telluro *core:* **12** centrosphere *god:* **3** Geb, Keb, Seb **5** Dagan *goddess:* **4** Erda, Gaea **5** Ceres, Nintu **6** Kishar **7** Demeter, Nerthus *relating to:* **8** telluric **9** planetary **11** terrestrial *satellite:* **4** moon *science:* **7** geology **9** geography
earthenware 4 clay **5** china, delft **7** biscuit, faience, pottery **8** clayware, crockery, majolica **9** porcelain, stoneware **10** terra-cotta
earthlike 11 terrestrial
earthly 6 likely, mortal **7** mundane,

worldly **8** feasible, material, physical, possible, probable, temporal **9** corporeal, potential, practical **10** imaginable **11** conceivable, terrestrial, unspiritual
earthquake 5 shake, shock **6** tremor **7** temblor *measuring device:* **11** seismograph, seismometer *relating to:* **7** seismic *science:* **10** seismology **11** seismometry
earthwork 4 bank, wall **7** bulwark, rampart **10** embankment **13** fortification
earthworm 7 annelid **12** night crawler
earthy 3 low **4** base, real **5** crude, dirty, dusty, gross, muddy, sandy **6** clayey, coarse, common, simple **7** mundane, worldly **8** temporal **9** corporeal, inelegant, practical, pragmatic, realistic, unrefined **10** hard-boiled, hardheaded, indelicate, uncultured, unpolished **11** down-to-earth, terrestrial **12** matter-of-fact **13** materialistic, unsentimental
earwax 7 cerumen
ease 3 aid **4** bate, calm, dull, free, help, rest **5** allay, loose, peace, poise, relax, slack **6** assist, deaden, loosen, relief, repose, soften **7** assuage, comfort, fluency, improve, leisure, lighten, mollify, relieve, slacken **8** calmness, deftness, diminish, dispatch, facility, idleness, mitigate, moderate, pleasure, security, serenity **9** abundance, affluence, alleviate, expertise, reduction, untighten, well-being **10** ameliorate, artfulness, efficiency, expertness, facilitate, inactivity, mitigation, moderation, prosperity, relaxation, smoothness **11** alleviation, contentment, nonchalance, spontaneity, tranquility **12** satisfaction, skillfulness, tranquillity *off:* **3** ebb **4** bate, fade, fall, flag, wane **5** abate, let up, loose, relax, slack **6** lessen, loosen, relent, unbend, unwind **7** die away, die down, slacken, subside **8** diminish, loosen up, moderate **9** untighten
easel 4 desk **5** frame, stand **7** support **9** workbench, worktable
easement 6 relief **7** comfort **10** mitigation, palliative **11** alleviation, consolation, restorative **13** mollification
easily 6 simply **7** handily, lightly, readily **8** facilely, smoothly **11** dexterously, efficiently **12** effortlessly
East 4 Asia **6** Levant, Orient
Easter 5 Pasch *relating to:* **7** paschal *symbol:* **3** egg **4** lamb **5** bunny **6** rabbit
eastern 8 oriental **9** Levantine *countries:* **6** Orient
East Indian country 8 Malaysia **9** Indonesia, Singapore
East Timor *capital:* **4** Dili *monetary unit:* **6** dollar *neighbor:* **9** Indonesia

easy 3 lax **4** calm, cozy, glib, mild, soft, snug **5** basic, clear, comfy, cushy, light, loose, naive, plain, suave **6** breezy, facile, fluent, kindly, placid, poised, polite, secure, serene, simple, smooth, urbane **7** amiable, courtly, cursive, evident, flowing, lenient, obvious, patient, relaxed **8** apparent, composed, familiar, graceful, gullible, in clover, informal, manifest, merciful, obliging, peaceful, pleasant, sociable, tolerant, tranquil, trusting **9** collected, credulous, forgiving, indulgent, possessed **10** charitable, diplomatic, effortless, elementary, forbearing, gregarious, permissive **11** comfortable, complaisant, good-humored, good-natured, susceptible, sympathetic, unconcerned **12** good-tempered **13** compassionate, mollycoddling, self-possessed, uncomplicated

easygoing 3 lax **4** calm, cool, lazy **5** quiet **6** breezy, casual, dégagé, folksy, placid, poised, sedate, serene **7** affable, offhand, patient, relaxed, unfussy **8** amenable, carefree, composed, down home, fainéant, flexible, indolent, informal, laid-back, slothful, together, tranquil **9** apathetic, indulgent, offhanded, unhurried **10** nonchalant, permissive, unaffected **11** comfortable, complaisant, indifferent, low-pressure, pococurante, unconcerned, unflappable, uninhibited **12** devil-may-care, even-tempered, happy-go-lucky, lighthearted **13** self-possessed, unconstrained

easy mark 3 sap **4** butt, dupe, fool, gull **5** chump, patsy, sport **6** pigeon, softie, sucker, turkey, victim **7** fall guy **8** pushover **9** soft touch **11** sitting duck

eat 3 sup, vex **4** bite, chow, dine, gnaw, meal, pick, take, wolf **5** annoy, erode, feast, gorge, graze, hound, lunch, mouth, munch, scarf, scoff, scour, snack, use up **6** bother, devour, feed on, gobble, harass, hassle, ingest, inhale, nibble, pester, pick at, pig out, plague, take in **7** banquet, consume, corrode, exhaust, gorge on, swallow, torment **8** chow down, dissolve, take food, wear away **9** breakfast, decompose, masticate, partake of, polish off **10** break bread, gormandize, nibble away

eatable 6 edible **8** esculent, harmless **9** palatable **10** comestible, digestible

eatery 4 café **5** diner, grill **10** coffee shop, restaurant **11** greasy spoon **12** luncheonette

eating place 3 pub **4** café, mess **5** diner, grill, joint **6** bistro, tavern **7** automat,

beanery, canteen, dinette, tearoom **8** cookshop, messroom, pizzeria, snack bar **9** brasserie, cafeteria, chophouse, hash house, lunchroom, trattoria **10** coffee shop, restaurant, steak house **11** greasy spoon **12** luncheonette

eavesdrop 3 bug, tap **4** lurk **7** monitor **8** listen in, overhear

ebb 4 drop, fade, fall, flag, tide, wane **5** abate, droop, let up **6** lessen, recede, reduce, relent, shrink, wither **7** decline, descent, die away, die down, ease off, retreat, slacken, subside **8** decrease, diminish, languish, moderate, withdraw **10** retrograde

Eblis 5 Satan *son:* **3** Tir **4** Awar **5** Dasim **8** Zalambur

ebon, ebony 3 jet **4** inky **5** black, jetty, raven, sable **6** brunet **8** brunette, jet-black **9** pitch-dark **10** pitch-black

ebullience 3 vim, zip **4** brio, élan, zing **5** gusto **6** gaiety **7** abandon, elation **8** buoyancy, vitality, vivacity **9** animation **10** enthusiasm, excitement, exuberance, liveliness **11** high spirits **12** exhilaration, spiritedness **13** effervescence

ebullient 3 mad **4** gaga **5** brash, zingy, zippy **6** bouncy, bubbly, elated, frothy, geeked, pumped, raring **7** boiling, chipper, excited, gleeful, gushing, vibrant **8** hopped-up **9** sprightly, vivacious **11** exhilarated **12** enthusiastic, high-spirited **13** irrepressible

eccentric 3 odd, nut **4** coot, kook **5** crank, crazy, droll, flaky, freak, funky, funny, goofy, kooky, nutty, queer, wacky, weird **6** far out, oddity, quaint, quirky, screwy, weirdo, whacko, whacky **7** bizarre, curious, deviant, erratic, heretic, oddball, offbeat, strange, unusual **8** aberrant, abnormal, bohemian, cockeyed, crackpot, goofball, maverick, original, peculiar, singular, uncommon **9** anomalous, character, deviating, fantastic, fruitcake, grotesque, irregular, off-center, screwball, unnatural, whimsical **10** elliptical, off-balance, unbalanced, uncentered **11** exceptional **13** idiosyncratic, nonconformist

eccentricity 4 kink **5** quirk, twist **8** crotchet, quiddity **9** deviation, weirdness **10** aberration **11** strangeness **12** idiosyncrasy

ecclesiastic see CLERGYMAN

ecclesiastical 4 holy **5** papal **6** church, sacred **8** churchly, clerical, pastoral, priestly **9** apostolic, canonical, episcopal, spiritual, synagogal **10** churchlike, pontifical, rabbinical, sacerdotal

11 ministerial, patriarchal, theological
12 episcopalian, evangelistic, tabernacular
ecdysiast see STRIPTEASER
echelon 3 row 4 file, line, rank, tier
5 grade, group, level, order, queue
6 string 7 chevron 9 formation
echidna 8 anteater 9 monotreme
13 spiny anteater
Echidna *father:* 7 Phorcys 8 Chrysaor
mother: 4 Ceto 10 Callirrhoë *offspring:*
5 Hydra 6 dragon, Orthus, Sphinx
7 Chimera 8 Cerberus, Chimaera
echinoderm 6 urchin 7 crinoid, sea star
8 starfish 9 coelomate, sea urchin
11 sea cucumber
echo 3 ape 4 mime, ring 5 evoke, mimic,
trace 6 mirror, parrot, repeat, result,
reverb, second 7 imitate, iterate,
reflect, resound, revoice, vestige 8 resonate, response 9 duplicate, imitation,
reiterate 10 reflection, repetition
11 reverberate 12 repercussion
13 reverberation
Echo 5 nymph, oread *beloved:* 9 Narcissus
echoic 7 mimetic 9 imitative 10 derivative 12 onomatopoeic 13 onomatopoetic
éclat 4 bang, dash, fame, pomp 5 glory,
honor, kudos 6 luster, lustre, praise,
renown, repute 7 acclaim, display, laurels, stardom, success 8 applause, eminence, prestige, standing 9 celebrity,
notoriety, publicity 10 brilliance, brilliancy, exaltation, prominence, reputation 11 distinction, ostentation
eclectic 5 broad, fussy, mixed, picky
6 choosy, select, varied 7 diverse,
finicky, mingled 8 assorted, catholic,
elective 9 inclusive, selective 10 discerning, fastidious, particular 11 diversified 12 dilettantish, multifarious
13 heterogeneous
eclipse 3 dim 5 bedim, cloud, cover,
excel, outdo, shade 6 darken, exceed,
shadow 7 becloud, decline, obscure,
surpass 8 downfall, outshine 9 adumbrate, obfuscate, overcloud 10 extinguish, overshadow
eclogue 3 ode 4 idyl, poem 5 idyll, lyric
8 pastoral
ecological 5 green 8 bionomic *community:* 5 biome
ecology 9 bionomics 11 environment
economic 6 fiscal 8 material, monetary
9 budgetary, financial, pecuniary
10 mercantile, profitable *doctrine:*
12 laissez-faire *system:* 9 communism,
socialism 10 capitalism 11 syndicalism
12 mercantilism

economical 4 mean 5 canny, close, spare
6 frugal, saving, stingy 7 careful, miserly, prudent, sparing, thrifty 8 skimping
9 efficient, niggardly, penny-wise, penurious, provident, scrimping 10 unwasteful 12 cheeseparing, parsimonious
13 penny-pinching
economist *American:* 5 Arrow (Kenneth), Simon (Herbert, Julian), Solow
(Robert), Tobin (James) 6 Becker
(Gary), George (Henry), Thurow
(Lester), Veblen (Thorstein), Walker
(Amasa), Weaver (Robert) 7 Krugman
(Paul), Kuznets (Simon), Stigler
(George), Volcker (Paul) 8 Friedman
(Milton), Stiglitz (Joseph) 9 Galbraith
(John Kenneth), Greenspan (Alan),
Samuelson (Paul) 10 Schumpeter
(Joseph) *Austrian:* 5 Hayek (Friedrich
von), Mises (Ludwig von) *Canadian:*
7 Leacock (Stephen) *Dutch:* 9 Tinbergen (Jan) *English:* 3 Sen (Amartya)
4 Mill (John Stuart) 5 Coase (Ronald),
Hayek (Friedrich von), Pigou (Arthur)
6 Engels (Friedrich), Keynes (John
Maynard) 7 Bagehot (Walter), Malthus
(Thomas), Ricardo (David) *French:*
3 Say (Jean-Baptiste) 6 Monnet (Jean),
Turgot (Anne-Robert-Jacques), Walras
(Léon) 7 Quesnay (François) *German:*
4 Marx (Karl) 5 Weber (Max) 6 Engels
(Friedrich) 7 Schacht (Hjalmar) *Indian:*
3 Sen (Amartya) *Scottish:* 4 Mill
(James) 5 Smith (Adam) *Swedish:*
6 Myrdal (Gunnar) *Swiss:* 8 Sismondi
(Simonde de)
economize 4 save 5 skimp, stint 6 manage, scrimp 7 husband 8 conserve
10 cut corners 12 pinch pennies
economy 6 saving, thrift 8 prudence,
skimping 9 concision, frugality, husbandry, parsimony, restraint, scrimping
10 discretion, efficiency, providence,
stinginess 11 carefulness, conciseness,
miserliness, thriftiness 13 niggardliness
Eco novel 13 Name of the Rose (The)
17 Foucault's Pendulum
ecru see BEIGE
ecstasy 3 joy 5 bliss 6 frenzy, heaven,
trance 7 delight, elation, madness, rapture 8 euphoria, paradise, rhapsody
9 beatitude, transport 10 exaltation,
joyfulness 11 blessedness, derangement,
enchantment, high spirits, inspiration
12 blissfulness, exhilaration, intoxication 13 seventh heaven
ecstatic 6 elated, joyful 7 gleeful
8 euphoric, exultant, jubilant, thrilled
9 delirious, delighted, entranced, overjoyed, rapturous 11 exhilarated, transported

Ecuador *capital:* **5** Quito *city:* **6** Ambato, Cuenca **7** Machala **9** Guayaquil *Indian people:* **7** Quechua *island group:* **9** Galápagos *language:* **7** Spanish *monetary unit:* **5** sucre **6** dollar *mountain range:* **5** Andes *neighbor:* **4** Peru **8** Colombia *volcano:* **6** Sangay **7** Cayambe **8** Cotopaxi **10** Chimborazo

ecumenical 6 cosmic, global **7** general, generic **8** catholic **9** inclusive, planetary, universal, worldwide **12** all-inclusive, cosmopolitan **13** comprehensive

ecumenical council 4 Lyon **5** Basel, Lyons, Trent **6** Nicene **7** Ephesus, Ferrara, Lateran, Vatican **8** Florence **9** Chalcedon, Constance

eczema 6 tetter

edacious see VORACIOUS

eddy 4 purl **5** swirl, twirl, whirl, whorl **6** vortex **8** backwash **9** backwater, maelstrom, whirlpool **11** counterflow

edema 5 croup, tumor **6** dropsy **8** anasarca, swelling

Eden 6 heaven, utopia **7** arcadia, elysium **8** paradise *river:* **5** Gihon **6** Pishon **8** Hiddekel **9** Euphrates

edentate 5 sloth **8** aardvark, anteater, pangolin **9** armadillo, toothless

Edessa's king 5 Abgar

edge 3 cut, end, hem, lip, rim **4** bank, bite, brim, cusp, draw, ease, hone, inch, lead, limb, line, pink, side, whet, worm **5** arris, bound, brink, bulge, force, ledge, picot, point, ridge, sidle, skirt, sting, strop, verge **6** border, fringe, margin, nosing **7** acidity, contour, chamfer, outline, serrate, sharpen, vantage **8** acerbity, acridity, boundary, emborder, handicap, keenness, surround, thinness **9** acuteness, advantage, extremity, harshness, head start, perimeter, periphery, sharpness, threshold, upper hand **10** causticity, shrillness, stringency **11** astringency **12** incisiveness **13** effectiveness

edge city 5 exurb **6** suburb

edged 4 acid, tart **5** acute, sharp **6** strong **7** cutting **8** incisive, piercing

edge in 6 inject **9** interject, interpose, insinuate **10** infiltrate **11** interpolate

edging 3 hem **4** lace **5** braid, frill, limit **6** border, fringe, lacing, margin, piping **7** flounce, selvage **8** rickrack, selvedge, trimming

edgy 3 hip **5** funky, nervy, sharp, tense, testy **6** daring, touchy, uneasy **7** excited, keyed up, offbeat, restive, uptight **8** Bohemian, out-there, renegade, restless, skittery, skittish, volatile **9** excitable, impatient, irascible, irrita-

ble **10** high-strung, outlandish **11** provocative

edible 8 esculent **9** palatable **10** comestible *root:* **3** oca, yam **4** beet, taro, yuca **6** carrot, daikon, ginger, jicama, potato, radish, turnip, wasabi **7** burdock, cassava, ginseng, malanga, parsnip, salsify **8** celeriac, galangal, kohlrabi, rutabaga **11** horseradish, sweet potato *seed:* **3** nut, pea **4** bean **6** peanut

edibles 4 chow, eats, feed, food, grub **6** viands **7** aliment, goodies, nurture **8** victuals **9** provender **10** provisions, sustenance **11** comestibles

edict 3 law **4** bull, fiat, rule **5** canon, order, ukase **6** decree, dictum, ruling **7** command, dictate, mandate, precept, statute **9** directive, manifesto, ordinance, prescript **10** injunction, regulation **12** proclamation **13** pronouncement *Islamic:* **5** fatwa *papal:* **4** bull **8** decretal

Edict of ___ 5 Milan, Worms **6** Nantes

edifice 4 pile **8** building, erection **9** structure

edify 5 teach **6** better, fill in, illume, inform, update, uplift **7** educate, elevate, enhance, improve **8** illumine, instruct **9** elucidate, enlighten **10** illuminate

edit 3 cut **4** cull, omit **5** adapt, alter, amend, emend, fix up **6** delete, doctor, excise, polish, redact, refine, review, revise, reword, select **7** abridge, compile, correct, rewrite **8** annotate, assemble, condense, copyread, fine-tune **9** proofread, rearrange **10** blue-pencil, bowdlerize

edition 4 copy, form **5** issue, print **7** reissue, reprint, version **8** printing, variorum **10** impression, reprinting **12** reproduction

editor 8 redactor **9** scrivener, wordsmith **10** copyreader **11** proofreader

Edomite's ancestor 4 Esau

educate 4 rear **5** brief, coach, drill, edify, nurse, teach, train, tutor **6** inform, school **7** explain, nurture **8** instruct **9** brainwash, enlighten **10** discipline **12** indoctrinate

education 7 culture, tuition **8** breeding, coaching, guidance, learning, literacy, pedagogy, teaching, training, tutelage, tutorage, tutoring **9** erudition, knowledge, schooling, tutorship **11** instruction, learnedness, scholarship **13** enlightenment

educational 11 informative, instructive **13** informational, instructional *institu-*

tion: 6 school 7 academy, college 10 university 12 conservatory

educator 5 tutor 7 teacher 9 professor 10 instructor *American:* 4 Mann (Horace) 5 Dewey (John) 6 Butler (Nicholas Murray), Conant (James Bryant), Harris (William Torrey) 7 Barnard (Henry), Beecher (Catharine), Peabody (Elizabeth) 8 Hutchins (Robert Maynard), McGuffey (William) 10 Washington (Booker T.) *Czech:* 8 Comenius (John Amos) *English:* 6 Arnold (Thomas) 7 Spencer (Herbert) *German:* 7 Froebel (Friedrich), Herbart (Johann) *Italian:* 10 Montessori (Maria) *Swiss:* 10 Pestalozzi (Johann Heinrich)

educe 4 drag, draw, milk, pull 5 evoke, wrest, wring 6 derive, elicit, evince, evolve, extort, obtain, secure 7 distill, draw out, extract, procure 8 bring out 10 excogitate

eel 5 moray, siren 6 conger 7 hagfish, lamprey, sniggle *young:* 5 elver

eelpout 6 blenny, burbot 10 muttonfish

eely 5 slimy 6 slippy, wiggly 7 elusive, wriggly 8 slippery, slithery 9 wriggling

eerie 5 scary, weird 6 creepy, spooky 7 bizarre, strange, uncanny 8 chilling, spectral 9 fantastic, grotesque, unearthly 10 mysterious 11 frightening, hair-raising 12 otherworldly

efface 4 dele, x out 5 annul, erase 6 cancel, delete, rub out 7 blot out, destroy, expunge, scratch, wipe out 8 black out, wear away 9 eliminate, eradicate, extirpate 10 obliterate

effect 3 end 4 make 5 cause, enact, event, fruit 6 create, draw on, induce, intent, invoke, render, result, secure, sequel, upshot 7 achieve, bring on, enforce, execute, fulfill, outcome, perform, produce, purport, realize, turn out 8 bring off, carry out, complete, conceive, generate, sequence 9 actualize, aftermath, corollary, discharge, implement, influence, operation, outgrowth, pursuance 10 accomplish, appearance, bring about, conclusion, consummate, denouement, effectuate 11 consequence, development, eventuality, precipitate 12 carry through, ramification, repercussion

effective 4 able 5 sound, valid 6 causal, cogent, direct, potent, useful 7 capable 8 adequate 9 competent, operative 10 compelling, convincing, productive

effectiveness 5 clout, force, point, power, vigor 6 weight 7 cogency, potency 8 strength, validity 10 capability

effects 4 gear 5 goods, stuff 6 things

8 chattels, movables, property 9 equipment, moveables, trappings 10 belongings 11 impedimenta, possessions 13 accoutrements

effectual 5 sound, valid 6 potent, strong, useful 7 capable 8 decisive, powerful, workable 10 conclusive, fulfilling, productive 11 influential, practicable 13 authoritative, determinative

effectuate see EFFECT

effeminate 5 sappy, sissy 6 chichi, prissy 7 epicene, foppish 8 delicate, overnice, precious 9 sissified 10 old-maidish 11 overrefined

effervescence 5 giddy 7 fizzing, foaming, sparkle 8 bubbling, buoyancy, vivacity 9 animation 10 ebullience, ebullition, exuberance, exuberancy, liveliness 12 exhilaration

effervescent 3 gay 4 airy 5 jolly 6 bouncy, bubbly, lively 7 boiling, buoyant, excited 8 animated, mirthful, volatile 9 sparkling, sprightly, vivacious 10 carbonated 12 high-spirited 13 irrepressible

effete 4 soft, weak 5 frail, spent 6 barren 6 sickly 7 decayed, drained, sterile, worn-out 8 decadent, decaying, delicate, depleted, fatigued, pampered 9 declining, dissolute, enfeebled, exhausted, infertile, washed-out 10 degenerate, unfruitful 11 debilitated

efficacious 6 active, potent, strong 8 forceful, powerful, puissant 9 operative 10 productive 11 influential

efficacy see EFFECTIVENESS

efficiency see EFFECTIVENESS

efficient 4 able 5 adept 6 expert 7 capable, skilled 8 economic, masterly, skillful 9 competent 10 economical, productive

effigy 3 guy 4 icon, idol 5 dummy, image 6 figure 7 waxwork 8 likeness

effloresce 4 blow 5 bloom, burst 6 flower, sprout 7 blossom, burgeon 9 bear fruit

effluvium 3 air 4 odor, reek 5 smell, vapor, waste 6 miasma 7 exhaust 8 effusion, emission 9 by-product, discharge, emanation 10 exhalation

efflux see EFFLUVIUM

effort 3 job, try 4 feat, push, task, toil, work 5 chore, essay, force, labor, might, nisus, pains, sweat, while 6 energy, strain 7 attempt, travail, trouble, venture 8 endeavor, exertion, industry, struggle 11 application, elbow grease

effortful 4 hard 6 tiring, uphill 7 arduous, labored, operose 8 exacting, toilsome 9 ambitious, difficult, laborious, strenuous 11 challenging

effortless 4 easy 5 adept, light, ready 6 expert, facile, fluent, simple, smooth 8 masterly, skillful 10 proficient 11 undemanding

effrontery 4 face, gall 5 brass, cheek, nerve 8 audacity, boldness, chutzpah, temerity 9 arrogance, assurance, brashness, hardihood, impudence, insolence 10 brazenness 11 presumption 12 impertinence

effulgence 4 glow 5 blaze, glory 6 luster, lustre 8 radiance, splendor 9 splendour 10 brightness, brilliance, brilliancy, luminosity

effulgent 5 vivid 6 bright, lucent 7 beaming, glowing, lambent, radiant, shining 8 dazzling, glorious, luminous, lustrous, splendid 9 brilliant 11 resplendent 12 incandescent

effuse 4 flow, gush, pour, shed 5 exude, issue 6 stream 7 emanate, enthuse, flow out, radiate

effusive 5 gushy 6 lavish, sloppy, smarmy 7 cloying, fulsome, gushing, profuse, verbose 9 expansive, exuberant 10 loquacious, outpouring, unreserved 11 extravagant 12 enthusiastic, unrestrained 13 demonstrative, unconstrained

eft 4 newt 6 triton 10 salamander

e.g. 10 for example 13 exempli gratia

egad 6 zounds 7 criminy 8 gadzooks 11 odds bodkins

egg 3 ova (plural) 4 ovum, seed 5 ovule *case:* 5 shell 7 ootheca *combining form:* 3 ovi, ovo *dish:* 6 omelet 8 omelette *fertilized:* 6 zygote 7 oospore *fish:* 3 roe 6 caviar *French:* 4 oeuf *immature:* 6 oocyte *part:* 4 yolk 5 glair, shell, white *shaped:* 5 ovate, ovoid *white:* 5 glair 7 albumen

egghead 6 pundit 8 highbrow 10 doubledome 12 intellectual

egg on 4 goad, prod, spur, urge 5 prick, rally 6 arouse, exhort, excite, incite, prompt, stir up 7 agitate 9 instigate, stimulate

eggplant 6 purple 9 aubergine 10 nightshade

egg-shaped 4 oval 5 ovate, ovoid 7 oviform

Eglah *husband:* 5 David *son:* 7 Ithream

eglantine 7 dog rose 10 sweetbriar, sweetbrier

Eglantine *father:* 5 Pepin *husband:* 9 Valentine

Eglon *king:* 5 Debir *slayer:* 4 Ehud

ego 4 self 5 pride 6 vanity 7 conceit 10 self-esteem

egocentric 7 selfish 9 conceited 10 self-loving 11 self-seeking 12 narcissistic, self-absorbed, self-affected, self-centered, self-involved, vainglorious 13 individualist, self-conceited, self-concerned, self-indulgent

egoism 5 pride 6 vanity 7 conceit 8 self-love 9 self-glory, self-pride, vainglory 10 narcissism, self-regard 11 selfishness, self-opinion

egoistic 4 smug, vain 7 selfish 9 conceited 12 self-absorbed, self-centered 13 self-concerned, self-contented, self-satisfied

egomaniacal 12 self-exalting, vainglorious

egotism 5 pride 6 vanity 7 conceit 8 boasting, bragging, self-love, vainness, vaunting 9 arrogance, pomposity, self-glory, self-pride, vainglory 10 narcissism, self-esteem 11 megalomania, self-opinion 12 boastfulness 13 conceitedness

egotistic 4 vain 5 cocky, proud 7 selfish, stuck-up 8 arrogant, boastful, inflated, puffed-up 9 conceited 11 pretentious, self-serving 12 self-absorbed, self-centered, self-involved 13 self-concerned, self-satisfied

egregious 4 rank 5 gross, stark 6 arrant, brazen 7 blatant, glaring, heinous 8 flagrant, infamous, outright, shocking 9 atrocious, notorious, shameless 10 deplorable, outrageous 11 conspicuous

egress, egression 4 door, exit 5 issue, leave 6 depart, escape, exodus, outlet 7 doorway, exiting, opening, passage 9 departure, emergence

egret 5 heron, wader

Egypt *ancient city:* 6 Thebes 7 Memphis *capital:* 5 Cairo *city:* 4 Giza 8 Port Said 10 Alexandria *dam:* 5 Aswan *desert:* 6 Libyan 7 Arabian, Western *gulf:* 4 Suez 5 Aqaba *lake:* 6 Nasser *language:* 6 Arabic *leader:* 5 Sadat (Anwar el-) 6 Nasser (Gamal Abdul) 7 Mubarak (Hosni) *monetary unit:* 5 pound *neighbor:* 5 Libya, Sudan 6 Israel *oasis:* 4 Siwa 6 Dakhla, Kharga 7 Farafra *peninsula:* 5 Sinai *river:* 4 Nile *sea:* 3 Red 13 Mediterranean

Egyptian *burial jar:* 7 canopic *Christian:* 4 Copt *cross:* 4 ankh *dam:* 5 Aswan *dynasty:* 5 Saite, Xoite 6 Hyksos, Tanite, Theban 7 Persian, Thinite 8 Memphite 9 Bubastite, Ethiopian 10 Diospolite *god:* *chief:* 6 Amen-Ra *crocodile-headed:* 5 Sebek *falcon-headed:* 4 Ment 5 Horus, Mentu 6 Sokari 7 Sokaris *ibis-headed:* 5 Thoth 6 Dhouti *jackal-headed:* 6 Anubis *of creation:* 4 Ptah 5 Phtha *of day:* 5 Horus *of earth:* 3 Geb, Keb, Seb *of evil:* 3 Set 4 Seth

5 Sebek *of life:* **4** Amen, Amon
5 Ammon *of magic:* **5** Thoth **6** Dhouti
of Memphis: **4** Ptah **5** Phtha **6** Sokari
7 Sokaris *of the heavens:* **5** Horus *of the
morning sun:* **5** Horus **7** Khepera *of the
sun:* **6** Amen-Ra *of Thebes:* **4** Amen
6 Khensu, Khonsu *of the underworld:*
6 Osiris *of war:* **4** Ment **5** Mentu *of wisdom:* **5** Thoth **6** Dhouti *ram-headed:*
4 Amen, Amon **5** Ammon, Khnum
6 Khnemu *snake:* **4** Apep **5** Apepi
goddess:
　cat-headed: **4** Bast **5** Pakht *cow-headed:*
　5 Athor **6** Hathor *lioness-headed:*
　4 Bast **5** Pakht **6** Sekhet *of fertility:*
　4 Isis *of love and mirth:* **5** Athor
　6 Hathor *of motherhood:* **4** Apet, Isis
　of Thebes: **3** Mut *of the heavens:*
　3 Nut *queen of the gods:* **4** Sati *vulture-headed:* **3** Mut **7** Nekhebt **8** Nekhebet
king: (see KING entry) *language:* **6** Arabic, Coptic *native:* **4** Arab, Copt
5 Nilot *president:* **5** Sadat **6** Nasser
7 Mubarak *queen:* **9** Cleopatra, Nefertiti *sacred bird:* **4** ibis *solar disk:* **4** Aten
sultan: **7** Saladin *talisman:* **6** scarab
underworld: **4** Aaru, Duat **6** Amenti
wind: **7** khamsin, sirocco
eider 4 down, duck **7** sea duck
eidetic 5 exact, vivid **7** perfect, precise
8 absolute, lifelike
eidolon 4 icon **5** ghost, ideal, image,
model, shade **6** mirage, vision, wraith
7 epitome, fantasm, figment, paragon,
phantom, specter, spectre **8** exemplar,
illusion, paradigm, phantasm **9** archetype, prototype **10** apparition
eight *group of:* **5** octet **6** octave
eight bells 4 noon
eighth note 6 quaver
eighty-six 4 boot, toss **5** chuck, eject,
evict, scrap **6** bounce **7** discard, kick
out **8** get rid of, jettison, throw out
Einstein, Albert *birthplace:* **3** Ulm *theory:*
10 relativity
Eire see IRELAND
eject 4 boot, bump, dump, fire, oust,
sack **5** chuck, evict, expel **6** banish,
bounce **7** boot out, cast out, dismiss,
kick out **8** disgorge, throw out **9** discharge
eke out 6 extend **7** augment, enhance,
fill out, squeeze, stretch **8** increase
10 supplement
elaborate 4 busy **5** fancy, showy
6 daedal, dressy, evolve, expand, knotty, minute, ornate, refine, unfold
7 amplify, build up, careful, clarify,
comment, complex, develop, discuss,
elegant, enlarge, explain, expound,
profuse, work out **8** detailed, involved,
overdone, thorough **9** Byzantine, deco-

rated, embellish, extensive, interpret,
intricate **10** overworked **11** complicated, embellished, extravagant, painstaking **12** labyrinthine
Elaine *father:* **6** Pelles *lover:* **8** Lancelot
9 Launcelot *son:* **7** Galahad
Elam *capital:* **4** Susa **7** Shushan *father:*
4 Shem *king:* **12** Chedorlaomer
élan 3 pep, vim, zip **4** brio, dash, fire,
life, zeal, zest, zing **5** ardor, flair, gusto,
oomph, verve, vigor **6** energy, esprit,
fervor, spirit **7** impetus **8** vivacity **9** animation, eagerness, intensity **10** enthusiasm
élan vital 4 soul **5** anima **6** animus, pneuma, psyche, spirit
elapse 4 go by, pass **6** expire, run out,
slip by **8** pass away
elastic 6 bouncy, limber, pliant, rubber,
supple **7** ductile, pliable, rubbery,
springy **8** animated, flexible, moldable,
stretchy, volatile **9** adaptable, expansive, malleable, resilient **10** extendable,
extensible, rubber band, rubberlike
11 stretchable
elate 4 buoy **5** cheer, exalt, flush, set up
6 excite, perk up, uplift **7** cheer up,
delight, enliven, gladden, gratify, hearten, inspire, overjoy **8** brighten, embolden, inspirit, spirit up **9** encourage
10 exhilarate, invigorate
elated 4 glad, high **5** happy **7** exalted,
excited **8** ecstatic, euphoric, exultant,
gladsome, jubilant **9** overjoyed
10 enraptured **11** exhilarated, intoxicated **12** high-spirited
elation 3 joy **4** glee **7** delight, ecstasy, rapture **8** buoyancy, euphoria **9** happiness,
transport **10** exaltation, excitement,
jubilation **12** exhilaration, intoxication
Elbe *tributary* **4** Eger, Iser, Ohre **5** Saale
6 Moldau, Vltava
elbow 4 push **5** joint, nudge, shove
6 hustle, jostle
eld 4 yore **6** old age **8** old times
elder 6 senior **8** old-timer **9** patriarch,
presbyter **10** golden-ager
elderliness 3 age **6** old age **8** caducity
10 senescence **11** senectitude
elderly 3 old **4** aged, gray **5** aging, hoary
7 ancient **9** declining, venerable
eldritch 5 eerie, weird **7** uncanny
Eleanor's husband 7 Henry II **8** Franklin
elect 3 opt, tap **4** name, pick **5** co-opt,
saved **6** choice, choose, chosen, decide,
opt for, ordain, picked, vote in
7 resolve, vote for **8** destined, nominate, ordained, redeemed **9** delivered,
designate, determine, exclusive, single
out **10** designated, singled out
election 6 ballot, choice, voting **7** primary **8** choosing, decision **9** balloting

10 preference, referendum 11 alternative

electioneer 5 stump 7 canvass 8 campaign, politick 9 barnstorm

elective 6 chosen 8 optional 9 voluntary 11 sympathetic 13 discretionary, noncompulsory, nonobligatory

Electra *brother:* 7 Orestes *father:* 9 Agamemnon *husband:* 7 Pylades *mother:* 12 Clytemnestra *sister:* 9 Iphigenia *victim:* 9 Aegisthus 12 Clytemnestra

electric *appliance:* 3 fan 4 iron, oven 5 clock, drier, dryer, mixer, range, stove 6 stereo, washer 7 blender, freezer, toaster 10 dishwasher, television 12 refrigerator *coil:* 5 tesla 8 solenoid *device:* 4 coil, fuse, plug 6 dynamo, magnet, switch 7 battery 8 resistor, rheostat, varistor 9 amplifier, capacitor, condenser, generator 11 transformer *generator:* 6 dynamo *particle:* 3 ion *unit:* 3 amp, ohm 4 volt, watt 5 farad, henry, joule 6 ampere 7 coulomb, faraday 8 kilowatt

electric current *kind:* 6 direct 11 alternating *power:* 7 wattage *strength:* 8 amperage

electricity 5 juice, spark 7 current 9 galvanism, lightning *kind:* 6 static 7 current

electrify 3 jar 4 jolt, stun 5 amaze, power, shock 6 charge, excite, thrill 7 astound, enthuse, inflame, provoke, stagger, startle 8 astonish, energize

electrode 6 dynode *negative:* 7 cathode *positive:* 5 anode

electron 3 ion 7 polaron *stream:* 10 cathode ray *tube:* 6 triode 7 tetrode 8 dynatron, klystron

Electryon *brother:* 6 Mestor *daughter:* 7 Alcmene *father:* 7 Perseus *mother:* 9 Andromeda *wife:* 5 Anaxo

eleemosynary 6 humane 8 generous 10 altruistic, beneficent, benevolent, charitable, munificent, openhanded 12 humanitarian 13 philanthropic

elegance 4 chic, pomp, tone 5 charm, grace, style, taste 6 luxury, polish 7 culture, dignity 8 chicness, poshness, richness, splendor, urbanity 9 gentility, precision 10 ornateness, refinement 11 cultivation 12 magnificence, tastefulness 13 sumptuousness

elegant 4 chic, fine, posh 5 fancy, grand, noble, swank 6 choice, classy, dainty, lovely, modish, ornate, swanky, urbane 7 courtly, genteel, opulent, refined, stately, stylish 8 cultured, polished, splendid, tasteful 9 exquisite, luxurious, recherché, sumptuous 10 cultivated 11 fashionable

elegiac 7 pensive 8 dactylic 9 lamenting, sorrowful 10 melancholy

elegy 4 poem, song 5 dirge 6 lament, monody 8 threnody

___ **eleison** 5 Kyrie

Elektra *composer:* 7 Strauss (Richard)

element 4 item, part 5 basic, facet, piece, point 6 aspect, detail, factor, member, sector 7 article, feature, portion, section 8 division, particle, rudiment 9 component, essential, principle 10 ingredient, particular 11 constituent, fundamental *chemical:* 3 tin 4 gold, iron, lead, neon, zinc 5 argon, boron, radon, xenon 6 barium, carbon, cerium, cesium, cobalt, copper, curium, erbium, helium, indium, iodine, nickel, osmium, oxygen, radium, silver, sodium 7 arsenic, bismuth, bohrium, bromine, cadmium, calcium, dubnium, fermium, gallium, hafnium, hassium, holmium, iridium, krypton, lithium, mercury, niobium, rhenium, rhodium, silicon, sulphur, terbium, thorium, thulium, uranium, yttrium 8 actinium, aluminum, antimony, astatine, chlorine, chromium, europium, fluorine, hydrogen, illinium, lutecium, masurium, nitrogen, nobelium, platinum, polonium, rubidium, samarium, scandium, selenium, tantalum, thallium, titanium, tungsten, vanadium 9 americium, berkelium, beryllium, columbium, germanium, lanthanum, magnesium, manganese, neodymium, neptunium, palladium, plutonium, potassium, ruthenium, strontium, tellurium, virginium, ytterbium, zirconium 10 dysprosium, gadolinium, lawrencium, meitnerium, molybdenum, seaborgium 11 californium, einsteinium, mendelevium, phosphorous 12 darmstadtium, praseodymium 13 rutherfordium, protoactinium

elemental 3 key 4 pure 5 basal, basic, crude, prime 6 inborn, innate, primal, simple 7 central, connate, primary, radical 8 cardinal, inherent, integral, intimate, simplest 9 beginning, essential, ingrained, intrinsic, primitive 10 deepseated, primordial, underlying 11 fundamental 13 uncomplicated

elementary 4 easy 5 basal, basic 6 simple 7 initial 9 beginning, essential, primitive 10 rudimental, underlying 11 fundamental, preliminary, rudimentary 12 introductory

elemi 5 resin 9 oleoresin

elephant 6 tusker 9 pachyderm *boy:* 4 Sabu *driver:* 6 mahout *enclosure:* 5 kraal *extinct:* 7 mammoth 8 mastodon *female:* 3 cow *group:* 4 herd *keeper:* 6 mahout *male:* 4 bull *maverick:* 5 rogue *nose:* 5 trunk 9 proboscis *seat:* 6 how-

dah *sound:* 6 bellow 7 trumpet *tooth:* 4 tusk *tusk:* 5 ivory *young:* 4 calf
elephant-headed god 6 Ganesa 7 Ganesha
elephantine 4 huge 6 clumsy 7 awkward, hulking, mammoth, massive 8 colossal, enormous, gigantic 9 graceless, humongous, monstrous, ponderous 10 gargantuan, mastodonic, prodigious, ungraceful 11 heavy-footed
Elephant Man 7 Merrick (Joseph)
elevate 4 lift, rear, rise 5 boost, elate, erect, exalt, hoist, raise 6 buoy up, jack up, lift up, pick up, uplift 7 advance, dignify, ennoble, glorify, hearten, improve, inspire, promote, upgrade 8 heighten 10 exhilarate
elevated 4 high 5 grand, lofty, moral, noble 6 aerial, formal, superb 7 ethical, refined, soaring, stately, sublime 8 eloquent, majestic, virtuous 9 dignified, grandiose, high-flown, honorable, righteous 10 high-minded, upstanding 13 grandiloquent
elevation 4 hill, rise 5 boost 6 ascent, height, uplift 7 advance, raising 8 altitude, mountain 9 acclivity, promotion, upgrading 10 apotheosis, preference, preferment 11 advancement, ennoblement *indication:* 9 benchmark
elevator 4 cage, lift, silo 5 hoist *maker:* 4 Otis
elf 3 fay, imp 4 peri, puck 5 fairy, gnome, pixie, troll 6 goblin, sprite 7 brownie, gremlin 10 leprechaun
elfin 5 antic 6 frisky, impish 7 implike, playful, puckish 8 pixieish 11 mischievous
Elgin ___ 7 Marbles
Eli 4 Yale 5 Yalie
Eli ___ 4 Yale 5 Lilly 7 Whitney
Elia 4 Lamb (Charles)
Eliab *brother:* 5 David *daughter:* 7 Abihail *father:* 5 Helon, Pallu *son:* 6 Abiram, Dathan
Eliada *father:* 5 David *son:* 5 Rezon
Eliam's daughter 9 Bathsheba
elicit 5 educe, evoke 6 derive, evince, extort 7 extract, provoke 8 bring out 9 call forth, draw forth
elide 4 fail, omit, skip 6 excise, forget, ignore, remove, slight 7 abridge, curtail, neglect 8 condense, cross out, discount, overlook, pass over, suppress 9 disregard
eligible 3 fit 6 fitted, likely, nubile, seemly, suited, worthy 7 capable 8 entitled, suitable 9 desirable, qualified 10 acceptable 11 appropriate 12 marriageable
Elihu ___ 4 Root, Yale
Elijah 5 Elias 7 prophet 8 Tishbite *father:* 5 Harim 7 Jeroham

Elimelech's wife 5 Naomi
eliminate 3 bar 4 bate, drop, oust, void 5 debar, eject, erase, evict, expel, purge 6 delete, except, remove 7 discard, dismiss, exclude, expunge, obviate, rule out, take out 8 count out 9 clear away, eradicate, liquidate 11 exterminate
Eliot, George *lover:* 5 Lewes (George Henry) *novel:* 6 Romola 8 Adam Bede 11 Middlemarch, Silas Marner 13 Daniel Deronda 14 Mill on the Floss (The) *pseudonym of:* 5 Evans (Mary Ann)
Eliot, T.S. *play:* 13 Cocktail Party (The) *poem:* 9 Gerontion, Hollow Men (The), Waste Land (The) 12 Ash Wednesday, Four Quartets
Eliphaz *father:* 4 Esau *mother:* 4 Adah *son:* 5 Teman
Elisabeth *husband:* 9 Zacharias *son:* 4 John (the Baptist)
Elisha *father:* 7 Shaphat *servant:* 6 Gehazi
Elisheba *brother:* 7 Nahshon *father:* 9 Amminadab *husband:* 5 Aaron *son:* 5 Abihu, Nadab 7 Eleazar, Ithamar
elite 3 top 4 best, pick 5 cream, elect, pride, prime, prize 6 choice, flower, gentry, select 7 quality, society 9 exclusive, gentility, patrician 10 upper class, upper crust 11 aristocracy 12 aristocratic
elixir 4 balm, cure 6 potion 7 arcanum, cure-all, nostrum, panacea, philter 10 catholicon
Elizabeth I, name for 6 Oriana 8 Gloriana
elk 4 deer 5 moose 6 sambar, wapiti 7 red deer
ell 3 arm 4 wing 5 annex, elbow, joint 8 addition 9 extension
ellipse 4 oval 5 curve, orbit
elliptical 5 brief, ovate, short 6 gnomic 7 concise, cryptic, laconic, obscure, summary 9 condensed, enigmatic 11 abbreviated
elm 5 wahoo
elocution 7 diction, oratory 8 delivery, rhetoric 11 declamation, speechcraft
elongate 4 draw 6 extend 7 draw out, lengthy, spin out, stretch 8 extended, lengthen 10 lengthened
elope 4 flee 6 escape, run off 7 abscond, run away 9 steal away
eloquence 5 force, power 6 fervor, spirit 7 fluency, oratory, passion 8 rhetoric 10 expression 12 expressivity, forcefulness
eloquent 5 lofty 6 ardent, fervid, fluent, moving 7 fervent, voluble 8 elevated, forceful, powerful, stirring 9 affecting 10 articulate, expressive, impressive, meaningful, passionate, persuasive,

rhetorical **11** impassioned, sententious **12** smooth-spoken **13** silver-tongued
El Salvador *capital:* **11** San Salvador *city:* **8** Santa Ana **9** San Miguel *ethnic group:* **5** Pipil *lake:* **8** Ilopango *language:* **7** Spanish *monetary unit:* **5** colón **6** dollar *neighbor:* **8** Honduras **9** Guatemala *river:* **5** Lempa
else 5 if not **7** besides, further **9** otherwise **10** additional **11** differently **12** additionally
elucidate 7 clarify, clear up, explain, expound **8** annotate, spell out **9** exemplify, explicate, interpret **10** illuminate, illustrate
elude 4 defy, duck, flee, foil **5** avert, avoid, dodge, evade **6** baffle, escape, outwit, thwart **8** confound **9** frustrate **10** circumvent
elusive 6 subtle, tricky **7** evasive, phantom **8** baffling, fleeting, fugitive, slippery **10** evanescent, intangible, mysterious **13** insubstantial
elute 7 extract
elver 3 eel
elvish see ELFIN
Elysium 5 bliss **6** heaven **7** nirvana **8** empyrean, paradise
elytron 4 wing
emaciated 4 bony, lean, thin **5** gaunt **6** skinny, wasted **7** scrawny, starved, wizened **8** skeletal, underfed **10** cadaverous
emaciation 5 tabes **7** atrophy **8** marasmus **10** starvation **11** attenuation
emanate 4 emit, flow, rise, stem **5** arise, exude, issue **6** derive, emerge, spring **7** come out, give off, give out, proceed, radiate **9** originate **10** derive from
emanation 4 aura, flow **6** efflux **8** effusion, emission **9** effluence
emancipate 4 free **5** let go, loose **6** loosen, redeem, unbind **7** manumit, release, set free, unchain **8** liberate, unfetter **9** discharge, unshackle **11** enfranchise
emancipation 7 release **10** liberation **11** deliverance
emancipator 5 Moses **7** Lincoln (Abraham) **9** deliverer, liberator
emasculate 3 fix **4** geld **5** alter, unman **6** neuter, soften, weaken **7** unnerve **8** castrate, enervate, unstring **10** debilitate, devitalize
embalm 7 mummify, perfume **8** preserve
embankment 4 berm, bund, dike, quay **5** levee, mound
embargo 3 ban, bar **5** edict, order **8** blockade, stoppage **10** impediment **11** prohibition
embark 5 board, enter, start **6** set out **7** set sail **8** commence

embarrass 4 faze **5** abash, upset **6** flurry, hamper, hinder, impede, rattle **7** confuse, flummox, fluster, mortify, nonplus, perturb **8** confound, distress **9** discomfit, humiliate **10** complicate, discomfort, discompose, disconcert
embarrassment 5 shame, upset **7** chagrin **8** distress **9** confusion **10** discomfort **11** humiliation **12** discomfiture, perturbation **13** mortification
embassy 5 envoy **7** mission **8** legation **10** ambassador, delegation, deputation
embay 4 trap **5** catch, seize **7** capture **8** encircle, surround
embed 3 fix, set **4** bury, root **5** infix, inlay, lodge **7** implant, ingrain **8** entrench
embellish 3 pad **4** deck, gild, trim **5** adorn, color **6** bedeck, blazon, emboss, enrich **7** amplify, dress up, enhance, festoon, garnish **8** beautify, decorate, ornament **9** elaborate, embroider **10** exaggerate **11** romanticize
embellishment 7 garnish, gilding, melisma, mordent **8** coloring, ornament **9** fioritura, floridity, hyperbole **10** decoration **11** elaboration **12** embroidering, exaggeration **13** ornamentation
ember 3 ash **6** cinder
embezzle 4 loot **5** filch, steal **6** pilfer **7** purloin **8** peculate **9** defalcate
embitter 4 sour **6** poison **7** envenom **9** acidulate
emblazon 4 laud **5** extol **7** glorify **8** inscribe **9** celebrate
emblem 4 arms, flag, logo, mace, seal, sign **5** badge, brand, crest, image, token **6** banner, device, symbol **7** pennant **8** colophon, hallmark, insignia, monogram, standard **9** attribute, trademark **10** coat of arms
emblematic 8 symbolic **10** figurative, indicative **11** allegorical **12** illustrative, metaphorical
embodiment 6 avatar **7** epitome **8** exemplar **9** archetype **11** incarnation **13** manifestation
embody 5 reify **6** evince, mirror, typify **7** compose, contain, exhibit, realize, subsume **9** manifest **9** actualize, encompass, epitomize, exemplify, incarnate, integrate, objectify, personify, represent, symbolize **10** constitute, illustrate **11** emblematize, externalize, hypostatize, incorporate, materialize **12** substantiate
embolden 5 steel **7** fortify, hearten, inspire **8** inspirit **9** encourage **10** strengthen
embolus 4 clog, clot
embosom 3 hug **7** embrace, enclose, envelop, shelter

embouchure 10 mouthpiece
embowel 3 gut **4** draw **10** eviscerate, exenterate
embrace 3 hug **4** hold, lock, love, wrap **5** admit, adopt, clasp, cling, press **6** accept, cradle, cuddle, embody, enfold, fondle, nuzzle, take in, take on, take up **7** cherish, contain, embosom, enclose, entwine, envelop, espouse, include, receive, snuggle, squeeze, subsume, welcome **8** comprise, encircle **9** encompass **10** comprehend **11** accommodate, incorporate **12** encirclement
embrangle see EMBROIL
embrocation 5 salve **7** unguent **8** liniment
embroider 3 pad, sew, tat **4** gild **5** color **6** expand, overdo, play up, stitch **7** amplify, build up, enhance, garnish, magnify, stretch **8** decorate, ornament **9** dramatize, elaborate, embellish **10** exaggerate **11** hyperbolize, romanticize
embroidery 6 crewel **7** cutwork, orphrey **8** bargello, couching, smocking, tapestry **10** crewelwork, needlework **11** needlepoint
embroil 4 mire **6** tangle **7** confuse, ensnare, involve **8** disorder, entangle **9** implicate
embroilment 4 tiff **6** fracas **7** dispute, quarrel, wrangle **8** squabble **9** bickering **10** falling-out **11** altercation, controversy
embryo 3 bud **4** germ, seed **5** fetus, spark **7** nucleus **8** blastula, gastrula
emend 4 edit **5** alter, right **6** polish, revise **7** correct, improve, rectify, retouch
emerald 3 gem **5** beryl, green, stone **8** gemstone
Emerald Isle 4 Eire, Erin **7** Ireland
emerge 4 flow, loom, rise, stem **5** arise, issue **6** appear, derive, evolve, spring **7** come out, develop, emanate, proceed, surface **9** originate, transpire **11** come to light, materialize
emergency 3 fix **4** hole, pass **5** pinch **6** climax, clutch, crisis, crunch, strait **7** squeeze **8** accident, exigency
emeritus 7 retired
Emerson, Ralph Waldo *essay:* **12** Self-Reliance *forte:* **5** essay *home:* **7** Concord *friend:* **7** Thoreau (Henry David)
emery 6 powder **8** abrasive, corundum
emetic 8 vomitive **9** cathartic, purgative
émeute 4 riot **6** mutiny, revolt, tumult **8** outbreak, upheaval, uprising **9** rebellion **12** insurrection
emigrant 7 pioneer, settler **8** colonist **10** expatriate
émigré 5 alien, exile, expat **7** evacuee, migrant, refugee **8** colonist **10** expatriate

Emilia *husband:* **4** Iago **7** Palamon *slayer:* **4** Iago
eminence 3 VIP **4** fame, peak, rise **5** honor, power **6** bigwig, esteem, height, leader, renown, repute **7** dignity, notable **8** altitude, big-timer, luminary, prestige, standing **9** authority, dignitary, elevation, greatness, loftiness **10** importance, projection, prominence, promontory, reputation **11** distinction, superiority
eminent 4 high **5** famed, grand, great, large, lofty, noble, noted **6** august, famous **7** exalted, notable **8** esteemed, renowned, towering **9** important, well-known **10** celebrated, noteworthy, projecting **11** conspicuous, illustrious, outstanding, prestigious **13** distinguished
eminently 4 very **6** highly **7** notably **9** extremely **10** remarkably, strikingly **11** exceedingly **12** surpassingly **13** exceptionally
emir 5 chief, ruler, sheik, title **6** sheikh **9** chieftain, commander
emissary see ENVOY
emission 4 flow **7** venting **9** discharge, effluvium, emanation, radiation
emit 4 beam, glow, ooze, pour, shed, spew, vent, void **5** eject, expel, exude, issue, loose, utter **6** exhale, let out **7** emanate, excrete, extrude, give off, give out, radiate, release, secrete, send out **8** evacuate, throw off **9** circulate, discharge
emmer 5 grain, spelt, wheat
emmet 3 ant **7** pismire
emollient 4 balm **5** salve **7** lenient **8** lenitive, liniment, sedative, soothing **9** analgesic, softening **10** mollifying
emolument 3 fee, pay **4** wage **5** wages **6** income, reward, salary **7** guerdon, stipend **8** earnings **10** recompense **11** pay envelope **12** compensation
emotion 3 ire, joy **4** fear, glee, hate, love **5** agony, ardor, grief, shame **6** affect, hatred, relief, sorrow, warmth **7** ardency, despair, disgust, ecstasy, feeling, passion, sadness **8** jealousy, surprise **9** affection, agitation, happiness, sentiment **11** affectivity, sensibility, sensitivity **12** excitability
emotional 4 warm **6** ardent, fervid, heated, moving **7** feeling, fervent, intense, soulful, zealous **8** effusive, stirring, touching, vehement **9** affecting, affective, excitable, heartfelt, impetuous, rhapsodic, sensitive **10** hysterical, passionate **11** impassioned, overwrought, rhapsodical, softhearted, susceptible, sympathetic
emotionless 3 icy **4** cold, cool **5** chill, staid, stoic, stony **6** frigid, remote, tor-

pid **7** callous, deadpan, distant, glacial **8** detached, reserved **9** apathetic, immovable, impassive, unfeeling **10** impersonal **11** cold-blooded, indifferent **12** matter-of-fact **13** dispassionate, unimpassioned
empathy 4 pity **6** lenity, warmth **7** rapport **8** affinity, sympathy **9** communion **10** compassion **12** congeniality **13** compatibility, comprehension, fellow feeling, understanding
emperor 4 czar, shah, tsar, tzar **5** ruler **6** caesar, kaiser **7** monarch **8** autocrat, dictator **9** potentate, sovereign *French:* **8** Napoleon (Bonaparte) **9** Bonaparte (Napoleon) **11** Charlemagne *Indian:* **5** Babur *Japanese:* **6** mikado **7** Akihito **8** Hirohito *Mexican:* **8** Iturbide (Agustín de) **10** Maximilian *Roman:* **4** Nero **5** Galba, Nerva, Titus **6** Decius, Julian, Trajan **7** Gratian, Hadrian, Severus **8** Augustus, Aurelian, Caligula, Claudius, Commodus, Domitian, Honorius, Tiberius, Valerian **9** Antoninus, Caracalla, Justinian **10** Diocletian, Elagabalus **11** Constantine
emphasis 5 focus, force **6** accent, stress, weight **9** attention, intensity **10** insistence, prominence **12** accentuation
emphasize 6 accent, play up, stress **7** feature **8** pinpoint **9** highlight, italicize, spotlight, underline **10** accentuate, underscore
emphatic 4 firm **6** marked **7** decided, earnest, pointed **8** accented, decisive, forceful, positive, stressed, vigorous **9** assertive, energetic, insistent **10** resounding, underlined **11** accentuated
empire 5 realm **6** domain **7** demesne, kingdom **8** dominion *ancient:* (see ANCIENT EMPIRE)
Empire State 7 New York
empirical 7 factual **9** fact-based, pragmatic **12** experiential, experimental **13** observational
emplacement 7 battery **8** position
employ 3 job, use **4** busy, hire, work **5** apply, avail **6** devote, engage, occupy, retain, secure, take on **7** exploit, utilize **8** exercise, practice **9** make use of **10** occupation
employee 4 hand, help **5** agent **6** worker **7** servant **8** factotum **9** underling *bank:* **5** clerk, guard **6** teller *hotel:* **7** bellboy, bellhop, doorman **9** concierge, desk clerk **11** chambermaid
employer 4 boss **6** master **10** supervisor
employment 3 job, use **4** line, post, task, toil, work **5** trade, usage **6** hiring, métier, office **7** calling, mission, purpose, pursuit **8** business, exercise, function,

position, vocation **9** appliance, operation, situation **10** engagement, occupation **11** application, recruitment, utilization **12** exploitation
emporium 4 mall, mart, shop **5** store **6** bazaar, market **8** exchange **11** marketplace
empower 5 endow **6** charge, enable, invest **7** entitle, entrust, license **8** accredit, delegate, deputize, sanction **9** authorize, privilege **10** commission
empress 5 queen *Byzantine:* **3** Zoe *French:* **7** Eugénie **9** Josephine *Japanese:* **5** Suiko *of India:* **8** Victoria *Mexican:* **7** Carlota *Roman:* **6** Fausta *Russian:* **4** Anna **7** czarina, tsarina, tzarina **9** Alexandra, Catherine, Elizabeth
empressement 6 fervor, warmth **10** cordiality
emprise 4 feat, gest **5** geste **7** exploit, venture **9** adventure **11** undertaking
emptiness 4 void **5** blank **6** hunger, vacuum **7** inanity, vacancy, vacuity
emptor 5 buyer **6** vendee **8** consumer, customer **9** purchaser
___ **emptor 6** caveat
empty 3 rid **4** bare, dump, pour, vain, void **5** blank, clear, drain **6** barren, devoid, hollow, unload, vacant, vacate **7** deplete, drained, exhaust, vacated, vacuous **8** depleted, deserted, evacuate, forsaken **9** abandoned, destitute **10** unoccupied, untenanted *Scottish:* **4** toom
empty-headed 6 simple, vacant **7** vacuous, witless **8** ignorant, untaught **9** benighted, brainless, frivolous **10** illiterate, uneducated, unlettered, unschooled **11** know-nothing **12** uninstructed **13** rattlebrained
empyreal 4 airy, holy **6** aerial, divine **7** sublime **8** beatific, ethereal, heavenly **9** celestial, spiritual, unearthly **12** transcendent
empyrean 3 sky **4** Zion **5** bliss, ether **6** heaven, welkin **7** Elysium, heavens, nirvana **8** paradise **9** firmament
emu 4 bird, rhea **5** ratite **9** cassowary
emulate 3 ape **4** copy **5** equal, mimic, rival **6** follow, mirror **7** compete, imitate **9** challenge
emulation 7 rivalry **8** striving, tug-of-war **9** imitation **10** contention **11** competition
emulous 5 vying **8** aspiring, striving, vaulting **9** ambitious **11** competitive
emulsifier 4 soap **5** algin
enable 3 fit, let **5** allow, ready **6** permit **7** empower, entitle, license, prepare, qualify **8** accredit, sanction **9** authorize,

condition 10 commission, facilitate 12 make possible

enact 4 pass, play 6 decree, depict, effect, ordain, ratify 7 execute, perform, portray 8 proclaim 9 authorize, discourse, establish, institute, legislate, represent 10 accomplish, bring about, constitute, effectuate 11 impersonate

enactment 3 law 6 action, decree 7 statute 9 depiction, ordinance, portrayal 11 legislation, performance 12 ratification

enamel 5 glaze, gloss, japan, paint 7 lacquer

enamored 4 fond 6 loving 7 devoted, smitten 8 besotted 9 bewitched, enchanted, entranced, infatuate 10 captivated, infatuated

encamp 4 tent 6 settle 7 bivouac

encampment 6 billet, laager 7 bivouac, hutment

encase 3 box 4 pack 7 confine, enclose, envelop, sheathe

enceinte 6 gravid 8 pregnant 9 expectant, expecting 10 parturient

enchain 4 bind 6 fetter 7 manacle, shackle

enchant 3 hex 4 lure, wile 5 charm, spell, witch 6 allure, enamor, seduce, thrill, voodoo 7 attract, beguile, bewitch, delight 8 ensorcel, enthrall 9 captivate, enrapture, ensorcell, fascinate, hypnotize, magnetize, mesmerize, spellbind

enchanter 4 mage 5 magus 6 wizard 7 charmer, warlock 8 conjurer, conjuror, magician, sorcerer 11 necromancer, spellbinder

enchanting 5 siren 9 glamorous, seductive 10 attractive, delectable, delightful, intriguing

enchantment 3 hex 5 charm, magic, spell 6 allure 7 glamour, sorcery 8 witchery, wizardry 9 conjuring, seduction 10 necromancy, witchcraft 11 incantation

enchantress 3 hex 5 bruja, Circe, lamia, Medea, siren, witch 9 sorceress

enchiridion 4 text 5 guide 6 manual 8 Baedeker, handbook 9 guidebook, vade mecum

encipher 4 code

encircle 3 hem 4 band, gird, halo, hoop, ring 5 girth 6 begird, engird, enlace, girdle 7 compass, embrace, enclose, environ, wreathe 8 surround 9 encompass 12 circumscribe

enclave 6 colony, ghetto, sector 7 quarter 8 district, homeland

enclose 3 box, hem, mew, pen, rim 4 cage, coop, mure, wall, wrap

5 bound, fence, hedge, limit 6 circle, closet, corral, hold in, immure, shroud, shut in, wall in 7 compass, confine, contain, embosom, include 8 fence off, imprison, surround 9 capsulize 12 circumscribe

enclosed 6 obtect

enclosure 3 box, mew, pen, sty 4 cage, camp, cell, coop, cote, fold, jail, pale, quad, tank, trap, wall, weir, yard 5 court, fence, kraal, pound, stall 6 aviary, corral, cowpen, kennel, paling, prison 7 chamber, paddock 8 cloister, stockade 9 courtyard 10 quadrangle

encomiast 7 praiser 8 eulogist 10 panegyrist

encomiastic 9 adulatory, laudative, laudatory 10 eulogistic 11 panegyrical

encomium 4 laud 5 kudos, paean 6 eulogy, homage, praise 7 acclaim, plaudit, tribute 8 accolade, citation, plaudits 9 laudation, panegyric 10 compliment, salutation 11 acclamation 12 commendation

encompass 3 hem 4 belt, gird, ring 5 bound 6 begird, circle, girdle, take in 7 contain, embrace, enclose, include, subsume 8 encircle, surround 10 accomplish, bring about, comprehend

encore 6 recall, repeat, return 10 repetition

encounter 4 face, find, fray, meet 5 brush, clash, fight, run-in, scrap, set-to 6 battle, engage, take on 7 collide, contest, meeting, quarrel, run into 8 argument, bump into, come upon, conflict, confront, meet with, skirmish, struggle 10 contention, experience

encourage 4 abet, back, buoy, push, spur, stir, urge 5 boost, cheer, egg on, rally, rouse, serve, steel 6 assist, assure, buck up, excite, foster, incite, induce, praise 7 advance, animate, approve, bolster, cheer up, endorse, fortify, further, hearten, improve, inspire, promote, provoke, quicken, support, sustain 8 advocate, embolden, energize, inspirit, reassure, sanction 9 enhearten, galvanize, instigate, patronize, reinforce, stimulate, subsidize 10 invigorate, strengthen

encouragement 4 lift, push 5 boost 7 backing, support 8 approval 11 inspiration

encouraging 4 rosy 6 bright, likely 7 hopeful 9 favorable, promising 10 auspicious, propitious

encroach 5 poach 6 invade, meddle, trench 7 impinge, intrude 8 entrench, infringe, overstep, trespass

encrypt 4 code **6** cipher, encode **7** convert **8** disguise, encipher

encumber 4 lade, load **6** burden, charge, fetter, hamper, hinder, impede, saddle, weight **7** freight, oppress **8** handicap, obstruct, overload **9** weigh down **10** overburden **13** inconvenience

encumbrance 4 lien, load, onus **5** claim **6** burden **7** baggage **8** handicap, mortgage **9** albatross, millstone **10** impediment

encyclical 6 letter **7** general **8** circular

encyclopedic 5 broad **7** general **8** complete, thorough **9** extensive, inclusive, universal **11** compendious, wide-ranging **12** all-embracing, all-inclusive **13** comprehensive

encyclopedist 7 Diderot (Denis)

end 3 aim, tip **4** coda, doom, goal, halt, quit, stop, tail, term **5** cease, close, death, finis, limit **6** demise, expire, finale, finish, object, period, result, scotch, windup, wrap up **7** abolish, closing, closure, extreme, lineman, outcome, purpose **8** boundary, complete, conclude, confines, curtains, finality, surcease, terminal, terminus **9** cessation, extremity, objective, terminate **10** borderline, completion, conclusion, denouement, expiration, extinction, limitation **11** culmination, discontinue, termination **12** consummation

endanger 4 risk **5** peril **6** expose **7** imperil **8** threaten **10** compromise, jeopardize

endeavor 3 aim, try **4** push, seek, toil, work **5** assay, essay, labor, trial **6** effort, intend, strain, strive **7** attempt, purpose, travail, venture **8** exertion, striving, struggle **9** determine, undertake **10** enterprise **11** undertaking

ended 4 done, over, past **7** through **8** complete

endemic 5 local **6** innate, native **8** homebred, inherent, primeval **9** homegrown, prevalent **10** aboriginal, indigenous, native-born

ending 4 stop **5** close **6** finale, finish, period, windup **7** closing, closure **8** terminus **9** cessation **10** completion, conclusion, denouement **11** termination

endive 7 lettuce, witloof **8** escarole

endless 7 eternal, undying **8** constant, enduring, immortal, infinite, unending **9** ceaseless, continual, incessant, limitless, perpetual, unbounded, unceasing, unlimited **10** continuous, indefinite, unmeasured **11** everlasting, illimitable, measureless **12** immeasurable, interminable

endmost 4 last **5** final **8** farthest, furthest, ultimate **10** concluding

endocrine gland 5 gonad, ovary **6** pineal, testis, thymus **7** adrenal, thyroid **8** pancreas **9** pituitary **11** parathyroid **12** hypothalamus

endomorphic 5 beefy, heavy, husky, stout **6** portly, pyknic, rotund

endorse 4 back, okay, sign **5** bless, vouch **6** attest, ratify, second, uphold **7** approve, certify, command, confirm, stand by, support, witness **8** accredit, advocate, champion, inscribe, make over, notarize, sanction **9** autograph, recommend **10** underwrite **12** authenticate

endorsement 7 backing, support **8** approval, sanction **9** signature **12** confirmation, ratification **13** authorization

endow 4 back, fund **5** found **6** bestow, confer, enrich, supply **7** empower, enhance, finance, furnish, promote, provide, sponsor, support **8** bequeath **9** subsidize

endowment 4 fund, gift **5** award, dower, dowry, grant, power, skill **6** legacy, talent **7** ability, bequest **8** appanage, aptitude, bestowal, capacity, donation **11** benefaction

end product 5 fruit, issue **6** effect, payoff, result, upshot **7** outcome **11** consequence

endue 3 don **4** vest **5** dower, equip, imbue, put on **6** clothe, invest, outfit **7** furnish, provide **8** accouter **9** crown with, transfuse

endurance 4 grit, guts, wind **5** moxie, pluck **6** mettle **7** stamina **8** patience, strength, tenacity **9** fortitude **10** permanence, resolution **11** persistence **12** perseverance

endure 4 bear, bide, go on, last **5** abide, brook, stand **6** accept, hold on, linger, pocket, remain, suffer **7** carry on, persist, ride out, stomach, survive, sustain, swallow, undergo, weather **8** continue, submit to, tolerate, tough out **9** withstand

enduring 3 old **4** fast, firm, sure **6** steady **7** abiding, durable, eternal, lasting, staunch **8** constant, lifelong **9** long-lived, perennial, permanent, steadfast **10** continuing, inveterate, persistent **11** long-lasting, unfaltering **12** never-failing

Endymion *father:* **8** Aethlius *lover:* **5** Diana **6** Selene *author:* **5** Keats (John)

enemy 3 foe **5** rival **8** attacker, opponent **9** adversary, assailant **10** antagonist, competitor

energetic 4 spry **5** brisk, fresh, hardy, lusty, peppy, zippy **6** active, lively **7** driving, dynamic, vibrant **8** spirited, tireless, vigorous 9 sprightly, strenuous, vivacious 13 indefatigable

energize 3 pep 4 fuel, stir 5 liven, pep up, rouse, spark 6 enable, excite, stir up, turn on 7 empower, enliven, fortify, inspire, juice up 8 activate, inspirit, vitalize 9 electrify, galvanize, stimulate 10 invigorate, strengthen

energy 3 pep, vim, zip 4 dash, life, tuck 5 drive, force, juice, moxie, pluck, power, sinew, steam, verve, vigor 6 effort, muscle, spirit 7 current, potency, stamina, voltage 8 activity, dynamism, efficacy, exertion, strength, vitality 9 animation, intensity, puissance 10 enterprise, get-up-and-go, initiative 11 application *unit:* 3 erg 4 dyne, volt 5 joule 7 quantum 10 horsepower

enervate 3 sap 4 jade, tire 5 weary 6 soften, weaken 7 disable, exhaust, fatigue, unnerve 8 enfeeble, unstring 10 debilitate, devitalize

enfant terrible 3 imp 5 scamp 6 urchin 9 skeezicks

enfeeble 3 sap 6 soften, weaken 7 deplete, disable, exhaust, fatigue 8 enervate 9 attenuate, undermine 10 debilitate, devitalize

enfold 3 hug 4 wrap 5 clasp, cover, press 6 shroud, swathe 7 contain, embrace, squeeze 8 surround

enforce 5 exact, impel 6 compel, effect, impose, invoke, oblige 7 execute, fulfill 8 carry out 9 constrain, discharge, implement, prosecute 10 accomplish, administer, strengthen

enfranchise 4 free 6 rescue 7 deliver, manumit, release, set free 8 liberate 10 emancipate

engage 4 bind, grip, hire, mesh 5 fight, troth 6 absorb, arrest, attack, battle, commit, employ, enlist, occupy, pledge, take on 7 assault, betroth, engross, immerse, involve, promise 8 affiance, enthrall, interact 9 captivate, encounter, fascinate, interlace, interlock, intermesh, interplay, preoccupy, undertake

engaged 4 busy, rapt 6 intent 7 working 8 absorbed, employed, immersed, intended, occupied, plighted 9 affianced, betrothed, committed, engrossed, wrapped up 10 contracted 11 preoccupied *person:* 6 fiancé 7 fiancée

engage in 4 wage 5 enter 6 pursue, tackle, take up 7 conduct 8 embark on, practice 9 prosecute, undertake

engagement 3 gig 4 date, fray, word 5 fight, troth, tryst 6 action, battle, combat, hiring, pledge, plight 7 booking, meeting, promise 8 espousal, skirmish 9 betrothal, encounter 10 commitment, employment, rendezvous 11 appointment, assignation

engaging 7 likable, winning, winsome 8 charming, pleasant, pleasing 9 appealing 10 attractive 13 prepossessing

engender 4 sire, stir 5 beget, breed, cause, hatch, rouse, spawn 6 arouse, create, excite, father, induce, lead to, work up 7 develop, produce, provoke 8 generate 9 originate, procreate, stimulate

engine 5 motor, turbo 7 turbine 10 locomotive *kind:* 3 gas, jet 5 steam 6 diesel 7 turbine 8 gasoline 9 hydraulic *jet:* 8 turbofan, turbojet *part:* 3 cam, rod 4 gear, plug, pump 5 choke 6 filter, piston, tappet 8 cylinder, manifold, throttle 9 condenser, crankcase 10 carburetor 12 transmission *siege:* 3 ram 6 onager 8 ballista, catapult 9 trebuchet 12 battering ram *sound:* 4 chug, roar 6 rattle

engineer 4 plan, plot 5 set up, swing 6 devise, driver, manage, scheme, wangle 7 arrange, finagle 8 contrive, intrigue, maneuver, motorman 9 machinate, negotiate 10 manipulate, mastermind 11 orchestrate *kind:* 5 civil 6 mining 8 chemical, sanitary 10 electrical, mechanical 12 aeronautical *military:* 6 sapper

engineers' group *abbreviation:* 4 IEEE

England 6 Albion 7 Britain 9 Britannia 12 Great Britain see also UNITED KINGDOM

English 7 British *cathedral city:* 3 Ely 4 York 5 Wells 6 Durham, Exeter 7 Lincoln, Norwich 8 Coventry, Hereford 9 Salisbury, Worcester 10 Canterbury, Winchester *coin:* 5 crown, groat, pence 6 florin, guinea 8 farthing, shilling, sixpence, twopence 9 fourpence, half crown, halfpenny, sovereign 10 threepence *combining form:* 5 Anglo *farm:* 5 croft *forest:* 5 Arden 8 Sherwood *letter:* 3 zed *measure:* 3 rod, tun 4 gill, hand, peck, span 5 chain 6 barrel, bushel, fathom, firkin 7 furlong 8 hogshead 10 barleycorn *military college:* 9 Sandhurst *patron saint:* 6 George *person:* 4 chap, mate 5 bloke 6 Briton *pirate:* 4 Kidd (Capt. William) 5 Avery (Henry), Teach (Edward) 6 Morgan (Henry) 7 Dampier (William) 10 Blackbeard *prince:* 5 Harry 6 Andrew, Edward, Philip 7 Charles, William *princess:* 4 Anne 5 Diana 8 Margaret *professor:* 3 don *royal family:* 5 Tudor 6 Stuart 7 Hanover, Windsor *saint:*

7 Dunstan 8 Cuthbert *spa:* 4 Bath *sport:*
5 rugby 7 cricket *tavern:* 3 pub *university:* 5 Leeds 6 Oxford 9 Cambridge
weight: 5 stone 6 firkin 7 quintal 8 quartern

English Channel swimmer 6 Ederle
(Gertrude)

engrave 3 cut, fix 4 etch 5 carve, chase
6 incise, scrive 7 instill 8 inscribe

engraver 6 chaser, etcher *German:*
5 Dürer (Albrecht) 10 Schongauer
(Martin) *Italian:* 8 Raimondi (Marcantonio)

engraving 7 etching, linecut, woodcut
8 drypoint, intaglio 9 xylograph

engross 4 bury, busy, copy, grip 5 apply,
write 6 absorb, engage, indite, occupy,
scribe 7 consume, immerse, involve
8 enthrall, inscribe 9 captivate, preoccupy 10 transcribe

engrosser 6 scribe 7 copyist 9 scrivener
12 calligrapher 13 calligraphist

engulf 4 bury 5 drown, flood, swamp,
whelm 6 deluge, devour 7 immerse,
overrun, swallow 8 flow over, inundate,
overflow, submerge 9 overwhelm, swallow up

enhance 4 lift 5 add to, adorn, exalt,
raise 6 deepen 7 amplify, augment,
build up, elevate, enlarge, flatter,
improve, magnify 8 beautify, heighten,
increase 9 aggravate, embellish,
embroider, intensify, reinforce 10 exaggerate, strengthen

enigma 4 crux, knot 5 poser, rebus
6 puzzle, riddle, sphinx, teaser 7 mystery, problem, puzzler 9 conundrum
10 closed book, perplexity, puzzlement
12 question mark 13 Chinese puzzle,
mystification

enigmatic 6 mystic 7 cryptic, Delphic,
obscure 8 Delphian, oracular, puzzling
9 ambiguous 10 mysterious, mystifying,
perplexing 11 inscrutable

enisle 6 cut off 7 isolate 8 insulate, separate 9 segregate, sequester

enjoin 3 ban, bid 4 deny, rule, tell, urge,
warn 5 order, taboo 6 adjure, charge,
decree, direct, forbid, impose, outlaw
7 caution, command, counsel, dictate,
inhibit 8 admonish, disallow, forewarn,
instruct, prohibit 9 interdict, prescribe,
proscribe

enjoy 4 like, love 5 eat up, fancy, savor
6 relish 9 delight in 10 appreciate

enjoyable 3 fun 8 pleasant, pleasing
9 agreeable 10 delightful, satisfying
11 pleasurable 12 entertaining

enjoyment 4 zest 5 gusto, savor 6 relish
7 benefit, delight 8 felicity, fruition,
pleasure 9 diversion 10 indulgence,

recreation, relaxation 11 delectation
12 satisfaction 13 gratification

Enki *consort:* 5 Nintu *son:* 6 Ninsar

enkindle 4 fire 5 flame, light 6 ignite
7 inflame 8 touch off 9 set fire to

enlarge 3 wax 4 grow, rise 5 add to,
boost, build, mount, widen 6 beef up,
dilate, expand, extend 7 amplify, augment, broaden, develop, greaten,
inflate, magnify, stretch 8 heighten,
increase, multiply 9 elaborate, embroider 10 exaggerate

enlargement 4 node 5 tumor 6 blowup,
growth, nodule 7 buildup 8 addition,
increase, swelling 9 accretion, expansion, extension 12 augmentation
13 amplification

enlighten 5 edify, guide, teach 6 advise,
illume, inform, uplift 7 educate, improve 8 illumine, instruct 10 illuminate

enlist 4 join 5 draft, enter 6 employ,
enroll, join up, muster, sign on, sign up
7 attract, recruit 8 register 9 volunteer
11 participate

enliven 3 pep 4 buoy, fire, warm
5 amuse, cheer, pep up, renew, rouse
6 excite, jazz up, perk up, vivify, wake
up 7 animate, cheer up, inspire, quicken, refresh, restore, spice up 8 energize, recreate 9 entertain, galvanize,
stimulate 10 exhilarate, invigorate,
rejuvenate

en masse 5 as one 6 bodily 8 together
12 collectively

enmesh 4 hook, mire, trap 5 catch,
snare 6 draw in, tangle 7 embroil,
ensnarl, involve, trammel 8 drag into,
entangle 9 embrangle, implicate

enmity 4 hate 6 animus, hatred, rancor,
spleen 7 ill will 8 aversion, bad blood,
loathing 9 animosity, antipathy, hostility 10 abhorrence, antagonism 11 detestation

ennoble 5 exalt, honor, raise 6 uplift,
uprear 7 dignify, elevate, glorify, magnify, sublime 10 aggrandize 11 distinguish

ennui 6 apathy, tedium 7 boredom,
fatigue, languor 8 doldrums, dullness,
lethargy 9 jadedness, lassitude, tiredness, weariness 11 languidness 12 listlessness

Enoch *father:* 4 Cain *son:* 10 Methuselah
Enoch Arden author 8 Tennyson (Alfred)

enormity 6 infamy 7 outrage 8 atrocity,
hugeness, rankness, savagery, vastness
9 barbarity, depravity, flagrancy, graveness, greatness, grossness, immensity,
magnitude 11 abomination, heinousness, massiveness, monstrosity, seriousness, weightiness

enormous 4 huge, vast **5** great
7 immense, mammoth, massive, titanic
8 colossal, gigantic **9** humongous, monstrous **10** astronomic, gargantuan, prodigious, stupendous, tremendous
12 astronomical
Enos *father:* **4** Seth *grandfather:* **4** Adam
grandmother: **3** Eve *uncle:* **4** Abel, Cain
enough 5 ample **6** fairly, plenty **8** adequate, decently, passably **9** competent, tolerably **10** acceptably, adequately, sufficient **11** comfortable, sufficiency
12 satisfactory, sufficiently *poetic:*
4 enow
enounce 3 say **5** state, utter **6** intone
8 proclaim, set forth **10** articulate
enrage 3 ire **4** rile **5** anger **6** madden
7 incense, inflame, steam up **9** infuriate
enrapture 5 charm, elate **6** ravish, trance
7 delight, enchant, rejoice **8** enthrall, entrance **9** captivate, transport
enraptured 6 elated **7** charmed **8** ecstatic, thrilled **9** bewitched, delighted, enchanted, entranced **10** captivated, enthralled, mesmerized, spellbound
11 transported
enrich 5 adorn, endow **6** fatten
7 enhance, improve **8** beautify, ornament **9** embellish, fertilize **10** supplement
enroll 4 book, file, join, list **5** draft, enter
6 enlist, induct, join up, muster, record, sign on, sign up, wrap up **7** catalog, engross, recruit **8** inscribe, register
9 conscript, subscribe **10** transcribe
11 matriculate
ensconce 4 bury, hide **5** cache, cover, place, plant, stash **6** hole up, locate, settle **7** conceal, install, secrete, shelter
9 establish
ensemble 3 duo **4** band, crew, suit, trio
5 choir, combo, decor, group, suite, troop, whole **6** chorus, outfit, septet, sextet, troupe **7** chorale, company, costume, en masse, quartet, quintet
8 together **9** aggregate, orchestra
enshrine 6 hallow, revere **7** cherish
8 dedicate, preserve, sanctify, treasure
10 consecrate **11** memorialize
enshroud 4 hide, veil, wrap **5** cloak
6 clothe, enfold, enwrap, invest **7** blanket, conceal, envelop, obscure
ensign 4 flag, jack, sign **5** badge, crest
6 banner, colors, emblem, pennon
7 officer, pennant **8** gonfalon, insignia, standard, streamer **9** oriflamme
enslave 4 yoke **5** chain **6** fetter, thrall
7 enchain, oppress, shackle, subject
8 dominate, enthrall **9** indenture, subjugate **12** disfranchise
enslavement 4 yoke **6** thrall **7** bondage,

helotry, peonage, serfdom, slavery
9 servitude, thralldom
ensnare 3 bag, net **4** hook, lure, mesh, snag, trap **5** benet, catch, decoy
6 enmesh, entrap, tangle **7** capture
8 entangle, inveigle
ensnarl 4 mire **6** enmesh, tangle
7 embroil, perplex, trammel **8** entangle
9 embrangle
ensorcell 3 hex **5** charm, spell, witch
6 allure, voodoo **7** beguile, bewitch, enchant **8** enthrall **9** captivate, enrapture, hypnotize, magnetize, mesmerize, spellbind
ensorcellment 5 magic **7** sorcery
8 witchery, wizardry **9** conjuring
10 necromancy, witchcraft **11** bewitchment, enchantment
ensphere 4 ball **8** conglobe **10** conglobate
ensue 4 stem **5** issue **6** attend, derive, follow, result **7** emanate, proceed, succeed **9** supervene
ensuing 4 next **5** later **9** resultant **10** consequent, subsequent, succeeding
ensure 5 cinch **6** clinch, secure **7** certify, confirm, warrant **9** establish, guarantee
enswathe 4 roll, wrap **5** cloak, drape
6 bundle, enwrap, shroud, wrap up
7 envelop, swaddle
entail 5 imply **6** assign, confer, demand, impose, lead to **7** call for, involve, require **8** occasion, restrict, result in, transmit **11** necessitate
entangle 4 mesh, mire, trap **5** catch, ravel, snare, snarl, tie up, twist
6 enmesh, entrap **7** capture, catch up, embroil, ensnare, ensnarl, involve, perplex, trammel **10** complicate, intertwine, interweave
entanglement 3 web **4** knot, mesh, mess, toil **5** skein, snare **6** affair, cobweb, muddle **8** intrigue **9** confusion, imbroglio **11** embroilment, involvement **12** complication
entente 4 pact **6** league, treaty **7** compact **8** alliance, covenant **9** agreement, coalition, concordat **13** understanding
enter 4 go in, join, list, open **5** admit, begin, start **6** come in, enlist, enroll, go into, insert, join up, muster, record, sign on, sign up **7** intrude **8** come into, embark on, inscribe, register **9** introduce, penetrate **10** embark upon
enterprise 4 deed, feat, firm, push, task
5 cause, drive, pluck, vigor **6** action, daring, effort, energy, hustle, outfit, scheme **7** attempt, company, concern, courage, exploit, project, pursuit, venture **8** activity, ambition, audacity, boldness, business, campaign, endeav-

or, gumption, industry **9** adventure, eagerness **10** enthusiasm, get-up-and-go, initiative **11** corporation, undertaking **12** organization, self-reliance **13** establishment

enterprising 4 bold **5** eager **6** daring, hungry **7** driving, go-ahead **8** aspiring, hustling **9** ambitious, audacious, energetic **10** aggressive **11** adventurous, hardworking, industrious, up-and-coming, venturesome

entertain 4 host **5** amuse **6** divert, regale **7** delight, receive **8** consider

entertainer 4 mime **5** actor, clown, comic **6** busker, dancer, jester, singer **7** actress, artiste, diseuse, trouper **8** comedian, minstrel **10** comedienne

entertaining 6 lively **7** amusing **8** engaging **9** diverting, enjoyable

entertainment 4 fete, play, show, skit **5** revue, sport **6** circus **7** banquet, concert, pastime, ridotto **8** pleasure **9** amusement, diversion, enjoyment **10** recreation **11** distraction, performance

enthrall 4 grip **5** charm **6** absorb, subdue **7** beguile, bewitch, enchant, engross, enslave **9** fascinate, hypnotize, mesmerize, spellbind, subjugate

enthralling 8 exciting, gripping, riveting **9** absorbing, arresting **10** enchanting, engrossing, entrancing **11** captivating, charismatic, provocative **12** spellbinding

enthuse 4 gush, rave **6** excite, thrill **7** animate, delight, inspire **8** energize **10** rhapsodize

enthusiasm 4 élan, fire, zeal, zest **5** ardor, craze, fever, mania, verve **6** fervor, spirit **7** ardency, passion, rapture **9** eagerness, intensity **10** ebullience, excitement, fanaticism

enthusiast 3 bug, fan, nut **4** buff **5** fiend, freak, lover, maven **6** addict, junkie, maniac, votary, zealot **7** booster, devotee, fanatic, groupie, habitué **8** believer, partisan **9** extremist **10** aficionado

enthusiastic 4 avid, gaga, keen **5** eager, rabid **6** ardent, fervid, gung ho, hearty, hipped, raring **7** devoted, excited, fervent, intense, zealous **8** hopped-up, obsessed, spirited, vascular **9** fanatical **10** passionate

entice 4 bait, coax, draw, lure, toll, wile **5** charm, decoy, tempt **6** allure, cajole, entrap, invite, lead on, seduce **7** attract, wheedle **8** inveigle, persuade

enticement 4 bait, lure, trap **5** decoy, snare **6** come-on **9** seduction **10** allurement, attraction, seducement, temptation **12** blandishment, inveiglement

enticer 4 bait, vamp **5** Circe, decoy, siren **7** Lorelei **9** attractor, temptress **10** attraction, seductress **11** enchantress, femme fatale

enticing 5 siren **8** fetching, witching **9** seductive **10** attractive, bewitching, intriguing **11** captivating, fascinating

entire 3 all **4** full **5** gross, total, whole **6** intact **7** perfect, plenary, unified **8** complete, integral, outright **10** integrated **12** consolidated

entirely 5 fully, quite **6** wholly **7** utterly **9** perfectly **10** altogether, completely, thoroughly **11** exclusively

entirety 3 sum **5** total, whole **8** sum total, totality **9** aggregate, wholeness **10** everything **12** completeness, universality

entitle 3 dub, let **4** call, name, term **5** allow **6** enable, permit **7** baptize, empower, license, qualify **8** christen **9** authorize, designate **10** denominate

entity 3 sum **4** body, item, unit **5** being, thing, whole **6** object **7** article, integer **8** quiddity, totality **9** existence, something, substance **10** individual

entomb 4 bury **5** inter **6** inhume, shrine **7** mummify **8** enshrine **9** sepulcher, sepulchre

entombment 6 burial **7** obsequy **9** obsequies, sepulture **10** inhumation

entourage 5 staff, suite, train **6** escort, milieu **7** cortege, coterie, retinue **8** henchmen **9** courtiers, followers, following, hangers-on, retainers **10** associates, attendants **12** surroundings

entr'acte 8 interval **9** interlude **12** intermission

entrails 4 guts **5** pluck, tripe **6** bowels, tripes, vitals **7** giblets, innards, insides, viscera **8** stuffing **10** intestines

entrance 4 adit, door, gate, port **5** charm, foyer, inlet, lobby, mouth **6** access, portal, ravish **7** arrival, attract, bewitch, delight, doorway, enchant, gateway, ingress, opening **8** aperture, enthrall, open door **9** admission, captivate, enrapture, fascinate, hypnotize, mesmerize, spellbind, threshold, transport, vestibule **10** admittance, ingression **11** penetration

entrant 7 starter **10** competitor, contestant **11** participant

entrap 3 bag, net **4** bait, lure, toll **5** catch, decoy, snare, tempt **6** allure, ambush, entice, entoil, lead on, seduce, tangle **7** beguile, catch up, ensnare **8** entangle, inveigle

entre ___ 4 nous

entreat 3 ask, beg, bid **4** pray, urge **5** crave, plead, press **6** adjure, appeal

7 beseech, implore, wheedle **8** blandish
9 importune **10** supplicate
entreaty 4 plea, suit **6** appeal, orison,
prayer **7** request **8** petition **11** application, importunity **12** supplication
entrechat 4 leap
entrée 6 access **7** ingress **8** main dish
9 admission **10** admittance, main course
entrench 3 fix **4** root **5** embed, lodge
6 define, furrow, ground, hole up,
invade, settle **7** confirm, impinge,
implant, intrude **8** encroach, ensconce,
infringe, trespass **9** establish
10 strengthen
entrenched 3 set **4** firm **5** rigid, sworn
8 accepted, deep-dyed **9** hard-shell
10 deep-rooted, deep-seated, inveterate
13 bred-in-the-bone, dyed-in-the-wool
entrepôt 3 hub **4** mart **5** depot **6** bazaar,
market **8** emporium, exchange **9** concourse, warehouse **10** depository, storehouse **11** marketplace
entrepreneur 10 capitalist, contractor,
impresario
entresol 9 mezzanine
entropy 5 chaos, decay **7** decline **8** disorder **10** randomness **11** degradation
entrust 4 give **5** allot, leave **6** assign,
charge, commit, confer, impose **7** commend, confide, consign, deliver,
deposit **8** allocate, delegate, hand over,
relegate, turn over
entry 3 way **4** adit, door, gate, item, port
5 debit, foyer, inlet, lobby **6** access,
credit, portal, record **7** doorway,
ingress, opening **8** headword **9** admission, threshold, vestibule **10** admittance, enlistment, enrollment, ingression
entryway 4 door, gate **5** foyer, lobby
6 portal **7** ingress, narthex, portico
9 vestibule
entwine 4 coil, wind **5** braid, plait, twist
6 enmesh **7** wreathe **8** entangle **9** interlace **10** interweave
enumerate 3 sum, tot **4** cite, list, tell,
tote **5** add up, count, tally, total, tot up
6 detail, number, recite, reckon, tote
up **7** compute, itemize, recount, specify, tick off **8** identify **9** calculate, inventory **13** particularize
enunciate 3 say **5** speak, state, utter,
voice **6** affirm, intone **7** declare,
express, lay down **8** announce, proclaim, propound, vocalize **9** formulate,
postulate, pronounce, verbalize
10 articulate
envelop 3 hem **4** hide, roll, veil, wrap
5 cloak, cover, drape **6** cocoon, enfold,
engulf, enwrap, invest, sheath, shield,
shroud, swathe, wrap up **7** blanket,

embrace, enclose, swaddle **8** encircle,
enshroud, enswathe, surround **10** circumfuse
envenom 6 poison **8** embitter **10** exacerbate
envious 7 jealous **8** coveting, covetous,
grudging **9** green-eyed, invidious,
resentful **10** begrudging
environment 6 medium, milieu **7** ambient, climate, context, habitat, setting,
terrain **8** ambiance, ambience, backdrop **9** situation **10** atmosphere, background **11** mise-en-scène **12** surroundings *science:* **7** ecology
environmentalist 4 Muir (John) **6** Brower (David), Carson (Rachel), Nelson
(Gaylord), Wilson (Edward O.)
7 Ehrlich (Paul), Thoreau (Henry
David) **8** Commoner (Barry), Cousteau
(Jacques-Yves) **9** ecologist, Roosevelt
(Theodore)
environs 6 bounds, limits **7** compass,
fringes, suburbs **8** boundary, confines,
locality, purlieus, vicinity **9** districts,
outskirts, precincts **12** neighborhood,
surroundings
envisage 4 view **5** dream, fancy, grasp,
image, think **6** regard, vision **7** dream
up, feature, foresee, imagine, picture,
realize **8** conceive, look upon, summon
up **9** conjure up, objectify, visualize
envoy 5 agent **6** bearer, consul, deputy,
legate, nuncio **7** attaché, carrier, courier **8** diplomat, emissary, minister **9** messenger **10** ambassador **11** internuncio
12 intermediary
envy 5 covet **6** grudge **8** begrudge,
grudging, jealousy **10** resentment
12 covetousness **13** invidiousness
enwrap 4 roll, veil **5** clasp, drape
6 enfold, invest, shroud, swathe
7 enclose, engross, envelop, sheathe,
swaddle **8** enshroud, enswathe
enzyme 3 ase **5** ficin, lyase, renin, urase
6 kinase, ligase, lipase, mutase, papain,
pepsin, rennin, urease, zymase **7** amidase, amylase, cyclase, enolase, guanase, hydrase, inulase, isozyme, lactase,
maltase, oxidase, pectase, pepsine, plasmin, ptyalin, rennase, sucrase, trypsin,
zymogen **8** aldolase, diastase, elastase,
esterase, fumarase, lyzozyme, nuclease,
protease, steapsin, thrombin, zymogene **9** cellulase, invertase
eon see AEON
Eos see AURORA
épée 5 sword
epergne 5 stand **11** centerpiece
ephemeral 5 brief, short **7** passing
8 episodic, fleeting, fugitive, volatile
9 fugacious, momentary, temporary,

transient **10** evanescent, short-lived, transitory **11** impermanent

Ephialtes 5 giant *brother:* **4** Otus *father:* **6** Aloeus **8** Poseidon *mother:* **9** Iphimedia *slayer:* **6** Apollo

Ephraim *brother:* **8** Manasseh *father:* **6** Joseph *grandfather:* **5** Jacob *mother:* **7** Asenath

epic 4 poem, saga **5** grand, Iliad **6** Aeneid, heroic **7** Beowulf, Odyssey **8** imposing, sweeping **9** Gilgamesh, narrative **12** Heimskringla

epicene 10 effeminate **11** intersexual **13** hermaphrodite

epicure 7 gourmet **8** aesthete, hedonist, sybarite **9** bon vivant **10** gastronome **11** connoisseur **12** gastronomist

epicurean 7 gourmet, sensual **8** aesthete, hedonist, sensuous, sybarite **9** bon vivant, luxurious **10** gastronome, voluptuous **11** connoisseur **12** gastronomist, sensualistic

epidemic 3 flu **4** rash, wave **6** plague **7** rampant, scourge **8** catching, outbreak **9** contagion, prevalent **10** contagious, pestilence

epidermis 4 skin **7** cuticle **10** integument

epigram 3 saw **4** poem **5** adage, axiom, maxim **6** bon mot, dictum, saying, truism **7** proverb **8** aphorism, apothegm

epigrammatic 5 meaty, pithy, terse, witty **6** cogent **7** compact, concise, marrowy, piquant, pointed

epigraph 5 motto **9** quotation **11** inscription

epilogue 4 coda **5** close **6** ending, finale, windup **7** closing **8** postlude **9** afterword **10** conclusion, postscript

Epimetheus *brother:* **10** Prometheus *father:* **7** Iapetus *wife:* **7** Pandora

epiphany 6 aperçu, vision **7** insight **9** discovery, intuition **10** appearance, disclosure, revelation **11** inspiration, realization **13** manifestation

episode 5 event, phase **7** passage **8** incident, occasion **9** happening, interlude **10** occurrence **12** circumstance

episodic 5 brief **7** passing **8** fleeting, sporadic **9** ephemeral, irregular, temporary, transient **10** evanescent, occasional, short-lived **12** intermittent

epistaxis 9 nosebleed

epistle 4 note **6** letter **7** lection, missive **13** communication

epitaph 3 R.I.P. **5** elegy **6** eulogy **8** hic jacet **11** inscription

epithet 4 name **5** label, title **7** agnomen, moniker **8** cognomen, nickname **9** sobriquet **11** appellation

epitome 3 sum **4** acme, type **5** brief, short **6** digest, précis, résumé **7** essence, example, outline, summary **8** abstract, breviary, exemplar, synopsis, ultimate **9** archetype, summation, summing-up **10** abridgment, apotheosis, conspectus, embodiment **11** abridgement **12** condensation, quintessence

epitomize 5 sum up **6** digest, embody, mirror, typify **7** abridge, outline, summate **8** abstract, boil down, condense, manifest, tabulate **9** capsulize, exemplify, incarnate, inventory, objectify, personify, represent, summarize, symbolize, synopsize **10** abbreviate, illustrate **11** concentrate, emblematize, incorporate, personalize

epoch 3 age, eon, era **4** aeon, term, time **6** period **8** interval, time span

equable 4 calm, even, just **6** serene, stable, steady **7** orderly, regular, stabile, uniform **8** composed, constant **9** immutable, temperate, unvarying **10** consistent, invariable, unchanging **12** unchangeable

equal 3 tie **4** even, fair, like, mate, peer, same, twin **5** agree, alike, match **7** uniform **8** alter ego, amount to, parallel **9** duplicate, identical, impartial, objective **10** fifty-fifty **11** counterpart, symmetrical **12** commensurate, correspond to, proportional **13** commensurable, proportionate *combining form:* **3** iso **4** equi, pari *French:* **4** égal

equality 3 par **6** equity, parity **7** balance, égalité **8** evenness, fairness, sameness **10** uniformity

Equality State 7 Wyoming

equalize 4 even **5** level **6** square **7** balance **9** harmonize

equalizer 3 gun **6** pistol **8** handicap **10** tying score

equally 10 fifty-fifty **11** impartially

equanimity 4 calm, cool **5** poise **6** aplomb, phlegm **7** balance **8** calmness, coolness, evenness, serenity **9** assurance, composure, equipoise, placidity, sangfroid **10** detachment, steadiness **11** tranquility **12** tranquillity

equate 4 even **5** liken, match, treat **6** adjust, regard, relate, square **7** compare **8** consider, equalize, parallel **10** assimilate

Equatorial Guinea *capital:* **6** Malabo *island, island group:* **5** Bioko **6** Elobey, Pagulu **7** Corisco *language:* **5** Bantu **6** French **7** Spanish *mainland:* **5** Mbini **7** Río Muni *monetary unit:* **5** franc *neighbor:* **5** Gabon **8** Cameroon

equestrian 5 rider **6** horsey **8** horseman, knightly **10** horsewoman

equidistant 3 mid **6** medial, median,

middle, midway **7** central, halfway, midmost

equilibrium 5 poise **6** aplomb, stasis **7** balance **8** evenness, symmetry **9** composure, stability **10** steadiness **12** counterpoise **13** stabilization

equine 4 colt, mare **5** filly, horse, steed **6** horsey **8** stallion **9** horselike

equip 3 arm, fit, rig **5** array, dress, endow, rig up **6** attire, fit out, outfit, rig out, supply **7** appoint, furnish, prepare, provide **8** accouter, accoutre **9** provision

equipment 3 rig **4** gear **5** traps **6** attire, outfit, tackle, things **7** baggage, panoply **8** fittings, material, matériel, ordnance, supplies, tackling **9** apparatus, endowment, machinery, trappings **10** provisions **11** accessories, attachments, habiliments, impedimenta **12** accouterment, accoutrement, provisioning **13** accouterments, accoutrements, appurtenances, paraphernalia

equitable 4 even, fair, just **5** level **6** proper, square **7** condign **8** balanced, deserved, unbiased **9** identical, impartial, objective, uncolored **10** evenhanded, impersonal **12** unprejudiced **13** dispassionate

equity 3 law **7** justice **8** equality, interest, justness

equivalence 3 par **6** parity, simile **7** analogy **8** equality, identity, likeness, sameness **10** conformity **11** correlation

equivalent 4 akin, copy, like, peer, same, twin **5** alike, match **6** agnate **7** identic, similar **8** parallel **9** analogous, duplicate, identical **10** comparable, homologous, substitute, tantamount **11** convertible, correlative, counterpart **12** commensurate **13** corresponding, proportionate

equivocal 4 hazy **5** fishy, vague **6** unsure **7** clouded, dubious, obscure, suspect, unclear **9** doubtful **9** ambiguous, debatable, enigmatic, uncertain, undecided **10** ambivalent, indecisive, indistinct, irresolute, unresolved **11** problematic **12** disreputable, inconclusive, questionable **13** indeterminate

equivocate 3 fib, lie **5** cavil, dodge, evade, fudge, hedge **6** palter, waffle, weasel **7** shuffle **8** sidestep **9** pussyfoot **11** prevaricate **12** tergiversate

equivocation 3 fib **7** evasion, fibbing, hedging, sophism **8** waffling **9** ambiguity, casuistry, duplicity, sophistry **12** speciousness

equivoque 3 pun **8** wordplay

era 3 age, day **4** date, term, time **5** epoch, stage **6** period

eradicate 4 dele, raze **5** abate, erase, purge **6** delete, efface, remove, uproot **7** abolish, blot out, destroy, expunge, root out, weed out, wipe out **8** demolish, stamp out **9** eliminate, extirpate, liquidate **10** annihilate, do away with, extinguish, obliterate **11** exterminate

erase 4 dele, void, x out **6** cancel, delete, efface, excise, remove, rub out **7** abolish, blot out, expunge, nullify, scratch, take out, wipe out **8** black out, blank out, cross off, cross out **9** eliminate, extirpate, sponge out, strike out **10** obliterate

Erato see MUSE

Erbin *father:* **9** Custennin *nephew:* **6** Arthur *son:* **7** Geraint

ere 6 before

Erebus *daughter:* **3** Day **6** Hemera *father:* **5** Chaos *home:* **5** Hades *sister, wife:* **3** Nox, Nyx *son:* **6** Aether, Charon

Erec et ___ 5 Enide

Erechteus *daughter:* **8** Chthonia *father:* **6** Vulcan **10** Hephaestus *mother:* **4** Gaea *slayer:* **4** Zeus **7** Jupiter

erect 4 form **5** build, put up, raise, set up **6** create, raised **7** build up, stand-up, upright **8** assemble, elevated, standing, straight, vertical **9** construct, establish **10** upstanding **13** perpendicular

eremite 6 hermit **7** ascetic, recluse, stylite **9** anchoress, anchorite

Erewhon 6 utopia **7** nowhere *author:* **6** Butler (Samuel)

ergo 4 then, thus **5** hence **9** therefore **11** accordingly **12** consequently

Erichthonius *father:* **8** Dardanus *son:* **4** Tros

Eridanus star 8 Achernar

Erin see EIRE

Erinyes 6 Alecto, Furies **7** Megaera **9** Eumenides, Tisiphone

Eris *brother:* **4** Ares, Mars *daughter:* **3** Ate *fruit:* **5** apple *goddess of:* **6** strife **7** discord *mother:* **3** Nox, Nyx

Eritrea *archipelago:* **6** Dahlak *capital:* **6** Asmara *island:* **5** Zuqar *monetary unit:* **5** nakfa *neighbor:* **5** Sudan **8** Djibouti, Ethiopia *river:* **6** Baraka *sea:* **3** Red

ermine 3 fur **5** stoat **6** weasel

erode 3 eat, rub **4** wear **5** decay, scour **6** abrade, rub off **7** consume, corrade, crumble, eat away, rub away **8** wear away **9** scrape off **10** scrape away **11** deteriorate **12** disintegrate

Eroica composer 9 Beethoven (Ludwig van)

Eros see CUPID

erose 6 jagged, uneven **9** irregular

erotic 4 lewd, racy, sexy **5** bawdy, spicy **6** carnal, earthy, ribald, risqué **7** fleshly, obscene, profane, sensual **8** off-color, prurient, sensuous **9** salacious **10** voluptuous **11** aphrodisiac, titillating

err 3 sin **4** goof, slip, trip **5** lapse, stray **6** bungle, foul up, mess up, slip up **7** blunder, deviate, screw up, stumble **8** trespass **10** transgress

errand 3 job **4** task **5** chore **7** mission **10** assignment

errand boy 4 page **5** gofer **7** bellboy, bellhop, courier **9** go-between

errant 5 stray **6** fickle, roving **7** aimless, deviant, erratic, naughty, ranging, roaming, wayward, willful **8** drifting, fallible, rambling, shifting, straying **9** deviating, itinerant, traveling, wandering **10** meandering, unreliable **11** mischievous

erratic 5 flaky **6** fitful **7** wayward **8** freakish, shifting, unstable, variable, volatile **9** arbitrary, desultory, eccentric, fluctuant, irregular, mercurial, spasmodic, uncertain, wandering, whimsical **10** capricious, changeable, inconstant, meandering **12** inconsistent **13** idiosyncratic, unpredictable

erring see ERRANT

erroneous 3 off **4** awry **5** amiss, askew, false, wrong **6** untrue **7** unsound **8** mistaken, specious, spurious **9** defective, incorrect, misguided **10** fallacious, inaccurate, misleading

error 4 flub, goof, muff, slip, trip **5** boner, botch, fault, fluff, gaffe, lapse **6** boo-boo, bungle, fumble, howler, miscue, slipup **7** blooper, blunder, fallacy, falsity, faux pas, misstep, mistake, screwup, stumble, untruth **8** delusion, illusion, screamer **9** falsehood, indecorum, oversight **10** inaccuracy, misreading **11** impropriety, misjudgment *printing:* **4** typo **6** errata (plural) **7** erratum

ersatz 4 copy, fake, sham **5** bogus, dummy, faked, false, phony **6** pseudo **8** spurious **9** imitation, simulated, synthetic **10** artificial, factitious, simulacrum, substitute **11** counterfeit

Erse 5 Irish **6** Celtic, Gaelic

erstwhile 3 old **4** late, once, past **5** prior **6** before, bygone, former, whilom **7** already, earlier, onetime, quondam **8** formerly, previous **10** heretofore, previously

eruct 4 burp, emit, gush, spew **5** belch, eject, expel **7** explode **8** detonate, disgorge

erudite 7 bookish, learned **8** lettered, literate, studious, well-read **9** scholarly **10** scholastic

erudition 7 culture **8** learning, literacy **9** knowledge **11** bookishness, cultiva-

tion, learnedness, scholarship **12** studiousness **13** scholarliness

erupt 3 jet **4** spew **5** belch, burst, eject, expel, go off, spout, spurt **7** explode **8** break out, burst out, detonate **9** discharge **10** break forth, burst forth

eruption 4 gust, rush **5** blast, burst, flare, sally **6** access **7** flare-up **8** outbreak, outburst **9** commotion, explosion *skin:* **3** zit **4** rash **6** pimple

Esau *brother:* **5** Jacob *country:* **4** Edom *descendant:* **7** Edomite *father:* **5** Isaac *father-in-law:* **4** Elon *grandson:* **6** Amalek *mother:* **7** Rebekah *new name:* **4** Edom *son:* **5** Korha, Reuel **7** Eliphaz *wife:* **4** Adah **10** Aholibamah

escalade 5 climb, mount, scale **6** ascend **7** scaling

escalate 4 grow, rise, soar **5** boost, climb, mount, widen **6** expand, extend, spread, step up **7** amplify, augment, broaden, enlarge, inflate **8** heighten, increase, multiply **9** intensify **11** proliferate

escapade 4 lark, romp **5** antic, caper, fling, folly, prank, spree, stunt **6** frolic, vagary **7** roguery, rollick **8** mischief **9** adventure

escape 3 fly, lam **4** bolt, duck, flee, shun, skip, slip **5** avoid, break, dodge, elude, evade, shake **6** bypass, depart, eschew, flight, hegira, outlet **7** abscond, duck out, evasion, get away, make off, release, run away, skip out **8** breakout **9** avoidance, desertion, disappear, steal away **10** circumvent, liberation **11** deliverance, evasiveness *artist:* **7** Houdini (Harry) *narrow:* **9** close call **10** close shave

escargot 5 snail

escarole 6 endive

escarpment 5 bluff, cliff, slope

eschar 4 scab **5** crust **6** lesion

eschew 4 shun **5** avoid, elude, evade, forgo, spurn **6** abjure, forego, pass up, refuse, reject **7** decline **8** turn down

eschewal 7 elusion, evasion, refusal **8** shunning, spurning **9** avoidance, rejection

escort 4 beau, date, lead, show **5** guard, guide, pilot, steer, usher **6** attend, convoy, direct, gigolo, squire **7** company, conduct, consort, retinue **8** cavalier, chaperon, henchman, shepherd **9** accompany, bodyguard, chaperone, companion, entourage, safeguard **13** accompaniment

escritoire 4 desk **9** secretary **11** writing desk

escrow 4 bond, deed, fund **7** deposit

esculent 6 edible **7** eatable **10** comestible, digestible

escutcheon 6 flange, shield
Eshcol *ally:* 7 Abraham *brother:* 4 Aner
5 Mamre
esker 4 kame 5 mound, ridge
Eskimo 4 Inuk 5 Aleut, Inuit *boat:*
5 kayak, umiak *boot:* 6 mukluk *dog:*
5 husky 8 malamute *dwelling:* 5 igloo
outer garment: 5 parka 6 anorak *sledge:*
7 komatik
esophagus 6 gullet
esoteric 5 inner 6 arcane, mystic, occult,
orphic, secret 7 cryptic, private
8 abstruse, hermetic, profound 9 recondite 10 cabalistic, mysterious 12 confidential
ESP 9 telepathy 10 sixth sense 12 clairvoyance, precognition
espadrille 4 shoe 6 sandal
espalier 7 lattice, railing, trellis
esparto 5 grass
especial 4 main 5 close 7 express,
notable, unusual 8 dominant, intimate,
peculiar, singular, specific, uncommon
9 paramount 10 individual, particular
11 exceptional
especially 7 notably 8 markedly
9 expressly, primarily, unusually
10 peculiarly, remarkably, singularly
11 principally 12 particularly, specifically 13 distinctively, exceptionally
espial 6 notice 9 detection, discovery
11 observation
espionage 6 spying 9 sleuthing 12 surveillance
espousal 5 troth, union 6 mating
7 embrace, support, wedding 8 adoption, advocacy, approval, ceremony,
marriage 9 betrothal, embracing, matrimony, promotion 10 acceptance
espouse 3 wed 4 back 5 adopt, marry
6 accept, take on, take up 7 approve,
embrace, support 8 advocate
esprit 3 vim, wit 4 brio, dash, élan, zest,
zing 5 oomph, verve, vigor 6 fervor,
gaiety, mettle, morale, spirit 7 courage,
loyalty, panache, passion, sparkle
8 devotion, vibrancy, vitality 9 animation 10 brightness, enthusiasm, fellowship 11 camaraderie
esprit de corps see MORALE
espy 3 see 4 mark, spot 5 sight 6 descry,
detect, notice 7 discern, make out
9 recognize
___ es Salaam 3 Dar
essay 3 try 4 seek, test 5 labor, paper,
piece, study, theme, tract, trial 6 effort,
strive, thesis 7 article, attempt, venture
8 endeavor, treatise 9 undertake 10 discussion, exposition 11 composition,
undertaking 12 dissertation
essayist *American:* 4 Agee (James), Will

(George) 5 Baker (Russell), Cooke
(Alistair), Gould (Stephen Jay), White
(E. B.) 6 Brooks (Cleanth), Fisher
(M. F. K.), Holmes (Oliver Wendell),
Lowell (James Russell), Sontag (Susan),
Thomas (Lewis) 7 Buckley (William F.),
Cousins (Norman), Emerson (Ralph
Waldo), Mencken (Henry Louis),
Thoreau (Henry David) 8 Benchley
(Robert), Lippmann (Walter), Repplier
(Agnes) 10 Crèvecoeur (Jean de) *Eng-
lish:* 4 Elia, Lamb (Charles) 5 Bacon
(Francis), Cecil (Lord David), Pater
(Walter), Smith (Sydney) 6 Arnold
(Matthew), Cowley (Abraham), Morris
(Jan), Ruskin (John), Steele (Richard)
7 Addison (Joseph), Hazlitt (William)
8 Beerbohm (Max) 9 De Quincey
(Thomas) 12 Chesterfield (Lord)
French: 9 Montaigne (Michel de) *Scottish:* 7 Carlyle (Thomas)
essence 3 nub 4 base, core, crux, gist,
odor, pith, root, soul 5 basis, being,
fiber, fibre, point, stuff 6 center, entity,
kernel, marrow, nature, spirit 7 extract,
perfume, quality 9 substance 10 distillate 12 distillation, significance
essential 4 main, must 5 basal, basic,
chief, prime, vital 6 inborn, inbred,
innate, primal 7 connate, crucial, element, primary 8 cardinal, foremost,
inherent, required, rudiment 9 condition, elemental, intrinsic, necessary,
necessity, principal, requisite, substance 10 congenital, deep-seated, elementary, idiopathic, imperative, sine
qua non, underlying 11 fundamental,
requirement 12 precondition, prerequisite 13 indispensable, part and parcel
essentially 6 almost, au fond, really
7 largely 8 actually, as good as, as
much as, well-nigh 9 basically, virtually
11 practically 13 fundamentally, substantially
essonite 6 garnet 13 cinnamon stone
establish 3 fix, lay, put, set 4 base, form,
root, show 5 build, enact, endow, erect,
found, place, prove, set up, start
6 attest, create, decree, effect, ground,
impose, secure, settle, verify 7 build
up, certify, clarify, confirm, find out,
implant, install, instill, provide, set
down 8 document, ensconce, organize
9 authorize, construct, determine, formulate, institute, legislate, originate,
prescribe 10 bring about, constitute,
inaugurate 11 corroborate, demonstrate 12 authenticate, substantiate
establishment 4 firm 6 outfit 7 company,
concern 8 business, old guard 9 insti-

tute, workplace 10 enterprise, foundation 11 institution, ruling class
estate 4 farm, land 5 manor, ranch, villa 6 domain, legacy, quinta 7 demesne 8 dominion, hacienda, property 10 plantation *feudal:* 4 fief 7 fiefdom *first:* 6 clergy *fourth:* 5 press *manager:* 7 steward 8 executor, guardian *second:* 6 nobles 8 nobility *third:* 7 commons
esteem 4 deem 5 favor, honor, prize, think, value 6 admire, liking, regard, revere 7 account, believe, cherish, idolize, respect, worship 8 approval, consider, treasure, venerate 9 valuation 10 admiration, appreciate 12 appreciation 13 consideration
ester 6 oleate 7 acetate 8 compound 9 phosphate
Esther *cousin:* 8 Mordecai *enemy:* 5 Haman *father:* 7 Abihail *festival:* 5 Purim *Hebrew name:* 8 Hadassah *husband:* 6 Xerxes 9 Ahasuerus
estimable 5 noble 6 august, valued, worthy 7 admired 8 laudable, sterling 9 admirable, deserving, honorable, reputable, respected, venerable 10 creditable 11 commendable, meritorious, respectable 12 praiseworthy
estimate 3 put 4 call, rank, rate 5 assay, gauge, guess, infer, judge, price, set at, value 6 assess, deduce, figure, rating, reckon, survey 7 imagine, opinion, project, suppose, surmise 8 appraise, conclude, discover, evaluate, forecast, judgment, round off 9 appraisal, calculate, determine, reckoning, valuation 10 assessment, conjecture, evaluation, impression, projection 11 approximate, calculation, measurement
estimation 4 fame 5 favor, honor, stock 6 esteem, regard 7 account, opinion, respect 8 figuring, judgment 9 appraisal, reckoning, valuation 10 admiration, assessment, evaluation, impression 11 calculation 13 consideration
Estonia *capital:* 7 Tallinn *city:* 5 Tartu *gulf:* 4 Riga 7 Finland *island:* 4 Muhu 6 Vormsi 7 Hiiumaa 8 Saaremaa *lake:* 5 Pskov 6 Peipus 9 Vorts-Jarv *monetary unit:* 5 kroon *neighbor:* 6 Latvia, Russia *river:* 5 Narva, Pärnu 6 Kasari *sea:* 6 Baltic
estop 3 bar 6 enjoin, forbid 7 prevent 8 disallow, preclude, prohibit, restrain
estrange 4 part 5 split 7 break up, divorce 8 alienate, disunite, separate 9 disaffect
estrangement 4 rift 5 split 6 breach, schism 7 breakup, cooling, divorce, rupture 8 disunity, division 10 alien-

ation, falling-out, withdrawal 12 disaffection
estuary 5 firth, frith, mouth 10 tidal river
esurient 4 avid 6 greedy, hungry 8 covetous, grasping, ravening, ravenous 9 rapacious, voracious 10 avaricious, gluttonous 11 acquisitive
étagère 7 cabinet, whatnot
Etats-___ 4 Unis
etch 3 cut 5 carve, stamp 6 depict, incise 7 engrave, impress, imprint, portray 8 inscribe 9 delineate, represent
etcher *American:* 7 Pennell (Joseph) 8 Whistler (James McNeil) *Dutch:* 9 Rembrandt (van Rijn) *French:* 5 Redon (Odilon) 6 Villon (Jacques) *Italian:* 8 Piranesi (Giambattista) *Spanish:* 6 Ribera (José) *Swiss:* 4 Zorn (Anders)
Eteocles *brother:* 9 Polynices *father:* 7 Oedipus *mother:* 7 Jocasta *slayer:* 9 Polynices
eternal 7 abiding, ageless, endless, lasting, undying 8 constant, enduring, immortal, infinite, timeless, unending 9 ceaseless, continual, deathless, immutable, incessant, permanent, perpetual, unceasing 10 immemorial, unchanging 11 amaranthine, everlasting, illimitable, inalterable, never-ending, unalterable, unremitting 12 imperishable, interminable
Eternal City 4 Rome
eternally 3 e'er 4 ever 6 always 7 forever 8 evermore, for keeps 11 forevermore, in perpetuum 12 in perpetuity
eternity 3 age, eon 4 aeon 7 dog's age 8 blue moon, coon's age, infinity 9 afterlife 10 infinitude, perpetuity 11 endlessness, immortality 12 infiniteness, timelessness
Etesian 4 wind 6 annual
Ethan ___ 5 Allen, Brand, Frome
Ethbaal's daughter 7 Jezebel
ether 3 air, gas, sky 6 heaven 7 heavens 8 airwaves, empyrean 10 anesthetic, atmosphere
ethereal 4 aery, airy 5 filmy, light 6 aerial 7 fragile 8 delicate, empyreal, empyrean, gossamer, heavenly, rarefied, vaporous 9 celestial, spiritual, unearthly, unworldly 10 immaterial, intangible 13 unsubstantial
ethical 4 good 5 moral, noble 6 decent 7 upright, virtual 8 elevated, virtuous 9 righteous 10 principled, upstanding 11 right-minded 13 conscientious
ethics 5 mores 6 morals, values 8 morality 9 moral code, standards 10 principles
Ethiopia *battle site:* 5 Adowa *biblical name:* 4 Cush *capital:* 10 Addis Ababa

city: 6 Gonder 8 Dire Dawa *desert:* 4 Haud 7 Danakil *emperor:* 7 Menelik, Menilek 8 Selassie 9 Ras Tafari 13 Haile Selassie *former name:* 9 Abyssinia *language:* 5 Oromo 7 Amharic *monetary unit:* 4 birr *mountain:* 9 Ras Dashen *neighbor:* 5 Kenya, Sudan 7 Eritrea, Somalia 8 Djibouti *region:* 5 Tigre 6 Ogaden, Tigray 7 Danakil *river:* 4 Abay 5 Awash 6 Tekeze 8 Blue Nile

ethnic 6 racial, tribal 8 minority

etiolate 4 fade, pale 6 bleach, weaken 7 lighten, wash out 8 enfeeble

etiquette 4 code, form 5 mores 7 conduct, customs, decency, decorum, manners 8 behavior, protocol 9 amenities, propriety 10 civilities, convention, deportment, seemliness 11 conventions, formalities, proprieties

Etruscan *city, town:* 4 Roma, Veii 5 Caere, Vulci 6 Arezzo 7 Clusium, Felsina, Perugia 8 Volsinii 9 Florentia, Tarquinia, Vetulonia *deity:* 3 Tin, Tiv, Uni 4 Turm, Usil 5 Tinia, Turan, Turms 6 Menfra, Menrva, Nethun, Trithn 7 Velchan 8 Sethlans, Voltumna *king:* 7 Porsena, Tarquin 10 Tarquinius 11 Lars Porsena *kingdom:* 7 Etruria

étude 5 study 8 exercise 11 composition

etui 4 case

etymology 11 word history

etymon 4 root 5 radix 6 source 8 morpheme

eucalyptus eater 5 koala

Eucharist *container:* 3 pyx *plate:* 5 paten *service:* 4 Mass 9 Communion *vessel:* 8 ciborium *wafer:* 4 host 8 viaticum

Euclid *subject:* 8 geometry *work:* 8 Elements

___ **Eulenspiegel** 4 Till, Tyll

eulogistic 9 adulatory, laudative, laudatory 11 encomiastic, panegyrical 12 commendatory 13 complimentary

eulogize 4 hymn, laud 5 cry up, exalt, extol 6 praise 7 acclaim, applaud, commend, glorify, magnify 9 celebrate 10 panegyrize

eulogy 5 paean 6 praise 7 oration, tribute 8 accolade, citation, encomium 9 laudation, panegyric 10 salutation 12 commendation 13 glorification

Eumenides see ERINYES

eunuch 7 gelding 8 castrate, castrato

euphony 7 harmony 8 lyricism 9 sweetness 10 consonance

euphoria 3 joy 4 glee 5 bliss 7 ecstasy, elation, rapture 9 transport 10 exaltation, jubilation 11 high spirits 12 exhilaration, intoxication

Euphrosyne see GRACES

euphuistic 5 fancy, tumid 6 florid, ornate, prolix, purple, turgid 7 elegant, flowery, fustian, orotund, verbose 8 colorful, elevated, inflated, sonorous 9 bombastic, elaborate, high-flown, overblown 10 figurative, flamboyant, rhetorical 11 highfalutin, overwrought 12 magniloquent 13 grandiloquent

eureka 3 aha

Euridice's husband 7 Orpheus

Euripides play 3 Ion 5 Helen, Medea 6 Hecuba 7 Bacchae (The), Cyclops, Electra, Orestes 8 Alcestis 10 Andromache, Hippolytus, Suppliants (The) 11 Trojan Women (The)

Europa *brother:* 6 Cadmus *father:* 6 Agenor 7 Phoenix *husband:* 8 Asterius *son:* 5 Minos 8 Sarpedon

Europe 9 continent *country:* 4 Eire 5 Italy, Malta, Spain 6 France, Greece, Latvia, Monaco, Norway, Poland, Russia, Sweden, Turkey 7 Albania, Andorra, Armenia, Austria, Belarus, Belgium, Croatia, Denmark, Estonia, Finland, Georgia, Germany, Hungary, Iceland, Ireland, Moldova, Romania, Rumania, Ukraine 8 Bulgaria, Portugal, Slovakia, Slovenia 9 Lithuania, Macedonia, San Marino 10 Azerbaijan, Luxembourg, Yugoslavia 11 Netherlands, Switzerland, Vatican City 13 Czech Republic, Liechtenstein, United Kingdom *ethnic group:* 4 Celt, Finn, Lapp, Lett, Pole, Serb, Sorb, Turk, Wend 5 Croat, Czech, Dutch, Greek, Gypsy, Irish, Latin, Swede, Swiss, Welsh 6 Basque, Celtic, French, German, Magyar, Polish, Scotch, Slovak 7 Bosnian, Catalan, English, Finnish, Fleming, Italian, Lettish, Maltese, Russian, Slovene, Spanish, Swedish, Walloon 8 Albanian, Andorran, Armenian, Croatian, Romanian 9 Belarusan, Bulgarian, Hungarian, Ukrainian 10 Belarusian, Macedonian, Monegasque, Phoenician 11 Belarussian 12 Byelorussian, Scandinavian *language:* 4 Lapp 5 Czech, Dutch, Greek, Irish, Latin, Welsh 6 Basque, Breton, Danish, French, Gaelic, German, Magyar, Polish, Slovak 7 Catalan, English, Finnish, Flemish, Italian, Maltese, Romansh, Russian, Serbian, Slovene, Spanish, Swedish, Turkish, Wendish 8 Albanian, Croatian, Lusatian, Romanian, Rumanian 9 Bulgarian, Hungarian, Icelandic, Norwegian 10 Macedonian, Portuguese 13 Serbo-Croatian *mountain range:* 4 Alps 8 Pyrenees 11 Carpathians

Euryale see GORGON

Eurytus *daughter:* 4 Iole *slayer:* 8 Hercules

Euterpe see MUSE

evacuate 4 exit, void **5** clear, empty, expel, leave **6** decamp, depart, remove, vacate **7** abandon, excrete, exhaust, pull out, retreat **8** clear out, pull back, withdraw **9** eliminate

evacuee 6 émigré **7** refugee **8** fugitive

evade 4 duck, flee, foil **5** avoid, dodge, elude, hedge, parry, shirk, skirt **6** baffle, bypass, escape, eschew, outwit, thwart, weasel **7** shuffle **8** sidestep, slip away **9** pussyfoot, turn aside **10** circumvent, equivocate **11** prevaricate **12** tergiversate

evaluate 4 rank, rate **5** assay, class, gauge, grade, set at, weigh **6** assess, figure, reckon, size up, survey **7** eyeball **8** appraise, classify, estimate **9** calculate, criticize

evaluation 6 rating **7** judging, opinion **8** estimate, judgment **9** appraisal **10** assessment **12** appreciation

Evander *father:* **6** Hermes **7** Mercury *mother:* **8** Carmenta **9** Carmentis *son:* **6** Pallas

evanesce 4 fade **5** clear **6** vanish **7** scatter **8** disperse, dissolve, melt away **9** disappear, dissipate, evaporate **13** dematerialize

evanescent 6 fading **7** elusive, melting, passing **8** fleeting, fugitive, volatile **9** ephemeral, fugacious, momentary, transient, vanishing **10** dissolving, short-lived, transitory **12** disappearing

evangelical 6 ardent, fervid **7** fanatic, fervent, zealous **8** militant **9** crusading **10** missionary **13** proselytizing

Evangeline *author:* **10** Longfellow (Henry Wadsworth) *beloved:* **7** Gabriel *home:* **6** Acadia

evangelist 4 John, Luke, Mark **5** Moody (Dwight) **6** Bakker (Jim, Tammy Faye), Graham (Billy, Franklin), Sunday (Billy), Wesley (John) **7** apostle, Edwards (Jonathan), Falwell (Jerry), Matthew, Roberts (Oral) **8** Schuller (Robert), Swaggart (Jimmy) **9** McPherson (Aimee Semple), missioner, Robertson (Pat) **10** colporteur, missionary, revivalist, Whitefield (George)

evangelistic 9 crusading, reforming **10** missionary, revivalist **13** proselytizing

evangelize 6 preach **7** convert **9** sermonize

evaporate 4 fade, melt **5** clear **6** vanish **8** diminish, disperse, dissolve, evanesce, melt away, vaporize **9** disappear, dissipate

evasion 5 dodge, fudge **6** escape, excuse **7** dodging, elusion, fudging **8** escaping **9** avoidance **13** circumvention

evasive 3 sly **5** cagey, dodgy, vague **6** shifty **7** elusive **8** slippery **9** ambiguous, equivocal

Eve *home:* **4** Eden *husband:* **4** Adam *son:* **4** Abel, Cain, Seth *temptation:* **5** apple, fruit

even 3 tie **4** fair, flat, just, same, tied **5** align, equal, exact, flush, grade, level, plane, still, truly **6** as well, equate, smooth, square, stable, steady **7** balance, equable, flatten, uniform **8** balanced, constant, equalize, smoothen, straight **9** equitable, expressly, identical, precisely, unvarying **10** absolutely, comparable, consistent, continuous, fifty-fifty, unchanging **13** fair and square, proportionate

evening 4 dusk **6** soiree, sunset **7** sundown **8** gloaming, twilight **9** nightfall *French:* **4** soir *Italian:* **4** sera *service:* **7** vespers *star:* **5** Venus **6** Vesper **8** Hesperus

evenness 6 equity, parity **7** balance **8** equality **9** stability **10** equanimity, uniformity **11** consistency, equilibrium

event 3 act **4** case, deed, fact, feat, meet **5** issue, match **6** action, affair, chance, effect, result, upshot **7** contest, episode, outcome, product **8** accident, function, incident, occasion **9** aftermath, happening **10** occurrence, phenomenon **11** achievement, competition, consequence, eventuality **12** circumstance, happenstance

eventful 4 busy **6** lively **9** important, momentous

eventual 4 last **5** final **6** ending **7** closing, endmost, ensuing **8** terminal, ultimate **9** resulting **10** concluding, consequent, inevitable, succeeding

eventuality 4 case **6** effect, result **7** outcome **11** consequence, contingency, possibility

eventually 6 at last, one day **7** finally, someday **8** sometime **9** hereafter **10** ultimately **13** sooner or later

eventuate 5 ensue, occur **6** befall, follow, happen, result **9** come about, take place

ever 4 once **5** at all **6** always **7** forever **9** at any time, eternally, regularly **10** constantly, invariably **11** perpetually **12** consistently, continuously

evergreen 3 fir, ivy, yew **4** ilex, pine, tree **5** cedar, holly, savin **6** laurel, myrtle, spruce **7** conifer, cypress, hemlock, juniper, lasting, redwood, sequoia, undying **8** magnolia, mangrove, timeless, unfading **9** mistletoe, perennial **10** arborvitae **12** rhododendron

Evergreen State 10 Washington
everlasting 7 abiding, endless, eternal, forever, lasting, undying **8** constant, immortal, infinite, termless, timeless, unending **9** boundless, ceaseless, continual, deathless, limitless, permanent, perpetual, unceasing **10** continuous, perdurable **11** amaranthine, never-ending, unremitting **12** imperishable
evermore 6 always **7** for good **8** for keeps **9** eternally **12** in perpetuity
every 3 all **4** each *prefix:* **3** pan
everybody 3 all **4** each
everyday 5 banal, plain, usual **6** common, normal **7** mundane, prosaic, routine **8** familiar, habitual, ordinary **9** customary, quotidian **11** commonplace **12** conventional, run-of-the-mill, unremarkable
everything 3 all *French:* **4** tout *German:* **5** alles
everywhere 7 all over, overall **8** all round, wherever **9** all around **10** far and near, far and wide, high and low, throughout
evict 3 out **4** oust **5** eject, expel **6** bounce, put out **7** boot out, dismiss, extrude, kick out **8** dislodge, force out, throw out **10** dispossess
evidence 4 clue, mark, show, sign **5** goods, proof, prove **6** attest, evince, expose, reveal **7** confirm, display, exhibit, symptom, testify, witness **8** indicate **9** testament, testimony **10** indication, smoking gun **11** attestation, demonstrate, testimonial **12** confirmation **13** documentation
evident 5 clear, overt, plain **6** marked, patent **7** obvious, visible **8** apparent, distinct, manifest, palpable, tangible **9** prominent **10** noticeable, pronounced **11** conspicuous, perceptible, unambiguous
evidently 9 outwardly, seemingly **10** officially, ostensibly
evil 3 bad, sin **4** foul, vice, vile **5** black **6** infamy, malice, sinful, wicked **7** badness, baleful, baneful, devilry, hateful, heinous, malefic, satanic, vicious **8** damnable, iniquity, satanism, villainy **9** atrocious, diablerie, diabolism, execrable, loathsome, malicious, malignant, nefarious **10** flagitious, iniquitous, maleficent, malevolent, pernicious, sinfulness, wickedness **11** maleficence *combining form:* **3** mal
evildoer 6 sinner **7** villain **8** criminal **9** miscreant **10** malefactor
evil spirit 3 imp **5** demon, devil, fiend, Satan **6** daemon
evince 4 mark, show **5** educe, evoke,

prove **6** attest, betray, elicit, expose, reveal **7** bespeak, betoken, confirm, display, exhibit, signify **8** evidence, indicate, manifest, proclaim **10** illustrate **11** demonstrate
eviscerate 3 gut **4** draw **5** bowel **7** embowel **8** protrude **10** disembowel, exenterate
evocative 6 moving **8** redolent, stirring **9** affecting, emotional, nostalgic **10** expressive, meaningful, suggestive **11** stimulating
evoke 4 cite, stir **5** educe, raise, waken **6** arouse, awaken, call up, elicit, evince, excite, induce, recall **7** conjure **8** recreate, summon up **9** call forth, conjure up, stimulate **11** summon forth
evolution 6 change, growth **8** progress, upgrowth **9** flowering, phylogeny, unfolding **10** biogenesis, maturation **11** development, progression
evolve 4 grow **5** educe, ripen **6** change, derive, emerge, mature, open up, unfold **7** advance, develop, work out **8** progress **9** elaborate
ewe 5 sheep
ewer 3 jug **4** vase **7** pitcher
ex 4 from, past **5** prior **6** former **7** earlier, without **9** erstwhile
exacerbate 6 worsen **7** envenom, inflame, provoke **8** embitter, heighten **9** aggravate, intensify
exact 4 levy, true **5** claim, force, gouge, pinch, screw, wrest, wring **6** coerce, compel, dead-on, demand, extort, spot-on, strict **7** correct, extract, literal, precise, require, solicit, squeeze **8** accurate, rigorous, selfsame **9** identical, postulate, shake down **10** meticulous, scrupulous **11** painstaking, punctilious, requisition
exacting 5 fussy, rigid, stern, tough **6** severe, strict, taxing, trying **7** exigent, finicky, onerous **8** critical, rigorous **9** demanding, stringent **10** fastidious, nitpicking, particular, scrupulous **11** persnickety **13** hypercritical
exactitude 5 rigor **8** accuracy **9** precision **10** definitude **11** correctness, preciseness **12** definiteness
exactly 4 bang, just **5** quite, right, sharp, spang **6** bang on, square, to a tee, wholly **7** totally, utterly **8** entirely, smackdab, squarely **9** on the nose, precisely **10** absolutely, accurately, altogether, completely, positively **12** specifically
exaggerate 6 overdo **7** amplify, enlarge, inflate, magnify, overact, romance **8** overdraw, overrate **9** embellish, embroider, overstate **11** hyperbolize **13** overemphasize

exaggeration 8 travesty **9** hyperbole
10 caricature, stretching **11** enlargement, overdrawing **12** embroidering
13 embellishment, overstatement
exalt 4 fete, laud, lift **5** boost, elate,
extol, honor, raise **6** praise, uplift
7 acclaim, adulate, build up, dignify,
elevate, enhance, ennoble, glorify,
inspire, magnify, promote **8** eulogize,
heighten, inspirit **9** intensify **10** aggrandize **11** apotheosize
exaltation 3 joy **5** bliss, glory **6** homage,
praise **7** delight, ecstasy, elation, rapture, tribute **8** euphoria, rhapsody
9 panegyric, transport, uplifting
10 apotheosis, jubilation **11** deification
12 exhilaration, intoxication **13** glorification
exalted 4 high **5** grand, lofty, noble
6 august **7** eminent, highest, sublime
9 venerable **11** high-ranking, illustrious,
outstanding, prestigious
examination 4 quiz, scan, test **5** assay,
probe, trial **6** review, survey **7** canvass,
checkup, hearing, inquest, inquiry,
perusal, sifting, testing **8** analysis,
scrutiny **9** breakdown, check-over,
diagnosis **10** dissection, inspection
11 inquisition **13** catechization, investigation, perlustration *kind:* **4** oral **5** final
7 medical, midterm **8** physical *of
accounts:* **5** audit *of a corpse:* **7** autopsy
10 postmortem
examine 3 con, vet **4** pump, quiz, scan,
sift, test **5** audit, check, grill, probe,
query, study **6** go over, look at, peruse,
survey **7** canvass, check up, inquire,
inspect, observe **8** check out, look into,
look over, question **9** catechize, check
over **10** scrutinize **11** interrogate, investigate
examiner 6 censor **7** auditor, coroner
9 inspector **10** inquisitor, prosecutor
12 investigator
example 4 case **5** ideal, model **7** paragon,
pattern **8** instance, paradigm, specimen,
standard **9** archetype, precedent, prototype **11** case history **12** illustration
exanimate 4 dead **5** inert **8** lifeless, listless, sluggish, stagnant **9** lethargic
10 spiritless
exasperate 3 irk, vex **4** gall, rile, roil
5 anger, annoy, peeve, pique, upset
6 enrage, madden, nettle, rankle **7** agitate, incense, inflame, provoke **8** irritate **9** aggravate, infuriate
exasperation 8 vexation **9** annoyance
10 irritation **11** aggravation
ex cathedra 8 official **9** ex officio
13 authoritative
excavate 3 dig **4** grub **5** scoop, spade

6 dig out, dredge, expose, hollow, quarry, shovel **7** unearth **8** gouge out, scoop
out **9** hollow out, scrape out
excavation 3 dig, pit **4** hole, mine
5 ditch, stope **6** dugout, hollow, quarry,
trench, trough
exceed 3 cap, top **4** beat, best, pass
5 break, excel, outdo **6** better, outrun,
overdo **7** eclipse, outpace, overrun, surpass **8** go beyond, outreach, outshine,
outstrip, outweigh, overstep, overtake
9 overreach, transcend
exceedingly 4 very **6** hugely, vastly
7 awfully, notably, vitally **9** extremely
10 remarkably, strikingly **12** surpassingly **13** exceptionally *prefix:* **5** ultra
excel 3 cap, top **4** beat, best, pass
5 outdo, shine **6** better, exceed, outrun,
overdo **7** eclipse, outpace, overrun, surpass **8** go beyond, outclass, outreach,
outshine, outstrip, outweigh, overstep,
overtake **9** overreach, transcend
excellence 5 class, merit, value, worth
6 virtue **7** quality **8** fineness **9** greatness **10** perfection **11** distinction, superiority
excellent 3 top **4** fine **5** bully, prime
6 bang-up, banner, famous, Grade A,
superb, tip-top **7** capital, premium,
supreme **8** champion, five-star, splendid, stunning, superior, terrific, top-
notch **9** classical, first-rate, high-class,
high-grade, marvelous, number one,
wonderful **10** blue-ribbon, first-class
11 exceptional, magnificent, meritorious, sensational, superlative, unsurpassed **12** incomparable
except 3 bar, but, yet **4** omit, only, save
6 beside, exempt, object, reject, unless
7 barring, besides, exclude, however,
outside, rule out, suspend **8** pass over
9 apart from, aside from, eliminate,
excluding, outside of **11** exclusive of
exception 5 demur **7** anomaly, dissent
8 question **9** allowance, deviation,
exclusion, objection **10** aberration
exceptionable 8 unwanted **9** unwelcome
10 unsuitable **11** regrettable, undesirable **12** unacceptable **13** objectionable
exceptional 4 rare **6** scarce, unique
7 notable, special, unusual **8** abnormal,
atypical, distinct, singular, superior,
uncommon, unwonted **9** anomalous,
excellent, marvelous, wonderful
10 infrequent, noteworthy, phenomenal, remarkable **11** outstanding, uncustomary **13** extraordinary
exceptionally 4 very **6** hugely **7** notably
9 extremely **10** especially, remarkably,
strikingly **11** exceedingly **12** particularly, stupendously

excerpt 4 cite, cull, pick **5** glean, quote **6** choose, sample, select **7** extract, passage, pick out, portion, snippet **8** fragment **9** quotation

excess 3 fat **4** glut, rest **5** extra, flood, spare, waste **7** nimiety, overage, surfeit, surplus **8** leavings, leftover, overflow, overkill, overmuch **9** indulgent, overstock, redundant, remainder **10** oversupply, surplusage **11** dissipation, prodigality, superfluity, superfluous, unessential **12** extravagance, immoderation, intemperance **13** overabundance, supernumerary

excessive 4 over **5** dizzy, steep, super, undue **6** too-too **7** extreme, sky-high **8** overmuch, prodigal **10** exorbitant, immoderate, inordinate, profligate **11** extravagant, intemperate, overweening, superfluous **12** supernatural, unrestrained

excessively 3 too **6** overly, unduly **8** overmuch *prefix:* **5** hyper

exchange 4 swap, swop **5** bandy, trade, truck **6** barter, market, switch **7** bargain, commute, convert, pay back, replace, traffic **8** displace **9** transpose **10** conversion, substitute **11** reciprocate

exchequer 5 funds **8** treasury

excise 3 fee, tax **4** toll **5** elide, slash **6** cut out, delete, remove, resect **9** expurgate, extirpate, strike out, surcharge

excision 3 cut **7** removal, surgery **8** deletion **9** resection **11** extirpation

excitable 4 rash **8** volatile **9** impetuous **10** high-strung

excite 4 fire, goad, move, spur, stir **5** elate, evoke, key up, pique, prime, rouse, waken **6** appeal, arouse, elicit, fire up, induce, kindle, stir up, thrill, turn on **7** agitate, animate, commove, inflame, inspire, provoke, quicken **8** activate, charge up, energize, motivate **9** galvanize, impassion, innervate, stimulate **10** exhilarate

excited 3 hot **4** avid **5** eager **6** aflame **7** fevered **8** aflutter, worked up **10** passionate **12** enthusiastic

excitement 3 ado **4** buzz, stir, to-do **5** fever, furor **6** flurry, frenzy, furore, hubbub, thrill **7** turmoil **8** delirium, hysteria **9** agitation, commotion **10** enthusiasm, hullabaloo **11** disturbance, pandemonium **12** exhilaration

exclaim 4 blat, bolt **5** blurt **6** cry out **8** blurt out, burst out **9** ejaculate

exclamation 3 aah, aha, bah, boo, cry, eek, feh, fie, gee, hah, hey, huh, oho, ooh, pah, tsk, tut, ugh, wow **4** ahem, alas, amen, damn, dang, darn, drat, egad, gosh, heck, hell, oops, ouch, phew, pish, posh, rats, whew, yell **5** alack, bravo, faugh, golly, humph, pshaw, shout **6** clamor, hurrah, indeed, outcry, phooey, shucks **7** doggone, gee whiz, hosanna, jeepers, whoopee **9** expletive **10** hallelujah **12** interjection *of disappointment:* **4** damn, darn, rats *of disapproval:* **3** tsk **6** tsk-tsk *of disgust:* **3** bah, boo, feh, fie, ugh **4** yech, yuck **5** faugh, yecch **6** phooey *of dismay:* **4** oh no, uh-oh **5** yikes *of enthusiasm:* **4** whee **5** wahoo **7** whoopie *of fear:* **3** eek *of pain:* **4** ouch *of relief:* **4** phew *of sorrow:* **3** woe **4** alas **5** alack *of surprise:* **3** wow **4** gosh **5** golly *of triumph:* **3** aha, hah **5** yahoo **6** eureka (see also INTERJECTION)

exclude 3 ban, bar **4** oust **5** block, debar **6** banish, disbar, reject **7** keep out, lock out, obviate, prevent, rule out, shut out, suspend **8** count out, preclude, prohibit **9** blackball, blacklist, eliminate, ostracize

excluding 3 bar, but **4** less, save **6** except **7** barring, besides **9** apart from, aside from, other than, outside of

exclusion 3 bar **6** ouster **7** barring, lockout, removal **8** ejection, eviction, omission **9** blackball, expulsion, ostracism **10** banishment **12** blackballing, nonadmission

exclusive 4 lone, only, sole **5** elect, elite, prime, scoop, smart, swank, swish **6** choice, chosen, picked, select, single **7** cliquey, high-hat, stylish **8** clannish, cliquish, selected, snobbish **9** preferred, undivided **10** privileged **11** fashionable, prohibitive, restrictive **12** aristocratic, concentrated, preferential

exclusively 4 only **5** alone **6** wholly **8** entirely **10** completely **12** particularly

excogitate 6 derive, devise, invent **7** develop, think up **8** contrive, think out

excommunicate 7 cast out **8** unchurch

excoriate 4 flay, lash, skin **5** roast, slash **6** abrade, scathe, scorch **7** blister, censure, scarify, scourge **8** chastise, lambaste, lash into **9** castigate

excrement 6 ordure *of animals:* **4** dung, muck **6** manure *of sea birds:* **5** guano

excrescence 4 blot, lump, mole, wart **5** tumor **6** growth, nodule, pimple **7** blemish, process **9** by-product, outgrowth

excrete 4 emit, spew **5** eject, expel, exude **9** discharge

excruciate 4 rack **6** martyr **7** afflict, crucify, torment, torture **9** martyrize

excruciating 5 acute, sharp **6** severe **7** extreme, intense **8** piercing, shooting,

stabbing 9 agonizing, harrowing, torturous 10 unbearable 11 unendurable
exculpate 4 free 5 clear, remit 6 acquit, excuse, let off, pardon 7 absolve, amnesty, condone, forgive, justify 9 exonerate, vindicate 11 rationalize
excursion 4 ride, tour, trek, trip, walk 5 aside, drive, jaunt, paseo, sally, tramp 6 cruise, junket, outing, ramble, safari 7 day trip, journey 9 round trip 10 digression, divagation, expedition 11 parenthesis 12 pleasure trip
excusable 6 venial
excuse 3 out 4 plea 5 alibi, clear, remit 6 acquit, cop-out, defend, exempt, let off, pardon, reason, wink at 7 absolve, apology, condone, defense, forgive, justify, pretext, regrets, relieve 8 mitigate, overlook, palliate, pass over, shrug off, tolerate 9 discharge, exculpate, exonerate, extenuate, gloss over, makeshift, vindicate, whitewash 10 substitute 11 explanation, rationalize 13 justification
execrable 4 base, foul, vile 7 heinous 8 accursed, damnable, horrific, infernal, wretched 9 abhorrent, atrocious, loathsome, monstrous, repulsive, revolting 10 abominable, deplorable, despicable, detestable, horrifying
execrate 4 damn, hate 5 abhor, curse 6 detest, loathe, revile, vilify 7 censure, condemn, despise 8 denounce 9 abominate, imprecate 12 anathematize
execute 3 act 4 do in, kill, play, slay 5 cause, lynch 6 effect, finish, murder, render 7 achieve, bump off, conduct, enforce, fulfill, perform, realize 8 carry out, complete, dispatch, knock off, transact 9 discharge, eliminate, implement, liquidate 10 accomplish, administer, bring about, put through, put to death 11 assassinate 12 administrate
execution 6 murder 7 killing 11 performance
executioner 7 hangman, headman 8 headsman
executive 4 dean, suit 6 leader 7 manager 8 director, governor 9 president 10 supervisor 13 administrator
exegesis 5 gloss 8 analysis 9 construal 10 commentary, exposition 11 elucidation, explanation, explication 12 construction
exemplar 4 copy 5 ideal, model 7 epitome, paragon, pattern 8 instance, paradigm, specimen, standard 9 archetype, criterion, prototype 12 illustration
exemplary 4 pure 5 ideal, model 7 classic, typical 8 laudable, monitory, virtuous 9 admirable, blameless, classical,

estimable, faultless, honorable, righteous 10 impeccable, inculpable, prototypal 11 commendable, meritorious 12 illustrative, paradigmatic, praiseworthy, prototypical
exemplify 4 copy 6 embody, mirror, typify 7 clarify 9 enlighten, epitomize, personify, represent, symbolize 10 concretize, illuminate, illustrate
exempt 4 free 5 spare 6 except, excuse, let off, spared 7 absolve, excused, relieve 8 dispense 9 discharge
exemption 7 freedom, release 8 immunity, impunity 9 discharge, exception
exenterate 3 gut 4 draw 7 embowel 10 disembowel, eviscerate
exercise 3 use, vex 4 fret, gall, hone 5 alarm, annoy, apply, drill, étude, exert, sit-up, train, upset, wield 6 chin-up, crunch, employ, pull-up, push-up 7 agitate, develop, exploit, improve, prepare, problem, provoke, utilize, work out 8 activity, maneuver, practice, rehearse 9 athletics, condition, cultivate, discharge, operation 10 employment 11 application 12 calisthenics
exert 3 use 5 apply, wield 6 employ, expend, put out, strain 8 exercise, put forth
exertion 4 toil, work 5 labor, pains 6 effort, strain 7 trouble 8 activity, exercise, striving 11 application, elbow grease
exfoliate 4 peel, shed 5 scale 7 cast off, leaf out 8 flake off 10 desquamate
exhalation 6 breath 8 emission 9 breathing, effluvium, emanation
exhale 4 blow, emit 6 expire, let out 7 breathe, respire 10 breathe out
exhaust 3 fag, sap 4 do in, tire 5 drain, eat up, empty, spend, use up, waste, weary 6 expend, finish, tucker, wash up, weaken 7 burn out, consume, deplete, fatigue, frazzle, tire out, wear out 8 draw down, enervate, squander, wear down 9 discharge, dissipate, prostrate, tucker out 10 debilitate, overextend, run through
exhausted 4 beat, limp, weak 5 all in, spent, tired 6 bushed 7 run-down, worn out 8 dog-tired
exhaustion 7 burnout, fatigue 8 collapse 9 lassitude, tiredness, weariness 11 prostration
exhaustive 8 complete, sweeping, thorough 9 full-blown, full-scale, intensive 10 scrupulous 11 painstaking 13 comprehensive, thoroughgoing
exhibit 4 fair, show 6 evince, expose, flaunt, parade, reveal 7 display, feature,

show off **8** evidence, manifest, proclaim, showcase **10** exposition **11** demonstrate

exhibition 4 fair, show **7** display, pageant, showing **12** presentation **13** demonstration, manifestation

exhibitionist 3 fop **4** toff **6** hot dog **7** peacock, show-off **8** showboat **12** grandstander

exhilarate 4 buoy, lift **5** boost, cheer, elate, exalt, pep up **6** buck up, excite, thrill, uplift **7** animate, cheer up, commove, delight, enliven, gladden, inspire, refresh **8** inspirit, vitalize **9** stimulate **10** invigorate

exhilaration 3 joy **4** glee **7** ecstasy, elation **8** euphoria, gladness **10** exaltation, excitement **11** inspiration **12** vitalization, vivification **13** galvanization

exhort 4 goad, prod, spur, urge, warn **5** egg on, plead, press, prick **6** adjure, call on, incite, prompt, propel **7** beseech, entreat **8** admonish, call upon **9** stimulate

exhortation 4 plea **6** advice, urging **7** caution, warning **8** entreaty, jeremiad **10** admonition, incitement, injunction **11** inspiration **13** encouragement

exhume 5 dig up **6** redeem **7** reclaim, recover, unearth **8** disinter **9** resurrect

exigency 3 fix, jam **4** need, pass **5** pinch, rigor **6** crisis, demand, pickle, plight, strait **7** urgency **8** juncture, pressure, zero hour **9** extremity, necessity **10** compulsion, constraint, crossroads, difficulty, insistence **11** predicament, requirement

exigent 5 acute, vital **6** crying, taxing **7** burning, clamant, instant, onerous **8** exacting, grievous, pressing **9** clamorous, demanding, insistent, necessary **10** burdensome, imperative **11** importunate

exiguous 4 poor, puny, thin, tiny **5** scant, spare, token **6** meager, meagre, measly, paltry, scanty, shabby, skimpy, slight, sparse **7** minimal, scrimpy **9** miserable **10** inadequate, straitened

exile 4 oust **5** eject, expel **6** banish, deport, emigré **7** cast out, outcast, refugee **8** diaspora, displace, drive out, evacuate, expellee **9** exclusion, expulsion, extradite, migration, ostracism, ostracize **10** banishment, dispossess, expatriate, scattering **11** deportation, extradition **12** displacement, expatriation *place of:* **4** Elba **7** Siberia

exist 3 are, lie **4** live **5** occur

existence 4 life **5** being **7** reality **8** duration **9** actuality

existent 4 live, real **5** being, thing **6** actual, entity, extant, living **7** current, instant, present **10** present-day **12** contemporary

existentialist writer 5 Buber (Martin), Camus (Albert) **6** Marcel (Gabriel), Sartre (Jean-Paul) **7** Jaspers (Karl) **8** Beauvoir (Simone de) **9** Heidegger (Martin), Nietzsche (Friedrich) **11** Kierkegaard (Søren)

existing 5 alive, being, ontic **6** extant, living *from birth:* **6** innate **10** congenital *Latin:* **6** in esse

exit 3 die **4** door, gate, quit **5** death, going, leave, scram, split **6** depart, egress, escape, outlet, portal, retire **7** doorway, get away, off-ramp **8** withdraw **9** departure, egression **10** withdrawal

___ ex machina 4 deus

exodus 6 flight **9** migration **10** emigration

Exodus author 4 Uris (Leon)

exonerate 4 free **5** clear, remit **6** acquit, excuse, exempt, let off, pardon **7** absolve **8** reprieve **9** exculpate, vindicate

exorbitant 5 undue **7** extreme **9** excessive **10** immoderate, inordinate, outrageous **11** extravagant, unwarranted **12** preposterous

exordium 5 intro, proem **6** lead-in **7** opening, preface, prelude **8** foreword, overture, preamble, prologue **12** introduction, prolegomenon

exotic 4 rare **5** alien **7** bizarre, foreign, strange, unusual **8** alluring, enticing, imported, romantic **9** different, glamorous, nonnative **10** introduced, mysterious **11** fascinating

expand 3 wax **4** grow, open, rise **5** boost, mount, swell, widen **6** beef up, bulk up, dilate, pad out, spread, unfold **7** amplify, augment, bolster, develop, distend, enlarge, inflate, magnify, prolong, stretch **8** escalate, increase, lengthen, multiply, mushroom, protract **9** discourse, elaborate, expatiate, spread out

expanse 4 area, room **5** field, ocean, range, reach, scope, space, sweep, tract **6** domain, extent, sphere, spread **7** breadth, stretch **8** distance **9** territory

expansion 6 growth, spread **8** increase **9** unfolding **11** enlargement **12** augmentation

expansive 3 big **4** wide **5** ample, broad, large, roomy **6** lavish **7** buoyant, elastic, liberal, sizable **8** effusive, extended, generous, outgoing, spacious **9** capacious, garrulous, talkative **10** gregarious, openhanded, unreserved 11 extroverted 13 demonstrative

expatiate 6 ramble, wander 7 dissert, enlarge 8 dilate on, perorate 9 discourse, elaborate, sermonize 10 dilate upon, dissertate

expatriate 5 exile, expel 6 banish, deport, émigré 8 displace, expellee, relegate

expect 4 feel, hope, take 5 await, sense, think, trust 6 assume, divine, gather, look to 7 believe, count on, foresee, imagine, look for, predict, presume, suppose, surmise 8 forecast, foreknow 9 apprehend, count upon 10 anticipate, presuppose

expectant 5 alert 6 gravid 7 anxious, hopeful 8 enceinte, pregnant, vigilant, watchful 10 breathless, parturient 12 anticipatory, apprehensive

expectation 4 hope 5 hunch 8 prospect 9 assurance, intuition 10 assumption, likelihood 11 presumption, probability 12 anticipation, presentiment

expectorate 4 spit

expediency 5 means 6 resort, tactic 7 aptness, fitness, measure, stopgap 8 meetness, recourse, resource, strategy 9 makeshift, propriety, rightness 11 opportunism, suitability 12 appositeness, practicality, suitableness

expedient 3 fit 5 ad hoc, means, shift 6 resort, timely, useful 7 fitting, politic, prudent, stopgap 8 feasible, recourse, resource, suitable, tactical 9 advisable, judicious, makeshift, opportune, practical, pragmatic, well-timed 10 convenient 11 appropriate, practicable, utilitarian 12 advantageous

expedite 4 send 5 hurry, issue, speed 6 hasten 7 quicken, speed up 8 dispatch 10 accelerate, facilitate

expedition 4 trek, trip 5 hurry, speed 6 voyage 7 journey 8 campaign, dispatch 9 excursion, swiftness 10 efficiency, speediness 11 punctuality

expeditious 4 fast 5 brisk, quick, rapid, swift 6 prompt, speedy 9 efficient 11 efficacious

expeditiousness 5 hurry, speed 6 hustle 8 dispatch

expel 4 boot, oust, spew 5 eject, evict, exile 6 banish, bounce, deport, disbar 7 cast out, dismiss, drum out, kick out, turn out 8 disgorge, displace, throw out 9 discharge, eliminate 10 expatriate

expellee 5 exile 6 émigré 7 outcast 8 deportee, emigrant

expend 3 pay, sap 4 blow 5 drain, spend, use up, waste 6 lay out, outlay, pay out 7 consume, deplete, dig into, dole out,

exhaust, fork out, utilize 8 disburse, dispense, shell out, squander 9 dissipate 10 run through

expendable 10 disposable 11 dispensable, inessential, replaceable 12 nonessential

expenditure 4 cost 6 outlay, payoff, payout 12 disbursement

expense 4 cost, loss, toll 5 debit, price 6 burden, charge, outlay 7 forfeit, payment 8 overhead 9 decrement, sacrifice 10 forfeiture 12 disbursement

expensive 4 dear, high, posh 5 fancy, ritzy, steep, stiff 6 costly, deluxe, lavish, pricey 7 upscale 8 precious, valuable, wasteful 9 big-ticket, luxurious 10 exorbitant, high-priced, overpriced 11 extravagant 12 uneconomical

experience 4 know, live 5 event, savor, skill, trial 6 ordeal, suffer, wisdom 7 episode, know-how, sustain, undergo 8 incident, practice 9 encounter, go through 10 background 11 familiarity, savoir faire *anew:* 6 relive

experienced 4 wise 6 mature, versed 7 old-line, veteran, worldly 8 broken in, seasoned 9 practiced, qualified 12 accomplished

experiential see EMPIRICAL

experiment 3 try 4 test 5 assay, probe, trial 6 try out 7 test out 8 research, trial run 13 trial and error

experimental 9 empirical, tentative 10 innovative 11 exploratory, preliminary, preparatory, provisional 13 developmental, trial-and-error

experimentation 4 test 5 trial 7 testing 8 research, trial run 13 trial and error

expert 3 ace, pro, wiz 4 deft, whiz 5 adept, crack, doyen, maven 6 adroit, master, wizard 7 skilled 8 masterly, skillful, virtuoso 9 authority, dexterous, masterful, virtuosic 10 past master, proficient, specialist 11 crackerjack 12 passed master, professional

expertise 5 craft, skill 7 ability, command, know-how, mastery 8 facility 10 adroitness, competence 11 proficiency 12 skillfulness

expertness see EXPERTISE

expiate 6 offset, pay for, redeem 7 redress 8 atone for

expiation 9 atonement, indemnity 10 recompense, reparation 11 restitution 12 satisfaction

expiatory 7 atoning, lustral 9 purgative 11 penitential, purgatorial 12 propitiatory

expiration 3 end 5 death 10 exhalation 11 termination

expire 3 die, end **4** pass **5** lapse **6** elapse, exhale, pass on, perish, run out **7** decease **8** pass away **9** terminate **10** breathe out

explain 5 gloss, solve **7** analyze, clarify, clear up, condone, expound, justify, resolve, unravel **8** construe, decipher, spell out, unriddle, untangle **9** break down, elucidate, interpret **10** account for, illuminate, illustrate, unscramble **11** disentangle, rationalize

explain away 6 excuse **7** justify **8** minimize **9** extenuate **10** account for **11** rationalize

explanation 3 key **5** gloss **6** excuse, motive, reason **7** account, example, grounds, meaning **8** exegesis **9** construal, rationale **11** elucidation **12** significance **13** clarification

explanatory 10 discursive, exegetical **12** enlightening, illuminating, illustrative, interpretive

expletive 4 cuss, oath **5** curse, swear **8** cussword **9** swearword **12** interjection (see also EXCLAMATION)

explicate 7 amplify, develop, explain, expound **8** construe, spell out **9** elucidate, interpret

explication 5 gloss **8** exegesis **9** construal **10** commentary **11** development

explicative 10 discursive, exegetical, scholastic **12** interpretive **13** hermeneutical

explicit 4 open, sure **5** clear, exact, frank, lucid, overt, plain **7** certain, correct, express, obvious, precise **8** clearcut, definite, distinct, specific **10** definitive **11** categorical, perspicuous, unambiguous, unequivocal

explode 3 pop **4** fire **5** blast, burst, erupt, go off **6** blow up, debunk, negate, refute **7** burgeon, deflate **8** break out, burst out, detonate, disprove, dynamite, mushroom, puncture **9** discharge, discredit **10** burst forth **11** proliferate

exploit 3 act, use **4** coup, deed, feat, gest, play **5** abuse, geste, stunt **6** bestow, effort, employ, parlay, play on **7** emprise, utilize, venture **8** escapade, exercise **9** adventure, cultivate **10** enterprise, manipulate **11** achievement, performance, tour de force

explore 5 probe, scout **6** burrow, go into, search **7** dig into, examine **8** look into, prospect, traverse **9** delve into **11** inquire into, investigate

explorer African: 3 Cam, Cão (Diogo) **4** Park (Mungo) **5** Grant (James), Laird (Macgregor), Speke (John Hanning) **6** Akeley (Carl, Mary), Burton (Richard), Lander (John, Richard)

7 Covilhâ (Pero da), Stanley (Henry) **8** Covilhâo (Pero da) **10** Clapperton (Hugh) **11** Livingstone (David) *American:* **4** Byrd (Richard), Hall (Charles Francis), Kane (Elisha Kent), Pike (Zebulon) **5** Beebe (Charles William), Clark (William), Lewis (Meriwether), Peary (Robert) **6** Henson (Matthew), Powell (John Wesley), Wilkes (Charles) **7** Frémont (John Charles) *Antarctic:* **4** Byrd (Richard), Cook (Frederick), Ross (James Clark) **5** Fuchs (Vivian), Ronne (Finn), Scott (Robert Falcon) **6** Palmer (Nathaniel), Rymill (John Riddoch), Wilkes (Charles) **7** Weddell (James), Wilkins (George) **8** Amundsen (Roald), d'Urville (Dumont) **9** Ellsworth (Lincoln) **10** Shackleton (Ernest) *Arctic:* **3** Rae (John) **4** Byrd (Richard), Cook (Frederick) **5** Davis (John), Peary (Robert) **6** Baffin (William), Bering (Vitus), Henson (Matthew), Hudson (Henry), Nansen (Fridtjof), Nobile (Umberto) **7** Barents (Willem), Bennett (Floyd), Wilkins (George), Wrangel (Ferdinand von) **8** Amundsen (Roald) **9** Mackenzie (Alexander), MacMillan (Donald) **10** Stefansson (Vilhjalmur) *Australian:* **7** Wilkins (George) *Austrian:* **9** Weyprecht (Carl) *Canadian:* **9** Mackenzie (Alexander) **10** Stefansson (Vilhjalmur) *Danish:* **9** Rasmussen (Knud) *Dutch:* **6** Tasman (Abel Janszoon) *English:* **4** Cook (James) **5** Cabot (John, Sebastian), Drake (Francis), Scott (Robert Falcon), Smith (John) **6** Baffin (William), Burton (Richard), Hudson (Henry) **7** Raleigh (Walter), Stanley (Henry) **9** Vancouver (George) **10** Shackleton (Ernest) **12** Younghusband (Francis) *French:* **7** Cartier (Jacques), La Salle (Sieur de), Nicolet (Jean) **8** Cousteau (Jacques-Yves) **9** Champlain (Samuel de), La Perouse (Comte de), Marquette (Jacques) *French Canadian:* **6** Joliet (Louis) **7** Jolliet (Louis) **9** Iberville (Sieur d') *German:* **6** Peters (Carl) **8** Humboldt (Alexander von) *Italian:* **5** Cabot (John) **6** Nobile (Umberto) **8** Vespucci (Amerigo) *New Zealand:* **7** Hillary (Edmund) *Norwegian:* **6** Nansen (Fridtjof) **8** Amundsen (Roald), Sverdrup (Otto) **9** Heyerdahl (Thor) *Portuguese:* **4** Gama (Vasco da) **5** Cunha (Tristão da) **6** Cabral (Pedro) **8** Cabrilho (João Rodrigues), Magellan (Ferdinand) *Scottish:* **3** Rae (John) **4** Park (Mungo), Ross (James Clark) **7** Thomson (Joseph) **11** Livingstone (David) *Span-*

ish: 6 Balboa (Vasco Núñez de), Cortés (Hernán, Hernando), de Soto (Hernando), Pinzón (Martín Alonso, Vicente Yáñez) 7 Mendoza (Pedro de), Pizarro (Francisco) 8 Bastidas (Rodrigo de), Coronado (Francisco de) 11 Ponce de León (Juan)

explosion 3 pop, pow 4 bang, boom, clap 5 blast, burst, crack, crash, sally, salvo, storm 6 report, volley 7 barrage, blowout, torrent 8 eruption, outburst, paroxysm 9 discharge 10 detonation

explosive 3 TNT 5 nitro, tense 6 charge, petard, powder 7 cordite, violent 8 dynamite 9 gunpowder 13 nitroglycerin *device:* 3 cap 4 bomb, mine 5 shell 6 petard 7 grenade 8 firework *expert:* 5 Maxim (Hudson), Nobel (Alfred) *sound:* 3 pop, pow 4 bang, boom 5 crack

exponent 6 backer 7 booster 8 advocate, champion, defender, partisan, promoter, upholder 9 supporter 12 practitioner

expose 3 air 4 bare, open, show 5 dig up, flash 6 debunk, flaunt, parade, reveal, show up, unmask, unveil 7 abandon, display, exhibit, lay open, publish, show off, subject, uncover, undress 8 brandish, disclose, discover, endanger, unclothe

exposé 10 disclosure, revelation, uncovering

exposed 4 bare, open 5 naked 6 liable 7 evident, subject, visible 8 manifest, stripped, unhidden 9 uncovered 11 susceptible, unconcealed, unprotected

exposition 4 fair, show 6 bazaar 7 display, exhibit

expostulate 5 argue 6 debate, reason 7 discuss, dispute

exposure 4 risk 5 peril 6 airing, baring, danger 8 betrayal, jeopardy, openness 9 liability, publicity 10 revelation 12 helplessness 13 vulnerability

expound 5 state 6 defend 7 clarify, comment, explain, present 8 construe, set forth, spell out 9 discourse, explicate, interpret

expounder 7 teacher 8 advocate, champion, defender, promoter 9 proponent, supporter

express 3 air, say 4 mean, tell, vent 5 couch, crush, frame, state, utter 6 broach, convey, denote, impart, intend, voiced 7 connote, declare, signify, special, uttered 8 announce, clearcut, definite, disclose, explicit, intended, proclaim, specific 9 enunciate, formulate, high-speed, pronounce, symbolize, ventilate 10 definitive, particular 11 categorical, communicate,

intentional, unambiguous *gratitude:* 5 thank *regret:* 9 apologize

expression 4 cast, face, form, look, mien, sign, vent, word 5 idiom, issue, motto, token, voice 6 symbol, visage 7 diction, gesture 8 locution 9 eloquence, statement, utterance, verbalism, vividness 10 embodiment, indication 11 countenance, enunciation, observation 13 demonstration, manifestation *facial:* 4 grin, phiz, pout 5 frown, scowl, smile, smirk, sneer, wince 7 grimace *of assent:* 3 aye, nod, yea, yes 4 okay *of sorrow:* 4 alas, tear *trite:* 6 cliché 7 bromide 8 banality *witty:* 4 quip 5 sally 6 bon mot

expressionless 5 blank 6 stolid, vacant, wooden 7 deadpan 9 impassive 10 poker-faced 11 inscrutable

expressive 5 vivid 7 graphic 8 eloquent 9 revealing 10 meaningful, passionate

expressly 9 precisely, purposely 10 explicitly 12 particularly, specifically 13 intentionally

expressway 4 road 7 freeway, highway, parkway 8 turnpike 12 thoroughfare

expropriate 4 take 5 annex, seize 7 impound, preempt 8 arrogate 9 sequester 10 commandeer, confiscate, dispossess

expulse see EXPEL

expulsion 5 exile, purge 6 ouster 7 ousting, removal 8 ejection, eviction 9 ostracism 10 banishment, relegation 11 deportation 12 displacement

expunge 4 dele, x out 5 annul, erase 6 cancel, delete, efface 7 blot out, destroy, exclude, wipe out 8 black out 9 eliminate, eradicate, strike out 10 annihilate, obliterate

expurgate 4 blip 5 bleep, purge 6 censor, purify, screen 7 cleanse 8 sanitize 10 bowdlerize

expurgation 8 ablution 9 catharsis, cleansing 10 lustration 12 purification

exquisite 3 fop 4 fine, keen, rare 5 acute, dandy 6 choice, dainty, select, superb 7 coxcomb, elegant, extreme, intense, refined 8 delicate, finished, flawless, macaroni 9 recherché 10 fastidious, immaculate, impeccable

exsiccate 3 dry 4 sear 5 parch

extant 4 live 5 alive 6 actual, living 7 current, present 9 surviving 10 present-day 12 contemporary

extemporaneous 5 ad-lib 6 casual 7 offhand 8 ad-libbed, informal 9 impromptu, impulsive, makeshift, unplanned 10 improvised, unprepared, unscripted 11 spontaneous, unrehearsed 12 unthought-out

extempore see EXTEMPORANEOUS

extemporize 5 ad-lib 7 dash off, toss off 8 knock off 9 improvise

extend 4 draw, span, vary 5 award, grant, offer, range, reach 6 accord, attain, bestow, spread, tender, unbend, unfold 7 advance, amplify, augment, broaden, drag out, draw out, enlarge, further, hold out, present, proceed, proffer, project, prolong, spin out, stretch 8 continue, elongate, increase, lengthen, multiply, protract 10 outstretch, stretch out

extension 3 arm, ell 4 wing 5 annex, delay, range, reach, scope, sweep 6 radius, spread 7 adjunct, compass, purview 8 addition, increase 9 appendage, magnitude 10 broadening, elongation 11 enlargement, lengthening, protraction 12 augmentation, continuation, postponement, prolongation

extensity 5 ambit, orbit, range, reach, scope, sweep 6 radius 7 compass, purview

extensive 3 big 4 long, vast, wide 5 broad, large, major 7 general, immense, lengthy, sizable 8 far-flung, sizeable, spacious, sweeping, thorough 9 wholesale 10 large-scale, widespread 11 far-reaching, wide-ranging 12 considerable

extent 4 size 5 ambit, limit, orbit, range, reach, scope, sweep, width 6 amount, degree, domain, radius 7 breadth, compass, measure, purview 8 vicinity 9 magnitude 10 dimensions, proportion

extenuate 6 dilute, excuse, lessen, soften, temper, weaken 7 explain, justify, qualify, varnish 8 diminish, enervate, mitigate, moderate, palliate 9 gloss over 11 rationalize

exterior 4 skin 5 outer, shell 6 facade 7 outmost, outside, outward, surface 8 apparent 9 outermost 11 superficial

exterminate 4 kill 6 rub out 7 destroy, wipe out 8 massacre 9 eliminate, eradicate, finish off, liquidate, slaughter 10 annihilate, extinguish, obliterate

external 3 out 4 over 5 outer 7 foreign, outside, outward, surface 9 outermost 10 peripheral 11 superficial

externalize 4 show 6 embody, evince, excuse, expose, reveal 7 exhibit, justify 8 manifest 9 extenuate, incarnate, objectify, personify 11 rationalize 12 substantiate

extinct 4 cold, dead, gone, late 5 passé 6 bygone 7 archaic, defunct 8 deceased, departed, obsolete, perished, vanished 10 superseded

extinction 3 end 4 doom 5 death 6 demise 11 destruction, eradication, liquidation 12 annihilation, obliteration 13 disappearance, extermination

extinguish 3 end 5 crush, douse, erase, quash, quell 6 put out, quench, squash, stifle 7 abolish, blot out, blow out, destroy, eclipse, expunge, nullify, put down, wipe out 8 snuff out, stamp out, suppress 9 eliminate, eradicate, extirpate 10 annihilate, obliterate

extirpate 5 erase 6 cut out, efface, excise, resect, uproot 7 abolish, blot out, destroy, expunge, kill off, root out, wipe out 8 demolish 9 eliminate, eradicate 10 annihilate, deracinate, extinguish

extol 4 hymn, laud 5 cry up, exalt 6 praise 7 acclaim, applaud, commend, glorify, magnify 8 eulogize 9 celebrate 10 panegyrize

extort 5 wrest, wring 7 extract

extortion 8 exaction 9 blackmail

extra 3 odd 4 more, over 5 added, spare 6 de trop, rarely 7 reserve, surplus 8 leftover 9 lagniappe, redundant, unusually 10 additional, especially 11 superfluous 12 particularly, supplemental 13 supernumerary, supplementary

extract 4 pull, yank 5 evoke, glean, quote, wring 6 derive, eke out, elicit, remove 7 abridge, distill, essence, excerpt, passage, pull out, squeeze, take out 8 citation, condense, infusion 9 quotation, selection 11 concentrate

extraction 5 birth, blood, stock 6 origin 7 descent, essence, lineage 8 ancestry, pedigree 9 parentage 10 derivation 12 distillation

extraneous 5 alien, outer 6 exotic 7 foreign, outside 8 external 9 unrelated 10 immaterial, inapposite, incidental, irrelevant, peripheral 11 impertinent, inessential, superfluous, unessential 12 adventitious, inapplicable, nonessential

extraordinary 3 odd 4 rare 6 unique 7 amazing, notable, special, unusual 8 abnormal, atypical, singular, terrific, uncommon, unwonted 9 wonderful 10 noteworthy, phenomenal, remarkable, stupendous, tremendous 11 exceptional, outstanding

extravagance 5 frill, waste 6 excess, luxury 9 hyperbole, profusion 10 indulgence, lavishness 11 ostentation, prodigality, superfluity 12 immoderation, wastefulness

extravagant 4 wild 5 outré, undue 6 lavish 7 bizarre, extreme, profuse 8 over-

done, prodigal, reckless, wasteful
9 elaborate, excessive, fantastic,
grandiose, overblown 10 exorbitant,
hyperbolic, immoderate, inordinate,
profligate 11 exaggerated, implausible,
intemperate, nonsensical 12 ostentatious, preposterous, unrestrained
extreme 3 top 4 apex, dire, last, peak,
wild 5 crown, final, limit, ultra, undue
6 climax, excess, height, summit,
utmost, zenith 7 drastic, fanatic,
intense, maximal, maximum, outmost,
radical, violent 8 farthest, furthest, pinnacle, remotest, ultimate 9 desperate,
excessive, outermost, uttermost
10 immoderate, inordinate, outlandish,
outrageous 11 culmination, furthermost, unwarranted 12 unmeasurable,
unreasonable 13 revolutionary *degree:*
3 nth
extremely 4 very 5 ultra 6 highly, hugely,
mighty, overly, plenty 7 acutely, awfully, greatly, utterly 8 severely, terribly
9 immensely, seriously, unusually
10 remarkably, strikingly 11 exceedingly 12 terrifically
extremist 5 rabid, ultra 6 zealot 7 die-
hard, fanatic, radical 8 militant, ultraist
9 fanatical 10 monomaniac, ultraistic
11 reactionary 13 revolutionary
extremity 3 arm, end, leg, tip 4 acme,
apex, foot, hand, tail 5 limit, verge
6 apogee, vertex, zenith 8 terminal, terminus
extricate 4 free 5 loose 6 detach, redeem,
rescue 7 bail out, deliver, resolve, set
free, untwine 8 liberate, untangle 9 disengage 11 disencumber, disentangle,
distinguish, individuate 12 discriminate, disembarrass 13 differentiate
extrinsic 5 alien, outer 6 exotic 7 foreign, outside, outward 8 exterior, external, imported 10 incidental, extraneous
extrude 4 spew 5 eject 7 push out 8 press
out 10 squeeze out
exuberance 4 glee, life, zest 5 ardor
6 gaiety, spirit 7 abandon 8 buoyancy,
hilarity, vivacity 9 profusion 10 ebullience, enthusiasm, friskiness, liveliness
11 flamboyance, high spirits, zestful-
ness 12 exhilaration 13 effervescence,
sprightliness
exuberant 3 gay 4 lush, rank 5 happy
6 bouncy, elated, fecund, lavish, lively
7 buoyant, profuse, rampant, riotous,
zestful 8 fruitful, prodigal, prolific,
spirited 9 ebullient, luxuriant, sprightly, vivacious 10 flamboyant 11 exhilarated 12 effervescent, enthusiastic,
high-spirited

exude 4 emit, leak, ooze, seep, shed
5 issue 7 diffuse, display, emanate,
excrete, exhibit, give off, ooze out,
radiate, secrete 9 discharge
exult 4 crow 5 cheer, gloat, glory, revel
7 delight, rejoice 8 jubilate 9 celebrate
exultant 6 elated, joyful, joyous 7 gleeful
8 ecstatic, euphoric, jubilant 9 cock-a-
hoop, overjoyed, rejoicing, triumphal
10 triumphant
exultation 3 joy 4 glee 7 delight, ecstasy,
elation, rapture, triumph 8 euphoria,
gloating 9 jubilance, rejoicing 10 jubilation
eye 3 orb 4 lamp, ogle, scan, view
5 sight, watch 6 behold, goggle, look at,
ocular, oculus, peeper, regard, look up,
vision 7 inspect 8 check out, consider,
gaze upon, scrutiny 9 headlight
10 scrutinize *defect:* 6 myopia 9 hyper-
opia 10 emmetropia, presbyopia
11 astigmatism *disease:* 8 cataract, glaucoma, trachoma *doctor:* 7 oculist
11 optometrist *opening:* 5 pupil *part:*
4 iris, lens, uvea 5 pupil 6 cornea, reti-
na, sclera *relating to:* 5 optic 7 optical
socket: 5 orbit *Spanish:* 3 ojo
eyeball 4 scan 5 check, study 6 go over,
look at, peruse, survey 7 examine,
inspect, observe 8 appraise, check out,
evaluate, pore over 10 scrutinize
eye-catching 4 bold 5 gaudy, showy
6 flashy 7 salient 8 striking 9 arresting,
prominent 10 noticeable, remarkable
11 conspicuous
eyeful 6 looker 7 stunner 8 knockout
eyeglass 7 monocle
eyeglasses 5 specs 6 lenses 7 lorgnon
8 bifocals, pince-nez 9 lorgnette
10 spectacles
eyelash 6 cilium 11 hairbreadth
eyelet 4 hole 7 grommet 8 loophole,
peephole
eyepiece 4 lens 6 ocular
eye-popping 7 amazing 8 exciting, stirring 9 thrilling 10 astounding 11 astonishing, mind-blowing, spectacular
12 breathtaking
eyesore 4 blot, dump, mess 6 blight
7 blemish 8 atrocity 11 monstrosity
eyespot 6 blight, fungus 7 ocellus
eyetooth 6 canine
eyewash 3 rot 4 bunk 5 bilge, hooey,
tripe 6 bunkum 7 baloney, garbage,
hogwash, rubbish, twaddle 8 malarkey,
nonsense 9 poppycock 10 balderdash
13 horsefeathers
eyewitness 8 observer, onlooker
9 bystander, spectator
eyrie see AERIE

F

Fabergé product 3 egg **9** Easter egg
Fabian 4 Shaw (George Bernard), Webb (Beatrice, Sidney) **7** politic **8** cautious, dilatory **9** socialist **11** circumspect, calculating
fable 4 myth, tale, yarn **5** story **6** legend **7** fantasy, fiction, figment, parable **8** allegory *animal:* **8** bestiary
fabled 5 famed **6** famous, unreal **7** storied **8** fanciful, mythical, renowned **9** fictional, imaginary, legendary, pretended **10** fictitious **11** make-believe **12** mythological
fabric 3 aba, rep, web **4** lamé, repp **5** cloth, fiber, grain **7** texture **8** building, material, shirting **9** structure *coarse:* **5** crash, gunny **6** burlap, linsey, ratiné **7** cheviot, hopsack **8** homespun *corded:* **3** rep **4** repp **5** piqué **6** calico, moreen, poplin **7** pinwale **8** corduroy, paduasoy **9** bengaline *cotton:* **4** jean, leno **5** baize, chino, domet, drill, scrim, wigan **6** chintz, dimity, faille, madras, muslin **7** etamine, gingham, nankeen, percale, ticking **8** chambray, dungaree, nainsook, tarlatan *cotton and linen:* **4** huck **7** fustian **9** huckaback *crepe:* **8** marocain *dealer:* **6** draper, mercer *durable:* **4** huck, jean **5** chino, denim, drill **6** frieze, moreen **7** lasting, ticking **8** cretonne, dungaree *embroidered:* **9** baldachin **10** baldachino *finishing process:* **8** lustring **9** mercerize *flag material:* **7** bunting *glazed:* **6** chintz **7** cambric, holland *knitted:* **6** tricot **10** balbriggan *linen:* **7** cambric, lockram *looped:* **6** bouclé *lustrous:* **4** silk **5** moiré, satin, surah **7** taffeta **12** brilliantine *metallic:* **4** lamé *net:* **5** tulle **6** bobbinet, illusion *openwork:* **4** lace **8** filigree *ornamental:* **4** lace **5** braid **6** ribbon **7** bunting *pebbly-surface:* **8** barathea *pile-surface:* **5** panne, plush, terry **6** velour, velvet **7** duvetyn, velours **8** chenille, moleskin **9** velveteen *plaid:* **6** tartan *printed:* **5** batik, toile **6** calico, chintz, damask **7** allover, challis **8** cretonne, jacquard **11** toile de Jouy *puckered:* **6** plissé *raised pattern:* **4** lamé **7** brocade **10** brocatelle *satin weave:* **5** panne *sheer:* **4** lawn, mull **5** gauze, ninon, voile **6** dimity **7** batiste, chiffon, organdy, organza, tiffany **8** tarlatan *silk:* **6** faille, pongee, samite **7** foulard, grogram **8** paduasoy, sarcenet, sarsenet, shantung **9** bombazine *striped:* **3** aba **7** ticking **8** bayadere *synthetic:* **5** ninon, nylon, Orlon, rayon **6** Dacron *twill:* **4** jean **5** chino, drill, serge **7** foulard, nankeen, ticking **8** dungaree, shalloon **9** bombazine **10** broadcloth *unfinished:* **6** greige *waterproof:* **7** oilskin *wool:* **5** baize, loden, tweed **6** alpaca, caddis, camlet, duffel, duffle, melton, merino, wadmal, wadmel, wadmol, woolen **7** woollen **8** mackinaw, prunella **9** cassimere *wool, poor quality:* **5** mungo **6** shoddy *wool mixture:* **6** saxony **7** drugget, ratteen **8** moquette, shalloon, zibeline **9** zibelline *woven:* **4** weft **7** textile
fabricate 4 form, make **5** build, erect, frame, set up, shape **6** cook up, create, devise, invent, make up **7** concoct, dream up, fashion, produce, think up **8** assemble, contrive **9** construct, structure **11** manufacture, put together
fabrication 3 fib, lie **4** bull, jive **6** canard, deceit **7** fiction, figment, hogwash, product, untruth **8** assembly, building, creation **9** deception, fairy tale, falsehood, invention **10** concoction, production **11** manufacture **12** construction
fabulist *French:* **10** La Fontaine (Jean de) *Greek:* **5** Aesop *Roman:* **8** Phaedrus *Russian:* **6** Krylov (Ivan)
fabulous 5 super **7** amazing **8** mythical, terrific, wondrous **9** fantastic, legendary, marvelous, wonderful **10** astounding, fictitious, incredible, outrageous, phenomenal, prodigious, remarkable, stupendous **11** astonishing, extravagant, spectacular **12** mythological *animal:* **6** dragon **7** centaur, unicorn *bird:* **3** roc *serpent:* **8** basilisk **10** cockatrice
facade 4 face, mask **5** color, front, guise, put-on **6** veneer **8** disguise, exterior, frontage, pretense **10** appearance, camouflage, false front
face 3 mug, pan **4** dare, defy, dial, meet, phiz, puss, show, side **5** abide, brave, front, guise, honor, image, nerve **6** endure, facade, kisser, makeup,

mazard, oppose, resist, suffer, take on, visage **7** compete, contend, dignity, surface **8** confront, cope with, deal with, disguise, features, prestige, war paint **9** assurance, encounter, lineament, semblance, withstand **10** appearance, confidence, experience, expression, maquillage, reputation **11** countenance, self-respect

face-off 5 clash, set-to **13** confrontation

facet 4 edge, item, part, side **5** angle, bezel, front, phase, plane, point, trait **6** aspect, detail **7** element, feature, surface **9** attribute, component **10** appearance, particular

facetious 4 flip **5** comic, droll, smart, witty **6** blithe, joking **7** amusing, comical, jesting, jocular, joshing, kidding, risible, waggish **8** flippant, humorous **9** ludicrous, unserious, whimsical **10** irreverent, ridiculous **12** wisecracking **13** tongue-in-cheek

face-to-face 6 direct **7** contact, present, vis-à-vis **8** directly, in person, personal **10** personally

facile 4 deft, easy, glib, snap **5** light, quick, ready **6** adroit, expert, fluent, poised, simple, smooth **7** assured, cursory, offhand, shallow, voluble **8** skillful, untaxing **9** dexterous **10** effortless, simplistic **13** uncomplicated

facilitate 3 aid **4** abet, ease, help **6** assist, enable, smooth **7** advance, forward, further, promote **8** expedite, make easy, simplify

facility 3 aid, wit **4** bent, ease **5** knack, privy, skill **6** talent, toilet **7** ability, amenity, comfort, fluency, leaning **8** aptitude, bathroom, building, capacity, lavatory, washroom **9** advantage, dexterity **10** adroitness, competence, smoothness **11** convenience, institution, proficiency **12** installation **13** accommodation, establishment

facing 5 front, panel **6** contra, lining, toward, veneer **7** surface, vis-à-vis **8** covering, opposite, paneling **11** over against **down: 5** prone **up: 6** supine

facsimile 4 copy, dupe, fake, twin **5** clone, ditto, match, repro **6** carbon, double **7** replica **8** knockoff, likeness **9** duplicate, imitation, photocopy **10** carbon copy, dead ringer, similitude **11** counterpart, duplication, replication **12** reproduction

fact 4 dope **5** datum, event, truth **6** detail, gospel, truism, verity **7** episode, reality **8** evidence, incident **9** actuality **10** occurrence, particular, phenomenon **11** information **12** circumstance, intelligence

faction 4 band, bloc, camp, part, ring, sect, side, wing **5** cabal, group, party **6** caucus, circle, clique, sector, strife **7** combine, coterie, discord, machine, section **8** alliance, disunity, splinter **10** contingent, disharmony

factious 7 warring **8** contrary, divisive, partisan **9** dissident, insurgent, sectarian, seditious, turbulent **10** contending, malcontent **11** contentious, disaffected, dissentious, quarrelsome **12** disputatious **13** troublemaking

factitious 4 sham **5** bogus, false, phony **6** ersatz, forced, made-up, unreal **7** assumed, created, feigned, manmade, shammed **8** affected, invented, spurious **9** concocted, contrived, fashioned, pretended, simulated, synthetic, unnatural **10** artificial, fabricated **11** constructed, counterfeit **12** manufactured **13** counterfeited

___ **facto 4** ipso **6** ex post

factor 4 gene, item **5** agent, cause, proxy **6** broker, lender, number, symbol **7** divisor, element, exclude, include, resolve **8** attorney, emissary, quantity **9** component, majordomo, substance **10** antecedent, ingredient, multiplier **11** determinant **12** intermediary

factory 4 mill, shop **5** plant, works **8** workshop **9** sweatshop **11** machine shop

factotum 4 grub **5** gofer **6** drudge **7** servant **9** assistant, operative **11** functionary

factual 4 real, true **5** exact, valid **6** actual **7** certain, genuine, literal **8** absolute, positive **9** authentic, undoubted **10** undisputed **12** indisputable

faculty 4 bent, body, gift **5** flair, knack, power **6** talent **7** ability, college **8** aptitude, capacity, facility, function, instinct **9** educators, lecturers **10** department, professors **11** instructors

fad 4 chic, kick, mode, rage, whim **5** craze, furor, style, trend **6** furore, latest, whimsy **7** caprice, fashion **9** bandwagon **10** dernier cri

faddish 3 hot **4** chic **5** today **6** modish, red-hot, trendy, with-it **7** stylish, voguish **8** contempo **9** au courant **11** cutting-edge, fashionable

fade 3 die, dim, ebb **4** fail, pale, wane, wilt **6** lessen, vanish, weaken, wither **7** decline, lighten, wash out **8** decrease, discolor, diminish **9** disappear, evaporate

faded 3 dim, wan **4** drab, dull, pale **6** pallid **8** bleached, vanished, withered **9** etiolated, washed-out

Faerie Queene, The *author:* 7 Spenser (Edmund) *character:* 3 Ate, Una 4 Alma 5 Guyon, Talus 6 Abessa, Amavia, Amoret, Arthur, Cambel, Duessa, Palmer 7 Artegal, Corceca, Fidessa, Maleger, Sansloy 8 Calidore, Florimel, Fradubio, Gloriana, Lucifera, Orgoglio, Satyrane 9 Archimago, Britomart 11 Britomartis

Fafnir 6 dragon *brother:* 5 Regin 6 Fasolt, Reginn *father:* 8 Hreidmar *slayer:* 6 Sigurd 9 Siegfried *victim:* 6 Fasolt 8 Hreidmar

fag 4 do in, moil, tire, toil 5 serve, smoke, stick, weary 6 drudge, overdo, tucker 7 exhaust, fatigue, servant, wear out 8 drudgery, knock out 9 cigarette

fag end 4 butt, edge, fray 7 remnant

faience 11 earthenware

fail 3 die, end 4 bomb, fade, lack, lose, miss, sink, slip, stop, wane 5 break, flunk 6 fizzle, forget, ignore, lessen, weaken 7 decline, default, founder, give out, go under, neglect 8 fall flat, languish, miscarry 9 break down, fall short 10 disappoint, go bankrupt 11 deteriorate

failing 4 flaw, vice 5 fault 6 defect 8 weakness 9 weak point 10 deficiency 11 shortcoming 12 imperfection

failure 3 bum, dud 4 bomb, bust, flop, miss 5 decay, loser 6 fiasco, fizzle, nogood, outage 7 default, washout 8 collapse, fracture, omission 9 breakdown, cessation, oversight, unconcern 10 bankruptcy, deficiency, insolvency, negligence 11 defalcation, dysfunction, miscarriage 12 interruption 13 deterioration

fain 3 apt 5 eager, prone, ready 6 gladly, minded 7 willing 8 amenable, inclined 9 agreeable

fainéant 3 bum 4 idle, lazy 5 idler, sloth 6 loafer, torpid 7 goof-off, slacker 8 deadbeat, inactive, indolent, layabout, slothful, sluggard, sluggish 9 do-nothing, lazybones, shiftless 11 couch potato, ineffectual 13 lackadaisical

faint 3 dim, low, wan 4 hazy, pale, soft, weak, wilt 5 dizzy, light, swoon, vague, woozy 6 feeble 7 conk out, obscure, pass out, shadowy, syncope, unclear 8 black out, collapse, keel over 9 undefined 10 ill-defined, indistinct

fair 3 due 4 even, expo, fine, join, just, mild, okay, open, so-so 5 ample, blond, bonny, clear, equal, fresh, light, sunny 6 bazaar, blonde, comely, decent, honest, kermis, lovely, market, pretty, square 7 cricket 8 adequate, all right, balanced, carnival, festival, mediocre, middling, pleasant, pleasing, rainless, rational, sunshiny, unbiased 9 beautiful, cloudless, equitable, favorable, fortunate, impartial, objective, tolerable, unclouded 10 aboveboard, acceptable, attractive, evenhanded, exhibition, exposition, open-minded, reasonable 11 good-looking, indifferent, nonpartisan, respectable, sportsmanly 12 satisfactory, unprejudiced 13 disinterested, dispassionate, sportsmanlike

fair food 10 candy apple, candy floss, fried dough, funnel cake 11 cotton candy, elephant ear

fair-haired 3 pet 5 blond 6 blonde 7 beloved, darling, favored 8 favorite 9 fortunate

fairly 5 quite 6 nearly, rather 7 plainly 8 passably, properly, somewhat 9 tolerably 10 acceptably, deservedly, distinctly, moderately, reasonably 11 practically

fairness 6 candor 7 honesty 8 justness 9 good faith 12 impartiality

fairy 3 elf, imp, nix 4 puck 5 elfin, nixie, nymph, pixie, sylph 6 goblin, kobold, sprite 7 brownie, gremlin 10 leprechaun *king:* 6 Oberon *queen:* 3 Mab 7 Titania 8 Gloriana *shoemaker:* 10 leprechaun

fairy tale *author:* 4 Lang (Andrew) 5 Grimm (Jacob, Wilhelm), Wilde (Oscar) 7 Kipling (Rudyard) 8 Andersen (Hans Christian), Perrault (Charles) *character:* 4 Jack, Puck 6 Gretel, Hansel 8 Rapunzel, Tom Thumb 9 Snow White 10 Cinderella, Goldilocks, Thumbelina

faith 4 cult, sect 5 credo, creed, stock, troth, trust 6 belief, church, credit 8 credence, reliance, religion 9 certainty, certitude, communion, credulity 10 confidence, persuasion 12 denomination *article of:* 5 tenet

faithful 4 fast, just, true 5 liege, loyal, pious, tried 6 steady, trusty 7 devoted, dutiful, staunch 8 constant, follower, reliable, resolute, true-blue 9 religious, steadfast 10 dependable, scrupulous, unwavering 11 truehearted, trustworthy

faithfulness 5 piety, troth 6 fealty 7 loyalty 8 devotion, fidelity 9 adherence, constancy 10 allegiance, attachment

faithless 5 false, Punic 6 fickle, untrue 8 disloyal, recreant 10 perfidious, traitorous 11 treacherous 13 untrustworthy

faithlessness 7 perfidy, treason 8 betrayal 9 falseness, treachery 10 disloyalty, infidelity

fake 3 act, gyp **4** hoax, mock, sham **5** bluff, bogus, false, feign, fraud, phony, put on, spoof **6** affect, doctor, ersatz, forged, framed, humbug, pseudo **7** falsify, pretend **8** impostor, invented, simulate, spurious **9** brummagem, charlatan, concocted, fabricate, imitation, imposture, pinchbeck, pretended, simulated **10** artificial, fabricated, fictitious, fraudulent, simulation **11** counterfeit *combining form:* **5** pseud **6** pseudo

faker 4 sham **5** fraud, phony, quack **6** con man, hoaxer **8** deceiver, impostor **9** charlatan, con artist, pretender **10** mountebank **11** four-flusher **12** double-dealer **13** confidence man

fakir 7 ascetic, dervish **9** mendicant

falcon 4 hawk **5** hobby, saker **6** lanner, merlin **7** kestrel **9** peregrine *eye cover:* **4** seel *male:* **4** jack **6** tercel **7** tiercel **8** lanneret *mature:* **7** haggard *young:* **4** eyas

falcon-headed god see at EGYPTIAN

falconry 7 hawking *equipment:* **4** bell, hood, jess, lure *procedure:* **3** imp **4** cope, seel

Falkland Islands *capital:* **7** Stanley *colony of:* **7** Britain

fall 3 dip, ebb, sag **4** dive, drip, drop, dump, hang, plop, sink, slip, trip, wane **5** abate, crash, lapse, slide, slump, spill **6** autumn, drowse, give up, go down, header, plunge, sprawl, tumble **7** cascade, decline, descend, descent, devolve, go under, plummet, scatter, stumble, subside **8** collapse, decrease, diminish, keel over, nose-dive **9** hairpiece **10** depreciate **11** precipitate

fallacious 6 untrue **7** invalid **8** delusive, delusory **9** deceitful, deceptive, erroneous, sophistic **10** fraudulent

fallacy 5 error **6** canard **7** falsity, sophism, untruth **8** delusion **9** falsehood **11** non sequitur **13** misconception

fall apart 6 lose it **7** crumble **9** break down, decompose **10** go to pieces **11** come unglued, deteriorate **12** disintegrate

fall back 6 recede, recoil, retire **7** retract, retreat **8** withdraw **9** disengage, retrocede **10** retrograde

fall behind 3 lag **4** drag **5** delay, tarry, trail **6** dawdle, linger, loiter

fall flat 4 bomb, fail, flop, miss **6** fizzle

fall guy 4 dupe, fool, goat, gull **5** chump, front, patsy **6** stooge, sucker **8** front man **9** scapegoat **11** whipping boy

fallible 4 iffy, weak **5** dicey, frail, human **6** errant, erring, faulty **9** imperfect **10** unreliable

falling-out 3 row **4** beef, feud, fuss, spat, tiff **5** break, run-in, words **6** bicker, fracas, hassle **7** dispute, quarrel, rhubarb, wrangle **8** argument, conflict, squabble **9** brannigan **11** altercation, controversy **12** disagreement, estrangement

falloff 3 sag **4** drop, slip **5** slump **7** decline **8** downturn **9** downslide, downswing, downtrend **13** deterioration

fall out 5 argue, break, leave, occur **6** bicker **7** brabble, quarrel, wrangle **8** disagree, squabble

fallow 4 idle **5** inert **6** unsown **7** dormant, resting **8** inactive, unseeded, untilled **9** neglected, quiescent, unplanted **12** uncultivated

false 4 fake, mock, sham **5** bogus, dummy, hokey, lying, phony, wrong **6** ersatz, forged, hollow, pseudo, untrue **7** crooked, devious, feigned, seeming, unloyal **8** apostate, apparent, deluding, delusive, delusory, disloyal, recreant, specious, spurious **9** brummagem, deceitful, deceiving, deceptive, dishonest, distorted, erroneous, faithless, illogical, imitation, incorrect, pinchbeck, simulated **10** artificial, fictitious, fraudulent, inaccurate, misleading, perfidious, traitorous, unfaithful, untruthful **11** counterfeit, treacherous *combining form:* **5** pseud **6** pseudo

falsehood 3 fib, lie **5** fable **6** canard **7** fallacy, untruth, whopper **8** roorback **9** mendacity **11** fabrication **12** misstatement **13** prevarication

falseness 7 fallacy, perfidy **8** apostasy **9** treachery **10** disloyalty, infidelity **11** insincerity

false teeth 8 dentures

falsify 3 fib, lie **4** cook, deny **5** belie, fudge, slant **6** doctor, refute **7** deceive, distort, mislead **8** disprove, misstate **10** contradict **11** prevaricate **12** misrepresent

falsity 3 fib, lie **4** tale, yarn **5** fable **6** canard **7** untruth, whopper **9** falsehood, mendacity **11** fabrication **13** prevarication

Falstaff *companion:* **3** Nym **4** Peto **6** Pistol **8** Bardolph *composer:* **5** Verdi (Giuseppe) *creator:* **11** Shakespeare (William) *play:* **7** Henry IV *prince:* **3** Hal *tavern:* **9** Boar's Head

Falstaffian 3 fat **6** jovial **7** roguish **8** boastful **9** convivial, dissolute

falter 4 halt, limp, reel, sway, trip **5** quail, waver **6** flinch, teeter, totter, wobble **7** give way, stagger, stammer, stumble **8** hesitate **9** vacillate **12** shilly-shally

fame 4 note **5** éclat, glory, honor, kudos **6** esteem, regard, renown, repute **7** acclaim, stardom **8** standing **9** celebrity, notoriety **10** popularity, prominence, reputation **11** acclamation, immortality, recognition

famed 5 noted **6** marked **7** eminent, notable **8** renowned **9** notorious, prominent, well-known **10** celebrated **11** illustrious **13** distinguished

familiar 4 cozy **6** common, folksy **8** domestic, everyday, frequent, informal, intimate, standard **10** accustomed **11** comfortable, commonplace **12** conventional, recognizable **13** garden-variety

familiarity 4 ease **8** intimacy **9** closeness, knowledge **11** informality **12** acquaintance

family 3 kin **4** clan, folk, home, line, race **5** brood, folks, house, issue, stirp, stock, tribe **6** ménage, strain **7** dynasty, kindred, lineage, progeny **8** pedigree **9** bloodline, household, offspring *branch:* **5** stirp *lineage:* **4** tree **6** stemma **8** pedigree **9** genealogy

famine 4 want **6** dearth, hunger **10** starvation

famished 6 hungry **7** starved **8** ravenous, starving

famous 5 famed, noble, noted **6** fabled **7** eminent, notable, popular **8** historic, renowned **9** legendary, notorious, prominent, well-known **10** celebrated **11** illustrious, prestigious, redoubtable

fan 3 bug, nut **4** blow, buff, open, wind **5** lover, rouse **6** addict, arouse, expand, extend, kindle, rooter, ruffle, spread, stir up, unfold, votary, whip up, winnow **7** admirer, devotee, habitué **8** adherent, enkindle, follower, railbird **9** stimulate **10** aficionado, enthusiast *horseracing:* **7** turfman *India:* **6** punkah *movie:* **7** cineast **8** cineaste

fanatic 3 bug, nut **4** buff **5** fiend, freak, rabid **6** addict, maniac, votary, zealot **7** devotee, die-hard, habitué **10** aficionado, enthusiast

fanatical 5 fiery, rabid **6** ardent, fervid **7** extreme, fervent, zealous **8** frenetic, frenzied, maniacal, obsessed **9** perfervid **10** passionate **11** impassioned

fanaticism 4 zeal **5** mania **6** frenzy **8** zealotry **9** extremism, monomania

fancier 6 grower **7** amateur, admirer, breeder, devotee

fanciful 6 absurd, unreal **7** bizarre, fictive **8** fabulous, illusory, imagined, mythical, notional, romantic **9** fantastic, fictional, grotesque, imaginary

10 chimerical, fictitious **11** fantastical **12** preposterous

fancy 3 bee **4** posh, whim **5** dream, ritzy, shine, smart, taste **6** liking, megrim, notion, relish, snazzy, swanky, vision, whimsy **7** caprice, chimera, conceit, concept, dream up, elegant, fantasy, feature, imagine, picture **8** conceive, daydream, envision, fondness, judgment, velleity **9** capriccio, elaborate, intricate, inventive, visualize, whimsical **10** decorative, ornamental, partiality, propensity **11** extravagant, highfalutin, imagination, inclination

fandango 5 dance **9** malaguena

fanfare 4 pomp, show **5** array **7** display, panoply **8** flourish *trumpet:* **6** tucket

fanlike 7 plicate

fanny 3 bum, can **4** buns, butt, duff, moon, rear, rump, seat, tail, tush **5** booty, nates **6** behind, bottom, breech, heinie **7** caboose, hind end, keister, rear end, tail end **8** backside, buttocks, derriere **9** fundament, posterior

fantasia 6 vision **8** daydream, illusion, rhapsody **9** fairyland **10** apparition

fantasize 4 moon **5** dream, fancy **7** imagine **8** daydream **10** woolgather

fantastic 3 odd **4** wild **6** absurd, unreal **7** bizarre, surreal **8** fanciful, singular **9** eccentric, grotesque, imaginary, marvelous, monstrous, unearthly, whimsical **10** chimerical, far-fetched, improbable, incredible, outlandish, outrageous, prodigious, stupendous, tremendous **11** implausible, nonsensical, sensational, superlative **12** preposterous, unbelievable

fantasy 4 moon, whim **5** dream, fancy, freak **6** vagary, vision, whimsy **7** caprice, chimera, fiction, reverie **8** daydream, delusion, phantasm **9** imagining, invention, pipe dream **10** bizarrerie **11** imagination **12** grotesquerie

far 4 long **6** remote **7** distant **8** outlying *combining form:* **3** tel **4** tele, telo

far and wide 7 all over **10** everyplace, everywhere, throughout

faraway 4 lost **5** moony **6** absent, dreamy, remote **7** distant, removed **8** outlying **9** oblivious, unheeding **10** abstracted, distracted **11** preoccupied, inattentive **12** absentminded

farce 6 comedy, satire **7** mockery **8** travesty **9** burlesque, slapstick **10** caricature

farceur 5 clown, cutup, joker **7** buffoon

farcical 5 comic **6** absurd **7** comical, foolish, risible **9** laughable, ludicrous **10** ridiculous **12** preposterous

fare 4 diet, dine, food, pass, rate, toll **5** get on, price, track **6** manage, travel **7** come off, journey, make out, proceed, succeed **8** get along, progress, victuals **9** passenger, surcharge **10** provisions **11** comestibles

farewell 3 ave, bye **4** ta-ta **5** adieu, adios, aloha, congé **6** bye-bye, pip-pip, shalom, so long **7** aloha oe, cheerio, good-bye **8** swan song **9** bon voyage, departure **11** arrivederci, leave-taking, valediction, valedictory

far-fetched 5 fishy **6** absurd **7** dubious **8** doubtful, strained, unlikely **10** improbable, incredible **11** implausible, unrealistic **12** preposterous, unbelievable

far-flung 6 remote **7** distant, removed **8** outlying **10** widespread

farinaceous 5 mealy **6** floury **7** starchy *food:* **4** meal **5** flour, grits **6** cereal, hominy **7** polenta, pudding, tapioca

farm 4 till **5** croft, ranch **6** grange, rancho **7** hennery **8** estancia, hacienda, hatchery **9** cultivate, farmstead **10** plantation *building:* **4** barn, shed, silo *Dutch:* **6** bowery *Israeli collective:* **7** kibbutz *Russian:* **7** kolkhoz, sovkhoz

farmer 6 grower, tiller, yeoman **7** granger, planter, rancher **8** ranchero, ranchman **13** agriculturist *Russian:* **5** kulak *South African:* **4** Boer *tenant:* **6** cottar, cotter **7** crofter **12** sharecropper

farming 7 tillage **8** agronomy **9** husbandry **11** agriculture, cultivation

faro 5 monte *bet:* **7** sleeper *card:* **4** case, hock, soda

far-off 6 remote **7** distant, removed **8** outlying

far-out 3 rad **4** cool **5** outré, weird **6** groovy **7** bizarre, offbeat, radical **9** eccentric **10** avant-garde, off-the-wall, outlandish

farrago 4 hash, mess, olio **5** gumbo **6** jumble, medley, muddle **7** goulash, mélange, mixture **8** mishmash, shambles **9** potpourri **10** hodgepodge, miscellany

far-reaching 5 broad **8** sweeping **9** extensive, momentous, pervasive **10** portentous, widespread **11** significant, wide-ranging **13** comprehensive, consequential

farrier 5 smith **10** blacksmith, horseshoer

farsighted 4 sage, wise **9** hyperopic, prescient, sagacious **10** discerning

farthest 6 utmost **7** apogean, extreme, outmost **8** remotest, ultimate **9** outermost, uttermost

Fasching 8 carnival

fascinate 4 draw, wile **5** charm **6** allure, enamor, entice, please **7** attract, beguile, bewitch, enchant **8** enthrall, intrigue, transfix **9** captivate, enrapture, magnetize, mesmerize, spellbind

fascination 5 charm **6** allure, appeal **7** glamour **8** charisma **9** magnetism **10** attraction, witchcraft **11** enchantment **12** enthrallment

Fascist 4 Nazi **6** despot, Hitler (Adolf), tyrant **8** autocrat **9** Falangist, Mussolini (Benito) **10** Blackshirt

fashion 3 fad, fit, ton, way **4** chic, form, mode, mold, suit, tone, vein, wear **5** craze, shape, style, trend, usage, vogue **6** create, custom, design, devise, manner, method, sculpt, tailor **7** compose, costume, pattern **8** contrive **9** bandwagon, construct, fabricate **10** dernier cri **12** haute couture

fashionable 3 hip **4** chic, cool, posh, tony **5** fresh, ritzy, sharp, smart, swank, swish **6** chichi, du jour, modish, trendy, with-it **7** à la mode, current, dashing, faddish, popular, stylish, voguish **8** up-to-date **9** au courant, exclusive, happening **12** silk-stocking

fashion designer *American:* **4** Head (Edith) **5** Beene (Geoffrey), Blass (Bill), Dache (Lilly), Ellis (Perry), Karan (Donna), Klein (Anne, Calvin) **6** Jacobs (Marc), Lauren (Ralph), Mackie (Bob) **7** Galanos (James), Halston, Mizrahi (Isaac) **8** Galliano (John), Hilfiger (Tommy) **9** Claiborne (Liz), de la Renta (Oscar), Gernreich (Rudi) *Anglo-French:* **5** Worth (Charles Frederick) *Dominican:* **9** de la Renta (Oscar) *English:* **5** Quant (Mary) **8** Westwood (Vivienne) *French:* **4** Dior (Christian) **5** Bohan (Marc) **6** Cardin (Pierre), Chanel (Coco), Poiret (Paul) **6** Ungaro (Emanuel) **7** Balmain (Pierre), Lacroix (Christian), Montana (Claude) **8** Givenchy (Hubert de) **9** Courrèges (André), Lagerfeld (Karl) **12** Saint-Laurent (Yves), Schiaparelli (Elsa) *German:* **9** Lagerfeld (Karl) *Israeli:* **7** Mizrahi (Isaac) *Italian:* **5** Pucci (Emilio), Ricci (Nina) **6** Armani (Giorgio) **7** Cassini (Oleg), Versace (Gianni) **12** Schiaparelli (Elsa) *Japanese:* **6** Miyake (Issey) *Spanish:* **10** Balenciaga (Cristóbal)

fast 3 set **4** diet, easy, firm, Lent, soon, sure, true, wild **5** fixed, fleet, hasty, hitch, loose, loyal, quick, rapid, swift **6** firmly, prompt, snappy, speedy, stable **7** abstain, hastily, hurried, lasting, quickly, rapidly, staunch, swiftly **8** chop-chop, constant, faithful, full tilt, immobile, promptly, resolute, speedily

9 breakneck, dissolute, immovable, libertine 10 abstinence, profligate, recklessly, stationary 11 expeditious, promiscuous 12 lickety-split 13 expeditiously

fasten 3 fix, peg, pin, set, sew, tie, zip 4 bind, bolt, clip, hook, join, lace, lash, link, lock, moor, nail, seal, shut, weld 5 affix, cable, catch, chain, cinch, clamp, clasp, close, cramp, dowel, girth, hitch, latch, rivet, screw, stake, stick, strap, tie up, truss 6 anchor, attach, batten, buckle, button, couple, secure, skewer, solder, staple, tether 7 connect, mortise 8 buckle up

fastener 3 nut, peg, pin, tie 4 bolt, brad, clip, cord, frog, hasp, link, lock, nail, rope, snap, stud, tack, tape 5 catch, clamp, clasp, dowel, girth, hinge, hitch, latch, rivet, screw, spike, stake, strap 6 buckle, button, cotter, skewer, staple, tether, toggle, zipper 7 grommet, padlock, netsuke, shackle 8 coupling, cuff link, handcuff, seat belt, shoelace 9 connector, cotter pin, safety pin, thumbtack 10 clothespin

fastidious 5 fussy, picky 6 choosy, dainty, queasy 7 choosey, finical, finicky, refined 8 exacting 9 demanding, squeamish 10 meticulous, particular, pernickety 11 persnickety

fastness 4 fort, hold, keep 6 bunker, castle, refuge 7 alcazar, bastion, citadel, crannog, redoubt, sanctum 8 casemate, fortress, presidio 10 stronghold, tower house 11 strongpoint

fast-talking 4 glib 5 slick 6 facile 8 slippery 13 silver-tongued

fat 3 big, oil 4 flab, lard, suet, wide 5 beefy, broad, bulky, burly, cream, dumpy, gross, heavy, husky, large, lipid, obese, plump, pudgy, round, stout, thick, tubby 6 chunky, excess, fleshy, grease, portly, rotund, stocky, stubby, tallow 7 adipose, blubber, paunchy, porcine, surfeit, surplus, weighty 8 heavyset, oversize, thickset 9 corpulent 10 full-bodied, overweight, potbellied 11 superfluity

fatal 6 deadly, lethal, mortal 7 deathly, ruinous 8 terminal 9 incurable, pestilent 10 pernicious 12 pestilential

fatality 4 doom 5 death 8 casualty 10 deadliness

fata morgana 6 mirage 8 illusion

fat cat 5 mogul, nabob 6 big gun, bigwig, tycoon 7 big shot, magnate, pooh-bah 8 big wheel 9 moneybags, plutocrat 11 muckety-muck 13 high-muck-a-muck

fate 3 end, lot 4 doom, luck, ruin

5 death, karma 6 chance, kismet, upshot 7 destiny, fortune, outcome, portion 13 inevitability

fateful 6 deadly 7 ominous, ruinous 8 decisive 9 momentous, prophetic 10 portentous

Fates see at GREEK; NORSE; ROMAN

fathead 3 ass, oaf 4 boob, clod, dodo, dope, dolt, gawk, goof, goon, jerk, lump, mutt, yo-yo 5 cluck, clunk, dummy, dunce, idiot, moron, stock, stupe, yahoo 6 cretin, dimwit, donkey, doofus, dum-dum, nitwit, noodle, schlub, turkey 7 buffoon, dullard, jackass, schnook 8 dumbbell, imbecile, numskull 9 birdbrain, ignoramus, lamebrain, numbskull, simpleton

fatheaded 4 dull, dumb 5 dense, dopey, thick 6 obtuse, simple, stupid 7 doltish, idiotic 8 gormless 9 brainless, dimwitted, imbecilic 10 numskulled 11 numbskulled, thick-witted

father 3 dad, pop 4 dada, papa, père, sire 5 beget, breed, daddy, hatch, padre, pappy, pater, poppa, spawn 6 author, create, old man, parent, priest 7 builder, creator, founder, produce 8 ancestor, engender, generate, inventor, producer 9 architect, initiator, originate, patriarch, procreate 10 originator, prime mover *combining form:* 4 patr 5 patri, patro

Father Brown creator 10 Chesterton (Gilbert Keith)

fatherland 4 home, soil 7 country

Father Time's implement 6 scythe

fathom 4 know 5 probe, sound 7 discern, explore, measure 9 apprehend, figure out, penetrate 10 comprehend, understand 11 investigate

fathomless 7 abysmal, abyssal 8 profound 12 immeasurable

fatidic 5 vatic 6 mantic 7 Delphic, sibylic 8 Delphian, oracular, sibyllic 9 prophetic, prescient, sibylline, vaticinal 10 divinatory, predictive

fatigue 3 fag 4 poop, tire, wear 5 drain, weary 6 tucker 7 deplete, burn out, exhaust, frazzle, wear out 8 drudgery, wear down 9 tiredness, weariness 10 enervation, exhaustion *combat:* 7 frazzle 10 shell shock

Fatima *father:* 8 Mohammed, Muhammad *husband:* 9 Bluebeard *son:* 5 Hasan 6 Husayn *stepbrother:* 3 Ali

fatness 7 obesity 9 adiposity 10 corpulence, overweight

fatty 4 oily, rich 6 greasy 7 adipose 8 unctuous 10 oleaginous *combining form:* 4 lipo 5 adipo

fatuous 4 dumb, fond 5 inane, sappy,

silly **6** jejune, simple **7** asinine, foolish, puerile, witless

faucet 3 tap **4** bung, cock, gate **5** valve **6** spigot **7** hydrant, petcock **8** stopcock

Faulkner, William *character:* **3** Ike (Snopes), Joe (Christmas) **4** Eula (Varner Snopes), Flem (Snopes), Mink (Snopes) **5** Benjy (Compson), Caddy (Compson), Gavin (Stevens), Henry (Sutpen), Jason (Compson), Lucas (Beauchamp) **6** Dilsey, Temple (Drake) **7** Candace (Compson), Quentin (Compson) **8** Benjamin (Compson) *county:* **13** Yoknapatawpha *family:* **6** Benbow, Snopes, Sutpen **7** Compson **8** McCaslin, Sartoris **9** Beauchamp *novel:* **4** Town (The) **6** Hamlet (The) **7** Mansion (The), Reivers (The) **8** Sartoris **9** Sanctuary, Wild Palms (The) **11** As I Lay Dying **13** Light in August **14** Absalom, Absalom **15** Sound and the Fury (The) **17** Intruder in the Dust

fault 3 err, nag, sin **4** flaw, rift, slip, spot, vice, want **5** blame, break, knock, error, scold **6** accuse, defect, foible, miscue **7** censure, demerit, failing, fissure, frailty, mistake, upbraid **8** fracture, weakness **9** criticize, infirmity **10** San Andreas **11** culpability, dereliction, shortcoming **12** imperfection *line:* **4** rift **5** split **6** breach **7** fissure **8** crevasse

faultfinder 4 crab **5** grump **6** critic, griper, grouch, nagger, whiner **7** grouser **8** grumbler **10** bellyacher, complainer, criticizer, crosspatch

faultfinding 7 carping **8** captious, critical, nitpicky **9** criticism **10** censorious, nit-picking, pernickety **11** persnickety **12** overcritical **13** hypercritical

faultless 4 pure **7** perfect **8** innocent, unerring **9** guiltless **10** immaculate, impeccable, inculpable

faulty 4 awry **5** amiss, wrong **6** flawed, marred **7** botched, damaged, defaced, inexact, unsound **8** fallible, specious **9** blemished, defective, deficient, erroneous, imperfect, incorrect **10** fallacious, inaccurate *prefix:* **3** dys

faun 5 satyr

fauna 7 animals

Faunus *grandfather:* **6** Saturn *son:* **4** Acis **7** Latinus

Faust *author:* **6** Goethe (Johann Wolfgang von) *beloved:* **8** Gretchen *composer:* **6** Gounod (Charles)

faux 4 fake, sham **5** bogus, false, phony **6** ersatz **9** imitation, pretended, simulated, synthetic **10** substitute

faux pas 4 flub, goof, slip **5** boner, error, gaffe **6** boo-boo, howler, miscue, slipup **7** blooper, blunder, misstep, mistake, stumble **8** pratfall, solecism **9** gaucherie **11** impropriety

favor 4 baby, back, bias, boon, gift, okay **5** bless, bribe, grace, mercy, token, value **6** accept, behalf, choose, oblige, pamper, prefer, regard **7** indulge, present, support, sustain **8** courtesy, goodwill, interest, keepsake, kindness, resemble, sanction, sympathy **9** attention, patronage, privilege, take after **10** admiration, facilitate, indulgence, partiality **11** approbation, benevolence, countenance

favorable 4 fair **5** lucky **6** benign, biased, golden, timely, toward, useful **7** helpful, partial **8** pleasant, pleasing, positive **9** agreeable, benignant, fortunate, promising **10** auspicious, benevolent, propitious, prosperous **11** affirmative **12** advantageous **13** complimentary

favoring 4 rosy **6** timely, toward, useful **7** helpful **9** opportune **10** auspicious, beneficial, propitious **12** advantageous *prefix:* **3** pro

favorite 3 pet **7** dearest, popular, special **8** precious **9** preferred, well-liked **10** fair-haired, preference **11** frontrunner, teacher's pet, white-haired

favoritism 4 bias **8** cronyism, nepotism **10** partiality **12** one-sidedness

fawn 3 kid **4** deer, ecru **5** beige, toady **6** bister, grovel, kowtow **7** flatter, truckle, wheedle **8** blandish, bootlick **9** sweet-talk **11** apple-polish

fawning 6 smarmy **8** unctuous **9** parasitic **10** obsequious **11** sycophantic

fay 3 elf **4** puck **5** elfin, fairy, pixie **6** elfish, goblin, sprite **7** brownie **10** leprechaun

faze 3 cow **5** abash, daunt, throw **6** dismay, rattle **7** confuse, disturb, nonplus, perturb **8** befuddle, bewilder, confound, unsettle **9** discomfit, dumbfound, embarrass **10** disconcert **11** flabbergast

FBI director 5 Freeh (Louis) **6** Hoover (J. Edgar) **7** Mueller (Robert)

fealty 5 faith, troth **7** loyalty **8** devotion, fidelity **9** adherence, constancy, vassalage **10** allegiance, attachment **11** devotedness **12** faithfulness

fear 3 awe **5** alarm, angst, dread, panic, qualm, scare, worry **6** dismay, fright, horror, phobia, terror **7** anxiety, jitters **8** cold feet, disquiet, timidity **9** agitation, cowardice, misgiving **10** foreboding **11** disquietude, trepidation **12** apprehension, cowardliness, perturbation, presentiment, timorousness *of animals:* **9** zoophobia *of being buried* *alive:* 11 taphephobia *of cats:* 12 ailuro-phobia *of crowds:* 11 ochlophobia *of darkness:* 11 nyctophobia *of dirt:* 10 mysophobia *of fire:* 10 pyrophobia *of heights:* 10 acrophobia *of men:* 11 androphobia *of new things:* 9 neo-phobia *of open areas:* 11 agoraphobia *of pain:* 10 algophobia *of strangers:* 10 xenophobia *of thunder:* 12 bronto-phobia *of water:* 11 hydrophobia *of women:* 10 gynophobia

fearful 5 timid 6 afraid, aghast, scared, trepid 7 alarmed, anxious, jittery, pan-icky 8 alarmist, paranoid, timorous 9 terrified, tremulous 12 apprehensive

fearless 4 bold 5 brave 6 daring 7 gal-lant, valiant 8 intrepid, unafraid 9 dauntless 10 courageous 11 lionheart-ed 12 greathearted, stouthearted

Fear of Flying author 4 Jong (Erica)

fearsome 3 shy 5 scary, timid 6 afraid 7 extreme, intense 8 daunting, timorous 9 frightful 10 terrifying 11 frightening 12 intimidating

feasible 6 doable, likely, viable 8 possi-ble, suitable, workable 10 reasonable 11 practicable 12 tried-and-true

feast 3 eat 4 dine, meal 5 gorge 6 dinner, regale, repast, spread 7 banquet, indulge 8 potlatch *Hawaiian:* 4 luau *Scottish:* 3 foy

Feast of Lights 8 Hanukkah

Feast of Lots 5 Purim

Feast of Tabernacles 6 Sukkot 7 Sukkoth

feat 3 act 4 deed, gest 5 stunt, trick 6 action 7 exploit 11 achievement, per-formance, tour de force

feather 3 ilk 4 down, kind, sort, type 5 breed, order, pinna, plume, quill 6 fledge, fletch, pinion 7 species, vari-ety *kind:* 4 down 6 covert 7 contour, plumule, rectrix 8 scapular *part:* 3 web 4 barb, vane 5 shaft 7 barbule, calamus 8 barbicel

featherbrained 5 dizzy, giddy, silly 7 flighty, foolish 8 heedless 9 frivolous 11 light-headed, thoughtless

feathered 7 plumose

feathers 4 down 7 plumage

feature 4 item, mark, part 5 add-on, trait 6 aspect, detail, factor 7 article, ele-ment, fixture, gimmick, quality 8 hall-mark, property 9 attribute, component, lineament 10 attraction, ingredient 11 drawing card, peculiarity

febrile 3 hot 5 fiery 7 fevered, pyretic 8 feverish

feckless 4 weak 7 useless 8 carefree, impotent 11 incompetent, ineffective,

ineffectual 12 undependable 13 irre-sponsible

fecund 4 rich 7 fertile 8 fruitful, prolific 9 inventive 10 productive

fecundity 9 abundance, fertility 11 prod-igality 12 fruitfulness, productivity

Federalist writer 3 Jay (John) 7 Madison (James) 8 Hamilton (Alexander)

federation 5 union 6 league, nation 7 council 8 alliance 10 government 11 confederacy

fed up 4 sick 9 disgusted 11 exasperated

fee 3 cut, pay, tax 4 bill, cost, dues, hire, toll, wage 5 price 6 charge 7 expense, payment, rake-off, stipend, tuition 8 retainer 9 emolument 10 commission, recompense *minting:* 10 seignorage 11 seigniorage *wharf:* 7 quayage

feeble 4 puny, weak 5 frail 6 infirm, sickly, weakly 7 doddery 8 decrepit 9 doddering, unhealthy 10 inadequate

feebleminded 4 daft, dull, slow 5 dense, thick 6 stupid 7 doltish, foolish, idiotic, moronic, witless 8 imbecile, retarded 9 brainless, dim-witted, imbecilic 10 half-witted, slow-witted 11 hare-brained, thickheaded

feebleness 7 frailty 8 debility 9 fragility, infirmity 10 enervation, inadequacy 11 decrepitude

feed 3 eat 4 grub, hand, meal 5 feast, gorge, graze, stuff 6 browse, devour, fatten, fodder, ingest, regale, repast, supply, viands 7 banquet, consume, deliver, dish out, edibles, furnish, nour-ish, nurture, provide, sustain 8 dis-pense, hand over, victuals 9 partake of, provender, provision, refection 10 pro-visions

feedback 8 critique, reaction, response 9 criticism 10 evaluation

feed the kitty 4 ante

feel 5 grope, sense, touch 6 caress, fon-dle, handle, stroke 7 palpate

feeler 4 palp 5 probe 6 palpus 7 antenna 8 proposal, tentacle 12 trial balloon

feeling 3 air 4 aura, mood 5 hunch, sense, touch 6 notion, temper 7 emo-tion, inkling, opinion, outlook, passion, sensate 8 attitude, instinct, sentient 9 affection, emotional, intuition, sem-blance, sensation, sentiment, suspicion 10 atmosphere, impression, persuasion 11 affectivity, palpability, sensibility, sensitivity, tangibility

feign 3 act 4 fake, play, sham 5 bluff, put on 6 affect, assume 7 pretend 8 simu-late 9 dissemble 11 counterfeit, make believe

feigned 4 fake, sham 5 false, phony, put-on 7 assumed 8 imagined 9 imitation, insincere, pretended, simulated **10** fabricated, fictitious **11** counterfeit

feint 4 fake, hoax, play, ploy, ruse, sham, wile **5** trick **6** gambit **8** maneuver **9** stratagem *hockey:* **4** deke

feisty 6 frisky, plucky, spunky, touchy **7** bristly, fidgety **8** petulant, snappish, spirited **9** fractious, irascible **10** aggressive **11** quarrelsome

feldspar 6 albite **8** andesine **9** anorthite, moonstone **10** microcline, orthoclase **11** plagioclase *clay:* **6** kaolin

felicitate 6 salute **7** commend **10** compliment **12** congratulate

felicitous 3 apt, fit **4** meet **5** happy **6** proper, timely **7** apropos, fitting **8** apposite, pleasant, suitable **9** agreeable **10** delightful **11** appropriate

feline 3 cat, sly, tom **4** lion, lynx, pard, puma, puss **5** catty, felid, pussy, sleek, tiger **6** bobcat, cougar, jaguar, margay, ocelot, serval, slinky, sneaky, tomcat **7** caracal, catlike, cheetah, furtive, leonine, leopard, lioness, panther, tigress, wildcat **8** pussycat, stealthy *hybrid:* **5** liger, tigon **6** tiglon

fell 3 cut, hew, mow **4** down, drop, kill, raze **5** floor **6** poleax **7** cut down, flatten **8** knock off **9** bring down, knock down

Fellini film 8 Amarcord, Casanova, La Strada **9** Satyricon **10** I Vitelloni **11** La Dolce Vita **15** Nights of Cabiria **18** Juliet of the Spirits

fellow 3 bub, guy, joe, lad, man **4** buck, chap, dude, gent, mate, peer, twin **5** bloke, match **6** codger, cohort, hombre, person **7** comrade, consort, partner **8** confrere **9** associate, companion, copartner, gentleman **10** coordinate, reciprocal

fellow feeling 5 agape **7** concern, empathy, rapport **8** affinity, kindness, sympathy **9** affection **10** compassion, kindliness **11** consolation **13** understanding

fellowship 4 club **5** guild **6** league **7** coterie, society, stipend **8** sodality **9** communion, community **10** fraternity **11** association, brotherhood

felon 3 con **7** convict, whitlow **8** criminal **10** malefactor

felt 6 groped, sensed

felt hat 3 fez **5** derby, terai **6** fedora, trilby **7** homburg, stetson **8** snap-brim **9** wideawake

female 4 girl **5** woman **7** girlish, womanly **8** feminine *suffix:* **3** ess **4** ette, trix

Feminine Mystique author 7 Friedan (Betty)

feminist 10 suffragist

femme fatale 5 siren **7** Lorelei **8** Mata

Hari **9** temptress **10** seductress **11** enchantress

femur 9 thighbone

fen 3 bog **4** mire, quag, wash **5** marsh, swamp **6** morass, muskeg, slough **9** marshland

fence 3 bar, pen **4** cage, rail, pale, weir **5** hedge, parry **6** corral, paling, picket **7** barrier, enclose, railing **8** backstop, boundary, hoarding, palisade, receiver, sidestep, stockade **9** barricade, stone wall

fencer 7 duelist, épéeist **8** foilsman **9** swordsman

fencing 9 swordplay *attack:* **5** lunge **6** thrust **7** reprise, riposte *cry:* **6** touché *defense:* **5** parry *movement:* **4** volt *term:* **4** jury **5** forte, lunge **6** flèche, foible, touché *touch:* **3** cut, hit *weapon:* **4** épée, foil **5** blade, guard, saber, sabre **6** pommel

fender 4 skid **5** guard **6** buffer, bumper, shield **7** cushion, railing **8** mudguard

fennec 3 fox

Fenrir chain: **8** Gleipnir *father:* **4** Loki *form:* **4** wolf *mother:* **9** Angerboda **10** Angerbotha *slayer:* **5** Vidar **6** Vithar *victim:* **4** Odin

Fenway Park site 6 Boston

feral 4 wild **5** brute **6** brutal, savage **7** beastly, bestial, brutish, inhuman, untamed

Ferber novel 5 Giant, So Big **8** Cimarron, Show Boat **9** Ice Palace **13** Saratoga Trunk

Ferdinand beloved: **7** Miranda *father:* **6** Alonso

Ferdinand, King conquest: **7** Granada *daughter:* **6** Joanna *wife:* **8** Germaine, Isabella

fermata 4 hold **5** pause

ferment 4 boil, brew, stir **5** rouse, sweat **6** clamor, enzyme, excite, incite, leaven, seethe, simmer, unrest, work up **7** smolder, turmoil **9** agitation, commotion **12** restlessness

fermentation 7 zymosis **13** bioconversion

fern 4 tree **5** brake, holly, royal **6** Boston **7** bracken **8** polypody **10** maidenhair, spleenwort *leaf:* **5** frond

ferocious 4 fell, grim, wild **5** brute, cruel **6** brutal, fierce, savage **7** bestial, extreme, inhuman, intense, vicious, violent **8** barbaric, inhumane, ruthless **9** barbarous, rapacious, truculent

ferret out 4 find **5** dig up, flush **6** elicit **7** unearth **8** discover **9** ascertain

ferrule 3 cap, tip **4** band, ring, virl **6** collet

ferry 5 carry **6** convey **7** shuttle **9** transport

ferryman 6 Charon 9 gondolier
fertile 4 lush, rich 6 fecund 8 abundant, creative, fruitful, pregnant, prolific 9 bountiful, ingenious, inventive, luxuriant, plenteous 10 productive 12 reproductive
fertilize 5 beget, breed 6 enrich 8 generate 9 fecundate, pollinate 10 impregnate, inseminate
fertilizer 4 dung 5 guano, mulch 6 manure 7 compost 9 plant food
ferule 3 rod 5 stick
fervent 3 hot 4 keen 5 eager, fiery 6 ardent, devout, gung-ho 7 blazing, burning, earnest, glowing, intense, zealous 8 vehement 9 heartfelt 10 hot-blooded, passionate 11 impassioned, warm-blooded 12 enthusiastic, wholehearted
fervor 4 fire, heat, zeal 5 ardor 6 warmth 7 passion 8 devotion, violence 9 vehemence 10 devoutness, enthusiasm
fescennine 7 obscene 10 scurrilous
fess up 3 own 5 admit 9 come clean
fester 3 rot 6 rankle 7 inflame, putrefy 8 ulcerate 9 suppurate
festina ___ 5 lente
festival 4 fair, fete, gala 5 feast 6 fiesta 7 jubilee 8 carnival, jamboree 11 celebration, merrymaking
festive 3 gay 4 gala 5 jolly, merry 6 joyful, joyous 7 gleeful 8 mirthful 11 celebratory
festivity 4 bash, fair, fete, gala 5 feast, party, revel 6 affair, frolic, gaiety 7 blowout, revelry, whoopee 8 carnival, jamboree 9 rejoicing, merriment 11 celebration, merrymaking
festoon 4 deck, hang 5 adorn 6 bedeck 7 garland 8 decorate, ornament 9 embellish
fetch 3 get 4 draw, earn 5 bring, yield 6 take in 7 attract, bring in, realize 8 retrieve
fetching 4 fair 6 comely, lovely, pretty 7 winsome 8 alluring, charming, enticing, engaging, handsome, pleasing 9 appealing 10 attractive
fete 4 ball, bash, fair, gala 5 feast, honor, party 6 affair, fiesta, soiree 7 banquet, jubilee, shindig 8 carnival, festival, jamboree, wingding 9 celebrate, entertain 11 celebration, commemorate 13 entertainment
fetid 4 foul, high, rank 5 funky 6 putrid, rancid, smelly, strong 8 mephitic, stinking 10 malodorous
fetish 4 idol, juju, luck 5 charm 6 amulet 7 periapt 8 fixation, gris-gris, talisman 10 phylactery
fetor 4 odor, reek 5 stink 6 stench

fetter 3 tie 4 bind, bond, gyve 5 chain, check, irons 6 hobble, hog-tie, impede 7 enchain, manacle, shackle, trammel 8 handcuff, restrain 9 restraint
fettle 5 shape 6 health 7 fitness 9 condition 12 constitution
feud 6 enmity, strife 7 dispute, quarrel 8 argument, vendetta 9 hostility 11 controversy
feudal *estate:* 3 fee 4 feud, fief *jurisdiction:* 4 soke *laborer:* 4 serf *lord:* 5 laird, liege, thane 8 suzerain *status:* 9 vassalage *tax:* 7 tallage *tenant:* 6 vassal 7 homager, socager, vavasor 8 vavasour *tenure of land:* 6 socage *tribute:* 6 heriot
feuilleton 5 essay
fever 4 ague, fire, heat 5 flush, Lassa 6 dengue, frenzy 7 ferment, passion, pyrexia 8 delirium 9 calenture *recurrent:* 7 malaria, quartan, tertian
fevered 6 crazed, heated 7 burning, febrile, flushed 8 agitated, frenetic, restless 9 delirious 10 distracted, overheated 11 overwrought
feverish 3 hot 5 fiery 6 hectic 7 burning, febrile, flushed, pyretic 8 frenetic, frenzied 10 passionate 11 overwrought
fever tree 6 acacia 7 blue gum
few 4 rare 5 scant 6 meager, meagre, scanty, scarce, sparse 7 handful, limited 8 sporadic 9 scattered 10 infrequent, occasional, scattering, smattering, spattering, sprinkling *combining form:* 4 olig 5 oligo
fey 4 daft 5 campy, crazy, vatic 7 touched 8 oracular, precious 9 pixilated, prophetic, sibylline, visionary 11 clairvoyant 12 otherworldly
___-**fi** 3 sci
fiasco 3 dud 4 bomb, flop 5 farce, flask 6 bottle, defeat 7 blunder, debacle, failure, washout 8 abortion, disaster 11 miscarriage 13 embarrassment
fiat 5 edict, order 6 decree 7 command, dictate, mandate, warrant 8 sanction 11 endorsement 12 proclamation 13 authorization
fib 3 lie 4 tale 5 story 7 falsify, falsity, untruth 9 falsehood, mendacity 10 taradiddle 11 fabrication, prevaricate
fiber 3 web 4 noil, pita 5 grain, istle 6 fabric, strand, thread 7 texture *basketry:* 5 istle *brain:* 4 pons *coarse:* 4 jute 8 piassava *coconut husk:* 4 coir *rope:* 4 bast, hemp 5 sisal 8 henequen *silky:* 5 kapok *small:* 6 fibril *substructure:* 7 micelle, spongin *synthetic:* 5 nylon, Orlon, rayon, saran, vinal 6 Dacron 7 spandex *woody:* 4 bast *woollike:* 7 lanital

fibrous 4 ropy, wiry 5 tough, woody
6 sinewy 7 stringy
fibula 4 bone 5 clasp
fichu 5 scarf
fickle 7 flighty 8 unstable, variable,
volatile 9 mercurial 10 capricious,
changeable, inconstant, unfaithful,
unreliable 12 undependable 13 temperamental, unpredictable
fiction 4 tale, yarn 5 fable, story 7 fantasy, figment 8 pretense 9 fish story,
invention, narrative 10 concoction
11 fabrication
fictional 6 made-up, unreal 8 notional
9 imaginary 11 make-believe 12 suppositious
fictitious 4 fake, mock, sham 5 bogus,
faked, false, phony 6 ersatz, made-up,
unreal, untrue 7 assumed, created
8 cooked-up, fanciful, illusory, imagined, invented, mythical, spurious
9 concocted, fantastic, imaginary, simulated, trumped-up 10 apocryphal, artificial, chimerical, fabricated 11 make-
believe 12 suppositious
fiddle 3 toy 4 play, rack 5 alter, cheat
6 dawdle, diddle, doodle, finger, meddle, monkey, potter, putter, tamper, tinker, trifle, violin 7 swindle 9 interfere
10 fool around, manipulate, mess
around
fiddle-faddle 3 rot 4 bosh, bull, bunk,
nuts 5 fudge, drool, hokum, hooey
6 bunkum, drivel, hoodoo, humbug,
piffle 7 baloney, blarney, hogwash, rubbish, twaddle 8 nonsense, pishposh,
tommyrot 9 poppycock 10 applesauce,
balderdash, flapdoodle
___ **Fideles** 6 Adeste, Semper
Fidelio *composer:* 9 Beethoven (Ludwig
van) *hero:* 9 Florestan *heroine:*
7 Leonora
fidelity 5 ardor, piety, troth 6 fealty
7 loyalty 8 devotion 9 adherence, constancy 10 allegiance, attachment
11 staunchness 12 faithfulness
13 dependability, steadfastness
fidget 6 fantod, fiddle, jitter, squirm,
twitch 7 wriggle
fidgety 5 antsy, jumpy 6 uneasy 7 jittery,
nervous, restive, squirmy, twitchy
8 restless
field 3 lea 4 area, mead, turf 5 green,
milpa, orbit, range 6 domain, meadow,
métier, region, sphere 7 demesne, pasture, purview, terrain 8 dominion, gridiron, precinct, vocation 9 bailiwick,
champaign, specialty, territory
10 department, discipline, occupation
field crop 3 hay 4 corn, oats 5 grain,
wheat 6 cotton 7 alfalfa 8 soybeans

field deity 3 Pan 4 Faun 5 Fauna
6 Faunus
field glasses 10 binoculars
field hand 4 hoer 5 sower 6 picker
7 laborer, planter
Fielding novel 6 Amelia 8 Tom Jones
13 Joseph Andrews
field marshal *Austrian:* 8 Radetzky
(Joseph) *British:* 6 Napier (Robert),
Raglan (Baron), Wavell (Archibald),
Wilson (Henry) 7 Roberts (Frederick)
8 Wolseley (Garnet) 9 Kitchener (Horatio) 10 Montgomery (Bernard) *French:*
4 Foch (Ferdinand) 6 Joffre (Joseph-
Jacques-Césaire), Pétain (Philippe) *German:* 6 Keitel (Wilhelm), Paulus
(Friedrich), Rommel (Erwin), Rupert
(Prince) 9 Mackensen (August von),
Rundstedt (Karl von), Waldersee
(Alfred von) 10 Kesselring (Albert)
Japanese: 8 Sugiyama (Hajime) *Prussian:* 6 Moltke (Helmuth von) *Russian:*
7 Kutuzov (Mikhail), Suvorov (Aleksandr) 8 Potemkin (Grigory)
field mouse 4 vole
field officer 5 major 7 colonel
fiend 3 bug, imp, nut 5 demon, devil,
freak, Satan 6 addict, Belial, diablo,
maniac, zealot 7 devotee, fanatic,
habitué, Lucifer, monster, Old Nick,
serpent 8 Apollyon, succubus 9 Beelzebub 10 enthusiast, Old Scratch 13 Old
Gooseberry
fiendish 3 bad 4 evil 5 cruel 6 malign,
savage, wicked 7 baleful, demonic,
hellish, inhuman, malefic, satanic,
vicious 8 demoniac, devilish, diabolic,
infernal, sinister 9 barbarous, difficult,
ferocious, malicious, malignant 10 diabolical
fierce 4 fell, grim, wild 5 cruel 6 brutal,
savage, wicked 7 brutish, hostile, inhuman, intense, vicious, violent, wolfish
8 inhumane, pitiless, ruthless, terrible,
vehement 9 barbarous, bellicose, ferocious, merciless, truculent 10 aggressive, determined
fiery 3 hot, red 5 afire 6 ablaze, aflame,
ardent, fervid, fierce, heated, red-hot,
torrid 7 burning, febrile, fervent, flaming, flaring, igneous, intense, peppery
8 broiling, feverish, spirited, vehement,
white-hot 9 flammable, hotheaded, irritable, perfervid 10 mettlesome, passionate 11 combustible, inflammable,
impassioned
fiesta 4 fete 5 party 6 frolic 8 carnival,
festival, jamboree 9 merriment
fife 4 pipe 5 flute
fifth *combining form:* 5 quint

fig *genus:* 5 Ficus *sacred:* 5 pipal *variety:* 5 elemi 6 Smyrna
fight 3 row, war 4 bout, buck, duel, feud, fray, spat, tiff 5 brawl, broil, clash, joust, match, melee, repel, scrap, set-to 6 affray, attack, battle, combat, fracas, oppose, oppugn, resist, rumble, tussle 7 contend, contest, dispute, quarrel, scuffle, wrangle, wrestle 8 conflict, skirmish, slugfest, squabble, struggle, traverse 10 aggression, donnybrook, free-for-all 11 altercation
fighter 3 pug 5 boxer 7 brawler, soldier, warrior 8 champion, pugilist, scrapper 9 combatant, gladiator, man-at-arms, mercenary 11 interceptor
fighter plane 3 MiG, Roc 4 Zero 5 Sabre 6 bomber, Fokker, Hawker, Mirage, Voodoo 7 Corsair, Harrier 8 Spitfire 11 interceptor
fighting fish 5 betta
figment 5 dream, fable, fancy 7 chimera, fiction 8 daydream, illusion, phantasm 9 invention, unreality 11 contrivance, fabrication
figure 3 add, sum, tot 4 cast, form, mold, rule, tote 5 count, digit, frame, image, model, motif, shape, total 6 cipher, decide, design, device, effigy, motive, number, reckon, settle, symbol 7 compute, integer, numeral, outline, pattern, resolve 8 conclude, estimate, physique 9 calculate, character, determine, enumerate *geometric:* 4 cone, cube 5 rhomb 6 circle, isogon, square 7 decagon, ellipse, hexagon, nonagon, octagon, polygon, rhombus 8 pentacle, pentagon, rhomboid, tetragon, triangle 9 rectangle 10 hexahedron, octahedron 11 icosahedron 12 dodecahedron, rhombohedron *human:* 4 nude 5 atlas 7 telamon 8 caryatid *ornamental:* 6 statue 8 gargoyle
figurehead 4 pawn, tool 5 front 6 minion, puppet 7 cat's-paw 8 creature 10 instrument, mouthpiece
figure of speech 5 trope 6 aporia, simile 7 litotes 8 metaphor, metonymy 10 synecdoche
figure out 5 crack, learn, solve 6 decide, decode, fathom 7 resolve, unravel 8 decipher, discover, unriddle 9 ascertain, determine
figure skating *jump:* 4 axel, loop, lutz 5 split 6 rocker 7 bracket, counter, salchow 11 spreadeagle *spin:* 5 camel
figurine 9 statuette
Fiji *capital:* 4 Suva *explorer:* 4 Cook (Capt. James) 6 Tasman (Abel) *island:* 3 Gau 4 Koro 6 Ovalau 8 Viti Levu 9 Vanua Levu *island group:* 3 Lau

6 Yasawa *language:* 6 Fijian 7 English *monetary unit:* 6 dollar *neighbor:* 5 Samoa 7 Vanuatu
filch 3 cop, nip 4 crib, lift, take 5 boost, pinch, steal, swipe 6 pilfer, snitch 7 purloin
file 3 row, rub 4 line, rank, rasp, tier 5 lodge, march, place, queue 6 smooth 7 archive, arrange, corrupt, dossier 10 emery board
filial 5 sonly 7 duteous, dutiful
filibuster 5 delay, stall 10 adventurer
filigree 4 lace 6 design 7 pattern 8 fretwork, openwork, ornament 10 decoration 13 embellishment, ornamentation
fill 3 jam 4 clog, cloy, cram, glut, heap, lade, load, pack, pile, plug, sate, stop 5 block, choke, close, gorge, stock, stuff 6 charge, stodge 7 congest, engorge, inflate, occlude, pervade, satiate, satisfy, stopper, surfeit 8 permeate *interstices:* 4 calk 5 caulk, chink, putty
filled 5 awash, flush, sated 6 packed 7 replete 9 saturated
filler 5 squib 7 packing, padding, tobacco, wadding 8 stuffing
fillet 4 band 5 slice, snood, strip 6 ribbon, stripe 7 bandeau, banding 8 headband *anatomical:* 9 lemniscus *architectural:* 6 listel, reglet, taenia *meat:* 10 tenderloin
fill in 3 sub 4 clew, clue, post 6 advise, detail, insert, notify 7 apprise 8 acquaint, complete 10 substitute
fill-in 3 sub 4 temp 6 backup 7 stopgap 9 alternate, expedient, makeshift, surrogate, temporary 10 substitute 11 locum tenens, pinch hitter, replacement, succedaneum
fillip 3 tap 4 goad, kick, spur 5 boost, tonic 6 buffet, strike 7 impetus, wrinkle 8 catalyst, stimulus 9 incentive, stimulant, stimulate 10 inducement, motivation 13 embellishment
film 4 coat, scum, show, skim, skin 5 flick, glaze, layer, movie, Mylar, shoot 6 cinema, lamina, patina 7 tarnish 8 membrane, pellicle 9 celluloid, photoplay 11 picture show 13 motion picture, moving picture
filmy 4 hazy 5 gauzy, misty, sheer, wispy 6 dainty 8 delicate, gossamer 10 diaphanous 11 transparent
fils 3 son
filter 4 sift 5 clean, leach, sieve 6 purify, refine, screen, strain 7 clarify, cleanse 9 percolate
filth 4 crud, dirt, dung, muck, slop, smut 5 dreck, grime, slime, trash 6 ordure, refuse, sludge 7 squalor 9 obscenity
filthy 4 base, foul, vile 5 black, dirty,

grimy, gross, gunky, mucky, muddy, nasty **6** coarse, cruddy, grubby, ribald, scuzzy, skanky, smutty, sordid **7** obscene, raunchy, squalid, unclean **8** indecent **9** loathsome, offensive, repulsive, revolting **12** scatological

filthy lucre 4 cash, loot, pelf **5** bread, bucks, dough, money, moola **6** boodle, riches, moolah, wampum **7** cabbage, scratch **8** currency

fin 3 arm **4** bill **5** fiver, pinna **7** airfoil, flipper *type:* **6** caudal, dorsal **7** ventral **8** pectoral

finagle 5 cheat, trick **6** wangle **7** snaffle, swindle, wheedle **8** fast-talk, maneuver, scrounge **9** bamboozle, machinate

final 3 end **4** last **6** ending, latest **7** closing **8** hindmost, terminal, ultimate **10** concluding, conclusive, definitive **11** examination

finale 3 end **4** coda **5** close, finis **6** capper, climax, ending, payoff, windup, wrap-up **7** closing **10** conclusion, denouement **11** culmination, termination

finalize 3 end **5** close, sew up, tie up **6** decide, finish, wind up, wrap up **7** approve **8** complete, conclude, solidify **9** terminate **10** consummate

finally 6 at last, lastly **7** someday **8** at length **9** belatedly **10** at long last, eventually, ultimately **12** subsequently

finance 4 back, bank, fund **5** endow, funds, money, stake **6** credit **7** banking, promote, revenue, sponsor, support **8** bankroll **9** grubstake, patronize, subsidize **10** capitalize, investment, underwrite

financial 6 fiscal, pocket **8** business, economic, monetary **9** pecuniary **10** commercial *plan:* **6** budget *statement:* **12** balance sheet

financier *American:* **4** Hill (James Jerome), Ryan (Thomas Fortune), Sage (Russell) **5** Astor (John Jacob), Baker (George Fisher), Eaton (Cyrus), Field (Cyrus West), Gould (Jay), Grace (William Russell), Green (Hetty) **6** Biddle (Nicholas), Boesky (Ivan), Girard (Stephen), Mellon (Andrew), Morgan (John Pierpont, Junius Spencer), Morris (Robert), Rogers (Henry Huttleston), Yerkes (Charles Tyson) **7** Peabody (George) **10** Vanderbilt (Cornelius, William) *British:* **6** Baring (Alexander), Rhodes (Cecil) **7** Gresham (Thomas) *French:* **6** Necker (Jacques) **7** Colbert (Jean-Baptiste) *German:* **7** Schacht (Hjalmar) **10** Rothschild (Amschel, Jakob, Karl, Mayer, Nathan, Salomon)

finch 4 pape **5** junco, serin, zebra **6** canary, linnet, siskin, towhee

7 bunting, chewink, redpoll, sparrow **8** cardinal, grosbeak, longspur **9** crossbill, seedeater

find 3 gem **4** gain, meet, spot **5** catch, dig up, hit on, reach, sight **6** attain, detect, locate, supply, turn up **7** discern, furnish, scare up, uncover, unearth **8** bump into, come upon, discover, meet with, perceive, treasure **9** determine, discovery, encounter **10** experience **13** treasure trove

find out 4 hear **5** catch, learn **6** detect **7** catch on **8** discover, perceive **9** ascertain, determine

fine 3 end, top **4** fair, keen, levy, pure, thin **5** bonny, close, clear, dandy, mulct, sheer **6** amerce, choice, minute, ornate, punish, purify, subtle **7** clarion, damages, elegant, forfeit, penalty **8** all right, delicate, penalize, pleasant, splendid, superior **9** beautiful, enjoyable, excellent, first-rate **10** punishment, reparation

finery 5 array **6** attire **7** apparel, regalia **8** clothing, frippery, glad rags, ornament **9** caparison, full dress, trappings, trimmings **10** decoration, Sunday best

finesse 5 dodge, evade, skill, skirt **6** jockey **7** beguile, cunning, exploit **8** maneuver, subtlety **9** dexterity **10** adroitness, artfulness, manipulate

Fingal's Cave island 6 Staffa

finger 5 blame, digit, index, pinky, strum, touch **6** accuse, pinkie **7** palpate **8** identify, pinpoint *bone:* **7** phalanx *combining form:* **6** dactyl

finicky 5 fussy, picky **6** choosy, dainty, prissy **7** choosey **8** exacting **9** squeamish **10** fastidious, meticulous, particular, pernickety **11** persnickety

finis 3 end **5** close **6** finale **10** completion, conclusion

finish 3 end **4** do in, kill, slay, stop **5** cease, close, glaze, use up **6** cut off, ending, finale, murder, patina, polish, windup, wrap up **7** closing, consume, destroy, execute, exhaust, surface **8** complete, conclude, dispatch, finalize, terminus **9** cessation, liquidate, terminate **10** completion, conclusion, denouement, run through **11** termination *dull:* **3** mat **4** matt **5** matte *second:* **5** place *third:* **4** show

finished 4 done, over, ripe **5** ideal **7** done for, perfect, refined, through **8** achieved, complete, over with, polished, washed-up **9** perfected **10** consummate

finite 5 bound, fixed **7** bounded, limited, precise **9** definable **10** restricted **12** determinable

fink 3 rat **5** Judas **6** betray, snitch, squeal **7** traitor **8** betrayer, informer, quisling, snitcher **11** backstabber **13** strikebreaker

Finland 5 Suomi *Arctic region:* **7** Lapland *capital:* **8** Helsinki *city:* **5** Espoo, Turku **6** Vantaa **7** Tampere *ethnic group:* **4** Lapp, Sami *gulf:* **7** Bothnia *invader:* **9** Alexander *island:* **5** Karlö **6** Kimito **9** Vallgrund *island group:* **5** Åland *lake:* **5** Inari **6** Saimaa **7** Keitele **8** Pielinen *language:* **7** Finnish, Swedish *monetary unit:* **4** euro *monetary unit, former:* **6** markka *neighbor:* **6** Norway, Russia, Sweden

Finlandia composer 8 Sibelius (Jean)

Finnigans Wake author 5 Joyce (James)

Finnish *bath:* **5** sauna *epic:* **8** Kalevala *god:* **6** Jumala

fir 4 pine **6** balsam, Fraser **7** conifer, Douglas **9** evergreen *genus:* **5** Abies

fire 3 can, pep, vim, zip **4** bake, brio, burn, cast, dash, hurl, sack, stir, toss, zeal, zest, zing **5** ardor, blaze, drive, flame, flare, fling, glare, ingle, light, pitch, rouse, salvo, shoot, spark, throw, torch, verve, vigor **6** arouse, energy, excite, fervor, flames, ignite, kindle, spirit **7** animate, boot out, dismiss, enthuse, inferno, inflame, inspire, kick out, passion, provoke **8** enkindle **9** calenture, discharge, holocaust, terminate **10** combustion, enthusiasm, liveliness **13** conflagration *combining form:* **3** pyr **4** igni, pyro *god:* **4** Agni, Loki **6** Vulcan **10** Hephaestus

firearm see GUN

firebrand 8 agitator **10** incendiary, instigator

firebug 5 torch **8** arsonist **10** incendiary, pyromaniac

firecracker 5 squib **6** banger **9** explosive **10** cherry bomb, noisemaker

firedog 7 andiron

firedrake 6 dragon

firefly 12 lightning bug

fire opal 7 girasol

fireplace 5 grate, ingle *equipment:* **6** fender, screen **7** andiron *part:* **3** hob **6** hearth, mantel

fireplug 7 hydrant

fire up 5 anger, annoy, rouse, spark **6** excite, ignite, incite, kindle **7** enliven, inflame, inspire, provoke **8** enkindle, irritate

firework 6 petard, rocket **8** pinwheel, sparkler **11** pyrotechnic, Roman candle *cluster:* **9** girandole

firkin 3 keg, tun, vat **4** butt, cask, pipe **6** barrel, vessel **8** hogshead

firm 3 set **4** fast, hard, sure **5** fixed, rigid, solid, sound, stiff, tight, tough **6** harden, outfit, secure, settle, stable, steady, strong, sturdy **7** abiding, adamant, certain, company, concern, improve, settled, staunch, unmoved **8** business, constant, definite, enduring, faithful, resolute, specific, vigorous **9** steadfast, tenacious **10** determined, enterprise, inflexible, stipulated, strengthen, unwavering, unyielding **11** established, partnership, substantial, unfaltering, well-founded **13** establishment

firmament 3 sky **5** vault **6** sphere, welkin **7** expanse, heavens **8** empyrean

firmness 7 resolve **8** decision, security, solidity, strength, tenacity **9** constancy, stability **10** durability, resolution **13** determination

first 4 arch, head **5** alpha, chief, prime **6** maiden, primal **7** highest, initial, leading, lead-off, opening, pioneer, premier, primary, supreme **8** champion, dominant, earliest, foremost, headmost, original **9** inaugural, initially, paramount, principal, sovereign **10** aboriginal, preeminent, primordial *prefix:* **4** prot **5** proto

firstborn 4 heir **6** eldest, oldest

first-class 3 top **4** A-one, best, fine **5** prime **6** tip-top **7** capital, supreme **8** five-star, superior, top-notch **9** excellent, top-drawer

firsthand 6 direct **7** primary **9** immediate

first man in space 7 Gagarin (Yury)

first showing 5 debut **7** opening **8** premiere

First State 8 Delaware

firth 3 arm, bay **4** cove, gulf **5** inlet **6** harbor, slough **7** estuary

fiscal 8 monetary **9** budgetary, financial

fish 3 bob, net **4** cast, gill, hint **5** angle, seine, trawl, troll **7** gillnet, sniggle *angler:* **9** goosefish *aquarium:* **4** barb **5** betta, danio, guppy, platy, tetra **7** cichlid, gourami, rasbora **8** goldfish **9** angelfish *basket:* **5** creel *catfish:* **8** bullhead, hornpout *cod:* **4** cusk, hake, ling **6** burbot, tomcod **7** pollack, pollock *combining form:* **6** ichthy *croaker:* **4** drum **7** corbina **8** kingfish, sea trout, weakfish **10** squeteague *eellike:* **5** moray **6** conger **7** hagfish, lamprey *eggs:* **3** roe **5** spawn *electric:* **7** torpedo **9** stargazer *flatfish:* **3** dab **4** butt, dace, sole **5** bream, brill, fluke **6** plaice, turbot **7** halibut **8** flounder *food:* **3** cod, eel **4** bass, carp, cero, hake, ling, scup, shad, sole, tuna **5** jurel, perch, scrod, skate, smelt, trout **6** bonito, caviar, kipper, mullet, plaice, pompon, salmon, tautog, wrasse **7** alewife, catfish, cavalla, escolar,

grouper, haddock, halibut, herring, pollack, pollock, pompano, sardine, sea carp, snapper **8** brisling, crevalle, flounder, mackerel *game:* **4** bass, pike, tuna **5** cobia, perch, trout **6** grilse, marlin, salmon, tarpon **8** pickerel **9** swordfish *grunt:* **7** pigfish *herring:* **4** shad, sild **5** sprat **7** alewife, sardine **8** brisling, pilchard *kind:* **3** gar, ray **4** bass, cero, chub, dory, goby, jack, opah, pike, rudd, scup, tuna **5** bream, cisco, loach, perch, porgy, shark, skate, smelt, snook, tench, tunny, wahoo **6** blenny, bonito, dorado, marlin, minnow, mullet, permit, puffer, remora, sauger, sucker, tarpon, tautog, warsaw, wrasse **7** anchovy, buffalo, capelin, cavalla, chimera, cowfish, crappie, dolphin, grunion, haddock, hogfish, jewfish, mudfish, oarfish, piranha, pupfish, sardine, sawfish, sculpin, snapper, sunfish, tilapia, whiting **8** albacore, blowfish, bluefish, bluegill, bonefish, chimaera, filefish, gambusia, grayling, halfbeak, ladyfish, lookdown, lumpfish, lungfish, mackerel, menhaden, moonfish, pickerel, pipefish, rockfish, sailfish, seahorse, skipjack, stingray, sturgeon, tilefish, warmouth, wolffish **9** amberjack, barracuda, greenling, jacksmelt, killifish, mummichog, pilotfish, spadefish, swordfish, topminnow, trunkfish, whitebait, whitefish **10** butterfish, flying fish, needlefish, parrotfish, silverside, tripletail, yellowtail **11** muskellunge, pumpkinseed, stickleback, triggerfish **12** schoolmaster *luminescent:* **11** hatchetfish, lanternfish *minnow:* **3** koi **4** carp, chub, dace **6** shiner *pan:* **5** bream, perch, trout **7** crappie, sunfish **8** bluegill, rock bass **11** pumpkinseed *porgy:* **4** scup **7** pinfish **10** sheepshead *relating to:* **7** piscine *rockfish:* **8** bocaccio, lionfish, rosefish *salmon:* **3** dog **4** chum, coho **6** sebago **7** chinook, sockeye *spear:* **3** gig **7** harpoon, trident *stew:* **8** cioppino, matelote **13** bouillabaisse *trap:* **4** weir *trout:* **4** char **5** charr **7** rainbow **9** cutthroat **11** Dolly Varden *voracious:* **6** caribe **7** piranha *young:* **3** fry **4** parr **5** larva, smolt **6** alevin, grilse
fisherman 6 angler
fish hawk 6 osprey
fishhook *adjunct:* **5** snell *part:* **4** barb **5** shank
fishing line 4 trot **7** setline **8** longline, trotline *float:* **3** bob **5** quill *leader:* **5** snell
fishing lure 3 fly **4** bait **5** spoon **7** spinner
fishing net 5 seine, trawl
fishlike mammal 4 orca **5** whale

6 dugong, sea cow **7** dolphin, grampus, manatee, narwhal **8** cetacean, porpoise
fish story 3 fib, lie **4** bunk, yarn **11** fabrication **12** exaggeration **13** overstatement
fishwife 5 harpy, scold, shrew, vixen **6** virago **9** termagant, Xanthippe
fishy 7 dubious, suspect **8** doubtful, unlikely **9** ambiguous, dubitable, equivocal, uncertain **10** suspicious **11** problematic **12** questionable
fission element 7 uranium **9** plutonium
fissure 3 gap **4** gash, hole, part, rent, rift **5** break, chasm, chink, cleft, crack, split **6** breach, cleave, divide, schism **7** crevice, discord, opening, rupture **8** crevasse, fracture **10** disharmony, separation
fist 4 duke, grip, hand **5** clamp, grasp **6** clench, clinch, clutch
fit 3 apt, set **4** hale, jibe, just, sane, suit, turn **5** adapt, agree, frame, ready, sound, spasm, spell, tally, throe **6** access, accord, adjust, attack, become, belong, decent, go with, proper, seemly, square, tailor, useful **7** capable, conform, healthy, prepare, qualify, seizure, tantrum **8** assemble, decorous, dovetail, eligible, paroxysm, suitable **9** agree with, congruous, consonant, harmonize, reconcile **10** applicable, convenient, correspond, felicitous, go together **11** accommodate, appropriate
fitful 6 random, spotty **7** erratic **8** periodic, sporadic, variable **9** haphazard, hit-or-miss, irregular, spasmodic, uncertain **10** changeable, convulsive, herky-jerky, inconstant **12** intermittent
fitness 4 trim **5** order, shape **6** fettle, health, kilter, repair **7** account, decorum, service, utility **8** capacity **9** condition, propriety, relevance **11** eligibility, suitability **13** applicability
fit out 3 arm, rig **5** equip **6** outfit **7** appoint, furnish **8** accouter, accoutre
fitting 3 apt, due **4** able, just, meet, part, true **5** happy, right **6** proper, seemly **7** apropos, germane **8** apposite, relevant, suitable **9** accessory, befitting, pertinent, qualified **10** applicable, attachment, felicitous, harmonious **11** appropriate
fit together 4 hook, join, mesh **6** hook up **7** connect **8** dovetail **9** integrate
Fitzgerald novel 10 Last Tycoon (The) **11** Great Gatsby (The) **16** Tender Is the Night **17** All the Sad Young Men, Tales of the Jazz Age **18** This Side of Paradise **21** Beautiful and the Damned (The)
five *combining form:* **4** pent **5** penta

6 quinqu 7 quinque *group of:* 6 pentad 7 quintet

five-dollar bill 3 fin

fivefold 9 quintuple

Five Nations 8 Iroquois *member:* 7 Cayugas, Mohawks, Oneidas, Senecas 9 Onondagas

five-sided figure 8 pentagon

five-star 6 deluxe, superb 8 superior, top-notch 9 excellent, first-rate 10 first-class 11 outstanding

five-year period 6 luster, lustre 7 lustrum

fix 3 jam, rig, set 4 cook, cure, geld, mend, mess, moor, root, spay, spot, work 5 affix, alter, catch, patch, ready, renew, rivet, solve, state, stick 6 adjust, anchor, assign, attach, change, decide, doctor, fasten, neuter, pickle, plight, repair, revamp, scrape, secure, settle, square, steady 7 appoint, arrange, correct, dilemma, resolve, restore, specify, work out 8 castrate, discover, overhaul, position, renovate, solution 9 condition, establish, stabilize, sterilize 11 predicament

fixation 5 craze, mania 6 fetish 9 obsession 11 fascination, infatuation

___ **fixe** 4 idée, prix

fixed 3 pat, set 4 fast, firm, sure 6 frozen, secure, stable, stated, steady 7 abiding, certain, limited, precise, settled 8 constant, definite, enduring, immobile, resolute 9 exclusive, immovable, immutable, permanent, steadfast, tenacious 10 inflexible, invariable, restricted, stationary, stipulated, unswerving, unwavering 11 determinate, unalterable 12 concentrated, unchangeable 13 circumscribed

fizz 4 buzz, foam, hiss 5 froth 6 bubble, spirit 7 bubbles, sparkle, sputter 10 effervesce, liveliness 13 effervescence

fizzle 4 bomb, fail, flop 6 fiasco 7 failure, misfire 8 miscarry, peter out 10 effervesce 11 fall through

fjord *Baffin Island:* 9 Admiralty *Denmark:* 3 Ise, Lim 5 Lamme *Iceland:* 4 Axar, Eyja 5 Horna, Skaga, Vopna *Norway:* 3 Tys 4 Bokn, Nord, Salt, Stor, Tana, Vest 5 Lakse, Ranen, Sogne 9 Stavanger, Trondheim *Spitsbergen:* 3 Ice *Svalbard:* 4 Stor

flab 3 fat 4 bulk, lard 5 flesh 7 blubber, fatness 9 cellulite 10 corpulence 11 love handles

flabbergast 3 awe 4 stun 5 amaze, shock, throw 7 astound, nonplus 8 astonish, bowl over, surprise 9 dumbfound, overwhelm

flabby see FLACCID

flaccid 4 limp, soft, weak 6 feeble, flabby, floppy 8 flexible

flag 3 ebb, lag, sag, tag 4 fade, fail, hail, iris, jack, sign, swag, tail, tire, waft, wane, wave, wilt 5 abate, color, droop, stone 6 banner, burgee, colors, ensign, guidon, pennon, signal, weaken 7 bunting, decline, pendant, pennant 8 bannerol, gonfalon, languish, Old Glory, penalize, registry, standard, streamer, tricolor 9 banderole, blue peter, oriflamme, Union Jack 10 Jolly Roger 11 deteriorate 12 Stars and Bars

flagellate 4 beat, flog, hide, lash, whip 5 whale 6 larrup, lather, stripe, switch, thrash 7 scourge 9 horsewhip

flagitious 4 evil 6 sinful, wicked 7 corrupt, vicious 8 criminal, depraved, infamous, perverse, shameful 9 miscreant, nefarious, perverted 10 degenerate, scandalous, villainous 11 disgraceful

flagon 3 jug 4 ewer 5 stoup 6 vessel 7 tankard

flagpole 4 mast 5 staff *rope:* 7 halyard

flagrant 4 bold, rank 5 gross 6 wanton 7 blatant, glaring, heinous, obvious 8 striking 9 atrocious, egregious, monstrous 10 outrageous 11 conspicuous

flagstone 5 shale, slate

flag-waver 7 patriot 8 jingoist, loyalist 10 chauvinist 11 nationalist 12 superpatriot

flail 4 club, beat, flog, whip 6 strike, thrash, thresh 7 scourge 8 flounder, thresher

flair 4 bent, chic, élan, gift 5 knack, style 6 genius, talent 7 ability, aptness, faculty 8 aptitude, tendency 10 proclivity 11 inclination

flak 4 fire 5 abuse 6 shells 7 censure, vitriol 9 brickbats, criticism, hostility 10 opposition 11 disapproval 12 condemnation, fault-finding

flake 3 bit 4 chip, kook, peel 5 scale 6 lamina 7 oddball 8 crackpot, fragment 9 eccentric

flake off 4 chip, peel 5 scale 9 exfoliate 10 desquamate

flaky 3 odd 5 goofy, nutty, wacky, weird 6 fickle, screwy 7 bizarre, erratic, offbeat 9 eccentric

flambé 6 ablaze, aflame, alight 7 blazing, flaming

flamboyant 4 loud 5 gaudy, showy 6 flashy, florid, ornate, rococo 7 baroque, splashy 8 colorful, luscious 10 over-the-top 12 ostentatious

flame 4 beau, dear, fire, glow, love 5 ardor, blaze, flare, flash, honey, light, lover 7 beloved, darling, passion, sweetie 8 ladylove, truelove 9 boyfriend, inamorata, inamorato 10 brilliance, brightness, girlfriend, heartthrob, sweetheart

flamen 6 priest

flaming 5 afire, fiery 6 ablaze, alight, ardent, red-hot 7 blazing, burning, fervent, flaring, ignited, intense 10 hot-blooded, passionate 11 conflagrant, impassioned

flammable 8 burnable 9 ignitable 10 incendiary 11 combustible *liquid:* 3 gas, oil 7 acetone, alcohol, ethanol 8 gasoline, kerosene 9 petroleum 10 turpentine

Flanders *capital:* 5 Lille *language:* 7 Flemish

flaneur 12 boulevardier, man-about-town

flank 4 abut, side 6 adjoin, border

flap 3 tab, tap 4 beat, flog, fold, slap, stew, wave, wing 5 fling, panel 6 crisis, dither, lather, pother, tumult, uproar 7 aileron, flutter, turmoil 9 agitation, commotion, confusion

flapdoodle 3 rot 4 bosh, bull, nuts 5 drool, fudge, hokum, hooey 6 bunkum, drivel 7 baloney, blarney, hogwash, rubbish 8 malarkey, nonsense, tommyrot 9 poppycock 10 applesauce, balderdash 12 blatherskite, fiddle-faddle, fiddlesticks

flapjack 7 hotcake, pancake 11 griddle cake

flare 4 burn 5 blaze, burst, flame, flash 6 signal 7 flicker 8 outburst

flare-up 5 blaze, burst, flame, flash, surge 8 eruption, outburst 9 explosion

flaring 5 afire, fiery 6 ablaze, aflame, alight 7 blazing, burning 11 conflagrant

flash 3 ray 4 beam, rush, snap, show 5 blaze, blink, crack, flame, flare, glare, gleam, glint, jiffy, shake, shine, showy, spark, speed 6 dazzle, expose, flaunt, glance, minute, moment, second 7 display, disport, exhibit, flicker, glamour, glimmer, glisten, glitter, instant, pizzazz, shimmer, show off, spangle, sparkle, twinkle 8 brandish 9 coruscate 11 coruscation, scintillate, split second 13 scintillation

flashy 4 loud 5 gaudy, jazzy, showy 6 brazen, florid, garish, glitzy, ornate, snazzy, sporty, tawdry, tinsel 7 blatant, chintzy, glaring, insipid 9 sparkling 10 flamboyant, glittering 12 meretricious, ostentatious

flask 6 bottle, fiasco, flacon 7 ampulla, canteen, costrel, thermos

flat 3 dim, mat 4 dead, drab, dull, even 5 banal, bland, exact, fixed, flush, level, muted, plane, prone, rooms, stale,

vapid 7 insipid, prosaic 8 lodgings, tenement, unsavory 9 apartment, colorless, innocuous 10 flavorless, lackluster, monotonous

flatfish see at FISH

flatland 4 mesa 5 plain 6 steppe, tundra 7 plateau 9 tableland

flat-out 8 absolute 9 downright 10 absolutely

flatten 4 deck, down, dull, even, fell, raze 5 crush, floor, level 6 smooth, squash 9 knock down, prostrate

flattened at the poles 6 oblate

flatter 4 coax, suit 5 toady 6 become, cajole, praise, stroke 7 adulate, blarney, gratify, wheedle 8 blandish, bootlick, butter up, soft-soap 9 sweet-talk

flattery 5 smarm 6 butter, praise 7 blarney 8 cajolery, soft soap, toadyism 9 adulation, sweet talk 10 sycophancy 11 compliments 12 blandishment, ingratiation, unctuousness

Flaubert, Gustave *birthplace:* 5 Rouen *heroine:* 4 Emma (Bovary) *novel:* 8 Salammbô 12 Madame Bovary

flaunt 4 show, wave 5 flash, flout, vaunt 6 expose, parade 7 display, disport, exhibit, show off 8 brandish, flourish

flavor 4 race, tang, zest, zing 5 smack, spice, taste, tinge 6 relish, season 7 variety, version

flavorless 4 flat 5 bland, stale 7 insipid 8 unsavory 11 unpalatable

flavorsome 5 sapid, tasty, yummy 6 savory 9 delicious, palatable 10 appetizing, delectable 11 good-tasting

flaw 3 gap, rip, sin 4 blot, chip, tear, vice 5 crack, fault 6 defect 7 blemish 8 weakness 9 deformity 12 imperfection

flawed 5 amiss 6 faulty, marred 7 damaged, spoiled 8 impaired 9 defective, imperfect

flawless 4 pure 5 ideal, model 6 intact 7 perfect 8 seamless, unmarred 9 exquisite 10 immaculate, impeccable 11 unblemished

flax 5 linen *fiber:* 3 tow *prepare:* 3 ret 4 card 5 dress 6 hackle, scutch

flaxen 4 fair 5 blond, straw 6 blonde, golden, yellow 7 towhead

flay 4 beat, lash, peel, skin 7 blister, censure, lambast, upbraid 8 lambaste 9 castigate, criticize, excoriate

flea 6 chigoe, jigger 7 chigger *water:* 7 daphnid

Fleance's father 6 Banquo

flèche 5 spire

fleck 3 dot 4 mark, mote, spot 5 flake, speck 6 dapple, mottle, streak, stripe 7 spatter, speckle, stipple 8 particle 9 bespeckle

Fledermaus, Die 3 bat *character:* **5** Adele, Falke, Frank **6** Alfred **9** Rosalinde **10** Eisenstein *composer:* **7** Strauss (Johann)

fledge 4 rear **7** feather

fledgling 4 colt, tyro **6** novice, rookie **8** beginner, freshman, neophyte, newcomer **10** apprentice

flee 3 fly, lam, run **4** bolt, scat, skip **5** elude, scoot, scram, skirr, steal **6** decamp, escape **7** abscond, make off, run away, scamper, vamoose **8** stampede, turn tail **9** skedaddle **10** make tracks

fleece 3 rob **4** bilk, clip, gaff, milk, rook, skin, soak, wool **5** bleed, cheat, cozen, mulct, shear, stick, sweat **6** extort, hustle, rip off **7** defraud, swindle **8** flimflam **10** overcharge

fleecy 5 downy **6** fluffy, pilose, woolly **7** hirsute **9** whiskered **10** flocculent

fleer 4 gibe, gird, jeer, jest, mock, quip **5** flout, laugh, scoff, scout, sneer, taunt

fleet 4 fast, navy, spry **5** agile, brisk, group, hasty, quick, rapid, swift **6** argosy, armada, nimble, speedy **8** flotilla **9** breakneck **10** harefooted

fleeting 5 brief **7** passing **8** fugitive, volatile **9** ephemeral, fugacious, momentary, temporary, transient **10** evanescent, short-lived, transitory

Fleming, Ian *hero:* **9** James Bond *novel:* **4** Dr. No **9** Moonraker **10** Goldfinger **11** Thunderball **12** Casino Royale **13** Live and Let Die **16** You Only Live Twice **18** From Russia with Love

flesh 4 beef, meat, skin **5** stock **7** kindred **9** offspring, relatives, substance

fleshly 5 obese **6** animal, bodily, carnal **7** lustful, profane, secular, sensual **8** corporal, physical, sensuous, temporal **9** corporeal, epicurean, luxurious, sybaritic **10** voluptuous

fleshy 3 fat **5** ample, beefy, burly, gross, heavy, hefty, husky, meaty, obese, plump, pudgy, stout, tubby **6** chubby, chunky, portly, rotund **7** porcine, weighty **9** corpulent **10** overweight, well-padded *fruit:* **4** pome **5** berry, drupe

Fletcher's partner 8 Beaumont (Francis)

fleur-de-lis 4 iris

flex 4 bend **5** tense

flexible 5 lithe, loose **6** docile, floppy, limber, pliant, supple **7** elastic, pliable, springy, willowy **8** amenable, bendable, stretchy, yielding **9** adaptable, compliant, malleable, tractable

flexion 3 bow **4** bend, fold, turn **5** angle

flexuous 5 fluid, lithe, snaky **7** sinuous, winding **8** tortuous **10** circuitous, convoluted, meandering, serpentine **11** anfractuous

flick 4 film, show **5** movie **13** motion picture, moving picture

flicker 4 bird, film, flit, hint **5** flash, gleam, glint, movie, waver **6** quiver **7** twinkle **10** woodpecker **13** motion picture, moving picture

flickering 7 lambent **8** unsteady

flier 3 ace **5** pilot **6** airman **7** aviator, birdman, handout **8** aviatrix, brochure, circular **9** throwaway

flight 3 hop, lam **4** rout, soar, slip, wing **5** flock, floor, flush, flyby, story **6** escape, flying, series **7** getaway **8** breakout

flighty 5 dizzy, giddy, silly, swift **7** foolish **8** freakish, skittish, unstable, volatile **9** frivolous, mercurial, transient **10** capricious, changeable, inconstant **11** empty-headed, harebrained **13** irresponsible

flimflam 3 con, gyp **4** bilk, dupe, fake, fool, gull, hoax, jazz, sham **5** cheat, cozen, fraud, hokum, trick **6** chouse, deceit, diddle, humbug **7** chicane, deceive, defraud, swindle **8** hoodwink, trickery **9** bamboozle, deception, moonshine **10** balderdash, double-talk **11** hornswoggle

flimflammer 3 gyp **5** cheat **6** con man **7** diddler, sharper **8** swindler **9** defrauder **11** four-flusher **12** double-dealer

flimsy 4 limp, weak **5** cheap, filmy, frail, gauzy, sheer **6** feeble, flabby, sleazy, slight, spindly **7** flaccid, fragile, rickety, tenuous, unsound **8** decrepit, delicate, gossamer **10** diaphanous, improbable **11** implausible, transparent **12** unconvincing **13** insubstantial

flinch 5 quail, start, wince **6** blench, cringe, recoil, shrink

fling 3 peg **4** cast, emit, fire, flap, hurl, plop, rush, shot, slap, stab, tear, toss **5** binge, chuck, heave, pitch, shoot, spree, throw **6** affair, charge, hurtle, launch **7** splurge **8** catapult

flip 4 glib, leaf, pert, riff, toss, wise **6** breezy, riffle, ruffle **8** turn over **10** somersault **11** impertinent, smart-alecky

flip-flop 5 U-turn, waver **6** sandal, switch, waffle **7** reverse **8** reversal **9** about-face, turnabout, vacillate, volte-face **10** turnaround **11** vacillation

flippancy 5 cheek **6** levity **8** archness, pertness **9** cockiness, freshness, frivolity **10** cheekiness, impishness **11** roguishness

flippant 4 glib, pert **5** sassy, saucy

6 breezy, cheeky 11 impertinent, smart-
alecky 13 disrespectful

flirt 3 toy 4 flit, fool, minx, ogle, vamp
5 dally, tease 6 coquet, trifle, wanton
8 coquette 10 experiment, mess around

flit 3 fly, zip 4 dart, pass, rush, sail, scud,
whiz, wing 5 flash, hurry, scoot, speed
7 flicker, flutter, twinkle

flitter 4 dart, flap, wing 5 hover, waver
6 quiver 7 skitter 9 fluctuate

flivver 6 jalopy 9 tin lizzie

float 3 bob, fly 4 buoy, cork, hang, raft,
ride, sail, scud, swim, waft 5 drift,
hover 6 wander 7 pontoon, propose
8 levitate 9 negotiate

floater 3 bum, vag 4 hobo, raft 5 tramp
7 drifter, vagrant 8 derelict, vagabond
10 roustabout

floating 5 fluid, loose 6 adrift 7 buoyant,
movable 8 moveable, shifting, variable
10 adjustable 11 fluctuating

flocculent 5 flaky 6 fleecy, fluffy, woolly

flock 3 mob 4 army, bevy, herd, host,
mass, pack, rout 5 brood, bunch,
cloud, covey, crowd, drove, group
6 flight, gaggle, gather, legion, scores,
throng 8 assemble, assembly, converge
9 multitude 11 aggregation 12 congregation

floe 3 ice 4 berg 7 glacier, iceberg 8 ice
field

flog 3 tan 4 beat, cane, flap, hide, lash,
slog, whip 5 birch, drive, flail, whale
6 larrup, lather, stripe, switch, thrash
7 cowhide, leather, scourge 10 flagellate

flood 4 fill, flow, flux, glut, pour, rush,
tide 5 burst, drown, float, spate, swamp
6 deluge, engulf, stream 7 current,
freshet, immerse, Niagara, torrent
8 alluvion, cataract, inundate, overflow,
submerge 9 avalanche, cataclysm, overwhelm 10 inundation, outpouring

floor 4 base, down, drop, fell 5 amaze,
level, shock, story 6 ground 7 astound,
flatten 8 astonish, audience, bowl
down, bowl over, surprise 9 dumbfound, knock down 11 flabbergast

flop 3 dud 4 bomb, bust, fail, fall
5 lemon, loser 6 bummer, fizzle, turkey
7 clinker, failure

floppy 4 limp 6 flimsy 7 flaccid
8 diskette, flexible

flora 6 plants 10 vegetation

flora and fauna 5 biota

Florence *bridge:* 12 Ponte Vecchio *cathedral:* 5 Duomo *family:* 6 Medici *museum:*
6 Uffizi 8 Bargello *palace:* 5 Pitti *river:*
4 Arno

florid 3 red 5 flush, gaudy, ruddy, showy
6 ornate, rococo 7 baroque, flowery,
flushed, glowing 8 rubicund, sanguine,

sonorous 9 bombastic, elaborate,
overblown 10 euphuistic, flamboyant,
rhetorical 11 declamatory 12 magniloquent 13 grandiloquent

Florida *capital:* 11 Tallahassee *city:*
5 Miami, Tampa 6 Naples, Venice
7 Hialeah, Key West, Orlando 8 Sarasota 9 Palm Beach 11 St. Augustine
12 Jacksonville, St. Petersburg *college,
university:* 7 Rollins, Stetson *key:*
4 Long, Vaca, West 5 Largo 7 Big Pine
9 Matecumbe, Sugarloaf *lake:* 9 Kissimmee 10 Okeechobee *nickname:* 8 Sunshine (State) *park:* 10 Everglades *river:*
6 Indian 7 St. Johns 8 Suwannee
12 Apalachicola *state bird:* 11 mockingbird *state flower:* 13 orange blossom
state tree: 9 sabal palm

florilegium 5 album 6 reader 7 garland,
omnibus 8 analects 9 anthology 10 collection, miscellany

Florimel's husband 7 Marinel

floss 4 down, fuzz, lint 5 fluff 6 thread

flotilla 5 fleet 6 argosy, armada

Flotow opera 5 Indra 6 L'Ombre,
Martha

flotsam 6 debris, jetsam 7 remains
8 wreckage 9 driftwood

flounce 5 frill, mince, strut, waltz
6 bounce, prance, ruffle, sashay

flounder 3 dab 5 slosh 6 fumble, muddle,
splash, thrash, wallow 7 blunder,
flounce 8 flatfish, struggle

flour 4 meal 6 pinole, powder *beetle:*
6 weevil

flourish 3 wax 4 grow, wave 5 adorn,
bloom 6 flower, stroke, thrive 7 blossom, burgeon, develop, fanfare, prosper, succeed 8 brandish, curlicue, ornament 13 embellishment, ornamentation

flout 4 defy, mock 5 scorn, spurn
6 deride, insult 7 scoff at

flow 4 emit, flux, gush, ooze, pour, rill,
rise, rush, stem, tide, well 5 arise, drift,
flood, issue, spate, spill, surge, swarm
6 course, deluge, onrush, sluice, spring,
stream 7 cascade, current, emanate,
give off, outflow, proceed 8 inundate,
sequence 9 discharge, originate 10 continuity, inundation, succession 11 progression 12 continuation

flower 4 best, blow, pick, posy 5 bloom,
cream, elite, pride, prime, prize
6 choice, thrive 7 blossom, burgeon,
develop 10 effloresce 13 inflorescence
buttonhole: 11 boutonniere *cluster:*
4 cyme 5 spike, umbel 6 corymb, floret,
raceme, spadix 7 panicle 8 spikelet
9 capitulum, dichasium, glomerule
11 monochasium 13 inflorescence *cup:*
5 calyx *garden:* 4 iris, lily, pink, rose

5 aster, canna, daisy, pansy, peony, phlox, poppy, tulip 6 azalia, cosmos, crocus, dahlia, orchid, violet 7 jonquil, petunia 8 camellia, daffodil, gardenia, geranium, gloxinia, hyacinth, larkspur, marigold, primrose 9 carnation, gladiolus, narcissus 10 delphinium, heliotrope 13 chrysanthemum *opening:* 8 anthesis *part:* 5 bract, calyx, ovary, ovule, petal, sepal, style 6 anther, pistil, spathe, stamen, stigma 7 corolla, nectary, pedicel, petiole 8 calyptra, filament, peduncle, perianth *spike:* 5 ament 6 catkin, spadix *stalk:* 7 pedicel 8 peduncle *type:* 3 ray 4 disk 6 annual, simple 9 composite, perennial *wild:* 4 flag 5 bluet, daisy, vetch 6 lupine 7 anemone, arbutus, cowslip, gentian, vervain 8 bluebell, hepatica, trillium 9 buttercup, columbine, dandelion, saxifrage 10 cinquefoil 12 lady's slipper

flower arranging 7 ikebana

flowering 6 growth 8 progress 9 evolution 11 development, florescence, progression

flowerless plant 4 fern, moss 6 lichen 9 liverwort

flowery 5 wordy 6 florid, ornate, prolix 7 aureate, diffuse, verbose 8 sonorous 9 overblown 10 euphuistic, rhetorical 11 declamatory 12 magniloquent 13 grandiloquent

Flowery Kingdom 5 China

flowing 4 easy 5 fluid 6 fluent, liquid, smooth 7 cursive, running 10 effortless *back:* 6 reflux 8 refluent *in:* 6 influx 8 influent *together:* 7 conflux 9 confluent

flow regulator 4 cock, gate 5 valve 8 throttle

flub 4 goof, mess, muff, slip 5 boner, botch, error, fluff, gaffe, lapse, snarl 6 bollix, bungle, foul up, goof up, mess up 7 blunder, faux pas, louse up

fluctuate 4 sway, yo-yo 5 swing, waver 6 seesaw 8 undulate 9 alternate, oscillate, vacillate

flue 4 pipe, vent 6 funnel, uptake 7 channel, chimney, outtake

fluent 4 easy, glib 5 fluid 6 facile, liquid, smooth, supple 7 cursive, flowing, voluble 8 eloquent, polished 10 articulate, effortless

fluff 4 down, flub, fuzz, goof, lint, mess, muff, slip, trip 5 boner, botch, error, floss, gaffe, lapse, whisk 6 bobble, bollix, bungle, goof up, mess up 7 blooper, blunder, faux pas, louse up, mistake

fluffy 5 downy 6 flossy 7 cursory, shallow 8 puffed up 10 flocculent 11 superficial 13 unsubstantial

fluid 4 free 5 lymph, water 6 liquid, mobile, molten, serous, watery 7 mutable, protean 8 flexible, shifting, unstable, unsteady, variable 9 adaptable, changeful, unsettled 10 changeable *excessive:* 5 edema

fluke 3 hap 4 lobe, worm 5 quirk 6 chance 8 flatfish, fortuity 9 trematode

fluky 3 odd 6 casual, chance, chancy, random 9 arbitrary 10 accidental, fortuitous

flume 5 chute 6 sluice, stream 7 channel 8 aqueduct 11 watercourse

flummox 5 abash, addle 6 baffle, rattle, stymie 7 confuse, fluster, perplex 8 befuddle, bewilder, confound 9 discomfit, embarrass 10 disconcert

flunk 4 fail

flunky 4 peon 5 gofer, toady 6 drudge, lackey, stooge, yes-man 7 footman, servant, steward 8 factotum, follower

flurry 3 ado, fit 4 fuss, gust, spit, stir, to-do 5 haste, whirl 6 bother, bustle, furore, pother, tumult 7 barrage, flutter, turmoil 8 snowfall 9 agitation, commotion, confusion, whirlpool, whirlwind 10 excitement, turbulence

flush 4 even, flat, glow, pink, rich, rose, wash 5 bloom, color, level, plane, raise, rinse, rouge 6 florid, filled, mantle, redden, sluice 7 cleanse, crimson, glowing, inflame, opulent, suffuse, wealthy 8 abundant, abutting, irrigate, rubicund, sanguine, squarely 9 turn color

fluster 5 addle, dizzy, shake, upset 6 ball up, bother, fuddle, muddle, rattle, ruffle 7 agitate, confuse, disturb, nonplus, perturb, unhinge 8 befuddle, bewilder, confound, disquiet, distract 10 discompose

flustered 5 upset 7 abashed, anxious, rattled 8 agitated, confused, troubled 9 chagrined, disturbed, flummoxed, perplexed, perturbed 10 bewildered, disquieted, distracted, distraught, distressed, nonplussed 11 discomposed, embarrassed 12 disconcerted

flute 4 fife, roll 5 pleat 6 goffer, groove 7 chamfer, channel, piccolo 8 recorder 9 wineglass *Japanese:* 10 shakuhachi *player:* 5 piper 7 flutist 8 flautist

flutist *American:* 5 Baker (Julius), Baron (Samuel) 7 Robison (Paula) 8 Zukerman (Eugenia) *British:* 6 Galway (James) *French:* 6 Rampal (Jean-Pierre)

flutter 4 beat, flap, flit 5 hover, quake, shake 6 flurry, quaver, quiver, wobble 7 flicker, flitter, pulsate, tremble, vibrate 9 agitation, commotion, confusion, palpitate, vibration 11 fluctuation

flu type 5 Asian, swine

flux 3 run **4** flow, fuse, melt, rush, thaw, tide **5** drift, flood, spate **6** change, stream **7** current, flowing, outflow **8** dissolve

fly 3 zip **4** bolt, dart, dash, flee, flit, lure, scud, skip, soar, whiz, wing **5** fleet, float, glide, hover, hurry, pilot, scoot, shoot, skirr, sweep, whish, whisk **6** aviate, escape, hasten, hustle **7** abscond, flutter *insect:* **4** gnat **5** midge **6** botfly, gadfly, mayfly, tsetse **7** deerfly, sandfly **8** blackfly, dipteron, horsefly, housefly, tachinid **10** bluebottle *larva:* **6** maggot

fly-by-night 5 shady **7** passing **9** transient **10** transitory, unreliable **12** disreputable, undependable **13** untrustworthy

flycatcher 5 pewee **6** phoebe, tyrant **8** bellbird, kingbird **9** passerine

flying 5 aloft **6** volant **8** airborne

Flying Dutchman, The *composer:* **6** Wagner (Richard) *heroine:* **5** Senta

flying fish 7 gurnard

flying fox 3 bat **8** fruit bat

flying horse 7 Pegasus **10** hippogriff

flying island 6 Laputa

flying lemur 6 colugo

flying mammal 3 bat

flying saucer 3 UFO

fly in the ointment 5 catch **8** drawback

foam 4 head, scud, scum, suds, surf **5** churn, froth, spume **6** bubble, lather, seethe **7** bubbles **10** effervesce

fob 4 seal **5** chain **6** pocket, ribbon **8** ornament

fob off 5 foist **6** put off **7** palm off, pass off

focus 3 fix, hub **4** zoom **5** heart, rivet **6** adjust, center, fixate, home in **8** converge, emphasis, meditate, polestar **9** concenter, epicenter **10** hypocenter **11** concentrate, nerve center

fodder 4 feed, food **6** forage, silage **9** provender *crop:* **3** hay, oat, rye **4** corn **5** maize, vetch, wheat **6** barley, clover, millet **7** alfalfa, sorghum *storage structure:* **4** silo *store:* **6** ensile

foe 5 enemy, rival **8** opponent **9** adversary **10** antagonist

fog 4 blur, daze, foam, haze, mist, murk, soup **5** brume, cloud, vapor **6** miasma, muddle **7** pea soup, pogonip

foggy 4 hazy **5** dirty, grimy, misty, murky, soupy, vague **7** brumous, muddled, obscure, tenuous **8** confused, pea soupy, vaporous

fogy 6 fossil, square **7** diehard **8** mossback **10** fuddy-duddy **12** antediluvian, conservative **11** standpatter **13** stick-in-the-mud

fogyish 7 old-line **8** outmoded, standpat **9** hidebound, out-of-date **10** antiquated,

fuddy-duddy, mossbacked **11** reactionary **12** conservative, old-fashioned

foible 4 vice **5** fault **6** defect **7** failing, frailty **8** weakness **11** shortcoming **12** imperfection

foil 4 balk, beat, curb, dash, faze **5** check, sword **6** baffle, defeat, rattle, thwart **7** buffalo **8** contrast, restrain **9** discomfit, embarrass, frustrate **10** circumvent, disappoint, disconcert **11** straight man

foist 6 fob off **7** palm off, pass off

fold 3 pen, ply **4** bend, fail, tuck **5** drape, flock, pleat, plica, ridge **6** crease, double, furrow, pucker **7** flexure, plicate **9** plication **11** corrugation *skin:* **4** ruga **5** plica, rugae (plural) **6** dewlap, plicae (plural)

folder 4 file **6** binder **9** portfolio

foliage 6 growth, leaves **7** verdure **8** greenery, lushness **10** vegetation

folk 4 race **6** people **9** community

folklore 4 myth, tale **5** fable **6** belief, custom, legend, mythos, wisdom **9** mythology, tradition **12** superstition

folks 6 family **7** parents **9** relatives

folksinger 4 Baez (Joan), Ives (Burl) **5** Dylan (Bob), Niles (John Jacob), White (Josh) **6** Odetta, Seeger (Pete) **7** Collins (Judy), Guthrie (Arlo, Woody), Robeson (Paul) **9** Belafonte (Harry), Ledbetter (Huddie)

folksy 5 homey **6** casual, earthy, mellow, rustic, simple **7** natural **8** down-home, familiar, informal, laid-back, sociable **9** easygoing, ingenuous **10** unaffected, unpolished **13** unpretentious

folktale 4 myth **5** fable **6** legend **7** märchen

follow 3 dog, spy, tag **4** hunt, keep, obey, seek, tail, walk **5** catch, chase, ensue, grasp, hound, trace, track, trail **6** accept, comply, convoy, pursue, search, shadow, travel **7** conform, imitate, proceed, replace, succeed **8** postdate, practice, supplant **9** accompany, supersede **10** comprehend, understand

follower 3 fan **5** toady **6** addict, cohort, minion, sequel, votary **7** apostle, devotee, groupie, habitué, sectary, trailer **8** adherent, advocate, disciple, faithful, hanger-on, henchman, myrmidon, parasite, partisan, tagalong **9** dependent, satellite, supporter, sycophant **10** aficionado

following 4 next **5** after, below, later, since **6** behind, public **7** ensuing, retinue **8** audience, partisans **9** adherents, afterward, believers, disciples, entourage **10** afterwards, sequential, supporters, subsequent, succeeding,

successive **12** subsequently, subsequent to
follow-up 6 sequel
folly 4 whim **6** lunacy, vanity **7** fatuity, foolery, inanity, madness **8** insanity, nonsense **9** absurdity, craziness, dottiness, silliness, stupidity **10** indulgence **11** foolishness **12** extravagance
foment 3 sow **4** brew, goad, spur **5** rouse, set on **6** arouse, excite, foster, incite, stir up, whip up **7** agitate, nurture, provoke **9** cultivate, encourage, instigate
fond 4 dear, warm **5** silly **6** doting, loving, tender **7** devoted, fatuous, foolish, partial **8** desirous, enamored, romantic **9** indulgent **10** infatuated **11** sentimental **12** affectionate
fondle 3 paw, pet **5** grope, touch **6** caress, cosset, dandle, stroke **7** embrace **8** canoodle
fondness 4 love **5** fancy, taste **6** liking, relish **8** appetite, devotion, penchant, soft spot, weakness **9** affection, tendresse **10** attachment, partiality, preference, propensity **11** inclination **12** predilection
font 4 root, type **6** origin, source **8** fountain **10** receptacle
food 3 pap **4** chow, diet, eats, fare, grub, meal, meat **5** bread, manna **6** fodder, viands **7** aliment, cuisine, edibles, nurture, pabulum, vittles **8** delicacy, victuals **9** nutriment, provender **10** provisions, sustenance **11** comestibles, nourishment *disorder:* **7** bulimia **8** anorexia *divine:* **8** ambrosia *element:* **5** fiber, fibre, sugar **6** starch **7** mineral, protein, vitamin **12** carbohydrate *from heaven:* **5** manna *lover:* **7** epicure, gourmet **8** gourmand *provision:* **4** mess **6** ration **7** serving *scarcity:* **6** famine *waste:* **7** garbage
foofaraw 3 ado **4** fuss, stir, to-do **5** stink **6** bother, finery, frills, furore, hurrah, pother, ruckus, rumpus **8** brouhaha **9** commotion **11** disturbance
fool 3 ass, kid, oaf, rag, rib, sap, toy **4** boob, butt, clod, dolt, dope, dupe, fish, gull, hoax, jerk, jest, joke, josh, zany **5** chump, clown, comic, dally, dummy, dunce, goose, idiot, loser, moron, ninny, patsy, schmo, trick **6** banter, cretin, dawdle, delude, diddle, dimwit, doodle, galoot, gammon, jester, lead on, meddle, monkey, motley, nitwit, pigeon, schmoe, stooge, sucker, tamper, trifle, victim **7** beguile, buffoon, chicane, deceive, fake out, fall guy, fritter, half-wit, jackass, mislead, pinhead, saphead, schmuck **8** bonehead, comedian, dumbbell, flim-

flam, hoodwink, imbecile, lunkhead, numskull, pushover **9** bamboozle, birdbrain, blockhead, interfere, simpleton **10** nincompoop **11** hornswoggle, merry-andrew, string along **13** laughingstock *around:* **4** futz, idle, laze, loaf, loll **5** flirt **6** dawdle, diddle, lounge **8** lollygag, womanize **9** philander
foolhardy 4 bold, rash **6** daring, madcap **8** headlong, reckless **9** audacious, daredevil, impetuous **11** precipitate, temerarious
foolish 3 mad **4** daft, gaga, rash, zany **5** balmy, batty, crazy, dippy, dizzy, dorky, dotty, goofy, inane, inept, kooky, loony, loopy, nutty, sappy, silly, wacky **6** absurd, insane, simple, stupid, unwise **7** asinine, doltish, fatuous, idiotic, lunatic, meshuga, moronic, witless **8** clueless, reckless, trifling **9** half-baked, brainless, fantastic, frivolous, half-baked, imbecilic, insensate, laughable, ludicrous, senseless **10** cockamamie, half-cocked, half-witted, irrational, ridiculous **11** harebrained, nonsensical **12** feebleminded
foolishness 4 bull, bunk **5** folly, fudge **6** bêtise, bunkum, lunacy **7** fatuity, inanity, rubbish **8** claptrap, drollery, insanity, nonsense, tommyrot **9** absurdity, craziness, silliness, stupidity **10** imbecility, imprudence **12** fiddlefaddle **13** horsefeathers
fool's gold 6 pyrite
foot 3 paw **4** hoof *ailment:* **4** corn **6** bunion, callus *animal:* **3** pad, paw **4** hoof *bones of:* **5** talus, tarsi (plural) **6** cuboid, tarsal, tarsus **7** phalanx **9** calcaneus, cuneiform, navicular, phalanges (plural) **10** metatarsal *combining form:* **3** ped, pod **4** podo *doctor:* **10** podiatrist **11** chiropodist *metric:* **4** iamb **5** arsis **6** dactyl, thesis **7** anapest, pyrrhic, spondee, trochee *part:* **3** toe **4** arch, ball, claw, nail **5** ankle, digit, talon **6** hallux, instep
football 5 rugby **6** rugger, soccer **7** pigskin *field:* **8** gridiron *foul:* **7** holding, offside **8** clipping **12** interference *official:* **6** umpire **7** referee **8** linesman **9** back judge, line judge **10** field judge *play:* **4** dive, trap **5** sneak, sweep **6** option, screen **7** audible, counter, handoff, rollout, runback **8** dropback **9** crossbuck, off-tackle **10** buttonhook *player position:* **3** end **4** back **5** guard **6** center, safety, tackle **7** flanker, lineman, wideout **8** fullback, halfback, slotback, split end, tailback, tight end, wingback **9** noseguard **10** cornerback, linebacker, nose tackle **11** quarterback

12 defensive end, wide receiver *scoring:*
6 safety 9 field goal, touchdown 10 conversion *starting play:* 7 kickoff *team:*
6 eleven *term:* 4 down, kick, pass, punt,
rush, snap 5 blitz, block, squad 6 fumble, huddle, kicker, onside, option,
safety, spiral 7 end zone, handoff, kickoff, offside, pigskin, quarter, spinner,
tweener, yardage 8 clipping, crossbar,
goal line, goalpost, gridiron, halftime
9 backfield, defensive, field goal, intercept, offensive, placekick, scrimmage,
touchback, touchdown 11 broken field
12 interception
footballer 3 end 4 half, Kemp (Jack),
Long (Howie), Lott (Ronnie), Levy
(Marv), Monk (Art), Moon (Warren),
Reed (Andre), Rice (Jerry), wing
5 Allen (Marcus), Baugh (Sammy),
Berry (Raymond), Brady (Tom), Brown
(Bob, Jim), Clark (Gary), Ditka (Mike),
Elway (John), Eller (Carl), Favre
(Brett), Gibbs (Joe), Groza (Lou),
guard, Jones (Bert, Deacon), Kelly
(Jim), Kosar (Bernie), Leahy (Pat),
Lomax (Neil), Muñoz (Anthony), Shula
(Don), Simms (Phil), Smith (Emmitt),
Starr (Bart), Stram (Hank), Swann
(Lynn), Young (Steve) 6 Aikman (Troy),
Blanda (George), Butkus (Dick), Carter
(Chris, Ki-Jana), center, Csonka
(Larry), Dawson (Len), Ellard (Henry),
Graham (Otto), Grange (Red), Greene
(Joe), Harris (Franco), Jaeger (Jeff),
Joiner (Charlie), kicker, Lofton
(James), Lowery (Nick), Marino (Dan),
Murray (Eddie), Namath (Joe), Payton
(Walter), player, Rypien (Mark), safety,
Sayers (Gale), Slater (Jackie), tackle,
Taylor (Lawrence), Thorpe (Jim), Tittle
(YA.), Turner (Jim), Unitas (Johnny),
Walker (Herschel) 7 Bledsoe (Drew),
Dorsett (Tony), Esiason (Boomer),
flanker, Gifford (Frank), Hornung
(Paul), Johnson (Norm), Largent
(Steve), lineman, Luckman (Sid), Man-
ning (Peyton), Montana (Joe), New-
some (Ozzie), Riggins (John), Sanders
(Barry, Deion), Simpson (O. J.), Stabler
(Ken), Thurman (Thomas), tweener
8 Andersen (Morten), Anderson (Gary,
Ottis), Bradshaw (Terry), defender, full-
back, halfback, linesman, Nagurski
(Bronko), Plunkett (Jim), receiver, scat-
back, split end, Staubach (Roger), tail-
back, tight end, wingback 9 Dickerson
(Eric), Jurgensen (Sonny), Hostetler
(Jeff), noseguard, Tarkenton (Fran)
10 cornerback, linebacker, Stallworth
(John), Singletary (Mike), Stephenson
(Dwight), Youngblood (Jack) 11 ball-

carrier, placekicker, quarterback, running back, snapper-back 12 strong safety, triple threat, wide receiver
Foote play 15 Trip to Bountiful (The)
19 Young Man from Atlanta (The)
footfall 4 step 5 tread
footing 4 base, rank, seat, term 5 basis,
place, state 6 bottom, ground, status
7 bedrock, seating, station, warrant
8 basement, capacity, pedestal, position, standing 9 character, situation
10 foundation, groundwork, substratum 12 underpinning
footless 4 dull, dumb 5 crass, dense,
inept, unfit 6 stupid 7 foolish
foot lever 5 pedal 7 treadle
footman 7 servant 10 pedestrian
11 infantryman
footpad 5 thief 6 mugger, robber 8 criminal 10 highwayman, pickpocket
footprint 3 pug 4 sign, step 5 spoor,
trace, track, tract 7 pugmark, vestige
footslog 4 plod, slop, toil 5 tramp,
tromp 6 trudge
footstone 6 ledger, marker 8 monument
11 grave marker
footstool 7 cricket, hassock, ottoman
fop 3 jay 4 beau 5 blade, blood, dandy,
spark, swell 7 coxcomb, gallant 8 cavalier, macaroni, popinjay 9 exquisite,
ladies' man, pretty boy 10 lady-killer
11 Beau Brummel, petit-maître 12 fashion plate, lounge lizard
foppish 6 chichi 8 dandyish, peacocky
10 peacockish
for 3 pro
forage 4 beat, comb, grub, prog, raid,
rake, sack 5 scour 6 browse, fodder,
ravage, rustle, search 7 plunder, ransack, rummage 8 finecomb, scrounge
9 pasturage (see also FODDER)
foray 4 raid 6 inroad, sortie 8 invasion
9 incursion, irruption
forbear 4 shun 5 avoid, forgo, spare
6 endure, eschew, resist, suffer
7 abstain, decline, refrain 8 hold back,
restrain, tolerate
forbearance 5 grace, mercy 6 lenity
7 charity 8 clemency, lenience, leniency, mildness, patience 9 restraint, tolerance 10 abstinence, toleration 13 consideration
forbearing 4 easy, kind, mild 6 gentle
7 clement, lenient, patient 8 merciful,
tolerant 9 indulgent 10 charitable,
thoughtful 11 considerate, magnanimous
Forbes hero 8 Tremaine (Johnny)
forbid 3 ban, bar, nix 4 curb, deny, halt,
stop, veto 5 block, check, debar
6 enjoin, hinder, impede, outlaw, refuse

7 inhibit, prevent, rule out, shut out
8 disallow, obstruct, preclude, prohibit, restrain 9 interdict, proscribe

forbidden 5 taboo 6 banned 7 illegal, illicit 8 verboten 10 prohibited

Forbidden City 5 Lhasa 6 Gu Gong 7 Beijing

forbidding 4 grim 5 drear, harsh 6 dreary, severe 8 daunting, menacing, sinister 9 repellent 10 formidable 11 threatening

force 3 jam 4 cram, push 5 drive, foist, impel, might, power, press, vigor, wreak, wreck, wrest 6 coerce, compel, demand, duress, effort, energy, extort, impose, legion, muscle, oblige 7 command, impetus, inflict, potency, require, sandbag 8 coercion, manpower, momentum, obligate, pressure, shoehorn, strength, violence 9 constrain, intensity, puissance, strong-arm 10 compulsion, constraint *apart:* 5 wedge *unit:* 4 dyne

forced 8 strained 9 contrived, unnatural 10 artificial, compulsory 11 involuntary

forceful 5 stiff, stout 6 mighty, potent, punchy, strong, virile 7 dynamic 8 emphatic, powerful, puissant, vigorous 9 assertive 10 compelling

forceless 4 lame, weak 5 wimpy 6 feeble 8 impotent, nugatory 9 powerless 10 inadequate 11 ineffective, ineffectual

force out see EXPEL

forcible 8 coercive 9 compelled 10 compulsory, obligatory, peremptory

ford 5 cross

Ford's folly 5 Edsel

for each 3 per 6 apiece

forearm bone 4 ulna 6 radius

forebear 8 ancestor 9 precursor 10 antecedent, progenitor 11 predecessor 12 primogenitor

forebode 5 augur 7 betoken, portend, predict, presage 8 foretell, prophesy, soothsay 13 prognosticate

foreboding 4 omen, sign 5 dread 6 augury 7 anxiety, portent, presage, warning 10 prediction, prognostic 11 premonition 12 apprehension, presentiment

forecast 5 augur 6 divine 7 foresee, portend, predict, presage 8 estimate, foretell, indicate, prophecy, prophesy 9 adumbrate, calculate, prevision, prognosis 10 prediction 13 prognosticate

forecaster 4 seer 5 augur 6 oracle 7 diviner, prophet 8 haruspex 9 predictor 10 prophesier, soothsayer, weatherman 11 Nostradamus 13 meteorologist, weatherperson

foreclose 3 bar 5 debar 6 cut off, hinder 7 prevent, shut out 8 preclude

forefather see FOREBEAR

forefeel 6 divine 9 apprehend, prevision

forefinger 5 index

forefront 3 van 4 lead 8 vanguard 10 avant-garde, firing line 11 cutting edge

foregoer 6 herald 8 ancestor, forebear 9 harbinger, precursor, prototype 10 antecedent, antecessor, forerunner, progenitor 11 predecessor 12 primogenitor

foregoing 5 prior 6 former 7 earlier 8 anterior, previous 9 precedent, preceding 10 antecedent

forehanded 7 prudent, thrifty 8 well-to-do 9 provident 10 prosperous

forehead 4 brow 5 frons, front 8 sinciput 9 sincipita (plural)

foreign 5 alien 6 exotic 7 strange 8 external, offshore, overseas 9 extrinsic, nonnative 10 accidental, extraneous, immaterial, irrelevant 11 incongruous 12 adventitious, inapplicable, incompatible, inconsistent 13 inappropriate *prefix:* 4 xeno

foreigner 5 alien 8 outsider, stranger 9 outlander 10 tramontane

foreknow 6 divine 9 apprehend, prevision 10 anticipate

foreland 4 beak, cape, head, ness 5 point 10 promontory

forelock 5 bangs, quiff

foreman 4 boss 5 chief 6 gaffer, ganger, honcho, leader 7 captain, manager, steward 8 overseer 10 supervisor

foremost 4 arch, head, high, main 5 chief, first, front, grand 7 leading, premier, supreme 9 number one, paramount, principal 10 preeminent 11 cutting-edge, outstanding

forenoon 4 morn 7 morning 12 ante meridiem

forensic 8 judicial 9 debatable 10 rhetorical 13 argumentative

foreordain 4 doom, fate 9 determine 10 predestine 12 predetermine

forerunner 4 omen, sign 5 envoy 6 augury, herald 7 pioneer, portent, presage, symptom, warning 8 ancestor, exemplar, outrider 9 announcer, harbinger, initiator, messenger 10 antecedent, originator, prognostic 11 anticipator, predecessor

foresee 6 divine 7 predict, presage 8 perceive, prophesy 9 apprehend, prefigure, prevision 10 anticipate 13 prognosticate

foreseer 5 augur 6 auspex, oracle 7 diviner, prophet 8 haruspex 9 predictor 10 soothsayer 11 Nostradamus

foreshadow 4 bode, hint 5 augur 6 herald 7 betoken, portend, predict, presage, promise, suggest 8 forecast, intimate 9 adumbrate, prefigure 13 prognosticate

foresight 6 vision 7 caution 8 prudence, sagacity 10 discretion, perception, precaution, prescience, providence

forest 4 bosk, wood 5 copse, grove, weald, woods 6 bosque 7 coppice, thicket, woodlot 8 wildwood, woodland 10 timberland, wilderness *deity:* 5 dryad 6 sylvan 8 Sylvanus *English:* 5 Arden 8 Sherwood *opening:* 5 glade *relating to:* 6 sylvan *subarctic:* 5 taiga *tropical:* 5 selva 6 jungle

forestall 5 avert, block, deter 6 hinder 7 obviate, preempt, prevent, rule out, ward off 8 preclude, stave off 10 anticipate

Forester, C. S. *hero:* 10 Hornblower (Horatio) *novel:* 12 African Queen (The)

foretell 4 bode, warn 5 augur 6 divine 7 portend, predict, presage, promise 8 proclaim, prophesy, soothsay 9 adumbrate, apprehend, prefigure 10 anticipate, vaticinate 13 prognosticate

forethought 8 judgment, planning, prudence 10 discretion, precaution 12 deliberation 13 premeditation

foretoken 4 bode, hint, omen, sign, warn 5 augur 6 augury, herald 7 portend, portent, presage, promise, symptom, warning 8 forecast 9 harbinger, precursor 10 intimation

forever 3 aye 6 always 7 endless 8 eternity, evermore 9 endlessly, eternally 10 in aeternum 11 ad infinitum, ceaselessly, continually, everlasting, incessantly, permanently, perpetually, unceasingly 12 in perpetuity 13 everlastingly

forewarning 6 caveat, tip-off 7 caution 8 monition 11 premonition

foreword 5 intro, proem 7 preface, prelude 8 exordium, overture, preamble, prologue 12 introduction, prolegomenon

for example 6 such as

for fear that 4 lest

forfeit 4 fine, lose 5 mulct 6 give up 7 penalty 9 sacrifice 10 amercement

forfend 4 ward 5 avert, deter 6 secure 7 obviate, prevent, protect, rule out, ward off 8 preclude, preserve, stave off

forge 4 copy, fake, form, make 5 pound, shape 6 smithy 7 advance, fashion, imitate, produce, turn out 8 continue 9 construct, fabricate 11 counterfeit, manufacture

forget 4 fail, omit 6 ignore, slight 7 neglect 8 discount, overlook, pass over 9 disregard

forgetful 3 lax 5 slack 6 absent, remiss 7 amnesic 8 amnesiac, careless, heedless 9 negligent, oblivious, unwitting 10 abstracted, neglectful 11 inattentive, thoughtless 12 absentminded

forgetfulness 5 lethe 7 amnesia 8 oblivion 10 negligence 11 inattention

forgivable 6 venial 10 remissible

forgive 5 remit 6 excuse, pardon 7 absolve, condone 8 overlook

forgiveness 6 pardon 7 amnesty 9 remission 10 absolution

forgo 3 bag 5 leave, waive, yield 6 eschew, give up, resign 7 abandon 8 abnegate, jettison, renounce 9 sacrifice, surrender 10 relinquish

fork 6 bisect, branch, crotch 7 diverge, utensil 9 branch off *prong:* 4 tine

fork out 3 pay 5 spend 10 contribute

forlorn 5 alone 6 bereft, futile, lonely 8 desolate, forsaken, hopeless, lonesome, solitary, wretched 9 abandoned, depressed, destitute, miserable 10 despairing, despondent 12 disconsolate

form 3 way 4 body, cast, make, mode, mold 5 build, forge, found, frame, image, model, shape, style 6 create, design, devise, figure, make up, manner 7 compose, contour, develop, fashion, outline, process, produce, profile 8 comprise, organize, practice 9 construct, establish, fabricate, framework, procedure, structure, take shape 10 constitute, convention, regulation 11 materialize 13 configuration *combining form:* 5 morph

formal 3 set 4 prim 5 exact, legal, rigid, stiff 6 dressy, lawful, proper, seemly, solemn 7 distant, orderly, regular, stately, starchy, stilted 8 abstract, black-tie, decorous, elevated, official, reserved 10 ceremonial, methodical, systematic 11 ceremonious, syntactical 12 conventional

formality 4 form, rite 6 ritual 7 liturgy, service 8 ceremony, insignia 10 ceremonial, convention, observance

formalize 6 codify 9 establish, normalize 10 regularize 11 standardize

format 4 plan, size 5 shape, style 6 makeup, method 11 arrangement 12 organization

formation 4 rank 6 design, makeup 9 structure 11 arrangement, composition, development 12 architecture, construction

former 3 old 4 late, once, past 5 prior 6 bygone, whilom 7 earlier, onetime, quondam **8** anterior, previous, sometime **9** erstwhile, precedent, preceding **10** antecedent

formerly 4 erst, once **6** before, whilom **7** already, earlier **9** erstwhile **10** heretofore, previously

formidable 8 daunting **9** difficult **10** impressive **11** redoubtable

formless 5 vague **7** chaotic, obscure, unclear **8** inchoate, nebulous, unshaped **9** amorphous, undefined, unordered **10** immaterial, indefinite, indistinct **11** unorganized

Formosa 6 Taiwan *capital:* **6** Taipei

formula 4 rite, rule **5** canon, maxim, tenet **6** method, recipe, ritual **7** precept, theorem **8** equation **9** algorithm, blueprint, principle, yardstick **10** touchstone **12** prescription

formulate 5 couch, draft, frame, hatch **6** codify, devise, invent, make up, phrase **7** concoct, dream up, express, prepare, work out **8** contrive

forsake 4 quit **5** avoid, leave, spurn **6** defect, depart, desert, give up, reject, resign **7** abandon **8** abdicate, renounce **9** throw over **10** relinquish

forsaken 4 lorn **6** bereft **7** forlorn **8** derelict, deserted, desolate, solitary **9** abandoned

Forseti *father:* **6** Balder *palace:* **7** Glitnir

forswear 4 deny **5** unsay **6** abjure, recall, recant, reject **7** perjure, retract **8** renounce, take back, withdraw

fort 6 castle **7** bastion, bulwark, citadel, redoubt **8** fastness, fortress, garrison, martello, stockade **10** stronghold *Baltimore:* **7** McHenry *California:* **3** Ord *New Jersey:* **3** Dix *New York:* **7** Niagara, Stanwix **8** Schuyler **11** Ticonderoga *Ontario:* **9** Frontenac *San Antonio:* **5** Alamo *South Carolina:* **6** Sumter *Spanish:* **7** alcazar **8** presidio

forte 3 bag **4** loud **5** thing **6** métier **8** long suit, strength **9** specialty **10** strong suit **11** strong point

forthcoming 7 pending **8** imminent **9** impending, proximate **10** responsive **11** approaching

for the most part 9 generally, typically **10** on the whole

for the time being 3 now **6** pro tem **9** at present, currently, presently **10** pro tempore

forthright 4 open **5** blunt, frank, plain **6** candid, direct **7** up-front **8** straight **10** aboveboard, foursquare **11** openhearted, straight-out, undisguised, unvarnished

forthwith 3 now **6** at once **8** directly **9** instantly, right away, thereupon

11 immediately, straightway **12** straightaway

fortification 4 moat, wall **6** abatis, buffer, glacis **7** barrier, bastion, bulwark, citadel, parapet, rampart, redoubt **8** barbican, enceinte, fastness, garrison, palisade, presidio, stockade **9** barricade, earthwork **10** breastwork, stronghold *part:* **7** salient

fortify 3 arm **4** gird, stir **5** brace, rally, ready, renew, rouse, steel **6** enrich, secure **7** hearten, prepare, protect, refresh, restore **8** embolden, energize **9** encourage, reinforce **10** invigorate, strengthen

fortitude 4 grit, guts, pith **5** fiber, heart, nerve, pluck, spunk, valor **6** mettle, phlegm, spirit **7** bravery, courage, stamina **8** backbone, boldness, strength, tenacity **9** constancy, endurance, tolerance **10** resolution **11** intrepidity **12** fearlessness, perseverance, resoluteness, staying power **13** dauntlessness, determination

fortress see FORT

fortuitous 5 fluky, happy, lucky **6** casual, chance **10** accidental, auspicious **12** providential

fortuity 3 hap **4** luck **5** fluke **6** chance **8** accident **9** happening **10** occurrence

Fortuna 5 Tyche *symbol:* **5** wheel **6** rudder

fortunate 5 happy, lucky **9** favorable **10** auspicious, propitious **12** providential

Fortunate Islands 8 Canaries

fortune 3 lot, pot, wad **4** doom, fate, luck, mint, pile, ship **5** worth **6** boodle, bundle, chance, happen, hazard, packet, riches, wealth **7** destiny, success, weather **8** property **9** resources

Fortune founder 4 Luce (Henry)

fortune-teller 4 seer **5** augur, sibyl **7** diviner, palmist **9** wisewoman **10** soothsayer (see also FORESEER)

fortune-telling see DIVINATION

forty winks 3 nap **6** catnap, siesta, snooze **7** shut-eye

forum 5 court, panel **6** medium **8** congress, tribunal **9** symposium **10** colloquium, conference, roundtable **11** convocation, marketplace

forward 3 aid **4** abet, bold, send, ship **5** ahead, brash, eager, pushy, ready, relay, remit, sassy, saucy **6** cheeky, foster, onward, uphold **7** address, advance, consign, further, promote, support **8** advanced, champion, dispatch, impudent, transmit **9** encourage, in advance **11** smart-alecky **12** presumptuous **13** self-assertive *prefix:* **4** ante

For Whom the Bell Tolls *author:* 9 Hemingway (Ernest) *character:* 5 Maria, Pablo, Pilar 6 Jordan

Forza del Destino composer 5 Verdi (Giuseppe)

fossa 3 pit 5 fovea 6 cavity, groove 10 depression

fosse 4 dike, moat 5 canal, ditch 6 trench 7 acequia, channel

fossil 4 fogy 5 amber, relic 7 antique 8 calamite, conodont, mossback 10 antiquated, fuddy-duddy 12 antediluvian 13 stick-in-the-mud *fuel:* 3 gas, oil 4 coal, peat 9 petroleum 10 natural gas

foster 4 back, help, rear, tend 5 nurse 6 assist, harbor, parent 7 advance, bring up, nourish, nurture, promote, support, sustain 8 champion 9 cultivate, encourage

fou 5 crazy, drunk

foul 4 base, rank, soil, vile 5 botch, dirty, fetid, funky, muddy, nasty, yucky 6 coarse, defile, filthy, grubby, horrid, impure, odious, putrid, rotten, scuzzy, smutty, stormy, turbid, vulgar, wicked 7 abusive, noisome, obscene, pollute, profane, raunchy, squalid, tarnish, unclean 8 indecent, obstruct, polluted, stinking, wretched 9 collision, loathsome, obnoxious, offensive, repellent, repugnant, repulsive, revolting 10 abominable, detestable, disgusting, malodorous 11 contaminate, treacherous 12 dishonorable, scatological

foul play 3 hit 5 blood 6 murder 7 killing, outrage 8 homicide, violence 12 manslaughter

found 4 base, cast, rear 5 begin, erect, raise, set up, start 6 bottom, create, invent 7 fashion, support 8 commence, initiate, organize 9 establish, institute, originate, predicate

foundation 3 bed 4 base, rock 5 basis 6 bottom, corset, makeup 7 bedding, footing, support 8 pedestal 9 endowment 10 groundwork, substratum 11 institution 12 organization, substructure, underpinning

foundational 5 basic 6 bottom 7 primary 10 supportive, underlying 11 fundamental

founder 4 fail, sink 5 wreck 6 author, father, go down 7 creator 8 collapse, inventor, submerge, submerse 9 architect, generator, patriarch, shipwreck 10 originator

fountain 3 jet 4 head, root 5 spout 6 geyser, origin, source, spring 7 bubbler 8 wellhead 9 inception, reservoir 10 wellspring *nymph:* 6 Egeria

four 6 tetrad 7 quartet 10 quaternion *bagger:* 5 homer 7 home run *combining form:* 4 tetr 5 quadr, tetra 6 quadri, quadru, quater, tessar 7 tessara, tessera *gills:* 4 pint *hundred:* 5 elite 10 upper crust *inches:* 4 hand *pecks:* 6 bushel *quarts:* 6 gallon

four-flush 4 dupe 5 bluff 6 betray, delude, humbug, take in 7 beguile, deceive 11 doublecross

four-footed animal 8 tetrapod 9 quadruped

Four Horsemen 3 War 5 Death 6 Famine 8 Conquest 10 Pestilence

four-in-hand 3 tie 5 coach 7 necktie

fourpence 5 groat

four-poster 3 bed

fourscore 6 eighty

four-sided figure 5 rhomb 6 square 7 rhombus 9 rectangle 13 quadrilateral, parallelogram

foursquare 8 straight 10 forthright 13 quadrilateral

fourteen pounds 5 stone

fourth 7 quarter 8 quadrant, quartern *combining form:* 5 quadr, quart 6 quadri, quadru

fowl 3 hen 4 bird, cock, duck 5 chick, goose, poult 6 bantam, pullet, turkey 7 chicken, rooster (see also CHICKEN; POULTRY)

Fowles novel 5 Magus (The) 9 Collector (The) 22 French Lieutenant's Woman (The)

fox 4 fool 5 trick 6 baffle, outwit 7 confuse, reynard 8 bewilder *African:* 4 asse *female:* 5 vixen *kind:* 3 kit, red 5 swift 6 arctic, fennec, silver 8 bat-eared *Scottish:* 3 tod *young:* 3 cub

foxglove 9 digitalis

fox grape 9 muscadine 11 scuppernong

foxiness 4 wile 5 craft, guile 7 cunning, slyness 8 wiliness 10 artfulness, craftiness, cleverness

foxlike 7 vulpine

foxy 3 sly 4 wily 5 canny, slick 6 artful, astute, clever, crafty, shrewd, tricky 7 cunning, vulpine 8 guileful 9 insidious

foyer 5 lobby 8 anteroom, entrance 9 vestibule

fracas 3 row 4 feud, fray 5 brawl, broil, fight, melee, run-in, set-to 6 affray, hassle, shindy, uproar 7 dispute, quarrel, ruction 8 squabble 9 bickering 10 donnybrook, free-for-all 11 altercation

fraction 3 bit, cut 4 part 5 piece, scrap 6 divide, little 7 portion, section 8 fragment

fractious 4 wild 6 unruly 7 peevish, pettish, willful 8 contrary 9 bellicose, irritable 10 headstrong, pugnacious, refractory **11** belligerent, contentious, intractable, quarrelsome **12** recalcitrant, ungovernable, unmanageable

fracture 4 rent, rift, tear **5** break, cleft, crack, split **6** breach, schism **7** rupture

Fra Diavolo composer 5 Auber (Esprit)

fragile 4 weak **5** frail **6** feeble, flimsy, infirm **7** brittle, friable, tenuous, unsound **8** decrepit, delicate **9** breakable, frangible

fragment 3 bit **4** chip, iota, part, rive **5** burst, crumb, flake, grain, piece, scrap, shard, shred, smash **6** morsel, shiver, sliver **7** break up, flinder, shatter **8** fraction, particle, splinter **9** fall apart **12** disintegrate

fragmentary 6 broken **7** partial **10** fractional, incomplete, unfinished

fragrance 4 musk, nose, odor **5** aroma, attar, scent, smell, spice **7** bouquet, cologne, incense, perfume **9** redolence **11** eau de parfum, toilet water **13** eau de toilette

fragrant 7 odorous, scented **8** aromatic, perfumed, redolent **11** odoriferous

frail 4 puny, slim, thin, weak **5** petty, reedy, wispy **6** feeble, flimsy, infirm, sickly, slight **7** brittle, fragile, slender, spindly, tenuous, unsound **8** decrepit, delicate **9** breakable, frangible

frailty 4 vice **5** fault **6** foible **7** failing **8** delicacy, weakness **9** infirmity **10** feebleness **11** tenuousness **12** imperfection

frame 4 body, form, mold, plan, sash **5** build, draft, erect, forge, mount, shape, shell **6** border, casing, cook up, devise, draw up, figure, invent, make up, sketch, system **7** arrange, chassis, concoct, fashion, imagine, prepare **8** assemble, casement, conceive, contrive, regulate, skeleton **9** cartouche, construct, fabricate, formulate, structure *part:* **4** sill, stud **5** joist, plate

framework 4 rack **5** shell, truss **7** trestle **8** cribbing, cribwork, scaffold, skeleton, studding, studwork, trussing **9** bare bones, structure *of crossed strips:* **7** lattice, trellis

France bay: **6** Biscay *capital:* **5** Paris *channel:* **6** Manche (La) **7** English *city:* **4** Caen, Lyon, Metz, Nice **5** Brest, Lyons **6** Amiens, Calais, Nantes, Rennes **8** Bordeaux, Grenoble, Toulouse **9** Marseille **10** Marseilles, Strasbourg, Versailles **11** Montpellier *conqueror:* **6** Caesar (Julius) *emperor:* **5** Pepin (III, the Short) **8** Napoleon (Bonaparte) **11** Charlemagne *enclave:* **6** Monaco *former name:* **4** Gaul **6** Gallia *historic province:* **4** Foix **5** Anjou, Aunis, Bearn, Berry, Maine **6** Alsace, Artois,

Marche, Poitou, Vendée **7** Gascony, Guyenne, Picardy **8** Auvergne, Bretagne, Brittany, Burgundy, Dauphine, Flanders, Gascogne, Limousin, Lorraine, Lyonnais, Normandy, Picardie, Provence, Touraine **9** Angoumois, Bourgogne, Champagne, Languedoc, Nivernois, Orléanais, Saintonge, Venaissin **10** Roussillon **11** Bourbonnais, Île-de-France **12** Franche-Comté *island:* **3** Yeu **6** Hyères, Oléron, Ushant **7** Corsica **8** Belle-Île **11** Noirmoutier *monarch:* **5** Henri, Henry, Louis **6** Philip **7** Charles **8** Philippe *monetary unit:* **4** euro *monetary unit, former:* **3** sou **5** franc *mountain, range:* **4** Alps, Jura **6** Vosges **8** Auvergne, Pyrenees **9** Mont Blanc *neighbor:* **5** Italy, Spain **7** Andorra, Belgium, Germany **10** Luxembourg **11** Switzerland *president:* **8** de Gaulle (Charles) **10** Mitterrand (François) *region:* **5** Corse **6** Alsace, Centre **7** Corsica, Picardy **8** Auvergne, Bretagne, Brittany, Burgundy, Limousin, Normandy, Picardie **9** Aquitaine, Bourgogne, Champagne, Languedoc, Normandie **10** Rhône-Alpes **11** Île-de-France **12** Franche-Comté, Midi-Pyrénées *river:* **4** Aire, Aude, Oise **5** Adour, Isère, Loire, Marne, Rhone, Saône, Seine, Somme, Yonne **7** Garonne *sea:* **13** Mediterranean *strait:* **5** Dover

Francesca's lover 5 Paolo

franchise 4 vote **6** ballot **7** freedom, license **8** suffrage **9** privilege

frangible 7 brittle, fragile, friable **8** delicate **9** breakable

frank 3 dog **4** fair, free, open **5** blunt, plain **6** candid, direct, honest, hot dog, weenie, wiener, wienie **7** upright **8** man-to-man, out-front, straight **9** barefaced, outspoken **10** forthright, scrupulous, unreserved **11** openhearted, plainspoken, transparent, unconcealed, undisguised, uninhibited, unvarnished, wienerwurst **12** heart-to-heart, unmistakable

Frankenstein author 7 Shelley (Mary)

frankfurter 3 dog **6** hot dog, weenie, wiener, wienie **11** wienerwurst

Frankie's lover 6 Johnny

Frankish hero 6 Roland

Franklin, Benjamin *birthplace:* **6** Boston *invention:* **5** stove **8** bifocals *pen name:* **11** Poor Richard

frankness 6 candor **7** honesty

frantic 3 mad **4** wild **5** upset, wired **7** fraught, shook up, unglued **8** feverish, frenetic, frenzied, maniacal, worked up **10** distraught **11** overwrought

Franzen novel 11 Corrections (The)

frappe 7 chilled, liqueur **9** milk shake
fraternal 6 clubby **8** sociable **9** brotherly, comradely, dizygotic **10** like-minded
fraternal society 3 FOE **4** BPOE, Elks **5** Lions, Moose **6** Eagles, Masons **7** Woodmen (of the World) **8** Shriners **10** Freemasons, Hibernians, Odd Fellows
fraternity 4 club **5** guild, order, union **6** league **7** company **8** sodality **10** fellowship **11** association, brotherhood **13** brotherliness
fraud 3 gyp **4** fake, gaff, hoax, sham **5** cheat, faker, phony, quack, trick **6** deceit, dupery, humbug, hustle **7** chicane, swindle **8** cozenage, flimflam, impostor, operator, trickery **9** charlatan, chicanery, deception, imposture, pretender, shell game, trickster **10** dishonesty, mountebank, subterfuge **11** counterfeit **12** double-dealer **13** double-dealing, sharp practice
fraudulence 6 deceit **8** quackery, trickery **9** chicanery, deception, phoniness **10** dishonesty
fraudulent 4 fake **5** false, phony **7** crooked **8** cheating, guileful **9** deceitful, deceptive, dishonest **10** fallacious **11** duplicitous
fraught 4 full **5** laden, tense **6** filled, uneasy **7** charged, replete, stuffed **8** pregnant **9** stressful
fräulein 4 maid, Miss **6** maiden **9** governess **12** mademoiselle
fray 3 row **4** fret **5** brawl, broil, brush, clash, fight, melee, ravel, shred **6** combat, fracas, strain, strife **7** dispute, frazzle, ruction, scuffle **8** irritate, skirmish, struggle **9** commotion, scrimmage **10** donnybrook **11** disturbance
frayed 4 worn **6** ragged, shabby **8** tattered **9** moth-eaten **10** threadbare
frazzle 4 do in, fray, poop, tire, wear **5** upset **6** tucker **7** exhaust, fatigue, wear out
frazzled 4 beat **5** upset **6** bushed, sapped **7** drained, rattled **8** agitated, confused, fatigued, tired out **9** exhausted, fagged out, unsettled **10** distressed **11** overwrought **12** disconcerted
freak 3 bug, nut **4** buff, geek, whim **5** go ape, fancy, fiend, maven **6** addict, hippie, maniac, megrim, oddity, vagary, weirdo, whimsy, zealot **7** anomaly, caprice, chimera, conceit, deviate, fanatic, monster **8** crotchet, flimflam **9** androgyne, curiosity **10** aberration, enthusiast **11** abnormality, monstrosity **12** lusus naturae, malformation
freakish 3 odd **5** kooky, outré, weird **6** far-out, quirky **7** bizarre, erratic, oddball, strange **8** aberrant, abnormal

9 arbitrary, eccentric, grotesque, whimsical **10** capricious, outlandish
freckle 3 dot **4** mole, spot **5** fleck **7** speckle, stipple
free 3 rid **4** comp, open **5** frank, loose, untie **6** acquit, exempt, gratis, loosen, unbind, untied **7** absolve, at large, liberal, manumit, movable, release, unbound, unchain, unleash, unloose **8** detached, generous, liberate, relieved, separate, unburden, unfasten, unloosen **9** at liberty, discharge, exculpate, exonerate, extricate, sovereign, unchained, unchecked, unimpeded, unshackle, unsparing **10** autonomous, democratic, emancipate, gratuitous, unconfined, unfastened, unfettered, unhampered, unshackled, voluntary **11** disentangle, emancipated, independent, spontaneous, untrammeled **12** unrestrained, unrestricted **13** complimentary, self-directing, self-governing, unconstrained
freebie 4 gift, pass **7** present **8** giveaway
freebooter 5 rover **6** bandit, pirate, raider **7** brigand, corsair **8** marauder, picaroon, pillager, rapparee, sea rover **9** buccaneer, pickaroon, plunderer, ransacker
freedom 5 right **7** liberty, license, release **8** autonomy, immunity, latitude **9** exemption, franchise, privilege **11** prerogative **12** emancipation, independence **13** outspokenness
free-for-all 4 fray **5** brawl, broil, melee **6** affray, fracas, rumble **7** ruction **10** donnybrook
freehanded 7 liberal **8** generous **9** bounteous, bountiful **10** munificent
freeloader 5 bum **5** leech **6** sponge **7** moocher **8** barnacle, hanger-on, parasite **11** bloodsucker
Free State 8 Maryland
free ticket 4 pass **11** Annie Oakley
freeze 4 halt, stop **5** chill, stall **6** benumb **7** congeal **8** glaciate, solidify, stoppage **10** immobilize
freezing 3 icy **4** cold **5** chill, gelid, nippy, polar **6** arctic, bitter, chilly, frigid, frosty, wintry **7** glacial, shivery **combining form: 4** cryo, kryo
freight 4 haul, lade, load **5** cargo **6** burden, charge, lading **7** payload **9** transport
freighter 4 scow, ship **7** carrier, shipper
Freischütz composer 5 Weber (Carl Maria von)
French article: 3 les, une **attendant: 9** concierge **back: 3** dos **bed: 3** lit **6** couche **boy: 6** garçon **brother: 5** frère **cap: 5** beret **cardinal: 7** Mazarin (Jules) **9** Richelieu (Duc de) **castle: 7** château

cathedral city: 4 Albi 5 Paris, Reims, Rouen 6 Amiens, Nantes, Rheims 8 Chartres *clergyman:* 4 abbé, curé, père *coin:* 3 ecu *combining form:* 5 Gallo 6 Franco *conjunction:* 4 mais *daughter:* 5 fille *day:* 5 jeudi, lundi, mardi 6 samedi 8 dimanche, mercredi, vendredi *dear:* 4 cher *department head:* 7 prefect *direction:* 3 est, sud 4 nord 5 ouest *down with:* 4 à bas *dream:* 4 rêve *drink:* 5 boire *dynasty:* 5 Capet 6 Valois 7 Bourbon *egg:* 4 oeuf *emblem:* 10 fleur-de-lis *empress:* 7 Eugénie 9 Joséphine *evening:* 4 soir *exclamation:* 3 zut 4 eheu, hein 9 sacrebleu *farewell:* 5 adieu 8 au revoir *father:* 4 père *forest:* 7 Argonne, Belleau *friend:* 3 ami 4 amie *game:* 3 jeu 4 jeux (plural) *God:* 4 dieu *good:* 3 bon 5 bonne *hat:* 7 chapeau *here:* 3 ici *income:* 5 rente *king:* 3 roi *language:* 9 Provençal *month:* 3 mai 4 août, juin, mars, mois 5 avril 7 février, janvier, juillet *mother:* 4 mère *national anthem:* 12 Marseillaise (La) *opera:* 5 Faust, Lakmé, Manon, Thaïs 6 Carmen, Mignon 7 Werther *pancake:* 5 crêpe *pastry:* 6 éclair 8 napoleon *policeman:* 4 flic 8 gendarme *porcelain:* 6 Sèvres 7 Limoges *preposition:* 3 par, sur 4 avec, dans, pour, sans, sous *pretty:* 4 joli 5 jolie *prison:* 8 Bastille *pronoun:* 3 eux, ils, mes, moi, toi, une 4 elle, nous, vous *Protestant:* 6 Calvin (John) 8 Huguenot *pupil:* 5 élève *queen:* 5 reine *rabbit:* 5 lapin *railroad station:* 4 gare *resort:* 3 Pau 4 Nice 5 Vichy 6 Cannes, Menton 7 Antibes 8 Biarritz *resort area:* 7 Riviera *restaurant:* 6 bistro *revolutionist:* 5 Marat (Jean-Paul) 6 Danton (Georges) 11 Robespierre (Maximilien) *Revolution party:* 7 Gironde, Jacobin 8 Mountain *Revolution song:* 5 Ça Ira *saint:* 4 Joan (of Arc) 5 Denis 6 Martin (of Tours) 7 Thérèse (of Lisieux) *school:* 5 école, lycée *sea:* 3 mer *season:* 3 été 5 hiver 7 automne 9 printemps *servant:* 5 valet *shop:* 8 boutique *shrine:* 7 Lourdes *singer:* 4 Piaf (Edith) 8 chanteur 9 chanteuse *sister:* 5 soeur *small:* 5 petit 6 petite *soldier:* 5 poilu 6 soldat, Zouave 8 chasseur *son:* 4 fils *song:* 7 chanson *soup:* 6 potage *star:* 6 étoile *state:* 4 état *stock exchange:* 6 bourse *street:* 3 rue *subway:* 5 metro *there!:* 5 voilà *too much:* 4 trop *very:* 4 très *wartime capital:* 5 Vichy *water:* 3 eau *well:* 4 bien *wineshop:* 6 bistro *wood:* 4 bois *yesterday:* 4 hier

French Guiana *capital:* 7 Cayenne *department of:* 6 France *ethnic group:* 6 Creole *island:* 6 Devil's *mountain range:* 10 Tumac-Humac *neighbor:* 6 Brazil

8 Suriname *river:* 4 Mana 6 Maroni 7 Oyapock

French Polynesia *archipelago* 7 Tuamotu *capital:* 7 Papeete *island, island group:* 6 Tahiti 7 Austral, Gambier, Society 9 Marquesas *territory of:* 6 France

frenetic 3 mad 4 loco, wild 5 crazy, wired 6 crazed, hectic 7 berserk, frantic 8 agitated, feverish, frenzied, maniacal 9 delirious, orgiastic 10 corybantic

frenzied see FRENETIC

frenzy 4 amok, fury, rage 5 amuck, craze, furor, mania 6 madden 7 derange, madness, unhinge 8 delirium, distract, hysteria, insanity, paroxysm 9 unbalance 11 derangement

frequency unit 5 hertz 7 fresnel 9 gigahertz, megahertz

frequent 5 haunt, often, usual, visit 6 common, hourly 7 regular 8 everyday, familiar, habitual 9 customary

frequenter 7 denizen, habitué, haunter

frequently 5 often 8 commonly 9 routinely 10 oftentimes, repeatedly 11 customarily, recurrently

fresh 3 new, raw 4 rude 5 green, naive, novel, sassy, saucy, smart 6 callow, cheeky, recent, unused, vernal, virgin 8 brand-new, impudent, insolent, original 9 unspoiled 11 impertinent, smartalecky 12 invigorating 13 inexperienced

freshet 5 flood, spate 6 influx

freshman 4 tyro 5 frosh, plebe 6 novice, rookie 8 beginner, neophyte, newcomer 10 apprentice, tenderfoot 13 underclassman

fret 4 fume, fuss, stew 5 brood, chafe, worry 6 dither, pother

fretful 5 angry, cross 6 crabby, cranky 7 carping, chafing, peevish, pettish, whining 8 captious, caviling, critical, perverse, petulant, restless, snappish 9 fractious, impatient, irascible, irritable, querulous

Frey *father:* 5 Njörd 6 Njörth *god of:* 3 sun 4 rain 5 peace 9 fertility *sister:* 5 Freya *wife:* 4 Gerd 5 Gerda, Gerth

Freya *brother:* 4 Frey *domain:* 9 Folkvangr *father:* 5 Njörd 6 Njörth *husband:* 4 Odin

friable 5 mealy 7 brittle, crumbly, fragile 9 frangible

friar 7 brother 8 cenobite 9 mendicant

fribble 3 toy 5 dally, flirt 6 coquet, trifle 7 trifler 8 trifling 9 dalliance, frivolity 10 dillydally, fool around

friction 4 drag 7 discord, rubbing 8 abrasion 9 animosity, attrition 10 disharmony, dissension, resistance 12 disagreement

friction match 5 vesta 7 lucifer 8 vesuvian

Friday's rescuer 6 Crusoe (Robinson)
friend 3 pal 4 ally, chum, mate 5 buddy,
crony, matey, serve 6 cohort 7 comrade, partner 8 alter ego, compadre,
confrere, familiar, intimate, playmate,
sidekick 9 associate, colleague, companion, confidant 10 confidante
11 cater-cousin 12 acquaintance *French:*
3 ami 4 amie *Spanish:* 5 amiga, amigo
Friend 6 Quaker *founder:* 3 Fox (George)
friendly 5 happy 6 amical, chummy,
folksy, genial 7 affable, amiable, cordial
8 amicable, cheerful, familiar, sociable
9 congenial, favorable 10 buddy-buddy,
compatible, hospitable, neighborly
12 affectionate, well-disposed
13 accommodating
Friendly Islands 5 Tonga
friends and neighbors 4 kith
friendship 5 amity 6 accord, comity
7 concord, empathy, harmony 8 affinity, alliance, goodwill
frigate bird 3 ioa, iwa 8 alcatras 11 man-
o'-war bird *genus:* 7 Fregata
Frigga, Frigg *husband:* 4 Odin *son:*
6 Balder
fright 4 fear 5 alarm, dread, panic, scare,
shock 6 dismay, horror, terror 11 trepidation
frighten 3 cow 5 alarm, bully, daunt,
scare, shock, spook 6 appall, dismay
7 horrify, perturb, scarify, startle, terrify, unnerve 9 terrorize 10 intimidate
frightful 4 ugly 6 awful, scary 6 horrid
7 fearful, ghastly, hideous 8 alarming,
dreadful, fearsome, horrible, horrific,
shocking, terrible, terrific 9 appalling,
startling 10 formidable, horrendous,
terrifying
frigid 3 icy 4 cold 5 chill 6 arctic, chilly,
frosty 7 glacial 8 freezing 11 emotionless, indifferent, passionless, unemotional 12 unresponsive
frijoles 5 beans
frill 4 ruff 5 jabot, ruche 6 doodad, luxury, ruffle 7 flounce, ruching 8 furbelow
11 affectation, superfluity 12 extravagance
fringe 3 hem, rim 4 brim, ruff 5 bound,
brink, skirt, thrum, verge 6 border,
edging, margin 7 fimbria 8 penumbra,
trimming 9 perimeter, periphery
10 borderland
frippery 6 finery, frills, tawdry 7 regalia
8 foofaraw, trumpery 9 trappings
11 ostentation
frisée 6 endive 7 lettuce
frisk 4 leap, play, romp, skip 5 caper,
dance 6 cavort, frolic, gambol, search
7 disport, pat down, rollick
frisky 3 gay 5 antic 6 feisty, lively

7 coltish, playful 8 animated, game-
some, sportive 9 sprightly, vivacious
10 frolicsome
fritter away 4 blow 5 spend, waste 7 consume 8 squander 9 dissipate
frivolity 3 fun 4 play 6 gaiety, levity,
whimsy 8 nonsense 12 childishness
frivolous 3 gay 5 dizzy, giddy, light, silly
6 frothy, yeasty 7 flighty, playful, shallow, trivial 8 carefree, careless, heedless, trifling 11 light-headed, superficial
frizzy 5 kinky 6 coiled, curled 7 twisted
frock 4 gown 5 dress, habit 6 jersey,
mantle
frog 4 toad 5 ranid 6 anuran 7 croaker
9 amphibian 10 batrachian *family:*
7 Ranidae *genus:* 4 Rana *kind:* 4 hyla
6 peeper 7 leopard 8 bullfrog, tree toad
larva: 7 tadpole
frolic 3 fun 4 lark, play, romp 5 antic,
caper, dance, frisk, party, prank, revel,
sport, spree 6 cavort, didoes, gaiety,
gambol, prance 7 disport, skylark
8 escapade, hilarity 9 festivity, merriment 10 shenanigan, tomfoolery
frolicsome 3 gay 5 antic 6 frisky, impish
7 coltish, jocular, playful, roguish
8 sportful, sportive 9 sprightly 10 rollicking 11 mischievous
from *German:* 3 von *Scottish:* 4 frae
From Here to Eternity author 5 Jones
(James)
frondeur 5 rebel 8 mutineer, renegade
9 anarchist, dissident, insurgent 10 malcontent
front 3 bow, van 4 face, fore, lend, look,
mask, prow 5 beard 6 facade, facing
7 forward 8 anterior, disguise 9 challenge, encounter 10 appearance, figurehead 11 countenance
frontier 5 bound, field, march 6 border
8 backland, backwash, boundary 9 up-
country 10 borderland, hinterland
11 backcountry
frontiersman 5 Boone (Daniel), Clark
(George Rogers, William) 6 Carson
(Kit) 7 pioneer, settler 8 Crockett
(Davy) 10 bushranger
fronton game 7 jai alai
frontward 8 anterior
frost 4 hoar, rime 6 freeze
frostfish 5 smelt 6 tomcod
frost heave 5 pingo
frosting 5 icing 7 topping 8 trimming
Frost poem 11 Mending Wall 12 Road
Not Taken (The) 18 Death of the Hired
Man (The) 30 Stopping By Woods on a
Snowy Evening
frosty 3 icy 4 cold, rimy 5 chill, frore,
hoary, nippy 6 chilly, frigid 7 glacial
8 freezing 10 unfriendly

froth 4 foam, head, suds **5** cream, spume, yeast **6** lather **8** airiness **9** frivolity, lightness

froufrou 6 frills **8** rustling

froward 5 balky **6** mulish, ornery **7** peevish, restive **8** contrary, perverse, petulant, stubborn **9** obstinate **10** headstrong, refractory **11** disobedient

frown 4 pout, sulk **5** glare, lower, scowl **6** glower

frowsy 5 dowdy, funky, fusty, messy, musty, stale **6** shabby, smelly, sordid, untidy **7** squalid, unkempt **8** slattern, slovenly **10** disheveled, disordered, slatternly **13** draggletailed

frozen 4 cold, hard **5** fixed, frore, rigid, stiff **6** frigid, numbed **7** chilled **8** benumbed, immobile **9** congealed, petrified

frugal 4 mean **5** canny, scant, spare **6** Scotch, stingy **7** careful, prudent, scrimpy, sparing, thrifty **8** discreet, stinting **9** niggardly, penurious, provident **10** economical, unwasteful **12** cheeseparing, parsimonious **13** penny-pinching

frugality 6 thrift **7** economy **8** prudence **9** husbandry **10** providence **11** thriftiness

fruit 5 issue, young **6** result **7** outcome, progeny **9** offspring *citrus:* **4** lime **5** lemon **6** citron, orange, pomelo **7** kumquat, tangelo **8** bergamot, mandarin, shaddock **9** tangerine **10** calamondin, grapefruit *dried:* **5** prune **6** raisin *drink:* **3** ade **5** juice, punch *fleshy:* **7** syconia (plural) **8** syconium *hard-shelled:* **3** nut **4** seed **5** gourd **7** coconut *residue:* **4** marc **6** pomace *seed:* **3** pip *study of:* **8** pomology **9** carpology *subtropical:* **3** fig **4** date, lime **5** lemon, olive **6** citron, orange **7** avocado, kumquat **9** tangerine **10** grapefruit *sugar:* **7** glucose **8** fructose, levulose *temperatezone:* **4** pear, plum, sloe **5** apple, grape, melon, papaw, peach, prune **6** casaba, cherry, loquat, pawpaw, quince **7** apricot, currant **8** dewberry **9** blueberry, cranberry, muskmelon, nectarine, raspberry **10** blackberry, gooseberry, loganberry, strawberry **11** boysenberry, huckleberry, pomegranate *tropical:* **5** guava, mango **6** banana, papaya **7** acerola **8** rambutan, tamarind **9** cherimoya, persimmon, pineapple **10** calamondin, mangosteen *type:* **3** nut **4** pepo, pome **5** berry, drupe **6** achene, legume, loment, samara **7** capsule, silique, utricle **11** hesperidium *undeveloped:* **6** nubbin

fruitful 6 fecund **7** copious, fertile

8 abundant, prolific **9** bountiful, fructuous, plenteous, plentiful **10** productive **11** proliferant

fruition 7 delight **8** pleasure **9** enjoyment **10** attainment, conclusion **11** achievement, delectation, fulfillment, realization

fruitless 4 vain **6** barren, futile **7** sterile, useless **8** abortive **10** unavailing **11** ineffective, ineffectual **12** unproductive, unsuccessful

frumpy 4 drab, dull **5** dated, dowdy, tacky **6** stodgy **8** outmoded **9** out-of-date, unstylish **12** old-fashioned

frustrate 4 balk, bilk, dash, foil, halt **5** block, check, stump **6** arrest, baffle, defeat, hinder, impede, stymie, thwart **7** inhibit, prevent **8** confound, obstruct, preclude, prohibit **9** discomfit, forestall, interrupt **10** disappoint

frustration 6 defeat, dismay **7** chagrin, letdown **8** vexation **9** annoyance, hindrance **10** impediment, irritation **11** displeasure, obstruction

fry 4 burn, sear **5** frizz, grill, sauté **6** fishes, picnic **7** frizzle **11** electrocute

frying pan 6 spider **7** griddle, skillet

fuddle 5 befog, booze **6** ball up, jumble, tipple **7** confuse, fluster, stupefy **8** bewilder **10** intoxicate

fuddy-duddy 4 fogy **6** fossil, square, stodgy **8** mossback, outdated, outmoded **12** antediluvian, Colonel Blimp, old-fashioned, stuffed shirt **13** stick-in-the-mud

fudge 3 pad **4** blur, bosh, fake **5** candy, cheat, color, dodge, hedge, hooey, welsh **6** bunkum **7** distort, falsify, hogwash, penuche **8** contrive, divinity, nonsense **9** embellish, embroider, overstate, poppycock **10** equivocate, flapdoodle **11** foolishness

fuel 3 gas, oil **4** coal, coke, fire, peat, wood **5** stoke **6** biogas, diesel, petrol **7** ethanol, gasohol, inflame, propane **8** charcoal, gasoline, kerosene **9** petroleum, stimulate **10** natural gas **13** reinforcement

fugacious 7 brittle, passing **8** fleeting, fugitive, volatile **9** ephemeral, momentary, transient **10** evanescent, short-lived, transitory

fugitive 5 exile **6** outlaw **7** escapee, lamster, nomadic, passing, refugee, runaway **8** deserter, fleeting, runagate, vagabond **9** ephemeral, fugacious, momentary, transient, wandering **10** evanescent, short-lived, transitory

fugue master 4 Bach (Johann Sebastian)

Führer, der 6 Hitler (Adolf)

fulcrum 3 hub 4 axis, prop 5 hinge, nexus, pivot 7 support

fulfill 4 meet 5 honor 6 effect, finish, redeem 7 achieve, execute, perform, satisfy 8 complete 9 discharge, implement 10 accomplish

fulgent 6 bright 7 beaming, glowing, radiant, shining 8 luminous, lustrous 9 brilliant

fuliginous 4 dark 5 dingy, dusky, grimy, murky, sooty 7 obscure

full 5 sated, total, whole 6 entire, gorged, jammed, loaded, packed, utmost 7 crammed, crowded, glutted, maximum, plenary, replete, stuffed 8 brimming, complete, satiated 9 jam-packed, plentiful, surfeited 11 chockablock

full-blooded 4 rich 5 flush, ruddy 6 ardent, florid 7 flushed, genuine, glowing 8 forceful, purebred, rubicund, sanguine 9 pedigreed, pureblood 10 compelling 12 thoroughbred

full-blown 4 lush, ripe 5 adult, total 6 all-out, mature 7 grown-up

full-bodied 4 rich 5 husky, lusty, stout 6 potent, robust, strong 9 corpulent 10 meaningful 11 significant, substantial

full dress 6 finery 7 regalia 8 frippery, glad rags 10 Sunday best

full-figured 5 ample, buxom, plump 6 zaftig 10 curvaceous, Rubenesque, statuesque, voluptuous

full-fledged 4 ripe 5 adult, grown, total 6 mature 7 genuine, grown-up 8 complete 9 full-blown

full-grown 4 ripe 5 adult 6 mature

fullness 6 plenty 7 satiety 9 abundance, amplitude, repletion 10 perfection 12 completeness

full-scale 5 total 6 all-out 8 complete, life-size 9 unlimited

full tilt 7 flat-out, rapidly, swiftly 8 pell-mell, speedily 9 posthaste 12 lickety-split

fulminate 4 boil, burn, foam, fume, rage, rave 5 curse, flare 7 bluster, explode, inveigh

fulsome 4 oily 5 plump, slick, soapy, suave 6 lavish, smarmy, smooth 7 buttery, cloying, copious, profuse 8 abundant, effusive, generous, overdone, unctuous 9 excessive 10 flattering, oleaginous 11 extravagant, pharisaical 12 ingratiating, Pecksniffian

Fulton's steamboat 8 Clermont

fumarole 4 vent

fumble 3 bob, paw 4 feel, flub, mess, muff 5 botch, grope 6 bobble, bollix, bungle, muddle 7 blunder, misplay 8 flounder

fume 3 gas 4 boil, burn, odor, rage, rant, rave, reek, snit, stew 5 smoke, vapor 6 seethe, swivet 7 sputter

fun 4 play 5 sport 6 frolic, gaiety 7 amusing, jollity, pastime, whoopee 8 hilarity, pleasant, ridicule 9 amusement, diversion, diverting, enjoyment, frivolity, horseplay, jocundity, joviality, merriment 10 pleasantry 12 entertaining 13 entertainment

function 3 act, job, run, use 4 duty, goal, mark, role, task, work 5 party, power, react, serve 6 affair, behave, object, office, target 7 concern, faculty, operate, perform, purpose, service 8 activity, behavior, business, capacity, ceremony, occasion, province 9 objective, officiate, operation, reception *trigonometric:* 4 sine 6 cosine, secant 7 tangent 8 cosecant 9 cotangent

functional 5 handy, utile 6 useful 7 working 9 practical 11 practicable, serviceable, utilitarian 12 occupational

functioning 6 active 7 dynamic 9 operative

fund 4 bank, pool 5 endow, stake, stock, store 6 coffer, supply 7 capital, finance, reserve 8 bankroll, treasury 9 inventory, subsidize 10 accumulate, capitalize

fundament 4 butt, rear, rump, seat 5 basis, fanny 6 behind, bottom 8 backside, buttocks, derriere 9 posterior, principle 10 foundation, groundwork

fundamental 3 key 5 axiom, basal, basic, prime, vital 6 bottom, factor, primal, simple 7 bedrock, organic, primary, radical, theorem 8 absolute, cardinal, dominant, ultimate 9 component, essential, important, necessary, paramount, primitive, principal, principle, requisite 10 deep-rooted, elementary, grassroots, primordial, rock-bottom, underlying 11 constituent, irreducible, nitty-gritty 12 constitutive, foundational

fund-raiser 8 telethon

funeral 6 burial 7 obsequy 9 obsequies *car:* 6 hearse *director:* 9 mortician 10 undertaker *oration:* 6 eulogy 8 encomium 9 panegyric *procession:* 7 cortege *service:* 7 requiem 9 obsequies *song:* 5 dirge, elegy 8 threnody

funereal 3 sad 4 dark 5 black, bleak, grave 6 dismal, dreary, gloomy, solemn, somber, sombre 7 elegiac 8 mournful 9 deathlike, sorrowful 10 depressing, depressive, lugubrious, oppressive, sepulchral

fungus 4 conk, mold, rust, smut 5 ergot, yeast 6 agaric, dry rot, mildew 7 candida, truffle 8 mushroom, puffball 9 earthstar, stinkhorn, toadstool *combining form:* 4 myco 5 myces, mycet

6 mycete, myceto *part:* **3** cap **4** gill
5 ascus, hypha, stipe, volva **7** annulus
8 basidium, conidium, mycelium

fungus disease 3 rot **4** mold, rust, scab, smut **5** ergot, tinea **6** blight, mildew, thrush **7** mycosis **8** lumpy jaw, ringworm **12** athlete's foot

funk 4 odor, reek **5** blues, dolor, dumps, ennui, gloom, smell, stink, slump **6** recoil, stench **7** sadness **9** dejection **10** depression, melancholy

funky 3 hip, odd **4** foul, rank **5** fetid, reeky **6** earthy, frowsy, grungy, quaint, quirky, smelly, stinky **7** natural, noisome, oddball, offbeat **8** down-home **10** malodorous

funnel 4 flue, pipe **5** stack **6** hopper **7** channel, conduct, tundish **8** transmit **10** smokestack

funny 3 odd **4** joke, zany **5** antic, comic, droll, fishy, queer **7** amusing, bizarre, comical, jocular, risible, strange **8** farcical, humorous, peculiar **9** facetious, fantastic, hilarious, laughable, ludicrous **10** ridiculous

Funny Girl 5 Brice (Fanny) *composer:* **5** Styne (Jule)

funnyman 3 wag, wit **5** clown, comic, cutup, droll, joker **6** gagman, jester **8** comedian, humorist, jokester, quipster **10** comedienne

fur 4 down, hide, pelt, pile **5** floss, fluff, stole **6** pelage, peltry *kind:* **3** fox **4** mink, seal **5** fitch, otter, sable **6** ermine, fisher, marten, nutria, tanuki **7** raccoon **10** chinchilla *lamb:* **7** caracul, karakul **9** broadtail *medieval:* **4** vair **7** miniver

furbelow 5 frill **7** flounce

furbish 4 buff **5** fix up, renew, shine **6** polish, revive **7** burnish, refresh, restore **8** renovate

Furies 6 Alecto **7** Erinyes, Megaera **9** Eumenides, Tisiphone

furious 3 mad **4** wild **5** angry, livid, irate, rabid, upset **6** crazed, fierce, insane, raging, stormy **7** enraged, excited, extreme, frantic, intense, violent **8** feverish, frenetic, frenzied, incensed, maddened, vehement, wrathful **9** impetuous, turbulent **10** boisterous, corybantic

furl 4 curl, fold, roll, wrap **6** take in

furlough 4 pass **5** leave **6** lay off **7** liberty **10** shore leave **13** authorization

furnace 4 kiln, oven **5** forge, stove **6** heater **7** smelter **8** tryworks **11** incinerator *part:* **4** port, vent **6** tuyere *tender:* **6** stoker

furnish 3 arm, rig **4** give, hand, lend **5** endow, endue, equip **6** fit out, outfit, supply **7** apparel, appoint, deliver, provide, turn out **8** accouter, accoutre, dispense, hand over, transfer **9** provision **10** contribute

furnishings 4 gear **5** decor **9** equipment, trappings **10** housewares **11** appointment **13** accouterments, accoutrements, paraphernalia

furniture designer *American:* **5** Eames (Charles, Ray), Phyfe (Duncan) **7** Goddard (John, Stephen, Thomas), Haldane (William) **8** Stickley (Gustav) *British:* **6** Morris (William) **7** Gibbons (Grinling), Shearer (Thomas) **8** Sheraton (Thomas) **11** Chippendale (Thomas), Hepplewhite (George) *French:* **5** Marot (Daniel) **6** Boulle (André-Charles) *German:* **6** Breuer (Marcel) *Scottish:* **4** Adam (James, Robert)

furniture style 4 Adam **6** Empire, Shaker **7** Bauhaus, Federal, Mission **8** Colonial, Georgian, Jacobean, Sheraton, Stickley **9** Queen Anne **11** chinoiserie, Chippendale, Duncan Phyfe, Hepplewhite **13** Arts and Crafts

furor 3 ado, cry, fad, wax **4** chic, mode, rage, stir, to-do **5** anger, craze, mania, style, vogue **6** flurry, frenzy, pother, ruckus, rumpus, uproar **7** fashion, madness **8** foofaraw **9** commotion **10** dernier cri, excitement **11** controversy

furrow 3 rut **4** ruck **5** plica, ridge, sulci (plural) **6** course, crease, groove, sulcus, trench **7** channel, crinkle, wrinkle **8** entrench **9** corrugate **11** corrugation

furrowed 5 lined **6** rugose **7** grooved, sulcate **8** wrinkled **10** corrugated

further 4 abet, also, help **5** again, fresh **6** beyond **7** advance, besides, forward, promote **8** engender, moreover **9** encourage, propagate **10** additional, in addition **12** additionally

furthermore 3 and, too **4** also **6** as well, withal **7** besides **8** likewise, moreover **9** what's more **12** additionally

furthermost 4 last **7** extreme **8** farthest, remotest, ultimate

furtive 3 sly **4** foxy, wary, wily **6** artful, covert, crafty, feline, masked, secret, shifty, sneaky, stolen, tricky **7** catlike, cunning, evasive, sub-rosa **8** guileful, hush-hush, scheming, stealthy **9** disguised, insidious **11** circumspect, clandestine **12** hugger-mugger **13** surreptitious, under-the-table *look:* **4** peek, peep

fur trader 8 voyageur

furuncle 4 boil **7** abscess

fury 3 ire **4** burn, rage **5** anger, furor, wrath **6** frenzy **7** madness, passion **8** violence **9** vehemence **10** fierceness

furze 4 whin **5** gorse *genus:* **4** Ulex **7** Genista

fuse 3 mix **4** flux, meld, melt, weld **5** blend, merge, smelt, unify, unite

6 anneal, solder **7** liquefy **8** coalesce, conflate, dissolve, intermix **9** commingle, integrate **10** amalgamate **11** consolidate, incorporate

fusillade 4 hail **5** burst, salvo **6** shower, volley **7** barrage **8** drumfire, outburst **9** broadside, cannonade **11** bombardment

fusion 5 alloy, blend, union **6** merger **7** amalgam, mixture **8** compound **9** coalition, immixture, synthesis

fuss 3 ado, nag, row **4** beef, crab, flap, fret, miff, stew, stir, to-do, wail **5** gripe, stink, upset, whine, worry **6** bother, bustle, hassle, hurrah, pother, ruckus, rumpus, squawk **7** protest, quarrel **8** complain, foofaraw, squabble **9** commotion, complaint, kerfuffle, objection **10** excitement **11** controversy **12** perturbation

fussbudget 3 hen **6** granny **8** stickler **10** fuddy-duddy **13** perfectionist

fusspot 8 stickler **9** nitpicker, worrywart

fussy 5 picky **6** cranky, dainty, ornate **7** careful, finicky, fretful **9** crotchety, irritable, querulous **10** fastidious, meticulous, particular, pernickety, scrupulous **11** painstaking, persnickety, punctilious **13** conscientious

fustian 4 rant **7** bombast, pompous **8** affected, inflated **9** high-flown **11** exaggerated, highfalutin, pretentious **13** grandiloquent

fusty 4 rank **5** close, dated, fetid, moldy, passé, stale **6** bygone, old-hat, smelly **7** archaic **8** outdated **10** antiquated, malodorous **11** reactionary **12** old-fashioned **13** superannuated

futile 4 idle, vain **5** empty **6** hollow, otiose **7** useless **8** abortive, bootless, hopeless, nugatory **9** fruitless, worthless **10** unavailing **11** ineffective, ineffectual **12** unproductive, unsuccessful

future 5 later **6** offing, to come **7** by-and-by **8** oncoming, tomorrow **9** hereafter

Futurism *founder:* **9** Marinetti (Filippo Tommaso) *painter:* **5** Balla (Giacomo), Carra (Carlo) **7** Russolo (Luigi) **8** Boccioni (Umberto), Severini (Gino) *sculptor:* **8** Boccioni (Umberto)

fuzz 3 cop **4** down, lint **6** police

fuzzy 3 dim **5** faint, gauzy, linty, vague, woozy **6** bleary, blurry **7** blurred, muddled, obscure, shadowy, unclear **8** confused **9** distorted, undefined **10** ill-defined, incoherent, indefinite, indistinct

fylfot 8 swastika

G

gab 3 jaw, rap, yak **4** blab, chat, talk **5** clack, drool, prate, speak **6** babble, drivel, gibber, gossip, jabber, natter, yammer **7** blabber, blather, chatter, palaver, prattle, twaddle **8** chitchat, converse, idle talk **9** gibberish, small talk

gabber 6 gossip, magpie **7** blabber **9** chatterer **10** chatterbox **12** blabbermouth, gossipmonger

gabby 4 glib **5** talky, windy **6** chatty **7** voluble **8** effusive **9** garrulous, talkative **10** long-winded, loquacious **11** loose-lipped **12** loose-tongued

gaberdine 4 coat, suit **5** cloak, cloth **6** capote, fabric **7** garment, manteau **8** material

gable 4 wall **8** pediment *ornament:* **6** finial

Gabon *capital:* **10** Libreville *city:* **10** Port-Gentil *ethnic group:* **4** Fang **5** Bantu *language:* **6** French *monetary unit:* **5** franc *neighbor:* **5** Congo **8** Cameroon *river:* **6** Ogooué

gad 3 bat **4** flit, roam, rove **5** amble, drift, mooch, range, stray, tramp **6** chisel, ramble, wander **7** maunder, meander, traipse **9** gallivant

Gad *brother:* **5** Asher *father:* **5** Jacob *mother:* **6** Zilpah *son:* **3** Eri **5** Ezbon, Haggi

Gaddis *novel* **12** Recognitions (The) **14** Frolic of His Own (A) **16** Carpenter's Gothic

gadfly 3 nag **4** pest, pill **6** bother, critic, insect, nudnik **8** nuisance

gadget 4 tool **5** gizmo, thing **6** device, dingus, doodad, hickey, jigger, widget **7** concern, gimmick, utensil **9** apparatus, appliance, doohickey, implement, mechanism **10** instrument **11** contraption, thingamabob, thingamajig, thingumajig

gadwall 4 bird, duck, fowl 9 waterfowl

gadzooks 4 drat, egad 6 crikey, zounds

Gaea *husband:* 6 Uranus *offspring:* 6 Furies, Giants, Titans, Typhon, Uranus 7 Erinyes 8 Cyclopes 9 Eumenides *parent:* 5 Chaos

Gaelic 4 Erse 5 Irish 6 Celtic 8 Scottish *god:* 3 Ler 5 Dagda *hero:* 5 Oisin 6 Ossian 11 Finn MacCool *king:* 9 Conchobar, Conchobor *language:* 4 Manx *poet:* 4 bard 6 Ossian *queen:* 4 Medb *soldier:* 4 kern 6 Fenian *spirit:* 7 banshee

gaff 3 fix, rig 4 hoax, hook, spar, spur 5 abuse, fraud, spear, trick 6 fleece, ordeal 7 deceive, gimmick 8 raillery 12 climbing iron

gaffe 4 flub, goof, muff 5 boner, error, fault, fluff, lapse 6 bollix, boo-boo, bungle, foul-up, howler, slipup 7 blooper, blunder, clinker, faux pas, misstep, mistake 8 solecism 9 gaucherie 11 impropriety, misjudgment 12 indiscretion

gag 4 balk, gasp, hoax, jape, jest, joke, quip 5 choke, crack, heave, prank, retch, trick 6 muffle, muzzle, shtick, stifle, strain 7 repress, silence, squelch 8 throttle 9 restraint, wisecrack, witticism

gaga 4 agog, wild 5 crazy, giddy, nutty, wacky 6 doting, fervid, gung ho 7 foolish, gushing, excited, smitten 8 animated, enamored, obsessed, thrilled 9 ebullient, exuberant 10 captivated, infatuated 12 enthusiastic

gage 3 vow 4 bond 5 token 6 pledge, surety 8 gauntlet, security (see also GAUGE)

gaggle 4 crew, gang, pack 5 array, bunch, flock, group 6 clutch, number 7 cluster 10 assemblage, collection 11 aggregation

Gaheris *brother:* 6 Gareth, Gawain *father:* 3 Lot *mother:* 8 Margawse, Morgause *uncle:* 6 Arthur *victim:* 8 Margawse, Morgause

gaiety 3 fun, joy 4 glee 5 mirth, revel 6 finery, frolic, hoopla 7 elation, jollity, revelry, whoopee 8 elegance, hilarity, reveling, vivacity 9 animation, festivity, happiness, joviality, merriment 10 ebullience, exuberance, hullabaloo, joyousness, jubilation, liveliness 11 high spirits, merrymaking 12 conviviality

gain 3 get, net, win 4 earn, land, make, reap 5 clear, cover, lucre, reach, score 6 attain, expand, obtain, pick up, profit, rack up, return, secure 7 achieve, acquire, advance, attract, augment, ben-

efit, bring in, enlarge, procure 8 draw down, earnings, increase, overtake, persuade, proceeds, traverse, windfall 10 accomplish 11 move forward

gainful 6 paying 8 fruitful, generous 9 lucrative, rewarding 10 beneficial, productive, profitable, well-paying, worthwhile 12 advantageous, remunerative

gainsay 4 buck, defy, deny 6 impugn, negate, oppose, refute, resist 7 dispute 8 disclaim, disprove, negative, traverse 9 disaffirm, repudiate, withstand 10 contradict, contravene, controvert

Gainsborough *painting* 7 Blue Boy

gait 3 air, run 4 clip, dash, lope, pace, rate, step, trot, walk 5 amble, speed, strut, train, tread 6 canter, gallop, stride 7 bearing 8 demeanor

gaiter 4 boot, shoe, spat 7 legging 8 overshoe

gal 4 babe, doll 5 chick

gala 4 ball, bash, fete, prom 5 merry, party 6 lively 7 festive, jubilee, pageant, shindig 8 festival, jamboree, wingding 9 festivity, spectacle 11 celebration 13 entertainment

galago 5 lemur 8 bush baby

Galahad *father:* 8 Lancelot 9 Launcelot *mother:* 6 Elaine *quest:* 5 Grail 9 Holy Grail

Galatea *father:* 6 Nereus *husband:* 9 Pygmalion *lover:* 4 Acis *mother:* 5 Doris

galaxy 6 nebula 8 Milky Way, universe

Galba *predecessor:* 4 Nero *successor:* 4 Otho

gale 4 blow, gust, wind 5 blast, storm 6 squall 7 cyclone, tempest, typhoon 8 outburst 9 hurricane

galena 3 ore

Galen's *forte* 7 healing 8 medicine

galilee 5 porch 6 chapel

Galilee *town* 4 Cana 7 Gergesa 8 Nazareth, Tiberias 9 Bethsaida, Capernaum

Galileo's *birthplace* 4 Pisa 5 Italy 7 Tuscany

gall 3 irk, nag, rub, vex 4 bile, fray, fret, rile, roil, sore, wear 5 annoy, brass, chafe, cheek, erode, grate, graze, nerve 6 abrade, bother, burn up, harass, pester, plague, rancor, ruffle, scrape 7 conceit, disturb, frazzle, inflame, provoke, scratch, torment 8 audacity, boldness, chutzpah, irritate, temerity 9 aggravate, arrogance, brashness, impudence, insolence 10 bitterness, effrontery

gallant 3 fop 4 beau, bold, buck, dude, hero 5 blade, blood, brave, civil, dandy, lover, manly, Romeo, showy, suave, swain, wooer 6 daring, heroic, suitor, urbane 7 courtly, coxcomb, dashing, Don Juan, stately, valiant 8 Casanova, gracious, lothario, paramour, spirited, valorous 9 attentive, courteous, dauntless, ladies' man 10 chivalrous, courageous

gallantry 5 honor, poise, valor 6 daring, mettle, spirit 7 amenity, bravery, courage, heroism, prowess, suavity 8 boldness, chivalry, courtesy, urbanity, valiance, valiancy 9 attention, manliness 10 resolution 11 courtliness 12 fearlessness

galleon 7 warship 12 square-rigger

gallery 5 patio, porch, salon 6 arcade, loggia, museum, piazza 7 balcony, passage, portico, veranda 8 audience, corridor, showroom 9 colonnade, onlookers, promenade *ancient Greek:* 4 stoa

galley 3 gig 4 boat, mess, ship, tray 5 cuddy, proof 6 bireme 7 canteen, kitchen, trireme, warship 8 scullery 9 cookhouse

Gallic 6 French

gallimaufry 3 mix 4 hash, mess, olio, stew 5 chaos 6 jumble, medley 7 clutter, goulash, mélange, mixture, variety 8 mishmash, pastiche 9 patchwork, potpourri 10 assortment, hodgepodge, hotchpotch, miscellany, salmagundi

gallinaceous bird 3 hen 5 quail 6 grouse, turkey 7 chicken, hoatzin, peacock 8 curassow, pheasant 9 partridge 10 guinea fowl

galling 6 bitter, vexing 8 rankling 9 upsetting, vexatious 10 afflictive, irritating, nettlesome 11 aggravating, distressing, troublesome 12 exasperating

gallivant 3 bat, bum, gad 4 flit, roam, rove 5 amble, drift, jaunt, mooch, range, stray 6 cruise, ramble, travel, wander 7 meander, traipse 8 vagabond 10 knock about

gallop 4 dash, race 6 sprint

gallows 6 gibbet *bird:* 7 villain 8 criminal

galore 4 full, lush, rich 5 ample, great 6 lavish 7 aplenty, copious, endless, profuse 8 abundant, generous 9 bountiful, expansive, plentiful 11 overflowing

galosh 4 boot, shoe 6 rubber 8 overshoe

Galsworthy work 7 Justice 11 Forsyte Saga (The)

galumph 4 plod 5 barge, clomp, clump, stomp, stump, tramp 6 lumber, trudge

galvanize 3 jar, zap 4 coat, fire, jolt, stir, spur, stun 5 pep up, pique, prime, react, rouse, shock 6 arouse, excite, perk up, thrill 7 animate, enliven, immerse, inspire, provoke, quicken 8 activate, astonish, energize, motivate,

vitalize 9 electrify, innervate, magnetize, stimulate 10 invigorate

gam 3 leg, pin, pod, rap 4 chat, flap, limb, talk 5 visit 6 confab 9 drumstick 12 conversation

Gambia *capital:* 6 Banjul *city:* 9 Serekunda *language:* 7 English *monetary unit:* 6 dalasi *neighbor:* 7 Senegal

gambit 3 con, jig 4 move, play, ploy, ruse, wile 5 dodge, topic, trick 6 design, device, remark, tactic 7 gimmick 8 artifice, maneuver, trickery 9 expedient, stratagem 10 subterfuge

gamble 3 bet, lay, set 4 dare, game, play, punt, risk 5 put on, stake, wager 6 chance, hazard, plunge, raffle 7 imperil, lottery, venture 8 cast lots, long shot 9 crapshoot, speculate 10 jeopardize

gambler 5 dicer, shark, sharp 7 sharper 9 cardsharp 10 cardplayer 11 cardsharper

gambling place 3 den 4 club, dive, Reno 5 joint, Vegas 6 casino 8 Las Vegas, pool hall 9 roadhouse 10 Monte Carlo 12 Atlantic City, betting house

gambol 3 hop 4 jump, lark, leap, romp, skip 5 bound, caper, frisk, revel, sport 6 cavort, frolic, prance, spring 7 carry on, roister, rollick

Gambrinus' invention 3 ale 4 beer 5 lager

game 3 bet, fun, lay 4 bold, jest, joke, lark, play, prey, romp 5 brave, chase, eager, hardy, sport, stake, trick, wager 6 gamble, quarry, spunky 7 contest, pastime, valiant, willing 8 fearless, intrepid, resolute, unafraid, valorous 9 amusement, dauntless, diversion, undaunted 10 courageous, recreation *ball:* 4 golf, polo, pool 5 fives, rogue, rugby 6 hockey, pelota, soccer, squash, tennis 7 cricket, croquet, jai alai 8 baseball, football, handball, hardball, lacrosse, racquets, rounders, softball 9 billiards 10 basketball, volleyball 11 racquetball *Basque:* 6 pelota 7 jai alai *bird:* 4 duck 5 quail 6 chukar, turkey 7 bustard 8 bobwhite, pheasant 9 partridge *board:* 5 chess 7 pachisi 8 checkers, Scrabble 9 crokinole, Parcheesi 10 backgammon *card:* 3 gin, loo, Uno, war 4 faro, fish, skat, solo 5 monte, ombre, pitch, poker, rummy, whist 6 Boston, bridge, casino, écarté, euchre, fan-tan, hearts, piquet 7 auction, bezique, canasta, cooncan, old maid, primero 8 baccarat, Canfield, conquian, cribbage, gin rummy, pinochle 9 blackjack, solitaire, twenty-one, vingt-et-un 11 chemin de fer *child's:* 3 tag 5 jacks 7 marbles

8 leapfrog, peekaboo **9** hopscotch *confidence:* **4** scam **5** bunco, bunko, sting *court:* **5** roque **6** pelota, squash, tennis **7** jai alai **8** handball, racquets **9** badminton **10** basketball, volleyball **11** racquetball *electric:* **7** pinball *English:* **5** rugby **7** cricket **8** draughts *Irish:* **7** hurling *of chance:* **4** faro, keno **5** beano, bingo, boule, craps, lotto, rondo **6** fan-tan, hazard, policy, raffle **7** lottery, rondeau **8** roulette *parlor:* **8** charades *racket:* **6** squash, tennis **8** lacrosse, ping-pong, racquets **9** badminton **11** racquetball, table tennis *roulette-like:* **6** boule *rule maker:* **5** Hoyle (Edmond) *string:* **10** cat's cradle *table:* **4** pool **5** craps **7** mah-jong, snooker **8** dominoes, mah-jongg, ping-pong, roulette **9** bagatelle, billiards **11** table tennis *word:* **5** rebus **6** crambo **7** anagram, hangman **8** acrostic, charades, Scrabble **9** crossword, logograph
game plan 6 scheme, tactic **8** scenario, strategy **9** blueprint **10** big picture
gamete 3 egg **4** ovum **5** sperm **8** germ cell
gamin 3 elf, imp, tad **4** brat, tyke, waif **5** scamp **6** monkey, rascal, urchin **11** guttersnipe **12** street urchin
gamine 3 elf, imp **4** brat, waif **5** scamp **6** hoyden, rascal, tomboy, urchin **11** guttersnipe **12** street urchin
gaming cubes 4 dice **5** bones
gammon 3 ham **4** dupe, fool, rook **5** bacon, feign **6** delude, fleece, humbug **7** deceive, pretend, swindle **8** flimflam, hoodwink **9** bamboozle **11** hornswoggle
gamut 5 range, scale, scope, sweep **6** extent, series, spread **7** compass **8** diapason, spectrum
gamy 3 off **4** foul, racy, rank, vile **5** brave, fetid, funky **6** plucky, putrid, rancid, rotten, smelly, sordid, stinky, strong **7** corrupt, decayed, noisome, noxious, reeking **10** decomposed, malodorous, scandalous **12** disagreeable, disreputable
gander 4 look, peek **5** goose **6** glance **7** glimpse **9** simpleton, waterfowl
___ **Gandhi 5** Rajiv **6** Indira **7** Mahatma **8** Mohandas
gandy dancer 10 railroader, tracklayer
ganef 5 thief **6** rascal **9** scoundrel
Ganesa, Ganesh *father:* **4** Siva **5** Shiva *head:* **8** elephant *mother:* **7** Parvati
gang 3 lot, mob, set **4** band, clan, club, crew, pack, ring, team **5** bunch, crowd, group, horde **6** circle, clique, outfit **7** arrange, cluster, collect, combine, company, coterie **8** assemble **10** accumulate, assemblage **11** combination
gangling 4 bony, lean, slim **5** gaunt,

lanky, rangy **6** meager, meagre, skinny **7** angular, scrawny, slender, spindly, stringy **8** rawboned **9** spindling
ganglion 5 tumor **7** nucleus
gangrene 3 rot **5** decay **7** mortify, putrefy **8** necrosis **9** decompose
gangster 4 goon, hood, thug **5** rough, thief, tough **6** bandit, gunman **7** hoodlum, mafioso, mobster, ruffian **8** criminal **9** cutthroat, racketeer *girlfriend:* **4** moll
gangway 4 hall, path **5** aisle **7** passage, walkway **8** corridor **10** passageway
ganja 3 kef, kif, pot, tea **4** hemp, herb, weed **5** grass, smoke **7** hashish **8** cannabis, Mary Jane **9** marijuana
gannet 4 bird **5** booby **7** seabird
ganoid fish 3 gar **6** beluga, bowfin **7** dogfish, garfish, teleost **8** billfish, sturgeon **10** paddlefish
Ganymede *abductor:* **4** Zeus **7** Jupiter *brother:* **4** Ilus *father:* **4** Tros *function:* **9** cupbearer
gaol 3 jug, pen **4** jail **5** clink, joint, pokey **6** cooler, lockup, prison **7** slammer **8** bastille **9** calaboose, jailhouse **12** penitentiary
gap 3 cut, pit **4** gash, gulf, hole, lull, pass, rent, rift, skip, slit, slot, tear, vent, void, yawn **5** abyss, blank, break, chasm, chink, cleft, clove, crack, gorge, gulch, gully, pause, space, split **6** arroyo, breach, canyon, cavity, cranny, divide, hiatus, hollow, lacuna, ravine, recess, schism, vacuum **7** caesura, crevice, fissure, interim, opening, orifice, rupture, vacancy, vacuity **8** aperture, cleavage, division, fracture, interval **9** disparity, interlude **10** deficiency, difference, interstice, separation **12** intermission, interruption **13** discontinuity
gape 3 eye, yaw **4** bore, gawk, gawp, gaze, glom, leer, look, ogle, open, part, peer, yawn **5** crack, glare, gloat, space, split, stare **6** glance, goggle **7** eyeball **10** rubberneck
gaping 4 huge, open, vast, wide **5** broad, great **7** chasmal **9** cavernous
gar 4 fish, pike **8** billfish **10** needlefish
garage 4 shop **7** cabinet, car park, carport, shelter
Garand 5 rifle
garb 4 clad, duds **5** array, cover, dress, getup, style **6** attire, clothe, outfit **7** apparel, clothes, garment, raiment, threads **8** trappings **10** appearance
garbage 4 junk, muck, slop **5** dreck, dregs, filth, offal, trash, waste **6** debris, litter, refuse, sewage **7** rubbish **8** detritus, riffraff *heap:* **6** midden

garble 4 sift, warp 5 alter, belie, color, twist 6 jumble, mangle, muddle 7 becloud, confuse, contort, distort, falsify, obscure, pervert 8 miscolor, misstate, mutilate 9 obfuscate 10 impurities 12 misrepresent

garçon 3 boy 6 waiter 7 servant

garden 4 Eden, park 7 nursery *shelter:* 5 arbor 6 arbour

gardener 6 grower 7 yardman 9 topiarist

garden house 6 alcove, gazebo 9 belvedere

Garden State 9 New Jersey

garden tool 3 hoe 4 claw, fork, rake 5 mower, spade 6 dibble, pruner, scythe, shears, shovel, sickle, trowel, weeder 8 clippers

Gardner character 10 Perry Mason

Gareth *brother:* 6 Gawain 7 Gaheris *father:* 3 Lot *mother:* 8 Margawse, Morgause *slayer:* 8 Lancelot 9 Launcelot *uncle:* 6 Arthur *wife:* 6 Liones

Gargamelle's son 9 Gargantua

Gargantua *abbey:* 7 Thélème *author:* 8 Rabelais (François) *father:* 12 Grandgousier *first word:* 5 drink *mother:* 10 Gargamelle *son:* 10 Pantagruel

gargantuan see GIGANTIC

Garibaldi follower 8 redshirt

garish 4 loud 5 gaudy, showy, vivid 6 brassy, brazen, flashy, tawdry, tinsel, vulgar 7 blatant, chintzy, glaring, raffish 12 meretricious

garland 3 ana, lei 5 album, crown 6 anadem, digest, laurel, wreath 7 chaplet, coronal, coronet, laurels, omnibus 8 analects 9 anthology, selection 10 collection, compendium, miscellany 11 florilegium

garlic 4 moly, ramp 5 clove 6 allium

garment 4 garb, gear 5 array, habit 6 attire 7 apparel, raiment 8 clothing, vestment 10 habiliment *African:* 6 kaross 7 dashiki *Arab:* 3 aba 4 haik *British:* 10 mackintosh *clergy's:* 3 alb 4 cope 7 cassock, soutane 8 vestment *close-fitting:* 6 girdle, tights 7 leotard *for sleeping:* 6 pajama 7 nightie 9 nightgown *Greek:* 5 tunic 6 chiton, peplos 7 chlamys 8 himation *Hindu:* 4 sari *hooded:* 8 djellaba *Japanese:* 6 kimono *lace:* 10 chemisette *Malay:* 6 sarong *men's:* 3 tie 4 vest 5 pants, shirt, socks 6 jacket, slacks 7 drawers 8 trousers *outer:* 4 cape, coat, robe, wrap 5 cloak, parka, shawl, smock, stole 6 capote, jacket, kimono, poncho, sarong, ulster, wammus 7 overall, pelisse, surtout, sweater, topcoat 8 overcoat, pinafore, pullover, scapular 9 coveralls, gaberdine, polonaise *Polynesian:* 5 pareo,

pareu *rain:* 6 poncho 7 oilskin, slicker *Roman:* 4 toga 5 tunic *Scottish:* 4 jupe, kilt 7 sporran *sleeveless:* 3 aba 4 cape 6 mantle, tabard *Turkish:* 6 dolman *women's:* 4 gown 5 dress, skirt 6 blouse, vestee 7 blouson, nightie, partlet 8 negligee, peignoir, pelerine

garner 4 cull, earn, hive, reap 5 amass, glean, hoard, lay up, store 6 gather, pick up, roll up 7 collect, extract, harvest, store up 8 cumulate, ingather 9 stockpile 10 accumulate

garnet 5 jewel, stone 6 pyrope 8 essonite 9 hessonite *black:* 8 melanite *red:* 9 almandine, almandite

garnish 4 deck, trim 5 adorn 6 bedeck 7 dress up, enhance 8 beautify, decorate, ornament 9 embellish

garret 4 loft, room 5 attic 8 cockloft

garrison 4 camp, fort, post 6 assign, billet, occupy, troops 7 station 8 fortress 10 stronghold

garrote 5 choke 8 strangle, throttle 11 strangulate

garrulous see GABBY

garter 4 band, belt 5 strap 7 support 9 supporter

garth 4 yard 5 close 9 enclosure

gas 4 fuel, fume 5 fumes, steam, vapor 6 petrol 8 gasoline 9 petroleum *atmospheric:* 4 neon 5 argon, oxide, ozone, xenon 6 helium, oxygen 7 krypton, methane 8 hydrogen, nitrogen *flammable:* 6 butane, ethane, ethyne 7 methane, propane, propene 8 ethylene *inert:* 4 neon 5 argon, radon, xenon 6 helium 7 krypton *mine:* 8 firedamp 9 black damp *oxygen:* 5 ozone *toxic:* 5 sarin, soman, tabun 6 arsine, ketene 7 mustard 8 phosgene 9 phosphine

gasconade 4 brag 7 bravado 8 boasting, bragging 11 braggadocio

gash 3 cut, rip 4 rend, slit, tear 5 carve, cleft, gouge, slash, slice, split 6 incise 8 lacerate 10 depression, laceration

gasket 4 ring, seal 5 O-ring 6 sealer

gasoline 4 fuel 6 petrol *rating:* 6 octane

gasp 4 blow, huff, pant, puff 5 heave 6 wheeze 11 exclamation

Gaspar *companion:* 8 Melchior 9 Balthazar *gift:* 12 frankincense

gassy 5 windy 7 verbose 8 inflated, vaporous 9 flatulent

gastronome 7 epicure, gourmet 8 gourmand 9 bon vivant 11 connoisseur

gastropod 4 slug 5 conch, murex, snail, whelk 6 cowrie, limpet, volute 7 abalone, mollusc, mollusk, sea slug 8 pteropod, univalve 10 periwinkle

gat 3 gun 6 pistol, roscoe 7 channel, firearm, handgun, passage 8 revolver

gate 3 tap **4** cock, door, exit, port **5** entry, hatch, toril, valve **6** faucet, portal, spigot, switch, wicket **7** hydrant, opening, petcock **8** entrance, entryway, stopcock **9** turnstile **10** attendance

gâteau 4 cake

gatefold 6 insert **7** foldout

Gates of Hercules 9 Gibraltar **12** promontories

gateway 4 arch, door, exit **5** pylon, toril **6** portal **7** archway, doorway, opening **8** entrance

gather 4 brew, cull, gain, grow, heap, herd, loom, mass, meet, pick, pile, pool, reap **5** amass, bunch, flock, glean, group, horde, infer, judge, pluck, shirr, swarm **6** assume, deduce, derive, expect, garner, muster, pick up, pucker, summon, take in **7** cluster, collect, convene, extract, harvest, marshal, round up, suppose, surmise, suspect **8** assemble, conclude, converge, increase **9** aggregate, intensify **10** accumulate, congregate, understand **11** concentrate

gathering 4 bevy, crew, gang, herd, mass, ruck **5** bunch, crowd, crush, drove, flock, group, horde, party, press, rally, swarm **6** caucus, klatch, muster, throng **7** company, harvest, klatsch, meeting, reunion, turnout **8** assembly, congress, junction **9** concourse, congeries **10** assemblage, collection, conference, confluence **11** aggregation, get-together **12** congregation

Gath's giant 7 Goliath **10** Philistine

gauche 5 crude, gawky, inept **6** clumsy **7** awkward, halting, loutish, uncouth **8** bumbling, tactless **9** graceless, hamhanded, inelegant, maladroit **10** blundering

gaucho 6 cowboy **8** herdsman *weapon:* **4** bola **5** bolas **7** machete

gaudeamus ___ 6 igitur

gaudy 4 loud **5** showy **6** brassy, brazen, coarse, flashy, garish, tawdry, tinsel, vulgar **7** blatant, chintzy, glaring **9** brummagem, tasteless **10** outlandish **12** meretricious, ostentatious

Gaugamela *loser:* 6 Darius, Persia *victor:* **9** Alexander (the Great)

gauge 4 bore, rule, size **5** check, judge, meter, scale, weigh, width **6** assess, degree **7** compute, measure **8** diameter, estimate, evaluate, quantify, standard **9** benchmark, criterion, dimension, thickness, yardstick **10** instrument, touchstone **11** measurement

Gauguin's island 6 Tahiti

Gaul 4 Celt **6** France **9** Frenchman

Gaulish 6 French *god:* **4** Esus **7** Taranis *goddess:* **8** Belisama *priest:* **5** druid

gaunt 4 bare, bony, grim, lank, lean, thin **5** harsh, lanky, spare **6** barren, gangly, skinny, wasted **7** angular, scraggy, scrawny **8** gangling, rawboned, skeletal **9** emaciated **10** cadaverous

gauntlet 4 dare, test **5** glove, trial **6** attack, ordeal **9** challenge, onslaught

Gautama 6 Buddha **10** Siddhartha *mother:* **4** Maya **8** Mahamaya *son:* **6** Rahula *wife:* **9** Yasodhara

gauze 4 film, haze, leno, mesh, mist **5** cloth, crepe, tulle **6** fabric, tissue **7** bandage, chiffon, tiffany **8** compress, dressing **11** cheesecloth

gauzy 4 thin **5** filmy, fuzzy, sheer, vague **6** flimsy **8** delicate, pellucid **9** gossamery **10** diaphanous **11** transparent

gavel 6 hammer, mallet

gavial 7 gharial, reptile **9** crocodile

gavotte 4 tune **5** dance

Gawain *brother:* 6 Gareth **7** Gaheris *father:* **3** Lot *mother:* **8** Margawse, Morgause *slayer:* **8** Lancelot **9** Launcelot *uncle:* **6** Arthur *victim:* **6** Uwayne **7** Lamerok **9** Pellinore

gawk 3 oaf **4** bore, gape, gaze, hick, look, lout, lump, peer, rube **5** churl, glare, gloat, klutz, looby, stare, yokel **6** goggle, lubber

gawky 5 inept, splay **6** clumsy, coarse, gauche, oafish **7** awkward, loutish, lumpish, uncouth **8** bumbling, bungling, lubberly, ungainly **9** graceless, ham-handed, lumbering, maladroit

gay 4 glad, keen, wild **5** bonny, brash, happy, jolly, merry, queer, showy, sunny, vivid **6** blithe, bouncy, bright, cheery, festal, frisky, jocund, jovial, joyful, joyous, lively, rakish, sporty **7** animate, chipper, excited, festive, forward, gleeful, lesbian, playful, raffish **8** animated, cheerful, colorful, mirthful, rakehell, spirited, sportive **9** brilliant, exuberant, homophile, sparkling, sprightly, vivacious **10** blithesome, frolicsome, homoerotic, homosexual, insouciant, licentious, nonchalant **12** light-hearted

___ Gay 4 John **5** Enola

Gaza victor 7 Allenby (Edmund)

gaze 3 eye **4** bore, gape, gawk, leer, look, ogle, peer, pore, scan, view **5** glare, gloat, stare, watch **6** goggle **7** eyeball, observe **8** consider **10** rubberneck **11** contemplate

gazebo 6 alcove **8** pavilion **9** belvedere **11** garden house, summerhouse

gazelle 4 kudu, oryx **5** eland, nyala **7** gemsbok **8** antelope

gazette 5 paper **6** record **7** journal, publish 9 newspaper 10 periodical 11 publication 12 announcement

gazetteer 5 atlas, guide, index

Ge see GAEA

gear 3 cam, cog, rig 5 dress, goods, shift, stuff, wheel 6 adjust, tackle, things 7 apparel, harness, rigging 8 clothing, cogwheel, garments, materiel, property, sprocket, tackling, trapping 9 apparatus, equipment, machinery 10 belongings 11 accessories, habiliments, possessions 13 accouterments, accoutrements, paraphernalia

Geats *king:* 7 Hygelac *prince:* 7 Beowulf

Geb *daughter:* 4 Isis 8 Nephthys *father:* 3 Shu *mother:* 6 Tefnut *sister:* 3 Nut *son:* 3 Set 6 Osiris *wife:* 3 Nut

gecko 6 lizard 7 reptile

Gedaliah *father:* 6 Ahikam 7 Pashhur 8 Jeduthun *slayer:* 7 Ishmael

gee 3 wow 4 gosh, turn 5 golly, right 8 goodness, gracious 9 turn right

geek 4 buff, guru, nerd, whiz 5 carny, fiend, freak 6 carney, carnie, expert, pundit, weirdo 7 devotee, egghead, fanatic, oddball 9 authority, eccentric 10 enthusiast 12 intellectual

Gehenna 3 pit 4 hell 5 abyss, hades, Sheol 6 Tophet 7 inferno 8 Tartarus 9 perdition 10 underworld 11 netherworld

Geisel *pseudonym* 7 Dr. Seuss

geisha wear 3 obi 6 kimono

gel 3 dry, set 4 clot 6 harden, mousse 7 colloid, congeal, thicken 8 solidify 9 coagulate

gelatin 3 jam 4 agar 5 jelly 7 sericin

geld 3 cut, fix, tax 5 alter, desex, unsex 6 change, neuter 7 deprive 8 castrate, mutilate 9 sterilize 10 emasculate 11 desexualize

gelid 3 icy 4 cold 5 chill, nippy, polar 6 arctic, chilly, frigid, frosty, frozen, steely 7 glacial 8 freezing

gelt 5 money

gem 3 jet 4 jade, onyx, opal, rock, ruby, sard 5 agate, amber, beryl, bijou, coral, jewel, pearl, stone, topaz 6 amulet, garnet, jasper, scarab, sphene, spinel, zircon 7 bejewel, cat's-eye, citrine, diamond, emerald, enjewel, olivine, peridot 8 amethyst, corundum, diopside, fluorite, intaglio, lazurite, obsidian, sapphire, sardonyx, sparkler, tigereye 9 carnelian, moonstone, phenakite, scapolite, spodumene, tiger's-eye, turquoise 10 aquamarine, cordierite, tourmaline 11 alexandrite, chrysoberyl, chrysoprase, lapis lazuli, masterpiece *blue:* 6 zircon 8 sapphire 9 turquoise 10 aquamarine 11 lapis lazuli *carved:*

8 intaglio *changeable:* 9 chatoyant *cut:* 7 marquis 8 baguette, cabochon, marquise 9 brilliant *face:* 5 facet *green:* 4 jade 7 emerald, peridot, smaragd 10 chrysolite 11 chrysoprase *red:* 4 ruby, sard 6 garnet, pyrope, spinel 9 carnelian *support:* 7 setting *weight:* 5 carat *yellow:* 5 amber, topaz 6 sphene 7 citrine

Gemini star 6 Castor, Pollux

gemmule 3 bud

gemsbok 4 oryx 8 antelope

Gem State 5 Idaho

gemütlich see GENIAL

gendarme 3 cop 5 bobby 7 officer, soldier 8 flatfoot 9 constable, patrolman, policeman

gender 3 sex 4 kind, male, sort, type 5 class 6 female, neuter 8 feminine 9 masculine

genealogy 5 roots, stirp, stock 6 origin, stemma 7 descent, history, lineage 8 ancestry, heredity, pedigree 9 bloodline 10 family tree

general 4 wide 5 broad, usual, vague 6 common, global, normal, public 7 blanket, generic, overall, regular, routine, typical 8 catholic, everyday, sweeping 9 all-around, inclusive, prevalent, universal 10 collective, prevailing, unspecific, widespread 11 commonplace 13 comprehensive *American:* 3 Lee (Robert E.) 4 Haig (Alexander), Pike (Zebulon), Wood (Leonard) 5 Clark (Mark, Wesley, William), Grant (Ulysses S.), Meade (George), Scott (Charles, Hugh, Winfield), Smith (Andrew Jackson, Giles, Holland, Morgan, Samuel, Walter Bedell), Stark (John), Worth (William) 6 Abrams (Creighton), Custer (George Armstrong), Franks (Tommy), Hooker (Joseph), Kearny (Philip, Stephen), Patton (George S.), Porter (Fitz-John), Powell (Colin), Slocum (Henry), Spaatz (Carl), Taylor (Maxwell, Richard, Zachary) 7 Bradley (Omar), Frémont (John Charles), Houston (Samuel), Jackson (Andrew, Thomas "Stonewall"), Lejeune (John), Ridgway (Matthew B.), Sherman (William Tecumseh), Twining (Nathaniel), Wallace (Lewis), Wheeler (Joseph) 8 Burnside (Ambrose), Goethals (George Washington), Marshall (George), Mitchell (Billy), Pershing (John J.), Sheridan (Philip), Stilwell (Joseph) 9 MacArthur (Arthur, Douglas), McClellan (George), Rosecrans (William), Schofield (John), Wilkinson (James) 10 Beauregard (P. G. T.), Eisenhower (Dwight D.), Vandegrift

(Alexander), Wainwright (Jonathan) **11** Schwarzkopf (Norman) **12** Westmoreland (William) *American Revolutionary:* **4** Knox (Henry), Ward (Artemas) **5** Gates (Horatio), Wayne ("Mad Anthony") **6** de Kalb (Baron), Greene (Nathanael), Morgan (Daniel), Putnam (Israel, Rufus) **8** Moultrie (William), Sullivan (John) **10** Washington (George) *Austrian:* **11** Wallenstein (Albrecht von) *British:* **4** Gage (Thomas), Howe (William) **5** Clive (Robert), Monck (George), Wolfe (James) **6** Rupert (Prince) **7** Amherst (Jeffery), Wingate (Orde Charles, Reginald) **8** Burgoyne (John), Cromwell (Oliver) **10** Abercromby (Ralph, Robert), Cornwallis (Charles), Wellington (Duke of) *Carthaginian:* **8** Hamilcar, Hannibal **9** Hasdrubal *Chinese:* **3** Yan (Xishan), Yen (Hsi-shan) **4** Feng (Guozhang, Kuo-chang, Yü-hsiang, Yuxiang) **5** Chang (Tso-lin), Zhang (Zuolin) *Confederate:* **3** Lee (Robert E.) **4** Hill (Ambrose), Hood (John Bell) **5** Bragg (Braxton), Ewell (Richard Stoddart), Price (Sterling), Smith (Edmund Kirby) **6** Morgan (John Hunt), Stuart (Jeb) **7** Forrest (Nathan Bedford), Hampton (Wade), Jackson (Thomas "Stonewall"), Pickett (George) **8** Johnston (Albert Sidney, Joseph Eggleston) **9** Pemberton (John) **10** Beauregard (Pierre G. T.), Longstreet (James) *French:* **3** Ney (Michel) **4** Foch (Ferdinand) **6** Moreau (Victor), Pétain (Philippe) **7** Weygand (Maxime) **8** de Gaulle (Charles), Lefebvre (Pierre), Montcalm (Marquis de), Saint-Cyr (Laurent de Gouvion-) **9** Frontenac (Comte de) **10** Rochambeau (Comte de) *German:* **4** Jodl (Alfred) **6** Kleist (Paul Ludwig von), Rommel (Erwin) **9** Rundstedt (Gerd von) **10** Kesselring (Albert), Ludendorff (Erich) *Greek:* **6** Nicias **9** Miltiades **10** Alcibiades **12** Themistocles *Japanese:* **4** Tojo (Hideki) **5** Koiso (Kuniaki) **6** Yasuda (Yoshisada) **8** Yamagata (Aritomo) **9** Yamashita (Tomoyuki) *Mexican:* **9** Santa Anna (Antonio López de) *Prussian:* **11** Scharnhorst (Gerhard von) *Roman:* **5** Sulla (Lucius Cornelius) **6** Caesar (Julius), Fabius (Quintus), Marius (Gaius), Pompey (the Great), Scipio (Gnaeus Cornelius, Publius Cornelius) **7** Regulus (Marcus Atilius), Ricimer (Flavius) **8** Agricola (Gnaeus Julius), Lucullus (Lucius Licinius), Stilicho (Flavius) **9** Marcellus (Marcus Claudius), Sertorius (Quintus) **10** Theodosius (the Great) **11** Cincinnatus (Lucius Quinctius) *Russian:* **6** Zhukov (Georgy) **7** Kutuzov (Mikhail), Trotsky (Leon), Wrangel (Pyotr), Zhdanov (Andrey) **9** Yeremenko (Andrey) *Spanish:* **4** Alba (Duke of), Alva (Duke of) **6** Franco (Francisco) *Swedish:* **7** Wrangel (Karl Gustav)

general assembly 4 diet **6** plenum **8** congress **10** parliament **11** legislature

generalize 5 infer, widen **6** derive, extend, induce, spread **7** broaden **8** conclude **12** universalize

generally 6 mainly, mostly, widely **7** all told, as a rule, broadly, chiefly, en masse, largely, overall, usually **8** all in all, commonly, normally **9** on average, primarily, typically **10** altogether, by and large, frequently, on the whole, ordinarily **11** customarily, principally **12** almost always **13** predominantly

generate 4 bear, make, sire **5** beget, breed, cause, get up, hatch, spawn, yield **6** create, effect, father, induce, whip up, work up **7** achieve, develop, produce, provoke **8** engender, initiate, multiply, muster up **9** originate, procreate, propagate, reproduce **10** bring about, bring forth

generic 5 broad **6** common, global **7** blanket **9** inclusive, unbranded, universal **10** indistinct **12** nonexclusive

___ **generis 3** sui

generosity 7 charity **8** altruism, kindness, largesse **9** abundance **10** liberality **11** beneficence, benevolence, magnanimity, munificence **12** philanthropy **13** unselfishness

generous 4 free, kind **5** ample **6** lavish **7** copious, helpful, liberal, profuse, willing **8** abundant **9** bounteous, bountiful, plenteous, plentiful, unselfish, unsparing **10** altruistic, benevolent, bighearted, charitable, munificent, openhanded, ungrudging, unstinting **11** considerate, kindhearted, magnanimous, overflowing **12** greathearted

genesis 4 dawn, root **5** alpha, birth, start **6** origin, outset, source **7** dawning, opening **8** creation **9** beginning, formation, inception **10** provenance **12** commencement

genetic 10 congenital, hereditary *material:* **3** DNA, RNA **7** cistron **9** chromatid **10** chromosome *term:* **8** synapsis **9** backcross

genial 4 kind, warm **5** jolly, merry **6** benign, blithe, hearty, jocund, jovial, kindly, mellow, social **7** affable, amiable, cordial **8** amicable, friendly, gracious, pleasant, sociable **9** agreeable,

congenial, convivial, easygoing
10 neighborly **11** good-humored, good-natured, warmhearted
genie 3 imp **4** jinn, puck **5** afrit **6** afreet, spirit, sprite **7** servant
geniture 4 dawn **5** birth, start **6** origin **8** nativity **9** beginning, inception
genius 4 bent, gift, head, turn **5** flair, jinni, knack **6** acumen, brains, master, spirit, talent, wizard **7** aptness, faculty, prodigy **8** aptitude, capacity, penchant **9** ingenuity, intellect **10** brilliance, creativity, mastermind, propensity **12** intelligence **13** inventiveness
Genoa's liberator 5 Doria (Andrea)
genre 3 ilk **4** kind, sort, type **5** class, style **6** family, stripe **7** species, variety **8** category, division
gens 3 kin **4** clan **5** group **6** family, people **7** kinfolk **9** relations, relatives
Genseric's subjects 7 Vandals
genteel 4 nice, prim **5** civil **6** formal, ladi-da, polite, prissy, strict, stuffy, urbane **7** courtly, elegant, prudish, refined, stilted, stylish **8** affected, cultured, graceful, gracious, ladylike, mannerly, polished, precious, priggish, well-bred **9** courteous **10** artificial, cultivated **11** fashionable, gentlemanly, pretentious, straitlaced, well-behaved **12** aristocratic, well-mannered **13** distinguished
gentile 3 goy **5** pagan **7** heathen **9** Christian, non-Jewish
gentility 5 elite **6** gentry **7** decorum, manners, quality, society **8** breeding, courtesy, nobility **9** blue blood **10** aristocrat, refinement, upper class, upper crust **11** aristocracy
gentle 4 calm, easy, kind, meek, mild, soft, tame **5** balmy, bland, quiet, tamed **6** benign, docile, genial, kindly, mellow, placid, serene, smooth, tender **7** amiable, lenient **8** delicate, merciful, peaceful, pleasant, pleasing, soothing, tranquil **9** agreeable **11** softhearted, sympathetic, warmhearted **13** compassionate *creature:* **4** lamb
gentleman 3 sir **6** aristo, fellow, mister **8** cavalier **9** blue blood, chevalier, patrician **10** aristocrat *English:* **6** milord *French:* **8** monsieur *Hindu:* **4** babu *Spanish:* **3** don **5** señor
gentleman friend 4 beau **5** lover, swain **6** fiancé, squire, suitor **7** gallant
gentlemanly 5 civil, noble, suave **6** polite, urbane **7** elegant, gallant, genteel, refined **8** mannerly, well-bred **9** courteous, honorable **10** chivalrous, cultivated **11** considerate
gentry 5 elite, folks **7** quality, society

8 nobility **9** gentility, patrician **10** gentlefolk, patriciate, upper class, upper crust **11** aristocracy, high society, ruling class
genuflect 3 bow **4** fawn **5** kneel **6** kowtow
genuine 4 pure, real, true **5** plain, pukka, valid **6** actual, dinkum, honest, tested **7** factual, natural, sincere **8** absolute, bona fide, positive, trueborn **9** authentic, certified, unalloyed, undoubted, unfeigned, veritable **10** sure-enough, unaffected
genus 3 ilk **4** kind, mode, sort, type **5** class, group, order **6** family **7** species, variety **8** category
geode 4 rock **5** stone **6** cavity, nodule
geoduck 4 clam
geographer *American:* **10** Huntington (Ellsworth) *Flemish:* **8** Mercator (Gerardus) *German:* **6** Ratzel (Friedrich) *Greek:* **6** Strabo **7** Ptolemy *Italian:* **8** Vespucci (Amerigo)
geologic period 5 azoic **6** Eocene, Hadean **7** Archean, Miocene, Permian **8** Cambrian, Cenozoic, Devonian, Holocene, Jurassic, Mesozoic, Pliocene, Silurian, Triassic **9** Oligocene, Paleocene, Paleozoic **10** Cretaceous, Ordovician **11** Phanerozoic, Pleistocene, Precambrian, Proterozoic **13** Mississippian, Pennsylvanian
geometer 6 Euclid **13** mathematician
geometric *coordinate:* **8** abscissa, ordinate *curve:* **3** arc **6** spiral **7** ellipse, evolute **8** parabola *figure:* **5** rhomb **6** circle, oblong, square **7** ellipse, hexagon, octagon, polygon, rhombus **8** heptagon, pentagon, rhomboid, triangle **9** rectangle *solid:* **4** cone, cube **5** prism **6** sphere **7** pyramid **8** cylinder, spheroid, spherule *surface:* **5** nappe, torus **6** toroid
geometry letters 3 QED
geophagy 4 pica
Georgia *capital:* **7** Atlanta *city:* **5** Macon **6** Albany, Athens **7** Augusta **8** Columbus, Savannah *college, university:* **5** Clark, Emory **6** Mercer **7** Spelman **8** Valdosta **9** Morehouse *founder:* **10** Oglethorpe (James) *nickname:* **5** Peach (State) **21** Empire State of the South *river:* **8** Ocmulgee **13** Chattahoochee *state bird:* **13** brown thrasher *state flower:* **12** Cherokee rose *state tree:* **7** live oak *swamp:* **10** Okefenokee
Georgia, Republic of *ancient kingdom:* **6** Iberia **7** Colchis *capital:* **6** Tiflis **7** Tbilisi *city:* **7** Kutaisi, Rustavi *includes:* **6** Ajaria **8** Abkhazia, Adzharia **12** South Ossetia *monarch:* **6** Tamara (Queen)

monetary unit: 4 lari *mountain range:*
8 Caucasus *neighbor:* 6 Russia, Turkey
7 Armenia 10 Azerbaijan *river:* 4 Kura
5 Rioni *sea:* 5 Black
Georgics *author* 6 Virgil
Geraint's wife 4 Enid
Gerda's husband 4 Frey
geriatric 3 old 4 aged 5 aging 6 senior
7 elderly 8 outmoded 12 old-fashioned
13 superannuated
germ 3 bud, bug 4 seed 5 spark, spore,
virus 6 embryo, origin, source
7 microbe, nucleus 8 pathogen 9 bacterium *cell:* 3 egg 4 ovum 5 sperm
German 3 Hun 4 Goth 6 Teuton *article:*
3 das, der, des, die *bomber:* 5 Gotha,
Stuka *child:* 4 Kind *coin:* 4 Mark 5 Taler
6 Thaler 7 Pfennig *empire:* 5 Reich
head: 4 Kopf *highway:* 8 Autobahn
leader: 6 Führer, Kaiser *measles:*
7 rubella *mister:* 4 Herr *no:* 4 nein
nobleman: 6 Junker *pronoun:* 3 ich, sie,
wir *rifle:* 6 Mauser *weight:* 3 Lot
5 Pfund, Stein 8 Vierling *woman:* 4 Frau
8 Fräulein
germane 3 apt 5 ad rem 7 apropos, fitting, related 8 material, relevant 9 pertinent 10 applicable 11 appropriate
Germany 11 Deutschland *capital:*
6 Berlin *city:* 3 Ulm 4 Bonn, Jena, Kiel
5 Essen, Mainz 6 Bremen, Erfurt,
Lübeck, Munich 7 Cologne, Dresden,
Hamburg, Hanover, Leipzig, München,
Potsdam 8 Augsburg, Dortmund, Duisburg, Freiburg, Hannover, Schwerin
9 Frankfurt, Nuremberg, Stuttgart,
Wiesbaden 10 Baden Baden, Düsseldorf
leader: 4 Kohl (Helmut) 6 Brandt
(Willy), Hitler (Adolf) 7 Schmidt (Helmut), Wilhelm (Kaiser) 8 Bismarck
(Otto) *monetary unit:* 4 euro *monetary
unit, former:* 4 mark 5 taler 6 thaler
12 deutsche mark *mountain, range:*
4 Harz 7 Brocken *neighbor:* 6 France,
Poland 7 Austria, Belgium, Denmark
10 Luxembourg 11 Netherlands,
Switzerland 13 Czech Republic *region:*
4 Ruhr 6 Saxony 7 Bavaria 11 Black
Forest *river:* 4 Eder, Elbe, Isar, Main,
Oder, Ruhr 5 Rhein, Rhine 6 Danube
7 Moselle *sea:* 5 North 6 Baltic *state:*
5 Hesse 6 Saxony 7 Bavaria 8 Saarland
9 Thuringia 11 Brandenburg
germinate 3 bud 6 evolve, spring, sprout
7 blossom, develop 9 originate, pullulate
Gerontion *poet* 5 Eliot (T. S.)
Gershom, Gershon *father:* 4 Levi *son:*
5 Libni 6 Shimei
Gershwin 3 Ira 6 George *opera:* 12 Porgy
and Bess *piece:* 14 Rhapsody in Blue

15 American in Paris (An) *show:* 5 Oh
Kay 9 Funny Face, Girl Crazy 10 Lady
Be Good 11 Of Thee I Sing 15 Strike
Up the Band *song:* 10 I Got Rhythm,
Summertime
Gertrude *husband:* 8 Claudius *son:*
6 Hamlet
Gervaise's daughter 4 Nana
Geryon *dog:* 6 Orthus *father:* 8 Chrysaor
mother: 10 Callirrhoë *slayer:* 8 Hercules
gestalt 4 form 5 shape 6 figure 7 pattern
9 structure 13 configuration
Gestapo chief 7 Himmler (Heinrich)
geste 4 deed, feat 7 emprise, exploit,
romance, venture 9 adventure 10 enterprise 11 undertaking
gesticulate 3 nod 4 move, wave 6 beckon, motion, signal
gesticulation 4 wave 6 motion 7 gesture
8 high sign 9 pantomime 12 body language, sign language
gesture 3 nod 4 sign, wave 5 shrug,
token 6 motion, salute, signal
8 reminder 9 signalize 10 expression,
indication *graceful:* 9 beau geste
get 3 bag 4 draw, earn, gain, land
5 catch, cause, seize 6 access, attain,
become, elicit, extort, obtain, pick up,
secure 7 achieve, acquire, bring in,
capture, chalk up, deliver, extract, procure, receive 8 contract 10 understand
12 come down with
get around 4 roam, rove, tour, trek,
walk 5 avoid, dodge, elude, evade, skirt
6 cruise, detour, escape, ramble, travel,
wander 8 ambulate, outflank, sidestep
10 circumvent
get away see GET OUT
getaway 3 lam 4 exit, slip 6 escape, flight
7 retreat 8 breakout, vacation
get back 6 go home, recoup, regain,
return, revert 7 recover, reclaim,
revenge, revisit 8 retrieve 9 repossess,
retaliate
get by 4 cope, fare 5 slide 6 eke out,
endure, manage 7 carry on, survive
8 maintain
get off 4 walk 5 leave 6 alight, depart, go
free, launch 7 pull out 8 dismount
9 disembark 10 beat the rap
get out 4 exit, kite, leak 5 break, issue,
leave, scram, split 6 alight, beat it,
begone, decamp, depart, egress, escape
7 buzz off, publish, skiddoo, take off,
vamoose 8 dispatch, hightail 9 circulate, skedaddle 10 make tracks
Gettysburg *general* 3 Lee (Robert E.)
5 Meade (George)
get up 4 gain 5 arise, breed, cause, dress,
hatch, mount, raise, stand 6 create,
induce, summon 7 acquire, prepare,

produce **8** engender, generate **12** rise and shine

getup 3 rig **4** duds, garb, togs **5** array, dress, guise **6** outfit **7** costume, threads

get-up-and-go 3 pep, vim, zip **4** bang, push, snap, zeal, zest **5** drive, moxie, oomph, punch, spunk, steam, verve, vigor **6** energy, spirit, starch **8** ambition **10** enterprise, initiative

gewgaw 3 toy **4** dido **5** bijou, curio **6** bangle, bauble, doodad, trifle **7** bibelot, novelty, trinket, whatnot **8** gimcrack, kickshaw **9** bagatelle, objet d'art **10** knickknack

geyser 3 jet, spout, spurt **6** gusher, spring **8** fountain **10** wellspring **11** Old Faithful

Ghana *capital:* **5** Accra *city:* **4** Tema **6** Kumasi, Tamale *ethnic group:* **4** Akan **5** Mossi *former name:* **9** Gold Coast *gulf:* **6** Guinea *lake:* **5** Volta *language:* **7** English *monetary unit:* **4** cedi *neighbor:* **4** Togo **10** Ivory Coast **11** Burkina Faso *river:* **5** Volta

ghastly 4 grim, pale **5** awful, lurid **6** grisly, horrid, pallid **7** ghostly, hideous, macabre **8** dreadful, ghoulish, gruesome, horrible, shocking, spectral, terrible **9** appalling, deathlike, frightful, ghostlike, repulsive, sickening **10** cadaverous, corpselike, disgustful, disgusting, horrifying, nauseating, terrifying **11** frightening

ghee 3 fat **6** butter

gherkin 4 vine **6** pickle **8** cucumber

ghetto 4 slum

ghost 4 soul **5** demon, haunt, shade, spook, trace **6** kelpie, shadow, spirit, wraith, zombie **7** eidolon, phantom, specter **8** phantasm **10** apparition **11** poltergeist

ghostly 5 eerie, scary **6** spooky **7** shadowy **8** ethereal, spectral **9** deathlike, spiritual, unearthly, unworldly **10** cadaverous, corpselike, phantasmal **12** supernatural

Ghosts author 5 Ibsen (Henrik)

ghoul 4 ogre **5** fiend **7** monster **11** grave robber

GI 5 grunt **7** dogface, fighter, soldier, warrior **8** doughboy **9** man-at-arms **10** serviceman

Gianni Schicchi composer 7 Puccini (Giacomo)

giant 4 huge, hulk, ogre, Otus, vast **5** gross, Gyges, Hymir, jumbo, titan, whale **6** Cottus, Typhon **7** Aloadae (plural), Antaeus, Cyclops, Goliath, immense, mammoth, monster, titanic, whopper **8** behemoth, Briareus, colossal, colossus, enormous, gigantic,

Orgoglio **9** cyclopean, Enceladus, Ephialtes, Gargantua, Herculean, humongous, leviathan, monstrous **10** gargantuan, prodigious **11** elephantine *biblical:* **4** Anak **7** Goliath *cactus:* **7** saguaro *killer:* **4** Jack **5** David *one-eyed:* **5** Arges **7** Cyclops **10** Polyphemus *100-armed:* **9** Enceladus *100-eyed:* **5** Argus *rime-cold:* **4** Ymer, Ymir *sea god:* **5** Aegir

Giant author 6 Ferber (Edna)

giaour 7 infidel **10** unbeliever **11** nonbeliever

gib 6 tomcat

gibber 3 gab, yak **4** blab **5** prate **6** babble, drivel, gabble, jabber, yammer **7** blabber, blather, chatter, palaver, prattle, twaddle

gibberish 3 gab **5** Greek, hokum **6** babble, bunkum, burble, drivel, gabble, jabber, yammer **7** blabber, blather, chatter, palaver, prattle, twaddle **8** claptrap, flimflam, nonsense **10** balderdash, double-talk, hocus-pocus, mumbo jumbo **11** abracadabra, jabberwocky **12** gobbledygook

gibbet 4 hang **5** lynch, noose, scrag **7** execute, gallows **8** string up

gibbon 3 ape **7** primate, siamang **10** anthropoid

gibbous 6 arched, convex, humped **7** bulging, rounded, swollen **10** humpbacked **11** protuberant

gibe 4 gird, jeer, jest, mock, quip, rail **5** fleer, flout, scoff, scorn, scout, sneer, taunt, tease **6** deride, insult **8** ridicule

Gibraltar *colony of:* **7** Britain, England *conqueror:* **5** Tarik, Tariq *neighbor:* **5** Spain *opposite:* **5** Ceuta

giddy 4 gaga **5** dizzy, inane, light, silly, woozy **6** elated, yeasty **7** flighty, foolish, vacuous **8** euphoric **9** frivolous, slaphappy **10** hoity-toity **11** empty-headed, harebrained, light-headed, vertiginous **12** bubbleheaded **13** rattlebrained

___ **Gide 5** André

Gideon *father:* **5** Joash *servant:* **5** Purah *son:* **9** Abimelech

gift 3 set, tip **4** alms, bent, boon, head, turn **5** award, bonus, endow, favor, flair, forte, grant, knack **6** genius, legacy, reward, talent **7** ability, aptness, cumshaw, faculty, freebie, handout, present, subsidy **8** aptitude, bestowal, capacity, donation, gratuity, largesse, oblation, offering **9** endowment, lagniappe **11** benefaction, benevolence **12** contribution, presentation

gifted 4 able **5** smart **6** expert **7** hotshot,

skilled **8** masterly, skillful, talented **9** ingenious, masterful

gig 3 jab, job, top **4** boat, fool, goad, prod, spur **5** annoy, freak, rotor, spear **6** chaise, harass **7** demerit, provoke, rowboat **8** carriage **10** engagement

gigantic 4 huge, vast **5** giant, jumbo **7** hulking, immense, mammoth, massive, titanic **8** behemoth, colossal, enormous, king-size, whopping **9** cyclopean, humongous, king-sized, monstrous, walloping **10** gargantuan, prodigious, stupendous **11** elephantine

giggle 5 laugh **6** guffaw, hee-haw, titter **7** chortle, chuckle, snicker, snigger, twitter

Gigi author 7 Colette

Gilbert and Sullivan opera 6 Mikado (The) **8** Iolanthe, Patience, Sorcerer (The) **9** Grand Duke (The), Ruddigore **10** Gondoliers (The) **11** H.M.S. Pinafore, Princess Ida, Trial by Jury

Gil Blas author 6 Lesage (Alain-René)

gild 4 coat, deck **5** adorn, cover, tinge **6** bedeck, tinsel **7** enhance, overlay **8** brighten, ornament **9** embellish, embroider

Gilda's father 9 Rigoletto

Gilead *father:* **6** Machir *grandfather:* **8** Manasseh *son:* **7** Jephtha **8** Jephthah

Gilgamesh 4 epic *companion:* **6** Eabani, Enkidu *home:* **4** Uruk **5** Erech *mother:* **6** Ninsun *victim:* **6** Huwawa **7** Humbaba

gill 4 race **5** brook, creek **6** runnel, stream, wattle **7** rivulet *relating to:* **9** branchial

gillyflower 4 pink **9** carnation, clove pink

Gilroy play 15 Subject Was Roses (The)

gilt 3 hog, pig, sow **4** bond, gold **5** swine **6** gilded, golden **10** brilliance

gimcrack 5 cheap **6** bauble, gewgaw, shoddy, trifle **7** bibelot, chintzy, trinket **8** kickshaw **10** knickknack

gimlet 4 tool **5** drill, drink **8** cocktail *ingredient:* **3** gin **5** vodka **9** lime juice

gimmick 3 con **4** ploy, ruse, wile **5** angle, catch, dodge, feint, gizmo, trick **6** device, gadget, gambit, jigger, scheme, widget **8** artifice, maneuver **9** stratagem **10** subterfuge

gimp 3 vim **4** cord, halt **5** braid, hitch **6** dodder, falter, hobble, spirit **7** cripple **8** lameness

gimpy 4 game, halt, lame **7** hobbled, limping **8** crippled

gin 3 net **4** sloe, trap **5** catch, rummy, snare **6** device, liquor **7** springe **8** beverage, generate, separate

ginger 3 fig, pep, vim, zip **4** herb, stir, zing **5** liven, spice, verve, vigor **6** energy, mettle, revive, spirit **7** sparkle *cookie:* **4** snap

gingerly 4 safe, wary **5** canny, chary **7** careful, guarded **8** cautious, delicate, discreet

gingery 4 tart **5** fiery, peppy, sharp, spicy, tangy, zesty **6** snappy, spunky **7** peppery, piquant, pungent **8** spirited **10** mettlesome **12** high-spirited

gingham 5 cloth **6** fabric **7** textile **8** material

gingiva 3 gum

gin mill 3 bar, pub **4** dive **5** joint **6** saloon, tavern **7** barroom, taproom **8** alehouse **9** roadhouse **11** public house **12** watering hole

Ginsberg poem 4 Howl **7** Kaddish

ginseng 4 herb, root

Gioconda, La 8 Mona Lisa *composer:* **10** Ponchielli (Amilcare) *painter:* **7** da Vinci (Leonardo)

giraffe 8 ruminant **9** quadruped **10** camelopard

girandole 7 earring **10** candelabra **11** candelabrum, candlestick, composition

girasol 3 gem **4** opal **5** jewel, stone **7** mineral **8** fire opal **9** artichoke

gird 3 hem **4** band, belt, bind, ring, wrap **5** brace, equip, hem in, ready, round, steel **6** circle **7** bolster, enclose, fortify, prepare, provide, shore up, wreathe **8** buttress, cincture, encircle, surround **9** encompass, reinforce **10** strengthen

girder 4 beam **5** brace **7** support **8** crossbar **9** crossbeam **10** crosspiece, transverse

girdle 4 band, belt, ring, sash **6** cestus, circle **8** ceinture, cincture, encircle, surround **9** encompass, waistband *of Aphrodite:* **6** cestus

girl 4 babe, bird, coed, doll, lass, maid, miss **5** chick, filly, missy, wench **6** damsel, lassie, maiden **8** daughter **10** sweetheart

girth 4 band, belt, bind, size **5** brace, cinch, strap **6** circle, fasten, girdle **7** measure **8** cincture, encircle, surround **9** thickness **10** dimensions **13** circumference

Giselle composer 4 Adam (Adolphe)

gist 3 nub, sum **4** core, meat, pith **5** sense **6** burden, ground, kernel, marrow, matter, thrust, upshot **7** essence **9** main point, substance

give 3 pay **4** deal, hand **5** allot, allow, award, grant, issue, offer, remit **6** accord, afford, assign, bestow, commit, confer, convey, devote, direct, donate, extend, market, pony up, render, supply, tender **7** deliver, dish out, display, dole out, fall out, fork out, furnish, hand out, mete out, present, produce, proffer, provide 8 allocate, bequeath, disburse, dispense, give away, hand over, shell out, turn over 9 apportion, sacrifice 10 administer, contribute, distribute

give-and-take 6 banter 8 exchange, repartee, trade-off 10 compromise 11 cooperation, reciprocity

give away 4 blab, leak 5 award, grant, spill 6 bestow, betray, confer, devote, donate, expose, reveal, tattle 7 deliver, divulge, hand out, let slip, present 8 bequeath, disclose

giveaway 4 deal, gift, leak 5 steal, value 6 tip-off 7 bargain, freebee, freebie, premium, present, sellout 8 betrayal, exposure 10 disclosure, revelation

give back 6 refund, retire, return 7 replace, restore, retreat 8 withdraw 9 reinstate

give in 4 fold, quit, stop 5 yield 6 assent, comply, desist, relent, submit 7 concede, deliver, indulge, succumb 8 back down, cry uncle 9 surrender 10 relinquish

given 5 prone 6 donnée 7 assumed, granted 8 inclined 9 presented, specified 10 particular 11 considering, susceptible

give off 4 beam, emit, flow, vent 5 exude, issue 6 effuse 7 emanate, radiate, release 9 discharge

give out 4 deal, dole, emit, fail, mete, vent 5 issue 6 cave in 7 declare, release, succumb 8 collapse, throw off 9 break down 10 distribute

giver 5 donor 7 donator, grantor

give up 4 cede, quit 5 allow, cease, forgo, waive, yield 6 abjure, devote, resign, vacate 7 abandon, despair 8 abdicate, hand over, renounce, withdraw 9 sacrifice, surrender 10 relinquish

give way 5 yield 6 buckle, cave in 7 retreat, succumb 8 collapse 9 surrender

gizmo see GADGET

glabrous 4 bald, bare 6 shaven, smooth 8 hairless 9 beardless 10 bald-headed 12 smooth-shaven

glacial 3 icy, raw 5 chill, gelid, nippy, polar 6 arctic, biting, chilly, frigid, frosty, frozen, wintry 8 freezing

glacier 3 ice 6 ice cap 8 ice field, ice sheet *Alaska:* 4 Muir, Taku 6 Bering 10 Mendenhall *Antarctica:* 9 Beardmore *deposit:* 4 kame 5 esker 6 placer 7 moraine *fissure:* 8 crevasse *fragment:* 4 berg 7 iceberg *Greenland:* 8 Humboldt

hill: 7 drumlin *Karakoram:* 5 Biafo 7 Baltoro *New Zealand:* 6 Tasman *pinnacle:* 5 serac

glacis 5 grade, slope 7 incline 10 buffer zone 11 buffer state

glad 3 gay 4 fain 5 happy, jolly, merry 6 blithe, bright, cheery, genial, jocund, jovial, joyful, joyous 7 beaming, gleeful, pleased, radiant, tickled, willing 8 cheerful, mirthful, pleasant, rejoiced 9 delighted, gratified, overjoyed 11 exhilarated 12 lighthearted

gladden 4 buoy 5 cheer, elate 6 buck up, perk up, please, uplift 7 cheer up, delight, gratify, hearten

glade 6 meadow 8 clearing 9 open space

gladiator 7 fighter 9 combatant, Spartacus

gladly 4 fain, lief 6 freely 7 happily, readily 8 heartily 9 willingly 10 cheerfully, with relish 12 with pleasure

gladness 3 joy 4 glee 5 bliss, cheer, mirth 6 gaiety 7 delight, jollity 9 happiness, merriment

gladstone 3 bag 8 suitcase

glamorous 7 elegant 8 alluring, charming, dazzling, enticing, magnetic 9 seductive 10 attractive, bewitching, enchanting 11 captivating, fascinating 13 sophisticated

glamour 5 charm, magic, spell 6 allure, appeal 7 romance 8 charisma, witchery 9 magnetism, sex appeal 10 attraction, witchcraft 11 fascination 12 razzle-dazzle

glance 4 peek, peep, skim, skip 5 brush, carom, flash, glaze, graze, shine 6 bounce, careen 7 glimpse 8 ricochet *lascivious:* 4 leer

gland 5 gonad, liver, organ 6 pineal, thymus 7 adrenal, mammary, parotid, thyroid 8 exocrine, pancreas, prostate, salivary 9 endocrine, pituitary 11 parathyroid *secretion:* 7 hormone *swelling:* 4 bubo

glare 4 gaze, glow, peer 5 blaze, flame, flash, frown, gleam, light, lower, scowl, shine, stare 6 dazzle, glower 7 obtrude 8 stand out 10 garishness

glaring 4 loud, rank 5 gaudy, plain, vivid 6 brazen, flashy, garish, tawdry, tinsel 7 blatant, obvious 8 blinding, flagrant 9 audacious, egregious, obtrusive 10 noticeable 11 conspicuous, outstanding 12 ostentatious

Glasgow's patron saint 5 Mungo 9 Kentigern

glass 4 lens, pane 5 image, lense, prism 6 mirror 7 reflect 9 barometer, telescope *combining form:* 5 vitro *container:* 3 jar 6 beaker, bottle *decorative:*

7 schmelz **8** schmelze *drinking:* **4** pony
5 flute **6** goblet, jigger, rummer, seidel
7 snifter, tumbler **8** schooner *gem:*
5 paste **6** strass *magnifying:* **5** loupe
milky: **7** opaline *volcanic:* **7** perlite
8 obsidian

glasses 5 specs **6** shades **7** goggles
8 bifocals, pince-nez, tumblers
9 lorgnette, trifocals **10** spectacles

glass-like 5 clear **6** glazed, limpid,
smooth **8** pellucid, vitreous **9** vitrified
11 translucent, transparent

glassmaker 6 Blenko (William)
7 Lalique (René), Tiffany (Louis Comfort) **9** Waterford

glassmaking tool 5 punty **6** pontil
8 blowpipe

Glass Menagerie author 8 Williams
(Tennessee)

glassy 5 blank, dazed, shiny **6** glazed,
smooth, vacant **7** hyaloid **8** polished,
vitreous **9** burnished

glaucous 4 waxy **7** frosted, powdery

Glaucus *beloved:* **6** Scylla *father:* **5** Minos
8 Sisyphus *mother:* **6** Merope **8** Pasiphaë
son: **11** Bellerophon

glaze 3 rub **4** buff, coat, film **5** cover,
glint, gloss, sheen, shine **6** enamel, finish, luster, patina, polish **7** burnish,
coating, furbish, lacquer, overlay

glazed 5 blank **6** glassy

gleam 3 ray **4** beam, burn, glow **5** flare,
flash, glint, sheen, shine **6** glance
7 glimmer, glisten, glitter, radiate,
shimmer, sparkle, twinkle **8** radiance
11 coruscation, scintillate **13** scintillation

gleaming 5 aglow, shiny **6** glossy, sheeny
7 beaming, burning, glowing, lambent,
radiant, shining **8** flashing, luminous,
lustrous, polished **9** brilliant, burnished, refulgent, sparkling, twinkling
10 glimmering, glistening, glittering,
shimmering **13** scintillating

glean 4 cull, reap, sift **5** amass, learn
6 garner, gather, pick up **7** extract, find
out, harvest

glebe 4 land **5** field, tract **7** acreage
8 cropland, farmland

glee 4 joy **5** mirth **6** gaiety, levity
7 delight, elation, jollity **8** gladness,
hilarity, part-song **9** enjoyment, festivity, good cheer, happiness, jocundity,
joviality, merriment **10** exuberance,
joyfulness, jubilation **12** exhilaration

gleeful 3 gay **5** jolly, merry **6** blithe, elated, jocund, jovial, joyous **8** cheerful,
exultant, jubilant, mirthful **9** exuberant
12 lighthearted

glen 4 dale, vale **5** swale **6** dingle, valley
deep: **5** gorge **6** ravine

glengarry 3 cap **6** bonnet

glib 4 easy **5** slick **6** facile, fluent,
smooth **7** offhand, shallow, voluble
8 eloquent, flippant **10** articulate, nonchalant **11** superficial

glide 3 fly **4** flow, sail, skim, slip, soar,
waft **5** coast, creep, drift, float, skate,
skirr, skulk, slide, slink, sneak, steal
7 descend, slither **8** glissade, volplane
10 portamento

glimmer 4 glow, hint **5** blink, flash,
gleam, glint, shine, spark, trace
6 glance **7** flicker, glisten, glitter,
inkling, shimmer, sparkle, twinkle
9 coruscate **10** suggestion **11** coruscation, scintillate **13** scintillation

glimpse 4 peek, peep **5** flash, glint, stime
6 glance

glint 3 ray **5** flash, glaze, gleam, sheen,
shine, trace **6** glance, luster **7** glimmer,
glisten, glitter, shimmer, sparkle, twinkle **9** coruscate **11** coruscation, scintillate **13** scintillation

glissade 4 skim, slip **5** glide, slide

glissando 3 run **5** slide **7** gliding, sliding

glisten 4 glow **5** flash, gleam, glint, shine
6 glance **7** flicker, glimmer, glitter,
shimmer, spangle, sparkle, twinkle
9 coruscate **11** coruscation, scintillate
13 scintillation

glitch 3 bug **4** flaw, snag **5** fault **6** defect
7 failing, failure, gremlin, problem
8 obstacle **10** difficulty **11** malfunction

glitter 5 flash, gleam, glint, shine **7** glimmer, glisten, shimmer, spangle, sparkle,
twinkle **9** coruscate **11** coruscation,
scintillate **13** scintillation

glittering 5 gaudy, shiny, showy **6** flashy
7 fulgent **9** brilliant, clinquant, coruscant, effulgent **11** spectacular

gloaming 3 eve **4** dusk **5** gloom
7 evening **8** eventide, twilight **9** nightfall

gloat 4 crow **5** exult, revel, vaunt **6** relish
7 triumph **9** celebrate

glob 4 clot, lump **6** dollop

global 5 grand **6** cosmic **7** blanket, general, overall **8** all-round, catholic
9 inclusive, planetary, spherical, universal, worldwide **12** encyclopedic **13** comprehensive

globe 3 orb **4** ball **5** earth, round, world
6 planet, sphere **7** rondure *half:*
10 hemisphere

globule 4 ball, bead, drip, drop **6** gobbet,
pellet **7** driblet, droplet **8** spherule

gloom 3 dim **4** dusk, funk, loom, murk
5 bedim, blues, cloud, dumps, frown,
lower, mopes, scowl **6** darken, glower,
shadow **7** becloud, despair, dimness,
obscure, sadness **8** darkness, overcast,

twilight 9 adumbrate, bleakness, dejection 10 blue devils, depression, melancholy, overshadow 11 despondency, unhappiness 12 mournfulness

gloomy 3 dim, dun, sad 4 cold, dark, dour, down, drab, dull, glum 5 black, bleak, drear, dusky, mopey, murky, muzzy, sulky, surly 6 dismal, dreary, morose, solemn, somber, sullen 7 forlorn, joyless, obscure, stygian, unhappy 8 dejected, desolate, downcast, funereal, mournful 9 cheerless, depressed, mirthless, oppressed, saturnine, tenebrous, woebegone 10 caliginous, chapfallen, depressing, depressive, dispirited, despondent, forbidding, lugubrious, melancholy, oppressive, tenebrific 11 dispiriting, pessimistic 12 disconsolate, discouraging

glorify 4 hymn, laud 5 bless, cry up, erect, exalt, extol, honor 6 admire, praise, revere 7 acclaim, dignify, elevate, ennoble, light up, lionize, magnify, sublime, worship 8 eulogize, venerate 9 celebrate 10 aggrandize

glorious 5 grand, great, noble, proud 6 august, divine, superb 7 eminent, exalted, radiant, sublime 8 esteemed, gorgeous, lustrous, majestic, renowned, splendid, stunning 9 beautiful, brilliant, effulgent, excellent, marvelous, ravishing, wonderful 11 illustrious, magnificent, resplendent, splendorous

glory 4 crow, fame, halo, pomp 5 exalt, exult, gloat, honor, revel 6 heaven, praise, relish, renown 7 acclaim, aureole, delight, majesty, rejoice, triumph 8 eminence, eternity, grandeur, jubilate, radiance, splendor 9 greatness, hereafter 10 effulgence, exaltation, exultation 11 distinction 12 magnificence, resplendence

gloss 4 buff 5 glaze, glint, sheen, shine 6 define, enamel, facade, finish, luster, patina, polish, veneer 7 burnish, comment, explain, furbish, varnish 8 annotate 9 interpret, sleekness, slickness, translate 10 annotation, appearance, brilliance, commentary, definition 11 elucidation, explanation, translation

glossary 7 lexicon 8 wordbook 9 wordhoard 10 dictionary, vocabulary

gloss over 4 mask 5 slant 6 veneer 7 conceal, cover up, distort, falsify, varnish 8 disguise, palliate 9 dissemble, extenuate, sugarcoat, whitewash 10 camouflage

glossy 5 shiny, sleek, slick 7 shining 8 gleaming, lustrous, polished 9 burnished 10 glistening *fabric:* 4 silk 5 satin *paint:* 6 enamel

glove 4 gage, mitt 5 catch, cover 6 mitten, sheath 8 covering, gauntlet

glow 4 burn, pink, rose 5 bloom, blush, flush, gleam, rouge, shine 6 mantle, redden 7 blossom, crimson, fox fire, glisten, glitter, radiate 8 brighten, radiance 10 brilliance, luminosity 13 incandescence

glower 5 frown, scowl, stare 11 look daggers

glowing 3 hot, red 4 avid 5 flush, ruddy, shiny 6 ardent, fervid, florid, heated, red-hot 7 beaming, burning, fervent, flushed, lambent, radiant, vibrant 8 blushing, dazzling, gleaming, luminous, lustrous, rubicund, sanguine, suffused 9 brilliant 10 candescent, hot-blooded, passionate 11 impassioned 12 enthusiastic, incandescent

Gluck opera 5 Orfeo 6 Armide 7 Alceste

glucose 5 sugar, syrup

glue 3 fix, gum 4 bind, join 5 epoxy, paste, stick 6 adhere, attach, cement, fasten 7 plaster, stickum 8 adhesive, mucilage

gluey 5 gummy, tacky 6 sticky, viscid 7 viscous 8 adhesive 12 mucilaginous

glum 3 sad 4 blue, dour, down 5 moody, sulky, surly 6 dismal, dreary, gloomy, morose, sullen, woeful 7 crabbed 8 brooding, dejected, downcast, taciturn 9 depressed, oppressed, saturnine, sorrowful, woebegone 10 despondent, dispirited, melancholy 11 downhearted, melancholic

glut 4 clog, cloy, cram, fill, pack, pall, sate 5 feast, flood, gorge, stuff 6 deluge, excess, stodge 7 satiate, surfeit, surplus, swallow 8 saturate 10 oversupply 13 overabundance

glutinous 4 ropy 5 gluey, gooey, gummy, pasty, tacky, thick 6 sticky, viscid 7 viscous 10 gelatinous 12 mucilaginous

glutton 3 hog, pig 8 gourmand 9 chowhound, wolverine 11 gormandizer

gluttonous 7 hoggish, piggish 8 edacious, ravening, ravenous 9 dissolute, indulgent, rapacious, voracious 10 insatiable 11 intemperate 13 overindulgent

gluttony 6 excess 7 edacity 8 gulosity, rapacity, voracity 11 piggishness

glyph 6 figure, groove, symbol 7 graphic 9 character

G-man 3 fed 4 narc, Ness (Eliot) 5 agent 6 Hoover (J. Edgar)

gnarl 4 bend, knot, warp 5 growl, snarl, twist 6 deform 7 contort, distort

gnash 4 bite 5 grind

gnat 3 bug, fly 4 pest 5 midge 6 insect 7 no-see-um

gnaw 3 eat, nag, vex **4** bite, chaw, chew **5** annoy, chomp, erode, munch, scour, tease, worry **6** bother, crunch, nibble, pester, plague, rankle **7** bedevil, corrode, eat away **8** irritate, wear away **9** masticate

gnome 3 elf, saw **4** rule **5** adage, axiom, dwarf, maxim, moral, troll, truth **6** dictum, goblin, saying, truism **7** proverb **8** aphorism, apothegm **10** shibboleth

gnostic 6 occult, secret **8** abstruse **10** mysterious

gnu 10 wildebeest

go *against:* **4** defy **5** fight **6** oppose, resist **7** counter, protest **10** contradict *ahead:* **4** lead **7** precede, proceed **8** continue, progress *along:* **5** agree, yield **6** accede, comply, concur **7** consent **9** acquiesce *around:* **5** avoid, skirt **6** bypass, detour **7** compass **8** outflank, sidestep **10** circumvent *at:* **6** assail, attack, tackle **7** assault *away:* **3** git **4** exit, scat, shoo **5** leave, scram, split **6** beat it, begone, cut out, depart, move on, retire **7** buzz off, get lost, pull out, take off **8** clear out, run along, shove off, withdraw **9** skedaddle *back:* **6** recede, return, revert **7** regress, retreat *back on:* **6** betray, renege **7** abandon **8** abrogate *back over:* **6** rehash, review, rework **7** recheck, retrace *before:* **4** lead **7** precede, predate **8** antedate *beyond:* **4** pass **5** excel, outdo **6** exceed, outrun **7** eclipse, surpass **8** outshine, outstrip, overtake **9** transcend *forward:* **6** move on, push on **7** advance, press on, proceed **8** continue, progress *in:* **5** enter **9** penetrate *out:* **4** exit **5** leave **6** expire *Scottish:* **3** gae *through:* **4** bear **5** audit, brave, check, spend **6** endure, suffer **7** consume, deplete, examine, exhaust, ride out, survive, sustain, undergo **8** squander **9** penetrate, withstand **10** experience *together:* **3** fit **4** date, jibe, suit **5** agree, match, tally **6** accord, square **7** conform **8** dovetail **9** accompany, harmonize **10** correspond *with:* **4** suit **5** befit, match **9** accompany

goad 3 egg, rod, sic **4** prod, push, spur, urge **5** drive, egg on, impel, prick, thorn **6** coerce, exhort, incite, motive, needle, prompt, propel **7** impetus, impulse **8** catalyst, motivate, stimulus **9** encourage, impulsion, incentive, stimulant, stimulate **10** inducement

go-ahead 4 okay **7** consent **8** spirited **9** ambitious, authority, clearance, energetic **10** green light, permission **11** progressive, up-and-coming **12** enterprising **13** authorization

goal 3 aim, end, use **4** duty, hope, mark **5** score **6** design, intent, object, target **7** mission, purpose **8** ambition, function **9** intention, objective

goat 3 kid, ram **4** lech **5** billy, letch, nanny **6** alpaca, angora, lecher, Saanen **8** cashmere **10** Toggenburg *female:* **3** doe **5** nanny *genus:* **5** Capra *Himalayan:* **4** tahr *male:* **4** buck **5** billy *neutered:* **6** wether *relating to:* **7** caprine *wild:* **4** ibex *wool:* **6** mohair **8** pashmina

goat antelope 5 serow **7** chamois

goatee 5 beard **7** Vandyke **8** imperial, whiskers

goatfish 6 mullet

goatish 3 hot **4** lewd **6** carnal **7** caprine, lustful, satyric **8** prurient **9** indulgent, lecherous, lickerish **10** lascivious, libidinous, passionate **12** concupiscent

goat-man deity 3 Pan

goat nut 6 jojoba, pignut

gob 3 wad **4** blob, clod, glob, hunk, lump, mass **5** chunk, mouth **6** nugget, sailor **7** extract

gobbet 4 drib, drip, drop, hunk, lump, mass **5** chunk, piece **7** driblet, droplet, globule, portion **8** fragment

gobble 3 eat **4** bolt, cram, grab, glut, gulp, slop, wolf **5** gorge **6** devour, guzzle **7** swallow **11** ingurgitate

gobbledygook see GIBBERISH

go-between 5 agent, envoy, proxy **6** broker, deputy, factor **7** liaison **8** emissary, mediator, procurer **9** middleman **10** arbitrator, interagent, interceder, matchmaker, negotiator, procurator **11** intercessor **12** intermediary, intermediate

goblet 3 cup **5** glass, grail **6** vessel **7** chalice

goblin 3 elf, fay, hob, imp **4** puck **5** bogey, bogle, fairy, ghost, gnome **6** sprite **7** brownie, bugbear **8** bogeyman

___ go bragh 4 Erin

gobs 4 lots, tons, wads **5** heaps, loads, lumps, piles, rafts, reams, scads **6** oodles **8** slathers **10** quantities

god 4 idol **5** deity **7** creator **8** Almighty, divinity, immortal *combining form:* **4** theo *false:* **4** baal *French:* **4** dieu *Hebrew:* **6** Elohim, Yahweh *Latin:* **4** deus *Spanish:* **4** dios (see specific entries (as GREEK; ROMAN) for names of specific gods and goddesses)

god-awful 4 foul **6** horrid, rotten **7** beastly **8** dreadful, horrible, shameful, shocking, terrible, wretched **9** appalling, atrocious, miserable **10** abominable, deplorable, despicable, detestable, disgusting, outrageous

God Bless America composer 6 Berlin (Irving)

goddess 4 idol 5 deity 8 divinity, immortal *Latin:* 3 dea (see note at GOD)

godfather 3 don 4 boss, capo 6 leader 7 sponsor

Godfather, The 8 Corleone (Don) *actor:* 6 Brando (Marlon), De Niro (Robert), Pacino (Al) *author:* 4 Puzo (Mario) *director:* 7 Coppola (Francis Ford)

God-fearing 5 pious 6 devout 8 faithful, reverent 9 pietistic, religious, righteous

godforsaken 4 bare 5 bleak 6 barren, dismal, gloomy, remote 7 pitiful 8 deserted, desolate, pitiable, wretched 9 miserable, neglected 11 unfortunate

Godiva's husband 7 Leofric

godless 5 pagan 6 unholy, wicked 7 heathen, impious, infidel, profane 8 agnostic 9 atheistic 11 irreligious, unreligious

godlike 4 holy 6 divine 7 blessed, supreme 8 almighty, immortal 10 omniscient 11 all-powerful

godliness 5 piety 6 purity 8 devotion, divinity, holiness, sanctity 9 beatitude, reverence 10 devoutness, sacredness 11 religiosity, saintliness 12 spirituality, virtuousness 13 righteousness

godly 4 holy 5 pious 6 devout, divine 7 angelic, blessed, saintly, supreme 8 almighty, hallowed, immortal, virtuous 9 pietistic, prayerful, religious 10 omniscient 11 all-powerful

go down 3 dip, set 4 drop, fall, fold, lose, sink 5 ensue, lower, occur, pitch, slide, slump 6 cave in, happen, plunge, settle, topple, tumble 7 crumple, decline, descend, founder, succumb 8 collapse, keel over, submerge, submerse 9 surrender, take place

God's acre 8 boneyard, catacomb, cemetery 9 graveyard 10 churchyard, necropolis 12 burial ground, memorial park, potter's field

godsend 4 boon, gift, good 5 manna 7 benefit 8 blessing, windfall 9 advantage 11 benevolence, serendipity

Goethe work 5 Faust 6 Egmont, Stella 7 Clavigo 10 Prometheus

gofer 4 aide, peon 5 toady 6 drudge, flunky, helper, lackey, menial 7 courier, servant 8 factotum 9 assistant, attendant

goffer 5 crimp, flute, pinch, plait, pleat

go-getter 6 dynamo 7 hustler, rustler 8 live wire 10 ball of fire, powerhouse 11 self-starter

goggle 3 eye 4 bore, gape, gawk, gaze, look, ogle, peer 5 glare, gloat, stare 10 rubberneck

goggles 5 specs 7 glasses 10 eyeglasses, spectacles

go-go 5 hyper 6 hectic 7 frantic 8 frenetic, frenzied

Gogol *novel:* 9 Dead Souls *story:* 8 Overcoat (The) 10 Taras Bulba 14 Diary of a Madman

goiter 6 struma 8 swelling

Golconda see GOLD MINE

gold 4 gilt 5 money 6 riches, wealth, yellow 7 bullion 8 treasure *bar:* 5 ingot *combining form:* 4 auri, auro 5 chrys 6 chryso *fool's:* 6 pyrite *imitation:* 6 ormolu *measure:* 5 carat, karat *Spanish:* 3 oro

goldbrick 3 bum 4 idle, laze, lazy, loaf, loll 5 cheat, dally, idler, shirk, slack 6 dawdle, loafer, loiter, lounge 7 lounger, shirker, slacker, swindle 8 lollygag, malinger, sluggard 9 lazybones 10 dillydally, malingerer

Gold Bug author 3 Poe (Edgar Allan)

gold cloth 4 lamé

gold-covered 4 gilt 6 gilded

golden 4 gilt, rich 5 auric, blond, shiny, straw 6 blonde, flaxen, gilded, mellow, superb, yellow 7 aureate, honeyed, shining 8 glorious, lustrous, resonant 9 favorable 10 auspicious, prosperous 11 flourishing

golden-ager 5 elder 6 senior 7 ancient, oldster, retiree 8 old-timer 13 senior citizen

golden-apples guardian 5 Ithun 6 Ithunn

golden bough 9 mistletoe

Golden Bough author 6 Frazer (James George)

Golden Boy playwright 5 Odets (Clifford)

golden-crowned accentor 7 warbler 8 ovenbird

goldeneye 3 bug 4 duck, fowl 6 insect 8 lacewing

Golden Fleece seeker 5 Jason 8 Argonaut

Golden Hind captain 5 Drake (Francis)

Golden Horde 6 Tatars 7 Mongols *leader:* 4 Batu

golden horse 7 Trigger 8 palomino

golden shiner 4 dace, fish

Golden State 10 California

goldfinch 4 bird 8 songbird 12 yellowhammer

gold mine 7 bonanza, pay dirt 8 El Dorado, Golconda, treasure, treasury 13 treasure trove

golem 3 oaf 4 clod, dolt, dope 5 dunce, idiot, robot 6 nitwit 7 halfwit, machine 8 imbecile 9 automaton, blockhead 10 nincompoop 11 blunderhead

golf *assistant:* 5 caddy 6 caddie *club:* 4 iron, wood 5 billy, spoon, wedge

6 driver, mashie, putter 7 niblick, pitcher 9 metal wood, sand wedge *club part:* 3 toe 4 face, grip, head, heel, neck, sole 5 hosel, shaft *course:* 5 links *cup:* 5 Ryder 6 Curtis, Walker *hazard:* 4 trap 6 bunker 8 sand trap *mound:* 3 tee *score:* 3 ace, par 5 bogey, eagle 6 birdie *stroke:* 4 baff, chip, draw, fade, hook, putt 5 drive, pitch, shank, slice 6 sclaff *target:* 3 cup, par, pin 4 flag 5 green 7 fairway *term:* 3 lie 4 club, fore, hole, loft 5 divot, rough, swing 6 hazard, marker, stance, stroke 8 foursome, handicap 9 backswing, downswing, flagstick

golfer 8 linksman *man:* 3 Els (Ernie) 4 Daly (John), Ford (Doug), Kite (Tom), Lyle (Sandy), Mize (Larry), Tway (Bob) 5 Boros (Julius), Faldo (Nick), Floyd (Ray), Grady (Wayne), Green (Hubert), Hagen (Walter), Hogan (Ben), Jones (Bobby), Irwin (Hale), North (Andy), Pavin (Corey), Peete (Calvin), Price (Nick), Shute (Denny), Singh (Vijay), Snead (Sam), Woods (Tiger) 6 Casper (Billy), Graham (David), Janzen (Lee), Langer (Bernhard), Miller (Johnny), Nelson (Byron, Larry), Norman (Greg), Ouimet (Francis), Palmer (Arnold), Player (Gary), Sluman (Jeff), Sutton (Hal), Vardon (Harry), Watson (Tom) 7 Azinger (Paul), Couples (Fred), Guldahl (Ralph), Mayfair (Billy), Sarazen (Gene), Simpson (Scott), Stewart (Payne), Strange (Curtis), Trevino (Lee), Woosnam (Ian), Zoeller (Fuzzy) 8 Crenshaw (Ben), Nicklaus (Jack), Olazabal (José), Weiskopf (Tom) 9 Rodriguez (Chi Chi), Elkington (Steve) 10 Middlecoff (Cary) 11 Ballesteros (Seve) *woman:* 4 Berg (Patty), King (Betsy) 5 Baker (Kathy), Lopez (Nancy), Rawls (Betsy), Stacy (Hollis), Suggs (Louise) 6 Alcott (Amy), Carner (Joanne), Daniel (Beth), Davies (Laura), Geddes (Jane), Mallon (Meg), Merten (Lauri), Wright (Mickey) 7 Bradley (Pat), Inkster (Juli), Mochrie (Dottie), Sheehan (Patty) 8 Zaharias (Babe) 9 Didrikson (Babe), Sorenstam (Annika), Whitworth (Kathy) 10 Stephenson (Jan)

Golgotha 7 Calvary

Goliath 5 giant 10 Philistine *deathplace:* 4 Elah *home:* 4 Gath *slayer:* 5 David

Gollum creator 7 Tolkien (J. R. R.)

gonad 5 gland, ovary 6 testis 8 testicle

gondola 3 car 4 boat 7 ski lift 11 railroad car

gone 4 away, dead, left, lost, past 5 flown 6 absent 7 defunct, extinct, lacking, missing 8 departed, vanished

gonef see GANEF

goner 8 dead duck 9 lost cause

Goneril *father:* 4 Lear (King) *husband:* 6 Albany *sister:* 5 Regan 8 Cordelia *victim:* 5 Regan

Gone with the Wind *author:* 8 Mitchell (Margaret) *character:* 5 Rhett (Butler) 6 Ashley (Wilkes) 7 Melanie (Wilkes) 8 Scarlett (O'Hara) *plantation:* 4 Tara

gonfalon 4 flag, jack 6 banner, ensign 7 pendant, pennant 8 banderol, standard 9 banderole

gong 6 cymbal, tam-tam

gonzo 6 far-out 7 bizarre, offbeat 9 wigged-out 10 outrageous

goo 4 crud, glop, guck, gunk, muck 5 slime

goober 6 peanut

good 4 pure 5 right, sound, whole 6 decent, humane, kindly, toward, worthy 7 benefit, healthy, upright, welfare 8 innocent, virtuous 9 admirable, advantage, blameless, exemplary, favorable, healthful, honorable, righteous, well-being, wholesome 10 altruistic, beneficent, beneficial, benevolent, charitable, worthwhile 11 respectable, well-behaved 12 humanitarian 13 philanthropic *French:* 3 bon 5 bonne *German:* 3 gut *Spanish:* 5 bueno

good-bye 4 ciao, ta-ta 5 adieu, congé, later 6 so long 7 cheerio, parting, send-off, toodles 8 farewell, toodle-oo 9 departing, departure 11 leave-taking, valediction, valedictory *French:* 5 adieu 8 au revoir 9 bon voyage *German:* 8 lebe wohl *Italian:* 11 arrivederci *Japanese:* 8 sayonara *Spanish:* 5 adios 12 hasta la vista

Good Earth author 4 Buck (Pearl S.)

good-for-nothing 3 bum 6 rascal, waster 7 inutile, rounder, useless, wastrel 8 feckless, rascally, unworthy 9 dissolute, scoundrel, valueless, worthless 10 ne'er-do-well, profligate, scapegrace 11 purposeless

good-looking 4 cute, fair, foxy 5 bonny, dishy, hunky 6 comely, lovely, pretty 8 alluring, drop-dead, fetching, handsome 9 beauteous, beautiful, bodacious, ravishing 10 attractive

goodly 4 fair, tidy 5 ample, hefty, large 7 sizable 8 generous 9 bountiful, plentiful 11 significant, substantial 12 considerable

good-natured 4 easy, kind, mild, warm 6 genial, jovial, mellow 7 affable, amiable, cordial, lenient 8 cheerful, friendly, laid-back, obliging, pleasant, pleas-

ing, sanguine 9 agreeable, congenial, easygoing, gemütlich 10 altruistic, benevolent, charitable 11 complaisant
goodness 5 honor, merit, worth 6 purity, virtue 7 decency, honesty, probity, quality 8 morality 9 integrity, rectitude 11 benevolence
goods 4 gear 5 cargo, stock, stuff, wares 7 effects 8 chattels, movables, property 9 vendibles 10 belongings 11 commodities, merchandise, possessions 13 paraphernalia *smuggled:* 10 contraband *stolen:* 4 loot, swag 5 booty 6 boodle, spoils 7 plunder *thrown overboard:* 5 lagan 6 jetsam
good-tasting 5 sapid, yummy 6 delish, savory, toothy 8 luscious 9 delicious, palatable, relishing, toothsome 10 appetizing, delectable, flavorsome 11 scrumptious 13 mouthwatering
goodwill 5 amity, favor 6 comity 7 charity, rapport 8 altruism, kindness, sympathy 9 tolerance 10 compassion, friendship, generosity, kindliness 11 benevolence, helpfulness 12 friendliness
goody 5 candy, treat 6 bonbon, dainty, morsel, tidbit 8 delicacy, kickshaw
goody-goody 4 prig 5 prude 6 Grundy 7 prudish, puritan, uptight 8 bluenose, Comstock, priggish 9 Mrs. Grundy, nice-nelly 11 puritanical
gooey 5 gluey, gummy, mushy, sappy, soupy 6 cloggy, drippy, slushy, sticky, viscid 7 maudlin, viscous 8 adhesive 9 glutinous 11 sentimental 12 mucilaginous
goof 3 err, kid 4 boob, dolt, flub, fool, mess, muff 5 boner, booby, botch, chump, dunce, error, fluff, gaffe, gum up, idiot, put on 6 bobble, boggle, bollix, bumble, bungle, fumble, mess up, slip-up 7 blooper, blunder, fathead, louse up, mistake 8 dolthead, lunkhead 9 blockhead
go off 4 blow 5 blast, burst, erupt, leave, sound 6 blow up, depart 7 explode 8 detonate
goofy 5 balmy, batty, crazy, daffy, dippy, loony, nutty, potty, silly 6 simple, stupid 7 foolish, idiotic 9 ludicrous 10 ridiculous 11 harebrained
gook 4 crud, glop, gunk, muck 5 gumbo, slime 6 debris, sludge
go on 4 last, stay 5 occur 6 endure, happen, keep up 7 persist, proceed 8 continue 9 persevere
goon 3 oaf, sap 4 boob, dodo, dolt, dope, fool, hood, thug 5 dummy, idiot 6 dimwit, hit man, nitwit 7 hoodlum 8 dumbbell, enforcer 10 triggerman

gooney 7 seabird 9 albatross
goop 4 crud, gunk, muck 5 gumbo, tripe
Goops author 7 Burgess (Gelett)
goose 4 poke, spur 9 stimulate *cry:* 4 honk 5 clang *flock:* 3 vee 5 skein 6 gaggle *genus:* 5 Anser *Hawaiian:* 4 nene *male:* 6 gander *wild:* 5 brant 7 greylag 8 barnacle *young:* 7 gosling
gooseberry 7 currant
Goosebumps author 5 Stine (R. L.)
goose egg 3 nil, zip 4 nada, zero 5 aught, zilch 6 cipher, naught, nought 7 no score, nothing
gooseflesh 5 bumps 7 pimples
go over 4 scan, skim 5 study 6 peruse, review 7 examine, inspect
gopher 6 rodent 8 tortoise
Gopher State 9 Minnesota
Gordian knot cutter 9 Alexander
Gordius' son 5 Midas
gore 3 jab 4 stab 5 blood, slime, wound 6 gusset, pierce 7 carnage 12 gruesomeness
gorge 3 gap 4 cloy, fill, glut, jade, pall, sate 5 abyss, chasm, cleft, clove, flume, gulch, stuff 6 arroyo, canyon, clough, defile, pig out, ravine 7 couloir, overeat, satiate, surfeit 11 overindulge *Arizona:* 11 Grand Canyon *Colorado:* 5 Royal
gorgeous 5 grand, plush 6 comely, lavish, lovely, pretty, superb 7 opulent, sublime 8 alluring, dazzling, glorious, splendid 9 beautiful, brilliant, exquisite, luxurious, sumptuous 10 attractive, glittering 11 magnificent, resplendent, splendorous
gorgon 3 hag 5 crone, harpy, witch 6 Medusa, ogress, virago 8 battle-ax, fishwife, harridan, slattern 9 battle-axe, termagant *father:* 7 Phorcus, Phorcys *mother:* 4 Ceto
gorilla 3 ape 4 goon, hood, thug 5 tough 6 simian 7 primate 8 gangster 10 anthropoid
Gorky drama 11 Lower Depths (The)
gormless 4 dumb, slow 6 stupid
gorse 4 whin 5 furze, shrub 6 legume
gory 5 lurid 6 bloody, grisly 8 gruesome, sanguine 10 sanguinary 11 ensanguined, sanguineous, sensational 12 bloodstained 13 bloodcurdling
gosh 3 gee, wow 4 dang, darn, drat, egad, geez, heck 5 golly 6 crikey, cripes, shucks 7 doggone 8 goodness, gracious
gospel 5 truth 6 truism 7 message 8 doctrine 9 scripture 11 evangelical
gossamer 4 airy, film, fine, webs 5 filmy, gauzy, sheer 6 flimsy 7 cobwebs, tenu-

ous 8 delicate 10 diaphanous 11 transparent

gossip 4 blab, buzz, chat, dirt, talk 5 clack, prate, rumor 6 babble, rumble, tattle 7 babbler, chatter, hearsay, prattle, tattler 8 bigmouth, busybody, informer, prattler, quidnunc, telltale 10 talebearer 11 rumormonger, scandalizer, scuttlebutt 12 blatherskite

gossipy 5 gabby, talky 6 chatty 8 babbling, blabbing 9 garrulous, talkative

Gotham 7 New York (City)

Gothic 4 dark, wild 5 crude 6 brutal, coarse, savage 7 uncouth 8 barbaric, Germanic, medieval, Teutonic 9 barbarian, barbarous, sans serif 11 black letter, uncivilized

Götterdämmerung composer 6 Wagner (Richard)

Gouda 6 cheese

gouge 3 dig 4 milk, ream, tool 5 cheat, exact, pinch, screw, wrest, wring 6 chisel, coerce, extort, groove, wrench 7 squeeze 8 scoop out 9 blackmail, extortion, shake down 10 overcharge

goulash 4 stew 6 jumble, medley 7 mélange 8 mishmash 9 potpourri 10 bridge hand, hodgepodge, salmagundi 11 gallimaufry

go under 4 fall, flop, fold, lose, sink 5 drown 6 plunge, submit 7 founder, immerse, succumb 8 collapse, submerge, submerse 9 surrender 10 capitulate

Gounod work 5 Faust 8 Ave Maria

gourd 4 pepo 5 fruit, melon 6 bottle, squash, vessel 7 chayote, gherkin, pumpkin 8 calabash, cucumber, cucurbit *instrument:* 6 maraca

gourmand see GLUTTON; GOURMET

gourmet 7 epicure 9 bon vivant 10 gastronome 11 connoisseur 12 gastronomist

gout 4 blob, clot, gush 5 spurt 6 splash 7 disease, podagra 8 eruption, swelling

govern 4 head, lead, rule 5 guide, order, reign, steer 6 direct, manage, master 7 command, conduct, control, execute, oversee 8 dominate, hold sway, regulate 9 supervise 10 administer 11 superintend

governess 5 nanny, nurse 6 duenna 8 mistress 9 nursemaid 10 babysitter 11 Mary Poppins

government 4 rule 5 power 6 polity, regime 7 regency, regimen 8 monarchy, republic, Uncle Sam 9 authority, autocracy, democracy, hierarchy, oligarchy 10 Big Brother 11 aristocracy, sovereignty *autocratic:* 7 czarism, fascism, tyranny 9 despotism 10 absolutism

12 dictatorship *by a few:* 9 oligarchy *by one:* 8 monarchy *by three:* 8 triarchy 11 triumvirate *by women:* 8 gynarchy *official:* 10 bureaucrat 11 functionary *without:* 7 anarchy

government agency 3 ATF, BIA, BLM, CDC, CIA, DEA, EPA, FAA, FBI, FCC, FDA, FEC, FHA, GAO, GPO, HUD, ICC, INS, IRS, NBS, NEA, NIH, NRC, TVA 4 FDIC, FEMA, FEPC, NASA, NOAA, NTSB, OSHA

governor 3 bey 4 head 5 chief, nabob, ruler 6 leader, regent 7 manager, viceroy 8 director 9 executive, regulator 10 commandant, magistrate *Chinese:* 6 tuchun *of a fort:* 7 alcaide, alcayde 9 castellan, chatelain *Persian:* 6 satrap

gown 4 robe, toga 5 dress, frock, habit, tunic 6 camise, kimono, kirtle, mantua 7 cassock, chemise 8 peignoir *dressing:* 8 bathrobe *hospital:* 6 johnny

goy 6 non-Jew 7 gentile

grab 3 nab 4 glom, grip, snag, take 5 catch, clasp, grasp, pluck, seize 6 clutch, collar, snatch, tackle 7 capture, grapple, seizure

grabby 6 greedy 8 covetous, desirous, grasping 9 rapacious 10 avaricious, prehensile 11 acquisitive

grace 4 ease 5 adorn, charm, favor, mercy, poise 6 allure, lenity, pardon, polish, prayer, thanks, virtue 7 charity, dignify, dignity, enhance 8 approval, blessing, clemency, easiness, elegance, goodness, kindness, leniency, petition, reprieve 9 embellish, privilege 10 indulgence, invocation, refinement 11 benediction, forbearance 12 thanksgiving

graceful 4 airy, deft, easy 5 agile, lithe 6 nimble, poised, seemly, smooth, urbane 7 elegant, flowing, genteel, refined 8 debonair, elegance, pleasing, polished

graceless 4 rude 5 crude, gawky, inept 6 clumsy, coarse, gauche, klutzy, vulgar 7 awkward, boorish, uncouth 8 barbaric, ungainly 9 barbarian, barbarous 10 outlandish, unmannered 12 infelicitous

Graces 6 Charis 8 Charites (plural) *brilliance:* 6 Aglaia *bloom:* 6 Thalia *joy:* 10 Euphrosyne *mother:* 5 Aegle

gracious 4 kind 5 suave 6 benign, genial, kindly, urbane 7 affable, amiable, cordial, courtly, gallant, stately, tactful 8 charming, generous, mannered, merciful, obliging, sociable 9 congenial, courteous 11 complaisant, good-natured 13 compassionate

grackle 5 mynah 7 jackdaw 8 starling 9 blackbird

gradation 4 rank, step 5 order, range, scale, shade, stage 6 ablaut, change, degree, nuance, series 8 ordering, position, spectrum 9 continuum, variation 10 difference, succession

grade 3 peg 4 cant, form, kind, lean, mark, rank, rate, rung, sort, step, tier, tilt 5 blend, class, group, level, notch, order, pitch, place, slant, slope, stage 6 assess, assort, degree, league, rating 7 arrange, caliber, echelon, incline, leaning, quality 8 appraise, category, classify, division, evaluate, grouping, position, standard 10 categorize 11 inclination

Grade A 3 ace, top 4 best, boss, fine, tops 5 grand, great, prime, primo, super 6 choice, tip-top 7 capital, supreme 8 five-star, superior, top-notch 9 excellent, first-rate, nonpareil, number one, top-drawer 10 first-class 11 outstanding 13 par excellence

gradient 4 lean, ramp, rise, tilt 5 angle, pitch, slant, slope 7 incline, leaning 9 acclivity, declivity 11 inclination

gradual 4 even, slow 6 Psalms, steady 7 ongoing 8 bit-by-bit, creeping 9 piecemeal, prolonged 10 continuous, developing, protracted, step-by-step 11 progressive

gradually 6 slowly 7 by steps 8 bit by bit 9 by degrees, piecemeal 10 step by step 12 deliberately 13 imperceptibly, incrementally

graduate 4 alum *female:* 6 alumna 7 alumnae (plural) *male:* 6 alumni (plural) 7 alumnus

Graeae, Graiae 4 Enyo 5 Deino 8 Pephredo *father:* 7 Phorcus, Phorcys *mother:* 4 Ceto *sisters:* 7 Gorgons

graft 4 join, mend, scam, skim 5 affix, crime, fraud, scion, unite 6 attach, boodle, fasten, payola, splice 7 implant, swindle, topwork 8 kickback 10 corruption

Grafton, Sue *character:* 8 Millhone (Kinsey) *novel:* 11 A Is for Alibi

Grahame, Kenneth *character:* 3 Rat 4 Toad, Mole 6 Badger *novel:* 16 Wind in the Willows (The)

grail 3 cup, end 4 goal 6 goblet, object, target 7 chalice 9 objective

grain 3 bit, jot, rye 4 corn, flax, iota, meal, mite, oats, rice 5 crumb, fiber, kamut, maize, speck, spelt, trace, wheat 6 barley, cereal, millet, quinoa, tittle 7 granule, smidgen, sorghum, texture 8 amaranth, molecule, particle 9 buckwheat, triticale *bundle:* 4 bale

5 sheaf *chute:* 6 hopper *ear:* 5 spike *elevator:* 4 silo *mixture:* 6 fodder *row:* 5 swath 7 windrow

grainy 5 rough 6 coarse 8 granular 10 unfinished, unpolished

grammarian *Roman:* 7 Donatus (Aelius)

grammatical case 6 dative 7 oblique 8 ablative, genitive, locative, vocative 9 objective 10 accusative, nominative, possessive, subjective

grampus 5 whale 7 dolphin 8 cetacean, porpoise, scorpion 9 blackfish 12 whip scorpion

Granada *building:* 8 Alhambra *citadel:* 8 Alcazaba *last Moorish king:* 7 Boabdil

granary 3 bin 4 silo 9 grain area 10 repository, storehouse

grand 3 fab 4 epic, fine, huge, vast 5 gaudy, lofty, noble, regal, royal, showy, super 6 august, flashy, garish, lavish, lordly, mighty, ornate, superb 7 exalted, opulent, pompous, stately, sublime 8 baronial, elevated, foremost, gorgeous, imposing, majestic, princely, splendid 9 first-rate, inclusive, luxurious, principal, sumptuous, wonderful 10 first-class, impressive, monumental, prodigious, stupendous, tremendous 11 magnificent 12 ostentatious 13 comprehensive

Grand Canyon *explorer:* 6 Powell (John Wesley) *state:* 7 Arizona

grande dame 5 queen 6 matron 7 dowager 9 matriarch

grandee 4 duke, earl, king, lord, peer 5 baron, noble, pasha 6 bashaw, prince 8 mandarin, marquess, nobleman, viscount 11 muckety-muck

grandeur 4 pomp 5 glory 7 dignity, majesty 8 nobility, opulence, splendor, vastness 9 greatness, immensity, largeness, loftiness, nobleness, sublimity 10 augustness 11 stateliness 12 magnificence

grandiloquent 5 lofty 7 aureate, bloated, fustian, pompous 8 inflated 9 bombastic, flatulent, high-flown, overblown 10 histrionic, portentous 11 declamatory, highfalutin, pretentious 12 magniloquent

grand inquisitor *Spanish:* 10 Torquemada (Tomás de)

grandiose 4 epic, vast 5 lofty, noble, regal, royal, showy 6 august, cosmic, lavish, lordly 7 pompous, stately, sublime, utopian 8 affected, imposing, majestic, princely, splendid 9 ambitious, high-flown 11 extravagant, highfalutin, magnificent, pretentious 12 ostentatious

grand mal 7 seizure 8 epilepsy

grandmother *Russian:* 8 babushka
grange 4 farm 9 farmhouse, farmstead
granite 3 ore 4 rock 5 stone 6 aplite
7 mineral 11 igneous rock
Granite State 12 New Hampshire
grant 3 aid 4 alms, avow, cede, dole, gift,
give 5 admit, allow, award, endow, yield
6 accord, assert, assign, assume,
bestow, confer, convey, donate, permit
7 charity, concede, consent, entitle,
handout, present, property, subsidy,
suppose 8 bequeath, donation, transfer
9 endowment, vouchsafe 10 assistance,
concession, relinquish, subvention
11 acknowledge, benefaction 12 contribution 13 appropriation
granular 5 rough, sandy 6 coarse, grainy
7 powdery 8 powdered 10 unfinished,
unpolished
granule 3 bit, jot 4 iota, pill, spot 5 grain
6 pellet 8 fragment, particle
grape 3 fox, uva 4 Bual 5 Gamay, Pinot,
Syrah 6 Arinto, Burger, Gentil, merlot,
muscat, Shiraz 7 Albillo, Aligote, Barbera, Catawba, Concord, Furmint, Niagara, sultana 8 Aleatico, Cabernet,
Charbono, Delaware, Friularo,
Grenache, Isabella, malvasia, mus-
cadel, Muscadet, Nebbiolo, Riesling,
Semillon, Sylvaner, Thompson, Tramin-
er, vinifera, Viognier 9 Carmenère,
Chasselas, Lambrusco, Malvoisie, muscadine, Pinot Gris, pinot noir, Sauvignon, Trebbiano, zinfandel 10 chardonnay, Grignolino, muscadelle, pinot
blanc, Sangiovese, Verdicchio
11 Chenin Blanc, Petite Sirah, pinot
grigio, scuppernong *disease:* 4 esca
dried: 6 raisin *drink:* 4 wine *pulp:* 4 rape
6 pomace *residue:* 4 marc
grapefruit 6 pomelo
Grapes of Wrath, The *author:* 9 Steinbeck
(John) *family:* 4 Joad *people:* 5 Okies
grapevine 4 buzz 5 rumor 6 gossip
7 hearsay 9 rumor mill 11 scuttlebutt
graph 3 map 4 plot 5 chart 6 sketch
7 diagram, outline 8 nomogram, pie
chart
graphic 3 map 5 clear, lucid, photo,
vivid 6 cogent, visual 7 picture, precise,
telling, written 8 clear-cut, definite,
detailed, explicit, incisive, striking
9 pictorial, realistic 10 compelling, photograph 11 descriptive, picturesque
graphite 4 lead 6 carbon 8 plumbago
grapnel 4 hook 6 anchor
grappa 6 brandy
grapple 3 nab 4 bind, cope, grab, grip,
hold 5 catch, clamp, clasp, fight, grasp,
seize 6 battle, bucket, clench, clinch,

clutch, fasten, tackle, tussle 7 contest,
scuffle, wrestle 8 struggle
grasp 3 dig, ken, see 4 glom, grip, hold,
know, take 5 catch, clamp, clasp, seize
6 accept, clench, clinch, clutch, fathom, follow, handle, take in, tenure
7 cognize, compass, control, embrace,
grapple, realize 8 envisage, perceive
9 apprehend, awareness 10 appreciate,
comprehend, take hold of, understand
12 apprehension 13 comprehension,
understanding
graspable 5 clear, lucid 6 lucent 8 coherent, knowable, palpable 10 fathomable
11 perspicuous 12 intelligible 13 apprehensible
grasping 4 avid 6 grabby, greedy 8 covetous, desirous 9 rapacious 10 avaricious, prehensile 11 acquisitive
grass 3 pot, sod, tea 4 lawn, reed, turf,
weed 6 redtop 7 herbage, panicum, pasture 8 cannabis, Mary Jane 9 cocks-
foot, marijuana *African:* 6 imphee *annual:* 6 darnel 8 teosinte *Asian:* 7 vetiver,
whangee *Australian:* 8 spinifex *beach:*
6 marram *cereal:* 3 oat, rye 4 milo, teff
5 kafir, maize, proso, sorgo, wheat
6 millet 7 sorghum 8 triticum *clump:*
4 tuft 7 tussock *dried:* 3 hay 5 straw
European: 7 Bermuda, timothy *fiber:*
4 flax *fragrant:* 10 citronella *pasture:*
5 Bahia, grama *perennial:* 6 fescue,
quitch, zoysia 7 esparto, galleta *prairie:*
8 bluestem *second growth:* 5 rowen *tropical:* 5 cogon 6 bamboo
grasshopper 6 locust 7 katydid 8 cocktail
grassland 3 lea 5 field 6 meadow 7 pasture, prairie *African:* 4 veld 5 veldt *flat:*
7 savanna 8 savannah *South American:*
5 pampa 6 pampas
Grass novel 7 Tin Drum (The)
grate 3 irk, jar, rub, vex 4 file, fray, fret,
gall, rasp, rile 5 annoy, chafe, gnash,
grind, peeve, pique 6 abrade, grille,
nettle, rankle, scrape 7 provoke,
scratch 8 irritate 9 aggravate, fireplace
grateful 7 obliged, pleased, restful, welcome 8 beholden, indebted, pleasant,
pleasing, thankful 9 agreeable, congenial, favorable 10 refreshing 11 restorative 12 appreciative
Gratiano *brother:* 9 Brabantio *friend:*
7 Antonio 8 Bassanio *niece:* 9 Desdemona *wife:* 7 Nerissa
gratify 4 baby, sate 5 favor, humor, spoil
6 coddle, oblige, pamper, pander,
please 7 appease, cater to, content,
delight, gladden, indulge, satisfy
gratin 5 crust
grating 3 dry 4 grid, rasp 5 grill, harsh,

rough 6 grille, hoarse 7 irksome, jarring, lattice, rasping, raucous 8 gridiron, strident 9 vexatious 10 stridulous

gratis 4 comp, free 6 comped 8 costless 10 chargeless 13 complimentary, without charge

gratitude 6 thanks 12 appreciation, gratefulness, thankfulness

gratuitous 6 wanton 8 baseless 9 unfounded, voluntary 10 groundless, reasonless, ungrounded 11 uncalled-for, unnecessary, unwarranted 12 indefensible

gratuity 3 tip 4 gift, perk 5 bonus 6 reward 7 cumshaw, douceur 8 donation, largesse, offering 9 baksheesh, lagniappe, pourboire 10 perquisite 11 benefaction 12 contribution

grave 3 pit, sad 4 dire, dour, fell, grim, tomb 5 acute, awful, crypt, fatal, heavy, major, sober, staid, vault 6 burial, deadly, gloomy, sedate, severe, solemn, somber, sombre, urgent 7 austere, ghastly, ominous, ossuary, serious, subdued, weighty 8 catacomb, critical, dreadful, perilous, pressing, terrible 9 dangerous, mausoleum, momentous, ponderous, saturnine, sepulcher, sepulchre, sepulture, unsmiling *marker:* 5 stela, stele 8 memorial, monument 9 footstone, headstone, tombstone 11 sarcophagus *mound:* 6 barrow 7 tumulus *robber:* 5 ghoul

gravel 4 dirt, grit, sand *ridge:* 5 esker

gravelly 5 raspy, rough 6 gritty, hoarse 7 rasping, grating 8 abrasive, granular, gutteral, scratchy

graven image 4 icon, idol

graver 4 tool 5 burin 8 sculptor

graveyard 8 boot hill, catacomb, cemetery, God's acre 10 necropolis 12 burial ground, memorial park, potter's field

gravid 5 heavy 8 enceinte, pregnant 9 expectant, expecting, with child 10 parturient 12 childbearing

gravity 5 force 6 weight 7 dignity, urgency 8 sobriety 9 heaviness, solemnity 10 importance, somberness 11 consequence, seriousness 12 significance

gravlax 3 lox 6 salmon

gravy 4 perk 5 bonus, bribe, graft, juice, sauce 6 payola 8 dressing, windfall *French:* 3 jus

gray 3 ash, old 4 aged, ashy, blah, drab, dull 5 ashen, bleak, color, hoary, slate, slaty 6 dismal, gloomy, leaden 7 elderly, grizzly, neutral 8 grizzled, gunmetal, overcast 9 cinereous, colorless *brownish:* 5 taupe 7 fuscous

gray duck 7 gadwall, pintail

grayfish 5 shark 7 dogfish

gray matter 3 wit 4 head, mind 5 brain 6 brains, noddle, noggin, noodle 8 cerebrum 9 intellect 10 encephalon 12 intelligence, neural tissue

graze 3 eat, rub 4 feed, gall, kiss, skim, skip, wear 5 brush, chafe, erode, shave, touch 6 abrade, browse, bruise, forage, glance, scrape 7 contuse, corrade, pasture 8 abrasion, ricochet

grazier 7 rancher

grease 3 fat, oil 4 lard 5 smear 6 smooth 7 lanolin 9 lubricant, lubricate *combining form:* 4 sebi, sebo

greasy 4 oily 5 fatty, slick 8 slippery, unctuous 10 lubricious, oleaginous

greasy spoon 4 café 5 diner, grill 6 eatery 7 beanery, hashery 9 chophouse, hash house, lunchroom 10 coffee shop 12 luncheonette

great 3 big, fat 4 huge, vast 5 famed, grand, jumbo, large, noble 6 famous, heroic 7 eminent, exalted, extreme, immense, mammoth, notable, sublime, supreme, titanic 8 colossal, enormous, gigantic, glorious, oversize, renowned, terrific, towering 9 excellent, fantastic, humongous, paramount, prominent, wonderful 10 celebrated, impressive, noteworthy, prodigious, remarkable, stupendous, surpassing, tremendous, voluminous 11 illustrious, magnificent, outstanding, superlative 13 distinguished *combining form:* 4 mega 6 megalo

Great Bear 9 Big Dipper, Ursa Major 13 constellation

Great Britain see ENGLAND

Great Commoner, the 4 Pitt (William) 5 Bryan (William Jennings) 7 Lincoln (Abraham)

Great Emancipator, the 7 Lincoln (Abraham)

greater 4 more 5 metro 6 better, bigger, higher, larger 8 superior 9 exceeding 10 surpassing 12 metropolitan

greatest 4 best, most 6 utmost 7 maximum, supreme 8 foremost

Great Expectations *author:* 7 Dickens (Charles) *character:* 3 Joe (Gargery), Pip 5 Biddy 7 Estella, Jaggers 8 Havisham (Miss), Magwitch (Abel)

greathearted 4 bold, kind 5 brave, lofty, noble 6 heroic 7 gallant 8 fearless, generous, princely 10 benevolent, chivalrous, courageous, high-minded 11 considerate, magnanimous

Great Lake 4 Erie 5 Huron 7 Ontario 8 Michigan, Superior *acronym:* 5 HOMES

Great Lake State 8 Michigan

greave 7 legging

grebe 4 bird, fowl 8 dabchick 10 diving bird
Greece *ancient city-state:* 5 Argos
6 Athens, Sparta, Thebes 7 Corinth *capital:* 6 Athens *city:* 6 Patras 7 Larissa, Piraeus 8 Salonika 12 Thessaloníki *conqueror:* 6 Philip (of Macedonia)
9 Alexander (the Great) *island, island group:* 5 Crete 6 Aegean, Euboea, Ionian 8 Cyclades, Sporades *monetary unit:* 4 euro *mountain, range:* 3 Ida 4 Ossa
6 Pindus 7 Olympus 9 Parnassus *neighbor:* 6 Turkey 7 Albania 8 Bulgaria, Macedonia *part of:* 7 Balkans *peninsula:* 6 Balkan 10 Chalcidice 11 Peloponnese *region:* 6 Epirus, Thrace 8 Thessaly *sea:* 6 Aegean, Ionian 13 Mediterranean
greed 6 excess, hunger 7 avarice, avidity, craving 7 edacity, longing 8 cupidity, gluttony, rapacity, voracity 12 covetousness, ravenousness
greedy 4 avid 5 itchy 6 grabby 7 hoggish, miserly, selfish 8 covetous, desirous, edacious, esurient, grasping 10 avaricious, gluttonous 11 acquisitive
Greek 6 babble, drivel, jabber 7 Achaean 8 Hellenic, nonsense 9 gibberish *assembly:* 5 agora, boule *coin:* 4 obol 6 lepton, stater *column:* 5 Doric, Ionic
10 Corinthian *contest:* 4 agon *counselor:* 6 Nestor *dictator:* 7 Metaxas (Ioannis) *dragon:* 9 Eurython *drink:* 4 ouzo *epic:* 5 Iliad 7 Odyssey *Fates:* 6 Clotho, Moirae 7 Atropos 8 Lachesis *god:*
  chief: 4 Zeus *messenger:* 6 Hermes *of agriculture:* 6 Cronus *of death:* 8 Thanatos *of dreams:* 8 Morpheus *of fire:* 10 Hephaestus *of healing:* 9 Asclepius 11 Aesculapius *of love:* 4 Eros *of marriage:* 5 Hymen *of the sun:* 6 Apollo *of physicians:* 6 Hermes *of the sea:* 6 Nereus, Triton 7 Oceanus 8 Poseidon *of the sun:* 6 Helios *of the underworld:* 5 Pluto *of the winds:* 5 Eurus, Notus 6 Aeolus, Boreas 8 Zephyrus *of war:* 4 Ares *of wine:* 8 Dionysus *of woods:* 3 Pan
goddess:
  of agriculture: 7 Demeter *of beauty:* 9 Aphrodite *of dawn:* 3 Eos *of discord:* 4 Eris *of fertility:* 6 Cybele *of flowers:* 7 Chloris *of harvests:* 4 Rhea *of hunting:* 7 Artemis *of justice:* 7 Astraea *of love:* 9 Aphrodite *of marriage:* 7 Hera *of night:* 3 Nyx *of peace:* 5 Irene *of retribution:* 7 Nemesis *of ruin:* 3 Ate *of the earth:* 4 Gaea, Gaia *of the hearth:* 6 Hestia *of magic:* 6 Hecate, Hekate *of the moon:* 6 Hecate, Hekate, Selena, Selene 7 Artemis, Astarte *of the rain-*

bow: 4 Iris *of the seasons:* 5 Horae *of the underworld:* 6 Hecate, Hekate
10 Persephone *of vengeance:* 7 Nemesis *of victory:* 4 Nike *of wisdom:* 6 Athena *of witchcraft:* 6 Hecate, Hekate *of womanhood:* 4 Hera *of youth:* 4 Hebe
hero:
  4 Aias, Ajax 5 Jason 7 Theseus
  8 Achilles, Argonaut, Heracles, Hercules, Odysseus 9 Achilleus *historian:* 8 Xenophon 9 Herodotus 10 Thucydides *lawgiver:* 5 Draco, Solon *leader:* 9 Agamemnon *letter:* 3 chi, eta, phi, psi, rho, tau 4 beta, iota, zeta 5 alpha, delta, gamma, kappa, omega, sigma, theta 6 lambda 7 epsilon, omicron, upsilon *magistrate:* 6 archon *marketplace:* 5 agora *porch:* 4 stoa *sandwich:* 4 gyro *soldier:* 7 hoplite *theater:* 5 odeon, odeum *underworld:* 5 Hades *war cry:* 5 alala *warrior:* 4 Ajax
7 Ulysses 8 Achilles, Diomedes, Odysseus 9 Agamemnon, Palamedes *wine:* 7 retsina
green 3 raw 4 jade, lime, moss 5 alive, fresh, kelly, leafy, naive, virid, young
6 callow, forest, unripe 7 avocado, celadon, emerald, untried, verdant
8 immature, juvenile, unversed, youthful 9 unfledged 10 unseasoned
11 unpracticed 13 inexperienced *bluish:* 8 glaucous *combining form:* 4 verd
6 chloro *grayish:* 5 olive *yellowish:* 7 luteous 10 chartreuse
greenbacks 4 cash, jack, loot 5 bread, bucks, dough, lucre, money, moola
6 moolah, wampum 7 dollars, scratch
8 currency, smackers 11 legal tender
greenery 7 foliage, leafage 8 verdancy
green-eyed 6 envious, jealous 9 invidious *monster:* 8 jealousy
greenfly 5 aphid
greengage 4 plum
greenhead 3 fly 8 horsefly
greenheart 6 laurel 9 evergreen
greenhorn 4 babe, hick, jake, naif, rube, tyro 5 clown 6 newbie, novice, rookie
7 bumpkin, ingenue 8 beginner, newcomer 10 clodhopper, provincial
greenhouse 7 nursery 12 conservatory
Greenland *capital:* 4 Nuuk 7 Godthåb *city:* 5 Thule *ethnic group:* 5 Inuit 6 Eskimo *explorer:* 4 Eric (the Red), Erik (the Red), Leif (Eriksson) 9 Rasmussen (Knud) *language:* 6 Danish *monetary unit:* 5 krone *possession of:* 7 Denmark
green light 3 nod 4 okay 5 leave 6 assent
7 consent, go-ahead, mandate
8 approval, blessing, sanction, thumbs-up 9 authority, clearance 10 permission
11 endorsement 13 authorization

Green Mansions *author:* 6 Hudson (W. H.) *character:* 4 Rima
green monkey 6 guenon, simian, vervet
Green Mountain State 7 Vermont
greenness 5 youth 6 spring 7 puberty 8 verdancy, viridity 9 youthhood 10 immaturity, juvenility, pubescence, springtide, springtime 11 adolescence 12 inexperience
green osier 6 willow 7 dogwood
green plover 7 lapwing 9 shorebird
greenroom 6 lounge
greenstone 4 jade 7 diabase 8 nephrite 9 tremolite 10 actinolite
greet 3 bow 4 hail, meet 6 accost, call to, salaam, salute 7 address, react to, receive, welcome
greeting 3 ave, bow, nod 4 ciao, hail 5 aloha, hello, howdy 6 salaam, salute 7 address, welcome 9 handshake, reception 10 salutation
gregarious 6 clubby, genial, social 7 affable 8 outgoing, sociable 9 clubbable, congenial, convivial 11 extroverted 13 companionable
gremlin 3 bug, elf, imp 5 dwarf, gnome 6 defect, glitch 7 brownie
Grenada *capital:* 9 St. George's *discoverer:* 8 Columbus (Christopher) *former name:* 10 Concepción *language:* 7 English *location:* 10 West Indies *nickname:* 11 Isle of Spice
grenade 4 bomb 5 shell 7 missile 9 explosive, pineapple
grenadier 7 rattail, soldier
grenadine 4 pink, yarn 5 syrup 6 fabric 9 carnation
Grendel's slayer 7 Beowulf
Gretchen's lover 5 Faust
greylag 5 goose
Grey's forte 7 Western
grid 3 net 5 grate, grill 6 grille 7 grating, lattice, network, trellis
griddle 3 pan 5 grill
griddle cake 7 hotcake, pancake 8 flapjack
gridiron 3 net 5 field, grate, grill 7 grating, network
grief 3 rue, woe 4 care 5 agony, dolor, gloom, tears 6 mishap, regret, sorrow 7 anguish, chagrin, sadness, trouble 8 disaster, distress, hardship 9 adversity, heartache, suffering 10 affliction, heartbreak, misfortune 11 despondency
Grieg work 8 Peer Gynt
grievance 4 beef 5 cross, gripe, trial, wrong 6 burden, grouse, injury, squawk 8 hardship, jeremiad 9 complaint, injustice 10 affliction, allegation, unfairness 11 tribulation
grieve 3 cry 4 ache, keen, moan, wail,

weep 5 mourn 6 burden, lament, sadden, sorrow, suffer 7 afflict, agonize 8 distress
grievous 3 sad 4 dire, fell, sore 5 cruel, grave, great, major 6 bitter, severe, taxing, tragic, woeful 7 galling, heinous, onerous, painful, serious, weighty 9 egregious 10 abominable, burdensome, calamitous, deplorable, lamentable, oppressive 11 distressing, regrettable, troublesome, unfortunate 12 heartrending
grift 3 con, gyp 4 bilk, rook 7 defraud, swindle 8 flimflam
grifter 3 gyp 5 cheat, crook, thief 6 con man, gouger 7 cheater, scammer, sharper, slicker 8 swindler 9 defrauder, trickster 13 confidence man
grill 3 fry, vex 4 cook, grid, pump, quiz 5 broil, grate, sauté, toast 6 eatery 7 afflict, debrief, grating, griddle, torment 8 gridiron, question 10 restaurant 11 interrogate 12 cross-examine
grilse 6 salmon
grim 3 set 4 cold, dour, fell, firm, hard 5 bleak, cruel, fixed, grave, harsh, rigid, stern 6 dismal, dogged, dreary, fierce, grisly, intent, savage, severe, somber 7 adamant, austere, inhuman 8 gruesome, inhumane, obdurate, resolute, ruthless, stubborn 9 merciless, offensive, truculent 10 determined, forbidding, implacable, inevitable, inexorable, inflexible, melancholy, relentless, unyielding, vindictive 11 unforgiving, unrelenting
grimace 3 mow, mug 4 face, moue, pout 5 frown, lower, mouth, scowl, sneer
grimalkin 3 cat 5 tabby 6 feline 9 female cat
grime 4 crud, dirt, gunk, muck, smut, soot 5 filth
grim reaper 5 death
grimy 5 dingy, dirty 6 filthy, grubby, grungy, soiled, scuzzy, smutty 10 besmirched
grin 4 beam 5 smile, smirk
grind 3 rut, vex 4 chew, grub, mill, moil, pace, plod, plug, rote, slog, toil, whet 5 crank, crush, gnash, grate, labor, slave, sweat 6 abrade, crunch, drudge, groove, harass, kibble, powder, rotate 7 oppress, routine, travail 8 drudgery, monotony, wear down 9 pulverize, treadmill 10 donkeywork
grinder 3 sub 4 gyro, hero 5 molar, tooth 6 hoagie 8 sandwich 9 submarine
grinding 5 harsh 6 severe 7 arduous, grating, wearing 9 fatiguing, strenuous *stone:* 4 mano 6 mortar, muller, pestle
griot 11 storyteller

grip 4 glom, hold, take **5** clamp, clasp, grasp, seize **6** clench, clinch, clutch, handle, tenure, valise **7** grapple **8** enthrall, suitcase **9** fascinate, mesmerize, restraint, spellbind, stagehand **10** constraint

gripe 3 bug, vex **4** beef, carp, crab, fuss, yawp **5** annoy, bitch, bleat, cavil, croak, groan, whine **6** bother, grouch, grouse, kvetch, murmur, mutter, object, squawk, yammer **7** afflict, grumble **8** complain, distress, irritate **9** bellyache, complaint, grievance, objection

griper see GRUMBLER

grippe 3 flu **9** influenza

gripper 4 clip, hand, vise **5** clamp, clasp, tongs **6** pliers

gris-gris 5 charm, spell **6** amulet, fetish **8** talisman **11** incantation

Grisham novel 4 Firm (The) **6** Broker (The), Client (The) **7** Chamber (The), Partner (The) **8** Brethren (The) **12** Pelican Brief (The)

grisly 4 gory, grim **5** awful, lurid **6** horrid **7** ghastly, hideous, macabre **8** fearsome, god-awful, gruesome, horrible, terrible, **9** frightful, repellent, repulsive, sickening **10** disgusting, horrifying, terrifying

grist 3 lot **5** grain, input, stint **6** amount, output **7** product **8** quantity

gristle 9 cartilage

grit 4 guts, sand **5** grate, grind, heart, moxie, nerve, pluck, spunk **6** gravel, mettle, powder, smooth, spirit **7** bravery, courage, granule **8** backbone, tenacity **9** fortitude **10** doggedness **13** determination

gritty 4 game **5** dirty, gutsy, rough, sandy **6** dogged, plucky, spunky **8** abrasive, gravelly, resolute, spirited **9** steadfast, tenacious **10** courageous, determined

groan 4 beef, carp, moan **5** cavil, creak, gripe **6** bemoan, grouse, lament, object, repine **7** grumble **8** complain **9** bellyache

grocery 5 store **11** supermarket *Spanish:* **6** bodega

grog 3 rum **5** booze, drink, hooch, juice, sauce **6** liquor, tipple **7** alcohol, spirits **9** firewater

groggy 4 dull, hazy, logy, weak **5** dazed, dopey, foggy, muzzy, tired, woozy **6** dulled, sleepy **7** muddled **8** befogged, confused, sluggish **9** befuddled, slaphappy, stupefied **10** punch-drunk

groin 4 fold **6** crotch

grok 6 intuit

grommet 6 eyelet **7** cringle

groom 4 comb, tend, tidy **5** brush, clean,

curry, primp, ready, shave **6** neaten, ostler, polish **7** hostler, prepare, servant **8** benedict **9** attendant *Indian:* **4** syce

groove 3 rut **4** pace, rote, slot **5** canal, flute, glyph, gouge, grind, niche, score, stria **6** furrow, gutter, hollow, rabbet, rhythm **7** chamfer, channel, routine, top form **8** monotony **10** depression

groovy 3 hip **4** cool, neat **5** ducky, great, nifty, sharp, slick, super, swell **6** choice, gnarly, peachy **7** right-on **8** smashing **9** copacetic, excellent, hunky-dory, marvelous, wonderful **10** delightful, marvellous, peachy keen

grope 4 feel, grub, poke, root **6** fondle, fumble, search **7** grabble **8** scrabble

grosbeak 5 finch **8** hawfinch, songbird

gross 3 fat, raw, sum **4** earn, foul, mass, rude **5** brute, bulky, crude, obese, rough, utter, whole **6** carnal, coarse, entire, vulgar **7** blatant, boorish, capital, extreme, glaring, hulking, obscene, overall, porcine, uncouth **8** absolute, complete, flagrant, ignorant, improper, indecent, outright, sum total, tangible, totality **9** aggregate, before tax, corporeal, corpulent, downright, egregious, excessive, loathsome, offensive, out-and-out, repulsive, revolting, unrefined **10** disgusting, exorbitant, immoderate **11** twelve dozen

grotesque 6 absurd, rococo, unreal **7** baroque, bizarre, extreme **8** aberrant, abnormal, deformed, fanciful, freakish **9** distorted, fantastic, ludicrous, misshapen, monstrous **11** incongruous

grotto 4 cave, hole **5** crypt, vault **6** cavern *Capri:* **4** Blue

grouch 4 beef, carp, crab, kick, sulk, yawp **5** crank, croak, growl, grump, pique **6** carper, griper, grouse, grudge, kicker, kvetch, murmur, mutter, repine, squawk, whiner, yawper **7** crabber, grouser, growler, grumble **8** complain, grumbler, kvetcher, sorehead, sourpuss, squawker **9** bellyache, complaint **10** bellyacher, complainer, crosspatch, malcontent

ground 3 bed, sod **4** base, dirt, land, root, seat, soil, turf **5** basis, cause, earth, floor, proof **6** bottom, reason **7** bedrock, dry land, footing, support, sustain, terrain **8** argument, buttress, evidence **9** establish, testimony **10** foundation, terra firma

groundbreaking 10 innovative, innovatory, pioneering **11** cutting-edge, leading-edge

grounded 6 stable **7** beached **8** marooned, sensible, stranded **9** realistic **13** unpretentious

groundhog 6 marmot 9 woodchuck

grounding 8 practice, training, tutelage 11 instruction, preparation

groundless 4 idle 5 empty, false 6 hollow 8 baseless 9 causeless, unfounded 10 gratuitous 11 uncalled-for, unjustified, unwarranted

groundwork 3 bed 4 base, foot, root 5 basis 6 bottom 7 bedrock, footing, support 8 basement 10 foundation, substratum 11 cornerstone, preparation 12 substruction, substructure, underpinning

ground zero 5 focus, get-go 6 center, outset, target 8 bull's-eye 9 epicenter, square one

group 3 lot, set 4 band, bevy, body, club, crew, gang, pack, push, ruck, sect, team, tier 5 array, batch, bunch, class, clump, covey, crowd, grade, horde, squad, suite, troop 6 adjust, assort, bundle, cartel, circle, clique, clutch, gather, huddle, league, passel 7 battery, brigade, cluster, combine, company, coterie, council, dispose, echelon, platoon 8 assemble, assembly, category, classify, ensemble, organize 9 congeries, gathering, syndicate 10 assemblage, categorize, collection *of angels:* 4 host *of ants:* 6 colony *of bees:* 4 hive 5 swarm *of birds:* 6 flight *of cats:* 7 clowder, clutter *of cattle:* 5 drove *of chicks:* 5 brood 6 clutch *of clams:* 3 bed *of crows:* 6 murder *of ducks:* 5 brace *of eight:* 5 octet *of elephants:* 4 herd *of elks:* 4 gang *of fish:* 5 shoal 6 school *of five:* 5 quint 6 pentad 7 quintet *of four:* 6 tetrad 7 quartet *of foxes:* 5 leash, skulk *of geese:* 5 flock, skein 6 gaggle *of gnats:* 5 cloud, horde *of goats:* 5 tribe *of gorillas:* 4 band *of greyhounds:* 5 leash *of grouse:* 5 covey *of hares:* 4 down, husk *of hawks:* 4 cast *of hounds:* 3 cry 4 mute, pack *of kangaroos:* 3 mob 5 troop *of kittens:* 6 litter *of larks:* 10 exaltation *of lions:* 5 pride *of locusts:* 6 plague *of monkeys:* 5 troop *of mules:* 4 span *of nine:* 5 nonet *of oysters:* 3 bed *of partridges:* 5 covey *of peacocks:* 6 muster *of pheasants:* 4 nest *of plovers:* 4 wing 12 congregation *of quail:* 4 bevy 5 covey *of seals:* 3 pod 5 patch *of seven:* 6 pleiad, septet *of sheep:* 5 drove, flock *of six:* 6 sextet *of swans:* 4 bevy *of teals:* 6 spring *of three:* 4 trio 5 triad 7 ternary, trinity, triplet *of vipers:* 4 nest *of whales:* 3 gam, pod *of wolves:* 4 pack

grouper 8 rockfish

grouse 4 beef, carp 5 croak, gripe, quail, scold 6 mutter, yammer 7 grumble 8 complain, pheasant 9 bellyache,

blackcock, ptarmigan 12 capercaillie *extinct:* 8 heath hen *red:* 8 moorfowl *strut:* 3 lek

grout 4 lees, lute 5 dregs 6 cement, filler, mortar 7 grounds, plaster 8 concrete

grove 4 holt, wood 5 copse 7 boscage, coppice, orchard, thicket

grovel 4 fawn 5 abase, cower, crawl, creep, toady 6 cajole, cringe, kowtow, snivel, wallow 7 eat dirt, truckle 8 blandish, bootlick 9 brownnose 10 curry favor, ingratiate 11 apple-polish

grow 3 age, wax 4 flow, gain, rise, tend 5 amass, breed, nurse, raise, ripen, swell 6 abound, become, expand, foster, mature, sprout, thrive 7 burgeon, care for, develop, enlarge, gestate, nurture, produce 8 escalate, flourish, increase, multiply, mushroom, spring up 9 cultivate, propagate

growl 4 beef, carp, crab, fuss, roar 5 bitch, gripe, groan, snarl 6 grouse, kvetch, mutter, repine, rumble, yammer 7 grumble 8 complain 9 bellyache

growler 3 can 4 crab, floe 5 crank, grump 6 grouch, vessel 7 ice floe, iceberg, pitcher 8 sorehead, sourpuss 9 container 10 crosspatch, malcontent 11 faultfinder

grown-up 5 adult 6 mature 8 seasoned 9 developed 11 full-fledged

grow old 3 age 4 wane 5 ripen, wizen 6 mature, mellow

growth 4 gain, rise 5 surge, swell, tumor 7 buildup 8 increase, progress, swelling 9 accretion, evolution, expansion, flowering, unfolding 11 development, enlargement, progression *malignant:* 6 cancer *skin:* 3 tag, wen 4 corn, cyst, mole, wart 5 nevus 6 bunion, callus, keloid 7 verruca

grow up 3 age 5 ripen 6 evolve, mature, mellow 7 advance, develop 8 maturate 9 come of age

grub 3 dig 4 chow, comb, eats, feed, food, hack, moil, plod, poke, rake, root, slog, toil 5 grind, larva, scour, slave, spade, stump 6 burrow, drudge, forage, menial, shovel, slavey, uproot, viands 7 edibles, ransack, rummage, unearth, vittles 8 excavate, hireling, victuals 9 provender 11 comestibles

grubby 4 foul 5 dirty, grimy, messy, seedy 6 filthy, frowsy, frowzy, grungy, scuzzy, shabby, sloppy, soiled 7 scruffy, squalid, unclean, unkempt 8 slovenly, unwashed

grubstake 3 aid 4 back, fund, help, loan 5 funds 6 assist 7 backing, capital, finance, support 8 bankroll 9 financing 10 assistance, capitalize, underwrite

grudge 4 deny, envy **5** spite **6** refuse, spleen **7** ill will **9** grievance **10** resentment **12** hard feelings, spitefulness
gruel 4 mush **5** atole, kasha **6** burgoo, congee, sowens **8** flummery, loblolly, porridge **9** stirabout
gruesome see GRISLY
gruff 4 curt, dour **5** bluff, blunt, cross, harsh, husky, stern, surly **6** abrupt, crabby, crusty, hoarse, morose, sullen **7** bearish, brusque, crabbed, grating, grouchy **8** churlish, croaking, snappish, snippety **9** saturnine **10** ill-natured **11** bad-tempered
grumble 4 beef, carp, crab, fuss, moan, yawp **5** bitch, croak, gripe, groan, growl, snarl, whine **6** bemoan, grouch, grouse, murmur, mutter, repine, squawk **8** complain **9** bellyache
grumbler 4 crab **5** crank, grump **6** grouch **8** sorehead **10** crosspatch, malcontent
grump 3 pet **4** beef, carp, crab, pout, sulk **5** crank, gripe, growl **6** griper, grouch **7** growler, grumble **8** complain, sorehead, sourpuss **9** bellyache **10** bellyacher, malcontent
grumpy 4 dour, sour **5** cross, moody, sulky, surly, testy **6** crabby, cranky, sullen **7** crabbed, peevish **8** petulant, vinegary **9** crotchety, irascible **11** bad-tempered **12** cantankerous
grunion 10 silverside
grunt 5 groan, growl, snort **7** dogface, draftee, soldier
guacharo 7 oilbird
Guadeloupe *capital:* **10** Basse-Terre *department of:* **6** France *dependency:* **8** Désirade, St. Martin **12** Marie-Galante, St. Barthélemy *discoverer:* **8** Columbus (Christopher) *island:* **10** Basse-Terre **11** Grande-Terre *location:* **10** West Indies *volcano:* **9** Soufrière
Guam *capital:* **5** Agana *ethnic group:* **8** Chamorro *island group:* **7** Mariana
guanaco 5 llama **6** alpaca *kin:* **5** camel
guano 6 manure **9** excrement
guarantee 3 vow **4** bail, bond, oath, seal, word **5** token, vouch **6** assert, assure, ensure, insure, pledge, surety **7** certify, earnest, promise, warrant **8** security, warranty **9** agreement, assurance, insurance, undertake **11** stand behind, undertaking
guarantor 5 angel **6** backer, patron, surety **7** ensurer, insurer, sponsor **8** bondsman **11** underwriter
guard 4 fend, mind, tend, ward **5** aegis, alert, armor, cover, watch **6** convoy, defend, escort, jailer, keeper, minder, patrol, picket, police, screen, secure,

sentry, shield, warden, warder **7** bulwark, defense, lookout, oversee, protect, turnkey **8** chaperon, overseer, preserve, security, sentinel, shepherd, watchdog, watchman **9** chaperone, custodian, look after, patrolman, protector, watch over **10** protection
guarded 4 safe, wary **5** cagey, chary, leery **7** careful, politic, prudent **8** cautious, discreet, gingerly, reserved **11** circumspect, considerate
guardhouse 4 brig, jail, keep **5** clink **6** lockup, prison **8** stockade
guardian 6 escort, keeper, patron, warden, warder **7** curator, trustee **8** Cerberus, defender, overseer, watchdog **9** custodian, protector **11** conservator
guardianship 4 care, keep, ward **5** aegis, trust **6** charge **7** custody, keeping **8** auspices **10** protection **11** safekeeping
Guare play 17 House of Blue Leaves (The) **22** Six Degrees of Separation
Guatemala *capital:* **9** Guatemala (City) *ethnic group:* **4** Maya **5** Mayan *lake:* **6** Izabal **7** Atitlán **9** Petén Itzá *language:* **7** Spanish *monetary unit:* **8** quetzal *mountain, range:* **6** Tacaná **9** Tajumulco **10** Acatenango, Santa María **11** Sierra Madre *neighbor:* **6** Belize, Mexico **8** Honduras **10** El Salvador *peninsula:* **7** Yucatán *river:* **7** Motagua **8** Polochic, Sarstoon **10** Usumacinta
guck 3 bog, goo, mud **4** clay, crud, dirt, glop, goop, mire, ooze, smut **5** filth, slime **7** stickum
gudgeon 3 pin **4** fish **5** pivot **6** socket **7** journal
Gudrun *brother:* **6** Gunnar **7** Gunther *father:* **5** Hetel *husband:* **4** Atli **5** Etzel **6** Sigurd **9** Siegfried
guerrilla 8 partisan **9** irregular *Greek:* **6** klepht
guess 4 call, shot, stab **5** fancy, hunch, infer **7** believe, predict, presume, suppose, surmise **8** estimate **9** speculate **10** conjecture, prediction **11** presumption, supposition, speculation
guest 6 caller, lodger, roomer **7** boarder, company, visitor **9** sojourner
guff 3 jaw, lip **4** bosh, sass **5** bilge, cheek, hokum, hooey, mouth, sauce, trash **6** bunkum, drivel, hot air, humbug **7** baloney, hogwash, palaver, twaddle **8** back talk, claptrap, malarkey, nonsense, tommyrot **9** poppycock **10** balderdash **13** horsefeathers
guffaw 6 cackle, hee-haw **7** chortle
guidance 6 advice **7** control, counsel **8** handling **9** direction, oversight **10** leadership, management **11** instruction, supervision

guide 4 dean, guru, help, lead, show **5** doyen, pilot, route, steer, usher **6** beacon, convoy, direct, docent, escort, handle, leader, manage, manual, mentor **7** adviser, conduct, control, marshal, oversee **8** Baedeker, chaperon, director, handbook, instruct, maneuver, navigate, shepherd, signpost **9** accompany, chaperone, conductor, vade mecum, Sacagawea **10** bellwether, compendium, instructor, pathfinder **11** enchiridion

guidebook 6 Fodor's, manual **8** Baedeker, Frommer's, handbook, Michelin **9** itinerary, vade mecum **10** compendium **11** enchiridion

guided missile 3 ABM **4** Hawk, ICBM, IRBM, Nike, Thor, Zuni **5** Atlas, drone, Snark, Titan **6** Bomarc, cruise, Exocet, Falcon, Navaho, rocket **7** Bullpup, Matador, Polaris, Regulus, Terrier **8** Redstone, Tomahawk **9** Minuteman **10** projectile, Sidewinder

Guiderius *brother:* **9** Arviragus *father:* **9** Cymbeline

guidon 4 flag **6** banner, burgee, ensign, pennon

guild 4 club **5** lodge, order, union **6** cartel, league **7** society **8** sodality **10** fellowship, fraternity **11** association, brotherhood *medieval:* **5** Hansa, Hanse

guile 4 wile **5** craft, fraud **6** deceit **7** cunning **8** artifice, trickery, wiliness **9** deception, duplicity, stratagem **10** cleverness **13** dissimulation

guileful 3 sly **4** foxy, wily **5** cagey, canny, slick **6** artful, astute, crafty, shifty, shrewd, sneaky, tricky **7** cunning, devious **8** indirect, slippery, sneaking **9** designing, insidious, underhand **11** calculating, duplicitous, underhanded

guileless 4 open **5** frank, naive **6** candid, direct, honest **7** genuine, natural, sincere, up-front **8** innocent, truthful **9** ingenuous **10** aboveboard, forthright

guillemot 3 auk **5** murre **7** seabird

guillotine 6 behead **9** decollate **10** decapitate

guilt 4 onus **5** blame, fault, shame **6** regret, stigma **7** offense, remorse **10** contrition **11** culpability **12** self-reproach

guiltless 4 pure **5** clean **6** chaste **8** innocent, virtuous **9** blameless, exemplary, faultless, righteous, stainless **10** immaculate, inculpable

guilty 6 liable, rueful, sinful **7** ashamed, at fault **8** blamable, contrite, culpable, indicted, penitent **9** impeached, regretful **10** answerable, remorseful

11 accountable, blameworthy, responsible

guimpe 6 blouse

Guinea *capital:* **7** Conakry *city:* **4** Labé **6** Kankan, Kindia *ethnic group:* **6** Fulani **7** Malinke *island, island group:* **3** Los **5** Tombo *language:* **6** French *monetary unit:* **5** franc *mountain:* **5** Nimba *neighbor:* **4** Mali **7** Liberia, Senegal **10** Ivory Coast **11** Sierra Leone **12** Guinea-Bissau *river:* **5** Niger **6** Gambia **7** Senegal

Guinea-Bissau *archipelago:* **7** Bijagós *capital:* **6** Bissau *ethnic group:* **6** Fulani **7** Malinke **8** Mandyako *language:* **10** Portuguese *monetary unit:* **5** franc *neighbor:* **6** Guinea **7** Senegal *river:* **4** Gêba

guinea fowl *genus:* **6** Numida *young:* **4** keet

guinea pig 4 cavy **6** rodent *genus:* **5** Cavia

Guinevere *court:* **7** Camelot *husband:* **6** Arthur *lover:* **8** Lancelot **9** Launcelot

guise 4 mask **5** cloak, cover, dress, getup **6** aspect, facade, outfit, veneer **7** costume, pretext **8** coloring, pretense **9** posturing, semblance **10** appearance, false front

guitar *accessory:* **4** capo *Mexican:* **5** tiple **6** cuatro **8** charango *part:* **3** nut, peg **4** fret, neck **5** brace **6** bridge, string **7** peghead *small:* **3** uke **7** ukulele *tool:* **4** pick **8** plectrum

guitarist *American:* **4** Byrd (Charlie), King (B. B., Freddie), Page (Jimmy), Pass (Joe) **5** Ellis (Herb), Isbin (Sharon) **6** Kessel (Barney), Kottke (Leo), Watson (Doc) **7** Burrell (Kenny), Hendrix (Jimi), Metheny (Pat), Vaughan (Stevie Ray) **9** Christian (Charlie), Parkening (Christopher) **10** Montgomery (Wes), Pizzarelli (Bucky, John) *Australian:* **8** Williams (John) *British:* **4** Beck (Jeff) **5** Bream (Julian) **8** Richards (Keith) *French:* **9** Reinhardt (Django) *Italian:* **7** Ghiglia (Oscar) *Spanish:* **5** Yepes (Narciso) **6** Romero (Celedonio) **7** Segovia (Andrés)

guitarlike instrument 3 uke **4** lute, vina **5** banjo, sitar **7** bandore, pandora, samisen, ukulele **8** mandolin, shamisen

gulch 3 gap **4** glen **5** gorge, gully **6** arroyo, canyon, coulee, hollow, ravine, valley **7** couloir

gules 3 red

gulf 3 bay, pit **4** cove **5** abysm, abyss, bayou, bight, chasm, firth, gorge, gulch, inlet **6** cavity, harbor, hollow, ravine, slough **8** crevasse *Adriatic Sea:* **6** Venice *Aegean Sea:* **7** Saronic **8** Salonika *Africa:* **6** Guinea *Arabian Sea:*

4 Oman 7 Persian *Australia:* 9 Van Diemen 11 Carpentaria *Baltic Sea:* 4 Riga 6 Danzig, Gdansk 7 Bothnia, Finland *Bering Sea:* 6 Anadyr *Canada:* 13 Saint Lawrence *Central America:* 7 Fonseca *Djibouti:* 6 Tajura 8 Tadjoura *Europe:* 7 Bothnia, Gascony 8 Gascogne *Greece:* 7 Corinth, Lepanto *Indian Ocean:* 4 Aden *Ionian Sea:* 4 Arta 7 Taranto *Iran:* 7 Arabian *Italy:* 5 Genoa *Mediterranean Sea:* 5 Sidra, Tunis 8 Valencia 10 Khalij Surt 11 Syrtis Major *New Guinea:* 5 Papua 7 McCluer *New Zealand:* 7 Hauraki *North America:* 6 Mexico *Northwest Territories:* 7 Boothia 8 Amundsen 9 Queen Maud *Philippines:* 4 Asid 5 Davao, Leyte, Panay, Ragay *Red Sea:* 4 Suez 5 Aqaba 11 Aelaniticus *Russia:* 8 Sakhalin *Solomon Sea:* 4 Huon, Kula 5 Vella *South China Sea:* 4 Siam 6 Tonkin 8 Lingayen *Tyrrhenian Sea:* 7 Paestum *Yellow Sea:* 6 Chihli

Gulf State 5 Texas 7 Alabama, Florida 9 Louisiana 11 Mississippi

gull 3 con, mew, sap 4 bird, dupe, fool, hoax, scam 5 chump, cozen 6 fleece, pigeon, stooge, sucker, take in 7 chicane, fall guy 8 flimflam, hoodwink 9 bamboozle 11 hornswoggle

gullet 3 maw 4 crop, tube 6 dewlap, throat 7 channel 9 esophagus

gullible 4 easy 5 green, naive 8 innocent, trusting 9 believing, credulous 11 susceptible 12 unsuspecting

Gulliver's Travels *author:* 5 Swift (Jonathan) *horses:* 10 Houyhnhnms *land:* 6 Laputa 8 Lilliput 11 Brobdingnag *people:* 6 Yahoos

gully 3 gap 4 glen 5 gorge, gulch 6 arroyo, coulee, hollow, ravine, valley 7 couloir

gulp 4 bolt, chug, cram, glut, slop, swig, wolf 5 gorge, quaff, scarf, scoff, stuff, swill 6 devour, gobble, guzzle 7 swallow 8 mouthful 11 ingurgitate

gum 4 chew 5 botch 6 bobble, bollix, bungle, chicle, gluten, goof up, tupelo 7 exudate, gingiva, louse up 8 adhesive, mucilage 9 sapodilla 10 eucalyptus *kind:* 6 acacia, Arabic, balata, bubble 7 chewing, dextrin *resin:* 5 myrrh 7 gamboge 8 ammoniac, galbanum, scammony 9 asafetida 10 asafoetida 12 frankincense

gumbo 3 mud 4 okra, soil, soup 6 creole 7 mélange, mixture

gummy 5 gooey, pasty 6 cloggy, sticky, viscid 7 viscous 8 adhesive 9 glutinous 10 gelatinous 12 mucilaginous

gumption 5 drive, nerve, savvy 6 energy

8 industry 10 enterprise, get-up-and-go, initiative

gumshoe 3 cop 4 bull, dick, fuzz, G-man, heat, narc 6 copper, peeler, shamus, sleuth 7 officer 8 flatfoot, hawkshaw, Sherlock 9 detective, policeman 10 bloodhound, private eye 12 investigator

gun 3 gat, rod 4 Colt 5 rev up, rifle 6 cannon, Garand, heater, mortar, musket, pistol, weapon 7 bazooka, carbine, firearm 8 Browning, howitzer, revolver 9 derringer, Remington 10 Winchester *antiaircraft:* 6 ack-ack, Bofors *Austrian:* 5 Glock *British:* 4 Sten *French:* 8 arquebus 9 harquebus *German:* 5 Glock, Luger *Italian:* 7 Beretta *mount:* 6 turret *part:* 3 pin 4 bolt, bore, butt, lock 5 sight, stock 6 barrel, breech, hammer, muzzle, safety 7 chamber, trigger 8 cylinder, magazine 9 buttstock

gunfire 4 shot 5 blast, salvo 6 volley 7 barrage 9 broadside, discharge, fusillade

gung ho 4 avid, keen 6 ardent, fervid, raring 7 fervent, zealous 9 exuberant 11 impassioned 12 enthusiastic

Guni's father 8 Naphtali

gunk 3 goo 4 crud, glop, gook, goop, muck 5 slime

gunman 5 bravo 6 hit man, killer 7 shooter, torpedo 8 assassin, enforcer

Gunnar *brother-in-law:* 6 Sigurd *father:* 5 Hetel *sister:* 6 Gudrun *wife:* 8 Brunhild, Brynhild

gunner 6 sniper 7 shooter 8 marksman, rifleman 9 musketeer 11 infantryman 12 artilleryman

Gunther *sister:* 7 Gutrune 9 Kriemhild *slayer:* 5 Hagen *uncle:* 5 Hagen *wife:* 8 Brunhild 9 Brynhild

gurgle 3 lap 4 flow, purl, wash 5 plash, slosh, swash 6 babble, bubble, burble, ripple

Gurkha knife 5 kukri

gurney 3 cot 9 stretcher

guru 4 sage 5 guide, swami, tutor 6 expert, leader, master, mentor 7 teacher 9 maharishi

gush 3 jet 4 emit, flow, pour, rave, roll, rush, spew, teem, well 5 burst, flood, flush, issue, spout, spurt, surge 6 babble, effuse, sluice, spring, stream 7 cascade, emanate 10 effervesce, outpouring

gushy 5 gooey, mushy, sappy, soppy 6 sloppy, slushy, sticky 7 cloying, maudlin, mawkish, tearful 8 bathetic, effusive 9 schmaltzy, sickening 10 nauseating, saccharine 11 sentimental

gusset 4 fold, gore, tuck 5 armor, plate, pleat 6 insert 7 bracket

gussy up 5 adorn 6 bedeck 7 furbish 8 decorate, renovate

gust 3 fit 4 blow, gale, rush, wind 5 blast, burst, draft, sally, surge, whiff 6 breeze, flurry, squall 7 bluster, delight, flare-up 8 eruption, outburst, paroxysm

gusto 3 vim 4 brio, élan, zeal, zest 5 ardor, heart, oomph, taste, verve 6 fervor, palate, relish, spirit 7 delight, passion 9 enjoyment 10 enthusiasm

gusty 5 blowy, windy 6 breezy 8 blustery

gut 4 draw, loot 5 belly, bowel, dress, empty, tummy 6 bowels, paunch 7 abdomen, ransack, stomach 8 clean out, entrails, visceral 9 intestine 10 disembowel, eviscerate, exenterate, intestines 11 instinctive

Gutenberg, Johannes *city:* 5 Mainz *invention:* 11 movable type *partner:* 4 Fust (Johann)

gutless 5 sissy, wimpy, wussy 6 coward, craven, yellow 7 chicken, unmanly 8 cowardly, timorous 9 spineless, spunkless, weak-kneed 11 lily-livered, poltroonish 12 fainthearted 13 pusillanimous

guts 4 grit, sand 5 bowel, heart, moxie, nerve, pluck, spunk, tripe 6 bowels, mettle, spirit 7 bravery, courage, innards, insides, stamina, viscera 8 backbone, entrails, stuffing 9 fortitude, intestine 10 intestines, resolution

gutsy 4 bold 5 brave 6 plucky, spunky 7 valiant 8 intrepid, resolute 10 courageous, determined, mettlesome

gutter 5 chase, ditch, flume, gully 6 furrow, groove, trench, trough 7 channel, conduit

guttersnipe 3 bum 4 hobo, scum, waif 5 gamin 6 beggar, gamine, urchin 7 outcast, vagrant, wastrel 8 derelict, riffraff, vagabond 10 ragamuffin

guttural 4 deep 5 gruff, harsh, husky, rough, velar 6 croaky, hoarse 7 grating, palatal, rasping, throaty 8 gravelly

guy 3 cat, lad, man 4 buck, chap, dude, male, rope, stud, wire 5 bloke, brace, chain, guide 6 effigy, fellow, steady 7 support

Guyana *capital:* 10 Georgetown *language:* 7 English *monetary unit:* 6 dollar *mountain range:* 9 Pacaraima *neighbor:* 6 Brazil 8 Suriname 9 Venezuela *river:* 9 Essequibo

Guys and Dolls *author:* 6 Runyon (Damon) *composer:* 7 Loesser (Frank)

guzzle 4 belt, gulp, slop, soak, swig, toss, tope 5 booze, drink, quaff, slosh, swill 6 imbibe, tank up, tipple 7 consume, swizzle

Gwendolen's husband 7 Locrine

gymnast 7 acrobat, athlete, tumbler *American:* 4 Hamm (Paul) 5 Rigby (Cathy) 6 Conner (Bart), Miller (Shannon), Retton (Mary Lou), Thomas (Kurt) *Romanian:* 8 Comaneci (Nadia) *Russian:* 3 Kim (Nelly) 6 Korbut (Olga)

gymnastics 5 sport 8 exercise, tumbling 9 athletics 10 acrobatics 12 calisthenics *apparatus:* 3 bar 4 bars, beam, buck, ring, rope 5 horse 11 balance beam *feat:* 3 kip 4 flip 5 vault 6 tumble 9 handstand, headstand 10 handspring, headspring, somersault

gyp 3 con 4 bilk, dupe, fake, hoax, rook, scam, sham 5 bunco, cheat, cozen, cross, fraud, spoof, trick 6 chisel, chouse, con man, diddle, fleece, humbug, rip off 7 cheater, deceive, defraud, diddler, finagle, sharper, swindle 8 chiseler, hoodwink, swindler 9 bamboozle, defrauder, imposture, trickster 10 mountebank 11 double-cross, flimflammer 12 double-dealer

gypsum 7 drywall, mineral 8 selenite 9 alabaster, wallboard

gypsy 3 Rom 5 caird, nomad, rover 6 roamer, Romany, tinker 7 drifter, tzigane 8 Bohemian, vagabond, wanderer *Spanish:* 6 gitano

gyrate 4 coil, purl, roll, spin, turn, wind 5 orbit, twirl 6 circle, rotate 7 revolve 9 oscillate, pirouette

gyration 4 coil, turn 5 cycle, orbit, twirl, wheel, whirl 6 circle 7 circuit, turning 8 rotation 10 revolution

gyre 4 coil, gird, ring, spin, wind 5 cycle, orbit, twirl, whirl 6 circle, girdle, rotate, spiral, vortex 7 circuit, revolve 8 rotation 10 revolution

gyro 8 sandwich

gyve 4 bond, iron 5 chain 6 fetter 7 shackle 8 restrain 9 restraint

H

Habakkuk 7 prophet
habeas corpus 4 writ 5 right 7 mandate
habiliments 4 gear 5 dress 6 attire, outfit 7 apparel, clothes 8 clothing 9 apparatus, equipment, trappings
habilitate 5 dress 6 clothe 7 qualify
habit 3 rut 4 bent, form, garb, mode, rote, wont 5 dress, quirk, style, usage 6 attire, clothe, custom, groove, manner, outfit 7 costume, fashion, pattern, routine 8 behavior, clothing, practice, tendency 9 addiction, mannerism 10 consuetude, convention, proclivity 11 disposition, inclination *riding:* 8 jodhpurs *wearer:* 3 nun 5 rider
habitable 7 livable
habitant 5 liver 7 denizen, dweller, resider 8 occupant, resident
habitat 4 home, site, turf 5 abode, haunt, range 6 locale, milieu 7 terrain 8 domicile 9 territory 11 environment 12 surroundings
habitation 3 pad 4 digs, flat, home, nest, seat 5 abode, haunt, haven, house, place, roost 7 housing, lodging, tenancy 8 domicile, dwelling, lodgment, quarters 9 homestead, residence, residency 10 settlement
habitual 3 set 5 fixed, usual 6 addict, inborn, native, normal, steady, wonted 7 chronic, regular, routine, settled 8 accepted, addicted, constant, familiar, frequent, inherent 9 automatic, confirmed, continual, customary, ingrained 10 accustomed, inveterate, persistent 11 established, instinctive, involuntary
habitually 8 commonly, normally, wontedly 9 generally, regularly, routinely 10 ordinarily 11 customarily 12 consistently
habituate 4 bear 5 inure, train 6 addict, adjust, endure, harden, school, season, take to 7 break in, prepare, support 8 accustom, tolerate 9 acclimate, condition 11 familiarize
habitué 3 fan 4 buff, user 5 hound, lover 6 addict, patron 7 denizen, devotee, haunter 8 adherent, customer 10 enthusiast, frequenter
hacienda 4 farm 5 manor, ranch, villa

6 estate, quinta 8 dwelling 9 residence 10 plantation
hack 3 cab, cut, hew, try, vex 4 blow, chip, chop, dull, gash, grub, jade, loaf, mean, ride, taxi 5 annoy, cabby, cough, grind, horse, petty, sever, slave, usual 6 cabbie, cliché, drudge, lackey, mangle, stroke, writer 7 clichéd, grating, machine, plodder, taxicab, trivial, vehicle 8 inferior, low grade, mediocre, tolerate 9 cabdriver, mercenary, potboiler 10 second-rate, uninspired 11 commonplace
hacker 4 geek, nerd 6 duffer
hackney 3 cab 4 taxi 5 horse 6 jitney 7 taxicab 8 carriage
hackneyed 3 old 4 dull, worn 5 banal, corny, stale, stock, tired, trite 6 cliché, common, old hat, old saw 7 archaic, clichéd, worn-out 8 everyday, obsolete, outdated, overused, outmoded, timeworn 9 out-of-date 10 antiquated, overworked, pedestrian 11 commonplace, meaningless
Hadad *father:* 5 Bedad 7 Ishmael *victim:* 6 Midian
Hades 4 Hell 5 Pluto, Sheol 6 blazes, Tophet 7 Gehenna, inferno 8 Tartarus 9 perdition 10 underworld 11 netherworld *Babylonian:* 5 Aralu *god:* 3 Dis 5 Orcus, Pluto *goddess:* 10 Persephone *guard:* 8 Cerberus *lake:* 7 Avernus *river:* 4 Styx 5 Lethe 7 Acheron, Cocytus 10 Phlegethon
haft 4 grip, hilt, knob 5 helve 6 handle
hag 3 hex 5 biddy, crone, harpy, shrew, vixen, witch 6 beldam, gorgon, virago 8 battle-ax, fishwife, harridan, slattern 9 hobgoblin
Hagar 9 concubine *lover:* 7 Abraham *rival:* 5 Sarah, Sarai *son:* 7 Ishmael
Hagen *father:* 8 Alberich *nephew:* 7 Gunther *slayer:* 9 Kriemhild *victim:* 9 Siegfried
haggard 3 wan 4 hawk, lank, pale, thin, weak, wild, worn 5 ashen, drawn, faded, gaunt, tired 6 fagged, pallid, skinny, wasted 7 angular, pinched, scraggy, scrawny, starved, wearied 8 careworn, fatigued, shrunken, worndown 9 emaciated, exhausted

Haggard, H. Rider *novel:* 3 She 17 King Solomon's Mines

Haggith *husband:* 5 David *son:* 8 Adonijah

haggle 4 deal 5 argue, cavil, trade 6 barter, bicker, dicker 7 bargain, dispute, quibble, stickle, wrangle 8 squabble 10 horse-trade

hagiography subject 5 saint

hail 3 ave 4 ahoy, call 5 greet, salvo, shout, storm 6 accost, call to, holler, praise, salute, shower, volley 7 acclaim, address, applaud, barrage, call out, commend 8 greeting 9 broadside, cannonade, fusillade, originate, recommend 10 salutation 11 acclamation, bombardment

Haile Selassie 9 Rastafari *follower:* 11 Rastafarian *nation:* 8 Ethiopia

hair 3 bit, jot 4 hint, mite, wool 5 cilia (plural), pilus, trace 6 cilium, trifle 7 eyelash, whisker 8 fraction, particle *animal:* 3 fur 4 mane, pelt, wool 8 vibrissa 9 vibrissae (plural) *braid:* 5 queue 7 pigtail *clip:* 8 barrette *coarse:* 7 bristle *covering of:* 3 wig *cream:* 6 pomade 7 pomatum 12 brilliantine *facial:* 5 beard, patch 6 goatee 7 Vandyke 8 mustache, whiskers 9 burnsides, handlebar, moustache, sideburns, soul patch 11 muttonchops *fine:* 6 lanugo *fringe:* 4 bang *head of:* 9 chevelure *knot:* 3 bun *lock of:* 4 curl 5 tress 7 cowlick *loose roll:* 4 pouf *matted:* 6 dreads 10 dreadlocks *ornament:* 7 topknot *preparation:* 3 gel 6 mousse, pomade 12 brilliantine *root:* 6 fibril *set:* 4 perm *stiff:* 4 seta 5 setae (plural) *style:* 4 flip, pomp, shag 5 butch, taper, wedge 6 Caesar, mullet 7 bowl cut, buzz cut, crew cut, flattop, pageboy 8 ducktail 9 pompadour *tangled:* 7 elflock *tuft of:* 7 fetlock *unruly:* 3 mop *without:* 4 bald

haircutter 6 barber 7 stylist 8 coiffeur 9 coiffeuse

hairdo 3 bob, bun 4 afro, flip, perm, trim 5 bangs, braid 6 Mohawk, mullet 7 beehive, bowl cut, buzz cut, chignon, crew cut, flattop, pageboy 8 brush cut, coiffure, cornrows, ducktail, pigtails, ponytail, razor cut 9 permanent, pompadour 10 dreadlocks

hairdresser see HAIRCUTTER

hair-raising 5 eerie, scary 6 spooky 7 amazing, awesome 8 exciting 9 thrilling 10 terrifying 11 astonishing, frightening

hairsplitting 7 finicky 8 exacting 9 quibbling 10 nit-picking 12 overcritical 13 hypercritical

hairstyle see HAIRDO

hairy 5 bushy, downy, furry, fuzzy, nappy, risky, rough 6 chancy, fleecy, fluffy, shaggy, tufted, woolly 7 bristly, hirsute, scraggy, unshorn, villous 8 perilous, strigose 9 dangerous, difficult, hazardous, tomentose, whiskered 11 treacherous

Haiti *capital:* 12 Port-au-Prince *island:* 7 Tortuga 10 Hispaniola *language:* 6 Creole, French *leader:* 8 Aristide (Jean-Bertrand), Duvalier (François, Jean-Claude) *location:* 10 West Indies *monetary unit:* 6 gourde *passage:* 8 Windward *peninsula:* 7 Tiburon *river:* 10 Artibonite

hake 4 fish, ling 7 codling, whiting *relative:* 3 cod

halcyon 4 calm 5 happy, lucky, quiet, still 6 golden, hushed, placid, serene 8 affluent, peaceful, tranquil 9 favorable 10 auspicious, felicitous, kingfisher, prosperous, untroubled

Halcyone *father:* 6 Aeolus *husband:* 4 Ceyx

hale 3 fit 4 sane, well 5 sound, stout 6 hearty, robust 7 healthy 8 vigorous 9 strapping, wholesome

Hale character 5 Nolan (Philip)

Haley epic 5 Roots

half 6 moiety *prefix:* 4 demi, hemi, semi

half-baked 8 slapdash, slipshod 9 imbecilic, senseless, underdone 11 harebrained, impractical, nonsensical, unrealistic 12 ill-conceived, shortsighted 13 irresponsible

half-cocked 4 rash 5 brash 8 reckless 9 foolhardy, imprudent, impulsive, misguided, premature 10 incautious, unprepared 11 precipitate

halfhearted 4 weak 5 tepid 6 feeble 8 lukewarm 12 uninterested

half-moon 4 arch 5 curve 6 lunule 8 crescent

halfway 3 mid 6 center, medial, median, middle 7 midmost 10 centermost 11 equidistant 12 intermediate

half-wit 4 dolt, dope, fool 5 dunce, idiot, moron 6 cretin 8 imbecile 9 blockhead, simpleton

half-witted 4 dull, slow 7 moronic 8 backward, imbecile 9 imbecilic 12 feebleminded, simpleminded

hall 4 dorm 5 foyer, lobby 6 lyceum 7 passage 8 corridor 9 dormitory 10 auditorium, passageway *exhibition:* 5 salon *Salvation Army:* 7 citadel

Halley's ___ 5 comet

hallmark 4 logo, seal, sign 5 badge, stamp, trait 6 device, emblem, symbol, virtue 7 feature, imprint, quality

8 logotype, property 9 attribute 11 distinction 13 certification

hallow 5 bless, honor 6 anoint, devote, revere 8 dedicate, make holy, sanctify, venerate 10 consecrate

hallowed 4 holy 6 sacred

hallucination 4 trip 5 ghost 6 mirage, vision, wraith 7 fantasy, phantom, specter 8 delusion, illusion, phantasm 10 apparition 11 fata morgana, ignis fatuus

hallucinogen 3 LSD 9 mescaline 10 psilocybin 11 scopolamine

halo 4 aura 5 nimbi (plural) 6 corona, nimbus 7 aureole

halogen 6 iodine 7 bromine, element 8 astatine, chlorine, fluorine

halt 3 bar, end 4 lame, limp, quit, stay, stop 5 cease, check, close, hitch, lapse, stall, waver 6 arrest, desist, dither, falter, finish, pull up 7 adjourn, bring up, stagger, suspend 8 conclude, cut short, hesitate, knock off, leave off 9 determine, interrupt, terminate, vacillate 10 standstill 11 discontinue

halter 3 bit 4 hang, rope 5 noose 6 blouse, bridle, hamper 8 restrain, trammels 9 hackamore, headstall, restraint

ham 4 hock 5 bacon, emote, thigh 7 buttock, overact 8 overplay, strutter 10 scene-eater 13 exhibitionist

Ham *brother:* 4 Shem 7 Japheth *father:* 4 Noah *son:* 4 Cush, Phut 6 Canaan 7 Mizraim

Haman's adversary 6 Esther

ham-handed 5 inept 7 clumsy, gauche 8 bumbling 9 all thumbs, graceless, inelegant, maladroit 10 blundering, unskillful

Hamilcar *conquest:* 5 Spain *home:* 8 Carthage *son:* 8 Hannibal *surname:* 5 Barca

hamlet 7 village *Irish, Scottish:* 7 clachan

Hamlet *author:* 11 Shakespeare (William) *beloved:* 7 Ophelia *castle:* 8 Elsinore *country:* 7 Denmark *friend:* 7 Horatio *mother:* 8 Gertrude *slayer:* 7 Laertes *uncle:* 8 Claudius *victim:* 7 Laertes 8 Claudius, Polonius

Hamlet, The *author:* 8 Faulkner (William) *family:* 6 Snopes

hammer 4 drub, maul, peen 5 forge, gavel, pound 6 batter, mallet, pummel, sledge 7 malleus 8 lambaste *type:* 3 air 4 claw, maul 6 sledge 8 ball-peen 9 pneumatic

hammerhead 4 dolt, dope, fool 5 dunce, idiot, shark 8 clodpoll, numskull 9 numbskull 10 thickskull

hamper 3 bin, tie 4 balk, curb, snag

5 block, check, cramp, crimp, leash, limit 6 baffle, basket, fetter, hinder, hobble, hold up, impede, retard, stymie, thwart 7 inhibit, manacle, pannier, prevent, trammel 8 encumber, handicap, obstacle, obstruct, restrain, restrict, slow down 9 frustrate

hamstring 4 lame 6 muscle, tendon 7 cripple, disable 10 immobilize 12 incapacitate

Hamutal *father:* 8 Jeremiah *husband:* 6 Josiah *son:* 8 Jehoahaz, Zedekiah

hand 3 aid, paw 4 fist, pass 5 manus 6 script, worker 7 deliver, dish out, laborer, workman 8 employee, transfer 10 assistance, penmanship 11 calligraphy, chirography *clenched:* 4 fist *combining form:* 4 chir 5 chiro *counting zero:* 8 baccarat *covering:* 5 glove 6 mitten *down:* 8 bequeath *gesture:* 5 mudra *on hip:* 6 akimbo *part:* 4 palm 5 thumb 6 finger *poker:* 5 flush 8 straight 9 full house *protector:* 5 glove 7 gantlet 8 gauntlet

handbag 4 grip 5 purse 6 clutch 8 reticule, suitcase 10 pocketbook

handbill 5 flier, flyer 6 poster 7 affiche, leaflet, placard 8 circular

handbook 5 guide 6 manual 8 Baedeker 9 vade mecum 10 compendium 11 enchiridion *religious:* 9 catechism

handcuff 6 fetter 7 manacle, shackle *British:* 7 darbies (plural)

hand down 4 will 6 bestow, pass on 7 deliver 8 bequeath, transmit

Handel, George Frideric *aria:* 5 Largo *birthplace:* 5 Halle 7 Germany *opera:* 4 Nero 5 Serse 6 Admeto, Alcina, Almira, Ottone, Xerxes 7 Arminio, Orlando, Rinaldo, Rodrigo 8 Berenice 9 Agrippina, Ariodante 12 Giulio Cesare, Julius Caesar *oratorio:* 4 Saul 6 Esther, Joshua, Samson, Semele 7 Athalia, Deborah, Jephtha, Messiah, Solomon 8 Theodora

handicap 4 edge, load, odds 6 burden, hamper, hinder, impede 8 drawback, encumber, restrict 9 advantage, allowance, detriment, head start, hindrance 10 disability, limitation 11 encumbrance 12 disadvantage

handicraft 5 skill 8 artefact, artifact

hand in 6 submit, tender 7 deliver, present

handkerchief 5 hanky 6 hankie 7 bandana 8 bandanna, mouchoir 9 accessory

handle 3 paw, use 4 feel, grip, haft, hilt, knob, name, test 5 crank, touch, trade, treat, wield 6 manage 7 control, moniker, operate 8 deal with, doorknob, exercise, maneuver, nickname 10 manipulate *scythe:* 5 snath 6 snathe

handling 4 care 6 charge 9 packaging, treatment *partner:* 8 shipping

hand out 4 give, mete 6 bestow, donate 7 deliver, present, provide 8 disburse, dispense, give away 10 administer, distribute

hand over 4 cede, feed, give 5 leave, yield 6 commit, donate, fork up, give up, supply 7 commend, confide, consign, deliver, entrust, present 8 dispense, give back, relegate, transfer 9 deliver up, surrender 10 relinquish

handrail 8 banister

handsome 4 buff, cute, fair 5 ample, hunky, noble 6 comely, lavish 7 dashing, liberal, sizable, stately, stylish 8 abundant, generous, gracious, majestic 9 beautiful, bounteous, bountiful 10 attractive, munificent 11 fashionable, good-looking 12 considerable

handspring 6 tumble *lateral:* 9 cartwheel

handwriting 6 script 8 longhand 10 autography, manuscript, penmanship 11 calligraphy, chirography *bad:* 10 cacography *study of:* 10 graphology

handy 4 able, deft, near 5 adept, close, utile 6 adroit, clever, nearby, nimble, useful 7 close-by, skilled 8 adjacent, skillful 9 adaptable, available, dexterous 10 accessible, convenient, proficient 11 practicable, within reach

handyman 6 helper 7 go-to guy 8 factotum

hang 3 jut, sag 4 hook, idle, loll 5 cling, drape, droop, float, hoist, knack, lynch, sling, swing 6 dangle, depend 7 suspend *back:* 3 lag 4 drag, poke 5 trail 6 dawdle, schlep 7 schlepp 8 straggle *loosely:* 3 sag 6 dangle

hang around 4 stay, wait 5 abide, dally, tarry 6 dawdle, linger, loiter 7 goof off 8 frequent

hangdog 3 sad 4 blue, glum 5 cowed 6 guilty 7 ashamed, pitiful, unhappy 8 dejected, sheepish 9 chagrined, depressed 11 embarrassed

hanger-on 5 leech 6 sponge, sucker 7 sponger 8 barnacle, follower, parasite 9 sycophant 10 freeloader 11 bloodsucker

hanging 5 arras, slope 7 curtain, drapery, pendant, pendent 8 covering, tapestry 9 declivity, execution, pendulous, suspended

Hanging Gardens 7 Babylon

hang on 4 grip 5 grasp 6 clutch, endure, remain 7 persist, survive 8 continue, hold fast 9 persevere

hang out 4 idle, loaf 5 chill, dally, relax 6 loiter, lounge 7 goof off

hangout 5 haunt, joint 6 resort 7 purlieu, retreat 10 rendezvous 12 watering hole

hang up 4 mire, snag 5 delay 6 detain, impede, retard 7 bog down, set back, suspend 8 slow down

hang-up 5 block 7 dilemma, problem 9 obsession 10 difficulty, inhibition

hank 4 clip, coil, loop, ring 6 bundle

hanker 3 yen 4 ache, itch, long, lust, want, wish 5 covet, crave, yearn 6 desire, hunger, thirst

hankering 3 yen 4 ache, itch, lust, urge 5 ardor 6 desire, hunger, pining, thirst 7 craving, longing, passion 8 appetite, yearning

hanky-panky 5 fraud, trick 7 chicane 8 mischief, trickery 9 chicanery, dalliance, deception 13 double-dealing, sharp practice

Hannibal *defeat:* 4 Zama *father:* 8 Hamilcar *home:* 8 Carthage *surname:* 5 Barca *vanquisher:* 6 Scipio *victory:* 6 Cannae

Hansa 5 guild 6 league

Hans Brinker author 5 Dodge (Mary Mapes)

Hanseatic League city 6 Bremen, Lübeck, Wismar 7 Cologne, Hamburg, Rostock

Hänsel und Gretel composer 11 Humperdinck (Engelbert)

Hansen's disease 7 leprosy

hansom 5 coach 8 carriage

haole 5 white

haphazard 6 casual, chance, random 7 aimless 8 at random, careless, slipshod 9 desultory, hit-or-miss, irregular, unplanned 10 accidental, willy-nilly 11 unorganized 12 unsystematic 13 helter-skelter

hapless 4 poor 6 woeful 7 unhappy, unlucky 8 ill-fated, wretched 9 miserable 10 ill-starred 11 star-crossed, unfortunate

happen 4 pass 5 occur 6 befall, betide 7 develop, fall out, turn out 8 bechance 9 transpire *again:* 5 recur *together:* 6 concur 8 coincide

happening 3 new 5 event, scene, thing 7 episode 8 incident, occasion 9 adventure 10 experience, occurrence, phenomenon 11 fashionable 12 circumstance

happen on 4 find 8 bump into, discover

happenstance 5 event 6 chance 8 incident, occasion 9 condition, situation 11 coincidence

happiness 3 joy 4 glee 5 bliss, cheer, mirth 6 gaiety 7 aptness, content, delight, elation, jollity 8 felicity, gladness, pleasure **9** enjoyment, well-being **11** contentment **12** satisfaction

happy 4 glad **5** jolly, lucky, merry **6** joyful, joyous, upbeat **7** blessed, content, pleased **8** friendly, jubilant **9** contented, favorable, satisfied **12** enthusiastic, lighthearted

happy-go-lucky 4 easy **6** blithe, breezy, casual **8** carefree, careless, cheerful, heedless, laid-back, reckless **9** easygoing, unworried **10** insouciant, nonchalant **11** unconcerned **12** devil-may-care, light-hearted

hara-kiri 7 seppuku, suicide **8** felo-de-se

Haran *brother:* **7** Abraham *daughter:* **5** Iscah **6** Milcah *father:* **5** Terah **6** Shimei *son:* **3** Lot

harangue 4 rant, rave **5** orate, spiel **6** exhort, hassle, tirade **7** declaim, lecture, oration **8** bloviate, diatribe, jeremiad **9** discourse, philippic **11** declamation, exhortation

harass 3 irk, vex **4** bait, raid, ride **5** annoy, beset, bully, chivy, harry, hound, tease, worry **6** badger, chivvy, hassle, heckle, hector, pester, plague, stress **7** bedevil, exhaust, fatigue, torment, trouble **8** bullyrag, distress **9** beleaguer, persecute

harbinger 4 omen, sign **5** augur **6** augury, herald **7** apostle, portent **9** messenger, precursor **10** forerunner, indication

harbor 3 bay **4** cove, port **5** haven, inlet, lodge, put up **6** billet, refuge, shield, take in **7** nurture, protect, seaport, shelter **9** anchorage, safeguard, sanctuary *Hawaii:* **5** Pearl

hard 4 firm, iron **5** cruel, harsh, solid, tough **6** brutal, knotty, packed, rugged, tiring, trying **7** arduous, callous, onerous **8** absolute, concrete, exacting, granitic, grinding, indurate, pitiless, rigorous **9** demanding, difficult, fatiguing, intensely, intensive, laborious, unfeeling **10** adamantine, exhausting, spirituous, thoroughly, vigorously **11** complicated, intensively, intractable, troublesome, unrelenting, unremitting **12** backbreaking *to please:* **7** finicky

hard-boiled 4 grim **5** rough, stoic, tough **6** coarse **7** callous **8** seasoned **9** impassive, pragmatic, unfeeling **11** insensitive, unemotional **12** stonyhearted, thick-skinned **13** unsympathetic

harden 3 dry, set **5** inure, steel **6** anneal, freeze, ossify, season, temper **7** calcify, compact, congeal, densify, lithify, petrify, stiffen, toughen **8** solidify **9** acclimate, fossilize, habituate **10** strengthen

hardfisted 4 mean **5** close, tight **6** stingy, strict **13** penny-pinching

hardheaded 5 sober, tough **6** mulish, shrewd **7** willful **8** obdurate, perverse, stubborn **9** obstinate, practical, pragmatic, realistic **10** determined **11** down-to-earth, intractable

hardhearted 4 cold **8** pitiless, uncaring **9** merciless, unfeeling

hard-hitting 6 strong **8** emphatic, forceful, powerful **9** effective

hardihood 3 pep **4** gall, grit, guts **5** cheek, moxie, nerve, pluck, vigor **6** daring **7** courage **8** audacity, boldness, temerity **9** assurance, brashness, cockiness, fortitude, impudence, insolence **10** brazenness, robustness

hard-line 4 firm **5** fixed, rigid, tough **8** obdurate **9** obstinate, unbending **10** inflexible, unyielding **11** stiff-necked **12** intransigent

hardness 5 rigor **7** density **8** rigidity, severity **10** difficulty, resistance

hardscrabble 6 barren **8** marginal **9** infertile, unbearing, unfertile **12** impoverished, unproductive

hardship 4 need, toil **5** rigor, trial **6** burden **7** travail **8** asperity, distress, drudgery **9** adversity, privation, suffering **10** affliction, difficulty, discomfort, misfortune **11** tribulation

Hard Times author 7 Dickens (Charles)

hard up 4 poor **5** broke, needy **6** bad off **8** beggared, bankrupt, deprived, indigent, strapped **9** desperate, destitute, penniless **10** down-and-out **11** necessitous **12** impoverished

hardy 4 bold, hale **5** brave, tough **6** daring, robust, rugged, strong **7** healthy **8** intrepid, resolute **9** audacious

Hardy, Thomas *character:* **3** Sue (Bridehead) **4** Alec (D'Urberville), Clym (Yeobright), Jude (Fawley), Tess (Durbeyfield) **5** Angel (Clare) **7** Gabriel (Oak) **8** Arabella (Donn), Eustacia (Vye), Henchard (Michael) **9** Bathsheba (Everdene) *novel:* **11** Woodlanders (The) **14** Jude the Obscure **17** Return of the Native (The) **19** Mayor of Casterbridge (The) **21** Tess of the D'Urbervilles **22** Far from the Madding Crowd *setting:* **6** Wessex

hare 5 lapin **6** rabbit *female:* **3** doe *genus:* **5** Lepus *male:* **4** buck *tail:* **4** scut *young:* **7** leveret

harebrained 5 crazy, loony, silly, wacky **6** absurd, insane, stupid **7** asinine, foolish **9** frivolous **10** ridiculous **12** preposterous

harem 5 serai **6** zenana **8** seraglio *concubine:* **9** odalisque

haricot 3 pod **4** bean **10** kidney bean

hark 4 hear, heed, mind, note 6 attend, listen, notice

harlequin 5 clown, joker 6 jester, mottle 7 buffoon 9 prankster

Harlequin *beloved:* 9 Columbine *rival:* 7 Pierrot

harm 3 mar 4 hurt, maim, ruin 5 abuse, spoil, wound, wrong 6 damage, ill-use, impair, injure, injury, misuse, molest 7 tarnish 8 ill-treat, maltreat, mischief, mistreat 9 undermine 10 disservice, misfortune

harmful 3 bad 4 evil 5 risky, toxic 6 malign, unsafe 7 noisome, noxious 8 damaging 9 dangerous, hazardous, injurious, malignant, unhealthy 10 pernicious 11 deleterious, detrimental, unhealthful

harmless 4 safe 6 benign 8 innocent, nontoxic 9 innocuous 11 inoffensive

Harmonia *daughter:* 3 Ino 5 Agave 6 Semele 7 Autonoë *father:* 4 Ares, Mars *husband:* 6 Cadmus *mother:* 5 Venus 9 Aphrodite *son:* 9 Polydorus

harmonious 5 sweet 7 chiming, chordal, musical, pacific 8 blending, friendly, in accord, peaceful, pleasing 9 agreeable, congenial, congruous, consonant, symphonic 10 compatible, concordant 11 cooperative, symmetrical, sympathetic

harmonize 3 fit 4 jibe, sing 5 agree, blend, match 6 accord, attune 7 arrange, concert, conform 8 coincide, dovetail 10 integrate 10 coordinate, correspond, synthesize 11 orchestrate

harmony 5 grace, peace, unity 6 accord 7 balance, concert, concord, oneness, rapport 8 affinity, sonority, symmetry 9 agreement, congruity, polyphony 10 accordance, concinnity, conformity, consonance, proportion 11 concordance, consistency, cooperation *lack of:* 7 discord 10 dissonance *of movement:* 8 eurythmy

harness 4 curb, gear, yoke 5 hitch, leash 6 bridle, tackle 7 utilize 11 domesticate *part:* 3 bit 4 rein 5 girth, trace 6 collar 7 blinder, crupper 9 bellyband, breeching, checkrein 12 breast collar *ring:* 6 terret

harp 4 lyre 9 harmonica *Greek:* 7 cithara, kithara

harpsichord 7 cembalo 8 clavecin

harpsichordist *American:* 6 Fuller (Albert, David), Kipnis (Igor), Newman (Anthony) 7 Marlowe (Sylvia), Pinkham (Daniel), Pinnock (Trevor), Valenti (Fernando) 11 Kirkpatrick (Ralph) *English:* 7 Malcolm (George) *German:* 7 Richter (Karl) 9 Leonhardt

(Gustav) *Italian:* 7 Sgrizzi (Luciano) *Polish:* 9 Landowska (Wanda)

harpy 3 nag 5 leech, scold, shrew, vixen 6 virago 8 fishwife, harridan 9 termagant

Harpy 5 Aello 7 Celaeno, Ocypete *father:* 7 Thaumas *mother:* 7 Electra *sister:* 4 Iris

harridan 3 hag 4 fury 5 biddy, harpy, shrew, vixen, witch 6 dragon, gorgon, ogress, virago 7 hellcat 8 battle-ax, fishwife 9 battle-axe, termagant

harrier 3 dog 4 hawk 6 hector, runner 10 persecutor

harrow 3 try, vex 4 bait, rack 5 devil, tease 6 badger, heckle, hector, needle, pester, suffer 7 afflict, bedevil, torment, torture, trouble 8 distress, irritate 9 cultivate 10 excruciate

harry 3 dog, irk, vex 4 gnaw, raid, sack 5 annoy, tease, upset, worry 6 attack, badger, harass, hassle, pester, plague, ravage 7 assault, bedevil, despoil, perturb, pillage, plunder, torment 8 desolate, maltreat 9 beleaguer, depredate

harsh 5 cruel, gruff, rough, stern 6 biting, brutal, coarse, severe, uneven, unkind 7 austere, caustic, grating, jarring, painful, pungent, raucous, stubbly 8 exacting, grinding, jangling, scraping, scratchy, strident, unsmooth 9 dissonant, inclement 10 discordant, irritating, unpleasant

hart 4 deer, stag 7 red deer *mate:* 4 hind

hartebeest 8 antelope *family:* 7 Bovidae

Harte story 17 Luck of Roaring Camp (The) 19 Outcasts of Poker Flat (The)

Hartford *college:* 7 Trinity *specialty:* 9 insurance

Hart, Moss *autobiography:* 6 Act One *collaborator:* 7 Kaufman (George S.) *musical:* 13 Lady in the Dark *play:* 15 Once in a Lifetime 18 Man Who Came to Dinner (The) 20 You Can't Take It with You

haruspex 5 augur 7 diviner, prophet 8 foreseer 9 predictor 10 forecaster, foreteller, soothsayer

harvest 4 crop, pick, reap 5 amass, cache, glean, hoard, stash, yield 6 garner, gather 7 collect, reaping, store up, vintage 8 ingather, squirrel, stow away 9 garnering, gathering *bug:* 4 mite 7 chigger *fly:* 6 cicada *festival:* 6 Lammas 7 Cerelia 10 Michaelmas 12 Thanksgiving *god, goddess:* 3 Ops 5 Ceres 8 Consus 7 Demeter

harvester 7 gleaner *grain:* 6 header *of grapes:* 8 vintager

Harvey 5 pooka 6 rabbit *author:* 5 Chase (Mary) *character:* 6 Elwood (P. Dowd)

hash 4 chop, mess, stew **5** botch, mince, mix-up **6** jumble, medley, muddle, review **7** clutter, confuse, mélange, mixture **8** consider, shambles **9** patchwork **10** assortment, hodgepodge, miscellany

hash house 4 café **5** diner **6** bistro, eatery **7** pit stop **10** coffee shop **12** luncheonette

hashish 5 bhang, ganja **6** charas **8** cannabis, narcotic *plant:* **4** hemp

hash out 6 review **7** discuss **8** talk over **9** talk about

hasp 5 catch **6** fasten **8** fastener **9** fastening

hassle 3 row **4** beef, to-do **5** annoy, argue, brawl, fight, run-in **6** bicker, clamor, harass, hubbub, tumult, uproar **7** dispute, problem, quarrel, rhubarb, turmoil, wrangle **8** argument, squabble, struggle **9** commotion **11** altercation, controversy

hassock 4 pouf **7** cushion, kneeler, ottoman **9** footstool

haste 3 run **4** dash, rush **5** hurry, speed **6** barrel, bustle, flurry, hustle **7** beeline, hotfoot **8** celerity, dispatch, rapidity, velocity **9** fleetness, quickness, swiftness **10** speediness **11** hurriedness, impetuosity

hasten 3 fly, hie, run **4** rush, urge **5** hurry, press, speed **6** barrel, hustle, step up, urge on **7** hurry up, quicken, speed up **8** expedite **10** accelerate

hasty 4 fast, rash **5** brisk, eager, fleet, quick, rapid, swift **6** abrupt, rushed, speedy, sudden **7** cursory, hurried, rushing **8** careless, fleeting, headlong, heedless, reckless, slapdash **9** hotheaded, impatient, impetuous, irritable, quickened **10** ill-advised, incautious **11** expeditious, perfunctory, precipitate, precipitous, superficial, thoughtless

hat 5 derby, tuque **6** boater, cloche, fedora, panama, topper **7** bicorne, chapeau, homburg, porkpie, Stetson, tricorn **8** sombrero, tricorne **9** headpiece **11** deerstalker *ancient Greek:* **7** petasos, petasus *brimless:* **7** pillbox *close-fitting:* **4** kufi **5** toque, tuque **6** cloche, turban *felt:* **5** busby, derby **6** bowler, trilby *fur:* **5** busby **6** castor *helmetlike:* **4** topi **5** topee *maker:* **7** modiste **8** milliner *Middle Eastern:* **3** fez *military:* **4** kepi **5** busby, shako *Muslim:* **3** fez **6** turban **8** tarboosh *sheepskin:* **6** calpac **7** calpack *soft:* **5** toque *straw:* **6** boater, panama, sailor **7** bangkok, leghorn, skimmer **8** sombrero *sun:* **5** terai *tall:* **9** stovepipe *waterproof:* **9** sou'wester *woman's:* **4** coif **5** toque **6** bonnet **7** pillbox

hatch 4 door, plan, plot **5** breed, brood, cover, inlay, spawn **6** cook up, create, design, devise, emerge, invent, make up, work up **7** concoct, dream up, opening, produce, think up **8** contrive, engender, generate, incubate, occasion **9** floodgate, formulate, give birth, give forth, originate, procreate **11** compartment

hatchet 3 axe **8** tomahawk

hatchet man 6 killer **7** torpedo **8** assassin, enforcer, murderer **9** attack dog, cutthroat **10** eliminator

hate 5 abhor, scorn, spite **6** animus, detest, enmity, horror, loathe, malice, rancor **7** despise, disgust **8** aversion, execrate, loathing **9** abominate, animosity, antipathy, deprecate, repulsion, revulsion **10** abhorrence, repugnance **11** abomination, detestation

hateful 4 evil, foul, mean, vile **5** nasty **6** horrid, malign, odious, scurvy **7** vicious **8** accursed, damnable, infamous **9** abhorrent, execrable, malicious, obnoxious, repellent, repulsive **10** abominable, despicable, detestable, malevolent **11** blasphemous, opprobrious, unspeakable **13** reprehensible

Hatfields vs. ___ 6 McCoys

hatred 5 odium, spite **6** animus, enmity, rancor **7** dislike **8** aversion, loathing **9** animosity, antipathy, hostility, repulsion, revulsion **10** abhorrence, repugnance **11** abomination, detestation, malevolence *of change:* **9** misoneism *of humankind:* **11** misanthropy *of marriage:* **8** misogamy *of men:* **8** misandry *of women:* **8** misogyny

hats 9 millinery

hauberk 5 armor **9** chain mail, habergeon

haughtiness 4 airs **5** pride, scorn **7** conceit, disdain, hauteur **9** arrogance, insolence, pomposity **12** snobbishness

haughty 5 aloof, proud **6** lordly, sniffy **7** distant **8** arrogant, cavalier, scornful, snobbish, superior **9** egotistic **10** disdainful **11** overbearing **12** contemptuous, supercilious

haul 3 lug, tow, tug **4** cart, drag, draw, hump, lift, load, loot, pull, swag, take, tote **5** boost, booty, cargo, hoist, raise, truck **6** burden, lading, schlep, spoils **7** freight, payload, schlepp *with a tackle:* **5** bowse

haul up 5 hoise, hoist *with a rope:* **5** trice

haunch 3 hip **11** hindquarter

haunches 4 rump **7** hind end, rear end **8** backside, buttocks **9** posterior **12** hindquarters

haunt 4 site **5** spook **6** obsess, prey on

7 habitat, hang out, inhabit, torment, trouble 8 frequent 9 preoccupy 10 hang around, rendezvous, stay around, visit often

haunter 5 ghost 7 denizen, habitué

hautbois 4 oboe

hauteur see HAUGHTINESS

haut monde 5 elite 6 jet set 7 society, who's who 10 glitterati, upper crust 11 aristocracy, high society 13 carriage trade

have 3 own 4 hold 7 contain, include, possess

haven 4 port, roof 5 house 6 asylum, harbor, refuge 7 retreat, shelter 9 anchorage, sanctuary

haversack 3 bag 4 pack 8 backpack

havoc 4 loss, ruin, sack 5 chaos, waste 6 mayhem 8 calamity, disorder, ravaging 9 confusion, ruination 11 catastrophe, destruction, devastation, pandemonium

haw 4 left, tree 5 berry, fruit, shrub 8 turn left 10 equivocate

Hawaii *author:* 8 Michener (James A.) *capital:* 8 Honolulu *city:* 4 Hilo *coast:* 4 Kona *discoverer:* 4 Cook (Capt. James) *island:* 4 Maui, Oahu 5 Kauai, Lanai 6 Niihau 7 Molokai *mountain:* 7 Kilauea 8 Mauna Kea, Mauna Loa *nickname:* 5 Aloha (State) *park:* 9 Haleakala *state bird:* 4 nene *state flower:* 8 hibiscus *state tree:* 5 kukui 9 candlenut

Hawaiian *dance:* 4 hula *feast:* 4 luau *food:* 3 poi *god:* 4 Kane, Lono 5 Wakea 7 Kanaloa *goddess:* 4 Pele *goose:* 4 nene *instrument:* 3 uke 7 ukulele *neckwear:* 3 lei *nonnative:* 5 haole 8 malihini *resident:* 8 kamaaina *shaman:* 6 kahuna *soup:* 6 saimin *tree:* 3 koa

hawk 4 kite, sell, vend 5 buteo 6 falcon, monger, osprey, peddle 7 Cooper's, goshawk, haggard, harrier 8 caracara, huckster, roughleg 9 accipiter, redtailed, warmonger 10 militarist 11 ferruginous, rough-legged *male:* 6 tercel 7 tiercel *young:* 4 eyas

hawker 6 coster, monger, seller, vendor 7 packman, peddler 8 pitchman 12 costermonger

hawkeyed 11 keen-sighted 12 sharp-sighted

Hawkeye State 4 Iowa

hawkish 7 martial, warlike 9 combative 10 aggressive 11 belligerent 12 militaristic

___ Hawley Tariff 5 Smoot

Hawthorne, Nathaniel *birthplace:* 5 Salem *character:* 6 Hester (Prynne) 8 Clifford (Pyncheon), Hepzibah (Pyncheon), Pyncheon (Judge) 10 Dimmesdale (Rev. Arthur) 13 Chillingworth (Roger) *novel:* 10 Marble Faun (The) 13 Scarlet Letter (The) 21 House of the Seven Gables (The)

hay 3 bed 4 feed 5 grass 6 fodder, reward 7 herbage *crops:* 6 clover 7 alfalfa, timothy

Haydn oratorio 7 Seasons (The) 8 Creation (The)

hay fever 7 allergy 10 pollenosis, pollinosis *cause:* 6 pollen 7 ragweed

haying machine 5 baler

haymaker 3 box 4 blow, sock 5 clout, punch 6 wallop

hayseed see HICK

haywire 4 amok, awry 5 amuck, crazy, upset 6 faulty 8 confused 10 out of order 12 out of control

hazard 3 bet, try 4 dare, game, luck, risk 5 peril, shoal, wager 6 chance, danger, gamble, menace 7 fortune, imperil, venture 8 accident, endanger, jeopardy, obstacle

hazardous 5 hairy, risky 6 chancy, unsafe 7 unsound 8 perilous 9 dangerous, unhealthy 10 precarious

haze 3 fog 4 film, mist, murk, smog 5 brume, cloud, drive, smoke, vapor 6 harass 7 dimness, obscure 8 dullness, initiate, overcast 9 mistiness, murkiness, vagueness 10 cloudiness

hazel 4 wood 5 birch, shrub 7 filbert

hazy 3 dim 5 faint, filmy, foggy, fuzzy, misty, murky, vague 6 cloudy, unsure 7 blurred, clouded, obscure, unclear 8 nebulous, vaporous 9 uncertain 10 indefinite, indistinct

head 3 nut 4 boss, john, main, pate, poll 5 brain, caput, chief, first, prime, privy, scalp, skull 6 climax, honcho, leader, master, noggin, noodle, set out, talent, toilet 7 cranium, faculty, latrine, leading, premier, proceed, supreme 8 director, foremost, lavatory, light out 9 chieftain, principal, strike out 10 promontory *area:* 5 crown 6 temple *back part:* 7 occiput *bone:* 5 skull 7 cranium 8 parietal *combining form:* 6 cranio 7 cephalo *covering:* 3 cap, hat 6 bonnet 8 kerchief *monastery:* 4 dean 5 abbot 8 superior *nunnery:* 6 abbess 8 superior *of hair:* 4 mane 6 fleece 9 chevelure *relating to:* 8 cephalic *shaving of:* 7 tonsure *skin:* 5 scalp *top:* 4 pate 5 crown

headache 4 pain 5 worry 6 bother, megrim 7 problem 8 migraine, nuisance, vexation 9 annoyance 10 irritation

headband 7 bandeau, circlet, coronal *ancient Greek:* 6 taenia 7 taeniae (plural)

headdress 7 topknot *American Indian:*
9 warbonnet *Arab:* **8** kaffiyeh *bishop's:*
5 miter, mitre *medieval:* **4** barb *Eastern:*
6 turban *nobleman's:* **7** coronet *royal:*
5 crown, tiara **6** diadem *Spanish*
women's: **8** mantilla *women's:* **6** bonnet
(see also HAT)
headland 4 cape **5** point **10** promontory
headline 6 banner **7** feature, promote
8 screamer **9** emphasize, publicize,
spotlight **10** noteworthy
headlong 4 rash **5** hasty **6** abrupt, daring, rashly, sudden **7** hurried, rushing
8 heedless, reckless **9** foolhardy,
impetuous, impulsive **10** heedlessly,
recklessly **11** precipitate, precipitous
headmaster 6 leader **9** principal
head off 4 stop **5** avert, block **6** thwart
7 deflect, obviate, prevent, ward off
8 stave off, turn back **9** forestall, intercept
headquarters 3 hub **4** base, seat **6** center
head start 4 edge, jump, lead, odds
5 boost **7** advance, vantage **8** handicap
9 advantage, allowance
headstone 8 memorial, monument
11 grave marker
headstrong 6 dogged, mulish, unruly
7 willful **8** contrary, perverse, stubborn
9 obstinate **10** bullheaded, refractory,
self-willed **11** intractable, stiff-necked
heads-up 5 alarm, alert **6** signal, tip-off
7 warning **8** high sign **11** resourceful
headway 4 gain **6** growth **7** advance
8 anabasis, progress **11** advancement,
improvement
heady 4 rash, rich **5** giddy **6** elated,
potent **7** willful **8** exciting **9** impetuous
11 exhilarated, intoxicated **12** intoxicating
heal 3 fix **4** cure, mend **5** sew up, treat
6 cement, remedy, repair **7** patch up,
restore **8** make well
healer 6 doctor, shaman
healing 8 curative, remedial, salutary,
sanative **9** vulnerary, wholesome
10 salubrious **11** restorative, therapeutic **12** convalescent *goddess of:* **3** Eir
health 7 fitness, welfare **8** haleness, vitality, wellness **9** soundness, well-being,
wholeness *club:* **3** gym, spa
healthful 8 curative, hygienic, remedial,
salutary **9** favorable, wholesome
10 beneficial, corrective, profitable,
salubrious **11** restorative
healthy 3 fit **4** hale, spry, well **5** sound,
tonic **6** benign, robust, strong, sturdy
7 chipper **8** blooming, hygienic, positive, salutary, thriving, vigorous
9 wholesome **10** able-bodied, beneficial,
prosperous, salubrious **11** flourishing

heap 3 lot **4** cock, fill, gobs, hill, load,
lump, mass, much, pack, pile, rick,
scad **5** amass, bunch, clump, crate,
loads, mound, shock, stack, wreck
6 barrel, charge, gather, jalopy, junker,
lumber, oodles **7** clunker, collect,
deposit, jillion **8** assemble, mountain,
slathers **9** abundance, great deal, profusion, stockpile **10** quantities *combustible:* **4** pyre
hear 4 heed **5** learn **8** listen to, perceive
9 apprehend
hearing 4 test **5** trial **6** tryout **7** earshot,
inquiry **8** audience, audition **9** interview **10** conference, discussion *distance:* **7** earshot
hearken 4 heed, mind, note **6** attend, listen, notice **7** observe
hearsay 4 buzz, news, talk **5** rumor
6 gossip, report **7** account, chatter
9 grapevine **11** scuttlebutt
heart 3 hub **4** core, crux, gist, guts, love,
pith, root, seat, soul, zest **5** ardor,
bosom, focus, gusto, moxie, pluck,
spunk **6** breast, center, kernel, mettle,
relish, spirit, ticker **7** courage, resolve
8 feelings, sympathy **9** character, fortitude **10** affections, compassion, conscience, enthusiasm *combining form:*
6 cardio *contraction:* **7** systole *dilation:*
8 diastole *part:* **5** valve **6** atrium, septum
9 ventricle
heartache 3 rue, woe **4** care, pain, pang
5 grief **6** regret, sorrow **7** anguish, sadness **8** distress **10** affliction
heartbeat 5 flash, jiffy, pulse, throb,
trice **6** moment, second **9** pulsation
irregular: **10** arrhythmia
heartbreak 3 rue, woe **5** agony, grief
6 misery, regret, sorrow **7** anguish,
despair, torment, torture **9** suffering
10 desolation **12** wretchedness
heartbreaking 6 bitter, tragic **8** grievous
9 agonizing **10** calamitous, deplorable,
lamentable **11** devastating, distressing
heartbroken 7 crushed, grieved
8 mournful, overcome, wretched **9** sorrowful **10** despairing, despondent
12 disconsolate
heartburn 7 pyrosis
hearten 4 buoy, stir **5** cheer, rally, rouse
6 arouse, buck up, buoy up, perk up
7 animate, cheer up, enliven, inspire
8 embolden, energize, inspirit **9** encourage
heartfelt 4 deep, true **6** honest **7** earnest,
fervent, genuine, sincere **8** profound
9 unfeigned
hearth 4 home **5** abode **8** domicile,
dwelling, fireside **9** fireplace, residence

heartily 6 wholly 9 sincerely, with gusto, zestfully 10 completely, thoroughly

heartless 4 cold, hard 5 cruel 6 unkind 7 callous 8 uncaring 9 unfeeling 10 hard-boiled 11 insensitive, unemotional 13 unsympathetic

Heart of Dixie 7 Alabama

heartsease 5 pansy, viola 6 violet 11 peace of mind, tranquility 12 johnny-jump-up, tranquillity

heart-shaped 7 cordate

heartsick 4 blue, down 8 dejected, desolate, dismayed, downcast 9 depressed 10 despondent, dispirited 11 demoralized 12 disconsolate

heartthrob 4 idol, love 5 flame, honey, sweet 7 beloved, darling, passion 10 sweetheart

heart-to-heart 4 open, talk 5 frank 6 candid, honest 7 sincere 8 truthful 12 conversation

hearty 4 hale, warm 5 ample 6 jovial, robust, sailor, strong 7 cordial, healthy, profuse, sincere 8 abundant, vehement, vigorous 9 approving, energetic, exuberant, flavorful, unfeigned 12 enthusiastic, unrestrained

heat 4 cook, rage, warm, zeal 5 ardor, fever 6 fervor, simmer, warmth 7 caloric, inflame, passion, swelter 8 pyrolyze *combining form:* 4 pyro 6 calori, thermo 7 thermia *measuring device:* 11 calorimeter, thermometer *quantity:* 3 BTU

heated 3 hot, mad 5 angry, fiery, irate 6 ardent, fervid, fierce, ireful, raging, steamy 7 boiling, burning, fevered, furious 8 broiling, feverish, scalding, sizzling, vehement, wrathful 9 indignant, scorching 10 passionate 11 acrimonious

heater 3 gun, rod 5 stove 6 boiler, pistol 7 furnace 8 fastball, radiator

heath 4 moor 5 shrub 9 wasteland

heathen 5 pagan 7 infidel 8 barbaric 11 irreligious, uncivilized

heat-producing 9 calorific

heave 3 lob 4 cast, draw, fire, gasp, haul, heft, huff, hurl, lift, pant, puff, pull, push, toss 5 fling, hoist, labor, pitch, raise, retch, sling, surge, throw, vomit 6 launch

heave-ho 4 boot 6 ouster 8 bum's rush 9 dismissal

heaven 3 God 4 Zion 5 bliss, glory 6 utopia 7 arcadia, delight, ecstasy, elysium, nirvana, rapture 8 empyrean, eternity, paradise 9 firmament, Shangri-la 10 wonderland 11 immortality, kingdom come 12 promised land

heavenly 4 lush 6 divine, sacred 7 blessed 8 beatific, empyreal, empyrean, ethereal 9 ambrosial, celestial, delicious 10 delectable, delightful, enchanting

heavy 3 big, fat 4 rich 5 beefy, bulky, gross, hefty, obese, stout 6 bad guy, chunky, drowsy, fleshy, gravid, leaden, portly 7 arduous, intense, labored, massive, porcine, villain, weighty 8 burdened, cumbrous, enceinte, pregnant, sluggish, unwieldy 9 corpulent, expectant, expecting, laborious, lumbering, ponderous, strenuous 10 burdensome, cumbersome, formidable, oppressive, overweight

heavy-handed 5 crude, harsh, inept 6 clumsy, gauche, klutzy 7 awkward 8 bumbling, despotic 9 maladroit 10 oppressive 11 domineering, overbearing

heavyhearted 3 sad 4 glum 5 sorry 7 unhappy 8 dejected, downcast, mournful, saddened 9 depressed, miserable, sorrowful 10 despondent, dispirited, melancholy

heavyset 5 beefy, husky, stout, thick 6 chunky, portly, stocky 11 thickbodied

heavyweight 3 VIP 4 lion 5 boxer, chief 6 big gun, bigwig, leader 7 big shot, notable 8 big-timer

Hebe *father:* 4 Zeus 7 Jupiter *husband:* 8 Hercules *mother:* 4 Hera, Juno *successor:* 8 Ganymede

hebetude 6 stupor, torpor 7 languor 8 dullness, lethargy 9 lassitude, torpidity 10 drowsiness

hebetudinous 4 dull, logy 5 dopey 6 drowsy, stupid, torpid 8 listless, sluggish 9 lethargic

Hebrew 3 Jew 6 Jewish *coin:* 6 lepton, shekel *festival:* 5 Purim 6 Pesach, Sukkot 7 Hanukah, Sukkoth 8 Chanukah, Lag b'Omer, Passover, Shabuoth 9 Tishah-b'Ab, Yom Kippur 12 Rosh Hashanah, Simchas Torah *God:* 6 Adonai, Elohim, Yahweh 7 Jehovah *judge:* 6 Gideon *lawgiver:* 5 Moses *letter:* (see at ALPHABET) *measure:* 5 cubit, ephah *month:* 4 Adar, Elul, Iyar 5 Nisan, Sivan, Tebet 6 Kislev, Shebat, Tammuz, Tishri 6 Veadar (in leap year) 7 Heshvan *patriarch:* 3 Dan, Gad 4 Cain, Levi, Seth 5 Asher, David, Isaac, Jacob, Judah 6 Joseph, Reuben, Simeon 7 Abraham, Zebulun 8 Benjamin, Issachar, Naphtali *sacred city:* 5 Safad, Safed 6 Hebron 8 Tiberias 9 Jerusalem (see also JEWISH)

Hebrides island 4 Eigg, Rhum, Skye, Uist 5 Lewis 6 Harris

Hecate *father:* 6 Perses *goddess of:*

5 night **10** underworld, witchcraft *mother:* **7** Asteria

hecatomb 7 killing, slaying **8** butchery **9** bloodbath, sacrifice, slaughter

heck 4 darn, drat, geez, gosh, hell, jeez **5** golly **6** shucks

heckle 3 nag **4** bait, faze, gibe, ride **5** annoy, chivy, hound, tease, worry **6** badger, bother, harass, hassle, hector, molest, needle, pester, plague, rattle **7** disrupt, disturb, torment **9** interrupt **10** disconcert

hectic 3 red **6** fervid **7** burning, excited, fevered, flushed **8** confused, exciting, feverish, frenetic, restless **9** turbulent **10** persistent

hector 3 cow, nag **4** bait, ride **5** bully, chivy, hound **6** badger, harass, lean on **7** bedevil, swagger **8** browbeat, bullyrag, domineer **10** intimidate

Hector *brother:* **5** Paris **7** Helenus, Troilus **9** Deiphobus, Polydorus *father:* **5** Priam *mother:* **6** Hecuba *sister:* **5** Creusa **8** Polyxena **9** Cassandra *slayer:* **8** Achilles *victim:* **9** Patroclus *wife:* **10** Andromache

Hecuba *daughter:* **6** Creusa **8** Polyxena **9** Cassandra *father:* **5** Dymas *husband:* **5** Priam *son:* **5** Paris **6** Hector **7** Helenus, Troilus **9** Deiphobus, Polydorus *victim:* **11** Polymnestor

hedge 4 trim **5** avoid, evade, fence, guard, hem in, limit **6** hinder **7** barrier, defense, enclose, evasion, protect **8** boundary, encircle, restrict **9** shrubbery **10** protection

hedgehog 9 porcupine **10** stronghold

hedonist 4 rake **7** epicure, gourmet **8** gourmand, sybarite **9** bon vivant, epicurean, libertine **10** sensualist, voluptuary

heebie-jeebies 5 jumps **6** creeps, nerves, shakes **7** jitters, shivers, willies **11** nervousness

heed 4 care, hark, mark, mind, note, obey **5** watch **6** attend, harken, listen, notice, regard, remark **7** be aware, concern, hearing, hearken, observe, respect **8** consider, interest **9** attention **10** observance

heedful 5 alert, aware **7** on guard **8** vigilant **9** attentive, observant, observing **10** interested, meticulous, scrupulous **13** conscientious

heedless 9 negligent, oblivious, unmindful **10** unthinking **11** inadvertent, inattentive, unobservant **12** unreflective **13** inconsiderate

heedlessness 7 neglect **9** disregard, unconcern **11** disinterest, inattention, insouciance **12** indifference

hee-haw 4 bray **5** laugh **6** guffaw **10** horse laugh

heel 3 bum, cad, tip **4** cant, hock, lean, list, tilt **5** creep, knave, louse, rogue, skunk, slope **6** rascal, rotter **7** incline, lowlife, villain **9** scoundrel *bone:* **8** calcanea (plural), calcanei (plural) **9** calcaneum, calcaneus

heft 4 lift, load **5** hoist, raise, weigh **6** weight **7** heave up **9** heaviness, influence **10** importance

hefty 3 big **5** beefy, burly, bulky, heavy, husky, large, major **6** brawny, mighty, rugged, strong **7** massive, sizable **8** imposing, powerful **9** extensive, goodsized, plentiful, ponderous, strapping **11** substantial

hegira 6 escape, exodus, flight **7** journey **10** emigration, evacuation **11** deliverance

Heidi *author:* **5** Spyri (Johanna) *goatherd:* **5** Peter *setting:* **4** Alps

heifer 4 calf

___ Heifetz 6 Jascha

height 3 top **4** acme, apex, cusp, peak, rise **6** apogee, climax, heyday, summit, vertex, zenith **7** stature **8** altitude, pinnacle **9** elevation, loftiness **10** prominence *combining form:* **4** acro

heighten 3 wax **5** boost, mount, raise **6** beef up, expand, extend **7** amplify, augment, build up, elevate, enhance, enlarge, improve, magnify **8** increase **9** highlight, intensify **10** aggrandize

heinie 3 bum **4** butt, rear, rump **5** fanny **6** bottom **7** rear end **8** backside

heinous 4 evil **6** odious **7** hateful **8** infamous, shocking **9** abhorrent, atrocious, execrable, monstrous **10** abominable, detestable, outrageous

heinousness 4 evil **6** horror, infamy **8** atrocity, enormity **13** monstrousness

heir 4 scion **7** grantee, heritor, legatee **9** inheritor, successor **11** beneficiary *joint:* **8** parcener **10** coparcener

heist 3 cop, rob **4** lift, loot **5** boost, caper, filch, pinch, steal, swipe, theft **6** holdup, rip off **7** larceny, purloin, robbery **8** burglary **9** strong-arm

Helen of Troy *abductor:* **5** Paris *husband:* **8** Menelaus

Helenus *brother:* **5** Paris **6** Hector **7** Troilus **9** Deiphobus, Polydorus *father:* **5** Priam *mother:* **6** Hecuba *sister:* **6** Creusa **8** Polyxena **9** Cassandra *wife:* **10** Andromache

Hel, Hela *father:* **4** Loki *hall:* **7** Niflhel **8** Niflheim *mother:* **9** Angerboda

helical 6 spiral

helicopter 7 chopper **9** eggbeater

10 whirlybird *armed:* 7 gunship *blade:* 5 rotor

Helios 6 Apollo *daughter:* 5 Circe 8 Pasiphaë *father:* 8 Hyperion *mother:* 5 Theia *sister:* 3 Eos 6 Aurora, Selene *son:* 8 Phaethon

heliotrope 4 herb 5 shrub 6 borage 10 bloodstone

hell 5 hades, Sheol 6 blazes, Tophet 7 Gehenna, inferno 9 perdition

hell-bent 6 driven, intent 8 obsessed, resolved 10 determined

Hellen *father:* 9 Deucalion *mother:* 6 Pyrrha *son:* 5 Dorus 6 Aeolus, Xuthus

hellhole 3 pit 8 dystopia, snake pit 9 mare's nest

hellion 3 elf, imp 4 puck, punk 5 demon, rogue, scamp 6 rascal 7 gremlin

hellish 6 horrid 7 ghastly, hideous, satanic, stygian 8 damnable, diabolic, dreadful, gruesome, horrible, infernal, terrible 9 appalling, frightful, monstrous, plutonian 10 diabolical

Hellman play 11 Little Foxes (The) 13 Children's Hour (The) 15 Watch on the Rhine

hello 3 hey 4 ciao, hail 5 aloha, howdy 7 hi there, welcome 8 greeting 9 greetings

helm 5 wheel 7 cockpit 8 controls

helmet 6 casque, sallet, tin hat 7 morrion 8 burgonet, headgear *medieval:* 6 sallet 7 basinet *part:* 7 ventail 8 aventail *sun:* 4 topi 5 topee

helmsman 5 pilot

Heloïse *husband:* 7 Abelard (Peter) *son:* 9 Astrolabe

helot 4 peon, serf 5 slave 6 vassal 7 laborer, peasant, servant

helotry 4 yoke 6 thrall 7 bondage, peonage, serfdom, slavery 9 servitude, thralldom 11 enslavement

help 3 aid 4 abet, back, mend 5 avail, boost, guide, serve 6 assist, relief, remedy, succor 7 advance, benefit, bolster, further, promote, relieve, secours, service, support 8 mitigate, palliate 9 alleviate, meliorate 10 ameliorate, assistance, facilitate 11 cooperation *forward:* 7 further *hired:* 5 labor

helper 4 aide 6 server 7 ancilla, servant 8 employee 9 assistant, associate, attendant, auxiliary 10 apprentice 11 subordinate

helpful 5 of use 6 usable, useful 8 salutary, valuable 9 effective, favorable, practical 10 beneficial, profitable, propitious 11 encouraging 12 advantageous, constructive

helping 4 dose 5 share 7 portion, serving 9 auxiliary

helpless 4 weak 6 feeble, futile, unable 7 forlorn 8 desolate 9 abandoned, dependent 11 unprotected

helter-skelter 6 anyhow 7 anywise, flighty, hastily, turmoil 8 at random, disorder, pell-mell, randomly 9 confusion, haphazard, hit-or-miss 11 any which way, haphazardly, in confusion, precipitate

helve 4 haft 6 handle

Helvetian 5 Swiss

hem 3 pen, rim 4 brim, edge, gird, ring, seam, shut 5 bound, brink, fence, hedge, skirt, verge 6 border, circle, corral, edging, fringe, immure, margin, stitch 7 close in, enclose, selvage, shorten 8 encircle, surround 9 encompass, perimeter, periphery *turned-back:* 4 cuff

Heman *father:* 4 Joel *grandfather:* 6 Samuel

hematite 3 ore 7 mineral 12 black diamond

Hemingway, Ernest *novel:* 9 In Our Time 12 Sun Also Rises (The) 13 Moveable Feast (A) 14 Farewell to Arms (A) 15 Old Man and the Sea (The) 16 To Have and Have Not 18 Islands in the Stream, Snows of Kilimanjaro (The) 19 For Whom the Bell Tolls *sobriquet:* 4 Papa

hemlock 4 drug, herb, tree, wood 6 poison

hemophiliac 7 bleeder

hemp 3 kef, kif 7 hashish 8 cannabis 9 marijuana *fiber:* 5 oakum *kind:* 4 aloe

hen 5 biddy *broody:* 6 sitter *spayed:* 8 poularde *young:* 6 pullet

hence 4 away, ergo, thus 5 since 9 as a result, from now on, therefore, thereupon 11 accordingly 12 consequently

henceforth 9 from now on, hereafter

henchman 6 cohort, lackey, minion, stooge 7 abettor 8 adherent, disciple, follower, partisan, retainer 9 attendant, supporter 10 accomplice

Henley poem 8 Invictus

henpeck 3 nag 4 carp, fuss 5 annoy 6 badger, carp at, harass, hector 8 domineer 9 find fault

Henry II *adversary:* 6 Becket (Thomas à) *son:* 7 Richard (Lionheart) *surname:* 5 Anjou 11 Plantagenet *wife:* 7 Eleanor

Henry IV *surname:* 9 Lancaster *victim:* 10 Richard III

Henry VIII *archbishop:* 7 Cranmer (Thomas) 10 Thomas More *daughter:* 9 Elizabeth *son:* 6 Edward *surname:* 5 Tudor *victim:* 4 Anne (Boleyn) 9 Catherine (Howard) 10 Thomas More *wife:* 4 Anne (Boleyn, of Cleves), Jane

(Seymour) **9** Catherine (Howard, of Aragon, Parr)

hepatic 9 liverwort

Hephaestus 6 Vulcan *father:* **4** Zeus **7** Jupiter *mother:* **4** Hera, Juno *wife:* **5** Venus **6** Charis **9** Aphrodite

Hephzibah *husband:* **8** Hezekiah *son:* **8** Manasseh

hepped up 5 eager **7** excited, fervent **12** enthusiastic

Hera 4 Juno *father:* **6** Cronus, Saturn *husband:* **4** Zeus **7** Jupiter *messenger:* **4** Iris *mother:* **4** Rhea

Heracles *beloved:* **4** Iole *brother:* **8** Iphicles *charioteer:* **6** Iolaus *father:* **4** Zeus **7** Jupiter *mother:* **7** Alcmene *son:* **6** Hyllus *victim:* **5** Hydra, Ladon **6** Geryon, Megara, Orthus **10** Nemean lion *wife:* **4** Hebe **6** Megara **8** Deianira

herald 4 hail, tout **5** crier, greet **6** signal **7** courier, declare, portend, precede, presage, trumpet **8** announce, ballyhoo, exponent, outrider, proclaim **9** advertise, harbinger, messenger, precursor, publicize, spokesman **10** forerunner, foreshadow

heraldic *border:* **7** bordure *cross:* **6** fleury, formée, moline, pommée **8** fourchée *term:* **4** bend, fess, orle, pale, seme, vert **5** crest, flank, gules **6** argent, blazon, canton, charge, device, dexter, emblem, impale, manche, sejant, voided, volant **7** chevron, nombril, passant, purpure, rampant, saltire, statant **8** guardant, sinister, tincture **9** regardant **10** escutcheon

heraldry 6 armory **9** pageantry

herb 3 oca **4** dill, flax, forb, hemp, leek, mint, nard, sage, wort **5** basil, chive, tansy, thyme **6** allium, arnica, borage, catnip, endive, eryngo, fennel, garlic, hyssop, lovage, orpine, squill, yarrow **7** boneset, caraway, catmint, chervil, chicory, comfrey, episcia, ginseng, milfoil, mullein, oregano, parsley, pinesap, pussley, salsify, sanicle **8** angelica, camomile, capsicum, cardamom, centaury, cilantro, costmary, feverfew, freewort, hepatica, lungwort, mandrake, marjoram, origanum, pokeweed, purslane, rapeseed, selfheal, tarragon, turmeric, euphrasy, valerian, woodruff, wormwood **9** birthwort, bush basil, chamomile, patchouli, spikenard **10** basil thyme **12** balm of Gilead *mythical:* **4** moly *poisonous:* **7** aconite, dogbane, hemlock, henbane **8** veratrum **9** hellebore

herbicide 6 dioxin, diquat, diuron **7** monuron **8** picloram, simazine **11** Agent Orange

Herculean 4 huge, vast **5** giant **7** arduous, immense, mammoth, titanic **8** colossal, enormous, gigantic, powerful **10** formidable, superhuman

Hercules see HERACLES

herd 3 mob **4** bevy, lead **5** covey, crowd, drive, drove, flock, swarm **6** gather, throng **9** associate, multitude

herdsman 6 Boötes, cowboy **7** breeder **8** shepherd

here and there 6 passim **7** at times **9** sometimes **11** irregularly

hereditary 6 inborn, inbred, innate, lineal **7** genetic **9** ancestral, inherited **10** congenital **11** traditional, transmitted

heredity 7 lineage **8** ancestry **9** tradition **11** inheritance *unit:* **4** gene

heresy 6 schism **7** dissent, fallacy, impiety **9** defection, deviation, misbelief **10** dissidence, heterodoxy, infidelity, radicalism **11** revisionism, unorthodoxy **13** nonconformism, nonconformity

heretic 7 infidel **8** apostate, defector, recusant, renegade **9** dissenter, dissident **10** iconoclast, schismatic, separatist, unbeliever **11** misbeliever, nonbeliever, revisionist **13** nonconformist

heretical 7 infidel **8** apostate **9** dissident, heterodox, miscreant, sectarian **10** dissenting, schismatic, unorthodox **11** revisionist **12** misbelieving **13** nonconformist

heritage 6 legacy **7** bequest **9** patrimony, tradition **10** birthright

Hermes 7 Mercury *attribute:* **7** petasos, petasus **8** caduceus *father:* **4** Zeus **7** Jupiter *mother:* **4** Maia

hermetic 6 closed, occult, secret **7** recluse **8** abstruse, airtight, profound, secluded, solitary **9** recondite **10** cloistered, impervious **11** sequestered

Hermia *beloved:* **8** Lysander *father:* **5** Egeus

Hermione *father:* **8** Menelaus *husband:* **7** Orestes, Pyrrhus **11** Neoptolemus *mother:* **5** Helen

hermit 5 loner **6** cookie **7** eremite, recluse **8** solitary **9** anchorite

hermitage 7 retreat **8** cloister, hideaway **9** monastery

hernia 6 breach **7** rupture **10** protrusion *support:* **5** truss *type:* **6** cystic, hiatal **7** femoral **9** umbilical **10** incisional

hero 4 idol **6** knight **7** demigod, paladin **8** champion **11** protagonist *American:* **6** Bunyan (Paul) **8** Superman *Armenian:* **10** Skanderbeg *Babylonian:* **9** Gilgamesh *Celtic-French:* **7** Tristan **8** Tristram *Crusades:* **7** Tancred **8** Tancredi *English:* **6** Arthur **7** Beowulf **9** Robin Hood

French: 6 Roland **11** Charlemagne **German: 5** Etzel **8** Arminius **9** Siegfried **Greek: 4** Ajax **5** Jason **7** Perseus, Ulysses **8** Achilles, Heracles, Hercules, Leonidas, Odysseus **11** Bellerophon **Hebrew: 5** David **6** Daniel, Samson **Hungarian: 5** Arpad **7** Hunyadi (János) **Irish: 9** Cuchulain, Cuchulinn, Cuchullin **Italian: 7** Orlando **Roman: 7** Romulus **8** Horatius **Scandinavian: 6** Sigurd **9** Siegfried **Scottish: 5** Bruce (Robert) **6** Rob Roy **Spanish: 5** El Cid **Spartan: 8** Leonidas **Trojan: 6** Aeneas, Hector

Herod *daughter:* **6** Salome *father:* **7** Antipas **9** Antipater *kingdom:* **5** Judea **6** Judaea *mother:* **6** Cyprus *son:* **5** Herod (Antipas) **6** Joseph **7** Pheroas **9** Phasaelus

Herodias *daughter:* **6** Salome *father:* **11** Aristobulus *husband:* **5** Herod (Antipas)

heroic 4 bold, huge **5** brave, noble **6** daring, mighty **7** drastic, extreme, radical, valiant **8** colossal, enormous, fearless, gigantic, intrepid, unafraid, valorous **9** dauntless, Herculean, undaunted **10** courageous

heroin 4 gear, skag **5** horse, smack **8** narcotic **11** diamorphine

heroism 5 valor **6** daring, spirit **7** bravery, courage, prowess **8** boldness, chivalry, nobility, valiance **9** gallantry **11** intrepidity

heron relative 5 egret **7** bittern

Hero's lover 7 Leander

herring 7 sardine **8** brisling, pilchard *smoked:* **7** bloater

Herse *father:* **7** Cecrops *sister:* **8** Aglauros *son:* **8** Cephalus

Hersey *novel:* **4** Wall (The) **12** Bell for Adano (A) *town:* **5** Adano

Hesione *brother:* **5** Priam *father:* **8** Laomedon *husband:* **7** Telamon *rescuer:* **8** Heracles, Hercules *son:* **6** Teucer

hesitant 4 slow **5** chary, loath, timid **6** afraid, averse, unsure **7** halting, uneager **9** faltering, reluctant, tentative, uncertain, unwilling **10** irresolute **11** disinclined, vacillating

hesitate 4 balk **5** delay, demur, hedge, pause, stall, stick, waver **6** dawdle, dither, falter, waffle **7** stammer, stutter **8** hang back, hold back **9** temporize, vacillate **12** shilly-shally

Hesperides 6 nymphs

Hesperus 5 Venus **11** evening star *father:* **8** Astraeus *mother:* **3** Eos

Hesse *novel* **6** Demian **10** Siddhartha **11** Steppenwolf **12** Magister Ludi

Hestia 5 Vesta *father:* **6** Cronus, Saturn *mother:* **4** Rhea

heterodox 9 dissident, heretical, sectarian **10** schismatic, unorthodox **13** nonconformist

heterodoxy 6 heresy, schism **7** dissent **9** misbelief **10** dissidence **13** nonconformism, nonconformity

heterogeneous 5 mixed **6** motley, sundry, varied **7** diverse, various **8** assorted **9** disparate **12** conglomerate

het up 5 irate, upset **7** excited **8** agitated

hew 3 axe, cut **4** chop, fell, form **5** shape, stick **6** adhere **7** conform, cut down

hex 4 jinx **5** charm, curse, spell, witch **6** voodoo, whammy **7** bad luck, bewitch, enchant **9** sorceress **11** enchantment, enchantress

heyday 4 acme, peak **5** prime **6** height, zenith **9** high point

Hezekiah *father:* **4** Ahaz **7** Neariah *mother:* **3** Abi *son:* **8** Manasseh *wife:* **9** Hephzibah

hiatus 3 gap **5** break, space **6** breach, lacuna **7** interim **8** aperture, downtime, interval **10** suspension **12** interruption **13** discontinuity

Hiawatha *author:* **10** Longfellow (Henry Wadsworth) *grandmother:* **7** Nokomis *mother:* **7** Wenonah *tribe:* **6** Ojibwa, Ojibwe **7** Ojibway *wife:* **9** Minnehaha

hibernal 6 wintry **8** winterly

Hibernia 4 Eire, Erin **7** Ireland

hick 4 rube **5** yokel **6** rustic **7** bumpkin, hayseed **8** cornball **10** clodhopper, provincial

hidden 5 privy **6** buried, covert, occult, secret, veiled **7** obscure **8** obscured, shrouded, ulterior **9** concealed **11** undisclosed *combining form:* **6** crypto, krypto

hide 3 fur **4** bury, lurk, mask, pelt, skin, veil **5** cache, cloak, cover, inter, shade, stash **6** harbor, lie low, screen, shroud **7** conceal, cover up, leather, obscure, seclude, secrete, shelter **8** ensconce

hideaway see HIDEOUT

hidebound 8 obdurate **9** parochial **10** inflexible, provincial **11** reactionary, straitlaced **12** conservative, narrow-minded **13** straightlaced

hideous 4 ugly **5** awful, gross, lurid, nasty **6** grisly, horrid **7** ghastly, hateful **8** gruesome, horrible, shocking, terrible **9** appalling, dismaying, frightful, loathsome, monstrous, offensive, repellent, repugnant, repulsive, revolting, sickening **10** disgusting, horrifying

hideout 3 den **4** lair **5** cache, haven **6** covert, refuge **7** retreat, shelter **9** hermitage, safe house, sanctuary

hie 3 run **4** dash, push, trot **5** hurry, scoot **6** hasten, hustle

hierarch 4 boss, head **5** chief **6** honcho, leader, master **7** headman **9** chieftain **10** high priest

hierarchy 5 group, order, ranks **6** ladder, system **7** pyramid **9** food chain, structure **11** bureaucracy **12** pecking order

hieratic 6 formal **8** priestly, stylized **10** priestlike, sacerdotal

high 4 tall **5** drunk, giddy, grand, lofty, noble, tipsy **6** elated, raised, stoned, treble, zonked **7** drugged, keyed up, soaring, supreme **8** abstruse, elevated, eloquent, euphoric, hopped-up, piercing, towering **9** climactic, delirious, prominent, spaced-out **11** extravagant, intoxicated *combining form:* **4** alti

high ___ 3 hat, tea **4** five, noon, road, sign, tech, tide, time **5** chair, heels, jinks **6** priest, roller, school

high-and-mighty 5 bossy, proud **6** lordly **7** haughty **8** arrogant, cavalier, insolent, superior **9** imperious **10** disdainful **11** domineering, overbearing **12** supercilious

highball 3 fly, run **4** dash, rush, whiz **5** hurry, speed **6** barrel, hustle, signal **7** hotfoot **8** cocktail

highboy 5 chest **6** bureau **7** dresser **9** furniture

highbrow 4 snob **7** egghead **8** cerebral, cultured, educated **9** intellect **12** intellectual

high-class 7 elegant **8** five-star, superior **9** exclusive, exquisite, first-rate, patrician **11** fashionable **12** aristocratic **13** sophisticated

highest 3 top **5** chief **6** apical, upmost **7** exalted, supreme, topmost **9** topdrawer, uppermost **10** top-ranking *point:* **4** acme, apex **5** crest **6** summit, zenith **8** pinnacle

highfalutin 5 fancy, windy **6** florid **7** aureate, flowery, fustian, orotund, pompous **8** affected **9** bombastic, grandiose, overblown, rhapsodic **10** oratorical, rhetorical **11** declamatory, pretentious

high-flown 5 showy, tumid, windy **6** turgid **7** aureate, flowery, fustian, orotund, pompous, swollen **8** elevated, inflated, sonorous **9** bombastic, grandiose, overblown **10** flamboyant **11** declamatory, pretentious **12** magniloquent, ostentatious **13** grandiloquent

high-handed 5 bossy **8** dogmatic, imperial **9** arbitrary, imperious **10** autocratic, disdainful, imperative, peremptory **11** dictatorial, domineering, magisterial, overbearing

high-hat 4 snub **6** slight, snobby, snooty **7** disdain, haughty **8** arrogant, snobbish **9** conceited, disregard **11** pretentious **12** supercilious

high jinks 3 fun **6** antics **7** fooling, revelry **9** horseplay, rowdiness, whoop-de-do

Highlander 4 Gael, Scot

highlight 4 mark **5** focus **6** accent, stress **7** feature **8** point out **9** emphasize, underline **10** accentuate, focal point

high-minded 5 lofty, moral, noble **7** ethical, upright **8** elevated **10** principled

high-muck-a-muck 3 VIP **5** nabob **6** bigwig **7** big shot, notable

high-pitched 6 shrill **7** excited **8** agitated, feverish, frenetic, piercing

high point 3 top **4** acme, peak **6** apogee, summit, zenith **8** best part, pinnacle

high-powered 6 driven, strong **7** dynamic **8** animated, forceful, vigorous **9** energetic, strenuous **10** aggressive, compelling **12** enterprising

high-pressure 8 forceful **9** insistent, stressful **10** aggressive

high roller 7 gambler, spender, wastrel **8** prodigal **10** big spender, profligate, squanderer **11** spendthrift

high sign 3 nod, tip **4** wink **5** alarm **6** signal, tipoff **7** gesture, warning

Highsmith novel 11 Ripley's Game **16** Talented Mr. Ripley (The)

high-sounding 7 pompous **8** affected, imposing, inflated, puffed-up **9** grandiose, overblown **11** pretentious

high-spirited 4 bold **5** brash, fiery, jolly, merry **6** bubbly, daring, joyful, lively, plucky, spunky **7** excited, gleeful **9** ebullient, energetic, exuberant, vivacious **12** effervescent, lighthearted

high-strung 4 edgy, taut **5** hyper, jumpy, nervy, tense, tight, wired **6** touchy **7** fidgety, jittery, keyed up, nervous, uptight **8** restless **9** excitable, sensitive

hightail it 3 run **4** bolt, dash, flee **5** scoot, scram **6** get out, run off **7** take off **8** clear out **9** skedaddle

highway 4 pike, road **5** track **6** artery **8** corridor, turnpike **10** interstate **12** thoroughfare *German:* **8** autobahn *Italian:* **10** autostrada

highwayman 5 thief **6** bandit, robber **7** brigand

hijack 5 seize, steal **6** abduct, kidnap **8** take over **10** commandeer **11** appropriate

hike 4 jump, rove, snap, trek, walk **5** boost, raise, tramp, tromp **6** jack up, rise up, travel **7** journey, traipse, upgrade **8** backpack, increase

hilarious 5 funny, merry **7** comical

8 humorous, mirthful 9 laughable, priceless 10 rollicking

hilarity 4 glee 5 cheer, mirth 6 gaiety 7 delight 8 jocosity, laughter 9 merriment 12 cheerfulness

hill 4 bank, bump, cock, dune, heap, knob, pile, rick, rise 5 bluff, butte, knoll, mound, ridge, shock, slope, stack 6 cuesta, height 7 hummock, incline 8 mountain 9 elevation, monadnock *African veld:* 5 kopje 6 koppie *Boston:* 6 Bunker *craggy:* 3 tor *Cuba:* 7 San Juan *D.C.:* 7 Capitol *elongate:* 7 drumlin *level-topped:* 4 mesa 5 butte *of stratified drift:* 4 kame *rounded:* 5 swell *sand:* 4 dune *small:* 5 knoll, kopje, mound 6 koppie *surrounded by ice:* 7 nunatak

hillbilly 4 rube 5 yokel 6 rustic 7 bumpkin, hayseed 10 clodhopper 12 backwoodsman

hillock 4 rise 5 knoll, mound

hillside 5 slope *Scottish:* 4 brae

hilt 4 grip, haft 6 handle 8 handgrip

Himalayan country 5 Nepal 6 Bhutan

hind 3 doe 4 back, deer, rear 5 after 7 grouper 9 posterior *mate:* 4 hart

hinder 4 balk, curb, mire 5 block, check, delay, deter 6 baffle, burden, fetter, hamper, hold up, impede, retard, thwart 7 inhibit, prevent, shackle, trammel 8 handicap, hold back, obstruct, restrain 9 frustrate, hamstring, interfere, interrupt

hindmost 3 end 4 back, last, rear 5 after, final 6 latter 7 closing 8 farthest, terminal, ultimate 9 posterior 10 concluding

hindquarters 8 haunches

hindrance 3 bar 4 snag 8 obstacle 9 impedance 10 impediment 11 obstruction

Hindu *age:* 4 yuga *ascetic:* 4 yogi 5 fakir, swami *caste (varna):* 5 Sudra 6 Vaisya 7 Brahman 9 Kshatriya *class:* 5 caste, varna *community:* 6 ashram *demon:* 4 Rahu 6 Ravana *essence:* 5 atman *force:* 5 karma *garment:* 4 sari *gentleman:* 4 babu *god:* 4 deva, Siva 5 Shiva 6 Brahma, Vishnu *goddess:* 4 devi *goddess of beauty:* 7 Lakshmi *goddess of destruction:* 4 Kali *god of destruction:* 4 Siva 5 Shiva *god of fire:* 4 Agni *god of love:* 4 Kama *god of the heavens:* 7 Krishna *god of war:* 6 Skanda 10 Karttikeya *god of wisdom:* 6 Ganesa, Ganesh *hell:* 6 Naraka *holy man:* 5 sadhu *instrument:* 5 sitar, tabla *leader:* 6 Gandhi (Mahatma) *lowest caste:* 5 Sudra *nobleman:* 4 raja 5 rajah *philosophy:* 7 Vedanta *precept:* 5 sutra *prince:* 4 raja 5 rajah 8 maharaja 9 maharajah *queen:* 4 rani 5 ranee 8 maharani 9 maharanee *salvation:* 7 nirvana *scripture:* 4 Veda 6 Purana 12 Bhagavad Gita *social group:* 5 caste, varna *teacher:* 4 guru 5 swami 9 maharishi *term of respect:* 5 sahib *title:* 3 sri *treatise:* 9 Upanishad *twice-born:* 6 Vaisya 7 Brahman 9 Kshatriya

hinge 4 pawl 5 joint, mount 12 turning point *kind:* 4 butt 5 piano 10 hook-and-eye

hint 3 cue, tip 4 clue, dash, sign, wisp 5 imply, taste, tinge, touch, trace 6 allude, notion, shadow, tipoff 7 inkling, soupçon, suggest 8 allusion, indicate, innuendo, intimate 9 insinuate, scintilla, suspicion 10 indication, intimation, suggestion 11 implication, insinuation

hinterland 4 bush 6 sticks 8 frontier, interior 9 backwater, backwoods, boondocks, up-country 10 wilderness 11 backcountry

hip 3 hot 4 chic, coxa 5 aware, savvy 6 haunch, trendy, with-it 7 tuned in 11 fashionable *bone:* 5 ilium, pubis 6 pelvis 7 ischium *cattle:* 5 thurl *disorder:* 8 sciatica

hippie 8 bohemian, longhair 11 flower child 13 nonconformist

Hippocratic ___ 4 oath

Hippodamia *father:* 8 Oenomaus *husband:* 6 Pelops 9 Pirithous 10 Peirithous *son:* 6 Atreus 8 Thyestes

Hippolytus *father:* 7 Theseus *mother:* 7 Antiope 9 Hippolyte *stepmother:* 7 Phaedra

hire 3 fee, pay 4 rent, wage 5 lease, wages 6 employ, engage, retain, sign on, take on 7 charter, payment, recruit 8 contract 10 employment 11 contract for

hireling 4 hack 6 worker 7 servant 8 employee 9 mercenary

Hirschfeld's daughter 4 Nina

hirsute 5 hairy 6 shaggy, woolly 9 whiskered

Hispania 6 Iberia 9 peninsula *part:* 5 Spain 8 Portugal

Hispaniola country 5 Haiti

hiss 3 boo 4 hoot, jeer 5 decry 6 deride, revile, sizzle, wheeze 7 catcall, whisper, whistle 8 sibilate

historian 8 annalist 10 chronicler *American:* 4 Webb (Charles Richard) 5 Adams (Brooks, Charles Kendall, Hannah, Henry, Herbert Baxter), Beard (Charles, Mary), Foote (Shelby) 6 Brooks (Van Wyck), Catton (Bruce), DeVoto (Bernard), Durant (Ariel, Will), Malone (Dumas), Miller (Perry), Muzzey (David), Nevins (Allen), Sarton (George Alfred), Shirer (William), Sparks (Jared), Turner (Frederick Jackson) **7** Ambrose (Stephen), Morison (Samuel Eliot), Parkman (Francis), Ridpath (John Clark), Tuchman (Barbara), Woodson (Carter G.) **8** Bancroft (George), Boorstin (Daniel), Channing (Edward), Commager (Henry Steele), Prescott (William H.), Robinson (James Harvey), Woodward (C. Vann) **10** McCullough (David) **11** Schlesinger (Arthur) *Arab:* **10** Ibn Khaldun *Danish:* **4** Saxo (Grammaticus) *Dutch:* **8** Huizinga (Johan) *English:* **4** Bede (Venerable), Stow (John), Ward (Adolphus) **5** Acton (Lord), Grote (George), Wells (Herbert George) **6** Camden (William), Gibbon (Edward), Keegan (John), Namier (Lewis Bernstein), Stubbs (William), Taylor (A. J. P.) **7** Hakluyt (Richard), Raleigh (Walter), Toynbee (Arnold), Whewell (William) **8** Geoffrey (of Monmouth), Macaulay (Thomas Babington) **9** Holinshed (Raphael), Trevelyan (George) *French:* **5** Bloch (Marc), Renan (Ernest), Taine (Hippolyte) **6** Guizot (François), Thiers (Louis-Adolphe), Volney (Comte de) **7** Braudel (Ferdinand) **8** Hanotaux (Gabriel), Michelet (Jules) *German:* **5** Ranke (Leopold von) **7** Mommsen (Theodor), Niebuhr (Barthold Georg) **8** Spengler (Oswald) *Greek:* **8** Plutarch, Polybius, Xenophon **9** Dionysius, Herodotus **10** Thucydides *Italian:* **4** Vico (Giovanni) **5** Croce (Benedetto) **9** Salvemini (Gaetano) *Jewish:* **8** Josephus (Flavius) *Roman:* **4** Livy **7** Sallust, Tacitus (Cornelius) **9** Suetonius *Scottish:* **7** Carlyle (Thomas) **9** Robertson (William) *Swiss:* **6** Müller (Johannes von) *Welsh:* **7** Nennius

historical period 3 age, era **5** epoch

history 4 past, saga **5** diary **6** annals, memoir, record **7** account, done for, journal **9** chronicle, narrative, treatment **10** chronology

histrionic 5 showy, stagy **6** staged **8** affected, dramatic **10** artificial, theatrical

hit 3 bop, jab, rap **4** bang, bash, bean, biff, blow, bump, bunt, butt, conk, cuff, ding, lick, slap, slug, sock, swat **5** clout, knock, paste, pound, punch, smack, smash, smite, swipe, whack **6** batter, buffet, chance, larrup, strike, stroke, thwack, wallop **7** clobber, sellout, success **8** bludgeon, lambaste **9** collision, sensation *baseball:* **5** homer, liner **6** double, single, triple **7** home run **9** line drive *golf ball:* **5** shank

hitch 4 jerk, join, halt, hook, knot, lift, limp, snag, yoke **5** delay, thumb, unite **6** attach, couple, fasten, hobble, tether **7** connect, harness **8** make fast, stoppage **10** connection, difficulty, impediment **11** obstruction **12** entanglement

Hitchcock, Alfred *film:* **4** Rope **5** Birds (The), Topaz **6** Frenzy, Marnie, Psycho **7** Rebecca, Vertigo **8** Lifeboat, Sabotage **9** Notorious, Suspicion **10** Rear Window, Spellbound **12** Lady Vanishes (The) **13** To Catch a Thief **14** Shadow of a Doubt **16** North by Northwest *forte:* **8** suspense

hitchhike 5 thumb

hither 4 here **6** nearer **11** to this place

hitherto 5 as yet, so far **7** earlier, thus far, till now **8** formerly, until now **10** previously

Hitler, Adolf *follower:* **4** Nazi *title:* **6** Führer **7** Fuehrer *wife:* **5** Braun (Eva)

hit man 5 bravo **6** killer **7** torpedo **8** assassin, enforcer, murderer **9** cutthroat

hit-or-miss 6 casual, chance, random **7** aimless, erratic **8** careless **9** desultory, haphazard, irregular, unplanned

hive 6 apiary, colony **7** cluster **9** stockpile

HMS Pinafore *composer:* **8** Sullivan (Arthur) *librettist:* **7** Gilbert (W. S.)

hoagie 3 sub **4** hero **5** po'boy **7** grinder, torpedo **8** sandwich **9** submarine

hoar 4 rime **5** frost

hoard 4 save **5** amass, cache, lay by, lay up, stash, stock, store, trove **6** supply **7** collect, lay away, nest egg, reserve **8** squirrel, treasure **9** stockpile **10** accumulate, collection, cumulation **11** aggregation **12** accumulation

hoarder 5 miser **7** scrooge

hoarse 5 gruff, husky, rough, thick **6** croaky **7** grating, rasping, raucous, throaty **8** croaking, gravelly, guttural

hoary 3 old **4** aged **5** stale **6** age-old **7** ancient, antique **8** timeworn **9** venerable

hoax 3 con **4** dupe, fake, fool, gull, sham **5** fraud, phony, trick **6** befool, delude, humbug, take in **7** deceive, mislead **8** flimflam, hoodwink, trickery **9** bamboozle, deception, imposture

Hobbit creator 7 Tolkien (J. R. R.)

hobble 4 lame, limp **6** fetter, hamper, hinder, hog-tie, impede **7** cripple, trammel **8** handicap

hobby 6 falcon **7** pastime, pursuit **8** activity, sideline **9** avocation, diversion

hobgoblin 5 bogey **7** bugaboo

hobnob 3 mix **6** mingle **7** consort **9** associate, rub elbows, socialize 10 fraternize 11 get together

hobo 3 bum 5 gypsy, tramp 7 drifter, floater, swagman, vagrant 8 derelict, vagabond

hock 4 debt, pawn 5 ankle 6 prison

hockey 6 shinny *arena:* 4 rink *cup:* 7 Stanley *implement:* 4 puck 5 stick *official:* 7 referee 8 linesman *player:* 3 Orr (Bobby), Roy (Patrick) 4 Bure (Pavel), Fuhr (Grant), Howe (Gordie), Hull (Bobby, Brett), Jagr (Jaromir), wing 5 Bossy (Mike), Bucyk (John), Hasek (Dominik), Kurri (Jari), Maruk (Dennis), Sakic (Joe), Shore (Eddie), Shutt (Steve) 6 center, Clarke (Bobby), Coffey (Paul), Dionne (Marcel), Dryden (Ken), goalie, Harvey (Doug), Juneau (Joe), Kariya (Paul), Leetch (Brian), Mikita (Stan), Morenz (Howie), Parent (Bernie), Potvin (Denis), Recchi (Mark), Savard (Denis), Sundin (Mats) 7 Belfour (Ed), Bourque (Ray), Brodeur (Martin), Chelios (Chris), Fedorov (Sergei), forward, Francis (Ron), Gretzky (Wayne), Lafleur (Guy), Lemieux (Claude, Mario), Lindros (Eric), Messier (Mark), Mogilny (Alexander), Richard (Maurice), Richter (Mike), Selanne (Teemu), Stastny (Peter), Yzerman (Steve) 8 Beliveau (Jean), Esposito (Phil, Tony), Forsberg (Peter), Nicholls (Bernie), pointman, Shanahan (Brendan), Trottier (Bryan), Ysebaert (Paul) 9 Hawerchuk (Dale) 10 Carbonneau (Guy), defenseman, goalkeeper *team:* 4 Jets 5 Blues, Kings, Stars 6 Bruins, Devils, Flames, Flyers, Oilers, Sabres, Sharks 7 Canucks, Rangers, Whalers 8 Capitals, Panthers, Penguins, Red Wings, Senators 9 Canadiens, Islanders, Lightning, Nordiques 10 Black Hawks, Maple Leafs, North Stars 11 Mighty Ducks *term:* 3 box 4 cage, goal, puck, rink 5 bandy, bench, check, icing, stick 6 charge, crease, shinny 7 face-off, offside 8 blue line 9 back-check, body-check 10 center line, penalty box *variation of:* 9 broomball

hocus-pocus 4 sham 8 artifice, nonsense, trickery 9 conjuring, deception, imposture 10 mumbo jumbo 11 abracadabra, incantation, legerdemain 13 sleight of hand

hod 4 tray 6 trough 7 scuttle 11 coal scuttle

Hoder, Hoth *brother:* 6 Balder *slayer:* 4 Vali *victim:* 6 Balder

hodgepodge 4 hash 6 jumble, medley 7 mélange, mixture 8 mishmash, mixed

bag 9 patchwork, potpourri 10 assortment, miscellany 11 gallimaufry

hoe 4 till, weed 6 tiller, weeder 9 cultivate

hoedown 9 barn dance 11 contra dance, square dance

hog 3 pig, sow 4 boar 5 swine *family:* 6 Suidae *female:* 3 sow 4 gilt *genus:* 3 Sus *red:* 5 duroc *young:* 5 shoat

hogback 5 crest, ridge

hogshead 3 keg, tun 4 butt, cask 6 barrel 9 container

hog-tie 4 bind 6 fetter 7 shackle, trammel

hogwash 3 rot 4 bunk, slop 5 bilge, hokum, hooey, swill 6 piffle 7 baloney, garbage, rubbish 8 nonsense 9 moonshine, poppycock 10 applesauce, balderdash, flapdoodle, taradiddle 12 gobbledygook

hog wild 5 crazy 6 crazed, madcap 7 berserk

ho-hum 4 dull 5 bored 6 boring 7 tedious 8 tiresome 10 unexciting 11 indifferent

hoi polloi 3 mob 5 horde 6 masses 8 populace 9 multitude 10 lower class 11 proletariat

hoist 4 lift 5 drink, raise, winch 6 lift up, pick up, take up 7 derrick, elevate 8 windlass

hoity-toity 4 smug 5 dizzy, giddy, silly 7 flighty, pompous 9 conceited, frivolous 11 highfalutin

hokey 4 fake, mock, sham 5 banal, bogus, corny, hammy, phony, stale, stagy, trite 6 ersatz, pseudo 7 clichéd 8 cornball, outdated 9 contrived, hackneyed 12 melodramatic

hokum 4 bosh 5 hooey 7 baloney, hogwash 8 malarkey, nonsense 9 moonshine, poppycock 10 applesauce, balderdash, flapdoodle, taradiddle 11 foolishness 12 gobbledygook

hold 3 own 4 bear, deem, grab, grip, keep 5 carry, clamp, clasp, cling, grasp, gripe, judge, sense, think, value 6 arrest, clench, clinch, clutch, detain, harbor, regard, retain 7 contain, convene, convoke, fermata, grapple, keep out, possess, reserve, support, sustain 8 keep back, maintain, preserve, restrict *close:* 6 cuddle *dear:* 7 cherish *in check:* 7 repress *in common:* 5 share *out:* 4 last 6 endure *together:* 4 bond 5 clamp 6 fasten *wrestling:* 6 nelson 8 headlock, scissors 10 full nelson, half nelson

hold back 4 curb, keep, stop 5 check, delay 6 bridle, detain, impede, retain 7 inhibit, keep out, prevent, refrain, reserve 8 restrain, suppress, withhold 9 constrain

hold forth 4 rant 5 orate, speak, spout
7 declaim, expound, lecture
8 harangue, proclaim 9 expatiate
10 dilate upon

hold off 4 stay, wait 5 defer, delay, pause,
repel 6 rebuff, resist 7 abstain, adjourn,
repulse, suspend 8 hesitate, postpone,
prorogue 9 withstand 11 discontinue

hold up 3 rob 4 halt, lift, stay 5 check,
defer, delay, raise 6 hinder, impede, put
off, retard 7 support, suspend 8 postpone, prorogue, slow down

hole 3 den, gap, jam, pit 4 cave, flaw,
lair, rent, spot, void 5 fault, niche
6 breach, burrow, cavity, cranny,
defect, eyelet, lacuna, outlet 7 dilemma, opening, orifice 8 aperture, weakness 9 perforate 10 excavation, interstice 11 perforation, predicament

hole in one 3 ace

holiday 5 leave 6 May Day 7 Flag Day
8 Labor Day, New Year's, vacation
9 Christmas, Halloween 10 Father's
Day, Mother's Day 11 Memorial Day,
Veterans Day 12 All Saints' Day,
Groundhog Day, Thanksgiving 13 Presidents' Day, St. Patrick's Day, Valentine's Day *British:* 9 Boxing Day *Canadian:* 11 Dominion Day, Victoria Day
Jewish: 8 Passover

holiness 5 piety 6 purity 8 devotion,
divinity, sanctity 9 beatitude 11 religiosity 12 consecration, spirituality

Holland see NETHERLANDS

holler 3 cry 4 call, yell 5 shout 6 bellow,
clamor, cry out, outcry 7 call out
8 complain 9 complaint

hollow 3 dip, sag 4 void 5 basin, empty,
false 6 cavity, ravine, sunken, vacant
7 concave, echoing, sinkage 8 sinkhole,
thorough 9 cavernous, concavity
10 depression, sepulchral *out:* 3 dig, gut
4 mine 5 gouge 8 excavate

holly 4 tree 5 shrub *genus:* 4 Ilex

holocaust 4 fire 7 inferno 8 genocide
9 sacrifice 10 mass murder 11 destruction 13 conflagration

Holofernes' slayer 6 Judith

holy 6 adored, divine, sacred 7 angelic,
blessed, revered, sainted, saintly, sublime 8 hallowed 9 glorified, religious,
spiritual, venerated, worshiped 10 reverenced, sacrosanct, sanctified 11 consecrated *combining form:* 5 hagio, hiero
communion: 9 Eucharist *oil:* 6 chrism
person: 5 saint 6 zaddik 7 tzaddik *Spirit:*
9 Paraclete *vessel:* 5 grail 7 chalice
8 ciborium

holy place 6 church, shrine, temple
7 sanctum 9 sanctuary

Holy Roman Emperor 4 Karl, Otto

5 Adolf, Franz, Henry, Louis 6 Albert,
Arnulf, Conrad, Joseph, Lothar, Ludwig, Philip, Rudolf, Rupert, Wenzel
7 Charles, Francis, Leopold, Lothair
8 Heinrich 9 Ferdinand, Frederick,
Friedrich, Sigismund 10 Maximilian
11 Charlemagne

Holy Thursday 6 Maundy (Thursday)
9 Ascension (Day)

holy writ 5 Bible 9 Scripture

homage 5 honor 6 praise 7 respect, tribute 9 deference, obeisance, reverence

hombre 3 cat, guy, lad, man 4 buck,
chap, dude, gent, stud 6 fellow, honcho
7 comrade

home 4 digs, land, site 5 abode, haunt,
house, range 6 family, hearth 7 country,
habitat, housing 8 domicile, dwelling,
locality 9 household, residence
10 fatherland, habitation, motherland
12 headquarters *country:* 5 cabin 7 cottage 8 bungalow

homeless 5 stray 6 exiled 7 outcast,
vagrant 8 derelict 9 abandoned, displaced, wandering 12 dispossessed

homely 4 cozy 5 plain 6 direct, modest,
simple 7 natural 8 familiar, ordinary
11 comfortable, commonplace 12 unattractive 13 unpretentious

Homer epic 5 Iliad 7 Odyssey

homesickness 7 longing 9 nostalgia

homespun 5 plain 6 fabric, folksy, simple 8 ordinary 9 practical 13 unpretentious

Home, Sweet Home *music:* 6 Bishop
(Henry) *words:* 5 Payne (John Howard)

homicidal 6 bloody 8 sanguine 9 murdering, murderous 10 sanguinary
11 sanguineous 12 bloodthirsty

homicide 5 blood 6 killer, murder, slayer
7 killing 8 foul play, murderer 9 manslayer 12 manslaughter

homily 6 sermon 7 lecture 9 discourse

homogeneous 7 uniform 10 consistent

Homo sapiens 3 man 7 mankind
8 humanity 9 humankind, human race

homunculus 5 dwarf, pygmy 6 midget,
peewee 7 manikin 8 Tom Thumb

honcho 4 boss, head 5 chief 6 leader,
master 7 big shot, foreman, headman
8 hierarch, overseer 9 chieftain

Honduras *capital:* 11 Tegucigalpa *city:*
7 La Ceiba 9 Choluteca 10 El Progreso
12 San Pedro Sula *coast:* 8 Mosquito
discoverer: 8 Columbus (Christopher)
Indian people: 4 Maya 5 Mayan *language:* 7 Spanish *monetary unit:* 7 lempira *neighbor:* 9 Guatemala, Nicaragua
10 El Salvador *river:* 4 Coco, Ulúa
5 Aguán 6 Patuca *sea:* 9 Caribbean

hone 4 edge, whet 6 finish, polish,

refine, smooth 7 perfect, sharpen
9 whetstone
honest 4 fair, just, open, real, true
5 frank, plain 6 candid, simple 7 genuine, sincere, upright 8 innocent, reliable, truthful 9 objective, reputable, unfeigned, veracious 10 creditable, forthright, legitimate, scrupulous
11 respectable 12 praiseworthy 13 conscientious, dispassionate, unimpeachable
honesty 4 herb 5 honor 6 candor, virtue
7 probity 8 fairness, goodness, justness, veracity 9 integrity, rectitude, sincerity
11 uprightness 12 truthfulness
honey *combining form:* 4 meli, mell
5 melli *drink:* 4 mead
honeybee genus 4 Apis
honeycomb 3 pit 4 fill, fret 5 cells
6 impair, infest, riddle, weaken 7 subvert 9 perforate
honeydew 5 melon
honeyed 5 sweet 6 golden, liquid, mellow 9 sweetened 10 flattering 11 mellifluous
honeysuckle 6 azalea 9 columbine
13 pinxter flower
honk 4 blow, toot 5 blare, blast 7 trumpet
honky-tonk 4 dive 5 joint 7 hangout
9 juke joint, roadhouse 11 barrelhouse
honor 4 fete, laud 5 adorn, asset, award, badge, exalt, glory, kudos, medal
6 credit, esteem, homage, praise, purity, regard, trophy 7 commend, dignify, ennoble, fulfill, glorify, laurels, respect
8 accolade, approval, carry out, chastity, decorate, devotion, good name
9 adulation, deference, integrity, privilege, recognize, reverence 10 admiration, decoration, reputation, veneration
11 distinction, distinguish, recognition
12 commendation
honorable 4 just, true 5 moral, right
6 honest, worthy 7 ethical, upright
8 laudable 9 dignified 10 creditable, scrupulous 11 illustrious 13 conscientious
honorarium 7 payment 8 gratuity 10 recompense 12 compensation 13 consideration
hooch 6 liquor, rotgut 7 bootleg
8 dwelling, home brew 9 firewater, moonshine 11 bathtub gin
hood 4 cowl, thug 5 tough 6 bonnet, helmet 7 capuche 8 covering, gangster, hooligan 10 delinquent
hoodlum 4 punk, thug 5 bully 7 mobster, ruffian 8 criminal, gangster, hooligan
10 delinquent
hoodoo 3 hex 4 jinx, juju, rock 5 curse,

haunt, hokum, magic, spell, spook
6 harass, voodoo, whammy 7 bewitch, evil eye, sorcery, terrify, torment
8 nonsense 9 conjuring 10 black magic, hocus-pocus, mumbo jumbo, witchcraft
hoodwink 3 con 4 dupe, fool, gull, hoax
5 trick 6 befool 7 deceive, mislead
8 flimflam 9 bamboozle
hooey 3 rot 4 bunk 5 bilge 6 bunkum
7 baloney, hogwash 8 claptrap, malarkey, nonsense
hoof 4 foot, walk 5 troop 7 traipse
8 ambulate *cloven:* 5 cloot
hoofer 6 dancer 7 danseur 8 coryphée, danseuse 9 ballerina, tap dancer
hooflike 6 ungual
hook 3 nab, nip 4 gore, hasp 5 catch, curve, hitch, pinch, steal 6 anchor, fasten, pilfer 7 hamulus 8 crotchet *a fish:*
4 gaff, snag *for keys:* 10 chatelaine
hooklike 7 falcate 8 unciform, uncinate
part: 5 uncus 7 hamulus
hookup 7 circuit, linkage 8 alliance
10 assemblage, connection 11 affiliation, association, combination, conjunction, partnership
hooky 6 truant 7 truancy 8 truantry
hooligan see HOODLUM
hoop 4 band, ring 6 circle 7 circlet
hoopla 4 bash, fuss, stir, to-do 6 bustle, frolic 7 revelry, shindig, whoopee 8 ballyhoo, wingding 9 commotion, festivity, merriment, promotion 13 entertainment
hoops 5 b-ball 10 basketball
hooray 3 rah, yay 5 cheer, huzza 6 huzzah, yippee 7 acclaim 10 hallelujah
hoosegow 3 jug, pen 4 brig, cage, coop, jail, keep, stir 5 clink, pokey 6 cooler, lockup, prison 7 slammer 8 bastille, big house 9 calaboose, jailhouse 12 penitentiary
Hoosier State 7 Indiana
hoot 3 bit, boo, jot 4 hiss, iota, jeer, whit
5 laugh, scrap, shout, whoop 6 assail, deride, heckle 7 catcall, modicum
8 particle
hooter 3 owl 5 owlet
Hoover Dam lake 4 Mead
hop 4 jump, leap, trip, vine 5 bound, dance 6 bounce, spring, wait on
7 rebound 8 jump over
hope 4 goal, wish 5 await, dream, faith, trust 6 aspire, desire, expect 7 count on, longing, promise 8 ambition, optimism, prospect 9 count upon 10 anticipate, aspiration, confidence *loss of:*
7 despair
hopeful 4 rosy 5 eager, sunny 6 bright, cheery, golden, seeker, upbeat

7 assured **8** aspirant, aspiring **9** candidate, confident, expectant, promising **10** auspicious, contestant, optimistic, propitious **11** encouraging **12** advantageous

hopeless 4 glum, lost, vain **6** futile, gloomy, morose **7** forlorn **8** downcast **9** desperate, incurable, insoluble **10** despairing, despondent, impossible **11** ineffectual, irreparable, pessimistic **12** incorrigible, irredeemable, irremediable

hoper 7 truster **8** optimist **9** expectant, Pollyanna

hopped-up 4 high **5** giddy **6** stoned, zonked **7** drugged, excited **9** delirious **12** enthusiastic

hopper 3 box, mix **4** frog, hare, tank, toad **5** bunny, chute **6** rabbit **7** cricket **10** freight car, receptacle

___ **Hopper 5** Grace (Murray), Hedda **6** Edward

hopping 4 busy **5** irate, livid **6** lively **7** furious **9** extremely, violently **10** infuriated

Horae 4 Dike **6** Eirene **7** Eunomia, seasons

Horam *kingdom:* **5** Gezer *slayer:* **6** Joshua

horde 3 mob **4** army **5** crowd, crush, drove, press, swarm **6** throng **9** multitude

horizon 4 goal **5** limit, range, reach, scope, vista **6** extent **7** purview, skyline **8** prospect **11** perspective

horizontal 4 flat **5** level **8** parallel

hormone 4 ACTH **5** kinin **6** estrin **7** estriol, estrone, gastrin, insulin, relaxin **8** autacoid, estrogen, glucagon, kallidin, secretin *female:* **8** estrogen *insect:* **8** ecdysone *pituitary:* **8** oxytocin

horn 4 toot **5** cornu **6** antler, klaxon, shofar **7** trumpet **10** cornucopia, projection *ancient Greek:* **5** rhyta (plural) **6** rhyton *animal:* **6** antler

___ **Hornblower 7** Horatio

horn in 6 meddle **7** intrude, obtrude **9** insinuate, interfere, interlope, interrupt

hornlike 8 corneous **10** keratinous

hornswoggle 3 con **4** dupe, fool, gull, hoax **5** trick **7** deceive **8** flimflam, hoodwink **9** bamboozle

horrendous 5 awful **7** fearful, ghastly, heinous, hideous **8** alarming, dreadful, gruesome, horrible, horrific, shocking, terrible **9** abhorrent, appalling, execrable, frightful, repugnant, revolting **11** distressing, unspeakable

horrible 4 grim **5** awful, lurid **6** grisly **7** fearful, ghastly, hateful, hellish, hideous **8** dreadful, gruesome, shocking **9** abhorrent, appalling, frightful, loathsome, repellent, repugnant, repulsive, revolting **10** abominable, disgusting, terrifying

horrid 5 nasty **7** noisome **8** shocking **9** loathsome, offensive, repulsive, sickening **10** detestable, disgusting

horrific 5 awful **7** fearful **8** dreadful, shocking, terrible **9** appalling, dismaying, frightful, harrowing

horrify 5 daunt, shock **6** appall, dismay **7** disgust

horrifying 4 grim **5** awful, lurid **6** grisly **7** ghastly, hideous **8** gruesome, terrible **9** appalling, atrocious

horror 4 fear, hate, pain **5** alarm, dread, panic, shock **6** dismay, fright, hatred, terror **7** disgust **8** aversion, loathing **9** repulsion, revulsion **10** abhorrence, repugnance **11** abomination, detestation, trepidation

hors d'oeuvre 4 whet **6** canape **7** crudité **9** antipasto, appetizer

horse 4 buck, roan **5** bronc, pacer, steed **6** bronco, brumby, equine **7** cavalry, palfrey, sawbuck, trestle, trotter **8** footrope, jackstay, palomino, skewbald, stallion, traveler *Australian-bred:* **5** waler *battle:* **7** charger *breed:* **5** pinto **6** Morgan **7** Arabian, Belgian, Iceland **8** Palomino, Shetland **9** Appaloosa, Percheron **10** Lippizaner **12** standardbred, Thoroughbred *champion:* **7** Man o' War **8** Affirmed, Citation **10** Seabiscuit **11** Seattle Slew, Secretariat, Smarty Jones *collar part:* **4** hame *color:* **3** bay **6** sorrel **8** chestnut *combining form:* **4** hipp **5** hippo *covering:* **8** trapping *draft:* **10** Clydesdale *extinct:* **8** eohippus *farm:* **6** dobbin *female:* **4** mare **5** filly *foot part:* **7** pastern *gait:* **4** trot **6** canter, gallop *gear:* **3** bit **4** rein **6** saddle **7** harness **9** checkrein *leg joint:* **7** fetlock *leg part:* **6** gaskin **7** gambrel *male:* **4** colt **8** stallion *mark:* **5** blaze *of the movies:* **4** Fury **6** Flicka, Silver **7** Trigger **8** Champion **11** Black Beauty *race:* **5** Ascot, derby **7** Belmont **9** Preakness *rump:* **7** crupper *small:* **4** pony **6** garron, jennet *spotted:* **5** pinto **7** piebald *tan:* **8** palomino *thoroughbred:* **8** hotblood *war:* **8** destrier *wild:* **7** mustang

horsefeathers 3 rot **4** bull, bunk **5** bilge, hokum, hooey, trash **6** bunkum, drivel, piffle **7** baloney, garbage, hogwash, rubbish, twaddle **8** claptrap, flimflam, nonsense, tommyrot **9** poppycock **10** applesauce, balderdash

horseman 5 rider **6** cowboy **7** vaquero **8** cavalier **9** caballero, chevalier **10** equestrian

horsemanship 6 manège 10 equitation

horse opera 5 oater 7 western

horseplay 7 fooling 8 clowning, rowdyism 9 high jinks, rowdiness 10 buffoonery, roughhouse 11 shenanigans 12 roughhousing

horseshoer 6 smithy 10 blacksmith

hortative 8 advisory 9 exhorting, homiletic

horticulturist 7 Burbank (Luther)

Horus *brother:* 6 Anubis *father:* 6 Osiris *mother:* 4 Isis *victim:* 3 Set 4 Seth

hose 4 sock, tube, wash 5 cheat, spray, trick, water 6 tights 8 stocking

hoser 6 barfly, boozer 7 redneck

hospice see HOSTEL

hospitable 4 kind, open 6 social 7 cordial 8 friendly, generous, gracious 9 convivial, receptive, welcoming 10 gregarious

hospital 6 clinic 7 lazaret 9 infirmary, lazaretto *attendant:* 7 orderly *ship's:* 7 sickbay

Hospitallers' island 5 Malta 6 Rhodes

host 4 army 5 array, cloud, crowd, emcee, flock, horde 6 angels, legion, myriad, scores, server 7 present, receive 8 assemble 9 innkeeper, introduce, moderator, multitude, presenter

hostage 4 pawn 5 token 6 pledge, surety 7 captive, earnest 8 guaranty, prisoner, security 9 guarantee

hostel 3 inn 4 stay 5 lodge 6 tavern, travel 7 auberge, lodging 11 caravansary, public house

hostile 4 anti, mean 5 enemy 6 bitter, fierce 7 adverse, opposed, warlike 8 contrary, inimical, opposite 9 bellicose, combative, resistant, resisting 10 malevolent, pugnacious, unfriendly 11 belligerent, contentious 12 antagonistic 13 argumentative

hostility 3 war 6 animus, enmity, hatred, rancor 7 ill will 8 conflict 9 antipathy 10 aggression, antagonism, opposition, resistance 12 belligerence

hot 3 new 4 fast, heat, sexy 5 angry, close, eager, fiery, lucky, spicy 6 ardent, baking, banned, heated, hectic, on fire, raging, stolen, sultry, torrid, urgent 7 boiling, burning, excited, fevered, illicit, lustful, peppery, popular, pungent, zealous 8 broiling, feverish, in demand, scalding, sizzling, tropical, vehement 9 energized, lecherous, scorching 10 blistering, contraband, passionate, sweltering 11 radioactive

hot air 4 bosh 6 bunkum 7 blather, prattle, twaddle 8 malarkey, nonsense 9 empty talk, poppycock 10 double-talk

hotbed 3 hub 4 core, seat 5 heart 6 center 7 nucleus 10 focal point 11 nerve center

hot-blooded 5 fiery 6 ardent 7 burning, fervent, flaming 9 excitable, impetuous, impulsive 10 passionate 11 impassioned 12 high-spirited

hotchpotch see HODGEPODGE

hot dog 5 frank 6 weenie, wiener, wienie 7 sausage, show-off 11 frankfurter, wienerwurst

hotel 3 inn 5 lodge 6 tavern 7 auberge, hospice, pension 8 motor inn 11 public house 12 lodging house, rooming house 13 boardinghouse *chain:* 5 Hyatt 6 Hilton, Ramada, Westin 7 Days Inn 8 Marriott, Radisson, Sheraton, Stouffer 10 Holiday Inn 11 Best Western, Four Seasons *inferior:* 7 fleabag 9 flophouse

hothead 5 rebel 7 fanatic, inciter, radical 8 agitator 9 demagogue, firebrand 10 incendiary 12 rabble-rouser, troublemaker 13 revolutionary

hotheaded 4 rash 5 brash, fiery, hasty 6 madcap 8 reckless 9 excitable, impetuous, imprudent, impulsive, irritable

hotshot 3 ace 4 star, whiz 5 comer 6 expert, master, wizard 8 virtuoso 10 powerhouse 11 heavyweight

hot-tempered see QUICK-TEMPERED

hot water 3 box, fix, jam 4 bind, hole 6 corner, pickle 7 dilemma, problem, trouble 9 tight spot 10 difficulty 11 predicament

___ Houdini 5 Harry

hound 3 dog, fan 4 bait, buff, ride 5 chivy 6 badger, basset, beagle, bowwow, canine, harass, hassle, heckle, hector, pester, pursue, Talbot 7 devotee 8 bullyrag 9 dachshund, persecute 10 aficionado *Russian:* 6 borzoi

hourglass 5 timer

house 3 cot, hut, ken 4 home, shed 5 abode, board, cabin, dwell, hovel, lodge, put up, shack 6 billet, chalet, harbor, shanty 7 contain, cottage, enclose, mansion, quarter, saltbox, shelter, theater 8 audience, bungalow, domicile, dwelling, quarters 9 residence *clergyman's:* 5 manse 7 rectory 9 parsonage *country:* 5 manor 7 cottage 8 bungalow *dog:* 6 kennel *earth:* 5 adobe *Eskimo:* 5 igloo *mean:* 5 hovel, shack *of prostitution:* 4 crib 6 bagnio 7 brothel 8 bordello *religious:* 5 abbey 6 priory 7 convent, nunnery 9 monastery *rooming:* 5 lodge *Russian:* 5 dacha *small:* 4 camp 5 cabin, shack 6 shanty 7 cottage 8 bungalow *Spanish:* 4 casa

housebreaker 4 yegg **5** thief **7** burglar, prowler **8** picklock

household 4 home **5** folks **6** family, ménage **8** domestic, familiar *gods (Roman):* **5** lares **7** penates

house of worship 6 bethel, chapel, church, mosque, pagoda, shrine, temple **7** chantry, minster, oratory **8** basilica **9** cathedral, sanctuary, synagogue **10** tabernacle **11** conventicle

housing 4 case, room **7** shelter **8** barracks, quarters **9** enclosure

hovel 3 hut, sty **4** dump, shed **5** hutch, shack **6** burrow, pigpen, pigsty, shanty **7** shelter

hover 4 flit, hang **5** dance, drift, float, poise, waver **7** flitter, flutter, suspend **9** fluctuate, hang about

howbeit 3 yet **4** when **5** still, while **6** even if, much as, though **7** whereas **8** after all, although **11** nonetheless **12** nevertheless

however 3 but, yet **4** only **5** still **6** except, though **8** after all **11** nonetheless

howl 3 bay, cry **4** bark, keen, wail, yell, yelp **6** cry out **9** caterwaul

howler 4 flub, gaff, goof **5** boner, fluff, gaffe **6** boo-boo **7** blooper, blunder

huarache 6 sandal

hub 4 axis, core **5** focus, heart, pivot **6** center **8** polestar **10** focal point **11** nerve center *opposite:* **3** rim

hubbub 3 din **4** fuss, stir, to-do **5** babel, furor, hoo-ha, noise **6** clamor, furore, hassle, jangle, pother, racket, rumpus, tumult, uproar **7** turmoil **8** brouhaha, foofaraw **9** commotion, confusion **10** hullabaloo, hurly-burly **11** disturbance, pandemonium

hubris 3 ego **4** gall **5** brass, cheek, nerve, pride **7** conceit, hauteur, swagger **8** audacity, chutzpah **9** arrogance, cockiness, vainglory **11** braggadocio

hubristic 4 vain **5** cocky, proud **7** haughty **8** arrogant, insolent, superior **11** overbearing, overweening **13** overconfident

Huckleberry Finn *author:* **5** Twain (Mark) **7** Clemens (Samuel) *character:* **3** Jim, Tom (Sawyer) **4** Duke, King *river:* **11** Mississippi

huckster 4 hawk, plug, vend **5** pitch **6** dicker, haggle, hawker, peddle, vendor **7** bargain, chaffer, haggler, packman, peddler, promote **8** pitchman

huddle 4 lump, mass **5** bunch, crowd, group, hunch **6** confab, confer, crouch, curl up, gather, parley, powwow **7** cluster, consult, meeting **8** assemble **10** conference, discussion

Hudson's ship 8 Half Moon

hue 4 cast, tint, tone **5** color, shade, shape, tinge, value **6** aspect, manner **8** coloring, tincture **10** coloration, complexion

huff 3 pet **4** blow, gasp, pant, rile, roil, snap, snit, tiff **5** annoy, grate, heave, peeve, pique, storm **6** nettle, put out **7** bluster, inflate **8** irritate

huffy 5 angry, proud, testy **6** piqued, touchy **7** annoyed, fretful, haughty, peevish, prickly, waspish **8** arrogant, petulant, snappish **9** irritable, irritated, querulous

hug 4 hold **5** clasp, press, prize, value **6** clinch, clutch, cuddle, enfold **7** cherish, embrace, envelop, squeeze **8** hold fast, hold onto **12** congratulate

huge 4 vast, wide **5** bulky, giant, grand, great, jumbo **6** heroic, mighty, untold **7** immense, mammoth, massive, titanic **8** colossal, enormous, gigantic, whopping **9** extensive, monstrous **10** monumental, prodigious, stupendous, tremendous **11** magnificent, mountainous

hugeness 8 enormity **9** immensity, magnitude

hugger-mugger 4 hash **6** jumble, muddle, secret, tangle **7** clutter, furtive, jumbled, secrecy **8** confused, covertly, disorder, secretly **9** by stealth, confusion, furtively **10** disordered, disorderly, stealthily, undercover **11** clandestine **13** clandestinely

Hugo, Victor *character:* **6** Javert (Inspector) **7** Cosette, Fantine, Valjean (Jean) **9** Esmeralda, Quasimodo *novel:* **13** Les Misérables **20** Hunchback of Notre Dame (The)

Huguenot 10 Protestant *leader:* **5** Condé (Prince de), Rohan (Henri) **6** Mornay (Philippe) **7** Coligny (Gaspard II de)

Huguenots composer 9 Meyerbeer (Giacomo)

hulk 4 body, loom, ship **5** shell, wreck **8** skeleton **9** shipwreck

hulking 4 huge **5** beefy, bulky, burly, husky **7** immense, mammoth, massive **8** colossal, enormous, gigantic, oversize **9** humongous, lumbering, monstrous, ponderous, strapping **11** heavyweight

hull 3 pod **4** bark, body, case, husk, peel, rind, skin **5** chaff, frame, shell, shuck **6** casing **8** covering **11** decorticate

hullabaloo 3 din **4** to-do **5** hoo-ha, noise **6** clamor, hubbub, jangle, pother, racket, tumult, uproar **8** ballyhoo, foofaraw **9** commotion, hue and cry **11** pandemonium

hum 4 buzz, purr, sing, zing **5** drone **6** murmur **7** vibrate

human 5 being, party **6** mortal, person **7** hominid **8** hominoid **10** individual *race:* **7** mankind

Human Comedy author 6 Balzac (Honoré de) **7** Saroyan (William)

humane 4 kind **6** gentle, kindly, tender **8** merciful **10** altruistic, benevolent, charitable **11** considerate, kindhearted, soft-hearted, sympathetic, warmhearted **13** compassionate, philanthropic

humanitarian 5 giver **8** generous **10** altruistic, benefactor, beneficent, benevolent, charitable **13** compassionate, philanthropic

humanity 6 people **7** mankind **8** kindness, sympathy **10** compassion, generosity **11** benevolence, Homo sapiens

humble 3 low **4** meek **5** abash, crush, lowly, quiet **6** demean, modest, simple **7** chagrin, deflate, degrade, subdued **8** cast down, disgrace, ordinary **9** compliant, diffident, discomfit, embarrass, humiliate **10** submissive, unassuming **11** acquiescent, deferential **13** insignificant, unpretentious

humbug 3 con, rot **4** fake, fool, hoax, sham **5** faker, fraud, hokum, phony, spoof, trick **6** bunkum, delude, drivel, take in **7** beguile, deceive, mislead **8** flimflam, impostor, malarkey, nonsense, pretense, quackery **9** deception, hypocrite, imposture, pretender, trickster **10** balderdash

humdinger 3 gem **5** beaut, dandy, dilly, doozy, jewel, prize **6** doozie **8** jimdandy **11** crackerjack

humdrum 4 blah, dull, flat **6** boring, dreary, stodgy **7** prosaic, tedious **8** monotone, monotony, plodding, unvaried, workaday **10** monotonous, uneventful **13** uninteresting

humid 3 wet **4** damp, dank **5** close, moist, muggy, soggy **6** clammy, sodden, steamy, sticky, stuffy **10** oppressive

humidify 6 dampen **7** moisten

humiliate 5 abase, crush, lower, shame **6** bemean, debase, demean, humble **7** chagrin, degrade, mortify **8** belittle, cast down, disgrace **9** embarrass

humiliation 5 shame **7** chagrin, put-down **8** disgrace, ignominy, reproach **9** abasement, disrepute, indignity **11** degradation **13** embarrassment, mortification

humility 7 modesty, shyness **8** meekness **9** abasement, lowliness **10** diffidence, submission **12** subservience **13** self-abasement

humming 4 busy **5** brisk **6** active, lively **8** bustling, hustling **9** energetic

hummock 4 hump **5** couch, knoll, mound **7** hillock

humongous 4 huge, vast **5** giant, jumbo **7** immense, mammoth, massive, titanic **8** colossal, enormous, gigantic **9** monstrous **10** gargantuan, prodigious, tremendous

humor 3 wit **4** baby, bent, mind, mood, tone, vein, whim **5** fancy, fluid, spoil, yield **6** banter, coddle, comedy, cosset, esprit, joking, levity, nature, pamper, temper **7** caprice, cater to, conceit, gratify, indulge, jesting, kidding **8** crotchet, drollery, jocosity, repartee **9** character, drollness, flippancy, funniness, witticism, wittiness **10** complexion, jocularity, pleasantry **11** disposition, temperament

humorist 3 Ade (George), wag, wit **4** card, Nash (Ogden), Shaw (Henry Wheeler), Ward (Artemus, Edward) **5** Adams (Franklin Pierce), Allen (Fred), Barry (Dave), clown, comic, cutup, droll, Dunne (Finley Peter), joker, Twain (Mark), White (E. B.) **6** Blount (Roy), Browne (Charles Farrar), Diller (Phyllis), gagman, jester, kidder, Parker (Dorothy), Rogers (Will), Rourke (P. J.), Runyon (Damon), Thorpe (Thomas Bangs) **7** buffoon, Bombeck (Erma), Burgess (Gelett), Clemens (Samuel Langhorne), gagster, Hubbard (Kin), Keillor (Garrison), Marquis (Don), punster, Sedaris (David), Thurber (James), Trillin (Calvin) **8** Aleichem (Shalom), Benchley (Robert), comedian, funnyman, jokester, Perelman (S. J.), quipster **9** jokesmith, prankster, Wodehouse (P. G.) *Canadian:* **7** Leacock (Stephen)

humorous 5 comic, droll, funny, jokey, merry, witty **6** jocose **7** amusing, comical, jocular, risible, waggish **8** mirthful **9** facetious, laughable, whimsical

hump 3 lug **4** bump, race, tote **5** bulge, carry, hunch, mound, range **6** hustle, schlep **7** hummock, schlepp **8** mountain, obstacle, swelling **9** transport **10** protrusion

humpback 5 whale **8** kyphosis **10** pink salmon

humpbacked 6 convex, curved **7** gibbous

Humperdinck opera 15 Hansel and Gretel

humus 3 mor **4** mull, soil **7** compost **8** material

hunch 4 arch, clod, idea, lump, hump, push **5** chunk, clump, crook, squat, stoop **6** crouch, curl up, huddle, jostle, notion, nugget **7** feeling, inkling **9** intuition

Hunchback of Notre Dame *author:* **4** Hugo (Victor) *character:* **9** Esmeralda, Quasimodo

hundred *combining form:* **5** centi, hecto
Hungary *capital:* **8** Budapest *city:* **4** Pécs
6 Szeged **7** Miskolc **8** Debrecen *ethnic group:* **6** Magyar *lake:* **7** Balaton *monetary unit:* **6** forint *mountain range:* **10** Carpathian *national hero:* **5** Árpád *neighbor:* **6** Serbia **7** Austria, Croatia, Romania, Ukraine **8** Slovakia, Slovenia *plain:* **11** Great Alföld *river:* **5** Tisza **6** Danube
hunger 3 yen **4** ache, itch, long, lust, need, pine, want **5** crave, greed, yearn **6** desire, hanker, thirst **7** craving, longing
hungry 4 avid, keen, poor **5** eager **6** barren **7** craving, starved, thirsty **8** desirous, famished, ravenous, starving, underfcd, yearning **9** hankering, motivated
hunk 3 gob, wad **4** clod, lump **5** chunk, clump, piece, wedge **6** nugget **7** portion
hunker down 5 dig in, squat **6** crouch **8** settle in
hunky 4 buff **5** burly **6** buffed **8** athletic, muscular **9** strapping, well-built
hunky-dory 4 fine, okay **5** dandy, ducky, nifty, swell **6** peachy **10** peachy keen **12** satisfactory
Hunnish 4 rude, wild **6** savage **7** fearful, uncivil **9** barbarian, barbarous, ferocious **11** uncivilized
hunt 3 dog, run **4** hawk, seek **5** chase, hound, prowl, quest, shoot, snare, stalk, track, trail **6** battue, course, dig out, prey on, pursue, safari, search **7** explore, pursuit, rummage **9** ferret out, search for, search out *birds:* **4** fowl *illegally:* **5** poach
hunter 6 jaeger, nimrod **8** predator *biblical:* **6** Nimrod *cap:* **7** montero *constellation:* **5** Orion *mythological:* **5** Orion **7** Actaeon
hunting 5 chase **6** venery **7** gunning, hawking **8** coursing, falconry **9** predatory **10** predacious *bird:* **6** falcon *call:* **7** recheat *cry:* **6** yoicks **7** tallyho **10** view halloo *dog:* **5** hound **6** basset, beagle, borzoi, saluki, setter, vizsla **7** harrier, pointer, spaniel **9** ridgeback, wolfhound **10** bloodhound *expedition:* **6** safari *horn:* **5** bugle
huntress 5 Diana **7** Artemis **8** Atalanta
hurdle 3 bar **4** leap, snag **5** bound, clear, vault **6** hamper, spring **7** barrier **8** leap over, obstacle, overcome, overleap surmount, traverse **9** negotiate **10** difficulty, impediment **11** obstruction
hurl 4 cast, fire **5** chuck, fling, heave, pitch, sling, throw, vomit **6** launch, thrust **8** catapult
hurly-burly 3 din **4** riot, to-do **5** melee

6 clamor, furore, hassle, hubbub, racket, rumpus, tumult, uproar **7** turmoil **8** confused **9** commotion, confusion
hurrah 4 fuss, to-do, zeal **5** cheer **6** fervor, rumpus **7** fanfare, ovation **8** approval **9** commotion **10** enthusiasm **11** acclamation
hurricane 7 typhoon
hurried 4 fast, sped **5** hasty, quick, swift **6** abrupt, rushed, sudden **7** cursory, rushing **8** headlong **9** impetuous **11** precipitant, precipitate
hurry 3 fly, hie, jog, run, zip **4** post, prod, push, rush **5** fleet, haste, scoot, speed, whirl, whish, whisk **6** barrel, breeze, bullet, bustle, hasten, hustle, rocket, rustle, step up, tumult **7** beeline, hotfoot, quicken, shake up, skelter, speed up, swiften **8** celerity, dispatch, expedite, highball, make time **9** commotion, make haste, swiftness **10** accelerate, speediness
hurt 3 mar **4** ache, blow, harm, pain **5** wound, wrong **6** damage, grieve, hamper, harmed, impair, injure, injury, in pain, misuse, offend, pained, suffer **7** afflict, anguish, blemish, damaged, wounded **8** aggrieve, distress, mischief, mistreat **9** constrain, detriment, prejudice, resentful, suffering **10** resentment
hurtful 4 mean, sore **6** aching, unkind **7** harmful, painful **8** damaging, wounding **9** injurious **11** deleterious, destructive, detrimental, distressing, prejudicial
hurtle 3 fly **4** race, rush, tear **5** fling, shoot, speed, throw **6** charge, plunge, rocket
husband 3 man **4** mate, save **6** manage, mister, spouse **7** consort, partner **8** conserve, helpmate, helpmeet **9** economize, other half **10** bridegroom
husbandry 6 thrift **7** control, economy, farming **8** prudence **9** frugality **10** management **11** agriculture, thriftiness **12** conservation, preservation
hush 4 calm **5** quell, quiet **6** shut up, stifle **7** cover up, mollify, secrecy, silence **8** choke off, suppress **9** cessation, quietness, stillness
hush-hush 6 covert, secret **7** private, sub-rosa **9** top secret **11** clandestine **12** confidential **13** surreptitious, under-the-table
husk 3 pod **4** case, peel, rind, skin **5** shell, shuck, strip **6** casing
husky 3 big, dog **5** beefy, burly, great, hefty, large, rough, stout **6** brawny, croaky, hoarse, mighty, robust, strong, sturdy **7** throaty **8** muscular, oversize, stalwart, thickset **9** strapping

hustings 5 stump

hustle 3 fly, rob, run **4** earn, move, push, rush, sell, urge, work **5** cheat, elbow, fraud, haste, hurry, press, shove, speed **6** hasten **7** hotfoot, promote, solicit, swindle **8** bulldoze, deception, dispatch **9** swiftness

hustler 4 doer **6** dynamo, vendor **8** go-getter, live wire **10** powerhouse

hustling 4 busy **5** eager **6** active, lively, speedy **7** hopping, humming **9** energetic **10** aggressive

hut 3 cot **4** camp, crib, shed **5** cabin, dacha, hooch, hovel, hutch, jacal, lodge, roost, shack **6** cabana, chalet, lean-to, shanty **7** cottage **8** bungalow *American Indian:* **6** wigwam **7** wickiup *Scottish:* **5** bothy, shiel **8** shieling

hutch 3 bin, pen **4** cage, coop **5** chest, shack **6** locker, shanty **8** cupboard **9** enclosure

Huxley novel 8 Antic Hay **11** Crome Yellow **13** Brave New World, Eyeless in Gaza

Hyacinthus *father:* **7** Amyclas *slayer:* **6** Apollo

hybrid 5 blend, cross, mixed **7** amalgam, mixture **8** combined, compound **9** composite, crossbred **10** crossbreed **11** combination

hybridize 4 join **5** blend, cross **7** combine **10** crossbreed, interbreed, intercross

Hydra 5 polyp **6** plague **7** monster, serpent **13** constellation *father:* **6** Typhon *mother:* **7** Echidna *slayer:* **8** Heracles, Hercules

hydrant 3 tap **4** pipe **5** valve **6** faucet, spigot **7** petcock **8** fireplug

hydraulic device 3 ram **4** jack, lift, pump **5** brake, press **8** elevator

hydrocarbon 5 xylol **6** dioxin, ethane, xylene **7** benzene, methane, styrene, toluene **8** biphenyl, butylene, ethylene *liquid:* **6** octane **7** retinol, styrene **8** menthene

hydroid 5 polyp **6** medusa, obelia **9** jellyfish

hydrometer scale 4 Brix **5** Baumé

hydrophobia 5 lyssa **6** rabies

hyena 5 dingo **6** jackal **9** scavenger

Hygeia 5 Salus *father:* **9** Asclepius **11** Aesculapius *goddess of:* **6** health

hygiene 6 health **10** sanitation **11** cleanliness

hygienic 5 clean **7** aseptic, healthy, sterile **8** sanitary **9** healthful **10** antiseptic, unpolluted

Hyllus' father 8 Heracles, Hercules

hymeneal 6 bridal, wedded **7** marital, married, nuptial, spousal **8** conjugal **9** connubial **11** matrimonial

hymn 4 laud, song **5** bless, carol, chant, extol, paean, psalm **6** anthem, choral, praise **7** chorale, glorify **8** canticle, doxology, eulogize

hype 4 plug, tout **5** boost, thump **7** acclaim, enliven, glorify, promote, puffery, trumpet **8** ballyhoo, increase **9** advertise, excellent, publicity, publicize, stimulate **11** advertising

hyper 4 edgy **5** antsy, jumpy, wired **6** on edge **7** anxious, frantic **8** agitated, frenetic, hopped-up **9** excitable **10** highstrung, overactive **11** overwrought

hyperbole 6 excess **12** embroidering, exaggeration **13** embellishment, overstatement

hypercritical 6 severe **7** carping **8** captious, exacting **10** censorious, nitpicking **12** faultfinding

Hyperion *daughter:* **3** Eos **6** Aurora, Selene *father:* **6** Uranus *mother:* **4** Gaea *son:* **6** Helios *wife:* **5** Theia

hypnotic 6 opiate, sleepy **8** mesmeric, narcotic, sedative **9** somnolent, soporific **11** mesmerizing, somniferous **12** somnifacient, spellbinding

hypnotize 4 drug **5** charm **6** dazzle, trance **8** enthrall, entrance, overcome **9** captivate, mesmerize, overpower, spellbind

hypocorism 7 pet name **8** nickname **9** sobriquet

hypocrisy 4 cant, sham **6** deceit, humbug **7** falsity, pietism **8** quackery **9** deception, duplicity, phoniness **10** sanctimony **11** insincerity, religiosity

hypocrite 4 fake, sham **5** actor, faker, fraud, phony, poser **6** humbug, poseur **7** bluffer, pietist **8** deceiver, impostor, pharisee **9** charlatan, pretender **10** dissembler **11** masquerader **12** dissimulator

hypocritical 5 false **7** canting **8** affected, specious, two-faced **9** deceitful, insincere, pietistic **10** Janus-faced **11** dissembling, double-faced, duplicitous **12** mealymouthed, xpecksniffian **13** sanctimonious

hypothesis 6 belief, theory **7** premise **8** position, supposal **9** condition, inference **10** antecedent, assumption, conjecture **11** explanation, speculation, supposition

hypothetical 7 assumed **8** abstract, academic, supposed **10** assumptive **11** conditional, conjectural, suppositous, theoretical **12** suppositious **13** suppositional

hyrax 4 cony **5** coney **6** dassie, mammal **8** ungulate

hysteria 4 fear **5** craze, furor, mania, panic **6** excess, frenzy **7** madness **8** delirium
hysterical 5 rabid **6** crazed, madcap, raving **7** berserk, frantic **8** agitated, frenzied, neurotic **9** delirious, disturbed, hilarious, impetuous **10** convulsive, distraught, uproarious **11** impassioned, overexcited, overwrought **13** side-splitting

I

Iago *general:* **7** Othello *victim:* **6** Cassio, Emilia **7** Othello **9** Desdemona *wife:* **6** Emilia
Iapetus *father:* **6** Uranus *mother:* **4** Gaea *son:* **5** Atlas **9** Menoetius **10** Epimetheus, Prometheus *wife:* **7** Clymene
Iasion *brother:* **8** Dardanus *father:* **4** Zeus **7** Jupiter *lover:* **5** Ceres **7** Demeter *mother:* **7** Electra *son:* **6** Plutus
ibex 4 tahr **8** wild goat *family:* **7** Bovidae *genus:* **5** Capra
Ibhar's father 5 David
ibis-headed god 5 Thoth
ibis relative 5 heron, stork
Ibsen, Henrik *character:* **3** Ase **4** Nora (Helmer) **5** Brack (Judge), Brand, Hedda (Gabler), Helen (Alving), Werle (Gergers) **6** Ejlert (Lovberg), Hedvig (Ekdal), Jorgen (Tesman), Oswald (Alving) **7** Solness (Halvard), Solveig, Torvald (Helmer) **8** Peer Gynt **9** Stockmann (Thomas) *country:* **6** Norway *play:* **6** Ghosts **8** Peer Gynt, Wild Duck (The) **10** Doll's House (A) **11** Hedda Gabler, Little Eyolf, Rosmersholm **13** Master Builder (The) **16** Enemy of the People (An)
Icarus' father 8 Daedalus
ice *area:* **4** rink *dessert:* **6** sorbet **7** sherbet *floating:* **4** berg, floe *hanging:* **6** icicle *pinnacle:* **5** serac
icebox 6 cooler, fridge **12** refrigerator
ice cream 7 spumoni, tortoni *dish:* **6** sundae **11** baked Alaska *drink:* **4** soda **6** frappe
iced 5 glacé **6** glazed **7** chilled
ice field 4 floe **7** glacier
ice game 6 hockey **7** curling
ice house 5 igloo
Iceland *capital:* **9** Reykjavik *monetary unit:* **5** krona *sea:* **9** Norwegian *snow-*

field: **11** Vatnajökull *strait:* **7** Denmark *volcano:* **5** Hekla
Icelandic *epic:* **4** Edda, saga *hero:* **5** Njáll **6** Gunnar **7** Grettir
Ichabod Crane's beloved 7 Katrina
icing 7 topping **8** frosting
icky 4 vile **5** awful, gross, nasty **9** loathsome, offensive, repellent, repulsive, revolting, sickening **10** disgusting **11** distasteful
icon 4 idol, sign **5** image **6** emblem, symbol
iconoclastic 9 dissident, heretical **10** rebellious, unorthodox **13** nonconformist
icy 4 cold **5** gelid, polar **6** arctic, chilly, frigid, frosty, steely **7** glacial **8** freezing **11** emotionless, unemotional
Idaho *capital:* **5** Boise *city:* **6** Moscow **9** Pocatello, Twin Falls **10** Idaho Falls **11** Coeur d'Alene *mountain:* **5** Borah (Peak) *nickname:* **3** Gem (State) *river:* **5** Snake **6** Salmon *state bird:* **8** bluebird *state flower:* **9** syringa *state tree:* **9** white pine
Idas *brother:* **7** Lynceus *father:* **8** Aphareus *slayer:* **4** Zeus *victim:* **6** Castor *wife:* **8** Marpessa
idea 4 whim **5** fancy, guess, motif **6** belief, notion, theory, thesis, vagary **7** caprice, conceit, concept, inkling, meaning, opinion, subject, surmise, thought **8** estimate **9** sentiment, suspicion **10** assumption, brainstorm, conception, conclusion, conjecture, conviction, estimation, hypothesis, impression, perception, reflection **11** abstraction, formulation, supposition
ideal 4 best, goal **5** model **7** chimera, classic, epitome, paragon, perfect, utopian **8** absolute, ensample, exem-

plar, flawless, nonesuch, paradigm, standard, ultimate **9** archetype, classical, exemplary, nonpareil **10** archetypal, conceptual, consummate **11** theoretical

idealist 7 dreamer, quixote, utopian **9** ideologue, visionary

idealistic 6 dreamy **7** utopian **8** poetical, quixotic, romantic **9** visionary **10** starry-eyed **11** impractical, unrealistic

idealize 5 deify, exalt, extol **7** elevate, ennoble, glorify, worship **8** venerate

ideate 5 think **7** imagine **8** conceive, envisage, envision

idée fixe 5 mania **6** fetish, phobia **7** complex **8** fixation **9** obsession **13** preoccupation

identical 3 one **4** like, same, very **5** alike, equal, exact **8** selfsame **9** duplicate **10** equivalent, synonymous

identification mark 4 logo **5** badge, brand, label **6** emblem

identify 3 tag **4** mark, name, spot **5** brand, place **6** finger, select **7** make out, pick out **8** pinpoint **9** determine, recognize **11** distinguish

identity 4 name, self **7** oneness **8** sameness, selfhood **9** character **10** congruence, uniformity, uniqueness **11** personality, singularity **13** individuality, particularity

ideological 8 notional **10** conceptual, ideational **11** speculative **13** philosophical

ideologue 8 believer, idealist, partisan, theorist

ideology 3 ism **5** credo, creed **7** beliefs **8** doctrine **10** philosophy, principles

idiocy 7 fatuity **9** cretinism, stupidity **10** imbecility **11** foolishness

idiomatic 7 demotic **8** peculiar **9** dialectal **10** colloquial, vernacular

idiosyncrasy 5 quirk **6** oddity **7** anomaly **11** peculiarity, singularity **12** eccentricity

idiosyncratic 3 odd **5** kooky, queer, weird **6** quirky **7** erratic, oddball, offbeat, unusual **8** peculiar, singular **9** eccentric **11** distinctive

idiot 3 ass **4** dolt, fool, jerk, simp **5** dummy, dunce, moron, ninny **6** cretin, nitwit, stupid **7** airhead, dullard, half-wit, jackass, natural, tomfool **8** dumbbell, imbecile, numskull **9** ignoramus, numbskull, simpleton **10** nincompoop

idiotic 5 dopey **6** stupid **7** foolish, moronic **8** ignorant **9** brainless, imbecilic, senseless

idle 3 bum **4** laze, lazy, loaf, loll, rest, vain **5** dally, drone, empty, inert, slack,

tarry **6** asleep, dawdle, diddle, fallow, futile, linger, loiter, lounge, otiose, unused, vacant **7** aimless, dormant, passive **8** inactive, indolent, slothful **9** shiftless **10** unoccupied

idleness 4 ease **5** sloth **6** vanity **7** leisure, loafing **8** lethargy **9** indolence **10** inactivity

idler 3 bum **4** slug **5** drone **6** loafer, slouch **7** dawdler **8** deadbeat, fainéant, loiterer, slugabed, sluggard **9** do-nothing, lazybones **11** couch potato

Idmon *daughter:* **7** Arachne *father:* **6** Apollo *mother:* **6** Cyrene

idol 3 god **4** hero, icon, star **5** deity, image, totem **6** fetish, minion, symbol **8** likeness *Chinese:* **4** joss

idolatry 7 worship **8** devotion **9** adoration **10** exaltation, veneration **11** deification **13** glorification

idolize 5 adore, deify, exalt **6** revere **7** glorify, worship **8** venerate

Idomeneo *composer:* **6** Mozart (Wolfgang Amadeus)

idyllic 5 ideal **6** rustic **7** bucolic, halcyon, perfect, utopian **8** arcadian, heavenly, pastoral, peaceful, romantic **9** idealized, unspoiled **11** picturesque, sentimental

Idylls of the King *author:* **8** Tennyson (Alfred) *character:* **4** Enid **6** Arthur, Elaine, Gareth, Merlin, Vivien **7** Geraint, Lynette **8** Lancelot

iffy 5 dicey, risky **6** chancy, unsure **7** dubious, erratic **8** doubtful **9** uncertain **10** unreliable **12** inconsistent **13** unpredictable

igneous rock 4 lava **5** magma **6** basalt, gabbro **7** diabase, granite **8** porphyry

ignis fatuus 6 mirage **7** chimera **8** delusion, illusion, phantasm **9** pipe dream **12** will-o'-the-wisp **13** hallucination

ignitable 7 burnable **9** excitable, flammable **10** incendiary **11** combustible, inflammable

ignite 4 fire **5** light, spark **6** excite, kindle **7** inflame **8** enkindle, touch off

ignited 3 lit **5** afire, fiery **6** ablaze, aflame, alight **7** blazing, burning, flaming, flaring **11** conflagrant

ignoble 3 low **4** base, mean, poor, vile **5** lowly **6** abject, coarse, common, scurvy, sordid, vulgar **7** lowborn, servile **8** baseborn, indecent, inferior, plebeian, shameful, unwashed, wretched **10** despicable, inglorious **11** disgraceful **12** contemptible, dishonorable

ignominious 6 odious **8** infamous, shameful **9** degrading **10** despicable, inglorious **11** disgraceful, humiliating, opprobrious **12** contemptible, dishonorable, disreputable **13** discreditable, unrespectable

ignominy 5 odium, shame **6** infamy **7** obloquy, scandal **8** disgrace, dishonor **9** discredit, disesteem, disrepute **10** opprobrium **11** humiliation **13** mortification

ignoramus 4 dolt **5** dummy, dunce, idiot, moron **6** dimwit, nitwit, stupid **7** airhead, dullard, half-wit **8** dumbbell, imbecile, numskull **9** numbskull, simpleton

ignorance 7 naiveté **9** innocence, nescience, stupidity **10** illiteracy, simpleness, simplicity **11** unawareness **12** incognizance

ignorant 5 naive **6** simple **7** unaware **8** nescient, untaught **9** benighted, ingenuous, oblivious, unknowing, unlearned, untutored, unwitting **10** illiterate, uncultured, uneducated, uninformed, unlettered, unschooled **11** incognizant, know-nothing **12** uninstructed **13** unenlightened

ignore 4 omit, snub **5** avoid **6** forget, reject, slight **7** neglect **8** overlook **9** disregard

Igraine *husband:* **5** Uther **7** Gorlois *son:* **6** Arthur

iguana 5 anole **6** lizard **8** basilisk **10** chuckwalla

ilex 4 maté **5** holly **6** yaupon **7** holm oak **8** inkberry

Iliad 4 epic *author:* **5** Homer *character:* **4** Ajax **5** Helen, Paris, Priam **6** Aeneas, Hector **8** Achilles, Diomedes, Odysseus **9** Agamemnon, Patroclus *city:* **4** Troy

Ilium 4 Troy

ilk 4 kind, sort, type **5** breed, class, genre **6** family, kidney, nature, stripe **7** variety

ill 4 sick **6** ailing, infirm, laid up, malady, peaked, queasy, unwell **7** ailment, disease, trouble, unlucky **8** diseased, disorder, distress, feverish, nauseous, scarcely, sickness, syndrome **9** afflicted, infirmity, nauseated, unhealthy **10** misfortune

ill-adapted 8 unfitted, unsuited **10** unsuitable

ill-advised 4 rash **5** brash, hasty **6** madcap, unwise **7** foolish **8** careless, heedless, reckless **9** foolhardy, impolitic, imprudent **10** incautious, indiscreet, unthinking **11** inexpedient, injudicious, thoughtless

ill at ease 3 shy **4** edgy **6** on edge **7** anxious, awkward, fidgety, nervous **8** insecure, restless **9** unsettled **11** discomfited **12** apprehensive **13** self-conscious, uncomfortable

ill-boding 4 dire **7** baleful, doomful, fateful, ominous, unlucky **8** sinister **10** portentous **11** apocalyptic **12** inauspicious, unpropitious

ill-bred 4 rude **5** crude **7** boorish, loutish, uncivil, uncouth **8** impolite **9** unrefined **10** uncultured, ungracious, unmannered, unmannerly, unpolished **11** uncivilized **12** discourteous

ill-defined 5 faint, fuzzy, vague **7** shadowy **10** indistinct

illegal 3 hot **6** banned **7** bootleg, illicit, lawless **8** criminal, outlawed, unlawful, wrongful **9** felonious, forbidden **10** actionable, prohibited, proscribed, unlicensed **12** illegitimate *act:* **5** crime **6** felony *scheme:* **4** scam

illegible 8 scrawled **10** unreadable **11** inscrutable

illegitimacy 8 bastardy **11** bar sinister **12** unlawfulness

illegitimate 7 bastard, bootleg, erratic, invalid, lawless, natural **8** criminal, improper, spurious, unlawful **11** misbegotten **12** unauthorized

ill-fated 6 cursed, doomed **7** unhappy, unlucky **8** accursed, luckless, untoward **10** disastrous **11** star-crossed, unfortunate

ill-favored 4 ugly **5** plain **6** homely **12** unattractive

ill-humored 4 dour, sour **5** cross, surly, testy **6** crabby, cranky, crusty, grumpy, morose, ornery, sullen, tetchy, touchy **7** crabbed, grouchy, peevish, prickly **8** choleric, churlish, snappish **9** dyspeptic, irascible, irritable, saturnine, splenetic **12** cantankerous, disagreeable, misanthropic

illiberal 6 biased, narrow **7** bigoted, insular **9** hidebound, parochial, penurious **10** intolerant, prejudiced, provincial **11** reactionary, small-minded **12** conservative, narrow-minded, uncharitable

illicit 7 bootleg, crooked, lawless **8** criminal, unlawful **9** forbidden **10** contraband, prohibited **11** black-market, clandestine **12** unauthorized

illimitable 7 endless **8** infinite, unending **9** boundless **11** measureless

Illinois *capital:* **11** Springfield *city:* **6** Aurora, Cicero, Joliet, Peoria **7** Chicago **8** Rockford *college, university:* **4** Knox **6** DePaul **7** Wheaton **12** Northwestern *nickname:* **7** Prairie (State) *river:* **6** Wabash *state bird:* **8** cardinal *state flower:* **6** violet *state tree:* **8** white oak

illiterate 6 unread **8** untaught **9** untutored **10** uneducated, unlettered, unschooled

ill-mannered 4 rude **6** coarse **7** boorish, loutish, uncivil, uncouth **8** churlish, impolite **10** ungracious **12** discourteous

ill-natured 4 sour **5** cross, huffy, surly, testy **6** bitchy, crabby, grumpy, ornery, tetchy **7** grouchy, peevish, waspish **8** choleric, churlish, snappish, spiteful **9** dyspeptic, fractious, irascible, irritable **10** malevolent **11** belligerent, contentious, quarrelsome **12** cantankerous, disagreeable

illness 6 malady **7** ailment, disease, malaise **8** cachexia, disorder, sickness **9** infirmity **10** affliction **13** indisposition

illogical 6 absurd **7** invalid, unsound **8** specious **9** plausible, senseless, sophistic **10** fallacious, irrational, unreasoned **11** nonrational **12** preposterous, unreasonable

ill-starred 6 cursed, doomed, malign **7** fateful, ominous, unhappy, unlucky **8** luckless, untoward **10** disastrous, foreboding, portentous **11** unfavorable, unfortunate, unpromising **12** inauspicious, unpropitious

ill-tempered 4 sour **5** cross, huffy, surly **6** crabby, bitchy, grumpy, ornery, snippy **7** grouchy, peevish, waspish **8** choleric, churlish, petulant, shrewish, snappish, spiteful **9** dyspeptic, fractious, irascible, irritable **11** belligerent, contentious, quarrelsome **12** cantankerous, disagreeable

ill-timed 11 inopportune **12** unseasonable

ill-treat 4 harm, hurt **5** abuse **6** injure, misuse, molest **7** torment **8** aggrieve **10** traumatize

illuminate 5 clear, edify, exalt, gloss, light **6** uplift **7** clarify, clear up, explain, lighten **8** brighten, decorate **9** elucidate, embellish, enlighten, highlight, irradiate, spotlight

illuminati 5 elite **7** clerisy, scholar **8** academic **11** academician **13** intellectuals

illumination 8 lighting *unit of:* **3** lux **4** phot **5** lumen **6** candle **7** candela **10** footcandle

illusion 4 myth **5** dream, fancy, ghost **6** facade, mirage **7** chimera, fantasy **8** phantasm, phantasy **9** invention, pipe dream, semblance **11** ignis fatuus **12** will-o'-the-wisp **13** hallucination

illusionist 8 conjurer, magician **9** trickster

illusive see ILLUSORY

illusory 4 sham **6** unreal **7** seeming **8** apparent, fanciful **9** deceptive, fictional, imaginary, visionary **10** chimerical, fallacious, fictitious, misleading, ostensible

illustrate 4 mark, show **6** depict, evince, expose, reveal **7** clarify, display, exhibit, explain, picture, portray **8** decorate, describe, evidence, instance, manifest **9** elucidate, epitomize, exemplify **11** demonstrate

illustration 4 case **6** sample **7** diagram, drawing, example, picture, problem **8** instance

illustrative 7 graphic **9** pictorial **10** clarifying **11** descriptive **12** iconographic

illustrator *American:* **4** Kent (Rockwell), Pyle (Howard) **5** Abbey (Edwin Austin), Flagg (James Montgomery), Smith (Jessie Willcox), Wyeth (Newell Convers) **6** Gibson (Charles Dana) **7** Burgess (Gelett), Parrish (Maxwell) **8** Rockwell (Norman) **9** Remington (Frederic) *English:* **5** Crane (Walter) **6** Morris (William), Potter (Beatrix) **7** Nielsen (Kay), Rackham (Arthur), Tenniel (John) **9** Beardsley (Aubrey), Caldecott (Randolph), du Maurier (George), Greenaway (Kate) *French:* **4** Doré (Gustave) **5** Dulac (Edmund) *German:* **5** Dürer (Albrecht)

illustrious 5 famed, great, lofty, noted **6** famous **7** eminent, exalted, notable, sublime **8** glorious, renowned, splendid **9** acclaimed, prominent **10** celebrated, preeminent **11** outstanding, prestigious **13** distinguished

illustriousness 4 fame **5** glory **6** renown **8** eminence, prestige **9** celebrity **10** prominence **11** distinction, preeminence

ill will 5 spite, venom **6** animus, enmity, malice, rancor, spleen **7** despite, dislike **8** acrimony, aversion, bad blood **9** animosity, antipathy, hostility, malignity **10** resentment **11** malevolence **12** spitefulness **13** maliciousness

Ilus *father:* **4** Tros *grandson:* **5** Priam *mother:* **10** Callirrhoë *son:* **8** Laomedon

image 4 copy, form, icon, idea, idol **5** equal, match **6** double, effigy, figure, mirror, notion, ringer, vision **7** concept, fantasm, feature, picture **8** likeness, phantasm, portrait **9** facsimile, semblance **10** conception, equivalent, impression, reflection, simulacrum **12** illustration *Polynesian:* **4** tiki *Semitic:* **6** teraph **8** teraphim (plural)

imaginary 5 ideal **6** made-up, unreal **7** fancied, fictive **8** abstract, fabulous, fanciful, illusive, illusory, notional, quixotic **9** dreamlike, fantastic, fictional, legendary, visionary **10** apocryphal, chimerical, fictitious, phantasmal **11** make-believe **12** hypothetical, suppositious

imagination 5 fancy **7** fantasy **8** phantasy

9 invention 10 creativity 11 inspiration
13 inventiveness

imaginative 5 false **7** blue-sky, fictive
8 artistic, creative, fanciful, original,
poetical **9** ingenious, inventive, visionary, whimsical **11** resourceful **12** enterprising

imagine 5 dream, fancy **6** assume,
invent, make up **7** dream up, feature,
picture, suspect **8** conceive, envisage,
envision **9** fabricate, visualize **10** conjecture

imbecile 4 dodo, dolt, dull, fool, jerk
5 dunce, idiot, moron, ninny **6** cretin,
dimwit, nitwit **7** half-wit, jackass,
moronic, pinhead, tomfool **8** numskull
9 birdbrain, blockhead, numbskull
10 dunderhead, nincompoop

imbibe 3 sip, sup **4** chug, soak, swig, toss
5 booze, drink, quaff, swill **6** absorb,
guzzle, tipple **7** consume, swallow,
swizzle **10** assimilate

imbricate 3 lap **7** overlap, shingle
11 overlapping

imbroglio 3 row **4** maze, mess, spat, to-
do **5** brawl, mix-up **6** fracas, muddle,
tangle **7** dispute, quarrel, rhubarb,
scandal, wrangle **8** argument, disorder,
squabble **9** confusion, intricacy
10 falling-out **11** altercation, predicament **12** complication, entanglement

imbrue 4 soil **5** stain **8** discolor

imbue 3 dye **4** soak **5** bathe, endow,
steep, tinge **6** infuse, invest, leaven
7 ingrain, instill, pervade, suffuse **8** permeate, saturate **9** influence, inoculate

imitate 3 ape **4** copy, echo, mime, mock
5 forge, mimic, spoof **6** parody **7** emulate, take off **8** resemble, simulate, travesty **9** burlesque, duplicate, replicate,
reproduce **11** counterfeit, impersonate

imitation 4 copy, fake, mock, sham
5 clone, ditto, dummy, false, match,
phony **6** ersatz, parody, ringer **7** forgery, replica **8** likeness, parallel, spurious, travesty **9** duplicate, semblance,
simulated **10** artificial, simulacrum,
simulation, substitute **11** counterfeit,
counterpart **12** reproduction, substitution

imitative 4 mock **5** apish **6** echoic
7 copycat, mimetic, parodic, slavish
11 counterfeit **12** onomatopoeic **13** onomatopoetic

immaculate 4 pure **5** clean **6** chaste, virgin **7** cleanly, perfect, sinless **8** flawless,
spotless, unsoiled, virtuous **9** stainless,
undefiled, unsullied **11** spic-and-span,
unblemished **12** spick-and-span

immaterial 7 trivial **8** bodiless, ethereal
10 extraneous, inapposite, intangible,

irrelevant **11** disembodied, incorporeal,
nonphysical, unimportant **12** inapplicable **13** insignificant, insubstantial,
unsubstantial

immature 3 raw **5** crude, green, young
6 callow, infant, unripe **7** puerile
8 childish, juvenile, youthful **9** infantile, primitive, unfledged **10** unfinished
11 undeveloped

immaturity 6 nonage **7** infancy **8** minority **9** childhood, salad days **11** adolescence **12** juvenescence

immeasurable 4 vast **6** untold **7** endless
8 infinite **9** boundless, extensive, limitless, unbounded, unlimited **11** illimitable, inestimable, uncountable
12 incalculable, unfathomable

immediate 4 next, nigh **5** close **6** at hand,
direct, nearby, urgent **7** current,
instant, ongoing, primary **9** firsthand,
proximate **10** unmediated **12** straightaway **13** instantaneous

immediately 3 now, PDQ **4** anon, stat
6 at once, presto, pronto **8** directly,
promptly **9** forthwith, instanter, instantly, right away **11** straightway
12 straightaway

immense 4 huge, vast **5** great, large
6 mighty **7** mammoth, massive, titanic
8 colossal, enormous, gigantic
9 humongous, monstrous **10** gargantuan, monumental, prodigious, tremendous **11** elephantine

immensely 4 a lot **8** terribly **9** extremely
11 exceedingly **12** inordinately

immensity 8 enormity, hugeness, vastness **9** greatness **12** enormousness

immerse 3 dip **4** duck, dunk, sink, soak
5 bathe, douse **6** drench, engage,
plunge **7** baptize, engross, involve **8** saturate, submerge

immigrant 5 alien **7** settler **8** newcomer
10 transplant *Japanese:* **5** issei

imminent 6 at hand **6** coming **7** brewing,
nearing, ominous, pending **8** upcoming
9 gathering, proximate **11** approaching,
overhanging

immobile 3 set **5** fixed, inert, still
6 frozen, stable, static **9** unmovable
10 motionless, stationary

immobilize 5 still **7** cripple, disable **8** paralyze **9** hamstring **12** incapacitate

immoderate 5 undue **7** extreme **9** excessive **10** exorbitant, inordinate, untempered **11** extravagant, intemperate
12 unreasonable, unrestrained
13 extraordinary, overindulgent

immoderation 6 excess **11** exorbitance,
prodigality **12** extravagance, intemperance

immodest 4 lewd, vain **7** stuck-up

8 arrogant, boastful, indecent, puffed-up, unchaste 9 conceited, egotistic 11 pretentious

immolate 4 burn, kill 7 destroy 9 sacrifice

immoral 4 evil, vile 5 dirty, wrong 6 sinful, wanton, wicked 7 corrupt, unclean, vicious 8 depraved, indecent, unchaste 9 dissolute, reprobate, uncleanly 10 degenerate, iniquitous, licentious

immorality 3 sin 4 vice 8 iniquity 9 depravity 10 corruption, unchastity, wickedness

immortal 7 endless, eternal, godlike, undying 8 timeless, unending 9 ceaseless, deathless, perpetual 11 amaranthine, everlasting, sempiternal

immotile 5 fixed, inert 6 rooted, static 9 paralyzed 10 stationary

immovable 3 pat, set 4 fast, firm 5 fixed, rigid 6 rooted, stable 7 adamant 8 constant, obdurate, stubborn 9 steadfast 10 inflexible, invariable, stationary, unyielding

immune 4 free, safe 6 exempt, secure 9 protected 10 impervious 12 invulnerable, unassailable

immunity 7 defense, freedom 9 exemption, privilege 10 protection

immure 3 pen 4 cage, coop, jail, wall 6 entomb, intern, shut in 7 confine, enclose 8 imprison 11 incarcerate

immutable 4 firm 5 fixed 8 constant 9 permanent, steadfast 10 changeless, inflexible, invariable, unchanging 11 inalterable, unalterable 12 unchangeable

Imogen *father:* 9 Cymbeline *husband:* 9 Posthumus

imp 3 elf 4 brat, puck 5 demon, devil, fiend, gamin, gnome, pixie, scamp 6 goblin, kobold, sprite, urchin 7 gremlin 9 hobgoblin

impact 3 hit, jar, rap 4 blow, bump, jolt, rock, slam, slap 5 brunt, embed, pound, punch, shock, smash, smite 6 affect, buffet, strike, wallop 9 collision, influence 10 concussion, percussion

impair 3 mar, sap 4 harm, hurt 5 spoil 6 damage, injure, lessen, weaken, worsen 7 cripple, tarnish, vitiate 8 enfeeble 9 prejudice, undermine 10 debilitate

impala 8 antelope

impale 4 gore, spit, stab 5 lance, prick, spear, spike, stick 6 pierce, skewer 8 puncture, transfix 11 transpierce

impalpable 4 fine 7 powdery 8 ethereal 10 intangible 11 disembodied, incorporeal 12 imponderable 13 imperceptible, indiscernible

impart 4 cede, give, lend, tell 5 grant, share, yield 6 afford, bestow, confer, convey, pass on, relate, render 8 disclose, transmit 11 communicate *knowledge:* 5 teach 6 inform 7 educate 8 instruct

impartial 4 even, fair, just 5 equal 7 neutral 8 detached, unbiased 9 equitable, objective, uncolored 10 evenhanded 12 unprejudiced 13 disinterested, dispassionate

impassable 6 closed 7 blocked 10 obstructed 12 impenetrable

impasse 3 box, fix, jam 6 aporia, corner, logjam, pickle, pocket 7 catch-22, dead end, dilemma 8 cul-de-sac, deadlock, standoff 9 stalemate 10 blind alley, bottleneck

impassioned 3 hot 5 fiery 6 ardent, fervid, fierce, heated, red-hot, torrid 7 blazing, burning, fervent, flaming, intense, violent, zealous 8 feverish, romantic, vehement, white-hot 9 emotional, perfervid 10 hot-blooded, overheated 11 dithyrambic 12 melodramatic 13 overemotional

impassive 4 calm, cold, cool 5 stoic 6 stolid, vacant 7 deadpan 8 composed, hardened, reserved, reticent, taciturn 9 heartless 10 insensible, insentient, phlegmatic, poker-faced 11 cold-blooded, emotionless, insensitive, passionless, unconcerned, unemotional, unexcitable, unflappable 12 inexpressive, unexpressive, unresponsive 13 dispassionate, self-possessed, unsusceptible

impassivity 6 apathy, phlegm 8 stoicism 9 stolidity 12 indifference 13 insensibility

impatient 4 edgy 5 antsy, eager, hasty 7 anxious, fretful, restive 8 restless 9 irascible, irritable 10 intolerant

impeach 5 blame, doubt 6 accuse, charge, indict 7 censure 9 inculpate, reprehend 11 incriminate

impeccable 4 pure 5 exact 7 perfect, precise 8 absolute, accurate, flawless, unerring 9 blameless, errorless, faultless, guiltless 10 infallible 11 unblemished

impecunious 4 poor 5 broke, needy 7 pinched 8 bankrupt, beggarly, indigent 9 destitute, insolvent, penniless, penurious 10 down-and-out 11 necessitous

impecuniousness 4 need, want 6 penury 7 poverty 9 indigence, neediness, pauperism, privation 11 destitution

impedance 3 bar 4 clog 5 block 8 blockage, obstacle 9 hindrance 10 opposition 11 obstruction impede 3 bar, dam 4 clog, slow 5 block, check, debar, delay, deter, stall 6 hinder, hang up, hold up, stymie, thwart 7 bog down 8 encumber, obstruct 9 embarrass, interfere, stonewall

impediment 3 bar 4 clog, snag 5 block, hitch 6 hurdle 7 barrier 8 obstacle 9 barricade, hindrance, roadblock 10 difficulty 11 encumbrance, obstruction

impel 4 goad, prod, push, spur, urge 5 drive, force, rouse 6 excite, incite, prompt 7 actuate, inspire 8 mobilize, motivate 9 instigate, stimulate

impend 4 loom, near 6 menace 8 approach, overhang, threaten

impenetrable 5 dense 6 arcane 7 obscure 9 enigmatic, recondite 10 impervious, invincible, mysterious, unknowable 11 impermeable, bulletproof, inscrutable, ungraspable 12 unfathomable

imperative 4 duty, need, rule, writ 5 acute, vital 6 crying, urgent 7 burning, clamant, command, crucial, exigent 8 critical, pressing, required 9 clamorous, essential, insistent, mandatory, necessary, necessity, requisite 10 compulsory, obligation, obligatory 11 fundamental, necessitous 12 prerequisite

imperceptible 3 dim 5 faint, vague 6 slight, subtle 7 gradual 9 invisible 10 impalpable, indistinct, insensible, intangible, unapparent 12 undetectable, unnoticeable, unobservable 13 inappreciable, inconspicuous, indiscernible

imperceptive 4 dull 7 shallow, unaware 11 inattentive, insensitive

imperfect 6 faulty, flawed 9 defective, deficient, irregular 10 defeasible, inadequate

imperfection 3 sin 4 flaw, wart 5 fault 6 defect, foible 7 blemish, demerit, failing, frailty 8 weakness 10 deficiency 11 shortcoming

imperial 5 regal, royal 6 kingly, lordly 7 haughty 8 absolute, majestic 9 masterful, sovereign 10 high-handed, peremptory 11 domineering, magisterial, monarchical

imperil 4 risk 6 hazard, menace 7 venture 8 endanger, threaten 10 jeopardize

imperious 5 bossy 6 urgent 7 haughty 8 absolute, arrogant, despotic, dominant 9 arbitrary, masterful 10 autocratic, commanding, high-handed, oppressive, peremptory, tyrannical 11 dictatorial, domineering, heavy-handed, magisterial, overbearing

impermanent 7 passing 8 fleeting, fugitive 9 ephemeral, fugacious, momentary, temporary, transient 10 evanescent, short-lived, transitory

impersonal 4 cold 5 aloof 8 abstract, detached 11 cold-blooded, emotionless 13 dispassionate, unimpassioned

impersonate 3 ape 4 play 5 mimic 6 act out 7 imitate, playact, portray 9 represent 11 counterfeit

impersonator 4 mime 5 actor, mimic 6 mummer, player, ringer 7 actress, copycat 8 thespian

impertinence 3 lip 4 gall, guff, sass 5 brass, cheek 8 audacity, boldness, chutzpah, rudeness, temerity 9 brashness, impudence, insolence 10 brazenness, effrontery, incivility 11 discourtesy, irrelevance

impertinent 4 bold, busy, rude 5 brash, fresh, sassy, saucy 6 brazen, cheeky 7 uncivil 8 insolent, meddling 9 audacious, intrusive, obtrusive, officious 10 inapposite, irrelative, irrelevant, meddlesome 11 ill-mannered 12 discourteous, inapplicable, presumptuous

imperturbability 5 poise 6 aplomb, phlegm 8 calmness, coolness, serenity, stoicism 9 composure, placidity, sangfroid 10 dispassion, equanimity 11 equilibrium, nonchalance 12 tranquillity

imperturbable 4 calm, cool 5 stoic 6 placid, poised, serene, smooth, steady, stolid 7 unmoved 8 composed, tranquil 9 collected, unruffled 10 nonchalant, phlegmatic, unaffected 11 unflappable

impervious 4 safe 6 immune 8 hardened 10 inviolable 12 inaccessible, invulnerable

impetuous 3 hot 4 rash, wild 5 fiery, hasty 6 ardent, fervid, madcap, sudden 8 headlong, vehement, volatile 9 hotheaded, mercurial 10 irrational, passionate 11 precipitant, precipitate, precipitous, spontaneous 13 temperamental

impetus 4 goad, push, spur 5 force 6 motive 8 catalyst, momentum, stimulus 9 incentive, stimulant 10 incitement, motivation 13 encouragement

impinge 5 press 6 border 7 intrude, obtrude 8 encroach

impious 6 sinful, unholy, wicked 7 godless, infidel, profane, secular, ungodly 8 agnostic, apostate 9 atheistic 10 irreverent, unfaithful, unhallowed 11 blasphemous, irreligious, unrighteous 12 iconoclastic, sacrilegious 13 unconsecrated

impish 4 arch 5 elfin 6 elvish 7 playful,

puckish, roguish, waggish **11** mischievous

impishness 7 devilry, roguery, waggery **8** deviltry, mischief **9** devilment **11** roguishness, waggishness

implacable 4 grim **8** ruthless **9** merciless **10** inexorable, unyielding **11** intractable **12** unappeasable

implant 3 fix **4** root **5** embed, graft, infix **6** enroot, infuse, insert **7** ingrain, inspire, instill **9** establish, inculcate, inoculate, introduce **10** inseminate **12** augmentation

implausible 5 fishy **6** flimsy **7** dubious, suspect **8** doubtful, fanciful, unlikely **10** far-fetched, incredible **12** questionable, unbelievable, unconvincing

implement 4 tool **6** device, effect, enable, gadget **7** enforce, execute, fulfill, perform, realize, utensil **8** carry out, complete, make good **9** actualize, apparatus, appliance **10** accomplish, instrument, supplement **11** contraption, contrivance *carpentry:* **3** die, saw **4** file **5** brace, clamp, drill, punch, tongs **6** chisel, hammer, pliers, reamer, sander, wrench **7** hacksaw, scraper **9** blowtorch **11** screwdriver *cleaning:* **3** mop **5** broom, brush, whisk **6** duster, vacuum **7** sweeper **10** whiskbroom *cutting:* **5** knife, mower, razor **6** scythe, shears, sickle **8** scissors *digging:* **5** spade **6** dibber, dibble, shovel *drawing:* **3** pen **6** eraser, pencil **7** compass **8** template *eating:* **4** fork **5** knife, spoon *engraving:* **5** burin **6** graver *farm:* **4** plow **6** binder, harrow, plough, scythe, seeder, sickle **8** gangplow, reaphook, spreader, thresher **9** pitchfork **10** cultivator *fireplace:* **5** poker, tongs **7** andiron *fishing:* **3** rod **4** hook, lure, reel **6** sinker **7** harpoon, trident *garden:* **3** hoe **4** rake **5** spade **6** dibber, dibble, digger, tiller, trowel **7** mattock **11** wheelbarrow *grooming:* **4** comb, file **5** brush, razor **7** clipper **8** clippers, nail file, tweezers **10** toothbrush *kitchen:* **3** pan, pot **4** mold **5** mixer, whisk **6** grater, kettle, mortar, pestle **7** blender, skillet, spatula **8** colander, saucepan, stockpot *logging:* **5** peavy **6** peavey **8** cant hook *measuring:* **3** cup **4** gage, rule **5** gauge, ruler, scale **7** caliper, divider, trammel, T-square **10** micrometer, protractor *stone:* **5** burin **7** neolith **9** paleolith

implicate 4 link, mire **5** blame **6** tangle **7** concern, embroil, entwine, include, involve **8** entangle, intimate **11** incriminate

implication 4 hint **8** allusion, overtone **9** inference, undertone **10** connection, intimation, suggestion **11** association, connotation **12** significance

implicit 5 tacit **6** unsaid **8** inherent, unspoken **9** doubtless, potential, unuttered **10** undeclared, understood **11** unexpressed **13** unquestioning

implied 5 tacit **6** unsaid **8** unspoken **9** suggested **10** undeclared, understood **11** unexpressed

implore 3 ask, beg **4** coax, pray **5** crave, plead **6** adjure, appeal **7** beseech, entreat, solicit **10** supplicate

imply 4 hint, mean **7** connote, include, involve, signify, suggest **8** indicate, intimate **9** insinuate

impolite 4 rude **5** crude **7** ill-bred, uncivil, uncouth **10** ungracious, unladylike, unmannered, unmannerly **11** ill-mannered **12** discourteous **13** ungentlemanly

impolitic 5 brash **6** unwise **8** tactless **9** imprudent, maladroit, untactful **10** ill-advised, indiscreet **11** inadvisable, inexpedient, injudicious **12** shortsighted, undiplomatic

import 4 bear, gist, mean, pith **5** sense, value, worth **6** convey, denote, intend, intent, matter, moment, stress, thrust, weight **7** concern, connote, express, meaning, message, purpose, signify **8** emphasis, indicate, transfer **9** magnitude, substance **10** intendment **11** acceptation, consequence **12** significance **13** signification

importance 4 mark, note, pith **5** value, worth **6** moment, weight **7** account, gravity **8** eminence, priority, salience, standing **9** greatness, magnitude, substance **10** prominence, worthiness **11** consequence, distinction, seriousness, weightiness **12** significance

important 3 big **5** chief, grave, great, heavy, major, noted, vital **6** famous, marked, potent, urgent, worthy **7** bigtime, capital, crucial, eminent, fateful, notable, salient, serious, telling, weighty **8** critical, eventful, foremost, material, powerful, pressing, valuable **9** essential, estimable, imperious, memorable, momentous, prominent **10** meaningful, noteworthy, preeminent, worthwhile **11** outstanding, significant, substantial **12** considerable **13** consequential, distinguished, indispensable

importune 3 beg **4** pray, urge **5** annoy, plead, worry **6** appeal, invoke, plague **7** beseech, besiege, entreat, solicit, trouble **8** petition

impose 3 fob **4** lade, levy **5** abuse, enact, exact, foist, force, order, place, put on,

visit, wreak 6 assess, burden, charge, compel, decree, demand, enjoin, fob off, ordain, saddle 7 command, dictate, exploit, inflict, intrude, lay down, obtrude, palm off, pass off, require 8 encroach, encumber, infringe, trespass 9 authorize, constrain, establish
imposing 4 huge 5 grand, noble, regal, royal 6 august 7 awesome, massive, pompous, stately 8 baronial, majestic, towering 9 dignified 10 commanding, monumental 11 magnificent, outstanding 12 high-sounding 13 distinguished
imposition 3 tax 4 duty, fine, levy 6 burden, demand 7 penalty 9 deception 13 inconvenience
impossible 6 absurd 8 hopeless 10 infeasible, unfeasible, unworkable 11 unthinkable 12 preposterous, unacceptable, unattainable, unbelievable, unimaginable, unrealizable, unreasonable 13 inconceivable
impost 3 fee, tax 4 duty, levy, toll 6 charge, tariff 7 tribute 9 surcharge 10 assessment
impostor 4 fake, sham 5 actor, cheat, faker, fraud, mimic, phony, poser, quack 6 humbug, poseur 8 deceiver 9 charlatan, con artist, hypocrite, pretender 10 dissembler, mountebank 11 masquerader 12 impersonator
imposture 4 fake, hoax, sell, sham, wile 5 cheat, fraud 6 deceit, humbug 8 flimflam 9 deception, mare's nest, stratagem 11 counterfeit
impotence 8 weakness 9 sterility 10 inadequacy 12 helplessness 13 powerlessness
impotent 4 lame, weak 6 effete, feeble 7 sterile 8 helpless 9 forceless, incapable, powerless 11 ineffective, ineffectual 12 invertebrate
impound 5 seize 6 immure, lock up 7 confine, enclose, put away 8 imprison 10 confiscate
impoverish 4 bust, ruin 5 break 6 beggar 8 bankrupt 9 pauperize
impoverished 4 poor 5 broke, needy 8 bankrupt, indigent 9 destitute, penniless, penurious
impoverishment 4 need, want 6 penury 9 indigence, neediness, privation 11 destitution
impracticable 8 unusable 10 infeasible, unfeasible, unworkable 11 insuperable, unrealistic 12 inaccessible, unattainable
impractical 7 utopian 8 quixotic, romantic, unusable 9 visionary 10 idealistic, infeasible, ivory-tower, starry-eyed, unfeasible, unworkable 11 theoretical, unrealistic

imprecation 3 hex 4 cuss 5 curse 7 malison 8 anathema 11 malediction
imprecise 5 rough, vague 7 inexact 9 estimated 10 indefinite 11 approximate, unspecified
impregnable 4 safe 6 immune, secure 9 protected 10 invincible, inviolable, unbeatable 11 indomitable, insuperable 12 unassailable 13 unconquerable
impregnate 3 sop 4 fill, soak 5 imbue, souse, steep 6 drench, infuse 7 pervade 8 conceive, permeate, saturate 9 fecundate, fertilize, penetrate, transfuse 10 inseminate
impresario 4 Bing (Rudolf) 5 Carte (Richard D'Oyly), Hurok (Sol) 6 Pastor (Tony) 7 manager 8 director, Kirstein (Lincoln), producer, promoter 9 Diaghilev (Sergei) 10 D'Oyly Carte (Richard)
impress 3 fix, set 4 dent, etch, mark, move, seal, sway 5 brand, carry, drive, exert, force, grave, infix, print, stamp, touch 6 affect, effect, excite, strike 7 engrave, ingrain, inspire 8 inscribe, transfer, transmit 9 establish, influence, stimulate
impressible 8 gullible, immature, moldable 9 malleable, receptive, sensitive 10 affectable, susceptive, vulnerable 11 persuadable, suggestible, susceptible
impression 4 dent, idea, mark, sign 5 image, print, stamp, trace, track 6 effect, hollow, notion 7 concept, edition, feeling, reissue, thought, vestige 8 printing, reaction 9 influence
impressionable 8 sensible, sentient 9 malleable, receptive, sensitive 10 responsive 11 suggestible, susceptible
impressionist *composer:* 5 Ravel (Maurice) 7 Debussy (Claude) *mimic:* 6 Carvey (Dana), Little (Rich) *painter:* 5 Degas (Edgar), Manet (Edouard), Monet (Claude) 6 Renoir (Auguste), Sisley (Alfred) 7 Cassatt (Mary), Morisot (Berthe) 8 Pissarro (Camille) (see also POSTIMPRESSIONIST)
impressive 5 grand, noble 6 moving, superb 7 amazing, awesome, notable, stately, sublime 8 dazzling, dramatic, gorgeous, majestic, powerful, splendid, stirring, striking, touching 9 admirable, affecting, arresting, inspiring 11 magnificent
imprimatur 6 permit 7 license 8 approval, sanction 10 permission 13 authorization
imprint 3 fix 4 dent, etch, mark 5 grave, press, stamp 6 dimple, effect 7 engrave 8 inscribe 9 engraving, influence

10 depression 11 indentation, inscription

imprison 3 jug 4 cage, jail 6 coop up, detain, immure, intern, send up 7 confine, enclose 8 restrain, restrict, stockade 9 constrain 11 incarcerate

improbable 5 fishy 7 dubious 8 doubtful, fanciful, unlikely 10 far-fetched 11 implausible

impromptu 5 ad-lib 7 offhand 9 extempore, makeshift, unplanned, unstudied 10 off-the-cuff, unprepared, unscripted 11 extemporary, spontaneous, unrehearsed

improper 5 inapt, inept, outré, undue, wrong 6 gauche, risqué 7 illicit, naughty 8 ill-timed, indecent, tactless, unseemly, untimely, untoward 9 incorrect, unethical, unfitting 10 inaccurate, inapposite, indecorous, indelicate, malapropos, unbecoming, undecorous, unsuitable 11 impertinent, unbefitting 12 illegitimate, inadmissible, inapplicable, infelicitous, unseasonable 13 inappropriate

impropriety 5 gaffe 7 blooper, blunder, faux pas 8 solecism 9 barbarism, gaucherie, indecorum, vulgarism 12 unseemliness 13 incorrectness

improve 4 edit, help, mend 5 amend, boost, edify, emend, raise 6 better, enrich, look up, perk up, refine, reform, remedy, revise, revive, uplift 7 advance, amplify, augment, build up, correct, develop, enhance, enlarge, further, perfect, recover, rectify, upgrade 8 increase, progress 9 cultivate, intensify, meliorate 10 aggrandize, ameliorate, recuperate, strengthen

improvident 4 rash 6 lavish 8 careless, feckless, heedless, prodigal, reckless, wasteful 9 impetuous, negligent, unthrifty 10 profligate 11 extravagant, spendthrift 12 shortsighted, uneconomical

improvise 5 ad-lib 6 cook up, invent, make up 7 concoct 8 contrive 9 fabricate 11 extemporize

improvised 7 offhand 9 extempore, unstudied 10 off-the-cuff, unprepared, unscripted 11 extemporary, unrehearsed

imprudent 4 rash 6 unwise 7 foolish 8 reckless 9 foolhardy 10 ill-advised, incautious, indiscreet 11 inadvisable, inexpedient, injudicious 12 shortsighted

impudence 4 gall 5 brass, cheek, nerve 8 audacity, boldness, chutzpah, temerity 9 brashness, cockiness, hardihood, insolence, nerviness 10 disrespect, effrontery 11 presumption

impudent 4 bold, flip, pert, wise 5 brash, cocky, fresh, nervy, sassy, saucy, smart 6 brassy, brazen, cheeky 7 blatant, forward 8 flippant, insolent, overbold 9 audacious, barefaced, bold-faced 11 brazen-faced, smart-alecky 12 contumelious 13 disrespectful

impugn 5 cross 6 assail, attack, defame, malign, oppose, vilify 7 asperse, gainsay, impeach 8 chastise, reproach, traverse 9 castigate, denigrate, deprecate, disparage, reprehend 9 criticize, denigrate

impugnable 5 fishy, shady 6 guilty 7 suspect 8 doubtful 9 equivocal, uncertain 10 assailable, suspicious 11 problematic 12 disreputable

impulse 4 goad, push, spur, urge, whim 5 drive, force 6 motive, thrust, whimsy 7 caprice, passion 8 catalyst, excitant, stimulus 9 actuation, incentive, stimulant 10 incitation, incitement, motivation 11 inspiration, instigation

impulsive 4 rash 5 hasty 6 abrupt, fickle, sudden 7 erratic, flighty, offhand 8 headlong, volatile 9 automatic, extempore, mercurial, unplanned, whimsical 10 capricious 11 instinctive, involuntary, precipitate, spontaneous

impunity 7 freedom, liberty, license 8 immunity 9 exception, exemption, indemnity, privilege 10 absolution, protection 12 dispensation

impure 3 raw 5 mixed 6 soiled, sordid, unholy 7 alloyed, defiled, profane, sullied, unclean 8 indecent, polluted, unchaste 9 uncleanly, unrefined 10 desecrated, unhallowed 11 adulterated

impute 3 lay 4 cite 5 blame, refer 6 accuse, adduce, assign, charge, credit, indict 7 ascribe 8 accredit 9 attribute, implicate

inaccessible 5 aloof 6 arcane, closed, far-off, remote 7 cryptic, distant, faraway, obscure 8 abstruse, esoteric, hermetic 9 recondite 11 unavailable, unreachable 12 unattainable, unobtainable

inaccurate 5 false, wrong 6 all wet, faulty, untrue 7 unsound 8 specious 9 distorted, erroneous 10 fictitious

inaction 6 repose 7 latency 8 dormancy, idleness, lethargy 9 indolence, passivity, slackness, torpidity 10 quiescence 12 slothfulness

inactive 4 idle, lazy 5 inert, quiet, slack, still 6 asleep, latent, sleepy, static, torpid 7 abeyant, dormant, passive, resting 8 slothful, sluggish 9 do-nothing, lethargic, quiescent, sedentary

in addition 4 also 6 as well, to boot,

withal **7** besides, further **8** moreover **11** furthermore

inadequacy 4 lack, want **6** dearth **7** deficit, failure, paucity **8** shortage, weakness **9** impotence **10** deficiency, scantiness **11** shortcoming

inadequate 3 shy **5** scant, short **6** meager, scanty, scarce, skimpy **7** lacking, scrimpy, wanting **8** impotent **9** defective, deficient **10** emasculate

inadmissible 5 unapt, unfit **8** unusable, unworthy **9** unwelcome **10** unsuitable **11** unqualified **12** unacceptable

inadvertent 8 careless, heedless **9** negligent, unmindful, unplanned, unwitting **10** accidental, unintended, unthinking **13** unintentional

inadvisable 4 rash **6** unwise **7** foolish **8** careless, reckless **9** foolhardy, impolitic, imprudent, pointless **10** illadvised **11** harebrained

inalterable 5 fixed **6** stable **8** constant **9** immovable, immutable, steadfast, unmovable, unvarying **12** unchangeable

inamorata, inamorato 4 beau, dear **5** flame, honey, lover **6** steady **7** beloved, darling, squeeze, sweetie **8** ladylove, mistress, paramour, truelove **9** boyfriend **10** girlfriend, heartthrob, sweetheart

inane 4 flat, idle, vain **5** blank, dotty, empty, silly, vapid **6** absurd, hollow, jejune, vacant **7** asinine, fatuous, foolish, idiotic, insipid, lunatic, trivial, vacuous, witless **8** mindless **9** frivolous, pointless, senseless

inanimate 4 dead, dull **5** inert **5** still **6** asleep, torpid **7** dormant **8** immotile, lifeless **9** quiescent **10** motionless **11** unconscious

inanity 5 folly **6** idiocy, lunacy **7** fatuity, vacuity **8** vapidity **9** absurdity, dottiness, emptiness, silliness **10** hollowness **11** foolishness, vacuousness, witlessness **13** senselessness

inappreciable 6 meager, scanty, skimpy, slight **10** impalpable, unapparent **13** imperceptible

inappropriate 5 amiss, undue, unfit **6** unmeet **8** improper, unseemly, untimely, untoward **9** ill-suited **10** malapropos, unsuitable **11** impertinent

inapt 5 unfit **6** clumsy, gauche, jejune, unmeet **7** awkward, unhandy **8** improper, unfitted, unsuited, untimely **9** maladroit, unfitting, unskilled **10** amateurish, irrelevant, malapropos, unskillful, unsuitable

inarticulate 4 dumb, mute **5** tacit **6** silent **7** halting, unvocal **8** mumbling, unspo-

ken, wordless **9** voiceless **10** maundering, speechless, tongue-tied, undeclared **11** unexpressed

inasmuch as 5 since **7** because, whereas **11** considering

inattentive 6 absent, remiss **8** distrait, heedless **9** forgetful, negligent, unheeding, unmindful **10** abstracted, distracted, unthinking **12** absentminded

inaugural 5 first **6** maiden, speech **7** address, initial, leading, opening, premier **8** foremost **9** beginning

inaugurate 5 begin, set up, start **6** launch **7** kick off **8** commence, dedicate, initiate **9** establish, institute, originate **10** consecrate

inauspicious 4 dire **7** adverse, baleful, direful, fateful, ominous, unlucky **8** sinister **9** ill-boding **11** threatening, unfavorable, unpromising **12** unpropitious

inborn 6 innate, native **7** connate, natural **8** inherent **9** intrinsic **10** congenital, connatural, hereditary, unacquired

inbred 7 connate, genetic, natural **8** inherent **9** intrinsic **10** congenital, connatural, deep-seated, hereditary

Inca *capital:* **5** Cuzco *conqueror:* **7** Pizarro (Francisco) *god:* **4** Inti **9** Viracocha **10** Pachacamac *language:* **7** Quechua *record:* **5** quipu *ruler:* **9** Atahualpa, Pachacuti **10** Atahuallpa

incalculable 4 huge, iffy, vast **6** untold **8** enormous **9** boundless, countless, limitless, uncertain **10** tremendous, unnumbered **11** illimitable, measureless, uncountable **12** immeasurable, unmeasurable **13** unpredictable

in camera 7 privily, sub rosa **8** covertly, secretly **9** furtively, privately **10** stealthily **13** clandestinely

incandescent 3 hot **5** lucid **6** ardent, bright, lucent **7** beaming, fulgent, glowing, intense, lambent, radiant **8** dazzling, luminous **9** brilliant, effulgent, refulgent **11** resplendent

incantation 3 hex **4** rune **5** chant, charm, magic, spell **10** hocus-pocus, mumbojumbo, necromancy **11** abracadabra, conjuration, enchantment *Buddhist, Hindu:* **6** mantra

incapable 5 unfit **6** unable **8** impotent, unexpert, unfitted **9** powerless, unskilled **10** unequipped, unskillful **11** unqualified **12** disqualified

incapacitate 6 disarm **7** cripple, disable **8** paralyze **10** debilitate, devitalize, disqualify, immobilize

incapacity 9 impotence, unfitness **10** impairment **11** disablement **12** fecklessness

incarcerate 3 jug 4 jail 6 coop up, immure, intern, send up 7 confine, enclose, impound 8 imprison

incarnadine 3 red 4 rosy 5 ruddy 6 redden 7 pinkish 8 bloodred

incarnate 5 human, reify 6 embody 7 realize 8 embodied, manifest 9 actualize, corporeal, personify 11 materialize, personalize 12 substantiate

incarnation 6 avatar 10 embodiment 11 reification *of Christ:* 7 kenosis

incautious 4 rash 5 brash, hasty 6 daring, madcap, unwary 8 careless, heedless, reckless 9 daredevil, foolhardy, impetuous, imprudent, negligent, unmindful 10 ill-advised, neglectful, regardless 11 precipitate, thoughtless

incendiary 5 fiery, torch 7 firebug 8 agitator, arsonist, arsonous 9 explosive, firebrand, ignitable 10 pyromaniac 12 pyromaniacal

incense 3 ire, mad, oil 4 balm, burn, rile 5 anger, aroma, scent, spice 6 arouse, enrage, homage, incite, madden 7 inflame, provoke 8 irritate 9 infuriate *vessel:* 6 censer 8 thurible

incentive 4 goad, spur 5 spark 6 motive 7 impetus, impulse 8 catalyst, stimulus 9 stimulant 10 inducement, motivation 11 provocation 13 encouragement

inception 4 root 5 birth, start 6 origin, outset, source 7 genesis, kickoff, opening 9 beginning 10 derivation, provenance 11 provenience 12 commencement

inceptive 7 initial, leadoff, nascent 9 beginning 10 initiatory

incertitude 5 doubt 7 dubiety 8 mistrust 9 suspicion 10 skepticism 11 dubiousness, uncertainty, vacillation 12 irresolution

incessant 6 steady 7 endless, eternal, nonstop 8 constant 9 ceaseless, continual, perpetual, unceasing 10 continuous 11 everlasting, unremitting 12 interminable 13 uninterrupted

inch 3 bit 5 crawl, creep 7 modicum

inchoate 8 formless, immature, unformed, unshaped 9 amorphous, embryonic, incipient, potential, shapeless 10 disjointed, incoherent 11 rudimentary, unorganized 12 disconnected

incident 5 event 6 moment 7 episode 8 occasion 9 ancillary, attendant, happening, satellite 10 affiliated, collateral, consequent, occurrence 11 concomitant, subordinate 12 circumstance

incidental 5 fluky, minor 6 casual, chance 9 accessory 10 contingent, fortuitous 11 subordinate 12 nonessential

incidentally 7 by the by 8 by the bye, by the way, casually 12 fortuitously

incinerate 4 burn 7 cremate

incipient 7 nascent 9 beginning, embryonic 10 commencing

incipit 5 start 7 opening 9 beginning

incise 3 cut 4 etch, gash, kerf, slit 5 carve, slash, slice 6 chisel, pierce 7 engrave

incision 3 cut 4 gash, slit 5 blaze, notch 10 laceration

incisive 4 keen 5 acute, crisp, sharp, terse 6 direct 7 cutting, mordant 8 clear-cut, piercing, slashing, succinct 9 trenchant 11 penetrating 13 perspicacious

incite 3 egg 4 abet, goad, prod, spur, urge 5 egg on, raise, rouse, set on 6 arouse, exhort, foment, kindle, set off, spur on, stir up, whip up 7 actuate, agitate, provoke, trigger 8 motivate 9 instigate, stimulate

incitement see INCENTIVE

inclement 3 raw 5 harsh, rough 6 bitter, brutal, severe, stormy 8 rigorous

inclination 3 bow, nod 4 bent, bias, lean, tilt, will 5 fancy, grade, pitch, slant, slope, taste, trend 6 ascent, liking 7 descent, incline, leaning 8 affinity, appetite, fondness, gradient, penchant, soft spot, tendency, velleity, weakness 9 affection 10 attachment, partiality, proclivity, propensity 11 disposition 12 predilection

incline 3 tip 4 bend, bias, cant, cast, heel, lean, list, sway, tend, tilt, turn 5 grade, impel, slant, slide, slope 6 affect, induce 7 dispose, leaning 8 gradient, persuade 9 influence, prejudice

inclined 3 apt 5 given, prone, raked 6 liable, likely, minded 7 dipping, leaning, oblique, sloping, tilting, willing 8 diagonal, pitching 11 predisposed *way:* 4 ramp

include 5 admit, bound, cover 6 enfold, number, take in 7 confine, contain, embrace, enclose, receive, subsume 8 comprise, encircle 9 encompass 10 comprehend 11 accommodate

inclusive 5 broad 6 global 7 general, overall 8 complete, sweeping 9 allaround, embracive 11 compendious 12 encompassing, encyclopedic 13 comprehensive

incognito 6 veiled 7 cloaked 9 anonymous, disguised 11 camouflaged

incognizant 7 unaware 8 ignorant 9 oblivious, unknowing, unmindful, unwitting 10 unfamiliar, uninformed 11 unconscious 12 unacquainted

incoherent 5 loose 6 broken, raving

7 muddled, unclear 8 confused 9 illogical 10 disjointed, disordered, irrational, maundering, tongue-tied 11 unconnected, unorganized 12 disconnected, disorganized 13 discontinuous
incombustible 9 fireproof 10 unburnable 12 nonflammable
income 4 gain, take 5 wages 6 profit 7 revenue 8 entrance, proceeds, receipts 9 emolument
incommode 3 irk, vex 5 annoy, upset 6 bother, burden, hinder, plague, put out 7 disturb, perturb, trouble 8 disquiet, distress, irritate 9 disoblige 10 disconcert
incommodious 7 awkward, cramped, crowded 8 confined 9 congested
incommunicable 8 reserved, taciturn 9 ineffable, withdrawn 11 unspeakable, unutterable 13 undescribable, unexpressible
incomparable 6 unique 7 supreme 8 peerless, singular, ultimate 9 matchless, nonpareil, paramount, unequaled, unmatched, unrivaled 10 preeminent, surpassing, unequalled, unrivalled 11 outstanding, superlative, unequalable, unmatchable 12 transcendent, unparalleled 13 unsurpassable
incompatible 7 adverse, counter 8 contrary, opposite 9 dissonant, unmixable 10 discordant, discrepant 11 conflicting, disagreeing, uncongenial, unfavorable 12 antagonistic, antithetical 13 contradictory, unsympathetic
incompetence 9 unfitness 10 disability, ineptitude 12 fecklessness
incompetent 5 inept, unfit 6 clumsy 8 helpless, inexpert, unfitted 9 incapable, maladroit, unskilled 10 unequipped 11 inefficient, unqualified
incomplete 4 part 5 short 6 broken, undone 7 partial, sketchy 8 abridged, immature 9 truncated 10 unfinished 11 fragmentary
incompliant 5 rigid, stiff 6 mulish 7 defiant 8 perverse, stubborn 9 obstinate, pigheaded, resistant, unbending 10 bullheaded, headstrong, inflexible, self-willed, unyielding 11 intractable 12 pertinacious, recalcitrant
incomprehensible 7 cryptic, obscure, unclear 8 abstruse, baffling, esoteric 9 fantastic 10 fathomless, mysterious, mystifying, unknowable 11 ungraspable 12 impenetrable, unfathomable, unimaginable
inconceivable 10 improbable, unknowable 11 implausible, unthinkable 12 unbelievable, unconvincing, unimaginable

in conclusion 6 lastly 7 finally
inconclusive 4 open 9 equivocal, uncertain, undecided, unsettled 10 unfinished
incongruous 5 alien 6 absurd 7 foreign, variant 9 anomalous, dissonant 10 discordant, discrepant, unsuitable 11 conflicting, disagreeing 12 disconsonant
inconsequential 5 petty, small 6 measly, paltry 7 trivial 8 picayune, trifling 9 illogical, small-time 10 immaterial, irrelevant, negligible 11 impertinent, superficial, unimportant
inconsiderable 4 puny 5 minor, petty 6 meager, meagre, paltry, scanty, skimpy, slight 7 scrimpy, trivial 8 picayune, trifling 9 frivolous, small-beer 10 negligible 11 unimportant
inconsiderate 4 rash 5 brash, hasty 6 unkind 8 careless, heedless, impolite, reckless 9 hotheaded, impulsive 10 ill-advised, ungracious 11 precipitate, thoughtless 12 discourteous, uncharitable
inconsistent 6 fickle 8 contrary 9 dissonant, illogical, mercurial 10 capricious, changeable, discordant, discrepant 11 conflicting 13 contradictory
inconsolable 7 forlorn 8 desolate 9 heartsick 11 comfortless, heartbroken
inconspicuous 6 hidden, subtle 7 obscure 9 concealed 11 unobtrusive 12 unnoticeable
inconstant 6 fickle, untrue 7 erratic, mutable, protean, vagrant 8 unstable, unsteady, variable, volatile, wavering 9 changeful, faithless, fluctuant, irregular, mercurial, uncertain, unsettled 10 capricious, changeable, irresolute, perfidious, unfaithful 11 chameleonic, vacillating 13 temperamental
incontestable 4 sure 7 certain 8 absolute, clear-cut, ironclad, positive 9 apodictic, undoubted 10 conclusive, inarguable, undeniable 11 irrefutable, unequivocal 12 unassailable, undisputable 13 unimpeachable
incontinent 5 loose 6 wanton 9 dissolute 10 licentious, profligate 12 unrestrained
incontrovertible 4 sure 7 certain 8 absolute, clear-cut, definite, positive 10 conclusive, undeniable 11 irrefutable, unequivocal 12 undisputable
inconvenience 3 irk, vex 5 annoy 6 bother, meddle, put out 7 disrupt, disturb, trouble 8 handicap, vexation 9 aggravate, annoyance, disoblige 10 discomfort, discommode, disruption, exasperate 11 aggravation, awkwardness 12 disadvantage, discomfiture, exasperation 13 embarrassment

inconvenient 7 awkward, unhandy 8 annoying 10 bothersome, unsuitable 11 pestiferous, troublesome

incorporate 3 mix 4 form, fuse, join 5 blend, merge, unite 6 absorb, embody, imbibe, mingle 7 combine 8 organize 9 establish 10 amalgamate, assimilate

incorporeal 8 bodiless, formless 9 spiritual 10 discarnate, immaterial, unphysical 11 disembodied, nonmaterial, nonphysical 12 metaphysical 13 unsubstantial

incorrect 5 false, wrong 6 faulty, untrue 7 unsound 8 improper, specious 9 erroneous, imprecise 10 fallacious, inaccurate, unbecoming

incorrigible 6 unruly 8 depraved 9 incurable 10 delinquent, inveterate 11 unalterable 12 irredeemable

increase 3 add, eke, wax 4 gain, grow, hike, jump, plus, push, rise, teem 5 boost, build, mount, put up, raise, run up, surge, swarm, swell 6 accrue, amount, beef up, dilate, expand, extend, gather, growth, jack up, markup 7 accrual, advance, amplify, augment, burgeon, distend, enhance, enlarge, inflate, magnify, prolong, upsurge 8 addition, compound, escalate, flourish, heighten, lengthen, manifold, multiply, protract, snowball 9 accession, accretion, aggravate, expansion, extension, increment, inflation, intensify, pullulate, reinforce 10 accelerate, accumulate, aggrandize, appreciate, strengthen 11 enlargement 12 augmentation, breakthrough 13 amplification

incredible 7 amazing, awesome 8 unlikely 9 cockamamy, fantastic 10 astounding, cockamamie, far-fetched, impossible, improbable, outlandish, phenomenal, remarkable 11 astonishing, implausible 12 preposterous, unbelievable, unconvincing, unimaginable 13 extraordinary

incredulity 7 unfaith 8 distrust, mistrust, unbelief 9 disbelief, nonbelief, suspicion 10 skepticism

incredulous 6 show-me 7 dubious 8 doubting 9 quizzical, skeptical 10 suspicious 11 distrustful, mistrustful, questioning, unbelieving, unconvinced 12 disbelieving

increment 4 gain, hike, rise, step 5 raise 6 degree, growth 7 quantum 8 addition 9 accession, accretion 11 enlargement 12 augmentation

incriminate 6 accuse, charge 7 arraign, impeach 9 implicate

incrustation 4 film, rime, scab 5 scale 6 tartar 7 coating

incubus 5 demon, fiend 9 nightmare

inculcate 5 teach, train 6 impart 7 educate, implant, impress, instill

inculpable 4 pure 5 clean 8 innocent, spotless, virtuous 9 blameless, guiltless, righteous 10 impeccable

incumbent 7 leaning, resting 8 occupant, required 9 overlying 10 obligatory 12 officeholder

incur 7 acquire, bring on 8 contract

incurable 5 fatal 6 deadly, lethal 8 hopeless, terminal 9 immutable 11 immedicable, irreparable 12 irremediable, unchangeable 13 uncorrectable

incursion 4 raid 5 blitz, foray, sally 6 attack, sortie 7 assault 9 irruption

incus 4 bone 5 anvil

indebted 5 bound 7 obliged 8 beholden 9 obligated

indebtedness 3 due, IOU 7 arrears 9 arrearage, gratitude, liability 10 obligation 11 delinquency 12 thankfulness

indecent 4 blue, foul, lewd, racy 5 bawdy, dirty, gross, nasty 6 coarse, filthy, impure, risqué, smutty, vulgar 7 obscene, profane, raunchy 8 immodest, improper, off-color, unseemly, untoward 9 offensive 10 malodorous, scurrilous 12 scatological 13 objectionable

indecision 5 doubt 8 wavering 9 hesitancy 11 ambivalence, uncertainty, vacillation 12 equivocation, irresolution, shilly-shally

indecisive 5 vague 6 unsure 7 dubious, unclear 8 wavering 9 equivocal, tentative, uncertain, undecided, unsettled 10 irresolute 11 problematic, vacillating

indecorous 4 rude 5 gross, rough 6 coarse, vulgar 7 uncivil 8 impolite, improper, unseemly, untoward 9 graceless, irregular, offensive, tasteless, unrefined 10 unbecoming 11 ill-mannered, undignified 12 discourteous

indecorum 5 gaffe 6 breach 7 blooper, blunder, faux pas, offense 8 solecism 11 impropriety

indeed 4 amen 5 truly 6 really, surely, verily 8 forsooth, honestly 9 assuredly, certainly 10 positively, undeniably 11 doubtlessly, undoubtedly 13 unequivocally

indefatigable 6 dogged 8 tireless, untiring, vigorous 9 energetic, tenacious 10 persistent, relentless, unflagging, unwearying 11 unrelenting

indefensible 9 unguarded, untenable 10 assailable, vulnerable 11 unprotected **12** unforgivable, unpardonable **13** unjustifiable

indefinable 5 vague **7** elusive **9** uncertain **11** unspeakable, unutterable **13** undescribable

indefinite 4 wide **5** broad, loose, vague **7** endless, general, inexact, obscure, unclear, unfixed **8** infinite **9** ambiguous, boundless, imprecise, limitless, unbounded, uncertain, undefined, unlimited **10** indistinct, inexplicit, unmeasured, unspecific **12** inconclusive **13** indeterminate *pronoun:* **3** all, any, few **4** each, many, most, none, some **6** anyone, nobody **7** anybody, several, someone **8** everyone, somebody **9** everybody

indehiscent fruit 3 key, nut **4** pepo **5** berry, grain, grape, melon **6** achene, loment, samara, squash **7** pumpkin **8** cucumber **9** caryopsis **10** schizocarp

indelible 4 fast **5** fixed **7** lasting **8** enduring **9** memorable, permanent **13** unforgettable

indelicate 3 raw **4** lewd, rude **5** crude, gross, rough **6** coarse, vulgar **7** uncouth **8** impolite, improper, tactless, unseemly, untoward **9** unrefined **10** unbecoming

indemnify 5 repay **6** secure **7** redress, requite **9** reimburse **10** compensate, recompense, remunerate

indemnity 6 amends **7** redress **8** requital, security **9** exemption, quittance, reprisals **10** protection, recompense, reparation **11** restitution **12** compensation, remuneration **13** fee-for-service

indentation 4 dent, nick **5** notch **6** dimple, recess **10** depression

indenture 4 nick **5** notch **8** contract **9** agreement **11** certificate

indentured 5 bound **10** controlled **11** apprenticed

independent 4 free **8** absolute, autarkic, separate **9** autarchic, sovereign **10** autonomous **11** self-reliant **13** self-contained

indescribable 11 unspeakable, unutterable **13** unexplainable

indestructible 7 lasting **8** enduring, immortal **9** permanent **12** imperishable, irrefragable, unperishable

indeterminate 5 vague **9** imprecise, uncertain, unlimited

index 4 list, mark, sign **5** ratio, table **7** catalog, symptom **8** classify, evidence, regulate **9** catalogue **11** systematize

India *bay:* **6** Bengal *capital:* **8** New Delhi *city:* **5** Delhi **6** Bombay, Kanpur, Madras, Mumbai, Nagpur **7** Chennai, Kolkata, Lucknow **8** Calcutta **9** Ahmadabad, Bangalore, Hyderabad *coast:*

7 Malabar **10** Coromandel *European discoverer:* **4** Gama (Vasco da) *language:* **5** Hindi *leader:* **5** Nehru (Jawaharlal) **6** Gandhi (Indira, Mohandas, Rajiv) *monetary unit:* **5** rupee *mountain range:* **7** Vindhya **9** Himalayas *neighbor:* **5** Burma, China, Nepal **6** Bhutan **7** Myanmar **8** Pakistan **10** Bangladesh *pass:* **5** Bolan, Gumal **6** Khyber *plateau:* **6** Deccan *river:* **5** Indus **6** Ganges, Yamuna **7** Krishna **11** Brahmaputra *sea:* **7** Arabian

Indian *bread:* **3** nan **4** naan **7** chapati *butter:* **3** ghi **4** ghee *caste:* **5** Sudra **6** Vaisya **7** Brahman **9** Kshatriya *female dancer:* **8** bayadere *groom:* **4** syce *harem:* **6** zenana *instrument:* **4** vina **5** sarod, sitar, tabla **7** tambura *lady:* **4** bibi **5** begum **8** memsahib *nurse:* **4** amah, ayah *outcast:* **6** pariah *prince:* **4** raja, rana **5** rajah **8** maharaja **9** maharajah *princess:* **4** rani **5** begum, ranee *scholar:* **6** pandit, pundit *screen:* **6** purdah *seal, stamp:* **4** chop *soldier:* **4** peon **5** sepoy *teacher:* **4** guru *viceroy:* **5** nabob, nawab *weight unit:* **3** ser **4** cash, dhan, pank, pice, powe, rati, tank, tola **5** adpao, fanam, hubba, masha, maund, pally, pouah, ratti **6** dhurra, pagoda, pollam **7** chinnam, chittak

Indiana *capital:* **12** Indianapolis *city:* **4** Gary **6** Muncie **9** Fort Wayne, South Bend **10** Evansville, Terre Haute **11** Bloomington *college, university:* **6** DePauw, Purdue **9** Ball State, Notre Dame *nickname:* **7** Hoosier (State) *river:* **5** White **6** Wabash *state bird:* **8** cardinal *state flower:* **5** peony *state tree:* **5** tulip

Indian, American *baby:* **7** papoose *ball game:* **8** lacrosse *carrier:* **7** travois *Central and South American:* **3** Ona **4** Cuna, Inca, Maya **5** Arara, Aztec, Carib, Huave, Olmec, Yagua **6** Arawak, Aymara, Jivaro, Omagua, Toltec, Yahgan **7** Chibcha, Quechua, Zapotec **8** Tarascan, Yanomamo **10** Araucanian **11** Tupi-Guaraní *food:* **4** samp **5** maize **8** pemmican *home:* **5** hogan, lodge, tepee **6** pueblo, teepee, wigwam **7** wickiup *leader:* **4** Popé **6** Wovoka **7** Cochise, Osceola, Pontiac, Sequoia, Sequoya **8** Geronimo, Hiawatha, Powhatan, Sequoyah, Tecumseh **9** Black Hawk, Massasoit **10** Crazy Horse **11** Cornplanter, Sitting Bull *money:* **6** wampum *North American:* **3** Fox, Oto, Sac, Ute **4** Cree, Crow, Erie, Hopi, Hupa, Iowa, Otoe, Pima, Pomo, Sauk, Taos, Yuma, Zuni **5** Aleut, Caddo, Creek, Haida, Huron, Kansa, Kiowa, Maidu, Miami, Modoc, Omaha, Osage, Sioux, Uinta

6 Apache, Cayuga, Dakota, Lenape, Mandan, Micmac, Mohawk, Munsee, Navaho, Navajo, Nootka, Oglala, Ojibwa, Oneida, Paiute, Pawnee, Pueblo, Quapaw, Salish, Santee, Seneca, Siwash **7** Anasazi, Arapaho, Arikara, Bannock, Chilkat, Chinook, Choctaw, Dakotah, Esselen, Klamath, Kutenai, Mohican, Naskapi, Natchez, Ojibway, Pontiac, Shawnee, Tlingit **8** Cherokee, Cheyenne, Chippewa, Comanche, Delaware, Illinois, Iroquois, Kickapoo, Kwakiutl, Nez Percé, Onondaga, Powhatan, Seminole, Shoshoni **9** Blackfoot, Chickasaw, Menominee, Tsimshian, Tuscarora, Wampanoag, Winnebago **10** Assiniboin, Chiricahua, Gros Ventre, Potawatomi **11** Massachuset, Narraganset *pipe:* **7** calumet *spirit:* **5** totem **6** manitu **7** kachina, manitou

Indian paintbrush 8 hawkweed **10** painted cup

indicate 4 bode, hint, mark, mean, show **5** augur, imply, point, prove **6** attest, convey, denote, evince, import, reveal **7** bespeak, betoken, connote, display, exhibit, express, presage, signify, suggest **8** disclose, evidence, foretell, manifest, register **9** designate **10** foreshadow, illustrate **11** demonstrate

indication 3 cue **4** clue, hint, mark, sign **5** proof, token, trace **6** augury, signal **7** gesture, inkling, portent, symptom **8** evidence, reminder, telltale **9** testimony **10** expression, suggestion **13** foreshadowing, manifestation

indicative 10 expressive, suggestive **11** evidentiary, symptomatic **12** illustrative **13** demonstrative

indicia 5 marks, signs **8** imprints, markings

indict 5 blame **6** accuse, charge **7** arraign, censure, impeach **9** criticize

indifference 6 apathy **9** aloofness, unconcern **10** detachment, dispassion **11** disinterest **12** carelessness, impartiality

indifferent 4 cold, cool, numb, so-so **5** aloof, blasé, stoic **6** casual, remote **7** average, neutral **8** careless, detached, mediocre, middling, moderate, ordinary, passable, unbiased, uncaring **9** apathetic, impartial, impassive, objective **10** nonchalant, unaffected **11** unconcerned, unemotional **12** uninterested, unprejudiced **13** disinterested, dispassionate

indigence 4 need, want **6** penury **7** poverty **9** neediness, pauperism, privation **11** deprivation, destitution

indigene 6 native **9** aborigine **10** aboriginal

indigenous 6 native **7** endemic, natural **10** aboriginal, congenital, connatural, unacquired **13** autochthonous

indigent 4 poor **5** broke, needy **9** destitute, penniless **11** impecunious, necessitous **12** impoverished

indigestion 9 dyspepsia, heartburn

indignant 3 mad **5** irate, riled, upset, vexed **6** galled, heated **7** annoyed **8** offended, outraged, provoked **9** affronted, irritated, resentful

indignation 5 pique **7** dudgeon **10** irritation, resentment

indignity 3 cut **4** slap **6** injury, insult, slight **7** affront, outrage **9** contumely, grievance **10** disrespect **11** humiliation **13** disparagement, embarrassment

indigo 4 blue **8** deep blue

indigo bird 5 finch **7** bunting

Indira's father 5 Nehru (Jawaharlal)

indirect 7 devious, oblique, vagrant, winding **8** circular, sidelong, tortuous **9** deceitful, underhand, wandering **10** backhanded, circuitous, collateral, meandering, roundabout **11** duplicitous, underhanded

indiscreet 5 gabby **6** unwise **7** foolish, gossipy **8** tactless **9** impolitic, imprudent, untactful **10** ill-advised **11** loose-lipped

indiscretion 4 slip **5** folly, gaffe, lapse **7** blunder, faux pas, mistake, misstep **8** solecism **10** imprudence **11** impropriety

indiscriminate 5 mixed **6** hybrid, motley, random, varied **7** aimless, jumbled, vagrant **8** assorted, careless **9** arbitrary, desultory, haphazard, hit-or-miss, unplanned, wholesale **10** uncritical **11** promiscuous **12** conglomerate, multifarious, unrestrained **13** heterogeneous, miscellaneous

indispensable 5 basic, vital **6** needed **7** crucial, needful, pivotal **8** cardinal, critical **9** essential, necessary, requisite **10** imperative, obligatory **11** fundamental

indisposed 3 ill **4** down, sick **5** loath **6** ailing, averse, poorly, sickly, unwell **7** uneager **8** hesitant **9** reluctant, resistant, unwilling **11** disinclined

indisposition 6 malady **7** ailment, dislike, illness, malaise **8** aversion, disfavor, distaste, sickness, unhealth **10** affliction, reluctance

indisputable 4 sure, true **7** certain, evident, obvious **8** absolute, ironclad, positive **9** apodictic **10** undeniable **11** irrefutable, unequivocal **12** irrefragable, unassailable

indistinct 3 dim **4** hazy **5** faint, foggy,

misty, murky, vague **6** bleary, blurry, cloudy **7** blurred, obscure, shadowy, unclear **8** confused **9** uncertain, undefined **12** undetermined

indistinguishable 4 same **5** alike, equal, vague **7** unclear **9** duplicate, identical **10** equivalent

indite 3 pen **5** write **6** record, scribe **7** compose, engross **10** transcribe

individual 3 one **4** body, lone, self, sole, soul, unit **5** being, human, party, thing **6** entity, mortal, person, proper, single **7** special **8** creature, discrete, distinct, peculiar, personal, separate, singular, solitary, specific **10** particular, respective **11** distinctive **13** idiosyncratic *combining form:* **4** idio

individualist 5 loner **6** hermit **8** lone wolf, maverick **13** nonconformist

individuality 4 self **7** essence, oneness **8** identity, selfhood **9** character **10** uniqueness **11** personality, singularity **12** idiosyncrasy, separateness

individualize 4 mark **7** specify **9** customize **10** specialize **11** distinguish, personalize, singularize **12** characterize **13** differentiate, particularize

Indochinese country 4 Laos **5** Burma **7** Myanmar, Vietnam **8** Cambodia, Thailand **9** Kampuchea

indoctrinate 5 teach, tutor **7** educate, program **8** convince, persuade **9** brainwash, inculcate

indolence 4 laze **5** sloth **7** inertia, languor **8** idleness, laziness, lethargy **9** torpidity **12** slothfulness, sluggishness **13** shiftlessness

indolent 4 idle, lazy **6** torpid **8** fainéant, slothful, sluggish **9** lethargic, shiftless

indomitable 7 staunch **9** steadfast **10** invincible, unbeatable **11** impregnable **13** unconquerable

Indonesia *archipelago:* **5** Malay *capital:* **7** Jakarta **8** Djakarta *city:* **5** Medan **7** Bandung, Cilacap **8** Semarang, Surabaja, Surabaya **9** Palembang *island group:* **5** Sunda **8** Moluccas *language:* **6** Bahasa *leader:* **7** Suharto, Sukarno *monetary unit:* **6** rupiah *regions:* **4** Bali, Java **5** Ceram, Timor **6** Bangka, Borneo, Flores, Lombok, Madura **7** Celebes, Sumatra **8** Sulawesi **9** Irian Jaya *volcano:* **8** Krakatau, Krakatoa

indubitable 4 sure **6** patent **7** certain, evident, obvious **8** definite, ironclad, positive **9** apodictic, veritable **10** undeniable **11** irrefutable, self-evident, unequivocal **12** irrefragable

induce 5 cause **6** effect, elicit, prompt **7** actuate, procure **8** convince, engender, generate, motivate, occasion, persuade **9** encourage

inducement 4 bait, lure **6** come-on, motive **10** attraction, motivation **13** consideration

induct 4 lead **5** admit **6** enlist, enroll **7** appoint, install

inductance unit 5 henry

induction 8 entrance **9** accession, reasoning **10** enlistment **11** appointment **13** ratiocination

inductive 7 logical **9** prefatory, prelusive **11** a posteriori

indulge 3 pet **4** baby, bask **5** allow, favor, humor, spoil **6** cocker, coddle, cosset, oblige, pamper, permit, please, wallow **7** cater to, delight, gratify, satisfy **9** luxuriate **11** mollycoddle

indulgence 5 favor, mercy, treat **6** luxury **7** charity **8** clemency, courtesy, kindness, lenience, leniency **9** allowance, remission, tolerance **10** compassion, kindliness, permission, toleration **11** forbearance, forgiveness **12** dispensation, mercifulness **13** gratification

indulgence seller 5 Tezel (Johann) **6** Tetzel (Johann)

indulgent 4 easy, kind **7** clement, lenient **8** generous, merciful, tolerant **9** forgiving **10** charitable, permissive

indurate 6 harden **7** callous, confirm, congeal **8** hardened, solidify, stubborn **9** unfeeling **11** hard-hearted

industrialist 6 tycoon **7** magnate **12** manufacturer

industrious 4 busy **8** diligent, sedulous **9** assiduous, laborious

industry 4 work **5** labor **8** business, commerce **9** assiduity, diligence **10** enterprise

inebriant see INTOXICANT

inebriate 3 sot **4** lush, soak **5** drunk, souse, tight, tipsy, toper **6** bibber, boozer **7** stupefy, tippler, tosspot **8** drunkard **10** intoxicate

inebriated 3 lit **5** drunk, lit up, oiled, stiff, tight, tipsy **6** blotto, juiced, loaded, plowed, potted, soused, stewed, tanked, wasted **7** crocked, pickled, pie-eyed, sloshed, smashed **8** polluted **9** plastered

inedible 9 poisonous **12** unappetizing

ineffable 5 taboo **9** forbidden **11** unspeakable, unutterable **13** undescribable

ineffaceable 7 lasting **8** enduring **9** indelible, permanent

ineffective 4 vain, weak **6** futile **7** useless **8** abortive, bootless, feckless, impotent **9** fruitless, powerless **10** emasculate, unavailing **12** unproductive, unsuccessful

ineffectiveness 8 futility **9** impotence

ineffectual see INEFFECTIVE

inefficient 5 slack **6** clumsy **8** careless, slipshod, wasteful **9** negligent

inelastic 5 rigid, stiff **7** brittle **9** unbending **10** unyielding

inelegant 5 crass, crude, gross, rough **6** coarse, gauche, vulgar **7** awkward, uncouth **9** graceless, unrefined **10** uncultured, ungraceful **12** uncultivated

ineligible 5 unfit **8** unfitted, unworthy **10** unequipped, unsuitable **11** unqualified **12** disqualified

ineluctable 4 sure **5** bound, fated **6** doomed **7** certain **8** destined **9** necessary **10** inevitable, unevadable **11** unavoidable, unescapable **13** unpreventable

inept 5 unfit **6** clumsy, gauche, klutzy **7** artless, awkward, foolish, halting, unhandy **8** bumbling, bungling **9** all thumbs, ham-handed, maladroit, unskilled **10** malapropos, unskillful, unsuitable **11** heavy-handed, undexterous, unfortunate

inequality 8 imparity **9** disparity **10** unevenness **12** irregularity, variableness **13** disproportion, heterogeneity

inequitable 6 biased, unfair, unjust **7** partial **10** prejudiced **11** unjustified, unrighteous

inequity 4 bias **5** wrong **9** prejudice **10** unfairness, unjustness

ineradicable 6 innate **7** chronic **8** constant, inherent, stubborn **9** ingrained **10** deep-rooted, deep-seated, entrenched, inveterate **11** established, ever-present, never-ending

inert 4 calm, dead, idle **5** quiet, still **6** asleep, sleepy **7** dormant, passive **8** immobile, lifeless, sluggish **9** apathetic, lethargic **10** motionless

inert gas 4 neon **5** argon, radon, xenon **6** helium **7** krypton

inertia 5 sloth **6** apathy, stupor, torpor **7** languor **8** idleness, laziness, lethargy **9** indolence, inertness, lassitude, passivity, torpidity **10** immobility, inactivity **11** disinterest **12** listlessness, sluggishness

inescapable see INEVITABLE

inessential see UNESSENTIAL

inestimable 9 priceless **11** measureless **12** immeasurable, unmeasurable, unfathomable

inevitable 4 sure **5** bound, fated **6** doomed **7** certain **8** destined **9** necessary **11** unavoidable, unescapable **12** foreordained **13** unpreventable

inevitably 8 perforce **10** willy-nilly **11** like it or not, unavoidably

inexcusable 6 guilty **8** blamable, culpable **9** untenable **10** censurable **11** blameworthy, condemnable **12** criticizable, unforgivable, unpardonable **13** reprehensible, unjustifiable

inexhaustible 8 tireless, untiring **9** unfailing, weariless **10** bottomless, unflagging **13** indefatigable

inexorable 5 rigid **6** strict **7** adamant **8** immobile, obdurate, stubborn **9** immovable, unbending **10** relentless, unyielding **11** unrelenting

inexpensive 3 low **5** cheap **7** cut-rate **8** moderate **10** reasonable

inexperience 7 naïveté, rawness **8** verdancy **9** freshness, greenness **10** callowness

inexperienced 3 raw **5** fresh, green, naive, young **6** callow **7** untried **8** unversed **9** unskilled, untrained, unworldly **10** amateurish, unseasoned

inexpert 9 maladroit, unskilled, untrained **10** amateurish

inexplicable 6 arcane, obtuse, opaque **7** cryptic **9** enigmatic **10** mysterious, mystifying, unsolvable **11** undefinable **12** impenetrable, unfathomable **13** unaccountable, unexplainable

inexpressible 8 nameless **11** unspeakable, unutterable **13** undescribable, unexplainable

inexpressive 5 blank, stoic **6** stolid, vacant, wooden **7** deadpan **9** impassive **10** poker-faced **13** straight-faced

inextricable 9 insoluble **10** unsolvable

infallible 4 sure **5** exact **6** trusty **7** certain, correct, perfect **8** absolute, accurate, flawless, surefire, unerring **9** errorless, unfailing **10** dependable, impeccable **11** trustworthy **12** tried-and-true **13** unimpeachable

infamous 4 evil, vile **6** odious **7** hateful, heinous **8** flagrant, shameful **9** abhorrent, miscreant, nefarious, notorious **10** abominable, despicable, detestable, flagitious, scandalous, villainous **11** disgraceful, ignominious, opprobrious **12** contemptible, disreputable

infamy 5 odium, shame **7** obloquy **8** disgrace, dishonor, ignominy **9** disrepute, notoriety **10** opprobrium

infancy 8 babyhood **9** childhood

infant 4 babe, baby **5** bairn, child, green **7** bambino, neonate, newborn, papoose, toddler **8** bantling, immature, nursling **9** unfledged *bed:* **4** crib **6** cradle **8** bassinet *food:* **3** pap **4** milk **7** pabulum *room:* **7** nursery

infanta 8 princess

infantile 7 babyish, puerile **8** childish, immature

infantryman 7 dogface **8** doughboy **11** foot soldier *Algerian:* **6** Zouave

infatuated 5 dotty, silly **7** foolish **8** besotted, enamored, obsessed **9** bewitched, rapturous **10** captivated, passionate

infatuation 4 rage **5** ardor, craze, crush, folly **7** passion, rapture **8** devotion **9** obsession, puppy love **11** fascination

infect 5 taint **6** defile, poison **7** corrupt, pollute **11** contaminate

infection 3 bug **6** sepses (plural), sepsis *fungous:* **8** mycetoma

infectious 8 catching, epidemic, virulent **9** pestilent **10** contagious, corrupting **12** communicable **13** contaminating, transmittable

infelicitous 5 unapt, unfit **6** unmeet **7** awkward, unhappy **8** improper **9** imperfect **10** malapropos, unsuitable **11** regrettable, unfortunate

infer 5 judge **6** deduce, deduct, derive, gather, reason **7** collect, make out, suppose, surmise **8** conclude, construe **10** conjecture **11** hypothesize

inference 7 surmise **8** illation, sequitur **9** deduction **10** assumption, conclusion, conjecture, derivation **11** presumption, supposition

inferior 3 low **4** base, fair, hack, mean, poor, puny **5** cheap, lousy, lower, minor, petty, scrub, sorry, under, worse **6** common, deputy, feeble, impure, junior, lesser, nether, no-good, paltry, satrap, shoddy, sleazy, tawdry, tinpot, vassal **7** average, subject, unequal **8** declassé, low-grade, mediocre, middling, ordinary, unworthy, wretched **9** attendant, auxiliary, no-account, satellite, secondary, subaltern, subjacent, underling, worthless **10** inadequate, second-rate **11** substandard *prefix:* **3** sub **4** demi **5** infra

infernal 6 Hadean **7** hellish, satanic **8** chthonic, damnable, demoniac, devilish, diabolic, plutonic **9** chthonian, plutonian, Tartarean **10** diabolical, sulphurous

inferno 3 pit **4** fire, hell **5** Hades, Sheol **6** blazes, Tophet **7** Gehenna **9** holocaust, perdition **10** underworld **11** netherworld **13** conflagration

Inferno *division:* **5** canto *poet:* **5** Dante (Alighieri) *verse form:* **9** terza rima

infertile 6 barren, effete **7** sterile **8** impotent **10** unfruitful **12** hardscrabble, unproductive

infest 4 teem **5** beset, swarm **6** plague **7** overrun **10** parasitize

infidel 5 pagan **7** atheist, heathen,

heretic, skeptic **8** agnostic **10** unbeliever

infidelity 7 perfidy, treason **8** adultery, betrayal, cheating **9** disbelief, treachery **10** disloyalty **13** faithlessness

infinite 4 vast **7** endless, eternal, immense **8** unending **9** boundless, countless, limitless, perpetual, unlimited **11** everlasting, illimitable, measureless, sempiternal **12** immeasurable

infinity 8 eternity **10** perpetuity **11** endlessness **12** sempiternity **13** boundlessness, limitlessness

infirm 4 lame, sick, weak **5** frail **6** ailing, feeble, sickly **7** failing, fragile, unsound **8** decrepit, unstable **9** doddering **11** debilitated

infirmity 3 ill **4** flaw **5** decay **6** malady **7** ailment, disease, frailty, illness, malaise **8** debility, disorder, sickness, syndrome, weakness **9** complaint, condition **10** affliction, feebleness, sickliness **11** decrepitude **12** debilitation, enfeeblement

infix 4 root **5** embed, lodge **6** fasten, pierce **7** engrave, implant, impress

inflame 4 fire, gall, goad, rile, roil **5** anger, light, rouse **6** arouse, enrage, excite, foment, ignite, kindle, madden, redden, stir up **7** provoke **8** enkindle, irritate **9** aggravate **10** exacerbate, exasperate

inflammable 5 fiery **6** ardent **8** burnable, volatile **9** excitable, ignitable, irascible **11** combustible

inflammation 4 gout, sore **6** otitis, quinsy **7** catarrh, colitis **8** adenitis, bursitis, cystitis, neuritis, pleurisy, rachitis, swelling **9** arthritis, chilblain, gastritis, nephritis, phlebitis **10** bronchitis, cellulitis, combustion, dermatitis, gingivitis, laryngitis, tendinitis **12** encephalitis **13** poliomyelitis *eye:* **6** iritis **7** pinkeye **9** keratitis *horse:* **7** fistula, quittor *intestines:* **7** ileitis **9** enteritis *suffix:* **4** itis

inflammatory 8 exciting **9** explosive, seditious **11** provocative **13** rabble-rousing, revolutionary

inflate 4 fill **5** bloat, elate, swell **6** expand **7** amplify, distend **10** aggrandize

inflated 5 tumid, windy **6** turgid **7** bloated, swollen, verbose **9** bombastic, distended, dropsical, flatulent, overblown **10** heightened **11** exaggerated, pretentious

inflection 4 bend, tone **5** curve, pitch **6** accent, change, stress, timbre **8** emphasis, tonality **9** accidence **10** modulation

inflexible 3 set **4** grim, hard, iron **5** fixed, rigid, stiff **6** strict **7** adamant, die-hard

8 granitic, hard-line, immobile, iron-clad, obdurate, stubborn **9** immovable, immutable, obstinate, steadfast, unbending **10** adamantine, brassbound, implacable, rock-ribbed, unbendable, unyielding **11** unalterable, unrelenting **12** unchangeable **13** dyed-in-the-wool

inflict 5 visit, wreak **7** mete out, subject **8** dispense **10** administer

inflow 4 rush **7** arrival

influence 4 move, pull, sway **5** alter, bribe, clout, force, impel, lobby, touch **6** affect, compel, impact, modify, moment, strike, weight **7** command, control, impress, mastery **8** dominate, militate, persuade, prestige **9** authority, dominance

influenceable 8 gullible **9** malleable, receptive, tractable **11** persuadable, persuasible, suggestible

influential 6 potent **8** forceful, powerful **9** effective **10** persuasive **13** authoritative

influx 7 arrival **8** entrance, invasion **9** accession

inform 3 rat **4** blab, clue, leak, post, tell, warn **5** brief, edify, endow, endue, imbue, teach **6** advise, betray, fill in, impart, leaven, notify, reveal, snitch, squeal, tattle, turn in, update **7** animate, apprise, caution, educate **8** acquaint, disclose, forewarn **9** advertise, enlighten **10** illuminate **11** familiarize

informal 6 casual, dégagé, folksy **7** natural, offhand, relaxed **8** down-home, familiar, laid-back **9** easygoing **10** colloquial, unofficial **13** unceremonious

information 4 data, fact, lore, news, poop, word **5** scoop **6** advice, notice, skinny, wisdom **7** lowdown, tidings **9** knowledge **12** intelligence *second-hand:* **7** hearsay

information bureau *abbreviation:* **4** USIA, USIS

informative 8 edifying, exegetic **10** exegetical **11** educational, elucidative, explanatory **12** enlightening, illuminating

informed 4 wise **5** aware **6** au fait, versed **7** abreast, knowing **8** apprised, educated **9** au courant, cognizant **10** acquainted, conversant **11** enlightened **13** knowledgeable

informer 3 rat, spy **4** fink, mole **5** stool **6** canary, gossip, snitch **7** rat fink, stoolie, tattler, tipster **8** squealer, telltale **10** deep throat, talebearer, tattletale **11** stool pigeon **13** whistle-blower

infra 5 after, below, later, under **7** beneath

infract 3 sin **6** breach, offend **7** violate **8** trespass **10** contravene, transgress

infraction 3 sin **4** foul **5** crime, error **6** breach **7** faux pas, misdeed, offense **8** trespass **9** violation **12** encroachment **13** contravention, transgression

infrastructure 4 base **5** basis **9** framework **10** foundation, groundwork, substratum **12** underpinning

infrequent 3 odd **4** rare **6** scarce, seldom **7** unusual **8** isolated, sporadic, uncommon, unwonted **10** occasional **11** exceptional

infringe 6 breach, impose, meddle, offend **7** disturb, obtrude, violate **8** encroach, entrench, trespass **10** transgress

infuriate 3 ire, mad **4** rile **5** anger, pique **6** enrage, madden, rankle **7** incense, inflame, outrage, provoke, steam up

infuse 4 fill, soak **5** imbue, steep **6** leaven **7** animate, implant, pervade, suffuse **8** permeate, saturate **10** impregnate

ingenious 5 acute, canny, sharp, smart **6** adroit, clever, crafty **7** cunning, fertile **8** creative, original **11** imaginative, resourceful

ingenuity 5 knack, savvy, skill **6** acumen, smarts, talent **7** know-how, mastery **8** deftness, keenness **9** adeptness, handiness **10** adroitness, capability, cleverness, perception, shrewdness **11** proficiency **12** intelligence, skillfulness **13** inventiveness

ingenuous 4 open **5** naive **6** simple **7** artless, natural **8** innocent **9** childlike, guileless, unstudied **10** unaffected

ingest 3 eat **4** feed **6** devour **7** consume, partake, swallow

Inge work 6 Picnic **7** Bus Stop **18** Splendor in the Grass **19** Come Back Little Sheba

inglorious 8 shameful **11** disgraceful, ignominious, opprobrious **12** dishonorable, disreputable **13** discreditable, unrespectable

ingot 3 bar, rod **4** mold **6** billet

ingrained 6 innate **8** inherent **9** essential **10** congenital, deep-rooted, deep-seated

ingratiating 5 silky **6** silken, smarmy **7** fawning **8** pleasing, unctuous **9** adulatory **10** flattering **11** sycophantic

ingredient 4 part **5** piece **6** factor **7** element **9** component **11** constituent

ingress 4 door **5** entry **6** access, entrée, portal **7** doorway, passage **8** entrance, entryway **9** admission, vestibule **10** admittance **11** entranceway

ingurgitate 4 bolt, cram, gulp, slop, wolf **5** gorge, scarf, stuff, swill **6** devour, gobble, guzzle **7** swallow

inhabit 4 live **5** dwell, haunt **6** occupy, people, settle, tenant **8** populate
inhabitant 5 liver **6** inmate, native **7** citizen, denizen, dweller, resider **8** indigene, resident **9** aborigine **10** autochthon *foreign:* **5** alien *indigenous:* **6** native **9** aborigine
inhale 7 breathe, consume, respire, swallow
inharmonious 6 atonal **7** jarring **9** dissonant, unmusical **10** discordant **11** cacophonous, conflicting, conflictive, disagreeing, quarrelsome, uncongenial **12** antagonistic
inhere 3 lie **5** dwell **6** belong, reside
inherent 4 born **5** basic **6** native **7** built-in, connate, natural **8** immanent **9** elemental, essential **10** congenital, deep-seated **11** fundamental
inherit 7 acquire, receive, succeed
inheritance 3 DNA **4** gene, gift **6** devise, estate, legacy **7** bequest **8** heirloom, heritage **9** patrimony, tradition **10** birthright **13** primogeniture
inherited 6 native **7** connate, genetic, natural **10** bequeathed, congenital, connatural, handed-down, hand-me-down
inheritor 4 heir **7** heiress, legatee **11** beneficiary
inhibit 4 curb, slow **5** check **6** arrest, bridle, enjoin, fetter, hamper, hinder, hobble, impede **7** prevent, repress, trammel **8** hold back, obstruct, restrain, suppress, withhold **9** constrain **10** discourage
inhibition 4 curb **5** taboo **6** hang-up **7** barrier **9** hindrance, restraint, stricture **10** impediment, repression **11** suppression
inhuman 5 cruel, feral **6** brutal, savage **7** beastly, bestial, brutish **8** fiendish **9** barbarous, monstrous **10** diabolical
inhumane 4 fell, grim **5** cruel **6** brutal, fierce, malign, savage **8** ruthless, sadistic **9** barbarous, ferocious, heartless, merciless, truculent
inhumation 6 burial **9** interment, sepulture **10** entombment
inhume 4 bury **5** plant **6** entomb **7** put away **9** lay to rest
inimical 7 adverse, harmful, hostile **10** malevolent, unfriendly **11** belligerent, contentious **12** antagonistic, antipathetic
iniquitous 3 bad **4** base, evil, vile **5** wrong **6** sinful, unjust, wicked **7** immoral, vicious **9** nefarious
iniquity 3 sin **4** evil **5** crime, wrong **7** offense **9** turpitude **8** trespass **10** immorality, wickedness, wrongdoing **13** transgression

initial 5 first, prime **6** anlage, letter, maiden **7** approve, engrave, leading, opening, primary **8** earliest, foremost, monogram, original **9** beginning
initiate 4 open **5** begin, enter, set up, start **6** enroll, get off, induct, invest, launch, take up **7** install, kick off, usher in **8** commence **9** originate **10** inaugurate
initiation 5 debut **7** baptism **9** admission, beginning, induction **10** admittance **11** investiture, origination **12** commencement, introduction
initiative 4 push **5** drive, spunk **6** energy **8** ambition, aptitude, gumption **9** beginning **10** enterprise, get-up-and-go
inject 3 add **6** insert **7** implant, instill **9** inoculate, introduce, vaccinate
injection 3 fix **4** hypo, shot **5** serum **7** booster, vaccine **10** hypodermic **11** inoculation, vaccination
injudicious 4 rash **5** hasty **6** unwise **8** heedless, reckless **9** ill-judged, impolitic, imprudent **10** ill-advised, indiscreet **11** inexpedient **12** short-sighted
injunction 3 ban, bar **4** writ **5** order **6** behest, charge **7** bidding, command, dictate, mandate **9** direction **11** prohibition
injure 3 mar **4** foul, harm, hurt, maim, pain **5** spoil, wound, wrong **6** blight, bruise, damage, deface, deform, foul up, impair, mangle **7** afflict, contort, cripple, disable, torture **8** distress, maltreat, mutilate **9** disfigure **12** incapacitate
injurious 6 nocent **7** abusive, adverse, harmful, hurtful **8** damaging **9** offensive **10** defamatory **11** detrimental
injury 3 ill **4** harm, hurt **5** wound, wrong **6** bruise, damage, trauma **8** distress **9** detriment
injustice 4 tort **5** crime, wrong **6** breach, damage **7** outrage **8** inequity, trespass **9** grievance, violation **10** favoritism, wrongdoing
ink 3 dye, pen **4** sign **8** inscribe **9** autograph, signature, subscribe
inkling 3 cue, tip **4** clue, hint, idea, lead, wind **5** hunch **6** notion, tip-off **8** telltale **9** suspicion **10** indication, intimation, suggestion
inky 3 jet **4** ebon **5** black, ebony, jetty, raven, sable **9** Cimmerian, pitch-dark **10** pitch-black
inlaid 5 piqué **6** boolle **7** hatched **8** enchased, nielloed **9** damascene, incrusted
Inland Empire 8 Illinois
inlet 3 arm, bay **4** cove, gulf **5** bayou,

bight, creek, fiord, firth, fjord, sound
6 harbor, slough, strait 7 estuary *Admiralties:* 4 Kali *Adriatic Sea:* 5 Vlorë
Aegean Sea: 7 Saronic *Africa:* 6 Walvis
Alaska: 4 Cook 5 Cross, Taiya 7 Glacier
8 Chilkoot *Aleutians:* 5 Holtz, Nazan
Angola: 5 Bengo, Tiger 6 Tigres *Antarctica:* 3 Ice 7 McMurdo 8 Amundsen
10 Shackleton *Arabian Sea:* 4 Qamr
5 Kamar *Australia:* 4 King 6 Botany
9 Discovery 10 Broad Sound *Baffin Bay:*
8 Melville *Baffin Island:* 9 Admiralty
Baltic Sea: 4 Hano 6 Danzig, Gdansk
9 Pomerania 10 Pomeranian *Barents
Sea:* 4 Kola 7 Pechora *Beaufort Sea:*
7 Prudhoe 9 Mackenzie *Bismarck Sea:*
5 Kimbe *Brazil:* 9 Guanabara *Bristol
Channal:* 10 Carmarthen *California:*
5 Morro 8 Monterey *Canada:* 5 Fundy
9 Howe Sound *Cape Breton Island:*
4 Mira *Caribbean Sea:* 5 Limón *Central
America:* 7 Fonseca *Chile:* 5 Otway
Crete: 4 Suda 5 Canea *Denmark:* 3 Ise
Djibouti: 6 Tajura 8 Tadjoura *East River:*
8 Flushing *Ecuador:* 5 Manta *Eire:*
4 Clew 7 Brandon *English Channel:*
3 Tor *Florida:* 8 Biscayne 10 Saint Lucie
Georgia: 8 Altamaha *Greenland:* 6 Baffin
Gulf of Alaska: 3 Icy 5 Woman 12 Resurrection *Gulf of Mexico:* 7 Aransas
8 Suwannee 9 Matagorda, Pensacola
10 Terrebonne 11 Atchafalaya
12 Apalachicola *Gulf of St. Lawrence:*
5 Bonne *Hawaii:* 11 Pearl Harbor *Honshu:* 3 Ise 5 Owari 6 Atsuta *Hudson Bay:*
7 Repulse *Iceland:* 4 Axar, Eyja, Huna
5 Horna, Skaga, Vopna 8 Hunafloi
Indonesia: 4 Bima 5 Saleh *Ionian Sea:*
7 Taranto *Irish Sea:* 4 Luce 7 Dundalk
Japan: 4 Tosa *Java:* 4 Lada 5 Peper *Java
Sea:* 7 Batavia *Kara Sea:* 6 Enisei 7 Yenisei *Labrador:* 8 Hamilton *Lake Erie:*
8 Put-in-Bay, Sandusky *Lake Huron:*
7 Saginaw, Thunder *Lake Ontario:*
11 Irondequoit *Lake Superior:* 5 Huron
8 Keweenaw 9 Whitefish *Long Island:*
8 Rockaway *Long Island Sound:* 6 Oyster *Madagascar:* 8 Antongil *Maine:*
5 Casco 7 Machias *Maryland-Virginia:*
10 Chesapeake *Massachusetts:* 8 Buzzards, Plymouth 9 Annisquam *Massachusetts Bay:* 10 Lynn Harbor *Mediterranean Sea:* 8 Valencia 9 Famagusta
10 Khalij Surt 11 Syrtis Major *Mozambique:* 5 Memba, Pemba *Nantucket
Sound:* 5 Lewis *Newfoundland:* 4 Hare
5 White 7 Fortune *New Guinea:* 3 Oro
5 Berau, Hansa 11 McCluer Gulf *New
Jersey:* 7 Raritan 8 Barnegat 9 Little
Egg *New Zealand:* 5 Hawke 6 Tasman
North Carolina: 9 Albemarle *Northern Ire-*

land: 12 Belfast Lough *North Sea:* 4 Lyse
9 Hardanger *Northwest Territories:*
5 Wager 8 Bathurst, Franklin 9 Frobisher 12 Prince Albert *Norway:* 3 Tys
4 Bokn, Tana 5 Lakse, Sogne *Norwegian
Sea:* 4 Nord, Salt, Stor, Vest 5 Ranen
8 Scoresby 9 Trondheim *Ontario:*
4 Owen *Oregon:* 4 Coos *Philippines:*
5 Baler, Pilar, Sogod 6 Butuan 9 Davao
Gulf, Leyte Gulf, Panay Gulf *Puget
Sound:* 4 Carr, Case *Quebec:* 6 Ungava
Red Sea: 4 Foul *Rhode Island:* 12 Narragansett *Russia:* 5 Chaun 8 Sakhalin
Santo Cruz Islands: 8 Basilisk *Solomon
Islands:* 4 Deep 8 Huon Gulf *South
Africa:* 5 Table *South Carolina:* 4 Bull
South China Sea: 4 Bias, Datu, Siam,
Taya 5 Dasol, Subic, Subig 6 Brunei,
Paluan 7 Camranh 8 Lingayen *Spain:*
5 Cádiz *Spitsbergen:* 3 Ice 4 Bell 5 Kings
Sumatra: 5 Bajur 10 Koninginne
Tyrrhenian Sea: 6 Naples 7 Paestum
Wales: 5 Burry *Washington:* 5 Dabob
6 Skagit 11 Grays Harbor
inmate 7 convict 8 occupant, prisoner,
resident 10 inhabitant
inmost part 4 core, pith 5 heart 6 center,
depths, kernel, marrow 7 nucleus
inn 5 hotel, lodge, motel, serai 6 hostel,
tavern 7 auberge, hospice, pension
8 hostelry 9 roadhouse 11 caravansary,
public house 12 caravansarai 13 boardinghouse *German:* 7 Gasthof 8 Gasthaus
Spanish: 5 fonda 6 posada 7 parador
Turkish: 6 imaret
innards 4 guts 5 belly 6 bowels, tripes
7 viscera 8 entrails, stuffing 10 intestines
innate see INHERENT
inner 3 gut 5 focal 6 hidden, middle,
secret 7 central, nuclear, private
8 familiar, interior, internal, personal,
visceral 9 concealed, essential
innervate 4 jolt, move 5 pique, rouse
6 excite 7 animate, provoke, quicken
8 motivate, vitalize 9 electrify, galvanize, stimulate
Innisfail 4 Eire, Erin 7 Ireland
innkeeper 4 host 8 boniface, hosteler,
hotelier, landlord, publican
innocence 6 purity 7 naiveté 8 chastity
10 simplicity 11 artlessness, sinlessness
innocent 4 good, lamb, naïf, pure, void
5 clean, legal, licit, naive 6 chaste,
devoid, lawful 7 artless, natural,
unaware 8 harmless, ignorant, virtuous
9 blameless, childlike, exemplary, faultless, guileless, guiltless, ingenuous,
innocuous, righteous, stainless,
unstained, unsullied, untainted

10 inculpable, legitimate 12 unsuspecting
innocuous 5 banal, bland 6 pallid
7 insipid 8 harmless 11 inoffensive,
unoffending 13 insignificant
innovation 6 change 7 novelty
innovative 3 new 5 novel 8 creative, original 9 inventive 10 newfangled 11 cutting-edge, leading-edge 12 trailblazing
innovator 9 architect, developer 10 originator 11 trailblazer 13 revolutionary
innuendo 4 clue, hint, slur 7 calumny
8 allusion 9 aspersion 10 backbiting,
intimation 11 implication, insinuation
innumerable 4 many 6 legion, myriad,
untold 7 umpteen 9 countless, uncounted 10 numberless 13 multitudinous
Ino *brother:* 9 Polydorus *father:* 6 Cadmus *grandfather:* 6 Agenor *husband:*
7 Athamas *mother:* 8 Harmonia *sister:*
5 Agave 6 Semele 7 Autonoë *son:*
8 Learchus, Palaemon 10 Melicertes
inobtrusive 5 muted, quiet 6 modest
7 subdued 8 discreet, tasteful 10 restrained
inoculate 5 imbue, shoot, steep 6 infuse
7 implant, suffuse 9 vaccinate
inoffensive 5 bland 7 neutral 8 harmless
9 innocuous, peaceable
inopportune 8 ill-timed, mistimed,
untimely 12 unseasonable
inordinate 5 undue 6 wanton 7 extreme
8 overmuch 9 excessive 10 exorbitant,
gratuitous, immoderate, irrational
11 extravagant, intemperate, superfluous, uncalled-for 12 unreasonable
13 extraordinary
inorganic 7 mineral 10 artificial
in passing 5 aside 6 obiter 7 by the by
8 by the bye, by the way 12 incidentally
in perpetuum 4 ever 6 always 7 forever,
for good 8 evermore, for keeps 9 eternally 10 enduringly 11 forevermore
input 4 data 6 advice, energy 7 comment,
counsel, opinion 8 feedback, guidance,
material, stimulus 11 information
inquest 5 probe 7 hearing, inquiry
11 examination 13 investigation
inquietude 5 angst 6 unease, unrest
7 anxiety, ferment, turmoil 8 distress
10 uneasiness 11 restiveness 12 restlessness 13 Sturm und Drang
inquire 3 ask, pry 4 seek 5 probe, query
7 examine 8 question 9 catechize
11 interrogate, investigate
inquiry 5 audit, probe, query 7 hearing
8 grilling, question, research, scrutiny
11 examination, questioning 13 investigation

inquisition 4 hunt 5 probe, quest, trial
6 search 7 inquiry 8 grilling, research
11 examination 13 interrogation, investigation
inquisitive 4 nosy 6 prying, snoopy
7 curious 8 meddling, snooping 9 intrusive 10 meddlesome 11 questioning
inquisitor 10 Torquemada (Tomás de)
in re 4 as to 5 about, as for 7 apropos
9 as regards, regarding 10 as respects,
concerning, respecting 12 with regard
to 13 with respect to
in respect to see IN RE
inroad 4 raid 5 foray 7 advance 8 invasion 9 incursion 12 encroachment
ins and outs 5 ropes 6 quirks 7 details
8 minutiae, oddities 11 incidentals, particulars 12 lay of the land 13 peculiarities, ramifications
insane 3 mad, off 4 daft, nuts 5 batty,
crazy, daffy, dotty, loony, manic, nutsy,
nutty, rabid, silly, wacky 6 absurd,
crazed, cuckoo, maniac, raving, schizo,
screwy, teched 7 berserk, bonkers,
cracked, haywire, lunatic, tetched,
touched, unsound 8 demented,
deranged, unhinged 9 eccentric, psychotic 10 disordered, irrational, moonstruck, unbalanced 11 harebrained
12 crackbrained, preposterous, unreasonable
insane asylum 6 bedlam 8 loony bin,
madhouse, nuthouse, snake pit 10 sanatorium, sanitarium
insanity 5 folly, mania 6 frenzy, lunacy
7 madness 8 delirium, delusion, dementia, hysteria, illusion 9 craziness, dottiness, psychosis 11 derangement, psychopathy
insatiable 6 crying, greedy, urgent 7 exigent 8 pressing, ravenous 9 clamorous,
demanding, voracious 10 quenchless
11 importunate 12 unappeasable,
unquenchable
inscribe 4 etch, list 5 carve, enter, print,
write 6 enroll, record 7 engrave,
engross, impress, imprint 8 dedicate,
enscroll, register
inscription 5 title 6 legend 7 epigram,
epitaph, heading 8 epigraph 10 dedication
inscrutable 6 arcane 7 deadpan 10 mysterious, poker-faced, sphinxlike,
unknowable, unreadable 12 impenetrable, unfathomable
insect 3 bee, bug, fly 6 beetle *adult:*
5 imago *antenna:* 4 palp 6 feeler, palpus
combining form: 5 entom 6 entomo *covering:* 6 chitin *immature:* 4 grub, pupa
5 larva, nymph 6 larvae (plural), maggot 8 wriggler 9 chrysalis 11 caterpillar

kind: 3 ant, bee 4 flea, moth, wasp 5 aphid, scale 6 bedbug, beefly, beetle, cicada, earwig, hornet, mantid, mantis, mayfly 7 ant lion, cricket, firefly, June bug, katydid, ladybug, termite 8 honeybee, horsefly, housefly, lacewing, mosquito, stinkbug 9 bumblebee, butterfly, damselfly, dragonfly 10 silverfish, springtail 11 grasshopper 12 walkingstick *luminous:* 7 firefly 8 glowworm *molt:* 7 ecdysis *moth:* 4 luna 5 gypsy 6 miller, sphinx 7 noctuid, pyralid, tortrix, tussock 8 cecropia, cinnabar, forester, sphingid 9 clearwing, geometrid, saturniid, tortricid 10 Polyphemus *multi-legged:* 8 diplopod 9 centipede, millipede *part:* 4 palp 5 cerci (plural) 6 cercus, labium, labrum, ocelli (plural), palpus, thorax 7 antenna, maxilla, ocellus 8 antennae (plural), mandible, maxillae (plural) 9 proboscis, spiracles 10 ovipositor 11 exoskeleton *pest:* 4 flea, lice (plural), mite 5 louse, midge, scale 7 blowfly, termite 8 horsefly, housefly, mealybug 9 cockroach, gypsy moth 10 boll weevil, Hessian fly, silverfish *science:* 10 entomology *winged:* 5 alate *wingless:* 4 flea, lice (plural) 5 louse 8 firebrat 10 silverfish, springtail 11 bristletail
insecticide 3 DDT 5 mirex, naled 6 aldrin, endrin 7 lindane, phorate 8 carbaryl, dieldrin, rotenone 9 chlordane, malathion, parathion 10 permethrin
insecure 5 shaky 6 unsafe, unsure, wobbly 7 anxious 8 unstable 9 uncertain 10 precarious 11 unconfident 12 apprehensive
inseminate 7 implant, instill 9 fertilize, pollinate 10 impregnate
insensate 4 dull, hard, numb 5 stony 6 brutal, numbed 7 callous 8 comatose 9 bloodless, heartless, impassive, unfeeling
insensibility 4 coma 6 apathy, torpor 8 lethargy, stoicism 12 indifference
insensible 4 cold, dead, dull, hard, numb, rapt 5 stoic 6 asleep, intent, numbed, obtuse, stolid 7 callous 8 absorbed, comatose, deadened, hardened, obdurate 9 apathetic, bloodless, engrossed, impassive, unfeeling 11 unconscious 12 anesthetized
insensitive 4 dull, hard, numb, rude 5 crass 6 numbed, obtuse, unkind 7 callous 8 benumbed, deadened, hardened, tactless, uncaring 9 bloodless, heartless, unfeeling 10 anesthetic, impossible 11 indifferent, unconcerned 12 anesthetized, unresponsive

insert 5 enter 7 implant, obtrude 9 interpose 10 interleave 11 intercalate, interpolate
insertion 8 addendum, addition 13 interpolation
in short 7 briefly, tersely 9 concisely 10 succinctly
inside 6 closet, secret, within 7 private 8 hush-hush, interior 12 confidential *combining form:* 4 endo
insidious 3 sly 4 foxy, wily 6 artful, crafty, subtle, tricky 7 cunning, gradual 8 creeping, guileful 9 deceitful 13 surreptitious
insight 6 acumen, aperçu, wisdom 8 sagacity, sapience 9 intuition 11 discernment, penetration 13 understanding
insightful 4 keen, sage, wise 7 gnostic, knowing 9 intuitive, sagacious 10 discerning, perceptive 11 penetrating
insignia 4 mark, sign 5 badge 6 emblem 8 brassard 10 decoration
insignificant 4 puny 5 dinky, minor, petty, small 6 casual, little, minute, paltry 7 minimal, trivial 8 nugatory, trifling 9 secondary, small-time 10 negligible 11 minor-league, unimportant
insincere 5 false, lying, phony 6 double, forced, hollow, shifty, tricky 7 feigned 8 mala fide, slippery, spurious 9 deceitful, deceptive, dishonest, pretended, simulated 10 left-handed, mendacious, untruthful 11 dissembling, double-faced 12 hypocritical
insinuate 4 hint 5 imply 6 inject, insert, work in, worm in 7 implant, instill, suggest 9 introduce
insipid 3 dry 4 arid, dull, flat, mild, pale, thin, weak 5 banal, bland, vapid 6 jejune, watery 7 mundane, prosaic, subdued, tedious 8 bromidic, lifeless, ordinary 9 innocuous, tasteless 10 flavorless, monotonous, namby-pamby, wishy-washy 11 commonplace
insist 4 hold 5 argue, claim, swear 6 affirm, assert, demand, stress 7 certify, contend, declare, require, testify 8 maintain
insistent 6 crying, dogged, urgent 7 adamant, burning, clamant, exigent 8 emphatic, forceful, pressing, resolute 9 assertive, clamorous, obtrusive 10 determined, imperative, relentless 11 persevering
insolence 4 gall, guff, sass 5 brass, cheek, nerve 8 audacity, boldness, chutzpah, contempt, rudeness 9 arrogance, impudence 10 brazenness, disrespect, effrontery 11 haughtiness, presumption 12 impertinence

insolent 4 bold, flip, pert, rude 5 cocky, lofty, sassy, saucy 6 brazen, cheeky 7 haughty, uncivil 8 arrogant, cavalier, flippant, impolite, impudent, superior 9 audacious, barefaced, bold-faced 10 disdainful, peremptory 11 impertinent, overbearing 12 contumelious, discourteous, supercilious 13 high-and-mighty

insouciance 6 aplomb 9 disregard, unconcern 10 breeziness 11 disinterest, nonchalance 12 carelessness, heedlessness, indifference

insouciant 4 airy, flip 6 blithe, breezy, casual, jaunty 8 carefree, flippant, heedless 9 easygoing 10 nonchalant, untroubled 11 indifferent, thoughtless, unconcerned 12 devil-may-care, happy-go-lucky, lighthearted

inspect 3 con, vet 4 scan, view 5 audit, check, probe, study 6 review, size up, survey 7 canvass, examine, observe 8 appraise, check out, look over, question 9 check over 10 scrutinize 11 investigate

inspiration 4 muse 6 animus, genius, vision 7 insight 8 afflatus 9 brainwave, influence 10 brainchild, brainstorm, creativity 13 enlightenment

inspire 4 fire, stir 5 elate, exalt, imbue, rouse 6 arouse, excite, foment, incite, prompt, strike 7 animate, enliven, impress, instill, quicken 8 motivate 9 encourage, galvanize, influence, stimulate 10 exhilarate

inspiring 6 moving 7 awesome, rousing 8 exalting, stirring 9 animating, uplifting 10 vitalizing

inspirit 4 fire, lift, spur, stir 5 cheer, exalt, liven, rally, rouse, spark, steel 6 arouse, excite, incite, kindle, revive, uplift, vivify 7 animate, comfort, console, delight, enliven, gladden, hearten, nourish, quicken, refresh, restore 8 activate, embolden, energize, revivify, vitalize 9 encourage, stimulate 10 invigorate, strengthen

instability 8 fluidity 9 shakiness 10 insecurity, volatility 11 inconstancy 12 unsteadiness

install 4 seat, vest 5 put in, set up 6 induct, invest 8 ensconce, enthrone, entrench 9 establish

instance 4 case, cite, item 6 detail, ground, reason, sample 7 example 8 specimen 10 particular 12 illustration

instant 3 sec 4 wink 5 flash, jiffy, point, shake, trice 6 moment, second, urgent 7 current, exigent, present 8 existent, occasion, pressing 9 heartbeat, immedi-ate, insistent, twinkling 10 imperative, present-day

instantaneous 4 fast 5 quick, rapid 9 immediate, ligntning, momentary 11 hair-trigger, split-second

instanter 3 now 6 at once 8 directly 9 forthwith, right away 11 immediately

instantly 3 now 6 at once 8 directly 9 forthwith, right away 11 immediately

instead 4 else 6 in lieu, rather 11 alternately 13 alternatively

instigate 4 abet, fire, goad, plan, plot, prod, spur, urge 5 egg on, impel, raise 6 excite, foment, incite, stir up, whip up 7 provoke, suggest 8 motivate 9 stimulate 10 bring about

instill 5 imbue 6 impart, infuse, inject 7 implant, suffuse 8 engender 9 inculcate, introduce

instinct 4 nose 5 hunch, sense 7 feeling, impulse 8 aptitude, behavior 9 intuition 10 proclivity, sixth sense 11 gut reaction

instinctive 3 gut 6 inborn, innate, normal 7 natural 8 habitual, inherent, visceral 9 automatic, ingrained, intrinsic, intuitive, reflexive, unlearned 10 congenital, unprompted 11 involuntary, spontaneous, unmeditated

instinctual 6 reflex 7 natural, routine 8 habitual, knee-jerk, untaught 9 automatic, impulsive, intuitive, reflexive 10 mechanical, unthinking 11 involuntary, spontaneous, unconscious

institute 5 begin, found, set up, start 6 decree, launch, ordain 7 academy, pioneer, usher in 8 initiate, organize 9 establish, introduce, originate 10 inaugurate 12 organization

institution 4 firm, rite 5 habit 6 custom 9 enactment 10 foundation 13 establishment *kind:* 6 asylum, school 7 academy, college 8 hospital 10 sanatorium, sanitarium, sanitorium, university

instruct 4 show 5 coach, drill, guide, order, steer, teach, train, tutor 6 direct, enjoin, inform, school 7 apprise, command, counsel, educate, lecture 9 enlighten, prescribe

instruction 5 drill 6 advice, lesson 7 precept 8 coaching, guidance, teaching, training, tutelage 9 catechism, education, schooling 10 directions *place of:* 6 school 7 academe, academy, college 10 university

instructive 8 didactic, edifying, pedantic 9 pedagogic 11 educational, explanatory, explicative, informative 12 enlightening

instructor 3 don 4 guru 5 coach, guide, swami, tutor 6 mentor 7 teacher, trainer 8 educator, lecturer 9 pedagogue, preceptor

instrument 4 deed, gear, mean, tool 5 agent, means, organ 6 agency, device, gadget, medium 7 utensil, vehicle 9 apparatus, appliance, machinery, mechanism 11 contraption, contrivance 13 paraphernalia *aircraft:* 5 radar, radio 7 compass 9 altimeter, gyroscope 10 altazimuth, tachometer 11 transponder *calculating:* 6 abacus 8 computer 9 slide rule *graphic:* 6 camera 8 otoscope 9 telescope 10 binoculars, microscope 11 fluoroscope, stethoscope, stroboscope 12 bronchoscope, oscilloscope, spectrograph, spectroscope *measuring:* 4 gage 5 clock, gauge, radar, scale, sonar 7 alidade, ammeter, balance, caliper, sextant, transit 8 quadrant 9 altimeter, astrolabe, barometer, bolometer, manometer, pedometer, sonometer, voltmeter 10 anemometer, Fathometer, hydrometer, hygrometer, micrometer, radiometer, radiosonde, spirometer, tachometer, theodolite 11 chronometer, lie detector, range finder, seismograph, speedometer, thermometer 12 electroscope, galvanometer, oscillograph, oscilloscope 13 Geiger counter, potentiometer *medical:* 6 lancet, trocar 7 curette, forceps, specula (plural) 8 tenacula (plural) 9 tenaculum *radiation-producing:* 5 laser, maser (see also IMPLEMENT; MUSICAL INSTRUMENT; TOOL)

instrumental 5 vital 6 useful 7 crucial, helpful 9 conducive, essential, necessary, requisite 10 imperative 13 indispensable

instrumentality 5 agent, force, means, organ 6 agency, energy, medium 7 channel, vehicle 8 ministry 9 mechanism

insubordinate 6 unruly 8 factious, mutinous 9 fractious, seditious 10 headstrong, rebellious, refractory 11 disobedient, intractable, uncompliant 12 contumacious, recalcitrant, ungovernable

insubstantial 4 airy, weak 5 frail 6 feeble, flimsy 7 fragile, tenuous 8 bodiless, ethereal 9 imaginary, unfleshly 10 intangible 11 disembodied 12 apparitional

insufferable 10 unbearable 11 intolerable, unendurable 13 insupportable

insufficiency 4 lack 6 dearth 7 paucity, poverty 8 scarcity, shortage 10 deficiency, inadequacy, scantiness, scarceness 11 defalcation

insufficient 5 scant 6 scanty, scarce, skimpy 7 lacking, wanting 10 inadequate, incomplete

insular 5 local 6 narrow 7 bigoted, limited 8 confined, isolated, secluded 9 illiberal, parochial, sectarian, small-town 10 prejudiced, provincial, restricted

insulate 6 cut off, enisle 7 isolate 8 close off 9 segregate, sequester

insult 4 gibe, jeer, mock, slap, slur 5 abuse, fleer, scoff, scorn, shame, sneer, taunt 6 debase, deride, offend, revile 7 affront, disdain, obloquy, offense, outrage 8 derision, disgrace, ignominy, ridicule 9 contumely, humiliate 10 opprobrium 12 vituperation

insurance 8 guaranty, warranty 10 protection *agency:* 7 actuary 8 adjuster 11 underwriter *term:* 6 policy 7 annuity 8 coverage 9 bordereau 11 beneficiary

insure 5 cinch, guard 6 shield 7 confirm, protect 9 guarantee, safeguard 10 underwrite

insurgent 5 rebel 6 anarch 8 factious, frondeur, mutineer, mutinous, revolter 9 anarchist, seditious 10 incendiary, rebellious 12 contumacious 13 insubordinate, revolutionary

insurrection 4 coup 6 mutiny, putsch, revolt, rising 8 uprising 9 rebellion

insurrectionist 5 rebel 6 anarch 8 frondeur, mutineer, revolter 10 malcontent

insusceptible 6 exempt, immune 9 resistant 10 impervious 11 unreceptive

intact 5 sound, whole 6 entire, unhurt, virgin 7 perfect 8 complete, unbroken, unmarred, virginal 9 undamaged, uninjured, untouched 10 unimpaired

intangible 4 airy 5 vague 7 elusive, ghostly 8 ethereal 10 evanescent, immaterial, impalpable 11 incorporeal

integer 4 unit 5 digit 6 entity, figure, number 7 numeral 11 whole number

integral 4 full 5 whole 6 entire 7 perfect 8 complete, inherent 9 composite, elemental, essential, necessary, requisite 11 constituent 13 indispensable

integrate 3 mix 4 fuse, join, link 5 blend, merge, unify, unite 6 embody, mingle 7 combine, conjoin 8 coalesce 9 harmonize, reconcile 10 amalgamate, assimilate, coordinate, synthesize 11 consolidate, desegregate

integrity 5 honor 6 virtue 7 honesty, probity 8 cohesion 9 coherence, constancy, rectitude, soundness, wholeness 12 completeness

integument 4 coat 5 testa 7 coating, cuticle 8 covering, envelope

intellect 3 wit 4 mind 5 brain 6 acumen, brains, genius, reason, smarts 9 intu-

ition, mentality **12** intelligence **13** comprehension, understanding
intellectual 5 brain **6** brainy, mental, pundit **7** bookish, egghead, erudite, psychic, thinker **8** academic, cerebral, highbrow, longhair **9** scholarly
intelligence 3 wit **4** dope, info, mind, news, word **5** brain, savvy, sense **6** acuity, acumen, brains, notice, reason, smarts, wisdom **7** hearsay, tidings **8** aptitude, judgment, learning, sagacity **9** knowledge, mentality, mother wit **10** brainpower, shrewdness
intelligent 4 keen, wise **5** acute, alert, aware, quick, sharp, smart, sound **6** adroit, astute, brainy, bright, clever, shrewd **7** cunning, knowing, logical **8** rational, sensible **9** brilliant, ingenious, sagacious **10** reasonable **11** quick-witted, ready-witted **13** perspicacious
intelligentsia 7 clerisy **8** literati, vanguard **10** avant-garde, illuminati
intelligible 5 clear, lucid, plain
intemperance 6 excess **7** license **9** depravity **10** debauchery, profligacy **11** dissipation, drunkenness **12** immoderation, incontinence
intemperate 5 harsh **6** bitter, brutal, severe **7** drunken, extreme, violent **8** bibulous **9** crapulous, dissolute, excessive **10** dissipated, exorbitant, gluttonous, immoderate, inordinate, profligate **12** unrestrained **13** overindulgent
intend 3 aim, try **4** mean, plan **5** essay, spell **6** assign, denote, design, scheme, strive **7** attempt, connote, propose, purpose, signify **8** endeavor **9** designate
intended 6 fiancé **7** engaged, fiancée **8** destined, plighted, promised, proposed **9** affianced, betrothed **10** calculated, deliberate
intense 4 keen **5** acute, vivid **6** ardent, fervid, fierce, severe, strong **7** extreme, fervent, furious, violent, zealous **8** powerful, vehement **9** assiduous, excessive, exquisite **10** heightened **12** concentrated
intensify 4 rise **5** mount, rouse **6** accent, heat up, stress **7** enhance, sharpen **8** escalate, heighten, increase, redouble **9** aggravate, aggrandize, exacerbate **11** concentrate
intensity 6 energy, fervor **7** passion **8** emphasis, ferocity, fervency, loudness **9** vehemence
intensive 6 all-out **7** zealous **8** sweeping, thorough **10** exhaustive **12** concentrated *pronoun:* **6** itself, myself **7** herself, himself **8** yourself **9** ourselves **10** themselves, yourselves
intent 3 aim, set **4** goal, plan, rapt, will

5 eager, fixed **6** design, import, object **7** decided, earnest, engaged, meaning, purport, purpose, riveted, wrapped **8** absorbed, conation, decisive, diligent, immersed, resolute, resolved, sedulous, volition **9** engrossed, objective, wrapped up **10** determined
intention 3 aim, end **4** goal, hope, plan, wish **6** design, desire, object **7** meaning, purpose **8** ambition **9** objective **10** aspiration
intentional 5 meant **7** advised, studied, willful, willing, witting **8** designed, proposed **9** voluntary **10** considered, deliberate **12** premeditated
intentionally 9 on purpose, purposely
inter 4 bury **5** plant **6** entomb, inhume **9** lay to rest
interact 9 cooperate **11** collaborate
interbreed 5 cross **9** hybridize **10** mongrelize
intercede 6 step in **7** mediate **9** arbitrate
intercept 4 grab **5** catch, seize, steal **6** cut off, hijack
intercessor 5 agent **6** broker **8** advocate, mediator **9** go-between, middleman
interconnect 4 join, link **5** unite **6** couple, hook up, link up
intercourse 3 sex **5** trade, truck **7** contact, dealing, traffic **8** business, commerce, dealings **9** communion **10** connection, networking **11** give-and-take **12** conversation **13** communication
intercross 9 hybridize **10** mongrelize
interdict 3 ban, bar **4** veto **5** block, taboo **6** cut off, enjoin, forbid, outlaw **7** censure, condemn, embargo **8** disallow, prohibit, sanction **9** proscribe **11** prohibition
interest 4 gain, grab, hook, lure, pull **5** pique, stake, tempt **6** appeal, arouse, behalf, engage, profit, regard **7** attract, concern, engross, involve, welfare **8** appeal to, intrigue **9** attention, curiosity, fascinate, tantalize, well-being **10** prosperity
interested 4 rapt **5** drawn **7** curious, partial **8** invested, partisan **9** attentive
interface 3 GUI **6** border **8** boundary **9** cooperate **11** communicate
interfere 6 butt in, horn in, meddle, step in **7** barge in, intrude
interim 3 gap **5** break, pause **6** acting, breach, hiatus, lacuna, pro tem **7** stopgap, time-out **8** downtime, meantime **9** makeshift, temporary **10** pro tempore **11** provisional
interior 3 gut **4** pith **5** belly, bosom, heart, inner **6** center, inland, inside, inward, marrow **8** visceral **9** heartland **10** hinterland

interject 3 add 6 fill in, insert 7 throw in
interjection *agreement:* 4 amen 5 roger
6 righto 7 right on *attention-getter:* 3 hey
4 ahem, ahoy, psst 6 yoo-hoo *calling
pigs:* 5 sooey *cheer:* 3 rah 5 wahoo
6 hooray, hurrah, hurray *contempt:*
4 pooh 5 pshaw *disappointment:* 4 rats
5 shoot 6 shucks *disapproval:* 3 boo, fie
disbelief: 3 huh *disgust:* 3 bah, boo,
pah, ugh 4 rats, yuck 5 faugh, yecch
6 phooey *dismay:* 4 oh no, uh-oh *dismissal:* 3 git 4 shoo *farewell:* 3 bye 4 ciao
5 adios 6 bye-bye, so long 7 cheerio
greeting: 4 ciao 5 aloha, hello, howdy *in
golf:* 4 fore *in hunting:* 6 yoicks *in march-
ing:* 3 hup, hut *joy:* 4 whee 6 hooray,
hurrah, hurray, yippee 7 hosanna,
whoopee 8 alleluia 10 hallelujah *mild
apology:* 4 oops 6 whoops *mild oath:*
3 gad 4 darn, drat, egad, geez, gosh,
heck, jeez 5 egads, golly, zooks
6 jiminy, zounds 7 begorra, gee whiz,
jeepers 8 gadzooks 13 gee whillikers
O.K.: 5 roger, wilco *pain:* 4 ouch *peace:*
6 shalom *regret:* 3 woe 4 alas 5 alack
8 lackaday *relief:* 4 phew *request:*
7 prithee *silence:* 3 shh *sneeze:* 5 achoo
6 atchoo 7 kerchoo *sorrow:* 4 alas
5 alack 8 lackaday *stop:* 4 whoa *surprise:* 3 aha, huh, oho, wow 4 gosh,
oops 5 blimy, yikes, yipes, zowie
6 blimey *to a horse:* 4 whoa 7 giddyap
toast: 5 salud, skoal 6 cheers, prosit,
l'chaim 7 l'chayim *triumph:* 3 aha, hah
6 eureka (see also EXCLAMATION)
interlace 3 mix 5 braid, plait, twine,
weave 7 entwine 9 alternate
interlard 3 mix 6 mingle
interlocuter 4 host 5 emcee
interlope 6 butt in, horn in, meddle 7 intrude 8 encroach, infringe 9 interfere
interlude 4 halt, lull, rest 5 break, idyll,
letup, pause, spell 6 recess 7 episode,
respite 8 breather, entr'acte, meantime,
stoppage 9 meanwhile 10 suspension
intermediary 3 mid 4 mean 5 agent,
envoy, organ 6 agency, broker, center,
medium, middle, midway 7 central,
channel, vehicle 8 delegate, emissary,
mediator, ministry 9 go-between, middleman
intermediate 3 mid 4 fair, mean, so-so
6 broker, center, medium, middle, midway, step in 7 average, between, central
8 middling 9 arbitrate, go-between,
middleman
intermediator 6 broker 7 liaison, referee
9 go-between, middleman
interment 6 burial 9 sepulture 10 inhumation
intermesh 4 lock 6 engage 8 dovetail

interminable 7 endless, eternal, lasting
8 constant, infinite, unending 9 boundless, ceaseless, continual, limitless, permanent, perpetual, unceasing 10 protracted 11 everlasting, never-ending
intermission 4 lull, rest, stop 5 break,
pause, spell 6 recess 7 latency, respite,
time-out 8 abeyance, dormancy, interval 10 quiescence, suspension 11 parenthesis
intermit 4 halt, stay 5 break, defer, delay
6 arrest, hold up, put off 7 suspend
8 postpone, prorogue 9 interrupt 11 discontinue
intermittent 6 broken, cyclic, fitful, serial
8 cyclical, metrical, periodic, seasonal,
sporadic 9 irregular, recurrent, recurring, spasmodic, stop-and-go 10 occasional
intermix 4 meld 5 blend 6 mingle
8 comingle, compound 9 commingle,
integrate 10 amalgamate 11 intermingle
intermixture 4 brew 5 blend 7 amalgam
8 compound 9 composite, synthesis
12 amalgamation 13 miscegenation
intern 4 jail 6 immure 7 confine,
impound, put away, trainee 8 imprison
11 incarcerate
internal 6 native 7 private 8 visceral
10 subjective *prefix:* 5 intra
internal organs 4 guts 6 bowels, vitals
7 innards, viscera 8 entrails 10 intestines, penetralia
international organization 3 FAO, IAM,
ICJ, IFC, ILO, ITO, ITU, OAS, WHO,
WMO, WTO 4 IAAF, IABA, IAEA,
IARU, IATA, ICAO, IFIP, IMCO,
NATO 5 ICFTU, SEATO 6 UNESCO,
UNICEF
internuncio 5 envoy 6 bearer, legate
7 carrier, courier 8 delegate, emissary
9 go-between, messenger, middleman
interpolate 3 add 5 admit, annex, enter
6 append, fill in, inject, insert 7 throw
in 9 introduce
interpose 6 butt in, fill in, insert, meddle, step in 7 intrude, mediate, obtrude,
throw in 8 moderate 9 arbitrate, insinuate, introduce, negotiate 11 come
between
interpret 5 gloss 6 decode 7 explain,
expound 8 annotate, construe 9 elucidate, explicate 10 paraphrase
interpretation 5 gloss 7 meaning, reading, version 8 exegesis 9 construal, rendering 11 explanation, translation
interpretive 8 exegetic 10 diagnostic,
exegetical, expository 11 explanatory,
explicatory
interregnum 5 break, lapse, pause 6 hiatus 7 time-out

interrogate 3 ask **4** pump, quiz **5** grill, query **7** examine **8** question **9** catechize **12** cross-examine

interrupt 4 halt, stay, stop **5** abort, break, cut in **7** break in, chime in, suspend **8** cut short

interruption 3 gap **4** halt **5** break, pause, split **6** breach, cutoff, hiatus, lacuna, recess **7** caesura **8** stoppage

intersect 4 meet **5** cross **9** decussate **10** crisscross

intersection 8 crossing, junction **10** crossroads

intersperse 7 diffuse, scatter **8** sprinkle

interstice 3 gap **4** slit, slot, vent **5** chink, cleft, crack, space **6** breach, cavity, cranny **7** crevice, fissure, opening, orifice **8** aperture

intertwine 4 mesh **5** braid, plait, twist, weave **7** network **9** convolute **10** crisscross

interval 3 gap **4** lull, wait **5** break, comma, delay, letup, pause, space **6** breach, hiatus, lacuna **7** caesura, interim, respite, time-out **8** downtime **9** pausation **11** parenthesis *music:* **4** rest

intervene 6 butt in, meddle, step in **7** intrude, mediate, obtrude

interweave 3 mix **4** fuse, join, knit, link, mesh **5** blend, plait, twine **6** enmesh **7** entwine, wreathe

intestinal fortitude 4 grit, guts **5** nerve, pluck, spunk **6** mettle, spirit **7** courage **8** backbone **10** resolution

intestine 3 gut **4** tube **5** bowel, canal **7** viscera (plural) *combining form:* **4** coli, colo **6** entero *part:* **5** cecum, colon, ileum **7** jejunum **8** duodenum

in the same place 6 ibidem

intimacy 9 closeness **11** familiarity **12** acquaintance

intimate 3 gut **4** cozy, dear, fond, hint **5** amigo, close, crony, imply, inner, privy **6** attest, friend, impart, loving, secret **7** comrade, connote, devoted, nearest, suggest **8** familiar, inherent **9** close-knit, companion, confidant, ingrained, insinuate, intrinsic **12** confidential

intimation 3 cue **4** clue, hint **5** shade, tinge, trace **6** breath **7** inkling **8** telltale **10** suggestion

intimidate 3 awe, cow **4** bait **5** bully, chivy, daunt, scare **6** badger, coerce, hector **7** buffalo, overawe **8** browbeat, bulldoze, bullyrag **9** strong-arm, terrorize

intolerable 10 unbearable **11** unendurable **12** insufferable **13** insupportable

intolerant 6 narrow **7** bigoted **8** dogmatic **9** hidebound, illiberal **10** inflexible,

prejudiced **11** small-minded **12** narrow-minded

intonation 5 chant, pitch **6** accent, timbre **7** cadence **8** chanting **10** inflection, modulation, recitation

intone 5 chant, croon, drone **10** cantillate

in toto 3 all **6** wholly **7** all told, en masse **10** altogether

intoxicant 5 booze, drink, hooch, sauce **6** hootch, liquor, rotgut **7** alcohol, spirits **9** aqua vitae, firewater, moonshine

intoxicated 3 lit, wet **4** high **5** blind, drunk, fried, giddy, lit up, oiled, stiff, tight, tipsy **6** blotto, bombed, canned, elated, juiced, loaded, looped, potted, sodden, soused, stewed, stoned, tanked, tiddly, zonked **7** blitzed, crocked, drunken, excited, maudlin, muddled, pickled, pie-eyed, sloshed, smashed, sozzled **8** cockeyed, polluted, squiffed **9** crapulous, plastered **11** exhilarated

intoxication 3 joy **5** bliss **6** frenzy **7** ecstasy, elation, rapture **8** delirium, euphoria **9** transport **10** exaltation **11** drunkenness, inebriation

intractable 4 wild **5** balky **6** mulish, ornery, unruly **7** froward, willful **8** mutinous, obdurate, perverse, stubborn **9** fractious, obstinate, pigheaded, unbending **10** bullheaded, headstrong, inflexible, rebellious, refractory, unyielding **12** pertinacious, recalcitrant, ungovernable **13** undisciplined

intransigent 5 rigid, tough **7** willful **8** obdurate, resolute, stubborn **9** obstinate, unbending, unpliable **10** refractory, self-willed, unyielding **12** contumacious, pertinacious

intrepid 4 bold, game **5** brave, gutsy, hardy **6** daring, heroic **7** doughty, gallant, valiant **8** fearless, resolute, stalwart, unafraid, valorous **9** audacious, dauntless, undaunted **10** courageous **11** adventurous, temerarious

intricate 4 mazy **6** daedal, knotty **7** complex, gordian, tangled **8** abstruse, involved, tortuous **9** Byzantine, elaborate **10** circuitous, convoluted **11** complicated **12** labyrinthine **13** sophisticated

intrigue 4 plot, wile **5** amour, cabal, cheat, pique, trick **6** affair, appeal, excite, scheme **7** attract, beguile, collude, connive, liaison, romance **8** cogitate, conspire, contrive, interest **9** machinate **10** conspiracy **11** machination

intriguing 8 enticing **9** absorbing, beguiling **10** engrossing, entrancing **11** captivating, fascinating, stimulating

intrinsic see INHERENT

intrinsically 5 per se **6** as such **7** at heart **10** inherently

introduce 5 begin, enter, found, set up **6** broach, fill in, insert, launch, unveil, work in **7** bring up, implant, install, instill, pioneer, precede, preface, present, throw in, usher in **8** initiate, innovate, organize **9** establish, insinuate, institute, interject, interpose, originate

introduction 5 debut, proem **6** lead-in **7** introit, opening, preface, prelude **8** entrance, exordium, foreword, overture, preamble, prologue, protases (plural), protasis **12** prolegomenon

introductory 5 basic **7** initial, nascent, opening **8** proemial **9** beginning, prefatory **10** elementary **11** preliminary, preparatory

intrude 5 cut in **6** butt in, horn in, impose, invade, meddle **7** barge in, burst in, presume **8** encroach, infringe, trespass **9** interfere, interlope, interrupt

intrusive 4 busy, nosy **5** nosey **6** prying, snoopy **7** curious **8** meddling, snooping **9** officious **10** meddlesome **11** impertinent

in truth 6 indeed, really, verily **8** actually, candidly **9** veritably

intuit 5 infer, sense **6** deduce, divine **7** surmise

intuition 5 hunch **7** feeling, inkling, insight **8** instinct **10** sixth sense **11** second sight **12** presentiment

intuitive 6 innate **7** natural **8** unwilled, visceral **10** unthinking **11** instinctive, instinctual, involuntary, spontaneous, unconscious

Inuit 6 Eskimo

inundate 4 glut **5** drown, flood, swamp, whelm **6** deluge, engulf **7** overrun **8** overflow, submerge **9** overwhelm

inundation 5 flood, spate **6** deluge **7** Niagara, torrent **8** cataract, flooding, overflow **9** avalanche, cataclysm, landslide **10** cloudburst

inure 5 steel, train **6** harden, season **7** prepare, toughen **8** accustom **9** acclimate, habituate **10** discipline **11** familiarize

inutile 6 no-good **7** useless **8** unusable **9** valueless, worthless

invade 4 loot, raid **6** breach, occupy, ravage **7** overrun, pillage, plunder **8** encroach, infringe, trespass **9** penetrate

invader 8 intruder **10** encroacher, interloper, trespasser **11** infiltrator

invalid 3 bad **4** null, sick, void **5** false **6** ailing, infirm, shut-in, sickly **7** unsound **8** baseless, disabled **9** bedrid-den, illogical, sophistic **10** fallacious, irrational **11** null and void **12** convalescent

invalidate 4 undo, void **5** annul, quash **6** cancel, offset, vacate **7** abolish, nullify **9** discredit, repudiate **10** counteract, disqualify, neutralize

invaluable 7 crucial **8** precious **9** essential, priceless **11** beyond price, inestimable **13** irreplaceable

invariable 4 same **5** fixed **6** static, steady **7** uniform **8** constant **9** continual, immovable, immutable, unfailing, unvarying **10** changeless, consistent, unchanging **11** inalterable, unalterable **12** unchangeable

invariably 4 ever **6** always **7** forever

invasion 4 raid **5** foray **6** attack, inroad **7** assault, offense **8** trespass **9** incursion, intrusion, offensive, onslaught **12** encroachment

invective 5 abuse **6** tirade **7** abusive, obloquy **8** diatribe, jeremiad **9** contumely, philippic, truculent **10** opprobrium, scurrility, scurrilous **11** opprobrious **12** billingsgate, contumelious, vituperation, vituperative

inveigh 4 kick, rail, rant **6** object **7** protest **8** complain **9** fulminate **11** expostulate, remonstrate

inveigle 4 coax, lure **5** decoy, snare, tempt **6** allure, cajole, entice, entrap, lead on, rope in, seduce, wangle **7** blarney, win over **8** blandish, butter up, maneuver, persuade

invent 4 coin, mint **6** cook up, create, design, devise, make up, patent, vamp up **7** concoct, dream up, fashion, hatch up, pioneer, think up **8** conceive, contrive, discover, engineer, envision **9** fabricate, formulate, originate

invention 7 coinage, fiction **8** creation **10** brainchild, innovation **11** contrivance

inventive 7 fertile, teeming **8** creative, fruitful, original **9** demiurgic, ingenious **10** innovative, innovatory **11** imaginative

inventor 5 maker **6** author, father, mother **7** creator, founder **8** engineer **9** architect, generator, innovator **10** discoverer, introducer, originator *air brake:* **12** Westinghouse (George) *air conditioning:* **7** Carrier (Willis) *automobile:* **7** Daimler (Gottlieb) *ballpoint pen:* **4** Loud (John) *barbed wire:* **7** Glidden (Joseph Farwell) *barometer:* **10** Torricelli (Evangelista) *bifocal lens:* **8** Franklin (Benjamin) *camera:* **7** Eastman (George) *cash register:* **5** Ritty (James) *cotton gin:* **7** Whitney (Eli) *cylinder lock:* **4** Yale

(Linus) *dirigible:* 8 Zeppelin (Ferdinand von) *dynamite:* 5 Nobel (Alfred) *electric battery:* 5 Volta (Alessandro) *electric fan:* 7 Wheeler (George) *electric organ:* 7 Hammond (Laurens) *electric razor:* 6 Schick (Jacob) *electric stove:* 7 Hadaway (W. S.) *elevator:* 4 Otis (Elisha) *fountain pen:* 8 Waterman (Lewis) *friction match:* 6 Walker (John) *gyrocompass:* 6 Sperry (Elmer) *helicopter:* 8 Sikorsky (Igor) *hot-air balloon:* 11 Montgolfier (Jacques, Joseph) *incandescent lamp:* 6 Edison (Thomas Alva) *induction motor:* 5 Tesla (Nikola) *lawn mower:* 5 Hills (Amariah) *Linotype:* 12 Mergenthaler (Ottmar) *logarithm:* 6 Napier (John) *machine gun:* 7 Gatling (Richard) *microphone:* 8 Berliner (Emile) *microwave oven:* 7 Spencer (Percy) *movable type:* 9 Gutenberg (Johannes) *parachute:* 9 Blanchard (Jean-Pierre) *pendulum clock:* 7 Huygens (Christiaan) *phonograph:* 6 Edison (Thomas Alva) *photography:* 6 Niepce (Nicéphore), Talbot (W. H. Fox) 8 Daguerre (Louis) *piano:* 10 Cristofori (Bartolomeo) *radio:* 7 Marconi (Guglielmo) *reaper:* 9 McCormick (Cyrus) *revolver:* 4 Colt (Samuel) *rocket engine:* 7 Goddard (Robert) *safety pin:* 4 Hunt (Walter) *safety razor:* 8 Gillette (King) *sewing machine:* 4 Howe (Elias) *sleeping car:* 7 Pullman (George) *spinning jenny:* 10 Hargreaves (James) *steamboat:* 5 Fitch (John) 6 Fulton (Robert), Miller (Patrick), Rumsey (James) 8 Jouffroy (Claude de) *steam engine:* 4 Watt (James) *steam locomotive:* 10 Stephenson (George) *stethoscope:* 7 Laënnec (René) *submarine:* 7 Holland (John Philip) *synthesizer:* 4 Moog (Robert) *tank:* 7 Swinton (Ernest) *telegraph:* 5 Morse (Samuel F. B.) *telephone:* 4 Bell (Alexander Graham) *telescope:* 10 Lippershey (Hans) *television:* 5 Baird (John) 6 Nipkow (Paul) 8 Zworykin (Vladimir) 10 Farnsworth (Philo) *thermometer:* 7 Galileo (Galilei) *torpedo:* 9 Whitehead (Robert) *tractor:* 5 Deere (John) *transistor:* 7 Bardeen (John) 8 Brattain (Walter), Shockley (William) *vulcanized rubber:* 8 Goodyear (Charles) *writing for the blind:* 7 Braille (Louis) *zipper:* 6 Judson (Whitcomb)

inventory 3 sum 4 fund, list 5 hoard, stock, store, tally 6 assets, digest, record, supply, survey 7 account, backlog, catalog, itemize, reserve, specify, summary 8 register, tabulate 9 catalogue, checklist, enumerate, reservoir, stockpile, summarize, synopsize

inverse 8 contrary, opposite

inversion 7 reverse 8 flipping, reversal, upending 9 about-face, turnabout, volte-face

invert 4 flip 5 upend 7 reverse 8 overturn, turn over 9 transpose

invertebrate 4 weak 5 timid 7 chicken, doormat, milksop 8 boneless, impotent, weakling 9 jellyfish, spineless 10 namby-pamby 11 ineffectual, milquetoast *kind:* 4 worm 6 insect, sponge 7 mollusc, mollusk 8 arachnid 9 arthropod 12 coelenterate

invest 4 gird, veil, wrap 5 adorn, array, dress, endow, imbue 6 clothe, confer, enfold, induct, infuse, ordain 7 empower, enclose, envelop, ingrain, install, suffuse

investigate 3 pry 4 sift 5 audit, probe, study 6 go into, search 7 dig into, examine, explore, inquire, inspect 8 check out, look into, muckrake, prospect, research 9 delve into 10 scrutinize 11 inquire into

investigation 5 audit, probe 6 survey 7 inquest, inquiry 8 research, scrutiny 11 fact-finding, inquisition

investigator 3 spy 4 dick 5 hound 6 shamus, sleuth 7 gumshoe 8 hawkshaw, sherlock 9 detective

investiture 9 inaugural, induction 10 initiation, ordination 12 inauguration, installation, ratification

inveterate 3 old, set 5 fixed, sworn 6 rooted 7 abiding, chronic, settled 8 deep-dyed, enduring, habitual, hardcore, hardened, lifelong 9 confirmed, ingrained, perennial 10 continuing, deep-rooted, deep-seated, entrenched, habituated, persistent, persisting 11 established 12 incorrigible 13 dyed-in-the-wool

Invictus author 6 Henley (William Ernest)

invidious 7 envious, envying, jealous 9 green-eyed, obnoxious, resentful

invigorate 4 stir 5 brace, pep up, rally, renew, rouse 6 perk up, vivify 7 animate, brace up, enliven, fortify, juice up, refresh, restore 8 energize, vitalize 9 reinforce, stimulate 10 rejuvenate, revitalize, strengthen

invincible 10 inviolable, unbeatable 11 impregnable, indomitable, insuperable 12 invulnerable, unassailable, undefeatable 13 unconquerable

in vino ____ 7 veritas

inviolable 4 safe 6 secure 10 impervious, sacrosanct 11 consecrated, impregnable 12 unassailable 13 incorruptible

invisible 6 hidden 9 concealed 10 intangible 12 unnoticeable 13 imperceptible

Invisible Man *author:* 5 Wells (H. G.) 7 Ellison (Ralph) *character:* 7 Griffin

Invisible Man, The *author:* 5 Wells (Herbert George) *character:* 7 Griffin (Herbert)

invitation 4 call, lure 6 come-on 7 bidding, proffer 8 entreaty, proposal 10 enticement 11 proposition 12 solicitation

invite 3 ask, bid 4 call, lure 5 tempt 6 allure, call in, entice, summon 7 propose, request, solicit

inviting 8 engaging, enticing, tempting 9 appealing, beguiling, seductive 10 attractive, intriguing

invocation 6 appeal, prayer 8 entreaty, petition 11 conjuration, incantation 12 supplication

invoice 3 tab 4 bill, list 5 score 7 account 8 manifest 9 reckoning, statement 11 consignment

invoke 3 beg 4 pray 5 crave, plead 6 appeal, call on, effect 7 beseech, conjure, enforce, entreat, implore, solicit 8 call upon, petition 9 call forth, conjure up, implement, importune 10 supplicate

involuntary 6 forced, reflex 8 knee-jerk 9 automatic, impulsive, reflexive, unwitting 10 compulsory, unintended, unprompted 11 instinctive, spontaneous, unconscious, unmediated 13 unintentional

involve 4 mire 6 affect, embody, engage, entail, take in 7 call for, concern, contain, embrace, embroil, include, require, subsume 8 comprise, entangle 9 encompass, implicate 10 complicate, comprehend 11 necessitate

involved 6 daedal, knotty 7 complex, gordian 8 confused 9 Byzantine, elaborate, intricate 10 convoluted 11 complicated 12 labyrinthine

invulnerable 6 immune, secure 10 impervious, invincible, unbeatable 11 impregnable, indomitable 12 unassailable

Io *father:* 7 Inachus *guard:* 5 Argus *son:* 7 Epaphus

iodine source 4 kelp

Iolanthe *composer:* 8 Sullivan (Arthur) *librettist:* 7 Gilbert (W. S.)

Iolcus king 5 Aeson 6 Pelias

Iole *captor:* 8 Heracles, Hercules *father:* 7 Eurytus *husband:* 6 Hyllus

ion 6 ligand *kind:* 5 anion 6 cation 8 thermion

Ion *father:* 6 Apollo *mother:* 6 Creusa *stepfather:* 6 Xuthus

Ionesco, Eugène *play:* 6 Chairs (The), Lesson (The) 10 Rhinoceros 11 Bald Soprano (The)

iota 3 bit, jot, ray 4 atom, hint, mite, whit 5 crumb, grain, ounce, scrap, shred, speck, trace 6 tittle 7 smidgen 8 molecule, particle 9 scintilla

IOU 4 chit, debt *part:* 3 owe, you

Iowa *capital:* 9 Des Moines *city:* 4 Ames 7 Dubuque 8 Waterloo 9 Davenport, Sioux City 11 Cedar Rapids 13 Council Bluffs *college, university:* 5 Drake 8 Grinnell *nickname:* 7 Hawkeye (State) *river:* 9 Des Moines *state bird:* 9 goldfinch *state flower:* 15 wild prairie rose *state tree:* 3 oak

Iphicles *brother:* 8 Heracles, Hercules *mother:* 7 Alcmene *son:* 6 Iolaus

Iphigenia *avenger:* 12 Clytemnestra *brother:* 7 Orestes *father:* 9 Agamemnon *mother:* 12 Clytemnestra *sister:* 7 Electra

Iran *ancient civilization:* 4 Elam 5 Medes, Media 6 Persia *capital:* 6 Tehran 7 Teheran *city:* 3 Qom, Qum 6 Shiraz, Tabriz 7 Esfahan, Isfahan, Mashhad *conqueror:* 9 Alexander (the Great) *gulf:* 4 Oman 7 Persian *island:* 5 Qeshm *language:* 5 Farsi 7 Persian *leader:* 7 Pahlavi (Mohammad Reza, Reza Shah) 8 Khomeini (Ayatollah Ruholla) *monetary unit:* 4 rial *mountain, range:* 6 Elburz, Zagros 8 Damavand 9 Hindu Kush *neighbor:* 4 Iraq 6 Turkey 7 Armenia 8 Pakistan 10 Azerbaijan 11 Afghanistan 12 Turkmenistan *river:* 5 Atrek, Karun, Safid 7 Karkheh *sea:* 7 Caspian *strait:* 6 Hormuz

Iranian 7 Persian *parliament:* 6 Majlis *religious movement:* 5 Baha'i *sect:* 4 Shia *sect member:* 6 Shiite

Iraq *ancient civilization:* 5 Akkad, Sumer 8 Akkadian, Sumerian 9 Babylonia 10 Babylonian *ancient name:* 11 Mesopotamia *capital:* 7 Baghdad *city:* 5 Basra, Mosul, Najaf 6 Kirkuk 7 Falluja, Karbala 8 Fallujah *conqueror:* 9 Alexander (the Great) *desert:* 6 Syrian *gulf:* 7 Persian *leader:* 6 Faisal 7 Hussein (Saddam) *monetary unit:* 5 dinar *neighbor:* 4 Iran 5 Syria 6 Jordan, Kuwait, Turkey 11 Saudi Arabia *river:* 6 Tigris 9 Euphrates

irascible 4 tart 5 huffy, surly, testy 6 crabby, cranky, feisty, tetchy, touchy 7 bristly, grouchy, peevish, peppery, prickly 8 choleric, petulant, snappish 9 crotchety, fractious, irritable, querulous, splenetic 11 hot-tempered 12 cantankerous 13 quick-tempered

irate 3 mad 5 angry, livid, riled, vexed,

wroth **6** fuming **7** enraged, furious, steamed **8** choleric, incensed, provoked, wrathful **9** indignant **10** infuriated

ire 4 fury, rage, rile **5** anger, wrath **6** choler, enrage, madden, temper **7** incense, steam up, umbrage **9** infuriate **10** exasperate **11** indignation **12** exasperation

Ireland 4 Eire, Erin **8** Hibernia *capital:* **6** Dublin *city:* **4** Cork **5** Kerry, Louth, Meath, Sligo **6** Galway **7** Donegal, Kildare, Wexford, Wicklow **8** Kilkenny, Limerick **9** Waterford **12** Dun Laoghaire *county:* **4** Mayo **5** Clare **6** Galway **8** Limerick *island group:* **4** Aran **8** Hibernia *lake:* **3** Ree (Lough) **4** Derg (Lough) **5** Neagh (Lough) **6** Corrib (Lough) *language:* **5** Irish **6** Gaelic **7** English *monetary unit:* **4** euro *monetary unit, former:* **5** pound *nickname:* **11** Emerald Isle *river:* **6** Barrow, Liffey **7** Shannon

Irene 3 Pax *father:* **4** Zeus **7** Jupiter *mother:* **6** Themis

irenic 4 calm **7** pacific **8** pacifist **9** peaceable, placative, placatory **10** nonviolent **12** conciliatory, propitiatory

Iris *father:* **7** Thaumas *mother:* **7** Electra

Irish 4 Erse **6** Celtic, Gaelic *accent:* **6** brogue *cattle:* **4** Kerry *clan:* **4** sept *combining form:* **7** Hiberno *coronation stone:* **7** Lia Fail *cudgel:* **10** shillelagh *death spirit:* **7** banshee *dog:* **6** setter **7** terrier *elf:* **10** leprechaun *flag color:* **5** green, white **6** orange *flower:* **8** shamrock *girl:* **4** lass **6** lassie **7** colleen *god:* **3** Ler **5** Dagda **6** Aengus *goddess:* **4** Badb, Bodb **6** Brigit **8** Morrigan *hero:* **9** Cuchulain **10** Cú Chulainn *heroine:* **7** Deirdre *king:* **9** Brian Boru *lake:* **5** lough *language:* **6** Gaelic *legislature:* **4** Dail *militant force:* **3** IRA *nationalist:* **4** Tone (Wolfe) **6** Pearse (Padraig) **7** Collins (Michael), Parnell (Charles) **8** De Valera (Eamon), O'Connell (Daniel) **9** Sarsfield (Patrick) *nationalist society:* **8** Sinn Fein *patron saint:* **7** Patrick *theater:* **5** Abbey *writing system:* **4** ogam **5** ogham (see also GAELIC; CELTIC)

Irish moss 7 seaweed **9** carrageen

irk 3 try, vex **4** fret, gall, pain, rile **5** annoy, peeve, pique, upset **6** abrade, bother, harass, nettle, ruffle, strain, stress **7** provoke, trouble **8** exercise, irritate **10** exasperate

irksome 6 vexing **7** tedious **8** annoying, rankling **9** provoking, upsetting, vexatious **10** bothersome, irritating, nettle-

some, unpleasant **11** aggravating, troublesome, unpalatable

iron 4 firm, gyve, hard **5** press, rigid **6** fetter, strong **7** adamant, manacle, shackle **8** handcuff, obdurate **9** unbending **10** inexorable, inflexible, *combining form:* **5** ferro **6** sidero *German:* **5** Eisen *relating to:* **6** ferric **7** ferrous

ironbound 5 harsh, rocky, rough, stern **6** craggy, jagged, rugged, severe, strict, uneven **7** scraggy **8** asperous, exacting, rigorous, scabrous **9** stringent **10** inflexible

Iron City 10 Pittsburgh

ironclad 5 fixed **7** binding **8** constant **9** immovable, immutable **10** inflexible, invariable **11** inalterable, irrefutable, unalterable **12** indisputable, irrefragable, unchangeable **13** unimpeachable

ironfisted 4 grim, hard, mean **5** harsh **6** brutal, severe, stingy **7** callous, miserly **8** pitiless, ruthless **9** penurious **10** implacable, unmerciful **11** hardhearted, intractable, remorseless **12** unappeasable

ironhanded 5 harsh, rigid **6** severe, strict **8** despotic, rigorous **9** draconian, stringent **10** tyrannical **12** unpermissive

ironhearted 5 stony **7** callous **8** hardened, obdurate, ruthless **9** merciless, unfeeling **10** hard-boiled **11** cold-blooded **13** unsympathetic

iron horse 10 locomotive

ironic 3 wry **6** biting **7** caustic, cutting, cynical, mordant, satiric **8** sardonic **9** sarcastic, trenchant

iron ore 8 goethite, hematite, limonite, siderite, taconite **9** magnetite

Iron Pants 6 Patton (George)

irons 5 bonds, gyves **6** chains **7** bilboes, darbies, fetters **8** manacles, shackles

Iroquois tribe 6 Cayuga, Mohawk, Oneida, Seneca **8** Onondaga **9** Tuscarora

irradiate 4 beam, glow **5** edify, light, shine **6** uplift **7** light up **8** illumine **9** enlighten **10** illuminate

irrational 3 mad **5** crazy **6** absurd, insane **7** invalid **8** demented **9** illogical, senseless, sophistic **10** cockamamie, fallacious, ridiculous **12** preposterous, unreasonable

irrefutable 4 sure **6** proven **7** certain **8** airtight, ironclad, positive **9** apodictic, veracious **10** conclusive, inarguable **11** indubitable **12** indisputable **13** incontestable

irregular 3 odd **5** queer **6** fitful, patchy, random, spotty, uneven **7** aimless, erratic, unequal **8** aberrant, abnormal, atypical, informal, lopsided, peculiar, singular, sporadic, unstable, unsteady, variable **9** anomalous, desultory, divergent, eccentric, guerrilla, haphazard, hit-or-miss, spasmodic, unregular, unsettled **10** asymmetric, capricious, changeable, inconstant, off-balance, unbalanced, unofficial **11** exceptional, fluctuating **12** intermittent, unsystematic

irregularity 5 freak, quirk **6** oddity **7** anomaly **8** deviance **9** deviation, roughness **10** aberration, inequality, unevenness **11** abnormality

irrelevant 5 inapt **9** unrelated **10** extraneous, immaterial, inapposite, peripheral **11** inessential, unessential, unimportant **12** inapplicable **13** insignificant

irreligious 6 unholy **7** godless, impious, profane, ungodly **11** blasphemous

irreparable 8 cureless, hopeless **9** incurable **11** immedicable **12** irredeemable, irremediable **13** irretrievable, unrecoverable

irreproachable 4 pure **8** flawless, innocent, spotless, virtuous **9** blameless, errorless, exemplary, faultless, guiltless, righteous **10** immaculate, impeccable, inculpable **11** unblamable

irresolute 5 shaky **6** fickle, unsure, wobbly **7** halting **8** doubtful, hesitant, unstable, waffling, wavering **9** equivocal, faltering, tentative, uncertain, undecided **10** ambivalent, changeable, inconstant, wishy-washy **11** fluctuating, half-hearted, vacillating

irresponsible 4 rash, wild **8** carefree, careless, feckless, reckless **10** incautious, unreliable **12** undependable **13** unaccountable, untrustworthy

irreverent 4 flip **7** impious, profane, ungodly **8** flippant **9** satirical **11** blasphemous **12** sacrilegious

irrevocable 4 firm **5** final **9** immutable **11** unalterable **12** irreversible, unchangeable **13** nonreversible

irrigation ditch 5 flume **6** sluice **7** acequia

irritability 5 pique **6** choler **8** edginess **9** petulance **10** crabbiness, impatience **11** fretfulness, peevishness *abnormal:* **8** erethism

irritable 4 edgy, sour **5** cross, huffy, testy, waspy, whiny **6** crabby, cranky, crusty, grumpy, ornery, snappy, tetchy, touchy **7** fretful, grouchy, peevish, pettish, prickly, waspish **8** captious, choleric, petulant, snappish **9** crotchety, fractious, impatient, irascible, querulous, splenetic **12** cantankerous, disagreeable

irritant 4 itch, pest **5** nudge **6** bother, gadfly, noodge, nudnik, pester, plague

8 headache, nuisance, vexation **9** annoyance **11** botheration

irritate 3 bug, irk, rub, vex **4** fret, gall, goad, rile, roil **5** anger, annoy, chafe, grate, peeve, pique, spite **6** abrade, badger, bother, burn up, harass, hector, madden, needle, nettle, offend, ruffle **7** inflame, provoke **9** aggravate, stimulate **10** exacerbate, exasperate

irritated 5 irate, testy **7** fretful, peevish **8** choleric **9** impatient, irascible

irritation 4 itch, pest, rash, sore **6** bother, plague **7** chagrin **8** nuisance, vexation **9** annoyance

irrupt 5 belch, eruct, surge **6** invade **7** intrude

irruption 4 raid **5** foray **6** inroad **7** upsurge **8** invasion **9** incursion, intrusion

I.R.S. employee 7 auditor **10** accountant

Irving novel 15 Cider House Rules (The) **17** Hotel New Hampshire (The) **20** World According to Garp (The)

Isaac *father:* **7** Abraham *mother:* **5** Sarah *son:* **4** Esau **5** Jacob *wife:* **7** Rebekah

Isabella I *country:* **5** Spain *home:* **7** Castile *husband:* **9** Ferdinand

Isaiah 7 prophet *father:* **4** Amoz

Iscah *brother:* **3** Lot *father:* **5** Haran *sister:* **6** Milcah

Iseult, Isolde *beloved:* **7** Tristan **8** Tristram *husband:* **4** Mark

Ishbak *father:* **7** Abraham *mother:* **7** Keturah

Ishbosheth's father 4 Saul

Ishmael 6 pariah **7** outcast **8** castaway, outsider **11** untouchable *father:* **7** Abraham *mother:* **5** Hagar

Ishtar *brother:* **7** Shamash *father:* **3** Anu, Sin *lover:* **6** Tammuz

Ishui's father 4 Saul **5** Asher

Isis *brother:* **6** Osiris *father:* **3** Geb *husband:* **6** Osiris *mother:* **3** Nut *son:* **4** Sept **5** Horus

Islam *adherent:* **6** Moslem, Muslim *founder:* **8** Mohammed, Muhammad *god:* **5** Allah *holy city:* **5** Mecca *holy month:* **7** Ramadan *law:* **6** Sharia *place of worship:* **6** mosque *priest:* **4** imam *scriptures:* **5** Koran, Quran *sect:* **4** Shia, Sufi **5** Sunni **6** Shiite, Sufism **7** Ismaili, Wahhabi (see also MUSLIM)

island 3 ait, cay, key **4** holm **5** atoll, oasis **6** skerry **7** crannog *Admiralty group:* **5** Manus *Adriatic Sea:* **3** Vis **4** Brac, Cres, Hvar **5** Brach, Ciovo, Mljet, Solta **6** Lesina, Pharus *Aegean Sea:* **4** Scio **5** Chios, Khios, Samos, Thira **6** Ikaria, Lemnos, Lesbos, Limnos **7** Nikaria **8** Mitilini, Mytilene, Santorin **10** Sakis-Adasi, Susam-Adasi *Alaska:* **4** Adak,

Atka, Attu, Kuiu 8 Wrangell *Aleutian group:* 3 Rat 4 Adak, Akun, Attu 5 Amlia, Kiska, Umnak 6 Kanaga, Tanaga, Unimak 8 Amchitka, Unalaska *American Samoa:* 3 Ofu, Tau 4 Rose 6 Swains *Andaman Sea:* 4 Mali 5 Tavoy *Antarctica:* 5 Scott, Young *Apostle group:* 3 Oak 4 Long, Sand 5 Outer 8 Madeline, Michigan, Stockton *Arafura Sea:* 5 Dolak *Arctic Archipelago:* 6 Baffin 8 Victoria *Arctic Ocean:* 5 Senja *Australian:* 5 Cocos 8 Tasmania *Azores:* 4 Pico 5 Corvo, Faial *Bahamas:* 3 Cat, Rum 4 Long 5 Abaco, Exuma 6 Andros, Inagua 7 Acklins, Crooked 8 Watlings 9 Eleuthera, Mayaguana 11 San Salvador *Bahrain:* 5 Sitra 8 Muharraq *Balearic group:* 5 Ibiza 7 Majorca, Menorca, Minorca 8 Mallorca *Baltic Sea:* 4 Moon, Muhu 5 Faron, Mukhu, Rugen, Worms 6 Vormsi 7 Gotland 8 Bornholm, Gothland, Gottland *Barents Sea:* 4 Bear *Bay of Naples:* 5 Capri *Bay of Panama:* 4 Naos *Bering Sea:* 5 Medny 7 Nunivak 10 Big Diomede 13 Little Diomede *Bismarck Archipelago:* 5 Lihir 10 New Britain *Bristol Channel:* 5 Lundy *Buzzards Bay:* 9 Cuttyhunk *Canadian:* 5 Banks, Devon 6 Baffin 8 Bathurst, Melville, Somerset, Victoria 9 Anticosti, Ellesmere 10 Cape Breton 11 Axel Heiberg, Southampton 12 Newfoundland, Prince Edward *Canaries:* 6 Gomera 7 La Palma 8 Tenerife 9 Lanzarote *Cape Verde:* 4 Fogo, Maio, Mayo 5 Brava, Rombo *Caribbean Sea:* 4 Cuba 5 Aruba, Utila, Vache 6 Tobago 7 Antigua, Curaçao, Jamaica 8 Barbados, Dominica, Trinidad 10 Guadeloupe, Martinique, Puerto Rico (see also VIRGIN GROUP) *Carolines:* 5 Sorol 6 Ponape 9 Ascension *Chagos Archipelago:* 11 Diego Garcia *Channel group:* 4 Herm, Sark 5 Lihou, Sercq 6 Jersey 8 Guernsey *Chesapeake Bay:* 4 Deal, Kent 5 Smith, Watts *Chukchi Sea:* 6 Herald *Comoro group:* 7 Mayotte *Congo River:* 4 Bamu *Cook group:* 4 Atiu 5 Mauke *Croatia:* 3 Krk, Pag, Rab 5 Susak, Unije *Cyclades:* 3 Ios, Kea, Nio 4 Ceos, Keos, Milo 5 Delos, Melos, Milos, Naxos, Paros, Siros, Syros 6 Andros, Dhilos 7 Amorgos, Cythnos, Kithnos, Kythnos, Mykonos *Denmark:* 3 Als, Fyn, Mon 4 Aero, Fano, Moen, Mors 5 Alsen, Funen, Moers, Samso 8 Bornholm 13 Fanum Fortunae *D'Entrecasteaux group:* 8 Kaluwawa 9 Fergusson *Dodecanese group:* 3 Coo, Cos, Kos 4 Caso, Lero, Simi, Syme 5 Kasos,

Leros, Lipso, Lisso, Patmo, Telos 6 Calino, Lipsos, Nisiro, Patmos 7 Calimno, Nisiros, Nisyros 8 Kalymnos *East River:* 5 Ward's 7 Welfare 9 Roosevelt *England's:* 7 Britain 9 Britannia 12 Great Britain *English Channel:* 5 Wight *Faeroes:* 4 Vago 5 Bordo, Sando *Fiji:* 4 Koro 5 Mango, Vatoa *Florida Keys:* 4 Long, Vaca, West 5 Largo 7 Big Pine 9 Matecumbe, Sugarloaf *Fox group:* 5 Umnak 6 Akutan, Unimak 8 Unalaska *French:* 7 Corsica 12 New Caledonia *French Polynesia:* 4 Rapa, Reao, Ua Pu 5 Ua Pau *Frisian group:* 3 Rom 4 Föhr, Sylt 5 Amrum, Juist, Mando, Texel 6 Borkum 7 Ameland 8 Langeoog, Pellworm, Vlieland 9 Helgoland, Norderney *Futunas:* 5 Alofi *Galápagos:* 5 Pinta 7 Chatham, Isabela 8 Abingdon 10 Albermarle *Georgia:* 5 Tybee *Germany:* 4 Fohr 7 Fehmarn 9 Helgoland 10 Heligoland *Greater Antilles:* 4 Cuba 7 Jamaica 10 Hispaniola, Puerto Rico *Greece:* 4 Milo, Rodi 5 Creta, Crete, Hydra, Idhra, Kriti, Rodos, Tenos, Tinos 6 Euboea, Evvoia, Hydrea, Lesbos, Rhodes, Rhodus 9 Negropont 10 Negroponte *Grenadines:* 5 Union *Gulf of Alaska:* 6 Kodiak *Gulf of Bothnia:* 5 Karlö *Gulf of Carpentaria:* 5 Maria 6 Groote 7 Eylandt *Gulf of Guinea:* 7 Sao Tomé 8 Príncipe, Sao Thomé 11 Saint Thomas *Gulf of Mexico:* 3 Cat 5 Lobos *Gulf of Panama:* 3 Rey *Gulf of St. Lawrence:* 5 Brion *Gulf of Thailand:* 3 Kut 5 Samui *Haiti:* 6 Gonâve *Hawaii:* 4 Maui, Oahu 5 Kauai, Lanai 6 Niihau 7 Molokai 9 Kahoolawe *Hudson Bay:* 5 Coats *Indian Ocean:* 4 Mahé, Nias 5 Heard, Pemba 7 La Dique, Praslin, Réunion 8 Sri Lanka, Zanzibar 9 Mauritius 10 Madagascar *Indonesia:* 4 Bali, Biak, Java, Maja, Muna, Nias, Rhio, Riau, Roma, Roti, Savu, Sawu 5 Batam, Boano, Buton, Djawa, Japen, Lakor, Moena, Riouw, Rotti, Rupat, Sawoe, Solor, Sumba, Wetar, Wokam 6 Butung, Flores, Jappen, Lombok, Madura, Padang, Roepat, Romang, Soemba 7 Celebes, Madoera, Sumatra, Sumbawa 8 Boetoeng, Soembawa, Sulawesi 10 Bandanaira, Banda Neira, Sandalwood *Inner Hebrides:* 4 Coll, Eigg, Iona, Jura, Muck, Mull, Skye 5 Canna, Gigha, Islay, Tiree, Tyree *Ionian group:* 5 Corfu, Paxos, Zante 6 Cerigo, Ithaca, Leukas, Levkas 10 Santa Maura *Iran:* 5 Shahi *Ireland:* 4 Aran *Irish Sea:* 3 Man *Italy:* 4 Elba 6 Sicily 8 Sardinia *Japan:* 3 Iki, Uku 4 Naru, Yezo

5 Awaji, Fukae, Fukue, Hondo, Shodo 6 Honshu, Kyushu 7 Shikoku 8 Hokkaido 10 Shodoshima *Java Sea:* 4 Laut *Kiribati:* 6 Tarawa *Kuril group:* 4 Urup 5 Ketoi, Matua 6 Iturup 7 Etorofu, Matsuwa 8 Kunashir 9 Kunashiri *Lake Champlain:* 5 Grand *Lake Erie:* 9 North Bass, South Bass 10 Middle Bass *Lake Huron:* 8 Drummond 10 Manitoulin *Lake Michigan:* 3 Hog 4 High 6 Beaver *Lake Ontario:* 5 Wolfe *Lake Superior:* 4 Sand 6 Royale 7 Manitou *Lake Winnipeg:* 5 Hecla *largest:* 9 Greenland *Leeward group:* 5 Nevis 7 Antigua, Barbuda, Redonda 8 Anguilla, Sombrero 10 Montserrat, Saint Kitts 13 St. Christopher *legendary:* 7 Cipango *Lesser Sundas:* 4 Alor 5 Ombai *Leti group:* 3 Moa 5 Lakor *Line group:* 5 Flint 6 Malden, Vostok 7 Fanning, Palmyra 8 Starbuck 9 Christmas *Long Island Sound:* 4 City, Hart 5 Goose, Harts *Loyalty group:* 3 Uea 4 Lifu, Maré, Uvea 5 Lifou *Malay Archipelago:* 5 Kisar, Larat, Timor 6 Borneo 9 New Guinea *Malaysia:* 6 Penang, Pinang 13 Prince of Wales *Malta:* 4 Gozo *Marianas:* 4 Maug, Rota 5 Pagan 6 Saipan *Marquesas group:* 4 Eiào, Ua Pu 6 Hatutu, Hiva Oa, Ua Huka 7 Tahuata 8 Fatu Hiva, Nuku Hiva *Marshall group:* 5 Wotho, Wotje 8 Eniwetok 9 Kwajalein *Massachusetts:* 9 Nantucket *Mediterranean Sea:* 4 Elba 5 Corfu, Crete, Malta 6 Cyprus, Euboea, Rhodes, Sicily 7 Corsica 8 Sardinia *Midway group:* 4 Sand 7 Eastern *Moluccas:* 4 Buru 5 Ambon, Ceram, Seram 6 Boeroe *Mozambique channel:* 10 Juan de Nova *Myanmar:* 5 Daung, Kadan, Lanbi *Narragansett Bay:* 5 Rhode 8 Prudence 9 Aquidneck, Conanicut *Netherlands:* 5 Texel 7 Ameland 8 Vlieland *Netherlands Antilles:* 7 Curaçao *New York:* 4 Fire, Long 9 Gardiners, Roosevelt *New York Bay:* 5 Ellis 6 Staten 7 Liberty 9 Governors, Manhattan *New Zealand:* 5 South, White 7 Chatham, Stewart 8 D'Urville *Niagara River:* 4 Goat *Nile River:* 4 Argo, Roda, Ruda 5 Rhoda 6 Rawdah 11 Elephantine *North Channel:* 3 Mew *Northern Cook group:* 7 Penrhyn 8 Manihiki 9 Tongareva *North Pacific:* 4 Wake *Northwest Territories:* 5 Banks, Bylot, Devon 8 Bathurst, Melville 9 Ellesmere 10 Cornwallis, Resolution 13 Prince of Wales *Norwegian:* 8 Jan Mayen *Norwegian Sea:* 5 Donna, Smola, Vikna *Nova Scotia:* 5 Sable 10 Cape Breton *off Alaska:* 4 Dall 5 Kayak *off Albania:* 5 Sazan 6 Saseno *off Australia:* 4 Dunk *off Belize:*

9 Ambergris *off Brazil:* 4 Apeu 5 Rocas *off British Columbia:* 4 King, Pitt 9 Vancouver *off Cape Cod:* 8 Muskeget 9 Nantucket *off Chile:* 5 Guafo, Mocha *off China:* 4 Amoy 5 Ma-tsu 6 Hainan, Quemoy, Taiwan *off Crete:* 3 Dia *off Ecuador:* 4 Puna *off England:* 3 Man 5 Wight 6 Walney *off Florida:* 3 Dog 4 Pine 6 Amelia 7 Pelican, Sanibel 9 Anastasia *off French Guiana:* 6 Devil's *off Georgia:* 10 Cumberland 11 Saint Simons *off Germany:* 4 Sylt *off Greenland:* 5 Disko *off Guinea:* 5 Tombo *off Hispaniola:* 5 Beata *off Honduras:* 5 Tigre *off Iceland:* 7 Surtsey *off India:* 5 Sagar *off Ireland:* 4 Tory 5 Clare, Clear *off Kenya:* 4 Lamu *off Long Island:* 7 Fishers *off Louisiana:* 5 Marsh *off Maine:* 4 Deer, Orrs 5 Swans 8 Monhegan 11 Mount Desert *off Malay Peninsula:* 6 Phuket 9 Singapore *off Maryland:* 10 Assateague *off Massachusetts:* 4 Plum 7 Naushon *off Mexico:* 7 Cozumel *off Mississippi:* 4 Horn, Ship *off Mozambique:* 3 Ibo *off New Brunswick:* 10 Campobello *off Newfoundland:* 4 Bell *off Nigeria:* 5 Lagos *off North Carolina:* 5 Bodie *off Norway:* 5 Bomlo, Froya, Hitra, Sotra, Stord, Vardo 8 Hitteren *off Panama:* 5 Coiba 6 Parida *off Poland:* 5 Wolin 6 Wollin *off Puerto Rico:* 4 Crab 7 Culebra, Vieques *off Rhode Island:* 5 Block *off Scotland:* 4 Bute 5 Arran *off South Carolina:* 5 North 6 Parris 10 Hilton Head *off Sri Lanka:* 5 Delft *off Staten Island:* 7 Hoffman *off Sumatra:* 3 Weh *off Sweden:* 5 Graso, Oland, Vaddo *off Syria:* 5 Arvad, Arwad, Rouad 6 Aradus *off Tanzania:* 5 Mafia, Pemba *off Tasmania:* 5 Bruni, Bruny *off Tunisia:* 5 Jerba 6 Djerba, Meninx *off Venezuela:* 5 Aruba 7 Bonaire 8 Buen Aire *off Virginia:* 5 Wreck *off Wales:* 5 Caldy 6 Caldey *Okinawa group:* 4 Kume *Orkneys:* 3 Hoy *Outer Hebrides:* 5 Barra, Scarp *Palmer Archipelago:* 6 Anvers 7 Antwerp, Brabant *Pearl Harbor:* 4 Ford *Persian Gulf:* 4 Qeys 5 Kharg, Khark *Philippines:* 4 Buad, Cebu, Fuga, Ilin, Poro, Sulu 5 Balut, Batan, Bohol, Coron, Daram, Leyte, Luzon, Panay, Samal, Samar, Sugbu, Talim, Ticao, Verde 6 Negros 7 Masbate, Mindoro, Palawan, Paragua 8 Limasawa, Mindanao 10 Corregidor *Phoenix group:* 4 Hull, Mary 6 Birnie, Canton 9 Enderbury *Puerto Rico:* 4 Mona *Quebec:* 4 Alma *Queen Charlotte group:* 7 Moresby *Red Sea:* 5 Tiran, Zugur, Zuqar *Russia:* 7 Wrangel *Ryukyu group:* 7 Okinawa *St. Lawrence River:* 4 Hare 5 Jesus

8 Montreal *San Francisco Bay:* 5 Angel *Santa Cruz:* 5 Anuda, Ndeni 6 Cherry *Sea of Japan:* 4 Sado 5 Rebun *Sea of Marmara:* 4 Avsa *second largest:* 9 New Guinea *Senegal:* 5 Gorée *Seychelles:* 4 Mahé 7 La Digue, Praslin *Shetland archipelago:* 4 Unst, Yell 5 Foula *Shumagin group:* 4 Unga *Sierra Leone:* 5 Tasso *Society group:* 5 Eimeo, Tahaa, Tahao, Taiti 6 Moorea, Tahiti 8 Otaheite *Solomon group:* 4 Buka, Gizo, Savo 7 Malaita 11 Guadalcanal 12 Bougainville *South Atlantic:* 5 Gough 6 Gough's 11 Saint Helena *South Korea:* 5 Cheju *South of Tokyo:* 3 Iwo 7 Iwo Jima, Naka Iwo *South Orkneys:* 10 Coronation *South Pacific:* 3 Hiu 4 Niue 5 Raoul 6 Savage, Sunday 7 Norfolk 8 Pitcairn *Spitsbergen archipelago:* 4 Edge *Strait of Hormuz:* 5 Qeshm, Qishm *Sulu Archipelago:* 4 Jolo 5 Lapac *Svalbard:* 4 Hope *Sverdrup:* 11 Axel Heiberg 12 Amund Ringnes *Swedish:* 3 Ven 4 Hven 5 Hveen, Orust *Tanzania:* 8 Zanzibar *Texas:* 5 Padre *Thames River:* 7 Sheppey *third largest:* 6 Borneo *Tierra del Fuego:* 5 Hoste *Tonga:* 3 Eua, Foa 4 Uiha 5 Haano *Treasury group:* 4 Mono *Truk group:* 3 Tol 4 Haru, Moen, Udot, Uman 5 Fefan *Tuamotu Archipelago:* 4 Anaa 5 Chain *Turkish:* 5 Imroz 6 Imbros *Tuvalu:* 7 Nanumea 9 Nukufetau *Tyrrhenian Sea:* 6 Ischia 11 Montecristo *Vanuatu:* 3 Api, Epi, Oba 4 Aoba, Gaua, Tana, Vate 5 Efate, Maewo, Tanna *Venezuelan:* 5 Patos 9 La Tortuga *Virgin group, American:* 9 Saint John 10 Saint Croix 11 Saint Thomas *Virgin group, British:* 5 Peter 6 Norman 7 Anegada, Tortola 11 Jost Van Dyke *volcanic:* 5 Tofua 7 Iwo Jima *Wales:* 8 Anglesea, Anglesey, Holyhead *Weddell Sea:* 4 Ross 6 Hearst *Western Samoa:* 5 Upolu 6 Savaii *West Indies:* 4 Mona, Saba, Salt 5 Nevis, Peter, Saona 6 Tobago, Tortue 7 Grenada, Tortuga 8 Trinidad 9 Santa Cruz 10 Concepción, Hispaniola, Montserrat, Saint Croix (see also BAHAMAS; GREATER ANTILLES; LEEWARD GROUP; VIRGIN GROUP; WINDWARD GROUP) *West of England:* 7 Ireland *West Pacific:* 5 Dyaul, Fauro, Ocean 6 Banaba, Marcus 7 Iwo Jima, Kita Iwo 9 Minami Iwo *Windward group:* 10 Martinique *with former penitentiary:* 8 Alcatraz

island group *Alaska:* 3 Rat 8 Aleutian, Pribilof 9 Andreanof, Catherine *Aleutians:* 4 Near *American Samoa:* 5 Manua *Arabian Sea:* 9 Laccadive *Arctic Archipel-*ago: 8 Sverdrup *Arctic Ocean:* 8 Svalbard 12 Novaya Zemlya *Bahamas:* 5 Berry, Exuma 6 Bimini *Banda Sea:* 5 Damar *Bangladesh:* 5 Hatia, Hatya *Bay of Bengal:* 7 Andaman, Nicobar *between England and France:* 7 Channel *Bismarck Archipelago:* 4 Feni 5 Tabar, Tanga *Bismarck Sea:* 4 Vitu *British:* 7 Bermuda *Caribbean Sea:* 4 Swan 5 Pearl 6 Cayman, Perlas, Pigeon 8 Pichones 10 Grenadines, West Indies *Carolines:* 3 Uap, Yap 4 Truk 5 Nomoi 7 Hogoleu *Central Pacific Ocean:* 4 Line 5 Samoa, Union 6 Danger, Midway 7 Phoenix, Tokelau 8 Manihiki 9 Polynesia 12 Northern Cook *Coral Sea:* 4 Huon *Cuba:* 8 Camagüey *east of Philippines:* 10 Micronesia *East Siberian Sea:* 4 Bear 8 Medvezhi *Ecuador:* 5 Colón 9 Galápagos *England:* 5 Farne *Fiji:* 3 Lau 7 Eastern *Formosa Strait:* 4 Hoko 6 Peng hu 10 Pescadores *French:* 5 Salut 6 Safety 9 Kerguelen *French Polynesia:* 3 Low 6 Tubuai 7 Austral, Paumotu, Société, Society, Tuamotu 9 Marquesas, Touamotou *Germany:* 8 Halligen *Greece:* 6 Aegean, Ionian 8 Cyclades 11 Dodecanese 11 Dodecanesus *Hudson Bay:* 7 Belcher *Indian Ocean:* 7 Aldabra *Indonesia:* 4 Asia, Batu, Pagi, Sula 5 Babar, Batoe, Pagai, Pageh, Penju, Spice, Wakde 6 Maluku *Ireland:* 4 Aran *Japan:* 5 Osumi *largest:* 5 Malay 6 Malaysia *Lesser Antilles:* 8 Windward *Malay Archipelago:* 5 Sunda 6 Soenda *Mediterranean Sea:* 8 Baleares, Balearic *Moluccas:* 3 Kai, Kei, Obi 4 Leti 5 Banda, Letti 8 Tanimbar 9 Timorlaut *New Caledonia:* 7 Loyalty 9 Loyalties *north of Australia:* 9 Melanesia *north of British Isles:* 5 Faroe 7 Faeroes *north off Fiji:* 5 Hoorn 6 Futuna *north of Madagascar:* 7 Aldabra 8 Farquhar *north of New Caledonia:* 5 Belep *north of New Guinea:* 8 Bismarck 9 Admiralty 11 Admiralties *Northwest Territories:* 5 Parry *off Alaska:* 3 Fox *off Alaska Peninsula:* 8 Shumagin *off Cape Cod:* 9 Elizabeth *off eastern Asia:* 5 Kuril 6 Kurile *off England:* 5 Scilly *off Florida:* 11 Dry Tortugas *off Guinea:* 3 Los 4 Loos *off Honduras:* 5 Bahia *off Morocco:* 7 Madeira *off New Guinea:* 3 Aru 4 Aroe *off Nicaragua:* 4 Corn *off northern Africa:* 6 Canary 8 Canaries *off northern Australia:* 6 Wessel 7 Dampier *off Sicily:* 5 Egadi 6 Aegadian *Outer Hebrides:* 4 Uist *Papua New Guinea:* 5 Green *Persian Gulf:* 4 Tunb *Philippines:* 4 Cuyo 5 Tapul 6 Lubang 7 Basilan, Bisayas, Visayan *Portuguese:* 6 Azores

Quebec: 8 Magdalen 9 Madeleine
Ryukyus: 5 Amami *St. Lawrence River:*
8 Thousand *Sea of Japan:* 3 Oki *Sea of
Marmara:* 5 Kizil 7 Princes 11 Kizil
Adalar *South Atlantic Ocean:* 8 Falkland,
Malvinas *South China Sea:* 6 Hirata
7 Paracel, Spratly *south of New Zealand:*
8 Auckland *South Pacific:* 11 Austrone-
sia *Sulu Sea:* 7 Cagayan 9 Cagayanes
Tonga: 5 Vavau *Tyrrhenian Sea:* 5 Ponza
Venezuelan: 4 Aves, Bird 9 Los Roques
West Europe: 12 British Isles *West Indies:*
6 Virgin 10 Guadeloupe *west of French
Polynesia:* 4 Cook *west of Scotland:*
7 Western 8 Hebrides *west Pacific
Ocean:* 4 Duff 5 Bonin, Mapia, Palau,
Pelew 7 Ladrone, Mariana, Solomon,
Vanuatu 8 Marshall, Treasury 9 Oga-
sawara 10 Saint David
island nation *Atlantic Ocean:* 9 Cape
Verde *Indian Ocean:* 8 Malagasy, Mal-
gache, Sri Lanka 9 Mauritius 10 Madagascar, Seychelles *Mediterranean Sea:*
6 Cyprus *Mozambique Channel:*
6 Comoro 7 Comores *off southern
China:* 6 Taiwan *south of Greenland:*
7 Iceland *West Indies:* 4 Cuba 7 Jamaica
8 Barbados 10 Saint Lucia *West Pacific
Ocean:* 5 Nauru *Windward group:*
8 Dominica
island province 12 Prince Edward
island state 6 Hawaii
isle see ISLAND
Ismene *brother:* 9 Polynices *father:*
7 Oedipus *mother:* 7 Jocasta *sister:*
8 Antigone *uncle:* 5 Creon
isochronous 7 regular 8 cyclical, periodic, rhythmic 9 recurrent, recurring
10 periodical 12 intermittent
isolate 6 cut off, detach, enisle 7 seclude
8 close off, insulate, pinpoint, separate,
set apart 9 segregate, sequester 10 quarantine
isolated 5 alone 6 random, remote,
unique 7 unusual 8 solitary, sporadic
9 separated, withdrawn 11 exceptional,
quarantined
Isolde see ISEULT
Israel *ancient name:* 4 Zion 5 Judea
6 Canaan, Judaea 9 Palestine *capital:*
9 Jerusalem *city:* 4 Acre 5 Haifa, Jaffa
7 Tel Aviv 9 Beersheba *desert:* 5 Negeb,
Negev *gulf:* 5 Aqaba *lake:* 8 Tiberias
12 Sea of Galilee *language:* 6 Arabic,
Hebrew *monetary unit:* 6 shekel *neighbor:* 5 Egypt, Syria 6 Jordan 7 Lebanon
plain: 9 Esdraelon *river:* 6 Jordan *sea:*
4 Dead 13 Mediterranean
Israeli 5 Sabra
Israelite see HEBREW; JEWISH
Issachar *father:* 5 Jacob *mother:* 4 Leah

issue 4 emit, flow, gush, pour, rise, seed,
stem, vent 5 arise, birth, brood, child,
fruit, scion, topic 6 affair, appear,
effect, emerge, get out, matter, put out,
result, scions, sequel, source, spring,
upshot 7 concern, descent, edition,
emanate, give off, give out, outcome,
problem, proceed, progeny, publish,
release, subject 8 bulletin, children,
question, throw off 9 come forth, offspring, originate, posterity 10 derive
from, distribute, end product, promulgate 11 consequence, descendants,
progeniture, publication
Istanbul *ancient name:* 9 Byzantium *business section:* 6 Galata *country:* 6 Turkey
foreign quarter: 4 Pera 7 Beyoglu *park:*
8 Seraglio *residential section:* 7 Uskudar
isthmus *Africa-Asia:* 4 Suez *Greece:*
7 Corinth *America:* 6 Panama *Malay
Peninsula:* 3 Kra
Italian *automobile:* 4 Fiat 6 Lancia 7 Ferrari 8 Maserati 9 Alfa Romeo 11 Lamborghini *cathedral:* 5 duomo *dialect:*
6 Tuscan 8 Sicilian *dictator:* 9 Mussolini
(Benito) *family:* 4 Este 5 Cenci, Savoy
6 Borgia, Medici, Orsini, Pepoli,
Savoia, Sforza 7 Colonna, Gonzaga,
Spinola 8 Visconti *fascist:* 10 Blackshirt
game: 5 bocce, bocci 6 boccie *gentleman:* 6 signor 7 signore *highway:*
10 autostrada *lady:* 5 donna 7 signora
9 signorina *magistrate:* 7 podestà *meat:*
6 salami 8 pancetta 9 pepperoni, salsi-
ccia 10 mortadella, prosciutto *opera
house:* 7 La Scala *patriot:* 6 Cavour
(Conte di), Rienzo (Cola di) 7 Mazzini
(Giuseppe) 9 Garibaldi (Giuseppe) *religious reformer:* 10 Savonarola (Girolamo) *resort:* 4 Lido 5 Abano, Capri
8 Sorrento, Taormina *road:* 6 strada
soup: 10 minestrone *square:* 6 piazza
street: 3 via 5 corso *weight:* 5 libra,
oncia
Italy *bay:* 6 Naples *capital:* 4 Rome *city:*
4 Asti, Bari, Pisa 5 Aosta, Genoa,
Milan, Padua, Parma, Siena, Turin
6 Genova, Mantua, Milano, Modena,
Naples, Napoli, Padova, Torino, Venice,
Verona 7 Bergamo, Bologna, Bolzano,
Catania, Cremona, Firenze, Leghorn,
Livorno, Mantova, Palermo, Perugia,
Ravenna, Salerno, Taranto, Trieste,
Venezia 8 Florence, Siracusa, Syracuse
enclave: 9 San Marino 11 Vatican City
gulf: 5 Gaeta 7 Salerno, Taranto 11 Sant'
Eufemia *island, island group:* 4 Elba
5 Capri 6 Ischia, Lipari, Sicily 7 Aeolian, Capraia 8 Sardinia *lake:* 4 Como
5 Garda 7 Bolsena 8 Maggiore 9 Brac-
ciano *leader:* 9 Mussolini (Benito)

monetary unit: 4 euro **monetary unit, former:** 4 lira **mountain, range:** 4 Alps, Etna 9 Apennines, Mont Blanc, Monte Rosa 10 Monte Corno **neighbor:** 6 France 7 Austria 8 Slovenia 11 Switzerland **peninsula:** 9 Salentina **river:** 4 Arno, Liri 5 Adige, Piave, Tiber 6 Isonzo, Tevere 8 Volturno **sea:** 6 Ionian 8 Adriatic, Ligurian 10 Tyrrhenian 13 Mediterranean **strait:** 7 Messina, Otranto **volcano:** 4 Etna 8 Vesuvius **wine region:** 4 Asti

itch 3 yen 4 ache, long, lust, pine 5 crave, yearn 6 desire, hanker, hunger, thirst 7 craving, longing 8 appetite, pruritus, yearning 9 hankering

itchy 4 avid, edgy, keen 5 antsy, eager, jumpy 7 fidgety, restive 8 prurient, pruritic, restless 9 impatient

item 3 bit 5 entry, point, scrap, story, thing, topic 6 detail, matter 7 account, article, element, feature, product 8 clipping 9 commodity 10 particular

itemize 4 list 5 count, tally 6 number 7 catalog, run down, specify, tick off 8 document, spell out 9 catalogue, enumerate, inventory

iterate 5 drill, recap, renew 6 rehash, repeat, replay, retell 7 reprise, restate 12 recapitulate

Ithaca king 8 Odysseus

Ithamar's father 5 Aaron

itinerant 5 gypsy, nomad 6 roving 7 migrant, nomadic, roaming, vagrant 8 drifting, rambling, traveler, vagabond, wanderer 9 migratory, transient, unsettled, wandering, wayfaring 11 peripatetic

itty-bitty 3 wee 4 tiny 5 teeny, weeny 6 teensy 10 teeny-weeny 12 teensy-weensy

Ivanhoe author: 5 Scott (Walter) **character:** 5 Isaac 6 Cedric, Rowena, Ulrica 7 Rebecca, Wilfred 9 Robin Hood

Ivory Coast 11 Côte d'Ivoire **capital:** 7 Abidjan 12 Yamoussoukro **city:** 6 Bouaké **language:** 6 French **monetary unit:** 5 franc **mountain:** 5 Nimba **neighbor:** 4 Mali 5 Ghana 6 Guinea 7 Liberia 11 Burkina Faso **river:** 7 Bandama 9 Sassandra

ivory-tower 8 academic 11 conjectural, impractical, theoretical, unrealistic

J

jab 3 hit 4 blow, poke, prod, sock, stab 5 nudge, prick, punch 6 pierce, strike, thrust 8 puncture

jabber 3 gab, jaw, yak 6 babble, drivel, gabble 7 blather, chatter, prattle 8 nonsense 9 gibberish

jabberer 6 gabber, magpie 7 babbler, blabber, gabbler 8 prattler 9 chatterer 10 chatterbox

Jabberwocky author 7 Carroll (Lewis)

jabot 4 fall 5 frill 6 ruffle

___ jacet 3 hic

jack 3 tar 4 bird, card, fish, flag, hike, lift, move, salt 5 boost, brace, bread, dough, knave, knife, money, put up, raise 6 brandy, cheese, device, donkey, rabbit, sailor, seaman 7 laborer, mariner, servant 8 increase, standard 9 criticize, mechanism 10 take to task

jackal 4 dupe, pawn 5 agent, canid, patsy

6 canine, flunky, lackey, minion, stooge 7 cat's-paw 9 accessory, auxiliary 10 accomplice 11 stool pigeon **god:** 4 Anpu 6 Anubis

jackanapes 3 ape 4 brat, fool 6 monkey

jackass 4 dolt, dope, fool, jerk 5 burro, dunce, idiot, schmo 6 donkey, nitwit 7 nebbish 8 bonehead, imbecile, numskull 9 blockhead, numbskull 10 nincompoop **deer:** 3 kob 8 antelope

jackdaw 7 grackle 9 blackbird

jacket 4 Eton 5 parka, tunic 6 anorak, blazer, bolero, jerkin, reefer, sacque, tuxedo 7 doublet, Norfolk, peacoat, spencer 8 camisole 10 roundabout **armored:** 7 hauberk 9 habergeon **sleeveless:** 4 vest 6 bolero, jerkin 9 waistcoat

jackhammer 5 drill 9 rock drill

jackknife 4 dive 6 barlow **game:** 11 mumblety-peg

jackleg 6 make-do, novice 7 amateur,

shyster, stopgap **9** dishonest, greenhorn, makeshift, temporary, unskilled
10 substitute **11** pettifogger
12 unscrupulous
jack-of-all-trades 6 tinker **7** go-to guy
8 factotum, handyman
jack-o'-lantern 6 fungus **7** pumpkin
jackpot 3 sum **4** pool **5** award, kitty,
prize **6** reward, stakes **7** bonanza, success **8** windfall
jackrabbit 4 hare
jackstay 3 bar, rod **4** rope **7** rigging, support
Jacob *brother:* **4** Esau *daughter:* **5** Dinah
father: **5** Isaac *father-in-law:* **5** Laban
mother: **7** Rebekah *new name:* **6** Israel
son: **3** Dan, Gad **4** Levi **5** Asher, Judah
6 Joseph, Reuben, Simeon **7** Zebulun
8 Benjamin, Issachar, Naphtali *variant:*
5 James *wife:* **4** Leah **6** Rachel
Jacobin 7 radical **9** Dominican, extremist
Jacob's ladder 4 herb **5** phlox **9** perennial
jade 3 gem, nag **4** bore, cloy, dull, minx,
pall, tire, wear **5** color, drain, flirt,
green, hussy, jewel, stone, tramp,
weary, wench **6** wanton **7** fatigue,
jezebel, mineral, trollop, wear out
8 gemstone, nephrite, strumpet,
wear down
jaded 4 worn **5** blasé, bored, sated, tired,
weary **6** dulled **7** cynical, wearied,
worn-out **8** fatigued, satiated, worn
down **9** apathetic, exhausted, surfeited
10 overworked
jaeger 4 skua **6** hunter **8** huntsman
Jael *husband:* **5** Heber *victim:* **6** Sisera
jag 3 cut **4** barb, jerk, load, pink, tear
5 binge, notch, prick, spell, spree
6 bender, indent, thrill, thrust **7** serrate
jagged 5 harsh, rough, sharp **6** broken,
craggy, rugged, spiked, uneven **7** scraggy **8** serrated, unsmooth **9** irregular
___ **Jagger 4** Mick
jai alai 6 pelota *basket:* **5** cesta *court:*
6 cancha **7** fronton
jail 3 can, jug, pen **4** coop, gaol, poky
5 clink, pokey **6** cooler, lockup, prison
7 confine, freezer, slammer **8** hoosegow,
imprison, stockade **9** constrain **11** confinement, incarcerate
jailbird 3 con **5** felon, loser **7** convict
8 criminal, prisoner, repeater **10** recidivist
jailer 5 guard, screw **6** keeper, warden
7 turnkey **8** overseer
jakes 5 privy **8** outhouse **9** backhouse
jalopy 3 car **4** auto, heap **5** crate, wreck
6 beater, junker **7** clunker, vehicle
10 automobile, rattletrap

jalousie 5 blind **6** window **7** shutter
jam 3 box, fix **4** bind, clog, cram, dunk,
pack, push **5** block, crowd, crush,
force, jelly, press, stuff, wedge **6** bruise,
impede, plight, scrape, squash, squish
7 dilemma, squeeze **8** compress, conserve, obstacle, preserve **9** confiture,
preserves **10** difficulty **11** predicament
Jamaica *capital:* **8** Kingston *cay:* **5** Pedro
6 Morant *city:* **10** Montego Bay
11 Spanish Town *discoverer:* **8** Columbus (Christopher) *language:* **7** English
location: **10** West Indies *mountain range:*
4 Blue **10** Dry Harbour *sea:*
9 Caribbean
Jamaican *export:* **3** rum **5** sugar *hair
style:* **10** dreadlocks *music:* **3** dub, ska
6 reggae *musician:* **5** Cliff (Jimmy)
6 Marley (Bob, Ziggy) **7** Wailers *nationalist:* **6** Garvey (Marcus)
jambalaya 4 olio **5** gumbo **7** mélange,
mixture **8** mishmash
jamboree 4 gala **5** revel **6** fiesta, frolic
7 carouse, shindig **8** carnival, festival,
wingding **9** merriment **11** celebration
13 entertainment
James *brother:* **4** John **5** Jesus, Joses
cousin: **5** Jesus *father:* **7** Zebedee
8 Alphaeus *mother:* **4** Mary **6** Salome
James novel 8 American (The) **9** Euro-
peans (The) **10** Bostonians (The), Confidence, Golden Bowl (The), Tragic
Muse (The) **11** Ambassadors (The),
Daisy Miller **14** Turn of the Screw
(The), Wings of the Dove (The) **15** Portrait of a Lady (The) **16** Washington
Square
Jammu and ___ 7 Kashmir
Jane Eyre *author:* **6** Brontë (Charlotte)
lover: **9** Rochester
jangle 3 jar **4** ring **5** babel, clash **6** clam-
or, excite, hubbub **7** discord, quarrel
8 conflict **11** discordance, discordancy
12 disharmonize
jangling 5 harsh, noisy, tense **7** grating
9 dissonant **10** discordant, quarreling
janitor 5 super **6** porter **7** cleaner **9** caretaker, concierge, custodian **10** door-
keeper
japan 4 coat **7** coating, varnish **11** lac-
querware
Japan 5 Nihon **6** Nippon *capital:* **3** Edo
5 Tokyo *city:* **4** Kobe **5** Kyoto, Osaka,
Otaru **6** Nagoya **7** Fukuoka, Okinawa,
Sapporo **8** Kawasaki, Nagasaki, Yokohama **9** Hiroshima *island:* **6** Honshu,
Kyushu **7** Shikoku **8** Hokkaido *lake:*
4 Biwa **8** Chuzenji *monetary unit:* **3** yen
mountain: **4** Fuji **8** Fujiyama
Japanese *aborigine:* **4** Ainu *art:* **6** bonsai
6 ukiyo-e *baron:* **6** daimyo *battle cry:*

6 banzai *Buddha:* **5** Amida, Amita *cartoons:* **5** anime *comics:* **5** manga *dancing girl:* **6** geisha *dish:* **4** miso, soba **5** gyoza, katsu, kombu, sushi **7** sashimi, tempura **8** sukiyaki, teriyaki *drama:* **3** Noh **6** Bugaku, Kabuki **7** Bunraku *drink:* **4** sake, saki *emperor:* **6** Mikado **7** Akihito **8** Hirohito *fencing:* **5** kendo *festival:* **3** Bon *fish:* **4** fugu *flower arrangement:* **7** ikebana *garment:* **6** kimono *gateway:* **5** torii *god:* **5** Ebisu, Hotei **7** Daikoku, Jurojin **8** Bishamon *goddess:* **6** Benten **9** Amaterasu *governor:* **6** shogun *grill:* **7** hibachi *immigrant:* **5** issei *instrument:* **4** biwa, koto **7** samisen **8** shamisen **10** shakuhachi *martial art:* **4** judo **5** kendo **6** aikido, karate **7** jujitsu *martial artist:* **5** ninja *money:* **3** sen, yen *plum:* **6** loquat *poem:* **5** haiku, tanka *porcelain:* **5** imari *pottery:* **4** raku **7** satsuma *radish:* **6** daikon *religion:* **6** Shinto **8** Buddhism **9** Shintoism *rice wine:* **4** sake, saki *robe:* **6** kimono *samurai clan:* **5** Taira **8** Minamoto *sash:* **3** obi *song:* **3** uta *suicide:* **7** seppuku **8** harakiri, kamikaze *theater:* **3** Noh **6** Bugaku, Kabuki **7** Bunraku *tidal wave:* **7** tsunami *vehicle:* **8** rickshaw *warrior:* **7** samurai *warrior code:* **7** bushido *wrestling:* **4** sumo *writing:* **4** kana **8** hiragana, katakana *zither:* **4** koto

Japanese-American 5 Issei, Nisei *second-generation:* **6** Sansei

jape 3 gag, kid, rib **4** gibe, jest, jibe, joke, mock, quip **5** crack, laugh, prank, tease **7** waggery **8** drollery **9** wisecrack, witticism

Japheth *brother:* **3** Ham **4** Shem *father:* **4** Noah *son:* **5** Gomer, Javan, Madai, Magog, Tiras, Tubal **7** Meshech

jar 4 bump, jolt, olla **5** cruse, quake, shake, shock, upset **6** jangle, jounce **7** tremble, vibrate **8** mismatch **9** container *ancient:* **6** krater **7** amphora *Egyptian:* **7** canopic

jardiniere 5 stand **6** holder **7** garnish

jargon 4 cant **5** argot, idiom, lingo, slang **6** patois, pidgin **7** dialect, lexicon, palaver **8** language **9** gibberish **10** mumbo-jumbo, vernacular, vocabulary **11** terminology *lawyer's:* **8** legalese

jarl 4 earl **5** noble **8** nobleman **12** Scandinavian

jarring 5 harsh, rough **6** hoarse, jangly **7** grating, rasping, raucous **8** strident **9** dissonant **10** discordant, unsettling

jasmine 3 tea **4** vine **5** shrub **6** flower, yellow **7** perfume

Jason *father:* **5** Aeson *helper:* **5** Medea *lover:* **6** Creusa, Glauce, Glauke *quest:* **6** Fleece **12** Golden Fleece *ship:* **4** Argo

shipmate: **8** Argonaut *teacher:* **6** Chiron **7** Cheiron *uncle:* **6** Pelias *wife:* **5** Medea

jasper 6 morlop, quartz **9** stoneware **10** chalcedony

jaundice 4 bias **7** disease, icterus **9** prejudice

jaundiced 6 biased, warped, yellow **7** colored, cynical, envious, hostile, jealous **9** distorted **10** suspicious

jaunt 4 ride, trip **5** drive, sally **6** junket, outing, ramble **7** journey **9** excursion

jaunty 4 airy, pert **5** fresh, light, peppy, perky **6** breezy, lively **7** buoyant **8** debonair **9** sprightly **10** nonchalant

java 6 coffee

Java *almond:* **7** talisay *cotton:* **5** kapok *jute:* **5** kenaf *plum:* **5** jaman **6** jambul **7** jambool

Javanese *civet:* **5** rasse *orchestra:* **7** gamelan *tree:* **4** upas

Javan squirrel 8 jelerang

javelin 5 lance, shaft, spear **6** weapon **7** assagai, assegai, harpoon

Javert's prey 7 Valjean (Jean)

jaw 3 gab, yak **4** chat, rail, talk **5** clack, prate **6** babble, gabble **7** chatter, prattle **9** yakety-yak

jawbone 7 maxilla **8** arm-twist, mandible, persuade, talk into

jawbreaker 9 hard candy

jay 4 bird, blue, hick, rube **5** dandy **6** rustic **7** bumpkin, hayseed **9** chatterer, greenhorn

Jayhawker 9 guerrilla *State:* **6** Kansas **8** Missouri

jazz 3 bop **4** guff, jive **5** bebop, stuff, swing **6** boogie **7** ragtime **8** malarkey, nonsense *up:* **5** rouse **6** vivify **7** animate, enliven **9** stimulate

jazz musician 4 Cole (Nat "King"), Getz (Stan), Hirt (Al), Monk (Thelonious), O'Day (Anita), Rich (Buddy), Shaw (Artie) **5** Baker (Chet), Basie (Count), Brown (Clifford), Corea (Chick), Davis (Miles), Evans (Bill, Gil), Hines (Earl "Fatha"), Jones (Hank), Krall (Diana), Krupa (Gene), McRae (Carmen), Roach (Max), Smith (Jimmy), Sun Ra, Tatum (Art), Tormé (Mel), Young (Lester) **6** Bechet (Sidney), Blakey (Art), Burton (Gary), Carter (Benny), Dorsey (Jimmy, Tommy), Farmer (Art), Garner (Erroll), Gordon (Dexter), Herman (Woody), Jordan (Louis), Kenton (Stan), Mingus (Charles), Morton (Jelly Roll), Oliver (King), Parker (Charlie), Pepper (Art), Powell (Bud), Puente (Tito), Silver (Horace), Waller (Fats) **7** Brubeck (Dave), Coleman (Ornette), Connick (Harry), Goodman (Benny), Hampton (Lionel), Hancock (Herbie),

Hawkins (Coleman), Holiday (Billie), Jarrett (Keith), Metheny (Pat), Rollins (Sonny), Rushing (Jimmy), Shorter (Wayne), Vaughan (Sarah), Webster (Ben) **8** Adderley (Cannonball), Calloway (Cab), Coltrane (John), Eldridge (Roy), Marsalis (Wynton), Mulligan (Gerry), Peterson (Oscar), Williams (Mary Lou) **9** Armstrong (Louis), Ellington (Duke), Gillespie (Dizzy), Reinhardt (Django) **10** Fitzgerald (Ella), Montgomery (Wes), Washington (Dinah) **11** Beiderbecke (Bix)

jazzy 5 gaudy **6** brassy, flashy, glitzy, lively, rakish **7** raffish, splashy **8** animated, colorful, exciting, spirited **9** vivacious **10** flamboyant

jealous 5 green **7** envious, hostile **8** doubting, vigilant **9** demanding, green-eyed, invidious, resentful **10** intolerant, possessive, suspicious **11** distrustful, mistrustful

jeer 4 gibe, jibe, mock **5** fleer, flout, scoff, scorn, sneer, taunt **6** deride, heckle, hector, insult **7** contemn, laugh at, mockery **8** derision, ridicule

Jeeves *creator:* **9** Wodehouse (P. G.) *employer:* **7** Wooster (Bertie) *position:* **5** valet **6** butler

jeez 4 gosh, heck **5** golly, shoot **6** shucks **7** jeepers

jefe 4 boss, head, lord **5** chief, ruler **6** honcho, leader **9** chieftain, commander

Jefferson, Thomas *home:* **10** Monticello *lover:* **5** Sally (Hemings) *state:* **8** Virginia

Jehoram *brother:* **7** Ahaziah *father:* **4** Ahab **11** Jehoshaphat *kingdom:* **5** Judah *slayer:* **4** Jehu *wife:* **8** Athaliah

Jehoshaphat *father:* **3** Asa **6** Ahilud, Nimshi, Paruah *father-in-law:* **4** Ahab *son:* **4** Jehu **7** Jehoram *wife:* **8** Athaliah

Jehovah 3 God **6** Adonai, Elohim, Yahweh

Jehu 6 driver *father:* **6** Hanani **11** Jehoshaphat *grandfather:* **6** Nimshi *son:* **8** Jehoahaz *victim:* **5** Joram **7** Jehoram

jejune 4 dull, flat **5** banal, bland, empty, inane, silly, trite, vapid **7** insipid, puerile **8** childish, juvenile, lifeless **9** colorless, innocuous **10** spiritless **13** uninteresting

Jekyll's alter ego 4 Hyde (Mr.)

jell 3 set **4** form **6** cohere, gelate **7** congeal, thicken **8** coalesce **9** coagulate, take shape

jelly 3 set **4** mass **5** aspic **6** spread **7** congeal, thicken **9** coagulate

jellyfish 6 coward, medusa **7** doormat, medusan **8** medusoid, pushover, weak-

ling **10** ctenophore **12** coelenterate, invertebrate, siphonophore

je ne ___ quoi 4 sais

jennet 3 ass **5** hinny, horse **6** donkey

jenny 4 bird **6** donkey (female) **7** machine

jeopardize 4 risk **5** peril **6** chance, expose, hazard **7** imperil **8** endanger

jeopardy 4 risk **5** peril **6** danger, hazard, menace **8** exposure **9** liability **12** endangerment

jeremiad 6 lament, tirade **7** lecture **8** diatribe, harangue **9** complaint, philippic **11** declamation, lamentation

Jeremiah *scribe:* **6** Baruch

Jericho's conqueror 6 Joshua

jerk 3 ass, lug, tic, tug **4** dolt, dope, fool, jolt, pull, push, snap, twit, yank **5** brute, idiot, lurch, ninny, spasm, twist, wrest **6** bounce, nitwit, thrust, twitch, wrench **7** jackass **8** preserve **10** nincompoop

jerkin 6 jacket

jerky 4 meat **5** inane **6** abrupt, stupid, sudden **7** foolish, idiotic, jolting **8** saccadic **9** senseless

Jerome's Bible 7 Vulgate

jersey 3 cow **6** fabric **7** garment, sweater **8** pullover

Jerusalem 4 Sion, Zion **5** Salem **8** Holy City *hill:* **4** Sion, Zion **6** Moriah *mosque:* **4** Omar **6** Al-Aqsa **13** Dome of the Rock *pool:* **6** Siloam **8** Bethesda

Jerusalem artichoke 5 tuber **8** girasole **9** sunflower

Jerusalem thorn 5 shrub **9** horsebean

jess 5 strap

Jesse *daughter:* **7** Abigail, Zeruiah *father:* **4** Obed *grandfather:* **4** Boaz *son:* **4** Ozem **5** David, Eliab, Elihu **6** Raddai **7** Shammah **8** Abinadab, Nethanel *youngest son:* **5** David

Jessica *father:* **7** Shylock *husband:* **7** Lorenzo

jest 3 fun, gag, kid, rag, rib **4** butt, game, gibe, jape, jeer, joke, josh, mock, quip, razz **5** crack, fleer, flout, humor, prank, scoff, sneer, spoof, sport, tease **6** banter, gaiety **7** mockery, waggery **8** derision, drollery, ridicule **9** merriment, wisecrack, witticism

jester 3 wag, wit **4** fool **5** actor, clown, comic, joker **7** buffoon **8** comedian, funnyman, humorist, jokester, quipster **9** prankster **11** entertainer

Jesuit *founder:* **6** Loyola (Ignatius) *leader:* **6** Xavier (St. Francis)

jet 4 coal, ebon, emit, gush, inky, rush, spew **5** black, ebony, plane, spout, spurt **6** engine, nozzle, squirt, stream,

travel 7 current, jewelry 8 airplane
9 pitch-dark 10 pitch-black
Jethro *daughter:* 8 Zipporah *son-in-law:*
5 Moses
jetsam 7 flotsam 8 wreckage 9 driftwood
jet set 5 A-list, elite 9 beau monde, haut
monde 10 glitterati
jettison 4 drop, dump, junk, omit
5 eject, forgo, scrap 6 reject, remove
7 deep-six, discard 8 disposal, get rid
of, throw out 9 sacrifice, throw away
jetty 4 dock, ebon, inky, pier, quay
5 black, ebony, groin, wharf 7 project
9 pitch-dark 10 pitch-black
Jew 6 Essene, Hebrew, Semite 7 Israeli,
Judaist 9 Israelite
jewel 3 gem 4 rock 5 adorn, bijou, ideal,
prize, stone 7 bearing 8 gemstone,
ornament, treasure 9 embellish
jeweler 8 lapidary *famous:* 7 Tiffany
(Charles Lewis)
jewelry 10 bijouterie *artificial:* 5 glass,
paste 6 strass 7 costume *piece:* 3 pin
4 ring 6 brooch 7 earring 8 bracelet,
cufflink, necklace, tieclasp 9 lavaliere
set: 6 parure
Jewish *bread:* 5 matzo 6 matzoh *ceremony:* 4 bris 8 havdalah 10 bar mitzvah,
bas mitzvah *combining form:* 5 Judeo
6 Judaeo *credo:* 5 shema *doctrine:*
6 Mishna 7 Mishnah *New Year:* 12 Rosh
Hashanah *organization:* 8 Hadassah
9 B'nai B'rith *prayer:* 7 kaddish, kiddush *prayer book:* 6 siddur *sabbath:*
8 Saturday *scripture:* 5 Torah 8 Talmud
synagogue: 4 shul *teacher:* 5 rabbi,
rebbe 6 Hillel *village:* 6 shtetl (see also
HEBREW)
Jezebel 4 slut 5 hussy, tramp, trull,
wench 6 wanton 7 trollop 8 slattern,
strumpet *father:* 7 Ethbaal *home:*
5 Sidon *husband:* 4 Ahab *slayer:* 4 Jehu
victim: 6 Naboth
jib 3 arm, shy 4 balk, boom, sail, stop
5 demur 6 refuse 9 stop short
jibe 5 agree, fit in, match, shift, tally
6 accord, concur, square 7 conform
8 dovetail 9 harmonize 10 correspond,
go together 12 change course
jiffy 3 sec 4 tick, wink 5 flash, hurry,
shake, trice 6 minute, moment, second
7 instant 11 split second
jig 4 fish, game, hoax, hook, jerk, play,
ploy, ruse, sham, wile 5 catch, dance,
feint, trick 6 device, gambit 7 gimmick
9 deception
jigger 4 jerk, mold, sail 5 alter, gizmo
6 device, dingus, doodad, gadget, widget 7 gimmick, machine, measure
9 doohickey, rearrange, shot glass,
thingummy 10 manipulate

jiggle 4 jerk 5 shake 7 agitate 9 oscillate
jigsaw 3 cut 4 tool 6 puzzle 7 arrange,
machine
jihad 3 war 6 strife 7 crusade, holy war
8 campaign, struggle
jilt 4 drop 5 ditch, leave 6 desert, reject
7 abandon, cast off, discard
jim-dandy 5 great, ideal, nifty, super
7 perfect 8 knockout 9 excellent, first-
rate, humdinger 11 outstanding
jimmy 3 bar, pry 4 open 5 crack, force,
lever 7 crowbar 9 break open,
force open
jimsonweed 6 datura 10 thorn apple
jingle 4 call, ring, song 5 clink, rhyme,
sound, verse 6 tinkle
jingoistic 7 hawkish 11 belligerent
12 chauvinistic, militaristic 13 national-
istic
jinn 5 afrit, genie 6 afreet, spirit
jinx 3 hex 5 charm, curse, spell 6 plague,
whammy 7 bad luck, evil eye 8 fore-
doom 10 affliction, misfortune
jitters 5 jumps, panic 6 nerves, shakes
7 anxiety, shivers, willies 9 whim-
whams 11 nervousness, stage fright
13 heebie-jeebies
jittery 5 jumpy, nervy 6 goosey, spooky
7 anxious, fearful, fidgety, nervous,
panicky 10 high-strung
jive 3 kid 4 fool, jazz, talk 5 dance,
music, swing, tease 6 cajole, hot air,
jargon
Joab *brother:* 6 Asahel 7 Abishai *father:*
7 Seraiah, Zeruiah *slayer:* 7 Benaiah
uncle: 5 David *victim:* 5 Abner, Amasa
Joan of Arc *birthplace:* 7 Domremy *epithet:* 7 Pucelle (La) 13 Maid of Orléans
king: 10 Charles VII *victory:* 7 Orléans
Joan's husband 5 Darby
Joash *father:* 4 Ahab 7 Ahaziah 8 Jehoahaz *son:* 6 Gideon 7 Amaziah 8 Jeroboam *victim:* 9 Zechariah
job 4 duty, hire, item, post, role, spot,
task, work 5 chore, stint, trade 6 effort,
office 7 calling, deprive, posting, pursuit, robbery 8 business, function,
penalize, position, vocation 9 situation,
speculate, victimize 10 assignment, difficulty, employment, engagement,
livelihood, occupation, profession
11 undertaking
Job *daughter:* 6 Keziah 7 Jemimah
father: 8 Issachar *friend:* 6 Bildad,
Zophar 7 Eliphaz
jobber 6 broker, dealer, seller, trader
8 merchant 10 contractor, wholesaler
job-safety agency 4 OSHA
job-training program 4 JTPA
Jocasta *daughter:* 6 Ismene 8 Antigone

husband: 5 Laius 7 Oedipus *son:* 7 Oedipus 8 Eteocles 9 Polynices

jock 5 pilot 7 athlete

jockey 4 play 5 rider, trick 7 beguile, exploit, finesse 8 maneuver 10 manipulate *famous:* 5 Baeza (Braulio) 6 Arcaro (Eddie), Bailey (Jerry), Murphy (Isaac), Pincay (Laffit) 7 Cauthen (Steve), Cordero (Angel), Hartack (Bill), Longden (Johnny), Stevens (Gary) 8 McCarron (Chris), McHargue (Darrel), Turcotte (Ron) 9 Shoemaker (Willie)

jocular 5 comic, funny, jolly, merry, witty 6 jocose, jocund, jovial, lively 7 amusing, comical, jesting, playful 8 cheerful, humorous 9 facetious

jocularity 3 fun, wit 4 glee 5 humor, mirth 6 gaiety 7 jollity 8 hilarity 9 jocundity, joviality, merriment 11 high spirits, playfulness

jocund 3 gay 5 happy, jolly, merry 6 elated, jovial, lively 7 festive, gleeful, playful 8 mirthful 12 lighthearted

joe 3 guy 4 java 6 coffee, fellow

jog 3 dig, jab, run 4 lope, move, pace, poke, prod, push, ride, stir, trot 5 nudge, punch, rouse, shake 6 bounce, change, jounce, prompt, remind

joggle 4 join, trot 5 dowel, joint, notch, shake, tooth 6 jostle

john 4 head 5 privy 6 toilet 7 latrine 8 bathroom, lavatory 11 water closet

John Hancock 9 autograph, signature

Johnson, Samuel *biographer:* 7 Boswell (James) *work:* 8 Rasselas 10 dictionary

John the Baptist *father:* 9 Zacharias *mother:* 9 Elisabeth

John the Evangelist *brother:* 5 James *father:* 7 Zebedee *mother:* 6 Salome

join 3 tie, wed 4 abut, ally, bind, bond, fuse, line, link, mate, yoke 5 affix, align, blend, marry, merge, piece, touch, unify, union, unite 6 attach, border, couple, engage, enlist, enroll, sign on, sign up, splice 7 combine, connect 8 compound, side with 9 affiliate, associate, integrate 12 come together

joint 3 bar, ell, hip, tie 4 butt, crux, dive, knee, link, node, seam 5 ankle, elbow, hinge, nexus, union, wrist 6 common, mutual, public, shared, suture, united 7 hangout, knuckle, shiplap 8 abutment, combined, communal, conjunct, coupling, junction, juncture, shoulder 9 concerted, honky-tonk 10 collective, connection 11 cooperative 12 articulation *combining form:* 5 arthr 6 arthro, condyl 7 condylo *disease:* 9 arthritis 10 rheumatism

joist 4 beam 6 rafter, timber 7 support

joke 3 gag, kid, pun, rag, rib, yak 4 fool, jape, jest, josh, quip, razz 5 crack, humor, prank, sally 6 banter, corker, parody 7 mockery, sarcasm, waggery 8 drollery, one-liner 9 burlesque, wisecrack, witticism 11 monkeyshine *stale:* 8 chestnut

joker 3 guy, wag, wit 4 card, fool 5 catch, clown, comic, cutup 6 fellow, jester, kicker 7 proviso 8 comedian, humorist 9 condition 10 limitation 11 stipulation

jollity 3 fun, joy 4 glee 5 cheer, mirth 6 gaiety, revels 7 revelry, whoopee 8 hilarity 9 festivity, jocundity, joviality, merriment 10 ebullience, jocularity, liveliness 11 high spirits, merrymaking 12 cheerfulness, conviviality

jolly 3 fun, gay, kid 4 glad, jest, josh, very 5 humor, merry 6 banter, blithe, jocund, jovial, joyful, joyous 7 festive, gleeful, jocular, playful, roguish, waggish 8 cheerful, mirthful, splendid 9 convivial 10 frolicsome 12 lighthearted

Jolly Roger 4 flag 6 ensign *user:* 6 pirate

jolt 3 hit, jar 4 blow, bump, jerk, shot, slug, stun 5 check, clash, crash, knock, lurch, shake, shock, snort, upset 6 impact, jounce, rattle 7 disturb, reverse, shake up, startle 8 astonish, surprise 9 collision

Jonah 7 prophet *swallower:* 4 fish 5 whale

Jonathan *brother:* 7 Johanan *father:* 4 Saul *friend:* 5 David

Jones, John Paul *ship:* 15 Bonhomme Richard *victim:* 7 Serapis

Jones novel 11 Thin Red Line (The) 15 Some Came Running 18 From Here to Eternity

jongleur 4 bard 6 singer 7 juggler 8 minstrel 10 troubadour 11 entertainer

jonquil 8 daffodil 9 narcissus, perennial

Jonson play 7 Volpone 9 Alchemist (The) 15 Bartholomew Fair

Joplin creation 3 rag 7 ragtime

Joram *brother:* 7 Ahaziah *father:* 3 Toi 4 Ahab 11 Jehoshaphat *slayer:* 4 Jehu *son:* 7 Ahaziah

Jordan *capital:* 5 Amman *city:* 5 Irbid, Zarqa *gulf:* 5 Aqaba *language:* 6 Arabic *monarch:* 7 Hussein *monetary unit:* 5 dinar *mountain:* 4 Ramm *neighbor:* 4 Iraq 5 Syria 6 Israel 11 Saudi Arabia *river:* 6 Jordan *sea:* 4 Dead

jorum 3 cup, jug 6 vessel

Joseph *brother:* (see JACOB son) *buyer:* 8 Potiphar *father:* 5 Asaph, Jacob 9 Zacharias 10 Mattathias *mother:* 6 Rachel *son:* 5 Jesus 7 Ephraim 8 Manasseh *wife:* 4 Mary 7 Asenath

josh 3 kid, rag, rib 4 jest, joke, razz
5 chaff, jolly, tease 6 banter
Joshua's victory 7 Jericho
Joshua tree 5 yucca
joss 4 idol 5 image
Jo's sister 3 Amy, Meg 4 Beth
jostle 3 jar, jog 4 bump, push 5 crowd,
elbow, nudge, press, shove 7 agitate,
collide, compete, contend, vie with
8 shoulder
jot 3 bit 4 atom, iota, note, whit 5 grain,
minim, speck, write 6 tittle 7 smidgen
8 particle
joule component 3 erg
jounce 3 bob, jar, jog 4 bump, jolt
5 shake, shock, thump 6 impact
journal 3 log 5 diary, organ, paper
6 ledger, record, review 7 account,
gazette, minutes 8 magazine, register
9 chronicle, newspaper 10 periodical
journalist 3 Bly (Nellie) 4 Dowd (Maureen), Drew (Elizabeth), King (Larry),
Pyle (Ernie), Reed (John), Rose (Charlie), Will (George F.), Zahn (Paula)
5 Baker (Russell), Brown (George),
Cooke (Alistair), Dunne (Finley Peter),
Evans (Rowland), Hersh (Seymour),
Novak (Robert), Rowan (Carl), Royko
(Mike), Safer (Morley), Smith
(Hedrick), Stahl (Lesley), Stone (I. F.),
Szulc (Tad), White (William Allen),
Wolfe (Tom) 6 Arnett (Peter), Bierce
(Ambrose), Broder (David), Brokaw
(Tom), Ephron (Nora), Koppel (Ted),
Kuralt (Charles), Lehrer (Jim), Moyers
(Bill), Murrow (Edward R.), Osgood
(Charles), Rather (Dan), Reston
(James), Reuter (Paul Julius), Rivera
(Geraldo), Runyon (Damon), Safire
(William), Shirer (William L.), Thomas
(Helen, Lowell), Zenger (John Peter)
7 Blitzer (Wolf), Bradlee (Benjamin),
Breslin (Jimmy), Cousins (Norman),
Greeley (Horace), Gunther (John),
Huntley (Chet), Kempton (Murray),
McGrory (Mary), Mencken (H. L.),
Pearson (Drew), Royster (Vermont),
Russert (Tim), Tarbell (Ida), Trillin
(Calvin), Wallace (Chris, Mike), Walters (Barbara) 8 Amanpour (Christiane), Anderson (Jack, Terry), Atkinson (Brooks), Brinkley (David),
Cronkite (Walter), Garrison (William
Lloyd), Jennings (Peter), Lippmann
(Walter), Pulitzer (Joseph), Salinger
(Pierre), Sevareid (Eric), Steffens (Lincoln), Thompson (Dorothy, Hunter),
Winchell (Walter), Woodward (Bob)
9 Bernstein (Carl), Donaldson (Sam),
Frederick (Pauline), Salisbury (Harrison), Schieffer (Bob)

journey 3 hie 4 hike, roam, tour, trek,
trip 5 jaunt, quest 6 cruise, junket,
push on, safari, travel, voyage 7 caravan, odyssey, proceed, travels
8 progress 9 excursion 10 expedition,
pilgrimage *route:* 9 itinerary *stage:* 3 leg
joust 4 duel, feud, spar, tilt 5 clash, fight
6 combat 7 contest 8 conflict 10 tournament *arena:* 5 lists 8 tiltyard
Jove see JUPITER
jovial 5 happy, jolly, merry 6 cheery
7 amiable 8 cheerful 9 convivial
11 good-humored, good-natured
jowl 3 jaw 5 cheek 6 dewlap, wattle
8 mandible
joy 4 glee 5 bliss, mirth 6 gaiety
7 delight, elation 8 felicity, fruition,
gladness, pleasure 9 enjoyment, happiness, merriment 11 delectation
Joyce, James *birthplace:* 6 Dublin *character:* 5 Bloom (Leopold), Bloom
(Molly) 7 Dedalus (Stephen) *work:*
6 Exiles 7 Ulysses 9 Dubliners
13 Finnegans Wake
joyful 3 gay 4 glad 5 happy, jolly, merry
6 elated, jocund 7 buoyant, festive,
gleeful, pleased 8 ecstatic, jubilant,
mirthful 9 delighted, rapturous
12 lighthearted
jubilant 5 happy 6 elated, joyful, joyous
8 euphoric, exultant, exulting 9 cock-a-hoop, delighted, overjoyed, triumphal
10 triumphant
jubilate 5 exult, glory 7 delight, rejoice
9 celebrate
jubilation 3 joy 4 glee 7 ecstasy, rapture
8 euphoria, rhapsody 9 rejoicing, transport 10 exaltation, exultation, joyfulness, joyousness 11 celebration
12 exhilaration
jubilee 6 flambé 8 festival 9 festivity
10 indulgence 11 anniversary, celebration 13 commemoration
Judah *brother:* (see JACOB son) *father:*
5 Jacob *king:* 3 Asa 4 Ahaz, Amon
5 Joash 6 Abijam, Josiah, Jotham,
Uzziah 7 Ahaziah, Amaziah, Jehoram
8 Hezekiah, Jehoahaz, Manasseh,
Rehoboam, Zedekiah 9 Jehoiakim
10 Jehoiachin 11 Jehoshaphat *mother:*
4 Leah *son:* 4 Onan 6 Shelah
Judas 7 traitor 8 informer, turncoat
father: 5 Simon 7 Chalphi 10 Mattathias
replacement: 8 Matthias *suicide place:*
8 Aceldama, Akeldama
judge 3 ref, try, ump 4 call, deem, rule,
test 5 infer 6 critic, decide, deduce,
jurist, reckon, settle, umpire 7 arbiter,
justice, mediate, referee 8 assessor, critique, estimate, mediator 9 arbitrate,
criticize, determine, moderator

judgment 10 adjudicate, arbitrator, chancellor, magistrate, negotiator 11 conciliator 12 intermediary *bench:* 4 banc *chamber:* 6 camera *in Hades:* 5 Minos 6 Aeacus 12 Rhadamanthus *mallet:* 5 gavel *Muslim:* 5 mufti

judgment 5 award, sense 6 acumen, decree, ruling, result, wisdom 7 finding, insight, opinion, verdict 8 decision, sagacity, sentence 9 appraisal, deduction, good sense, inference 10 assessment, conclusion, discretion, estimation, evaluation, horse sense, punishment 11 common sense, discernment 13 determination

judgmental 7 carping 8 captious, critical 10 belittling, censorious, derogatory 11 disparaging, reproachful 12 disapproving, faultfinding 13 hypercritical

Judgment Day 8 doomsday

___ **judicata** 3 res

judicial *assembly:* 5 court *document:* 4 writ

judicious 3 apt 4 fair, just, sage, sane, wise 5 right, sound 6 astute 7 careful, prudent, sapient 8 accurate, discreet, rational, sensible 9 equitable, objective, sagacious 10 discerning, reasonable

Judith *father:* 5 Beeri *home:* 8 Bethulia *husband:* 4 Esau *victim:* 10 Holofernes

judo 10 martial art *teacher:* 6 sensei

Judy's husband 5 Punch

jug 3 jar, pen 4 coop, ewer, gaol, jail, stew, stir, toby 5 pokey 6 cooler, flagon, immure, intern, lockup, prison, vessel 7 confine, pitcher, slammer 8 demijohn, imprison 9 constrain, container 11 incarcerate

jug-band instrument 5 kazoo 6 bottle 7 washtub 9 stovepipe, washboard

juggernaut 11 steamroller

juggle 3 fix 4 fool, toss 5 bluff, trick 6 change, delude, doctor, handle, humbug, take in 7 balance, beguile, deceive, mislead, shuffle 9 rearrange 10 manipulate

juice 3 sap 4 fuel, must 5 fluid 7 current, essence 8 vitality 10 succulence 11 electricity *fermented:* 4 wine 5 cider, perry

juicy 3 fat 4 racy, rich 5 lusty, vital 7 piquant 8 colorful, dripping, exciting 9 delicious, rewarding, succulent 10 profitable 11 fascinating, sensational

juju 4 luck 5 charm, magic 6 amulet, fetish, mascot 8 talisman 10 lucky charm

jujube 4 tree 5 fruit 7 gumdrop, lozenge

julep 5 drink

Juliet *betrothed:* 5 Paris *father:* 7 Capulet *lover:* 5 Romeo

July 14 11 Bastille Day

jumble 3 mix 4 cake, hash, mess, olio 5 chaos, mix up, shake 6 cookie, medley, mess up, muddle, muss up 7 clutter, confuse, disturb, mélange, rummage, shuffle 8 disarray, disorder, mishmash, pastiche, scramble 9 confusion, patchwork, potpourri 10 assortment, hodgepodge, hotchpotch, miscellany

jumbo 4 huge, vast 5 giant 6 mighty 7 immense, mammoth, massive 8 colossal, enormous, gigantic, oversize 9 oversized 10 prodigious 11 elephantine

jump 3 hop 4 bolt, hike, leap, move, trip 5 avoid, begin, boost, bound, clear, flush, hurry, leave, put up, raise, shift, start, vault 6 attack, bounce, bustle, change, hurdle, hustle, jack up, pounce, spring 7 bail out, elevate, startle 8 increase, leap over 9 advantage

jumper 4 sled 5 dress, horse, smock 6 blouse, jacket

jumping-frog county 9 Calaveras

jumpy 6 on edge 7 anxious, jittery, nervous 9 excitable 10 high-strung

junction 4 seam 5 joint, union 7 joining, meeting 8 coupling 9 interface 10 confluence, connection, crossroads 12 intersection

juncture 4 seam 5 joint, point, union 6 crisis, moment 7 instant, joining 8 coupling 10 connection, crossroads 11 concurrence, convergence 12 turning point

jungle 3 web, zoo 4 hash, mash, maze 5 snarl 6 jumble, morass, muddle, tangle 7 clutter, thicket 8 mishmash 9 labyrinth

Jungle Books, The *author:* 7 Kipling (Rudyard) *bear:* 5 Baloo *boy:* 6 Mowgli *panther:* 8 Bagheera *python:* 3 Kaa *tiger:* 9 Shere Khan *wolf:* 5 Akela

Jungle, The *author:* 8 Sinclair (Upton) *locale:* 7 Chicago 10 stockyards

junior 3 son 5 lower, minor, sonny, youth 6 lesser 7 student, younger 8 inferior, young man, youthful 9 secondary, youngster 11 subordinate

juniper 4 cone 5 cedar, fruit, savin, shrub 7 conifer 9 evergreen

junk 4 boat, dope, drug, ship 5 scrap, trash, waste 6 debris, heroin, litter, refuse, reject 7 cashier, clutter, discard, rubbish, rummage 8 get rid of, jettison, throw out 9 narcotics, throw away

junker 4 heap 5 crate, wreck 6 jalopy

junket 4 trip 5 feast, jaunt, spree 6 outing, picnic 7 banquet, dessert, journey 9 excursion

junk mail 4 spam

Juno *bird:* 7 peacock *epithet:* 6 Moneta *Greek equivalent:* 4 Hera *husband:* 7 Jupiter (see also HERA)

Junoesque 7 stately 10 curvaceous, statuesque

junta 5 cabal, group 7 council, faction 9 committee

Jupiter 4 Jove, Zeus *angel:* 7 Zadkiel *cupbearer:* 8 Ganymede *daughter:* 5 Venus 7 Minerva *epithet:* 6 Fidius, Fulgur, Stator, Tonans 7 Pluvius *father:* 6 Saturn *lover:* 6 Europa 8 Callisto *mother:* 3 Ops *satellite:* 6 Europa 8 Callisto, Ganymede *son:* 5 Arcas 6 Castor, Pollux *temple:* 7 Capitol *wife:* 4 Juno

Jurgen *author:* 6 Cabell (James Branch) *trade:* 10 pawnbroker

juridical 5 legal 6 lawful 8 juristic 10 legalistic

jurisdiction 3 law, see 4 sway, zone 5 might, orbit, power, range, reach, scope, venue 6 county, domain, parish, sphere 7 circuit, command, compass, control, diocese, mastery, purview 8 dominion, hegemony, province 9 authority, bailiwick, territory 10 domination 11 supervision

jurisprudence 3 law

jurist 5 judge

jury 5 panel *decision:* 7 verdict

jury-rigged 6 make-do 7 stopgap 9 makeshift, temporary 10 improvised

just 3 apt, due, fit 4 even, fair, good, meet, only, true, very 5 equal, legal, quite, right 6 barely, hardly, honest, lawful, nearly, proper, simply, square 7 correct, ethical, exactly, fitting, merited, perhaps, precise, totally, upright 8 accurate, deserved, directly, possibly, recently, rightful, scarcely, squarely, suitable, unbiased 9 equitable, expressly, honorable, impartial, justified,

objective, precisely, requisite, righteous 10 accurately, completely, legitimate, reasonable, scrupulous 11 appropriate, immediately, well-founded 12 unprejudiced 13 conscientious

justice 3 law 5 court, judge, right 6 equity 7 honesty 8 evenness, fairness, fair play 10 lawfulness, magistrate 11 correctness 12 impartiality

justification 6 excuse, reason 7 account, apology, defense, grounds 8 apologia 9 rationale 10 validation 11 explanation, vindication

justify 5 argue, claim, prove 6 assert, defend, uphold, verify 7 account, bear out, confirm, contend, explain, support, warrant 8 maintain, make even, validate 9 vindicate 10 legitimate, legitimize 11 corroborate, rationalize 12 authenticate, legitimatize, substantiate

jut 4 hang, poke 5 bulge, pouch 6 beetle, thrust 7 project 8 extend up, overhang, protrude, stand out, stick out 9 extend out, extension 10 projection, protrusion 12 protuberance

jute 5 gunny 6 burlap 7 sacking

Juvenal 4 poet 5 Roman *forte:* 6 satire

juvenile 3 kid 5 actor, child, green, young, youth 6 callow, jejune, junior, moppet 7 preteen, puerile 8 childish, immature, youthful 9 childlike, fledgling, youngling, youngster 11 undeveloped

juvenility 5 youth 9 childhood, greenness 10 immaturity, springtide, springtime 12 youthfulness

juxtaposed 4 next 8 abutting, adjacent, neighbor, proximal, touching 9 adjoining, bordering 10 appositive, contiguous, side-by-side 11 coterminous, neighboring 12 conterminous

K

kabob see KEBAB

kachina 4 doll 6 spirit 12 impersonator

kaddish 6 prayer

Kafka, Franz *character:* 4 Olga 6 Gregor (Samsa), Joseph (K.) *novel:* 5 Trial

(The) 6 Castle (The) 7 Amerika *story:* 8 Judgment (The) 12 Hunger Artist (A) 13 Metamorphosis (The)

kaiser 5 ruler 7 emperor, monarch 8 autocrat 9 sovereign

kaka 6 parrot
kale 4 cash, cole 5 bucks, money, moola
6 moolah 7 cabbage 8 colewort
kaleidoscopic 8 changing, colorful
10 variegated
Kali *aspect:* 5 Durga 7 Parvati *husband:*
4 Siva 5 Shiva
Kama *god of:* 4 love *mount:* 6 parrot
7 sparrow *wife:* 4 Rati
kamikaze 7 suicide 8 suicidal
kampong 6 hamlet 7 village
Kampuchea see CAMBODIA
kangaroo 6 leaper 7 wallaby 8 wallaroo
9 marsupial *herd:* 3 mob *young:* 4 joey
Kansas *capital:* 6 Topeka *city:* 6 Olathe,
Salina, Topeka 7 Abilene, Emporia,
Shawnee, Wichita 8 Lawrence *nickname:* 9 Jayhawker (State), Sunflower
(State) *prison:* 11 Leavenworth *river:*
8 Arkansas *state bird:* 10 meadowlark
state flower: 9 sunflower *state tree:*
10 cottonwood
kaolin 4 clay
kaput 5 spent 6 ruined 7 done for, useless 8 defeated, finished, outmoded
9 destroyed
karakul 5 sheep 9 broadtail
karma 4 fate 9 emanation
kaross 3 rug 7 garment
kasha 5 grain 8 porridge 9 buckwheat
Katharina *father:* 8 Baptista *suitor:*
9 Petruchio
Katrina's suitor 9 Brom Bones 12 Ichabod Crane
katydid 3 bug 6 insect 11 grasshopper
katzenjammer 3 din 5 noise 6 clamor,
hubbub, racket 8 distress, hangover,
headache 9 commotion
kava 5 shrub 6 pepper 8 beverage
kayo 6 defeat, finish 8 knockout 9 finish
off 11 coup de grace
Kazakhstan *capital:* 6 Akmola, Astana
city: 5 Semey 6 Pavlodar, Shymkent
lake: 6 Tengiz 8 Balkhash *language:*
6 Kazakh 7 Russian *monetary unit:*
5 tenge *mountain:* 10 Khan-Tengri *neighbor:* 5 China 6 Russia 10 Kyrgyzstan,
Uzbekistan 12 Turkmenistan *river:*
4 Ural 6 Irtysh 8 Syr Dar'ya *sea:* 4 Aral
7 Caspian
Kazantzakis hero 5 Zorba (Alexis)
kea 6 parrot
Keats poem 5 Lamia 8 Endymion, Hyperion, Isabella, To Autumn 11 Ode to
Psyche 12 Eve of St. Agnes (The)
16 Ode on a Grecian Urn 17 Ode to a
Nightingale
kebab 8 shashlik
kedge 6 anchor
keel 4 boat, lean, ship 5 barge, pitch,

ridge, slump 6 carina 7 capsize 8 overturn 11 centerboard
keen 4 avid, fine, wail, yowl 5 acute,
alert, eager, honed, mourn, sharp,
smart 6 ardent, astute, bewail, bright,
clever, gung ho, intent, lament, shrewd
7 anxious, fervent, intense, whetted,
zealous 8 animated, spirited 9 fine-
edged, impatient, sensitive, wonderful
10 perceptive, razor-sharp 11 lamentation, penetrating, quick-witted, sharp-
witted 12 enthusiastic, sharp-sighted
keenness 3 wit 4 edge, zeal 6 acuity,
acumen 10 enthusiasm 11 discernment,
penetration 12 incisiveness, perspicacity
keep 3 own 4 hold, jail, mind, obey,
save, stay, tend 5 lodge, stock 6 castle,
comply, detain, living, lockup, manage,
prison, retain 7 abstain, conduct, confine, forbear, fulfill, possess, refrain,
reserve 8 conserve, fortress, maintain,
preserve, withhold 9 constrain 10 livelihood, sustenance 11 maintenance, subsistence
keep back 3 bar, dam 4 curb, hold, save,
stay 6 detain, retain, retard, stifle 7 contain, inhibit, repress, reserve 8 restrain,
restrict, suppress, withhold
keeper 5 guard 6 warden 7 big fish,
curator 8 Cerberus, guardian, watchdog 9 custodian, protector
keeping 4 care, ward 5 aegis, trust
6 charge 7 custody, support 8 wardship
9 provision 10 caretaking, conformity,
observance 11 maintenance 12 conservation, guardianship
keep on 4 last 5 abide 6 endure 7 persist
8 continue 9 hang tough, persevere
keep out 3 ban, bar 4 hold, stop 5 block,
check, debar 6 forbid 7 embargo,
exclude 8 prohibit, turn back 9 blackball
keepsake 5 token 6 trophy 7 memento
8 memorial, reminder, souvenir
11 remembrance
keep up 7 persist, prolong, sustain 8 continue, maintain, preserve 9 persevere
kef 4 hash, hemp 7 hashish 10 dreami-
ness 12 tranquillity
keg 3 tun 4 butt, cask, pipe 6 barrel,
firkin, vessel 8 hogshead 9 container
kegler 6 bowler
keister 3 bum, end 4 buns, duff, rear,
rump, seat, tail, tush 5 fanny 6 behind,
bottom 8 backside, buttocks, derriere
9 posterior
keloid 4 scar
kelp 4 alga 7 seaweed
kelpie 3 dog 5 naiad, nixie 6 sprite
ken 4 view 5 grasp, range, reach, scope,

sight **7** horizon, purview **9** knowledge **10** perception **13** comprehension, understanding

kenaf 5 fiber, plant **8** hibiscus

Kenilworth author 5 Scott (Walter)

Kennedy novel 8 Ironweed

kennel 4 pack **5** board **6** gutter **7** shelter **9** enclosure

keno 4 game *similar to:* **5** beano, bingo, lotto

Kentucky *capital:* **9** Frankfort *city:* **9** Lexington **10** Louisville **12** Bowling Green *nickname:* **9** Bluegrass (State) *park:* **11** Mammoth Cave *racecourse:* **14** Churchill Downs *river:* **4** Ohio *state bird:* **8** cardinal *state flower:* **9** goldenrod *state tree:* **11** tulip poplar

Kentucky bluegrass 3 Poa

Kenya *capital:* **7** Nairobi *city:* **6** Kisumu, Nakuru **7** Mombasa *lake:* **7** Turkana **8** Victoria *language:* **7** English, Swahili *monetary unit:* **8** shilling *mountain:* **5** Elgon, Kenya *neighbor:* **5** Sudan **6** Uganda **7** Somalia **8** Ethiopia, Tanzania *river:* **4** Tana

kepi 3 cap

kerchief 6 hankie **7** bandana **8** babushka, bandanna, kaffiyeh *Scottish:* **5** curch

kerf 3 cut **4** nick, slit **5** cleft, notch **6** groove

kerfuffle 3 ado, row **4** flap, fuss, stir, to-do **5** hoo-ha **6** dust-up, ruckus, rumpus **7** turmoil **8** foofaraw **11** disturbance

kermis 4 fair **8** carnival, festival

kernel 3 nub, nut **4** core, crux, gist, meat, pith, seed **5** grain **6** nubbin, upshot **7** essence, nucleus **9** substance

Kerouac novel 6 Big Sur **9** On the Road **10** Dharma Bums (The) **13** Subterraneans (The)

Kesey novel 21 Sometimes a Great Notion **25** One Flew over the Cuckoo's Nest

kestrel 4 bird, hawk **6** falcon **9** windhover

ketch 4 boat **6** vessel **8** sailboat **10** watercraft

ketone 7 acetone, camphor

kettle 3 pot **6** hollow, vessel **7** caldron, marmite, pothole **8** cauldron

kettledrum 5 naker **7** timpani (plural), timpano

key 4 clue, isle, reef **5** basic, islet, vital **6** cotter, island, legend, master, opener, samara, spline, ticket, tip-off **7** central, crucial, digital, pivotal **8** critical, passport, password, skeleton, solution, tonality **9** essential, important **10** open sesame **11** fundamental *combining form:* **5** clavi, clavo *notch:* **4** ward

keyboard 6 manual **7** clavier

key fruit 6 samara

key man 5 chief **7** kingpin **9** locksmith

keynote 4 core, crux, gist, pith, tone **5** theme, tonic

keynoter 6 orator **7** speaker

Keystone State 12 Pennsylvania

khaki 3 tan **6** brown, cloth, color **7** garment, uniform

khamsin 4 wind

khan 5 chief, ruler **9** chieftain, sovereign **11** caravansary

khedive 5 ruler **7** viceroy

Khomeini 4 imam **9** ayatollah

Ki *mother:* **5** Nammu *son:* **5** Enlil

kiang 3 ass

kibble 4 meal **5** grain, grind **9** pulverize

kibbutz 4 co-op, farm **7** commune **10** collective, settlement **11** cooperative

kibe 4 heel, sore **8** swelling **9** chilblain

kibitz 4 chat **6** banter, butt in, meddle **7** comment, intrude, obtrude **9** interfere

kibitzer 7 meddler **8** busybody, observer **9** buttinsky, spectator **10** rubberneck

kibosh 3 hex **4** jinx, stop **5** check, curse

kick 4 bang, boot, carp, fuss, punt, wail **5** gripe, rebel, whine **6** object, recoil, repine, resist, thrill, wallop **7** grumble, protest **8** complain

kicker 5 catch **6** clause, punter **9** condition, fine print

kick in 3 die, pay **4** give **5** begin, put up, start **6** donate, pony up **7** cough up, fork out **8** fork over, hand over **10** contribute

kick off 3 die **4** open **5** begin, croak, start **6** launch **8** commence, drop dead, embark on, initiate **10** inaugurate

kick out 3 axe, can **4** fire, oust, sack **5** eject, evict **6** bounce **7** boot out, cashier, dismiss **8** throw out **9** discharge

kickshaw 5 goody, treat **6** bauble, dainty, gewgaw, morsel, tidbit, trifle **7** bibelot, trinket **8** delicacy **9** bagatelle

kid 3 guy, rag, rib **4** dupe, fool, gull, hoax, jest, joke, josh, razz **5** child, jolly, trick, youth **6** banter, befool, moppet, nipper **7** deceive, younger **8** flimflam, hoodwink, juvenile **9** bamboozle, youngling, youngster

kidnap 4 abduct, snatch **8** shanghai

kidney 5 gland, organ *combining form:* **4** reni, reno **5** nephr **6** nephro

kidney-shaped 8 reniform

kielbasa 7 sausage

kilderkin 3 keg **4** cask **6** barrel **9** container

kilim 3 mat, rug **6** carpet

kill 3 end, off, zap **4** do in, prey, slay, stop, veto **5** creek, croak, scrag, snuff, waste **6** defeat, delete, finish, murder, quarry, stifle **7** bump off, butcher, channel, destroy, execute **8** blow away, carry off, dispatch, knock off, massacre **9** sacrifice, slaughter **10** annihilate **11** assassinate, exterminate

killer 6 gunman, hit man **7** butcher, torpedo **8** assassin, homicide *combining form:* **4** cide

Killer Angels author 6 Shaara (Michael)

killer whale 4 orca **8** cetacean

killing 5 blood, fatal **6** deadly, lethal, mortal, murder **7** carnage **8** butchery, foul play, homicide **9** bloodbath, bloodshed, slaughter **12** manslaughter *of a race:* **8** genocide *of bacteria:* **11** bactericide *of a brother:* **10** fratricide *of a father:* **9** patricide *of a king:* **8** regicide *of a mother:* **9** matricide *of a relative:* **9** parricide *of a sister:* **10** sororicide *of oneself:* **7** suicide *of plants:* **9** herbicide

killjoy 6 downer, grinch, grouch **7** spoiler **8** doomster, sourpuss **9** Cassandra, defeatist, doomsayer, gloomy Gus, pessimist, worrywart **10** spoilsport, wet blanket

Kilmer poem 5 Trees

kiln 4 oast, oven **7** furnace

kilt 5 skirt *accessory:* **7** sporran *fabric:* **5** plaid **6** tartan

kilter 4 trim **5** order, shape **6** fettle, repair **7** fitness **9** condition

kimono 4 gown, robe *sash:* **3** obi

kin 3 sib **4** clan, folk, sept **5** blood, flesh, house, stock, tribe **6** family **7** lineage, related **8** relation, relative

kind 3 ilk **4** good, like, sort, type, warm **5** breed, class, genre **6** benign, genial, gentle, humane, loving, nature, stripe, tender **7** affable, amiable, clement, essence, feather, helpful, lenient, quality, species, variety **8** category, merciful, tolerant **9** character **10** altruistic, benevolent, charitable, forbearing, responsive **11** considerate, description, good-hearted, good-humored, good-natured, openhearted, softhearted, sympathetic, warmhearted **12** affectionate, good-tempered, humanitarian **13** compassionate, philanthropic

kindle 4 bear, fire, stir, wake, whet **5** light, rally, rouse, spark, start, waken **6** arouse, awaken, bestir, excite, foment, ignite, incite **7** inflame, provoke **8** activate **9** instigate, stimulate **10** illuminate

kindliness 8 goodwill, sympathy **9** affection **10** solicitude **11** benevolence

kindly 6 benign, gentle **7** benefic **8** friendly, generous, gracious, pleasant **9** agreeable, attentive, benignant **10** beneficent, beneficial, neighborly

11 considerate, good-hearted, sympathetic

kindness 5 favor, mercy **7** service **8** clemency, courtesy, goodwill, sympathy **10** compassion, generosity, indulgence **11** benevolence **13** consideration

kind of 5 quite **6** fairly, pretty, rather **8** passably, somewhat **9** tolerably **10** more or less, reasonably, relatively

kindred 3 sib **4** clan, folk, like, sept **5** alike, blood, flesh, house, stock, tribe **6** agnate, allied, family **7** cognate, connate, lineage, related, similar **9** relatives **10** affiliated, connatural **11** consanguine

king 3 rex **4** czar, tsar **5** mogul, ruler **6** tycoon **7** magnate, monarch **9** sovereign *Albanian:* **3** Zog **7** William *Assyrian:* **6** Sargon **11** Sennacherib, Shalmaneser *Babylonian:* **6** Sargon **9** Hammurabi **10** Belshazzar *Belgian:* **6** Albert **7** Leopold **8** Baudouin *Bohemian:* **9** Wenceslas **10** Wenceslaus *Bulgarian:* **5** Boris **6** Simeon *Damascus:* **8** Benhadad *Danish:* **4** Abel, Eric, Gorm, Hans, John, Olaf **5** Sweyn **6** Canute, Harold, Magnus **8** Nicholas, Waldemar **9** Christian, Frederick **11** Christopher *Dutch:* **7** William *Egyptian:* **3** Tut **4** Pepi, Seti **5** Khufu, Menes, Necho **6** Cheops, Ramses **7** Harmhab, Osorkon, Psamtik, Ptolemy **8** Ikhnaton, Thothmes, Thutmose **9** Amenhotep, Sesostris **11** Tutankhamen *English:* **4** John **5** Henry, James **6** Alfred, Canute, Edmund, Edward, Egbert, George, Harold **7** Charles, Richard, Stephen, William **8** Ethelred **9** Athelstan, Ethelbald, Ethelbert *French:* **3** Odo, roi **4** Jean, John **5** Henri, Henry, Louis, Pepin, Raoul **6** Philip, Robert, Rudolf **7** Charles, Francis, Lothair **8** François **9** Hugh Capet **11** Charlemagne *German:* **4** Carl, Karl **5** König, Louis **6** Lothar, Ludwig **7** Charles, Lothair *Greek (modern):* **4** Paul **6** George **10** Alexander **11** Constantine *Hawaiian:* **10** Kamehameha *Hungarian:* **6** Attila *Indian:* **4** raja **5** rajah *Irish:* **9** Brian Boru *Italian:* **7** Humbert, Umberto *Jordanian:* **5** Talal **7** Hussein **8** Abdullah *Judah:* (see at JUDAH) *Judean:* **5** Herod *Lydian:* **5** Gyges **7** Croesus **8** Alyattes *Norwegian:* **4** Eric, Erik, Inge, Olaf **5** Sweyn **6** Haakon, Harald, Harold, Magnus, Sigurd, Sverre *Ostrogothic:* **9** Theodoric *Persian:* **5** Cyrus **6** Darius, Xerxes *Portuguese:* **4** John **5** Henry, Louis, Peter **6** Carlos, Edward, Manuel, Sancho **7** Alfonso **9** Ferdinand, Sebastian *Prussian:* **7** Wilhelm, William **9** Frederick, Friedrich *relating to:* **5** regal, royal

Saudi Arabian: **4** Saud **6** Faisal **9** Abdul-Aziz *Scottish:* **4** John **5** David, Edgar, James **6** Duncan **7** Macbeth, Malcolm, William **9** Alexander, Donalbane **10** David Bruce **11** Robert Bruce *Spanish:* **3** rey **5** Louis **6** Philip **7** Alfonso, Amadeus, Charles **9** Ferdinand **10** Juan Carlos *Spartan:* **8** Leonidas *Swedish:* **4** Eric, John **5** Oscar **6** Birger, Gustav, Haakon, Magnus **7** Charles **8** Gustavus, Waldemar **9** Frederick, Sigismund, Sten Sture *Visigothic:* **6** Alaric

King Arthur *birthplace:* **8** Tintagel *chronicler:* **8** Geoffrey (of Monmouth) *court site:* **7** Camelot **8** Caerleon *deathplace:* **6** Camlan *father:* **5** Uther *father-in-law:* **9** Laodogant, Leodegran **11** Leodegrance *foster father:* **5** Ector *jester:* **7** Dagonet *knight:* **3** Kay **4** Bors **5** Balan, Balin **6** Gareth, Gawain, Modred **7** Galahad, Geraint, Lamerok, Mordred, Tristan **8** Bedivere, Lancelot, Parsifal, Percival, Tristram **9** Launcelot *lance:* **3** Ron *last abode:* **6** Avalon *last name:* **9** Pendragon *magician:* **6** Merlin *mother:* **6** Ygraine **7** Igraine *nephew:* **6** Gareth, Modred **7** Mordred *queen:* **9** Guinevere *shield:* **7** Pridwin *sister:* **7** Morgain **11** Morgan le Fay *slayer:* **6** Modred **7** Mordred *son:* **6** Modred **7** Mordred *steward:* **3** Kay *sword:* **9** Excalibur *victim:* **6** Modred **7** Mordred *wife:* **9** Guinevere

king crab 7 limulus

kingdom 5 realm **6** domain, empire **7** demesne **8** monarchy

kingdom come 4 Zion **6** heaven **8** paradise **9** hereafter **10** afterworld

kingfish 4 boss **6** bigwig, honcho, master **7** big shot, croaker **8** mackerel

kingfisher 7 halcyon **10** kookaburra

kingly 5 regal, royal **6** august, lordly, regnal **7** exalted **8** imperial, majestic **9** imperious, masterful, monarchal, sovereign **10** monarchial **11** monarchical

King novel 6 Carrie **7** Shining (The) **8** Dead Zone (The) **9** Dark Tower (The), Green Mile (The), Salem's Lot **11** Firestarter, Pet Sematary

King Philip 9 Metacomet

kingpin 4 boss, guru, head **5** chief, mogul **6** bigwig, top dog **7** magnate **9** top banana **10** mastermind

Kings Peak range 5 Uinta

Kingu *consort:* **6** Tiamat *slayer:* **6** Marduk

kink 4 bend, curl, knot, whim **5** cramp, crick, quirk, snarl, spasm, twist **6** tangle **11** peculiarity **12** eccentricity, imperfection

kinky 3 odd **4** bent **5** curly, outré, ultra,

weird **6** curled, far-out, frizzy, quirky **7** bizarre, deviant, knotted, strange, twisted **9** eccentric **10** outlandish

kiosk 5 booth **8** pavilion **9** newsstand **11** summerhouse

kip 3 bed, nap **4** hide, pelt, skin **5** sleep

Kipling, Rudyard *work:* **3** Kim **6** L'Envoi **8** Gunga Din, Mandalay **10** Fuzzy Wuzzy **11** Jungle Books (The), Recessional **13** Just So Stories, Soldiers Three **15** Light That Failed (The), Puck of Pook's Hill **18** Captains Courageous

Kiribati *capital:* **6** Tarawa *island, island group:* **4** Line **6** Banaba **7** Gilbert, Phoenix *language:* **7** English *location:* **7** Oceania *monetary unit:* **6** dollar

kirk 6 church

kirsch 6 brandy, liquor

kirtle 4 coat, gown **5** dress, tunic **7** garment

Kish *father:* **3** Ner **4** Abdi **5** Abiel, Jeiel **6** Jehiel *son:* **4** Saul

kismet 3 lot **4** doom, fate, luck **5** weird **6** Moirai **7** destiny, fortune

kiss 4 buss, neck, peck **5** graze, smack **6** cookie, glance, smooch **7** lip-lock **8** osculate, pucker up **10** osculation

kisser 3 mug **4** face, lips **5** mouth

Kiss sculptor 5 Rodin (Auguste)

kit 3 set **4** gear, pelt **5** group **6** outfit, tackle, violin **7** package **8** caboodle **9** container **10** collection

kitchen 4 mess **6** galley **7** cuisine **8** scullery *appliance:* (see at APPLIANCE) *boss:* **4** chef (see also COOKING)

kite 4 hawk, sail, soar **5** check, glede, hurry, mosey **7** saunter, take off **8** clear out, hightail, predator **9** spinnaker

kith 3 kin, sib **4** clan, folk **6** family **7** friends, kindred, kinfolk **9** neighbors, relatives

kitsch 4 camp, junk **9** vulgarity

kittenish 3 coy **6** elvish, frisky, impish **7** coltish, playful **10** frolicsome **11** mischievous

kitty 3 cat, pot **4** fund, pool, puss **5** pussy **6** feline, stakes **7** jackpot

kiwi 4 bird **5** fruit **7** Apteryx **12** New Zealander

klatch 5 bunch, group **7** meeting **9** gathering **11** get-together

kleptomaniac 5 thief **7** booster **10** shoplifter

klutz 3 oaf **4** boob, clod, gawk, lout, lump **5** looby **6** lubber, lummox **7** bungler, palooka **8** shlemiel **9** schlemiel **10** stumblebum

klutzy 5 inept **6** clumsy **7** awkward **9** all thumbs, maladroit **10** blundering

knack 4 bent, gift, head **5** flair, forte, skill, trick **6** genius, talent **7** ability, aptness, command, faculty, know-how, mastery **8** aptitude, capacity, facility **9** dexterity, expertise, stratagem **10** expertness

knapsack 4 pack **8** backpack

knave 4 heel, jack **5** fraud, rogue, scamp **6** rascal, varlet **7** lowlife, villain **8** scalawag, swindler **9** scoundrel **10** blackguard **11** rapscallion

knavery 5 fraud **6** deceit **8** mischief, trickery, villainy **9** chicanery, deception, rascality **10** dishonesty

knavish 5 lying **6** shifty, tricky **7** devious, roguish **8** rascally **9** deceitful, deceptive, dishonest **10** mendacious **12** unscrupulous

knead 4 form, mold, work **5** press, shape **7** massage **10** manipulate

knee 5 joint *bend:* **9** genuflect **12** genuflection *bone:* **7** patella

kneeler 5 stool **7** cushion **8** prie-dieu **9** footstool

knell 4 bong, peal, ring, toll **5** chime **6** summon **7** warning **8** announce, proclaim

knickknack 3 toy **4** dido **5** curio **6** bauble, gadget, gewgaw, trifle **7** bibelot, novelty, trinket, whatnot, whatsit **8** gimcrack, ornament, souvenir **9** bagatelle, bric-a-brac, objet d'art

knife 4 bolo, shiv, snee **5** blade, bowie, panga, shank, sword **6** barong, cutter, dagger, parang, sickle **7** cleaver, machete, scalpel **8** stiletto, yataghan **11** switchblade *case:* **6** sheath *handle:* **4** haft, hilt *maker:* **6** cutler **7** grinder

knifelike 4 keen **5** acute, sharp **7** cutting **8** piercing, stabbing **11** penetrating

knight 3 dub, sir **5** eques **8** cavalier, chessman, horseman **9** caballero, chevalier *code:* **8** chivalry *competition:* **7** listing, tilting **8** jousting **10** tournament *German:* **6** Ritter *servant:* **4** page **5** valet **6** squire *title:* **3** sir *wife:* **4** lady

knighthood 8 chivalry

knightly 4 bold **5** brave, noble **6** heroic **7** gallant, valiant **10** chivalrous

Knight of the Round Table see KING ARTHUR

Knight of the Rueful Countenance 10 Don Quixote

knit 4 bind, heal, join, link, mend, purl **5** plait, unite, weave **6** fabric, stitch **7** conjoin, crochet **8** contract **9** interlace **10** intertwine

knitting *material:* **4** yarn *stitch:* **3** rib **4** purl **6** garter *tool:* **6** needle

knob 3 bun, bur, nub **4** bump, burl, burr, dial, hill, hump, lump, node, umbo **5** bulge, gnarl, knoll, mound

6 button, finial, handle, nubble, pommel **7** hillock **12** protuberance

knobkerrie 3 bat **4** club, mace **5** billy **6** cudgel, weapon **7** war club **8** bludgeon **9** billy club, truncheon

knock 3 bob, hit, rap, tap **4** bash, blow, bump, cuff, lick, swat **5** blame, clout, fault, pound, swipe, thump **6** strike **7** censure, condemn, setback **8** denounce, reversal **9** criticize **10** denunciate

knock down 4 drop, earn, fell, gain, raze **5** floor, level, lower **6** lay low, reduce **7** acquire, bring in, flatten **9** dismantle **11** disassemble

knocker 6 carper, critic **7** caviler **8** quibbler **10** complainer, criticizer **11** faultfinder

knock off 3 rob **4** copy, do in, halt, kill, quit, slay, stop **5** cease **6** deduct, defeat, desist, finish, murder **7** execute, imitate, take out **8** discount, overcome, subtract **9** liquidate **11** assassinate, call it quits, counterfeit

knockout 4 kayo **5** dandy, final **6** beauty, eyeful, looker, lovely **7** stunner **8** decisive, jim-dandy, striking, stunning **9** deathblow, finishing, humdinger **10** attractive **11** coup de grace, crackerjack

knock over 3 rob **4** down, drop, fell **5** amaze, floor, steal, upset **6** boggle, hijack, hold up, lay low, topple **7** flatten, stick up **9** bring down, eliminate, overpower, overthrow, overwhelm, prostrate

knoll 4 hill, knob **5** mound **7** hillock

knot 3 bow, tie **4** bond, burr, link, loop, lump, node **5** bunch, gnarl, hitch, nexus **6** jungle, tangle **8** ligament, ligature, vinculum *in fiber:* **3** nep *kind:* **4** bend, loop, slip **5** hitch **6** granny, splice, square **7** bowline **9** sheet bend **10** clove hitch, sheepshank

knotty 4 hard **6** sticky **7** complex, gnarled, Gordian **8** involved **9** byzantine, difficult, elaborate, intricate **10** formidable **11** complicated, problematic

knout 4 flog, lash, whip **7** scourge

know 3 wot **5** grasp **6** fathom, intuit **7** discern, realize **9** apprehend, recognize **10** appreciate, comprehend, experience, understand *Scottish:* **3** ken

knowable 9 graspable **10** cognizable, fathomable **12** intelligible **13** apprehensible

know-how 5 craft, knack, skill **6** talent **7** ability, cunning, faculty, mastery **8** aptitude **9** dexterity, expertise **10** adroitness, expertness **11** proficiency

knowing 3 hep, hip **4** sage, wise **5** aware, blasé, canny, smart **6** bright, clever **7** witting, worldly **8** sentient **9** cognizant, conscious, sagacious **10** conversant, discerning, insightful, perceptive **11** worldly-wise **13** sophisticated
know-it-all 6 smarty **7** wise guy **8** wiseacre **10** smart aleck **11** smartypants, wisenheimer
knowledge 3 ken **4** lore, news **5** facts **6** wisdom **7** science **8** learning **9** cognition, education, erudition **10** cognizance **11** information, scholarship **12** intelligence **13** enlightenment *lack of:* **9** ignorance *mystical:* **6** gnosis
knowledgeable 5 savvy **8** educated, informed
know-nothing 4 dolt, dope, fool **5** dummy, dunce, idiot, yahoo **6** dimwit **7** pinhead **8** agnostic, ignorant, numskull **9** benighted, blockhead, brainless, ignoramus, lamebrain, numbskull **10** illiterate, uneducated **11** emptyheaded
knuckle 5 joint *combining form:* **6** condyl **7** condylo
knucklehead 4 dolt, dope, fool **5** dummy, dunce, idiot, yahoo **6** dimwit **8** clodpole, numskull **9** ignoramus, lamebrain, numbskull
knuckle under 3 bow **4** cave **5** yield **6** cave in, give in, submit **7** succumb **8** say uncle **9** surrender **10** capitulate
knurl 3 nub **4** bead, knob **5** ridge **12** protuberance
KO 4 kayo **8** knockout
koan 7 paradox
kobold 5 dwarf, gnome **6** goblin, spirit, sprite
Kohinoor 3 gem **7** diamond
kohlrabi 7 cabbage
kola 3 nut **4** tree
komatik 4 sled **6** sledge
kook 3 nut **5** crank, loony, wacko **6** cuckoo, weirdo **7** dingbat, lunatic, oddball **8** crackpot **9** ding-a-ling, fruitcake, screwball **10** crackbrain
kooky 4 daft, nuts **5** batty, crazy, daffy, dotty, flaky, loony, nutty, silly, wacky, weird **6** freaky, fruity, insane, screwy **7** bizarre, idiotic, lunatic, offbeat, touched **8** demented **9** eccentric, fantastic **10** flipped out, freaked-out, off-the-wall, outlandish
kopeck 4 coin *one hundred:* **5** ruble
Koran *chapter:* **4** sura *revealer of:* **7** Gabriel *scholar:* **5** ulama, ulema
Korea see *Korea, North; Korea, South*
Korean *dynasty:* **5** Silla **7** Koguryo *national dish:* **6** kimchi
Korea, North *capital:* **9** P'yongyang *city:*

7 Hamhung **8** Ch'ongjin *leader:* **9** Kim Il-sung, Kim Jong Il **10** Kim Chong-Il *monetary unit:* **3** won *mountain:* **6** Paektu *neighbor:* **5** China **6** Russia **10** South Korea *sea:* **6** Yellow
Korea, South *captial:* **5** Seoul *city:* **5** Pusan, Taegu **6** Inch'on, Taejon **7** Kwangju *island:* **5** Cheju *monetary unit:* **3** won *neighbor:* **10** North Korea *river:* **3** Han **7** Naktong *sea:* **5** Japan **6** Yellow
kosher 3 fit **4** pure **5** clean **6** proper **10** acceptable, legitimate, sanctioned **12** satisfactory
Kosinski novel 5 Steps **10** Being There **11** Painted Bird (The)
Koussevitzky 5 Serge **6** Sergei **9** conductor
kowtow 3 bow **4** fawn **5** cower, defer, kneel, toady **6** cringe, grovel **7** honey up, truckle **8** bootlick **11** apple-polish
kraal 3 pen **6** corral **7** village **9** enclosure
kraken 5 squid **9** leviathan **10** giant squid, sea monster
krater 3 jar **4** vase **6** vessel
Kriemhild *brother:* **7** Gunther *husband:* **5** Etzel **8** Attila **9** Siegfried *slayer:* **10** Hildebrand *victim:* **5** Hagen
kris 6 dagger
Krishna *avatar of:* **6** Vishnu *brother:* **8** Balarama *father:* **8** Vasudeva *mother:* **6** Devaki *uncle:* **5** Kansa *victim:* **5** Kansa
Krupp works site 5 Essen
kudos 4 bays, fame **5** award, glory, honor **6** honors, praise, renown **7** acclaim, bouquet, laurels **8** accolade, bouquets **10** compliment **11** distinction, recognition
kudu 8 antelope
kukri 5 sword
kumquat 5 fruit *kin:* **6** orange
Kushner play 15 Angels in America
Kuwait *capital:* **6** Kuwait *gulf:* **7** Persian *island:* **7** Bubiyan **8** Faylakah *language:* **6** Arabic **7** Persian *monetary unit:* **5** dinar *neighbor:* **4** Iraq **11** Saudi Arabia *oasis:* **8** Al-Jahrah
kvass 4 beer
kvetch 4 beef, crab, fret, fuss **5** gripe, whine **6** grouch, grouse **7** grumble **8** complain **9** bellyache
___ **kwon do 3** tae
kyphosis 8 humpback **9** curvature, hunchback
Kyrgyzstan *capital:* **7** Bishkek *city:* **3** Osh *conqueror:* **9** Jöchi Khan *lake:* **8** Issyk-Kul *language:* **6** Kyrgyz **7** Russian *monetary unit:* **3** som *mountain, range:* **4** Alai **6** Pobedy **7** Victory **8** Tian Shan **10** Khan-Tengri **11** Kok Shaal-Tau *neighbor:* **5** China **10** Kazakhstan, Tajikistan, Uzbekistan *river:* **5** Naryn

L

Laadah *father:* 6 Shelah *grandfather:*
5 Judah
laager 4 camp 6 encamp 7 bivouac
lab 13 proving ground
Laban *daughter:* 4 Leah 6 Rachel *father:*
7 Bethuel *grandfather:* 5 Nahor *sister:*
7 Rebekah
label 3 tag 4 band, mark 6 marker, ticket
7 epithet, hallmark, sticker 8 classify,
identify, insignia
labium 3 lip
labor 4 moil, task, toil, work 5 chore,
grind, sweat 6 drudge, effort, strain,
strive 7 slavery, travail 8 drudgery,
endeavor, exertion, struggle 10 birth
pangs, childbirth, donkeywork
12 childbearing *group:* 3 AFL, CIO
5 ILGWU, union 6 AFL-CIO *leader:*
5 Hoffa (James, Jimmy), Lewis (John
L.), Meany (George) 6 Chavez (Cesar)
7 Gompers (Samuel), Reuther (Walter),
Sweeney (John J.) 8 Kirkland (Lane),
Randolph (A. Philip)
laboratory *device:* 5 flask 6 beaker, mortar, pestle, retort 7 burette, pipette
8 crucible, test tube 12 Bunsen burner
labored 4 hard 6 forced, taxing, tiring
7 arduous 8 strained 9 difficult, effortful, fatiguing, strenuous
laborer 4 hack, hand, peon 5 grind,
navvy 6 coolie, menial 7 workman
10 roustabout, workingman *Mexican:*
7 bracero
laborious 4 hard 6 tiring, uphill 7 arduous, onerous, operose 8 diligent, grueling, sedulous, toilsome 9 assiduous, difficult, effortful, strenuous
10 burdensome, unflagging 11 hardworking, industrious, persevering
12 backbreaking
La Brea 4 pits 7 tar pits *fossil:* 7 mammoth 8 mastodon 10 saber-tooth
labyrinth 3 web 4 coil, knot, maze, mesh
5 skein, snarl 6 jungle, morass, tangle
builder: 8 Daedalus *hero:* 7 Theseus
monster: 8 Minotaur
labyrinthine 4 mazy 6 daedal, knotty
7 complex, gordian 8 involved, maze-
like, tortuous 9 Byzantine, elaborate,
intricate 10 convoluted, perplexing
11 bewildering, complicated
lace 3 net, tat, tie 4 cord, trim 5 adorn,

braid, frill, plait, twine 6 fasten, string
7 entwine, netting, tatting 8 filigree,
openwork 9 embroider 10 embroidery,
intertwine 11 needlepoint *edge:* 5 picot
ground: 6 reseau *into:* 5 abuse 6 attack
7 condemn *kind:* 6 bobbin 7 Alençon,
guipure, macramé, Maltese, Mechlin,
torchon 8 Brussels, Venetian 9 Chantil-
ly 11 needlepoint 12 Valenciennes
make: 3 tat *pattern:* 5 toilé
Lacedaemon 6 Sparta
lacerate 3 cut, rip 4 gash, rend, tear
5 slash, wound 6 mangle, pierce
7 afflict, mangled, torment 8 distress
lachrymose 3 sad 5 teary, weepy 7 doleful, tearful, weeping 8 dolorous,
mournful 11 tear-jerking
lack 4 need, want 6 dearth, defect
7 absence, default, deficit, failure,
paucity, poverty, require 8 scarcity,
shortage 9 privation 10 deficiency, inadequacy, scantiness 13 insufficiency
lackadaisical 4 idle, lazy, limp, slow
5 moony 6 dreamy 7 languid, passive
8 fainéant, indolent, listless, slothful
9 apathetic, enervated 10 languorous,
spiritless 11 daydreaming, halfhearted,
languishing
lackey 5 toady 6 fawner, flunky, minion,
vassal 7 footman, servant 8 truckler
9 attendant, sycophant
lacking 3 shy 4 sans 5 minus, short
6 absent, flawed, needed 7 missing,
needing, omitted, wanting, without
8 devoid of, impaired 9 defective, deficient 10 deprived of, inadequate,
incomplete 11 halfhearted 12 insufficient
lackluster 3 dim 4 arid, blah, drab, dull,
flat 5 blind, ho-hum, matte, muted,
prosy, rusty, vapid 6 boring, leaden
7 prosaic 8 lifeless, mediocre 9 colorless, tarnished, wearisome 10 uninspired 13 unimaginative
Laconian 7 Spartan *king:* 5 Lelex, Myles
8 Menelaus
laconic 4 curt 5 bluff, blunt, brief, pithy,
short, terse 7 brusque, concise 8 succinct
lacquer 5 glaze, gloss 6 enamel, finish
7 shellac, varnish
lacrosse *related game:* 7 jai alai *term:*

5 clamp 6 crease, crosse, pocket 7 face-off *team:* 3 ten

lactate 4 salt 5 ester, nurse 6 suckle 7 secrete 8 wet-nurse 10 breast-feed

lacteal 5 milky 6 cloudy, pearly

lacuna 3 gap, pit 4 void 5 blank, break, space 6 breach, cavity, hiatus 7 caesura 10 deficiency 12 interruption 13 discontinuity

lacy 5 meshy 6 dainty 7 netlike 8 delicate, gossamer 9 filigreed

lad 3 boy, son, tad 5 youth 6 shaver 9 shaveling, stripling *Irish:* 4 boyo 5 bucko *Scottish:* 5 chiel 7 callant

ladder 3 run 5 ranks, scale 6 series 7 ranking 9 hierarchy *adjunct:* 4 rung 6 rundle

ladderlike 6 scalar, scaled 7 stepped 11 scalariform

lade 3 dip, tax 4 bail, load, pack, ship, stow 5 ladle, scoop 6 burden, saddle, weight 8 encumber

la-di-dah 6 too-too 7 elegant, genteel, stuck-up 8 affected, snobbish 9 conceited, grandiose, high-flown 10 hoity-toity 11 pretentious

lading 4 haul, load 5 cargo, goods 6 burden 7 bailing, dipping, freight, loading, payload 8 shipment 11 consignment

ladle 3 dip 4 bail 5 scoop, spoon 6 dipper

Ladon 6 dragon *father:* 7 Phorcus, Phorcys *mother:* 4 Ceto *slayer:* 8 Heracles, Hercules

lady 4 dame 5 madam, woman 6 female, matron *French:* 4 dame *German:* 4 Frau *Italian:* 5 donna 7 signora *Muslim:* 5 begum *Spanish:* 4 doña 6 señora

lady ___ 4 luck 5 apple 6 beetle, chapel

ladybug 6 beetle *Australian:* 7 vedalia

Lady Chatterley's Lover *author:* 8 Lawrence (David Herbert) *character:* 6 Connie 7 Mellors (Oliver) 9 Constance

lady-killer 4 dude, hunk, roué, stud 7 playboy, seducer 8 Casanova, lothario 12 heartbreaker

Lady of the Lake, The 5 Ellen (Douglas), Nimue 6 Vivien *author:* 5 Scott (Walter)

Lady Windermere's Fan *author:* 5 Wilde (Oscar)

Laertes *father:* 8 Acrisius, Polonius *sister:* 7 Ophelia *son:* 7 Ulysses 8 Odysseus *victim:* 6 Hamlet *wife:* 8 Anticlea

La Fontaine's forte 5 fable

lag 4 drag, flag, last, poke, slow, tire 5 dally, delay, tarry, trail 6 dawdle, linger, loiter 7 slacken 8 hang back, hindmost, interval 10 dillydally 13 procrastinate

lager 4 beer, brew, malt, suds 7 brewski

laggard 3 lax 4 slow 5 tardy 6 loafer

7 dawdler 8 dallying, dawdling, delaying, dilatory, flagging, lingerer, loiterer, slowpoke, sluggish, tarrying 9 apathetic, lazybones, lethargic, loitering, straggler 10 behindhand

La Gioconda 8 Mona Lisa *composer:* 10 Ponchielli (Amilcare) *painter:* 7 da Vinci (Leonardo) 8 Leonardo (da Vinci)

lagniappe 3 tip 4 gift, perk 5 bonus 7 cumshaw, largess 8 dividend, gratuity 9 baksheesh, pourboire 10 perquisite

lagomorph 4 hare, pika 6 rabbit

lagoon 4 pond, pool 5 bayou, sound 6 strait 7 channel, narrows

___ La Guardia 8 Fiorello

Lahmi *brother:* 7 Goliath *slayer:* 7 Elhanan

laid-back 4 cool 6 breezy, casual 7 relaxed 8 carefree, informal 9 easygoing, hang-loose 10 nonchalant

lair 3 den 4 cave 5 haunt, lodge 6 burrow, refuge 7 hideout, retreat 8 hideaway 9 sanctuary

Laius *father:* 8 Labdacus *slayer, son:* 7 Oedipus *wife:* 7 Jocasta

lake 4 loch, mere, pond, pool, tarn 5 lough 6 lagoon *Adriatic:* 6 Varano *Alberta:* 6 Louise *Algeria:* 5 Hodna *Alps:* 6 Annecy *Arizona-Nevada:* 4 Mead *Armenia:* 5 Sevan 6 Gokcha, Sevang 9 Lychnitis *Aswan's:* 6 Nasser *Australia:* 4 Eyre 5 Carey, Cowan, Frome, Wells 6 Barlee 7 Amadeus, Everard, Torrens 8 Gairdner *Austria:* 5 Atter, Traun 6 Kammer 8 Attersee 9 Kammersee *Bolivia:* 5 Poopó *Botswana:* 5 Ngami *British Columbia:* 4 Pitt 5 Atlin *California:* 4 Mono, Tule 5 Clear, Eagle, Honey *Cambodia:* 8 Tonle Sap *Canada:* 4 Dyke 8 Manitoba *central Africa:* 4 Kivu 5 Mweru 6 Albert *Central America:* 5 Guija *central Europe:* 5 Leman 6 Geneva, Lugano 7 Ceresio 8 Bodensee 9 Constance *central North America:* 5 Rainy *Chile:* 4 Laja 5 Ranco *China:* 6 Poyang 8 Dongting *Colorado:* 5 Grand *Denmark:* 5 Esrum *east Africa:* 6 Rudolf 7 Turkana *east Asia:* 6 Khanka 7 Xingkai 8 Hsingkai *east central Africa:* 8 Victoria 10 Tanganyika *east China:* 3 Tai 5 Dalai, Hulun *Ethiopia:* 4 Tana, Zwai 5 Abaya, Shala, Shamo, Tsana 8 Stefanie 9 Chew Bahir *Finland:* 5 Inari *Florida:* 5 Worth 10 Okeechobee *Germany:* 5 Ammer, Chiem 8 Ammersee, Chiemsee *Ghana:* 5 Volta *Great:* 4 Erie 5 Huron 7 Ontario 8 Michigan, Superior *Greece:* 5 Bolbe, Volvi *Guatemala:* 7 Atitlán *Honduras:* 5 Yojoa *Honshu:* 3 Omi 4 Biwa, Suwa, Yodo *Hungary:* 7 Balaton 10 Plattensee *Idaho:* 4 Waha

5 Grays 6 Priest 11 Coeur d'Alene, Pend Oreille *India:* 3 Dal 5 Wular 6 Chilka *Indonesia:* 4 Poso, Toba 5 Ranau *Iowa:* 5 Storm *Iran:* 5 Niriz, Shahi, Urmia 8 Matianus, Urumiyeh 9 Bakhtigan *Ireland:* 3 Gur, Ree 4 Conn, Derg, Mask 5 Allen, Arrow, Leane *Israel:* 12 Bahr Tabariya, Sea of Galilee *Israel-Jordan:* 7 Dead Sea *Italy:* 4 Como, Iseo, Nemi 5 Garda 6 Albano 7 Bolsena, Perugia 8 Maggiore 9 Trasimene *Japan:* 4 Imba 8 Imbanuma *Kazakhstan:* 7 Balqash 8 Balkhash *Louisiana:* 4 Soda 9 Catahoula 13 Pontchartrain *Maine:* 6 Sebago 9 Moosehead *Mali:* 4 Debo *Manitoba:* 4 Gods 5 Cedar, Moose 8 Winnipeg *Mexico:* 7 Chapala *Michigan:* 4 Burt *Minnesota:* 3 Red 4 Cass, Gull, Swan 5 Leech 6 Itasca 9 Mille Lacs 10 Minnetonka, of the Woods 11 Lac qui Parle *Minnesota-Wisconsin:* 5 Pepin *Mongolian:* 3 Har 5 Har Us, Khara 8 Khara Usu *Montana:* 8 Medicine *mountain:* 4 tarn *Myanmar:* 4 Inle *Nevada:* 4 Ruby 7 Pyramid *New Hampshire:* 5 Squam 13 Winnipesaukee *New Jersey:* 5 Union *New York:* 4 Long 5 Chazy, Keuka 6 Cayuga, George, Oneida, Otsego, Owasco, Placid, Seneca 7 Crooked, Saranac 8 Onondaga, Saratoga 10 Chautauqua 11 Canandaigua, Skaneateles *New Zealand:* 4 Ohau 5 Hawea, Taupo 6 Pukaki, Wanaka 8 Wakatipu *Nicaragua:* 7 Managua *North Africa:* 4 Chad *Northern Ireland:* 5 Neagh *Northwest Territories:* 4 Gras 5 Baker, Garry, Pelly 9 Great Bear 10 Great Slave *Norway:* 5 Mjosa *Nova Scotia:* 7 Bras d'Or *Ontario:* 4 Rice, Seul 5 Trout *Oregon:* 5 Abert 6 Crater 7 Malheur, Wallowa *Paraguay:* 4 Ypoá *Peru:* 5 Junín 13 Chinchaycocha *Philippines:* 4 Bato, Taal 5 Lanao 6 Bombon *Poland:* 5 Mamry, Mauer *Quebec:* 5 Minto, Payne *Russia:* 3 Seg 5 Chany, Ilmen, Lacha, Onega 6 Baikal, Ladoga 7 Rybinsk 10 Eltonskoye 11 Ladozhskoye *Saskatchewan:* 4 Cree 5 Ronge *Scotland:* 3 Ard, Awe 4 Doon, Earn, Ness, Oich, Shin, Sloy 5 Leven, Lochy, Maree, Morar, Shiel 6 Lomond *Siberia:* 6 Baikal, Baykal *South Africa:* 4 Kosi *South America:* 5 Merin, Mirim 8 Titicaca *South Carolina:* 7 Wateree *South Dakota:* 5 Andes *southeast Africa:* 5 Nyasa 6 Nyassa *southwest Europe:* 5 Ohrid 7 Okhrida *Sweden:* 5 Asnen, Roxen 6 Siljan, Vänern, Vetter 7 Malaren, Vattern *Switzerland:* 3 Zug 4 Biel, Joux 5 Zuger 6 Bieler, Bienne, Brienz, Sarnen, Sarner, Zurich

7 Lucerne, Lungern 8 Brienzer, Züricher 9 Neuchâtel, Zürichsee *Tajikistan:* 7 Karakul *Tanzania:* 5 Rukwa *Texas-Louisiana:* 5 Caddo *Tibet:* 4 Na-mu 6 Nam Tso, Tengri *Turkey:* 3 Tuz, Van 4 Bafa, Nice 5 Iznik, Sugla 6 Nicaea *Uganda:* 5 Kyoga *Utah:* 6 Powell, Sevier 9 Great Salt *Wales:* 4 Bala *Washington:* 4 Omak 5 Moses 6 Chelan 9 Wenatchee *western China:* 4 Ai-pi 6 Ebinur *western United States:* 4 Bear 5 Tahoe *Wisconsin:* 5 Green 9 Winnebago *Yellowstone National Park:* 5 Heart, Lewis 8 Shoshone *Zaire:* 5 Tumba *Zambia:* 9 Bangweolo, Bangweulu

lake group *central North America:* 5 Great *Connecticut:* 4 Twin *Egypt:* 5 Balah *Maine:* 8 Rangeley *New Hampshire:* 11 Connecticut *New York:* 6 Finger *Saskatchewan:* 5 Quill *Twin:* 8 Washinee 9 Washining *Wisconsin:* 4 Four

lake herring 5 cisco

Lake poet 7 Southey (Robert) 9 Coleridge (Samuel Taylor) 10 Wordsworth (William)

Lake Wobegon Days author 7 Keillor (Garrison)

Lakmé *aria:* 8 Bell Song *composer:* 7 Delibes (Léo)

Lakshmi *husband:* 6 Vishnu *son:* 4 Kama

lam 3 hit 4 beat, blow, bolt, drub, flay, flee, flog, pelt, skip, whip 5 baste, paste, pound, scram, smack, split, whale 6 batter, beat it, buffet, cut out, decamp, escape, flight, hammer, pummel, strike, thrash, wallop 7 getaway, take off, vamoose 8 breakout, escaping 9 skedaddle

La Mancha's knight 10 Don Quixote

lamb 4 cade 5 sheep 6 cosset 8 yeanling *leg of:* 5 gigot

lambaste 3 pan 4 beat, drub, flay, flog, lash, lick, pelt, slam, slap, trim, whip 5 paste, pound, roast, scold, score, slash, smear 6 assail, attack, berate, cudgel, hammer, pummel, scathe, scorch, thrash, wallop 7 assault, blister, censure, clobber, reprove, scourge, shellac, upbraid 8 bludgeon, denounce, harangue, lash into 9 castigate, criticize, excoriate 10 tongue-lash

lambent 5 aglow 6 ardent, bright, lucent 7 beaming, glowing, radiant, shining 8 gleaming, luminous, lustrous 9 brilliant, effulgent, refulgent, twinkling 10 flickering, glittering, shimmering 12 incandescent

lamblike 4 meek 6 docile

lamb of God 5 Jesus 6 Christ 8 Agnus Dei

Lamb's pseudonym 4 Elia

lame 4 gimp, halt, limp 5 gimpy, stiff

6 feeble, flimsy 7 cripple, disable, halting, limping 8 crippled, disabled, hobbling, inferior 10 inadequate 11 ineffectual 12 contemptible, unconvincing 13 incapacitated

lamebrain 3 oaf 4 dolt, dope, goof, mutt, simp, yo-yo 5 chump, dummy, dunce, idiot, moron, ninny, noddy, stupe 6 dimwit, donkey, dum-dum, nitwit, noodle 7 airhead, dullard, pinhead, schnook 8 bonehead, clodpoll, dumbbell, dumbhead, imbecile, lunkhead, meathead, numskull 9 blockhead, ignoramus, numbskull, simpleton, thickhead 10 dunderhead, hammerhead, nincompoop 11 chowderhead, chucklehead, knucklehead

Lamech *daughter:* 6 Naamah *father:* 10 Methuselah *son:* 4 Noah 5 Jabal, Jubal 9 Tubalcain *wife:* 4 Adah 6 Zillah

lament 3 cry, rue 4 keen, moan, pine, wail, weep 5 dirge, elegy, mourn 6 bemoan, bewail, grieve, plaint, regret, repent, sorrow 7 deplore, elegize, wailing 8 jeremiad, threnody 9 complaint, ululation

lamentable 6 rueful, woeful 7 doleful, pitiful 8 dolorous, grievous, mournful 9 plaintive, sorrowful 10 afflictive, deplorable, lugubrious, melancholy 11 distressing, regrettable, unfortunate 13 heartbreaking

lamentation 5 elegy, grief 7 anguish, remorse, wailing 8 grieving, mourning, threnody 9 sorrowing, ululation 13 mortification

Lamerok *father:* 9 Pellinore *lover:* 8 Margawse *slayer:* 6 Gawain

lamia 3 hag, hex 5 witch 7 hellcat, vampire 9 sorceress 11 enchantress, necromancer

Lamia *country:* 5 Libya *form:* 7 serpent *lover:* 4 Zeus

lamina 5 blade, flake, layer, plate, scale

lamp 3 arc 4 bulb 5 klieg, light, torch 7 lantern 10 candelabra 11 candelabrum *floor:* 8 torchère 9 torchiere *hanging:* 10 chandelier

lampblack 4 soot 6 carbon

Lampetia *father:* 6 Apollo, Helios *husband:* 9 Asclepius *mother:* 6 Neaera *sister:* 9 Phaethusa

lampoon 4 mock 5 roast, spoof, squib 6 parody, satire, send-up 7 take off 8 ridicule, satirize 9 burlesque 10 caricature, pasquinade

lamprey 3 eel

lanai 5 patio, porch 6 piazza 7 terrace, veranda

lance 4 gash, hurl 5 slash, spear 6 impale, pierce, skewer 7 javelin 8 transfix

Lancelot, Launcelot *father:* 3 Ban *lover:* 6 Elaine 9 Guinevere *son:* 7 Galahad *victim:* 6 Gawain

lancer 10 cavalryman *Prussian:* 5 uhlan

lancet 4 arch 5 blade, knife 6 cutter, window 7 scalpel

land 4 dirt, dock, gain, soil 5 acres, berth, earth, light, manor, shore, terra, tract 6 alight, estate, ground, obtain, pick up, secure 7 acquire, acreage, country, expanse, grounds, procure, set down, terrain, terrene 9 touch down 10 terra firma *alluvial:* 5 delta *barren:* 5 waste 6 desert *cultivated:* 4 farm 5 tilth 7 tillage *for grazing:* 3 lea, ley 5 range 6 meadow 7 pasture *high:* 4 hill, mesa 7 plateau 8 mountain *level:* 4 mesa 5 plain 7 plateau *low:* 4 vale 6 valley 9 intervale *measure:* 3 rod 4 acre *open:* 3 lea 5 field, green, plain 6 meadow 7 pasture *piece:* 3 lot 4 plot 5 tract 6 estate, parcel *reclaimed:* 6 polder *sloping:* 6 cuesta *strip:* 7 isthmus *wet:* 3 bog, fen 5 marsh, swamp 6 marish

land east of Eden 3 Nod

landed 4 alit

landlord 6 lessor, squire 9 innkeeper 10 freeholder

landmark 5 cairn, guide 9 benchmark, milestone, watershed 11 achievement 12 breakthrough, turning point

Land of Enchantment 9 New Mexico

Land of Lakes 8 Michigan

Land of Opportunity 3 USA 8 Arkansas 12 United States

Land of the Midnight Sun 6 Norway

landowner 6 squire, yeoman *Anglo-Saxon:* 5 thane, thegn *Dutch:* 7 patroon *Scottish:* 5 laird

landscape 5 scene, vista 7 scenery, setting, terrain 8 backdrop, prospect

lane 3 way 4 path, road 5 aisle, alley, byway, track 6 street 7 pathway, roadway 8 footpath 10 passageway

lang syne 4 past, yore 10 yesteryear

language 4 cant 5 argot, idiom, lingo, prose, slang 6 jargon, patois, speech, tongue 7 dialect, lexicon, palaver 10 vernacular, vocabulary 11 terminology *ambiguous:* 8 newspeak 10 doubletalk *ancient:* 5 Greek, Latin 6 Hebrew 8 Etruscan, Sanskrit *artificial:* 3 Ido 7 Volapük 9 Esperanto *classical:* 5 Greek, Latin *combining form:* 5 gloss, glott 6 glosso, glotto *expert:* 8 linguist *informal:* 4 jive 5 lingo, slang *meaningless:* 6 babble, jabber 7 blather 9 gibberish 10 mumbo-jumbo *mixed:* 6 creole, pidgin *pretentious:* 7 bombast, fustian 8 claptrap *regional:* 7 dialect *relating to:* **10** linguistic *Romance:* **6** French **7** Catalan, Italian, Spanish **8** Romanian, Rumanian **10** Portuguese *secret:* **4** cant, code **5** argot *structure:* **6** syntax **7** grammar *suffix:* **3** ese *written:* **5** prose

languid 4 lazy, limp **5** inert **6** draggy, supine, torpid **8** drooping, flagging, inactive, listless, slothful, sluggish **9** apathetic, enervated, impassive, lethargic **10** languorous, phlegmatic, spiritless **13** lackadaisical

languish 4 fade, fail, pine, tire, wilt **5** brood, droop **6** weaken **7** decline **9** waste away

languishing 4 limp, weak **6** feeble, pining **7** languid **8** fainéant, indolent, listless, weakened **9** depressed, enervated, enfeebled **10** dispirited, languorous, spiritless **11** debilitated, devitalized **13** lackadaisical

languor 3 kef, kif **5** ennui **6** stupor, tedium, torpor **7** fatigue **8** doldrums, dullness, hebetude, lethargy **9** heaviness, inertness, lassitude, torpidity, weariness **10** exhaustion

languorous 4 lazy, limp **5** inert **6** draggy, supine, torpid **7** laggard, languid, passive, relaxed **8** dilatory, drooping, fainéant, flagging, inactive, indolent, indulged, listless, pampered, slothful, sluggard **9** apathetic, enervated, impassive, lethargic **10** phlegmatic, spiritless **11** languishing **13** lackadaisical

lank 4 bony, lean, thin **5** rangy, spare **6** gangly **7** angular, scraggy, slender **8** gangling **10** attenuated

lanky 4 lean, thin **5** gaunt, spare **6** gangly **7** scrawny **8** gangling, rawboned

lanyard 4 cord, line, rope **7** cordage

Laocoön *city:* **4** Troy *killer:* **8** serpents

Laodamia *father:* **7** Acastus *husband:* **11** Protesilaus

Laomedon *daughter:* **7** Hesione *father:* **4** Ilus *kingdom:* **4** Troy *mother:* **8** Eurydice *slayer:* **8** Heracles, Hercules *son:* **5** Priam **8** Tithonus

Laos *capital:* **9** Vientiane *city:* **11** Savannakhet *ethnic group:* **5** Hmong *monetary unit:* **3** kip *neighbor:* **5** Burma, China **7** Myanmar, Vietnam **8** Cambodia, Thailand **9** Kampuchea *river:* **6** Mekong

lap 3 sip **4** fold, join, wind **6** cuddle, splash, swathe **7** circuit, control, custody, shingle **9** imbricate

lapidary 6 cutter **7** elegant, jeweler **8** engraver, polisher

lapillus 4 lava **6** cinder

lapin 6 rabbit

Lapiths *foes:* **8** centaurs *king:* **5** Ixion

lappet 4 flap, fold **5** lapel

Lapsang 3 tea **6** Fujian

lapse 3 err, gap, sin **4** fall, flub, goof, sink, slip, vice **5** boner, cease, error, fluff, gaffe, slide **6** breach, bungle, expire, foible, miscue **7** blooper, blunder, decline, descend, failing, failure, faux pas, forfeit, frailty, mistake, screwup, subside **8** apostasy, interval, trespass **9** backslide, deviation, oversight, violation **10** apostatize **11** backsliding, impropriety **12** indiscretion, interruption **13** retrogression, transgression

lapsed 4 sunk **5** ended **6** ceased **7** expired **8** obsolete **9** forfeited

Laputan 6 absurd **9** visionary

Lar 3 god **6** spirit

larboard 4 left, port **8** leftward

larcenist 5 thief **6** bandit, robber **7** burglar, filcher, stealer **8** pilferer **9** embezzler, plunderer, purloiner **10** pickpocket, shoplifter

larcenous 7 robbing **8** thieving **9** pilfering **10** plunderous **13** light-fingered

larceny 5 theft **7** looting, robbery **8** burglary, stealing, thievery, thieving *kind:* **5** grand, petty

lard 3 fat **6** fatten, grease **10** shortening

larder 6 pantry

large 3 big, fat **4** bull, huge, vast **5** ample, bulky, giant, grand, great, gross, hefty, husky, jumbo, major **6** goodly **7** copious, extreme, immense, mammoth, massive, outsize, sizable **8** colossal, enormous, gigantic, king-size, oversize, spacious, whopping **9** capacious, excessive, extensive, humongous, monstrous **10** exorbitant, immoderate, inordinate, large-scale, monumental, prodigious, stupendous, tremendous, voluminous **11** extravagant, substantial *combining form:* **4** macr, mega **5** macro **6** megalo

largesse 4 alms, gift **6** bounty **7** bequest, charity, cumshaw, gifting, present **8** donation, gratuity **9** endowment, pourboire **10** almsgiving, generosity, liberality **11** benefaction, benevolence, benificence, magnanimity, munificence **12** philanthropy

largo 4 slow **5** broad, tempo

lariat 4 rope **5** lasso, noose, reata, riata *user:* **6** cowboy, drover **10** cowpuncher

lark 4 bird, dido, romp **5** antic, caper, prank, shine, stunt, trick **6** frolic **7** rollick **8** escapade, songbird **9** diversion **10** tomfoolery **11** distraction, shenanigans **12** monkeyshines

larrup 3 tan **4** beat, cane, drub, dust, flay, flog, hide, lash, lick, whip, whup **5** pound, spank, whale **6** cudgel, lather, paddle, thrash, wallop **7** clobber,

scourge, shellac, trounce **8** lambaste
10 flagellate
larva 3 bot **4** grub, worm **6** dobson, maggot **8** cercaria, hornworm, mealworm
10 casebearer **11** caterpillar **12** hellgrammite *amphibian:* **7** tadpole *crustacean:* **4** zoea *flatworm:* **5** redia *freeswimming:* **7** planula *mollusk:* **7** veliger
moth: **8** leafworm *tapeworm:* **6** measle
larynx 7 trachea **8** voice box
lasagna 5 pasta **7** noodles
lascivious 4 lewd **5** bawdy, loose, randy
6 carnal, coarse, rakish, wanton **7** fleshly, goatish, immoral, lustful, satyric
8 depraved, prurient **9** lecherous, libertine, lickerish, salacious **10** libidinous,
licentious, lubricious, profligate
12 concupiscent
lash 4 beat, bind, dash, flay, flog, hide,
whip **5** baste, birch, fling, pound, scold,
slash, whale **6** assail, berate, buffet,
pummel, scathe, strike, stripe, switch,
thrash **7** blister, scarify, scourge,
upbraid **8** lambaste **9** castigate, excoriate, horsewhip **10** flagellate
lass 3 gal **4** girl, maid **5** wench **6** damsel,
maiden **7** colleen
lassitude 5 ennui, sloth **6** apathy, stupor,
tedium, torpor **7** fatigue, languor
8 debility, doldrums, dullness, hebetude, laziness, lethargy **9** indolence,
tiredness, torpidity, weariness
10 exhaustion **11** disinterest, insouciance **12** heedlessness, indifference,
listlessness, sluggishness
lasso see LARIAT
last 3 end, lag **5** abide, final **6** endure,
latest, latter, utmost **7** closing, extreme,
perdure, persist **8** continue, crowning,
eventual, farthest, furthest, hindmost,
rearmost, remotest, terminal, ultimate
9 umpteenth, uttermost **10** concluding,
conclusive **11** terminating *French:*
7 dernier *next to:* **6** penult **11** penultimate
last-ditch 5 final **7** defiant **8** ultimate
9 desperate **10** concluding
lasting 6 stable **7** abiding, durable, undying **8** enduring, lifelong, long-term,
longtime **9** continual, indelible, perennial, permanent, unceasing **10** continuing, continuous, perdurable, persisting
12 indissoluble, long-standing
Last of the Mohicans, The 5 Uncas
author: **6** Cooper (James Fenimore)
character: **4** Cora **5** Alice, Magua, Uncas
11 Natty Bumppo **12** Chingachgook
Last Supper, The *painter:* **7** da Vinci
(Leonardo)
latch 4 bolt, hasp, hook **5** catch **6** fasten,
secure **8** fastener *British:* **5** sneck

latchet 4 band, cord, lace **5** strap, thong
8 shoelace
late 4 dead, past, slow **5** tardy **6** former,
recent, whilom **7** defunct, delayed, onetime, overdue, quondam **8** deceased,
departed, sometime **9** preceding
Late George Apley, The *author:* **8** Marquand (John P.)
latent 4 idle **5** inert **6** covert, fallow, hidden, innate, unripe **7** abeyant, dormant, lurking **8** immature, inactive,
inherent **9** concealed, intrinsic, potential, quiescent
later 4 anon, soon **5** after, infra **6** behind
7 by and by, ensuing **9** afterward, following, posterior **10** subsequent, succeeding **12** subsequently
lateral 4 pass, side **6** branch **8** crabwise,
flanking, sidelong, sideward, sideways,
sidewise
laterally 8 crabwise, sideward, sideways,
sidewise
latest 6 newest, red-hot **7** current **8** contempo **9** au courant **10** dernier cri
13 up-to-the-minute
latex 6 balata **8** emulsion *product:* **5** paint
6 chicle, rubber
lath 4 slat **5** board, frame, stave, stick,
strip
lather 4 flap, flog, foam, hide, lash, soap,
stew, suds, whip **5** froth, spume, tizzy,
yeast **6** dither, hoopla, pother, thrash,
welter **7** scourge, turmoil **8** soapsuds
Latin 5 Roman **7** Italian **8** Hispanic *after:*
4 post *always:* **6** semper *before:* **4** ante,
prae *book:* **5** liber *boy:* **4** puer *brother:*
6 frater *but:* **3** sed *day:* **4** dies *dog:*
5 canis *foot:* **3** pes *friend:* **6** amicus *god:*
4 deus *goddess:* **3** dea *grammarian:*
7 Donatus (Aelius) *hand:* **5** manus *is:*
3 est *law:* **3** ius, jus, lex *light:* **3** lux *love:*
3 amo **4** amas, amat, amor *peace:* **3** pax
pronoun: **3** ego, nos, vos *road:* **3** via *see:*
4 vide *that is:* **5** id est *thing:* **3** res *this:*
3 hic, hoc **4** haec *thus:* **3** sic *war:* **6** bellum *wife:* **4** uxor *woman:* **6** femina *year:*
5 annus
Latin American *country:* **4** Cuba, Peru
5 Chile **6** Belize, Brazil, Guyana, Mexico, Panama **7** Bolivia, Ecuador,
Uruguay **8** Colombia, Honduras,
Paraguay, Suriname **9** Argentina, Costa
Rica, Guatemala, Nicaragua,
Venezuela **10** El Salvador *revolutionary:*
6 Castro (Fidel) **7** Bolívar (Simón),
Guevara (Ché), Hidalgo (Father
Miguel) **8** O'Higgins (Bernardo) **9** San
Martín (José de)
Latinus *daughter:* **7** Lavinia *father:*
6 Faunus **8** Odysseus *son-in-law:*
6 Aeneas *wife:* **5** Amata

latitude 4 play, room 5 range, scope, space, width 6 leeway, margin 7 breadth, compass, freedom, liberty, license 9 elbowroom 10 discretion 12 independence

latke 7 pancake 13 potato pancake

Latona 4 Leto *daughter:* 5 Diana 7 Artemis *father:* 5 Coeus *mother:* 6 Phoebe *son:* 6 Apollo

Latter-day Saint 6 Mormon

lattice 4 grid, mesh 5 grate, grill 7 grating, network, trellis 12 reticulation

Latvia *capital:* 4 Riga *city:* 7 Liepaja 10 Daugavpils *gulf:* 4 Riga *monetary unit:* 3 lat *neighbor:* 6 Russia 7 Belarus, Estonia 9 Lithuania *river:* 7 Daugava 12 Western Dvina *sea:* 6 Baltic

Latvian 4 Lett 7 Lettish

laud 5 adore, bless, cry up, extol, glory, honor 6 admire, praise, revere 7 acclaim, flatter, glorify, magnify, worship 8 eulogize, venerate 9 celebrate, reverence

laudable 6 worthy 9 admirable, deserving, estimable 11 commendable, meritorious, thankworthy 12 praiseworthy

laudatory 7 glowing 9 adulatory, approving 10 eulogistic, flattering 11 approbative, encomiastic, panegyrical 12 commendatory 13 complimentary

laugh 3 yuk 4 ha-ha, roar, yuck 5 tehee, whoop 6 cackle, giggle, guffaw, heehaw, titter 7 chortle, chuckle, snicker 10 cachinnate

laughable 4 rich 5 comic, droll, funny, goofy, witty 6 absurd, jocose 7 amusing, comical, jocular, mocking, risible 8 derisive, derisory, farcical, humorous 9 ludicrous 10 ridiculous

laughing 5 merry, riant 6 blithe 8 mirthful 9 sparkling

laughingstock 4 butt, dupe, fool, jest, joke, mark, mock 5 sport 6 target 7 mockery 8 derision

launch 4 boat, cast, fire, hurl 5 begin, debut, fling, heave, pitch, sling, start, throw 6 get off 7 jump off, kick off, lift off, release, take off, usher in 8 blast off, catapult, commence, embark on, initiate 9 inception, institute, introduce, motorboat, set afloat 10 inaugurate, initiation 12 inauguration

launder 4 wash 5 clean 6 trough 7 cleanse 8 sanitize, transfer

Laura's lover 8 Petrarch

laurels 4 bays, fame 5 award, honor, kudos, prize 6 awards, badges, honors, prizes, renown 7 acclaim 8 accolade, citation 9 accolades, citations 10 decoration, reputation 11 decorations, distinction 12 achievements, distinctions

laurel-tree nymph 6 Daphne

lava 4 slag 5 magma 6 scoria 8 andesite, trachyte *fragment:* 8 lapillus *stream:* 4 flow 6 coulee

lavalava 5 cloth, skirt

lavaliere 7 pendant 8 necklace

lavatory 4 head, john 5 basin, potty, privy 6 johnny, toilet 7 latrine 8 bathroom, restroom, washroom 11 water closet

lave 4 pour, wash 5 bathe

Lavinia *father:* 7 Latinus *husband:* 6 Aeneas *mother:* 5 Amata

Lavinium's founder 6 Aeneas

lavish 4 lush, pour 5 plush, spend, waste 6 swanky 7 liberal, opulent, profuse 8 effusive, prodigal, splendid, squander 9 bountiful, excessive, exuberant, luxuriant, luxurious, sumptuous 10 immoderate, inordinate, munificent 11 extravagant

law 3 act, lex 4 bill, code, rule 5 axiom, canon, edict, Torah 6 assize, decree, equity 7 dictate, justice, mandate, precept, statute, theorem 8 exigency 9 enactment, ordinance, principle 10 principium, regulation 11 commandment, fundamental 12 prescription *body of:* 4 code 7 pandect 12 constitution *degree:* 3 LLB, LLD *expert:* 5 judge 6 jurist 7 justice *practitioner:* 6 lawyer 7 counsel 8 attorney 9 barrister, solicitor *relating to:* 5 jural, legal 7 canonic 8 forensic, juristic 9 judiciary *violation of:* 4 tort 5 crime 6 felony 11 misdemeanor

law-abiding 6 decent 7 duteous, dutiful, orderly, upright 8 obedient, obliging, straight 9 compliant, peaceable 10 forthright, respectful 11 respectable, well-behaved

lawbreaker 3 con 4 hood, thug 5 crook, felon 6 outlaw, sinner 7 convict, hoodlum, mobster 8 criminal, gangster, hooligan, jailbird, offender, scofflaw, violator 9 desperado, wrongdoer 10 malefactor, trespasser 12 transgressor

lawful 3 due 4 just 5 legal, legit, licit, valid 6 kosher 7 condign 8 bona fide, innocent, mandated, ordained 9 allowable, canonical, juridical, legalized 10 authorized, legitimate 11 permissible

lawgiver 5 Draco, Moses, solon 7 senator 8 alderman 10 councilman, legislator 11 congressman

lawlessness 5 chaos 6 strife 7 anarchy, discord, misrule, turmoil 8 conflict, disorder 9 mobocracy 10 illegality, misconduct, ochlocracy, unruliness, wrongdoing 11 criminality, pandemonium

lawman 7 marshal, officer, sheriff 9 policeman

Lawrence novel 7 Rainbow (The) 8 Kangaroo, Lost Girl (The) 9 Aaron's Rod 11 Women in Love 13 Sons and Lovers

lawsuit 4 case 5 cause, claim 6 action 8 replevin 9 assumpsit 10 litigation, proceeding 11 presentment, prosecution

lawyer 6 jurist, legist 7 counsel, pleader 8 advocate, attorney 9 barrister, counselor, solicitor *dishonest:* 7 shyster 11 pettifogger *fictional:* 7 Matlock (Ben) 10 Perry Mason *French:* 6 avocat

lax 5 loose, slack 6 casual, remiss, sloppy 7 lenient 8 careless, derelict, lacrosse 9 deficient, forgetful, negligent 10 neglectful 11 inattentive

lay 3 bet, put, set 5 apply, hatch, place, wager 6 assert, assign, ballad, charge, credit, devise, impute, settle, spread 7 amateur, arrange, ascribe, concoct, deposit, prepare, present 11 nonclerical

lay by 4 keep, save 5 amass, hoard, store 7 deposit, discard, store up 8 preserve, salt away, set aside 10 accumulate

lay down 3 set 4 rule 5 order, store, yield 6 assert, decree, define, give up, impose, ordain, record, resign 7 abandon, command, dictate, specify 8 hand over, preserve, proclaim 9 establish, prescribe, surrender 10 relinquish

layer 3 hen, ply 4 coat, film, seam, tier 5 paver, sheet 6 folium, lamina, veneer 7 coating, stratum 8 covering, laminate, membrane, sandwich, stratify *inner:* 6 lining *of skin:* 6 dermis 9 epidermis *outer:* 4 skin 6 veneer

lay for 6 ambush 8 surprise

lay in see LAY BY

layman 6 novice 7 amateur, secular 11 parishioner

lay off 4 halt, quit, stop 5 avoid, cease, let go, lie by 6 desist 7 dismiss, measure, release 9 discharge, terminate 10 inactivity 11 discontinue

lay out 3 pay 4 give, plan 5 chart, dummy, place, spend 6 design, expend 7 arrange, display, exhibit, prepare 8 disburse

lay waste 4 ruin 6 ravage 7 destroy 8 desolate 9 devastate

lazar 5 leper

Lazarus' sister 4 Mary 6 Martha

laze 3 bum, lag 4 bask, hang, idle, loaf, loll 5 chill 6 dawdle, loiter, lounge, slouch 7 goof off, hang out 8 chill out 9 goldbrick 10 hang around

laziness 5 sloth 6 torpor 7 inertia, languor, laxness, loafing 8 idleness, lethargy, otiosity 9 indolence, lassitude, loitering, slackness 10 inactivity 11 languidness 12 listlessness

lazy 3 lax 4 idle 5 inert, slack 6 droopy, remiss, supine, torpid 7 languid, loafing, passive 8 fainéant, inactive, indolent, listless, slothful, sluggish 9 lethargic, negligent, shiftless, slowgoing 10 languorous

lazy Susan 4 tray 9 turntable

leach 4 drip, leak, ooze, perk, seep, suck, weep 5 bleed, drain, exude, issue 7 draw out, dribble, trickle 8 filtrate, perspire 9 discharge, lixiviate, percolate

lead 3 tip 4 head, hint, show, star 5 guide, metal, plumb, route, steer, trace, usher 6 bullet, ceruse, direct, escort, leader 7 captain, conduct, precede, preface 8 graphite, persuade, shepherd 10 bellwether *combining form:* 5 plumb 6 plumbo *ore:* 6 galena 9 anglesite *oxide:* 6 sinter *sounding:* 5 plumb 7 plummet

lead astray 6 seduce 7 corrupt

leaden 4 drab, dull, flat, gray 5 heavy, inert 6 gloomy, somber 7 languid, weighty 8 dragging, lifeless, sluggish 9 ponderous

leader 4 boss, dean, duce, guru, head, jefe, lord 5 chief, guide, pilot 6 despot, honcho, rector 7 captain, foreman, general, headman, manager, warlord 8 chairman, director, hierarch, superior 9 chieftain, commander, conductor, demagogue, harbinger, precursor, president, principal, straw boss 10 bellwether, forerunner, pacesetter *authoritarian:* 10 Big Brother *Cossack:* 6 ataman, hetman *German:* 6 führer 7 fuehrer *Japanese:* 6 shogun *military:* 7 admiral, general, warlord 9 commander 12 field marshal *Muslim:* 3 aga 4 agha, emir 6 caliph, mullah *national:* 7 premier 9 president 12 chief of state

leading 4 arch, head, main 5 chief, first, major 6 famous, master 7 premier, primary 8 champion, foremost, headmost, peerless 9 paramount, principal, prominent, well-known 10 preeminent

lead on 3 con 4 bait, dupe, fool, gull, hoax, lure, scam, tole, toll, wile 5 cozen, flirt, tempt 6 allure, betray, cajole, coquet, delude, entice, entrap, humbug, seduce, suck in, take in, trifle 7 beguile, deceive, toy with 8 coquette, hoodwink, inveigle 9 bamboozle 11 string along

leaf 4 flip, foil, page, riff, scan, skim 5 blade, bract, folio, frond, petal, scale, sepal, thumb 6 browse, glance, riffle, spathe *aperture:* 5 stoma *axis:* 6 rachis *combining form:* 5 phyll 6 phyllo 7 phyllum *edge:* 9 crenation *lily:* 3 pad *part:* 4 lobe, vein 5 blade, costa, stoma 7 petiole, stipule, tendril *pine:* 6 needle *vein:* 5 costa

leafage 7 foliage, umbrage, verdure

leaflet 5 flier, flyer, pinna, sheet, tract 6 folder 7 handout 8 circular, handbill, pamphlet

leafy 4 lush 5 green, shady 6 shaded, wooded 7 foliate, verdant 8 foliated, laminate 9 verdurous

league 4 band, bond, club, crew 5 class, grade, group, guild, order, union, unite 6 circle 7 circuit, combine, society 8 alliance, category, division, grouping, sodality 9 coalition 10 conference, consortium, federation, fellowship, fraternity 11 association, brotherhood, confederacy 13 confederation

Leah *daughter:* 5 Dinah *father:* 5 Laban *husband:* 5 Jacob *sister:* 6 Rachel *son:* 4 Levi 5 Judah 6 Reuben, Simeon 7 Zebulun 8 Issachar

leak 4 drip, ooze, seep 5 break, crack, spill 6 escape, get out, reveal, source 7 come out, divulge, seepage 8 disclose 9 discharge 10 make public

leaky 6 broken, faulty, porous 7 cracked, damaged

lea, ley 4 veld 5 field, veldt 6 fallow, meadow 7 pasture 9 grassland, pasturage

lean 3 sag, tip 4 bend, bony, cant, heel, lank, list, slim, thin, tilt 5 gaunt, lanky, shift, slant, slope, spare 6 meager, meagre, skinny, slight, wasted 7 angular, deviate, haggard, incline, pinched, scraggy, scrawny, slender, stringy, wizened 8 gradient, rawboned 9 deficient 11 inclination

Leander's beloved 4 Hero

Leaning Tower site 4 Pisa

lean-to 3 hut 4 shed 5 shack 6 shanty 7 bivouac, shelter

leap 3 hop 4 buck, jump, loup, rise, soar 5 bound, caper, clear, mount, vault 6 ascend, gambol, hurdle, spring 7 saltate 8 capriole, surmount *ballet:* 4 jeté 9 entrechat *by a horse:* 7 gambado

Lear, King *daughter:* 5 Regan 7 Goneril 8 Cordelia *servant:* 4 Kent

learn 3 con 4 hear 5 grasp, study 6 attain, detect, master, pick up 7 acquire, catch on, discern, find out, realize, uncover, unearth 8 discover, memorize 9 ascertain, determine 10 comprehend, understand 11 stumble onto

learned 4 sage, wise 6 expert, versed 7 bookish, erudite, sapient, studied 8 abstruse, academic, cultured, educated, esoteric, highbrow, lettered, pedantic, well-read 9 recondite, scholarly 10 cultivated, scholastic 12 intellectual

learner 4 tyro 5 pupil 6 novice, rookie 7 student, trainee 8 beginner, disciple, initiate, neophyte 9 greenhorn, postulant 10 apprentice, catechumen 11 abecedarian

learning 4 lore 6 wisdom 7 science, tuition 8 booklore, pedantry 9 education, erudition, knowledge 11 scholarship *person of:* 7 egghead, scholar 9 professor 12 intellectual

lease 3 let 4 hire, rent 6 sublet 7 charter, compact 8 contract, covenant, document 11 continuance

leash 3 tie 4 bind, cord, curb, rein, rope 5 strap 6 bridle, fetter, hamper, tether 7 shackle, trammel 8 restrain 9 entrammel

least 6 fewest 7 minimal, minimum 8 smallest

leather 3 tan 4 hide, skin, whip 6 thrash *kind:* 3 kid, kip, oak 4 bock, buff, calf, roan 5 crown, grain, mocha, strap, suede, whang 6 castor, latigo, oxhide, patent, roller, saddle, skiver 7 buffalo, chamois, morocco, ostrich, peccary 8 capeskin, cordovan, cordwain, shagreen *maker:* 5 tawer 6 tanner 7 tannery *piece:* 4 welt 5 strap, thong *prepare:* 3 tan, taw 5 curry *soft:* 5 mocha, suede 8 cabretta

leatherneck 6 marine

Leatherstocking Tales, The *author:* 6 Cooper (James Fenimore) *hero:* 5 Natty (Bumppo) *title:* 7 Prairie (The) 8 Pioneers (The) 10 Deerslayer (The), Pathfinder (The) 17 Last of the Mohicans (The)

leave 3 fly, let 4 blow, cede, exit, flee, move, part, quit, will 5 allow, scram, split 6 assent, assign, beat it, commit, cut out, decamp, depart, desert, devise, escape, get off, legate, permit, resign, retire, set out, vacate 7 abandon, abscond, absence, consent, consign, entrust, forsake, get away, liberty, pull out, take off, vamoose 8 bequeath, clear out, farewell, furlough, hand down, transmit, vacation, withdraw 9 departure, disappear, surrender, terminate 10 permission, relinquish, sabbatical 13 authorization

leaved 5 green 7 foliate, verdant 8 foliated

leaven 5 imbue, steep, yeast 6 infuse, invest, modify, temper, vivify 7 enliven,

ingrain, lighten, suffuse **8** moderate **9** alleviate, inoculate, sourdough **12** baking powder
leave of absence 8 furlough
leave off 3 end **4** halt, quit, stop **5** cease **6** desist, give up **7** abstain **8** give over, surcease **9** terminate **11** discontinue
leave out 4 omit, skip **5** elide **7** exclude
Leaves of Grass author **7** Whitman (Walt)
leavings 4 lees, orts, rest **5** dregs, scrap **6** debris, grouts **7** balance, remains, remnant, residue, rubbish **8** discards, oddments, remnants, residual, residuum **9** fragments, leftovers, remainder
Lebanon capital: **6** Beirut city: **4** Tyre **5** Sidon **6** Zahlah **7** Tripoli language: **6** Arabic, French monetary unit: **5** pound mountain: **6** Hermon neighbor: **5** Syria **6** Israel river: **6** Litani **7** Orontes sea: **13** Mediterranean valley: **5** Bekáa
Le Carré, John character: **6** Smiley (George) novel: **11** Russia House (The) **17** Little Drummer Girl (The) **22** Tinker, Tailor, Soldier, Spy **23** Spy Who Came in from the Cold (The)
lecher 4 rake, roué, wolf **7** Don Juan, seducer **8** Casanova, lothario **9** debauchee, reprobate, libertine, womanizer **10** degenerate, profligate, voluptuary **11** philanderer
lecherous 4 lewd **5** bawdy, loose, randy **6** carnal, coarse, rakish, wanton **7** fleshly, goatish, immoral, lustful, satyric **8** depraved, prurient, scabrous **9** debauched, libertine, lickerish, salacious **10** lascivious, libidinous, licentious, lubricious, profligate **11** promiscuous **12** concupiscent
lectern 4 desk **5** stand **6** podium
lecture 4 talk **5** chide, scold, speak **6** berate, preach, rebuke, sermon, speech **7** address, declaim, expound, oration, reproof, reprove, upbraid **8** admonish, briefing, harangue, scolding **9** chalk talk, criticism, criticize, discourse, hold forth, reprimand, talking-to **10** allocution **12** disquisition, dressing-down
lecturer 3 don **6** docent, fellow, master, orator, reader **7** scholar, speaker, teacher, trainer **9** pedagogue, preceptor, professor **10** instructor **11** academician
Leda daughter: **5** Helen **12** Clytemnestra father: **8** Thestius husband: **9** Tyndareus lover: **4** swan, Zeus son: **6** Castor, Pollux
ledge 3 bar, rim **4** berm, lode, reef, sill, vein **5** bench, ridge, shelf **6** mantle **7** bedrock, molding **10** projection

ledger 4 book **5** tally **6** record **7** account, balance **8** register **9** reckoning
lee 5 haven **7** shelter **9** protected, sheltered
leech 4 milk, worm **5** bleed, drain **6** sponge, sucker **7** exhaust, sponger **8** barnacle, hanger-on, parasite **10** freeloader **11** bloodsucker **12** lounge lizard
leer 3 eye **4** ogle **5** fleer, gloat, smirk, sneer, stare **6** glance, goggle, squint **7** grimace
leery 4 wary **5** chary **6** unsure **7** dubious, guarded **8** cautious, doubtful, doubting **10** suspicious **11** circumspect, distrustful, mistrustful
lees 5 dregs **6** grouts, refuse **7** deposit, grounds, residue **8** leavings, residual, residuum, sediment **9** settlings **11** precipitate
leeward 8 downwind opposite: **8** windward
leeway 4 play, room **5** scope, space **6** margin **7** breadth, compass, freedom, liberty **8** latitude **9** elbowroom, tolerance
left 4 port **7** liberal, radical **8** departed, deserted, larboard, residual, sinister **9** abandoned, discarded, remaining, sinistral
left-handed 5 inept **6** clumsy, gauche **7** awkward, dubious **8** fumbling, southpaw **9** ambiguous, equivocal, insincere, maladroit **10** morganatic
left-hand page 5 verso
leftover 5 extra, spare **6** excess, unused **7** remnant, reserve, residue, surplus, uneaten, vestige **8** residual, unneeded **9** redundant, remainder, remaining **10** unconsumed **11** superfluous
leftovers see LEAVINGS
leftward 4 levo **5** aport go: **3** haw
leg 3 gam **4** limb **5** shank **7** support, upright **8** cabriole **9** appendage, drumstick bone: **4** shin **5** femur, tibia **6** fibula **7** patella part: **4** calf, crus, foot, knee, shin **5** ankle, thigh
legacy 4 gift **5** trust **6** devise, estate **7** bequest **8** heirloom, heritage **9** endowment, patrimony, tradition **10** birthright **11** benefaction, inheritance
legal 5 legit, licit **6** lawful **7** allowed **8** innocent **9** juridical, statutory **10** legitimate, sanctioned matter: **3** res **4** case, suit order: **4** writ **7** summons **8** subpoena party: **6** suitor **8** litigant **9** defendant, plaintiff restraint: **8** estoppel
legal tender 3 wad **4** cash **5** bread, dough, money, moola, notes **6** moolah, specie **7** coinage **8** banknote, currency **9** long green

legate 4 will 5 endow, envoy, grant, leave 6 bestow, commit, devise, deputy, devise, pass on 7 entrust, leave to 8 bequeath, delegate, emissary, hand down, transmit 10 ambassador
legatee 4 heir 7 devisee 9 inheritor
legato 5 fluid 6 smooth 7 flowing
legend 3 key 4 lore, myth, saga, tale, yarn 5 fable, motto, story 6 mythos 7 caption, fiction 8 epigraph, folklore, folktale 9 mythology, tradition 11 inscription
legendary 5 famed 6 fabled, famous, mythic 7 fabular, fancied, fictive, storied 8 fabulous, mythical, renowned, supposed 9 well-known 10 apocryphal, celebrated 11 illustrious, traditional 12 mythological
legerdemain 5 magic 8 trickery 9 chicanery, conjuring, deception 13 sleight of hand
leggings 5 chaps 7 puttees 9 gambadoes
leghorn 3 hat 4 fowl 5 straw 7 chicken
legible 5 clear 8 distinct, readable 12 decipherable, intelligible
legion 4 army, host, many, mass, rout 5 cloud, crowd, drove, flock, horde 6 myriad, scores, sundry, throng 7 phalanx, various 8 numerous, populous 9 countless, multitude 10 numberless
legislate 5 enact, order 6 codify, decree, ordain, permit, ratify 7 empower, mandate 8 legalize, regulate, sanction 9 establish
legislation 3 act, law 4 acts, bill, code, laws 5 bills, codes, rules 6 edicts 7 statute 8 charters, dictates, statutes 9 enactment, lawmaking 10 enactments, ordinances, regulation 11 regulations 12 codification
legislator 5 solon 7 senator 8 alderman, lawgiver, lawmaker 10 councilman 11 assemblyman, congressman
legislature 4 diet 5 house, junta 6 senate 7 council 8 assembly, congress 10 parliament *Communist:* 6 soviet 9 politburo, presidium *czarist Russian:* 4 duma *Danish:* 9 Folketing *Finnish:* 9 Eduskunta *German:* 9 Bundesrat, Bundestag *Iceland:* 7 Althing *Israel:* 7 Knesset *Norway:* 8 Storting *one-house:* 10 unicameral *Poland:* 4 Sejm *Spain:* 6 Cortes *Sweden:* 7 Riksdag *two-house:* 9 bicameral
legitimate 4 fair, just, true 5 legal, licit, sound, usual, valid 6 kosher, lawful, normal, proper 7 genuine, regular, typical 8 accepted, innocent, orthodox, rightful 9 allowable, authentic, canonical, customary 10 admissable, autho-

rized, reasonable, recognized 11 justifiable, well-founded
Le Guin novel 7 Telling (The) 18 Left Hand of Darkness (The)
legume 3 pea, pod 4 bean, guar, seed 5 pulse 6 clover, lentil 7 soybean
leg up 3 aid 4 edge, lift 5 boost 6 assist 9 advantage, head start
lei 6 wreath 7 garland 8 necklace
Leibniz's invention 8 calculus
Leif Eriksson *discovery:* 7 Vinland *father:* 4 Eric, Erik (the Red)
leisure 4 ease, rest, time 6 casual, chance, repose 7 freedom, liberty 10 relaxation 11 opportunity
leisurely 4 easy, slow 6 lazily, slowly 7 relaxed, restful 8 laid-back 9 unhurried
leitmotiv 4 idea 5 theme, topic 6 burden, motive, thesis 7 subject
lemma 5 bract, theme 7 heading, premise, theorem 8 argument 11 proposition
lemon 3 dud 4 bomb, bust, flop 5 fruit, loser, scent 6 flavor, yellow 7 failure
lemur 5 indri, loris, potto 6 aye-aye, colugo, galago 7 tarsier 8 bush baby
lend 4 give, loan 5 allow, grant 6 afford, oblige, supply 7 advance, furnish, provide 11 accommodate
length 4 span 5 ambit, range, reach, realm, scope 6 extent, radius 7 compass, expanse, measure, purview, section, stretch, yardage 8 distance, duration
lengthen 6 expand, extend, let out 7 draw out, prolong, spin out, stretch 8 elongate, increase, protract 9 string out *Scottish:* 3 eke
lengthy 4 long 8 dragging, drawn-out, extended, overlong 9 elongated, prolonged 10 long-winded, protracted, voluminous 12 interminable
leniency 5 mercy 7 quarter 8 clemency 9 tolerance 10 indulgence, toleration 11 forbearance
lenient 4 easy, kind, mild, soft 6 benign, gentle, kindly 7 amiable, clement 8 merciful, obliging, tolerant 9 benignant, forgiving, indulgent 10 forbearing, permissive
lenity 5 mercy 7 quarter 8 clemency 9 tolerance 10 humaneness, indulgence 11 forbearance
lens 5 glass 6 lentil 8 meniscus *kind:* 5 toric 6 convex 7 bifocal, concave 8 trifocal
lento 4 slow 5 tempo
Leofric's wife 6 Godiva
Leoncavallo opera 9 Pagliacci (I) 10 Chatterton
leonine 8 lionlike

Leonora 7 heroine *alias:* 7 Fidelio *husband:* 9 Florestan
leopard 3 cat **4** pard **5** ounce **7** panther
leper 6 pariah **7** Ishmael, outcast **8** castaway, derelict **9** incurable **10** Ishmaelite **11** untouchable
Leper Priest 6 Damien (Father)
lepers' hospital 9 lazaretto
lepers' island 7 Molokai
lepidoptera 5 moths **8** skippers **11** butterflies **12** caterpillars
Leporello's master 11 Don Giovanni
leprechaun 3 elf **5** dwarf, fairy **6** sprite **7** brownie *trade:* **8** cobbling
Lesage hero 7 Gil Blas
Lesbos poet 6 Sappho **7** Alcaeus
___ **LeShan 3** Eda
lesion 3 cut **4** boil, flaw, harm, sore **5** ulcer, wound **6** injury **7** blister
Lesotho *capital:* **6** Maseru *ethnic group:* **5** Sotho *former name:* **10** Basutoland *language:* **5** Sotho *monetary unit:* **4** loti *mountain:* **9** Ntlenyana *neighbor:* **11** South Africa *river:* **6** Orange **7** Caledon
lessen 3 cut **4** clip, crop, ease, thin, wane **5** abate, erode, lower, taper **6** dilute, impair, minify, recede, reduce, shrink, weaken **7** abridge, assuage, curtail, degrade, dwindle, lighten, relieve, subside **8** decrease, diminish, minimize, mitigate, taper off **9** attenuate
lessening 4 drop, fall **5** letup **8** decrease, slowdown **9** abatement, reduction **10** curtailing, diminution **11** degradation
lesser 5 lower, minor **7** smaller **8** inferior **9** secondary, small-time, subjacent **11** minor-league, subordinate **13** insignificant
lesson 4 text **5** chide, moral, study **6** rebuke **7** example, lecture, reading, reprove, warning **8** admonish, exercise, homework, reproach **9** reprimand **10** admonition, assignment **11** instruction
lessor 8 landlady, landlord **9** landowner **10** freeholder
let 4 make, rent **5** allow, grant, lease, leave **6** assign, permit, suffer **9** authorize **11** obstruction
letdown 5 slump **7** decline, descent, failure, reverse, setback **10** anticlimax, depression, misfortune **11** frustration
let go 3 can **4** boot, fire, free, sack **5** remit **6** unhand **7** dismiss, neglect, release, set free **8** liberate **9** discharge, terminate
lethal 4 fell **5** fatal **6** deadly, mortal, poison **7** baleful, deathly **8** poisoned, virulent **9** murderous, poisonous **11** destructive, devastating
lethargic 4 dull, idle, slow **5** dopey, heavy, inert **6** draggy, supine, torpid **7** dormant, laggard, languid, passive **8** comatose, dilatory, inactive, listless, slothful, sluggish **9** apathetic, impassive **10** languorous, phlegmatic, spiritless **11** indifferent **12** hebetudinous **13** lackadaisical
lethargy 5 sloth **6** apathy, phlegm, stupor, torpor **7** inertia, languor, slumber **8** dullness, hebetude, idleness, laziness **9** disregard, inanition, indolence, inertness, lassitude, torpidity **10** inactivity, supineness **11** impassivity, passiveness **12** listlessness
lethe 7 amnesia **8** oblivion **13** forgetfulness
Leto see LATONA
let off 5 spare **6** excuse, exempt **7** absolve, relieve **8** dispense **9** discharge
let on 3 own **5** admit, allow, grant, own up, spill **6** betray, fess up, reveal **7** concede, confess, confirm, divulge, pretend **8** disclose, give away
let out 5 blurt, loose **6** exhale **7** release, set free, unloose **8** lengthen, liberate, set loose **9** discharge, turn loose
letter 3 bee, cee, cue, dee, ess, gee, jay, kay, pee, tee, vee, wye, zed, zee **4** line, mail, memo, note, rune **5** aitch, print, vowel **6** report, screed, symbol **7** epistle, message, missive **8** dispatch, inscribe **9** consonant *airmail:* **8** aerogram *Anglo-Saxon:* (see ANGLO-SAXON) *Arabic:* (see ALPHABET) *Greek:* (see ALPHABET) *Hebrew:* (see ALPHABET) *kind:* **5** chain, roman **6** italic, uncial **8** Dear John *large:* **7** capital **9** majuscule, uppercase *small:* **9** lowercase, minuscule
lettuce 3 cos **4** Bibb, head **6** Boston **7** iceberg, romaine, Simpson **10** butterweed
let up 3 ebb **4** fall, stop, wane **5** abate, cease **6** lessen, relent **7** die away, die down, ease off, slacken, subside **8** decrease, diminish, moderate, taper off
letup 4 lull **5** break, pause **7** respite **9** abatement, cessation, lessening, reduction **10** slackening
levee 4 dike, dock, pier, quay **5** jetty, ridge, wharf **7** seawall **8** assembly, function **9** reception **10** breakwater, embankment, riverfront
level 3 aim, lay, par **4** calm, even, flat, raze, same, tier **5** equal, floor, flush, grade, plane **6** direct, ground, smooth, status, steady **7** aligned, flatten, mow down **8** balanced, bulldoze, demolish,

equalize, parallel, smoothen, standing
9 bring down, intensity, knock down,
magnitude 10 equivalent, horizontal,
reasonable 11 equilibrium
lever 3 bar, pry 4 jack, tool 5 jimmy,
peavy, prize 6 peavey, tappet 7 crowbar
leverage 5 clout, power 7 exploit
9 advantage, dominance, influence
11 superiority 13 effectiveness
leveret 4 hare
Levi *father:* 5 Jacob *mother:* 4 Leah *son:*
6 Kohath, Merari 7 Gershon
leviathan 4 huge 5 giant, jumbo, large,
titan, whale 7 Goliath, immense, mammoth, massive, monster, titanic 8 behemoth, colossal, colossus, enormous,
gigantic 9 cyclopean, monstrous 10 formidable, gargantuan 11 elephantine,
monstrosity
Leviathan author 6 Hobbes (Thomas)
levitate 4 lift, rise 5 float, raise 7 elevate,
suspend
levity 5 folly, humor 8 buoyancy
9 absurdity, flippancy, frivolity, giddiness, lightness, silliness 10 jocularity,
volatility
levy 3 tax 4 duty, toll, wage 5 exact, lay
on 6 assess, charge, custom, enlist,
impose, impost, tariff 7 carry on, collect 9 conscript 10 assessment, enlistment 12 conscription
lewd 5 bawdy, gross 6 coarse, ribald,
smutty, vulgar 7 fleshly, goatish, lustful, obscene, satyric 8 depraved,
improper, indecent, prurient, unchaste
9 debauched, lecherous, libertine, lickerish, salacious 10 indelicate, lasciv-
ous, libidinous, licentious, lubricious
Lewis and Clark interpreter 9 Sacagawea
Lewis novel 7 Babbitt 9 Dodsworth
10 Arrowsmith, Main Street 11 Elmer
Gantry
Lewis work 18 Chronicles of Narnia
(The)
lexicographer 8 compiler *American:*
6 Porter (Noah) 7 Webster (Noah)
9 Worcester (Joseph) *English:* 4 Wyld
(Henry) 6 Fowler (Francis, Henry),
Murray (James), Onions (Charles)
7 Craigie (William), Johnson (Samuel)
9 Partridge (Eric) *French:* 6 Littré
(Paul-Emile) 8 Larousse (Pierre) *German:* 5 Grimm (Jakob, Wilhelm)
lexicon 4 cant 6 jargon 8 glossary, language, wordbook 9 inventory, word-
hoard 10 dictionary, repertoire, vocabulary 11 terminology
liable 3 apt 4 open 5 given, prone 6 likely
7 exposed, subject 8 inclined 9 sensitive
10 answerable, assailable, vulnerable
11 accountable, responsible, susceptible

liaison 4 bond, link 5 amour, fixer
6 affair, broker, hookup 7 contact,
romance 8 intrigue 9 go-between
10 connection 12 entanglement, intermediary, relationship 13 communication
liana 4 vine
liar 6 fibber 7 Ananias 8 fabulist, perjur-
er 9 falsifier 12 prevaricator *female:*
8 Sapphira
libation 5 drink 6 liquid, liquor 7 potable
8 beverage, oblation, offering, potation
libel 4 slur 5 smear 6 defame, malign,
vilify 7 asperse, calumny, obloquy,
slander, traduce 8 bad-mouth, tear
down 9 aspersion, denigrate 10 calumniate, defamation, scandalize 11 denigration
libelous 6 untrue 9 injurious, invidious,
maligning, traducing, vilifying 10 backbiting, calumnious, defamatory, dero-
gative, derogatory, detracting, detractive, malevolent, pejorative,
scandalous, slanderous
liberal 4 full, open 5 ample, broad, loose
6 lavish 7 copious, profuse, radical
8 abundant, generous, prodigal, tolerant 9 bounteous, bountiful, indulgent,
plentiful, unsparing 10 benevolent, bighearted, charitable, freehanded, munificent, openhanded, permissive,
unorthodox 11 broad-minded
liberate 4 free 5 loose 7 manumit,
release, unchain 9 discharge, unshackle
10 commandeer, emancipate 11 appropriate, expropriate
liberator 6 savior 7 messiah 9 deliverer *of
Argentina:* 9 San Martín (José de) *of
Chile:* 8 O'Higgins (Bernardo) *of
Ecuador:* 5 Sucre (Antonio José de) *of
Scotland:* 5 Bruce (Robert the) *of South
America:* 7 Bolívar (Simón)
Liberia capital: 8 Monrovia *coast:* 3 Kru
5 Grain *language:* 7 English *neighbor:*
6 Guinea 10 Ivory Coast 11 Sierra
Leone
Liberian language: 3 Kwa *native:* 3 Kru,
Vai 4 Gola, Toma 5 Bassa, Grebo
6 Kruman
libertine 4 lewd, rake, roué 5 bawdy,
loose, randy 6 carnal, rakish, wanton
7 lustful, raffish, satyric 9 debauched,
debauchee, dissolute, lecherous, salacious 10 degenerate, dissipated, lascivious, libidinous, licentious, profligate
11 promiscuous
liberty 4 risk 5 leave 6 chance 7 freedom,
license 8 autonomy 9 franchise, privilege 10 permission 11 familiarity
12 emancipation, independence
libidinous 4 lewd 5 bawdy, loose, randy

6 carnal, rakish, wanton 7 fleshly, goatish, lustful, satyric 8 depraved, prurient 9 debauched, lecherous, libertine, lickerish, salacious 10 lascivious, licentious, lubricious, profligate 11 promiscuous 12 concupiscent

librarian 5 Dewey (Melvil)

library 7 archive 8 atheneum 9 athenaeum 11 bibliotheca *desk:* 6 carrel

Libya *capital:* 7 Tripoli *city:* 8 Benghazi *desert:* 6 Sahara *gulf:* 5 Sidra *language:* 6 Arabic 7 Hamitic *leader:* 7 Gadhafi, Qaddafi (Mu'ammar) *monetary unit:* 5 dinar *neighbor:* 4 Chad 5 Egypt, Niger, Sudan 7 Algeria, Tunisia *sea:* 13 Mediterranean

lice 7 cooties

license 3 let, tag 5 allow, grant, leave 6 enable, laxity, permit, suffer, ticket 7 certify, empower, freedom, go-ahead, liberty 8 accredit, document, sanction, variance 9 authority, authorize, slackness 10 permission, profligacy 11 certificate, impropriety 12 carte blanche 13 authorization

licentious 4 lewd 5 bawdy, loose, randy 6 amoral, carnal, rakish, wanton 7 fleshly, goatish, immoral, lustful, satyric 8 depraved, prurient, scabrous 9 abandoned, debauched, dissolute, lecherous, libertine, salacious 10 lascivious, libidinous, lubricious, profligate 11 promiscuous 12 concupiscent

lichen 4 moss 6 archil, litmus 7 oakmoss *genus:* 5 Usnea

licit 4 okay 5 legal 6 lawful 7 allowed 8 approved, innocent, licensed 9 allowable, permitted 10 admissible, authorized, legitimate, sanctioned 11 permissible

lick 3 bit, dab, dig, hit, lap, rap, tan 4 beat, dash, deck, down, drub, hint, swat, whip, wipe 5 cream, pinch, pound, smack, smear, spank, taste, touch, trace, whiff 6 defeat, master, punish, thrash, tongue, wallop 7 clobber, conquer, shellac, trounce 8 lambaste, outstrip, overcome, surmount 9 overwhelm

lickerish see LIBIDINOUS

lickety-split 4 fast 5 apace 6 presto, pronto 7 flat out, hastily, quickly, rapidly, swiftly 8 chop-chop, full tilt, headlong, pell-mell, speedily 9 posthaste 13 expeditiously, precipitately

licorice 4 root 5 candy *pill:* 6 cachou

lid 3 cap, top 5 cover 8 covering *moss:* 9 operculum

lie 3 fib 4 rest, tale 5 exist, fable, libel 6 belong, canard, covert, delude,

extend, inhere, remain, repose, reside 7 consist, falsify, falsity, perjure, recline, untruth 8 misspeak, misstate 9 dissemble, falsehood, fish story, mendacity 10 inaccuracy, taradiddle 11 prevaricate 12 misstatement

Liechtenstein *capital:* 5 Vaduz *language:* 6 German *monetary unit:* 4 euro *mountain range:* 4 Alps *neighbor:* 7 Austria 11 Switzerland *river:* 5 Rhein, Rhine

lied 4 song 7 art song

lief 4 fain, soon 6 freely, gladly 7 happily, readily 9 willingly 11 contentedly

liege 4 lord, true 5 loyal 6 ardent, master, vassal 7 abiding, staunch 8 constant, enduring, faithful, reliable, resolute, stalwart 9 dedicated, steadfast 10 dependable

lien 5 claim 6 charge, demand 8 interest, mortgage 10 imposition

lieu 5 place, stead

lieutenant 4 aide 6 backup, deputy 7 officer 9 assistant, coadjutor 10 aide-de-camp, coadjutant 11 subordinate

life 3 vim 4 brio, dash, élan, soul 5 verve 6 energy, esprit, spirit 8 vitality 9 animation, existence *animal:* 5 fauna *animal and plant:* 5 biota *combining form:* 3 bio *plant:* 5 flora *relating to:* 5 vital 8 biologic 10 biological *science:* 7 biology

life jacket 7 Mae West

lifeless 4 dead, drab, dull 5 inert 6 asleep, barren, torpid, wasted 7 defunct, extinct 8 comatose, deceased, departed 9 inanimate, inorganic, insensate 10 lackluster

lifelike 5 exact 7 natural, precise 8 accurate, faithful, veristic 9 realistic

life of ___ 5 Riley 8 the party

Life with Father *author* 3 Day (Clarence)

lift 4 heft, hike, jack, load, rear, rise 5 boost, exalt, filch, heave, hoist, pinch, raise, steal, swipe, theft 6 assist, pick up, pilfer, repeal, revoke, snitch, take up 7 elevate, purloin, rescind, reverse, support 8 levitate, stealing, thievery 10 plagiarize

lift-off 6 ascent, launch 7 takeoff 9 launching

ligament 3 tie 4 band, bond, link, yoke 5 nexus 8 ligature, vinculum 10 connection

ligature see LIGAMENT

Ligeia *author* 3 Poe (Edgar Allan)

light 4 airy, dawn, deft, easy, fair, fire, lamp, land, luck, neon 5 blond, flash, minor, perch, roost, sunny, torch 6 beacon, blithe, bright, candle, casual, facile, flimsy, fluffy, ignite, kindle, settle, simple, slight, strobe 7 lantern, sunrise, trivial **8** cheerful, daybreak, enkindle, illumine, luminous, trifling **9** frivolous, touch down **10** chandelier, effortless, illuminate *combining form:* **4** luci, phos, phot **5** lumin, photo **6** lumini, lumino *measure:* **3** lux **4** phot **5** lumen **6** candle **7** candela *refractor:* **5** prism *relating to:* **6** photic *ring:* **4** halo **6** corona **7** aureola, aureole *science:* **6** optics *source:* **3** sun **4** lamp

light-emitting 6 lucent **7** fulgent, lambent, shining **8** luminous **9** effulgent, refulgent

lighten 4 dawn, ease, fade **5** allay, cheer **6** bleach, lessen, reduce **7** assuage, gladden, hearten, mollify, relieve **8** decrease, mitigate, unburden **9** alleviate, attenuate, extenuate **11** disencumber

light-headed 5 dizzy, faint, giddy, silly **6** swimmy **7** flighty **9** frivolous, slaphappy **10** unbalanced **11** disoriented, vertiginous

lighthearted 3 gay **4** glad **5** happy, jolly, merry, sunny **6** blithe, jocund, jovial, joyful, joyous, lively, upbeat **7** buoyant, festive, gleeful, playful, winsome **8** carefree, cheerful, mirthful, spirited, volatile **9** easygoing, expansive, resilient, sprightly, vivacious **10** blithesome, insouciant **12** effervescent, happy-go-lucky, high-spirited

lighthouse 6 beacon **7** warning

lightless 4 dark **5** unlit **7** aphotic, stygian **9** tenebrous, pitch-dark **10** caliginous, pitch-black **11** unillumined

lightness 6 bounce, gaiety, levity **8** buoyancy, vivacity **9** animation, frivolity **10** cheeriness, liveliness, resiliency, volatility **12** cheerfulness **13** effervescence

lightning bug 7 firefly

lignite 4 coal **9** brown coal

likable 4 nice **6** genial **7** affable, amiable, popular, winning, winsome **8** charming, engaging, friendly, pleasant, pleasing **9** agreeable, appealing, congenial **10** attractive, personable **11** good-natured

like 3 à la, dig **4** akin, same, such **5** close, enjoy, equal, match **6** admire, agnate, allied, prefer, relish **7** approve, cognate, kindred, related, similar, uniform **8** parallel, selfsame **9** analogous, consonant, identical **10** appreciate, comparable, comprehend, equivalent, resembling

likelihood 6 chance **8** prospect **11** eventuality, possibility, presumption, probability

likely 3 apt **5** given, prone **6** liable, odds-on **7** assumed **8** credible, inclined, possible, presumed, probable, probably, reliable, suitable **9** doubtless, plausible, promising **10** achievable, attractive, believable, presumably

liken 5 match **6** equate **7** compare **8** parallel **10** assimilate

likeness 4 copy, twin **5** clone, image **6** double, effigy **7** analogy, picture, replica **8** affinity, portrait, sameness **9** depiction, facsimile, look-alike, semblance **10** appearance, photograph, similarity, similitude, uniformity **11** resemblance

likewise 3 and, too **4** also **6** as well, withal **7** besides **8** moreover **9** similarly **10** in addition **11** furthermore

liking 4 bent **5** fancy, taste **6** desire **8** affinity, appetite, fondness, penchant, pleasure, soft spot, weakness **9** affection **10** attraction, partiality **11** inclination **12** appreciation, predilection

Lilith *husband:* **4** Adam *successor:* **3** Eve

lilliputian 3 wee **4** runt, tiny **5** dwarf, petty, pygmy, small **6** bantam, little, midget, peanut, peewee, shrimp **7** manikin **8** pint-size, Tom Thumb **9** miniature, pint-sized, undersize **10** diminutive, homunculus

lilt 3 air **4** flow, purl, sing, song, tune **5** carol, pulse, swing, tempo **6** melody, rhythm **7** cadence **8** buoyancy

lily 3 pad **4** aloe, sego **5** calla, tiger, yucca **6** flower **7** leopard **8** mariposa

lily-livered 5 sissy, wimpy **6** craven, yellow **7** caitiff, chicken, fearful, gutless **8** cowardly, cowering, poltroon, recreant, timorous **9** spineless, spunkless, weak-kneed **12** fainthearted, poor-spirited **13** pusillanimous

lily-white 4 pure **7** upright **8** innocent, virtuous **9** blameless, estimable, exclusive, exemplary, guiltless, righteous, untainted **10** inculpable **11** uncorrupted

limb 3 arm, fin, gam, leg **4** lobe, twig, wing **5** bough, shoot, spray, sprig **6** branch, member, pinion **7** flipper **8** offshoot **9** appendage, dismember, extremity

limber 4 spry **5** agile, lithe, loose **6** nimble, pliant, supple **7** elastic, lissome, pliable, springy **8** flexible **9** lithesome, resilient

limbo 5 dance **7** neglect **8** oblivion **9** detention, purgatory **11** confinement, uncertainty

lime 4 tree **5** color, fruit, green **6** citrus, linden **7** calcium

limen 8 doorsill, doorstep **9** threshold

limerick 4 poem **5** verse *writer:* **4** Lear (Edward)

limestone 4 tufa, tuff **5** chalk **6** marble, oolite **7** coquina **10** travertine

lime tree 6 linden

limit 3 bar, cap, end, fix, set **4** curb **5** check, quota **6** border, bounds, curfew, define, extent, hinder, lessen **7** confine, curtail, enclose, extreme, mark out, measure **8** boundary, deadline, restrain, restrict **9** constrict, demarcate, determine, extremity, prescribe **12** circumscribe

limitless 4 vast **7** endless **8** infinite, wide-open **9** boundless, unbounded **10** indefinite **11** illimitable, innumerable, measureless **12** immeasurable, incalculable **13** inexhaustible

limn 4 draw **5** image, paint **6** depict, render, sketch **7** outline, picture, portray **8** describe **9** delineate, interpret, represent

Limoges product 9 porcelain

limp 3 lax **4** bent, halt, lame, wilt **5** hitch, loose, slack, spent, weary **6** dodder, droopy, falter, hobble **7** flaccid, languid, shamble, shuffle, slumped **8** drooping **9** enervated, exhausted **10** spiritless

limpid 4 pure **5** clear, lucid **6** glassy, serene **8** pellucid **10** see-through, untroubled **11** crystalline, translucent, transparent, unambiguous **12** crystal clear

limping 4 halt, lame **5** gimpy **7** halting **8** hobbling, lameness **9** faltering **12** claudication

linchpin 8 backbone, mainstay

Lincoln *assassin:* **5** Booth (John Wilkes) *biographer:* **8** Sandburg (Carl) *debater:* **7** Douglas (Stephen) *law partner:* **7** Herndon (William) *mother:* **5** Nancy (Hanks) *nickname:* **9** Honest Abe **12** Railsplitter *photographer:* **5** Brady (Mathew) *secretary of state:* **6** Seward (William) *secretary of war:* **7** Stanton (Edwin) *wife:* **8** Mary Todd

line 3 row **4** file, rank, rope **5** array, goods, queue, route **6** border, column, series, strain, string **7** contour, descent **8** business, pedigree, sequence **10** employment, occupation, succession *curved:* **3** arc *mathematical:* **6** vector *metrical:* **5** verse **6** verset **8** versicle *weather map:* **6** isobar

lineage 3 kin **4** clan, folk, race **5** birth, blood, breed, house, stirp, stock, tribe **6** family, origin, strain **7** descent, kindred **8** ancestry, breeding, pedigree **9** forebears, genealogy **10** derivation, extraction, succession **11** forefathers, progenitors

lineal 6 direct **8** familial **9** ancestral, inherited **10** bequeathed, hereditary

lineament 4 form **6** figure, relief **7** contour, feature, outline, profile **10** figuration, silhouette

lined 5 drawn, ruled **7** aligned, striate, striped **8** streaked, wrinkled

linen 4 lawn **5** cloth, toile **6** byssus, damask, fabric, napery, sheets **7** batiste, bedding, cambric, taffeta **8** cretonne, lingerie *fiber:* **3** tow *source:* **4** flax

linger 3 lag **4** bide, drag, loll, mope, poke, stay, wait **5** abide, dally, delay, mosey, tarry **6** dawdle, loiter, put off, remain **7** saunter **10** dillydally **11** stick around **13** procrastinate

lingerie 8 negligee

lingo 4 cant **5** argot, idiom, slang **6** jargon, patois, patter, speech, tongue **7** dialect **10** vernacular, vocabulary

linguist 8 polyglot **11** philologist

linguistics 9 philology

liniment 3 oil **4** aloe, balm **5** salve **6** lotion **7** anodyne, unction, unguent **8** aloe vera, lenitive, ointment **9** demulcent **11** embrocation

lining 6 facing, insert **8** wainscot

link 3 tie **4** bind, bond, join, knot, ring, yoke **5** hitch, nexus, unite **6** attach, copula, couple, hookup, relate, splice **7** bracket, combine, conjoin, connect, contact, joining **8** catenate, division, vinculum **9** associate, conjugate **10** attachment, connection **11** association **12** relationship

linksman 6 golfer

linnet 5 finch

lint 3 fur, nap **4** down, fuzz, pile **5** floss, fluff **9** ravelings

lion 3 cat **4** puma **6** cougar **7** notable **8** eminence, luminary **9** carnivore, personage *group:* **5** pride *young:* **3** cub

lionhearted 4 bold **5** brave **6** heroic **7** valiant **8** fearless, intrepid, stalwart, unafraid, valorous **9** dauntless **10** courageous

lionize 4 fete **5** exalt, extol, honor **7** glorify **8** venerate **9** celebrate

lion monkey 7 tamarin **8** marmoset

Lion of Judah 8 Selassie (Haile)

lip 3 rim **4** brim, edge, guff, sass **6** labium, labrum, margin **8** back talk *relating to:* **6** labial

lipid 3 fat, wax

lipped 7 labiate **9** bilabiate

liquefy 3 run **4** flux, melt, thaw **5** smelt **6** render **8** dissolve **10** deliquesce

liqueur 4 arak, ouzo, raki **5** crème **6** brandy, Kahlua, kirsch, kummel, pastis, Pernod **7** cordial, curaçao,

ratafia, sambuca, sloe gin **8** absinthe, amaretto, anisette, Drambuie, Galliano **10** Chartreuse, pousse-café
liquid 5 drink, fluid, sauce, water **6** watery **7** flowing **8** beverage, emulsion **11** mellifluous *container:* **3** cup, jug, keg, mug **4** vial **5** glass **6** bottle, goblet **7** pitcher, tumbler *flammable:* **3** gas, oil **5** ether, furan **6** butane, toluol **7** alcohol, toluene **8** gasoline, pyridine *measure:* **3** cup, gal **4** pint **5** liter, ounce, quart **6** gallon *thick:* **5** syrup **8** molasses
liquidate 3 pay **4** do in, kill **5** pay up, purge **6** murder, remove, rub out, settle, square **7** bump off, convert, gun down, satisfy **8** amortize, dispatch, dissolve, knock off **9** eliminate, terminate **10** annihilate **11** assassinate
liquor 5 booze, drink, hooch **7** alcohol, potable, spirits **8** potation **9** firewater, inebriant **10** intoxicant *add:* **4** lace **5** spike *Asian:* **4** arak **6** arrack *homemade:* **9** moonshine **10** bathtub gin *inferior:* **5** hooch **6** red-eye, rotgut *Japanese:* **4** sake, saki *kind:* **3** gin, rum, rye **5** vodka **6** brandy, geneva, scotch **7** aquavit, bourbon, schnaps, whiskey **8** schnapps, vermouth **9** aqua vitae **10** barley-bree *malt:* **3** ale **4** beer **5** nappy, stout **6** porter *measure:* **4** dram, shot **6** jigger **7** shooter *Mexican:* **5** sotol **6** mescal **7** tequila
lissome 5 agile, lithe **6** limber, nimble, supple, svelte **7** slender **8** flexible, graceful
list 3 tip **4** book, cant, file, heel, lean, menu, note, post, roll, tilt **5** arena, count, index, slant, slate, slope, tally **6** agenda, census, docket, lineup, record, roster **7** catalog, incline, itemize, specify **8** calendar, glossary, manifest, register, roll call, schedule, tabulate **9** chronicle, enumerate, inventory **13** particularize
listen 4 hark, hear, heed, note **5** audit **6** attend, harken **7** hearken, monitor **8** overhear **9** eavesdrop
listeners 8 audience
listless 4 dull, limp, weak **5** inert, slack **6** torpid, vacant **7** languid **8** indolent, sluggish **9** apathetic, enervated, lethargic, lymphatic **10** languorous, phlegmatic, spiritless **11** indifferent, languishing **13** lackadaisical
listlessness 6 apathy, stupor, torpor **7** fatigue, inertia, languor **8** doldrums, lethargy **9** indolence, lassitude, torpidity **10** enervation
litany 4 list **5** chant **6** prayer **7** account, listing, recital, refrain **8** petition, roga-

tion **9** catalogue **10** invocation, recitation **11** enumeration **12** supplication
literal 4 bald, bare **5** blunt, exact, stark **6** actual, simple, strict **7** precise **8** accurate, bona fide, faithful, verbatim **9** authentic **11** unvarnished, word-for-word **13** unembellished
literally 5 truly **6** direct, indeed, openly, simply **7** plainly, totally, utterly **8** candidly, directly, verbatim **9** genuinely, virtually **11** word for word
literary 7 bookish, erudite, learned **8** lettered, well-read **9** authorial, scholarly **12** belletristic
literary work 4 book, opus, play, poem **5** drama, essay, novel **10** short story
literature 5 prose **6** poetry **7** fiction **13** belles-lettres
lithe 4 lean, slim **5** agile, spare **6** limber, supple, svelte **7** lissome, pliable, slender **8** flexible, graceful
lithographer 4 Ives (James Merritt) **7** Currier (Nathaniel)
Lithuania *capital:* **7** Vilnius *city:* **6** Kaunas **8** Klaipeda *monetary unit:* **5** litas *neighbor:* **6** Latvia, Poland, Russia **7** Belarus *river:* **5** Neman, Venta **7** Lielupe *sea:* **6** Baltic
litigant 4 suer **6** suitor **9** defendant, disputant, plaintiff
litigate 3 sue **6** indict **7** arraign, contest, dispute **9** prosecute
litigation 4 case, suit **7** lawsuit **11** prosecution, proceedings
litter 3 bed **4** cubs, junk **5** brood, couch, issue, strew, trash, waste, young **6** clutch, debris, refuse **7** bedding, clutter, garbage, kittens, piglets, progeny, puppies, rubbish, scatter **8** detritus **9** offspring, stretcher **10** scattering
little 3 bit, dab, toy, wee **4** dash, hint, mean, puny, tiny **5** brief, dinky, minor, petty, pinch, short, small, taste, trace, young **6** bantam, meager, meagre, minute, narrow, paltry, petite, skimpy **7** limited, trivial **8** dwarfish, slightly, smallish, trifling **9** miniature, smallbeer **10** diminutive, short-lived, undersized **11** microscopic, unimportant
Little Bighorn *state:* **7** Montana *victim:* **6** Custer (George Armstrong) *victor:* **11** Sitting Bull
little by little 6 slowly **8** inchmeal, steadily **9** gradually, piecemeal
Little Dipper *constellation:* **9** Ursa Minor *star:* **5** North **7** Polaris
Little Women *author:* **6** Alcott (Louisa May) *character:* **3** Amy, Meg **4** Beth **6** Laurie, Marmee *surname:* **5** March
littoral 5 beach, coast, shore **6** strand

7 coastal, seaside 8 seaboard, sea front, seashore 9 shoreline 10 oceanfront

liturgy 4 rite 6 ritual 7 service 8 ceremony 9 sacrament 10 ceremonial, observance, repertoire

livable 6 viable 8 adequate, bearable, passable 9 endurable, habitable, tolerable 11 inhabitable, supportable

live 4 fare, stay 5 abide, dwell, exist, vital, vivid 6 actual, reside, thrive 7 breathe, current, subsist, survive

livelihood 3 job 4 game, keep, work 5 craft, trade 7 support 8 business, vocation 10 employment, handicraft, occupation, profession, sustenance 11 subsistence

liveliness 3 pep, zip 4 brio, élan, zing 5 verve, vigor 6 energy, hustle, spirit 8 dispatch, vibrance, vibrancy, vitality, vivacity 9 animation

lively 3 gay 4 busy, keen, pert, spry, yare 5 agile, alert, brisk, fresh, jazzy, jolly, merry, peppy, zippy 6 active, bouncy, bright, chirpy, frisky, jocund, nimble 7 animate, buoyant, chipper, intense, rousing 8 animated, bustling, hustling, spirited, vigorous, volatile 9 energetic, resilient, sparkling, sprightly, vivacious 11 stimulating

liven 5 pep up 6 jazz up, vivify 7 animate, freshen, quicken 8 energize, inspirit, vitalize 10 invigorate

liver 7 denizen 8 habitant, occupant, resident 10 inhabitant *combining form:* 5 hepat 6 hepato *disease:* 9 cirrhosis, hepatitis *French:* 4 foie *lobster's:* 8 tomalley

liverwort 8 hepatica 9 bryophyte

livestock 4 cows, hogs, pigs 5 bulls, goats, sheep 6 beasts, calves, cattle 7 animals *feed:* 6 silage 8 ensilage

live wire 6 dynamo 7 hustler, rustler 8 go-getter, promoter 9 energizer, generator 11 self-starter

livid 3 hot, mad, wan 4 ashy, pale 5 ashen, lurid, waxen 6 fuming, leaden, pallid, sultry 7 boiling, bruised, enraged, furious, reddish 8 blanched, contused, incensed 9 colorless 10 discolored, infuriated 12 black-and-blue 13 beside oneself

living 5 means, vital 6 extant, income 8 animated, existent 10 livelihood, sustenance

living room 6 parlor 10 lebensraum

lizard 3 eft 4 gila, newt 5 anole, gecko, skink, teiid 6 dragon, goanna, iguana 7 monitor, reptile, saurian 8 basilisk, mosasaur, slowworm, squamate, whiptail 9 alligator, blindworm, chameleon,

crocodile 10 chuckwalla, salamander *combining form:* 4 saur 5 saura, sauro

llama 6 alpaca, vicuña 7 camelid, guanaco *country:* 4 Peru *habitat:* 5 Andes

Lloyd's business 9 insurance

lo 4 hark, heed, look, mark, mind 6 attend 7 observe

load 3 tax 4 bias, copy, fill, haul, heap, lade, onus, pack, pile, task 5 cargo, laden, swamp, weigh 6 burden, debase, doctor, dope up, eyeful, lading, saddle, weight 7 freight 8 encumber, shipment, transfer 9 liability, millstone, transport 11 consignment, encumbrance

loaded 4 full, high, rich 5 awash, doped 6 aboard, biased, filled, packed, stoned 7 boarded, brimful, crowded, wealthy 8 affluent, brimming, chockful, tripping, turned on 9 chock-full

loaf 3 bum, bun 4 idle, laze, lazy, loll 5 bread, dough 6 dawdle, lounge 7 goof off 8 lollygag 9 bum around, goldbrick 10 fool around

loafer 3 bum 4 shoe, slug 5 idler 6 slouch 7 goof-off, lounger 8 deadbeat, dolittle, fainéant, slugabed, sluggard 9 do-nothing, goldbrick, lazybones 11 beachcomber, lollygagger

loam 4 clay, dirt, sand, silt, soil 7 topsoil *deposit:* 5 loess

loan 3 pay 4 lend 6 credit 7 advance, imprest 9 grubstake

loan shark 6 lender, usurer 7 Shylock 10 pawnbroker 11 moneylender

loath 6 afraid, averse 8 hesitant 9 reluctant, unwilling 10 indisposed 11 disinclined 12 antipathetic

loathe 4 hate 5 abhor, scorn, spurn 6 detest, refuse, reject 7 despise 8 execrate 9 abominate

loathsome 4 foul, ugly, vile 5 gross, nasty 6 odious 7 beastly, hateful, hideous 8 horrible 9 abhorrent, execrable, obnoxious, offensive, repellent, repugnant, repulsive, revolting 10 abominable, deplorable, detestable, disgusting, nauseating

lob 4 loft, toss 5 chuck, fling, heave, pitch, sling, throw 6 propel

lobby 4 hall 5 foyer 7 promote 8 anteroom, corridor 9 influence, vestibule 10 passageway 11 waiting room

lobe 4 flap 7 pendant

lobo 4 wolf 8 gray wolf 10 timber wolf

lobster 8 crawfish 10 crustacean *claw:* 5 chela 6 pincer *female:* 3 hen *male:* 4 cock *trap:* 3 pot 5 creel

local 6 native 7 endemic, insular, topical 9 parochial 10 provincial

locale 4 area, belt, site, turf, ward 5 place, scene, venue 6 milieu, parish, region, sector **7** commune, quarter, setting **8** district, precinct, vicinage, vicinity **9** community, territory **11** mise-en-scène **12** neighborhood

locality 4 area, belt, city, site, turf, zone **5** block, field, haunt, place, tract **6** county, domain, hamlet, region, sector, sphere, square **7** habitat, section **8** district, environs, precinct, province, purlieus, township, vicinage, vicinity **9** bailiwick, situation, territory **12** neighborhood

localize 4 mass **5** amass, focus **7** cluster, collect **8** coalesce, pinpoint **10** accumulate **11** concentrate, consolidate **12** conglomerate

locate 3 fix, spy **4** espy, find, site, spot **5** dwell, place, trace **6** detect, reside, settle **7** nose out, situate, station, uncover **8** come upon, discover, pinpoint, position **9** establish, ferret out, search out **10** come across

location 4 area, site, post, spot **5** locus, place, point, scene, venue, where **7** bearing, habitat, setting **8** position **9** situation **11** mise-en-scène, whereabouts

loch 3 bay **4** lake

lock 4 bolt, curl, hank, hold, tuft **5** latch, tress **6** fasten, secure **7** ringlet **8** fastener **9** enclosure, fastening

lockjaw 7 tetanus, trismus

lockup 3 jug, pen **4** brig, cell, coop, jail, stir, tank **5** clink, pokey, pound **6** cooler, prison **7** slammer **8** bastille

loco 3 ape, mad **4** nuts **5** balmy, batty, crazy, kooky, loony, nutty **6** crazed, insane, screwy **7** bananas, berserk, bonkers, cracked, flipped, lunatic **8** demented, deranged, frenzied, unhinged **10** flipped out

locomotive 5 cheer, dolly, train **6** engine *small:* **5** dinky **6** dinkey *type:* **5** steam **6** diesel **8** electric

locum tenens 3 sub **5** proxy **6** backup, fill-in, supply **7** stand-in **9** alternate, auxiliary, surrogate **10** substitute **11** pinch hitter, replacement, succedaneum

locus 3 hub **4** seat, site **5** focus, heart, stage **6** center **7** setting **8** cynosure, location, polestar **10** focal point **11** nerve center **12** headquarters

locust 4 tree, wood **5** carob **6** cicada, insect **11** grasshopper

locution 4 word **5** argot, idiom, lingo **6** jargon, patois, phrase **7** dialect **8** parlance, phrasing **9** utterance **10** expression **11** phraseology

lode 4 seam, vein **5** store **6** source, supply **7** deposit

lodestar 4 guru **5** gauge, guide, ideal, model **6** beacon, leader, mentor **7** epitome **8** exemplar, paradigm **9** archetype, guidepost **11** inspiration

lodestone 6 magnet **9** magnetite

lodge 3 den, fix, inn **4** bunk, camp, club, file, lair, nest, root, stay **5** abide, abode, board, cabin, couch, dwell, embed, guild, hotel, house, motel, order, put up **6** billet, burrow, hostel, league, remain, shanty, tavern, wigwam **7** auberge, contain, cottage, deposit, hospice, quarter, receive, shelter **8** domicile, hostelry, sodality **9** gatehouse **10** fellowship **11** accommodate, brotherhood, caravansary, public house

lodger 5 guest **6** renter, roomer, tenant **7** boarder, resider

lodging 3 inn, pad **4** dorm, room **5** abode, hotel, motel, place **7** shelter **8** chambers, diggings, domicile, dwelling, quarters **9** apartment, residence **10** pied-à-terre **13** accommodation

loess 4 clay, loam, marl **7** deposit

loft 4 rise **5** attic, raise **6** dormer, garret, propel **7** gallery

loftiness 5 pride **6** height **7** disdain, hauteur, stature **8** altitude, eminence **9** aloofness, arrogance, elevation, pomposity, sublimity **11** haughtiness, superiority **13** condescension

lofty 4 airy, epic, high, tall **5** grand, noble, proud **6** aerial, august, raised, remote, superb **7** exalted, haughty, soaring, stately, sublime, utopian **8** arrogant, cavalier, elevated, eloquent, imposing, insolent, majestic, superior, towering **9** ambitious, grandiose, visionary **10** disdainful **11** overbearing, pretentious, skyscraping **12** supercilious

log 5 diary, tally **6** record, timber **7** journal **8** register *mover:* **5** peavy **6** peavey **7** cant dog

loge 3 box **5** booth, stall **7** balcony **9** mezzanine

logger 9 lumberman **10** lumberjack, woodcutter *legendary:* **10** Paul Bunyan

loggerhead 6 shrike, turtle

loggia 6 arcade **7** balcony, gallery, veranda

logic 6 reason **9** reasoning **10** syntactics *specious:* **7** sophism **9** sophistry

logical 5 sound, valid **6** cogent **8** analytic, sensible **9** deducible, deductive, plausible **10** analytical, compelling, convincing, diagnostic, reasonable, scientific, systematic

logjam 5 crowd **7** impasse **8** blockage, deadlock, stoppage **11** obstruction

logo 5 badge, brand, motto **6** cipher, device, emblem, symbol **8** colophon, hallmark, monogram **9** trademark

logogriph 6 puzzle **7** anagram

logroll 4 birl

logy 4 dull, slow **5** dopey, heavy **6** drowsy, groggy, torpid **8** listless, sluggish

Lohengrin *composer:* **6** Wagner (Richard) *father:* **8** Parsifal, Parzival *wife:* **4** Elsa

loincloth 5 dhoti **11** breechcloth, breechclout

Loire city 5 Blois, Tours **6** Nantes **7** Orléans

loiter 3 bum, lag **4** drag, idle, laze, lazy, loaf, loll, poke **5** dally, delay, tarry, trail **6** dawdle, diddle, linger, lounge, put off, putter **8** lollygag **10** dillydally, fool around, hang around **11** screw around **13** procrastinate

Loki *father:* **8** Farbauti *mother:* **3** Nal **6** Laufey *offspring:* **3** Hel **4** Hela **6** Fenris **7** Midgard *slayer:* **8** Heimdall *victim:* **6** Balder *wife:* **5** Sigyn **9** Angurboda

Lolita *author* **7** Nabokov (Vladimir)

loll 3 bum, lag **4** drag, idle, laze, lazy, loaf, poke **5** chill, dally, delay, droop, slump, tarry, trail **6** dawdle, diddle, linger, lounge, putter, slouch **8** chill out **10** dillydally, fool around, hang around **13** procrastinate

Lollards' leader 8 Wycliffe (John)

lollygag 4 idle, loaf, loll, poke, drag **6** dawdle, diddle, loiter, piddle, putter **10** dilly-dally, fool around **11** horse around **12** monkey around

Lombard 6 banker **11** moneylender *king:* **5** Cleph **6** Alboin, Audoin **7** Aistulf, Aripert, Authari **9** Liudprand

London *borough:* **5** Brent **6** Barnet, Bexley, Ealing, Harrow, Sutton **7** Barking, Bromley, Chelsea, Croydon, Enfield, Hackney, Lambeth **8** Haringey, Havering, Hounslow, Lewisham **9** Greenwich, Islington, Redbridge **10** Kensington **11** Westminster *cathedral:* **7** St. Paul's *clock:* **6** Big Ben *district:* **4** Soho **5** Acton **7** Chelsea, Mayfair **9** Belgravia, Southwark *gallery:* **4** Tate *policeman:* **5** bobby *prison:* **7** Newgate *river:* **6** Thames *square:* **9** Leicester, Trafalgar *street:* **4** Bond **5** Fleet **6** Strand **7** Downing **9** Whitehall **10** Piccadilly *subway:* **4** tube

London novel 7 Sea Wolf (The) **8** Iron Heel (The) **9** White Fang **10** Martin Eden **13** Call of the Wild (The)

lone 4 only, sole, solo **5** alone **6** single, unique **8** deserted, forsaken, isolated, secluded, separate, singular, solitary **13** unaccompanied

lonely 4 left, lorn **5** alone **7** forlorn **8** deserted, forsaken, homesick, lonesome, rejected, solitary **9** abandoned

loneness 8 solitude **9** isolation **10** detachment **12** separateness, solitariness

loner 6 hermit **7** isolate, outcast, recluse **8** outsider, solitary **13** individualist

Lone Ranger, The *creator:* **7** Striker (Fran) *companion:* **5** Tonto *horse:* **6** Silver *trademark:* **4** mask **12** silver bullet

Lone Star State 5 Texas

long 3 far, yen **4** ache, itch, lust, pine, sigh, tall **5** large, wordy, yearn **6** hanker, hunger, prolix, strong, thirst **7** endless, lengthy, tedious **8** dragging, drawn-out, extended, unending **9** extensive **10** full-length, protracted

long-drawn-out 7 endless, lengthy **8** dragging, unending **10** protracted **12** interminable

Longfellow poem 8 Christus, Hiawatha, Hyperion, Kavanagh **10** Evangeline **11** My Lost Youth, Psalm of Life (A)

long for 4 want **5** covet, crave, mourn **6** desire **8** aspire to

longing 3 yen **4** itch, lust, urge, wish **5** greed **6** desire, hunger, thirst **7** avidity, craving, passion **8** appetite

longshoreman 9 stevedore **10** roustabout

long-suffering 7 patient, stoical **8** enduring, resigned **9** compliant **10** forbearing, submissive **13** accommodating, uncomplaining

long suit 3 bag **4** gift **5** forte, thing **6** métier, talent **8** strength **9** specialty

long-winded 5 wordy **6** prolix **7** diffuse, lengthy, verbose **8** rambling **9** garrulous, redundant **10** loquacious

look 3 air, eye **4** gape, gawk, leer, mien, ogle, peek, peep, peer, seem, view **5** glare, stare, watch **6** admire, appear, aspect, behold, expect, eyeful, glance, glower, goggle, regard, squint, survey, visage **7** bearing, examine, eyeball, glimpse, observe **8** demeanor, onceover **10** appearance, expression, rubberneck **11** countenance, physiognomy

look after 4 mind, tend **5** nurse, serve, watch **8** attend, wait on **7** care for, husband **8** wait upon **9** watch over **10** provide for

look-alike 4 twin **5** clone **6** double **7** similar **8** matching **9** duplicate

look at 3 eye, see **4** face, ogle, scan, view **5** check **6** behold, ponder **7** examine, inspect **8** confront, consider **11** investigate

look back 6 recall, review **7** reflect **8** remember **9** reminisce

look down on 5 abhor, scorn, scout,

spurn **7** contemn, despise, disdain **8** dominate **9** tower over **10** tower above

looker 6 beauty, eyeful, lovely, vision **7** stunner, witness **8** knockout, ornament **9** bystander, sightseer, spectator **10** eyewitness

looker-on 5 gaper **6** viewer **7** watcher, witness **8** beholder, observer **9** bystander, spectator **10** eyewitness **12** rubbernecker

look for 4 seek **5** await **6** expect, plan on **9** search out **10** anticipate

looking glass 6 mirror **9** reflector

look into 5 check, probe, study **6** pursue, survey **7** examine, explore, inspect **8** check out, question, research **10** scrutinize **11** investigate

look out 4 mind **6** beware

lookout 4 view **5** guard, scout, tower, vista, watch **6** affair, cupola, picket, sentry **7** spotter **8** panorama, prospect, sentinel, watchman **9** belvedere, crow's nest, firetower **10** watchtower, widow's walk **11** observatory, perspective

look over 3 vet **4** read **5** check **6** review, size up **7** examine, inspect **8** appraise, evaluate

loom 4 brew, bulk, near, rear **5** hover, mount, tower **6** appear, come on, emerge, gather, impend **7** portend **8** approach, overhang, stand out, threaten **9** take shape *part:* **6** heddle **7** harness, shuttle, treadle, trundle

loon 3 nut, oaf **4** bird, clod, dodo, dolt, goof, lout, yo-yo **5** chump, dummy, dunce, ninny, noddy, stupe, yokel **6** dimwit, dum-dum, nitwit **7** airhead, buffoon, dullard, pinhead **8** bonehead, dumbbell, crackpot, imbecile, lunkhead, meathead, numskull **9** birdbrain, blockhead, ignoramus, lamebrain, numbskull, simpleton **10** dunderhead, nincompoop **11** chowderhead, chucklehead

loony 3 nut **5** balmy, batty, crazy, daffy, dippy, goofy, inane, nutty, silly, wacky **6** absurd, insane, madman, maniac, screwy **7** fatuous, foolish, idiotic, lunatic **8** demented, reckless **9** bedlamite, half-baked, ludicrous, senseless **10** ridiculous **11** harebrained **12** preposterous

loony bin 6 asylum, bedlam **8** bughouse, madhouse, nuthouse **9** funny farm **10** booby hatch, crazy house

loop 3 arc, eye **4** ring **5** curve, noose, picot **6** circle, eyelet, league, staple **7** circlet, circuit **13** circumference

looped 4 high **5** bowed, drunk, stiff **6** blotto, bombed, curved, juiced,

loaded, potted, stewed, tanked, zonked **7** crocked, pickled, pie-eyed, sloshed, smashed **9** plastered **10** inebriated **11** curvilinear, intoxicated

loophole 3 out **6** escape, outlet **7** opening

loopy 4 daft, nuts, wavy **5** arced, batty, bowed, crazy, daffy, dotty, flaky, nutty, silly, snaky, wacky **6** arched, curved, freaky, fruity, screwy, swirly **7** bizarre, idiotic, lunatic, offbeat, sinuous, touched **8** demented **9** eccentric **10** flipped out, off-the-wall, outlandish

loose 3 lax **4** easy, fast, free, lewd, limp **5** baggy, slack, vague **6** flabby, wanton **7** flaccid, relaxed **8** flexible **9** debauched, desultory, dissolute, imprecise **10** disjointed, dissipated, illdefined, licentious, unattached, unconfined **12** disconnected, unrestrained

loose end 6 detail **8** fragment

loose-lipped see LOQUACIOUS

loosen 4 ease, free, undo **5** relax, slack, untie **6** unbind **7** ease off, manumit, release, slacken, unchain **8** liberate, unbuckle, unfasten **10** emancipate

loosen up 5 relax **6** unbend, unwind **7** ease off, stretch

loot 3 rob **4** haul, lift, pelf, raid, sack, swag **5** boost, booty, dough, lucre, money, moola, reave, rifle, spoil **6** boodle, moolah, ravish, spoils **7** despoil, pillage, plunder, ransack, stick up **9** knock over

looter 5 thief **7** brigand **8** marauder

lop 3 cut **4** chop, clip, crop, trim **5** prune, sever **6** excise **8** amputate, truncate **9** dismember **10** guillotine

lope 3 jog, run **4** gait, romp, trot **5** amble **6** canter

lopsided 4 awry **5** askew **6** uneven **7** crooked, leaning, tilting **8** top-heavy **10** asymmetric, off-balance, unbalanced **12** asymmetrical **13** unsymmetrical

loquacious 5 gabby, talky, wordy **6** chatty, mouthy, prolix **7** verbose, voluble, yakking **8** babbling **9** garrulous, jabbering, talkative **10** blathering, chattering, long-winded **11** loose-lipped **12** motormouthed

lord 3 sir **4** boss, duke, earl, peer **5** noble, ruler **6** master **7** marquis **8** governor, marquess, nobleman, viscount **9** sovereign, tyrannize *feudal:* **5** liege **8** seigneur, suzerain *Muslim:* **6** sayyid

Lord High Executioner 4 Koko

Lord Jim author 6 Conrad (Joseph)

lordly 5 grand, lofty, noble, proud **6** august, uppity **7** exalted, haughty, pompous, stately, swollen **8** affected, arrogant, cavalier, gracious, imposing, insolent, majestic, princely, snobbish, superior **9** dignified, egotistic, grandiose **10** disdainful, high-handed **11** dictatorial, magisterial, magnificent, overbearing, patronizing **12** aristocratic, supercilious **13** authoritarian, high-and-mighty

Lord of the Flies *author:* **7** Golding (William) *character:* **4** Jack **5** Piggy, Ralph

Lord's Prayer 9 Our Father **11** Paternoster

lore 6 mythos, wisdom **7** history **8** folkways, learning **9** knowledge, mythology, tradition **11** information **12** superstition

Lorelei 5 siren **9** temptress **10** seductress **11** femme fatale *poet:* **5** Heine (Heinrich) *river:* **5** Rhein, Rhine *victim:* **6** sailor **7** mariner

lorgnette 10 eyeglasses, spectacles **12** opera glasses

Lorna Doone *author:* **9** Blackmore (Richard) *hero:* **4** Ridd (John)

___ **Lorraine 6** Alsace

lorry 3 rig, van **4** semi **5** truck

lose 4 miss **5** evade, shake, waste, yield **6** escape, give up, mislay **7** destroy, forfeit, succumb **8** misplace, shake off, throw off **9** sacrifice, surrender

lose it 7 crack up, flip out, go crazy **8** freak out

loser 3 dud **4** bomb, bust, flop **5** lemon **6** bummer, fiasco, misfit, turkey **7** also-ran, debacle, failure, washout **8** deadbeat **11** incompetent

loss 4 harm, ruin **5** waste **6** damage, defeat, injury **7** deficit, failure, forfeit **8** casualty, decrease, fatality **9** depletion, privation, sacrifice, shrinkage **10** divestment, forfeiture, misfortune, misplacing **11** bereavement, deprivation, destruction **13** disappearance

lost 4 dead, gone, rapt **6** absent, astray, bygone, damned, doomed, futile, hidden, wasted **7** defunct, faraway, lacking, mislaid, missing **8** absorbed, departed, distrait, helpless, hopeless, vanished **9** condemned, desperate, destroyed **10** abstracted, insensible, overlooked **11** irrevocable, preoccupied **12** irredeemable, unregenerate

Lost Horizon *author:* **6** Hilton (James) *character:* **6** Conway (Hugh) *land:* **9** Shangri-La

lot 3 cut, ilk, set **4** doom, fate, give, heap, kind, mass, part, plat, sort, type, yard **5** allow, batch, block, bunch, field, group, moira, patch, quota, share, slice, tract, weird **6** assign, barrel, bundle, clutch, kismet, parcel, stripe **7** acreage, cluster, destiny, fortune, mete out, portion, species **8** allocate, clearing, frontage **9** aggregate, allowance, apportion

Lot *father:* **5** Haran *sister:* **5** Iscah **6** Milcah *son:* **4** Moab **5** Ammon *uncle:* **7** Abraham

lothario 4 stud, wolf **5** letch, Romeo **6** lecher, tomcat **7** amorist, Don Juan, gallant, seducer **8** Casanova, paramour **9** debaucher, womanizer **10** lady-killer **11** philanderer

lotion 3 oil **4** balm **5** cream, salve **6** cerate **7** unguent **8** ablution, cosmetic, lenitive, liniment, ointment **9** demulcent **11** embrocation

lottery 6 raffle **7** drawing **11** sweepstakes

lotus-eater 7 dreamer **8** escapist, romantic **10** daydreamer **13** castle-builder

loud 5 forte, gaudy, noisy, showy **6** brassy, brazen, flashy, garish, glitzy, tawdry, vulgar **7** blaring, blatant, booming, chintzy, glaring, pealing, raucous, roaring **8** piercing, resonant, sonorous, strident **9** clamorous, deafening, obnoxious, obtrusive, offensive, tasteless **10** bigmouthed, boisterous, flamboyant, resounding, stentorian, thunderous, vociferous **12** earsplitting

loudmouth 6 ranter **7** stentor **8** blowhard, braggart **9** blusterer

loudspeaker 6 woofer **7** tweeter **9** amplifier

Louisiana *capital:* **10** Baton Rouge *city:* **10** New Orleans, Shreveport *college, university:* **6** Tulane *county:* **6** parish *lake:* **13** Pontchartrain *nickname:* **7** Pelican (State) *river:* **11** Mississippi *state bird:* **12** brown pelican *state flower:* **8** magnolia *state tree:* **11** bald cypress

lounge 3 bar, bum, lie, pub, tap **4** idle, laze, loaf, loll, sofa **5** couch, dally, drift, lobby, relax **6** dawdle, loiter, parlor, repose, saloon **7** barroom, goof off, lie down, recline, taproom **8** restroom, kill time **10** living room

lounge lizard 3 fop **4** rake, toff **5** blade, dandy, leech **6** gigolo, sponge **9** ladies' man

Lourdes saint 10 Bernadette

louse 3 cur, dog, rat **4** toad **5** aphid, creep, skunk, snake **6** cootie, psylla, rotter, slater, wretch **7** stinker *egg:* **3** nit

louse up 4 blow, flub, muff, ruin **5** botch, spoil, wreck **6** bobble, bollix, bumble, bungle, fumble

lousy 3 ill **4** poor, rife **5** awful **6** shoddy, rotten **7** replete, teeming **8** crawling, horrible, inferior, infested, terrible **9** miserable, repulsive **10** despicable **12** contemptible

lout 3 oaf **4** boob, boor, dolt, gawk, hick, rube **5** brute, chuff, churl, klutz, looby, scorn, yokel **6** galoot, lubber, lummox, rustic **7** bumpkin, hayseed, palooka **9** simpleton **10** clodhopper

Louvre masterpiece 8 Mona Lisa **11** Venus de Milo

lovable 4 dear **5** sweet **6** cuddly **7** winning, winsome **8** adorable **9** appealing, endearing **11** embraceable

love 4 zeal **5** adore, ardor, crush, Cupid, exalt, prize, value **6** desire, dote on, fervor, revere **7** adulate, cherish, idolize, passion, romance, worship **8** devotion, fondness, idolatry, treasure, venerate, yearning **9** adoration, adulation, affection, delight in, sentiment **10** allegiance, appreciate, attachment, enthusiasm **11** amorousness, infatuation *combining form:* **5** phily **6** philia *French:* **5** amour *Italian:* **5** amore

love apple 6 tomato

lovebird 6 budgie, parrot **10** budgerigar

love feast 5 agape

love god 4 Amor, Eros, Kama **5** Bhaga, Cupid

love goddess 5 Athor, Freya, Venus **6** Hathor, Inanna, Ishtar **7** Astarte **9** Aphrodite, Ashtoreth

love letter 8 mash note **9** valentine **10** billet-doux

lovely 4 fair **5** sweet, swell **6** comely, dainty, pretty **7** elegant **8** adorable, alluring, charming, delicate, engaging, graceful, knockout **9** beauteous, beautiful, exquisite **10** attractive, delightful, enchanting, entrancing **11** captivating, good-looking

love potion 7 philter, philtre **11** aphrodisiac

lover 3 fan **4** beau, buff **5** flame, leman, Romeo, swain **6** addict, steady, suitor, votary **7** amorist, darling, devotee, Don Juan, gallant, habitué, squeeze **8** fancy man, lothario, mistress, paramour **9** boyfriend, inamorata, inamorato **10** aficionado, girlfriend, sweetheart

lovey-dovey 5 mushy **6** doting **7** amorous **12** affectionate

loving 4 dear, fond **6** ardent, erotic, tender **7** amatory, amorous, cordial, devoted, fervent **8** attached, enamored, faithful **10** benevolent, infatuated, passionate, solicitous **11** impassioned **12** affectionate

low 3 moo **4** base, blue, dead, deep, down, flat, mean, neap, poor, weak **5** cheap, short **6** abject, ailing, humble, hushed, lesser, nether, poorly, sickly, sordid, sparse, unwell **7** cut-rate, reduced, scrubby **8** cast down, deject-ed, depleted, downcast, inferior, mediocre, wretched **9** declining, depressed, miserable, subnormal, woebegone **10** economical, inadequate, indisposed, marked down, spiritless **11** crestfallen, downhearted, substandard, unfavorable

lowbred 4 base, rude **6** coarse, oafish, vulgar **7** boorish, brutish, loutish, uncouth **8** churlish, cloddish, lubberly **11** uncivilized

low-cost 5 cheap **6** budget, cheapo **7** bargain, cut-rate **10** affordable, reasonable **11** inexpensive

low-down 4 base, mean, ugly, vile **6** odious, scurvy **7** ignoble **8** shameful, wretched **9** abhorrent, worthless **10** despicable, disgusting **11** ignominious **12** contemptible

lowdown 4 dope, info **5** facts, scoop, specs **6** skinny **8** briefing **11** information

lower 3 cut **4** clip, drop, fall, sink **5** frown, gloom, scowl, shave, slash, under **6** debase, demean, demote, humble, lesser, menace, nether, reduce **7** cut down, deflate, degrade, demerit, depress, descend, devalue, let down **8** inferior, mark down, overcast, submerge, threaten **9** devaluate, downgrade *prefix:* **5** infra

Lower Depths author 5 Gorki, Gorky (Maksim, Maxim)

lowest point 5 nadir *in the U.S.:* **11** Death Valley *on earth:* **7** Dead Sea

low-grade 4 hack **5** junky, lousy **6** cheesy, cruddy, shabby, shoddy, sleazy, tawdry **8** below par, déclassé, inferior, mediocre **9** deficient **10** second-rate **11** second-class, substandard **12** second-drawer

low-key 4 soft **5** muted, quiet **7** relaxed, subdued **8** laid-back, softened, tasteful **9** easygoing, minimized, temperate, toned down **10** played down, restrained **11** understated

lowland 4 flat, sump, vale **5** basin **6** bottom, slough, valley **7** bottoms *Scottish:* **6** lallan **7** lalland

lowlife 4 fink, heel **5** knave, rogue **6** nogood, outlaw, rascal, wretch **7** hoodlum, ruffian, villain **9** miscreant, reprobate, scoundrel **10** blackguard, black sheep, sleazeball **11** rapscallion, slimebucket **12** bottom-feeder

lowly 4 base, mean, meek **6** abject, humble, menial, modest **7** ignoble, mundane, obscure, prosaic, servile **8** baseborn, plebeian, unwashed

low-pressure 4 calm **6** casual, dégagé, folksy, mellow **7** relaxed **8** flexible,

informal, laid-back **9** easygoing **10** nonchalant
low-spirited 3 sad **4** blue, down, glum **6** abject, droopy, gloomy, morose **7** doleful **8** cast down, dejected, downcast, saddened **9** bummed out, cheerless, depressed, woebegone **10** dispirited, melancholy **11** discouraged, downhearted **12** disheartened, heavyhearted
low tide 3 ebb **4** neap
loyal 4 firm, true **5** liege **6** ardent, trusty **7** devoted, dutiful, staunch **8** constant, faithful, resolute, true-blue **9** allegiant, steadfast, unfailing **10** dependable **11** trustworthy
loyalist 4 Tory **7** patriot **8** partisan **10** countryman **11** nationalist
loyalty 6 fealty **8** adhesion, devotion, fidelity **9** adherence, constancy **10** allegiance, attachment, dedication **11** staunchness **12** faithfulness **13** dependability, steadfastness
lozenge 4 pill **6** troche **7** diamond, rhombus **8** pastille
LSD 4 acid *user:* **8** acidhead
lubricate 3 oil **6** grease, smooth **7** moisten
lubricious 4 lewd, oily **5** slick **6** carnal, greasy, slippy, wanton **8** prurient, slippery, slithery, ticklish **9** lecherous, salacious **10** lascivious, libidinous **12** concupiscent
lucent 5 clear **6** bright, limpid **7** beaming, crystal, glowing, lambent, radiant, shining **8** clear-cut, luminous, pellucid **9** brilliant, effulgent, refulgent **11** unambiguous
Lucia di Lammermoor *character:* **7** Edgardo *composer:* **9** Donizetti (Gaetano) *novelist:* **5** Scott (Walter)
lucid 4 sane **5** clear **6** bright, limpid **7** crystal, lambent, radiant **8** clear-cut, knowable, luminous **9** brilliant, effulgent, graspable, refulgent, unblurred **10** articulate, fathomable **11** translucent, transparent, unambiguous **12** compos mentis, incandescent, intelligible, transpicuous **13** apprehensible
lucidity 6 acumen, sanity **7** clarity **8** sagacity, saneness **9** clearness, plainness, soundness **10** cognizance, perception **12** clairvoyance
Lucifer 5 devil, fiend, Satan, Venus **7** Old Nick **8** Apollyon **9** archfiend, Beelzebub **10** Old Scratch **13** Old Gooseberry
Lucinde *beloved:* **7** Leandre **9** Clitandre *father:* **7** Geronte **10** Sganarelle
luck 3 hap, hit **4** juju, meet **5** fluke, light **6** chance, happen, hazard, kismet **7** fortune, godsend, stumble **8** fortuity,

occasion, windfall **9** advantage **11** opportunity *token:* **5** charm **6** amulet, clover, fetish, mascot **8** talisman **9** horseshoe **11** rabbit's foot
luckless 7 adverse, hapless, unhappy **8** ill-fated, untoward, wretched **9** miserable **10** ill-starred **11** star-crossed, unfavorable, unfortunate **12** misfortunate, unpropitious
lucky 6 golden, timely **7** favored **9** favorable, fortunate **10** auspicious, beneficial, felicitous, fortuitous, propitious **12** advantageous, providential **13** serendipitous *Scottish:* **5** canny
Lucky Jim *author* **4** Amis (Kingsley)
lucrative 6 paying **7** gainful **8** fruitful **10** high-income, productive, profitable, well-paying, worthwhile **11** moneymaking **12** advantageous, remunerative
lucre 3 pay **4** cash, gain, jack, loot **5** dough, green, money, moola **6** dinero, do-re-mi, moolah, profit, wampum **7** cabbage, revenue **9** long green **10** greenbacks
Lucrezia ___ 6 Borgia
ludicrous 4 zany **5** antic, comic, droll, funny, goofy, nutty, silly **6** absurd **7** amusing, bizarre, comical, foolish, risible **8** farcical **9** fantastic, grotesque, laughable **10** off-the-wall, outlandish, ridiculous **11** incongruous **12** preposterous
Ludlum novel 14 Bourne Identity (The) **15** Bourne Supremacy (The) **16** Holcroft Covenant (The) **19** Prometheus Deception (The)
lug 3 nut, oaf, tow, tug **4** bear, buck, drag, draw, haul, hump, jerk, pull, tote **5** carry, ferry, shlep **6** convey, schlep **9** transport
luggage 4 bags, gear **7** baggage
lugubrious 3 sad **4** blue, dour, down, glum **5** bleak **6** dismal, dreary, gloomy, morose, rueful, somber, sullen, woeful **7** doleful, joyless **8** cast down, dejected, dolesome, downcast, mournful **9** cheerless, depressed, plaintive, saturnine, sorrowful, woebegone **10** depressing, despondent, lamentable, melancholy, oppressive **11** discouraged, dispiriting, downhearted **12** disconsolate
lukewarm 5 blasé, tepid **7** dubious, offhand **8** hesitant **9** uncertain, undecided **10** wishy-washy **11** halfhearted, indifferent
lull 3 ebb **4** balm, calm, hush, wane **5** letup, pause, quiet, still **6** becalm, pacify, soothe, temper **7** compose, decline, ease off, slacken **8** abeyance, interval **9** stillness **10** quiescence **11** tranquilize
lullaby 8 berceuse **10** cradlesong

lulu 3 ace 5 dandy, doozy, dream 6 doozie, wonder 7 delight 8 knockout 9 sensation

lumber 3 tax 4 clog, lade, load, logs, plod, slog, wood 5 barge, clump, stump, weigh 6 burden, charge, rumble, saddle, timber, trudge 8 encumber

lumberjack see LOGGER

luminance 10 brightness

luminary 3 sun, VIP 4 lion, name, star 5 celeb, light, nabob 6 leader, worthy 7 big name, notable 8 big-timer, eminence, somebody 9 celebrity, dignitary, superstar 10 notability 12 leading light

luminous 5 clear, lucid 6 bright, lucent 7 beaming, crystal, fulgent, lambent, radiant, shining 8 clear-cut, lustrous, pellucid 9 brilliant, effulgent, refulgent 11 illustrious, translucent, transparent 12 enlightening, incandescent

lummox 3 oaf 4 boor, clod, gawk, lout 5 klutz, looby 6 lubber 7 palooka

lump 3 gob, lot, oaf, wad 4 blob, bulk, chip, clod, gawk, glob, heap, hunk, lout, mass, pile, welt 5 abide, batch, block, brook, bulge, bunch, chunk, hunch, klutz, knurl, looby, piece, scrap, stand, tumor 6 digest, endure, entire, lubber, morsel, nugget 7 handful, palooka, portion, stomach, swallow 8 swelling, totality 9 aggregate 10 protrusion, tumescence 12 protuberance

lumpy 5 crude, gawky, rough 6 choppy, clumsy, coarse, oafish 8 clumpish, unformed 9 roughhewn

lunacy 5 folly, mania 6 idiocy 7 fatuity, foolery, inanity, madness 8 delirium, dementia, silliness, insanity 9 absurdity, craziness, stupidity 10 imbecility 11 derangement, foolishness 13 senselessness

lunar *dark area:* 4 mare 5 maria (plural) *valley:* 4 rill 5 rille

lunatic 3 mad, nut 4 daft, kook, loco, yo-yo, zany 5 balmy, batty, crank, crazy, nutty, raver, wacko, wacky 6 absurd, crazed, cuckoo, insane, madman, maniac, nitwit, psycho, screwy 7 bonkers, cracked, foolish 8 crackpot, demented, demoniac, deranged, frenzied, maniacal, paranoid, schizoid, unhinged 9 bedlamite, ding-a-ling, fruitcake, harebrain, screwball 10 crackbrain 11 nonsensical

lunch 3 eat 4 meal, nosh 5 snack

luncheonette 4 café 5 diner 6 bistro, eatery 7 beanery, canteen, tearoom 8 snack bar 9 cafeteria 10 coffee shop, restaurant 11 greasy spoon

lune 3 bow 5 curve 6 sickle 8 crescent, meniscus

lung *combining form:* 5 pneum, pulmo 6 pneumo, pulmon *disease:* 9 emphysema, pneumonia 10 byssinosis 12 tuberculosis

lunge 3 jab 4 dash, dive, stab 5 bound, drive, pitch, surge 6 charge, plunge, pounce, thrust

lunkhead 3 oaf 4 boob, clod, dodo, dolt, goof, yo-yo 5 booby, chump, dummy, dunce, idiot, moron, ninny, noddy, stupe 6 dimwit, dum-dum, nitwit 7 dullard 8 dumbbell, imbecile, numskull 9 birdbrain, ignoramus, lamebrain, numbskull, simpleton 10 nincompoop

lupine 5 feral 6 brutal, fierce 7 wolfish 8 ravening 9 predatory, rapacious 10 bluebonnet, sanguinary

lurch 3 bob, yaw 4 jerk, lean, list, reel, rock, roll, sway, tilt, toss 5 heave, pitch, slide, swing 6 bumble, careen, falter, plunge, seesaw, swerve, teeter, totter 7 blunder, stagger, stumble 8 flounder

lure 3 bag 4 bait, call, draw, fake, hook, pull, rope, toll, trap, wile 5 blind, catch, charm, decoy, snare, tempt, trick 6 appeal, cajole, come-on, draw in, draw on, entice, entrap, invite, lead on, seduce 7 attract, beguile, bewitch, capture, con game, enchant, ensnare, gimmick, wheedle 8 blandish, delusion, illusion, inveigle 9 captivate, fascinate, incentive, seduction, siren song 10 attraction, camouflage, enticement, inducement, seducement, temptation *fishing:* 3 fly 4 worm 5 spoon 6 minnow 8 bucktail

lurid 3 wan 4 ashy, gory, gray, grim, pale 5 ashen, fiery, gross, livid, waxen 6 doughy, grisly, malign, sultry, yellow 7 baleful, ghastly, graphic, hideous, macabre, malefic, tabloid 8 blanched, gruesome, horrible, shocking, sinister, terrible 9 colorless 10 horrifying, maleficent, terrifying 11 sensational 12 melodramatic

Lurie *novel* 14 Foreign Affairs 18 War Between the Tates (The)

lurk 4 hide, slip 5 creep, prowl, skulk, slide, slink, sneak, snoop, steal 9 pussyfoot

luscious 4 rich, sexy 5 sapid, sweet, tasty, yummy 6 delish, divine, ornate, savory 7 opulent, piquant, sensual 8 sensuous 9 ambrosial, epicurean, exquisite, flavorful, luxurious, seductive, sumptuous, toothsome 10 delectable, delightful, flamboyant, flavorsome, voluptuous 11 scrumptious 13 mouth-watering

lush 3 sot **4** rank, rich, wino **5** dense, drink, drunk, yummy **6** bibber, boozer, deluxe, lavish, savory **7** fertile, opulent, profuse, sensual, teeming, tippler **8** abundant, drunkard, palatial, prodigal, sensuous, thriving **9** ambrosial, delicious, epicurean, exuberant, inebriate, luxuriant, luxurious, plentiful, sumptuous, toothsome **10** boozehound, delectable, delightful, profitable, prosperous, voluptuous **11** extravagant, flourishing
Lusitania 8 Portugal
lust 3 rut, yen **4** ache, itch, pine, urge, wish, zeal, zest **5** ardor, crave, drive, greed, letch, yearn **6** desire, fervor, hanker, hunger, libido **7** avidity, craving, lechery, longing, passion **8** appetite, coveting, cupidity, lewdness, priapism, salacity, satyrism, yearning **9** carnality, eagerness, eroticism, lubricity, prurience, pruriency **10** enthusiasm, excitement, satyriasis, wantonness **11** nymphomania **13** concupiscence, lecherousness, salaciousness
luster 4 glow **5** glaze, gleam, glint, gloss, sheen, shine **6** polish **7** burnish, shimmer **8** lambency, radiance **9** afterglow **10** brightness, brilliance, brilliancy, effulgence, luminosity, refulgence **11** candescence, iridescence
lusterless 3 dim, wan **4** blah, drab, dull, flat, gray, matt **5** brown, dingy, dusky, faded, matte, muddy, muted, vapid **6** boring **10** uninspired
lustful 3 hot **4** lewd **5** bawdy, horny **6** carnal, erotic, wanton **7** burning, goatish, itching, ruttish, satyric **8** prurient **9** debauched, lecherous, libertine, lickerish, salacious **10** hot-blooded, lascivious, libidinous, licentious, lubricious, passionate **12** concupiscent
lustrate 5 purge **6** purify **7** cleanse
lustration 6 ritual **8** ablution **9** catharsis, cleansing, purgation **10** sprinkling **12** purification
lustrous 5 nitid, shiny **6** bright, gleamy, glossy, sheeny **7** fulgent, glowing, lambent, radiant, shining **8** gleaming, luminous, polished, splendid **9** brilliant, burnished, effulgent, refulgent **10** glimmering, glistening **11** resplendent **12** incandescent
lusty 4 hale **5** hardy, vital **6** brawny, hearty, mighty, potent, robust, strong, virile **7** dynamic, healthy, rousing **8** vigorous **9** energetic, strapping, strenuous **10** prodigious, red-blooded **12** enthusiastic

lute 4 clay, seal **5** grout **6** cement **7** bandora **8** mandolin **10** chitarrone, instrument *Arabic:* **3** oud *two-necked:* **7** theorbo
lutenist 5 Bream (Julian) **7** Dowland (John) **8** Gaultier (Denis)
Lutetia 5 Paris
Luxembourg *capital:* **10** Luxembourg *monetary unit:* **4** euro *mountain range:* **8** Ardennes *neighbor:* **6** France **7** Belgium, Germany *river:* **4** Sûre **7** Alzette
luxuriant 4 lush, rank, rich **5** dense **6** fecund, lavish **7** copious, fertile, opulent, profuse, rampant, riotous, teeming **8** abundant, fruitful, luscious, prodigal, prolific **9** excessive, exuberant, sumptuous
luxuriate 4 bask **5** bloom, enjoy, feast, revel **6** abound, relish, thrive, wallow **7** delight, indulge **8** flourish
luxurious 4 lush, posh, rich **5** fancy, grand, plush, ritzy, showy **6** costly, deluxe, lavish, plushy **7** opulent, sensual, stately **8** imposing, majestic, palatial, splendid **9** elaborate, epicurean, expensive, grandiose, sumptuous **10** impressive **11** extravagant, magnificent *situation:* **7** fat city **10** bed of roses, easy street
luxury 5 frill, treat **6** dainty **7** amenity, comfort **8** delicacy, opulence **9** abundance, affluence **10** indulgence **11** superfluity **12** extravagance
lycée 6 school **10** high school
lyceum 4 hall **6** school **7** academy, chamber **9** institute
Lycidas author 6 Milton (John)
Lycomedes *daughter:* **8** Deidamia *victim:* **7** Theseus
Lycus *brother:* **7** Nycteus *father:* **7** Pandion *slayer:* **6** Zethus **7** Amphion *wife:* **5** Dirce
Lydian *king:* **5** Gyges **7** Croesus **8** Alyattes *queen:* **7** Omphale
lye 7 caustic **9** hydroxide
lynch 4 hang **5** scrag **6** gibbet, murder **7** execute **8** string up
Lynette see LINE
lynx 4 puma **6** bobcat, cougar **7** caracal, wildcat **9** catamount
Lyra star 4 Vega
lyre 4 harp
lyric 3 ode **4** odic, poem **5** melic, verse **6** poetic **7** melodic, musical **8** operatic **9** exuberant, rhapsodic
lyrical 7 lilting, melodic, musical, songful, tuneful **8** operatic
lyricist 4 poet **10** librettist
Lysander's beloved 6 Hermia

M

Maacah *father:* 5 Nahor 6 Talmai 7 Absalom *husband:* 5 David 6 Jehiel, Machir 8 Rehoboam *son:* 5 Hanan 6 Abijam, Achish 7 Absalom 10 Shephatiah

macabre 4 grim 5 lurid 6 grisly, horrid, morbid 7 deathly, ghastly, hideous 8 ghoulish, gruesome, horrible 9 deathlike 10 horrifying

macadam 3 tar 7 asphalt, roadway 8 pavement

macaque 6 monkey, rhesus

macaroni 3 fop 4 beau, buck, dude, toff 5 dandy, pasta, swell 7 coxcomb, gallant

macaw 6 parrot

Macbeth *character:* 4 Ross 5 Angus 6 Hecate, Lennox 7 Fleance *slayer:* 7 Macduff *successor:* 7 Malcolm *title:* 5 thane *victim:* 6 Banquo, Duncan

mace 4 club 5 baton, staff 6 cudgel, nutmeg 8 bludgeon

Macedonia *capital:* 6 Skopje *city:* 6 Tetovo *monetary unit:* 5 denar *neighbor:* 6 Greece, Serbia 7 Albania 8 Bulgaria *part of:* 7 Balkans *peninsula:* 6 Balkan

macerate 4 soak 5 steep 6 drench, soften 7 immerse, suffuse 8 saturate

machete 4 bolo 5 knife 6 scythe

Machiavellian 4 wily 6 shrewd 7 cunning, devious 8 guileful, scheming 9 conniving, deceitful, insidious 10 conspiring 11 duplicitous, treacherous 12 unscrupulous

Machiavelli *work* 6 Prince (The) 8 Mandrake (The) 10 Mandragola (La)

machinate 4 plot 6 scheme 7 connive, finagle 8 conspire, intrigue, maneuver

machination 4 plot, ploy, ruse 5 cabal, dodge 6 gambit, scheme 8 artifice, intrigue, maneuver, scheming, trickery 9 chicanery, collusion, deception, dirty work, expedient, stratagem 10 hanky-panky, subterfuge 11 contrivance, skulduggery 12 gamesmanship, skullduggery

machine 6 device, engine, gadget 9 apparatus, appliance, automaton 11 contraption

machine-gun 4 rake 6 strafe 8 enfilade 9 rapid-fire

machine-gun inventor 7 Gatling (Richard)

machinery 5 works 9 apparatus, equipment, mechanism

machismo 7 swagger 8 virility 9 manliness 11 masculinity

macho 5 manly 6 virile 9 masculine

Machu Picchu resident 4 Inca

mackinaw 4 coat 5 cover, trout 7 blanket

mackintosh 7 slicker 8 raincoat

macrocosm 5 world 6 cosmos 8 creation, universe

mad 4 daft, nuts, rash, sore, wild 5 angry, crazy, irate, irked, kooky, livid, loony, nutty, rabid, wacky 6 absurd, crazed, cuckoo, heated, insane, ireful, screwy 7 berserk, bonkers, cracked, enraged, foolish, frantic, furious, lunatic 8 choleric, demented, deranged, frenetic, frenzied, incensed, offended, outraged, unhinged, worked up, wrathful 9 delirious, fanatical, fantastic, hilarious, illogical, senseless 10 distracted, infuriated, irrational, unbalanced

Madagascar *capital:* 12 Antananarivo *channel:* 10 Mozambique *city:* 9 Mahajanga, Toamasina *language:* 6 French 8 Malagasy *monetary unit:* 5 franc *mountain range:* 9 Ankaratra

madame 3 Mrs. 4 wife 6 milady, missus

Madame Bovary *author:* 8 Flaubert (Gustave) *character:* 4 Emma (Bovary) 7 Charles (Bovary) 8 Rodolphe

Madame Butterfly *character:* 9 Cho-Cho-San, Cio-Cio-San, Pinkerton, Sharpless *composer:* 7 Puccini (Giacomo)

madcap 4 rash, wild 5 antic 7 foolish 8 reckless 9 frivolous, hotheaded 10 capricious, incautious

Mad Cavalier 6 Rupert (Prince)

madden 3 ire, vex 4 goad 5 anger, craze 6 enrage 7 derange, incense, inflame, outrage, possess, steam up, unhinge 9 infuriate, unbalance

Madeira Islands *capital:* 7 Funchal *export:* 4 wine *part of:* 8 Portugal

mademoiselle 4 girl, Miss 6 maiden 9 governess 10 yellowtail 11 silver perch

made-to-order 6 custom 7 bespoke 10 customized 11 custom-built

made-up 5 bogus, false 7 painted 8 invented, mythical, specious 9 fictional, imaginary, pretended, trumped-up 10 fabricated, fictitious 11 make-believe 12 cosmeticized

madhouse 6 asylum, bedlam 8 loony bin 9 funny farm 10 booby hatch

madman 3 nut 4 kook, loon 5 loony, raver 6 cuckoo, maniac, psycho 7 lunatic, nutcase 9 bedlamite, psychotic, fruitcake

madness 4 rage 5 folly 6 lunacy 8 insanity 9 psychosis 11 derangement

Madonna initials 3 BVM

Madras 9 Tamil Nadu *founder:* 3 Day (Francis)

Madrid museum 5 Prado

madrigal 4 glee, poem, song 8 part-song

madrigalist *English:* 4 Byrd (William) 6 Morley (Thomas), Wilbye (John) 7 Tomkins (Thomas), Weelkes (Thomas) *Flemish:* 8 Willaert (Adriaan) *Italian:* 8 Marenzio (Luca) 10 Monteverdi (Claudio)

maelstrom 4 eddy 5 whirl 6 vortex 7 turmoil 9 whirlpool

maenad 9 bacchante, priestess

maestro see CONDUCTOR

Mafia 3 mob 4 ring 6 clique 7 rackets 8 gangland 9 Black Hand, syndicate 10 Cosa Nostra, underworld

mafioso 4 goon 6 hit man 7 mobster 8 gangster 9 racketeer

magazine 4 dump 5 cache, depot, organ, store 6 armory, digest, review, weekly 7 arsenal, gazette, journal, monthly 8 biweekly 9 bimonthly, quarterly, warehouse 10 depository, periodical, repository, storehouse 11 publication

mage 6 priest 8 magician, sorcerer

maggot 4 grub, whim 5 fancy, larva 6 vagary 7 caprice, conceit

Magi 6 Caspar, Gaspar 8 Melchior 9 Balthasar, Balthazar *gift:* 4 gold 5 myrrh 7 incense 12 frankincense

Magian see MAGUS

magic 4 juju 5 wicca 6 hoodoo, voodoo 7 alchemy, devilry, sorcery 8 satanism, witchery, witching, wizardry 9 conjuring, diablerie, diabolism, occultism, sortilege 10 hocus-pocus, mumbo jumbo, necromancy, witchcraft 11 abracadabra, bewitchment, enchantment, legerdemain, thaumaturgy

magical 6 occult 8 wizardly 10 bewitching, entrancing 11 necromantic 12 thaumaturgic

Magic Flute composer 6 Mozart (Wolfgang Amadeus)

magician 5 brujo, witch 6 shaman, wizard 7 Houdini, warlock 8 conjurer, satanist, sorcerer 9 diabolist, enchanter, trickster, voodooist 11 medicine man, necromancer, thaumaturge *Arthurian:* 6 Merlin *Shakespearean:* 8 Prospero

stage: 5 Randi (James) 11 Copperfield (David), illusionist *Tolkien's:* 7 Gandalf

Magic Mountain, The *author:* 4 Mann (Thomas) *character:* 7 Castorp (Hans)

magisterial 6 lordly 7 pompous 8 dogmatic 9 imperious, masterful 10 highhanded 11 doctrinaire, domineering, overbearing 13 authoritative, self-important

Magister Ludi author 5 Hesse (Hermann)

magistrate 5 court, judge 7 bencher, justice 8 official *ancient Greek:* 5 ephor 6 archon *ancient Roman:* 6 aedile 7 duumvir, praetor, questor 8 quaestor *Italian:* 7 podesta *Scottish:* 6 bailie

Magna Carta *king:* 4 John *place signed:* 9 Runnymede

magnanimous 5 noble 7 liberal 8 generous, princely 9 forgiving, unselfish 10 benevolent, bighearted, charitable, chivalrous, high-minded, munificent

magnate 5 baron, mogul, nabob 6 fat cat, prince, tycoon 9 personage, plutocrat

magnet 9 lodestone 10 attraction

magnetic 8 alluring 9 appealing, seductive 10 attractive 11 captivating, charismatic, fascinating 12 irresistible *substance:* 4 iron 7 ferrite

magnetism 4 draw, lure, pull 5 charm 6 allure, appeal 7 glamour 8 charisma 10 attraction 11 fascination

magnetize 4 draw, lure, wile 5 charm 7 attract, bewitch, enchant 9 captivate, fascinate

magnification unit 8 diameter

magnificence 4 pomp 7 majesty 8 grandeur, splendor 9 pageantry 13 sumptuousness

magnificent 5 grand, noble, regal, royal 6 august, lavish, lordly, superb 7 exalted, opulent, stately, sublime 8 glorious, imposing, majestic, palatial, princely, splendid 9 brilliant, grandiose, luxurious, sumptuous 11 extravagant, resplendent, splendorous 13 splendiferous

magnifier 4 lens 9 telescope *jeweler's:* 5 loupe

magnify 4 hymn, laud 5 add to, boost, cry up, exalt, extol, honor, swell 6 expand, extend, praise 7 amplify, augment, enhance, enlarge, ennoble, glorify, inflate 8 eulogize, heighten, increase, maximize, multiply, overplay 9 aggravate, celebrate, embellish, embroider, intensify, overstate 10 aggrandize, exaggerate, panegyrize 13 overemphasize

magniloquent 5 tumid, windy 6 florid, turgid 7 aureate, flowery, fustian, orotund, pompous, swollen **8** sonorous **9** bombastic, high-flown, overblown, rhapsodic **10** euphuistic, rhetorical **11** declamatory

magnitude 4 size **5** order, range **6** extent, import, number, volume **7** bigness, caliber, measure, quality **8** enormity, hugeness, quantity, vastness **9** greatness, immensity, largeness **10** dimensions, importance, proportion **11** consequence

Magnolia State 11 Mississippi

magnum opus 7 classic **10** masterwork **11** chef d'oeuvre, masterpiece, tour de force

Magog's king 3 Gog

magpie 3 jay **4** bird **6** gabber, prater **7** blabber, hoarder **8** jabberer, prattler **9** chatterer, collector **10** chatterbox **12** blabbermouth

maguey 5 agave, fiber **7** cantala *relative:* **4** aloe

magus 6 wizard **7** diviner, warlock **8** conjurer, sorcerer **9** enchanter **10** astrologer **11** necromancer

Magyar 9 Hungarian

Mahalath *father:* 7 Ishmael **8** Jerimoth *husband:* **4** Esau **8** Rehoboam

mah-jongg piece 4 tile

Mahlon *father:* 9 Elimelech *mother:* **5** Naomi *wife:* **4** Ruth

Maia *father:* 5 Atlas *mother:* **7** Pleione *sisters:* **8** Pleiades *son:* **6** Hermes **7** Mercury

maid 4 amah, girl, lass, miss **5** biddy, bonne, wench **6** au pair, damsel, lassie, live-in, virgin **7** servant **8** domestic **9** charwoman, hired girl **10** au pair girl *Indian:* **4** ayah *lady's:* **7** abigail *stage:* **9** soubrette

maiden 3 gal **4** girl, lass, miss **5** first, fresh, missy, prime, wench **6** damsel, lassie, unused, virgin **7** initial, pioneer, primary **8** earliest, original, spinster, virginal **10** spinsterly *Norse mythological:* **8** valkyrie

maidenhair tree 6 ginkgo

maidenhead 5 hymen **6** purity **9** virginity

maidenhood 9 virginity

Maid of Astolat 6 Elaine

Maid of Orleans, The 4 Joan (of Arc) **7** Pucelle (La) *author:* **8** Schiller (Friedrich von)

mail 4 post **5** armor **7** hauberk, letters **8** messages

___ mail 3 air **4** junk **5** chain

maim 4 maul **6** mangle **7** cripple, disable **8** mutilate, paralyze **9** disfigure

main 3 sea **5** chief, great, major, ocean, prime, trunk, vital **7** central, high sea, leading, premier, primary **8** cardinal, foremost, high seas **9** essential, paramount, principal **10** preeminent, prevailing **11** fundamental, outstanding, predominant

Maine *capital:* 7 Augusta *city:* **6** Bangor **8** Lewiston, Portland *college, university:* **5** Bates, Colby **7** Bowdoin *lake:* **6** Sebago *motto:* **6** Dirigo *mountain:* **8** Cadillac, Katahdin *nickname:* **8** Pine Tree (State) *park:* **6** Acadia *river:* **8** Kennebec **9** Penobscot *state bird:* **9** chickadee *state flower:* **22** white pine cone and tassel *state tree:* **9** white pine

mainly 6 mostly **7** chiefly, largely **8** above all **9** primarily **10** especially **11** principally **13** predominantly

mainstay 4 prop **5** brace **6** pillar **7** bulwark, standby, support **8** backbone, buttress **9** supporter, sustainer

Main Street author 5 Lewis (Sinclair)

maintain 4 aver, avow **5** argue, claim **6** affirm, allege, assert, back up, defend, insist, keep up, manage, stress, uphold **7** care for, carry on, contend, declare, justify, persist, profess, support, sustain, warrant **8** continue, preserve **9** cultivate, emphasize, look after **10** provide for

maintenance 4 care, keep **6** living, upkeep **7** alimony, support **10** livelihood **11** subsistence **12** alimentation *worker:* **7** janitor **9** custodian

maize 4 corn, milo **10** Indian corn

majestic 5 grand, noble, regal, royal **6** august, kingly, lordly, superb **7** exalted, stately **8** elevated, imperial, imposing, princely, splendid **9** dignified, grandiose, sumptuous **11** ceremonious, magnificent

majesty 4 pomp **5** glory **8** eminence, grandeur, splendor **9** greatness, loftiness **11** stateliness **12** magnificence

major 3 big **4** main, star **5** chief, grave, large **6** higher, larger **7** capital, greater, notable, primary, serious, sizable **8** sizeable, superior **9** principal, prominent **10** large-scale, preeminent **11** outstanding, predominant, significant **12** considerable

Major Barbara author 4 Shaw (George Bernard)

majority 4 bulk, edge **6** margin **13** preponderance

make 3 act, net, set **4** earn, form, gain, mold **5** build, cause, erect, forge, frame, hatch, shape, spawn **6** compel, create, derive, draw up, effect, output, parent **7** achieve, bring in, compose, fashion, prepare, produce **8** comprise, conclude, draw down, generate **9** construct, establish, fabricate, originate **10** constitute **11** manufacture, put together *amends:* **5** atone *believe:* **7** pretend *certain:* **6** assure **8** convince *fast:* **3** fix **4** gird

6 secure *good:* 7 succeed 9 indemnify
known: 3 air 6 expose, reveal, spread
7 declare, divulge, uncover 8 announce,
disclose, proclaim *use of:* 6 employ
make-believe 4 mock, sham 7 charade,
feigned, fiction 8 disguise, pretense
9 fictional, imaginary, insincere, pretended, simulated 10 fictitious
make do 4 cope 5 get by, get on, shift
6 endure, fake it, manage, wing it
7 survive 8 get along 9 improvise
11 extemporize 13 muddle through
make off 3 fly, run 4 flee, skip 5 leave,
scoot, scram 6 decamp, depart, escape
7 abscond, run away 9 skedaddle
make out 3 see 4 fare, neck 5 grasp, infer
6 accept, deduce, derive, follow, gather,
manage, take in, thrive 7 discern, prosper, succeed 8 conclude, flourish, get
along, perceive 9 apprehend, determine, establish, interpret 10 comprehend, understand
make over 4 cede, deed 6 assign, convey,
reform 7 remodel, reshape 8 renovate,
transfer
maker 7 builder, creator 8 borrower,
designer, inventor, producer 10 originator 11 constructor 12 manufacturer
makeshift 6 resort 7 stopgap 8 recourse,
resource 9 expedient, temporary
10 expediency, substitute 11 provisional
13 quick-and-dirty, rough-and-ready
make up 4 form 5 atone 6 devise, invent
7 arrange, compile, compose, concoct,
fashion, prepare 8 comprise, contrive
9 apologize, construct, fabricate, formulate, improvise, reconcile 10 compensate
makeup 4 cast, form, kohl, mold
5 blush, fiber, gloss, grain, paint, rouge,
shape, stamp, style 6 design, nature,
powder, stripe, temper 7 blusher, mascara 8 lip gloss, war paint 9 character,
formation 10 complexion, maquillage
11 arrangement, composition, disposition, greasepaint, personality, temperament 12 architecture, constitution,
construction, organization
maladroit 5 inept 6 clumsy, gauche,
klutzy 7 awkward, unhandy 8 bumbling, bungling, tactless 9 ham-handed,
impolitic 10 blundering, ungraceful
11 heavy-handed 12 undiplomatic
malady 3 ill 7 ailment, disease, illness
8 disorder, sickness, syndrome 9 complaint, condition, infirmity 10 affliction
malaise 4 funk 5 dumps, ennui 8 debility, doldrums 10 enervation
Malamud, Bernard *novel:* 5 Fixer (The)
7 Natural (The) 9 Assistant (The) *story:*
11 Magic Barrel (The)
malapert 4 rude 5 brash, fresh, nervy,

sassy, saucy, smart 6 brassy, brazen,
cheeky 7 forward 8 impudent, insolent
12 presumptuous
Malaprop creator 8 Sheridan (Richard
Brinsley)
malapropos 5 inapt, undue 8 improper,
unseemly, untimely 10 unsuitable
11 inopportune 13 inappropriate, inop-
portunely
malaria 4 ague 6 miasma *medicine:* 7 quinine 8 cinchona *mosquito:* 9 anopheles
malarkey 4 guff 5 bilge, hokum, hooey,
tripe 6 bunkum, drivel 7 hogwash, rubbish, twaddle 8 nonsense 9 poppycock
10 balderdash 12 blatherskite
Malawi *capital:* 8 Lilongwe *city:* 8 Blantyre *explorer:* 11 Livingstone (David)
former name: 9 Nyasaland *lake:* 5 Nyasa
6 Malawi *language:* 7 English
8 Chichewa *monetary unit:* 6 kwacha
neighbor: 6 Zambia 8 Tanzania
10 Mozambique *river:* 5 Shire
Malaysia *capital:* 11 Kuala Lumpur *city:*
4 Ipoh 6 Penang 11 Johor Baharu
island: 6 Borneo *monetary unit:* 7 ringgit
neighbor: 8 Thailand 9 Indonesia *peninsula:* 5 Malay *sea:* 10 South China *strait:*
7 Malacca
malcontent 5 rebel 6 griper, grouch,
unruly 8 agitator, factious, frondeur,
grumbler, mutinous, restless 9 alienated 10 bellyacher, complainer, rebellious 11 disaffected, disgruntled, disobedient, ungratified 12 contumacious,
dissatisfied
mal de mer 6 nausea 8 vomiting 10 quea-
siness 11 seasickness
Maldives *capital:* 4 Male *language:*
6 Divehi *monetary unit:* 7 rufiyaa
male 3 guy, tom 4 gent 5 macho, manly
6 manful, virile 7 manlike 9 masculine,
staminate
malediction 4 jinx, oath 5 curse 7 malison 8 anathema 10 execration 11 imprecation
malefactor 5 felon, knave, rogue 6 sinner 8 criminal, evildoer, offender 9 miscreant, reprobate, scoundrel, wrongdoer 10 blackguard, lawbreaker
maleficent 4 evil, vile 5 toxic 6 malign,
sinful, wicked 7 baleful, baneful, beastly, harmful, noxious, vicious
8 damnable, sinister, virulent 9 execrable, injurious, nefarious, repugnant
10 pernicious, villainous 11 destructive
malevolence 4 evil 5 spite 6 grudge, malice, spleen 7 ill will 9 hostility, malignity 12 spitefulness 13 maliciousness
malevolent 4 evil 6 malign, wicked
7 baleful, hateful, hurtful, vicious 8 sinister, spiteful, venomous 9 injurious,
malicious, malignant, poisonous

malfunction 6 glitch 7 misfire

Mali *capital:* 6 Bamako *city:* 5 Mopti, Ségou 7 Sikasso 8 Timbuktu 10 Tombouctou *desert:* 6 Sahara *former name:* 11 French Sudan *language:* 6 French *monetary unit:* 5 franc *neighbor:* 5 Niger 6 Guinea 7 Algeria, Senegal 10 Ivory Coast, Mauritania 11 Burkina Faso *river:* 5 Niger

malice 4 bile, hate 5 spite, venom 6 animus, enmity, grudge, hatred, poison, spleen 7 ill will 8 meanness 9 animosity, antipathy 10 bitterness, resentment 11 hatefulness, malevolence 12 spitefulness 13 invidiousness

malicious 4 evil, mean 5 nasty, petty 6 wicked 7 baneful, hateful, heinous, jealous 8 spiteful, vengeful, venomous, virulent 9 poisonous, poison-pen, rancorous 10 malevolent

maliciousness see MALEVOLENCE

malign 4 evil, soil 5 abuse, decry, libel, smear, stain, sully, taint 6 befoul, defame, defile, revile, smirch, vilify, wicked 7 asperse, baleful, baneful, blacken, detract, hateful, hostile, noxious, slander, tarnish, traduce, vicious 8 besmirch, derogate, inimical, sinister, spiteful, tear down, virulent 9 denigrate, disparage, injurious, rancorous 10 calumniate, depreciate, maleficent, malevolent, pernicious, scandalize, vituperate 11 deleterious, opprobriate 12 antagonistic, antipathetic

malignant 4 evil 5 fatal 6 deadly, lethal, wicked 7 baleful, hateful, vicious 8 devilish, fiendish, spiteful 9 injurious, rancorous 10 diabolical, malevolent

malison 5 curse 8 anathema 11 commination, imprecation, malediction

mall 4 lane 5 alley, plaza, strip 7 passage 9 concourse, esplanade, promenade 10 passageway 11 median strip

malleable 6 pliant, supple 7 ductile, plastic, pliable 8 flexible 9 adaptable

mallet 6 hammer

malodorous 4 foul, gamy, rank 5 fetid, fuggy, funky, fusty, musty, stale 6 frowsy, putrid, rancid, rotten, smelly, stinky 7 noisome, noxious, reeking, spoiled 8 mephitic, stinking 9 offensive 10 nauseating 11 ill-smelling 12 pestilential

Malta *capital:* 8 Valletta *city:* 5 Qormi 10 Birkirkara *island:* 4 Gozo 6 Comino *language:* 6 French 7 Maltese *monetary unit:* 4 lira *sea:* 13 Mediterranean

Maltese Falcon, The *actor:* 5 Astor (Mary), Lorre (Peter) 6 Bogart (Humphrey) 11 Greenstreet (Sydney)

author: 7 Hammett (Dashiell) *detective:* 5 Spade (Sam) *director:* 6 Huston (John)

maltreat 5 abuse 6 ill-use, misuse, molest

mama 4 dame, doll, wife 5 broad, femme, hussy, madam, woman 6 matron, mother

Mamet *play* 7 Oleanna 14 Boston Marriage 15 American Buffalo 17 Glengarry Glen Ross

mammal 3 ass 5 camel, hippo, hyrax 6 alpaca, colugo, dassie, rabbit 7 primate 8 elephant 12 hippopotamus *African:* 5 okapi, zebra 8 aardvark, aardwolf *aquatic:* 6 dugong, sea cow 7 cowfish, manatee, narwhal, platypi (plural) 8 cetacean, platypus, porpoise, sirenian *arboreal:* 5 lemur 6 sifaka 7 opossum 8 kinkajou *Australian:* 5 koala 8 kangaroo *burrowing:* 8 starnose *carnivorous:* 3 cat, dog, fox 4 bear, lion, mink, seal, wolf 5 genet, hyena, otter, panda, ratel, sable, tiger 6 badger, grison, marten, racoon, walrus 7 linsang, polecat, raccoon 8 mongoose *catlike:* 5 civet *doglike:* 6 jackal *extinct:* 6 quagga 8 mastodon, stegodon *feline:* 4 lion 5 tiger, tigon 6 ocelot, tiglon 7 leopard, lioness, tigress *flying:* 3 bat *gnawing:* 3 rat 6 beaver, rodent 8 squirrel *goatlike:* 4 tahr 5 takin *harelike:* 5 hyrax 7 hyraces (plural) *hoofed:* 3 cow, pig 4 deer, goat, oxen (plural) 5 camel, sheep, tapir 6 alpaca 7 peccary 8 ruminant, ungulate 12 hippopotamus *horned:* 4 goat *insect-eating:* 4 mole 5 shrew 6 tenrec 8 hedgehog *longnecked:* 7 giraffe *marine:* 4 orca, seal 6 walrus 7 dolphin, grampus *marsupial:* 9 bandicoot *nocturnal:* 6 wombat *raccoon-like:* 10 cacomistle *ruminant:* 4 deer 5 llama, moose, sheep 6 vicuña *small:* 4 pika 8 hedgehog, hedgepig *South American:* 7 guanaco *toothless:* 5 sloth 8 edentate, pangolin 9 armadillo *tropical:* 5 coati *unweaned:* 8 suckling *with flippers:* 8 pinniped *wolflike:* 5 hyena

mammon 4 pelf 5 lucre 6 riches, wealth 8 treasure 9 abundance, affluence 10 prosperity 11 possessions

mammoth 4 huge, vast 5 giant, jumbo 6 mighty 7 immense, massive, monster, titanic 8 colossal, enormous, gigantic 9 leviathan, monstrous 10 gargantuan, mastodonic, monumental 11 elephantine

man 3 guy 4 buck, chap, cuss, dude, gent 5 being, bloke 6 fellow, mister, mortal, person 7 husband 8 creature, paramour 9 boyfriend, mortality, personage 10 individual 11 Homo sapiens *castrated:* 6 eunuch *combining form:*

4 andr 5 andro, homin 6 homini *French:* 5 homme *Italian:* 4 uomo *Latin:* 3 vir 4 homo *old:* 6 codger, geezer *Spanish:* 6 hombre *Yiddish:* 6 mensch *young:* 3 boy, lad 6 shaver 9 stripling

manage 3 run 4 cope, fare, head, keep 5 get by, get on, guide, shift 6 afford, direct, effect, govern, handle 7 achieve, carry on, conduct, control, execute, finagle, operate, oversee, succeed 8 carry out, contrive, cope with, deal with, dominate, engineer, get along, maintain 9 cultivate, supervise 10 accomplish, administer, bring about 11 superintend

manageable 6 docile 8 amenable, bearable, biddable, passable 9 agreeable, compliant, endurable, tractable 10 responsive 11 cooperative, supportable, sustainable 13 accommodating

management 4 care 5 brass 6 charge 7 conduct, control, running 8 guidance, handling 9 direction, oversight 10 conducting 11 front office, supervising, supervision

manager 4 boss, exec 6 gerent 7 handler, officer 8 director, official, overseer, producer 9 conductor, executive 10 impresario, supervisor 13 administrator *museum:* 7 curator

mañana 7 someday 8 sometime, tomorrow

Man and Superman author 4 Shaw (George Bernard)

Manassas battle 7 Bull Run

Manasseh, Manasses *brother:* 7 Ephraim *father:* 6 Hashum, Joseph 8 Hezekiah 10 Pahathmoab *grandfather:* 5 Jacob *grandson:* 6 Gilead *mother:* 7 Asenath *son:* 6 Machir

man-at-arms 7 fighter, soldier, warrior 10 serviceman

Mandalay author 7 Kipling (Rudyard)

mandarin 5 elder 6 orange 8 official 9 tangerine 10 bureaucrat, panjandrum

mandate 4 fiat, word 5 edict, order, ukase 6 behest, charge, decree 7 bidding, command, dictate 9 authority, directive 10 imperative, injunction 13 authorization

mandatory 6 forced 7 binding 8 required 9 de rigueur, necessary, requisite 10 compulsory, imperative, obligatory 11 involuntary

mandible 3 jaw 8 lower jaw

man-eater 4 lion, ogre 5 shark, tiger 8 cannibal 13 mackerel shark

Manette's daughter 5 Lucie

maneuver 3 ply 4 move, plan, plot, ploy, step 5 feint, trick, wield 6 design, device, gambit, handle, jockey, scheme,

tactic, wangle 7 exploit, finagle, finesse 8 artifice, démarche, engineer, exercise, intrigue, movement, navigate 9 machinate, procedure, stratagem 10 manipulate, proceeding, subterfuge 11 contrivance, machination 12 manipulation *maneuvering room* 8 latitude

Man for All Seasons, A *author:* 4 Bolt (Robert) *subject:* 4 More (Thomas)

manganese *ore:* 10 pyrolusite

manger 4 rack 6 cratch, feeder, trough

mangle 3 mar 4 iron, maim, maul 5 press 6 damage, deface, deform, impair, injure 7 butcher, contort, distort 8 lacerate, mutilate 9 disfigure

mangy 5 seedy 6 ragtag, shabby 7 scruffy, squalid 8 decrepit, tattered 9 moth-eaten 10 down-at-heel, threadbare

manhandle 5 abuse 6 batter 7 rough up 8 maltreat, mistreat 10 push around, slap around

Manhattan *building:* 11 Empire State *district:* 4 Soho 6 Harlem 7 Chelsea, Tribeca *entertainment district:* 11 Times Square *financial district:* 10 Wall Street *museum:* 7 Whitney 10 Guggenheim 12 Metropolitan *opera house:* 12 Metropolitan *purchaser:* 6 Minuit (Peter) *river:* 4 East 6 Hudson *school:* 3 NYU 8 Columbia 9 Juilliard

mania 4 rage, zeal 5 craze, fancy 6 frenzy, lunacy 7 madness, passion 8 fixation, idée fixe, insanity 9 cacoëthes, obsession 10 compulsion, enthusiasm 11 infatuation

maniac 3 bug, nut 4 loon 5 fiend, freak 6 madman, psycho, zealot 7 fanatic, lunatic, nutcase 8 crackpot 9 bedlamite 10 enthusiast

manifest 4 show 5 clear, overt, plain, shown, utter, voice 6 appear, embody, evince, expose, patent, reveal 7 display, evident, evinced, exhibit, express, invoice, obvious, visible 8 apparent, distinct, evidence, palpable, proclaim, revealed 9 evidenced, incarnate, objectify, prominent 10 illustrate, noticeable, observable 11 demonstrate, exteriorize, externalize, perceptible, unambiguous

manifestation 4 show, sign 5 proof 7 display, symptom 8 epiphany 10 appearance, revelation

manifesto 4 fiat, rule, writ 5 credo, creed, edict, ukase 6 decree, dictum, gospel, notice, policy, ruling 7 mandate, statute 8 doctrine, document, platform 9 affidavit, directive, statement, testament, testimony, ultimatum 10 deposition, indictment, injunction, regulation, resolution 11 declaration

12 announcement, denunciation, notification, proclamation 13 pronouncement

manifold 7 diverse, various 8 compound, multiple, multiply, numerous 9 multiform, multiplex 10 multiphase 12 multifarious

manikin 4 runt 5 dummy, dwarf, gnome, model, pygmy 6 midget, peewee 8 Tom Thumb 10 homunculus

Manila *founder:* 7 Legazpi (Miguel López de) *site:* 11 Phillipines *victor:* 5 Dewey (George)

manipulate 3 ply, rig 4 play 5 steer, swing, wield 6 direct, doctor, handle, jockey, juggle, manage 7 beguile, conduct, control, exploit, finagle, finesse, massage 8 engineer, maneuver 9 machinate 10 tamper with

Man, Isle of *capital:* 7 Douglas *cat:* 4 Manx *possession of:* 7 Britain *sea:* 5 Irish

Manitoba *capital:* 8 Winnipeg *lake:* 8 Winnipeg 12 Winnipegosis *mountain:* 5 Baldy *provincial flower:* 13 prairie crocus *river:* 6 Nelson 9 Churchill

mankind 6 humans, people 8 humanity 11 Homo sapiens

manlike 4 male 6 virile 8 hominoid, humanoid 9 masculine 10 anthropoid

manly 4 male 5 macho 6 virile 9 masculine

man-made 9 synthetic 10 artificial, factitious *object:* 8 artefact, artifact

Mann character 6 Joseph 10 Aschenbach (Gustav von), Felix Krull 11 Hans Castorp, Tonio Kröger

manner 3 air, use, way 4 form, kind, look, mien, mode, sort, vein, wont 5 habit, modus, style, usage 6 aspect, custom, method 7 bearing, conduct, fashion, p's and q's 8 behavior, demeanor, habitude, practice, presence 9 demeanour, etiquette, technique 10 consuetude, deportment 11 affectation, comportment, peculiarity 12 idiosyncrasy

mannered 7 stilted 8 affected 10 artificial 13 self-conscious

mannerism 3 tic 4 pose 5 quirk 10 preciosity 11 affectation, peculiarity, singularity 12 eccentricity, idiosyncrasy 13 artificiality

mannerless 4 rude 6 coarse 7 boorish, ill-bred, uncivil, uncouth 8 impolite 12 discourteous

mannerly 5 civil 6 polite 7 genteel, refined 8 decorous, gracious, well-bred 9 civilized, courteous 10 respectful

Manon composer 8 Massenet (Jules)

Manon Lescaut *author:* 7 Prévost (Abbé)

composer: 7 Puccini (Giacomo) 8 Massenet (Jules) *lover:* 9 des Grieux

manor 5 villa 6 estate, quinta 7 château, demesne 12 landed estate

manservant 5 valet 6 butler

mansion 4 hall 5 villa 6 palace 7 château

manslayer 6 killer 8 homicide, murderer

manta 3 ray 5 cloak, cloth, shawl 7 blanket

manteau 4 coat, robe, wrap 5 cloak 6 capote, mantle, tabard

mantic 5 vatic 7 Delphic, fatidic 8 Delphian, oracular 9 prophetic, sibylline, vaticinal 10 divinatory

mantilla 4 cape, wrap 5 cloak, fichu, scarf, shawl

mantle 4 cope, glow, pink, robe, rose 5 blush, cloak, color, cover, flush, rouge 6 capote, casing, pinken, redden 7 crimson

man-to-man 4 open 5 frank, plain 6 candid, direct, honest 10 forthright, unreserved 11 openhearted

mantra 5 chant, motto 6 prayer, slogan 9 watchword 10 invocation 11 incantation

manual 4 text 5 guide 6 primer 8 Baedeker, handbook, hornbook, textbook 9 guidebook, vade mecum 10 compendium 11 abecedarium, enchiridion *religious:* 9 catechism *worker:* 6 menial 7 laborer

manufacture 4 form, make 6 create, invent 7 fashion, produce 8 assemble 9 fabricate 11 put together

manumit 4 free 6 unbind 7 release, set free, unchain 8 liberate 9 unshackle 10 emancipate

manure 4 dung 6 ordure 7 excreta 9 excrement 10 fertilizer

manuscript 4 hand 6 scrawl 8 longhand 9 autograph 10 penmanship 11 calligraphy, handwriting *ancient:* 5 codex 6 scroll 7 codices (plural) *red part:* 6 rubric

Man Without a Country, The *author:* 4 Hale (Edward Everett) *character:* 5 Nolan

many 5 scads 6 divers, legion, myriad, sundry 7 copious, diverse, umpteen, various 8 abundant, manifold, multiple, numerous 9 abounding, bounteous, bountiful, countless, multitude, plentiful 12 multifarious 13 multitudinous *combining form:* 4 poly 5 multi, pluri

many-sided 7 diverse 8 all-round, talented 9 all-around, versatile 10 variegated 11 diversified 12 multifaceted, multifarious 13 comprehensive

Mao's successor 3 Hua (Guofeng, Kuofeng) **4** Deng (Xiaoping), Teng (Hsiao-p'ing)

map 4 plan, plat **5** chart, draft, globe, graph **6** design, lay out, set out, sketch, survey **7** arrange, diagram, drawing, outline, tracing **9** delineate *collection:* **5** atlas *line:* **6** isobar **7** contour, isogram, isohyet **8** isogloss, isogonic, isopleth, isotherm *maker:* **12** cartographer *making:* **11** cartography

maple *genus:* **4** Acer *product:* **5** syrup *type:* **3** red **5** sugar **8** box elder

map projection 5 conic **8** Mercator **9** polyconic **10** sinusoidal **12** orthographic **13** stereographic

maquillage 6 makeup

mar 4 ding, harm, hurt, scar, warp **5** spoil, stain **6** bruise, damage, deface, deform, impair, injure **7** blemish, scratch, tarnish, vitiate **9** disfigure

marabou 5 stork

Marat/Sade author **5** Weiss (Peter)

Marat, Jean-Paul *colleague:* **6** Danton (Georges) **11** Robespierre (Maximilien) *slayer:* **6** Corday (Charlotte)

maraud 4 loot, raid, sack **5** foray, harry **6** harass, ravage, ravish **7** despoil, pillage, plunder, ransack

marauder 6 bandit, pirate **7** brigand, spoiler, wrecker **9** buccaneer, desperado **10** freebooter

marble 3 mib, mig, taw **4** immy, migg **5** agate, aggie, alley, rance **6** blotch, miggle, mottle, streak **7** cipolin, glassie, steelie **9** limestone

marbled 6 veined **7** dappled, flecked, mottled **8** speckled, streaked

Marble Faun, The *author:* **9** Hawthorne (Nathaniel) *character:* **5** Hilda **6** Kenyon, Miriam **9** Donatello *setting:* **4** Rome

marcel 4 wave

march 3 hem, rim **4** abut, file, line **5** skirt **6** adjoin, border, parade **7** advance, headway, proceed **8** anabasis, boundary, frontier, outlands, progress, traverse **9** periphery **10** borderland

March *date:* **4** ides *mother:* **6** Marmee *sisters:* **3** Amy, Meg **4** Beth

March Hare creator **7** Carroll (Lewis)

March King 5 Sousa (John Philip)

Mardi Gras 8 carnival **10** Fat Tuesday *city:* **10** New Orleans

Marduk *city:* **7** Babylon *consort:* **8** Zarbanit, Zarpanit *victim:* **5** Kingu **6** Tiamat

mare 3 sea **5** horse **6** equine

mare's nest 3 con, din **4** hoax, scam **5** babel, cheat, fraud, put-on, spoof **6** bedlam, clamor, hubbub, humbug, racket, ruckus, tumult, uproar **7** swin-

dle, turmoil **8** brouhaha, flimflam, illusion **9** confusion, imposture **10** hullabaloo **11** pandemonium

margarine 4 oleo

margin 3 hem, rim **4** brim, edge, join, line, play, room, side **5** bound, brink, frame, scope, shore, skirt, verge **6** border, fringe, leeway **7** minimum, outline, selvage **8** boundary, latitude, selvedge, surround, trimming **9** elbowroom, perimeter, periphery **13** circumference *tiny:* **4** hair

marginal 5 minor **7** limited, minimal **9** bordering **10** borderline, negligible, peripheral, subsidiary **13** insignificant

Marguerite's lover **5** Faust

Maria ___ 5 Elena **7** Stuarda

Marianas *discoverer:* **8** Magellan (Ferdinand) *island:* **4** Guam, Rota **5** Pagan **6** Guguan, Saipan, Tinian **7** Agrihan, Aguijan

marijuana 3 pot **4** hash, hemp, weed **5** bhang, grass **6** reefer **7** hashish **8** cannabis

marina 4 dock, pier, quay **5** basin, berth, wharf **8** boatyard

marinate 4 soak **5** steep **6** drench, pickle **7** immerse **8** macerate

marine 5 naval **7** abyssal, aquatic, deepsea, oceanic, pelagic **8** nautical, seagoing **9** seafaring, thalassic **10** oceangoing **12** hydrographic **13** oceanographic *crustacean:* **6** shrimp **7** lobster **8** barnacle *deposit:* **5** coral *plant:* **4** kelp, nori **5** dulse **6** wakame **7** seaweed

mariner 3 gob, tar **4** jack, salt, swab **5** limey **6** hearty, rating, sailor, sea dog, seaman **7** jack-tar, old salt, swabbie **8** seafarer **9** sailorman, shellback, tarpaulin **10** bluejacket

marital 6 wedded **7** married, nuptial, spousal **8** conjugal, hymeneal **9** connubial

maritime 7 oceanic, pelagic **8** nautical **9** thalassic **12** navigational

mark 3 aim, jot, sap **4** butt, dupe, fool, goal, gull, heed, look, nick, note, pick, show, sign, view **5** blaze, bound, brand, chart, chump, elect, grade, label, notch, stamp, token, trait **6** behold, choose, denote, evince, lay off, notice, object, opt for, rating, record, select, sucker, target, victim, virtue **7** betoken, delimit, discern, exhibit, fall guy, feature, gudgeon, indicia, initial, measure, observe, qualify, scratch, signify, symptom **8** function, indicate, perceive, register **9** attribute, character, designate, objective, single out **10** indication **11** differentia, distinction, distinguish **12** characterize *distinctive:* **7** indicia **8** indicium *identifying:* 4 logo, seal 6 emblem, signet, symbol 8 colophon, logotype *of insertion:* 5 caret *of omission:* 8 ellipsis 10 apostrophe *over a vowel:* 5 breve 6 accent, macron *over n:* 5 tilde *punctuation:* 4 dash 5 brace, colon, comma, slant, slash 6 hyphen, period 7 bracket, solidus 9 backslash, guillemet, semicolon 10 apostrophe *under a letter:* 7 cedilla

Mark 6 Gospel *cousin:* 8 Barnabas *mother:* 4 Mary

mark down 3 cut 4 pare 5 shave, slash 6 reduce 7 devalue 8 discount 9 devaluate 10 depreciate, undervalue

marked 5 noted 6 patent, signal 7 evident, notable, obvious, pointed, salient 8 distinct, manifest, striking 9 arresting, prominent 10 noticeable, remarkable 11 conspicuous, outstanding 12 considerable 13 distinguished *man:* 4 Cain

market 4 fair, mall, sell, shop, vend 5 store 6 bazaar, outlet, retail 8 emporium, exchange, showroom 9 advertise, traffic in, wholesale 11 merchandise *kind:* 4 flea 5 money, stock

marketable 5 sound 7 salable 8 vendible 10 commercial

marketplace 4 mall, souk 5 agora 6 bazaar, rialto 8 emporium

marksman 4 shot 7 deadeye, shooter 12 sharpshooter

marl 4 clay, silt

marlin 8 billfish 9 spearfish

Marlowe play 8 Edward II 9 Dr. Faustus 10 Jew of Malta (The) 11 Tamburlaine 13 Doctor Faustus

marmot 6 rodent 9 woodchuck 10 prairie dog

maroon 3 red 6 claret, desert, strand 7 abandon, crimson, forsake, isolate, outcast 8 burgundy, castaway

Marquand character 4 Gray (Charles), Moto (Mr.) 5 Apley (George), Wayde (Willis) 6 Pulham (H.M.) 7 Goodwin (Melville)

Marquis, Don *cat:* 9 Mehitabel *cockroach:* 5 Archy

marriage 5 match, union 6 bridal 7 nuptial, spousal, wedding, wedlock 8 coupling, espousal, monogamy, nuptials, polygamy 9 matrimony 11 conjugality 12 connubiality *combining form:* 4 gamy 6 gamous *notice:* 5 banns *outside a group:* 7 exogamy *within a group:* 8 endogamy

marriageable 6 nubile 8 eligible

marriage broker 9 go-between 10 matchmaker

Marriage of Figaro composer 6 Mozart (Wolfgang Amadeus)

marrow 4 core, meat, pith, soul 5 heart, stuff 6 kernel 7 essence 12 quintessence

marry 3 tie, wed 4 join, link, mate, wive, yoke 5 hitch, merge, unite 6 couple, splice, spouse 7 combine, conjoin, espouse 9 conjugate

Mars 4 Ares 6 planet *lover:* 5 Venus *mission:* 6 Viking 7 Mariner 10 Pathfinder *moon:* 6 Deimos, Phobos *relating to:* 7 martian (see also ARES)

Marseillaise composer 13 Rouget de Lisle (Claude-Joseph)

marsh 3 bog, fen 4 mire, ooze, quag 5 bayou, glade, swale, swamp 6 morass, muskeg, slough 7 wetland 8 quagmire 9 swampland

marshal 5 align, array, guide, order, rally, usher 6 deploy, direct, escort, muster 7 arrange, officer, round up 8 assemble, mobilize, organize, shepherd 9 methodize, systemize

Marshall Islands *atoll:* 6 Bikini 8 Enewetak 9 Kwajalein *capital:* 6 Majuro *ethnic group:* 11 Micronesian *island chain:* 5 Ralik, Ratak 6 Sunset 7 Sunrise *language:* 7 English 11 Marshallese *monetary unit:* 6 dollar

marsupial 5 koala 6 possum, wombat 7 opossum 8 kangaroo 9 bandicoot

marten 6 fisher, weasel

Martha *brother:* 7 Lazarus *sister:* 4 Mary

martial 7 warlike 8 militant, military, spirited 9 bellicose, combative, soldierly 11 belligerent 12 militaristic

martial art 4 judo 5 kendo 6 aikido, karate, kung fu, tai chi 7 shaolin 8 capoeira, jiujitsu 9 tae kwon do 11 tai chi chuan *school:* 4 dojo

Martial's forte 7 epigram

Martin Chuzzlewit author 7 Dickens (Charles)

Martinique *capital:* 12 Fort-de-France *department of:* 6 France *discoverer:* 8 Columbus (Christopher) *island group:* 8 Windward *location:* 10 West Indies *neighbor:* 8 Dominica 10 Saint Lucia *volcano:* 5 Pelée

martyr 4 Paul, rack 5 Agnes, Alban, James, Peter, saint, wring 6 George, harrow, Justin 7 afflict, agonize, Clement, crucify, Cyprian, Stephen, torment, torture 8 Ignatius, Lawrence, Polycarp, sufferer 9 Joan of Arc, Sebastian 10 excruciate, Thomas More *Protestant:* 6 Ridley (Nicholas) 7 Cranmer (Thomas), Latimer (Hugh)

marvel 4 gape 6 wonder 7 miracle, portent, prodigy, stunner 9 curiosity, sensation 10 phenomenon 12 astonishment

marvelous 5 super, swell 6 divine 7 amazing, awesome, ripping 8 glorious, striking, stunning, superior, terrific, wondrous 9 excellent, wonderful 10 astounding, incredible, miraculous, phenomenal, prodigious, remarkable, staggering, stupendous, surprising 11 astonishing, exceptional, sensational, spectacular 12 awe-inspiring, supernatural 13 extraordinary

Marx brother 5 Chico, Harpo, Zeppo 7 Groucho

Marxist 9 socialist 9 communist

Marx, Karl *book:* 7 Kapital (Das) *collaborator:* 6 Engels (Friedrich)

Mary *husband:* 6 Clopas, Joseph 8 Alphaeus *kinswoman:* 9 Elisabeth *son:* 4 Mark 5 James, Jesus

Maryland *bay:* 10 Chesapeake *capital:* 9 Annapolis *city:* 9 Baltimore, Frederick *college, university:* 6 Towson 7 Goucher 9 Annapolis 12 Johns Hopkins 12 Naval Academy (U.S.) *fort:* 7 McHenry *nickname:* 7 Old Line (State) *river:* 7 Potomac 8 Patuxent *state bird:* 15 Baltimore oriole *state flower:* 14 black-eyed Susan *state tree:* 8 white oak

mascot 4 juju 5 charm 6 amulet, fetish, symbol 8 talisman

masculine 4 male 5 macho, manly 6 manful, virile 7 manlike

masculinity 8 machismo, virility 9 manliness

mash 4 pulp 5 crush, smash 6 squish 8 macerate 9 pulverize

masher 4 wolf 5 flirt 6 chaser 7 Don Juan, seducer 8 Casanova 9 ladies' man, womanizer 10 lady-killer 11 philanderer

mash note 10 billet-doux, love letter

mask 4 hide, pose, sham, veil 5 cover, front, guard, guise, visor 6 facade, screen, vizard 7 dress up, frisket, pretext 8 coloring, disguise, pretense 9 dissemble, semblance 10 appearance, camouflage, false front, simulation 11 dissimulate 13 dissimulation

masonry 9 brickwork, stonework *in a frame:* 7 nogging

masquerade 4 pose 6 facade 7 costume, posture 8 carnival, disguise 10 camouflage, masked ball 11 costume ball

mass 3 lot, sum, wad 4 bank, body, bulk, clot, core, glob, heap, hill, lump, pack, peck, pile 5 clump, group, mound 6 corpus, volume 7 expanse, globule, wadding 8 assemble 9 aggregate, great deal, stockpile, substance 11 aggregation 12 conglomerate *for the dead:* 7 requiem *of individuals:* 3 mob 4 host 5 crowd, crush, flock, horde, swarm 6 throng 12 congregation 13 agglomeration *part:* 6 proper 8 ordinary

Massachusetts *cape:* 3 Ann, Cod *capital:*

6 Boston *city:* 6 Lowell, Quincy 9 Cambridge, Worcester 10 New Bedford 11 Springfield *college, university:* 3 MIT 5 Clark, Smith, Tufts 6 Boston 7 Amherst, Berklee, Harvard 8 Brandeis, Williams 9 Hampshire, Radcliffe, Wellesley 12 Mount Holyoke, Northeastern *island:* 9 Nantucket 15 Martha's Vineyard *mountain, range:* 8 Greylock 9 Berkshire *nickname:* 3 Bay (State) 9 Old Colony (State) *river:* 11 Connecticut *state bird:* 9 chickadee *state flower:* 9 mayflower *state tree:* 3 elm (American)

massacre 4 kill 6 mangle, murder, pogrom 7 butcher, carnage 8 butchery, decimate, genocide, mangling, mutilate 9 bloodbath, bloodshed, slaughter 10 annihilate, blood purge, decimation, mutilation 11 exterminate 12 annihilation

massage 3 rub 5 knead 7 flatter, rubdown 8 blandish 10 manipulate

Massenet opera 5 Le Cid, Manon, Sapho, Thaïs 7 Werther

massive 4 huge, vast 5 bulky, giant, jumbo, solid 6 mighty 7 hulking, immense, mammoth, weighty 8 colossal, cumbrous, enormous, gigantic, towering 9 humongous, monstrous 10 gargantuan, monumental, prodigious, stupendous, tremendous 11 elephantine, mountainous

master 4 best, boss, guru, head, lick, rule, tame 5 adept, bwana, chief, crack, learn, ruler, sahib, tutor 6 artist, expert, genius, honcho, leader, subdue, victor 7 captain, conquer, headman, maestro, padrone, prevail, skilled, triumph 8 dominant, dominate, employer, governor, overcome, overlord, overseer, regulate, skeleton, skillful, superior, surmount, virtuoso 9 authority, chieftain, conqueror, dominator, paramount, principal, sovereign 10 proficient 11 predominant

masterful 4 deft 5 adept, bossy 6 adroit, expert 7 skilled 8 despotic, skillful 9 imperious 10 autocratic, high-handed, proficient, tyrannical 11 dictatorial, domineering, magisterial, overbearing 13 authoritarian, authoritative, high-and-mighty

masterly 5 adept, crack 6 adroit, expert 7 skilled 8 skillful 9 dexterous 10 proficient 11 crackerjack 12 accomplished

Master of Ballantrae, The 6 Durrie *author:* 9 Stevenson (Robert Louis)

masterpiece 7 classic 10 magnum opus 11 chef d'oeuvre, tour de force

mastery 5 knack, skill 7 ability, com-

mand, control, know-how, prowess
8 dominion **9** authority, expertise
10 ascendancy, domination, expertness, virtuosity **11** proficiency, superiority
masticate 4 chaw, chew, pulp **5** champ, chomp, crush, munch **6** crunch
7 scrunch **8** macerate, ruminate
9 break down
mat 3 rug **4** felt **6** border, carpet
matador 6 torero **8** toreador **11** bullfighter *adjunct:* **6** muleta *move:* **4** pase
5 faena **8** veronica
Mata Hari 3 spy
match 3 pit **4** bout, game, like, meet, peer, suit, twin **5** array, equal, liken, rival, touch, union **6** double, equate, oppose **7** compare, compeer, contest, counter, opposer, paragon, play off
8 alliance, analogue, marriage, opponent, parallel **9** adversary, correlate, duplicate, encounter, measure up, partake of **10** antagonist, complement, coordinate, engagement, equivalent, reciprocal, supplement, tournament
11 counterpart **12** correspond to **13** correspondent, harmonize with *a bet:* **3** see *friction:* **7** lucifer
matchless 6 unique **7** supreme **8** peerless, singular **9** nonpareil, unequaled, unrivaled **10** inimitable **12** incomparable, unparalleled
matchmaker see MARRIAGE BROKER
mate 3 pal, tie, wed **4** chum, pair, twin
5 amigo, breed, buddy, crony, equal, hitch, marry **6** cohort, couple, double, fellow, friend, helper, splice, spouse
7 compeer, comrade, consort, partner
8 confrere, sidekick **9** associate, companion, copartner, duplicate, procreate
10 complement, equivalent, reciprocal
11 concomitant
maté 3 tea **5** holly **8** beverage
mater 3 mom, mum **6** mother **9** matriarch
____ **mater 4** alma
material 4 real, true **5** cloth, stuff **6** actual, fabric, matter, object **7** earthly, element, germane, worldly **8** apposite, palpable, physical, relevant, sensible, tangible **9** component, corporeal, equipment, essential, important, objective, pertinent, substance **10** applicable, individual, ingredient, meaningful, phenomenal **11** appreciable, constituent, fundamental, perceptible, significant, substantial **12** considerable
13 consequential *building:* **5** adobe, brick **6** stucco **7** lagging, plaster, plywood, shingle **8** concrete
materialistic 7 secular, worldly
11 acquisitive

materialize 4 loom, rise **5** arise, issue, reify **6** appear, embody, emerge, evolve, show up, typify **7** develop, surface
8 manifest **9** come about, incarnate, objectify, take shape **11** exteriorize
12 substantiate
matériel 4 gear **5** stock **8** supplies **9** apparatus, equipment, machinery **10** provisions **13** accouterments, accoutrements, paraphernalia
maternal 8 motherly
matey 5 pally, tight **6** clubby **7** affable
8 amicable, familiar, friendly, intimate, sociable **9** congenial
mathematician *American:* **5** Wiles
(Andrew) **6** Peirce (Charles S.), Veblen
(Oswald), Wiener (Norbert) *Austrian:*
5 Gödel (Kurt) *British:* **6** Stokes
(George) *Dutch:* **7** Huygens (Christiaan)
English: **6** Newton (Isaac), Taylor
(Brook), Turing (Alan), Wallis (John)
7 Pearson (Karl), Russell (Bertrand)
8 Hamilton (James Rowan) **9** Sylvester
(James Joseph), Whitehead (Alfred
North, Henry) *French:* **5** Borel (Emile),
Comte (Auguste), Viète (François)
6 Galois (Evariste), Pascal (Blaise),
Picard (Charles-Emile) **7** Fourier (Jean-Baptiste), Laplace (Marquis de),
Vernier (Pierre) **8** Painlevé (Paul), Poincaré (Jules-Henri) **9** Descartes (René)
German: **5** Gauss (Carl), Wolff (Freiherr
von) **6** Staudt (Karl von) **7** Leibniz
(Gottfried Wilhelm), Riemann (Georg)
11 Weierstrass (Karl) *Greek:* **6** Euclid
10 Archimedes, Pythagoras *Hungarian:*
5 Erdos (Paul) *Italian:* **8** Volterra (Vito)
10 Torricelli (Evangelista) *Norwegian:*
7 Stormer (Fredrik) *Russian:*
11 Lobachevsky (Nikolay) *Scottish:*
4 Tait (Peter) **6** Napier (John) **8** Stirling
(James) *Swiss:* **5** Euler (Leonhard),
Sturm (Jacques) **7** Steiner (Jakob)
mathematics *branch:* **4** trig **7** algebra
8 calculus, geometry, topology **10** arithmetic, statistics **12** trigonometry *proven
statement in:* **7** theorem
____ **Mather 6** Cotton **7** Richard
8 Increase
matriarch 4 dame **6** mother **7** dowager
10 grande dame
matriculate 4 join **5** enter **6** enroll, sign
on **8** register
matrimonial 6 bridal, wedded **7** marital,
married, nuptial, spousal **8** conjugal,
hymeneal **9** connubial **11** epithalamic
matrimony 7 wedlock **8** marriage **11** conjugality **12** connubiality
matrix 3 die, net, web **4** grid, mesh
5 array **6** cradle, gangue **7** complex,
network **10** groundmass, truth table

matron 4 dame **7** dowager **8** chaperon **9** chaperone **10** grande dame
Mattathias *father:* **5** Simon **6** Ananos **7** Absalom, Boethus **10** Theophilus *son:* **8** Josephus
matter 4 body, core, gist, meat, pith, text **5** being, cause, point, sense, stuff, theme, thing, topic, value, weigh **6** affair, amount, burden, entity, import, object **7** concern, signify, subject **8** argument, material **9** grievance, magnitude, substance **11** constituent **12** circumstance
matter-of-fact 3 dry **5** plain, prose, prosy, sober, stoic **6** stolid **7** prosaic **9** impassive, objective, practical, pragmatic, realistic **10** hard-boiled, hardheaded, impersonal, phlegmatic, unaffected **11** cold-blooded, down-to-earth, emotionless **13** unimpassioned, unsentimental
mattress 3 pad **4** sack *case:* **4** tick *fabric:* **7** ticking *straw:* **6** pallet
mature 3 age, due **4** grow, ripe **5** adult, grown, owing, ready, ripen **6** flower, grow up, mellow, season, unpaid **7** advance, blossom, decline, develop, grown-up, overdue, payable, ripened **8** progress **9** developed, full-blown, full-grown **11** full-fledged
maudlin 5 gushy, mushy, silly, sappy, soppy **6** slushy, sticky **7** cloying, gushing, mawkish **8** bathetic **11** sentimental, tear-jerking
Maugham character 4 Kear, Liza **5** Carey, Rosie, Sadie **7** Mildred **8** Ashenden, Craddock **10** Strickland
maul 4 bang, bash, beat, club, drub, flog, whip **5** abuse, flail, pound **6** batter, bruise, buffet, cudgel, hammer, injure, mangle, molest, pummel, sledge, thrash **7** clobber, rough up **8** bludgeon, lambaste, maltreat **9** manhandle
Mauna ___ 3 Kea, Loa
maunder 3 bat, gad **4** rove **5** drift, mooch, range **6** mumble, mutter, ramble, wander **7** blather, digress, traipse **8** divagate
Mauritania *capital:* **10** Nouakchott *desert:* **6** Sahara *language:* **5** Wolof **6** Arabic, Fulani **7** Soninke *monetary unit:* **7** ouguiya *neighbor:* **4** Mali **6** Guinea **7** Senegal **7** Algeria **13** Western Sahara *river:* **7** Senegal
Mauritius *capital:* **9** Port Louis *island group:* **9** Mascarene *language:* **6** Creole **7** English *monetary unit:* **5** rupee
Maurois biographee 4 Hugo (Victor), Sand (George) **5** Byron (Lord), Dumas (Alexandre) **6** Balzac (Honoré de),

Proust (Marcel) **7** Shelley (Percy Bysshe) **8** Disraeli (Benjamin)
mauve 5 lilac **6** purple, violet
maven 3 ace **4** buff, whiz **5** adept, freak, shark **6** addict, expert, master, savant **7** devotee, fanatic, hotshot **8** virtuoso **9** authority **10** enthusiast **11** connoisseur
maverick 5 stray **7** heretic **8** unmarked **9** dissident, unbranded **10** iconoclast **11** independent **13** nonconformist
maw 4 crop **5** chasm, mouth **6** cavity, gullet **7** stomach
mawkish 5 gushy, mushy, sappy, soppy **6** sloppy, slushy, sticky, syrupy **7** cloying, gushing, insipid, maudlin **8** bathetic, romantic **9** schmaltzy, sickening **10** lovey-dovey, nauseating **11** sentimental, tear-jerking
maxilla 3 jaw **4** bone
maxim 3 law, saw **4** rule **5** adage, axiom, gnome, moral, motto, tenet, truth **6** byword, dictum, saying, truism **7** precept, proverb, theorem **8** aphorism, apothegm **9** platitude, prescript, principle **11** commonplace
maximal 3 top **6** utmost **7** highest, largest, supreme, topmost **8** complete, greatest, ultimate **9** paramount
maximum 3 top **6** utmost **7** highest, largest, supreme, topmost **8** extremum, greatest, ultimate **9** paramount
may 5 might, shrub **6** spirea **8** hawthorn
maybe 7 perhaps **8** possibly **9** perchance **11** conceivably, uncertainty
Mayflower *document:* **7** Compact *passengers:* **8** Pilgrims
mayhem 4 maim, riot **5** chaos, havoc **7** cripple, dislimb **8** mutilate **9** dismember **10** mutilation
mayor 11 burgomaster *Chicago (former):* **5** Daley (Richard) *New York (former):* **4** Koch (Edward) **6** Walker (Jimmy) **7** Lindsay (John) **8** Giuliani (Rudolph) **9** La Guardia (Fiorello) *Spanish:* **7** alcalde
Mayor of Casterbridge, The *author:* **5** Hardy (Thomas) *character:* **8** Henchard (Michael)
maze 3 web **4** knot, mesh **5** skein, snarl **6** jungle, morass, tangle **7** confuse, network, perplex **8** bewilder, mishmash **9** labyrinth
Mazel ___! 3 tov
McCarthy novel 8 Crossing (The) **16** Cities of the Plain **18** All the Pretty Horses
McCullers, Carson *novel:* **18** Ballad of the Sad Cafe (The) **18** Member of the Wedding (The) **20** Heart Is a Lonely Hunter (The) **23** Reflections in a Golden Eye

McCullough novel 10 Thorn Birds (The)
McMurtry novel 12 Buffalo Girls, Lonesome Dove 14 Horseman Pass By
15 Last Picture Show (The) 17 Terms of Endearment
McTeague author 6 Norris (Frank)
MD 3 doc 6 doctor, medico 8 sawbones
9 physician
mea culpa 5 error, fault 7 apology
9 admission 10 concession, confession
meadow 3 lea, ley 5 green 7 pasture
9 grassland *historic:* 9 Runnymede *lowlying:* 5 haugh
meadow mushroom 6 agaric
meager 4 bare, bony, lean, mere, thin
5 gaunt, lanky, scant, short, spare 6 paltry, scanty, shabby, skimpy, skinny,
slight, sparse 7 angular, minimum,
scraggy, scrawny, scrimpy 8 exiguous,
rawboned 9 deficient, miserable
10 inadequate 12 insufficient
meal 4 chow, fare, feed, grub 5 board,
feast, lunch, snack 6 brunch, dinner,
farina, picnic, repast, spread, supper
7 high tea, nooning 8 victuals 9 breakfast, collation, refection *army:* 4 mess
mealy 6 spotty, uneven 11 farinaceous
mean 3 low, mid, par 4 base, fair, hint,
norm, poor, want, wish 5 cheap, cruel,
imply, lousy, lowly, mingy, petty,
rough, small, snide, spell, tight, weigh
6 attest, center, common, denote,
design, humble, intend, matter, medial,
medium, middle, paltry, scummy,
scurvy, shabby, shoddy, sleazy, stingy,
unwell 7 average, betoken, connote,
express, lowborn, miserly, pitiful, portend, propose, purport, signify, suggest,
vicious 8 déclassé, indicate, inferior,
mediocre, middling, midpoint, moderate, ordinary, pitiable, plebeian, stand
for 9 designate, penurious, represent,
symbolize 10 despicable, second-rate
11 closefisted, tightfisted 12 contemptible, intermediary, intermediate
meander 4 roam, rove, turn, wind
5 amble, drift, range, snake, stray, twist
6 ramble, wander 7 traipse, winding
8 vagabond 9 gallivant, labyrinth
meandering 5 snaky 7 sinuous 8 flexuous, tortuous 10 convoluted, serpentine
11 anfractuous
meaning 3 aim 4 gist, pith 5 drift, force,
point, sense 6 effect, import, intent
7 essence, message, purport 9 intention,
substance 10 definition, denotation,
intimation 11 connotation, implication
12 significance 13 signification
meaningful 5 valid 7 pointed, serious,
weighty 8 eloquent, material 9 important, momentous 10 expressive 11 sen-

tentious, significant, substantial 13 consequential
meaningless 5 empty, inane 6 absurd,
futile, hollow 7 trivial 8 nugatory
11 nonsensical 13 insignificant
meanings *diverse:* 8 polysemy *study of:*
9 semantics
means 5 funds, money 6 agency, assets,
avenue, income 7 backing, capital
8 finances, holdings, property, reserves
9 apparatus, equipment, resources,
substance 10 instrument 11 wherewithal
meantime 7 interim 8 interval
measly 4 poor, puny 5 petty, scant
6 meager, meagre, paltry, scanty 7 pitiful, trivial 8 niggling, pathetic,
picayune, piddling, trifling 9 miserable
10 picayunish 13 insignificant
measure 3 bar 4 bill, size, step, test
5 bound, gauge, index, quota, scale,
share, shift, weigh 6 amount, bounds,
degree, effort, extent, figure, ration,
reckon, resort, size up, survey
7 caliper, compute, delimit, mark out,
portion, stopgap 8 calliper, estimate,
regulate, resource, standard 9 allotment, benchmark, calculate, calibrate,
criterion, demarcate, determine, expedient, magnitude, yardstick 10 dimensions, indication, proceeding, proportion, touchstone 11 proposition
13 apportionment *area:* 4 acre 7 hectare
capacity: 4 gill, peck, pint 5 liter,
minim, quart 6 bushel, gallon 8 fluidram 9 fluid dram 10 fluid ounce, milliliter *cloth:* 3 ell *combining form:* 6 metric
8 metrical *depth:* 5 plumb, sound *dry:*
4 peck 6 bushel *electrical:* 3 amp 4 watt
6 ampere 7 coulomb *horse height:*
4 hand *interstellar space:* 6 parsec
length: 3 rod 4 foot, inch, link, mile,
yard 5 chain, cubit, meter 6 league
7 furlong 9 kilometer 10 centimeter *liquid:* 4 gill, pint 5 minim, quart 6 gallon
mixed drinks: 6 jigger *of comparison:*
8 standard *paper:* 4 ream *printer's:*
4 pica 5 point *radioactive decay:*
8 halflife *rotation:* 5 angle *strength of
solution:* 7 titrate *surface:* 3 are *thermodynamic:* 7 entropy 8 enthalpy
measured 7 regular, stately 8 metrical
9 regulated, temperate, unhurried
10 calculated, controlled, deliberate,
restrained 13 proportionate
Measure for Measure *character:* 6 Angelo, Juliet 7 Claudio, Mariana 8 Isabella
9 Vincentio *setting:* 6 Vienna
measurement 4 area 6 degree 8 capacity,
quantity 9 dimension, magnitude
11 calibration, mensuration

measure up to 3 tie 4 meet 5 equal, match, rival, touch 7 emulate 10 qualify for

measuring device 4 gage 5 buret, gauge, scale 7 burette, caliper, sextant, venturi 8 calipers 8 dipstick 9 altimeter, barometer, dosimeter, pedometer 11 tensiometer, velocimeter

meat 4 core, food, gist, pith, pork, veal 5 flesh, jerky, steak 6 thrust, upshot 7 edibles 8 victuals 9 foodstuff, provender, substance 10 provisions 11 comestibles *broth:* 8 bouillon *cake:* 6 burger 9 hamburger *cured:* 7 biltong *cut:* 3 rib 4 loin, rump 5 chuck, flank, plate, round, shank 7 brisket, sirloin 8 rib roast 9 club steak, rump roast, short loin, short ribs 10 blade roast, flank steak, round steak, T-bone steak 12 boneless neck, pinbone steak, sirloin steak 13 blade rib roast, crosscut shank *dealer:* 7 butcher *deer:* 7 venison *dried:* 5 jerky *fastening pin:* 6 skewer *holding rod:* 4 spit 10 rotisserie *juices:* 5 gravy *packer:* 5 Swift 6 Armour *raw:* 6 gobbet *roasted:* 8 barbecue *roasting shop:* 10 rotisserie *seasoned:* 7 sausage 8 pastrami, scrapple *sheep:* 6 mutton *side:* 8 sowbelly *skewered:* 5 kebab, kebob *slice:* 6 cutlet, rasher *small portion:* 6 collop *tough part:* 7 gristle

meat-eating 11 carnivorous

meathead 3 lug, oaf 4 clod, dodo, dolt, gawk, goon, lout 5 chump, klutz, looby 6 dimwit, lubber 7 bungler, palooka 8 dumbbell, numskull 9 birdbrain, ignoramus, lamebrain, numbskull 10 nincompoop

Mebd *husband:* 6 Ailill *victim:* 10 Cuchulainn

Mecca 4 goal *country:* 11 Saudi Arabia *pilgrimage:* 4 hadj, hajj *port:* 5 Jedda, Jidda 6 Jeddah, Jiddah *shrine:* 5 Kaaba

mechanic 7 artisan 9 machinist

mechanical 4 cold 7 cursory, robotic 8 lifeless 9 automated, automatic, unfeeling 10 impersonal 11 emotionless, instinctive, involuntary, perfunctory, unemotional

mechanism 4 gear 5 gizmo, means, works 6 agency, doodad, jigger, medium, widget 7 whatsit 8 dohickey 9 apparatus, appliance, procedure, technique, thingummy 10 instrument 11 contraption, contrivance, thingamabob, thingamajig, thingumajig

medal 5 badge, honor, prize 6 reward 7 laurels 8 accolade 10 decoration 13 commemoration

meddle 3 pry 4 fool, nose 5 snoop 6 butt in, dabble, horn in, kibitz, monkey,

putter, tamper, tinker 7 intrude, obtrude 8 trespass 9 interfere, interlope, intervene 10 mess around

meddler 5 snoop, yenta 7 snooper 8 busybody, intruder, kibitzer 9 buttinsky 12 troublemaker

meddlesome 4 busy, nosy 6 prying 9 intrusive, obtrusive, officious 11 impertinent, interfering

Medea 5 witch 9 sorceress 11 enchantress *aunt:* 5 Circe *brother:* 8 Absyrtus *father:* 6 Aeëtes *husband:* 5 Jason 6 Aegeus *sister:* 5 Circe *son:* 6 Medeus *victim:* 6 Creusa, Glauce, Glauke

medial 3 mid 4 mean 6 center, middle 7 average, central, halfway, midmost 8 middling, moderate 10 centermost, middlemost 11 equidistant 12 intermediary, intermediate

median see MEDIAL

mediate 5 judge 6 broker, convey, liaise, settle, step in, umpire 7 adjudge, referee, resolve 8 moderate, transmit 9 arbitrate, intercede, interfere, interpose, intervene, negotiate 10 conciliate

mediator 5 judge 6 broker, umpire 7 arbiter, liaison, referee 9 go-between, middleman 10 interceder, negotiator, peacemaker 11 intercessor

medical instrument 6 needle 7 forceps, scalpel, scanner, syringe 8 otoscope 9 endoscope, speculum 11 cardiograph, stethoscope

medical practitioner 3 doc 5 nurse 6 doctor, intern 7 surgeon 9 physician

medicament 4 cure, pill 6 elixir, physic, remedy 7 nostrum 8 antidote, curative 10 palliative *inert:* 7 placebo

medicate 4 cure, dose, drug, heal 5 treat

medicinal 8 curative, remedial, salutary, sanative 9 healthful 12 health-giving, pharmaceutic

medicine 4 cure, pill 5 bromo 6 physic, remedy 7 anodyne, nostrum 8 busulfan, poultice 11 antipyretic *bottle:* 4 vial *branch:* 7 surgery 8 oncology 9 neurology, pathology 10 bariatrics, cardiology, geriatrics, gynecology, nephrology, obstetrics, pediatrics, psychiatry *cathartic:* 8 evacuant 9 purgative *combining form:* 5 iatro 8 pharmaco *quantity of:* 4 dose 6 dosage *shell:* 7 capsule *soothing:* 7 anodyne 8 lenitive, narcotic, sedative 9 calmative, soporific

medicine man 6 doctor, kahuna, shaman 9 curandero

medieval study 5 logic 7 grammar, trivium 8 rhetoric 10 quadrivium

mediocre 4 dull, fair, hack, so-so 6 common 7 average, fairish 8 inferior, mid-

dling, moderate, ordinary, passable
9 tolerable 10 pedestrian, uninspired
11 commonplace, indifferent 12 run-of-
the-mill 13 unexceptional
meditate 4 mull, muse 5 weigh 6 intend,
ponder 7 purpose, reflect, revolve
8 cogitate, consider, mull over, ruminate, turn over 9 reflect on 10 deliberate 11 contemplate
meditative 6 broody 7 pensive 8 brooding
10 reflective, ruminative, thoughtful
meditator 4 yogi
Mediterranean 11 Mare Nostrum
12 Mare Internum *coastal region:* 7 Riviera *eastern shores:* 6 Levant *island:*
(see at ISLAND) *wind:* 7 mistral, sirocco
medium 3 par 4 fair, mean, so-so
5 agent, organ 6 agency, métier, milieu,
normal 7 ambient, average, channel,
climate, culture, neutral, vehicle
8 ambience, middling, moderate, passable, standard 9 tolerable 10 atmosphere 11 clairvoyant, environment
12 run-of-the-mill *of exchange:* 5 money
8 currency 11 legal tender
medley 4 brew, olio 5 combo, gumbo
6 jumble, ragout 7 farrago, mélange,
mixture 8 mishmash, pastiche 9 pasticcio, patchwork, potpourri 10 assortment, hodgepodge, miscellany, salmagundi 11 gallimaufry
Medusa 6 Gorgon *father:* 7 Phorcus,
Phorcys *hair:* 6 snakes *mother:* 4 Ceto
offspring: 7 Pegasus 8 Chrysaor *sister:*
6 Stheno 7 Euryale *slayer:* 7 Perseus
medusa 9 jellyfish
meed 3 due 4 part 5 quota, share
6 amount, desert, ration, return,
reward 7 guerdon, measure, portion
8 dividend 9 allotment, allowance
10 recompense 13 apportionment
meek 3 shy 4 mild, tame 5 lowly, timid
6 docile, gentle, humble, modest
7 patient 8 tolerant 10 submissive,
unassuming 11 deferential 13 long-
suffering
meerschaum 4 pipe 9 sepiolite
meet 3 apt, fit 4 face, fair, fill, find, join,
just, open, spot 5 cross, event, hit on,
match, right, touch, unite 6 answer,
chance, engage, oppose, proper, settle,
take on, useful 7 contest, convene, fitting, fulfill, hit upon, satisfy, stumble,
undergo 8 approach, assemble, come
upon, concours, conflict, confront,
converge, suitable 9 encounter,
impinge on, measure up 10 congregate,
provide for 11 appropriate, competition *a bet:* 3 see *a need:* 7 suffice *athletic:* 8 gymkhana 10 tournament *by
appointment:* 10 rendezvous

meeting 4 moot, talk 5 tryst 6 huddle,
parley, powwow 7 session 8 assembly,
conclave, concours, congress, junction
9 concourse, encounter, gathering, rencontre 10 conference, confluence, convention, rendezvous 11 competition,
convocation, get-together 12 intersection *Anglo-Saxon:* 5 gemot 6 gemote
place: 5 forum *spiritual:* 6 séance
Mefistofele composer 5 Boito (Arrigo)
Megaera see ERINYES
megaphone 8 bullhorn 10 mouthpiece
Megara *father:* 5 Creon *husband:* 8 Heracles, Hercules *king:* 5 Nisus
megillah 5 story 7 account
megrim 4 urge, whim 5 fancy, freak,
humor 6 notion, vagary, whimsy
7 caprice, conceit, impulse, vertigo
8 crotchet, migraine 9 dizziness
Mehitabel 3 cat *creator:* 7 Marquis (Don)
friend: 5 Archy
Mein Kampf author 6 Hitler (Adolf)
meiosis 7 litotes 12 cell division
Meissen 5 china 8 ceramics 9 porcelain
Meistersinger 5 Sachs (Hans) 9 Frauen-
lob
Meistersinger, Die *beloved:* 3 Eva *composer:* 6 Wagner (Richard) *hero:* 6 Walter *mentor:* 5 Sachs (Hans)
melancholia 5 gloom 6 sorrow 7 despair,
sadness 9 dejection, morbidity
10 depression, desolation, gloominess
11 despondency, dolefulness
melancholic 3 low, sad 4 blue, glum
6 gloomy, morose, triste 7 joyless
8 dejected, downcast, mournful
9 depressed, saddening 10 depressing,
despondent, dispirited
melancholy 3 low, sad 4 blue, funk,
glum 5 blues, dumps, ennui, gloom
6 dismal, dreary, gloomy, misery,
morose, rueful, somber, tedium, triste,
woeful 7 boredom, despair, doleful,
joyless, pensive, sadness, unhappy
8 dejected, dolorous, downcast, funereal, mournful, saddened 9 black bile,
dejection, depressed, plaintive, saddening, sorrowful 10 depressing, depression, despondent, dispirited, lachrymose, lamentable, lugubrious,
reflective, thoughtful 11 despondency,
unhappiness 12 heavyhearted, wretchedness
mélange see MEDLEY
Melanippus *father:* 7 Theseus *slayer:*
10 Amphiaraus *victim:* 6 Tydeus
Melchior *companion:* 6 Caspar, Gaspar
9 Balthasar, Balthazar *gift:* 4 gold
Melchizedek's kingdom 5 Salem
meld 3 mix 4 fuse 5 blend, merge 6 mingle 7 combine, mixture 8 compound

9 commingle, interfuse **10** amalgamate **11** intermingle

Meleager *beloved:* **8** Atalanta *father:* **6** Oeneus *mother:* **7** Althaea *victim:* **4** boar

melee 3 row **4** fray, riot **5** brawl, broil, clash, fight **6** affray, fracas, ruckus, rumpus **7** scuffle **8** skirmish **9** scrimmage **10** donnybrook, free-for-all

meliorate 4 help **5** amend **6** better, soften **7** improve **8** mitigate, palliate

Mélisande's lover 7 Pelléas

melisma 7 cadenza, descant

mellifluous 5 sweet **6** dulcet, fluent, golden, liquid, smooth **7** flowing, honeyed, silvery **8** euphonic, soothing **10** euphonious **13** silver-tongued

mellow 3 age **4** aged, ripe **5** ripen **6** genial, golden, grow up, mature, season, smooth **7** honeyed, matured, ripened **8** laid-back, pleasant, seasoned **9** agreeable

melodic 5 sweet **6** dulcet **7** musical, songful, tuneful **8** canorous, euphonic **10** euphonious

melodious 5 lyric, sweet **6** dulcet **7** musical, songful, tuneful **8** euphonic **9** cantabile **10** euphonious

melody 3 air, lay **4** aria, song, tune **5** canto, music, theme **6** chorus, strain, warble **7** descant, refrain **11** tunefulness

melon 4 pepo **5** gourd **6** casaba, profit **8** crenshaw, honeydew, windfall **10** cantaloupe

Melpomene see MUSE

melt 3 run **4** flux, fuse, thaw **6** relent, soften **7** liquefy **8** dissolve, liquesce, unfreeze **9** disappear **10** deliquesce *down:* **6** render *together:* **4** fuse

Melville, Herman *character:* **3** Pip **4** Ahab, Toby **5** Bembo, Chase **6** Cereno (Benito), Jermin, Pierre **7** Fayaway, Ishmael **8** Bartleby, Queequeg, Starbuck *work:* **4** Omoo **5** Mardi, Typee **6** Pierre **7** Redburn **8** Moby Dick **11** White-Jacket **12** Benito Cereno **13** Confidence-Man (The)

member 3 cut **4** part **5** piece **6** clause, parcel **7** portion, section, segment **8** division **9** appendage, component **10** ingredient *political party:* **4** Tory, Whig **7** Liberal **8** Democrat, Laborite **9** Labourite **10** Republican **12** Conservative *service club:* **4** Lion **8** Kiwanian, Rotarian

membrane 4 film **6** pleura **7** pleurae (plural) *bodily:* **6** serosa *brain:* **3** pia *diffusion through:* **7** osmosis *dividing:* **5** septa (plural) **6** septum *ear:* **8** tympanum *enclosing:* **8** indusium *thin:* **6** lami-

na **7** lamella, laminae (plural) **8** lamellae (plural) *wing:* **8** patagium

memento 5 relic, token, trace **6** trophy **7** vestige **8** keepsake, reminder, souvenir **11** remembrance

Memnon *father:* **8** Tithonus *mother:* **3** Eos **6** Aurora *slayer:* **8** Achilles

memoir 3 bio **4** life **5** diary **6** record, report, thesis **7** account, journal **8** anecdote **9** biography **11** confessions **12** recollection, reminiscence **13** autobiography

memoirist 7 Boswell, diarist **10** biographer

memorable 7 lasting, notable **8** historic **9** deathless, indelible, momentous, redletter **10** noteworthy **11** significant **13** distinguished

memorandum 4 chit, note **6** minute, notice, record **7** tickler **8** notation, reminder **12** announcement

memorial 4 note **5** relic, token, trace **6** record, trophy **7** relique **8** keepsake, monument, reminder, souvenir **10** dedicatory **11** celebrative, remembrance **12** consecrative, remembrancer **13** commemoration, commemorative *mound:* **5** cairn

memorial park see CEMETERY

memorize 3 con, get **6** retain **8** remember

memory 6 recall **8** mind's eye, souvenir **9** anamnesis, awareness, flashback, retention **10** reflection **11** remembrance **12** recollection, reminiscence **13** retentiveness, retrospection *assisting:* **8** mnemonic *loss:* **7** amnesia

menace 4 risk **5** alarm, peril, scare **6** danger, hazard, threat **7** imperil, jeopard, torment **8** endanger, frighten, jeopardy, threaten **9** terrorize **10** intimidate, jeopardize

ménage 4 clan **5** house **6** family **8** quarters **9** household **12** housekeeping

menagerie 3 zoo **7** mixture

mend 3 fix, sew **4** cure, darn, heal **5** patch, renew **6** cobble, doctor, look up, perk up, reform, remedy, repair, revamp **7** correct, improve, patch up, rebuild, rectify, redress, restore **8** overhaul, renovate **9** condition, refurbish **10** ameliorate, convalesce, recuperate **11** recondition, reconstruct

mendacious 5 false, lying **6** shifty **7** fibbing **9** deceitful, deceptive, dishonest, paltering **10** untruthful **11** dissembling **13** prevaricating

mendacity 3 lie **6** deceit **9** deception, duplicity, falsehood **10** dishonesty **12** equivocation **13** truthlessness

mendicancy 7 beggary, begging, bumming, cadging 8 mooching, sponging 11 panhandling

mendicant 5 friar 6 beggar 7 begging

Mending Wall author 5 Frost (Robert)

Menelaus *brother:* 9 Agamemnon *father:* 6 Atreus *kingdom:* 6 Sparta *mother:* 6 Aerope *wife:* 5 Helen

menial 4 dull 5 lowly 6 humble 7 servant, servile, slavish 8 obeisant, retainer 9 unskilled 10 obsequious 11 subservient, undignified

meniscus 4 lens 9 cartilage

Menlo Park inventor 6 Edison (Thomas Alva)

menopause 11 climacteric 12 change of life

menorah 10 candelabra

Menotti, Gian Carlo *character:* 5 Amahl *opera:* 6 Consul (The), Medium (The) 9 Telephone (The)

men's store 12 haberdashery

mental 5 inner 7 psychic 8 cerebral, rational, thinking 9 reasoning, spiritual 10 immaterial, telepathic 11 intelligent 12 intellective, intellectual 13 psychological *faculty:* 6 memory

mentality 3 wit 5 sense 6 brains 7 mindset, outlook 9 intellect, mother wit 10 brainpower 12 intelligence

mention 4 cite, name, note 7 refer to, specify 8 advert to, allude to, citation, instance 9 reference

mentor 4 guru 5 coach, guide, tutor 7 teacher 9 counselor 10 counsellor

Mentor's pupil 10 Telemachus

menu 4 card, diet 5 carte 10 bill of fare 11 carte du jour *item:* 4 soup 5 salad 6 entrée 7 dessert 9 appetizer

Mephibosheth *father:* 4 Saul 8 Jonathan *mother:* 6 Rizpah

Mephistophelian 7 satanic 8 devilish, diabolic 10 diabolical

mephitic 4 rank 5 fetid, funky, musty 6 putrid, smelly 7 noisome, noxious, reeking 8 stinking 9 poisonous 10 malodorous

Merab *father:* 4 Saul *husband:* 6 Adriel

mercenary 4 hack 5 venal 6 greedy 7 corrupt, soldier 8 hireling

merchandise 4 line, sell 5 cargo, goods, stock, trade, wares 6 deal in, job lot, market, retail 7 effects, promote, staples, traffic 8 products 9 publicize, vendibles 11 commodities

merchandiser 6 dealer, trader, vendor 8 retailer 9 tradesman 10 wholesaler 11 businessman 13 businesswoman

merchant 5 buyer 6 dealer, jobber, seller, trader, vendor 7 peddler 8 purveyor, retailer 9 tradesman 10 trafficker, wholesaler 11 businessman, storekeep-

er *guild:* 5 Hansa, Hanse *League:* 9 Hanseatic *ship:* 5 oiler 6 argosy, coaler, galiot, packet, tanker, trader 7 collier, galliot, steamer 8 Indiaman 9 freighter *wine:* 7 vintner

Merchant of Venice, The 7 Antonio *character:* 6 Portia 7 Jessica, Lorenzo, Nerissa, Shylock 8 Bassanio

merciful 4 kind 6 benign, humane, kindly 7 clement, lenient 8 tolerant 9 forgiving, indulgent 10 charitable, forbearing 11 softhearted 13 compassionate

merciless 4 grim 5 cruel, harsh 6 brutal, savage, wanton 9 cutthroat, ferocious, unfeeling 10 gratuitous, implacable, ironfisted, unyielding 11 hardhearted, unrelenting 12 unappeasable

mercurial 5 flaky 6 fickle, mobile 7 erratic 8 unstable, variable, volatile 9 impulsive 10 capricious, changeable, inconstant 13 temperamental, unpredictable

mercury 5 azoth 11 quicksilver *ore:* 8 cinnabar

Mercury 6 planet (see also HERMES)

Mercutio *friend:* 5 Romeo *slayer:* 6 Tybalt

mercy 4 pity, ruth 5 grace 6 lenity 7 caritas, charity 8 clemency, goodwill, kindness, leniency 9 benignity, tolerance 10 compassion, generosity, kindliness 11 benevolence, forbearance 13 commiseration *petition for:* 5 kyrie 8 miserere

mere 4 bare, lake, pool, pure 8 boundary, landmark 9 undiluted

merely 4 just, only 6 simply, solely, wholly

meretricious 4 loud, sham 5 gaudy, phony, showy 6 flashy, garish, glitzy, sleazy, tawdry, tinsel, trashy 7 chintzy 8 delusive, delusory, illusory 9 contrived, deceptive 10 misleading 11 counterfeit, pretentious

merganser 4 duck, smew

merge 3 mix 4 fuse, join 5 blend, unify, unite 6 mingle 7 combine 8 coalesce, compound 9 commingle, interfuse 10 amalgamate, assimilate 11 consolidate, intermingle

merger 5 union 6 fusion 7 melding 8 alliance, takeover 9 coalition 10 absorption 11 combination, unification 12 amalgamation 13 consolidation

meridian 4 acme, apex, peak 6 apogee, climax, summit, zenith 8 pinnacle

merit 3 due 4 earn, rate 5 arete, value, worth 6 virtue 7 caliber, deserts, deserve, entitle, justify, quality, stature, warrant 10 excellence, perfection, recompense 11 achievement

merited 3 due 4 fair, just 5 right

7 condign, fitting 8 deserved, rightful, suitable 9 justified, requisite 11 appropriate

meritorious 6 worthy 8 laudable 9 admirable, deserving, estimable, honorable 10 creditable 11 commendable, thankworthy 12 praiseworthy

Merlin 4 seer 5 augur, magus 6 shaman, wizard 7 prophet 8 magician 10 soothsayer 11 necromancer, thaumaturge

merlin 6 falcon 10 pigeon hawk

mermaid 3 nix 5 Ariel, nixie 7 manatee 8 sirenian 10 water nymph 11 water sprite

Merope *father:* 5 Atlas 8 Oenopion *husband:* 7 Polybus 8 Sisyphus 11 Cresphontes *lover:* 5 Orion *mother:* 7 Pleione *sisters:* 8 Pleiades *son:* 7 Aepytus, Glaucus

merriment 4 glee 5 mirth, revel 6 gaiety 7 jollity, revelry, whoopee 8 hilarity, reveling 9 festivity, jocundity, joviality 10 jocularity, jubilation 13 entertainment

merry 3 gay 4 glad 5 happy, jolly 6 blithe, jocund, jovial, joyful, joyous, lively 7 festive, gleeful 8 animated, cheerful, mirthful 9 hilarious, sprightly, vivacious 12 high-spirited, lighthearted

merry-andrew 4 fool, zany 5 clown, joker 6 jester, madcap 7 buffoon 9 harlequin 10 mountebank

merrymaker 7 partyer, reveler 8 carouser

merrymaking 5 party, revel 6 frolic, gaiety 7 jollity, revelry, whoopee 8 hilarity 9 festivity 12 conviviality

Merry Widow composer 5 Lehár (Franz)

Merry Wives of Windsor, The *character:* 3 Nym 4 Ford, Page 5 Caius 6 Fenton, Pistol 7 Slender 8 Falstaff

mesa 5 bench, butte 7 plateau 9 tableland

mescal 5 agave 6 cactus, liquor, maguey, peyote

mesh 3 net, web 4 jibe, maze 5 skein, snare, snarl 6 engage, morass, tangle 7 netting, network 8 dovetail, entangle 9 harmonize, interlock, labyrinth 10 coordinate 12 reticulation

meshuga 3 mad 4 nuts 5 crazy, goofy, kooky, loony, nutty, wacky 6 insane, screwy 7 foolish

mesmeric 8 alluring, hypnotic 9 glamorous 10 bewitching, enchanting 11 captivating

mesmerize 4 vamp 6 dazzle, seduce 7 bewitch 8 ensorcel, enthrall, entrance 9 captivate, ensorcell, fascinate, hypnotize, spellbind

Mesopotamia 4 Iraq *civilization:* 4 Elam

5 Akkad, Sumer 7 Assyria, Elamite 8 Akkadian, Assyrian, Sumerian 9 Babylonia 10 Babylonian *river:* 6 Tigris 9 Euphrates

mess 4 hash 5 botch, snafu 6 fright, jumble, muddle 7 eyesore 8 botchery, disarray, disorder, shambles, wreckage 9 confusion 10 hodgepodge, miscellany *around:* 4 idle 5 chill, dally 6 dawdle, doodle, fiddle, potter, putter 7 goof off, hang out 8 chill out, lollygag 10 dillydally *up:* 4 blow, flub, muff, ruin 5 botch, fluff, fudge, spoil, touse 6 bungle, fumble, tousle 7 butcher

message 4 note 5 sense, theme 6 letter, report 7 epistle, meaning, mission, missive, purport 8 bulletin, dispatch, telegram 9 directive, telegraph 10 communiqué 12 significance 13 communication, signification

Messalina's husband 8 Claudius

mess around 4 fool, idle 5 flirt 6 dabble, dawdle, fiddle, meddle, monkey, potter, putter, tamper, tinker 8 womanize 9 associate, interfere, interlope, philander

messenger 4 post 5 envoy 6 herald, runner 7 apostle, courier 8 emissary 9 go-between, harbinger 10 ambassador 11 internuncio 12 intermediary *God's:* 5 angel *of the gods:* 6 Hermes 7 Mercury *Turkish:* 6 chiaus

messiah 6 savior 7 saviour 8 defender 9 deliverer, liberator

Messiah composer 6 Handel (George Frideric)

messy 6 frowsy, frowzy, sloppy, unneat, untidy 7 chaotic, rumpled, unkempt 8 careless, confused, ill-kempt, slapdash, slipshod, slovenly 10 disheveled, disorderly 11 dishevelled *abode:* 3 sty 6 pigpen, pigsty

mestizo 5 métis 6 ladino 10 mixed-blood

Mestor *father:* 7 Perseus *mother:* 9 Andromeda

metal 4 gold, iron 5 steel 6 bronze *alloy:* (see ALLOY) *casting mold:* 5 ingot *corrosion:* 4 rust *fuse:* 6 solder *in mass:* 7 bullion *layer:* 7 plating *lump:* 6 nugget *magnetic:* 4 iron *refuse:* 4 slag 5 dross 6 scoria *sheath:* 5 armor *thin:* 4 foil, leaf 5 plate *worker:* 5 smith 10 blacksmith

metallic element 3 tin 4 gold, iron, lead, zinc 6 barium, cobalt, copper, nickel, radium, silver, sodium 7 arsenic, bismuth, cadmium, calcium, lithium, mercury, uranium 8 aluminum, chromium, platinum, titanium, tungsten, vanadium 9 magnesium, manganese, potassium, strontium 10 molybdenum

metamere 6 somite **7** segment

metamorphic rock 5 slate **6** gneiss, marble, schist **9** quartzite, soapstone

metamorphose 6 change, mutate **7** convert, develop **9** transform, translate, transmute **11** transfigure **12** transmogrify

metamorphosis 6 change **8** changing, mutation **9** evolution, sea change **10** changeover **13** transmutation

Metamorphosis author 5 Kafka (Franz)

___ **me tangere 4** noli

metaphor 5 trope **6** simile, symbol **7** analogy **8** allegory **10** comparison, similitude

metaphorical compound 7 kenning

metaphysical 8 bodiless, numinous **9** unearthly, unfleshly **10** immaterial, suprahuman **12** supermundane, supramundane, supranatural, transcendent **13** preternatural *poet:* **5** Donne (John) **6** Cowley (Abraham) **7** Crashaw (Richard), Herbert (George), Marvell (Andrew), Vaughan (Henry) **9** Cleveland (John)

mete 4 deal, dole, give **5** allot, bound **6** border, parcel, ration **7** portion **8** allocate, boundary, disburse, dispense **9** apportion **10** distribute

meteor 8 fireball **12** shooting star *exploding:* **6** bolide *shower:* **5** Lyrid **6** Leonid, Taurid **7** Aquarid, Geminid, Orionid, Perseid **10** Quadrantid ·

meteorite 8 aerolite **10** siderolite

meter 4 beat, scan **6** rhythm **7** cadence, measure, pattern

metheglin 4 mead **8** beverage *ingredient:* **5** honey

method 3 way **4** mode, modi (plural), plan **5** means, modus, order, style **6** course, design, manner, schema, scheme, system **7** fashion, formula, pattern, process, routine, wrinkle **8** practice **9** procedure, technique **11** orderliness **13** modus operandi *careful:* **8** strategy *of employing troops:* **6** tactic **7** tactics *of procedure:* **4** game

methodical 5 exact **7** careful, logical, orderly, precise, regular **9** efficient, organized **10** deliberate, scrupulous, systematic, systemized **12** systematized

Methuselah *father:* **5** Enoch *grandson:* **4** Noah *son:* **6** Lamech

meticulous 5 exact, fussy, picky **6** strict **7** careful, finicky, precise **8** detailed, thorough **10** fastidious, nitpicking, pernickety, scrupulous **11** microscopic, painstaking, persnickety, punctilious **13** conscientious

métier 4 work **5** craft, field, forte, trade **7** calling, pursuit **8** business, strength,

vocation **9** specialty **10** employment, occupation, profession

metrical foot 4 iamb **5** ionic, paeon **6** cretic, dactyl, iambic, iambus **7** anapest, pyrrhic, pyrrhus, spondee, triseme, trochee **8** bacchius, choriamb, dactylic, spondaic, tribrach, trochaic **9** anapestic **10** tribrachic

metric unit *area:* **3** are **7** hectare *capacity:* **5** liter, litre **9** decaliter, deciliter, kiloliter **10** centiliter, hectoliter, milliliter *length:* **5** meter **9** decameter, decimeter, dekameter, kilometer **10** centimeter, hectometer, millimeter *mass and weight:* **4** gram **7** quintal **8** decagram, decigram, dekagram, kilogram **9** centigram, hectogram, metric ton, milligram

metro 4 tube **6** subway **11** underground

metropolis 4 city **7** capital

metropolitan 5 urban **6** urbane **7** primate **9** municipal **10** archbishop

mettle 4 fire, grit, guts **5** heart, moxie, nerve, pluck, spunk, steel, valor, vigor **6** daring, spirit, starch, temper **7** cojones, courage, resolve, stamina **8** backbone, boldness, tenacity, vitality **9** fortitude **10** resolution

mettlesome 4 bold, game **5** brave, fiery, gutsy **6** plucky, spunky **7** staunch, valiant **8** intrepid, resolute, spirited, vigorous **9** tenacious **10** courageous, determined

mew 3 hem, pen **4** cage, coop, gull **5** alley, fence **6** corral, immure, shut in, stable **7** enclose **8** hideaway

mewl 4 moan, pule **5** whine **6** snivel **7** whimper

Mexican *crop:* **5** sisal *estate:* **8** hacienda *food:* **4** masa, taco **5** chili, salsa **6** tamale **7** burrito, panocha, penuche, tostada **8** frijoles, tortilla **9** enchilada, guacamole **10** quesadilla **11** chimichanga *house:* **5** jacal *liquor:* **7** tequila

Mexico *ancient city:* **12** Tenochtitlán *ancient culture:* **4** Maya **5** Aztec, Mayan, Olmec **6** Toltec *bay:* **8** Campeche *capital:* **10** Mexico City *city:* **4** León **6** Juárez, Mérida, Oaxaca, Puebla **7** Nogales, Tijuana **8** Acapulco, Mexicali, Saltillo **9** Chihuahua, Matamoros, Monterrey **10** Cuernavaca **11** Guadalajara **12** Ciudad Juárez *conqueror:* **6** Cortés (Hernán, Hernando) *discoverer:* **7** Córdoba (Fernández de) *emperor:* **10** Maximilian *gulf:* **10** California *island:* **7** Cozumel *island group:* **13** Revillagigedo *lake:* **7** Chapala, Cuitzeo, Texcoco **9** Pátzcuaro *language:* **7** Spanish *leader:* **4** Díaz (Porfirio) **6** Juárez (Benito) **8** Carranza (Venustiano) *monetary unit:* 4 peso *mountain, range:* 8 Malinche 11 Sierra Madre *neighbor:* 6 Belize 9 Guatemala *peninsula:* 4 Baja 7 Yucatán *port:* 7 Tampico 8 Ensenada, Mazatlán, Veracruz *resort:* 6 Cancún 8 Acapulco *revolutionist:* 5 Villa (Pancho) 6 Zapata (Emiliano) 7 Hidalgo (Padre Miguel) *river:* 4 Mayo 5 Bravo, Yaquí 6 Balsas, Grande, Pánuco 7 Conchos 8 Grijalva, Río Bravo, Santiago 9 Rio Grande 10 Usumacinta *ruined city:* 5 Uxmal 7 Mayapán 8 Palenque 11 Chichén Itzá *sea:* 9 Caribbean *volcano:* 6 Colima 9 Paricutín 11 Ixtacihuatl 12 Citlaltépetl, Ixtaccíhuatl, Popocatépetl

mezzanine 5 story 7 balcony 8 entresol

mezzo 4 half 6 singer 7 soprano

mezzo-soprano *American:* 5 Elias (Rosalind), Horne (Marilyn), Jones (Sissieretta) 6 Bumbry (Grace), Graves (Denyce) 7 Stevens (Risë), Verrett (Shirley) 8 Troyanos (Tatiana), von Stade (Frederica) *Austrian:* 6 Ludwig (Christa) *English:* 5 Baker (Janet) *Italian:* 7 Bartoli (Cecilia) 8 Cossotto (Fiorenza)

Miami *bowl:* 6 Orange *chief:* 12 Little Turtle *county:* 4 Dade *stadium:* 9 Joe Robbie *team:* 4 Heat 7 Marlins 8 Dolphins, Panthers

miasma 3 fog 4 haze, mist, murk, smog 5 brume, vapor 9 effluvium

mica 7 biotite 8 silicate 9 isinglass, muscovite

Michelangelo Buonarotti *painting:* 10 Holy Family (The) 12 Last Judgment (The) *statue:* 5 David, Moses, Pietà 7 Bacchus

Michener novel 5 Space, Texas 6 Hawaii, Poland, Source (The) 8 Caravans, Covenant (The), Drifters (The), Sayonara 10 Centennial, Chesapeake 13 Fires of Spring (The) 15 Bridges at Toko-Ri (The)

Michigan *capital:* 7 Lansing *city:* 5 Flint 7 Detroit, Lansing, Pontiac 8 Ann Arbor, Dearborn 9 Kalamazoo 11 Grand Rapids 13 Sault Ste. Marie 16 Sault Sainte Marie *college, university:* 6 Calvin 9 Kalamazoo 10 Wayne State *lake:* 4 Erie 5 Huron 8 Michigan, Superior *nickname:* 9 Wolverine (State) 10 Great Lakes (State) *state bird:* 5 robin *state flower:* 12 apple blossom *state tree:* 9 white pine

mickey 5 flask, split

microbe 3 bug 4 germ 5 virus 8 bacillus, pathogen 9 bacterium 13 microorganism

microfilm sheet 5 fiche

Micronesia *capital:* 7 Palikir *island, island group:* 3 Yap 5 Chuuk 6 Kosrae 7 Pohnpei 8 Caroline *language:* 7 English

microorganism 4 germ 5 virus 6 aerobe 7 bacilli (plural), microbe, protist 8 bacillus, bacteria (plural), pathogen, protozoa (plural) 9 bacterium, protozoan, protozoon

microphone 3 bug 4 mike *shield:* 4 gobo

microscope 9 magnifier *inventor:* 11 Leeuwenhoek (Antoni van) *part:* 5 stage 6 mirror 8 eyepiece 9 objective

microscopic 4 tiny 5 small 6 minute

Mid-Atlantic state 7 New York 8 Delaware, Maryland, Virginia 9 New Jersey 12 Pennsylvania, West Virginia

midday 4 noon, sext 8 high noon, noontide, noontime

middle 4 core, mean 5 mesne, waist 6 center, medial, median 7 average, central, halfway 8 interior 10 centermost 11 equidistant, intervening 12 intermediary, intermediate

Middle American country 4 Cuba 5 Haiti 6 Belize, Mexico, Panama 7 Bahamas, Grenada, Jamaica 8 Barbados, Dominica, Honduras 9 Costa Rica, Guatemala, Nicaragua 10 El Salvador

middlebrow 7 Babbitt

middle class 11 bourgeoisie

middle-class 9 bourgeois

middle ear *bone:* 5 incus 6 stapes 7 malleus *membrane:* 7 eardrum 8 tympanum

Middle Eastern country 4 Iran, Iraq, Oman 5 Egypt, Qatar, Sudan, Syria, Yemen 6 Cyprus, Israel, Jordan, Kuwait, Turkey 7 Bahrain, Lebanon 11 Saudi Arabia

Middle Kingdom 5 China

middleman 5 agent 6 broker 8 mediator 9 go-between 11 intercessor 12 intermediary, intermediate

Middlemarch author 5 Eliot (George), Evans (Mary Ann)

middle-of-the-road 7 neutral 8 moderate 9 impartial 11 nonpartisan

middling 4 fair, okay, so-so 6 fairly, medium, rather 7 average, fairish, typical 8 adequate, mediocre, moderate, ordinary, passable 9 tolerable 10 moderately, second-rate 11 indifferent 12 intermediate, run-of-the-mill

midge 3 fly 6 punkie 7 no-see-um 8 dipteran 10 chironomid *larva:* 9 bloodworm

midget 4 runt 5 dwarf, pygmy 6 bantam, peewee 7 manikin 8 Tom Thumb 10 homunculus 11 hop-o'-my-thumb, Lilliputian

Midian *father:* 7 Abraham *mother:* 7 Keturah

midpoint 3 par 4 mean, norm 6 center, median, middle 7 average, centrum, halfway 8 bull's-eye, standard

midwife 6 granny, Lucina 10 accoucheur

mien 3 air, set 4 look 6 aspect, manner 7 address, bearing 8 carriage, demeanor, presence 9 mannerism 10 appearance, deportment, expression 11 comportment

miff 3 fit, irk, vex 4 beef, flap, spat 5 annoy, pique, run-in, upset 6 bother, fracas, nettle, offend, put out 7 dispute, provoke, quarrel, rhubarb 8 irritate, squabble 10 conniption, falling-out 11 altercation

might 3 may 4 sway 5 brawn, clout, force, means, power 6 energy, muscle 7 ability, command, control, mastery, potency 8 capacity, strength 9 authority, resources 12 forcefulness

mighty 4 huge, very 5 grand, great 6 heroic, potent, strong 7 eminent, immense, massive, titanic 8 enormous, forceful, gigantic, imposing, powerful, puissant 10 impressive, monumental, prodigious, stupendous, tremendous 11 illustrious 13 extraordinary

Mignon *composer* 6 Thomas (Ambroise)

mignonette 4 herb 5 sauce 6 annual 6 reseda

migrant 5 exile, mover, nomad 7 drifter, nomadic, refugee 8 traveler, wanderer 9 itinerant, transient 10 expatriate

migrate 4 move, trek 5 drift, range, shift 6 wander 8 transfer

migration 6 exodus 8 diaspora *of professionals:* 10 brain drain

migratory 5 nomad 6 errant, mobile, moving, roving 7 nomadic, ranging 9 wandering

Mikado, The *composer:* 8 Sullivan (Arthur) *librettist:* 7 Gilbert (W. S.)

milady 6 madame 10 noblewoman 11 gentlewoman

Milan *family:* 6 Sforza 8 Visconti *opera house:* 7 La Scala

Milcah *brother:* 3 Lot *father:* 5 Haran 10 Zelophehad *husband:* 5 Nahor *son:* 7 Bethuel

mild 4 calm, easy, meek, soft, tame 5 balmy, bland, faint, tepid 6 benign, docile, gentle, placid, serene, smooth, tender 7 amiable, clement, equable, insipid, lenient, patient, subdued 8 moderate, obliging 9 benignant, temperate 10 forbearing, submissive

mildew 4 mold, rust 6 fungus, growth

___ **mile** 7 statute 8 nautical

mileage recorder 8 odometer

milestone 5 event 6 marker 8 landmark, occasion

milieu 5 scene 6 medium, sphere 7 ambient, climate, setting 8 ambience 10 atmosphere, background 11 environment, mise-en-scène 12 surroundings

militant 7 fighter, martial, warlike, warrior 8 activist, fighting 9 assertive, bellicose, combatant, combative, truculent 10 aggressive, pugnacious 11 belligerent, contentious, quarrelsome 12 gladiatorial

military 5 troop 6 forces, troops 7 martial, warlike 8 soldiery 9 soldierly 10 servicemen 11 armed forces, soldierlike *alliance:* 4 NATO *base:* 4 camp, fort, post 5 depot, field 6 billet 8 barracks, garrison, quarters 10 encampment *officer:* 5 major 7 captain, colonel, general 9 brigadier 10 lieutenant *prisoner:* 3 POW *school:* 3 OCS, OTS 4 ROTC, USMA 9 Annapolis, West Point *sector:* 10 combat zone, front lines 11 battlefront *store:* 10 commissary *storehouse:* 5 depot 6 armory 7 arsenal *supplies:* 8 matériel, ordnance *unit:* 5 corps, squad, troop 7 company, platoon 8 division, regiment 9 battalion 11 battle group *vehicle:* 4 jeep, tank 6 Abrams, Humvee 7 Bradley 9 Blackhawk, half-track

militate 4 tell 5 count, weigh 6 matter 11 carry weight

militia 7 reserve

milk 4 pump, rook, suck 5 drain, educe, empty, evoke, exact, mulct, nurse, wring 6 elicit, extort, fleece 7 exhaust, exploit, extract *coagulated:* 4 curd *combining form:* 4 lact 5 lacti, lacto *curdled:* 7 clabber *fermented:* 5 kefir 6 kumiss, yogurt 7 koumiss, yoghurt *liquid part:* 4 whey *store:* 5 dairy *sugar:* 7 lactose

milk shake 6 frappe 7 frosted

milky 4 fair, meek, mild, pale, tame 5 white 6 chalky, cloudy, gentle 7 lacteal, whitish 8 timorous

mill 5 grind, plant, shape, works 7 factory, machine 9 circulate, pulverize 11 manufactory

millenary 8 thousand

Miller, Arthur *film:* 7 Misfits (The) *play:* 5 Price (The) 9 All My Sons 8 Crucible (The) 12 After the Fall 16 Death of a Salesman 17 View from the Bridge (A) *salesman:* 5 Loman (Willy)

milliner 6 hatter

million *combining form:* 3 meg 4 mega

millionth *combining form:* 4 micr 5 micro

Mill on the Floss *author* 5 Eliot (George), Evans (Mary Ann)

millstone 4 duty, load, onus 6 burden,

charge, weight **9** albatross **10** affliction, deadweight

Milne bear 4 Pooh

milord 8 nobleman **9** gentleman, patrician **10** aristocrat **12** silk stocking

Milquetoast, Caspar *creator:* **7** Webster (Harold Tucker) (see also MILKSOP)

Miltiades' victory 8 Marathon

Milton work 5 Comus **7** Lycidas **8** L'Allegro **12** Areopagitica, Paradise Lost

mime 3 act **5** actor **6** act out **7** Marceau (Marcel) **9** performer, represent **11** impersonate **12** impersonator

mimic 3 act, ape **4** copy, mock, play **5** actor, enact **6** mummer, parody, parrot, player **7** copycat, imitate **8** resemble, simulate, travesty **9** burlesque, pantomime **11** impersonate **12** impersonator

mimicry 4 echo **6** parody **8** travesty **9** imitation, parroting **10** caricature **13** impersonation

minatory 4 dire, grim **7** baleful, baneful, direful, hostile, malefic, ominous **8** menacing, sinister **9** ill-boding **10** forbidding, foreboding, maleficent **11** frightening, threatening **12** intimidating

mince 4 chop, dice, hash **5** cut up, strut **6** prance, sashay, soften **8** moderate, restrain, tone down **9** euphemize

mincing 5 fussy **6** dainty, la-di-da, tootoo **7** finical, finicky, stilted **8** affected, delicate **10** fastidious, pernickety **11** persnickety

mind 3 wit **4** mood, obey, soul, tend, will, wits **5** brain, fancy, watch, weigh **6** attend, belief, beware, brains, follow, memory, notice, psyche, reason, senses, spirit **7** care for, discern, dislike, feeling, observe, oversee, purpose **8** consider **9** intellect, intention, mentality, supervise **10** brainpower, gray matter **11** disposition, temperament **12** intelligence **13** consciousness *combining form:* **5** psych **6** psycho

mindful 5 alert, awake, aware **7** knowing **8** sensible, vigilant **9** attentive, cognizant, conscious, observant **10** conversant **13** conscientious

mindless 4 rash **5** silly **6** simple, stupid **7** asinine, foolish, unaware, vacuous **9** nitwitted, oblivious **10** irrational, unthinking **13** unintelligent

mine 3 dig, pit, sap **4** fund, lode, vein, well **5** delve, drill, hoard, stock, store **6** burrow, quarry, spring **7** bonanza, deposit, extract **8** eldorado, excavate, Golconda **10** excavation, wellspring **13** treasure trove *coal:* **8** colliery *entrance:* **4** adit

miner 6 pitman **7** collier

mineral 5 beryl, topaz, trona **6** augite, barite, garnet, iolite, pinite, rutile, sphene, spinel, sulfur, zircon **7** apatite, azurite, bornite, calcite, citrine, coesite, cyanite, jadeite, kernite, kunzite, olivine, zeolite **8** boracite, cinnabar, dolomite, epsomite, fayalite, feldspar, fluorite, hematite, lazulite, lazurite, siderite, sodalite, stibnite, triplite, wellsite **9** aragonite, celestite, cerussite, danburite, fosterite, kaolinite, lawsonite, magnetite, malachite, muscovite, phenakite, scapolite, tridymite, turquoise, wulfenite **10** chalcedony, orthoclase, pyrrhotite, tourmaline **11** alexandrite, chrysoberyl, melanterite **12** brazilianite, chalcopyrite, tincalconite **13** rhodochrosite *flaky:* **4** mica *greasy:* **4** talc **10** serpentine *hard:* **6** spinel **7** diamond **8** corundum *iridescent:* **4** opal *nonmetallic:* **5** boron **6** gypsum, halite **8** asbestos, graphite *shiny:* **4** gold **6** galena, pyrite, silver *soft:* **4** talc **6** gypsum **8** graphite *transparent:* **6** quartz

mineral water 7 seltzer **8** club soda

Minerva see ATHENA

mingle 3 mix **4** meld **5** blend, merge **6** commix **7** combine **8** intermix **9** associate, socialize

mingy 4 mean **5** cheap, tight **6** stingy **7** chintzy, miserly, scrimpy **8** grudging, ungiving **9** niggardly, penurious **10** pinchpenny **11** closefisted, tightfisted

miniature 3 wee **4** tiny **5** small, teeny, weeny **6** little, minute, petite, teensy **9** itsy-bitsy, itty-bitty **10** diminutive, small-scale, teeny-weeny **11** Lilliputian **12** illumination

minify 4 trim **6** lessen, shrink **7** abridge, curtail **8** decrease, diminish **10** abbreviate

minim 3 bit, jot **4** atom, iota **5** grain, speck **7** modicum, smidgen **8** particle *music:* **8** half note

minimal 5 basic, least, token **6** lowest **7** nominal **8** littlest, smallest **9** slightest

minimize 5 decry **6** reduce **7** run down **8** belittle, derogate, discount, downplay, play down **9** disparage, soft-pedal, underrate **10** depreciate **13** underestimate

minimum 3 dab, jot **4** iota, whit **5** least, speck **6** lowest, margin **7** smidgen **8** particle, pittance, smallest

minion 4 idol **5** toady **6** flunky, lackey, vassal, yes-man **7** darling, devotee, spaniel **8** creature, favorite, follower, parasite, truckler **9** sycophant, toad-

eater, underling 10 bootlicker 11 lickspittle, subordinate
minister 4 tend 5 agent, clerk, serve
6 cleric, curate, divine, parson 8 clerical, preacher, reverend 9 churchman,
clergyman 10 ambassador 12 ecclesiastic *of state:* 10 chancellor *plenipoten-
tiary:* 5 envoy 6 consul 8 diplomat,
emissary
ministry 5 agent, organ 6 agency, clergy,
medium 7 cabinet 10 department,
instrument 11 bureaucracy
Minnehaha's husband 8 Hiawatha
Minnesota *capital:* 6 St. Paul *city:* 5 Edina
6 Duluth 9 Rochester 11 Minneapolis
college, university: 8 Carleton 9 Saint
Olaf 10 Macalester *nickname:* 6 Gopher
(State) 9 North Star (State) *park:*
9 Voyageurs *river:* 7 St. Croix 9 Minnesota 11 Mississippi *state bird:* 4 loon
(common) *state flower:* 12 lady's slipper
state tree: 7 red pine
minor 5 lower, petty, small, youth
6 casual, lesser, little, paltry, slight
7 trivial 8 inferior, mediocre, piddling,
small-fry, trifling, underage 9 dependent, secondary, small-beer, small-time
10 bush-league, second-rate, shoestring
11 indifferent, unimportant 13 insignificant
minority 5 youth 6 nonage 7 infancy
9 childhood 10 immaturity
minor-league 5 small 6 lesser 9 secondary, small-time 11 unimportant
Minos *daughter:* 7 Ariadne, Phaedra
father: 4 Zeus 7 Jupiter *kingdom:* 5 Crete
monster: 8 Minotaur *mother:* 6 Europa
son: 9 Androgeos *wife:* 8 Pasiphaë
Minotaur *father:* 4 bull *home:* 9 labyrinth
mother: 8 Pasiphaë *slayer:* 7 Theseus
minstrel 4 bard, wait 6 harper, singer
7 gleeman 8 jongleur 9 balladist
10 troubadour *end man:* 5 Bones (Mr.),
Tambo (Mr.) *instrument:* 4 lute, lyre
5 rebec, shawm, tabor 6 crumhorn,
psaltery 9 krummhorn 10 tambourine
mint 3 pot 4 cast, coin, heap, pile, sage
5 basil, bugle, forge, issue, stamp, trove
6 boodle, bundle, create, intact, packet,
savory, strike, unused 7 fortune, like-
new, menthol, perfect, produce
8 brand-new, lavender, marjoram, original 9 blue curls, bugleweed, undamaged
Minuit's purchase 9 Manhattan
minus 4 flaw, lack, less, sans 6 absent,
defect 7 lacking, missing, wanting,
without 8 drawback, negative, subtract
10 deficiency
minuscule 4 tiny 5 small 6 letter, little,
minute 7 trivial 9 lowercase, miniature

10 negligible, small-scale 11 meaningless, microscopic 13 imperceptible,
inappreciable, insignificant
minute 3 wee 4 jiff, memo, note, tiny
5 draft, flash, jiffy, small, teeny, weeny
6 little, moment, record, teensy 7 careful, instant, precise, trivial 8 detailed,
itemized, thorough, trifling 9 itsy-bitsy,
itty-bitty, miniature, minuscule
10 diminutive, memorandum, meticulous, scrupulous, teeny-weeny 11 Lilliputian, punctilious 13 infinitesimal
minutes 3 log 6 annals, record 7 summary 10 transcript 11 proceedings
minutiae 6 trivia 7 details 10 fine points,
triviality 11 particulars
minx 4 bawd, moll, slut, tart 5 bimbo,
tramp, wench, whore 6 floozy, harlot,
hooker 7 hustler, trollop 8 strumpet
10 prostitute
miracle 4 boon, feat 6 marvel, wonder
7 godsend, portent, prodigy, stunner
8 windfall 9 sensation 10 phenomenon
miraculous 7 amazing 8 wondrous
9 marvelous, unearthly, wonderful
10 astounding, prodigious, superhuman
11 astonishing, spectacular 12 inexplicable, supernatural 13 preternatural
mirage 6 vision, wraith 8 delusion, illusion, phantasm 11 fata morgana, ignis
fatuus 13 hallucination
Miranda *father:* 8 Prospero *lover:* 9 Ferdinand
mire 3 bog, fen, mud 4 muck, ooze,
sink, trap 5 delay, marsh, slush, swamp
6 detain, enmesh, entrap, hang up,
morass, slough, tangle 7 bog down,
embroil, ensnare, involve, set back
8 entangle 9 imbroglio, implicate,
quicksand
Miriam's brother 5 Aaron, Moses
mirror 5 glass 6 embody, typify 7 reflect
8 speculum 9 exemplify, personify,
reflector, represent 10 illustrate
11 cheval glass 12 looking glass *signal-
ing:* 10 heliograph
mirth 3 fun, joy 4 glee 5 cheer 6 gaiety,
levity 7 jollity, revelry 8 gladness, hilarity 9 festivity, frivolity, happiness,
jocundity, joviality, merriment 10 jocularity 11 merrymaking 12 cheerfulness
mirthful 3 gay 5 jolly, merry, riant 6 joc-
und, jovial 7 festive 9 exuberant, hilarious 12 lighthearted
miry 4 oozy 5 boggy, mucky, muddy
6 marshy, slushy, swampy
misadventure 4 slip 5 boner, error, lapse
6 howler, mishap 7 blunder, faux pas
8 accident, calamity, casualty, disaster
9 cataclysm 10 misfortune 11 catastrophe

misanthrope 5 cynic, grump, loner **6** grinch **7** killjoy, recluse, scoffer **10** curmudgeon

misanthropic 7 cynical **10** antisocial

misappropriate 5 filch, steal **6** pilfer **7** purloin **8** embezzle, peculate **9** defalcate

misbegotten 7 bastard, illicit, natural **8** baseborn, deformed, spurious **10** fatherless, unfathered **12** contemptible, disreputable, ill-conceived, illegitimate

misbehave 5 act up, cut up, lapse, rebel, stray **6** act out, offend **7** carry on, disobey **8** trespass **10** roughhouse, transgress

misbehavior 7 misdeed **8** rudeness **9** high jinks **10** misconduct, wrongdoing **11** delinquency, dereliction, naughtiness **13** transgression

miscalculate 3 err **8** miscount, misgauge

miscarry 4 fail, flop **5** abort **6** fizzle **7** go wrong

miscellaneous 3 odd **5** mixed **6** motley, sundry, varied **7** diverse **8** assorted **9** different, disparate, scrambled **13** heterogeneous

miscellany 3 ana **4** hash, olio, stew **5** salad **6** jumble, medley, motley, muddle **7** farrago, mélange, mixture, omnibus **8** mixed bag, pastiche **9** anthology, congeries, pasticcio, patchwork, potpourri **10** assortment, hodgepodge, hotchpotch, salmagundi **11** aggregation, gallimaufry, odds and ends, olla podrida, smorgasbord

mischance 6 mishap **7** bad luck, tragedy **8** accident, casualty **9** adversity **10** misfortune **11** contretemps

mischief 3 ill **4** evil, harm **5** prank **6** damage, strife **7** devilry, roguery, trouble, waggery **8** deviltry, sabotage **9** devilment, diablerie, vandalism **10** wrongdoing **11** naughtiness, shenanigans **12** monkeyshines

mischief-maker 3 imp **4** puck **5** devil, knave, rogue, scamp **6** rascal **7** villain **8** agitator, scalawag **9** prankster, trickster **11** rapscallion **12** rabble-rouser

mischievous 3 sly **4** arch, foxy **5** antic, saucy **6** artful, bratty, impish, tricky, vexing **7** harmful, irksome, larkish, naughty, playful, puckish, roguish, tricksy, waggish **8** annoying, damaging, perverse, prankish, rascally, sportive **9** injurious, malicious **10** bothersome, frolicsome, ill-behaved

misconception 5 error **7** fallacy, mistake **8** delusion, illusion

misconduct 8 adultery **10** wrongdoing **11** dereliction, impropriety, malfea-

sance, malpractice, misbehavior **12** malversation **13** transgression

miscreant 4 heel **5** felon, knave, rogue **6** outlaw, rascal, sinner, wretch **7** corrupt, culprit, heretic, hoodlum, infidel, lowlife, vicious, villain **8** apostate, criminal, depraved, infamous, perverse **9** heretical, nefarious, scoundrel, unhealthy, wrongdoer **10** blackguard, degenerate, delinquent, unbeliever, villainous

miscue 4 goof, miss, slip, trip **5** error, fluff, lapse **6** slipup **7** blooper, blunder, mistake

misdeed 3 sin **5** crime, wrong **6** breach **7** offense **9** violation **10** infraction **13** transgression

misdoubt 4 fear **5** dread **7** suspect

mise-en-scène 3 set **4** site **6** locale, medium, milieu **7** ambient, climate, context, scenery, setting **8** ambience, stage set **10** atmosphere, background **11** environment **12** stage setting, surroundings

miser 5 piker **7** hoarder, niggard, scrooge **8** tightwad **9** skinflint **10** cheapskate, pinchpenny

miserable 6 gloomy, meager, meagre, paltry, rueful, sordid, woeful **7** doleful, forlorn, piteous, pitiful, squalid **8** desolate, dolorous, downcast, hopeless, shameful, tortured, wretched **9** afflicted, destitute, sorrowful, worthless **10** despairing, despondent, melancholy **12** contemptible

Miserables, Les *author:* **4** Hugo (Victor) *character:* **6** Javert (Inspector) **7** Cosette, Fantine, Valjean (Jean)

miserly 4 mean **5** close, tight **6** greedy, stingy **7** scrimpy **8** covetous, grasping **9** niggardly, penurious, scrimping **10** avaricious **11** closefisted, tightfisted **12** cheeseparing, parsimonious **13** penny-pinching

misery 3 woe **5** agony, dolor, grief **6** sorrow **7** anguish, squalor **8** calamity, distress **9** adversity, dejection, suffering **10** affliction, depression, desolation **11** despondency **12** wretchedness

misfit 6 oddity, weirdo, zombie **7** oddball **8** maverick **9** eccentric, screwball

misfortune 3 woe **4** blow, harm, loss **5** cross, trial **7** reverse, setback, tragedy, trouble **8** accident, calamity, casualty, disaster, hardship **9** adversity, cataclysm **10** affliction, visitation **11** catastrophe, contretemps, tribulation

misgiving 4 fear **5** doubt, dread, qualm **6** unease **7** anxiety **8** distrust **9** suspicion **10** foreboding **11** premonition, trepidation **12** apprehension, presentiment

misguided 5 wrong **9** erroneous **10** ill-advised **11** injudicious **12** short-sighted

mishandle 4 flub **5** abuse, botch **6** bungle, fumble, mess up **7** rough up **8** maltreat **10** knock about, slap around

mishap 7 bad luck, tragedy **8** accident, casualty **9** adversity **11** contretemps

mishmash 6 jumble, litter, medley, muddle **7** clutter, mélange, mixture, rummage **8** pastiche, scramble **9** pasticcio, patchwork, potpourri **10** hodgepodge, hotchpotch

misidentify 5 mix up **7** confuse **8** confound

misinterpret 7 confuse, misread

mislay 4 lose

mislead 4 dupe, fool, gull, lure **5** bluff, cheat **6** betray, delude, entice, seduce, take in **7** beguile, deceive **8** hoodwink, inveigle **11** double-cross

misleading 5 false, wrong **8** delusive, delusory, specious **9** deceitful, deceptive **10** fallacious, inaccurate **11** casuistical, sophistical

mismatch 3 jar **5** clash **6** jangle **7** discord **8** conflict

misplace 4 lose

misprint 4 typo

misprision 5 scorn **7** despite, disdain, neglect **8** contempt, sedition **9** contumely, disregard **10** misconduct, negligence **11** concealment, dereliction, impropriety, malpractice

misrepresent 4 warp **5** twist **6** garble **7** distort, falsify, varnish **8** disguise **9** embellish, embroider **10** camouflage **11** counterfeit

misrepresentation 3 fib, lie **4** tale **5** story **6** canard **7** falsity, untruth **9** falsehood **10** distortion

miss 3 err, gal **4** fail, girl, lass, maid, omit, skip **5** avoid **6** damsel, escape, forget, ignore, lassie, maiden **7** failure, misfire, neglect **8** discount, leave out, overlook **9** disregard

Missa Solemnis composer 9 Beethoven (Ludwig van)

misshape 4 warp **6** deform **7** contort, distort, torture **9** disfigure

missile 4 bolt, dart **5** arrow, shell, spear **6** bullet, rocket **10** cannonball, projectile *underwater:* **7** torpedo (see also GUIDED MISSILE)

missing 4 AWOL **6** absent

mission 3 aim, job **4** duty, goal, task **5** quest **6** charge, errand, object **7** calling, embassy, purpose **8** legation, lifework, ministry, vocation **9** objective **10** assignment

missionary 7 apostle **8** emissary **10** evangelist, revivalist **12** propagandist, proselytizer

Mississippi *capital:* **7** Jackson *city:* **6** Biloxi **8** Gulfport **10** Greenville *college, university:* **12** Jackson State **8** Millsaps *nickname:* **8** Magnolia (State) *river:* **5** Pearl **11** Mississippi *state bird:* **11** mockingbird *state flower:* **8** magnolia *state tree:* **8** magnolia

missive 4 memo, note **6** letter, report **7** epistle, message **8** dispatch

Miss Julie author 10 Strindberg (August)

Miss Lonelyhearts author 4 West (Nathanael)

Missouri *capital:* **13** Jefferson City *city:* **7** St. Louis **11** Kansas City **11** Springfield **12** Independence *college, university:* **10** Washington *lake:* **15** Lake of the Ozarks *nickname:* **6** Show Me (State) *river:* **8** Missouri **11** Mississippi *state bird:* **8** bluebird *state flower:* **8** hawthorn *state tree:* **7** dogwood

misstate 4 warp **5** color, twist **6** garble **7** distort, falsify

misstatement 3 fib, lie **4** tale **7** falsity, untruth **9** falsehood **13** prevarication

misstep 4 flub, goof, slip **5** boner, error, fluff, gaffe, lapse **6** slipup **7** blooper, blunder, faux pas

mist 3 dim, fog **4** blur, film, haze, murk **5** befog, brume, cloud **7** becloud, obscure

mistake 4 flub, slip **5** boner, error, fluff, folly, gaffe, lapse **6** boo-boo, bungle, howler, slipup **7** blooper, blunder, confuse, faux pas, take for **8** confound **10** inaccuracy

mistaken 5 false, wrong **6** all wet, faulty, flawed, untrue **7** invalid **8** specious **9** defective, incorrect, misguided, unfounded **10** fallacious, fraudulent, inaccurate **11** misinformed

mister 3 sir **7** husband *French:* **8** monsieur *German:* **4** Herr *Italian:* **6** signor *Spanish:* **5** señor

Mister Roberts author 6 Heggen (Thomas)

mistreat 5 abuse **6** ill-use, molest **7** rough up **8** brutalize, manhandle

mistress 4 doxy, moll **5** lover, woman **7** hetaira **8** dulcinea, ladylove, paramour **9** concubine, courtesan, inamorata, kept woman **10** chatelaine, girl friend *of Charles II:* **4** Gwyn (Nell) **8** Villiers (Barbara) *of Edward III:* **7** Perrers (Alice) *of Henry II (England):* **8** Clifford (Rosamund) *of Henry II (France):* **9** de Poiters (Diane) *of Louis XV:* **9** Pompadour (Madame de)

mistrust 5 doubt **7** concern, dispute, dubiety, surmise, suspect **8** wariness

9 apprehend, misgiving, suspicion **10** foreboding, skepticism **11** incertitude, uncertainty **12** apprehension
mistrustful 4 wary **5** leery **6** uneasy **7** dubious, jealous **8** doubting **9** skeptical **10** disquieted, suspicious **12** apprehensive
misty 3 dim **4** hazy **5** foggy, vague **6** cloudy, vapory **7** blurred, obscure, tearful, unclear **8** confused, nebulous, vaporous **10** indistinct
misunderstanding 4 rift, spat, tiff **5** mix-up **6** breach **7** dispute, quarrel, rupture **8** squabble **10** falling-out **12** disagreement
misuse 5 waste *of a word:* **8** malaprop **11** malapropism
mite 3 bit, jot **4** atom, iota **5** grain, minim, ounce, speck **6** acarid, tittle **7** chigger, modicum, smidgen **8** molecule, particle *family:* **8** oribatid
miter 5 crown, joint **9** headdress
mitigate 4 ease **5** abate, allay, relax, slake **6** lessen, soften, subdue, temper **7** assuage, lighten, mollify, relieve **8** palliate, moderate, tone down **9** alleviate, extenuate, meliorate
mitigation 4 ease **6** relief **8** easement
mitosis 12 cell division, karyokinesis *stage:* **8** anaphase, prophase **9** metaphase, telophase
mix 4 fuse, link, lump, meld, stir **5** blend, merge, unite **6** fusion, jumble, mingle, tangle, work in **7** amalgam, combine, concoct, confuse, conjoin **8** coalesce, compound, confound **9** associate, commingle, interfuse **10** amalgamate, crossbreed **11** intermingle **12** amalgamation
mixed 6 hybrid, impure, motley, sundry, varied **7** diluted, diverse, mongrel **8** assorted, compound **9** composite, interbred, irregular **12** multifarious **13** heterogeneous, miscellaneous
mixed bag 4 olio **5** salad **6** jumble, medley **7** mélange **8** mishmash, pastiche **9** potpourri **10** assortment, hodgepodge, miscellany **11** gallimaufry
mixed-up 5 fazed **7** jumbled **8** confused **9** flustered, perplexed **10** bewildered, disjointed, distracted, incoherent, nonplussed **12** disconcerted
mixologist 6 barman **7** tapster **9** barkeeper, bartender
mixture 4 brew, hash, olio, stew **5** alloy, blend **6** fusion, hybrid, jumble, medley **7** amalgam, farrago, mélange **8** compound, mishmash, solution **9** composite, potpourri **10** concoction, confection, miscellany, salmagundi **11** combination **12** amalgamation

mix up 5 addle **6** fuddle, jumble, muddle **7** confuse, fluster, mistake **8** befuddle, bewilder, confound **10** disarrange, discompose **11** disorganize, misidentify
mix-up 4 hash, mess, muss **5** botch, chaos, error, melee **6** muddle, tangle **7** mistake **8** shambles **9** commotion, confusion
mks unit 3 lux, ohm **4** mole, volt, watt **5** farad, henry, hertz, joule, lumen, meter, metre, tesla, weber **6** ampere, kelvin, newton, pascal, second **7** candela, coulomb, siemens **8** kilogram
Mnemosyne 6 Memory *daughters:* **5** Muses *father:* **6** Uranus *lover:* **4** Zeus *mother:* **4** Gaea
Moabite *city:* **3** Kir *god:* **7** Chemosh *king:* **5** Eglon, Mesha
Moab's father 3 Lot
moan 4 wail, weep **5** gripe, groan, whine **6** bewail, grieve, grouse, lament **7** deplore **8** complain
mob 3 jam **4** clan, gang, herd, pack, push, ring, riot **5** crowd, crush, horde, mafia, press, swarm **6** jostle, masses, rabble, throng **8** canaille, riffraff **9** hoi polloi, multitude **11** proletariat
mobile 5 fluid **6** moving **7** migrant, movable, protean **8** cellular, moveable, unstable, unsteady, variable **9** adaptable, changeful, itinerant, mercurial, migratory, unsettled, versatile **10** ambulatory, capricious, changeable, inconstant **11** peripatetic
mobile home 6 camper **7** trailer **9** Airstream
mobile-phone area 4 cell
mobilize 5 drive, impel, rally, ready, rouse **6** arouse, call up, muster, prompt, propel **7** actuate, animate, marshal **8** activate, assemble, organize **9** circulate
mobster 4 goon, thug **6** hit man **7** mafioso **8** criminal, gangster **9** godfather, racketeer
Moby Dick 5 whale **10** white whale *author:* **8** Melville (Herman) *character:* **3** Pip **4** Daggoo, Parsee **7** Ishmael **8** Queequeg, Starbuck, Tashtego *pursuer:* **4** Ahab *ship:* **6** Pequod
moccasin 6 loafer **7** slipper **8** larrigan
mock 3 ape **4** defy, fake, gibe, jape, jeer, razz, twit **5** bogus, chaff, dummy, false, feign, mimic, phony, quasi, sneer, taunt, tease **6** deride, ersatz, parody, pseudo, send up **7** deceive, feigned, imitate, lampoon, mislead **8** ridicule, satirize, so-called, spurious **9** imitation, simulated **10** artificial **11** counterfeit
mockery 4 sham **5** farce, scorn, sport **6** japery, parody, satire **7** take-off **8** con-

tempt, derision, raillery, ridicule, travesty **9** burlesque, imitation **10** caricature **13** laughingstock

mocking 8 derisive, sardonic, scornful **9** sarcastic

mode 3 fad, way **4** chic, rage **5** state, style, vogue **6** custom, manner, method, status, system **7** fashion **9** condition, procedure, situation, technique **10** convention, dernier cri

model 4 copy, type **5** dummy, ideal, shape **6** design, effigy, mirror, mockup, symbol **7** classic, epitome, example, imitate, manikin, paragon, pattern, perfect, replica, typical **8** ensemble, exemplar, flawless, mannikin, maquette, nonesuch, paradigm, standard **9** archetype, beau ideal, blueprint, classical, criterion, exemplary, miniature, nonpareil **10** apotheosis, embodiment, prototypal, touchstone **12** paradigmatic, prototypical, reproduction

moderate 3 ebb **4** calm, cool, curb, even, fair, mild, slow, so-so, wane **5** abate, bland, let up, sober **6** gentle, lessen, medium, paltry, reduce, relent, slight, soften, steady, subdue, temper **7** average, chasten, control, cushion, die away, die down, ease off, equable, lighten, limited, neutral, relieve, slacken, subside, trivial **8** centrist, constant, decrease, diminish, discreet, mediocre, middling, mitigate, restrain **9** alleviate, constrain, temperate **10** abstemious, controlled, reasonable, restrained **11** indifferent **12** conservative

moderation 7 control, measure **9** restraint **10** abstinence, constraint, limitation, temperance **13** temperateness

moderator 5 judge **7** arbiter **8** chairman, examiner, governor, mediator **10** peacemaker **11** chairperson

modern 3 new **5** fresh, novel **6** recent **7** current **8** neoteric, up-to-date **10** newfangled, present-day **12** contemporary

modernize 5 renew **6** update **8** renovate **9** refurbish **10** rejuvenate

modest 3 coy, shy **4** meek, prim **5** lowly, plain, timid **6** decent, demure, humble, prissy, proper, seemly, simple **7** bashful, prudish **8** decorous, discreet, moderate, priggish, reserved, reticent, retiring **9** diffident **10** unassuming **11** puritanical, straitlaced, unassertive, unelaborate **12** self-effacing, unornamented **13** unembellished, unembroidered, unpretentious

Modest Proposal author 5 Swift (Jonathan)

modesty 7 decency, reserve **8** chastity, humility, timidity **9** propriety, reticence **10** diffidence

modicum 3 bit, jot **4** atom, iota, mite, whit **5** grain, minim, ounce, pinch, scrap, speck, trace **7** smidgen, soupçon **8** particle

modify 4 vary **5** adapt, alter, amend, limit, tweak **6** adjust, change, mutate, revise, rework, temper **7** qualify **8** mitigate, moderate, restrain **9** refashion

modish 4 chic **5** smart, swank **6** chichi, trendy, with-it **7** dashing, stylish **11** fashionable

Modred *father:* **6** Arthur *mother:* **8** Margawse *slayer, victim:* **6** Arthur

modulate 4 vary **5** tweak **6** adjust, attune, temper **8** fine-tune, regulate, restrain

modus ___ **7** vivendi **8** operandi

modus operandi 5 style **6** custom, manner, method, system **7** process, program, routine **8** approach, practice, strategy **9** procedure, technique

mogul 4 czar, king, lord **5** baron, nabob, ruler **6** bigwig, prince, sachem, tycoon **7** kingpin, magnate **9** plutocrat, potentate

Mohammed see MUHAMMAD

Mohawk chief 5 Brant (Joseph) **8** Hiawatha

Mohican chief 5 Uncas

moiety 3 cut **4** half, part **5** piece **7** element, portion, section, segment **8** division **9** component

moil 3 tug, wet **4** grub, to-do, work **5** churn, dirty, drive, grind, labor, swirl **6** bustle, clamor, drudge, hubbub, lather, seethe, strain, strive, uproar **7** ferment, travail, trouble, wrangle **8** drudgery **9** agitation, commotion, confusion **10** hurly-burly, turbulence

moist 3 wet **4** damp, dank, dewy **5** humid **6** clammy, steamy, sticky **7** dampish, maudlin, tearful, wettish

moisten 3 wet **6** dampen **8** humidify, saturate

moisture 4 damp **5** vapor **7** wetness **8** humidity **13** precipitation

mojo 3 hex **4** jinx **5** charm, magic, power, spell **6** hoodoo, whammy

molar 5 tooth **7** grinder *neighbor:* **6** canine

molasses 7 treacle **10** blackstrap

mold 3 die **4** cast, form, sort, type **5** forge, knead, shape, stamp **6** design, fungus **7** fashion, pattern **8** template **9** construct **11** description

moldable 6 pliant, supple **7** ductile, plastic, pliable **9** adaptable, malleable

molder 3 rot **5** decay, waste **7** crumble

9 break down, decompose **11** deteriorate **12** disintegrate

molding 4 bead, ogee **5** congé, ogive, talon, torus **6** reglet **7** annulet, beading, cavetto, cornice, reeding **8** cincture **9** baseboard *compound:* **4** beak, cyma, ogie **10** serpentine *edge:* **5** arris *flat:* **5** bevel, splay **6** fascia, fillet, listel, regula **7** chamfer *simple curve:* **4** roll **5** flute, ovolo, torus **6** scotia **8** astragal

Moldova *capital:* **8** Chisinau, Kishinev *former name:* **8** Moldavia *language:* **8** Romanian *monetary unit:* **3** leu *neighbor:* **7** Romania, Ukraine *river:* **8** Dniester

moldy 5 dated, fusty, musty, passé **6** bygone, old hat **7** ancient, antique, archaic, outworn **8** mildewed, outdated **9** crumbling, moth-eaten **10** antiquated **12** old-fashioned

mole 3 spy **4** pier, quay **5** jetty, nevus **6** burrow, tunnel **9** birthmark **10** breakwater

molecule 3 bit, jot **4** iota **5** minim, speck **7** modicum **8** particle

molest 3 vex **4** bait **5** abuse, annoy, harry, tease **6** badger, bother, harass, heckle, hector, pester, plague **7** disturb, torment, trouble **9** persecute

Moll Flanders author 5 Defoe (Daniel)

mollify 4 calm, ease **5** allay **6** pacify, soften, soothe, temper **7** appease, assuage, lighten, placate, relieve, sweeten **8** mitigate **9** alleviate **10** ameliorate, conciliate, propitiate

mollusk 6 chiton *bivalve:* **4** clam **6** cockle, mussel, oyster, teredo **7** geoduck, scallop **8** shipworm *cephalopod:* **5** squid **7** octopus **8** argonaut, nautilus **10** cuttlefish *part:* **6** mantle, radula, siphon *tooth shell:* **9** dentalium *univalve:* **4** slug **5** conch, cowry, murex, snail, whelk **6** cowrie, limpet, triton **7** abalone **10** nudibranch, periwinkle

Molly ___ 7 Maguire, Pitcher

mollycoddle 3 pet **4** baby **5** humor, spoil **6** cocker, cosset, dandle, pamper **7** cater to, indulge

Moloch's pit 6 Tophet

molt 4 cast, shed, slip **6** change, slough **7** cast off, discard, ecdysis **9** slough off

molted skins 7 exuviae

molten 6 melted **7** glowing **9** liquefied

molten rock 4 lava **5** magma

moment 5 flash, jiffy, point, shake, trice **6** import, minute, second **7** instant **8** juncture, occasion **9** magnitude **10** importance **11** consequence, split second **12** significance

momentary 5 brief, quick **8** fleeting, fugitive **9** ephemeral, fugacious, transient **10** evanescent, short-lived, transitory

momentous 5 grave **7** epochal, fateful, serious, weighty **9** important **10** meaningful **11** significant, substantial **12** considerable **13** consequential

momentousness 6 import, weight **9** magnitude **10** importance **11** consequence, weightiness **12** significance

momentum 5 drive **6** energy, thrust **7** impetus, impulse **10** propulsion

Momo author 4 Ende (Michael)

momus 6 carper, critic, mocker **7** caviler **8** caviller **9** detractor **11** faultfinder

Monaco *commune:* **10** Monte Carlo *language:* **6** French *monetary unit:* **4** euro *neighbor:* **6** France *prince:* **6** Albert **7** Rainier *princess:* **5** Grace

monad 3 one **4** atom, unit **8** zoospore **9** protozoan

Mona Lisa 10 La Gioconda *painter:* **7** da Vinci (Leonardo) **8** Leonardo (da Vinci)

monarch 4 czar, king, raja, tsar, tzar **5** queen, rajah, ruler **6** kaiser, prince **7** emperor, empress, majesty **9** butterfly, potentate, sovereign

monarchical 5 regal, royal **6** kingly **8** imperial, kinglike, majestic **9** sovereign

monarch's daughter 8 princess *Portuguese, Spanish:* **7** infanta

monarch's son 6 prince *French:* **7** dauphin *Portuguese, Spanish:* **7** infante

monarchy 4 rule **5** realm, reign **7** kingdom **8** kingship **9** autocracy, monocracy **11** sovereignty

monastery 5 abbey **6** friary, priory **7** convent, nunnery **8** cloister *Buddhist:* **8** lamasery *Eastern Orthodox:* **5** laura *head:* **5** abbot, prior

monastic 4 abbé, monk **7** ascetic, brother **8** isolated, secluded **9** reclusive **10** cloistered **11** sequestered

___ Mondrian 4 Piet

monetary 6 fiscal **9** financial, pecuniary **10** numismatic

monetary rate 7 millage

monetary unit see at individual countries

money 4 cash, coin, gelt, jack, kale, loot, pelf, swag **5** bread, chips, dough, funds, lucre, moola, rhino **6** boodle, change, dinero, do-re-mi, mammon, moolah, riches, specie, wampum, wealth **7** cabbage, capital, coinage, lettuce, needful, scratch, stipend **8** bankroll, currency, finances, treasure **9** resources **10** greenbacks **11** filthy lucre, legal tender

moneyed 4 rich **5** flush **6** loaded **7** opulent, wealthy, well-off **8** affluent, well-to-do **10** prosperous, well-heeled

money-grubber 5 miser 7 hoarder, niggard, scrooge 8 tightwad 9 skinflint 10 cheapskate 12 penny-pincher
moneymaking 6 paying 7 gainful 9 lucrative 10 profitable, well-paying, worthwhile 12 advantageous, remunerative
monger 4 hawk, sell, vend 6 broker, dealer, hawker, peddle, trader, vendor 7 higgler, packman, peddler 8 huckster
Mongol conqueror 9 Tamerlane 10 Kublai Khan 11 Genghis Khan, Tamburlaine
Mongolia *capital:* 9 Ulan Bator 11 Ulaanbaatar *conqueror:* 6 Ögödei 11 Genghis Khan *desert:* 4 Gobi *lake:* 6 Baikal *monetary unit:* 6 tugrik *mountain range:* 5 Altai, Altay 6 Kentai 7 Hentiyn 9 Altai Shan, Altay Shan *neighbor:* 5 China 6 Russia *river:* 5 Orhun 7 Selenga
mongrel 3 cur 4 mule, mutt 5 cross 6 hybrid 7 bastard, mixture 8 half-bred 9 crossbred, half blood, half-breed 10 crossbreed
moniker 3 tag 4 name 6 handle 8 cognomen, nickname 9 sobriquet 11 appellation, designation
monish 4 warn
monition 6 caveat 7 caution, portent, warning 11 forewarning
monitor 4 test 5 check, watch 6 screen 7 adviser, observe, oversee 8 watchdog 11 keep track of
Monitor *designer:* 8 Ericsson (John) *opponent:* 8 Virginia 9 Merrimack
monitory 7 warning 8 advisory 10 cautionary
monk 4 abbé 5 friar 7 brother 8 cenobite, monastic 9 anchorite *Buddhist:* 4 lama 5 bonze *Hindu:* 8 sannyasi *Roman Catholic:* 8 Capuchin, Salesian, Trappist 9 Carmelite, Dominican 10 Carthusian, Cistercian, Franciscan 11 Augustinian *room:* 4 cell *shaven crown:* 7 tonsure *title:* 3 Dom, Fra 5 Padre
monkey 3 imp 4 mess 5 gamin 6 meddle, simian, tamper, urchin 8 busybody 9 interfere, interlope *New World:* 4 titi 6 howler, spider, uakari, woolly 7 sapajou, tamarin 8 capuchin, marmoset, squirrel 11 douroucouli *Old World:* 5 Diana, drill 6 guenon, langur, rhesus, vervet 7 colobus, hanuman, macaque 8 mandrill, mangabey 9 proboscis 10 Barbary ape
monkeyshine 3 gag 4 dido, jape, lark 5 antic, caper, prank, stunt, trick 6 frolic 10 shenanigan, tomfoolery
monocratic 8 absolute, despotic 9 arbitrary, autarchic, tyrannous 10 autocratic, tyrannical

monogram 8 initials
monograph 5 study 6 thesis 8 tractate, treatise 9 discourse 12 disquisition, dissertation
monopolize 3 hog 5 sew up 6 absorb, corner 7 control, engross 8 dominate, take over
monopoly 5 trust 6 cartel, corner 7 control 9 ownership, syndicate 10 consortium, domination 11 exclusivity
monotone 5 drone
monotonous 4 blah, dull 6 boring, dreary 7 droning, humdrum, one-note, uniform 8 singsong, unvaried 9 unvarying 10 pedestrian, repetitive 11 repetitious
monotony 6 tedium 7 humdrum 8 flatness, sameness 10 uniformity
monsoon 6 deluge 8 downpour 9 rainstorm 10 cloudburst
monster 4 ogre 5 beast, freak, giant, whale 6 mutant, ogress 8 behemoth, bogeyman, colossus, giantess 9 hellhound, leviathan, manticore *biblical:* 5 Rehab 8 Behemoth 9 Leviathan *female:* 6 Gorgon, Medusa, Scylla *fire-breathing:* 6 dragon, Typhon 7 Chimera 8 Chimaera *fowl-dragon:* 10 cockatrice *French:* 8 Tarasque *horse-fish:* 11 hippocampus *hundred-armed:* 9 Enceladus *hundred-eyed:* 5 Argus *hundred-handed:* 8 Briareus *lion-eagle:* 7 griffin *serpent-headed:* 6 gorgon *study of:* 10 teratology *three-bodied:* 6 Geryon *three-headed dog:* 8 Cerberus *two-headed dog:* 6 Orthos *water:* 6 kraken *woman-bird:* 5 Harpy *woman-lion:* 6 Sphinx *woman-serpent:* 7 Echidna (see also DRAGON)
___ monster 4 Gila
monstrosity 4 mess 5 freak 6 fright, horror 7 eyesore, outrage, prodigy 8 atrocity, enormity 11 abomination 12 malformation
monstrous 4 huge, vast 5 awful, giant, large 7 glaring, heinous, hellish, hideous, immense, mammoth, massive, titanic 8 aberrant, abnormal, colossal, deformed, dreadful, enormous, fiendish, freakish, gigantic, god-awful, gruesome, horrible, infamous, shocking, towering 9 atrocious, egregious, fantastic, frightful, grotesque, loathsome, malformed, unnatural 10 diabolical, flagitious, gargantuan, horrendous, impressive, monumental, outrageous, prodigious, scandalous, stupendous, tremendous 11 elephantine
montage 6 jumble, medley 7 mélange, mixture 9 composite, patchwork, potpourri 10 assortment, miscellany 12 conglomerate
Montagues' enemies 8 Capulets

Montaigne's forte 5 essay
Montana *capital:* **6** Helena *city:* **5** Butte **7** Bozeman **8** Billings, Missoula **10** Great Falls *lake:* **8** Flathead *motto:* **9** Oro y plata *mountain:* **7** Granite (Peak) *nickname:* **8** Treasure (State) *park:* **7** Glacier *river:* **8** Missouri **11** Yellowstone *state bird:* **10** meadowlark *state flower:* **10** bitterroot *state tree:* **13** ponderosa pine
Monteverdi *opera* **5** Orfeo **7** Arianna
Montezuma *capital:* **12** Tenochtitlán *conqueror:* **6** Cortés, Cortéz (Hernán, Hernando) *people:* **6** Aztecs *revenge:* **8** diarrhea
month *Hindu:* **3** Pus **4** Asin, Jeth, Magh **5** Aghan, Chait, Sawan **6** Asargh, Bhadon, Kartik, Phagun **7** Baisakh *Jewish:* **4** Adar, Elul, Iyar **5** Nisan, Sivan, Tebet **6** Kislev, Shebat, Tammuz, Tishri **7** Heshvan *Muslim:* **4** Rabi **5** Rajab, Safar **6** Jumada, Sha'ban **7** Ramadan, Shawwal **8** Muharram **9** Dhu'l-Hijja, Dhu'l-Qa'dah
Montmartre *church* **10** Sacré Coeur
Montserrat *capital:* **8** Plymouth *discoverer:* **8** Columbus (Christopher) *location:* **10** West Indies *territory of:* **7** Britain *volcano:* **9** Soufrière
monument 5 cairn, stela, stupa **7** memento, tribute **8** archives, cenotaph, document, memorial **9** footstone, headstone, tombstone **10** gravestone **11** grave marker, testimonial *prehistoric:* **6** dolmen, menhir **8** cromlech, megalith
monumental 4 huge, vast **6** mighty, mortal **7** awesome, immense, mammoth, massive **8** enormous, gigantic, historic, majestic, towering **9** monstrous **10** prodigious, stupendous, tremendous **11** mountainous, outstanding **12** overwhelming
mooch 3 bat, beg, bum **4** grub, roam, rove **5** amble, cadge, drift, range, slink, sneak, steal, stray **6** ramble, sponge, wander **7** maunder, meander, saunter **8** freeload, scrounge **9** panhandle
mooching 7 beggary **9** mendicity **10** mendicancy
mood 3 air **4** aura, feel, tone, whim **5** fancy, humor **6** spirit, temper, vagary **7** caprice, emotion, feeling, mind-set **8** ambiance, ambience **9** character, semblance **10** atmosphere **11** disposition, personality, temperament
moody 4 glum **5** mopey **6** fickle, gloomy **7** pensive **8** unstable **9** mercurial, whimsical **10** capricious, changeable, depressive, inconstant, melancholy **13** temperamental

moola 4 cash, coin, pelf, swag **5** bread, dough, money **6** dinero, specie, wampum **7** cabbage, scratch **9** long green
moon 4 gape, mope **5** dream **6** dawdle **8** languish **9** satellite *dark area:* **4** mare **5** maria (plural) **7** farside *god:* **3** Sin **5** Nanna **6** Meztli *goddess:* **4** Luna **5** Diana, Tanit **6** Hecate, Hekate, Selena, Selene, Tanith **7** Artemis, Astarte *valley:* **4** rill *vehicle:* **3** LEM (see also SATELLITE)
Moon and Sixpence *author* **7** Maugham (W. Somerset)
mooncalf 4 dolt, fool **5** dunce, ninny **7** jackass, tomfool **9** simpleton
Moon River *composer* **7** Mancini (Henry)
moonshine 4 bosh, jake **5** hokum **6** bunkum, humbug **7** bootleg, eyewash, hogwash **8** homebrew, malarkey, nonsense, tommyrot **9** poppycock **10** balderdash, bathtub gin, contraband, flapdoodle **11** mountain dew **12** blatherskite
Moonstone, The *author:* **7** Collins (Wilkie) *detective:* **4** Cuff
moonstruck 4 daft, nuts **5** batty, corny, flaky, kooky, mushy, nutty, sappy, wacko, wacky **6** crazed, cuckoo, fruity, insane, screwy **7** berserk, bonkers, lunatic, maudlin, touched **8** romantic **9** nostalgic, schmaltzy **10** lovey-dovey, saccharine, unbalanced **11** sentimental
moor 3 bog, fen **4** dock, fell **5** berth, catch, tie up **6** anchor, Berber, fasten, Muslim, secure, tether **7** peat bog **8** make fast, Moroccan *fictional:* **7** Othello
moose 6 cervid *female:* **3** cow *male:* **4** bull *relative:* **3** elk **4** deer
moot 5 argue, plead **6** broach, debate **7** agitate, bring up, canvass, discuss, dispute, dubious, suggest, suspect **8** abstract, academic, arguable, disputed, doubtful **9** debatable, introduce, thrash out, uncertain, unsettled, ventilate **10** disputable, unresolved **11** problematic **12** questionable **13** controversial
mop 4 swab, wipe
mope 4 fret, idle, moon, pine, pout, sigh, stew, sulk **5** brood, drift, mosey **6** dawdle, linger **7** maunder, meander, saunter **8** languish
mopes 4 funk **5** blues, dumps, ennui, slump **7** dismals, malaise, sadness **8** dolefuls **10** depression, melancholy **11** unhappiness
mopey 3 low **4** blue, down, glum **6** broody, droopy, morose **7** doleful

8 cast down, dejected, downcast
9 depressed 10 dispirited, melancholy,
spiritless
moppet 3 kid, tot 4 tyke 5 chick, child
7 toddler 8 juvenile 9 youngster
mop up 4 beat, drub, dust, lick, whip
6 absorb, garner, gather 7 shellac,
trounce 8 complete, lambaste 9 overwhelm
moral 3 saw 4 good, just, pure, rule
5 adage, axiom, gnome, maxim, noble,
right 6 chaste, decent, dictum, honest,
lesson, proper, saying, truism 7 epigram, ethical, preachy, precept,
proverb, upright, virtual 8 aphorism,
apothegm, didactic, elevated, sermonic,
virtuous 9 honorable, righteous
10 high-minded, principled, scrupulous, upstanding 11 right-minded
13 conscientious
morale 4 mood 5 heart 6 esprit, mettle,
spirit, temper 7 resolve 10 confidence
13 esprit de corps
moralistic 5 noble, pious 7 canting, ethical 8 didactic, virtuous 9 righteous
10 principled 11 pharisaical, right-
minded 13 sanctimonious
morality 5 ethic, honor, mores 6 purity,
virtue 7 decency, probity 8 goodness
9 integrity, rectitude, rightness 11 saintliness, uprightness 13 righteousness
moralize 6 preach 7 lecture 9 preachify,
sermonize 11 pontificate
morals 5 mores 6 ethics, ideals 8 scruples 9 integrity, standards 10 principles
morass 3 bog, fen, web 4 knot, maze,
mesh, mire, quag, trap 5 marsh, skein,
snarl, swamp 6 jungle, muddle, tangle
8 quagmire 9 imbroglio
moratorium 3 ban 5 delay 8 interval
10 suspension
moray 3 eel
morbid 4 dark, sick 5 moody 6 gloomy,
grisly, morose, sickly, sullen 7 unsound
8 diseased, gruesome 9 saturnine,
unhealthy 11 melancholic, unwholesome 12 pathological
mordancy 7 acidity 8 acerbity, acridity,
acrimony, asperity, pungency 9 harshness, sharpness 10 causticity, tren-
chancy 11 astringency, sardonicism
12 incisiveness
mordant 4 keen 5 acrid, salty, sharp
6 biting 7 burning, caustic, cutting,
pungent 8 incisive, sardonic, scathing
9 sarcastic, trenchant
Mordecai *cousin:* 6 Esther *father:* 4 Jair
mother: 6 Esther
more 3 new, too 4 also, else, plus
5 added, again, along, extra, fresh,
older, other, spare 6 as well, better,

nearer, withal 7 another, besides, farther, further, greater 8 likewise, moreover 9 increased 10 additional
More book 6 Utopia
more or less 5 about 7 roughly
13 approximately
moreover 3 and, too 4 also 6 as well,
withal 7 besides, further 8 likewise
10 in addition 11 furthermore 12 additionally
mores 6 ethics, habits, values 7 beliefs,
customs, manners 8 folkways 9 amenities, etiquette 10 civilities 11 proprieties
Morgana's brother 6 Arthur
Morgan le Fay 9 sorceress *brother:*
6 Arthur (King)
moribund 5 dying 6 ebbing, fading 7 dormant, outworn 8 decaying, expiring,
inactive 9 declining 11 obsolescent
13 deteriorating
Mormon Church *administrative unit:*
4 ward 5 stake *founder:* 5 Smith
(Joseph) *leader:* 5 Young (Brigham)
priest: 5 elder
Mormon State 4 Utah
morning 4 dawn 5 sunup 6 aurora
7 dawning, sunrise 8 cockcrow, daybreak, daylight, forenoon *moisture:*
3 dew 8 dewdrops *song:* 6 aubade
Morocco *capital:* 5 Rabat *city:* 3 Fès
6 Meknès 9 Marrakech, Marrakesh
10 Casablanca *coast:* 7 Barbary *language:* 6 Arabic, Berber *monetary unit:*
6 dirham *mountain:* 7 Toubkal *mountain
range:* 3 Rif 5 Atlas *neighbor:* 5 Spain
7 Algeria 13 Western Sahara *sea:*
13 Mediterranean
moron 4 dodo, dolt, dope, fool
5 dummy, dunce, idiot 6 cretin, dimwit,
stupid 7 dullard, half-wit 8 dumbbell,
imbecile, numskull 9 ignoramus, lamebrain, numbskull, simpleton
moronic 4 dull, dumb 6 simple, stupid
8 backward, retarded 9 brainless, dim-
witted, imbecilic 10 half-witted, slow-
witted 12 feebleminded, simpleminded
morose 4 dour, glum, sour 5 moody,
sulky 6 cranky, crusty, gloomy, morbid,
sullen 7 crabbed, unhappy 9 depressed,
saturnine 10 depressive, ill-humored,
melancholy
morph 6 change, mutate 7 convert
9 transform, transmute 12 metamorphose, transmogrify
Morpheus *father:* 6 Hypnos *god of:*
5 sleep
Morrison novel 4 Jazz, Love, Sula
7 Beloved 9 Bluest Eye (The) 13 Song
of Solomon
Morse code *dash:* 3 dah *dot:* 3 dit
morsel 3 bit 4 bite 5 crumb, goody,

piece, scrap, snack, taste, treat **6** dainty, nibble, tidbit **7** soupçon **8** delicacy, fragment, kickshaw, mouthful

mortal 3 man **5** awful, being, fatal, frail, human, party **6** deadly, lethal, person **7** deathly, earthly, extreme, fleshly, tedious, worldly **8** creature, ruthless, temporal **9** merciless, personage **10** implacable, individual, perishable **11** conceivable

mortality 5 flesh **7** mankind **8** fatality, humanity **9** death rate, humankind, lethality **10** deadliness

mortar 5 grout **6** binder, cannon, cement, vessel **7** plaster, sealant **8** howitzer, ordnance

Morte d'Arthur author 6 Malory (Thomas)

mortgage 4 hock, lien, pawn **6** pledge **10** obligation

mortician 8 embalmer **10** undertaker

mortified 6 shamed **7** ascetic, ashamed, austere **8** red-faced **9** chagrined **10** humiliated, shamefaced **11** embarrassed

mortify 5 abash, shame **6** dismay **7** chagrin, perturb **8** disgrace **9** discomfit, embarrass, humiliate

mortuary 8 funereal **10** sepulchral **11** funeral home

mosaic 5 inlay **7** chimera **8** terrazzo **9** composite, patchwork **12** tessellation *piece:* **6** smalto **7** tessera **8** tesserae (plural)

Moscow *cathedral:* **11** Saint Basil's *citadel:* **7** Kremlin *resident:* **9** Muscovite

Moses *brother:* **5** Aaron *brother-in-law:* **5** Hobab *deathplace:* **4** Nebo *father-in-law:* **6** Jethro *sister:* **6** Miriam *son:* **7** Eliezer, Gershom *spy:* **5** Caleb *successor:* **6** Joshua *wife:* **8** Zipporah

mosey 4 mope **5** amble, drift **6** dawdle, linger, ramble, stroll, wander **7** maunder, meander, saunter

mosh 4 slam **9** slam-dance

Moslem see MUSLIM

mosque 6 masjid *niche:* **6** mihrab *prayer caller:* **7** muezzin *turret:* **7** minaret

mosquito 5 culex *genus:* **5** Aëdes, Culex **9** Anopheles

moss 9 bryophyte *kind:* **4** peat **8** sphagnum *part:* **4** seta **7** capsule, rhizoid *study of:* **8** bryology

mossback 4 fogy **6** fossil **10** fuddy-duddy **11** reactionary **12** antediluvian, conservative **13** stick-in-the-mud

mostly 6 mainly **7** chiefly, largely, overall, usually **9** generally, primarily **11** principally **13** predominantly

mote 3 bit, dot, jot **4** iota, whit **5** grain, point, speck, trace **8** flyspeck, particle

moth *immature:* **5** larva **6** larvae (plural) **11** caterpillar *kind:* **4** luna **7** codling, tussock **8** Cecropia, silkworm **9** browntail *order:* **11** Lepidoptera

moth-eaten 4 worn **5** dated, dingy, faded, mangy, moldy, musty, passé, ratty, seedy **6** bygone, old hat, patchy, shabby **7** antique, archaic, raggedy, run-down, unkempt **8** decrepit, outdated, outmoded, tattered, timeworn **10** antiquated, down-at-heel, threadbare **11** dilapidated

mother 3 dam, mom **4** mama, root **5** fount, mammy, mater, momma, mommy, mummy, nurse **6** origin, source **7** care for, nurture **9** prototype, rootstock **10** provenance, wellspring *combining form:* **4** matr **5** matri, matro

mother country 8 homeland **10** fatherland

Mother Courage author 6 Brecht (Bertolt)

motherly 8 maternal **9** nurturing **10** protective

mother-of-pearl 5 nacre

Mother of Presidents 8 Virginia

Mother of the Gods 3 Ops **4** Rhea **6** Cybele

motif 4 idea, text **5** point, theme, topic **6** design, device, figure, matter **7** pattern, subject **13** subject matter

motion 4 stir, sway **6** signal **7** gesture **8** movement, proposal, stirring **9** agitation

motionless 5 fixed, inert, still **6** frozen, static **7** stalled **8** becalmed, immobile, stagnant, unmoving **9** immovable, steadfast **10** stationary, stock-still

motion picture see MOVIE

motivate 4 fire, goad, move, spur **5** impel, pique, rouse **6** arouse, excite, incite, induce, prompt **7** actuate, inspire, provoke, quicken, trigger **8** inspirit, persuade **9** galvanize, influence, stimulate

motivation 4 spur **5** drive **7** impetus, impulse **8** ambition, catalyst, stimulus **9** impulsion, incentive, stimulant **10** incitation, incitement **11** inspiration, instigation, provocation

motive 3 aim, end **4** spur **5** cause, point, theme, topic **6** design, device, figure, intent, matter, object, reason, spring **7** impulse, pattern, purpose, subject **8** stimulus **9** incentive, intention, rationale **10** incitement, inducement **11** inspiration

motley 5 mixed, salad **6** jumble, medley, varied **7** dappled, diverse, piebald **8** assorted, pastiche **9** disparate, multihued **10** assortment, hodgepodge, miscellany, multicolor, variegated **11** galli-maufry, varicolored **12** conglomerate, multicolored, multifarious, parti-colored **13** heterogeneous, miscellaneous, polychromatic

motor 3 car **4** auto, ride **5** buggy, drive **6** cruise, engine **7** machine **10** automobile

motorboat 6 launch **7** cruiser, inboard **8** outboard, runabout **12** cabin cruiser

motorcycle 7 chopper **8** minibike **9** trail bike *adjunct:* **7** sidecar

Motown 7 Detroit

mottle 4 spot **5** fleck **6** blotch, dapple, marble **7** spatter, speckle, stipple, splotch

mottled 5 tabby **7** blotchy, dappled, flecked, spotted **8** blotched, brindled, speckled **9** checkered **10** variegated

motto 3 cry **5** adage, axiom, maxim **6** byword, saying, slogan, war cry **7** precept, proverb **8** aphorism **9** battle cry, catchword, watchword **10** shibboleth **11** catchphrase

moue 3 mow, mug **4** face, pout **7** grimace

mound 4 bank, cock, heap, hill, hump, mass, pile **5** cairn, drift, knoll, shock, stack **6** barrow, tumuli (plural) **7** bulwark, hillock, rampart, tumulus **9** elevation **10** embankment *Buddhist:* **5** stupa *burial, Eastern Europe:* **6** kurgan *of detritus:* **4** kame *of sand:* **4** dune *of stones:* **5** cairn

mount 3 alp, wax **4** lift, peak, rise, show, soar **5** arise, build, climb, frame, horse, put on, raise, rouse, scale, set up, stage, steed, swell **6** ascend, aspire, deepen, expand, launch, uprear **7** advance, augment, display, enhance, enlarge, install, magnify, produce, support, upsurge **8** bestride, escalade, escalate, heighten, increase, multiply, redouble **9** aggravate, intensify **10** promontory

mountain 3 alp, lot **4** bank, crag, dome, heap, hill, hulk, lump, mass, mesa, much, peak, pile, slew **5** bluff, butte, drift, mound, shock, stack **6** height *Alaska:* **4** Bona **6** Denali **7** Foraker, Sanford **8** McKinley, Wrangell *Alberta:* **6** Castle **10** Eisenhower *Alps:* **4** Rosa (Monte) **5** Blanc, Eiger **8** Jungfrau **10** Matterhorn *Angola:* **4** Moco *Antarctica:* **4** Mohl **6** Vinson (Massif) **7** Gardner **9** Elizabeth *Appalachians:* **8** Mitchell **10** Kittatinny **10** Washington **13** Clingmans Dome *Argentina:* **9** Aconcagua *Australia:* **4** Ziel **5** Bruce **6** Cradle **9** Kosciusko *biblical:* **5** Horeb, Tabor **6** Hermon **8** Har Tavor *Black Hills:* **6** Harney (Peak) *Bolivia:* **6** Sorata **8** Illi-

mani *Borneo:* **8** Kinabalu, Kinabulu *California:* **5** Guyot **6** Shasta, Sonora (Peak) **7** Palomar, Whitney **8** Tuolumne **10** Buena Vista, Stanislaus *Canada:* **5** Logan *China:* **4** Emei, Song *Colorado:* **5** Pikes (Peak) **9** Purgatory (Peak) *Costa Rica:* **6** Blanco **14** Chirripó Grande *Cyprus:* **7** Olympus, Troodos *depression:* **3** col *Dominican Republic:* **6** Duarte **8** Trujillo *Egypt:* **4** Musa **5** Sinai *Fiji:* **8** Victoria **9** Tomaniivi *foot:* **8** piedmont *France:* **5** Blanc (Mont) *Gabon:* **8** Iboundji *Georgia:* **8** Springer **10** Oglethorpe *Germany:* **7** Zollern **9** Zugspitze **11** Fichtelberg *Greece:* **3** Ida **5** Athos, Levka **7** Helicon, Olympus **9** Parnassus, Psiloriti **10** Pendelikon, Pentelicus *Greenland:* **9** Gunnbjorn *Himalayas:* **6** Lhotse **7** Everest **9** Annapurna *India:* **5** Japvo *Indonesia:* **4** Lawu **5** Kwoka, Lawoe, Raung **6** Raoeng, Semeru **7** Kerinci *Israel:* **5** Meron **6** Carmel *Ivory Coast:* **5** Nimba *Japan:* **4** Fuji **5** Iwate **7** Fujisan **8** Fujiyama *Java:* **5** Liman *Jordan:* **3** Hor **5** Hārūn *Maine:* **8** Katahdin *Malaysia:* **5** Ophir, Tahan **6** Ledang *Mediterranean entrance:* **5** Calpe **9** Gibraltar *Mexico:* **7** Orizaba (Pico de) *New York:* **4** Bear **5** Marcy *North America's highest:* **6** Denali **8** McKinley *North Carolina:* **8** Mitchell *Oman:* **4** Sham *Oregon:* **4** Hood *Pakistan:* **9** Tirich Mir *Papua New Guinea:* **7** Wilhelm *Pennine Alps:* **4** Rosa (Monte) *Philippines:* **3** Apo, Iba **4** Labo **5** Silay *ridge:* **4** spur **5** arête, crest **7** sawbuck *Romania:* **11** Moldoveanul *South America:* **7** Roraima **9** Aconcagua *South Dakota:* **6** Custer (Peak) *Switzerland:* **3** Dom **4** Rosa (Monte) **5** Eiger **8** Jungfrau **10** Matterhorn *Syria:* **4** Druz **5** Duruz *Tanzania:* **11** Kilimanjaro *Tasmania:* **4** Ossa *Tennessee:* **13** Clingmans Dome *Togo:* **5** Agou *Utah:* **5** Kings *Vermont:* **9** Mansfield *Vietnam:* **8** Ngoo Linh *Virginia:* **6** Rogers *Western Hemisphere's highest:* **9** Aconcagua *world's highest:* **7** Everest *Wyoming:* **5** Cloud **7** Gannett (Peak) (see also PEAK)

mountain climbing *equipment:* **3** axe, nut **5** piton **7** crampon **9** carabiner *maneuver:* **6** rappel **10** rappelling

mountain dew see MOONSHINE

mountain formation 7 orogeny **10** orogenesis

mountainous 4 huge, vast **6** alpine, mighty **7** immense, mammoth, massive **8** enormous, gigantic, towering **10** monumental, prodigious

mountain pass 3 col *Afghanistan-Pakistan:* **6** Khyber *Alps:* **5** Gries *Califor-*

nia: 4 Muir 6 Sonora *China-Myanmar:* 5 Namni *Colorado:* 3 Ute 5 Mosca, Muddy, Music, Raton *Europe:* 8 Moravian *Greece:* 5 Rupel *Hindu Kush Mts.:* 5 Dorah, Durah *Pakistan:* 5 Bolan, Gomal, Gumal *Sierra Nevada:* 4 Mono *Switzerland:* 5 Furka, Gemmi 7 Grimsel 8 Lötschen *Tunisia:* 4 Faïd *Ukrainian:* 5 Uzhok *Wyoming:* 5 Union

mountain range *Asia:* 5 Altai, Altay 8 Himalaya, Tien Shan 9 Altai Shan, Altay Shan, Himalayan, Himalayas, Hindu Kush *Australia:* 8 Flinders *Europe:* 4 Alps 10 Carpathian *Germany:* 4 Harz 5 Hartz *Greece:* 4 Oeta *India:* 5 Ghats *Iran:* 6 Zagros *Italy:* 9 Apennines *Mexico:* 11 Sierra Madre *North Africa:* 5 Atlas *North America:* 5 Rocky 7 Rockies 11 Appalachian *Russia:* 4 Ural *Scotland:* 9 Grampians *Sinai:* 9 Gebel Musa *Slovakia:* 5 Tatra, Tatry 9 High Tatra *South America:* 5 Andes *Turkey:* 6 Taurus *United States:* 5 Rocky, White 6 Brooks 7 Cascade, Olympic, Rockies, Sawatch, Wasatch 8 Absaroka, Aleutian, Catskill, Wrangell 9 Blue Ridge, Wind River 10 Adirondack, Bitterroot, Black Hills, Clearwater, Grand Teton *Zimbabwe:* 6 Matopo (Hills) 7 Matoppo (Hills)

Mountain State 7 Montana 12 West Virginia

mountebank 5 quack 6 con man 8 swindler 9 charlatan 11 flimflammer, quacksalver 13 confidence man

Mount St. Helens 7 volcano

mourn 3 rue 6 bemoan, bewail, grieve, lament, sorrow 7 deplore, protest

mournful 3 sad 6 dismal, gloomy, rueful, somber, triste, woeful 7 doleful, forlorn, joyless, unhappy 8 dejected, desolate, dolorous, funereal, grievous, wretched 9 dirgelike, plaintive 10 depressing, despondent, dispirited, lugubrious, melancholy 11 distressing, melancholic, regrettable, unfortunate 12 heavyhearted

mournfulness 5 blues, dumps, gloom 7 dismals, sadness 9 dejection 10 depression, melancholy

mourning 5 grief 7 keening, remorse, wailing, weeping 8 grieving 9 lamenting, morbidity, sorrowing, ululation 10 heartbreak 11 bereavement, lamentation

Mourning Becomes Electra *author:* 6 O'Neill (Eugene)

mourning period, Jewish 5 shiva 6 shivah

mourning symbol 7 armband

mouse 6 rodent, shiner 8 black eye

mousy 3 shy 4 drab, dull 5 plain, quiet,

timid 7 bashful 8 retiring, timorous 9 colorless, diffident, shrinking 11 unassertive 12 self-effacing

mouth 3 gob 4 trap 5 chops 6 kisser 8 entrance 10 embouchure

mouthlike opening 5 stoma 7 stomata (plural)

mouthpiece 5 organ 6 puppet 7 speaker 8 front man 9 spokesman 10 figurehead 11 spokeswoman 12 spokesperson

mouthwatering 5 sapid, tasty, yummy 6 savory, toothy 8 tasteful 9 delicious, palatable, succulent, toothsome 10 appetizing, delectable 11 good-tasting

mouthy 4 glib 5 gabby, talky, windy 7 verbose, voluble 8 effusive 9 bombastic, garrulous, talkative

movable 5 loose 6 mobile, motile, roving 8 portable 10 changeable

movables 5 goods 7 effects 8 chattels 10 belongings 11 furnishings

move 3 act 4 lead, spur, stir, sway 5 bring, budge, carry, drive, impel, leave, march, rouse, shift, start, touch 6 affect, convey, depart, excite, incite, induce, kindle, prompt, propel 7 actuate, advance, animate, conduct, impress, inspire, migrate, proceed, propose, provoke, request, suggest 8 activate, dislodge, displace, evacuate, get along, maneuver, motivate, persuade, progress, relocate, resettle, transfer, withdraw 9 dislocate, galvanize, influence, instigate, stimulate, transport

movement 4 flow, stir 5 tempo, trend 6 action, motion 7 crusade 8 activity, campaign, dynamism, maneuver, progress, stirring, tendency, velocity 9 migration *music:* 4 moto *reflex:* 5 taxis *stimulated:* 7 kinesis

movie 4 cine, film, show 5 flick 6 cinema, talkie 7 picture 9 photoplay 11 picture show 13 motion picture *cowboy:* 5 oater 7 western *short:* 4 clip 8 newsreel

movie director *American:* 3 Lee (Spike), Ray (Nicholas) 4 Coen (Joel), Ford (John), Hill (George Roy), Mann (Anthony), Penn (Arthur), Ritt (Martin), Ross (Herbert), Sirk (Douglas), Wise (Robert) 5 Allen (Woody), Ashby (Hal), Brown (Clarence), Capra (Frank), Cukor (George), Demme (Jonathan), Donen (Stanley), Fosse (Bob), Hawks (Howard), Ivory (James), Jonze (Spike), Kazan (Elia), LeRoy (Mervyn), Logan (Joshua), Lucas (George), Lumet (Sidney), Lynch (David), Moore (Michael), Roach (Hal), Stone (Oliver), Vidor (King),

Walsh (Raoul), Whale (James), Wyler (William), Zwick (Ed) **6** Altman (Robert), Beatty (Warren), Benton (Robert), Brooks (Richard), Burton (Tim), Cimino (Michael), Curtiz (Michael), Fuller (Samuel), Gibson (Mel), Hanson (Curtis), Howard (Ron), Huston (John), Kramer (Stanley), Malick (Terrence), Pakula (Alan), Parker (Alan), Welles (Orson), Wilder (Billy) **7** Borzage (Frank), Cameron (James), Chaplin (Charlie), Coppola (Francis Ford, Sofia), Costner (Kevin), De Mille (Cecil B.), De Palma (Brian), Fleming (Victor), Gilliam (Terry), Jewison (Norman), Kubrick (Stanley), McCarey (Leo), Nichols (Mike), Pollack (Sydney), Redford (Robert), Siodmak (Robert), Stevens (George), Sturges (Preston), Van Sant (Gus), Wellman (William) **8** Avildsen (John), Eastwood (Clint), Flaherty (Robert), Friedkin (William), Griffith (David Wark), Jarmusch (Jim), Levinson (Barry), Lubitsch (Ernst), Marshall (Penny), Minnelli (Vincente), Mulligan (Robert), Scorsese (Martin), Zemeckis (Robert) **9** Carpenter (John), Hitchcock (Alfred), Milestone (Lewis), Peckinpah (Sam), Preminger (Otto), Spielberg (Steven), Sternberg (Josef von), Streisand (Barbra), Tarantino (Quentin), Zinnemann (Fred) **10** Cassavetes (John), Heckerling (Amy), Mankiewicz (Joseph), Soderbergh (Steven) **11** Bogdanovich (Peter) **13** Frankenheimer (John) *Australian:* **4** Weir (Peter) **6** Noonan (Chris) **9** Armstrong (Gillian), Beresford (Bruce) *Austrian:* **4** Lang (Fritz) **8** Stroheim (Erich von) **9** Sternberg (Josef von) *British:* **4** Lean (David), Reed (Carol) **5** Leigh (Mike), Losey (Joseph), Reisz (Karel), Scott (Ridley) **6** Figgis (Mike), Frears (Stephen), Jordan (Neil), Newell (Mike), Parker (Alan), Powell (Michael) **7** Boorman (John), Branagh (Kenneth), Forsyth (Bill) **8** Anderson (Lindsay) **9** Hitchcock (Alfred) **10** Richardson (Tony) **11** Schlesinger (John) *Chinese:* **3** Lee (Ang) **4** Chen (Kaige) **5** Zhang (Yimou) *French:* **4** Demy (Jacques), Tati (Jacques), Vigo (Jean) **5** Malle (Louis) **6** Godard (Jean-Luc), Ophüls (Marcel), Renoir (Jean), Rohmer (Eric) **7** Bresson (Robert), Chabrol (Claude), Cocteau (Jean), Resnais (Alain), Rivette (Jacques) **8** Truffaut (François) *German:* **6** Herzog (Werner), Ophüls (Max) **7** Winders (Wim) **8** Petersen (Wolfgang) **10** Fass-

binder (Rainer Werner) **11** Riefenstahl (Leni), Schlöndorff (Volker) *Italian:* **5** Leone (Sergio) **6** De Sica (Vittorio) **7** Fellini (Federico) **8** Pasolini (Pier Paolo), Visconti (Luchino) **9** Antonioni (Michelangelo) **10** Bertolucci (Bernardo), Rossellini (Roberto), Wertmüller (Lina), Zeffirelli (Franco) *Japanese:* **3** Ozu (Yasujiru) **5** Itami (Juzo) **8** Kurosawa (Akira), Miyazaki (Hayao) **9** Mizoguchi (Kenji) *New Zealand:* **7** Campion (Jane) *Polish* **5** Wajda (Ardrzej) **7** Holland (Agnieszka) **8** Polanski (Roman) *Russian:* **9** Tarkovsky (Andrei) **10** Eisenstein (Sergei) *Spanish:* **6** Buñuel (Luis) **9** Almodóvar (Pedro) *Swedish:* **7** Bergman (Ingmar) **10** Zetterling (Mai)

movie producer *American:* **3** Fox (William) **4** Cohn (Jack) **5** Lasky (Jesse), Mayer (Louis B.), Zukor (Adolph) **6** Warner (Jack L.), Zanuck (Darryl, Richard) **7** Goldwyn (Samuel), Laemmle (Carl) **8** Selznick (David O.) *Austrian:* **9** Reinhardt (Max)

moving 5 astir **6** mobile **7** emotive, rousing **8** arousing, exciting, gripping, pathetic, poignant, stirring, touching **9** affecting, emotional, inspiring, transient **11** stimulating

moving stairs 9 escalator

mow 3 cut **4** clip, crop, fell, heap, moue, pile, raze, rick **5** level, shave, shear, stack **7** grimace **9** knock down

moxie 3 pep, vim, zip **4** grit, guts **5** brass, heart, nerve, oomph, pluck, savvy, spunk, vigor **6** energy, mettle, spirit, starch **7** cojones, courage, know-how **8** backbone **9** fortitude **10** get-up-and-go, resolution **13** determination

Mozambique *capital:* **6** Maputo *language:* **5** Bantu **7** Swahili **10** Portuguese *monetary unit:* **7** metical *neighbor:* **6** Malawi, Zambia **8** Tanzania, Zimbabwe **9** Swaziland **11** South Africa *river:* **6** Ruvuma **7** Limpopo, Zambezi

Mozart, Wolfgang Amadeus *birthplace:* **8** Salzburg *cataloger:* **6** Köchel (Ludwig) *deathplace:* **6** Vienna *opera:* **8** Idomeneo **10** Magic Flute (The) **11** Don Giovanni, Il Rè Pastore **12** Così Fan Tutte **16** Marriage of Figaro (The)

MP's prey 4 AWOL **8** deserter

Mr. Moto star 5 Lorre (Peter)

Mrs. Grundy 4 prig **5** prude **7** puritan **8** bluenose

much 3 oft **4** long, many, most **5** often **6** highly, hugely, plenty **7** greatly, notably **8** abundant **9** eminently, extremely, great deal **10** frequently,

oftentimes, repeatedly *combining form:*
4 poly 5 multi
Much Ado About Nothing *character:*
4 Hero 7 Claudio, Don John 8 Beatrice,
Benedick, Dogberry
muck 3 goo, mud 4 crap, crud, dirt,
dung, gook, goop, grub, gunk, junk,
mess, mire, murk, plod, slog, slop, soil,
toil 5 dirty, dreck, filth, grime, gumbo,
slave, slime, swill, trash, waste
6 drudge, litter, manure, meddle, putter, sleaze, sludge, smirch, tinker
7 garbage, rubbish 8 nonsense 9 interfere
muckety-muck 3 VIP 5 nabob 6 bigwig,
fat cat 7 big shot, kingpin, notable
8 kingfish, somebody 9 dignitary
mucky 4 foul 5 dirty, grimy, muddy,
muggy, murky, nasty, soggy 6 cruddy,
filthy, grubby, grungy 7 squalid,
unclean
mucous 5 slimy 6 viscid
mud 4 dirt, mire, muck, ooze 5 dregs,
slime 6 depths, sludge
muddle 3 mix 4 hash, mess, muck, rile,
roil 5 addle, botch, mix up, snarl
6 ataxia, bungle, drivel, foul up, fumble, jumble, jungle, litter, mess up, tangle, tumble 7 clutter, confuse, fluster,
perplex, rummage, shuffle, snarl up,
stumble, stupefy 8 befuddle, bewilder,
confound, disarray, disorder, distract,
entangle, mishmash, scramble, shambles, throw off, unsettle 9 confusion,
throw away 10 complicate, disarrange,
discompose 11 disorganize
muddled 5 drunk, tight, tipsy, vague
7 mixed-up 8 inchoate 10 disjointed,
disordered, incoherent, inebriated
11 intoxicated, unorganized
muddle through 4 cope, fare 5 get by,
get on 6 manage 7 carry on, make out
8 get along
muddy 3 dim, fog 4 base, blur, drab,
dull, fade, foul, hazy, oozy, roil, soil
5 befog, cloud, dingy, dirty, grime,
grimy, murky 6 cloudy, gloomy, grubby, sordid, turbid 7 becloud, begrime,
confuse, obscure, squalid, tarnish,
unclean, unclear 8 confused
muff 4 blow, flub 5 botch, fluff 6 bobble,
bollix, bungle, fumble, goof up, mess
up 7 louse up, misplay, screw up 9 mishandle
muffle 4 dull, mute, veil 5 shush 6 damp-
en, deaden, lessen, shroud, soften, stifle, subdue, wrap up 7 envelop, repress,
silence, smother, squelch 8 bundle up,
suppress, tone down
muffled 5 muted 6 dulled 7 stifled, subdued 8 deadened, obscured, silenced

9 distorted, enveloped 10 indistinct,
suppressed
muffler 4 mask, veil 5 cloak, scarf
mug 3 cup, ham, mop, mow, rob 4 boob,
dolt, dope, face, fool, moue, phiz,
punk, puss, thug 5 dunce, idiot, mouth,
rowdy, stein, tough 6 ambush, dimwit
7 assault, grimace, tankard 8 bullyboy,
dumbbell, features, numskull 9 blockhead, bushwhack, ignoramus, roughneck
mugger 4 thug 6 robber 9 assailant,
crocodile
muggy 4 damp 5 humid, moist 6 sticky,
sultry 7 dampish
Muhammad *adopted son:* 3 Ali *birthplace:*
5 Mecca *camel:* 5 Kaswa *daughter:*
6 Fatima *deathplace:* 6 Medina *deity:*
5 Allah *father:* 8 Abdallah, Abdullah
father-in-law: 7 Abu Bakr *flight:* 6 hegira,
hejira *follower:* 6 Moslem, Muslim
horse: 5 Buraq 7 Alborak *religion:*
5 Islam *son:* 7 Ibrahim *son-in-law:* 3 Ali
successor: 6 caliph 7 Abu Bakr *tribe:*
7 Koreish, Quraysh *uncle:* 8 Abu Talib
wife: 5 Aisha 6 Ayesha 7 Khadija
mulatto 5 métis, mixed 7 mestizo 9 half-
breed, half-caste 10 crossbreed
mulberry 3 fig 10 breadfruit *type:*
6 banyan 11 India rubber, osage orange
mulct 4 fine, milk, rook 5 bleed, cheat,
gouge 6 extort, fleece 7 deceive,
defraud, forfeit, penalty, swindle
8 penalize 9 blackmail
mule 5 cross, scuff 6 bagman, hybrid
7 bastard, courier, mongrel 8 smuggler
9 crossbred, half blood, half-breed
10 crossbreed
mulish 8 contrary, perverse, stubborn
9 obstinate, pigheaded 10 bullheaded,
headstrong, inflexible, refractory,
unyielding 11 stiff-necked
mull 4 hash, muse 5 brood, think, weigh
6 ponder 7 reflect 8 cogitate, consider,
meditate, ruminate, turn over 9 pulverize 10 deliberate 11 contemplate
multicolored 4 pied 6 motley 7 dappled
9 prismatic 10 variegated 13 polychromatic
multifarious 5 mixed 6 motley, sundry,
varied 7 diverse, various 8 assorted,
manifold 13 heterogeneous, miscellaneous
multiform 6 sundry, varied 7 diverse,
various 8 assorted, manifold 9 disparate
12 multifarious
multilateral 9 many-sided
multiple 4 many 6 shared, sundry
7 diverse, several, various 8 assorted,
manifold, numerous 9 composite
multiplicity 3 lot 4 heap, load, mass,

peck 5 flood, hoard, horde 6 barrel
7 variety 8 mountain, plethora 9 diversity, great deal, profusion
multiply 3 wax 4 rise 5 boost, breed,
build, mount 6 expand, extend, spread
7 amplify, augment, enlarge, magnify
8 generate, heighten, increase 9 procreate, propagate, reproduce 10 aggrandize 11 proliferate
multitude 3 mob 4 army, herd, host,
mass, slew 5 crowd, crush, drove,
flock, horde, swarm 6 legion, myriad,
public, throng 8 populace
multitudinous 4 many 6 legion, myriad,
sundry 7 copious, various 8 abundant,
manifold, numerous, populous
9 countless 10 numberless, voluminous
11 innumerable
mum 4 dumb, mute 5 quiet 6 silent
8 wordless 10 speechless, tongue-tied
mumble 6 murmur, mutter 7 maunder
mumbo jumbo 4 juju 6 fetish 9 gibberish
10 hocus-pocus 11 abracadabra 12 gobbledygook, superstition
mummer 4 mime 5 actor, mimic
12 impersonator
mummify 5 dry up, wizen 6 embalm,
wither 7 shrivel 9 desiccate
munch 3 eat 4 chaw, chew 5 champ,
chomp, snack 6 crunch 9 masticate
mundane 5 lowly 6 earthy, normal
7 earthly, humdrum, prosaic, routine,
terrene, worldly 8 banausic, day-to-day,
everyday, familiar, ordinary, telluric,
workaday 9 practical, sublunary, tellurian 11 commonplace, terrestrial,
uncelestial 13 materialistic
municipal 5 civic, local, urban 12 metropolitan
munificent 6 lavish 7 liberal 8 generous,
handsome 9 bounteous, bountiful
10 benevolent, freehanded, openhanded 11 magnanimous 13 philanthropic
munitions maker 5 Krupp
muralist 4 Sert (José María) 6 Benton
(Thomas Hart), Giotto, Orozco (José
Clemente), Rivera (Diego) 7 La Farge
(John) 9 Siqueiros (David Alfaro)
12 Michelangelo (Buonarotti)
murder 3 hit, off 4 do in, kill, slay
5 blood, lynch, scrag, snuff, waste 6 rub
out 7 bump off, execute, garrote,
killing, smother, take out 8 foul play,
homicide, knock off, strangle 9 eradicate, liquidate, slaughter 10 annihilate,
asphyxiate, decapitate, extinguish
11 assassinate, electrocute, exterminate
12 manslaughter *brother:* 10 fratricide
father: 9 patricide *king:* 8 regicide *mother:* 9 matricide *parent:* 9 parricide *sister:*
10 sororicide

murderer 6 hit man, killer, slayer
7 butcher 8 assassin, homicide 9 cutthroat, manslayer 11 slaughterer
Murder in the Cathedral *author:* 5 Eliot
(Thomas Stearns) *character:* 5 Henry
(II) 6 Becket (Thomas à)
murderous 6 deadly, lethal 10 sanguinary 12 bloodthirsty
murk 3 fog 4 haze, mist 5 brume, gloom
6 miasma 8 darkness 9 obscurity
murky 3 dim 4 dark, dull, foul, gray
5 dirty, dusky, foggy, misty, muddy,
roily, vague 6 cloudy, gloomy, opaque,
somber, turbid 7 obscure 8 nebulous
9 ambiguous, equivocal, tenebrous
10 caliginous
murmur 3 hum 4 buzz, purr 5 drone,
rumor 6 grouch, grouse, mumble, mutter, rumble 7 grumble, whisper 8 complain 9 grumbling, undertone 11 scuttlebutt, susurration
Muscat sultanate 4 Oman
muscle 4 beef, thew 5 brawn, force,
might, power, sinew 6 energy 7 potency
8 strength 9 strong arm *abdomen:*
7 abdomen *arm:* 6 biceps 7 triceps *back:*
9 trapezius *calf:* 6 soleus *chest:* 10 pectoralis *jaw:* 8 masseter *kind:* 6 flexor,
tensor 7 dilator, evertor, levator, rotator 8 abductor, adductor, extensor *loin:*
5 psoas *neck:* 8 platysma *shoulder:*
7 deltoid 10 deltoideus *study of:* 7 myology *thigh:* 8 gracilis 9 sartorius
muscle-bound 5 rigid, stiff 6 wooden
muscular 4 ropy 5 beefy, burly, husky
6 brawny, mighty, robust, sinewy,
strong, sturdy 8 athletic, forceful, powerful, resolute, stalwart, vigorous 9 Herculean, strapping, well-built
muse 5 angel, brood, guide, think
6 genius, ponder, trance 7 reflect,
reverie 8 cogitate, meditate, mull over,
ruminate, turn over 10 deliberate
11 contemplate
Muse *father:* 4 Zeus 7 Jupiter *mother:*
9 Mnemosyne *of astronomy:* 6 Urania *of
choral song:* 11 Terpsichore *of comedy:*
6 Thalia *of dancing:* 11 Terpsichore *of
epic poetry:* 8 Calliope *of history:* 4 Clio
of love poetry: 5 Erato *of lyric poetry:*
5 Erato *of music:* 7 Euterpe *of pastoral
poetry:* 6 Thalia *of sacred poetry:*
8 Polymnia 10 Polyhymnia *of tragedy:*
9 Melpomene
museum 5 salon 7 archive, exhibit,
gallery 8 atheneum 10 collection,
repository
mush 4 slop 5 grits, gruel, hokum
6 bathos, drivel, hominy 8 porridge,
schmaltz
mushroom 4 grow 6 expand, spread

7 burgeon, explode, inflate 8 snowball 11 proliferate *combining form:* 3 myc 4 myco 5 mycet 6 myceto *edible:* 5 enoki, morel 6 bolete 7 cremini, crimini, porcini 8 shiitake 9 mousseron 10 champignon, portabella, portabello, portobello 11 chanterelle *kind:* 6 agaric, bolete 7 inky cap, russula *part:* 3 cap 4 gill, ring 5 stipe, volva 6 pileus 7 annulus 8 mycelium *poisonous:* 7 amanita 8 death cap 9 fly agaric, toadstool
mushy 4 soft 5 pulpy, soppy, vague 6 quaggy, spongy 7 amorous, maudlin, mawkish, squashy, squishy 8 bathetic, effusive, romantic, squooshy 9 schmaltzy 10 lovey-dovey, saccharine 11 sentimental
music *abbreviation:* 3 fff, ppp, sfz 5 cresc *bass staff lines:* 5 GBDFA *bass staff spaces:* 4 ACEG *characteristic phrase:* 9 leitmotif, leitmotiv *chord:* 5 major, minor, tonic 7 harmony 8 dominant 9 augmented 10 diminished *embellishment:* 3 run 4 turn 5 trill 7 cadenza, mordent, roulade 8 arpeggio, flourish 9 grace note *for eight:* 5 octet *for five:* 7 quintet *for four:* 7 quartet *for nine:* 5 nonet *for one:* 4 solo *for seven:* 6 septet *for six:* 6 sextet *for three:* 4 trio *for two:* 3 duo 4 duet *god:* 6 Apollo *hall:* 7 cabaret, theater *instrumental form:* 3 jig 4 jazz, reel 5 étude, fugue, gigue, march, polka, rondo, suite, swing, waltz 6 minuet, pavane, sonata 7 bourrée, gavotte, mazurka, prelude, ragtime, toccata 8 chaconne, concerto, courante, fantasia, galliard, nocturne, overture, rhapsody, ricercar, saraband, serenade, symphony, tone poem 9 allemande, polonaise 11 rock and roll *medley:* 4 olio *morning:* 6 aubade *Muse:* 7 Euterpe *night:* 8 nocturne, serenade *note:* 4 half 5 breve, minim, neume, whole 6 eighth, quaver 7 quarter 8 crotchet 9 sixteenth 10 semiquaver *patron saint:* 7 Cecilia *period:* 6 Modern, Rococo 7 Baroque 8 Medieval, Romantic 9 Classical *symbol:* 3 bar, key 4 clef, flat, note, rest, slur, turn 5 sharp, staff 7 fermata, mordent 9 alla breve 10 accidental *treble staff lines:* 5 EGBDF *treble staff spaces:* 4 FACE *vocal form:* 3 air 4 aria, hymn, lied, mass, song 5 chant, motet, opera, round 6 anthem, ballad 7 cantata, chanson, chorale 8 cavatina, madrigal, operetta, oratorio, serenade 9 cabaletta
musical 4 show 5 revue 6 choral 7 lyrical, melodic, songful, tuneful 8 har-

monic, operetta, zarzuela 9 melodious, symphonic 10 euphonious, harmonious
musical composition 4 aria, hymn, lied, opus, song, trio 5 chant, canon, carol, étude, fugue, march, motet, opera, rondo, suite 6 anthem, ballad, sextet, sonata 7 cantata, chanson, chorale, prelude, quartet, quintet, requiem, scherzo, toccata 8 concerto, fantasia, madrigal, nocturne, operetta, oratorio, overture, postlude, serenade, sonatina, symphony 9 bagatelle, cabaletta, interlude 10 intermezzo, recitative
musical direction *accented:* 7 marcato 8 sforzato 9 sforzando *all:* 5 tutti *brisk:* 4 vivo 6 vivace 7 allegro, animato *connected:* 6 legato *detached:* 8 spiccato, staccato *dignified:* 8 maestoso *disconnected:* 8 staccato *emotional:* 12 appassionato *emphatic:* 7 marcato *excited:* 7 agitato *fast:* 4 vite, vivo 6 presto, veloce, vivace 7 allegro *faster:* 7 stretto 11 accelerando *fluctuating tempo:* 6 rubato *forcefully:* 7 furioso *freely:* 9 ad libitum *gay:* 7 giocoso *gentle:* 5 dolce 7 amabile, amoroso 10 affettuoso *graceful:* 8 grazioso *half:* 5 mezzo *heavy:* 7 pesante *held firmly:* 6 tenuto *less:* 4 meno *little:* 4 poco *little by little:* 9 poco a poco *lively:* 4 vite 6 vivace 7 allegro, animato, giocoso *loud:* 5 forte *louder:* 9 crescendo *majestic:* 8 maestoso *moderate:* 7 andante 8 moderato *moderately loud:* 10 mezzo forte *moderately soft:* 10 mezzo piano *playful:* 10 scherzando *plucked:* 9 pizzicato *quick:* 4 vite, vivo 6 presto, veloce, vivace 7 allegro *quickening:* 11 affrettando *repeat:* 3 bis 6 da capo *run:* 8 arpeggio 9 glissando *sad:* 7 dolente 8 doloroso *separate:* 6 divisi *silent:* 5 tacet *singing:* 9 cantabile *sliding:* 9 glissando *slow:* 5 grave, largo 6 adagio 7 andante 9 larghetto *slowing:* 3 rit 6 ritard 10 ritardando 11 rallentando *smooth:* 6 legato *soft:* 5 dolce, piano *softening:* 10 diminuendo 11 decrescendo *solemn:* 5 grave *spirited:* 4 vivo 6 vivace 7 animato 9 spiritoso *stately:* 7 pomposo 8 maestoso *sustained:* 6 tenuto 9 sostenuto *sweet:* 5 dolce *tender:* 7 amabile, amoroso 10 affettuoso *together:* 4 a due 5 tutti *very:* 5 assai *very fast:* 11 prestissimo *very loud:* 10 fortissimo *very soft:* 10 pianissimo
musical drama 5 opera 8 operetta, zarzuela 9 singspiel
musical group 4 band, trio 5 choir, combo 6 chorus, sextet 7 quartet, quintet 8 ensemble, glee club 9 orchestra
musical instrument *African:* 5 mbira

7 kalimba *ancient:* 4 lyre, rote 5 crwth
6 syrinx 7 cithara, kithara, panpipe,
sistrum *Arabic:* 3 oud *bagpipe:*
7 musette, pibroch *biblical:* 6 cymbal
7 timbrel 8 psaltery *brass:* 4 horn, tuba
5 bugle 6 cornet 7 althorn, clarion, helicon, saxhorn, trumpet 8 trombone
10 French horn *Indian:* 4 vina 5 sarod,
sitar, tabla *Japanese:* 4 biwa, koto
7 samisen 8 shamisen 10 shakuhachi
keyboard: 5 organ, piano 6 spinet
7 celesta, cembalo, clavier 8 calliope,
melodeon, virginal 9 accordion
10 clavichord, concertina, pianoforte
11 harpsichord *medieval:* 4 lute 5 naker,
rebab, rebec, shawm, tabor 7 gittern,
mandola, panpipe 8 cornetto, dulcimer,
gemshorn, hornpipe, Jew's harp,
oliphant, recorder 9 monochord
10 clavichord, hurdy-gurdy *percussion:*
4 bell, drum 5 anvil, güiro, piano
6 cymbal, maraca 7 marimba, timbrel,
timpani, tympani 8 bass drum, castanet, triangle 9 snare drum, xylophone
10 kettledrum, tambourine, vibraphone
Persian: 6 santir *pipe:* 6 syrinx 7 bagpipe, musette, panpipe *reed:* 4 oboe
7 bassoon 8 clarinet 9 harmonica, saxophone 11 English horn *Renaissance:*
4 viol 5 regal, shawm 6 curtal, spinet
7 bagpipe, bandora, cittern, rackett,
sackbut, serpent, theorbo, vihuela, vio-
lone 8 crumhorn, recorder, virginal
10 chitarrone, colascione 11 harpsichord *Russian:* 9 balalaika *stringed:*
3 oud 4 harp, lute, lyre, vina, viol
5 banjo, cello, piano, rebec, sitar, viola
6 fiddle, guitar, violin, zither 7 bandora,
cittern, gittern, kantele, pandura,
ukulele 8 autoharp, dulcimer, mandolin 10 contrabass, double bass
11 harpsichord, violoncello *toy:* 5 kazoo
7 ocarina *two-necked:* 7 theorbo *woodwind:* 4 oboe 5 flute 7 bassoon, piccolo
9 flageolet, saxophone 11 English horn
musical interval 5 fifth, major, minor,
sixth, third 6 fourth, octave, second
7 perfect, seventh, tritone
musical syllable 3 sol
musician 4 bard 5 piper 6 player
7 jazzman, maestro 8 minstrel, virtuoso
9 performer 10 troubadour
muskeg 3 bog, fen 4 mire, quag 5 marsh,
swamp 6 morass, slough 8 quagmire
musket 5 fusil 7 flintlock, matchlock
12 muzzleloader
Musketeer 5 Athos 6 Aramis 7 Porthos
author: 5 Dumas (Alexandre) *friend:*
9 d'Artagnan
muskmelon 10 cantaloupe
Muslim *ascetic:* 4 Sufi 5 fakir 7 dervish

8 marabout *body of scholars:* 5 ulama,
ulema *branch:* 4 Shia 5 Sunni 6 Shiite
caller to prayer: 7 muezzin *decree:*
5 fatwa, irade *devil:* 5 Iblis *garment:*
6 chador *god:* 5 Allah *holy city:* 5 Mecca
6 Medina *holy war:* 5 jihad *judge:*
5 mufti *leader:* 3 aga 4 agha, amir, emir
5 ameer *mendicant:* 5 fakir *messiah:*
5 Mahdi *month:* (see at MONTH) *month
of fasting:* 7 Ramadan *mosque:* 6 masjid
mystic: 4 Sufi *pilgrim:* 5 hajji *pilgrimage:*
4 hajj *prayer:* 5 salat *priest:* 4 imam
prophet: 8 Mohammed, Muhammad
religion: 5 Islam *scripture:* 5 Koran,
Quran *shrine:* 5 Kaaba *temple:*
6 mosque *title:* 3 aga 4 emir 6 caliph *tradition:* 5 sunna (see also MOSQUE;
MUHAMMAD)
muss 3 row 4 mess 5 botch, chaos, mix-
up, upset 6 jumble, mess-up, muddle,
rumple, tousle 7 disrupt, rummage
8 disarray, dishevel, disorder, shambles
9 confusion 10 disarrange 11 disorganize
mussel 5 naiad *genus:* 4 Unio 7 Mytilus
8 Anodonta *larva:* 9 blackhead
Mussolini, Benito 4 Duce (Il) *son-in-law:*
5 Ciano (Galeazzo)
mussy 6 sloppy, untidy 7 tousled,
unkempt 8 slovenly 9 cluttered
10 disheveled
must 4 duty, mold, need, want 5 juice,
ought 6 devoir, should 9 condition,
essential, necessity, requisite 10 obligation, sine qua non 11 requirement
12 precondition, prerequisite
muster 4 call, roll 5 crowd, group, raise,
rally, rouse 6 enlist, enroll, gather,
induce, invoke, join up, roster, sample,
sign on, sign up, summon, work up
7 collect, convene, develop, include,
marshal, produce 8 assemble, assembly,
comprise, congress, generate, mobilize,
organize, roll call, specimen 9 gathering, inventory, nose count 10 accumulate, assemblage, collection, congregate, rendezvous 12 accumulation,
congregation
muster out 5 demob, let go 9 discharge
10 demobilize
musty 4 dank, dull, sour 5 funky, moldy,
stale, tired, trite 6 frowsy, frowzy, old
hat, smelly 7 airless, antique, mildewy,
squalid 8 shopworn, timeworn 10 antiquated, malodorous, threadbare
Mut *husband:* 4 Amen, Amon *son:*
5 Chons 6 Chonsu, Khonsu
mutable 5 fluid 6 fickle, mobile, shifty
7 erratic, protean 8 slippery, unstable,
unsteady, variable, volatile, wavering
9 changeful, mercurial, unsettled

10 capricious, changeable, inconstant **11** fluctuating, vacillating **12** inconstent
mutate 4 vary **5** alter, morph **6** change, modify **9** refashion, transform, transmute **11** transfigure **12** metamorphose, transmogrify
mutation 5 sport **6** change **7** novelty **9** deviation, variation **10** alteration **11** vicissitude **12** modification **13** metamorphosis
mute 3 mum **4** dumb **5** quiet **6** dampen, deaden, muffle, muzzle, reduce, silent, soften, stifle, subdue **7** silence **8** silencer, wordless **9** voiceless **10** speechless, tongue-tied
muted 3 dim, mat **4** dull **6** low-key, silent **10** speechless
mutilate 3 mar **4** maim **6** damage, deface, injure, mangle **7** cripple **9** disfigure, dismember
mutineer 5 rebel
mutinous 6 unruly **8** factious **9** insurgent, seditious, turbulent **10** rebellious **12** contumacious **13** insubordinate
mutiny 5 rebel **6** revolt, rise up **8** uprising **9** rebellion **12** insurrection
mutt 3 cur, dog **4** mule **5** cross **6** hybrid **7** mixture, mongrel **9** half blood, halfbreed **10** crossbreed
Mutt and ___ 4 Jeff
mutter 5 growl **6** grouch, grouse, mumble, murmur **7** grumble **9** undertone
muttonchops 9 burnsides, sideburns **10** sideboards **11** dundrearies **12** sidewhiskers
mutual 5 joint **6** common, public, shared, united **7** related **8** communal, conjoint, conjunct **9** bilateral, connected **10** associated, reciprocal, respective *prefix:* **5** inter
muumuu 6 caftan
muzzle 3 gag **4** hush, mute, nose, phiz **5** snout **7** silence, squelch
muzzy 3 dim **4** dull, hazy **5** faint, vague **6** blurry, gloomy **7** blurred, muddled, unclear **8** confused, nebulous **9** imprecise
myalgia 4 ache, pain **5** cramp **6** strain **8** soreness
Myanmar 5 Burma *bay:* **6** Bengal *capital:* **6** Yangon **7** Rangoon *monetary unit:* **4** kyat *neighbor:* **4** Laos **5** China, India **8** Thailand **10** Bangladesh *peninsula:* **9** Indochina *river:* **7** Salween **9** Irrawaddy *sea:* **7** Andaman
My Antonia author 6 Cather (Willa)
My Last Duchess author 8 Browning (Robert)
My Lost Youth author 10 Longfellow (Henry Wadsworth)

Myra Breckenridge author 5 Vidal (Gore)
myriad 3 lot **4** heap, host, raft, slew **5** flood, horde, swarm **6** throng **9** countless, multitude **10** infinitude, numberless **11** innumerable **12** incalculable **13** multitudinous
myrmecology subject 3 ant **4** ants
myrmidon 6 minion **8** follower, retainer **9** attendant, underling **11** subordinate
Myron's statue 10 Discobolos, Discobolus **13** Discus Thrower (The)
Myrrha's son 6 Adonis
mysterious 6 arcane, mystic, occult, secret **7** cryptic, obscure, strange **8** abstruse, esoteric, numinous **9** ambiguous, enigmatic, equivocal, recondite **10** cabalistic, unknowable **11** inscrutable **12** impenetrable, inexplicable, unfathomable **13** unaccountable
mystery 5 poser **6** enigma, puzzle, riddle, secret **7** arcanum, problem, stumper **8** whodunit **9** conundrum **10** closed book, perplexity, puzzlement **13** Chinese puzzle
mystic 4 seer **6** arcane, medium, occult, oracle, secret **7** obscure **8** anagogic, esoteric, hermetic, numinous **9** enigmatic, visionary **10** cabalistic, unknowable **11** inscrutable, necromantic **12** impenetrable, thaumaturgic **13** unaccountable
mystical 4 holy **6** arcane, covert, divine, occult, orphic, sacred, secret **7** cryptic, sub-rosa **8** anagogic, esoteric, hermetic, oracular, profound **9** recondite, spiritual **10** miraculous, symbolical **11** clandestine **12** supernatural, supranatural
mysticism 7 Orphism **8** cabalism, quietism **11** hermeticism
mystify 6 baffle, puzzle **7** confuse, obscure, perplex **8** befuddle, bewilder, confound **9** obfuscate
mystifying 7 cryptic, delphic **8** Delphian **9** enigmatic
mystique 5 charm, magic **7** glamour **8** charisma **9** magnetism
myth 4 lore, saga, tale **5** fable, story **6** legend **7** fiction, figment, parable **8** allegory, folklore **9** tradition **11** fabrication
mythical 6 fabled, made-up, unreal **7** created, fictive **8** fabulous, fanciful, invented **9** fantastic, fictional, imaginary, legendary **10** apocryphal, fictitious
mythologist 4 Jung (Carl Gustav), Ovid **5** Tylor (Edward Burnett) **6** Eliade (Mircea), Frazer (James George), Müller (Friedrich Max) **8** Campbell (Joseph) **9** Euhemerus **10** Malinowski (Bronislaw)
mythology see MYTH

N

Naamah *brother:* 9 Tubalcain *father:* 6 Lamech *husband:* 7 Solomon *mother:* 6 Zillah *son:* 8 Rehoboam

nab 4 grab 5 catch, pinch, run in, seize 6 arrest, clutch, collar, pick up, pull in, snatch 7 capture 9 apprehend

nabob 3 VIP 5 mogul, noble 6 bigwig, fat cat, tycoon 7 big shot, magnate, notable 8 big chief, eminence, governor 9 big cheese, dignitary, personage 10 notability

Nabokov novel 3 Ada 4 Gift (The), Pnin 6 Lolita 7 Defense (The), Despair 8 Pale Fire 14 King Queen Knave

nacre 13 mother-of-pearl

nada 3 nil, zip 5 zilch 6 naught 7 nothing, nullity 11 nothingness

nadir 4 base, foot 5 depth 6 bottom 8 low point *opposite:* 6 zenith

nag 3 irk, vex 4 bait, carp, goad, ride 5 annoy, chivy, harry, horse, hound, worry 6 badger, bother, carp at, harass, heckle, hector, needle, peck at, pester, plague 7 henpeck, torment 8 complain, harangue, irritate

naiad 5 nymph

naïf 7 ingenue

nail 3 bag, get, nab 4 brad, grab, stud, tack, trap 5 catch, clone, spike, sprig 6 arrest, collar, secure 7 capture 9 apprehend

naive 6 simple 7 artless, natural 8 gullible, innocent, wide-eyed 9 childlike, credulous, guileless, ingenuous, unstudied 10 self-taught, unaffected, unschooled 11 susceptible

naked 3 raw 4 bald, bare, mere, nude, pure 5 clear, sheer 6 peeled, scanty, simple, unclad 7 denuded, evident, exposed, obvious 8 revealed, stripped 9 au naturel, disclosed, unclothed, uncovered, undressed *combining form:* 4 gymn 5 gymno

Naked and the Dead author 6 Mailer (Norman)

namby-pamby 4 weak 5 banal, bland, inane, sissy, vapid 6 effete, jejune 7 insipid 8 nebbishy, weakling 9 spineless 10 effeminate, indecisive, pantywaist, wishy-washy 12 milk-and-water 13 characterless

name 3 dub, nom, tab, tag, tap 4 call, cite, race, term 5 alias, label, nomen, quote, state, style, title 6 byword, finger, handle, report, repute, rubric 7 appoint, baptize, declare, entitle, epithet, mention, moniker, publish, specify 8 announce, christen, identify, instance, nominate 9 advertise, character, designate, incognito, recognize, sobriquet, stipulate 10 denominate, reputation 11 appellation, appellative, designation *ancient Rome:* 7 agnomen 8 prenomen *assumed:* 5 alias 9 sobriquet *family:* 8 cognomen *fictitious:* 9 pseudonym *giver:* 6 eponym

nameless 6 unsung 7 obscure, unknown 9 anonymous 11 indefinable, unutterable 12 uncelebrated, unidentified

namely 3 viz. 5 to wit 6 that is 8 scilicet 9 expressly, specially, videlicet 10 especially 12 particularly, specifically

Namibia *capital:* 8 Windhoek *city:* 8 Oshakati, Rehoboth *desert:* 5 Namib 8 Kalahari *language:* 5 Bantu 6 German 9 Afrikaans *neighbor:* 6 Angola 8 Botswana 11 South Africa *river:* 6 Cunene, Orange 8 Okavango

nana 7 grandma 11 grandmother

Nana *author:* 4 Zola (Emile) *mother:* 8 Gervaise

Nanna *brother:* 6 Nergal, Ninazu *father:* 5 Enlil *husband:* 6 Balder *mother:* 6 Ninlil *son:* 3 Utu *wife:* 6 Ningal

nanny 5 nurse 9 caregiver, governess, nursemaid

Naomi 4 Mara *daughter-in-law:* 4 Ruth 5 Orpah *husband:* 9 Elimelech *son:* 6 Mahlon 7 Chilion

nap 4 doze, pile, rest, shag, wale, warp, weft, woof 5 sleep, weave 6 drowse, nod off, siesta, snooze 7 drop off, surface 10 forty winks

nape 6 scruff

Naphtali *brother:* 3 Dan *father:* 5 Jacob *mother:* 6 Bilhah *son:* 4 Guni 5 Jezer 7 Jahzeel, Jahziel, Shallum

naphtha 7 solvent 9 petroleum

napkin 5 cloth, doily, towel 9 serviette

napoleon 4 boot 6 pastry 8 card game 9 solitaire *bid:* 7 blucher 10 wellington

Napoleon *adversary:* 6 Nelson (Horatio) 7 Kutuzov (Mikhail) 10 Wellington (Duke of) *birthplace:* 7 Ajaccio, Corsica *brother:* 5 Louis 6 Jérome, Joseph, Lucien *brother-in-law:* 5 Murat (Joachim) *deathplace:* 8 St. Helena *defeat:* 7 Leipzig 8 Waterloo 9 Trafalgar *father:* 5 Carlo *island of exile:* 4 Elba 8 St. Helena *marshal:* 3 Ney (Michel) 5 Murat (Joachim), Soult (Nicolas-Jean) 6 Suchet (Louis-Gabriel) *sister:* 5 Maria 8 Carlotta, Carolina *victory:* 3 Ulm 4 Jena, Lodi 5 Ligny 6 Abukir, Abu Qir, Arcole, Wagram 7 Bautzen, Dresden, Marengo 8 Borodino 10 Austerlitz *wife:* 9 Josephine 11 Marie Louise

narcissism 6 egoism, vanity 7 conceit, egotism 8 self-love, vainness 9 vainglory 11 egocentrism, self-conceit 13 conceitedness

narcissistic 4 vain 7 stuck-up 9 conceited, egotistic 10 self-loving 11 egotistical 12 self-absorbed, self-admiring, self-centered, vainglorious

Narcissus *admirer:* 4 Echo *father:* 9 Cephissus *mother:* 7 Liriope

narcotic 3 hop 4 dope, drug, junk 5 opium 6 heroin, opiate 7 anodyne, cocaine, hashish 8 hypnotic, morphine, nepenthe 9 somnolent, soporific 10 somnorific 11 somniferous *peddler:* 6 dealer, pusher

narrate 4 tell 5 state 6 depict, detail, recite, relate, report 7 express, outline, portray, recount 8 describe, rehearse 9 chronicle, delineate

narrative 4 epic, myth, saga, tale, yarn 5 fable, story 6 legend, report 7 account, history, recital, version 8 anecdote 9 chronicle *medieval French:* 5 roman 7 romance *prose:* 5 novel 7 novella

narrator 6 teller 7 reciter 8 reporter 9 describer, performer 10 chronicler

narrow 5 close, small, taper 6 lessen, strait 7 bigoted, limited, precise, slender 8 contract, decrease, straiten 9 confining, constrict, hidebound, illiberal 10 brassbound, inflexible, intolerant, prejudiced, restricted

narrowly 6 barely 7 closely 8 scarcely, strictly

narrow-minded 5 petty 7 bigoted, insular 9 hidebound, illiberal 10 brassbound, intolerant, prejudiced, provincial

nasal 6 rhinal, twangy 9 nosepiece *combining form:* 4 rhin 5 rhino

nascency 5 birth 6 origin 7 genesis 8 birthing, creation, nativity 9 inception 11 parturition

nascent 7 budding, growing, newborn 8 emergent 9 beginning, embryonic, fledgling, incipient, sprouting 10 blossoming, burgeoning, initiative, initiatory

Naseby victor 7 Fairfax (Thomas) 8 Cromwell (Oliver)

___ **Nastase** 4 Ilie

nasty 4 evil, foul, icky, mean, vile 5 awful, dirty, gross, snide 6 coarse, filthy, grubby, horrid, malign, odious, wicked 7 beastly, harmful, hateful, illbred, painful, raunchy, squalid, vicious 8 god-awful, improper, indecent, spiteful 9 hazardous, loathsome, malicious, malignant, obnoxious, offensive, repugnant, repulsive, vexatious 10 disgusting, malevolent 11 distasteful 12 disagreeable

natant 8 floating, swimming

Nathan *father:* 4 Bani 5 Attai, David *son:* 5 Zabad

nation 4 race 5 realm, state, tribe 6 domain, people, polity 7 country, kingdom, society 8 dominion, populace, republic 11 sovereignty 12 commonwealth, principality

national 6 native 7 citizen, federal, subject 8 resident 10 countryman 11 countrywide

National Basketball Association *Atlanta:* 5 Hawks *Boston:* 7 Celtics *Charlotte:* 7 Hornets *Chicago:* 5 Bulls *Cleveland:* 9 Cavaliers *Dallas:* 9 Mavericks *Denver:* 7 Nuggets *Detroit:* 7 Pistons *Golden State:* 8 Warriors *Houston:* 7 Rockets *Indiana:* 6 Pacers *Los Angeles:* 6 Lakers 8 Clippers *Miami:* 4 Heat *Milwaukee:* 5 Bucks *Minnesota:* 12 Timberwolves *New Jersey:* 4 Nets *New York:* 6 Knicks *Orlando:* 5 Magic *Phoenix:* 4 Suns *Portland:* 12 Trail Blazers *Sacramento:* 5 Kings *San Antonio:* 5 Spurs *Seattle:* 11 SuperSonics *Toronto:* 7 Raptors *Utah:* 4 Jazz *Vancouver:* 9 Grizzlies *Washington:* 7 Bullets

National Football League *Arizona:* 9 Cardinals *Atlanta:* 7 Falcons *Baltimore:* 6 Ravens *Buffalo:* 5 Bills *Carolina:* 8 Panthers *Chicago:* 5 Bears *Cincinnati:* 7 Bengals *Cleveland:* 6 Browns *Dallas:* 7 Cowboys *Denver:* 7 Broncos *Detroit:* 5 Lions *Green Bay:* 7 Packers *Houston:* 5 Oilers *Indianapolis:* 5 Colts *Jacksonville:* 7 Jaguars *Kansas City:* 6 Chiefs *Miami:* 8 Dolphins *Minnesota:* 7 Vikings *New England:* 8 Patriots *New Orleans:* 6 Saints *New York:* 4 Jets 6 Giants *Oakland:* 7 Raiders *Philadelphia:* 6 Eagles *Pittsburgh:* 8 Steelers *St. Louis:* 4 Rams *San Diego:* 8 Chargers *Seattle:* 8 Seahawks *Tampa Bay:* 4 Bucs 10 Buccaneers *Tennessee:* 6 Oilers *Washington:* 8 Redskins

national historical park *Alaska:* 5 Sitka

Idaho: 8 Nez Percé *Kentucky-Tennessee:* 13 Cumberland Gap *Maryland-West Virginia:* 12 Harpers Ferry *Massachusetts:* 9 Minute Man *New York:* 8 Saratoga

National Hockey League *Anaheim:* 11 Mighty Ducks *Atlanta:* 9 Thrashers *Boston:* 6 Bruins *Buffalo:* 6 Sabres *Calgary:* 6 Flames *Carolina:* 10 Hurricanes *Chicago:* 10 Blackhawks *Colorado:* 9 Avalanche *Columbus:* 11 Blue Jackets *Dallas:* 5 Stars *Detroit:* 8 Red Wings *Edmonton:* 6 Oilers *Florida:* 8 Panthers *Los Angeles:* 5 Kings *Minnesota:* 4 Wild *Montreal:* 9 Canadiens *Nashville:* 9 Predators *New Jersey:* 6 Devils *New York:* 7 Rangers 9 Islanders *Ottawa:* 8 Senators *Philadelphia:* 6 Flyers *Phoenix:* 7 Coyotes *St. Louis:* 5 Blues *San Jose:* 6 Sharks *Tampa Bay:* 9 Lightning *Toronto:* 10 Maple Leafs *Vancouver:* 7 Canucks *Washington:* 8 Capitals

nationalism 8 jingoism 10 chauvinism, patriotism

National League *Arizona:* 12 Diamondbacks *Atlanta:* 6 Braves *Chicago:* 4 Cubs *Cincinnati:* 4 Reds *Colorado:* 7 Rockies *Florida:* 7 Marlins *Houston:* 6 Astros *Los Angeles:* 7 Dodgers *Milwaukee:* 7 Brewers *New York:* 4 Mets *Philadelphia:* 8 Phillies *Pittsburgh:* 7 Pirates *St. Louis:* 9 Cardinals *San Diego:* 6 Padres *San Francisco:* 6 Giants *Washington:* 9 Nationals

national military park *Alabama:* 13 Horseshoe Bend *Arkansas:* 8 Pea Ridge *Mississippi:* 9 Vicksburg *Pennsylvania:* 10 Gettysburg *South Carolina:* 13 Kings Mountain *Tennessee:* 6 Shiloh

national monument *Alabama:* 11 Russell Cave *Alaska:* 9 Aniakchak *Arizona:* 5 Tonto 6 Navajo 7 Saguaro, Wupatki 8 Tuzigoot 10 Chiricahua, Pipe Spring, Tumacacori 11 Hohokam Pima 12 Sunset Crater, Walnut Canyon *California:* 8 Cabrillo, Lava Beds 9 Muir Woods, Pinnacles 10 Joshua Tree 11 Death Valley *Colorado:* 10 Yucca House *Colorado-Utah:* 8 Dinosaur 9 Hovenweep *Florida:* 12 Fort Matanzas 13 Fort Jefferson *Georgia:* 8 Ocmulgee 11 Fort Pulaski 13 Fort Frederica *Iowa:* 12 Effigy Mounds *Louisiana:* 12 Poverty Point *Maryland:* 11 Fort McHenry *Minnesota:* 9 Pipestone 12 Grand Portage *Nebraska:* 9 Homestead 11 Scotts Bluff *New Mexico:* 5 Pecos 7 El Morro 9 Bandelier, El Malpais, Fort Union 10 Aztec Ruins, White Sands *New York:* 11 Fort Stanwix 13 Castle Clinton *South Carolina:* 10 Fort Sumter 13 Congaree Swamp *South Dakota:* 9 Jewel Cave *Utah:*

11 Cedar Breaks 13 Rainbow Bridge *Wyoming:* 11 Devils Tower, Fossil Butte

national park *Alaska:* 6 Denali, Katmai 9 Lake Clark 10 Glacier Bay 11 Kenai Fjords, Kobuk Valley *Angola:* 4 Iona, Mupa *Arizona:* 11 Grand Canyon *Arkansas:* 10 Hot Springs *Botswana:* 5 Chobe *California:* 7 Redwood, Sequoia 8 Yosemite 11 King's Canyon *Chad:* 5 Manda *Colombia:* 5 Uraba *Colorado:* 9 Mesa Verde 13 Rocky Mountain *eastern Africa:* 10 Mount Kenya *Florida:* 8 Biscayne 10 Everglades *Hawaii:* 9 Haleakala *India:* 5 Kanha *Japan:* 5 Nikko *Kentucky:* 11 Mammoth Cave *Kenya:* 4 Meru 5 Tsavo 10 Royal Tsavo *Lake Superior:* 10 Isle Royale *Maine:* 6 Acadia *Malaysia:* 8 Kinabalu *Minnesota:* 9 Voyageurs *Montana:* 7 Glacier *Nevada:* 10 Great Basin *Oregon:* 10 Crater Lake *Poland:* 5 Ojcow, Tatra *South Africa:* 6 Kruger *South Dakota:* 8 Badlands, Wind Cave *Sri Lanka:* 5 Yala *Sweden:* 5 Sarek *Tanzania:* 5 Ruaha 9 Serengeti *Texas:* 7 Big Bend *Utah:* 4 Zion 6 Arches 11 Bryce Canyon, Canyonlands, Capitol Reef *Virginia:* 10 Shenandoah *Washington:* 7 Olympic 12 Mount Rainier 13 North Cascades *Wyoming:* 10 Grand Teton *Wyoming-Idaho-Montana:* 11 Yellowstone *Zambia:* 5 Kafue *Zimbabwe:* 13 Rhodes Inyanga, Victoria Falls

native 3 raw 4 wild 5 local 6 inborn, innate 7 connate, endemic, natural 8 domestic, indigene, inherent, internal, national 9 inherited 10 aboriginal, congenital, connatural, indigenous, unacquired *Acadian Louisiana:* 5 Cajun *China:* 3 Han 9 Celestial *India:* 5 sepoy *Japan:* 9 Nipponese *London:* 7 Cockney *New England:* 4 Yank 6 Yankee *New York:* 13 Knickerbocker

Native Son author 6 Wright (Richard)

Nativity 4 Noel, Xmas, yule 8 yuletide 9 Christmas

nativity 5 birth, start 6 origin, outset 7 genesis 8 delivery 9 beginning, horoscope, inception 11 parturition

natter 3 gab, jaw, yak, yap 4 blab, buzz, chat, go on 5 prate, run on 6 babble, gabble, gossip, tattle 7 chatter, prattle, twaddle 8 chitchat, converse

natty 4 neat, tidy, trim 5 doggy, sassy, smart, swank 6 classy, dapper, jaunty, snazzy, spiffy, spruce, sprucy, swanky 7 bandbox, doggish, stylish 9 turned out 11 well-groomed

natural 4 pure, wild 5 naive, usual 6 candid, inborn, innate, native, normal, simple 7 artless, connate, organic

8 homespun, inherent, innocent
9 childlike, ingenuous, ingrained, primitive 10 congenital, indigenous, legitimate, unaffected 11 commonplace, instinctive, spontaneous
naturalist *American:* 4 Muir (John) 5 Hyatt (Alpheus) 7 Audubon (John James), Verrill (Addison, Alpheus) *English:* 3 Ray (John) 5 White (Gilbert) 6 Darwin (Charles) 7 Wallace (Alfred) 10 Williamson (William) *French:* 5 Fabre (Jean-Henri) 7 Lamarck (Chevalier de), Réaumur (René-Antoine) *Scottish:* 6 Wilson (Alexander) 10 Richardson (John)
nature 3 ilk, way 4 kind, sort, type 6 makeup, manner, stripe, temper 7 essence, scenery 8 creation, tendency, universe 9 character, landscape 10 complexion 11 description, disposition, personality, temperament 12 constitution
naught 3 nil, zip 4 love, nada, zero 5 zilch 6 cipher 7 nothing, nullity 8 goose egg 11 nothingness
naughty 3 bad 4 lewd 5 bawdy 6 unruly, ribald, risqué, smutty, vulgar 7 froward, obscene, raunchy, wayward, willful 8 contrary, improper, perverse, rascally 10 ill-behaved 11 disobedient, mischievous 12 obstreperous, recalcitrant
Nauru *capital:* 5 Yaren *former name:* 8 Pleasant (Island) *monetary unit:* 6 dollar
nauseate 5 repel 6 offend, sicken 7 disgust, repulse
nauseated 6 queasy 7 carsick 8 qualmish 9 disgusted, squeamish 10 grossed out
nauseating 6 putrid 7 noisome 9 loathsome, offensive, repellant, repugnant, repulsive, revolting, sickening 10 disgusting
Nausicaa *father:* 8 Alcinous *mother:* 5 Arete
nautical 5 naval 6 marine 7 oceanic 8 maritime 12 navigational *instrument:* 3 aba 7 compass, pelorus, sextant
Navajo *dwelling* 5 hogan
naval hero 5 Jones (John Paul), Perry (Matthew, Oliver Hazard) 8 Farragut (David, George), Lawrence (James)
navel 6 middle 7 nombril 9 umbilicus 11 belly button *combining form:* 6 omphal 7 omphalo
navigate 4 helm, plot, sail 5 guide, pilot, steer 6 cruise 8 maneuver, traverse
navigation 8 piloting 10 seamanship 12 helmsmanship
navigational system 5 loran
navigator 5 flyer, pilot 6 airman 7 co-

pilot *Danish:* 6 Bering (Vitus) *Dutch:* 6 Tasman (Abel) 7 Barents (Willem) *English:* 4 Cook (Captain James) 5 Cabot (John, Sebastian), Drake (Francis) 6 Hudson (Henry) 7 Gilbert (Humphrey), Raleigh (Walter) 9 Vancouver (George) *French:* 7 Cartier (Jacques) 9 La Perouse (Comte de) *Italian:* 6 Caboto (Giovanni) 8 Columbus (Christopher), Vespucci (Amerigo) 9 Verrazano (Giovanni) 10 Verrazzano (Giovanni) *Norwegian:* 4 Eric (the Red) 8 Ericsson (Leif) 12 Leif Ericsson, Leif Eriksson *Portuguese:* 4 Dias (Bartolomeu, Dinis) 6 Cabral (Pedro Alvares), da Gama (Vasco) 8 Magellan (Ferdinand) *Spanish:* 9 Fernández (Juan)
navy 4 blue 5 fleet 6 argosy, armada 8 flotilla
Nazi 9 Hitlerite 10 brownshirt *admiral:* 6 Dönitz (Karl), Raeder (Erich) 7 Doenitz (Karl) *air force:* 9 Luftwaffe *armed forces:* 9 Wehrmacht *collaborator:* 5 Laval (Pierre) 8 Quisling (Vidkun) *concentration camp:* 6 Belsen, Dachau 9 Auschwitz, Treblinka 10 Buchenwald, Nordhausen *field marshal:* 5 Model (Walter) 6 Keitel (Wilhelm), Paulus (Friedrich), Rommel (Erwin) 9 Rundstedt (Karl von) 10 Kesselring (Albert) *greeting:* 4 heil *leader:* 3 Ley (Robert) 4 Hess (Rudolf), Röhm (Ernst) 5 Roehm (Ernst) 6 Führer, Göring (Hermann), Hitler (Adolf) 7 Fuehrer, Goering (Hermann), Himmler (Heinrich) 8 Goebbels (Joseph), Heydrich (Reinhard) 9 Rosenberg (Alfred) *police:* 7 Gestapo *propagandist:* 5 U-boat *surrender signer:* 4 Jodl (Alfred) 6 Keitel (Wilhelm) *symbol:* 6 fylfot 8 swastika *tactic:* 10 blitzkrieg *tank:* 6 Panzer
NCO 3 cpl, sgt 8 corporal, sergeant
neap 3 low 4 tide
near 4 nigh 5 about, circa, close, round 6 almost, around 7 close by, close on 8 adjacent, approach 9 immediate, proximate 11 approximate
nearby 4 nigh 5 about, aside, close, handy 6 around, beside 8 adjacent 9 adjoining, proximate 10 contiguous, convenient 11 neighboring
nearest 4 next 7 closest 8 adjacent, proximal 9 proximate 10 contiguous
nearsighted 6 myopic
neat 4 deft, nice, prim, snug, tidy, trig, trim 5 clean, clear, kempt 6 clever, smooth, spruce 7 orderly, precise, unmixed 8 straight, well-kept 9 shipshape, undiluted 10 methodical, sys-

tematic **11** spic-and-span, uncluttered, well-groomed **12** spic-and-span **13** unadulterated

neb 3 tip **4** beak, bill, nose, prow **5** snoot, snout **9** proboscis

Nebraska *capital:* **7** Lincoln *city:* **5** Omaha *college, university:* **9** Creighton *nickname:* **10** Cornhusker (State) *river:* **6** Platte **8** Missouri *state bird:* **10** meadowlark *state flower:* **9** goldenrod *state tree:* **10** cottonwood

nebula 6 galaxy

nebulous 4 hazy **5** vague **6** cloudy, turbid **7** clouded, obscure, unclear **9** ambiguous, amorphous, uncertain **10** indefinite, indistinct **13** indeterminate

necessary 5 basic, vital **6** needed **7** crucial, needful **8** cardinal, integral, required **9** de rigueur, essential, mandatory, requisite **10** compulsory, imperative, inevitable, obligatory, undeniable **11** fundamental, ineluctable, inescapable, unavoidable **12** all-important, prerequisite **13** indispensable

necessitate 5 cause, exact, force **6** compel, demand, entail **7** call for, involve, require **8** occasion

necessity 4 must, need **6** crisis, duress **7** poverty **8** exigency **9** essential, privation, requisite **10** compulsion, imperative, obligation, sine qua non **11** dire straits, needfulness, requirement **12** precondition, prerequisite

neck 3 pet **4** kiss **6** fondle, smooch *back of:* **4** nape **5** nucha **6** scruff *ornament:* **6** gorget, torque

necklace 5 chain **6** choker **7** rivière **8** carcanet

necktie 5 ascot **6** cravat **10** four-in-hand

necrology 4 obit **8** obituary

necromancy 4 juju **5** magic, vodun **6** hoodoo, voodoo **7** devilry, sorcery **8** witchery, wizardry **9** conjuring, diabolism, magicking **10** black magic, witchcraft **11** bewitchment, conjuration, enchantment, incantation, thaumaturgy

necropolis 8 boneyard, boot hill, cemetery, God's acre **9** graveyard **10** churchyard **12** memorial park, potter's field

necropsy 7 anatomy, autopsy **10** dissection, postmortem

née 4 born **10** originally

need 3 use **4** call, duty, lack, must, want **5** crave **6** demand, devoir, hunger, penury, thirst **7** poverty, require **8** distress, exigency, occasion, shortage **9** indigence, necessity, privation, requisite **10** compulsion, deficiency, obligation **11** deprivation, destitution, requirement

neediness 4 want **6** penury **7** poverty **9** indigence, privation **11** deprivation, destitution **13** insufficiency

needle 3 rib **5** annoy, tease **6** harass, pester, plague **7** bedevil, hagride, obelisk, pricker, syringe **10** hypodermic *case:* **4** etui *hole:* **3** eye

needlefish 3 gar **8** pipefish

needlelike 7 styloid **8** belonoid *part:* **7** acicula

needlepoint 4 lace **7** alençon, crochet, tatting **8** bargello **10** embroidery **11** cross-stitch

needlework 4 lace **6** sewing **7** alençon, crochet, sampler, tatting **8** bargello, knitting **9** stitching **10** crocheting, embroidery **11** cross-stitch

needy 4 poor **5** broke **6** hard up **8** beggared, dirt-poor, indigent, strapped **9** destitute, penniless, penurious **10** down-and-out **11** impecunious, necessitous **12** impoverished

ne'er-do-well 3 bum, dud **5** loser **6** loafer, no-good **7** failure, wastrel **8** derelict **9** shiftless **10** profligate, scapegrace

nefarious 4 evil, vile **6** savage, wicked **7** heinous, impious, noxious **8** depraved, dreadful, flagrant, infamous, perverse **9** execrable, miscreant, monstrous, offensive **10** abominable, degenerate, detestable, iniquitous, outrageous, villainous **11** opprobrious **13** reprehensible

negate 4 deny, undo, void **5** annul, quash, rebut **6** cancel, impugn, refute, vacate **7** abolish, gainsay, nullify, redress, vitiate **8** abrogate, disallow, disprove, overturn, traverse **9** cancel out, disaffirm, repudiate **10** contradict, contravene, counteract, invalidate, neutralize **12** countercheck

negative 3 nix **4** deny, kill, veto **5** annul, cross, minus **6** impugn **7** adverse, gainsay, nullify, redress, refusal **8** abrogate, disprove, traverse **9** cancel out, frustrate **10** contradict, contravene, counteract, invalidate, neutralize **11** detrimental, unfavorable *battery terminal:* **5** anode *ion:* **5** anion *Scottish:* **3** nae *sign:* **5** minus

neglect 4 fail, omit **5** let go, shirk **6** forget, ignore, laxity, slight **7** failure, laxness **8** omission, overlook, overpass, pass over **9** avoidance, disregard, oversight, pretermit **10** negligence **11** dereliction, inattention **12** carelessness **13** pretermission

neglectful see NEGLIGENT

negligee 4 gown **5** teddy **7** chemise, nightie **8** camisole, peignoir **9** nightgown

negligent 3 lax **5** slack **6** remiss **8** careless, derelict, heedless **9** forgetful, imprudent **10** delinquent, neglectful, nonchalant, regardless, unthinking **11** inattentive, pococurante, unconcerned **12** disregardful **13** irresponsible, lackadaisical

negligible 4 puny, slim **5** minor, petty, small **6** meager, meagre, minute, remote, paltry, skimpy, slight **7** minimal, slender, trivial **8** nugatory, picayune, trifling **9** minuscule **11** meaningless, unimportant **13** imperceptible, insignificant

negotiable 8 passable **11** convertible **12** transferable

negotiate 4 cash **6** confer, dicker, hurdle, manage, parley, settle **7** arrange, bargain, develop, mediate, work out, wrangle **8** contract, covenant, moderate, surmount, transact, transfer **9** arbitrate **10** horse-trade

neigh 6 nicker, whinny

neighbor 4 abut **5** flank, frame, skirt **6** adjoin, border **7** abutter **8** border on

neighborhood 4 area, turf, ward **5** block, range **6** parish **8** district, locality, precinct, purlieus, vicinage, vicinity **9** community, proximity

neighborly 6 genial **7** amiable, cordial, helpful **8** amicable, friendly, obliging, sociable **9** congenial **10** gregarious, hospitable **11** considerate, cooperative, good-natured **13** accommodating

nematode 4 worm **7** eelworm **9** roundworm

Nemean predator 4 lion

nemesis 4 bane, doom **5** curse, enemy, rival **8** opponent **9** bête noire **11** retribution

neologism 7 coinage, new word

neophyte see NEWCOMER

Neoptolemus 7 Pyrrhus *father:* **8** Achilles *slayer:* **7** Orestes *victim:* **5** Priam *wife:* **8** Hermione

neoteric 6 modern, recent

Nepal *capital:* **8** Katmandu **9** Kathmandu *city:* **7** Pokhara **8** Lalitpur *monetary unit:* **5** rupee *mountain, range:* **7** Everest **8** Himalaya **9** Himalayan, Himalayas **10** Dhaulagiri **11** Gauri Sankar **12** Kanchenjunga *neighbor:* **5** China, India *river:* **6** Ganges

nepenthe 6 opiate, potion **7** anodyne **8** lenitive, narcotic **9** analgesic **10** anesthetic, painkiller

Nephthys *brother, husband:* **3** Set **4** Seth

nepotism 10 favoritism, partiality

Neptune 6 planet *satellite:* **6** Nereid, Triton (see also POSEIDON)

nerd 4 drip, geek **6** misfit **7** egghead, nebbish, oddball **10** pointy-head

Nereid 6 Thetis **7** Galatea **10** Amphitrite *father:* **6** Nereus *mother:* **5** Doris

Nereus *daughters:* **8** Nereides *emblem:* **7** trident *father:* **6** Pontus *mother:* **4** Gaea *wife:* **5** Doris

Nergal *brother:* **5** Nanna **6** Ninazu *father:* **5** Enlil *mother:* **6** Ninlil

Nero *birthplace:* **4** Rome *mother:* **9** Agrippina *successor:* **5** Galba *tutor:* **6** Seneca *victim:* **5** Lucan **6** Seneca **7** Octavia, Poppaea **9** Agrippina *wife:* **7** Octavia, Poppaea

Nero Wolfe *creator* **5** Stout (Rex)

nerve 4 face, gall, grit, guts **5** brass, cheek, crust, heart, moxie, spunk **6** daring **7** sciatic **8** audacity, backbone, boldness, chutzpah, temerity **9** assurance, brashness, fortitude, hardihood, hardiness **10** confidence, effrontery **11** presumption *cell:* **6** neuron *cell group:* **7** ganglia (plural) **8** ganglion *combining form:* **4** neur **5** neura, neuro *cranial:* **4** vagi (plural) **5** optic, vagus **8** abducens *ending:* **8** receptor *lesion:* **8** neuritis

nerve center 3 hub **4** core, seat **5** focus, heart, locus **7** capital **8** cynosure, polestar **10** crossroads, focal point **12** headquarters

nerve gas 5 sarin, soman, tabun

nervous 4 edgy **5** jerky, jumpy, tense, timid **6** fitful, goosey, on edge, spooky, uneasy **7** erratic, fidgety, fretful, jittery, restive, twitchy, uptight **8** aflutter, agitated, forcible, skittery, skittish, spirited, twittery, unsteady, vigorous, volatile **9** excitable, irregular, irritable **10** high-strung **12** apprehensive

nervy 4 bold, edgy, pert **5** brash, cocky, fresh, jerky, jumpy, sassy, tense **6** brassy, cheeky, goosey, plucky, spooky, uneasy **7** fidgety, forward, jittery, restive, twitchy, uptight **8** impudent, intrepid, twittery **9** excitable **10** high-strung **11** smart-alecky

ness 4 cape **8** foreland, headland **9** peninsula **10** promontory

Nessus' victim 8 Heracles, Hercules

nest 3 den **4** aery, home, lair, nidi (plural) **5** aerie, eyrie, nidus **7** hangout, shelter **11** aggregation *eagle's:* **4** aery **5** aerie, eyrie *wasp's:* **8** vespiary

nest egg 5 cache, funds, hoard, kitty, stash **6** assets **7** reserve

nestle 4 snug **6** bundle, burrow, cuddle, huddle, nuzzle **7** snuggle

Nestor *father:* **6** Neleus *kingdom:* **5** Pylos

net 4 gain, gist, mesh **5** basic, catch, clear, seine, tulle, yield **6** maline **7** clean

up, essence, malines *conical:* 5 trawl
fishing: 5 seine *hair:* 5 snood
Nethanel *brother:* 5 David *father:* 5 Jesse
7 Pashhur 8 Obededom *son:* 8 Shema-
iah
nether 3 low 4 down 5 below, lower,
under 6 lesser 8 chthonic, inferior
9 subjacent 10 underworld 11 underground 12 subterranean
Netherlands 7 Holland *capital:* 9 Amsterdam *city:* 5 Hague (The) 7 Utrecht
8 The Hague 9 Rotterdam *former inlet:*
9 Zuider Zee *island group:* 11 West
Frisian *lake:* 10 IJsselmeer *language:*
5 Dutch *monetary unit:* 4 euro *monetary
unit, former:* 7 guilder *neighbor:* 7 Belgium, Germany *river:* 4 Maas 5 Meuse,
Rhein, Rhine 7 Scheldt *sea:* 5 North
Netherlands Antilles *capital:* 10 Willem-
stad *discoverer:* 8 Columbus (Christopher) *former name:* 7 Curaçao *capital:*
4 Saba 7 Bonaire 7 Curaçao *location:*
10 West Indies *part of:* 11 Netherlands
netherworld 3 pit 4 hell 5 abyss, hades,
Sheol 6 blazes, Tophet 7 Gehenna,
inferno 8 hellfire 9 perdition 10 no-
man's-land, underworld 11 underground
netlike 9 reticular 10 reticulate
nettle 3 nag, vex 4 gall, huff, rile, roil
5 annoy, chafe, peeve, pique, upset
6 abrade, badger, harass, incite, put
out, pester, ruffle, stir up 7 agitate, disturb, perturb, provoke 8 irritate
10 exasperate
nettle rash 5 hives 9 urticaria
nettlesome 5 pesky 6 vexing 7 galling,
irksome, prickly 8 annoying, rankling
9 irritable, upsetting, vexatious 10 irritating
network 3 web 4 mesh 8 gridiron 9 reticulum *anatomical:* 4 rete 5 retia (plural)
neurotic 6 phobic, touchy 7 anxious
8 abnormal, unstable 9 disturbed,
obsessive 10 compulsive, disordered
neuter 3 fix 4 geld, spay 5 alter, unsex
7 sexless 8 castrate, mutilate 9 sterilize
11 desexualize 12 intransitive
neutral 7 hueless 8 detached, middling,
unbiased 9 colorless, impartial,
unaligned 10 achromatic, disengaged,
even-handed, impersonal, nonaligned,
pokerfaced 11 indifferent, nonpartisan
13 disinterested, dispassionate
neutralize 4 undo 5 annul 6 negate, offset 7 balance, nullify, redress, reverse
9 cancel out 10 counteract, invalidate
11 countervail 12 countercheck, counterpoise
Nevada *capital:* 10 Carson City *city:*
4 Elko, Reno 8 Las Vegas *dam:*

6 Hoover 7 Boulder *lake:* 4 Mead
5 Tahoe *mountain:* 8 Boundary (Peak)
nickname: 6 Silver (State) *river:* 8 Humboldt *state bird:* 8 bluebird (mountain)
state flower: 9 sagebrush *state tree:*
5 piñon 6 pinyon 15 bristlecone pine
névé 4 firn, snow
never-ending 7 eternal 8 immortal
9 ceaseless 11 everlasting
Never-Ending Story author 4 Ende
(Michael)
nevertheless 3 but, yet 5 still 6 anyhow,
anyway, though, withal 7 howbeit,
however 8 after all 10 regardless
11 nonetheless, still and all
nevus 4 mole 9 birthmark
new 5 fresh, novel 6 modern, recent
7 another, revived 8 neoteric, pristine
10 additional, unfamiliar 11 modernis-
tic 12 contemporary *combining form:*
3 neo, nov 4 novo *word:* 7 coinage
9 neologism
New Brunswick *capital:* 11 Fredericton
city: 6 St. John 7 Moncton *mountain:*
8 Carleton *provincial flower:* 12 purple
violet *river:* 9 Miramichi, Saint John
10 Nepisiguit 11 Restigouche
New Caledonia *capital:* 6 Nouméa *department of:* 6 France *discoverer:* 4 Cook
(Capt. James) *island:* 7 Loyalty, Walpole
11 Isle of Pines
newcomer 4 colt, tyro 6 novice, rookie
8 beginner, freshman, initiate, neophyte 9 greenhorn, immigrant, novitiate 10 apprentice, tenderfoot
New Deal agency 3 CCC, NRA, SEC,
TVA, WPA 4 FDIC, NLRB
Newfoundland and Labrador *capital:*
7 St. John's *mountain:* 8 Caubvick
provincial flower: 12 pitcher plant *river:*
6 Gander 8 Exploits 9 Churchill
New Hampshire *capital:* 7 Concord *city:*
6 Nashua 10 Manchester, Portsmouth
college, university: 9 Dartmouth *motto:*
13 Live Free or Die *mountain, range:*
5 White 10 Washington *nickname:*
7 Granite (State) *river:* 9 Merrimack
11 Connecticut *state bird:* 11 purple
finch *state flower:* 11 purple lilac *state
tree:* 10 white birch
New Jersey *capital:* 7 Trenton *city:*
6 Camden, Newark 7 Cape May
8 Paterson 9 Elizabeth 10 Jersey City
college, university: 4 Drew 7 Rutgers
9 Princeton, Seton Hall 18 Fairleigh
Dickinson *nickname:* 6 Garden (State)
river: 6 Hudson 7 Raritan 8 Delaware
state bird: 9 goldfinch *state flower:* 6 violet *state tree:* 6 red oak
New Mexico *capital:* 7 Santa Fe *caverns:*
8 Carlsbad *city:* 4 Taos 7 Roswell 9 Las

Cruces, Los Alamos **10** Farmington **11** Albuquerque *mountain, range:* **7** Wheeler (Peak) **14** Sangre de Cristo *nickname:* **17** Land of Enchantment *river:* **5** Pecos **9** Rio Grande *state bird:* **10** roadrunner *state flower:* **5** yucca *state tree:* **5** piñon **6** pinyon

news 4 dope, poop, word **5** rumor **6** advice, gossip, report, tattle **7** lowdown, tidings **9** knowledge, speerings **11** information, scuttlebutt **12** announcement, intelligence **4** TASS **7** Reuters **8** ITAR-TASS

newspaper 5 daily, organ **6** review **7** journal, tabloid **8** magazine **10** periodical *publisher:* **6** Hearst (William Randolph) **7** Murdoch (Rupert) **11** Beaverbrook (Lord)

newt 3 eft **6** triton *green:* **5** ebbet

New Testament see at BIBLE

New York *capital:* **6** Albany *city:* **4** Rome, Troy **5** Utica **6** Elmira, Ithaca **7** Buffalo, Yonkers **8** Saratoga, Syracuse **9** Rochester **11** New York City *college, university:* **3** RPI **4** Pace, CUNY, SUNY **5** Pratt, Siena **6** CW Post, Hunter, Vassar **7** Adelphi, Barnard, Colgate, Cornell, Fordham, Hofstra, St. Johns, Yeshiva **8** Columbia, Skidmore, Syracuse **9** Juilliard, West Point **13** Sarah Lawrence *island:* **4** Long, Fire *lake, lake group:* **4** Erie **6** Cayuga, Finger, Oneida **7** Saranac **9** Champlain *mountain, range:* **5** Marcy **8** Catskill **10** Adirondack *nickname:* **6** Empire (State) *river:* **6** Hudson **7** Niagara **10** St. Lawrence *state bird:* **8** bluebird *state flower:* **4** rose *state tree:* **10** sugar maple

New York City 6 Gotham **8** Big Apple *borough:* **5** Bronx **6** Queens **8** Brooklyn, Richmond **9** Manhattan **12** Staten Island

New Zealand *capital:* **10** Wellington *city:* **8** Auckland **12** Christchurch *ethnic group:* **5** Maori *explorer:* **4** Cook (Capt. James) **6** Tasman (Abel) *island:* **5** North, South **7** Chatham, Stewart *island group:* **4** Cook **8** Manihiki **12** Northern Cook *lake:* **5** Taupo *language:* **5** Maori **7** English *monetary unit:* **6** dollar *mountain, range:* **4** Cook **6** Egmont **12** Southern Alps *native:* **4** Kiwi *strait:* **4** Cook *volcano:* **7** Ruapehu **9** Ngauruhoe

next 3 then **5** after, later **6** behind, beside, second **7** closest, ensuing, nearest **8** abutting, adjacent, touching **9** adjoining, afterward, alongside, following, proximate **10** contiguous, subsequent, succeeding **11** neighboring

next to 4 near **6** almost, beside **7** abreast, close by **8** abutting, adjacent, opposite,

touching **9** adjoining, alongside, bordering **11** neighboring

nexus 3 tie **4** bond, knot, link, yoke **5** focus **6** center **8** ligament, ligature, vinculum **10** connection

Nez Percé chief 6 Joseph

Niagara 5 flood, spate **6** deluge **7** torrent **8** alluvion, cataract, flooding, overflow **9** cataclysm, waterfall **10** inundation

nib 3 neb, tip **4** beak, bill, nose, prow **5** prong, snoot, snout, tooth **8** pen point **9** proboscis

nibble 3 eat, nip **4** bite, chew, crop, gnaw, nosh, peck, pick **5** graze, munch, snack, taste **6** morsel, tidbit

Nicaragua *capital:* **7** Managua *city:* **4** León **6** Masaya *coast:* **8** Mosquito *ethnic group:* **4** Maya **5** Mayan *discoverer:* **8** Columbus (Christopher) *language:* **7** Spanish *monetary unit:* **7** córdoba *neighbor:* **8** Honduras **9** Costa Rica *sea:* **9** Caribbean

nice 4 fine, good, kind, mild, neat **5** right **6** benign, comely, dainty, decent, polite, proper, seemly **7** affable, clement, cordial, correct, fitting, refined **8** becoming, charming, decorous, obliging, pleasant, pleasing, suitable, virtuous, well-bred **9** admirable, agreeable, courteous, congenial, enjoyable, favorable, judicious **10** attractive, personable **11** appropriate, respectable

niche 4 nook **6** alcove, corner, cranny, recess **7** calling **8** vocation **9** cubbyhole **11** compartment

Nicholas Nickleby *author* **7** Dickens (Charles)

nick 3 cut **4** chip, gash **5** cheat, notch, score **6** groove, record **10** overcharge **11** indentation

nickname 3 tag **5** label **6** byword, handle **7** agnomen, epithet, moniker **8** cognomen **9** sobriquet **10** diminutive, hypocorism

Nicomede *conquest:* **10** Cappodocia *dramatist:* **9** Corneille (Pierre) *half-brother:* **6** Attale *stepmother:* **7** Arsinoë

nictitate 3 bat **4** wink **5** blink **7** flutter, twinkle

nifty 4 cool, keen, neat **5** dandy, ducky, super, swell **6** clever, groovy, peachy **7** stylish **8** jim-dandy, splendid, terrific **9** ingenious

Niger *capital:* **6** Niamey *city:* **6** Maradi, Zinder *desert:* **5** Sahel **6** Sahara *ethnic group:* **5** Hausa *language:* **5** Hausa **6** Arabic, French *monetary unit:* **5** franc *neighbor:* **4** Chad, Mali **5** Benin, Libya **7** Algeria, Nigeria **11** Burkina Faso *river:* **5** Niger

Nigeria *capital:* **5** Abuja, Lagos *city:*

4 Kano 6 Ibadan, Ilorin 7 Oshogbo
9 Ogbomosho *ethnic group:* 4 Igbo
5 Hausa 6 Fulani, Yoruba *gulf:* 6 Guinea
lake: 4 Chad *language:* 5 Hausa 7 English *monetary unit:* 5 naira *neighbor:*
4 Chad 5 Benin, Niger 8 Cameroon
river: 5 Benue, Niger 6 Kaduna

niggard 5 churl, miser, piker, screw
7 hoarder, scrooge 8 tightwad 9 skinflint 10 cheapskate, curmudgeon
12 money-grubber, penny-pincher

niggardly 5 tight 6 scanty, stingy
7 chintzy, miserly 9 penurious
10 begrudging 11 closefisted, tightfisted
12 cheeseparing, parsimonious
13 penny-pinching

niggling 5 minor, petty 6 measly, paltry,
two-bit 7 trivial 8 picayune, piddling,
tiresome, trifling 9 small-time 10 bothersome, picayunish 11 small-minded

nigh 4 near 5 about, close, round 6 all
but, almost, around, beside, nearby,
nearly 7 close to 8 approach 9 immediate, just about, proximate, virtually
10 near at hand, pretty much 11 practically

night blindness 10 nyctalopia

nightclub 5 disco 6 bistro, casino
7 cabaret 9 honky-tonk, speakeasy
11 discotheque

nightfall 3 eve 4 dusk, even 6 sunset
7 evening, sundown 8 eventide, gloaming, twilight

nighthawk 6 petrel 7 bullbat 10 goatsucker

nightjar 9 nighthawk 10 goatsucker
12 whip-poor-will

nightly 9 nocturnal

nightmare 5 dream, fancy, worry
6 fright, horror, ordeal, vision 7 bugbear, fantasy, incubus, torment 8 phantasm, phantasy, succubus 12 apprehension 13 hallucination

nightshade 6 tomato 7 henbane 10 belladonna 11 bittersweet

nightstick 3 bat 4 club, mace 5 baton,
billy, staff 6 cudgel 8 bludgeon 9 billy
club, blackjack, truncheon 10 shillelagh

Nike *father:* 6 Pallas *goddess of:* 7 victory
mother: 4 Styx

nil 3 nix, zip 4 love, wind, zero 5 zilch
6 naught 7 nothing

Nile 6 Al-Bahr *dam:* 5 Aswan 6 Makwar
10 Gebel Aulia *explorer:* 5 Baker (Sir
Samuel), Bruce (James), Grant (James
Augustus), Speke (John Hanning)
queen: 4 Cleo 9 Cleopatra *section:*
4 Abay 5 Abbai

nilgai 8 antelope

nimble 4 deft, spry, yare 5 agile, alert,
fleet, handy, light, quick, zippy

6 adroit, limber, lively 7 lissome 9 dexterous, sprightly 10 responsive
11 quick-witted

Nimrod 6 hunter *father:* 4 Cush

Ninazu *brother:* 5 Nanna 6 Nergal *father:*
5 Enlil *mother:* 6 Ninlil

nincompoop 3 oaf 4 boob, clod, dodo,
fool, goof, mutt, simp, yo-yo 5 chump,
dummy, dunce, idiot, moron, ninny,
noddy, stupe 6 dimwit, donkey, dumdum, nitwit 7 airhead, dullard, pinhead, schnook, tomfool 8 bonehead,
clodpoll, dumbbell, dumbhead, imbecile, lunkhead, meathead, numskull
9 birdbrain, blockhead, ignoramus,
lamebrain, numbskull, simpleton,
thickhead 10 dunderhead, hammerhead 11 chowderhead, chucklehead,
knucklehead

nine 12 baseball team *combining form:*
3 non 4 nona *goddesses:* 5 Muses
group: 6 ennead *inches:* 4 span *instruments:* 5 nonet

Nine Worlds 3 Hel 6 Asgard 7 Alfheim,
Midgard 8 Niflheim, Vanaheim
10 Jotunnheim 12 Muspellsheim
13 Svartalfaheim

ninny see NINCOMPOOP

Ninsum's son 9 Gilgamesh

Nintu *consort:* 4 Enki *son:* 6 Ninsar

Ninurta *father:* 5 Enlil *victim:* 3 Kur

Ninus *father:* 5 Belus *wife:* 9 Semiramis

Niobe *brother:* 7 Pelops *father:* 8 Tantalus
husband: 7 Amphion *sister-in-law:*
5 Aedon

nip 3 bit, nab, sip 4 bite, dart, dash,
dram, drop, jolt, peck, shot, slug, swig
5 chill, clamp, hurry, pinch, sever,
snort, steal 6 imbibe, snatch, thwart,
tipple 7 cabbage, snifter, swallow
9 frustrate

nipper 3 kid 4 tyke 5 child 6 moppet,
shaver 7 pincers 8 young one
9 youngling, youngster

nipple 3 pap 4 teat

Nippon 5 Japan

nippy 3 icy, raw 4 cold, cool 5 algid,
chill, crisp, sharp 6 arctic, biting, bitter,
chilly, frosty, wintry 7 caustic, glacial,
numbing, shivery 8 chilling, freezing

nirvana 5 bliss, dream 6 heaven 7 Elysium 8 empyrean, oblivion, paradise
9 Shangri-la

Nisus *betrayer, daughter:* 6 Scylla *father:*
7 Pandion

nitid 6 bright, glossy, lucent 7 fulgent,
glowing, shining 8 gleaming, glinting,
luminous, lustrous, polished 9 burnished

nitpick 4 carp 5 cavil 7 quibble 10 split
hairs

nitrogen 5 azote *combining form:* **3** azo
nitwit 3 oaf **4** boob, clod, dodo, dolt,
dope, goof, mutt, simp **5** chump, cluck,
dummy, dunce, idiot, moron, ninny,
noddy, stupe **6** donkey, dum-dum **7** airhead, dullard, pinhead, schnook
8 bonehead, clodpoll, dumbbell, imbecile, lunkhead, meathead, numskull
9 birdbrain, blockhead, ignoramus,
lamebrain, numbskull, simpleton,
thickhead **10** dunderhead, hammerhead, nincompoop **11** chowderhead,
chucklehead, knucklehead
nix 3 nay, zap **4** kill, nope, veto **5** quash
6 cancel, naught, reject, scotch, sprite
7 call off, nothing, nullify
Njord, Njorth *daughter:* **5** Freya *son:*
4 Frey *wife:* **6** Skadhi, Skathi
no 3 nay, nix **6** denial **7** refusal **8** negative **10** thumbs-down *German:* **4** nein
no-account see NO-GOOD
Noachian 3 old **4** aged **5** fusty, hoary
6 age-old **7** ancient, antique, archaic
8 timeworn **9** venerable **10** antiquated,
oldfangled **12** antediluvian, old-fashioned **13** superannuated
Noah *father:* **6** Lamech **10** Zelophehad
grandson: **4** Aram **6** Canaan *great-grand-
son:* **3** Hul *landing place:* **6** Ararat *son:*
3 Ham **4** Shem **6** Canaan **7** Japheth
Nobel Prize winner
chemistry:
1901: **8** van't Hoff (Jacobus) *1902:*
7 Fischer (Emil) *1903:* **9** Arrhenius
(Svante) *1904:* **6** Ramsay (William)
1905: **9** von Baeyer (Adolf) *1906:*
7 Moissan (Henri) *1907:* **7** Buchner
(Eduard) *1908:* **10** Rutherford (Ernest)
1909: **7** Ostwald (Wilhelm) *1910:* **7** Wallach (Otto) *1911:* **5** Curie (Marie) *1912:*
8 Grignard (François), Sabatier (Paul)
1913: **6** Werner (Alfred) *1914:*
8 Richards (Theodore) *1915:* **11** Willstatter (Richard) *1918:* **5** Haber (Fritz)
1920: **6** Nernst (Walther) *1921:* **5** Soddy
(Frederick) *1922:* **5** Aston (Francis)
1923: **5** Pregl (Fritz) *1925:* **9** Zsigmondy (Richard) *1926:* **8** Svedberg
(Theodor) *1927:* **5** Wieland (Heinrich)
1928: **7** Windaus (Adolf) *1929:* **6** Harden (Arthur) **12** Euler-Chelpin (Hans
von) *1930:* **7** Fischer (Hans) *1931:*
5 Bosch (Karl) **7** Bergius (Friedrich)
1932: **8** Langmuir (Irving) *1934:* **4** Urey
(Harold) *1935:* **11** Joliot-Curie
(Frédéric, Irene) *1936:* **5** Debye (Peter)
1937: **6** Karrer (Paul) **7** Haworth (Walter) *1938:* **4** Kuhn (Richard) *1939:*
7 Ruzicka (Leopold) **9** Butenandt
(Adolf) *1943:* **6** Hevesy (Georg de)
1944: **4** Hahn (Otto) *1945:* **8** Virtanen

(Artturi) *1946:* **6** Sumner (James)
7 Stanley (Wendell) **8** Northrop (John
Howard) *1947:* **8** Robinson (Robert)
1948: **8** Tiselius (Arne) *1949:*
7 Giauque (William) *1950:* **5** Alder
(Kurt), Diels (Otto) *1951:* **7** Seaborg
(Glenn) **8** McMillan (Edwin) *1952:*
5 Synge (Richard) **6** Martin (Archer)
1953: **10** Staudinger (Hermann) *1954:*
7 Pauling (Linus) *1955:* **10** du
Vigneaud (Vincent) *1956:* **7** Semenov
(Nikolay) **11** Hinshelwood (Cyril)
1957: **4** Todd (Alexander) *1958:*
6 Sanger (Frederick) *1959:* **9** Hey-
rovsky (Jaroslav) *1960:* **5** Libby
(Willard) *1961:* **6** Calvin (Melvin) *1962:*
6 Perutz (Max) **7** Kendrew (John)
1963: **5** Natta (Giulio) **7** Ziegler (Karl)
1964: **7** Hodgkin (Dorothy) **8** Woodward (Robert) *1966:* **8** Mulliken
(Robert) *1967:* **5** Eigen (Manfred)
6 Porter (George) **7** Norrish (Ronald)
1968: **7** Onsager (Lars) *1969:* **6** Barton
(Derek), Hassel (Odd) *1970:* **6** Leloir
(Luis) *1971:* **8** Herzberg (Gerhard)
1972: **5** Moore (Stanford), Stein
(William) **8** Anfinsen (Christian) *1973:*
7 Fischer (Ernst) **9** Wilkinson (Geoffrey) *1974:* **5** Flory (Paul) *1975:* **6** Pre-
log (Vladimir) **9** Cornforth (John)
1976: **8** Lipscomb (William) *1977:*
9 Prigogine (Ilya) *1978:* **8** Mitchell
(Peter) *1979:* **5** Brown (Herbert) **6** Wittig (Georg) *1980:* **4** Berg (Paul)
6 Sanger (Frederick) **7** Gilbert (Walter) *1981:* **5** Fukui (Kenichi) **8** Hoffmann (Roald) *1982:* **4** Klug (Aaron)
1983: **5** Taube (Henry) *1984:* **10** Merri-
field (R. Bruce) *1985:* **5** Karle
(Jerome) **8** Hauptman (Herbert)
1986: **3** Lee (Yuan) **7** Polanyi (John)
10 Herschbach (Dudley) *1987:* **4** Cram
(Donald), Lehn (Jean-Marie) **8** Peder-
sen (Charles) *1988:* **5** Huber (Robert)
6 Michel (Hartmut) **11** Deisenhofer
(Johann) *1989:* **4** Cech (Thomas) **6** Altman (Sidney) *1990:* **5** Corey (Elias)
1991: **5** Ernst (Richard) *1992:* **6** Marcus
(Rudolph) *1993:* **5** Smith (Michael)
6 Mullis (Kary) *1994:* **4** Olah (George)
1995: **6** Molina (Mario) **7** Crutzen
(Paul), Rowland (F. Sherwood) *1996:*
4 Curl (Robert) **5** Kroto (Harold)
7 Smalley (Richard) *1997:* **4** Skou
(Jens) **5** Boyer (Paul) **6** Walker (John)
1998: **4** Kohn (Walter) **5** Pople (John)
1999: **6** Zewail (Ahmed) *2000:* **6** Heeger
(Alan) **9** Shirakawa (Hideki) **10** Mac-
Diarmid (Alan) *2001:* **6** Noyori (Ryoji)
7 Knowles (William) **9** Sharpless (K.
Barry) *2002:* **4** Fenn (John) **6** Tanaka

(Koichi) **8** Wüthrich (Kurt) *2003:* **4** Agre (Peter) **9** MacKinnon (Roderick) *2004:* **4** Rose (Irwin) **7** Hershko (Avram) **11** Ciechanover (Aaron)

economics:

1969: **6** Frisch (Ragnar) **9** Tinbergen (Jan) *1970:* **9** Samuelson (Paul) *1971:* **7** Kuznets (Simon) *1972:* **5** Arrow (Kenneth), Hicks (John) *1973:* **8** Leontief (Wassily) *1974:* **5** Hayek (Friedrich von) **6** Myrdal (Gunnar) *1975:* **8** Koopmans (Tjalling) **11** Kantorovich (Leonid) *1976:* **8** Friedman (Milton) *1977:* **5** Meade (James), Ohlin (Bertil) *1978:* **5** Simon (Herbert) *1979:* **5** Lewis (Arthur) **7** Schultz (Theodore) *1980:* **5** Klein (Lawrence) *1981:* **5** Tobin (James) *1982:* **7** Stigler (George) *1983:* **6** Debreu (Gerard) *1984:* **5** Stone (Richard) *1985:* **10** Modigliani (Franco) *1986:* **8** Buchanan (James) *1987:* **5** Solow (Robert) *1988:* **6** Allais (Maurice) *1989:* **8** Haavelmo (Trygve) *1990:* **6** Miller (Merton), Sharpe (William) **9** Markowitz (Harry) *1991:* **5** Coase (Ronald) *1992:* **6** Becker (Gary) *1993:* **5** Fogel (Robert), North (Douglass) *1994:* **4** Nash (John) **6** Selten (Reinhard) **8** Harsanyi (John) *1995:* **5** Lucas (Robert) *1996:* **7** Vickrey (William) **8** Mirrlees (James) *1998:* **3** Sen (Amartya) *1999:* **7** Mundell (Robert) *2000:* **7** Heckman (James) **8** McFadden (Daniel) *2001:* **6** Spence (Michael) **7** Akerlof (George) **8** Stiglitz (Joseph) *2002:* **5** Smith (Vernon) **8** Kahneman (Daniel) *2003:* **5** Engle (Robert) **7** Granger (Clive) *2004:* **7** Kydland (Finn) **8** Prescott (Edward)

literature:

1901: **9** Prudhomme (Sully) *1902:* **7** Mommsen (Theodor) *1903:* **8** Bjornson (Bjornstjerne) *1904:* **7** Mistral (Frédéric) **9** Echegaray (José) *1905:* **11** Sienkiewicz (Henryk) *1906:* **8** Carducci (Giosue) *1907:* **7** Kipling (Rudyard) *1908:* **6** Eucken (Rudolf) *1909:* **8** Lagerlof (Selma) *1910:* **5** Heyse (Paul) *1911:* **11** Maeterlinck (Maurice) *1912:* **9** Hauptmann (Gerhart) *1913:* **6** Tagore (Rabindranath) *1915:* **7** Rolland (Romain) *1916:* **10** Heidenstam (Verner von) *1917:* **9** Gjellerup (Karl) **11** Pontoppidan (Henrik) *1919:* **9** Spitteler (Carl) *1920:* **6** Hamsun (Knut) *1921:* **6** France (Anatole) *1922:* **9** Benavente (Jacinto) *1923:* **5** Yeats (William Butler) *1924:* **7** Reymont (Wladyslaw) *1925:* **4** Shaw (George Bernard) *1926:* **7** Deledda (Grazia) *1927:* **7** Bergson (Henri) *1928:* **6** Undset

(Sigrid) *1929:* **4** Mann (Thomas) *1930:* **5** Lewis (Sinclair) *1931:* **9** Karlfeldt (Erik Axel) *1932:* **10** Galsworthy (John) *1933:* **5** Bunin (Ivan) *1934:* **10** Pirandello (Luigi) *1936:* **6** O'Neill (Eugene) *1937:* **12** Martin du Gard (Roger) *1938:* **4** Buck (Pearl) *1939:* **9** Sillanpää (Frans Eemil) *1944:* **6** Jensen (Johannes) *1945:* **7** Mistral (Gabriela) *1946:* **5** Hesse (Hermann) *1947:* **4** Gide (André) *1948:* **5** Eliot (Thomas Stearns) *1949:* **8** Faulkner (William) *1950:* **7** Russell (Bertrand) *1951:* **10** Lagerkvist (Pär) *1952:* **7** Mauriac (François) *1953:* **9** Churchill (Winston) *1954:* **9** Hemingway (Ernest) *1955:* **7** Laxness (Halldór) *1956:* **7** Jiménez (Juan Ramón) *1957:* **5** Camus (Albert) *1958:* **9** Pasternak (Boris) *1959:* **9** Quasimodo (Salvatore) *1960:* **5** Perse (Saint-John) *1961:* **6** Andric (Ivo) *1962:* **9** Steinbeck (John) *1963:* **7** Seferis (George) *1964:* **6** Sartre (Jean-Paul) *1965:* **9** Sholokhov (Mikhail) *1966:* **5** Agnon (Shmuel Yosef), Sachs (Nelly) *1967:* **8** Asturias (Miguel Angel) *1968:* **8** Kawabata (Yasunari) *1969:* **7** Beckett (Samuel) *1970:* **12** Solzhenitsyn (Alexander) *1971:* **6** Neruda (Pablo) *1972:* **4** Böll (Heinrich) *1973:* **5** White (Patrick) *1974:* **7** Johnson (Eyvind) **9** Martinson (Edmund) *1975:* **7** Montale (Eugenio) *1976:* **6** Bellow (Saul) *1977:* **10** Aleixandre (Vicente) *1978:* **6** Singer (Isaac Bashevis) *1979:* **6** Elytis (Odysseus) *1980:* **6** Milosz (Czeslaw) *1981:* **7** Canetti (Elias) *1982:* **13** García Márquez (Gabriel) *1983:* **7** Golding (William) *1984:* **7** Seifert (Jaroslav) *1985:* **5** Simon (Claude) *1986:* **7** Soyinka (Wole) *1987:* **7** Brodsky (Joseph) *1988:* **7** Mahfouz (Naguib) *1989:* **4** Cela (Camilo José) *1990:* **3** Paz (Octavio) *1991:* **8** Gordimer (Nadine) *1992:* **7** Walcott (Derek) *1993:* **8** Morrison (Toni) *1994:* **2** Oe (Kenzaburo) *1995:* **6** Heaney (Seamus) *1996:* **10** Szymborska (Wislawa) *1997:* **2** Fo (Dario) *1998:* **8** Saramago (José) *1999:* **5** Grass (Günter) *2000:* **3** Gao (Xingjian) **11** Gao Xingjian *2001:* **7** Naipaul (V. S.) *2002:* **7** Kertész (Imre) *2003:* **7** Coetzee (J. M.) *2004:* **7** Jelinek (Elfriede)

peace:

1901: **5** Passy (Frédéric) **6** Dunant (Jean-Henri) *1902:* **5** Gobat (Charles Albert) **8** Ducommun (Elie) *1903:* **6** Cremer (William) *1905:* **7** Suttner (Bertha von) *1906:* **9** Roosevelt (Theodore) *1907:* **6** Moneta (Ernesto)

7 Renault (Louis) *1908:* 5 Bajer (Fredrik) 9 Arnoldson (Klas Pontus) *1909:* 9 Beernaert (Auguste) 13 d'Estournelles (Paul) *1911:* 5 Asser (Tobias), Fried (Alfred) *1912:* 4 Root (Elihu) *1913:* 10 La Fontaine (Henri) *1919:* 6 Wilson (Woodrow) *1920:* 9 Bourgeois (Léon) *1921:* 5 Lange (Christian Louis) 8 Branting (Karl Hjalmar) *1922:* 6 Nansen (Fridtjof) *1925:* 5 Dawes (Charles) 11 Chamberlain (Austen) *1926:* 6 Briand (Aristide) 10 Stresemann (Gustav) *1927:* 6 Quidde (Ludwig) 7 Buisson (Ferdinand) *1929:* 7 Kellogg (Frank) *1930:* 9 Soderblom (Nathan) *1931:* 6 Addams (Jane), Butler (Nicholas Murray) *1933:* 6 Angell (Norman) *1934:* 9 Henderson (Arthur) *1935:* 9 Ossietzky (Carl von) *1936:* 13 Saavedra Lamas (Carlos de) *1937:* 5 Cecil (Robert) *1945:* 4 Hull (Cordell) *1946:* 4 Mott (John) 5 Balch (Emily Greene) *1949:* 3 Orr (John Boyd) *1950:* 6 Bunche (Ralph) *1951:* 7 Jouhaux (Léon) *1952:* 10 Schweitzer (Albert) *1953:* 8 Marshall (George) *1957:* 7 Pearson (Lester) *1958:* 4 Pire (Dominique Georges) *1959:* 9 Noel-Baker (Philip) *1960:* 7 Luthuli (Albert John) *1961:* 12 Hammarskjold (Dag) *1962:* 7 Pauling (Linus) *1964:* 4 King (Martin Luther) *1968:* 6 Cassin (René) *1970:* 7 Borlaug (Norman) *1971:* 6 Brandt (Willy) *1973:* 8 Le Duc Tho 9 Kissinger (Henry) *1974:* 4 Sato (Eisaku) 8 MacBride (Sean) *1975:* 8 Sakharov (Andrey) *1976:* 8 Corrigan (Mairead), Williams (Betty) *1978:* 5 Begin (Menachem), Sadat (Anwar el-) *1979:* 12 Mother Teresa *1980:* 8 Esquivel (Adolfo Pérez) *1982:* 6 Myrdal (Alva) 12 García Robles (Alfonso) *1983:* 6 Walesa (Lech) *1984:* 4 Tutu (Desmond) *1986:* 6 Wiesel (Elie) *1987:* 12 Arias Sánchez (Oscar) *1989:* 9 Dalai Lama *1990:* 9 Gorbachev (Mikhail) *1991:* 13 Aung San Suu Kyi *1992:* 6 Menchú (Rigoberta) *1993:* 7 de Klerk (F. W.), Mandela (Nelson) *1994:* 5 Peres (Shimon), Rabin (Yitzhak) 6 Arafat (Yasir) *1995:* 7 Rotblat (Joseph) *1996:* 10 Ramos-Horta (José) 11 Ximenes Belo (Carlos Felipe) *1997:* 8 Williams (Jody) *1998:* 4 Hume (John) 7 Trimble (David) *2000:* 3 Kim (Daejung) 10 Kim Dae-jung *2001:* 5 Annan (Kofi) *2002:* 6 Carter (Jimmy) *2003:* 5 Ebadi (Shirin) *2004:* 7 Maathai (Wangari)
physics:
1901: 8 Roentgen (Wilhelm) *1902:*

6 Zeeman (Pieter) 7 Lorentz (Hendrik Antoon) *1903:* 5 Curie (Marie, Pierre) 9 Becquerel (Antoine-Henri) *1904:* 6 Strutt (John) 8 Rayleigh (Lord) *1905:* 6 Lenard (Philipp von) *1906:* 7 Thomson (Joseph) *1907:* 9 Michelson (Albert) *1908:* 8 Lippmann (Gabriel) *1909:* 5 Braun (Karl) 7 Marconi (Guglielmo) *1910:* 11 van der Waals (Johannes) *1911:* 4 Wien (Wilhelm) *1912:* 5 Dalen (Nils) *1914:* 4 Laue (Max von) *1915:* 5 Bragg (William) *1917:* 6 Barkla (Charles) *1918:* 6 Planck (Max) *1919:* 5 Stark (Johannes) *1920:* 9 Guillaume (Charles) *1921:* 8 Einstein (Albert) *1922:* 4 Bohr (Niels) *1923:* 8 Millikan (Robert) *1924:* 8 Siegbahn (Karl) *1925:* 5 Hertz (Gustav) 6 Franck (James) *1926:* 6 Perrin (Jean-Baptiste) *1927:* 6 Wilson (Charles) 7 Compton (Arthur) *1928:* 10 Richardson (Owen) *1929:* 7 Broglie (Louis-Victor de) *1930:* 5 Raman (Chandrasekhara) *1932:* 10 Heisenberg (Werner) *1933:* 5 Dirac (Paul) 11 Schrödinger (Erwin) *1935:* 8 Chadwick (James) *1936:* 4 Hess (Victor) 8 Anderson (Carl) *1937:* 7 Thomson (George) 8 Davisson (Clinton) *1938:* 5 Fermi (Enrico) *1939:* 8 Lawrence (Ernest) *1943:* 5 Stern (Otto) *1944:* 4 Rabi (Isidor Isaac) *1945:* 5 Pauli (Wolfgang) *1946:* 8 Bridgman (Percy) *1947:* 8 Appleton (Edward) *1948:* 8 Blackett (Patrick) *1949:* 6 Yukawa (Hideki) *1950:* 6 Powell (Cecil) *1951:* 6 Walton (Ernest) 9 Cockcroft (John) *1952:* 5 Bloch (Felix) 7 Purcell (Edward) *1953:* 7 Zernike (Frits) *1954:* 4 Born (Max) 5 Bothe (Walther) *1955:* 4 Lamb (Willis) 5 Kusch (Polykarp) *1956:* 7 Bardeen (John) 8 Brattain (Walter), Shockley (William) *1957:* 3 Lee (Tsung Dao) 4 Yang (Chen Ning) *1958:* 4 Tamm (Igor) 5 Frank (Ilya) 9 Cherenkov (Pavel) *1959:* 5 Segrè (Emilio) 11 Chamberlain (Owen) *1960:* 6 Glaser (Donald) *1961:* 9 Mossbauer (Rudolf) 10 Hofstadter (Robert) *1962:* 6 Landau (Lev) *1963:* 5 Mayer (Maria) 6 Jensen (J. Hans), Wigner (Eugene) *1964:* 5 Basov (Nikolay) 6 Townes (Charles) 9 Prochorov (Alexander) *1965:* 7 Feynman (Richard) 8 Tomonaga (Shinichiro) 9 Schwinger (Julian) *1966:* 7 Kastler (Alfred) *1967:* 5 Bethe (Hans) *1968:* 7 Alvarez (Luis) *1969:* 8 Gell-Mann (Murray) *1970:* 4 Néel (Louis) 6 Alfven (Hannes) *1971:* 5 Gabor (Dennis) *1972:* 6 Cooper (Leon) 7 Bardeen (John) 10 Schrieffer

(John) *1973:* 5 Esaki (Leo) 7 Giaever (Ivar) 9 Josephson (Brian) *1974:* 4 Ryle (Martin) 6 Hewish (Antony) *1975:* 4 Bohr (Aage) 9 Mottelson (Ben), Rainwater (L. James) *1976:* 4 Ting (Samuel) 7 Richter (Burton) *1977:* 4 Mott (Nevill) 8 Anderson (Philip), Van Vleck (John) *1978:* 6 Wilson (Robert) 7 Kapitsa (Pyotr), Penzias (Arno) *1979:* 5 Salam (Abdus) 7 Glashow (Sheldon) 8 Weinberg (Steven) *1980:* 5 Fitch (Val) 6 Cronin (James) *1981:* 8 Schawlow (Arthur), Siegbahn (Kai) 11 Bloembergen (Nicholaas) *1982:* 6 Wilson (Kenneth) *1983:* 6 Fowler (William) 13 Chandrasekhar (Subrahmanyan) *1984:* 6 Rubbia (Carlo) 11 van der Meere (Simon) *1985:* 8 Klitzing (Klaus von) *1986:* 5 Ruska (Ernst) 6 Binnig (Gerd), Rohrer (Heinrich) *1987:* 6 Müller (K. Alex) 7 Bednorz (J. Georg) *1988:* 8 Lederman (Leon), Schwartz (Melvin) 11 Steinberger (Jack) *1989:* 4 Paul (Wolfgang) 6 Ramsey (Norman) 7 Dehmelt (Hans) *1990:* 6 Taylor (Richard) 7 Kendall (Henry) 8 Friedman (Jerome) *1991:* 8 De Gennes (Pierre-Gilles) *1992:* 7 Charpak (Georges) *1993:* 5 Hulse (Russell) 6 Taylor (Joseph) *1994:* 5 Shull (Clifford) 10 Brockhouse (Bertram) *1995:* 4 Perl (Martin) 6 Reines (Frederick) *1996:* 3 Lee (David) 8 Osheroff (Douglas) 10 Richardson (Robert) 3 Chu (Steven) 8 Phillips (William) 14 Cohen-Tannoudji (Claude) *1998:* 4 Tsui (Daniel) 7 Störmer (Horst) 8 Laughlin (Robert) *1999:* 6 't Hooft (Gerardus) 7 Veltman (Martinus) *2000:* 5 Kilby (Jack) 7 Alferev (Zhores), Kroemer (Herbert) *2001:* 6 Wieman (Carl) 7 Cornell (Eric) 8 Ketterle (Wolfgang) *2002:* 5 Davis (Raymond) 7 Koshiba (Masatoshi) 8 Giacconi (Riccardo) *2003:* 7 Leggett (Anthony) 8 Ginzburg (Vitaly) 9 Abrikosov (Alexei) *2004:* 5 Gross (David) 7 Wilczek (Frank) 8 Politzer (David)

physiology or medicine:
1901: 7 Behring (Emil von) *1902:* 4 Ross (Ronald) *1903:* 6 Finsen (Niels Ryberg) *1904:* 6 Pavlov (Ivan) *1905:* 4 Koch (Robert) *1906:* 5 Golgi (Camillo) 11 Ramón y Cajal (Santiago) *1907:* 7 Laveran (Alphonse) *1908:* 7 Ehrlich (Paul) 11 Metchnikoff (Elie) *1909:* 6 Kocher (Emil) *1910:* 6 Kossel (Albrecht) *1911:* 10 Gullstrand (Allvar) *1912:* 6 Carrel (Alexis) *1913:* 6 Richet (Charles) *1914:* 6 Barany

(Robert) *1919:* 6 Bordet (Jules) *1920:* 5 Krogh (August) *1922:* 4 Hill (Archibald) 8 Meyerhof (Otto) *1923:* 7 Banting (Frederick), Macleod (John) *1924:* 9 Einthoven (Willem) *1926:* 7 Fibiger (Johannes) *1927:* 13 Wagner-Jauregg (Julius) *1928:* 7 Nicolle (Charles) *1929:* 7 Eijkman (Christiaan), Hopkins (Frederick) *1930:* 11 Landsteiner (Karl) *1931:* 7 Warburg (Otto) *1932:* 6 Adrian (Edgar) 11 Sherrington (Charles) *1933:* 6 Morgan (Thomas) *1934:* 5 Minot (George) 6 Murphy (William) 7 Whipple (George) *1935:* 7 Spemann (Hans) *1936:* 4 Dale (Henry) 5 Loewi (Otto) *1937:* 12 Szent-Györgyi (Albert) *1938:* 7 Heymans (Corneille) *1939:* 6 Domagk (Gerhard) *1943:* 3 Dam (Henrik) 5 Doisy (Edward) *1944:* 6 Gasser (Herbert) 8 Erlanger (Joseph) *1945:* 5 Chain (Ernst) 6 Florey (Howard) 7 Fleming (Alexander) *1946:* 6 Muller (Hermann) *1947:* 4 Cori (Carl, Gerty) 7 Houssay (Bernardo) *1948:* 7 Mueller (Paul) *1949:* 4 Hess (Walter) 5 Moniz (Antonio) *1950:* 5 Hench (Philip) 7 Kendall (Edward) 10 Reichstein (Tadeus) *1951:* 7 Theiler (Max) *1952:* 7 Waksman (Selman) *1953:* 5 Krebs (Hans) 7 Lipmann (Fritz) *1954:* 6 Enders (John), Weller (Thomas) 7 Robbins (Frederick) *1955:* 8 Theorell (Hugo) *1956:* 8 Cournand (André), Richards (Dickinson) 9 Forssmann (Werner) *1957:* 5 Bovet (Daniel) *1958:* 5 Tatum (Edward) 6 Beadle (George) 9 Lederberg (Joshua) *1959:* 5 Ochoa (Severo) 8 Kornberg (Arthur) *1960:* 6 Burnet (Macfarlane) 7 Medawar (Peter) *1961:* 6 Bekesy (Georg von) *1962:* 5 Crick (Francis) 6 Watson (James) 7 Wilkins (Maurice) *1963:* 6 Eccles (John), Huxley (Andrew) 7 Hodgkin (Alan) *1964:* 5 Bloch (Konrad), Lynen (Feodor) *1965:* 5 Jacob (Francois), Monod (Jacques) 5 Lwoff (André) *1966:* 4 Rous (Francis) 7 Huggins (Charles) *1967:* 4 Wald (George) 6 Granit (Ragnar) 8 Hartline (H. Keffer) *1968:* 6 Holley (Robert) 7 Khorana (H. Gobind) 9 Nirenberg (Marshall) *1969:* 5 Luria (Salvador) 7 Hershey (Alfred) 8 Delbruck (Max) *1970:* 4 Katz (Bernard) 5 Euler (Ulf von) 7 Axelrod (Julius) *1971:* 10 Sutherland (Earl) *1972:* 6 Porter (Rodney) 7 Edelman (Gerald) *1973:* 6 Frisch (Karl von), Lorenz (Konrad) 9 Tinbergen (Nikolaas) *1974:* 4 Duve (Christian)

6 Claude (Albert), Palade (George) *1975:* 5 Temin (Howard) 8 Dulbecco (Renato) 9 Baltimore (David) *1976:* 8 Blumberg (Baruch), Gajdusek (D. Carleton) *1977:* 5 Yalow (Rosalyn) 7 Schally (Andrew) 9 Guillemin (Roger) *1978:* 5 Arber (Werner), Smith (Hamilton) 7 Nathans (Daniel) *1979:* 7 Cormack (Allan) 10 Hounsfield (Godfrey) *1980:* 5 Snell (George) 7 Dausset (Jean) 10 Benacerraf (Baruj) *1981:* 5 Hubel (David) 6 Sperry (Roger), Wiesel (Torsten) *1982:* 4 Vane (John) 9 Bergstrom (Sune) 10 Samuelsson (Bengt) *1983:* 10 McClintock (Barbara) *1984:* 5 Jerne (Niels) 7 Koehler (Georges) 8 Milstein (Cesar) *1985:* 5 Brown (Michael) 9 Goldstein (Joseph) *1986:* 5 Cohen (Stanley) 14 Levi-Montalcini (Rita) *1987:* 8 Tonegawa (Susumu) *1988:* 5 Black (James), Elion (Gertrude) 9 Hitchings (George) *1989:* 6 Bishop (J. Michael), Varmus (Harold) *1990:* 6 Murray (Joseph), Thomas (E. Donnall) *1991:* 5 Neher (Erwin) 7 Sakmann (Bert) *1992:* 5 Krebs (Edwin) 7 Fischer (Edmond) *1993:* 5 Sharp (Phillip) 7 Roberts (Richard) *1994:* 6 Gilman (Alfred) 7 Rodbell (Martin) *1995:* 5 Lewis (Edward) 9 Wieschaus (Eric) 15 Nüsslein-Volhard (Christiane) *1996:* 7 Doherty (Peter) 11 Zinkernagel (Rolf) *1997:* 8 Prusiner (Stanley) *1998:* 5 Murad (Ferid) 7 Ignarro (Louis) 9 Furchgott (Robert) *1999:* 6 Blobel (Günter) *2000:* 6 Kandel (Eric) 8 Carlsson (Arvid) 9 Greengard (Paul) *2001:* 4 Hunt (Tim) 5 Nurse (Paul) 8 Hartwell (Leland) *2002:* 7 Brenner (Sydney), Horvitz (Robert), Sulston (John) *2003:* 9 Lauterbur (Paul), Mansfield (Peter) 4 Axel (Richard), Buck (Linda)
Nobel's invention 8 dynamite
nobility 6 virtue 7 dignity, peerage, royalty 8 eminence, noblesse 9 loftiness 10 exaltation, excellence, worthiness 11 aristocracy, superiority, uprightness
noble 4 peer 5 grand, lofty, moral 6 august, lordly, titled, worthy 7 courtly, eminent, exalted, notable, stately, sublime, upright 8 baronial, elevated, generous, gracious, heroical, highborn, highbred, imposing, magnific, majestic, princely, sterling, virtuous, wellborn 9 dignified, estimable, excellent, grandiose, honorable, righteous 10 high-minded, impressive, principled 11 illustrious, magnanimous, magnifi-

cent, outstanding, right-minded 12 aristocratic
nobleman 4 duke, earl, peer 5 baron, count 6 prince 7 baronet, marquis 8 marquess, viscount *French:* 5 comte 7 vicomte *German:* 4 Graf 8 margrave 9 landgrave *Indian:* 6 sardar, sirdar 8 maharaja 9 maharajah *Italian:* 8 marchese *Japanese (former):* 6 daimyo *Scandinavian:* 4 jarl *Spanish:* 7 hidalgo
noblewoman 4 lady 7 baronne, duchess, peeress 8 baroness, countess, princess 11 marchioness, viscountess *French:* 8 marquise *Italian:* 8 marchesa
nobody 4 zero 6 cipher 7 nothing, nullity, upstart 9 nonentity 11 lightweight, small potato
nocturnal 7 nightly 9 nighttime
nocuous 3 bad 6 nocent 7 harmful, hurtful 8 damaging 9 injurious 11 deleterious, destructive, detrimental, mischievous
nod 3 bob, err 4 doze, okay 5 agree, droop, slump 6 assent, invite, signal 7 approve 8 approval 10 acceptance
nodding 6 casual, slight 7 passing 8 drooping 9 pendulous 11 superficial
noddle 3 nob, nut 4 bean, head, pate, poll 6 noggin
noddy 3 oaf 4 boob, clod, dodo, dolt, dope, fool, goof, mutt, simp, yo-yo 5 chump, dummy, dunce, moron, ninny, stupe 6 dimwit, donkey, dumdum 7 airhead, dullard, pinhead, schnook 8 bonehead, clodpoll, dumbbell, dumbhead, imbecile, lunkhead, meathead, numskull 9 birdbrain, blockhead, ignoramus, lamebrain, numbskull, simpleton, thickhead 10 dunderhead, hammerhead, nincompoop 11 chowderhead, chucklehead, knucklehead
node 4 bump, burl, knob, knot, lump, mass 5 bulge, point 6 growth, vertex 8 swelling 11 enlargement, predicament 12 entanglement, protuberance
Noel 4 Xmas 5 carol 9 Christmas
nog 3 ale 4 beer, brew, malt, suds 5 lager, stout
noggin 3 cup, mug, nip, nob, nut 4 bean, gill, head, pate, poll 6 noddle, noodle
no-good 3 bum, dud 4 base, vile, worm 5 loser 6 scurvy, wretch 7 dirtbag, inutile, lowlife, rounder, wastrel 8 deadbeat, shameful, unworthy, wretched 9 no-account, valueless, worthless 10 ne'er-do-well, profligate, scapegrace 11 ignominious 12 contemptible, disreputable 13 reprehensible
noise 3 din 4 blab, talk 5 babel, rumor,

sound **6** clamor, gossip, hubbub, racket, ruckus, rumpus, tattle, uproar **7** ruction, sonance, stridor **8** resonant **11** pandemonium

noiseless 4 hush, mute **5** muted, quiet, still, whist **6** hushed, silent, stilly **9** soundless

noisemaker 4 horn **6** rattle **7** clapper

noisome 4 foul, rank, vile **5** fetid, funky, fusty, musty, nasty **6** filthy, horrid, putrid, rancid, smelly **7** harmful, noxious, squalid **8** stinking **9** obnoxious, offensive, repulsive, revolting, sickening **10** disgusting, malodorous, nauseating

noisy 4 loud **5** rowdy **7** blatant, booming, clamant, rackety, raucous, squeaky **8** clattery, strident **9** clamorous, deafening, turbulent **10** boisterous, chattering, clangorous, tumultuous, uproarious, vociferous **11** conspicuous **12** earsplitting, obstreperous

nomad 5 gypsy, rover **7** migrant, rambler **8** vagabond, wanderer *Arabic:* **7** bedouin

nomadic 5 gypsy **6** roving **7** roaming, vagrant **8** drifting, vagabond **9** itinerant, migratory, wandering, wayfaring **11** peripatetic **13** perambulatory

nom de plume see PEN NAME

nomen 4 name **7** moniker **11** appellation, designation

nomenclature 4 list, name **7** catalog **8** glossary, taxonomy **11** appellation, designation, phraseology, terminology **12** codification

nominal 3 low **5** given, named, rated, small **6** formal, puppet **7** alleged, minimal, seeming, titular **8** apparent, so-called, trifling **9** pretended, professed **10** ostensible **11** approximate, inexpensive **12** satisfactory, substantival **13** insignificant

nominate 3 tap **4** call, name **5** offer, put up **7** appoint, propose, suggest **9** designate, recommend

nominee 6 choice **8** aspirant **9** candidate, contender **10** contestant

nonage 5 youth **7** infancy **8** minority **9** childhood **10** immaturity, juvenility

nonchalant 4 cool, easy **5** blase **6** casual, mellow, serene **7** offhand **8** carefree, careless, cheerful, composed, laid-back **9** collected, easygoing, incurious, unruffled **10** effortless, insouciant, untroubled **11** indifferent, unconcerned, unflappable, unperturbed **12** lighthearted **13** dispassionate, imperturbable, lackadaisical

noncommittal 7 neutral **8** reserved **9** impassive **10** disengaged

nonconformist 5 rebel **7** beatnik, heretic, oddball, offbeat, radical **8** bohemian, maverick **9** dissenter, dissident, eccentric, heretical, heterodox, protester, sectarian **10** schismatic, separatist, unorthodox **11** misbeliever, schismatist

nonconformity 6 heresy, schism **7** dissent **9** misbelief, recusancy **10** dissidence, heterodoxy, opposition **11** unorthodoxy **12** disaffection **13** individualism, noncompliance

nonentity 4 zero **5** aught, zilch **6** cipher, nobody **7** nothing, nullity, whiffet **8** unperson **10** figurehead, mouthpiece

nonesuch 5 ideal **7** epitome, paragon, pattern **8** exemplar, paradigm, standard **9** archetype, matchless, nonpareil, unequaled, unrivaled

nonetheless 3 yet **5** still **6** anyway, though, withal **7** howbeit, however **8** although, after all **10** regardless **11** still and all

nonexistence 4 nada, void **7** nullity, vacuity **11** nothingness

nonflammable 9 fireproof **10** unburnable **13** incombustible

non-Hawaiian 5 haole

non-Jewish 3 goy **6** goyish **7** gentile

non-Muslim 6 giaour

no-nonsense 5 grave, sober **6** solemn **7** earnest, serious **8** resolute **9** pragmatic, realistic **10** determined, hardheaded, sobersided **11** plainspoken **12** businesslike **13** unsentimental

nonpareil see NONESUCH

nonpartisan 7 neutral **8** unbiased **9** equitable, impartial, objective, uncolored **10** nonaligned **11** independent **12** unprejudiced

nonplus 4 faze **5** stump **6** baffle, boggle, muddle, puzzle, rattle, stymie **7** buffalo, confuse, dilemma, flummox, fluster, mystify, perplex, stagger **8** bewilder, confound, distract, overcome, paralyze, quandary **9** discomfit, dumbfound, frustrate **10** disconcert

nonresistant 6 docile, pliant **7** passive, pliable **8** resigned, yielding **9** complying, tractable **10** conforming, submissive **11** acquiescent, conformable **13** accommodating

nonsense 3 rot **4** blah, bosh, bull, bunk, crap, gook, guff, jazz, punk, tosh **5** bilge, crock, drool, folly, fudge, Greek, hokum, hooey, trash **6** babble, blague, bunkum, drivel, hot air, humbug, jabber, piffle **7** baloney, blather, eyewash, flubdub, foolery, fooling, hogwash, inanity, rubbish, trifles, twaddle **8** buncombe, claptrap, falderal, folderol, flimflam, malarkey, pishposh, slipslop, tommyrot, trumpery **9** gibberish, moonshine, poppycock **10** applesauce, balderdash, double-talk, flapdoodle, tomfoolery **11** jabberwocky **12** blatherskite, fiddle-faddle, fiddlesticks **13** horsefeathers *British:* **10** codswallop

nonsensical 5 crazy, daffy, flaky, goofy, inane, kooky, loony, nutty, silly, wacky **6** absurd, screwy **7** foolish, idiotic, risible **9** illogical, laughable, ludicrous, senseless **10** irrational **12** preposterous, unreasonable

nonviolent 6 irenic **7** pacific **8** pacifist **9** peaceable **10** pacifistic

noodle 3 oaf **4** bean, boob, clod, dodo, dope, goof, head, mutt, poll, simp, yo-yo **5** chump, dummy, dunce, idiot, moron, ninny, noddy, stupe **6** dimwit, donkey, dum-dum, nitwit, noggin **7** airhead, dullard, pinhead, schnook **8** bonehead, clodpoll, dumbbell, dumbhead, imbecile, lunkhead, meathead, numskull **9** birdbrain, blockhead, ignoramus, lamebrain, numbskull, simpleton **10** dunderhead, hammerhead, nincompoop **11** chowderhead, chucklehead, knucklehead

nook 3 bay **4** cove **5** hutch, niche **6** alcove, cavity, corner, cranny, recess **9** cubbyhole **11** compartment

noose 3 tie **4** bait, bind, hang, loop, lure, trap **5** lasso, snare **6** entrap, secure

norm 3 par **4** mean, rule, type **5** gauge, maxim, model **6** median **7** average, measure, pattern **8** paradigm, standard **9** benchmark, criterion **10** touchstone

Norma *composer:* **7** Bellini (Vincenzo) *librettist:* **6** Romani (Felice)

normal 4 sane **5** usual **6** common **7** average, general, natural, regular, typical **8** ordinary, standard **9** customary, prevalent **11** commonplace, traditional **12** conventional **13** perpendicular

Normandy's capital 5 Rouen

Norns 5 fates, Skuld, Urdur **9** Verthandi

Norris novel 3 Pit (The) **4** Blix **7** Octopus (The) **8** McTeague

Norse *abode of the dead:* **8** Niflheim *alphabet:* **5** Runic *archer:* **4** Egil *bard:* **5** scald, skald *chieftain:* **4** jarl, Rolf **5** Rollo *demon:* **4** Mara, Surt **5** Surtr *dragon:* **6** Fafnir **7** Nithhogg *epic:* **4** Edda *explorer:* **4** Erik, Leif **8** Ericsson (Leif), Eriksson (Leif) *first man:* **3** Ask **4** Askr *first woman:* **5** Embla *giant:* **4** Egil, Wade, Wate, Ymer, Ymir **5** Aegir, Egill, Hymir, Jotun, Mimir **6** Fafnir, Jotunn *giantess:* **4** Egia, Norn, Nott *god:* **3** Asa, Ass **4** Surt, Vali, Vili

5 Aesir (plural), Surtr, Vanir (plural) **6** Hoenir, Vithar **7** Vitharr *blind:* **4** Hoth **5** Hoder, Hodur, Hothr *chief:* **4** Odin **5** Othin, Wodan, Woden, Wotan *guardian:* **7** Heimdal **8** Heimdall **9** Heimdallr *messenger:* **6** Hermod **7** Hermodr *of beauty:* **5** Baldr **6** Balder, Baldur *of evil:* **4** Loke, Loki *of fertility:* **4** Frey **5** Freyr *of justice:* **7** Forsete, Forseti *of light:* **3** Dag *of peace:* **5** Baldr **6** Balder, Baldur *of poetry:* **5** Brage, Bragi *of the hunt:* **3** Ull **4** Ullr *of the seas:* **5** Njord **6** Njoerd, Njorth **4** Hler **5** Aegir, Gymir *of the sky:* **4** Odin **5** Othin *of thunder:* **4** Thor **5** Donar *of war:* **3** Tiu, Tiw, Tyr, Zio, Ziu *wolf:* **6** Fenrir *goddess:* **3** dis **4** Saga **5** disir (plural) **7** Asynjur *of fate:* **3** Urd **4** Norn, Urth, Wyrd **5** Skuld **9** Verthandi *of healing:* **3** Eir *of love:* **5** Freya *of marriage:* **5** Frigg **6** Frigga *of night:* **4** Natt, Nott *of storms:* **3** Ran *of the earth:* **5** Joerd, Jorth *of the moon:* **5** Nanna *of the sea:* **3** Ran *of the sky:* **5** Frigg **6** Frigga *of the underworld:* **3** Hel **4** Hela *of youth:* **4** Idun **5** Ithun **6** Ithunn *gods' abode:* **6** Asgard *hall of heroes:* **8** Valhalla *king:* **4** Atli, Olaf *nobleman:* **4** jarl *patron saint:* **4** Olaf *poem:* **4** rune *poet:* **5** scald, skald *rainbow bridge:* **7** Bifrost *sea serpent:* **4** Wade, Wate **6** kraken **7** Midgard *smith:* **6** Völund *tale:* **4** saga *toast:* **5** skoal *watchdog:* **4** Garm **5** Garmr *world's destruction:* **8** Ragnarok *world tree:* **8** Ygdrasil **10** Yggdrasill

north *combining form:* **4** arct **5** arcto

North African *country:* **5** Egypt, Libya **7** Algeria, Morocco, Tunisia *fruit:* **3** fig **4** date *garment:* **4** haik *grass:* **4** alfa **7** esparto *jackal:* **4** dieb *language:* **6** Arabic, Berber *Muslim sect:* **6** Sanusi **7** Senussi *people:* **6** Berber, Hamite **7** bedouin *seaport:* **4** Oran, Sfax **6** Annaba **7** Tangier **10** Casablanca

North America *country:* **6** Canada, Mexico, Panama **8** Honduras **9** Costa Rica, Guatemala, Nicaragua **10** El Salvador **12** United States

North Carolina *capital:* **7** Raleigh *city:* **6** Durham **9** Asheville, Charlotte **10** Greensboro **12** Winston-Salem *college, university:* **4** Duke, Elon **10** Wake Forest *mountain, range:* **8** Mitchell **9** Blue Ridge **10** Great Smoky *nickname:* **7** Tar Heel (State) *state bird:* **8** cardinal *state flower:* **7** dogwood *state tree:* **4** pine

North Dakota *capital:* **8** Bismarck *city:* **5** Fargo, Minot **10** Grand Forks *nickname:* **5** Sioux (State) **11** Flickertail (State) *river:* **3** Red **8** Missouri *state bird:*

10 meadowlark *state flower:* **11** prairie rose *state tree:* **3** elm (American)

northern 4 pike **6** boreal **11** hyperborean

Northern Mariana Islands *commonwealth of:* **12** United States *discoverer:* **8** Magellan (Ferdinand) *island:* **4** Rota **6** Saipan, Tinian

North Star State 9 Minnesota

Northwest Passage author 7 Roberts (Kenneth)

Northwest Territories *capital:* **11** Yellowknife *gulf:* **8** Amundsen *island:* **5** Banks **8** Victoria *lake:* **9** Great Bear **10** Great Slave *river:* **9** Mackenzie *sea:* **8** Beaufort

north wind see at WIND

Norway *Arctic region:* **7** Lapland *cape:* **7** Nordkyn *capital:* **4** Oslo *city:* **6** Bergen **9** Stavanger, Trondheim *inlet:* **9** Skagerrak *island:* **5** Senja **6** Sørøya **8** Magerøya, Steinsøy **10** Nord-Kvaløy, Ringvassøy *island group:* **7** Lofoten **10** Vesterålen *lake:* **5** Mjøsa *monetary unit:* **5** krone *mountain range:* **6** Kjølen **11** Jotunheimen *neighbor:* **6** Russia, Sweden **7** Finland *part of:* **11** Scandinavia *port:* **5** Vardø **6** Tromsø **8** Kirkenes **10** Hammerfest *river:* **4** Tana **5** Glåma, Lågen **9** Dramselva *sea:* **5** North

Norwegian *goblin:* **5** nisse *language:* **5** Norse **6** Bokmal **7** Bokmaal, Nynorsk, Riksmal **8** Landsmal, Riksmaal **9** Landsmaal

nose 3 pry **4** beak, bent, bump, gift, head, poke **5** aroma, flair, knack, scent, smell, sniff, snift, snoop, snoot, snout, snuff **6** genius, muzzle, nuzzle, talent **7** aptness, faculty, smeller, sneezer **8** smell out **9** olfaction, proboscis, schnozzle *French:* **3** nez *kind:* **3** pug **5** Roman **8** aquiline *lengthener:* **3** lie *opening:* **7** nostril

nosebleed 9 epistaxis

nosedive 4 drop, fall **6** header, plunge **7** plummet

nosegay 4 posy **6** flower **7** bouquet, corsage **11** boutonniere

nosh 4 bite **5** graze, munch, snack **6** nibble

Nostradamus 7 prophet

Nostromo author 6 Conrad (Joseph)

nostrum 4 cure **6** elixir, remedy **7** cure-all, panacea **8** antidote, medicine **10** catholicon, corrective **11** restorative

nosy 6 prying, snoopy **7** curious, peeping **8** snooping **9** intrusive **11** inquisitive, inquisitory

notability 3 VIP **4** lion, star **5** celeb, chief **6** leader, worthy **7** big name, big shot **8** big-timer, eminence, luminary, presence, somebody **9** celebrity, chieftain, dignitary, personage, superstar **11** personality

notable 3 VIP **4** star **5** celeb, chief, famed, mogul, nabob, power **6** big boy, biggie, big gun, bigwig, famous, fat cat, leader, prince **7** big name, big shot, eminent, magnate, pooh-bah **8** big chief, big-timer, big wheel, eminence, luminary, renowned, somebody, striking **9** big cheese, celebrity, character, dignitary, distingué, personage, prominent, superstar **10** celebrated, celebrious, noteworthy, remarkable **11** conspicuous, heavyweight, illustrious, muckety-muck, personality **13** distinguished, high-muck-a-muck

notarize 7 certify, endorse **8** validate **12** authenticate

notch 3 cut, gap, jag **4** gash, mark, nick, nock, rung, slit, step **5** cleft, grade, score, stage **6** degree, groove, indent, rabbet, record **7** achieve, scratch **8** incision, undercut **11** indentation

note 3 jot **4** bond, chit, heed, mark, memo, show, sign, tone **5** catch, sound, token **6** letter, notice, record, regard **7** comment, discern, jotting, missive, observe, promise, set down **8** eminence, indicate, perceive, reminder **9** attention, knowledge **10** cognizance, commentary, memorandum, observance, reputation **11** distinction, distinguish, observation

notebook 3 log **5** diary **7** journal

noted 6 famous **7** eminent, leading, popular **8** esteemed, renowned, striking **9** acclaimed, prominent, well-known **10** celebrated, recognized, remarkable **11** illustrious **13** distinguished

noteworthy 7 salient **8** singular, striking **9** arresting, bodacious, memorable, prominent, red-letter **10** impressive, meaningful, remarkable **11** conspicuous, exceptional, high-profile, major-league, outstanding, significant **12** considerable **13** extraordinary

nothing 3 nil, nix **4** zero **5** aught, nihil, zilch **6** cipher, naught, nobody, nought, trifle **7** nullity, whiffet **8** goose egg, whipster **9** no-account, nonentity *French:* **4** rien *German:* **6** nichts *Latin:* **5** nihil *Spanish:* **4** nada

nothingness 4 nada, void **5** death **6** vacuum **7** nullity, vacuity **9** emptiness **12** nonexistence

notice 3 see **4** espy, heed, mark, memo **5** catch, sight **6** descry, regard, review **7** discern, observe, respect **8** handbill, perceive **9** attention, directive, recognize **10** cognizance, evaluation **11** dec-

laration, information, observation
12 announcement, proclamation
13 communication
noticeable 6 marked, patent, signal
7 evident, obvious, pointed, salient
8 apparent, manifest, striking **9** arresting, prominent **10** noteworthy, observable, remarkable **11** appreciable, conspicuous, eye-catching, outstanding, perceptible, significant **12** unmistakable
notify 3 cue **4** tell, warn **5** alert, brief
6 advise, clue in, fill in, inform
7 apprise **8** acquaint **9** enlighten
notion 4 clue, hint, idea, whim **5** fancy
6 belief, maggot, theory, vagary
7 caprice, conceit, concept, inkling, thought **8** crotchet **10** conception, impression, intimation, perception
11 inclination
notional 5 ideal **6** unreal **7** fancied, fictive **8** fanciful, illusory, imagined
9 imaginary, visionary, whimsical
10 capricious, conceptual **11** speculative, theoretical **12** hypothetical
notoriety 4 fame **6** infamy, renown
7 obloquy **9** disrepute **10** opprobrium, prominence **11** recognition
notorious 5 noted **6** famous **8** ill-famed, infamous **9** prominent, well-known
10 outrageous, scandalous **12** disreputable
Notus 6 Auster *brother:* **5** Eurus **6** Boreas
8 Zephyrus *father:* **6** Aeolus **8** Astraeus *mother:* **3** Eos
noun 4 name **7** nominal **11** substantive *inflectional form:* **4** case *verbal:* **6** gerund
nourish 4 feed, rear **5** nurse, raise **6** foster **7** bring up, build up, nurture, promote, support **8** maintain **9** cultivate, encourage **10** provide for, strengthen
nourishment 3 pap **4** diet, eats, feed, food, grub **6** viands **7** aliment, pabulum, vittles **8** victuals **9** nutriment, provender **10** sustenance
____ **nous 5** entre
nouveau riche 7 parvenu, upstart
9 arriviste
Nova Scotia *capital:* **7** Halifax *city:*
9 Dartmouth *island:* **10** Cape Breton *lake:* **7** Bras D'Or *provincial flower:*
9 mayflower
novel 3 new, odd **5** fresh **6** unique **7** offbeat, unusual **8** atypical, original, peculiar, singular, uncommon **9** different, narrative **10** avant-garde, innovative, newfangled
novelist see AUTHOR
novelty 5 curio **6** bauble, gewgaw, oddity, trifle **7** bibelot, gimmick, newness, trinket, whatnot **8** gimcrack, souvenir

9 bagatelle, curiosity, objet d'art
10 innovation, knickknack
novice 3 cub **4** colt, punk, tyro **6** rookie
7 amateur, learner, recruit, student, trainee **8** aspirant, beginner, freshman, neophyte, newcomer, prentice **9** fledgling, greenhorn, novitiate, postulant
10 apprentice, tenderfoot **11** probationer
Novum Organum author 5 Bacon (Francis)
now 3 PDQ **4** soon **5** today **6** at once, pronto **7** anymore, present **8** directly, first off, promptly **9** forthwith, instanter, instantly, presently, right away, sometimes **11** immediately, straightway
12 straightaway
now and then 7 at times, betimes
9 sometimes **12** infrequently, occasionally, periodically, sporadically
Nox *brother:* **6** Erebus *daughter:* **3** Day
4 Eris **5** Light *father:* **5** Chaos *husband:*
6 Erebus *son:* **6** Charon, Hypnos
8 Thanatos
noxious 4 foul **5** fetid, toxic **6** deadly, putrid **7** baneful, harmful, noisome
8 stinking **9** dangerous, pestilent, poisonous, unhealthy **10** corrupting, pernicious **11** deleterious, destructive, detrimental, pestiferous **12** disagreeable, pestilential
nozzle 4 nose, vent **5** spout **7** channel
nuance 4 hint **5** shade, tinge, touch, trace **6** nicety **7** shading, soupçon
8 overtone, subtlety **9** gradation, suspicion **10** refinement, suggestion **11** distinction
nub 4 core, crux, gist, knob, knot, lump, meat, node, pith **5** bulge, point, short
6 kernel, upshot **8** swelling **9** substance
10 projection **12** protuberance
Nubian 5 Mahas **6** Birked, Kenuzi, Midobi **7** Dongola **8** Cushitic
9 Chari-Nile
nubile 4 ripe **10** attractive **12** marriageable
nuchal 4 nape
nuclear agency 3 AEC, NRC
nuclear particle 5 meson **6** proton **7** neutron
nucleus 3 bud **4** core, germ, head, kern, ring, seed **5** focus, spark **6** embryo *material:* **8** karyotin
nude 3 raw **4** bald, bare **5** naked, stark
6 barren, peeled, unclad **8** disrobed, stripped **9** au naturel, buck naked, unattired, unclothed, uncovered, undressed **10** stark naked
nudge 3 dig, jab, jog **4** near, poke, prod, push **5** elbow, punch, shove **8** approach
nudnik 4 bore, drip, pill, twit **8** nuisance

nugatory 4 idle, vain **5** empty, inane, vapid **6** futile, hollow, otiose **7** invalid, vacuous **8** trifling **9** fruitless, worthless **11** inoperative, meaningless

nugget 3 gob, wad **4** hunk, lump, plum **5** chunk **6** tidbit

nuisance 4 pain, pest, pill **6** bother, nudnik **8** headache, irritant, pesterer, vexation **11** botheration

nuke 4 bomb **5** crush, smash **6** attack **7** destroy **8** demolish **9** eradicate, microwave **10** annihilate **11** exterminate

null 4 void, zero **5** annul, empty **6** futile **7** invalid, useless **8** nugatory **9** worthless **10** invalidate, obliterate, unavailing **11** ineffective, ineffectual, inoperative

nullify 3 zap **4** undo, veto, void **5** abate, annul, limit, quash, scrub, trash **6** cancel, efface, negate, offset, repeal, revoke, squash **7** abolish, rescind, scratch, take out, wipe out **8** abrogate **10** annihilate, compensate, counteract, invalidate, neutralize **11** countervail

nullity 4 nada, zero **5** zilch **6** cipher, nobody **7** nothing, vacuity, whiffet **9** annulment, nonentity **11** nothingness **12** nonexistence

numb 5 chill, dazed **6** deaden, freeze **7** callous **8** deadened, detached **9** insensate, paralyzed, stupefied, unfeeling **10** insensible, insentient **11** desensitize, indifferent **12** anesthetized, desensitized

number 5 add up, count, digit, run to, sum to, tally, total **6** amount, cipher, come to, figure **7** chiffer, include, integer, numeral, ordinal, run into, several, sum into **8** cardinal, numerate, paginate **9** aggregate, enumerate **added to another: 6** augend **resulting from division: 8** quotient **resulting from multiplication: 7** product **resulting from subtraction: 10** difference **science: 11** mathematics

number one 4 best, main **5** chief, major **6** finest, Grade A, top dog **7** capital, highest, leading, primary, stellar **8** dominant, five-star, foremost, superior **9** excellent, first-rate, front-rank, numero uno, principal, top-drawer **10** blue-ribbon, first-class, preeminent **11** first-string, outstanding, predominant

numbness 5 shock **6** stupor **10** anesthesia **12** stupefaction **combining form: 4** narc **5** narco

numeral 5 digit **6** cipher, figure, number **7** integer **11** whole number

numerate 4 list **5** count, tally **6** number **7** compute, itemize, tick off **8** tabulate **9** calculate

numerous 4 many **6** legion **7** profuse,

umpteen **8** abundant, populous **9** plentiful **10** voluminous **13** multitudinous

Numitor brother: 7 Amulius **daughter: 9** Rea Silvia **10** Rhea Silvia **grandson: 5** Remus **7** Romulus

numskull 3 oaf **4** boob, clod, dodo, dolt, dope, goof, mutt, simp **5** chump, dummy, dunce, idiot, moron, ninny, noddy, stupe **6** dimwit, donkey, dumdum, nitwit **7** airhead, dullard, pinhead, schnook **8** bonehead, clodpate, clodpoll, dumbbell, dumbhead, imbecile, lunkhead, meathead **9** birdbrain, blockhead, ignoramus, lamebrain, simpleton, thickhead **10** dunderhead, hammerhead, nincompoop **11** chowderhead, chucklehead, knucklehead

nun 6 sister **headcloth: 6** wimple

Nunavut capital: 7 Iqaluit **island: 5** Devon **6** Baffin **9** Ellesmere **11** Southampton **mountain: 7** Barbeau (Peak) **peninsula: 7** Boothia **8** Melville **provincial flower: 11** Arctic poppy

nunnery 7 convent **10** sisterhood **head: 8** superior

nuptial 6 bridal, wedded **7** marital, married, spousal, wedding **8** conjugal, espousal, hymeneal, marriage **9** connubial **11** matrimonial

nurse 4 feed, nana, rear, suck **5** nanny, serve **6** attend, foster, pamper, suckle **7** care for, cherish, nourish, nurture **9** cultivate **10** minister to **children's: 5** nanny **English: 11** Nightingale (Florence) **Indian: 4** ayah **Chinese: 4** amah

nursemaid 4 nana **5** nanny **6** minder, sitter **9** governess **10** babysitter **Indian: 4** ayah **Chinese: 4** amah

nursery 6 crèche **7** brooder **8** hothouse **9** fosterage **10** greenhouse **12** conservatory

nurture 4 care, feed, rear, tend **5** nurse, raise, train **6** cradle, foster **7** bring up, care for, develop, educate, nourish, rearing **8** breeding, instruct, training, tutelage **9** cultivate **10** upbringing

nut 3 bug **4** kook, loon **5** acorn, crank, fiend, freak, loony, pecan **6** almond, cashew, cuckoo, madman, maniac, zealot **7** fanatic, filbert, hickory, lunatic **8** crackpot **9** bedlamite, ding-a-ling, macadamia, pistachio, screwball **10** enthusiast, Tom o' Bedlam **of a violin bow: 4** frog, heel

Nut consort: 3 Geb, Keb **daughter: 4** Isis **8** Nephthys **son: 6** Osiris

nuthouse 6 asylum, bedlam **8** loony bin **9** funny farm **10** booby hatch **11** institution **12** insane asylum

Nutmeg State 11 Connecticut

nutria 5 coypu

nutriment 4 diet, fare, food, grub, keep **6** viands **7** aliment, pabulum **8** victuals **9** provender **10** provisions, sustenance **11** comestibles, nourishment, subsistence

nutrition 4 diet **7** vittles **8** victuals **10** sustenance **11** nourishment

nutritious 9 healthful, wholesome **10** alimentary, nourishing

nuts 3 mad **4** daft, keen, wild **5** batty, crazy, kooky, loony, rabid, wacky **6** absurd, cuckoo, insane, screwy **7** bonkers, cracked, excited, foolish, idiotic **8** animated, demented, deranged **9** exuberant, fanatical, screwball **10** passionate, unbalanced **12** enthusiastic

nutty see NUTS

nuzzle 3 rub **4** root, snug **5** nudge **6** burrow, cuddle, nestle **7** snuggle

Nycteus *brother:* **5** Lycus *daughter:* **7** Antiope

nymph 3 nix **5** dryad, larva, naiad, nixie, sylph **6** kelpie, maiden, sprite **7** mermaid *changed into a bear:* **8** Callisto *changed into a laurel:* **6** Daphne *changed into a rock:* **4** Echo *mountain:* **5** oread *sea:* **6** Nereid **7** Calypso *water:* **5** naiad **6** undine *wood:* **5** dryad

Nyx see NOX

O

oaf 4 boob, boor, bull, clod, dodo, dolt, goof, goon, hulk, lout, lump, slob **5** booby, chump, clown, dummy, dunce, klutz **6** dum-dum, galoot, lubber, lummox **7** fathead, palooka **8** bonehead, lunkhead, meathead **9** blockhead, blunderer, lamebrain, simpleton

oafish 5 dense **6** clumsy, klutzy, rustic **7** boorish, doltish, loutish **8** bungling, churlish, clownish, lubberly

oak *African:* **7** turtosa *fruit:* **5** acorn *genus:* **7** Quercus *kind:* **3** bur, pin, red **4** bear, cork, holm, ilex, live **5** black, holly, roble, white **6** barren, cerris, encina **7** durmast, English, moss-cup, valonia **9** blackjack *Mexican:* **8** chaparro *young:* **8** flittern

oar 3 row **4** pole, pull **5** rower, scull **6** paddle **7** paddler *part:* **4** loom, palm **5** blade, shaft **6** button, collar *pin:* **5** thole

oarsman 3 bow **5** rower **6** stroke **7** sculler *director:* **3** cox **8** coxswain

oasis 3 spa **4** wadi **6** refuge, relief *ancient:* **4** Merv *Egypt:* **4** Siwa **5** Gafsa **6** Dakhla **7** Farafra **8** Ammonium *Libya:* **5** Mizda, Sebha **6** Sabhah **7** Gadames **8** Ghudamis *Niger:* **5** Bilma *Saudi Arabia:* **5** Hofuf, Taima **7** Al-Hufuf

oast 4 kiln, oven

oat 5 grain, grass **6** cereal *genus:* **5** Avena *Scottish:* **3** ait

oater 7 western **10** horse opera

oath 3 vow **4** cuss **5** curse, swear **6** pledge **7** promise **8** cussword **9** expletive, profanity, swearword *mild:* **3** gee **4** darn, drat, egad, geez, gosh, jeez **5** golly **6** jiminy **7** gee whiz

oatmeal 5 gruel **6** burgoo **8** porridge *Scottish:* **8** drammock

obdurate 3 set **4** firm, hard **5** harsh, rigid, stony **6** dogged, mulish **7** adamant, callous **8** stubborn **9** heartless, immovable, unbending, unfeeling **10** hard-boiled, inflexible, unshakable, unyielding **11** coldhearted, hardhearted, insensitive, unemotional **12** intransigent, stonyhearted **13** unsympathetic

obeah 5 charm, magic

Obed *father:* **4** Boaz **6** Ephlal **8** Shemaiah *mother:* **4** Ruth *son:* **5** Jesse **7** Azariah

obedient 5 loyal **6** docile **7** devoted, duteous, dutiful, willing **8** amenable, biddable, obliging, yielding **9** compliant, tractable **10** law-abiding, manageable, respectful, submissive **11** acquiescent, cooperative, deferential, subservient

obeisance 3 bow **5** honor **6** curtsy, esteem, fealty, homage, kowtow, salaam **7** gesture, loyalty, respect **9** deference, reverence **10** allegiance, submission

obelisk 6 dagger, pillar, symbol

Oberon *messenger:* 4 Puck *wife:* 7 Titania
Oberto composer 5 Verdi (Giuseppe)
obese 3 fat 5 bulky, gross, heavy, tubby
6 fleshy 7 adipose, outsize, porcine
9 corpulent 10 overweight
obey 3 bow 4 heed, keep, mind 5 agree,
defer, serve, yield 6 accede, accept,
assent, comply, follow, regard, submit
7 abide by, conform, execute, fulfill,
observe, satisfy 8 adhere to, carry out
9 acquiesce
obfuscate 4 blur 5 cloud, muddy 6 darken 7 becloud, conceal, confuse, cover
up, obscure 9 adumbrate
obi 4 sash
obiter dictum 4 note 6 remark 7 comment, opinion 10 commentary, incidental 11 observation
obituary 9 necrology 11 death notice
object 3 aim, end, use 4 goal, idea, item,
kick, view, wish 5 being, cause, demur,
focus, frown, point, thing 6 design,
entity, except, intent, matter, motive,
oppose, target 7 article, dissent, protest,
purpose 8 complain, disagree, function,
material 9 criticize, intention, something 10 disapprove
objection 5 demur 7 protest 8 argument, demurral, demurrer, question
9 challenge, complaint, exception
10 difficulty, opposition 11 disapproval
12 disagreement, remonstrance
13 remonstration
objectionable 5 unfit 8 unwanted
9 abhorrent, invidious, loathsome,
obnoxious, offensive, repellent, repugnant, repulsive, revolting, unwelcome
10 ill-favored, unpleasant 11 displeasing, distasteful, undesirable 12 disagreeable
objective 3 aim, end 4 fair, goal, just,
lens, mark 6 actual, design, intent, target 7 mission, purpose 8 ambition,
function, material, physical, sensible,
unbiased 9 corporeal, equitable, impartial, intention 10 impersonal 11 independent, substantial 12 unprejudiced
13 dispassionate
objet d'art 5 curio, virtu (plural)
7 bibelot, novelty 10 knickknack
objurgate 5 chide, decry, scold 6 rebuke
7 censure, reprove, upbraid 8 admonish, reproach 9 castigate, reprimand
oblate 7 lay monk 9 flattened, religious
oblation 4 gift 6 corban 8 holy gift, offering 9 sacrifice 12 presentation
obligate 4 bind 7 require 8 encumber,
restrict 9 constrain
obligated 5 bound, owing 6 liable
8 beholden, indebted 11 accountable,
responsible

obligation 3 IOU, vow 4 bond, call, debt,
dues, duty, need, oath 5 cause 6 burden, charge, pledge 7 promise 8 business, contract 9 committal, liability,
necessity, restraint 10 commitment,
compulsion, constraint 11 requirement
12 indebtedness
obligatory 7 binding 8 required 9 essential, mandatory, necessary, requisite
10 compulsory, imperative 11 unavoidable
oblige 3 aid 4 bind, help, make 5 avail,
favor, force 6 assist, coerce, compel,
please, profit 7 benefit, command, gratify, require 9 constrain 10 contribute
11 accommodate, necessitate
obliged 4 made 5 bound 6 forced
8 beholden, grateful, indebted, thankful 11 constrained 12 appreciative
obliging 4 kind 5 civil 7 amiable, helpful,
willing 8 friendly, pleasant 11 complaisant, considerate, cooperative,
good-humored, good-natured 12 good-tempered
oblique 6 sloped, tilted 7 devious, leaning, obscure, sloping, tilting 8 inclined,
indirect 9 inclining 10 roundabout
obliterate 4 raze, x out 5 erase 6 cancel,
delete, efface, remove, rub out 7 blot
out, destroy, expunge, wipe out 8 black
out, cross out 10 annihilate
oblivion 5 lethe, limbo 7 amnesia, nirvana, nowhere 9 emptiness 11 nothingness 13 forgetfulness, insensibility
oblivious 4 lost 5 blind 7 unaware
8 absorbed, heedless, ignorant 9 forgetful, unknowing, unmindful, unwitting
10 unfamiliar, uninformed 11 inattentive, incognizant, unconscious
oblong 4 oval 5 ovate 7 ellipse 8 elongate
9 elongated, rectangle 11 rectangular
obloquy 4 slam, slur 5 abuse, odium,
shame 6 infamy, rebuke 7 calumny,
censure 8 disgrace, dishonor, ignominy
9 aspersion, contumely, discredit, disrepute, invective, stricture 10 defamation, opprobrium, scurrility 11 disapproval 12 billingsgate, condemnation,
vituperation
obnoxious 4 vile 5 awful 6 odious, rotten 7 hateful 9 abhorrent, invidious,
loathsome, offensive, repellent, repugnant, revulsive, sickening 10 abominable, detestable, disgusting
oboe 4 reed 7 hautboy 8 hautbois,
woodwind 10 double reed *early:*
5 shawm *relative:* 7 bassoon
11 English horn
O'Brian character 6 Aubrey (Jack)
7 Maturin (Stephen)
obscene 4 foul, lewd, rank, vile

5 bawdy, crass, crude, dirty, gross, lurid, taboo **6** coarse, filthy, impure, ribald, risqué, smutty, vulgar **7** immoral, noisome, profane, raunchy **8** indecent, scabrous **9** abhorrent, appalling, excessive, offensive, repellent, repugnant, repulsive, salacious **10** disgusting, lascivious, scurrilous **11** foulmouthed, unprintable **12** pornographic, scatological

obscure 3 dim **4** blur, hide, mask, veil **5** blind, cloak, cloud, cover, dusky, faint, minor, murky, shade, shady, vague **6** cloudy, darken, hidden, opaque, remote, screen, secret, shadow, shroud, veiled **7** clouded, conceal, cryptic, eclipse, removed, shadowy, unclear, unknown, unnoted **8** disguise, nameless, overcast, puzzling, secluded, shrouded **9** ambiguous, enigmatic, tenebrous, uncertain, undefined **10** camouflage, ill-defined, indefinite, indistinct, mysterious, overshadow **11** out-of-the-way, unimportant **12** inaccessible, unnoticeable **13** inconspicuous

obscurity 3 fog **4** haze, mist, murk **5** gloom **6** enigma, miasma, puzzle **7** dimness, mystery, shadows **8** darkness **9** ambiguity

obsequies 4 rite **5** rites **7** funeral **10** burial rite

obsequious 4 oily **6** abject **7** fawning, servile, slavish **8** obedient, obeisant, toadying, unctuous **9** parasitic **10** flattering, submissive **11** deferential, subservient, sycophantic

observance 4 rite, rule **6** custom, notice, regard, ritual **7** liturgy, service **8** ceremony, practice **9** adherence, attention, formality **10** ceremonial

observant 4 keen **5** alert, awake, aware, sharp **7** heedful, mindful **8** watchful **9** advertent, attentive **10** perceptive

observation 4 note **6** notice, record, regard, remark **7** comment, finding, opinion **8** judgment, notation **9** attention, inference **10** commentary **12** obiter dictum

observatory 5 tower **7** lookout, outlook **8** overlook *famous:* **4** Lick **6** Wilson, Yerkes **7** Palomar *instrument:* **9** telescope

observe 3 see **4** espy, keep, look, mark, mind, note, obey, twig, view **5** honor, opine, sight, state, study, watch **6** behold, comply, follow, look at, notice, remark **7** abide by, comment, conform, discern, respect **8** perceive **9** celebrate, solemnize **10** comply with **11** commemorate

obsess 5 beset, haunt, hound, rivet

6 absorb, plague **7** consume, possess **9** captivate, preoccupy

obsessed 6 dogged, driven, hipped, hooked **7** gripped, haunted, plagued **8** overcome, troubled **9** dominated, possessed **11** preoccupied **12** prepossessed

obsession 5 craze, mania **6** fetish, hangup **8** fixation, idée fixe **11** infatuation **13** preoccupation

obsessive 5 rabid **8** frenetic, maniacal, neurotic **9** fanatical, possessed **10** passionate **11** preoccupied

obsolete 3 old **5** dated, passé, stale **6** old hat **7** disused, worn-out **8** outmoded, time-worn **9** out-of-date **10** antiquated, superseded **12** antediluvian, old-fashioned

obstacle 3 bar **4** bump, clog, snag **5** block, catch, check, crimp, hitch **6** hurdle **7** barrier **8** handicap, hardship **9** hindrance, impedance, roadblock **10** difficulty, impediment **11** encumbrance, vicissitude **12** interference

obstinate 4 deaf, firm **5** balky, fixed **6** dogged, mulish **7** staunch, willful **8** obdurate, perverse, resolute, stubborn **9** pigheaded, resistant, unbudging, immovable **10** hardheaded, headstrong, inflexible, persistent, refractory, unyielding **11** intractable, opinionated, stiff-necked, wrongheaded **12** intransigent, pertinacious, recalcitrant

obstreperous 4 loud **5** noisy, rowdy **6** unruly **7** blatant, raucous **8** strident **9** clamorous, insistent **10** boisterous, disorderly, vociferant, vociferous **11** disobedient, loudmouthed **12** rambunctious

obstruct 3 bar, dam **4** clog, hide, plug, stop **5** block, check, choke, close **6** cut off, hamper, hinder, impede, stymie, thwart **7** congest, occlude, prevent, shut off, shut out, trammel **9** interfere

obstruction 3 bar **4** snag **5** hitch **6** hamper, hurdle **7** barrier **8** blockage, obstacle, stoppage **9** hindrance, impedance **10** impediment

obtain 3 buy, get, win **4** earn, gain, have, reap **5** annex, reach **6** pick up, secure **7** achieve, acquire, chalk up, procure **8** purchase

obtrude 5 cut in **6** butt in, horn in, impose, meddle **7** presume, push out **8** chisel in, infringe **9** interfere, thrust out

obtrusive 4 nosy **5** pushy **6** prying **7** forward **8** meddling **9** bumptious, officious **10** meddlesome, protruding **11** impertinent, interfering

obtuse 4 dull, dumb, slow **5** blunt,

dense, thick 6 stupid 7 rounded, unclear 11 insensitive

obverse 4 face, side 5 front 8 opposite 9 other side 10 complement 11 counterpart

obviate 4 ward 5 avert, deter, block 7 forfend, prevent, rule out 8 preclude, stave off 9 forestall, interfere, interpose, intervene 10 anticipate

obvious 5 clear, overt, plain 6 patent, simple 7 blatant, evident, glaring 8 apparent, clear-cut, distinct, manifest, palpable 10 undeniable 11 conspicuous, self-evident, transparent, unambiguous, unequivocal

oca 5 tuber 6 sorrel

O'Casey, Sean 9 dramatist 10 playwright *plays:* 17 Juno and the Paycock, Plough and the Stars (The)

occasion 4 call, need, shot, show, time 5 basis, break, cause, event 6 chance, demand, effect, excuse, ground, lead to, moment, reason 7 episode, instant, opening, produce 8 ceremony, incident, instance 9 condition, happening, necessity 10 bring about, foundation, obligation, occurrence 11 celebration, determinant, opportunity 12 circumstance 13 justification

occasional 3 few, odd 4 rare 6 casual, random, scarce, seldom 7 special, unusual 8 specific, sporadic, uncommon 9 irregular 10 incidental, infrequent

Occidental 7 Western 8 European 9 Westerner

occlude 4 clog, fill, hide, plug, stop 5 block, choke, close, cover 6 screen, stop up 7 close up, conceal, congest, 8 block off, obstruct

occult 5 eerie, magic 6 arcane, orphic, secret 8 abstruse, esoteric, hermetic, mystical 9 recondite, unearthly 10 cabalistic, mysterious 12 supernatural

occupant 5 liver 6 inmate, tenant 7 denizen, dweller, resider 8 habitant, resident 10 inhabitant

occupation 3 job, use 4 line, work 5 trade 6 career, métier, office 7 calling, control, pursuit, seizure 8 activity, business, position, vocation 9 occupancy, residence 10 employment, habitation, possession, settlement

occupy 3 use 4 busy, fill, hold, take 5 seize, tie up 6 absorb, employ, engage, live in, people, take up, tenant 7 control, engross, immerse, inhabit, involve, possess 8 populate, reside in, take over

occur 3 hap 4 pass 5 arise, ensue, pop up 6 appear, befall, betide, chance, dawn

on, happen, result, strike 7 come off, develop 9 take place, transpire

occurrence 3 hap 4 pass 5 event, state 7 episode 8 exigency, incident, juncture, occasion 9 adventure, condition, emergency, happening, situation

ocean 3 sea 4 blue, deep, main 5 brine, drink 6 Arctic, Indian 7 Pacific 8 Atlantic 9 Antarctic *movement:* 4 tide, wave

Oceania *country:* 4 Fiji 5 Belau, Nauru, Palau, Samoa, Tonga 6 Tuvalu 7 Vanuatu 8 Kiribati 9 Australia 10 New Zealand *territory:* 7 Tokelau 12 New Caledonia 13 American Samoa *ethnic group:* 6 Fijian, Papuan, Samoan 10 Melanesian, Polynesian 11 Micronesian *language:* 5 Maori 6 Fijian, Papuan, Pidgin, Samoan 10 Melanesian

oceanic 4 huge, vast 5 great 6 marine 7 immense, pelagic 8 enormous, maritime 9 saltwater, thalassic

Ocean State 11 Rhode Island

Oceanus *daughter:* 5 Doris 7 Oceanid 8 Eurynome *father:* 6 Uranus *mother:* 4 Gaea *sister:* 6 Tethys *son:* 6 Peneus 7 Alpheus *wife:* 6 Tethys

ocellus 3 eye 7 eyespot

ocelot 3 cat 7 wildcat

octave 5 eight, scale 6 eighth, stanza 8 interval

Octavia *brother:* 8 Augustus *grandson:* 8 Caligula *husband:* 4 Nero 6 Antony

octopus 7 mollusc, mollusk 9 devilfish 10 cephalopod *arm:* 8 tentacle *genus:* 7 Polypus *kin:* 5 squid 10 cuttlefish

ocular 4 seen 5 optic 6 visual 7 eyelike, optical, visible 8 eyepiece, viewable 9 perceived

Odalisque painter 6 Ingres (Jean-Auguste-Dominique) 7 Matisse (Henri)

odd 4 lone, rare 5 extra, fluky, queer, rummy, weird 6 casual, chance, single, uneven 7 curious, erratic, strange, unusual 8 peculiar, singular 9 eccentric, unmatched 13 idiosyncratic

oddball 4 kook 5 kooky, weird 6 weirdo 7 bizarre, curious, offbeat, strange, unusual 8 original, peculiar 9 character, eccentric 10 outlandish 13 idiosyncratic

oddity 5 freak, quirk 6 weirdo 7 anomaly 9 character, curiosity, departure, deviation, eccentric, weirdness 10 aberration, difference 11 abnormality, peculiarity, strangeness 12 eccentricity, idiosyncrasy, irregularity

odds 4 edge 5 favor, ratio 7 benefit, chances 8 handicap, variance 9 advantage, allowance, disparity 10 difference, likelihood, partiality 11 probability 12 disagreement

odds and ends 4 bits, olio 6 jumble, medley, motley, scraps 7 mélange, mixture 8 remnants, sundries 9 etceteras, leftovers, potpourri 10 assortment, hodgepodge, miscellany 13 paraphernalia

ode 4 hymn, poem 5 lyric, psalm, verse *part:* 5 epode 7 strophe 11 antistrophe

Odets play 9 Golden Boy 11 Country Girl (The) 12 Awake and Sing 15 Waiting for Lefty

odeum 4 hall 7 theater 11 concert hall

Odin *brother:* 4 Vili *daughter-in-law:* 5 Nanna *father:* 3 Bor *hall:* 8 Valhalla *horse:* 8 Sleipnir *maiden:* 8 Valkyrie *mansion:* 9 Gladsheim *mother:* 6 Bestla *raven:* 5 Hugin, Munin *ring:* 8 Draupnir *son:* 3 Tyr 4 Thor, Vali 6 Balder *spear:* 7 Gungnir *sword:* 4 Gram *wife:* 4 Fria, Rind 5 Frigg 6 Frigga *wolf:* 4 Geri 5 Freki

odious 4 foul, vile 6 horrid 7 hateful 8 horrible 9 abhorrent, execrable, invidious, loathsome, malicious, repellent, repugnant 10 abominable, despicable, detestable

odium 4 hate, onus 5 shame 6 hatred, infamy, stigma 7 censure, obloquy 8 contempt, disgrace, dishonor, ignominy, loathing 9 disrepute 10 abhorrence, opprobrium 11 detestation 12 condemnation

odor 4 funk 5 aroma, scent, smell, stink, whiff 6 stench 7 bouquet, perfume 9 fragrance, redolence

odorous 5 heady, sweet 6 smelly, strong 7 pungent, scented 8 aromatic, fragrant, perfumed, redolent, unsavory 9 offensive

Odysseus 7 Ulysses *dog:* 5 Argos *enchantress:* 5 Circe *father:* 7 Laertes *friend:* 6 Mentor *harasser:* 8 Poseidon *herb:* 4 moly *kingdom:* 6 Ithaca *mother:* 8 Anticlea *son:* 9 Telegonus 10 Telemachus *swineherd:* 7 Eumaeus *voyage:* 7 odyssey *wife:* 8 Penelope

odyssey 4 trek 5 quest 6 voyage 7 journey 9 wandering 13 peregrination

Odyssey author 5 Homer

Oedipus *brother-in-law:* 5 Creon *daughter:* 6 Ismene 8 Antigone *father:* 5 Laius *foster father:* 7 Polybus *foster mother:* 8 Periboea *kingdom:* 6 Thebes *mother:* 7 Jocasta *son:* 8 Eteocles 9 Polynices 10 Polyneices *victim:* 5 Laius *wife:* 7 Jocasta

Oeneus *kingdom:* 7 Calydon *son:* 8 Meleager *wife:* 7 Althaea

Oenomaus *charioteer:* 8 Myrtilus *daughter:* 10 Hippodamia *kingdom:* 4 Pisa *slayer:* 6 Pelops

Oenone *husband:* 5 Paris *rival:* 5 Helen

oeuvre 4 work 6 corpus, output 8 lifework 10 collection 11 compilation

of *German:* 3 aus, von *Italian:* 5 degli, della, delle

off 4 away, kill 5 aside 6 depart, murder, remote, slight 7 seaward, spoiled 9 eccentric, incorrect

offal 4 guts 4 junk 5 gurry, trash, waste 6 debris, litter, refuse, spilth 7 carrion, garbage, innards, rubbish, viscera 8 entrails 9 sweepings 10 intestines

offbeat 3 odd 5 fresh, outré, weird 6 way out 7 bizarre, oddball, strange, unusual 8 bohemian, peculiar, singular, uncommon 9 different, eccentric, whimsical 10 outlandish, unorthodox 11 distinctive 13 idiosyncratic

off-color 3 ill, low 4 blue, racy 5 bawdy, broad, salty, shady 6 ailing, peaked, poorly, risqué, sickly, unwell 7 dubious, naughty 8 improper, indecent 10 indisposed, suggestive

offend 3 sin, vex 4 gall, hurt, miff, pain 5 anger, annoy, pique, repel, shock, upset 6 appall, breach, insult, nettle 7 affront, disturb, provoke, violate 8 aggrieve, distress, irritate 9 displease 10 antagonize, transgress

offender 5 felon 6 sinner 7 culprit 8 criminal, violator 9 wrongdoer 10 lawbreaker, malefactor 12 transgressor

offense 3 sin 4 huff, hurt, miff, tort, vice 5 crime, fault, pique, wrong 6 attack, breach, felony, injury, insult 7 affront, assault, dudgeon, misdeed, mistake, outrage, umbrage 9 indignity, onslaught, violation 10 aggression, infraction, resentment 11 displeasure, indignation, misdemeanor

offensive 3 bad 4 foul, rank, vile 5 drive, onset 6 attack, odious 7 assault, noisome, obscene, painful 8 nauseous, unsavory 9 loathsome, obnoxious, onslaught, repellent, repugnant, repulsive, sickening 10 aggression, aggressive, disgusting, nauseating, unpleasant 11 uncongenial, unpalatable, unwholesome 12 disagreeable, unappetizing 13 objectionable

offer 3 bid, try 4 seek, show 5 assay, essay, pitch, put up 6 afford, extend, submit, tender 7 advance, attempt, display, exhibit, hold out, present, propose, provide, suggest 8 endeavor, proposal, threaten 9 sacrifice 10 submission 11 proposition

offering 4 alms, gift 5 grant 6 course, corban 7 charity, present 8 donation, oblation 9 sacrifice 11 benefaction, beneficence 12 contribution

offhand 5 ad-lib 6 blithe, breezy, casual 8 informal 9 extempore, impromptu, unstudied 10 improvised, nonchalant, unprepared 11 extemporary, spontaneous, unrehearsed

office 3 job 4 duty 5 berth, suite 6 agency, billet, bureau 7 station 8 business, cube farm, function, province 9 situation, workplace 10 department *head:* 4 boss 7 manager *machine:* 3 fax 6 copier 7 printer 8 computer 10 calculator, fax machine 11 photocopier *seeker:* 9 candidate 10 politician *worker:* 5 clerk 6 typist 9 file clerk, secretary 10 bookkeeper

officer 3 cop 4 exec 6 noncom, police 7 John Law, manager 8 official 9 executive *abbreviation:* 3 Adm., Col., Ens., Gen., Maj. 4 Capt., Cmdr. 5 Comdr., Lieut. *army:* 5 major 7 captain, colonel, general 10 lieutenant *British:* 9 brigadier *court:* 7 bailiff *king's:* 11 chamberlain *law-enforcement:* 3 cop 6 deputy, police 7 marshal, sheriff 9 constable, patrolman, policeman *naval:* 4 mate 6 ensign 7 admiral, captain 9 commander, commodore 10 lieutenant *noncommissioned:* 5 sarge 8 corporal, sergeant *petty:* 5 bosun 6 yeoman 9 boatswain *prison:* 5 guard 6 warden

official 4 exec 7 cleared, manager 8 approved, bona fide, endorsed 9 authentic, canonical, cathedral, certified, executive 10 accredited, authorized, ex cathedra, magistrate, sanctioned 13 administrator, authoritative *city or town:* 5 mayor 8 alderman 9 councilor, selectman 10 councillor *diplomatic:* 5 envoy 6 consul 7 attaché 10 ambassador *governmental:* 6 syndic *parish:* 6 beadle *sports:* 3 ref, ump 6 umpire 7 referee 8 linesman *university:* 4 dean 6 bursar 7 provost 9 registrar 10 chancellor

officiate 5 chair, serve 6 direct, umpire 7 conduct, oversee, preside, referee 9 supervise 11 superintend

officious 4 busy, nosy 5 pushy 7 forward 8 meddling 9 assertive, intrusive, obtrusive 10 meddlesome 11 impertinent 13 self-important

offing 6 future 7 by-and-by 9 aftertime, hereafter 10 near future

off-key 3 odd 4 sour 7 jarring 9 anomalous, dissonant, unnatural 10 discordant 12 inharmonious

off-putting 8 daunting 9 dismaying, offensive, repellent 10 forbidding, foreboding 11 distasteful 12 disagreeable,

discouraging 13 disconcerting, disheartening, objectionable

offscouring 5 trash 6 pariah, refuse, reject 7 outcast 8 castaway, derelict 11 untouchable

offset 6 square 7 balance 8 equalize 10 balance out, compensate, neutralize 11 counterpose, countervail 12 counterpoise, displacement

offshoot 4 twig 5 scion 6 branch 7 product, spin-off 9 affiliate, by-product, outgrowth 10 derivative, descendant

offspring 3 kid 4 kids, seed 5 brood, child, hatch, issue, scion, spawn, swarm, young 7 produce, product, progeny 8 children 9 posterity 10 descendant 11 progeniture

off-the-wall 3 odd 5 kooky, weird 6 farout, way-out 7 bizarre, oddball, unusual 8 freakish 9 eccentric, fantastic, grotesque 10 outlandish

off-white 4 bone 5 cream, ivory 6 oyster, vellum 9 parchment

Of Human Bondage author 7 Maugham (W. Somerset)

Of Mice and Men *author:* 9 Steinbeck (John) *character:* 6 George (Milton), Lennie (Small)

often 9 generally 10 frequently, habitually, repeatedly 11 recurrently

ogee 3 ess 4 arch 5 curve 7 molding

Ogier the ___ 4 Dane

ogive 3 rib 4 arch 5 graph

ogle 3 eye 4 gape, gaze, leer, look 5 stare 6 goggle 10 rubberneck

ogre 5 bogey, giant 7 bugbear, monster 8 bogeyman 9 boogeyman *Algonquian:* 7 windigo

ogress 5 harpy, scold, shrew, vixen 6 amazon, virago 8 fishwife 9 termagant, Xanthippe

O'Hara novel 7 Pal Joey 12 Butterfield 8 17 Ten North Frederick

Ohio *capital:* 8 Columbus *city:* 5 Akron, Xenia 6 Canton, Dayton, Toledo 9 Cleveland 10 Cincinnati *college, university:* 5 Miami 6 Kenyon 7 Antioch, Denison, Oberlin 8 Kent State 12 Bowling Green *nickname:* 7 Buckeye (State) *river:* 4 Ohio 6 Maumee 8 Sandusky *state bird:* 8 cardinal *state flower:* 16 scarlet carnation *state tree:* 7 buckeye

Oholibamah *father:* 4 Anah *husband:* 4 Esau

oil 3 fat, gas 4 balm, fuel, lube, oleo 5 oleum, slick 6 anoint, grease, pomade 7 blarney, incense, lanolin 8 flattery, soft soap 9 adulation, lubricant, lubricate, petroleum *combining form:* 3 ole 4 olei, oleo *consecrated:* 6 chrism *fra-*

grant: 5 attar 6 neroli **fuel:** 3 gas 6 petrol 8 gasoline, kerosene **relating to:** 5 oleic **ship:** 6 tanker **source:** 5 olive, shale **well:** 6 gusher

Oil! author 8 Sinclair (Upton)

oilbird 8 guacharo

oily 5 fatty, slick, soapy, suave 6 greasy, smarmy, smooth 7 fulsome 8 slippery, unctuous 10 lubricious, obsequious, oleaginous

ointment 4 balm 5 cream, salve 6 lotion 7 unction, unguent 8 calamine, liniment 9 emollient 11 embrocation

Okinawa capital 4 Naha

Oklahoma capital: 12 Oklahoma City **city:** 3 Ada 4 Enid 5 Tulsa 6 Norman **college, university:** 11 Oral Roberts **mountain:** 9 Black Mesa **nickname:** 6 Sooner (State) **river:** 3 Red 8 Arkansas, Canadian **state bird:** 10 flycatcher **state flower:** 9 mistletoe **state tree:** 6 redbud

OK, okay 3 aye, yea, yes 4 fine, good, safe, well 5 agree, allow, favor 6 agreed, assent, decent, permit 7 approve, certify, endorse, support 8 accredit, adequate, all right, blessing, high sign, passable, sanction, thumbs-up 9 authorize, hunky-dory 10 acceptable, permission 11 endorsement 12 satisfactory

okra 4 herb, soup 5 gumbo 6 mallow

old 4 aged, gray, late, past 5 dated, hoary, passé, stale 6 bygone, démodé, former, mature, senior, whilom 7 ancient, antique, archaic, elderly, lasting, onetime, overage, quondam, veteran 8 enduring, lifelong, Noachian, outmoded, timeworn 9 erstwhile, geriatric, long-lived, perennial, perpetual, primitive, venerable 10 antiquated, inveterate 13 superannuated **Scottish:** 4 auld

old age 6 dotage 8 caducity 10 senescence 11 decrepitude, elderliness, senectitude

Old Bailey 5 court

Old Colony State 13 Massachusetts

Old Curiosity Shop author 7 Dickens (Charles)

Old Dominion State 8 Virginia

Old Faithful 6 geyser

old-fashioned 4 aged 5 dated, dowdy, fusty, moldy, passé, stale, tired 6 bygone, démodé, quaint, stodgy 7 ancient, antique, archaic, outworn, vintage 8 cocktail, obsolete, outdated, outmoded 9 out-of-date, unstylish 10 antiquated

old hand 3 pro, vet 6 expert, master 7 veteran 9 authority 10 past master, specialist

old hat 5 dated, passé, stale, tired, trite 6 démodé 7 antique, clichéd, vintage 8 outmoded, timeworn, well-worn 9 hackneyed, out-of-date 10 antiquated

Old Ironsides 12 Constitution (U.S.S.) **poet:** 6 Holmes (Oliver Wendell)

Old Line State 8 Maryland

old maid 6 fusser 7 fusspot 8 card game, spinster 10 fussbudget

Old North State 13 North Carolina

Old Rough and Ready 6 Taylor (Zachary)

Olds' car 3 Reo

old-time 5 dated 6 bygone 7 antique, vintage 10 antiquated 12 long-standing

old-timer 3 vet 5 elder 6 senior 7 ancient, antique, veteran

Old World 6 Europe

oleaginous see OILY

oleaster 5 shrub 12 Russian olive

olecranon 9 funny bone

oleo 9 margarine

oleoresin 10 turpentine

oleum 3 oil

olfaction 5 sense, smell 8 smelling

olid 4 rank 5 fetid 6 putrid, rancid, rotten 7 stenchy 8 stinking 9 offensive 10 malodorous

olio 3 mix 4 stew 5 umble 6 medley 7 mélange, mixture 8 mishmash, mixed bag 9 potpourri 10 assortment, collection, hodgepodge, miscellany

Oliver Twist author: 7 Dickens (Charles) **character:** 5 Fagin, Nancy, Sikes (Bill) 6 Bumble (Mr.) 12 Artful Dodger

Ollie's partner 4 Stan

Olympian 3 god 5 lofty, noble 6 lordly 7 athlete, exalted, godlike 8 majestic, superior 10 competitor

Olympics 5 games 6 sports 9 athletics **place of origin:** 6 Greece **symbol:** 5 flame, torch

Oman capital: 6 Masqat, Muscat **language:** 6 Arabic 7 Baluchi **monetary unit:** 4 rial **mountain range:** 7 Al-Hajar **neighbor:** 5 Yemen 11 Saudi Arabia **peninsula:** 7 Arabian **sea:** 7 Arabian

Omar 4 poet 7 Khayyám **country:** 6 Persia **father:** 7 Eliphaz **poem:** 8 Rubaiyat

omega 3 end 6 ending, finale, letter **kin:** 3 zed, zee

omen 4 sign 5 augur, token 6 augury, boding 7 auspice, portent, presage, warning 8 bodement, prophecy 9 foretoken 10 foreboding, prediction, prognostic

ominous 4 dark, dire, grim 6 dismal 7 baleful, direful, doomful, fateful 8 alarming, lowering, menacing, sinister 9 ill-boding, prophetic 10 forbidding, foreboding, portentous 11 frightening, threatening **12** inauspicious, unpropitious

omission 3 cut, gap **4** lack, skip, slip **5** blank, break, chasm, error, lapse **6** hiatus, lacuna **7** elision, failure **8** eclipsis, ellipsis, overlook **9** exclusion *mark:* **5** caret **8** ellipsis **10** apostrophe

omit 4 drop, fail, skip **5** elide **6** except, forget, ignore, slight **7** exclude, neglect **8** leave out, overlook, pass over **11** leave undone

omnibus 3 ana **4** posy **5** album **7** garland **8** analects, treasury **9** anthology **10** miscellany **11** florilegium

omnipotent 6 divine **7** godlike, supreme **8** almighty **9** unlimited **11** all-powerful

omnipresent 7 allover, endless **8** infinite, unending **9** boundless, limitless, universal **10** ubiquitous

omniscient 4 wise **7** learned **9** know-it-all **10** all-knowing

omnium-gatherum see OLIO

Omphale *domain:* **5** Lydia *slave:* **8** Heracles, Hercules

omphalos 3 hub **5** navel **9** umbilicus **10** focal point

on 4 atop, over **5** above, along **7** working **9** operating **11** functioning

onager 3 ass **5** kiang **8** catapult

Onan's father 5 Judah

once 4 ever, late, past **5** at all **6** before, bygone, former, whilom **7** already, earlier, long ago, onetime, quondam **8** formerly, sometime

once-over 4 look **5** check **6** gander, glance, survey **10** inspection **11** examination

one 4 lone, only, sole, unit **5** monad **6** single, unique **7** numeral **8** separate, singular, solitary **9** undivided **10** individual, particular *combining form:* **4** mono *French:* **3** une *German:* **3** ein **4** eine *prefix:* **3** uni *Scottish:* **3** ane *Spanish:* **3** una, uno

one and a half *combining form:* **6** sesqui

one-eyed giant 7 Cyclops **10** Polyphemus

one-handed god 3 Tiu, Tyr

one-horse town 4 burg **6** hamlet, Podunk **11** whistle-stop

one hundred 6 centum *years:* **7** century

O'Neill, Eugene *heroine:* **4** Anna, Nina *play:* **3** Ile **4** Gold **8** Hairy Ape (The) **12** Ah Wilderness, Anna Christie, Emperor Jones, Iceman Cometh (The) **13** Great God Brown (The), Marco Millions **16** Strange Interlude **18** Desire Under the Elms **22** Mourning Becomes Electra **24** Long Day's Journey into Night

oneiric 6 dreamy **8** anagogic **9** dreamlike

oneness 3 all **5** union, unity, whole

7 harmony **8** entirety, identity, sameness, totality **9** integrity, unanimity **10** singleness, uniformity **11** singularity, unification **13** individuality

onerous 4 hard **5** heavy, tough **6** taxing, trying **7** arduous, exigent, wearing, weighty **8** exacting, grievous, imposing, pressing, toilsome **9** demanding, difficult, laborious **10** burdensome, cumbersome, oppressive **11** troublesome

one-sided 6 biased, uneven **7** colored, partial, unequal **8** inclined, partisan, weighted **10** prejudiced, unbalanced, unilateral

onetime 3 old **4** once, past **6** bygone, former, whilom **7** quondam **8** previous **9** erstwhile

ongoing 7 current, growing **8** evolving **9** advancing, in process **10** continuing, continuous, developing, in progress, unfinished **11** progressing

on hand 4 here **5** ready **6** nearby **7** pending, present **9** available

onion 4 bulb **7** shallot *bulb:* **3** set *genus:* **6** Allium *kin:* **4** leek **6** garlic *kind:* **7** Bermuda, Danvers, Spanish *roll:* **5** bialy *young:* **8** scallion

online 5 wired **9** connected *business:* **5** e-tail *guffaw:* **3** LOL *system:* **3** Web **8** Internet

onlooker 6 viewer **7** watcher, witness **8** beholder, kibitzer, observer **9** bystander, spectator **10** eyewitness **12** rubbernecker

only 3 but, few, one, yet **4** just, lone, mere, save, sole, solo **5** alone **6** and yet, at most, except, merely, simply, single, solely, unique **7** however, utterly **8** entirely, singular, solitary **11** exclusively

onomasticon 7 lexicon **8** wordbook

onomatopoeic 5 mimic **6** echoic **7** mimetic **9** emulative, imitative **10** simulative

onset 4 dawn, rush **5** birth, start **6** attack, coming, origin **7** arrival, assault, dawning, offense, opening **8** invasion **9** beginning, inception, offensive **10** aggression **12** commencement

onslaught 5 blitz **6** attack, charge, deluge **7** assault, barrage, offense, torrent **8** invasion **9** offensive **10** aggression

on-target 5 exact, right **7** correct, perfect, precise **8** accurate **11** appropriate

Ontario *bay:* **8** Georgian *capital:* **7** Toronto *city:* **4** York **6** London, Ottawa **7** Markham, Windsor **8** Hamilton **9** Etobicoke, Kitchener, North York **10** Thunder Bay **11** Mississauga, Scarborough **13** Sault Ste. Marie *lake:* **4** Erie

5 Huron 7 Nipigon, Ontario 8 Superior *provincial flower:* 13 white trillium *river:* 5 Moose 6 Albany, Severn, Winisk

on the house 4 free 6 gratis 13 complimentary

on the nose 5 bingo 6 dead-on, spot-on 7 exactly 8 accurate 9 precisely 10 accurately

on the other hand 3 but 7 however

on the rocks 4 iced 7 with ice, wrecked

on the whole 6 mainly, mostly 7 usually 8 all in all 9 generally, in general, typically 10 altogether, by and large

onus 3 tax 4 duty, load, task 5 blame, brand, fault, guilt, odium, stain 6 burden, charge, stigma, weight 8 black eye 9 liability 10 obligation, oppression

onward 5 ahead, along, forth 7 forward 9 advancing

onyx 5 agate 10 chalcedony

oodles 4 gobs, lots, tons 5 heaps, loads, rafts, scads 6 plenty

oolong 3 tea

oomph 3 pep, vim, zip 4 brio, dash, élan, life, push, zest, zing 5 charm, drive, punch, verve, vigor 6 esprit, pizazz, spirit 7 glamour, pizzazz 8 strength, vitality 9 magnetism, sex appeal

ooze 3 goo, mud 4 emit, goop, leak, seep, weep 5 bleed, exude, issue, marsh, slime, sweat 7 secrete, seepage 8 transude

opacity 8 dullness 9 murkiness, obscurity 10 obtuseness

opal 3 gem 5 jewel, stone 6 silica 7 girasol, hyalite, mineral 8 gemstone

opaque 3 dim 4 dull, hazy 5 dense, filmy, murky, vague 6 cloudy 7 clouded, obscure, unclear 8 abstruse

OPEC nation 3 UAE 4 Iran, Iraq 5 Libya, Qatar 6 Kuwait 7 Algeria, Nigeria 9 Indonesia, Venezuela 11 Saudi Arabia

open 4 ajar, bare, free, wide 5 frank, naked, overt 6 broach, candid, expand, expose, public, reveal, spread, unfold, unlock, unseal, unveil 7 convene, outdoor, uncover, unlatch 8 disclose, outdoors, stripped, unclothe, unlocked, unsealed 9 available, uncovered 10 out-of-doors, unfastened 11 susceptible, unconcealed, undisguised 12 unrestricted

open-air 7 outdoor, outside 8 alfresco, outdoors 9 out-of-door 10 out-of-doors

open-and-shut 4 easy 5 clear, plain 6 patent, simple 7 evident, obvious

openhanded 6 giving, lavish 7 liberal 8 generous 9 bounteous, bountiful, unselfish, unsparing 10 beneficent, bighearted, charitable, munificent 11 magnanimous

openhearted 4 kind, warm 5 frank, plain 6 candid, honest 8 generous 10 responsive 11 sympathetic

opening 3 gap 4 dawn, door, gate, hole, pass, pore, slit, slot, vent 5 break, chasm, chink, cleft, crack, debut, mouth, onset, start, stoma 6 breach, chance, lacuna, outlet, outset 7 crevice, dawning, fissure, orifice, pinhole 8 aperture, overture 9 beginning 11 opportunity *ship's:* 5 hatch 8 hatchway, porthole

open-minded 7 liberal 8 tolerant, unbiased 9 receptive 12 freethinking, unprejudiced

openmouthed 4 agog, awed, rapt 5 agape 6 amazed, gaping 7 stunned 9 astounded, surprised 10 astonished, speechless

open sesame 3 key 5 charm 6 ticket 8 passport, password

open up 4 fire, talk 5 shoot 6 reveal 7 cut into, divulge 8 disclose 9 make plain, spread out 11 communicate

opera *comic:* 5 buffa 6 bouffe *glasses:* 9 lorgnette *kind:* 4 soap 5 comic, grand, horse, space *part:* 3 act 4 aria 5 scena *solo:* 4 aria *star:* 4 diva 10 prima donna *text:* 8 libretto (see also individual titles and composers)

operant 8 behavior 9 effective 10 measurable, observable, productive 12 conditioning

operate 3 act, cut, run, use 4 work 5 drive, exert, steer 6 behave, direct, effect, handle, manage 7 carry on, conduct, control, perform, produce 8 function, maneuver 9 influence 10 bring about, manipulate

operation 3 use 4 step 6 action 7 concern, mission, process, surgery 8 activity, business, exercise, exertion, function, maneuver 9 procedure 10 employment, engagement, enterprise 11 performance, transaction

operative 3 key 4 hand, live, open 5 agape, alive 6 active, artisan, moving, usable, worker 7 dynamic, in force, laborer, running, working, workman 8 mechanic, relevant 9 effective, essential, important 10 functional 11 efficacious, influential, secret agent, significant

operator 5 agent, fixer, pilot 6 doctor, driver 7 schemer, surgeon 9 conductor

operculum 3 lid 4 flap 8 covering

operetta composer 5 Friml (Rudolf), Lehár (Franz), Suppé (Franz von) 6 Straus (Oscar) 7 Gilbert (William S.), Herbert (Victor), Romberg (Sigmund),

Strauss (Johann) **8** Sullivan (Arthur) **9** Offenbach (Jacques)

operose 4 dull **6** boring, tiring **7** tedious **8** tiresome, toilsome, wearful **9** difficult, laborious, wearisome

Ophelia *beloved:* **6** Hamlet *brother:* **7** Laertes *father:* **8** Polonius

ophidian 5 snake **9** snakelike

opiate 4 dope, drug **7** anodyne **8** hypnotic, narcotic, nepenthe, sedative **9** analgesic, soporific **10** anesthetic, painkiller **11** somniferous **12** somnifacient, tranquilizer *type:* **7** codeine **8** morphine

opine 4 deem, hold, view **5** judge, state, think **6** advise, assert **7** believe, express, suppose **8** point out **9** recommend

opinion 4 idea, view **5** tenet **6** belief, notion, theory **7** feeling, thought **8** attitude, estimate, judgment, reaction **9** sentiment **10** assumption, conclusion, conjecture, conviction, estimation, hypothesis, persuasion **11** speculation, supposition *express an:* **4** vote **5** judge **9** criticize

opium 4 dope, drug **8** narcotic *derivative:* **6** heroin **7** codeine **8** laudanum, morphine **9** paregoric *source:* **5** poppy

opossum 9 marsupial *kin:* **8** kangaroo

opponent 3 con, foe **4** anti **5** enemy, rival **6** muscle **7** nemesis **9** adversary, assailant, combatant **10** antagonist, challenger, competitor **12** counteragent

opportune 3 apt, fit **6** timely **8** suitable **9** favorable, well-timed **10** auspicious, convenient, felicitous, propitious **11** appropriate

opportunity 4 turn **5** break, space, spell **6** chance **7** opening **8** juncture, occasion, prospect **12** circumstance

oppose 4 buck, defy, deny, duel **5** cross, fight, repel **6** attack, combat, debate, differ, object, refute, resist **7** assault, contest, counter, dispute, prevent, protest **8** confront, contrast, disagree, obstruct **9** withstand **10** contradict, contravene, controvert, disapprove

opposite 4 foil **5** polar **6** contra, facing **7** antonym, counter, inverse, obverse, opposed, reverse **8** antipode, antipole, contrary, contrast, converse **9** antipodal, diametric **10** antipodean, antithesis **11** contrasting, counterpole **12** antithetical, counterpoint **13** contradictory *prefix:* **3** dis **5** retro **6** contra **7** counter

opposition 3 con, foe **5** enemy **7** rivalry **8** conflict, defiance **9** adversary, animosity, hostility, other side **10** antagonism, antithesis, resistance **11** contrariety, disapproval

oppress 5 abuse, crush, wrong **6** burden, injure, sadden, subdue **7** afflict,

torment, torture, trouble **8** aggrieve, distress, overload **9** persecute, subjugate, weigh down

oppressive 5 harsh, heavy **6** brutal, dismal, gloomy, severe, somber, sombre, taxing **7** exigent, onerous, weighty **8** crushing, exacting, grievous, stifling **9** demanding **10** burdensome, depressing, tyrannical **11** dispiriting, overbearing, suffocating **12** discouraging, overwhelming

oppressive force 4 onus, yoke **6** burden, weight

oppressor 5 bully **6** despot, tyrant **8** autocrat, dictator **9** strongman

opprobrious 4 evil, vile **6** odious, vulgar **7** abusive, hateful **8** infamous **9** notorious, truculent **10** despicable, scurrilous **11** disgraceful, ignominious **12** contemptible, contumelious, vituperative

opprobrium 5 abuse, blame, odium, scorn, shame **6** infamy **7** obloquy **8** contempt, disgrace, dishonor, ignominy, reproach **9** discredit, disesteem, disrepute **10** scurrility **12** vituperation

oppugn 5 argue, fight **6** battle, combat **7** contend, contest, dispute **8** question

Ops 4 Rhea *consort:* **6** Cronus, Saturn *daughter:* **5** Ceres **7** Demeter

opt 3 tap **4** pick **5** elect, favor **6** choose, decide, prefer, select

optical 6 ocular, visual **8** visional *instrument:* **4** lens **5** scope **7** transit **9** magnifier, periscope, telescope **10** microscope

optimal 4 best **5** ideal **6** choice, finest **7** perfect **8** choicest, superior

optimist 5 hoper **7** dreamer **8** idealist, Micawber **9** Pollyanna **10** positivist

optimistic 4 rosy **5** happy, merry, sunny **6** bright, hoping, upbeat **7** assured, buoyant, hopeful **8** cheerful, positive, sanguine, trusting **9** confident, promising **11** rose-colored **12** Pollyannaish

option 4 pick **5** claim, extra, grant, right **6** choice **7** license **8** contract, election **9** accessory, privilege, selection **10** preference **11** alternative, prerogative

optional 4 free **5** extra **8** elective **9** voluntary **11** alternative **13** discretionary *item:* **5** add-on, extra

opulence 6 bounty, luxury, plenty, riches, wealth **7** fortune **9** abundance, affluence, plenitude, profusion

opulent 4 lush, rich **5** plush, showy, swank **6** deluxe, lavish **7** moneyed, profuse, wealthy **8** affluent, palatial **9** luxuriant, luxurious, plentiful, sumptuous **11** extravagant **12** ostentatious

opuntia 6 cactus

opus 4 work **5** piece **6** oeuvre **7** product **8** creation **11** composition or **4** else, gold **6** golden, yellow **9** otherwise

oracle 4 sage, seer **5** augur, sibyl **6** augury, medium, Pythia, vision **7** prophet **8** haruspex, prophecy **10** apocalypse, revelation, soothsayer *site:* **6** Claros, Delphi, Didyma, Dodona **7** Olympia **9** Epidaurus

oracular 5 vatic **6** mantic, orphic **7** cryptic, Delphic, fatidic, obscure **8** Delphian, dogmatic **9** ambiguous, arbitrary, prophetic, sibylline, vaticinal

oral 4 exam **5** vocal **6** spoken, verbal, voiced **8** narrated, viva voce **9** unwritten **11** examination

orange 6 citrus *brownish:* **6** Titian *deep:* **11** bittersweet *genus:* **6** Citrus *kin:* **4** lime **5** lemon **7** kumquat, satsuma **8** mandarin **9** tangerine **10** grapefruit *kind:* **4** sour **5** blood, chino, navel, Osage, sweet **7** Seville **8** bergamot, mandarin, Valencia *oil:* **6** neroli *seed:* **3** pip *skin:* **4** rind

orangutan 3 ape **6** pongid **7** primate **10** anthropoid

orate 4 rant **5** mouth, speak, spiel **6** preach **7** address, declaim, lecture **8** bloviate, harangue, perorate **9** discourse, sermonize, speechify **11** pontificate

oration 6 homily, sermon, speech **7** address, lecture **9** discourse *funeral:* **6** eulogy

orator 7 speaker *American:* **4** Clay (Henry) **5** Bryan (William Jennings), Henry (Patrick) **7** Calhoun (John C.), Douglas (Stephen), Webster (Daniel) *British:* **5** Burke (Edmund) **8** Disraeli (Benjamin) **9** Churchill (Winston), Gladstone (William) *French:* **8** Mirabeau (Comte de) *Greek:* **5** Corax **8** Pericles **11** Demosthenes *Roman:* **6** Cicero

oratory 6 chapel, speech **7** bombast **8** rhetoric **9** discourse, elocution, eloquence **10** expression **11** exhortation, speechcraft

orb 3 eye **4** ball **5** globe, round **6** circle, sphere

orbit 4 path **5** ambit, range, reach, scope, sweep, track **6** extent, radius **7** ellipse *farthest point:* **5** apsis **6** apogee **8** aphelion *nearest point:* **5** apsis **7** perigee **10** perihelion

orchard 5 trees **10** plantation

orchestra 4 band **7** gamelan **8** ensemble, symphony **12** philharmonic *leader:* **9** conductor *section:* **5** brass **6** string **7** brasses, strings **8** woodwind **9** woodwinds **10** percussion

orchestrate 5 blend, score, unify **6** man-

age **7** arrange, compose **8** organize **9** harmonize, integrate **10** coordinate

orchid *kind:* **7** calypso, pogonia **8** cattleya, oncidium **9** cymbidium **11** cypripedium *petal:* **3** lip **8** labellum *product:* **5** salep *tuber:* **5** salep

ordain 4 will **5** enact, order **6** decree, direct, impose, invest **7** appoint, command, conduct, destine, dictate, install, lay down **9** establish, prescribe, pronounce **10** predestine

ordeal 4 test **5** agony, cross, trial **7** calvary, torment, trouble **8** crucible **9** suffering **10** affliction, difficulty, visitation **11** tribulation

order 4 book, rank **5** array, caste, class, genre, range **6** decree, lineup, method, scheme, series, system **7** command, harmony, mandate, marshal, pattern, reserve **8** classify, neatness, position, shipment, tidiness **9** directive, hierarchy, procedure, structure **10** injunction, regularity **11** progression *lack of:* **5** chaos **6** ataxia **7** anarchy, clutter **9** confusion **11** pandemonium *of business:* **6** agenda, docket *of preference:* **8** priority

orderly 4 aide, calm, neat, tidy, trim **6** batman **7** correct, precise, regular, soldier, uniform **8** methodic, peaceful **9** attendant, organized, peaceable, regulated, shipshape **10** methodical, systematic **11** uncluttered, well-behaved **12** businesslike

ordinance 3 law **4** code, rule **5** edict **6** decree **7** precept, statute **9** direction, prescript **10** regulation

ordinary 4 so-so **5** banal, cheap, judge, plain, trite, usual **6** common, normal **7** average, humdrum, mundane, natural, popular, prelate, prosaic, regular, routine, typical **8** everyday, familiar, inferior, mediocre, workaday **9** clergyman, customary, quotidian **10** uneventful, unoriginal **11** commonplace **12** unnoteworthy

ordnance 4 arms, guns **6** cannon **7** weapons **8** armament, supplies, weaponry **9** artillery, munitions **10** ammunition

ore 4 gold, rock **5** metal **6** copper, silver **7** mineral **8** platinum *analysis:* **5** assay *deposit:* **4** lode, vein *excavation:* **5** stope *iron:* **5** ocher, ochre **8** goethite, hematite, limonite *lead:* **6** galena *process:* **8** leaching, smelting *refuse:* **4** slag **5** dross, matte **6** scoria *smelted:* **7** regulus

oread 5 nymph

Oregon *capital:* **5** Salem *city:* **4** Bend **6** Eugene **7** Coos Bay, Medford **8** Portland *college, university:* **4** Reed *lake:*

6 Crater *mountain, range:* 4 Hood 7 Cascade *nickname:* 6 Beaver (State) *river:* 5 Snake 8 Columbia *state bird:* 10 meadowlark *state flower:* 11 Oregon grape *state tree:* 10 Douglas fir

Orestes *father:* 9 Agamemnon *friend:* 7 Pylades *mother:* 12 Clytemnestra *sister:* 7 Electra 9 Iphigenia *victim:* 9 Aegisthus 12 Clytemnestra *wife:* 8 Hermione

organ 5 agent, means 6 agency, medium, review 7 channel, journal, vehicle 8 magazine, ministry 9 newspaper 10 instrument, periodical *ancient:* 9 hydraulus *barrel:* 10 hurdy-gurdy *bodily:* 3 ear, eye 4 lung, nose, skin 5 gland, heart, liver 6 kidney, larynx, spleen, tongue, tonsil, viscus 9 intestine *mouth:* 9 harmonica *part:* 4 pipe, reed, stop 5 pedal, valve 6 blower 7 console, tremolo 8 keyboard 9 wind chest *reed:* 8 melodeon 9 harmonium *stop:* 4 oboe, sext 5 gamba, quint, viola 6 dulcet 7 bassoon, celesta, melodia, subbass, tertian 8 carillon, diapason, dulciana, gemshorn *tactile:* 6 feeler 8 tentacle

organ cactus 7 saguaro

organic 5 basic 6 innate 7 natural, primary 8 inherent, integral 9 essential 10 structural 11 fundamental

organism 5 being, plant 6 animal *disease-producing:* 4 germ 5 virus 8 pathogen 9 bacterium *single-celled:* 5 monad 6 amoeba 9 protozoan

organist *American:* 3 Fox (Virgil) 5 Biggs (E. Power) 6 Newman (Anthony) *Dutch:* 9 Sweelinck (Jan) *English:* 6 Wesley (Samuel) 7 Gibbons (Christopher, Edward, Ellis, Orlando) *French:* 5 Alain (Marie-Claire), Widor (Charles) 6 Franck (César) 8 Messiaen (Olivier) 10 Schweitzer (Albert) *German:* 4 Bach (Johann Sebastian) 6 Handel (George Frideric), Walcha (Helmut) 7 Richter (Anton, Ernst, Ferdinand, Johann, Karl) *Swiss:* 4 Rogg (Lionel)

organization 4 body, club, unit 5 group, guild, setup 6 agency, system 7 pattern 9 framework, structure 11 arrangement, association, corporation, institution 13 establishment *college:* 4 frat 8 sorority 10 fraternity *criminal:* 4 gang 5 Mafia *fraternal:* (see FRATERNAL SOCIETY) *government:* (see GOVERNMENT AGENCY) *lack of:* 5 chaos *political:* 4 bloc 5 party 7 apparat, machine

organize 4 form 5 array, group, order, rally, set up, start 6 create, line up 7 arrange 8 classify, unionize 9 construct, establish, institute, integrate 10 constitute, coordinate 11 put together

orgulous 5 proud

orgy 4 rite 5 binge, revel, spree 7 blowout, carouse, debauch, rampage, revelry, splurge 8 carousal 9 bacchanal 10 indulgence, saturnalia 11 bacchanalia

oriel 3 bay 6 window

orient 3 set 4 face 5 adapt, align, pearl, sheen 6 adjust, direct, inform, locate, luster 7 arrange 8 acquaint, lustrous 9 sparkling 11 accommodate, familiarize

Orient 4 Asia, East 7 Far East

Oriental 3 rug 5 Asian 6 carpet 7 Eastern 10 Far Eastern

orientation 7 bearing 8 location, position 9 alignment, direction 10 adjustment 11 arrangement

orifice see OPENING

oriflamme 4 flag 5 ideal 6 banner, pennon, symbol 7 pendant, pennant 8 standard, streamer

origami 12 paper folding *bird:* 5 crane

origin 4 root, seed, well 5 birth, blood, start 6 source 7 descent, genesis, lineage 8 ancestry, fountain, pedigree 9 beginning, inception, maternity, parentage, paternity 10 derivation, extraction, provenance, wellspring

original 3 new 5 first, model, novel, prime 6 native, unique 7 initial, pattern, pioneer, primary 8 creative, earliest 9 archetype, ingenious, innovator, inventive, precursor, primitive, prototype 10 archetypal, forerunner, innovative

originally 5 first 7 at first 8 formerly 9 initially, primarily

originate 4 coin, flow, hail, make, rise, stem 5 arise, begin, found, hatch, issue, set up, start 6 create, derive, invent, launch, spring 7 emanate, proceed, produce, think up 8 commence, generate, initiate, innovate 9 institute, introduce

originator 5 maker 6 author 7 creator, founder, planner 8 inventor, producer 9 initiator, innovator 10 institutor, introducer

oriole 4 bird 8 troupial *European:* 6 loriot *genus:* 7 Icterus *golden:* 6 loriot *kind:* 6 golden 7 orchard 8 Bullock's 9 Baltimore

Orion 6 hunter 13 constellation *beloved:* 3 Eos *belt:* 7 Ellwand *father:* 7 Hyrieus 8 Poseidon *slayer:* 5 Diana 7 Artemis *star:* 5 Rigel 9 Bellatrix 10 Betelgeuse

orison 6 prayer 8 entreaty, petition 12 supplication

Orithyia *lover:* 6 Boreas *son:* 5 Zetes 6 Calais

Orlando author 5 Woolf (Virginia)
Orlando Furioso author 7 Ariosto (Ludovico)
Orléans heroine 9 Joan of Arc
orlop 4 deck
ormolu 5 brass 6 bronze
ornament 3 gem 4 bead, deck, trim 5 adorn, jewel 6 bedeck, finial, tassel 7 dress up, garnish, jewelry, pendant, whatnot 8 beautify, decorate, filigree 9 embellish, embroider, lavaliere *Christmas tree:* 4 bulb 5 angel 6 tinsel *lip:* 6 labret *shoulder:* 7 epaulet
ornamental case 4 etui
ornate 4 lush, rich 5 fancy, gaudy, showy 6 florid, frilly, gilded, glitzy, rococo 7 baroque, flowery, opulent 8 overdone 9 elaborate, luxuriant, sumptuous 10 flamboyant
ornery 5 balky, cross, testy 6 crabby, cranky, crusty, grumpy 7 bearish, froward, grouchy 8 contrary, perverse, stubborn, vinegary 9 crotchety, difficult, irascible, irritable 10 inflexible, vinegarish 12 cantankerous
ornithic 5 avian 8 birdlike
ornithologist *American:* 4 Bond (James) 7 Audubon (John James), Bartram (William) 8 Peterson (Roger Tory) *English:* 5 Gould (John) *Scottish:* 6 Wilson (Alexander)
orotund 4 full, loud 5 round 7 flowery, pompous, ringing 8 resonant, sonorous 9 bombastic, high-flown, overblown 10 euphuistic, oratorical, resounding, rhetorical, stentorian 11 declamatory 12 magniloquent 13 grandiloquent
Orpah *husband:* 7 Chilion *sister-in-law:* 4 Ruth
orphan 4 waif 5 Annie, gamin, stray 6 bereft, gamine, urchin 7 cast-off, ignored 8 forsaken, homeless 9 abandoned, foundling, neglected 10 motherless, parentless
Orpheus *father:* 6 Apollo 7 Oeagrus *home:* 6 Thrace *instrument:* 4 lyre *mother:* 8 Calliope *wife:* 8 Euridice
orphic 6 arcane, mystic, occult 7 cryptic, Delphic, obscure 8 abstruse, Delphian, esoteric, hermetic, mystical, oracular, profound 9 enigmatic, recondite
ort 3 bit 4 bite 5 crumb, piece, scrap 6 morsel 7 remnant 8 leftover
orthodox 6 proper 8 accepted, approved, official, received, standard 9 canonical, customary 10 conformist, recognized, sanctioned 11 established, traditional 12 acknowledged, conservative, conventional 13 authoritative
orthography 7 writing 8 spelling
ortolan 7 bunting

Orwell novel 10 Animal Farm 18 Nineteen Eighty-four
oryx 7 gemsbok 8 antelope
os 3 ora (plural) 4 bone, ossa (plural) 5 mouth 7 orifice
Osborne play 15 Look Back in Anger
oscillate 4 sway, vary 5 swing, waver 6 change, seesaw 7 vibrate 9 alternate, fluctuate
oscillation 4 sway 5 swing 9 variation, vibration 10 undulation 11 fluctuation, periodicity
osculate 3 lip 4 buss, kiss, peck 5 smack 6 smooch
osier 3 rod 6 willow 7 dogwood
Osiris *brother:* 3 Set 4 Seth *father:* 3 Geb, Keb, Seb *mother:* 3 Nut *scribe:* 5 Thoth *sister:* 4 Isis *slayer:* 3 Set 4 Seth *son:* 5 Horus 6 Anubis *wife:* 4 Isis
osmosis 4 flow 8 transfer 9 diffusion 10 absorption 12 assimilation 13 incorporation
osprey 4 hawk 8 fish hawk
osseous 4 bony 8 bonelike
ossicle 4 bone 5 incus 6 stapes 7 malleus
ossify 3 set 6 harden 7 stiffen 8 solidify 9 fossilize
osso ___ 4 buco
ossuary 4 tomb 5 vault 8 boneyard, cemetery 9 sepulcher, sepulchre
ostensible 6 stated 7 alleged, seeming 8 apparent, asserted, illusive, illusory, so-called, supposed 9 pretended, professed, purported, semblable 11 superficial
ostentation 4 show 5 flash, swank 7 display 9 pomposity, showiness, vainglory 10 flashiness, pretension 11 flamboyance
ostentatious 4 loud 5 gaudy, showy, swank 6 flashy, garish, swanky 7 pompous, splashy 8 overdone, peacocky 10 flamboyant, peacockish 11 pretentious 12 vainglorious
ostiole 4 pore 7 orifice 8 aperture
ostracism 5 exile 7 removal 9 exclusion 10 banishment, relegation 11 deportation
ostracize 3 bar, cut 4 shun, snub 5 exile 6 banish, deport 7 exclude, keep out, shut out 8 throw out 9 blackball 10 expatriate 12 cold-shoulder
ostrich 6 ratite
Ostrogoth king 9 Theodoric
otalgia 7 earache
Otello composer 5 Verdi (Giuseppe) 7 Rossini (Gioacchino)
O tempora! O ___! 5 mores
Othello *author:* 11 Shakespeare (William) *ensign:* 4 Iago *lieutenant:* 6 Cassio *maid:* 6 Emilia *victim, wife:* 9 Desdemona

others 4 rest 9 remainder *and:* 4 et al
6 et alia, et alii 7 et aliae
other than 3 but 4 save 6 except
7 besides 9 apart from, aside from,
except for, excepting, excluding
otherwise 3 not 5 if not 6 or else
7 changed 9 different 11 differently
12 anything else 13 alternatively
otic 5 aural 8 auditory 9 auricular
otiose 4 idle, vain 5 empty 6 futile, hollow 7 surplus, useless 8 nugatory
9 fruitless, pointless, worthless 11 ineffective, purposeless, superfluous
12 functionless 13 supernumerary
Ottawa chief 7 Pontiac
ottoman 4 seat 5 couch 6 fabric 9 footstool
Ottoman 4 Turk 7 Turkish *ruler:*
5 Osman, Selim 8 Suleiman, Süleyman
Otus 5 giant *brother:* 9 Ephialtes *father:*
6 Aloeus 8 Poseidon *mother:* 9 Iphimedia *slayer:* 6 Apollo
ouch 3 cry 5 bezel, jewel 6 brooch,
buckle 7 setting 8 ornament 11 exclamation
ounce 3 bit, cat 4 dram 5 pinch, scrap,
shred 6 amount, splash, weight 7 measure, modicum, smidgen 8 fraction, particle 11 snow leopard
our *French:* 5 notre *Italian:* 6 nostra
Our Town author 6 Wilder (Thornton)
oust 4 fire, sack 5 eject, evict, expel
6 banish, deport, remove, topple,
unseat 7 boot out, cast out, deprive,
dismiss, kick out 8 displace, drive out,
force out, relegate, supplant, take
away, throw out 10 dispossess
ouster 7 removal 8 ejection, eviction
9 discharge, dismissal, expulsion
10 banishment
out 4 away, exit 5 forth, loose 6 absent,
excuse *of control:* 4 wild 7 chaotic *of
gas:* 5 tired 7 drained 9 exhausted *of
line:* 4 awry, rude 5 askew, fresh *of
place:* 13 inappropriate *of sorts:* 5 cross
7 grouchy, peevish 9 irritable *of the ordinary:* 3 odd 7 bizarre, strange, unusual
outage 4 loss 5 break 7 failure 8 blackout 12 interruption
out-and-out 5 gross, sheer, total, utter
7 perfect 8 absolute, complete, positive
9 downright 10 consummate 11 unmitigated, unqualified 13 thoroughgoing
outback 4 bush 6 sticks 7 boonies
9 boondocks 10 hinterland, wilderness
outboard 4 boat 5 motor 6 engine
outbreak 4 rash, rise, rush 5 burst, flare,
spike, surge 6 attack, blowup, plague,
revolt 7 flare-up 8 epidemic, eruption,
increase, uprising 9 rebellion 12 insurrection

outburst 3 fit 4 gush, gust 5 flare, sally,
scene, spasm, storm, surge 6 frenzy,
tirade 7 flare-up, tantrum, torrent
8 eruption, paroxysm, upheaval
9 explosion
outcast 4 hobo 5 exile, leper, tramp
6 pariah 7 Ishmael, vagrant 8 castaway,
derelict, vagabond 9 reprobate 10 expatriate, Ishmaelite 11 offscouring,
untouchable
outclass 3 top 4 best 5 excel 6 exceed
7 surpass
outcome 3 end 5 event, fruit, issue
6 effect, result, sequel, upshot 9 aftermath 10 conclusion 11 aftereffect, consequence, development
outcrop 4 rock 5 ledge 6 appear 7 project 8 protrude 10 projection, protrusion 12 protuberance
outcry 4 yell 5 noise, shout 6 clamor,
tumult, uproar 7 auction, ferment,
protest 8 upheaval 9 commotion, objection 11 exclamation
outdated 3 old 5 passé 6 démodé, old hat
7 antique 12 old-fashioned
outdistance 3 top 4 beat, best, pass
5 trump 6 better 7 eclipse, surpass
outdo 3 top 4 beat, best 5 excel, trump
6 better, defeat, exceed 7 eclipse, surpass, triumph 8 overcome 9 transcend
outdoor 7 open-air 8 alfresco
outer 6 remote 7 surface 8 exoteric,
exterior, external 9 extrinsic 10 extraneous 11 superficial
outermost 4 last 5 final 6 far-off 7 distant, extreme 8 farthest, furthest,
remotest
outfit 3 kit, rig, set 4 band, firm, gear,
suit, team, togs, unit 5 corps, dress,
equip, getup, group, squad, troop
6 clothe, supply, tackle, troupe
7 appoint, company, concern, costume,
furnish 8 accouter, accoutre, business,
clothing, ensemble, matériel, tackling
9 equipment, provision 10 enterprise
12 organization 13 accouterments,
accoutrements, establishment
outflank 5 evade 6 bypass 9 get around
10 circumvent
outflow 6 efflux 8 drainage, effluent
9 effluence
out-front 4 open 5 frank 6 candid, honest
10 forthright
outgoing 4 open 7 affable 8 friendly,
sociable 9 departing, expansive 10 gregarious, responsive 11 extroverted
outgrowth 6 effect, result 7 product,
spin-off 8 offshoot 9 by-product, offspring 10 derivative 11 aftereffect, consequence
outhouse 5 jakes, privy 7 latrine

outing 4 spin, trip **5** drive, jaunt, sally **6** junket, picnic **9** excursion **10** appearance, disclosure

outlandish 3 odd **4** wild **5** alien, outré, ultra, weird **6** exotic, quaint, remote, vulgar **7** bizarre, curious, extreme, foreign, offbeat, strange, uncouth, unusual **8** peculiar, singular **9** eccentric, fantastic, tasteless **10** ridiculous, unorthodox **11** extravagant

outlast 6 endure **7** survive, weather **9** withstand

outlaw 3 ban, con **4** wild **5** crook **6** bandit, banned, enjoin, forbid **7** exclude, illegal **8** criminal, disallow, fugitive, prohibit, renegade, restrict **9** desperado, illegalize, interdict, proscribe **10** rebellious

outlay 3 pay, tab **4** cost, give **5** spend **6** amount, expend **7** expense, payment **8** disburse **11** expenditure **12** disbursement

outlet 4 exit, hole, mart, shop, vent **5** issue, store **6** avenue, egress, escape, market **7** channel, opening, passage, release **8** aperture **10** discounter, receptacle

outline 4 edge, form, limn, plan **5** brief, draft, shape, trace **6** bounds, border, précis, schema, sketch **7** contour, profile, summary **8** abstract, boundary, skeleton, syllabus, synopsis **9** delineate, summarize **10** figuration, silhouette **11** skeletonize

outlive 7 survive, weather

outlook 4 side, view **5** angle, scope, sight, slant, vista **6** aspect, future **7** promise **8** attitude, forecast, position, prospect **9** direction, viewpoint **10** standpoint **11** expectation, observatory, perspective, point of view

outlying 3 far **6** far-off, remote **7** distant, faraway, removed **8** far-flung

outmoded 4 dead **5** dated, passé, tired **8** obsolete **9** moth-eaten, unstylish **10** oldfangled **11** obsolescent **12** old-fashioned

Out of Africa author 7 Dinesen (Isak)

out-of-date 3 old **4** past **5** passé, stale **6** démodé, old hat, square **7** antique, archaic, old-time, vintage **8** obsolete **9** unstylish **10** antiquated **12** old-fashioned

out of it 4 lost **5** dazed **7** muddled **8** confused **10** bewildered

out-of-the-way 4 rare **6** remote **7** distant, obscure, removed, unusual **8** secluded, uncommon

outpost 4 base **6** branch, colony **8** foothold **10** detachment, settlement

outpouring 4 flow, gush, rush **5** burst, flood, spate, spurt **6** deluge, stream **7** torrent **8** effusion

output 4 crop, gain, take **5** power, yield **6** amount, profit **7** harvest, produce, product **10** production **11** achievement, information

outrage 4 fury, rape **5** abuse, shock, wrong **6** injury, insult, offend **7** affront, incense, violate **8** aggrieve, atrocity, illtreat, mischief, violence **9** brutality, infuriate **10** resentment, scandalize

outrageous 5 awful, gross **6** horrid, insane, odious, unholy, wicked **7** beastly, ghastly, heinous, ignoble, obscene **8** dreadful, flagrant, horrible, shocking, terrible **9** atrocious, egregious, excessive, fantastic **10** abominable, inordinate, scandalous **11** intolerable

outré 3 odd **5** ultra **6** far-out **7** bizarre, extreme, off-beat, strange **8** peculiar **9** eccentric

outrigger 4 beam, boat, prau, proa, spar

outright 4 pure **5** total, utter, whole **6** entire **7** perfect **8** absolute, complete, entirely, positive **9** on the spot **10** completely, consummate **11** unequivocal, unmitigated, unqualified **13** thoroughgoing

outrun 3 top **4** beat, pass **6** exceed **7** surpass

outset 4 dawn **5** birth, start **7** opening **9** beginning, inception **12** commencement

outshine 3 top **4** beat, best **5** excel **6** exceed **7** surpass

outside 5 alien **7** foreign, open-air **8** alfresco, exterior, external

outsider 5 alien **7** inconnu **8** newcomer, stranger **9** foreigner

outsmart see OUTWIT

outspoken 4 free, open **5** blunt, frank, plain, vocal **6** candid, direct, honest **7** up front **8** explicit **10** forthright, point-blank, unreserved **11** unequivocal

outstanding 3 due **4** star **5** noted, owing **6** signal, superb, unpaid **7** capital, eminent, notable, salient, stellar **8** dominant, striking, superior **9** arresting, excellent, prominent, unsettled **10** noticeable, preeminent, remarkable, unresolved **11** conspicuous, distinctive, exceptional, magnificent, superlative, uncollected **13** extraordinary

outstrip 3 top **4** beat, best, pass **5** excel **6** better, exceed **7** surpass **8** distance, go beyond, overtake **9** transcend **11** leave behind

outward 5 overt **7** evident, visible **8** apparent, exterior, external **10** noticeable, ostensible **11** superficial

outweigh 6 exceed 8 overbear 10 overshadow 11 overbalance 12 preponderate

outworn see OUTMODED

ouzel 6 dipper, thrush 9 blackbird

oval 5 track 6 oblong 7 ellipse 8 elliptic 9 egg-shaped, racetrack 10 elliptical 11 ellipsoidal

ovation 5 kudos 6 homage, praise 7 acclaim, tribute 8 applause, approval, cheering, clapping, plaudits 11 acclamation

oven 4 kiln, oast 5 range, stove

over 4 anew, atop, done, past, upon 5 above, again, aloft, ended 6 across, beyond 8 finished, once more *French:* 3 sur *German:* 4 über *prefix:* 3 epi, sur 5 extra, hyper, super, supra *Spanish:* 5 sobre

overabundance 4 glut 6 excess 7 surfeit, surplus 8 plethora 10 surplusage 11 superfluity

overact 3 ham, mug 4 rant 5 emote 10 exaggerate

overage 6 excess 7 surplus

overall 5 smock, total 6 global, mainly, mostly 7 chiefly, general, largely 8 as a whole, sweeping 9 generally, inclusive, in general, primarily 10 far and wide 11 principally 13 comprehensive, predominantly

overalls 5 pants 8 trousers

over and above 4 also 6 as well, beyond 7 besides 8 as well as 10 in addition

over and over 3 oft 5 often 8 ofttimes 10 frequently, oftentimes, repeatedly 11 continually, recurrently

overbearing 5 bossy 6 lordly 7 haughty, pompous 8 absolute, arrogant, despotic, dogmatic, dominant, imperial, insolent, scornful, superior 9 imperious, tyrannous 10 autocratic, disdainful, dominating, high-handed, oppressive, peremptory, tyrannical 11 dictatorial, domineering, magisterial 12 supercilious 13 high-and-mighty

overblown 6 turgid 7 flowery, hyped up, orotund, pompous 8 inflated 9 bombastic, excessive, high-flown 10 euphuistic, oratorical, rhetorical 11 declamatory, exaggerated, pretentious 12 magniloquent 13 grandiloquent

overcast 3 sew 4 dull, gray, hazy 5 cloud, cover 6 cloudy, darken, shadow 7 becloud, blanket, clouded, obscure 8 covering, lowering 9 adumbrate

overcharge 3 pad 4 bilk, clip, skin, soak 5 cheat, stick 6 fleece 7 inflate

overcoat 5 paint 6 capote, raglan, ulster 7 surtout 9 balmacaan, outerwear 12 chesterfield

overcome 4 beat, best, lick 5 drown, throw 6 defeat, hurdle, master 7 conquer, prevail, triumph 8 surmount 9 prostrate

overconfident 4 rash 5 brash, cocky, pushy 8 arrogant, cocksure, reckless 9 hubristic, presuming 12 presumptuous

overdo 7 exhaust, fatigue, wear out 9 embellish 10 exaggerate

overdue 4 late 5 owing, tardy 6 behind, unpaid 7 belated, delayed, payable 8 dilatory 9 unsettled 10 behindhand, delinquent, unpunctual 11 outstanding

overemphasize 7 magnify 8 heighten 9 dramatize, embellish 10 exaggerate

overflow 4 pour 5 cover, drown, flood, slosh, spate, spill, swamp 6 deluge, engulf, excess, outlet 7 surfeit, surplus, torrent 8 flooding, inundate, spillage, submerge 10 inundation, surplusage 11 superfluity

overgrown 4 lush 5 dense, thick 6 brushy 7 hulking 8 ungainly 9 excessive, ponderous 10 junglelike

overhang 3 jut 4 loom 5 bulge 6 beetle, extend, impend 7 project 8 protrude, stick out, threaten 10 projection

overhaul 3 fix 4 mend, redo 5 patch, renew 6 doctor, remake, repair, revamp, revise 7 rebuild, restore 8 renovate 11 recondition, reconstruct

overhead 4 atop 5 above, aloft, smash 7 ceiling, expense 8 expenses

overheated 5 fiery 7 fervent 8 inflated 9 perfervid 11 impassioned

overindulgence 6 excess 7 surfeit 8 gluttony 11 dissipation 12 immoderation, intemperance

overjoyed 6 elated 7 gleeful 8 ecstatic, euphoric, exultant, jubilant, thrilled 9 rapturous 11 transported

overkill 4 glut 6 excess 7 surfeit, surplus, too much 8 plethora 10 obliterate, redundancy, surplusage 11 superfluity

overlap 7 shingle 9 imbricate

overlay 3 cap 4 coat 5 cover, glaze 6 finish, veneer 7 blanket, coating, lacquer, varnish 8 covering 11 superimpose 12 transparency

overload 4 glut 5 stuff 6 burden, excess, pile on, strain 7 surfeit

overlook 4 fail, miss, omit, skip 5 check, let go 6 excuse, forget, ignore, pass by, slight, slip up, survey, wink at 7 blink at, condone, forgive, inspect, let pass, neglect 8 discount, dominate, surmount 9 disregard, supervise 11 superintend

overlord 4 czar, tsar, tzar 5 chief, mogul, ruler 6 tycoon 7 magnate 8 suzerain 9 potentate, sovereign

overly 3 too **6** unduly **11** exceedingly, excessively **12** immoderately, inordinately

overpass 5 cross **6** bridge **8** crossing, traverse **9** traversal **11** interchange

overplay 4 hype **6** expand **7** enlarge, inflate, magnify, point up, stretch **8** maximize **9** dramatize **10** exaggerate **11** hyperbolize

overpower 4 rout **5** crush, swamp, whelm **6** defeat, master, subdue **7** conquer **8** vanquish **9** prostrate, subjugate

overreach 3 con **4** beat, bilk **5** cheat, outdo **6** defeat, outfox, outwit **7** defraud **8** flimflam, outsmart **10** exaggerate **11** outmaneuver

override 4 veto **5** annul **6** cancel **7** nullify **10** counteract, neutralize

overriding 3 key **4** main **5** chief, major, prime, vital **7** central, crucial, pivotal, primary, supreme **8** cardinal, dominant, foremost **9** paramount, principal

overrule 4 undo, veto **5** upset **6** negate, revoke **7** reverse **8** set aside **11** countermand

overrun 4 beat, raid, teem, whip **5** swamp, swarm **6** defeat, excess, infest, invade, occupy, ravage, spread, thrash **7** clobber, conquer

overseas 6 abroad **11** transmarine, ultramarine **12** transoceanic

oversee 3 run **4** boss **5** watch **6** direct, manage, survey **7** command, examine, inspect **8** supervise **11** superintend

overseer 4 boss, exec, head **5** chief **7** foreman, manager **8** director **9** executive **10** supervisor **13** administrator

overshadow 4 veil **5** cloud, dwarf, shade **6** darken, exceed **7** becloud, eclipse, obscure, surpass **8** dominate, outshine, outweigh **9** adumbrate

overshoe 4 boot **6** arctic, galosh, patten, rubber

oversight 4 care, slip **5** aegis, check, error, lapse **6** charge, slip-up **7** control, failure, mistake, neglect **8** omission **10** intendance, management **11** supervision

overspread 3 cap **5** beset, cover, flood, swarm **6** infest, invade **7** blanket, obscure, pervade **8** permeate

overstate 3 pad **7** amplify, enlarge, magnify **9** embellish, embroider **10** exaggerate

overstep 6 exceed, offend **7** surpass, violate **8** infringe, trespass **10** transgress

overstock 4 glut **5** extra **6** excess **7** surplus **9** remainder **10** surplusage

overstress 7 magnify **8** maximize **10** exaggerate

overt 4 open **5** clear **6** patent **7** evident,

obvious, outward, visible **8** apparent, manifest **10** observable

overtake 4 pass **5** catch **6** pass by **7** outpace, surpass **8** come upon, outstrip **11** outdistance

Over the Rainbow *composer:* **5** Arlen (Harold) **7** Harburg (E. Y.) *singer:* **7** Garland (Judy)

over there 3 yon **6** yonder

over-the-top 7 extreme **8** reckless **9** egregious, excessive **10** exorbitant, flamboyant, outrageous **11** extravagant

overthrow 4 fell, oust, rout **5** purge, upset **6** defeat, depose, remove, topple, unseat **7** conquer **8** dethrone, downfall **9** bring down

overtone 4 hint **5** sense **8** coloring, harmonic **9** inference **10** suggestion **11** association, connotation, implication **12** undercurrent

overture 3 bid **5** proem **7** advance, preface, prelude, present **8** approach, foreword, preamble, prologue, proposal **9** prelusion **10** initiative **11** proposition **12** introduction, presentation

overturn 3 tip **4** flip, void **5** upend, upset **6** topple, tumble **7** capsize, nullify, reverse **8** set aside **10** invalidate

overused 5 stale, tired, trite **7** clichéd, worn-out **9** hackneyed

overview 6 aperçu, précis, survey **7** epitome, summary **10** conspectus

overweening 5 brash, pushy **6** lordly, uppish, uppity **7** forward **8** arrogant **9** conceited, presuming **10** immoderate **11** exaggerated **12** presumptuous

overweight 3 fat **5** beefy, burly, dumpy, gross, heavy, husky, obese, plump, pudgy, stout **6** chubby, chunky, flabby, fleshy, portly, rotund **7** outsize **8** heavyset, thickset **9** corpulent

overwhelm 4 beat, bury, rout, ruin, sink, whip **5** crush, drown, flood, swamp, upset, wreck **6** defeat, deluge, engulf, thrash **7** conquer, destroy, oppress, shatter, shellac, smother **8** inundate, submerge **9** devastate, prostrate **10** demoralize **11** subordinate

overwhelmed 6 aghast, **7** shocked, stunned, touched **8** defeated, helpless **10** distressed **13** thunderstruck

overwhelming 4 huge **5** great **7** extreme **8** numerous

overwrought 5 hyper, upset **7** anxious, frantic, wound up **8** agitated, frenetic, stressed, troubled **9** disturbed, emotional **10** distracted, freaked out, highstrung, hysterical **11** discomposed

Ovid work 5 Fasti **6** Amores **7** Tristia **8** Heroides **13** Metamorphoses

ovine 5 sheep **9** sheeplike

ovoid 4 oval 5 ovate 9 egg-shaped
ovule 3 egg *fertilized:* 4 seed
ovum 3 egg 6 gamete 7 egg cell
11 macrogamete
owing 3 due 6 in debt, mature, unpaid
7 overdue, payable 9 unsettled 11 outstanding
owing to 4 over 7 through 9 because of
10 by reason of 11 on account of
owl *cry:* 4 hoot *genus:* 4 Otus *kind:* 3 elf
4 barn, gray, lulu 5 eagle, gnome,
madge, pygmy, snowy 6 barred, horned
7 saw-whet, screech 9 long-eared
10 short-eared 11 great horned
Owl and the Pussycat author 4 Lear
(Edward)
own 4 avow, have, hold 5 admit, allow,
enjoy, grant, let on 6 accept, fess up,
retain 7 concede, confess, possess 8 disclose 9 recognize 11 acknowledge
owner 6 holder 8 landlady, landlord
9 possessor, purchaser 10 proprietor
ownership 4 hand 5 title 8 dominion,
property 10 possession 11 proprietary
perpetual: 8 mortmain
ox 3 yak 4 anoa, gaur, musk, zebu
5 bison, steer 6 bovine 7 banteng, buffalo *Asian:* 4 zebu *attachment:* 4 yoke
extinct: 4 urus 7 aurochs *family:* 7 Bovidae *relating to:* 6 bovine *wild:* 4 anoa,
gaur 7 banteng
oxeye 5 daisy 6 flower
oxford 4 shoe 5 cloth, sheep 6 cotton,
fabric
oxide *calcium:* 4 lime 9 quicklime *ferric:*
4 rust *sodium:* 4 soda
oxidize 4 rust
oxygen 3 air, gas 5 ozone 7 element *discoverer:* 9 Lavoisier (Antoine) *form:*
5 ozone *liquid:* 3 lox
oyster 7 bivalve, mollusc, mollusk *bed:*
4 park 6 claire, cultch *eggs:* 5 spawn
genus: 6 Ostrea *Long Island:* 9 bluepoint
product: 5 pearl *shell:* 4 test 5 shuck
young: 4 spat
oyster plant 7 salsify
Oz *creator:* 4 Baum (L. Frank) *inhabitant:*
8 Munchkin *princess:* 4 Ozma
Ozark State 8 Missouri
Ozem *brother:* 5 David *father:* 5 Jesse
9 Jerahmeel
Ozymandias author 7 Shelley (Percy
Bysshe)

P

pabulum 3 pap 4 food 7 aliment 8 nutrient 9 blandness, nutriment 10 insipidity, sustenance 11 nourishment
paca 4 cavy
pace 3 set 4 beat, clip, gait, lead, rate,
step, time, walk 5 speed, tempo, tread,
troop 6 motion, stride, timing 7 example, fluency, measure, precede, proceed, routine, step off 8 ambulate,
antecede, movement, progress, regulate
pachyderm 8 elephant
pacific 4 calm, mild 6 gentle, irenic,
placid, serene 8 dovelike, peaceful,
soothing, tranquil 9 peaceable, temperate 12 conciliatory
Pacificator, Great 4 Clay (Henry)
Pacific nation 5 Belau, Japan, Nauru,
Palau, Tonga 6 Tuvalu 7 Vanuatu
8 Kiribati
Pacific Ocean discoverer 6 Balboa
(Vasco Núñez de)
pacifist 4 dove 6 irenic 8 appeaser,
peaceful, peacenik 9 peaceable 10 nonviolent 11 peacemonger
pacify 4 calm, cool, ease, lull 5 allay,
quell, quiet, still 6 disarm, settle, soften, soothe, subdue, temper 7 appease,
assuage, mollify, placate 9 subjugate
10 conciliate, propitiate
pack 3 jam, kit, lot, lug, ram, set, wad
4 band, bear, cram, deck, fill, gang,
heap, load, lump, mass, pile, stow,
tamp, tote, unit 5 bunch, carry, cover,
crowd, ferry, group, store, stuff, troop
6 bundle, charge, clique, convey,
depart, gather 7 possess 8 assemble,
compress, knapsack 9 container, equipment, influence, transport 10 collection, congregate

package 3 box **4** deal, unit, wrap **5** array, combo, whole **6** bundle, parcel **7** enclose, present, wrapper **8** shipment **9** container **10** collection **11** combination

pack animal 3 ass **4** mule **5** burro, camel, horse, llama **6** donkey **7** jackass **13** beast of burden

packed 4 full **5** awash, dense, flush **6** filled, jammed **7** brimful, crowded, stuffed **8** brimming **9** chock-full **10** compressed

packet 3 wad **4** boat, mass, pile **5** group **6** bundle, parcel **7** cluster

pact 4 bond, deal **6** accord, treaty **7** bargain, concord **8** alliance, contract, covenant **9** agreement

pad 3 bed, mat, wad **4** foot, mute **5** fudge, guard, paper, stuff **6** buffer, expand, muffle, shield, tablet **7** augment, bolster, cushion, stretch **8** dressing, increase **9** embellish, embroider, overstate **10** exaggerate, overcharge

paddle 3 oar, row **4** beat, stir **5** spank **6** propel, thrash

paddock 5 field **7** pasture **9** enclosure

paddy wagon 10 Black Maria

padre 3 Fra **6** father, priest **8** chaplain, minister **9** clergyman, confessor

paean 4 hymn, song **6** anthem, eulogy, praise **7** tribute **8** accolade, encomium **9** panegyric

page 4 book, call, leaf **5** folio, sheet **6** locate, summon **7** bellhop, equerry *left-hand:* **5** verso *right-hand:* **5** recto

pageant 4 sham, show **7** charade, display, tableau **8** pretense **9** spectacle **10** exhibition

pageantry 4 pomp, show **7** display, panoply **8** flourish, splendor **9** spectacle **10** exhibition **11** flamboyance, ostentation **12** magnificence

Pagliacci, I *character:* **5** Canio, Nedda, Tonio **6** Silvio *composer:* **11** Leoncavallo (Ruggero)

pagoda 6 temple

pail 6 bucket, piggin, vessel

pain 3 irk **4** ache, care, hurt, pang **5** agony, cramp, grief, throe, upset **6** grieve, harass, stitch, twinge **7** afflict, anguish, torture, travail, trouble **8** aggrieve, distress **9** suffering **10** affliction, discomfort *back:* **7** lumbago *muscular:* **7** myalgia

painful 3 raw **4** hard, sore **5** acute, sharp **6** aching, trying **7** arduous, irksome **8** annoying, piercing, stinging **9** agonizing, difficult, laborious, torturous, upsetting, vexatious **10** afflictive, tormenting

painkiller 4 drug **6** opiate **7** anodyne,

codeine **8** morphine, narcotic **9** analgesic **10** anesthetic

painstaking 5 exact **7** careful, heedful **8** diligent, exacting, thorough **9** assiduous, diligence, laborious **10** meticulous, scrupulous **11** punctilious

paint 4 coat, daub, limn, swab, tint **5** adorn, brush, color, cover, horse, pinto, rouge, stain **6** depict, makeup **7** coating, pigment, portray, produce, touch up **8** cosmetic, decorate **9** delineate, represent **10** maquillage

painter 6 artist *American:* **4** Cole (Thomas), Haas (Richard), West (Benjamin), Wood (Grant) **5** Abbey (Edwin Austin), Davis (Stuart), Gorky (Arshile), Grosz (George), Henri (Robert), Hicks (Edward), Homer (Winslow), Johns (Jasper), Kline (Franz), Kroll (Leon), Marin (John), Marsh (Reginald), Moses (Grandma), Peale (Anna, Charles Willson, James, Raphaelle, Rembrandt, Sarah, Titian), Ryder (Albert Pinkham), Shahn (Ben), Sloan (Eric, John), Weber (Max), Wyeth (Andrew, Jamie, Newell Convers) **6** Albers (Josef), Benton (Thomas Hart), Catlin (George), Church (Frederick Edwin), Coburn (Alvin Langdon), Copley (John Singleton), Durand (Asher), Eakins (Thomas), Hassam (Childe), Hopper (Edward), Inness (George), Leutze (Emanuel), Martin (Agnes, Homer), Newman (Barnett), Rivers (Larry), Rothko (Mark), Stella (Frank), Stuart (Gilbert), Tanguy (Yves), Thorpe (Thomas), Warhol (Andy) **7** Allston (Washington), Bearden (Romare), Bellows (George), Bingham (George Caleb), Cassatt (Mary), Duchamp (Marcel), Harnett (William), Hartley (Marsden), Kinkade (Thomas), La Farge (John), O'Keeffe (Georgia), Parrish (Maxfield), Pollock (Jackson), Sargent (John Singer), Sheeler (Charles), Tiffany (Louis Comfort), Tworkov (Jack), Wiggins (Carleton) **8** Melchers (Gari), Rockwell (Norman), Sullivan (Patrick), Trumbull (John), Whistler (James McNeill) **9** Bierstadt (Albert), de Kooning (Willem), Feininger (Lyonel), Reinhardt (Ad), Remington (Frederic), Twachtman (John Henry), Vanderlyn (John) **10** Motherwell (Robert), Whittredge (Thomas) **12** Lichtenstein (Roy), Rauschenberg (Robert) *Austrian:* **5** Klimt (Gustav) **9** Kokoschka (Oskar) *Belgian:* **5** Ensor (James) **6** Campin (Robert) **8** Magritte (René) *Canadian:* **4** Kane (Paul) **6** Harris (Lawren), Watson (Homer) **7** Jackson (Alexander Young), Thomson (Tom) **9** MacDonald (James Edward Hervey) *Chinese:* **4** Wu Li **6** Ma Yüan **7** Wang Wei **8** Yen Li-pen *Dutch:* **3** Dou (Gerrit) **4** Hals (Frans), Lely (Peter), Maas (Nicolas) **5** Bosch (Hieronymus), Hooch (Pieter de), Steen (Jan) **6** Potter (Paul) **7** de Hooch (Pieter), de Witte (Emanuel), Hobbema (Meindert), van Gogh (Vincent), Vermeer (Jan) **8** Mondrian (Piet), Ruisdael (Jacob van, Salomon), Ruysdael (Salomon), Terborch (Gerard) **9** de Kooning (Willem), Rembrandt (van Rijn), Wouwerman (Philips) **11** Terbrugghen (Hendrik) *English:* **4** John (Augustus), Lear (Edward) **5** Bacon (Francis), Blake (William), Brown (Ford Madox), Lewis (Wyndham), Watts (George Frederick) **6** Romney (George), Turner (Joseph Mallord William), Wilson (Richard) **7** Hogarth (William), Kneller (Godfrey), Millais (John) **8** Lawrence (Thomas), Reynolds (Joshua), Rossetti (Dante Gabriel) **9** Constable (John), Nicholson (Ben, William) **12** Gainsborough (Thomas) *Finnish:* **9** Järnefelt (Edvard) *Flemish:* **4** Eyck (Hubert van, Jan van), Goes (Hugo van der) **6** Rubens (Peter Paul), Weyden (Rogier van der) **7** Memling (Hams), Teniers (David), Van Dyck (Anthony), van Eyck (Hubert, Jan) **8** Breughel, Brueghel (Abraham, Ambrose, Jan, Pieter) *French:* **4** Doré (Gustave), Dufy (Raoul), Erté **5** Corot (Camille), David (Jacques-Louis), Degas (Edgar), Léger (Fernand), Manet (Edouard), Monet (Claude), Redon (Odilon), Vouet (Simon) **6** Braque (Georges), Breton (André), Claude (of Lorrain), Clouet (François, Jean), Gérôme (Jean-Léon), Greuze (Jean-Baptiste), Ingres (Jean-Auguste-Dominique), Le Brun (Charles), Le Nain (Antoine, Louis, Mathieu), Millet (Jean-François), Renoir (Pierre-Auguste), Seurat (Georges), Sisley (Alfred), Tanguy (Yves), Vernet (Carle, Horace, Joseph) **7** Balthus, Bonheur (Rosa), Bonnard (Pierre), Boucher (François), Cézanne (Paul), Chardin (Jean-Baptiste), Courbet (Gustave), Daumier (Honoré), Duchamp (Gaston, Marcel), Gauguin (Paul), Matisse (Henri), Morisot (Berthe), Poussin (Nicolas), Rouault (Georges), Utrillo (Maurice), Watteau (Antoine) **8** Dubuffet (Jean), Magritte (René), Pissarro (Camille), Rousseau (Henri, Théodore), Vlaminck (Maurice de), Vuillard

(Edouard) **9** Delacroix (Eugène), Fragonard (Jean-Honoré), Géricault (Théodore), Laurencin (Marie) **10** Bouguereau (William), Meissonier (Jean-Louis) **11** Caillebotte (Gustave) **13** Claude Lorrain *German:* **5** Dürer (Albrecht), Ernst (Max), Grosz (George), Nolde (Emil) **6** Albers (Josef), Müller (Friedrich "Maler") **7** Cranach (Lucas), Holbein (Hans), Lochner (Stefan), Schwind (Moritz von), Zoffany (Johann) **8** Kirchner (Ernst), Kollwitz (Käthe) **9** Grünewald (Matthias), Kandinsky (Wassily) **10** Schongauer (Martin), Wohlgemuth (Michael) *Greek:* **6** Zeuxis **7** Apelles **10** Polygnotus *Irish:* **5** Yeats (Jack, John Butler) *Italian:* **4** Reni (Guido), Rosa (Salvator), Tura (Cosme) **5** Campi (Antonio, Bernardino, Giulio, Vincenzo), Lippi (Fra Filippo, Filippino, Lorenzo), Piero (della Francesca, di Cosimo), Sarto (Andrea del) **6** Andrea (del Sarto), Cosimo (Agnolo di, Piero di), Giotto, Romano (Giulio), Sodoma (Il), Titian, Vasari (Giorgio) **7** Bellini (Gentile, Giovanni, Jacopo), Chirico (Giorgio De), Cimabue, da Vinci (Leonardo), Fiesole (Giovanni da), Martini (Simone), Orcagna, Peruzzi (Baldassare), Raphael, Tiepolo (Giovanni), Uccello (Paolo), Zuccari (Taddeo) **8** del Sarto (Andrea), Fabriano (Gentile da), Giordano (Luca), Leonardo (da Vinci), Mantegna (Andrea), Masaccio, Montagna (Bartolommeo), Perugino, Pontorno (Jacopo da), Severini (Gino), Veronese (Paolo), Vivarini (Alvise, Antonio, Bartolomeo) **9** Carpaccio (Vittore), Correggio, Francesca (Piero della) **10** Caravaggio, Modigliani (Amedeo), Signorelli (Luca), Tintoretto, Verrocchio (Andrea del), Zuccarelli (Francesco) **11** Ghirlandaio (Domenico), Ghirlandajo (Domenico) **12** Michelangelo (Buonarotti), Parmigianino *Japanese:* **5** Korin **6** Sesshu *Lithuanian:* **7** Soutine (Chaim) *Mexican:* **6** Orozco (José), Rivera (Diego), Tamayo (Rufino) **9** Siqueiros (David) *Norwegian:* **5** Munch (Edvard) *Russian:* **7** Chagall (Marc), Roerich (Nikolay) **9** Kandinsky (Wassily) *Scottish:* **6** Ramsay (Allan) **7** Nasmyth (Alexander), Raeburn (Henry) *Spanish:* **4** Dalí (Salvador), Goya (Francisco), Gris (Juan), Miró (Joan), Sert (José Maria) **6** Ribera (José), Rincón (Antonio del), Tapiés (Antonio) **7** El Greco, Herrera (Francisco de), Murillo (Bartolomé Este-

ban), Picasso (Pablo), Zuloaga (Ignacio) **8** Zurbarán (Francisco de) **9** Velázquez (Diego) *Swedish:* **4** Zorn (Anders) **6** Roslin (Alexander) *Swiss:* **4** Klee (Paul), Witz (Konrad)
painting 3 oil **7** acrylic, picture **10** watercolor *circular:* **5** tondo *one-color:* **8** monotint **10** monochrome *plaster:* **5** secco **6** fresco *style:* **4** Dada **5** fauve **6** cubism, cubist, Gothic, pop art, rococo **7** baroque, Bauhaus, dadaism, fauvism, fauvist, realism, realist **8** Barbizon, futurism, futurist, romantic **9** Byzantine, geometric, mannerism, mannerist **10** classicism, classicist, surrealism, surrealist **11** romanticism **13** expressionism, expressionist, impressionism, impressionist *technique:* **3** oil **6** fresco, pastel **7** gouache, polymer, tempera **9** encaustic **10** watercolor *tool:* **5** brush, easel, knife, paint **6** canvas **7** palette *wall:* **5** mural
pair 3 duo, two **4** dyad, join, mate, span, team, twin, yoke **5** brace, match, twins, unite **6** couple **7** doublet, twosome **8** geminate
Pakistan *capital:* **9** Islamabad *city:* **6** Lahore, Multan **7** Karachi **9** Hyderabad **10** Faisalabad, Rawalpindi *language:* **4** Urdu *leader:* **6** Bhutto (Benazir) *monetary unit:* **5** rupee *mountain, range:* **8** Himalaya **9** Himalayan, Himalayas **11** Nanga Parbat *neighbor:* **4** Iran **5** China, India **11** Afghanistan *sea:* **7** Arabian
pal 4 chum, mate **5** amigo, buddy, crony **6** comate, friend **7** comrade, partner **9** companion
palace 5 court, manor, manse **6** castle **7** alcazar, château, mansion
paladin 6 leader **8** advocate, champion, defender, official
Palamedes *brother:* **6** Sforza **8** Achilles *father:* **8** Nauplius *slayer:* **7** Corinda, Ulysses **8** Odysseus
palatable 5 sapid, tasty **6** savory **8** pleasing, savorous, tasteful **9** agreeable, appealing, delicious, toothsome **10** acceptable, appetizing **12** satisfactory
palate 5 taste **6** liking **6** relish
palatial 4 rich **5** grand, large, noble, plush, regal **6** deluxe, ornate **7** opulent, stately **8** imposing, majestic, splendid **9** grandiose, luxuriant, luxurious, sumptuous **10** impressive **11** magnificent
Palau *capital:* **5** Koror *former name:* **5** Pelew *island:* **5** Koror **6** Angaur **7** Eli Malk **10** Babelthuap, Urukthapel *language:* **7** English, Palauan
palaver 3 gas, yak **4** blab, cant, chat,

guff, talk **6** babble, cajole, hot air, jargon, parley, powwow, speech **7** chatter, prattle **8** colloquy, converse, dialogue **10** conference, discussion, rap session **12** conversation
pale 3 dim, wan **4** area, ashy, dull, fade, sick, weak **5** ashen, faded, faint, fence, field, light, livid, pasty, stake, waxen **6** anemic, blanch, chalky, doughy, feeble, pallid, picket, sallow, sickly, weaken, whiten **7** enclose, ghastly, insipid **8** blanched, district, encircle **9** bloodless, colorless, enclosure
palinode 10 retraction **11** recantation
pall 4 bore, cloy, damp, jade, sate, tire **5** cloak, cloth, cloud, drape, ennui, gloom, weary **6** coffin, damper, mantle, shadow **7** dwindle, satiate, surfeit **8** covering
palladium 9 safeguard
Pallas 6 Athena *brother:* **6** Aegeus *father:* **7** Pandion *slayer:* **7** Theseus *wife:* **4** Styx (see also ATHENA)
palliate 4 ease, help **5** cover, salve **6** excuse, lessen, reduce, soften, soothe, temper **7** assuage, cover up, lighten **8** mitigate, moderate **9** alleviate, sugarcoat, whitewash **10** ameliorate
pallid 3 wan **4** ashy, dull, pale, weak **5** ashen, pasty, waxen **6** anemic, doughy, sickly **8** blanched, lifeless **9** bloodless, colorless
pallor 8 lividity, paleness **9** pastiness, whiteness **10** etiolation **12** glaucousness
pally 4 cozy **5** close, matey **6** chummy **7** devoted **8** familiar, friendly, intimate
palm 5 prize, steal, swipe **6** trophy **7** conceal, triumph, victory *beverage:* **4** nipa *fiber:* **4** bass, bast **8** piassava *fruit:* **4** date **7** coconut **11** coquilla nut *kind:* **3** fan, wax **4** coco, date, doom, hemp, nipa, sago **5** areca, betel, ivory, royal **6** raffia, rattan **7** cabbage, feather, palmyra **8** carnauba, palmetto, piassava **12** Washingtonia *leaf:* **4** olla **5** frond *starch:* **4** sago *vine:* **6** rattan
palmer 7 pilgrim
Palmetto State 13 South Carolina
palmistry 6 augury **8** prophecy **10** divination **11** soothsaying
palm off 5 foist **7** deceive, pretend **8** disguise
palmy 6 golden **7** booming, halcyon, opulent **8** affluent, thriving **10** prospering, prosperous **11** flourishing
Palmyra's queen 7 Zenobia
palooka 3 oaf **4** boob, dolt, goon, lout, lump **5** boxer, klutz **6** baboon, galoot, lummox **7** bruiser
palpable 4 real, sure **5** clear, plain **6** patent **7** certain, concrete, evident,

obvious, tactile 8 apparent, definite, distinct, manifest, material, positive, tangible 10 noticeable 11 discernible, perceptible, unequivocal

palpate 4 feel 5 touch 6 finger 7 examine

palpitate 4 beat 5 pulse, throb 6 quiver 7 flutter, pulsate 12 pitter-patter

palsy-walsy 4 cozy 5 close, thick, tight 6 chummy 8 intimate 10 buddy-buddy

palter 3 fib, lie 5 evade 6 dicker, haggle 7 bargain, chaffer, deceive, falsify, wrangle 10 equivocate 11 prevaricate 12 misrepresent

paltry 3 low 4 base, mean, poor, puny, vile 5 cheap, petty, tatty 6 meager, measly, narrow, shabby, shoddy, sleazy, trashy 7 low-down, pitiful, trivial 8 beggarly, inferior, picayune, piddling, rubbishy, trifling 9 worthless 10 despicable, picayunish 11 unimportant 12 contemptible 13 insignificant

paludal place 3 fen 5 marsh

Pamela author 10 Richardson (Samuel)

pampa 5 plain 7 prairie 9 grassland

pamper 3 pet 4 baby 5 humor, spoil 6 caress, cocker, coddle, cosset, cuddle, dandle, fondle 7 cater to, cherish, gratify, indulge 9 spoon-feed 11 mollycoddle

pamphlet 5 flier, flyer, tract 6 folder 7 leaflet 8 brochure, circular 9 throwaway 10 broadsheet

pan 3 pot, rap 4 slam, wash 5 basin, knock, roast, trash 6 attack, vessel 7 censure, condemn, skillet 8 denounce, ridicule 9 betel leaf, container, criticism, criticize 10 receptacle

Pan 5 Inuus 6 Faunus *father:* 6 Hermes *invention:* 6 syrinx *lower part:* 4 goat *mother:* 8 Penelope *pipe:* 6 syrinx *seat of worship:* 7 Arcadia *son:* 7 Silenus

panacea 4 cure 6 remedy 7 cure-all, nostrum 10 catholicon

Panacea's father 9 Asclepius 11 Aesculapius

panache 4 brio, dash, élan, tuft, zest 5 ardor, crest, flair, style, verve, vigor 6 esprit, polish, spirit 8 aigrette, flourish, vivacity 11 flamboyance

panama 3 hat

Panama *capital:* 10 Panama City *discoverer:* 6 Balboa (Vasco Núñez de) 8 Columbus (Christopher) *gulf:* 7 San Blas 8 Mosquito *language:* 7 Spanish *leader:* 7 Noriega (Manuel) *monetary unit:* 6 balboa *neighbor:* 8 Colombia 9 Costa Rica *peninsula:* 6 Azuero *sea:* 9 Caribbean *volcano:* 8 Chiriquí

pancake 8 flapjack, slapjack *French:* 5 crepe *Jewish:* 5 latke 6 blintz 7 blintze *Russian:* 5 blini

Pandarus 6 archer 8 procuror *father:* 6 Lycaon *slayer:* 8 Diomedes

pandect 4 code, laws 8 treatise 10 compendium 11 compilation

pandemic 4 rife 7 general, rampant 9 contagion, extensive, prevalent 10 contagious, widespread 11 wide-ranging

pandemonium 3 din 5 babel, chaos, furor 6 bedlam, clamor, hubbub, tumult, uproar 7 anarchy, discord, inferno, misrule, turmoil 8 disorder 9 confusion 10 hullabaloo

pander 4 pimp 5 cater 9 exploiter, go-between

Pandion *daughter:* 6 Procne 9 Philomela *son:* 6 Pallas

Pandora *creator:* 10 Hephaestus *husband:* 10 Epimetheus

pane 4 side 5 sheet 7 section

panegyric 6 eulogy, praise 7 tribute 8 citation, encomium 9 laudation 10 compliment 12 commendation

panegyrical 8 praising 9 laudative, laudatory 10 eulogistic 11 encomiastic 12 commendatory 13 complimentary

panel 4 jury 5 board, frame 6 hurdle 7 section 9 dashboard

panfry 5 sauté

pang 4 ache, pain, stab 5 agony, prick, spasm, throe 6 stitch, twinge 7 anguish, torment 8 distress

Pangloss's pupil 7 Candide

panhandle 3 beg, bum, tap 5 cadge, hit up, touch 6 hustle 7 solicit

panhandler 6 beggar

panic 4 fear, riot, rush 5 alarm, scare 6 dismay, frenzy, fright, horror, terror 7 anxiety, terrify 8 frighten, hysteria, stampede

pannier 4 hoop, pack 6 basket, hamper 9 overskirt

panoply 4 pomp, show 5 armor, array 6 attire 7 display, fanfare 9 trappings

panorama 4 view 5 range, reach, scene, scope, sweep, vista 7 display, expanse, picture, purview 12 presentation

panoramic 8 sweeping, synoptic 12 all-inclusive, unobstructed 13 comprehensive

pan out 4 work 5 click, prove, score 7 come off, succeed

pant 4 blow, gasp, gulp, huff, puff 5 chuff, heave 6 wheeze

Pantagruel 5 giant *companion:* 7 Panurge *father:* 9 Gargantua *mother:* 7 Badebec

pantaloon 7 buffoon, trouser

Pantaloon's daughter 9 Columbine

pantheon 4 gods 5 Aesir 6 temple 9 hierarchy 10 hall of fame

panther 4 pard, puma **6** cougar, jaguar **7** leopard **12** mountain lion
pantomime 5 drama, mimic **6** act out, ballet, dancer **7** charade **12** harlequinade *clown:* **7** Pierrot
pantry 6 closet, larder **7** buttery **9** storeroom
pants 5 jeans **6** slacks **7** drawers, garment **8** breeches, britches, knickers, trousers
Panurge's companion 10 Pantagruel
Paolo's lover 9 Francesca
pap 4 food, mash, mush **7** aliment, pabulum **8** soft food **9** blandness, nutriment **10** sustenance **11** nourishment
papal 8 pontific **9** apostolic **10** pontifical *court:* **5** Curia *decree:* **8** decretal *envoy:* **6** nuncio *letter:* **4** bull **10** encyclical
paper 5 essay, sheet, theme **6** letter, report **7** article **8** document **9** monograph, newsprint **10** memorandum **11** composition, publication **12** dissertation *measure:* **4** ream **5** quire *roll:* **6** scroll *scrap:* **4** chad *size:* **3** cap **5** atlas, crown, folio, legal, royal, sexto, sixmo **6** octavo, quarto **7** emperor **8** elephant, foolscap, imperial *stiff:* **7** bristol **9** cardboard **12** bristol board *strong:* **5** kraft **6** manila *thin:* **6** tissue **9** onionskin *transparent:* **8** glassine *writing:* **3** rag **6** vellum **9** parchment
paper folding 7 origami
paperwork 7 red tape
papillon 7 spaniel **9** butterfly
Papua New Guinea *archipelago:* **8** Bismarck *capital:* **11** Port Moresby *city:* **3** Lae *island:* **12** Bougainville *language:* **4** Motu **8** Tok Pisin *monetary unit:* **4** kina *neighbor:* **9** Indonesia, Irian Jaya
par 4 mean, norm **5** equal, score, usual **6** median, normal **7** average, typical **8** equality, standard
parable 4 myth, tale **5** fable, moral, story **7** example **8** allegory
parachute 7 bailout, skydive *part:* **5** riser **6** canopy **7** harness, ripcord
Paraclete 9 Holy Ghost **10** Holy Spirit
parade 4 brag, pomp, show **5** array, boast, flash, march, shine, strut **6** expose, flaunt, ground, reveal, review **7** display, disport, exhibit, fanfare, marshal, panoply, show off, trot out **8** brandish, ceremony, movement, proclaim **9** advertise, cavalcade, pageantry, promenade **10** exhibition, masquerade, procession **11** demonstrate
paradigm 5 ideal, model **6** mirror **7** example, pattern **8** exemplar, standard **9** archetype, beau ideal, framework, prototype
paradise 4 Eden, Zion **5** bliss **6** heaven,

utopia **7** arcadia, elysium, nirvana **8** empyrean **9** Shangri-la **10** wonderland **12** New Jerusalem, promised land
Paradise Lost author 6 Milton (John)
paragon 3 gem **4** tops **5** champ, cream, ideal, jewel, match, model, peach, saint **6** beauty **7** compare, epitome **8** champion, exemplar, last word, nonesuch, parallel, ultimate **9** archetype, beau ideal, nonpareil **10** apotheosis
Paraguay *capital:* **8** Asunción *lake:* **4** Ypoá *language:* **7** Guarani, Spanish *monetary unit:* **7** guarani *neighbor:* **6** Brazil **7** Bolivia **9** Argentina *river:* **9** Pilcomayo
parallel 4 akin, copy, even, like **5** agree, align, alike, along, equal, liken, match **6** double, equate, line up **7** aligned, compare, similar **8** analogue **9** alongside, analogous, companion, consonant, corollary, correlate, duplicate **10** comparable, comparison, correspond, equivalent, similarity **11** coextensive, counterpart, duplication, resemblance **13** correspondent, corresponding
parallelogram 5 rhomb **6** oblong, square **7** rhombus **8** rhomboid **9** rectangle **13** quadrilateral
paralysis 5 palsy **7** inertia **9** impotence
paralyze 3 awe **4** daze, numb, stun **6** benumb, deaden, dismay **7** cripple, disable, nonplus, petrify, stupefy **8** shut down **10** immobilize **12** incapacitate
paramount 5 chief, ruler **6** master **7** capital, leading, primary, regnant, supreme **8** cardinal, crowning, dominant, foremost, headmost, superior **9** principal, sovereign, uppermost **10** commanding, preeminent **11** predominant
paramour 5 lover, Romeo **7** Don Juan, gallant **8** Casanova, lothario, mistress **9** courtesan, inamorata, inamorato
parapet 4 wall **7** bastion, bulwark, rampart **10** battlement, breastwork *part:* **6** merlon **12** crenellation
paraphernalia 4 gear **5** items **6** outfit, tackle **7** effects **8** property **9** equipment, trappings **10** belongings **11** accessories, furnishings **13** accouterments, accoutrements, appurtenances
paraphrase 6 reword **7** restate, version **9** interpret, rendering, translate **11** restatement, translation
parasite 5 leech, toady **6** sponge, sucker **7** sponger **8** barnacle, deadbeat, hanger-on **9** dependent, exploiter, sycophant **10** freeloader, self-seeker **11** bloodsucker
parasitic 8 sponging, toadying **9** leech-

like 11 freeloading, sycophantic
12 bloodsucking
parasol 8 umbrella
___ **paratus** 6 semper
Parcae 5 Fates, Norns 6 Moirai *name:*
4 Nona 5 Morta 6 Decuma
parcel 3 box, cut, lot 4 body, deal, land,
mete, pack, part, plot, wrap 5 allot,
array, batch, bunch, group, piece,
share, tract 6 assign, bundle, divide,
packet, ration 7 package, partial, portion, prorate, section, segment 8 allocate, disburse, disperse, division, part-
time 9 apportion, partition 10 distribute
parch 3 dry 4 burn, sear 5 dry up, roast,
toast 6 dry out, scorch 7 shrivel 9 dehydrate, desiccate
parched 3 dry 4 arid, sere 5 dusty
7 bone-dry, thirsty 8 scorched, withered
9 shriveled, waterless 10 dehydrated
parchment 4 skin 5 paper 6 vellum
7 diploma 8 document
pardon 4 free 5 remit, spare 6 excuse, let
off 7 absolve, amnesty, condone, forgive, release 8 liberate, reprieve, tolerate 9 acquittal, exculpate, indemnity,
remission 10 absolution, indulgence
11 exculpation, exoneration, forgiveness
pardonable 6 venial 9 allowable, excusable 11 permissible
pare 3 cut 4 clip, crop, peel, trim
5 lower, prune, shave 6 reduce, remove
7 curtail, cut back, cut down, trim off,
whittle 8 diminish
parent 4 make, rear 5 beget, cause,
hatch, raise, spawn 6 author, create,
father, mother, origin 7 bring up, care
for, produce 8 begetter, generate 9 originate, procreate 10 progenitor
parenthetically 7 by the by 8 by the bye,
by the way 9 in passing 12 incidentally
parentless 6 orphan 8 orphaned
par excellence 3 top 5 prime 7 premier,
supreme 8 foremost, peerless, superior
9 number one, unmatched 10 first-
class, preeminent 11 outstanding
pariah 5 leper 7 Ishmael, outcast 8 castaway 10 Ishmaelite 11 offscouring,
untouchable *Japanese:* 3 eta
Paris *ancient name:* 7 Lutetia *avenue:*
13 Champs-Elysées *basilica:* 10 Sacré
Coeur *cathedral:* 9 Notre Dame *city hall:*
12 Hôtel de Ville *college:* 8 Sorbonne
garden: 9 Tuileries 10 Luxembourg
island: 11 Île de la Cité *museum:*
5 Cluny 6 Louvre *palace:* 6 Louvre
7 Bourbon *patron saint:* 9 Geneviève
racecourse: 7 Auteuil *river:* 5 Seine *section:* 8 Left Bank 9 Right Bank
10 Montmartre 12 Latin Quarter *stock*

exchange: 6 Bourse *subway:* 5 Métro
tower: 6 Eiffel
Paris *beloved:* 5 Helen *betrothed:* 6 Juliet
father: 5 Priam *mother:* 6 Hecuba *slayer:*
11 Philoctetes *wife:* 6 Oenone
parish 6 county 8 district 9 community
12 congregation, neighborhood
Parisina *author:* 5 Byron (Lord) *husband:*
3 Azo *lover:* 4 Hugo *slayer:* 3 Azo
parity 8 equality, sameness, symmetry
10 similarity, similitude 11 equivalence,
equivalency, parallelism
park 4 stop 5 green, plaza 7 deposit, fun-
fair, reserve 8 carnival, preserve
9 esplanade 11 reservation
parka 6 anorak, jacket 7 garment
8 pullover 9 outerwear
park designer 4 Vaux (Calvert) 6 Paxton
(Joseph) 7 Alphand (Jean), Le Nôtre
(André), Olmsted (Frederick Law)
parlance 4 talk 5 idiom, style, usage
6 phrase, speech 7 wording 8 language,
locution, phrasing 9 verbalism
11 phraseology
parlay 3 bet 4 risk 5 bid up, boost, stake,
wager 6 expand, extend, hazard 7 build
up, enhance, enlarge, exploit, venture
8 increase, leverage 9 transform
parley 4 talk 5 speak 6 confab, confer,
huddle, powwow 7 discuss, meeting
8 colloquy, converse, dialogue 9 discourse, negotiate 10 conference, discussion 11 confabulate 12 conversation
13 confabulation
parliament *see* legislature
parlor 4 room 5 salon 11 drawing room
13 reception room
parlous 5 hairy, risky 6 chancy, unsafe
8 critical 9 dangerous, hazardous
10 precarious
Parnassian 4 poet 6 poetic
parochial 5 local 6 narrow 7 insular, limited 9 sectarian, small-town 10 provincial, restricted
parody 3 rib 4 mock 5 mimic, spoof
6 satire 7 imitate, lampoon, mockery,
takeoff 8 ridicule, travesty 9 burlesque,
imitation 10 caricature
parole 4 free, word 6 let out, pledge
7 promise, release 9 discharge, proba-
tion, watchword 11 performance
paronomasia 3 pun 11 play on words
paroxysm 3 fit 4 bout 5 spasm, throe
6 attack, frenzy 7 flare-up, seizure
8 eruption, outbreak, outburst 9 explosion 10 conniption, convulsion
parrot 3 ape 4 aper, copy, echo 5 mimic
6 repeat 7 chatter, copycat, imitate
kind: 3 ara, kea 4 kaka, lory 5 macaw
6 Amazon, budgie, kakapo 8 cockatoo,

lorikeet, lovebird, parakeet 9 cockatiel
10 budgerigar
parrot fever 11 psittacosis
parry 4 duck, fend 5 avert, avoid, block,
dodge, elude, evade 7 counter, deflect,
evasion, fend off, prevent, respond,
ward off 8 sidestep, stave off 9 turn
aside 10 circumvent
parse 4 scan 7 analyze, dissect, examine,
resolve 8 construe 9 anatomize, explicate, interpret
Parsi 11 Zoroastrian
Parsifal *composer:* 6 Wagner (Richard)
magician: 8 Klingsor *quest:* 5 Grail *son:*
9 Lohengrin *temptress:* 6 Kundry
parsimonious 4 mean 5 cheap, close,
tight 6 frugal, stingy 7 chintzy, miserly,
sparing, thrifty 9 penurious
10 restrained 11 closefisted, tightfisted
13 penny-pinching
parsley 4 herb 7 garnish *family:* 6 carrot
piece: 5 sprig
parson 6 cleric, pastor, rector 8 clerical,
minister, preacher, reverend 9 clergyman 12 ecclesiastic
parsonage 5 manse 7 rectory
part 3 bit, cut 4 chip, unit 5 chunk,
piece, quota, scrap, sever, share, slice
6 detail, divide, member, moiety,
ration, sector 7 element, measure, portion, quantum, quarter, section, segment 8 division, fraction, fragment,
function, separate 9 component
partake 3 eat 5 savor, share 6 accept,
sample 7 acquire, consume, receive
9 enter into 11 participate
Parthenon *sculptor:* 7 Phidias 8 Pheidias
sculpture: 6 frieze *site:* 9 Acropolis
partial 6 biased, unfair, warped 7 colored, half-way 8 inclined, one-sided
9 jaundiced 10 fractional, incomplete,
prejudiced 11 fragmentary, predisposed
partiality 4 bent, bias 5 favor, taste 6 liking 7 leaning 8 affinity, fondness, tendency 10 favoritism, preference
11 inclination 12 one-sidedness,
predilection
participant 5 party 6 fellow, member,
player, sharer 7 partner, sharing 11 contributor, shareholder
participate 4 join, play 5 share 6 engage,
join in 7 partake 8 take part
particle 3 ace, bit, dot, jot, tad 4 atom,
doit, dram, drop, hint, hoot, iota, mite,
mote, spot, whit 5 atomy, crumb, fleck,
grain, minim, ounce, scrap, shred,
speck 6 morsel, tittle 7 granule, modicum, smidgen, soupçon 8 fragment
9 scintilla *atomic:* 3 ion 5 anion 6 cation
elementary: 3 psi, tau 4 kaon, muon,
pion 5 boson, meson 6 baryon, hadron,

lambda, lepton, photon, proton
7 fermion, hyperon, neutron, nucleon,
upsilon 8 electron, mesotron, neutrino,
positron *hypothetical:* 5 gluon, quark
6 parton 8 graviton *virus:* 6 virion *with
negative charge:* 8 electron *with positive
charge:* 6 proton 8 positron
particular 3 one 4 fact, full, item, lone
5 exact, fussy, picky, point, thing
6 detail, marked, minute, single, unique
7 careful, correct, element, feature,
finicky, notable, precise, several, special, unusual 8 accurate, concrete,
detailed, distinct, especial, exacting,
itemized, separate, solitary, specific,
uncommon 10 blow-by-blow, fastidious, individual, meticulous, pernickety,
scrupulous 11 distinctive, exceptional,
persnickety, punctilious 12 circumstance
particularize 4 list 6 detail 7 catalog,
itemize, specify 8 spell out 9 enumerate, inventory 13 individualize
parting 4 last 5 adieu, break, congé, final
6 good-by 7 good-bye 8 division,
farewell 10 divergence, separation
11 leave-taking, valedictory
partisan 6 backer, biased, warped
7 devotee, die-hard, fanatic, patriot,
sectary 8 adherent, advocate, disciple,
follower, one-sided, stalwart, upholder
9 factional, guerrilla, irregular, satellite, sectarian, supporter
partition 4 wall 6 divide, screen
7 divider, section, wall off 8 disunion,
division, fence off, separate 10 separation
partner 4 ally, chum, mate 5 buddy,
crony 6 cohort, fellow 7 comrade
8 confrere, sidekick 9 assistant, associate, colleague, companion 10 accomplice 11 confederate
partnership 4 firm 5 union 7 cahoots,
company, sharing 8 alliance, business,
marriage, relation 11 affiliation, association, combination 12 consociation,
togetherness 13 participation
parturient 6 gravid, parous 8 enceinte,
pregnant 9 expecting
parturition 5 birth 8 delivery 10 childbirth 12 childbearing
party 4 ball, band, bash, bevy, bloc,
crew, fete, gala, orgy, side 5 actor,
corps, covey, feast, group, revel, troop
6 fiesta, frolic, kegger, mortal, person,
social, soiree, troupe 7 blowout,
carouse, faction, roister, shindig
8 carousal, litigant, wingding 9 bacchanal, gathering, make merry, raise hell
10 detachment, individual, saturnalia
11 bacchanalia, celebration, participant

parvenu 7 upstart 9 arriviste 12 nouveau riche

Pascal essay 6 Pensée

Pasiphaë *daughter:* 7 Ariadne, Phaedra *husband:* 5 Minos *son:* 8 Minotaur

pass 3 die, end 4 fare, hand 5 cease, lapse, occur, relay, spend, while 6 crisis, depart, elapse, exceed, expire, hand on, happen, permit, push on, slight, slip by, strait 7 come off, develop, journey, proceed, succumb 8 bequeath, fork over, hand down, juncture, outshine, outstrip, transmit 9 while away *Afghanistan:* 5 Murgh *Afghanistan-Pakistan:* 6 Khyber *Alaska:* 5 White *Alps:* 3 col 5 Cenis, Loibl 7 Brenner, Ljubelj, Simplon 9 St. Bernard *California:* 5 Cajon *China-India:* 9 Karakoram *Colorado:* 3 Ute *Pakistan:* 5 Kilik *Russian:* 12 Caspian Gates *Tennessee:* 10 Cumberland *Turkey:* 13 Cilician Gates

passable 4 okay, open, so-so 6 decent 8 adequate, all right 9 tolerable, unblocked 10 accessible, good enough 12 satisfactory

passably 6 enough 8 all right, somewhat 10 moderately

passage 3 way 4 exit, fare, hall, path, text 5 route, shift 6 access, arcade, avenue, course, egress, strait, travel, tunnel, voyage 7 channel, excerpt, hallway, journey, transit 8 corridor, transfer, traverse 9 enactment, quotation 10 transition 11 transmittal 12 transference, transmission *air:* 7 windway *arched:* 6 arcade *Atlantic-Pacific:* 9 Northwest *roofed:* 6 arcade 9 breezeway

Passage to India author 7 Forster (E. M.)

pass away 3 die, end 6 demise, depart, elapse, expire, perish 7 decease, succumb 9 disappear

pass by 4 miss, omit 6 forget, ignore 7 neglect 8 overlook 9 disregard

passé 4 dead 5 dated, stale 6 démodé, old hat 7 demoded, disused, extinct, outworn 8 obsolete, outdated, outmoded 9 out-of-date 10 antiquated, superseded 12 old-fashioned

passel 3 lot 4 heap, pack 5 bunch 6 bundle 9 multitude

passing 5 brief, death, quick 6 demise, highly 7 cursory, decease 8 fleeting 9 ephemeral, fugacious, extremely, momentary, transient 10 evanescent, short-lived, transitory 11 exceedingly, superficial 12 satisfactory

passion 4 fire, fury, heat, itch, love, lust, rage, urge, zeal 5 agony, amour, anger, ardor, craze, crush, drive 6 desire, fervor, hunger 7 avidity, craving, ecstasy, emotion, feeling, rapture 8 appetite, devotion, outburst, yearning 9 affection, eagerness, suffering, transport 10 enthusiasm, excitement, heartthrob 11 amorousness, infatuation

passionate 3 hot 5 angry, fiery 6 ardent, fervid, heated 7 amorous, aroused, blazing, burning, excited, fervent, furious, intense 8 incensed, vehement 9 impetuous, steamed up 10 hot-blooded, stimulated 11 hot-tempered 12 enthusiastic 13 quick-tempered

passive 4 idle 5 inert 6 docile, latent 8 enduring, immobile, inactive, listless, resigned, yielding 9 apathetic, compliant, lethargic, quiescent 10 motionless, nonviolent, phlegmatic, submissive 11 acquiescent, complaisant, indifferent, unresistant

pass out 3 die 5 faint, swoon 7 divvy up 8 disburse, keel over 10 distribute

pass over 4 miss, omit, skip 6 forget, ignore 7 dismiss, neglect 8 discount, leave out 9 disregard

Passover 5 Pasch 6 Pesach *bread:* 5 matzo 6 matzoh *meal:* 5 seder

pass up 5 forgo 6 refuse, reject 7 decline

past 3 ago, old 4 gone, late, once, yore 5 above, after, prior 6 beyond, bygone, former, whilom 7 onetime, quondam 8 anterior, foretime, lang syne, previous, sometime 9 antiquity, erstwhile, foregoing, precedent, preceding, yesterday 10 antecedent, yesteryear

pasta 5 dough *kind:* 4 ziti 7 gnocchi, lasagna, ravioli 8 linguine, linguini, macaroni, rigatoni 9 canneloni, fettucine, fettucini, manicotti, spaghetti 10 cannelloni, fettuccine, fettuccini, tortellini, vermicelli 11 cappelletti

paste 3 fix, hit 4 beat, clay, drub, food, glue, sock 5 affix, dough, pound, stick, stuff 6 adhere, attach, cement, defeat, fasten, thrash, wallop 7 trounce 8 adhesive, material

Pasternak hero 7 Zhivago (Dr.)

pastiche 4 olio 6 jumble, medley 7 farrago, mélange, mixture 8 mishmash 9 potpourri 10 assortment, hodgepodge, hotchpotch, miscellany, salmagundi 11 gallimaufry

pastime 4 game 5 hobby, sport 9 amusement, diversion 10 recreation 13 entertainment

past master 4 whiz 5 adept, maven 6 expert, wizard 9 authority

pastor 5 padre 6 cleric, parson 8 minister, preacher, reverend, sky pilot 9 clergyman

pastoral 5 idyll, rural 6 rustic 7 bucolic,

country, crosier, idyllic **8** agrarian, clerical, innocent, peaceful **10** campestral
pastor's assistant 6 curate
pastry 3 bun, pie **4** baba, cake, flan, tart **5** torte **6** cornet, Danish, éclair, gâteau, pirogi **7** baklava, beignet, bouchée, dariole, fritter, gâteaux (plural), palmier, savarin, strudel, tartlet **8** napoleon, papillon, piroshki, pirozhki, turnover **9** barquette, cream puff, madeleine, petit four, vol-au-vent **10** cheesecake **11** profiterole **12** millefeuille *kind:* **4** filo, puff **5** flaky **6** phyllo *shell:* **7** timbale **8** meringue
pasture 3 lea, ley **4** feed, land **5** field, grass, graze **6** browse, meadow **9** grassland
pasty 3 wan **4** pale **6** doughy, pallid, sickly **7** meat pie **8** turnover **9** unhealthy
pat 3 apt, dab, set **4** firm **5** fixed, slice, stiff, trite **6** dead-on **7** apropos, fitting **8** apposite, standard, suitable **9** contrived, pertinent, rehearsed
patch 3 bit, fix **4** area, fill, mend, plot **5** cover, piece, scrap, spell **6** doctor, emblem, fill up, repair, shield **7** connect, plaster **8** material **10** connection
patchwork 4 olio **5** quilt **6** jumble **7** mixture **8** covering, mishmash, mixed bag **10** assortment, hodgepodge, hotchpotch, miscellany, salmagundi
patchy 6 fitful, random, spotty, uneven **7** erratic **8** sporadic **9** haphazard, hit-or-miss, irregular **12** intermittent
pate 4 bean, dome, head, poll **5** brain, crown **6** noddle, noggin, noodle
pâté de ___ 8 foie gras
patella 7 kneecap, kneepan
patent 4 open **5** clear, plain, right **6** secure **7** evident, license, obvious, visible **8** apparent, distinct, manifest, unclosed **9** exclusive, privilege, prominent, protected **11** proprietary **12** intelligible, unobstructed
paternal 8 fatherly *relative:* **6** agnate
paternity 7 lineage **8** ancestry **10** fatherhood, provenance **11** progenitors
Pater Noster 9 Our Father
path 3 way **4** lane, line, road, tack, walk **5** byway, orbit, route, track, trail **6** avenue, bridle, course **7** passage, walkway **9** direction **10** trajectory
pathetic 3 sad **4** poor **5** sorry **6** absurd, moving, paltry, rueful **7** piteous, pitiful, risible, useless **8** inferior, pitiable, poignant, touching **9** affecting, laughable, miserable **10** inadequate, lamentable, ridiculous
Pathfinder *author:* **6** Cooper (James Fenimore) *hero:* **6** Bumppo (Natty)

pathogen 4 germ **5** virus **9** bacterium
pathological 7 deviant **8** aberrant, abnormal, diseased, maniacal, schizoid **9** psychotic
pathos 4 pity **7** emotion **8** sympathy **9** poignance, poignancy
pathway 4 line, walk **5** route, track, trail **6** course **7** channel, conduit, network, passage
patience 4 cool **8** calmness, stoicism **9** composure, endurance **10** equanimity, sufferance **11** forbearance, resignation, self-control
Patience *composer:* **8** Sullivan (Arthur) *librettist:* **7** Gilbert (W. S.)
patient 4 case, meek **8** enduring **9** easygoing **10** persistent **11** susceptible **13** long-suffering *man:* **3** Job
patina 4 aura, coat, film **6** finish, polish **7** coating **8** covering **10** appearance, coloration
patio 5 court **6** atrium **7** terrace **9** courtyard
patois 4 cant **5** argot, lingo, slang **6** jargon **7** dialect **10** colloquial, vernacular
patriarch 4 sire **6** father **7** creator, founder **9** architect, graybeard *biblical:* **5** David, Isaac, Jacob **7** Abraham
patrician 5 noble **6** aristo **9** blue blood, gentleman **10** aristocrat, upper-class
patriciate 5 elite **6** gentry **9** blue blood, gentility **10** upper crust **11** aristocracy
patrimony 6 estate, legacy **8** heritage **9** endowment **10** birthright **11** inheritance
patriot 5 jingo **8** jingoist, loyalist **9** flagwaver **10** chauvinist **11** nationalist
patriotism 8 jingoism **10** chauvinism **11** nationalism
Patroclus *friend:* **8** Achilles *slayer:* **6** Hector
patrol 5 guard, round, scout, troop, watch **7** protect **8** sentinel **9** keep watch
patrolman 3 cop **5** guard **6** police **7** officer
patrol wagon see PADDY WAGON
patron 5 angel **6** backer, client **7** sponsor **8** customer, guardian **9** protector, supporter **10** benefactor
patronage 4 help **5** aegis, trade **6** custom **7** backing, subsidy, support, traffic **8** activity, advocacy, auspices, business, cronyism **9** clientage, clientele, influence **10** pork barrel, protection **11** benefaction, sponsorship **12** guardianship
patronize 3 aid, use **4** back **5** deign, favor **6** assist, shop at **7** protect, support **8** frequent **10** condescend
patron saint *of beggars, cripples:* **5** Giles *of children:* **8** Nicholas *of England:*

6 George *of fishermen:* 5 Peter *of France:* 5 Denis *of Ireland:* 7 Patrick *of lawyers:* 4 Ives *of musicians:* 7 Cecilia *of Norway:* 4 Olaf *of physicians:* 4 Luke *of sailors:* 4 Elmo 8 Nicholas *of Scotland:* 6 Andrew *of shoemakers:* 7 Crispin *of Spain:* 5 James 8 Santiago *of Wales:* 5 David *of winegrowers:* 7 Vincent *of workers:* 6 Joseph

patsy 3 sap 4 dupe, fool, mark 5 chump 6 pigeon, sucker, victim 8 easy mark, pushover

patter 4 cant 5 argot, lingo, slang, spiel 6 babble, jargon, patois 7 chatter, prattle

pattern 4 copy, form, plan 5 guide, ideal, model, motif, order, shape 6 design, figure, follow, method, mirror, system 7 diagram, emulate, example, imitate 8 exemplar, grouping, paradigm, standard, template 9 archetype, incidence, prototype 10 flight path 11 arrangement, orderliness 12 distribution 13 configuration

paucity 4 lack, want 6 dearth 7 poverty 8 scarcity, shortage 9 scantness, smallness 10 deficiency, meagerness, meagreness 13 insufficiency

___ **Paulo** 3 São

Paul the Apostle *birthplace:* 6 Tarsus *companion:* 5 Silas, Titus 7 Artemas, Timothy 8 Barnabas *original name:* 4 Saul *place of conversion:* 8 Damascus *prosecutor:* 9 Tertullus *teacher:* 8 Gamaliel *tribe:* 8 Benjamin

paunch 3 gut, pot 5 belly, tummy 7 abdomen, stomach 8 potbelly 9 bay window, beer belly 11 breadbasket

paunchy 3 fat 5 beefy, plump, tubby 6 chunky, portly, rotund 8 thickset 10 overweight, potbellied

pauper 6 beggar 7 have-not 8 bankrupt, indigent 9 mendicant

pauperism 4 need, ruin, want 6 penury 7 beggary, poverty 9 indigence, neediness, privation 11 destitution

pause 3 gap 4 halt, hush, lull, rest, stop, wait 5 break, comma, delay, lapse, letup 6 hiatus, linger, recess 7 caesura, respite, time out 8 breather, hesitate, inaction, interval, take five 9 cessation, interlude 10 hesitation, suspension 12 intermission, interruption

pave 3 lay, tar 5 cover 7 asphalt, surface 8 blacktop, concrete

pavement 6 tarmac 7 asphalt, macadam, surface 8 concrete, sidewalk

pavilion 4 tent 5 kiosk 6 canopy, gazebo 9 belvedere 11 summerhouse

paw 4 feel, foot, grab, hand 5 grope, touch 6 fondle, handle, molest, scrape

pawn 4 hock, tool 6 pledge, puppet, stooge, victim 7 deposit, hostage, warrant 8 guaranty, security 9 guarantee 10 chess piece, instrument

pax 5 peace 6 tablet

Pax ___ 3 Dei 6 Romana 10 Britannica

pay 3 fee 4 wage 5 clear, offer, remit, serve, spend 6 answer, defray, employ, expend, kick in, lay out, pony up, profit, render, return, salary, settle, square, tender, reward 7 benefit, bring in, cough up, forfeit, fork out, requite, satisfy, stipend 8 defrayal, disburse, earnings, shell out 9 discharge, emolument, indemnify, liquidate, reimburse 10 compensate, recompense, remunerate 12 compensation, remuneration

payable 3 due 4 owed 5 owing 6 mature, unpaid 7 overdue 9 unsettled 10 obligatory 11 outstanding, uncollected

paycheck 5 wages 6 salary

payload 4 haul 5 cargo, goods 6 burden, lading, weight 7 freight, tonnage 8 shipment

payment 3 fee 4 dues 5 award, money 6 amends, outlay, return, reward 7 penance 8 defrayal, requital 11 restitution 12 compensation, remuneration, satisfaction

payoff 3 fix 5 bribe 6 climax, profit, result, reward, upshot 7 outcome 8 clincher, decisive 10 conclusion, conclusive, denouement 11 retribution

payola 5 bribe

PDQ 4 ASAP 6 at once, pronto 8 directly, right now, right off 9 forthwith, instanter, instantly, right away 11 immediately, straightway 12 straightaway

peace 3 pax 4 calm, ease, pact 5 amity, order, quiet 6 accord, repose 7 concord, harmony, silence 8 serenity 11 tranquility 12 tranquillity

peaceable 6 dovish, irenic 7 amiable, pacific 8 amicable, friendly, pacifist, tranquil 10 nonviolent 11 complaisant 12 conciliatory

peaceful 4 calm 5 still, quiet 6 irenic, placid, serene 7 equable, pacific 8 composed, tranquil 9 unruffled 10 harmonious, nonviolent, untroubled

peacemaker 7 arbiter 8 mediator, pacifier, placater 10 arbitrator, negotiator 11 conciliator, pacificator

peace officer 3 cop 6 police 9 policeman 11 policewoman

peach 3 rat 4 blab, tree 5 fruit 6 betray, inform, reveal, snitch, squeal 9 freestone, humdinger, nectarine 10 clingstone 11 crackerjack *family:* 4 rose

Peach State 7 Georgia

peachy 4 fine, good, nice 5 dandy, nifty,

super, swell **8** pleasant, pleasing
9 excellent, hunky-dory, marvelous,
wonderful
peacockish 5 showy, swank **6** chichi,
flashy, swanky **7** splashy **8** show-offy
10 flamboyant **11** pretentious **12** ostentatious
peak 3 alp, top, tor **4** acme, apex, bill,
crag, roof **5** crest, crown, mount, visor
6 apogee, summit, vertex, zenith **8** capsheaf, capstone, meridian, mountain,
pinnacle *Adirondack:* **9** Whiteface
Africa's highest: **4** Kibo *Alaska-Canada:*
12 Mt. Saint Elias *Andes:* **4** Ruiz **5** Torrá
Apennines: **5** Amaro *Argentina:* **4** Azul
5 Negra, Payún *Bavaria:* **5** Arber *Berkshires:* **8** Greylock *Black Hills:* **8** Rushmore *Bolivia:* **5** Cuzco, Tahua, Ubina
6 Sajama *Borneo:* **4** Raja *California:*
6 Shasta, Sonora **7** Palomar, Whitney
8 Half Dome **9** Excelsior *Canada:*
5 Keele *Canaries:* **5** Teide **8** Tenerife
Carpathian: **4** Rysy *Cascades:* **7** Rainier
Catskill: **6** Pisgah *Caucasus:* **5** Ushba
6 Elbrus *Chile:* **4** Mayo, Pili **5** Paine,
Pular *Colombia:* **4** Tama **5** Neiva *Colorado:* **3** Ute **5** Pikes **9** Purgatory *Cuba:*
8 Turquino *Ecuador:* **10** Chimborazo
England: **11** Scafell Pike *Ethiopia:*
4 Guna **5** Holla *France:* **5** Pilat *French
Guiana:* **5** Amana *Georgia:* **8** Springer
Glacier National Park: **8** Kootenai
Greece: **4** Ossa **6** Pelion *Himalayas:* **3** Api
5 Kamet **6** Lhotse **10** Gasherbrum *Honshū:* **4** Yari **10** Yarigatake *Idaho:* **11** Pend
Oreille *Iran:* **8** Damavand *Italy:* **4** Etna
8 Vesuvius *Japan:* **5** Oyama
7 Sobozan *Java:* **6** Slamet *Jordan:*
6 Gilead *Karakoram Range:* **7** Dapsang
10 Masherbrum **12** Godwin Austen
Maine: **8** Katahdin **10** Saddleback *Montana:* **8** Gallatin *Nevada:* **3** Ely *Newfoundland:* **9** Gros Morne *New Hampshire:*
9 Monadnock *New Zealand:* **3** Una
4 Cook **7** Aorangi **8** Aspiring *Oahu:*
5 Kaala *Oregon:* **4** Hood *Papua New
Guinea:* **8** Victoria *Pennine Alps:* **10** Matterhorn, Mont Cervin *Philippines:*
4 High *Pyrenees:* **11** de Vignemale *Russia's highest:* **6** Elbrus *Scotland:* **8** Ben
Nevis *Sicily:* **4** Etna *Spain:* **5** Yelmo
8 Mulhacén *Switzerland:* **3** Dom **4** Dôle,
Tödi **5** Eiger, Mönch **6** La Dôle, Rusein
7 Pilatus **8** Jungfrau *Tanzania:* **11** Kilimanjaro *Utah:* **5** Kings *Venezuela:*
5 Icutú *Vermont:* **8** Haystack, Stratton
8 Ascutney **9** Mansfield *Washington:*
7 Olympus, Rainier **11** Saint Helens
White Mts.: **10** Washington *Wyoming:*
3 Elk **10** Grand Teton *Yukon:* **4** King
5 Logan

peaked 3 ill, wan **4** ashy, pale, sick
5 acute, ashen, drawn, sharp **6** ailing,
pallid, sickly **7** pointed **9** emaciated
peal 4 bell, bong, ring, toll **5** chime,
knell, sound **7** ringing **8** ding-dong
peanut 6 goober, legume **10** foam pellet
pear 4 Bosc **5** Anjou, Hardy **6** Comice,
Garber, Seckel **7** Kieffer, LeConte
8 Bartlett *cider:* **5** perry
pearl 3 gem **4** dear **5** jewel **7** paragon
8 treasure
Pearl Mosque site 4 Agra
pearly 8 lustrous, nacreous, precious
10 iridescent, opalescent
pear-shaped 8 pyriform
peasant 4 carl, kern, peon, serf **5** churl
6 rustic **7** bumpkin, hayseed, villein
Arab: **6** fellah *Latin-American:*
9 campesino *Russian:* **6** muzhik
peccary 4 javelina *genus:* **7** Tayassu
peck 3 lot, nag **4** buss, carp, fuss, heap,
kiss, load, mess, pile, poke **6** carp at,
nibble, pick at, pick up, pierce, strike
8 quantity
pecking order 6 ladder **7** pyramid **9** food
chain, hierarchy
peculate 6 steal **8** embezzle **9** defalcate
11 appropriate
peculiar 3 odd **4** rare **5** queer, weird
6 unique **7** bizarre, curious, oddball,
offbeat, special, strange, unusual
8 abnormal, singular, specific, uncommon **9** eccentric **10** individual, particular **11** distinctive
peculiarity 4 mark **5** quirk, trait **6** oddity
7 feature, quality **8** property **9** attribute, character, mannerism **12** eccentricity, idiosyncrasy
pecuniary 6 fiscal **8** economic, monetary
9 financial
pedagogue 5 tutor **6** pedant **7** teacher
8 educator **12** schoolmaster
pedagogy 8 teaching **9** education
pedal 5 lever **7** bicycle, treadle *digit:*
3 toe
pedant 7 teacher **9** formalist **10** schoolmarm **12** precisionist
pedantic 3 dry **4** arid, dull **6** stodgy
7 bookish, donnish, erudite, learned,
tedious **8** academic, didactic, priggish
9 ponderous **10** pedestrian, scholastic
11 pedagogical **13** unimaginative
peddle 4 hawk, push, sell, vend **5** pitch
6 monger **8** huckster
peddler 6 coster, dealer, hawker, monger, vendor **8** huckster, merchant, promoter **9** tradesman **12** costermonger
pedestal 4 base, foot **5** stand **7** footing,
support **10** foundation **12** underpinning
part: **4** dado **6** plinth **7** subbase
pedestrian 4 blah, dull **5** banal **6** dreary,

stodgy, walker **7** humdrum, mundane, prosaic **8** everyday, ordinary **11** commonplace **13** unimaginative
pedigree 6 origin, purity **7** descent, history, lineage **8** ancestry, purebred **9** bloodline, genealogy **10** background, extraction, family tree
peduncle 4 stem **5** stalk **7** pedicel
peek 3 spy **4** look **6** glance **7** glimpse
peel 4 bark, pare, rind, skin **5** flake, scale, strip **7** take off **8** flake off **9** break away, exfoliate
peeled 4 bare, open **5** naked **7** denuded, exposed **8** stripped **9** uncovered
peep 3 see, spy **4** look **5** chirp, tweet, watch **6** glance, squeak **7** glimpse, twitter **9** sandpiper
Peeping Tom 5 snoop **6** voyeur **7** prowler, snooper
peer 3 pry **4** gaze, lord **5** equal, glare, noble, stare **6** goggle, squint **9** associate
British: **4** duke, earl **5** baron **7** marquis **8** marquess, viscount
Peer Gynt *author:* **5** Ibsen (Henrik) *beloved:* **7** Solveig **composer:* **5** Grieg (Edvard) *mother:* **3** Ase **4** Aase
peerless 4 best **6** unique **7** perfect, supreme **8** superior **9** matchless, nonpareil, paramount, unequaled, unmatched, unrivaled **12** incomparable, unparalleled
peeve 3 bug, irk, vex **4** miff, rile **5** anger, annoy, pique **6** bother, nettle, put out **7** disturb, provoke **8** irritate, nuisance, vexation **9** aggravate, annoyance, grievance **10** exasperate **11** aggravation
peevish 4 sour **5** cross, testy **6** cranky, grumpy, ornery **7** fretful, whining **8** petulant **9** fractious, irritable, obstinate, querulous **11** ill-tempered
peewee 4 runt, tyke **5** dwarf, pygmy, small **6** midget, shaver, shrimp, squirt **9** miniature **10** diminutive, flycatcher **11** lilliputian
Peewee ___ 5 Reese
peg 3 fix, pin **4** hold, mark, plod, plug, step, work **5** dowel, place, prong, stake, throw **6** attach, degree, fasten, hustle, marker, reason **7** pin down, pretext, support **8** identify, restrict
Pegasus 5 horse, steed *rider:* **11** Bellerophon
pejorative 7 adverse **8** critical, debasing **9** slighting **10** belittling, derogatory, detractive **11** denigrating, deprecatory, disparaging, opprobrious, unfavorable **12** depreciatory
pelagic 6 marine **7** oceanic **8** maritime
Peleus *brother:* **7** Telamon *father:* **6** Aeacus *half brother:* **6** Phocus *son:* **8** Achilles *victim:* **8** Eurytion *wife:* **6** Thetis

pelf 4 loot, swag **5** booty, money, moola **6** boodle, moolah, riches, spoils **7** plunder
Pelias *country:* **6** Iolcus *father:* **8** Poseidon *half brother:* **5** Aeson *son:* **7** Acastus
Pelican State 9 Louisiana
Pelléas *beloved:* **9** Mélisande *brother, slayer:* **6** Golaud
Pelles *daughter:* **6** Elaine *grandson:* **7** Galahad
pellet 3 wad **4** ball, shot **6** sphere **10** projectile
Pellinore *slayer:* **6** Gawain *son:* **5** Torre **6** Dornar **7** Lamerok **8** Percival **9** Agglovale
pell-mell 5 chaos, snarl **6** muddle, rashly **7** chaotic, clutter, hastily **8** confused, disarray, disorder, headlong, reckless **9** confusion, haphazard, hurriedly **10** carelessly, heedlessly **11** hurry-scurry **13** helter-skelter
pellucid 5 clear, plain, sheer **6** limpid **7** crystal, evident, obvious **8** clear-cut, luminous **9** unblurred **10** see-through **11** crystalline, transparent
Pelops *father:* **8** Tantalus *son:* **6** Atreus **8** Pittheus, Thyestes *wife:* **10** Hippodamia
pelota 4 ball **7** jai alai
pelt 3 fur, run **4** beat, blow, dash, drub, hide, hurl, rush, skin, whop **5** hurry, pound, scoot, speed, strip, throw, whack **6** assail, batter, pepper, pummel, strike, wallop **7** bombard, hotfoot
pen 3 sty **4** cage, coop, jail, swan **5** pound, quill, write **6** cooler, corral, indite, prison, shut in, stylus, writer **7** close in, confine, enclose, fence in **9** ballpoint, enclosure
penal 8 punitive **12** correctional, disciplinary
penalize 4 dock, fine **5** mulct **6** punish **7** deprive **8** handicap **10** discipline **12** disadvantage
penalty 4 fine, loss **5** mulct **7** damages, forfeit **8** hardship **10** amercement, forfeiture, punishment **12** disadvantage
penance 4 rite **7** penalty **8** hardship **9** atonement **10** punishment
penchant 4 bent **5** taste **6** liking **7** leaning **8** affinity, fondness, tendency **9** inclining **10** partiality, proclivity, propensity **11** inclination **12** predilection
pendant 4 flag, jack, rope **7** fixture **8** ornament **10** supplement
pendent 7 hanging **9** suspended, undecided, unsettled **11** overhanging **12** undetermined
pending 6 during **8** awaiting, imminent **9** undecided, unsettled **12** undetermined

___ **Pendragon 5** Uther
pendulous 7 hanging **8** dangling, drooping, wavering **9** faltering, suspended,
tentative, uncertain **10** hesitating, indecisive **11** vacillating
Penelope *father:* **7** Icarius *father-in-law:*
7 Laertes *husband:* **7** Ulysses
8 Odysseus *mother:* **8** Periboea *son:*
10 Telemachus *suitor:* **7** Agelaus
penetrable 6 porous **8** pervious **9** permeable
penetrate 3 jab **4** bore, go in, stab
5 break, drive, enter, probe, touch
6 affect, charge, invade, pierce **7** pervade **8** discover, encroach, perceive,
permeate, puncture, saturate **9** percolate, perforate **10** understand
penetrating 4 keen **5** acute, sharp
6 astute, shrewd **8** incisive, piercing
9 trenchant **10** discerning, insightful,
perceptive **11** quick-witted, sharp-witted **12** sharp-sighted
Peneus *daughter:* **6** Daphne *father:*
7 Oceanus *mother:* **6** Tethys
penguin type 6 Adélie
___ **Penh 5** Phnom
peninsula 4 neck **10** chersonese *Alaska:*
5 Kenai **6** Seward *Australia:* **6** Tasman
Barents Sea: **5** Kanin *British colony:*
9 Gibraltar *Canada:* **8** Labrador *Chile:*
5 Swett *Costa Rica:* **3** Osa *Croatia:*
6 Istria *Denmark:* **7** Jutland *eastern United States:* **8** Delmarva *Estonia:* **5** Sorve
Florida: **8** Pinellas **9** Canaveral *France:*
5 Giens *Greece:* **4** Acte **10** Chalcidice
11 Peloponnese **12** Peloponnesus *Guam:*
5 Orote *Hong Kong:* **7** Kowloon *Honshu:*
3 Izu **5** Miura *Massachusetts:* **7** Cape
Ann, Cape Cod *Mexico:* **7** Yucatan
14 Baja California *Michigan:*
8 Keweenaw *Middle East:* **5** Sinai *New
Guinea:* **4** Huon *New Jersey:* **9** Sandy
Hook *New Zealand:* **5** Banks, Mahia
Nunavut: **7** Boothia **8** Melville *Ontario:*
5 Bruce *Persian Gulf:* **9** Ras Tanura *Quebec:* **5** Gaspé *Russia:* **4** Kola **5** Taman,
Yamal **6** Kolski, Taimyr **9** Kamchatka
Scotland: **7** Kintyre *South Australia:*
4 Eyre **5** Yorke *Southeast Asia:* **5** Malay
9 Indochina *southeastern Europe:*
6 Balkan *southwestern Asia:* **6** Arabia
7 Arabian *southwestern Europe:* **7** Iberian *Texas:* **9** Matagorda *Tierra del
Fuego:* **5** Mitre *Turkey:* **8** Anatolia
9 Asia Minor *Ukraine:* **5** Kerch *Wales:*
5 Gower, Lleyn *Washington:* **7** Olympic
Wisconsin: **4** Door
Peninsular State 7 Florida
penitence 3 rue **4** ruth **6** regret, sorrow
7 anguish, remorse **8** distress, humbling

10 contrition, repentance **11** compunction, self-reproof **12** self-reproach
penitent 5 sorry **6** rueful **8** contrite
9 regretful, repentant **10** apologetic,
remorseful
penitentiary see PRISON
penman 5 clerk **6** author, scribe, writer
7 copyist **9** scrivener **12** calligrapher
penmanship 4 hand **5** style **6** script
7 writing **11** calligraphy, chirography,
handwriting
pen name 6 anonym **9** pseudonym
10 nom de plume *Addison, Joseph:*
4 Clio *Arouet, François-Marie:* **8** Voltaire
Beyle, Marie-Henri: **8** Stendhal *Blair, Eric:*
12 George Orwell *Brontë, Anne:* **9** Acton
Bell *Brontë, Charlotte:* **10** Currer Bell
Brontë, Emily: **9** Ellis Bell *Clemens,
Samuel:* **9** Mark Twain *Dickens, Charles:*
3 Boz *Dodgson, Charles Lutwidge:*
12 Lewis Carroll *Dupin, Amandine-
Aurore:* **10** George Sand *Evans, Mary
Ann:* **11** George Eliot *Faust, Frederick:*
8 Max Brand *Franklin, Benjamin:*
11 Poor Richard *Geisel, Theodore:* **7** Dr.
Seuss *Glidden, Frederick:* **9** Luke Short
Lamb, Charles: **4** Elia *Munro, Hector
Hugh:* **4** Saki *Poquelin, Jean-Baptiste:*
7 Molière *Porter, William Sidney:*
6 O. Henry *Ramé, Maria Louise:* **5** Ouida
Thibault, Jacques-Anatole-François:
13 Anatole France *Viaud, Louis-Marie-
Julien:* **10** Pierre Loti
pennant 4 flag, jack **5** color **6** banner,
ensign **8** standard, streamer **9** banderole
12 championship
penniless 4 poor **5** broke, needy **8** bankrupt, indigent **9** destitute, insolvent
11 impecunious
pennon 4 flag, jack, wing **5** color **6** banner, ensign **8** bannerol, gonfalon,
streamer **9** banderole, oriflamme
Pennsylvania *capital:* **10** Harrisburg *city:*
4 Erie **6** Reading **8** Scranton **9** Allentown **10** Pittsburgh **12** Philadelphia *college, university:* **6** Drexel, Lehigh, Temple **7** LaSalle **8** Bryn Mawr, Bucknell
9 Dickinson, Lafayette, Penn State, Villanova **10** Swarthmore **14** Carnegie
Mellon *mountain range:* **6** Pocono *nickname:* **8** Keystone (State) *river:*
9 Allegheny **10** Schuylkill **11** Monongahela, Susquehanna *state bird:* **12** ruffed
grouse *state flower:* **14** mountain laurel
state tree: **7** hemlock
penny-pincher 5 miser **7** niggard, scrooge
8 tightwad **9** skinflint **10** cheapskate
penny-pinching 4 mean **6** frugal, stingy,
thrift **7** miserly, thrifty **9** frugality, niggardly, parsimony, penurious **11** tightfisted **12** cheeseparing, parsimonious

penny-wise 5 canny, tight 6 frugal, stingy 7 prudent, sparing, thrifty 9 provident 10 economical 12 parsimonious

pen point 3 neb, nib

pension 3 inn 5 hotel, lodge 6 hostel, reward 7 annuity, auberge, payment, stipend 8 gratuity 9 allowance 12 room and board, roominghouse 13 boardinghouse

pensioner 7 retiree

pensive 3 sad 6 dreamy, musing 7 wistful 10 meditative, melancholy, reflective, ruminative, thoughtful 11 preoccupied 13 contemplative

Pentateuch 5 Torah *books:* 6 Exodus 7 Genesis, Numbers 9 Leviticus 11 Deuteronomy

Penthesilea *queen of:* 7 Amazons *slayer:* 8 Achilles

Pentheus *grandfather:* 6 Cadmus *king of:* 6 Thebes *mother:* 5 Agave

penumbra 4 veil 5 cover, shade 6 fringe, screen, shadow, shroud 7 curtain

penurious 4 mean, poor 5 needy, tight 6 frugal, stingy 7 miserly 8 indigent, stinting 9 destitute, niggardly 11 impecunious, tightfisted 12 impoverished, parsimonious 13 penny-pinching

penury 4 need, want 7 beggary, poverty 8 distress 9 indigence, privation, pauperism 11 destitution, needfulness

peon 4 serf 5 slave 6 drudge, toiler 7 laborer, peasant 11 galley slave *Anglo-Saxon:* 4 esne

peonage 4 yoke 6 thrall 7 bondage, helotry, serfdom, slavery 9 servitude, thralldom, villenage 11 enslavement

people 3 kin 4 folk 5 plebs 6 public 7 society 8 populace 9 commoners, community, plebeians 10 commonalty 11 inhabitants, rank and file, third estate

pep 3 vim 4 brio, dash 5 moxie, punch, verve, vigor 6 energy 7 sparkle 8 vitality, vivacity 10 get-up-and-go, liveliness 11 high spirits

pepo 5 gourd, melon 6 squash 7 pumpkin 8 cucumber

pepper 4 pelt 5 chili 6 season, shower 7 cayenne, paprika, pimento, tabasco 8 capsicum, cascabel, chipotle, habanero, jalapeño, pimiento, sprinkle 9 condiment, seasoning 12 Scotch bonnet

peppery 3 hot 5 cross, fiery, sharp, spicy, testy, zesty 6 biting, lively, snappy, touchy 7 piquant, pungent 8 choleric, poignant, seasoned, stinging 9 irascible, irritable 11 hot-tempered 13 quick-tempered

peppy 5 alert, perky 6 active, bright, lively 7 vibrant 8 animated, spirited, vigorous 9 energetic, sprightly, vivacious

___ **Pepys** 6 Samuel

Pequod *cabin boy:* 3 Pip *captain:* 4 Ahab *harpooner:* 6 Daggoo 8 Queequeg, Tashtego *mate:* 8 Starbuck

per 3 via 4 a pop, each, with 6 apiece 7 by way of, for each, through 9 by means of 12 individually

perambulate 4 walk 6 ramble, stroll 8 traverse 9 promenade

per capita 4 each 6 apiece, by each 7 equally, for each

perceive 3 see 4 espy, feel, know, mark, note 5 grasp, seize, sense 6 detect, notice, remark 7 discern, observe, realize 8 identify 9 apprehend, recognize 10 comprehend, understand

percentage 3 cut 4 part 5 piece, share, slice 6 profit 7 portion 9 advantage 10 commission, proportion 11 probability

perceptible 5 clear 6 marked 7 visible 8 apparent, definite, distinct, palpable, sensible, tangible 10 detectable, noticeable, observable 11 appreciable, discernible 12 recognizable

perception 4 idea 5 grasp, image 6 acumen, notion 7 concept, feeling, insight, thought 9 awareness, cognition 10 impression 11 discernment, observation 12 appreciation 13 understanding

perceptive 4 keen, sage, wise 5 acute, alert, aware, sharp 7 knowing 9 intuitive, observant, sagacious, sensitive 10 discerning, insightful, responsive 13 understanding

perch 3 bar, peg, set 4 fish, land, rest, seat 5 light, roost, sit on 6 alight, settle 7 set down, sit atop, sit down

perchance 5 maybe 7 perhaps 8 possibly 11 conceivably

percipience 6 acumen 8 keenness 9 cognition, intuition 10 astuteness 11 discernment 12 appreciation, perspicacity 13 comprehension

percolate 4 drip, ooze, seep 5 exude 6 charge, filter, simmer, spread 7 pervade, trickle 9 penetrate

percussion 3 jar 4 bump, jolt 5 clash, crash, shock 6 impact 9 collision 10 concussion *instrument:* (see at MUSICAL INSTRUMENT)

Perdita *father:* 7 Leontes *mother:* 8 Hermione

perdition 4 hell 5 hades 7 inferno 9 damnation 10 underworld 11 netherworld

Père Goriot author 6 Balzac (Honoré de)

peregrination 4 trek, trip, walk **7** journey, travels **9** traversal **10** expedition
peremptory 5 bossy, final **7** haughty **8** absolute, arrogant, decisive, dogmatic, imperial **9** imperious, masterful **10** autocratic, commanding, disdainful, high-handed, imperative **11** dictatorial, domineering, magisterial, overbearing
perennial 7 durable **8** constant, enduring, lifelong **9** continual, long-lived, permanent, perpetual, recurrent, unceasing **10** continuing, persistent, persisting, unchanging **11** long-lasting
Perez brother: 5 Zerah **father: 5** Judah **mother: 5** Tamar
perfect 4 full, pure **5** exact, ideal, model, right, sound, total, utter, whole **6** entire, expert, intact, polish, proper, refine **7** correct, improve, precise **8** absolute, accurate, complete, finished, flawless, outright, peerless, spotless, unbroken, unflawed **9** downright, excellent, faultless, matchless, stainless, unalloyed, undamaged, undiluted **10** consummate, impeccable, proficient **11** unequivocal, unmitigated, unqualified
perfection 4 acme **5** ideal **6** purity, virtue **7** paragon **9** integrity, wholeness **10** excellence, excellency **11** saintliness **12** completeness, flawlessness, transcendence **13** faultlessness
perfectly 5 fully, quite **6** wholly **7** to a turn, utterly **8** entirely **10** altogether, completely, thoroughly
perfidious 5 false **6** untrue **8** disloyal **9** deceitful, dishonest, faithless **10** treasonous, traitorous, unfaithful, unreliable **11** treacherous
perfidy 6 deceit **7** falsity, sellout, treason **8** betrayal **9** falseness, treachery **10** disloyalty, infidelity **13** faithlessness
perforate 3 pit **4** bore **5** drill, prick, punch **6** pierce **8** puncture **9** penetrate
perform 3 act **4** play, work **5** enact **6** behave, comply, effect **7** achieve, execute, fulfill, operate, playact, present, satisfy **8** bring off, carry out, complete, function **9** discharge, entertain, implement **10** accomplish
performance 3 act **4** deed, feat, show, work **6** acting, action **7** conduct, display **8** behavior, efficacy, exercise **9** discharge, execution, operation **10** efficiency, exhibition **11** achievement, fulfillment **12** presentation
performer 4 doer, mime **5** actor, mimic **6** mummer, player **7** actress, artiste, trouper **8** thespian **9** playactor **12** impersonator
perfume 4 balm **5** aroma, cense, scent,

smell, spice **6** sachet **7** bouquet, incense, odorize **9** aromatize, fragrance, redolence **source: 4** musk **5** attar, myrrh, orris **8** bergamot
perfumer 6 Chanel (Coco)
perfunctory 7 cursory, routine **8** careless **9** automatic **10** impersonal, mechanical **11** superficial
pergola 5 arbor, bower **7** trellis
perhaps 5 maybe **8** feasibly, possibly **9** perchance **11** conceivably
periapt see AMULET
Pericles father: 10 Xanthippus **mistress: 7** Aspasia **mother: 8** Agariste
peril 4 risk **6** danger, hazard, menace **8** exposure, jeopardy **9** liability **12** endangerment
perilous 5 hairy, risky **6** chancy, unsafe **7** unsound **9** dangerous, desperate, hazardous, uncertain **11** treacherous
___ **Perilous 5** Siege
perimeter 4 edge **5** limit, verge **6** border, bounds, margin **8** boundary
period 3 age, end, era **4** span, stop, term, time **5** cycle, phase, point, spell, stage **6** extent **8** division, duration, interval, sentence
periodic 6 cyclic, fitful **7** regular **8** cyclical, repeated, sporadic **9** recurrent, recurring **10** occasional **11** fluctuating **12** intermittent
periodical 5 organ **6** cyclic, review **7** journal **8** cyclical, magazine **9** alternate, newspaper, recurrent, recurring **10** isochronal **11** isochronous, publication **12** intermittent
peripatetic 6 moving, roving **7** nomadic, walking **8** ambulant, vagabond **9** itinerant, traveling, wayfaring **10** ambulatory, pedestrian, travelling **13** perambulatory
peripheral 6 remote **7** lateral, surface **8** far-flung, marginal, outlying **9** auxiliary, secondary **10** borderline, tangential **11** out-of-the-way **13** supplementary
perish 3 die, end **4** pass **5** cease **6** be lost, demise, depart, expire, vanish **7** decease, decline, go under, succumb **8** collapse, pass away **9** disappear
perjure 3 lie **6** delude **7** deceive, distort, falsify, mislead **8** forswear **9** misinform **10** equivocate **11** prevaricate
perk 4 gain, mend, plus **5** cheer, extra **7** benefit, freshen, improve, refresh, smarten **8** brighten
perky 5 alert, cocky, happy **6** bouncy, bubbly, cheery, chirpy, frisky, jaunty, lively, upbeat **7** buoyant, chipper **8** animated, cheerful, spirited, sportive **9** energetic, sparkling, sprightly, vivacious **12** effervescent, high-spirited

permanent 5 fixed **6** stable **7** abiding, durable, lasting **8** constant, enduring, hair wave **9** continual, perennial **10** changeless, invariable, unchanging **11** established, everlasting **12** imperishable

permeable 6 porous, spongy **8** pervious **9** diffusive **10** penetrable

permeate 5 imbue **6** drench, infuse, spread **7** diffuse, pervade, suffuse **8** saturate **9** penetrate, percolate **10** impregnate, infiltrate **11** pass through

permissible 4 okay **5** legal **7** allowed **8** approved **9** allowable, tolerable, tolerated **10** acceptable, authorized, sanctioned

permission 5 leave **6** assent, permit **7** consent, license **8** approval, sanction **9** agreement, allowance **11** approbation, endorsement **12** acquiescence **13** authorization

permissive 3 lax **4** open **7** lenient, liberal **8** tolerant **9** easygoing, forgiving, indulgent **10** forbearing **11** acquiescent, complaisant

permit 3 let **4** okay, pass **5** agree, allow, grant, leave **6** accede, enable, say yes, suffer **7** consent, license, warrant **8** sanction, tolerate **9** allowance, authorize, give leave **10** permission **13** authorization

permutation 6 change **7** variety, version **9** variation **10** alteration, innovation **11** arrangement, vicissitude **12** modification

pernicious 4 evil **5** fatal, toxic **6** deadly, lethal, malign, wicked **7** baleful, baneful, harmful, hurtful, killing, malefic, noxious, ruinous **8** damaging, sinister, virulent **9** injurious, malignant, offensive, poisonous **10** maleficent **11** deleterious, destructive, detrimental, devastating

Pernod flavor 5 anise **8** licorice

perorate 5 speak **7** declaim, lecture **8** bloviate, harangue, proclaim **9** hold forth

perpend 5 study, weigh **6** ponder **7** examine, reflect **8** consider, think out **9** reflect on, think over **10** excogitate, think about **11** contemplate

perpendicular 5 plumb, sheer, steep **7** upright **8** straight, vertical **11** precipitate, precipitous

perpetrate 6 commit, effect **7** inflict, execute, perform **8** carry out **10** bring about

perpetual 7 endless, eternal, undying **8** constant, unending **9** ceaseless, continual, incessant, perennial, recurrent, unceasing **10** continuous **11** everlasting, unremitting

perpetuate 7 sustain **8** conserve, continue, eternize, maintain, preserve **9** keep alive **10** eternalize **11** immortalize

perplex 5 befog, mix up, stump **6** baffle, bemuse, muddle, puzzle **7** buffalo, confuse, mystify, nonplus, perturb **8** befuddle, bewilder, confound, distract, entangle **9** dumbfound **10** discompose

perquisite 3 tip **4** gain **5** right **6** profit **7** benefit, payment **8** gratuity **9** privilege

per se 6 as such, solely **8** in itself **11** essentially **13** intrinsically

persecute 4 bait, ride **5** annoy, harry, hound, worry, wrong **6** badger, harass, hector, injure, molest, pester, pick on, plague, punish, pursue **7** afflict, oppress, torment, torture **8** aggrieve

Persephone 4 Kore **10** Proserpina *father:* **4** Zeus **7** Jupiter *husband:* **5** Hades, Pluto *mother:* **5** Ceres **7** Demeter

Perseus *father:* **4** Zeus **7** Jupiter *grandfather:* **8** Acrisius *mother:* **5** Danaë *victim:* **6** Medusa **8** Acrisius *wife:* **9** Andromeda

perseverance 8 tenacity **9** diligence, endurance **10** dedication **11** persistence **13** steadfastness

persevere see PERSIST

Persia 4 Iran

Persian *ancient:* **4** Mede *fairy:* **4** peri *governor:* **6** satrap *language:* **5** Farsi, Parsi *mystic:* **4** sufi *poet:* **5** Hafez, Hafiz **7** Firdusi **8** Ferdowsi, Firdausi, Firdawsi, Firdousi **11** Omar Khayyám *prophet:* **9** Zoroaster *robe:* **6** caftan *sacred books:* **6** Avesta *sun-god:* **7** Mithras *title:* **4** shah *writing:* **9** cuneiform

persiflage 6 banter, joking **7** jesting, kidding, ribbing **8** badinage, raillery, repartee

persist 4 go on, last **5** abide **6** endure, hang on, keep on, linger **7** carry on, prevail **8** continue **9** persevere

persistence 8 duration **9** endurance **10** continuity **11** continuance **12** continuation

persistent 6 dogged **7** lasting **8** enduring, obdurate, stubborn **9** continual, steadfast, tenacious **10** continuing, determined, relentless, unshakable **11** persevering, unremitting

persnickety 5 fussy, picky **6** choosy **7** finicky **8** exacting **10** fastidious, particular

person 3 guy **4** self, soul **5** being, human **6** entity, mensch, mortal **8** creature, specimen **10** individual

personable 4 nice **6** genial **7** affable, amiable **8** charming, friendly, pleasant,

pleasing **9** appealing, congenial
10 attractive
personage 3 VIP **5** human **6** bigwig, figure **7** big shot, notable **8** creature, luminary, somebody **9** celebrity, character, dignitary **10** individual
personal 3 own **5** privy **7** private, special **8** peculiar **10** individual, particular
personal effects 5 stuff **10** belongings **11** possessions
personality 3 ego, VIP **4** self **6** makeup, nature, temper, traits **7** notable **8** identity, selfhood, selfness **9** celebrity, character, dignitary, qualities **10** complexion **11** disposition, singularity, temperament **13** individualism, individuality
personate 3 act **4** play **5** enact **6** embody, typify **7** perform **9** epitomize, exemplify, represent **10** illustrate
personify 6 embody, typify **8** stand for **9** actualize, epitomize, exemplify, incarnate, represent, symbolize **11** emblematize
perspective 4 view **5** angle, scene, slant, vista **7** outlook **8** position, prospect **9** viewpoint **10** standpoint **11** point of view
perspicacious 4 keen **5** acute, quick, savvy, sharp **6** astute, clever, shrewd **9** observant, sagacious **10** discerning, insightful, perceptive **11** penetrating
perspicacity 6 acumen **7** insight **8** keenness **10** astuteness, shrewdness **11** discernment, penetration, percipience
perspicuous 5 clear, lucid, plain **6** lucent, simple **7** crystal, precise **8** clear-cut, pellucid **11** unambiguous
perspiration 5 sweat
perspire see SWEAT
persuadable 4 open **7** willing **9** receptive **11** suggestible, susceptible
persuade 3 win **4** coax, lead, sell, sway, urge **5** argue **6** entice, induce, prompt **7** convert, impress, win over **8** convince **9** influence, prevail on **11** bring around
persuasion 4 kind, mind, sort, type, view **5** group **6** belief, school **7** faction, opinion **8** argument **9** character, prejudice, sentiment **10** connection, conviction **11** affiliation, description
Persuasion author 6 Austen (Jane)
persuasive 6 cogent **7** telling, winning **8** credible **10** compelling, convincing **11** influential
pert 4 bold, chic, flip, trim **5** alert, cocky, fresh, sassy, saucy, smart **6** brazen, bright, cheeky, jaunty, lively **7** forward **8** animated, flippant, spirited **9** audacious, sprightly, vivacious
pertain 5 apply, refer **6** affect, bear on,

belong, regard, relate **7** concern **8** bear upon **9** touch upon
pertinacious 4 firm **5** fixed **6** dogged, mulish **7** willful **8** resolute, stubborn **9** obstinate, tenacious **10** inflexible, persistent, unshakable, unyielding
pertinent 3 apt, fit **5** ad rem **7** apropos, fitting, germane **8** apposite, material, relevant **10** applicable **11** appropriate
perturb 5 upset, worry **6** bother **7** agitate, disturb, fluster, trouble **8** disorder, disquiet, unsettle **10** discompose, disconcert
Peru *ancient civilization:* **4** Inca *capital:* **4** Lima *city:* **5** Cusco, Cuzco **6** Callao **8** Arequipa, Trujillo *conqueror:* **7** Pizarro (Francisco) *ethnic group:* **7** Quechua *lake:* **8** Titicaca *language:* **6** Aymara **7** Quechua, Spanish *leader:* **8** Fujimori (Alberto) *monetary unit:* **3** sol *mountain, range:* **5** Andes **9** Huascarán *neighbor:* **5** Chile **6** Brazil **7** Bolivia, Ecuador **8** Colombia *river:* **6** Amazon **7** Marañón *volcano:* **5** Misti **7** El Misti **8** Yucamani
peruse 4 read, scan **5** study **6** survey **7** examine **8** consider, look over, pore over
pervade 5 imbue **6** spread **7** diffuse **8** permeate, saturate **9** penetrate, percolate, transfuse **10** impregnate
perverse 5 balky **6** cranky, mulish, ornery **7** corrupt, deviant, froward, peevish, wayward, willful **8** contrary, depraved, improper, stubborn **9** incorrect, irritable, obstinate **10** degenerate, headstrong, refractory **11** stiff-necked, wrongheaded **12** cross-grained, unreasonable
pervert 4 ruin, skew, warp **5** abuse, twist **6** debase, divert, garble, misuse **7** corrupt, debauch, deprave, distort, deviant, falsify, vitiate **8** misstate, mistreat **9** misdirect **11** misconstrue **12** misinterpret, misrepresent
pervious 4 open **6** porous **9** permeable **10** accessible, penetrable
pesky 6 vexing **7** irksome **8** annoying **9** vexatious **10** bothersome **11** troublesome
pessimist 5 cynic **9** Cassandra, defeatist, doomsayer, worrywart **11** misanthrope
pessimistic 6 gloomy, morose **7** cynical **10** despairing **11** distrustful **12** misanthropic
pest 4 bane **5** trial, worry **6** bother, plague, vermin **7** nudnick, trouble **8** irritant, nuisance, vexation **9** annoyance, tormentor
pester 3 bug, irk, nag **4** ride **5** annoy, harry, tease, worry **6** badger, bother,

harass, hassle, plague **7** bedevil, disturb, torment **8** irritate

pestiferous 7 baneful, noxious **8** annoying, infected **9** infective, pestilent **10** pernicious **11** troublesome **12** pestilential

pestilence 5 curse **6** plague **7** scourge

pestilential 5 fatal **6** deadly, lethal, vexing **7** baneful, deathly, noxious, ruinous **8** annoying **10** pernicious

pestle 4 mano **6** muller *vessel:* **6** mortar

pet 3 cat, dog, hug **4** dear, kiss, love, neck, pout, sulk **5** loved **6** caress, cosset, dandle, fondle, pamper, stroke **7** beloved, cherish, darling, indulge **8** favorite, treasure **9** cherished, endearing, sulkiness

petcock 3 tap **5** valve **6** faucet, spigot

Peter Grimes composer 7 Britten (Benjamin)

peter out 4 fade, wane **5** abate, cease **6** lessen, recede, run dry **7** dwindle **8** decrease, diminish, taper off **9** drain away

Peter Pan *author:* **6** Barrie (James) *character:* **5** Wendy **7** Michael **9** Tiger Lily **10** Tinker Bell *dog:* **4** Nana *pirate:* **4** Hook, Smee

Peter the Apostle *brother:* **6** Andrew *father:* **5** Jonah *original name:* **5** Simon

Peter the Great *father:* **6** Alexis *wife:* **7** Eudoxia **9** Catherine

petite 5 small **6** little **8** smallish **10** diminutive

petition 3 ask **4** plea **5** plead **6** appeal **7** beseech, entreat, implore, request, solicit **8** entreaty **10** supplicate **11** application **12** supplication

Petrarch's beloved 5 Laura

Petrified Forest author 8 Sherwood (Robert)

petrify 4 daze, numb, stun **5** chill, scare **6** benumb, deaden, harden **7** startle **8** confound, frighten, paralyze

Petruchio's wife 9 Katharina, Katharine

pettifogger 7 shyster **8** quibbler **9** nitpicker

petty 4 mean **5** minor, small **6** measly, narrow, paltry **7** trivial **8** niggling, picayune, piddling, trifling **9** frivolous, secondary **10** irrelevant, negligible **11** small-minded, subordinate, unimportant **13** insignificant

petty officer 6 noncom

petulant 5 huffy, moody, sulky, testy, whiny **6** touchy **7** grouchy, peevish **8** snappish, irritable, querulous **10** ill-humored

pew 3 row **4** seat **5** bench

peyote 6 cactus, mescal *drug:* **9** mescaline

Phaedra *father:* **5** Minos *husband:* **7** Theseus *mother:* **8** Pasiphaë *sister:* **7** Ariadne *stepson:* **10** Hippolytus

Phaëthon's father 6 Helios **7** Phoebus

phalanx 4 army, host, mass **5** horde **6** myriad, throng **6** troops

phantasm 5 dream, fancy, ghost **6** spirit, vision **7** fantasy, fiction, figment, specter, spectre **8** daydream, delusion, illusion **9** invention **10** apparition **11** fabrication **13** hallucination

phantom 5 dummy, ghost, shade, spook **6** goblin, shadow, spirit, vision **7** bugbear, chimera, eidolon, specter, spectre **8** illusory **9** imaginary **10** apparition, fictitious **12** will-o'-the-wisp

pharaoh 3 Tut **4** Seti **5** Menes, ruler **6** Ahmose, Ramses, tyrant **7** Harmhab **8** Ikhnaton, Thutmose **9** Amenhotep, Merneptah **11** Tutankhamen

pharisee 9 hypocrite

pharmacist 8 druggist **10** apothecary *British:* **7** chemist

pharos 6 beacon **10** lighthouse

Pharsalus, battle of *vanquished:* **6** Pompey *victor:* **6** Caesar (Julius)

phase 4 part, side, view **5** point, stage, state **6** adjust, aspect **7** conduct **8** carry out, position **9** condition, situation, viewpoint **10** appearance

PhD exam 5 orals

Phèdre author 6 Racine (Jean)

phenomenal 6 actual **7** unusual **8** material, physical, sensible, singular, tangible, uncommon **9** corporeal, fantastic, objective **10** remarkable **11** exceptional, outstanding, perceivable, perceptible, substantial **13** extraordinary

phenomenon 4 fact **5** event **6** marvel, object, rarity, wonder **7** miracle, reality **9** actuality, sensation **10** experience, uniqueness **11** peculiarity, singularity

Phi ___ Kappa 4 Beta

philander 8 womanize

philanthropic 6 giving, humane **8** generous **10** altruistic, benevolent, bighearted, charitable **11** magnanimous **12** eleemosynary, humanitarian

philanthropist *American:* **5** Gates (Bill) **6** Cooper (Peter), Girard (Stephen), Mellon (Andrew) **7** Cornell (Ezra), Eastman (George), Packard (David), Whitney (Gertrude Vanderbilt) **8** Carnegie (Andrew), Stanford (Leland) **9** Rosenwald (Julius) **10** Vanderbilt (Cornelius) **11** Rockefeller (J. D.) *English:* **11** Wilberforce (William) *Swedish:* **5** Nobel (Alfred)

Philemon's wife 6 Baucis

philharmonic 8 symphony **9** orchestra, symphonic

Philip of Macedonia *father:* 7 Amyntas *son:* 9 Alexander

philippic 6 tirade 8 diatribe, harangue, jeremiad 12 condemnation

Philippics author 6 Cicero

Philippines *capital:* 6 Manila *city:* 4 Cebu 5 Davao 10 Quezon City *discoverer:* 8 Magellan (Ferdinand) *island:* 4 Cebu 5 Leyte, Luzon, Panay, Samar 6 Negros 7 Masbate, Mindoro, Palawan 8 Mindanao *language:* 7 Ilocano, Tagalog 8 Filipino, Pilipino *leader:* 6 Aquino (Corazon), Marcos (Ferdinand) *liberator:* 9 MacArthur (Douglas) *patriot:* 5 Rizal (José) *monetary unit:* 4 peso *sea:* 4 Sulu 5 Samar 7 Celebes, Sibuyan, Visayan 8 Mindanao 10 Philippine, South China *volcano:* 4 Taal 5 Mayon

Philippi victor 6 Antony (Marc, Mark) 8 Octavian

Philip the Tetrarch *father:* 5 Herod *mother:* 9 Cleopatra

philistine 4 boob 7 Babbitt 9 bourgeois, vulgarian 10 capitalist 11 materialist

Philistine *champion:* 7 Goliath *city:* 4 Gath, Gaza 5 Ekron 6 Ashdod 8 Ashkelon *foe:* 5 David 6 Samson *god:* 5 Dagon

Philoctetes *father:* 5 Poeas *victim:* 5 Paris

Philomela 11 nightingale *father:* 7 Pandion *ravisher:* 6 Tereus *sister:* 6 Procne

philosopher *American:* 5 Adler (Mortimer), Dewey (John), James (William), Quine (Willard), Rorty (Richard), Royce (Josiah) 6 Langer (Susanne), Peirce (C. S.) 7 Marcuse (Herbert), Mumford (Lewis), Strauss (Leo) 9 Santayana (George) *Arab:* 8 Averroës, Avicenna *Austrian:* 6 Popper (Karl) 12 Wittgenstein (Ludwig) *Chinese:* 5 Laoxi 6 Lao-tsu 7 Dai Zhen, Mencius, Tai Chen 9 Confucius *Danish:* 11 Kierkegaard (Soren) *Dutch:* 7 Erasmus (Desiderius), Spinoza (Baruch de) *English:* 4 Ayer (A. J.), Mill (John Stuart), More (Henry, Thomas), Watt (James) 5 Bacon (Francis), Burke (Edmund), Locke (John), Moore (G. E.), Occam (William of), Paine (Thomas) 6 Berlin (Isaiah), Hobbes (Thomas), Huxley (Thomas), Ockham (William), Popper (Karl) 7 Bentham (Jeremy), Russell (Bertrand), Spencer (Herbert), Whewell (William) 9 Whitehead (Alfred North) 12 Wittgenstein (Ludwig) *Finnish:* 11 Westermarck (Edward) *French:* 4 Weil (Simone) 5 Comte (Auguste), Taine (Hippolyte) 6 Pascal (Blaise), Sartre (Jean-Paul), Valéry (Paul) 7 Abelard (Peter), Bergson (Henri), Derrida (Jacques), Diderot (Denis), Fourier (Charles) 8 Foucault (Michel), Maritain (Jacques), Rousseau (Jean-Jacques), Voltaire 9 Descartes (René), Montaigne (Michel de) 10 Saint-Simon (Comte de) 11 Montesquieu (Baron de) 12 Merleau-Ponty (Maurice) *German:* 4 Kant (Immanuel), Marx (Karl) 5 Frege (Gottlob), Hegel (Georg Wilhelm Friedrich), Wolff (Christian von) 6 Carnap (Rudolf), Fichte (Immanuel, Johann), Herder (Johann von) 7 Husserl (Edmund), Jaspers (Karl), Leibniz (Gottfried) 8 Spengler (Oswald) 9 Heidegger (Martin), Nietzsche (Friedrich), Schelling (Friedrich von) 12 Schopenhauer (Arthur) 14 Albertus Magnus *Greek:* 4 Zeno 5 Plato, Timon 6 Thales 7 Gorgias, Proclus 8 Diogenes, Epicurus, Longinus, Socrates 9 Aristotle, Epictetus 10 Anaxagoras, Democritus, Empedocles, Heraclitus, Parmenides, Protagoras, Pythagoras, Xenocrates, Xenophanes 11 Anaximander 12 Theophrastus *Irish:* 8 Berkeley (George) *Italian:* 5 Croce (Benedetto) 6 Ficino (Marsilio) 11 Machiavelli (Niccolo) *Jewish:* 5 Buber (Martin), Philo 10 Maimonides (Moses) 12 Philo Judaeus *Roman:* 6 Seneca (Lucias Annaeus) 8 Boethius (Anicius), Plotinus 9 Lucretius *Scottish:* 4 Hume (David), Mill (James), Reid (Thomas) 7 Stewart (Dugald) *Spanish:* 6 Suárez (Francisco) 7 Unamuno (Miguel de) 13 Ortega y Gasset (José) *Swedish:* 10 Swedenborg (Emanuel)

philosopher's stone 3 key 6 elixir

philosophical 4 calm 7 stoical 8 composed, rational, resigned 9 unruffled 10 thoughtful

philosophy 6 system, theory, values 7 beliefs, inquiry 8 attitude, calmness 10 discipline *component:* 5 logic 6 ethics 10 aesthetics 11 metaphysics 12 epistemology

philter 4 drug 5 charm, tonic 6 potion 9 stimulant 10 love potion 11 aphrodisiac, restorative

Phineas *beloved:* 9 Andromeda *tormentors:* 7 Harpies *wife:* 9 Cleopatra

phlegm 5 humor, mucus 6 apathy 8 calmness, coolness, dullness 9 composure, sangfroid 10 equanimity 11 impassivity, nonchalance 12 indifference

phlegmatic 4 calm, cool, dull 5 aloof, stoic 6 stolid 8 detached 9 apathetic, impassive, lethargic 11 indifferent, unconcerned

Phlegyas *daughter:* 7 Coronis *father:* 4 Ares, Mars *son:* 5 Ixion

phobia see FEAR
Phobos 4 moon **9** satellite *brother:*
6 Deimos *father:* **4** Ares, Mars
Phocus *father:* **6** Aeacus **8** Ornytion *half brother:* **6** Peleus **7** Telamon *mother:*
8 Psamathe *slayer:* **6** Peleus **7** Telamon *wife:* **7** Antiope
Phoebe 5 Diana **7** Artemis *daughter:*
4 Leto *father:* **9** Leucippus *mother:*
4 Gaea
Phoebus see APOLLO
Phoenician *city:* **4** Acre, Tyre **5** Sidon *colony:* **8** Carthage *god:* **4** Baal **6** Eshmun *goddess:* **6** Baltis **7** Astarte
Phoenix *pupil:* **8** Achilles *sister:* **6** Europa *team:* **4** Suns **7** Coyotes **9** Cardinals
12 Diamondbacks
phony 4 fake, sham **5** bogus, cheat, faker, false, fraud **6** humbug, pseudo
8 impostor, specious, spurious **9** charlatan, dishonest, pretender **10** ficticious, suspicious **11** counterfeit **12** hypocritical
photograph 3 pic **4** film, snap **5** shoot
6 glossy **7** picture, tintype **8** snapshot
three-dimensional: **8** hologram
photographer 8 photoist **9** cameraman
10 shutterbug *famous:* **3** Ray (Man)
4 Capa (Cornell, Robert), Haas (Ernst), Hine (Lewis), Penn (Irving), Riis (Jacob) **5** Adams (Ansel), Arbus (Diane), Atget (Eugène), Brady (Mathew), Evans (Frederick, Walker), Horst (Horst Peter), Karsh (Yousuf), Lange (Dorothea), Model (Lisette), Nadar, Parks (Gordon), Ritts (Herb), Smith (W. Eugene), Weber (Bruce), White (Clarence, Minor) **6** Abbott (Berenice), Avedon (Richard), Beaton (Cecil), Brandt (Bill), Coburn (Alvin), Curtis (Edward S.), Newton (Helmut), Porter (Eliot), Rowell (Galen), Siegel (Eliot), Strand (Paul), Talbot (William Henry Fox), Weegee, Wegman (William), Weston (Brett, Edward) **7** Brassaï, Cameron (Julia Margaret), Emerson (Peter), Halsman (Philippe), Jackson (William Henry), Kertész (André), Salomon (Erich), Siskind (Aaron), Snowdon (Earl of), Thomson (John), Watkins (Carleton) **8** Callahan (Harry), Cosindas (Marie), Daguerre (Louis-Jacques-Mandé), Kasebier (Gertrude), Scavullo (Francesco), Steichen (Edward), Steinert (Otto) **9** Caponigro (Paul), Feininger (Andreas), Leibovitz (Annie), Meyrowitz (Joel), Muybridge (Eadweard), O'Sullivan (Timothy), Rejlander (Oscar), Rothstein (Arthur), Stieglitz (Alfred), Winogrand (Garry)
10 Cunningham (Imogen), Heartfield

(John), Moholy-Nagy (Laszlo)
11 Bourke-White (Margaret), Eisenstaedt (Alfred) **12** Mapplethorpe (Robert)
photographic 5 exact, vivid **7** graphic
8 accurate, detailed **9** pictorial **11** picturesque *solution:* **4** hypo **5** fixer, toner
7 reducer **9** developer
phrase 5 couch, frame, idiom **6** slogan
7 diction, express, styling, wording
8 locution, verbiage **9** catchword, formulate, verbalism, watchword
10 expression
Phrygian *god:* **4** Atys **5** Attis *goddess:*
6 Cybele *king:* **5** Midas **7** Gordius
phylactery 5 charm **6** amulet **7** periapt
8 talisman
physic 4 cure, heal **5** purge **6** remedy
8 medicine **9** cathartic, purgative
10 medication
physical 4 real **5** lusty, rough **6** actual, bodily, carnal, sexual **7** fleshly, natural, somatic **8** concrete, corporal, material, sensible, tangible **9** corporeal, objective
10 phenomenal **11** perceivable, perceptible, substantial
physician 3 doc **5** medic **6** doctor, medico **7** surgeon **8** sawbones *American:*
4 Rush (Benjamin), Salk (Jonas)
5 Minot (George), Spock (Benjamin), Still (Andrew) **6** Jarvik (Robert), Murphy (John), Weller (Thomas) **7** Huggins (Charles), Robbins (Frederick), Theiler (Max) **8** Richards (Dickinson) **9** Sternberg (George Miller) *Arab:* **8** Avicenna *Canadian:* **5** Osler (William) *English:*
4 Ross (Ronald) **6** Harvey (William), Jenner (Edward, William), Willis (Thomas) **8** Sydenham (Thomas)
French: **5** Widal (Fernand) **7** Laveran (Charles) **10** Schweitzer (Albert) *German:* **7** Sylvius (Franciscus) *Greek:*
5 Galen **11** Hippocrates *Italian:* **7** Galvani (Luigi) *South African:* **7** Barnard (Christiaan) *Swiss:* **10** Paracelsus (see also NOBEL PRIZE WINNER *physiology or medicine;* SURGEON)
physicist *American:* **4** Rabi (I. I.), Ting (Samuel) **5** Fermi (Enrico), Gibbs (J. Willard), Kusch (Polykarp), Mayer (Maria-Goeppert), Pauli (Wolfgang), Pupin (Michael), Segré (Emilio), Smyth (Henry DeWolf), Stern (Otto) **6** Teller (Edward), Townes (Charles), Wigner (Eugene) **7** Alvarez (Luis), Feynman (Richard), Goddard (Robert), Purcell (Edward) **8** Einstein (Albert), Gell-Mann (Murray), McMillan (Edwin), Millikan (Clark, Robert), Mulliken (Robert), Shockley (William), Van Allen (James) **9** Michelson (Albert),

Schwinger (Julian) **11** Oppenheimer (J. Robert) **Austrian:** **4** Mach (Ernst) **7** Doppler (Christian) **11** Schrödinger (Erwin) **British:** **4** Snow (C. P.) **5** Dirac (P. A. M.), Jeans (James), Joule (James) **6** Dalton (John), Kelvin (Baron), Newton (Isaac), Powell (Cecil), Stokes (George) **7** Faraday (Michael), Hodgkin (Dorothy), Thomson (George, Joseph, William), Tyndall (John) **8** Rayleigh (Lord), Robinson (Robert), Thompson (Benjamin, Silvanus) **9** Wollaston (William) **10** Richardson (Owen), Rutherford (Ernest), Wheatstone (Charles) **Chinese:** **4** Yang (Chen Ning) **Danish:** **4** Bohr (Aage, Niels) **Dutch:** **6** Zeeman (Pieter) **7** Huygens (Christian), Lorentz (Hendrik), Zernike (Frits) **11** Van der Waals (Johannes) **French:** **4** Néel (Louis) **5** Arago (François) **6** Ampère (André-Marie), Perrin (Jean-Baptiste) **7** Coulomb (Charles-Augustin de), Kastler (Alfred), Réaumur (René-Antoine de) **8** Lippmann (Gabriel) **German:** **3** Ohm (Georg) **4** Laue (Max von), Wien (Wilhelm) **5** Hertz (Gustav, Heinrich), Stark (Johannes) **6** Jensen (Hans), Lenard (Philipp), Nernst (Walther), Planck (Max) **7** Meitner (Lise) **8** Roentgen (Wilhelm) **9** Helmholtz (Hermann von), Kirchhoff (Gustav), Mossbauer (Rudolf) **10** Fahrenheit (Daniel), Hofstadter (Robert) **Indian:** **5** Raman (Chandrasekhara) **Irish:** **6** Walton (Ernest) **Italian:** **5** Rossi (Bruno), Volta (Alessandro) **7** Galileo (Galilei), Galvani (Luigi) **10** Torricelli (Evangelista) **Japanese:** **6** Yukawa (Hideki) **8** Tomonaga (Shinichiro) **Mexican:** **8** Vallarta (Manuel) **Russian:** **4** Tamm (Igor) **6** Landau (Lev) **9** Prokhorov (Aleksandr) **Scottish:** **4** Tait (Peter) **6** Wilson (Charles) **7** Maxwell (James Clerk) **Swedish:** **7** Rydberg (Johannes) **8** Angstrom (Anders), Siegbahn (Kai, Karl) **Swiss:** **6** Zwicky (Fritz) **7** Piccard (Auguste) (see also NOBEL PRIZE WINNER *physics*)

physiognomy **3** mug **4** face **5** front **6** aspect, visage **7** profile **8** features **9** character **10** lineaments **11** countenance, temperament

physiologist *English:* **8** Starling (Ernest) *German:* **5** Weber (Ernst), Wundt (Wilhelm) **7** Schwann (Theodor) **9** Helmholtz (Hermann von) *Italian:* **11** Spallanzani (Lazzaro) (see also NOBEL PRIZE WINNER *physiology or medicine*)

physique **4** body, form **5** build, shape

6 figure, makeup **7** anatomy **9** structure **12** constitution

pianist *American:* **4** Nero (Peter), Wild (Earl) **5** Arrau (Claudio), Janis (Byron), Watts (André) **6** Duchin (Peter), Joplin (Scott), Serkin (Peter, Rudolf) **7** Cliburn (Van), Istomin (Eugene), Ohlsson (Garrick), Perahia (Murray), Winston (George) **8** Graffman (Gary), Horowitz (Vladimir), Pennario (Leonard) **9** Fleischer (Leon) **10** Johannesen (Grant), Rubinstein (Arthur) *Argentinian:* **8** Argerich (Martha) *Austrian:* **6** Czerny (Karl) **7** Brendel (Alfred) **8** Schnabel (Artur) *Bulgarian:* **11** Weissenberg (Alexis) *Canadian:* **5** Gould (Glenn) *Cuban:* **5** Bolet (Jorge) *English:* **4** Hess (Myra) **5** Ogdon (John) **6** Curzon (Clifford) *French:* **6** Cortot (Alfred) **7** Cziffra (Gyorgy) **9** Casadesus (Robert), Entremont (Philippe) **10** Saint-Saëns (Camille) *German:* **6** Kempff (Wilhelm) **8** Schumann (Clara) **9** Gieseking (Walter) *Hungarian:* **5** Liszt (Franz) **7** Cziffra (Gyorgy) *Italian:* **6** Busoni (Ferruccio) **7** Pollini (Maurizio) **8** Clementi (Muzio) *Japanese:* **6** Uchida (Mitsuko) *Polish:* **6** Chopin (Frédéric) **7** Hofmann (Josef) **10** Paderewski (Ignacy), Rubinstein (Arthur) *Romanian:* **4** Lupu (Radu) **7** Lipatti (Dinu) *Russian:* **6** Berman (Lazar), Gilels (Emil), Kissin (Evgeny) **7** Richter (Sviatoslav) **8** Horowitz (Vladimir), Pachmann (Vladimir von) **9** Ashkenazy (Vladimir) **10** Rubinstein (Anton) **12** Rachmaninoff (Sergey) *Spanish:* **6** Iturbi (José) **8** Granados (Enrique) **10** de Larrocha (Alicia) *Swiss:* **4** Anda (Geza)

piano **5** grand **6** softly, spinet **7** quietly, upright **9** baby grand *builder:* **5** Knabe (William), Stein (Johann), Zumpe (Johann) **7** Baldwin (Dwight) **8** Steinway (Henry) **9** Bechstein (Friedrich) **10** Chickering (Jonas), Silbermann (Johann) *inventor:* **10** Cristofori (Bartolomeo) *pedal:* **6** damper **9** sostenuto

piazza **5** patio, plaza, porch **6** square **7** balcony, gallery, portico, terrace, veranda **9** courtyard

picaroon **5** rogue, rover, thief **6** pirate **7** brigand, corsair **8** sea rover **9** buccaneer **10** freebooter

picayune **5** petty **6** measly, paltry, trifle **7** trivial **8** piddling **11** small-minded **13** insignificant

pick **3** rob, tap **4** best, carp, cull, open, pull, take, tool **5** elect, pluck, probe, prize **6** choice, choose, chosen, option, pierce, pilfer, remove, select, unlock

7 harvest, provoke **8** selected **9** exclusive, single out

picket 4 pale, post **5** fence, guard, stake, watch **6** sentry, tether **7** enclose, lookout, protest **8** palisade, sentinel, watchman **11** demonstrate

pickle 3 fix, jam **4** dill, spot **5** brine, treat **6** plight, scrape **7** dilemma, gherkin, trouble **8** marinate, preserve **10** difficulty **11** predicament

pick on 5 bully, harry, taunt, tease **6** hector, pester **9** criticize, single out

pick out 4 espy, name, spot **6** choose, descry, detect, select, take in **7** discern **8** identify, perceive **9** apprehend, ascertain, recognize **11** distinguish

pickpocket 3 dip **5** thief **6** dipper **8** cutpurse

pick up 3 buy, get **4** cull, gain, earn, land, lift, tidy **5** catch, glean, hoist, learn, raise, run in **6** arrest, detain, gather, notice, obtain, pull in, resume, revive **7** acquire, clean up, collect, restart **8** perceive **9** apprehend **10** appreciate, understand

pickup 5 truck **9** detention **10** hitchhiker **11** improvement **12** acceleration

picky 5 fussy **6** choosy **7** finicky **10** fastidious, particular, pernickety **11** persnickety

picnic 4 snap **5** cinch **6** breeze, outing **7** cookout **8** cakewalk **11** piece of cake

picture 4 limn, show **5** image, photo, pinup **7** drawing, tableau **8** describe, painting, portrait **9** depiction, portrayal **10** simulacrum **11** delineation, description **13** spitting image *stand:* **5** easel

picturesque 5 vivid **6** quaint, scenic **8** artistic, charming

piddling 4 puny **5** petty **6** meager, meagre, measly, paltry **7** trivial **8** picayune, trifling **11** Mickey Mouse, unimportant **13** insignificant

pie 4 flan, tart **5** pasty **6** pastry **7** cobbler, dessert **8** turnover

piebald 5 mixed **6** motley **7** mottled **10** multicolor

piece 4 part **5** patch, slice **6** member, parcel **7** firearm, portion, section, segment **8** division, fraction, fragment **9** allotment **10** allocation

pièce de résistance 8 main dish **9** showpiece **11** centerpiece, chef d'oeuvre, masterpiece

piecemeal 5 apart **6** slowly **7** gradual **8** bit by bit **9** by degrees, gradually **11** fragmentary

pied 6 motley **7** blotchy, brindle, dappled, mottled **8** brindled, speckled **9** multihued **10** variegated **11** varicolored **12** parti-colored

pier 4 anta, dock, quay, slip **5** berth, jetty, levee, wharf **6** column, pillar **8** pilaster *architectural:* **4** anta

pierce 3 cut **4** stab **5** probe, spear **6** impale, incise, skewer **8** puncture **9** penetrate, perforate **10** run through

piercing 4 high, keen **5** acute, sharp **6** piping, shrill **8** shooting, stabbing, strident **9** knifelike **12** earsplitting *tool:* **3** awl

piety 6 fealty **7** loyalty **8** devotion, fidelity, sanctity **9** reverence **10** allegiance, dedication, devoutness **12** faithfulness

piffle 4 bosh, bunk **5** hooey **6** drivel **7** baloney, rubbish, twaddle **8** malarkey, nonsense **10** balderdash

pig 3 hog **4** slob **5** shoat, swine **6** farrow, piglet, porker **7** casting, glutton *breed:* **5** Duroc **8** Tamworth **9** Berkshire, Hampshire, Yorkshire *female:* **3** sow **4** gilt *feral:* **9** razorback *litter:* **6** farrow *male:* **4** boar **6** barrow *meat:* **3** ham **4** pork **5** bacon **7** sausage **8** chitlins **12** chitterlings *wild:* **7** peccary, warthog **8** babirusa

pigeon 3 sap **4** dupe, fool, gull, mark **5** chump, decoy, patsy **6** culver, stooge, sucker **7** fall guy **8** rock dove *genus:* **7** Columba *house:* **4** cote, loft *kind:* **4** barb, rock **5** homer **6** homing, pouter, roller **7** carrier, crowned, fantail, tumbler *relative:* **4** dove *young:* **5** squab

pigeon hawk 6 merlin

pigeonhole 4 slot, sort **5** class, cubby, grade, group, niche **6** recess, shelve **7** catalog **8** category, classify, grouping **10** categorize **11** compartment

piggish 6 greedy **7** selfish, swinish **10** gluttonous

pigheaded 5 rigid **6** dogged, mulish **7** willful **8** contrary, perverse, stubborn **9** obstinate **10** inflexible, unyielding

piglet 5 shoat

pigment 3 dye **4** tint **5** color, paint, stain **8** colorant, dyestuff, tincture *black:* **9** lampblack *blue:* **4** cyan **5** azure, smalt **6** indigo **7** cyanine **8** cerulean **9** verdigris **11** ultramarine *brown:* **5** sepia *umber:* **6** bister, sienna *combining form:* **5** chrom **6** chromo *dark:* **7** melanin *green:* **7** celadon **8** viridian **10** biliverdin *orange:* **7** realgar **8** carotene *red:* **4** lake *toxic:* **8** gossypol *yellow:* **5** ocher, ochre **6** flavin, lutein **7** flavine, xanthin

pigpen 3 sty **4** dump, mess **5** hovel

pigskin 6 saddle **8** football

pike 4 dive, fish **5** spear **7** highway **8** pickerel

piker 5 miser **7** scrooge **8** tightwad **9** skinflint **10** cheapskate **12** pennypincher

pilaster 4 pier 6 column, pillar
pilchard 7 herring, sardine
pile 3 fur, lot, nap 4 coat, fill, heap, hill, load, mass, much, pack, peck, pyre 5 amass, crowd, drive, stack 6 bundle, column, jumble 7 collect, fortune, reactor 8 quantity 9 great deal 10 assemblage, collection 11 aggregation 12 accumulation
pileup 4 mass 5 crash, smash 8 accident 9 collision 12 accumulation
pilfer 3 rob 4 lift, take 5 filch, pinch, steal, swipe 6 finger, snitch, thieve 7 purloin 11 appropriate
pilgarlic 4 butt 8 baldhead 13 laughingstock
Pilgrim 5 Alden (John) 6 Carver (John) 7 Puritan, Winslow (Edward) 8 Bradford (William), Brewster (William), Standish (Myles)
pilgrim 5 hadji, hajji 6 palmer 8 traveler, wanderer, wayfarer
pilgrimage 4 hajj, trip 7 journey
Pilgrims' interpreter 7 Squanto
Pilgrim's Progress 8 allegory *author:* 6 Bunyan (John) *hero:* 9 Christian
pill 4 ball, bore, pain, pest 5 bolus 6 pellet 7 capsule, lozenge 8 medicine, nuisance 9 annoyance
pillage 4 lift, loot, sack 5 booty, prize, spoil, steal 6 maraud, ravage, thieve 7 despoil, plunder, purloin 8 spoliate 9 depredate, desecrate
pillar 4 pier, post, prop 5 pylon, shaft, stela, stele 6 column, stelae (plural) 7 obelisk, support, upright 8 backbone, mainstay, pedestal, pilaster
pillory 6 stocks
pillow 3 pad 4 rest 7 bolster, cushion, support
pilot 4 lead, show, tool 5 drive, flier, guide, steer 6 airman, direct, leader 7 aviator, conduct, guiding, tracing 8 aviatrix, helmsman, shepherd
pimple 3 dot, zit 4 acne, boil, spot, stud 6 papule 7 blemish, blister, pustule, speckle 8 sprinkle, swelling
pin 3 leg, peg 4 clip, hold, join 5 affix, blame, stake 6 attach, broach, brooch, cotter, emblem, fasten, secure, trifle 8 fastener, hold down, ornament, restrain
pinafore 5 apron, dress, frock
pinch 3 bit, nab, nip 4 dash, lift, pain, take 5 filch, press, prune, run in, skimp, steal, swipe, taper, theft, tweak 6 arrest, crisis, narrow, pilfer, snatch, stress 7 confine, deficit, larceny, squeeze, straits 8 compress, exigency, hardship, juncture, pressure, stealing, straiten 9 apprehend, constrict, emer-

gency, privation, tight spot 10 substitute
pinchbeck 4 fake, sham 5 alloy, bogus, false, phony 6 pseudo 8 spurious 9 brummagem 11 counterfeit
pinch hitter 3 sub 6 backup, fill-in, relief 7 stand-in 9 alternate, surrogate 10 substitute 11 alternative, replacement
pinchpenny 4 mean 5 cheap, close, mingy, tight 6 stingy 7 chintzy, costive, miserly, scrimpy 9 niggardly, penurious 11 closefisted, tightfisted 12 parsimonious
Pindar *home:* 6 Thebes *poem:* 3 ode
pine 4 ache, long, mope, sigh, tree, wish, wood 5 brood, crave, dream, yearn 6 desire, grieve, hanker, hunger, lament, thirst 7 conifer 8 languish 9 evergreen
Pine Tree State 5 Maine
pinhead 4 dolt, dope, fool 5 dunce 6 dimwit, nitwit 7 dullard 8 dumbbell 9 birdbrain
pinion 3 cog 4 bind, gear, wing 5 quill, tie up, truss 6 fetter, tether 7 disable, feather, shackle 8 cogwheel, restrain 9 hamstring
pink 3 cut 4 best, peak, stab 5 blush 6 flower, height, pierce 7 excited, paragon 9 perforate
pinna 3 ear, fin 4 wing 7 feather, leaflet
pinnacle 3 top, tor 4 acme, apex, peak 5 crest, crown, serac, spire 6 apogee, climax, height, summit, zenith 7 steeple 8 capsheaf, meridian 11 culmination
pinniped 4 seal 6 walrus
Pinocchio author 7 Collodi (Carlo) 9 Lorenzini (Carlo)
pinochle *card:* 3 ace, ten 4 jack, king, nine 5 queen *term:* 4 meld 5 widow 7 auction *two-handed:* 7 goulash
pinpoint 3 aim, fix 4 spot, tiny 5 exact, place 6 locate 7 precise 8 identify, stand out 9 determine, highlight, recognize 11 distinguish
Pinter play 8 Betrayal 9 Caretaker (The) 10 Homecoming (The)
pinto 4 pied, pony 5 horse, paint 7 mottled, piebald 8 skewbald
pint-size 3 wee 5 dwarf, small 6 midget, pocket 9 miniature 10 diminutive
pioneer 5 first, prime 6 maiden 7 explore, founder, initial, primary, settler 8 colonist, earliest, explorer, original 9 innovator 10 avant-garde, pathfinder 11 trailblazer 12 frontiersman *famous:* 5 Boone (Daniel), Bowie (Jim), Clark (William), Lewis (Meriwether) 6 Carson (Kit), Colter (John) 7 Bridger (Jim), Chapman (John),

Frémont (John C.), Whitman (Marcus) 8 Crockett (Davy)

pious 4 holy 5 godly 6 devout, worthy 7 devoted, dutiful 8 reverent, virtuous 9 hypocrite, pietistic, prayerful, religious 10 devotional 12 hypocritical

pip 3 dot 4 blip, peep, seed, spot 5 speck 9 break open

pipe 3 keg, tun 4 butt, cask, duct, hose, tube 6 barrel, convey, funnel, siphon 7 channel, conduct, conduit 8 aqueduct, hogshead *ceremonial:* 7 calumet *part:* 4 bowl, stem

pipe down 4 hush 5 dry up, quiet 6 shut up 7 be quiet

pipe dream 4 wish 7 chimera, fantasy 8 illusion

pipeline 5 works 6 system 7 channel, conduit, process 8 activity, supplier 10 connection

pipsqueak 6 shaver, squirt 7 tadpole 8 half-pint, small fry

piquant 4 tart 5 sharp, spicy, tangy, zesty 6 biting, lively, savory, snappy 7 peppery, pungent 8 poignant, spirited 9 flavorful, sparkling 10 appetizing 11 provocative, stimulating

pique 3 irk, vex 4 huff, miff, move 5 anger, annoy, peeve, pride, rouse 6 arouse, excite, nettle, offend, put out 7 dudgeon, offense, provoke, quicken 8 irritate, motivate, vexation 9 aggravate, annoyance, challenge, stimulate 10 exasperate, irritation, resentment

piracy 5 theft 7 lifting, looting, pillage, plunder, robbery 8 stealing, thievery 10 plagiarism

piranha 6 caribe

pirate 5 rover 6 looter, raider, robber, sea dog 7 brigand, corsair, sea wolf 8 marauder, picaroon, pillager, sea rover 9 buccaneer, plunderer, privateer, sea robber 10 freebooter *English:* 4 Read (Mary) 5 Bonny (Anne), Teach (Edward) 6 Morgan (Henry) 7 Dampier (William) 10 Blackbeard *flag:* 10 Jolly Roger *French:* 7 Laffite (Jean), Lafitte (Jean) *Scottish:* 4 Kidd (William)

Pirates of Penzance, The *composer:* 8 Sullivan (Arthur) *librettist:* 7 Gilbert (W. S.)

pirogue 5 canoe 6 dugout

pirouette 4 spin, turn 5 twirl, whirl

piscator 6 angler 9 fisherman

pismire 3 ant

pistol 3 gat, rod 4 Colt 5 Glock, Luger 6 Magnum, Mauser, roscoe 7 bulldog, handgun 8 revolver, small arm 9 derringer, pepperbox *case:* 7 holster

pit 3 vie 4 dent, hell, hole, scar 5 arena, hades, match, shaft, stone 6 cavity, hol-

low, oppose 7 counter, play off 8 pockmark 11 indentation

Pit and the Pendulum author 3 Poe (Edgar Allan)

pitch 3 dip, set 4 buck, dive, drop, fall, hurl, line, play, plug, tilt, tone, toss 5 erect, fling, heave, lurch, put up, resin, slant, sling, slope, spiel, throw 6 encamp, go down, plunge 7 discard, incline, present, promote 8 distance 9 advertise, declivity 13 advertisement

pitch-dark 3 jet 4 ebon, inky 5 black, ebony, jetty

pitcher 4 ewer, olla, toby 5 cruse 6 beaker, flagon 7 creamer *area:* 5 mound *handle:* 3 ear 4 ansa (see also BASEBALLER)

pitch in 3 aid 4 help 5 begin, set to, start 6 fall to 8 commence, get going, start off 9 subscribe, volunteer 10 contribute

piteous 3 sad 4 poor 8 pathetic 9 affecting 10 lamentable 11 distressing

pitfall 4 risk, snag, trap 5 catch, peril, snare 6 danger, hazard 9 booby trap 10 difficulty 12 entanglement

pith 3 nub 4 core, kill, meat, pulp 5 focus, heart 6 center, import, kernel 7 essence, nucleus 9 substance 10 importance 12 significance

pith helmet 5 topee

pithy 5 brief, crisp, meaty, short, terse 6 cogent 7 compact, concise, pointed 8 succinct 12 epigrammatic 13 short and sweet

pitiable 4 poor 5 cheap, sorry 8 shameful 10 deplorable, lamentable 12 contemptible

pitiful 3 sad 4 mean, poor 5 cheap, sorry 6 meager, meagre, paltry, shabby 7 forlorn 8 beggarly, pathetic, wretched 9 miserable 10 despicable, inadequate 12 contemptible 13 heartbreaking

pitiless 4 cold, hard 5 cruel, harsh, stony 6 brutal 8 inhumane, uncaring 9 barbarous, unfeeling 10 unmerciful 11 coldhearted, hardhearted

pittance 4 wage 5 scrap, trace 6 trifle 7 modicum, peanuts 9 allowance

pity 3 rue 4 ache, ruth 5 mercy 6 regret, sorrow 7 empathy, feel for, sadness 8 distress, sympathy 10 compassion, condolence, sympathize 11 commiserate 13 commiseration

pivot 3 pin 4 turn 5 hinge, shaft, swing, wheel 6 center, swivel

pivotal 3 key 5 chief, vital 7 central, crucial 8 critical, decisive 9 essential, important

pixie 3 elf, fay, imp 5 antic, fairy, scamp 6 elvish, impish, rascal, sprite 7 brownie, coltish, playful, puckish **8** prankish **11** mischievous

pixilated 3 fey **7** bemused, erratic, flighty, muddled, touched **9** eccentric, whimsical **10** capricious

Pizarro, Francisco *brother:* **7** Gonzalo *city founded:* **4** Lima *conquest:* **4** Peru *victims:* **5** Incas **9** Atahualpa **10** Atahuallpa

pizzazz 3 pep, vim, zip **4** bang, brio, dash, snap, zest, zing **5** éclat, flair, flash, gusto, moxie, oomph, punch, verve **6** dazzle, energy, hoopla, sizzle, spirit **7** glamour, panache **8** vitality **10** excitement

placard 4 bill, post **6** notice, plaque, poster **7** affiche **8** handbill

placate 4 calm, ease **6** pacify, soothe **7** appease, assuage, comfort, mollify, satisfy, sweeten, win over **10** conciliate, propitiate

place 3 lay, put, set **4** area, lieu, loci (plural), post, rank, site, spot, zone **5** locus, point, stead, tract **6** region, status **7** situate, station **8** district, identify, locality, location, pinpoint, position, standing **9** establish, recognize *combining form:* **3** top **4** loco, topo, topy

placid 4 calm, easy, mild **5** quiet, still **6** gentle, serene **7** halcyon **8** composed, peaceful, tranquil, waveless, windless **9** unruffled **10** complacent, unagitated, untroubled **11** undisturbed **13** imperturbable

plagiarize 4 copy, crib **5** steal **6** pirate **11** appropriate

plague 3 vex **4** bane, evil, pest **5** annoy, beset, curse, harry, hound, smite, trial, worry **6** blight, bother, infest, harass, hassle, hector, pester **7** afflict, bedevil, disease, disturb, scourge, torment, trouble **8** calamity, distress, epidemic, invasion, irritant, irritate, nuisance, outbreak, pandemic **9** annoyance, beleaguer **10** affliction, black death, pestilence **11** infestation

plaid 6 tartan

plain 3 lea **4** bald, bare, open, pure **5** blunt, clear, field, frank, usual **6** candid, common, homely, modest, patent, severe, simple, tundra **7** expanse, evident, obvious, prairie, savanna **8** apparent, distinct, everyday, homespun, manifest, ordinary, straight **9** outspoken, unadorned **10** absolutely, forthright, unaffected **11** undecorated, unvarnished **13** uncomplicated

plainclothesman 4 dick **6** shamus, sleuth **7** gumshoe **8** hawkshaw **9** detective **12** investigator

___ **Plaines 3** Des

plainness 6 candor, purity **7** clarity, honesty **8** lucidity **10** simplicity

plainsong 5 chant **12** cantus firmus

plainspoken 4 open **5** frank **6** candid, direct, honest **8** straight, truthful **10** forthright **11** undisguised, unvarnished

plaintive 3 sad **4** glum **6** woeful **7** doleful, piteous, pitiful **8** dolorous, downcast, mournful **9** sorrowful **10** dispirited, lamentable, lugubrious, melancholy

plait 4 fold **5** braid, pleat, weave **7** pigtail **10** intertwine, interweave

plan 3 aim, map, way **4** cast, goal, idea, mean, plot **5** chart, frame **6** design, devise, intend, intent, lay out, map out, method, scheme, set out **7** arrange, diagram, drawing, outline, pattern, program, project, propose, purpose, work out **8** contrive, engineer, organize, strategy, think out **9** blueprint, formulate, intention, procedure **11** arrangement, formulation

plane 3 fly, jet **4** even, flat, tool, tree **5** flush, level **6** smooth **8** aircraft, airliner

planet 4 Mars **5** Earth, Pluto, Venus **6** Saturn, Uranus **7** Jupiter, Mercury, Neptune *path:* **5** orbit *satellite:* **4** moon *shadow:* **5** umbra *small:* **8** asteroid

planetary 4 vast **6** global **7** erratic, immense **8** colossal, enormous **9** universal, wandering, worldwide **11** terrestrial

plangent 7 orotund, ringing, vibrant **8** resonant, sonorous **9** consonant, plaintive **10** expressive, resounding **11** reverberant

plank 4 item, wood **5** board, floor **6** lumber, timber **7** article, support

plant 3 fix, pot, set, sow **4** bury, grow, hide, mill, park, root, seed, tomb **5** cache, cover, imbed, inter, place, plunk, put in, stash, works **6** entomb, inhume, occult, screen **7** conceal, factory, install, lay away, put away, secrete **8** colonize, populate **9** cultivate *angiosperm:* **5** dicot **7** monocot *aquatic:* **4** reed **5** lotus, sedge **7** awlwort, cattail, fanwort, papyrus **8** duckweed, eelgrass, hornwort, pondweed **9** water lily **10** watercress **11** bladderwort **12** pickerelweed *Australian:* **6** mallee **7** banksia **8** blackboy **10** eucalyptus *body:* **4** stem **7** thallus *bulbous:* **4** lily **5** camas, onion, tulip **7** jonquil **8** hyacinth **9** narcissus *carnivorous:* **6** sundew **10** butterwort **12** pitcher plant, Venus flytrap *cell layer:* **7** phellem *climbing:* **3** ivy **4** vine **5** betel, liana, vetch **6** bryony, derris, smilax **7** creeper, jasmine **8** bignonia, fumitory, moonseed, scammony, wisteria 12 morning glory *coloring agent:* 8 carotene 11 chlorophyll, xanthophyll *combining form:* 4 phyt 5 phyto *cone-bearing:* 3 fir, yew 4 pine 5 cedar, cycad 6 ginkgo, spruce 7 conifer, cypress, redwood 10 arborvitae, gymnosperm *desert:* 4 aloe 5 agave 6 cactus, cholla 8 mesquite, ocotillo 9 paloverde 11 brittlebush *disease:* 3 rot 4 gall, mold, rust, scab, smut, wilt 5 ergot 6 blight, mildew, mosaic 7 blister 8 clubroot 9 black spot 10 black heart *extinct:* 8 calamite *flowerless:* 4 alga, fern, kelp, moss 5 algae (plural), fungi (plural) 6 fungus, lichen 7 seaweed 8 clubmoss 9 bryophyte, equisetum, horsetail, liverwort *fluid:* 3 gum, sap 4 milk 5 latex, resin *gland:* 7 nectary *hallucinogenic:* 4 hemp 5 poppy 6 mescal 8 cannabis 9 marijuana *largest:* 7 sequoia *life:* 5 flora *marine:* 4 kelp, nori 5 dulse, fucus 6 wakame 7 seaweed 8 gulfweed 10 sea lettuce *marsh:* 4 reed 5 carex, sedge 7 bogbean, bulrush, calamus, cattail 8 red maple, sphagnum 11 loosestrife *medicinal:* 4 aloe, sage 5 poppy, senna, tansy 6 catnip, fennel, garlic, hyssop, ipecac, nettle 7 aconite, boneset, burdock, camphor, comfrey, ginseng, hemlock, henbane, juniper, lobelia, mullein, mustard, parsley 8 camomile, capsicum, cinchona, feverfew, licorice, pilewort, plantain, wormwood 9 asafetida, chamomile, dandelion, echinacea, fenugreek, monkshood 10 asafoetida, goldenseal, peppermint *microscopic:* 4 mold 6 diatom 7 euglena 8 bacteria (plural) 9 bacterium *oldest:* 11 bristlecone *onion-like:* 4 leek 5 chive 7 shallot 8 scallion *opening:* 5 stoma 7 stomata (plural) *parasitic:* 6 dodder, fungus 7 pinesap 8 gerardia 9 broomrape, mistletoe, rafflesia, witchweed 10 beechdrops *part:* 3 bud, nut, sap 4 bark, bulb, cell, cone, corm, leaf, pome, root, seed, stem, wood 5 drupe, fruit, grain, spore, thorn, tuber, xylem 6 catkin, flower, nectar, phloem, raceme 7 rhizome 8 lenticel 9 cellulose, cotyledon 11 chlorophyll, chloroplast 13 inflorescence *pest:* 5 aphid, scale 6 chafer, thrips, weevil 7 cutworm 8 fruit fly, wireworm 9 gypsy moth 10 cankerworm, leafhopper, phylloxera 11 codling moth *poisonous:* 4 poke, upas 5 sumac 6 castor, croton, datura 7 amanita, cassava, cowbane, henbane, lobelia, tobacco 8 foxglove, larkspur, locoweed, mayapple, oleander, pokeweed 9 baneberry, monkshood 10 belladonna, jimsonweed, manchineel, nightshade *saprophytic:* 5 fungi (plural) 6 fungus 7 pinesap 9 pinedrops, snow plant 10 beechdrops, Indian pipe *succulent:* 4 aloe 5 agave 6 cactus 10 bitterroot *thorny:* 4 rose 5 briar 6 cactus, nettle, teasel 7 caltrop, thistle 9 cocklebur *tissue:* 5 xylem 6 phloem 7 cambium, medulla 8 meristem *young:* 5 scion, shoot 6 sprout 7 cutting 8 seedling

plantain 5 fruit 6 banana

plantation 5 manor 6 colony, estate, quinta 7 acreage, demesne 8 hacienda 10 encampment, habitation, settlement

plant louse 5 aphid

plaque 4 film 5 badge, patch 6 brooch, lesion, tablet 7 tribute 8 bacteria, memorial 13 commemoration

plaster 3 dab 4 coat 5 affix, cover, gesso 6 stucco 7 coating, conceal, overlay 8 dressing *of paris:* 5 gesso 6 gypsum

plastered 3 lit 4 high 5 drunk, lit up, oiled 6 bashed, blotto, bombed, juiced, potted, soaked, soused, stewed, stoned, tanked, wasted, zonked 7 crocked, drunken, pickled, pie-eyed, sloshed, smashed, sottish 10 inebriated, liquored up 11 intoxicated

plastic 4 soft 5 vinyl 6 pliant, supple 7 ductile, pliable 8 creative, flexible, moldable, workable 9 adaptable, formative, malleable, synthetic 10 artificial, credit card, sculptural

plat 3 lot, map 4 plan 5 chart, tract 6 parcel 7 quadrat

plate 4 base, coat, disc, dish, disk, gild, tile 5 layer, paten, scute, slice 6 enamel, fascia, lamina, plaque 7 anodize, lamella, overlay

plateau 4 mesa 5 table 6 upland 9 altiplano, tableland *arid:* 4 puna *barren:* 5 field 6 paramo *dry:* 5 karoo 6 karroo

platform 3 map 4 bank, base, dais, deck, plan 5 bimah, forum, ledge, riser, shelf, stage, stump 6 design, perron, podium, pulpit, scheme 7 balcony, pattern, rostrum 8 hustings, scaffold 9 banquette, manifesto 11 declaration *temporary:* 7 staging 8 scaffold *wooden:* 9 boardwalk

Plath, Sylvia *novel:* 7 Bell Jar (The) *poem:* 5 Ariel, Daddy

platitude 6 cliché, truism 7 bromide 8 banality, prosaism 10 shibboleth

Plato *father:* 7 Ariston *literary form:* 6 dialog 8 dialogue *original name:* 10 Aristocles *school:* 7 Academy *work:* 3 Ion 4 Meno 5 Crito, Lysis 6 Laches, Phaedo 7 Apology, Gorgias 8 Phaedrus, Republic (The) 9 Charmides, Symposium

platter 5 plate 6 record 8 trencher

platypus 8 duckbill
plaudits 5 kudos **6** cheers, praise **7** acclaim, ovation **8** applause, approval, encomium **9** accolades **11** acclamation
plausible 8 credible, specious **10** believable, convincing, creditable, persuasive, reasonable
play 3 act, fun **4** game, jest, joke, romp **5** drama, feint, serve, sport, treat, trick, wager **6** cavort, comedy, fiddle, frolic, gambit, gambol, leeway, margin **7** delight, disport, perform, twiddle **8** latitude, maneuver, pleasure **9** amusement, diversion, enjoyment, stratagem **10** manipulate, recreation *kind:* **5** farce **6** comedy **7** musical, tragedy **8** oneacter **9** melodrama, pantomime *part:* **3** act **5** scene **8** epilogue, prologue
playact 5 put on **7** perform, posture, pretend **9** personate **11** impersonate, make believe
playboy 4 rake, roué **8** hedonist **9** bon vivant
play down 8 minimize **9** deprecate, softpedal, underrate **11** de-emphasize
player 5 actor **6** mummer **7** actress, athlete, trouper **8** musician, thespian **9** contender, performer **10** competitor, contestant **11** participant
playful 5 antic, jolly, merry, pixie **6** elvish, frisky, impish, jocund, joking, jovial, lively **7** coltish, jocular, puckish, waggish **8** humorous, sportive **9** kittenish, sprightly **10** frolicsome
play off 3 pit, vie **5** match **6** oppose **7** counter **8** contrast
plaything 3 toy
play up 6 stress **7** feature **9** dramatize, emphasize, highlight, overstate, underline **10** accentuate, exaggerate, underscore
playwright 9 dramatist **10** dramaturge (see also DRAMATIST)
plaza 6 circus, common, square, zocalo **9** carrefour **11** marketplace
plea 4 suit **5** alibi **6** appeal, excuse, orison, prayer **7** apology, defense, pretext, request **8** entreaty, overture, petition **11** application, imploration **12** supplication *defendant's:* **4** nolo **6** guilty **8** innocent **9** not guilty
plead 3 beg **4** pray **5** argue **6** allege, answer, appeal **7** beseech, entreat, implore **8** advocate, maintain **9** importune **10** supplicate
pleasant 4 fair, fine, good, nice **5** clear, sunny, sweet **6** cheery, genial, pretty **7** amiable, clarion, likable, welcome **8** amicable, charming, cheerful, engaging, gracious, grateful, likeable, pleas-

ing, sunshine, sunshiny **9** agreeable, appealing, cloudless, congenial, convivial, enjoyable, favorable, unclouded **10** delightful, gratifying
pleasantry 3 fun **4** jest, joke **6** banter, levity **8** badinage, repartee **9** wittiness **10** jocularity
please 4 like, suit, wish **5** agree, amuse, enjoy, serve **6** choose **7** content, delight, gladden, gratify, indulge, satisfy *French:* **12** s'il vous plait *German:* **5** bitte *Spanish:* **8** por favor
pleasing 4 good, nice **6** pretty **7** welcome **8** suitable **9** agreeable, congenial, favorable, palatable **10** attractive, delightful, gratifying **12** satisfactory
pleasure 3 fun, joy **4** will **5** bliss, fancy **6** desire, liking, relish **7** delight, gladden, gratify **8** felicity, gladness, hedonism **9** amusement, diversion, enjoyment, happiness, merriment **11** inclination
pleat 4 fold **5** crimp **6** crease
plebe 5 frosh **8** freshman
plebeian 3 low **4** base **5** crude, lowly **6** coarse, common, humble, menial **8** commoner, everyday, ordinary **10** lower-class
plectrum 4 pick
pledge 3 vow **4** bail, bind, bond, gage, hock, oath, pawn, seal, sign, word **5** drink, swear, toast, token **6** parole, plight, surety **7** chattel, earnest, promise, warrant **8** bailment, contract, covenant, guaranty, security, warranty **9** agreement, assurance, certainty, guarantee, undertake
pledget 3 pad **8** compress
Pleiades 4 Maia **6** Merope **7** Alcyone, Celaeno, Electra, Sterope, Taygeta **8** Asterope *brightest star:* **7** Alcyone
plenary 4 full **5** whole **6** entire **7** general **8** absolute, complete **9** inclusive **11** unqualified **12** unrestricted
plenitude 4 glut **6** excess **7** satiety, surfeit **8** fullness **9** abundance, profusion, repletion **11** copiousness, sufficiency, superfluity **12** completeness
plenteous 7 fertile **8** abundant, fruitful, prolific **9** abounding **10** productive
plentiful 4 full, rich **5** ample, flush **7** copious, profuse **8** abundant, affluent, generous **9** abounding, bounteous, unstinted **10** sufficient
plenty 3 lot **4** heap, pack, peck, pile **6** stacks, wealth **8** adequacy, fullness, mountain **9** abundance, affluence, great deal **10** cornucopia
pleonasm 8 verbiage **9** prolixity, tautology, verbosity, wordiness **10** redundancy **11** periphrasis, superfluity

plethora 4 glut **5** flood **6** excess **7** overrun, surfeit, surplus **8** fullness, overflow **9** abundance, profusion, repletion **11** superfluity **13** overabundance

plexus 4 rete **7** network

pliable 6 supple **7** plastic **9** adaptable **10** adjustable **11** complaisant, manipulable

pliant 5 lithe **6** limber, supple **7** ductile, plastic, springy **8** flexible, moldable, workable, yielding **9** adaptable, malleable, tractable **10** manageable

plica 4 fold **6** crease, groove

plight 3 fix, jam, vow **4** hole, spot, word **5** swear **6** engage, pickle, pledge, scrape **7** betroth, dilemma, promise **8** quandary **9** betrothal **10** difficulty, engagement **11** predicament

plod 4 slog, toil **5** grind, slave, tramp, tread, tromp **6** drudge, lumber, trudge **8** plug away

plot 3 map **4** area, land, mark, note, plan **5** cabal, chart, story, tract **6** design, devise, invent, lay out, locate, parcel, scheme **7** collude, compact, connive, diagram, outline **8** conspire, contrive, intrigue, scenario **9** collusion, conniving, machinate **10** complicity, connivance, conspiracy **11** machination

plover 5 pewit, stilt **6** peewit **7** lapwing **8** dotterel, killdeer *relative:* **9** sandpiper, turnstone

plow 3 dig **4** till, turn **5** break **6** furrow, harrow, trench **8** turn over **9** cultivate *part:* **4** beam, frog **5** share **7** coulter **8** landside **9** moldboard

ploy 4 ruse, scam, wile **5** feint, trick **6** device, frolic, gambit, tactic **7** gimmick **8** artifice, escapade, maneuver **9** stratagem **11** contrivance

pluck 3 rob, tug **4** grit, guts, pick, pull, yank **5** cheek, grasp, heart, moxie, nerve, spunk **6** daring, fleece, mettle, remove, snatch, spirit, tweeze **7** bravery, courage, pull out **8** gameness **10** resolution

plucky 4 bold, game **5** brave **6** feisty, spunky **7** doughty **8** fearless, spirited, unafraid **9** dauntless **10** courageous

plug 3 tap **4** bung, clog, core, cork, fill, hype, pack, push, stop, tout **5** block, blurb, boost, choke, close, cry up, shoot **6** device, remedy **7** congest, fitting, hydrant, promote, stopper **8** obstruct **9** advertise, publicity, publicize **10** connection

plug-ugly 4 thug **5** bully, rowdy, tough **7** hoodlum, ruffian **9** roughneck

plum 5 prize **6** purple, reward **7** guerdon, premium **8** dividend *dried:* **5** prune

kind: **6** damson **7** bullace **9** greengage *spiny:* **10** blackthorn

plumage 8 feathers *early:* **4** down

plumb 5 delve, probe, sound **6** fathom, weight **7** exactly, examine, explore, install, measure **8** absolute, complete, thorough, vertical **10** absolutely, vertically **11** immediately **13** perpendicular

plume 4 tail **5** array, preen, pride, prize **6** column **7** feather **8** aigrette

plummet 4 dive, drop, fall **5** crash **6** plunge, tumble **8** collapse, nose-dive **11** precipitate

plump 3 fat **4** drop, fall, full **5** ample, buxom, favor, pudgy, round, stout, tubby **6** chubby, portly, rotund **7** rounded, support **8** abundant, directly, roly-poly **10** Rubenesque

plumply 7 frankly, plainly **8** candidly **12** forthrightly

plunder 3 rob **4** loot, sack, swag, take **5** booty, prize, seize, spoil, steal, strip **6** boodle, rapine, spoils **7** despoil, pillage, ransack, relieve, stick up **9** pillaging

plunge 3 bet, ram, run **4** dive, drop, fall, jump, rush, sink, stab, swim **5** drive, lunge, pitch, stick **6** charge, gamble, hasten, hurtle, thrust, topple, tumble **7** descend, immerse, plummet **8** nose-dive, submerge **9** penetrate

plus 3 and **4** more, perk **5** added, asset, bonus, boost, extra **6** excess **7** benefit **8** addition, increase, positive

plush 4 full, rich **6** deluxe, fabric, lavish, velvet **7** opulent **8** luscious, palatial **9** expensive, luxuriant, luxurious, sumptuous

Pluto 3 Dis **5** Hades *brother:* **4** Zeus **7** Jupiter, Neptune **8** Poseidon *father:* **6** Cronus, Saturn *mother:* **3** Ops **4** Rhea *wife:* **10** Persephone, Proserpina

plutocrat 5 mogul **6** fat cat, tycoon **7** magnate **9** financier, moneybags **10** capitalist

plutonian 8 infernal **10** underworld

Plutus *father:* **6** Iasion *god of:* **6** riches, wealth *mother:* **5** Ceres **7** Demeter

ply 3 use **4** bias, sail **5** apply, exert, layer, wield **6** employ, handle, strand, supply, travel, voyage **7** furnish, perform **8** maneuver, practice **11** inclination

pneuma 4 soul **5** anima **6** psyche, spirit

pneumatic 4 airy **5** ample, buxom, plump **6** aerial, zaftig **9** spiritual **10** curvaceous **11** atmospheric

poach 4 cook **5** steal **6** coddle, simmer **7** intrude **8** encroach, trespass **9** interlope **11** appropriate

Pocahontas *father:* **8** Powhatan *husband:* **5** Rolfe (John)

pock 3 pit 4 hole, spot 7 pustule
pocket 3 bag 4 lift, sack 5 filch, pinch, pouch, purse, steal, swipe 6 cavity 7 capsule, dead end, impasse 8 cul-de-sac 9 condensed 10 blind alley *billiards:* 4 pool
pocketbook 3 bag 4 poke 5 purse 6 clutch, income, wallet 7 handbag 8 billfold 9 clutch bag
pocket bread 4 pita
pocket money 6 change 9 petty cash 11 small change
pocket-size 4 tiny 5 small 9 miniature 10 diminutive
pod 3 bag, gam, sac 4 boll, case, hull, husk, skin 5 shell, shuck 6 cocoon 7 capsule, silique 8 seedcase *plant:* 3 pea 4 bean, okra 5 chili, gumbo 6 cassia, cowpea, legume, lentil, peanut, pepper 8 capsicum, mesquite, milkweed 9 lespedeza
pod-bearing tree 5 carob 6 locust 7 catalpa
podiatry 9 chiropody
podium 4 dais 6 pulpit 7 lectern, rostrum 8 platform
___ podrida 4 olla
Poe, Edgar Allan *detective:* 5 Dupin (C. Auguste) *poem:* 5 Bells (The), Raven (The) 6 Lenore 7 Israfel, To Helen, Ulalume 8 Eldorado, For Annie 10 Annabel Lee *tale:* 6 Ligeia, Shadow 7 Gold-Bug (The), Morella, Silence 8 Black Cat (The) 13 Tell-tale Heart (The) 15 Purloined Letter (The) 17 Cask of Amontillado (The), Pit and the Pendulum (The) 19 Masque of the Red Death (The) 21 Fall of the House of Usher (The)
poem 3 ode 4 epic, epos, idyl, rime, rune, song 5 ditty, elegy, epode, idyll, lyric, rhyme, verse 6 ballad, epopee, jingle, rondel, sonnet 7 eclogue, rondeau 8 limerick, madrigal *closing:* 5 envoi, envoy *division:* 4 foot, line 5 canto, epode, stich, verse 6 stanza 7 refrain 8 epilogue, prologue *Japanese:* 5 haiku, tanka *of eight lines:* 6 octave 7 triolet *of four lines:* 8 quatrain *of fourteen lines:* 6 sonnet *of three lines:* 7 triplet *pastoral:* 7 eclogue, georgic *short:* 5 ditty 7 epigram
poet 4 bard, muse, scop 5 skald 6 lyrist 7 elegist 8 idyllist, lyricist 9 balladist, sonneteer 10 Parnassian *American:* 3 Poe (Edgar Allan) 4 Dove (Rita), Hass (Robert), Nash (Ogden), Read (Thomas), Rich (Adrienne), Tabb (John Banister), Tate (Allen) 5 Auden (Wystan Hugh), Benét (Stephen Vincent), Crane (Hart), Field (Eugene), Frost (Robert),

Guest (Edgar), Moore (Marianne), Plath (Sylvia), Pound (Ezra), Riley (James Whitcomb), Wylie (Elinor) 6 Barlow (Joel), Bishop (Elizabeth), Brooks (Gwendolyn), Bryant (William Cullen), Ciardi (John), Dickey (James), Dunbar (Paul Laurence), Hughes (Langston), Kilmer (Joyce), Lanier (Sidney), Lowell (Amy, James Russell, Robert), McKuen (Rod), Millay (Edna St. Vincent), Pinsky (Robert), Ransom (John Crowe), Seeger (Alan), Strand (Mark), Taylor (Edward), Warren (Robert Penn), Wilbur (Richard) 7 Angelou (Maya), Ashbery (John), Emerson (Ralph Waldo), Freneau (Philip), Halleck (Fitz-Greene), Jeffers (Robinson), Lindsay (Vachel), Markham (Edwin), Merrill (James), Nemerov (Howard), Roethke (Theodore), Shapiro (Karl), Stevens (Wallace), Whitman (Walt) 8 Berryman (John), Cummings (E. E.), Ginsberg (Allen), MacLeish (Archibald), Robinson (Edwin Arlington), Sandburg (Carl), Teasdale (Sara), Wheatley (Phillis), Whittier (John Greenleaf), Williams (C. K., William Carlos) 9 Dickinson (Emily), Santayana (George) 10 Bradstreet (Anne), Longfellow (Henry Wadsworth) 12 Wigglesworth (Michael) *Anglo-Saxon:* 7 Caedmon, Cynwulf 8 Cynewulf, Kynewulf *Arab:* 5 Jarir 6 Hariri 8 al-Hariri *Australian:* 8 Paterson (Andrew Barton) *Belgian:* 11 Maeterlinck (Maurice) *Canadian:* 5 Pratt (Edwin John) 6 Hébert (Anne) 7 Roberts (Charles G. D.), Service (Robert) 8 Drummond (William Henry) 9 Fréchette (Louis-Honoré) *Chilean:* 6 Neruda (Pablo) 7 Mistral (Gabriela) *Chinese:* 4 Li Po, Tu Fu 7 Wang Wei *Danish:* 4 Rode (Helge) 5 Ewald (Johannes) *English:* 3 Gay (John) 4 Gray (Thomas), Owen (Wilfred), Pope (Alexander), Rowe (Nicholas), Tate (Nahum), Wyat (Thomas) 5 Blake (William), Byron (Lord), Carew (Thomas), Clare (John), Donne (John), Eliot (Thomas Stearns), Gower (John), Hardy (Thomas), Keats (John), Noyes (Alfred), Wilde (Oscar), Wyatt (Thomas), Young (Edward) 6 Arnold (Matthew), Austin (Alfred), Belloc (Hilaire), Brooke (Rupert), Butler (Samuel), Clough (Arthur Hugh), Cowper (William), Dryden (John), Graves (Robert), Larkin (Philip), Milton (John), Savage (Richard), Sidney (Philip), Surrey (Earl of), Symons (Arthur), Waller (Edmund), Warton

(Thomas), Watson (William), Wotton (Henry) **7** Bridges (Robert), Campion (Thomas), Chaucer (Geoffrey), Gilbert (W. S.), Herbert (George), Herrick (Robert), Hopkins (Gerard Manley), Housman (A. E.), Kipling (Rudyard), Layamon, Marvell (Andrew), Patmore (Coventry), Quarles (Francis), Shelley (Percy Bysshe), Skelton (John), Southey (Robert), Spender (Stephen), Spenser (Edmund) **8** Betjeman (John), Browning (Elizabeth Barrett, Robert), de la Mare (Walter), Langland (William), Lovelace (Richard), Meredith (George), Rossetti (Christina, Dante Gabriel), Suckling (John), Tennyson (Alfred Lord), Thompson (Francis) **9** Coleridge (Samuel Taylor), Masefield (John), Swinburne (Algernon Charles) **10** Chatterton (Thomas), FitzGerald (Edward), Wordsworth (William) **11** Shakespeare (William) *Finnish:* **8** Runeberg (Johan Ludvig) *French:* **5** Marot (Clément) **6** Musset (Alfred de), Valéry (Paul), Villon (François) **7** Bourget (Paul), Chénier (André de, Marie-Joseph), Gautier (Théophile), Rimbaud (Arthur), Ronsard (Pierre de) **8** Malherbe (François de), Mallarmé (Stéphane), Verlaine (Paul) **9** Lamartine (Alphonse de) **10** Baudelaire (Charles) **11** Apollinaire (Guillaume) *German:* **5** Heine (Heinrich), Rilke (Rainer Maria), Sachs (Hans), Storm (Theodor) **6** Brecht (Bertolt), Goethe (Johann Wolfgang von), Uhland (Ludwig) **7** Walther (von der Vogelweide), Wolfram (von Eschenbach) **8** Schiller (Friedrich von) **9** Klopstock (Friedrich Gottlieb) *Greek:* **5** Arion, Homer **6** Elytis (Odysseus), Erinna, Hesiod, Pindar, Ritsos (Yannis), Sappho **7** Agathon, Alcaeus, Orpheus, Seferis (George), Thespis **8** Anacreon **9** Simonides **10** Apollonius, Theocritus *Hindu:* **5** Naidu (Sarojini) **6** Tagore (Rabindranath) **8** Kalidasa, Tulsidas *Hungarian:* **6** Petofi (Sandor), Zrinyi (Miklos) *Irish:* **5** Moore (Thomas), Wolfe (Charles), Yeats (William Butler) **6** Heaney (Seamus) **7** Dunsany (Lord) **8** Drummond (William Henry), MacNeice (Louis) *Italian:* **4** Rosa (Salvator), Vida (Marco) **5** Dante (Alighieri), Tasso (Torquato) **7** Ariosto (Ludovico), Manzoni (Alessandro), Montale (Eugenio) **8** Carducci (Giosuè), Leopardi (Giacomo), Petrarch **9** Boccaccio (Giovanni), D'Annunzio (Gabriele), Marinetti (Filippo Tommaso), Quasimodo (Salvatore), Ungaretti (Giuseppe) *Japanese:*

5 Basho **6** Matsuo *medieval:* **8** minstrel, trouvère **10** troubadour *Mexican:* **3** Paz (Octavio) *nonsense:* **4** Lear (Edward) *Norwegian:* **8** Bjornson (Bjornstjerne), Welhaven (Johan) **9** Wergeland (Henrik) *Persian:* **4** Sadi **5** Attar, Hafez, Hafiz **11** Omar Khayyám *Roman:* **4** Ovid **6** Horace, Vergil, Virgil **7** Juvenal, Martial, Statius **8** Catullus, Tibullus **9** Lucretius *Russian:* **4** Blok (Aleksandr) **7** Brodsky (Joseph), Pushkin (Aleksandr), Yesenin (Sergey) **9** Akhmatova (Anna), Kheraskov (Mikhail), Pasternak (Boris), Tsvetaeva (Marina) **10** Mandelstam (Osip), Mayakovsky (Vladimir) **11** Yevtushenko (Yevgeny) *Saint Lucian:* **7** Walcott (Derek) *Scottish:* **4** Hogg (James), Muir (Edwin) **5** Burns (Robert), Scott (Alexander, Walter) **6** Dunbar (William), Ramsay (Allan) **7** Thomson (James) **10** MacDiarmid (Hugh) *Spanish:* **5** Lorca (Federico García) **7** Jiménez (Juan Ramón) **8** Figueroa (Francisco) **10** Aleixandre (Vicente) **11** García Lorca (Federico) *Swedish:* **5** Sachs (Nelly) **6** Tegner (Esaias) **8** Snoilsky (Carl Johan) **9** Karlfeldt (Erik Axel) *Swiss:* **5** Amiel (Henri Frédéric) **9** Spitteler (Carl) *Welsh:* **6** Thomas (Dylan) **7** Aneurin, Watkins (Vernon)

poetic 5 lyric **6** dreamy **8** romantic **9** aesthetic, beautiful

poet laureate *British:* **3** Pye (Henry) **4** Rowe (Nicholas), Tate (Nahum) **6** Austin (Alfred), Cibber (Colley), Dryden (John), Hughes (Ted), Jonson (Ben), Motion (Andrew) **7** Bridges (Robert), Southey (Robert) **8** Betjeman (John), Davenant (William), Day-Lewis (Cecil), Shadwell (Thomas), Tennyson (Alfred) **9** Masefield (John), Whitehead (William) **10** Wordsworth (William) *American:* **4** Dove (Rita), Hass (Robert) **5** Glück (Louise) **6** Kooser (Ted), Kunitz (Stanley), Merwin (W. S.), Pinsky (Robert), Strand (Mark), Warren (Robert Penn), Wilbur (Richard) **7** Brodsky (Joseph), Collins (Billy), Nemerov (Howard), Van Duyn (Mona)

Pogo creator 5 Kelly (Walt)

poi 4 taro

poignancy 6 pathos **7** emotion, sadness **9** sentiment

poignant 3 sad **4** keen **5** acute, sharp **6** biting, moving **7** painful, piquant, pointed, pungent **8** incisive, piercing, stirring, touching **9** affecting, emotional **11** penetrating, stimulating

point 3 aim, bit, dot, end, jag, nib, tip **4** apex, barb, crux, goal, item, mark,

show, site, spot, step, tine, turn, unit
5 brink, motif, place, stage, theme,
topic, trace, verge 6 credit, detail,
direct, intent, moment, motive, object,
period, reason 7 cogency, decimal, element, essence, feature, instant, meaning, purpose, sharpen, subject 8 headland, juncture, locality, location,
particle, position 9 direction, emphasize, punctuate 10 promontory 12 significance
Point Counter Point author 6 Huxley
(Aldous)
pointed 5 acute, sharp 6 barbed,
marked, signal 7 salient 8 incisive,
striking 9 arresting, pertinent, prominent 11 conspicuous, penetrating
pointer 3 dog, tip 4 clue, hint 5 arrow,
guide 6 gundog 9 indicator 10 suggestion
pointillist 6 Seurat (Georges), Signac
(Paul) 8 Pissarro (Camille)
pointless 4 idle, vain 5 inane, silly
6 futile 7 useless 8 bootless 9 fruitless,
senseless, worthless 10 immaterial,
irrelevant, unavailing, unfruitful
11 meaningless 12 unprofitable
point of view 5 angle, slant 7 outlook
8 position, prospect 11 perspective
poise 4 ease, hang, tact 5 brace, grace,
hover, skill 6 aplomb, steady 7 address,
balance, bearing, dignity, support, suspend 8 calmness, carriage, elegance,
serenity 9 assurance, composure, diplomacy 10 confidence, equanimity 11 del-
icatesse, equilibrium, savoir faire, tactfulness
poised 4 calm 6 at ease, serene, steady
7 assured, equable 8 composed, tranquil 9 collected, confident 13 self-possessed
poison 4 bane, upas 5 toxin, venom
6 toxoid 7 arsenic, botulin, cyanide,
envenom 8 toxicant 9 botulinum, contagion 10 strychnine 13 contamination
arrow: 4 inée, upas 6 curare 7 ouabain
combining form: 3 tox 4 toxi, toxo 6 tox-
ico
poisoning *food:* 8 botulism *lead:*
8 plumbism
poisonous 5 toxic 7 baneful, miasmal,
nocuous, noxious 8 mephitic, venomous, virulent 9 pestilent 10 pernicious
poke 3 dig, hit, jab, jut, lag, pry 4 cuff,
nose, prod, push, sock, stab, stir, urge
5 bulge, dally, delay, elbow, nudge,
punch, snoop, tarry 6 dawdle, meddle,
pierce, putter, thrust 7 intrude, project,
rummage 8 stick out 9 interfere, interject, interpose

poker *bet total:* 3 pot *form:* 4 stud *hand:*
4 pair 5 flush 8 straight 9 full house
10 royal flush 13 straight flush *stake:*
4 ante *term:* 3 see 4 call, draw, open
5 raise *token:* 4 chip
poker-faced 5 blank, staid 7 deadpan,
neutral 9 impassive 11 inscrutable, noncommittal 12 inexpressive
pokey 3 can, jug, pen 4 brig, coop, jail,
stir 5 clink 6 cooler, prison 7 slammer
9 calaboose
poky 4 slow 5 dingy, seedy 6 dreary,
shabby 7 cramped, laggard, run-down
8 dilatory, plodding, sluggish
Poland *capital:* 6 Warsaw *city:* 4 Lódz
6 Gdansk, Kraków, Poznan 7 Wroclaw
8 Katowice, Szczecin *leader:* 6 Walesa
(Lech) *monetary unit:* 5 zloty *mountain
range:* 10 Carpathian *national hero:*
10 Kosciuszko (Thaddeus) *neighbor:*
6 Russia 7 Belarus, Germany, Ukraine
8 Slovakia 9 Lithuania 13 Czech
Republic *river:* 4 Oder 7 Vistula *sea:*
6 Baltic
polar 6 arctic 7 pivotal 8 opposite 9 diametric
pole 4 punt, spar 5 shaft, staff, stick, stilt
Indian: 5 totem *Scottish:* 5 caber
polecat 5 fitch, skunk 6 ferret 7 fitchet
polemic 6 attack, debate, screed, tirade
7 defense, dispute 8 argument, diatribe,
harangue, jeremiad 9 assertion, philippic 10 contention, refutation 11 controversy, disputation 12 denunciation,
remonstrance
polemical 7 scrappy 10 pugnacious
11 contentious, opinionated 12 disputatious 13 argumentative, controversial
polestar 3 hub 5 focus, guide 10 focal
point
police 3 cop, law, man 4 fuzz, heat
6 copper, govern, lawman, patrol
7 control, monitor, trooper 8 bluecoat,
flatfoot, gendarme, regulate 9 patrolman 12 peace officer
police officer 3 cop 4 fuzz, heat 5 bobby
6 copper, peeler 7 John Law, sheriff,
trooper 8 bluecoat, Dogberry, flatfoot,
gendarme 9 constable, patrolman *Italian:* 11 carabiniere *Parisian:* 4 flic 8 gendarme
policy 4 plan 6 course, method, number
7 lottery, program 8 contract, practice
9 procedure 10 management
polio vaccine developer 4 Salk (Jonas)
5 Sabin (Albert)
polish 3 rub, wax 4 buff 5 glaze, glint,
gloss, sheen, shine 6 luster, refine,
smooth, soften 7 burnish, culture,
enhance, improve, perfect, touch up
8 brighten 10 refinement

Polish *dumpling:* 7 pierogi *leader:* 6 Walesa (Lech) *patriot:* 9 Kosciusko (Thaddeus) *pope:* 8 John Paul *sausage:* 8 kielbasa *soldier:* 7 Pulaski (Casimir)

polish off 5 eat up 6 devour 7 consume, put away 8 dispatch 9 dispose of

polite 5 civil 7 courtly, genteel, refined 8 cultured, mannerly, polished, wellbred 9 attentive, courteous 10 thoughtful 11 considerate 12 well-mannered

politeness 7 manners 8 civility, courtesy 10 refinement

politic 4 wise 5 suave 6 adroit, shrewd, smooth 7 prudent, tactful 8 tactical 9 advisable, expedient, judicious, sagacious 10 diplomatic

political *meeting:* 6 caucus *party:* 3 GOP 10 Democratic, Republican *system:* 7 fascism 9 communism, democracy, socialism

poll 4 cast, clip, crop, head, nape 5 count, shear, tally, votes 6 record, sample, survey 7 canvass, pollard 8 question 9 interview 10 canvassing

pollack 4 fish 6 saithe 8 bluefish *family:* 3 cod

pollard 3 top 4 crop, tree 7 cut back

pollen-producing organ 6 stamen

pollex 5 thumb

___ polloi 3 hoi

pollster 5 Zogby (John) 6 Gallup (George), Harris (Lou)

pollute 4 foul, soil 5 dirty, spoil, stain, sully, taint 6 befoul, damage, debase, defile 7 corrupt, profane 10 adulterate 11 contaminate

pollution 4 smog 5 abuse 8 impurity 10 defilement

Pollux 10 Polydeuces *brother:* 6 Castor *father:* 4 Zeus *mother:* 4 Leda *sister:* 5 Helen 12 Clytemnestra

Pollyanna 8 optimist *author:* 6 Porter (Eleanor)

Pollyannaish 6 blithe, cheery, upbeat 8 cheerful, positive 10 optimistic 11 rose-colored

pollywog 7 tadpole

Polonius *daughter:* 7 Ophelia *slayer:* 6 Hamlet *son:* 7 Laertes

poltergeist 5 ghost 6 spirit

poltroon 6 coward, craven, yellow 7 chicken, dastard, gutless 8 cowardly 9 dastardly 11 lily-livered

Polydorus *father:* 5 Priam 6 Cadmus *mother:* 6 Hecuba 8 Harmonia *slayer:* 8 Achilles 10 Polymestor 11 Polymnestor

polygon *eight-sided:* 7 octagon *five-sided:* 8 pentagon *four-sided:* 8 tetragon *nine-sided:* 7 nonagon *seven-sided:* 8 heptagon *six-sided:* 7 hexagon *ten-sided:*

7 decagon *three-sided:* 8 triangle *twelve-sided:* 9 dodecagon

Polyhymnia 4 Muse *invention:* 4 lyre

Polynesian 5 Maori 6 Samoan, Tongan 8 Hawaiian, Tahitian 9 Marquesan

Polynices *brother:* 8 Eteocles *father:* 7 Oedipus *mother:* 7 Jocasta *wife:* 5 Argia 6 Argeia

polyp 5 tumor, zooid 6 growth 7 hydroid *freshwater:* 5 hydra

Polyphemus 7 Cyclops *beloved:* 7 Galatea *father:* 8 Poseidon *victim:* 4 Acis

pome 4 pear 5 apple, fruit

pommel 4 knob 6 handle

pomp 4 show 5 array 6 parade, ritual 7 display, fanfare, panoply 8 ceremony, grandeur, splendor 9 pageantry, vainglory 11 ostentation

pompano 4 fish 8 carangid 10 butterfish

Pompeii's volcano 8 Vesuvius

pompous 4 vain 5 proud, showy 6 lordly, ornate, stuffy 7 stuck-up 8 arrogant, boastful, inflated 9 bombastic, conceited, important, overblown 10 egocentric, flamboyant, pontifical 11 magisterial, pretentious 12 ostentatious, vainglorious

pond 4 mere, pool, tarn 5 stank 6 lagoon

ponder 4 mull, muse 5 study, think, weigh 6 reason 7 examine, perpend, reflect 8 appraise, cogitate, consider, evaluate, meditate, mull over, ruminate 9 reflect on, speculate 10 deliberate, think about 11 contemplate

ponderous 4 dull 5 heavy 6 clumsy, dreary, stodgy, wooden 7 labored, massive, weighty 8 cumbrous, lifeless, plodding, unwieldy 9 lumbering 10 burdensome, cumbersome, oppressive

poniard 6 dagger

Ponte Vecchio *city:* 8 Florence *river:* 4 Arno

Pontiac 5 chief *tribe:* 6 Ottawa

pontiff 4 pope

pontifical 7 pompous 8 dogmatic 9 episcopal 11 magisterial

pony 4 crib, trot 5 horse 6 bronco, cayuse 7 mustang *breed:* 6 Exmoor 8 Shetland

pony up 3 pay 6 lay out, pay out 7 dish out, dole out, fork out 8 hand over, shell out, turn over 10 compensate, remunerate

pooch 3 dog, pup 4 tyke 5 hound, puppy 6 bowwow, canine

Pooh *creator:* 5 Milne (A. A.) *illustrator:* 7 Shepard (Ernest)

pooh-bah 3 VIP 4 czar, king, star, tsar, tzar 5 baron, heavy, mogul 6 big gun, bigwig, honcho, kahuna, prince, worthy 7 big name, big shot, kingpin, magnate, notable 8 big wheel, eminence, luminary 9 big cheese, personage, superstar 11 heavyweight

pooh-pooh 5 scorn 6 deride 7 disdain, dismiss, sneer at 8 minimize, play down

pool 3 pot 4 mere, pond, tarn 5 chain, group, kitty, merge, trust 6 cartel, lagoon, laguna, puddle 7 combine, jackpot 9 syndicate *player:* 7 Mosconi (Willie) 13 Minnesota Fats

poop 4 dirt, info, tire 7 fatigue

poor 4 base, mean 5 broke, needy, scant, skimp, spare 6 humble, meager, meagre, paltry, scanty, skimpy, sparse 8 bankrupt, beggarly, indigent, strapped 9 destitute, insolvent, penniless, penurious 10 down-and-out, pauperized, stone-broke 11 impecunious, necessitous

poorly 3 ill, low 4 sick 5 badly 6 ailing, sickly, unwell 10 indisposed 11 imperfectly

pop 3 dad, dot, gun, hit, try 4 dada, dart, ding, shot, slap, slog, sock, soda 5 catch, crack, daddy, drink, fling, shoot, whack, whirl 6 attack, bug out, effort, father, strike 7 assault, attempt, explode 8 backfire

pop artist 5 Blake (Peter), Johns (Jasper) 6 Warhol (Andy) 7 Hockney (David), Indiana (Robert) 9 Oldenburg (Claes), Wesselman (Tom) 10 Rosenquist (James) 12 Lichtenstein (Roy)

pope 3 Leo 4 John, Mark, Paul, Pius 5 Caius, Conon, Donus, Felix, Gaius, Lando, Linus, Peter, Soter, Urban 6 Adrian, Agatho, Fabian, Julius, Lucius, Martin, Sixtus, Victor 7 Anterus, Clement, Damasus, Gregory, Hadrian, Hyginus, Marinus, Paschal, Pontian, Romanus, Sergius, Stephen, Zosimus 8 Agapetus, Anicetus, Benedict, Boniface, Calixtus, Eugenius, Eusebius, Formosis, Gelasius, Hilarius, Honorius, Innocent, John Paul, Liberius, Nicholas, Pelagius, Siricius, Theodore, Vigilius, Vitalian 9 Adeodatus, Alexander, Anacletus, Callistus, Celestine, Cornelius, Densdedit, Dionysius, Eutychian, Evaristus, Hormisdas, Marcellus, Miltiades, Severinus, Silverius, Silvester, Sisinnius, Sylvester, Symmachus, Valentine, Zacharias 10 Anastasius, Melchiades, Sabinianus, Simplicius, Zephyrinus 11 Christopher, Constantine, Eleutherius, Eutychianus, Marcellinus, Telesphorus

Pope poem 7 Dunciad (The) 10 Essay on Man (An) 13 Rape of the Lock (The)

Popeye *accessory:* 4 pipe *baby:* 7 Swee'-

Pea 8 Sweet Pea *energizer:* 7 spinach *friend:* 5 Wimpy 8 Olive Oyl *occupation:* 6 sailor *rival:* 5 Bluto

pop in 4 call 5 visit 6 drop by, look up, stop by 8 come over

popinjay 3 fop 4 toff 5 dandy, swell 7 peacock 8 macaroni

poplar 5 abele, alamo, aspen 6 balsam 9 tulip tree 10 cottonwood 12 balm of Gilead

Poppaea's husband 4 Nero

poppycock 3 rot 4 bosh, bunk, guff 5 bilge, hokum 6 bunkum 7 baloney 8 malarkey, nonsense 10 balderdash

populace 5 plebs 6 masses, people, public 9 citizenry, commonage, commoners, plebeians 10 commonalty 11 commonality, rank and file, third estate

popular 5 cheap, noted 6 common, famous 7 admired, current, favored, general, leading 8 accepted, approved, favorite, ordinary 9 preferred, prevalent, prominent, well-known, well-liked 10 democratic, prevailing, widespread 11 inexpensive

populate 6 occupy, people, settle 7 inhabit

populous 6 packed 7 crowded, teeming 8 numerous 9 congested 13 multitudinous

porcelain *Chinese:* 9 Lowestoft *English:* 3 Bow 5 Derby, Spode 6 Minton 7 Aynsley, Belleek, Bristol, Chelsea 8 Caughley, Wedgwood *French:* 6 Sèvres 7 Limoges *German:* 7 Dresden, Meissen *ingredient:* 6 kaolin *Italian:* 6 Doccia *Japanese:* 5 Imari

porch 4 deck 5 lanai 6 piazza 7 gallery, veranda 8 verandah

porcupine 8 hedgehog

pore 6 outlet 7 opening, orifice, reflect 8 meditate 10 interstice

pore over 4 read, scan 5 study 6 peruse 10 scrutinize

porgy 4 fish, scup 6 sparid 8 menhaden

Porgy and Bess *composer:* 8 Gershwin (George) *librettist:* 7 Heyward (DuBose) 8 Gershwin (Ira)

Po River city 5 Milan, Padua, Turin 6 Milano, Padova, Torino, Verona 7 Brescia

pork 3 ham, pig 5 bacon, swine 8 sowbelly *cut:* 3 ham 4 jowl, loin, side 7 fatback 8 forefoot, hind foot, spare rib 9 picnic ham 10 Boston butt

pork-barreling 9 patronage

pornographic 7 obscene

porous 5 leaky 6 spongy 8 pervious 9 permeable 10 penetrable

porpoise 5 whale 7 dolphin

porridge 4 mush 5 gruel, kasha 6 bur-

goo, cereal, congee, pablum, sowens
7 oatmeal, pabulum 8 flummery, loblolly 9 stirabout

port 4 hole, jack, left, wine 5 cover, haven 6 harbor, refuge 7 bearing, opening, retreat, shelter 8 larboard, left side 9 anchorage, harborage, roadstead, sanctuary 11 comportment *opposite:* 9 starboard

portable 5 handy 6 mobile, wieldy

portal 4 door, gate 5 entry 7 doorway, gateway 8 approach, entrance, entryway

portcullis 4 gate 7 grating, lattice

portend 4 bode 5 augur 6 signal 7 betoken, predict, presage, promise, signify 8 forebode, forecast, foretell, indicate, prophesy 9 adumbrate, foretoken 10 foreshadow, vaticinate

portent 4 omen, sign 6 augury, boding 7 presage, prodigy 9 foretoken, sensation 10 foreboding, indication 11 premonition

portentous 5 grave 6 solemn 7 ominous, pompous, serious, weighty 8 inflated 9 marvelous, momentous, ponderous 10 prodigious

porter 5 hamal, stout 6 bearer, redcap, skycap 7 bellboy, bellhop, carrier 9 transport 10 doorkeeper

Portia 6 lawyer *husband:* 6 Brutus 8 Bassanio *maid:* 7 Nerissa

portico 4 stoa 9 colonnade

portion 3 cut, lot 4 bite, part 5 dower, moira, piece, quota, share, slice 6 moiety, parcel 7 measure, quantum, segment 8 division *largest:* 10 lion's share *unused:* 8 leftover

portly 3 fat 5 bulky, heavy, large, stout 6 fleshy 7 rotund, stately, weighty 8 imposing 9 corpulent 10 overweight

portmanteau 8 carryall, suitcase

portrait 4 bust 5 image 6 figure, statue 7 picture 8 painting 9 depiction

portray 4 draw, limn, play 5 enact, paint 6 depict, render 7 picture 8 describe 9 delineate, interpret, represent

portrayal 5 image 7 account, picture 8 likeness, painting 9 depiction 11 delineation, description, performance 12 illustration

Portugal *capital:* 6 Lisbon *city:* 5 Porto 6 Oporto 7 Amadora *former name:* 9 Lusitania *island group:* 6 Azores 7 Madeira *leader:* 7 Salazar (Antonio de) *monetary unit:* 4 euro *monetary unit, former:* 6 escudo *neighbor:* 5 Spain *peninsula:* 7 Iberian *river:* 5 Tagus

pose 3 act, air, ask, set, sit 4 airs, fake, role, sham 5 feign, front, offer, place, stand, state, strut 6 affect, assume, pass

as, stance 7 pass for, pass off, present, pretend, show off, suggest 8 attitude, pretense, set forth 9 mannerism 10 pretension 11 affectation

Poseidon 7 Neptune *brother:* 4 Zeus 5 Hades, Pluto 7 Jupiter *consort:* 4 Tyro 6 Medusa 7 Demeter *father:* 6 Cronus *mother:* 4 Rhea *offspring:* 7 Pegasus *son:* 5 Orion 6 Neleus, Pelias, Triton 7 Antaeus 10 Polyphemus *weapon:* 7 trident *wife:* 10 Amphitrite

poser 6 puzzle, riddle 7 problem 9 conundrum 11 brainteaser

poseur 4 fake 5 bluff, decoy, fraud, phony, quack 7 bluffer 8 deceiver, imposter 9 charlatan, hypocrite, pretender 10 mountebank 11 masquerader 12 impersonator

posh 4 chic, rich, tony 5 fancy, grand, smart, swank 7 elegant, stylish 9 exclusive, expensive, luxurious 11 fashionable, highfalutin, pretentious

posit 3 fix 5 offer 6 affirm, assert, assume 7 premise, present, presume, propose, suggest 9 postulate

position 3 job 4 rank, site, spot 5 locus, place, point, situs, stand, state 6 belief, locate, stance 7 emplace, footing, stature 8 attitude, capacity, location, prestige, standing 10 standpoint

positive 4 firm, real, sure 5 clear, sound 6 actual, useful 7 assured, certain, decided, factual, genuine, helpful, reality 8 absolute, complete, constant, definite, forceful, outright 9 confident, doubtless, downright, effective, favorable, realistic 10 beneficial, inarguable, optimistic, prescribed, undeniable 11 categorical, irrefutable, unequivocal, unmitigated, unqualified 12 indisputable, unmistakable 13 incontestable

possess 3 own 4 have, hold, keep 5 carry 6 retain 7 acquire, control

possessed 3 mad 6 crazed, hooked 8 frenzied 9 bewitched

possession 7 control 8 property 9 occupancy, ownership 10 occupation

possessive 7 jealous 8 watchful 10 protective 11 proprietary

possibility 4 odds 6 chance 8 instance 9 potential 10 likelihood 11 contingency, feasibility

possible 6 doable, likely, viable 7 earthly 8 feasible 9 expedient, potential 10 imaginable, realizable 11 practicable

possibly 5 maybe 7 perhaps 8 by chance 9 perchance 11 conceivably

post 3 set 4 camp, mail, pole, ride, spot, task 5 affix, hurry, newel, place, put up, score, stage, stake 6 advise, column, fill in, inform, notify, office, pillar

7 apprise, express, placard, publish, station 8 announce, denounce, position 9 advertise 10 assignment

poster 4 bill, sign 6 notice 7 affiche, placard 9 broadside, signboard 12 announcement 13 advertisement

posterior 4 back, hind, rear, rump, seat, tail 5 after, fanny, later 6 behind, caudal, dorsal, hinder 7 ensuing, rear end, tail end 8 backside, buttocks, derriere, hindmost, rearward 9 following 10 subsequent

posterity 6 future 7 progeny 8 children 9 offspring 11 descendants

posthaste 4 fast 6 at once, pronto 7 fleetly, quickly, rapidly, swiftly 8 promptly, speedily 11 immediately

Postimpressionist painter 6 Seurat (Georges) 7 Cezanne (Paul), Gauguin (Paul), Van Gogh (Vincent) 8 Pissarro (Camille), Rousseau (Henri)

postmortem 7 autopsy 8 necropsy

postpone 5 defer, delay, table 6 hold up, put off, shelve 7 hold off, lay over, suspend 8 hold over, prorogue

postulate 5 axiom, claim 6 assert, assume, demand, thesis 7 premise, suppose 10 assumption, hypothesis, presuppose 11 hypothesize, presumption, supposition

posture 4 mode, pose 5 state 6 affect, assume, manner, stance, status 7 bearing, outlook 8 attitude, carriage, position 9 condition, situation 12 attitudinize

posy 5 bloom 6 flower 7 blossom, bouquet, corsage, nosegay 9 sentiment

pot 3 bet, pan, wad 4 ante, hemp, olla 5 grass, kitty, stake, wager 6 boodle, bundle, pipkin 8 cannabis 9 marijuana

potable 5 clean, drink, fresh 6 liquid, liquor 8 beverage 9 drinkable

potassium ore 7 sylvite

potato 3 yam 4 spud 5 tater *bud:* 3 eye

pot-au-___ 3 feu

potbelly 3 gut 5 stove 6 paunch 9 bay window, spare tire

potency 3 pep 5 force, might, power, vigor 6 energy, muscle 8 strength 9 influence, puissance 10 capability 13 effectiveness

potent 4 rich 6 mighty, robust, strong, virile 7 dynamic 8 forceful, forcible, powerful 9 effective 10 persuasive 11 influential

potential 6 latent, likely 7 ability, promise 8 capacity, possible 9 plausible, promising 10 imaginable 11 conceivable, possibility

pother 3 ado 4 flap, fret, fuss, stir, to-do 5 furor, whirl, worry 6 bustle, flurry,

furore, hassle, hubbub, tumult, uproar 7 fluster, turmoil 9 agitation, annoyance, commotion, confusion

potion 6 liquid 7 mixture, philter, philtre 8 medicine 10 concoction

Potiphar's slave 6 Joseph

Potiphera *daughter:* 7 Asenath *son-in-law:* 6 Joseph

Potok novel 6 Chosen (The) 16 My Name Is Asher Lev

potpourri 4 olio 5 blend 6 medley 7 grab bag, mélange, variety 8 mishmash, pastiche 10 assortment, collection, hodgepodge, miscellany, salmagundi

potshot 3 cut, dig 4 gibe, jibe 5 crack, shoot, swipe 6 attack, insult 9 criticism

potter see PUTTER

Potter character 5 Mopsy, Mr. Tod 6 Flopsy, Jemima (Puddleduck) 10 Cotton-tail, Hunca Munca 11 Peter Rabbit 12 Jeremy Fisher

potter's field 8 cemetery, God's acre 9 graveyard

pottery 4 raku 5 delft 7 redware 8 ceramics, clayware, slipware 10 lusterware, terra-cotta, yellowware 11 earthenware

pouch 3 bag, sac 4 sack 5 bulge, bursa, burse 6 pocket 7 saccule 8 sacculus

pouf 5 quilt 7 ottoman 9 comforter

poultry 4 fowl *type:* 4 duck, swan 5 goose, quail 6 grouse, pigeon, turkey 7 chicken, ostrich, peacock 8 pheasant 9 partridge

pounce 5 seize, swoop, talon 6 attack, powder 7 assault, stencil

pound 4 bang, bash, beat, slam, slug, sock 5 drive, money, stamp, throb, thump, tramp 6 batter, buffet, hammer, pummel, strike, thrash, wallop 7 belabor, impress, pulsate 9 enclosure

Pound work 6 Cantos (The)

poupée 4 doll

pour 4 flow, gush, rain, rill, rush, teem 5 flood, issue, skink, spate, surge, swarm 6 decant, deluge, drench, sluice, spring, stream 7 cascade, torrent 8 inundate, overflow

pourboire 3 tip 7 cumshaw 8 gratuity

pout 3 pet 4 fish, moue, sulk 5 grump 8 protrude 10 expression, protrusion

poverty 4 need, want 6 dearth, penury 7 beggary, paucity 8 hardship, poorness, scarcity, shortage 9 indigence, neediness, pauperism, privation 10 mendicancy, scarceness 11 destitution 13 pennilessness

POW camp 6 stalag

powder 4 bray, dust, talc 5 crush 6 talcum 8 sprinkle 9 comminute, pulverize, triturate 10 besprinkle

power 3 vis 4 sway 5 force, might, sinew,

steam, vigor, vires (plural) **6** energy, muscle **7** command, ability, control, potency, voltage **8** dominion, dynamism, imperium, strength **9** authority, influence, privilege, puissance, strong arm **10** ascendancy, domination **11** prerogative, sovereignty, superiority **12** jurisdiction, potentiality *combining form:* **5** dynam **6** dynamo *unit:* **4** watt

powerful 5 great **6** mighty, potent, strong **7** dynamic **8** dominant, puissant, vigorous **9** energetic, strenuous **10** convincing, impressive, invincible, persuasive **11** efficacious, influential, prestigious **13** authoritative

powerless 4 weak **5** inert **6** feeble, unable **7** passive **8** impotent **9** incapable **11** incompetent, ineffective

powwow 4 chat, talk **6** confab, confer, huddle, parley **7** discuss, meeting **8** ceremony **9** gathering **10** discussion **11** confabulate, get-together

practicable 5 utile **6** doable, likely, usable, useful **8** feasible, possible **9** operative **10** functional

practical 5 handy, utile **6** active, useful, versed **7** applied, skilled, trained, virtual **8** sensible **9** pragmatic, realistic **10** functional **11** down-to-earth, experienced **12** businesslike

practically 5 about **6** all but, almost, near to, nearly **7** close to **8** in effect **9** in essence, just about

practice 3 use, way **4** form, mode, wont **5** drill, habit, usage **6** custom, manner, method, repeat, system, tryout, warm up **7** perform, process **8** drilling, engage in, exercise, habitude, rehearse **9** procedure, rehearsal **10** convention

pragmatic 7 factual, logical **8** rational **9** practical, realistic **11** down-to-earth

prairie 4 veld **5** plain, veldt **7** plateau **9** grassland

prairie chicken 6 grouse

prairie wolf 6 coyote

praise 4 hail, hymn, laud, puff **5** bravo, cry up, exalt, extol, honor, kudos **6** belaud, kudize **7** acclaim, adulate, applaud, commend, enhance, flatter, glorify, hosanna, magnify, ovation, plaudit, puffery, sublime **8** accolade, applause, approval, citation, encomium, eulogize, flattery **9** celebrate, laudation, panegyric, recommend **10** aggrandize, compliment, panegyrize **11** acclamation **12** commendation

praiseworthy 8 laudable **9** admirable, deserving, estimable **11** commendable, meritorious

prance 4 step **5** mince, strut **6** sashay, spring **8** cakewalk

prank 3 gag **4** deck, dido, lark, whim **5** adorn, antic, caper, fancy, spiff, sport, trick **6** doll up, frolic, gambol, levity, shavie, vagary, whimsy **7** caprice, deck out, doll out, dress up, garnish, rollick, spiff up **8** beautify, decorate, escapade, ornament, spruce up **9** embellish, frivolity, horseplay, smarten up **10** shenanigan, tomfoolery **11** monkeyshine

prankster 3 wag **5** cutup, joker

prate 3 gab, jaw, yak **4** blab, chat, go on **5** run on **6** babble, gabble, jabber **7** blabber, blather, chatter **9** yakety-yak

prater 6 gossip, magpie **10** chatterbox **12** blabbermouth

pratfall 6 mishap, tumble **7** blunder, stumble **11** humiliation

prawn 6 shrimp **11** langoustine *French:* **8** crevette

praxis 5 habit **6** action, custom, manner **7** conduct **8** exercise, habitude, practice

Praxiteles statue 5 Satyr **6** Hermes **9** Aphrodite

pray 3 ask, beg **5** plead **6** appeal **7** beseech, entreat, implore, request **8** petition **10** supplicate

prayer 4 plea, suit **6** appeal, litany, orison **7** angelus, begging, worship **8** blessing, devotion, entreaty, petition, pleading, rogation **9** adoration **11** application, imploration, imprecation **12** supplication *beads:* **6** rosary *ending:* **4** amen *for the dead:* **7** requiem *Jewish:* **7** kaddish, kiddush *period:* **6** novena **7** triduum *shawl:* **7** tallith

prayer book 6 missal, siddur **8** breviary

prayerful 4 holy **5** godly, pious **6** devout **7** earnest, sincere

preach 4 urge **6** exhort **7** address, deliver, lecture **8** admonish, advocate, moralize **9** sermonize **10** evangelize

preacher 5 padre **6** cleric, divine, parson, pastor **8** chaplain, clerical, minister, reverend **9** churchman, clergyman **10** evangelist, sermonizer **12** ecclesiastic

preaching friar 9 Dominican

preachy 4 smug **7** donnish **8** didactic, sermonic, unctuous **9** homiletic, hortative, pedagogic, pietistic **10** moralizing **11** exhortative, sermonizing **13** sanctimonious, self-righteous

preamble 5 intro, proem **8** exordium, foreword, overture, prologue **12** introduction

precarious 4 iffy **5** dicey, risky, shaky **6** chancy, touchy, tricky, unsafe **7** dubious **8** delicate, doubtful, insecure, ticklish, unstable **9** dangerous, hazardous, sensitive, uncertain **10** unreliable

precaution 4 care 8 prudence 9 foresight, insurance, provision, safeguard 11 forethought

precede 4 lead, rank 5 usher 6 herald 7 forerun, outrank, surpass 8 announce, antedate, go before 9 introduce

precedence 5 order 8 priority 9 seniority

precedent 4 past, rule 5 model, prior 6 former 7 earlier, example 8 anterior 9 foregoing 10 convention

preceding 4 past 5 prior 6 before, former 7 ahead of, prior to 8 anterior, hitherto 9 erstwhile 10 heretofore 11 in advance of *prefix:* 4 ante

precept 3 law 4 rule 5 axiom, edict, order, tenet 6 behest, decree 7 bidding, command 8 doctrine 9 principle 10 injunction, regulation 11 fundamental

preceptive 8 didactic

preceptor 4 head 5 tutor 7 teacher 9 principal 10 headmaster

precinct 4 area 6 domain, region, sector, sphere 7 quarter, section 8 district, division, township 9 bailiwick, enclosure

precious 3 pet 4 dear, nice, rare, rich, very 5 fussy, great, loved, showy 6 adored, choice, costly, la-di-da, prized 7 beloved, darling 8 affected, esteemed, favorite, valuable 9 cherished, exquisite, extremely, priceless 10 invaluable

precipice 5 brink, cliff 8 overhang

precipitancy 4 rush 5 haste, hurry 9 hastiness 10 abruptness, suddenness 11 hurriedness

precipitate 4 fall, hurl 5 hasty, sheer, steep, throw 6 abrupt, madcap, result, sudden, upshot 7 bring on, deposit, falling, flowing, grounds, hurried, outcome, product 8 condense, headlong, sediment, separate 9 breakneck, impatient, impetuous, impulsive 10 unexpected, unforeseen 11 consequence

precipitation 4 hail, mist, rain, snow 5 sleet 7 deposit 8 sediment

precipitous 4 rash 5 hasty, sheer, steep 6 abrupt, sudden 7 hurried, rushing 8 headlong, heedless, plunging 9 breakneck 13 perpendicular

précis 6 digest, survey 7 summary 8 abstract, overview, syllabus 10 abridgment, compendium 11 abridgement 12 condensation

precise 4 nice 5 exact, fixed, right 6 narrow, strict 7 correct, limited 8 accurate, clear-cut, definite, rigorous, specific 9 clocklike, stringent 10 particular

precisely 4 just 5 right 7 exactly 8 strictly

precision 4 care 5 rigor 8 accuracy

9 exactness 10 exactitude, refinement 11 correctness

preclude 5 avert, deter 7 forfend, obviate, prevent, rule out 8 prohibit, stave off 9 forestall

precocious 5 smart 6 brainy, bright, mature 7 forward 8 advanced

precondition 4 must, need 7 proviso 9 essential, necessity, provision, requisite 10 sine qua non 11 requirement, stipulation

precursor 6 herald 8 ancestor, forebear 9 harbinger, indicator, prototype 10 antecedent, forerunner

predator 6 hunter, preyer, raptor 7 stalker 8 devourer 9 destroyer 10 bird of prey

predatory 6 greedy 9 pillaging, rapacious 10 plundering 12 exploitative

predecessor 8 ancestor, forebear 9 precursor, prototype 10 antecedent, forerunner

predicament 3 fix, jam 4 bind, hole, spot 5 pinch, state 6 corner, muddle, pickle, plight, puzzle, scrape, strait 7 dilemma, impasse, trouble 8 hardship, nuisance, quagmire 9 condition, situation 10 difficulty

predicate 4 aver, avow, base, rest 5 found, imply 6 affirm, assert, avouch 7 declare, profess 9 establish

predict 5 augur, guess, infer 6 expect 7 forbode, foresee, portend, surmise 8 announce, conclude, forebode, forecast, foretell, indicate, prophesy, soothsay 10 conjecture, vaticinate 13 prognosticate

prediction 6 augury 8 forecast, prophecy 9 prognosis 10 expectancy 11 expectation

predilection 4 bent, bias 5 fancy, taste 6 liking 7 leaning 8 fondness, penchant, tendency 9 inclining 10 partiality, proclivity, propensity 11 inclination

predispose 4 bend, bias, tend, sway 5 prime 6 affect 7 incline 9 influence

predisposed 5 prone, ready 6 biased 7 partial, willing 8 inclined 11 susceptible

predisposition 4 bent, bias 7 leaning 8 penchant, tendency 9 inclining 10 partiality, proclivity, propensity 11 inclination

predominant 4 main 5 chief, major 6 master, ruling 7 capital, general, leading, primary 8 reigning, superior 9 number one, paramount, principal, sovereign 10 prevailing 11 outstanding

predominate 4 rule 5 reign 6 govern, master 7 command, control, prevail 8 outweigh

preeminence 6 renown 7 primacy 8 dominion, prestige 9 supremacy 10 ascendancy, domination, excellence, importance 11 distinction, superiority

preeminent 4 main 5 chief 7 capital, stellar, supreme 8 dominant, foremost, peerless, towering, ultimate 9 matchless, number-one, paramount, principal, unrivaled 10 surpassing, unrivalled 11 outstanding, unmatchable 12 incomparable, transcendent *prefix:* 4 arch

preempt 4 bump, take 5 annex, seize, usurp 6 assume 7 acquire, replace 8 arrogate 9 forestall 10 confiscate, substitute 11 appropriate, expropriate

preen 5 gloat, groom, pride, primp, swell 6 smooth

preface 4 lead, open 5 begin, proem, usher 6 herald 8 exordium, foreword, overture, preamble, prologue 9 introduce 11 preliminary 12 introduction

prefatory 7 opening 8 proemial 12 introductory

prefect 7 head boy, monitor 8 head girl 10 magistrate

prefer 5 elect, favor 6 choose, opt for, select 7 advance, elevate, promote, upgrade

preferable 5 finer 6 better 8 superior, worthier

preference 4 pick 6 choice, option 8 election, priority 9 advantage, elevation, promotion, selection, upgrading 10 favoritism, partiality

prefigure 4 hint 7 foresee 8 indicate 9 adumbrate 10 foreshadow

pregnancy 9 gestation, gravidity

pregnant 4 full, rich 5 heavy 6 gravid, parous 7 teeming, weighty 8 eloquent, enceinte, profound 9 expectant, expecting, gestating, inventive, momentous, with child 10 expressive, meaningful, parturient 11 significant

prehensile 8 grasping

prejudice 3 mar 4 bias, harm, hurt, sway 5 color, favor 6 damage, injure, injury, racism, sexism 7 bigotry, leaning 8 aversion 9 antipathy, hostility, influence 10 partiality 11 intolerance 12 one-sidedness

prejudicial 6 biased 7 bigoted 8 damaging 9 injurious 11 deleterious, detrimental

prelate 5 abbot 6 bishop 7 primate 8 cardinal, diocesan 9 patriarch 10 archbishop 12 ecclesiastic

preliminary 4 heat 5 basic, match, trial 7 initial, opening 8 proemial 9 beginning 10 qualifying 11 fundamental 12 introductory

prelude 5 intro, proem 8 exordium, fore-word, overture, prologue 12 introduction, prolegomenon

premature 5 early 8 untimely 10 before-hand

premeditated 5 set up 7 planned, studied, willful 8 designed, intended 9 conscious 10 calculated, considered, deliberate, thought-out 11 intentional

premier 4 head, main 5 chief, first 7 leading, primary 8 earliest, foremost, original 9 principal 13 prime minister

premiere 5 debut 7 opening 8 earliest, original 9 beginning 10 first night

premise 4 base 5 posit 6 assume, thesis 8 building, property, set forth 9 postulate 10 assumption 11 postulation, proposition, supposition

premium 5 bonus, extra, prize 6 reward 8 dividend, superior 9 excellent 10 recompense 11 exceptional

premonition 4 omen 9 misgiving, suspicion 10 foreboding 11 forewarning 12 apprehension, presentiment

preoccupied 4 deep, lost, rapt 6 absent, intent 7 engaged, faraway, worried 8 absorbed, immersed 9 concerned, engrossed, wrapped up 10 abstracted, distracted 11 inattentive 12 absent-minded

prep 5 basic, coach, drill, equip, groom, prime, ready, train, trial 8 get ready 11 preliminary 12 introductory

preparation 4 base, plan 5 study 7 fitness, measure 8 compound, medicine, training 9 alertness, foresight, readiness 10 background, concoction

preparatory 5 basic 11 preliminary, rudimentary 12 introductory

prepare 3 fit, fix 4 gird 5 draft, prime, ready, train 6 draw up, make up, outfit 7 fortify, furnish 9 formulate

prepared 3 set 4 up on 5 fixed, ready 6 primed 7 treated 9 processed

preponderance 4 bulk 8 dominion, majority, main part 9 ascendant, dominance, supremacy 10 ascendancy, domination 11 superiority

preponderant 7 supreme 8 dominant, superior 9 paramount 10 prevailing

preponderate 4 rule 5 reign 6 exceed 7 command, dictate, outrank, prevail 8 dominate, outweigh

prepossess 4 bias, sway 5 favor 6 absorb, engage, occupy 7 engross, immerse, involve 9 influence

prepossessing 7 likable 9 appealing 10 attractive

preposterous 4 wild 5 crazy, wacky 6 absurd, insane 7 asinine, foolish, idiotic 9 fantastic, laughable, senseless

10 irrational, ridiculous 11 harebrained 12 unreasonable

prerequisite 4 must, need 5 vital 8 required 9 condition, essential, mandatory, necessary, necessity 10 imperative, sine qua non 11 requirement 13 indispensable

prerogative 5 power, right 8 appanage, immunity 9 authority, exemption, privilege 10 birthright, perquisite

presage 4 bode, omen, warn 5 augur, sense 6 augury, boding, herald, intuit 7 portend, portent, predict, promise, warning 8 announce, forebode, forecast, foretell, forewarn, indicate, prophesy, soothsay 9 foretoken, harbinger, intuition, misgiving 10 foreboding, foreshadow, prediction, prognostic, vaticinate

presbyter 5 elder 6 priest

prescience 9 foresight 12 anticipation, clairvoyance 13 foreknowledge

prescribe 3 fix, set 4 rule 5 guide, order 6 assign, choose, decide, decree, define, direct, impose, ordain, select 7 dictate, lay down, pick out, require, specify 9 designate, determine, stipulate

prescript 3 law 4 rule 5 edict, order 6 decree 10 regulation

prescription 4 drug, rule 5 claim, right, title 6 custom, remedy 8 medicine 9 direction 10 medication

presence 3 air 4 look, mien 5 poise 6 aspect, spirit 7 address, bearing 8 carriage, demeanor 9 composure

present 3 act, aim, now 4 boon, gift, give, here, pose, show 5 award, bring, favor, offer, point, stage, tense, today 6 at hand, bestow, confer, convey, direct, donate, extend, in view, modern, submit, tender 7 hand out, largess, perform, proffer 8 existing, nominate 9 introduce 12 contemporary

presentable 3 fit 6 decent, proper 8 becoming 9 befitting 10 acceptable 11 appropriate 12 satisfactory

present-day 6 living, recent 7 current, ongoing, popular, topical 8 contempo, existent, existing, pressing, up-to-date 9 prevalent, surviving 10 prevailing 12 contemporary

presently 3 now 4 anon, soon 5 today 6 in time, one day 7 by and by 9 forthwith, these days 10 before long

preservation 4 care 6 saving, shield 7 defense, keeping 8 pickling 10 husbanding, protection 11 conservancy, maintenance, safekeeping

preserve 3 can, jam 4 save 5 jelly, put up 6 keep up, pickle 7 protect, shelter, sustain 8 keep safe, maintain 9 confiture

preside 3 run 4 head, lead 5 chair 6 direct, handle, manage 7 conduct, control, operate, oversee 8 moderate 9 officiate

president *United States:* 4 Bush (George, George W.), Ford (Gerald R.), Polk (James K.), Taft (William H.) 5 Adams (John, John Quincy), Grant (Ulysses S.), Hayes (Rutherford B.), Nixon (Richard M.), Tyler (John) 6 Arthur (Chester A.), Carter (Jimmy), Hoover (Herbert), Monroe (James), Pierce (Franklin), Reagan (Ronald), Taylor (Zachary), Truman (Harry S.), Wilson (Woodrow) 7 Clinton (Bill), Harding (Warren), Jackson (Andrew), Johnson (Andrew, Lyndon), Kennedy (John F.), Lincoln (Abraham), Madison (James) 8 Buchanan (James), Coolidge (Calvin), Fillmore (Millard), Garfield (James), Harrison (Benjamin, William Henry), McKinley (William), Van Buren (Martin) 9 Cleveland (Grover), Jefferson (Thomas), Roosevelt (Franklin D., Theodore) 10 Eisenhower (Dwight D.), Washington (George)

presidio 4 fort 7 bastion, citadel 8 fastness, fortress, garrison 10 stronghold 13 fortification

press 3 hug, jam, ram 4 cram, iron, mass, pack, pile, push, rush, urge 5 clasp, crowd, crush, drive, force, horde, hurry, media, shove 6 demand, hustle, insist, jostle, propel, squash, stress, throng, thrust 7 beseech, entreat, imprint, printer, squeeze 9 constrain, influence, multitude

pressing 5 acute, vital 6 urgent 7 crucial, earnest, exigent, serious 8 critical 9 immediate, important, insistent 10 compelling, imperative

pressure 4 push, rush 5 drive, impel 6 burden, strain, stress 7 tension 10 constraint *combining form:* 5 piezo *instrument:* 9 barometer *unit:* 3 bar 6 pascal

prestige 4 fame, rank, sway 5 power 6 cachet, credit, esteem, regard, renown, repute, status, weight 7 dignity, stature 8 eminence, position, standing 9 authority, influence 10 importance, prominence 11 consequence, distinction

prestigious 5 famed, great 6 famous 7 eminent, honored, notable 8 esteemed, renowned 9 prominent, respected 10 celebrated 11 influential 13 distinguished

presto 4 fast 7 hastily, quickly, rapidly 8 suddenly 9 posthaste 11 immediately

presumably 6 likely, surely 8 probably 9 doubtless

presume 4 dare 5 guess, imply, infer, think, trust 6 expect, gather, impose, reason 7 believe, intrude, suppose, surmise, venture 8 infringe 9 postulate 10 conjecture

presumption 4 gall 5 brass, cheek, nerve 6 belief, daring, ground, reason, thesis 7 conceit 8 audacity, chutzpah, evidence 9 brashness, inference, postulate 10 confidence, effrontery

presumptuous 4 bold, smug 5 brash, fresh, pushy 6 cheeky, uppity 7 forward 8 arrogant 9 audacious, confident 11 overweening, self-assured

presuppose 5 posit 6 assume, expect 7 imagine, require, surmise 9 postulate

pretend 3 act 4 fake, pose, sham 5 bluff, claim, false, feign, guess, put on 6 affect, assume, delude, invent 7 deceive, imitate, mislead, playact, profess, purport, suppose, surmise 8 simulate 9 imaginary 11 counterfeit, make-believe

pretender 4 fake, sham 5 actor, faker, fraud, phony 6 humbug 8 claimant, impostor 9 hypocrite

pretense 3 act, air 4 face, fake, mask, pose, sham 5 claim, cloak, cover, front, guise 6 deceit, facade, humbug 7 charade, fiction 8 disguise 9 deception, false show, imposture 10 masquerade, simulation 11 affectation, make-believe, ostentation

pretension 5 claim, right 6 vanity 8 ambition 10 allegation, aspiration 11 affectation

pretentious 5 lofty, put-on, showy 6 chichi, la-di-da, too-too 7 pompous, stilted 8 affected, inflated, puffed up, snobbish, specious 9 bombastic, conceited, grandiose, overblown 10 euphuistic, rhetorical 11 highfalutin 12 high-sounding, magniloquent, vainglorious

preternatural 7 psychic, unusual 8 abnormal, atypical 9 anomalous, unearthly, untypical 10 mysterious 12 inexplicable, supernatural 13 extraordinary

pretext 4 mask, ploy 5 alibi, cloak, cover, front, guise 6 device, excuse 7 apology 10 subterfuge

pretty 3 apt, pat 4 cute, fair, nice, some 5 bonny, quite 6 adroit, artful, clever, comely, fairly, kind of, lovely, mainly, rather, seemly, sort of 7 cunning, darling 8 graceful, handsome, pleasant, pleasing, skillful, somewhat 9 appealing, beautiful 10 attractive, moderately,

more or less 11 good-looking 12 considerable

prevail 4 beat, rule 5 reign 6 master 7 conquer, impress, persist, triumph 8 convince, dominate, domineer, overcome, override, persuade 9 influence

prevalent 4 rife 6 ruling 7 favored, popular, regnant 8 accepted, dominant, superior 9 ascendant, customary, paramount, sovereign 10 accustomed, widespread

prevaricate 3 fib, lie 5 avoid, evade 6 palter 7 confuse, deceive, distort, falsify, quibble 12 misrepresent

prevarication 3 fib, lie 4 tale 5 lying, story 6 canard, deceit 7 falsity 9 deception, falsehood

prevent 3 bar, dam 4 balk, foil, ward 5 avert, avoid, block, check, debar, deter 6 arrest, baffle, forbid, hinder, impede, thwart 7 forfend, head off, inhibit, obviate 8 obstruct, prohibit, stave off 9 forestall, frustrate, interdict 10 anticipate

previous 4 fore, past 5 early, prior 6 before, former 7 earlier, onetime 8 anterior 9 erstwhile, foregoing, in advance 10 antecedent, beforehand

previously 4 once 5 afore, ahead 6 before 7 already, earlier 8 formerly 9 erstwhile 10 heretofore

prewar 10 antebellum

prey 4 feed, game, mark 5 chase 6 quarry, target, victim 8 casualty, distress

Priam *daughter:* 6 Creusa 8 Polyxena 9 Cassandra *father:* 8 Laomedon *grandfather:* 4 Ilus *kingdom:* 4 Troy *slayer:* 7 Pyrrhus 11 Neoptolemus *son:* 5 Paris 6 Hector, Lycaon 7 Helenus, Troilus 9 Deiphobus, Polydorus *wife:* 6 Arisbe, Hecuba

Priapus *father:* 7 Bacchus 8 Dionysus *mother:* 5 Venus 9 Aphrodite

price 3 fee, fix, tab 4 cost, fare, rate, toll 6 amount, assess, charge, figure, outlay, reward, tariff 7 expense, payment 8 appraise

priceless 4 rare, rich 5 droll, funny, witty 6 absurd, costly, prized, valued 7 amusing 8 precious, valuable 9 cherished, treasured 10 invaluable

pricey 4 dear 5 steep 6 costly 9 expensive

prick 3 jab 4 goad, mark, prod, spur, urge 5 egg on, point, sting, thorn 6 affect, excite, exhort, pierce, prompt 7 pinhole 8 puncture 9 perforate

prickly 5 burry, sharp, spiny 6 briary, thorny, tingly, touchy, trying 7 brambly, waspish 8 annoying, nettling, snappish, stinging 9 difficult, fractious, irritable, vexatious 10 bothersome, irritating, nettlesome 11 troublesome

pride 3 ego, top 4 best, brag, pack, pick 5 boast, cream, elite, exult, group, preen, prime, prize, vaunt 6 choice, egoism, vanity 7 conceit, delight, elation, dignity, disdain, egotism 8 smugness, treasure 9 arrogance, cockiness, vainglory 10 self-esteem, self-regard 11 self-respect 12 congratulate

Pride and Prejudice author 6 Austen (Jane)

prideful 6 elated 7 haughty 8 exultant 10 disdainful

prier 5 snoop 7 meddler 8 busybody, quidnunc 9 buttinsky

priest 6 cleric, divine, rector 8 chaplain 9 clergyman, presbyter *ancient Roman:* 6 flamen 8 pontifex *Buddhist:* 4 lama *Celtic:* 5 druid *French:* 4 abbé, curé *Muslim:* 4 imam *tribal:* 6 shaman

priestly 8 clerical, hieratic 10 sacerdotal

prig 5 prude, thief 6 pedant 8 bluenose 9 Mrs. Grundy 10 goody-goody

priggish 5 fussy 6 stuffy 7 genteel, pompous, prudish 8 affected, pedantic 11 puritanical, straitlaced

prim 4 neat, nice, snug, tidy, trig 5 stiff 6 formal, proper, strict, stuffy, wooden 7 correct, genteel, orderly, precise, prudish 8 decorous, priggish 11 straitlaced

prima donna 4 diva, snob, star 7 artiste 9 chanteuse 10 narcissist 11 leading lady

prima facie 4 true 5 valid 8 apparent 11 self-evident

primal 5 basic 6 age-old 7 ancient, premier 8 cardinal, original 9 atavistic, paramount, primitive 10 preeminent 11 prehistoric

primary 4 main 5 basal, basic, chief, first 6 direct 7 initial, pioneer, radical 8 cardinal, earliest, original 9 elemental, essential, firsthand, immediate, number-one, paramount, principal 10 aboriginal, underlying 11 fundamental, rudimentary 12 foundational, introductory *combining form:* 4 prot 5 proto *prefix:* 4 arch 5 archi

primate 3 ape, man 5 human, lemur, loris 6 aye-aye, bonobo, monkey 7 gorilla 10 anthropoid, chimpanzee, human being 11 Homo sapiens *nocturnal:* 5 loris 7 tarsier *small:* 6 galago

prime 3 top 4 best, dawn, fill, load, morn, peak, pick, rate 5 coach, cream, elite, first, paint, sunup, tonic, youth 6 choice, excite, height, spring, symbol 7 capital, highest, initial, morning, prepare, provoke, quicken 8 earliest, moti-

vate, original, superior 9 excellent, first-rate, principal, stimulate 10 first-class

primer 4 book 5 guide 6 manual, reader 8 hornbook

primeval 7 ancient 8 earliest, original 10 aboriginal

primitive 3 raw 4 rude 5 basic, crude, early 6 savage 7 archaic, Spartan 8 barbaric, original, primeval 9 atavistic, barbarian, barbarous, elemental, essential, unevolved 10 elementary, primordial, underlying 11 fundamental, preliterate, uncivilized, undeveloped 12 uncultivated *combining form:* 5 palae, paleo 6 archae, archeo, palaeo 7 archaeo *prefix:* 4 arch 5 arche, archi

primogenitor 8 ancestor, forebear 9 precursor 10 forefather

primordial 5 basic, early, first 7 ancient 8 earliest, original

primp 4 fuss 6 adorn, dress, fix up, preen 7 dress up

prince *Anglo-Saxon:* 8 atheling *Arab:* 4 amir, emir *Austrian:* 8 archduke *Ethiopian:* 3 ras *Indian:* 4 raja 5 rajah *of demons:* 9 Beelzebub *of Monaco:* 7 Rainier *of the church:* 8 cardinal *of Wales:* 7 Charles

Prince and the Pauper author 5 Twain (Mark) 7 Clemens (Samuel)

Prince ___ Coast, Antarctica 4 Olav

Prince Edward Island *capital:* 13 Charlottetown *provincial flower:* 12 lady's slipper

Prince Igor composer 7 Borodin (Aleksandr)

princely 5 grand, noble, royal 8 generous, imposing, majestic 9 dignified 11 magnificent

princess 7 infanta *mythical:* 3 Ino *of Monaco:* 5 Grace

Prince Valiant *artist:* 6 Foster (Hal) *son:* 3 Arn *wife:* 5 Aleta

principal 4 arch, dean, head, main, star 5 chief, first, major, prime 6 assets 7 capital, leading, premier, primary, stellar 8 cardinal, champion, dominant, foremost 9 paramount 10 headmaster, preeminent 11 outstanding, predominant *combining form:* 4 prot 5 proto *prefix:* 4 arch 5 archi

principium 3 law 5 axiom, basis 7 element, theorem 10 foundation 11 fundamental

principle 3 law 4 code, form, rule 5 axiom, basis, canon, ethic, tenet 6 ground, origin, source 7 conduct, faculty, precept 8 doctrine, polestar, rudiment 10 assumption, convention, foundation 11 fundamental

principled 5 moral, noble 6 honest 7 ethical, upright 8 virtuous 9 righteous 10 moralistic

print 4 type 5 issue, litho, stamp, write 7 engrave, impress, publish, typeset 10 impression *style:* 4 bold 5 roman 6 italic 7 cursive 8 boldface

printer *English:* 6 Caxton (William) *German:* 9 Gutenberg (Johann, Johannes) *Italian:* 6 Bodoni (Giambattista) 8 Manutius (Aldus)

printing 7 edition, reissue 10 impression *measure:* 4 pica 5 agate *process:* 4 roto 7 gravure

priority 4 lead 5 order 8 ordering 9 supremacy 10 importance, precedence, preference

prison 3 can, pen 4 brig, coop, jail, keep 5 clink 6 cooler, lockup 7 dungeon, slammer 8 bastille, big house, stockade 9 calaboose 11 reformatory 12 penitentiary *California:* 8 Alcatraz 10 San Quentin *New York:* 6 Attica 8 Sing Sing 12 Rikers Island *Northern Ireland:* 4 Maze *resident:* 6 inmate 7 convict 8 jailbird

prisoner 7 captive, convict, hostage 8 criminal, detainee, jailbird

prissy 5 picky 7 finicky, precise, prudish 8 exacting 10 fastidious, particular 11 straitlaced

pristine 4 pure 5 clean, fresh 8 earliest, original 9 unspoiled

privacy 6 secret 7 retreat, secrecy 9 seclusion 11 concealment

private 5 inner 6 secret 7 soldier 8 eyes-only, hush-hush, intimate, personal 9 concealed 10 closed-door, restricted, unofficial 11 independent, sequestered 12 confidential

privateer 4 ship 7 gunship 9 mercenary

private eye 3 spy 4 G-man, tail 6 sleuth, shamus 7 gumshoe 9 detective 12 investigator

privately 7 sub rosa 8 covertly, in camera, in secret, secretly

privation 4 lack, loss, need, want 6 dearth, penury 7 absence, poverty 8 distress 9 indigence, neediness, suffering

privilege 4 boon 5 favor, grant, right 7 license 8 appanage 9 allowance, exemption 10 birthright, concession, perquisite 11 entitlement, opportunity, prerogative *pope-granted:* 6 indult

privy 3 can, loo 4 head, john 5 jakes 6 secret, toilet 7 latrine 8 bathroom, informed, lavatory, outhouse, personal 9 concealed, withdrawn 11 water closet

prize 3 pry, top 4 best, loot, pick, plum, rate, swag 5 award, booty, cream, elite, force, lever, spoil, value 6 choice, esteem, reward, spoils, trophy 7 capture, cherish, jackpot, plunder, premium 8 treasure 10 appreciate 11 outstanding

prizefighting 6 boxing 8 pugilism

pro 3 for 6 expert, master 8 skillful 9 authority, in favor of 11 affirmative

probable 6 likely 7 seeming 8 apparent, credible, expected, feasible, rational, reliable 10 reasonable

probe 4 poke, quiz, test 5 query, study 6 search 7 dig into, examine, explore, feel out, inquest, inquire, inquiry 8 check out, look into, research, sound out 9 delve into, penetrate 11 exploration, investigate, reconnoiter 13 investigation

probity 5 honor 6 virtue 7 honesty 8 fairness, goodness 9 integrity, rectitude 11 uprightness

problem 4 mess 5 hitch, issue, poser 6 enigma, puzzle, riddle 7 dilemma, example, mystery, puzzler, trouble 8 hardship, headache, question 10 difficulty

problematic 4 iffy, moot, open 7 dubious 8 arguable, doubtful 9 debatable, uncertain, unsettled 10 precarious 12 questionable

proboscis 4 beak, nose 5 snoot, snout, trunk

procedure 4 plan, step 6 course, custom, method, policy, system 7 formula, measure, routine 8 protocol 9 operation 11 instruction

proceed 4 flow, move, rise, stem, wend 5 arise, get on, issue, segue 6 emerge, push on, spring, travel 7 advance, carry on, emanate, journey 8 continue, get along 9 originate 10 derive from

proceedings 8 goings-on *recorded:* 4 acta 6 annals 7 minutes

proceeds 4 gain, take 5 yield 6 profit, result, return 8 earnings

process 3 way 4 mode, wise 5 modus, treat 6 handle, manner, method, refine, system 7 fashion, prepare, recycle, routine 8 workings 9 evolution, operation, outgrowth, procedure, technique 11 development

procession 5 march, order, train 6 parade, series, string 7 caravan, cortege 8 sequence 9 cavalcade, marchpast, motorcade 11 consecution

proclaim 5 extol 6 assert, insist 7 declare, exhibit, glorify, publish 8 announce, evidence, manifest 9 advertise, broadcast, make known 10 annunciate, bruit about

proclivity 4 bent **6** liking **7** leaning **8** penchant **9** proneness **11** inclination

Procne *father:* **7** Pandion *husband:* **6** Tereus *sister:* **9** Philomela *son:* **4** Itys

procrastinate 5 dally, delay **6** dawdle

procreate 5 beget, breed **7** produce **8** conceive, generate, multiply **9** reproduce

Procris' husband 8 Cephalus

Procrustean ___ **3** bed

proctor 7 monitor, oversee **9** supervise **10** supervisor

procure 3 buy, get **4** gain **6** obtain, pick up **7** achieve, acquire **8** purchase **10** bring about

prod 3 dig, jab, jog **4** goad, poke, push, spur, stir, urge **5** elbow, nudge, point, prick, rouse **6** excite, exhort, incite, thrust **8** motivate **9** stimulate **10** incitement

prodigal 4 lush **6** lavish **7** opulent, profuse, riotous, spender, wastrel **8** reckless, wasteful **9** exuberant, luxuriant **10** profligate, squanderer **11** extravagant, spendthrift

prodigious 4 huge, vast **6** mighty, unreal **7** amazing, immense, mammoth, massive, strange, unusual **8** colossal, enormous, gigantic **9** fantastic, marvelous, wonderful **10** astounding, impressive, monumental, phenomenal, remarkable, staggering, stupendous, surprising **11** astonishing **13** extraordinary

produce 4 bear, form, grow, make, show, sire **5** beget, breed, build, cause, erect, frame, hatch, mount, put on, raise, spawn, stage, yield **6** create, effect, father, output, parent, secure, work up **7** deliver, fashion, turn out **8** engender, generate, multiply **9** construct, fabricate, originate, procreate, propagate **10** bring about **11** manufacture, put together

product 5 fruit, issue, yield **6** effect, legacy, output, result, upshot **7** harvest, outcome, turnout **8** artifact, creation, multiple, offshoot **9** handiwork, outgrowth **11** consequence, manufacture

production 5 fruit, yield **6** output **7** staging, turnout **8** artifact, assembly, creation **9** execution, handiwork, rendering **11** achievement, manufacture, realization

productive 4 rich **6** fecund, useful **7** fertile **8** abundant, fruitful, prolific **9** rewarding **10** beneficial

proem 7 preface, prelude **8** exordium, foreword, overture, prologue **11** preliminary

profane 3 lay **4** damn, foul **5** abuse, dirty, pagan **6** coarse, debase, defile,

filthy, impure, unholy, vulgar **7** impious, obscene, secular **8** indecent, temporal, unsacred **9** desecrate **10** irreverent, unhallowed **11** blasphemous, irreligious **12** sacrilegious, unsanctified

profanity 4 oath **5** abuse, curse **7** cursing, cussing **8** swearing **9** blasphemy, sacrilege **10** execration **11** imprecation, irreverence

profess 4 aver, avow **5** claim, teach **6** affirm, allege, assert, avouch **7** declare, pretend, protest, purport **8** maintain, practice

profession 3 art, job, vow **5** craft, trade **6** avowal, career, métier **7** calling **8** business, vocation **9** assertion, specialty, statement, testimony **10** handicraft, occupation **11** affirmation

professional 4 paid **6** expert, master **7** learned, skilled **9** authority **10** proficient, specialist **11** experienced **12** businesslike

professor 3 don **6** expert **7** teacher **8** academic, educator

proffer 4 give, pose **6** extend, submit, tender **7** hold out, present, suggest **10** invitation, suggestion

proficiency 5 savvy, skill **7** ability, advance **8** progress **9** adeptness, expertise, knowledge **10** competence

proficient 4 able **5** adept **6** expert **7** capable, skilled **8** advanced, masterly, skillful **9** authority, competent, effective, masterful, qualified **11** crackerjack, experienced **12** accomplished

profile 5 chart **6** sketch, survey **7** contour, diagram, outline **8** exposure, portrait, side view **9** biography **10** silhouette **11** description

profit 3 net **4** gain, take **5** serve, yield **6** excess, income, payoff, return **7** benefit, receipt **8** earnings, proceeds **10** percentage **12** compensation

profitable 6 paying, useful **7** gainful **8** fruitful **9** lucrative, rewarding **10** beneficial, well-paying, worthwhile **11** moneymaking **12** advantageous, remunerative

profligate 4 wild **6** waster **7** immoral, spender, wastrel **8** prodigal, reckless, wasteful **9** abandoned, dissolute, indulgent, reprobate **10** dissipated, immoderate, licentious, squanderer **11** extravagant, promiscuous, spendthrift **13** self-indulgent

profound 4 deep, wise **5** heavy, total, utter **7** abysmal, intense **8** absolute, abstruse, complete, esoteric, thorough **9** intensive **10** deep-seated, insightful

profundity 5 depth **6** wisdom **7** insight **8** deepness **12** abstruseness

profuse 4 lush 6 lavish 7 copious, fulsome, liberal, opulent 8 abundant, generous, prodigal 9 abounding, bounteous, bountiful, excessive, exuberant, luxuriant, plentiful 10 munificent 11 extravagant

profusion 4 glut, riot 5 flood, spate, surge 6 bounty, deluge, excess, wealth 7 nimiety, satiety, surfeit, surplus, torrent 8 overflow, overload, plethora 9 abundance, plenitude 10 lavishness, luxuriance, oversupply, plentitude, redundancy 11 copiousness, prodigality, sufficiency, superfluity 12 extravagance 13 overabundance

progenitor 4 sire 6 author, father, mother 8 ancestor, forebear 9 initiator, precursor 10 antecessor, forefather, forerunner, originator 11 predecessor

progeny 4 line 5 issue 6 litter, result, scions 7 outcome, product 8 children 9 offspring, posterity 11 descendants

prognosis 8 estimate, forecast, prophecy 9 prevision 10 estimation, prediction 11 expectation 12 anticipation

prognostic 4 omen, sign 6 augury 7 portent, presage 10 foreboding, indication

prognosticate 6 divine 7 foresee, predict, presage 8 forecast, foretell, prophesy

program 4 bill, book, plan, show 5 plans, slate 6 agenda, course, docket, lineup, policy 7 listing 8 calendar, playbill, schedule, syllabus 9 broadcast, procedure, timetable 10 bill of fare, curriculum

progress 4 fare, gain, grow 5 get on, march 6 course, growth 7 advance, headway, passage, proceed 8 anabasis, get along, momentum 9 evolution, flowering, unfolding 11 advancement, development, improvement *planned:* 7 telesis

progressing 5 afoot 7 en route 8 under way

progression 5 chain 6 course, growth, series 7 advance 8 sequence 9 evolution, unfolding 11 development

progressive 6 modern 7 growing, liberal, radical 8 advanced, tolerant 9 advancing 10 developing, increasing

prohibit 3 ban, bar 4 stop 5 block, debar 6 enjoin, forbid, outlaw 7 prevent 8 preclude 9 interdict

prohibited 5 taboo 6 banned, barred 7 illegal, illicit 8 verboten 9 forbidden

prohibition 3 ban, bar 5 taboo 7 embargo 8 sanction 9 interdict 10 constraint, forbidding, injunction 12 disallowance, interdiction, proscription

prohibitive 5 steep 6 costly 7 sky-high

9 excessive 10 exorbitant, forbidding 11 restrictive

project 3 jut 4 cast, feat, plan 5 bulge 6 affair, design, devise, extend, intend, scheme, vision 7 arrange, concern, emprise, exploit, feature, imagine, propose, purpose, venture 8 business, conceive, envisage, envision, game plan, overhang, protrude, stand out, stick out, strategy 9 blueprint, visualize 10 enterprise 11 proposition, undertaking

projection 3 jut 4 bump, knob, view 5 bulge 7 display 8 estimate, forecast, overhang, scheming, swelling 9 extension 10 jutting out, perception 11 expectation

proletariat 6 masses 7 workers 8 laborers 9 commoners, hoi polloi 12 working class

prolific 4 rich 6 fecund, gifted, lavish 7 fertile 8 abundant, creative, fruitful 9 abounding, bountiful, inventive 10 generating, generative 11 reproducing 12 reproductive

prolix 4 long 5 windy, wordy 7 diffuse, lengthy, tedious, verbose 8 drawn out, rambling, tiresome 9 redundant, wearisome 10 long-winded

prologue 7 opening, preface, prelude 8 exordium, foreword, overture, preamble 9 beginning 12 introduction

prolong 6 extend 7 drag out, draw out, spin out, stretch 8 continue, elongate, lengthen

prolonged 7 lasting, lengthy 8 drawn-out 9 lingering 10 continuing, persistent, persisting

prom 4 ball, fete, gala 5 dance 6 formal

promenade 4 deck, walk 6 parade, stroll 9 boardwalk

Prometheus *brother:* 5 Atlas 9 Menoetius 10 Epimetheus *creation:* 3 man 7 mankind *father:* 7 Iapetus *gift:* 4 fire *mother:* 7 Clymene *rescuer:* 8 Heracles, Hercules *tormentor:* 5 eagle

prominence 4 crag, fame, rise, spur 5 bulge 6 height, renown, status 8 eminence, headland, prestige, salience, standing 9 celebrity, elevation 10 importance, projection 11 distinction

prominent 5 famed, great, noted 6 famous, marked, signal 7 eminent, jutting, leading, notable, popular, salient 8 renowned, striking 9 arresting, notorious, well-known 10 celebrated, noticeable, pronounced, remarkable 11 conspicuous, eye-catching, illustrious, outstanding 13 distinguished *person:* 3 VIP 4 BMOC, lion 5 mogul, nabob 6 bigwig, honcho 7 big shot,

grandee 8 luminary, mandarin, somebody 9 dignitary 13 high-muck-a-muck
promiscuous 5 mixed 6 casual, random,
varied 7 immoral 8 careless 9 haphazard, hit-or-miss, irregular 10 licentious
11 unselective 12 unrestrained
promise 3 vow 4 bode, bond, oath
5 agree, augur, swear, vouch 6 assure,
engage, ensure, expect, insure, parole,
pledge, plight 7 betroth, compact, consent, declare, outlook, portend,
presage, suggest 8 contract, covenant,
indicate 9 assurance, betrothal, potential, undertake 11 declaration, expectation
promised land 4 Zion 6 Canaan, heaven
8 paradise 11 kingdom come
promising 6 likely 7 hopeful 9 favorable
10 auspicious 11 encouraging
promissory note 3 IOU
promontory 4 beak, bill, cape, head,
ness 5 bulge, point 8 foreland, headland
promote 3 aid 4 help, plug, puff, push,
sell, tout 5 boost, favor, raise 6 foster,
launch, prefer 7 advance, build up, elevate, endorse, forward, further, nurture, present, support 8 advocate,
champion 9 advertise, encourage, publicize, recommend
promotion 6 step up 7 advance, buildup,
puffery 9 elevation, publicity, upgrading 10 preference, preferment
11 advancement, advertising, improvement 13 advertisement
prompt 3 apt, cue, jog 4 fast, goad, help,
hint, move, spur, urge 5 alert, quick,
rapid, ready 6 assist, incite, induce, on
time, remind, speedy, stir up, timely
7 suggest 8 convince, persuade, punctual, reminder 10 responsive
promulgate 5 issue 6 decree 7 declare,
publish 8 announce, proclaim 9 advertise, broadcast 10 annunciate 11 disseminate
prone 3 apt 4 flat, open 5 given, level
6 liable, likely, supine 7 subject, tending, willing 8 disposed, facedown,
inclined 9 lying down, reclining,
recumbent 10 horizontal 11 predisposed, susceptible
prong 4 barb, fang, fork, spur, stab, tine
5 point, thorn 6 pierce
pronghorn 8 antelope
___ **pro nobis** 3 ora
pronoun *archaic:* 3 thy 4 thou 5 thine
demonstrative: 4 that, this 5 these, those
indefinite: 3 all, any, few, one 4 both,
each, none, some 5 no one, other
6 anyone, either, nobody 7 another,
anybody, neither, nothing, someone
8 anything, somebody 9 everybody,

something 10 everything *personal:*
3 her, him, she, you 4 them, they *possessive:* 3 her, his, its, our 4 hers, mine,
ours, your 5 their, yours 6 theirs *reflexive:* 6 itself, myself 7 herself, himself,
oneself, ourself 8 yourself 9 ourselves
10 themselves, yourselves *relative:*
3 who 4 that, what, whom 5 which,
whose, whoso 6 whomso 7 whoever
8 whatever, whomever 9 whichever,
whosoever 10 whatsoever, whomsoever
11 whichsoever
pronounce 3 say 5 judge, sound, speak,
utter 6 affirm, assert, decree, recite
7 declare 9 enunciate 10 articulate
pronounced 5 clear 6 marked, strong
7 assured, decided, evident, obvious
8 clear-cut, definite, distinct 12 unmistakable
pronouncement 5 edict 6 decree 9 manifesto, statement 11 declaration, publication 12 notification
pronto 3 now, PDQ 4 ASAP, fast, stat 6 at
once 7 quickly 8 directly 9 forthwith,
posthaste, right away 11 immediately
pronunciation *distinctive:* 4 burr, lilt
5 drawl, twang 6 accent, brogue *study:*
8 orthoepy 9 phonetics
proof 4 test 5 facts, goods 6 galley
8 argument, evidence 9 testament, testimony 10 impression 11 attestation
12 confirmation
proofreaders' mark 4 dele, stet 5 caret
prop 4 stay 5 brace, shore 6 buoy up,
hold up 7 bolster, shore up, support,
sustain 8 buttress 10 strengthen
12 underpinning
propaganda 4 hype 8 agitprop, lobbying
propagandize 4 tout 5 boost, extol
7 advance, promote, trumpet 9 brainwash, catechize, inculcate 10 promulgate 11 proselytize 12 indoctrinate
propagate 5 beget, breed, raise, strew
6 extend, spread 7 diffuse, publish,
radiate 8 disperse, generate, increase,
multiply, transmit 9 circulate, cultivate,
publicize, reproduce 10 distribute
11 disseminate
propel 4 goad, move, push, spur, urge
5 drive, egg on, power, shoot, shove
6 exhort, launch, thrust 7 actuate
8 activate
propellant 3 gas 4 fuel, spur 7 impetus,
impulse 8 catalyst, stimulus 9 explosive,
incentive, stimulant 10 motivation
propensity 7 leaning 8 penchant 10 preference 11 inclination
proper 3 apt, due, fit 4 good, just, meet,
nice, prim, true 5 exact, happy, right
6 au fait, decent, prissy, seemly, useful
7 correct, desired, fitting, genteel, pre-

cise 8 accurate, becoming, decorous, peculiar, priggish, rightful, rigorous, suitable 9 befitting 10 applicable, convenient, felicitous, individual 11 appropriate, comme il faut, distinctive *combining form:* 4 orth 5 ortho

property 4 land, mark 5 acres, trait, worth 6 assets, estate, realty, riches, virtue, wealth 7 acreage, chattel, effects, feature, fortune, quality 8 chattels, dominion, hallmark, holdings, premises 9 attribute, ownership, resources, substance 10 belongings, possession, real estate *conveyor:* 7 alienor *recipient:* 7 alienee *seller:* 7 Realtor *transfer:* 8 alienate

prophecy 6 vision 8 forecast 10 divination, prediction 11 foretelling

prophesy 5 augur 6 divine, preach 7 foresee, portend, predict, presage 8 forecast, foretell, instruct, soothsay 9 adumbrate, prefigure 10 vaticinate 13 prognosticate

prophet 4 seer 5 augur, sibyl 6 auspex, oracle 7 diviner, seeress 8 foreseer, haruspex 9 predictor 10 forecaster, foreteller, prophesier, soothsayer 11 Nostradamus 13 fortune-teller *Arthurian:* 6 Merlin *Major:* 6 Daniel, Isaiah 7 Ezekiel 8 Jeremiah *Minor:* 4 Amos, Joel 5 Hosea, Jonah, Micah, Nahum 6 Haggai 7 Malachi, Obadiah 8 Habakkuk 9 Zechariah, Zephaniah **Prophet author** 6 Gibran (Khalil)

prophetess 5 sibyl 7 Deborah 9 Cassandra

prophetic 5 vatic 6 orphic 7 Delphic 8 Delphian, oracular 9 presaging, prescient, sibylline, vaticinal 10 predictive, revelatory 11 apocalyptic, foretelling

propinquity 7 kinship 8 nearness 9 closeness, proximity 10 contiguity

propitiate 5 adapt, atone 6 adjust, pacify, soothe 7 appease, assuage, gratify, mollify, placate, satisfy 9 intercede, reconcile 10 conciliate

propitious 4 good, rosy 5 lucky 6 benign, bright 7 benefic, helpful 8 favoring 9 favorable, fortunate, opportune, promising 10 auspicious, beneficent, beneficial, benevolent 12 advantageous

proponent 6 backer 8 advocate, champion, defender 9 expounder, supporter 10 enthusiast

proportion 4 rate, size 5 allot, ratio, quota, share 6 adjust, divide 7 balance, conform, harmony 8 symmetry 9 dimension 10 percentage 12 relationship

proportional 5 scale 7 in scale 8 relative 9 equalized 10 contingent, equivalent,

reciprocal 11 correlative, symmetrical 12 commensurate 13 commensurable, corresponding

proposal 3 bid 4 idea, plan 6 motion, scheme 7 outline, proffer, project 8 scenario 10 invitation, suggestion 11 proposition *final:* 9 ultimatum

propose 3 aim, ask, put 4 name, plan, pose 5 offer 6 design, intend, submit, tender 7 advance, move for, present, request, solicit, suggest 8 nominate, put forth, set forth, theorize 9 recommend 10 put forward

proposition 4 plan 5 offer 6 scheme, thesis 7 premise, suggest, theorem 10 invitation, suggestion

propound 3 put 4 pose 5 offer 7 present, suggest 8 put forth

proprietor 5 owner 8 landlord 9 possessor

propriety 7 aptness, decency, decorum, manners 8 behavior, civility, good form 9 etiquette, rightness 10 seemliness 11 correctness, fittingness, suitability 12 decorousness

propulsion 4 fuel, push 5 drive, force, power 6 energy, thrust

prorate 5 allot, divvy, quota, share, split 6 assess, divide, parcel, ration 7 divvy up, portion 9 apportion, partition 10 distribute

prorogue 3 end 4 rise, stay 5 defer, delay 6 hold up, put off, recess, shelve 7 adjourn, hold off, suspend 8 dissolve, hold over, postpone 9 terminate

prosaic 4 dull, flat 5 banal, prose, prosy, trite, vapid 6 boring, common 7 factual, literal, mundane, tedious 8 everyday, lifeless, ordinary, workaday 9 colorless 10 lackluster, uneventful 11 commonplace 13 unimaginative

proscenium 5 frame, stage 9 forestage 10 foreground

proscribe 3 ban 4 damn 6 enjoin, forbid, outlaw 7 condemn 8 prohibit, sentence 9 interdict

proscription 3 ban 5 taboo 11 prohibition 12 condemnation, interdiction

prosecute 3 sue 4 wage 5 press 6 charge, indict, pursue 7 carry on, perform 8 continue 9 bring suit, persevere

proselyte 7 convert, recruit 8 neophyte

proselytize 5 draft 6 enlist, enroll, sign up 7 convert, recruit, win over 8 convince 9 brainwash, catechize 11 prevail upon 12 indoctrinate

___ **prosequi** 5 nolle

prospect 4 mine, view 5 scene, vista 6 chance, survey, vision 7 dig into, explore, lookout, outlook 8 customer, exposure 9 candidate 10 expectancy

11 expectation, possibility 12 anticipation

prospective 6 coming, future, likely 7 awaited, ensuing, nearing, pending, planned, would-be 8 destined, eventual, expected, hoped-for, intended, proposed, soon-to-be 9 impending, looked-for, potential, scheduled 10 consequent, succeeding 11 anticipated, approaching, predestined, forthcoming

prospectus 4 list, plan 6 design, layout, précis 7 epitome, outline, program, summary 8 bulletin, synopsis 9 catalogue, timetable 10 projection 11 description 12 announcement

prosper 5 score, yield 6 arrive, do well, thrive 7 make out, produce, succeed, turn out 8 flourish, grow rich

prosperity 4 ease 6 riches, wealth 7 success 8 thriving 9 abundance, advantage, affluence, well-being

Prospero *daughter:* 7 Miranda *servant:* 5 Ariel *slave:* 7 Caliban

prosperous 4 rich, well 5 happy, lucky 6 robust, strong 7 booming, halcyon, opulent, wealthy, well-off 8 affluent, thriving, well-to-do 9 desirable, favorable, fortunate, promising, well-fixed 10 auspicious, successful, well-heeled 11 comfortable, flourishing

prostitute 4 bawd, doxy, drab, moll 5 abuse, B-girl, madam, quean, whore 6 callet, debase, floozy, harlot, hooker, misuse, wanton 7 chippie, cocotte, corrupt, cyprian, floozie, hustler, Paphian 8 call girl, meretrix, strumpet 9 courtesan, party girl 11 fille de joie, nightwalker 12 camp follower, streetwalker *reformed:* 8 magdalen 9 magdalene

prostitution 8 harlotry, whoredom 13 streetwalking *house of:* 4 crib, stew 6 bagnio 7 brothel, lupanar 8 bordello, cathouse 10 bawdy house 13 sporting house

prostrate 4 fell, flat 5 abase, level, prone 6 humble, lay low, submit, supine 7 exhaust, wear out 8 helpless, overcome 9 decumbent, exhausted, overpower, overwhelm, powerless, recumbent 10 procumbent, submissive

protagonist 4 hero, lead, star 5 actor 6 leader 7 heroine, sponsor 8 advocate, champion 9 principal

protean 6 mobile, varied 7 diverse, mutable 8 variable 9 adaptable, versatile 10 changeable

protect 4 save 5 cover, guard 6 defend, screen, secure, shield 7 shelter 8 preserve, restrict 9 safeguard

protection 4 care 5 aegis, armor, bribe, graft, guard 6 safety, shield 7 bulwark,

defense, shelter, support 8 armament, coverage, immunity, security 9 extortion, insurance, safeguard 11 supervision

protector 5 armor, guard 6 patron, regent, shield 8 guardian 9 caretaker

protégé 4 ward 5 pupil 7 student, trainee 8 disciple

protein 4 zein 5 actin, opsin 6 avidin, enzyme, fibrin, globin 7 albumin, elastin, fibroin, histone, keratin, legumin, sericin 8 creatine, globulin, glutelin, prolamin, protamin, proteose, vitellin *complex:* 6 mucoid *derivative:* 7 peptone *poisonous:* 5 abrin, ricin

pro tem 6 acting 7 interim 9 ad interim, temporary

protest 4 aver, avow, beef 6 affirm, assert, avouch, except, object, oppose, picket, resist 7 declare, profess 8 maintain 9 challenge, complaint, objection 10 disapprove 11 demonstrate, disapproval 13 demonstration

Protestant 5 Amish 6 Mormon, Quaker, Shaker 7 Baptist, Lollard, Pilgrim, Puritan 8 Anglican, Lutheran, Moravian 9 Adventist, Mennonite, Methodist, Unitarian 11 Pentecostal 12 Episcopalian, Presbyterian *Bohemian:* 7 Hussite *French:* 8 Huguenot

protocol 4 code, form, rule 6 custom, ritual 7 compact, conduct, decorum, manners 8 courtesy 9 concordat, etiquette, politesse, propriety 11 conventions, formalities

prototype 4 norm 5 model 6 design 7 example, pattern 8 original, paradigm, standard

prototypical 5 ideal, model 7 classic 9 classical, exemplary 10 archetypal

protozoan 4 cell 5 ameba 6 amoeba 7 ciliate, stentor 10 flagellate, paramecium

protract 6 drag on, extend 7 drag out, draw out, prolong, stretch 8 continue

protrude 3 jut 4 poke, pout 5 bulge 6 jut out 7 project 8 overhang, stand out, stick out

protrusion 3 jut, nub 4 bump 5 bulge 8 swelling 10 projection

protuberant 5 bulgy 7 bulging 9 prominent 11 conspicuous

proud 4 vain 5 huffy, lofty, noble 6 lordly, stuffy, superb 7 haughty, pleased, pompous, stuck-up, stately 8 arrogant, exultant, glorious, scornful, snobbish, spirited, splendid, superior, vigorous 9 conceited, delighted, imperious 10 disdainful, high-handed 11 magnificent, pretentious, resplendent 12 ostentatious, supercilious

Proulx novel 9 Postcards 12 Shipping News (The)
prove 3 try 4 show, test 5 argue, check 6 attest, pan out, verify 7 bear out, certify, confirm, examine, explain, turn out 8 document, indicate, validate 9 determine, establish 11 corroborate, demonstrate 12 substantiate
provenance 4 root, well 6 origin, source 7 history 9 inception 10 derivation
provender 4 feed, food 8 victuals 10 provisions
proverb 3 saw 5 adage, axiom, maxim 6 byword, saying 7 epigram 8 aphorism
provide 4 give, hand 5 endow, equip, serve, state 6 afford, outfit, supply 7 deliver, furnish, prepare, specify, support 8 dispense, hand over, maintain 9 stipulate
provided 5 given 6 if only 8 equipped, supplied
providence 4 care 6 thrift 7 caution, economy 8 prudence 9 foresight, frugality 11 forethought, thriftiness
provident 5 canny, chary 6 frugal, saving 7 careful, prudent, sparing, thrifty 8 prepared 10 economical, unwasteful 11 foresighted
providential 5 happy, lucky 9 benignant, fortunate 10 auspicious, fortuitous
province 4 area, duty, role, work 5 field, shire 6 canton, county, domain, office, region, sphere 7 demesne, pursuit, terrain 8 district, dominion, function 9 bailiwick, champaign, territory 10 department 12 jurisdiction
provincial 5 local, rural 6 narrow, rustic, simple 7 country, insular, limited 8 pastoral 9 parochial, sectarian, small-town 11 countrified
provision 5 stock, store 6 supply 9 condition 11 preparation, requirement, reservation, stipulation
provisional 5 stamp 6 acting, pro tem 9 temporary 10 contingent 11 conditional
provisions 4 feed, food, grub 5 stock 6 viands 7 aliment, edibles, nurture, vittles 8 supplies, victuals 9 provender 10 sustenance 11 comestibles *dealer:* 8 chandler
proviso 6 clause 7 article 9 condition 11 stipulation
provocation 5 cause, wrong 7 offense 8 stimulus, vexation 9 annoyance, incentive 10 incitement 11 instigation
provocative 5 heady 8 alluring, annoying, arousing, exciting 9 offensive 10 intriguing 11 challenging, stimulating
provoke 3 bug, irk, vex 4 abet, rile, stir,

wake 5 anger, annoy, cause, evoke, pique, rouse, upset, waken 6 arouse, awaken, bother, excite, foment, harass, incite, induce, kindle, nettle, stir up, whip up 7 incense, inflame, inspire, outrage, quicken 8 generate, irritate, motivate, occasion 9 challenge, galvanize, instigate, stimulate
provost 4 head 6 keeper 7 marshal 8 director 10 magistrate 13 administrator
prow 3 bow 4 stem 5 front 10 projection
prowess 5 skill, valor 7 bravery, command, courage, heroism, mastery 9 expertise, gallantry 10 excellence
prowl 4 hunt, roam 5 skulk, slink, sneak, steal 6 search, wander
proximate 4 near, next 5 close 6 nearby 8 adjacent, imminent 9 following, immediate, preceding 10 near-at-hand 11 forthcoming
proximity 8 nearness, vicinity 9 adjacency, closeness, immediacy 10 contiguity 11 propinquity
proxy 5 agent 6 deputy 7 stand-in 8 attorney 9 surrogate 10 substitute
pro ___ 3 tem 4 bono, rata 5 forma 7 tempore
prude 4 prig 7 old maid, Puritan 8 bluenose 9 Mrs. Grundy
prudence 4 care 5 skill 6 acumen, reason, thrift, wisdom 7 caution, economy 8 sagacity 9 foresight, frugality 10 astuteness, discretion, expediency, precaution, providence, shrewdness 11 calculation, forethought, thriftiness
prudent 4 sage, sane, wary, wise 5 canny, chary 6 frugal 7 careful, politic 8 cautious, discreet, sensible 9 expedient, judicious 11 circumspect
prudish 4 prim 5 stern 6 narrow, prissy, proper, severe, strict, stuffy 7 austere, genteel 8 affected, decorous, priggish 11 puritanical, straitlaced
prune 3 cut, lop 4 clip, crop, pare, plum, thin, trim 5 shear 6 cut off, reduce, remove 7 cut away, cut back, shorten 8 pare down, truncate
prurience 4 lust 6 desire, libido 7 lechery, passion 8 cupidity 9 carnality, eroticism 11 lustfulness 13 concupiscence
prurient 4 lewd 5 bawdy 6 erotic 7 goatish, lustful, satyric, sensual 9 lickerish 10 lascivious, libidinous, passionate 12 concupiscent
pruritic 5 itchy
Prussian *aristocrat:* 6 Junker 12 Hohenzollern *prime minister:* 8 Bismarck (Otto von) *ruler:* 7 Wilhelm 9 Frederick (the Great)

pry 4 nose, open, poke **5** jimmy, lever, snoop **6** meddle **7** inquire **9** interfere
prying 4 nosy **6** snoopy **7** curious **8** meddling, snooping **9** intrusive, obtrusive, officious **10** meddlesome **11** impertinent, inquisitive
psalm 3 ode **4** hymn, poem, song **5** paean *book:* **7** psalter *selection:* **6** Hallel *word:* **5** selah
psalmist 4 poet **5** Asaph, David **6** cantor
pseudo 4 fake, mock, sham **5** bogus, false, phony **7** pretend **8** spurious **9** imitation **10** artificial **11** counterfeit
pseudonym 5 alias **7** pen name **9** false name, stage name **10** nom de plume **11** nom de guerre
psyche 4 mind, soul **5** anima **6** animus, pneuma, spirit *part:* **3** ego **8** superego
Psyche's beloved 4 Eros **5** Cupid
psychiatrist 6 shrink **8** alienist **11** neurologist *American:* **3** May (Rollo) **5** Reich (Wilhelm) **6** Kramer (Peter), Rogers (Carl) **7** Erikson (Erik) **8** Sullivan (Harry Stack) **9** Menninger (Karl) **10** Bettelheim (Bruno) *Austrian:* **5** Adler (Alfred), Freud (Anna, Sigmund), Reich (Wilhelm) *British:* **5** Laing (R. D.) *French:* **5** Lacan (Jacques) *German:* **5** Fromm (Erich) **6** Horney (Karen) *Swiss:* **4** Jung (Carl) **9** Rorschach (Hermann)
psychic 4 seer **6** medium, mental, occult **8** cerebral **9** mentalist, prophetic, spiritual **10** mind reader, telepathic **11** clairvoyant, telekinetic **12** intellectual, supersensory *American:* **5** Cayce (Edgar), Dixon (Jeane) **10** Montgomery (Ruth) *power:* **3** ESP
psycho 3 nut **5** crazy, sicko, wacko **6** madman, maniac, mental, schizo, weirdo **7** berserk, haywire, lunatic, nutcase **8** crackpot, demented, deranged, head case **9** fruitcake, screwball, sociopath
psychoanalyst 4 Jung (Carl Gustav), Rank (Otto) **5** Adler (Alfred), Freud (Sigmund), Fromm (Erich), Klein (Melanie), Kohut (Heinz), Lacan (Jacques) **6** Horney (Karen) **7** Erikson (Erik) **8** Ferenczi (Sandor)
psychologist 6 shrink **9** therapist *American:* **5** James (William) **6** Terman (Lewis), Watson (John), Yerkes (Robert) **7** Skinner (B. F.) **9** Thorndike (Edward L.) *English:* **4** Ward (James) **8** Spearman (Charles), Tichener (Edward) *German:* **5** Wundt (Wilhelm) **6** Müller (Georg), Stumpf (Carl) **10** Wertheimer (Max)
psychotic 3 mad **5** crazy **6** insane

8 demented, deranged, schizoid **13** schizophrenic
ptarmigan 6 grouse
ptomaine 6 poison
pub 3 bar, inn **4** dive **5** joint **6** tavern **7** barroom, gin mill, taproom **8** grogshop **9** roadhouse **11** rathskeller
puberty 11 adolescence
public 4 open **5** civic, civil, state **6** common, mutual, people, shared, social **7** general, popular, society **8** communal, national, populace **9** community, municipal, universal **10** accessible, government
publican 7 barkeep **8** landlord, licensee, taverner **9** bartender, collector, innkeeper **12** tax collector
publication 4 book **7** article, journal **8** magazine, pamphlet **9** broadside, newspaper **10** periodical *list:* **12** bibliography
public house 3 bar, inn **6** hostel, saloon, tavern **7** auberge, hospice **8** hostelry
publicity 3 ink **4** hype, plug **5** blurb, press, promo **6** hoopla, notice **7** billing, write-up **8** ballyhoo **9** attention, promotion **11** advertising **12** announcement **13** advertisement
publicize 4 bill, hype, plug, puff, push, tout **5** boost **7** promote, trumpet **8** announce **9** advertise, broadcast **10** press-agent, promulgate
publish 3 air **5** issue, print **6** get out, inform, put out, report **7** release **8** announce, bring out, proclaim **9** advertise, broadcast, make known **10** distribute, promulgate **11** disseminate
Puccini, Giacomo *opera:* **5** Tosca **7** Le Villi **8** La Bohème, Turandot **12** Manon Lescaut **15** Madame Butterfly
puck 3 elf, imp **4** disk **5** fairy **6** spirit, sprite **9** hobgoblin, prankster
pucker 4 fold **5** purse **6** cockle, crease **7** wrinkle **8** compress, contract **9** constrict
puckish 5 antic, elfin, larky, pixie **6** elvish, impish **7** playful **8** prankish **9** whimsical **11** mischievous
Puck's master 6 Oberon
pudding 4 duff **6** burgoo **7** custard, tapioca *baked:* **5** kugel **10** brown Betty
pudgy 3 fat **5** plump, round, stout, tubby **6** chubby, chunky, flabby, rotund **8** plumpish, roly-poly
pueblo 4 town **7** village **8** dwelling *ceremonial room:* **4** kiva
puerile 5 inane, silly **6** jejune **7** foolish **8** childish, immature, juvenile
Puerto Rico *capital:* **7** San Juan *city:* **5** Ponce **7** Bayamon **8** Mayagüez *discov-*

erer: 8 Columbus (Christopher) **language:** 7 Spanish **location:** 10 West Indies

puff 3 pad 4 blow, brag, crow, drag, emit, huff, pant, plug, pouf, push, tout, waft 5 blurb, boast, boost, elate, expel, quilt, swell, vaunt, whiff 6 exhale, pastry, praise 7 flatter, inflate 8 swelling 9 advertise, comforter, publicize 10 exaggerate

puffer 8 blowfish 9 globefish, swellfish

puffery 4 hype, plug 9 promotion, publicity 11 advertising 12 exaggeration, press-agentry

puffin 4 bird 7 seabird 9 sea parrot 10 shearwater **cousin:** 3 auk

puffy 7 swollen 8 inflated

pug 3 bun, dog 4 nose 5 boxer, track 9 footprint

pugilism 6 boxing 13 prizefighting

pugilist 5 boxer 7 fighter 12 prizefighter

pugnacious 7 defiant, scrappy 8 brawling, fighting, militant 9 bellicose, combative, truculent 10 aggressive, rebellious 11 belligerent, contentious, quarrelsome 13 argumentative

pugnacity 9 hostility 10 aggression, truculence, truculency 12 belligerence 13 combativeness

puisne 6 junior 8 inferior

puissance 5 force, might, power 6 energy 7 potency 8 strength

puissant 6 mighty, potent, strong 8 forceful, powerful

pukka 4 real, tops 7 genuine 8 bona fide 9 authentic 10 first-class

pule 3 cry 4 mewl 5 whine 7 whimper

Pulitzer Prize fiction winner *1918:* 5 Poole (Ernest) *1919:* 10 Tarkington (Booth) *1921:* 7 Wharton (Edith) *1922:* 10 Tarkington (Booth) *1923:* 6 Cather (Willa) *1924:* 6 Wilson (Margaret) *1925:* 6 Ferber (Edna) *1926:* 5 Lewis (Sinclair) *1927:* 9 Bromfield (Louis) *1928:* 6 Wilder (Thornton) *1929:* 8 Peterkin (Julia) *1930:* 7 La Farge (Oliver) *1931:* 6 Barnes (Margaret) *1932:* 4 Buck (Pearl) *1933:* 9 Stribling (T. S.) *1934:* 6 Miller (Caroline) *1935:* 7 Johnson (Josephine) *1936:* 5 Davis (Harold) *1937:* 8 Mitchell (Margaret) *1938:* 8 Marquand (John) *1939:* 8 Rawlings (Marjorie Kinnan) *1940:* 9 Steinbeck (John) *1942:* 7 Glasgow (Ellen) *1943:* 8 Sinclair (Upton) *1944:* 6 Flavin (Martin) *1945:* 6 Hersey (John) *1947:* 6 Warren (Robert Penn) *1948:* 6 Michener (James) *1949:* 7 Cozzens (James Gould) *1950:* 7 Guthrie (A. B.) *1951:* 7 Richter (Conrad) *1952:* 4 Wouk (Herman) *1953:* 9 Hemingway (Ernest) *1955:* 8 Faulkner (William) *1956:* 6 Kantor (MacKinlay) *1958:* 4 Agee (James) *1959:* 6 Taylor (Robert Lewis) *1960:* 5 Drury (Allen) *1961:* 3 Lee (Harper) *1962:* 7 O'Connor (Edwin) *1963:* 8 Faulkner (William) *1965:* 4 Grau (Shirley Ann) *1966:* 6 Porter (Katherine Anne) *1967:* 7 Malamud (Bernard) *1968:* 6 Styron (William) *1969:* 7 Momaday (N. Scott) *1970:* 8 Stafford (Jean) *1972:* 7 Stegner (Wallace) *1973:* 5 Welty (Eudora) *1975:* 6 Shaara (Michael) *1976:* 6 Bellow (Saul) *1978:* 9 McPherson (James Alan) *1979:* 7 Cheever (John) *1980:* 6 Mailer (Norman) *1981:* 5 Toole (John Kennedy) *1982:* 6 Updike (John) *1983:* 6 Walker (Alice) *1984:* 7 Kennedy (William) *1985:* 5 Lurie (Alison) *1986:* 8 McMurtry (Larry) *1987:* 6 Taylor (Peter) *1988:* 8 Morrison (Toni) *1989:* 5 Tyler (Anne) *1990:* 8 Hijuelos (Oscar) *1991:* 6 Updike (John) *1992:* 6 Smiley (Jane) *1993:* 6 Butler (Robert Olen) *1994:* 6 Proulx (E. Annie) *1995:* 7 Shields (Carol) *1996:* 4 Ford (Richard) *1997:* 10 Millhauser (Steven) *1998:* 4 Roth (Philip) *1999:* 10 Cunningham (Michael) *2000:* 6 Lahiri (Jhumpa) *2001:* 6 Chabon (Michael) *2002:* 6 Russo (Richard) *2003:* 9 Eugenides (Jeffrey) *2004:* 5 Jones (Edward P.)

pull 3 oar, row, tow, tug 4 drag, draw, haul, lure, root, yank 5 clout, draft, drive, force, pluck, put on 6 appeal, assume, entice 7 attract, draw out, extract, stretch 9 advantage, influence 10 attraction

pull back 6 rein in 7 retreat 8 withdraw

pull down 4 draw, earn, raze, ruin 5 lower, wreck 6 reduce 7 depress, destroy 8 demolish, overcome 9 dismantle

pullet 3 hen 5 chick 7 chicken

pulley 5 wheel 6 sheave **watch's:** 5 fusee

pull in 3 nab 4 stop 5 check, pinch 6 arrest, arrive, collar, detain, pick up 7 inhibit 8 hold back, restrain 9 apprehend

pulling 6 towage 7 draught, haulage 8 traction **cable:** 7 towline

Pullman 3 car 7 sleeper 8 suitcase 11 railroad car

pull off 6 attain, manage 7 achieve, succeed 8 carry out 10 accomplish

pull out 4 exit, quit 5 leave 6 depart 7 abandon, retreat, take off 8 shove off, withdraw

pull through 5 rally 7 get over, recover, ride out, survive, weather 9 get better

pullulate 4 teem 5 breed, crawl, swarm

6 abound, sprout 7 produce 9 germinate
pull up 4 halt, stop 5 check 6 rebuke
8 draw even 9 reprimand
pulp 4 mash, pith 5 crush 6 bruise, squash 7 tabloid 8 soft part
pulpit 4 ambo, dais 6 podium 7 lectern, rostrum 8 ministry, platform
pulpy 4 soft 5 cheap, juicy, lurid, mushy 6 spongy 11 sensational
pulsate 4 beat, pump 5 pound, throb 7 vibrate 9 oscillate, palpitate
pulse 4 beat 5 throb 6 rhythm
pulverize 4 beat, ruin 5 crush, grind, smash, wreck 6 crunch, powder 7 atomize, destroy 8 demolish 9 micronize 10 annihilate
puma 3 cat 6 cougar 7 panther 12 mountain lion
pumice 5 glass, stone 8 polisher
pummel 3 hit 4 beat, drub 5 pound, punch 6 batter, buffet, hammer, thrash, wallop 7 belabor
pump 4 draw, shoe, quiz 5 exert, grill, heart, raise 6 device, elicit 7 operate 8 energize, question
pumpernickel 3 rye 5 bread
pumpkin 4 pepo 6 orange, squash 12 jack-o'-lantern *family:* 5 gourd
pump up 4 fill 6 excite, expand 7 enthuse, inflate 8 energize, increase, motivate 9 stimulate
pun 4 joke 11 paronomasia, play on words 13 double meaning
punch 3 box, cut, die, dig, hit, jab, jog, pep 4 bang, blow, cuff, poke, prod, push, snap, sock 5 clout, drive, notch, smack, vigor 6 buffet, emboss, energy, impact, pummel, strike, thrust 8 uppercut, vitality 9 emphasize, perforate
punch bowl 8 monteith
punch-drunk 5 dazed, dizzy, woozy 6 addled, groggy 8 unsteady 9 befuddled, slaphappy 10 staggering 11 disoriented
puncheon 3 log 4 cask, slab, tool 6 timber
puncher 5 boxer 6 cowboy
Punch's wife 4 Judy
punchy 5 dazed, dizzy, vivid 6 addled, lively 7 dynamic, vibrant 8 forceful, spirited, vigorous 9 befuddled, energetic, slaphappy 11 light-headed
punctilious 5 exact, fussy 7 careful, precise 9 attentive, observant 10 meticulous, particular, scrupulous 11 painstaking
punctual 5 ready 6 on time, prompt, timely
punctuate 4 mark 5 point 6 accent,

divide, stress 8 separate 9 emphasize, interrupt 10 accentuate
punctuation mark 4 dash 5 brace, colon, comma, slant, slash 6 hyphen, parens, period 7 bracket, solidus, virgule 8 diagonal, ellipsis 9 backslash, guillemet, semicolon 10 apostrophe 11 parenthesis
puncture 3 jab 4 bore, flat, hole, stab 5 burst, drill, prick, punch 6 blow up, debunk, riddle 7 deflate, explode 8 disprove 9 discredit, perforate 11 perforation
pundit 4 guru, sage 5 maven, swami 6 critic, expert 7 teacher, wise man 9 authority
pungency 4 bite 5 sting 8 piquancy 9 intensity, sharpness
pungent 5 acrid, acute, harsh, sharp, spicy, tangy, zesty 6 barbed, biting 7 caustic, cutting, intense, mordant, painful, peppery, piquant, pointed 8 exciting, incisive, poignant, stinging 9 trenchant 10 irritating 11 provocative, stimulating
punish 4 fine, hurt 5 mulct, spank 6 amerce, avenge 7 chasten, correct, put down, reprove, revenge, scourge, torture 8 chastise, penalize 9 castigate, criticize 10 discipline
punishment 3 rod 4 fine 5 lumps, mulct 7 penalty, reproof 10 amercement, chastening, correction, discipline 11 castigation, comeuppance, just deserts 12 chastisement
punitive 5 penal 11 castigating, vindictive 12 correctional, disciplinary
punk 4 hood, thug 5 rowdy, tough 6 novice, rookie, tinder 7 hoodlum, ruffian, toughie 8 beginner, gangster, inferior 9 roughneck 10 delinquent
punkah 3 fan
punt 4 boat, boot, kick, play 6 gamble, propel
Punta del ___ 4 Este
puny 4 weak 5 dinky, petty, small 6 feeble, little, measly, paltry, slight 7 trivial 8 inferior, niggling, picayune, piddling, trifling
pupa 9 chrysalid, chrysalis
pupil 5 cadet, tutee 7 learner, scholar, student 8 disciple 9 schoolboy 10 apprentice, schoolgirl *French:* 5 élève
puppet 4 doll, dupe, pawn, tool 6 figure, stooge 10 figurehead, marionette
puppy 3 dog 5 whelp
Purcell opera 13 Dido and Aeneas
purchase 3 buy 4 hold 6 obtain, pay for 7 acquire, procure 9 advantage 11 acquisition
pure 5 clean, fresh, plain, sheer, total,

utter 6 chaste, decent 7 a priori, genuine, perfect, unmixed 8 absolute, abstract, innocent, spotless, virtuous 9 authentic, continent, exemplary, inviolate, stainless, unalloyed, undiluted, untainted 10 immaculate 11 theoretical, unblemished, unmitigated, unqualified 13 unadulterated

purebred 8 pedigree 9 full-blood, pedigreed 10 registered 11 full-blooded

puree 4 soup 5 paste

purely 4 just 5 quite 6 merely, simply, wholly 7 exactly, totally, utterly 8 entirely 10 altogether, completely 11 exclusively

purfle 4 trim 6 border 8 decorate, ornament

purgation 9 catharsis, cleansing 10 lustration

purgative 5 jalap 7 lustral 9 cathartic

purge 3 rid 4 oust 5 clear, expel 6 purify, remove 7 cleanse, wipe out 8 get rid of, lustrate 9 eliminate, liquidate

purification 8 ablution 9 catharsis, cleansing, expiation, purgation 10 absolution, lustration 11 expurgation 12 regeneration *sacrament:* 7 baptism

purify 5 clean, purge 6 filter, refine 7 clarify, cleanse

Purim 11 Feast of Lots *queen:* 6 Esther

puritan 4 prig 5 prude 8 bluenose 9 Mrs. Grundy

puritanical 4 prim 5 rigid 6 severe, strict 7 ascetic, austere, prudish 8 priggish 9 bluenosed 11 straitlaced

purity 8 chastity 9 innocence

purl 4 eddy, edge, knit 5 swirl, whirl 6 border, murmur, stitch 9 embroider

purlieu 5 haunt 7 hangout

purlieus 6 bounds, limits 7 suburbs 8 boundary, confines, environs 9 outskirts, precincts 12 neighborhood

purloin 3 nip 4 lift, take 5 filch, pinch, steal, swipe 6 pilfer, remove, rip off, snitch 11 appropriate

purloiner 5 crook, thief 8 larcener 9 larcenist

purple 4 plum, robe 5 cloth, grape, lilac, mauve, regal 6 florid, maroon, orchid, ornate, turgid, violet 7 flowery, pigment, pompous 8 imperial, lavender 9 bombastic, high-flown, overblown 10 rhetorical

Purple Heart 5 award, medal 10 decoration

purport 4 gist, mean 5 claim, drift, sense, tenor 6 allege, intend, thrust 7 meaning, message, profess, purpose 8 maintain 9 substance 11 connotation, implication 12 significance, significancy

purported 7 alleged, reputed, seeming

8 apparent, so-called, supposed 9 professed 10 ostensible

purpose 3 aim, end, use 4 goal, plan 5 point 6 action, design, intent, object 7 meaning, mission, resolve, subject 8 ambition, function, proposal 9 direction, intention, objective 10 aspiration, resolution 13 determination

purposeful 6 driven, intent 7 earnest, planned, studied, willful 8 resolute 9 conscious, dedicated 10 calculated, considered, deliberate, determined 11 intentional 12 premeditated

purposeless 6 random 9 desultory, haphazard, hit-or-miss, irregular, unplanned

purposely 9 expressly 10 explicitly 12 deliberately 13 intentionally

purr 3 hum 6 murmur

purse 3 bag, sum 4 knit 5 money, pouch, prize 6 pucker, wallet 7 handbag 8 reticule 9 clutch bag 10 pocketbook, prize money *Scottish:* 7 sporran

pursue 3 woo 4 hunt, seek 5 chase, haunt, hound, stalk, track, trail 6 badger, follow 7 afflict, go after, proceed 8 continue, engage in 9 persecute, persevere

pursuit 3 job 4 hunt, work 5 chase, quest, trade 6 search 8 activity, business, vocation 9 avocation, following 10 employment, occupation, profession

purvey 6 obtain, peddle, supply 7 furnish, provide 9 provision

purview 3 ken 5 ambit, limit, orbit, range, reach, scope, sweep 6 extent 8 boundary

push 3 pep 4 goad, plug, prod, sell, spur, urge 5 boost, drive, elbow, exert, force, impel, press, punch, shove, vigor 6 attack, effort, energy, expand, peddle, propel, throng, thrust 7 advance, assault, impetus, promote 8 ambition, pressure, vitality 9 incentive, influence, offensive 10 enterprise, get-up-and-go, initiative

Pushkin, Alexander *novel:* 12 Eugene Onegin *play:* 10 Stone Guest (The) 12 Boris Godunov *story:* 13 Queen of Spades (The)

push off 4 exit 5 leave, start 6 depart, set out

push on 6 travel 7 advance, journey, proceed 8 continue, progress

pushover 4 snap 5 chump, cinch, softy 6 breeze, picnic, stooge, sucker 9 soft touch

pushy 4 bold 5 brash, nervy 7 forward 8 forceful 9 assertive, obnoxious 10 aggressive 12 presumptuous

pusillanimous 5 timid 6 coward, craven

7 chicken, gutless **8** cowardly, poltroon, timorous **9** spineless **11** lily-livered
puss 3 cat, mug **4** face **6** kisser, kitten
pussycat 5 sissy, softy **6** softie **8** pushover, weakling **9** soft touch **10** namby-pamby **13** bleeding heart
pussyfoot 5 creep, dodge, evade, glide, skulk, slink, sneak, steal **6** tiptoe **10** equivocate
pustule 4 boil **6** pimple **7** abscess, blister **8** furuncle **9** carbuncle
put 3 lay, set **4** park **5** place **8** position
putative 7 assumed, reputed **8** accepted, believed, presumed, supposed **11** conjectural **12** hypothetical
put away 3 eat **4** stow **5** eat up, swill **6** commit, devour, lock up **7** confine, consume **9** polish off **11** incarcerate
put by 4 save **5** lay in, store **7** lay away **8** lay aside, salt away
put down 5 crush, quash, quell **6** demean, demote, depose, squash, subdue **7** squelch **8** belittle, suppress **9** criticize, disparage, downgrade, humiliate
put forth 5 issue **6** assert **7** present, propose
put off 5 defer, delay **7** suspend **8** hold over, postpone
put on 3 act, don, kid **4** fake **5** apply, bluff, feign, mount, stage **6** affect, assume **7** mislead, perform, pretend, produce
put-on 3 act **4** fake, sham, show **5** faked, phony, spoof **6** parody **7** assumed, feigned **8** affected, disguise **9** pretended **10** artificial, false front
put out 3 vex **4** gall **5** annoy, douse, issue, upset **6** bother, quench **7** disturb, produce, publish, trouble **8** irritate **9** aggravate, displease, embarrass **10** disconcert, exasperate, extinguish **13** inconvenience
putrefy 3 rot **5** decay, spoil, taint **6** molder **7** corrupt **9** break down, decompose
putrid 4 foul **5** fetid **6** rancid, rotten **7** corrupt, decayed, noisome, spoiled
putsch 4 coup **6** revolt **8** takeover, uprising **9** coup d'état, overthrow, rebellion **10** usurpation
putter 4 club, idle **6** fiddle, golfer, tinker **8** golf club
putting area 5 green
putto 6 cherub **8** amoretto
put together 4 form, join, make **5** build, unite **7** combine, connect, fashion, produce **8** assemble **9** construct, fabricate

putty 3 mud **4** clay **6** cement
put up 4 bunk **5** board, build, erect, house, lodge, raise **6** billet, harbor **7** quarter **8** domicile **9** construct
put up with 4 bear **5** stand **6** endure **8** tolerate
Puzo novel 6 Omerta **7** Last Don (The) **8** Fools Die, Sicilian (The) **9** Godfather (The)
puzzle 3 why **4** foil **5** poser, rebus **6** baffle, enigma, fuddle, muddle, riddle **7** anagram, confuse, mystery, mystify, nonplus, perplex, problem, tangram **8** acrostic, befuddle, bewilder, confound **9** conundrum, crossword, dumbfound, frustrate **10** disconcert **11** brainteaser
puzzle out 5 solve **6** answer, decode **7** clarify, clear up, explain, unravel **8** decipher, unriddle
puzzling 6 knotty **7** cryptic **8** baffling **9** confusing, difficult, enigmatic **10** mystifying, perplexing **11** bewildering, paradoxical **12** inexplicable
Pygmalion *beloved:* **7** Galatea *father:* **5** Belus *playwright:* **4** Shaw (George Bernard) *sister:* **4** Dido *victim:* **8** Sichaeus
pygmy 4 tiny **5** dwarf **6** bantam, little, midget **8** dwarfish **10** diminutive, homunculus **11** lilliputian
Pylades *companion:* **7** Orestes *father:* **9** Strophius *wife:* **7** Electra
pylon 4 post **5** tower **6** marker **7** gateway
Pym's creator 3 Poe (Edgar Allan)
Pynchon novel 15 Gravity's Rainbow
pyramid builder 5 Khufu **6** Cheops
Pyramus' beloved 6 Thisbe
pyre 4 heap, pile
pyretic 3 hot **7** burning, febrile, fevered **8** feverish
pyromaniac 5 torch **8** arsonist **10** incendiary
pyrosis 9 heartburn
pyrotechnics 7 display **9** fireworks, spectacle
Pyrrha's husband 9 Deucalion
Pyrrhonist 7 doubter, skeptic **10** unbeliever
Pyrrhus *kingdom:* **6** Epirus *victory:* **7** Asculum
Pythias' friend 5 Damon
python 3 boa **5** snake *slayer:* **6** Apollo
pyx 3 box **4** case **6** vessel **9** container **10** receptacle

Q

Qatar *capital:* 4 Doha *gulf:* 7 Persian *language:* 6 Arabic *monetary unit:* 5 riyal *neighbor:* 11 Saudi Arabia *peninsula:* 7 Arabian

QED word 4 erat, quod 13 demonstrandum

q.t., on the 8 covertly, secretly 13 under the table

quack 3 cry 4 honk, sham 6 con man, humbug 7 shammer 9 charlatan 10 mountebank 12 saltimbanque

quackery 4 hoax, scam 5 fraud, hokum 6 deceit 8 flimflam, pretense 9 deception, duplicity, imposture 11 dissembling

quad see QUADRANGLE

quadrangle 4 yard 5 close, court, patio 6 square 7 polygon 9 courtyard, curtilage, enclosure

quadrant 3 arc 6 fourth 9 one-fourth 10 instrument

quadratic 4 boxy 6 square 7 boxlike 10 foursquare

quadriga 7 chariot

quadrille 5 dance, ombre 8 card game

quadrivium subject 5 music 8 geometry 9 astronomy 10 arithmetic

quaestor 6 bursar 8 official 9 paymaster, treasurer

quaff 3 sip 4 swig, toss 5 drink, sup up 6 guzzle, imbibe, sup off 7 carouse, swallow

quagga 3 ass

quaggy 4 soft 5 boggy, mushy, pulpy 6 flabby, marshy, spongy 7 flaccid, squashy, squishy 8 squooshy, yielding

quagmire 3 bog, fen, fix, jam 4 mire 5 marsh, pinch, swamp 6 morass, pickle, plight, scrape, slough 7 dilemma 8 quandary 9 imbroglio, marshland, swampland 11 predicament

quahog 4 clam 7 mollusc, mollusk 9 shellfish 11 cherrystone

quail 5 cower, wince 6 blanch, blench, cringe, flinch, recoil, shrink 7 shudder, squinch, tremble 8 bobwhite *flock of:* 4 bevy

quaint 3 odd 5 funny, queer 7 antique, archaic, curious, oddball, strange, unusual 8 peculiar, singular 9 different, eccentric, whimsical 10 antiquated, unfamiliar 12 old-fashioned

quake 5 shake, waver 6 dither, quaver, quiver, shiver, tremor 7 shudder, temblor, tremble, twitter, vibrate 8 trembler

Quaker 6 Friend *city:* 12 Philadelphia *colonizer:* 4 Penn (William) *founder:* 3 Fox (George) *poet:* 6 Barton (Bernard) 8 Whittier (John Greenleaf) *State:* 12 Pennsylvania

qualification 6 caveat 7 ability, fitness 8 adequacy, aptitude, capacity, criterion, standard 9 condition 10 capability, competence 11 requirement, restriction, stipulation

qualified 3 fit 4 able 6 au fait, proper, proved, proven, tested 7 capable, limited, partial, skilled, trained 8 eligible, modified, reserved 9 competent 10 restricted 11 conditional 12 accomplished

qualify 3 fit 5 limit 6 lessen, modify, reduce, soften, temper 7 certify, entitle, license, mollify, prepare 8 describe, mitigate, moderate 9 authorize 12 characterize

quality 4 rank 5 class, elite, grade, merit, prime, savor, state, trait, value, worth 6 factor, flower, gentry, status, virtue 7 caliber, element, feature, stature 8 position, property, standing 9 attribute, blue blood, character, gentility, parameter 10 excellence, patriciate, perfection

qualm 4 fear 5 demur, doubt 6 nausea, unease 7 illness, scruple 8 mistrust 9 faintness, misgiving, objection 10 conscience, foreboding, reluctance, uneasiness 11 compunction, nervousness, uncertainty 12 apprehension, remonstrance 13 unwillingness

qualmish 3 ill 4 sick 6 queasy, uneasy, unwell 8 hesitant, nauseous 9 nauseated, reluctant, squeamish, uncertain 10 scrupulous 12 apprehensive

quandary 3 fix, jam 4 bind, hole, spot 5 pinch 6 pickle, plight, scrape 7 dilemma 8 quagmire 10 difficulty 11 predicament

quantity 4 body, bulk, dose 5 total 6 amount, degree, volume 9 abundance, aggregate, magnitude *fixed:*

8 constant *small:* **3** bit **7** modicum, smidgen

Quantrill's ___ **7** Raiders

quantum 5 quota, share, total **6** amount, budget, ration **7** measure, portion **9** aggregate, allotment, allowance, increment **13** apportionment *of gravity:* **8** graviton *of radiant energy:* **6** photon *of vibrational energy:* **6** phonon *theory originator:* **6** Planck (Max)

quarantine 6 detain **7** confine, isolate **8** restrain **9** isolation, restraint **10** detainment **11** confinement

quarrel 3 row **4** beef, bolt, dust, feud, fray, fuss, miff, spar, spat, tiff **5** argue, arrow, brawl, broil, clash, fight, melee, run-in, scrap, set-to **6** affray, battle, bicker, differ, dustup, fracas, ruckus, squall, strife **7** brabble, discord, dispute, dissent, fall out, rhubarb, ruction, scuffle, wrangle **8** argument, catfight, conflict, disagree, skirmish, squabble **9** altercate, bickering, brannigan, disaccord, lock horns, imbroglio, scrimmage **10** contention, difference, dissension, donnybrook, falling-out, free-for-all **11** altercation, battle royal, embroilment **12** disagreement

quarrelsome 6 brawly **7** adverse, counter, hostile, scrappy, warlike **8** brawling, choleric, inimical, militant **9** bellicose, combative, irascible, irritable, rancorous, truculent **10** pugnacious **11** bad-tempered, belligerent, contentious **12** cantankerous, disputatious **13** argumentative

quarry 3 dig, pit **4** game, mine, pane, prey **5** chase, delve **6** source, victim **8** excavate **10** excavation

quarter 4 area, bunk, part **5** board, house, lodge, mercy, put up **6** barrio, billet, canton, fourth, ghetto, harbor, sector **7** barrack, section, shelter **8** clemency, district, division, locality, precinct, quadrant *circle:* **8** quadrant *note:* **8** crotchet *pint:* **4** gill *ship's:* **6** fo'c'sle **10** forecastle

quarterback 4 boss, head, lead **6** direct, leader, player **7** athlete, oversee **8** director, overseer **9** supervise **10** footballer, supervisor

quartet 4 four **5** group **6** tetrad **8** ensemble, foursome **10** quadruplet, quaternion **11** composition

quart, metric 5 liter, litre

quartz 4 onyx, sard **5** agate **6** jasper **7** citrine, mineral **8** amethyst, sardonyx **9** cairngorm, carnelian **10** chalcedony

quash 4 undo, void **5** annul, crush, quell **6** defeat, negate, quench, stifle, subdue **7** abolish, nullify, put down, repress, smother, squelch **8** abrogate, dissolve, suppress **10** extinguish, invalidate

quasi 6 almost **7** nominal, seeming, virtual **8** apparent

Quasimodo 9 hunchback *creator:* **4** Hugo (Victor) *occupation:* **10** bell ringer *residence:* **9** Notre Dame

quaver 4 note **5** quake, shake, trill, waver **6** dither, shiver, tremor **7** shudder, tremble, twitter **10** eighth note

quay 4 dock, pier, slip **5** berth, jetty, levee, wharf **6** marina **7** moorage

quean 4 bawd, slut, tart **5** tramp, wench, whore **6** harlot, hooker **7** chippie, hustler **8** strumpet **9** courtesan **10** prostitute **12** streetwalker

queasy 3 ill **4** sick **6** qualmy, uneasy, unwell **7** dubious **8** delicate, doubtful, hesitant, nauseous, qualmish, troubled **9** hazardous, nauseated, reluctant, squeamish

Quebec province *capital:* **6** Quebec *city:* **5** Laval **8** Montreal **9** Longueuil *island:* **9** Anticosti *mountain:* **9** Tremblant **10** D'Iberville *peninsula:* **5** Gaspé *provincial flower:* **10** fleur-de-lys **11** madonna lily *river:* **10** St. Lawrence

Queeg's ship 5 Caine

queen *Austria-Hungary:* **12** Maria Theresa *Belgian:* **6** Astrid *Danish:* **8** Margaret, Margrete *Egyptian:* **9** Cleopatra **10** Hatshepsut *English:* **4** Anne, Mary **8** Victoria **9** Elizabeth *French and English:* **7** Eleanor *Netherlands:* **7** Beatrix, Juliana **10** Wilhelmina *of heaven:* **4** Mary, moon **7** Astarte *of Isles:* **6** Albion *of Ithaca:* **8** Penelope *of Navarre:* **8** Margaret *of Scots:* **4** Mary *of Sheba:* **6** Balkis *of the Adriatic:* **6** Venice *of the Antilles:* **4** Cuba *of the East:* **7** Zenobia *of the fairies:* **3** Mab **7** Titania *of the gods:* **4** Hera, Juno, Sati *of the Nile:* **9** Cleopatra *of the North:* **9** Edinburgh *of the underworld:* **3** Hel **4** Hela **10** Persephone, Proserpina *Spanish:* **8** Isabella *Swedish:* **9** Christina

Queen Anne's lace 6 carrot **10** wild carrot

Queen of Spades *author:* **7** Pushkin (Alexander) *composer:* **11** Tchaikovsky (Peter Ilyich)

Queensland *capital:* **8** Brisbane *explorer:* **4** Cook (Captain James)

queer 3 odd **4** ruin **5** bogus, droll, funny, spoil, weird **6** qualmy, queasy, unwell **7** bizarre, curious, dubious, oddball, strange, touched, unusual **8** doubtful, obsessed, peculiar, qualmish, singular **9** eccentric, squeamish, worthless **10** outlandish, suspicious **11** counterfeit **12** questionable

quell 4 calm, stop 5 check, crush, quash, quiet 6 pacify, quench, squash, subdue 7 conquer, put down, squelch 8 overcome, suppress, vanquish 9 overwhelm, subjugate 10 extinguish

Quemoy's neighbor 4 Amoy 5 Matsu

quench 4 sate 5 allay, douse, quash, quell, slake 6 lessen, put out, reduce 7 appease, assuage, gratify, lighten, put down, relieve, satiate, satisfy 8 mitigate, suppress 9 alleviate, eliminate 10 extinguish

quenelle 8 dumpling, meatball 9 forcemeat

quern 4 mill

querulous 5 whiny 7 fretful, peevish, pettish, whining 8 petulant 9 lamenting 10 whimpering 11 complaining

query 3 ask 4 quiz 5 doubt, grill 7 dubiety, inquire, inquiry 8 question 9 catechize 11 interrogate 13 interrogation

quest 4 hunt 5 probe 6 pursue, search 7 delving, inquire, inquiry, probing, pursuit, seeking 8 research 9 pursuance 11 inquisition 13 investigation

question 3 ask, pry 4 poll, pump, quiz 5 doubt, grill, issue, probe, query 6 chance, matter 7 debrief, dispute, examine, inquire, inquiry, problem, suspect 8 distrust, mistrust 9 catechize, challenge, objection 10 difficulty, puzzle over 11 interrogate, possibility 13 interrogation, interrogatory

questionable 4 iffy, moot 5 shady, vague 6 unsure 7 dubious, obscure, suspect 8 arguable, doubtful, unproven 9 debatable, equivocal, refutable, uncertain 10 disputable, fly-by-night, improbable, unreliable 11 problematic 12 undependable

questioning 5 probe, query 6 show-me 7 delving, dubious, inquiry, probing 8 doubtful, grilling 9 inquiring, quizzical, skeptical, uncertain 11 incredulous, inquisitive, unbelieving 12 disbelieving 13 interrogation, interrogatory, investigative

quetzal 4 bird, coin 6 trogon

queue 3 row 4 file, line, rank, wait 5 braid 6 column 8 sequence

quibble 4 carp 5 argue, cavil 6 argufy, bicker, niggle, object 7 dispute, evasion, nitpick, wrangle 8 squabble 9 criticism, criticize, objection 10 split hairs

quick 4 core, deft, fast, keen, pith, root 5 acute, agile, brisk, fleet, hasty, rapid, sharp, smart, swift 6 abrupt, clever, nimble, prompt, speedy, sudden 7 hurried 9 breakneck, impetuous 10 harefooted 11 expeditious 12 lickety-split *combining form:* 5 tachy

quick bread 6 muffin 7 biscuit

quicken 4 goad, grow, move, spur, stir, wake 5 hurry, liven, pique, rouse, speed 6 arouse, awaken, excite, hasten, incite, induce, kindle, revive, step up, vivify 7 actuate, animate, enliven, provoke, shake up, sharpen, speed up 8 activate, energize, motivate, vitalize 9 galvanize, stimulate 10 accelerate, exhilarate, invigorate

quickly 5 apace 6 at once, pronto 9 forthwith, posthaste 12 straightaway

quickness 5 haste, speed 8 alacrity, celerity, dispatch, legerity, rapidity, velocity 9 fleetness, rapidness, swiftness 10 promptness

quicksand 3 bog 4 mire 6 morass

quicksilver 7 mercury 9 mercurial 10 inconstant

quick-tempered 5 cross, fiery, ratty, testy 6 cranky, touchy 7 peppery 8 choleric, petulant 9 irascible, irritable, splenetic 10 passionate

quick-witted 3 apt 4 keen 5 acute, agile, alert, canny, ready, sharp, smart 6 astute, brainy, bright, clever, prompt 9 brilliant 10 perceptive 11 intelligent, penetrating

quid 3 cut, wad 4 chew, coin 5 money, pound 9 sovereign

quiddity 3 nub 4 gist, meat, pith 6 trifle 7 essence, quibble 8 crotchet 12 eccentricity, quintessence

quidnunc see RUMORMONGER

quiescent 4 calm 5 quiet, still 6 benign, hushed, latent, placid, serene, stilly 7 abeyant, dormant, halcyon, lurking 8 inactive, tranquil 10 untroubled

quiet 4 calm, hush, idle, lull, mute, stop 5 abate, allay, inert, muted, shush, still, whist 6 asleep, becalm, gentle, hushed, lessen, placid, serene, settle, silent, sleepy, soothe, subdue 7 compose, halcyon, pacific, passive, restful, silence, subdued 8 decrease, inactive, peaceful, reserved, secluded, taciturn, tranquil 9 cessation, easygoing, noiseless, soundless, stillness, unruffled 10 restrained, untroubled 11 tranquility, tranquilize, unobtrusive 12 tranquillity

quietus 3 end 5 death, sleep 6 damper, demise, finish 7 decease, passing, silence 8 curtains 10 inactivity, settlement 11 termination

quill 3 pen 5 float, shaft, spine, spool 6 bobbin 7 feather, spindle

quilt 4 pouf, puff 5 duvet 8 coverlet 9 comforter, eiderdown 11 counterpane *design:* 8 trapunto

quintessence 4 gist, meat, pith, soul

5 ideal, model, stuff 6 marrow 7 epitome 8 exemplar, last word, quiddity, ultimate 9 substance 10 apotheosis 12 essentiality

quintessential 5 ideal, model 7 classic, typical 8 ultimate 9 classical, exemplary 10 archetypal, consummate, prototypal 12 prototypical

quintuple 8 fivefold

quip 3 dig, gag, kid 4 gibe, gird, jape, jeer, jest, jibe, joke 5 crack, fleer, sally, scoff, sneer, tease 6 banter, oddity, retort 7 quibble 8 drollery, repartee 9 wisecrack, witticism 12 equivocation

quipster 3 wag, wit 4 card 5 clown, comic, droll, joker 6 jester 8 comedian, funnyman, humorist, jokester 11 wisecracker

quirk 3 tic 4 bend, kink, quip, whim 5 crook, curve, twist 6 groove, oddity, vagary 7 caprice 8 accident, crotchet 9 mannerism 11 peculiarity 12 idiosyncrasy

quirky 3 odd 7 erratic, offbeat 8 peculiar 9 eccentric, irregular, whimsical 10 capricious 13 idiosyncratic

quirt 4 lash, whip

quisling 5 Judas, rebel 7 traitor 8 apostate, betrayer, defector, turncoat 10 copperhead 11 backstabber 12 collaborator

quit 3 end, pay 4 drop, free, halt, stop 5 cease, chuck, leave 6 depart, desert, desist, give up, resign, retire, settle 7 abandon, drop out, forsake, release, relieve, satisfy 8 knock off, leave off, released, renounce, withdraw 9 discharge, liquidate, surrender, terminate 10 relinquish 11 discontinue

quite 3 all 4 just, very, well 5 fully, in all 6 in toto, purely, rather, wholly 7 exactly, totally, utterly 8 entirely 9 perfectly 10 absolutely, altogether, completely, positively, thoroughly 12 considerably

quittance 6 amends 7 redress 8 reprisal, requital 9 atonement, discharge, expiation, repayment 10 recompense, reparation 11 restitution 12 compensation

quitter 4 funk 6 coward, craven 7 chicken, dastard 8 poltroon, recreant 9 defeatist 11 yellowbelly

quiver 4 beat, case 5 pulse, quake,

shake, throb, waver 6 arrows, dither, jitter, quaver, shiver, tremor 7 pulsate, shudder, tremble, twitter, vibrate 9 palpitate, vibration

Quixote see DON QUIXOTE

quixotic 7 foolish 8 fanciful, illusory, romantic 9 fantastic, imaginary, visionary 10 capricious, chimerical, idealistic 11 impractical 13 unpredictable

quiz 3 ask 4 exam, test 5 grill, query 7 examine, inquire 8 question 9 catechize 11 interrogate 12 cross-examine

quizzical 3 odd 5 queer 6 quaint, showme 7 curious, dubious, mocking, probing, puzzled, teasing 8 doubtful, doubting, sardonic 9 inquiring, skeptical 11 incredulous, inquisitive, questioning, unbelieving 12 disbelieving

quodlibet 5 issue, point 6 debate, medley 7 mélange 8 fantasia, question 11 disputation

quoin 5 angle, block, wedge 6 corner 8 keystone, voussoir

quoit 4 game, ring 6 circle

quoits peg 3 hob

quondam 4 late, once, past 6 bygone, former, whilom 7 defunct, onetime 8 sometime 9 erstwhile 10 occasional

quorum 4 body 5 group 7 council 8 majority

quota 3 cut, lot 4 bite, meed, part 5 share, slice, whack 6 amount, parcel, ration 7 measure, portion, quantum 9 allotment, allowance 10 allocation, percentage, proportion

quotation 3 bid 5 offer, price 7 excerpt, extract, passage 8 citation

quotation mark, French 9 guillemet

quote 3 bid 4 cite, list 5 offer, price, refer 6 adduce, borrow, repeat 7 excerpt, extract, passage 8 citation

quotidian 5 daily, plain, usual 6 common 7 average, diurnal, prosaic, regular, routine, vanilla 8 day-to-day, everyday, ordinary, workaday 9 circadian 11 commonplace 12 unremarkable

quotient 5 ratio, share 7 caliber, portion 9 allotment, magnitude 10 percentage, proportion

Quo Vadis *author:* 11 Sienkiewicz (Henryk) *character:* 4 Nero 5 Lygia, Peter 8 Vinicius 9 Petronius

R

Ra *son:* 6 Khonsu *wife:* 3 Mut
Raamah *father:* 4 Cush *son:* 5 Dedan, Sheba
Rabbi Ben Ezra author 8 Browning (Robert)
rabbit 4 cony, hare 5 bunny, coney *female:* 3 doe *fictional:* 5 Fiver, Hazel, Mopsy, Peter 6 Flopsy, Harvey 7 Thumper 8 Crusader, Ricochet 9 Bugs Bunny 10 Cotton-tail 11 Easter Bunny *food:* 5 salad 6 carrot 7 lettuce *neutered:* 5 lapin *tail:* 4 scut
rabble 3 mob 4 mass, rout 5 crush, horde 6 masses 8 canaille, populace, riffraff, unwashed 9 hoi polloi 10 lower class 11 proletariat, rank and file
rabble-rouser 7 inciter 8 agitator, fomenter 9 demagogue 10 incendiary 12 troublemaker
Rabelais character 7 Panurge 9 Gargantua 10 Pantagruel
rabid 3 mad 4 wild 5 crazy, ultra 6 crazed, insane 7 extreme, fanatic, frantic, furious, radical, zealous 8 demented, deranged, frenetic, frenzied, obsessed, ultraist 9 delirious, extremist 10 corybantic 11 hydrophobic
rabies 11 hydrophobia
raccoon 8 ringtail *dog:* 6 tanuki *relative:* 5 civet, coati, panda 8 civet cat, kinkajou 10 cacomistle, coatimundi
race 4 bolt, dart, dash, gill, lash, meet, rush, tear, type 5 brook, chase, creek, fling, hurry, match, rally, relay, shoot, speed, spurt 6 charge, course, gallop, runnel, scurry, sprint, stream 7 channel, contest, rivalry, rivulet, scamper 8 marathon 9 grand prix 11 competition, watercourse
racecourse 4 oval, turf 5 track
racehorse 5 Alsab, Kelso 6 Forego 7 Assault, Man O' War 8 Affirmed, Citation 9 Riva Ridge, War Emblem 10 War Admiral 11 Forward Pass, Seattle Slew, Secretariat, Smarty Jones 12 Native Dancer
Rachel *father:* 5 Laban *husband:* 5 Jacob *servant:* 6 Bilhah *sister:* 4 Leah *son:* 6 Joseph 8 Benjamin
rachis 4 back 5 chine, spine 8 backbone 12 spinal column

rachitic 5 shaky 6 wobbly 7 rackety, rickety, tenuous 9 tremulous 10 ramshackle, rattletrap
___ **Rachmaninoff** 6 Sergei, Sergey
racing enthusiast 8 railbird
racism 7 bigotry, jim crow 9 apartheid, prejudice 11 segregation
racist 4 nazi 5 bigot 7 bigoted 10 intolerant, prejudiced 11 supremacist
rack 3 bed 4 buck, bunk, pace, pain, sack, scud 5 frame, wring 6 harass, harrow, martyr, strain, wrench 7 afflict, agonize, antlers, crucify, ratchet, sawbuck, stretch, torment, torture 8 distress, sawhorse 9 framework, persecute 10 excruciate
racket 3 con, din 4 game 5 babel, fraud, hoo-ha, noise 6 clamor, hubbub, rattle, scheme, tumult, uproar 7 pursuit, swindle 8 ballyhoo, brouhaha, foofaraw 10 hullabaloo 11 pandemonium
racketeer 7 mafioso, mobster 8 extorter, gangster 9 godfather
rack up 3 win 4 gain 5 reach, score 6 attain 7 achieve, realize 10 accomplish
raconteur 11 storyteller
racy 4 blue, gamy 5 bawdy, broad, juicy, salty, spicy, vampy, zesty 6 purple, risqué, smutty, snappy, vulgar, wicked 7 piquant, pungent 8 indecent, offcolor, vigorous 10 suggestive
Radames' beloved 4 Aïda
radar image 3 pip 4 blip, spot 5 trace
Raddai *brother:* 5 David *father:* 5 Jesse
radiance 3 ray 4 glow 5 glory, shine 6 luster 7 aureola, aureole 8 splendor 10 brightness, brilliance
radiant 4 glad 5 beamy, shiny 6 bright, cheery, lucent 7 beaming, fulgent, glowing, lambent 8 cheerful, luminous, lustrous 9 brilliant, effulgent 10 effulgence 12 incandescent
radiate 4 beam, glow 5 gleam, shine, strew 6 spread 7 diverge 8 illumine 10 illuminate
radiation unit 3 rad, rem, rep 7 langley, sievert 8 roentgen
radiator 6 cooler, heater 9 convector 11 transmitter 13 heat exchanger
radical 4 acyl, root 5 basal, basic, rebel, ultra 7 extreme, fanatic, primary 8 agitator, cardinal, inherent, militant, ultra-

ist **9** anarchist, essential, extremist, intrinsic **10** subversive, underlying **11** fundamental **12** foundational, iconoclastic **13** revolutionary *mathematical:* **4** surd

radicle 4 root **5** radix **9** hypocotyl

radio 8 wireless *frequency range:* **8** wave band

radioactive 3 hot **7** nuclear

radius 5 ambit, orbit, range, reach, sweep **6** extent **7** compass, purview **9** extension

radix 4 base, root **6** source

raffish 6 coarse, jaunty, rakish, sporty, vulgar **9** dissolute **12** devil-may-care

raffle 7 drawing, lottery

raft 3 lot, ton **4** heap, mess, pile, scad, slew **5** balsa, float **6** bundle

rafter 4 balk, beam, viga

rag 3 jaw, kid, rib **4** bait, jive, josh, rail, razz, rock **5** baste, cloth, scold, tease **6** berate, harass, hector, needle, pester **7** tabloid, torment **9** newspaper

ragamuffin 3 bum **4** hobo, waif **5** gamin, tramp **6** beggar, gamine, orphan, urchin **7** wastrel **8** vagabond **9** scarecrow **11** guttersnipe

rage 3 cry, fad, ire, mad, wax **4** chic, fume, fury, mode, rant **5** anger, craze, fancy, furor, mania, storm, style, vogue, wrath **6** blow up, frenzy, furore, seethe **7** fashion, madness, passion **8** boil over, hysteria, violence **10** dernier cri **11** indignation

ragged 4 rent, torn **5** seedy **6** frayed, jagged, shabby, uneven **7** unkempt, worn-out **8** frazzled, straggly, tattered **10** threadbare

raging 4 wild **6** stormy **7** furious, extreme, intense, violent **8** blustery **9** ferocious, turbulent **10** blustering **11** tempestuous

ragout 4 stew **5** salmi **6** burgoo, jumble, medley **7** farrago, goulash, mélange, mixture **8** mishmash **9** potpourri **10** hodgepodge, salmagundi **11** gallimaufry

rags 4 duds, garb **5** dress **6** attire, shreds **7** apparel, clothes, raiment, threads **8** clothing **10** attirement **11** habiliments

ragtag see RABBLE

ragwort 7 senecio **9** cineraria, groundsel **10** butterweed

raid 4 bust, loot, sack **5** foray, harry **6** attack, forage, harass, inroad, invade, maraud, ravage, sortie **7** assault, despoil, overrun, plunder **8** invasion, spoliate **9** incursion, onslaught

raider 6 pirate **10** freebooter

rail 3 bar, jaw **5** fence, scold, track **6** berate, revile **7** barrier, inveigh,

upbraid **8** banister **10** tongue-lash, vituperate

rail bird 4 sora **5** crake **7** clapper **8** marsh hen, water hen

railing 8 banister **10** balustrade *part:* **8** baluster

raillery 5 scorn **6** banter **7** mockery, teasing **8** badinage, derision, ridicule, taunting **10** lampoonery, persiflage

railroad *branch:* **6** siding *car:* **5** coach, diner, stock **6** hopper **7** caboose, gondola, Pullman *engine:* **10** locomotive *locomotive:* **9** iron horse *station:* **5** depot *underground:* **4** tube **5** metro **6** subway *worker:* **6** porter **7** fireman **8** brakeman, engineer **9** conductor **11** gandy dancer

raiment 4 duds, garb, gear, togs **5** array, dress **6** attire **7** apparel, clothes, threads, vesture **8** clothing, garments, glad rags, vestiary **9** caparison **10** attirement **11** habiliments

rain 6 deluge, mizzle, shower **7** drizzle **8** downpour, sprinkle **10** cloudburst **13** precipitation

rainbow 3 arc **4** iris **5** array, gamut **7** fantasy **8** illusion, spectrum **9** pipe dream *bridge:* **7** Bifrost *chaser:* **9** visionary *goddess:* **4** Iris

rainbow fish 5 guppy, trout **6** wrasse

raincoat 3 mac **4** mack **6** poncho, trench **7** oilskin, slicker **10** mackintosh

rain leader 9 downspout

rain tree 9 monkeypod

raise 4 ante, grow, hike, jack, jump, lift, pump, rear **5** boost, breed, erect, exalt, hoist, put up **6** foment, incite, jack up, muster **7** augment, bring up, collect, elevate, enhance, inflate, produce **8** heighten, increase **9** construct, cultivate, increment, propagate

raisin 5 grape **7** currant, sultana **10** dried grape

Raisin in the Sun author 9 Hansberry (Lorraine)

raison d'____ 4 état, être

raja 4 king **5** chief, ruler **6** prince **9** dignitary

rake 3 rip **4** comb, roué **5** angle, blood, pitch, rifle, scamp, scour, slope **6** forage, glance, lecher, rascal, scrape, search, strafe **7** incline, playboy, ransack, rummage, scratch **8** enfilade, lothario **9** debauchee, libertine **10** profligate

rakehell 4 fast, wild **5** blood **6** rascal, sporty **7** playboy, raffish **8** lothario, rascally **9** debauchee, dissolute, lecherous, libertine **10** licentious, profligate

rake-off 3 cut **4** bite, take **5** chunk, share **7** portion **9** baksheesh, lagniappe **10** commission, percentage

rake's look 4 leer, ogle
Rake's Progress artist 7 Hogarth (William)
rakish see RAKEHELL
rally 4 race, stir, wake 5 harry, renew, rouse, waken 6 arouse, awaken, bestir, kindle, muster, perk up, pick up, repair, volley 7 convene, enliven, marshal, rebound, recover 8 assemble, clambake, comeback, mobilize, recovery 9 challenge, re-collect 10 invigorate, reorganize
rallying cry 5 motto 6 byword, slogan 9 watchword 10 shibboleth 11 catchphrase
ram 5 Aries, crash, crowd, drive, pound, sheep, stuff 6 batter, plunge, strike, thrust 7 warship
Rama's wife 4 Sita
ramble 3 gad 4 roam, rove 5 drift, range, stray, troll 6 stroll, wander 7 blather, digress, diverge, maunder, meander, saunter, traipse 8 divagate, straggle 9 gallivant
rambler 4 rose 5 gypsy, hiker, nomad, rover 6 roamer, walker 7 drifter, vagrant 8 stroller, vagabond, wanderer 9 itinerant 10 ranch house
rambunctious 5 rowdy 6 unruly 7 raucous, willful 10 boisterous, headstrong 11 intractable 12 recalcitrant, ungovernable
ramification 5 shoot 6 branch, offset 8 offshoot 9 outgrowth, offspring 11 consequence
ramify 6 branch, divide, extend 7 develop, radiate 9 branch out, propagate 11 proliferate
Ramona author 7 Jackson (Helen Hunt)
ramose 8 branched
ramp 5 apron 7 incline
rampage 4 rage, riot, tear 5 binge, fling, spree, storm
rampageous 4 wild 6 unruly 7 riotous
rampant 4 rank, rife, wild 7 rearing, regnant 9 prevalent, unbridled 10 widespread 12 uncontrolled, unrestrained
rampart 4 wall 5 ridge 7 bulwark, parapet 9 barricade 10 breastwork
ramshackle 6 flimsy 7 rickety, run-down 8 decrepit 10 tumbledown 11 dilapidated
ram's mate 3 ewe
ranch 5 finca 8 estancia, hacienda *worker:* 6 cowboy, gaucho 7 cowgirl, cowhand, cowpoke 10 cowpuncher
rancher 6 cowboy 7 breeder 9 cattleman
rancid 4 high, rank, sour 5 fetid 6 putrid, skunky, smelly 7 noisome, spoiled 8 stinking 9 offensive 10 malodorous
rancor 4 gall 6 animus, enmity, hatred

7 ill will 9 animosity, antipathy, hostility 10 antagonism, bitterness
rancorous 6 bitter 7 hateful, hostile 8 spiteful, venomous 9 malicious, malignant, vitriolic 10 malevolent 11 acrimonious 12 antagonistic
Rand, Ayn *novel:* 6 Anthem 12 Fountainhead (The) 13 Atlas Shrugged
random 6 casual 7 aimless 8 slapdash 9 arbitrary, desultory, haphazard, hit-or-miss, unplanned 10 accidental, contingent, hit-and-miss, incidental 11 purposeless
randy 4 lewd 5 bawdy, lusty 7 lustful, satyric 9 lecherous, libertine, lickerish, salacious 10 lascivious, libidinous, licentious
range 3 row, run 4 area, band, roam, rove, shot, site, sort, span, vary 5 align, ambit, carry, drift, field, gamut, orbit, order, reach, realm, ridge, scale, scope, space, stove, stray, sweep, width 6 assort, domain, extent, length, limits, ramble, sierra, sphere, spread, wander 7 compass, earshot, expanse, eyeshot, habitat, meander, purview, stretch 8 confines, distance, latitude, locality, panorama, province, stovetop, traverse, vicinity 9 amplitude, extension, gallivant, magnitude, territory 12 distribution
range finder 9 telemeter
ranger 3 spy 5 scout 6 lawman, patrol, warden 8 overseer 9 caretaker, protector
rangy 4 lean 5 lanky 6 gangly 7 spindly 8 gangling
rani's mate 4 raja 5 rajah
rank 3 row 4 file, foul, lush, rate, sort, tier 5 class, fetid, funky, grade, gross, humid, order, place, queue 6 assort, cachet, coarse, filthy, lavish, putrid, rancid, rating, smelly, status 7 arrange, dignity, echelon, footing, noisome, perfect, profuse, rampant, reeking, station, stature 8 absolute, classify, evaluate, flagrant, outright, position, standing, stinking 9 downright, egregious, loathsome, luxuriant, overgrown, repulsive 10 consummate, malodorous 11 conspicuous, outstanding, unmitigated
rank and file 5 plebs 6 people, plebes 8 populace 9 commonage, commoners, plebeians 10 commonalty 11 enlisted men
rankle 3 irk, vex 4 rile 5 annoy 6 bother, fester, nettle, seethe 8 embitter, irritate 9 aggravate 10 exasperate
ransack 3 rob 4 comb, grub, loot, rake 5 rifle, scour 6 forage, ravage 7 plunder, rummage

Ran's husband 5 Aegir
ransom 3 buy **4** free **6** redeem, regain, rescue **7** deliver, recover **8** liberate **13** consideration
rant 3 jaw, rag **4** huff, rage, rail, rate, rave **5** mouth, scold **7** bluster, bombast, declaim, fustian **8** bloviate, harangue, perorate **10** vituperate **11** rodomontade
ranula 4 cyst
rap 3 hit, tap **4** blow, chat, swat, talk, wipe **5** blame, chide, knock, swipe **6** charge, patter, rebuke **7** censure, condemn, reproof **8** causerie, denounce, reproach, sentence **9** criticize, criticism, reprehend, reprimand, reprobate **10** discussion **12** conversation
rapacious 6 greedy **8** covetous, grasping, ravening, ravenous **9** predatory, raptorial, voracious **10** gluttonous, predaceous
rapacity 5 greed **7** avarice, avidity **8** cupidity, voracity **10** greediness **12** covetousness, ravenousness
rape 4 ruin **5** colza, force, spoil **6** canola, defile, ravage, ravish **7** assault, debauch, despoil, outrage, plunder, violate **9** violation **10** ravishment, spoliation
Rape of the Lock, The *author:* **4** Pope (Alexander) *heroine:* **7** Belinda
Raphael *birthplace:* **6** Urbino *subject:* **7** Madonna *teacher:* **8** Perugino
rapid 4 fast **5** brisk, chute, fleet, hasty, quick, swift **6** speedy **7** hurried **9** breakneck **11** expeditious
rapidity 5 haste, hurry, speed **8** celerity, velocity
rapids 5 chute **8** cataract **10** white water
rapine 4 loot, swag **5** booty, prize, spoil **6** boodle, spoils **7** pillage, plunder **10** spoliation
Rappaccini's Daughter 8 Beatrice *author:* **9** Hawthorne (Nathaniel)
rapport 5 unity **6** accord **7** concord, harmony **8** affinity **9** communion **13** communication
rapscallion see RASCAL
rap session 6 confab, parley **7** palaver **8** colloquy **10** discussion
rapt 6 intent **7** engaged **8** absorbed, immersed **9** engrossed **11** carried away, preoccupied, transported
raptor 3 owl **4** hawk **5** eagle **6** condor, falcon, merlin, osprey **7** kestrel, vulture **9** gyrfalcon **10** bird of prey **11** deinonychus
rapture 5 swoon **6** heaven **7** delight, ecstasy, nirvana **9** transport **10** exaltation **13** seventh heaven
rara ___ 4 avis
rare 3 few, red **4** pink, thin **6** choice,

dainty, exotic, scarce, seldom, select **7** elegant, unusual **8** delicate, singular, sporadic, superior, uncommon, unwonted **9** exquisite, recherché, underdone **10** infrequent, occasional **11** distinctive, exceptional **13** extraordinary
rarefied 4 fine, thin **7** tenuous **8** esoteric **10** attenuated
rarefy 4 thin **6** refine **9** attenuate
rarely 6 little, seldom **9** extremely, unusually **12** infrequently
raring 4 avid, keen **5** eager **6** gung-ho **12** enthusiastic
rarity 5 curio **6** oddity **7** curiosa **8** scarcity **9** curiosity **10** aberration **11** collectible
rascal 3 imp **4** rake **5** devil, knave, rogue, scamp **7** lowlife, villain, wastrel **8** scalawag **9** miscreant, reprobate, scoundrel, skeezicks **10** blackguard **11** rapscallion *Irish:* **8** spalpeen
rash 5 hasty, heady **6** abrupt, daring, madcap, plague, sudden, unwary, unwise **7** foolish **8** careless, epidemic, eruption, headlong, heedless, outbreak, reckless **9** audacious, daredevil, foolhardy, hotheaded, impetuous, imprudent, impulsive **10** ill-advised, incautious, indiscreet, unthinking **11** injudicious, precipitate, temerarious, thoughtless
rasp 4 file, fret **5** annoy, chafe, grate **6** abrade, scrape **7** scratch **8** irritate
raspberry 7 catcall **8** blackcap **10** Bronx cheer
raspy 3 dry **5** harsh, rough **6** hoarse **7** grating, jarring, raucous **8** scrabbly, scratchy
rat 4 fink, heel, scab **5** louse **6** defect, desert, inform, rodent, snitch, squeak, squeal, tattle **7** stoolie **8** apostate, defector, informer, recreant, renegade, squealer, turncoat **9** bandicoot, repudiate, turnabout **11** stool pigeon **12** tergiversate *female:* **3** doe
rate 3 fee, set, tab **4** cost, earn, rank **5** assay, class, grade, merit, price, scale, set at, value **6** amount, assess, charge, degree, esteem, regard, survey, tariff **7** apprize, deserve, valuate **8** appraise, classify, consider, estimate, evaluate, price tag **9** valuation **10** proportion
rather 4 a bit **5** quite **6** fairly, in lieu, kind of, pretty, sort of **7** instead **8** somewhat **9** tolerably **10** moderately, more or less, preferably **11** alternately **12** considerably **13** alternatively
rathskeller 3 bar, inn, pub **4** dive **6** saloon, tavern **7** barroom, taproom **8** alehouse, basement

ratify 4 seal 5 enact 7 approve, certify, confirm, endorse, license 8 accredit, sanction, validate

rating 4 mark, rank 5 class, grade 6 number 8 estimate, standing

ratio 5 scale 7 percent 8 fraction, quotient 10 percentage, proportion

ratiocination 8 judgment, sequitur 9 inference, reasoning 10 conclusion

ration 4 dole, food, meal, mete 5 allot, divvy, quota, share 6 divide, parcel 7 measure, mete out, prorate 8 allocate 9 allotment, allowance 10 provisions 13 apportionment

rational 4 calm, cool, sane 5 lucid, sober, sound 6 stable 7 logical, prudent 8 sensible, thinking 9 judicious 10 consequent, reasonable 11 circumspect, intelligent, level-headed 12 intellectual

rationale 5 basis, logic 6 reason 7 grounds 9 reasoning 11 explanation 13 justification

rationalize 7 explain, justify 10 account for 11 externalize

ratite 3 emu, moa 4 kiwi, rhea 7 ostrich

rattail 3 cod 9 grenadier

rattan 4 cane, palm 6 switch 7 malacca

Rattigan play 10 Winslow Boy (The) 14 Separate Tables

rattle 3 gab, jaw, yak 4 chat, faze 5 abash, addle, clack, noise, rouse, run on, upset 6 babble, gabble, jangle, racket 7 chatter, clatter, confuse, disturb, flummox, perplex 8 bewilder, confound, distract 9 discomfit, embarrass 10 noisemaker

rattlebrained 5 dizzy, giddy, silly 7 flighty 8 skittish 9 frivolous

rattling 4 very 5 brisk, quick 6 damned, lively, mighty 8 whacking, whopping 9 energetic, extremely 11 exceedingly

ratty 4 mean 5 dowdy, dumpy, tacky 6 cheesy, scurvy, shabby 7 unkempt 8 slovenly 10 despicable 11 treacherous 12 contemptible

raucous 4 loud 5 harsh, noisy, rough, rowdy 6 hoarse, unruly 7 grating, jarring, squawky 8 rowdyish, strident 9 termagant, turbulent 10 boisterous, disorderly, stridulent, stridulous, tumultuous 11 cacophonous 12 rambunctious

raunchy 4 foul 5 dirty, nasty 6 coarse, filthy, sloppy, smutty, vulgar 7 obscene 8 indecent 9 salacious

ravage 4 loot, raze, ruin, sack 5 foray, harry, spoil, strip, waste, wreck 6 forage, invade, ravish 7 despoil, overrun, pillage, plunder, ransack, scourge 8 desolate, spoliate 9 depredate, desecrate, devastate

rave 4 gush, rant 5 storm 6 babble, jabber 7 enthuse 10 rhapsodize

ravel 3 run 4 fray 5 snarl 6 muddle, tangle 7 perplex, untwine 8 entangle 9 extricate 10 complicate 11 disentangle

ravelings 4 lint 7 threads

Ravel work 6 Boléro 7 La Valse 14 Daphnis et Chloé 17 Rapsodie espagnole

raven 3 jet 4 ebon, inky, prey 5 black, ebony, jetty, sable 7 despoil, plunder 9 pitch-dark 10 pitch-black *relative:* 3 jay 4 crow 6 magpie 7 blue jay

Raven, The *author:* 3 Poe (Edgar Allan) *lost love:* 6 Lenore *refrain:* 9 Nevermore

ravenous 6 greedy, hungry 7 starved 8 edacious, famished, starving 9 rapacious, voracious 10 gluttonous

ravine 3 cut, gap 4 gulf, pass 5 abyss, chasm, cleft, clove, flume, gorge, gulch, gully, notch 6 arroyo, canyon, clough, coulee, defile, gutter, nullah 7 crevice, fissure 8 barranca, crevasse *Mt. Washington's:* 9 Tuckerman

raving 3 mad 5 manic, rabid, upset 6 crazed 7 frantic, lunatic, unglued 8 demented, deranged, frenetic, frenzied, maniacal, obsessed, unhinged, worked up 9 ravishing 10 distraught, flipped out, hysterical, irrational 11 overwrought

ravish 4 rape 5 force, spoil 6 defile 7 assault, despoil, outrage, pillage, plunder, violate 8 deflower, entrance, overcome 9 enrapture, transport

raw 4 cold, nude, rude 5 bleak, chill, crass, crude, fresh, green, naked, rough, young 6 callow, coarse, impure, native, unclad, unripe, vulgar 7 uncouth 8 immature, uncooked, unformed 9 au naturel, inelegant, irritated, run-of-mine, unbridled, unclothed, undressed, unrefined 10 unfinished, unpolished 13 inexperienced

rawboned 4 bony, lank, lean 5 gaunt, gawky, lanky, spare 6 skinny 7 angular, scraggy, scrawny

ray 4 beam 5 gleam, manta, shaft, skate, trace 6 radius, streak, stream 7 radiate, sawfish, sunbeam, torpedo 8 moonbeam 9 devilfish, thornback 10 guitarfish

raze 4 ruin 5 level 7 destroy 8 demolish, pull down, tear down

razor 6 shaver

razz 3 rag, rib 4 bait, josh, mock, twit 5 scout, taunt 6 badger, banter, deride, heckle, hector 8 ridicule (see also RASPBERRY)

RBI 11 run batted in 12 runs batted in

re 4 as to 5 as for 7 apropos 9 apropos

of, as regards, regarding 10 as respects, concerning, relating to, respecting 12 with regard to 13 with respect to

reach 4 beat, gain, pass, span, tack 5 carry, get at, get to, grasp, level, range, scope, sweep, touch 6 arrive, attain, extend, extent, rack up, thrust 7 achieve, horizon, project, stretch 9 encompass, influence 10 accomplish, get through

___ **reaction** 4 dark 5 alarm, chain, light 7 nuclear 8 chemical

reactivate 5 renew 6 revive 8 rekindle, revivify 9 resurrect 10 revitalize 11 resuscitate

read 4 scan, skim 6 peruse 8 pore over *inability to:* 8 dyslexia

readable 7 legible

reader 6 lector, primer 7 proofer, scanner 8 bookworm 9 anthology

readily 4 well 6 easily, freely 7 lightly 9 willingly 12 effortlessly

readiness 4 ease 5 skill 7 aptness 8 alacrity, dispatch, facility 9 dexterity, quickness 10 promptness 11 inclination, promptitude 12 preparedness

reading 6 lesson 7 lection, version, vulgate 9 rendition 10 recitation

ready 3 set 4 prep, ripe 5 equip 6 active, gear up, make up, primed, prompt 7 prepare 8 prepared 9 available, inclined

real 4 true, very 5 pukka, sound, valid 6 actual, honest 7 certain, genuine, sincere 8 bona fide, concrete, existent, tangible 9 authentic, undoubted, veridical 10 sure-enough, undeniable 11 substantive 12 indisputable

realism 6 verism 7 verismo 10 naturalism, pragmatism 11 objectivism, objectivity

realistic 4 sane 5 sober, sound 7 genuine, natural 8 lifelike, rational, sensible, veristic 9 practical, pragmatic 10 bottom-line, hard-boiled, hardheaded, reasonable, unromantic 11 down-to-earth 12 matter-of-fact 13 unsentimental

reality 4 fact, true 5 being, sooth, truth 9 actuality, existence, substance 13 flesh and blood

realize 4 gain 5 grasp, reach, score 6 attain, rack up 7 achieve, feature, imagine, reflect 8 conceive, envisage, envision 9 actualize, recognize 10 accomplish, comprehend

really 4 very 5 truly 6 indeed, verily 7 awfully, clearly 8 actually, honestly 9 assuredly, certainly, decidedly, genuinely 10 definitely, positively 11 exceedingly, indubitably, undoubtedly 12 unmistakably

realm 5 orbit, range, scope, sweep 6 domain, empire, estate, extent, radius, sphere 7 compass, demesne, kingdom, purview 8 dominion

ream 4 load, scad 5 widen 7 enlarge 11 countersink

reanimation 7 rebirth, revival 10 renascence, resurgence 11 reawakening, renaissance 12 risorgimento

reap 3 cut 4 earn, gain 5 glean, shear 6 garner, gather, obtain, sickle, thresh 7 harvest

rear 3 aft 4 back, butt, hind, lift, ramp, rump, seat, tail 5 after, breed, build, erect, fanny, hoist, nurse, put up, raise, set up 6 behind, bottom, fledge, foster, uphold 7 bring up, caboose, elevate, nurture 8 backside, buttocks, hindmost 9 construct, posterior

rear end 3 bum, bun, can 4 duff, moon, rump, seat, tail, tush 5 booty, fanny 6 behind, bottom, heinie 7 caboose, keister, tail end 8 backside, buttocks, derriere 9 posterior

rearmost 3 end 4 last 5 final 8 terminal, ultimate

rearrange see READJUST

rearward 3 aft 4 back 6 behind 8 backward 9 posterior 10 retrograde

Rea Silvia *father:* 7 Numitor *son:* 5 Remus 7 Romulus

reason 3 why, wit 4 mind, nous 5 basis, cause, infer, proof, think 6 excuse, ground, motive, sanity, senses 7 account, reflect 8 argument, cogitate, conceive, persuade 9 inference, intellect, rationale, soundness, speculate, wherefore 10 antecedent, deliberate 11 determinant, explanation 12 intelligence 13 consideration, justification, ratiocination, understanding

reasonable 4 fair, just 5 cheap, level, sound 6 modest 7 logical, low-cost, tenable 8 credible, feasible, moderate, rational, sensible 9 equitable, plausible 10 acceptable, affordable, restrained 11 inexpensive, intelligent

reasoning 4 case 5 logic 8 argument 9 deduction

reasonless 7 invalid 8 baseless 9 illogical, senseless, unfounded 10 fallacious, groundless, irrational 11 meaningless, purposeless

reawaken 5 renew 6 revive 7 refresh 8 revivify 9 reanimate 10 regenerate 12 reinvigorate

rebate 6 lessen, refund, return 8 decrease, diminish, give back 9 deduction, reduction

Rebecca *beloved:* 7 Ivanhoe *father:* 5 Isaac

Rebekah *brother:* 5 Laban *father:*
7 Bethuel *husband:* 5 Isaac *nurse:*
7 Deborah *son:* 4 Esau 5 Jacob

rebel 6 anarch, mutiny, resist, revolt
7 disobey 8 frondeur, mutineer 9 insurgent 10 malcontent 13 revolutionary, revolutionist

rebellion 6 émeute, mutiny, revolt, rising
8 defiance, intifada, sedition, uprising
10 insurgence, insurgency, resistance, revolution 12 insurrection

rebellious 6 unruly 8 mutinous, stubborn 9 insurgent 10 refractory 11 disaffected, disobedient 12 contumacious, unmanageable 13 insubordinate

rebirth 7 revival 9 awakening 10 conversion, renascence, resurgence 11 reanimation, reawakening, renaissance 12 resurrection, risorgimento

rebound 5 rally 6 bounce, reecho, recoil, repeat 7 recover 8 comeback, recovery, ricochet, snap back 10 convalesce

rebozo 5 scarf, shawl

rebuff 4 slap, snub 5 repel 6 reject 7 fend off, repulse, ward off 8 turn away

rebuild 6 repair, revamp 7 remodel, restore 8 overhaul, renovate, retrofit 9 modernize, refurbish 11 recondition, reconstruct 12 rehabilitate

rebuke 3 rap 4 snub 5 chide, scold, scorn 6 bawl out, berate, earful, lesson, rebuff 7 lecture, reproof, reprove 8 admonish, call down, reproach, scolding 9 reprimand, talking-to 10 tongue-lash 11 comeuppance, objurgation 12 admonishment, dressing-down 13 tongue-lashing

rebut 5 repel 6 refute, reject 7 confute, fend off, repulse, ward off 8 confound, disprove, stave off 10 controvert, disconfirm

rebuttal 5 reply 6 answer, retort 7 defense, riposte 8 argument, comeback, response 9 rejoinder 10 refutation 11 repudiation

recalcitrant 6 unruly 7 froward, willful 8 contrary, perverse, stubborn, untoward 9 fractious, obstinate, resistant 10 headstrong 11 intractable 12 ungovernable, unmanageable

recall 4 stir 5 evoke, renew, rouse, waken 6 arouse, awaken, cancel, memory, remind, repeal, revive, revoke 7 bethink, rescind, restore, retract, reverse 8 callback, remember, resemble, take back, withdraw 9 anamnesis, recollect, reinstate, reminisce, represent, reproduce 10 revocation 11 bring to mind, countermand, remembrance 12 recollection, reminiscence

recant 5 unsay 6 abjure, revoke 7 retract 8 forswear, renounce, take back, withdraw 9 backtrack, repudiate

recap 5 sum up 6 précis, résumé 7 reprise, retread, summary 8 overview 9 summarize 10 retrograde

recapitulate 5 sum up 6 resume 9 summarize 10 retrograde

recapitulation 5 sum-up 6 précis, résumé 7 epitome, reprise, summary 9 summing-up

recede 3 ebb 4 back 5 abate, taper 6 lessen, reduce, retire 7 dwindle, regress, retract, retreat 8 decrease, diminish, fall back, withdraw 10 retrograde, retrogress

receipts 4 gate, take 5 sales 6 income 7 revenue, takings 8 earnings, proceeds

receive 4 host 5 admit, catch, greet 6 accept, endure, suffer, take in 7 acquire, sustain, welcome 10 experience

received 5 plain, sound 6 common 7 popular 8 accepted, familiar, ordinary, orthodox 12 acknowledged, conventional

receiver 4 dish 5 donee, fence, pager 6 aerial 7 antenna, catcher, scanner 9 recipient, treasurer

recent 3 new 4 late 5 fresh, novel 6 latest, modern 8 neoteric

receptacle 6 hamper, holder, hopper, trough, vessel 9 container 10 repository

receptive 4 open 7 passive 8 amenable 9 sensitive 10 accessible, hospitable, open-minded, responsive 11 persuadable, persuasible, suggestible, susceptible

recess 4 cove, nook 5 break, cleft, niche 6 alcove, grotto, hiatus 7 adjourn 8 prorogue 9 prorogate, terminate 11 indentation

Recessional *author* 7 Kipling (Rudyard)

recessive 3 shy 8 retiring 9 reclusive, withdrawn 10 unsociable

recherché 4 rare 5 novel 6 choice, dainty, exotic, select 7 elegant, unusual 8 affected, delicate, original, superior, uncommon 9 exquisite 11 pretentious

recipe 7 formula 9 procedure 12 prescription

reciprocal 4 mate, twin 5 match 6 double, fellow, mutual 8 requited 9 companion, duplicate 10 coordinate 11 interactive *prefix:* 5 inter

reciprocate 5 repay 6 retort, return 7 requite 8 exchange 9 retaliate 10 compensate, recompense 11 interchange

recital 5 story 6 soiree 7 concert, reading 9 discourse, narration 10 recounting 11 enumeration, performance

recite 4 tell 5 chant, count, state 6 detail, number, relate, repeat, report, set out 7 declaim, narrate, recount, reel off 8 describe, rehearse 9 pronounce

reckless 4 rash, wild 5 brash, hasty 6 daring, madcap 8 carefree, heedless 9 audacious, daredevil, foolhardy, hot-headed 10 ill-advised, incautious 11 harebrained, temerarious, thought-less 12 devil-may-care 13 irresponsible

reckon 3 sum 5 count, gauge, guess, judge, tally, total 6 cipher, figure, number, regard 7 account, compute, suppose, surmise 8 consider, estimate 9 calculate, enumerate 10 conjecture 11 approximate

reckoning 3 tab 4 bill 5 tally, score 7 account, invoice 9 statement 10 arithmetic, estimation 11 calculation, computation

reclaim 4 save, tame 6 redeem, reform, rescue 7 deliver, recover, restore 9 restitute 11 recondition, reconstruct 12 rehabilitate

recline 3 lie 4 rest, tilt 5 couch, slant, slope 6 lounge, repose 7 lie down 10 stretch out

reclining 4 flat 5 prone 6 supine 9 decumbent, prostrate, recumbent

recluse 5 loner 6 hermit, shut-in 7 eremite 8 cenobite, solitary 9 anchorite *female:* 7 ancress 9 anchoress

reclusive 8 eremitic, hermetic, reserved, solitary 9 withdrawn 10 antisocial, eremitical, unsociable 12 misanthropic

recognition 6 credit, esteem, notice 9 attention, awareness, gratitude 10 cognizance, perception 11 realization 12 appreciation

recognize 4 note, spot 5 admit 6 notice 7 observe, realize 8 diagnose, identify 9 apprehend 10 appreciate 11 acknowledge, determinate, distinguish

recoil 4 balk, kick 5 cower, dodge, quail, start, wince 6 blench, cringe, flinch, shrink 7 rebound, retract, squinch 8 reaction

recollect 5 evoke 6 recall, remind, revive 7 bethink 8 remember 9 reminisce

recollection 6 memory, recall 9 anamnesis, flashback 11 remembrance 12 reminiscence

recommence 5 renew 6 pick up, reopen, resume, take up 7 restart 8 continue

recommend 4 tout 6 advise, praise, prefer 7 acclaim, commend, counsel, endorse, entrust, propose, suggest 8 advocate

recommendation 4 plug 5 pitch 6 advice 7 counsel 11 endorsement, testimonial

recompense 3 pay 4 wage 5 repay 6 amends, reward 7 guerdon, premium, redress, requite 8 gratuity, requital 9 indemnify, indemnity, quittance, reimburse, repayment 10 compensate, remunerate, reparation 11 reciprocate, restitution, retribution 12 compensation, remuneration 13 consideration, gratification

reconcile 4 suit, tune 5 adapt 6 accept, accord, adjust, attune, make up, resign, settle, square, submit, tailor 7 conform, get over, resolve 9 harmonize, integrate 10 conciliate, coordinate 11 accommodate

recondite 4 deep 6 hidden, mystic, occult, orphic, secret 7 cryptic, erudite, learned, obscure 8 abstruse, academic, esoteric, hermetic, profound 9 concealed, difficult, enigmatic, scholarly

recondition 3 fix 4 mend 6 doctor, repair, revamp 7 rebuild, restore 8 make over, overhaul, retrofit 9 restitute 10 rejuvenate 12 rehabilitate

reconnoiter 5 scout 6 survey

reconsider 6 review, revise 7 rethink, reweigh 8 reassess 9 reexamine 10 reevaluate 13 think better of

reconstruct 6 recast, re-form, remake, revamp 7 rebuild, reclaim, remodel, restore 8 make over, overhaul, readjust, renovate 9 refashion, restitute 10 reassemble, reorganize

record 4 disc, disk 5 album 6 annals, enroll 7 archive, journal, platter 8 archives, document, register 9 chronicle 10 transcript *of a meeting:* 7 minutes *of proceedings:* 4 acta *ship's:* 3 log 7 logbook

recorder 5 flute 9 registrar *flight:* 8 black box

record player 5 phono 8 Victrola 9 turntable 10 gramophone, phonograph

recount 4 tell 5 state 6 recite, relate, report, retail 7 narrate 8 describe, rehearse 9 enumerate

recoup 6 regain 7 get back, reclaim, recover 8 retrieve 9 repossess

recourse 6 backup, refuge, resort 7 standby, stopgap, support 8 resource 9 expedient, makeshift

recover 4 heal, mend 5 evict, rally, renew 6 recoup, redeem, regain, revive 7 get back, get over, improve, rebound, recycle, reclaim, restore 8 retrieve, snap back 9 come round, reacquire, recapture, re-collect, repossess, restitute 10 bounce back, convalesce, recuperate

recreant 3 rat 5 false 6 coward, craven,

untrue 7 chicken, dastard, unloyal
8 apostate, cowardly, defector, deserter,
disloyal, poltroon, renegade, turncoat
9 dastardly, faithless, turnabout 10 perfidious, traitorous, unfaithful 13 pusillanimous

recreate 4 play 5 evoke, renew 7 freshen,
refresh, restore 11 reconstruct

recreation 4 play 5 hobby, sport
7 leisure, pastime 8 activity 9 avocation, diversion 10 relaxation 13 entertainment

recrudesce 5 recur 6 return, revert,
revive 7 reoccur 8 break out

recruit 4 boot, hire 5 raise 6 engage,
enlist, enroll, muster, novice, rookie
7 draftee 8 beginner, enlistee, freshman,
headhunt, neophyte, newcomer 9 conscript, fledgling, reinforce, replenish
10 apprentice, tenderfoot

rectifier 4 tube 5 diode 8 detector, igni-
tron

rectify 3 fix 4 mend 5 amend, emend
6 adjust, remedy, repair 7 correct

rectitude 6 virtue 7 honesty, probity
8 morality 9 rightness 11 uprightness
13 righteousness

rector 6 parson, pastor, priest 9 clergyman 10 headmaster

rectory 5 manse 8 benefice 9 parsonage

recumbent 4 flat 5 prone 6 supine 7 leaning, resting 8 reposing 9 lying down,
prostrate, reclining

recuperate 4 heal, mend 5 rally 6 regain,
revive 7 rebound, recover 8 snap back
10 convalesce

recur 5 cycle, haunt 6 repeat, resort,
return 7 iterate, revolve 8 turn back

recurring 7 chronic 8 periodic 10 continuous, isochronal, periodical, persistent
11 isochronous 12 intermittent

red 4 puce, ruby 5 coral, gules, rouge,
ruddy 6 cerise, claret, florid, maroon
7 carmine, crimson, flushed, glowing,
magenta, oxblood, scarlet, vermeil
8 burgundy, sanguine 9 vermilion *combining form:* 4 rhod 5 rhodo

Red 6 Bolshy, commie 7 Bolshie, comrade 9 Bolshevik, Communist

redact 4 edit 6 censor, revise

Red and the Black author 8 Stendhal

red ape 9 orangutan

red arsenic 7 realgar

red-backed sandpiper 6 dunlin

Red Badge of Courage *author:* 5 Crane
(Stephen) *hero:* 7 Fleming (Henry)

red-bellied snipe 9 dowitcher

redbird 7 tanager 8 cardinal 13 summer
tanager

red blood cell 11 erythrocyte

red-blooded 5 juicy, lusty, manly
6 hearty, robust, virile 8 vigorous
9 energetic

redbreast 4 knot 5 robin 7 sunfish

red-breasted snipe 9 dowitcher

Redburn author 8 Melville (Herman)

red carp 8 goldfish

red cobalt 9 erythrite

red copper ore 7 cuprite

Red Cross *founder:* 6 Barton (Clara)
Knight: 6 George

redden 5 blush, color, flush, rouge
6 mantle, ruddle 11 incarnadine

red dog 5 blitz

redecorate 4 redo 5 fix up 9 refurbish

redeem 4 free, save 5 atone, loose,
renew 6 offset, pay off, ransom, reform,
rescue 7 expiate, reclaim, recover,
restore 9 exonerate

redeemer 5 Jesus 6 Christ, savior 7 messiah, saviour

redemption 6 ransom 7 release 9 atonement, expiation, salvation 11 deliverance

red-eye 5 hooch 6 flight, rotgut
7 whiskey 8 rock bass 9 moonshine

red-faced 5 ruddy 6 florid, shamed
7 abashed, flushed, glowing 8 blushing,
rubicund, sanguine, sheepish 9 mortified 11 embarrassed

redfish 4 bass, drum 5 perch 6 salmon
10 ocean perch 11 channel bass

red hickory 6 pignut

red-hot 5 fiery 6 ardent, fervid 7 blazing,
boiling, burning, fervent, flaming,
glowing 8 brand-new, scalding, sizzling
9 scorching 10 blistering, passionate,
sweltering 11 impassioned

red Indian paint 9 bloodroot 11 san-
guinaria

red ink 7 arrears, deficit 8 shortage

red inkberry 8 pokeweed

red ironbark 8 eucalypt 10 eucalyptus

red iron ore 5 ocher, ochre 8 hematite

red lauan 8 mahogany

red-legged crow 6 chough

red-legged sandpiper 9 turnstone

red-letter 7 notable 8 historic 9 important, memorable 10 noteworthy,
observable, remarkable 11 significant

red-light district 5 stews 10 tenderloin

red mite 7 chigger

redneck 4 clod, hick, rube 5 Bubba,
yahoo, yokel 6 rustic 7 bumpkin, hayseed 9 hillbilly 10 clodhopper, good old
boy, good ole boy

redo 5 renew 6 repeat, revamp 7 remodel, restyle 8 make over, overhaul, refin-
ish, renovate 9 refurbish 10 redecorate

red ocher 8 hematite

redolence 4 balm, odor **5** aroma, attar, scent, spice **7** bouquet, incense, perfume **9** fragrance

redolent 5 balmy, spicy, sweet **7** odorous, scented **8** aromatic, fragrant, perfumed **9** ambrosial, evocative **10** suggestive **11** reminiscent

redouble 4 dupe **7** dualize, enhance, magnify **8** heighten **9** duplicate, intensify, reinforce **10** strengthen

redoubt 4 fort **7** bastion, citadel **8** fastness, fortress **10** stronghold

redoubtable 5 famed, great **6** famous, mighty **7** awesome, eminent **8** imposing, puissant, renowned **9** prominent **10** celebrated, formidable, impressive **11** illustrious **12** intimidating, overwhelming **13** distinguished

redound 6 accrue, recoil **7** conduce, reflect **10** contribute

red pigment 5 ocher, ochre **6** ruddle

Red Planet 4 Mars

redpoll 5 finch **6** linnet

redraft 6 revamp, revise, rework **7** restyle, rewrite **8** make over, overhaul, rescript, revision, work over **9** recension

redress 4 heal **6** amends, avenge, negate, offset, relief, remedy **7** correct **8** reprisal, requital **9** cancel out, indemnity, quittance, vindicate **10** compensate, counteract, correction, neutralize, recompense, reparation **11** restitution, retribution **12** compensation

red roe 5 coral **6** caviar

redroot 7 alkanet, pigweed **9** bloodroot **12** New Jersey tea

red sable 8 kolinsky

red silver ore 9 proustite

red squirrel 9 chickaree

reduce 3 cut **4** cull, diet, melt, pare **5** abate, force, lower, shade, shave, slash, smelt **6** humble, lessen, recede, weaken **7** abridge, curtail, cut back, cut down, dwindle, liquefy, squeeze **8** boil down, compress, contract, decrease, diminish, discount, mark down, minimize, simplify, taper off **10** depreciate, slenderize **11** consolidate

reductio ad ___ 8 absurdum

reduction 6 digest, précis, rebate **7** cutback, cutdown, epitome, summary **8** abstract, discount, markdown, synopsis **9** abatement **10** shortening **11** curtailment **12** condensation

redundancy 6 excess **7** nimiety, surfeit **8** pleonasm **9** abundance, profusion, prolixity, tautology **10** repetition **11** periphrasis, reiteration, superfluity **13** supernumerary

redundant 5 extra, spare, windy, wordy

6 prolix **7** surplus, verbose **9** duplicate, excessive, iterative **11** duplicative, reiterative, repetitious, superfluous, tautologous **13** supernumerary

redux 7 revived **8** restored

redwing 6 thrush **9** blackbird

redwood 7 amboyna, sequoia **8** mahogany

reed 4 pipe **5** arrow, grass

reedy 4 thin **6** skinny, stalky, twiggy **7** spindly

reef 3 bar, cay, key **4** lode, vein **5** atoll, ledge **6** reduce, skerry **7** sandbar

reek 4 funk **5** fetor, smell, stink **6** stench **9** effluvium

reeking 4 rank **5** fetid, funky, fusty **6** putrid, rancid, smelly, stinky **7** noisome, stenchy **10** malodorous

reel 4 spin, sway, turn **5** lurch, spool, weave, whirl **6** bobbin, careen, teeter, totter, waggle, wobble **7** stagger, stumble **8** fall back

reestablish 5 renew **6** revive **7** restore **9** reinstate **10** reinscribe **11** reintroduce

reevaluate 6 review **7** rethink, reweigh **8** reassess **9** reexamine **10** reconsider

reeve 4 ruff **6** thread **9** sandpiper **10** magistrate

reexamine see REEVALUATE

refashion 5 alter **6** change, modify, recast, remake, revamp **7** remodel **8** make over, overhaul **9** transmute

refection 4 feed, meal **6** repast **11** nourishment, refreshment

refectory 10 dining hall

refer 6 advert, allude, assign, relate, submit **7** ascribe **9** attribute

referee 3 ump **5** judge **6** umpire **7** adjudge, arbiter, mediate **8** mediator **9** arbitrate, officiate **10** adjudicate, arbitrator

reference 5 atlas **6** credit, source **7** almanac, meaning, mention **8** allusion, citation, innuendo, relation, resource **9** directory **10** dictionary **11** testimonial **12** encyclopedia

reference book 5 atlas, bible, guide **6** manual **7** almanac **8** handbook **9** guidebook **10** dictionary **11** enchiridion **12** encyclopedia

reference guide 5 index **12** bibliography

referendum 4 poll, vote **10** plebiscite

refine 5 smelt, prune **6** polish, purify, smooth **7** elevate, improve, perfect, process **8** civilize **9** cultivate

refined 4 pure **6** subtle, urbane **7** elegant, genteel, raffiné **8** cultured, elevated, ladylike, raffinée, well-bred **9** civilized **10** cultivated, fastidious **13** sophisticated

refinement 5 couth, grace, taste **6** finish,

polish **7** culture, finesse, suavity **8** breeding, civility, courtesy, elegance, subtlety, urbanity **9** politesse **10** politeness **11** cultivation **12** civilization, distillation, purification **13** clarification

reflect 4 echo, pore, show **5** weigh **6** bounce, mirror, ponder, reason, return **7** redound **8** chew over, cogitate, consider, ruminate **9** cerebrate **10** deliberate, retrospect **11** contemplate, demonstrate

reflection 4 slur **5** image **6** musing **7** replica, thought **8** reproach **9** aspersion **10** cogitation, meditation, rumination, simulacrum **11** cerebration **12** deliberation, reproduction **13** animadversion, consideration, contemplation

reflective 7 pensive **9** reflexive **10** cogitative, indicative, meditative, ruminative, thoughtful **12** deliberative **13** contemplative

reflux 3 ebb **4** GERD **8** backflow

reform 5 amend, emend **6** redeem, revise **7** correct, improve, reclaim, shape up **8** make over **10** correction, houseclean, regenerate

Reformation leader 4 Knox (John) **6** Calvin (John), Luther (Martin) **7** Zwingli (Huldrych)

reformatory 3 pen **6** prison **7** borstal **8** big house, remedial **10** corrective **12** penitentiary

refractory 6 mulish, unruly **7** froward, restive **8** contrary, perverse, stubborn **9** obstinate **10** bullheaded, headstrong, rebellious, unyielding **11** intractable, stiff-necked **12** unmanageable

refrain 4 keep, stop **6** burden, chorus, shrink **7** abstain, forbear **8** hold back

refresh 5 renew **6** revive **7** animate, enliven, quicken, restore **8** irrigate, recreate, renovate **9** replenish, stimulate **10** rejuvenate

refresher 5 drink, tonic **6** bracer **8** reminder **9** stimulant **11** restorative

refreshing 5 brisk, tonic **7** bracing **8** reviving **9** analeptic, animating **10** delightful, energizing **11** restorative, stimulating **12** invigorating, rejuvenating

refrigerant 3 ice **5** freon **7** coolant, cryogen **12** fluorocarbon **13** sulfur dioxide

refrigerator 6 cooler, fridge, icebox, walk-in **9** condenser **10** Frigidaire

refuge 4 lair, port **5** cover, haven **6** asylum, covert, harbor, resort **7** hideout, protect, retreat, shelter **8** hideaway, recourse, resource **9** expedient, harborage, sanctuary, safe house

refugee 5 exile **6** émigré **7** evacuee

8 emigrant, fugitive **10** boat person, expatriate

refulgent 6 bright **7** glowing, radiant **8** luminous **9** brilliant

refund 5 repay **6** rebate **8** give back **9** reimburse, repayment, restitute **11** restitution

refurbish 4 redo **5** fix up, renew **6** revamp **7** restore **8** make over, overhaul, renovate **10** redecorate, rejuvenate **11** recondition

refusal 4 veto **6** denial **7** regrets **8** negative, negation **9** disavowal **10** abnegation **11** declination, repudiation

refuse 3 jib, nix **4** deny, junk, scum **5** dreck, dross, offal, spurn, swill, trash, waste **6** debris, litter, reject, scraps, spilth **7** decline, garbage, residue, rubbish **8** disallow, leavings, remnants, turn down, withhold **9** reprobate, repudiate, sweepings **10** disapprove

refutation 8 disproof, elenchus, rebuttal

refute 4 deny **5** rebut **7** confute **8** confound, disprove **10** controvert, disconfirm

regain 6 recoup **7** get back, recover **8** reoccupy, retrieve **9** recapture, repossess *possession:* **7** replevy **8** replevin

regal 5 grand **6** august, kingly, purple **7** queenly, stately, sublime **8** glorious, imperial, imposing, kinglike, majestic, princely, splendid **9** monarchal, sovereign **10** monarchial **11** magnificent, monarchical, resplendent

regale 4 feed **5** amuse, feast **6** dinner, divert, spread **7** banquet **9** entertain

regalia 5 array **6** finery **8** frippery, insignia **10** caparison, full dress, trappings **10** decoration **11** habiliments

Regan *father:* **4** Lear *husband:* **8** Cornwall *sister:* **7** Goneril **8** Cordelia

regard 4 deem, heed, mark, note, rate, view **5** assay, favor, honor, judge, value **6** admire, assess, esteem, homage, liking, notice, reckon, repute **7** account, concern, respect **8** approval, consider, devotion, estimate, fondness **9** attention **10** admiration, cognizance, estimation, observance, solicitude **11** approbation, contemplate, observation **12** appreciation, satisfaction **13** consideration

regardful 7 heedful **8** watchful **9** advertent, attentive, observant **10** perceptive, respectful

regarding 4 as to, in re **5** about, anent, as for **7** apropos **8** touching **9** apropos of **10** as respects, concerning, relative to, respecting **11** in respect to **13** with respect to

regatta 4 race

regenerate 5 renew **6** reform, revive **7** rebirth, restore **8** recreate **9** reproduce

regent 5 ruler **6** warden **8** governor **9** protector

regicide's victim 4 king

regime 4 rule, term **5** reign **6** empire, tenure **7** dynasty **10** government, leadership

regimen 4 diet, plan, rule **6** course **10** government

region 4 area, belt, part, zone **5** field, tract **6** domain, locale, sector, sphere **7** demesne, terrain **8** locality, province, vicinity **9** bailiwick, territory **12** neighborhood

regional 5 local **9** localized, sectional **10** provincial **11** territorial

register 4 file, list, note, roll, till **5** enter, range, tally **6** annals, docket, enroll, ledger, record, roster **7** catalog, check in, express **8** indicate **9** catalogue

regnant 4 rife **6** ruling **7** current, popular **8** dominant, reigning **9** paramount, prevalent, sovereign **10** prevailing, widespread

regress 6 revert **9** backslide **10** retrograde

regret 3 rue, woe **4** care **5** grief, mourn **6** bemoan, bewail, excuse, grieve, lament, repent, sorrow **7** anguish, apology, deplore, remorse **9** heartache, penitence **10** contrition, heartbreak **11** compunction

regretful 5 sorry **6** rueful **8** contrite, mournful, penitent **9** repentant, sorrowful **10** apologetic, remorseful **11** penitential

regrettable 3 sad **6** too bad, woeful **8** grievous **10** lamentable **11** distressing, unfortunate **13** heartbreaking

regular 3 due, set **4** even **5** fixed, usual **6** common, normal, steady **7** average, equable, general, natural, orderly, typical, uniform **8** complete, constant, everyday, methodic, ordinary, standard **9** clocklike, customary, prevalent **10** methodical, systematic **11** commonplace **12** run-of-the-mill

regulate 5 order, scale **6** adjust, direct, govern, police, square, temper **7** arrange, control **8** organize **9** methodize, systemize **11** systematize

regulation 3 law **4** rule **5** canon, edict, order **6** decree **7** precept, statute **9** ordinance, prescript **11** restriction **12** codification

regulator 8 governor

rehabilitate 4 cure, heal **7** reclaim, recover, restore **8** renovate **9** reeducate, restitute **11** recondition

rehash 5 reuse **6** repeat, review, rework **7** restate, version **8** chew over, rehearse, talk over **9** rendering, rendition, rewording **11** restatement **12** recapitulate

rehearse 5 drill, train **6** repeat **7** run over **8** exercise, practice **10** run through

Rehoboam *father:* **7** Solomon *kingdom:* **5** Judah **6** Israel *mother:* **6** Naamah

reign 4 rule, sway **6** govern **7** prevail **8** dominate, dominion **11** predominate, sovereignty

reimburse 3 pay **5** repay **6** recoup, refund **7** requite **9** indemnify **10** compensate, remunerate

rein 4 curb, stem **5** check **6** bridle **7** compose, control, repress **8** hold back, restrain, suppress

reinforce 4 prop **5** brace **7** augment, bolster, enlarge, fortify, recruit, sustain **8** buttress, increase, redouble **10** invigorate, strengthen

reinstate 6 recall **7** restore **11** reestablish, reintroduce **12** rehabilitate

reintroduce 6 recall, revive **7** restore **9** reinstate **11** reestablish

reinvestment 4 DRIP **8** plowback

reiterate 5 renew, resay **6** repeat, resume, retell **7** reprise

reject 3 nix **4** jilt, junk, shed **5** debar, scorn, scrap, spurn **6** abjure, pariah, pass up, rebuff, refuse **7** cashier, castoff, decline, discard, dismiss, exclude, outcast, repulse, shut out **8** castaway, jettison, throw out, turn away, turn down **9** eliminate, repudiate, shoot down, throw away **10** disapprove

rejoice 5 cheer, exult, glory **7** delight, gladden **8** jubilate

rejoinder 5 reply **6** answer, retort **8** comeback, rebuttal, repartee, response

rejuvenate 5 green, renew **7** refresh **8** renovate **9** modernize **10** revitalize

rekindle 5 renew **6** revive **7** restart **8** reawaken, reignite, revivify **10** reactivate, revitalize

relate 4 link, tell **5** apply, refer **6** assign, detail, recite, report **7** connect, express, pertain, recount **8** describe, disclose, interact, rehearse **9** appertain, chronicle

related 4 akin **5** alike, enate **6** agnate, allied **7** cognate, connate, germane, kindred **8** incident **9** analogous, connected, identical, pertinent **10** associated, connatural, homologous **11** consanguine

relation 3 kin **6** agnate **7** hinship, kinsman **8** affinity **9** kinswoman, reference **11** propinquity

relationship 3 tie 4 bond, link 5 ratio, tie-in, union 6 affair 7 analogy, contact, liaison 8 affinity, alliance 10 connection 11 affiliation, association 13 confederation, consanguinity

relative 3 mom, sib, sis, son 4 aunt, mama, papa 5 blood, madre, mamma, momma, niece, pappy, pater, poppa, uncle 6 agnate, cousin, father, mother, nephew, parent, sister 7 apropos, brother, cognate, germane, kinsman, sibling 8 ancestor, daughter, grandson, relation, relevant 9 ascendant, dependent, kinswoman, pertinent 10 applicable, collateral, descendant, grandchild 11 comparative, conditional, grandfather, grandmother, grandparent 13 granddaughter

relatives 3 kin 4 kith 5 folks 7 kindred, kinfolk 8 kinfolks 9 relations

relax 4 bask, ease, loll, rest 5 chill, let go, loose, remit 6 loosen, lounge, modify, unkink, unwind 7 slacken 8 chill out, kick back, loosen up, unbuckle, wind down 9 untighten 10 decompress

relaxation 3 fun 4 ease, rest 5 hobby 6 repose 7 leisure, pastime 9 amusement, diversion, enjoyment 10 recreation

relaxed 5 loose, slack 6 casual, dégagé, mellow 8 informal 9 easygoing 11 low-pressure

release 4 emit, free, vent 5 issue, loose, untie, yield 6 acquit, loosen, pardon, ransom, unbind, uncage 7 give off, give out, manumit, set free, unchain, unleash 8 liberate, unfetter 9 acquittal, discharge, exculpate, exonerate, surrender 10 emancipate 11 manumission 12 emancipation *conditional:* 6 parole

relegate 5 exile, expel 6 assign, banish, charge, commit, demote, resign 7 commend, confide, consign, entrust 8 delegate, hand over, transfer, turn over

relent 3 ebb 4 cave, ease, wane 5 abate, let up, yield 6 give in, submit 7 die away, die down, ease off, slacken, subside 8 moderate 9 acquiesce 10 capitulate

relentless 5 cruel, rigid, stern 6 dogged 7 adamant, nonstop 8 constant, obdurate, rigorous, unabated 9 ferocious, incessant, stringent 10 implacable, inexorable, inflexible, unyielding 11 remorseless, unfaltering

relevant 3 apt, fit 5 ad rem 6 cogent 7 apropos, germane 8 apposite, material, relative 9 pertinent 10 admissible, applicable 11 applicative, appropriate 12 proportional

reliable 4 safe, sure 5 solid, sound, tried,

valid 6 proven, secure, trusty 7 bedrock, certain 8 constant, verified 9 foolproof, validated 10 dependable 11 trustworthy 12 tried-and-true

reliance 4 hope 5 faith, stock, trust 10 dependence

relic 5 token 6 corpse 7 antique, memento, remains, remnant, vestige 8 artifact, fragment, keepsake, memorial, reminder, souvenir 11 remembrance

relict 5 widow 8 survivor

relief 3 aid 4 ease, fret, hand, help, lift 5 break, cameo 6 assist, raised, remedy, succor 7 comfort, redress, respite, support, welfare 8 breather, fretwork, repoussé 9 abatement, diversion 10 assistance, mitigation 11 alleviation, deliverance *pitcher:* 6 closer 7 fireman, stopper

relieve 3 rid 4 calm, ease, free, help, quit, vent 5 allay, relax, spell 6 assist, exempt, lessen, reduce, remedy, soften, solace, soothe, succor, supply 7 absolve, assuage, comfort, deprive, lighten, mollify,

religion 4 cult, sect 5 cause, creed, dogma, faith 6 belief, church 8 devotion, doctrine

religious 3 nun 4 holy, monk 5 friar, godly, pious 6 devout, priest, sacred, votary 7 staunch, upright 8 cenobite, faithful, monastic, priestly, reverent 9 pietistic, prayerful, spiritual, steadfast 10 scriptural, scrupulous, worshipful

relinquish 4 cede, quit, shed 5 forgo, leave, waive, yield 6 desert, give up, resign 7 abandon, discard, lay down, release 8 abdicate, hand over, renounce 9 quitclaim, sacrifice, surrender

relish 4 like, tang, zest 5 enjoy, fancy, flair, gusto, savor, taste 6 flavor, liking, palate 7 delight 8 fondness, penchant, pleasure, sapidity 9 appetizer, condiment, enjoyment 10 appreciate 11 delectation, hors d'oeuvre

relucent 6 bright 7 glaring, radiant, shining 10 reflecting

reluctant 3 shy 4 wary 5 chary, loath 6 afraid, averse 8 cautious, grudging, hesitant 9 unwilling 10 indisposed 11 disinclined *prophet:* 5 Jonah

rely 3 bet 4 bank, plan 5 count 6 depend, gamble, reckon

rely on 5 trust 6 expect 10 anticipate

remain 4 bide, last, live, stay, wait 5 abide, tarry 6 endure, linger, loiter 7 persist, survive 8 continue 10 hang around 11 stick around

remainder 4 rest 5 dregs, trace 6 excess 7 balance, residue, remnant, surplus, vestige 8 leavings, leftover, residual, residuum

remains 4 body 5 ashes, bones, ruins 6 corpse, debris, relics 7 balance, cadaver, carcass, flotsam 8 leavings, remnants 9 reliquiae

remand 8 send back

remark 4 gibe, note 5 aside, crack 7 comment, mention 9 utterance, wisecrack, witticism 10 annotation 11 observation 12 obiter dictum

remarkable 4 rare 5 great 6 signal, unique 7 salient, strange, unusual 8 singular, striking, uncommon 9 arresting, bodacious, momentous, prominent 10 impressive, noteworthy, noticeable 11 conspicuous, exceptional, outstanding, significant 13 extraordinary

___ **Remarque** 5 Erich (Maria)

remedial 8 curative, salutary, sanative 9 medicinal 10 corrective 11 restorative, therapeutic 12 recuperative

remedy 3 fix 4 cure, drug, heal 5 salve, solve 6 elixir, relief, repair 7 correct, cure-all, nostrum, panacea, rectify, redress, relieve 8 antidote, medicine, specific 9 alleviate, treatment 10 corrective, medicament, medication

remember 5 educe, evoke 6 recall, record, relive, retain, reward 7 bethink 9 flash back, recollect, reminisce 10 bear in mind 11 commemorate, memorialize

remembrance 4 gift 5 favor, relic, token 6 memory, recall, trophy 7 memento, present, thought 8 keepsake, memorial, reminder, souvenir 9 anamnesis, flashback 12 recollection, reminiscence

remind 6 advise, prompt 7 bethink 8 admonish

reminder 4 hint, memo 5 relic, token 6 prompt, trophy 7 memento 8 keepsake, memorial, monument, souvenir 9 refresher 10 admonition, memorandum 11 remembrance

reminisce see REMEMBER

reminiscence 6 memory, recall 8 anecdote 9 anamnesis, flashback 11 remembrance 12 recollection

remise 4 cede, deed 5 alien, grant 6 assign, convey 8 make over, transfer 9 quitclaim

remiss 3 lax 4 lazy 5 slack 8 careless, derelict, heedless, indolent, slothful 9 negligent 10 delinquent, neglectful, slatternly 11 inattentive

remit 4 send, ship, stay, stop 5 abate, defer, delay, relax 6 desist, hold up, pardon, put off, remand, shelve 7 condone, consign, forgive, forward, hold off 8 dispatch, moderate, postpone

remnant 3 end 4 heel, husk, part, rest, rump 5 relic, trace, wrack 6 fag end, relict 7 balance, oddment, residue 8 leavings, leftover, residuum 9 remainder

remodel 4 redo 6 recast, revamp 8 make over, overhaul, redesign 9 refashion 11 reconstruct

remonstrance 5 demur 7 protest 8 demurral, demurrer 9 challenge, objection

remonstrate 5 argue, demur, plead 6 combat, object, oppose, reason 7 protest 9 challenge

remora 4 clog, drag 6 sucker 9 hindrance 10 impediment 11 encumbrance, shark sucker

remorse 3 rue 4 ruth 5 guilt, smart 6 regret, sorrow 9 penitence 10 contrition, repentance 11 compunction 12 self-reproach

remorseful see REGRETFUL

remote 3 far, off 4 slim 5 aloof 6 far-off, slight 7 distant, faraway, obscure, outside, slender 8 detached, far-flung, frontier, isolated, lonesome, off-lying, outlying, secluded 9 backwoods, withdrawn 10 negligible 11 godforsaken, out-of-the-way *combining form:* 3 tel 4 tele

remotest 6 utmost 7 extreme, outmost 8 farthest 9 outermost, uttermost 11 furthermost

remove 4 doff, skim 5 purge 6 unseat 7 extract, take off, take out 8 dislodge, evacuate, take away, withdraw 9 clear away, eliminate *from office:* 6 depose *hair:* 8 depilate *surgically:* 6 resect

removed 5 aloof, apart 6 far-off, remote 7 devious, distant, faraway, obscure 8 detached, far-flung, isolated, outlying, separate 10 distracted 11 unconnected

remunerate 3 pay 5 repay 7 requite 9 indemnify, reimburse 10 compensate, recompense

remunerative 6 paying 7 gainful, payable 9 lucrative 10 productive, profitable 11 moneymaking

Remus *brother:* 7 Romulus *father:* 4 Mars *mother:* 9 Rea Silvia 10 Rhea Silvia *slayer:* 7 Romulus

renaissance see REBIRTH

renal 7 nephric 9 nephritic

rend 3 rip 4 rive, tear 5 split 6 cleave, divide

render 3 pay 4 cede, limn 5 yield 6 depict, give up, impart, return, submit 7 deliver, execute, pay back, picture, portray, provide, restore 8 carry out, describe, hand over, turn over

9 delineate, interpret, represent, translate, transpose 10 administer, relinquish 12 administrate

rendering 4 copy 7 version 9 depiction 10 paraphrase 11 description, performance, restatement, translation 12 reproduction

rendezvous 4 date 5 haunt, tryst 6 gather, muster 7 collect, hangout, meeting 8 assemble 10 congregate, engagement 11 appointment, assignation, gettogether

rendition 7 reading, version 10 adaptation 11 performance, translation

renegade 3 rat 5 rebel 6 outlaw 7 heretic 8 apostate, defector, deserter, maverick, recreant, turncoat 9 turnabout 10 schismatic

renege 4 deny 5 welsh 6 cry off, recall, recant, revoke 7 back off, back out, retract 8 renounce, withdraw 9 backpedal

renew 6 redeem, reform, revamp, revive 7 freshen, refresh, remodel 8 make over, overhaul, recharge, recreate, rekindle, renovate, revivify 9 refurbish, resurrect 10 reactivate, recommence, regenerate, rejuvenate, revitalize

rennet 8 abomasum

renounce 4 deny, quit 5 demit 6 abjure, defect, desert, give up, recant, renege, resign 7 abandon, decline, forsake, put away, retract 8 abdicate, abnegate, disclaim, forswear, swear off 9 repudiate, sacrifice 10 apostatize

renovate 4 redo 5 renew 6 remake, repair, revamp, revive 7 furbish, refresh, restore 8 overhaul, revivify 9 modernize, refurbish, resurrect 10 rejuvenate, revitalize 12 rehabilitate

renown 4 fame 5 éclat, glory, kudos 6 repute 7 acclaim 8 eminence, prestige 9 celebrity, notoriety 10 prominence, reputation 11 distinction

renowned 5 famed, great, noted 6 fabled, famous 7 eminent, notable 8 extolled 9 acclaimed, legendary, notorious, prominent, well-known 10 celebrated 11 illustrious, outstanding 13 distinguished

rent 3 let, rip 4 hire, rift, tear, torn 5 lease, split 6 breach, sublet 7 charter, fissure, rupture 8 fracture

rental 4 hire 7 tenancy

renter 6 lessee, tenant 11 leaseholder

renunciation 6 denial 7 refusal 8 apostasy, eschewal, forgoing 9 disavowal, sacrifice, surrender 10 abdication, abnegation, disclaimer, self-denial 11 abandonment, forswearing, repudiation, resignation

reorder 5 shift 7 permute 9 rearrange, reshuffle

reorganization 7 shake-up 8 turnover

repair 3 fix 4 mend 5 patch 6 cobble, doctor 7 fitness, service 8 overhaul 9 condition 11 recondition

reparations 6 amends 7 redress 9 indemnity, quittance 10 recompense, settlement 11 restitution 12 satisfaction

repartee 4 quip 6 banter, retort 7 riposte 8 backchat, badinage, comeback 9 cross talk, rejoinder 10 persiflage

repast 3 eat 4 feed, meal 5 feast 9 refection

repay 6 offset, return, reward 7 requite 9 indemnify, reimburse 10 compensate, recompense, remunerate 11 get even with

repeal 4 lift, void 5 annul 6 recall, revoke 7 abandon, abolish, nullify, rescind, reverse 8 abrogate, renounce

repeat 4 copy, echo 5 recap, recur, rerun, resay 6 go over, parrot, reecho, recite, rehash, relate, retell 7 imitate, iterate, reprise, restate 9 duplicate, reiterate, replicate 11 reduplicate 12 recapitulate

repeater 7 firearm 10 recidivist

repeating 7 iterant 9 perennial, recurrent 11 reiterative, repetitious

repel 5 rebut 6 rebuff, reject, revolt, sicken 7 disgust, fend off, hold off, repulse, ward off 8 nauseate, stave off

repellent 4 foul, vile 5 nasty 7 noisome 8 aversive 9 abhorrent, loathsome, obnoxious, offensive, repulsive, revolting 10 forbidding, disgusting, off-putting 11 rebarbative

repent 3 rue 6 regret

repentance 3 rue 4 ruth 6 sorrow 7 remorse 10 contrition 11 compunction

repentant see REGRETFUL

repetition 4 copy, echo 5 rerun 7 recital, reprise 11 duplication

rephrase 6 recast, reword 7 restate

repine 4 beef, fuss, kick, long, moan, wail 5 gripe, yearn 6 grouse, hanker, murmur 7 grumble 8 complain

replace 7 put back, restore 8 exchange, supplant 9 supersede 10 substitute

replacement 3 sub 6 fill-in, makeup 7 stand-in 9 alternate, surrogate, temporary 10 substitute 11 locum tenens, pinch hitter, succedaneum

replenish 4 fill 5 renew, stock 6 refill 7 refresh, restore

replete 4 full, rife 5 awash, lousy 7 brimful, crammed, stuffed 8 brimming 9 chock-full 11 overflowing

replica 4 copy, dupe, fake 5 clone, ditto 6 carbon 9 duplicate, facsimile, imitation 10 carbon copy, simulacrum 12 reproduction

replicate 4 copy 5 clone 6 repeat 9 reproduce

reply 4 echo 6 answer, rejoin, retort 7 respond 8 comeback, repartee, response 9 rejoinder

report 4 bang, boom, news, tell 5 crack, relay, rumor, study 6 record, relate, return, review, show up 7 account, article, check in, hearsay, narrate, recount, rundown 8 advisory, bulletin, describe, dispatch 9 broadcast, chronicle, narrative, statement 11 compte rendu

reporter 7 newsman 8 pressman 9 newshound, newswoman 10 journalist *inexperienced:* 3 cub

repose 3 lie 4 calm, rest 5 peace, poise, quiet, sleep 7 lie down, recline 8 quietude 9 composure, stillness 10 inactivity, quiescence, relaxation 11 restfulness, tranquility 12 tranquillity

repository 3 ark 5 depot, store 7 archive, arsenal 8 magazine, treasury 10 storehouse

repossess see REGAIN

reprehend 3 rap 4 rate, skin 5 blame, chide, fault, knock, scold 6 berate, rebuke 7 censure, condemn, upbraid 8 admonish, denounce 9 criticize 10 denunciate

reprehensible 4 base, evil 6 guilty, sinful, unholy, wicked 8 blamable, criminal, culpable 10 censurable 11 blameworthy, disgraceful

represent 3 act 6 denote, depict, embody, mirror, recall, relate, render, sketch, typify 7 display, exhibit, express, hold out, imitate, make out, narrate, outline, picture, portray, present, protest, realize, signify, suggest 8 describe, stand for 9 delineate, epitomize, exemplify, interpret, personify, symbolize 10 constitute, illustrate, substitute 11 emblematize, impersonate

representation 5 draft, image 6 effigy, symbol 7 picture 8 likeness 9 portrayal, statement 10 caricature, delegation

representative 5 agent, envoy, model, proxy 6 deputy, sample 7 burgess, example, typical 8 delegate, emissary, sampling, specimen 9 exemplary, spokesman 10 ambassador, legislator, prototypal, substitute 11 congressman 12 illustrative, prototypical 13 congresswoman

repress 4 curb 5 check, sit on 6 bridle, muffle, stifle, subdue 7 smother, squelch, swallow 8 keep down, restrain, suppress

repression 4 curb 7 amnesia, control 8 stifling 9 clampdown, crackdown, restraint 10 constraint

reprieve 4 stay 5 grace 7 respite, suspend

reprimand 3 rap 4 rate, ream, task 5 chide, scold 6 rebuke 7 bawl out, censure, chew out, reproof, reprove 8 admonish, call down, reproach, scolding 9 reprimand, talking-to 10 admonition 12 admonishment, dressing-down 13 tongue-lashing

reprisal 7 redress, revenge 8 revanche 9 vengeance 11 counterblow, retaliation, retribution

reprise 5 recap 6 repeat 9 reiterate 10 recurrence, repetition

reproach 3 rap 4 rail 5 blame, chide, scold 6 berate, rebuke 7 bawl out, censure, chew out, remorse, reprove, upbraid 8 admonish, call down 9 reprimand 10 admonition, opprobrium 12 admonishment

reprobate 3 rap 4 skin 5 blame, scamp, spurn 6 refuse, reject, sinner 7 censure, condemn, lowlife, villain 8 denounce, scalawag 9 miscreant, scoundrel 10 blackguard, degenerate

reproduce 4 bear, copy 5 beget, breed, spore 7 imitate 8 multiply 9 duplicate, procreate, propagate, replicate 10 regenerate 11 reduplicate

reproduction see REPLICA

reproductive cell 3 egg 4 ovum 5 sperm, spore 6 gamete 12 spermatozoid, spermatozoon

reproof 3 rap 6 rebuke 7 censure, lecture 8 scolding 9 criticism, reprimand 10 admonition 11 castigation 12 admonishment, reprehension 13 remonstration

reprove 5 chide, scold 6 rebuke 7 censure, chasten 8 admonish, call down, lambaste, reproach 9 criticize, dress down, reprimand

reptile 5 snake 6 caiman, cayman, gavial, iguana, lizard, turtle 7 tuatara 8 tortoise 9 alligator, crocodile, sphenodon *combining form:* 6 herpet 7 herpeto *extinct:* 8 dinosaur

republic 5 state 6 nation 9 democracy

Republican Party 3 GOP *mascot:* 8 elephant

Republic author 5 Plato

repudiate 4 deny 5 spurn 6 abjure, disown, recant, refuse, reject 7 decline, disavow, dismiss 8 disclaim, renounce 9 disaffirm 10 apostatize, disapprove

repugnance 6 horror 7 disgust 8 aversion, loathing 9 repulsion, revulsion 10 abhorrence, antagonism, odiousness 11 abomination, detestation

repugnant 4 foul, vile **5** nasty, yucky **6** creepy, horrid, skanky **7** noisome **8** aversive, gruesome **9** abhorrent, loathsome, obnoxious, offensive, repulsive, revolting **10** disgusting

repulse 5 rebut, repel, spurn **6** rebuff, reject, revolt, sicken **7** disgust, fend off, hold off, ward off **8** nauseate, stave off

repulsion see REPUGNANCE

repulsive see REPUGNANT

reputable 7 eminent, upright **8** esteemed **9** estimable, honorable **10** creditable, legitimate, recognized, sanctioned **11** respectable, trustworthy **13** well-thought-of

reputation 4 fame, name, note **5** éclat, honor **6** esteem, renown, report **8** position, prestige, standing **9** celebrity, character, notoriety

reputed 6 honest **7** alleged **8** putative, supposed **9** estimable, purported **10** creditable, ostensible **11** respectable **12** hypothetical

request 3 ask, dun, sue **4** pray, seek **5** plead, press **6** appeal, demand, invite **7** entreat, solicit **8** entreaty, petition **10** invitation

Requiem for a Nun author 8 Faulkner (William)

require 3 ask, beg **4** lack, need, want **5** claim, crave **6** demand, desire **7** call for, dictate, mandate, solicit **11** necessitate

required 3 due **5** vital **7** crucial **9** essential, mandatory, necessary, requisite **10** compulsory, obligatory **11** fundamental

requirement 4 must, need, want **5** claim **6** charge, demand **9** condition, essential, necessity, requisite **10** imperative, sine qua non **11** stipulation

requisite 3 due **4** must **5** vital **7** crucial, needful **8** cardinal **9** condition, essential, necessity **10** imperative, sine qua non **11** fundamental **12** precondition **13** indispensable

requisition 4 call **5** claim, exact **6** demand **7** solicit **11** application

requite 3 pay **5** repay **6** return **7** revenge, satisfy **9** indemnify, reimburse **10** compensate, recompense, remunerate **11** reciprocate

reredos 6 screen **9** partition

rescind 3 lift **5** annul **6** cancel, recall, repeal, revoke **7** retract, reverse **8** roll back, take back

rescue 4 free, save **6** ransom, redeem **7** bailout, deliver, reclaim, recover, release, salvage **8** liberate, preserve **9** extricate **11** deliverance

rescuer 6 savior **7** saviour

research 5 probe, study **7** inquest, inquiry **8** look into **9** delve into **10** experiment **11** examination, inquisition, investigate **13** investigation

resect 6 cut out, excise **8** amputate **9** extirpate

resemblance 7 analogy **8** likeness **9** alikeness **10** comparison, similarity, similitude **11** parallelism

resemble 5 favor **6** recall **8** look like, simulate **9** take after **11** approximate

resembling 4 like **6** akin to

resentful 4 sore **6** bitter, piqued, sullen **7** envious

resentment 5 pique **6** animus, grudge, malice, rancor **7** dudgeon, offense, umbrage **9** animosity **11** indignation

reservation 5 doubt **7** booking, proviso **8** homeland, preserve **9** condition, misgiving, sanctuary **10** limitation

reserve 4 book, fund, hold, keep **5** hoard, put by, stash, stock, store, tract **6** retain, supply **7** nest egg, savings, standby **8** contract, distance, fallback, hold back, postpone, set aside, squirrel, withhold **9** inventory, restraint, reticence, stockpile **10** constraint, discretion, diffidence **13** qualification

reserved 4 cool **5** aloof, stiff **6** demure, formal, remote **7** distant **8** reticent, retiring, taciturn **9** diffident, reclusive, secretive, withdrawn **10** unsociable **11** tight-lipped **12** closemouthed **13** self-contained

reservoir 5 hoard, stock, store **6** supply **7** nest egg **9** inventory, stockpile

reside 3 lie **4** live, stay **5** dwell, exist **6** inhere **7** consist

residence 4 home, stay **5** abode, house **7** address **8** domicile, dwelling **9** occupancy **10** habitation

resident 5 liver **6** inmate, lodger, native, tenant **7** citizen, denizen, dweller, present **8** inherent, occupant **10** inhabitant **11** householder

residential area 9 community **12** neighborhood

residual 7 balance, payment, remnant **8** leavings, leftover **9** remainder

residue 3 ash **4** heel, lees, rest, silt, slag **5** ashes, dregs, grout **6** debris, excess, scraps **7** balance, grounds, remains, remnant, surplus **8** leavings, remnants, residuum **9** leftovers, remainder, scourings

resign 4 cede, quit **5** demit, leave, yield **6** give up, retire, submit **7** abandon, consign **8** abdicate, hand over, relegate, renounce, step down 9 reconcile, surrender 10 relinquish

resignation 8 meekness 9 demission, surrender 10 abdication, compliance, submission 12 acquiescence, renunciation

resigned 9 compliant 10 submissive 11 acquiescent, complaisant

resile 6 recede, recoil, spring 7 rebound, retract, retreat 8 draw back, snap back

resilient 6 bouncy, supple, whippy 7 buoyant, elastic, springy 8 flexible, stretchy 9 adaptable

resin 4 balm 5 copal, damar, roset 6 dammar 7 acrylic, copaiba *aromatic:* 6 balsam, mastic 8 sandarac *fragrant:* 5 elemi 6 storax, styrax 7 ladanum 8 labdanum *gum:* 5 myrrh 7 benzoin *medicinal:* 6 guaiac 8 guaiacum *of an insect:* 3 lac *synthetic:* 8 phenolic *used by bees:* 8 propolis

resist 4 buck, defy, kick 5 rebel 6 baffle, combat, oppose, revolt 7 contest, counter, gainsay 8 traverse 10 contradict, contravene

resistance 7 dissent 8 defiance, variance 10 dissension, dissidence, opposition 11 contrariety, obstruction

resistance unit 3 ohm

resistor 8 rheostat, varistor 10 thermistor

resolute 3 set 4 bent, bold, fast, firm, true 6 intent, steady, sturdy 7 decided, staunch 8 constant, decisive, faithful, intrepid, stubborn 9 obstinate, steadfast, tenacious, undaunted 10 determined, persistent 12 pertinacious, single-minded

resolution 4 guts 5 heart, nerve, pluck, spunk 6 mettle, spirit 7 courage, outcome 8 decision, firmness, tenacity 10 conclusion 12 perseverance 13 determination, steadfastness

resolve 5 clear, crack 6 decide, settle 7 clear up, iron out, unravel, work out 8 boldness, conclude, decipher, firmness 9 breakdown, determine, intention, reconcile 10 unscramble 13 determination, steadfastness

resonant 4 deep, full, rich 6 silver 7 booming, echoing, orotund, vibrant 8 powerful, sonorous 11 reverberant

resonate 4 echo, peal, ring 7 resound, vibrate 11 reverberate

resort 3 spa 5 haven, hotel, lodge, shift 6 harbor, refuge 7 retreat, riviera, stopgap 8 recourse 9 expedient, makeshift 10 substitute

resound 4 boom, echo, peal, ring 11 reverberate

resounding 7 booming, echoing, oro-

tund, vibrant 8 emphatic, sonorous 10 clangorous, resonating, thunderous 11 unequivocal

resource 3 aid 5 asset, means, shift 6 supply 7 standby

resourceful 5 adept 6 adroit, artful, clever, shrewd 7 capable, cunning 8 creative, skillful 9 ingenious, inventive 10 innovative 11 imaginative 12 enterprising

resources 5 funds, means, purse 6 assets, riches, wealth 7 capital, fortune, reserve 8 bankroll, finances, property, reserves 9 substance 11 wherewithal

respect 3 awe 5 favor, honor, props 6 admire, detail, devoir, esteem, homage, regard, revere 7 account, concern 8 venerate 9 deference 10 admiration, estimation, particular, veneration

respectable 4 fair 5 ample 6 decent, proper, worthy 8 adequate 9 admirable, estimable, honorable 10 sufficient 11 appropriate, presentable 12 satisfactory 13 well-thought-of

respectful 5 civil 6 polite 8 obeisant, reverent 9 courteous 11 deferential, reverential

respecting 3 per 4 as to, in re 5 about 7 apropos 9 as regards, regarding 10 as concerns, concerning, relating to 11 considering

respire 7 breathe

respite 4 lull, rest 5 break, delay, pause, spell, truce 6 hiatus, recess, relief 8 breather, reprieve, surcease 12 intermission

resplendent 5 regal 7 glowing, shining 8 glorious, gorgeous 9 brilliant, refulgent 11 magnificent

respond 5 react, reply 6 answer, rejoin, retort 8 come back

response 5 reply 6 answer, retort, return 7 riposte 8 antiphon, comeback, reaction 9 rejoinder

responsibility 4 buck, duty, onus 5 blame, brief, fault 6 burden, charge, devoir 10 obligation 11 reliability

responsible 6 liable 8 amenable, reliable 10 answerable, chargeable, dependable 11 accountable, trustworthy

responsive 4 open 8 sentient 9 sensitive 11 susceptible, sympathetic

rest 3 sit 4 calm, ease, loaf, loll, lull, stay 5 let up, pause, peace, quiet, relax, spell 6 depend, excess, lounge, repose 7 balance, leisure, lie down, recline, remains, remnant, surplus 8 breather, interlude, leavings, vacation 9 predicate, remainder

restate 4 echo 6 reword 8 rephrase 9 translate 10 paraphrase 12 recapitulate

restatement 10 paraphrase 11 translation

restaurant 4 café 5 diner 6 eatery 7 beanery 9 brasserie, cafeteria 10 coffee shop 11 coffeehouse, greasy spoon *price:* 8 à la carte, prix fixe 10 table d'hôte *worker:* 4 chef, cook 6 busboy, server, waiter 7 maître d', waitron 8 waitress 10 dishwasher, headwaiter, waitperson 12 maître d'hôtel

___ **Restaurant** 6 Alice's

restful 4 calm 5 quiet 6 placid 8 peaceful, tranquil

restitute 6 refund, return 7 reclaim, recover, restore 8 give back 11 recondition, reconstruct 12 rehabilitate

restitution 6 amends, refund, return 7 redress 8 reprisal 9 indemnity, quittance 10 recompense, reparation 11 restoration 12 remuneration, satisfaction

restive 4 edgy 5 balky, nervy, tense 6 ornery, uneasy 7 fidgety, froward, uptight, wayward 8 contrary, perverse, skittish

restiveness 7 anxiety, ferment, turmoil 8 disquiet 9 balkiness 10 inquietude, perversity 11 contrariety, disquietude, waywardness 12 contrariness

restless 5 antsy, itchy, jumpy 6 fitful, uneasy 7 anxious, fidgety, fretful, jittery, nervous, unquiet 8 agitated, troubled 9 disturbed, perturbed, unsettled 12 discontented, dissatisfied

restorative 4 balm 5 tonic 7 healing 8 curative, remedial, sanative 12 recuperative

restore 4 cure, heal, mend 5 amend, remit, renew, right 6 recall, recoup, reform, remedy, render, repair, return, revive 7 get back, improve, reclaim, recover, rectify, refresh, replace 8 give back, recreate, renovate, revivify 9 refurbish, reinstate, replenish, restitute 10 regenerate, rejuvenate 11 recondition, reestablish 12 rehabilitate

restrain 3 bit, gag 4 curb, rein 5 check, leash 6 arrest, bridle, halter, hamper, hinder, hold in, impede, muzzle, temper 7 collect, control, harness, inhibit, repress 8 hold back, hold down, moderate, suppress *trade:* 7 embargo

restrained 4 cool 5 low-key 5 canny, quiet 6 modest 7 subdued 8 discreet, reserved, reticent, retiring, tasteful 9 contained, inhibited, temperate 10 controlled, reasonable

restraint 6 bridle 7 durance, embargo, reserve 8 estoppel, pullback 9 hin-

drance 10 deterrence, inhibition, limitation, moderation 11 confinement, forbearance 12 straitjacket

restrict 3 bar, tie 4 bind, curb 5 hem in, limit 6 hamper, hobble, impede, narrow, shrink 7 confine, curtail, delimit, inhibit, trammel 8 hold back, prelimit 10 delimitate 12 circumscribe *a will:* 6 entail

restriction 4 curb 5 check, limit, stint 7 control 9 restraint 10 constraint, limitation, regulation 11 confinement, prohibition 12 proscription 13 qualification

restyle 4 redo 6 revamp, revise, rework 8 make over

result 3 end 4 flow, stem 5 close, ensue, fruit, issue 6 effect, emerge, finish, follow, payoff, sequel, upshot 7 outcome, product 8 sequence, solution 9 aftermath, come about, eventuate 10 conclusion, denouement, production 11 aftereffect, consequence, eventuality *incidental:* 7 spinoff

resume 4 go on 5 renew 6 pick up, reopen 7 carry on, proceed, restart 8 continue 10 recommence

résumé 4 vita 5 sum-up 7 summary 9 summation, summing-up

resurgence 5 rally 7 rebirth, revival 8 comeback, recovery 10 renascence 11 renaissance 12 risorgimento

resurrect 5 raise, renew 6 come to, revive 8 retrieve, revivify 10 reactivate

resurrection 7 rebirth, revival 10 renascence 11 renaissance 12 risorgimento

resuscitate see RESURRECT

retail 4 sell, tell, vend 6 market 7 narrate 11 merchandise

retailer 6 dealer, seller, trader, vendor 8 merchant 9 tradesman 10 shopkeeper 11 storekeeper 12 merchandiser

retain 3 own 4 hire, hold, keep 6 detain 7 reserve 8 hold over, preserve, remember, withhold

retainer 3 fee 6 lackey, menial, minion, yeoman 7 deposit, servant 8 employee, follower 9 bite plate, dependent, pensioner

retaliate 7 get back, get even

retaliation see REPRISAL

retaliatory 8 punitive, vengeful 10 vindictive

retard 4 clog, mire, slow 5 delay, stunt 6 detain, fetter, hamper, hang up, hinder, impede, slow up 7 set back, slacken 8 decrease, hold back, restrain 10 decelerate

retarded 3 dim 4 dull, dumb, slow 6 opaque, simple, stupid 8 backward 9 dim-witted 10 half-witted, slow-witted 11 exceptional

retch 3 gag **4** barf, hurl, puke, spew **5** heave, vomit **6** spit up **7** bring up, throw up, upchuck **8** disgorge

retention 6 memory **7** storage

reticent see RESERVED

reticulate 4 vein **5** veiny **6** meshed, netted **7** netlike **10** crisscross

retinue 4 band, tail **5** suite, train **6** livery **7** company, cortege **9** entourage, following

retire 4 exit, quit **5** leave, yield **6** bow out, depart, recede, resign, turn in **7** dismiss, pension **8** step down, withdraw **9** discharge, strike out, terminate **10** relinquish

retired person 7 emerita **8** emeritus **9** pensioner

retiree 9 pensioner **10** golden-ager **13** senior citizen

retirement allowance 3 SEP **7** pension

retiring 3 shy **5** mousy, timid **6** demure, modest **7** bashful **8** reserved **9** diffident, withdrawn **11** unassertive

retool 7 reequip **10** reengineer

retort 5 reply, sally **6** answer, rejoin **7** counter, respond, riposte **8** comeback, repartee, response **9** rejoinder, retaliate, wisecrack

retouch 5 alter, emend, renew **6** repair **7** correct, enhance, improve, restore

retract 4 deny **5** unsay **6** abjure, recall, recant, recede, renege, resile, revoke **7** disavow, rescind, retreat, swallow **8** forswear, renounce, take back, withdraw

retreat 3 den, ebb **4** flee, quit **5** cover, haven, leave **6** ashram, asylum, bow out, covert, decamp, depart, escape, recede, recoil, refuge, shrink, vacate **7** abandon, back off, back out, pull out, shelter **8** back down, draw back, evacuate, fall back, hideaway, withdraw **9** backtrack, climb down, sanctuary **10** give ground, withdrawal

retrench 3 cut **4** pare **5** slash **6** excise, lessen, reduce **7** abridge, curtail **9** economize

retribution 6 return, reward **7** deserts, revenge **8** avenging, reprisal, requital, revanche **9** vengeance **10** punishment, recompense **11** counterblow, retaliation
goddess of: **3** Ate **4** Fury **7** Nemesis

retrieve 5 fetch **6** recall, recoup, redeem, rescue **7** get back, recover, restore, salvage **9** resurrect

retro 7 antique, revival, vintage **9** nostalgic **12** old-fashioned

retrograde 4 back **7** inverse, reverse **8** backward, inverted, rearward

retrogress see REVERT

retrospect 9 hindsight **12** recollection **13** reexamination

retrospective 6 review **8** backward **10** exhibition, reflective, ruminative

return 5 recur, repay, reply, yield **6** answer, rebate, regain, rejoin, render, repeat, retort, revert **7** bring in, get back, rebound, recover, reprise, requite, respond, reverse, riposte **8** comeback, dividend, earnings, give back, proceeds, reappear, response **9** rejoinder, repayment, reversion **10** recompense, recurrence **11** reciprocate, restitution

Return of the Native *author:* **5** Hardy (Thomas) *character:* **4** Clym **8** Eustacia

Reuben *brother:* **6** Joseph *father:* **5** Jacob *mother:* **4** Leah *son:* **5** Carmi **6** Hanoch, Hezron, Phallu

Réunion *capital:* **7** St.-Denis *city:* **6** St.-Paul **7** St.-Louis **8** St.-Pierre *department of:* **6** France *ethnic group:* **6** Creole *former name:* **7** Bourbon **9** Bonaparte *island group:* **9** Mascarene

revamp 4 redo **5** renew **6** remake, repair, revise, rework **7** remodel, restyle, rewrite **8** make over, overhaul, redesign, renovate **9** refurbish **11** recondition

reveal 4 bare, blab, jamb, leak, open, show, tell **5** admit, let on, peach, spill **6** betray, evince, expose, impart, unmask, unveil **7** confess, declare, display, divulge, exhibit, publish, uncover, undress **8** announce, decipher, disclose, discover, give away, unclothe **9** broadcast **11** acknowledge, communicate **12** bring to light

revel 4 bask, orgy, riot **5** binge, feast, party, spree **6** boogie, frolic, gaiety, hoopla, wallow **7** carouse, delight, indulge, jollity, roister, rollick, wassail, whoopla **8** carnival, carousal, festival **9** bacchanal, celebrate, festivity, luxuriate, merriment, whoop-de-do **11** bacchanalia, celebration, merrymaking

revelation 6 kicker **8** epiphany, giveaway, prophecy, surprise **9** discovery **10** apocalypse, disclosure **13** manifestation

reveler 7 orgiast **8** bacchant, carouser **9** bacchante, wassailer **10** merrymaker

revelry 4 orgy, riot **6** gaiety **7** carouse, jollity, wassail, whoopee, whoopla **8** carousal, partying **9** festivity, high jinks, merriment, whoop-de-do **10** whoop-de-doo **11** merrymaking

revenant 5 ghost, haunt, shade, spook **6** shadow, spirit, wraith, zombie **7** phantom, specter, spectre **8** phantasm, prodigal, visitant **10** apparition

revenge 5 right **6** defend **7** get back, get even, redress, requite **8** reprisal,

requital, revanche **9** retaliate, vindicate **11** retaliation, retribution
revenue 4 rent **5** gains, issue, yield **6** income, profit, return **7** comings **8** earnings, interest, proceeds, receipts, taxation
reverberant 6 hollow **7** booming, echoing **8** resonant **10** resounding
reverberate 4 echo, ring **6** reecho **7** resound
revere 4 laud **5** adore, exalt, extol, honor, prize, value **6** admire, esteem, regard **7** cherish, magnify, respect, worship **8** treasure, venerate **10** appreciate
revered 9 venerable
reverence 4 awe **5** adore, dread, honor, piety **6** esteem, fealty, homage **7** loyalty, respect, worship **8** devotion, venerate **9** deference, obeisance, solemnity **10** veneration *gesture of:* **3** bow **6** kowtow **8** kneeling **12** genuflection
reverend 4 abbé, holy **5** clerk, vicar **6** clergy, cleric, deacon, divine, parson, rector **8** chaplain, clerical, minister, preacher **9** churchman, clergyman **11** clergywoman **12** ecclesiastic
reverent 5 godly **6** devout **7** dutiful **9** prayerful **10** God-fearing, respectful, worshipful
reverie 4 muse **5** dream **6** trance, vision **7** fantasy **8** daydream **10** absorption, brown study, meditation **11** abstraction **13** woolgathering
reversal 4 turn **5** U-turn **6** double, switch **7** setback, undoing **8** backfire, flip-flop **9** about-face, inversion, turnabout, volte-face **10** switcheroo **12** solarization **13** change of heart
reverse 4 lift **6** change, contra, defeat, invert, recall, repeal, revoke **7** capsize, counter, rescind, setback **8** antipode, backward, contrary, disaster, exchange, opposite, overrule, overturn **9** aboutface, backwards, diametric, overthrow, transpose, turnabout, volte-face **10** antithesis, misfortune
reversion 4 turn **5** lapse **6** return **7** atavism, escheat **9** about-face, throwback, turnabout, volte-face **10** regression, succession
revert 4 turn **6** return **7** decline, devolve, escheat, inverse, regress **8** turn back **9** backslide **10** degenerate, retrograde, retrogress
revetment 6 bunker, riprap **9** barricade, earthwork **10** embankment
review 4 scan **5** audit, recap, study **6** assess, go over, parade, report, revise, survey **7** analyze, journal, rethink **8** analysis, critique, magazine, revision, scrutiny, talk over **9** criticism, reexam-

ine, refresher **10** evaluation, inspection, periodical, reconsider, reevaluate **11** examination **13** reexamination, retrospective
revile 4 rail, rate **5** abuse, scold **6** attack, berate, defame, malign, vilify **7** asperse, bawl out, chew out, upbraid **8** belittle, disgrace, execrate **9** blaspheme **10** tongue-lash, vituperate
revise 4 edit **5** alter, amend, emend, proof, renew **6** change, polish, redraw, reform, retool, revamp, rework **7** correct, improve, redraft, restore, restyle, rewrite **8** overhaul, redesign, work over **9** red-pencil **10** blue-pencil
revision 6 change, revamp, update **7** redraft **8** facelift, overhaul, updating **10** alteration, correction, emendation **11** overhauling **12** modification
revitalize see REVIVE
revival 7 rebirth, renewal **8** comeback **10** renascence, resurgence **11** reanimation, renaissance, restoration **12** regeneration, rejuvenation, resurrection, risorgimento **13** recrudescence, resuscitation
revive 4 wake **5** rally, renew, rouse **6** arouse, awaken, come to, recall **7** bring to, enliven, freshen, quicken, refresh, restore **8** reawaken, rekindle, renovate, retrieve **9** reanimate, resurrect **10** reactivate, recuperate, regenerate, rejuvenate **11** bring around, reintroduce, resuscitate **12** reinvigorate
revoke 4 lift, void **5** annul, erase **6** abjure, cancel, recall, recant, renege, repeal **7** abolish, nullify, rescind, retract, reverse **8** abrogate, call back **10** invalidate **11** countermand
revolt 4 riot **5** rebel, repel, shock **6** mutiny, resist, sicken **7** disgust, repulse **8** nauseate, outbreak, uprising **9** jacquerie, rebellion **10** insurgence, insurgency **12** insurrection
revolter 5 rebel **6** anarch **8** frondeur, mutineer **9** anarchist, insurgent **10** malcontent
revolting 4 foul, ugly, vile **5** nasty **6** horrid **7** hideous, noisome, obscene **8** shocking **9** atrocious, loathsome, repellent, repugnant, repulsive **10** disgusting, nauseating
revolution 4 gyre, reel, riot, roll, spin, turn **5** cycle, orbit, twirl, wheel, whirl **6** mutiny **7** circuit **8** gyration, rotation, uprising **9** pirouette, rebellion **10** barrel roll, changeover, somersault **12** insurrection
revolutionary 5 rebel, ultra **7** extreme, radical **8** mutineer, rotating, ultraist **9** extremist, insurgent *American:* **4** Reed

(John) **5** Shays (Daniel) *French:* **5** Marat (Jean-Paul) **6** Danton (Georges) **8** Mirabeau (Comte de) **9** Saint-Just (Louis) **11** Robespierre (Maximilien) *Irish:* **4** Tone (Wolfe) **6** Pearse (Padraig, Patrick) **7** Collins (Michael), Parnell (Charles Stewart) **8** Casement (Roger), de Valera (Eamon), Griffith (Arthur), O'Connell (Daniel) *Mexican:* **5** Villa (Pancho) **6** Zapata (Emiliano) **7** Hidalgo (Padre Miguel) *Russian:* **5** Kirov (Sergey), Lenin (Vladimir Ilyich) **7** Trotsky (Leon) **8** Kerensky (Aleksandr) **9** Kropotkin (Pyotr)

revolutionize 9 transform **11** transfigure

revolve 4 spin, turn **5** twirl, wheel, whirl **6** circle, gyrate, rotate

revolver 3 gun, rod **4** Colt **5** Glock, Luger, Ruger **6** Magnum, pistol, sixgun **7** firearm, handgun, shooter, sidearm **10** six-shooter

revue 4 show **9** burlesque **10** production, vaudeville **13** entertainment

revulsion 4 hate **6** hatred, horror **7** disgust **8** aversion, loathing **10** abhorrence, repugnance **11** abomination, detestation

reward 5 bonus, booty, crown, medal, price, prize **6** bounty, carrot, payoff, trophy **7** guerdon, jackpot, premium **8** dividend **10** compensate, honorarium, recompense, remunerate **12** compensation, remuneration

rewarding 7 gainful **8** edifying, fruitful, valuable **9** lucrative **10** beneficial, fulfilling, gratifying, productive, profitable, satisfying, worthwhile **12** advantageous, remunerative

reword see RESTATE

rework 6 revamp, revise **7** restyle, rewrite

Reynard 3 fox

rhadamanthine 3 due **4** just **5** right **6** strict **7** condign, fitting, merited **8** deserved, rigorous, rightful, suitable **9** requisite, stringent **11** appropriate

Rhadamanthus 5 judge *brother:* **5** Minos *father:* **4** Zeus **7** Jupiter *mother:* **6** Europa

rhapsodic 5 lyric **8** ecstatic, effusive **9** emotional, exuberant

rhapsodize 4 gush, rave **5** drool **6** effuse **7** enthuse

Rhea 3 Ops *daughter:* **4** Hera, Juno **5** Ceres, Vesta **6** Hestia **7** Demeter *father:* **6** Uranus *husband:* **6** Cronus, Saturn *mother:* **4** Gaea *son:* **4** Zeus **5** Hades, Pluto **7** Jupiter, Neptune **8** Poseidon

Rheingold, Das *character:* **4** Loki **5** Freya, Wotan **6** Fafner, Fafnir, Fasolt

8 Alberich *composer:* **6** Wagner (Richard)

rheostat 8 resistor

rhesus 6 monkey **7** macaque

rhetoric 4 rant **6** speech **7** bombast, fustian, oratory **8** rhapsody **9** elocution, eloquence, verbosity **11** rodomontade, speechcraft *term:* **6** aporia, simile **7** litotes **8** metaphor **10** apostrophe, digression **12** alliteration, onomatopoeia

rhetorical 4 glib **5** gassy, grand, tumid, windy **6** florid, fluent, ornate, purple, turgid **7** aureate, flowery, orotund, pompous, stilted **8** eloquent, forensic, inflated, overdone, sonorous **9** bombastic, grandiose, high-flown, overblown, tumescent **10** euphuistic, flamboyant, oratorical **11** declamatory, highfalutin, overwrought, pretentious **12** highsounding, magniloquent **13** grandiloquent

rhetorician 6 orator, writer **7** speaker *Roman:* **10** Quintilian

Rhine River *city:* **4** Bonn, Köln **5** Basel, Mainz **7** Coblenz, Cologne, Koblenz **8** Duisburg, Mannheim **9** Rotterdam, Weisbaden **10** Düsseldorf *nymph:* **7** Lorelei *tributary:* **3** Aar, Ill, Lek **4** Aare, Lahn, Main, Ruhr, Waal

rhizome 4 root **5** tuber

Rhode Island *bay:* **12** Narragansett *capital:* **10** Providence *city:* **7** Newport, Warwick **9** Pawtucket *college, university:* **4** RISD **5** Brown *island:* **5** Block *nickname:* **5** Ocean (State) **11** Little Rhody *river:* **8** Pawtuxet *state bird:* **14** Rhode Island red *state flower:* **6** violet *state tree:* **8** red maple

Rhodesia 8 Zimbabwe

rhombus 7 diamond, lozenge **13** parallelogram

rhonchus 5 snore

Rhône River *city:* **4** Lyon **5** Arles, Lyons **6** Geneva **7** Avignon *lake:* **6** Geneva *mountain range:* **4** Jura *tributary:* **5** Isère, Saône

rhubarb 3 row **4** flap **5** run-in **6** ruckus, tangle **7** dispute, quarrel, wrangle **8** argument, pieplant **11** altercation, controversy

rhyme 4 poem, song **5** agree, ditty, verse **6** accord, jingle, poetry **7** conform **8** dovetail **9** harmonize **10** coordinate, correspond

rhymer 4 bard, poet **5** odist **7** metrist **9** poetaster, rhymester, sonneteer, versifier

rhythm 4 beat, flow, lilt, time **5** meter, pulse, swing **6** accent, groove **7** cadence, measure, pattern **8** sequence

rhythmic 7 pulsing, regular **8** measured, metrical

rialto 6 market **8** district, exchange **11** marketplace

riant 3 gay **5** jolly, merry **6** blithe, bright, jocund, jovial **7** buoyant, gleeful **8** cheerful, mirthful **10** blithesome

riata 4 rope **5** lasso **6** lariat

rib 3 fun, kid, rag **4** band, bone, dike, fool, jape, jest, joke, josh, purl, razz, stay, wale **5** chaff, costa, ridge, tease **6** banter, costae (plural), lierne, needle

ribald 3 raw **4** blue, racy, rude **5** bawdy, crude, dirty **6** coarse, earthy, filthy, purple, risqué, smutty, vulgar **7** obscene, profane, raunchy **8** indecent, off-color **9** offensive, reprobate **10** suggestive

ribbon 3 bow **4** band, tape **5** braid, shred, strip **6** cordon, fillet, stripe, tatter **7** bandeau

rice 7 arborio, risotto *dish:* **5** pilaf **6** congee **7** risotto **9** jambalaya *drink:* **4** sake, saki **5** mirin **6** arrack *field:* **5** paddy *husk:* **5** lemma

rich 4 dear, lush, oily, posh **5** ample, fatty, flush, grand, heavy, plush, swank, vivid **6** costly, creamy, deluxe, fecund, gilded, lavish, loaded, monied, ornate, potent, rococo **7** baroque, copious, elegant, fertile, filling, moneyed, opulent, orotund, profuse, wealthy, well-off **8** abundant, affluent, eloquent, fruitful, palatial, well-to-do **9** abounding, bountiful, elaborate, luxuriant, luxurious, plentiful, sumptuous, well-fixed **10** productive, prosperous, well-heeled **11** extravagant *person:* **5** Midas, mogul, nabob **6** fat cat **7** Croesus, magnate **9** moneybags, plutocrat

Richardson work 6 Pamela **8** Clarissa

Richelieu's successor 7 Mazarin

riches 4 gold, pelf **5** booty, lucre, worth **6** mammon, wealth **7** fortune **8** opulence, property, treasure **9** resources *demon of:* **6** Mammon

rick 4 cock, heap, pile **5** shock, stack

rickety 4 weak **5** shaky **6** wobbly **7** unsound **8** decrepit, insecure, rachitic, unstable, unsteady **10** ramshackle, rattletrap

ricochet 4 ping, skim, skip **5** carom **6** bounce, glance **7** rebound **9** boomerang

rid 6 divest **7** relieve **8** unburden **11** disencumber

riddle 5 rebus **6** enigma, puzzle **7** mystery, perplex, problem **9** conundrum, perforate **10** closed book, puzzlement **11** brainteaser

ride 4 spin, tour, trip **5** drive, jaunt, mount **7** journey **8** carousel **9** excursion

ride out 6 endure **7** outlast, survive, weather **9** withstand

rider 6 clause, cowboy, jockey **7** codicil **8** addendum, addition, appendix, horseman, reinsman **9** amendment **10** equestrian, horsewoman, supplement

ridge 3 rib, top **4** bank, brow, fold, keel, reef, roll, ruck, seam, wave **5** arête, arris, chine, crest, knurl, plica, spine **6** crease, divide, furrow, rimple, saddle, summit **7** annulet, breaker, crinkle, hogback, wrinkle **8** shoulder **9** razorback **11** corrugation *gravelly:* **5** esker *on the skin:* **4** welt *sharp:* **7** hogback

ridicule 3 pan **4** gibe, haze, jape, jeer, mock, razz, ride, twit **5** chaff, flout, mimic, roast, scoff, scout, sneer, squib, taunt **6** deride, satire **7** lampoon, mockery, pillory, sarcasm **8** derision, raillery, satirize, travesty **9** burlesque **10** caricature *god of:* **5** Momus *object of:* **4** butt **13** laughingstock

ridiculous 5 comic, daffy, dotty, goofy, silly, wacky **6** absurd, insane **7** bizarre, comical, foolish, risible **8** derisory, farcical **9** cockamamy, fantastic, grotesque, laughable, ludicrous, monstrous **10** cockamamie, outrageous **11** for the birds, harebrained **12** preposterous, unbelievable

riding *academy:* **6** manège *costume:* **5** habit *pants:* **8** jodhpurs *whip:* **4** crop **5** quirt

Rienzi composer 6 Wagner (Richard)

rife 4 full **5** flush **6** common **7** replete, teeming **8** abundant, swarming **9** abounding, plentiful, prevalent **10** widespread **11** overflowing

riff 4 flip, leaf, scan, skim **5** thumb **6** browse **8** ostinato

riffle 4 flip, leaf, fret, scan, skim, wave **5** shoal, sluice, thumb **6** browse **7** shallow, shuffle **10** interstice

riffraff 3 mob **5** trash, waste **6** debris, kelter, litter, masses, rabble, refuse **7** garbage, rubbish **8** canaille, unwashed **11** proletariat

rifle 3 arm, gun, rob **4** loot, sack **5** steal **6** burgle, groove, weapon **7** carbine, despoil, firearm, pillage, plunder, ransack, rummage **9** chassepot *accessory:* **6** ramrod *kind:* **6** Garand, Mauser **7** Enfield **8** Browning **9** Remington **10** Winchester **11** Springfield

rift 3 gap **4** rent **5** break, chasm, chink, cleft, crack, fault, space, split **6** breach, cleave, divide, hiatus, schism **7** fissure, opening, rupture **8** crevasse, division, fracture, interval **9** fault line **10** separation **12** estrangement

rig 3 arm, fit, fix **4** fake, gear **5** dress, equip, getup, trick **6** adjust, clothe, doctor, outfit, tackle **7** apparel, arrange, costume, derrick, furnish, turn out **8** accouter, accoutre, clothing, equipage **9** apparatus, construct, equipment **10** manipulate

rigging 3 net **4** duds, gear, togs **5** dress, lines, ropes **6** attire, chains, tackle, things **7** apparel, clothes, raiment **8** clothing **9** apparatus, equipment

right 3 apt, due, fit **4** fair, just, sane, true, well **5** amend, amply, claim, droit, emend, exact, sound, title **6** at once, common, decent, dexter, direct, equity, honest, lawful, proper, square, strict **7** condign, correct, exactly, fitting, freedom, genuine, healthy, liberty, license, merited, old-line, rectify, redress **8** accurate, becoming, bona fide, decorous, easement, faithful, interest, orthodox, smack-dab, straight, suffrage, suitable **9** authentic, befitting, equitable, forthwith, honorable, privilege, requisite, veracious, veritable **10** altogether, applicable, felicitous, perquisite, scrupulous **11** appropriate, correctness, prerogative *combining form:* **4** orth, rect **5** dextr, ortho, recti **6** dextro *feudal:* **4** soke *legal:* **5** droit **8** usufruct *royal:* **7** regalia (plural)

right away 3 now **6** at once, pronto **8** directly, promptly **9** forthwith, instanter, instantly **11** immediately, straight off, straightway **12** then and there

righteous 4 good, holy, just, pure **5** godly, moral, noble, pious **6** devout, worthy **7** ethical, genuine, sinless, upright **8** innocent, virtuous **9** blameless, guiltless **10** inculpable, principled

righteousness 6 equity, virtue **7** justice, probity **8** holiness, morality **9** rectitude

rightful 3 apt, due, fit **4** fair, just, true **5** legal **6** honest, lawful, proper **7** condign, fitting **8** deserved, suitable **9** befitting, equitable, impartial **10** applicable, legitimate **11** appropriate

right-handed 6 dexter **7** dextral **9** clockwise

right-hand page 5 recto

rightist 4 tory **11** reactionary **12** conservative

right-minded 5 moral, noble **6** decent, honest **7** ethical **8** virtuous **10** upstanding

Rights of Man author 5 Paine (Thomas)

rigid 3 set **4** firm, hard, taut **5** fixed, stiff, tense **6** severe, strict **7** austere, precise, hard-set **8** cast-iron, ironclad, obdu-

rate, rigorous **9** draconian, immovable, inelastic, rockbound, stringent, unbending **10** adamantine, brassbound, inflexible, relentless, unyielding **11** unbudgeable **13** rhadamanthine

rigidity 6 turgor **7** buckram **8** hardness **9** stiffness *muscular:* **8** myotonia

rigmarole 6 bunkum, drivel, ramble **8** nonsense **9** gibberish, procedure **10** balderdash, mumbo jumbo

Rigoletto *composer:* **5** Verdi (Giuseppe) *daughter:* **5** Gilda

rigor 7 cruelty **8** asperity, hardness, hardship, severity **9** austerity, exactness, harshness, roughness, sharpness, sternness **10** affliction, difficulty, exactitude, strictness **11** tribulation **13** inflexibility

rigorous 5 exact, harsh, rigid, rough, stern, stiff **6** bitter, brutal, proper, rugged, severe, strict **7** ascetic, drastic, onerous, precise **8** accurate, exacting **9** draconian, ironbound, stringent **10** burdensome, inflexible, ironhanded, oppressive **13** rhadamanthine

rile 3 bug, rub, vex **4** roil **5** anger, annoy, grate, muddy, peeve, pique, upset **6** muddle, nettle, put out, rankle **7** agitate, disturb, fluster, inflame, perturb, provoke **8** disorder, disquiet, irritate **9** aggravate **10** discompose, exasperate

rill 3 run **4** burn, purl **5** bourn, brook, creek **6** runnel, stream, valley **7** freshet, rivulet **8** brooklet **9** streamlet **11** watercourse

rim 3 hem, lip **4** bank, boss, brim, edge, ring **5** bezel, bezil, bound, brink, skirt, verge **6** border, flange, fringe, margin, shield **7** annulus, horizon, outline **8** boundary, surround **9** perimeter, periphery *of a basket:* **4** hoop *of a cask:* **5** chime *of an insect's wing:* **6** termen *of a spoked wheel:* **5** felly **6** felloe

rime 3 ice **4** hoar **5** crust, frost **7** coating, encrust **9** hoarfrost, Jack Frost **12** incrustation

Rinaldo *beloved:* **8** Angelica *cousin:* **7** Orlando *father:* **5** Aymon *horse:* **6** Bayard *mother:* **3** Aya *sister:* **10** Bradamante *uncle:* **11** Charlemagne

rind 4 bark, husk, peel, skin **5** crust **9** crackling

ring 3 eye, hem, rim **4** band, bloc, bong, echo, gird, gyre, hoop, loop, peal, toll **5** arena, bezel, cabal, chime, clang, cycle, group, knell, knoll, round, sound **6** circle, clique, collar, girdle, staple **7** annulus, clangor, combine, compass, resound, vibrate **8** bracelet, cincture, encircle, surround **9** coalition, encompass **11** combination, reverberate *around sun or moon:* **6** corona

curtain: 3 eye *for a compass:* 6 gimbal
harness: 3 dee 6 button, terret *heraldic:*
7 annulet *in a hinge:* 7 gudgeon *of chain:*
4 link *of color:* 8 stocking *of leaves or*
flowers: 6 wreath 7 garland *of light:*
4 halo 5 glory 6 corona, nimbus 7 aureole 8 halation *of rope or metal:* 4 hank
6 becket 7 garland, grommet, thimble
of two hoops: 6 gimmal *relating to:*
7 annular *used as a valve or diaphragm:*
5 wafer *wedding:* 4 band
Ring and the Book author 8 Browning
(Robert)
ringed 8 annulate, bordered 9 encircled
10 surrounded
ringer 4 fake, spit 5 clone, image 6 double 7 clapper, picture 8 impostor, portrait 10 simulacrum 13 spitting image
ringing 7 orotund, vibrant 8 decisive,
emphatic, plangent, resonant, sonorous
10 clangorous, resounding 11 reverberant, unequivocal
ringleader 4 boss 5 chief 6 honcho
7 kingpin 9 godfather 10 head honcho,
instigator, mastermind
ringlet 4 curl, lock 5 crimp, tress 7 circlet, earlock, tendril
Ring of the Nibelung composer 6 Wagner (Richard)
rinse 4 dunk, lave, wash 5 bathe, douse,
swill 6 shower, sluice 7 cleanse *the*
mouth: 6 gargle
riot 5 brawl, melee, revel, spree 6 bedlam, émeute, jumble, revolt, tumult,
uproar 7 carouse, debauch, rampage,
revelry, roister, wassail 8 carousal, disorder, uprising 9 commotion
10 debauchery, donnybrook, revolution
11 disturbance
riotous 4 lush, wild 6 stormy, unruly,
wanton 7 bacchic, profuse 8 abundant
9 abounding, clamorous, exuberant,
luxuriant, plentiful, turbulent 10 boisterous 11 saturnalian, tempestuous
12 unrestrained
rip 4 gash, hole, rend, rent, rive, spit,
tear 5 shred, slash, split 6 attack, cleave
7 current, sputter 8 lacerate, undertow
9 criticize, disparage 12 undercurrent
into: 5 go for 6 assail, attack 8 lambaste
off: 3 con, rob 4 copy 5 cheat, steal,
theft 7 defraud, imitate, swindle 9 imitation
ripe 4 aged, full, late 5 adult, grown,
ready, ruddy, plump 6 mature, mellow,
smelly, timely 7 grown-up 8 prepared,
suitable 9 developed, full-blown, full-
grown, offensive, opportune 10 seasonable 11 appropriate, full-fledged
ripen 3 age 4 cure, grow 6 better, grow
up, mature, mellow, season 7 develop,

enhance, improve, perfect 8 heighten,
maturate
riposte 5 parry, reply 6 retort, return,
thrust 8 back talk, comeback, repartee
13 counterattack
ripping 4 fine 5 grand, nifty, super, swell
6 divine, peachy 7 capital 8 glorious,
splendid, terrific 9 admirable, delicious, excellent, fantastic, marvelous,
wonderful 10 delightful, delectable,
remarkable 11 scrumptious, sensational
ripple 3 lap 4 curl, fret, riff, wave
6 cockle, dimple, lipper, popple, ruffle,
spread, wimple 7 crinkle, wavelet,
wrinkle 8 undulate
rip-roaring 5 noisy 6 lively 8 exciting
9 hilarious 10 boisterous, rollicking,
uproarious
ripsnorter 5 dandy 6 hummer 8 jim-
dandy 9 humdinger 11 crackerjack
riptide 7 current 8 undertow 12 undercurrent
Rip Van Winkle *author:* 6 Irving (Washington) *dog:* 4 Wolf
rise 3 wax 4 flow, grow, lift, rear, soar,
stem, well 5 awake, begin, climb, get
up, issue, mount, rouse, stand, surge,
swell, tower 6 ascend, ascent, awaken,
emerge, expand, growth, spring, thrive,
uprear 7 advance, augment, develop,
emanate, enhance, enlarge, stand up,
succeed, surface, upsurge 8 eminence,
heighten, increase 9 ascension, increment, intensify, originate, terminate
above: 8 surmount *again:* 7 resurge
9 resurrect *against:* 5 rebel 6 mutiny,
revolt *and fall:* 4 tide 5 heave 6 welter
and shine: 5 get up *gradually:* 4 loom
Rise and Fall of the Third Reich author
6 Shirer (William)
Rise of Silas Lapham author 7 Howells
(William Dean)
riser 4 step 8 platform
risible 4 rich 5 comic, droll, funny, jokey
6 absurd 7 comical 8 farcical 9 laughable, ludicrous 10 ridiculous
risk 4 ante, dare, defy 5 peril, stake,
throw, wager 6 chance, danger, gamble,
hazard, menace, stakes 7 imperil, jeopard, venture 8 endanger, exposure,
jeopardy 9 adventure, encounter, liability 10 jeopardize
risky 4 bold 5 dicey, hairy 6 chancy, daring, touchy, tricky 7 parlous, unsound
8 delicate, perilous, ticklish 9 dangerous, hazardous, unhealthy 10 jeopar-
dous, precarious 11 adventurous, speculative, treacherous
risqué 4 blue, lewd, racy, sexy 5 broad,
crude, dirty, salty, spicy, vampy
6 coarse, daring, earthy, purple, ribald,

vulgar 7 naughty, obscene, raunchy 8 indecent, off-color, scabrous 9 salacious 10 indecorous, indelicate, suggestive
rite 6 office 7 liturgy, mystery, service 8 ceremony 9 formality, ordinance, sacrament, solemnity 10 ceremonial, initiation, observance 11 celebration, sacramental *funeral:* 6 exequy 7 obsequy 8 exequies 9 obsequies *Jewish:* 4 bris *of initiation or purification:* 7 baptism *of knighthood:* 8 accolade (see also SACRAMENT)
ritual see RITE
ritzy 4 posh 5 fancy, swank 6 chichi, classy, modish, snazzy, swanky 7 elegant, high-hat, stylish 9 au courant, exclusive, expensive, luxurious 11 fashionable 12 ostentatious
rival 3 tie, try, vie 4 even, peer, side 5 equal, match 6 strive 7 attempt, compete, contend, contest, emulate 8 approach, opponent 9 adversary, competing, contender, measure up 10 antagonist, competitor, contending, contestant 11 comparative, competition
rivalry 6 strife 7 contest, warfare 8 conflict, jealousy, tug-of-war 9 emulation 10 contention, opposition 11 competition
rive 3 rip 4 rend, tear 5 break, burst, crack, sever, smash, split 6 cleave, divide, shiver, sunder 7 fissure, shatter 8 fracture, fragment, lacerate, separate, splinter
river *Africa:* 4 Bomu, Juba 5 Chari, Congo, Shari, Tsavo, Zaire 6 Atbara, Mbomou, Songwe, Ubangi 7 Aruwimi, Limpopo, Zambesi, Zambezi 9 Astaboras, Crocodile *Alabama:* 5 Coosa 6 Mobile 7 Conecuh, Perdido 9 Tombigbee 10 Tallapoosa *Alaska:* 5 Kobuk 6 Copper, Noatak, Tanana 7 Koyukuk, Susitna 9 Kuskokwim *Albania:* 4 Drin 5 Drini *Argentina:* 5 Negro 6 Paraná 7 Matanza *arm:* 6 branch 9 tributary *Asia:* 3 Ili 4 Amur, Oxus 5 Indus 6 Jayhun, Sutlej 7 Oedanes 8 Amu Darya 9 Dyardanes 11 Brahmaputra *Australia:* 4 Daly 5 Roper, Yarra 6 Barwon, Culgoa, Dawson, DeGrey, Murray 7 Darling, Fitzroy, Lachlan 8 Victoria 10 Yarra Yarra *Austria:* 4 Enns *bank:* 5 levee *Belgium:* 5 Rupel, Senne, Weser 6 Dender, Dindar, Ourthe 8 Visurgis *Bolivia:* 4 Beni 5 Abuná 6 Mamoré *Borneo:* 5 Kajan *bottom:* 3 bed *Brazil:* 3 Ica 4 Pará, Paru 5 Negro, Xingu 6 Paraná 7 Madeira, Tapajos, Tapajoz *British Columbia:* 6 Skeena 10 Bella Coola *California:* 3 Eel, Pit 4 Kern, Yuba 6 Merced

7 Feather, Salinas, Trinity 8 Tuolumne *Cambodia:* 8 Tonle Sap *Canada:* 3 Bow 4 Back 5 Moose, Peace, Slave 6 Beaver, Fraser, Nelson 8 Gatineau, Saguenay 9 Athabasca, Great Fish, Mackenzie, Richelieu 11 Assiniboine *Carolinas:* 7 Catawba *central United States:* 3 Fox 5 Grand 6 Neosho, Platte, Wabash 8 Keya Paha, Missouri, Niobrara 9 Tennessee, Verdigris 10 Republican, Saint Croix 11 Mississippi *channel:* 6 alveus *Chile:* 3 Loa 5 Itata, Maule 6 Bío-Bío 8 Valdivia *China:* 3 Bei, Hun, Wei 4 Dong 5 Baihe, Chang, Huang, Tarim 6 Yellow 7 Kashgar, Yangtze *China-North Korea:* 4 Yalu *Colombia:* 4 Tomo 6 Atrato 9 Magdalena *Colorado:* 5 Yampa 8 Gunnison *Connecticut:* 6 Thames 7 Niantic, Shepaug 9 Naugatuck 10 Farmington, Housatonic, Quinnipiac 11 Willimantic *crossing:* 4 ford *current:* 4 eddy 6 rapids *Czech Republic:* 4 Iser 6 Jizera, Moldau, Vltava *dam:* 4 weir *Denmark:* 4 Stor *dried bed:* 4 wadi *East Asia:* 4 Yalu 5 Amnok 7 Oryokko *Ecuador:* 4 Napo 10 Esmeraldas *England:* 3 Esk, Exe, Nen, Ure 4 Aire, Avon, Eden, Nene, Ouse, Tees, Tyne, Wear, Yare 5 Swale, Trent 6 Mersey, Ribble, Thames *Ethiopia:* 3 Omo 4 Baro, Dawa *Europe:* 4 Eger, Elbe, Labe, Oder, Ohre 5 Albis, Saale 6 Danube, Ticino *Florida:* 6 Indian 9 Kissimmee 10 Saint Johns 12 Apalachicola *France:* 3 Ain, Lot, Var 4 Aire, Aude, Cher, Eure, Gers, Loir, Oise, Orne, Saar, Tarn, Yser 5 Adour, Marne, Rhône, Saare, Sâone, Seine, Somme, Yonne 6 Allier, Ariège, Scarpe, Vienne 7 Durance, Garonne, La Riège 8 Charente, Dordogne *Georgia:* 6 Etowah, Oconee 8 Altamaha, Ocmulgee 13 Chattahoochee *Germany:* 3 Ems, Rur 4 Eder, Eger, Elbe, Isar, Main, Rems, Ruhr 5 Hunte, Lippe, Rhine, Spree, Werra, Weser 6 Neckar *Germany-Poland:* 4 Oder *Ghana:* 5 Volta *god:* 7 Alpheus, Inachus 8 Achelous *Greece:* 3 Iri 4 Arta 5 Lerna, Lerne 7 Alpheus, Eurotas 8 Achelous 9 Arakhthos *Honduras:* 4 Ulúa 5 Aguán 6 Patuca *Iberian:* 5 Douro, Duero *Idaho:* 5 Lemhi *Illinois:* 8 Mackinaw *India:* 4 Sind 5 Sindh, Tapti 6 Chenab, Ganges, Jhelum, Kaveri, Kistna 7 Cauvery, Krishna 8 Acesines, Godavari *inlet:* 5 bayou 6 slough *Iran:* 3 Kor 4 Mand, Mund 5 Karun 8 Safid Rud, Sefid Rud *Ireland:* 3 Lee 4 Deel, Erne, Suir 5 Boyne, Clare, Foyle 6 Barrow, Liffey 7 Shannon *Italy:* 4 Adda,

Arno, Liri, Nera 5 Adige, Arnus, Etsch, Liris, Oglio, Padus, Piave, Tiber 6 Ollius, Rapido, Tevere, Trebia 7 Athesis, Rubicon, Secchia, Tiberis, Trebbia 8 Rubicone, Volturno *Kansas:* 6 Pawnee *Kazakhstan-Russia:* 4 Ural 5 Tobol 6 Irtysh *Kenya:* 4 Athi, Tana *Kubla Khan's:* 4 Alph *land:* 4 holm 5 flats 7 bottoms *Latvia:* 5 Gauja *Latvia-Lithuania:* 7 Lielupe *Lebanon:* 6 Litani *Little Rock's:* 8 Arkansas *living on the bank of:* 8 riparian *longest:* 4 Nile *Louisiana:* 11 Atchafalaya *Maine:* 8 Kennebec 9 Aroostook, Penobscot *Malaysia:* 9 Trengganu *Maryland:* 8 Monocacy, Patapsco, Patuxent 9 Nanticoke *Massachusetts:* 7 Charles, Taunton 9 Westfield 10 Housatonic *Mexico:* 6 Pánuco, Sonora 7 Tabasco 8 Grijalva *Michigan:* 4 Cass 5 Huron 7 Saginaw 8 Manistee, Muskegon 9 Cheboygan, Kalamazoo 10 Michigamme, Shiawassee *Mississippi:* 5 Pearl, Yazoo 10 Pascagoula *Moldova-Ukraine:* 8 Dneister *Missouri:* 5 Osage *mouth:* 5 delta *Myanmar (Burma):* 4 Pegu 8 Chindwin, Irrawady *Nebraska:* 4 Loup 6 Nemaha, Platte 7 Elkhorn *Netherlands:* 4 Waal 5 Issel, Yssel 6 IJssel 7 Vahalis *New England:* 4 Saco 6 Nashua 9 Merrimack 10 Blackstone 11 Connecticut 12 Androscoggin *New Jersey:* 6 Rahway 7 Passaic, Raritan 8 Tuckahoe *New York:* 5 Tioga 6 Hudson, Mohawk, Oneida, Oswego, Seneca 7 Chemung, Niagara 8 Chenango *New Zealand:* 7 Waikato *Nicaragua:* 4 Coco 7 Segovia *Nigeria:* 5 Benin *North Carolina:* 3 Haw, Tar 5 Neuse 6 Chowan 8 Alamance *northeast United States:* 4 Ohio 6 Hoosic 7 Genesee, Hocking 8 Delaware, Mahoning 9 Allegheny 11 Monongahela, Susquehanna *Northern Ireland:* 4 Bann 6 Mourne *North Korea:* 5 Daido 7 Taedong *northwest United States:* 5 Snake 7 Klamath 8 Columbia 11 Pend Oreille *Norway:* 4 Tana, Teno *nymph:* 5 naiad *of fire:* 10 Phlegethon *of forgetfulness:* 5 Lethe *of ice:* 7 glacier *of woe:* 7 Acheron *Ohio:* 5 Miami 8 Cuyahoga, Sandusky 9 Muskingum 10 Tuscarawas *Oklahoma:* 8 Cimarron *Oregon:* 5 Rogue 6 Owyhee 7 Malheur 8 McKenzie 9 Clackamas, Deschutes 10 Willamette *Panama:* 5 Tuira 7 Chagres *Papua New Guinea:* 3 Fly 5 Sepik *Paraguay:* 3 Apa 9 Pilcomayo *Pennsylvania:* 6 Lehigh 10 Schuylkill *Peru:* 5 Rímac, Santa 7 Marañón 8 Apurímac, Huallaga, Urubamba *Philippines:* 4 Abra, Agno 5 Pasig 7 Cagayan 8 Cotabato, Min-

danao, Pampanga *Poland:* 3 San 7 Vistula *Portugal:* 4 Sado 7 Mondego *relating to:* 7 fluvial *Rhode Island:* 7 Seekonk 8 Sakonnet 10 Providence *Romania:* 5 Arges *Russia:* 3 Don, Oka, Ufa, Usa 4 Kama, Kara, Lena, Msta, Neva, Sura, Svir 5 Onega, Terek, Volga 6 Anadyr, Angara, Belaya, Kolima, Kolyma, Ussuri, Vyatka 7 Dnieper, Pechora, Yenisey 8 Barguzin, Kostroma, Voronezh, Vychegda *Russia-Ukraine:* 6 Donets *sacred:* 6 Ganges *Scotland:* 3 Dee, Don, Esk, Tay 4 Doon, Nith, Spey, Tyne 5 Afton, Annan, Clyde, Forth, Tweed 6 Teviot 7 Deveron 8 Findhorn *Shanghai's:* 7 Huangpu, Hwang Pu *Sicily:* 5 Salso 6 Simeto *siren:* 7 Lorelei *Slovakia:* 3 Vag, Vah 4 Gran, Hron, Waag 5 Garam, Nitra 6 Neutra, Nyitra *South Africa:* 4 Vaal 6 Orange *South America:* 3 Apa 6 Amazon 8 Amazonas, Orellana 9 Pilcomayo *South Carolina:* 6 Saluda, Santee 7 Wateree 8 Congaree *South Dakota:* 3 Bad *Southeast Asia:* 6 Dza-chu, Mekong 7 Salween 8 Lan-ts'ang *southeast United States:* 6 Pee Dee 7 Noxubee, Washita 8 Escambia, Ouachita, Suwannee 10 Okanoxubee *southern United States:* 6 Sabine *South Korea:* 3 Kum *southwest United States:* 4 Gila, Zuni 5 Pecos 8 Colorado *Spain:* 4 Ebro 6 Aragon 12 Guadalquivir *Sweden:* 4 Göta 5 Kalix *Switzerland:* 3 Aar 4 Aare 5 Reuss *Syria:* 6 Khabur 7 Orontes *Tasmania:* 4 Huon *Tbilisi's:* 4 Kura *Texas:* 5 Llano 6 Brazos, Nueces 7 San Saba, Trinity 9 Guadalupe *Texas-Mexico:* 8 Rio Bravo 9 Rio Grande *tidal:* 7 estuary *Tokyo's:* 6 Sumida *Turkey:* 4 Aras 5 Araks 6 Seihun, Seyhan *Ukrainian:* 3 Bug 4 Alma *underworld:* 4 Styx 5 Lethe 7 Acheron, Cocytus 10 Phlegethon *Uruguay:* 5 Negro *Utah:* 5 Provo, Uinta, Weber 6 Jordan, Sevier *valley:* 6 strath *Venezuela:* 5 Apure, Caura 6 Caroní 7 Orinoco *Vermont:* 3 Mad 5 Onion, White 8 Winooski *Virginia:* 3 Dan 5 James 7 Rapidan 9 Nansemond 10 Appomattox, Shenandoah 12 Chickahominy, Rappahannock *wailing:* 7 Cocytus *Wales:* 4 Dyfi 5 Clwyd, Dovey, Teifi *Washington:* 6 Skagit, Yakima 9 Klickitat, Snohomish, Wenatchee *West Africa:* 5 Niger 6 Gambia 7 Senegal *western United States:* 7 Laramie 8 Columbia, Flathead 11 Yellowstone *West Virginia:* 7 Kanawha *Wisconsin:* 8 Kickapoo 9 Menominee *Wyoming:* 8 Shoshone 10 Gros Ventre 11 Medicine Bow

___ **Rivera 5** Diego
river duck 4 teal **6** wigeon **7** dabbler, mallard, widgeon **8** shoveler **9** greenwing
river horse 5 hippo **12** hippopotamus
riverine 8 riparian
river island 3 ait
rivet 3 fix, pin **4** bolt, brad, stud **5** affix **6** absorb, attach, clinch, fasten **7** engross **8** fastener
Riviera city 4 Nice **6** Cannes, Monaco **7** Antibes, San Remo **8** St. Tropez **10** Monte Carlo
rivulet 3 run **4** beck, burn, gill, race, rill **5** bourn, brook, creek **6** runlet, runnel, stream **9** streamlet
Rizpah *father:* **4** Aiah *lover:* **4** Saul *son:* **6** Armoni **12** Mephibosheth
roach 3 hog **6** shiner **7** sunfish
road 3 way **4** fare, lane, line, path **5** drive, going, route, track **6** artery, avenue, career, causey, course, street **7** highway, journey, passage **8** causeway, chaussée, crossway, highroad, pavement, speedway, turnpike **9** boulevard **12** thoroughfare *along a cliff:* **8** corniche *around a city:* **6** bypass **7** beltway *bend:* **7** hairpin *edge:* **4** berm **8** shoulder *French:* **6** chemin *Irish:* **6** boreen *machine:* **5** paver **6** grader **9** bulldozer *Roman:* **3** via **4** iter *side:* **6** branch **8** shunpike *Spanish:* **6** camino *surface:* **3** tar **6** gravel **7** macadam **8** pavement
roadblock 7 barrier **8** blockade **9** barricade **11** obstruction
road book 3 map **5** atlas **9** gazetteer, itinerary
roadhouse 3 bar, inn **4** dive **5** hotel, lodge **6** tavern **9** nightclub
roadrunner 6 cuckoo **13** chaparral cock
road rut 6 kettle **7** pothole **9** chuckhole
roam 3 bat, bum, gad, run **4** rove, walk **5** drift, prowl, range, stray **6** ramble, stroll, travel, wander **7** meander, traipse **8** straggle, vagabond **9** gallivant
roamer 3 bum **5** gipsy, gypsy, nomad, rover **6** ranger, walker **7** drifter, prowler, rambler, vagrant **8** marauder, stroller, traveler, vagabond, wanderer **11** nightwalker
roar 3 din **4** bawl, bell, boom, bray, howl, yell **5** shout **6** bellow, clamor, outcry **7** bluster **10** vociferate *bullring:* **3** olé
roast 4 bake, mock, rack, sear **5** broil, grill, joint, parch **6** scathe, scorch **7** banquet, blister, mockery, swelter **8** barbecue, ridicule **9** criticize
rob 3 cop, mug **4** lift, loot, nick, raid, roll, sack **5** boost, filch, heist, pinch, pluck, reave, steal **6** burgle, fleece,

hijack, hold up, pilfer, rip off, snitch, thieve **7** defraud, deprive, despoil, pillage, plunder, purloin, ransack, stick up, swindle **8** knock off **9** knock over **10** burglarize
robber 4 yegg **5** crook, thief **6** bandit, looter, mugger, pirate, reiver **7** brigand, burglar, footpad, rustler **8** hijacker, swindler **9** holdup man **10** cat burglar, highwayman, sandbagger, stickup man **12** housebreaker *grave:* **5** ghoul
robbery 5 heist, theft **6** holdup, piracy **7** larceny, mugging, stickup **8** banditry
robe 3 aba **4** cape, gown, wrap **5** cloak, habit **6** caftan, mantle **7** garment, manteau **8** covering, dalmatic, vestment *baptismal:* **7** chrisom *bishop's:* **7** chimere *of Roman emperors:* **6** purple *Turkish:* **6** dolman
Robinson Crusoe *author:* **5** Defoe (Daniel) *character:* **6** Friday
robot 5 golem **7** android **8** automata (plural) **9** automaton
Rob Roy author 5 Scott (Walter)
robust 4 hale, rude **5** hardy, husky, lusty, rough, sound, stout **6** hearty, potent, rugged, sinewy, strong, sturdy **7** healthy **8** athletic, muscular, vigorous **9** strapping **10** boisterous, red-blooded, full-bodied, prosperous
robustious 4 rude **5** lusty, rough, rowdy, wooly **6** rugged **7** boorish, ill-bred, loutish **8** churlish, clownish **9** unrefined **10** boisterous, unpolished
rock 4 crag, reel, roll, sway, toss **5** geode, pitch, quake, shake, swing **6** totter **7** boulder, breccia **8** astonish, convulse, undulate **9** oscillate *basaltic:* **5** wacke *cavity:* **3** vug *combining form:* **4** lite, lith, lyte, petr **5** clast, petri, petro *decomposed:* **6** gossan *fissile:* **5** shale *formation:* **5** nappe **6** pluton **7** rimrock, terrane **8** isocline, syncline *fragment:* **8** xenolith *igneous:* **4** lava **6** basalt, gabbro, pumice **7** diabase, diorite, granite **8** eruptive, felstone, obsidian, porphyry, traprock **10** travertine *layer:* **10** mantlerock *mass:* **5** scree **9** batholith *metamorphic:* **5** slate **6** gneiss, marble, schist **9** quartzite, soapstone *molten:* **4** lava *sedimentary:* **4** clay, coal **5** chalk, chert, coral, flint, shale **8** mudstone **9** limestone, sandstone, siltstone *volcanic:* **4** tuff **6** basalt
rock bass 7 sunfish
rock-bottom 4 root **6** lowest **8** cheapest **9** lowermost **11** fundamental
rocket 3 fly, zip **4** soar, whiz, zoom **5** mount **6** ascend, bullet **7** missile, shoot up **8** firework, starship **10** projectile *landing:* **7** reentry **10** splashdown

launcher: 7 bazooka *launching:* 7 liftoff 8 blastoff *scientist:* 5 Braun (Wernher von) 7 Goddard (Robert)

rockfish 4 cony, hind 5 coney 7 grouper, jewfish, sea bass 8 bocaccio 10 scorpaenid 11 striped bass

Rockies resort 4 Vail 5 Aspen 8 Snowmass 9 Telluride

___ **Rockne** 5 Knute

rock rabbit 4 cony, pika 5 coney, hyrax 6 dassie

rock-ribbed 5 rigid 8 dogmatic, obdurate 9 unbending 10 inflexible, unyielding

rockweed 5 algae, fucus 7 seaweed 12 bladder wrack

rocky hill 3 tor 5 kopje

rococo 4 busy 5 showy 6 florid, frilly, ornate 7 baroque, elegant, opulent 9 elaborate, intricate 10 decorative, flamboyant 11 overwrought

rod 3 bar 4 cane, pole, wand 5 baton, dowel, spoke, staff, stave, stick 6 pistol 7 scepter 8 revolver 10 correction, discipline, punishment 11 castigation 12 chastisement *bundle of:* 6 fasces

rodent 3 rat 4 cavy, cony, mole, paca, pika, vole 5 cavie, coney, coypu, mouse, shrew 6 agouti, beaver, gerbil, gopher, jerboa, marmot, murine, nutria, rabbit 7 hamster, lemming, leveret, muskrat 8 capybara, chipmunk, dormouse, squirrel, tuco tuco, viscacha, vizcacha, water rat 9 guinea pig, porcupine 10 chinchilla, field mouse, prairie dog 11 kangaroo rat, meadow mouse, pocket mouse 12 pocket gopher *aquatic:* 5 coypu 6 beaver, nutria 7 muskrat 8 musquash *burrowing:* 6 gerbil, gopher 7 hamster 8 viscacha, vizcacha *family:* 5 murid 6 murine 7 sciurid *genus:* 3 Mus 5 Lepus

rodeo 7 contest, roundup 9 enclosure 10 exhibition 11 competition *animal:* 5 horse, steer 10 Brahma bull *event:* 10 calf roping 11 bulldogging 12 bronco riding *performer:* 5 clown 6 cowboy

___ **Rodin** 7 Auguste

rodomontade 4 blow, brag, rant 5 boast, swash, vaunt 7 bluster, swagger 9 gasconade 11 braggadocio

Rodomonte *beloved:* 8 Doralice *slayer:* 8 Ruggiero

Rodrigo Díaz de Bivar 5 El Cid

rod-shaped 7 virgate 8 bacillar 9 bacillary

roe 4 deer, eggs 6 beluga, caviar, osetra 7 sevruga

Roentgen's discovery 4 X-ray

rogation 6 litany, prayer 8 entreaty, petition 10 beseeching 12 supplication

___ **Rogers** 3 Roy 4 Carl, Fred, Will 6 Ginger, Robert

rogue 5 cheat, gypsy, knave, scamp 6 rascal 7 lowlife, sharper, villain 8 picaroon, scalawag, swindler 9 defrauder, miscreant, reprobate, scoundrel, skeezicks, trickster 10 blackguard, mountebank 11 rapscallion *relating to:* 10 picaresque

roguery 5 fraud 7 devilry, knavery, waggery 8 deviltry, mischief, trickery 9 devilment, diablerie 11 waggishness 12 sportiveness

roguish 3 sly 4 arch 6 impish, wicked 7 knavish 8 devilish, espiègle, scampish 10 picaresque 11 mischievous

roil 3 mud, vex 4 foul, rile, romp 5 annoy, dirty, grate, muddy, peeve, upset 6 befoul, muddle, nettle, stir up 7 agitate, disturb 8 disorder, irritate 9 aggravate 10 exasperate

roily 5 muddy, riley 6 turbid 9 turbulent

roister 4 riot 5 revel 6 frolic 7 carouse, reveler, wassail 9 wassailer

Roland 7 Orlando *beloved:* 4 Aude *betrayer:* 4 Gano 7 Ganelon *friend:* 6 Oliver 7 Olivier *horn:* 7 Olivant *sword:* 8 Durandal, Durendal *uncle:* 11 Charlemagne

role 3 bit 4 duty, lead, part, pose 5 cameo, cloak, guise, niche 6 aspect, office 7 quality 8 capacity, function, position 9 character 13 impersonation

roll 3 bun, rob 4 bolt, coil, flow, furl, gyre, list, pour, rock, toss, turn, wind, wrap 5 heave, pitch, surge 6 bundle, roster, rotate, stream, swathe, wallow, wrap up 7 biscuit, brioche, envelop, revolve, swaddle, trundle 8 involute, register, schedule, turn over

roll about 6 wallow, welter

roll back 5 lower 6 reduce, repeal 7 curtail, rescind

roller 3 rod 4 bowl, drum, wave 6 canary, caster, platen 7 breaker, carrier, tumbler 8 cylinder

Roller-Derby round 3 jam

rollick 4 lark, play, romp 5 caper, frisk, party, revel, sport 6 cavort, frolic, gambol 7 disport, skylark 8 escapade 9 merriment

rollicking 4 wild 5 antic, merry 6 frisky, lively 8 sportive 10 boisterous, frolicsome 12 high-spirited

rolling stock 4 cars 7 coaches, engines 8 cabooses, Pullmans, sleepers, trailers 11 locomotives

rolling stone 5 rover 6 roamer 7 drifter, rambler, vagrant 8 wanderer, vagabond

roly-poly see ROTUND

Roman 5 Latin 7 Italian *amphitheater:* 9 Colosseum *assembly:* 5 forum 6 senate 7 comitia *building:* 5 Forum 6 Circus 8 basilica, Pantheon *clan:* 4 gens *comedy writer:* **7** Plautus (Titus), Terence *conspirator:* **6** Brutus (Marcus Junius) **7** Cassius (Gaius) **8** Catiline *date:* **4** Ides **7** calends, kalends *emperor:* **4** Nero, Otho **5** Galba (Servius Sulpicius), Nerva (Marcus Cocceius), Titus, Verus (Lucius Aurelius) **6** Julian, Trajan **7** Hadrian, Maximus (Magnus Clemens, Marcus Clodius, Petronius), Severus (Lucius Septimius) **8** Augustus, Caligula, Claudius, Commodus (Lucius Aelius), Domitian, Tiberius, Valerian **9** Caracalla, Vespasian **10** Diocletian, Theodosius **11** Constantine, Valentinian *entrance hall:* **5** atria (plural) **6** atrium *epic:* **6** Aeneid *epigrammatist:* **7** Martial *family:* **7** Gracchi *Fates:* **4** Nona **5** Morta **6** Decuma, Parcae *founder:* **5** Remus **7** Romulus *fountain:* **5** Trevi **6** Triton *garment:* **4** toga **5** tunic *general:* **5** Sulla (Lucius Cornelius), Titus **6** Antony (Marc), Marius (Gaius), Scipio (Publius Cornelius) **8** Agricola (Gnaeus Julius) *god:* **4** deus *blind:* **6** Plutus *chief:* **4** Jove **7** Jupiter *messenger:* **7** Mercury *of agriculture:* **6** Saturn *of animals:* **6** Faunus *of death:* **4** Mors *of dreams:* **8** Morpheus *of fire:* **6** Vulcan *of gates and doors:* **5** Janus *of healing:* **9** Asclepius **11** Aesculapius *of heaven:* **6** Uranus *of households:* **5** Lares **7** Penates *of love:* **4** Amor **5** Cupid *of medicine:* **9** Asclepius **11** Aesculapius *of mirth:* **5** Comus *of regeneration:* **6** Priapus *of sleep:* **6** Somnus *of the sea:* **6** Pontus **7** Neptune, Proteus *of the sun:* **3** Sol **6** Apollo *of the underworld:* **3** Dis **5** Orcus, Pluto **8** Dispater *of the wind:* **5** Eurus, Notus **6** Aeolus, Aquilo, Auster, Boreas **8** Favonius, Zephyrus *of war:* **4** Mars **8** Quirinus *of wealth:* **6** Plutus *of wine:* **7** Bacchus *of woods:* **6** Faunus *two-faced:* **5** Janus *goddess:* **3** dea *of agriculture:* **5** Ceres *of beauty:* **5** Venus *of dawn:* **5** Aurora *of flowers:* **5** Flora *of handicrafts:* **7** Minerva *of harvests:* **3** Ops *of health:* **7** Minerva *of hope:* **4** Spes *of hunting:* **5** Diana *of justice:* **7** Astraea *of love:* **5** Venus *of marriage:* **4** Juno *of night:* **3** Nox *of peace:* **3** Pax *of springs:* **7** Juturna *of strife:* **9** Discordia *of the earth:* **6** Tellus *of the hearth:* **5** Vesta *of the moon:* **4** Luna *of the sea:* **10** Amphitrite *of the underworld:* **10** Proserpina *of victory:* **6** Vacuna *of war:* **7** Bellona *of wisdom:* **7** Minerva *of womanhood:* **4** Juno *greeting:* **3** ave *hero:* **6** Caesar (Julius) **11** Cincinnatus (Lucius Quinctius) *hill:* **7** Caelian, Viminal **8** Aventine, Palatine, Quirinal **9** Esquiline **10** Capitoline *historian:* **4** Livy **5** Nepos **7** Sallust, Tacitus **9** Suetonius *king:* **7** Romulus, Servius, Tullius

12 Ancus Martius **13** Numa Pompilius *marketplace:* **5** agora *military formation:* **3** ala **6** alares (plural) **7** phalanx *miltary unit:* **6** cohort, legion **7** maniple *officer:* **9** centurion *official:* **5** augur, edile **6** aedile, censor, consul, lictor **7** praetor, prefect, tribune **8** quaestor *people:* **5** Laeti, plebs **6** populi (plural) **7** populus, Sabines **9** plebeians *philosopher:* **4** Cato **6** Seneca **8** Apuleius **9** Epictetus, Lucretius *physician:* **9** Asclepius **11** Aesculapius *port:* **5** Ostia *procurator:* **6** Pilate (Pontius) *racecourse:* **6** circus *road:* **4** iter *slave:* **9** Spartacus *statesman:* **4** Cato **5** Pliny **6** Caesar, Cicero, Pompey, Seneca **7** Agrippa **8** Augustus, Gracchus, Maecenas **9** Flaminius *symbol of authority:* **6** fasces

roman à ___ **4** clef
romance 3 woo **4** gest, love **5** amour, court, fling, geste, novel **6** affair **7** fantasy, fiction **8** stardust **10** love affair **12** bodice ripper
Romance language 6 French **7** Catalan, Italian, Spanish **8** Romanian, Rumanian **9** Sardinian **10** Portuguese
Romania capital: **9** Bucharest *city:* **4** Iasi **6** Brasov, Galati **7** Craiova **9** Constanta, Timisoara *monetary unit:* **3** leu *mountain range:* **10** Carpathian *neighbor:* **6** Serbia **7** Hungary, Moldova, Ukraine **8** Bulgaria *part of:* **7** Balkans *peninsula:* **6** Balkan *river:* **5** Tisza **6** Danube *sea:* **5** Black
romantic 5 gauzy, ideal, idyll, mushy **6** ardent, dreamy, exotic, gothic, poetic, unreal **7** amorous, maudlin, mawkish **8** fanciful, quixotic **9** fantastic, imaginary, visionary **10** idealistic, lovey-dovey **11** sentimental
Romany 5 Gipsy, Gypsy
Romeo 7 amorist, Don Juan, gallant **8** Casanova, lothario, paramour *beloved:* **6** Juliet *enemy:* **6** Tybalt *father:* **8** Montague *friend:* **8** Mercutio
Rommel, Erwin 9 Desert Fox
romp 4 lark, play **5** caper, frisk, sport **6** cavort, frolic, gambol, hoyden **7** rollick, runaway, skylark **8** escapade
Romulus brother: **5** Remus *father:* **4** Mars *mother:* **9** Rea Silvia **10** Rhea Silvia *victim:* **5** Remus
rondure 3 arc, orb **4** arch, ball, ring **5** curve, globe, round **6** circle, sphere **9** curvature
rood 5 cross **8** crucifix
roof 3 hip, top **4** apex, peak **5** cover, crest, crown **6** summit **7** ceiling **8** covering, housetop *material:* **3** tar, tin **4** tile **5** slate, straw, terne **6** copper, thatch **7** shingle *of a cavern:* **4** dome *of the mouth:* **6** palate *part:* **3** hip **4** eave *structure:* **9** penthouse *type:* **5** gable **7** gam-

brel, mansard **9** butterfly *vaulted:*
4 dome
roofer 5 tiler
rook 4 bilk, colt, crow, scam, tyro
5 cheat, mulct, raven, stick **6** castle,
fleece, novice **7** amateur, defraud,
recruit, swindle, trainee **8** beginner,
flimflam, freshman, neophyte, newcomer **10** apprentice, tenderfoot
rookery 5 roost **6** colony
rookie 4 colt, tyro **6** novice **7** amateur,
recruit, trainee **8** beginner, freshman,
neophyte, newcomer **10** apprentice,
tenderfoot
room 3 den **4** cell, hall, play, rein
5 divan, house, lodge, put up, salon,
scope, space **6** alcove, billet, leeway,
margin, reside, studio **7** chamber, cubicle, expanse, gallery, lodging **9** clearance *ancient Roman:* **5** atria (plural)
6 atrium *eating:* **4** nook **6** alcove **7** commons, kitchen **8** mess hall **9** refectory
food storage: **6** larder, pantry *for paint-
ings:* **7** gallery *in a monastery:* **4** cell
9 refectory **11** calefactory *in a prison:*
4 cell *on a ship:* **5** cabin **6** galley *round:*
7 rotunda
roomer 5 guest **6** lodger, renter, tenant
7 boarder
roomy 4 wide **5** ample, broad, large
8 spacious **9** capacious **10** commodious
Roosevelt, Franklin D. *birthplace:* **8** Hyde
Park *dog:* **4** Fala *message:* **12** fireside
chat *mother:* **4** Sara *predecessor:*
6 Hoover (Herbert) *program:* **7** New
Deal *successor:* **6** Truman (Harry) *wife:*
7 Eleanor
roost 3 sit **4** land, nest, rest **5** perch
6 alight, settle **7** rookery **8** dovecote
rooster 4 cock **5** capon **8** cockerel, game-
cock **10** cockalorum **11** chanticleer
root 3 dig, fix **4** base, bulb, core, grub,
pith, stem, well **5** basis, cheer, embed,
grout, lodge, plant, radix, tuber **6** bottom, etymon, ground, marrow, origin,
settle, source **7** applaud, bedrock,
essence, footing, radical **8** radicate
9 beginning, establish, inception
10 foundation *aromatic:* **7** ginseng *edible:* **3** oca, yam **4** beet **6** carrot, daikon,
ginger, jicama, potato, radish, turnip
7 burdock, parsnip, salsify **8** celeriac,
kohlrabi, rutabaga, tuckahoe **11** horseradish *fragrant:* **5** orris **7** vetiver *main:*
7 taproot *medicinal:* **5** jalap **7** ginseng
relating to: **7** radical *starch:* **4** arum *tropical:* **4** taro *word:* **6** etymon
rootlet 7 radicle, rhizoid
root out 4 grub **9** eradicate, extirpate
10 deracinate
Roots author 5 Haley (Alex)
rope 3 guy, tie **4** bind, cord, line, stay

5 belay, bight, brace, cable, chord,
lasso, riata, sheet **6** binder, fasten, halter, hawser, lariat, marlin, shroud,
strand, string, tether **7** halyard, lashing,
marline, painter, towline **8** buntline,
lifeline *loop:* **7** cringle *mooring:*
6 hawser *ship's:* **6** marlin, parral, parrel
7 lanyard, marline, ratline
ropedancer 11 funambulist
rope off 6 cordon
ropes 10 ins and outs, procedures, tech-
niques
ropy 4 wiry **6** sinewy **7** stringy, viscous
8 muscular
roque 7 croquet
rorqual 5 whale **7** finback **8** fin whale
11 baleen whale
Rosalind's beloved 7 Orlando
rosary 5 beads **7** chaplet **8** beadroll,
devotion **11** prayer beads
rose 4 glow, pink **5** blush, color, flush,
rouge **6** mantle, pinken, redden **7** crimson **10** erysipelas *Chinese:* **8** Cherokee
cotton: **7** cudweed *feature:* **5** thorn *kind:*
4 moss **5** Peace, Vogue **6** Circus,
damask **7** Fashion, Granada, Iceberg,
New Dawn, Pascali, Tiffany **8** Rubaiyat
9 Floradora, Montezuma, polyantha,
Tropicana **10** Floribunda **11** grandiflo-
ra, Mount Shasta **12** Crimson Glory
roseate 3 red **4** pink **5** sunny **6** bright,
upbeat **7** beamish **8** cheerful, sanguine
10 optimistic
rose-colored see ROSEATE
Rosenkavalier composer 7 Strauss
(Richard)
rose of ___ 6 Sharon
rose oil 5 attar
Rose Tattoo author 8 Williams (Tennessee)
rosette 7 cockade **8** ornament
Rosinante's master 7 Quixote (Don)
Rosmersholm author 5 Ibsen (Henrik)
___ Rossetti 5 Dante (Gabriel) **9** Christina *work:* **8** Sing-Song **11** Annus Domini,
House of Life (The), Seek and Find,
Sister Helen **12** Beata Beatrix, Goblin
Market
Rossini opera 6 Otello **8** Tancredi
11 Cenerentola (La), William Tell
14 Siege of Corinth (The) **15** Barber of
Seville (The)
Rostand hero 6 Cyrano (de Bergerac)
roster 4 list, roll, rota **5** slate **6** muster,
scroll **8** register, roll call, schedule
9 honor roll **10** muster roll **11** waiting list
rostrum 4 dais **5** bimah **6** pulpit
7 lectern, tribune **8** platform
rosy see ROSEATE
rot 4 bosh, bull, mold **5** decay, hooey,
spoil, taint, trash **6** fester, molder **7** cor-

rupt, crapola, crumble, garbage, hogwash, putrefy, rubbish **8** gangrene, nonsense **9** break down, decompose, poppycock **10** balderdash, degenerate **11** deteriorate, putrescence **12** disintegrate, putrefaction **13** decomposition

rotary 6 circle **8** gyratory, spinning, whirling **10** roundabout **11** vertiginous **13** traffic circle

rotate 4 gyre, roll, spin, turn **5** pivot, twirl, wheel, whirl **6** gyrate, swivel **7** revolve, trundle **9** alternate, pirouette

a log: **4** birl

rotation 4 gyre, loop, turn **5** cycle, orbit, pivot, round, wheel, whirl **7** circuit, turning **8** gyration **10** revolution, succession

rote 5 crowd, grind **6** custom, groove, memory **7** routine **8** practice **9** automatic, treadmill **10** mechanical, repetition **12** memorization

Roth novel 11 Call It Sleep **15** Goodbye Columbus **16** American Pastoral **17** Portnoy's Complaint

rotten 4 foul **5** fetid, lousy **6** crummy, putrid **7** corrupt, decayed, spoiled, tainted **9** nefarious, offensive, putrified **10** decomposed, degenerate, putrescent

rotter 3 cad, cur **4** lout **5** creep, louse **7** bounder **9** scoundrel **10** blackguard

rotund 3 fat **5** obese, plump, podgy, pudgy, round, stout, thick, tubby **6** chubby, chunky, portly, stocky **7** rounded **8** heavyset, roly-poly, thickset **9** corpulent **10** potbellied

roué 4 lech, rake, wolf **6** lecher **7** Don Juan, seducer, swinger **8** Casanova, lothario, sybarite **9** bon vivant, debauchee, libertine, womanizer **10** sensualist, voluptuary **11** philanderer

rouge 3 red **4** glow, pink, rose **5** blush, color, flush **6** mantle, pinken, redden **7** crimson

rough 3 raw **4** rude, wild **5** brute, bumpy, crass, crude, hairy, harsh, raspy, rowdy, yahoo **6** choppy, coarse, craggy, crusty, hoarse, jagged, rugged, stormy, uneven **7** cragged, grating, jarring, rasping, raucous, ruffian, scraggy, uncivil, uncouth **8** bullyboy, churlish, impolite, scabrous, unformed **9** difficult, imperfect, strenuous, turbulent, unrefined **10** boisterous, tumultuous, unfinished, unpolished **11** approximate, tempestuous

rough-and-ready 5 crude **6** make-do **7** stopgap **8** slapdash **9** expedient, impromptu, makeshift **10** improvised **11** provisional **13** quick-and-dirty

rough-hewn 4 rude **5** crude, plain **10** unfinished, unpolished **12** uncultivated

roughly 5 about **9** virtually **10** more or less **13** approximately

roughneck see RUFFIAN

rough out 5 block, chalk, draft **6** sketch **7** outline **9** adumbrate **11** skeletonize

rough up 4 beat, maul **6** batter, pummel **8** maltreat **9** brutalize, manhandle **10** slap around

round 4 gyre, tour, turn **5** bowed, cycle, globe, wheel **6** circle, curved, rotund **7** annular, circuit **8** circular, globular, roly-poly, rotation **9** orbicular, spherical **10** conglobate

roundabout 6 circle, detour, rotary **7** circuit, compass, curving, devious, oblique, winding **8** circular, indirect **10** circuitous, meandering **13** traffic circle

rounded 5 bowed, plump **6** arched, convex, curved, zaftig **7** concave **9** developed **10** curvaceous, Rubenesque **13** well-developed

rounder 4 rake, roué, waif **6** no-good, waster **7** wastrel **8** vagabond **9** libertine **10** profligate

roundly 4 well **5** fully, quite **6** widely, wholly **7** bluntly, sharply, smartly, utterly **8** candidly, entirely **9** brusquely **10** altogether, completely, rigorously, scathingly, thoroughly, vigorously

round off 3 cap, top **5** crown **6** climax, finish **8** conclude **9** culminate

round-robin 6 appeal, letter, series **7** protest **8** petition, sequence **9** statement **10** tournament

round trip 4 tour **7** circuit **9** excursion

round up 4 herd **5** drive, group **6** gather **7** cluster, collect **8** assemble

rouse 3 jog **4** call, goad, rock, stir, wake, whet **5** alarm, awake, pique, rally, roust, waken **6** awaken, bestir, excite, foment, incite, kindle, muster, rattle, recall, revive, vivify, work up **7** agitate, animate, commove, disturb, enliven, provoke, quicken **8** motivate **9** aggravate, challenge, galvanize, instigate, stimulate

rousing 5 brisk, peppy **6** lively **8** animated, exciting, spirited, stirring **9** inspiring **11** stimulating **12** exhilarating, intoxicating

Rousseau work 5 Émile

roustabout 4 hand **6** worker **7** laborer, workman **8** deckhand **10** workingman **12** longshoreman, troublemaker

route 3 way **4** path, road, send, ship **5** guide, pilot, steer, track, trail **6** avenue, bypass, course, detour, direct, divert, escort, flyway, seaway, skyway **7** channel, circuit, conduct, consign, forward, highway, journey, passage, portage, sea-lane 8 corridor, dispatch, transmit, traverse 9 direction, itinerary

routine 3 act, bit, rut 4 dull, pace, rote 5 chore, drill, grind, habit, ho-hum, plain, round, trial, usual 6 course, groove, improv, shtick, wonted 7 chronic, formula, program, regular, utility 8 accepted, everyday, habitual, ordinary, standard, workaday 9 customary, procedure, quotidian, treadmill 10 accustomed, donkeywork, mechanical, monologue 11 commonplace, cut-and-dried, housekeeping, perfunctory 12 unremarkable

rove 3 gad 4 roam 5 drift, range, stray 6 ramble, wander 7 meander, traipse 8 straggle, vagabond 9 gallivant

rover 5 stray 6 pirate, roamer, viking 7 corsair, drifter, floater, rambler, vagrant 8 picaroon, runabout, traveler, wanderer 9 buccaneer, meanderer 10 freebooter 12 rolling stone

roving 6 errant, mobile 7 movable, nomadic, vagrant 8 straying, vagabond 9 itinerant, migratory, wayfaring 11 peripatetic

row 3 oar, way 4 bank, crew, file, fray, fuss, line, muss, rank, spat, tier, tiff 5 align, brawl, broil, chain, fight, melee, order, queue, range, run-in, scrap, scull, strip, swath 6 bicker, clamor, column, dustup, fracas, kickup, paddle, propel, ruckus, series, string, stroke 7 brabble, dispute, quarrel, rhubarb, wrangle 8 argument, diagonal, sequence, squabble 9 commotion 10 falling-out, single file, succession 11 altercation, disturbance, progression

rowdy 4 punk, rude 5 bully, crude, rough, yahoo 6 unruly 7 hoodlum, rackety, raffish, raucous, ruffian 8 bullyboy, hooligan 9 roughneck 10 boisterous, disorderly, robustious 11 rumbustious 12 rambunctious

Rowena *father:* 7 Hengist *guardian:* 6 Cedric *husband:* 7 Ivanhoe 9 Vortigern

Rowling character 11 Harry Potter

Roxana *husband:* 9 Alexander *rival:* 7 Statira

royal 5 grand, noble, regal 6 kingly, lordly 7 stately 8 glorious, imperial, imposing, majestic, princely, splendid 9 grandiose, monarchal, sovereign 10 monarchial 11 magnificent, monarchical

rub 4 buff 5 chafe, grate, shine 6 abrade, polish, smooth, stroke 7 burnish, massage

Rubaiyat author 4 Omar (Khayyám)

rubber 4 buna 5 crepe 6 eraser

10 caoutchouc *basis:* 5 latex *hard:* 7 ebonite *synthetic:* 8 neoprene *tree:* 4 Para

Rubber City 5 Akron

rubberneck 3 eye 4 gape, gawk, gaze 5 snoop, stare 6 goggle 8 sightsee

rubber-stamp 7 approve, certify, endorse 9 authorize

rubbish 3 rot 4 bosh, crap, crud, junk, muck, slop 5 bilge, dreck, hooey, offal, trash, truck, waste 6 debris, litter, refuse, raffle, rubble, spilth 7 crapola, garbage, hogwash 8 nonsense, riffraff, tommyrot 9 poppycock, sweepings 11 foolishness

rubbishy 5 cheap, tatty 6 paltry, shoddy, sleazy, trashy 9 worthless

rubble 5 ruins, scree 6 debris, litter 8 detritus, wreckage

rube 4 boor, hick, naïf 5 churl, cluck, swain, yahoo, yokel 6 rustic 7 bumpkin, hayseed, redneck 9 greenhorn, hillbilly 10 clodhopper 12 apple-knocker, backwoodsman

rubicund 3 red 5 flush, ruddy 6 florid 7 glowing, reddish 8 sanguine 11 fullblooded, incarnadine

___ **Rubik** 4 Erno

rub out 3 ice, off, zap 4 do in, kill, slay 5 erase, smoke, waste, whack 6 finish, murder 7 bump off, destroy, put away 8 dispatch, knock off 9 liquidate, terminate 10 extinguish, obliterate 11 assassinate

rubric 4 name, rule 5 canon, class, gloss, style, title 6 custom 7 concept, heading 8 category, headline 9 tradition 11 appellation, designation 13 interpolation

ruck 3 mob 4 fold, heap, mass, pile 5 crimp, crowd, group, purse, ridge 6 cockle, crease, furrow, gather, jumble, pucker, rumple 7 crinkle, crumple, scrunch, wrinkle 10 generality 11 corrugation

rucksack 4 pack 6 kit bag 7 musette 8 backpack

ruckus 3 row 4 fuss, to-do 5 brawl, melee, scrap 6 fracas, furore, hassle, pother, rumpus, shindy, uproar 7 dispute, quarrel, rhubarb, shindig, wrangle 8 squabble 9 commotion 10 fallingout 11 altercation, controversy, disturbance

ruddle see REDDEN

ruddy 3 red 4 ripe, rosy 5 flush 6 blowsy, florid 7 flushed, glowing 8 rubicund, sanguine 11 full-blooded, incarnadine

rude 3 raw 4 curt 5 crass, gross, gruff, harsh, rough, rowdy, surly 6 abrupt, callow, clumsy, coarse, crusty, robust,

rugged, rustic, sturdy, unhewn, vulgar
7 boorish, brusque, ill-bred, loutish,
lowbred, uncivil, uncouth **8** arrogant,
churlish, clownish, impolite, tactless
9 barbarian, barbarous, elemental, inelegant, primitive, rough-hewn, unrefined **10** ungracious, unmannered,
unmannerly, unpolished **11** ill-mannered, impertinent, uncivilized **12** discourteous, uncultivated **13** disrespectful

rudimentary 5 basal, basic **6** simple **7** initial, primary **8** simplest **9** beginning,
elemental, vestigial **10** elementary
11 fundamental, undeveloped **12** introductory

rudiments 6 basics **10** essentials **12** fundamentals

rue 3 woe **4** pity, ruth **5** dolor, grief,
mourn, prick **6** grieve, lament, regret,
repent, sorrow **7** anguish, deplore,
remorse **8** sympathy **9** heartache, penitence **10** affliction, compassion, contrition, heartbreak, repentance **11** compunction

rueful 5 sorry **6** woeful **8** contrite, penitent **9** regretful, sorrowful **10** remorseful

ruff 5 frill, perch, trump **6** collar, fringe
9 sandpiper **11** pumpkinseed *female:*
5 reeve

ruffian 4 goon, hood, punk, thug **5** beast,
brute, bully, rowdy, tough, yahoo
6 Apache, hector **7** gorilla, hoodlum
8 bullyboy, hooligan **9** muscleman,
roughneck, swaggerer

ruffle 3 bug, irk, rub, vex **4** fret, gall,
wear **5** annoy, brawl, chafe, frill, graze,
jabot, pleat, ruche **6** abrade, bother,
nettle, ripple **7** agitate, bristle, disturb,
flounce, provoke, trouble, wrinkle
8 drumbeat, furbelow, irritate, skirmish
9 commotion

rug 3 mat **6** carpet, runner **7** laprobe
kind: **3** rag, rya **6** hooked **7** braided,
dhurrie, flokati, Persian **8** Aubusson,
bearskin, Oriental **10** Savonnerie

rugby *formation:* **5** scrum **9** scrummage
goal: **7** dropped, penalty *period:* **4** half
player: **6** center, hooker, winger **8** standoff **9** scrum half *scoring:* **3** try **4** goal
10 conversion *team:* **7** fifteen *term:*
4 heel **5** match **7** convert, dribble, hand
off, knock on **9** fair catch *time-out:*
8 stoppage *version:* **5** union **6** league

rugged 5 burly, hardy, harsh, heavy,
husky, rough, tough **6** brawny, coarse,
craggy, jagged, robust, severe, stable,
stormy, strong, sturdy, uneven **7** arduous, austere, scraggy **8** leathery, muscular, rigorous, scabrous, stalwart, vigor-

ous **9** difficult, inclement, strenuous,
unrefined, weathered **10** formidable,
unpolished **11** tempestuous

Ruggiero *guardian:* **7** Atlante *sister:*
7 Marfisa *slayer:* **11** Tisaphernes *wife:*
10 Bradamante

rug rat 3 tot **4** tyke **6** moppet **7** toddler

Ruhr industrial city 5 Essen

ruin 4 bane, bust, dash, do in, doom,
fall, loss, rape, raze, sack, undo
5 decay, havoc, smash, spoil, trash, use
up, waste, wrack, wreck **6** beggar, finish, pauper, perish, ravage **7** corrupt,
deplete, despoil, destroy, exhaust, failure, nemesis, pillage, shatter, undoing,
wipe out **8** bankrupt, collapse, decimate, demolish, downfall, spoliate
9 depredate, devastate, disrepair, overthrow, pauperize, shipwreck **10** desolation, impoverish **11** destruction, devastation, dissolution **12** degeneration
13 deterioration

ruination 4 bane, loss, rack **5** havoc
7 undoing **8** calamity, disaster, downfall
10 decimation **11** destruction, devastation

ruinous 5 fatal **7** baneful **10** calamitous,
disastrous, pernicious **11** destructive
12 catastrophic

rule 3 law **4** lead, sway **5** axiom, bylaw,
canon, edict, habit, judge, maxim,
moral, order, reign **6** assize, custom,
decree, deduce, dictum, direct, govern,
regime, truism **7** brocard, command,
control, precept, prevail, regency, regimen, resolve, statute **8** decretum, doctrine, dominate, domineer, dominion
9 authority, determine, etiquette, ordinance, principle, procedure **10** regulation *absolute:* **7** autarky **8** autarchy *by a*
god: **8** theonomy

Rule Britannia composer 4 Arne
(Thomas)

rule out 3 bar **5** block, debar **6** forbid,
refuse, reject **7** exclude, forfend, head
off, obviate, prevent **8** preclude, prohibit, stave off **9** eliminate

ruler 4 king, lord **5** queen **6** archon,
dynast, ferule, gerent, prince, regent,
satrap, sultan **7** emperor, monarch,
viceroy **8** governor, hierarch, oligarch,
pentarch, princess, theocrat **9** dominator, imperator, matriarch, patriarch,
potentate, sovereign **12** straightedge
absolute: **6** despot, tyrant **8** autocrat,
dictator, overlord *Arab:* **4** amir, emir
5 sheik **6** sharif, sheikh, sultan *Asian:*
4 khan *Byzantine Empire:* **6** exarch
Egyptian: **7** pharaoh *family:* **7** dynasty
Iranian: **4** shah *one of four:* **8** tetrarch
one of seven: **8** heptarch *one of three:*

7 triarch 8 triumvir *Persian:* 6 satrap
Russian: 4 czar, tsar, tzar *Turkish:*
3 bey, dey
ruling 3 law 4 call 5 chief, edict, order,
ukase 6 decree 7 current, finding, popular, regnant, verdict 8 decision, judgment 9 directive, judgement, prevalent,
statement 10 prevailing, widespread
11 predominant 12 adjudication
Rumania see ROMANIA
rumble 4 buzz, roar, roll 5 brawl, drone,
fight, growl, rumor 6 murmur, report
7 hearsay, quarrel, resound, thunder
8 feedback 9 complaint 11 altercation,
disturbance, reverberate, scuttlebutt
ruminant 3 cow, yak 4 deer, goat, tahr
5 bison, camel, okapi, serow, sheep,
takin 6 alpaca, cattle, musk ox, vicuña
7 buffalo, chamois, chewing, giraffe,
guanaco 8 antelope *stomach:* 5 rumen
6 omasum 8 abomasum 9 reticulum
ruminate 4 chew, mull, muse 5 champ,
chomp, weigh 6 ponder 7 reflect 8 cogitate, consider, meditate 9 masticate
10 deliberate 11 contemplate
ruminative 7 pensive 8 thinking 9 pondering 10 cogitative, meditative, reflective, thoughtful 11 speculative 13 contemplative, introspective
rummage 4 comb, fish, grub, hash,
hunt, poke, rake, rout, seek 5 delve,
scour 6 ferret, forage, jumble, litter,
search 7 clutter, ransack 8 mishmash
9 potpourri 10 hodgepodge, hotchpotch, miscellany
rummy 3 gin, odd, sot 4 lush, soak, wino
5 drunk, souse, toper 6 boozer
7 bizarre, canasta, curious, guzzler,
strange, swiller, tippler, tosspot
8 drunkard, peculiar 9 eccentric, inebriate 10 boozehound
rumor 4 blab, buzz, talk 5 bruit, story
6 canard, gossip, murmur, mutter,
report, rumble, tattle 7 hearsay, tidings,
whisper 9 grapevine 11 scuttlebutt,
susurration
rumormonger 6 gossip 8 gossiper,
informer, quidnunc, telltale 9 whisper-
er 10 talebearer, tattletale
rump 3 can 4 beam, butt, duff, hind,
rear, tush 5 fanny 6 behind, bottom,
breech, heinie 7 keister, rear end
8 backside, buttocks, derriere, haunches 9 posterior
rumple 4 fold, muss, ruck 5 crimp,
screw, touse 6 pucker, tousle 7 crimple,
crinkle, scrunch, wrinkle 8 dishevel,
disorder
rumpus see RUCKUS
run 3 fly, hie, jog 4 bolt, dart, dash, flee,
flow, race, rush, scud, tear 5 chase,

haste, hurry, scoot, skirr, speed
6 career, gallop, hasten, scurry, sprint,
streak, stream 7 scamper, scuttle,
smuggle 9 skedaddle
run across 4 meet 8 bump into, discover
9 encounter, stumble on
runagate 4 hobo 5 tramp 6 outlaw
7 drifter, floater, lamster, vagrant,
wastrel 8 bohemian, fugitive, rapparee,
vagabond, wanderer 11 guttersnipe
run along 5 leave, scram 6 beat it,
begone, cut out, depart 7 get lost, skiddoo, take off, vamoose 8 shove off
9 skedaddle 10 make tracks
runaround 4 duck, slip 5 dodge 7 elusion, evasion
run away 4 bolt, flee, skip 5 elope, leave,
scram, skirr, split, steal 6 depart,
desert, escape 7 abscond, make off
8 clear out, light out, stampede
9 skedaddle 10 make tracks
runaway 4 wild 5 loose 6 outlaw
7 escapee, lamster 8 deserter, fugitive
10 delinquent 12 uncontrolled
run down 3 hit, ram, tag 5 catch, knock,
trace 6 pursue 7 decline 8 belittle, derogate, diminish 9 apprehend, disparage
10 depreciate 11 catch up with
run-down 5 dingy, seedy, tacky, tired
6 beat-up, bushed, shabby 7 rickety,
ruinous, worn-out 8 decrepit, tattered,
untended 9 burned-out, exhausted,
neglected 10 bedraggled, down-at-heel,
ramshackle, uncared-for 11 dilapidated
rundown 4 dope, poop 5 recap, scoop
6 report, review, skinny, update 7 outline, summary 8 briefing, synopsis
runes 4 ogam 5 ogham 7 futhark
rung 3 bar 4 step 5 grade, notch, round,
spoke, staff, stage, stair, tread 6 degree,
rundle 10 crosspiece
run-in 3 row 4 tiff 5 brush, fight, set-to
6 hassle, scrape, tangle 7 dispute, quarrel, rhubarb, wrangle 8 skirmish,
squabble 9 encounter 10 falling-out
11 altercation
run into 3 hit, ram 4 meet 9 encounter,
stumble on 11 collide with
runner 3 rug 5 miler, racer 6 carpet,
stolon 7 carrier, courier 8 smuggler,
sprinter 9 go-between, messenger
10 marathoner 11 ballcarrier
running 6 active, fluent 7 cursive,
dynamic, flowing, working 9 operative
10 continuous 11 functioning
run-of-the-mill 4 dull, so-so 5 usual
6 common, normal 7 average, humdrum, regular, typical 8 everyday,
familiar, mediocre, middling, moderate, ordinary 9 prevalent 10 monoto-

nous 11 commonplace, indifferent 12 intermediate 13 unexceptional
run on 3 gab, yak 4 blab 5 clack 6 babble, cackle, gabble, jabber, rattle 7 chatter, prattle 8 continue
run out of 5 use up 6 finish 7 exhaust
run over 5 spill 6 exceed, repeat 7 examine 8 overfill, overflow, rehearse
runt 5 dwarf, pygmy 6 midget, peanut, peewee, shrimp, squirt 7 manikin 8 Tom Thumb 10 homunculus 11 hopo'-my-thumb, lilliputian
run through 3 jab 4 blow, gore, read, scan, stab 5 spend, use up, waste 6 expend, finish, impale, pierce 7 consume, examine, exhaust 8 rehearse, squander, transfix
runty 3 wee 4 puny 6 peewee 7 stunted 8 dwarfish 10 diminutive, undersized
run up 5 build, erect, mount 6 expand 7 augment, enlarge 8 increase, multiply 9 construct 10 accumulate
runway 4 duct, path 5 strip, track, trail 6 sluice, tarmac 7 channel, conduit 8 airstrip, platform
rupture 4 rend, rent, rift, rive 5 break, burst, cleft, sever, split 6 breach, cleave, hernia, schism, sunder 7 blowout, break up, disrupt, divorce, fissure, parting, split-up 8 division, fracture, separate 9 partition 10 separation 11 dissolution 12 estrangement
R.U.R. *author:* 5 Capek (Karel) *character:* 5 robot
rural 6 rustic 7 bucolic, country, idyllic 8 agrarian, arcadian, down-home, pastoral 10 campestral 11 countrified
ruse 3 con, jig 4 hoax, ploy, wile 5 dodge, feint, fraud, stall, trick 6 deceit, gambit 7 gimmick, swindle 8 artifice, maneuver, trickery 9 deception, stratagem 10 subterfuge 13 double-dealing
rush 3 fly, rip, run 4 boil, bolt, dart, dash, flit, flow, hurl, lash, race, roar, scud, tear, tide, whiz 5 blitz, break, carry, chase, court, daily, flash, haste, hurry, lunge, onset, sally, scoot, shoot, spate, speed, storm, surge 6 attack, barrel, beat it, bustle, career, charge, course, hasten, hurtle, hustle, irrupt, plunge, streak, stream, thrill, whoosh 7 assault, cattail, current, rampage, torrent 8 stampede 9 whirlwind, wire grass 13 precipitation
Rushdie novel 5 Shame 13 Satanic Verses (The) 17 Midnight's Children
rushing 5 hasty 6 abrupt, sudden 7 hurried 8 headlong 9 impetuous 11 precipitate, precipitous
rusk 7 biscuit 8 biscotto

Russia *capital:* 6 Moscow *city:* 3 Ufa 4 Omsk, Perm' 5 Kazan', Kursk 6 Grozny, Samara 7 Groznyy, Izhevsk, Ivanovo 8 Murmansk 9 Leningrad, Volgograd 10 Stalingrad 11 Chelyabinsk, Novosibirsk, Vladivostok 12 St. Petersburg 13 Yekaterinburg *emperor:* 5 Boris (Godunov), Peter (the Great) 7 Godunov (Boris), Michael (Romanov), Romanov (Michael) 8 Nicholas *empress:* 4 Anna (Ivanovna) 9 Catherine (the Great), Elizabeth (Petrovna) *ethnic group:* 7 Cossack *island:* 8 Sakhalin *island group:* 5 Kuril 6 Kurile *lake:* 5 Il'men', Onega 6 Baikal, Ladoga *leader:* 5 Lenin (Vladimir), Putin (Vladimir) 6 Stalin (Joseph) 7 Trotsky (Leon) 8 Brezhnev (Leonid) 10 Khrushchev (Nikita) *monetary unit:* 5 ruble *mountain, range:* 4 Ural 5 Altai, Altay, Sayan 6 Elbrus, Kolyma, Koryak 8 Caucasus, Stanovoy *neighbor:* 5 China 6 Latvia, Norway 7 Belarus, Estonia, Finland, Georgia, Ukraine 8 Mongolia 9 Kazakstan 10 Azerbaijan, Kazakhstan, North Korea *peninsula:* 4 Kola 5 Gydan, Kanin, Yamal 6 Taymyr 7 Chukchi 9 Kamchatka *region:* 7 Siberia 9 Circassia 11 Golden Horde *revolution:* 9 Bolshevik *river:* 3 Don 4 Amur, Lena, Ural 5 Desna, Dvina, Vitim, Volga 6 Belaya, Kolyma, Vilyui, Vilyuy 7 Pechora, Yenisey 9 Indigirka *sea:* 4 Azov, Kara 5 Black, White 6 Laptev, Okhotsk 7 Barents, Caspian, Chukchi *strait:* 6 Bering
Russian *aristocrat:* 5 boyar *family:* 7 Romanov 9 Stroganov *grandmother:* 8 babushka *monk:* 8 Rasputin *peasant:* 5 kulak, mujik 6 moujik, muzhik *ruler:* (see CZAR) *saint:* 15 Alexander Nevsky *urn:* 7 samovar *vehicle:* 6 troika *villa:* 5 dacha
rustic 4 hick, rube, rude 5 churl, clown, plain, rough, rural, swain, yokel 6 farmer 7 bucolic, bumpkin, country, granger, hayseed, peasant, plowboy, plowman, red-neck, uncouth 8 agrarian, pastoral 9 chawbacon, hillbilly 10 campestral, clodhopper, countryman, husbandman 11 countrified 12 apple-knocker, backwoodsman
rustle 5 haste, hurry, speed, steal, swish 6 forage, swoosh 7 crackle, crinkle 8 susurrus
rustler 5 thief 6 duffer, robber 7 forager 8 marauder
Rustum's son 6 Sohrab
rusty 4 slow 6 bygone, creaky 7 outworn 8 outdated, outmoded 10 antiquated, discolored 12 old-fashioned

rut 5 gouge, grind, track **6** furrow, groove **7** channel, routine **9** treadmill

rutabaga 5 swede **6** turnip

ruth 3 rue, woe **4** pity **5** grief, mercy **6** regret, sorrow **7** anguish, remorse, sadness **8** distress, sympathy **9** attrition, penitence **10** compassion, contrition, repentance **11** compunction **13** commiseration

Ruth *husband:* **4** Boaz **6** Mahlon *mother-in-law:* **5** Naomi *son:* **4** Obed

ruthful 6 woeful **7** doleful **8** dolorous, wretched **9** miserable, sorrowful

ruthless 4 hard **5** cruel, harsh **6** brutal, savage **7** inhuman **8** pitiless **9** barbarous, cutthroat, dog-eat-dog, ferocious, heartless, merciless, unsparing **10** implacable, ironfisted

ruttish 4 lewd **5** lusty, randy **6** wanton **7** goatish, lustful, satyric **9** lecherous, lickerish, salacious **10** lascivious, libidinous **12** concupiscent

Rwanda *city:* **6** Kigali *ethnic group:* **4** Hutu **5** Tutsi *language:* **6** French, Rwanda *monetary unit:* **5** franc *neighbor:* **5** Congo **6** Uganda **7** Burundi **8** Tanzania

S

___ **Saarinen 4** Eero **5** Eliel

Sabatini novel 11 Scaramouche **12** Captain Blood

sabbatical 4 rest **5** leave **7** time off **8** vacation

saber 5 sword **7** cutlass **8** scimitar

sabertooth 3 cat **5** tiger

sable 3 fur **4** dark, inky **5** black, ebony, raven **6** gloomy, somber, sombre, weasel **8** mourning

sabot 4 clog, shoe **10** wooden shoe

sabotage 5 wreck **6** damage, hamper, hinder **7** cripple, disable, subvert, torpedo **8** obstruct, wreckage, wrecking **9** frustrate, undermine, vandalize **10** subversion **11** undermining

Sabra *father:* **7** Ptolemy *rescuer:* **8** St. George *son:* **3** Guy **5** David **9** Alexander

sac 4 caul, cyst **5** pouch **7** vesicle

saccharine 5 mushy, sweet **6** sugary, syrupy **7** candied, cloying, honeyed, maudlin, mawkish, sugared **9** oversweet, schmaltzy **11** sentimental, sugar-coated **12** ingratiating

sacerdotal 8 hieratic, pastoral, priestly **10** priestlike **11** ministerial

sachem 4 boss **5** chief **6** leader

sachet 3 bag **6** powder **7** perfume **9** potpourri

sack 3 bag, bed, can **4** bunk, drop, fire, loot, raid, wine **5** expel, pouch, strip, waste **6** pocket, ravage **7** boot out, cashier, despoil, dismiss, hammock, kick out, pillage, plunder **8** desolate, spoliate **9** container, depredate, desecrate, devastate, white wine

sackbut 8 trombone

sacque 6 jacket

sacrament 4 rite **6** ritual **7** baptism, penance **8** ceremony, marriage **9** Communion, Eucharist, matrimony **10** holy orders **12** confirmation

sacrarium 6 chapel, shrine **7** oratory, piscina **8** sacristy **9** sanctuary

sacred 4 holy **5** godly **6** divine, immune **7** angelic, blessed, saintly **8** hallowed, numinous **9** inviolate, spiritual **10** inviolable, sacrosanct, sanctified **11** consecrated, sacramental *combining form:* **4** hagi, hier, sacr **5** hagio, hiero, sacro *monkey:* **6** baboon, rhesus **7** hanuman *place:* **7** sanctum *weed:* **7** vervain

sacrifice 4 bunt, cede, lose, loss **5** forgo, yield **6** devote, donate, eschew, give up, martyr, victim **7** forfeit, offer up **8** dedicate, hecatomb, immolate, oblation, offering **12** renunciation

sacrilege 6 heresy **7** impiety, offense **9** blasphemy, violation **11** desecration, irreverence, profanation

sacrilegious 7 impious, profane, ungodly **10** irreverent **11** blasphemous

sacristan 6 sexton

sacristy 6 vestry

sacrosanct 9 inviolate **10** inviolable

sad 4 blue, down **5** sorry **6** dismal, drea-

ry, gloomy, morose, triste, woeful
7 doleful, joyless, piteous, pitiful,
unhappy 8 dejected, desolate, dolorous,
downbeat, downcast, grieving, mournful, pathetic, pitiable 9 depressed, sorrowful, woebegone 10 depressing,
dispirited, lamentable, melancholy
11 melancholic 12 heavyhearted
sadden 7 depress, oppress, trouble
8 aggrieve, dispirit 9 weigh down 10 discourage
saddle 3 tax 4 lade, load, task 5 weigh
6 burden, charge, hamper, impede,
impose, weight 7 aparejo, inflict
8 encumber, restrict *adjunct:* 7 stirrup
part: 6 cantle, pommel *strap:* 5 cinch,
girth 6 latigo 7 harness
sadness 3 woe 4 funk 5 blues, dolor,
dumps, gloom, grief, mopes 6 misery,
sorrow 7 dismals, megrims 8 doldrums,
glumness, mourning 9 dejection, dysphoria, heartache 10 blue devils,
depression, desolation, melancholy
11 despondency, melancholia, unhappiness
safari 4 hunt, trek, trip 7 caravan, journey 10 expedition
safe 4 snug, wary 5 chary 6 secure,
unhurt 7 careful, guarded 8 cautious,
defended, shielded, unharmed
9 innocuous, protected, sheltered,
uninjured, unscathed 10 inviolable,
sheltering 11 impregnable 12 invulnerable, unassailable
safecracker 4 yegg 8 picklock 9 cracks-
man
safeguard 4 ward 6 convoy, defend,
escort, shield, surety 7 bulwark,
defense, protect 8 armament, preserve
10 precaution, protection
safety 6 asylum, refuge 7 defense, shelter 8 immunity, security 9 assurance,
sanctuary 10 protection 13 inviolability
sag 3 dip 4 bend, drop, flag, flap, flop,
hang, sink, slip, wilt 5 droop, slide,
slump 6 dangle, hollow, slouch
7 decline, drop off, falloff, sinkage,
sinking 8 downturn, settling, sinkhole
9 concavity, downswing 10 depression
saga 4 edda, epic, myth, tale 5 story
6 legend 9 chronicle, narrative
12 Heimskringla
sagacious 4 keen, wise 5 acute, smart
6 astute, clever, shrewd 7 knowing,
prudent, sapient 8 critical 9 far-seeing,
judicious 10 discerning, insightful, perceptive 11 intelligent 13 perspicacious
sagacity 5 grasp 6 acuity, acumen, wisdom 7 insight 8 judgment, keenness,
prudence, sapience 10 perception,
shrewdness 11 discernment, penetra-

tion, percipience, perspicuity 12 perspicacity 13 comprehension, judiciousness, understanding
sagamore 5 chief 6 sachem
Sagan work 6 Cosmos 16 Bonjour
tristesse
sage 4 guru, mint, wise 6 expert, master,
nestor, pundit, savant, shrewd 7 gnostic, knowing, learned, prudent, sapient,
scholar, wise man 8 polymath, profound, sensible 9 judicious 10 discerning, insightful, perceptive 11 penetrating, philosophic *Hindu:* 6 pandit
7 mahatma
Sage *of Chelsea:* 7 Carlyle (Thomas) *of
Concord:* 7 Emerson (Ralph Waldo) *of
Emporia:* 5 White (William Allen) *of Fer-
ney:* 8 Voltaire *of Monticello:* 9 Jefferson
(Thomas) *of Pylos:* 6 Nestor
Sagebrush State 6 Nevada
Sagittarius 6 archer 7 centaur 13 constellation
sago 4 palm 6 starch
saguaro 6 cactus
sahib 3 sir 6 master 9 gentleman
sail 3 fly 4 dart, flit, scud, skim, wing
5 fleet, float, shoot, skirr, sweep
6 cruise, mizzen 7 spencer 9 spinnaker
triangular: 3 jib 5 genoa
sailboat 4 bark, yawl 5 ketch, skiff,
sloop, yacht 6 dinghy 8 schooner, skipjack
sailing vessel 4 bark, brig 5 xebec
6 barque 7 frigate, galleon 8 schooner
10 barkentine, brigantine 11 bar-
quentine
sailor 3 gob, tar 4 jack, mate, salt, swab
6 hearty, sea dog, seaman 7 jack-tar,
mariner, matelot, old salt, swabbie
8 flatfoot, seafarer, shipmate, water
dog 9 shellback, tarpaulin, yachtsman
10 bluejacket *British:* 5 limey *fictional:*
6 Sinbad *patron saint:* 4 Elmo *song:*
6 chanty 7 chantey 9 barcarole
saint 7 paragon *biography:* 11 hagiography *list:* 9 hagiology (see also PATRON
SAINT)
Saint, The 12 Simon Templar *creator:*
9 Charteris (Leslie)
Saint Anthony's cross 3 tau
Saint Elmo's Fire 9 corposant
Saint Helena *capital:* 9 Jamestown *colony
of:* 7 Britain *island:* 9 Ascension
Saint Joan author 4 Shaw (George
Bernard)
Saint John's bread 5 carob
Saint Kitts and Nevis *capital:* 10 Basse-
terre *island group:* 7 Leeward *language:*
7 English *location:* 10 West Indies *mone-
tary unit:* 6 dollar
Saint Lucia *capital:* 8 Castries *island*

group: 8 Windward *language:* 6 French 7 English *location:* 10 West Indies *monetary unit:* 6 dollar *volcano:* 8 Quilabou

saintly 4 holy, pure 5 godly, pious 6 devout, worthy 7 angelic, blessed, upright 8 beatific, seraphic, virtuous 9 righteous

Saint Paul's architect 4 Wren (Christopher)

Saint Peter's Basilica *architect:* 7 Bernini (Gian Lorenzo) 12 Michelangelo (Buonarotti) *sculpture:* 5 Pietà

Saint-Pierre and Miquelon *capital:* 8 St.-Pierre *department of:* 6 France

Saint Vincent and the Grenadines *capital:* 9 Kingstown *island group:* 8 Windward *language:* 6 French 7 English *location:* 10 West Indies *monetary unit:* 6 dollar *volcano:* 9 Soufrière

Saint Vitus' dance 6 chorea

sake 3 end 4 good 5 drink 7 benefit, purpose, welfare

Saki 5 Munro (H. H.)

salaam 3 bow 6 kowtow 8 greeting 9 obeisance

salacious 4 fast, lewd 5 bawdy 6 erotic, ribald, risqué 7 lustful, satyric 8 indecent, prurient 9 lecherous, libertine 10 lascivious, libidinous, licentious

salad *item:* 3 egg 4 bean, cuke, herb 5 cress, olive, onion 6 carrot, celery, cheese, endive, pepper, potato, radish, tomato 7 anchovy, cabbage, crouton, lettuce, parsley, spinach 8 chickpea, coleslaw, cucumber, garbanzo, mushroom, scallion 10 watercress *type:* 5 chef's 6 Caesar

salamander 3 eft 4 newt 7 urodele 8 mud puppy, water dog 10 hellbender *Mexican:* 7 axolotl

salary 3 pay 4 take, wage 6 income 7 stipend 8 earnings 9 emolument 10 recompense 12 compensation, remuneration

sale 6 bazaar, demand 7 auction 8 closeout, disposal, transfer 9 clearance 11 transaction

salient 4 marked, signal 7 obvious, weighty 8 striking 9 arresting, important, obtrusive, pertinent, prominent 10 impressive, noticeable, projecting, pronounced, remarkable 11 conspicuous, outstanding, significant

saline 5 briny, salty 8 brackish

Salinger, J. D. *character:* 4 Esmé 6 Holden (Caulfield) *novel:* 14 Franny and Zooey 15 Catcher in the Rye

saliva 4 spit 6 slaver, sputum 7 spittle

salivate 5 drool 6 drivel, slaver 7 slobber

___ **Salk** 5 Jonas

sallow 3 wan 4 pale, waxy 5 pasty 6 pallid, sickly, willow, yellow 7 bilious 9 jaundiced

sally 3 gag 4 gust, jape, jest, joke, quip 5 blast, burst, crack, jaunt 6 depart, junket, outing, set out, sortie, volley 7 barrage, flare-up 8 drollery, eruption, outbreak, outburst, paroxysm 9 discharge, excursion, explosion, wisecrack, witticism

salmagundi see HODGEPODGE

salmon 4 parr, pink 5 smolt 6 grilse 7 sockeye 9 brandling *cured:* 7 gravlax 8 gravlaks *male:* 6 kipper *smoked:* 3 lox

Salome *composer:* 7 Strauss (Richard) *father:* 5 Herod *husband:* 6 Philip 7 Zebedee 11 Aristobulus *mother:* 8 Herodias *son:* 4 John 5 James *victim:* 4 John (the Baptist)

salon 4 hall, shop 5 suite 6 parlor 7 gallery 9 apartment, reception 10 exhibition

saloon 3 bar, pub 6 tavern 7 barroom, cantina, gin mill, taproom 9 beer joint 12 watering hole

salt 3 tar 4 jack, keep, NaCl 5 brine 6 sailor, saline, seaman 7 jack-tar, mariner 8 salinize 9 sailorman

salt away 4 bank, save 5 hoard, lay by, lay up, put by, stash, store 7 deposit 8 lay aside, squirrel

saltpeter 5 niter, nitre

salty 4 blue, racy 5 briny, crude, spicy, tangy 6 earthy, purple, risqué, salt 7 caustic, mordant, pungent 8 brackish, off-color, scathing 9 trenchant

salubrious 5 tonic 7 bracing, healthy 8 hygienic, salutary 9 healthful, wholesome 10 beneficial 11 restorative 12 invigorating

Salus see HYGEIA

salutary 5 tonic 6 benign 7 bracing, healing 8 curative, remedial, sanative 9 analeptic, healthful, vulnerary, wholesome 10 beneficial, salubrious 11 restorative, therapeutic 12 advantageous, health-giving

salutation 4 hail 5 hello, howdy 7 welcome 8 greeting *Arab:* 6 salaam *French:* 5 salut *Hawaiian:* 5 aloha *Italian:* 4 ciao *Latin:* 3 ave *Spanish:* 4 hola

salute 4 hail 5 greet, honor 6 praise 7 address, commend 8 greeting 12 congratulate

salvage 4 save 6 ransom, recoup, redeem, regain, rescue 7 deliver, reclaim, recover 8 retrieve

salvation 6 saving 7 keeping 10 redemption 11 deliverance 12 conservation, preservation

Salvation Army founder 5 Booth (General William)

salve 4 balm **5** cream, quiet **6** cerate, chrism, lotion, remedy **7** assuage, unction, unguent **8** ointment **9** emollient
salver 4 tray
salvo 4 hail **5** burst, spray, storm **6** attack, shower, volley **7** barrage, proviso **9** broadside, cannonade, discharge, fusillade **11** bombardment
Samaritan 6 helper **10** benefactor
same 4 idem, like, very **5** equal, exact **7** coequal, similar **8** constant **9** duplicate, identical, unvarying **10** consistent, equivalent, invariable, unchanging
Samoa *capital:* **4** Apia *island:* **5** Upolu **6** Savai'i *language:* **6** Samoan **7** English *monetary unit:* **4** tala
samovar 3 urn
samp 6 cereal, hominy
sampan 4 boat **5** skiff
sample 3 try **4** case, part, test, unit **5** piece, taste **7** element, example, excerpt, portion, segment **8** fragment, instance, specimen **10** indication **11** case history, constituent **12** illustration
Samson *betrayer:* **7** Delilah *birthplace:* **5** Zorah *deathplace:* **4** Gaza *father:* **6** Manoah *tribe:* **3** Dan
Samson Agonistes *author* **6** Milton (John)
Samuel *father:* **7** Elkanah *grandson:* **5** Heman *mother:* **6** Hannah
samurai *code* **7** Bushido
San Antonio *team:* **5** Spurs *landmark:* **5** Alamo
sanatorium 3 spa **8** hospital, rest home
sanctify 5 bless **6** hallow, ordain, purify **8** dedicate **10** consecrate
sanctimonious 5 pious **7** canting, preachy **8** unctuous **9** pharisaic **11** pharisaical **12** hypocritical, Pecksniffian **13** self-righteous
sanction 4 fiat, okay **5** bless, leave **6** assent, decree, permit, ratify **7** approve, backing, boycott, certify, consent, embargo, endorse, license, penalty, support **8** accredit, approval **9** allowance, authorize **10** commission, permission, sufferance **11** approbation, endorsement **12** confirmation, ratification **13** authorization, encouragement
sanctity 8 holiness **9** godliness **11** saintliness, uprightness **13** inviolability, righteousness
sanctuary 5 haven, oasis **6** asylum, covert, harbor, refuge, shrine, temple **7** reserve, retreat, shelter **8** preserve **9** holy place
sanctum 4 lair **6** shrine **7** retreat, shelter **9** holy place, sanctuary
sand 3 tan **4** buff, ecru, fawn, grit

5 beach, beige, camel, grind, khaki, scour, shore **6** gravel, polish, smooth **7** burnish **8** granules
sandal 4 clog, zori **5** sabot, thong **6** patten **8** flip-flop, huarache **10** espadrille
sandbag 6 ambush, waylay
sandbar 4 reef, spit **7** tombolo
Sand County Almanac *author* **7** Leopold (Aldo)
sandpiper 4 knot, ruff **5** reeve **6** dunlin **9** shorebird
sandstone deposit 6 flysch
sandwich 3 BLT, sub **4** club, gyro, roti **5** butty, Cuban **6** Denver, hoagie, Reuben **7** grinder, Western **9** submarine **10** muffuletta *shop:* **4** deli
sandy 4 fair **5** blond **6** blonde, grainy, gritty
sane 3 fit **4** good, hale, sage, well, wise **5** lucid, right, sober, sound **6** cogent, normal **7** healthy, logical, prudent, sapient **8** all there, balanced, oriented, rational, sensible **9** judicious, wholesome **10** reasonable **11** levelheaded **12** compos mentis
San Francisco *hill:* **3** Nob **7** Russian *tower:* **4** Coit
sangfroid 4 calm **5** poise **6** aplomb, phlegm **9** composure **10** equanimity **11** self-control
sanguinary 4 gory **6** bloody **9** homicidal, murdering, murderous **12** bloodstained, bloodthirsty
sanguine 4 gory **5** flush, ruddy **6** bloody, florid, secure, upbeat **7** assured, buoyant, flushed, glowing, hopeful **8** bloodred, cheerful, rubicund **9** confident, homicidal, murdering, murderous **10** optimistic **11** self-assured **12** bloodstained, bloodthirsty, Pollyannaish **13** self-confident
sanitary 5 clean **7** sterile **8** hygienic **9** healthful **10** antiseptic, salubrious
sanitize 5 clean, purge **6** bleach, censor, purify **7** cleanse, launder **8** black out **9** disinfect, expurgate, sterilize **10** bowdlerize
sanity 6 health, reason **7** balance **8** lucidity, prudence **9** normality, soundness, stability
San Marino *capital:* **9** San Marino *monetary unit:* **4** euro *monetary unit, former:* **4** lira *neighbor:* **5** Italy
sans 7 lacking, missing, wanting, without
Sanskrit *dialect:* **4** Pali *epic:* **8** Ramayana *Scripture:* **4** Veda
Santa Lucia *composer* **5** Denza (Luigi)
São Tomé and Príncipe *capital:* **7** São Tomé *language:* **10** Portuguese *location:*

12 Gulf of Guinea *monetary unit:*
5 dobra

sap 4 dupe, fool, gull, mark **5** chump, drain **6** pigeon, sucker, weaken **7** cripple, deplete, disable, exhaust, fall guy **8** enervate, enfeeble **9** attenuate, schlemiel, undermine **10** debilitate

sapid 5 tasty **6** savory **9** delicious, flavorful, palatable, toothsome **10** appetizing **11** scrumptious

sapience see SAGACITY

sapient see SAGACIOUS

sapling 4 tree **5** child, youth **9** youngster

Sapphira's husband 7 Ananias

Sappho *forte:* **6** poetry *island:* **6** Lesbos

sappy 5 ditzy, flaky, mushy, silly, soupy **6** drippy, slushy, sticky, syrupy **7** cloying, foolish, maudlin, mawkish **8** bathetic **11** sentimental

Saracen hero 9 Rodomonte

Sarah *husband:* **7** Abraham *maid:* **5** Hagar *son:* **5** Isaac

sarcasm 3 wit **4** gibe **5** irony, scorn **6** satire **7** mockery **8** acerbity, mordancy, ridicule, sneering **10** causticity

sarcastic 4 acid, tart **5** acerb, sharp **6** biting, ironic **7** acerbic, caustic, cutting, cynical, jeering, mocking, mordant, satiric **8** sardonic, scathing, scornful, stinging **9** corrosive

sarcophagus 4 tomb **6** coffin

sardine 4 sild **7** anchovy, herring **8** pilchard

Sardinia's capital 8 Cagliari

sardonic 3 wry **6** ironic **7** caustic, cynical, jeering, mocking, satiric **8** derisive, scornful, sneering **9** corrosive, sarcastic **10** disdainful **12** contemptuous

sarong 5 skirt **7** garment

Sarpedon *brother:* **5** Minos **12** Rhadamanthus *father:* **4** Zeus **7** Jupiter *mother:* **6** Europa **8** Laodamia

Sartor ___ 8 Resartus

Sartre work 4 Wall (The) **5** Flies (The) **6** Nausea, No Exit **8** Huis Clos **10** Saint Genet

sash 4 belt **6** girdle **8** ceinture, cincture **9** waistband **10** cummerbund

sashay 5 mince, strut **6** prance **7** flounce, saunter, swagger

Saskatchewan *capital:* **6** Regina *city:* **8** Moose Jaw **9** Saskatoon **12** Prince Albert *mountain range:* **12** Cypress Hills *provincial flower:* **7** red lily **11** prairie lily *river:* **9** Churchill **11** Assiniboine

sass 3 lip **4** guff **5** brass, cheek, mouth, sauce **8** back talk **9** impudence, insolence **12** impertinence

sassy 4 bold, flip, pert, wise **5** fresh, lippy, nervy, smart **6** brazen, cheeky **7** forward **8** flippant, impudent, insolent, malapert **9** audacious, unabashed **11** smart-alecky

Satan 5 demon, devil, fiend **6** diablo **7** Lucifer, Old Nick, serpent, villain **9** archfiend, Beelzebub **10** Old Scratch

satanic 4 evil **6** wicked **7** demonic, hellish **8** demoniac, devilish, diabolic, fiendish, infernal

satanism 9 diabolism

satchel 3 bag **4** case, tote **5** pouch **6** valise **7** handbag **9** briefcase

sate 4 cloy, fill, glut, jade, pall **5** gorge, stuff **6** stodge **7** appease, overeat, placate, surfeit **8** overfill **9** overstuff **10** conciliate

sated 4 full **6** filled, gorged **7** glutted, overfed, replete, stuffed **8** appeased, chockful **9** chock-full, surfeited

satellite 4 moon **5** toady **6** cohort, minion **7** Sputnik **8** adherent, disciple, follower, henchman, partisan **9** attendant, supporter, sycophant, tributary *of Jupiter:* **6** Europa **8** Callisto, Ganymede *of Mars:* **6** Deimos, Phobos *of Neptune:* **6** Nereid, Triton *of Saturn:* **4** Rhea **5** Dione, Janus, Mimas, Titan **6** Phoebe, Tethys **7** Iapetus **8** Hyperion **9** Enceladus *of Uranus:* **5** Ariel **6** Oberon **7** Miranda, Titania, Umbriel

satiate see SATE

satire 3 wit **5** irony, spoof, squib **6** parody **7** lampoon, mockery, takeoff **8** raillery, ridicule, spoofery, travesty **9** burlesque **10** caricature, lampoonery, pasquinade, persiflage

satiric 6 ironic **7** mocking **8** farcical, ironical

satirist *English:* **5** Swift (Jonathan) **7** Marston (John) *French:* **8** Rabelais (François), Voltaire *Greek:* **8** Menippus *Italian:* **7** Aretino (Pietro) *Roman:* **6** Horace **7** Juvenal, Martial, Persius **9** Petronius

satirize 4 mock **5** spoof **6** parody, send up **7** lampoon **8** ridicule **10** caricature

satisfaction 6 amends **7** redress **8** pleasure, serenity **9** atonement **10** reparation **11** contentment, fulfillment, restitution, vindication **12** propitiation **13** gratification

satisfactory 4 fair, good, okay **5** sound **6** decent **8** adequate, all right, passable **9** competent, tolerable **10** acceptable, sufficient **13** unexceptional

satisfy 3 pay **4** fill, meet, sate, suit **5** clear, humor, pay up, serve **6** answer, assure, dispel, pacify, please, settle, square **7** appease, content, fulfill, gladden, gratify, indulge, placate, satiate, suffice, win over **8** convince, persuade

9 conform to, discharge, indemnify **10** comply with

satori 12 illumination **13** enlightenment

satrap 5 ruler **6** cohort **7** viceroy **8** governor, henchman, sidekick **11** subordinate

saturate 3 sop, wet **4** fill, soak **5** bathe, douse, imbue, souse, steep **6** charge, drench, infuse **7** pervade, suffuse **8** permeate, waterlog **9** transfuse

Saturn *moon:* **4** Rhea **5** Dione, Janus, Mimas, Titan **6** Phoebe, Tethys **7** Iapetus **8** Hyperion **9** Enceladus see also CRONUS

saturnalia 4 orgy **5** party, revel **6** excess **7** debauch **9** bacchanal **11** bacchanalia, dissipation

saturnine 4 dour, glum, grim **5** sulky, surly **6** gloomy, moping, morose, somber, sombre, sullen **7** crabbed **8** funereal, sardonic

satyr 4 goat, rake, wolf **6** lecher **9** butterfly

satyric 4 lewd **5** randy **6** wanton **7** goatish, lustful **8** prurient **9** lecherous, libertine, lickerish, salacious **10** lascivious, libidinous, licentious, lubricious **11** promiscuous **12** concupiscent

sauce 4 guff, sass **5** mouth **6** relish **7** topping **8** back talk **9** condiment, impudence *kind:* **3** soy **4** hard, mole **5** chili, curry, gravy, melba, pesto, salsa **6** Mornay, panada, tamari, tartar **7** chutney, marengo, Newburg, piquant, soubise, tartare, velouté **8** béchamel, duxelles, marinara, matelote, noisette, normande **9** béarnaise, lyonnaise, rémoulade **10** bordelaise, Provençale **11** hollandaise, vinaigrette

saucy *see* SASSY

Saudi Arabia *capital:* **6** Riyadh *city:* **5** Jedda, Jidda, Mecca **6** Jeddah, Jiddah, Medina *desert:* **7** Arabian **10** Rub Al-Khali **12** Empty Quarter *gulf:* **7** Persian *monetary unit:* **5** riyal *neighbor:* **3** UAE **4** Iraq, Oman **5** Qatar, Yemen **6** Jordan *peninsula:* **7** Arabian *sea:* **3** Red

Saul *concubine:* **6** Rizpah *cousin:* **5** Abner *daughter:* **5** Merab **6** Michal *father:* **4** Kish *son:* **8** Jonathan *successor:* **5** David *uncle:* **3** Ner *wife:* **7** Ahinoam

saunter 4 mope, roam, rove **5** amble, drift, mosey **6** loiter, ramble, sashay, stroll, wander **7** meander, traipse

sausage 5 wurst **6** banger, kishke, salami, Vienna, wiener **7** baloney, bologna, boloney, chorizo, saveloy **8** cervelat, kielbasa **9** andouille, bratwurst, frankfurt, pepperoni, Thuringer **10** knack-

wurst, knockwurst, liverwurst, mortadella **11** frankfurter

sauté 3 fry **4** sear **5** brown, grill **6** sizzle **7** frizzle

savage 4 grim, wild **5** brute, cruel, feral **6** bloody, brutal, fierce, Gothic, rugged **7** bestial, brutish, inhuman, untamed, vicious, wolfish **8** barbaric, inhumane, primeval, ravenous, unbroken **9** barbarian, barbarous, ferocious, heartless, murderous, primitive, rapacious, truculent, voracious **10** implacable, relentless **11** uncivilized **12** bloodthirsty, uncontrolled, uncultivated, unsocialized

savagery 7 cruelty **8** atrocity **9** barbarity, brutality, depravity **10** bestiality, inhumanity **11** abomination, monstrosity, viciousness **12** ruthlessness

savanna 5 plain **9** grassland

savant 4 sage **7** scholar, thinker, wise man

save 3 bar, but, yet **4** bank, keep, only, stow **5** amass, avoid, cache, guard, hoard, lay by, lay in, lay up, put by, set by, skimp, spare, store **6** defend, except, gather, keep up, manage, ransom, redeem, rescue, scrimp, shield, unless **7** barring, besides, collect, deliver, deposit, however, husband, lay away, protect, reclaim, reserve, salvage, set free, store up **8** conserve, lay aside, liberate, maintain, preserve, salt away, set aside, squirrel **9** aside from, economize, excluding, safeguard, stash away, stockpile **10** accumulate

savior 7 messiah, paladin, rescuer **8** defender **9** deliverer, liberator, preserver, protector, salvation **11** white knight

savoir faire 4 tact **5** grace, poise **6** aplomb **7** address, dignity, finesse, manners **8** urbanity **10** confidence, refinement **13** self-assurance

savor 4 odor, tang **5** enjoy, scent, smack, smell, spice, taste, tinge **6** flavor, relish, season **8** sapidity

savory 5 sapid, spicy, tangy, tasty **7** piquant **9** flavorful, palatable, toothsome **10** appetizing

savvy 4 deft **5** adept, craft, handy, knack, skill **6** clever, talent **7** ability, know-how, skilled **8** deftness **9** adeptness, expertise, handiness, ingenuity **10** capability, cleverness, competence

saw 3 cut, hew **5** adage, axiom, maxim **6** byword, cliché, saying **7** precept, proverb **8** aphorism, apothegm

____ **saw 3** bow, jig, pit, rip **4** band, buck, buzz, fret, hack, whip **5** chain, crown, saber **6** coping, scroll **7** compass, keyhole **8** circular, crosscut

sawbones 3 doc 6 doctor 7 surgeon 9 physician

sawbuck 6 tenner 7 trestle

sawhorse see SAWBUCK

saw-toothed 7 serrate, serried 8 serrated 11 denticulate

Saxon *assembly:* 4 moot 5 gemot 6 gemote *nobleman:* 8 atheling *serf:* 4 esne *warrior:* 5 thane

say 4 talk, tell 5 mouth, speak, state, utter, voice 6 affirm, assert, assume, recite, remark 7 comment, declare, express 8 announce, proclaim 9 enunciate, pronounce 10 articulate

Sayers character 6 Wimsey (Lord Peter)

saying 3 mot, saw 5 adage, axiom, maxim 6 byword, dictum, truism 7 precept, proverb 8 apothegm

scab 5 crust 6 eschar 13 strikebreaker

scabbard 6 sheath

scabrous 4 lewd 5 harsh, rough, salty, scaly 6 craggy, grubby, jagged, knobby, knotty, rugged, scabby, scurfy, sordid, uneven 7 bristly, prickly, scraggy, squalid 8 indecent 10 scandalous

scads 4 gobs, lots, wads 5 loads, piles, reams 6 oodles 8 slathers 10 quantities

scaffold 5 stage, truss 7 staging 8 platform 9 framework

Scala, La *city:* 5 Milan *production:* 5 opera

scalawag see SCAMP

scald 4 boil, burn 6 scorch

scale 4 peel, rate, skin 5 climb, flake, gamut, gauge, mount, ratio, scute, strip 6 ascend, degree, extent, ladder, lamina, scutum, squama 7 measure, ranking 8 escalade, flake off, spall off 9 exfoliate, hierarchy 10 desquamate, proportion 11 decorticate *auxiliary:* 7 vernier *earthquake:* 7 Richter *temperature:* 6 Kelvin 7 Celsius 10 centigrade, Fahrenheit *wind:* 8 Beaufort

scallion 4 leek 5 onion 7 shallot 10 green onion

scalp 4 flay, skin 5 cheat 6 resell, trophy

scam 3 con, gyp 4 bilk, dupe, fool, hoax 5 cheat, fraud, stick, trick 6 delude, diddle, take in 7 beguile, deceive, defraud, swindle 8 flimflam, hoodwink 11 double-cross

scamp 3 imp 4 brat, rake, tyke 5 devil, joker, knave, rogue 6 rascal, urchin 7 hellion 9 scalawag, slyboots 9 prankster, skeezicks 11 rapscallion

scamper 3 run 4 dash, skip 5 scoot 6 scurry 7 scuttle

scan 3 eye 4 skim, view 5 audit, check 6 browse, review, survey 7 examine, eyeball, inspect 8 glance at 10 run through, scrutinize

scandal 5 rumor 6 gossip, infamy 7 calumny, obloquy, offense, slander 8 disgrace, dishonor, reproach 9 aspersion, discredit, disrepute 10 backbiting, defamation, detraction, opprobrium

scandalize 5 libel, shock, smear 6 defame, malign 7 asperse, slander 9 denigrate 10 calumniate

scandalmonger 6 gossip 8 busybody, gossiper, quidnunc, telltale 9 backbiter, muckraker 10 talebearer

scandalous 7 heinous 8 infamous, libelous, shameful, shocking 9 notorious, offensive 10 defamatory, outrageous, scurrilous 11 disgraceful

Scandinavian see NORSE

Scandinavian country 6 Norway, Sweden 7 Denmark, Finland, Iceland

scant 5 short, skimp, spare, stint, tight 6 meager, meagre, paltry, scarce, scrimp, skimpy, slight, sparse 7 scrimpy, wanting 8 exiguous 10 inadequate 12 insufficient

scantiness 4 lack 6 dearth 7 deficit, paucity 8 scarcity, shortage, sparsity 10 deficiency, inadequacy, scarceness, sparseness 13 insufficiency

scanty see SCANT

scapegoat 6 target, victim 7 fall guy 9 sacrifice 11 whipping boy

scapegrace 5 knave, rogue, scamp 6 bad egg, rascal 7 ruffian, varmint, villain 8 hooligan, recreant, scalawag 9 miscreant, reprobate, scoundrel 10 blackguard, black sheep, delinquent 11 rapscallion

Scapin 5 rogue, valet 6 rascal *author:* 7 Molière *employer:* 7 Léandre

scar 3 mar 4 flaw 5 score 6 deface, defect, keloid 7 blemish, scratch 8 cicatrix, pockmark 9 cicatrize, disfigure *on a seed:* 5 hilum

scarab 6 beetle

scaramouch see SCAMP

scarce 3 few 4 rare 5 scant 6 barely, hardly, scanty, sparse 7 limited, wanting 8 sporadic, uncommon 9 deficient 10 inadequate, infrequent, occasional 12 insufficient

scarcity see SCANTINESS

scare 5 alarm, panic, spook 6 fright 7 horrify, petrify, shake up, startle, terrify 8 frighten, paralyze 9 terrorize

scaredy-cat 4 wimp, wuss 5 mouse, sissy 6 coward 7 chicken, dastard 8 alarmist, poltroon 11 milquetoast, yellowbelly

scare up 4 find, snag 5 rally 6 corral, gather, locate, obtain, secure 7 acquire, collect, procure, unearth 8 smoke out 9 ferret out, track down

scarf 4 gulp, wolf 5 ascot, fichu, plaid,

shawl, stole **6** cravat, devour, gobble, inhale **8** babushka, liripipe, mantilla, puggaree **10** lambrequin *Mexican:* **6** rebozo

Scarlet Letter, The *author:* **9** Hawthorne (Nathaniel) *character:* **5** Pearl **6** Hester (Prynne) **10** Dimmesdale (Arthur) **13** Chillingworth (Roger)

Scarlet Pimpernel author 5 Orczy (Baroness Emmuska)

Scarlett's home 4 Tara

scary 6 creepy, spooky **8** chilling **9** frightful

scathe 4 burn, flay, flog, harm, lash, sear **5** roast, slash **6** assail, berate, scorch, thrash **7** blister, scarify, scourge, upbraid **8** lambaste **9** castigate, excoriate

scathing 6 biting, brutal **7** caustic, mordant **8** stinging **9** trenchant

scatter 3 sow **4** cast, part, shed **5** strew **6** divide, spread **7** bestrew, break up, diffuse, disband, diverge **8** disperse, sprinkle **9** broadcast, dissipate **10** besprinkle, distribute **11** disseminate

scatterbrained 5 dizzy, giddy, silly **7** flighty, foolish **8** heedless **9** frivolous

scattering 8 diaspora **10** dispersion

scavenger 5 hyena **6** jackal **7** vulture

scenario 4 plot **6** script **7** outline **8** libretto, synopsis **10** screenplay

scene 3 row, set **4** fuss, site, spot, view **5** arena, field, place, sight, vista **6** locale, milieu, sphere **7** episode, outlook, setting, tableau, tantrum **8** backdrop, locality, location, stage set **9** commotion, landscape, situation **10** background **11** environment **12** stage setting

scenery 3 set **5** decor, props **7** setting **8** stage set **10** properties **11** furnishings **12** stage setting

scent 4 nose, odor **5** aroma, smell, sniff, snuff, whiff **7** bouquet, essence, incense, odorize, perfume **9** aromatize, fragrance, redolence

scepter 4 mace **5** baton, staff **11** sovereignty

schedule 4 list, roll **5** chart, slate, table **6** agenda, docket, record, roster **7** catalog, program, reserve **8** calendar, register, roll call **9** catalogue, timetable

scheme 4 plan, plot, ploy, ruse **5** cabal, order **6** design, device, devise **7** collude, connive, diagram, program, project **8** cogitate, conspire, contrive, game plan, intrigue, proposal, strategy **9** blueprint, expedient, machinate **10** conspiracy **11** arrangement, contrivance, machination

schism 4 rent, rift **5** break, chasm, cleft, split **6** breach, heresy **7** discord, dissent, fissure, rupture **8** cleavage, division, fracture **10** disharmony, dissidence, divergence, falling-out, heterodoxy, separation **11** unorthodoxy **12** estrangement

schlemiel 4 fool **5** chump, klutz **7** bungler

schlep 3 lug, tow **4** drag, haul, hump, plod, pull, slog, tote **5** carry, truck **6** trudge **7** shamble, shuffle **8** straggle

schlock 4 junk, mean **5** cheap, dreck, gaudy, junky, tacky, tatty **6** cheesy, common, kitsch, shoddy, sleazy, tawdry, trashy **8** inferior, low-grade **11** second-class, substandard

schmaltzy 5 mushy, soppy **6** drippy **7** maudlin, mawkish **11** sentimental

schmo 4 dolt, dope, dork, fool, goof, jerk, mutt, simp, twit, yo-yo **5** brute, chump, idiot, moron, ninny, noddy, scamp **6** dimwit, donkey, dumdum, nitwit, noodle, nudnik, rascal **7** dullard, halfwit, jackass, schmuck, schnook **8** bonehead, clodpoll, imbecile, lunkhead, meathead, numskull **9** birdbrain, blockhead, ignoramus, lamebrain, numbskull, thickhead **10** dunderhead, hammerhead, nincompoop **11** chowderhead, chucklehead, knucklehead

schmooze 3 gab, yak **4** chat **6** chat up **8** converse

schnoz 4 beak, nose **6** honker

scholar 4 sage, wonk **5** pupil **6** savant **7** bookman, egghead, student, wise man **8** bookworm, polymath **12** intellectual *Hindu:* **6** pandit, pundit *Muslim:* **5** ulama, ulema

scholarly 7 bookish, erudite, learned **8** academic, educated, studious **10** scholastic **12** intellectual

scholarship 5 award, grant **7** stipend **8** learning **9** education, erudition, knowledge **11** learnedness

scholastic 7 bookish, erudite, learned **8** academic, lettered, literary, pedantic **9** scholarly *life:* **8** academia

school 3 gam, pad **5** shoal, teach, train, tutor **7** academy, borstal, college, educate **8** instruct **9** alma mater, institute **10** discipline, university *French:* **5** école, lycée *grounds:* **6** campus *Jewish:* **5** heder **7** yeshiva *judo:* **4** dojo *organization:* **3** PTA, PTO *religious:* **8** seminary *term:* **7** quarter **8** semester **9** trimester

schoolbook 4 text **6** primer, reader **7** speller

School for Scandal author 8 Sheridan (Richard Brinsley)

schooner 4 ship **5** stoup **6** goblet, seidel **7** tumbler **8** sailboat

Schubert forte 4 lied, song

science *of agriculture:* **8** agronomy *of animals:* **7** zoology *of armorial bearings:* **8** heraldry *of criminal punishment:* **8** penology *of environment:* **7** ecology *of fermentation:* **8** zymology *of health:* **7** hygiene **9** hygienics *of heredity:* **8** genetics *of human behavior:* **10** psychology *of measuring time:* **8** horology **11** chronometry *of motion:* **8** kinetics *of mountains:* **7** orology *of plants:* **6** botany *of projectiles:* **10** ballistics *of the earth:* **7** geology

scientific classification 8 taxonomy

sci-fi writer 3 Lem (Stanislaw) **4** Card (Orson Scott), Dick (Philip K.), Pohl (Frederik) **5** Disch (Thomas M.), Lewis (C. S.), Niven (Larry), Verne (Jules), Wells (H. G.) **6** Aldiss (Brian), Asimov (Isaac), Bester (Alfred), Bishop (Michael), Butler (Octavia), Clarke (Arthur C.), Delany (Samuel), Farmer (Philip José), Gibson (William), Le Guin (Ursula), Leiber (Fritz), Miller (Walter) **7** Ballard (J. G.), Clement (Hal), Ellison (Harlan), Herbert (Frank), Hubbard (L. Ron), Van Vogt (A. E.), Zelazny (Roger) **8** Anderson (Poul), Bradbury (Ray), Heinlein (Robert A.), Sterling (Bruce), Sturgeon (Theodore), Vonnegut (Kurt) **9** Gernsback (Hugo), Kornbluth (C. M.) **10** Silverberg (Robert)

scimitar 5 saber, sabre, sword **7** cutlass

scintilla 3 bit, jot **4** iota, whit **5** grain, spark, speck, trace **8** particle

scintillate 5 flash, gleam, glint, spark **6** glance **7** glimmer, glisten, glitter, shimmer, sparkle, twinkle **9** coruscate

scion 4 heir **5** child, graft, issue **7** progeny **8** offshoot **9** inheritor, offspring, successor **10** descendant

scoff at 4 mock, twit **5** fleer, scorn **6** deride **7** contemn, disdain **8** belittle, pooh-pooh, ridicule

scold 3 rag **4** chew, lash, rail, rant **5** baste, blame, chide, grill, harpy, hound, shrew, vixen **6** berate, grouch, grouse, harass, murmur, mutter, rebuke, revile, virago **7** bawl out, blister, censure, chasten, chew out, grumble, lecture, reprove, tell off, upbraid **8** admonish, execrate, fishwife, lambaste, reproach, Xantippe **9** criticize, dress down, excoriate, objurgate, reprehend, reprimand, termagant, Xanthippe **10** tongue-lash, vituperate

scoop 3 dig, dip **4** bail, beat, lift **5** gouge, ladle, spade **6** dig out, pick up, shovel **8** excavate **9** exclusive

scoot 3 fly, run, zip **4** dash, flee, race, rush, skip **5** hurry, scram, skirr, slide **6** hustle, scurry, sprint **7** scamper **9** skedaddle

scope 4 area, room **5** ambit, gamut, orbit, range, reach, sweep **6** extent, leeway, margin, radius **7** breadth, compass, purview **8** capacity, fullness, latitude **9** amplitude, extension

Scopes trial lawyer 5 Bryan (William Jennings) **6** Darrow (Clarence)

scorch 4 bake, burn, char, flay, sear **5** broil, roast, singe **6** scathe **7** blacken, blister, scarify, scourge, swelter **8** lambaste **9** castigate, excoriate

score 3 cut, tab, win **4** bill, gain, goal, line, mark, nick, slit **5** cleft, count, notch, reach, tally, total **6** attain, furrow, groove, grudge, rack up, record, thrive, twenty **7** account, achieve, invoice, prosper, scratch, succeed **8** flourish **9** reckoning **10** accomplish

scorn 4 gibe, jeer, mock **5** abhor, flout, scoff, spurn, taunt **6** deride **7** contemn, despise, despite, disdain, jeering, mockery **8** contempt, derision, ridicule, scoffing, taunting **9** contumely

Scorpius star 7 Antares

Scotch cocktail 6 Rob Roy **9** Rusty Nail

scoter 7 sea coot, sea duck

Scotland *capital:* **9** Edinburgh *city:* **6** Dundee **7** Glasgow **8** Aberdeen **9** Inverness **11** Dunfermline *firth:* **5** Clyde, Forth, Moray **6** Solway *former capital:* **5** Perth *island, island group:* **4** Iona, Jura, Mull, Skye, Uist **5** Arran, Islay **7** Orkneys **9** Shetlands **8** Hebrides *lake:* **8** Loch Ness **10** Loch Lomond *mountain, range:* **8** Ben Nevis **9** Grampians *patron saint:* **6** Andrew *river:* **3** Dee, Esk

Scott, Sir Walter *novel:* **5** Abbot (The) **6** Rob Roy **7** Ivanhoe **8** Talisman (The), Waverley **9** Woodstock **10** Kenilworth **11** Redgauntlet **12** Old Mortality **14** Quentin Durward *poem:* **7** Marmion **13** Lady of the Lake (The)

____ Scott case 4 Dred

Scottish *cap:* **3** tam **9** glengarry **11** tam-o'-shanter *child:* **5** bairn *dance:* **4** reel **5** fling **10** strathspey *guide:* **6** gillie *hero:* **5** Bruce (Robert) **7** Wallace (William) *hill:* **4** brae *lake:* **4** loch *landowner:* **5** laird *outlaw:* **6** Rob Roy *patron saint:* **6** Andrew *plaid:* **6** tartan *pudding:* **6** haggis *skirt:* **4** kilt *spirit:* **6** kelpie **7** banshee *sword:* **8** claymore *trousers:* **5** trews

scoundrel see SCAMP

scour 4 comb, rake **5** erode, purge,

range, scrub **6** forage, search **7** corrode, eat away, ransack, rummage **8** wear away **9** ferret out

scourge 4 bane, flay, flog, hide, lash, whip, whop **5** curse, flail, slash, whale **6** plague, ravage, scathe, stripe, thrash **7** afflict, blister, despoil, pillage, scarify **8** chastise, lambaste **9** castigate, depredate, desecrate, devastate, excoriate **10** affliction, flagellate, pestilence

Scourge of God 6 Attila

scout 3 spy **6** ranger, survey **7** explore, lookout **8** searcher, watchman **11** investigate, reconnoiter

scouting group 3 BSA, GSA

scow 3 hoy **5** barge **6** garvey **7** lighter

scowl 5 frown, glare, lower **6** glower

scrabble 5 grope **6** scrawl **7** clamber **8** flounder

scraggly 6 ragged, shaggy, uneven **7** unkempt **9** irregular

scraggy 4 bony, lank, lean **5** gaunt, harsh, lanky, rocky, rough **6** jagged, rugged, skinny, uneven **7** angular, scrawny, spindly, unlevel **8** gangling, rawboned, scabrous

scram 5 scoot, split **6** beat it, get out **7** buzz off, get lost, skiddoo, take off, vamoose **8** clear out **9** skedaddle

scramble 4 hash **6** jumble, jungle, muddle, scurry, tumble **7** clamber, clutter, rummage, scuttle, shuffle **8** mishmash, scrabble, straggle **9** confusion

scrambled 7 chaotic, jumbled, mixed-up **8** confused **9** corrupted **10** disordered, disorderly

scrap 3 bit, jot, row **4** chip, dump, fray, junk, spat, tiff, whit **5** brawl, chuck, crumb, fight, melee, piece, set-to, shred, speck **6** bicker, fracas, reject, sliver, tittle **7** brabble, cutting, discard, fall out, quarrel, scuffle, smidgen, wrangle **8** fragment, jettison, leftover, particle, squabble, throw out **9** throw away

scrape 3 fix, jam, rub **4** mess, rasp, spot **5** chafe, fight, grate, graze, pinch, scour, scuff, shave, skimp, spare, stint **6** abrade, pickle, plight, scrimp **7** dilemma, scratch, trouble **8** abrasion, struggle **11** predicament

scrappy 6 feisty **8** brawling **9** combative, truculent **10** pugnacious **11** belligerent, contentious, quarrelsome

scratch 4 claw, rake, rasp **5** grate, score, scrup **6** scotch, scrape, scrawl **7** call off **8** scrabble, scribble

scratchy 5 rough **6** gritty **7** itching, prickly, rasping **8** abrasive, granular, tingling **10** irritating

scrawl 6 doodle **7** scratch **8** scrabble, scribble

scrawny 4 bony, lank, lean **5** gaunt, lanky **6** skinny **7** scraggy **8** rawboned

scream 3 cry **4** yell, yowl **5** shout **6** screak, shriek, shrill, squeal **7** screech

screech 6 screak, scream, shriek, shrill, squeal

screed 5 level, spiel **6** letter, tirade **8** diatribe, harangue, jeremiad **9** discourse, philippic **11** disputation **12** disquisition

screen 4 cull, sift, veil **5** blind, sieve **6** facade, filter, movies, shroud, winnow **7** conceal, obscure, pick out **9** partition **10** camouflage *Japanese:* **5** shoji

screw 9 propeller

screwball 3 nut, wag **4** kook, zany **5** clown, crazy, cutup, flake, flaky, freak, gonzo, joker, kooky, loony, nutty, silly, wacko, wacky **6** madcap, weirdo **7** buffoon, dingbat, farceur **8** crackpot, jokester **9** ding-a-ling, eccentric, fruitcake, whimsical

Screwtape Letters author 5 Lewis (C. S.)

screwy 3 mad **4** daft, nuts **5** batty, crazy, goofy, loony, nutty, wacky **6** absurd, insane **7** bizarre, cracked, lunatic **9** eccentric **10** unbalanced

scribble 5 write **6** scrawl **7** scratch **8** squiggle

scribe 5 clerk, write **6** author, writer **7** copyist **9** scrivener, secretary

scrimmage 4 fray **5** brawl, broil, clash, fight, melee, scrap, set-to **6** battle, fracas, ruckus, rumpus **7** scuffle **8** skirmish **10** donnybrook, free-for-all

scrimp 4 save **5** stint **6** save up, scrape **8** conserve **9** economize

script 4 hand, text **5** write **8** longhand, scenario **10** penmanship, screenplay **11** calligraphy, chirography, handwriting, orchestrate

scrivener 6 notary, scribe, writer **7** copyist

scrooge 5 miser **7** niggard **8** tightwad **9** skinflint **10** cheapskate **12** moneygrubber

scrounge 3 beg, bum, tap **4** grub, hunt, loot **5** cadge, filch, mooch, pinch, steal, swipe, touch **6** forage, hustle, pilfer, snitch, sponge, thieve **7** finagle, solicit, wheedle **8** freeload **9** panhandle

scroungy 5 dirty, seedy **6** grubby, grungy, scurvy, scuzzy, shabby, sleazy, sordid **7** scruffy, squalid, unkempt **8** slovenly **10** slatternly

scrub 3 rub **4** buff, drop, wash **5** abort, brush, scour **6** cancel, mallee, maquis, polish **7** abandon, call off, cleanse, scratch **9** chaparral, eliminate

scrubby 4 drab, mean **5** dingy, dowdy,

runty **6** paltry, ragged, shabby, shoddy **7** rundown, runtish, stunted **8** inferior **9** neglected **10** bedraggled, broken-down

scruff 4 nape, neck

scruffy 5 mangy, seedy, tacky **6** frowsy, frowzy, shabby, shaggy **7** run-down, scrubby, unkempt **8** slovenly, tattered **10** down-at-heel, threadbare

scrumptious 5 tasty, yummy **8** heavenly, luscious **9** ambrosial, delicious, succulent, toothsome **10** delectable, delightful **13** mouthwatering

scruple 3 bit, jot **4** balk, iota **5** demur, doubt, grain, qualm, scrap, shred, worry **7** concern, modicum **8** particle, question **9** hesitancy **11** compunction

scrupulous 5 exact, fussy **6** honest, minute, strict **7** careful, heedful, upright **8** critical, punctual, rigorous **9** honorable **10** fair-minded, fastidious, meticulous, principled, upstanding **11** painstaking, punctilious **12** conscionable **13** conscientious

scrutinize 4 comb, scan **5** audit, probe, study **6** peruse **7** analyze, canvass, dig into, dissect, examine, eyeball, inspect **8** look over, pore over **9** check over **11** contemplate, investigate

scrutiny 4 scan **5** audit **6** review, survey **7** perusal **8** analysis **10** inspection **11** examination **12** surveillance

scuba diver 7 frogman **8** aquanaut

scud 3 fly **4** race, rain, rush, sail, skim **5** brume, froth, scoot, speed, spray, spume **6** clouds, scurry, shower

scuff 6 scrape **7** scratch, shamble, shuffle

scuffle 3 row **4** fray **5** brawl, broil, fight, scrap, set-to **6** affray, fracas, hubbub, tussle **7** bobbery, grapple, shamble, shuffle, wrestle **10** roughhouse

scull 3 oar, row **4** boat **5** shell **6** propel

sculpt 3 hew **5** carve, shape **6** chisel

sculptor *American:* **3** Lin (Maya) **4** Gabo (Naum), Taft (Lorado) **5** Andre (Carl), Koons (Jeff), Pratt (Bela), Segal (George), Serra (Richard), Smith (David), Story (William) **6** Aitkin (Robert), Calder (Alexander), French (Daniel Chester), Powers (Hiram), Zorach (William) **7** Borglum (Gutzon), Cornell (Joseph), Noguchi (Isamu) **8** Lachaise (Gaston), Lipchitz (Jacques), Nadelman (Elie), Nevelson (Louise) **9** Bourgeois (Louise), Mestrovic (Ivan), Oldenburg (Claes), Remington (Frederic) **12** Saint-Gaudens (Augustus) *Czech:* **6** Stursa (Jan) *Danish:* **11** Thorvaldsen (Bertel), Thorwaldsen (Bertel) *Dutch:* **6** Sluter (Claus) *English:* **5** Moore (Henry), Watts (George)

7 Epstein (Jacob), Flaxman (John) **8** Hepworth (Barbara) *French:* **3** Arp (Hans, Jean) **4** Bloc (André) **5** Rodin (Auguste) **6** Dubois (Paul), Houdon (Jean-Antoine) **7** Maillol (Aristide), Pevsner (Antoine) **9** Bartholdi (Frédéric-Auguste), Roubillac (Louis-François) *Greek:* **5** Myron **7** Phidias **8** Pheidias **10** Polyclitus, Praxiteles **11** Polycleitus *Italian:* **5** Leoni (Leone), Salvi (Niccolò, Nicola) **6** Canova (Antonio), Pisano (Andrea, Nino), Robbia (Andrea, Giovanni, Girolamo, Luca della) **7** Bernini (Gian Lorenzo), Cellini (Benvenuto), da Vinci (Leonardo), Orcagna, Quercia (Jacopo della) **8** Ghiberti (Lorenzo), Leonardo (da Vinci), Vittoria (Alessandro) **9** Donatello, Sansovino (Jacopo) **10** Verrocchio (Andrea del) **12** Michelangelo (Buonarroti) *Rhodian:* **9** Polydorus *Romanian:* **8** Brancusi (Constantin) *Russian:* **7** Zadkine (Ossip) *Swedish:* **6** Milles (Carl) **9** Oldenburg (Claes) *Swiss:* **10** Giacometti (Alberto)

scum 5 algae, dregs, dross **6** refuse, vermin **8** riffraff

scummy 3 low **4** base, mean, vile **5** dirty, mucky, slimy **6** grubby, odious, sleazy, sordid **7** squalid **10** despicable **12** contemptible

scurrilous 4 foul **5** dirty, gross, nasty **6** coarse, filthy, vulgar **7** abusive, obscene, profane **8** indecent **9** insulting, offensive **10** outrageous **11** opprobrious **12** contumelious, vituperative

scurry 3 run **4** dart, dash **5** scoot, shoot **6** bustle **7** scamper, scuffle, scuttle

scurvy see SCUMMY

scut 4 tail

scuttlebutt 4 buzz, talk **5** rumor **6** gossip, report **7** chatter, hearsay **9** grapevine

Scylla 4 rock *counterpart:* **9** Charybdis *father:* **5** Nisus *lover:* **5** Minos

scythe handle 5 snath **6** snathe

sea 4 blue, deep, main **5** brine, drink, ocean *Antarctica:* **4** Ross **5** Davis **7** Weddell **8** Amundsen *Arctic:* **4** Kara **7** Chukchi **8** Beaufort, Karskoye **9** Chuckchee, Norwegian **11** Chukotskoye **12** East Siberian *Asia-Europe:* **5** Black *Asia Minor:* **7** Icarian *Atlantic:* **5** North **7** Weddell **9** Caribbean *Australia-Indonesia:* **7** Arafura *Balkan Peninsula-Italy:* **8** Adriatic *Bay of Bengal:* **7** Andaman *China-Korea:* **5** Huang, Hwang **6** Yellow *combining form:* **3** mer **4** mari **5** pelag **6** pelago **7** thalass **8** thalasso *Corsica-Italy:* **10** Tyrrhenian *Denmark-Norway:* **9** Skagerrak *Denmark-Sweden:* **8** Kattegat *England-Ireland:*

5 Irish *Fiji:* **4** Koro *France-Italy:* **8** Ligurian *Greece:* **5** Crete *Greece-Italy:* **6** Ionian *Greece-Turkey:* **6** Aegean **8** Thracian *Honshu:* **6** Sagami *Indian Ocean:* **5** Timor **7** Arabian *Indonesia:* **4** Bali **6** Flores *inland:* **3** Red **4** Aral **7** Caspian *Japan:* **3** Suo **6** Inland *Malay Archipelago:* **5** Banda *Mexico:* **6** Cortés *Netherlands:* **6** Wadden *North Atlantic:* **8** Sargasso *Northern Europe:* **6** Baltic, Ostsee **8** Suevicum *North Pacific:* **6** Bering *off Scotland:* **8** Hebrides *off Sweden:* **5** Aland *Pacific:* **4** Java **5** China, Coral **6** Maluku **7** Celebes, Eastern, Molucca, Solomon **9** East China **10** South China *Philippine:* **4** Sulu *Russia:* **5** White **7** Okhotsk *Russia-Ukraine:* **4** Azov *South Pacific:* **4** Ross **6** Tasman **8** Amundsen *Turkey:* **7** Marmara **9** Propontis *West Pacific:* **5** Ceram, Japan **8** Bismarck **10** Philippine

sea anemone 5 polyp

seabird see BIRD *aquatic*

seacoast 5 beach, coast, shore **6** strand **8** littoral **9** shoreline

sea cucumber 7 trepang **11** holothurian

sea dog see SAILOR

sea duck 5 eider, scaup **6** scoter **9** merganser

sea eagle 4 erne **6** osprey **8** fish hawk

seafarer 3 tar **4** salt **6** sailor **7** jack-tar, mariner

seafood dish 4 clam, crab **5** clams, squid **6** mussel, oyster, shrimp **7** lobster, mussels, oysters, scallop **8** calamari, scallops

seagoing 8 maritime, nautical

seal 5 sigil, stamp **6** cachet, signet **7** sticker *female:* **3** cow *herd:* **3** pod **5** patch *young:* **3** pup

sealant 4 lute **5** caulk, grout **6** luting, mastic **8** caulking

sea lily 7 crinoid

seam 4 bond **5** joint, union **8** coupling, juncture **10** connection

seaman see SAILOR

sea monster 3 Orc **6** kraken **9** leviathan

seamount 5 guyot

seamy 5 dirty, rough, seedy **6** sordid **7** squalid **12** disreputable

séance 7 meeting, session, sitting *holder:* **6** medium

seaport *Alaska:* **6** Juneau **9** Anchorage *Albania:* **5** Vlorë **6** Durres, Valona *Algeria:* **4** Bône, Oran **6** Annaba *Angola:* **6** Lobito, Luanda **7** Cabinda **8** Benguela *Argentina:* **11** Buenos Aires, Mar del Plata *Australia:* **4** Eden **5** Bowen, Perth **6** Darwin, Hobart, Sydney **8** Brisbane **9** Melbourne **10** Wollongong *Azores:* **5** Horta *Balearic:* **5** Ibiza *Belgium:* **6** Ostend **7** Antwerp *Benin:* **7** Cotonou

9 Porto-Novo *Black Sea:* **5** Varna **6** Burgas, Odessa **9** Constanta *Brazil:* **3** Rio **4** Pará **5** Bahia, Belém, Natal **6** Recife, Santos **7** Vitoria **8** Salvador **9** Fortaleza **10** Pernambuco **11** Pôrto Alegre, São Salvador **12** Rio de Janeiro *Bulgaria:* **5** Varna **6** Burgas *Cameroon:* **6** Douala *Canaries:* **8** Arrecife **9** Las Palmas *Chile:* **5** Arica **8** Coquimbo **10** Valparaíso *China:* **4** Amoy **6** Dalian, Fuzhou, Lüshun, Xiamen **7** Foochow, Hsia-men, Qingdao, Tianjin **8** Shanghai, Tientsin, Tsingtao **9** Guangzhou, Zhenjiang **10** Chen-chiang, Port Arthur *Colombia:* **6** Lorica **9** Cartagena **12** Barranquilla *Corsica:* **5** Calvi **7** Ajaccio *Costa Rica:* **5** Limón **10** Puntarenas *Crimean:* **5** Kerch, Yalta **10** Sebastopol, Sevastopol *Croatia:* **5** Rieka, Split **6** Rijeka **9** Dubrovnik, Santiago *Cuba:* **6** Havana **8** Matanzas, Santiago *Cyprus:* **9** Famagusta *Denmark:* **5** Arhus **6** Aarhus, Alborg **7** Aalborg **8** Elsinore **10** Copenhagen *Ecuador:* **9** Guayaquil *Egypt:* **4** Said **10** Alexandria *England:* **4** Hull **5** Dover **9** Liverpool **10** Portsmouth **11** Southampton *Equatorial Guinea:* **4** Bata *Eritrea:* **4** Aseb *Estonia:* **5** Pärnu **7** Tallinn *Finland:* **3** Abo **4** Kemi, Oulu, Pori, Vasa **5** Hango, Kotka, Rauma, Turku, Vaasa **6** Vyborg *Florida:* **5** Miami, Tampa **9** Pensacola **12** Apalachicola, Jacksonville *France:* **4** Nice **5** Brest, Havre **6** Calais, Cannes, Toulon **7** Dunkirk, Le Havre **8** Bordeaux, Boulogne **9** Cherbourg, Dunkerque, Marseille **10** Marseilles *French Polynesia:* **7** Papeete *Georgia:* **8** Savannah **9** Brunswick *Georgia, Republic of:* **4** Pot'i *Germany:* **4** Kiel **5** Emden **6** Bremen, Lübeck, Wismar **7** Hamburg, Rostock **8** Cuxhaven **11** Bremerhaven *Ghana:* **4** Tema **5** Accra *Greece:* **5** Pylos, Syros, Volos **7** Piraeus *Guatemala:* **7** San José **10** Livingston *Haiti:* **5** Cayes **10** Cap Haitien *Honduras:* **7** La Ceiba **8** Trujillo *India:* **3** Goa **4** Puri **5** Marud **6** Bombay, Madras, Mumbai, Old Goa **7** Calicut, Chennai **8** Calcutta **9** Jagannath **10** Trivandrum *Iran:* **4** Jask **7** Bushehr *Iraq:* **5** Basra *Ireland:* **4** Cork **5** Sligo **6** Dingle, Dublin, Galway, Tralee **8** Drogheda, Limerick **9** Waterford **10** Balbriggan *Israel:* **4** Acre, Akko, Elat, Yafo **5** Accho, Eilat, Haifa, Jaffa, Joppa **6** Ashdod **8** Ashqelon *Italy:* **4** Bari **5** Anzio, Gaeta, Genoa **6** Naples, Pesaro, Rimini, Venice **7** Leghorn, Livorno, Marsala, Messina, Rapallo, Salerno, Taranto, Trieste **8** Brindisi, Sorrento, Syracuse *Ivory Coast:* **5** Tabou

7 Abidjan *Jamaica:* 8 Kingston 10 Montego Bay *Japan:* 4 Kobe 5 Kochi, Osaka, Rumoi, Ujina, Uraga 6 Sasebo 7 Fukuoka 8 Nagasaki, Yokohama 9 Hiroshima *Java:* 5 Tegal, Tuban 7 Cilacap, Jakarta 8 Semarang, Surabaya *Jordan:* 5 Aqaba, Elath 6 Aelana *Latvia:* 4 Riga *Lebanon:* 4 Tyre 5 Saida, Sidon 6 Beirut 7 Tripoli *Libya:* 6 Tobruk 7 Tripoli 8 Benghazi *Lithuania:* 5 Memel 8 Klaipeda *Madagascar:* 8 Tamatave *Maine:* 7 Belfast 8 Portland *Malaysia:* 4 Miri, Weld 5 Pekan 6 Melaka, Pinang 7 Malacca 10 George Town *Massachusetts:* 6 Boston 9 Fall River 10 New Bedford *Mauritius:* 9 Port Louis *Mediterranean:* 4 Gaza, Oran 5 Genoa, Haifa, Jaffa 6 Beirut, Naples, Venice 7 Algiers, Bizerte, Catania, Palermo, Piraeus, Tripoli 8 Benghazi, Port Said 9 Barcelona, Marseille 10 Alexandria, Marseilles *Mexico:* 7 Tampico 8 Acapulco, Mazatlán, Veracruz *Minorca:* 5 Mahón *Moluccas:* 5 Ambon *Montenegro:* 5 Kotor *Morocco:* 4 Safi, Salé 5 Ceuta 6 Agadir 7 Tangier, Tétouan 10 Casablanca *Mozambique:* 5 Beira, Pemba 6 Amelia, Maputo, Xai Xai 11 Porto Amelia *New Hampshire:* 10 Portsmouth *New Zealand:* 8 Auckland 10 Wellington *Nicaragua:* 5 Brito *Nigeria:* 5 Lagos 8 Harcourt *Niger mouth:* 5 Bonny *North Korea:* 4 Yuki 5 Nampo, Unggi 6 Wonsan *Norway:* 4 Bodo, Moss 5 Vadso 6 Bergen, Tromso 9 Stavanger, Trondheim 11 Fredrikstad *Oman:* 6 Masqat, Muscat *Pakistan:* 5 Pasni 6 Gwadar 7 Karachi *Papua New Guinea:* 3 Lea *Peru:* 3 Ilo 4 Eten 5 Paita, Pisco 6 Callao *Philippines:* 4 Cebu 5 Davao, Laoag 6 Aparri, Cavite, Iloilo, Manila 7 Legaspi 8 Tacloban 9 Zamboanga *Poland:* 6 Danzig, Gdansk, Gdynia 7 Stettin 8 Szczecin *Portugal:* 4 Faro 5 Porto 6 Oporto 7 Funchal *Puerto Rico:* 5 Ponce 7 Arecibo, San Juan 8 Mayagüez *Russia:* 6 Vyborg 8 Murmansk 11 Kaliningrad, Vladivostok *Ryukyu:* 4 Naha, Nawa *Sakhalin Island:* 8 Korsakov *Saudi Arabia:* 5 Jedda, Jidda, Yanbu, Yenbo 6 Jeddah, Jiddah *Scotland:* 3 Ayr 5 Leith, Leven 6 Dundee 7 Glasgow 8 Aberdeen *Sicily:* 7 Catania, Marsala, Messina, Palermo 8 Syracuse *Slovenia:* 5 Kopar, Koper, Piran *Somalia:* 7 Berbera 9 Mogadishu *South Africa:* 5 Natal 6 Durban 8 Cape Town *South Carolina:* 8 Savannah 10 Charleston *South Korea:* 5 Masan, Mokpo, Pusan 6 Inchon 7 Incheon, Masampo *Spain:* 5 Cádiz, Gijón

6 Abdera, Málaga 8 Alicante 9 Algeciras, Barcelona, Cartagena, Las Palmas *Sri Lanka:* 7 Colombo 10 Batticaloa *Sumatra:* 5 Medan 6 Padang 9 Banda Aceh *Sweden:* 4 Umea 5 Gavle, Lulea, Malmö, Pitea, Ystad 8 Göteborg 9 Stockholm 10 Gothenburg 11 Helsingborg *Tanzania:* 5 Lindi, Tanga 8 Zanzibar 11 Dar es Salaam *Thailand:* 4 Trat 8 Bang Phra *Tunisia:* 5 Sfax 5 Gabès 6 Sousse 7 Bizerta, Bizerte *Turkey:* 4 Rize 5 Izmir, Sinop 6 Samsun, Smyrna 7 Antalya 8 Istanbul *Ukraine:* 5 Kerch, Yalta 6 Odessa 7 Kherson *Vanuatu:* 4 Vila 8 Port-Vila *Vietnam:* 3 Hue 6 Da Nang 7 Tourane 8 Haiphong, Nha Trang *Virginia:* 7 Norfolk 10 Portsmouth *Yemen:* 4 Aden 5 Mocha **seaport capital** 4 Aden, Apia, Dili, Lomé, Suva 5 Accra, Adana, Dakar, Lagos 6 Banjul, Belize, Bissau, Dublin, Havana, Kuwait, Lisbon, Maputo, Masqat, Muscat, Roseau 7 Algiers, Batavia, Colombo, Jakarta, Moresby, San Juan 8 Castries, Djakarta, Freetown, Hamilton, Helsinki, Honolulu, Kingston, Monrovia, Valletta 9 Mogadishu, Nuku'alofa, Porto-Novo, Reykjavík, Singapore 10 Bridgetown, Daressalem, Libreville, Mogadiscio, Paramaribo 11 Dar es Salaam, Port of Spain 12 Port-au-Prince

sear 3 dry 5 parch, singe 6 burn up, scorch, sizzle 7 shrivel 9 cauterize, dehydrate, desiccate

search 4 beat, comb, grub, hunt, scan, seek 5 chase, check, delve, frisk, grope, quest, rifle, scour 6 ferret, forage 7 fossick, hunting, manhunt, pursuit, ransack, rummage, run down 8 finecomb, scavenge, scout out 9 cast about, ferret out 10 scrutinize

searing 3 hot 5 harsh 6 severe 7 blazing, burning, intense 8 scathing 9 agonizing, scorching 10 blistering 12 excruciating

sea robber 5 rover 6 pirate 7 corsair 8 picaroon 9 buccaneer 10 freebooter

seasickness 6 nausea 8 mal de mer

season 3 fit 4 fall, term, time 5 spice, train, treat 6 autumn, harden, pepper, period, school, spring, summer, winter 7 prepare, toughen 8 marinade, marinate 9 acclimate 10 case-harden, discipline 11 acclimatize

seasonable 3 apt 6 timely 7 welcome 9 favorable, opportune, pertinent, well-timed 10 auspicious, convenient, propitious 11 appropriate

seasoned 6 inured, mature, tested, versed 7 adapted, matured, veteran 8 flavored, hardened 9 flavorful, prac-

ticed **10** acclimated, habituated
11 experienced **12** acclimatized, accomplished
seasoning 3 bay **4** dill, herb, mace, sage, salt **5** anise, basil, chili, clove, cumin, spice, thyme **6** cloves, fennel, garlic, ginger, nutmeg, pepper, savory **7** cayenne, chervil, mustard, oregano, paprika, parsley, saffron **8** allspice, cardamom, cinnamon, rosemary, tarragon, turmeric **9** condiment, coriander
seat 3 hub **4** base, beam, duff, rear, rest, rump **5** basis, chair, place, usher **6** behind, bottom, center, settee **7** fulcrum **8** backside, buttocks, derriere **9** fundament, posterior **10** foundation *church:* **3** pew *on a camel or elephant:* **6** howdah *upholstered:* **9** banquette
sea urchin 7 echinus **8** echinoid
seaweed 4 kelp, nori, ulva **5** dulse, fucus, kombu **6** fucoid, wakame **8** sargasso **9** carrageen, Irish moss **12** bladder wrack
Sea Wolf, The *author:* **6** London (Jack) *captain:* **10** Wolf Larsen *ship:* **5** Ghost
Sebastian *brother:* **6** Alonso *sister:* **5** Viola
secco 3 dry **8** painting, staccato
secede 4 quit **5** leave **8** separate, withdraw
seclude 4 hide **6** closet, immure, retire, screen **7** confine, enclose, isolate, shut off **8** cloister, separate, withdraw **9** sequester
secluded 6 hidden, remote **7** private, recluse, shut off **8** hermetic, isolated, screened, solitary **9** concealed, reclusive, withdrawn **10** cloistered, tucked away **11** out-of-the-way, quarantined, sequestered
seclusion 7 privacy **8** solitude **9** isolation **10** separation, withdrawal
second 4 wink **5** flash, jiffy, trice **6** moment **7** endorse, instant, support **9** twinkling
secondary 3 sub **6** lesser **7** derived **8** borrowed, inferior **9** resultant, tributary **10** collateral, derivative, subsequent **11** subordinate, subservient
second-class 6 common **8** déclassé, inferior, low-grade, mediocre
secondhand 4 used, worn **7** derived **8** borrowed **10** derivative
second-string 3 sub **6** backup **9** alternate **10** substitute
secrecy 7 silence, stealth **10** covertness, subterfuge **11** concealment, furtiveness
secret 5 sneak **6** arcane, closet, covert, hidden, occult **7** cryptic, furtive, obscure, sub-rosa **8** abstruse, backdoor, discreet, hermetic, hush-hush, stealthy **9** concealed, recondite **10** classified, restricted, undercover **11** clandestine, out-of-the-way, underhanded **12** confidential, hugger-mugger **13** surreptitious, under-the-table *combining form:* **5** crypt, krypt **6** crypto, krypto
secret agent 3 spy **8** emissary
secretary 4 aide, desk **5** clerk **6** scribe **9** assistant **10** amanuensis, escritoire *king's:* **10** chancellor
secrete 4 bury, emit, hide **5** cache, exude, plant, stash **6** screen **7** conceal, deposit, emanate
secretive 7 furtive **8** reticent, taciturn **10** backstairs, buttoned-up **11** tight-lipped **12** close-mouthed **13** unforthcoming
secretly 7 sub rosa **9** furtively **10** stealthily
secret society 3 KKK **4** tong **5** cabal, Mafia, Triad **6** Mau Mau, Yakuza **7** camorra **9** camarilla, Carbonari **10** Cosa Nostra, Freemasons, Ku Klux Klan
sect 4 cult **5** creed, party **7** faction **8** division, religion **12** denomination
sectarian 5 local **8** splinter **9** dissident, heretical, heterodox, parochial **10** provincial, schismatic, unorthodox **13** nonconformist
sectary 5 rebel **7** heretic **8** adherent, disciple, follower, partisan **9** dissenter, dissident **10** schismatic, separatist **13** nonconformist, revolutionary
section 3 cut **4** area, belt, part, zone **5** chunk, piece, slice, tract **6** member, moiety, parcel, region, sector, sphere **7** portion, quarter, segment **8** district, division, locality, precinct **11** subdivision
sector 4 area, zone **7** quarter, section **8** district, precinct **11** subdivision
secular 3 lay **7** earthly, profane, worldly **8** temporal, unsacred **11** nonclerical, terrestrial **12** nonreligious
secure 3 fix **4** bind, fast, firm, gain, land, lock, moor, nail, safe **5** catch, cinch, clamp, cover, fixed, guard, solid, sound, tried **6** anchor, assure, cement, clinch, defend, effect, ensure, fasten, insure, obtain, shield, stable **7** acquire, assured, capture, procure, protect, tie down **8** reliable, sanguine **9** confident, safeguard **10** batten down, bring about **11** established, impregnable
security 4 bail, bond, pawn **5** guard, token **6** pledge, safety, shield, surety **7** defense, earnest, warrant **8** guaranty, immunity, warranty **9** assurance, guarantee, safeguard, soundness, stability

10 collateral, protection, steadiness
13 certification
sedate 4 calm 5 grave, sober, staid
6 placid, proper, seemly, serene, steady
7 earnest, serious 8 composed, decorous, tranquil 9 collected, dignified,
unruffled 10 sobersided 13 dispassionate, imperturbable
sedative 4 balm 6 downer, Valium
7 calmant, Librium, Miltown, Seconal
8 barbital, hyoscine, Nembutal 9 calmative 10 depressant 11 barbiturate
12 sleeping pill, tranquilizer
sedentary 4 lazy 6 seated 7 settled, sitting 8 inactive 10 stationary
sediment 4 lees, silt 5 dregs, dross 7 bottoms, deposit, grounds, heeltap, residue
8 residuum 9 settlings 11 precipitate
layer: 5 varve
sedition 4 coup 6 mutiny, putsch, revolt,
strike 7 protest, treason 8 intrigue,
uprising 9 coup d'état, rebellion 10 revolution 12 insurrection
seditious 8 disloyal, factious, mutinous
9 dissident, insurgent 10 rebellious,
traitorous 11 treacherous
seduce 4 bait, coax, lure 5 decoy, tempt
6 allure, betray, delude, entice, entrap,
lead on, ravish 7 corrupt, debauch,
deceive 8 entrance, inveigle
seducer 4 roué, vamp 7 Don Juan, playboy 8 lothario 9 libertine
seduction 4 lure 8 conquest 9 siren song
10 allurement, attraction, ravishment,
temptation
seductive 5 siren 8 alluring, magnetic,
tempting 9 beguiling 10 attractive,
bewitching, enchanting 11 captivating
seductress 5 siren 7 Lorelei 9 temptress
11 femme fatale
sedulous 8 diligent, tireless 9 assiduous,
laborious 10 persistent 11 industrious,
persevering, unremitting
see 4 call, date, espy, gape, gaze, look,
mark, peer, scan, view 5 grasp, sight,
visit, watch 6 behold, come by, descry,
divine, drop by, drop in, go with, look
in, notice, stop by, stop in, take in
7 discern, examine, find out, glimpse,
imagine, make out, observe, realize
8 conceive, consider, envisage, envision, perceive 9 apprehend, ascertain,
determine, recognize, visualize 10 comprehend, scrutinize, understand
seed 3 sow 4 core, germ 5 brood, grain,
issue, ovule, plant, spark, spawn
6 embryo, kernel, notion 7 concept,
nucleus, progeny 8 children 9 offspring
11 descendants *aromatic:* 6 fennel *coating:* 5 testa 6 testae (plural) *covering:*
4 aril *of a bean:* 7 haricot *of a vine:*

6 peanut *poisonous:* 10 castor bean *vessel:* 3 pod 5 fruit, pyxis 7 silicle, silique
seedcase 3 pod
seedy 5 dingy, faded, mangy, ratty, tired
6 droopy, frowsy, frowzy, shabby, used
up, wilted 7 run-down, scruffy, squalid,
unkempt, wilting 8 decaying, decrepit,
drooping, flagging, inferior, slovenly,
tattered 9 neglected, overgrown
10 bedraggled, down-at-heel, threadbare 12 disreputable
seek 3 try 4 fish, hunt, root 5 assay,
delve, essay, offer, quest, sniff 6 pursue,
strive 7 attempt, inquire, look for,
request 8 endeavor, smell out 9 search
for, search out, undertake
seem 3 act 4 look 5 imply 6 appear,
behave 7 suggest 8 resemble
seemly 3 fit 6 decent, proper, suited
7 apropos, correct, fitting 8 becoming,
decorous, suitable 9 befitting, congenial, congruous 10 compatible, conforming 11 appropriate, comme il faut
seep 4 drip, leak, ooze, weep 5 bleed,
exude, leech, sweat 6 filter, strain 7 diffuse, dribble, trickle 8 transude 9 percolate
seer 5 augur, sibyl 6 oracle 7 diviner,
prophet 8 foreseer, haruspex 9 predictor 10 forecaster, foreteller, soothsayer
11 clairvoyant, Nostradamus
seesaw 3 yaw 4 rock, veer 5 lurch,
pitch, swing 6 teeter 7 bascule 8 flip-
flop 9 alternate, fluctuate, oscillate
11 teeterboard
seethe 3 sop 4 boil, burn, foam, fret,
fume, rage, soak, stew 5 churn, erupt,
froth, souse, steam, steep 6 bubble,
drench, simmer, sizzle 7 bristle, ferment, parboil, smolder 8 saturate,
smoulder, waterlog
see-through 5 clear 6 limpid 8 pellucid
11 translucent, transparent
segment 3 cut 4 part 5 piece 6 divide,
member, moiety 7 portion, section
8 division, separate 10 categorize
sego 4 lily
segregate 6 enisle, select 7 isolate 8 separate 9 sequester 10 disconnect
segregation 9 apartheid, isolation 10 jim
crowism, separatism 13 ghettoization
segue 7 proceed 8 continue 10 transition
11 progression
seidel 5 stoup 8 schooner
seine 3 net 5 trawl
Seine tributary 4 Oise 5 Marne, Yonne
seismologist 7 Richter (Charles)
seize 3 bag, nab 4 grab, take 5 annex,
catch, clasp, grasp, usurp 6 abduct,
arrest, clinch, clutch, kidnap, occupy,
secure, snatch 7 capture, grapple,

impound 8 arrogate, carry off 9 apprehend, sequester 10 commandeer, confiscate 11 appropriate, expropriate
seizure 3 fit 4 turn 5 spasm, spell, throe 6 access, attack, taking 7 capture 8 paroxysm, takeover 9 breakdown 10 annexation, convulsion, usurpation 12 confiscation
seldom 6 hardly, rarely 8 scarcely 10 hardly ever 12 infrequently, occasionally, sporadically
select 4 best, cull, fine, pick, rare 5 cream, elite, prime 6 choice, choose, chosen, culled, opt for, picked 7 favored, pick out 8 screened, superior 9 exclusive, exquisite, preferred, recherché, single out
selection 6 choice 7 culling, excerpt, picking 8 choosing 10 assortment, preference
selective 5 fussy, picky 6 choosy 7 choosey, finicky 8 specific 10 discerning, particular, scrupulous 11 persnickety
Selene 4 Luna 6 Hecate 7 Artemis *beloved:* 8 Endymion *brother:* 6 Helios *father:* 8 Hyperion *mother:* 4 Thea
self 3 ego *combining form:* 3 aut 4 auto
self-absorbed 4 smug 6 egoistic 9 conceited, egotistic 10 complacent, egocentric 11 egotistical, introverted 12 narcissistic 13 inner-directed
self-acting 9 automatic
self-assertive 4 bold 5 brash, pushy 6 cheeky 7 forward 8 cocksure, militant 9 audacious, obtrusive, officious 10 aggressive 11 impertinent, overweening 12 presumptuous
self-assurance 5 poise 6 aplomb 8 coolness 9 composure, sangfroid 10 confidence, equanimity 13 collectedness
self-assured 4 smug 6 poised 8 sanguine 9 confident
self-centered 9 conceited, egotistic 10 egocentric 11 egotistical 12 narcissistic
self-composed 4 calm 6 poised, serene 7 assured 9 collected, confident, possessed 10 controlled
self-confidence 5 poise 6 aplomb 9 assurance
self-confident 5 cocky 6 jaunty, poised 7 assured 8 sanguine
self-conscious 4 prim 5 stiff 6 formal, uneasy 7 awkward, stilted, studied 8 affected, mannered 9 contrived, ill at ease 10 artificial
self-contained 6 closed, formal 7 built-in 8 composed, enclosed, reserved, reticent 9 exclusive 10 restrained 11 independent

self-control 7 balance, dignity, reserve 9 restraint, stability, willpower 10 abstinence, constraint, discipline, temperance 11 forbearance
self-defense art 4 judo 6 aikido, karate, kung fu 7 jujitsu 9 tai kwan do
self-destruction 7 suicide 8 felo-de-se, hara-kiri
self-discipline 4 will 8 stoicism 9 willpower 10 abstinence
self-educated 12 autodidactic
self-effacing 3 shy 5 timid 6 modest 7 bashful 8 retiring, sheepish 9 diffident, unassured 11 unassertive
self-esteem 5 pride 6 vanity 7 conceit, dignity, egotism 10 narcissism 11 amour propre
self-evident 5 clear, plain 6 patent 7 obvious 8 manifest, palpable 10 prima facie, undeniable 12 demonstrable, unmistakable
self-explanatory 5 clear, plain 7 evident, obvious 8 manifest 11 perspicuous, transparent
self-governing 7 popular 9 sovereign 10 autonomous, democratic
self-importance 3 ego 5 pride 6 egoism, hubris 7 conceit, egotism 9 arrogance, pomposity, vainglory
self-important 4 smug, vain 6 lordly 7 bloated, haughty, pompous 8 arrogant 9 conceited, egotistic 10 pontifical 11 magisterial, pretentious
self-indulgent 9 libertine, sybaritic 10 hedonistic
self-interest 6 egoism
selfish 6 stingy 8 egoistic 9 egotistic 10 egocentric, ungenerous 11 egomaniacal 12 self-centered 13 self-indulgent
selfless 8 generous 10 altruistic, benevolent, charitable
self-love 6 egoism, vanity 7 conceit, egotism 8 vainness 9 vainglory 10 narcissism 11 amour propre 13 conceitedness
self-possessed 4 calm 6 poised, serene 7 equable 8 composed, sanguine 9 collected, unruffled 11 unflappable 13 imperturbable
self-proclaimed 8 so-called 9 soi-disant 10 self-styled
Self-Reliance author 7 Emerson (Ralph Waldo)
self-respect 5 pride 7 dignity 11 amour propre
self-restraint 8 chastity, sobriety 9 willpower 10 abnegation, abstention, abstinence, continence, discipline 11 forbearance
self-righteous 5 pious 7 canting, preachy 8 unctuous 9 pharisaic 10 complacent,

goody-goody 11 pharisaical 12 hypocritical, pecksniffian 13 sanctimonious
self-sacrificing 8 generous, selfless 9 unselfish
self-satisfied 4 smug 8 priggish 10 complacent
self-seeking 6 greedy 7 selfish 8 egoistic 9 egotistic 10 egocentric 11 egotistical
self-serving see SELF-SEEKING
self-starter 7 hustler 8 go-getter
self-styled 7 nominal, would-be 8 so-called 9 soi-disant
self-taught 12 autodidactic
sell 4 hawk, vend 5 trade 6 barter, deal in, hustle, market, peddle, retail, unload 7 auction 8 exchange
sell out 4 dump, move 6 betray, turn in, unload 7 deceive 8 inform on 11 double-cross
selvage, selvedge 3 hem 4 edge 6 border
semblance 3 air 4 face, look, mask, pose, show, veil 5 front, guise, image 6 aspect, facade, simile, veneer 7 analogy, feeling, modicum 8 affinity, disguise, likeness, pretense 10 apparition, appearance, comparison, false front, masquerade, similarity, similitude, simulacrum 11 countenance
Semele *father:* 6 Cadmus *mother:* 8 Harmonia *sister:* 3 Ino 5 Agave 7 Autonoë *son:* 7 Bacchus 8 Dionysus
semi 3 rig 4 demi, half, hemi 5 truck 6 partly
seminar 5 forum 8 colloquy 10 colloquium, conference, roundtable
Seminole *chief* 7 Osceola
Semiramis *husband:* 5 Ninus *kingdom:* 7 Babylon
Semite 3 Jew 4 Arab 6 Hebrew 7 Moabite 8 Akkadian, Assyrian 9 Canaanite 10 Babylonian, Phoenician
Senapo *daughter:* 8 Clorinda *kingdom:* 8 Ethiopia
senate 7 chamber, council 8 assembly 11 legislature
senator 5 solon 8 lawmaker 10 legislator
send 4 mail, post, ship 5 relay, remit, route 6 commit, export, launch 7 address, advance, airmail, consign, forward, traject 8 dispatch, transmit *back:* 6 remand
Sendak *book* 17 In the Night Kitchen 21 Where the Wild Things Are
send in 6 submit
send-up 5 roast, spoof 6 parody, satire 7 lampoon, takeoff 9 burlesque 10 caricature, pasquinade
Senegal *capital:* 5 Dakar *enclave:* 6 Gambia *ethnic group:* 5 Wolof 6 Fulani 7 Malinke *language:* 6 French *monetary unit:* 5 franc *neighbor:* 4 Mali 6 Guinea

10 Mauritania 12 Guinea-Bissau *river:* 6 Gambia 7 Senegal
senescence 6 old age 8 caducity 11 elderliness, senectitude
senior 5 doyen, elder, older, prior 7 ancient, doyenne, oldster 8 higher-up, old-timer, superior 10 golden-ager
Sennacherib *domain:* 7 Assyria *father:* 6 Sargon *kingdom:* 7 Assyria *slayer, son:* 8 Sharezer 11 Adrammelech
sensation 4 bomb 6 marvel, tingle, wonder 7 feeling, miracle, prodigy, stunner 8 response 9 bombshell 10 impression, perception, phenomenon 13 consciousness
sensational 3 hot 5 boffo, juicy, lurid 6 purple, vulgar 7 tabloid 8 dramatic, exciting, fabulous, glorious, slambang, smashing, stunning 9 hunky-dory, marvelous, thrilling 10 astounding, impressive, incredible, remarkable, scandalous 11 astonishing, extravagant, outstanding, spectacular 12 electrifying
sense 3 wit 4 feel 5 sight, smell, taste, touch 6 divine, intuit, pick up 7 believe, discern, feeling, hearing, meaning, message, realize 8 consider, judgment, perceive, prudence 9 awareness, foresight, intuition 10 anticipate, cognizance, discretion, perception 12 intelligence, significance 13 comprehension, consciousness, understanding *sixth:* 3 ESP
Sense and Sensibility *author* 6 Austen (Jane)
senseless 4 cold, numb 5 silly 6 absurd, numbed, simple, stupid 7 fatuous, foolish, idiotic, moronic, trivial, witless 8 benumbed, comatose, deadened, mindless 9 brainless, pointless 10 irrational 11 meaningless, purposeless, unconscious
senselessness 5 folly 7 inanity 8 insanity 9 absurdity, stupidity 12 illogicality
sense organ 3 ear, eye 4 nose, skin 6 tongue 8 receptor
sensibility 5 taste 7 emotion, feeling, insight 8 judgment, keenness 9 affection, awareness, sensation 11 discernment, penetration 12 appreciation
sensible 4 sage, sane, wise 5 solid, sound 6 astute, shrewd 7 logical, prudent, sapient 8 rational 9 judicious, objective, sagacious 10 reasonable
sensitive 4 keen, sore 5 aware, prone 6 liable, tender, touchy, tricky 7 feeling, nervous 8 delicate, sensible, sentient, ticklish 9 emotional 10 high-strung, perceptive, precarious, responsive 11 susceptible 13 understanding
sensitive plant 6 mimosa *family:* 3 pea

sensual **4** lush **6** animal, carnal, earthy **7** fleshly, mundane, worldly **8** temporal **9** epicurean, luxurious, sybaritic **10** hedonistic, voluptuous **11** irreligious, unspiritual

sensuality **4** lust **6** desire, luxury **7** lechery, license **8** hedonism, lewdness, pleasure **9** carnality, depravity, eroticism, prurience **10** debauchery, degeneracy, immorality, indulgence, perversion, profligacy, sybaritism **11** dissipation **12** incontinence **13** dissoluteness, gratification, salaciousness

sensuous **4** lush **6** carnal **7** fleshly **8** luscious **9** epicurean, luxurious, sybaritic **10** hedonistic, voluptuous **13** self-indulgent

sentence **3** rap **4** damn, doom **5** blame, judge **6** dictum, ordain, punish **7** adjudge, condemn, convict, verdict **8** decision, denounce, judgment, penalize **10** adjudicate, punishment

sententious **5** crisp, pithy, terse **7** concise, piquant, pointed **8** eloquent, pregnant, succinct **10** aphoristic, expressive, meaningful, moralistic, moralizing

sentient **5** alert, aware, savvy **7** knowing **8** sensible **9** attentive, cognizant, conscious, receptive, sensitive **10** conversant, discerning, perceptive, percipient, responsive **12** appreciative

sentiment **4** view **6** belief **7** emotion, feeling, leaning, opinion, passion, posture **8** penchant, position, tendency **9** affection, inclining, sensation **10** conception, conviction, partiality, persuasion, propensity **11** disposition, inclination, sensibility

sentimental **4** soft **5** corny, gooey, gushy, mushy, sappy, soupy, sweet **6** dreamy, drippy, slushy, sticky, sugary, syrupy, tender **7** cloying, gushing, insipid, maudlin, mawkish **8** bathetic, effusive, romantic **9** misty-eyed, nostalgic, schmaltzy **10** idealistic, lovey-dovey, moonstruck, namby-pamby, saccharine, soft-boiled **11** tear-jerking **12** affectionate

sentimentality **4** mush **8** schmaltz

sentinel see SENTRY

sentry **5** guard, watch **6** picket **7** lookout **8** sentinel, watchman

separate **4** comb, only, part, sift, sole, sort **5** apart, sever, split **6** cut off, detach, divide, single, sunder, unique, winnow **7** asunder, disjoin, diverse, divided, divorce, isolate, several, split up, unravel, various **8** alienate, detached, discrete, disjoint, disperse, distinct, insulate, isolated, solitary, splinter, uncouple **9** different, diver-

gent, extricate, segregate, sequester **11** compartment, distinctive, distinguish, independent, unconnected **12** disconnected, discriminate **13** differentiate

separation **3** gap **4** rift **5** break, split **6** schism **7** breakup, divorce, parting, rupture, split-up **8** disunion, disunity, division **9** apartheid, dichotomy, partition **11** disjunction, dissolution, segregation **12** dissociation, estrangement **13** disconnection, sequestration

separatism **9** apartheid **11** segregation

separatist **10** schismatic **12** secessionist

sepia **3** ink **5** brown, umber **6** sienna

sepulchral **4** grim **5** bleak, grave **6** dismal, gloomy, solemn, somber **7** doleful, macabre **8** funereal, ghoulish, mortuary **9** tenebrous

sepulchre **4** tomb **5** grave, vault **9** mausoleum

sequel **3** end **5** close **6** effect, ending, finish, result, upshot **7** closing, outcome **8** epilogue **9** aftermath **10** succession **11** aftereffect, consequence, development, eventuality, progression, termination **12** continuation

sequence **3** row, run, set **4** flow **5** chain, order, train **6** course, series, string **8** disposal, ordering **9** placement **10** procession, succession **11** arrangement, disposition, progression **12** distribution

sequential **6** serial **9** succedent **10** continuous, succeeding, successive **11** consecutive **12** successional **13** chronological

sequester **4** hide, take **5** annex, seize **6** attach, cut off, enisle **7** impound, isolate, preempt, seclude, secrete **8** accroach, arrogate, cloister, close off, insulate, separate, set apart, withdraw **9** segregate **10** commandeer, confiscate, dispossess **11** appropriate, expropriate

sequoia **7** big tree, redwood **12** coast redwood

seraglio **5** harem

serape **5** shawl

seraph **5** angel **8** guardian **9** messenger

seraphic **4** pure **7** angelic, sublime **8** beatific, cherubic, ethereal

Serbia and Montenegro *capital:* **8** Belgrade *city:* **3** Bar **5** Kotar, Tivat **7** Novi Sad, Pancevo **9** Podgorica **11** Pristinauzi *monetary unit:* **4** euro **5** dinar *neighbor:* **6** Bosnia, Kosovo **7** Albania, Croatia, Hungary, Romania **8** Bulgaria **9** Macedonia *part of:* **7** Balkans *peninsula:* **6** Balkan *province:* **9** Vojvodina *province, former:* **6** Kosovo *river:* **4** Sava **6** Danube *sea:* **8** Adriatic

sere 3 dry 5 dried 7 parched, thirsty
8 withered 9 shriveled, unwatered
serenade 7 lullaby 8 shivaree 9 charivari
serene 4 calm 5 quiet, still 6 limpid,
placid, poised, sedate 7 halcyon 8 composed, tranquil 9 unruffled 10 untroubled
serenity 4 calm 5 peace 8 calmness, quietude 9 composure, placidity, stillness
10 equanimity 11 contentment, tranquility 12 peacefulness, tranquillity
serf 4 esne, peon 5 churl, helot, slave
6 thrall 7 bondman, villein *freeborn:*
7 colonus
serial 10 sequential, successive 11 consecutive, installment
series 3 row, run, set 4 list, tier 5 chain,
range, scale, train 6 catena, column,
parade, sequel, string 8 sequence 9 cavalcade, gradation 10 procession, succession 11 progression 12 continuation
serious 4 grim, hard 5 grave, heavy,
major, sober, staid, stern, tough
6 intent, sedate, severe, solemn,
somber, sombre, steady 7 austere,
earnest, intense, pensive, sincere,
unfunny, weighty 8 funeral, menacing,
resolute, sobering 9 difficult, humorless, important, laborious, strenuous,
unamusing 10 determined, formidable,
meditative, no-nonsense, poker-faced,
purposeful, reflective, sobersided,
thoughtful, unhumorous 11 significant,
threatening 12 businesslike 13 contemplative
sermon 6 homily, speech, tirade
7 address, lecture, oration 8 harangue
9 preaching 10 preachment 11 exhortation
sermonize 5 orate 6 dilate, exhort,
preach 7 dissert, lecture 8 moralize
9 discourse, expatiate, preachify 10 dissertate, evangelize 11 pontificate
serpent 5 fiend, Satan, snake *fabled:*
8 basilisk *mythical:* 10 cockatrice *sound:*
4 hiss
serpentine 4 rock, wily 5 snaky 7 cunning, devious, mineral, sinuous, winding 8 flexuous, tempting, tortuous
9 snakelike 10 circuitous, convoluted,
meandering
serrated 7 notched, toothed 8 sawedged, sawtooth 10 saw-toothed 11 denticulate
servant 4 maid, peon 5 slave, valet
6 butler, flunky, helper, lackey, menial
7 famulus, footman 8 domestic, handmaid, hireling, houseboy 9 attendant
11 chamberlain, chambermaid *India:*
4 syce *kitchen:* 8 scullion *Wodehouse:*
6 Jeeves

serve 3 act, fit, use 4 help, make, play,
suit, work 5 nurse, spend, treat 6 foster,
handle, wait on 7 advance, benefit,
care for, present, promote, provide,
satisfy, suffice, work for 8 deal with,
function 9 encourage, officiate 10 minister to
service 3 use 4 duty, help, rite 5 favor
6 employ, repair, ritual 7 account, benefit, fitness, liturgy 8 ceremony, courtesy, disposal, maintain 10 active duty,
assistance, ceremonial, observance,
usefulness 11 maintenance 12 dispensation
serviceable 5 handy, utile 6 decent,
usable, useful 7 durable, helpful 8 adequate, suitable 9 efficient, practical
10 acceptable, beneficial, convenient,
dependable, functional 11 utilitarian
12 satisfactory
servile 6 abject, craven, humble, menial
7 fawning, slavish 8 obedient, obeisant
9 groveling 10 obsequious, submissive
11 subservient
servility 7 bondage, helotry, peonage,
serfdom, slavery 9 thralldom
11 enslavement
serving 6 dollop 7 helping, portion
servitude 5 labor 6 corvée, thrall
7 bondage, helotry, peonage, serfdom,
slavery 9 captivity, indenture, thralldom, villenage 10 subjection
11 enslavement 12 enthrallment
sesame 3 til *grass:* 4 gama
sessile 5 fixed 6 rooted 7 settled
8 attached 11 established
session 6 assize, séance 7 meeting, sitting
set 3 aim, dry, fix, gel, lay, lot, put
4 firm, jell 5 array, batch, bunch, fixed,
group, place, put on, ready, rigid, scene
6 belong, harden, impose, placed, rooted, secure, stated 7 arrange, certain,
cluster, congeal, decided, deposit, dictate, jellify, lay down, located, prepare,
scenery, situate, specify, station 8 prepared, resolute, resolved, situated,
solidify, specific 9 confirmed, designate, establish, prescribe, specified,
stipulate, tenacious 10 assortment,
determined, gelatinize, inflexible, positioned, prescribed, stipulated 11 established, mise-en-scène *a gem:* 6 collet
right: 7 redress
set aside 4 void 5 annul 7 discard, dismiss, reserve 8 overrule
set back 4 mire 5 delay 6 detain, hang
up, hinder, retard, slow up
setback 5 check, hitch 6 defeat, rebuff
7 reverse 8 obstacle, reversal 9 hindrance 10 impediment, regression

set down 4 land **5** light, perch, roost **6** alight, record **9** establish, touch down
set fire to 4 burn **6** ignite **7** emblaze, inflame **8** enkindle, touch off
set forth 4 cite **5** state **6** adduce, affirm, allege, avouch, depart, embark, launch, submit **7** advance, declare, express, present, proffer, propose, take off **8** proclaim, spell out **9** introduce **10** account for
set free 5 loose **6** redeem, rescue, unbind **7** deliver, manumit, unchain, unloose **8** liberate, unloosen **9** unshackle **10** emancipate
Seth *brother:* **4** Abel, Cain *father:* **4** Adam *mother:* **3** Eve *son:* **4** Enos
set out 5 start **6** embark, intend **7** take off **9** undertake
Set's victim 6 Osiris
settee 4 seat, sofa **5** bench, divan **6** lounge
setting 5 scene **7** context, scenery **8** ambience **10** background **11** mise-en-scène *for a stone:* **4** ouch
settle 3 fix, lay, pay, put **4** calm **5** allay, judge, light, pay up, perch, place, quiet, roost, still **6** alight, clinch, decide, soothe, square, verify, wind up **7** arrange, compose, confirm, dispose, install, mediate, resolve, satisfy, work out **8** colonize, conclude, ensconce, nail down **9** determine, discharge, establish, negotiate, reconcile, touch down
settlement 4 deal **6** colony, hamlet **7** outpost, quietus, village **8** decision **9** agreement **10** conclusion, encampment, habitation, resolution **11** arrangement **13** determination *Israeli:* **6** moshav
settler 7 pioneer **8** colonist, squatter **9** colonizer
set-to 3 row **4** fray, spat **5** brawl, broil, brush, fight, run-in, scrap **6** affray, blowup, fracas, tussle **7** dispute, quarrel, rhubarb, scuffle **8** argument, skirmish **9** encounter **10** falling-out **11** altercation
set up 4 open **5** erect, found, raise, start **6** create, launch **7** arrange, install **8** assemble, generate, initiate, organize **9** construct, establish, institute, originate
setup 4 plan **5** array, trick **6** layout, scheme, shoo-in **7** pattern, project, setting **8** assembly, carriage, position, slam dunk **9** alignment, apparatus, structure, sure thing **11** arrangement, preparation **12** constitution
seven *combining form:* **4** hept, sept **5** hepta, septi *group of:* **6** heptad **8** hebdomad

seventeenth century 8 seicento
sever 3 cut, lop **4** part, rend **5** slice, split **6** cleave, cut off, detach, divide, sunder **7** break up, divorce **8** amputate, disjoint, separate
several 4 a few, many, some **6** divers, plural, sundry, varied **7** certain, diverse, various **8** assorted, discrete, distinct, manifold, numerous, separate, specific **9** different **10** respective
severe 4 dour, grim, hard **5** acute, grave, harsh, heavy, rigid, sober, stern, tough **6** bitter, brutal, rugged, strict **7** arduous, ascetic, austere, extreme, intense, onerous, serious, weighty **8** exacting, pitiless, rigorous **9** demanding, difficult, laborious, strenuous, stringent, unbending **10** forbidding, implacable, inflexible, iron-willed, oppressive, unyielding **11** disciplined, heavyhanded
severity 5 rigor **7** gravity, urgency **8** exigency, grimness, obduracy, rigidity **9** austerity, harshness, intensity, plainness, privation, restraint, spareness, starkness, sternness **10** strictness, stringency **11** seriousness
sew 4 darn, mend, seam **5** baste **6** needle, stitch, suture
sewer 4 duct **5** ditch, drain **6** tailor **7** cesspit, conduit **8** cesspool, stitcher
sewing *aid:* **7** thimble *case:* **4** etui *kit:* **9** housewife
sewing-machine inventor 4 Howe (Elias)
sexless 6 neuter **7** epicene **8** neutered
sex manual 9 Kama-sutra
sexton 6 deacon **9** custodian, sacristan
sexual 4 blue, lewd, racy **6** carnal, erotic, ribald, risqué, smutty **7** obscene **8** venereal **9** salacious **12** pornographic
sexual desire 4 eros, lust **6** libido
sexy 4 blue, racy **5** bawdy, spicy **6** erotic, purple, ribald, risqué, steamy, sultry **7** naughty **8** alluring, off-color, sensuous **9** appealing, salacious, seductive **10** attractive, suggestive
Seychelles *capital:* **8** Victoria *island:* **4** Mahé **7** La Digue, Praslin *language:* **6** Creole, French *monetary unit:* **5** rupee
Sganarelle *brother:* **6** Ariste *daughter:* **7** Lucinde *ward:* **7** Leonore **8** Isabelle *wife:* **7** Martine
shabby 5 dingy, dowdy, faded, mangy, ratty, seedy, sorry, tacky, tired **6** frayed, scurvy, shoddy, sleazy, sordid **7** outworn, rickety, run-down, scrubby, scruffy, squalid, worn-out **8** beggarly, decaying, decrepit, dog-eared, tattered **9** miserable, moth-eaten, neglected, worm-eaten **10** bedraggled, down-at-heel, ramshackle, threadbare **11** dilapi-

dated **12** deteriorated, disreputable
13 deteriorating, unrespectable

shack 3 cot, hut **4** camp, shed **5** cabin, hovel, lodge **6** shanty **7** cottage

shackle 4 gyve **5** bilbo, chain, leash, strap **6** fetter, hobble, hog-tie, impede, pinion, secure **7** enchain, leg-iron, manacle, trammel **8** handcuff **9** entrammel

shad 7 clupeid, herring

shade 3 hue **4** cast, tint, tone, veil **5** ghost, tinge, trace, umbra **6** awning, darken, nuance, screen **7** dimness, eclipse, phantom, shelter, specter, spectre, umbrage **8** darkness, penumbra, phantasm, tincture **9** gradation, intensity, obscurity **10** apparition **11** distinction

shadow 3 dim, dog, tag **4** haze, hint, tail **5** cloud, shade, tinge, touch, trace, trail, umbra **6** screen, spirit, wraith **7** eidolon, obscure, phantom, specter, umbrage, vestige **8** overcast, penumbra, phantasm, revenant, tincture **9** inumbrate, overcloud, suspicion **10** apparition, intimation, suggestion **11** adumbration

shadowy 3 dim **4** dark **5** dusky, faint, murky, vague **6** gloomy, shaded **7** ghostly, obscure **9** tenebrous **10** indistinct

shady 4 dark **5** bosky, dusky, fishy **6** purple, shabby, shoddy **7** clouded, dubious, suspect **8** doubtful, screened **9** equivocal, sheltered, uncertain **10** suggestive, suspicious, umbrageous, unreliable **12** disreputable

Shaffer play 5 Equus **7** Amadeus

shaft 3 jab, ray, rod **4** axle, barb, beam, dart, pole, stem **5** arrow, lance, shoot, spear, stalk, thill **6** thrust **7** chimney, spindle **8** short end

shag 3 nap, rug **4** pile **5** chase, fetch **7** thicket, tobacco **9** cormorant

shaggy 5 bushy **7** unkempt **8** uncombed

shake 3 jar, jog, rid **4** deal, jerk, jolt, lose, rock, roil, sway **5** avoid, churn, daunt, elude, jiffy, quail, quake, shock, upset, waver, worry **6** escape, frappe, jiggle, joggle, outwit, quaver, quiver, rattle, ruffle, shimmy, shiver, stir up, tremor **7** agitate, chatter, disturb, perturb, shingle, shudder, temblor, tremble, unnerve, vibrate **8** brandish, convulse, throw off, unsettle **9** oscillate, palpitate **10** earthquake

shake down 5 frisk, gouge, screw, wrest, wring **6** coerce, extort, fleece, search **7** squeeze **9** blackmail

shakedown 3 bed **4** test **5** dance, trial **6** pallet, search, tryout **7** pursuit, testing **8** exaction **9** blackmail, extortion **10** inspection

Shakers leader 3 Lee (Ann) **9** Mother Ann

Shakespearean actor 4 Kean (Edmund) **5** Booth (Edwin), Dench (Judi), Evans (Maurice), Terry (Ellen) **6** Irving (Henry) **7** Branagh (Kenneth), Burbage (Richard), Garrick (David), Gielgud (John), Olivier (Laurence), Siddons (Sarah) **8** Ashcroft (Peggy), Macready (William), Redgrave (Michael), Scofield (Paul) **9** Barrymore (Ethel, John, Lionel, Maurice) **10** Richardson (Ralph)

Shakespeare, William *mother:* **9** Mary Arden *play:* **6** Hamlet, Henry V **7** Henry IV, Henry VI, Macbeth, Othello, Tempest (The) **8** King John, King Lear, Pericles **9** Cymbeline, Henry VIII, Richard II **10** Coriolanus, Richard III **11** As You Like It, Winter's Tale (The) **12** Julius Caesar, Twelfth Night **13** Timon of Athens **14** Comedy of Errors (The), Romeo and Juliet **16** Love's Labour's Lost, Merchant of Venice (The), Taming of the Shrew (The) **17** Measure for Measure **18** Antony and Cleopatra **19** Much Ado About Nothing **20** All's Well That Ends Well, Midsummer Night's Dream (A) *theater:* **5** Globe *wife:* **12** Anne Hathaway

shaky 4 weak **6** infirm, unsure, wobbly **7** aquiver, dubious, jittery, quaking, rackety, rickety, suspect, trembly, unsound **8** doubtful, insecure, rachitic, unstable, unsteady, wavering **9** quivering, tottering, trembling, tremulous, uncertain, unsettled **10** indecisive, precarious, rattletrap, unreliable **11** problematic, vacillating

shale 4 rock **5** slate

shallot 4 herb **5** onion **10** green onion

shallow 4 idle, vain **5** petty, shoal **7** cursory, sketchy, trivial **8** trifling **9** depthless, frivolous **11** perfunctory, superficial

shallows 6 lagoon, shoals

Shallum *father:* **5** Shaul, Zadok **6** Jabesh, Josiah, Sismai, Tikvah **8** Colhozeh, Naphtali **9** Hallohesh *mother:* **6** Bilhah *nephew:* **8** Jeremiah *slayer:* **7** Menahem *son:* **6** Mibsam **7** Hilkiah **8** Maaseiah *victim:* **9** Zechariah

shalom 5 peace

sham 3 act, ape **4** fake, hoax, mock **5** bluff, bogus, bunco, cheat, dummy, false, farce, feign, fraud, phony, put on, spoof **6** deceit, ersatz, facade, fakery, forged, invent, pseudo **7** assumed, feigned, forgery, imitate, mislead, mockery, pretend **8** affected, flimflam, simulate, spurious, travesty **9** brummagem, burlesque, deception, hypocrisy, imitation, imposture, pinchbeck, simulated **10** artificial, caricature, false front, fictitious, fraudulent, sanctimony, substitute **11** counterfeit, make-believe **12** pecksniffery *combining form:* **5** pseud **6** pseudo

shaman 6 healer, priest, wizard **7** diviner **8** conjurer, conjuror, magician, sorcerer **9** enchanter, priestess **10** high priest, soothsayer **11** faith healer, necromancer, thaumaturge, witch doctor

Shamash 6 sun-god *father:* **3** Sin *sister:* **6** Ishtar *wife:* **3** Aya

shamble see SHUFFLE

shambles 4 mess **5** chaos **6** jumble, muddle **8** disarray, disorder, wreckage **9** confusion

shame 4 pity **5** abash, guilt, odium **6** infamy, stigma **7** chagrin, mortify, obloquy, remorse, scandal **8** disgrace, dishonor, ignominy **9** disrepute, embarrass, humiliate, ill repute **10** opprobrium **11** humiliation **12** self-reproach **13** embarrassment, mortification

shamefaced 7 abashed **8** blushing, sheepish **9** mortified **10** humiliated **11** crestfallen, embarrassed

shameless 6 arrant, brazen, wanton **7** blatant, immoral **8** depraved, flagrant, immodest, impudent **9** abandoned, bald-faced, barefaced, dissolute, unabashed **10** outrageous, profligate, unblushing **11** brazen-faced, disgraceful **12** presumptuous

Shammah *brother:* **5** David *father:* **4** Agee **5** Jesse, Reuel *grandfather:* **4** Esau **7** Ishmael *son:* **7** Jonadab **8** Jonathan

Shammua *father:* **5** David, Galal **6** Bilgah, Zaccur *mother:* **9** Bathsheba *son:* **4** Abda

shamus 3 cop **4** dick, tail **6** copper, shadow, sleuth **7** gumshoe **8** flatfoot, sherlock **9** constable, detective, operative, policeman **10** private eye **12** investigator **13** police officer

shanghai 6 abduct, hijack, kidnap

Shangri-la 5 Tibet **6** utopia **7** arcadia **8** paradise **9** Cockaigne, fairyland **10** wonderland

shank 3 leg **4** shin, stem **5** stalk, tibia

shanty 3 cot, hut **4** camp, shed **5** cabin, hovel, lodge, shack **7** cottage

shape 3 fit **4** case, cast, form, mold, plan, trim **5** forge, frame, state, whack **6** aspect, devise, fettle, figure, kilter, repair, sculpt, tailor, work up **7** contour, fitness, outline, pattern, profile **8** assemble **9** condition, construct, fab-

ricate, semblance **10** appearance, silhouette **12** conformation **13** configuration *combining form:* **5** morph **6** morpho

shapeable 6 pliant, supple **7** ductile, plastic, pliable **8** flexible **9** tractable

shapeless 8 inchoate, unformed **9** amorphous

shapely 4 trim **5** buxom **9** Junoesque **10** curvaceous, statuesque, well-turned **11** clean-limbed

shard 4 chip **5** chunk, scale, scrap, shell **6** sliver **7** elytron **8** carapace, fragment

share 3 cut, lot **4** part **5** chunk, claim, quota, slice, stake **6** divide, parcel, ration **7** dole out, give out, helping, partake, portion, prorate, quantum **8** dispense, fraction, interest, quotient **9** allotment, allowance, apportion **10** experience, percentage, proportion **11** participate

shared 5 joint **6** common, mutual, public **8** communal, conjoint, conjunct **9** concerted **10** collective **11** cooperative

Sharezer *father, victim:* **11** Sennacherib

shark 5 cheat **8** swindler *kind:* **4** mako, sand, tope **5** nurse, tiger **7** basking, dogfish, leopard **8** mackerel, man-eater, thresher **9** porbeagle **10** great white, hammerhead *skin:* **8** shagreen

sharp 3 sly **4** acid, keen, tony, trig **5** acrid, acute, alert, canny, crisp, honed, quick, slick, smart, swank **6** biting, bitter, brainy, bright, clever, jagged, nimble, peaked, shrewd, shrill, snappy **7** caustic, dashing, intense, pointed, prickly, stylish, whetted **8** clean-cut, clear-cut, incisive, piercing, shooting, stabbing, stinging **9** agonizing, brilliant, ingenious, knifelike, vitriolic **10** astringent, perceptive **11** intelligent, penetrating, quickwitted, resourceful **12** excruciating, nimble-witted

sharpen 4 edge, file, hone, whet **5** grind, strop

sharper 6 con man **7** diddler **8** chiseler, swindler **9** defrauder, trickster **10** mountebank **12** double-dealer

sharp-eyed 4 keen **5** alert **8** vigilant, watchful **9** attentive, observant **10** discerning, perceptive

sharpie see SHARPER

sharpness 4 edge **6** acumen **9** precision

sharpshooter 8 marksman

sharp-sighted 8 hawk-eyed, lynx-eyed **9** eagle-eyed

sharp-witted 4 keen **5** acute, canny, quick, smart **6** astute, clever, shrewd **11** intelligent

shatter 4 dash **5** break, burst, crush, smash **6** shiver **8** demolish, fragment,

splinter 9 pulverize 10 annihilate
11 fragmentize 12 disintegrate
shatterable 7 brittle, fragile 9 breakable,
frangible
shave 3 cut 4 clip, crop, pare, peel,
skim, trim 5 lower, prune, shear, skive
6 barber, cut off, deduct, reduce,
scrape, sliver 7 cut back, whittle
8 mark down
shaveling 3 boy, kid, lad, tad 6 laddie,
squirt 9 stripling, youngster
shaver 3 boy, kid, lad, tad 5 child, razor
6 barber, laddie, squirt 9 stripling,
youngster
shawl 4 wrap 5 fichu, manta 6 chador,
serape 7 tallith 8 mantilla
shawm's descendant 4 oboe
Shawnee chief 8 Tecumseh, Tecumtha
9 Cornstalk
Shaw play 6 Geneva 7 Candida 9 Pygmalion, Saint Joan 11 Misalliance
12 Major Barbara 13 Arms and
the Man
shay 6 chaise 8 carriage
shear 3 cut, mow 4 clip, crop, pare,
snip, trim 5 prune, shave, skive 6 barber
shears 8 scissors
shearwater 4 bird 6 petrel 7 skimmer
sheath 4 case, skin 5 cover 7 holster
8 scabbard
sheathe 4 case, clad, face, side, skin,
wrap 5 cover, panel 6 encase, jacket
Sheba *father:* 6 Bichri *queen:* 6 Balkis
shebang 4 mess 6 affair 7 schmear
8 business, caboodle 9 ball of wax,
enchilada
shed 3 hut 4 cast, doff, drop, emit, molt
5 exude, hovel, hutch, scrap, shack,
stall 6 divest, lean-to, reject, slough
7 cast off, diffuse, discard, radiate, take
off 8 jettison, throw out 9 throw away
sheen 5 glaze, gleam, glint, gloss, shine
6 finish, luster, lustre, polish 7 burnish,
glitter, shimmer 8 radiance 9 shininess
10 brightness
sheeny see SHINY
sheep 5 ovine *breed:* 5 Tunis 6 Dorper,
Dorset, Merino, Navajo, No-Tail,
Oxford, Panama, Romney 7 Cheviot,
Colbred, Karakul, Lincoln, Ryeland,
Suffolk 8 Columbia, Cotswold, Pol-
warth 9 Hampshire, Leicester, Mon-
tadale, Southdown 10 Corriedale,
Debouillet 11 Rambouillet *coat:* 4 wool
6 fleece *disease:* 3 gid *female:* 3 ewe
male: 3 ram 6 wether *meat:* 6 mutton
relating to: 5 ovine *Scottish:* 9 blackface
sound: 5 bleat *tender:* 8 shepherd *wild:*
5 urial 6 aoudad, argali, bharal
7 bighorn, mouflon *young:* 4 lamb

sheepish 4 meek 5 timid 7 abashed,
ashamed, bashful 8 timorous 9 diffident
10 shamefaced 11 embarrassed
sheepskin 4 roan 6 mouton 7 diploma
9 parchment *prepare:* 3 taw
sheer 4 pure, skew, thin, turn, veer
5 filmy, gauzy, steep, utter 6 abrupt,
arrant, flimsy, simple, swerve 7 chiffon,
deflect, deviate, perfect, unmixed
8 absolute, complete, gossamer, outright 9 out-and-out, unalloyed, undiluted 10 diaphanous, see-through
11 precipitate, precipitous, transparent,
unmitigated
sheet 3 ply 4 film, leaf, page, sail, slab
5 cover, linen, paper 6 lamina, veneer
8 membrane 9 newspaper
sheet ___ 3 ice 4 film 5 glass, metal,
music 6 anchor
shelf 3 hob 4 bank, edge, reef, sill
5 ledge, shoal 6 mantel 7 counter
8 sandbank
shell 3 pod 4 boat, bomb, case, hull,
husk, rake, skin 5 blitz, conch, shuck
6 pepper 7 bombard, capsule, grenade,
mollusc, mollusk 8 carapace 9 cannonade, cartridge *defective:* 3 dud *explosive:* 4 bomb *layer:* 5 nacre *ornamental:*
6 cowrie *study:* 10 conchology
shellac 4 beat, drub, flay, lick, rout,
trim, whap, whip, whop, whup 5 resin,
smear, whomp 6 defeat, thrash 7 clobber, smother, trounce 8 lambaste, vanquish
Shelley, Percy Bysshe *poem:* 5 Cloud
(The) 7 Adonais, Alastor 8 Queen Mab
10 Ozymandias, To a Skylark 16 Ode to
the West Wind
shellfish 4 clam, crab 5 conch, cowry,
prawn, snail, whelk 6 cockle, limpet,
mussel, oyster, quahog, triton
7 abalone, crawdad, geoduck, lobster,
mollusc, mollusk, scallop 8 barnacle,
crayfish, escargot 10 crustacean, periwinkle
shell out 3 pay 4 give 5 spend 8 fork
over, hand over
shell-shaped 6 spiral 9 cochleate
shelter 3 den, hut, lee 4 cote, fold, hide,
port, roof, shed, tent 5 arbor, bower,
cloak, cover, haven, house, shack,
tower 6 asylum, burrow, covert,
defend, harbor, refuge, shield 7 chamber, defense, foxhole, hideout, hospice,
housing, lodging, pergola, pillbox, protect, retreat 8 hideaway, hidy-hole,
security 9 dwellings, hermitage, hidey-
hole, sanctuary 10 retirement *for aircraft:* 6 hangar *for cows:* 4 barn, byre
toward: 4 alee
shelve 4 dish, drop, stay, tilt 5 defer,

delay, slope, stock, waive 6 freeze, give up, hold up, put off 7 hold off, suspend 8 hold over, mothball, postpone, prorogue, set aside

Shem *brother:* 3 Ham 7 Japheth *father:* 4 Noah

Shema's father 4 Joel 6 Hebron

Shemida's father 6 Gilead

shenanigan 4 dido, lark 5 antic, caper, prank, stunt, trick 6 frolic 8 escapade, mischief 10 tomfoolery 11 monkeyshine

Sheol see HADES

shepherd 4 lead, show, tend 5 guide, pilot, route, steer, watch 6 direct, escort, leader 7 conduct 8 guardian *dog:* 6 collie 12 border collie *stick:* 5 crook, staff

Sheridan *play* 6 Critic (The), Rivals (The) 7 Pizarro 16 School for Scandal (The)

sheriff 5 reeve 6 lawman 7 marshal, officer *aide:* 6 deputy

sherlock 4 dick, tail 5 snoop 6 shadow, shamus, sleuth 7 gumshoe 8 hawkshaw 9 detective 10 private eye 12 investigator

Sherlock Holmes *creator:* 5 Doyle (Arthur Conan) *sidekick:* 6 Watson (Dr.)

sherry 4 fino, wine 7 oloroso 10 manzanilla 11 amontillado

Sherwood *play* 10 Road to Rome (The) 13 Idiot's Delight 14 Waterloo Bridge 15 Petrified Forest (The)

shibboleth 3 saw, tag 5 axiom, maxim 6 byword, cliché, phrase, saying, slogan, truism 7 bromide 8 banality, chestnut, password, prosaism 9 catchword, platitude, watchword 11 catchphrase, commonplace

shield 4 fend, roof, ward 5 aegis, armor, cover, guard, haven, house 6 buffer, defend, harbor, screen, secure 7 buckler, bulwark, defense, protect, shelter 8 defilade 9 safeguard 10 escutcheon *band:* 4 fess *bullfighter's:* 9 burladero *light:* 5 targe *part:* 4 boss, umbo 7 bordure *Roman:* 7 testudo

shield-like 7 peltate

shift 3 yaw 4 bend, bout, move, stir, tack, time, tour, turn, vary, veer 5 alter, budge, get by, spell, stint, trick 6 change, make do, manage, remove, resort, swerve 7 deviate, replace, shuffle, stopgap 8 get along, relocate, resource, transfer 9 deviation, expedient, fluctuate 10 alteration, changeover, conversion, transition 11 fluctuation

shiftless 4 idle, lazy 5 inept 8 feckless, indolent, slothful 11 inefficient

shifty 3 sly 4 foxy, wily 5 cagey, lying, shady, slick 6 crafty, sneaky, tricky 7 cunning, devious, elusive, evasive, furtive 8 guileful, slippery, sneaking 9 conniving, deceitful, deceptive, dishonest, insidious, underhand 10 inconstant, untruthful 11 duplicitous, underhanded 12 equivocating

shill 5 blind, decoy, pitch 6 capper 8 promoter 10 accomplice, sales pitch

shillelagh 3 bat 4 club, cosh, mace 5 baton, billy, stick 6 cudgel 8 bludgeon 9 bastinado, billy club, blackjack, truncheon 10 nightstick

shilling 3 bob

shilly-shally 5 fudge, hedge, stall, waver 6 dawdle, dither, waffle 7 whiffle 8 hesitate 9 temporize, vacillate 11 prevaricate 12 tergiversate

Shimea *brother:* 5 David *father:* 5 David, Jesse *son:* 7 Jonadab 8 Jonathan

shimmer 5 flash, gleam, glint, sheen 6 luster, lustre 7 glimmer, glisten, glitter, spangle, sparkle, twinkle 9 coruscate 11 coruscation, scintillate 13 scintillation

shimmy 5 dance, shake 6 quiver, shiver, tremor 7 chemise, shudder, tremble, vibrate 9 vibration

shin 3 run 4 dash 5 scoot, tibia 6 scurry, sprint 7 scamper

shindig 4 ball, bash, fête, gala 5 binge, dance, party, revel 6 affair, frolic 7 blowout 8 wingding

shine 3 ray, rub 4 beam, buff, burn, glow 5 blaze, flare, flash, glare, glaze, gleam, glint, gloss, sheen 6 luster, lustre, polish 7 burnish, glimmer, glisten, glitter, radiate, shimmer, sparkle, twinkle 10 luminesce 10 incandesce

shiner 4 fish 8 black eye, cyprinid

shingle 5 beach, coast, shore 7 haircut, overlap, overlay 8 detritus 9 signboard

shiny 6 bright, glossy 7 fulgent, radiant 8 dazzling, gleaming, lustrous, polished 9 burnished, effulgent 10 glistening

ship 4 boat, send 5 remit, route 6 export 7 consign, forward, freight 8 dispatch, transfer, transmit *ancient:* 6 galley 7 galleon, trireme *attendant:* 7 steward *beam:* 7 keelson *berth:* 4 dock, slip *boat:* 6 dinghy *body:* 4 hull *cabin:* 9 stateroom *commercial:* 5 liner, oiler 6 argosy, tanker, trader 9 freighter *crew member:* 4 hand, mate 6 sailor *deck:* 4 boat, main, poop 5 orlop 6 bridge 10 forecastle *fishing:* 6 lugger 7 trawler *fleet:* 6 armada *floor:* 4 deck *front:* 3 bow 4 prow, stem 8 cutwater *hoister:* 4 boom 5 davit 7 capstan *kitchen:* 6 galley *left side:* 4 port 8 larboard *military:* 6 cutter,

PT boat 7 carrier, cruiser 9 destroyer, submarine *officer:* 4 mate 5 bosun 6 purser 7 captain, steward 9 boatswain *part:* 3 bow 4 beam, deck, helm, hold, hull, keel, mast, stem 5 bilge, hatch, stern 6 bridge, rudder 7 scupper *partition:* 7 bulwark 8 bulkhead *personnel:* 4 crew *platform:* 9 crow's nest, gangboard, gangplank *post:* 4 mast 7 bollard *prison:* 4 brig *projection:* 7 sponson *rear:* 5 stern *record:* 3 log *right side:* 9 starboard *room:* 4 brig 5 cabin 6 galley *rope:* 4 line 5 sheet 7 halyard *sailing:* 3 hoy 4 brig, dhow, prau, proa, yawl 5 ketch, sloop, xebec, yacht 6 lugger 7 caravel, galleon 8 schooner *steerer:* 4 helm 6 tiller *storage area:* 4 hold *to the rear of:* 3 aft 5 abaft 6 astern *valve:* 7 seacock *window:* 4 port 8 porthole
shipment 5 cargo 6 lading 7 freight, payload 8 delivery 11 consignment
Ship of Fools author 6 Porter (Katherine Anne)
Shipping News author 6 Proulx (Annie)
ships, group of 4 navy 5 fleet, flota 6 armada 8 flotilla
shipshape 4 neat, snug, tidy, trig, trim 7 orderly 11 spic-and-span, uncluttered 12 spick-and-span
shipworm 6 teredo
shire 5 horse 6 county 8 district 10 draft horse
shirk 4 duck, lurk, shun 5 avoid, creep, dodge, elude, evade, skulk, slink, sneak, steal 8 sidestep
shirker see SLACKER
shirt 4 polo, sark 5 dress, kurta, sport 6 blouse, jersey 9 guayabera
shirty 3 mad 5 angry, cross, irate 6 heated, ireful 7 annoyed 8 choleric, incensed, offended 9 indignant, irritated
shiv 5 blade, knife, shank 6 dagger 8 stiletto
Shiva *consort:* 3 Uma 4 Devi, Kali 5 Durga, Gauri 6 Ambika, Chandi 7 Parvati 9 Haimavati *son:* 6 Ganesa, Skanda 7 Ganesha 10 Karttikeya
shiver 5 burst, quake, shake, smash 6 quaver, quiver, tremor 7 shatter, shudder, tremble, twitter 8 fragment, splinter, splitter
shoal 3 bar 4 bank, hook, reef, spit 6 school 7 barrier, sandbar, shallow, tombolo 8 sandbank, sand reef
shoat 3 hog, pig 5 swine 6 piglet, porker
Shobab *father:* 5 Caleb, David *mother:* 6 Azubah 9 Bathsheba
shock 3 jar 4 blow, bump, daze, jolt, pile, rick, stun 5 amaze, clash, crash, mound, quake, shake, sheaf 6 appall,

dismay, impact, insult, offend, trauma, tremor 7 astound, disgust, horrify, outrage, stagger, startle, stupefy, temblor 8 astonish, surprise 9 collision, electrify 10 concussion, earthquake, percussion, scandalize, traumatize 11 flabbergast 12 stupefaction
shock absorber 6 spring 7 dashpot, snubber
shocker 4 blow 7 stunner 8 surprise, thriller 9 bombshell, eye-opener, sensation 11 showstopper
shocking 5 awful, lurid 6 horrid 7 glaring, heinous 8 dreadful, horrible, horrific, shameful, terrible 9 appalling, atrocious, frightful, monstrous, revolting 10 outrageous, scandalous 11 disgraceful, distressing, unspeakable
shoddy 4 base, mean, poor 5 cheap, dingy, gaudy, junky, seedy, tacky, tatty 6 cheesy, common, paltry, shabby, sleazy, tawdry, trashy 7 run-down, scruffy 8 inferior, rubbishy, shameful 9 makeshift 10 broken-down, down-at-heel 11 dilapidated, disgraceful, ignominious, pretentious 12 dishonorable, disreputable 13 discreditable
shoe 4 boot, clog, geta, mule, pump 5 sabot, wedge 6 brogan, brogue, buskin, gaiter, galosh, gillie, loafer, oxford, patten, sandal 7 chopine, ghillie, slipper, sneaker 8 balmoral, moccasin, platform, plimsoll 10 clodhopper, espadrille *armored:* 8 solleret *athlete's:* 7 sneaker *form:* 4 last, tree *kind:* 8 elevator, open-toed 10 high-heeled *part:* 3 tip, toe 4 arch, heel, lace, lift, sole, vamp 5 shank, upper 6 box toe, collar, foxing, insole, lining, throat, tongue 7 counter, outsole 8 backstay *protective:* 6 galosh, rubber *shiner:* 6 polish 9 bootblack *wooden:* 5 sabot 7 chopine
shoelace tip 5 aglet
shoeless 6 unshod 8 barefoot 9 discalced
shoemaker 7 cobbler *patron saint:* 7 Crispin *Scottish:* 6 souter
Shogun author 7 Clavell (James)
Sholem Aleichem character 5 Tevye
shoo 4 scat 5 drive, leave, scare, scram, split 6 beat it, begone, bug off, skidoo 7 buzz off, get lost, skiddoo, vamoose 8 clear out 9 skedaddle, take a hike 10 hit the road
shoo-in 6 winner 7 sure bet 8 slam dunk 9 sure thing
shoot 3 bud, fly, gun, ray 4 beam, bolt, dart, dash, fire, lash, race, rush, sail, scud, skim, spew, tear 5 blast, chase, fling, photo, shaft, skirr, snipe, spurt

6 branch 7 project 9 discharge 10 photograph

shoot down 3 pan, rap 4 bash, kill, slam 5 blast, decry, knock, scorn, trash 6 assail, deride, dump on, reject, squash 7 deflate, squelch, torpedo 8 bad-mouth, belittle, derogate, discount, disprove, puncture, ridicule 9 discredit

shooting 4 keen 5 acute, sharp 7 gunplay 8 piercing, stabbing

shooting star 6 meteor 8 fireball

shoot up 4 soar 6 inject, rocket 7 burgeon 8 mushroom 9 skyrocket

shop 4 hunt 5 store 6 browse, market, outlet, search 8 boutique, emporium, showroom

shoplift 3 bag, cop 4 lift, palm 5 filch, pinch, steal, swipe 6 pilfer, rip off, snitch

shop owner 8 merchant, retailer 9 tradesman 10 proprietor

shopworn 5 banal, faded, stale, tired, trite 6 cliché, soiled 7 clichéd 8 overused 9 hackneyed 10 threadbare

shore 4 bank, prop, stay 5 beach, brace, brink, coast 6 bear up, strand, uphold 7 bolster, shingle, support, sustain 8 buttress, littoral, seacoast 9 coastland, coastline, riverbank, riverside, waterside 10 embankment, waterfront

shorebird see at BIRD

short 3 shy 4 curt 5 blunt, brief, crisp, scant, skimp, spare, squat, stint, terse 6 abrupt, meager, meagre, scanty, scarce, skimpy, stubby 7 brusque, compact, concise, lacking, laconic, stunted, wanting 8 abridged, succinct 9 deficient 10 inadequate 11 abbreviated 12 insufficient

shortage 4 lack 5 pinch 6 dearth, ullage 7 deficit, paucity 8 scarcity 10 deficiency, inadequacy, scantiness

shortcoming 3 bug, sin 4 flaw, lack 5 fault, lapse 6 defect 7 demerit, failing 8 weakness 9 weak point 10 deficiency 12 imperfection

shortcut 6 bypass, cutoff

shorten 3 bob, cut 4 clip, dock 5 elide, slash 6 lessen, reduce, shrink 7 abridge, curtail, cut back, cut down, excerpt 8 boil down, compress, condense, contract, decrease, diminish, minimize, truncate 10 abbreviate

shorthand 11 stenography *method:* 5 Gregg 6 Pitman

shorthanded 7 wanting 11 undermanned 12 understaffed

short-lived 5 brief 7 passing 8 fleeting 9 ephemeral, fugacious, momentary, temporary 10 evanescent, transitory

shortly 4 anon, soon 6 pronto 7 briefly, by and by, in brief, quickly, tersely 8 directly 9 concisely, presently 10 succinctly 11 laconically

shortness 7 brevity 9 concision

shortsighted 6 myopic 8 heedless, reckless 10 astigmatic

short-spoken 4 curt 5 bluff, blunt, brief, gruff, terse 6 abrupt, crusty, snippy 7 brusque 8 snippety

short-tempered 5 testy 6 touchy 7 prickly 8 snappish 9 irascible, irritable

Shoshone chief 8 Washakie 9 Pocatello

shot 3 nip, pop, try 4 dose, dram, drop, jolt, stab 5 blast, break, carom, crack, fling, guess, ounce, photo, range, reach, snort, swipe, whack, whirl 6 chance, effort, stroke 7 attempt, snifter 8 marksman, occasion 9 discharge 11 opportunity

shoulder 4 bear, edge, push, side 5 elbow, press, shove 6 assume, hustle, jostle, take on 8 bulldoze *bone:* 7 scapula 8 clavicle *covering:* 6 tippet 8 scapular *muscle:* 7 deltoid *relating to:* 7 humeral 8 scapular

shoulder blade 7 scapula

shout 3 cry 4 bark, bawl, bray, call, roar, yell 5 blare, whoop 6 bellow, clamor, holler, scream 7 exclaim 10 vociferate

shove 3 dig, jab, jam 4 cram, prod, push 5 crowd, drive, elbow, press 6 jostle, propel, thrust 8 bulldoze, shoulder

shovel 3 dig 4 grub 5 delve, scoop, spade 6 dig out, dredge, trowel 8 excavate

shoveler 4 duck 9 broadbill

shove off 3 git 4 blow, exit 5 leave, scoot, scram, split 6 beat it, cut out, decamp, depart, move on 7 move out, pull out, vamoose 8 clear out, run along

show 4 fair, film, lead, pomp, sham 5 array, flick, front, guide, mount, movie, offer, prove, revue, sport, stage 6 appear, arrive, direct, effect, evince, expose, flaunt, lay out, parade, reveal, set out, submit, unveil 7 conduct, display, divulge, exhibit, explain, fanfare, panoply, picture, present, produce, project, trot out 8 brandish, disclose, evidence, illusion, indicate, instruct, manifest, proclaim 9 determine, establish, pageantry, represent, semblance, spectacle 10 appearance, exhibition, exposition, illustrate, production 11 demonstrate, materialize, performance 13 demonstration, manifestation

Show Boat *author:* 6 Ferber (Edna) *composer:* 4 Kern (Jerome) *lyricist:* 11 Hammerstein (Oscar)

showcase 6 flaunt, parade 7 cabinet, exhibit, feature, vitrine

shower 4 hail, rain, wash **5** bathe, burst, party, salvo, spray, storm **6** deluge, lavish, volley **7** barrage, cascade, shatter, spatter **8** cataract, downpour, fountain, rainfall **9** broadside, cannonade, fusillade **10** cloudburst **11** bombardment

showman 8 producer, promoter **10** impresario *famous:* **4** Cody (William F.) **6** Barnum (Phineas T.)

Show Me State 8 Missouri

show off 4 brag **5** boast, flash, model, vaunt **6** expose, flaunt, hotdog, parade **7** display, exhibit, swagger, trot out **8** brandish **10** grandstand

show-off 3 ham **6** hotdog **7** boaster, hotshot, peacock **8** blowhard, braggart **9** swaggerer **13** exhibitionist

showpiece 3 gem **5** jewel, prize **10** magnum opus, masterwork **11** chef d'oeuvre, masterpiece

show up 4 come **6** appear, arrive, debunk, expose, reveal, unmask **8** discover **9** discredit, embarrass **10** invalidate **11** materialize

showy 4 loud **5** gaudy, jazzy **6** flashy, garish, ornate, sporty, tawdry **7** opulent, splashy **8** gorgeous, overdone, striking **9** luxurious, sumptuous **10** flamboyant **11** overwrought, pretentious, resplendent, sensational **12** meretricious, orchidaceous, ostentatious

shred 3 bit, dag, jot, rag **4** iota, whit **5** crumb, grain, grate, ounce, scrap, shave, speck, trace **6** sliver, tatter **7** modicum, smidgen, snippet **8** demolish, fragment, particle **9** scintilla

shrew 3 nag **4** mole **5** harpy, scold, vixen, witch **6** dragon, gorgon, ogress, rodent, virago **7** hellcat **8** battle-ax, fishwife, harridan, she-devil, spitfire, Xantippe **9** battle-axe, termagant, Xanthippe

shrewd 3 sly **4** foxy, keen, wily, wise **5** acute, cagey, canny, savvy, sharp, slick, smart **6** artful, astute, clever, crafty, smooth **7** knowing, prudent **8** sensible **9** ingenious, judicious, sagacious **10** discerning **11** intelligent, penetrating, quick-witted **13** perspicacious

shrewish 5 cross, testy **6** cranky, snappy **7** peevish, peppery **8** choleric, petulant **9** crotchety, fractious, irascible, splenetic **10** ill-natured **11** contentious, intractable, quarrelsome **12** disputatious **13** quick-tempered, short-tempered

shriek 3 cry **4** yell **6** screak, scream, shrill, squawk, squeal **7** screech

shrill 4 keen **5** acute, sharp **6** piping **8** piercing, strident **9** deafening **12** ear-splitting

shrimp 4 runt **5** prawn **6** peanut, scampi **10** crustacean

shrine 5 altar **6** temple **7** sanctum **9** reliquary, sacrarium, sanctuary *Buddhist:* **5** stupa **7** chorten

shrink 3 shy **4** wane **5** cower, quail, slink, start, wince **6** blench, boggle, cringe, flinch, huddle, recede, recoil, wither **7** analyst, dwindle, refrain **8** compress, condense, contract, draw back, withdraw **9** constrict, shrivel up, therapist, waste away **12** psychiatrist, psychologist

shrinking 3 shy **5** mousy, timid **7** bashful **8** retiring, skittish **9** withdrawn

shrive 5 purge **6** pardon, purify **7** absolve, confess, expiate **8** lustrate

shrivel 4 wilt **5** dry up, parch, wizen **6** shrink, wither **7** dwindle, wrinkle **9** dehydrate, desiccate

Shropshire Lad author 7 Housman (A. E.)

shroud 4 hide, rope, veil, wrap **5** cloak, cover, shade **6** enfold, enwrap, screen **7** conceal, enclose, envelop, obscure **8** cerement, obstruct **9** cerecloth **12** winding-sheet

shrouded 5 privy **6** covert, hidden, secret **7** obscure **10** mysterious

shrub 4 bush **5** elder, erica, hazel **6** muskit, privet **7** arboret, dyeweed, guayule **8** barberry, bluewood, boxthorn, inkberry, ironweed, rosebush **9** bearberry **10** bladdernut *Asian:* **4** bago **6** kerria **8** caragana, japonica *desert:* **7** ephedra *dwarf:* **6** bonsai *East Indian:* **3** aal **4** sunn *European:* **4** cade **8** woodbine *evergreen:* **3** box, kat, yew **4** ilex, khat, titi **5** furze, heath, holly, pyxie, savin, taxus **6** kalmia, laurel, myrtle, nandin, protea, sabine, savine **7** boxwood, heather, jasmine, juniper, rosebay **8** lambkill, oleander, rosemary, tamarisk *flowering:* **5** ribes, tiara, wahoo **6** daphne, laurel, myrtle, spirea **7** chamise, chamiso, mahonia, maybush, rhodora, spiraea, weigela **8** magnolia, mezereon, nineback, oleander, oleaster, shadblow, shadbush, snowball, snowbush, tornillo, viburnum, wisteria *genus:* **4** Inga, Itea **7** Solanum **8** Euonymus *hardwood:* **6** cornel *Mexican:* **8** ocotillo *ornamental:* **6** privet **7** syringa **9** bluebeard *pasture:* **8** cowberry *prickly:* **5** briar, chico, furze, gorse **7** bramble **8** hawthorn, mesquite **9** buckthorn *thicket:* **6** maquis **7** macchia **9** chaparral *tropical:* **4** kava **5** henna **7** lantana **8** buddleia **10** frangipani *West Indian:* **4** anil **7** acerola

shrug off 8 belittle, downplay, minimize

shtick 3 act, bag, bit 5 spiel 6 number 7 routine 9 specialty 11 performance
Shuah *father:* 7 Abraham *mother:* 7 Keturah
shuck 3 pod 4 case, cast, hull, husk, junk, peel, shed, skin 5 ditch, scrap, shell, strip 6 reject, remove, slough 7 discard, peel off, take off 8 jettison 11 decorticate
shudder 5 quake, shake 6 quaver, quiver, shimmy, shiver, tremor 7 frisson, tremble, twitter, vibrate
shuffle 3 mix 4 hash 5 dodge, evade, hedge, scuff, shift 6 jumble, mess up, muddle, weasel 7 clutter, reorder, rummage, shamble 8 disarray, disorder, intermix, mishmash 9 rearrange 10 disarrange, equivocate 11 disorganize
shun 3 cut 4 duck, snub 5 avoid, dodge, elude, evade, scorn 6 escape, eschew, refuse, reject 7 decline, disdain
shunt 4 turn 5 avert, shift 6 change, divert, switch 7 deflect, shuttle 8 transfer 9 sidetrack
shush 4 hush 5 quiet, still 6 muffle, muzzle, shut up, stifle 7 repress, silence, squelch 8 suppress
shut 3 bar 4 lock, seal, slam 5 close 6 fasten 9 close down 10 batten down
Shute *novel* 10 On the Beach
shut in 3 hem, mew, pen 4 cage, coop, wall 5 fence 6 coop up, immure 7 confine, enclose 8 imprison
shut-in 7 invalid 8 confined 9 withdrawn 12 convalescent
shut out 3 bar 6 screen 7 exclude 9 ostracize
shutter 5 blind 6 screen
shuttle 5 ferry, shunt 6 bobbin 7 commute, spindle 9 alternate
shuttlecock 4 bird 5 bandy
shut up 3 gag, mew, pen 4 cage, hush, jail, mute 5 burke, choke, quiet, shush, still 6 muzzle, stifle 7 confine, enclose, impound, silence, squelch 8 choke off, imprison, pipe down, suppress 9 quiet down 11 incarcerate
shy 3 coy 4 balk, duck, meek, shun, wary 5 avoid, chary, elude, evade, mousy, quail, scant, short, timid 6 averse, blench, demure, modest, recoil, scanty, scarce, shrink 7 bashful, fearful, lacking, wanting 8 hesitant, reserved, reticent, retiring, sheepish, timorous 9 diffident 11 introverted, unassertive 12 apprehensive, insufficient, self-effacing 13 self-conscious
Shylock 6 usurer 9 loan shark *daughter:* 7 Jessica
shyster 11 pettifogger
Siam see THAILAND

sib 3 bro, kin, sis 4 akin 6 sister 7 brother, kindred, kinsman, related 8 relation, relative 9 relatives
Sibelius *composition* 9 Finlandia 11 Valse Triste
Siberian *dog:* 5 husky 7 Samoyed *native:* 5 Tatar, Yakut 6 Tartar, Tungus 7 Chukchi 9 Mongolian *plain:* 6 steppe *tent:* 4 yurt
sibilate 4 buzz, fizz, hiss, whiz 6 fizzle, sizzle 7 whisper
sibling 3 bro, sis 6 sister 7 brother
sibyl 4 seer 6 oracle 7 prophet 10 prophetess, soothsayer 13 fortune-teller
sic 3 set 4 thus 5 chase 6 attack
Sicilian *secret organization:* 5 Mafia *volcano:* 4 Etna
Sicily *capital:* 7 Palermo *city:* 7 Catania, Messina 8 Siracusa, Syracuse, Taormina *volcano:* 4 Etna
sick 3 ill 5 fed up, tired, weary 6 ailing, laid up, morbid, peaked, rotten, unwell, wobbly 7 fevered, invalid 8 confined, diseased 9 bedridden, defective, disgusted, unhealthy 10 indisposed 11 debilitated
sicken 5 upset 7 afflict, disgust, fall ill 8 nauseate
sickle 5 blade, mower 6 scythe 8 crescent
sickle-shaped 7 falcate
sickly 3 ill, low, wan 4 puny, weak 5 frail 6 ailing, anemic, feeble, infirm, morbid, peaked, poorly, unwell 8 delicate, diseased 9 unhealthy 10 indisposed 11 unhealthful, unwholesome 12 insalubrious
sickness 3 bug 6 malady 7 ailment, disease, illness 8 disorder, syndrome 9 complaint, condition, infirmity 10 affliction 13 indisposition
sic transit gloria ___ 5 mundi
side 4 clad, team 5 angle, facet, flank 6 aspect 9 direction 10 standpoint *combining form:* 5 later 6 lateri, latero *exposed:* 8 windward *sheltered:* 3 lee
sideboard 5 table 6 buffet 8 credence, credenza *for wine:* 8 cellaret 10 cellarette
sideburns 9 burnsides 10 sideboards 11 dundrearies, muttonchops
sidekick 3 pal 4 chum 5 buddy, crony 7 partner 9 assistant, companion 10 accomplice
sideline 5 eject, hobby 6 injure 7 disable, pastime, take out 9 avocation, diversion 10 recreation 11 distraction 12 incapacitate
sidereal 6 astral, starry 7 stellar
side road 5 byway 8 bystreet, shunpike

sideshow 9 diversion 11 distraction

sidestep 4 duck 5 avoid, burke, dodge, evade, hedge, skirt 6 bypass, swerve, weasel 10 circumvent, equivocate 12 tergiversate

sideswipe 5 brush, carom, graze, shave 6 glance, scrape

sidetrack 5 shunt 6 divert, switch 7 deflect

sidewhiskers see SIDEBURNS

side with 4 back 5 favor 6 second, uphold 7 endorse, support 8 backstop, champion

sidle 4 edge, slip

siege 4 bout 5 spell 6 attack 7 assault, seizure 8 blockade 9 onslaught

Siegfried *composer:* 6 Wagner (Richard) *lover:* 8 Brunhild *mother:* 9 Sieglinde *slayer:* 5 Hagen *sword:* 7 Balmung *vulnerable spot:* 4 back 8 shoulder *wife:* 9 Kriemhild

Sienkiewicz novel 8 Quo Vadis

sierra 3 saw 4 fish 5 range 8 mackerel 13 mountain range

Sierra Leone *capital:* 8 Freetown *ethnic group:* 5 Mende, Temne *language:* 4 Krio 7 English *monetary unit:* 5 leone *neighbor:* 6 Guinea 7 Liberia

Sierra Nevada lake 5 Tahoe

Sierra ___ 5 Ancha, Leone, Madre 6 Blanca, Nevada

siesta 3 nap 4 doze 5 sleep 6 catnap, snooze 10 forty winks

sieve 4 sift 6 filter, screen, winnow 8 colander, filtrate, strainer

Sif's husband 4 Thor

sift 3 pan 4 comb, cull, sort 5 glean, sieve 6 filter, screen, strain, winnow 8 filtrate, separate

sigh 3 sob 4 gasp, long, moan, pine 5 groan, sough, whine, yearn 6 exhale, grieve, hanker, murmur 7 breathe, respire, suspire

sight 3 aim, eye, spy 4 espy, view 5 scene, vista 6 notice, vision 7 make out, outlook *relating to:* 5 optic 6 ocular, visual 7 optical

sightseer 7 tourist 10 rubberneck 12 rubbernecker

sign 3 cue, ink 4 flag, hint, mark, omen 5 index, proof, token, trace 6 motion, signal, symbol 7 endorse, gesture, indicia, initial, symptom, vestige, warning 8 evidence, exponent, reminder 9 autograph, indicator 10 expression, indication, suggestion *directional:* 5 arrow *of the zodiac:* (see ZODIAC SIGN)

signal 3 cue, nod 4 flag 5 alarm, alert 6 beckon, wigwag 7 gesture 8 high sign 9 indicator *distress:* 3 SOS 6 Mayday

signature 4 name 9 autograph 11 John Hancock *flourish:* 6 paraph

signet 4 ring, seal 5 stamp 6 device 8 hallmark, intaglio

significance 4 pith 5 merit, point, sense 6 credit, import, moment, weight 7 gravity, meaning 9 authority, magnitude 10 importance 11 consequence, weightiness

significant 5 sound, valid 7 notable, telling, weighty 8 material, powerful 9 important, momentous 10 compelling, convincing, meaningful, noteworthy 11 substantial 12 considerable 13 consequential

signification 4 gist 5 point, sense 6 import 7 essence, meaning, message, purport 9 substance 10 intendment 11 implication 12 notification 13 understanding

signify 4 mean, show 5 count, imply, spell, weigh 6 convey, denote, intend, matter 7 add up to, bespeak, connote, express, purport, suggest 8 indicate

sign on 4 book, hire, join 5 draft 6 engage, enlist, enroll, induct, join up, retain, secure 7 recruit 9 conscript

sign over 4 cede, deed 5 alien, grant 6 assign, convey, remise 7 consign 8 alienate, transfer

sign up 4 join 5 enter 6 enlist, enroll, muster

Sigurd *horse:* 5 Grani *slayer:* 5 Hogni *victim:* 6 Fafner, Fafnir *wife:* 6 Gudrun

Sigyn's husband 4 Loki

Sikhism *deity:* 4 Akal *founder:* 5 Nanak 9 Guru Nanak *leader:* 5 Arjan 9 Guru Arjan 11 Gobind Singh *scripture:* 9 Adi Granth *shrine:* 12 Golden Temple

silage 6 fodder

silence 3 gag 4 calm, hush, lull, mute 5 quash, quell, quiet, shush, still 6 dampen, deaden, muffle, muzzle, shut up, squash, stifle 7 secrecy, squelch 8 choke off, muteness, quietude, suppress 9 quietness, reticence, stillness

silent 3 mum 4 dumb, mute 5 muted, quiet, still, tacit, whist 6 hushed, stilly 8 reticent, taciturn, unspoken, wordless 9 noiseless, soundless, voiceless 10 speechless 11 close-lipped, tight-lipped 12 closemouthed, tight-mouthed

silhouette 6 shadow 7 contour, outline, profile 9 lineament, lineation 10 figuration 11 delineation

Silicon Valley city 8 Palo Alto

silk 5 fiber 7 foulard 8 sarcenet, sarsenet *fabric:* 4 gros 5 caffa, ninon, Pekin, satin, surah, tulle 6 mantua, pongee, samite, sendal, tussah 7 taffeta *factory:*

8 filature *hat:* **6** topper *maker:* **4** worm *raw:* **6** greige *source:* **6** cocoon *waste:* **4** noil **5** floss *wild:* **6** tussah

sill 5 bench, ledge, shelf **9** threshold

silliness 5 folly **6** idiocy **7** inanity **9** absurdity, stupidity

silly 4 daft **5** balmy, crazy, daffy, dippy, dizzy, funny, giddy, inane, loony, sappy, wacky **6** absurd, simple **7** asinine, fatuous, flighty, foolish, idiotic, vacuous, witless **9** brainless, frivolous, ludicrous, nitwitted, senseless **10** irrational, ridiculous, weak-minded **11** emptyheaded, harebrained, light-headed **12** preposterous, simpleminded **13** rattlebrained

silt 5 dregs **7** deposit, residue **8** alluvium, sediment

silver 4 coin **5** money, shiny **6** argent, dulcet **7** bullion, element **8** flatware, lustrous, sterling **9** argentine, tableware *relating to:* **9** argentine

silverfish 6 insect, tarpon

silversmith 6 Revere (Paul) **11** metalworker

silver-tongued 4 glib **6** fluent **7** voluble **8** eloquent

silvery 6 argent **7** shining **9** argentine, brilliant **10** glittering, shimmering

Silvia's beloved 9 Valentine

___ **Simbel 3** Abu

Simenon character 7 Maigret (Inspector)

Simeon *father:* **5** Jacob *mother:* **4** Leah *son:* **4** Ohad **6** Nemuel

simian 3 ape **5** chimp, lemur, loris **6** baboon, bonobo, galago, monkey **7** apelike, gorilla, primate, tarsier **9** orangutan **10** anthropoid, chimpanzee, monkeylike

similar 4 akin, like **5** alike **6** agnate **7** uniform **8** parallel, suchlike **9** analogous, consonant **10** comparable, reciprocal **11** correlative **13** complementary, corresponding

similarity 6 parity **7** analogy, harmony, kinship **8** affinity, likeness, parallel, sameness **9** alikeness, closeness, congruity, semblance **10** conformity, congruence **11** coincidence, correlation, homogeneity, parallelism, resemblance

similarly 8 likewise

simile 7 analogy **8** affinity, likeness, metaphor **9** alikeness, semblance **10** comparison **11** correlation, resemblance *word:* **4** like

similitude 4 copy **5** image **6** double **7** analogy, kinship, replica **8** affinity, likeness, metaphor, relation, sameness **9** alikeness, congruity, semblance **10** comparison, similarity **11** correla-

tion, counterpart, equivalence, resemblance

simmer 4 boil, fret, fume, stew, stir **5** churn **6** bubble, seethe **7** ferment, smolder

simmer down 5 relax

Simon *brother:* **5** Jesus **6** Andrew *father:* **5** Jonah *new name:* **5** Peter *son:* **5** Judas, Rufus **9** Alexander

Simon ___ **5** Magus **6** Legree **8** of Cyrene **9** the Zealot

Simon Maccabaeus *father:* **10** Mattathias *nickname:* **6** Thassi *slayer:* **7** Ptolemy

Simon play 9 Odd Couple (The) **10** Chapter Two, Plaza Suite **11** Biloxi Blues **12** Sunshine Boys (The) **13** Lost in Yonkers **16** Come Blow Your Horn **17** Barefoot in the Park **20** Brighton Beach Memoirs **21** Last of the Red Hot Lovers **22** Prisoner of Second Avenue (The)

simp 4 dope **5** dunce, idiot, moron **6** dimwit, nitwit **7** pinhead **8** bonehead, imbecile, lunkhead, numskull **9** blockhead, lamebrain, numbskull **10** nincompoop

simple 4 easy, mere, pure **5** basic, lucid, naive, plain, sheer **6** modest **7** artless, natural, unmixed **8** absolute, trusting **9** childlike, credulous, ingenuous, unadorned **10** effortless, elementary, unaffected **11** fundamental, undecorated, unelaborate **13** unpretentious *combining form:* **4** hapl **5** haplo

simpleminded 4 dull, slow **5** naive **6** stupid **7** foolish, idiotic, moronic **8** gullible, retarded **9** dim-witted, imbecilic **10** half-witted, slow-witted

simpleton 4 dolt, dope, fool **5** dummy, dunce, idiot, moron **6** cretin, dimwit, nitwit **7** dullard, half-wit, pinhead **8** bonehead, dumbbell, imbecile, lunkhead **9** blockhead, ignoramus, lamebrain **10** nincompoop

simplify 4 ease **7** clarify, clear up **8** boil down **10** facilitate, streamline, unscramble **11** disentangle **13** straighten out

simply 4 just, only **6** merely

simulacrum 4 copy **5** clone, ditto, guise, image, trace **6** double, ersatz, mirror, ringer **7** picture, replica **8** likeness, portrait **9** facsimile, imitation, semblance **10** appearance **12** reproduction **13** impersonation, spitting image

simulate 3 ape **4** fake, sham **5** feign, mimic **6** embody, mirror, parody, parrot **7** imitate **8** resemble **9** incarnate **11** counterfeit

simulated 4 fake, mock, sham **5** bogus, dummy, false, phony **6** ersatz **8** spurious **9** imitation, insincere, pretended **10** artificial, fictitious, substitute **11** counterfeit

simultaneous 6 coeval **10** coexistent, coexisting, coincident, coinciding, concurrent, synchronic **11** synchronous **12** contemporary

simultaneously 6 at once **7** jointly **8** together **9** meanwhile

sin 3 err **4** debt, evil, tort, vice **5** crime, fault, guilt, lapse, stray, wrong **6** offend **7** demerit, misdeed, offense **8** hamartia, iniquity, trespass **10** deficiency, peccadillo, transgress, wickedness, wrongdoing **11** shortcoming **12** imperfection *deadly:* **4** envy, lust **5** anger, greed, pride, sloth **8** gluttony **12** covetousness

Sin 7 moon-god *daughter:* **6** Ishtar *son:* **7** Shamash *wife:* **6** Ningal

since 3 ago **5** after **6** behind **7** because, whereas **8** as long as **9** following **10** inasmuch as **11** considering *Scottish:* **4** syne

sincere 4 real, true **5** frank, plain **6** actual, candid, devout, honest **7** artless, earnest, genuine, serious **8** bona fide, truthful **9** authentic, heartfelt, ingenuous, unfeigned **10** aboveboard, forthright **12** wholehearted **13** unpretentious

sincerity 6 candor **7** honesty **8** goodwill, openness **9** frankness, good faith **11** artlessness, earnestness

sine qua non 4 must **9** condition, essential, necessity, requisite **11** requirement **12** precondition, prerequisite

sinew 6 tendon

sinewy 4 ropy, wiry **5** tough **6** brawny **7** fibrous, stringy **8** muscular

sinful 3 bad **4** base, evil, vile **5** wrong **6** guilty, unholy, wicked **7** immoral, peccant, vicious **8** blamable, culpable, damnable, depraved, shameful **9** reprobate **10** iniquitous **11** blameworthy, disgraceful **13** reprehensible

sing 3 rat **4** fink, hymn **5** carol, chant, chirp, croon, troll, yodel **6** inform, intone, snitch, squeal, warble **7** confess, descant, lullaby **8** serenade, vocalize **10** cantillate

Singapore *capital:* **9** Singapore *language:* **5** Malay, Tamil **8** Mandarin *monetary unit:* **6** dollar

singe 4 burn, char, sear **6** scorch

singer 4 alto, bass **5** mezzo, tenor **6** canary **7** crooner, soloist, soprano **8** baritone, choirboy, songbird, songster, vocalist **9** balladeer, chorister, contralto **10** troubadour *cabaret:* **11** chansonnier *female:* **9** chanteuse *opera:* **4** diva **10** cantatrice *religious:* **6** cantor

singing *exercise:* **7** solfège *group:* **3** duo **4** trio **5** choir **6** chorus **7** chorale, quartet, quintet *voice:* **4** alto, bass **5** mezzo,

tenor **7** soprano **8** baritone **9** contralto **12** mezzo-soprano

single 3 hit, odd, one **4** free, lone, only, sole **5** unwed **6** maiden, unique **7** base hit, unitary **8** distinct, isolated, separate, solitary, specific **9** exclusive, unmarried **10** individual, particular, unattached *combining form:* **3** mon **4** hapl, mono **5** haplo *prefix:* **3** uni

single-minded 5 rigid **6** dogged, driven, intent **7** adamant, devoted, diehard **8** hell-bent, obdurate, resolute, resolved, stubborn **9** dedicated, steadfast, unbending **10** brassbound, determined, inexorable, inflexible, purposeful, relentless, unyielding

single out 4 cull, mark, pick **5** elect, favor **6** choose, opt for, select **9** designate **11** distinguish

singular 3 odd **4** lone, only, rare, sole, solo **5** weird **6** unique **7** bizarre, oddball, strange, unusual **8** peculiar, solitary, uncommon **9** exclusive **10** individual, outlandish, particular, unexampled **11** exceptional **13** extraordinary

singularity 5 quirk, unity **6** oddity **7** anomaly, oneness **8** identity **9** exception **11** peculiarity, personality **12** idiosyncrasy **13** individuality, particularity

singularize 4 mark **11** distinguish, individuate **12** characterize **13** differentiate, individualize

sinister 4 dark, dire, evil, left **6** creepy, malign **7** baleful, fateful, malefic, ominous **8** lowering, menacing **9** ill-omened, malicious **10** foreboding, maleficent, portentous **11** apocalyptic, threatening **12** inauspicious, unpropitious

sink 3 dip, pit, sag **4** bore, bury, dive, drop, fall, sump, wane **5** basin, drill, droop, lower, sewer, slope, slump, stoop, swamp **6** hollow, invest, plunge, settle, thrust, worsen **7** capsize, cesspit, decline, depress, descend, founder, go under, immerse, let down, scuttle, subside, torpedo **8** cesspool, hellhole, submerge, submerse **9** concavity, disappear **10** depression

sinker 3 bob **5** plumb **6** weight **8** doughnut, fastball, plumb bob

sinkhole 3 dip, sag **4** bowl **5** basin **6** hollow **8** cesspool **9** concavity **10** depression

sinless 4 pure **6** chaste **8** innocent **9** righteous **10** impeccable

sinner 5 rogue, scamp **6** bad egg, outlaw, rascal, wretch **7** lowlife, villain **8** criminal, evildoer, offender **9** libertine, miscreant, reprobate, scoundrel, wrongdoer **10** black sheep, delinquent, profligate, malefactor **11** rapscallion

Sinn ___ 4 Fein

sinuous 4 wavy 5 lithe, snaky 7 winding 8 flexuous, tortuous 10 convoluted, meandering, serpentine 11 anfractuous, snake-shaped

sinus 6 cavity, hollow, recess

Sioux 6 Dakota *chief:* 8 Red Cloud 10 Crazy Horse 11 Sitting Bull *people:* 3 Ofo 4 Crow 6 Biloxi, Tutelo 7 Catawba, Hidatsa 9 Winnebago

sip 5 drink, savor, taste 6 imbibe

siphon 3 tap 4 draw, pipe, pump 5 draft, drain 6 convoy, divert, funnel 7 channel, conduct, draw off 8 transmit

sir 4 lord 5 title 6 knight, mister 9 gentleman

sire 4 lord 5 beget, breed, hatch, spawn 6 father, parent 7 founder 8 engender 9 patriarch, procreate, propagate 10 forefather

siren 4 vamp 5 alarm 7 Lorelei 9 temptress 10 seductress 11 femme fatale *film:* 4 Bara (Theda)

Siren 5 Ligea 8 Leucosia 10 Parthenope *German:* 7 Lorelei

sirenian 6 dugong, sea cow 7 manatee

siren song 4 lure 5 decoy, snare 6 come-on 10 allurement, enticement, temptation

Sirius 7 Dog Star

sister 3 nun 7 sibling *French:* 5 soeur *Latin:* 5 soror *Spanish:* 7 hermana

Sister Carrie author: 7 Dreiser (Theodore)

sisterly 7 sororal

Sisyphus *brother:* 7 Athamas 9 Salmoneus *father:* 6 Aeolus *mother:* 7 Enarete *son:* 7 Glaucus

sit 4 pose 5 perch, roost

Sita *abductor:* 6 Ravana *husband, rescuer:* 4 Rama

sitarist 7 Shankar (Ravi)

site 3 dig 4 home, spot 5 haunt, locus, place, point, scene, venue 6 locale 7 station 8 locality, location, position

sit-in 7 protest

sitting 6 séance 7 session *prolonged:* 8 sederunt

Sitting Bull's tribe 5 Sioux

sitting duck 4 butt, mark 6 target

situate 3 put, set 5 place 6 locate 7 install 8 position

situation 3 job 4 post, rank 5 point, state 6 plight, status 7 footing, setting, station 8 location, position, standing 9 condition 13 circumstances

situs 5 place, venue 6 locale

Siva see SHIVA

six *combining form:* 3 hex, sex 4 hexa, sexi 5 sexti *group of:* 6 sestet, sextet 9 sextuplet *relating to:* 6 senary

sixfold 8 sextuple

six-shooter 3 gun 6 pistol 8 revolver

sixth sense 3 ESP 7 insight 9 intuition, telepathy 12 clairvoyance

sizable 3 big 5 ample, hefty, large, major, roomy 8 spacious 9 capacious, extensive 10 commodious, large-scale 11 substantial 12 considerable

size 4 area, bulk, mass 5 range, scope, width 6 extent, height, length, spread, volume 7 bigness, breadth, caliber, expanse, measure, stature 9 amplitude, dimension, extension, greatness, largeness, magnitude 10 dimensions, proportion 11 measurement, proportions

size up 3 peg 4 rate, read 5 assay, gauge, judge, value 6 assess, review, survey 7 adjudge, dope out 8 appraise, estimate, evaluate 9 figure out

sizzle 3 fry 4 buzz, fizz, hiss, whiz 5 grill 6 hoopla, seethe 7 pizzazz 8 sibilate 10 excitement

sizzling 3 hot 6 red-hot, torrid 7 burning 8 scalding, white-hot 9 scorching

skald 4 bard, poet

Skanda 6 war-god *brother:* 6 Ganesa 7 Ganesha *father:* 4 Siva 5 Shiva

skate 3 nag, ray 4 skid, skim 5 glide, skirr, slide 8 glissade 11 Rollerblade *blade:* 6 runner *kind:* 6 figure, hockey

skating site 3 ice 4 rink

skedaddle 3 run 4 bolt, flee, skip 5 scoot, scram, split 6 beat it, begone, bug off, cut out, decamp, get out 7 make off, run away, scamper, skiddoo, take off, vamoose 8 clear out 10 make tracks

skein 4 coil 5 flock, snarl, twist 6 tangle 12 entanglement

skeletal 4 bony 5 gaunt 6 wasted 7 angular, scraggy, starved 8 rawboned 9 emaciated 10 cadaverous

skeleton 5 bones, draft, frame 6 sketch 7 diagram, outline 9 bare bones, framework *marine:* 5 coral, shell

skeptic 5 cynic 7 doubter, scoffer 8 agnostic 10 Pyrrhonist, questioner, unbeliever 11 disbeliever

skeptical 4 wary 5 leery 6 show-me 7 cynical, dubious 8 doubtful, doubting 9 quizzical 10 dissenting, suspicious 11 mistrustful, questioning, unbelieving 12 disbelieving, freethinking

skepticism 5 doubt 7 dubiety 8 distrust, mistrust, wariness 9 dubiosity, misgiving, suspicion 11 incertitude, uncertainty

skerry 4 isle, reef 6 island

sketch 4 draw, plot 5 draft, rough, trace 6 depict, design, doodle, lay out, map out, précis 7 develop, diagram, outline, portray 8 block out, chalk out, rough

out 9 blueprint, delineate 12 characterize
sketchy 4 iffy 5 crude, rough, vague
6 skimpy, slight 7 cursory, shallow
8 skeletal 10 incomplete 11 preliminary,
superficial 12 questionable
skew 4 bias, veer 5 angle, fudge, slant,
slide 6 swerve 7 distort
skewer 3 rod 4 spit 5 lance, spear, spike
6 impale, pierce 8 puncture, ridicule,
transfix 9 brochette, criticize
ski 5 glide, slide *lift:* 4 J-bar, T-bar 5 chair
7 gondola
skid 5 glide, skate, slide 6 pallet, runner
7 spinout 8 sideslip
skiddoo 4 scat 5 leave, scram, split
6 beat it, begone, bug off, decamp,
depart, vacate 7 buzz off, take off,
vamoose 8 clear out, shove off
9 skedaddle, take a hike 10 hit the
road, make tracks
skid row 6 bowery
skier *American:* 3 Moe (Tommy) 4 Kidd
(Billy) 5 Mahre (Phil, Steve) 6 Miller
(Bode) 7 Johnson (Bill) *Austrian:*
5 Maier (Hermann) 6 Proell
(Annemarie), Sailer (Toni) 7 Klammer
(Franz), Schranz (Karl) 10 Girardelli
(Marc) 11 Moser-Proell (Annemarie)
French: 5 Killy (Jean-Claude) *Italian:*
5 Tomba (Alberto) 6 Thoeni (Gustavo)
Luxembourg: 10 Girardelli (Marc)
Swedish: 8 Stenmark (Ingemar) *Swiss:*
10 Zurbriggen (Pirmin)
skiff 4 boat 7 rowboat
skiing *area:* 3 run 5 slope *cross-country:*
7 touring *event:* 6 schuss, slalom
8 downhill 11 giant slalom *horse-drawn:*
9 skijoring *kind:* 6 Alpine, Nordic *position:* 7 vorlage *technique:* 6 wedeln
8 snowplow, traverse *turn:* 7 christy
8 christie
skill 3 art 5 craft, knack 7 ability,
address, command, cunning, finesse,
know-how, mastery, prowess, sleight
8 deftness, facility 9 dexterity, expertise, ingenuity, readiness, technique
10 adroitness, competence 11 proficiency
skilled 3 apt 4 able 5 adept 6 expert
7 capable, trained 8 masterly, talented
9 competent, masterful, practiced
10 proficient 12 accomplished
skillet 3 pan 6 spider 9 frying pan
skillful 4 deft 5 adept, crack, handy
6 adroit, clever, daedal, expert 7 skilled
8 masterly 9 competent, dexterous,
masterful, practiced, workmanly
10 proficient 11 crackerjack, workman-
like 12 accomplished
skim 4 sail, scan, scud, skip 5 brush,

carom, glide, graze, skirr 6 browse
8 embezzle, ricochet
skimp 4 save 5 pinch, scant, spare, stint
6 meager, scanty, scrape, sparse 7 slender 8 begrudge, conserve, retrench,
withhold 9 economize
skimpy 5 scant, spare 6 meager, meagre,
paltry, scanty, scarce, sparse 7 limited,
wanting 8 exiguous 9 deficient 10 inadequate 12 insufficient
skim through 4 scan 6 browse
skin 3 fur, gyp, pod, rap 4 clad, clip,
husk, hide, pare, peel, pelt, rind, soak
5 blame, cheat, cover, scale, shell, stiff,
strip 6 fleece, sheath, slough 7 censure,
condemn, sheathe 8 denounce 9 epidermis, sheathing 10 integument, overcharge 11 decorticate *animal:* 4 coat,
hide, pelt 6 hackle, peltry *combining
form:* 3 cut 4 cuti, derm 5 derma,
dermo, dermy 6 dermat, dermia, dermis 7 cutaneo, dermata (plural), der-
mato, epiderm 8 epidermo *depression:*
6 dimple *disease:* 4 acne 5 hives, mange
6 eczema 10 dermatitis *dry:* 5 scurf *fold:*
5 plica *layer:* 5 derma 6 corium, dermis
7 cuticle 9 epidermis *opening:* 4 pore
protuberance: 3 tag, wen 4 mole, wart
6 pimple *rabbit:* 5 coney *relating to:*
6 dermal 9 cuticular, epidermal *spot:*
7 freckle
skin-deep 7 shallow, trivial 11 superficial
skinflint 5 miser 7 niggard, scrooge
8 tightwad 10 cheapskate, pinchpenny
skin game 3 con 4 scam 5 bunco, bunko,
cheat, fraud, sting, trick 6 hustle, racket 7 swindle 8 flimflam
skink 6 lizard
skinny 4 bony, dope, info, lank, lean,
thin 5 gaunt, lanky, scoop, spare,
weedy 6 twiggy 7 angular, lowdown,
scraggy, scrawny 8 rawboned, skeletal
9 emaciated
Skin of Our Teeth author 6 Wilder
(Thornton)
skip 3 hop, run 4 flee, jump, leap, omit,
trip 5 bound, caper, carom, frisk, leave,
scoot, skirr 6 cavort, gambol, pass up,
spring 7 misfire, scamper, skitter
8 leave out, overlook, pass over, ricochet 9 skedaddle
skipjack 4 boat, fish, tuna 8 bluefish,
ladyfish, sailboat
skipper 5 pilot 6 leader 7 captain 9 butterfly, commander
skirmish 3 row 4 fray 5 broil, brush,
clash, melee, run-in, scrap, set-to
6 affray, battle, fracas 7 assault, dispute
8 conflict, struggle 9 encounter, scrimmage
skirr 3 run 4 bolt, flee, sail, scud, skim,

skip **5** float, scoot, shoot **7** make off, scamper **9** skedaddle

skirt 3 hem, rim **4** brim, duck, edge **5** avoid, bound, brink, burke, dodge, elude, evade, hedge, verge **6** border, bypass, define, detour, escape, fringe, ignore, margin **8** sidestep, surround **9** perimeter, periphery **10** circumvent *ballet:* **4** tutu *feature:* **3** hem **4** slit *long:* **4** maxi *Scottish:* **4** kilt *short:* **4** mini *style:* **5** A-line **6** sheath

skit 6 shtick, sketch **9** burlesque

skitter 3 hop **4** flit, skip, trip **6** scurry, spring **7** scamper

skittery see SKITTISH

skittish 3 coy, shy **4** edgy, wary **5** chary, dizzy, jumpy, leery **6** fickle **7** bashful, fidgety, flighty, nervous, rabbity, restive **8** unstable, volatile **9** excitable, frivolous, impulsive, mercurial, whimsical **10** capricious, unreliable

skive 4 pare **5** carve, shave, slice

skivvies 9 underwear

skoal 5 toast **6** health

skua 4 bird **6** jaeger **7** seabird

skulduggery 5 fraud **8** foul play, trickery **9** chicanery, duplicity **10** hanky-panky

skulk 4 lurk, slip **5** creep, prowl, shirk, slink, sneak, steal

skull 4 head, mind **5** brain **7** cranium **8** brainpan **9** braincase *back of:* **7** occiput *bone:* **5** vomer **6** zygoma **7** ethmoid, frontal **8** parietal, sphenoid, temporal *jawless:* **9** calvarium *joint:* **6** suture *part:* **3** jaw **5** inion

skullcap 6 beanie, pileus **7** calotte **8** yarmulke **9** calvarium, zucchetto

skunk 4 beat, drub, lick, scum, whip, whup **6** thrash, wallop **7** clobber, polecat, shellac, stinker, trounce **8** civet cat, lambaste **9** overwhelm, slaughter *genus:* **8** Mephitis

sky 5 azure **6** heaven, welkin **7** heavens **8** empyrean **9** firmament

sky-blue 5 azure **8** cerulean

skylarking 5 revel **7** revelry, whoopee **9** high jinks, horseplay, rowdiness, whoop-de-do **10** roughhouse **12** roughhousing

skylight 6 window

skyline 7 horizon, outline

sky pilot 5 padre **6** cleric, parson, pastor **8** chaplain, minister, preacher **9** churchman, clergyman

skyrocket 4 rise, soar **7** shoot up **8** catapult

sky sighting 3 UFO

slab 5 block, chunk, slice, strip **8** pavement

slack 3 lax **4** lazy, slow, soft **5** inert, loose, relax **6** remiss **7** ease off, laggard,

passive, relaxed **8** careless, derelict, dilatory, inactive, indolent, slothful, sluggish, stagnant **9** leisurely, lethargic, negligent **10** neglectful

slacken 3 ebb, lax **4** ease, slow, wane **5** abate, let up, loose, relax **9** detain, ease up, lessen, loosen, relent, retard, slow up **7** die down, dwindle, ease off, subside **8** diminish, moderate, slow down **9** untighten **10** decelerate

slacker 3 bum **4** slug **5** idler, sloth **6** loafer **7** goof-off, shirker, wastrel **8** deadbeat, layabout, slugabed, sluggard **9** goldbrick, lazybones **10** delinquent **11** couch potato

slag 4 lava **5** dross **6** cinder, debris, scoria

slake 5 allay **6** deaden, quench **7** crumble, hydrate, relieve, satisfy **9** alleviate

slam 3 bat, hit, jab, pan, rap **4** bang, bash, beat, belt, blow, boom, dash, drub, flay, slug, slur, swat, wham **5** blast, crack, crash, fling, knock, pound, slash, smack, smash, swipe, whack **6** batter, cudgel, hammer, scathe, strike, thwack, wallop **7** clobber, potshot **8** lambaste **9** castigate

slam-dance 4 mosh

slam dunk 5 cinch, setup **6** shoo-in **7** safe bet **9** certainty, sure thing

slammer 3 can, jug, pen **4** brig, coop, jail, stir **5** clink, pokey **6** cooler, lockup, prison **9** calaboose **12** penitentiary

slander 4 slur, tale **5** libel, slime, smear, sully **6** defame, malign, smirch, vilify **7** calumny, scandal, tarnish, traduce **8** besmirch **9** denigrate **10** backbiting, calumniate, defamation, detraction, scandalize **11** mud-slinging **12** backstabbing

slang 4 cant, jive **5** argot, lingo **6** jargon, patois, patter **7** dialect **10** vernacular

slant 3 tip **4** bank, bias, cant, heel, lean, list, skew, tilt, veer, warp **5** angle, aside, bevel, grade, slope, splay **7** distort, incline, leaning, outlook **8** gradient **9** prejudice, viewpoint **10** standpoint **11** inclination **12** predilection *combining form:* **4** clin **5** clino

slap 3 hit, pop **4** bash, blow, cuff, shot, slam, swat **5** clout, smack, spank, whack **6** buffet, insult, rebuff, strike **7** affront, putdown **8** brickbat, lambaste, penalize **9** castigate

slapdash 5 hasty, messy **6** random, sloppy **7** cursory **8** careless, slipshod **9** halfbaked, haphazard, hit-or-miss, makeshift

slap down 5 quell **6** kibosh **7** squelch **8** prohibit, suppress

slaphappy 5 dazed, dizzy, woozy **6** punchy **10** punch-drunk

slash 3 cut **4** clip, gash, hack, pare, slit **5** lower, shave, slice **6** reduce, scathe, scorch **7** abridge, blister, curtail, cut back, cut down, scarify, scourge, shorten **8** lacerate, lambaste, mark down **9** castigate, excoriate **10** abbreviate

slat 4 lath **5** board, stave, strip **6** louver, louvre **7** airfoil

slate 4 gray, list, rock, tile **6** lineup, record, tablet, ticket **7** shingle **8** schedule **9** designate

slather 5 smear **6** spread **8** squander

slattern 4 bawd, moll, slut, tart **5** hussy, tramp, wench **6** floozy, harlot **7** chippie, jezebel, trollop **8** strumpet **10** prostitute **11** painted lady **12** scarlet woman, streetwalker

slaughter 4 kill, slay **6** murder **7** butcher, carnage, killing, wipe out **8** butchery, decimate, demolish, hecatomb, massacre **9** bloodbath, bloodshed, liquidate **10** annihilate, butchering **11** destruction, exterminate, liquidation **12** annihilation

slaughterhouse 8 abattoir

Slav 4 Pole, Serb, Sorb, Wend **5** Croat, Czech **6** Bulgar, Slovak **7** Russian, Serbian, Slovene **8** Bohemian, Croatian, Moravian **9** Bulgarian, Ruthenian, Ukrainian

slave 4 grub, help, peon, plod, serf, slog, toil **5** grind, helot, swink **6** drudge, menial, thrall, toiler, vassal **7** bondman, chattel, servant *feudal:* **4** serf *harem:* **9** odalisque *liberated:* **8** freedman *Muslim:* **6** Mamluk **8** Mameluke *Spartan:* **5** helot

slave driver 6 tyrant **7** foreman **8** martinet, overseer **10** taskmaster **11** Simon Legree

slaver 4 spit **5** drool, froth **6** drivel, saliva **7** dribble, slobber, spittle **8** salivate

slavery 6 thrall **7** bondage, helotry, peonage, serfdom **9** indenture, servitude, thralldom **11** subjugation

Slavic apostle 5 Cyril **9** Methodius

slavish 6 abject, menial **7** servile **8** obeisant, wretched **9** groveling, imitative, laborious **10** obsequious, unoriginal **11** subservient

slay 4 do in, kill **6** murder **7** bump off, butcher, execute, put away **8** dispatch, knock off **9** liquidate, slaughter **11** assassinate

slayer 7 butcher **11** executioner

sleazy 3 low **5** cheap, dingy, seedy, tacky, tatty **6** cheesy, flimsy, shabby, shoddy, trashy **7** run-down, squalid **8** gimcrack **10** down-at-heel **11** dilapidated **12** disreputable

sled 4 luge, pung **6** sleigh **7** coaster, travois **8** toboggan *Russian:* **6** troika

sled dog 5 husky **8** malamute

sledge 4 maul **6** hammer, sleigh *Eskimo:* **7** komatik

sleek 4 oily **6** glassy, glossy, smooth **7** elegant, stylish **8** lustrous, polished **10** glistening

sleep 3 nap **4** doze, rest **6** catnap, repose, siesta, snooze **7** shut-eye, slumber **11** slumberland *bringer:* **7** sandman *combining form:* **4** hypn, narc **5** hypno, narco, somni *god:* **6** Hypnos, Somnus

sleeper 4 beam, mole **7** Pullman **8** long shot **11** double agent, stringpiece

sleeping 7 dormant **8** comatose *disease:* **10** narcolepsy

sleepless 7 wakeful **8** vigilant **9** insomniac

sleeplessness 8 insomnia

sleepwalker 12 somnambulist

sleepy 4 dozy **6** drowsy **7** nodding **9** somnolent **10** slumberous

sleigh 4 pung **6** sledge

sleight 4 ploy, ruse, wile **5** skill, trick **7** gimmick, prowess **8** artifice, deftness, maneuver **9** dexterity, stratagem **10** adroitness

sleight of hand 11 legerdemain

slender 4 lean, slim, thin, trim **5** lithe, reedy, spare **6** skinny, slight, svelte, twiggy **7** spindly, willowy

sleuth 4 dick, Drew (Nancy) **5** Brown (Encyclopedia, Father), Kojak, Morse, Queen (Ellery), Saint (The), snoop, Spade (Sam), Tracy (Dick), Wolfe (Nero) **6** Hammer (Mike), Holmes (Sherlock), Marple (Miss), Poirot (Hercule), shamus, Wimsey (Peter) **7** Cadfael (Brother), Columbo, Fansler (Kate), gumshoe, Maigret, Marlowe (Philip) **8** hawkshaw, Millhone (Kinsey), Rockford (Jim), sherlock **9** Dalgliesh (Adam), detective, Scarpetta (Kay) **10** private eye **12** investigator

slew 3 lot, mob, ton **4** army, heap, host, load, mess, pile, raft, skid, turn, veer **5** batch, bunch, crowd, flock, pivot, twist **6** myriad, passel, swerve, throng **9** abundance, multitude

slice 3 cut **4** gash, slit **5** allot, carve, divvy, quota, sever, share, slash, split, wedge **6** cleave, divide, incise, sample **7** dissect, portion, segment **8** allocate **9** allotment, allowance

slick 4 film, glib, oily, slip, wily **5** sharp, sleek, soapy **6** crafty, glossy, greasy, shrewd, smarmy, smooth, tricky **7** cunning **8** slippery, slithery, unctuous **10** lubricious, oleaginous

slicker 4 dude **5** dandy, shark **6** con man

7 cheater, diddler, grifter, oilskin, sharper **8** raincoat, swindler **9** trickster **11** flimflammer

slide 3 dip, sag **4** flow, ramp, skid, slip **5** chute, coast, chute, drift, glide, skate, slump, spill **6** scooch, stream **7** decline, slither **8** downturn **9** downswing, downtrend **12** transparency

slight 4 omit, skip, slim, snub, thin **5** frail, reedy, scorn, small **6** flimsy, ignore, meager, meagre, modest, offend, paltry, remote, skinny **7** contemn, neglect, outside, put-down, slender, tenuous, trivial **8** brush-off, delicate, discount, overlook, smallish, trifling **9** disregard, pint-sized **10** disrespect, negligible

slim 4 thin **5** lithe, reedy, small, spare **6** meager, meagre, minute, narrow, paltry, remote, skinny, slight, svelte, twiggy **7** lissome, outside, slender, tenuous **9** lithesome **10** negligible

slim down 4 diet, fast **6** reduce **10** slenderize

slime 3 goo, mud **4** glop, gunk, muck, ooze, scum **5** filth **6** sleaze, sludge **7** slander

slimy 4 oozy **6** mucous **7** viscous

sling 3 lob **4** cast, fire, hang, hurl, sock, toss **5** chuck, heave, march, pitch, throw **6** dangle, launch **7** suspend **8** catapult

slink 4 lurk **5** creep, prowl, skulk, slide, sneak, steal **7** gumshoe

slinky 4 sexy **5** lithe, sleek **6** svelte **7** furtive, lissome, sinuous, slender, willowy **8** graceful, sensuous, stealthy

slip 3 sag **4** dock, drop, fall, flow, flub, goof, lurk, shed, sink, skid **5** berth, boner, creep, error, fluff, gaffe, glide, lapse, slide, slink, slump, sneak, steal **6** escape **7** blooper, blunder, decline, drop off, fall off, faux pas, mistake, slither **8** downturn, throw off **9** downswing, downtrend

slipper 4 mule, shoe **5** scuff **6** bootee, bootie, sandal **8** flip-flop, pantofle

slippery 3 icy **4** eely, oily **5** slick **6** greasy, shifty, smooth **7** devious, evasive **8** illusive, slithery **10** lubricious

slipshod 6 blowsy, blowzy, frowsy, frowzy, shabby, shoddy, sloppy, untidy **7** rumpled, scrubby, scruffy, unkempt **8** careless, ill-kempt, slapdash, slovenly, tattered **9** haphazard, negligent **10** bedraggled, disheveled, down-at-heel

slipup 4 goof **5** boner, error, fluff, lapse **6** bungle, glitch, miscue, mishap **7** blooper, blunder, faux pas, misstep, mistake, setback, stumble **8** accident

9 mischance, oversight **10** misfortune **11** misjudgment

slit 3 cut, gap **4** gash, rent **5** chink, crack, slash, slice **6** cranny, incise **7** crevice, fissure, opening

slither 4 slip **5** creep, glide, sidle, slide, slink, snake, sneak, steal **7** wriggle **8** undulate

slithery see SLIPPERY

sliver 5 scrap, shard, shave, shred, slice **6** paring **7** shaving, snippet **8** splinter

slob 3 oaf **4** boor, clod, goon, lout **6** galoot, sloven

slobber 4 gush **5** drool, froth **6** drivel, effuse, slaver **7** dribble, enthuse **8** salivate

sloe 4 plum **10** blackthorn

slog 4 grub, moil, plod, plug, toil **5** chore, grind, labor, slave, sweat **6** drudge, schlep, trudge **7** schlepp

slogan 5 motto **6** byword **9** catchword, watchword **10** shibboleth **11** catchphrase

sloop 4 boat **8** sailboat

slop 3 mud, pap **4** gush, muck **5** douse, dreck, dregs, offal, slosh, slush, spill, swill **6** guzzle, pablum, refuse, splash, sludge **7** garbage, pabulum, rubbish **8** splatter

slope 3 tip **4** bend, cant, heel, lean, list, rise, skew, swag, sway, tilt **5** grade, pitch, scarp, slant **6** ascent, glacis **7** descent, incline, leaning, recline **8** gradient **9** acclivity, declivity, obliquity **11** inclination *combining form:* **5** cline **6** clinal

sloppy 5 dowdy, gushy, messy **6** slushy, untidy **7** gushing, unkempt **8** careless, effusive, ill-kempt, slapdash, slipshod, slovenly **10** bedraggled, disheveled **11** dishevelled

slosh 4 gush, slop, wash **5** churn, swash **6** gurgle, splash **8** flounder, splatter

slot 4 vent **5** niche, notch **6** groove, keyway **7** keyhole, opening, passage **8** aperture **10** pigeonhole

sloth 4 laze **5** idler **6** acedia, apathy, idling, lazing, loafer, slouch, torpor **7** goof-off, languor, loafing, slacker **8** idleness, laziness, lethargy **9** heaviness, indolence, lassitude, lazybones, torpidity **11** couch potato **12** listlessness, sluggishness **13** shiftlessness

slothful 4 idle, lazy **8** fainéant, indolent **9** shiftless

slouch 3 bum, oaf, sag **4** laze, loaf, loll, lout, mope, slug **5** droop, idler, sloth, slump, stoop **6** loafer, loiter, lounge **7** saunter, shamble, shuffle **8** fainéant, slugabed, sluggard **9** do-nothing, lazybones

slough 3 bog, fen 4 cast, mire, molt, quag, shed, sump 5 inlet, marsh, scrap, swamp 6 morass, reject 7 discard 8 jettison, quagmire, throw out 9 backwater, marshland, swampland, throw away

Slovakia *capital:* 10 Bratislava *city:* 6 Kosice *monetary unit:* 6 koruna *mountain range:* 10 Carpathian *neighbor:* 6 Poland 7 Austria, Hungary, Ukraine 13 Czech Republic *river:* 3 Váh 4 Hron 6 Danube, Morava

Slovenia *capital:* 9 Ljubljana *city:* 7 Maribor *monetary unit:* 5 tolar *neighbor:* 5 Italy 7 Austria, Croatia, Hungary *part of:* 7 Balkans *peninsula:* 6 Balkan

slovenly 5 dingy, messy, mussy, seedy, slack 6 frowsy, frowzy, grubby, grungy, scuzzy, shabby, skanky, sleazy, sloppy, untidy 7 squalid, unkempt 8 careless, slapdash, slipshod 10 bedraggled, slatternly

slow 4 late, poky 5 brake, check, lento, tardy 6 adagio, hinder, impede, leaden, retard, torpid 7 halting, lagging, slacken 8 dilatory, dragging, plodding, sluggish, stagnant 9 leisurely, snaillike, unhurried 10 decelerate, snail-paced, straggling

slowpoke 5 snail 6 lagger 7 dawdler, laggard 8 lingerer, loiterer 9 straggler

sludge 3 mud 4 crud, gunk, mire, muck, ooze, slop 5 slime 6 sewage 8 sediment

slug 3 bum, hit, nip, tot 4 bash, belt, dram, drop, jolt, shot, slam, swat 5 blast, clout, idler, larva, pound, punch, smack, smash, snail, snort, thump 6 buffet, loafer, slouch, thwack, wallop 7 clobber, goof-off, slacker 8 fainéant, toothful 9 do-nothing, lazybones 11 couch potato *genus:* 5 Limax

slugfest 4 bout 5 brawl, set-to 6 rumble 8 dogfight 10 donnybrook, prizefight

sluggard 3 bum 5 idler 6 loafer, slouch 7 dawdler, goof-off, laggard, shirker, slacker 8 deadbeat, fainéant, slowpoke, slugabed 9 do-nothing, goldbrick, lazybones

slugger 5 boxer 6 batter, hitter 7 palooka

sluggish 4 lazy, logy, slow 5 inert, slack 6 draggy, leaden, stupid, torpid 7 lumpish 8 dragging, indolent, listless, slothful 9 apathetic, lethargic

sluice 4 duct, flow, gush, pour, race, wash 5 flush, surge 6 trough 7 channel 8 spillway 9 floodgate

slum 6 ghetto 7 skid row

slumber 3 nap 4 doze 5 sleep 6 catnap, drowse, snooze, stupor, torpor 8 dor-

mancy, hebetude, lethargy 9 lassitude, torpidity

slumberous see SLEEPY

slumgullion 4 stew 6 burgoo, ragout 7 goulash

slump 3 dip, sag 4 drop, fall, flag, funk, loll, sink, slip 5 droop, hunch, slide 6 slouch, trough 7 decline, drop off, falloff 8 collapse, downturn 9 downslide, downswing, downtrend, recession 10 depression, stagnation

slur 4 blot, blur, lisp, onus, slam, spot 5 brand, knock, libel, odium, smear, stain 6 befoul, defame, insult, malign, stigma, vilify 7 blacken, calumny, obloquy, obscure, slander, spatter, traduce 8 black eye, brickbat, innuendo, tear down 9 aspersion, bespatter, denigrate, discredit, disparage 10 accusation, calumniate

slurp 3 lap 4 gulp, suck 5 lap up, swill 6 guzzle

slush 3 mud 4 mire, muck, slop 6 drivel 8 schmaltz

sly 4 foxy, wily 5 cagey, saucy, shady, slick 6 artful, clever, crafty, shifty, shrewd, smooth, sneaky, subtle, tricky 7 cunning, devious, furtive, roguish, vulpine 8 guileful, scheming, slippery, stealthy 9 designing, insidious, underhand 11 mischievous, underhanded

slyboots see SCAMP

slyness 4 wile 5 guile 7 cunning 8 caginess, foxiness, wiliness 9 canniness 10 craftiness

smack 3 bat, bop, box 4 bang, bash, belt, biff, blow, buss, chop, clip, cuff, dash, hint, kiss, peck, reek, slam, slap, sock, tang, whop 5 clout, crack, plumb, punch, right, savor, smell, spank, stink, taste, tinge, trace, whack 6 buffet, heroin, relish, smooch, square, strike, thwack 7 clobber, soupçon

smack-dab 4 bang, just 5 plumb, right 7 exactly 8 squarely 9 perfectly, precisely

small 3 wee 4 mean, mini, puny, tiny 5 bitty, dinky, dwarf, micro, minor, petty, runty, short, teeny 6 bantam, little, meager, meagre, minute, monkey, narrow, paltry, petite, slight, teensy 7 cramped, stunted, trivial 8 picayune, piddling, pint-size, trifling 9 miniature, minuscule, pint-sized 10 diminutive, negligible, undersized 11 ineffectual, unimportant *combining form:* 4 micr, mini 5 micro

small fry 4 kids, tots 8 children 10 youngsters

small-minded 4 mean 5 petty 6 narrow 7 bigoted 9 hidebound, illiberal, parochial 10 brassbound, intolerant, provincial

smallpox 7 variola

small talk 4 chat 6 banter 7 chatter, palaver, prattle 8 badinage, chitchat, raillery, repartee 10 persiflage

small-time 5 minor, petty 6 paltry, two-bit 7 trivial 8 picayune, piddling, trifling 10 bush-league, negligible, shoestring 11 minor-league, unimportant 13 insignificant

smalt 4 blue

smarmy 4 glib, oily 5 slick 6 sleazy 7 buttery, fawning, fulsome 8 unctuous 10 obsequious, oleaginous 12 ingratiating

smart 3 apt 4 ache, chic, keen 5 acute, alert, canny, fresh, natty, quick, sassy, saucy, sharp, slick, sting, swank, throb 6 brainy, bright, cheeky, clever, dapper, shrewd, spruce, suffer 7 dashing, stylish 8 impudent 11 fashionable, intelligent, quick-witted, ready-witted, sharp-witted

smart aleck 7 show-off, wise guy 8 wiseacre 9 know-it-all 11 wisecracker, wisenheimer

smart-alecky 4 wise 5 fresh, sassy, saucy 6 cheeky 8 impudent, insolent 9 bold-faced 11 impertinent

smart set 5 elect, elite 6 bon ton, gentry 7 in crowd, quality, society, who's who 9 beau monde, haut monde 10 blue bloods, upper crust 11 aristocracy, Four Hundred, high society

smarty-pants 7 wise guy 9 know-it-all, swellhead 11 wisenheimer

smash 3 hit, jar 4 bang, bash, belt, blow, boom, clap, jolt, raze, ruin, slam, slug, sock, wham, whop 5 blast, burst, clash, crack, crash, crush, pound, shock, whack, wreck 6 batter, impact, pileup, shiver, wallop 7 clobber, crack-up, debacle, destroy, shatter, smashup, success 8 collapse, decimate, demolish, fragment, knockout, overhand, splinter, tear down 9 breakdown, collision, pulverize, sensation, succès fou 10 annihilate 12 disintegrate

smashup 5 crash, wreck 6 fiasco, pileup 7 crack-up, debacle 8 accident, collapse, disaster 9 breakdown, collision

smattering 3 few 7 handful 10 sprinkling

smear 3 dab, tar 4 beat, coat, daub, drub, lick, slur, soil, whip 5 cover, libel, stain, sully, taint 6 befoul, defame, defile, malign, smirch, smudge, spread, thrash, vilify 7 asperse, blacken, calumny, plaster, shellac, slander, tarnish, traduce 8 besmirch 9 bespatter, denigrate 10 calumniate

smell 4 funk, nose, odor, reek 5 aroma, scent, sense, smack, sniff, snuff, stink, trace, whiff 6 detect, stench 7 bouquet, perfume 9 fragrance, redolence

smell, sense of 9 olfaction

smelly 4 rank 5 fetid, funky, reeky 6 foetid, putrid, rancid, stinky 7 noisome, reeking, stenchy 8 mephitic, stinking 10 malodorous

smelt 4 flux, fuse, slag 6 reduce, refine, tomcod 8 sparling 9 sand lance, whitebait

smidgen see PARTICLE

smile 4 beam, grin 5 smirk 6 simper

smirch see SMUDGE

smirk 4 grin, leer 5 fleer, sneer 6 simper 7 grimace

smite 3 hit 4 belt, kill, sock 5 clout, whack 6 assail, attack, strike 7 afflict, assault, clobber, torment

smithereens 4 bits 6 pieces 9 fragments, particles

smitten 5 taken 6 hooked 8 besotted, enamored 9 enamoured, enchanted, entranced 10 captivated, enraptured, infatuated 11 intoxicated

smock 5 apron, dress, frock 8 pinafore

smoke 4 cure, fume 5 fumes, vapor 8 fastball, fumigate 9 cigarette

smoky 4 fumy, gray, hazy 5 murky, sooty 6 turbid 7 reeking 10 caliginous, smoldering

smolder 4 glow 5 churn 6 bubble, seethe, simmer 7 ferment 9 fulminate

smooch 4 buss, kiss, neck, peck 5 smack 8 osculate

smooth 4 easy, even, flat 5 fluid, flush, level, plane, sleek, slick, suave 6 facile, fluent, glassy, glossy, polish, urbane 7 cursive, flatten, flowing, running 8 glabrous, hairless, soothing, unbroken 10 effortless, unwrinkled

smooth-spoken 4 glib 6 fluent 8 eloquent 10 articulate 13 silver-tongued

smorgasbord 4 hash, olio 6 buffet, jumble, medley 7 farrago, mélange 8 mishmash, mixed bag, pastiche 9 potpourri 10 hodgepodge, miscellany, salmagundi 11 gallimaufry

smother 4 choke, douse, quell 6 hush up, muffle, quench, stifle 7 blanket, repress, squelch 8 inundate, restrain, suppress 9 overwhelm, suffocate 10 asphyxiate

smudge 3 dab 4 blot, blur, daub, foul, soil 5 dirty, smear, stain, sully, taint 6 bedaub, blotch, defile, smirch 7 begrime, besmear, blacken, blemish, splotch, tarnish 8 besmirch

smug 8 priggish 9 conceited 10 complacent 13 self-satisfied

smuggle 3 run 7 bootleg
smut 4 porn 5 filth 9 obscenity
11 pornography
smutty 4 blue, foul, lewd, racy 5 bawdy,
dirty, nasty, sooty 6 coarse, filthy,
risqué, vulgar 7 obscene, raunchy
8 indecent, off-color, prurient 9 salacious 12 pornographic, scatological
Smyrna 5 Izmir
snack 3 tea 4 bite, nosh, tapa 6 morsel,
nibble 11 refreshment
snaffle 3 bit, cop 4 lift 5 filch, pinch,
swipe 6 pilfer, pocket 7 purloin
snafu 5 botch, error, mix-up, snarl
6 bungle, foul up, mess up, muddle
7 chaotic, screwup 9 confusion
snag 3 nab 4 curb, grab, hook, nail, tear
5 catch, hitch 6 glitch, holdup, hurdle,
obtain, secure 7 capture 8 drawback,
obstacle 9 apprehend 10 impediment
11 obstruction
snail 5 whelk 6 limpet 7 mollusc, mollusk 8 escargot, ramshorn, slowpoke
9 gastropod 10 periwinkle
snake 3 boa 4 fink 5 crawl, creep, racer,
slide 6 python, writhe 7 hognose, serpent, slither 8 anaconda, ophidian,
undulate *poisonous:* 3 asp 5 adder,
cobra, coral, krait, mamba, viper
6 elapid, taipan 7 rattler 8 pit viper
10 bushmaster, copperhead, fer-de-
lance 11 cottonmouth 13 water moccasin
snakebird 6 darter 7 anhinga
snake-eater 8 mongoose
13 secretary bird
snakelike 7 sinuous 8 ophidian 10 serpentine
snakeroot 7 bugbane 10 wild ginger
11 blazing star
snakeweed 7 bistort 13 poison hemlock
snaky 7 sinuous, winding 8 flexuous,
tortuous 10 convoluted, meandering,
serpentine 11 anfractuous
snap 4 bang, bark 5 break, cinch, crack
6 breeze, picnic 7 crackle 8 duck soup,
kid stuff, pushover 10 child's play
snap back 6 revive 7 rebound, recover
10 convalesce, recuperate
snappy 4 edgy, fast, tart 5 brisk, hasty,
huffy, natty, quick, rapid, sharp, smart,
swank, swift, testy 6 lively, prompt,
speedy, touchy 7 dashing, stylish,
waspish 8 animated, petulant, vigorous
9 breakneck, fractious, irritable, vivacious
snare 3 bag 4 bait, hook, lure, trap
5 catch, decoy, tempt 6 come-on,
enmesh, entice, entrap, seduce, tangle
7 capture, catch up, chicane, embroil,
ensnare, ensnarl, involve, pitfall, tram-

mel 8 entangle, inveigle 9 chicanery,
deception 10 enticement, temptation
snarl 3 jam, web 4 bark, knot, maze,
mesh 5 chaos, growl, ravel, skein 6 jungle, morass, muddle, tangle 7 perplex
8 disarray, disorder, entangle, mishmash 9 confusion, labyrinth 10 com-
plexity, complicate 12 complication,
entanglement
snatch 3 bit, nab 4 grab, jerk, take, yank
5 catch, pluck, seize, swipe 6 abduct,
clutch, kidnap, wrench 8 fragment
snazzy 4 chic 5 fancy, gaudy, jazzy,
nobby, ritzy, sassy, sharp, smart, showy,
swank 6 chichi, classy, flashy, garish,
glitzy, jaunty, spiffy, swanky 7 elegant
sneak 3 cur, pad 4 lurk, slip, worm
5 crawl, creep, glide, mooch, prowl,
shirk, skulk, skunk, slide, slink, steal
6 covert, secret, tiptoe, weasel
7 furtive, gumshoe, slither, smuggle
8 hush-hush, slyboots, stealthy 9 pussyfoot, scoundrel 10 undercover 11 clandestine
sneaky 4 foxy 6 shifty, tricky 7 devious,
furtive 8 guileful, indirect, slippery,
stealthy 9 underhand 11 duplicitous,
underhanded
sneer 4 gibe, jeer 5 fleer, scoff, smirk
7 grimace, snigger
snicker 5 laugh 6 giggle, titter 7 chortle,
chuckle
snide 4 mean 5 nasty 8 spiteful 9 malicious 11 insinuating
sniff 4 jeer, nose 5 scent, scoff, smell,
snoop 6 inhale
sniffy 4 smug 5 aloof, lofty 6 lordly,
snooty, uppity 7 haughty, pompous,
stuck-up 8 scornful, superior 10 disdainful, hoity-toity 12 contemptuous,
supercilious
snifter 3 nip, sip, tot 4 dram, drop, jolt,
shot, slug 5 glass, snort 6 finger, goblet
snip 3 bit, cut 4 clip, crop, trim 5 notch,
scrap 8 fragment
snipe 4 carp 9 sandpiper
sniper 6 gunman, killer 7 shooter
8 marksman, rifleman 12 sharpshooter
snippety see SNIPPY
snippy 4 curt 5 bluff, blunt, brief, gruff,
short, terse 6 abrupt, crusty 7 brusque
8 snappish
snit 3 fit 4 flap, fume, huff, stew 5 panic,
pique, sweat, tizzy 6 dither, frenzy,
lather, pother, swivet 10 conniption
snitch 3 cop, nip, rat 4 beak, fink, hook,
lift, palm, sing, tell 5 filch, peach,
pinch, spill, steal, swipe 6 inform, pilfer, pocket, squeal, tattle 7 purloin, rat
fink, tattler, tipster 8 betrayer,
informer, squealer 11 stool pigeon

snivel 3 sob **4** weep **5** cower, whine **6** cringe, whinge **7** blubber, snuffle, whimper

snob 5 snoot **6** poseur **7** parvenu

snobbish 6 snooty, uppity **7** haughty, high-hat, stuck-up **10** hoity-toity **11** patronizing, pretentious **12** supercilious **13** condescending

snook 5 cobia **6** robalo **12** sergeant fish

snooker 3 con **4** dupe, fool, hoax, pool **5** trick **6** delude **7** beguile, deceive, defraud **8** flimflam, hoodwink **9** bamboozle **11** hornswoggle

snoop 3 pry, spy **4** nose, peek, peep, peer, poke **5** prier, pryer **6** ferret, meddle, sleuth **7** gumshoe, intrude, meddler **8** busybody, quidnunc **9** detective, inspector, interfere **10** rubberneck

snooper 3 spy **9** detective, inspector **12** investigator

snoopy 4 nosy **6** prying **7** curious **8** meddling **9** intrusive **10** meddlesome **11** inquisitive

snoot see SNOUT

snooty see SNOBBISH

snooze 3 kip, nap **4** doze **5** sleep **6** catnap, drowse, nod off, siesta **7** drop off, slumber **10** forty winks

snore 8 rhonchus

snort 3 nip, tot **4** dram, drop, jolt, shot, slug **5** scoff, snarl **6** exhale, inhale **7** snifter

snout 4 beak, nose **6** muzzle **9** proboscis

snow *glacial:* **4** firn, névé *melted:* **5** slush *pellet:* **7** graupel *ridge:* **8** sastruga

snow apple 8 mushroom

snowball 5 mount, run up **6** expand **7** augment, burgeon, explode, inflate **8** increase, multiply, mushroom, viburnum **10** accumulate **11** proliferate

snowbird 5 finch, junco **6** thrush **7** bunting **9** fieldfare, ivory gull

Snow-Bound author 8 Whittier (John Greenleaf)

snow finch 9 brambling

snow grouse 9 ptarmigan

snow leopard 5 ounce

Snow Leopard author 11 Matthiessen (Peter)

snowstorm 8 blizzard

snub 3 cut **4** shun **5** blunt, scorn, spite, spurn **6** rebuff, rebuke, slight, stubby **7** put down **9** ostracize, repudiate **12** cold-shoulder

snuff 3 ice, off **4** kill, nose **5** pinch, scent, smell **6** murder, rappee **7** execute **10** extinguish **11** exterminate

snug 4 cozy, neat, taut, tidy, trim **5** comfy, cushy, tight **6** burrow, cuddle, nestle, nuzzle, secure **7** orderly **9** sheltered, shipshape **11** comfortable

snuggle 5 spoon **6** burrow, cuddle, curl up, huddle, nestle, nuzzle

so 3 sae **4** ergo, then, thus **5** hence **6** indeed **9** similarly, therefore **11** accordingly **12** consequently

soak 3 sot, wet **4** bilk, clip, lush, skin, swig, wino **5** douse, drink, gouge, imbue, souse, steep **6** boozer, drench, fleece, infuse, seethe **7** drinker, guzzler, immerse **8** drunkard, permeate, saturate, submerge **9** alcoholic, penetrate **10** boozehound, impregnate, overcharge *flax:* **3** ret

soap 4 suds **6** stroke **7** flatter, wheedle **8** blandish, butter up, inveigle **9** sweet-talk *hard:* **7** castile *ingredient:* **3** lye

soapbox 4 dais **6** podium **7** rostrum **8** hustings, platform, scaffold

soap plant 5 amole

soapstone 8 steatite

soapwort 7 cowherd **11** bouncing bet

soar 3 fly **4** lift, rise **5** arise, climb, glide, hover, mount, shoot **6** ascend, rocket **7** shoot up **8** increase **9** skyrocket

sob 3 cry **4** bawl, blub, wail, weep **7** blubber, whimper

sober 4 calm, cool **5** grave, staid **6** low-key, proper, sedate, serene, solemn **7** austere, earnest, serious, subdued **8** composed, decorous, low-keyed, moderate, rational, reserved **9** abstinent, collected, practical, pragmatic, realistic, temperate **10** abstaining, abstemious, controlled, forbearing, hardheaded, no-nonsense, reasonable, restrained **11** disciplined, down-to-earth **12** matter-of-fact **13** imperturbable, self-possessed, unimpassioned

sobriety 7 gravity **10** abstinence, continence, sedateness, temperance **11** seriousness

sobriquet 3 tag **5** alias **6** byname **7** epithet, moniker **8** cognomen, nickname **10** hypocorism

so-called 6 formal **7** alleged, nominal, titular **8** supposed **9** pretended, professed, purported **10** ostensible, self-styled

soccer *cup:* **5** World *official:* **7** referee **8** linesman *player:* **6** booter, goalie, kicker, winger **7** forward, link man, striker, sweeper **8** defender, fullback, halfback **10** goalkeeper *star:* **4** Hamm (Mia), Pelé **5** Akers (Michelle) **7** Beckham (David), Ronaldo **8** Maradona (Diego) **11** Beckenbauer (Franz) *term:* **3** net **4** boot, chip, kick, trap **6** corner, header, tackle, volley **7** dribble, kickoff, throw-in **8** back-heel, free kick, goal kick, goal line **9** touchline **10** center spot, corner flag, corner kick

11 dropped ball, halfway line, penalty kick, penalty spot

sociable 5 close **6** genial **7** affable, amiable, cordial **8** familiar, gracious **9** clubbable, congenial, convivial **10** gregarious, hospitable **11** good-natured

social 5 civic, civil **8** communal **9** clubbable, convivial **10** collective, gregarious, hospitable **11** extroverted **13** companionable *class:* **5** caste

Social Contract author 8 Rousseau (Jean-Jacques)

socialist *American:* **4** Debs (Eugene) **6** Ripley (George), Thomas (Norman) *British:* **4** Owen (Robert, Robert Dale), Webb (Beatrice, Sidney) **6** Morris (William) *French:* **7** Fourier (Charles), Viviani (René) **10** Saint-Simon (Henri de) *German:* **4** Marx (Karl) **6** Engels (Friedrich) **9** Luxemburg (Rosa) **10** Liebknecht (Wilhelm)

socialize 3 mix **5** party **6** hobnob, mingle **7** consort **9** associate **10** fraternize

social worker 4 Riis (Jacob), Wald (Lillian D.) **6** Addams (Jane) **7** Alinsky (Saul), Lathrop (Julia C.)

society 4 club **5** elite, guild **6** gentry, league, people, public **7** company, quality, who's who **8** populace, sodality **9** beau monde, community, haut monde **10** fellowship, fraternity, upper class, upper crust **11** aristocracy, association, brotherhood **13** companionship

sociologist *American:* **4** Bell (Daniel), Ward (Lester Frank) **5** Balch (Emily Green), Whyte (William H.) **6** Du Bois (W. E. B.), Glazer (Nathan), Sumner (William Graham) **7** Johnson (Charles Spurgeon), Riesman (David) *English:* **7** Spencer (Herbert) *French:* **8** Durkheim (Emile) *German:* **5** Weber (Max) *Italian:* **6** Pareto (Vilfredo) *Swedish:* **6** Myrdal (Alva, Gunnar)

sock 3 bop, box, hit **4** bash, belt, blow, chop, cuff, ding, slap, slog **5** clout, punch, smack, smash, whack **6** argyle, buffet, strike, thwack **8** stocking

sock away 4 bank, save, stow **5** cache, hoard, lay by, put by, stash **8** lay aside

socks 4 hose **7** hosiery

Socrates *birthplace:* **6** Athens *poison:* **7** hemlock *pupil:* **5** Plato *wife:* **8** Xantippe **9** Xanthippe

Socratic 8 maieutic

sod 4 land, peat, turf **5** earth, grass **6** ground

soda 3 pop **4** cola **5** tonic **7** seltzer

sodality 4 club **5** guild, lodge, order, union **6** league **7** society **9** community **10** fellowship, fraternity **11** association, brotherhood

sodden 3 wet **5** soggy, soppy **6** soaked, soused **7** soaking, sopping **8** drenched, dripping **9** saturated **11** waterlogged, wringing-wet

Sodom and ___ 8 Gomorrah

sofa 5 couch, divan **7** ottoman **9** banquette, davenport

so far 3 yet **5** as yet, still **6** to date **7** till now **8** hitherto, until now **10** heretofore

Sofia native 6 Bulgar **9** Bulgarian

soft 4 cozy, easy, mild, snug **5** balmy, comfy, cushy, downy, faint, mushy, silky **6** doughy, flabby, gentle, low-key, pliant, satiny, silken, simple, smooth, spongy, tender **7** cottony, lenient, pillowy, pliable, squashy, squishy, subdued, velvety **8** cushiony, workable, yielding **9** malleable **11** comfortable

softcover 9 paperback

soften 4 ease, tame **5** abate, allay, blunt, relax **6** dampen, lessen, mellow, soothe, subdue, temper, weaken **7** assuage, lighten, mollify **8** diminish, enfeeble, mitigate, moderate, palliate, tone down, turn down **9** alleviate

soft hail 7 graupel

softhearted 4 kind, warm **6** humane, kindly, tender **7** lenient **10** responsive **11** sympathetic **13** compassionate

soft palate 5 velum

soft-pedal 4 mute **6** dampen, hush up, muffle, subdue **8** minimize, play down, suppress, tone down **9** underplay **11** deemphasize

soft-soap 3 con **4** coax **6** cajole, soothe, wangle **7** blarney, flatter, wheedle **8** blandish, butter up, inveigle **9** sweet-talk

soggy 3 wet **6** doughy, soaked, sodden **7** soaking, sopping **8** drenched, dripping **9** saturated **10** bedraggled **11** waterlogged

Sohrab and Rustum author 6 Arnold (Matthew)

soi-disant 7 alleged **8** putative, so-called, supposed **9** pretended, professed, purported **10** ostensible, self-styled

soil 3 mud, tar **4** daub, dirt, foul, land, loam, mess, muck, murk **5** dirty, earth, grime, muddy, smear, stain, sully, taint **6** defile, ground, smirch, smudge **7** blacken, country, pollute, tarnish **8** besmirch, discolor, homeland **10** fatherland, motherland, terra firma **11** contaminate *aggregate:* **3** ped *clay:* **5** gault *dark:* **9** chernozem *deposit:* **5** loess **7** eluvium *infertile:* **6** podzol *layer:* **4** gley, sola (plural) **5** solum *rich:* **6** hotbed *tropical:* **7** latosol

soiree 4 fete, gala **5** party **6** affair, social

7 shindig **8** function **9** festivity, reception **11** celebration **13** entertainment
sojourn 4 bide, stay, stop **5** abide, lodge, tarry, visit **6** linger **7** layover **8** stopover
Sol 3 sun **7** daystar, phoebus *horse:* **4** Eous **5** Ethon **9** Erythreos (see also HELIOS)
solace 5 allay, amuse, cheer **6** buck up **7** comfort, console, hearten **8** inspirit **10** condolence
solar disk 4 Aten, Aton
solarium 7 sunroom
solder 4 fuse, weld **5** braze
soldier 5 grunt, sepoy **7** dogface, draftee, fighter, private, recruit, trooper, veteran, warrior **8** bluecoat, doughboy, fusilier, rifleman **9** free lance, guerrilla, man-at-arms, mercenary **10** carabineer, carabinier, serviceman **11** condottiere, infantryman *ancient Greece:* **7** hoplite *British:* **5** Tommy **7** redcoat *cavalry:* **6** hussar **8** chasseur *Confederate:* **3** reb *French:* **5** poilu **6** Zouave *German:* **5** jerry *irregular:* **8** guerilla **9** guerrilla *Prussian:* **5** uhlan *Turkish:* **9** janissary
sole 3 one **4** lone, only **5** alone **6** bottom, single, unique **8** flatfish, singular **9** exclusive
solecism 4 goof, slip **5** boner, error, gaffe, lapse **6** misuse **7** blooper, blunder, faux pas, mistake **9** barbarism, indecorum, vulgarism **11** impropriety
solemn 5 grand, grave, sober, staid, stern **6** august, formal, ritual, sedate, somber, sombre **7** earnest, plenary, serious, stately, weighty **8** funereal, imposing, majestic **9** dignified **10** ceremonial, impressive, no-nonsense, sobersided **11** ceremonious, magnificent
solemnize 4 keep **5** bless, honor **6** hallow **7** dignify, observe **8** venerate **9** celebrate, ritualize **10** consecrate **11** commemorate
solicit 3 ask, beg **4** lure, tout, urge **5** apply **6** demand, drum up, entice **7** beseech, bespeak, canvass, entreat, implore, request **8** petition **9** importune **11** proposition, requisition
solicitor 6 jurist, lawyer, suitor **7** pleader **8** advocate, attorney **9** counselor
solicitous 4 avid, keen **5** eager, fussy **6** ardent, tender **7** anxious, careful, devoted, fearful, finicky, worried **8** rigorous **9** assiduous, attentive, concerned, impatient **10** fastidious, meticulous, scrupulous **11** considerate, punctilious, sympathetic **12** apprehensive **13** conscientious
solicitude 4 care, heed **5** qualm, worry **6** unease **7** anxiety, concern, scruple **9** attention, vigilance **10** uneasiness

11 compunction **12** watchfulness **13** consideration
solid 4 firm, hard **5** dense, sound, valid **6** cogent, secure, stable, sturdy, united **7** compact **8** reliable, unbroken **9** steadfast, unanimous, undivided **10** convincing **11** substantial
solidarity 5 union, unity **6** esprit **7** concord, oneness **8** cohesion **9** integrity **10** singleness **12** cohesiveness, togetherness **13** esprit de corps
solidify 3 dry, fix, gel, set **4** cake, jell **6** freeze, harden, secure **7** compact, congeal **8** compress, contract, indurate **11** consolidate
solitary 4 lone, lorn, only, solo **5** alone **6** hermit, lonely, single, unique **7** recluse **8** derelict, deserted, desolate, eremitic, forsaken, isolated, lonesome, separate, singular **9** abandoned, reclusive, withdrawn **10** antisocial, particular, unsociable **11** standoffish **12** misanthropic **13** unaccompanied
solitude 7 privacy **8** loneness **9** aloneness, isolation, seclusion **10** detachment, loneliness, quarantine, retirement, withdrawal **11** confinement **12** separateness
solo 4 lone **5** alone **6** single **7** unaided **8** solitary **13** independently, unaccompanied
Solomon *brother:* **8** Adonijah *daughter:* **7** Taphath **8** Basemath *father:* **5** David *kingdom:* **6** Israel *mother:* **9** Bathsheba *son, successor:* **8** Rehoboam *victim:* **4** Joab **8** Adonijah
Solomon Islands *capital:* **7** Honiara *ethnic group:* **10** Melanesian *island:* **7** Florida, Malaita, Rennell **8** Choiseul **11** Guadalcanal, Santa Isabel **12** San Cristóbal *language:* **5** Pijin **7** English *monetary unit:* **6** dollar
solon 8 lawgiver **10** legislator
so long 4 by-by, ciao, ta-ta **5** adieu, adios **6** bye-bye **7** cheerio, goodbye, toodles **8** farewell, Godspeed, toodle-oo
solution 6 answer, result *salt:* **6** saline
solve 3 fix **5** break, crack **6** decode, reveal, settle **7** clarify, clear up, dope out, explain, unravel, work out **8** construe, decipher, unriddle, untangle **9** elucidate, figure out, interpret, puzzle out **11** disentangle
Somalia *capital:* **9** Mogadishu *gulf:* **4** Aden *language:* **6** Arabic, Somali *location:* **12** Horn of Africa *monetary unit:* **8** shilling *neighbor:* **5** Kenya **8** Djibouti, Ethiopia
somatic 6 bodily, carnal **7** fleshly **8** corporal, parietal, physical **9** corporeal
somber 3 dim **4** dark, drab, dull, grim

5 bleak, dusky, grave, heavy, murky, staid 6 dismal, dreary, gloomy, sedate, solemn 7 doleful, joyless, obscure, serious, weighty 8 funereal, mournful 9 tenebrous 10 caliginous, depressing, depressive, lugubrious, melancholy, sepulchral, sobersided, tenebrific 11 dispiriting

somewhat 5 quite 6 fairly, kind of, rather, sort of 7 a little 8 slightly 9 partially, tolerably 10 moderately

sommelier's offering 4 wine

somniferous see SLEEPY

somnolent see SLEEPY

Somnus *brother:* 4 Mors *god of:* 5 sleep *mother:* 3 Nox

son *French:* 4 fils *Italian:* 6 figlio *Spanish:* 4 hijo

song 3 air, lay 4 aria, glee, hymn, lied, tune 5 carol, chant, ditty, lyric, paean 6 ballad, melody, number 7 chanson 8 madrigal *biblical:* 8 canticle *boat:* 9 barcarole 10 barcarolle *French:* 7 chanson *German:* 4 lied 6 lieder (plural) *lamentation:* 5 dirge 8 threnode, threnody *medieval:* 8 sirvente 9 sirventes *morning:* 6 aubade *of joy:* 5 paean *operatic:* 4 aria 8 cavatina 9 cabaletta *Portuguese:* 4 fado *sacred:* 5 psalm *sailor's:* 6 chanty, shanty 7 chantey *short:* 8 canzonet *wedding:* 8 hymeneal

song and dance 5 pitch, spiel

songbird see at BIRD

Song of Myself author 7 Whitman (Walt)

Song of Solomon 9 Canticles

songwriter 8 composer, lyricist

Sonja ___ 5 Henie

Sonnambula composer 7 Bellini (Vincenzo)

sonnet *developer:* 8 Petrarch *part:* 5 octet 6 octave, sestet

sonorous 7 ringing, vibrant 8 resonant 10 oratorical, resounding, rhetorical 11 declamatory 12 magniloquent 13 grandiloquent

Sontag novel 9 In America 12 Volcano Lover (The)

soon 4 anon 6 any day, pronto 7 betimes, quickly, rapidly, shortly 8 directly, promptly, speedily 9 forthwith, presently, right away 10 before long

Sooner State 8 Oklahoma

soothe 4 balm, calm, ease, hush, lull 5 allay, quiet, salve, still 6 becalm, pacify, settle, solace, subdue 7 appease, assuage, comfort, compose, console, massage, mollify, placate, relieve 8 calm down, reassure 9 alleviate 10 conciliate, propitiate 11 tranquilize

soothsay 5 augur 8 prophesy 9 adumbrate 10 vaticinate 13 prognosticate

soothsayer 4 seer 5 sibyl 6 oracle 7 diviner, prophet 8 foreseer 9 predictor 10 forecaster, foreteller *ancient Roman:* 5 augur 6 auspex 8 haruspex *blind:* 8 Tiresias (see also PROPHET)

sop 3 wet 4 gift, soak 5 bribe, douse, goody, souse, steep 6 deluge, drench, reward, seethe 7 douceur 8 gratuity, saturate, waterlog 9 incentive, lagniappe, sweetener 10 enticement

sophism see SOPHISTRY

sophistic 5 false, phony 7 invalid, seeming, unsound 8 delusive, illusory, spurious 9 beguiling, casuistic, deceptive, plausible 10 fallacious, fraudulent, misleading, ostensible

sophisticated 5 blasé, jaded, suave 6 smooth, svelte, urbane 7 complex, knowing, refined, worldly 8 cultured, involved, schooled, seasoned 9 Byzantine, elaborate, intricate, practiced 10 world-weary 11 complicated, experienced, worldly-wise 12 cosmopolitan

sophistry 9 casuistry 12 equivocation 13 dissimulation, prevarication

Sophocles play 4 Ajax 7 Electra 8 Antigone 10 Oedipus Rex

Sophonisba *brother:* 8 Hannibal *father:* 9 Hasdrubal *husband:* 6 Syphax

soporific 4 dozy 6 drowsy, opiate, sleepy 7 anodyne, calming, numbing 8 hypnotic, narcotic, sedative 9 calmative, deadening, somnolent 10 anesthetic, slumberous 11 somniferous 12 somnifacient 13 tranquilizing

soprano *American:* 4 Pons (Lily) 5 Costa (Mary), Gluck (Alma), Moffo (Anna), Moore (Grace), Price (Leontyne), Sills (Beverly) 6 Arroyo (Martina), Battle (Kathleen), Callas (Maria), Curtin (Phyllis), Donath (Helen), Farrar (Geraldine), Garden (Mary), Munsel (Patrice), Norman (Jessye), Peters (Roberta), Piazza (Marguerite), Resnik (Regina) 7 Farrell (Eileen), Fleming (Renée), Kirsten (Dorothy), Stevens (Risë), Traubel (Helen) 8 Ponselle (Rosa) *Australian:* 5 Melba (Nellie) 10 Sutherland (Joan) *Austrian:* 4 Popp (Lucia) 7 Rysanek (Leonie) 8 Sembrich (Marcella) *Canadian:* 7 Stratas (Teresa) *French:* 7 Crespin (Régine) *German:* 6 Leider (Frida) 7 Lehmann (Lilli, Lotte) 11 Schwarzkopf (Elisabeth) *Italian:* 5 Freni (Mirella), Grisi (Giuditta, Giulia), Patti (Adelina) 6 Scotto (Renata) 7 Bartoli (Cecilia), Tebaldi (Renata) 10 Tetrazzini (Luisa) 11 Ricciarelli (Katia) *Korean:* 6 Sumi Jo *Mexican:*

8 Cruz-Romo (Gilda) *New Zealand:* 8 Te Kanawa (Kiri) *Norwegian:* 8 Flagstad (Kirsten) *Romanian:* 8 Cotrubas (Ileana) *Spanish:* 7 Caballé (Montserrat) 8 Berganza (Teresa) 12 de los Angeles (Victoria) *Swedish:* 4 Lind (Jenny) 7 Nilsson (Birgit) (see also MEZZO-SOPRANO)

sorcerer 4 mage 5 magus 6 wizard 7 warlock 8 conjurer, conjuror, magician 9 enchanter 11 necromancer, thaumaturge 13 thaumaturgist

sorceress 3 hag, hex 5 Circe, witch

sorcery 5 magic 8 diablery, wizardry 9 conjuring 10 necromancy, witchcraft 11 bewitchment, enchantment, thaumaturgy *West Indian:* 5 obeah

sordid 3 low 4 base, foul, mean, vile 5 dirty, nasty, seamy, shady, venal 6 blowsy, blowzy, filthy, frowsy, frowzy, grubby, scurvy, shabby, sleazy 7 ignoble, low-down, squalid, unclean 8 degraded, shameful, wretched 9 loathsome, mercenary 10 despicable, scandalous, slatternly 11 disgraceful 12 contemptible, disreputable 13 reprehensible

sore 3 raw 4 boil 5 angry, irked, ulcer, upset, vexed 6 aching, bitter, canker, peeved, tender 7 abscess, chancre, hurting, painful 8 inflamed, smarting 9 chilblain, irritated, rancorous, resentful, sensitive 10 affliction

sorehead 4 crab 5 grump 6 griper, grouch 7 grouser 8 grumbler, sourpuss 10 bellyacher, complainer, crosspatch, malcontent

sorrel 4 dock 8 chestnut, sourwood

sorrow 3 rue, sob, woe 4 moan, ruth 5 dolor, grief, mourn 6 grieve, lament, misery, regret 7 anguish, remorse, sadness 8 distress, grieving, mourning 9 dejection, heartache, suffering 10 affliction, heartbreak, melancholy 11 lamentation, unhappiness 12 mournfulness

sorrowful 3 sad 6 rueful, triste, woeful 7 doleful, forlorn, piteous, ruthful, unhappy 8 dolorous, downcast, grieving, mournful, tristful, wretched 9 afflicted, miserable, plaintive, woebegone 10 lamentable, lugubrious, melancholy 11 heartbroken 12 disconsolate

sorry 3 bad, sad 4 mean, poor 5 cheap 6 cheesy, paltry, scummy, scurvy, shabby, shoddy 7 scruffy, unhappy 8 beggarly, contrite, mournful, penitent, pitiable, saddened, trifling, wretched 9 miserable, regretful, repentant 10 apologetic, despicable, inadequate, melancholy, remorseful 11 disgraceful,

penitential 12 contemptible, heavyhearted

sort 3 ilk, lot, set 4 comb, cull, kind, pick, sift, type 5 class, order 6 choose, screen, select, stripe, winnow 7 arrange, catalog, species, variety 8 classify, separate 9 catalogue, character 10 categorize, pigeonhole

sortie 4 dash, raid 5 foray, sally 7 assault, mission 9 excursion 10 expedition

sortilege 6 augury 7 sorcery 8 divining, witchery 10 divination, necromancy, witchcraft 11 thaumaturgy

so-so 4 fair, okay 6 decent, enough, fairly, medium, rather 7 average, fairish 8 adequate, mediocre, middling, moderate, passable, passably 9 tolerably 10 moderately 11 indifferent 12 run-of-the-mill

sot 4 lush, wino 5 drunk, souse 6 bibber, boozer 7 guzzler, tippler, tosspot 8 drunkard 9 alcoholic, inebriate 10 boozehound

sotto voce 3 low 5 aside 6 softly 7 faintly, mutedly, quietly 9 privately

souchong 3 tea

sough 4 sigh 7 suspire, whisper

soul 4 pith 5 anima, being, heart, stuff 6 animus, breast, marrow, pneuma, psyche, spirit 7 essence 9 élan vital, substance 10 conscience, vital force 12 quintessence *combining form:* 5 psych 6 psycho

soulful 6 moving, tender 7 emotive, fervent 8 poignant, stirring, touching 9 affecting, emotional 11 impassioned, sentimental

soul singer 4 Gaye (Marvin) 5 Bland (Bobby), Brown (James), Cooke (Sam), Flack (Roberta), Green (Al), Hayes (Isaac) 6 Butler (Jerry), Knight (Gladys), Sledge (Percy) 7 Charles (Ray), Pickett (Wilson), Redding (Otis) 8 Franklin (Aretha), Mayfield (Curtis)

sound 3 fit 4 firm, hale, safe, sane 5 audio, legit, noise, plumb, probe, right, sober, solid, valid, whole 6 cogent, fathom, intact, secure, stable, sturdy, unhurt 7 correct, earshot, healthy, logical, prudent 8 rational, reliable, sensible, unharmed 9 judicious, resonance, undamaged, vibration, wholesome 10 convincing, reasonable 11 well-founded 12 satisfactory, well-grounded 13 reverberation *combining form:* 3 son 4 phon, soni, sono 5 audio, audit, phone, phony 6 audito, phonia *high-pitched:* 4 ping, ting *pleasant:* 7 euphony *quality:* 6 timbre *repeating:* 7 rat-a-tat 8 rataplan 10 rat-a-tat-tat *science:* 6 sonics 7 phonics 9 acoustics

Sound *Alaska:* **5** Cross *Antarctica:*
7 McMurdo *Australia:* **4** King **5** Broad
Bahamas: **5** Exuma *Canada:* **4** Howe
6 Nansen *Connecticut-New York:* **10** Long
Island *English Channel:* **8** Plymouth
Georgia: **8** Altamaha *Greenland:* **5** Smith
Gulf of Mexico: **8** Suwannee **11** Mississippi *Massachusetts:* **8** Vineyard **9** Nantucket *New England:* **11** Block Island
North Carolina: **4** Core **5** Bogue **7** Pamli-
co, Roanoke **9** Albemarle, Currituck
Northwest Territories: **4** Peel **8** Melville
9 Lancaster **12** Prince Albert *Norwegian
Sea:* **8** Scoresby *Ontario:* **4** Owen *Scotland:* **3** Hoy **4** Jura, Mull **5** Inner *Spitsbergen:* **4** Bell *Washington:* **5** Puget
Sound and the Fury, The *author:*
8 Faulkner (William) *character:* **5** Benjy
(Compson), Caddy (Compson), Jason
(Compson) **6** Dilsey **7** Quentin (Compson)
soundness 6 health, sanity **7** balance
8 lucidity, prudence, security, solidity,
strength **9** integrity, stability **11** reliability **12** practicality
sound off 7 speak up **8** speak out
soup *beet:* **6** borsch **7** borscht *bowl:*
6 tureen *clear:* **5** broth **8** bouillon, consommé, julienne *cold:* **8** gazpacho
11 vichyssoise *curry:* **12** mulligatawny
okra: **5** gumbo *seafood:* **7** chowder *thick:*
5 gumbo, puree **6** bisque, burgoo *vegetable:* **10** minestrone
soupçon see PARTICLE
soupy 5 foggy, gooey, gushy, murky,
mushy **6** drippy, slushy, smoggy **7** cloying, maudlin, mawkish **8** cornball
9 schmaltzy **10** saccharine **11** sentimental, tear-jerking
sour 4 acid, dour, tart **5** acerb, acrid,
tangy, testy **6** acidic, bitter, crabby,
cranky, curdle, grumpy, morose, rancid, rotten, sullen, turned **7** acerbic,
grouchy, peevish, prickly, spoiled,
unhappy **8** embitter, vinegary **9** acidulous, fermented **12** disagreeable
source 4 font, root, well **5** basis, cause,
fount, model, onset, start **6** mother, origin, spring **7** dawning, genesis **8** begetter, fountain, wellhead **9** beginning,
inception, informant, precursor, prototype, reference, rootstock **10** antecedent, authorship, birthplace, derivation, originator, progenitor, provenance, wellspring **11** origination,
provenience **12** fountainhead
sourness 7 acidity **8** acerbity, asperity
sourpuss 4 crab **5** crank, grump
6 griper, grouch **7** grouser, killjoy
8 grumbler, sorehead **10** bellyacher,

complainer, crosspatch, curmudgeon
11 misanthrope
souse 3 dip, sop, sot **4** lush, soak, wino
5 binge, drown, steep **6** boozer, drench,
pickle, plunge, seethe **7** immerse
8 drunkard, inundate, marinate, preserve, saturate, submerge, submerse
9 alcoholic, immersion, inebriate
10 boozehound, intoxicate **11** dipsomaniac
soused 3 lit **4** high **5** drunk, lit up, oiled
6 bashed, blotto, bombed, juiced, potted, soaked, soused, stewed, stoned,
tanked, wasted, zonked **7** crocked,
drunken, pickled, pie-eyed, sloshed,
smashed, sottish **8** polluted **9** plastered
10 inebriated, liquored up **11** intoxicated
south *combining form:* **5** austr **6** austro
French: **3** sud *Spanish:* **3** sur
South Africa *capital:* **8** Cape Town, Pretoria **12** Bloemfontein *city:* **8** Durban
12 Johannesburg *desert:* **8** Kalahari
enclave: **7** Lesotho *grassland:* **4** veld
5 veldt *language:* **5** Bantu **7** English
9 Afrikaans *monetary unit:* **4** rand *mountain range:* **11** Drakensberg *neighbor:*
7 Namibia **8** Botswana **9** Swaziland,
Zimbabwe **10** Mozambique *plateau:*
5 Karoo **6** Karroo *river:* **6** Molopo,
Orange *settlers:* **5** Boers
South America *country:* **4** Peru **5** Chile
6 Brazil, Guyana **7** Bolivia, Ecuador,
Uruguay **8** Colombia, Paraguay, Suriname **9** Argentina, Venezuela *ethnic
group:* **6** Aymara, Creole, Indian **7** mestizo, mulatto, Quechua, Spanish
10 Amerindian, Portuguese *language:*
6 Aymara **7** Guaraní, Quechua, Spanish
10 Portuguese
South Carolina *capital:* **8** Columbia *city:*
10 Charleston, Greenville *college, university:* **7** Citadel, Clemson *fort:*
6 Sumter *island, island group:* **3** Sea
6 Edisto, Parris **10** Hilton Head *nickname:* **8** Palmetto (State) *river:* **6** Edisto,
Pee Dee, Santee **7** Tugaloo **8** Savannah
state bird: **12** Carolina wren *state flower:*
13 yellow jasmine *state tree:* **8** palmetto
South Dakota *capital:* **6** Pierre *city:*
9 Rapid City **10** Sioux Falls *mountain:*
6 Harney (Peak) **8** Rushmore **10** Black
Hills *nickname:* **6** Coyote (State) **10** Mt.
Rushmore (State) *park:* **8** Badlands,
Wind Cave *river:* **8** Missouri **11** Belle
Forche *state bird:* **18** ring-necked pheasant *state flower:* **12** pasqueflower *state
tree:* **6** spruce
southerly 7 austral
South-West Africa 7 Namibia
south wind see at WIND

souvenir 5 relic, token **6** trophy
7 memento **8** keepsake, memorial,
reminder **11** remembrance
sovereign 4 coin, czar, free, king, tsar
5 queen, regal, royal, ruler **6** kingly,
ruling **7** emperor, empress, highest,
monarch, regnant, supreme **8** absolute,
autarkic, autocrat, dominant, imperial,
kinglike, majestic **9** ascendant,
autarchic, monarchal, number one,
paramount, potentate **10** autonomous,
monarchial **11** independent, monarchical, predominant **12** self-governed
soviet 7 council **9** committee
sow 4 seed, toss **5** drill, fling, plant,
strew **7** bestrew, scatter **9** broadcast
11 disseminate
spa 5 baths, hydro, wells **6** hot tub,
resort, spring, waters **7** springs
13 watering place *Czech:* **6** Bilina
8 Karlsbad *English:* **4** Bath **6** Buxton
9 Harrogate *French:* **3** Dax **5** Evian *German:* **3** Ems **5** Baden **6** Bad Ems
9 Kissingen
space 3 gap **4** area, room **5** blank, scope
6 cavity, extent, spread, volume
7 breadth, expanse, stretch **8** capacity,
distance, interval, universe **9** amplitude, expansion
spaced-out 4 high **5** doped **6** stoned,
zonked **7** drugged **8** hopped-up,
turned on
spacious 3 big **4** vast, wide **5** ample,
large, roomy **7** immense **8** enormous,
extended **9** boundless, capacious, cavernous, expansive, extensive **10** commodious, voluminous
spade 3 dig **4** grub **5** dig up, scoop **6** dig
out, shovel **8** excavate
Spade, Sam 4 dick **6** shamus, sleuth
7 gumshoe **9** detective **10** private eye
creator: **7** Hammett (Dashiell) *novel:*
13 Maltese Falcon (The)
Spain *ancient name:* **8** Hispania *capital:*
6 Madrid *city:* **6** Málaga **7** Seville
8 Valencia, Zaragoza **9** Barcelona,
Saragossa *island group:* **6** Canary
8 Balearic *king:* **10** Juan Carlos *leader:*
6 Franco (Francisco) *monetary unit:*
4 euro *monetary unit, former:* **4** real
6 peseta *mountain:* **8** Mulhacén **11** Pico
de Aneto *mountain range:* **8** Pyrenees
neighbor: **6** France **8** Portugal *peninsula:*
7 Iberian *region:* **8** Valencia **9** Catalonia
river: **4** Ebro **12** Guadalquivir *sea:*
13 Mediterranean *strait:* **9** Gibraltar
spall 4 chip **5** flake **7** shaving **8** fragment
9 exfoliate
spam 8 junk mail
span 4 arch, term, time **5** cross, reach
6 extent, length, period, spread **7** compass, measure, stretch **8** duration, interval, lifetime, straddle, traverse
spangle 4 trim **5** flash, gleam **6** sequin
7 glitter, shimmer, sparkle, twinkle
9 coruscate **11** scintillate
Spaniard 9 Castilian
Spanish *boss:* **7** cacique *chaperone:*
6 duenna *combining form:* **7** hispano *dictator:* **8** caudillo *folksong:* **6** tonada
fortress: **7** alcazar *garrison:* **8** presidio
hors d'oeuvre: **4** tapa *inn:* **6** posada
mayor: **7** alcalde *national hero:* **3** Cid
(El) **5** El Cid *nobleman:* **7** grandee
operetta: **8** zarzuela *penal settlement:*
8 presidio *plain:* **5** llano, pampa *plantation:* **8** hacienda *princess:* **7** infanta
ranch: **5** finca **8** estancia *saint:*
7 Dominic **8** Ignatius *scarf:* **8** mantilla
shawl: **6** serape *title:* **3** don **4** doña
5 señor **6** señora **8** señorita *wine:* **4** sack
6 sherry
Spanish fly 9 cantharis
spank 4 cane, flog, lash, slap **5** smack
6 larrup, paddle, punish, thrash
7 scourge **8** chastise
spar 3 box, vie **4** pole **5** joust, stall **7** dispute, wrangle **8** longeron *ship's:*
4 boom, gaff, mast, yard **7** yardarm
8 bowsprit
spare 4 lank, lean, pity, save, slim
5 avoid, extra, gaunt, lanky **6** backup,
excess, excuse, exempt, let off, meager,
meagre, pardon, scanty, scrape, scrimp,
skimpy, skinny, slight, unused
7 absolve, relieve, reserve, scrawny,
scrimpy, surplus **8** leftover **10** additional **11** superfluous
sparing 4 bare, wary **5** canny, chary,
tight **6** frugal, meager, meagre, saving,
stingy **7** prudent, thrifty **9** provident
10 economical, restrained, unwasteful
11 tightfisted **12** parsimonious
spark 3 woo **5** court, ember, glint
6 foment, incite, kindle, set off **7** provoke, trigger **8** activate, touch off
9 instigate, scintilla
sparkle 4 zing **5** flash, gleam, glint, verve
7 glimmer, glisten, glitter, shimmer,
twinkle **8** vivacity **9** animation, coruscate **10** effervesce, liveliness **11** coruscation, scintillate **13** scintillation
sparkling 6 bubbly, lively **8** animated,
bubbling **9** brilliant **12** effervescent
Spark novel 11 Memento Mori **21** Prime
of Miss Jean Brodie (The)
sparse 4 rare, thin **5** scant **6** meager,
meagre, scanty, scarce, skimpy **7** limited, scrimpy **8** exiguous, sporadic,
uncommon **9** dispersed, scattered
10 inadequate, infrequent, occasional
12 insufficient

Sparta 10 Lacedaemon *country:* **7** Laconia *king:* **8** Leonidas *opponent:* **6** Athens

Spartacus *author:* **4** Fast (Howard) *slayer:* **7** Crassus

spasm 3 fit, tic **4** pang **5** burst, crick, throe **6** twitch **8** paroxysm **10** convulsion *muscular:* **6** clonus

spasmodic 5 jerky **6** fitful, spotty **7** erratic **8** sporadic **9** desultory, excitable **10** convulsive **12** intermittent

spat 3 row **4** flap, miff, tiff **5** fight, scene, scrap **6** bicker, gaiter, hassle, oyster **7** brabble, dispute, fall out, quarrel, rhubarb, wrangle **8** argument, outburst, squabble **10** falling-out **11** altercation

spate 4 flow, flux, gush, pour, rain, rush, tide **5** flood, river, spurt, surge **6** deluge, series, shower, stream **7** current, freshet, torrent **8** cataract, outburst, overflow **10** inundation, outpouring

spatter 4 slop, slur, spit **5** douse, fleck, plash, slosh, smear, spray, spurt, swash **6** befoul, defame, malign, splash, splosh, vilify **7** asperse, blacken, handful, slander, speckle, splurge, stipple, traduce **8** besmirch, sprinkle **9** denigrate, disparage

spawn 4 eggs, sire **5** beget, breed, brood, hatch, issue **6** create, father, parent **7** produce, product, progeny, provoke **8** engender, generate **9** offspring, originate, procreate, propagate, reproduce, stimulate

speak 3 gab, jaw, say, yak **4** blab, chat, chin, talk **5** blurt, drawl, mouth, orate, spiel, spout, utter, voice **6** assert, convey, intone, mumble, murmur, mutter, parley **7** address, declaim, declare, lecture, phonate, whisper **8** converse, dilate on, perorate, vocalize **9** discourse, enunciate, expatiate, hold forth, verbalize *confusedly:* **7** stammer, stutter **8** splutter *for:* **7** testify

speaker 5 voice **9** spokesman **10** mouthpiece **12** spokesperson

spear 3 gig **4** pike, spit **5** gouge, lance, spike **6** impale, pierce, skewer **7** harpoon, leister, trident **8** puncture, transfix **9** penetrate

special 4 rare **6** unique **7** express, notable, unusual **8** peculiar, uncommon **10** designated, individual, noteworthy, particular **11** distinctive, exceptional, outstanding

species 4 kind, sort, type **5** breed, class, order

specific 3 set **5** exact **6** strict, unique **7** express, limited, precise, special **8** clean-cut, clear-cut, definite, distinct,

especial, explicit **10** individual, particular **11** categorical, unambiguous

specify 3 fix, set **4** cite, list, name **6** detail **7** itemize, mention, pin down, tick off **8** instance, spell out **9** determine, enumerate, establish, inventory, stipulate **13** particularize

specimen 4 case, sort, type **6** sample **7** example, neotype, variety **8** exemplar, holotype, instance, sampling **12** illustration

specious 5 empty, false **6** hollow **8** spurious **9** casuistic, plausible, sophistic **10** misleading, ostensible **11** sophistical

speciousness 7 sophism **9** casuistry, sophistry

speck 3 bit, dot, jot **4** atom, iota, mite, mote, spot, tick, whit **5** crumb, fleck, grain, point, shred, trace **7** freckle, smidgen **8** molecule, particle, pinpoint

speckle 3 dot **4** spot **5** flake, fleck **6** dapple, pepper **7** stipple **8** sprinkle

spectacle 4 pomp, show **5** drama, sight **6** parade **7** display, pageant, panoply, tableau **10** exhibition, exposition **12** extravaganza

spectacular 5 stagy **7** amazing, pageant **8** dazzling, dramatic, striking, wondrous **9** marvelous, thrilling, wonderful **10** astounding, eye-popping, histrionic, miraculous, phenomenal, prodigious, staggering, stupefying, stupendous, theatrical **11** astonishing, sensational **12** extravaganza

spectator 5 gazer **6** viewer **7** watcher, witness **8** beholder, observer, onlooker **9** bystander **10** eyewitness

Spectator *author:* **6** Steele (Richard) **7** Addison (Joseph)

specter 5 ghost, shade **6** shadow, spirit, wraith **7** eidolon, phantom **8** phantasm, revenant, visitant **10** apparition

spectral 6 spooky **7** ghastly, ghostly, phantom **9** ghostlike, unearthly **10** shadowlike **11** disembodied, phantomlike

spectrum 5 ambit, gamut, range, scale, sweep **7** compass **8** diapason **9** continuum

speculate 4 muse **5** study, think, weigh **6** ponder, reason, review, wonder **7** reflect **8** cogitate, consider, meditate, ruminate, theorize **9** cerebrate **10** conjecture, deliberate **11** contemplate

speculation 5 guess, hunch **6** gamble, review, theory **7** surmise **9** brainwork **10** conjecture

speculative 7 curious, pensive **8** academic **10** thoughtful **11** conjectural, theoretical **12** hypothetical

speech 4 talk **5** idiom, spiel, voice

6 debate, homily, parley, sermon, tirade, tongue 7 address, dialect, diction, lecture, oration, palaver 8 dialogue, diatribe, harangue, language, parlance, rhetoric 9 discourse, monologue, utterance 10 allocution, expression, vernacular 11 declamation 12 articulation, disquisition, vocalization 13 verbalization *defect:* 4 lisp 7 stutter

speechcraft 7 oratory 8 rhetoric 9 elocution

speechless 3 mum 4 dumb, mute 6 silent 7 aphonic 10 dumbstruck, tongue-tied

speed 3 fly, run, zip 4 clip, gait, pace, race, rush, tear, whiz 5 chase, haste, hurry, tempo 6 barrel, burn up, career, hasten, hustle, whoosh 7 quicken 8 alacrity, celerity, dispatch, expedite, highball, legerity, momentum, rapidity, velocity 9 fleetness, quickness, swiftness 10 accelerate, cannonball, facilitate, promptness

speedway 5 track 8 turnpike 9 racetrack 10 racecourse

speedy 4 fast 5 brisk, fleet, hasty, quick, rapid, swift 6 nimble, prompt 8 headlong 9 breakneck 11 expeditious

spell 3 hex 4 bout, jinx, mojo, time, tour, turn 5 charm, hitch, shift, stint, throe, while 6 attack, period, streak, voodoo 7 relieve, stretch 11 conjuration, incantation

spellbind 3 hex 4 grip, vamp 5 charm 7 bewitch, catch up, enchant 8 enthrall, entrance 9 enrapture, fascinate, hypnotize, mesmerize

spelling 11 orthography *bad:* 10 cacography

spell out 7 clarify, explain, expound 8 construe, set forth 9 elucidate, explicate, interpret

spend 3 pay 4 blow, drop, pass 5 use up, waste 6 lavish, lay out, outlay 7 consume, exhaust, fork out, hand out, splurge 8 disburse, shell out, squander 9 dissipate, go through, throw away, while away 10 contribute, run through

spender 7 wastrel 8 prodigal 10 high roller, profligate, squanderer 11 scattergood

spendthrift see SPENDER

spent 4 shot 5 all in 6 effete, pooped, used-up, wasted 7 drained, worn-out 8 burnt out, consumed, depleted, washed-up 9 exhausted, washed-out

spew 4 gush, ooze 5 belch, eject, eruct, erupt, expel, exude, flood, heave, shoot, spray, vomit 6 irrupt, spit up, squirt 7 throw up, upchuck 8 disgorge

sphagnum 4 moss

sphere 3 orb 4 area, ball, star, turf, zone 5 arena, field, globe, range, realm, round, scope 6 circle, domain, planet 7 demesne, rondure, terrain 8 dominion, province 9 bailiwick, territory 12 jurisdiction

spherical 5 round 6 global 7 globose 8 globular 9 orbicular

Sphinx *builder:* 6 Khafre *father:* 6 Typhon *mother:* 7 Echidna *query:* 6 riddle *site:* 4 Giza 6 Thebes

spice 3 pep, zip 4 kick, mace, tang, zest 5 anise, aroma, clove, cumin, poppy, savor, scent, smack, smell, taste 6 cloves, fennel, ginger, nutmeg, pepper, relish, sesame 7 bouquet, caraway, perfume 8 cardamom, cinnamon, piquancy 9 fragrance, redolence, seasoning

Spice Islands 8 Moluccas

spick-and-span 3 new 4 mint, neat, snug, tidy, trig, trim 5 clean, fresh 6 spruce 7 orderly 8 brand-new, spotless 9 shipshape 10 immaculate 11 well-groomed

spicy 3 hot 4 racy 5 bawdy, fiery, salty, tangy, zesty 6 lively, purple, ribald, risqué, savory, snappy, wicked 7 gingery, peppery, piquant, pungent, scented, zestful 8 aromatic, fragrant, off-color, perfumed, redolent, seasoned, spirited 9 flavorful, salacious 10 scandalous, suggestive 11 titillating

spider 5 frypan 7 skillet 8 arachnid 9 frying pan 10 black widow

spiel 4 jive, line 5 pitch 6 patter 12 song and dance

spieler 4 tout 6 barker, hawker, talker 8 huckster

spigot 3 tap 4 cock, gate 5 valve 6 faucet 7 hydrant, petcock, shutoff 8 stopcock

spike 3 pin 4 heel, nail 5 lance, piton, spear 6 antler, impale, needle, skewer 7 spindle 8 increase, mackerel, puncture, transfix

spile 4 bung 5 spout

spill 3 blab, drip, drop, fall, flow, slop, tell 5 spray 6 betray, inform, reveal, splash, squeal, tattle 7 divulge, dribble, run over, spatter 8 disclose, overflow

Spillane detective 10 Mike Hammer

spilth 5 dregs, dross, swill, trash, waste 6 debris, refuse, scraps 7 garbage, rubbish 8 leavings

spin 4 gyre, reel, ride, swim, turn 5 dizzy, swirl, twirl, wheel, whirl 6 gyrate, rotate 7 revolve 8 rotation 9 pirouette, whirligig 10 revolution *a log:* 4 birl *out:* 4 draw 6 extend 7 pro-

long, stretch 8 elongate, lengthen, protract 10 prolongate
spinal column 5 chine 6 rachis *curvature:*
8 lordosis *part:* 8 vertebra (see also
SPINE)
spindle 3 pin, rod 5 newel, shaft, spike
6 impale, rachis
spindly 5 frail, lanky, rangy, shaky,
weedy 6 flimsy, gangly, skinny, twiggy,
wobbly 7 fragile, rickety, tottery 8 gangling, skeletal, unsteady 9 emaciated
10 jerry-built
spine 4 back 6 rachis 7 spicule 8 backbone 9 vertebrae
spineless 5 timid 8 cowardly, timorous
9 weak-kneed 10 weak-willed 12 invertebrate
spin-off 8 offshoot 9 by-product, outgrowth 10 derivative, descendant
___ **Spinoza** 6 Baruch
spinster 7 old maid 10 maiden lady
spiny 6 barbed, thorny 7 prickly 8 echi-
nate 10 nettlesome
spiral 4 coil, curl, wind 5 helix, twine,
twist 6 volute 7 helical, helices (plural)
8 gyroidal, volution 9 cochleate,
corkscrew *combining form:* 3 gyr 4 gyro
5 helic 6 helico
spire 4 coil 5 twist, whorl 7 steeple 8 pinnacle
spirit 3 pep, vim, zip 4 brio, dash, élan,
gimp, grit, guts, life, mood, snap, soul,
zeal, zest, zing 5 anima, ardor, drive,
force, heart, moxie, oomph, pluck,
shade, spunk, tenor, verve, vigor 6 animus, daimon, energy, esprit, fervor,
ginger, mettle, morale, pneuma,
psyche, starch, temper, wraith 7 passion, phantom, specter, spectre 8 phantasm, revenant, vitality 9 animation,
élan vital, substance 10 apparition,
enthusiasm, get-up-and-go, liveliness
away: 6 abduct, kidnap, snatch *evil:*
5 afrit, demon 6 afreet 7 erlking, shai-
tan *female:* 5 nymph 7 banshee *Hopi:*
7 kachina *Persian:* 4 peri
spirited 4 bold, game, keen 5 eager,
fiery, peppy 6 ardent, gritty, lively,
plucky, spunky 7 chipper, fervent, gingery, peppery, valiant, zealous 8 animated, cheerful, intrepid, resolute
9 audacious, dauntless, energetic,
sprightly, vivacious 10 courageous,
mettlesome, passionate 12 enthusiastic
spirits 5 booze, drink 6 liquor, tipple
9 aqua vitae, firewater *low:* 5 blues,
dumps, ennui 8 doldrums 10 blue devils, depression, melancholy
spiritual 6 sacred 7 saintly 8 churchly,
mystical, numinous, platonic 9 religious 10 high-minded, immaterial,

unphysical 11 disembodied, incorporeal, nonmaterial, nonphysical 12 metaphysical, supernatural, transcendent
spiritualist 6 medium, mystic 7 psychic
spit 5 spear 6 impale, saliva, skewer,
slaver, sputum 7 spatter, sputter
8 splutter 9 brochette 11 expectorate
spite 5 venom 6 grudge, malice, rancor,
spleen 7 ill will, revenge 9 pettiness,
vengeance 11 malevolence 13 maliciousness
spiteful 4 mean 5 catty, nasty, snide
6 malign, wicked 7 vicious, waspish
8 venomous 9 malicious, malignant,
rancorous 10 malevolent, vindictive
spitfire 4 fury 5 harpy, shrew, vixen
6 dragon, virago 7 hellcat, tigress 8 fishwife, harridan 9 termagant
spitting image 4 twin 5 clone 6 double,
ringer 9 duplicate 10 carbon copy, dead
ringer, simulacrum
spittoon 8 cuspidor
splash 3 sop, wet 4 slop, soak 5 douse,
slosh, spray, swash 6 drench 7 spatter
8 sprinkle
splashy 5 gaudy, jazzy, showy 6 flashy,
garish, glitzy, tawdry 7 blatant, dashing
8 colorful, dazzling, striking 10 flamboyant, theatrical 11 sensational
12 meretricious, ostentatious
splatter 4 slop 5 douse, plash, slosh,
spray, swash 6 splash 8 sprinkle
splay 4 cant, tilt 5 angle, bevel, gawky,
slant, slope 6 clumsy, extend, spread
7 awkward, incline 8 ungainly 9 expansion 11 inclination
spleen see SPITE
splendid 4 fine 5 grand, showy 6 superb
7 shining 8 glorious, gorgeous 9 brilliant, excellent, marvelous, wonderful
10 first-class, impressive 11 illustrious,
magnificent, outstanding 12 transcendent
splendor 4 pomp 5 glory 6 dazzle
7 panoply 8 grandeur, richness
9 pageantry, spectacle 10 brilliance,
brilliancy 12 magnificence
splenetic 5 cross, surly 6 fuming
8 incensed, spiteful 9 malicious 10 ill-
natured, malevolent 11 ill-tempered
splice 3 tie 4 join, mate, mesh 5 braid,
graft, plait, unite
splint 5 brace, strip 7 support 10 immobilize
splinter 4 rive 5 burst, smash 6 shiver,
sliver 7 faction, shatter 8 fragment
12 disintegrate
split 3 rip 4 part, rend, rent, rift, rima,
rime, rive, tear 5 break, carve, chasm,
chink, cleft, crack, sever, slice
6 breach, cleave, cloven, divide,

schism, sunder **7** break up, disjoin, dissect, diverge, divorce, divvy up, fission, fissure, rupture **8** cleavage, dissever, fracture, separate **11** dichotomize *combining form:* **5** schiz **6** schizo **7** schisto
splotch 4 blob, blot, spot **5** fleck, stain **6** smudge
splurge 4 orgy **5** binge, fling, spree **7** blowout, rampage **10** indulgence **12** extravagance
splutter 4 spit **6** babble, jabber **7** stammer
spoil 3 mar, rob, rot **4** baby, harm, prey, ruin, sack **5** decay, humor, taint, waste, wreck **6** coddle, cosset, curdle, damage, defile, impair, molder, pamper, ravish **7** blemish, cater to, destroy, indulge, pillage, putrefy, tarnish, vitiate **8** demolish **9** break down, decompose **11** mollycoddle
spoiled 4 rank, sour **6** putrid, rancid, rotten, ruined **7** coddled, decayed **8** impaired, indulged, pampered **9** indulgent
spoils 4 haul, loot, swag **5** booty **7** pillage, plunder
spoilsport 7 killjoy
spoken 4 oral, said, told **6** verbal, voiced **7** uttered **8** phonetic, viva voce **9** delivered, unwritten **11** articulated
sponge 4 grub **5** cadge, leech, mooch **7** moocher **8** freeload, parasite, scrounge **10** freeloader *material:* **8** mesoglea *opening:* **6** oscula (plural) **7** osculum, ostiole
sponger 5 leech **7** moocher **8** parasite **10** freeloader
spongy 4 soft **5** mushy, pulpy **6** porous, quaggy **7** squashy, squishy **9** absorbent
sponsor 4 back, fund **5** angel, stake **6** backer, patron, surety **7** endorse, finance **8** advocate, bankroll, champion, Maecenas, mainstay, promoter, vouch for **9** grubstake, guarantee, guarantor, patronize, subsidize, supporter **10** benefactor, underwrite **11** underwriter
sponsorship 5 aegis **7** backing, support **8** advocacy, auspices **9** patronage
spontaneous 5 ad-lib **7** natural, offhand **8** ad-libbed, unforced **9** automatic, extempore, impromptu, impulsive, unstudied **10** improvised, off-the-cuff, unprompted **11** instinctive, unmeditated **13** unconstrained
spontoon 4 pike **5** lance, spear
spoof 4 sham **5** farce, put-on **6** parody, satire, send-up **7** lampoon, takeoff **8** travesty
spook 3 spy **5** agent, alarm, ghost, haunt, scare **7** specter, spectre, startle, terrify **8** frighten

spooky 5 eerie, weird **6** creepy **7** ghostly, ominous, uncanny **9** unearthly
spool 4 wind **6** bobbin
spoon 3 pet, woo **4** neck **5** court, ladle, scoop **6** cuddle
spoonbill 4 ibis **8** shoveler **9** ruddy duck **10** paddlefish
Spoon River poet 7 Masters (Edgar Lee)
spoony 5 mushy, silly **6** simple, slushy, syrupy **7** fatuous, foolish, mawkish, smitten, witless **9** schmaltzy **10** saccharine **11** sentimental
spoor 5 scent, trace, track, tract, trail **7** vestige **8** footstep **9** droppings, footprint
sporadic 4 rare **6** catchy, fitful, random, scarce, sparse, spotty **7** erratic **8** episodic, isolated, uncommon **9** desultory, irregular, scattered, spasmodic **10** infrequent, occasional
sport 3 fun **4** game, jest, joke, mock, play **6** frolic, racing, trifle **7** mockery, show off **9** diversion, high jinks, horseplay **10** recreation *indoor:* **6** boxing, hockey, squash **7** bowling **8** handball **9** wrestling **10** acrobatics, basketball, gymnastics **11** racquetball, table tennis *Olympic:* **4** judo **6** boxing, diving, hockey, rowing **7** archery, cycling, fencing, shot put **8** canoeing, football, high jump, long jump, marathon, shooting, swimming, yachting **9** decathlon, pole vault, water polo, wrestling **10** basketball, gymnastics, pentathlon, triple jump, volleyball **11** discus throw, hammer throw **12** javelin throw, steeplechase **13** weightlifting *water:* **6** diving, rowing **7** sailing, surfing **8** canoeing, swimming, yachting *winter:* **4** luge **6** hockey, skiing **7** curling, lugeing, skating **8** biathlon, sledding **10** ski jumping **11** bobsledding, tobogganing
sporting house 6 bagnio **7** brothel **8** bordello
sportive 5 antic **6** frisky, impish **7** playful, roguish, waggish **10** frolicsome **11** mischievous
sportiveness 7 devilry, roguery, waggery **8** deviltry, mischief **9** devilment, rascality
sporty 4 fast **5** peppy **6** breezy, casual, jaunty, lively **7** dashing, relaxed **8** debonair, informal **10** insouciant **11** streamlined
spot 3 fix, jam, nip, see **4** espy, post, site **5** fleck, hit on, locus, place, point, speck **6** blotch, detect, pickle, plight, scrape **7** dilemma, smidgen, spatter, speckle **8** diagnose, flyspeck, identify, location, pinpoint, position **9** recognize, situation **11** predicament

spotless 4 pure 5 clean 6 chaste 8 hygienic, sanitary, unsoiled 9 undefiled, unstained, unsullied 10 immaculate 11 unblemished

spotlight 5 focus 6 notice 7 feature, point up 8 interest, point out 9 attention, emphasize, public eye, publicity 10 illuminate 12 illumination

spotted 4 seen 6 motley 7 brindle, dappled, piebald 8 brindled, speckled, stippled

spouse 4 mate, wife 5 bride, groom, hubby 7 consort, husband

spout 3 jet 4 gush 5 chute, eject, spray, spurt 6 nozzle, squirt

sprain 4 pull, tear, turn 5 twist 6 wrench 7 stretch

sprawl 4 flop, loll 5 drape, slump 6 extend, lounge, slouch, spread 7 stretch 11 spread-eagle

spray 3 fog 4 hose, mist 6 shower, spritz 7 aerosol, atomize, diffuse, spatter 8 atomizer, droplets, fumigate, nebulize 9 spindrift

spread 3 jam, lay, set, sow 4 deal, oleo, open, pâté, push 5 apply, feast, jelly, space, splay, strew, sweep 6 butter, expand, extend, fan out, pass on, retail 7 banquet, breadth, diffuse, expanse, overrun, pervade, radiate, scatter, slather, stretch, suffuse 8 bedcover, coverlet, dispense, disperse, mushroom, permeate 9 amplitude, broadcast, circulate, diffusion, dissipate, expansion, extension, profusion, propagate, radiation 10 dispersion, distribute, outstretch 11 counterpane, disseminate 12 transmission 13 proliferation

spree 3 jag 4 bash, bust, lark, orgy, riot, tear 5 binge, drunk, fling, revel 6 bender, frolic 7 blowout, carouse, rampage, splurge 8 carousal, wingding 10 indulgence 11 bacchanalia

sprig 4 brad, heir, twig 5 scion, shoot 7 pintail 9 ruddy duck

sprightly 3 gay 4 keen, spry, yare 5 agile, alert, antic, brisk, peppy, perky, zesty, zingy, zippy 6 active, breezy, chirpy, frisky, jaunty, lively, nimble 7 animate, chipper, coltish, piquant, playful, pungent 8 animated, cheerful, spirited, sportive 9 energetic, vivacious 10 frolicsome, rollicking 13 scintillating

spring 3 hop 4 flow, jump, leap, lope, rise, root, skip, stem, trip, well 5 arise, begin, bound, cause, fount, issue, start 6 appear, bounce, emerge, hurdle, reason, source, uncoil, vernal 7 come out, emanate, proceed, rebound, startle 8 commence, fountain, stimulus, well-

head 9 originate 10 incitement, resilience 12 fountainhead *back:* 6 resile

springe 4 trap 5 noose, snare 7 pitfall 9 booby trap

springlike 6 vernal

springy 6 supple 7 elastic 8 flexible, stretchy 9 recoiling, resilient

sprinkle 3 dot 4 rain, spot 5 shake, speck, spray, strew 6 pepper, powder, spritz 7 asperse, drizzle, freckle, scatter, speckle, stipple 9 bespeckle

sprint 3 run 4 dart, dash, race, shin, tear 5 scoot 6 gallop, hurtle, scurry 7 scamper

sprite 3 elf, fay, nix 4 puck 5 dryad, fairy, naiad, nixie, nymph, pixie, sylph 6 kelpie 7 brownie 9 hamadryad

spritz 3 jet 5 spray, spurt 6 shower, squirt

sprout 3 bud 4 grow 5 scion, shoot 6 ratoon, sucker 7 burgeon 8 offshoot 9 germinate

spruce 4 trim 5 natty, sassy, spiff 6 dapper, spiffy 11 well-groomed

spry 4 yare 5 agile, brisk, sound, zesty, zippy 6 active, lively, nimble, robust 7 healthy 8 animated, spirited, vigorous 9 energetic, vivacious

spud 6 potato

_____ **Spumante** 4 Asti

spume 4 fizz, foam, head, scum, suds 5 froth, spray, yeast 6 lather

spunk 4 grit, guts 5 heart, moxie, nerve, pluck 6 mettle, spirit, tinder 7 cojones, courage 8 backbone, gumption 9 fortitude, toughness 10 liveliness, resolution

spunky 4 bold 5 brave, fiery 6 daring 7 doughty, gingery, peppery 8 fearless, spirited 9 dauntless 10 courageous, mettlesome 12 high-spirited

spur 4 goad, prod, stir, urge 5 egg on, impel, prick, rally, rouse, spine 6 arouse, branch, exhort, motive, prompt, propel 7 impetus, impulse 8 buttress, catalyst, excitant, stimulus 9 actuation, incentive, instigate, stimulant, stimulate 10 incitement, inducement, motivation, projection *part:* 5 rowel

spurious 4 fake, mock, sham 5 bogus, dummy, false, phony, put-on 6 ersatz, pseudo 7 assumed, feigned, pretend 8 affected 9 brummagem, imitation, pinchbeck, pretended, simulated 10 apocryphal, artificial, substitute 11 counterfeit, make-believe 12 illegitimate *combining form:* 5 pseud 6 pseudo

spurn 4 snub 5 flout, scoff, scorn, scout, sneer 6 rebuff, refuse, reject 7 contemn, decline, despise, disdain, dismiss, repulse 8 turn down 9 disregard, reprobate, repudiate 10 disapprove 12 cold-shoulder

spurt 3 jet 4 gush, jump 5 burst, expel, spout, surge 6 shower, spritz, squirt 7 upsurge 8 eruption, increase 9 discharge

sputter 4 fizz, fume, rage, rant, rave, spew, spit 6 gibber, jabber 7 bluster, stammer

spy 5 agent, scout, snoop, spook 6 beagle, sleuth 7 gumshoe 8 informer, saboteur 9 detective 12 investigator 13 undercover man *name:* 4 Ames (Aldrich), Boyd (Belle), Hari (Mata) 5 André (John), Blunt (Anthony), Fuchs (Klaus) 6 Philby (Kim), Smiley (George) 7 Burgess (Guy), Hanssen (Robert), Maclean (Donald), Pollard (Jonathan)

spyglass 9 telescope

spying 9 espionage

Spyri's heroine 5 Heidi

squab 5 couch 6 pigeon 7 cushion

squabble see SPAT

squalid 3 low 4 base, foul, mean, vile 5 dingy, dirty, nasty, seedy 6 filthy, frowsy, frowzy, grubby, scurvy, shabby, shoddy, sleazy, sordid 7 ignoble, lowdown, run-down, scrubby, unclean, unkempt 8 slovenly, wretched 10 despicable, disheveled 11 dilapidated 12 disreputable

squall 3 caw, row, yap, yip 4 bark, bawl, beef, feud, fuss, gust, howl, roar, tiff, wail, yawp, yell, yelp, yowl 5 brawl, fight, hoo-ha, shout 6 bellow, clamor, flurry, fracas, hubbub, ruckus, rumpus, scream, shriek, squeal, yammer 7 dispute, flare-up, quarrel, rhubarb, screech 8 brouhaha, squabble 9 bickering, caterwaul, commotion 10 falling-out, hullabaloo 11 altercation

squalor 5 filth 6 misery 7 neglect, poverty 8 baseness, iniquity 9 depravity, dirtiness 10 sordidness 11 degradation 12 wretchedness

squander 4 blow 5 spend, waste 7 consume, exhaust, fritter, scatter 9 dissipate, throw away 10 trifle away 11 fritter away

squanderer see SPENDER

square 3 fit, fix 4 bang, boxy, even, fair, jibe, just, tied 5 adapt, agree, align, clear, equal, exact, fit in, match, pay up, plaza, right, sharp, spang, tally 6 accord, adjust, settle 7 balance, conform, exactly, satisfy, settled 8 check out, coincide, dovetail, orthodox, quadrate, smack-dab, straight, unbiased 9 discharge, equitable, harmonize, impartial, liquidate, objective, precise-

ly, quadratic, reconcile, rectangle 10 accurately, correspond

squash 3 jam 4 cram, mash, pepo, pulp 5 crush, gourd, press, quell 7 flatten, put down, squeeze, squelch 8 suppress *variety:* 5 acorn 6 cushaw, Sibley, turban 7 Hubbard, scallop 8 pattypan, zucchini 9 butternut, crookneck 10 Marblehead

squat 3 low 5 dumpy, hunch, stoop, stout, thick 6 chunky, crouch, hunker, stocky, stubby 8 heavyset, thickset 10 hunker down 11 thick-bodied

squawfish 4 chub 8 cyprinid 10 pikeminnow

squawk 3 caw, yap, yip 4 beef, crab, fuss, yawp 5 bleat, gripe 6 yammer 7 protest, screech 8 complain 9 bellyache, complaint

squeak 3 rat 4 blab, fink, peep, pipe, sing 5 cheep, creak 6 escape, inform, snitch, tattle 10 tattletale

squeal 3 rat, yip 4 blab, howl, sing, yell, yelp, yowl 5 bleat, creak, grate, gripe, peach 6 inform, screak, scream, shriek, shrill, snitch, squawk, tattle 7 protest, screech 8 complain 10 tattletale

squealer 3 rat 4 fink 6 canary, snitch, weasel 7 ratfink, stoolie, tattler, tipster 8 betrayer, informer 10 talebearer, tattletale 11 stool pigeon

squeamish 5 fussy, upset 6 queasy 7 finical, finicky 8 nauseous 9 nauseated 10 fastidious, particular, pernickety 11 persnickety

squeeze 3 hug, jam 4 bind, cram, grip, milk, pack, push 5 clasp, crowd, crush, exact, gouge, juice, pinch, press, screw, wring 6 clutch, coerce, compel, crunch, eke out, enfold, extort, jostle, squash, squish 7 dilemma, embrace, extract 8 compress, contract, pressure, quandary 9 shake down 11 compression, predicament

squelch 5 quell, shush, sit on 6 muffle, muzzle, squash, squish, stifle, subdue 7 repress, silence, smother 8 strangle, suppress 10 extinguish

squib 4 fire 6 filler 7 lampoon 8 shoot off 9 detonator 11 firecracker

squid 7 mollusc, mollusk 8 calamari, calamary 10 cephalopod *kin:* 7 octopus 10 cuttlefish

squiggle 4 worm 6 doodle, scrawl, squirm, writhe 7 scratch 8 curlicue, scrabble, scribble

squinch 5 quail, start, wince 6 blench, crouch, recoil, shrink

squint 4 peek, peep, peer 10 hagioscope, strabismus

squire 6 attend, escort, lawyer 7 consort,

gallant 8 cavalier, chaperon 9 accompany, landowner

squirm 4 worm 6 fidget, wiggle, writhe 7 wriggle

squirrel 4 stow 5 cache, hoard, stash 7 secrete *red:* 9 chickaree

squirt 3 jet, kid, pup, tot 4 brat, tyke 5 sprat, spray, spurt, twerp 6 shaver, shrimp, splurt, spritz 7 spatter

squish 3 jam 4 cram, mash, mush, pack, push 5 crush, press, quash, smash 7 flatten, scrunch, squeeze, squelch, trample

squishy 4 soft 6 flabby, quaggy, slushy, spongy

Sri Lanka *bay:* 6 Bengal *capital:* 7 Colombo *city:* 8 Moratuwa *ethnic group:* 9 Sinhalese *former name:* 6 Ceylon *language:* 5 Tamil 9 Sinhalese *monetary unit:* 5 rupee *shoals:* 11 Adam's Bridge *strait:* 4 Palk

SRO 7 sellout

SS chief 7 Himmler (Heinrich)

S-shaped 7 sigmoid

stab 3 dig, pop, try 4 pang, poke, shot 5 crack, drive, fling, prick, spear, stick, whack, whirl 6 effort, pierce, thrust, twinge 7 attempt 8 puncture 9 penetrate

Stabat ___ 5 Mater

stabile 6 steady 9 sculpture 10 stationary

stabilize 3 fix, set 4 prop 5 brace, poise 6 cement, firm up, fixate, prop up, secure, settle, steady 7 balance, ballast, support, sustain 8 solidify 9 reinforce

stable 3 set 4 barn, fast, firm, mews, safe, sure 5 fixed, solid, sound 6 secure, steady, sturdy 7 abiding, durable, lasting, staunch 8 balanced, constant, enduring, resolute 9 immutable, permanent, steadfast, unvarying 10 perdurable, stationary, unchanging, unshakable

stack 4 cock, heap, hill, load, mass, pile, pipe 5 mound, sheaf 7 chimney, pyramid

stack up 3 add 5 equal, total 6 equate, gather 7 compare, measure

stadium 4 bowl, rink, ring 5 arena 6 garden 8 coliseum 10 hippodrome 12 amphitheater

staff 3 rod 4 club, prop, rung, team, wand 5 baton, billy 6 cudgel 7 faculty, support 9 personnel *bishop's:* 7 crosier, crozier *medical:* 8 caduceus

stage 3 lot 4 play, rung, show, step 5 grade, level, mount, notch, phase, put on 6 degree, period, status 7 execute, perform, present, produce *direction:* 4 exit 5 enter 6 exeunt *scenery:* 3 set 8 backdrop *show:* 4 play 5 drama, revue 7 musical 9 burlesque 10 vaudeville *signal:* 3 cue *whisper:* 5 aside

stage set 5 decor, scene 7 scenery 8 backdrop 11 mise-en-scène

stagger 4 daze, reel, stun, sway 5 amaze, floor, lurch, pitch, stump, waver, weave 6 boggle, careen, dither, falter, teeter, topple, totter, wobble, zigzag 7 astound, nonplus, perplex, shatter, stumble, stupefy 8 astonish, bowl over 9 dumbfound, overwhelm, vacillate 11 flabbergast

stagnant 5 musty, stale 6 static 8 immobile, unmoving 10 motionless, stationary

stagnate 4 idle 5 stall 6 fester 8 languish, stultify, vegetate

stagy 10 artificial, histrionic, theatrical 11 pretentious 12 melodramatic

staid 5 grave, sober 6 formal, sedate, solemn, somber, sombre, stuffy 7 earnest, serious, starchy 8 composed, decorous, priggish 9 dignified

stain 3 dye, tar 4 blot, daub, onus, slur, soil, spot 5 brand, color, odium, shame, smear, sully, taint, tinge 6 blotch, defile, embrue, imbrue, smirch, smudge, stigma 7 blemish, pigment, tarnish 8 besmirch, colorant, discolor, dishonor, dyestuff, tincture

staircase *handrail:* 8 banister *outdoor:* 6 perron *post:* 5 newel 8 baluster

stake 3 bet, lay, pot, set 4 ante, back, game, pale, play, post, risk 5 claim, put on, share, wager 6 gamble, paling, picket, pledge, tether 7 finance 8 bankroll, interest 10 capitalize, investment

stalag 7 POW camp 10 prison camp

stale 5 banal, dusty, faded, fusty, moldy, musty, passé, tired, trite 7 clichéd, tedious, worn-out 8 overused, shopworn, timeworn 9 hackneyed, tasteless 11 commonplace, stereotyped

stalemate 3 tie 4 draw 7 impasse 8 deadlock, gridlock, standoff

stalk 4 hunt, prey 5 chase, track 6 ambush, follow, pursue, stride 8 flush out *flower:* 8 peduncle *leaf:* 7 petiole *short:* 5 stipe

stall 3 bay, pew 4 halt 5 booth, brake, check, delay, hedge, kiosk, stand 6 arrest, put off 7 conk out, counter, hold off 8 obstruct 9 stonewall 10 filibuster 11 compartment, prevaricate

stalwart 4 bold 5 brave, gutsy, husky, stout, tough 6 brawny, robust, sinewy, strong, sturdy 7 valiant 8 fearless, intrepid, unafraid, valorous, vigorous 9 dauntless, tenacious, undaunted 10 courageous

stamen part 6 anther 8 filament

stamina 8 tenacity **9** endurance, fortitude, tolerance **11** persistence **12** staying power

stammer 6 gibber, jabber **7** sputter, stutter **8** hesitate, splutter

stamp 3 ilk, lot **4** etch, kind, mark, mint, mold, seal, sort, type **5** clomp, clump, pound, print, tromp **6** hammer, stripe **7** impress, imprint, trample **8** hallmark, inscribe **9** character **10** impression **12** characterize

stampede 4 bolt, dash, rout, rush, tear **5** crush, panic, rodeo **6** charge

stamps 7 postage

stance 4 pose **7** bearing, posture **8** attitude, carriage, position **10** deportment

stanch 4 stem, stop **5** check **6** stop up **8** hold back

stanchion 4 post, prop **5** brace **7** support

stand 4 bear **5** abide, booth, brook, kiosk, stall, treat **6** endure, handle, suffer **7** counter, stomach, swallow, weather **8** attitude, platform, position, tolerate *artist's:* **5** easel *three-legged:* **6** tripod, trivet *ornamental:* **7** étagere

standard 3 law, par **4** flag, jack, mean, norm, rule **5** color, gauge, ideal, model, stock, usual **6** banner, belief, common, ensign, median, normal, pennon **7** average, classic, example, general, measure, pattern, pennant, regular, typical, uniform **8** accepted, everyday, exemplar, familiar, ordinary, orthodox, paradigm **9** archetype, benchmark, criterion, customary, principle, yardstick **10** definitive, prevailing, recognized, regulation, touchstone **11** established, fundamental

standardize 6 adjust **7** conform **8** regulate **9** reconcile

stand for 4 bear, mean **5** allow **6** denote, permit **7** signify **8** indicate, tolerate **9** put up with, represent, symbolize

stand-in 3 sub **5** proxy **6** backup, second **9** alternate, surrogate **10** substitute, understudy **11** pinch hitter, replacement **12** impersonator

standing 4 rank, term **5** erect, fixed, place **6** cachet, credit, repute, status **7** dignity, footing, station, stature, upright **8** capacity, duration, eminence, position, prestige, stagnant **9** character, permanent, situation **10** estimation, reputation **11** consequence, established

standoff see STALEMATE

standoffish 5 aloof **6** chilly **7** distant, haughty **8** detached, reserved **9** reclusive, withdrawn **10** unfriendly, unsociable **12** misanthropic

stand out 3 jut **4** bulk, loom **5** bulge **7** project **8** protrude

standpatter 4 fogy, tory **7** diehard

8 mossback **11** bitter-ender **12** conservative

standpoint 4 side **5** angle, slant **7** outlook **9** direction **11** perspective

standstill 4 halt, stop **5** check, pause **7** impasse **8** deadlock, dead stop **9** cessation, stalemate

Stanford site 8 Palo Alto

Stanley Kowalski's wife 6 Stella

Stanleys' car 7 steamer

Stan's partner 5 Ollie

stanza 7 strophe *combining form:* **5** stich *of eight lines:* **6** octave *of four lines:* **6** ballad **8** quatrain *of six lines:* **6** sestet *of three lines:* **6** tercet **7** triplet *Persian:* **8** rubaiyat

star 4 icon, idol, lead, main, nova **5** actor, chief, major **6** étoile **7** actress, capital **8** asterisk, dominant, luminary **9** celebrity, headliner, principal **10** preeminent **11** outstanding *bright:* **4** Vega **5** Deneb, Rigel, Spica **6** Altair, Pollux, Sirius **7** Antares, Canopus, Capella, Procyon **8** Arcturus **9** Aldebaran, Archernar, Fomalhaut **10** Beta Crucis, Betelgeuse **11** Alpha Crucis **12** Beta Centauri **13** Alpha Centauri *combining form:* **4** astr **5** aster, astro **6** astero, sidero *five-pointed:* **8** pentacle **9** pentagram *giant:* **10** Betelgeuse *six-pointed:* **8** hexagram

starch 3 pep **4** push, snap **5** drive, moxie, punch, spunk, vigor **7** stiffen **8** gumption, vitality **9** formality *combining form:* **4** amyl **5** amylo

starchy 4 prim **5** aloof, stiff **6** doughy, formal, wooden **7** stilted

star-crossed 6 doomed **7** hapless, unlucky **8** ill-fated, luckless **10** ill-starred **11** unfortunate **12** misfortunate

Stardust composer 10 Carmichael (Hoagy)

stare 3 eye **4** gape, gawk, gaze, ogle, peer **6** goggle **10** rubberneck

stark 3 raw **4** bare, nude, pure **5** bleak, blunt, clear, harsh, naked, quite, rigid, sheer, utter **6** barren, strict, unclad, vacant, wholly **8** absolute, complete, desolate, stripped **9** au naturel, out-and-out **10** absolutely

starry 6 astral **7** stellar **8** sidereal

starry-eyed 6 dreamy, unreal **7** utopian **8** ecstatic **9** rapturous, visionary **11** impractical, unrealistic **13** impracticable

Star-Spangled Banner writer 3 Key (Francis Scott)

start 4 bolt, dawn, draw **5** arise, begin, crank, found, issue, onset, quail, react, set up, wince **6** blench, create, embark, flinch, launch, outset, recoil, shrink, spring, take up **7** actuate, genesis, infancy, kickoff, opening, trigger **8** activate, commence, embark on, initiate, organize, reaction **9** beginning, establish, institute, originate **10** inaugurate **12** commencement

startle 4 jolt, jump **5** alarm, scare, shock, spook **8** astonish, frighten, surprise

starved 6 hungry **8** famished, ravenous, underfed

stash 4 bury, hide **5** cache, hoard, plant, store **7** conceal, lay away, nest egg, secrete **8** lay aside, sock away, squirrel **9** stockpile

stasis 7 balance, inertia **9** equipoise **10** immobility, stagnation **11** equilibrium

state 3 air, put, say **4** aver, mode, rank, tell, vent **5** utter **6** affirm, assert, recite, relate, report **7** declare, dignity, explain, expound, express, posture, recount **8** attitude, capacity, describe, position, set forth, standing **9** condition, enunciate, situation, ventilate *subdivison:* **6** county

state *easternmost:* **5** Maine *largest:* **6** Alaska *smallest:* **11** Rhode Island *southernmost:* **6** Hawaii

state abbreviation *Alabama:* **3** Ala. *Alaska:* **4** Alas. *Arizona:* **4** Ariz. *Arkansas:* **3** Ark. *California:* **3** Cal. **5** Calif. *Colorado:* **3** Col. **4** Colo. *Connecticut:* **4** Conn. *Delaware:* **3** Del. *Florida:* **3** Fla. *Idaho:* **3** Ida. *Illinois:* **3** Ill. *Indiana:* **3** Ind. *Kansas:* **3** Kan. **4** Kans. *Kentucky:* **3** Ken. *Massachusetts:* **4** Mass. *Michigan:* **4** Mich. *Minnesota:* **4** Minn. *Mississippi:* **4** Miss. *Montana:* **4** Mont. *Nebraska:* **3** Neb. **4** Nebr. *Nevada:* **3** Nev. *New Mexico:* **4** N. Mex. *North Carolina:* **4** N. Car. *North Dakota:* **4** N. Dak. *Oklahoma:* **4** Okla. *Oregon:* **3** Ore. **4** Oreg. *Pennsylvania:* **4** Penn. **5** Penna. *South Carolina:* **4** S. Car. *South Dakota:* **4** S. Dak. *Tennessee:* **4** Tenn. *Texas:* **3** Tex. *Vermont:* **4** Verm. *Virginia:* **4** Virg. *Washington:* **4** Wash. *West Virginia:* **3** W. Va. *Wisconsin:* **3** Wis. **4** Wisc. *Wyoming:* **3** Wyo.

stately 5 grand, lofty, noble, regal, royal **6** august, formal, kingly, lordly, solemn **7** courtly, elegant, gallant, haughty **8** gracious, imperial, imposing, majestic, palatial, princely **9** dignified **10** ceremonial, impressive, monumental **11** ceremonious, magnificent

statement 3 tab **4** bill **5** score **6** avowal, charge, dictum, remark, report **7** account, comment, invoice, recital **8** averment **9** affidavit, assertion, manifesto, narrative, reckoning, testimony,

utterance **10** deposition, expression **11** description *introductory:* **7** preface **8** foreword, prologue

stateroom 5 cabin

statesman 10 politician *American:* **3** Hay (John Milton) **4** Clay (Henry), Hull (Cordell), Otis (James), Root (Elihu) **5** Adams (Samuel), Henry (Patrick), Lodge (Henry Cabot), Vance (Cyrus) **6** Bunche (Ralph), Bunker (Ellsworth), Dulles (John Foster), Kennan (George F.), Morris (Gouverneur), Powell (Colin), Sumner (Charles) **7** Acheson (Dean), Hancock (John), Kellogg (Frank B.), Lansing (Robert), Sherman (John, Roger), Stimson (Henry L.), Webster (Daniel) **8** Franklin (Benjamin), Hamilton (Alexander), Harriman (Averell), Pinckney (Charles, Thomas), Randolph (Edmund Jennings, John, Payton), Rutledge (John), Trumbull (Jonathan, Joseph) **9** Kissinger (Henry), Stevenson (Adlai) **10** Stettinius (Edward Reilly) *Australian:* **9** Wentworth (William Charles) *Austrian:* **6** Renner (Karl) **7** Kaunitz (Wenzel von) **8** Dollfuss (Engelbert), Stevenson (Adlai) **10** Metternich (Klemens von) **13** Schwarzenberg (Felix zu) *Canadian:* **4** King (W. L. Mackenzie) **7** Laurier (Wilfrid) **8** Thompson (John Sparrow) **9** Macdonald (John Alexander, John Sandfield), Mackenzie (Alexander, William Lyon) *Chinese:* **3** Yen (Hsishan) **4** Deng (Xiaoping), Kung (Hsiang-hsi), Teng (Hsiao-p'ing), Wang (Anshih, Chingwei), Yuan (Shih-kai) **9** Sun Yat-Sen *Dutch:* **6** de Witt (Johan de) **7** Grotius (Hugo), Stikker (Dirk) *East German:* **8** Ulbricht (Walter) *English:* **3** Fox (Charles, Henry) **4** Eden (Anthony, George, William), More (Thomas), Peel (Arthur, Robert, William), Pitt (William), Vane (Henry) **5** Cecil (Robert, William), North (Francis, Frederick, Roger) **6** Morley (John), Sidney (Algernon, Henry, Philip, Robert), Temple (Henry, William), Wolsey (Thomas) **7** Halifax (Earl of), Reading (Marquis of), Russell (John, William), Stanley (Edward George, Edward Henry), Stewart (Robert), Warwick (Earl of) **8** Cromwell (Oliver, Thomas), Disraeli (Benjamin), Robinson (George Frederick Samuel), Villiers (George) **9** Cavendish (Spencer, William), Churchill (Randolph, Winston), Gladstone (William), Salisbury (Earl, Marquis of), Strafford (Earl of), Wellesley (Arthur, Richard Colley) **10** Palmerston (Lord), Rockingham

(Marquis of), Sunderland (Earl of), Walsingham (Francis), Wellington (Duke of) 11 Chamberlain (Austen, Joseph, Neville), Shaftesbury (Earl of) 12 Chesterfield (Earl of) *Finnish:* 9 Stahlberg (Kaarlo Juho) *French:* 5 Sully (Duc de) 6 Guizot (François-Pierre-Guillaume), Thiers (Louis-Adolphe), Turgot (Anne-Robert-Jacques) 7 Herriot (Edouard), Mazarin (Jules), Schuman (Robert), Viviani (René) 8 Hanotaux (Gabriel) 9 Lafayette (Marquis de), Millerand (Alexandre), Richelieu (Duc de) 10 Clemenceau (Georges) 11 Tocqueville (Alexis de) *German:* 5 Wirth (Joseph) 10 Stresemann (Gustav) *German-Danish:* 9 Struensee (Johann Friedrich) *Greek:* 6 Zaimis (Alexandros) 8 Pericles 9 Aristides 11 Cleisthenes, Demosthenes 12 Themistocles *Israeli:* 4 Eban (Abba) 5 Begin (Menachem), Dayan (Moshe) *Italian:* 6 Cavour (Conte di), Crispi (Francesco) 7 Orlando (Vittorio Emanuele) 11 Machiavelli (Niccolo) *Japanese:* 5 genro, Kanoe 6 Kanoye *Norwegian:* 6 Nansen (Fridtjof) *Polish:* 7 Zaleski (August) 9 Pilsudski (Jozef) 10 Paderewski (Ignacy) *Prussian:* 5 Stein (Karl) *Roman:* 4 Cato (Marcus Porcius) 6 Cicero (Marcus Tullius), Pompey, Seneca (Lucius Annaeus) 7 Agrippa (Marcus Vipsanius) 8 Gracchus (Gaius, Tiberius), Maecenas (Gaius) 9 Symmachus (Quintus Aurelius) *Russian:* 5 Witte (Sergey) 7 Molotov (Vyacheslav) 8 Potemkin (Grigory) 9 Vyshinsky (Andrey) *Scottish:* 4 Knox (John) *South American:* 7 Bolívar (Simón) 9 San Martín (José de) *Swiss:* 4 Ador (Gustave) 5 Welti (Emil)

static 5 fixed, inert 6 stable, steady 7 stabile, stalled, stopped 8 constant, immobile, inactive, stagnant, unmoving 9 immovable, unvarying 10 changeless, unchanging

station 4 post, rank, site, spot 5 depot, locus, place, point 6 assign 7 footing 8 capacity, standing 9 character 10 white noise

stationary 5 fixed 6 static 8 immobile, stagnant, unmoving 9 immovable 10 motionless, stock-still

statue *base:* 6 plinth 8 pedestal *gigantic:* 8 Colossus *Greek:* 5 atlas 7 telamon 8 caryatid *religious:* 5 Pietà *small:* 8 figurine

stature see STATUS

status 4 rank 5 merit, place, worth 6 cachet, rating, renown 7 caliber, dig-

nity, footing, posture, quality 8 capacity, eminence, position, prestige, standing 9 character, condition, situation 10 prominence 11 consequence, distinction

statute 3 act, law 4 bill 5 canon, edict 9 enactment, ordinance

staunch 4 fast, firm, sure, true 5 liege, loyal, solid, sound 6 secure, stable, strong, trusty 8 constant, faithful, reliable, resolute, stalwart 9 steadfast 10 dependable 11 substantial, trustworthy

stave off 4 foil 5 avert, block, deter, dodge, elude, parry, rebut, repel 6 rebuff, thwart 7 forfend, obviate, prevent, repulse 8 preclude 9 forestall 10 circumvent

stay 3 guy, lag 4 bide, halt, prop, rest, stop, wait 5 abide, brace, check, defer, delay, dwell, lodge, tarry, visit 6 linger, put off, remain 7 sojourn, support, suspend 8 hold over, postpone, stop over 9 interrupt 10 suspension 11 stick around

steadfast 4 firm, sure, true 5 fixed, liege, loyal 7 abiding, adamant, patient, staunch 8 constant, enduring, faithful, immobile, reliable, resolute, stubborn 9 immovable, unbending, unmovable 10 dependable, unwavering, unyielding 11 unfaltering, unflinching 12 never-failing, single-minded, wholehearted 13 unquestioning

steady 3 set 4 even, fast, firm, sure 5 fixed, liege, loyal, sober 6 stable, static 7 abiding, ballast, certain, durable, equable, nonstop, regular, stabile, staunch, uniform 8 constant, enduring, faithful, habitual, reliable, resolute, unbroken, unshaken 9 ceaseless, incessant, stabilize, unvarying 10 changeless, consistent, continuous, dependable, persistent, sweetheart, unchanging, unswerving, unwavering 11 unfaltering 12 unchangeable, wholehearted

steak 4 club, cube, loin 5 chuck, flank, round, T-bone 6 rib eye 7 brisket, sirloin 9 Delmonico, hamburger, Salisbury 10 tenderloin 11 filet mignon, London broil, porterhouse 13 chateaubriand

steal 3 bag, cop, nab, nip, rob 4 grab, hook, kite, lift, loot, lurk, slip, take 5 creep, filch, glide, heist, pinch, poach, prowl, seize, shirk, sidle, skulk, slide, slink, sneak, swipe 6 burgle, fleece, hijack, pilfer, pocket, snatch, snitch, thieve, tiptoe 7 bargain, pillage, plunder, purloin 8 embezzle, shanghai, shoplift 9 pussyfoot 10 burglarize, pla-

giarize 11 appropriate *a vehicle:*
6 hijack **8** highjack
stealing 5 theft **6** piracy **7** larceny, robbery **8** burglary
stealthy 3 sly **4** wily **6** covert, crafty, feline, secret, shifty, silent, slinky, sneaky **7** catlike, cunning, furtive, subrosa **8** hush-hush, skulking, slinking, sneaking **9** noiseless **10** undercover **11** clandestine **13** surreptitious
steam bath 5 sauna
steamboat structure 5 texas
steamer 4 boat, clam, ship
steam organ 8 calliope
steed 5 horse, mount **7** charger
steel 4 gird **5** brace, nerve, rally **6** buck up, harden **7** fortify, hearten, stiffen **8** embolden, inspirit **9** reinforce **10** strengthen
steep 3 sop **4** high, soak **5** bathe, dizzy, imbue, sheer **6** abrupt, drench, infuse **7** arduous, extreme, immerse, suffuse **8** elevated, marinate, saturate **9** excessive **10** exorbitant, immoderate, impregnate, inordinate **11** precipitate, precipitous
steeple 5 spire, tower **6** flèche
steer 4 helm, lead **5** guide, pilot, point, route **6** direct, escort, tip-off **7** channel, conduct, skipper **8** shepherd *a ship:* **4** conn, helm, luff
Stegner novel 13 Angle of Repose, Spectator Bird (The) **20** Big Rock Candy Mountain (The)
stein 3 mug **5** stoup **6** goblet **7** tankard
Steinbeck novel 5 Pearl (The) **10** Cannery Row, East of Eden **12** Of Mice and Men, Tortilla Flat **13** Grapes of Wrath (The)
Stein's companion 6 Toklas (Alice B.)
Steinway product 5 piano
stellar 6 astral, starry **7** leading, shining **8** sidereal, standout, starlike **10** preeminent **11** outstanding, predominant, superlative
stem 4 flow, head, rise, stop **5** arise, check, issue **6** arrest, derive, spring, stanch **7** control, develop, emanate, proceed **8** peduncle **9** originate *plant:* **5** haulm *underground:* **5** tuber **7** rhizome
stench 4 funk, reek **5** smell, stink
stentorian 4 loud **7** blaring, booming, orotund, raucous, roaring **8** sonorous, strident **9** clamorous, deafening **10** thundering **12** earsplitting
step 4 hoof, pace, rung, walk **5** grade, level, notch, stage, stair, track, tread **6** degree **7** measure, traipse **8** footfall **9** gradation *dance:* **3** pas
step-by-step 7 gradual **9** piecemeal

steppe 5 plain **6** tundra
Steppenwolf author 5 Hesse (Hermann)
stereotype 4 mold **7** pattern **10** categorize, pigeonhole **11** standardize
stereotypical 4 hack **5** banal, stale, trite **7** clichéd **8** shopworn, timeworn **9** hackneyed **11** commonplace
sterile 4 arid, bare, vain **6** barren, fallow **7** aseptic, worn-out **8** desolate, hygienic, impotent, lifeless, sanitary **9** fruitless, infertile **10** antiseptic, unfruitful, uninspired **11** disinfected **12** unproductive
sterilize 3 fix **4** geld, spay **5** alter **6** neuter, purify **7** cleanse **8** sanitize **9** disinfect **10** emasculate
sterilized 7 aseptic
sterling 4 pure, true **5** noble **6** worthy **8** virtuous **9** estimable, exemplary, honorable
stern 4 grim **5** harsh, rigid, sober, stony **6** gloomy, severe, strict **7** ascetic, austere **8** obdurate **10** forbidding, implacable, inexorable, inflexible **11** unrelenting
sternward 3 aft
Sterope *father:* **5** Atlas *mother:* **7** Pleione *sisters:* **8** Pleiades
Stevenson novel 9 Kidnapped
stew 4 boil, brew, flap, fret, fume, fuss, hash, olio, olla, snit **5** daube, salmi, sweat, tizzy, worry **6** burgoo, dither, jumble, lather, medley, pother, ragout, seethe, simmer, swivet, tumult **7** brothel, goulash, mélange, mixture, parboil, swelter, turmoil **8** bordello, mishmash, mulligan, pot-au-feu **9** Brunswick, cassoulet, commotion, confusion, pasticcio, potpourri **10** hodgepodge, hotchpotch, miscellany, turbulence **11** olla podrida, ratatouille, slumgullion **13** bouillabaisse
steward 6 manage **7** manager **8** overseer **10** supervisor
stewed 3 lit **4** high **5** drunk, lit up, oiled **6** bashed, blotto, bombed, cooked, juiced, potted, soaked, soused, stewed, stoned, tanked, wasted, zonked **7** crocked, drunken, pickled, pie-eyed, sloshed, smashed, sottish **8** simmered **9** plastered **10** inebriated, liquored up **11** intoxicated
Stheno see GORGON
stick 3 put, rod **4** glue, pole, stab **5** affix, baton, cling **6** adhere, attach, cleave, cohere, fasten **7** scruple **10** overcharge
stick around 4 bide, stay, wait **5** abide, dally, tarry **6** linger, remain
sticker 3 pin **4** barb, seal, shiv, spur **5** point, prong, shank, spike, spine, stamp **6** dagger **8** stiletto

stick-in-the-mud 4 fogy 6 fossil 8 moss-back 10 fuddy-duddy
stick out 3 jut 5 bulge 6 beetle 7 project 8 overhang, protrude
stick up 3 mug, rob 6 waylay 7 project 8 protrude
sticky 5 gluey, gooey, gummy, humid, muggy, mushy, soggy, tacky 6 clammy, knotty, slushy, sultry, thorny, viscid 7 awkward, cloying, maudlin, mawkish, viscous 8 adhesive, bathetic, clinging, romantic 9 difficult 11 problematic, sentimental, tear-jerking
stiff 3 guy, lit, set 4 body, firm, hard, lush 5 cheat, drunk, harsh, oiled, proud, rigid, stark, steep, stick, tense, tight, tipsy 6 buzzed, corpse, frozen, jelled, juiced, person, plowed, potent, potted, severe, soused, stewed, wooden 7 cadaver, carcass, sloshed, starchy, stilted 8 hardened, reserved, stubborn 9 cardboard, excessive, inelastic, obstinate, petrified, plastered, unbending 10 exorbitant, inebriated, inflexible, mechanical, unyielding 11 intoxicated, intractable
stiffen 5 tense 6 harden 7 thicken 8 rigidify, solidify 9 stabilize 10 immobilize
stifle 3 gag 4 hush, mute 5 burke, choke, deter 6 dampen, deaden, hush up, muffle, muzzle 7 repress, silence, smother, squelch 8 stultify, suppress 9 suffocate 10 asphyxiate, discourage
stigma 4 blot, onus, spot 5 brand, odium, shame, stain, taint 6 smudge, smutch 8 black eye, disgrace, dishonor, petechia, tainting
stigmatize 5 brand, label, stamp
still 3 yet 4 calm, even, hush, lull 5 allay, inert, quiet, shush, whist 6 becalm, hushed, placid, serene, settle, silent, though, withal 7 halcyon, however, silence 8 after all, likewise, peaceful, stagnant, tranquil 9 noiseless, quietness, soundless 10 motionless, stationary 11 furthermore, nonetheless, tranquility 12 nevertheless
stilt 4 bird, pile, pole 8 longlegs 9 shorebird
stilted 4 prim 5 stiff 6 formal, wooden 7 pompous, starchy 8 affected 9 cardboard
stilt-like bird 6 avocet
stimulant 4 goad, spur 5 tonic 7 impetus, impulse 8 caffeine, catalyst, excitant 9 analeptic, energizer, incentive 10 incitement, motivation
stimulate 4 fire, goad, move, prod, spur, urge, whet 5 impel, pique, rouse, set up, spark 6 arouse, excite, fire up, foment, incite, prompt, vivify, work up

7 agitate, enliven, inspire, provoke, quicken, trigger 8 activate, energize, motivate, vitalize 9 galvanize 10 exhilarate
stimulus 4 goad, kick, push, spur 5 boost, cause 6 charge, motive 7 impetus, impulse 8 catalyst 9 incentive 10 incitement, inducement, motivation 11 instigation, provocation 13 encouragement
sting 3 con 4 trap 5 cheat, prick, smart, snare 6 hustle, tingle 7 con game 8 skin game
stinging 8 aculeate
stingy 4 mean 5 close, tight 6 frugal, narrow, paltry, skimpy 7 chintzy, costive, miserly, niggard, scrimpy, sparing, thrifty 8 grudging 9 niggardly, pennywise, penurious 10 economical, ironfisted, pinchpenny, ungenerous 11 tightfisted 12 cheeseparing, parsimonious 13 penny-pinching
stink 4 flap, funk, fuss, reek 5 smell 6 stench
stinker 3 dog, dud 4 bomb, bust, flop 5 lemon, skunk 6 petrel
stinking see SMELLY
stinky see SMELLY
stint 3 job 4 bout, task, time, tour, turn 5 chore, cramp, pinch, scant, share, shift, skimp, spare, spell 6 amount, scrape, scrimp 8 quantity, restrict 9 allotment, stricture 10 assignment, limitation 11 restriction
stipend 3 fee, pay 4 hire, wage 5 award 6 salary 7 payment 9 allowance, emolument 13 consideration
stipple 3 dot 5 fleck, speck 6 pepper 7 freckle, speckle 8 sprinkle
stipulate 5 state 6 detail 7 specify 8 contract, spell out 13 particularize
stipulation 5 limit, terms 7 proviso, strings 9 condition, provision 11 requirement
stir 3 ado, din, mix 4 beat, fuss, rout, to-do, wake, whet 5 awake, blend, budge, churn, evoke, impel, raise, rally, rouse, roust, set on, spark, waken, whirl 6 arouse, awaken, bustle, excite, flurry, foment, hubbub, incite, kindle, pother, seethe, simmer, tumult, whip up 7 actuate, agitate, disturb, ferment, inspire, provoke, quicken 8 activate, activity, energize 9 agitation, commotion, galvanize, stimulate 11 disturbance
stirrup 6 stapes 8 footrest
stithy 5 anvil
stoat 6 ermine, weasel
stock 4 butt, fund, hope, race 5 brace, carry, faith, goods, hoard, store, trunk,

trust 6 family, supply 7 furnish, lineage 8 pedigree, reliance 9 inventory, selection 10 confidence, dependence 11 merchandise

stockade 4 jail 5 fence 6 paling, prison 8 palisade 9 enclosure, guardroom

stock exchange 6 bourse

stockings 4 hose 5 socks 7 hosiery

stockpile 4 bank, heap, mass 5 amass, cache, hoard, lay up, store 6 garner, supply 7 backlog, collect, nest egg, reserve, store up 9 inventory, reservoir 10 accumulate, repository

stocky 3 fat 5 beefy, burly, dumpy, husky, plump, pudgy, squat, stout, thick 6 chunky, stubby, stumpy 8 heavyset, thickset 9 corpulent

stodge 4 fill, sate 5 gorge, stuff 7 overeat, surfeit

stodgy 5 fusty 6 stuffy 9 hidebound, out-of-date 12 old-fashioned

stogie 4 shoe 5 cigar 6 brogan

stoic 6 stolid 7 Spartan 9 apathetic, impassive 10 phlegmatic 11 indifferent, unconcerned

stoicism 9 stolidity 11 impassivity *founder:* 4 Zeno

stoke 3 fan 4 feed, fuel, poke, stir, tend 6 supply

Stoker novel 7 Dracula

stolid 3 dry 4 dull, flat 5 stoic 6 wooden 8 rocklike 9 apathetic, impassive, unruffled 10 phlegmatic 11 unemotional

stomach 3 gut 4 bear, craw 5 abide, belly, brook, stand, taste, tummy 6 digest, endure, paunch, venter 7 abdomen, swallow 8 appetite, tolerate *combining form:* 5 gastr 8 gastro, ventri, ventro *enzyme:* 6 pepsin, rennin *muscle:* 7 pylorus *ruminant:* 6 omasum 8 abomasum 9 reticulum *Scottish:* 4 kyte

stomachache 5 colic, gripe 12 collywobbles

stomp 5 clomp, clump, pound, tramp, tromp 7 trample

stone 3 gem 4 rock 5 lapis 6 pebble 7 boulder *base:* 6 plinth *block of:* 8 monolith *chip:* 5 spall *combining form:* 4 lite, lith, lyte *cosmic:* 6 meteor 9 chondrite, meteorite *for grinding grains:* 6 metate *fruit:* 5 drupe *memorial:* 7 obelisk *monument:* 8 megalith *of a fruit:* 3 pit

___ **Stone** 7 Blarney, Rosetta

Stone novel 11 Lust for Life 18 Agony and the Ecstasy (The)

stonecrop 5 sedum

stoned 3 lit 4 high 5 boozy, doped, drunk, fried, oiled, tight, tipsy 6 buzzed, canned, juiced, loaded,

plowed, potted, soused, stewed, tanked, wasted, zonked 7 crocked, drugged, muddled, pickled, pie-eyed, sloshed, smashed 8 hopped-up, turned on, wiped out 9 pixilated, plastered, spaced-out, strung out 10 inebriated, tripped out 11 intoxicated

stooge 3 act, sap 4 dupe, foil, gull, mark, pawn, tool 5 chump, dummy, patsy, proxy 6 puppet, sucker, victim 7 fall guy 8 sidekick 9 represent 11 stool pigeon, straight man 12 second banana

Stooge 3 Moe (Howard) 5 Curly (Howard), Larry (Fine)

stool pigeon 3 rat 4 fink, nark 5 decoy 6 canary, snitch 7 ratfink, tipster 8 informer

stoop 3 dip 4 bend, duck, sink 5 deign, hunch, porch, slump 6 resort, slouch 7 descend, portico, veranda 8 stairway 10 condescend

stop 3 bar, can, dam, end 4 clog, fill, halt, plug, quit, stay, stem 5 block, brake, cease, check, close, stall, tarry 6 arrest, cut off, desist, draw up, ending, kibosh, stanch 7 disrupt, occlude, prevent, shut off, sojourn, suspend, turn off 8 knock off, leave off, obstruct 9 cessation, interrupt, terminate 10 conclusion, standstill 11 discontinue, refrain from, termination *up:* 4 cork, plug 7 occlude

stopgap 5 shift 6 resort 8 recourse, resource 9 expedient, makeshift 10 expediency, substitute

stopover 4 stay 5 visit 7 sojourn

stoppage 4 halt 6 cutoff, strike 7 walkout 8 shutdown 10 standstill 11 obstruction

stopper 4 bung, cork, fill, plug 5 close

store 3 bin 4 fund, mart, pack, shop, tank 5 amass, cache, depot, hoard, lay up, stash 6 ensile, garner, market, outlet, shoppe, supply 7 arsenal, backlog, bootery, deposit, reserve 8 boutique, cumulate, emporium, mothball, showroom, squirrel 9 abundance, chandlery, inventory, reservoir, stockpile, warehouse 10 accumulate, depository, five-and-ten, repository 11 five-and-dime 12 accumulation

storehouse 5 depot 7 arsenal, granary 8 magazine 9 stockpile 10 depository, repository

storekeeper 8 merchant, retailer 9 tradesman

storeroom 6 larder, pantry 7 buttery

storm 3 row 4 fury, gale, hail, rage, rant, rave, roar, rush, to-do 5 beset, blast, blitz, burst, furor, onset, salvo 6 assail, attack, charge, clamor, fall on, flurry, furore, hubbub, outcry, pother, racket, rumpus, shower, squall, strike, tumult, volley **7** assault, barrage, bluster, cyclone, monsoon, ruction, tempest, thunder, tornado, turmoil, twister, typhoon **8** blizzard, downpour, drumfire, fall upon, outbreak, outburst, paroxysm, upheaval **9** broadside, cannonade, commotion, discharge, fusillade, hurricane, nor'easter, onslaught **10** blitzkrieg, cloudburst, hurly-burly **11** bombardment, northeaster, northwester

storm trooper 10 brownshirt
stormy 4 foul **5** rainy, rough **6** raging **7** furious **8** blustery **9** turbulent **10** tumultuous **11** tempestuous, threatening
story 3 fib, lie **4** epic, saga, tale, yarn **5** conte, fable **6** canard, legend, report **7** account, fiction, märchen, parable, version **8** allegory, anecdote, folktale, megillah, tall tale **9** chronicle, fairy tale, narration, narrative **11** description, fabrication
storyteller 4 liar **6** fibber **8** fabulist **9** raconteur
stoup 4 font **5** basin **6** flagon, goblet **7** chalice, tankard
stout 3 ale, fat **4** brew **5** beefy, bulky, burly, heavy, husky, obese, plump, thick **6** fleshy, portly, strong, sturdy **9** corpulent **10** overweight
Stout detective 5 Wolfe (Nero)
stouthearted 4 bold, game **5** brave, gutsy **7** doughty, valiant **6** fearless, intrepid, resolute, stalwart, stubborn, unafraid **9** audacious, dauntless, undaunted **10** courageous
stove 4 kiln, oven **5** range **8** Franklin, potbelly
stow 4 load, pack **5** stash, store **7** deposit
stower 9 stevedore
Stowe work 4 Dred
strabismus 6 squint
straddle 4 span **6** sprawl **8** bestride **11** spread-eagle
strafe 4 rake **6** attack **8** enfilade **10** machine-gun
straggle 3 lag **4** poke, roam, rove **5** drift, range, stray **6** dawdle, loiter, ramble, wander **7** maunder, meander **8** trail off **9** string out
straight 4 even, fair, neat, pure, true **5** erect, plain, plumb, right **6** at once, candid, direct, honest, linear, square **7** unmixed, upright **8** orthodox **9** bourgeois, forthwith, undiluted **10** aboveboard, button-down, forthright **12** con-

ventional **13** unadulterated *combining form:* **4** orth, rect **5** ortho, recti
straightaway 3 now **6** at once **7** stretch **8** directly, first off, promptly **9** forthwith, instanter **11** immediately
straighten 4 even, tidy **5** align **6** neaten, unbend, uncurl **7** rectify
straightforward 5 frank, lucid **6** candid, direct, honest **7** genuine, precise, sincere **8** clear-cut **9** outspoken **10** forthright **11** undeviating
strain 3 air, tax, try **4** hint, kind, pull, sort, toil, tune, vein **5** exert, stock, sweat, tinge, touch, trace, twist **6** filter, melody, screen, streak, stress, strive, wrench **7** lineage, overtax, tension, trouble **8** ancestry, exertion, overwork, pedigree, pressure, struggle **9** overexert
strait 4 bind, pass **5** pinch **6** crisis, plight **7** channel, dilemma, narrows, squeeze **8** exigency, hardship, juncture **9** crossroad, emergency **10** difficulty **11** contingency *Adriatic Sea-Ionian Sea:* **7** Otranto *Alaska:* **3** Icy *Alaska-Russia:* **6** Bering *Albania-Greece:* **5** Corfu *Asia-Europe:* **11** Dardanelles *Atlantic-Baffin Island:* **5** Davis *Atlantic-Mediterranean:* **9** Gibraltar *Atlantic-Nantucket Sound:* **8** Muskeget *Atlantic-North Sea:* **7** English *Atlantic-Pacific:* **5** Drake **8** Magellan *Atlantic-Saint Lawrence:* **5** Cabot *Baffin Island-Quebec:* **6** Hudson *Bering Sea-Sea of Okhotsk:* **5** Kuril **6** Kurile *Bismarck Sea-Solomon Sea:* **6** Vitiaz *Canada:* **3** Rae **5** Dease *East China Sea:* **5** Korea **8** Tsushima *East China-South China:* **6** Taiwan **7** Formosa *England-France:* **5** Dover *Flores Sea-Indian Ocean:* **4** Sape *Flores Sea-Savu Sea:* **4** Alor *Indian Ocean-Java Sea:* **5** Sunda *India-Sri Lanka:* **4** Palk *Indonesia:* **4** Alas, Alor, Bali **5** Tioro **6** Lombok **7** Dampier **8** Macassar, Makassar, Surabaya *Inner Hebrides:* **5** Tiree *Iran-Oman:* **6** Hormuz *Italy:* **7** Messina *Japan:* **4** Yura **5** Bungo, Kitan **7** Hayasui *Japan-Sakhalin Island:* **4** Soya *Lake Huron:* **10** Mississagi *Lake Huron-Lake Michigan:* **8** Mackinac *Malay Archipelago:* **5** Wetar *Malaysia-Singapore:* **6** Johore *Malay-Sumatra:* **7** Malacca *New Jersey-Staten Island:* **7** van Kull *New South Wales-Tasmania:* **4** Bass *New Zealand:* **4** Cook *Northwest Territories:* **6** Barrow **8** Franklin, Victoria **13** Prince of Wales *Nova Scotia:* **5** Canso *Pacific-San Francisco Bay:* **10** Golden Gate *Pacific-South China Sea:* **5** Luzon *Philippines:* **5** Bohol, Tanon **6** Iloilo **7** Basilan *Russia:* **4** Kara *Suvu Sea-Timor Sea:* **4** Roti *Sea of Azov-Black Sea:* **5** Kerch **7** Enikale *Sea of Japan:* **5** Tatar *Solomon*

Islands: 12 Bougainville *South China Sea:* 7 Mindoro 9 Singapore *Turkey:* 8 Bosporus 9 Bosphorus, Karadeniz *Vancouver-Washington:* 10 Juan de Fuca *Wales:* 5 Menai *Washington Sound:* 4 Haro

straitened 7 lacking, pinched, wanting 8 deprived, strapped 9 deficient, destitute 10 distressed, inadequate 12 impoverished

straitlaced 4 prim 5 staid, stiff 6 formal, narrow, prissy, strict, stuffy 7 genteel, prudish, starchy, stilted 8 priggish 9 hidebound, Victorian 11 puritanical

strand 4 bank 5 beach, coast, fiber, leave, shore, wreck 6 desert, maroon, thread 7 abandon, shingle 8 cast away, littoral, seacoast, seashore 9 shipwreck 10 run aground, waterfront

strange 3 odd 5 alien, crazy, fishy, funny, kinky, kooky, nutty, outré, queer, weird 6 exotic, far-out, freaky 7 bizarre, curious, oddball, offbeat, uncanny, unknown, unusual 8 aberrant, abnormal, atypical, peculiar, singular, wondrous 9 eccentric, fantastic, grotesque 10 mysterious, off-the-wall, outlandish, surprising, unfamiliar 11 exceptional 12 unaccustomed

Strange Interlude author 6 O'Neill (Eugene)

stranger 5 alien, guest 7 visitor 8 newcomer, outsider, wanderer 9 auslander, foreigner, immigrant, transient

strangle 5 burke, choke, shush 6 muffle, quelch, stifle 7 garotte, garrote 8 suppress, throttle 10 asphyxiate

strap 4 band, beat, belt, bind 5 leash 6 attach, punish, secure, suffer 7 binding, leather 8 distress 9 constrict

strapping 5 beefy, burly, hardy, husky 6 brawny, robust, rugged, sturdy 8 muscular, vigorous 10 able-bodied

stratagem 4 play, plot, ploy, ruse, wile 5 feint, trick 6 device, gambit, scheme, tactic 8 artifice, intrigue, maneuver 10 conspiracy, subterfuge 11 machination

strategy 4 plan 6 design, method, scheme 7 project, tactics 8 game plan 9 blueprint

stratum 3 bed 4 rank 5 class, grade, layer, level

Strauss, Richard opera: 6 Salome 7 Elektra 13 Rosenkavalier (Der) 15 Ariadne auf Naxos 16 Frau ohne Schatten (Der) *tone poem:* 7 Don Juan 10 Don Quixote 11 Heldenleben (Ein) 20 Thus Spake Zarathustra 23 Death and Transfiguration

straw 3 hay 5 blond 6 flaxen, golden,

thatch *braided:* 6 sennit *mat:* 6 tatami *plaited:* 7 leghorn

stray 3 err, gad 4 lost, roam, rove, waif 5 drift, range 6 depart, errant, ramble, random, wander 7 deviate, digress, diverge, erratic, meander, runaway, traipse, vagrant 8 divagate, homeless, sporadic 9 gallivant

streak 4 hint, vein 5 fleck, tinge, trace 6 dapple, marble, mottle, strain, stripe 7 striate 8 tincture 9 suspicion, variegate 10 intimation, suggestion

streaked 5 upset 7 brindle, marbled, striped 8 brindled, grizzled 9 disturbed

stream 3 run 4 beck, burn, flow, flux, gill, gush, pour, race, rill, rush, sike, tide 5 bourn, brook, creek, spate, surge 6 bourne, branch, rindle, runnel, sluice 7 current, freshet, rivulet, torrent 8 affluent

streamer 4 flag, jack 6 banner, burgee, ensign, pennon 7 pennant 8 banderol, bannerol, standard 9 banderole

streamline 7 contour 8 organize, simplify 9 modernize

street 3 way 4 drag, road, wynd 5 alley, drive 6 artery, avenue 7 roadway 9 boulevard 12 thoroughfare *border:* 4 curb 7 curbing *material:* 6 cobble 7 asphalt, macadam 11 cobblestone

streetcar 4 tram 7 trolley

Streetcar Named Desire, A author: 8 Williams (Tennessee) *character:* 6 Stella (Kowalski) 7 Blanche (DuBois), Stanley (Kowalski)

Street Scene author 4 Rice (Elmer)

strength 5 brawn, force, might, power, sinew, vigor 6 energy, muscle 7 potency 8 firmness, security 9 fortitude, intensity, soundness, stability, toughness 10 steadiness, sturdiness

strengthen 4 gird 5 brace, steel 6 anneal, harden, prop up 7 bolster, enhance, fortify, support, toughen 8 buttress, embolden, energize 9 intensify, reinforce, undergird 10 invigorate, rejuvenate

strenuous 4 hard 5 tough 6 taxing, uphill 7 arduous, operose 9 demanding, difficult, effortful, Herculean, laborious 12 backbreaking

Strephon 8 shepherd *beloved:* 5 Chloe 6 Urania

stress 6 accent, burden, import, play up, strain, weight 7 anxiety, feature, tension, trouble, urgency 8 emphasis, pressure 9 emphasize, italicize, underline 10 accentuate, underscore 12 accentuation *in poetry:* 5 ictus

stretch 4 area, draw, time 5 range, reach, scope, space, spell, sweep, tract, while

6 extend, extent, length, limber, region, spread 7 breadth, compass, draw out, expanse, magnify, prolong, purview, spin out, tighten 8 distance, elongate, lengthen, protract 9 embellish, embroider, expansion, overstate 10 exaggerate *on a frame:* 6 tenter *out:* 6 sprawl 7 lie down, recline

stretchable 7 ductile, elastic, tensile

stretched 4 taut

stretcher 4 yarn 6 gurney, litter 8 tall tale

strew 3 sow 4 dust 5 cover 6 pepper, spread 7 scatter 8 disperse, sprinkle 9 broadcast, circulate, propagate 10 distribute 11 disseminate

stricken 3 hit, ill 4 hurt, sick 7 injured, wounded 9 afflicted 11 overwhelmed

strict 4 firm 5 exact, harsh, rigid, stern, tough 6 narrow, severe 7 precise 8 exacting, faithful, rigorous 9 draconian, stringent, unsparing 10 inflexible, ironhanded, meticulous, scrupulous 11 punctilious

stricture 5 cramp, stint 7 censure, reproof 8 reproach 9 aspersion, criticism, reprimand 10 constraint, limitation 11 restriction 13 animadversion

stride 4 gait, pace, step 5 march, stalk 7 advance 8 straddle

strident 4 loud 5 harsh 6 shrill 7 grating, jarring, rasping, raucous, squawky 8 piercing 9 clamorous, insistent, obtrusive 10 boisterous, discordant, stentorian, vociferous 11 loudmouthed 12 earsplitting, obstreperous

strife 4 fray 5 broil, fight 6 battle, combat 7 discord, dispute, dissent, quarrel, rivalry, warfare, wrangle 8 argument, conflict, disunity, friction, struggle, tug-of-war 10 contention, difference, dissension, dissidence 11 altercation, competition, controversy

strike 3 hit, pop, rap 4 bash, beat, find, poke, slam, slap, slug, sock, swat, whap, whop 5 clout, knock, punch, smack, smite, swipe, thump, whack 6 affect, assail, attack, cudgel, delete, hammer, pummel, thrash 7 assault, impress, inflict, inspire 8 discover, stoppage

striking 5 showy, vivid 6 cogent, marked, signal 7 salient, telling 8 forceful 9 arresting, prominent 10 compelling, noticeable, remarkable 11 conspicuous, outstanding

Strindberg play 6 Easter, Father (The) 8 Comrades 9 Creditors (The), Dream Play (A), Miss Julie 10 Master Olaf 11 Ghost Sonata (The) 12 Dance of Death (The), Gustavus Vasa

string 3 row 4 file, line, rank, tier 5 chain, order, queue, train, twine

6 sequel, series 7 echelon 8 recourse, resource, sequence 10 succession *up:* 4 hang 5 noose, scrag 6 gibbet

stringent see STRICT

stringy 4 lean, ropy, wiry 6 sinewy 7 fibrous 8 muscular

strip 4 band, bare, doff, flay, husk, peel, sack, skin 5 scale 6 billet, denude, divest, expose, fillet, ravage, ribbon 7 bandeau, deprive, disrobe, pillage, uncover, undress 8 unclothe *leather:* 5 thong *of wood:* 4 lath, slat *skin:* 6 flense

stripe 3 ilk 4 band, kind, lash, sort, type 5 order 6 strake, streak 7 banding, chevron, lineate, striate, variety

stripling 3 boy, lad 5 youth 9 youngster 10 adolescent

stripper 6 peeler, teaser 9 ecdysiast

stripteaser see STRIPPER

strive 3 try, vie 4 seek 5 labor 6 strain 7 attempt, contend 8 endeavor, struggle 9 undertake

stroke 3 fit, hit, pet, rub 4 blow, hone, whet 5 swing 6 attack, caress, fondle, soothe 7 flatter 8 apoplexy, ischemia 9 heartbeat

stroll 4 rove, turn, walk 5 amble, drift, mosey, paseo 6 cruise, linger, ramble, wander 7 saunter, traipse 9 promenade

stroller 4 pram 6 go-cart 8 carriage 12 baby carriage, perambulator

strong 4 fast, firm, hard 5 burly, hardy, lusty, solid, sound, stout, tough 6 brawny, hearty, heroic, mighty, potent, robust, rugged, secure, sinewy, stable, sturdy 7 durable, intense, staunch 8 forceful, muscular, powerful, stalwart, vigorous 9 resilient, strapping, tenacious 10 able-bodied, full-bodied, spirituous 12 concentrated

strong-arm 5 bully 6 bounce, hector, lean on 7 assault, dragoon 8 browbeat, bulldoze, bullyrag 9 terrorize 10 intimidate

strongbox 4 safe 5 chest 6 coffer 13 treasure chest

stronghold 4 fort 7 bastion, bulwark, citadel, redoubt 8 fastness, fortress

strong point 5 forte 6 métier

strong suit see STRONG POINT

strophe 5 verse 6 stanza

structure 4 form 5 frame 6 format, makeup, system 7 anatomy, complex, edifice, network 8 building, erection, skeleton 9 framework 10 morphology 11 arrangement, composition

struggle 3 try, vie 4 agon 5 trial 6 battle, effort, hassle, strain, strife, strive, tussle 7 attempt, compete, contest, grapple, scuffle 8 endeavor, exertion, flounder, skirmish, striving **9** undertake **11** undertaking

strumpet 4 bawd, jade, slut, tart **5** hussy, tramp, trull, wench **6** floozy, harlot, hooker, wanton **7** jezebel, trollop **8** slattern

strut 6 flaunt, parade, prance, sashay **7** flounce, peacock, show off, swagger

stub 3 end **4** butt, tail **5** stump **6** put out, strike **7** remnant **10** extinguish

stubborn 5 balky, rigid **6** cussed, dogged, mulish, ornery **7** adamant, lasting, willful **8** obdurate, perverse **9** obstinate, pigheaded, steadfast, unbending **10** bullheaded, determined, headstrong, inexorable, inflexible, persistent, rebellious, refractory, relentless, unyielding **11** intractable **12** cantankerous, contumacious, pertinacious, single-minded

stubby 5 dumpy, short, squat, stout **6** stocky, stumpy **8** heavyset, thickset

stuck 5 clung, glued **6** jammed, wedged **7** adhered, baffled, blocked, saddled, stabbed, stopped, stumped **8** attached, held fast **11** overcharged

stuck-up 4 vain **6** sniffy, snippy, snooty **7** haughty **8** snobbish **9** conceited **12** narcissistic, supercilious

stud 3 guy **4** dude, hunk, male, nail, post **5** cleat **6** button, pillar **7** earring, speckle, upright **8** sprinkle, stallion

student 5 pupil **6** novice **7** protégé, scholar **8** disciple **10** apprentice *college:* **9** undergrad **13** undergraduate *female:* **4** coed *first-year:* **5** frosh **8** freshman *fourth-year:* **6** senior *French:* **5** élève **8** étudiant *military:* **5** cadet, middy **10** midshipman *second-year:* **9** sophomore *third-year:* **6** junior *wandering:* **7** goliard

studio 4 shop **7** atelier **8** workroom, workshop

studious 7 bookish, learned **9** scholarly

Studs Lonigan creator 7 Farrell (James T.)

study 3 con, den, vet **4** cram, muse **6** ponder, survey **7** analyze, examine, inspect, reverie **8** consider **9** attention, think over **10** excogitate, scrutinize **11** application

stuff 3 jam, ram **4** cram, fill, glut, junk, pack, sate, tamp **5** crowd, gorge, shove **6** matter, things **7** essence, jam-pack, squeeze, surfeit **8** material, overfill **9** substance **11** possessions

stuffy 4 dull, prim **5** close, fuggy, heavy, humid, stale, thick **6** narrow, stodgy **7** airless, bloated, genteel, humdrum, pompous, prudish, stilted **8** priggish, stagnant, stifling **9** hidebound, Victorian **10** oppressive, pontifical **11** puritanical, suffocating **12** narrow-minded **13** self-important, self-righteous

stultify 4 dull **6** deaden, impair, stifle, weaken **7** inhibit, nullify, repress, smother, trammel **8** restrain, stagnate, suppress **9** suffocate **10** discourage, invalidate

stumble 3 err **4** reel, slip, trip **5** error, fluff, gaffe, lapse, lurch **6** falter, muddle, slipup, totter **7** blunder, faux pas, mistake, stagger, stammer **8** flounder

stump 3 end **4** beat, butt, dare, defy, plod, stub **5** barge, clomp, clump, stick **6** baffle, outwit, puzzle, stymie, trudge **7** buffalo, flummox, galumph, mystify, nonplus, perplex **8** bewilder, campaign, confound, hustings, politick **9** barnstorm, challenge **11** electioneer

stun 4 daze **5** amaze, floor, shock **6** dazzle **7** astound, nonplus, stagger, stupefy **8** astonish, bewilder, bowl over, knock out, paralyze **9** dumbfound **11** flabbergast

stunning 6 superb **7** amazing, awesome **8** gorgeous, striking **9** excellent, wonderful **10** astounding, impressive, remarkable, staggering, surprising **11** astonishing

stunt 4 curb, feat **5** antic, caper, check, dwarf, prank, trick **6** hinder, impair, retard **8** escapade, hold back, suppress

stupefy 4 daze, dull, faze, stun **5** addle, amaze **6** muddle, rattle **7** astound, nonplus, petrify, stagger **8** astonish, bewilder, paralyze **9** disorient, dumbfound **11** flabbergast

stupendous 7 amazing, awesome, massive, titanic **8** colossal, enormous, gigantic, stunning, towering, wondrous **9** fantastic, marvelous, monstrous, wonderful **10** astounding, miraculous, monumental, phenomenal, prodigious, staggering, tremendous **11** astonishing, spectacular **12** breathtaking, mindboggling, overwhelming

stupid 3 dim **4** dull, dumb, slow **5** dense, dopey, inane, silly, thick **6** oafish, obtuse, simple, torpid **7** asinine, doltish, fatuous, foolish, idiotic, moronic, witless **8** backward, ignorant, mindless, retarded **9** brainless, fatheaded, imbecilic, laughable, ludicrous, pinheaded, senseless **10** half-witted, slow-witted **11** blockheaded, thickheaded, thickwitted **13** chuckleheaded

stupor 6 torpor **7** languor **8** dullness, hebetude, lethargy, narcosis **9** lassitude, torpidity **10** anesthesia, somnolence **13** insensibility *combining form:* **4** narc **5** narco

sturdy 5 hardy, solid, sound, stout,

tough **6** robust, rugged, secure, strong **7** durable, healthy, staunch **8** stalwart, vigorous **9** strapping
sturgeon 6 beluga *roe:* **6** caviar
Sturm und Drang 5 angst **6** unease, unrest **7** anxiety, ferment, turmoil **8** disquiet **9** agitation **10** inquietude, turbulence **11** disquietude, restiveness **12** restlessness
St. Vitus' ___ 5 dance
sty 3 pen **4** coop, cyst **6** pigpen **7** piggery
stygian 4 dark **6** gloomy **7** hellish, sunless **8** infernal, plutonic **9** Cimmerian, plutonian
style 3 fad, way **4** élan, mode, rage, vein **5** craze, decor, flair, trend, vogue **6** manner **7** fashion, panache **10** dernier cri **11** savoir-faire *hair:* **4** coif **8** coiffure
stylish 3 mod **4** chic, posh, tony, trig **5** doggy, natty, ritzy, sassy, sharp, showy, sleek, slick, smart, swank, swell **6** chichi, dapper, dressy, modern, modish, snappy, snazzy, spiffy, trendy, with-it **7** à la mode, dashing, doggish **8** spiffing, up-to-date **10** newfangled **11** fashionable
stymie 4 stop **5** block **6** hamper, hinder, impede, thwart **7** flummox, prevent **8** confound, obstruct **9** frustrate, hamstring
Stymphalides' slayer 8 Heracles, Hercules
Styron novel 13 Sophie's Choice **22** Confessions of Nat Turner (The)
Styx *father:* **7** Oceanus *ferryman:* **6** Charon *location:* **5** Hades *mother:* **6** Tethys
Styx's counterpart 5 Lethe **7** Acheron, Cocytus **10** Phlegethon
suave 4 oily **5** slick **6** smooth, urbane **7** cordial, courtly, gallant, politic, refined, tactful, worldly **8** debonair, gracious, polished, unctuous, well-bred **9** courteous **10** cultivated, diplomatic **12** ingratiating **13** sophisticated
sub 5 below, proxy, under **6** backup, fill-in **7** stand-by, stand-in **8** pinch-hit **9** alternate, secondary, surrogate **10** understudy **11** locum tenens, pinch hitter, replacement
subaltern 8 inferior **9** secondary, underling
subdue 4 curb, tame **5** crush, quash, quell **6** defeat, master, quench **7** conquer, control, put down, repress, squelch **8** beat down, overcome, suppress, tone down, vanquish **9** overpower, overthrow, subjugate
subdued 4 soft, tame **5** muted, quiet, sober **6** low-key, mellow, subtle **7** neutral, serious **8** low-keyed, softened,

tasteful, tempered **9** moderated, toned down **10** controlled, restrained, submissive **11** unobtrusive
subjacent 3 low **5** lower, under **6** lesser, nether **8** inferior
subject 3 apt **4** core, open **5** motif, point, prone, theme, topic **6** expose, liable, likely, matter, motive, vassal **7** citizen, exposed, lay open, problem **8** argument, inferior, material, question **9** dependent, leitmotif, secondary, sensitive, subjugate, substance, tributary **11** subordinate, subservient, susceptible
subjective 6 biased **10** prejudiced
subjugate see SUBDUE
sublime 4 holy **5** ideal, lofty, noble, proud **6** august, divine, sacred, superb **7** blessed, exalted **8** elevated, glorious, heavenly, majestic, splendid **9** celestial, spiritual **11** magnificent, resplendent **12** transcendent
submarine 4 hero **5** po'boy, U-boat **6** hoagie **7** grinder *detector:* **5** sonar
submerge 3 dip **4** duck, dunk, sink **5** drown, flood, swamp **6** deluge, engulf, plunge **7** founder, go under, immerse **8** inundate, overflow
submerse see SUBMERGE
submissive 4 meek, tame **6** abject, docile, pliant **7** servile, slavish, subdued **8** amenable, obedient, obeisant, yielding **9** compliant, tractable **10** obsequious **11** acquiescent, deferential, subservient, unresisting **12** nonresisting
submit 3 bow **4** cave, fold, obey **5** defer, offer, yield **6** accede, comply, give in, hand in, relent, send in, tender **7** concede, deliver, go under, present, proffer, provide, subject, succumb, suggest **9** acquiesce, surrender **10** capitulate **11** buckle under **12** knuckle under
subordinate 5 minor, scrub, under **6** junior **7** adjunct, subject **8** inferior **9** accessory, ancillary, auxiliary, dependent, secondary, subaltern, tributary, underling **10** collateral, submissive, subsidiary **11** subservient
sub rosa 6 covert, secret **7** furtive, private **8** covertly, in camera, secretly, stealthy **9** by stealth, furtively, privately, secretive, underhand **10** stealthily **11** clandestine, underhanded **13** clandestinely, surreptitious
subscribe 3 ink **4** sign **5** agree **6** accede, adhere, assent, attest, pledge **7** approve, consent, endorse, support **8** sanction **9** acquiesce
subsequent 4 next **5** after, later **6** serial **7** ensuing **9** following, resultant, resulting **10** sequential, succeeding, successive **11** consecutive *prefix:* **4** post

subsequently 4 next, then 5 after, later 9 afterward 10 afterwards, thereafter

subservient 6 abject, docile 7 fawning, ignoble, servile, slavish 8 adjuvant, obeisant 9 accessory, ancillary, auxiliary, compliant, truckling 10 collateral, obsequious, submissive 11 acquiescent, deferential, subordinate, sycophantic

subside 3 ebb 4 ease, fall, lull, sink, wane 5 abate, let up, taper 6 ease up, recede, settle 7 decline, descend, die away, die down, dwindle, ease off, slacken 8 decrease, diminish, moderate

subsidiary 5 minor 6 backup, branch 7 subject 8 adjuvant 9 accessory, ancillary, auxiliary, secondary, tributary 10 collateral 11 subordinate 12 supplemental 13 supplementary

subsidize 4 back, fund 5 endow, stake 7 finance, promote, sponsor, support 8 bankroll 9 grubstake 10 underwrite

subsidy 4 gift 5 grant 6 reward 10 subvention 13 appropriation

subsistence 4 keep, salt 5 bread, means 6 income, living 7 support 9 resources 10 livelihood, sustenance 11 maintenance, wherewithal 12 alimentation

substance 3 nub 4 bulk, core, crux, gist, mass, meat, pith, soul 5 being, drift, focus, heart, point, sense, stuff, tenor 6 amount, burden, entity, import, kernel, marrow, matter, nubbin, object, thrust, upshot, wealth 7 essence, meaning, nucleus, purport 8 material, property, sum total 9 resources 12 essentiality, quintessence

substantial 3 big 4 full 5 ample, hefty, large, solid 6 strong, sturdy 7 massive, sizable, weighty 8 abundant, concrete, material, physical, sensible, tangible 9 corporeal, important, objective 10 meaningful, phenomenal 11 significant 12 considerable

substantiate 5 prove 6 embody, evince, verify 7 bear out, confirm, justify 8 evidence, manifest, validate 9 establish, incarnate, objectify, vindicate 11 corroborate, demonstrate 12 authenticate

substantive 4 firm, noun, real 5 solid 8 definite 9 essential

substitute 4 mock, sham, swap 5 dummy, locum, proxy, trade 6 acting, backup, deputy, double, ersatz, fill-in, refuge, resort, second, switch 7 replace, reserve, standby, stand-in, stopgap 8 exchange, recourse, resource, spurious 9 alternate, expedient, imitation, makeshift, simulated, surrogate, temporary 10 artificial, expediency, understudy 11 alternative, locum tenens,

pinch hitter, replacement, succedaneum

substratum 4 base 5 basis 6 bottom, ground 7 bedrock, footing 10 foundation, groundwork 12 underpinning

substructure 4 base, seat 5 basis 6 bottom 7 footing 10 foundation, groundwork 12 underpinning

subsume 6 embody, take in 7 contain, embrace, include, involve 8 comprise 9 encompass 10 comprehend

subterfuge 4 ploy, ruse, sham 5 cheat, feint, fraud 6 deceit, dupery 7 chicane 8 trickery 9 chicanery, deception 10 dishonesty

subterranean 11 underground

subtle 4 fine 5 faint 6 artful, astute 7 cunning, refined 8 delicate, finespun, guileful, skillful 9 insidious 10 indistinct 13 inconspicuous

subtract 6 deduct, remove 7 take off 8 discount, knock off, take away, withdraw, withhold

subtraction 6 rebate 8 discount 9 abatement, deduction 10 diminution, withdrawal *term:* 7 minuend 9 remainder 10 subtrahend

suburb 8 edge city

suburbs 7 fringes 8 environs, purlieus 9 outskirts

subversion 8 sabotage 11 undermining 12 undercutting

subvert 5 upset 6 debase 7 corrupt, deprave, vitiate 8 overturn, sabotage 9 overthrow, undermine

subway *British:* 4 tube 11 underground *French:* 5 métro

succeed 3 win 4 boom 5 click, ensue, score 6 arrive, follow, go over, make it, pan out, thrive, win out 7 catch on, come off, make out, prevail, prosper, replace, triumph 8 displace, flourish, get ahead, make good, supplant 9 supervene

succes ___ 3 fou 7 d'estime

success 3 hit 5 smash 7 arrival, fortune, killing, triumph, victory 8 fruition 10 attainment, prosperity 11 achievement, fulfillment

successful 5 smash 7 booming 8 fruitful, thriving 9 effective, lucrative 10 prosperous, triumphant, victorious 11 flourishing

succession 3 row 5 chain, cycle, march, order, round, suite, train 6 course, sequel, series, string 8 sequence 11 progression

successive 4 next 7 ensuing 9 following 10 subsequent

successor 4 heir 8 claimant, follower 9 inheritor 11 beneficiary

succinct 4 curt **5** blunt, brief, pithy, short, terse **7** brusque, compact, concise, laconic, summary **11** compendious

succor 3 aid **4** help, lift **6** assist, relief **7** comfort, relieve, support **10** assistance, sustenance

succulent 5 juicy **8** luscious

succumb 3 bow, die **4** cave, fold, wilt **5** defer, yield **6** accede, buckle, cave in, expire, give in, perish, relent, resign, submit **7** give out, go under, knuckle **8** collapse **9** break down, surrender **10** capitulate **11** buckle under **12** knuckle under

sucker 3 con, gyp, sap **4** bilk, dupe, fool, gull, mark, rook **5** cheat, chump, patsy, shoot **6** diddle, pigeon **7** defraud, fall guy, swindle **8** hoodwink, pushover **9** bamboozle

suckle 5 nurse **7** nourish, nurture **10** breast-feed

Sudan *capital:* **8** Khartoum *desert:* **6** Libyan *language:* **6** Arabic *monetary unit:* **5** dinar *neighbor:* **4** Chad **5** Congo, Egypt, Kenya, Libya **6** Uganda **7** Eritrea **8** Ethiopia *river:* **4** Nile *sea:* **3** Red

sudden 4 rash **5** hasty, swift **6** abrupt, prompt **7** hurried **8** headlong **9** impetuous, impromptu, impulsive **10** unexpected, unforeseen **11** precipitant, precipitate, precipitous

suddenly 5 aback **7** hastily, shortly, unaware **8** abruptly, promptly, unawares **10** by surprise **12** unexpectedly

suds 4 beer, fizz, foam, head, soap **5** froth, spume **6** lather

sue 8 litigate

suer 8 litigant

suet 3 fat **4** lard **6** tallow

Suez Canal *builder:* **7** Lesseps (Ferdinand de) *city:* **8** Ismailia, Port Said

suffer 4 ache, bear, lump **5** abide, admit, allow, brook, leave, stand, yield **6** accept, endure, permit, submit **7** agonize, anguish, stomach, sustain, swallow, undergo **8** tolerate **10** experience **11** countenance

sufferer 6 victim

suffering 4 ache **5** agony, dolor **6** misery, ordeal **7** anguish, passion, torment, torture **8** distress **10** affliction, misfortune

suffice 5 avail, serve

sufficient 3 due **5** ample **6** common, decent, enough, plenty **8** adequate, all right **9** competent, tolerable **10** acceptable **11** comfortable **12** commensurate, satisfactory **13** commensurable, proportionate *poetic:* **4** enow

suffocate 5 burke, choke **6** stifle **7** smother **8** snuff out, strangle **10** asphyxiate

suffrage 4 vote **5** voice **6** ballot **9** franchise

suffragist 4 Catt (Carrie Chapman), Howe (Julia Ward), Mott (Lucretia), Paul (Alice) **5** Stone (Lucy) **7** Anthony (Susan B.), Bloomer (Amelia), Stanton (Elizabeth Cady) **8** Woodhull (Victoria Claflin) **9** Pankhurst (Emmeline)

suffuse 4 fill **5** flush, imbue, steep **7** pervade **8** permeate, saturate **10** impregnate

sugar 6 aldose, fucose, xylose **7** glucose, lactose, maltose, mannose, pentose, sorbose, sucrose, sweeten **8** fructose, furanose, levulose **10** saccharose *combining form:* **4** gluc, glyc, sucr **5** gluco, glyco, sucro **7** sacchar **8** sacchari, saccharo *from palm sap:* **7** jaggery *Mexican:* **7** panocha, penuche *source:* **4** beet, cane, corn **5** maple

sugarcane refuse 7 bagasse

sugarcoat 5 candy **6** veneer **7** sweeten, varnish **8** palliate **9** extenuate, gloss over, gloze over, whitewash

sugary 6 syrupy **7** cloying, honeyed, mawkish **10** saccharine **11** sentimental

suggest 4 hint **5** evoke, imply **6** submit **7** connote, propose, signify **8** indicate, intimate **9** adumbrate, insinuate

suggestion 3 cue **4** clue, hint **5** shade, smack, tinge, trace **6** advice **7** inkling **8** allusion, innuendo, overtone, proposal, reminder **9** suspicion, undertone **10** indication, intimation **11** implication, insinuation

suggestive 4 racy **5** salty, spicy **6** ribald, risqué **8** off-color **9** evocative **10** indicative **11** reminiscent

suicidal pilot 8 kamikaze

suicide 8 felo-de-se, hara-kiri **10** self-murder **13** self-slaughter *Japanese:* **7** seppuku

suit 3 fit **4** case, jibe, plea **5** adapt, agree, befit, cause, check, serve, tally **6** accord, action, adjust, appeal, become, go with, please, prayer, square, tailor **7** conform, enhance, flatter, lawsuit, request, satisfy **8** entreaty, petition **9** agree with, reconcile **10** go together **11** accommodate, application, imploration, imprecation **12** solicitation, supplication *type:* **4** zoot **6** monkey, vested **9** paternity **10** pin-striped **11** class-action

suitable 3 apt, due, fit **4** just, meet **5** right **6** proper, seemly, useful **7** condign, fitting **8** apposite, becoming, deserved, eligible **9** pertinent, qualified, requisite **10** acceptable, felicitous **11** appropriate

suitcase 3 bag **4** grip **6** valise **7** carry-on, holdall **8** carryall

suite 3 lot, row, set **4** flat **5** array, group, rooms, staff, train **6** sequel, series, string **7** lodging, retinue **8** chambers, sequence **9** apartment, entourage, following

suitor 4 beau **5** lover, spark, swain, wooer **7** admirer, gallant, sparker **8** cavalier, paramour **9** boyfriend **10** petitioner

sulfur 9 brimstone

sulk 4 mope, pout **5** brood, gloom

sulky 4 cart, dour, glum **5** moody **6** gloomy, morose, sullen **7** crabbed **9** saturnine

sullen 4 dour, glum, mean, sour **5** moody, pouty, surly **6** crabby, dismal, gloomy, grumpy, morose, somber, sombre **7** crabbed, pouting **8** lowering, scowling **9** glowering, saturnine **10** ill-humored **11** pessimistic

Sullivan's partner 7 Gilbert (William Schwenk)

sully 3 tar **4** soil **5** dirty, shame, smear, stain, taint **6** defame, defile, malign, vilify **7** asperse, blacken, pollute, slander, tarnish, traduce **8** besmirch, disgrace, dishonor **9** denigrate

Sultan of Swat 8 Babe Ruth

sultry 3 hot **4** sexy **5** close, humid, muggy **6** steamy, sticky, stuffy, torrid **7** airless **8** stifling **9** seductive **10** passionate, sweltering, voluptuous

sum 3 add, all, tot **4** mass, tote **5** gross, total, whole **6** amount, digest, entity, figure, resumé **7** epitome **8** entirety, integral, nutshell, totality **9** aggregate, epitomize

Sumatra *country:* **9** Indonesia *highest peak:* **7** Kerinci **8** Kerintji *largest city:* **5** Medan *shrew:* **4** tana

Sumerian *city:* **4** Umma *dragon:* **3** Kur *god:* **3** Abu, Kur, Utu **4** Enki **5** Enlil, Lahar, Nanna, Nintu **6** Dumuzi, Nergal, Ninazu **7** Enkimdu *goddess:* **6** Ningal, Ninlil

summarize 5 recap **6** digest **7** abridge, outline **8** boil down, condense **9** epitomize, synopsize **11** encapsulate **12** recapitulate

summary 5 recap **6** aperçu, digest, précis, résumé, review, wrap-up **7** compend, epitome, outline, roundup, rundown **8** abstract, overview, scenario, synopsis **9** inventory **10** abridgment, compendium, conspectus **12** condensation

summer *French:* **3** été

summerhouse 6 alcove, gazebo, pagoda **9** belvedere

summery 7 estival

summit 3 top **4** acme, apex, peak, roof **5** crest, crown **6** apogee, climax, height, vertex, zenith **8** capstone, meridian, pinnacle **11** culmination

summon 3 bid **4** call, cite **5** evoke, order **6** beckon, call in, invite, muster **7** arraign, command, conjure, convene, convoke, send for **8** assemble, subpoena

sump 4 sink **8** cesspool

sumptuous 4 lush, rich **5** grand **6** costly, deluxe, lavish, superb **7** opulent **8** gorgeous, luscious, palatial, splendid **9** grandiose, luxurious **11** extravagant, resplendent **12** awe-inspiring

sun 3 orb, Sol **4** bask, star **7** daystar, phoebus **8** daylight, luminary, radiance **9** radiation *combining form:* **4** heli **5** helio *disk:* **4** Aten *god:* **3** Lug, Sol, Tem, Utu **4** Amen, Atmu, Atum, Inti, Lleu, Llew, Lugh, Utug **5** Horus, Sunna, Surya **6** Apollo, Babbar, Helios, Marduk **7** Khepera, Ninurta, Phoebus, Shamash **8** Hyperion, Merodach

Sun Also Rises, The *author:* **9** Hemingway (Ernest) *character:* **6** Ashley (Brett), Barnes (Jake)

sunder 3 cut **4** rend, rive **5** break, sever, slice, split **6** cleave, divide **8** dissever, disunite, separate

sundial part 6 gnomon

sundown 4 dusk **7** evening **8** eventide, gloaming, twilight

sundries 7 notions **8** oddments **9** etceteras **11** odds and ends

sundry 4 many, some **6** varied **7** diverse, several, various **8** assorted, manifold, numerous **9** different, disparate **12** multifarious **13** miscellaneous, multitudinous

sunfish 4 opah **7** pompano **8** bluegill **11** pumpkinseed

Sunflower State 6 Kansas

sun-god see at SUN

Sun King 8 Louis XIV

sunny 4 fair, fine, warm **5** clear, happy **6** blithe, bright, cheery, chirpy, golden **7** beaming, clarion, radiant **8** cheerful, pleasant, rainless **9** brilliant, cloudless, unclouded **10** optimistic

sunrise 4 dawn, morn **6** aurora **7** dawning, morning **8** cockcrow, daybreak, daylight *goddess:* **3** Eos **6** Aurora

sunroom 8 solarium

sunset 3 eve **4** dusk **7** evening **8** gloaming, twilight

Sunset State 6 Oregon

Sunshine State 7 Florida

sunup see SUNRISE

sup 3 eat **4** dine **5** feast

super 4 very **5** great **8** powerful, splendid, terrific **9** excellent, extremely, fantastic, first-rate, wonderful **11** outstanding

superannuated 4 aged **5** hoary, passé **6** bygone **7** ancient, archaic, elderly, outworn **8** obsolete, outdated, outmoded **9** out-of-date **10** antiquated **11** obsolescent **12** old-fashioned

superb 4 rich **5** grand, lofty, noble, prime, super **7** elegant, exalted, optimal, optimum, opulent, stately, sublime, supreme **8** glorious, gorgeous, imposing, majestic, peerless, splendid, standout **9** excellent, marvelous, matchless, wonderful **11** magnificent, outstanding, resplendent, sensational, splendorous, superlative **13** splendiferous

supercilious 5 lofty **6** lordly, sniffy, snippy **7** haughty, stuck-up **8** cavalier, snobbish, superior **10** disdainful **11** patronizing **13** condescending, high-and-mighty

superficial 5 hasty **6** casual, slight **7** cursory, shallow, sketchy, trivial **8** external, skin-deep **9** depthless **11** perfunctory

superfluity 4 glut **5** frill **6** excess **7** nimiety, overrun, surfeit, surplus **8** overflow, overkill, overload, overmuch, overplus, plethora **10** oversupply, redundancy, surplusage **11** prodigality **12** extravagance **13** overabundance

superfluous 5 extra, spare **6** de trop, excess **7** surplus **8** needless **9** excessive, redundant **10** gratuitous **11** uncalled-for, unnecessary

superintend 4 boss **6** direct, manage **7** control, oversee **10** administer

superintendence 4 care **6** charge **7** conduct, running **8** handling **9** authority, direction, oversight **10** management

superior 4 rare **5** above, lofty, major, prime, proud, upper **6** better, choice, higher, lordly, select, senior, sniffy, snippy, snooty **7** capital, greater, haughty, premium, stuck-up **8** arrogant, brass hat, cavalier, dominant, higher-up, insolent **9** excellent, first-rate, marvelous **10** disdainful, first-class, noteworthy, preeminent, preferable, remarkable **11** exceptional, overbearing, patronizing, predominant **13** condescending, high-and-mighty

superiority 9 advantage, dominance, seniority, supremacy, upper hand **10** ascendancy

superjacent 4 over **6** higher **7** greater **9** overlying

superlative 4 best **8** peerless, standout

10 consummate **11** magnificent, outstanding

Superman 9 Clark Kent *cartoonist:* **7** Shuster (Joe) *girlfriend:* **8** Lois Lane

supernatural 5 magic **6** divine, mystic **7** magical, psychic, uncanny **8** heavenly **9** celestial, unearthly **10** miraculous, paranormal, phenomenal **12** metaphysical, transcendent **13** extraordinary

supernatural being 3 elf, fay, god, hob, imp, nix **4** jinn, ogre, peri, puck **5** afrit, angel, bogle, deity, demon, fairy, gnome, jinni, lamia, naiad, nixie, nymph, pixie, satyr, sylph, Titan, troll **6** afreet, goblin, kelpie, seraph, spirit, sprite **7** banshee, brownie, bugbear, goddess, incubus, silenus, vampire **8** bogeyman, demiurge, succubus **9** hobgoblin **10** leprechaun

supernumerary 5 extra, spare **6** de trop, excess, walk-on **7** reserve, surplus **8** leftover **9** redundant

supersede 5 usurp **7** replace, succeed **8** displace, supplant

supervene 5 ensue, occur **6** befall, follow, result **7** succeed **9** eventuate, transpire

supervise 3 run **4** boss **5** steer **6** direct, govern, manage **7** conduct, control, monitor, oversee, proctor, referee **8** chaperon, overlook **10** administer

supervision 4 care **6** charge **7** control, running **8** auspices, handling **9** direction, oversight **10** intendance, management **11** stewardship

supervisor 7 foreman, manager **8** director, overseer **13** administrator

supine 5 inert, prone, slack **7** passive **8** inactive, indolent **9** prostrate, recumbent **10** horizontal **12** outstretched

supper club 6 nitery **7** cabaret **9** night spot

supplant 4 oust **5** usurp **6** cut out, unseat **7** replace, succeed **8** crowd out, displace, force out **9** overthrow, supersede

supple 5 agile, lithe, withy **6** limber, nimble, pliant, whippy **7** ductile, elastic, lissome, plastic, pliable, springy, willowy **8** flexible, graceful, moldable **9** adaptable, malleable, resilient

supplement 3 add, pad **5** rider **6** append, beef up, enrich, extend, sequel **7** adjunct, augment, codicil, enhance, fill out, fortify **8** addendum, addition, appendix, buttress, increase **9** accessory, reinforce **10** postscript, strengthen

suppliant 5 asker **6** beggar, suitor **9** solicitor **10** petitioner

supplicant see SUPPLIANT

supplicate 3 ask, beg, sue **4** pray **5** crave,

plead **6** appeal, invoke **7** beseech, entreat, implore, solicit **8** petition **9** importune

supplication 4 plea, suit **6** appeal, orison, prayer **8** entreaty, petition **11** application

supplies 6 stores **8** matériel **9** equipment, materials **10** provisions

supply 3 man **4** fund, hand, help **5** cache, equip, hoard, stock, store **6** afford, outfit, purvey **7** deliver, fulfill, furnish, provide, reserve, satisfy, surplus **8** dispense, hand over, transfer, turn over **9** inventory, provision, reservoir, stockpile **10** contribute **12** accumulation

support 3 aid **4** back, base, bear, hand, help, lift, prop, root, side, stay **5** abide, adopt, boost, brace, bread, brook, carry, favor, shore, strut, truss **6** anchor, assist, bear up, buoy up, column, crutch, defend, endure, girder, pillar, second, suffer, uphold, verify **7** alimony, applaud, approve, backing, bolster, comfort, confirm, embrace, endorse, espouse, fortify, fulcrum, nourish, nurture, pull for, shore up, stiffen, sustain **8** abutment, advocate, backstop, buttress, champion, mainstay, maintain, sanction, side with, underpin **9** encourage, reinforce, underprop **10** assistance, foundation, livelihood, provide for, strengthen, sustenance **11** corroborate, maintenance, subsistence **12** underpinning

supporter 4 ally **6** patron **7** booster, sectary **8** adherent, advocate, champion, disciple, exponent, follower, henchman, partisan **9** proponent

suppose 4 deem **5** allow, guess, infer, opine, posit, think **6** assume, expect, gather, reckon **7** believe, imagine, presume, pretend, surmise, suspect **8** consider **9** postulate, speculate **10** conjecture **11** hypothesize

supposed 7 alleged, seeming **8** apparent, putative **10** ostensible

supposition 5 guess, hunch, posit **6** notion, theory, thesis **7** premise, surmise **9** postulate **10** assumption, conjecture, hypothesis **11** postulation, presumption, speculation

supposititious 6 unreal **7** dubious, fictive, reputed **8** doubtful, fanciful, illusory, putative, spurious **9** fantastic, fictional, imaginary, pretended, simulated **10** chimerical, fictitious, fraudulent **11** conjectural **12** hypothetical, illegitimate, questionable

suppress 4 curb, stop **5** burke, check, choke, crush, drown, quash, quell, shush, spike, stunt **6** arrest, censor, cut

off, hush up, muffle, muzzle, quench, retard, squash, stifle, subdue **7** abolish, collect, conceal, control, prevent, put down, silence, smother, squelch, swallow **8** prohibit, restrain, snuff out, withhold **9** overthrow **10** extinguish

suppurate 6 fester

supra 5 above

supremacy 7 control, mastery **8** dominion **9** authority, dominance **10** ascendancy, domination, mastership, prepotency **11** preeminence, sovereignty **12** predominance **13** preponderance

supreme 4 best **5** chief, final, prime **6** superb, utmost **7** highest, leading, maximum, perfect **8** absolute, cardinal, crowning, foremost, greatest, peerless, towering, ultimate **9** matchless, paramount, principal, sovereign, unequaled, unmatched, unrivaled **10** preeminent, surpassing **11** culminating, predominant, superlative, unmatchable, unsurpassed **12** incomparable, transcendent, unparalleled **13** unsurpassable

Supreme Being 3 God **5** Allah **7** creator, Jehovah **8** Almighty

surcease 3 end **4** halt, quit, rest, stay, stop **6** desist **7** refrain, respite, suspend **8** knock off, leave off, postpone, stoppage **9** cessation, remission **10** suspension **11** discontinue **12** postponement

sure 3 set **4** fast, firm, safe **5** fixed **6** indeed, secure, stable, steady, strong **7** certain, staunch **8** absolute, definite, enduring, positive, reliable, unerring **9** confident, convinced, steadfast **10** convincing, dependable, inevitable, infallible, undeniable, unshakable, unwavering **11** indubitable, trustworthy, unequivocal, unfaltering **12** indisputable **13** incontestable, unquestioning

surefire 7 assured, certain **8** reliable **10** dependable, guaranteed

sure thing 6 shoo-in, winner **9** certainty

surety 4 bail, bond **5** angel **6** backer, patron, pledge **7** sponsor **8** guaranty, security, warranty **9** certainty, certitude, guarantee, guarantor **10** confidence, conviction

surface 3 top **4** face, pave, rise, skin **5** cover **6** appear, come up, facade, facing, finish, patina, show up, veneer **7** outside **8** covering, exterior **11** superficial

surfeit 4 cloy, fill, glut, jade, pall, sate **5** gorge, stuff **6** excess **7** replete, satiate, surplus **8** overfill, overflow, overkill, overmuch, overplus, plethora **10** surplusage **11** overindulge, superfluity **13** overabundance

surge 4 flow, gush, pour, rise, roll, rush, tide, wave **5** flood, swell **6** billow, deluge, sluice, stream **7** torrent
surgeon 8 sawbones *American:* **4** Mayo (Charles, William), Reed (Walter) **6** Thorek (Max) **7** Cushing (Harvey), DeBakey (Michael) **8** McDowell (Ephraim) *British:* **6** Hunter (John) *English:* **5** Paget (James) **6** Lister (Joseph) *French:* **4** Paré (Ambroise) **5** Broca (Paul) *South African:* **7** Barnard (Christiaan) *Swiss:* **6** Kocher (Emil Theodor)
surgery 9 operation *instrument:* **5** clamp, curet, lance, laser, probe **6** gorget, lancet, splint, stylet, trocar **7** forceps, scalpel
surgical removal 8 ablation *combining form:* **6** ectomy
Suriname *capital:* **10** Paramaribo *former name:* **11** Dutch Guiana *language:* **5** Dutch, Hindi **6** Sranan *monetary unit:* **7** guilder *mountain range:* **10** Tumac-Humac *neighbor:* **6** Brazil, Guyana **12** French Guiana *river:* **6** Maroni **8** Suriname **10** Courantyne
surly 4 dour, glum **5** cross, gruff, sulky **6** crusty, grumpy, morose, sullen **7** bearish, crabbed, grouchy **8** churlish, menacing, snappish **9** irritable, saturnine **10** ungracious **11** ill-mannered, threatening **12** discourteous
surmise see SUPPOSE
surmount 3 cap, top **4** best, down, leap, lick **5** clear, climb, crest, crown, excel, outdo, vault **6** better, hurdle, master **7** conquer, surpass **8** outstrip, overcome, vanquish **9** negotiate, transcend
surpass 3 cap, top **4** beat, best **5** excel, outdo, trump **6** better, exceed, outrun **7** eclipse, outpace **8** go beyond, outclass, outshine, outstrip, outweigh, overstep **9** transcend **10** overshadow **11** outdistance
surplice 5 cotta, ephod **8** vestment
surplus 4 extra, spare **6** excess **7** overage, overrun, reserve, surfeit **8** leftover, overflow, overkill, overmuch, plethora **9** overstock, remainder **10** oversupply **11** superfluity, superfluous **13** overabundance, supernumerary
surprise 4 faze, stun **5** amaze, floor **6** ambush, dismay, rattle, waylay, wonder **7** astound, capture, nonplus, stagger, startle, stupefy **8** astonish, bewilder, bowl over **9** amazement, dumbfound, overpower, take aback **11** flabbergast **12** astonishment, stupefaction
surreal 5 weird **7** bizarre **9** dreamlike, fantastic **10** outlandish **12** unbelievable
surrender 4 cave, cede, fold **5** waive, yield **6** cave in, give in, give up, resign,

submit 7 abandon, concede, succumb **8** cry uncle, hand over **10** abdication, capitulate, relinquish, submission **12** capitulation, renunciation *sign:* **7** hands up **9** white flag
surreptitious see STEALTHY
surrogate 3 sub **5** proxy **6** acting, deputy, fill-in **7** stand-in, stopgap **9** alternate, makeshift **10** substitute **11** alternative, locum tenens, pinch hitter, replacement, succedaneum
surround 3 hem, rim **4** edge, gird, loop, ring **5** beset, bound, hem in, limit, round, skirt, verge **6** border, circle, fringe, girdle, margin **7** besiege, compass, confine, enclose, envelop, outline **8** encircle **9** encompass **12** circumscribe
surrounding 5 about **7** ambient **12** circumjacent *prefix:* **4** peri **6** circum
surroundings 6 milieu **7** ambient **8** ambience **11** environment, mise-enscène
surveillance 3 eye, tab **4** tail **5** vigil, watch **7** lookout **8** scrutiny, stakeout **9** vigilance **11** supervision
survey 3 con, vet **4** case, scan, view **5** assay, audit **6** assess, précis, review, size up **7** canvass, examine, inspect, pandect, perusal, preview **8** analysis, appraise, estimate, evaluate, look over, overlook, overview, scrutiny, syllabus **9** check over **10** inspection, scrutinize **11** reconnoiter, superintend
survive 4 keep, last **6** endure **7** carry on, hold out, outlast, outlive, outwear, persist, recover, ride out, weather **8** continue, live down **9** withstand **11** come through, live through, pull through
Surya 6 sun-god *son:* **4** Manu, Yama **5** Karna **6** Asvins **7** Sugriva *temple site:* **7** Konarak
susceptible 4 open **5** naive, prone **6** liable **7** exposed, pliable, subject **8** disposed, inclined, sensible **9** malleable, receptive, sensitive **10** responsive, vulnerable **11** impressible, persuadable, predisposed **12** nonresistant
suspect 5 doubt, fishy, guess **6** assume, unsure **7** believe, dubious, imagine, suppose, surmise **8** distrust, doubtful, mistrust **9** doubtable, uncertain **10** disbelieve **11** problematic **12** questionable
suspend 3 bar **4** bate, halt, hang, stay, stop **5** debar, defer, delay, hover, sling **6** dangle, depend, hold up, put off, shelve **7** adjourn, hold off **8** intermit, postpone, prorogue **9** eliminate **11** discontinue
suspended 6 frozen **7** hanging, pendant, pendent, stopped **8** dangling, swinging **9** pendulous

suspenders 6 braces **8** galluses
suspense 7 anxiety, mystery, tension **10** expectancy **11** expectation, uncertainty **12** apprehension
suspension 4 halt, stay, stop **5** delay, letup, pause **6** cutoff, freeze **7** latency, respite, time-out **8** abeyance, dormancy, stoppage **9** remission **10** moratorium, quiescence **11** cold storage, withholding **12** intermission, interruption, postponement
suspicion 4 hint **5** doubt, dread, guess, hunch, qualm, shade, smell, tinge, touch, trace, whiff **7** concern, dubiety, surmise **8** distrust, mistrust, wariness **9** chariness, misgiving **10** foreboding, intimation, skepticism, suggestion **11** incertitude, premonition, supposition, uncertainty
suspicious 4 wary **5** chary, fishy, leery **7** dubious, jealous, suspect **8** doubtful, watchful **9** doubtable, skeptical **11** distrustful, mistrustful, problematic **12** apprehensive, questionable
suspire 4 sigh **5** sough
sustain 4 bear, feed, prop, save **5** brace, carry, stand **6** bear up, buoy up, endure, foster, hold up, keep up, succor, suffer, uphold **7** bolster, confirm, nourish, nurture, prolong, relieve, shore up, support, undergo **8** buttress, preserve, tolerate **9** withstand **10** experience, strengthen
sustenance 3 pap **4** food, keep, meat **5** bread, means **6** living, viands **7** aliment, alimony, pabulum, support **8** victuals **9** nutriment, provender **10** livelihood, provisions **11** maintenance, nourishment, subsistence, wherewithal **12** alimentation
susurration 4 purr **6** mumble, murmur, mutter, rustle **7** whisper **9** undertone
suture 3 sew **4** seam **6** stitch
suzerain 5 ruler **8** overlord **9** sovereign
svelte 4 slim **5** lithe, sleek, suave **6** smooth, urbane **7** elegant, slender **8** graceful
swab 3 mop **5** clean **6** sponge
swaddle 4 roll, wrap **5** drape **6** enfold, enwrap, swathe, wrap up **7** blanket, envelop **8** enshroud, enswathe
swag 3 yaw **4** loot, tilt **5** booty, droop, lurch, money, pitch, prize **6** boodle, seesaw, spoils **7** cluster, festoon, garland, pillage, plunder, profits **10** contraband
swagger 4 brag **5** boast, bully, strut, swank, swash, swell **7** bluster, bravado, peacock, saunter **9** arrogance, cockiness, gasconade **11** braggadocio, swashbuckle

swagman 4 hobo **5** rover, tramp **7** drifter, vagrant **8** vagabond, wanderer
swain 4 beau **5** lover, spark, wooer **6** rustic, suitor **7** admirer, peasant, sparker **8** shepherd **9** boyfriend
swallow 3 buy, sip **4** bear, belt, bolt, down, gulp, swig, take, toss, wolf **5** abide, brook, drink, quaff, slurp, stand, swill **6** absorb, accept, digest, endure, guzzle, imbibe, ingest, inhale **7** believe, consume, fall for, repress, retract, stomach **8** chugalug, take back, tolerate **11** ingurgitate
swamp 3 bog, fen **4** holm, mire, moss, muck, quag **5** drown, flood, glade, marsh, whelm **6** deluge, engulf, morass, muskeg, slough **7** bottoms **8** inundate, overcome, overflow, quagmire, submerge **9** everglade, marshland, overwhelm *Everglades:* **10** Big Cypress *Georgia:* **10** Okefenokee *North Carolina-Virginia:* **6** Dismal
Swamp Fox 6 Marion (Francis)
swan *female:* **3** pen *male:* **3** cob **4** cobb *young:* **6** cygnet
Swanhild *father:* **6** Sigurd *mother:* **6** Gudrun
swank 4 posh, tony, trig **5** boast, fancy, ritzy, sharp, showy, smart, swell, swish **6** chichi, classy, dapper, deluxe, lavish, plushy, snappy, trendy **7** elegant, peacock, show off, splashy, stylish, swagger **8** peacocky **9** glamorous, luxurious **10** flamboyant, peacockish **12** orchidaceous, ostentatious
swap 5 trade, truck **6** barter, change, switch **7** bargain, traffic **8** exchange **10** substitute
swarm 3 jam, mob **4** army, bevy, herd, host, mass, pack, push, shin, teem **5** crawl, crowd, crush, drove, flock, group, horde, mount, press **6** abound, gather, myriad, throng **7** climb up, cluster, overrun **9** multitude, pullulate **10** congregate
swarthy 4 dark **5** dusky, sooty **6** brunet **8** bistered **11** dark-skinned
swash 3 lap **4** brag, dash, gush, rush, slop **5** boast, churn, douse, froth, plash, slosh **6** bubble, burble, gurgle, seethe, splash **7** bluster, channel, saunter, spatter, splurge, swagger **8** splatter
swat 3 bat, box, hit, rap **4** bash, belt, blow, cuff, lick, slap, slog, slug, sock **5** blast, clout, homer, knock, smack, smash, smite, swipe, whack **6** buffet, larrup, strike, wallop **7** clobber, home run
swath 4 belt, path **5** strip, sweep **6** stroke
swathe see SWADDLE

sway 4 bend, bias, rock, rule **5** lurch, might, power, range, reach, reign, scope, sweep, swing, waver, weave **6** affect, direct, govern, induce, totter, wobble **7** command, control, dispose, impress, incline, mastery, stagger, win over **8** dominate, dominion, overrule, persuade, undulate **9** authority, dominance, fluctuate, influence, oscillate, prevail on, vacillate **10** domination, predispose **11** fluctuation

Swaziland *capital:* **7** Lobamba, Mbabane *city:* **7** Manzini *language:* **5** Swazi **7** English *monetary unit:* **9** lilangeni *neighbor:* **10** Mozambique **11** South Africa *river:* **5** Usutu **6** Komati **8** Umbeluzi

swear 3 vow **4** avow, bind, cuss, damn, oath, rail, rant **5** abuse, curse, vouch **6** adjure, affirm, assert, attest, depone, depose, pledge, plight **7** declare, promise, testify, warrant **8** covenant, maintain **9** blaspheme, imprecate **10** asseverate, vituperate

swearword 4 cuss, oath **5** curse **9** expletive, obscenity **10** scurrility

sweat 4 emit, glow, moil, ooze, seep, toil, weep **5** exude, grind, labor **6** strain, swivet **7** excrete **8** perspire, transude **12** perspiration

sweater 8 cardigan, pullover, slipover **10** turtleneck

sweaty 6 clammy, sticky **7** glowing **10** perspiring

Sweden *Arctic region:* **7** Lapland *capital:* **9** Stockholm *city:* **5** Malmö **8** Göteborg *gulf:* **7** Bothnia **8** Kattegat *island:* **5** Öland **7** Gotland *lake:* **6** Vänern **7** Mälaren, Vättern **9** Hjälmaren *monetary unit:* **5** krona *mountain range:* **5** Kölen *neighbor:* **6** Norway **7** Finland *part of:* **11** Scandinavia *river:* **3** Dal *sea:* **6** Baltic

Swedish Nightingale 4 Lind (Jenny)

sweep 3 arc, fly, mop, win **4** flit, sail, scud, skim, wing **5** ambit, broom, brush, clean, clear, curve, drive, orbit, range, reach, scope, surge, whisk **6** extent, radius, search **7** compass, purview, victory **9** extension

sweeping 5 broad **6** all-out **7** blanket, general, overall, radical **8** thorough, whole-hog **9** extensive, inclusive, out-and-out, universal, wholesale **12** all-embracing **13** comprehensive, thoroughgoing

sweepings 4 dust **5** trash, waste **6** debris, litter, refuse **7** garbage, residue, rubbish **8** detritus

sweet 5 candy, honey **6** bonbon, dulcet, lovely, sugary, syrupy **7** angelic, cloying, dessert, melodic, scented, sugared, winning, winsome **8** aromatic, fragrant, heavenly, luscious, perfumed **9** ambrosial, delicious **10** delectable, saccharine *combining form:* **4** glyc **5** glyco

Sweet ___ **7** Adeline, Charity **8** Caroline

sweeten 5 candy, honey, sugar **6** soften **7** appease, assuage, enhance, mollify, placate **9** sugarcoat, sugar over **10** conciliate, propitiate

sweet potato 3 yam

sweet-talk 4 coax **5** charm **6** banter, cajole, wangle **7** blarney, flatter, wheedle **8** blandish, butter up, inveigle, soft-soap

swell 4 fine, grow, keen, neat, pout, puff **5** bloat, bulge, dandy, nifty, pouch, super, surge, swank **6** abound, billow, blow up, dilate, expand, groovy **7** amplify, augment, balloon, distend, inflate, peacock, swagger, upsurge **8** increase, terrific **9** crescendo, marvelous, wonderful *British:* **3** nob **4** toff

swelled head 5 pride **6** egoism, vanity **7** conceit, egotism **8** smugness **9** arrogance, vainglory **10** narcissism **11** amour propre, self-conceit **13** conceitedness

swelling 3 sty **4** boil, bubo, bump, corn, gall, node **5** bulge, edema, tumid, tumor **6** bunion, growth, nodule **7** gibbous **8** tubercle **9** carbuncle, chilblain, expansion, tumescent **10** tumescence **11** excrescence **12** inflammation, protuberance

sweltering 3 hot **5** fiery **6** baking, sultry, torrid **7** burning, searing **8** broiling, roasting, sizzling, tropical **9** scorching

swerve 4 skew, turn, veer **5** sheer, shift, stray, waver **6** depart, wander **7** deflect, deviate, digress, diverge

swift 4 fast **5** fleet, hasty, quick, rapid, ready **6** prompt, snappy, speedy, sudden **8** full-tilt, headlong **9** breakneck

___ Swift 3 Tom **8** Jonathan *character:* **8** Gulliver

swiftness 4 gait, pace **5** haste, hurry, speed **6** hustle **8** celerity, dispatch, legerity, rapidity, velocity **9** quickness, rapidness **10** expedition, speediness

swig 4 belt, down, drag, gulp, pull, slug **5** booze, draft, drain, drink, quaff, swill **6** guzzle, imbibe, tipple **7** swallow, swizzle

swill 4 bolt, gulp, slop, swig, tope, wolf **5** booze, draft, drink, gorge, scarf, scoff, slops, trash, waste **6** debris, gobble, guzzle, ingest, inhale, refuse, spilth, tank up, tipple **7** consume, garbage, hogwash, put away, rubbish, swizzle **8** chow down **9** polish off

swim 3 dip **4** reel, spin, turn **5** bathe, crawl, float, swoon, whirl **9** dizziness, dog-paddle

swimmingly 6 easily **8** smoothly **10** splendidly

swimming stroke 5 crawl **7** dolphin, trudgen **9** butterfly, dog paddle

swindle 3 con, gyp **4** bilk, clip, dupe, fake, hoax, rook, scam, sell, sham, skin, soak **5** bunco, bunko, cheat, cozen, fraud, gouge, phony, rogue, shaft, skunk, sting **6** chouse, diddle, fleece, humbug, hustle, take in **7** defraud **8** flimflam, hoodwink **9** bamboozle, imposture, victimize **11** hornswoggle

swindler 5 cheat, crook, ganef, gonif, shark **6** con man, goniff **7** sharper, shyster **8** deceiver **9** charlatan, defrauder **10** mountebank

swine see HOG

swing 4 sway, veer **5** flail, lurch, pivot, twirl, waver, weave, whirl, wield **6** dangle, divert, rhythm, rotate, seesaw, stroke, swerve, switch **7** revolve, suspend **8** brandish **9** alternate, fluctuate, oscillate, vacillate

swinish 5 feral **6** animal, coarse **7** beastly, bestial, porcine

swipe 3 cop, hit, nab, rap **4** blow, clip, conk, grab, hook, lick, lift, nick, sock, swat, wipe **5** clout, filch, heist, knock, pinch, smack, steal **6** pilfer, snatch, snitch, strike, wallop

swirl 4 eddy, purl, roil **5** curve, twist, whirl, whorl **6** swoosh, vortex **9** whirlpool **11** convolution

swish 4 buzz, chic, fizz, hiss, posh, tony, whiz **5** ritzy, smart, swank, whisk **6** classy, dressy, sizzle, trendy, whoosh **7** elegant, stylish **8** sibilate **9** exclusive

Swiss Family Robinson author 4 Wyss (Johann David)

switch 3 rod, wag **4** beat, flay, flog, lash, swap, veer, wand, whip **5** shift, shunt, trade, whisk **6** change, strike, waggle **7** scourge **8** exchange, flip-flop, reversal **9** about-face, sidetrack **10** substitute **12** substitution

Switzerland *capital:* **4** Bern *city:* **5** Basel **6** Geneva, Zürich **8** Lausanne *lake:* **6** Geneva, Wallen **7** Lucerne **9** Constance, Neuchâtel, Thunersee, Zürichsee *language:* **6** French, German **7** Italian *monetary unit:* **5** franc *mountain, range:* **4** Alps, Jura **6** Monte Rosa *neighbor:* **5** Italy **6** France **7** Austria, Germany **13** Liechtenstein *resort:* **5** Davos, Vevey **7** Zermatt **8** Montreux, St. Moritz **10** Interlaken *river:* **4** Aare **5** Rhine, Rhône *state:* **6** canton

swivel 4 spin, turn **5** pivot, swing, twirl, whirl **6** rotate **7** revolve **9** pirouette

swivet see SNIT

swizzle see SWIG

swollen 5 puffy, tumid **6** turgid **7** bloated, bulbous, bulging, pompous **8** enlarged, inflated, varicose **9** bombastic, distended, tumescent **10** rhetorical **12** magniloquent **13** grandiloquent

swoon 4 coma, daze, fade **5** droop, faint **6** torpor **7** pass out, rapture, syncope **8** black out

swoosh 4 eddy, gush, purl, rush **5** swirl, whirl, whorl

sword 4 épée, foil **5** saber, sabre **6** barong, bilboa, rapier, Toledo **7** cutlass **8** claymore, falchion, scimitar, yataghan

sword of ___ 8 Damocles

sword-shaped 8 ensiform

sworn 6 avowed **7** devoted **8** affirmed **9** committed, confirmed **10** deep-rooted, deep-seated, entrenched, inveterate

sybarite 7 epicure **8** hedonist **9** libertine **10** sensualist, voluptuary

sybaritic 6 carnal **7** sensual **8** sensuous **9** epicurean, libertine, luxurious **10** hedonistic, voluptuous **13** self-indulgent

sycophancy 7 fawning **8** flattery, toadying **9** truckling **11** bootlicking

sycophant 5 leech, toady **6** flunky, lackey, minion, yes-man **8** groveler, hanger-on, parasite, truckler **9** easy rider, flatterer, toadeater **10** bootlicker, self-seeker **11** lickspittle **13** apple-polisher

sycophantic 7 fawning, servile, slavish **8** toadying, unctuous **9** groveling, kowtowing, parasitic, truckling **10** obsequious **11** bootlicking

Sycorax's son 7 Caliban

syllable *deletion:* **7** apocope *last:* **6** ultima *lengthening of:* **7** ectasis *next to last:* **6** penult *shortening:* **7** elision, systole *stressed:* **5** arsis

syllabus 6 aperçu, digest, précis, sketch, survey **7** epitome, outline, pandect, summary **8** abstract, headnote, synopsis **10** compendium

sylph 5 fairy, nymph **6** sprite

sylvan 5 bosky, woody **6** rustic, wooded *deity:* **3** Pan **4** Faun **5** dryad, satyr **6** Faunus **7** Silenus **8** Arethusa, Silvanus, Sylvanus

symbol 4 logo, mark, sign **5** badge, motif, stamp, token **6** design, device, emblem, mascot **9** attribute **10** indication *chemical:* see individual element *musical:* **4** clef, flat, hold, note, rest, turn **5** shake, sharp, trill **7** fermata,

mordent, natural 8 arpeggio 9 crescendo 10 diminuendo 11 decrescendo
symbolic 5 token 10 emblematic 11 allegorical
symbolist poet 7 Rimbaud (Arthur) 8 Mallarmé (Stéphane), Verlaine (Paul)
symbolize 4 mean 6 embody, mirror, typify 7 signify 8 stand for 9 epitomize, exemplify, personify, represent 10 illustrate 11 emblematize
symmetrical 5 equal 7 regular 8 balanced 12 commensurate, proportional 13 commensurable
symmetry 5 order 6 parity 7 balance, harmony 8 equality, evenness 9 agreement, congruity 10 conformity, proportion, regularity 11 arrangement
sympathetic 4 kind, warm 6 benign, caring, humane, kindly, tender 8 amenable, friendly 9 agreeable, approving, benignant, congenial, congruous, consonant, favorable, receptive 10 compatible, consistent, responsive 11 considerate, kindhearted, softhearted, warmhearted 12 well-disposed 13 compassionate, understanding
sympathize 4 pity 7 condole 11 commiserate 13 compassionate
sympathy 4 pity, ruth 5 heart 6 accord, solace, warmth 7 comfort, harmony, rapport 8 affinity, kindness 9 agreement 10 benignancy, compassion, condolence, kindliness, tenderness 11 consolation, sensitivity 13 commiseration
symphonic 10 orchestral
symphony 9 orchestra 12 philharmonic
symposium 5 forum 7 meeting, seminar 9 gathering 10 conference, discussion
symptom 4 mark, sign 5 index, token 8 evidence 10 indication
symptoms 7 indicia 8 syndrome
synagogue 6 temple
sync 4 jibe 5 agree, match 7 harmony 8 coincide 9 harmonize 10 concurrent 12 simultaneous
synchronize 5 agree 6 concur 8 coincide
synchronous 6 coeval 10 coetaneous, coexistent, coexisting, coincident, concurrent 11 concomitant 12 contemporary, simultaneous 13 geostational
syncope 4 coma 5 faint, swoon 8 blackout
syndicate 3 mob 4 pool 5 chain, group, mafia, trust, union 6 cartel, league 7 combine 11 association, partnership 12 conglomerate, organization 13 confederation
syndrome 3 ill 6 malady 7 ailment, disease 8 disorder, sickness 9 complaint, condition, infirmity

synergic 5 joint 6 shared 8 coacting, coactive, conjoint 9 collusive, concerted 11 cooperating, cooperative, coordinated
synod 4 body, diet 7 council, meeting 8 assembly, conclave, congress 10 conference, convention 11 convocation
synopsis 5 brief, recap 6 aperçu, digest, précis, review 7 capsule, epitome, outline, rundown, summary 8 abstract, breviary, syllabus 10 abridgment, compendium, conspectus 12 condensation
synopsize 5 recap, sum up 6 digest 7 outline, summate 8 abstract, boil down, compress, condense 9 epitomize, inventory, summarize 11 encapsulate
synthesis 5 blend, union 6 fusion, merger 7 amalgam 8 blending, compound 9 composite 11 combination 12 amalgamation 13 incorporation
synthesize 4 fuse, meld 5 blend, merge, unify 7 combine 8 compound 9 harmonize, integrate 10 amalgamate 11 incorporate
synthetic 6 ersatz 7 man-made 9 unnatural 10 artificial, fabricated 11 counterfeit
Syria *capital:* 8 Damascus *city:* 4 Homs 6 Aleppo *desert:* 6 Syrian *language:* 6 Arabic, French *monetary unit:* 5 pound *mountain range:* 7 Lebanon *neighbor:* 4 Iraq 6 Israel, Jordan, Turkey 7 Lebanon *plain:* 11 Mesopotamia *river:* 9 Euphrates *sea:* 13 Mediterranean
syringe 6 needle
Syrinx 5 nymph *pursuer:* 3 Pan
syrinx 7 panpipe 8 panpipes
syrup 6 orgeat 9 grenadine
syrupy 5 gooey, mushy, sappy, sweet 6 drippy, dulcet, slushy, sticky, sugary 7 cloying, maudlin, mawkish 9 schmaltzy 10 saccharine 11 sentimental
system 3 way 4 mode, plan 5 modus, order, setup 6 entity, manner, method, scheme 7 complex, network, pattern, process, regimen, routine 8 strategy 9 procedure, structure, technique 10 regularity 11 arrangement, disposition, orderliness
systematic 7 logical, ordered, orderly, regular 8 arranged 9 organized 10 analytical, methodical 12 businesslike
systematize 5 array, order 6 codify 7 arrange, catalog, dispose, marshal 8 classify, organize, regiment 9 catalogue, methodize
system of weights 4 troy 11 avoirdupois 12 apothecaries

T

tab 4 bill, cost, flap, list, loop, rate **5** check, count, price, score **6** charge, record **7** account, invoice **8** eagle eye, price tag, scrutiny **9** appendage, designate, extension, reckoning, statement **12** surveillance

tabard 4 cape, coat **5** tunic **10** coat of arms

tabby 3 cat **6** feline, cement **8** brindled

tabernacle 4 tent **5** hovel **6** church, temple

tabes 7 atrophy, wasting **12** degeneration

Tabitha's Greek name 6 Dorcas

table 4 fare, list **5** bench, board, chart, defer, stand **6** buffet, put off, record, shelve, teapoy **7** counter **8** mahogany, postpone **9** sideboard *ornament:* **7** epergne **11** centerpiece *writing:* **4** desk **9** secretary **10** escritoire

table d' ___ 4 hôte

tableland 4 mesa **5** butte **6** upland **7** plateau *Alabama-West Virginia:* **10** Cumberland *Arizona:* **5** Kanab **6** Kaibob *England:* **8** Dartmoor *India:* **5** Malwa (see also PLATEAU)

tablet 3 bar, pad **4** cake, disk, pill, slab **5** panel, slate **6** pellet, plaque, troche **7** lozenge, notepad **8** steno pad

Table Talk author 6 Selden (John)

tableware 4 cups **5** bowls, china, forks **6** dishes, knives, plates, silver, spoons **7** glasses, saucers **8** settings, utensils **9** stainless

tabloid 3 rag **5** lurid, pulpy **6** digest **7** summary **9** condensed, newspaper **11** sensational **12** scandal sheet

taboo 3 ban **4** no-no **6** banned, enjoin, forbid **7** inhibit, obscene **9** forbidden, ineffable, interdict, off-limits, restraint **10** inhibition **11** restriction, unspeakable **12** interdiction

tabor 4 drum

tabulate 4 list **5** count, order **6** codify, figure, record **7** arrange **9** enumerate **11** systematize

tabulation 4 list **5** chart, tally **6** record **7** account

tabula ___ 4 rasa

tacit 6 silent, unsaid **7** assumed, implied **8** implicit, inferred, unspoken **9** intimated, suggested **10** subtextual, unde-clared, underlying, understood **11** acquiescent, unexpressed **12** inarticulate

taciturn 4 dumb **6** silent **7** laconic **8** reserved, reticent, wordless **9** secretive **11** tight-lipped **12** closemouthed

Tacitus work 7 Annales **8** Dialogus, Germania **9** Historiae

tack 3 pin, yaw **4** beat, brad, gear, join, nail, stay, turn **5** baste, reach, shift **6** attach, double, stitch, swerve, turn up, zigzag **7** tangent **8** put about **9** come about, deviation **10** alteration, deflection, digression, sea biscuit **11** ship biscuit **12** pilot biscuit

tackle 3 cat, rig **4** gear, sack **6** outfit, take on, take up **7** halyard, lineman, rigging **8** set about **9** apparatus, equipment, machinery, undertake **10** footballer, linebacker, plunge into **13** paraphernalia

tacky 5 cheap, crude, dingy, dowdy, gaudy, messy, seedy, ratty, tatty **6** blowsy, frowsy, frumpy, kitsch, shabby, sleazy, sloppy, sticky, frumpy, tawdry, untidy, vulgar **7** run-down, unkempt **8** adhesive, frumpish, slovenly **9** inelegant, tasteless, unstylish **10** broken-down, down-at-heel, threadbare

tact 5 poise, touch **6** acumen **7** address, finesse, suavity **8** civility, courtesy, delicacy, urbanity **9** diplomacy, politesse **10** adroitness, politeness, smoothness **11** savoir faire, sensitivity

tactful 5 civil, suave **6** adroit, urbane **7** politic **8** delicate, discreet, polished **9** courteous, sensitive **10** diplomatic, perceptive, thoughtful **11** considerate

tactical 7 politic, prudent **9** advisable, expedient, strategic

tactics 4 plan **6** method, scheme **8** maneuver, playbook, strategy **9** stratagem

tactile 8 palpable, tangible **9** touchable

taction 4 feel **5** touch **7** contact **9** palpation

tactless 4 rude **5** blunt, crude, inept **6** candid, clumsy, gauche **7** awkward **8** impolite **9** impolitic, maladroit **10** indiscreet **11** insensitive

tad 3 bit, boy, lad, son **4** lick, mite, snap,

spot, whit **5** child, crumb, sonny, speck
6 laddie, nipper, shaver **7** smidgen
8 fraction
tadpole 8 polliwog, pollywog
taffy 5 candy **8** flattery
tag 3 bit, dog, end **4** cost, flag, game,
logo, mark, name, tail **5** aglet, brand,
label, price, trail **6** append, charge, follow, select, shadow, slogan, tassel, tatter, ticket **7** license, run down **8** graffi-
to, identify, insignia
Tahiti *city:* **7** Papeete *painter:* **7** Gauguin
(Paul)
tail 3 dog, end, tag **4** butt, rear **5** hound,
stalk **6** follow, pursue, shadow **7** hind
end, rear end **8** backside, buttocks
9 posterior *bone:* **6** coccyx *relating to:*
6 caudal *short:* **4** scut
tailed 7 caudate
tailor 3 fit, sew **4** suit **5** alter **8** clothier,
seamster **11** haberdasher
tailor-made 6 fitted, suited **7** bespoke,
fitting **8** suitable **10** well-suited
11 appropriate
taint 3 rot **4** blot, blur, foul, harm, hurt,
smut, soil, spot, turn, vice **5** brand,
cloud, color, decay, dirty, fault, smear,
spoil, stain, sully, touch **6** befoul, dark-
en, defile, poison, smudge, smutch
7 blacken, blemish, corrupt, pollute,
putrefy, tarnish **8** besmirch, discolor
9 discredit **10** adulterate, stigmatize
11 contaminate
taipan 5 snake **8** merchant **11** businessman
Taiwan 7 Formosa *capital:* **6** Taipei *channel:* **5** Bashi *city:* **6** T'ai-nan **8** Pan-
ch'iao, T'ai-chung **9** Kao-hsiung *language:* **8** Mandarin *leader:* **13** Chiang
Kai-shek *monetary unit:* **6** dollar *mountain:* **6** Yü Shan
Tajikistan *capital:* **8** Dushanbe *monetary
unit:* **5** ruble *mountain, range:* **6** Pamirs
9 Communism (Peak), Trans Alai
10 Revolution (Peak) *neighbor:* **5** China
10 Kyrgyzstan, Uzbekistan
11 Afghanistan *river:* **8** Amu Dar'ya, Syr
Dar'ya
Taj Mahal 9 mausoleum *builder:* **9** Shah
Jahan *site:* **4** Agra
take 3 get, nab **4** grab **5** annex, catch,
seize **6** gather, obtain, secure **7** capture,
receive **8** proceeds, receipts *account of:*
6 notice *advantage of:* **5** abuse **7** exploit
after: **6** follow **8** resemble *apart:* **7** analyze, dissect **9** dismantle *care:* **6** beware
care of: **3** fix **4** tend **5** nurse **6** attend
exception: **6** object *five:* **4** rest *from:*
7 deprive, detract **8** subtract *it easy:*
5 relax *on the:* **7** corrupt *part:* **4** join
5 share **11** participate *place:* **5** occur

6 happen *to task:* **5** scold **7** reprove
turns: **9** alternate *unawares:* **8** surprise
take away 4 grab **5** wrest **6** arrest, commit, deduct, detach, detain, remove
7 deprive, detract **8** diminish, discount,
minimize, subtract, withdraw
take back 5 unsay **6** abjure, recall,
recant, return **7** replace, restore,
retract, swallow **8** forswear, withdraw
9 repossess
take down 4 note **5** lower, write **6** humble, record, reduce **7** deflate **8** dismount **9** dismantle **11** disassemble
take in 3 con **4** dupe, fool, furl, jail
5 admit, bluff, board, house, trick
6 absorb, accept, arrest, attend, betray,
delude, embody **7** beguile, compass,
contain, deceive, embrace, include,
involve, mislead, observe, receive, shelter, snooker, subsume **8** flimflam,
hoodwink, perceive **9** apprehend, bamboozle, encompass, four-flush
10 assimilate, comprehend, understand
11 double-cross
take off 4 doff, exit, quit **5** leave, scram
6 begone, deduct, depart, remove, set
out **7** pull out, skiddoo, vamoose
8 clear out, discount, hightail, light out,
subtract, withdraw **9** skedaddle
takeoff 5 spoof **6** launch, parody, satire,
send-up **7** lampoon **8** travesty **9** burlesque **10** caricature *area:* **3** pad **6** runway
take on 3 don **4** face, hire, meet **5** adopt,
annex, fight **6** accept, append, assume,
attack, battle, employ, engage, strike,
tackle **7** contest, embrace, espouse,
venture **8** endeavor, set about
9 encounter, undertake
take out 4 date, kill, omit **5** loose
6 deduct, remove **7** destroy, release,
unleash **8** discount, knock off, separate, subtract, withdraw, withhold
9 eliminate **10** annihilate
take over 5 seize, spell, usurp **6** assume
7 capture, relieve
take up 3 use **4** fill, open **5** adopt, begin,
enter, raise, renew, set to, start
6 absorb, accept, assume, gather, occupy, resume, shrink, tackle **7** embrace,
espouse, kick off, restart, shorten,
tighten **8** commence, continue, initiate
10 recommence
talc 6 powder **8** steatite **9** soapstone
tale 3 fib, lie **4** myth, saga, yarn **5** fable,
rumor, story **6** canard, legend **7** fiction
8 anecdote **9** narration, narrative
talebearer 3 rat **4** fink **6** canary, gossip,
snitch **7** rat fink, tattler **8** busybody,
gossiper, informer, quidnunc, squealer,
telltale **9** informant **10** newsmonger, tat-

tletale 11 rumormonger, stool pigeon 12 blabbermouth 13 scandalmonger

talent 4 bent, gift, head, nose 5 craft, dowry, flair, forte, knack, skill 6 genius 7 ability, aptness, faculty 9 endowment, expertise

talented 4 able 6 clever, expert, gifted 8 skillful

Tale of Two Cities, A author: 7 Dickens (Charles) character: 5 Lucie (Manette) 6 Carton (Sidney), Darnay (Charles) 7 Defarge (Madame), Manette (Alexander)

Tales of a Traveller author 6 Irving (Washington)

Tales of a Wayside Inn author 10 Longfellow (Henry Wadsworth)

Tales of Hoffman composer 9 Offenbach (Jacques)

talisman 4 juju, luck 5 charm 6 amulet, fetish, mascot, scarab 7 periapt 10 phylactery

Talisman author 5 Scott (Walter)

talk 3 gab, rap, yak 4 blab, buzz, chat, chin, yarn 5 prate, rumor, run on, speak, utter, voice 6 babble, gabble, gossip, parley, patter, report, speech 7 address, chatter, declaim, hearsay, lecture, prattle 8 colloquy, converse, dialogue, harangue 9 discourse, utterance 10 discussion 12 conversation about: 7 discuss back: 4 sass foolish: 4 bunk 6 babble 7 chatter, palaver indistinctly: 6 mumble, mutter over: 7 discuss slowly: 5 drawl small: 8 chitchat wildly: 4 rant, rave

talkative 4 glib 5 gabby, vocal 6 chatty, fluent 7 gossipy, voluble 9 garrulous 10 loquacious 13 communicative

talk over 6 debate 7 discuss, hash out 8 consider 9 thrash out 10 deliberate

talky 5 gabby, windy, wordy 6 chatty, prolix 7 verbose, voluble

tall 4 high, long 5 lanky, large, lofty, rangy 6 absurd 7 pompous 8 towering 9 high-flown 10 far-fetched 11 skyscraping 12 altitudinous

tallow 3 fat 4 lard, suet 6 grease

tally 3 tab 4 list, tale 5 agree, count, match, score, total 6 accord, census, number, reckon, square 7 account, balance, catalog, compute, conform, itemize 8 check off, register, tabulate 9 agreement, catalogue, enumerate, harmonize, inventory, reckoning 10 complement, correspond

talon 4 claw, hand 5 stock 6 finger

talus 5 ankle, scree, slope 9 anklebone 10 astragalus

tam 3 cap

Tamar brother: 7 Absalom father: 5 David 7 Absalom father-in-law: 5 Judah half brother: 5 Amnon seducer: 5 Amnon son: 5 Perez, Zerah

tamarisk 9 salt cedar

tambour 3 cup 4 drum 9 embroider 10 embroidery

Tamburlaine the Great author 7 Marlowe (Christopher)

tame 4 bust, dull, meek, mild 5 break, train, vapid 6 bridle, docile, gentle, humble, soften, subdue 7 harness, insipid, reclaim, subdued 8 domestic, familiar, obedient 9 tractable 10 housebreak, submissive 11 domesticate, housebroken 12 domesticated

Taming of the Shrew, The character: 6 Bianca 8 Baptista 9 Katharina, Petruchio

Tammany boss 5 Tweed (William)

Tammuz's lover 6 Ishtar

tam-o'-shanter 3 cap

tamp 3 ram 4 pack 5 pound, press, stuff

tampion 4 plug 5 cover

tan 3 sun, taw 4 beat, ecru, flog, whip 5 beige, brown, tawny, toast 6 bronze, darken, thrash 7 biscuit

Tan novel 11 Joy Luck Club (The) 15 Kitchen God's Wife (The) 19 Bonesetter's Daughter (The)

tanager 7 redbird

Tancred, Tancredi beloved: 8 Clorinda father: 3 Odo mother: 4 Emma victim: 8 Clorinda

tandem 4 pair 7 bicycle, concert 8 carriage

tang 3 nip 4 bite, fang, odor, ring, zest 5 aroma, clang, prong, sapor, savor, shank, smack, taste, trace 6 flavor, relish 8 piquancy, pungency, sapidity 9 spiciness

tangible 4 real 7 tactile 8 concrete, material, palpable, physical, sensible 9 corporeal, touchable 10 detectable, observable, phenomenal 11 appreciable, discernible, perceptible, substantial

tangle 3 mat, web 4 foul, knot, maze, mesh, shag 5 clash, ravel, skein, snare, snarl 6 entrap, foul up, hamper, jumble, jungle, morass, muddle, pileup, raffle 7 dispute, embroil, ensnare, ensnarl, involve, perplex, seaweed, thicket 8 obstruct 9 embarrass, implicate 10 complicate 11 altercation, predicament 12 bewilderment, complication

Tanglewood Tales author 9 Hawthorne (Nathaniel)

tango 5 dance 8 circuity 11 indirection 13 deceitfulness

tangy 5 sharp 6 lively 7 piquant, pungent, zestful 9 flavorful

tank 3 vat 5 basin 7 cistern 8 aquarium 9 reservoir *American:* 6 Abrams 7 Bradley, Sherman *German:* 6 panzer *part:* 6 turret

tankard 3 mug 5 stoup 6 flagon 9 blackjack

tanked 3 lit 4 high, lost 5 drunk, lit up, oiled 6 bashed, blotto, bombed, failed, gave up, juiced, potted, soaked, soused, stewed, stoned, tanked, wasted, zonked 7 crocked, drunken, pickled, pie-eyed, sloshed, smashed, sottish 9 collapsed, plastered 10 inebriated, liquored up 11 intoxicated

tanker 4 ship 5 oiler

Tannhäuser composer 6 Wagner (Richard)

tantalize 3 rag 4 bait, lure 5 tease, tempt 6 entice, needle 7 torment 9 frustrate

Tantalus *daughter:* 5 Niobe *father:* 4 Zeus *son:* 6 Pelops

tantamount 4 same 5 alike, equal 8 parallel, selfsame 9 duplicate, identical 10 equivalent 12 commensurate

tantara 5 blare 7 fanfare

tantivy 3 run 6 gallop

tantrum 3 fit 6 blowup 8 outburst, paroxysm 9 hysterics 10 conniption

Tanzania *capital:* 6 Dodoma 11 Dar es Salaam *city:* 6 Arusha *former name:* 10 Tanganyika *island:* 5 Mafia, Pemba 8 Zanzibar *lake:* 5 Rukwa 6 Malawi 8 Victoria 10 Tanganyika *language:* 7 English, Swahili *monetary unit:* 8 shilling *mountain:* 11 Kilimanjaro *neighbor:* 5 Congo, Kenya 6 Malawi, Rwanda, Uganda, Zambia 7 Burundi 10 Mozambique *plain:* 9 Serengeti *river:* 6 Kagera, Rufiji, Ruvuma 7 Pangani *volcano:* 6 Lengai

Taoism founder 5 Laozi 6 Lao Tzu

tap 3 hit, pat 4 cock, draw, flap, name, plug, tick 5 chuck, draft, drain, nudge, touch, valve 6 faucet, select, siphon, spigot, strike 7 appoint, draw off, hydrant, percuss, petcock 8 drumbeat, half sole, nominate, stopcock 9 designate

tape 4 band, belt, bind 5 strip 6 fillet, ribbon 7 bandage *kind:* 5 inkle 6 ferret 7 masking 8 adhesive *machine:* 4 deck 8 recorder

taper 4 wane, wick 5 abate, close, draft, pinch, spire 6 candle, lessen, narrow, reduce 7 dwindle, glimmer 8 decrease, diminish

tapering 5 conic, spiry 6 spired, terete 7 conical 8 ensiform, fusiform, napiform, subulate 9 acuminate, attenuate 10 lanceolate

tapestry 5 arras, kilim 6 dossal 7 curtain, Gobelin, hanging *pattern:* 7 cartoon

Taphath's father 7 Solomon

tapioca 4 yuca 5 yucca 6 manioc 7 cassava, farinha, pudding

taproom 3 bar, pub 4 café 6 bodega, saloon, tavern 7 cantina 8 dramshop 9 roadhouse

tapster 6 barman 7 barkeep, barmaid, skinker 9 barkeeper, bartender 10 mixologist

tar 3 gob 4 jack, salt, soil, swab 5 pitch, smear, stain, sully, taint 6 defile, hearty, sailor, seaman 7 asphalt, besmear, mariner, shipman 8 besmirch, creosote, deckhand, flatfoot 9 shellback

taradiddle 3 fib, lie 5 hooey, story, trash 6 bunkum, canard 7 baloney, falsity 8 claptrap, nonsense 9 falsehood 10 balderdash 13 prevarication

tarantella 5 dance

tarantula 6 spider 10 wolf spider

Taras Bulba author 5 Gogol (Nikolai)

tarboosh 3 fez, hat

tardy 4 dull, late, lazy, slow 7 belated, delayed, laggard, overdue 8 dilatory, sluggish 10 behindhand, delinquent, unpunctual

tare 4 seed 5 vetch, weigh 6 weight 11 undesirable 13 counterweight

target 3 aim 4 butt, goal, mark, prey 5 aim at 6 object, quarry, victim 9 objective 11 sitting duck *center:* 8 bull's-eye *shooter's:* 10 clay pigeon

Tar Heel State 13 North Carolina

tariff 3 tax 4 cost, duty, levy, rate 5 price 6 charge, impost 7 tribute 10 assessment

Tarkington character 6 Penrod

tarn 4 lake, pool

tarnish 3 dim, mar 4 dull, foul, harm, hurt, soil 5 dirty, muddy, smear, spoil, stain, sully, taint 6 damage, darken, defile, injure, smirch, smudge, smutch 7 begrime, besmear, blemish, vitiate 8 besmirch, discolor

taro 5 aroid 6 yautia 7 dasheen, malanga *product:* 3 poi

tarpaulin 3 gob 4 jack, salt, swab 5 cover, sheet 6 hearty, sailor, seaman 7 mariner, shipman 9 shellback

tarpon 8 ladyfish 10 silverfish

tarry 3 lag 4 bide, drag, stay, wait 5 abide, dally, delay, visit 6 dawdle, linger, loiter, pitchy, remain 7 sojourn

tarsus 5 ankle

tart 3 pie 4 acid, bawd, moll, slut, sour 5 acerb, quean, sharp, tramp, trull, whore 6 biting, harlot, pastry 7 acerbic, cutting, piquant, pungent, tootsie 8 chess pie, strumpet 10 prostitute

tartar 5 argol **6** plaque **8** calculus
Tartar 6 Mongol, Turkic **7** Turkish
9 Mongolian
Tartuffe author 7 Molière
Tarzan *chimpanzee:* **7** Cheetah *creator:*
9 Burroughs (Edgar Rice) *mate:* **4** Jane
task 3 job **4** duty, lade, load, post, slog,
toil, work **5** chare, chore, labor, stint
6 assign, burden, charge, detail, devoir
7 mission, project **8** business, encumber, function **9** challenge, dress down,
reprimand **10** assignment, commission
11 undertaking **12** dressing-down
Tasmanian 4 wolf **5** devil *capital:*
6 Hobart *pine:* **4** Huon
tassel 3 tag **4** tuft **5** adorn **6** fringe **7** pendant, tzitzit **8** ornament **13** inflorescence
Tasso, Torquato *patron:* **4** Este (Alfonso
II d') *work:* **6** Aminta **7** Rinaldo
18 Jerusalem Delivered
taste 3 eat, sip, try **4** tang, zest **5** savor,
smack **6** flavor, liking, palate, relish
7 stomach **8** appetite, elegance, fondness, sapidity, soft spot, weakness
10 experience, partiality, refinement
11 inclination *kind:* **4** salt, sour **5** sweet
6 bitter *organ:* **3** bud
tasteful 4 fine **7** elegant, genteel, refined,
stylish **8** artistic, becoming **9** aesthetic
tasteless 4 dull, flat **5** bland, crass,
gaudy, showy, stale, tacky, vapid **6** vulgar **7** insipid **8** off-color, unsavory
9 inelegant, savorless, unrefined **10** flavorless
tasty 5 sapid, yummy **6** dainty, delish,
savory **8** luscious **9** delicious, flavorful,
palatable, succulent, toothsome
10 appetizing, delectable, flavorsome
tattered 4 torn **5** dingy, seedy **6** frayed,
ragged, ripped, shabby **7** raggedy, rundown, worn-out **10** bedraggled, threadbare **11** dilapidated
tattle 3 wag, yak **4** blab, buzz, dish, talk
5 clack, prate, rumor **6** gossip, inform,
report, snitch, squeal **7** chatter,
hearsay, prattle **8** chitchat **9** grapevine
11 scuttlebutt
tattletale see TALEBEARER
tatty 5 cheap, dingy, dowdy, dumpy,
seedy, tacky **6** beat-up, cheesy, paltry,
scuzzy, shabby, shoddy, sleazy, trashy
7 run-down, scrubby **8** rubbishy
10 threadbare **11** dilapidated
taunt 3 jab **4** gibe, jeer, mock, quip, razz,
skit, twit **5** scout, tease **6** deride, insult
7 affront, provoke **8** reproach, ridicule
9 challenge
taurine 6 bovine **8** bull-like
Taurus 4 bull *star:* **9** Aldebaran
taut 4 firm, snug, trim **5** rigid, tense,
tight **6** corded **10** high-strung

tautology 8 iterance, pleonasm **9** iteration **10** redundancy, repetition
tavern 3 bar, inn, pub **4** café, dive
6 bistro, bodega, saloon **7** barroom,
cantina, gin mill, taproom **8** alehouse,
pothouse, wineshop **9** roadhouse
11 public house, rathskeller **12** watering hole **13** watering place
taverner 7 barkeep **8** boniface, publican
9 barkeeper, bartender, innkeeper
12 saloonkeeper
taw 3 tan **6** marble **7** partner
tawdry 4 loud **5** cheap, gaudy, tacky
6 brazen, flashy, garish, tinsel **7** chintzy,
glaring, ignoble **9** brummagem, dimestore **12** meretricious
tawny 3 tan **4** buff **5** beige, brown, sandy
6 copper, tanned
tax 4 duty, lade, levy, load, onus, scot,
toll **5** drain, tithe **6** assess, burden,
cumber, impost, saddle, strain, tariff,
weight **7** tribute **8** encumber **10** imposition *agency:* **3** IRS *feudal:* **7** scutage, tallage *kind:* **4** geld **5** sales, tithe **6** excise,
income **8** property **9** surcharge *on salt:*
7 gabelle *rate:* **10** assessment
taxi 3 cab, car **4** hack **5** cyclo
taxing 5 tough **6** trying **7** exigent, onerous, wearing **8** exacting, grievous, grueling **9** demanding, difficult **10** burdensome, oppressive
Taygeta *father:* **5** Atlas *mother:* **7** Pleione
sisters: **8** Pleiades
tazza 3 cup **4** vase
Tchaikovsky, Pyotr Ilyich *ballet:* **8** Swan
Lake **10** Nutcracker (The) **14** Sleeping
Beauty *opera:* **12** Eugene Onegin
13 Queen of Spades (The)
tea 5 party **6** repast **8** beverage **9** reception *black:* **5** bohea, pekoe **8** souchong
cake: **6** cookie *genus:* **4** Thea *kind:*
4 herb, Java **5** Assam, black, bohea,
green, hyson, pekoe **6** Ceylon, congou,
oolong **7** cambric **8** Earl Grey, souchong **9** sassafras **10** Darjeeling
teach 5 coach, edify, guide, train, tutor
6 impart, school **7** educate, instill, profess **8** instruct **9** enlighten, inculcate
12 indoctrinate
teacher 4 guru, prof **5** coach, guide,
tutor **6** docent, master, mentor, pedant
7 maestro, trainer **8** educator **9** pedagogue, preceptor, professor **10** instructor **12** schoolmaster *Hindu:* **5** swami
Jewish: **5** rabbi, rebbe *Muslim:* **6** mullah
organization: **3** NEA *religious:* **9** catechist **10** mystagogue
Tea for Two composer 7 Youmans (Vincent)
team 4 band, club, crew, gang, join, pair,
side, yoke **5** group, squad, troop,

wagon 6 stable, troupe 8 carriage *baseball:* 4 nine *basketball:* 4 five 7 quintet *football:* 6 eleven *kind:* 6 jayvee 7 varsity

teamster 6 driver 7 trucker

tear 3 cry, cut, fly, rip, run 4 bolt, claw, dash, drop, flaw, gash, hole, lash, pull, race, rend, rift, rive, rush, slit, snag, weep 5 chase, hurry, shoot, shred, slash, speed, split, spree 6 career, charge, course, sunder, tatter, wrench 7 droplet, fissure, rupture 8 lacerate 10 laceration

tear down 4 raze, ruin, slur 5 knock, smash, smear, wreck 6 defame, malign, vilify 7 asperse, traduce, destroy, shatter, slander 8 demolish 9 denigrate, disparage, take apart 10 annihilate, calumniate 11 disassemble

tearful 3 sad 5 misty, moist, weepy 6 crying, watery, woeful 7 bawling, sobbing, weeping 8 mournful, pathetic 9 lamenting, sniveling, sorrowful 10 blubbering, lachrymose

tear-jerking 5 mushy 6 drippy, sticky 7 maudlin, mawkish 8 touching 9 schmaltzy 11 sentimental

teary-eyed 5 blear, moist

tease 3 bug, kid, rag, rip 4 bait, coax, comb, gibe, jive, josh, ride, tear, twit 5 annoy, chaff, chivy, harry, shred, taunt, worry 6 cajole, harass, needle, pester, pick on, plague 7 bedevil, torment 8 ridicule 9 tantalize

teaser 5 promo 7 preview

teched 3 mad 4 daft 5 batty, crazy 6 insane 7 cracked, lunatic 8 demented

technicality 6 detail 8 loophole

technique 4 mode 5 modus 6 method, system 8 approach 9 procedure 13 modus operandi

ted 5 strew 7 spread 7 scatter

tedious 3 dry 4 dull 5 ho-hum, stale 6 boring, dreary 7 irksome, operose 8 drudging, tiresome 9 dryasdust, wearisome 10 monotonous 11 mindnumbing 13 uninteresting

tedium 4 yawn 5 ennui 7 boredom 8 doldrums, dullness, monotony, sameness

teem 4 flow, pour 5 crawl, empty, swarm 6 abound, bustle 7 produce 9 pullulate

teeming 4 lush, rife 5 alive 6 aswarm 7 replete 8 abundant, swarming, thronged 9 abounding 11 overflowing

teen 5 youth 10 adolescent

tee off 4 open 5 begin, drive, enter, start 8 commence, initiate

teeter 4 rock, sway 5 waver 6 falter, seesaw, wobble 9 vacillate

telamon 5 atlas *counterpart:* 8 caryatid

Telamon *brother:* 6 Peleus *father:* 6 Aea-cus *half-brother:* 6 Phocus *son:* 4 Ajax 6 Teucer

Telegonus *father:* 7 Ulysses 8 Odysseus *mother:* 5 Circe

telegraph 4 wire 5 cable 6 signal *code:* 5 Morse

Telemachus *father:* 7 Ulysses 8 Odysseus *mother:* 8 Penelope

telephone 4 buzz, call, dial, ring 5 phone 6 ring up *inventor:* 4 Bell (Alexander Graham)

Telephus *father:* 8 Heracles, Hercules *mother:* 4 Auge

telescope 5 glass 6 finder 7 compact 8 compress, condense, contract, spyglass 9 reflector, refractor

television 4 tube 5 video 8 boob tube, idiot box *antenna:* 10 rabbit ears *award:* 4 Emmy *British:* 5 telly *children's:* 6 kidvid *frequency:* 3 UHF, VHF *interference:* 4 snow *network:* 3 ABC, BBC, CBS, Fox, NBC, NET, PBS *pioneer:* 5 Baird (John Logie) 8 De Forest (Lee), Zworykin (Vladimir) *program:* 4 news 5 rerun 6 series, sitcom 7 western 8 game show, talk show 9 broadcast, docudrama, soap opera 11 infomercial 12 infotainment *tube:* 9 kinescope

tell 3 say 4 blab, clue, warn 5 break, count, crack, mound, order, spill, state, utter 6 advise, betray, fill in, inform, notify, relate, report, retail, reveal 7 confess, declare, divulge, narrate, recount, reel off 8 describe, disclose, give away 9 come clean

teller 5 clerk 6 banker 7 cashier, counter 8 informer, narrator 12 communicator

telling 5 solid, sound, valid 6 cogent 7 weighty 8 powerful 9 effective 10 convincing, expressive

tell off 4 flay, rate, ream 5 chide, scold 6 berate, rebuke 7 bawl out, chew out, reprove, upbraid 8 admonish, call down 9 dress down, excoriate, reprimand 10 take to task, tongue-lash, vituperate

tell on 6 inform, snitch, tattle

telltale 3 cue 4 clue, fink, lead, sign 5 proof 6 canary, gossip, signal, snitch, tip-off 7 rat fink, tattler 8 evidence, gossiper, informer, quidnunc, signpost, squealer 9 indicator 10 indication, newsmonger 12 blabbermouth, gossipmonger 13 scandalmonger

telluric 6 earthy 7 earthly, mundane, terrene, worldly 9 sublunary 11 terrestrial

temblor 5 quake, shake, shock 6 tremor 8 upheaval 10 aftershock, earthquake

temerarious 4 rash 6 daring 8 heedless, reckless 9 audacious, daredevil, foolhardy, venturous 11 adventurous, venturesome 13 adventuresome

temerity 4 gall 5 cheek, nerve 6 daring 8 audacity, chutzpah, rashness 9 assurance, brashness, hardihood, hardiness 10 effrontery 12 recklessness 13 foolhardiness

temper 4 heat, mean, mind, mood, tone, vein 5 admix, alloy, anger, blood, grain, humor, trend 6 anneal, attune, dander, dilute, govern, hackle, makeup, medium, season, soften, spirit, strain 7 courage, mollify, passion, quality, toughen 8 hardness, moderate, modulate, restrain 9 character, composure, condition 10 resilience, resiliency 11 disposition, personality

temperament 4 mood 5 humor 6 manner, makeup, mettle, nature 9 character 10 complexion 11 disposition, personality

temperamental 5 moody 6 ornery, touchy 7 erratic 8 contrary, ticklish, unstable, variable, volatile 9 mercurial 10 capricious, changeable, high-strung, inconstant 13 unpredictable

temperance 8 sobriety 9 austerity, restraint 10 abstinence, continence, moderation, self-denial 11 self-control *advocate of:* 6 Nation (Carry) 7 Willard (Frances)

temperate 4 calm, even, mild, soft 5 balmy, sober 6 modest, steady 7 clement 8 discreet, moderate 9 abstinent, continent 10 abstemious, controlled, reasonable, restrained 11 abstentious

temperature 4 heat, mood 5 fever 6 degree, warmth 7 hotness 8 coldness 9 intensity

tempered 7 diluted, treated 8 adjusted, hardened, softened 9 mitigated, moderated, qualified 12 strengthened

tempest 3 din 4 blow, gale, rage, wind 5 furor, hurly, storm 6 hubbub, squall, tumult, uproar 8 brouhaha, foofaraw 9 commotion, hurricane 10 hullabaloo, hurly-burly

Tempest, The *character:* 5 Ariel 6 Alonso 7 Caliban, Miranda 8 Prospero 9 Ferdinand

tempestuous 4 wild 5 roily, rough 6 raging, stormy 7 furious, moiling, violent 8 blustery 9 turbulent 10 tumultuous

temple 4 fane 6 church 9 synagogue 10 tabernacle *ancient:* 8 pantheon *Aztec:* 8 teocalli *Buddhist:* 3 wat *Eastern:* 6 pagoda *Greek:* 9 Parthenon *sanctuary:* 5 cella 6 adytum 10 penetralia

tempo 4 pace, rate, time 5 speed 6 rhythm *fast:* 6 presto, vivace 7 allegro

moderate: 7 andante *slow:* 5 grave, lento 6 adagio

temporal 3 lay 5 civil 6 carnal 7 earthly, mundane, profane, secular, worldly 13 chronological, synchronistic

temporary 6 acting 7 Band-Aid, interim 8 fleeting 9 ad interim, makeshift, transient 10 short-lived, substitute, transitory 11 provisional

temporize 5 delay, stall, yield 6 palter 7 draw out 8 gain time 10 equivocate 11 prevaricate

tempt 3 woo 4 bait, lure, risk, sway 5 court, decoy 6 allure, entice, entrap, invite, lead on, seduce 7 provoke 8 inveigle 9 tantalize

temptation 4 bait, lure, trap 5 decoy, siren, snare 6 allure, come-on 9 seduction 10 attraction, enticement

tempting 8 alluring 9 appealing, delicious, seductive 10 attractive, come-hither

temptress 4 vamp 5 siren 7 Lorelei 10 seductress 11 femme fatale

ten *cents:* 4 dime *combining form:* 3 dec, dek 4 deca, deka 5 decem *dollars:* 7 sawbuck *mills:* 4 cent *thousand:* 6 myriad *years:* 6 decade

tenable 5 sound 8 rational 10 defendable, defensible, reasonable 12 maintainable

tenacious 3 set 4 fast, firm, true 5 fixed, stout 6 dogged, secure, sturdy 8 adhesive, clinging, resolute, stalwart, stubborn 9 obstinate, steadfast 10 persistent 11 persevering

tenacity 4 grit, guts 5 moxie, pluck, spunk 6 mettle, spirit 7 courage 8 firmness 10 resolution 11 persistence 13 determination

tenant 6 holder, lessee, lodger, renter 7 boarder, dweller 8 occupant *feudal:* 6 vassal

tenantable 7 livable 9 habitable 11 inhabitable

Ten Commandments 9 Decalogue

tend 4 lean, mind, till, work 5 guard, labor, nurse, serve, watch 6 foster 7 babysit, care for, conduce, incline, nurture, oversee 8 minister 9 cultivate, look after, watch over

tendency 4 bent, bias 5 drift, tenor, trend 7 current, leaning 8 penchant 10 partiality, proclivity, propensity 11 disposition, inclination 12 predilection

tendentious 6 biased 7 colored, partial 8 one-sided, partisan 10 prejudiced

tender 3 bid 4 fond, mild, soft, sore, warm 5 green, money, mushy, offer, young 6 callow, extend, gentle, humane, loving, submit, touchy **7** fragile, hold out, lenient, painful, present, proffer, propose **8** delicate, immature, proposal **9** sensitive, succulent **10** benevolent, solicitous **11** considerate, warmhearted **12** affectionate **13** compassionate

tenderfoot 4 colt, punk, tyro **6** novice, rookie **7** amateur **8** beginner, freshman, neophyte, newcomer **9** cheechako, fledgling, greenhorn, novitiate **10** apprentice

tenderhearted 6 kindly **11** sympathetic **13** compassionate

Tender Is the Night author 10 Fitzgerald (F. Scott)

tendon 4 band, cord **5** nerve, sinew **6** leader **9** hamstring

tendril 4 curl, vine **6** cirrus, spiral **7** ringlet

tenebrific 4 dark, glum, gray, grim **5** black, bleak, sable **6** dismal, dreary, gloomy, somber, sombre **8** desolate, funereal **10** depressing, oppressive **11** dispiriting

tenebrous 3 dim **4** dark, deep, dusk, hazy **5** dusky, foggy, muddy, murky, vague **6** cloudy, gloomy **7** cryptic, obscure, shadowy, unclear **9** ambiguous, lightless **10** caliginous

tenement 4 flat **6** rental, walk-up, warren **7** lodging, rookery **8** building **9** apartment, residence

tenet 3 ism **5** canon, creed, dogma **6** belief **7** paradox **8** doctrine **9** principle **10** empiricism

tenfold 7 decuple

Tennessee *capital:* **9** Nashville *city:* **7** Memphis **9** Knoxville **11** Chattanooga *college, university:* **10** Vanderbilt *mountain, range:* **7** Lookout **10** Great Smoky **13** Clingmans Dome *nickname:* **9** Volunteer (State) *public works:* **3** TVA **9** Norris Dam *river:* **9** Tennessee **11** Mississippi *state bird:* **11** mockingbird *state flower:* **4** iris *state tree:* **11** tulip poplar

tennis *award:* **8** Davis Cup *item:* **3** net **4** ball **6** racket **7** racquet *kind:* **5** table **7** doubles, singles **8** platform *score:* **4** love **5** deuce *serve:* **3** ace *shoe:* **7** sneaker *stroke:* **3** cut, lob **4** chop, drop **5** serve, slice **6** volley **8** backhand, forehand *term:* **3** let, set **5** court, fault **7** service **9** advantage, backcourt

tennis champ 4 Ashe (Arthur), Borg (Bjorn), Cash (Pat), Graf (Steffi), King (Billie Jean), Noah (Yannick), Wade (Virginia) **5** Budge (Don), Chang (Michael), Court (Margaret Smith), Evert (Chris), Gómez (Andres), Laver (Rod), Lendl (Ivan), Perry (Fred), Seles (Monica), Stich (Michael), Vilas (Guillermo), Wills (Helen) **6** Agassi (André), Austin (Tracy), Becker (Boris), Casals (Rosie), Edberg (Stephan), Fraser (Neale), Gibson (Althea), Hewitt (Lleyton), Hingis (Martina), Kramer (Jack), Muster (Thomas), Pierce (Mary), Stolle (Fred), Tilden (Bill) **7** Connors (Jimmy), Courier (Jim), Emerson (Roy), Federer (Roger), Lacoste (Rene), McEnroe (John), Nastase (Ilie), Novótna (Jana), Sampras (Pete) **8** Connolly (Maureen), González (Pancho), Martínez (Conchita), Newcombe (John), Rosewall (Ken), Sabatini (Gabriela), Wilander (Mats), Williams (Serena, Venus) **9** Davenport (Lindsay) **10** Mandlikova (Hana) **11** Navratilova (Martina) **14** Sánchez Vicario (Arantxa)

Tennyson poem 4 Maud **7** Ulysses **8** Princess (The), Tiresias **10** Enoch Arden, In Memoriam **12** Locksley Hall **23** Charge of the Light Brigade (The)

tenor 4 mood, tone **5** drift, voice **6** singer **7** meaning, purport **8** tendency **9** substance *American:* **5** Lanza (Mario) **6** Hadley (Jerry), Peerce (Jan), Tucker (Richard) **8** Melchior (Lauritz) **9** McCormack (John), McCracken (James) *Canadian:* **7** Vickers (Jon) *Czech:* **6** Slezak (Leo) *German:* **10** Wunderlich (Fritz) *Italian:* **5** Gigli (Beniamino) **6** Alagna (Roberto), Caruso (Enrico) **7** Bocelli (Andrea), Corelli (Franco) **8** Bergonzi (Carlo) **9** del Monaco (Mario), di Stefano (Giuseppe), Pavarotti (Luciano) *Spanish:* **5** Kraus (Alfredo) **7** Domingo (Plácido) **8** Carreras (José) *Swedish:* **5** Gedda (Nicolai) **8** Björling (Jussi) **9** Bjoerling (Jussi)

tenpins 7 bowling

tense 4 edgy, taut **5** nervy, rigid, tight, wired **6** uneasy **7** anxious, jittery, nervous, restive, uptight **8** strained, stressed **10** high-strung *grammatical:* **4** past **6** future **7** perfect, present **8** preterit **9** preterite **10** pluperfect **11** progressive

tension 5 state, steam **6** nerves, strain, stress, unease **7** anxiety, balance **8** edginess, pressure, tautness **9** agitation, hostility, stiffness **10** discomfort, opposition, uneasiness **11** nervousness, uptightness

tent 4 camp **6** canopy, encamp, laager **7** bivouac, shelter *kind:* **3** pup **4** yurt **5** Baker, tepee **6** wigwam **7** marquee **8** pavilion, umbrella *maker:* **4** Omar *material:* **6** canvas *part:* **3** fly, guy, peg **4** pole

tentacle 3 arm 6 barbel, feeler
tentative 4 test 5 chary, loath, probe,
trial 6 averse 7 halting 8 hesitant, insecure 9 diffident, makeshift, reluctant,
uncertain, undecided, unsettled
10 irresolute 11 conditional, disinclined, problematic, provisional
tenth 5 tithe *combining form:* 4 deci
tenuous 4 slim, thin, weak 5 reedy,
shaky 6 feeble, flimsy, slight, stalky
7 fragile, sketchy, slender 8 gossamer
10 precarious 11 implausible 13 insubstantial, unsubstantial
tenure 4 term 6 estate 10 incumbency
feudal: 7 burgage
tepid 4 mild, warm 7 warmish 8 lukewarm 9 apathetic 11 halfhearted, indifferent
tequila source 5 agave
Terentia's husband 6 Cicero
Tereus *son:* 4 Itys *wife:* 6 Procne
tergiversate 3 haw, hem, rat 5 dodge,
evade, hedge 6 defect, desert, waffle,
weasel 7 abandon, shuffle 8 renounce,
sidestep 9 pussyfoot, repudiate 10 apostatize, equivocate
term 3 dub, end 4 call, name, span, tour,
word 5 label, spell, stint, title 6 detail,
period, tenure 7 quarter, session
8 duration, semester 9 designate
10 conclusion, denominate, expression,
limitation, particular 11 appellation,
designation
termagant 5 harpy, scold, shrew, vixen
6 ogress, virago 8 fishwife, harridan
9 Xanthippe
terminable 6 finite
terminal 3 end, lag 4 last 5 depot, fatal,
final 6 finial, latest, latter, lethal 7 closing, extreme, station 8 eventual, hindmost, junction, ultimate 9 extremity
10 concluding *negative:* 7 cathode *positive:* 5 anode
terminate 3 end 4 boot, drop, fire, halt,
kill, quit, sack, stop 5 abort, cease,
close, issue, leave 6 cut off, finish, wind
up 7 abolish, dead-end, dismiss 8 complete, conclude, dissolve 9 determine,
discharge 10 extinguish 11 assassinate,
discontinue
terminology 4 cant 5 argot, idiom, lingo
6 jargon, patois 7 lexicon 8 language,
shoptalk 10 vernacular, vocabulary
12 nomenclature
termite 5 alate 8 white ant
ternary 5 third 6 triple 9 threefold
Terpsichore see MUSE
terrace 4 bank, deck, mesa, park, roof,
step 5 bench, porch, shelf 6 street 7 balcony, sundeck 8 platform 9 promenade
terra-cotta 4 clay 7 pottery

terra firma 4 dirt, land, soil 5 earth
6 ground
terrain 4 area, land, turf 5 field
6 domain, ground, milieu, sphere
8 province 9 bailiwick, territory
10 topography 11 environment
terrapin 6 turtle
terrestrial 4 land 6 earthy, ground
7 earthly, mundane, worldly 8 everyday, ordinary, telluric, workaday
9 earthlike, planetary, sublunary
10 earthbound
terrible 4 dire 5 awful, dread 6 fierce,
grisly, horrid, severe 7 dreaded, fearful,
furious, ghastly, hideous, intense,
macabre, vicious, violent 8 dreadful,
gruesome, horrible, horrific, shocking,
vehement 9 abhorrent, appalling, atrocious, desperate, frightful, harrowing,
laborious, loathsome, monstrous,
strenuous 10 disastrous, formidable,
horrendous, horrifying
terrier 3 dog *kind:* 3 fox 4 blue, bull,
Skye 5 cairn, Irish, Welsh 6 Boston
8 Airedale, Lakeland 9 Yorkshire
terrific 5 super, swell 6 superb 7 amazing, awesome 8 dreadful, dynamite,
glorious 9 appalling, frightful, marvelous, upsetting, wonderful 10 formidable 11 magnificent, sensational
13 extraordinary
terrify 5 alarm, scare 7 scarify, startle
8 affright, frighten 10 intimidate
terrifying 4 grim 5 scary 6 grisly, horrid
7 ghastly, hideous, macabre 8 alarming,
dreadful, fearsome, gruesome, horrible, terrible 9 frightful 10 formidable,
horrifying
territory 4 area, belt, land, turf, zone
5 field, route, state, tract 6 domain,
region, sphere 7 country, demesne, terrain 8 conquest, district, dominion,
province 9 bailiwick 10 borderland
12 jurisdiction
terror 4 brat, fear 5 alarm, dread, panic,
worry 6 dismay, fright, horror
7 scourge 9 nightmare 11 fearfulness,
trepidation
terrorize 3 cow 5 alarm, bully, scare
6 coerce, fright, menace 7 scarify
8 browbeat, bulldoze, frighten, threat-
en 9 strong-arm 10 intimidate
terry 4 loop 5 cloth 6 fabric 12 Turkish
towel
terse 4 curt 5 brief, crisp, pithy, short
6 abrupt 7 brusque, compact, concise,
elegant, laconic, summary 8 polished,
succinct 11 compendious, sententious,
telegraphic 12 monosyllabic
tertiary 5 third
terza ___ 4 rima

tessera 3 die **4** tile **6** tablet, ticket
test 3 try **4** exam, quiz **5** assay, check, essay, final, proof, prove, shell, taste, touch, trial, try on **6** sample, tryout, verify **7** confirm, examine, midterm **8** evaluate, gut check, sounding, trial run **9** benchmark, criterion **10** evaluation, experiment, touchstone **11** demonstrate, examination **12** experimental
testa 6 cupule **7** coating **8** envelope, seed coat, tegument **10** integument
testament 4 will **5** credo, creed, proof **7** tribute, witness **8** evidence **9** scripture **11** attestation **12** confirmation
tester 4 coin **6** canopy, prover **7** analyst, assayer **8** examiner **12** investigator
testifier 7 witness **8** deponent
testify 5 prove, swear **6** affirm, attest, depone, depose, evince **7** certify, witness **11** certificate
testimonial 5 proof **6** salute **7** tribute, witness **8** evidence, memorial, monument **9** affidavit, character, reference **11** attestation **12** appreciation, commendation, confirmation **13** commemoration
testimony 5 proof **6** avowal **7** witness **8** evidence **9** affidavit, authority **10** deposition, profession **11** affirmation, attestation, declaration **12** confirmation **13** corroboration, documentation
testy 4 edgy **5** cross, fussy, hasty **6** cranky, ornery, tetchy, touchy **7** fretful, grouchy, peevish **8** choleric **9** crotchety, irascible, irritable **10** ill-humored, out of sorts **12** cantankerous **13** quick-tempered
tetanus 7 lockjaw, trismus
tetchy see TESTY
tête-à-tête 4 chat, talk **5** à deux **7** private, vis-à-vis **8** causerie **10** face-to-face **12** conversation
tether 3 tie **4** bind, rope **5** cable, chain, stake **6** fasten, fetter, lariat, picket **8** restrain **9** restraint
Tethys *daughters:* **9** Oceanides *father:* **6** Uranus *husband:* **7** Oceanus *mother:* **4** Gaea **5** Terra
tetrad 4 four **7** quartet **8** foursome **10** quaternion
Teutonic 6 German **8** Germanic *language:* **5** Dutch **6** Danish, German, Gothic **7** English, Flemish, Frisian, Swedish **9** Afrikaans, Norwegian
Texas *capital:* **6** Austin *city:* **4** Waco **6** Dallas, El Paso **7** Houston **8** Amarillo **9** Arlington, Fort Worth **10** San Antonio *college, university:* **3** SMU **4** Rice **5** Lamar **6** Baylor **9** Texas Tech **15** Sam Houston State *island:* **5** Padre *mountain:*

9 Guadalupe (Peak) *nickname:* **8** Lone Star (State) *park:* **7** Big Bend *river:* **3** Red **5** Pecos **6** Brazos **8** Colorado **9** Rio Grande *state bird:* **11** mockingbird *state flower:* **10** bluebonnet *state tree:* **5** pecan
text 6 script
textbook 6 primer
textile 5 cloth **6** fabric *dealer:* **6** mercer *machine:* **8** calender *shop:* **7** mercery *treat:* **9** mercerize
texture 3 web **4** feel, hand, wale, woof **5** weave **6** fabric
Thackeray novel 9 Pendennis **10** Vanity Fair **11** Barry Lyndon, Henry Esmond
Thailand *capital:* **7** Bangkok *city:* **9** Chiang Mai *former name:* **4** Siam *island:* **6** Phuket *monetary unit:* **4** baht *neighbor:* **4** Laos **5** Burma **7** Myanmar **8** Cambodia, Malaysia *river:* **10** Chao Phraya *sea:* **7** Andaman
Thaïs 7 hetaera, hetaira **9** courtesan *author:* **6** France (Anatole) *composer:* **8** Massenet (Jules) *husband:* **7** Ptolemy *lover:* **9** Alexander (the Great)
thalassic 6 marine **7** oceanic **8** maritime
Thalia see GRACES; MUSE
Thanatopsis author 6 Bryant (William Cullen)
Thanatos 5 death *brother:* **6** Hypnos *mother:* **3** Nyx
thankful 4 glad **8** grateful **12** appreciative
thanks 5 grace **8** blessing **9** gratitude **11** benediction **12** appreciation, gratefulness
Thanksgiving 5 feast **7** holiday *first celebrant:* **6** Indian **7** Pilgrim *food:* **6** turkey
thatch 4 mop **4** hair, roof **5** cover
that is *Latin:* **5** id est
Thaumas *daughter:* **4** Iris **5** Aello, Harpy **7** Celaeno, Ocypete *daughters:* **7** Harpies *father:* **6** Pontus *mother:* **4** Gaea *wife:* **7** Electra
thaumaturgic 5 magic **6** Magian, mystic, witchy **7** magical **8** wizardly **9** marvelous **10** miraculous **11** necromantic **12** supernatural
thaumaturgy 5 magic **7** sorcery **8** cabbalah, kabbalah, witchery, wizardry **10** necromancy
thaw 4 melt **5** deice, relax **6** unbend **7** defrost, liquefy **8** dissolve, unfreeze **10** condescend, deliquesce
the 7 article *French:* **3** les *German:* **3** das, der, die *Spanish:* **3** las, los
Thea *daughter:* **6** Selene *father:* **6** Uranus *husband:* **8** Hyperion *mother:* **4** Gaea
theater 4 nabe **5** drama, stage **6** boards **9** playhouse **10** footlights *award:* **4** Tony *district:* **6** rialto *entrance:* **5** foyer, lobby *Greek:* **5** odeum *movie:* **6** cinema **8** cine-

plex, megaplex 9 multiplex *outdoor:*
7 drive-in *part:* 3 box, pit 4 loge
5 apron, stage, wings 7 balcony, par-
quet 8 parterre 9 greenroom, mezzanine, orchestra 10 proscenium
theatrical 5 stagy 6 staged 8 dramatic,
thespian 10 artificial, flamboyant,
histrionic 11 dramaturgic 12 melodramatic *agent:* 6 Morris (William) *device:*
4 prop *group:* 6 troupe
Theban Eagle 6 Pindar
Thebes *founder:* 6 Cadmus *king:* 5 Laius
7 Oedipus *queen:* 7 Jocasta
theft 5 heist, pinch 6 holdup, piracy
7 break-in, larceny, robbery 8 burglary,
stealing, thievery 9 pilferage *combining
form:* 5 klept 6 klepto
theme 4 stem, text, tune 5 essay, lemma,
motif, paper, point, topic, topos 6 burden, matter, melody, mythos, thesis
7 article, conceit, message, subject 8 argument 11 composition 12 dissertation
Themis *father:* 6 Uranus *goddess of:*
3 law 7 justice *husband:* 4 Zeus
7 Jupiter *mother:* 4 Gaea
then 4 also, anon, ergo, next, thus, when
5 again, hence, later 7 besides, further
8 moreover 9 therefore, thereupon
10 in addition 11 accordingly, furthermore 12 additionally, consequently
thence 4 away 7 thereof 9 from there,
therefrom
Theogony *poet* 6 Hesiod
theologian *American:* 6 Merton
(Thomas) 7 Edwards (Jonathan),
Niebuhr (Reinhold), Tillich (Paul),
Walther (Carl) *Dutch:* 6 Jansen (Cor-
nelis) *English:* 4 Bede (Venerable)
5 Pusey (Edward), Watts (Isaac)
6 Alcuin, Wesley (John) 7 Langton
(Stephen) 8 Pelagius, Wycliffe (John)
French: 6 Calvin (John) 7 Abelard
(Peter), William (of Auvergne, of Aux-
erre) 8 Maritain (Jacques), Sabatier
(Auguste), Teilhard (de Chardin,
Pierre) *German:* 6 Rahner (Karl) 7 Eck-
hart (Meister) 8 Albertus (Magnus)
9 Niemöller (Martin) 10 Bonhoeffer
(Dietrich) *Greek:* 9 Zygomalas
(Theodore) *Italian:* 6 Thomas (Aquinas)
7 Aquinas (Thomas), Socinus (Fausto,
Laelius) *Scottish:* 10 Duns Scotus
(John) *Spanish:* 6 Suárez (Francisco)
7 Vitoria (Francisco de) 8 Servetus
(Michael) *Swedish:* 9 Soderblom
(Nathan) *Swiss:* 4 Küng (Hans) 5 Barth
(Karl), Vinet (Alexandre-Rodolphe)
theological *school:* 8 seminary *virtue:*
4 hope 5 faith 7 charity
___ **Theologica** 5 Summa
theorbo 4 lute

theorem 3 law 4 rule 5 axiom 7 formula,
inverse, stencil 8 converse 9 principle
10 principium 11 fundamental, proposition
theoretical 4 pure 5 ideal 8 abstract, academic, notional, unproved 11 conjectural, speculative 12 hypothetical
13 problematical, suppositional
theorize 5 guess 6 submit 7 suggest 9 formulate, postulate, speculate 10 conjecture 11 hypothesize
theory 7 perhaps, premise, surmise
8 supposal 10 conjecture, hypothesis
11 speculation, supposition *astronomical:* 7 big bang *suffix:* 3 ism
therapeutic 5 tonic 7 healing, helpful
8 curative, remedial, salutary, sanative
9 healthful, medicinal, vulnerary,
wholesome 10 beneficial, corrective
11 restorative 12 health-giving
therapy 9 treatment
therefore 4 ergo, then, thus 5 hence
6 thence 11 accordingly 12 consequently
therefrom 4 away 6 thence
thereupon 4 ergo, then, thus 6 at once,
at that, thence 8 directly 9 right away,
therefore, wherefore 11 accordingly,
straightway 12 consequently
thermal unit 3 Btu 6 degree 7 calorie
thermometer 5 gauge 9 indicator *kind:*
7 Celsius, Réaumur 10 centigrade,
Fahrenheit
thermos 5 dewar 10 Dewar flask
Theroux *work* 9 Saint Jack 13 Mosquito
Coast (The) 14 Half Moon Street
18 Great Railway Bazaar (The)
Thersites' slayer 8 Achilles
thesaurus *editor* 5 Roget (Peter Mark)
Theseus *beloved:* 7 Ariadne *father:*
6 Aegeus *mother:* 6 Aethra *slayer:*
9 Lycomedes *son:* 10 Hippolytus *victim:*
6 Sciron 8 Minotaur 10 Procrustes *wife:*
7 Phaedra
thesis 5 essay, point, theme 6 belief
7 premise 8 downbeat, position, tractate, treatise 9 discourse, monograph,
postulate, synthesis 10 contention,
exposition 11 postulation, proposition,
supposition 12 disquisition, dissertation
thespian 5 actor 6 mummer, player
7 actress, trouper 8 dramatic 9 performer 10 histrionic, theatrical 11 dramaturgic 12 impersonator, melodramatic
Thespis' forte 5 drama 7 tragedy
Thessalian hero 5 Jason 8 Achilles
___ **the Terrible** 4 Ivan
Thetis 6 Nereid *father:* 6 Nereus *husband:* 6 Peleus *mother:* 5 Doris *son:*
8 Achilles

theurgist 5 witch **7** warlock **8** magician, sorcerer **12** wonder-worker
thew 4 beef **5** brawn, might, power, sinew, vigor **6** muscle **8** strength, vitality
thick 3 fat **4** wide **5** broad, bulky, burly, close, dense, dumpy, husky, squat, stout **6** chummy, chunky, packed, stocky **7** compact, crammed, crowded, viscous **8** familiar, heavyset, intimate **11** inspissated
thicken 3 set **4** blur, clot, jell **6** curdle **7** broaden, compact, congeal **8** condense **9** coagulate **10** inspissate **11** concentrate, consolidate
thicket 4 bosk, bush, shaw, wood **5** clump, copse, grove, hedge **6** bosket, covert, mallee, tangle **7** boscage, bosquet, coppice, spinney **8** hedgerow, quickset **9** brushwood, canebrake, chaparral
thickness 3 ply **4** loft **5** depth, gauge, layer, sheet **7** density **8** dullness **9** stupidity, viscosity
thickset 5 bulky, burly, husky, pudgy, stout **6** chunky, portly, stocky, sturdy **7** compact **9** corpulent
thief 3 dip **4** prig **5** ganef **6** bandit, lifter, looter, pirate, rascal, robber **7** booster, burglar, filcher, stealer **8** hijacker, larcener, pilferer, water rat **9** larcenist, purloiner **10** cat burglar, highwayman, pickpocket, shoplifter **12** housebreaker
thieve 3 rob **4** hook, lift, pick, roll **5** filch, pinch, pluck, steal, swipe **6** hijack, hold up, pilfer, rip off, snitch **7** purloin **8** knock off **9** knock over
thievery see THEFT
thievish 9 larcenous **13** light-fingered
thigh 3 ham **5** flank **6** gammon *bone:* **5** femur *relating to:* **6** crural **7** femoral
thimble 3 cup **5** cover
thin 4 fine, lank, lean, slim **5** gaunt, lanky, reedy, scant, sharp, spare **6** dilute, flimsy, meager, meagre, rarefy, scanty, skimpy, skinny, slight, sparse, stalky, treble, twiggy, watery **7** diluted, scraggy, scrawny, slender, spindly, squinny, subtile, tenuous **8** rarefied, skeletal **9** attenuate, extenuate **10** attenuated **11** watered-down **13** unsubstantial
thing 4 item **5** being, event **6** entity, matter, object **7** article, concern, element **8** business, incident, material, occasion **9** existence, happening **10** occurrence, phenomenon *in law:* **3** res
thingamajig 5 gizmo **6** dingus, doodad, gadget, jigger, widget **7** whatsit **9** doohickey
things 4 gear **5** goods, stock, stuff **7** baggage, clothes, effects, luggage **8** chat-

tels, clothing, matériel, movables, property, supplies **10** belongings, provisions **11** impedimenta, merchandise **13** accoutrements, paraphernalia
think 4 mull, muse **5** brood, study, weigh **6** ideate, ponder, reason **7** believe, imagine, reflect, suppose, surmise **8** cogitate, consider, meditate, ruminate **9** cerebrate, speculate **10** conjecture, deliberate, excogitate **11** contemplate
Thinker sculptor 5 Rodin (Auguste)
third 8 tertiary *combining form:* **3** tri *power:* **4** cube
third degree 7 torture **8** grilling **11** inquisition, questioning **13** interrogation
third estate 5 plebs **6** people, plebes **8** populace **9** commonage, commoners, plebeians **10** commonalty **11** rank and file
Third Man author 6 Greene (Graham)
Third of May painter 4 Goya (Francisco)
thirst 3 yen **4** itch, long, lust, pine **5** crave, yearn **6** desire, hanker, hunger **7** craving, dryness, longing **8** appetite
thirsty 3 dry **4** arid, avid **5** eager **6** ardent **7** anxious, bone-dry, parched **8** droughty **9** absorbent, waterless
this and that 8 oddments, sundries **9** etceteras **11** miscellanea, odds and ends
Thisbe's lover 7 Pyramus
This Side of Paradise author 10 Fitzgerald (F Scott)
thistle 4 weed **7** caltrop *Russian:* **10** tumbleweed
thistlebird 9 goldfinch
thither 3 yon **5** there **6** yonder
thole 3 peg, pin **6** endure
Thomas à ___ 6 Becket, Kempis
Thomas's Greek name 7 Didymus
Thomas opera 6 Mignon
Thompson 4 Emma **5** Sadie **6** Hunter **7** Dorothy, Francis, J. Walter **8** Benjamin
thong 4 band, lace, lash, rein, zori **5** lasso, strap, strip, whang **6** sandal **7** latchet **8** flip-flop
Thor 5 Donar *father:* **4** Odin **5** Wotan *god of:* **7** thunder *hammer:* **8** Mjollnir *mother:* **5** Jordh, Jorth
thorax 5 chest, trunk **6** pereon
Thoreau, Henry David *friend:* **7** Emerson (Ralph Waldo) *town:* **7** Concord *work:* **6** Walden
thorn 4 barb **5** briar, spike, spine **7** prickle, spinule **9** annoyance **10** irritation
thorny 5 sharp, spiny **6** briary, touchy, tricky **7** awkward, prickly, spinous **8** ticklish **9** difficult, vexatious **10** nettlesome **11** troublesome

thorough 4 full **6** minute **7** careful, in-depth **8** complete, detailed, diligent, whole-hog **9** downright **10** blow-by-blow, exhaustive, meticulous **11** painstaking **13** conscientious

thoroughbred 8 pedigree, purebred **9** pedigreed, pureblood **10** bloodstock **11** full-blooded

thoroughfare 3 way **4** road **5** track **6** artery, avenue, street **7** highway, parkway **8** corridor **9** boulevard

thoroughgoing 5 utter **6** all-out **7** extreme **8** absolute, complete, outright, whole-hog **9** out-and-out **10** consummate, exhaustive **11** straight-out, unmitigated **13** dyed-in-the-wool

thou 3 you **5** grand *French:* **5** mille

though 3 yet **5** still, while **6** albeit **7** however, whereas **8** after all **11** nonetheless **12** nevertheless

thought 4 idea **6** notion, reason **7** concept, opinion **8** ideation **9** brainwork **10** cogitation, conception, meditation, reflection, rumination **11** cerebration, speculation **12** deliberation, intellection **13** contemplation

thoughtful 6 polite **7** careful, gallant, heedful, mindful, pensive, serious, studied **8** gracious, studious, thinking **9** attentive, courteous, pondering, regardful **10** cogitative, meditative, reflective, ruminative, solicitous **11** considerate **12** deliberative, intellectual **13** contemplative

thoughtless 4 rash, rude **5** brash, hasty **6** madcap **7** selfish **8** careless, feckless, heedless, impolite, reckless, uncaring **9** insensate **10** incautious, ungracious **12** discourteous **13** inconsiderate

thousand *combining form:* **4** kilo *dollars:* **5** grand *years:* **10** millennium

thousandth 10 millesimal *combining form:* **5** milli

thrall 4 peon, serf, yoke **5** helot, slave **7** bondage, bondman, helotry, peonage, serfdom, slavery, villein **9** servitude, villenage **10** absorption **11** enslavement

thrash 3 tan **4** beat, belt, drub, flog, hide, lash, lick, maul, pelt, trim, whip **5** baste, flail, pound, smear, swing, thump, whale, whang **6** batter, buffet, larrup, pummel, stripe, wallop **7** scourge, shellac, trounce **8** flounder, lambaste, work over **10** flagellate

thrash out 4 moot **5** argue **6** debate **7** discuss **10** deliberate, kick around

thread 4 line, vein, yard **5** fiber, trail, weave **6** strand, stream, string **8** filament *ball of:* **4** clew *dental:* **5** floss *holder:* **6** bobbin *kind:* **4** silk, yarn **5** floss, lisle **6** cotton **8** surgical *loose:* **8** raveling **9** ravelling *surgical:* **6** catgut, suture

threadbare 4 hack, worn **5** dingy, faded, seedy, stale, tacky, tatty, tired, trite **6** beat-up, cheesy, cliché, frayed, ragged, shabby, shoddy **7** clichéd, run-down, tedious, worn-out **8** shopworn, slipshod, tattered, timeworn, well-worn **9** destitute, hackneyed **10** down-at-heel **11** commonplace, dilapidated, down-at-heels, stereotyped **13** down-at-the-heel

threadlike 11 filamentous

threads 4 duds **7** clothes **8** clothing, garments

threat 6 danger, duress, menace **7** assault, warning **8** big stick, coercion **11** thunderbolt

threaten 3 cow **4** warn **5** augur **6** coerce, menace **7** caution, portend, presage **8** endanger, forebode, forewarn, overhang **10** intimidate

three 4 trey **5** crowd *combining form:* **3** ter, tri

threefold 5 trine **6** thrice, treble, trinal, triple **7** triplex

Three Musicians artist 7 Picasso (Pablo)

Three Musketeers 5 Athos **6** Aramis **7** Porthos *author:* **5** Dumas (Alexandre) *friend:* **9** D'Artagnan

Threepenny Opera, The *author:* **6** Brecht (Bertolt) *music:* **5** Weill (Kurt)

threescore 5 sixty

Three Sisters, The 4 Olga **5** Irina, Masha *author:* **7** Chekhov (Anton)

threesome 4 trio **5** triad, trine **6** triple, triune, troika **7** trinity **8** triangle **11** triumvirate

three-wheeler 5 cycle, trike **7** pedicab **8** tricycle **10** velocipede

threnody 5 dirge, elegy **6** lament

thresh 3 lam, tan **4** beat, belt, drub, flog, hide, lash, lick, pelt, trim, wave, whip **5** baste, forge, flail, pound, slate, smear, swing, thump, whale, whang **6** batter, buffet, larrup, pummel, strike, stripe, wallop, winnow **7** scourge, shellac, trounce **8** lambaste, work over **10** flagellate

threshold 3 eve **4** door, edge, gate, sill **5** brink, limen, verge **6** outset **8** boundary

thrift 6 saving **7** economy, sea pink **8** prudence **9** frugality, parsimony

thrifty 5 canny **6** frugal, saving **7** sparing **9** provident **10** economical **12** parsimonious

thrill 3 wow **4** bang, boot, kick, rush, send **5** blast, throb **6** charge, excite, shiver, tingle, wallop **7** frisson, tremble, vibrate **9** electrify **10** excitement **11** titillation

thriller 6 gothic **7** chiller, mystery, shocker **8** whodunit **9** dime novel **10** hairraiser **13** penny dreadful

thrive 4 boom, grow **7** advance, burgeon, develop, prosper, succeed **8** flourish, get ahead

throat 3 maw **4** tube **5** gorge **6** groove, gullet **7** channel, weasand *inflammation:* **5** croup **6** angina, quinsy **10** laryngitis *relating to:* **8** guttural *warmer:* **5** scarf

throaty 5 gruff, husky, thick **6** hoarse **8** gravelly, guttural

throb 4 ache, beat, drum **5** pound, pulse **6** thrill **7** pulsate, vibrate **9** palpitate

throe 3 fit **4** pain, pang **5** agony, spasm **6** attack **7** seizure **9** suffering **10** convulsion **11** contraction

thrombus 4 clot **8** blockage, coagulum

throne 4 seat **5** chair, crown, power, reign **8** cathedra, dominion **11** sovereignty

throng 3 jam, mob **4** host, pack, push, rout **5** bunch, crowd, crush, drove, flock, group, horde, press, scrum, shoal, swarm **6** resort **9** multitude **10** assemblage

throttle 3 gun **5** choke **6** throat **7** garrote, trachea **8** strangle, suppress **11** accelerator, strangulate

through 3 per, via **4** done, past **5** due to, ended **6** direct **7** by way of, done for, nonstop, owing to **8** by dint of, complete, finished, washed-up **9** because of, by means of, completed, concluded **10** by virtue of, terminated, throughout *prefix:* **3** dia, per

throughout 3 mid **4** amid **5** midst **6** during **7** all over, overall **10** everywhere, far and near, far and wide, high and low

Through the Looking Glass *author:* **7** Carroll (Lewis) *character:* **5** Alice

throve 9 burgeoned, prospered **10** flourished

throw 3 lob, peg, put **4** cast, fire, hurl, toss **5** chuck, fling, heave, pitch, sling **6** launch, propel **7** buck off, project *in the towel:* **4** quit **6** give up

throw away 4 blow, cast, junk, shed **5** scrap, waste **7** discard, fritter **8** jettison, squander

throwback 7 atavism **9** reversion

throw down the gauntlet 4 defy **8** confront **9** challenge

throw off 4 lose, shed **5** addle, shake **7** confuse, fluster **8** befuddle, bewilder, distract *the track:* **6** derail **7** confuse, mislead

throw out 4 emit, junk, shed **5** chuck, eject, evict, scrap **6** reject **7** discard **8** jettison

throw up 4 barf, cast, hurl, lose, puke, quit, spew, toss **5** heave, retch, vomit **7** upchuck **8** disgorge **11** regurgitate

thrush 5 mavis, ouzel, robin, veery **6** mistle **8** bluebird **9** blackbird, fieldfare, mistletoe **11** nightingale

thrust 3 dig, jab, ram **4** barb, butt, core, cram, dash, dive, duck, gist, hurl, kick, pith, poke, prod, push, stab, tilt **5** barge, crowd, cut in, drive, force, lunge, press, punch, sense, shoot, shove, spear, stick, stuff **6** burden, extend, insert, pierce, plunge, propel, upshot **7** assault, obtrude, project, purport, riposte **8** pressure **9** substance

thud 3 jar **4** bump, jolt, plop **5** clunk, throb, thump **6** impact **10** concussion

thug 3 mug **4** goon, hood, punk **5** bully, rough, rowdy, tough **6** Apache, Capone, gunman, hit man **7** hoodlum, mobster, ruffian **8** enforcer, gangster, hooligan, plug-ugly **9** cutthroat, roughneck

thumb 4 leaf, turn **5** digit, hitch, ovolo **6** pollex, riffle **8** pollices (plural) **9** hitchhike

thumbs-up 3 AOK, nod **4** okay **7** goahead **10** green light

thumb through 4 scan **6** browse, riffle **7** dip into

thump 3 bop, hit **4** bash, beat, belt, blow, drub, jolt, pelt, whip **5** knock, paste, pound, punch, shock, smack, sound, whack **6** batter, buffet, impact, pummel, strike, thrash, thwack, wallop **7** clobber, endorse, promote, shellac, trounce **8** advocate

thunder 4 bang, boom, clap, peal, roar **6** rumble **7** resound **8** rumbling **9** fulminate

thunderbolt 9 lightning

thunder lizard 11 apatosaurus **12** brontosaurus

thunderstruck 5 agape **6** amazed **7** shocked, stunned **8** dismayed **9** astounded, staggered **10** astonished, bewildered, confounded **11** dumbfounded **13** flabbergasted

Thurber character 5 Mitty (Walter)

thus 3 sic **4** ergo, then **5** hence **9** therefore **11** accordingly **12** consequently *French:* **5** ainsi

Thus Spake Zarathustra author 9 Nietzsche (Friedrich)

thwack 3 bop **4** belt, biff, blow, pelt, sock, whop **5** crack, pound, smack, thump, whack

thwart 4 balk, beat, dash, foil **5** bench **6** baffle, hinder, oppose, scotch, stymie **9** checkmate, frustrate **10** circumvent, contravene, disappoint

Thyestes *brother:* 6 Atreus *daughter:* 7 Pelopia *father:* 6 Pelops *mother:* 10 Hippodamia *son:* 9 Aegisthus

Tiamat *husband:* 4 Apsu *slayer:* 6 Marduk

tiara 5 crown 6 diadem 8 headband

Tibetan *animal:* 3 yak 5 takin *capital:* 5 Lhasa *coin:* 5 tanga *monk:* 4 lama *people:* 6 Bhotia, Sherpa

tibia 8 shinbone

tic 5 quirk, spasm 6 twitch 9 twitching

tick 5 check 8 arachnid, parasite 9 checkmark 11 bloodsucker

ticker 4 bomb 5 clock, heart, watch

ticket 3 key, tag 4 comp, pass, vote 5 slate 6 ballot 7 receipt 8 passport, password 10 open sesame *seller:* 7 scalper

tickle 4 stir 5 amuse, tease, touch 6 arouse, excite, please, tingle 7 delight, gratify, provoke 9 stimulate, titillate

tickled 5 happy 6 amused 7 pleased 9 delighted

ticklish 6 tender, thorny, touchy, tricky 8 delicate, unstable 9 sensitive 10 precarious 13 oversensitive

tick off 3 ire, irk 5 anger 6 rankle 7 incense, provoke 9 aggravate

tidal flood 4 bore

tidbit 4 bite 5 goody, treat 6 dainty, morsel, nugget

tide 3 flow, flux, rush 5 drift, flood, spate, surge 6 stream 7 current, holiday *type:* 3 ebb, low 4 high, neap 5 flood 6 spring

tidings 4 news, word 6 advice 7 message 11 information 12 intelligence

tidy 4 fair, neat, smug, snug, trim 5 kempt 6 pick up 7 clean up, orderly, precise 9 shipshape 10 acceptable, methodical 11 respectable, spic-and-span, substantial, uncluttered, well-groomed 12 satisfactory, spick-and-span

tie 3 rod 4 band, bind, bond, cord, draw, gird, join, knit, knot, lash, link, moor, rope, yoke 5 equal, leash, match, truss 6 attach, cravat, fasten, fetter, hamper, oxford, ribbon, secure 7 connect, harness, shackle 8 dead heat, deadlock, fastener, ligament, ligature, restrain, shoelace, standoff, vinculum 9 constrain, stalemate 10 attachment, four-in-hand

tied 5 bound 6 joined, united 8 attached, fastened 9 connected

tier 3 row 4 bank, deck, file, line, rank 5 class, grade, group, story 6 league 7 echelon 8 category, grouping

tie-up 3 jam 4 snag 5 crimp, delay, hitch 6 glitch 7 problem 8 gridlock, slowdown, stoppage 10 connection, traffic jam 11 association

tiff 3 row 4 fuss, spat 5 run-in, scrap 6 bicker 7 brabble, dispute, quarrel, wrangle 8 argument, squabble 10 falling-out 11 altercation 12 disagreement

tiffany 5 gauze 11 cheesecloth

tiger 3 cat 6 feline 9 carnivore *young:* 3 cub

tight 4 fast, firm, snug, taut, trim 5 cheap, close, drunk, fixed, tipsy 6 firmly, secure, stingy 7 compact, crowded, drunken, miserly 8 intimate 9 tenacious 10 inebriated 11 closefisted, intoxicated 12 cheeseparing, parsimonious 13 penny-pinching

tighten 4 bind 5 choke, close, cramp, pinch, screw 6 clench, fasten, narrow, secure, shrink 8 compress, restrict 9 clamp down, constrict

tightfisted see STINGY

tight-lipped 6 silent 8 reserved, reticent, taciturn 12 closemouthed

tightwad 5 miser, piker 7 niggard, scrooge 9 skinflint 10 cheapskate 12 penny-pincher

tile 5 plate, slate 6 domino 7 tessera 8 linoleum

till 3 hoe, sow 4 disk, plow, tend, turn, up to, work 6 before, harrow 7 prior to 9 cultivate 11 in advance of 12 cash register

tillable 6 arable 10 cultivable 12 cultivatable

tillage 4 farm, land 5 tilth 7 culture 11 cultivation

tiller 4 helm 5 stalk 6 farmer, sprout 7 planter, steerer 9 sodbuster 10 cultivator

tilt 3 tip 4 bank, bent, bias, cant, cock, heel, lean, list, toss 5 grade, joust, level, lurch, pitch, slant, slope, speed 6 attack, charge, thrust 7 dispute, incline, leaning, recline 8 gradient 11 inclination

timbal 4 drum 10 kettledrum

timber 3 log 4 balk, beam, stud, tree, wood 5 board, joist, plank, trees, woods 6 forest, girder, lumber, rafter 8 woodland *uncut:* 8 stumpage *wolf:* 4 lobo

timbre 4 tone 6 temper 7 quality 9 resonance, tone color

timbrel 4 drum 10 tambourine

time 3 age, era 4 bout, date, hour, pace, span, term 5 clock, epoch, shift, space, spell, stint, tempo, while 6 moment, period, season 7 instant, stretch 8 duration, occasion 11 opportunity *combining form:* 5 chron 6 chrono *gone by:*

4 past 9 yesterday *long:* 3 age, eon, era 4 aeon *of day:* 4 dawn, dusk, noon 5 night 6 sunset 7 evening, morning, sunrise 8 daybreak, twilight 9 afternoon *olden:* 4 yore 10 yesteryear *period:* 3 age, day, eon, era 4 aeon, hour, week, year 5 epoch, month 6 decade, minute, moment, second 7 century, instant 9 fortnight 10 millennium *present:* 3 now *relating to:* 8 temporal *short:* 5 jiffy 6 moment, second 7 instant *to come:* 6 future 8 tomorrow *waste:* 4 loaf 5 dally 6 loiter

time and again 3 oft 5 often 6 hourly 8 commonly, ofttimes 10 constantly, frequently, oftentimes, repeatedly 11 continually, over and over 12 periodically

Time founder 4 Luce (Henry R.) 6 Hadden (Briton)

timeless 7 ageless, eternal, unaging 8 unageing 9 atemporal, perpetual 11 everlasting

timely 5 early 6 prompt, proper 8 punctual, suitable 9 opportune 10 seasonable 11 appropriate

Time Machine author 5 Wells (H. G.)

Time of Your Life author 7 Saroyan (William)

time-out 4 rest 5 break, pause 6 hiatus, recess 7 respite 8 breather 9 interlude 12 interruption

timepiece 5 clock, watch 7 sundial 8 horologe 9 clepsydra, stopwatch 10 water clock 11 chronograph, chronometer

timetable 6 agenda, docket 7 program 8 calendar, schedule

timeworn 3 old 4 aged, hack 5 hoary, stale, trite 6 age-old 7 ancient 8 dog-eared, Noachian 9 hackneyed 10 threadbare

time zone 7 Central, Eastern, Pacific 8 Mountain

timid 3 shy 4 wary 5 chary, mousy 6 afraid, yellow 7 bashful, chicken, fearful, halting, nervous, panicky 8 cowardly, retiring, timorous 9 diffident, tentative, trepidant, uncertain 11 unassertive 12 apprehensive, faint-hearted

timidity 4 fear 7 modesty, shyness 8 meekness 9 hesitancy, reticence 10 diffidence, hesitation

Timon's servant 7 Flavius

timorous 4 wary 5 timid 6 afraid 7 fearful 8 retiring 9 shrinking, tremulous 12 apprehensive

Timothy's associate 4 Paul

tin 3 box, can 5 metal 7 element 9 container *mining region:* 8 stannary *relating to:* 7 stannic 8 stannous *sheet:* 6 latten

tincture 3 dye 4 cast, hint, tint 5 color, shade, smack, stain, tinge, touch, trace 6 iodine, streak 8 colorant, dyestuff, laudanum 9 paregoric 10 intimation, suggestion

tinder 4 punk 5 spunk 8 kindling

tine 5 point, prong, spike 6 branch

tinge 3 dye, hue 4 cast, hint, tint, tone 5 color, imbue, shade, stain, tinct, touch 8 tincture 10 intimation

tingle 5 sting 6 thrill 7 prickle 9 sensation

tinker 3 fix 4 mend, mess, muck, play 5 gypsy 6 adjust, diddle, fiddle, mender, potter, putter, repair 7 bungler, twiddle 9 repairman

tinkle 4 ring, ting 5 chink, clink, plink 6 jingle

tinny 4 thin 5 cheap, harsh 8 metallic

Tin Pan Alley acronym 3 BMI 5 ASCAP

tinsel 5 gaudy 6 flashy, garish, tawdry 7 chintzy, glaring, trinket 8 ornament, specious 9 clinquant 11 superficial 12 meretricious

tint 3 dye, hue 4 cast, tone, wash 5 color, shade, tinge, touch 8 tincture 10 coloration 12 pigmentation

tiny 3 wee 5 bitsy, bitty, elfin, pygmy, teeny, weeny 6 minute, peewee, pocket, teensy, weensy 8 pint-size 9 itsy-bitsy, itty-bitty, miniature, minuscule 10 diminutive, pocket-size, teeny-weeny 11 lilliputian, microscopic 12 teensy-weensy 13 infinitesimal

tip 3 cap, cue, top 4 apex, cant, clue, cusp, heel, hint, lean, list, peak, perk, tilt 5 point, slant, slope, steer, upset 6 advice, topple 7 cumshaw, incline 8 gratuity, overturn, turn over 9 baksheesh, lagniappe, pourboire 11 information

tip-off 4 clue, hint, sign 6 advice 7 pointer, warning 8 giveaway, jump ball 10 indication

Tippecanoe and ___ too 5 Tyler

tippet 4 cape 5 scarf 8 liripipe

tipple 3 bib, sip 4 swig, tope 5 booze, drink 6 guzzle, imbibe 7 swizzle 8 liquor up

tippler 3 sot 4 lush, soak 5 drunk, toper 6 bibber, boozer 7 tosspot 8 drunkard 9 inebriate

tipstaff 7 bailiff

tipster 4 fink 6 canary, snitch 7 adviser, rat fink, stoolie, tattler 8 informer, squealer 11 stool pigeon

tipsy 3 lit 4 high 5 askew, drunk, lit up, oiled, tight 7 drunken, fuddled 8 unsteady 10 inebriated 11 intoxicated

tiptoe 5 creep, steal 9 pussyfoot

tirade 4 rant 6 screed 8 diatribe, harangue, jeremiad 9 philippic

12 denunciation, vituperation
13 tongue-lashing
tire 3 sap 4 bore, fail, flag, jade, pall, poop, wear 5 drain, droop, ennui, weary, wheel 6 tucker, weaken 7 exhaust, fatigue, wear out 8 enervate, wear down *airless:* 4 flat 7 blowout *kind:* 4 bias, snow 6 radial 7 retread 9 whitewall
tired 4 worn 5 spent, weary 6 done in 7 drained, run-down, worn out 8 fatigued, flagging 9 enervated, exhausted
tiredness 7 fatigue 8 collapse 9 lassitude 10 exhaustion 11 prostration
tireless 10 unflagging 13 indefatigable, inexhaustible
Tiresias 4 seer 10 soothsayer
tiresome 4 dull 5 stale 6 boring 7 irksome, lumpish, operose, tedious
Tirol *capital:* 9 Innsbruck *country:* 7 Austria *mountains:* 4 Alps
Tisiphone see ERINYES
tissue 3 web 4 film, mesh 5 fiber, gauze, paper 6 fabric *anatomical:* 4 tela 5 fiber 6 diploe 8 ganglion 10 epithelium *connective:* 6 stroma, tendon 9 cartilage *kind:* 3 fat 5 nerve 6 muscle 7 nervous 8 muscular 10 connective *layer:* 6 dermis 7 stratum *plant:* 4 bast, wood 5 xylem 6 phloem
titan 5 giant 8 colossus
Titan *father:* 6 Uranus *female:* 4 Rhea 6 Tethys, Themis *male:* 6 Cronus 7 Iapetus, Oceanus *mother:* 4 Gaea
Titan author 7 Dreiser (Theodore)
Titania's husband 6 Oberon
titanic 4 huge, vast 5 great 6 mighty 7 immense, mammoth, massive 8 colossal, enormous, gigantic 9 cyclopean, Herculean, monstrous 10 gargantuan, tremendous
tithe 3 tax 4 levy 5 tenth 12 contribution
Tithonus *beloved by:* 3 Eos *father:* 8 Laomedon
Titian painting 5 Danaë 8 Ecce Homo 10 Assumption (The), Holy Family (The) 12 Rape of Europa (The) 13 Maltese Knight, Medea and Venus, Venus and Cupid 14 Worship of Venus (The) 17 Bacchus and Ariadne
titillate 6 arouse, excite, stir up, thrill, tickle 9 stimulate
title 3 dub, due 4 call, deed, dibs, name, term 5 claim, merit, nomen 7 baptize, caption, heading 8 christen, cognomen, pretense 9 designate 10 denominate, pretension 11 appellation, appellative, designation 12 championship, compellation, denomination *Dutch:* 7 mynheer *ecclesiastic:* 8 reverend *feminine:* 3 Mrs.

4 dame, lady, ma'am, miss 5 madam 6 madame, milady, missus 8 mistress *French:* 6 madame 8 monsieur 12 mademoiselle *German:* 4 Frau, Herr 8 Fräulein *holder:* 5 noble 8 champion *Indian:* 3 sri 5 sahib *Islamic:* 5 hajji 6 sayyid 9 ayatollah *Italian:* 5 donna 6 signor 7 signora 9 signorina *monk's:* 3 fra 7 brother *of nobility:* 3 sir 4 duke, earl, king, lady, lord, sire 5 baron, count, queen 6 prince 7 baronet, duchess, marquis 8 Archduke, baroness, countess, marchesa, marchese, marquise, princess, viscount 11 marchioness, viscountess *Oriental:* 4 mirza *Persian:* 5 mirza *Portuguese:* 3 dom 4 dona 6 senhor 7 senhora 9 senhorita *Spanish:* 3 don 4 doña *Turkish:* 3 bey
titmouse 4 bird 6 tomtit 7 bushtit 9 chickadee
Tito 4 Broz (Josip)
titter 5 laugh 6 giggle 7 chortle, chuckle, snicker, snigger
tittle 3 bit, jot 4 atom, iota, mite 5 minim, speck 7 smidgen 8 particle 9 diacritic
titular 5 legal 6 titled 7 nominal 8 so-called 11 designative
Tityus *father:* 4 Zeus *slayer:* 6 Apollo
Tiu see TYR
tizzy 4 flap, fume, snit, stew 5 sweat 6 dither, swivet, uproar
T-man 5 agent 8 revenuer
to be sure: 6 indeed 7 granted 9 certainly *Scottish:* 3 tae *wit:* 3 viz 6 namely, that is 8 scilicet
toad 6 anuran, peeper 8 truckler 9 amphibian, brownnose, sycophant 10 batrachian, bootlicker 11 lickspittle *genus:* 4 Bufo
toady 4 fawn 5 cower, leech 6 cringe, flunky, grovel, kowtow, lackey, sponge 7 truckle 8 bootlick, parasite, truckler 9 brownnose, sycophant 10 bootlicker 11 apple-polish, lickspittle
toast 5 bread, drink, skoal 6 cheers, health, l'chaim, pledge, prosit, salute 7 wassail 8 mazel tov *kind:* 5 melba 6 French 8 zwieback
toastmaster 5 emcee
To a Waterfowl author 6 Bryant (William Cullen)
tobacco 4 leaf, weed *cask:* 8 hogshead *chewing:* 4 chaw, quid *ingredient:* 3 tar 8 nicotine *juice:* 6 ambeer *kind:* 4 shag 5 snuff 6 burley 7 caporal, perique, Turkish 9 broadleaf, mundungus *pipe:* 4 heel 6 dottle *rolled:* 5 cigar 9 cigarette *Turkish:* 7 latakia
Tobacco Road author 8 Caldwell (Erskine)

to be *Latin:* 4 esse
Tobias *father:* 5 Tobit *son:* 8 Hyrcanus
toby 3 jug, mug 7 pitcher
tocsin 3 SOS 5 alarm, alert 6 signal
today 3 now 9 currently, presently
toddler 3 tot 4 tyke
to-do 4 fuss, rout, stir 5 hoo-ha, rouse, stink, whirl 6 bother, bustle, clamor, furore, hubbub, hurrah, pother, ruckus, rumpus, uproar 7 turmoil 8 foofaraw 9 agitation, commotion 10 hurly-burly 11 disturbance
toe 5 digit *big:* 6 hallux *combining form:* 6 dactyl
toehold 7 footing
toff 3 fop 4 beau 5 blade, dandy, swell 7 coxcomb, peacock 8 macaroni, popinjay 9 exquisite 12 clotheshorse
toga 4 gown, robe, wrap
together 6 at once, joined, united 7 jointly 8 mutually 10 conjointly 11 concertedly 12 coincidently, collectively, concurrently *prefix:* 3 col, com, con, cor, sym, syn
togetherness 5 union 7 cahoots 8 alliance 10 connection, solidarity 11 affiliation, association, combination, conjunction, partnership
toggle 3 pin 6 fasten, switch 9 alternate 10 crosspiece
Togo *capital:* 4 Lomé *language:* 3 Ewe 6 French *monetary unit:* 5 franc *neighbor:* 5 Benin, Ghana 11 Burkina Faso
togs 3 rig 4 duds, suit 5 dress 6 attire, outfit 7 apparel, clothes, raiment, rigging 8 clothing, ensemble, garments
To His Coy Mistress *author* 7 Marvell (Andrew)
toil 3 fag, net, tug 4 grub, plod, plug, slog, trap, work 5 grind, labor, slave, snare, sweat 6 drudge 7 slavery, travail 8 drudgery
toiler 4 peon 5 slave 6 drudge, slavey 9 workhorse
toilet 3 loo 4 head, john 5 bidet, potty, privy 6 johnny 7 latrine 8 bathroom, lavatory 11 water closet
toilsome 4 hard 5 heavy 6 uphill 7 arduous, labored 9 difficult, effortful, laborious, strenuous
Tokay 4 wine
token 4 buck, chip, gift, mark, note, sign 5 badge, check, favor, index, piece, plume, prize, relic, scrip 6 copper, emblem, pledge, symbol, ticket, trophy 7 earnest, gesture, memento, symptom, warrant 8 evidence, keepsake, memorial, reminder, security, souvenir 9 indicator 10 expression, indication 11 perfunctory, remembrance

To Kill a Mockingbird *author* 3 Lee (Harper)
Tokyo *formerly:* 3 Edo *island:* 6 Honshu
tolerable 4 fair 6 common, decent 7 livable 8 adequate, all right, bearable, passable 9 endurable 10 acceptable, sufferable 11 respectable 12 satisfactory
tolerably 4 so-so 5 quite 6 fairly, pretty, rather 8 passably 9 averagely 10 moderately
tolerance 6 leeway 8 patience 9 allowance, endurance, deviation, fortitude, variation 10 indulgence, resistance, sufferance 11 forbearance, habituation
tolerant 4 easy 5 broad 7 lenient, liberal 8 placable 9 easygoing, eurytopic, forgiving, indulgent, tractable 10 open-minded, permissive 11 broad-minded, progressive, sympathetic 13 understanding
tolerate 4 bear, bide, hack 5 abide, allow, brook, stand 6 accept, endure, pardon, permit, suffer 7 condone, stomach, swallow 8 bear with, live with 9 put up with 11 countenance
Tolkien *creature* 3 Ent, Orc 5 Ainur 6 Balrog, Hobbit, Nazgul, Shelob 9 Oliphaunt
toll 3 fee, tax 4 bell, bong, cost, levy, peal, ring 5 chime, knell, price, sound 6 charge, summon, tariff 7 expense 8 casualty 10 assessment
tollbooth 11 customhouse
Tolstoy *novel* 8 Cossacks (The) 11 War and Peace 12 Anna Karenina 16 Death of Ivan Ilich (The)
tomato 9 love apple
tomb 5 crypt, grave 6 burial 9 mausoleum, sepulcher, sepulchre, sepulture *ancient Egyptian:* 7 mastaba *empty:* 8 cenotaph
tomboy 6 gamine, hoyden
tombstone 4 slab 8 memorial, monument 11 grave marker *inscription:* 3 RIP 8 hic jacet
tome 4 book 6 volume
___ Tomé and Príncipe 3 Sao
tomfool 3 ass 4 dolt, fool, jerk 5 crazy, idiot, loony, ninny, silly, wacky 6 absurd, donkey, stupid 7 doltish, foolish, jackass 8 clodpoll, dummkopf, imbecile 9 blockhead, fantastic, horse's ass, thickhead 10 dunderhead, nincompoop 11 chowderhead, chucklehead, harebrained 12 preposterous
tomfoolery 4 dido, lark 5 antic, caper, prank, shine, trick 6 frolic 8 escapade, fandango 9 high jinks 10 shenanigan 11 monkeyshine
Tom Jones *author* 8 Fielding (Henry)

tommyrot 4 bull 5 hooey, trash 7 baloney, hogwash, rubbish 8 claptrap, nonsense 10 balderdash 13 horsefeathers

Tom o'Bedlam 3 nut 4 loon 5 loony 6 madman, maniac 7 lunatic 9 bedlamite

tomorrow 6 future, mañana

Tom Sawyer *author:* 5 Twain (Mark) 7 Clemens (Samuel) *character:* 5 Becky (Thatcher) 8 Huck Finn, Injun Joe 9 Aunt Polly 10 Muff Potter

Tom Thumb 4 runt 5 dwarf, pygmy 6 midget, peanut, peewee 7 manikin 8 half-pint 10 homunculus 11 lilliputian

ton 3 lot 4 chic 5 bunch, style, trend, vogue 6 bundle 7 fashion

tone 3 hue 4 cast, mode, mood, note, tint, vein 5 color, pitch, shade, style, tinge 6 accent, manner, spirit, strain, temper, timbre 7 fashion 10 inflection

toned down 4 mute, soft 5 sober 6 lowkey, mellow 7 subdued 8 laid-back, low-keyed, softened

Tonga *capital:* 9 Nuku'alofa *ethnic group:* 10 Polynesian *explorer:* 4 Cook (Capt. James) 6 Tasman (Abel) *island group:* 5 Vava'u 6 Haapai 9 Tongatapu *language:* 6 Tongan 7 English *monetary unit:* 6 pa'anga

tongue 4 lick, pole, tang 6 glossa, lingua, speech 7 clapper, dialect, languet 8 language 10 vernacular *combining form:* 4 glot 5 gloss, lingu 6 glossa, glosso, lingua, lingui, linguo 7 glossia

tongue-lash 4 lash, rail 5 chide, scold 6 berate, rebuke, revile 7 bawl out, chew out, tell off, reprove, upbraid 8 admonish, call down, reproach 9 castigate, reprimand 10 vituperate

tongue-lashing 6 rebuke, tirade 7 censure, reproof 8 scolding 9 reprimand, talking-to 11 castigation 12 dressing-down

tongue-tied 3 mum, shy 4 mute 6 silent 7 bashful 9 diffident 10 speechless 12 inarticulate

tonic 3 pop 4 cola, soda 5 brisk 7 bracing, soda pop 8 curative, salutary 10 refreshing 11 restorative, stimulating 12 exhilarating, invigorating *extract:* 4 cola 9 berberine

tons 4 gobs, lots 5 heaps, loads, piles, scads

tony 4 chic, posh 5 smart, swank, swish 6 classy, modish, uptown 7 à la mode, elegant, stylish 9 exclusive 11 fashionable

too 4 also, ever, over, very 5 along 6 as well, overly, unduly, withal 7 awfully, besides, further, greatly 8 likewise,

moreover, overmuch 9 extremely, immensely 10 in addition, remarkably, strikingly 11 exceedingly, excessively, furthermore 12 additionally, exorbitantly, immoderately, inordinately 13 exceptionally

tool 4 pawn 5 means 6 puppet, rimmer, stooge 7 cat's-paw, hayfork, machine, rounder, utensil 8 picklock 9 appliance, implement, mechanism 10 instrument *axlike:* 4 adze *boring:* 5 auger, drill *carving:* 5 veiner *cleaving:* 4 froe *cobbler's:* 3 awl *cutting:* 3 axe, saw 4 adze 5 knife 6 shears 8 billhook *digging:* 4 pick 5 spade 6 shovel 7 mattock *engraving:* 5 burin *farm:* 6 seeder *filing:* 4 rasp 7 riffler *garden:* 3 hoe 4 rake 5 spade 6 trowel, weeder *grasping:* 6 pincer 7 tweezer 8 tweezers *mining:* 6 trepan *prehistoric:* 6 eolith *pruning:* 6 shears 8 secateur *rubbing:* 9 burnisher *scooping:* 6 router *toothed:* 3 saw 7 rippler *woodworking:* 3 saw 5 bevel, plane 6 chisel, hammer

toot 3 bat, jag 4 bout, bust, tear 5 binge, blast, drunk, snort, sound, souse, spree 6 bender 7 carouse

tooth 5 molar 7 incisor 8 bicuspid, premolar *combining form:* 4 dent 5 denti, dento *cuspid:* 6 canine 8 dogtooth, eyetooth *cutting:* 10 carnassial *decay:* 6 caries *doctor:* 7 dentist *pointed:* 4 fang 6 canine, cuspid *small:* 8 denticle

toothless 7 useless 8 edentate 10 edentulous 11 ineffective, ineffectual

toothsome 5 sapid, tasty 6 delish, savory 8 luscious, pleasant, pleasing, tasteful 9 agreeable, delicious, palatable, succulent 10 appetizing, attractive

too-too 6 la-di-da 7 extreme 8 affected, overdone, overmuch, precious 9 excessive 10 hoity-toity, inordinate 11 exaggerated, overrefined, pretentious

tootsie 3 pet 4 dear 5 honey 7 beloved, darling, sweetie 10 sweetheart

top 3 cap, tip 4 acme, apex, best, cusp, head, peak, pick, roof 5 cream, crest, crown, elite, point, prime, prize 6 apical, choice, climax, height, summit, utmost, vertex 7 capital, highest, maximal, maximum, surface 8 five-star, loftiest, pinnacle, superior 9 first-rate, uppermost 10 first-class 11 culmination

tope 3 nip 4 soak 5 booze, drink, shark, stupa 6 guzzle, imbibe, tipple 7 swizzle 8 liquor up

toper 3 sot 4 lush, soak, wino 5 drunk, rummy, souse 6 bibber, boozer 7 tippler, tosspot 8 drunkard 9 inebriate

Tophet 4 hell 5 hades, Sheol 6 blazes 7 Gehenna, inferno 9 perdition 10 underworld

topic 4 talk, text **5** issue, motif, point, score, theme **6** burden, matter, motive, thread **7** content, subject **8** argument **11** proposition

topical 5 local **7** current, nominal **8** regional **9** temporary **11** superficial

topmost 7 highest, leading, supreme **8** crowning, ultimate **9** paramount, principal **10** consummate, preeminent **11** culminating

top-notch 5 prime **6** choice **7** capital **8** five-star, superior **9** excellent, first-rate **10** first-class **11** first-string

top off 3 cap **5** crown **6** climax, finish, refill **8** complete, conclude, resupply **9** culminate

topography 7 surface, terrain **8** features

topple 3 tip **4** drop, fall **5** crash, lurch, pitch, slump, upset **6** defeat, falter, plunge, totter, tumble **8** collapse, keel over, overturn **9** overthrow

tops 4 best **5** primo **6** at most **7** highest **8** peerless, superior **9** at the most, first-rate, matchless **11** outstanding

topsy-turvy 7 chaotic, jumbled, mixed-up **8** cockeyed, confused, inverted **10** disjointed, disordered, upside down

toque 3 cap, hat

tor 4 crag, hill, peak **5** butte, cliff, mound, talus

Torah 10 Pentateuch

torch 4 fire **5** flame, light **6** ignite **7** firebug **8** arsonist, flambeau, guidance **10** flashlight, incendiary

toreador 6 torero **7** matador **11** bullfighter

torero 7 matador **11** bullfighter

torment 3 rag, try, vex **4** bait, bane, hell, hurt, pain, pang, rack **5** abuse, agony, curse, grill, harry, tease, worry, wring **6** harass, harrow, heckle, misery, molest, needle, plague **7** afflict, agonize, anguish, crucify, distort, hagride, torture, travail, trouble **8** distress **9** persecute, tantalize **10** affliction, excruciate

torn 4 rent **5** split **6** ragged, ripped, unsure **7** mangled **8** tattered, wrenched **9** lacerated, uncertain, undecided

tornado 6 funnel **7** cyclone, twister **9** windstorm, whirlwind

toro 4 bull

torpedo 3 gun, ray **4** mine, thug **5** blast, bravo, smash, wreck **6** gunman, gunsel, hit man, killer, weapon **7** destroy, nullify, scuttle **8** assassin, firework **9** explosive, shoot down **10** hatchet man, projectile, triggerman **11** electric ray

torpid 4 dull, lazy, numb **5** dopey, inert **6** sodden, stupid **7** dormant **8** comatose, inactive, sluggish **9** apathetic, lethargic **12** hebetudinous

torpor 4 coma, daze **5** swoon **6** apathy, stupor **7** languor **8** dopiness, dullness, hebetude, lethargy **9** lassitude, passivity, stolidity **10** stagnation **12** listlessness

torque 5 twist

torrent 4 rush **5** flood, spate **6** deluge, stream **7** cascade, Niagara **8** cataract, flooding **9** cataclysm **10** inundation, outpouring

torrid 3 hot **5** fiery **6** ardent, fervid, heated, red-hot, sultry **7** boiling, burning, flaming, parched **8** broiling, white-hot **9** scorching **10** hot-blooded, passionate, sweltering **11** impassioned

tort 5 crime, wrong **7** offense **10** wrongdoing

tortilla dish 4 taco **6** flauta **7** burrito, chalupa, tostada **9** enchilada **10** quesadilla **11** chimichanga

Tortilla Flat author 9 Steinbeck (John)

tortoise 6 turtle **8** terrapin **9** chelonian
  beak: **3** neb *shell:* **8** carapace

tortuous 5 snaky **6** cranky, tricky **7** crooked, devious, sinuous, winding **8** flexuous, indirect, involute, involved **9** meandrous **10** circuitous, convoluted, meandering, serpentine **11** anfractuous, vermiculate **12** labyrinthine

torture 4 pain, rack, warp **5** agony, wring **6** harrow, martyr **7** afflict, agonize, anguish, crucify, torment **9** martyrdom **10** excruciate **11** third degree

tortured 4 bent **6** racked, warped **7** twisted **8** deformed **9** distorted

tory 5 right **7** old-line **8** loyalist, old guard, orthodox, rightist, royalist **12** conservative

Tosca *character:* **5** Mario (Cavaradossi) **7** Scarpia (Baron) *composer:* **7** Puccini (Giacomo)

___ Toscanini 6 Arturo

tosh 3 rot **4** bosh, bunk **5** bilge, hooey **6** bunkum, drivel, humbug **7** baloney, eyewash, hogwash, twaddle **8** malarkey, nonsense, tommyrot, trumpery

toss 4 cast, flap, flip, hurl, rock, roll **5** chuck, drink, fling, heave, match, pitch, quaff, sling, surge, throw, vomit **6** imbibe, tumble, welter, writhe **7** discard **9** knock back, throw away

tosspot see TIPPLER

tot 3 add, kid, nip, sum **4** dram, shot, slug, tyke **5** child, snort **6** figure, infant, nipper, shaver, squirt **7** snifter, toddler

total 3 add, all, sum **4** foot, full **5** add up, equal, gross, run to, smash, sum to, utter, whole, wreck, yield **6** all-out, amount, budget, entire, figure, number **7** crack up, destroy, full-out, overall, perfect, plenary, quantum **8** absolute, complete, demolish, entirety, outright, positive, quantity **9** aggregate, full-blown, full-scale, inclusive, out-and-out, unlimited **10** consummate, unreserved **11** unmitigated **13** comprehensive, thoroughgoing

totalitarian 8 absolute, despotic **10** autocratic **11** dictatorial **13** authoritarian

totality 3 all, sum **4** lump **5** whole **7** oneness **8** entirety **9** aggregate, wholeness **12** completeness

totalize 3 add, sum **5** sum up **6** figure **7** summate

tote 3 lug **4** cart, haul, load, pack **5** carry, ferry, sum up **6** burden, convey, figure **7** summate **9** transport **10** pari-mutuel

totem 6 emblem, symbol

To the Lighthouse author 5 Woolf (Virginia)

totter 4 reel, sway **5** lurch, shake, waver **6** falter, toddle, topple, wobble **7** stagger

touch 4 abut, feel, meet, move, stir **5** brush, graze **6** adjoin, border, caress, finger, stroke **7** contact, palpate **9** palpation, tactility

touchable 7 tactile **8** palpable, tangible

touch down 4 land **5** light, perch, roost **6** alight, settle

touched 3 odd, off **5** batty, crazy, moved **7** stirred **8** affected **9** emotional

touching 4 as to, in re **5** about, anent, as for **6** moving, tender **7** against, apropos, emotive, meeting, piteous, pitiful, tangent **8** abutting, adjacent, pathetic, pitiable, poignant, stirring **9** adjoining, affecting, apropos of, as regards, bordering, immediate, impinging, regarding **10** as respects, back-to-back, concerning, contiguous, respecting, tangential **11** coterminous **12** conterminous

touch off 5 erupt, spark, start **6** ignite, incite, kindle **7** explode, inflame, provoke, trigger **8** initiate **9** instigate **11** precipitate

touchstone 4 test **5** check, gauge, proof, trial **7** measure **8** standard **9** barometer, benchmark, criterion, yardstick

touch up 3 fix **5** patch **6** rework **7** improve, perfect

touchy 5 dicey, huffy, risky, testy **6** tender, tricky **7** peppery **8** delicate, ticklish **9** explosive, hazardous, irascible, irritable, sensitive **10** precarious **11** inflammable, quarrelsome, thin-skinned **13** oversensitive, temperamental, unpredictable

tough 3 bad, mug **4** goon, hard, hood, lout, punk, stud, thug **5** bully, hardy, harsh **6** rugged, severe, sturdy, unruly **7** arduous, hoodlum, onerous, ruffian **8** bullyboy, exacting, hooligan, obdurate **9** arbitrary, demanding, difficult, effortful, hard-nosed, hidebound, immutable, laborious, resistant, roughneck, strenuous **10** hard-bitten, hard-boiled, hardheaded, inflexible, refractory, unyielding **11** intractable, unbreakable **12** pertinacious

toughen 5 inure **6** anneal, harden, season, temper **9** acclimate, habituate **10** strengthen **11** acclimatize

toughie 4 goon, hood, lout, punk, thug **5** poser, rowdy **7** hoodlum, ruffian, stumper **8** bullyboy, hooligan, plug-ugly **9** roughneck

toupee 3 rug, wig **6** peruke, wiglet **7** periwig **8** postiche **9** hairpiece

tour 4 bout, trip, turn **5** jaunt, round, shift, spell, stint **6** junket, period, travel, troupe **7** circuit, journey **8** progress **9** barnstorm, excursion **10** expedition, rubberneck

tour de force 4 deed, feat **7** classic, display, exploit **10** magnum opus, masterwork **11** achievement, chef d'oeuvre, masterpiece

tour guide 8 cicerone

tourist 7 tripper, visitor **8** traveler **9** sightseer, traveller **10** day-tripper, rubberneck, vacationer **12** excursionist, globe-trotter

tournament 4 open, tilt **5** pro-am **6** jousts, series **7** contest, tourney **8** carousel **10** round-robin **11** competition **12** championship

tourney 4 meet **5** event, games, match **7** compete, contest **8** concours **11** competition

tousle 4 mess, muss **6** rumple **8** dishevel, disorder

tout 3 spy, tip **4** brag, laud, plug **5** watch **6** blow up, peddle, praise, talk up **7** acclaim, crack up, promote, solicit **8** ballyhoo, persuade, proclaim **9** publicize

tovarich 7 comrade

tow 3 lug, tug **4** drag, draw, haul, pull, rope, yarn **5** chain, trail **6** hawser *truck:* **7** wrecker

towel word 3 his **4** hers

tower 4 loom **5** spire **6** turret **8** overlook *on a mosque:* **7** minaret

towering 4 high, tall **5** grand, great, lofty **6** aerial, mighty **7** extreme, soaring, stately **8** imposing, majestic **9** excessive, grandiose **10** exorbitant, immoderate, inordinate, monumental, prodigious **11** extravagant, magnificent, skyscraping **12** altitudinous, overwhelming

towhee 5 finch **7** chewink

to wit 3 viz **6** namely **8** scilicet **9** c'est-à-dire, videlicet

town 4 burg **6** hamlet, podunk **7** borough, village *medieval:* **5** bourg

town and ___ 4 gown **7** country

townsman 7 burgher, citizen

town square 5 plaza *Italian:* **6** piazza

toxic 6 poison **7** harmful **8** venomous, virulent **9** poisonous **10** infectious

toxin 5 venom **6** poison

toy 4 fool, play **5** antic, curio, dally, flirt, knack, mouse, tease **6** bauble, caress, coquet, diddle, fiddle, gewgaw, trifle **7** bibelot, novelty, pastime, trinket, whatnot **8** gimcrack **9** plaything **10** diminutive, knickknack

trace 3 jot, ray, run, tug **4** blip, echo, hint, iota, mark, path, scan, wisp **5** relic, shade, tinge, trail, tread **6** derive, detect, nuance, shadow, strain, streak **7** outline, remains, remnant, run down, soupçon, symptom, vestige **8** discover, tincture, traverse **9** delineate, footprint, remainder, scintilla, suspicion **10** intimation, suggestion

trachea 6 larynx, throat, vessel **7** weasand **8** throttle, windpipe

track 3 way **4** drag, path, road, sign, step, tail **5** chase, cover, print, spoor, trace, trail, tread **6** artery, follow, pursue, shadow, travel **7** footway, imprint, monitor, pathway, vestige **8** footpath, footstep **9** footprint

track-and-field event 4 dash **5** relay **6** discus **7** javelin, hurdles, shot put **8** footrace, high jump, long jump **9** broad jump, decathlon, pole vault **10** heptathlon, triple jump **11** discus throw **12** steeplechase

tract 3 lot **4** area, belt, farm, land, plat, plot, zone **5** block, claim **6** parcel, region **7** leaflet, portion, terrain **8** pamphlet, preserve **9** territory

tractable 4 tame **6** docile, gentle, pliant **7** ductile, plastic, pliable **8** amenable, biddable, flexible, obedient, workable **9** adaptable, breakable, malleable **10** manageable

tractate 5 summa **6** memoir, thesis **7** pandect **8** hornbook, monument, treatise **9** discourse, monograph **10** commentary **12** disquisition, dissertation, introduction

traction 4 drag, pull **5** force **7** drawing, tension **8** friction

tractor maker 5 Deere (John)

trade 4 deal, sell, swap **5** craft, truck **6** barter, change, custom, market, métier, peddle, switch **7** bargain, calling, pursuit, traffic **8** business, commerce, exchange, industry, vocation **10** employment, occupation, profession, substitute **11** merchandise, transaction *illicit:* **11** black market

trademark 3 tag **4** logo **5** brand, label, stamp **6** patent, symbol **8** colophon, logotype **9** brand name

trader 4 ship **6** broker, dealer, vendor **8** merchant

trade route 7 sea-lane

tradition 4 lore, myth **5** habit **6** belief, custom, legacy, legend, mythos, rubric **7** folkway **8** folklore, heredity, heritage, practice **9** mythology **10** convention **12** old wives' tale

traditional 4 oral **5** usual **6** common, spoken, verbal **7** classic, old-line, popular **8** habitual, orthodox **9** classical, customary, old-school, unwritten **10** button-down **11** established **12** acknowledged, buttoned-down, conservative, conventional

traditionalist 6 purist **12** conservative

traditionalistic 4 tory **7** die-hard, old-line **8** orthodox, standpat **12** conservative

traduce 4 slur **5** libel, smear, wrong **6** betray, breach, defame, malign, vilify **7** asperse, slander, violate **8** disgrace, tear down **9** denigrate **10** calumniate

Trafalgar commander 6 Nelson (Horatio)

traffic 4 deal **5** cargo, fence, trade, truck **6** barter, custom **7** bootleg, freight **8** commerce, dealings, exchange, movement **9** patronage, transport **11** black-market *circle:* **6** rotary **10** roundabout *cone:* **5** pylon *jam:* **5** tie-up **6** holdup **8** gridlock **10** bottleneck

trafficker 6 dealer, trader

tragedy 3 woe **6** mishap, plague **8** calamity, disaster **9** cataclysm, mischance **10** misfortune **11** catastrophe **12** misadventure

trail 3 dog, lag, tag **4** drag, flag, path, plod, poke **5** chase, dally, delay, tarry, trace, track **6** dawdle, follow, linger, pursue, shadow **7** draggle, gumshoe, pathway, traipse **8** footpath, footwalk **10** bridle path *emigrant:* **6** Oregon *Florida:* **7** Tamiami *Georgia-Maine:* **11** Appalachian *Indian:* **5** Great

trailer 5 truck **7** preview **9** motor home, transport **10** mobile home

trailer truck 4 semi

train 3 row **4** file, tame **5** coach, drill, teach, track **6** column, convoy, course, school, sequel, series, thread **7** caravan, cortege, educate, prepare, retinue **8** exercise, instruct, sequence **9** cultivate, entourage, following, habituate **10** succession **11** progression

trainee 6 novice 7 learner, new hire 8 beginner 10 apprentice

training 7 tuition 8 teaching, tutelage 9 education, schooling 11 instruction
horses: 6 manège

traipse 3 gad 4 pace, roam, rove, step, walk 5 amble, range, trail, tramp, tread 6 ramble, stroll, wander 7 maunder, meander 8 ambulate 9 gallivant

trait 4 mark 5 point, quirk, trace 6 oddity 7 feature, quality 8 hallmark, property, specific 9 attribute

traitor 5 Judas 8 apostate, betrayer, defector, deserter, quisling, renegade, turncoat 9 turnabout

traitorous 5 Punic 8 apostate, disloyal, mutinous, recreant, renegade 9 faithless 10 perfidious, rebellious, unfaithful 11 treacherous

traject 4 beam, pass, pipe, send 5 carry 6 convey, render 7 conduct, forward, impress 8 hand down, transfer, transmit 9 broadcast, transfuse

tram 3 car 7 trolley 9 streetcar

trammel 3 tie 4 bind, curb 5 check, gauge, leash 6 fetter, hamper, hobble 7 compass, confine, ensnare, manacle, pothook, shackle 8 entangle, handcuff 9 restraint

tramontane 8 outsider 9 foreigner, outlander 11 transalpine

tramp 3 bum 4 hike, hobo, jade, plod, slog, thud 5 bimbo, caird, clump, gypsy, march, stamp, stiff, stomp, tread 6 ramble, stroll, travel, trudge, wander 7 chippie, clochard, drifter, floater, saunter, stroller, traipse, vagrant 8 derelict, footslog, homeless, vagabond 10 prostitute

trample 4 mash 5 crush, pound, stamp, stomp, tread, tromp

trance 4 daze, muse 5 swoon 7 ecstasy, rapture, reverie 8 hypnosis 9 catalepsy, enrapture 10 absorption, brown study 11 abstraction

tranquil 4 calm, easy 5 quiet, still 6 dreamy, placid, poised, serene 7 restful 8 composed, peaceful 10 untroubled 13 self-possessed

tranquilize 4 calm, hush, lull 5 quiet, relax, still 6 becalm, pacify, sedate, settle, soothe, subdue 7 compose, mollify

tranquilizer 6 downer 8 diazepam, pacifier, sedative 10 depressant 11 barbiturate

tranquillity 4 calm 5 peace, quiet 8 calmness, serenity 9 composure, placidity

transaction 4 deal 5 trade 7 bargain, dealing 8 contract, covenant 9 agreement

transcend 3 top 4 beat, best 5 excel, outdo 6 better, exceed 7 surpass 8 outshine, outstrip, overcome, surmount

transcendent 5 ideal 7 perfect, sublime, supreme 8 abstract, immanent 10 consummate, surpassing

Transcendentalist 6 Alcott (Bronson), Fuller (Margaret) 7 Emerson (Ralph Waldo), Thoreau (Henry David)

transcribe 4 copy 5 write 6 record 8 transfer 9 translate, write down 13 transliterate

transfer 4 cede, deed, hand, pass, ship 5 carry, grant, shift 6 assign, convey, remove, supply 7 consign, convert, deliver, devolve, dispose 8 alienate, hand over, make over, relocate, turn over 9 carry over 10 assignment, conveyance 11 disposition

transfix 4 spit 5 lance, spear, spike, stick 6 impale, skewer 7 spindle 8 entrance 9 fascinate, hypnotize, mesmerize

transform 5 alter, morph 6 change, mutate 7 commute, convert 12 metamorphose

transformation 8 reaction 10 changeover, conversion 13 metamorphosis

transfuse 5 endue, imbue 7 pervade, suffuse, traject 8 permeate, saturate 9 penetrate, percolate 10 impregnate

transgress 5 err, sin 6 breach, exceed, offend 7 violate 8 infringe, overpass, overstep, trespass 10 contravene

transgression 3 sin 5 crime, error, wrong 6 breach 7 misdeed, offense 9 violation 12 infringement

transient 4 hobo 5 brief, tramp 7 drifter, migrant, passing 8 fleeting, flitting, fugitive, volatile 9 ephemeral, fugacious, momentary, temporary 10 evanescent, fly-by-night, short-lived 11 impermanent

transit 7 passage 8 traverse 10 conveyance

transition 4 leap 5 segue, shift 6 change 7 passage 10 conversion 13 metamorphosis

transitory *see* TRANSIENT

translate 6 render 7 convert 9 interpret, reproduce 10 paraphrase

translation 9 rendition 10 conversion, paraphrase

transmarine 7 oversea 8 overseas

transmission 7 gearbox 8 handover 9 broadcast, infection

transmit 3 air 4 beam, hand, pass, pipe, send 6 convey, hand on, impart, pass on, render, signal 7 channel, conduct, consign, diffuse, forward, traject 8 bequeath, dispatch, hand down 9 broadcast

transmogrify *see* TRANSFORM

transmute see TRANSFORM

transoceanic message 4 wire 5 cable 9 cablegram

transparent 5 clear, filmy, gauzy, sheer 6 limpid 7 crystal 8 clear-cut, gossamer, pellucid 10 diaphanous, see-through 11 crystalline

transpire 3 hap 4 leak 5 exude, occur, sweat 6 chance, emerge, happen 7 develop 9 come about, take place 11 come to light

transplant 8 relocate, resettle

transport 3 bus, fly, lag, lug, wow, zap, zip 4 haul, hump, lift, pack, pass, send, ship, taxi, tote 5 carry, ferry, motor, truck 6 convey, excite, ravish, remove, thrill 7 delight, ecstasy, freight, rapture, sealift, trundle, vehicle 8 carriage, displace, railroad, rhapsody 9 carry away, chauffeur, troopship 10 conveyance, helicopter

transportation 6 moving 7 freight, hauling, removal, vehicle 8 carriage, carrying 10 conveyance 12 displacement

transpose 6 invert 7 convert, permute, reorder, reverse 9 rearrange 11 interchange

transude 4 ooze, reek, seep, weep 5 bleed, sweat 7 diffuse, give off 8 permeate 9 transfuse

transverse 5 cross 6 across, thwart 8 crossbar, crossing 9 crossbeam, crosswise 10 crosspiece

trap 3 bag, net 4 bait, snag 5 catch, decoy, set up, snare 6 ambush, enmesh, tangle 7 ensnare, pitfall 8 birdlime, deadfall, entangle, quagmire 9 ambuscade

trappings 4 gear 5 dress 6 finery 8 equipage, ornament 9 adornment, caparison, equipment 10 decoration 11 habiliments 13 accouterments, accoutrements, embellishment, paraphernalia

Trappist 4 monk *writer:* 6 Merton (Thomas)

trash 3 rag, rot 4 bosh, junk, ruin, scum, slop 5 bilge, blast, dreck, dregs, hokum, offal, spoil, tripe, waste, wreck 6 bunkum, debris, insult, litter, refuse, rubble 7 clutter, destroy, garbage, hogwash, put down, rubbish 8 claptrap, malarkey, nonsense 9 disparage, throw away, vandalize 10 balderdash 11 guttersnipe, proletariat

trash can 7 dustbin

trashy 5 bawdy, cheap, tatty 6 cruddy, shoddy, sleazy, smutty, vulgar 8 rubbishy 9 third-rate

trauma 4 blow, pain 5 shock, upset,

wound 6 crisis, injury, stress 8 collapse 9 suffering

travail 4 grub, moil, task, toil, work 5 grind, labor, pains 6 drudge, effort 7 slavery, torment 8 drudgery, struggle

travel 4 fare, pass, roam, tour, trek, trip, wend 5 jaunt, tramp 6 junket, push on, voyage 7 explore, journey, passage, proceed, traffic, transit 8 movement, traverse 9 gallivant 10 hit the road

traveler 5 gypsy 7 drummer, tourist 8 salesman, vagabond 9 itinerant, sightseer 10 journeyman 11 peripatetic

traveling library 10 bookmobile

traverse 4 ride, walk 5 cover, cross, march, route, trace, track 6 course, thwart, travel, voyage 7 transit 8 crossing, navigate, pass over 10 crisscross 11 perambulate, peregrinate

travesty 3 ape 4 mock, sham 5 farce, mimic, spoof 6 parody 7 imitate, lampoon, mimicry, mockery, take off 8 ridicule 9 burlesque 10 caricature, distortion *satanic:* 9 Black Mass

Traviata, La *character:* 7 Alfredo (Germont), Germont 8 Violetta (Valéry) *composer:* 5 Verdi (Giuseppe)

trawl 3 net 4 fish 7 setline

tray 6 salver, server 7 platter 8 teaboard *revolving:* 9 lazy Susan

treacherous 5 false, Punic, risky 6 chancy, tricky 7 unsound 8 disloyal, perilous, recreant 9 dangerous, deceptive, faithless, hazardous, insidious 10 perfidious, traitorous, unfaithful, unreliable

treachery 7 perfidy, treason 8 bad faith, betrayal 10 disloyalty, infidelity 11 double-cross 13 dastardliness, double-dealing, faithlessness

treacle 4 mush 5 slush, syrup 8 molasses, schmaltz 11 golden syrup

tread 4 hoof, pace, plod, step, walk 5 dance, march, stamp, stomp, trace, track, tramp, tromp, troop 6 follow, stride 7 footing, traipse, trample 8 footstep

treadle 5 lever, pedal

treadmill 3 rut 4 rote 5 chore, grind 6 groove 7 routine 8 drudgery, turnspit

treason 7 perfidy 8 betrayal, sedition 9 treachery 10 disloyalty, misprision

treasure 4 haul, save 5 adore, cache, hoard, pearl, prize, trove, value 6 esteem, revere, riches, wealth 7 apprize, cherish, idolize, worship 8 conserve, preserve, venerate 9 reverence 10 appreciate

Treasure Island *author:* 9 Stevenson (Robert Louis) *character:* 7 Ben Gunn

8 Long John (Silver) *narrator:* **10** Jim Hawkins

treasurer 6 bursar, purser **7** curator **8** receiver **11** chamberlain

Treasure State 7 Montana

treasure trove 4 find, mine **7** bonanza, pay dirt **8** El Dorado, Golconda, gold mine

treasury 4 fisc, mine **5** cache, chest, hoard **6** argosy, coffer, museum **7** bonanza, gallery, omnibus **8** archives, El Dorado, Golconda, gold mine, war chest **9** anthology, exchequer **10** depositary, depository, repository, storehouse

treat 5 goody, nurse **6** bonbon, dainty, doctor, goodie, handle, manage, morsel, tidbit **7** care for **8** deal with, delicacy, medicate **10** minister to *animals:* **3** vet *leather:* **3** tan, taw **7** tanning

treatise 6 thesis **8** tractate **9** discourse, monograph **10** exposition **12** disquisition, dissertation

treatment 4 care **7** therapy

treaty 4 pact **6** accord **7** charter, compact, concord **8** alliance, contract, covenant **9** agreement, concordat **10** convention

treble 4 high **6** shrill, triple **7** descant, soprano **9** threefold **11** high-pitched

tree *African:* **4** akee, cola, shea **5** limba, sassy **6** baobab **7** avodire, bubinga **8** sasswood **9** berberine *Asian:* **4** dhak, upas **6** banyan, kamala *Australian:* **7** blue gum **8** lacewood, quandong **9** casuarina *branch:* **5** bough *Brazilian:* **3** apa, ule **7** arariba, seringa, wallaba *Chinese:* **4** tung **5** yulan **6** ginkgo, lychee **7** kumquat *citrus:* **4** lime **5** lemon **6** orange **8** bergamot *combining form:* **3** dry **4** dryo **5** arbor, dendr **6** arbori, dendra (plural), dendro *coniferous:* **3** fir, yew **4** pine **5** alder, cedar, larch **6** spruce **7** cypress, hemlock, juniper, redwood, sequoia *dwarf:* **8** arbuscle **10** chinquapin *East Indian:* **4** neem, poon, teak, toon **6** banyan, deodar **7** deodara *elm:* **4** wych *Eurasian:* **5** abele, rowan **6** medlar *European:* **5** osier **8** bourtree *European oak:* **7** murmast *evergreen:* **3** fir, yew **4** atle, pine, titi **5** athel, carob, cedar, piñon, taxus **6** arbute, loquat, mallee, sapota **7** arbutus, camphor, conifer, inkwood, juniper, lentisk, madrona, madrone, redwood, sequoia **8** loblolly, longleaf, tamarisk **9** balsam fir **12** balm of Gilead *evergreen oak:* **6** encina *fig:* **5** pipal *flowering:* **5** sumac **6** acacia **7** dogwood **8** sourwood *hardwood:* **3** oak **5** beech, birch, ebony, maple **6** cherry, cornel, walnut **7** hickory **8** chestnut, mahogany *Japanese:* **4** kaki **7** zelkova *linden:* **8** basswood *mulberry:* **8** sycamine *North African:* **5** babul *nut-bearing:* **4** cola, kola **5** hazel, pecan, piñon **6** almond, cashew **7** buckeye, filbert, hickory **9** pistachio *oak:* **5** roble **8** bluejack *ornamental:* **3** box **5** holly **6** ginkgo, mimosa, myrtle, redbud **8** laburnum, magnolia **9** poinciana **12** rhododendron *palm:* **4** coco, nipa **5** ratan **6** pinang, raffia, rattan **7** coquito **8** carnauba *Peruvian:* **8** cinchona *Philippine:* **4** dita, pili **6** bataan **10** calamondin *resinous:* **10** candlewood *rubber:* **3** ule *shade:* **3** elm, oak **5** maple **6** linden **8** sycamore **10** chinaberry *softwood:* **5** alamo **6** tupelo **8** black gum, corkwood (see also CONIFEROUS) *South American:* **3** apa **4** ombu **7** wallaba **9** Brazil nut *swamp:* **11** bald cypress *tropical:* **4** akee, ohia, palm, sago, teak **5** areca, assai, balsa, cacao, ceiba, lehua, mamey **6** acajou, balata, baobab, citrus **7** genipap, logwood, majagua, palmyra, quassia, soursop **8** allspice, barbasco, mahogany, mangrove, milkwood, palmetto, rosewood, soapbark, sweetsop, tamarind **9** candlenut, jacaranda **10** breadfruit, manchineel **11** candleberry, coconut palm *trunk:* **4** bole *willow:* **5** osier, sauch, saugh **6** poplar *young:* **7** sapling

trefoil 4 leaf **6** clover *part:* **3** arc

trek 4 hike, trip **6** travel, trudge **7** journey **9** migration **10** expedition

trellis 4 arbor **6** screen **7** lattice, pergola **8** espalier **11** latticework

tremble 5 quake, shake **6** dither, quaver, quiver, shiver **7** shudder, twitter, vibrate

tremblor see TEMBLOR

tremendous 4 huge, vast **6** mighty, raging **7** awesome, immense, massive, titanic **8** colossal, enormous, fearsome, gigantic, terrific, towering **9** fantastic, monstrous **10** formidable, gargantuan, incredible, monumental, prodigious, stupendous **13** extraordinary

tremolo 7 vibrato

tremor 5 quake, shock **6** quaver, quiver, shiver **7** shudder, temblor **10** earthquake *muscular:* **8** dystaxia

tremulous 5 shaky, timid **6** afraid **7** aquiver, fearful, quaking, shivery **8** timorous **9** quivering, shivering

trench 4 sink **5** ditch, fosse, gully, verge **6** border, furrow, trough *Caribbean:* **6** Cayman

trenchant 4 keen **5** crisp, sharp **6** biting **7** caustic, cutting, mordant, probing, satiric **8** clear-cut, distinct, incisive, sardonic, scathing 9 sarcastic 11 penetrating

trencher 4 tray 7 platter

trencherman 7 glutton

trend 3 fad, run 4 flow, mode 5 curve, drift, shift, style, swing, tenor, vogue 6 course, temper 7 current, fashion, incline 8 approach, movement, tendency 9 direction

trendy 3 hep, hip, hot 4 cool, tony 5 faddy 6 groovy, modish, with-it 7 à la mode, faddish, stylish 8 downtown, nouvelle, up-to-date 11 fashionable, ultramodern

trepang 10 bêche-de-mer

trepidation 4 fear 5 alarm, dread 6 dismay 7 anxiety 12 apprehension 13 consternation

trespass 3 err, sin 4 debt 5 lapse, poach 6 breach, invade, offend 7 impinge, intrude 8 encroach, entrench, infringe 9 interlope, violation 10 infraction, transgress 12 encroachment, infringement 13 transgression

tress 4 curl, lock 5 braid, plait

trestle 4 buck 6 bridge 7 sawbuck 8 sawhorse

trey 5 three

triad 4 trio 5 chord 6 triple, troika 7 harmony, trinity 9 threesome 11 triumvirate

trial 3 woe 4 care, test 5 agony, cross, essay, grief, rigor, worry 6 dry run, hassle, misery, ordeal, sorrow, tryput 7 anguish, attempt, contest, trouble 8 crucible, distress, endeavor, gauntlet, hardship, struggle, vexation 9 adversity, rehearsal, suffering 10 affliction, coup d'essai, difficulty, experiment, misfortune, proceeding, temptation 11 preliminary, tribulation 12 experimental

trial balloon 6 feeler, tryout

trial run 4 test 5 essay 7 break-in 10 experiment

triangle type 5 acute, right 6 obtuse 7 scalene 9 isosceles 11 equilateral

tribal unit 6 moiety 7 phratry

tribe 4 clan, folk, race 5 house, stock 6 family 7 kindred, lineage

tribulation 3 woe 5 cross, trial 6 burden, ordeal 9 adversity 10 affliction, oppression, visitation 11 persecution

tribunal 3 bar 4 dais 5 bench, court 8 platform 10 consistory 12 court of honor

tributary 5 bayou, creek 6 branch, feeder, stream 7 subject 8 affluent, influent 9 backwater, confluent, dependent, satellite 12 contributory

tribute 5 paean 6 eulogy 8 citation, encomium 9 panegyric 10 salutation

11 recognition, testimonial 12 appreciation

trice 4 lash, wink 5 blink, flash, jiffy, shake 6 moment, second, secure 7 instant 8 eyeblink 9 twinkling 11 split second

trick 3 jig 4 dido, dupe, fool, gull, hoax, lark, play, ploy, ruse, sham 5 antic, caper, dodge, feint, fraud, prank, stunt 6 gambit, outwit, scheme 7 chicane, finagle, gimmick, sleight 8 escapade, flimflam, hoodwink 9 bamboozle, deception, stratagem, victimize 10 red herring, shenanigan, tomfoolery 11 hornswoggle, monkeyshine 13 practical joke

trickery 4 scam, wile 5 cheat, fraud 6 deceit 7 chicane, dodgery 8 jugglery 9 chicanery, deception 10 subterfuge 11 double cross 13 double-dealing, jiggery-pokery, sharp practice

trickle 4 drip, seep 5 creep, trill 7 dribble

trickster 5 cheat, shark 7 cheater, diddler, grifter, sharper 8 conjurer, deceiver, magician, swindler 9 defrauder 11 flimflammer, illusionist 12 doubledealer

tricksy 5 rough 6 trying 7 arduous 8 prankish

tricky 3 sly 4 foxy, wily 5 dodgy 6 catchy, clever, crafty, shifty, sticky, thorny, touchy, trying 7 cunning, knavish 8 delusive, guileful, slippery, ticklish, tortuous, unstable 9 deceptive, difficult, dishonest, ingenious, intricate 10 misleading, nettlesome, precarious, unreliable 11 complicated, treacherous, troublesome 12 undependable

trident 5 spear

tried 6 proved, proven, secure, tested, trusty 7 staunch 8 approved, faithful, reliable, true-blue 9 certified, steadfast 10 dependable 11 trustworthy

tried and true 6 proven, secure, tested, trusty 8 reliable 10 dependable 11 trustworthy

trifle 3 bob, fig, pin, toy 4 doit, fool, mess, play 5 curio, dally, flirt, sport, waste 6 bauble, coquet, diddle, doodle, fiddle, fidget, footle, frivol, gewgaw, monkey, niggle 7 bibelot, conceit, fribble, fritter, novelty, trinket, twiddle, whatnot 8 folderol, gimcrack, kickshaw, nonsense, squander 9 bagatelle, cream puff, dalliance 10 knickknack, triviality 11 small change

trifling 4 tiny 5 petty 6 measly, paltry 7 trivial 8 niggling, picayune, piddling 9 frivolous, worthless 10 negligible 11 unimportant 13 insignificant

trifolium 6 clover 8 shamrock

trig 4 chic, neat, prim, snug, tidy, trim 5 sharp, smart, swank, trick 6 classy, modish, snappy 7 chipper, dashing, orderly, precise, stylish 9 shipshape

trigger 4 fire 5 cause, spark, start 6 ignite, kindle, set off 7 actuate, release 8 activate, initiate, touch off

triggerman 3 gun 5 bravo 6 gunsel, killer 7 torpedo 8 assassin 9 cutthroat, pistolero

trigonometric function see at FUNCTION

trill 4 burr, drop, roll 5 chirr, shake, twirl 6 quaver, warble 7 dribble, revolve, trickle, twitter, vibrato

trillion *combining form:* 4 tera, treg 5 trega

trillionth *combining form:* 4 pico

trim 3 cut, fit 4 clip, crop, deck, neat, pare, snug, tidy, trig 5 adorn, order, prune, shape, shave, shear, skive 6 barber, dapper, fettle, kilter, repair, spruce 7 chipper, dress up, garnish, orderly, shapely 8 clean-cut, decorate, manicure 9 shipshape 11 spic-and-span, streamlined, well-groomed 12 spick-and-span *a tree:* 5 prune 7 pollard

Trinidad and Tobago *capital:* 11 Port of Spain *language:* 7 English *monetary unit:* 6 dollar *sea:* 9 Caribbean

trinity see TRIAD

trinket 3 toy 5 curio, jewel 6 bauble, doodad, gewgaw, trifle 7 bibelot, novelty, whatnot 8 gimcrack, kickshaw 9 bagatelle, plaything, tchotchke 10 knickknack

trinkets 10 bijouterie

trio of goddesses 5 Fates 6 Furies, Graces

trip 3 hop, run 4 fall, ride, skip, slip, step, tour, trek 5 boner, caper, dance, error, lapse 6 bungle, junket, outing, sashay, travel, tumble, voyage 7 blooper, blunder, journey, mistake, misstep, stumble 9 excursion 10 expedition

tripe 4 guts 5 bilge, trash 6 waffle, viscus 7 innards, viscera (plural) 8 entrails, stuffing 9 internals

triple 4 trio 5 triad, trine 6 treble, triune, troika 7 triform, trilogy, trinity 8 trifecta 9 threefold, threesome 11 three-bagger, triumvirate

Triple Crown winner *1919:* 9 Sir Barton *1930:* 10 Gallant Fox *1935:* 5 Omaha *1937:* 10 War Admiral *1941:* 9 Whirlaway *1943:* 10 Count Fleet *1946:* 7 Assault *1948:* 8 Citation *1973:* 11 Secretariat *1977:* 11 Seattle Slew *1978:* 8 Affirmed

tripped out 4 high 5 doped 6 stoned, zonked 7 drugged 8 hopped-up, turned on, wiped out 9 spaced-out 10 freaked-out

Tristan's beloved 6 Iseult, Isolde

Tristan und Isolde composer 6 Wagner (Richard)

triste 3 sad 5 sorry 7 doleful, pensive, wistful 8 mournful 9 depressed, sorrowful 10 melancholy 11 melancholic

Tristram Shandy author 6 Sterne (Laurence)

trite 3 pat, set 4 dull, flat, hack 5 banal, corny, musty, slick, stale, stock, tired, vapid 6 cliché, common, jejune, old-hat 7 prosaic, worn-out 8 bathetic, bromidic, flyblown, ordinary, shopworn, timeworn, well-worn 9 hackneyed 10 threadbare 11 commonplace, stereotyped 13 platitudinous, stereotypical

triton 5 conch 7 mollusc, mollusk 9 shellfish

Triton 6 merman *attribute:* 5 conch *father:* 7 Neptune 8 Poseidon *mother:* 10 Amphitrite

triturate 4 bray 5 crush, grind 6 powder 9 comminute, pulverize

triumph 3 joy, win 4 crow, palm 5 exult, glory, vaunt 6 master 7 conquer, prevail, succeed, success, victory 8 conquest, overcome, surmount 10 exultation, jubilation

triumphant 8 exultant, exulting, jubilant 10 conquering, victorious

triumvirate see TRIAD

Triumvirate, First *member:* 6 Caesar (Julius), Pompey (the Great) 7 Crassus (Marcus Licinius)

Triumvirate, Second *member:* 6 Antony (Marc) 7 Lepidus (Marcus Aemilius) 8 Octavius (Gaius)

trivet 4 rack 5 stand 6 tripod

trivia 8 factoids, minutiae 9 small beer 11 small change 13 small potatoes

trivial 5 light, minor, petty, small 6 casual, measly, paltry, piddly, slight 8 picayune, piddling, piffling, trifling 9 small-beer 10 negligible 11 Mickey Mouse, unimportant 13 insignificant

troche 6 tablet 7 lozenge 8 pastille 9 cough drop

troglodyte 6 hermit 7 caveman, recluse 11 cave dweller

Troilus *beloved:* 8 Cressida, Criseyde *father:* 5 Priam *mother:* 6 Hecuba *slayer:* 8 Achilles

Trojan *horse builder:* 5 Epeus *king:* 5 Priam *priest:* 7 Laocoon *soothsayer:* 7 Helenus 9 Cassandra *warrior:* 5 Paris 6 Aeneas, Agenor, Hector 9 Euphorbus

Trojan Horse builder 5 Epeus 6 Epeius

troll 4 fish, lure, sing, spin 5 angle, dwarf, prowl 6 goblin, search

trolley 3 car 4 cart, tram 8 carriage 9 streetcar

Trollope novel 10 Claverings (The)

11 Ayala's Angel, Phineas Finn
12 Phineas Redux 12 Way We Live Now
(The) 15 Eustace Diamonds (The)
16 Barchester Towers
trombone 7 sackbut
tromp 4 beat, drub, hike, pelt, slog, walk
5 pound, stamp, stomp, stump, tramp,
tread 6 batter, buffet, pummel, thrash,
trudge 7 belabor, trample 8 lambaste
troop 4 army, band, crew, host, pace,
step, walk 5 corps, crowd, flock, tread
6 legion, outfit 7 brigade, company, soldier, traipse 8 assembly 9 associate, battalion, gathering, multitude 10 collection
trooper 3 cop 5 actor, horse 7 soldier
9 policeman 10 cavalryman
trope 6 cliché, simile 8 metaphor,
metonymy 10 synecdoche
Trophonius *brother:* 8 Agamedes *temple
site:* 6 Delphi
trophy 3 cup 5 award, prize, relic, scalp,
token 6 spoils 7 memento 8 hardware,
keepsake, memorial, reminder, souvenir 9 loving cup 11 remembrance
tropical 3 hot 4 lush, warm 5 balmy,
humid 6 jungly, steamy, sultry, torrid
10 equatorial
tropical storm see TYPHOON
Tropic of Cancer author 6 Miller (Henry)
Tros' son 4 Ilus 8 Ganymede
trot 3 jog 4 gait, lope, pony, rack
5 amble, hurry 7 setline 11 translation
troth 6 commit, engage, pledge 7 loyalty
8 affiance, contract, espousal, fidelity
10 engagement 12 faithfulness
trot out 4 show 6 expose, parade 7 display, disport, exhibit, show off
Trotsky, Leon *associate:* 5 Lenin
(Vladimir) *rival:* 6 Stalin (Joseph)
troubadour 4 bard, poet 6 singer 8 jongleur, minstrel, musician 9 balladist
10 folksinger
trouble 3 ado, ail, ill, irk, try, vex, woe
4 care, fret, fuss, pain 5 annoy, beset,
Dutch, grief, harry, haunt, pains, trial,
upset, worry 6 bother, doo-doo, effort,
harass, impose, kiaugh, misery, pester,
plague, put out, ruffle, strain, stress,
unrest 7 afflict, agitate, ailment, bedevil, concern, disturb, oppress, perturb,
torment 8 aggrieve, disquiet, distress,
exertion, hardship, hot water, irritate,
vexation 9 beleaguer, importune, suffering 10 difficulty, disconcert 11 disturbance, predicament
troubled 6 uneasy 7 anxious, worried
9 concerned, disturbed 10 distressed
troublemaker 7 hellion 8 agitator 9 firebrand 10 instigator 11 provocateur
12 rabble-rouser

troublesome 5 pesky 6 thorny, tricky,
trying, vexing 7 carking, onerous,
prickly 8 annoying 9 difficult, upsetting, vexatious 10 bothersome, burdensome, cumbersome, disturbing 11 dis-
quieting, importunate, pestiferous
troublous 5 pesky 6 rugged, stormy
7 onerous 9 turbulent, vexatious
10 tumultuous 11 tempestuous
trough 3 hod 4 bowl, tank 5 basin, drain
6 vessel 7 channel
trounce 4 beat, drub, lick, rout, whip,
whup 5 whomp 6 defeat, larrup, punish, thrash, thresh, wallop 7 clobber,
shellac 9 overwhelm
troupe 4 band 5 corps, party 6 outfit
7 company
trouper 4 mime 5 actor, mimic 6 mummer, player 7 actress, artiste 8 thespian
9 performer 11 entertainer
trousers 5 pants 6 slacks 7 drawers
8 breeches, britches *tartan:* 5 trews
trout *kind:* 3 sea 4 char, lake 5 brook,
brown, river 7 rainbow 8 speckled
9 steelhead
Trovatore, Il *character:* 7 Azucena,
Leonora, Manrico 11 Count di Luna
composer: 5 Verdi (Giuseppe)
trove 4 find, haul 5 hoard, store 8 treasure 10 collection 11 aggregation
12 accumulation
Troy 5 Ilium *epic of:* 5 Iliad *excavator:*
10 Schliemann (Heinrich) *founder:*
4 Ilus *modern site:* 9 Hissarlik (see also
TROJAN)
truant 4 idle 5 shirk 7 shirker, slacker
8 shirking 10 delinquent
truce 4 lull 5 letup, pause, peace
6 accord 7 respite 9 armistice,
cease-fire
truck 3 van 4 semi, swap 5 lorry, trade
6 barter, handle, peddle, retail 7 bargain, traffic 8 commerce, dealings,
exchange *military:* 6 camion
Truckee River city 4 Reno
truckle 4 fawn 5 cower, defer, toady
6 cringe, grovel, kowtow 8 bootlick
11 apple-polish
truckler 5 leech, toady 6 lackey, sponge
7 spaniel 8 parasite 9 sycophant
10 bootlicker 11 lickspittle 13 apple-
polisher
truculent 4 fell, grim 5 cruel, harsh,
rough, sharp 6 brutal, deadly, fierce,
savage, severe 7 abusive, warlike 9 barbarous, bellicose, combative, ferocious
10 pernicious, pugnacious 11 belligerent, contentious, destructive, opprobrious, quarrelsome
trudge 4 plod, slog, trek 5 march, tramp,
tromp 8 footslog

true 4 real, very 5 valid 6 actual, honest, trusty 7 factual, genuine, staunch, upright 8 accurate, bona fide, constant, faithful, resolute, rightful 9 authentic, honorable, steadfast, undoubted, veracious 10 dependable, legitimate, undeniable 11 indubitable, trustworthy 12 indisputable 13 authoritative

true-blue 5 loyal 6 proven, steady 7 genuine 8 bona fide, constant, faithful 9 steadfast 10 unswerving

truism 3 saw 4 rule 5 adage, axiom, gnome, maxim, moral 6 cliché, dictum, gospel, saying, verity 8 aphorism, apothegm 9 platitude 10 shibboleth 11 commonplace

Truk Island 3 Tol 4 Moen, Udot, Uman 5 Fefan 6 Dublon

truly 4 well 6 easily, indeed, really, surely, verily 7 de facto 8 actually 9 doubtless, genuinely, sincerely, veritably 10 absolutely, definitely, positively, truthfully, undeniably 11 confidently, doubtlessly, undoubtedly

Truman, Harry S *birthplace:* 5 Lamar (Missouri) *predecessor:* 3 FDR *successor:* 3 DDE

trump 3 cap, top 4 beat, best, pass, ruff 5 excel, outdo 6 better 7 manille, surpass 8 clincher, jew's harp, outstrip, override, spadille *up:* 6 invent 7 concoct 9 fabricate 11 manufacture

trumpery 4 bosh, junk, muck, slop, tosh 5 bilge, cheap, dreck, hokum, trash 6 bunkum, cheesy, common, humbug, paltry, piffle, shoddy, trashy 7 baloney, twaddle 8 claptrap, flimflam, malarkey, nonsense, rubbishy, tommyrot 10 double-talk

trumpet 4 horn, tout 6 herald 8 ballyhoo *call:* 6 sennet *ram's horn:* 6 shofar

trumpeter 4 Hirt (Al), swan 5 André (Maurice), Baker (Chet), Brown (Clifford), Davis (Miles), James (Harry) 6 Alpert (Herb), Bolden (Buddy), Farmer (Art), Voisin (Roger) 7 Schwarz (Gerard) 8 advocate, Eldridge (Roy), eulogist, Marsalis (Wynton), Masekela (Hugh) 9 Armstrong (Louis), encomiast, Gillespie (Dizzy), spokesman 10 mouthpiece, panegyrist, Severinsen (Doc)

truncate 3 lop, top 4 crop, trim 5 prune, shear 6 cut off 7 abridge, shorten 10 abbreviate

truncheon 3 bat 4 club 5 baton, billy 6 cudgel, warder 8 bludgeon 9 billy club 10 nightstick, shillelagh

trundle 3 bed, tub 4 cart, haul, roll, spin 5 churn, wheel 6 rotate 7 revolve 9 transport

trunk 3 box 4 body, case, stem 5 chest, torso 7 channel, circuit, luggage *elephant:* 9 proboscis *tree:* 4 bole 5 stump

truss 3 tie 4 band, bind 5 brace 7 bandage, bracket, support 9 framework, supporter 10 strengthen

trust 4 hope, pool, rely 5 faith, stock 6 assume, bank on, belief, cartel, charge, commit, credit, rely on 7 build on, combine, confide, consign, count on, custody, keeping, presume 8 bank upon, credence, depend on, reckon on, reliance, rely upon 9 assurance, certainty, certitude, syndicate 10 confidence, conviction, dependence, depend upon 11 safekeeping 12 conglomerate

trustee 8 guardian 9 custodian, protector 10 supervisor

trustworthy 4 sure, true 5 tried, valid 6 honest, proven, secure 8 accurate, credible, faithful, reliable 9 authentic, realistic, veracious 10 dependable 11 responsible 12 tried and true 13 authoritative

trusty 4 true 5 tried 6 proven, secure, stable, steady 7 certain, convict 8 faithful, reliable 9 truepenny 10 dependable 11 responsible 12 tried and true

truth 5 axiom, maxim, sooth 6 candor, gospel, verity 7 lowdown, reality, veritas 8 veracity 9 rightness 11 genuineness 12 authenticity *goddess:* 4 Maat *serum:* 11 scopolamine

truthful 5 frank 6 candid, honest 7 factual, sincere 8 accurate 9 realistic, veracious, veridical

truthfulness 6 candor, verity 7 honesty 8 veracity

try 3 aim, tax, vex 4 seek, shot, stab, test 5 annoy, assay, essay, judge, offer, prove, study, whack, whirl, worry 6 aspire, harass, harrow, strain, stress, strive 7 afflict, adjudge, attempt, trouble 8 endeavor, struggle 9 undertake 10 adjudicate, experiment

trying 6 taxing, thorny, tricky, vexing 7 arduous, onerous 8 annoying, exacting, grueling 9 demanding, difficult, strenuous, vexatious 10 irritating 11 aggravating, troublesome

try out 8 audition

tryst 4 date 7 meeting 10 engagement, rendezvous 11 appointment, assignation

tsunami 9 tidal wave

tub 3 vat 4 boat 9 container *hot:* 3 spa 7 Jacuzzi

tuba 7 helicon 9 bombardon, euphonium 10 sousaphone

Tubalcain *father:* 6 Lamech *mother:* 6 Zillah

tubby 3 fat 5 plump, podgy, porky, pudgy 6 chubby, chunky, rotund 8 roly-poly

tube 4 duct, hose, pipe 5 buret 6 siphon, subway, tunnel, vessel 7 burette, conduit, cuvette, pipette, syringe 8 pipeline *anatomical:* 3 vas 4 duct, vasa (plural) 7 salpinx 9 salpinges (plural)

tuber 3 set 4 bulb, corm, root, stem 6 potato 7 rhizome 10 prominence

tuberculosis 8 phthisis, scrofula 11 consumption 12 Pott's disease

tucker out 4 do in, poop, tire 5 drain, weary 7 exhaust

tuft 5 clump, mound 7 cluster *of feathers:* 7 panache *ornamental:* 6 pom-pom *vascular:* 6 glomus

tufted 7 crested

tug 3 tow 4 drag, draw, haul, moil, pull, toil 5 labor 6 strain, strive

tug-of-war 5 match 6 strife 7 contest, grapple, rivalry 8 conflict, struggle 10 contention 11 competition

tuition 3 fee 6 charge 8 teaching, training, tutelage 9 education, schooling 11 instruction

tumble 4 drop, fall, trip 5 upset 6 plunge, topple 8 collapse, keel over 9 bring down, overthrow 10 somersault

tumbledown 8 decrepit 10 ramshackle 11 dilapidated

tumbler 5 glass 6 roller 7 acrobat, gymnast 11 cartwheeler

tumbrel 4 cart 5 wagon 7 tipcart

tumescent 6 turgid 7 aureate, bloated, bulging, flowery, swollen 8 inflated, swelling 9 bombastic, dropsical, overblown 10 euphuistic, rhetorical 12 magniloquent 13 grandiloquent

tummy 3 gut 5 belly 6 paunch 7 abdomen, stomach 8 potbelly 9 bay window 11 breadbasket

tumult 3 din 4 flap, riot, to-do 5 babel, broil, hoo-ha, hurly, whirl 6 clamor, dither, hubbub, lather, outcry, pother, racket, strife, uproar 7 ferment, tempest, turmoil 8 disorder, foofaraw, outburst, paroxysm, upheaval 9 agitation, commotion, confusion, kerfuffle, maelstrom 10 convulsion, hullabaloo, hurly-burly, turbulence 11 disturbance, pandemonium

tumultuous 5 rowdy 6 stormy, unruly 7 raucous, riotous 9 clamorous, turbulent 10 boisterous, disorderly 11 rumbustious, tempestuous 12 rambunctious

tumulus 5 grave, knoll, mound 6 barrow 7 hillock

tun 3 keg, vat 4 butt, cask, pipe 6 barrel 8 hogshead, puncheon

tuna 3 ahi 4 pear 6 bigeye, bonito 7 bluefin 8 albacore, skipjack 9 scombroid, yellowfin

tune 3 air 4 dial, lilt, song 5 theme 6 accord, adjust, amount, attune, extent, jingle, melody, strain, temper 7 descant 8 modulate, regulate 9 harmonize 10 coordinate, intonation *out:* 6 ignore

tuneful 5 sweet 6 dulcet 7 melodic 9 melodious 10 euphonious

tungsten 7 wolfram 9 scheelite 10 wolframite

tunic 5 jupon 6 kirtle *Greek:* 6 chiton

tunicate 4 salp 8 ascidian, chordate 9 sea squirt 11 urochordate

Tunisia *capital:* 5 Tunis *city:* 4 Sfax 6 Ariana *island:* 5 Jerba *language:* 6 Arabic *monetary unit:* 5 dinar *neighbor:* 5 Libya 7 Algeria *ruins:* 8 Carthage *sea:* 13 Mediterranean

tunnel 4 tube 6 burrow 7 conduit 8 crawlway *Alps:* 7 Simplon *France:* 4 Rove *Hudson river:* 7 Holland, Lincoln *Nevada:* 5 Sutro *railroad:* 6 Hoosac 7 Cascade

Turandot *character:* 3 Liu 5 Calaf *author:* 5 Gozzi (Carlo) *composer:* 6 Busoni (Ferruccio) 7 Puccini (Giacomo)

turban 7 bandana, pugaree 8 bandanna 9 headdress

turbid 4 dark 5 dense, mucky, muddy, murky, riley, roily, smoky, thick 6 cloudy, opaque, roiled 7 clouded, obscure

turbot 8 flatfish

turbulence 3 din 4 flap, stew 5 babel, fight, hoo-ha 6 dither, fracas, lather, pother, tumult, uproar 7 turmoil 8 foofaraw 9 agitation, commotion, confusion 11 pandemonium

turbulent 4 wild 5 bumpy, roily, rough, rowdy 6 raging, stormy, unruly 7 furious, moiling, raucous, riotous, roaring 8 agitated, blustery, brawling, mutinous, rowdyish, swirling 9 clamorous 10 boisterous, disorderly, tumultuous 11 rumbustious, tempestuous 12 rambunctious

tureen 3 pot 4 bowl 5 crock 6 vessel 9 casserole

turf 3 sod 4 area, peat 5 grass, sward, track 6 domain, region 7 terrain 9 racetrack, territory 11 horse racing 12 neighborhood

turgid see TUMESCENT

Turkey *capital:* 6 Ankara *city:* 5 Adana, Bursa, Izmir, Konya 8 Istanbul 9 Gaziantep *enclave:* 8 Naxçivan *lake:* 3 Van *leader:* 7 Atatürk (Kemal) *monetary unit:* 4 lira *mountain, range:* 6 Ararat,

Taurus *neighbor:* 4 Iran, Iraq 5 Syria
6 Greece 7 Armenia, Georgia 8 Bulgaria
part of: 7 Balkans *peninsula:* 6 Balkan
9 Asia Minor *river:* 6 Tigris 8 Menderes
9 Euphrates 10 Kizil Irmak *sea:*
6 Aegean 7 Marmara 13 Mediterranean
turkey *buzzard:* 7 vulture *disease:*
9 blackhead *female:* 3 hen *head growth:*
5 snood 7 dewbill *male:* 3 tom 7 gobbler
throat pouch: 6 wattle *young:* 5 poult
Turkey in the ___ 5 Straw
Turkish *cavalryman:* 5 spahi *empire:*
7 Ottoman *governor:* 4 vali *inn:* 4 kahn
6 imaret *measure:* 3 ohe *music:* 9 janissary *soldier:* 5 nizam 9 janissary *sultan:*
5 Ahmed, Selim 7 Bajazet, Bayezid,
Ilderim *sword:* 8 yataghan *title:* 3 aga,
bey 4 agha 5 pasha 6 vizier 7 effendi
Turkmenistan *capital:* 8 Ashgabat
9 Ashkhabad *city:* 9 Chardzhou, Dashhowuz *desert:* 7 Kara-Kum *monetary
unit:* 5 manat *neighbor:* 4 Iran 10 Kazakhstan, Uzbekistan 11 Afghanistan
river: 6 Murgab 7 Murghab 8 Amu
Dar'ya *sea:* 7 Caspian
Turks and Caicos Islands *capital:*
9 Grand Turk *location:* 10 West Indies
passage: 6 Caicos 8 Mouchoir *territory
of:* 7 Britain
turmeric 3 dye 4 herb 5 spice 6 ginger
8 dyestuff
turmoil 4 coil, flap, moil, riot, stew, stir,
to-do 5 chaos, whirl 6 clamor, dither,
hassle, hubbub, lather, pother, strife,
tumult, unease, unrest, uproar, welter
7 anxiety, ferment 8 disorder, disquiet,
distress, upheaval 9 agitation, commotion, confusion 10 disruption, hurly-
burly, inquietude, storminess, turbulence, uneasiness 11 anxiousness,
disquietude, hurry-scurry, pandemonium, restiveness 12 restlessness 13 helter-skelter, Sturm und Drang
turn 3 yaw, zag, zig 4 bend, bias, bout,
cast, grow, gyre, reel, spin, tack, tour,
veer, whip, wind 5 angle, curve, pivot,
refer, shunt, spell, stint, swirl, train,
twirl, whirl 6 detour, divert, gyrate,
mutate, revert, rotate, switch, swivel
7 circuit, convert, deflect, deviate,
digress, diverge, reverse, revolve
8 gyration, rotation 9 about-face, deviation, pirouette, volte-face 10 deflection,
revolution, tergiverse 11 changeabout
12 tergiversate *to stone:* 8 lapidify
turnabout 3 rat 6 coward 7 reverse
8 apostate, defector, recreant, renegade, reversal 9 about-face, reversion,
volte-face 11 retaliation 12 merry-go-
round 13 tergiversator
turn aside 4 shun, sway, veer 5 avert,

repel, shunt, stave 6 divert, refuse,
reject, swerve 7 deflect, deviate,
digress, dismiss, diverge, fend off,
reflect, ward off 8 alienate, estrange,
separate 9 sidetrack
turncoat 3 rat, spy 5 Judas 7 traitor
8 apostate, betrayer, defector, deserter,
quisling, recreant, renegade 9 traitress,
turnabout 13 tergiversator
turn down 4 jilt, veto 5 spurn 6 rebuff,
refuse, reject 7 decline, dismiss 9 repudiate 10 disapprove
turned on 4 high 5 doped 6 stoned,
zonked 7 aroused, drugged, excited
8 hopped-up, tripping 9 activated,
spaced-out, zonked-out 10 passionate
12 enthusiastic
turn in 5 crash, rat on 6 betray, inform,
rat out, retire 7 deliver, produce, sack
out 8 hand over 10 hit the sack, relinquish
turning point 4 cusp 5 pivot 6 climax,
crisis 8 landmark 11 climacteric
turnip 5 swede 8 rutabaga *Scottish:* 4 neep
turnip-shaped 8 napiform
turnkey 6 jailer
turn left 3 haw
Turn of the Screw, The *author:* 5 James
(Henry) *character:* 5 Flora, Miles
10 Peter Quint *composer:* 7 Britten
(Benjamin)
turn on 5 start 6 excite, ignite 7 start up
8 activate, motivate 9 stimulate, titillate
turn over 4 plow, roll 5 upend, upset
6 assign, commit, give up, rotate 7 capsize, consign, deliver, entrust, furnish,
provide, revolve 8 delegate, transfer
9 overthrow, surrender 10 relinquish
turnpike 7 highway
turn right 3 gee
turn up 4 find 6 appear, arrive, reveal
7 uncover, unearth 8 discover
9 encounter 11 materialize
Turnus *beloved:* 7 Lavinia *slayer:*
6 Aeneas
Turow work 4 One L 13 Burden of Proof
14 Pleading Guilty 16 Personal Injuries,
Presumed Innocent
turpentine 7 galipot, solvent, thinner
ingredient: 6 pinene *tree:* 4 pine 9 tere-
binth
turret 5 tower 6 cupola, louver, louvre
7 mirador 8 bartizan 9 belvedere
turtle 8 terrapin, tortoise 9 chelonian
edible part: 7 calipee 8 calipash *sea:*
6 ridley 8 hawkbill *shell:* 8 carapace
shell part: 8 plastron
Tuscany *city:* 4 Pisa 8 Florence *river:*
4 Arno *tower:* 4 Pisa *wine:* 7 chianti
tusk 4 fang 5 ivory, tooth
tusker 6 dugong, walrus 7 mammoth,

muntjac, narwhal, warthog **8** elephant, musk deer **11** barking deer

tussle 4 spar **5** scrap, scrum **6** hassle, scrape **7** scuffle, wrangle, wrestle **8** argument, skirmish, struggle **9** scrimmage **11** controversy

tussock 4 tuft **5** clump, mound **7** cluster

tutelage see TUITION

tutor 3 don **5** coach, teach **6** docent, mentor **7** teacher **9** pedagogue, preceptor **10** instructor

Tut's tomb discoverer 6 Carter (Howard)

tutti 3 all

Tuvalu *capital:* **9** Fongafale *ethnic group:* **10** Polynesian *former name:* **6** Ellice (Islands) *monetary unit:* **6** dollar

twaddle 3 jaw, yak **4** bosh, bull, bunk, chat, guff, muck, talk, tosh **5** clack, drool, hooey, prate, run on **6** babble, bunkum, burble, drivel, gabble, hot air, humbug, jabber, tattle **7** baloney, blabber, blarney, blather, chatter, hogwash, prattle, rubbish **8** claptrap, malarkey, nonsense, tommyrot, trumpery **9** poppycock **10** applesauce, balderdash **12** blatherskite **13** horsefeathers

tweak 4 jerk, mock, pull, zing **5** annoy, pinch, pluck **6** adjust, bother, twitch **8** fine-tune **9** poke fun at

tweet 4 call, note **5** cheep, chirp **7** chirrup, twitter

Twelfth Night character 5 Viola **6** Olivia, Orsino (Duke) **7** Antonio, Cesario **8** Malvolio **9** Sebastian, Toby Belch

twelve *combining form:* **5** dodec **6** dodeca

twenty *combining form:* **4** icos **5** icosa, icosi

twerp 4 brat, drip, fool, jerk, nerd, twit **6** squirt

twice 3 bis **7** twofold *combining form:* **3** bis *prefix:* **3** dis

twice a day 3 b.i.d. **8** bis in die **11** semidiurnal

twice a year 8 biannual **10** semiannual, semiyearly

Twice-Told Tales author 9 Hawthorne (Nathaniel)

twig 4 shoot, sprig **6** branch *bundle of:* **5** fagot **6** faggot

twiggy 4 slim, thin **5** reedy **6** slight, stalky **7** slender **9** sticklike

twilight 3 eve **4** dusk **5** gloam, gloom **6** sunset **7** decline **8** gloaming **9** nightfall **10** crepuscule

Twilight of the Gods 8 Ragnarok *composer:* **6** Wagner (Richard)

twill 5 chino, cloth, serge, toile, tweed, weave **6** fabric **7** cheviot **8** dungaree **9** bombazine, gabardine **11** herringbone

twin 4 dual, like, mate **5** clone, match **6** bifold, binary, double, fellow, paired **7** matched, similar, twofold **8** matching **9** companion, duplicate, identical **10** coordinate, reciprocal

Twin Cities 6 St. Paul **11** Minneapolis

twine 4 coil, cord, curl, wind, wrap **5** twist, weave **6** spiral, string **7** embrace, meander, wreathe **8** entangle **9** interlace **10** interweave

twinge 4 ache, pain, pang **5** pluck, shoot, throe, tweak **6** stitch

twinkle 3 bat **4** flit, wink **5** blink, flash, flirt, gleam, glint, light, shake, shine, trice **6** moment, second, winkle **7** flicker, flutter, glimmer, glisten, glitter, instant, shimmer, sparkle **9** coruscate, nictitate **11** coruscation, scintillate, split second

twin stars 6 Castor, Pollux

twirl 4 coil, gyre, spin **5** pitch, trill, whirl, whorl **6** gyrate **7** revolve **9** pirouette

twist 3 wry **4** coil, curl, turn, warp, wind **5** belie, gnarl, pivot, twine, twirl, wring **6** garble, spiral, sprain, squirm, torque, wrench, writhe **7** contort, distort, entwine, falsify, pervert, wriggle **8** misstate **9** corkscrew **12** misrepresent

twisted 3 wry **4** awry, sick **5** askew, kinky **6** swirly, warped **9** perverted

twister 6 funnel **7** tornado **9** dust devil, whirlwind **10** waterspout

twit 4 dolt, fool, gibe, jeer, jive, josh, mock, quiz, razz **5** chide, rally, scout, taunt, tease, twerp **6** deride **8** bonehead, numskull, ridicule **9** blockhead, numbskull **10** nincompoop

twitch 3 tic **4** jerk, pang, pull, yank **5** pluck, spasm, throe, tweak **9** quiver **10** quack grass **11** contraction

twitter 4 chat, peep **5** cheep, chirp, quake, tweet **6** cackle, giggle, jargon, quiver, shiver, titter, tremor, warble **7** chatter, chirrup, chitter, flicker, flitter, flutter, tremble **9** vibration

twittery 6 giggly **8** chattery **9** flustered, tremulous

two 3 duo **4** duet, pair **5** twain **6** couple *combining form:* **3** bis, duo, dyo *divide into:* **4** fork **6** bisect **9** bifurcate *prefix:* **3** twi

two-faced 9 deceitful, dishonest, insincere **11** duplicitous **12** hypocritical **13** double-dealing *god:* **5** Janus

twofold 4 dual, twin **5** binal, duple **6** binary, double, duplex, dyadic, paired **9** dualistic

Two Gentlemen of Verona *author:* **11** Shakespeare (William) *character:* **5** Julia **6** Silvia, Thurio **7** Proteus **9** Valentine

twosome 3 duo 4 dyad, pair 5 brace 6 couple 7 doublet

two-time 4 dupe 6 betray, delude, humbug, take in 7 beguile, cheat on, deceive, mislead 9 bamboozle 11 double-cross

two-wheeler 4 bike 5 cycle 7 bicycle, scooter 10 motorcycle

Two Years Before the Mast author: 4 Dana (Richard Henry)

Tybalt *cousin:* 6 Juliet *family:* 7 Capulet *slayer:* 5 Romeo *victim:* 8 Mercutio

Tyche *goddess of:* 7 fortune

tycoon 5 mogul, nabob 7 magnate

tyke 3 dog, kid 5 child, hound, puppy 6 canine, moppet, nipper, shaver 7 mongrel

Tyler novel 16 Breathing Lessons 17 Accidental Tourist (The) 29 Dinner at the Homesick Restaurant

tympanum 7 eardrum 9 middle ear

Tyndareus *kingdom:* 6 Sparta *wife:* 4 Leda

type 3 cut, ilk, lot, way 4 cast, form, kind, mold, sort 5 breed, class, genre, order, print, serif, stamp 6 kidney, nature, stripe 7 feather, species, variety 8 category 9 character 10 persuasion 11 description *bar:* 4 slug *measure:* 4 pica 5 point *set:* 7 compose *setter:* 10 compositor *size:* 4 pica 5 agate, pearl *stroke:* 5 serif *style:* 4 bold 5 roman 6 Gothic, italic 7 Fraktur 8 boldface 9 lightface, sans serif *tray:* 6 galley

Typee *author:* 8 Melville (Herman) *character:* 4 Toby

typewriter *part:* 3 key 6 platen, spacer *type size:* 4 pica 5 elite

Typhon 3 Set 7 monster 8 Typhoeus *offspring:* 6 Sphinx 7 Chimera 8 Cerberus, Chimaera *wife:* 7 Echidna

typhoon 7 cyclone 9 hurricane 13 tropical storm

typical 5 ideal, model, usual 6 common, normal 7 classic, general, natural, regular 8 symbolic

typify 6 embody, mirror 9 epitomize, exemplify, personify, represent, symbolize 10 illustrate 11 emblematize 12 characterize

typo 5 error 7 erratum 8 misprint 11 corrigendum

typographer 7 printer 10 compositor

Tyr 3 Tiu *brother:* 4 Thor *father:* 4 Odin *god of:* 3 war *mother:* 5 Jordh, Jorth

tyrannical 8 absolute, despotic 9 arbitrary 10 absolutist, autocratic, oppressive 11 dictatorial 12 totalitarian

tyrannize 7 oppress 8 dominate, domineer, overbear 9 terrorize

tyrannous 5 harsh 6 brutal, severe 8 absolute, despotic 9 arbitrary, fascistic 10 autocratic 11 dictatorial 12 totalitarian

tyranny 7 cruelty, fascism 9 autocracy, despotism, monocracy 10 absolutism, domination, oppression 12 dictatorship

tyrant 4 czar, duce, tsar, tzar 5 ruler 6 despot, führer 7 fuehrer, pharaoh, usurper 8 autocrat, dictator 9 oppressor, strongman 10 absolutist 12 totalitarian

Tyrian ___ 6 purple

tyro 4 punk 6 novice, rookie 7 amateur, dabbler, student 8 beginner, freshman, neophyte, newcomer 9 novitiate 10 apprentice, dilettante, tenderfoot 11 abecedarian

Tyrol see TIROL

tzar see CZAR

tzigane 3 Rom 5 gypsy 6 Romany

U

übermensch 8 superman

ubiquitous 7 allover 9 pervasive, universal 10 everywhere, wall-to-wall, widespread 11 omnipresent

U-boat 3 sub 7 pigboat 9 submarine

Uganda *capital:* 7 Kampala *falls:* 5 Ripon *lake:* 5 Kyoga 6 Albert, Edward, George 8 Victoria *language:* 7 English, Swahili *leader:* 4 Amin (Idi) *monetary unit:* 8 shilling *mountain:* 5 Elgon *mountain range:* 9 Ruwenzori *neighbor:* 5 Congo, Kenya, Sudan 6 Rwanda 8 Tanzania *river:* 4 Nile

ugly 4 vile 7 hideous 8 deformed 9 loathsome, misshapen, offensive, repugnant, repulsive, unsightly 10 disfigured 12 unattractive

Ugly Duckling author 8 Andersen (Hans Christian)

ukase 4 fiat 5 edict, order 6 decree, dictum, ruling 7 command, dictate, mandate 9 directive 10 injunction 12 proclamation 13 pronouncement

Ukraine *capital:* 4 Kiev *city:* 4 Lviv, Lvov 5 Yalta 6 Odessa 7 Kharkiv 9 Chernobyl *ethnic group:* 7 Cossack *monetary unit:* 6 hryvny *mountain range:* 10 Carpathian *neighbor:* 6 Poland, Russia 7 Belarus, Hungary, Moldova 8 Slovakia *peninsula:* 5 Kerch 6 Crimea 7 Crimean *river:* 3 Bug 5 Tisza 6 Donets 7 Dnieper 8 Dniester *sea:* 4 Azov 5 Black

Ulalume author 3 Poe (Edgar Allan)

ulcer 4 sore 6 fester 7 corrupt *kind:* 6 peptic 8 duodenal *mouth:* 10 canker sore

ulna 7 forearm

Ulster hero 6 Fergus 7 Deirdre 9 Conchobar, Cuchulain, Cuchullin 10 Cú Chulainn

ulterior 5 privy 6 covert, future, hidden, latent 7 further, obscure, remoter 9 ambiguous, concealed 10 subsequent, succeeding 11 undisclosed

ultimate 3 end 4 acme, last, peak 5 basic, final 6 summit, utmost, zenith 7 closing, epitome, extreme, maximum, primary, supreme, topmost 8 absolute, deciding, decisive, eventual, farthest, furthest, greatest, original, terminal 9 elemental, paramount 10 apotheosis, concluding, conclusive, consummate, preeminent 11 categorical, fundamental, furthermost, indivisible 12 incomparable, quintessence

ultimatum 5 order 6 demand, threat 7 mandate 9 challenge 12 notification

ultra 5 kinky, outré, rabid 6 beyond, far-out, too-too 7 extreme, fanatic, radical 9 excessive, extremist, fanatical 10 outlandish 11 extravagant

ultraconservative 11 reactionary

ultraist 5 rabid 6 zealot 7 extreme, fanatic, radical 9 extremist

ultramarine 7 oversea, sea-blue 8 overseas 11 lapis lazuli

ululate 3 bay 4 howl, wail, yowl

Ulysses *author:* 5 Joyce (James) *character:* 5 Bloom (Leopold), Molly (Bloom) 6 Blazes (Boylan) 7 Dedalus (Stephen) (see also ODYSSEUS)

umber 5 brown, sepia, shade 6 darken, shadow

umbilicus 3 hub 4 core 5 heart, hilum, navel 6 center

umbra 5 shade 6 shadow

umbrage 4 hint, huff 5 anger, pique, shade 6 shadow 7 chagrin, dudgeon, foliage, leafage, offense 9 annoyance, suspicion 10 irritation, resentment 11 displeasure, indignation 12 exasperation

umbrageous 5 shady 6 shaded, touchy 7 shadowy 8 shadowed 9 defensive, sensitive

umbrella 5 cover, guard, shade 6 brolly, pileus, screen 7 parasol, protect, shelter 8 sunshade 10 protection 11 bumbershoot

umph see OOMPH

umpire 3 ref 5 judge 6 decide, settle 7 arbiter, referee 9 arbitrate 10 arbitrator *call:* 3 out 4 balk, ball, safe 6 strike

unabashed 5 blunt, brash, frank, naked, overt 6 arrant, brassy, brazen, candid 7 blatant, forward 8 outright 9 audacious, barefaced, shameless, undaunted 10 unblushing 11 undisguised, unmitigated 12 unapologetic

unabbreviated see UNABRIDGED

unable 5 inept, unfit 6 helpless, impotent 9 incapable, maladroit, powerless, unskilled 10 unequipped 11 incompetent, unqualified 13 incapacitated

unabridged 5 uncut, whole 6 entire, intact 8 complete 10 full-length 11 uncondensed 13 unabbreviated

unacceptable 8 unwanted 9 unwelcome 10 unsuitable 11 intolerable, undesirable 12 inadmissible 13 exceptionable, inappropriate, insupportable, objectionable

unaccompanied 4 lone, sole, solo, stag 5 alone, apart 6 single 8 detached, solitary 9 a cappella 10 unattended, unescorted

unaccountable 6 arcane, mystic 7 strange 8 baffling, puzzling 9 enigmatic 10 mysterious, mystifying, unknowable, unreliable 12 impenetrable, inexplicable, undependable, unfathomable 13 irresponsible, unexplainable

unaccustomed 3 new 5 alien, novel 6 unused 7 strange, unusual 8 singular, uncommon, unwonted 10 unexpected, unfamiliar

unadorned 4 bald, bare 5 naked, plain, spare, stark 6 rustic, severe, simple 7 artless, austere, natural, spartan 11 undecorated 13 unembellished, unembroidered, unpretentious

unadulterated 4 neat, pure 5 sheer, utter 7 genuine, unmixed 8 absolute, straight 9 unalloyed, undiluted 11 unmitigated, unqualified

unaffected 5 naive 6 candid, simple

7 artless, callous, genuine, natural, sincere, unmoved **9** guileless, impassive, ingenuous, unaltered, unchanged, unstudied, untouched **10** hard-boiled, impervious **13** unpretentious

unalloyed 4 pure **5** sheer, total **7** genuine, unmixed **8** absolute, straight **9** authentic, out-and-out, undiluted **11** unmitigated, unqualified **13** thoroughgoing, unadulterated

unalterable 5 fixed **7** binding, bounden, certain, decided **8** constant, required **9** immutable, mandatory, necessary **10** compulsory, invariable **12** unchangeable **13** predetermined

unambiguous 5 clear, lucid, plain **6** patent **7** evident, express, obvious, precise **8** apparent, clean-cut, clear-cut, decisive, definite, distinct, explicit, manifest, specific, univocal **10** definitive, forthright **11** categorical, translucent, transparent, unequivocal **12** transpicuous

unanimous 6 united **8** communal, univocal **9** unopposed **10** collective **11** uncontested **13** consentaneous

unanimously 5 as one **6** wholly **7** en masse **10** altogether

unanticipated 9 unplanned **10** surprising, unexpected, unforeseen **12** out of the blue

unappeasable 4 grim **7** adamant **8** obdurate, resolute **9** insatiate, unbending **10** implacable, insatiable, relentless, unyielding **11** unrelenting **12** unquenchable

unappetizing 4 icky **5** gross, yucky **7** insipid **8** unsavory **9** repugnant **11** unappealing, unpalatable **12** unattractive

unapproachable 5 aloof **6** remote, offish **7** distant **8** reserved **10** unfriendly, unsociable **11** standoffish, unreachable **12** inaccessible, unattainable

unasked 7 willing **8** unbidden, unsought, unwanted **9** uninvited, unwelcome, voluntary **10** gratuitous, unprompted **11** spontaneous, uncalled-for, unrequested, voluntarily

unassailable 6 secure **8** airtight **10** invincible, inviolable, undeniable **11** impregnable, irrefutable **12** indisputable, invulnerable **13** incontestable, unconquerable

unassertive 3 shy **4** meek **5** mousy, timid **6** modest, mousey **7** bashful **8** backward, reticent, retiring, sheepish, timorous **9** diffident, shrinking **10** submissive **12** self-effacing

unassuming 3 shy **6** humble, modest, simple **8** ordinary, retiring **9** diffident

11 unassertive **12** self-effacing **13** unpretentious

unattached 4 free **5** loose **6** single **8** separate **9** unmarried **10** unassigned **11** uncommitted, unconnected **12** disconnected, freestanding, unassociated

unattainable 7 elusive **10** impossible **12** inaccessible

unattractive 4 drab, dull, ugly **5** dowdy, plain **6** homely **8** frumpish **10** unalluring, unsuitable **11** unappealing, undesirable **12** unflattering

unauthentic 4 fake, mock, sham **5** bogus, dummy, faked, false, phony **6** ersatz, forged, pseudo **7** feigned **8** affected, spurious **9** contrived, imitation, pretended, simulated **10** apocryphal, artificial **11** counterfeit, make-believe **12** illegitimate

unavailable 4 busy **6** absent, tied up **7** missing **8** occupied

unavailing 4 idle, vain **5** empty **6** barren, futile **7** useless **8** abortive, bootless **9** fruitless, pointless **11** ineffective, ineffectual **12** unproductive

unavoidable 5 fated **7** certain **8** destined **9** impending, necessary **10** compulsory, inevitable, obligatory **11** ineluctable, inescapable

unavoidably 8 perforce **10** helplessly, inevitably, willy-nilly **11** inescapably, necessarily, whether or no

unaware, unawares 5 aback **7** unready **8** abruptly, heedless, ignorant, off guard, suddenly **9** oblivious, unknowing, unmindful, unwitting **10** by surprise, unfamiliar, uninformed, unprepared **12** unacquainted, unexpectedly

unbalance 11 destabilize

unbalanced 3 mad **4** daft **5** batty, nutty **6** crazed, insane, uneven, wobbly **7** unequal, unsound **8** demented, deranged, lopsided, unhinged, unstable **9** psychotic **10** disordered, moonstruck

unbearable 11 intolerable, unendurable **12** excruciating, insufferable

unbeautiful 4 ugly **5** plain **6** homely **8** uncomely, unlovely **9** unsightly **10** ill-favored, unbecoming, uninviting **12** unattractive

unbecoming 8 improper, unlovely, unseemly, untimely, untoward, unworthy **9** inelegant, tasteless, unfitting **10** indecorous, indelicate, malapropos, unsuitable **11** disgraceful **12** unattractive **13** inappropriate

unbelievable 7 amazing, awesome **8** fabulous **9** fantastic **10** astounding, improbable, incredible, phenomenal, staggering, stupendous **11** astonishing, implausible, spectacular **12** unconvincing, unimaginable **13** extraordinary, inconceivable

unbeliever 5 pagan **6** giaour **7** atheist, doubter, gentile, heathen, heretic, infidel, scoffer, skeptic **8** agnostic **10** Pyrrhonist **11** freethinker

unbelieving 5 leery **6** show-me **8** agnostic, apostate, doubting **9** quizzical, skeptical **10** dissenting, suspicious **11** incredulous, mistrustful, questioning

unbending 5 rigid, stern, stiff **8** hardline, obdurate, resolute **9** inelastic **10** brassbound, inexorable, inflexible, unyielding

unbiased 4 fair, just **5** equal **7** neutral **8** detached, tolerant **9** equitable, impartial, objective, unbigoted **10** even-handed, open-minded **11** broad-minded, uncommitted **12** unprejudiced **13** disinterested, dispassionate

unbidden 7 unasked, willing **8** unsought, unwanted **9** impromptu, uninvited, unwelcome, voluntary **10** gratuitous, unprompted **11** spontaneous, unrequested

unbind 4 free, undo **5** loose, untie **6** detach, loosen **7** manumit, release, unchain, unloose **8** dissolve, liberate, unfasten, unloosen **9** discharge, disengage, unshackle **10** emancipate

unblemished 4 pure **7** perfect **8** flawless, spotless, unmarred, virtuous **9** exemplary, faultless, stainless, undefiled, unspotted, unsullied **10** immaculate **11** untarnished

unbosom 4 bare, open, tell **6** betray, expose, reveal, unveil **7** divulge, express, uncover **8** disclose

unbound 4 free **5** freed, loose **6** loosed **10** unattached, unconfined, unfastened

unbounded 4 open **6** untold **7** endless **8** infinite, unending **9** excessive, limitless, unchecked, unlimited **10** immoderate, indefinite, inordinate **11** extravagant, measureless **12** immeasurable, incalculable, uncontrolled, unrestrained

unbreakable 7 durable, lasting **10** unyielding **11** everlasting

unbridled 4 free **5** loose **6** madcap **8** reckless, uncurbed **9** dissolute, unchecked **10** immoderate, licentious, unconfined, unfettered, ungoverned **11** spontaneous, uninhibited, unrepressed **12** uncontrolled, unrestrained, unrestricted **13** unconstrained

unbroken 5 solid, sound, whole **6** entire, intact, single **8** complete, constant, enduring **9** ceaseless, steadfast, unceasing, undamaged, undivided, unsub-

dued, unvarying **10** continuous, unimpaired **13** uninterrupted

unburden 3 rid **4** dump, ease, lose **5** shake **6** reveal, unload **7** cast off, confess, confide, off-load, relieve **8** shake off, throw off **9** discharge **10** relinquish **11** disencumber

uncalled-for 8 baseless, needless **9** officious, unfounded **10** gratuitous, groundless **11** unessential, unjustified, unnecessary, unwarranted **13** unjustifiable

uncanny 5 eerie, weird **6** creepy, spooky **7** ghostly, strange **9** unearthly, unnatural **10** mysterious, mystifying, superhuman **11** supernormal, supranormal **12** supernatural

uncared-for 5 dingy **6** beat-up, shabby **7** rickety, run-down, worn-out **8** decrepit, derelict, deserted, desolate, forsaken, tattered, untended **9** neglected **10** broken-down, down-at-heel, ramshackle, tumble-down **11** dilapidated

uncaring 4 cold **7** callous **9** heartless, negligent, oblivious, unfeeling, unheeding **11** coldhearted, hard-hearted, indifferent, insensitive, thoughtless, unconcerned **13** inconsiderate, unsympathetic

unceasing 7 abiding, endless, eternal, nonstop, undying **8** constant, enduring, unbroken, unending **9** continual, perennial, perpetual **10** continuous **11** amaranthine, everlasting, unremitting **12** imperishable, interminable **13** uninterrupted

unceremonious 4 curt, rude **5** bluff, blunt, frank, hasty, sharp, short, terse **6** abrupt, breezy, casual, sudden **7** brusque, hurried, offhand **8** familiar, informal **10** ungracious **11** precipitate, precipitous

uncertain 4 hazy, iffy, moot **5** vague **6** chancy, fitful, unsure, wobbly **7** dubious, erratic, halting, unclear **8** arguable, doubtful, insecure, slippery, unstable, unsteady, variable **9** ambiguous, debatable, undecided, unsettled **10** ambivalent, disputable, inconstant, indefinite, precarious **11** problematic, speculative **12** questionable, undependable **13** indeterminate, problematical, unforeseeable, unpredictable, untrustworthy

uncertainty 5 doubt **7** dubiety **8** distrust, mistrust **9** ambiguity, suspicion **10** indecision, perplexity, puzzlement, skepticism, uneasiness **11** ambivalence **12** doubtfulness, irresolution

unchain 4 free **5** loose **6** loosen, unbind **7** manumit, release **8** liberate, unfasten, unfetter 9 discharge, unshackle 10 emancipate 11 disenthrall

unchangeable 3 set 4 firm 5 fixed 7 settled 8 constant 9 immutable, permanent 10 continuing, inflexible, invariable 11 established, inalterable

unchanging 5 fixed 6 stable, static, steady 7 abiding, equable, eternal, settled, stabile, uniform 8 constant, enduring 9 immutable, steadfast, unvarying 10 consistent, continuing, invariable

unchaste 4 easy, lewd 5 bawdy, loose 6 impure, vulgar, wanton 7 immoral, lustful, obscene, scarlet, unclean 8 depraved, prurient 9 debauched, dissolute, lecherous, salacious 10 adulterous, lascivious, libidinous, licentious, profligate 11 promiscuous

unchecked 5 loose 7 rampant 9 spreading, unbounded, unbridled 10 widespread 11 uninhibited 12 unrestrained, unrestricted

uncivil 4 rude 5 crass, crude 6 coarse, savage, vulgar 7 boorish, ill-bred, uncouth 8 barbaric, impolite 9 barbarous 10 indecorous, uncultured, ungracious 11 ill-mannered, uncourteous 12 discourteous 13 disrespectful

uncivilized 4 rude, wild 5 crude 6 brutal, coarse, Gothic, savage 7 boorish, Hunnish, ill-bred, loutish, lowbred, uncouth 8 barbaric, churlish 9 barbarian, barbarous, primitive, unrefined 10 mannerless, uncultured, unmannerly, unpolished 12 uncultivated 13 unenlightened

unclad see UNCLOTHED

uncle *cry:* 6 give up 9 surrender *Scottish:* 3 eme *Spanish:* 3 tío *U.S. symbol:* 3 Sam

unclean 4 foul 5 dingy, dirty, grimy 6 filthy, grubby, grungy, impure, soiled, sordid 7 corrupt, defiled, immoral, obscene, squalid, stained, sullied, tainted 8 befouled, indecent, polluted, unchaste 9 tarnished 10 besmirched, desecrated 12 contaminated

unclear 3 dim 4 hazy 5 murky, vague 6 bleary, blurry, cloudy, opaque, unsure 7 clouded, cryptic, dubious, obscure, shadowy 8 doubtful, nebulous, overcast, puzzling 9 ambiguous, enigmatic, tenebrous, unsettled 10 ill-defined, indistinct, indefinite, inexplicit 13 indeterminate

Uncle Remus creator 6 Harris (Joel Chandler)

Uncle Tom's Cabin *author:* 5 Stowe (Harriet Beecher) *character:* 5 Eliza, Topsy 6 Legree (Simon) 9 Little Eva

Uncle Vanya author 7 Chekhov (Anton)

unclothe 5 strip 6 denude, divest, expose, unveil 7 display, disrobe, uncloak, uncover, undress

unclothed 4 bare, nude 5 naked 6 peeled, unclad 7 denuded, exposed 8 in the raw, stripped 9 au naturel, buck-naked, undressed 10 stark naked

unclouded 4 fair 5 clear, lucid, sunny 6 bright 7 halcyon 8 rainless, sunshiny

uncluttered 4 neat, tidy, trig, trim 7 orderly 9 organized, shipshape 11 spic-and-span, well-ordered 12 spick-and-span

uncombed 5 messy, mussy 6 matted, mussed 7 ruffled, snarled, tangled, tousled, unkempt 10 disheveled

uncommon 3 odd 4 rare 5 novel 6 choice, scarce, unique 7 special, unusual 8 esoteric, especial, singular, sporadic, unwonted 10 infrequent, noteworthy, remarkable 11 distinctive, exceptional 12 unaccustomed 13 extraordinary

uncommunicative 3 mum 4 dumb 5 aloof 6 offish, silent 7 distant, guarded, private 8 reserved, reticent, taciturn 9 reclusive, secretive, withdrawn 10 antisocial, poker-faced, speechless, tongue-tied, unsociable 11 inscrutable, standoffish, tight-lipped 12 close-mouthed, tight-mouthed, unresponsive 13 unforthcoming

uncompassionate 4 cold, hard 5 stony 7 callous 8 obdurate, pitiless, uncaring 9 heartless, unfeeling 10 hard-boiled 11 coldhearted, hardhearted, insensitive 12 stonyhearted 13 unsympathetic

uncomplicated 4 easy 5 basic, clear, plain 6 simple 8 clear-cut 10 effortless, elementary, manageable, uninvolved

uncomplimentary 7 adverse 8 critical 9 degrading 10 belittling, derogatory, pejorative 11 deprecatory, disparaging, unfavorable 12 depreciative, depreciatory, unflattering

uncompromising 4 firm 5 rigid 8 hardline, obdurate, resolute, stubborn 9 hard-nosed, immovable, insistent, unbending 10 brassbound, determined, inexorable, inflexible, unshakable, unyielding 12 intransigent, single-minded

unconcealed 4 bald, bare, open 5 frank, naked, overt, plain 6 candid 7 blatant, evident, exposed, express, obvious, visible 8 apparent, explicit, manifest, palpable 10 forthright 11 openhearted, transparent, undisguised, unvarnished

unconcern 6 apathy 7 neglect 9 aloofness, disregard 10 alienation, detachment, dispassion 11 disinterest, inattention, insouciance, nonchalance 12 carelessness, heedlessness, indifference 13 preoccupation

unconcerned 4 cool 6 remote 7 unmoved 8 careless, detached, heedless 9 alienated, apathetic, oblivious, unmindful, unruffled 10 insouciant, neglectful, untroubled 11 inattentive, indifferent, unperturbed 12 uninterested 13 disinterested, dispassionate

unconditional 5 sheer, total, utter 8 absolute, definite, explicit, outright 9 downright, out-and-out 10 unreserved 11 unequivocal, unqualified 12 unrestricted 13 thoroughgoing

unconfined 4 free, vast 5 loose 7 at large 9 at liberty, boundless, limitless, unlimited 12 unrestrained, unrestricted

uncongenial 6 at odds 8 unfitted 9 repellent, repugnant, unlikable 10 discordant, unsociable, unsuitable 11 conflicting, displeasing 12 antipathetic, disagreeable, incompatible, unattractive 13 unsympathetic

unconnected 5 alone, apart 8 discrete, detached, disjoint, disjunct, distinct, inchoate, rambling, separate 9 unrelated 10 unattached 11 independent 12 unassociated 13 discontinuous, noncontinuous

unconquerable 10 invincible, inviolable, unbeatable 11 bulletproof, impregnable, indomitable, insuperable 12 invulnerable, unassailable

unconscionable 5 undue 6 unfair, unholy, unjust, wanton, wicked 7 immoral, ungodly 8 barbaric, criminal 9 barbarous, unethical 10 exorbitant, inordinate, outrageous 11 inexcusable, uncivilized 12 unprincipled, unscrupulous

unconscious 3 out 6 asleep, chance 7 out cold, stunned, unaware 8 comatose 9 insensate, passed out, unplanned, unwitting 10 blacked out, insensible, knocked out 11 inadvertent, instinctual, involuntary 12 uncalculated 13 unintentional

unconsciousness 4 coma 5 faint 6 stupor, torpor, trance 7 syncope 13 obliviousness

unconsidered 4 rash 5 brash, hasty 6 casual 7 offhand 8 careless, reckless, slapdash 9 desultory, haphazard, hit-or-miss, hotheaded, impetuous, unplanned 10 ill-advised, incautious, unthinking 11 thoughtless

unconstrained 4 free, open 6 blithe, dégagé, wanton 7 buoyant, gushing, relaxed 8 animated, carefree, effusive, informal, outgoing 9 easygoing, expan-sive, liberated 10 expressive, nonchalant, unreserved

uncontrollable 4 wild 6 unruly 7 wayward, willful 9 fractious 10 headstrong, refractory, self-willed 11 intractable 12 overwhelming, recalcitrant, ungovernable, unmanageable 13 irrepressible, undisciplined

uncontrolled 4 free, wild 5 loose 6 wanton 9 automatic, excessive, unbounded, unlimited, unmanaged 10 autonomous, immoderate, licentious, ungoverned 11 independent, instinctual, involuntary, unconscious, uninhibited, unregulated 12 disorganized, unrestrained 13 self-governing

unconventional 3 odd 4 beat 5 kinky, kooky, outré 6 casual, far-out, freaky, quirky, unique, way-out, weirdo 7 bizarre, deviant, oddball, offbeat, unusual, wayward 8 aberrant, abnormal, atypical, bohemian, freakish, original, peculiar 9 anomalous, eccentric, irregular 10 avant-garde, unexpected, unorthodox 11 uncustomary 13 idiosyncratic

unconvinced 5 leery 6 unsure 7 dubious 8 doubtful 9 skeptical, undecided 10 suspicious

unconvincing 4 lame 6 feeble, flimsy, forced 7 dubious, suspect 8 doubtful, strained 10 farfetched, improbable, incredible 11 implausible, unrealistic 12 unbelievable 13 unsubstantial

uncooked 3 raw

uncouple 4 part 6 detach, divide 7 disjoin, divorce, unhitch 8 separate, unfasten 9 disengage 10 disconnect, dissociate 12 disaffiliate

uncouth 3 odd, raw 4 rude 5 crass, crude, gross, rough 6 clumsy, coarse, rugged, vulgar 7 awkward, bizarre, boorish, ill-bred, loutish, strange, uncivil 8 barbaric, clownish, impolite, ungainly 9 eccentric, graceless, inelegant, unrefined 10 outlandish, uncultured, unpolished 11 ill-mannered, uncivilized 12 discourteous, uncultivated *person:* 3 oaf 4 boor, dolt, lout 5 clown 7 bumpkin 9 barbarian

uncover 4 bare 5 strip 6 betray, detect, divest, expose, remove, reveal, unmask, unveil 7 display, divulge, unearth 8 disclose

uncritical 5 naive 9 credulous 11 perfunctory

unction 3 oil 4 balm 5 cream, salve 6 balsam, cerate, chrism 7 suavity, unguent 8 liniment, ointment 9 emollient 11 embrocation

unctuous 4 oily 5 fatty, slick, soapy,

suave 6 greasy, smarmy 7 cloying, fawning, fulsome 8 slippery 9 wheedling 10 flattering, oleaginous, saccharine 11 sycophantic

uncultivated 4 wild 5 crass, crude, gross 6 coarse, desert, fallow, savage, vulgar 7 boorish, lowbrow, uncouth 8 barbaric, unplowed, untilled 9 barbarian, barbarous, inelegant, unrefined 10 unpolished 11 uncivilized

uncultured 3 raw 4 rude 5 crass, crude, gross, rough 6 coarse, vulgar 7 artless, boorish, ill-bred, loutish, lowbred, lowbrow, natural, uncouth 8 barbaric, churlish, cloddish 9 barbarian, barbarous, benighted, inelegant, unrefined 10 unpolished 11 uncivilized 13 unenlightened

uncustomary 4 rare 7 special, strange, unusual 8 aberrant, abnormal, atypical, singular, uncommon 9 anomalous 10 surprising, unfamiliar, unorthodox 11 exceptional 13 extraordinary

uncut 5 whole 6 entire, intact 8 complete 9 undiluted 10 full-length, unabridged 11 uncondensed 13 unabbreviated

undamaged 5 sound, whole 6 intact, unhurt 8 unbroken, unmarred 9 uninjured, unscathed 10 unimpaired 11 unblemished

undaunted 4 bold 5 brave 6 daring, heroic 7 doughty, Spartan, valiant 8 fearless, intrepid, resolute, unafraid, valorous 9 audacious 10 courageous 11 lionhearted, unconquered, unflinching 12 stouthearted

___ **und Drang** 5 Sturm

undeceive 8 disabuse 11 disillusion

undecided 4 iffy, moot, open 6 unsure 7 dubious, pending 8 doubtful, wavering 9 equivocal, tentative, uncertain, unsettled 10 ambivalent, indefinite, unresolved 12 undetermined

undeclared 5 tacit 6 unsaid 7 assumed, implied 8 accepted, implicit, inferred, presumed, unspoken, unstated 10 understood

undecorated 4 bare 5 plain, stark 6 homely, severe, simple 8 no-frills 9 unadorned 12 unornamented 13 unembellished, unembroidered

undefiled 4 pure 6 chaste, intact, vestal, virgin 8 innocent, spotless, virginal, virtuous 9 stainless, unstained, unsullied, untainted 10 immaculate 11 unblemished, untarnished

undefined 3 dim 4 hazy 5 faint, vague 6 bleary 7 obscure, shadowy, unclear 8 inchoate, nebulous, unformed 9 amorphous, shapeless 10 indistinct 12 undetermined

undemonstrative 4 calm, cold, cool 5 aloof, chill 7 aseptic, distant, laconic 8 reserved, retiring 9 contained, inhibited, shrinking, withdrawn 10 restrained, unsociable 11 emotionless, passionless, standoffish, unemotional 12 matter-of-fact, unresponsive 13 self-contained

undeniable 6 patent 7 certain, evident, genuine, obvious 8 manifest 9 veridical 10 inarguable 11 indubitable, irrefutable, unequivocal 12 indisputable 13 incontestable

undependable 6 fickle, tricky, unsafe 7 erratic 10 capricious, fly-by-night, inconstant, unreliable 12 inconsistent, questionable 13 irresponsible, unpredictable, untrustworthy

under 3 low, sub 4 down, less 5 below, lower, short 6 lesser 7 beneath, covered, subject 8 downward, inferior 9 dependent, receiving, secondary, subjacent 11 subordinate *prefix:* 3 hyp, sub 4 hypo

undercarriage 5 frame 9 framework 11 landing gear

undercover 6 covert, hidden, secret 7 furtive, stealth, sub-rosa 8 hush-hush, stealthy 11 clandestine 12 confidential 13 surreptitious *person:* 3 spy 4 mole 5 agent, spook 6 sleuth 9 detective, operative 10 counterspy 11 double agent, secret agent 12 counteragent

undercroft 5 crypt, vault 7 chamber 8 catacomb

undercut 7 subvert 8 sabotage

underdeveloped 4 poor 7 dwarfed, stunted 8 backward, immature 9 unevolved 10 third-world

underdog 5 loser 6 victim 7 also-ran, fall guy 9 dark horse

underdone 3 raw, red 4 rare

underestimate 6 slight 7 dismiss 8 belittle, discount, disprize, minimize 9 deprecate, disparage, sell short 10 depreciate

undergarment 3 bra 4 BVDs, slip 5 teddy 6 bikini, bodice, briefs, corset, girdle, shorts, undies 7 chemise, drawers, panties, stammel, step-ins 8 lingerie, pretties, Skivvies, woollies 9 brassiere, jockstrap, long johns, petticoat, underwear 10 foundation

undergo 4 bear, face 5 abide, brave, brook 6 endure, suffer 7 sustain, weather 8 submit to, tolerate 9 withstand 10 experience

undergraduate 4 coed 5 frosh 6 junior, senior 8 freshman 9 collegian, sophomore

underground 4 tube 5 metro, train

6 buried, hidden, nether, secret, subway **7** illegal, off-beat, railway **8** hypogeal, hypogean **10** undercover **11** alternative, clandestine **12** subterranean **13** surreptitious

underhanded 3 sly **4** wily **5** shady **6** covert, crafty, secret, shifty, sneaky, tricky **7** cunning, devious, elusive, evasive, furtive, sub-rosa **8** guileful, sneaking, stealthy **9** deceitful, deceptive **10** circuitous **11** clandestine, duplicitous **13** surreptitious

underlie 4 bear **6** prop up **7** subtend, support **8** buttress

underline 4 mark **6** play up, stress **9** emphasize, italicize **10** accentuate, underscore

underling 4 aide, peon, serf **5** gofer, scrub, slave **6** flunky, gopher, lackey, menial, minion **7** fall guy **8** inferior **9** assistant, attendant, subaltern **11** subordinate

underlying 4 root **5** basal, basic **7** primary **8** implicit **9** elemental, essential **11** fundamental

Under Milk Wood author 6 Thomas (Dylan)

undermine 3 sap **4** foil **5** blunt, erode **6** impair, thwart, weaken **7** cripple, disable, subvert **8** sabotage **9** attenuate, frustrate **10** debilitate, demoralize

undermost 6 bottom, lowest **9** lowermost **10** bottommost, nethermost, rock-bottom

underneath 4 sole **5** below, lower **6** bottom **7** covered

underpin 4 back, base, prop, root **5** brace **6** uphold **7** bolster, justify, shore up, support **8** buttress, validate **10** strengthen **11** corroborate

underpinning 4 base, prop, root, stay **5** basis, brace **7** bedrock, footing, seating, support **8** buttress **10** foundation, groundwork **12** substructure

underprivileged 4 poor **5** needy **7** hapless, unlucky **8** deprived **11** handicapped, unfortunate **13** disadvantaged

underrate 7 devalue **8** discount, mark down, minimize, write off **9** devaluate, write down **10** depreciate

underscore 6 accent, play up, stress **9** emphasize, italicize **10** accentuate

underside 4 sole **6** bottom **7** reverse

undersized 3 toy **4** baby, mini, puny **5** dinky, dwarf, pygmy, runty, short, small **6** bantam, little, pocket, slight **7** scrubby, stunted **9** miniature **10** diminutive **11** Lilliputian

understand 3 con, ken, see **4** know **5** grasp, guess, infer, savvy, sense, think **6** accept, assume, deduce, expect, fathom, figure, follow, gather, reason, reckon, take in, take it **7** believe, discern, imagine, presume, realize, suppose, surmise, suspect **8** conceive, conclude, consider, perceive **9** apprehend, interpret **10** appreciate, comprehend, conjecture

understandable 5 clear, lucid, plain **8** clear-cut, coherent, knowable **9** excusable, graspable, plausible **10** articulate, believable, defensible, fathomable, reasonable **11** justifiable, perceivable, unambiguous **12** intelligible **13** apprehensible

understanding 3 ken, wit **4** deal, pact **5** grasp, sense **6** accord, humane, kindly **7** compact, empathy, entente, insight, mastery **8** sympathy **9** agreement, awareness, knowledge, tolerance **10** acceptance, impression, perception **11** considerate, discernment, explanation, sympathetic **12** apprehension, relationship **13** comprehension

understatement 7 litotes

understood 5 tacit **7** assumed, implied **8** accepted, implicit, inferred, unspoken

understudy 6 double, backup, fill-in **7** standby, stand-in **9** surrogate **10** substitute **11** replacement

undertake 3 try **4** dare **5** assay, begin, essay, start **6** accept, assume, pledge, strive, tackle, take on, take up **7** attempt, certify, execute, perform, promise, warrant **8** commence, contract, covenant, endeavor, set about, set forth, shoulder **9** guarantee

undertaker 8 embalmer **9** mortician

undertaking 3 job **4** task **6** affair, charge, effort **7** calling, emprise, exploit, mission, project, pursuit, venture **8** endeavor **9** adventure, guarantee, operation **10** enterprise **11** proposition, transaction

under-the-table 6 covert, hidden, secret, sneaky **7** furtive, sub-rosa **8** hush-hush, stealthy **9** concealed, underhand **10** undercover **11** clandestine **13** surreptitious

undertone 3 hue, hum **4** cast, hint, tint **5** shade **6** mumble, murmur, mutter **7** inkling **10** suggestion **11** association, connotation, implication

undertow 4 eddy **7** current, riptide, sea puss

undervalue see UNDERRATE

underwater 9 submarine **10** subaquatic, subaqueous ***breathing apparatus:* 5** scuba ***captain:* 4** Nemo ***chamber:* 7** caisson ***device:* 8** paravane ***missile:* 7** torpedo ***sound detector:* 5** sonar

underwear see UNDERGARMENT

underwood 5 brush, copse, hedge, scrub 7 boscage, coppice, thicket 9 shrubbery

underworld 4 hell 5 hades, Sheol 6 Erebus, Tophet 7 Gehenna, inferno 8 gangland 9 antipodes 11 Pandemonium *boatman:* 6 Charon *deity:* 3 Dis 4 Bran 5 Pluto 6 Osiris *goddess:* 6 Hecate 10 Persephone *organization:* 5 Mafia *relating to:* 8 chthonic *watchdog:* 8 Cerberus

underwrite 4 back, fund, sign 5 endow, stake 6 assure, insure, pay for, secure 7 agree to, endorse, finance, sponsor, support 8 bankroll 9 grubstake, guarantee 11 subscribe to

undesigning 5 frank 6 candid, honest 7 artless, earnest, genuine, sincere 9 guileless, ingenuous, unfeigned 10 aboveboard, forthright

undesirable 8 annoying, unwanted 9 offensive, unwelcome 10 ill-favored, unpleasant, unsuitable 11 displeasing, inadvisable, troublesome 12 disagreeable, unacceptable, unattractive 13 inappropriate, objectionable

undesired 8 needless, unsought, unwanted 9 uninvited, unwelcome 10 gratuitous 11 uncalled-for, unnecessary 12 nonessential

undetermined 5 vague 7 dubious, obscure, pending, unclear 8 doubtful 9 ambiguous, equivocal, uncertain, undecided, undefined, unsettled 10 ill-defined, indefinite, indistinct 12 inconclusive

undeveloped 5 crude, green, rough 6 latent 8 backward, immature, inchoate 9 embryonic, incipient, primitive, unevolved 10 unfinished

undiluted 4 neat, pure 5 sheer, utter 7 genuine, unmixed 8 absolute, straight 9 authentic, unalloyed 11 unmitigated, unqualified 13 unadulterated

undiplomatic 4 rash, rude 5 brash, cocky 6 brazen, cheeky 8 impudent, tactless 9 audacious, hotheaded, impolitic, impulsive, maladroit, untactful 10 ill-advised, indiscreet 11 impertinent, injudicious, insensitive, thoughtless 12 presumptuous

undisciplined 4 wild 6 unruly, wanton 7 froward, restive, wayward, willful 8 contrary, untoward 9 fractious 10 disorderly, rebellious, refractory 11 intractable 12 contumacious, noncompliant, obstreperous, recalcitrant, ungovernable, unmanageable

undisclosed 6 hidden, sealed, secret 7 unknown, unnamed 8 ulterior, withheld 9 anonymous 10 unreported, unrevealed 11 clandestine, unmentioned, unspecified 12 confidential, undesignated, unidentified

undisguised 4 bald, open, pure 5 frank, naked, overt, sheer, stark 6 candid, patent 7 obvious 8 apparent, explicit, manifest, palpable 9 barefaced 11 openhearted, unconcealed, unvarnished

undistinguished 5 cheap, stock 6 common 7 humdrum, obscure, routine 8 déclassé, everyday, inferior, low-grade, mediocre, middling, ordinary, workaday 10 second-rate 11 commonplace, nondescript, second-class 12 run-of-the-mill 13 insignificant

undivided 3 one 4 full 5 fixed, total, whole 6 entire, intact, united 8 complete, unbroken 9 unanimous 10 continuous, unswerving 11 indivisible 12 concentrated, undistracted

undo 4 free, open, ruin 5 annul, loose, untie, upset, wrack, wreck 6 cancel, defeat, loosen, negate, stymie, unbind, unsnap 7 abolish, destroy, nullify, release, reverse, vitiate, wipe out 8 abrogate, unfasten, unloosen 9 disengage 10 invalidate 11 disentangle, outmaneuver

undoing 4 bane, doom, ruin, slip 5 shame 7 misstep 8 downfall, reversal 9 destroyer, overthrow, ruination 10 misfortune 11 destruction, humiliation

undoubted 4 real, sure, true 7 certain, genuine 8 definite, positive 9 authentic 10 undisputed

undoubtedly 5 truly 6 indeed, really, surely 7 clearly 8 of course 9 assuredly, certainly 10 definitely, positively, presumably, undeniably 11 indubitably

undress see UNCLOTHE

undressed 4 nude, rude 5 naked 6 unclad 7 exposed 8 in the raw, stripped 9 au naturel, unclothed

undue 5 inapt 7 extreme 8 ill-timed, improper, needless, untimely 9 excessive, unfitting 10 immoderate, indecorous, inordinate, unsuitable 11 extravagant, uncalled-for, unnecessary, unwarranted 12 unreasonable 13 inappropriate, unjustifiable

undulant fever 11 brucellosis

undulate 4 roll, swag, sway, wave 5 heave, snake, swell, swing 6 billow, ripple 7 slither 9 fluctuate, oscillate

unduly 3 too 6 overly 9 extremely, immensely 11 excessively 12 immoderately, inordinately, unreasonably 13 unnecessarily

undying 7 abiding, ageless, endless, eternal 8 enduring, immortal, unending

9 continual, deathless, perennial, perpetual, unceasing **10** continuing **11** amaranthine, everlasting **12** imperishable, unquenchable

unearth 4 find, show **5** dig up, learn **6** exhume, expose, reveal **7** exhibit, find out, root out, uncover **8** come upon, disclose, discover, dredge up, excavate **9** ascertain, determine **10** come across

unearthly 5 eerie, weird **6** absurd, insane, spooky **7** awesome, ghostly, uncanny, ungodly **8** abnormal, ethereal, heavenly, numinous, spectral **9** appalling, fantastic **10** miraculous, mysterious, outlandish, superhuman, suprahuman **12** preposterous, supermundane, supernatural **13** preternatural

unease 4 care, fear **5** angst, worry **6** strain, stress, unrest **7** anxiety, concern, tension **8** disquiet, distress **9** abashment, confusion, misgiving **10** discomfort, discontent, solicitude **11** disquietude, fretfulness, nervousness, uncertainty, uptightness **12** apprehension, discomfiture, discomposure **13** embarrassment

uneasy 4 edgy **5** jumpy, tense **6** afraid **7** anxious, awkward, fearful, fidgety, fretful, nervous, restive, unquiet, uptight, worried **8** agitated, doubtful, insecure, restless, unstable **9** ambiguous, concerned, difficult, disturbed, perturbed, uncertain, unsettled **10** disquieted, precarious, solicitous **11** embarrassed **12** apprehensive **13** uncomfortable

uneducated 5 crude, rough **8** ignorant, untaught **9** benighted, untutored **10** illiterate, unlettered, unschooled **12** uncultivated, uninstructed

unembellished 4 bald, bare **5** blunt, plain, spare, stark **6** severe **7** austere **9** essential, unadorned **11** undecorated, unelaborate, ungarnished, unvarnished **12** unornamented **13** unembroidered, unpretentious

unemotional 4 cold, cool **5** chill, stoic, stony **6** frigid, sedate, serene **7** deadpan, equable, glacial, stoical **8** composed, obdurate, reserved, reticent **9** apathetic, impassive **10** hard-boiled, phlegmatic **11** insensitive, passionless, unexcitable **12** intellectual, thick-skinned, unresponsive **13** dispassionate

unemployed 4 idle **5** fired **6** otiose, unused **7** jobless, laid off, loafing **8** inactive, leisured, workless **10** unoccupied

unending 7 eternal, undying **8** constant, immortal, infinite, timeless **9** boundless, ceaseless, continual, incessant, limitless, perennial, perpetual, unceasing **10** continuous **11** amaranthine, everlasting, unremitting **12** interminable **13** uninterrupted

unenlightened 5 naive **6** unread **7** heathen, unaware **8** backward, ignorant, nescient **9** benighted, unknowing **10** uneducated, uninformed **11** uninitiated **12** uncultivated

unenthusiastic 4 cool **5** tepid **8** grudging, listless, lukewarm **9** apathetic, unexcited **10** lackluster, lacklustre, spiritless **11** halfhearted, indifferent, perfunctory **12** uninterested

unequal 3 odd **6** uneven, unfair **7** diverse **8** inferior, lopsided, one-sided **9** different, disparate, divergent, irregular **10** asymmetric, dissimilar, inadequate, mismatched, off-balance **12** insufficient

unequaled 6 unique **7** supreme **8** foremost, nonesuch, peerless **9** matchless, paramount, unmatched, unrivaled **10** preeminent, surpassing **12** incomparable, transcendent, unparalleled **13** unprecedented

unequivocal 5 clear **6** direct, patent **7** certain, evident **8** apparent, definite, distinct, explicit, manifest, palpable **10** undeniable **11** categorical, indubitable, unambiguous **12** indisputable, undisputable

unerring 5 exact **6** dead-on **7** certain, correct, perfect, precise **8** accurate, reliable **9** faultless, unfailing **10** dependable, infallible **11** trustworthy

unessential 8 marginal, needless, unneeded **9** redundant **10** expendable, gratuitous, irrelevant, peripheral, unrequired **11** dispensable, superfluous, uncalled-for, unimportant, unnecessary **13** insignificant, insubstantial

unethical 5 venal, wrong **7** corrupt, crooked, immoral **9** dishonest, reprobate **12** disreputable, unprincipled, unscrupulous

uneven 3 odd **4** wavy **5** bumpy, erose, harsh, jaggy, rough **6** craggy, jagged, patchy, ragged, random, rugged, spotty **7** scraggy, unequal, varying **8** lopsided, scabrous, scraggly, variable **9** haphazard, hit-or-miss, irregular **10** asymmetric, imbalanced, unbalanced

unevenness 4 bump, wave **7** anomaly **8** asperity, imparity **9** disparity, imbalance, roughness, variation **10** inequality **12** irregularity, lopsidedness **13** disproportion

uneventful 5 usual **6** placid **7** humdrum, prosaic, routine **8** ordinary **10** unexciting **11** commonplace **12** unremarkable

unexampled 4 lone, only, sole, solo **5** alone **6** unique **8** singular, solitary **9** matchless, unequaled, unmatched, unrivaled **10** consummate, inimitable, sui generis, unequalled, unrivalled **12** incomparable, unparalleled **13** unprecedented

unexcited 4 calm **5** blasé, stoic **6** placid, sedate, serene **7** relaxed, stoical **8** composed, tranquil **9** apathetic, collected, unruffled **10** nonchalant **11** indifferent **12** uninterested **13** dispassionate

unexciting 4 arid, dull, tame **5** banal, bland, ho-hum **6** boring, stodgy **7** humdrum, insipid, prosaic, tedious **8** lifeless, tiresome **10** monotonous **11** commonplace **13** uninteresting

unexpected 10 surprising, unforeseen **11** unpredicted **13** unanticipated

unexpectedly 5 aback, short **6** sudden **7** unaware **8** abruptly, suddenly, unawares **9** forthwith **11** unwittingly **12** accidentally **13** inadvertently

unexpended 5 saved **7** reserve, surplus **8** left over, reserved **9** remaining

unexpired 5 valid **9** operative

unexpressed 5 tacit **6** silent, unsaid **7** assumed, implied **8** implicit, presumed, unspoken, wordless **9** unuttered **10** undeclared, understood

unfailing 4 fast, sure **7** certain, devoted **8** constant, faithful, reliable, resolute, surefire, unerring **9** steadfast, unvarying **10** consistent, dependable, infallible, invariable, persistent, unchanging, unflagging, unwavering **11** everlasting, persevering, unrelenting **12** tried-and-true **13** inexhaustible

unfair 4 foul **5** wrong **6** biased, shabby, uneven, unjust **7** unequal **8** wrongful **9** arbitrary, dishonest, unethical **10** prejudiced **11** inequitable, underhanded, unrighteous

unfaithful 5 false **6** untrue **8** cheating, disloyal, recreant, turncoat **9** faithless, two-timing **10** adulterous, inaccurate, perfidious, traitorous **11** treacherous **13** untrustworthy

unfaltering 3 set **4** firm **6** steady **7** abiding **8** constant, enduring, resolute, tireless **9** steadfast, unfailing **10** continuous, unflagging, unwavering **11** persevering **12** never-failing, wholehearted

unfamiliar 3 new **5** alien, novel **6** exotic **7** foreign, strange, unaware, unknown **8** peculiar **11** incognizant, out-of-the-way **12** unaccustomed, unacquainted

unfashionable 5 dated, dowdy, passé, stale **6** bygone, démodé, old-hat, shabby **7** outworn **8** outdated, outmoded **9** out-of-date, unstylish **10** antiquated, oldfangled

unfasten 4 free, open, undo **5** loose, unbar, unfix, unpin, untie **6** detach, loosen, unbind, unbolt, unlace, unlock, unsnap **7** release, unclasp, unhitch, unlatch, unleash, unloose, unstrap **8** unbuckle, unfetter, unloosen, untether **9** disengage

unfathomable 7 abysmal, obscure **8** profound **9** boundless, enigmatic, unplumbed **10** bottomless, fathomless, unknowable **11** inscrutable **12** immeasurable, impenetrable

unfavorable 3 bad, ill **4** poor **6** averse, unfair, unkind **7** adverse, hostile, opposed **8** contrary, damaging, inimical, negative **9** disliking, troubling **11** detrimental, displeasing **12** antagonistic, disapproving, inauspicious *prefix:* **3** dys

unfavorably 4 awry **5** amiss, badly **6** astray, poorly **7** wrongly **10** negatively, unsuitably **13** unfortunately

unfeasible 8 quixotic **9** visionary **10** chimerical, impossible, unworkable **11** impractical, speculative, theoretical, unrealistic **12** unattainable, unrealizable **13** impracticable

unfeeling 4 cold, hard, numb **5** cruel, harsh, stern, stony **6** brutal, leaden, marble, numbed, severe, stolid, unkind **7** callous **8** benumbed, deadened, hardened, obdurate, pitiless, ruthless, uncaring **9** apathetic, heartless, indurated, insensate, senseless **10** hardboiled, insensible, insentient **11** coldblooded, coldhearted, hardhearted, insensitive, unemotional **12** anesthetized **13** unsympathetic

unfeigned 4 real, true **6** actual, hearty, honest **7** artless, earnest, genuine, natural, sincere **8** innocent **9** guileless, heartfelt, ingenuous **11** undesigning **12** wholehearted

unfinished 3 raw **5** crude, rough **7** sketchy **9** imperfect, roughhewn, undressed **10** incomplete, unpolished

Unfinished Symphony composer 8 Schubert (Franz)

unfit 4 sick, weak **5** inapt, inept **6** faulty **7** deprive, disable, unsound, useless **8** disabled, improper, unsuited **9** ill-suited, incapable, maladroit **10** disqualify, ill-adapted, inadequate, ineligible, unsuitable **11** incompetent, unqualified **12** disqualified, incompatible **13** inappropriate, incapacitated

unfitting 5 inapt **8** improper, unseemly **9** imprudent **10** ill-advised, inapposite, malapropos, unbecoming, unsuitable 11 inadvisable 13 inappropriate

unfix 4 part, undo **5** loose, sever **6** cut off, detach, loosen, sunder, unbind **7** unloose **8** uncouple, unfasten, unloosen **9** disengage **10** disconnect, dissociate

unflagging 6 steady **7** staunch **8** constant, tireless, untiring **9** unceasing, unfailing, unwearied **11** persevering, unfaltering, unrelenting, unremitting **13** indefatigable, inexhaustible

unflappable 4 calm **6** poised, serene **7** assured, equable **8** composed, laidback **9** collected, unruffled **10** deliberate, nonchalant **11** self-assured **13** imperturbable, self-possessed

unfledged 5 green, young **6** callow, jejune, unripe **7** puerile **8** immature, juvenile **10** unseasoned **11** undeveloped, unfeathered **13** inexperienced

unflinching 4 firm, grim **6** dogged **7** doughty, staunch, valiant **8** intrepid, resolute **9** dauntless, steadfast **10** relentless, unwavering, unyielding **11** unfaltering, unrelenting **12** stouthearted

unfold 4 open **6** deduce, evolve, expand, expose, extend, flower, mature, reveal, unwrap **7** blossom, burgeon, clear up, develop, display, dope out, exhibit, explain, resolve **8** decipher, disclose, evidence, manifest **9** elaborate, explicate, figure out, puzzle out, transpire **10** effloresce, outstretch **11** come to light

unforced 4 easy **7** natural, willing, witting **8** elective, optional **9** available, easygoing, voluntary **10** deliberate, volitional **11** intentional **12** unprescribed **13** discretionary, noncompulsory

unforeseeable 9 uncertain, unplanned **10** accidental

unforeseen 6 chance **8** surprise **10** accidental, surprising, unexpected **11** unlooked-for, unpredicted **13** unanticipated

unforgivable 9 untenable **10** censurable, inexpiable, outrageous **11** blameworthy, inexcusable, intolerable **12** indefensible, unacceptable, unpardonable **13** insupportable, reprehensible, unjustifiable

unformed 4 rude **5** crude, rough, vague **6** callow **8** immature, inchoate, nebulous, unshaped **9** amorphous, roughhewn, shapeless **10** indefinite, unfinished, unpolished **11** undeveloped, unfashioned **12** unstructured **13** indeterminate

unfortunate 3 bad, sad **4** dire, poor **6** woeful, wretch **7** adverse, awkward, hapless, unhappy, unlucky **8** grievous, ill-fated, luckless, untoward, wretched **9** desperate, graceless, ill-chosen, miserable **10** afflictive, calamitous, deplorable, disastrous, ill-starred, lamentable, unsuitable **11** distressing, regrettable, star-crossed, unfavorable **12** disagreeable, inauspicious, infelicitous, unsuccessful **13** heartbreaking

unfounded 4 idle, vain **5** false **8** baseless, spurious, unproven **9** fabricated, fallacious, gratuitous, groundless, mendacious, misleading, untruthful **11** uncalled-for, unsupported, unwarranted

unfriendly 4 cold, cool **5** alien, aloof, chill, gruff, surly **6** chilly, frosty, remote **7** distant, grouchy, hostile, opposed, warlike **8** inimical, unsocial **10** antisocial, censorious, inimicable, unsociable **11** ill-disposed, uncongenial **12** antagonistic, disagreeable, inhospitable, misanthropic, unneighborly **13** unsympathetic

unfruitful 4 arid, idle **5** empty, waste **6** barren, desert, effete, fallow, futile, wasted **7** parched, sterile, useless **8** abortive, bootless, depleted, impotent **9** infertile, pointless **10** unavailing **11** ineffective, ineffectual **12** impoverished, unproductive, unprofitable

unfurl 4 open **6** expose, reveal, spread, unfold, unroll, unwind **7** develop, display, exhibit, uncover **8** disclose **9** elaborate, spread out

unfurnished 4 bare **5** empty **6** vacant

unfussy 5 loose **6** breezy, casual, common, dégagé, folksy, mellow **7** cursory, relaxed **8** familiar, informal, laid-back **9** easygoing **10** unreserved **11** low-pressure, pococurante, unconcerned **12** unparticular **13** unceremonious, uncomplicated

ungainly 5 gawky, lanky, splay **6** clumsy, klutzy, oafish **7** awkward, boorish, hulking, loutish, lumpish, uncouth **8** bungling, clownish, lubberly, unwieldy **9** lumbering, maladroit **10** blundering

ungarnished 5 plain **6** modest, simple **9** unadorned **11** undecorated, unelaborate **12** unornamented **13** unembellished, unembroidered

ungenerous 4 mean **5** petty, tight **6** paltry, shabby, skimpy, stingy **7** chintzy, miserly **8** grudging, picayune, ungiving **9** illiberal, niggardly, penurious **11** closefisted, tightfisted **12** parsimonious **13** penny-pinching

ungodly see UNHOLY

ungovernable 4 wild **6** unruly **7** froward, lawless, willful **8** mutinous, untoward **9** fractious, turbulent, unbridled **10** disorderly, headstrong, rebellious, refractory, tumultuous **11** intractable **12** recalcitrant, uncontrolled, unmanageable **13** irrepressible, undisciplined

ungraceful 5 crude, gawky, inept, stiff **6** clumsy, gauche, klutzy, oafish, wooden **7** artless, awkward, halting, labored, stilted **8** bumbling, bungling, ungainly, untoward **9** all thumbs, inelegant, lumbering, maladroit **10** blundering

ungracious 4 rude **5** gruff **6** crusty **7** brusque, uncivil **8** churlish, impolite **9** offensive **10** unmannerly **11** disobliging, ill-mannered, impertinent, thoughtless, uncalled-for **12** disagreeable, discourteous **13** disrespectful, inconsiderate, unceremonious

ungraspable 6 opaque **7** obscure **8** baffling **9** enigmatic **10** unknowable **12** impenetrable, inexplicable, unfathomable

ungrateful 9 thankless

unguarded 5 frank, hasty **6** candid, direct, unwary **7** offhand **8** careless, heedless, reckless **9** impolitic, imprudent, impulsive **10** incautious, indiscreet, unthinking **11** defenseless, thoughtless, unprotected

unguent 4 balm **5** cream, salve **6** balsam, cerate, chrism, lotion **8** ointment **9** emollient, lubricant **11** embrocation

ungulate 3 hog, pig **4** deer **5** horse, tapir **6** hoofed **8** elephant **10** rhinoceros

unhallowed 4 evil **6** impure, unholy, wicked **7** immoral, impious, profane, ungodly **8** infernal **9** nefarious **10** desecrated, iniquitous, irreverent **13** unconsecrated

unhampered 4 free, open **5** frank, loose **6** direct **8** uncurbed **9** unbridled, unchecked, unimpeded, unlimited **10** unhindered **11** uninhibited, untrammeled **12** unrestrained, unrestricted, unobstructed **13** unconstrained

unhand 5 let go **7** release

unhandy 5 bulky, inept **6** clumsy, gauche, klutzy **7** awkward, halting, hulking **8** bumbling, bungling, cumbrous, unwieldy **9** all thumbs, hamhanded, maladroit, ponderous **10** cumbersome, unskillful **12** inconvenient

unhappiness 3 woe **5** blues, dolor, dumps, gloom, grief, worry **6** misery, mishap, sorrow **7** anxiety, sadness **8** distress **9** dejection **10** depression, desolation, discontent, heartbreak, melancholy **11** despondency, dolefulness **12** mournfulness, wretchedness **13** cheerlessness

unhappy 3 sad **4** down, grim **5** sorry **6** dismal, dreary, gloomy **7** joyless **8** dejected, downcast, mournful, saddened, troubled, wretched **9** cheerless, depressed, sorrowful, woebegone **10** despondent, dispirited, melancholy **11** melancholic, unfortunate **12** disconsolate, heavyhearted

unharmed 4 safe **5** sound **6** intact, secure, unhurt **8** unbroken, unmarred **9** protected, undamaged, undefiled, uninjured, unscathed **10** unimpaired **11** unblemished

unhealthiness 7 ailment, disease, illness, malaise **8** debility, sickness **9** infirmity **10** affliction, sickliness **11** decrepitude **13** indisposition

unhealthy 3 ill **4** sick **6** ailing, infirm, sickly, unwell **7** baneful, noisome, noxious, unsound **8** diseased **9** injurious **11** deleterious, unwholesome **12** insalubrious

unheard-of 3 new **6** unique **7** obscure, unknown, unnoted **8** nameless **10** phenomenal, unrenowned **12** uncelebrated **13** extraordinary, unprecedented

unhesitating 7 assured, earnest **8** decisive, positive, resolute **9** confident, immediate, unchecked **10** determined, forthright, purposeful **11** unflinching **12** wholehearted

unhinge 5 addle, craze **6** madden, ruffle **7** derange **9** unbalance

unhinged 3 mad **4** daft, loco, nuts **5** balmy, crazy, loony, wacky **6** insane **7** lunatic, unglued **8** demented, deranged **9** disturbed **10** unbalanced

unholy 4 base, evil, vile **6** impure, sinful, wicked **7** heinous, immoral, impious, profane, ungodly **8** dreadful, fiendish, god-awful, shocking **9** atheistic, barbarous **10** iniquitous, irreverent, outrageous, scandalous, unhallowed **11** irreligious, unbelieving **12** sacrilegious, unsanctified **13** reprehensible

unhorse 5 pitch, throw **6** topple, tumble, unseat **7** buck off **8** dislodge, dismount, overturn, unsaddle **9** overthrow

unhurried 4 easy, slow **7** laggard, relaxed **8** dilatory, laid-back **9** easygoing, leisurely **10** deliberate **11** low-pressure

unhurt 4 safe **5** sound, whole **6** entire, intact **7** perfect **8** unbroken, unharmed, unmarred **9** undamaged, uninjured, unscathed, untouched **10** unimpaired **11** unblemished

unification 5 union **6** fusion, hookup, merger **7** amalgam, joining, linkage, melding, merging **8** alliance, coupling

9 coalition 10 connection, federation 11 affiliation, coalescence, combination 12 amalgamation 13 confederation, consolidation

uniform 4 even, like, suit 5 alike, dress, equal, level 6 attire, outfit, stable, steady 7 ordered, orderly, regular, similar, stabile 8 constant, unvaried 9 consonant, unvarying 10 comparable, consistent, invariable, unchanging 11 homogeneous 13 unfluctuating *combining form:* 3 iso *type:* 5 blues, habit, khaki 6 livery, whites

uniformity 6 parity 7 oneness 8 equality, evenness, identity, monotony, sameness 9 agreement, congruity, constancy 11 consistency 13 invariability

uniformly 6 always, evenly 7 equally 8 smoothly 10 comparably 11 analogously, identically 12 equivalently

unify 3 tie, wed 4 bind, bond, fuse, knit, link, mesh 5 blend, marry, merge, unite 6 cement, couple 7 combine, conjoin 8 coalesce, compound, federate 9 integrate 10 amalgamate, centralize, synthesize 11 concatenate, consolidate

unimaginable 10 incredible, unknowable 11 unthinkable 12 mind-boggling, unbelievable 13 extraordinary, inconceivable, indescribable

unimaginative 4 dull, flat 5 banal, bland, trite, vapid 6 common 7 literal, prosaic, routine, vanilla 8 bromidic 10 derivative, pedestrian, uncreative, uninspired 11 commonplace

unimpaired 4 safe 5 sound 6 intact, unhurt 7 perfect 8 unbroken, unharmed, unmarred 9 undamaged, uninjured, unscathed 11 unblemished

unimpassioned 4 calm, cool 5 sober, stoic 6 placid, remote, stolid 7 deadpan 8 detached, lukewarm, reserved, tranquil 9 impassive, temperate 10 phlegmatic, spiritless 11 cold-blooded, emotionless 12 matter-of-fact

unimpeachable 5 valid 7 correct 8 flawless, reliable, virtuous 9 blameless, exemplary, faultless, unspotted, unsullied 10 conclusive, impeccable, undisputed 11 unblemished, untarnished 13 authoritative

unimportant 5 minor, petty 6 casual, minute, paltry 7 trivial 8 piddling 9 small-beer, worthless 10 expendable, immaterial, irrelevant, negligible 11 dispensable, meaningless, superfluous 13 insignificant

uninformed 7 unaware 8 ignorant, nescient 9 oblivious, unknowing, unwitting 10 unfamiliar 11 incognizant, superficial 12 unacquainted, undiscerning

uninhabited 5 empty, waste 6 barren, vacant 7 vacated 8 deserted, desolate, forsaken 9 abandoned, evacuated 10 unoccupied

uninhibited 3 lax 4 free 5 loose 8 uncurbed 9 expansive, fancy-free, liberated, unbridled 10 boisterous, ungoverned, unhampered, unreserved 11 spontaneous, unrepressed, untrammeled 12 unrestrained, unsuppressed 13 unconstrained

uninjured 4 safe 5 sound, whole 6 intact, unhurt 8 unharmed, unmarred 9 undamaged, undefiled, unscathed, untouched 10 unimpaired 11 unblemished

uninspired 4 blah, drab, dull 5 banal, stock, trite, vapid 6 boring, leaden, old-hat, stodgy 7 humdrum, insipid, plastic, sterile, vanilla 8 bromidic, lifeless, ordinary 9 colorless 10 lackluster, lacklustre, pedestrian, uncreative, unoriginal 11 commonplace 13 unimaginative

unintelligent 4 dumb 5 dense 6 obtuse, stupid 7 asinine, brutish, doltish, fatuous, foolish, moronic, vacuous, witless 8 mindless 9 brainless, ludicrous 10 half-witted, ill-advised, irrational, ridiculous, weak-minded 11 harebrained, lamebrained 12 feebleminded

unintentional 6 chance, random 9 haphazard, unplanned, unwitting 10 accidental, fortuitous, incidental, unexpected, unforeseen, unthinking 11 inadvertent, unconscious, unlooked-for 12 adventitious, coincidental 13 unanticipated

uninterested 5 aloof, blasé, bored, jaded 9 apathetic, incurious, unexcited 10 uninvolved 11 indifferent, unconcerned

uninteresting 3 dry 4 arid, blah, drab, dull, flat 5 banal, dusty, ho-hum, stale 6 boring, jejune 7 humdrum, insipid, prosaic, tedious 8 bromidic, plodding, tiresome 9 colorless, dryasdust, wearisome 10 monotonous, pedestrian, uneventful, unexciting 11 uninspiring

uninterrupted 6 direct 7 endless, nonstop 8 constant, unbroken, unending 9 ceaseless, continual, incessant, perpetual, sustained, unceasing 10 continuous 11 undisturbed, unremitting 12 interminable

uninvited 7 unasked 8 unbidden, unsought 9 intruding 10 gratuitous 11 uncalled-for, unrequested, unsolicited 12 presumptuous

union 4 bloc, bond, club 5 alloy, group, guild, joint 6 fusion, league, merger

7 amalgam, joining, melding, merging, society **8** alliance, congress, coupling, junction, juncture, marriage, sodality **9** coalition **10** connection, federation, fellowship **11** association, brotherhood, coalescence, combination, confederacy, cooperative, unification **13** confederation, consolidation *labor:* **3** AFL, CIO, UAW, UMW **5** ILGWU

unique 3 odd, one **4** lone, only, sole, solo **5** alone, novel **6** single **8** peculiar, peerless, singular, solitary, uncommon, unwonted **9** anomalous, exclusive, matchless, unequaled, unmatched, unrivaled **10** inimitable, particular, sui generis, unequalled, unexampled, unrivalled **11** distinctive, exceptional **12** incomparable, unparalleled, unrepeatable **13** extraordinary, idiosyncratic, unprecedented

uniqueness 8 identity **10** singleness **11** peculiarity, singularity **13** individuality

___-Unis 5 Etats

unit 3 arm, one **4** area, item, part, wing **5** digit, group, monad, piece, whole **6** entity **7** element, measure **8** molecule **9** component **10** individual **11** constituent *administrative:* **6** agency, bureau, sector **8** district *boy scout:* **5** troop *educational:* **6** course *military:* (see at MILITARY) *of acceleration:* **3** gal *of action:* **7** episode *of advertising space:* **4** line **6** column *of an element:* **4** atom **8** molecule *of angular measure:* **6** radian *of area:* **3** are **4** acre **6** morgen **7** hectare **9** square rod **10** square mile, square yard *of astronomical distance:* **6** parsec **9** light-year *of brightness:* **7** lambert *of capacity:* **3** cup, tun **4** cord, dram, gill, peck, pint **5** liter, litre, minim, ounce, quart **6** barrel, bushel, firkin, gallon *of computer information:* **3** bit, gig, meg **4** byte **8** gigabyte, megabyte *of conductance:* **3** mho **7** siemens *of distance:* **4** mile, yard **5** meter **6** league **7** furlong *of electricity:* **3** amp **4** volt, watt **6** ampere **7** coulomb *of energy:* **3** erg **5** joule **7** quantum **8** watt-hour *of explosive force:* **7** megaton *of fineness:* **5** carat, karat *of force:* **4** dyne **6** newton **7** poundal *of frequency:* **5** hertz **7** fresnel *of grain:* **5** sheaf *of heat:* **3** BTU **5** therm **7** calorie *of illumination:* **3** lux **5** lumen *of inductance:* **5** henry *of length:* **3** mil, rod **4** foot, hand, inch, mile, rood, yard **5** chain, fermi, meter **6** fathom, micron **7** furlong **9** kilometer *historic:* **5** cubit *of loudness:* **4** sone **7** decibel *of lumber:* **9** board foot *of magnetic flux:* **5** gamma, gauss, tesla, weber **7** maxwell *of mag-*

netic intensity: **7** oersted *of magnetomotive force:* **7** gilbert *of pressure:* **3** bar **4** torr **6** pascal **10** atmosphere *of radiation:* **3** rad **8** roentgen *of radioactivity:* **5** curie *of resistance:* **3** ohm *of solar radiation:* **7** langley *of sound absorption:* **5** sabin *of speech:* **4** word **6** toneme **7** phoneme **8** morpheme, syllable *of speed:* **3** CPS, MPH, RPM **4** knot *of temperature:* **6** degree, kelvin *of time:* **3** day **4** beat, bell, hour, week, year **5** month **6** minute, season, second **8** svedberg *of viscosity:* **5** poise *of volume:* **9** cubic foot, cubic yard **10** cubic meter *of weight:* **3** cwt, ton **4** dram, gram, tael **5** carat, grain, ounce, pound, tonne **6** drachm **7** gigaton, kiloton, quintal, scruple **8** kilogram, millieme **9** metric ton, microgram, milligram *historic:* **3** tod **5** gerah, libra *Indian:* **4** tola *Russian:* **4** pood *of work:* **3** erg **5** ergon, joule *social:* **4** clan **5** tribe **6** family **7** chapter

unite 3 mix, tie, wed **4** ally, band, bind, bond, fuse, join, knit, link, meld, pool, weld **5** blend, graft, marry, merge, unify **6** cement, couple, gather, league, mingle, splice **7** combine, conjoin, connect **8** assemble, coadjute, coalesce, compound, federate **9** affiliate, aggregate, commingle **10** amalgamate, federalize **11** confederate, incorporate

united 3 one, wed **5** joint **6** allied, linked, merged, wedded **7** made one **8** agreeing, combined, in accord **10** harmonious

United Arab Emirates *capital:* **8** Abu Dhabi *city:* **5** Dubai **6** Dubayy *coast:* **6** Pirate **7** Trucial *emirate:* **5** Dubai **6** Dubayy **8** Abu Dhabi *former name:* **13** Trucial States *gulf:* **4** Oman **7** Persian *monetary unit:* **6** dirham *neighbor:* **4** Oman **11** Saudi Arabia *peninsula:* **7** Arabian *strait:* **6** Hormuz

United Kingdom *capital:* **6** London *city:* **3** Ely **4** Bath **5** Derby, Dover, Leeds **6** Exeter, Oxford **7** Bristol, Cardiff, Glasgow, Paisley **8** Bradford, Brighton, Coventry, Plymouth **9** Cambridge, Edinburgh, Leicester, Liverpool, Newcastle, Sheffield **10** Birmingham, Manchester, Nottingham **11** Bournemouth *colony:* **8** Falkland (Islands) *component:* **5** Wales **7** England **8** Scotland **12** Great Britain *conqueror:* **6** Caesar (Julius) **7** William (the Conqueror) *island:* **3** Man **4** Jura, Skye **5** Islay, Lewis, Wight **6** Jersey **8** Anguilla, Guernsey, Mainland *island group:* **6** Orkney **7** Channel **8** Hebrides, Shetland *language:* **5** Welsh **6** Gaelic **7** English *leader:* 8 Cromwell (Oliver) 9 Churchill (Winston) *monarch:* 4 Anne, Mary 5 Henry, James 6 Alfred (the Great), Edward, George 7 Charles, Richard, William 8 Victoria 9 Elizabeth *monetary unit:* 5 pence, penny, pound *monetary unit, former:* 3 bob 5 crown, groat 6 florin, guinea 7 ha'penny 8 farthing, shilling, sixpence 9 halfpenny 10 threepence *mountain, range:* 7 Scafell (Peak), Snowdon 8 Ben Nevis, Cumbrian, Grampian 12 Cheviot Hills *peninsula:* 7 Kintyre *prehistoric site:* 7 Avebury 9 Skara Brae 10 Stonehenge *river:* 3 Dee, Exe, Wye 4 Aire, Avon, Ouse 5 Clyde 6 Mersey, Severn, Thames *sea:* 5 Irish, North 6 Celtic *territory:* 8 Anguilla

United Nations *secretary-general:* 3 Lie (Trygve) 5 Annan (Kofi), Thant (U) 8 Waldheim (Kurt) 12 Boutros-Ghali (Boutros), Hammarskjöld (Dag) 14 Pérez de Cuéllar (Javier)

United States *desert:* 6 Mojave 7 Sonoran 8 Colorado *highest point:* 6 Denali (Mt.) 8 McKinley (Mt.) *island:* 6 Hawaii, Kodiak, Unimak 7 Nunivak 9 Admiralty, Chichagof 10 St. Lawrence 13 Prince of Wales *island group:* 3 Fox 6 Hawaii 8 Aleutian, Pribilof, Thousand *lowest point:* 11 Death Valley *mountain range:* 5 Coast, Green, Ozark, Rocky, White 7 Cascade, Olympic 9 Blue Ridge, Catskills 10 Adirondack, Great Smoky 11 Appalachian 12 Sierra Nevada *national park:* 4 Zion 6 Denali 7 Glacier, Olympic, Redwood, Sequoia 8 Badlands, Carlsbad, Wind Cave, Yosemite 9 Mesa Verde, Mt. Rainier 10 Everglades, Grand Teton, Hot Springs, Isle Royale, Shenandoah 11 Dry Tortugas, Grand Canyon, Kenai Fjords, Mammoth Cave, Yellowstone *possession:* 10 Puerto Rico *state:* 4 Iowa, Ohio, Utah 5 Idaho, Maine, Texas 6 Alaska, Hawaii, Kansas, Nevada, Oregon 7 Alabama, Arizona, Florida, Georgia, Indiana, Montana, New York, Vermont, Wyoming 8 Arkansas, Colorado, Delaware, Illinois, Kentucky, Maryland, Michigan, Missouri, Nebraska, Oklahoma, Virginia 9 Louisiana, Minnesota, New Jersey, New Mexico, Tennessee, Wisconsin 10 California, Washington 11 Connecticut, Mississippi, North Dakota, Rhode Island, South Dakota 12 New Hampshire, Pennsylvania, West Virginia 13 Massachusetts, North Carolina, South Carolina *territory:* 4 Guam 13 American Samoa, Virgin Islands

unity 5 union 6 accord 7 concord, harmony, oneness 8 identity, soleness 9 agreement, consensus 10 continuity, singleness, solidarity

universal 3 all 5 broad, total, whole 6 common, cosmic, entire, global 7 general, generic 8 catholic 9 extensive, planetary, unlimited, worldwide 10 ecumenical, ubiquitous 11 omnipresent 12 all-embracing, all-inclusive, cosmopolitan 13 comprehensive *combining form:* 4 omni

universe 3 all 5 whole, world 6 cosmos, system 8 creation 9 macrocosm

unjust 5 wrong 6 biased, shabby, unfair 7 partial, unequal 8 one-sided, improper, wrongful 9 inequable 10 prejudiced, undeserved 11 inequitable, unrighteous

unjustifiable 5 undue 7 invalid 8 baseless 9 unfounded, untenable 10 groundless 11 inexcusable, unsupported, unwarranted 12 indefensible

unkempt 5 messy 6 frowsy, frowzy, shaggy, sloppy, untidy 7 ruffled, rumpled, scruffy, tousled 8 scraggly, slipshod, slovenly, uncombed 10 bedraggled, disarrayed, disheveled, disordered, unpolished 11 disarranged

unkind 4 mean, vile 5 cruel, harsh, rough, stern 6 severe 7 callous 8 uncaring 9 inclement, malicious 10 ungenerous, ungracious 11 insensitive, thoughtless, unfavorable 12 uncharitable 13 unsympathetic

unknowable 6 arcane, hidden, mystic, occult, secret 7 cryptic 8 mystical, numinous 9 enigmatic, recondite 10 mysterious 11 inscrutable, ungraspable 12 impenetrable, unfathomable

unknowing 6 unwary 7 unaware 8 heedless, ignorant 9 oblivious, unmindful, unwitting 10 insensible, unfamiliar, uninformed 11 incognizant 12 unsuspecting

unknown 6 hidden, nobody, secret 7 obscure, strange 8 nameless 9 anonymous, incognito

unlawful 6 banned 7 bootleg, corrupt, crooked, illegal, illicit, immoral 8 criminal, outlawed, wrongful 9 forbidden, felonious, nefarious 10 contraband, flagitious, indictable, iniquitous, prohibited, proscribed, unlicensed 11 black-market 12 illegitimate, unauthorized

unlearned 5 naive 6 unread 7 unaware 8 ignorant, nescient, untaught 10 illiterate, uneducated, unlettered, unschooled 11 instinctive 13 unenlightened

unleash 4 free, vent 5 let go, loose,

untie, visit, wreak **6** unbind **7** inflict, release **8** carry out, liberate **10** bring about

unless 3 but **4** save **6** except, saving **7** barring, but that, without **9** excepting, excluding

unlettered see UNEDUCATED

unlikable 9 obnoxious, offensive, repellent **10** unpleasant **11** displeasing, distasteful **12** disagreeable

unlike 5 mixed **7** diverse, unequal, various **8** assorted **9** different, disparate, divergent **10** dissimilar **11** distinctive, diversified **13** heterogeneous

unlikely 5 faint, unfit **6** remote, slight **7** distant, dubious **8** doubtful **10** farfetched, improbable, unsuitable **11** implausible, unpromising **12** questionable

unlimited 4 full, vast **5** total **6** untold **7** endless, immense **8** absolute, infinite, wide-open **9** boundless, countless, unbounded, universal **10** unconfined, unfettered **11** unqualified, untrammeled **12** immeasurable, interminable, unrestrained, unrestricted **13** comprehensive, unconditional, unconstrained

unlit 4 dark, inky **6** gloomy **9** lightless

unload 4 drop, dump, junk **5** chuck, ditch, empty **6** debark, remove **7** confess, confide, deep-six, deliver, discard, divulge, lighten, relieve **8** disclose, disgorge, jettison **9** disburden, discharge, disembark, eighty-six, stevedore **11** disencumber

unloose 4 free, undo **5** let go, relax, untie **6** detach, unbind **7** break up, manumit, release, set free, slacken **8** liberate, uncouple, unfasten **9** disengage, extricate, untighten **10** disconnect

unlucky 6 jinxed **7** hapless, ominous **8** ill-fated, untoward **9** ill-boding **10** ill-starred **11** detrimental, inopportune, regrettable, star-crossed, unfavorable, unfortunate **12** inauspicious, unpropitious

unmanageable 4 wild **5** balky, bulky **6** unruly **7** awkward **8** contrary, cumbrous, perverse, stubborn, unwieldy **9** fractious, obstinate **10** cumbersome, disorderly, headstrong, inflexible, rebellious, refractory **11** intractable **12** obstreperous, recalcitrant, ungovernable **13** uncooperative, undisciplined

unmannered 4 rude **5** crude, rough **6** coarse, gauche **7** boorish, ill-bred, loutish **8** impolite **10** indecorous, ungracious **12** discourteous **13** disrespectful

unmarred 5 sound, whole **6** intact,

unhurt 7 perfect **8** pristine, unflawed, unharmed **9** undamaged, undefiled, unscathed, unstained **10** unimpaired **11** unblemished, untarnished

unmask 6 debunk, detect, expose, reveal, show up, unveil **7** deflate, uncover **8** disclose, discover, disprove **9** demystify

unmatched 3 odd **4** only **5** alone **6** unique **8** peerless, singular **9** unequaled, unrivaled **10** inimitable, unequalled, unrivalled **11** exceptional **12** incomparable, unparalleled

unmerciful 5 cruel, harsh **6** brutal **7** callous, extreme **8** inhumane, pitiless, ruthless, uncaring, vengeful **9** heartless, unfeeling, unsparing **10** relentless

unmindful 7 unaware **8** careless, heedless **9** forgetful, negligent, oblivious, unheeding, unwitting **10** abstracted, distracted, neglectful **11** inattentive

unmistakable 5 clear, frank, plain **6** patent **7** certain, decided, evident, express, obvious **8** apparent, definite, distinct, explicit, manifest, palpable **11** unambiguous, unequivocal

unmitigated 4 pure, rank **5** gross, sheer, utter **6** arrant **7** perfect, unmixed **8** absolute, clearcut, complete, outright **9** downright, out-and-out, unalloyed, undiluted **10** consummate, unmodified, unrelieved **11** straight-out, unqualified **12** unalleviated **13** thoroughgoing, unadulterated

unmixed 4 mere, neat, pure **5** plain, sheer, utter **6** simple **7** perfect, sincere **8** absolute, straight **9** unalloyed, unblended, undiluted, undivided **11** unmitigated, unqualified **13** unadulterated

unmoved 4 calm, cool, firm **5** aloof, stony **6** stolid **7** adamant, callous, stoical **8** obdurate **9** impassive, untouched **10** insensible, untroubled **11** unconcerned, unemotional, unimpressed **12** unresponsive

unnamed 5 incog **6** secret **7** obscure, unknown **9** anonymous, incognito **11** unspecified **12** unidentified

unnatural 7 uncanny **8** aberrant, abnormal **9** anomalous, contrived, irregular, synthetic **10** artificial, fabricated, factitious

unnecessary 6 excess **7** surplus **8** needless, optional, prodigal **9** redundant **10** expendable, extraneous, gratuitous, unrequired **11** dispensable, inessential, superfluous, uncalled-for, unessential **12** nonessential

unnerve 5 daunt, shake, throw, upset **6** dismay, rattle **7** agitate, fluster, per-

turb, unhinge **8** bewilder, confound
9 undermine **10** demoralize, disconcert,
discourage, dishearten, intimidate
unobstructed 4 open **5** clear **8** passable
9 unblocked, unimpeded **10** unhampered, unhindered **12** unrestricted
unobtrusive 5 quiet **6** modest **7** subdued
8 reserved, retiring, tasteful
10 restrained **13** inconspicuous
unoccupied 4 free, idle **5** empty **6** vacant
7 jobless, vacated **8** deserted **9** abandoned, available **10** employable, unemployed **11** uninhabited
unofficial 7 pirated, private, wildcat
8 informal **9** irregular **10** unapproved,
unorthodox **12** unauthorized, unsanctioned
unorganized 7 aimless, chaotic, muddled **8** confused, inchoate, nebulous,
rambling, unformed **9** amorphous,
arbitrary, haphazard, shapeless,
unplanned **10** disjointed, disordered,
incoherent, incohesive **11** spontaneous
unoriginal 5 banal, stock **6** copied, oldhat **7** clichéd, humdrum, prosaic, sterile **8** borrowed, ordinary **9** hackneyed,
imitative **10** derivative, uninspired
11 commonplace, plagiarized, uninventive **12** conventional **13** unimaginative
unornamented 4 bare **5** plain, spare,
stark **6** chaste, modest, severe, simple
7 austere **9** unadorned **11** unelaborate,
ungarnished **13** unembellished, unembroidered
unorthodox 3 odd **5** kinky, novel, weird
6 far-out **7** strange, unusual **8** abnormal
9 different, dissident, eccentric, heretical, irregular, sectarian **10** schismatic,
unexpected **13** nonconformist
unorthodoxy 6 heresy, schism **7** dissent
8 variance **9** disbelief, ingenuity, recusancy **10** contention, dissidence, innovation **13** nonconformism, nonconformity
unpaid 3 due **5** owing **6** mature **7** donated, overdue, payable, pro-bono
8 freewill, honorary, wageless **9** unsettled, voluntary, volunteer **10** delinquent, gratuitous, receivable, unsalaried **11** contributed, outstanding
13 uncompensated, unremunerated
unpalatable 8 unsavory **10** flavorless
11 distasteful **12** unappetizing
unparalleled 6 unique **8** peerless, singular **9** matchless, unequaled, unmatched,
unrivaled **10** inimitable, unequalled,
unrivalled **11** exceptional **12** incomparable
unplanned 5 fluky **6** chance, random
7 aimless **9** desultory, haphazard, hitor-miss **10** accidental, unexpected,

unforeseen, unintended **11** inadvertent
12 adventitious, coincidental, unconsidered **13** unintentional
unpleasant 4 sour **5** seamy **7** painful
8 annoying **9** offensive, troubling **10** disturbing, irritating **11** displeasing, distasteful, distressing **12** disagreeable
13 objectionable
unpolished 4 rude **5** crude, gruff, rough
6 crusty, unhewn, vulgar **7** brusque,
uncivil, uncouth **8** homespun,
unworked **9** inelegant, roughhewn,
unrefined **10** amateurish, uncultured,
unfinished, ungracious **11** ill-mannered,
uncivilized **12** discourteous
unpredictable 4 iffy **5** dicey, fluky
6 chancy, fickle, random, touchy
7 erratic, mutable **8** unstable, variable,
volatile **9** arbitrary, mercurial, uncertain, whimsical **10** capricious, changeable **13** unforeseeable
unprejudiced 4 fair, just **5** equal **8** balanced, unbiased **9** equitable, impartial,
objective, unbigoted, uncolored
10 even-handed, fair-minded, openminded **11** nonpartisan **12** uninfluenced
13 disinterested, dispassionate
unpressed 7 rumpled, wrinkly **8** crinkled, puckered, wrinkled
unpretentious 5 frank, plain **6** candid,
honest, modest, simple **7** genuine
8 ordinary **9** unadorned **10** forthright,
unaffected, unassuming **11** plainspoken
unprincipled 5 venal **7** corrupt, crooked,
immoral **9** deceitful, dishonest, dissolute, mercenary, reprobate, unethical
10 inconstant, iniquitous, profligate,
unfaithful **11** underhanded
12 unscrupulous
unproductive 4 vain **6** barren, futile
7 sterile, useless **8** bootless, depleted,
feckless, impotent **9** fruitless, infertile
10 unavailing **11** ineffectual **12** hardscrabble
unprofitable 4 idle, vain **6** barren, futile
7 useless **8** bootless **9** fruitless
10 unavailing **11** ineffective **12** unproductive, unsuccessful
unprogressive 8 orthodox **9** illiberal
11 traditional **12** conservative
unpropitious 4 grim **5** bleak **7** ominous,
unlucky **9** ill-boding, ill-omened
10 foreboding **11** inopportune, threatening, unfavorable **12** discouraging
13 disheartening
unprosperous 4 poor **5** needy **8** strapped
9 penurious **11** impecunious
unprotected 6 unsafe **7** exposed **8** helpless, insecure **9** unguarded **10** endangered, undefended, unshielded, vulner-

able 11 defenseless, susceptible, unsheltered

unproved 7 untried 8 untested 10 postulated 11 conjectural, preliminary, provisional, speculative, theoretical 12 experimental, hypothetical

unpunctual 4 late 5 tardy 6 remiss 7 belated, delayed, overdue 10 behindhand, delinquent

unqualified 4 firm, rank 5 sheer, total, unfit, utter 7 express 8 absolute, explicit, unfitted 9 incapable, out-and-out, steadfast, unalloyed, undiluted, unskilled 10 ineligible, unequipped, unreserved, unsuitable 11 ill-equipped, incompetent, unmitigated 12 wholehearted 13 unadulterated, unconditional

unquenchable 6 crying 7 buoyant, exigent 8 pressing, yearning 9 demanding, insatiate, insistent 10 insatiable 12 effervescent, unrestrained 13 irrepressible, unconstrained

unquestionable 4 real, sure, true 7 certain, genuine 8 absolute, bona fide 9 authentic, undoubted 10 sureenough, undeniable 11 established, indubitable, self-evident, well-founded 12 indisputable, well-grounded 13 authoritative, incontestable, unimpeachable

unquestioning 4 firm, sure 5 fixed 6 steady 7 abiding 8 enduring, gullible, resolute, trusting, unshaken 9 accepting, believing, credulous, steadfast 10 uncritical, undoubting, unshakable, unwavering 11 unfaltering, unqualified 12 never-failing, unhesitating, unsuspecting, unsuspicious, wholehearted

unravel 5 break, solve 6 answer, decode, unknit, unwind 7 clear up, dope out, explain, resolve, unsnarl 8 decipher, dissolve, untangle 9 elucidate, extricate, figure out, interpret, puzzle out, translate 11 disentangle

unreadable 7 deadpan 9 illegible 10 poker-faced 11 inscrutable 12 hieroglyphic 13 cacographical

unreal 4 fake 5 false 6 fabled 7 fictive 8 chimeric, fanciful, illusory, mythical 9 fantastic, fictional, imaginary, imitation 10 artificial, chimerical, fictitious, improbable, incredible 11 nonexistent 12 unbelievable *combining form:* 5 pseud 6 pseudo

unrealistic 7 blue-sky, idyllic, utopian 8 fanciful, quixotic, romantic 9 distorted, idealized, overblown 10 farfetched, ivory-tower, overstated, starry-eyed, unworkable 11 exaggerated, extravagant, impractical, sensational

unreasonable 5 undue 6 absurd 7 invalid 9 arbitrary, excessive, illogical, senseless, sophistic 10 exorbitant, fallacious, headstrong, immoderate, inordinate, irrational, peremptory, ridiculous 11 extravagant, incongruous, nonsensical, uncalled-for, unwarranted 12 preposterous 13 unjustifiable

unreasoned 7 invalid, unsound 9 deceptive, illogical, sophistic, unfounded 10 fallacious, ill-founded, irrational, misleading, ungrounded 11 nonrational

unrefined 3 raw 4 rude 5 crass, crude, rough, tacky 6 coarse, earthy, impure, vulgar 7 natural, uncouth 9 graceless, inelegant, maladroit, roughhewn 10 uncultured, unpolished 11 ill-mannered, uncivilized, unprocessed 12 uncultivated

unreflective 6 casual 7 offhand 8 careless, feckless, heedless, mindless 9 imprudent, impulsive, oblivious, unheeding 10 indiscreet, nonchalant, unthinking 11 inadvertent, perfunctory, thoughtless 13 ill-considered

unrehearsed 7 offhand 8 informal 9 extempore, impromptu, unstudied 10 improvised, off-the-cuff, unprepared 11 extemporary, spontaneous 12 extemporized

unrelated 8 discrete, separate 9 different, disparate 10 dissimilar, extraneous, irrelevant 11 independent

unrelenting 3 set 4 grim 5 stern 7 adamant, endless 8 constant, resolute, ruthless, tireless 9 ceaseless, continual, hard-nosed, incessant, tenacious, unbending, unsparing 10 continuous, determined, implacable, inexorable, inflexible, persistent, unflagging, unshakable, unwavering, unyielding 12 unappeasable

unreliable 6 fickle, shifty, tricky, unsafe 7 dubious 8 fallible, slippery, two-faced 9 deceitful, deceptive, faithless, trustless, unassured, uncertain 10 capricious, fly-by-night, inaccurate, inconstant, perfidious, unfaithful 11 vacillating 12 falsehearted, questionable, unconvincing, undependable 13 irresponsible, unpredictable, untrustworthy

unremarkable 4 so-so 5 plain, usual 6 common, decent, normal 7 average, mundane, prosaic, routine, vanilla 8 adequate, everyday, familiar, habitual, mediocre, ordinary, workaday 9 customary, quotidian, tolerable 11 commonplace, nondescript 12 run-of-the-mill 13 unexceptional

unremitting 7 abiding, chronic, endless,

lasting, nonstop **8** constant, enduring, unending **9** ceaseless, continual, incessant, perennial, perpetual, sustained, unceasing **10** continuous, persistent, persisting, relentless **12** interminable **13** uninterrupted

unrepentant 10 impenitent **11** remorseless **12** unregenerate

unrepresentative 7 deviant, unusual **8** aberrant, abnormal, atypical **9** anomalous, divergent, eccentric, irregular, untypical **11** exceptional, heteroclite **13** nonconforming

unreserved 4 open **5** frank, plain **6** candid **7** sincere **8** effusive, explicit, informal, outgoing, outright **9** expansive, talkative **10** definitive **11** forthcoming, openhearted, unconcealed, undisguised, unqualified, unvarnished **13** demonstrative, unconstrained

unresolved 4 moot **7** pending **8** hesitant, wavering **9** faltering, tentative, uncertain, undecided, unsettled **10** ambivalent, hesitating, indecisive, irresolute, unanswered **11** vacillating

unrespectable 3 low **5** shady **6** shabby, shoddy **8** shameful, unworthy **10** inglorious **11** disgraceful, ignominious **12** dishonorable, disreputable **13** discreditable

unresponsive 4 cold **5** aloof, stoic **6** frigid, remote, stolid **7** distant, passive **8** detached, reserved **9** inhibited, withdrawn **10** forbidding, insentient **11** insensitive, passionless, unemotional **12** uninterested **13** insusceptible, unsusceptible

unrest 6 strife, tumult **7** anarchy, anxiety, ferment, tension, turmoil **8** disorder, disquiet, distress, edginess, upheaval **9** agitation, commotion, confusion **10** inquietude, turbulence, uneasiness **11** disquietude, disturbance, instability **12** perturbation **13** Sturm und Drang

unrestrained 5 bluff, blunt, frank **6** candid, wanton **7** rampant **8** outgoing, uncurbed **9** audacious, excessive, expansive, indulgent, unbridled **10** forthright, immoderate, implacable, inordinate, ungoverned, unhampered **11** extravagant, impassioned, intemperate, overwrought, plainspoken, spontaneous, uninhibited, untrammeled **12** uncontrolled **13** demonstrative, irrepressible, overindulgent

unrestricted 4 free, full, open **9** boundless, extensive, unlimited **10** accessible, unconfined, unfettered, unhampered **11** far-reaching, unqualified, wide-ranging **12** unobstructed **13** unconditional

unripe 3 raw **5** green, young **6** callow, jejune **7** untried **8** emergent, immature, juvenile, unformed, youthful **9** unfledged, untrained **10** unprepared, unseasoned **11** undeveloped **13** inexperienced

unrivaled 4 only, sole **5** alone **6** unique **7** leading, stellar, supreme **8** champion, foremost, greatest, peerless **9** matchless, paramount, principal, unequaled, unmatched **10** inimitable, preeminent, unequalled **11** outstanding, predominant, unsurpassed **12** incomparable, transcendent, unparalleled

unroll 6 expose, extend, reveal, unfurl, unwind **7** exhibit, open out **8** disclose **9** spread out

unromantic 5 sober **8** sensible **9** practical, pragmatic, realistic **10** hard-boiled, hardheaded **11** down-to-earth, levelheaded, utilitarian **12** businesslike, matter-of-fact **13** unsentimental

unruffled 4 calm, cool **6** poised, placid, serene, smooth **7** equable, unmoved **8** composed, tranquil **9** collected, unexcited **10** nonchalant, untroubled **11** unconcerned, undisturbed, unflappable **13** imperturbable, self-possessed

unruly 4 wild **5** rowdy **7** froward, naughty, raucous, wayward, willful **8** contrary, perverse, untoward **9** fractious, obstinate, turbulent **10** boisterous, disorderly, headstrong, illbehaved, rebellious, refractory, tumultuous **11** disobedient, indomitable, intractable **12** contumacious, incorrigible, obstreperous, rambunctious, recalcitrant, ungovernable, unmanageable **13** undisciplined

unsafe 5 risky, shaky **6** chancy **7** erratic, harmful, parlous, rickety, tottery, unsound **8** insecure, perilous, slippery, unstable **9** dangerous, hazardous, uncertain **10** precarious, ramshackle, unreliable, vulnerable **11** threatening, treacherous **12** undependable

unsaid 5 known, tacit **6** silent **7** assumed, implied **8** accepted, implicit, indirect, inferred, presumed, unspoken, unstated, wordless **9** customary, unuttered **10** insinuated, undeclared, understood **11** traditional, unexpressed

unsatisfactory 3 bum **4** lame **5** amiss **8** mediocre **9** defective, deficient **10** inadequate **11** displeasing, substandard **12** unacceptable **13** disappointing,

unsavory 4 rank **5** gross, shady **6** rancid **7** insipid **9** repugnant, repulsive, sickening, tasteless **10** disgusting, flavorless **11** distasteful, ill-flavored, unpalatable **12** disagreeable, unappetizing

unsay 4 lift, void 6 abjure, cancel, disown, recall, recant, revoke 7 nullify, rescind, retract, reverse, suspend 8 abnegate, abrogate, disclaim, forswear, renounce, take back, withdraw 11 countermand

unscathed 4 safe 5 sound, whole 6 intact, unhurt 8 unharmed 9 uninjured, unscarred, untouched 11 unscratched

unscented 8 odor-free, odorless

unschooled 5 naive 7 artless, natural, vacuous 8 ignorant, untaught 9 ingenuous, unstudied, untrained, untutored 10 illiterate, unaffected, uneducated, unlettered 11 empty-headed 12 unartificial, uninstructed

unscramble 5 solve, untie 6 unwind 7 clarify, resolve, restore, sort out, unravel, untwine 8 untangle 9 extricate 11 disentangle 12 disembarrass

unscrupulous 5 shady, venal 7 corrupt, crooked, knavish 8 scheming, wrongful 9 deceitful, dishonest, mercenary, shameless, underhand, unethical 11 underhanded 12 dishonorable, exploitative, unprincipled

unseasonable 8 ill-timed, untimely 12 inconvenient

unseasoned 3 raw 4 flat 5 bland, fresh, green, young 6 callow 7 untried 8 immature 9 credulous, tasteless, unfledged, untrained 10 flavorless 11 unpracticed 13 inexperienced

unseat 3 axe, can 4 boot, buck, fire, oust, sack 5 eject, pitch, purge, throw 6 depose, recall, remove 7 buck off, dismiss, unhorse 8 dethrone, dislodge, displace 9 ostracize

unseemliness 5 gaffe 7 blunder, faux pas 8 solecism 9 barbarism, gaucherie, immodesty, impudence, indecency, vulgarity 10 coarseness, imprudence, incivility, indelicacy 11 impropriety 12 indiscretion

unseemly 8 improper, untoward 9 inelegant, unrefined 10 indecorous, indelicate, malapropos, unbecoming, unsuitable 11 unbefitting 13 inappropriate

unseen 6 hidden 9 concealed, invisible, unnoticed 10 overlooked, unobserved 11 unsuspected

unsentimental see UNROMANTIC

unserviceable 7 useless 10 inoperable, unfeasible, unworkable 11 impractical, unrealistic 13 impracticable, nonfunctional

unsettle 3 vex 4 faze 5 spook, upset 6 bother, flurry, jumble, rattle, ruffle 7 agitate, disturb, fluster, perturb, trouble, unhinge, unnerve 8 bewilder, confound, disarray, disorder, disquiet 9 discomfit 10 disarrange, discompose, disconcert 11 disorganize

unsettled 3 due 4 open 5 fluid, owing, shaky 6 mobile, queasy, shaken, uneasy, unpaid 7 anxious, dubious, mutable, overdue, payable, pending, restive 8 agitated, bothered, doubtful, frontier, restless, troubled, unstable, unsteady, variable 9 disturbed, uncertain, undecided 10 changeable, indecisive, unbalanced, unresolved 11 outstanding, problematic 12 undetermined

unsex 3 fix 4 geld, spay 5 alter 6 change, neuter 8 castrate 9 sterilize 10 emasculate

unshackle 4 free 5 loose 6 loosen, unbind 7 manumit, release, unchain 8 liberate, unfetter 10 emancipate

unshakable 4 firm, sure 5 fixed 6 stable, steady 7 abiding, adamant, settled, staunch 8 resolute 9 steadfast, tenacious, unbending 10 determined, persistent, unwavering, unyielding 11 unfaltering, unrelenting 12 neverfailing 13 unquestioning

unshaped 5 vague 7 nascent 8 formless, inchoate, unformed 9 amorphous, embryonic 11 preliminary, undeveloped 13 indeterminate

unshared 4 sole 6 single, unique 7 private 8 singular 9 exclusive, undivided 10 individual 11 distinctive

unshod 8 barefoot, shoeless 9 discalced 10 barefooted

unsightly 4 ugly 5 gross 6 grisly 7 hideous 9 repulsive 10 ill-favored 12 unattractive

unskillful 5 inept 6 clumsy, gauche 7 awkward, unhandy 8 bumbling, bungling, inexpert 9 ham-handed, incapable, maladroit, stumbling, untrained 11 unpracticed 13 unworkmanlike

unsnarl see UNTANGLE

unsociable 3 shy 4 cold, cool 5 aloof, timid 6 offish, remote, shut-in 7 distant 8 reserved, secluded, solitary 9 diffident, reclusive, unbending, withdrawn 10 unfriendly 11 introverted, standoffish 12 inaccessible, unneighborly

unsoiled 5 clean 8 spotless 9 unspotted, unstained, unsullied, untainted 10 immaculate 11 unblemished, untarnished

unsophisticated 5 corny, green, naive 6 callow, folksy, rustic, simple 7 artless, natural, sincere, uncouth 8 gullible, innocent 9 childlike, ingenuous, unrefined, unworldly

unsorted 5 mixed 6 divers, motley, sundry, varied 7 diverse, jumbled, mingled 8 ungraded 9 disparate, scrambled, unmatched, unrefined 10 variegated 11 diversified 12 multifarious 13 heterogeneous, miscellaneous

unsought 7 unasked, willing 8 unbidden, unwanted 9 undesired, uninvited, unwelcome, voluntary 10 gratuitous, unprompted 11 spontaneous, unrequested, unsolicited

unsound 3 mad 4 weak 5 false, frail, shaky, wrong 6 faulty, flawed, flimsy, infirm, insane, sickly, untrue, weakly 7 cracked, damaged, fragile, invalid 8 decrepit, demented, deranged, specious 9 defective, erroneous, imperfect, incorrect, unhealthy 13 insubstantial

unsparing 5 ample, harsh, stern, tough 6 lavish, severe, strict 7 copious, liberal, onerous, profuse 8 abundant, exacting, generous, prolific, rigorous, ruthless 9 bounteous, bountiful, demanding, plenteous 10 freehanded, munificent, openhanded, unmerciful 11 magnanimous

unspeakable 4 dire, evil 5 awful 6 grisly 7 beastly, ghastly, hateful, heinous, hideous 8 dreadful, ghoulish, gruesome, horrific, shocking 9 appalling, atrocious, execrable, frightful, loathsome, monstrous, obnoxious, repugnant, repulsive, revolting 10 abominable, detestable, disgusting, horrendous, outrageous, scandalous 11 unutterable 13 inexpressible

unspoiled 5 ideal 6 intact, virgin 7 halcyon, idyllic, perfect, untamed 8 arcadian, pastoral, pristine, virginal 9 idealized, undamaged, undefiled, untouched 10 unimpaired 11 unblemished, uncorrupted

unspoken 4 mute 5 tacit 6 hinted, silent, unsaid 7 assumed, implied 8 implicit, inferred, presumed, unstated, wordless 9 intimated, suggested, unuttered 10 undeclared, understood 11 unexpressed

unstable 5 fluid, shaky 6 fickle, shifty, tricky, wobbly 7 dubious, protean, rickety, suspect 8 insecure, rootless, slippery, ticklish, unsteady, variable, volatile, wavering 9 ambiguous, changeful, fluctuant, irregular, mercurial, teetering, uncertain, unsettled 10 capricious, inconstant, precarious 11 vacillating 13 temperamental, unpredictable

unstated 5 tacit 6 latent, unsaid 7 assumed, implied 8 implicit 10 understood

unsteady 5 rocky, shaky, tippy 6 uneven, wobbly 7 erratic, mutable, rickety,

varying 8 shifting, unstable, variable 9 changeful, irregular, tottering 10 changeable, inconstant *British:* 5 wonky

unstudied 5 naive 6 casual, improv, simple 7 artless, natural, offhand 8 careless, informal, unforced, unversed 9 extempore, guileless, impromptu, ingenuous, makeshift, unlabored, unlearned, unplanned, untutored 10 improvised, nonchalant, unaffected, unpolished, unschooled 11 extemporary, spontaneous, uncontrived, unrehearsed 13 improvisatory

unstylish 4 drab, dull 5 dated, dowdy, fusty, passé, ratty, tacky 6 démodé, frumpy, old-hat, shabby, stodgy 7 vintage 8 outdated, outmoded 9 inelegant, moth-eaten, out-of-date 10 antiquated, oldfangled 12 old-fashioned 13 unfashionable

unsubstantial 4 thin 5 frail, shaky 6 feeble, flimsy, infirm 7 fragile, shadowy, tenuous, unsound 8 ethereal, illusory 9 dreamlike, imaginary, spiritual, unearthly 10 immaterial, impalpable, intangible 11 implausible, incorporeal, nonmaterial, nonphysical 12 metaphysical

unsuitable 5 inapt, undue, unfit 7 awkward, jarring 8 ill-timed, improper, unfitted, unseemly, untimely 9 ill-suited 10 ill-adapted, inadequate, inapposite, malapropos, mismatched, unbecoming 11 inadvisable, inopportune, unbefitting, unqualified 12 incompatible, infelicitous, unacceptable, unseasonable 13 inappropriate

unsullied 4 pure 5 clean 6 chaste 8 flawless, spotless, unsoiled 9 blameless, exemplary, guiltless, stainless, taintless, undefiled 10 immaculate 11 unblemished, untarnished

unsure 5 dicey, shaky 6 wobbly 7 dubious, unclear 8 doubtful, insecure, unstable, wavering 9 fluctuant, skeptical, uncertain, undecided 10 ambivalent, indecisive, irresolute, unreliable 11 unconvinced, vacillating 12 questionable, undependable 13 indeterminate, untrustworthy

unsurpassable 7 supreme 8 ultimate 9 matchless 10 consummate, preeminent 12 transcendent

unsusceptible 6 immune, inured 8 hardened 9 impassive, resistant 10 impervious 11 insensitive 12 invulnerable, unresponsive

unsuspecting 5 naive 6 unwary 8 gullible, trustful, trusting 9 confiding, credulous, imprudent 10 incautious

unswerving see UNFALTERING

unsympathetic 4 cold, cool 5 chill, stony 6 averse 7 callous, haughty, unmoved 8 detached, lukewarm 9 apathetic, unfeeling, unpitying 10 disdainful, hard-boiled 11 coldhearted, hardhearted, indifferent, insensitive, unconcerned, uncongenial 12 contemptuous, stonyhearted, unresponsive 13 disinterested

untactful 4 flip, rash, rude 5 brash, nervy 6 brazen 8 flippant, insolent 9 audacious, impolitic, imprudent, maladroit 10 indiscreet 11 impertinent, thoughtless 12 presumptuous, undiplomatic

untamed 4 wild 5 brute, feral 6 carnal, fierce, savage 7 bestial, brutish 8 barbaric 9 primitive 11 uncivilized

untangle 5 solve 7 clear up, explain, resolve, unravel, unsnarl, untwine, untwist 9 elucidate, extricate, interpret 10 disembroil, disentwine, straighten, unscramble 11 disencumber 12 disembarrass

untaught 5 naive 7 natural 8 ignorant, nescient 9 intuitive, untrained, untutored 10 uneducated, unlettered, unschooled 11 empty-headed, instinctive, instinctual, spontaneous 12 uncultivated, uninstructed

untempered 6 wanton 7 extreme 9 excessive 10 gratuitous, immoderate, inordinate 11 extravagant 12 unrestrained

untenable 5 wrong 6 faulty, flimsy 10 inadequate 12 indefensible

untended 5 seedy 7 rickety, run-down 8 decrepit, derelict, deserted, forsaken, tattered 9 neglected 10 ramshackle, tumbledown, uncared-for 11 dilapidated

Unter den ___ 6 Linden

untested 6 intact, unused 7 untried 8 unproved, unproven 11 unpracticed

unthinkable 10 impossible, incredible, outlandish 12 preposterous, unimaginable 13 extraordinary, inconceivable, unprecedented

unthinking 8 careless, feckless, habitual, heedless, knee-jerk, uncaring 9 automatic, reflexive, unheeding, unmindful 10 distracted, unintended 11 inattentive, inadvertent, instinctive, instinctual, involuntary, perfunctory, spontaneous, thoughtless 12 unreflective

unthrifty 6 lavish, wanton 7 ruinous 8 prodigal, wasteful 9 imprudent 10 profligate 11 extravagant, improvident 12 uneconomical

untidy 5 messy 6 sloppy 7 chaotic, jum-

bled, unkempt 8 confused, littered, slapdash, slipshod, slovenly 9 cluttered 10 disheveled, disordered, disorderly, topsy-turvy 11 disarranged, dishevelled 12 disorganized, unsystematic

untie 5 let go 6 loosen, unbind, unknot, unlace, unlash 7 release, resolve, set free 8 unstring 9 extricate 11 disencumber, disentangle 12 disembarrass

until 4 up to 6 before 7 prior to 11 in advance of

untimely 5 early, undue 9 premature 10 malapropos 11 ill-seasoned, inopportune 12 unseasonable 13 inappropriate

untiring 7 devoted, patient 8 diligent, enduring 9 assiduous, ceaseless, dedicated, energetic, unceasing 10 determined, persistent, unflagging, unwavering, unwearying 11 persevering, unfaltering 13 indefatigable, inexhaustible

untold 4 huge, vast 7 immense 8 enormous, gigantic 9 countless 10 prodigious 11 innumerable, uncountable 12 incalculable 13 indescribable

untouchable 5 leper 6 pariah 7 outcast 8 outcaste

untouched 4 pure 5 sound, whole 6 intact, virgin 7 unmoved 8 flawless, pristine, unharmed, unmarred, untapped, virginal 9 undamaged, unspoiled 10 unaffected 11 unblemished, unconcerned, unimpressed

untoward 6 unruly 7 adverse, awkward, froward, ungodly, unhappy, unlucky 8 ill-fated, improper, indecent, luckless, unseemly 9 fractious, unfitting, vexatious 10 ill-starred, indecorous, indelicate, refractory, unbecoming 11 detrimental, intractable, star-crossed, troublesome, unfortunate 12 inconvenient, recalcitrant, ungovernable, unmanageable, unpropitious

untrained see UNSKILLED

untrammeled 8 uncurbed 9 unimpeded 10 unconfined, unfettered, ungoverned, unhampered 11 uninhibited 12 unobstructed, unrestrained, unrestricted

untried 3 raw 5 fresh, green 6 callow, rookie 8 unproved, untested 10 innovative, pioneering, unseasoned 11 unpracticed 13 inexperienced, unprecedented

untroubled 4 calm 5 still 6 blithe, placid, serene 7 halcyon 8 carefree, composed, peaceful, tranquil 9 easygoing, unruffled 10 insouciant, nonchalant 11 unconcerned, unperturbed 12 lighthearted

untrue 4 fake 5 false, wrong 7 inexact 8 disloyal, specious 9 erroneous, faithless, imprecise, incorrect 10 fictitious,

inaccurate, unfaithful *combining form:*
5 pseud 6 pseudo

untrustworthy 5 shady 6 shifty, unsafe,
unsure 7 devious, dubious 8 disloyal,
slippery, two-faced 9 deceptive, negligent, two-timing 10 fly-by-night, unreliable 11 duplicitous 12 questionable,
undependable 13 double-dealing, irresponsible

untruth 3 fib, lie 4 sham 5 error 6 canard,
deceit 7 blarney, fallacy, falsity, fiction,
hogwash 9 deception, duplicity, falsehood, falseness, hypocrisy, mendacity
11 fabrication, insincerity 12 misstatement 13 prevarication

untruthful 4 sham 5 bogus, false, lying,
phony 7 knavish 8 specious 9 deceitful,
dishonest, erroneous, incorrect 10 fictitious, inaccurate, mendacious

untutored see UNSCHOOLED

unusable 7 outworn, useless 8 obsolete
9 worthless 10 inoperable, unavailing,
unworkable 11 impractical, unrealistic
12 inapplicable 13 nonfunctional

unused 3 new 4 idle 5 fresh 6 excess
7 dormant, surplus 8 leftover, residual
9 untouched

unusual 3 odd 4 rare 6 quaint, unique
7 bizarre, curious, special, strange
8 aberrant, abnormal, peculiar, singular, uncommon, atypical, unwonted
9 anomalous, different, eccentric, irregular 11 exceptional 13 extraordinary

unusually 4 very 5 extra 6 rarely, seldom
8 markedly 9 curiously, extremely,
strangely 10 abnormally, especially,
peculiarly, remarkably, strikingly,
uncommonly 11 exceedingly 12 infrequently, particularly

unutterable 5 taboo 7 awesome 9 ineffable 11 unspeakable 13 indescribable,
inexpressible

unvaried 4 like, same 5 alike 7 uniform
9 identical 10 consistent, unchanging
11 undeviating

unvarnished see UNDISGUISED

unvarying see UNCHANGING

unveil see UNCOVER

unversed 3 raw 5 fresh, green 6 callow
7 untried 8 inexpert 9 unfledged
10 unfamiliar, unseasoned 11 uninitiated, unpracticed 12 unaccustomed
13 inexperienced

unwanted see UNWELCOME

unwarranted 5 undue 8 baseless 9 misguided, unfounded 10 gratuitous,
groundless, immoderate, unprovoked
11 extravagant, inexcusable, injudicious, uncalled-for, unjustified 12 indefensible, unreasonable 13 insupportable, unjustifiable, unsupportable

unwary 5 brash, hasty 8 careless,
gullible, heedless, reckless 9 credulous,
impetuous, imprudent, unguarded
10 ill-advised, incautious, indiscreet
11 thoughtless 12 unsuspecting

unwavering see UNFALTERING

unwelcome 7 unasked 8 unsought,
unwanted 9 undesired, uninvited
11 undesirable 12 unacceptable
13 objectionable

unwell 3 ill 4 sick 5 frail, shaky 6 ailing,
feeble, infirm, offish, peaked, queasy,
sickly, wobbly 8 diseased, stricken
9 afflicted, enfeebled, unhealthy
10 indisposed 11 debilitated

unwholesome 4 foul 5 toxic 6 sickly
7 adverse, baneful, corrupt, harmful,
immoral, noisome, noxious, obscene,
ruinous, unsound 8 diseased 9 injurious, loathsome, offensive, unhealthy
10 disgusting, pernicious, subversive
11 deleterious, detrimental, unhealthful
12 insalubrious

unwieldy 5 bulky 7 awkward, massive
8 cumbrous 9 ponderous 10 burdensome, cumbersome 12 unmanageable

unwilling 5 loath 6 averse 8 grudging,
hesitant 9 obstinate, reluctant 10 indisposed 11 disinclined

unwind 4 rest, undo 5 let go, relax
6 loosen, unbend, uncoil, unfold,
unreel, unroll 7 ease off, slacken,
unravel 8 calm down, kick back,
loosen up

unwise 4 rash 5 silly 6 stupid 7 asinine,
fatuous, foolish, idiotic, witless 8 reckless 9 brainless, foolhardy, ill-judged,
imbecilic, impolitic, imprudent, ludicrous, misguided, senseless 10 ill-
advised, indiscreet, ridiculous
11 impractical, injudicious, thoughtless, undesirable, unfortunate 13 unintelligent

unwitting 6 chance 7 unaware 8 ignorant, innocent 9 haphazard, oblivious,
unknowing, unmindful, unplanned
10 unfamiliar, uninformed, unintended
11 inadvertent 12 unacquainted

unwonted 4 rare 6 signal, unique
7 notable, unusual 8 singular, uncommon 10 remarkable, unexpected
11 exceptional 12 unaccustomed
13 extraordinary

unworkable 7 useless 8 quixotic 9 half-
baked 10 impossible, infeasible, inoperable, unfeasible 11 impractical, unrealistic 12 inapplicable 13 impracticable,
nonfunctional

unworldly 5 naive 6 astral, dreamy, simple 7 artless, natural 8 ethereal, innocent, trusting 9 celestial, ingenuous,

spiritual, unearthly, visionary
11 impractical 13 inexperienced
unworthy 6 no-good 7 ignoble 8 shameful, unseemly 9 no-account, unmerited, worthless 10 unbecoming 11 disgraceful, inexcusable, undeserving
unwrap see UNCOVER
unwritten 4 oral 5 blank, tacit 6 latent, spoken, verbal 7 assumed 8 accepted, implicit 10 understood 11 traditional, word-of-mouth 12 conventional
unyielding 4 firm, grim, hard 5 fixed, rigid, stern, stiff, tough 6 dogged, mulish 7 adamant 8 hard-core, obdurate, stubborn 9 hard-nosed, insistent, obstinate, pigheaded, steadfast, unbending 10 determined, headstrong, implacable, inexorable, inflexible, persistent, relentless 11 intractable, unrelenting 12 pertinacious, single-minded, unappeasable
up 4 hike, jump, lift, rise 5 above, ahead, arise, boost, built, mount, raise, risen 6 ascend, arisen, lifted, versed 7 abreast, promote 8 familiar, increase, informed, positive 9 au courant, northward 10 acquainted, conversant *prefix:* 3 ana, sur
up-and-coming 7 go-ahead, hot-shot 8 aspiring 9 promising 11 presumptive, prospective 12 enterprising
upbeat 4 rosy 6 cheery 7 buoyant, hopeful 8 cheerful, positive, sanguine 9 confidant, expectant, promising 10 heartening, optimistic 12 Pollyannaish
upbraid 4 lash, rate 5 chide, scold 6 berate, rail at, rebuke, revile, scorch 7 bawl out, censure, chasten, chew out, reprove, scourge, tell off 8 admonish, chastise, reproach 9 castigate, criticize, dress down, reprimand 10 tongue-lash, vituperate
upbringing 7 nurture, rearing 8 training 9 schooling
upchuck 4 barf, hurl, puke, spew 5 heave, retch, vomit 6 spit up 7 bring up, throw up 8 disgorge 11 regurgitate
upcoming 7 looming, nearing, pending 8 expected, foreseen, imminent 9 advancing, impending, onrushing 11 anticipated, approaching, forthcoming, prospective
up-country 4 bush 6 inland, sticks, upland 7 outback 8 backland, frontier, interior, outlying, woodland 9 backwater, backwoods, boondocks 10 hinterland, timberland
update 5 amend, brief, renew 6 inform, revamp, revise, revive 7 apprise, enhance, improve, refresh, restore,

rundown, upgrade 8 renovate 9 modernize, refurbish 10 rejuvenate
upend 4 beat, best, drub, flip, lick, skin, trim, whip 5 cream, crush, upset 6 invert, subdue, thrash, topple, unseat, wallop 7 capsize, clobber, conquer, overrun, shellac, trounce 8 dethrone, lambaste, overcome, overturn, vanquish 9 overpower, overwhelm, subjugate
upgrade 4 hike, rise 5 boost, raise 6 prefer 7 advance, elevate, enhance, improve, promote 8 increase 9 promotion 10 betterment 11 advancement, improvement 12 breakthrough
upheaval 6 clamor, outcry, tumult, upturn 7 ferment, turmoil 8 churning, disaster, disorder 9 cataclysm, commotion 10 alteration, convulsion, disruption 11 catastrophe
uphill 4 hard 6 rising, rugged, taxing 7 arduous, labored, operose, tedious 8 climbing, grueling, toilsome 9 ascending, difficult, effortful, gruelling, laborious, punishing, strenuous, wearisome
uphold 3 aid 4 back, help, lift, prop 5 brace, carry, hoist, raise 6 assist, back up, bear up, buoy up, defend, second 7 bolster, elevate, justify, shore up, support, sustain 8 advocate, backstop, buttress, champion, maintain, side with 9 vindicate
upkeep 4 cost 7 expense 8 overhead 11 expenditure, maintenance
upland 4 mesa 5 table 7 plateau
uplift 4 buoy 5 cheer, hoist, raise 6 take up 7 animate, elevate, enliven, gladden, hearten 8 brighten, embolden, inspirit 9 encourage 10 exhilarate, strengthen
upon 4 atop *prefix:* 3 epi
upper class 4 rank 5 elite 6 gentry 7 peerage, quality, society, who's who 8 affluent, nobility, noblesse, well-to-do 9 blue blood, gentility, haut monde 10 patricians, patriciate 11 aristocracy 13 carriage trade, Establishment
upper hand 4 edge, sway 5 leg up 7 control, mastery 8 leverage 9 advantage, dominance 10 ascendancy 11 superiority 12 predominance
uppermost 3 top 6 apical 7 highest 8 loftiest
uppity 4 smug 5 aloof, brash 6 lordly, sniffy, snippy, snooty, snotty 7 forward, haughty, pompous 8 arrogant, cavalier 9 conceited, egotistic, imperious, know-it-all, presuming 10 disdainful, high-handed 11 overweening, pretentious 12 contemptuous, presumptuous, supercilious 13 self-asserting, self-assertive, self-important

upright 4 fair, good, just, pure, true **5** erect, moral, noble, piano **6** honest, raised **7** correct, ethical **8** elevated, goalpost, standing, vertical, virtuous **9** equitable, exemplary, honorable, impartial **10** principled, scrupulous **13** conscientious, perpendicular

uprightness 5 honor **6** repute, virtue **7** honesty, probity **8** morality, nobility **9** character, integrity, rectitude **13** righteousness

uprising 4 riot **6** mutiny, revolt **8** upheaval **9** rebellion **10** insurgence, revolution **12** insurrection

uproar 3 din, row **4** coil, fuss, to-do, riot **5** babel, brawl, broil, chaos, furor, hooha, melee, whirl **6** bedlam, clamor, fracas, furore, hassle, hubbub, mayhem, pother, racket, ruckus, rumpus, shindy, tumult **7** shindig, turmoil **8** brouhaha, disorder, foofaraw **9** commotion, confusion **10** hullabaloo, hurly-burly, turbulence **11** pandemonium

uproarious 5 noisy, rowdy **7** comical, rackety, raucous, riotous **8** brawling, clattery, mirthful, strident **9** clamorous, hilarious **10** clangorous, hysterical, resounding, rollicking, tumultuous **12** obstreperous **13** sidesplitting

uproot 4 grub, move, weed **8** displace, overturn, supplant **9** eradicate, extirpate, overthrow, supersede **10** annihilate, transplant **11** exterminate

upset 4 ail, ill **5** worry **6** bother, defeat, dismay, invert, jumble, muddle, topple, tumble **7** afflict, agitate, capsize, disturb, fluster, invalid, jittery, jumbled, muddled, perturb, rattled, reverse, tip over, toppled, trouble, unnerve, worried **8** agitated, bewilder, bothered, confound, confused, disarray, dismayed, disorder, distress, overturn, troubled, turn over, unnerved **9** afflicted, confusion, disturbed, flustered, knock over, overthrow, perturbed **10** bewildered, confounded, disconcert, disordered, distracted, distressed, indisposed, invalidate, overthrown, overturned, tipped over **11** overwrought **12** apprehensive, disconcerted

upshot 5 issue **6** burden, climax, effect, ending, finish, result **7** outcome, purport **9** substance **10** conclusion, denouement **11** consequence, culmination, termination **12** significance

upside-down 7 chaotic, haywire, jumbled **8** backward, confused, inverted, pell-mell, reversed **10** disordered, overturned, topsy-turvy **13** helter-skelter

upstanding see UPRIGHT

upstart 5 comer **7** parvenu **8** outsider

9 arriviste, pretender **12** nouveau riche **13** social climber

upsurge 4 gain, jump, rise, wave **5** boost, spurt **6** growth **7** advance **8** increase

uptight 4 edgy **5** riled, tense **6** uneasy **7** anxious, nervous, restive, worried

up to 4 till **5** until **6** before **11** in advance of

up-to-date 6 modern, modish, timely, trendy **7** abreast, à la mode, current, stylish **8** advanced, brand-new, contempo **9** au courant **10** avant-garde **11** cutting-edge, fashionable **12** contemporary **13** state-of-the-art

upturn 4 jump, rise **6** growth **8** increase **11** improvement

Urania see MUSE

Uranus 6 planet *mother, wife:* **4** Gaea *offspring:* **6** Titans **8** Cyclopes *overthrower, son:* **6** Cronus

urban 9 municipal **12** metropolitan

urbane 5 suave **6** poised, smooth **7** elegant, genteel, politic, refined **8** cultured, debonair, gracious, polished **9** civilized, distingué **10** cultivated, diplomatic **12** cosmopolitan **13** sophisticated

urbanize 6 citify

urchin 3 imp **4** brat **5** child, gamin, scamp **10** ragamuffin

Urdur see NORN

urge 3 egg, sic, yen **4** coax, goad, itch, lust, prod, push, spur, wish **5** drive, egg on, impel, press, prick, set on, tar on **6** adjure, cajole, compel, demand, desire, exhort, incite, induce, needle, prompt, propel **7** beseech, conjure, craving, entreat, implore, impulse, inspire, longing, passion, promote, propose, provoke, solicit, wheedle **8** advocate, appetite, blandish, pressure, yearning **9** encourage, instigate, stimulate **12** high-pressure

urgency 6 duress, stress **8** exigence, exigency, pressure **9** necessity **10** compulsion, insistence

urgent 5 vital **6** crying **7** burning, clamant, crucial, driving, exigent, instant, present **8** critical, pressing **9** clamorous, demanding, immediate, impelling, insistent, momentous **10** compelling, imperative **11** importunate

Uriel 9 archangel

Uris novel 3 Haj (The) **5** QB VII **6** Exodus **7** Trinity **9** Battle Cry, Mitla Pass **10** Angry Hills (The), Redemption

urn 4 vase **6** vessel **7** samovar *Greek:* **7** amphora

Ursa Major 9 Great Bear **11** Great Dipper

Ursa Minor 10 Little Bear **12** Little Dip-

per *star:* 7 Polaris 8 polestar
9 North Star
Uruguay *capital:* 10 Montevideo *language:* 7 Spanish *monetary unit:* 4 peso
neighbor: 6 Brazil 9 Argentina *river:*
7 La Plata 8 Río Negro
usable 6 liquid 7 running, working
9 adaptable, available, operative
10 accessible, applicable, employable,
expendable, functional, marketable,
negotiable 11 exploitable, operational,
serviceable
usage 3 way 4 form, mode, wont
5 habit, sense 6 action, amount, custom, manner, method, praxis 7 process
8 habitude, practice 9 formality, procedure 10 convention
use 3 ply 4 wont, work 5 apply, avail,
habit, serve, treat, value, wield, worth
6 custom, demand, employ, handle, liking, manage, manner 7 benefit, exploit,
operate, purpose, service, utility, utilize
8 deal with, exercise, exertion, function, impose on, occasion, practice,
regulate 9 advantage, habituate, objective, relevance 10 employment, manipulate 11 application
used 8 pre-owned, shopworn 10 second-hand
used up 5 all in, spent 6 bleary, effete,
sapped, wasted 7 drained, emptied, fargone, worn-out 8 consumed, depleted
9 exhausted, washed-out
useful 3 fit 4 meet 5 handy, utile 7 helpful 8 fruitful, suitable, valuable 9 favorable, practical 10 beneficial, convenient, functional, productive, profitable,
propitious, worthwhile 11 appropriate,
practicable, serviceable, utilitarian
12 advantageous
usefulness 5 value, worth 7 fitness, service, utility 8 function 9 advantage, relevance, substance 10 expedience, expediency 12 practicality 13 applicability
useless 4 idle, vain 5 inept 6 futile
7 inutile 8 bootless, hopeless, unusable
9 fruitless, pointless, worthless
10 unavailing, unworkable 11 impractical, ineffective, ineffectual, inoperative
12 unproductive, unprofitable
13 impracticable, nonfunctional
user 5 buyer 6 addict 8 consumer, customer, utilizer
use up 5 drain, spend 6 devour, expend
7 consume, deplete, exhaust 8 draw
down 10 run through
usher 4 lead, seat 5 guide 6 escort 7 conduct, precede 9 conductor 10 doorkeeper
usher in 5 begin, greet, start 6 launch
7 kick off, trumpet, welcome

8 announce, commence, initiate, proclaim 9 institute, introduce, originate
10 inaugurate
usual 5 stock, typic 6 common, kosher,
normal, wonted 7 average, regular,
routine, typical, vanilla 8 accepted,
everyday, expected, familiar, habitual,
ordinary, orthodox, standard, workaday 9 customary, prevalent, quotidian
10 accustomed, prevailing 11 commonplace, established 12 conventional,
unremarkable
usually 6 mainly, mostly 7 as a rule
8 commonly, normally 9 generally, routinely 10 habitually, ordinarily 11 customarily
usurer 7 Shylock 9 loan shark 11 moneylender
usurp 5 wrest 6 assume 7 preempt
8 arrogate, displace, supplant 10 commandeer 11 appropriate
Utah *capital:* 12 Salt Lake City *city:*
4 Orem 5 Ogden, Provo *college, university:* 12 Brigham Young *lake:* 6 Powell
9 Great Salt *motto:* 8 Industry *mountain:*
5 Kings (Peak) *nickname:* 7 Beehive
(State) *park:* 4 Zion 5 Bryce 6 Arches
11 Canyonlands *river:* 5 Green 6 Sevier
state bird: 14 California gull *state flower:*
8 sego lily *state tree:* 10 blue spruce
utensil 3 pan, pot 4 fork, tool 5 knife,
spoon 6 device, vessel 8 saucepan, teaspoon 9 implement 10 instrument
uterus 4 womb
Uther Pendragon *son:* 6 Arthur *wife:*
6 Ygerne 7 Igraine
utile 5 handy 6 useful 7 working 9 available, operative, practical 10 accessible,
convenient, dependable, functional
11 practicable, serviceable
utilitarian 6 useful 9 practical, pragmatic
10 functional *philosopher:* 4 Mill (John
Stuart) 7 Bentham (Jeremy)
utility 3 use 7 benefit, fitness, service
8 function 9 advantage, relevance
10 efficiency, usefulness 12 practicality
13 applicability
utilize 3 use 5 apply, spend 6 bestow,
deploy, employ, handle, occupy
7 exploit 8 exercise 11 appropriate
utmost 3 top 4 acme, apex, best, peak
6 height, zenith 7 extreme, highest,
maximal, maximum, supreme 8 farthest, furthest, greatest, pinnacle,
remotest, ultimate 9 damnedest,
extremity
utopia 4 Eden, Zion 5 bliss 6 heaven
7 Elysium 8 paradise 9 Cockaigne,
dreamland, Shangri-la 10 dreamworld
12 promised land 13 Elysian fields
Utopia author 4 More (Thomas)

utopian 5 ideal, lofty **6** edenic **7** dreamer **8** arcadian, fanciful, idealist, quixotic **9** grandiose, ideologue, visionary **10** chimerical, idealistic, impossible, millennial, unfeasible **11** impractical **12** otherworldly **13** castle-builder, impracticable

utter 3 say **4** damn, dang, darn, rank, talk, tell **5** sheer, speak, stark, state, total, voice **6** arrant, dashed, deuced, reveal **7** blasted, blessed, declare, deliver, divulge, flat-out **8** absolute, bring out, complete, crashing, disclose, infernal, outright, positive, throw out **9** downright, out-and-out, pronounce, verbalize **10** confounded, consummate **11** come out with, straight-out, unmitigated, unqualified **13** thoroughgoing

utterance 4 rant, vent, word **5** voice **6** speech **7** oration **8** delivery, speaking **9** assertion, discourse, statement **10** expression, revelation **11** declaration **12** announcement, articulation **13** pronouncement, verbalization

utterly 4 just **5** plumb, quite **6** in toto **7** totally **8** entirely **9** perfectly **10** absolutely, altogether, completely, thoroughly

uttermost 4 last **5** final **7** extreme, outmost **8** farthest, furthest, remotest

Utu see SHAMASH

Uzbekistan *capital:* **8** Tashkent *city:* **7** Bokhara, Bukhara **9** Samarkand, Samarqand *desert:* **8** Kyzyl Kum *enclave:* **10** Karakalpak *monetary unit:* **3** sum *neighbor:* **9** Kazakstan **10** Kazakhstan, Kyrgyzstan, Tajikistan **11** Afghanistan **12** Turkmenistan *river:* **8** Amu Dar'ya, Syr Dar'ya **9** Zeravshan *sea:* **4** Aral

V

vacancy 4 void **6** vacuum **7** opening **8** idleness **9** blankness, emptiness

vacant 4 bare, free, idle, open, void **5** blank, clear, empty, inane, stark **6** unused **7** deadpan, vacuous **8** deserted, unfilled **9** abandoned, impassive **10** tenantless, unoccupied **11** emptyheaded **12** inexpressive

vacate 4 quit, void **5** annul, clear, empty, leave **6** bow out, give up, repeal, revoke **7** abandon, rescind, retract, reverse **8** abrogate, check out, dissolve, evacuate **9** discharge **10** relinquish

vacation 4 rest, trip **5** break, leave **6** recess **7** holiday, leisure, respite, time off **8** furlough, interval **10** sabbatical **12** intermission

vacationer 7 tourist, tripper **9** weekender **10** rubberneck **12** holidaymaker

vaccination 4 shot **7** booster **9** injection **11** inoculation

vaccine 4 shot **5** serum **9** antiserum **11** preparation *inventor:* **6** Jenner (Edward)

vacillate 4 sway, yo-yo **5** waver **6** dither, falter, teeter, waggle **7** swither, whiffle **8** hesitate **9** alternate, fluctuate, oscillate **10** equivocate **12** shilly-shally

vacillating 4 weak **6** fickle, unsure, wobbly **8** hesitant, shifting, unstable, unsteady **9** fluctuant, tentative, uncertain, undecided, unsettled **10** changeable, inconstant, indecisive, irresolute **12** shilly-shally

vacillation 5 doubt **8** to-and-fro, wavering **9** hesitancy **10** fickleness, indecision **12** irresolution, shilly-shally

vacuity 4 hole, void **6** cavity, hollow, vacuum **7** inanity **9** black hole, blankness, ditsiness, ditziness, emptiness, stupidity **10** hollowness **11** nothingness

vacuous 4 idle, void **5** blank, empty, inane, silly **6** stupid, vacant **7** foolish, shallow **11** birdbrained, empty-headed, superficial

vacuum 4 void **5** space **7** suction **9** emptiness **11** nothingness *bottle:* **5** dewar **7** thermos

vacuum tube 5 diode **6** triode **7** tetrode *casing:* **4** bulb

vade mecum 5 guide **6** manual **8** Baedeker, handbook **9** guidebook **11** enchiridion

___ **Vadis** 3 Quo

vagabond 3 bum 4 hobo 5 gypsy, idler, rogue, rover, tramp 6 picaro, roamer 7 drifter, migrant, nomadic, vagrant, wastrel 8 bohemian, clochard, picaroon, runabout, runagate, traveler, wanderer 9 itinerant, transient, wandering 11 peripatetic

vagarious 6 fickle 7 erratic, flighty, mutable, wayward 8 unstable, volatile 9 impulsive, mercurial, whimsical 10 capricious, inconstant 13 unpredictable

vagary 3 bee 4 whim 5 crank, fancy, freak, humor, quirk 6 megrim, whimsy 7 caprice, fantasy 8 crotchet

vagrancy 6 roving 7 roaming 8 drifting, nomadism, rambling 9 wandering 10 itinerancy

vagrant see VAGABOND

vague 3 dim 4 hazy 5 blear, faint, foggy, fuzzy, gauzy, misty, muddy, woozy 6 bleary, blurry, cloudy, dreamy, slight, vacant 7 inexact, obscure, shadowy, unclear 8 confused, nebulous, vaporous 9 ambiguous, dreamlike, enigmatic, imprecise, uncertain 10 diaphanous, indefinite, indistinct 13 indeterminate, unsubstantial

vain 4 idle 5 empty, proud 6 futile, hollow, otiose 7 foppish, haughty, stuck-up, trivial, useless 8 abortive, arrogant, boastful, bootless, nugatory 9 conceited, fruitless, valueless, worthless 10 egocentric, profitless, sophomoric, unavailing 11 egotistical, ineffective, ineffectual 12 narcissistic, unproductive, unprofitable, unsuccessful 13 self-important

vainglorious 8 arrogant, boastful, bragging, puffed-up, vaunting 9 conceited, egotistic 10 swaggering 11 egotistical 12 supercilious

vainglory 4 pomp 5 pride 6 egoism, vanity 7 conceit, egotism 9 arrogance 10 pretension 11 haughtiness 12 boastfulness

valance 5 drape 6 pelmet 7 curtain, drapery 10 lambrequin

vale 4 dale, dell, glen 5 combe 6 dingle, hollow, valley

valediction 5 adieu 7 good-bye 8 farewell 11 leave-taking

valedictory see VALEDICTION

valentine 4 card, dear, love 7 beloved, darling, tribute 10 sweetheart

valet 7 servant 9 attendant 10 manservant

valiant 4 bold 5 brave 6 heroic, plucky 7 doughty, gallant, valiant 8 fearless, intrepid 10 chivalrous, courageous

11 lionhearted **12** greathearted, stouthearted

valid 4 just, true 5 legal, solid, sound 6 cogent, lawful, potent, proven 7 binding, in force, logical, telling 8 attested, bona fide, credible, forceful 9 effective, effectual, operative 10 acceptable, compelling, convincing, legitimate, persuasive 11 justifiable, trustworthy 12 well-grounded

validate 5 prove 6 affirm, ratify, verify 7 approve, bear out, certify, confirm, endorse, justify, probate 8 legalize, sanction 10 legitimate, legitimize 11 corroborate, rubber-stamp 12 authenticate, substantiate

validity 5 force, proof 7 cogency, potency 8 efficacy 9 soundness 10 lawfulness 13 effectiveness

valise 3 bag 4 grip 6 kit bag, suiter 7 handbag, Pullman 8 gripsack, suitcase 9 gladstone, two-suiter 10 weekend bag 11 portmanteau 12 overnight bag, traveling bag 13 traveling case

Valjean's pursuer 6 Javert

Valkyrie 6 maiden 8 Brynhild

valley 4 dale, dell, glen, vale, wadi 5 basin, combe, gulch, gully, swale 6 canyon, dingle, hollow, ravine 10 depression *Africa-Asia:* 4 Rift 9 Great Rift *Alps:* 11 Grindelwald *ancient Greece:* 5 Nemea *Asia:* 7 Fergana *California:* 4 Napa 5 Death, Squaw 7 Central 8 Imperial, Yosemite 11 San Fernando *Dead Sea area:* 6 Arabah *Dominican Republic:* 5 Cibao *Egypt:* 6 Kharga *England:* 5 Doone *Germany:* 4 Ruhr *Greece:* 5 Tembi, Tempe *India:* 4 Kulu 7 Kashmir (Vale of) *Ireland:* 5 Avoca, Ovoca *Israel:* 4 Elah *Lebanon:* 4 Biqa 5 Bekaa *moon:* 4 rill 5 rille *New York:* 12 Sleepy Hollow *Pennsylvania:* 7 Nittany *Scotland:* 7 Glen Roy *Switzerland:* 5 Hasli 8 Engadine 11 Grindelwald *Virginia:* 10 Shenandoah *Washington:* 11 Grand Coulee

Valmiki's epic 8 Ramayana

valor 4 guts 6 mettle, spirit, virtue 7 bravery, courage, heroism, prowess, stomach 8 chivalry, valiance, valiancy 9 fortitude, gallantry 10 resolution

valorous see VALIANT

valse 5 waltz

valuable 4 dear 6 costly, prized, useful, worthy 8 precious 9 expensive, important, rewarding, treasured 10 satisfying, worthwhile

valuate 4 rate 5 assay, price 6 assess, survey 7 adjudge 8 appraise, estimate

valuation 4 cost, rate 5 price, worth 6 rating 7 opinion 8 estimate, judgment

9 appraisal **10** assessment, estimation **12** appreciation

value 4 cost, rate **5** assay, gauge, judge, price, prize, scale, worth **6** assess, assign, charge, esteem, figure, reckon, regard, return, survey **7** account, apprize, care for, cherish, compute, quality, respect, utility **8** appraise, estimate, evaluate, quantity, treasure **9** appraisal, principle **10** appreciate, assessment, equivalent, importance **11** market price **12** denomination

valve 3 tap **4** cock, flap, gate **6** device, faucet, poppet, spigot **7** hydrant, petcock, shutoff **8** stopcock **9** regulator *cardiac:* **6** mitral **8** bicuspid

vamoose 3 git **4** scat **5** leave, scram, split **6** beat it, begone, cut out, decamp, depart, get out **7** run away, skiddoo, take off **8** clear out **9** skedaddle

vamp 3 fix **4** fake, lure, mend, wile **5** ad-lib, flirt, intro, patch, siren, tempt **6** cook up, entice, groove, lead-in, make up, repair, seduce **7** beguile, charmer, rebuild **8** inveigle **9** fabricate, formulate, improvise, refurbish, temptress **10** gold digger, seductress **11** enchantress, extemporize, femme fatale

vampire 3 bat **5** lamia **6** undead **7** Dracula **9** Nosferatu **11** bloodsucker

van 3 car **4** head, lead, wing **5** front, truck, wagon **7** minibus **11** cutting edge, leading edge

vandal 3 Hun **5** yahoo **6** looter **8** pillager **9** despoiler, destroyer, plunderer, spoliator

vandalize 5 smash, trash, wreck **6** damage, deface, ravage, tear up **7** destroy **8** demolish, sabotage

Vandal king 8 Gaiseric, Genseric

Vandyke 5 beard **6** border, collar, edging, goatee

vane 3 web **7** feather, wind tee **8** vexillum **10** bellwether **11** weathercock

vanguard 4 lead **5** front **9** forefront **11** cutting edge, leading edge

vanilla 4 tame **5** beige, cream, plain **7** extract **8** ordinary **9** innocuous **10** white-bread **12** conventional **13** garden-variety

vanish 3 die, fly **4** fade, flee, melt **5** clear **8** dissolve, evanesce **9** disappear, dissipate, evaporate **13** dematerialize

vanity 3 ego **5** pride **6** egoism **7** conceit, egotism **8** self-love, smugness **9** vainglory **10** narcissism, pretension **13** dressing table

Vanity Fair author 9 Thackeray (William Makepeace)

vanquish 4 beat, best, drub, lick, rout **5** cream, crush, quell **6** defeat, humble, subdue, thrash **7** clobber, conquer, destroy, smother, trounce **8** surmount **9** overpower, overthrow, subjugate **10** annihilate

vantage 4 edge, odds **8** handicap **9** head start, upper hand *point:* **3** POV **5** perch **7** lookout, outlook **8** position **10** watchtower

Vanuatu *capital:* **8** Port-Vila *ethnic group:* **10** Melanesian *explorer:* **4** Cook (Capt. James) *former name:* **11** New Hebrides *island:* **3** Epi **5** Efate, Maéwo, Tanna **6** Ambrim **8** Aneityum, Malekula **9** Erromango, Pentecost **13** Espíritu Santo *language:* **6** French *monetary unit:* **4** vatu

vapid 4 dull, flat, weak **5** banal, bland, ditsy, ditzy, inane, silly **6** jejune **7** fatuous, insipid, sapless, vacuous **9** brainless, colorless, innocuous **10** namby-pamby, wishy-washy **13** uninteresting

vapor 3 fog, gas **4** brag, haze, mist, smog **5** brume, cloud, smoke, steam **6** breath, miasma, nimbus **7** bluster **8** phantasm *condensed:* **3** dew *frozen:* **4** hoar, rime **5** frost **9** hoarfrost

vaporize 5 steam **6** ablate **8** disperse, dissolve, evanesce **9** dissipate, evaporate

vaporous 4 airy, hazy **5** foggy, misty, vague, wispy **6** cloudy, unreal **7** gaseous **8** ethereal, illusory, volatile **10** evanescent **13** unsubstantial

vaquero 5 waddy **6** cowboy, gaucho, herder, waddie **7** cowpoke **8** buckaroo, herdsman, wrangler **10** cowpuncher

varia 4 medley **7** mélange, mixture, omnibus **8** treasury **9** anthology **10** compendium, miscellany **11** compilation

variable 5 fluid **6** fickle, fitful, mobile, symbol **7** mutable, protean **8** unstable, unsteady, volatile **9** irregular, mercurial, uncertain, unsettled, versatile **10** capricious, changeable, inconstant **13** temperamental

variance 3 war **4** odds **6** change, strife **7** discord, dispute, dissent **8** conflict, disunity, division **9** variation **10** contention, difference, dissension, dissidence **11** fluctuation **12** disagreement

variation 4 riff **5** shade, shift **6** change, nuance **7** partita **8** mutation **9** disparity **10** alteration, difference, divergence **11** fluctuation, declination, discrepancy, oscillation **12** modification **13** dissimilarity

varicolored see VARIEGATED

varicose 7 bulging, dilated, swollen

varied 5 mixed **6** motley, sundry **7** diverse, various **8** assorted **9** different,

disparate, divergent 10 dissimilar
12 multifarious 13 heterogeneous,
kaleidoscopic, miscellaneous
variegated 4 pied 5 mixed, pinto 6 calico, motley 7 checked, dappled, diverse,
mottled, piebald, spotted 8 skewbald,
stippled, streaked 9 checkered, multihued 10 multicolor, parti-color, poly-
chrome 12 multicolored, parti-colored
13 kaleidoscopic, polychromatic
variety 3 ilk 4 kind, mode, sort, type
5 array, breed 6 flavor, medley, nature,
stripe 8 mixed bag 9 diversity, variation
10 assortment, collection, miscellany,
subspecies 12 multiformity, multiplicity
various 4 some 5 mixed 6 divers, sundry,
unlike 7 diverse, several, unalike
8 assorted, separate 9 different, disparate, divergent, unsimilar 10 dissimilar 12 multifarious 13 heterogeneous,
miscellaneous
varlet 3 cur 4 page 5 knave, rogue,
skunk 6 menial, rascal, wretch
8 coistrel 9 attendant, miscreant,
scoundrel 10 blackguard
varmint 4 pest 5 knave, rogue, scamp,
skunk, sneak 6 rascal 7 critter
9 scoundrel
varnish 4 coat 5 adorn, cover, glaze,
gloss, japan 6 veneer 7 coating, conceal, cover up, shellac 8 covering
9 embellish, gloss over, sugarcoat,
whitewash *component:* 5 resin
vary 5 alter, range 6 change, depart, differ, modify, mutate 7 deviate, digress,
diverge 8 modulate 9 diversify
vase 3 urn 5 tazza 6 crater, krater, vessel
7 amphora
Vashni's father 6 Samuel
Vashti's husband 6 Xerxes 9 Ahasuerus
vassal 4 leud, serf 5 helot, liege, slave
6 tenant 7 bondman, homager, peasant,
servant, subject 8 bondsman, liege
man 9 dependent, underling 11 subordinate
12 feudal tenant *high-ranking:* 7 vavasor
8 vavasour
vast 4 huge, mega 5 giant, great, jumbo
6 untold 7 immense, mammoth, oceanic, titanic 8 colossal, enormous, gigantic, spacious, whopping 9 boundless,
expansive, humongous 10 gargantuan,
tremendous, widespread 12 astronomical
vastness 5 sweep 8 enormity, hugeness
9 immensity, magnitude 13 expan-
siveness
vat 3 tub, tun 4 beck, butt, cask, kier,
tank 5 keeve, kieve 6 barrel, liquor,
vessel 7 cistern 8 cauldron *cheese:*
7 chessel
vatic 6 mantic 7 fatidic 8 oracular

9 fatidical, prophetic, sibylline 10 predictive 11 apocalyptic
Vatican City 10 papal state *army:* 11 Swiss
Guards *chapel:* 7 Sistine *church:*
11 Saint Peter's *ruler:* 4 Pope *site:*
4 Rome
vaticinal see VATIC
vaticinate 5 augur 6 divine 7 portend,
predict, presage 8 forebode, forecast,
foretell, prophesy, soothsay 9 adumbrate 13 prognosticate
vaudeville 5 revue 9 burlesque, music
hall 11 variety show 12 song and dance
vaudevillian 11 entertainer
vault 3 pit, sky 4 arch, cave, dome,
jump, leap, room, safe, tomb 5 bound,
crypt 6 cavern, cellar, cupola, hurdle,
spring, welkin 7 archway, dungeon
8 catacomb, overleap 9 firmament
10 undercroft
vaulting 4 arch, dome 7 emulous 8 aspiring 9 ambitious 12 enthusiastic
13 opportunistic
vaunt 4 blow, brag, crow, puff, rant
5 boast, strut 6 flaunt, parade 7 bluster,
display, exhibit, show off 8 brandish
9 gasconade 11 rodomontade
veal 4 calf *cutlet:* 9 schnitzel *roasted:*
10 fricandeau *shank:* 8 osso buco
vector 5 agent 7 carrier 9 direction
10 pollinator
Vedic religion *country:* 5 India *god:*
4 Agni, deva, Soma 5 Indra 6 Varuna
language: 8 Sanskrit *priest:* 7 Brahman
treatise: 9 Upanishad *writing:* 7 Rig
Veda, Samhita
veer 3 yaw 4 cast, chop, slew, sway, turn
5 fetch, sheer, shift, trend 6 depart,
swerve 7 deflect, deviate, digress,
diverge
vegetable 3 pea, soy, yam 4 bean, beet,
corn, kale, leek, okra, soya, taro, wort
5 chard, chive, cress, green, onion,
plant 6 carrot, celery, cowpea, endive,
garlic, legume, lentil, peanut, pepper,
potato, radish, sorrel, squash, tomato,
turnip 7 cabbage, chayote, dullard, lettuce, mustard, parsley, parsnip, pumpkin, rhubarb, salsify, shallot, soybean,
spinach 8 broccoli, collards, cucumber,
eggplant, kohlrabi, lima bean, rutabaga, scallion, snap bean 9 artichoke,
asparagus, muskmelon 10 watermelon
11 cauliflower, horseradish, sweet potato *bog:* 6 muskeg *dish:* 5 salad *mold:*
5 humus *seller:* 6 grocer 7 grocery
12 costermonger *sponge:* 5 luffa
6 loofah *spread:* 4 oleo 9 margarine
vegetarian 9 herbivore 11 herbivorous
vegetate 4 idle, laze, loaf, loll 5 chill,
slack 6 loiter, lounge 7 goof off, hang

out 8 languish, lollygag, slack off, stagnate 9 goldbrick, hibernate

vegetation 5 flora 6 growth, plants 7 verdure 8 greenery 9 plant life *floating:* 4 sudd 8 pleuston

vehement 3 hot 4 wild 5 fiery, rabid 6 ardent, bitter, fervid, fierce, heated 7 excited, fervent, vicious, violent, zealous 8 forceful, powerful 9 perfervid 10 passionate 11 impassioned 12 antagonistic

vehicle 3 ATV, bus, cab, car, SUV, van 4 auto, bike, taxi, tool 5 agent, buggy, means, organ, plane, sedan, train, truck, wagon 6 agency, binder, medium, vector 7 bicycle, carrier, channel, machine, solvent, travois 8 airplane, ministry 9 ambulance, implement, motor home, transport 10 automobile, conveyance, instrument, motorcycle *baby's:* 4 pram 8 carriage, stroller 9 baby buggy *child's:* 5 trike 7 scooter 8 tricycle *farm:* 4 wain 7 tractor *horsedrawn:* 4 cart, dray 5 buggy, lorry, sulky, wagon 6 hansom, landau, troika 7 calèche, phaeton 8 carriage 9 buckboard *military:* 4 jeep, tank 6 Humvee *one-wheeled:* 8 unicycle *passenger:* 3 bus, cab, car 4 auto, taxi 7 ricksha 8 cable car, rickshaw *public:* 3 bus 4 tram 5 train 6 subway 7 omnibus, trolley *Roman:* 7 chariot *winter:* 4 sled 6 sleigh 8 snowplow 10 snowmobile

veil 4 caul, hide, mask, wrap 5 cloak, cloth, cloud, cover, velum 6 mantle, screen, shield, shroud 7 conceal, cover up, curtain, obscure, secrete 8 covering, disguise, enshroud 10 camouflage, false front *Muslim:* 7 yashmak *netting:* 6 maline 7 malines

vein 3 bed, way 4 line, lode, mind, mode, mood, seam, tone, tube 5 style, tenor 6 manner, nature, spirit, strain, streak, vessel 7 channel, fashion, pattern, quality, stratum 8 aptitude 11 blood vessel *combining form:* 3 ven 4 veni, veno *deposit:* 3 ore *fluid:* 5 blood *heart:* 8 vena cava *leaf:* 3 rib *leg:* 7 saphena 9 saphenous *neck:* 7 jugular *small:* 6 venule *varicose:* 5 varix

velar 8 guttural

veld 7 prairie 9 grassland

velleity 4 bent, wish 5 fancy 6 desire, liking 7 leaning 10 propensity 11 inclination

velocipede 4 bike 5 cycle, trike 6 tandem 7 bicycle, pedicab 8 tricycle

velocity 4 pace 5 haste, speed, tempo 7 headway 8 celerity, rapidity 9 quickness, swiftness 12 acceleration

velum 4 caul, veil 8 membrane 10 soft palate

velvet 4 gain, mild, rich, soft 5 cloth 6 fabric, profit, smooth 8 winnings 10 antler skin

velvety 4 mild, soft 5 plush 6 smooth

venal 4 paid 6 sordid 7 corrupt 8 bribable 9 mercenary, unethical 11 corruptible, purchasable 12 unprincipled, unscrupulous

vend 4 hawk, sell, toot 6 market, monger, peddle, retail 8 huckster 9 advertise, broadcast

vendee 5 buyer 6 client 8 customer 9 purchaser

vendetta 4 feud 7 rivalry 9 blood feud

vendible 7 salable 8 sellable 10 marketable 12 merchantable

vendor 6 dealer, duffer, hawker, seller 7 packman, peddler 8 huckster, merchant, retailer, salesman

vendue 4 sale 7 auction 10 public sale

veneer 3 ply 4 burl, coat, face, mask, show, veil 5 cover, front, gloss, layer, plate 6 facade, facing 7 conceal, overlay 8 disguise

venerable 3 old 4 aged 5 hoary 6 sacred 7 ancient, antique, elderly, honored, revered, stately 8 esteemed 9 admirable, dignified, estimable, honorable, respected

venerate 5 adore, honor, prize 6 admire, esteem, revere 7 cherish, idolize, respect, worship 8 treasure 9 reverence

veneration 3 awe 5 honor 6 esteem, homage 7 respect, worship 9 adoration, reverence 10 admiration 11 hero worship

venery 3 sex 4 game, prey 5 chase 7 hunting

venesection 10 phlebotomy

Venetian *boat:* 7 gondola *boatman:* 9 gondolier *product:* 5 glass 9 glassware *ruler:* 4 doge *school:* 6 Titian 7 Bellini, Tiepolo 8 Veronese 9 Giorgione 10 Tintoretto *street:* 5 canal *suburb:* 6 Murano

Venezuela *capital:* 7 Caracas *city:* 8 Valencia 9 Maracaibo 12 Barquisimeto *island:* 9 Margarita *lake:* 8 Valencia 9 Maracaibo *language:* 7 Spanish *monetary unit:* 7 bolívar *mountain, range:* 5 Andes 6 Parima (Serra, Sierra) 7 Bolívar (Pico) 9 Pacaraima 11 Pico Bolívar, Serra Parima 12 Sierra Parima *neighbor:* 6 Brazil, Guyana 8 Colombia *peninsula:* 9 Paraguaná *river:* 7 Orinoco *sea:* 9 Caribbean *waterfall:* 10 Angel Falls

Venezuelan *herdsman:* 7 llanero *liberator:* 7 Bolívar (Simón) *people:* 5 Carib 6 Timote

vengeance 6 payoff **7** payback, redress, revenge **8** reprisal, revanche **9** repayment **10** punishment **11** retaliation, retribution

vengeful 8 punitive **10** vindictive **11** retaliatory

venial 5 minor **7** trivial **8** harmless, trifling **9** allowable, excusable, tolerable **10** condonable, forgivable, pardonable, remissible, remittable **13** insignificant

Venice of the East 7 Bangkok, Udaipur

Venice of the North 6 Bruges, Brugge **9** Amsterdam, Stockholm **12** St. Petersburg

Veni, Creator ___ 8 Spiritus

venison 4 deer

veni, vidi, ___ 4 vici

venom 4 bane, hate **5** spite **6** malice, poison, rancor **7** ill will, vitriol **8** embitter **9** contagion, malignity, virulence **11** malevolence

venomous 5 toxic **6** deadly, malign, poison **7** baneful, malefic, noxious **8** spiteful, viperish, viperous, virulent **9** malicious, malignant, poisonous **10** malevolent, pernicious **12** vituperative

vent 3 air **4** emit, flue, hole, pipe, pour, slit **5** burst, expel, issue, loose, utter, voice **6** broach, nozzle, outlet **7** chimney, exhaust, express, give off, opening, orifice, release, take out, unleash, volcano **8** breather, fumarole, spiracle **9** discharge **11** black smoker

venter 3 gut **5** belly **6** paunch **7** abdomen, stomach

ventilate 3 air **5** state, utter **6** aerate, expose **7** discuss, express **9** advertise, broadcast, circulate, verbalize **11** investigate

ventral area 7 abdomen, stomach

ventricle 6 cavity **7** chamber

ventriloquist 9 performer **11** entertainer *companion:* **5** dummy *famous:* **6** Bergen (Edgar)

venture 3 bet, try **4** dare, face, feat, gest, risk **5** brave, peril, stake, wager **6** chance, expose, gamble, hazard **7** attempt, daresay, emprise, exploit **8** endanger, jeopardy, long shot, make bold **9** challenge, crapshoot, speculate **10** enterprise **11** speculation, undertaking

venturesome 4 bold, rash **5** brave **6** daring **8** reckless **9** audacious, daredevil, foolhardy **11** adventurous, temerarious

venue 4 site **5** arena, forum, place, scene **6** locale, outlet **7** setting **8** locality

Venus 6 planet, Vesper **7** daystar, Lucifer **8** Hesperus (see also APHRODITE)

Venus de ___ 4 Milo

___ vera 4 aloe

veracious 4 just, true **5** exact, frank, right, valid **6** candid, honest **7** correct, factual, sincere **8** accurate, truthful

veracity 4 fact **5** truth **6** candor **7** honesty **8** accuracy, trueness **9** actuality, exactness **11** correctness **12** truthfulness

veranda 5 lanai, porch, stoop **6** piazza **7** gallery, portico

verb *auxiliary:* **3** are, can, did, had, has, may, was **4** have, must, were, will, word **5** could, might, shall, would **6** should *form:* **6** active, gerund **7** passive **10** infinitive, participle *kind:* **10** transitive **12** intransitive *linking:* **6** copula *mood:* **8** optative **10** imperative, indicative **11** subjunctive *tense:* **4** past **6** aorist, future **7** perfect, present **9** predicate **10** pluperfect

verbal 4 oral **5** wordy **6** gerund, spoken **7** literal **9** unwritten **10** infinitive, participle, rhetorical **11** word-for-word

verbalism 4 term **6** phrase **7** wording **8** phrasing **9** prolixity, windiness, wordiness **11** phraseology

verbalization 4 talk **6** speech **8** speaking **9** discourse, utterance **12** articulation, vocalization

verbalize 3 air, say **4** talk **5** speak, state, utter, voice, write **6** broach **7** express **8** bloviate, vocalize **9** ventilate

verbatim 5 exact **6** direct **7** exactly, literal, precise **8** directly **9** literally, literatim, precisely **10** accurately **11** word-for-word

verbiage 4 talk **6** phrase **7** diction, wording **8** parlance, phrasing, pleonasm **9** wordiness **10** redundancy **11** phraseology

verbose 5 gassy, windy, wordy **6** prolix **7** diffuse **9** garrulous, redundant, talkative **10** loquacious, pleonastic **11** tautologous

verbosity 9 prolixity, windiness, wordiness **10** redundancy

verboten 5 taboo **6** banned **7** illegal **8** outlawed **9** forbidden **10** prohibited

verdant 4 lush **5** green, leafy, naive **6** grassy, unripe

verdict 6 assize, ruling **7** finding, opinion **8** decision, judgment **9** judgement

Verdi opera 4 Aïda **6** Ernani, Oberto, Otello **7** Nabucco **8** Don Carlo, Falstaff, Lombardi (I), Traviata (La) **9** Don Carlos, Rigoletto, Trovatore (Il) **15** Simon Boccanegra

verdure 7 foliage **8** greenery **9** greenness **10** vegetation

verge 3 hem, lip, rim **4** abut, cusp, edge, sink **5** bound, brink, skirt, staff, touch

6 adjoin, border, fringe, margin 7 selvage 8 approach, shoulder 9 threshold 10 borderline

veridical see VERACIOUS

verifiable 4 true 6 proven 7 certain 8 provable 9 undoubted

verification 5 proof 10 validation 11 attestation 12 confirmation 13 corroboration

verify 4 aver, test 5 check, prove, vouch 6 attest, settle 7 bear out, confirm 8 document, validate 9 establish, factcheck 11 corroborate, demonstrate 12 authenticate, substantiate

verily 5 truly 6 indeed 7 in truth 9 assuredly, certainly 11 confidently, undoubtedly

veritable 4 real, true 6 actual 7 factual, genuine 8 bona fide 9 authentic, undoubted 10 sure-enough 11 indubitable

verity 5 truth 6 gospel, truism 7 honesty, reality 9 actuality 12 truthfulness

vermiform 8 wormlike

vermilion 3 red

vermin 4 lice, mice, pest, rats, scum 5 fleas, pests, trash 7 bedbugs, varmint

Vermont *capital:* 10 Montpelier *city:* 7 Rutland 10 Burlington *college, university:* 7 Norwich 8 Marlboro 10 Bennington, Middlebury *mountain, range:* 5 Green 9 Mansfield *nickname:* 13 Green Mountain (State) *river:* 11 Connecticut *state bird:* 12 hermit thrush *state flower:* 9 red clover *state tree:* 10 sugar maple

vernacular 4 cant 5 argot, idiom, lingo, slang 6 common, jargon, patois, patter, speech, tongue, vulgar 7 dialect, vulgate 8 language 9 dialectal 10 colloquial 12 mother tongue

vernal 5 fresh, green 6 spring 8 youthful 10 springlike

Verne, Jules *character:* 4 Fogg (Phileas), Nemo 12 Passepartout *submarine:* 8 Nautilus *work:* 16 Mysterious Island (The) 21 From the Earth to the Moon 26 Around the World in Eighty Days

versant see CONVERSANT

versatile 5 handy 6 adroit, facile 7 protean 8 variable 9 all-around, competent, many-sided 10 changeable 11 well-rounded 12 ambidextrous

verse 3 lay, ode 4 epic, poem, rune 5 lyric, poesy, rhyme 6 ballad, jingle, poetry, sonnet, stanza 7 passage 8 acquaint 11 composition, familiarize *analysis:* 8 scansion *four-line:* 8 quatrain *free:* 5 blank 8 unrhymed *six-line:* 6 sestet *three-line:* 6 tercet *two-line:* 7 couplet *writer:* 4 poet

versed 5 adept 6 au fait 7 abreast, skilled, veteran 8 familiar, informed, seasoned 9 au courant, competent, practiced 10 acquainted 11 experienced 13 knowledgeable

versifier 4 bard, poet 6 rhymer 9 poetaster, rhymester, sonneteer

version 4 copy 5 draft, model 6 flavor, remake 7 account, edition, reading, variant 8 revision 9 iteration, narrative, redaction, rendition, rewording 10 adaptation, paraphrase 11 arrangement, description, incarnation, restatement, translation

versus 4 anti 6 contra 7 against, vis-à-vis 11 over against

vertebra 7 segment *kind:* 6 dorsal, lumbar, sacral 8 cervical, thoracic 9 coccygeal

vertebrae 4 back 5 spine 6 coccyx, rachis, sacrum 8 backbone, tailbone 12 spinal column

vertebrate 6 animal *characteristic:* 5 spine 7 cranium 12 spinal column *kind:* 4 bird, fish, frog 6 mammal 7 reptile 9 amphibian

vertex 3 cap, top 4 acme, apex, peak 5 crest, crown 6 apogee, summit, tiptop, zenith

vertical 5 erect, plumb, sheer, steep 7 upright 8 straight 10 lengthwise, straight-up 13 perpendicular

vertiginous 5 dizzy, giddy, woozy 6 fickle, rotary 11 light-headed

vertigo 6 megrim 9 dizziness, giddiness

verve 3 pep, vim, zip 4 brio, dash, élan, fire, life, zest, zing 5 flair, gusto, moxie, oomph, style, vigor 6 bounce, energy, spirit, spring 7 panache 8 vitality, vivacity 10 enthusiasm, liveliness 13 sprightliness

very 3 too 4 bare, mere, most, much, pure, real, same, true 5 exact, ideal, model, plain, quite, sheer, super, truly, utter 6 actual, ever so, highly, hugely, mighty, really, simple 7 awfully, genuine, greatly, notably, perfect, precise, special 8 absolute, actually, bona fide, selfsame, terribly 9 authentic, extremely, genuinely, identical, undoubted 10 absolutely, particular 11 exceedingly *French:* 4 très *German:* 4 sehr *Italian:* 5 molto *Scottish:* 3 gey *Spanish:* 3 muy

vesicle 3 sac 4 cell, cyst 5 bulla 6 cavity 7 blister, vacuole

vespers 8 evensong

___ **Vespucci** 7 Amerigo

vessel 3 can, cup, jar, pan, pot, tub, urn 4 boat, bowl, cask, drum, duct, ewer, pail, ship, tank, tube, vase, vein 5 canal, craft, cruse 6 artery, barrel, bottle, bucket, firkin, flagon, kettle, krater, pottle **7** cresset, pitcher **8** crucible **9** container **10** receptacle, watercraft *combining form:* **3** vas **4** angi, vaso **5** angio *drinking:* **3** cup, mug **4** toby **5** flask, glass, gourd, stein, stoup **6** goblet, seidel **7** tankard, tumbler *Indian:* **4** lota **5** lotah *Scottish:* **6** quaich, quaigh

vest 6 weskit **9** waistcoat

Vesta see HESTIA

vestal 4 pure **6** chaste, virgin **8** celibate, virginal, virtuous

vestibule 5 entry, foyer, lobby **6** cavity **7** hallway, narthex, passage **8** anteroom, entrance, entryway **10** antechapel **11** antechamber

vestige 4 echo **5** dregs (plural), relic, scrap, stump, trace, track **6** shadow **7** memento, remains, remnant **8** leftover **9** remainder **10** hide or hair **11** hide nor hair

vestment 3 alb **4** cope, garb, gown, robe **5** amice, cotta, dress, habit, stole, tunic **6** attire, rochet **7** apparel, cassock, garment, maniple, pallium, tunicle **8** chasuble, cincture, clothing, covering, dalmatic, parament, surplice *ancient Hebrew:* **5** ephod **11** breastplate

vestry 6 closet **8** sacristy **9** sacrarium

vesture 4 robe **6** clothe **7** apparel, garment **8** clothing **10** habiliment

Vesuvius 7 volcano

vet 5 check **6** go over, review **7** analyze, examine, inspect **8** appraise, check out, evaluate, look over **10** old soldier

vetch 4 herb, tare **6** legume *type:* **4** milk (vetch) **5** crown (vetch), hairy (vetch)

veteran 4 ex-GI **5** adept **6** expert, master **7** old hand, skilled **8** old-timer, warhorse **9** practiced, shellback **10** past master **11** experienced

veto 3 nix **4** kill **6** defeat, forbid, refuse, reject **7** decline **8** disallow, negative, prohibit **9** blackball **10** disapprove **11** prohibition **12** interdiction

vex 3 bug, irk **4** fret, gall, itch, roil **5** annoy, chafe, gripe, harry, rowel, tease, worry **6** badger, baffle, bother, harass, harrow, nettle, pester, plague, puzzle, rankle, ruffle **7** chagrin, torment, trouble **8** bullyrag, distress, irritate

vexation 4 fret, sore **5** chafe, trial **6** bother **7** problem, torment **8** distress, headache **9** annoyance, troubling **10** affliction, harassment, irritation **11** aggravation, bedevilment, provocation

vexatious 5 pesky **7** prickly **8** annoying, tiresome **9** troublous **10** bothersome, irritating **11** distressing, troublesome **12** exasperating

vexed 6 sticky, touchy **7** debated, weighty **8** ticklish **9** difficult, discussed, troubling

vexing 5 tough **7** irksome **8** annoying **9** difficult, harassing, upsetting **10** bothersome, irritating **11** distressing, troublesome

via 3 per **4** over, with **5** along **7** by way of, through **9** by means of

viable 6 doable **7** capable **8** feasible, possible, workable **11** practicable, sustainable

vial 6 ampule **7** ampoule

viands 4 eats, fare, feed, food, grub **7** aliment, edibles, vittles **8** victuals **9** provender **10** provisions **11** comestibles

vibrant 5 alive, vital, vivid **6** bright, lively, punchy **7** ringing **8** resonant **9** consonant, pulsating **10** resounding **11** oscillating **12** effervescent

vibrate 3 jar **4** ring **5** quake, shake, swing, throb, waver **6** quiver, shimmy, thrill, tremor **7** flutter, pulsate **8** undulate **9** fluctuate, oscillate, vacillate

vibration 4 aura **5** quake, shake, trill **6** motion, quaver, quiver, shimmy, spirit, tremor **7** flutter, shaking **8** fremitus, wavering **9** emanation, trembling **11** fluctuation, oscillation, vacillation

vicar 6 pastor, priest **8** minister, reverend **9** clergyman

Vicar of Wakefield, The *author:* **9** Goldsmith (Oliver) *character:* **8** Primrose

vice 3 sin **4** evil, flaw **5** crime, fault **6** defect **7** devilry, failing, frailty, offense, scandal **8** iniquity **9** deformity, depravity, indecency **10** corruption, debauchery, immorality, perversion, wickedness **11** shortcoming

vice-president 4 veep **6** deputy **7** officer **9** executive *American:* **4** Burr (Aaron), Bush (George), Ford (Gerald), Gore (Albert), King (William) **5** Adams (John), Agnew (Spiro), Dawes (Charles), Gerry (Elbridge), Nixon (Richard), Tyler (John) **6** Arthur (Chester), Cheney (Richard), Colfax (Schuyler), Curtis (Charles), Dallas (George), Garner (John Nance), Hamlin (Hannibal), Hobart (Garret), Morton (Levi), Quayle (Dan), Truman (Harry), Wilson (Woodrow) **7** Barkley (Alben), Calhoun (John Caldwell), Clinton (George), Johnson (Andrew, Lyndon Baines, Richard Mentor), Mondale (Walter), Sherman (James Schoolcraft), Wallace (Henry), Wheeler (William) **8** Coolidge (Calvin), Fillmore (Millard), Humphrey (Hubert Horatio), Marshall (Thomas), Tompkins (Daniel),

Van Buren (Martin) **9** Fairbanks (Charles), Hendricks (Thomas), Jefferson (Thomas), Roosevelt (Theodore), Stevenson (Adlai) **11** Rockefeller (Nelson) **12** Breckinridge (John)

viceroy 5 nabob **6** exarch, satrap **7** khedive **8** alderman, governor **9** butterfly **11** stadtholder

vice versa 10 conversely **12** contrariwise

vicinity 4 area **5** range **6** extent, locale, region, shadow **7** suburbs **8** ballpark, district, environs, locality, nearness, precinct **9** closeness, magnitude, proximity **12** neighborhood

vicious 4 evil, mean, vile **5** cruel **6** fierce, malign, savage, sinful, wicked **7** brutish, corrupt, hateful, immoral, noxious, violent **8** depraved, horrible, perverse, spiteful **9** barbarous, ferocious, malicious, malignant, monstrous, nefarious, reprobate **10** degenerate, flagitious, iniquitous, malevolent, villainous, vindictive

vicissitude 5 rigor, trial **6** chance, change **7** weather **8** hardship, mutation, reversal **9** adversity, mischance **10** affliction, difficulty, misfortune, mutability **11** permutation, progression, tribulation

victim 4 butt, dupe, gull, mark, prey **5** chump, patsy **6** pigeon, martyr, quarry, sucker **7** fall guy **8** casualty, fatality, offering, underdog **9** sacrifice

victimize 4 dupe, fool, gull, hoax **5** cheat, cozen, trick **7** deceive, swindle **8** flimflam, hoodwink **9** bamboozle, sacrifice **11** hornswoggle

victor 5 champ **6** top dog, winner **7** subduer **8** champion **9** conqueror **10** vanquisher

Victorian 4 prim **6** prissy, stuffy **7** prudish **8** priggish **11** puritanical, straitlaced **12** old-fashioned

Victoria, Queen *family:* **7** Hanover *father:* **6** Edward *husband:* **6** Albert *prime minister:* **8** Disraeli (Benjamin) **9** Gladstone (William), Melbourne (Lord) *son:* **6** Edward

victory 3 win **5** sweep **6** defeat **7** mastery, success, triumph **8** conquest, walkaway, walkover **10** overcoming **11** superiority *costly:* **7** Pyrrhic *easy:* **8** cakewalk, walkaway *monument:* **4** arch **13** Arc de Triomphe *reward:* **6** spoils *sign:* **3** vee *symbol:* **4** flag **6** laurel, wreath

Victory author 6 Conrad (Joseph)

victuals 4 chow, eats, feed, food, grub, prog **6** viands **7** edibles, vittles **9** provender **10** provisions **11** comestibles

___ **Vidal 4** Gore

videlicet 3 viz **5** to wit **6** namely, that is **8** scilicet **11** that is to say

vie 3 pit **5** match **6** oppose, strive **7** compete, contend, contest, counter **8** struggle

Viennese *city hall:* **7** Rathaus *family:* **8** Habsburg, Hapsburg *palace:* **7** Hofburg *park:* **6** Prater *river:* **6** Danube

Vietnam *capital:* **5** Hanoi *city:* **3** Hue **6** Da Nang, Saigon **8** Haiphong **13** Ho Chi Minh City *delta:* **6** Mekong *gulf:* **6** Tonkin **8** Thailand *monetary unit:* **4** dong *mountain:* **8** Fan-si-pan *neighbor:* **4** Laos **5** China **8** Cambodia **9** Kampuchea *river:* **3** Red **6** Mekong *sea:* **10** South China

Vietnamese New Year 3 Tet

view 3 eye, see **4** espy, look, plan, scan **5** scene, sight, vista, watch **6** behold, belief, look at, notice, notion, regard, review, survey **7** close-up, examine, inspect, lookout, observe, opinion, outlook, picture, scenery, vantage **8** judgment, panorama, perceive, prospect, scrutiny, snapshot **10** conviction, inspection, scrutinize **11** contemplate, examination

viewer 7 witness **8** looker-on, onlooker **9** bystander, spectator **10** eyewitness

viewing instrument 5 glass, scope **6** binocs **7** glasses **9** telescope **10** binoculars, microscope **12** field glasses *combining form:* **5** scope

viewpoint 3 eye **5** angle, slant, stand **6** stance **7** outlook **8** attitude, position **9** direction **11** perspective

vigil 4 wake **5** watch **7** lookout, prayers **9** devotions **10** deathwatch **11** wakefulness **12** surveillance, watch and ward

vigilance 5 watch **9** alertness **12** surveillance, watchfulness

vigilant 4 keen, wary **5** alert, awake, aware, chary, sharp **7** careful, jealous, on guard **8** cautious, open-eyed, watchful **9** attentive, sharp-eyed, wide-awake

vignette 5 scene **6** sketch **7** glimpse, picture **8** ornament

vigor 3 pep, vim, zip **4** brio, push, snap, tuck **5** ardor, drive, force, gusto, moxie, oomph **6** energy, mettle, muscle, spirit, starch **7** potency **8** dynamism, strength, tonicity, virility, vitality **9** hardihood, lustiness, puissance **10** get-up-and-go, robustness, sturdiness

vigorous 5 brisk, hardy, lusty, stout, tough, vital **6** active, hearty, lively, potent, robust, strong, sturdy, virile **7** dashing, driving, dynamic, healthy **8** athletic, forceful, muscular, powerful, spirited, youthful **9** energetic, strenuous **10** mettlesome, red-blooded

Viking see NORSE

vile 4 base, evil, foul, mean, ugly **5** gross, nasty, slimy **6** filthy, horrid, sordid, vulgar, wicked **7** low-down, noisome, obscene, squalid **8** depraved, wretched **9** abhorrent, loathsome, obnoxious, offensive, perverted, repugnant, repulsive, revolting **10** despicable, disgusting **12** contemptible

vilify 5 abuse, libel, smear **6** assail, attack, berate, defame, malign **7** asperse, run down, slander, spatter, traduce **8** denounce, tear down **9** denigrate, disparage **10** calumniate

villa 5 dacha, manor **6** estate, quinta **7** château, mansion **9** residence

village 4 burg, town **5** bourg, thorp **6** hamlet **7** townlet *African:* **4** dorp **5** kraal *Indian:* **6** pueblo *Japanese:* **4** mura *Jewish:* **6** shtetl *Malay:* **7** kampong *Russian:* **3** mir

Village Blacksmith author 10 Longfellow (Henry Wadsworth)

villain 4 boor, heel **5** demon, devil, heavy, knave, rogue **6** rascal, sinner **7** lowlife **8** antihero, criminal, evildoer, offender, scalawag **9** character, miscreant, reprobate, scoundrel **10** blackguard, malefactor *classic:* **4** Iago **5** Judas (Iscariot) **6** Brutus (Marcus Junius) **8** Quisling (Vidkun)

villainous 4 evil **6** rotten, wicked **7** corrupt, debased, heinous, vicious **8** depraved, wretched **9** atrocious, felonious, miscreant, nefarious **10** detestable, diabolical, flagitious, iniquitous, perfidious, traitorous **11** treacherous

villainy 4 vice **5** crime **8** evilness **9** depravity, treachery, turpitude **10** corruption, wickedness

villein 7 peasant **8** villager

villenage 4 yoke **6** tenure, thrall **7** bondage, serfdom **9** servitude, thralldom

vim 3 zip **4** brio, dash, élan, gimp, zing **5** gusto, oomph, verve, vigor **6** bounce, energy, esprit, spirit **7** vinegar **9** animation **10** enthusiasm, razzmatazz

___ vincit omnia 4 Amor

vinculum 3 tie **4** bond, knot, link, yoke **5** nexus **8** ligament, ligature

vindicable 7 tenable **9** excusable **10** condonable, defendable, defensible, pardonable **11** justifiable, warrantable

vindicate 4 free **5** clear, guard, prove, right **6** acquit, avenge, defend, excuse, refute, shield, uphold, verify **7** absolve, bear out, confirm, deliver, justify,

redress, revenge, support, warrant **8** maintain **9** exculpate, exonerate, safeguard **11** corroborate **12** substantiate

vindictive 5 catty, nasty **6** malign **7** hateful, hurtful, vicious **8** punitive, spiteful, vengeful, venomous **9** malicious, malignant, poisonous

vine 3 hop, ivy, pea **5** grape, kudzu, liana, liane, maile, plant **6** maypop **7** chayote, climber, creeper **8** catbrier, clematis **11** bittersweet *Asian:* **6** pikake

vinegar 3 vim **6** liquid **8** ill humor, sourness **9** condiment **12** preservative *relating to:* **10** acetic acid *steep in:* **6** pickle

vinegarish 4 sour **6** bitter, cranky, ornery **7** bearish, waspish **8** snappish **9** crotchety, irascible **12** cantankerous, cross-grained, disagreeable

Vinegar Joe 8 Stilwell (Joseph)

vineyard *French:* **3** cru **7** château, domaine

Vinland discoverer 4 Leif (Ericsson, Eriksson) **12** Leif Ericsson, Leif Eriksson

vintage 3 age, old **4** crop, wine **5** yield **7** antique, classic, harvest **8** outdated **9** classical **10** antiquated **12** old-fashioned

Viola *brother:* **9** Sebastian *husband:* **6** Orsino *play:* **12** Twelfth Night

viola da ___ 5 gamba

violate 4 rape **5** break, wrong **6** breach, defile, offend, ravish **7** disturb, outrage, profane, traduce **8** fracture, infringe, trespass **9** desecrate, disregard **10** contravene, transgress

violation 4 foul, rape **5** break, crime, wrong **6** breach, injury **7** offense, outrage, perjury, scandal **8** trespass **9** blasphemy, injustice, sacrilege **10** illegality, infraction, ravishment **11** desecration, disturbance, misdemeanor, profanation **12** encroachment, infringement, interruption **13** contravention, transgression

violence 4 fury, riot **5** clash **6** frenzy, mayhem **7** assault, outrage, rampage **8** foul play, savagery **9** onslaught **10** distortion, roughhouse

violent 5 cruel, harsh, rabid **6** fierce, raging, savage, stormy **7** berserk, furious, intense, vicious **8** slam-bang, vehement **9** explosive, ferocious **10** hellacious **11** acrimonious, destructive

violet 7 mauve **6** purple **8** amethyst, lavender **10** heliotrope

violin 6 fiddle **10** instrument *kind:* **5** Amati, Strad **8** Guarneri **10** Guarnerius, Stradivari **12** Stradivarius *part:* **3** bow, nut, peg **4** neck **6** bridge, scroll, string **8** chin rest **9** tailpiece **10** sound-

board 11 fingerboard *precursor:* 5 rebec
6 rebeck
violinist *American:* 4 Hahn (Hilary)
5 Elman (Mischa), Fodor (Eugene),
Ricci (Ruggiero), Stern (Isaac)
6 Midori, Powell (Maud) 7 Heifetz
(Jascha), Menuhin (Yehudi), Szigeti
(Joseph) 8 Kreisler (Fritz), Milstein
(Nathan) 9 Zimbalist (Efrem) *Belgian:*
5 Ysaÿe (Eugene) 8 Grumiaux (Arthur)
Czech: 3 Suk (Josef) *English:* 7 Menuhin
(Yehudi) *French:* 12 Francescatti (Zino)
German: 6 Mutter (Anne-Sophie) *Hungarian:* 7 Joachim (Joseph) *Israeli:*
7 Perlman (Itzhak) 8 Zukerman (Pinchas) *Italian:* 6 Viotti (Giovanne Battista) 7 Corelli (Arcangelo), Vivaldi
(Antonio) 8 Paganini (Niccolo) 9 Geminiani (Francesco) *Romanian:* 6 Enescu
(George) *Russian:* 8 Oistrakh (David)
violin maker 4 Salò (Gasparo da)
5 Amati (Andrea, Antonio, Girolamo,
Nicolo) 7 Maggini (Giovanni Paolo),
Stainer (Jacob) 8 Guarneri (Andrea, del
Gesù, Giuseppe, Pietro) 10 Guarnerius
(Andrea, Giuseppe, Pietro), Stradivari
(Antonio, Francesco, Omobono)
12 Stradivarius (Antonio, Francesco,
Omobono)
VIP 4 BMOC, lion 5 mogul, nabob 6 big
gun, biggie, bigwig, fat cat, honcho
7 big shot, notable, someone 8 big
wheel, luminary, mandarin, somebody
9 big cheese, dignitary 10 panjandrum
13 high-muck-a-muck
viper 3 asp 5 adder, snake 7 serpent
10 bushmaster, copperhead, fer-de-lance 11 rattlesnake 13 water moccasin
virago 5 harpy, scold, shrew, vixen
6 amazon, dragon, gorgon, ogress
8 battle-ax, fishwife, harridan, Xantippe 9 battle-axe, termagant, Xanthippe
Virgil 4 poet 5 guide 6 orator 8 cicerone
epic: 6 Aeneid *poems:* 8 Eclogues,
Georgics
virgin 3 new 4 pure 5 first, fresh, unwed
6 chaste, intact, maiden, modest,
unused, vestal 7 initial 8 celibate, innocent, primeval, pristine, spotless
9 abstinent, undefiled, unmarried,
unspoiled, unsullied, untouched
10 immaculate
virginal 4 pure 5 fresh 6 chaste, intact,
maiden, spinet 8 pristine, virtuous
9 undefiled, unspoiled, unsullied,
untouched
Virgin Goddess 5 Diana 6 Hestia
7 Artemis
Virginia *capital:* 8 Richmond *city:* 7 Norfolk, Roanoke 10 Alexandria 11 New-

port News 13 Virginia Beach *college,
university:* 3 VMI 7 Hampton 10 Sweet
Briar 11 George Mason, Old Dominion
12 James Madison 13 Randolph-Macon
14 William and Mary *historical site:*
10 Monticello 11 Mount Vernon
12 Williamsburg *mountain, range:*
6 Rogers 9 Blue Ridge *nickname:* 11 Old
Dominion *river:* 5 James 7 Potomac
10 Shenandoah *state bird:* 8 cardinal
state flower: 7 dogwood (American)
state tree: 7 dogwood (American)
Virginian, The *author:* 6 Wister (Owen)
character: 7 Trampas
Virgin Island 5 Peter 6 Norman, St. John
7 Anegada, St. Croix, Tortola 8 St.
Thomas
Virgin Islands (U.S.) *capital:* 15 Charlotte
Amalie *island:* 6 St. John 7 St. Croix
8 St. Thomas *location:* 10 West Indies
territory of: 12 United States
Virgin Islands, British *capital:* 8 Road
Town *island:* 5 Peter 6 Norman 7 Anegada, Tortola 11 Jost Van Dyke, Virgin
Gorda *location:* 10 West Indies
virginity 6 purity 8 celibacy, chastity
10 chasteness, maidenhead, maidenhood
Virgin Queen 9 Elizabeth
Virgo star 5 Spica
virgule 5 comma, slant, slash 7 solidus
8 diagonal
viridity 5 green 7 naïveté 9 freshness,
greenness, innocence
virile 4 male 5 macho, manly 6 manful,
potent, robust 7 manlike 8 forceful,
vigorous 9 energetic, masculine
virtual 5 moral, tacit 7 de facto 8 implicit
9 essential, practical 10 electronic
11 fundamental
virtuality 4 core, pith, soul 5 being, juice,
stuff 6 effect, marrow, nature 7 essence,
makings 8 quiddity 9 substance
10 capability 12 essentiality, quintessence, potentiality
virtually 4 nigh 6 all but, almost, fairly,
nearly, next to 7 morally 8 as good as,
in effect, well-nigh 9 basically, in
essence, literally 10 implicitly 11 effectively, essentially, practically
13 approximately, fundamentally, substantially
virtue 5 merit, power, right, trait, valor,
value, vigor, worth 7 courage, feature,
potency, probity, quality 8 chastity,
goodness, morality, strength 9 attribute, character, puissance, rectitude,
rightness 10 excellence, excellency, perfection 11 uprightness *cardinal:* 4 hope,
love 5 faith 7 charity, justice 8 prudence 9 fortitude 10 temperance

virtuosic 5 showy 6 expert, flashy 7 hotshot, skilled 9 brilliant, masterful 10 consummate, prodigious 12 razzle-dazzle

virtuoso 4 whiz 6 expert, master, savant, wizard, wonder 7 artiste, hotshot, maestro, prodigy 10 past master, wunderkind

virtuous 4 good, pure 5 moral, noble, pious, right 6 chaste, decent, modest, proper 7 ethical, sinless 8 innocent, spotless 9 blameless, faultless, guiltless, righteous, unsullied, untainted 10 inculpable, moralistic 11 respectable, right-minded, untarnished

virulent 5 harsh, toxic 6 biting, bitter, malign, poison 7 cutting, hateful, hostile 8 scathing, spiteful, venomous 9 malicious, malignant, pestilent, poisonous, rancorous, vitriolic 10 pathogenic

virus 3 bug 8 pathogen 9 contagion, infection

vis 5 force, might, power

visage 3 mug, pan 4 cast, face, look, mien, phiz, puss 6 aspect, kisser 8 features 9 semblance 10 expression 11 countenance

vis-à-vis 4 date 6 escort, facing, toward 7 against 8 fronting, opposite, together 9 tête-à-tête 10 face-to-face 11 counterpart

visceral 3 gut 4 deep 5 inner 8 internal, intimate 9 intuitive 10 intestinal 11 instinctive, instinctual

viscid see VISCOUS

viscount 4 lord, peer 8 nobleman

viscous 4 limy, ropy 5 gluey, gooey, gummy, limey, slimy, thick 9 glutinous, semifluid 10 gelatinous 12 mucilaginous

vise 5 clamp, screw 7 squeeze

Vishnu 4 Hari *avatar:* 4 Rama 5 Kurma 6 Buddha, Matsya, Vamena, Varaha 7 Krishna 9 Narasinha *consort:* 3 Sri 4 Shri 7 Lakshmi *home:* 4 Meru

visible 6 patent 7 obvious 8 apparent, viewable 9 available, well-known 10 detectable 11 conspicuous, discernible, perceivable, perceptible 12 recognizable

Visigoth *conquest:* 4 Rome *king:* 6 Alaric

vision 3 eye 5 dream, fancy, image, sense, sight 6 beauty, seeing 7 concept, fantasy, feature, picture, specter 8 daydream, eyesight, phantasm, presence, prophecy 9 foresight, nightmare 10 apparition, perception, phenomenon, revelation 13 manifestation *combining form:* 4 opto 5 opsis *deceptive:* 6 mirage *relating to:* 5 optic 6 visual 7 optical

visionary 4 seer 5 ideal, lofty, noble 6 unreal 7 blue-sky, dreamer, utopian 8 fanciful, idealist, illusory, quixotic, romantic 9 ambitious, ideologue, imaginary 10 abstracted, daydreamer, idealistic, starry-eyed 11 impractical

visionless 5 blind

Vision of Sir Launfal author 6 Lowell (James Russell)

visit 3 gam, see 4 call, chat, stay, talk, tour 5 pop in, run in 6 call on, come by, drop by, drop in, look in, look up, stay at, stop by, stop in 7 force on, sojourn 8 come over, converse, stay with, stopover 10 social call

visitation 3 woe 4 wake 5 cross, trial 6 misery, ordeal, plague 8 calamity 9 martyrdom 10 affliction 11 tribulation

visitor 5 alien, guest 6 caller, drop-in 7 company, invitee 8 stranger, visitant 9 transient 10 houseguest

visor 4 bill, mask 6 domino 8 eyeshade, disguise, face mask, sunshade

vista 4 view 5 scene, sight 7 lookout, outlook 8 panorama, prospect 9 landscape 11 perspective

visual 5 optic 6 ocular 7 graphic, optical, seeable 8 viewable 9 pictorial 11 discernible, perceivable, perceptible

visualize 3 see 4 view 5 fancy, image 6 call up 7 feature, imagine, picture 8 conceive, envisage, envision 9 conjure up

vital 4 dire 5 alive 6 lively, living, mortal, urgent 7 animate, crucial, pivotal 8 animated, cardinal, critical, decisive, integral, pressing, required, vigorous 9 essential, important, necessary, requisite 10 imperative, red-blooded 11 fundamental, life-or-death 12 invigorating 13 indispensable

vitality see VIGOR

vitalize 5 liven 6 arouse, excite, infuse, perk up, spirit, vivify 7 animate, enliven, quicken 8 energize 9 encourage, galvanize, stimulate 10 invigorate

vitals see VISCERA

vitamin 6 biotin, niacin 7 choline, folacin, retinal, retinol 8 thiamine 9 carnitine, cobalamin, folic acid 10 calciferol, pyridoxine, riboflavin, tocopherol 12 ascorbic acid

Vita Nuova author 5 Dante (Alighieri)

vitelline 5 yolky 6 yellow

vitiate 3 mar 4 harm, soil, undo 5 annul, spoil, sully, taint 6 damage, debase, defile, impair, negate 7 blemish, corrupt, debauch, deprave, nullify, pervert, tarnish 8 abrogate 9 undermine 10 bastardize, demoralize, invalidate

vitreous 6 glassy

vitriol 4 bile **5** spite, venom **6** malice, rancor **7** sulfate **8** acrimony **9** virulence **12** sulfuric acid

vitriolic 4 acid **5** acrid **7** acerbic, caustic, cutting, mordant **8** scathing, stinging, virulent **9** rancorous, truculent

vituperate 3 rag **4** lash, rail, rant, rate **5** abuse, baste, curse, scold, score **6** berate, malign, revile, scorch **7** asperse, bawl out, chew out, condemn, cuss out, upbraid **8** lambaste **9** castigate **10** tongue-lash

vituperation 5 abuse **6** rebuke **7** censure, obloquy, reproof **8** scolding **9** contumely, invective **10** scurrility **11** fulmination, mudslinging **12** billingsgate **13** tongue-lashing

vituperative 7 abusive, railing, scurril **8** scathing, scolding, scurrile, venomous, viperish **9** invective **10** censorious, scurrilous **11** opprobrious **12** contumelious

vivace 5 brisk **6** lively **8** animated, spirited

vivacious 3 gay **4** airy, pert **5** perky, spicy, sunny, zesty **6** bouncy, breezy, bubbly, jaunty, lively, sparky **7** buoyant, chipper **8** animated, pixieish, spirited **9** ebullient, sprightly **12** effervescent, high-spirited

vivacity see VERVE

Vivaldi epithet 9 red priest (the)

___ **vivant 3** bon

vivarium 9 terrarium

viva voce 4 oral **6** orally, spoken **11** word-of-mouth

vivid 5 alive, sharp **6** bright, garish, lively, punchy, visual **7** graphic, intense, vibrant **8** animated, colorful, eloquent, lifelike **9** chromatic, pictorial **10** expressive **11** picturesque

vivify 5 liven, renew **6** excite, infuse, kindle, revive **7** animate, enliven, quicken, refresh, restore **9** stimulate

vixen 3 fox, nag **5** harpy, scold, shrew **6** ogress, virago **8** fishwife, harridan, Xantippe **9** termagant, Xanthippe

viz 5 to wit **6** namely, that is **8** scilicet **9** videlicet **12** in other words

vizard 4 face, mask **5** guise, visor **6** domino **8** disguise

vocabulary 4 cant **5** argot, lingo, slang, words **6** jargon, patois **7** lexicon **8** glossary **9** word-hoard **10** vernacular **11** terminology

vocal 4 oral **5** blunt, frank **6** phonic, spoken, voiced **7** uttered **8** eloquent **9** outspoken **10** articulate, expressive, freespoken

vocalic 5 vowel

vocalist 4 diva **6** belter, canary, singer **7** crooner, warbler, yodeler **8** minstrel, songbird **9** balladeer, chanteuse, chorister **10** cantatrice, prima donna

vocalization 4 song **5** voice **6** speech **7** diction **8** speaking **9** utterance **11** enunciation **12** articulation **13** pronunciation

vocalize 3 air, hem **4** sing, talk **5** chant, croon, speak, state, utter, voice **6** warble **7** express **9** enunciate, pronounce

vocal organ 6 larynx **8** voice box *bird:* **6** syrinx

vocation 3 art, job **4** call, work **5** craft, trade **6** career, métier **7** calling, mission, pursuit **8** business, lifework **10** employment, handicraft, occupation, profession

vociferate 3 bay, cry **4** bark, bray, call, roar, yawp, yell **5** shout **6** bellow, clamor, holler **7** thunder

vociferous 4 loud **5** noisy **6** shrill **7** blatant, clamant, raucous **8** strident **9** clamorous **11** openmouthed **12** obstreperous

vogue 3 cry, fad, ton **4** chic, mode, pose, rage **5** craze, favor, furor, style, trend **6** furore **7** fashion **10** dernier cri, popularity **11** stylishness

voice 3 put, say **4** part, talk, tell, vent **5** say-so, sound, speak, state, utter **6** assert, choice, medium, singer, speech **7** declare, express, opinion, present **8** vocalize **9** condition, enunciate, formulate, pronounce, statement, utterance, verbalize **10** articulate, expression, instrument *female:* **4** alto **5** mezzo **7** soprano **9** contralto *high:* **5** tenor **7** soprano **8** falsetto *in grammar:* **6** active **7** passive *Latin:* **3** vox *male:* **4** bass **5** tenor **8** baritone *quality:* **5** pitch **6** timbre *quiet:* **7** whisper *relating to:* **5** vocal **8** phonetic *without:* **4** dumb, mute

voice box 6 larynx

voiced 4 oral **5** vocal **6** sonant, spoken **7** uttered **8** phonated **9** expressed

voiceless 3 mum **4** dumb, mute, surd **6** silent **8** breathed **12** inarticulate

void 3 gap, nix **4** emit, hole, idle, lack, null, undo **5** abyss, annul, blank, clear, empty, inane, quash **6** bereft, cancel, cavity, hollow, negate, remove, vacant, vacate, vacuum **7** absence, give off, negated, nullify, rescind, reverse, vacuity, vacuous **8** abrogate, deserted, evacuate **9** black hole, discharge, eliminate, emptiness **10** extinguish **11** nothingness

volant 4 fast, spry, yare **5** agile, fleet, quick, zippy **6** flying, lively, nimble **9** dexterous, sprightly

volar 6 palmar

volatile 5 flaky **6** fickle, flying, lively **7** erratic, essence, flighty **8** fleeting, fugitive, skittery, skittish, unstable, variable, volcanic **9** ephemeral, explosive, fugacious, mercurial, momentary, transient **10** capricious, changeable, evanescent, inconstant, short-lived, transitory **11** impermanent **13** temperamental

volatility 10 fickleness **11** flightiness, inconstancy, instability **13** changeability

volcanic 7 violent **8** volatile **9** explosive *explosion:* **8** eruption *glass:* **8** obsidian *matter:* **3** ash **4** lava, tufa, tuff **5** magma **6** scoria *mound:* **4** cone *passage:* **6** throat **7** conduit *vent:* **8** fumarole **9** solfatara

volcano 4 hill, vent **8** mountain *Alaska:* **6** Katmai (Mount) **8** Wrangell (Mount) **9** Aniakchak (Crater) *Andes:* **5** Omate **12** Huaina Putina *Antarctica:* **6** Erebus (Mount) *Azores:* **4** Alto (Pico) *California:* **6** Lassen (Peak) *Canaries:* **5** Teide (Pico de), Teyde (Pico de) **8** Tenerife (Pico de) *Colombia:* **5** Huila (Nevado del), Pasto **6** Purace **7** Galeras *Costa Rica:* **4** Poás **5** Barba, Irazú *Ecuador:* **6** Sangay **8** Antisana, Cotopaxi *extinct:* **4** Popa (Mount) **5** Iriga, Kenya (Mount) **8** Mauna Kea **9** Haleakala (Crater) *Guatemala:* **4** Agua **5** Fuego **7** Atitlán *Hawaii:* **7** Kilauea **8** Mauna Loa *Honshu:* **4** Nasu **5** Asama, Azuma **6** Bandai **8** Nasudake **9** Asamayama *Iceland:* **5** Askja, Hecla, Hekla *Indonesia:* **3** Awu (Gunung) **5** Agung (Gunung) **7** Tambora (Gunung) *island:* **5** Thera, Thira **8** Krakatau, Krakatoa, Santorin **9** Santorini *Italy:* **8** Vesuvius **9** Stromboli *Iwo Jima:* **9** Suribachi (Mount) *Japan:* **3** Aso **5** Unzen **6** Asosan *Java:* **4** Gede (Gunung) **5** Bromo, Gedeh (Gunung), Kelud (Gunung), Salak (Gunung) *Madeira:* **5** Ruivo (Pico) *Martinique:* **5** Pelée (Mount) *Mexico:* **6** Colima **7** Orizaba **9** Paricutín **12** Popocatepetl *New Zealand:* **7** Ruapehu (Mount) **9** Ngauruhoe, Tongariro *Peru:* **5** Misti (El) *Philippines:* **3** Apo (Mount) **4** Taal **5** Mayon (Mount) **8** Pinatubo (Mount) *Sicily:* **4** Etna *Solomons:* **5** Balbi *South America:* **5** Lanín, Maipo, Maipu *Sumatra:* **5** Dempo (Gunung) **7** Kerinci **8** Kerintji *type:* **6** shield **10** cinder cone *Washington:* **11** Saint Helens (Mount) *West Indies:* **9** Soufrière

___ **volente 3** Deo

volition 4 will **6** choice, desire, intent, option **8** decision, election **9** selection **10** preference

volley 4 hail, shot **5** burst, round, salvo, storm **6** return, shower **7** barrage **8** drumfire **9** broadside, cannonade, discharge, fusillade

volplane 5 glide

Volpone 3 Fox (The) *author:* **6** Jonson (Ben) *servant:* **5** Mosca

Volsung *grandson:* **6** Sigurd **9** Siegfried *great-grandfather:* **4** Odin *son:* **7** Sigmund

voltage 5 power **6** energy **9** intensity

Voltaire *drama:* **5** Zaïre **6** Alzire, Brutus, Mèrope, Oedipe **7** Mahomet **8** Tancrède *novel:* **5** Zadig **7** Candide *real name:* **6** Arouet (François Marie)

volte-face 5 U-turn **8** flip-flop, reversal, turnover **9** about-face, inversion, turnabout **10** switcheroo **13** change of heart

voluble 4 glib **5** gabby, talky, windy **6** chatty, fluent, mouthy, prolix **7** verbose **8** effusive, vocative **9** garrulous, talkative **10** long-winded, loquacious

volume 4 body, book, bulk, mass, size, tome **5** album, flood, folio, space **6** amount, scroll **7** content **8** capacity, loudness, quantity **9** aggregate **12** displacement

voluminous 4 full **5** bulky **6** legion, prolix **7** copious **8** numerous, prolific **9** capacious **10** convoluted **13** multitudinous

Volumnia's son 10 Coriolanus

voluntary 4 free **7** willful, willing, witting **8** elective, freewill, optional **10** autonomous, deliberate, volitional **11** independent, intentional, spontaneous **13** discretionary

volunteer 5 offer **6** enlist, join up, sign up **7** present, propose, suggest *hospital:* **12** candy striper

Volunteer State 9 Tennessee

voluptuous 4 sexy **5** ample, buxom **6** wanton **7** languid, sensual **8** luscious, sensuous **9** bodacious, luxurious **10** curvaceous

volute 5 helix, shell **6** scroll, spiral **7** mollusc, mollusk **8** curlicue

vomit 3 gag **4** barf, cast, gush, hurl, lose, puke, spew, toss **5** expel, retch **6** spit up **7** bring up, throw up, upchuck **8** disgorge **11** regurgitate

vomiting 6 emesis

Vonnegut work 9 Galapagos, Timequake **10** Cat's Cradle, Hocus Pocus **11** Player Piano **13** Sirens of Titan (The) **18** Slaughterhouse Five **20** Breakfast of Champions **22** Happy Birthday Wanda June

voodoo 3 hex **4** jinx, juju, mojo **5** charm, magic, spell **6** amulet, whammy **7** bewitch, enchant, sorcery **8** ensorcel, wizardry **9** ensorcell **10** hocus-pocus,

mumbo jumbo, necromancy, witchcraft 11 abracadabra, implausible,
unrealistic
voracious 4 avid 5 eager 6 ardent,
greedy, hungry 7 piggish, starved 8 edacious, famished, ravenous, starving
9 rapacious 10 gluttonous, insatiable,
omnivorous, quenchless
vortex 4 eddy, gyre 5 swirl 7 tornado
9 hurricane, maelstrom, whirlpool,
whirlwind 11 tourbillion
votary 3 bug, fan, nut 4 buff 5 lover
6 addict, zealot 7 admirer, apostle,
devotee, groupie, habitué 8 adherent,
advocate, believer, disciple, follower
9 worshiper 10 aficionado, enthusiast,
worshipper
vote 3 opt 4 poll 5 elect, judge, offer
6 ballot, choice, choose, decide, ratify,
select, ticket 7 adjudge, declare,
endorse, express, opinion, propose,
suggest, verdict 8 election, suffrage
9 franchise 10 expression *affirmative:*
3 aye, nod, yea, yes 6 placet *kind:*
5 proxy, straw, voice 6 secret 7 write-in
8 absentee 10 plebiscite, referendum
negative: 3 nay *right to:* 8 suffrage
9 franchise
votive 8 grateful 10 devotional
vouch 5 prove 6 affirm, assert, assure,
attest, uphold, verify 7 certify, confirm,
support, witness 8 accredit 9 guarantee
11 corroborate 12 substantiate
voucher 3 IOU 4 chit 5 proof 6 coupon,
surety 7 receipt 9 affidavit, indenture
10 credential 11 certificate 13 authorization
vouchsafe 4 give 5 award, favor, grant
6 accord, bestow, confer, oblige 7 concede, furnish
vow 4 aver, oath, word 5 swear, troth
6 assert, attest, pledge, plight 7 confirm, declare, promise, warrant
8 covenant 9 assertion, guarantee
10 obligation 11 declaration

vowel 6 letter, symbol 11 speech sound
kind: 4 high, long 5 glide, schwa, short
9 diphthong 11 monophthong *omission:*
7 aphesis 11 contraction *variation:*
6 ablaut, umlaut
voyage 4 sail, trek, trip 5 jaunt 6 cruise,
junket, outing, travel 7 journey,
odyssey, set sail 8 traverse 9 excursion
10 expedition, pilgrimage
voyeur 6 peeper 10 peeping Tom
Vronski's lover 12 Anna Karenina
Vulcan see HEPHAESTUS
vulgar 3 low, raw 4 base, lewd, rude, vile
5 crass, crude, gaudy, gross, rough,
tacky 6 coarse, earthy, flashy, garish,
ribald, sordid, tawdry 7 kitschy, lowbred, lowbrow, obscene, profane,
uncouth 8 churlish, improper, indecent, off-color, unseemly 9 barbarous,
graceless, low-minded, offensive, tasteless, unrefined 10 indecorous, indelicate, scurrilous, unpolished, vernacular
11 pretentious
vulgate 10 vernacular
Vulgate translator 6 Jerome
vulnerability 8 exposure, soft spot,
weakness 10 underbelly
12 Achilles' heel
vulnerable 4 open, weak 6 liable
7 exposed 10 assailable 11 susceptible
vulnerary 4 balm 5 salve, tonic 7 healing,
unguent 8 curative, ointment, remedial, salutary, sanative 9 medicinal,
wholesome 10 salubrious 11 restorative,
therapeutic 12 healthgiving
vulpine 3 sly 4 foxy, wily 5 slick 6 artful,
astute, crafty, shrewd, tricky 7 cunning,
foxlike 8 guileful
vulture 4 bird 6 condor 11 lammergeier,
lammergeyer *food:* 7 carrion *relative:*
4 hawk 5 eagle 6 falcon 7 buzzard
vulturine 8 ravenous 9 predatory, rapacious, raptorial 10 predaceous, predacious, scavenging

W

wacky 3 fey, mad **4** daft, nuts **5** batty, daffy, crazy, flaky, kooky, loony, loopy, silly **6** absurd, fruity, insane, screwy **7** bonkers, cracked, foolish, idiotic, lunatic, offbeat **8** crackers, demented **9** eccentric **10** irrational **11** harebrained **12** preposterous

wad 3 gob **4** lump, mint, pile, plug, quid, roll, swab **5** chunk, stuff **6** boodle, bundle, packet, pellet **7** fortune **8** bankroll

waddle 6 toddle

waddy 4 club, cosh **6** cowboy, cudgel **7** rustler **8** bludgeon

wade 4 ford, plod **5** labor **6** drudge, trudge *into:* **5** set to **6** attack, plunge, tackle **9** undertake

wadi 3 bed **4** wash **5** gully **6** arroyo, coulee, course, ravine **9** streambed **10** depression **11** watercourse

wafer 4 chip, disk, host **5** matzo, slice **6** matzoh **7** cracker

waffle 4 yo-yo **5** tripe, waver **6** dither, drivel, seesaw **7** blather **8** flip-flop **9** fluctuate, vacillate **10** equivocate

waft 4 flag, gust, puff, wave **5** drift, float, hover **7** pennant

wag 3 bob, nod, wit **4** card, lash, wave **5** clown, cutup, joker, shake, swing, whisk **6** kidder, switch, twitch, waddle **8** brandish, comedian, funnyman, jokester

wage 3 fee, pay **6** income, reward, salary **7** carry on, payment, stipend **8** earnings, pittance, receipts **9** emolument **10** recompense **12** compensation, remuneration

wager 3 bet, lay, pot **4** ante, game, risk **5** stake **6** chance, gamble, hazard **7** venture

waggery 3 gag **4** jest, joke **5** prank, sport **7** devilry, kidding, roguery **8** deviltry, drollery, mischief **10** impishness, pleasantry **11** roguishness **12** sportiveness **13** practical joke

waggish 4 arch, pert **5** antic, comic, droll, saucy, witty **6** impish, jocose **7** comical, jocular, playful, puckish, roguish **8** humorous, prankish, sportive **9** facetious **10** frolicsome **11** mischievous

waggle 3 bob **4** reel, sway

Wagner, Richard *birthplace:* **7** Leipzig *father-in-law:* **5** Liszt (Franz) *festival site:* **8** Bayreuth *opera:* **4** Ring **6** Rienzi **8** Parsifal **9** Lohengrin, Rheingold (Das), Siegfried **10** Die Walküre, Tannhäuser **12** Das Rheingold **13** Meistersinger (Die) **14** Flying Dutchman (The) **15** Götterdämmerung **16** Tristan und Isolde **17** Ring of the Nibelung (The) *recurring theme:* **9** leitmotif, leitmotiv *wife:* **5** Minna **6** Cosima

wagon 3 van **4** cart, dray, tram, trek, wain **7** caravan, coaster, hayrack

wahoo 3 ono **8** mackerel **9** winged elm **11** burning bush

waif 5 gamin, stray **6** gamine, orphan, urchin **8** wanderer **9** foundling **10** ragamuffin **11** guttersnipe

wail 3 bay, cry **4** bawl, blub, fuss, howl, keen, weep, yowl **5** mourn, whine **6** bemoan, lament, plaint, repine **7** blubber, ululate **8** complain **9** complaint **11** lamentation

wain 5 wagon **9** Big Dipper

waistband 3 obi **4** belt, sash **6** girdle **8** ceinture, cincture **10** cummerbund

waistcoat 4 vest **6** jerkin, weskit

wait 4 bide, idle, stay **5** abide, dally, delay, serve, tarry, watch **6** expect, hold on, linger, remain **8** hang fire, mark time, sit tight **10** anticipate **11** stick around

waiter 4 tray **6** garçon, salver, server **7** servant **9** attendant

Waiting for ___ 5 Godot, Lefty

wait on 4 tend **5** serve **6** attend, tend to **7** care for, cater to **9** look after

waive 4 cede, stay **5** allow, defer, delay, forgo, table, yield **6** give up, hold up, put off, shelve **7** abandon, concede, dismiss, hold off, suspend **8** hand over, hold over, postpone **9** surrender **10** relinquish

wake 4 path, stir, wash **5** alert, arise, get up, rally, rouse, track, vigil, watch **6** arouse, bestir, excite, kindle, stir up **7** roll out **8** backwash **9** aftermath, stimulate

wakeful 5 alert **8** restless, vigilant **9** insomniac, sleepless

waken see WAKE

Walden author 7 Thoreau (Henry David)

wale 3 rib 4 bend, welt 5 brace, ridge 6 strake

walk 3 pad 4 gait, hike, hoof, pace, path, plod, roam, slog, step, trip 5 alley, amble, clump, mince, paseo, stave, strut, stump, trail, tramp, tread, troop 6 prance, ramble, sashay, stride, stroll, toddle, trudge, waddle, wander 7 saunter, shamble, shuffle, stumble, swagger, traipse 8 ambulate, traverse 9 promenade 11 base on balls, perambulate, peregrinate

walkaway 4 romp, rout

walking shorts 8 Bermudas

walking stick 4 cane 5 staff 6 crutch, insect 7 phasmid, whangee

walk out 5 leave 6 strike

walk out on 5 leave 6 desert 7 abandon, forsake

Walküre composer 6 Wagner (Richard)

walkway 4 path 7 passage 9 promenade

wall 3 bar, hem 4 side, stop 5 block, close, fence, hedge 6 immure 7 barrier, close in, enclose 8 blockade, surround 9 barricade, enclosure, roadblock, structure *bearing:* 7 support *hanging:* 8 tapestry *painting:* 5 mural *protective:* 7 parapet, rampart *top of:* 6 coping

wallaby 8 kangaroo

wallet 5 funds 6 folder 8 billfold 9 accessory, resources 10 pocketbook

Wallis and Futuna Islands *capital:* 7 Mata-Utu *island:* 4 Uvéa *territory of:* 6 France

wallop 3 bop, hit 4 bang, bash, beat, belt, blow, boil, bust, clip, drub, lick, pelt, slam, slug, sock, whip, whop, whup 5 baste, paste, pound, punch, smack, whack 6 buffet, pummel, thrash, thwack 7 shellac, trounce 8 lambaste

walloping 4 huge 5 giant 7 immense, mammoth, monster 8 colossal, enormous, gigantic, smashing 10 gargantuan, impressive, incredible, prodigious

wallow 4 bask, roll 5 enjoy, revel 6 billow, welter 7 delight, indulge 9 luxuriate

___ **Walpole** 4 Hugh 6 Horace

___ **Walton** 3 Sam 5 Izaak

waltz 5 dance, valse

Waltz King 7 Strauss (Johann)

Wampanoag chief 9 Massasoit, Metacomet 10 King Philip

wampum 5 beads, money 6 shells

wan 3 dim 4 ashy, gray, pale, waxy, weak, worn 5 ashen, faint, livid, lurid, pasty, waxen 6 anemic, doughy, feeble, infirm, pallid, peaked, sallow, sickly 7 ghastly, languid 8 blanched 9 bloodless, colorless, washed-out 10 cadaverous, white-faced

wand 3 rod 4 pole, tube 5 baton, staff

wander 3 bat, bum, gad 4 mill, roam, rove, swan 5 amble, dally, drift, float, gypsy, mooch, prowl, range, stray, tramp 6 ramble, stroll 7 deviate, digress, diverge, maunder, meander, saunter, traipse 8 divagate, straggle, vagabond 9 expatiate, gallivant 10 kick around

wanderer 4 waif 5 gypsy, nomad, rover, stray 7 pilgrim, vagrant 8 runabout, vagabond

wandering 7 erratic, migrant, nomadic, vagrant 8 vagabond 9 itinerant, migratory, walkabout, wayfaring 10 roundabout 11 peripatetic

wane 3 dim, ebb 4 fail, fall 5 abate, let up 6 lessen, recede, reduce, relent, shrink, weaken 7 decline, dwindle, slacken, subside 8 decrease, diminish, moderate, slack off, taper off

wangle 6 scheme 7 finagle, wheedle 8 inveigle, scrounge 10 manipulate

wannabe 5 clone 7 also-ran, copycat, hopeful, wishful 8 apparent, aspiring, desiring, desirous 9 ambitious, lookalike, potential

want 4 lack, like, need, void, wish 5 covet, crave, fault 6 dearth, desire, penury 7 absence, poverty, require 8 exigency 9 indigence, necessity, neediness, privation 10 deficiency, desiderate, inadequacy, scantiness 11 destitution, requirement 13 insufficiency

wanting 4 away, less, sans 5 minus, scant, short 6 absent, scanty, scarce 7 lacking, missing, without 9 deficient 10 inadequate, incomplete 12 insufficient

wanton 4 doxy, jade, lewd, minx, rank, slut 5 bawdy, cruel, hussy, loose, tramp, trull, wench 6 coquet, floozy, harlot, lavish, trifle, unruly 7 baggage, cyprian, immoral, jezebel, lustful, obscene, Paphian, sensual, trollop, wayward 8 inhumane, pitiless, ruthless, slattern, spiteful, sportive, strumpet 9 dissolute, luxuriant, malicious, merciless 10 gratuitous, lascivious, malevolent, outrageous, prostitute 11 extravagant, mischievous, uncalled-for

wapiti 3 elk 7 red deer

war 4 feud, odds 5 fight 6 battle, combat, strife 7 contest 8 conflict, struggle, variance 9 hostility 10 antagonism 11 competition *German:* 5 Krieg 10 blitzkrieg *god:* 3 Tiu, Tyr 4 Ares, Mars, Odin 5 Woden, Wotan *goddess:* 4 Enyo 5 Anath 6 Inanna, Ishtar 7 Bel-

lona *Latin:* 6 bellum *Muslim:* 5 jehad, jihad *relating to:* 7 martial
War and Peace *author:* 7 Tolstoy (Leo) *composer:* 9 Prokofiev (Sergey)
warble 4 sing 5 carol, chirp, trill, tweet 6 gadfly, maggot, quaver 7 descant, melisma, twitter
warbler 4 bird 6 singer 7 kinglet 8 songster 9 blackpoll 11 gnatcatcher *European:* 10 chiffchaff
war cry 5 motto 6 slogan *Greek:* 5 alala *Japanese:* 6 banzai
ward 4 care 5 aegis, stave 6 barrio, charge 7 custody, defense, keeping 8 district, division, precinct, security 9 bishopric 10 protection 11 safekeeping 12 guardianship
warden 6 jailer, keeper, regent 7 provost 8 governor, guardian, official 9 castellan, constable, custodian, protector 10 commandant, supervisor
ward off 5 avert, parry, rebut, repel 6 divert 7 deflect 8 turn away 9 forestall
wardrobe 5 trunk 6 closet 7 apparel, armoire, clothes 8 clothing 9 garderobe 12 clothespress
warehouse 4 stow 5 depot, lodge, stock, store 7 confine, deposit, shelter, storage, stowage 8 building 9 stockroom, storeroom 10 depository, repository 11 accommodate *oriental:* 6 godown
wares 4 line 5 goods, stock 9 vendibles 11 commodities, marketables, merchandise
warfare 6 battle, combat, strife 8 conflict, struggle 10 operations 11 hostilities *type:* 4 germ 6 trench 10 biological
warhorse 4 hack 7 charger, courser, veteran 8 chestnut, standard
warlike 7 hawkish, martial 8 militant, military 9 bellicose, combative, truculent 10 aggressive, pugnacious 11 belligerent
warlock 3 wiz 4 mage 5 magus 6 wizard 8 conjurer, conjuror, magician, satanist, sorcerer 9 diabolist, enchanter 11 necromancer
warm 4 bask, heat, kind 5 angry, fresh 6 ardent, genial, heated, heat up, loving, reheat, secure, tender 7 affable, cordial, excited, fervent, sincere 8 friendly, gracious, spirited 9 heartfelt 10 passionate, responsive 11 kindhearted, sympathetic 12 affectionate, enthusiastic, wholehearted 13 compassionate *air:* 7 thermal
warmed-over 5 banal, stale, tired, trite 6 old-hat 7 clichéd 8 shopworn, timeworn 9 hackneyed
warmhearted 4 kind 6 benign, kindly, loving, tender 7 cordial 8 generous

9 benignant, unselfish 10 benevolent 11 magnanimous, sympathetic 12 affectionate 13 compassionate
warmth 4 glow, heat 7 comfort 8 fondness 9 affection 10 cordiality
warn 3 tip 4 clew, clue 5 alert 6 advise, inform, notify, tip off 7 apprise, caution, counsel 8 admonish
warning 3 tip 4 hint 5 alarm, alert 6 caveat, notice, signal, tip-off 7 caution, counsel, summons 8 monition, monitory 10 admonition, cautionary 12 admonishment *legal:* 6 caveat
War of the Worlds author 5 Wells (H. G.)
warp 4 base, bend, cast, kink, rope, wind 5 color, curve, twist 6 buckle, debase, deform, wrench 7 confuse, contort, corrupt, deflect, distort, pervert, torture, vitiate 10 bastardize 12 misrepresent
warrant 4 pawn, writ 5 proof, prove, token 6 affirm, assert, assure, attest, avouch, ensure, ground, insure, pledge, secure 7 certify, contend, declare, justify, precept 8 guaranty, maintain, mittimus, sanction, security 9 assurance, authority, authorize, guarantee 10 foundation 11 certificate 12 confirmation 13 justification
warranty 4 bail, bond 6 surety 8 covenant, security 9 guarantee
warren 4 maze 7 network, rabbits 8 tenement
warrior 4 hero 7 battler, fighter, soldier 8 champion 9 combatant 10 serviceman *female:* 6 Amazon *Japanese:* 7 samurai
Warsaw *castle:* 5 Zamek *river:* 7 Vistula
wart 4 flaw 6 defect, growth 7 blemish, verruca 11 excrescence
wary 5 alert, cagey, canny, chary, leery 7 careful, dubious, guarded, mindful 8 cautious, skittish, vigilant, watchful 10 suspicious 11 circumspect, distrustful
wash 3 lap, pan, tub 4 hose, lave, suds, wadi 5 bathe, clean, creek, douse, drift, float, flush, marsh, scrub, slosh, swill 6 drench, shower, sluice, splash 7 cleanse, coating, launder, laundry, shampoo, suffuse 8 backwash
washed-out 4 beat 5 all in, faded, spent, tired, weary 6 bushed, effete, sapped, used-up, wasted 7 drained 8 depleted 9 exhausted
washed-up 4 beat, done 5 kaput, spent 6 done in 7 also-ran, defunct, done for, through 8 finished
washing 4 bath 6 lavage 7 laundry 8 ablution, lavation *ceremonial:* 6 lavabo
Washington *capital:* 7 Olympia *city:*

6 Tacoma 7 Seattle, Spokane 9 Vancouver 10 Walla Walla *college, university:* 7 Gonzaga, Whitman 9 Evergreen *dam:* 11 Grand Coulee *mountain, range:* 7 Cascade, Olympic, Rainier 8 St. Helens *nickname:* 9 Evergreen (State) *river:* 6 Yakima 8 Columbia *state bird:* 9 goldfinch *state flower:* 12 rhododendron *state tree:* 7 hemlock
Washington, D.C., designer 7 L'Enfant (Pierre-Charles)
Washington, George *home:* 11 Mount Vernon *wife:* 6 Martha
Washington Square author 5 James (Henry)
wasp 5 mason 6 digger, hornet, vespid 9 ichneumon, mud dauber 12 yellow jacket
waspish 5 testy 6 snappy, snarky, snippy, touchy 7 peevish, vespine 8 petulant, snappish, vinegary 9 crotchety, fractious, irritable, querulous 10 vinegarish 12 cantankerous, cross-grained
wassail 5 binge, carol, drink, revel, spree, toast 6 bender 7 carouse, revelry, roister 8 carousal, drinking
Wasserstein play 15 Heidi Chronicles (The) 17 Sisters Rosenzweig (The)
waste 4 arid, fail, kill, loss, ruin, sack, wild 5 empty, offal, scrap, trash 6 barren, damage, debris, desert, devour, litter, ravage, refuse, sewage, shrink, weaken 7 badland, consume, despoil, destroy, fritter, garbage, pillage, plunder, rubbish 8 decrease, desolate, emaciate, enfeeble, misspend, prodigal, spoilage, squander, wear away, wildland 9 devastate, dissipate, excrement, sweepings, throw away 10 desolation, wilderness 11 prodigality 12 extravagance, extravagancy *maker:* 5 haste *time:* 5 dally 6 dawdle, footle, piddle, trifle
waste away 4 fade, fail 6 molder, shrink 7 atrophy, decline, dwindle, shrivel 10 degenerate
wasted 3 lit 4 high 5 drunk, gaunt 6 peaked, sickly, stoned 7 elapsed, ravaged 8 skeletal 9 emaciated 10 cadaverous, skeletonic 11 intoxicated
wasteful 6 lavish 8 prodigal 9 throwaway 10 profligate, thriftless, uneconomic 11 extravagant, improvident, inefficient, spendthrift
wastefulness 6 excess 10 lavishness 11 prodigality 12 extravagance, immoderation
wasteland 4 wild 5 heath 6 barren 10 desolation, wilderness
Waste Land author 5 Eliot (T. S.)
wastrel 3 rip 4 rake, roué 7 rounder,

spender 8 prodigal 9 fritterer, libertine 10 dissipater, high roller, ne'er-do-well, profligate, squanderer 11 scattergood, spendthrift
watch 3 eye, see, spy 4 bide, look, tend, tout, wait, wake, ward 5 guard, shift, vigil 6 attend, follow, look at, notice, sentry 7 care for, lookout, monitor, observe, surveil 8 bulletin, eagle eye, scrutiny, sentinel, watchman 9 attention, timepiece, vigilance 10 duty period, observance 11 chronometer, observation 12 surveillance *chain:* 3 fob *maker:* 10 horologist
watchdog 5 guard 6 keeper 8 Cerberus, guardian 9 custodian, protector
watcher 6 viewer 7 guarder, lookout 8 beholder, follower, guardian, observer, onlooker 9 spectator
watchful 4 wary 5 alert, chary 7 on guard, wakeful 8 cautious, vigilant 9 attentive, observant, sleepless, wide-awake 10 unsleeping *Scottish:* 5 tenty 6 tentie
watchman 5 guard, scout 6 patrol, picket, sentry, warder 7 lookout 8 sentinel
watch out 6 beware 8 take care
watchtower 6 turret 7 lookout 8 barbican, bartizan 10 lighthouse
watchword 3 cry 5 motto 6 mantra, parole, signal, slogan 8 password 9 principle 10 shibboleth 11 catchphrase, countersign
water 4 soak, thin, tide 5 drink, fluid, spray 6 dilute, liquid, supply 7 moisten 8 irrigate, moisture, snowmelt, sprinkle 10 excellence 13 amniotic fluid *body:* 3 bay, sea 4 gulf, lake, pool 5 ocean 6 lagoon, strait 9 reservoir *combining form:* 4 aqui, aquo, hydr 5 hydro *French:* 3 eau *goddess:* 4 Nina 7 Anahita, Anaitis *Latin:* 4 aqua *Spanish:* 4 agua
water buffalo 4 arna 5 bovid 7 carabao *female:* 5 arnee
water clock 9 clepsydra
water closet 3 loo 4 head, john 5 privy 6 toilet 7 latrine 8 bathroom, lavatory
watercourse 4 dike, duct 5 bayou, canal, ditch 6 arroyo 7 channel, conduit 8 aqueduct, headrace, tailrace 9 streambed
water cow 6 dugong 7 manatee
watered-down 5 washy 6 dilute 7 diluted
waterfall 5 chute, sault, shoot 7 cascade 8 cataract *Brazil:* 6 Iguaçú (Falls), Iguazú (Falls) *California:* 8 Yosemite (Falls) *Canada:* 5 Grand (Falls) 8 Takkakaw 9 Churchill (Falls) *Canada-U.S.:* 7 Niagara (Falls) *Congo:* 6 Boyoma (Falls) 7 Stanley (Falls) *former Nile:* 4 Owen (Falls) 5 Ripon (Falls) *Ken-*

tucky: 10 Cumberland (Falls) *New Zealand:* 10 Sutherland (Falls) *Niagara:* 8 American, Canadian 9 Horseshoe *Norway:* 6 Rjukan (Falls) *Oregon:* 9 Multnomah (Falls) *South Africa:* 6 Tugela (Falls) *Snake River:* 4 Twin (Falls) 8 Shoshone (Falls) *Venezuela:* 5 Angel (Falls) *Washington:* 10 Snoqualmie (Falls) *world's highest:* 5 Angel (Falls) *Wyoming:* 11 Yellowstone (Falls) *Zambezi River:* 8 Victoria

water finder 6 dowser 11 divining rod

waterfront 8 seacoast 9 lakeshore, riverside

water hole 5 oasis

watering hole 3 bar, pub 4 café 5 oasis 6 lounge, nitery, resort, saloon, tavern 7 barroom, cabaret 9 nightclub, nightspot, roadhouse 10 supper club

waterless 3 dry 4 arid, sere 7 bone-dry 8 droughty 9 anhydrous 10 dehydrated

waterlog 8 saturate

waterloo 4 ruin 6 defeat 7 failure 8 disaster, downfall

water nymph 4 lily 5 naiad 6 mayfly, Nereid 7 Oceanid 9 dragonfly *female:* 3 nix 5 nixie

water oscillation 6 seiche

water pipe 4 bong 5 spout 6 hookah 8 narghile, nargileh 12 hubble-bubble

water plant 7 aquatic, seaweed 8 duckweed, wild rice 9 arrowhead, tape grass 10 hydrophyte, manna grass 11 bladderwort

water rat 6 nutria

watershed 6 crisis, divide 12 turning point

water spirit 3 nix 5 nixie, nymph 6 sprite, undine

water tank 7 cistern

watery 4 pale, thin, weak 5 banal, bland, vapid, washy 6 dilute, serous 7 diluted, insipid

wattle 4 gill, grid, jowl 5 frame 8 caruncle 9 framework, interlace 10 interweave

wattle and___ 4 daub

wave 3 wag 4 flag, flap 5 heave, ridge, surge, sweep, swell 6 comber, influx, marcel, motion, period, ripple, signal, waggle 7 breaker, dismiss, flutter, gesture, upsurge 8 activity, brandish, flourish, undulate 9 disregard *large:* 7 tsunami

waver 4 reel, sway 5 swing, weave 6 dither, falter, quaver, quiver, teeter, totter, wobble 7 flicker, stagger, whiffle 8 hesitate, undulate 9 oscillate, vacillate 12 shilly-shally

wavering 4 weak 5 shake, shaky 6 unsure, wobbly 7 halting 8 doubtful, insecure, to-and-fro, unstable 9 equivocal, faltering, fluctuant, hesitancy, undecided, vibration, whiffling 10 hesitating, hesitation, indecision, irresolute 11 fluctuating, vacillating, vacillation 12 irresolution, shilly-shally

Waverly author 5 Scott (Walter)

wavy 7 rolling 8 rippling, swelling 9 fluctuant 10 undulating 11 fluctuating

wavy pattern 5 moiré 8 squiggle 10 undulation 11 crenulation

wax 4 come, grow, rise 5 boost, build, mount 6 become, expand, record 7 augment, enlarge 8 heighten, increase, multiply, paraffin, simonize 9 secretion, substance

waxen 3 wan 4 ashy, pale 5 ashen, livid 6 pallid, smooth 7 pliable 8 blanched, moldable 9 colorless

way 3 ilk 4 door, kind, mode, much, path, road, sort, type, very 5 entry, habit, means, order, route, state, style, usage 6 access, artery, action, avenue, course, custom, degree, manner, method, street 7 ability, fashion, feature, ingress, opening, outcome, respect 8 distance, entrance, practice 9 boulevard, condition, direction, procedure, technique 11 opportunity, possibility 12 thoroughfare

wayfarer 5 gypsy, hiker, nomad, tramp 8 traveler 9 itinerant, journeyer

wayfaring 6 roving 7 nomadic, vagrant 8 vagabond 9 itinerant, traveling, wandering 10 travelling 11 peripatetic 13 perambulatory

waylay 5 brace 6 ambush, attack 8 surprise 9 bushwhack, still-hunt

Way of All Flesh author 6 Butler (Samuel)

Way of the World author 8 Congreve (William)

wayward 5 balky 6 fickle, unruly 7 froward, restive, vagrant 8 contrary, perverse, untoward 9 whimsical 10 capricious, headstrong 11 intractable, wrongheaded 12 ungovernable 13 unpredictable

we *French:* 4 nous *German:* 3 wir *Italian:* 3 noi *Spanish:* 8 nosotros

weak 3 dim, wan 4 puny, soft, thin 5 faint, frail, shaky, timid 6 dilute, feeble, flimsy, infirm, sickly, unsure, watery, wobbly 7 brittle, diluted, fragile, rickety, spindly, tenuous, unsound 8 decrepit, delicate, helpless, impotent, inferior, insecure, timorous, unstable, wavering 9 deficient, enfeebled, inaudible, powerless, spineless, uncertain 10 improbable, inadequate, unreliable, unstressed 11 debilitated, implausible, ineffective, ineffectual, vacillating, watered-down **12** unconvincing, undependable **13** insubstantial, unsubstantial

weaken 3 lag, sap **4** fail, flag, thin, wane **5** abate **6** damage, dilute, impair, lessen, reduce, soften **7** corrode, decline, disable, dwindle, subvert, unbrace **8** enervate, enfeeble, moderate **9** attenuate, grind down, honeycomb, undermine **10** debilitate, demoralize, invalidate

weak-kneed 5 timid **6** wobbly **7** gutless **8** cowardly, wavering **9** faltering, uncertain, whiffling **10** irresolute **11** lily-livered, vacillating **12** fainthearted, shilly-shally **13** pusillanimous

weakling 4 wimp, wuss **5** mouse, sissy **7** doormat, milksop, sad sack **8** pushover **9** jellyfish **10** namby-pamby **11** milquetoast, mollycoddle **12** invertebrate

weakness 4 flaw, hole, vice **5** crack, fault, taste **6** defect, desire, liking, relish **7** failing, frailty **8** appetite, debility, fondness, soft spot **9** infirmity **10** feebleness **11** decrepitude, shortcoming **12** Achilles' heel

weal 4 welt **5** ridge **7** welfare **9** well-being

weald 5 woods **6** forest **8** woodland **10** timberland, wilderness

wealth 5 goods, worth **6** assets, estate, plenty, riches **7** capital, fortune **8** holdings, opulence, property **9** abundance, affluence, profusion, resources **11** possessions

Wealth of Nations author 5 Smith (Adam)

wealthy 4 rich **5** flush **6** loaded **7** moneyed, opulent, well-off **8** affluent, well-to-do **9** well-fixed **10** prosperous, well-heeled **12** silk-stocking

wean 4 free, part **5** alien **6** detach **8** accustom, estrange, separate

weapon 3 bow, gun **4** bill, bolo, bomb, club, dart, dirk, mace, nuke, pike **5** A-bomb, arrow, H-bomb, knife, lance, prick, rifle, saber, sabre, sling, spear, steel, sword **6** dagger, Magnum, musket, pistol, poleax, rapier, rocket **7** bazooka, broadax, car bomb, carbine, firearm, gisarme, halberd, javelin, machete, missile, shotgun, sidearm, stun gun, torpedo, war club **8** battle-ax, bludgeon, broadaxe, catapult, crossbow, death ray, nerve gas, nunchaku, partisan, partizan, petronel, revolver, spontoon, tomahawk **9** battle-axe, blackjack, boomerang, derringer, slingshot **10** atomic bomb, machine gun, projectile **11** blunderbuss, depth charge, nuclear bomb **12** quarterstaff **13** brass knuckles

weapons 4 arms **7** arsenal, battery **8** ordnance **9** armaments, artillery, munitions **13** armamentarium

wear 3 rub **4** fray, tire **5** chafe, dress, erode, grind **6** abrade, attire, endure, impair **7** corrode, exhibit, fatigue, fashion **8** abrasion, clothing and tear: **12** depreciation thin: **4** fray **5** chafe **6** tatter **7** hackney

wear down 5 drain, erode, grind **6** abrade, weaken **7** corrode, degrade, exhaust, fatigue

weariness 5 ennui **7** boredom, fatigue, languor **8** lethargy **9** lassitude **10** enervation, exhaustion **12** taedium vitae

wearing 6 taxing, tiring, trying **9** difficult, fatiguing

wearisome see TIRESOME

wear out 3 fag **4** bust, do in, fray, poop, tire **5** drain **6** efface, tucker **7** consume, deplete, exhaust, frazzle **8** overstay

weary 4 beat, jade, limp, tire, worn **5** drain, jaded, spent, tired **6** bushed, done in, pooped, tucker, wasted **7** drained, fatigue, worn-out **8** dog-tired, fatigued, tiresome **9** apathetic

weasand 6 gullet, throat **7** trachea **8** windpipe **9** esophagus

weasel 5 dodge, evade, hedge, slink, sneak, stoat **6** ermine, escape, ferret, mammal **7** sneaker **8** sidestep **9** pussyfoot **10** equivocate Scottish: **8** whittret

weather 4 rain **5** storm **6** bear up, endure, expose **7** climate, ride out, undergo **9** withstand forecasting: **11** meteorology

weathercock 4 vane

weathered 8 hardened, seasoned, tempered

weave 4 cane, lawn, leno, spin, sway **5** braid, cloth, lurch, twine, waver **6** careen, fabric, pleach, raddle, wobble, zigzag **7** pattern, stagger, textile, texture **8** contrive **9** interlace **10** crisscross, intertwine

web 3 net **4** mesh, vane **5** snare, snarl **6** enmesh, fabric, tangle **7** ensnare, netting, network **8** entangle **10** enmeshment **12** entanglement

Weber opera 6 Oberon **9** Euryanthe **10** Freischütz (Der)

___ **Webster 4** Noah **6** Daniel

wed 4 join, link, mate, yoke **5** hitch, marry, merge, unite **6** splice **7** combine, conjoin, connect, espouse **10** tie the knot

wedded 7 marital, nuptial **8** conjugal, hymeneal **9** connubial **11** matrimonial

wedding 6 bridal 7 spousal 8 espousal, marriage, nuptials

wedding anniversary *fifteenth:* 7 crystal *fifth:* 6 wooden *fiftieth:* 6 golden *first:* 5 paper *seventy-fifth:* 7 diamond *tenth:* 3 tin *twentieth:* 5 china *twenty-fifth:* 6 silver

wedge 4 shim 5 chock, stuff 8 golf club, golf shot, keystone 10 force apart

wedge-shaped 7 cuneate 8 cottered, sphenoid 9 cuneiform

wedlock 4 knot, yoke 8 espousal, marriage 9 matrimony 11 conjugality 12 connubiality

wee 4 tiny 5 bitsy, bitty, early, small, teeny 6 little, minute, teensy 9 itty-bitty, miniature 10 diminutive, teeny-weeny 11 Lilliputian, little bitty 12 teensy-weensy

weed 4 dock, tare 5 chess, clear, plant 6 cockle, darnel, dodder, nettle, remove 7 burdock, burseed, ragweed, ruderal 8 amaranth, charlock, purslane 9 chickweed, cocklebur, dandelion, knotgrass, marijuana, poison ivy, poison oak, stickseed 10 cheatgrass, lady's thumb, sow thistle *European:* 6 spurry 7 spurrey *killer:* 8 paraquat 9 herbicide *Western:* 4 loco

weedy 4 lean, thin 5 lanky 6 skinny 7 scrawny, stringy, willowy 8 untended 9 overgrown

week 6 period 8 hebdomad *two weeks:* 9 fortnight

weep 3 cry, sob 4 drip, moan, ooze, tear, wail 5 bleed, exude, sweat 6 lament 7 blubber, dribble, trickle 8 transude

weepy 5 misty, moist, teary 7 tearful 10 lachrymose

weevil 7 billbug 8 curculio

weft 3 web 4 pick, woof, yarn 6 fabric, thread

weigh 3 way 4 heft, rate, tare 5 count, judge, scale, study 6 burden, ponder 7 balance, measure, oppress, perpend 8 appraise, bear down, consider, evaluate, militate 11 contemplate

weigh down 4 load 5 press 6 burden, sadden 7 depress, oppress 8 encumber 10 discourage, overburden

weight 3 tax 4 heft, lade, load, mass, onus, task 5 class, force, power 6 amount, assign, burden, charge, credit, import, moment, saddle 7 oppress, potency, quality 8 encumber, poundage, pressure, prestige, quantity 9 authority, influence, magnitude 10 corpulence, importance 11 consequence 12 significance *allowance:* 4 tare *apothecary:* 4 dram 5 grain, pound 7 scruple *Asian:* 6 cattie *gem:* 5 carat

measure of: 3 ton 4 dram, gram 5 grain, ounce, pound 7 long ton, scruple 8 kilogram, short ton 9 metric ton *system:* 3 net 4 troy 6 metric 10 apothecary 11 avoirdupois

weightiness 4 pith 6 import, moment 7 dignity, gravity 9 heaviness, magnitude, solemnity 10 importance 11 consequence, massiveness 12 significance 13 momentousness

weight lift 4 pull 5 clean, press, shrug 6 snatch 12 clean and jerk

weighty 3 fat 5 grave, gross, heavy, hefty, obese, sober, staid 6 fleshy, portly, sedate, severe, solemn, somber 7 massive, serious, telling 8 cumbrous, grievous, powerful 9 corpulent, effective, important, momentous, ponderous 10 burdensome, convincing, cumbersome 11 significant, substantial 12 considerable 13 consequential

weir 3 dam 5 stank

weird 3 odd 5 eerie, queer 6 creepy, freaky, spooky 7 bizarre, curious, oddball, strange, uncanny 8 freakish, peculiar, singular, sinister 9 eccentric, fantastic, unearthly 10 mysterious 11 inscrutable 12 supernatural 13 preternatural

weirdo 4 geek, kook 5 freak 7 nutcase, oddball 8 crackpot 9 eccentric, screwball

welcome 4 hail 5 cheer, greet, hello, howdy 6 accept, invite, salute 7 embrace, invited, receive 8 greeting, pleasant, pleasing 9 agreeable, favorable, reception 10 gratifying, hospitable 11 hospitality, pleasurable

weld 4 bond, fuse, join 5 braze, joint, merge, unite 6 solder

welfare 3 aid 4 dole, help, weal 5 pogey 6 health, relief, succor 7 benefit, fortune, success, support 8 interest 9 advantage, happiness, well-being 10 assistance, commonweal, prosperity

welkin 3 sky 5 ether, vault 6 heaven 7 heavens 8 empyrean 9 firmament

well 3 far, fit, pit 4 easy, emit, hale, hole, pool, rise, sane 5 amply, clear, cured, fully, quite, shaft, sound, truly 6 easily, freely, healed, indeed, justly, kindly, likely, nicely, origin, rather, really, source, spring, wholly 7 clearly, healthy, perhaps, readily, rightly 8 entirely, expertly, pleasing, possibly, probably, properly, sensibly, smoothly, suitably 9 advisable, correctly, desirable, elegantly, favorably, fittingly, fortunate, perfectly, wholesome 10 acceptably, adequately, affluently, becomingly, completely, pleasantly, pleasingly, prosperous, reasonably, thoroughly **11** attentively, comfortable, compartment, fortunately, substantial **12** considerably, prosperously, satisfactory, successfully **13** appropriately, significantly

well-being 4 weal **6** health **7** welfare **8** thriving **9** happiness **10** prosperity

well-bred 6 urbane **7** genteel, refined **8** cultured, highborn, polished **9** civilized, patrician **10** cultivated **11** blue-blooded, gentlemanly

well-built 4 buff **5** hunky, solid **8** muscular **9** strapping

well-developed 5 curvy **7** fulsome, rounded, shapely **8** advanced **9** Junoesque **10** curvaceous

well-disposed 7 amiable **8** friendly **9** favorable, receptive **11** sympathetic **13** understanding

Welles movie 5 Trial (The) **7** Macbeth, Othello **8** Jane Eyre, Stranger (The), Third Man (The) **11** Citizen Kane, Touch of Evil **15** Journey into Fear **16** Chimes at Midnight, Lady from Shanghai (The) **20** Magnificent Ambersons (The)

well-favored 4 fair **6** comely, lovely, pretty **8** gorgeous, handsome **9** beauteous, beautiful **10** attractive **11** good-looking

well-fixed see WELL-TO-DO

well-founded 5 sound, valid **6** cogent **8** rational **9** justified **10** convincing

well-groomed 4 neat, snug, tidy, trig, trim **5** natty, smart **6** dapper, snappy, spiffy, spruce, sprucy **7** orderly **8** clean-cut **9** shipshape

well-heeled see WELL-TO-DO

Wellington 4 duke **7** general **8** Iron Duke *horse:* **10** Copenhagen *original name:* **9** Wellesley (Arthur) *victory:* **7** Vitoria **8** Talavera, Waterloo **9** Salamanca

well-known 5 noted **6** famous **7** big-name, eminent, popular **8** renowned **9** notorious, prominent **10** celebrated **11** illustrious

well-liked 7 beloved, favored, popular **8** favorite **9** cherished, preferred

well-mannered 5 civil, suave **6** poised, polite, proper, urbane **7** genteel, tactful **9** courteous **10** diplomatic

well-nigh 6 all but, almost, fairly, nearly, next to **8** as good as **9** just about, virtually **11** essentially, practically

well-off see WELL-TO-DO

well-paying 7 gainful **9** lucrative, rewarding **10** profitable, worthwhile **11** moneymaking **12** advantageous, remunerative

wellspring 4 font, root **5** fount **6** origin,

source **7** genesis **8** fountain **10** provenance **11** provenience **12** fountainhead

well-thought-of 6 valued, worthy **7** admired, reputed **9** estimable, reputable **10** creditable **11** respectable

well-timed 6 timely **7** apropos, fitting, timeous **9** favorable, opportune **10** auspicious, felicitous, fortuitous, propitious, seasonable

well-to-do 4 rich **5** flush **6** loaded **7** mon-eyed, upscale, wealthy **8** affluent **10** prosperous **11** comfortable

well-turned 4 trim **5** plump **7** rounded, shapely **10** curvaceous, felicitous, Rubenesque, statuesque **11** clean-limbed

well-worn 5 banal, musty, stale, stock, tired, trite **6** frayed, old-hat, shabby **7** clichéd **8** bromidic, cobwebby, dog-eared, overused **9** hackneyed **10** thread-bare **11** commonplace, stereotyped

Welsh see CYMRIC

welsh 5 dodge **6** renege, resile **7** back out, default

welt 4 blow, edge, seam, wale, weal **5** ridge, wheal, whelk **6** insert

welter 4 coil, moil, toss **5** chaos, churn, steep, surge **6** flurry, hassle, hubbub, jumble, lather, ruckus, seethe, thrash, wallow, writhe **7** ferment, turmoil **8** disorder **9** confusion

___ **Welty 6** Eudora

wen 4 bleb, cyst **5** blain **6** growth **7** vesicle **11** excrescence

wench 3 gal **4** girl, jade, lass, maid, minx, miss, puss, slut, tart **5** hussy, nymph, tramp, trull, whore, woman **6** damsel, gamine, harlot, hoyden, lassie, maiden, wanton **7** jezebel, servant, trollop **8** slattern, strumpet

wend 3 hie **4** fare, pass **6** direct, push on, repair, travel **7** journey, proceed

werewolf 9 loup-garou **11** lycanthrope

Werther's beloved 5 Lotte **9** Charlotte

Wesleyan 9 Methodist

West 8 Occident

western 5 oater **9** Hesperian **10** horse opera, occidental *hemisphere:* **8** Americas, New World

Western novelist 5 Grey (Zane), Ross (Dana Fuller) **5** Brand (Max), Faust (Frederick), Short (Luke) **6** Judson (E. Z. C.), L'Amour (Louis), Patten (Lewis), Wister (Owen) **7** Guthrie (A. B.), Leonard (Elmore) **8** Buntline (Ned), McMurtry (Larry)

West Indies *country:* **4** Cuba **5** Haiti **7** Bahamas, Grenada, Jamaica **8** Barbados, Dominica **10** Guadeloupe, Martinique, Puerto Rico, Saint Lucia **17** Dominican Republic *island group:*

6 Virgin (Islands) 7 Bahamas, Leeward (Islands) 8 Antilles (Greater, Lesser), Windward (Islands)
West Point *father of:* 6 Thayer (Sylvanus) *freshman:* 5 plebe *student:* 5 cadet
West Side Story *composer:* 9 Bernstein (Leonard) *heroine:* 5 Maria *lyricist:* 8 Sondheim (Stephen)
West Virginia *capital:* 10 Charleston *city:* 8 Wheeling 10 Huntington *mountain:* 10 Spruce Knob *nickname:* 8 Mountain (State) *river:* 4 Ohio *state bird:* 8 cardinal *state flower:* 12 rhododendron *state tree:* 10 sugar maple
west wind see at WIND
wet 3 sop 4 damp, dank, rain, soak, wash, weak 5 douse, drown, drunk, humid, moist, rainy, soggy, soppy, souse, water 6 dampen, drench, soaked, sodden, soused, sweaty, watery 7 moisten, raining, soaking, sopping 8 drenched, dripping, humidify, irrigate, moisture, saturate, slippery 9 saturated, spineless *combining form:* 4 hygr 5 hygro
wet blanket 6 grinch 7 killjoy 8 sourpuss 9 pessimist 10 spoilsport 11 party pooper
wether 4 goat 5 sheep
wetland 3 bog, fen 4 mire, quag 5 marsh, swamp 6 morass, muskeg, slough
whack 3 bat, hit, pop, try 4 bash, belt, biff, blow, chop, cuff, kill, pelt, shot, sock, stab, wham, whap, whop 5 crack, punch, smack, smash 6 attack, defeat, murder, strike, wallop 7 bump off 8 knock off, lambaste *up:* 4 part 5 divvy, split 6 divide 7 portion 9 apportion
whale 3 hit 4 beat, flog, hide, lash, whip 5 giant 6 defeat, strike, stripe, thrash 7 mammoth 8 cetacean, behemoth 9 leviathan 10 flagellate *arctic:* 7 bowhead *group:* 3 pod *killer:* 4 orca *kind:* 3 sei 4 blue 5 right, sperm 6 baleen, beluga, killer 7 narwhal, rorqual 8 cachalot *tale:* 8 Moby Dick *toothed:* 5 pilot (whale) 9 blackfish *young:* 4 calf
whalebone 9 scrimshaw
wham 3 hit 4 bang, beat, blow, boom, clap, slam 5 blast, burst, crack, crash, smash, whack 6 impact, propel, strike 7 explode
whammy 3 hex, zap 4 jinx, juju 5 curse, spell 6 hoodoo, voodoo 7 evil eye
wharf 4 dock, pier, quay 5 jetty, levee
Wharton novel 10 Buccaneers (The), Ethan Frome 12 House of Mirth (The) 14 Age of Innocence (The) 18 Custom of the Country (The)
whatnot 7 étagère

wheal 4 lump, welt 5 ridge, whelk
wheat 4 crop 5 emmer, flour, grain, grass, spelt 6 cereal 7 einkorn *beard:* 3 awn *beat:* 6 thresh *chaff:* 4 bran *crushed:* 6 bulgur *disease:* 4 rust, smut *type:* 4 club 5 durum
wheedle 3 con 4 coax 5 cozen 6 cajole, entice, seduce 7 blarney, flatter 8 blandish, inveigle, scrounge, soft-soap 9 sweet-talk
wheel 3 VIP 4 auto, gyre, move, reel, spin, turn 5 cycle, drive, motor, pilot, pivot, round, whirl 6 bigwig, circle, gyrate, league, rotate, totter, travel 7 big shot, circuit, revolve 8 rotation 9 about-face, volte-face *part:* 3 hub, rim 4 tire 5 felly, spoke *spoke:* 6 radius *toothed:* 3 cog 4 gear
wheeze 3 saw, yuk 4 gasp, hiss, joke, puff, rasp 5 adage, cough 6 saying 7 proverb, whistle 8 chestnut, rhonchus
whelk 4 wale, weal, welt 5 wheal
whelm 4 bury, sink 5 cover, drown, flood, swamp 6 deluge, engulf 8 bear down, inundate, overbear, overcome, submerge 9 devastate
whelp 3 cub, kid, pup 4 bear 5 child, puppy 9 youngster
whereas 5 since, while 6 seeing, though 7 howbeit 8 although 11 considering
wherefore 3 why 4 thus 5 proof 6 ground, reason, whence 8 argument 11 explanation
wherewithal 5 funds, means, money 9 resources
wherry 4 boat 5 barge, scull 7 lighter, rowboat
whet 4 edge, goad, hone 5 drink, rally, rouse, waken 6 arouse, awaken, excite, kindle 7 sharpen, starter 8 aperitif 9 appetizer, challenge, stimulate 10 incitement 11 hors d'oeuvre
whiff 3 fan 4 blow, gust, hint, puff, waft 5 expel, smoke, tinge, trace 6 breath, exhale, inhale 7 soupçon, whisper 9 strikeout 10 indication, inhalation
whiffet 6 nobody, squirt 9 nonentity
whiffle 4 blow, gust, puff 5 waver 6 dither, falter 9 fluctuate, vacillate 12 shilly-shally
while 4 pass, time, when 5 spell 6 albeit, moment, though 7 howbeit, stretch, whereas 8 although, as long as, so long as
whilom 6 bygone, former 7 onetime, quondam 8 formerly, previous, sometime 9 erstwhile
whim 3 bee 4 idea, kink 5 dream, fancy, freak, humor 6 maggot, megrim, notion, vagary 7 caprice, capstan, conceit, thought 8 crotchet

whimper 3 cry **4** fret, mewl, pule, wail **5** bleat, whine **6** snivel

whimsical 4 iffy, zany **5** droll, fancy, flaky **6** chancy, fickle, fitful, quirky, random **7** erratic, flighty, mutable, puckish, wayward **8** fanciful, freakish, volatile **9** eccentric, impulsive, pixilated, screwball, uncertain, vagarious **10** capricious **13** unpredictable

whimsy 3 bee **4** play **5** dream, fancy, freak, humor **6** levity, maggot, megrim, notion, vagary **7** caprice, conceit, fantasy **9** capriccio, frivolity

whim-wham 4 dido **5** curio, fancy, frill **6** bauble, gewgaw, ruffle, trifle **7** bibelot, flounce, trinket **8** furbelow, gimcrack, kickshaw **9** objet d'art **10** knickknack

whine 3 cry **4** cant, fret, fuss, kick, moan, pule, wail **5** bleat, gripe **6** grouse, repine, snivel, whinge, yammer **7** grumble, snuffle, whimper **8** complain **9** bellyache

whinny 5 neigh **6** nicker **7** whicker

whiny 5 fussy **7** fretful, grouchy, peevish **8** petulant **9** irritable, querulous

whip 3 cut, hem, set **4** beat, cane, crop, dash, flog, hide, jerk, lash, lick, pull, rout, wind, wrap **5** abuse, mop up, quirt, spank, sting, whale, whisk **6** defeat, lather, snatch, strike, stroke, subdue, switch, thrash, urge on **7** agitate, dessert, provoke, rawhide, shellac, trounce, utensil **8** coachman, lambaste, overcome, vanquish **9** instigate, overwhelm **10** flagellate **13** cat-o'-nine-tails *braided:* **10** blacksnake

whippersnapper see WHIFFET

whipping boy 4 goat **5** patsy **7** fall guy **9** scapegoat

whippy 6 supple **7** elastic, springy **8** flexible **9** resilient

whir 3 fly, hum **4** burr, buzz, whiz **5** chirr, churr, drone, whizz **7** revolve, vibrate **9** bombinate

whirl 3 ado, gig, pop, try **4** eddy, flit, fuss, gyre, moil, reel, shot, spin, stab, stir, swim, turn, veer **5** hurry, pivot, swirl, whack, wheel **6** bustle, circle, gyrate, hassle, hubbub, pother, rotate **7** circuit, dervish, turmoil **8** ballyhoo, gyration, rotation **9** commotion, pirouette **10** revolution

whirligig 4 gyre, spin **6** beetle, gyrate **8** carousel **9** pirouette **12** merry-go-round

whirlpool 3 ado **4** eddy, fuss **6** bustle, flurry, furore, tumult, vortex **7** turmoil **8** vortices (plural) **9** commotion, maelstrom

whirlwind 4 rush, stir, to-do **5** hasty, spout, swift **6** bustle **7** cyclone, tornado, twister, typhoon **8** headlong **9** commotion, dust devil, dust storm, hurricane **10** waterspout **11** tourbillion

whish 4 fizz, hiss **6** fizzle **8** sibilate

whisk 3 mix, nip, wag, zip **4** beat, flit, whip **5** broom, brush, fluff, hurry, speed **6** switch

whisker 4 hair **7** bristle **8** filament, vibrissa **9** outrigger **11** hairbreadth

whiskered 5 hairy **6** pilose **7** bearded, bristly, hirsute **8** stubbled, unshaven

whiskers 5 beard **6** goatee **7** stubble, weepers **8** bristles **9** burnsides, peach fuzz, sideburns **11** muttonchops

whiskey 3 rye **6** liquor, Scotch **7** alcohol, bourbon *with beer chaser:* **11** boilermaker

whisper 4 buzz, hint, hiss, whiz **5** rumor, shade, tinge, touch, trace, whiff **6** breath, gossip, murmur, mutter **8** sibilate, susurrus **9** suspicion, undertone **11** susurration

whist 4 game, hush **5** quiet, still **6** silent **9** noiseless, soundless

whistle 4 pipe, toot **5** flute, whiff **6** signal, tootle, wheeze

whistle-stop 5 stump **8** campaign, politick **9** barnstorm **11** electioneer

whit 3 bit, fig, jot, rap **4** atom, damn, hoot, iota, mite **5** crumb, scrap, shred, speck, whoop **7** dribble, modicum, smidgen **8** molecule, particle

white 4 pure **5** livid, milky, snowy **6** albino, blanch, bleach, pallid **7** silvery **9** colorless *combining form:* **4** leuc, leuk **5** leuco, leuko *egg's:* **5** glair **6** glaire **7** albumen

White novel 12 Stuart Little **13** Charlotte's Web

white cliffs of___ 5 Dover

White Fang author 6 London (Jack)

White House *designer:* 5 Hoban (James) *first occupant:* **5** Adams (Abigail, John)

white lightning 5 hooch **7** bootleg, whiskey **9** moonshine **10** bathtub gin **11** mountain dew

whiten 4 fade, pale **5** frost **6** blanch, bleach, blench **8** etiolate **10** decolorize

white plague 8 phthisis **11** consumption **12** tuberculosis

whitewash 6 parget **7** cover up **9** gloss over, gloze over, sugarcoat

whither 5 where **7** whereto **9** whereunto

whiting 3 cod **4** hake **10** silver hake

Whitsunday 9 Pentecost

Whittier poem 9 Snow-Bound **10** Maud Muller **11** Barefoot Boy **16** Barbara Frietchie

whittle 4 chip, form, fret, pare, trim

5 carve, shape, shave, skive **6** reduce, sculpt **8** diminish

whiz 3 fly, hum, zip **4** buzz, flit, hiss, zoom **5** hurry, speed, swish, whirl **6** expert, fizzle, genius, phenom, rotate, whoosh **8** virtuoso **10** wunderkind

whoa 3 hey **4** slow, stop **6** hold up

whole 3 all, fit, sum **4** full, hale, sane **5** sound, total, uncut, unity **6** entire, entity, healed, intact, system, unhurt **7** healthy, perfect, plenary **8** complete, entirely, entirety, flawless, restored, totality, unbroken, unmarred **9** recovered, undamaged, undivided, uninjured, untouched **10** unimpaired, unmodified **11** unblemished **12** concentrated, undistracted *combining form:* **3** hol, pan **4** holo

wholehearted 6 ardent **7** devoted, earnest, fervent, sincere **8** bona fide **9** committed, heartfelt, steadfast, unfeigned **10** passionate, unwavering **11** impassioned **12** enthusiastic **13** unquestioning

whole-hog 6 all-out, gung-ho **8** complete, thorough **9** full-scale **11** straight-out **13** thoroughgoing

wholeness 7 oneness **8** entirety, totality **9** integrity, soundness **10** intactness, perfection

whole note 9 semibreve

whole number 5 digit **6** cipher **7** integer, numeral

wholesome 3 fit **4** good, hale, safe, sane, well **5** right, sound **6** benign **7** healthy **8** hygienic, salutary **9** favorable, healthful **10** beneficial, salubrious

wholly 3 all **4** only **6** in toto, singly, solely, purely **7** totally **8** entirely **10** altogether, completely **11** exclusively

whomp 3 hit **4** beat, drub, slap, whip, whup **5** crash, thump **6** crunch, strike, thrash, wallop **7** clobber, shellac, trounce **8** lambaste

whomp up 4 stir **5** rouse, spark **6** arouse, excite, foment

whoopee 3 fun **5** revel, yahoo **6** gaiety, hoopla, yippee **7** jollity, revelry, wassail, whoopla **8** hilarity **9** festivity, high jinks, merriment **10** hurly-burly **11** merrymaking

whoopla see HOOPLA

whop 3 bat, bop **4** bash, beat, biff, blow, drub, lick, sock **5** baste, pound, smack, thump, whack **6** batter, buffet, defeat, hammer, pummel, strike, thrash, thwack, wallop **7** trounce **8** lambaste

whopping 4 huge, vast **6** mighty **7** amazing, immense, massive **8** colossal, enormous, gigantic, whacking **9** bodacious,

humongous, monstrous **10** gargantuan, incredible, prodigious **13** extraordinary

whorl 4 coil, eddy, turn **5** swirl **6** spiral

why 5 cause **6** enigma, motive, puzzle, reason, riddle **7** mystery, problem, what for **9** conundrum, rationale, therefore, wherefore **10** puzzlement **11** explanation

wicked 4 evil, mean, very, vile **5** awful, black, wrong **6** fierce, malign, sinful, unholy **7** corrupt, hateful, heinous, immoral, naughty, ungodly, vicious **8** depraved, devilish, fiendish **9** atrocious, barbarous, dangerous, extremely, hazardous, injurious, malicious, malignant, nefarious **10** iniquitous, malevolent, outrageous **11** treacherous

wickedness 3 sin **4** evil, vice **7** devilry **8** enormity, iniquity, satanism **9** depravity **10** corruption, immorality **12** devilishness, fiendishness

wicker 4 twig **5** osier, withe **6** branch

wicket 4 arch, door, gate, hoop **6** window *sticky:* **3** fix, jam **4** knot **7** toughie **9** conundrum, tight spot

wide 4 vast **5** broad, fully **8** extended, spacious, straying, sweeping **9** deviating, expansive, extensive, inclusive **10** completely **13** comprehensive

widen 4 ream **6** dilate, expand, extend, open up, spread **7** broaden, distend, enlarge

widespread 4 rife, vast **6** common **7** current, general, popular, rampant, regnant **8** far-flung **9** extensive, pervasive, prevalent **10** far-ranging, ubiquitous

widget 5 gizmo **6** device, dingus, doodad, gadget, hickey, jigger **7** gimmick, whatsit **9** doohickey, thingummy **11** contraption, thingamabob, thingamajig, thingumajig

width 4 gape, kerf, span **5** depth, range **6** spread **7** breadth **9** extension

wield 3 use **5** exert **6** handle **7** control **8** exercise **10** manipulate *the gavel:* **7** preside

wiener 3 dog **5** frank **6** hot dog **7** sausage **11** frankfurter **13** Vienna sausage

wife 3 Mrs. **4** mate **5** bride, woman **6** female, matron, missis, missus, spouse **7** consort, partner **8** helpmate, helpmeet *Latin:* **4** uxor *of a rajah:* **4** rani **5** ranee

wifely 7 uxorial

wig 3 jaw, rap, rug **4** flip, rail, rate **5** chide, freak, scold **6** berate, peruke, rebuke, revile, toupee **7** bawl out, chew out, reproof, upbraid **8** postiche, reproach **9** hairpiece, reprimand **10** tongue-lash

wiggle 4 jerk **5** shake, twist **6** fidget, squirm, writhe *Scottish:* **5** hotch
wight 3 man **5** human **6** animal, mortal, person **7** critter **8** creature **10** human being, individual
wild 3 mad **4** fast **5** crazy **6** barren, raging, savage, stormy, unruly **7** erratic, frantic, furious, natural, untamed, vicious **8** barbaric, blustery, desolate, frenetic, frenzied, reckless **9** barbarian, barbarous, delirious, fantastic, turbulent, wasteland **10** incautious, outlandish **11** extravagant, intractable, sensational, tempestuous, uncivilized, uninhabited **12** preposterous, uncontrolled, uncultivated, ungovernable, unmanageable **13** irresponsible, undisciplined
wild ass 5 kiang **6** onager
Wild Duck author 5 Ibsen (Henrik)
wildebeest 3 gnu
wilderness 4 bush **5** heath, waste **6** barren, desert **9** backlands, wasteland **10** hinterland **11** backcountry
Wilder play 7 Our Town **10** Matchmaker (The) **14** Skin of Our Teeth (The)
wild-eyed 6 raving **7** blue-sky, radical **9** visionary
wile 4 ploy, ruse, vamp **5** charm, feint, guile, trick **6** allure, deceit, entice, gambit **7** attract, beguile, bewitch, chicane, cunning, enchant, gimmick **8** artifice, inveigle, maneuver, trickery **9** captivate, chicanery, fascinate, magnetize, stratagem **10** subterfuge
wiliness 5 guile **7** cunning
will 4 like, wish **5** cause, elect, leave, order **6** choice, choose, decree, desire, direct, intend, intent, liking, option, ordain, please **7** bequest, consent, control, passion, purpose **8** appetite, bequeath, pleasure, volition **9** intention, testament **10** discipline **11** disposition, inclination, self-control **13** determination, self-restraint *addition:* **7** codicil *maker:* **8** testator **9** testatrix *without:* **9** intestate
willful 5 heady **6** dogged, mulish, unruly **8** perverse, stubborn **9** obstinate, pigheaded, voluntary **10** deliberate, hardheaded, headstrong, purposeful, selfwilled **11** intentional, intractable, wrongheaded **12** contumacious, pertinacious, ungovernable
Williams play 10 Camino Real, Rose Tattoo (The) **14** Glass Menagerie (The), Summer and Smoke **16** Cat on a Hot Tin Roof, Night of the Iguana (The), Sweet Bird of Youth **18** Suddenly Last Summer **20** Streetcar Named Desire (A)

William Tell composer 7 Rossini (Gioacchino)
willies 6 creeps, shakes **7** jimjams, jitters, shivers **9** whim-whams **10** goose bumps **13** heebie-jeebies
willing 3 apt **4** fain, game, glad, open **5** prone, ready **6** minded **7** forward, witting **8** amenable, disposed, inclined, obliging, unforced **9** agreeable, compliant, favorable, receptive, voluntary **10** deliberate, volitional **11** intentional, predisposed
williwaw 4 gust, wind **5** blast **8** outburst, paroxysm **9** commotion
will-o'-the-wisp 7 fantasy, figment, phantom **8** daydream, delusion **11** ignis fatuus
willow 5 osier, salix **6** sallow **10** cricket bat *flower cluster:* **6** catkin *kind:* **5** crack, pussy, white **6** basket **7** weeping
willowy 4 tall **5** lithe **6** pliant, supple, svelte **7** lissome, pliable, slender **8** graceful
Wilson play 6 Fences **11** Piano Lesson (The) **12** Talley's Folly **13** Hot l Baltimore (The) **20** Ma Rainey's Black Bottom
wilt 3 sag **4** swag **5** droop, dry up, wizen **6** wither **7** shrivel **8** languish
wily 3 sly **4** foxy **5** cagey, canny, slick **6** artful, astute, clever, crafty, shrewd, tricky **7** cunning, devious, vulpine **8** guileful, scheming **10** serpentine
wimble 4 bore **5** auger, borer, brace, drill **6** gimlet
Wimbledon's game 6 tennis
wimp 4 nerd, wuss **5** sissy **7** doormat, nebbish **9** jellyfish **11** milquetoast
wimple 4 bend, veil, wrap **5** cover, curve **6** ripple *wearer:* **3** nun
wimp out 6 beg off, cave in, give in **8** back down
wimpy 4 lame, puny, weak **5** dinky, inept, timid **6** craven, feeble **7** gutless **8** cowardly, feckless, impotent, pathetic **9** spineless **10** namby-pamby, wishywashy **11** ineffective, ineffectual
win 3 get **4** beat, earn, gain **5** reach, score **6** attain, defeat, obtain, secure **7** achieve, acquire, conquer, procure, produce, realize, succeed, success, triumph, victory **8** conquest, persuade **9** influence **10** accomplish *over:* **6** disarm, induce **8** convince, persuade, talk into **9** prevail on
wince 5 cower, quail, start **6** blanch, blench, cringe, flinch, recoil, shrink **7** squinch
wind 3 air, dry, fan, gas **4** bend, blow, clue, coil, curl, gale, gird, gust, haul, hint, reel, rest, talk, turn, warp, wrap

5 cover, crank, curve, force, hoist, raise, sound, spool, twine, twist **6** breath, breeze, circle, enlace, girdle, notion, zephyr **7** enclose, entwine, envelop, inkling, involve, monsoon, nothing, tighten **8** easterly, encircle, entangle, surround, tendency, westerly **9** direction, idle words, influence, insinuate **10** indication, intimation, suggestion *cold:* **4** bora **7** mistral, pampero **8** williwaw *combining form:* **4** anem **5** anemo, venti, vento *gentle:* **6** breeze, zephyr *god:* **6** Boreas **8** Zephyrus *hot:* **6** simoom **7** sirocco *instrument:* **3** sax **4** horn, oboe, tuba, vane **5** flute **7** bassoon, trumpet **8** trombone **9** saxophone **10** anemometer **11** weather vane *into:* **8** aweather *measure of speed:* **4** knot *Mediterranean:* **7** sirocco **8** levanter, libeccio *scale:* **8** Beaufort *stormy:* **4** gale **7** cyclone, tornado, twister **9** hurricane **11** northeaster *warm:* **4** föhn **5** foehn **7** chinook

windbag 6 gabber **7** blabber **8** bigmouth, blowhard, braggart

windfall 4 boon, gain **5** break **7** jackpot **8** fortuity

winding 4 curl, kink **5** snaky **6** spiral **7** coiling, curving, devious, sinuous **8** flexuous, indirect, tortuous, twisting **9** meandrous **10** circuitous, convoluted, meandering, roundabout, serpentine **11** anfractuous **12** labyrinthine

windmill 4 spin **5** wheel **7** machine *fighter:* **10** Don Quixote

window 3 bay, eye **4** pane **5** oriel **6** dormer **7** opening **8** aperture, casement, jalousie *cover:* **5** blind **7** curtain, shutter *French:* **7** fenêtre *over a door:* **7** transom **8** fanlight *part:* **4** pane, sash, sill **5** frame *projecting:* **3** bay **5** oriel *roof's:* **6** dormer **7** lucarne **8** skylight *Scottish:* **7** winnock *ship's:* **4** port **8** porthole

windpipe 7 trachea *combining form:* **6** trache **7** tracheo

windrow 4 bank, heap, hill, mass, pile **5** mound, ridge, stack

wind up 3 end **4** halt **5** close **6** finish, settle **8** complete, conclude **9** terminate

windup 3 end **5** close **6** ending, finale, finish **9** backswing **10** completion, conclusion **11** termination

windy 4 airy **5** blowy, gassy, gusty, inane, tumid, wordy **6** breezy, prolix, stormy, turgid **7** diffuse, orotund, pompous, verbose **8** blustery, inflated **9** bombastic, overblown **11** tempestuous **13** grandiloquent

wine 4 vino **5** drink, juice **8** beverage *aromatized:* **8** vermouth **9** hippocras

beverage: **5** negus, punch **6** bishop, cooler **7** sangria **8** sangaree, spritzer **9** hippocras *bottle:* **6** fiasco, magnum **8** decanter, jeroboam **10** methuselah *cabinet:* **8** cellaret *cask:* **3** tun, vat **4** butt, pipe *cellar:* **6** bodega *combining form:* **3** eno, oen **4** oeno *discoverer:* **4** Noah *distillate:* **6** brandy, cognac *dry:* **3** sec **4** brut *flavor:* **4** mull *fortified:* **4** port **6** Malaga, sherry **7** Madeira, marsala, oloroso **8** muscatel *fragrance:* **4** nose **7** bouquet *lover:* **9** oenophile **11** oenophilist *maker:* **7** vintner **8** vigneron **10** winegrower **13** viticulturist *merchant:* **7** vintner *red:* **4** port **5** Gamay, Macon, Medoc, Rioja **6** Barolo, Beaune, claret, Shiraz **7** Chianti **8** Bordeaux, Burgundy, cabernet **9** Lambrusco, Pinot Noir, St. Emilion, zinfandel **10** Beaujolais, Sangiovese **11** Petite Sirah **12** Valpolicella *relating to:* **6** vinous *residue:* **4** marc *rice:* **4** sake *richness:* **4** body *sediment:* **4** lees **5** dregs *shop:* **6** bistro, bodega, tavern *sparkling:* **8** cold duck, sparkler, Spumante **9** champagne, Lambrusco *specialist:* **9** enologist **10** oenologist *spiced:* **6** mulled (wine) **9** hippocras *steward:* **9** sommelier *study of:* **7** enology **8** oenology *sweet:* **4** port **5** Tokay **6** canary, Malaga, muscat **7** Catawba, Madeira, malmsey, marsala, oloroso, Vouvray **8** Malvasia, muscatel, sauterne **9** Sauternes **11** scuppernong *sweeten:* **4** mull *vessel:* **7** chalice *white:* **4** hock **5** Rhine, Soave **7** Catawba, Chablis, Moselle, Orvieto, Vouvray **8** Bordeaux, Riesling, Semillon, vermouth **9** champagne, Hermitage, Meursault **10** chardonnay, Montrachet **11** Chenin Blanc, scuppernong **13** liebfraumilch **14** sauvignon blanc *year:* **7** vintage

wing 3 ala, arm, ell, fly **4** sail, unit, vane **5** annex, flank, fleet, pinna, wound **6** flight **7** airfoil, faction, flanker, section **8** appendage, expansion, extension, improvise *combining form:* **3** ali **4** pter **5** ptero *relating to:* **4** alar **5** alary

wingding 4 bash, fete, gala **5** binge, party **7** blowout, shindig **9** festivity

winged 4 alate, fleet, rapid, swift **7** soaring **8** elevated *deity:* **4** Amor, Eros, Nike **5** Cupid **6** Hermes **7** Mercury *horse:* **7** Pegasus *monster:* **5** harpy

wingless 8 apterous

winglike 4 alar **5** alary *part:* **3** ala **4** alae (plural)

wink 3 bat, nap **5** flash, jiffy, shake, trice **6** moment, second, signal **7** connive, flicker, instant, twinkle **9** nictitate, twinkling **11** split second

winner 3 ace **4** lulu **5** doozy **6** doozie, top dog, victor **7** success **8** champion **9** conqueror **11** titleholder

Winnie-the-Pooh *author:* **5** Milne (A. A.) *character:* **3** Roo **5** Kanga **6** Piglet, Tigger

winning 8 charming, engaging, pleasing **9** agreeable **10** delightful, successful, triumphant, victorious **11** captivating **13** prepossessing

winnow 3 fan **4** blow, cull, pare, sift, sort **6** delete, filter, narrow, reduce, remove, screen, select **8** separate

winsome 5 sweet **6** dulcet, lovely **8** charming, cheerful, engaging, pleasing **9** easygoing **12** lighthearted

winter 6 season **9** hibernate *French:* **5** hiver *Spanish:* **8** invierno

Winter's Tale, A *author:* **11** Shakespeare (William) *character:* **7** Camillo, Leontes, Paulina, Perdita **8** Florizel, Hermione **9** Antigonus, Autolycus, Polixenes

wintry 3 icy **4** cold **5** bleak, hoary, nippy, snowy **6** frigid, frosty **8** chilling, freezing, hibernal **12** bone-chilling

wipe 3 dry, rub **4** swab **5** towel, whisk **6** napkin, smudge, sponge **8** squeegee

wipe out 4 rout **5** crash, erase, smear, sweep **7** blot out, destroy, expunge **8** decimate **9** eradicate, extirpate **10** annihilate, obliterate

wipeout 4 fall, rout **5** crash **8** drubbing **11** destruction **12** annihilation

wire 3 rod **4** cord, line, send **5** cable, metal **6** thread **7** message **8** meshwork, telegram **9** cablegram, telegraph **10** finish line *measure:* **3** mil **5** gauge

wiry 4 lean, ropy **6** sinewy, supple **7** fibrous, stringy

Wisconsin *capital:* **7** Madison *city:* **6** Racine **7** Kenosha **8** Green Bay **9** Milwaukee *college, university:* **5** Ripon **6** Beloit **9** Marquette *lake:* **7** Mendota *motto:* **7** Forward *nickname:* **6** Badger (State) *peninsula:* **4** Door *river:* **7** St. Croix **9** Menominee, Wisconsin **11** Mississippi *state bird:* **5** robin *state flower:* **6** violet *state tree:* **10** sugar maple

wisdom 5 sense **7** insight, science **8** judgment, learning, sagacity, sageness, sapience **9** good sense, knowledge **10** horse sense **11** common sense, information

wise 3 hep, hip **4** bold, keen, sage, sane, tell, warn, wily **5** alert, aware, brash, cagey, canny, cocky, fresh, learn, nervy, quick, sassy, sharp, smart **6** artful, astute, bright, cheeky, clever, crafty, fill in, inform, notify, shrewd, sophic, tricky **7** cunning, gnostic, knowing, politic, prudent, sapient **8** discreet, flippant, impudent, insolent, sensible, tactical **9** advisable, bold-faced, expedient, judicious, sagacious, scholarly **10** discerning, insightful, perceptive, reflective, thoughtful **11** foresighted, impertinent, intelligent, quick-witted, sharp-witted, smart-alecky **13** contemplative, knowledgeable, perspicacious *old man:* **6** Nestor *person:* **4** sage **6** savant **7** scholar

wiseacre see WISE GUY

wisecrack 3 dig, gag **4** gibe, jape, jest, joke, quip **5** sally **9** witticism

wise guy 6 smarty **7** mobster **8** gangster, smart-ass **9** know-it-all, swellhead **10** smart aleck **11** smarty-pants, wisenheimer

wise man 4 guru, sage **5** magus **6** savant

Wise Men see MAGI

wish 3 bid **4** care, goal, like, long, lust, want **5** covet, crave, fancy, foist, order, yearn **6** desire, impose **7** request **10** desiderate

wishbone 7 furcula

wishful 5 eager **7** anxious, hopeful, longing **8** desirous

wishy-washy 4 lame, weak **5** banal, bland, vapid, wimpy **6** jejune, watery **7** insipid, languid **10** namby-pamby **11** ineffective, ineffectual **13** characterless

wisp 3 bit **5** shred, strip, trace **6** sliver, snatch, streak **7** smidgen, snippet **8** fragment **9** scintilla

wispy 4 slim **5** frail **6** flimsy, slight **7** slender, tenuous **8** fleeting, nebulous **10** evanescent

Wister novel 9 Virginian (The)

wistful 3 sad **6** dreamy, triste **7** longing, pensive **8** yearning **9** nostalgic **10** melancholy

wit 3 wag **5** brain, comic, droll, humor, irony, joker **6** banter, esprit, jester, reason, satire, wisdom **7** farceur, punster **8** banterer, comedian, funnyman, judgment, humorist, jokester, quipster, repartee **9** alertness, ingenuity, intellect **10** cleverness, persiflage

witch 3 hag, hex **5** dowse, spell **6** voodoo, Wiccan **7** charmer **8** magician, sorcerer **9** sorceress **11** enchantress *companion:* **3** cat *group:* **5** coven *male:* **6** wizard **7** warlock *meeting:* **6** sabbat *town:* **5** Endor *vehicle:* **5** broom

witchcraft 5 magic, wicca **6** hoodoo, voodoo **7** devilry, hexerei, sorcery **8** wizardry **9** diablerie, sortilege, voodooism **10** black magic, hocuspocus, mumbo jumbo, necromancy **11** abracadabra, thaumaturgy

witch hazel 5 shrub **6** lotion

witchy 6 Wiccan 7 magical 8 wizardly
9 sorcerous 11 necromantic 12 thaumaturgic

with 3 for, per, pro, via 4 over, upon
5 about 6 having 7 against, by way of,
through 8 as well as 9 by means of, in
favor of 10 by virtue of *French:* 4 avec
German: 3 mit *Italian, Spanish:* 3 con
Latin: 3 cum

withal 3 too, yet 4 also 5 still 6 as well,
though 7 besides, howbeit, however
8 after all, moreover 11 furthermore,
nonetheless 12 additionally, nevertheless

withdraw 4 exit, quit 5 demit, leave,
unsay 6 depart, bow out, call in, cash
in, desert, detach, recall, recant,
recede, recoil, retire, secede, shrink
7 back out, drop out, pull out, retract,
retreat, scratch, take off, take out
8 back down, evacuate, fall back, pull
away, push back, separate, take back,
turn away 9 disengage, stand down
10 disconnect, give ground

withdrawal 4 exit 6 exodus 7 exiting,
pullout, removal, retreat 9 departure
10 alienation, detachment, retirement,
retraction, revocation

withdrawn 4 cool 5 aloof 6 casual,
remote 7 distant, removed 8 detached,
isolated, reserved, retiring, solitary
9 incurious, unaffable, uncurious
10 unsociable 11 indifferent, introverted, standoffish, unconcerned, unex-
pansive 12 uninterested, unresponsive

wither 3 age, dry 4 fade, sear, wilt 5 dry
up, parch, quail, wizen 6 scorch
7 mummify, shrivel

withered 4 sere 7 sapless 8 shrunken,
wrinkled 9 shriveled

withhold 4 deny 5 check 6 deduct,
detain, refuse, retain 7 abstain, deprive,
forbear, inhibit, refrain, reserve
8 restrain, subtract 9 constrain

within 4 into 5 among 6 inside 7 indoors,
inwards 8 enclosed, interior, inwardly
10 inner place *prefix:* 5 infra, intra, intro

with-it 6 modern, modish, trendy 7 à la
mode, current, faddish, stylish 8 up-to-
date 11 fashionable 12 contemporary

without 4 open, past, sans 5 minus
6 absent 7 lacking, open air, outside,
wanting 8 outdoors 10 externally, out-
of-doors *Latin:* 4 sine

with respect to 4 as to, in re 5 as for
7 apropos 8 touching 9 as regards,
regarding 10 concerning

withstand 4 bear, buck, defy 5 fight,
repel 6 endure, oppose, resist, suffer
7 hold off, survive, sustain 8 tolerate,
traverse

withy 4 twig 5 osier 6 branch, willow
8 flexible 9 resilient

witless 3 mad 4 daft, nuts 5 crazy, daffy,
dotty, nutty, silly 6 insane, simple, stupid 7 asinine, cracked, foolish, idiotic
8 demented, deranged, mindless 9 bedlamite, brainless, senseless 10 weak-
minded, unbalanced

witlessness 5 folly 6 idiocy, lunacy
7 inanity 8 insanity 9 absurdity, stupidity

witness 3 see 4 note, sign, view 5 proof,
vouch 6 attest, depone, depose, notice,
viewer 7 bear out, confirm, betoken,
certify, testify, watcher 8 attester,
beholder, deponent, evidence, looker-
on, observer, onlooker 9 bystander,
spectator, testament, testifier, testimony 11 affirmation, attestation, corroborate, testimonial 12 confirmation

witticism 3 dig, gag, mot 4 gibe, jape,
jest, jibe, joke, quip 5 crack, sally 6 bon
mot 8 one-liner, repartee 9 throwaway,
wisecrack

witting 5 aware 7 knowing, willful 8 sensible, sentient 9 cognizant, conscious,
voluntary 10 deliberate 11 intentional

witty 5 funny 6 clever, jocose 7 amusing,
jocular 8 humorous 9 facetious 13 scintillating

wiz 3 ace 5 adept, fiend 6 artist, expert,
phenom 7 artiste 8 virtuoso

wizard 3 ace 4 mage 5 adept, druid,
fiend, magus 6 expert, phenom 7 warlock 8 conjurer, magician, sorcerer, virtuoso 9 enchanter 10 past master
11 necromancer, thaumaturge 13 thaumaturgist

wizardly 5 magic 6 mystic, witchy 7 magical 9 sorcerous 10 mysterious 11 necromantic 12 thaumaturgic

Wizard of Menlo Park 6 Edison (Thomas
Alva)

Wizard of Oz *author:* 4 Baum (L. Frank)
character: 7 Dorothy 9 Scarecrow
10 Tin Woodman 12 Cowardly Lion
dog: 4 Toto

wizardry 5 magic 6 voodoo 7 sorcery
8 witchery 9 diablerie, sortilege
10 black magic, necromancy, witchcraft 11 bewitchment, conjuration,
enchantment

wizen 3 dry 4 sere, wilt 5 dry up 6 shrink,
wither 7 dried-up, shrivel, wrinkle

wizened 4 aged, sere 5 dried 6 shrunk
7 pinched 8 shrunken, withered, wrinkled

wobble 4 reel, rock, sway 5 quake,
shake, waver, weave 6 dither, falter,
quaver, teeter, totter 7 stagger, stumble,
tremble 8 nutation 9 vacillate

wobbly 4 weak 5 rocky, shaky 6 unsure 7 rackety, rickety 8 insecure, rachitic, unstable, unsteady, wavering 9 faltering, teetering, tottering 10 nutational 11 vacillating

Wodehouse, P. G. *castle:* 9 Blandings *character:* 6 Bertie (Wooster), Gussie (Fink-Nottle), Jeeves, Psmith 7 Wooster (Bertie) 8 Emsworth (Lord), Mulliner (Mr.) 10 Threepwood (Clarence, Freddie) 12 Lord Emsworth *club:* 6 Drones

Woden see ODIN

woe 3 rue 4 bale, bane, care 5 grief 6 misery, regret, sorrow 7 anguish, sadness, trouble 8 calamity 9 heartache 10 affliction, heartbreak 11 lamentation, unhappiness 12 wretchedness

woebegone 3 low, sad 4 blue, down, worn 6 shabby 7 doleful, forlorn, ruthful 8 dejected, dolorous, downcast, wretched 9 depressed, miserable, sorrowful 10 despondent, melancholy 11 crestfallen, downhearted, low-spirited 12 disconsolate

woeful 3 sad 5 heavy, sorry 6 dismal, rueful, tragic, triste 7 ruthful 8 dejected, dolorous, downcast, grievous, mournful, stricken, tortured, wretched 9 afflicted, aggrieved, depressed, heartsick, miserable, plaintive, sorrowful 10 deplorable, lamentable, lugubrious, melancholy 11 distressing, downhearted, low-spirited 12 disconsolate 13 heartbreaking

wolf 4 bolt, lobo, rake, roué 5 canid 6 canine, coyote, devour, gobble, masher 7 Don Juan, poverty 8 Casanova, lothario 10 starvation *genus:* 5 Canis *group:* 4 pack *young:* 5 whelp

Wolfe *novel* 17 Look Homeward Angel, Of Time and the River 18 You Can't Go Home Again 20 Bonfire of the Vanities (The)

wolfish 4 wild 5 cruel, feral 6 fierce, lupine, savage 7 bestial, brutish, vicious 9 ferocious

wolverine *European:* 7 glutton *genus:* 4 Gulo

Wolverine State 8 Michigan

woman 4 dame, lady 5 madam 6 female, matron 8 mistress 10 girlfriend *attractive:* 5 belle 6 beauty, eyeful, looker 7 stunner 8 knockout *combining form:* 4 gyny 5 gynec 6 gynaec, gyneco, gynous 7 gynaeco *courageous:* 7 heroine *dignified:* 6 matron 7 dowager 10 grande dame *dowdy:* 5 frump *English:* 6 milady *first, biblical:* 3 Eve *first, mythological:* 7 Pandora *French:* 5 femme *German:* 4 Frau 8 Fräulein *Hawaiian:* 6 wahine *Indian:* 5 squaw *Ital-*

ian: 5 donna 7 signora *old:* 3 hag 4 dame 6 beldam, carlin, gammer, granny *pregnant:* 7 gravida *resembling:* 8 gynecoid *royal:* 5 queen 8 princess *sailor:* 4 Wave *servant:* 4 maid *soldier:* 3 Wac *Spanish:* 4 doña 6 señora *strong:* 6 amazon, virago *unmarried:* 4 miss 6 maiden 8 spinster *young:* 4 girl, lass 6 lassie, maiden

womanize 4 wolf 9 gallivant, philander 10 fool around, mess around

womanizer 4 stud, wolf 6 masher 7 Don Juan, gallant, playboy 8 Casanova, lothario 9 ladies' man 10 lady-killer 11 philanderer

womb 6 uterus *combining form:* 6 hyster 7 hystero

women *hatred of:* 8 misogyny *organization of:* 3 DAR, NOW 8 sorority

Women in Love *author* 8 Lawrence (D. H.)

wonder 3 awe 4 muse 5 doubt 6 marvel 7 dubiety, miracle, portent, prodigy 8 mistrust, question 9 amazement, speculate, suspicion 10 admiration, skepticism 11 incertitude, uncertainty 12 astonishment

wonderful 4 keen 5 grand, great, nifty, super, swell 6 divine, groovy, peachy, spiffy 7 amazing, strange, too much, topping 8 dynamite, fabulous, glorious, spiffing, terrific 9 admirable, excellent, marvelous, wunderbar 10 astounding, delightful, miraculous, out-of-sight, stupendous 11 astonishing, outstanding

wondrous 6 mystic 7 amazing, awesome, strange 9 marvelous 10 astounding, formidable, miraculous, portentous, prodigious, remarkable, stupendous, surprising 11 astonishing, spectacular 13 extraordinary

wonky 4 awry 5 geeky, nerdy, shaky 7 bookish 8 unsteady

wont 3 apt 4 used 5 habit, usage 6 custom, manner 8 accustom, habitude, inclined, practice 10 accustomed, consuetude

wonted 5 usual 7 routine 8 habitual, ordinary 9 customary 10 accustomed

woo 5 sue 6 court 6 pursue 7 address, entreat, solicit

wood 5 weald 6 forest, lumber, timber 8 golf club 10 timberland *combining form:* 3 xyl 4 lign, xylo 5 ligni, ligno *decayed:* 4 punk *eater:* 7 termite *for burning:* 5 fagot 6 tinder 8 kindling *golf:* 6 driver *hard:* 3 elm, oak 4 ebon, rata, teak 5 beech, birch, ebony, maple 6 cherry, walnut 8 chestnut, mahogany, sycamore *imperfection:* 4 knot 5 gnarl *light:* 5 balsa *made of:* 5 treen *pattern in:*

5 grain 6 figure *product:* 3 tar 5 paper 10 turpentine *soft:* 4 pine

wood alcohol 6 methyl 8 carbinol, methanol

woodchuck 6 marmot 9 groundhog

wood coal 7 lignite

wooded 5 bosky, treed 6 sylvan 8 forested, timbered

wooden 5 rigid, stiff 6 clumsy 7 awkward, stilted 8 ligneous 10 inflexible

woodland 5 copse, taiga, weald 6 forest, pinery 7 coppice 10 rain forest

wood nymph 5 dryad

woodpecker 4 bird 7 flicker, wryneck 9 sapsucker *genus:* 5 Picus *kind:* 5 downy, green, hairy 8 imperial, pileated 9 redheaded 11 ivory-billed

woodsman 6 logger 8 forester 10 bushranger 11 bushwhacker

wood sorrel 3 oca 6 oxalis 8 shamrock 9 carambola

woodsy 6 rustic, sylvan

woodwind 4 oboe, reed 5 flute, shawm 7 bassoon, piccolo 8 clarinet 9 saxophone 10 instrument 11 English horn 13 contrabassoon

woodworker 9 carpenter 12 cabinetmaker

woody 8 ligneous 12 station wagon

wooer 4 beau 5 lover, spark, swain 6 suitor 7 admirer, gallant, sparker

woof 4 bark, crow, weft, yarn 5 boast, weave 6 fabric, thread 7 texture

wool 3 fur 4 coat, hair 6 fabric, fleece *cut:* 5 shear *fabric:* 4 felt 5 baize, crepe, serge, tweed 6 covert, kersey, mohair, poplin, shoddy, velour 7 flannel, worsted 8 cashmere, chenille 9 gabardine 10 broadcloth *fat:* 7 lanolin *kind:* 4 hogg 6 angora, hogget, virgin *low-quality:* 5 mungo 6 shoddy *musk-ox:* 6 qiviut *process:* 7 carding *source:* 4 goat, lamb 5 camel, llama, sheep 6 alpaca

woolly 5 fuzzy, hairy, nappy 6 fleecy, shaggy 7 blurred, hirsute 9 roughness 10 indistinct

woozy 4 hazy, sick, weak 5 dazed, dizzy, faint, fuzzy, muzzy, vague 6 addled, blurry, groggy, punchy 8 confused, nauseous 9 nauseated, slaphappy 11 light-headed

word 3 vow 4 buzz, news, oath, term 5 logos, order, rumor 6 advice, gospel, gossip, phrase, pledge, plight, remark, report, saying, signal 7 command, message, promise 8 locution 9 assurance, directive, discourse, guarantee, statement, utterance 10 commitment, expression 11 declaration, information 12 announcement, conversation, intelligence *connective:* 11 conjunction *group:* 6 clause, phrase 8 sentence *misused:* 8 malaprop 11 malapropism *naming:* 4 noun *new:* 7 coinage 9 neologism *of action:* 4 verb *of honor:* 4 oath 7 promise *origin:* 9 etymology *part:* 8 syllable *root:* 6 etymon *scrambled:* 7 anagram *shortened:* 11 contraction 12 abbreviation *square:* 10 palindrome *with opposite meaning:* 7 antonym *with same meaning:* 7 synonym *with same pronunciation:* 7 homonym 9 homophone *with same spelling:* 7 homonym 9 homograph

wordbook 5 vocab 7 lexicon 8 glossary 9 thesaurus 10 dictionary, vocabulary

word-for-word 7 literal 8 ad verbum, verbally, verbatim

wordiness 8 verbiage 9 logorrhea, prolixity, verbosity 10 bloviation

word-of-mouth 4 oral 6 spoken, verbal 8 viva voce 9 unwritten

wordy 5 windy 6 prolix, verbal 7 diffuse, verbose 9 dictional, garrulous, iterative, redundant, vocabular 10 long-winded, logorrheic, loquacious, rhetorical

work 3 act, fix, job, run, tug, use 4 duty, line, make, opus, take, task, tend, till, toil 5 chore, craft, drive, forge, grind, guide, labor, shape, solve, sweat, trade 6 create, effect, effort, energy, excite, métier, result, strain, strive 7 arrange, calling, control, exploit, fashion, operate, perform, product, provoke, pursuit, resolve, succeed, travail 8 activity, business, contrive, drudgery, exertion, function, operate, slogging, striving, vocation 9 cultivate, embroider, execution 10 assignment, employment, handicraft, occupation, profession *together:* 9 cooperate 11 collaborate *unit:* 3 erg 5 joule

workaday 5 plain, usual 7 mundane, prosaic, routine 8 ordinary 9 quotidian 11 commonplace 12 run-of-the-mill

worker 4 doer, hand, serf 5 prole 6 toiler, wallah 7 artisan, laborer 8 employee, mechanic, operator 9 craftsman, operative 10 roustabout, wage earner 11 proletarian *fellow:* 7 comrade, partner 9 colleague *group:* 4 crew, gang 5 shift, staff, union *hard:* 5 slave 6 beaver, drudge *insect:* 3 ant, bee 4 wasp 7 termite *itinerant:* 6 boomer 7 migrant *slow:* 7 plodder *unskilled:* 4 peon 7 jackleg, laborer

working 4 busy, live 6 active, useful, viable 7 dynamic, engaged, running 8 employed, occupied 9 operative 11 functioning *not:* 5 kaput 6 broken

workman see WORKER

work out 3 fix 5 solve, train 6 devise, set-

tle **7** arrange, develop, resolve **8** exercise
workout 4 test **5** drill **8** exercise, practice **10** daily dozen
work over 4 beat, redo **5** scrag, study **6** beat up, mess up, redraw, rehash, revamp, revise **7** examine, redraft, restyle, rewrite, rough up **9** manhandle
workroom 3 lab **4** shop **6** studio **7** atelier **10** laboratory
works 4 mill **5** plant **7** factory **8** workshop **11** manufactory
Works and Days author **6** Hesiod
world 5 class, earth, globe, realm **6** career, cosmos, nature, planet, public, sphere, system **7** kingdom, society **8** creation, division, everyone, renowned, universe **9** human race, macrocosm, microcosm **13** distinguished *combining form:* **4** cosm **5** cosmo
worldly 5 blasé **6** carnal, earthy, urbane **7** earthly, fleshly, mundane, profane, secular, sensual, terrene **8** material, telluric, temporal **9** sublunary **11** terrestrial **12** cosmopolitan **13** sophisticated
worldly-wise 12 cosmopolitan **13** sophisticated
World War I *battle:* **5** Aisne, Marne, Somme, Ypres **6** Isonzo, Verdun **7** Jutland **9** Caporetto **10** Tannenberg **11** Dardanelles *battle line:* **9** Siegfried *general:* **4** Foch (Ferdinand), Haig (Douglas) **7** Allenby (Edmund) **8** Pershing (John) **10** Hindenburg (Paul von), Ludendorff (Erich) *hero:* **4** York (Alvin) **8** Red Baron (The) **10** Richthofen (Manfred von) **12** Rickenbacker (Eddie) *treaty:* **10** Versailles
World War II *admiral:* **6** Halsey (William "Bull"), Nimitz (Chester) *alliance:* **4** Axis **6** Allies *battle:* **4** St.-Lô **5** Anzio, Bulge **6** Bataan, Midway, Tarawa, Warsaw **7** Britain, Iwo Jima, Okinawa, Saint-Lô **8** Coral Sea, Normandy **9** El Alamein, Leyte Gulf **10** Stalingrad **11** Guadalcanal *general:* **6** Patton (George), Rommel (Erwin), Zhukov (Georgy) **7** Bradley (Omar) **9** MacArthur (Douglas) **10** Eisenhower (Dwight David), Montgomery (Bernard) *hero:* **6** Murphy (Audie) *journalist:* **4** Pyle (Ernie) *vehicle:* **4** jeep *weapon:* **5** A-bomb **6** rocket **8** buzz bomb
worldwide 6 cosmic, global **8** catholic **9** planetary, universal **10** ecumenical **12** cosmopolitan
worm 3 cad, cur **4** grub, lout **5** borer, creep, fluke, leech, louse, screw, treat **6** edge in, maggot, no-good, squirm,

thread, wiggle, wretch, writhe **7** extract, lowlife, serpent, triclad, wriggle **8** helminth, nematode, squiggle **9** insinuate, planarium, trematode **10** infiltrate *marine:* **6** nereid **7** annelid, tubifex *parasitic:* **5** fluke, leech **7** ascarid, ascaris, cestode, filaria **8** helminth, trichina **9** strongyle
worn 3 old, wan **4** aged, beat **5** drawn, jaded, tatty, tired, weary **6** eroded, frayed, ragged, shabby **7** haggard **8** fatigued **9** woebegone **10** threadbare
worn-out 4 beat **5** all in, spent, tired, weary **6** bleary, bushed, ragged, used-up **7** drained, run-down **8** decrepit, depleted, fatigued, overused **9** exhausted, worm-eaten **10** broken-down, threadbare, tumbledown **11** debilitated, dilapidated
worried 6 afraid, on edge **7** anxious, nervous **8** bothered, distrait, troubled **9** concerned, tormented **10** distracted, distraught, distressed **12** apprehensive
worry 3 nag, try, vex **4** care, fret, fuss, gnaw, goad, pain, stew, test **5** annoy, beset, shake, tease, trial, upset **6** assail, attack, bother, harass, needle, pester, plague, pull at, unease **7** afflict, anguish, anxiety, concern, disturb, oppress, torment, trouble **8** aggrieve, distress, irritate **9** agitation, annoyance, misgiving **10** irritation, uneasiness
worrywart 7 fusspot **9** Cassandra, doomsayer, pessimist **10** fussbudget
worse 8 inferior
worsen 4 sink **7** decline **10** degenerate **11** deteriorate
worship 4 love **5** adore, honor **6** admire, dote on, homage, revere **7** idolize, lionize, liturgy, respect **8** devotion, idolatry, venerate **9** adoration, affection, reverence **10** admiration, veneration **11** idolization *object of:* **3** god **4** icon, idol *place of:* **5** altar **6** church, mosque, shrine, temple **9** cathedral, synagogue
worshipper 3 fan **6** votary **7** admirer, devotee **8** adherent, believer, disciple **10** enthusiast
worsted 4 yarn **5** stuff **6** caddis, fabric **7** cheviot, etamine, flannel, lasting **8** shalloon **9** bombazine, sharkskin **10** broadcloth
worth 4 rate **5** merit, price, value **6** regard, riches, wealth **7** caliber, calibre, fortune, quality, stature **9** resources, substance, valuation **10** excellence
worthless 4 vain **6** futile, no-good **7** inutile **8** nugatory **9** no-account
worthwhile 6 paying **7** gainful **9** estimable, honorable, lucrative

10 profitable, well-paying 11 meritorious, moneymaking 12 advantageous, remunerative

worthy 4 good 5 noble 8 laudable, standout 9 admirable, deserving, desirable, estimable, honorable 10 acceptable, creditable 11 commendable, meritorious

Wotan see ODIN

Wouk novel 4 Hope (The) 5 Glory (The) 10 Winds of War (The) 11 Caine Mutiny (The) 19 Marjorie Morningstar

would-be 7 hopeful, wishful 8 apparent, aspiring, desiring, desirous 9 ambitious, potential

wound 3 cut 4 blow, harm, hurt, pain, rift 6 damage, injure, injury, insult, lesion, trauma 8 lacerate 10 laceration *discharge:* 3 pus *sign:* 4 scab, scar 5 blood 7 blister

wow 3 hit 4 boff, grab 5 amaze, boffo, smash 6 dazzle 7 astound, impress, success 8 bedazzle

Wozzeck composer 4 Berg (Alban)

wrack 4 kelp, raze, ruin 5 smash, total 7 destroy, flotsam, remnant, seaweed 8 decimate, demolish, shambles, wreckage 11 destruction

wraith 5 ghost, shade, spook 6 double, shadow, spirit 7 phantom, specter, spectre 8 phantasm 10 apparition

wrangle 3 row 4 spar, spat, tiff 5 argue, brawl, fight, scrap 6 bicker, fracas, haggle, hassle 7 brabble, dispute, fall out, finagle, quarrel, quibble 8 squabble 11 altercation

wrangler 6 cowboy 8 buckaroo 9 ranch hand

wrap 3 fur 4 bind, cape, coat, roll 5 cloak, drape, shawl, stole 6 bundle, clothe, enfold, invest, jacket, mantle, muffle, parcel, shroud, swathe 7 bandage, blanket, conceal, dress up, embrace, enclose, engross, envelop, involve, package, swaddle 8 bundle up, enshroud, surround

wrapped up 4 deep 6 intent 7 engaged 8 absorbed, consumed, immersed 9 engrossed 11 preoccupied

wrapper 5 cover 6 jacket 10 dust jacket 12 dressing gown

wrap up 6 muffle 8 close out, complete, conclude 9 summarize

wrap-up 4 coda 5 close 6 capper, closer, finale, report 7 closing 8 epilogue 9 summation 10 denouement

wrath 3 ire 4 fury, rage 5 anger 6 choler 8 ferocity 9 vengeance 10 punishment 11 retribution 12 chastisement

wrathful 3 mad 5 angry, irate 6 heated,

raging 7 enraged, furious 8 choleric, incensed, inflamed 10 infuriated

wreak 5 cause, exact, visit 6 effect, impose 7 inflict 10 bring about

wreath 3 bay, lei 5 crown 6 anadem, laurel 7 chaplet, circlet, coronal, coronet, garland, laurels

wreathe 4 coil, curl, wind 5 twine, twist 6 spiral 7 entwine 9 corkscrew 10 interweave

wreck 4 do in, heap, hulk, raze, ruin 5 beach, crack, crash, cream, smash, total 6 beater, damage, jalopy, junker, pileup, ravage, strand 7 clunker, crackup, destroy, scuttle, smashup, torpedo 8 decimate, demolish 9 vandalize 11 destruction

wreckage 5 wrack 6 debris 7 flotsam 8 detritus, shambles 11 destruction

wrecker 8 salvager, tow truck

wrench 4 jerk, pull, rack, tool, turn, warp, yank 5 force, twist, wrest, wring 6 change, injure, injury, snatch, socket, sprain, strain 7 disable, distort, pervert, squeeze 8 distress, twisting *kind:* 6 monkey 7 ratchet

wrest 4 rend, rive 5 exact, twist, wring 6 elicit, extort, snatch, wrench 7 extract, squeeze

wrestle 6 combat, strain, strive, tussle 7 contend, grapple, scuffle 8 struggle

wrestling *hold:* 4 lock 6 nelson 8 headlock, scissors *kind:* 4 sumo *term:* 3 pin 4 fall 5 throw 8 takedown

wretch 3 cur, dog 4 scum, toad, worm 5 devil, knave, louse, rogue, skunk, snake 6 rascal, rotter 7 caitiff, hangdog, lowlife, outcast, rat fink, stinker, villain 8 scalawag, stinkard 9 scoundrel 10 blackguard, sleazeball 11 rapscallion

wretched 3 low, sad 4 base, foul, mean, vile 6 abject, dismal, horrid, scurvy, sordid, woeful 7 abysmal, doleful, forlorn, ignoble, ruthful, servile, squalid, unhappy 8 dejected, dolorous, hopeless, inferior 9 afflicted, execrable, miserable, sorrowful 10 despairing, despicable, deplorable, despondent, melancholy, villainous

wretchedness 3 woe 6 misery 7 anguish 8 distress

wriggle 4 worm 5 slink 6 squirm, writhe

wring 3 wry 5 choke, exact, screw, twist, wrest 6 extort, squirm, wrench, writhe 7 afflict, draw out, extract, squeeze, torment *the neck:* 5 scrag

wringing-wet 5 soppy 6 soaked, sodden, soused 7 soaking, sopping 8 drenched, dripping 9 saturated

wrinkle 4 fold, ruck, ruga, seam 5 crimp, crisp, plica, ridge, wizen 6 cockle,

crease, fillip, furrow, pucker, rumple
7 crumple, novelty, scrunch, shrivel
8 contract 9 corrugate, crow's-foot,
worry line 10 innovation 11 corrugation 12 imperfection, irregularity
wrinkled 5 lined 6 rugose, rumply
7 creased 8 puckered, rugulose
Wrinkle in Time author 6 L'Engle
(Madeleine)
wrist 5 joint 6 carpus *bone:* 6 carpal,
hamate 8 pisiform
writ 5 brief, order 6 assize, capias,
decree, elegit, extent 7 mandate,
process, summons, warrant 8 detainer,
document, mandamus, mittimus,
praecipe, replevin, subpoena 9 execution 10 attachment, certiorari, court
order, injunction 11 fieri facias, scire
facias, supersedeas 12 habeas corpus,
venire facias 13 sequestration
write 3 ink, jot, pen 4 note 5 chalk, draft,
print, score, spell 6 answer, author,
byline, draw up, indite, ordain, pencil,
record, scrawl, scribe 7 compose, dissert, engross, fire off, put down,
scratch, set down 8 inscribe, scribble,
spell out 9 autograph, transpose 10 correspond, underwrite
write down 4 note 6 record, reduce
10 transcribe
write off 6 cancel 7 dismiss, expense
8 amortize, discount 9 eliminate
10 depreciate
write-off 4 debt, loss 7 expense 8 donation 9 allowance, deduction, reduction
writer 4 poet 6 author, penman, scribe
8 composer, novelist 9 scribbler, wordsmith *bad:* 4 hack
write-up 5 blurb, story 7 account, article
writhe 4 curl, worm 5 twist 6 squirm,
suffer, wallow, welter, wiggle, wrench
7 agonize, contort, distort, wriggle
8 convolve, squiggle 10 intertwine
writing 4 book, hand, note 5 essay,
paper, print, prose, style, words 6 letter,
notice, record, script 7 epistle 8 document, longhand 9 signature 10 authorship, literature, manuscript, penmanship 11 calligraphy, composition,
inscription, publication *character:* 6 letter 9 cuneiform 10 hieroglyph *combining form:* 4 gram 6 grapho, graphy *for
the blind:* 7 braille *instrument:* 3 pen
5 chalk, quill 6 pencil, stylus *kind:*
5 prose, verse 6 poetry *sacred:* 5 Bible,

Koran 6 Talmud, Tantra 9 scripture
secret: 4 code *surface:* 5 board, paper,
slate 6 scroll 9 parchment
wrong 3 bad, ill, off, sin 4 awry, evil,
harm, hurt, tort 5 abuse, amiss, badly,
crime, false, inapt, unfit 6 afield,
astray, injure, injury, malign, offend,
sinful, unfair, unjust, untrue 7 defraud,
immoral, oppress, outrage, violate
8 aggrieve, ill-treat, improper, inequity,
iniquity, maltreat, mistaken, mistreat,
opposite 9 discredit, erroneous, grievance, incorrect, injustice, misguided,
persecute, unethical, unfitting, violation 10 inaccurate, iniquitous, mistakenly, unfairness, unjustness, unsuitable,
wickedness 11 erroneously, incorrectly,
unfavorably 12 inaccurately, infelicitous 13 inappropriate
wrongdoer 5 felon 6 sinner 8 criminal,
offender 9 miscreant, reprobate
10 accomplice, delinquent, malefactor
12 transgressor
wrongdoing 3 sin 4 evil 5 crime 7 misdeed, offense 8 iniquity 10 misconduct
11 malefaction, malfeasance, misbehavior
wrongful 6 unjust, unfair 7 illegal, illicit,
lawless 8 criminal, improper, unlawful
12 illegitimate
wrongheaded 6 mulish 7 froward 8 contrary, perverse 9 obstinate
wrought 4 made 6 formed, shaped,
worked 7 created 8 finished, hammered
9 decorated, fashioned, processed
10 ornamented 11 embellished 12 manufactured *up:* 7 excited, stirred
wry 4 bent 5 askew, twist, wrest 6 ironic,
wrench 7 crooked, twisted 8 humorous,
sardonic 11 wrongheaded
wryneck 10 woodpecker 11 torticollis
wurst 7 sausage
Wuthering Heights *author:* 6 Brontë
(Emily) *character:* 5 Cathy 9 Catherine
10 Heathcliff *family:* 6 Linton 8 Earn-
shaw
Wycliffite 7 Lollard
Wyoming *capital:* 8 Cheyenne *city:*
6 Casper 7 Laramie *mountain, range:*
5 Rocky 7 Gannett (Peak) 9 Wind River
10 Grand Teton *nickname:* 8 Equality
(State) *river:* 5 Green, Snake 6 Powder
7 Bighorn 11 Yellowstone *state bird:*
10 meadowlark *state flower:* 16 Indian
paintbrush *state tree:* 10 cottonwood

X

x 3 chi, ten 4 kiss 5 annul, cross, erase, error, times, wrong 6 cancel, delete, efface 7 mistake, unknown 8 abscissa 9 signature

Xanthippe 3 nag 5 scold, shrew 6 nagger 9 termagant *husband:* 8 Socrates

Xenophon work 8 Anabasis 9 Cyropedia, Hellenica

xerophyte 6 cactus

Xerxes *crossing site:* 10 Hellespont *defeat:* 7 Plataea, Salamis *father:* 6 Darius *kingdom:* 6 Persia *mother:* 6 Atossa *victory:* 11 Thermopylae

Xmas 4 Noel, yule 8 Nativity, yuletide

X-ray *discoverer:* 8 Roentgen (Wilhelm) *science:* 9 radiology

xylophone relative 7 marimba

Y

yacht 4 race, sail 6 cruise 7 cruiser 8 sailboat 12 cabin cruiser

yahoo 3 hun, yay 4 boor, clod, dolt, hood, lout, punk, thug 5 brute, chuff, churl, clown, rough, rowdy, tough 6 hoorah, hooray, hurrah, savage, terror, vandal, yippie 7 buffoon, bumpkin, hoodlum, ruffian, toughie 8 bullyboy, hooligan 9 roughneck 10 clodhopper

Yahweh 3 God 6 Adonai, Elohim 7 Jehovah

yak 3 gab, jaw 4 blab, chat 5 clack, prate 6 babble, gabble, jabber, natter, yammer 7 blabber, blather, chatter, palaver, prattle 11 confabulate

Yalta participant 6 Stalin (Joseph) 9 Churchill (Winston), Roosevelt (Franklin Delano)

yam 7 boniato 11 sweet potato

yammer 3 cry 4 bawl, crab, fuss, moan, wail, yawp, yell 5 bleat, gripe, whine 6 babble, bellow, clamor, gabble, grouch, grouse, jabber, natter, snivel, squawk 7 blather, prattle, whimper 8 complain 9 bellyache, caterwaul

yank 3 tug 4 grab, jerk, pull, tear 5 hoick 6 snatch, wrench 7 extract

yap 3 gab 4 bark, hick 5 mouth, prate 6 babble, bowwow, gabble, jabber, natter, rustic, yammer 7 blather, bumpkin, chatter, hayseed, prattle 9 hillbilly 10 clodhopper

yard 3 pen 4 herd, quad, spar, unit 5 court, garth, glass 6 length 7 grounds, measure 9 curtilage, enclosure 10 playground, quadrangle *five and one-half:* 3 rod *part of:* 4 foot *two hundred and twenty:* 7 furlong

yardstick 4 norm, test 5 basis, gauge, model 7 measure, pattern 8 paradigm, standard 9 barometer, benchmark, criterion, guideline 10 touchstone

yare 4 deft, spry 5 agile, brisk, handy, lithe, quick, ready, zippy 6 lively, nimble, volant 7 lissome 9 sprightly

yarn 4 tale, talk 5 fiber, story 6 caddis, cotton, crewel, strand, thread 7 account, caddice 8 anecdote, tall tale 9 adventure, narration, narrative *ball of:* 4 clew *coil:* 5 skein 6 skeane *cotton:* 10 candlewick *for fastening a sail:* 6 roband *woolen:* 6 crewel 7 worsted 8 shetland

yaw 4 rock, swag, veer 5 lurch 6 swerve 7 deviate 9 alternate, deviation 10 deflection

yawn 3 gap 4 bore, gape 5 ennui 6 cavity,

tedium 7 boredom, bromide 10 dullsville
yawning 4 deep 5 agape 6 gaping
7 abyssal 9 cavernous
yawp 3 bay, cry, nag 4 bark, bawl, beef, crab, fuss, gape, wail 5 bleat, gripe 6 clamor, outcry, squall, squawk, yammer 8 complain 9 bellyache
yaws 9 frambesia
yclept 5 named 6 called
yea 3 aye, too 4 also, amen, even, more, okay 5 truly 6 agreed, assent, as well, indeed, really, verily 7 besides, granted 8 likewise, moreover, positive 9 certainly 10 definitely 11 affirmation, affirmative 12 additionally
yeanling 3 kid 4 lamb
year 4 time 5 cycle 6 period *academic division:* 4 term 7 quarter, session 8 semester 9 trimester *French:* 5 année *kind:* 4 leap 5 solar 6 fiscal 8 academic, calendar, sidereal *Latin:* 5 annus *Scottish:* 7 towmond *Spanish:* 3 año
yearbook 5 annal 6 annual 7 almanac
yearling 4 colt, foal 5 filly
Yearling, The *author:* 8 Rawlings (Marjorie Kinnan) *character:* 4 Jody *fawn:* 4 Flag
yearly 6 annual 8 annually
yearn 4 ache, burn, itch, long, lust, pant, pine, sigh, wish 5 dream, spoil 6 hanker, hunger, thirst
yearning 4 wish 5 ardor, drive, eager 6 desire, thirst 7 craving, wistful 8 appetite 10 aspiration
years 3 age, era *five:* 7 lustrum 12 quinquennial, quinquennium *four:* 11 quadrennial, quadrennium *one hundred:* 7 century 9 centenary 10 centennial *one thousand:* 10 millennium *ten:* 6 decade 9 decennial, decennium *three:* 9 triennial, triennium *two:* 8 biennial, biennium
yeast 4 barm, foam, suds 5 froth, spume 6 lather, leaven 7 ferment
yeasty 5 dizzy, giddy, light 6 frothy 7 flighty 8 immature, restless, seething 9 exuberant, frivolous, unsettled 11 light-headed
Yeats, William Butler *beloved:* 9 Maud Gonne *birthplace:* 6 Dublin *play:* 7 Deirdre 9 Herne's Egg (The) 16 Countess Cathleen (The) *poetry:* 5 Tower (The) 10 Easter 1916 12 Second Coming (The) 16 Wild Swans at Coole (The) 18 Sailing to Byzantium *theater:* 5 Abbey
yegg 5 thief 6 robber 7 burglar 8 picklock 11 safecracker
yell 3 cry 4 call, howl, roar, wail 5 cheer, hallo, hollo, shout, whoop 6 bellow,

clamor, holler, outcry, scream, shriek, squall 10 vociferate
yellow 3 age 4 buff, mean, weak, yolk 5 amber, blond, color, lemon, straw, tawny, topaz 6 coward, craven, flaxen, golden, sallow 7 gutless, ignoble, mustard, saffron 8 cowardly, discolor 9 dastardly, jaundiced, spunkless 11 sensational 12 dishonorable 13 pusillanimous *brownish:* 3 dun 5 amber, ocher *dye:* 7 annatto *greenish:* 5 olive 6 acacia 10 chartreuse
yellowhammer 5 finch 7 bunting, flicker
yelp 3 cry, yap 4 bark 6 outcry, squeal
Yemen *capital:* 4 Sana 5 Sanaa *city:* 4 Aden 5 Ta'izz *desert:* 10 Rub' al-Khali *gulf:* 4 Aden *island:* 7 Socotra *island group:* 7 Kamaran *language:* 6 Arabic *monetary unit:* 4 rial *neighbor:* 4 Oman 11 Saudi Arabia *peninsula:* 7 Arabian *sea:* 3 Red 7 Arabian
yen 4 ache, itch, long, lust, pine, sigh, urge 5 taste, yearn 6 desire, hanker, hunger, thirst 7 craving, longing, passion 8 appetite, yearning 9 hankering
yeoman 5 clerk 6 farmer 7 freeman 8 retainer 9 attendant, beefeater, landowner 10 freeholder 11 homesteader
yeomanly 5 loyal 6 sturdy 8 faithful
yes 3 aye, yea, yeh, yep, yup 4 okay, yeah 5 agree 6 agreed, assent, gladly 7 consent, exactly 8 all right 9 assuredly, certainly, willingly 11 affirmation, affirmative, undoubtedly *French:* 3 oui
yeshiva 6 school 8 seminary
yes-man 5 toady 6 minion, stooge 7 spaniel 8 groveler, truckler 9 flatterer, sycophant 10 bootlicker 13 applepolisher
yesterday 4 past, yore 8 recently 10 recent time *French:* 4 hier *Spanish:* 4 ayer
yesteryear 4 past, yore 7 history 8 foretime, lang syne
yet 3 but, too 4 also, even, more, only, save 5 so far, still 6 as well, though, withal 7 besides, earlier, finally, howbeit, however, someday, thus far 8 after all, hitherto, moreover, sometime 10 eventually, ultimately 11 furthermore, nonetheless, still and all 12 additionally, nevertheless
Yevtushenko poem 7 Babi Yar, Baby Yar
Ygerne see IGRAINE
yield 3 bow, net, pay 4 bear, bend, cave, cede, crop, fold 5 defer, grant, waive 6 accede, bounty, buckle, comply, impart, output, profit, relent, render, resign, return, reward, submit, supply, tender 7 abandon, bring in, concede,

consent, deliver, furnish, harvest, produce, product, proffer, provide, revenue, succumb **8** abdicate, collapse, generate, hand over **9** acquiesce, surrender **10** bring forth, capitulate, production, relinquish

yielding 4 soft **6** pliant, supple **7** bearing, passive, pliable **8** flexible **9** adaptable, tractable **10** manageable, productive, submissive **11** acquiescent, unresistant

yin and ___ 4 yang

yip 3 cry **4** bark, yelp

yippee 6 hoorah, hooray, hurrah, hurray

yoga posture 5 asana

yoke 3 bar, tie, wed **4** bond, join, link, pair, span, team **5** clamp, frame, hitch, marry, unite **6** attach, couple, inspan **7** bondage, connect, control, harness, peonage, serfdom, slavery **8** marriage **9** servitude **10** crosspiece, oppression *combining form:* **3** zyg **4** zygo *part:* **5** oxbow

yokel 3 oaf **4** boor, clod, hick, rube **5** churl, swain **6** rustic **7** bucolic, bumpkin, hayseed **9** chawbacon, hillbilly **10** clodhopper, countryman

yolk 4 food **6** yellow **10** ovum center

yon see YONDER

yonder 5 there **7** farther, further, thither **8** outlying

yore 3 old **7** history **8** foretime, lang syne **9** antiquity, yesterday **10** yesteryear

you 3 one **4** thee, thou *French:* **4** vous *German:* **3** Sie *Spanish:* **5** usted **7** ustedes

young 3 fry, new **4** baby, tyro **5** brood, fresh, green **6** babies, callow, infant, junior, litter, tender, unripe **7** untried **8** childish, immature, juvenile, unformed, youthful **9** unfledged **10** unfinished, unseasoned **11** unpracticed **13** inexperienced *animal:* **3** cub, fry, kid, kit, pup **4** calf, colt, fawn, foal, joey **5** puppy **6** kitten, heifer, piglet *bird:* **5** chick **7** gosling *hare:* **7** leveret *sheep, goat:* **4** lamb **8** yeanling

younger 6 junior

youngster 3 boy, cub, kid, lad, tad, tot **4** girl, lass, tike **5** chick, child **6** moppet, shaver **8** juvenile **9** fledgling

youth 5 prime **6** period, spring **8** juvenile, preadult, teenager **9** stripling **10** adolescent, springtide, springtime **12** inexperience *ancient Greek:* **6** ephebe **7** ephebus *goddess of:* **4** Hebe *mythological:* **6** Adonis, Apollo, Icarus **8** Ganymede *time of:* **9** salad days

youthful 5 fresh, green, young **6** boyish, callow, maiden, unripe **7** puerile **8** immature, juvenile, virginal **9** beardless, unfledged

yowl 3 bay, cry **4** bawl, howl, wail **6** scream, squall, squeal **7** ululate **9** caterwaul

yucca 7 cassava **9** bear grass

Yukon *bay:* **9** Mackenzie *capital:* **10** Whitehorse *city:* **6** Dawson *mountain:* **5** Logan *river:* **5** Yukon **8** Klondike

yule 4 Noel, Xmas **8** Nativity **9** Christmas **13** Christmastide

Z

Zambia *capital:* **6** Lusaka *city:* **5** Kitwe, Ndola **11** Livingstone *lake:* **5** Mweru **9** Bangweulu **10** Tanganyika *language:* **7** English *monetary unit:* **6** kwacha *mountain range:* **8** Muchinga *neighbor:* **5** Congo **6** Angola, Malawi **7** Namibia **8** Tanzania, Zimbabwe **10** Mozambique *river:* **5** Kafue **7** Luangwa, Zambezi *waterfall:* **13** Victoria Falls

zany 3 nut, wag **4** card, fool, kook **5** antic, campy, clown, comic, crazy, cutup, dotty, goofy, idiot, joker, kooky, loony, nutty, wacky **6** jester, madcap **7** buffoon, farceur, half-wit **8** clowning, clownish, comedian, funnyman, jokester **9** harlequin, prankster, screwball, simpleton, trickster **11** merry-andrew

zap 3 hit **4** blow, kill, nuke **5** blast, snuff **6** attack **7** destroy, wipe out **8** dissolve **9** eliminate, irradiate, liquidate **10** annihilate

Zauberflöte composer 6 Mozart (Wolfgang Amadeus)

zeal 4 brio, fire, zest **5** ardor, drive,

mania 6 desire, energy, esprit, fervor, spirit 7 avidity, passion, urgency 8 devotion, dynamism, keenness 9 eagerness, intensity, vehemence 10 enthusiasm, fanaticism, fierceness
zealot 3 bug, fan, nut 4 buff 5 fiend, freak 6 maniac, votary 7 devotee, fanatic, sectary 8 partisan 10 aficionado, enthusiast 12 true believer
zealous 4 avid, keen 5 afire, eager, fiery, fired, nutty, rabid 6 ardent, fervid, gung-ho 7 devoted, fanatic, fervent 8 frenetic, obsessed, wild-eyed 9 dedicated, fanatical, possessed 10 passionate 11 impassioned 12 enthusiastic
zebra 6 equine 7 referee 9 crosswalk *extinct:* 6 quagga *type:* 6 Grevy's 8 mountain 9 Burchell's
zebu 4 oxen
Zebulun 9 lost tribe *brother:* 4 Levi 5 Judah 6 Simeon *father:* 5 Jacob *mother:* 4 Leah
zecchino 6 sequin
Zechariah 7 prophet
Zedekiah 9 Mattaniah *father:* 6 Josiah
zenana 5 harem, serai 8 seraglio
zenith 3 top 4 acme, apex, peak 6 apogee, height, summit, vertex 8 capstone, pinnacle 11 culmination 12 highest point *opposite:* 5 nadir
Zenobia *husband:* 9 Odenathus *kingdom:* 7 Palmyra
Zeno follower 5 Stoic
Zephaniah 7 prophet 9 Sophonias
zephyr 6 breeze 8 west wind
Zephyrus *father:* 8 Astraeus *mother:* 3 Eos 6 Aurora
zeppelin 5 blimp 7 airship 9 dirigible
zero 3 aim, nil, zip 4 love, nada, none, null, void 5 aught, nadir, zilch 6 cipher, naught, nobody 7 nothing, nullity 8 goose egg 9 nonentity
zest 4 élan, peel, tang, zeal 5 ardor, gusto, taste 6 fervor, flavor, relish 7 delight, ecstasy, elation, passion, sparkle 8 appetite, dynamism, piquancy, pleasure 9 eagerness, enjoyment 10 enthusiasm 11 delectation 12 exhilaration, satisfaction
zesty 4 racy, tart 5 sharp, spicy, tangy 6 biting, lively, savory, snappy 7 peppery, piquant, pungent 8 exciting, poignant, seasoned, spirited 9 flavorful
Zetes *brother:* 6 Calais *father:* 6 Boreas *mother:* 8 Orithyia *slayer:* 8 Heracles, Hercules
Zethus *brother:* 7 Amphion *father:* 4 Zeus 7 Jupiter *mother:* 7 Antiope
Zeus 7 Jupiter *brother:* 5 Hades 8 Poseidon *daughter:* 3 Ate 4 Hebe 5 Helen 6 Athena 7 Artemis 9 Aphrodite

10 Persephone, Proserpina *father:* 6 Cronus *home:* 7 Olympus (Mt.) *lover:* 4 Leda, Leto, Maia 5 Danae, Dione, Metis 6 Aegina, Europa, Latona, Semele, Themis 7 Alcmene, Antiope, Demeter 8 Callisto, Eurynome *mother:* 4 Rhea *nurse:* 9 Almathaea *oracle:* 6 Dodona *shield:* 5 aegis *sister:* 4 Hera, Juno *son:* 4 Ares 5 Arcas, Argus, Minos 6 Aeacus, Apollo, Hermes, Zethus 7 Amphion, Perseus 8 Dionysus, Heracles, Hercules, Sarpedon, Tantalus *tree:* 3 oak *wife:* 4 Hera, Juno *weapon:* 11 thunderbolt
zigzag 4 tack, turn 5 angle, crank, weave 6 jagged 7 chevron 8 flexuous, indirect, serrated
zilch 3 nil, zip 4 zero 5 aught, squat 6 cipher, naught, nobody 7 nothing, nullity 8 goose egg 9 nonentity 11 diddly-squat
Zimbabwe *capital:* 6 Harare *city:* 5 Gweru 6 Kwekwe, Mutare 8 Bulawayo, Maxvingo 11 Chitungwiza *ethnic group:* 5 Shona 7 Ndebele *former name:* 8 Rhodesia *lake:* 6 Kariba *language:* 5 Bantu 7 English *monetary unit:* 6 dollar *neighbor:* 6 Zambia 8 Botswana 10 Mozambique 11 South Africa *river:* 4 Sabi 7 Limpopo, Zambezi *waterfall:* 13 Victoria Falls
zinc 7 element *ingot:* 7 spelter *ore:* 6 blende 10 sphalerite
zing 3 pan, pep, rap, vim, zap, zip 4 brio, dash, élan, slam, snap, zeal 5 ardor, flair, oomph, verve, vigor 6 energy, esprit, fervor, spirit 7 panache, passion, sparkle 8 dynamism, vitality 9 animation, eagerness 10 ebullience, enthusiasm
Zion 5 bliss 6 heaven, Israel 7 Elysium 8 eternity, paradise 12 New Jerusalem, promised land
Zionist *American:* 5 Szold (Henrietta) *English:* 7 Sokolow (Nahum) 8 Zangwill (Israel) *German:* 6 Nordau (Max Simon) *Hungarian:* 5 Herzl (Theodor) *Israeli:* 5 Buber (Martin) 8 Weizmann (Chaim)
zip 3 fly, nil, nix, pep, run, vim 4 brio, dash, hiss, rush, nada, snap, tear, whiz, zero, zest, zing, zoom 5 drive, gusto, hurry, oomph, speed, squat, whisk, zilch 6 bustle, energy, hasten, hustle 7 nothing 8 vitality 10 excitement, liveliness 11 diddly-squat
zippy 4 keen, spry, yare 5 agile, alert, brisk, peppy, quick, ready 6 lively, nimble, snappy, speedy 7 dynamic 8 spirited 9 sprightly
zircon 6 jargon 7 jargoon, mineral *variety:* 7 jacinth 8 hyacinth

zit 6 pimple

zither 10 instrument *Chinese:* 3 kin 4 ch'in *Japanese:* 4 koto *relative:* 8 autoharp, dulcimer

zodiac sign 3 Leo (the Lion) 5 Aries (the Ram), Libra (the Balance), Virgo (the Virgin) 6 Cancer (the Crab), Gemini (the Twins), Pisces (the Fishes), Taurus (the Bull) 7 Scorpio (the Scorpion) 8 Aquarius (the Water Bearer) 9 Capricorn (the Goat) 11 Sagittarius (the Archer)

Zola, Emile *work:* 4 Nana 7 J'accuse 8 Drunkard (The), Germinal 9 La Débâcle 10 L'Assommoir 13 Thérèse Raquin

zombie 5 robot 8 cocktail 9 automaton

zone 4 area, band, belt 5 layer, tract 6 region, sector 7 portion, quarter, section, segment, stretch 8 district, division, encircle, surround 9 partition, territory

zonked 4 high 5 dazed, doped, drunk, tight 6 ripped, stoned 7 drugged, drunken, smashed 8 hopped-up, tripping, turned on, wiped out 9 spacedout, strung out, stupefied 10 inebriated, tripped out 11 intoxicated

zoologist *American:* 5 Clark (Eugenie), Hyatt (Alpheus) 6 Carson (Rachel), Fossey (Dian), Osborn (Henry Fairfield), Yerkes (Robert) 7 Agassiz (Alexander), Ditmars (Raymond), Merriam (Clinton) 8 Hornaday (William) *Austrian:* 6 Frisch (Karl von) *British:* 6 Darwin (Charles), Huxley (Julian, Thomas) 7 Goodall (Jane), Medawar (Peter) 9 Lankester (Edwin) *Dutch:* 10 Swammerdam (Jan) *French:* 6 Buffon (G.-L. Leclerc), Cuvier (Georges) *German:* 7 Haeckel (Ernst) *Norwegian:* 6 Nansen (Fridtjof) *South African:* 5 Broom (Robert) *Swedish:* 8 Linnaeus (Carolus)

zoom 3 hum, zip 4 buzz, dash, whiz, zero 5 focus, speed, whizz 6 streak 7 shoot up 9 skyrocket

zoophyte 5 coral 6 sponge 8 bryozoan 9 gorgonian 10 sea anemone

Zoroastrian *demon:* 4 deva *god:* 10 Ahura Mazda *sacred writings:* 6 Avesta

zounds 3 gad 4 egad 8 gadzooks 11 odd's bodkins

zucchetto 7 calotte 8 skullcap

zwieback 5 toast 7 biscuit

zygomatic bone 5 malar 9 cheekbone

zygote 4 cell 6 oocyst